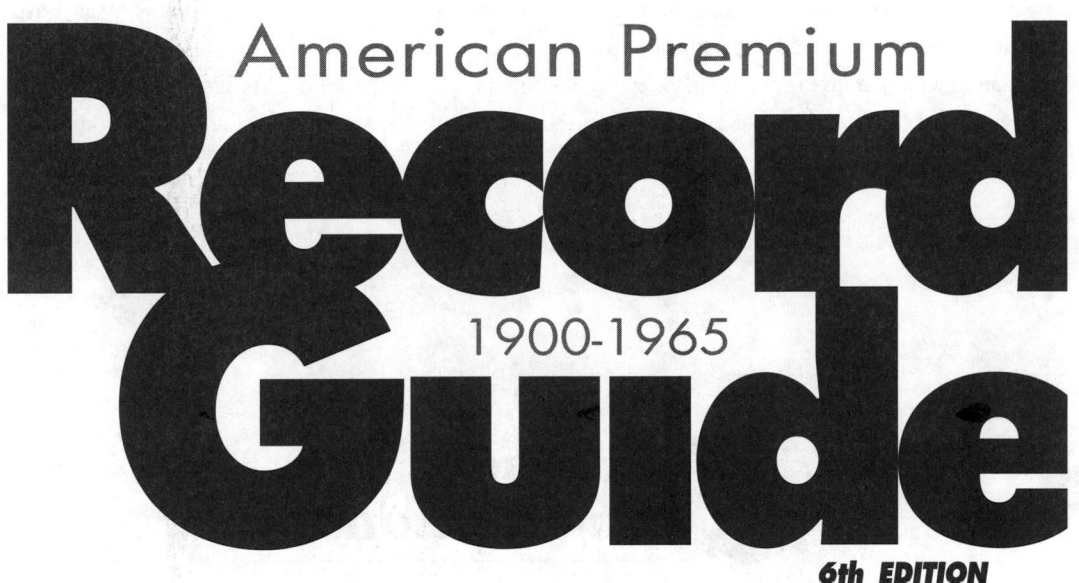

American Premium
Record Guide
1900-1965

6th EDITION

Les Docks

Published by

krause
publications

700 E. State Street • Iola, WI 54990-0001
Telephone: 715/445-2214
www.krause.com

Please call or write for our free catalog of publications. Our toll-free number to place an order or obtain a free catalog is 800-258-0929 or please use our regular business telephone, 715-445-2214.

Library of Congress Catalog Number: 2001088589
ISBN: 0-87349-282-X
Printed in the United States of America

TABLE OF CONTENTS

ACKNOWLEDGMENTS

Special thanks must be given to my wife, Pam, for her encouragement and indispensable assistance in compiling and revising this reference work, for the many hours she spent putting together and revising the index, and for her tolerant understanding during those periods when I was holed up in the "shellac shack," virtually incommunicado, compensating for earlier procrastination, getting ready to send everything to the publisher. I am indebted also to the following for furnishing records for photography and for contribution of data: James Apthorpe, Werner Beneke (whose contribution to a more accurate second and third edition is especially appreciated), George Blacker, Dan Campbell, Fred Chambers, Rex Clark, Scott Cleveland, F. Curran, Lou Curtiss, Rick Dembinsky, Ron Evry, Don Gray, Doug Gregory, Steve Gronda, Tom Hawthorne, E.J. Henke, The John Edwards Memorial Foundation (and Linda Painter, then editor of its *J.E.M.F. Quarterly*), Glenn Keck, Tim Lucy, Bob Mays, William C. (Bill) Menor, Jerry Nieporte, Charlie O'Haver, Robert R. Olson, Michael W. Sherman, Dan Stevens, Keith Titterington, Pete Whelan, and Morgan Wright.

There are a few contributors to whom I am also indebted, perhaps as much as to any of the foregoing, but to whom thanks must be given privately, it being their wish to remain anonymous.

My appreciation must also be expressed to Elaine Cary for her able typing services furnished on short notice, and to Dan Alexander, former president of Books Americana, Inc., for his patience each time this book and its revisions took shape.

INTRODUCTION

There is nothing "official" about this or any other price guide. Like other books on collectibles, it reflects the opinions of the author (opinions developed through many years of buying, selling, and trading records and consulting countless auction lists, sales lists, record publications, discographies, record company promotional literature, and collectors' want lists). Also important are the contributions of those who have supplied information, opinions on pricing, and photographs. Undoubtedly, many errors and omissions will be noted by knowledgeable collectors; it is hoped that these will be brought to my attention by writing to: **L.R. DOCKS, P.O. Box 691035, San Antonio, Texas 78269** Or, by e-mail to: **docks@texas.net**.

In this single volume are listed thousands of desirable records in the most widely-collected categories: jazz, dance bands, celebrity, blues, rhythm and blues, country and western, hillbilly, rockabilly, and rock 'n' roll. Included are 78s, 45s, EPs, and LPs. Emphasis is given to categories heretofore neglected and/or inadequately treated, such as early jazz, blues, and country 78s.

As in previous editions, the majority of records listed are unfamiliar to non-collectors. Indeed, many are so obscure as to be unfamiliar even to sophisticated collectors. Quick now: Who were Dubin's Dandies? Very few of the records listed are top-selling hits. This book is intended to be a guide to scarce, sought-after, and otherwise desirable discs that ought to be recognized as collectible. It is not meant to afford readers a "nostalgia trip," by listing thousands of familiar old favorites, complete with titles. Those seeking documentation and information about hit, or "charted," records should consult other references, such as those by Joel Whitburn (see bibliography). Those treasured records by Bing Crosby, Al Jolson, Glenn Miller, et al., even if they are indeed "originals," are probably not saleable to a knowledgeable collector, and certainly not at more than a nominal sum. Common sense ought to suggest that records that sold in the largest quantities remain relatively common and inexpensive today. But common sense sometimes seems uncommon: I get many callers who want to know what their original Bing Crosby's "White Christmas" is worth, but no calls offering me a store stock of 8000 series Okeh records.

Readers of previous editions will note, however, recent editions' inclusion of many more relatively common and inexpensive records (i.e., records valued at less than ten dollars), by the more familiar artists, on common labels such as red Columbia. They may well ask, "Has Docks sold out?" The answer is a resounding "no." Well, maybe not so resounding. This seeming concession is only slightly in response to popular demand. The real purpose is to illustrate the distinction between very common and very scarce records, and to avoid inquiries about why certain common records aren't listed. At least I shouldn't get any more letters from owners who think their Gene Autry red label Columbia records are unlisted rarities.

What kinds of records are regarded as desirable by knowledgeable collectors? Records in the categories mentioned above, regarded as excellent examples of their idiom; historically important records, such as those featuring the early work of a future star; and records issued on rare or interesting labels. Many of the records listed here were issued in special series or on labels aimed at limited markets. "Race" series and labels, aimed at the Negro, and hillbilly series (the "Songs From Dixie" series or the like), aimed at white rural folk, never attained the distribution levels of the more mainstream music popular in "polite" society. Music that was denigrated and segregated in its own time is today the music that is most appreciated and prized.

Definitions, Symbols and Terms

Following are brief explanations of the terms and symbols used by record collectors and dealers. Some of them are forthright and succinct. Others, attempting to define the various styles and idioms of music, are somewhat amorphous, if not downright evasive. Music appeals to the emotions and senses, and does not invite verbal analysis. Most people know jazz (or blues, or country/western music) when they hear it. "It Don't Mean A Thing If It Ain't Got That Swing" is better than any dictionary definition. If you have a record you're not familiar with (for example, "Four Or Five Times" by McKinney's Cotton Pickers), play it. You'll probably know what category it falls into without reading any definition. Or consult the artist index at the end of this book.

BLUES: *Webster's New Collegiate Dictionary* defines blues as "a song of lamentation characterized by 12-bar phrases, 3-line stanzas in which the words of the second stanza repeat those of the first, and continual occurrence of blue notes in melody and harmony." A bit of overdubbing: The songs relate to the troubles, hardships and common experiences of blacks (and poor whites). Often, humor, double-meanings, and lively rhythm were employed, as to dispel, rather than wallow in the blues. Nothing purposefully offensive was recorded. The use of the word "blues" in a song title does not necessarily identify a blues record; many such records are instrumental jazz, or even soulless "pop", e. g. Clyde McCoy's "Sugar Blues". Some blues are country style with accompaniments consisting of stringed or makeshift instruments; some blues are urbanized, closer to jazz, with wind instruments accompanying the vocalist. Sometimes, the choice of whether to include a given record in the first or second section of this book is little more than arbitrary. If all this seems meaningless, play a blues record: 12 bars of it will be worth a thousand words.

BOOTLEG: An unauthorized issue of a previously unreleased performance in derogation of the rights of the real owner of the tape or master and the artist. The term also is used in reference to an unauthorized copy or reissue of a previously issued record. Where the unauthorized copy closely resembles the original record in label design, the more correct term is "reproduction," or "counterfeit." Since the practice of bootlegging or reproducing rare and valuable 45 RPM records of the 1950s has become widespread, collectors are advised to exercise caution when spending large sums on records of that period. There is no substitute for personal familiarity with the subtle characteristics of the original records: such things as the distinctness of the lettering, the texture of the paper used for the label, the appearance of the grooves, master numbers in the wax, the thickness of the pressing, etc. For guidance in recognizing bootlegs of vocal group records, consult Lou Silvani's *Collecting Rare Records*, and Jeff Kreiter's *Group Collector's Record Price Guide*, both listed in the bibliography.

BUDGET LABELS: (See **COVER RECORDS**)

CONTEMPORANEOUS ISSUES: Contemporaneous issue of the same performance on two or more labels was common in the 1920s and 1930s. This was the result of contractual arrangement, corporate affiliation, or the ownership of several labels by the same company. The most frequently encountered grouping comprises Banner, Conqueror, Melotone, Oriole, Perfect, Romeo, and sometimes Vocalion. Many recordings of the 1930s for the American Record Company were issued at the same time on several if not all of the labels mentioned. The song titles, the artists' names, the typography, and even the catalog number of the record on many, would be identical on each label. Other examples from the 1930s are Champion and Decca; Bluebird, Electradisk, Montgomery Ward, Sunrise, and Timely Tunes (all RCA Victor products). In the 1920s, the following label affiliations commonly occurred: Cameo, Lincoln, Romeo; Harmony, Diva, Velvet-Tone (and later, about 1930, Clarion); Perfect and Pathe-Actuelle; Gennett, Champion, Challenge, Claxtonola, Herschel Gold Seal, Silvertone, Superior, Supertone; Harmograph, Paramount, Black Swan; Arto, Bell, Cleartone, Globe, Grey Gull, Radiex; Brunswick, Vocalion; Banner, Cameo, Jewel, Oriole, Regal, Romeo. The practice also existed in the 1950s; one example is the Sun and Flip labels. It should be noted that the affiliated labels may not have been issued at exactly the same time; technically, one might be regarded as the original issue. Collectors of 1950s records are far more particular in this regard than are collectors of vintage 78s. It should also be noted that the real name of the artist was not always used on all of the affiliated labels. The use of pseudonyms was extensive, often to evade exclusive recording artist contractual restrictions, or to avoid making royalty payments to artists. Performances by Irving Mills' groups were variously credited as by Jimmy Bracken's Toe Ticklers, Dixie Jazz Band, Kentucky Grasshoppers, The Lumberjacks and The Whoopee Makers on Banner, Jewel, Oriole, Regal and Romeo. The Wolverine Orchestra on Gennett became the Jazz Harmonizers on Claxtonola. Bradley Kincaid on Gennett became Dan Hughey on Champion. If this isn't confusing enough, one pseudonym, such as Dixie Jazz Band on Oriole, might conceal the true identity of a dozen or more bands, whose performances appeared on other labels, perhaps under different pseudonyms! Records listed in this volume are listed according to the label credits, without regard to pseudonyms. The real names behind pseudonyms should be sought in the various discographies listed in the bibliography. Those wishing to delve further into the complexities of label affiliation and the corporate evolution of record companies should consult Read and Welch's *From Tin Foil to Stereo*, Sutton and Nauck's *American Record Labels and Companies*, and Brian Rust's *The American Record Label Book*, all listed in the bibliography.

COUNTRY/WESTERN/HILLBILLY MUSIC: *Webster's New Collegiate Dictionary* defines this music as "derived from or imitating the folk style of the southern U. S. or of the Western cowboy." This definition, however, seems to exclude much of the watered down Nashville product. Is it broad enough to include Jimmie Rodgers, Bob Wills, Ernest Stoneman, Fiddlin' John Carson, et al.? Styles vary greatly, from country blues with minimal stringed instrumental accompaniment, to western swing, employing a full band, with piano and horns, the result being more like jazz. The inclusion of some artists in the third section of this book is almost arbitrary, e.g. The Hoosier Hot Shots.

"COVER" RECORDS: Re-recordings of popular hit tunes by artists other than those who did the original versions are frequently in accumulations of records, especially from the 1950s. Usually, these "cover" artists are relatively unknown (an exception is Pat Boone, who covered a number of rock 'n' roll and rhythm & blues tunes for the Dot label), and their recordings are of little interest to collectors (also true of Pat Boone's records!). The records are usually found on "budget" labels, most of which are multi-track (offering more than one tune on each side), including 78s and 45s. Some of these labels are Broadway (not related to the 1920s-early 1930s label of same name), Club 45, 18 Top Hits, Gateway, Gilmar, Prom, Tops, Top 30 Tunes, Value, and Variety ("The Nation's Top 18 Hits").

DISCOGRAPHY: A compilation of data concerning the recorded work of an artist, including recordings issued and unissued, recording dates, personnels, locations, and master numbers. Of course, discographies can vary as to completeness and accuracy. Discographies of a single artist or label usually are found in record collectors' publications. *78 Quarterly* No. 11 features an illustrated, extensively annotated *Black Patti* discography! The term may also refer to books such as the outstanding works by Brian Rust, which attempt to list all records by all artists in a given genre. Label discographies are numerical listings of particular labels, according to catalog number. Some offer only record numbers and song titles. See, for example, Roger Kinkle's (1974) four-volume encyclopedia on pop music. Kinkle offers numerical listings of nine major labels of the 1920s, 1930s, and 1940s. (Although the listings are often useful, abbreviation of titles and artists' names is often cause for puzzlement.) Ken Clee's five-volume directory consists of 45 RPM labels of the 1950s and later. Other label discographies are more thorough: in addition to song titles and record numbers, some offer master numbers, release dates, production figures, and more. See, for example, Dan Mahoney's *The Columbia 13000/14000-D Series*. Label discographies are also found in record collectors' publications.

DJ COPY: Refers to disc jockey or promotional records, which are issued to radio stations. The label color often differs from that of the regular issue, and usually bears the statement "Promotional Copy-Not For Sale" or words of similar import. The pressing quality of some DJ copies is higher than that of the regular issue. Some are pressed from translucent colored vinyl rather than black.

EP: Refers to extended play records. These are usually 45 RPM records containing four or more songs, issued in a stiff cardboard jacket similar to those for LPs. Some EPs were issued in a series of two and three, together containing the contents of an LP issued concurrently. Records issued in the early 1930s having extended playing time, such as some Clarion and Hit of the Week records, are not distinguished herein by the abbreviation EP.

HOME RECORDING DISCS; RECORDING/ AUDITION BLANKS: Frequently found among records of the 1930s-1950s, usually neither the unused disc nor the disc filled with a home or private recording is of interest to collectors. Often boasting cryptic handwritten labels, recordings of family members, amateur singers and musicians, most radio broadcasts, etc., have no value. The only possible exception would be recordings of live or off-the-air performances of desirable artists; and then only if specifically identified, of good recording quality, and not otherwise available to collectors. (Reference recordings of recording/sound studios/laboratories/services, similar physically to home recordings, may offer slightly greater possibilities.) Some of the labels (brand names) of these discs are: Audio Devices, Audiodisc, Presto, National (Hollywood), RCA Victor, Soundcraft, Wilcox-Gay (Recordio).

JAZZ: Again we consult *Webster's New Collegiate Dictionary* to find that jazz is defined as "American music developed ... from ragtime and blues and characterized by syncopated rhythms, contrapuntal ensemble playing, and ... improvisation often with special melodic features (as blue notes) peculiar to the individual interpretation of the player," or "popular dance music influenced by jazz and played in a loud rhythmic manner." You'll know it when you hear it. The second part of the definition is particularly noteworthy. Many records of jazz interest are ordinary fox trots having one or more hot solos by a jazz musician or some unknown stepping out of character and assuming that role. There are jazz records by the orchestras of Jan Garber, Guy Lombardo, and Clyde McCoy, believe it or not. Conversely, labels that suggest the presence of hot music should not necessarily be believed. The Missouri Jazz Band (often encountered on Banner and Regal discs of the 1920s) rarely produced anything sounding like jazz, and they probably weren't from Missouri, either. Take a few weeks off and study Rust's *Jazz Records, 1897-1942*.

JUNKING: The practice of visiting flea markets, garage sales, and second hand stores in quest of records.

LP: The abbreviation of long play, which refers to a record utilizing a finer groove, and therefore containing more playing time, than a single 45 or 78 RPM record of equivalent diameter. Most LPs have several or more songs on each side, but may instead have a single extended performance. Most modern LPs are 12 inches in diameter. Issues from the early 1950s are 10 inches in diameter. Playing speed is 33-1/3 RPM. Some early LPs issued by Edison in the 1920s contained as much as 20 minutes of playing time on each side at 80

RPM! These were failures, technically and commercially, and the records are quite scarce today. Musically, they contain little of interest to most collectors. In the early 1930s, RCA Victor issued 10-inch 33-1/3 RPM records called "Program Transcriptions" (see RCA Victor in **LABELS**). These too were technically inadequate and failed to sell well. Some of these scarce discs do have interesting musical content, and are listed herein.

PICTURE RECORD: This is a record displaying a picture over its entire surface, including the portion normally occupied by a label. The picture, which may be of the artist or a fanciful device (see Vogue picture record in **LABELS**), was printed on paper that was laminated between the clear plastic or vinyl that constituted the playing surface. The current mania for picture records may be unprecedented, but the idea is not new. Vogue picture records attained respectable sales briefly in the late 1940s. Picture records were commercially issued in the early 1930s, most successfully by RCA Victor, but even these are quite scarce (see Figure 1).

Figure 1

PICTURE SLEEVE: A record sleeve of a 45 RPM record having no center hole exposing the record, but rather having a picture, usually of the artist or group. Some picture sleeves are more highly valued than the subject record.

PROMOTIONAL COPY: (See DJ COPY)

"RACE" RECORDS: Records of the 1920s and 1930s produced for the black audience, utilizing primarily Negro talent. Musical content is usually blues, jazz, or gospel. Certain labels were almost entirely race-oriented (Black Swan and Black Patti) and were even owned and managed by blacks. Usually, however, race records were issued by the larger labels in special series bearing a special numerical sequence or even a variation in label design to distinguish the race records from the popular white-oriented series. Hillbilly records were similarly distinguished. Examples are the Victor V-38000 series, the Vocalion 1000 series, the Brunswick 7000 series (usually employing the distinctive "lightning" label design in addition to the special number series), the Columbia 13000-D and 14000-D series, and the Okeh 8000 series. While this musical segregation persisted well into the 1950s, the labels that were then the strongholds of black talent (Federal, DeLuxe, Vee Jay, and Jubilee, to name just a few) became "rhythm and blues" labels rather than race labels. Few white radio stations would play them, and their young, white purchasers would have to secrete them from their parents. The suppression of records was clearly offensive and unwarranted in those days. But today, with recorded pornography rampant, there are no strictures, no outrage!

R&B: (See RHYTHM & BLUES)

RED PLASTIC (or other colored plastic), RED WAX, etc.: Records made of other than the usual black material. The most frequent variation from black is translucent red vinyl. Many 45 RPM records from the 1950s issued in this form are highly prized. Other records were made of translucent green, blue or orange vinyl. Still others were made of opaque colored plastic, in the style of children's records. When a record occurs in both black and colored form, the colored version usually commands a substantial premium over the black. In the 1920s, some 78s were made of other than black material. Perfect and early Vocalion records were a brownish-orange; Pathe-Actuelle was mottled. In the early 1930s, Columbia attempted to spur lagging sales with its "Royal Blue" issues, which today are a favorite of collectors.

REISSUE: A re-release of a previously issued record by the owner of the performance or under license from such owner. A reissue may be on the original label with the same catalog number or with a different catalog number.

The label design may also have changed between the time of the original, or the reissue may be on an entirely different label than the original issue (see Figures 2 and 3.) Veteran collectors may note that some of the "reissues" are actually alternate takes issued for the first time years after being recorded. For guidance in recognizing reissues of 45 RPM vocal group records, consult Lou Silvani's *Collecting Rare Records* and Jeff Kreiter's *Group Collector's Record Price Guide.*

Figure 2   **Figure 3**

RHYTHM & BLUES (R&B): Music of the 1950s essentially for the Negro audience. R&B evolved from blues, jazz, and jump blues. This music was a major force in the emergence of rock 'n' roll and rockabilly.

ROCKABILLY: Rock 'n' roll sung by a hillbilly-sounding singer-, up-tempo country music. Other elements are a "slappin' bass," "hot" guitar and/or piano, and echo effects. Back-up voices or horns detract from desirability, according to rockabilly purists. The style is defined by early Elvis Presley records, as well as by such artists as Jerry Lee Lewis, Carl Perkins, and more obscure rockers such as Sonny Fisher and Pat Cupp.

ROCK 'N' ROLL: Popular, usually up-tempo, hard-driving music with solid rhythm, often having frantic vocals, wailing saxophones, hot piano, and elements of hillbilly boogie and jump blues and rhythm and blues from which it evolved. Although rock 'n' roll is identified with the 1950s and such artists as Chuck Berry, Elvis Presley, and Bill Haley, rock 'n' roll was actually being performed several years earlier by rhythm and blues artists such as Jackie Brenston and The Dominoes. Indeed, a case can be made for the existence of rock 'n' roll years, even decades, prior to the 1950s. Morgan Wright has done so, with a two-CD compilation of recordings from 1929 to 1951 (*Rock Before Elvis, Before Little Richard, Before Chuck Berry, Bo Diddley or Bill Haley,* Hoy Hoy CD 4050-2).

78 RPM (78s): The playing speed of most pre-1950 single records. Actually, many early 78 RPM records were intended to be played at 80 RPM, or some other speed, but these are treated in this guide as 78s, with no distinction.

TEST PRESSING: A record pressed to give the artist and/or record company executive a chance to hear and judge the merits of a recording and its commercial suitability. Test pressings were not distributed to the public. The record may be pressed on one side or on both sides. The label is usually plain white with the information handwritten, often cryptically, or printed (see Figures 4 and 4a). Test pressings should not be confused with the ubiquitous home recordings on "labels" such as Wilcox-Gay and Audio Disc.

   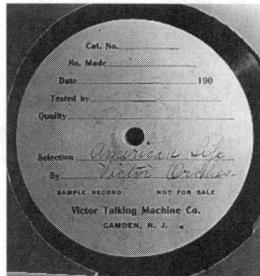

Figure 4   **Figure 4A**

The edge of the disc may be somewhat jagged and irregular, rather than smooth. All test pressings are scarce, but not every test pressing is valuable or highly collectible. If the next one you find is a previously unissued jazz, blues, or rockabilly performance, or an alternate take of an issued performance, let me know about it!

Organization of This Book

The main portion of this book is divided into four sections, each representing a genre or group of genres as well as a general time period during which the records were produced. The four sections are:

JAZZ: Jazz, dance bands, big bands, swing, and personality. These are primarily 78 RPM records from 1900 to about 1950.

BLUES: Blues and Rhythm & Blues records, primarily 78s, from the 1920s to the early 1950s.

COUNTRY/WESTERN: Country/western, hillbilly, old-time singing, string bands, and fiddling, primarily 78 RPM records from the 1920s to the early 1950s.

RHYTHM & BLUES: Rhythm & blues, blues, rock 'n' roll, rockabilly, etc. These records are primarily 45 RPMs, EPs and LPs, with selected 78s, mainly from the 1950s to about 1965.

The inclusion of a given artist in a particular section is often a matter of arbitrary choice. For example,

many records by blues artists are found in the jazz section due to the fact that their accompaniment is of jazz interest. Some artists are found in more than one section. When recordings were made in the 1930s and also in the 1950s, that artist might appear in both sections: Lonnie Johnson is an example. Use the artist index in the back of the book to find all listed records by an artist even when that artist appears in more than one section.

Within each category, the listings are alphabetical by artist. The listings for each artist are presented alphabetically by label, and by catalog number, from lowest to highest, within each label. This may not reflect the chronological order of issue. For example, Bluebirds are listed before Victors; but the Victors are almost always earlier issues than the Bluebirds. And the Gennett 3000 numbers are later than the 5000 numbers. The true order of recording and issue is left to the discographies. The intention here is to provide ease of usage.

Some listings embrace a number of issues on the same label, for example:

Bluebird, most other issues . . . . 5.00 - 8.00

Such a listing, while consisting of records of minimal scarcity and value, may well include some discs so common that they are virtually unsaleable to any real record collector.

Catalog number prefixes and suffixes (numbers or letters) common to all or most issues on a label or series are usually omitted. Thus, RCA Victor 47-6604 is listed as RCA Victor 6604. The prefix "47-" (or "20-" in the case of 78s) appears on the majority of RCA Victor 45 RPM records. Also omitted are the ubiquitous suffixes "-A" and "-B" (and variants such as "-L" and "-R" on Edison). Prefixes and suffixes do serve to distinguish between seemingly overlapping numerical series on Columbia records, and are therefore included.

All listings reflect the names as credited on the actual records, without regard to whether such names are actual or pseudonyms. Cross-references are kept to a minimum, it being assumed that interested collectors will seek any further information about pseudonyms (and any other matters beyond the scope of this reference, such as personnels, recording dates, additional recordings, reissues) from the discographics and other sources listed in the bibliography. (*A Guide to Pseudonyms on American Records, 1892-1942* by Allan Sutton, not yet in my library, would seem to be useful. To obtain this volume, inquire of booksellers listed in the back of this guide.)

Many records, especially the earlier 78s, have different artists on each side. Often only one side (the one deemed of interest to collectors) is listed in this book. It is advisable to check for listings of both sides of any dual-artist disc of possible interest.

Where to Buy, Sell or Trade Records

Every record collector, whether novice or veteran, obtains at least some discs by junking. The more avid the collector, the more time, effort and expense he or she devotes to junking. This is true even though the resultant finds often aren't worth the trouble, either for their musical enjoyment or their value. But there's always the possibility of that great find: King Oliver on Gennett; Charlie Spand on Paramount; Hank Williams on Sterling; Elvis Presley on Sun; or maybe a whole box of goodies. And getting up before daybreak to get first pick at the flea market or an estate sale certainly increases your chances!

Most collectors are not content to leave the acquisition of their wants to the fortuities of junking. The best source of collectible records is other collectors and dealers (in many instances the same persons). Often, a knowledgeable collector is easier to deal with than a casual or one-time vendor of records is. I've seen common, middle-of-the-road records at flea markets priced at $5.00 each, accompanied by a warning against handling the treasures! To get in contact with other collectors and/or dealers, begin with record collectors' publications (see the listing in the back of this guide).

Some leading record publications are largely marketplaces for selling, buying and trading records. It is advisable to utilize those most appropriate to your interests. If you specialize in rockabilly, you'll find little of interest in *VJM's Jazz & Blues Mart*. *Goldmine* contains little for the collector of Edison discs. Once you've gotten familiar with the appropriate publications and the terms and conditions of transacting business with advertisers, you might consider advertising your wants. In addition, you could contact other advertisers, particularly those who invite "want lists."

Record collectors' conventions have become fairly common in larger metropolitan areas. The publications usually contain a number of advertisements and notices about forthcoming conventions. The crowds often present at these conventions attest to the high level of enthusiasm record collectors have for their hobby. Nowhere was this more evident than at the record flea market (termed a "bizarre ritual" in *Goldmine*, November, 1980) that was, until several years ago, held in the parking lot of Capitol Records in Hollywood, California; it began in the middle of the night, and wouldn't break up until late morning. Today, the largest convention is *The Austin Record Convention*, held each spring and fall in Austin, Texas. These conventions appeal increasingly to collectors of modern records and peripheral memorabilia (albums, picture discs, and CDs of the 1960s and later). Usually there will be little of interest to the collector of vintage 78s.

Many cities are home to stores specializing in collectors' records. Unfortunately, the majority of these shops do not advertise in record collector publications. I have visited such shops in Bloomington, Indiana; Chicago; Detroit; Fort Worth, Texas; Glendale, California; Salt Lake City; San Diego and Santa Monica, California, and elsewhere. It might be helpful to go to the Internet.

Yes, it's true. I have bought a computer, and have gone "on-line" since the fifth edition of this book. If this "walking anachronism", whose motto is "not only am I not with it, I'm against it" finally accepted high-tech, there must have been good reason. And there was: A great deal of trading and information exchange in vintage records is now on the Internet. There are many thousands of records offered at any given time on *eBay*, including three to four thousand 78s. Usually, there are some very desirable discs to be found. Caution is advised with regard to grading and descriptions of records, which are largely the offerings of persons having little knowledge of grading or other elements of appropriately describing records. Pictures accompanying offerings often disclose defects and excessive wear that are not conveyed by written descriptions. Many record dealers, publications and sources now have e-mail addresses and Web sites. Mine are: **docks@texas.net** and **http://docks.home.texas.net** .

Valuation of Records

The prices in this guide are estimates of what records might reasonably be expected to bring in transactions between knowledgeable buyers and sellers. Most estimates are stated as a range ($10.00 to $15.00) rather than a specific figure. This method of pricing recognizes the partial validity of the widely held contention that it is impossible at this time, given the fluid and formative state of the market, to assign definite values to records. This assessment remains true, even though this and other price guides have been in print for over twenty years. The usefulness of price guides is greatest in identifying collectible records, and in suggesting relative desirability and value.

Although most of the really desirable records are bought and sold by mail, often at auction, the prices given here are not intended to reflect the highest sale prices or winning bids. A given record might bring $20.00 in one auction and $7.00 in the next. Indeed, in the same auction, the array of bids often demonstrates a wide disparity in bidders' estimations of value; and auction bidders are generally fairly knowledgeable. Widely differing prices on the same record are also found when comparing set sale lists or minimum bid figures in auction lists. Certainly these dealers in records must also be regarded as fairly knowledgeable. So, what is any record really worth? The only sure answer is, whatever you can get for it.

The casual seller of records, such as the flea market or garage sale vendor, who has no real knowledge of appreciation of records, who does not intelligently and selectively acquire records, who does not properly organize and preserve them, and who does not seek, by appropriate advertising, knowledgeable collectors as customers, will have difficulty realizing even a small fraction of the prices quoted herein for the better records, except, *possibly*, by auctioning on-line. There is nothing unfair about this situation. One not disposed to invest the time, effort and expense (beyond the cost of a price guide) necessary to deal with some expertise should perhaps be in another business. I have seen several such record vendors, compelled by economic realities, make just that decision.

Access to the on-line auction process, especially *eBay*, does give the casual seller of records a greater chance than heretofore of realizing a fair price for his desirable records. But, unless some basic steps are taken, the results are often disappointing. Records should be accurately described, with grading leaning toward conservative; digital pictures should be provided, and they should be clear and not blurry (in fairness, I have no standing to criticize others' digital photography!); and secure, sturdy packing should be over-emphasized. Laxity in any of these practices will probably lead to refunds, returns, and complaints ("negative feedback"), rather than a mutually satisfactory transaction.

One factor contributing to the difficulty in valuing records with more certainty is the reluctance of many collectors and dealers to divulge prices they have paid or received for records. Several prominent collectors and dealers I have contacted in the years since this book was conceived have expressly refused to furnish pricing information; a few others were very helpful, but only on condition of anonymity. The appearance of this book engendered hostile and unjustly critical letters, and even personal attacks. I can only conclude that some of these critics feel that they have a vested interest in being able to buy rare records for token sums, and that my dissemination of pricing information constitutes an infringement.

On the other hand, there is one area in which many dealers have no reluctance about publicizing record prices: in their own auctions. Anyone who peruses the ads in record publications will find that many of the offerings have "minimum bids" for some or all of the records listed. In some cases, these minimums are reasonable reserves, which will foreclose submission of bids that would only waste the time of both bidder and seller. But in most cases minimums are more like maximums, set at levels higher than the offeror thinks the records would bring without his bidding floors. I have seen "minimum bids" several times the amount comparable records have sold for in my own auctions and elsewhere. Access to on-line auctions allows users to observe that a large portion of records offered remain unsold, because no bid met the minimum or the hidden "reserve". Whether sellers employing these maximum minimums are motivated by greed, uncertainty as to their own pricing knowledge, or actual belief that their records are worth the exorbitant sums stated, no one can say. Perhaps if more bidders and would-be bidders would question the purpose and validity of the practice, sellers would be more likely to run sales that are sales, or auctions that are auctions.

Finally, I will address the criticism of those who have said that my prices are too low: that is, the criticisms of knowledgeable dealers and collectors. Those seeking to increase the value or marketability of certain records or categories of records in which they have an interest will find no accommodation here. First, I repeat, the intention is not to reflect the highest prices realized for records (i.e., winning bids at auction). Second, information about pricing should be submitted with specificity in a timely manner, as to be useful in revising this book, not as vague criticism after the fact. Third, it will become obvious from perusal of this book that many drastic price changes have been made in response to information received since the publication of the fifth edition. While most of the new information was supplied to me by others, some was the result of my own auctions and sales. When a record received a number of bids far above prices stated in this book, I had to suppress my embarrassment, accept the exorbitant sums, and resolve to do better next edition.

Grading of Records

The condition of a record is of paramount importance. An apparently new, (who can be certain?) unplayed copy might be worth many times the price of a worn junkshop copy. Indeed, a very worn or damaged copy may not be saleable at all. This is particularly true of common, low-value records.

The prices quoted in this guide are for records in excellent condition. "Excellent" is part of the standard grading code that has been in use for many years. Other standard grading terms follow.

NEW (N): Apparently unplayed and showing no signs of wear.

EXCELLENT (E): Showing only slight wear. Playing surfaces still retain much of their original shine. Surface noise is minimal.

VERY GOOD (V): Somewhat more worn than an excellent record, slight-grayness appearing in the grooves, especially in louder passages. Still a fairly clean and acceptable copy. Surface and extraneous noise is noticeable, but does not overwhelm the music.

GOOD (G): A misnomer. A "good" record is really not so good. It shows considerable wear and usage, grayness in the grooves, random mars and light abrasions from a sleeveless existence. Surface noise is prominent enough to impair enjoyment of music.

FAIR (F) and **POOR (P)** indicate the lowest grades of the condition code. Since only the rarest records would be saleable in these grades, they appear infrequently.

Plus and minus signs are often suffixed to above grades to indicate a somewhat better or worse grade, when appropriate.

Another grading code is often employed by persons and publications concerned with the music of the 1950s and later (primarily 45s, EPs, and LPs): Mint (M) is used in place of New (N); Very Good (VG) corresponds more closely to Excellent (E) than to the older system's Very Good (V); and Good (G) is roughly equivalent to the older system's Very Good (V).

In addition to the wear factor, defects and impairments can drastically affect the value and saleability of a record. Those typically affecting the playing surface are cracks, digs, and warps. A crack usually renders a record practically worthless; even the value of a rarity is generally reduced to a nominal sum by the presence of a crack. This is true even if the crack is "tight" and negotiable by a needle. There are exceptions, such as "lamination cracks," which affect only one side of a laminated record (having a cardboard core between the playing surfaces) such as Columbia or Okeh; these cracks severely affect, but do not necessarily destroy, the record's value. With most defects, the reduction of the record's value is a matter of degree. Is that scratch inaudible, or does it make the tone-arm jump half an inch? Does that dig allow the needle to negotiate the groove, or does the affected passage repeat? Other defects, such as damage to, or stickers on the label, affect only appearance and not play, but this can be very important. In short, the acknowledgment of defects is an essential part of the grading process.

Most auction lists and price lists will contain an explanation of the grading system and symbols used. It is also important that the system be applied fairly and objectively. Often it is not: overgrading has become commonplace in the collectors' record market. A reputable dealer will make an adjustment or refund if a record proves to be erroneously graded.

Trends and Fads in Record Collecting

Record collecting has undergone great change over the decades. Prior to 1935, most record collectors favored classical and operatic records. In the 1930s and 1940s, jazz and blues records (particularly blues records with jazz accompaniments) became the primary area of interest. Prior to the era of the LP as a vehicle for reissuing, some original 78s commanded prices higher than they did in the 1970s and 1980s (particularly if the decline in the value of the dollar is taken into account). The extensive reissuing of jazz undoubtedly affected the market for the original 78s. Many old-time collectors lost interest or relinquished their 78s in favor of LP reissues. On the other hand, many collectors insisted on owning the original 78s, including collectors who became acquainted with the classic recordings through reissues. In recent years, demand for, and prices of original 78s have increased, despite (or partly because of?) the proliferation of reissues, now largely on CD. Additional comments about the effects of advances in recording technology will follow.

Interest in jazz records has shifted somewhat in recent years. Demand for original 78 RPM jazz classics by big names has peaked, or even waned. The most intense demand, and the largest price increases, are for some of the more obscure bands, such as regional or "territory" bands. A record by Eddie & Sugar Lou's Hotel Tyler Orchestra will draw more bids than most Duke Ellington records of the same era. Also, there is increased interest in the semi-hot dance bands of the 1920s and 1930s.

Perhaps the most intense demand for early 78s is for obscure country blues by such artists as William Harris and Robert Johnson. The records are scarce to rare, and are infrequently offered (most auctions contain few or none), and even more infrequently found. Pursued by a relatively small number of hardcore, knowledgeable collectors, the records, when offered, command some of the highest prices in the world of collectible records. Yet, if the scarcity of the records (some are estimated to exist in quantities fewer than ten) is considered, one can only imagine what would happen if demand were to increase, and records were to gain the recognition of certain other collectibles.

Interest in early country and western records developed considerably later than did the mania for jazz. The reissuing of this music has also lagged far behind, and still has a long way to go to reach the point, which might be said of jazz, where most significant performances have been reissued. Contrary to the situation with jazz 78s, the demand for these records (and consequently their values) has yet to peak, much less decline. The long expected appearance of a country-western discography is certain to heighten interest in this field of collecting.

Seemingly the most active category of record collecting is the music of the 1950s and 1960s, including rock 'n' roll, rhythm and blues, rockabilly, and blues. In the early 1960s, rhythm and blues records, particularly vocal groups, were already being collected seriously, and obscure discs of only a few years earlier were commanding respectable premiums. Interest

spread to single-artist rhythm and blues, blues, rockabilly, and rock 'n' roll obscurities. Artists such as Elvis Presley, The Beatles, The Beach Boys, and The Four Seasons, have a following bordering on fanaticism, with some collectors seeking any tangible object relating to the artist, recorded or otherwise (see comment preceding Elvis Presley listing). Notable among many of the newer crop of collectors is their penchant for acquiring, displaying and preserving visual, graphic art souvenirs of recording artists, relegating the audio aspect to secondary importance. Thus, many albums remain sealed, and Elvis' Sun records find homes on collectors' walls. The jacket of an album is more important than the record in some cases (see The Beatles and Frank Ifield, in listings); picture sleeves can be worth more than the subject record; picture records find a market at exorbitant prices.

Advances in technology do not necessarily affect the market for vintage records. According to some, as CDs supplant LPs, there is a mad scramble underway to buy up LPs. But even if this is the case, in the long term the situation will be about the same as that surrounding old 78s. Each record will be regarded as collectible according to its recorded content, not the obsolescence of its technology. There are plenty of the thick Edison discs, discontinued in 1929, that can be bought for as little as two or three dollars because they lack the musical content that makes a record collectible. There are millions of "junk" 78s around, and there will be millions of junk LPs for many years to come.

This is a good place to insert my belief that the quality of the music recorded varies inversely with the technology used to record it. I will not engage in any correspondence seeking further explanation or seeking to dispute this matter. Suffice it to say that this book, ending as it does with the records of the mid-1960s, avoids documenting the transition from music to decibel-laden electronic anarchy.

The following information is presented in answer to some frequently asked questions. Answers to other questions might be pursued by reviewing the bibliography and the publications and sources listings at the back of this book. As a last resort, write to me.

Playing 78 RPM Records

An old wind-up player, such as those on which early 78s were originally played (and destroyed!), will play your records. If you don't care about the fact that your records will be damaged somewhat each time the nail-like needle negotiates the grooves, you'll be satisfied with the result, particularly when playing early acoustically recorded discs (pre-1925). When playing later electrically recorded records, the reproduction afforded by mechanical means will be rather tinny, and most of the richer sound provided by electrical recording will be lost. Also, playing records from the swing era and later on the old wind-ups seems incongruous. But if you want to play Perry Como records on a Victrola, that's your privilege. You'll save money on electricity, and get some exercise. See your local antiques dealer or flea marketer.

For the person wanting better sound and longer life from records, I recommend getting an older children's record player, many of which have 78 RPM speed; or better yet, get an older schoolroom record player. The schoolroom record players are more durable and offer better reproduction than the usual children's player. Sometimes these can be found at flea markets, at auction on the Internet, and for sale by dealers in vintage records and supplies (see Publications and Sources section of this book). An inquiry of your local school board, or whomever deals with school property and/or surplus property, could be fruitful.

Playing 78s on more sophisticated equipment, such as older stereo players (which often have 78 RPM speed), is usually less satisfactory, without special modifications and adaptations. Avid collectors of 78s, particularly those who want to do clean taping, obtain specially modified cartridges, needles (styli), and equalizers, from sources such as those listed in the back of this book.

Playing Edison Records

Edison records (the quarter-inch-thick ones) were recorded by a different process than ordinary 78s (vertically rather than laterally). They cannot-indeed, must not-be played on an ordinary wind-up record player. No sound will be reproduced, and irreparable damage to the record will result from just a single attempt at playing. Playing on high-fidelity or stereo players will not damage the record (at least, not noticeably), but will not give satisfactory results. Proper playing on high-fidelity or stereo players is accomplished with the use of special needles (styli), and specially "strapped" cartridges. See the sources listing for suppliers of this special equipment. If you

don't have this modified equipment, or an Edison phonograph (or other make designed for vertical recordings), you will not be able to obtain satisfactory results from Edison records.

Care and Restoration of Records

CLEANING RECORDS: Dusty and/or dirty records can be improved by washing in lukewarm (never hot) water with a mild liquid soap (such as Ivory Liquid). Rubbing with a soft cloth or paper towel in a circular motion (to follow the direction of the grooves) might help eliminate dirt deposited within the grooves. In more difficult cases, a soft-bristled brush might be more effective. Note that 78 RPM records will withstand a more vigorous scrubbing without the possibility of adding new scuffs and scratches than is the case with modern LPs, EPs, and 45 RPM records (vinyl microgroove records). Records should be cleaned and dried as quickly as possible, avoiding prolonged soaking that could result in label damage or even removal of the label: a common occurrence in the case of the thick Edison discs, more about which follows. Rinse, dry (with paper or other towel) sufficiently to take up most of the water, and set in a dish-drying rack to complete the drying process.

There are collectors who advise never to put water on Edison records, because, in addition to the possible removal of labels, there is a risk of causing flaking edges and lamination cracks if any moisture finds its way into the core of the record. (Presumably the same risk exists with other laminated records, such as Columbia.) A preferred method of cleaning laminated records is to use Windex applied to the cleaning cloth (not sprayed directly onto the record).

Commercial record cleaning preparations, sprays, anti-static applications and the like vary in effectiveness. In the case of records with dirty surfaces, commercial preparations are largely ineffective and should be used only after the above washing procedure.

There is no cleaning or restoration method that will completely remove all dirt from the grooves of records. Perhaps someone will adapt ultrasonic cleaning (such as the process used by jewelers to clean rings, etc.) to record cleaning. I'd be interested in the results. Records that have been subjected to moisture (floods, etc.) are particularly difficult to improve.

Microgroove records are more difficult, as a rule, to improve to a satisfactory level than are 78s.

SCRATCHED AND CRACKED RECORDS: There is no effective method of removing or minimizing the effects of scratches, scuffs, digs, and other defects resulting from the extensive use (or abuse, often from not replacing records in their sleeves/jackets) of records. The application of waxes, shoe polish, or the like might make a record look better to an unwary buyer, but it will not result in any net gain in playing enjoyment because the music will be dampened along with the extraneous noise. Also, the needle used to play records so treated will quickly become disabled by waxy buildup.

Cracks cannot be removed or mended in any way that will truly restore a record. If a crack is "tight," and the record is still playable, some protection against further damage might be afforded by application of an appropriate glue to the edge of the record (never within the playing surface). A cracked record has little, if any, value, and no efforts at repair or restoration can change that fact.

WARPED RECORDS: 78 RPM records can be straightened by at least two methods (note that the objective is to render playable unplayable records, not to render records totally free of audio and visual distortion, such as tell-tale heat marks):

(1) **THE RECIPE:** Basically, this is baking the record in an oven. The amount of time, as well as the temperature, are variable, depending upon the oven used, how many records are being baked, etc. Before trying this method on any prized disc, would-be shellac chefs are strongly advised to experiment with valueless records. The success of this method depends upon the fact that after a certain time at a certain temperature, most 78 RPM records (of the old shellac type) relax and become completely pliable, like a pancake. While in this state, records can be "poured" onto a perfectly smooth, flat surface and there be allowed to again become rigid.

The following procedure is suggested (again, experimentation with regard to time and temperature is advised):

A) Preheat oven to 200 degrees.

B) Place record to be straightened on a flat, smooth-surfaced utensil (the back of a cookie sheet, etc.) and place it in the oven.

C) In about two and a half minutes, look in the oven. If the record has "relaxed," and appears flat (no

vestiges of the warpage remain, even at the very edge), quickly remove it from the oven.

D) "Pour" (allow to slide) the now-soft, pliable record onto a perfectly smooth, cool surface (a cutting board, a piece of glass or marble), making sure that no part overhangs the edge.

E) Allow the record to cool somewhat in this position. Do not try to lift it or move it about. It will soon lose its pliability and become rigid (and flat, if you've done it right).

NOTE: If, when you pour the record onto the flat surface, some warping remains, you probably didn't allow the record to become hot enough to really relax. Try again. On the other hand, if you found that the record wouldn't pour, but rather remained stuck to the utensil, you've overcooked it, and have damaged the record irreparably.

(2) **SUNBATHING:** This method is slower, but involves basically the same principle. There is less risk of overcooking and ruining the record. Requirement: Bright sunshine.

A) Place the warped record on a piece of marble or thick glass.

B) Place another piece of glass over the record.

C) Put this sandwich in a place where it will remain undisturbed and will receive the sunshine.

D) Depending upon the temperature, brightness of the sun, etc., the record will be straightened.

E) When record is sufficiently straightened, leave it on the marble or glass and allow to cool in a shady place.

This method might also be tried on vinyl (45s, EPs, LPs) records, but the rate of success is less promising than on 78s. Microgroove records (45s, LPs, EPs) are more difficult to straighten. The application of weight for long periods (weeks, perhaps) while maintaining the record in a completely flat state has been known to work. Daring and skillful record restorers have used electric hair dryers, deftly applied, with varying degrees of success (and failure).

Mailing Records

Many correspondents express apprehension about mailing records, particularly 78s. (Even postal clerks have told me that records can't be mailed; can be mailed, but not insured; that there is no special postal rate applicable to records; and other nonsense.)

Records may be mailed, without undue risk of damage, if properly packed, and there is a "Media Mail" rate, lower than regular parcel post ("standard mail") and in most cases applicable to sound recordings. This special rate applies only to domestic parcels; there is no special rate for records sent to addressees outside of the United States. Packing is largely a matter of common sense. A sturdy carton should be used, large enough to hold the records with packing material on all sides (edge, top, and bottom). The records should not be able to shift about within the box. To get the "Media Mail" rate, clearly mark the parcel "Contents: Phonograph Records," and "Media Mail," and make sure that you are given this rate. Overcharges are common, even when the parcel is clearly labeled. One more rule (it shouldn't be necessary to say the following, but my experience dictates that it is): No records should be sent to anyone without prior authorization and approval. Unsolicited shipments of records, which usually prove to be unwanted junk, create no obligation on the part of the recipient, who need not acknowledge or pay for same.

Record Labels

What's on a record label? Referring to Figure 5, you'll find the name of the label (Columbia) and the logo; the song title in English and Spanish ("Mi Muchacha Linda"); composer/lyricist credits (Fulcher); the name of the artist/group/orchestra (Fletcher Henderson & His Orchestra); the record catalog number (2586-D); the master number (151276); the type of music and whether vocal or instrumental (Fox Trot, Vocal Refrain); copyright, patent or trademark registration numbers of dates; and the name and address of the manufacturer. Labels may also contain a picture of the artist (see Figure 7); the suggested retail price; and occasionally a release date (see Figure 8, "11-25" at the 3 o'clock position indicates November 1925); or a designation such as "Race Record" (see Figure 9). A common feature is a slogan referring to the use of electrical recording processes, such as "Electrically Recorded," "Electrical Process," "Super Electrical Recorded," "Viva-Tonal Recording," "Electrobeam," "Orthophonic Recording," "Truetone," and others. Starting in the early 1930s, an admonition against use for radio broadcast was commonly used (see Figure 6).

Information usually not found on record labels includes the date of recording, or release of the record. There are exceptions, such as Gennett (see Figure 8), Champion, and Mercury, and there are other instances where the date of release appears cryptically, such as the mid-1930s Banner, Melotone, Oriole, Perfect, and Romeo issues. With knowledge of various record labels, the date of their issue, and their usage of master numbers and catalog numbers, the collector can make a reasonably close estimate of recording and issue dates. Referring to a discography or to Steven Barr's *The (Almost) Complete 78 RPM Record Dating Guide* (1980), will provide the best information. Normally, dates appearing on the label relate to copyright, patent and trademark registration, and have little relation to the recording or issue date. For example, the 1921 copyright date on Regal records might appear on a record recorded and issued several years later.

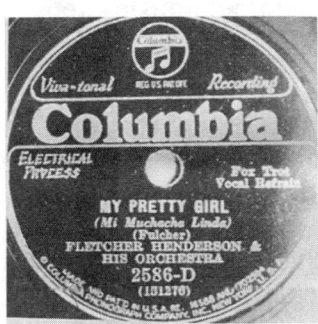 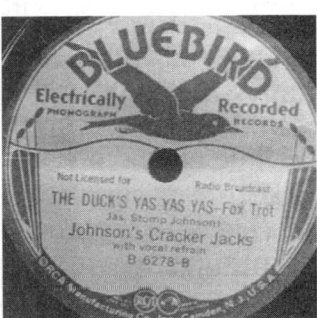

Figure 5   **Figure 6**

Figure 7

Figure 8   **Figure 9**

Personnels usually didn't appear on record labels until the late 1930s, when they were included on some original jazz and swing issues, principally by Columbia and Victor (which even had a special "Swing Classic" series).

Labels on collectors' reissues are likely to include personnels, recording dates, and the name and number of the original issue label, and many even credit the name of the artist differently than did the original issues. These reissues often were sold in album sets: Brunswick, Columbia and RCA Victor engaged in considerable amount of this type of reissuing in the late 1930s and 1940s. Few collectors' reissues will be found listed in this reference because of their minimal value, but they do contain many classic performances of vintage jazz that are practically unobtainable as original issues.

Apart from the musical value of records, labels themselves are often of interest for their artistic and historical value. Song titles can be amusing relics of different times and cultures. Some collectors even decorate their walls with interesting labels and titles.

Certain labels have an unusual attraction, or even mystique, which motivates their aficionados to collect by label rather than by artist or type of music. Most collectors are guilty of this tendency to some degree, even if only to the extent that they have favorite labels. But some collectors seek to obtain every issue on a certain label, regardless of artist or musical content. The label most commonly collected in this manner is the Sun label, which in the 1950s assumed a major role in producing first-class rockabilly and rock 'n' roll with such artists as Elvis Presley, Carl Perkins and Jerry Lee Lewis. Of course, not everything issued on that label was worthy of collecting, but collectors have paid substantial sums for scarce but musically mediocre Sun records in order to fill a numerical gap in their collections. Other labels of the 1950s collected in this manner include Atlantic, Federal, and Vee Jay, and probably any rhythm and blues label you can think of has its specialists. Among the 78 RPM labels, some of the most popular among label collectors are the Vogue picture record, Columbia 14000-D (Race) series, Victor 23000 and V-38000 series, Gennett, Paramount, and Okeh 8000 series. In recent years, Edison records, both the thick and thin types, have become the focus of some label collectors. Few collectors of the early 78s are really in earnest, however, about obtaining a complete numerical run as are Sun collectors. Incidentally, for the enlightenment,

amusement and perhaps frustration of Sun collectors, I offer the following photo of a Sun record from the early 1900s (having no relationship, of course, to the 1950s-1960s Memphis product).

SCARCE AND UNUSUAL LABELS: A relatively small number of collectors strive to obtain as many different labels as they can, often without regard to musical content. Auction lists of vintage 78s occasionally offer a "scarce and unusual label" (that's what I call it) section. A scarce label such as Autograph may bring several dollars even though the pipe-organ solo it offers is of no musical interest to the bidders. Other scarce labels (early 78s) include Black Patti, Black Swan, Blu-Disc, Buddy, Connorizcd, Claxtonola, Edison (thin), Electradisk, Everybody's, Gennett (Electrobeam), Harmograph, Herschel Gold Seal, Herwin, Hudson, Hy-Tone, Meritt, Mitchell, National (Iowa City label), New Flexo, Nordskog, Odeon (U.S. issue), Parlophone (U.S. issue), Q.R.S., Rich-Tone, Stark, Superior, Sunshine, Timely Tunes, and Up-To-Date. Some of these are so scarce that photographs for this book have only recently come to hand: two or three are still lacking. Some scarce 1950s labels include After Hours, Blue Lake, Chance, Club-51, Drexel, Great Lakes, Jax, J-V-B, Luna, Meteor, Parrot, Recorded in Hollywood, Red Robin, S.R.C., Sabre, States, Tin Pan Alley, and United. These are by no means all of the scarce labels. Particularly in the 1950s, a local or regional label might have been in existence for only one or two issues; the labels preceding are better known or of longer duration, but still scarce.

Following are some scarce labels that have value to label collectors regardless of musical content or lack thereof. All (except Vogue Picture Record, which is from the late 1940s) are pre1940, and should not be confused with more modern labels having the same or similar names. Prices are minimums, for the least desirable issues on each label; "better" issues, which should be found in the main listings, can be worth more, even multiples of the following prices. Labels should be free of significant damage (writing, stickers, needle scratches, stains, tears, etc.). While it is normally even more important that the playing surface of a record be free of defects or impairments, in the case of scarce labels a record might be saleable, even if unplayable, if labels are nice and clean. The price will be reduced, but some value remains in a good wall ornament.

Ajax (Canadian)...............................$10.00 - $15.00
Aurora (Canadian) ....15.00 -   20.00
Autograph (Marsh Laboratories, Chicago)
....5.00 -   8.00
Berliner (7-inch, single-sided, embossed 'label')
....15.00 -   30.00
Black Patti (Chicago Record Co.)...100.00 -   up
Black Swan ....10.00 -   15.00
Blu-Disc (#T-1001 through T-1009) 75.00 -   up
Buddy (six cities mentioned on label)
....20.00 -   30.00
Carnival (John Wanamker, New York)
....15.00 -   25.00
Chappelle & Stinnette ....50.00 -   75.00
Clover (Nutmeg Record Co.)..............5.00 -   8.00
Connorized ....5.00 -   8.00
Dandy...5.00 -   8.00
Davega ....4.00 -   8.00
Davis & Schwegler ....10.00 -   20.00
Domestic (Philadelphia).....................8.00 -   12.00
Edison ("Needle Cut Electric").........15.00 -   25.00
Edison (Long-playing, 24-minute)....20.00 -   30.00
Edison (Long-playing, 40-minute)....30.00 -   50.00
Edison (Sample record, 12-inch) ......50.00 -   up
Electradisk (RCA Victor product) ......4.00 -   8.00
Everybodys ....5.00 -   10.00
Flexo (small, flexible disc, by Pacific Coast Record
        Corp., San Francisco)............15.00 -   25.00
Golden (Los Angeles) ....10.00 -   20.00
Gramophone (see Berliner)
Harmograph ....10.00 -   15.00
Herschel Gold Seal ....10.00 -   20.00
Herwin (St. Louis) ....10.00 -   15.00
Hollywood Record (California) ....7.00 -   12.00
Homestead (Chicago Mail Order).......7.00 -   12.00
Improved (7-inch, single-sided)........20.00 -   30.00
Kalamazoo (single-sided) ....15.00 -   20.00
Marathon (7-inch, by Nutmeg Record Corp.)
....10.00 -   20.00
Meritt (Kansas City) ....50.00 -   up
Moxie ....20.00 -   30.00
Mozart (St. Louis).............................7.00 -   12.00
National (Iowa City) ....5.00 -   10.00
New Flexo (small, flexible disc).......10.00 -   20.00

Nordskog...15.00 -   30.00
Odeon (American "ONY" series) .....10.00 -   20.00
Paramount (12000-13000 series)......10.00 -   15.00
Parlophone (American "PNY" series)
....10.00 -   20.00
Par-O-Ket (7-inch, embossed "label")
....10.00 -   15.00
Pennington (Bamberger & Co., N J.)
....10.00 -   15.00
Q. R. S. (Cova Recording Co., New York)
....8.00 -   12.00
RCA Victor "Program Transcription" 8.00 -   12.00
Rialto (Rialto Music House, Chicago)
....20.00 -   30.00
Stark ....7.00 -   12.00
Sunrise (RCA Victor product) ....30.00 -   50.00
Sunset ("Made in California U.S.A.") 5.00 -   10.00
Sunshine (St. Petersburg, Florida) ....10.00 -   20.00
Sunshine (Los Angeles) ....50.00 -   up
Superior..10.00 -   15.00
Timely Tunes (RCA Victor product) 10.00 -   20.00
Tremont...4.00 -   8.00
Up-To-Date.......................................75.00 -   up
Vogue (The Picture Record) ....15.00 -   30.00
Yerkes..15.00 -   20.00

Knowledge of record labels is helpful in the intelligent acquisition of records, whether such acquisition consists of bidding in auctions by mail or just junking in local second-hand stores. if you know your labels, you're not likely to bid $50.00 on Bix & His Rhythm Jugglers on English Brunswick only to find out later that original issue is on Gennett. And you won't buy Chess (LP) 1433 by The Flamingos with an orange label if you require originals only (see Chess photos). Errors in junking purchases usually involve no great financial loss if it turns out that the supposed $20.00 record you've gotten for $.25 proves to be third pressing. But label knowledge can be handy when time is of the essence: for example, on your weekly visit to the Salvation Army Thrift Store you might find that a local radio station has just donated its record library, but another record sharpshooter is also there, shuffling vinyl. Of course, it's always a relief to find that he has beaten you to a choice copy of "The Chipmunk Song," leaving you to settle for all that unheard-of junk on labels such as Chess, Parrot and Red Robin. Or maybe you'd prefer "The Chipmunk Song."

Labels

Labels are presented in the following photo section in alphabetical order, without regard to vintage. 78s, 45s, EPs, and LPs are illustrated in the following section. For a given label, more than one speed or type of record may be shown first, followed by 45s, EPs, and finally LPs. The reader should use this section to identify most of the important, interesting and rare labels and significant variations thereof. Photos of a number of worthwhile labels could not be obtained in time for publication, and it is hoped that a seventh edition of this book will contain additional photographs. Of course, not every record label mentioned in the listings, much less every known record label, is represented.

In the 1950s, records were often issued in both 78 and 45 RPM form. Where the label design and/or logo is similar on the two speeds, only one is usually illustrated.

In the case of major, long-lived labels such as Okeh or Victor, significant changes in label design are shown in chronological order. Also, special race and hillbilly series, distinguishable by number series and/or label variation, are often illustrated and identified. See, for example, the Brunswick 7000-7233 series and the Brunswick 100 series, both (usually) having the "lightning" label.

Accompanying the photos are approximate issue dates (e.g., late 1920s). Where a label is primarily a race or rhythm and blues label, this is indicated.

For further information on pre-1943 labels, see Rust's *American Record Label Book* and Sutton and Nauck's *American Record Labels and Companies*.

For further information on post-war labels, see Galen Gart's *The American Record Label Directory & Dating Guide*. Ken Clee's *The Directory of American 45 R.P.M. Records* is a useful discography. All these volumes are listed in the bibliography. Also, illustrated essays on post-war labels may be found in current and back issues of the various record collectors' publications.

A-1 RECORDS
Ca. 1950 (78)

A-J
Ca. 1960 (45)

AA
Ca. 1950 (78)

AARDELL
Late 1950s (45)

ABBEY
Ca. 1950 (78)

ABBEY
D.J. copy, Ca. 1950 (78)

ABBOTT
Early 1950s (78)

ABCO
Rhythm & Blues (78)
Mid-1950s

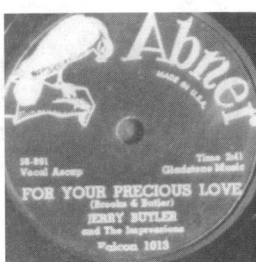

ABNER
Late 1950s (78)

ABC-PARAMOUNT
Late 1950s (78)

ABC-PARAMOUNT
Late 1950s (78)

ABC-PARAMOUNT
Late 1950s Early 1960s (45)

ACE
Ca. 1950 (78)

ACE
Ca. 1950 (78)

ACE
Ca. 1950 (78)

ACE
Mid to Late 1950s (45)

ACE
Mid to Late 1950s (78)

ACT IV
Ca. 1960 (45)

ACTUELLE
Ca. 1925 (78)

ADMIRAL
Late 1950s (45)

**AEOLIAN-
VOCALION**
Ca. 1918 (78)

**AEOLIAN-
VOCALION**
Ca. 1920 Lateral (78)

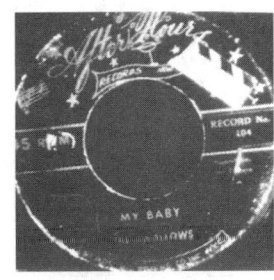

AFTER HOURS
Early 1950s (45)

AJAX
(Canadian) "Race" (78)
Early to Mid-1920s

ALADDIN
Rhythm & Blues, Jazz
Late 1940s

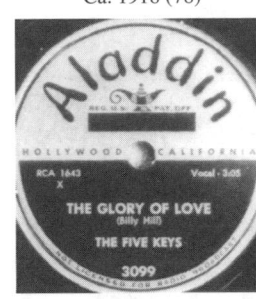

ALADDIN
Rhythm & Blues (78)
Early 1950s

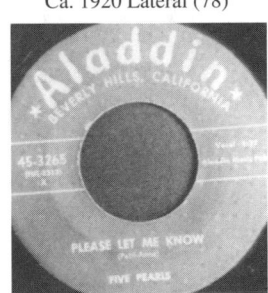

ALADDIN
Rhythm & Blues (45)
Mid-1950s

ALBEN
Ca. 1950 (78)

ALERT
Late 1940s (78)

ALERT
Late 1940s (78)

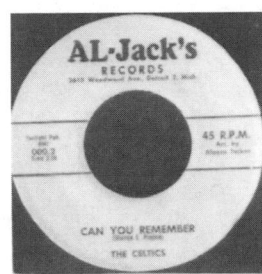

AL-JACK'S
Late 1950s (45)

ALLEN
Early 1950s (78)

ALLEN
Rhythm & Blues (45)
Mid-1950s

ALL STAR
Rhythm & Blues (45)
Late 1950s

ALL STAR
Rhythm & Blues
Late 1950s

ALLSTAR
Late 1950s (45)

ALMA
Ca. 1950 (78)

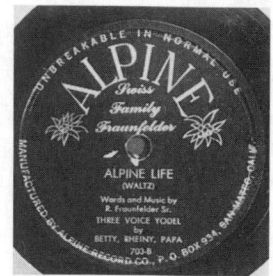

ALPINE
Ca. 1950 (78)

AL'S
Ca. 1960 (45)

ALTAIR
Ca. 1959 (45)

ALVERA
Early 1960s (45)

ALVIN
Ca. 1950 (78)

AMCO
Grey Gull Ca. 1925 (78)
Grey Gull affiliate

AMERICAN
Ca. 1950 (78)

AMERICAN MUSIC
1940s (78)

**AMERICAN RECORD
COMPANY**
Ca. 1916 (78)

**AMERICAN RECORD
CORP.**
Ca. 1930 (78)

**AMERICAN RECORD
CORP.**
Ca. 1932 (33 1/3)

AMMOR
Ca. 1940 (78)

AMMOR
Ca. 1940 (78)

ANDEX
Ca. 1960 (45)

ANDIE
Early 1960s (45)

ANDREA
78 rpm (mid-1950s)

ANNA
Rhythm & Blues (78)
Late 1959-60

ANNA
Rhythm & Blues (45)
Late 1959-60s

ANTHEM
Ca. 1960 (45)

ANTLER
Ca. 1960 (45)

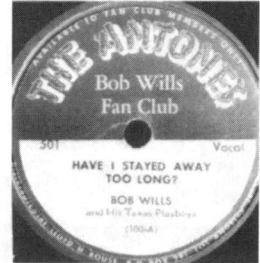

THE ANTONES
Country & Western (78)
Late 1940s

APEX
Mid-1920s (78)
Canadian

APEX
Late 1950s (45)

APOLLO
Perfect Affiliate
Ca. 1927 (78)

APOLLO
Late 1940s (78)

APOLLO
Rhythm & Blues (78)
Ca. 1950

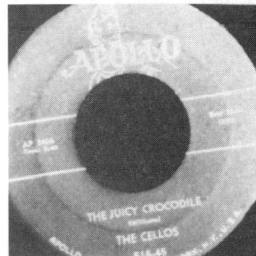
APOLLO
Rhythm & Blues (45)
Mid-1950s

APOLLO
Mid-1950s (45)

APPLAUSE
Ca. 1960 (45)

ARA
Ca. 1947 (78)

ARA
Late 1940s (78)

ARC
Late 1950s (45)

ARC
Late 1950s (45)

ARCADE
Late 1950s (45)

ARCADIA
Ca. 1950 (78)

ARCADIA
Ca. 1956 (45)

ARCTIC
Late 1950s (45)

ARGO
Late 1950s (78)

ARGO
Late 1950s (45)

ARGO
Late 1950s (78)

ARISTA
Ca. 1950 (78)

ARISTOCRAT
Rhythm & Blues (78)
Late 1940s

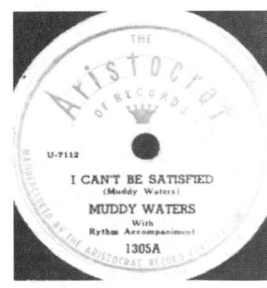
ARISTOCRAT
Rhythm & Blues (78)
Late 1940s

ARROW
Ca. 1918 (78)

ART
Ca. 1950 (78)

ARTISTIC
Late 1950s (78)

ARTO
Early 1920s (78)

ARVEE
Ca. 1960 (45)

ARWIN
Late 1950s (78)

ASCH
1940s (78)

ASCH
1940s (78)

ATCO
Late 1950s (78)

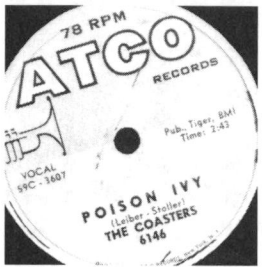

ATCO
Rhythm & Blues (78)
Late 1950s

ATHENS
Late 1950s (45)

ATLANTIC
Rhythm & Blues (78)
Early 1950s

ATLANTIC
Rhythm & Blues (45)
1950s

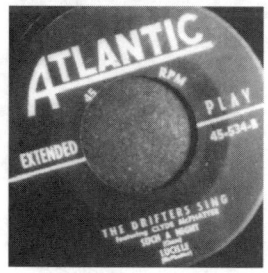

ATLANTIC
Rhythm & Blues (EP)
Mid-1950s

ATLANTIC
Rhythm & Blues (LP)
Mid-1950s

ATLANTIC
Rhythm & Blues (LP)
Later Pressing

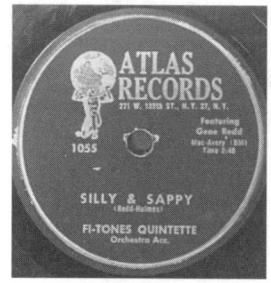

ATLAS
Mid-1950s (78)

ATLAS
Late 1940s (78)

ATOMIC
Late 1940s (78)

ATOMIC
Mid-1950s (45)

ATOMIC-H
Mid-1950s (45)

AURORA
Ca. 1933 (78)
Canadian

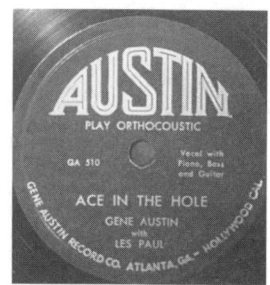

AUSTIN
Ca. 1950 (78)

AUTHENTIC
Early 1950s (78)

AUTOGRAPH
Ca. 1924 (78)

AUTOGRAPH
Electrically Recorded
Ca. 1925 (78)

AUTOGRAPH
Ca. 1925 (78)

AUTOGRAPH
Ca. 1925 (78)

AVALON
Early 1950s (78)

AYO
Late 1940s (78)

AZALEA
Late 1950s (45)

AZALEA CITY
78 rpm (ca. 1950)

B & S
Ca. 1950 (78)

BACK BEAT
Mid-1950s (78)

BACK BEAT
Mid-1950s (45)

BAMA
Early 1950s (78)

BAND BOX
Ca. 1960 (45)

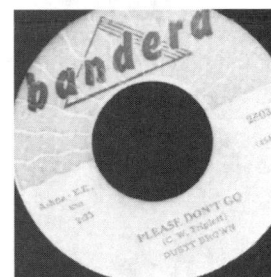

BANDERA
Rhythm & Blues (45)
Late 1950s

BANNER
Ca. 1910 (78)
Single-sided

BANNER
Ca. 1930 (78)

BANNER
Ca. 1948 (78)

BARBOUR
Ca. 1950 (78)

BATON
Mid 1950s (78)

BATON
Late 1950s (45)

BAYOU
Rhythm & Blues (45)
Mid-1950s

BAY-TONE
Late 1950s (45)

BBS
Early 1950s (78)

BEA & BABY
Rhythm & Blues (45)
Ca. 1960

BEACON
Late 1940s (78)

BELL
Early 1920s (78)

BELL
Early 1920s (78)

BELL
Mid-1920s (78)

BELL
Late 1940s (78)

BELL
Late 1940s (78)

BELL
Early 1950s (78)
7-inch record

BEL-TONE
Late 1940s (78)

BELVEDERE
Early 1920s (78)

BENNETT
Ca. 1950 (78)

**BERLINER'S GRA-
MOPHONE**
Late 1890s (78)

BERNARDO
Ca. 1929 (78)

BIG
Early 1960s (45)

BIG HOWDY
Late 1950s (45)

BIG TOWN
Rhythm & Blues (78)
Mid-1950s

BIG TOWN
Mid-1950s (45)

BILTMORE
1940s (78)
A reissue label for jazz
collectors

BINGO
Ca. 1960s (45)

BINGOLA
Ca. 1929 (78)
5-inch record

BLACK AND WHITE
Blues & Jazz (78)
Late 1940s

BLACK AND WHITE
Late 1940s (78)

BLACK AND WHITE
Late 1940s (78)

BLACK AND WHITE
Late 1940s (45)

BLACK PATTI
Ca. 1927 (78)
"Race" label

BLACK SWAN
"Race" (78)
Early 1920s

BLACK SWAN
"Race" (78)
Early 1920s

BLACK SWAN
"Race" (78)
Early 1920s

BLAZE
Early 1960s (45)

BLAZON
Late 1940s (78)

BLUE
Ca. 1950 (78)

BLUE BIRD
Early 1920s (78)
Unrelated to more familiar
RCA Victor product

BLUEBIRD
Ca. 1933 (78)

BLUEBIRD
Ca. 1935 (78)

BLUEBIRD
Late 1930s (78)

BLUEBIRD
Late 1930s-41 (78)

BLUE BONNET
Country & Western (78)
Late 1940s

BLUE-CHIP
Mid-1950s (78)

BLUE-CHIP
Late 1950s (45)

BLUE CHIP
Ca. 1960 (45)

BLUE RIVER
Late 1950s (45)

BLUE HEN
Mid-1950s (45)

BLUE MOUNTAIN
Ca. 1950 (78)

BLUES & RHYTHM
Ca. 1950 (78)

**BLUES BOYS
KINGDOM**
Rhythm & Blues (45)

BOBBIN
Rhythm & Blues (45)
Late 1950s

BO-KAY
Late 1950s (45)

BONNIE BLUE
Ca. 1950 (78)

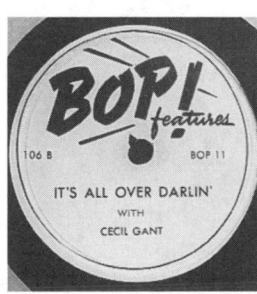

BOP!
Ca. 1950 (78)

BOULEVARD
Mid-1950s (45)

BRAX
Ca. 1960 (45)

BRENT
Rhythm & Blues (45)
Ca. 1960

BROADCAST
Ca. 1950 (78)

BROADWAY
Early 1920s (78)

BROADWAY
Mid-1920s (78)

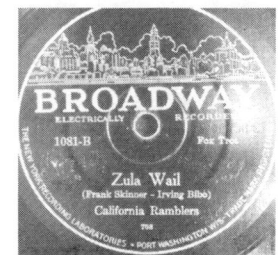

BROADWAY
Popular Series (78)
Late 1920s

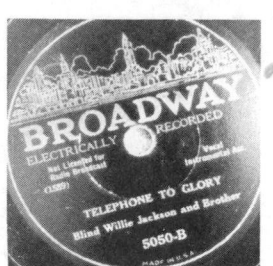

BROADWAY
"Race" (78)
5000 Series

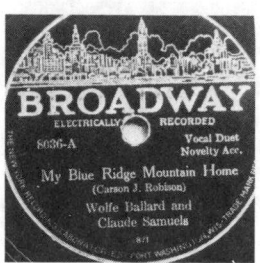

BROADWAY
8000 Series (78)
Country & Western
Late 1920s

BROKEN
Ca. 1950 (78)

BRONZE
Ca. 1940 (78)

BRUCE
Late 1950s (45)

BRUCE
Mid-1950s (78)

BRUNSWICK
Mid-1920s (78)

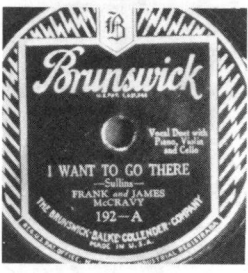

BRUNSWICK
100 Series-Hillbilly (78)
Late 1920s

BRUNSWICK
7000 Series "Race" (78)
Late 1920s

BRUNSWICK
1931 (78)

BRUNSWICK
Early 1930s (78)
(Special pressing)

BRUNSWICK
Mid-1930s (78)

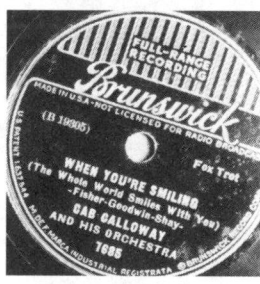

BRUNSWICK
Late 1930s (78)

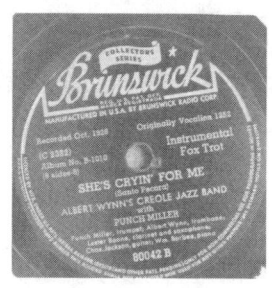

BRUNSWICK
1940s-Early 1950s (78)
Collectors Reissue Series

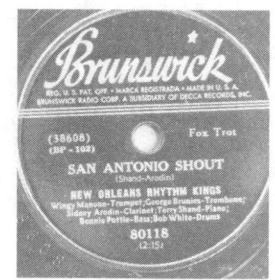

BRUNSWICK
Late 1940s (78)
Early 1950s

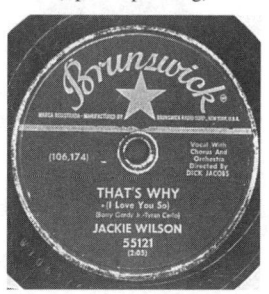

BRUNSWICK
Late 1950s (78)

BRUNSWICK
Late 1950s (45)

BRYAN
Ca. 1950 (78)

BRYTE
Late 1950s (45)

BUDDY
Ca. 1925 (78)

BULLET
Blues (78)
Late 1940s

BULL DOG
Late 1950s (45)

BULLSEYE
Ca. 1950 (78)

BULLSEYE
Late 1950s (45)

BUSY BEE
Ca. 1910 (78)

BUX-MONT
Ca. 1950 (78)

CADDY
Late 1950s (45)

CADENCE
Early 1950s (78)

CADENCE
Late 1950s (78)

CADENCE
Late 1950s (45)

CADET
Late 1940s (78)

CADILLAC
Early 1950s (78)

CALVERT
Early 1960s (45)

CAMEO
Ca. 1923 (78)

CAMEO
Ca. 1924 (78)

CAMEO-KID
Mid-1920s (78)
5-inch record

CAMEO
Late 1920s (78)

CAMEO
Late 1950s (78)

CAMEO
Late 1950s (45)

CAMEO
Early 1960s (45)

CANDIX
Early 1960s (45)

**CANDELIGHT
RECORDS**
Ca. 1960 (45)

CAPITOL
1950s (78)

CAPITOL
Early 1950s (78)

CAPITOL
Late 1950s (78)

CAPITOL
Ca. 1969 (78)
Special Commemorative
Record

CAPITOL
Late 1950s (45)

CAPITOL
Mid-1960s (45)

CAPITOL
Late 1950s (LP)

CAPITOL
7-inch (LP)
Mid-1960s

CAPROCK
Country & Western (45)
Late 1950s

CARAVAN
Early 1950s (78)

CARDINAL
Early 1920s (78)

CARDINAL
Early 1920s (78)

CARDINAL
Ca. 1950 (78)

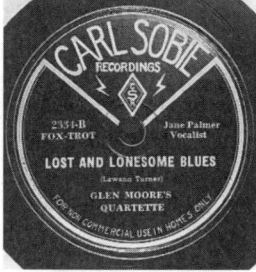

CARL SOBIE
Late 1940s (78)

CARLTON
Late 1950s (LP)

CARNIVAL
Ca. 1923 (78)

CARON
Ca. 1960 (45)

CASA GRANDE
Late 1950s (45)

CASH
Rhythm & Blues (45)
Mid-1950s

CASINO
Late 1950s (45)

CASTLE RECORDS
Ca. 1949 (78)

CAT
Late 1950s (78)

CAT
Late 1950s (45)

CAVALIER
Ca. 1950 (78)

CAVA-TONE
Ca. 1950 (78)

CELEBRITY
Late 1940s (78)

CENTRAL
Late 1950s (45)

CENTRAL
Late 1950s (45)

CHALLENGE
Late 1920s (78)

CHALLENGE
Late 1950s (78)

CHALLENGE
Late 1950s (45)

CHAMPION
Mid-1920s (78)
Early 1930s

CHAMPION
Mid-1930s (78)

CHAMPION
Ca. 1960 (45)

CHANCE
Rhythm & Blues (78)
Early 1950s

CHANCE
Rhythm & Blues (78)
Mid-1950s

CHANCE
Rhythm & Blues (45)
Mid-1950s

CHANCELLOR
Late 1950s (78)

CHANT
Early 1960s (45)

**CHAPPELLE AND
STINNETTE**
Ca. 1921 (78)

CHART
Late 1950s (45)

CHARTBUSTER
Ca. 1960 (45)

CHAUTAUQUA
Ca. 1922 (78)

CHECKER
Rhythm & Blues (78)
Early 1950s

CHECKER
Rhythm & Blues (45)
Mid-1950s

CHECKER
Rhythm & Blues (78)
Late 1950s

CHECKER
Rhythm & Blues (LP)
Late 1950s

CHECK-MATE
Early 1960s (45)

CHERRY
Ca. 1960 (45)

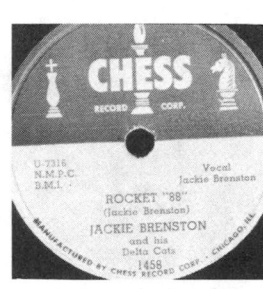

CHESS
Rhythm & Blues (78)
Early 1950s

CHESS
Rhythm & Blues (78)
Late 1950s

CHESS
Rhythm & Blues (78)
Late 1950s

CHESS
Rhythm & Blues (45)
Mid-1950s

CHESS
Late 1950s (45)

CHESS
Rhythm & Blues (78)
Late 1950s

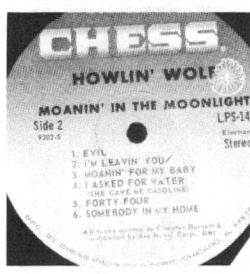

CHESS
Rhythm & Blues (LP)
Later pressing

CHIEF
Mid-1950s (45)

CHIEF
Late 1950s (45)

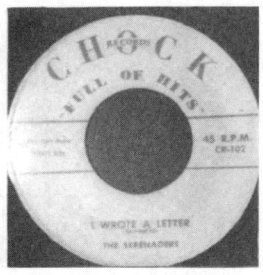

CHOCK FULL OF HITS
Late 1950s (45)

CHOICE
Ca. 1960 (45)

CIMARRON
Early 1960s (45)

CINDY
Ca. 1960 (45)

CIRCLE
Late 1940s (78)

CIRECO
Ca. 1948 (78)

CLARION
Ca. 1910 (78)

CLARION
Ca. 1921 (78)

CLARION
Early 1930s (78)

CLARION
Early 1930s (78)
"Double Track" record

CLASS
Late 1950s (78)

CLASSICS
Late 1940s (78)

CLAXTONOLA
Mid-1920s (78)

CLEARTONE
Early 1920s (78)

CLEARTONE
Early 1920s (78)

CLEAR TONE
Late 1940s (78)

CLIF
Mid-1950s (45)

CLIMAX RECORD
Ca. 1910 (78)

CLIMAX
Ca. 1910 (78)

CLOVER
Ca. 1926 (78)

CLUB "51"
Mid-1950s (45)

CLUB
Late 1950s (45)

CMI
Late 1950s (45)

COBRA
Late 1950s (78)

COBRA
Rhythm & Blues (45)
Late 1950s

COBRA
Early 1960s (45)

**COCKTAIL PARTY
SONGS**
Late 1940s (78)

COIN
Ca. 1960 (45)

COLEMAN
Ca. 1950 (78)

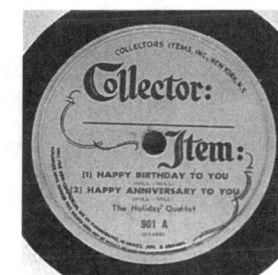

COLLECTOR ITEM
Early 1950s (78)

COLONIAL
Ca. 1950 (78)

COLONIAL
Late 1950s (78)

COLONIAL
Late 1950s (45)

COLONIAL
Late 1950s (45)

COLONY
Ca. 1950 (78)

COLPIX
Ca. 1960 (45)

COLUMBIA
Ca. 1904 (78)

**COLUMBIA DISC
RECORD**
Ca. 1905 (78)

COLUMBIA
Ca. 1905 (78)

COLUMBIA
Ca. 1905 (78)

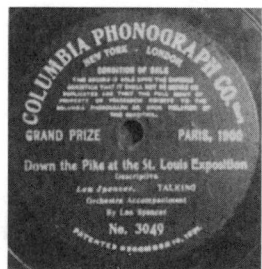

COLUMBIA
Ca. 1905 (78)

COLUMBIA
Ca. 1907 (78)

COLUMBIA
Ca. 1907 (78)

COLUMBIA
Ca. 1907 (78)

COLUMBIA
Ca. 1910 (78)

COLUMBIA
Advertising Record (obverse)
Ca. 1915 (78)

COLUMBIA
Advertising Record (reverse)
Ca. 1915

COLUMBIA
Personal
Ca. 1915 (78)

COLUMBIA
Ca. 1915 (78)
Panama-Pacific Exposition
souvenir record

COLUMBIA
Early 1920s (78)

COLUMBIA
Ca. 1923 (78)
"Exclusive Artist"

COLUMBIA
Personal
Ca. 1924 (78)

COLUMBIA
Mid-1920s (78)

COLUMBIA
14000-D Series is "Race"
15000-D Series is Country &
Western Late 1920s (78)

COLUMBIA
Picture Label (78)
Late 1920s
Ted Lewis

COLUMBIA
Spanish Series
Ca. 1930 (78)

COLUMBIA
Folk Series Ca. 1933 (78)

COLUMBIA
Ca. 1932 (78)
Rudy Vallee Logo

COLUMBIA
Rudy Vallee Logo
Ca. 1932 (78)

COLUMBIA
Ted Lewis Logo
Ca. 1933 (78)

COLUMBIA
Mid-1930s (78)

COLUMBIA
Mid-1930s (78)

COLUMBIA
1939-1950s (78)

COLUMBIA
Sacred Series
Ca. 1950 (78)

COLUMBIA
Early 1950s (45)

COLUMBIA
Late 1950s (78)

COLUMBIA
Late 1950s (45)

COLUMBIA
Early 1960s (45)

COMBO
Mid-1950s (78)

COMBO
Mid-1950s (45)

COMBO
Mid-1950s (45)

COMET
Late 1940s (78)

COMMODORE
Jazz (78)
Late 1930s, early 1940s

CONCERT RECORD
Ca. 1909 (78)

CONNORIZED
Ca. 1922 (78)
Vocal Series

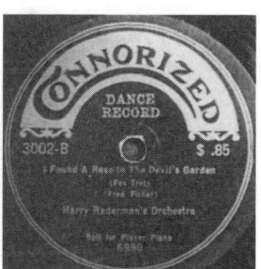

CONNORIZED
Dance Series
Ca. 1923 (78)

CONQUEROR
Late 1920s (78)

CONQUEROR
Early 1930s (78)

CONQUEROR
Late 1930s-1940 (78)

**CONSOLIDATED
RECORD**
Ca. 1912 (78)

CONTINENTAL
1940s (78)

CONTINENTAL
Ca. 1947 (78)

CONTRACT
Ca. 1950 (78)

THE COOK
Ca. 1922 (78)

CORAL
Late 1950s (78)

CORAL
Late 1950s (45)

CORAL
Late 1950s (LP)

CORMAC
Ca. 1950 (78)

CORMAC
Ca. 1950 (78)

CORT
Ca. 1915 (78)

CORT RECORD
Ca. 1915 (78)

COSMO
Ca. 1950 (78)

COSMO
Ca. 1950 (78)
Jazz Series

COURTNEY
Ca. 1950 (78)

COURTNEY
Ca. 1950 (78)

COVER
Late 1950s (45)

COWTOWN
Ca. 1950 (78)

COWTOWN
Late 1950s (45)

CREST
Early 1950s (78)
7-inch record

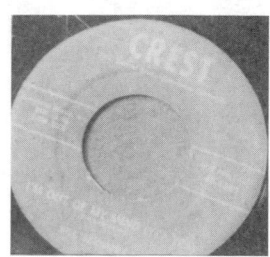

CREST
Late 1950s (45)

CREST
Early 1960s (45)

CROSS COUNTRY
Mid-1950s (45)

CROWN
Early 1930s (78)

CROWN
Canadian
Ca. 1928 (78)

CROWN
Ca. 1950 (78)

CRYSTAL
Ca. 1950 (78)

CRYSTALETTE
Early 1950s (78)

C SHARPE MINOR
Ca. 1950 (78)

CUB
Late 1950s to Early 1960s
(45)

CULLMAN
Ca. 1960 (45)

D
Late 1950s (45)

D
Ca. 1960 (45)

D & R
Ca. 1910 (78)

D & S
Ca. 1950 (78)

DALE
Late 1950s (45)

DAMON
Mid-1950s (45)

DANDY
Ca. 1924 (78)

DANISE
Mid-1950s (78)

DARL
Mid-1950s (45)

DARSA
Late 1950s (45)

DART
Early 1960s (45)

DAVEGA
Ca. 1924 (78)

DAVIS
Late 1940s (78)

DAVIS
Late 1950s (45)

DAWN
Late 1950s (45)

DAWN
Ca. 1960 (45)

D B C
Ca. 1960 (45)

DC
Rhythm & Blues (45)
Late 1950s

DEBUT
Ca. 1950 (78)

DEBUT
Ca. 1950 (78)

DECCA
7000 Series "Race" (78)
Mid-1930s

DECCA
"Race" Series
Ca. 1938 (78)

DECCA
Ca. 1941 (78)

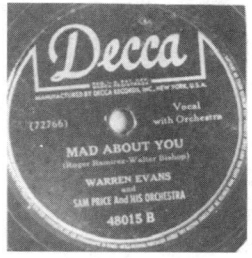
DECCA
Late 1940s (78)

DECCA
Mid-1950s (45)

DECCA
Late 1950s (78)

DECCA
Late 1950s (45)

DEL-CO
Late 1950s (45)

DEL-FI
Late 1950s (45)

DELTA
Mid-1950s (45)

DELTA
Ca. 1960 (45)

DELTONE
Early 1960s (45)

DE-LUXE
Late 1940s (78)

DeLUXE
Late 1940s (78)

DELUXE
Rhythm & Blues (78)
Mid-1950s

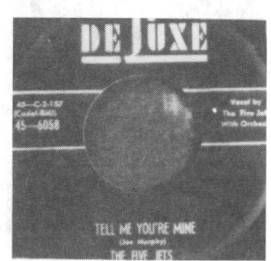
DELUXE
Mid-1950s (45)

DELVAR
Ca. 1950 (78)

DEMON
Late 1950s (78)

DERBY
Mid-1950s (45)

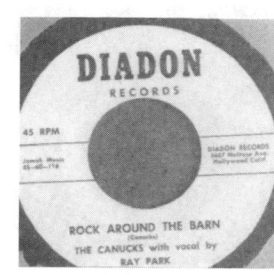
DIADON
Ca. 1960 (45)

DIAL
Late 1940s (78)

DIAL
Ca. 1960 (45)

DIAMOND
Ca. 1950 (78)

DIAMOND RECORD
Ca. 1912 (78)

DIG
Mid-1950s (78)

DIG
Late 1950s (45)

DIR
Late 1950s (45)

DISC-COVERY
Ca. 1950 (78)

DISCOVERY
Ca. 1950 (78)

DITTO
Late 1950s (45)

DIVA
Late 1920s (78)

DIX
Early 1950s (78)

DIXIE
Late 1950s (45)

DOKE
Late 1950s (45)

DOME
Ca. 1950 (78)

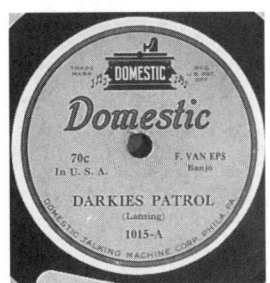

DOMESTIC
Ca. 1916 (78)

DOMINO
Mid-1920s (78)

DOMINO
Late 1920s (78)

DOMINO
Ca. 1933 (78)

DOMINO
Ca. 1928 (78)
Canadian

DOMINO
Late 1950s (45)

DONA
Late 1950s (45)

DON TAN
Ca. 1960 (45)

DOOTONE
Mid-1950s (78)

DOOTO
Mid-1950s (78)

DOOTONE
Mid-1950s (78)

DOOTONE
Late 1950s (45)

DOT
Ca. 1949 (78)

DOT
Mid-1950s (78)

DOT
Mid-1950s (45)

DOT
Late 1950s (78)

DOT
Ca. 1950 (78)

DOVE
Late 1950s (45)

DOWN BEAT
Rhythm & Blues (78)
Late 1940s

DOWN TOWN
Late 1940s (78)

DRAG RACE
Mid-1950s (78)

DREW-BLAN
Early 1960s (45)

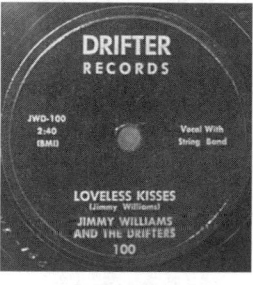

DRIFTER
Early 1950s (78)

DRUMFIRE
Ca. 1960 (45)

DRUMMOND
Mid-1950s (45)

D TOWN
Ca. 1960 (45)

DUB
Late 1950s (45)

DUCHESS
Early 1960s (45)

DUKE
Mid-1950 to Early 1960s (45)

DUKE
Mid-1950s (78)

DUNCAN
Ca. 1959 (45)

DUOPHONE
(English) Ca. 1929 (78)

DUPLEX
Late 1950s (78)

DURIUM JUNIOR
Early 1930s (78)
Paper Record, 4-inch diam.

DUROTONE
Ca. 1940 (78)
5-inch record

DYNAMIC
Ca. 1964 (45)

E & M
Early 1960s (45)

EAGLE
Ca. 1908 (78)

EAGLE
Ca. 1950 (78)

EAGLE
Early 1960s (45)

EAST-WEST
Late 1950s (45)

EBB
Rhythm & Blues (45)
Mid to Late 1950s

ECHO
Ca. 1950 (78)

ECHO
Late 1950s (45)

EDDIE'S
Late 1940s (78)

EDISON
Late Teens (78)
Embossed, not paper, label

EDISON
Late Teens (78)
Embossed, not paper, label

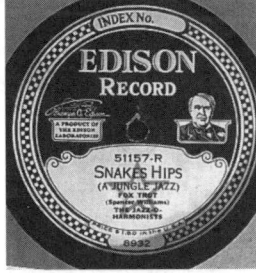
EDISON
Ca. 1923 (78)
Thick, with red star

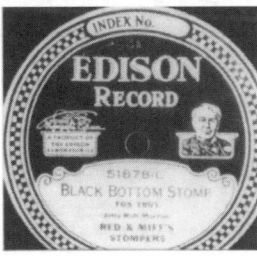
EDISON
1920s Thick (78)

EDISON
Special Pressing (thick)
Ca. 1924 (78)

EDISON
Ca. 1929 (thin) (78)

EDISON
Ca. 1926 (80) Long Play

EDISON
Ca. 1926 (80)
40-minute LP

**EDISON
INTERNATIONAL**
Late 1950s (45)

ELECTRA
Ca. 1925 (78)
Autograph/Marsh Laboratories affiliate

ELECTRADISK
Early 1930s (78)

**ELECTRIC
RECORDING LABS**
Mid-1920s (78)
Rudy Vallee personal

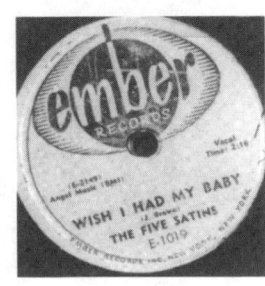
EMBER
Late 1950s (78)

EMBER
Ca. 1960 (45)

EMBER
Late 1950s (78)

EMBER
Late 1950s (45)

EMERALD
Early 1950s (78)

EMERSON
Late Teens (78)
7-inch record

EMERSON
Late Teens (78)
7-inch record

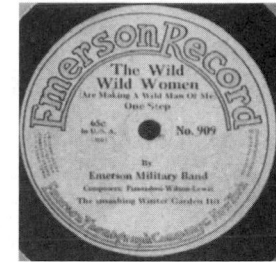
EMERSON
Late Teens (78)
9-inch record

EMERSON
Ca. 1918 (78)

EMERSON
Ca. 1922 (78)

EMERSON
Mid-1920s (78)

EMERSON
Ca. 1927 (78)
3000 Series

EMPIRE
Ca. 1919 (78)

EMPIRE
Ca. 1920 (78)

EMPIRE
Late 1950s (45)

EMPRESS
Ca. 1960 (45)

ENCINO
Mid-1950s (45)

END
Late 1950s (78)

END
Late 1950s (45)

END
Late 1950s (78)

ENSIGN
Ca. 1960 (45)

ENTERPRISE
Ca. 1950 (78)

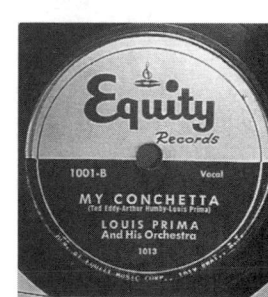
EQUITY
Ca. 1950 (78)

ERA
Ca. 1950 (78)

ERA
Mid-1950s (78)

ERA
Late 1950s (45)

ESSEX
Mid-1950s (78)

ESSEX
Mid-1950s (45)

EVEREST
Ca. 1960 (45)

EVERLAST
Late 1950s (45)

EVERYBODY'S
Mid-1920s (78)

EVERSTATE
Ca. 1948 (78)

EXCEL
Late 1950s (45)

EXCELLO
Mid-1950s (78)

EXCELSIOR
Ca. 1910 (78)

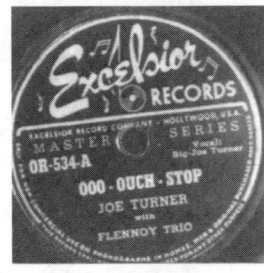

EXCELSIOR
Late 1940s (78)

EXCELSIOR
Late 1940s (78)

EXCLUSIVE
Late 1940s (78)

EXCLUSIVE
Ca. 1947 (78)

FABLE
Ca. 1957 (45)

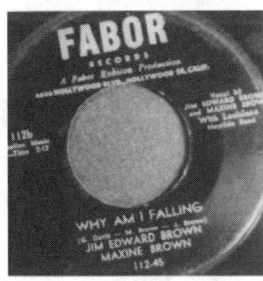

FABOR
Late 1950s (45)

FALCON
Late 1950s (45)

FAMOUS
Early 1920s (78)

FAN
Late 1950s (45)

FANTASY
Early 1950s (78)

FARGO
Ca. 1950 (78)

FASCINATION
Mid-1950s (45)

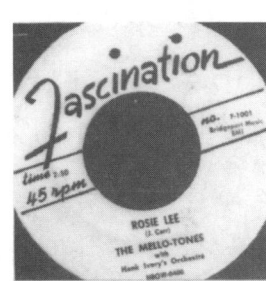

FASCINATION
Late 1950s (45)

FASCINATION
Late 1950s (45)

FAULTLESS CONCERT RECORD
Ca. 1910 (78)

FEATURE
Mid-1950s (45)

FEATURE
Late 1950s (45)

FEDERAL
Ca. 1923 (78)

FEDERAL
Mid-1950s (78)

FEDERAL
Mid-1950s (45)

FEDERAL
Mid-1950s (LP)

FEDERAL
Late 1950s (78)

FEDERAL
Late 1950s (45)

FEE BEE
Ca. 1956 (45)

FELSTED
Late 1950s (45)

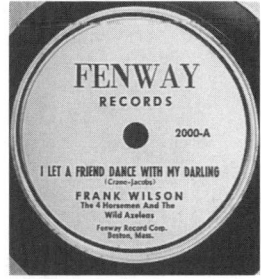

FENWAY
Early 1950s (78)

FERNWOOD
Late 1950s (45)

FIDELITY
Ca. 1950 (78)

FINE ARTS
Ca. 1950 (78)

FIRE
Ca. 1960 (78)

FIRE
Early 1960s (45)

FLAIR
Rhythm & Blues (78)
Mid-1950s

FLAIR
Mid-1950s (45)

FLAIR-X
Late 1950s (45)

FLASH
Ca. 1950 (78)

FLASH
Late 1950s (78)

FLASH
Late 1950s (45)

FLEXO
Ca. 1930 (78)
7-inch green plastic

FLIP
Mid-1950s (78)

FLIP
Mid-1950s (78)

FLIP
Mid-1950s (45)

FLIP
Late 1950s (78)

FLIP
Late 1950s (45)

FLICK
Late 1950s (45)

F M
Early 1950s (78)

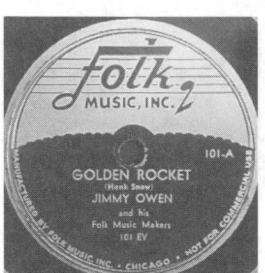

FOLK
Ca. 1950 (78)

FONSCA
Ca. 1960 (45)

FORD
Mid-1950s (78)

FORTUNE
Early 1950s (78)

FORTUNE
Mid-1950s (45)

4 STAR
Ca. 1950 (78)

FOX
Late 1950s (45)

FOX MOVIETONE
Mid-1930s (78)

FRANSIL
Mid-1950s (45)

FRATERNITY
Ca. 1923 (78)
Gennett pressing

FRATERNITY
Late 1950s (78)

FRATERNITY
Late 1950s (45)

FREEDOM
Ca. 1950 (78)

FREEDOM
Ca. 1950 (78)

FREEDOM
Late 1950s (45)

FREEMAN LANG
Ca. 1940 (78)

FURY
Late 1950s (45)

FURY
Late 1950s (45)

FURY
Ca. 1960 (45)

G & G
Late 1940s (78)

GAMETIME
Late 1950s (45)

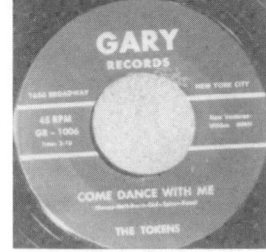

GARY
Late 1950s (45)

GATEWAY
Late 1950s (45)

GEE
Mid-1950s (45)

GEE
Late 1950s (78)

GEE
Late 1950s (78)

GEE
Ca. 1960 (45)

GEE-BEE
Ca. 1950 (78)

GEM
Ca. 1932 (78)
Crown pressing

GEM
Ca. 1950 (78)

GEM
Early 1950s (78)

GEM
Mid-1950s (45)

GENERAL
Ca. 1940 (78)

GENERAL TAVERN TUNES
Early 1940s (78)

GENNETT
Mid-1920s (78)

GENNETT
Early 1920s (78)
Personal

GENNETT
Late 1920s (78)

GENNETT
Ca. 1930 (78)
Transcription

GENNETT
1940s (78)

GENNETT SOUND EFFECTS
Early 1930s (78)

GILBERT
Mid-1950s (45)

GILT-EDGE
Late 1940s (78)

GILT-EDGE
Early 1950s (45)
DJ issue

GINA
Ca. 1960 (45)

GLOBAL
Early 1960s (45)

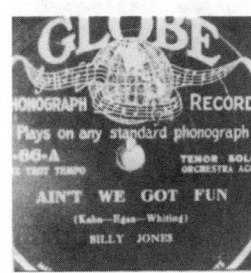

GLOBE
Ca. 1922 (78)

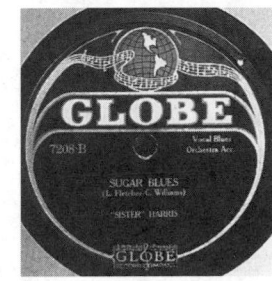

GLOBE
Ca. 1924 (78)

GLOBE
Mid-1920s (78)

GLOBE
Late 1940s (78)

GLOBE
Mid-1950s (45)

GOLDBAND
Late 1950s (45)

GOLDBAND
Late 1950s (45)

GOLDEN
Mid-1920s (78)

GOLDEN CREST
Early 1960s (45)

**GOLD MEDAL
RECORD**
Ca. 1950 (78)

GOLD-RAIN
Late 1940s (78)

GOLD STAR
Late 1940s (78)

GONE
Late 1950s (78)

GONE
Mid-1950s (45)

GONE
Late 1950s (45)

GOOD
Late 1950s (45)

GOODENOUGH
Mid-1920s (78)

GOOD TIME JAZZ
Mid-1950s (78)

**GOSPEL
TRUMPET CO.**
Mid-1920s (78)

GOTHAM
Late 1940s to Early 1950s
(78)

GOTHAM
Early 1950s (45)

GRAND
Ca. 1947 (78)

GRAND
Mid-1950s (45)

GRANITE
Late 1950s (45)

GREY CLIFF
Ca. 1960 (45)

GREY GULL
Ca. 1922 (78)

GREY GULL
Mid-1920s (78)

GREY GULL
1920s (78)

GREY GULL
Ca. 1929 (78)

**GREY GULL
YOUNGSTER**
Ca. 1928 (78)
5-inch record

GROOVE
Late 1950s (78)

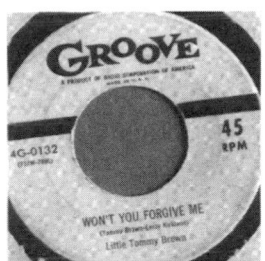

GROOVE
Mid-1950s (45)

GROOVE
Late 1950s (45)

GROOVY
Late 1940s (78)

GUARDSMAN
(English) Ca. 1917 (78)

GULF
Late 1940s (78)

GULF COAST
Ca. 1950 (78)

GUYDEN
Late 1950s (78)

GUYDEN
Late 1950s (45)

H.R.S.
Late 1940s (78)

HALL-WAY
Ca. 1960 (45)

HAMILTON
Late 1950s (45)

HANOVER
Ca. 1960 (45)

HARLEM
Late 1940s (78)

HARLEM
Late 1940s (78)

HARLEM
Late 1950s (78)

HARLEM
Ca. 1960 (45)

HARMOGRAPH
Early 1920s (78)

HARMOGRAPH
Early 1920s (78)

HARMONIA
Ca. 1950 (78)

**HARMONY DISC
RECORD**
Ca. 1908 (78)

HARMONY RECORD
Ca. 1912 (78)

HARMONY
1925 to Early 1930s (78)

HARMONY
Ca. 1958 (LP)

HART
Late 1950s (45)

HARVARD DISC RECORD
Ca. 1908 (78)

HARVARD DISC RECORD
Ca. 1908 (78)

HARVEY
Early 1960s (45)

HEART RECORDS
Ca. 1950 (78)

HEP
Ca. 1960 (45)

HERALD
Rhythm & Blues
Mid-1950s (45)

HERALD
Mid-1950s (45)

HERALD
Mid-1950s (78)

HERALD
Mid-1950s (45)

HERALD
Late 1950s (45)

HERSCHEL GOLD SEAL
Late 1920s (78)

HERMITAGE
Ca. 1960 (45)

HERWIN
Ca. 1926 (78)

HERWIN
Late 1920s (78)
Electrically recorded

HI
Late 1950s (45)

HICKORY
Late 1950s (45)

HI-LO
Ca. 1950 (78)

HIS MASTER'S VOICE
(Canadian) Ca. 1924 (78)

THE HIT
Ca. 1940 (78)

HIT RECORDS
Late 1950s (45)

HIT MAKER
Late 1950s (45)

HIT OF THE WEEK
Early 1930s (78)
Paper Record

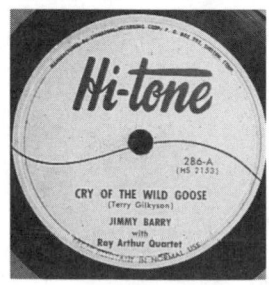

HI-TONE
Early 1950s (78)

HOB (HOUSE OF BEAUTY)
Early 1960s (45)

HOLIDAY
Late 1950s (45)

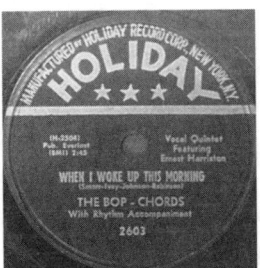
HOLIDAY
Late-1950s (78)

HOLIDAY INN
Early 1960s (45)

HOLLYWOOD
Mid-1920s (78)

HOLLYWOOD
Mid-1950s (45)

HOLLYWOOD HOT SHOTS
Ca. 1940 (78)

HOMESTEAD
Ca. 1930 (78)

HOOSIER
Ca. 1950 (78)

HORACE HEIDT
Ca. 1950 (78)
By Magnolia Records

HOT JAZZ CLUB OF AMERICA
1940s (78)
Collectors Reissue Series

HOT RECORD SOCIETY
Ca. 1939 (78)
Collectors Series

HOT WAX
Ca. 1948 (78)

HOWARD
Ca. 1950 (78)

HUB
Late 1940s

HUDSON
Ca. 1925 (78)

HULL
Late 1950s (45)

HULL
Late 1950s (78)

HULL
Late 1950s (45)

HUM
Ca. 1950 (78)

HUMMING BIRD
Ca. 1950 (78)

HUMMING BIRD
Early 1950s (45)

HUNTER
Late 1960s (45)

HYTONE
Early 1920s (78)

HY-TONE
Late 1940s (78)

HY-TONE
Late 1950s (45)

IMPERIAL
Ca. 1909 (78)

IMPERIAL
Late Teens (78)

IMPERIAL
Ca. 1950 (78)
Country Series

IMPERIAL
Early 1950s (78)

IMPERIAL
Mid-1950s (45)

IMPERIAL
Late 1950s (78)

IMPERIAL
Late 1950s (45)

IMPERIAL
Late 1950s (45)

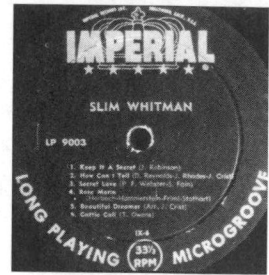

IMPERIAL
Late 1950s (LP)

IMPERIAL (LP)
Late 1950s to Early 1960s

IMPRA
Late 1950s (45)

IMPROVED RECORD
Ca. 1901 (78)
Victor-affiliated

INCO
Ca. 1940 (78)

INTERNATIONAL RECORD
Ca. 1910 (78)
Single-sided

INTRASTATE
Early 1950s (78)

INTRO
Early 1950s (78)

INTRO
Country & Western
Mid-1950s (45)

IRAGEN
1930s (78)

IRMA
Late 1950s (78)

IVORY
Ca. 1961 (45)

J & S
Ca. 1956 (45)

J-B
Ca. 1950 (78)

J-B
Early 1950s (45)

JACKPOT
Ca. 1960 (45)

JACKSON
Mid-1950s (45)

JAGUAR
Mid-1950s (45)

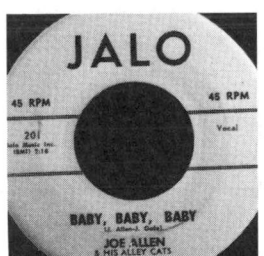

JALO
Late 1950s (45)

JALYNNE
Early 1950s (45)

JAMIE
Late 1950s (78)

JAMIE
Late 1950s (45)

JAMIE
Late 1950s (45)

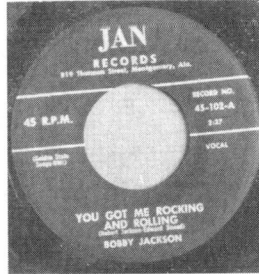

JAN
Late 1950s (45)

JAN
Late 1950s (45)

JAX
Ca. 1950 (78)

JAX
Early 1950s (45)

JAX
Mid-1950s (45)

JAX
Mid-1950s (78)

JAY
Ca. 1950 (78)
Collectors Reissue

JAY-DEE
Mid-1950s (78)

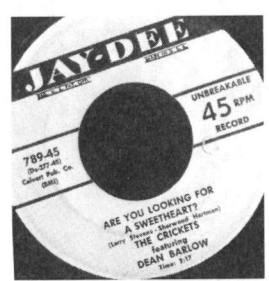

JAY-DEE
Mid-1950s (45)

JAY WING
Late 1950s (45)

JAZZ DISC
Late 1940s (78)

JAZZ MAN
Late 1940s (78)

JAZZ MAN
Late 1940s (78)

JAZZ RECORD
1940s (78)

JEWEL
Early 1920s (78)
Grey Gull affiliated

JEWEL
Ca. 1930 (78)

JEWEL
Late 1940s (78)

JEWEL
Late 1940s (78)

JEWEL
Early 1960s (45)

JIFFY
Mid-1950s (45)

JIFFY
Mid-1950s (45)

JIN
Late 1950s (45)

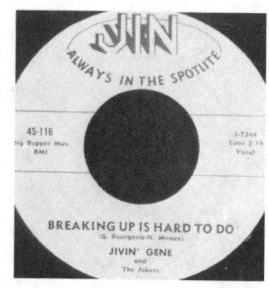

JIN
Late 1950s (45)

JIN
Ca. 1960 (45)

J.O.B.
Early 1950s (78)

J.O.B.
Mid-1950s (78)

J.O.B.
Late 1950s (45)

JOE DAVIS
Late 1940s (78)

JOHNSON
Ca. 1960 (45)

JOZ (JOSIE)
Late 1950s (78)

JOZ (JOSIE)
Late 1950s (45)

JOSIE
Ca. 1960 (45)

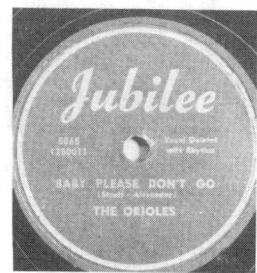

JUBILEE
Rhythm & Blues (78)
Early 1950s

JUBILEE
Early 1950s (45)

JUBILEE
Mid-1950s (78)

JUBILEE
Mid-1950s (45)

JUBILEE
Mid-1950s (78)

JUDD
Ca. 1960 (45)

JUMP
Ca. 1950 (78)

JUKE BOX
Late 1940s (78)

JVB
Ca. 1950 (78)

JVB
Rhythm & Blues
Late 1950s (45)

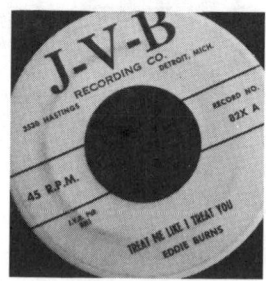

JVB
Late 1950s (45)

JVB
Rhythm & Blues
Late 1950s (78)

J-V-B
Late 1950s (78)

K-ARK
Late 1950s (45)

KAYBEE
Ca. 1950 (78)

KAYO
Late 1950s (45)

KEEN
Ca. 1950 (78)

KEEN
Late 1950s (78)

KEEN
Late 1950s (78)

KENT
Ca. 1960 (45)

KENTUCKY
Early 1950s (78)

KEY
Ca. 1950 (78)

KEY
Mid-1950s (78)

**KEYBOARD
RECORDS**
Ca. 1950 (78)

KHOURY'S
Early 1950s (78)

KHOURY'S
Mid-1950s (45)

KHOURY'S
Late 1950s (45)

KICK
Late 1950s (45)

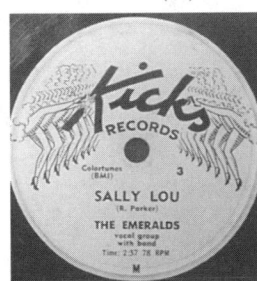

KICKS
Mid-1950s (78)

KICKS
Late 1950s (45)

KING
Late 1940s (78)

KING
Late 1950s (78)

KING
Late 1950s (45)

KING
Late 1950s (LP-33 1/3)

KKK
Mid-1920s (78)

KLIFF
Late 1950s (45)

KLIK
Mid-1950s (45)

KOOL
Early 1960s (45)

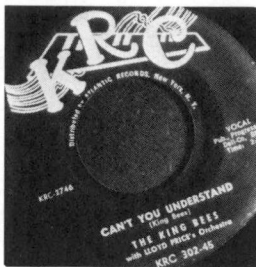

KRC
Late 1950s (45)

KUDO
Late 1950s (45)

LA BELLE
Ca. 1911 (78)

LAKESIDE
Ca. 1910 (78)

LAMB
Ca. 1950 (78)

LAMP
Mid-1950s (45)

LAMPLIGHTER
Ca. 1946 (78)

LA-PATRIE
Early 1920s(?) (78)

LASSO
Early 1950s (78)

LAURENT
Early 1950s (78)

LAURIE
Late 1950s (45)

LAURIE
Early 1960s (45)

LE CAM
Early 1960s (45)

LEE
Early 1950s (78)

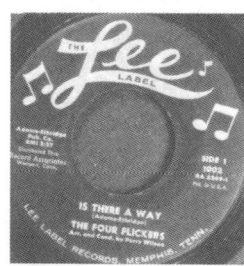

LEE
Late 1950s (45)

LEEDS
Ca. 1910 (78)
"Gold" foil label

LEGRAND
Ca. 1960 (45)

LENOX
Ca. 1950 (78)

LESLEY
Late 1950s (45)

LIBERTY
Late 1950s (78)

LIBERTY
Late 1950s (45)

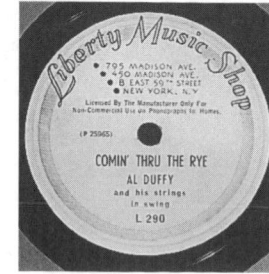

**LIBERTY MUSIC
SHOP**
Ca. 1939 (78)

LIDO
Late 1950s (45)

LIGHTNING
Mid-1950s (45)

LIN
Late 1950s (78)

LIN
Late 1950s (45)

LIN
Ca. 1960 (45)

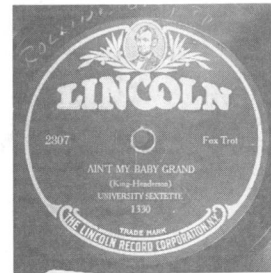

LINCOLN
Mid-1920s

LINCOLN
Ca. 1929 (78)

LINDWOOD
Early 1950s (78)

**LITTLE TOTS'
NURSERY TUNES**
Mid-1920s (78)
5-inch record; Regal pressing

LITTLE WONDER
Ca. 1915 (78)
5 1/2-inch record

LITTLE WONDER
Late Teens (78)
5 1/2-inch record

LITTLE WONDER
Ca. 1918 (78)
5 1/2-inch record

LLOYDS
Late 1950s (45)

LODE
Late 1950s (45)

LODE
Late 1950s (45)

LONDON
Early 1950s (78)

LONGHORN
Early 1960s (45)

LOST-NITE
Mid-1960s (45)
Reissue label

LUCKY
Late 1940s (78)

LUCKY
Mid-1950s (45)

LUCKY
Ca. 1960 (45)

LUCKY FOUR
Ca. 1960 (45)

LUCKY SEVEN
Ca. 1950 (45)

LUCKY STRIKE
Mid-1920s (78)
Canadian

LUDWIG
Late 1950s (45)

LUNA
Mid-1950s (45)

LUNIVERSE
Late 1950s (78)

LUNIVERSE
Late 1950s (45)

LUNIVERSE
Late 1950s (78)

LUNIVERSE
Late 1950s (45)

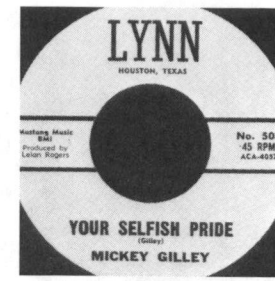

LYNN
Early 1960s (45)

LYRIC RECORD
Ca. 1919 (78)

LYRIC
Ca. 1919 (78)

LYRIC
Ca. 1920 (78)

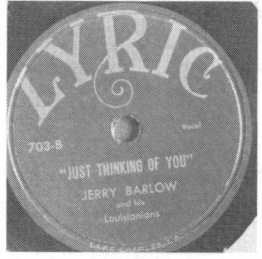

LYRIC
Early 1950s (78)

LYRIC
Ca. 1960 (45)

MGM
Late 1950s (78)

MGM
Late 1950s (45)

MGM
Mid-1950s (LP)

MacGREGOR
Mid-1930s (78)
Transcription

Mac GREGOR, C.P.
Mid-1930s (78)
Transcription

Mac GREGOR
1940s (78)

MACY'S
Ca. 1950 (78)

MADISON
Late 1920s (78)

MAGNOLIA
Ca. 1950 (78)

MAH'S
Early 1960s (45)

MAIL CALL
Early 1960s (45)

MAJESTIC
Ca. 1924 (78)

MAJESTIC
Late 1940s (78)

MAJOR
Late 1930s (78)

MAJOR
Late 1950s (45)

MAMBO
Mid-1950s (78)

MANCO
Ca. 1960 (45)

**MANHATTAN
RECORD**
Ca. 1910 (78)

MANOR
Late 1940s (78)

MARATHON
Ca. 1927 (78)
7-inch record

MARATHON
Ca. 1950 (78)

MARCONI
Ca. 1910 (78)

MARCONI
Reverse

MARDI-GRAS
Ca. 1950 (78)

MARGO
Ca. 1950 (78)
Latin label

MARS
Early 1950s (78)

MARTIN
Ca. 1950 (78)

MAR-VEL
Late 1950s (45)

MASTER
Late 1930s (78)

MASTER
Late 1940s (78)

MASTER
Ca. 1960 (45)

MASTERPIECE
Early 1950s (78)

MASTERTONE
Early 1920s (78)

MAXSA
Mid-1920s (78)

MELADEE
Late 1950s (45)

MEDALLION
Ca. 1919 (78)

MEDALLION
Ca. 1920 (78)

MEDIA
Mid-1950s (78)

MELBA
Late 1950s (45)

MELLOW
Ca. 1950 (78)

MELODISC
Late 1910s (78)

MELODY
Ca. 1923 (78)

MELODY
Ca. 1950 (78)

MELOTONE
Early 1930s (78)

MELOTONE
Ca. 1937 (78)

MEMO
Early 1950s (78)

MEMO
Ca. 1950 (78)

MERCER
Ca. 1950 (78)

MERCURY
Late 1940s (78)
Jazz label

MERCURY
8000 Series (78)
Rhythm & Blues Early 1950s

MERCURY POPULAR
Ca. 1950 (78)

MERCURY
Late-1950s (78)

MERCURY
Late 1950s (45)

MERCURY
Late 1950s (45)

MERCURY
Late 1950s (45)

MERCURY
Late 1950s (LP)

MERIDIAN
Ca. 1960 (45)

MERITT
Ca. 1927 (78)

METEOR
Mid Teens (78)

METEOR
Mid-1950s (78)

METEOR
Mid-1950s (45)

METEOR
Late 1950s (45)

METRO
Late 1950s (45)

**METRO-GOLDWYN-
MAYER**
Ca. 1929 (78)

METROTONE
Ca. 1950 (78)

LABELS

MICROPHONE
Mid-1920s (78)
Canadian

**MIDNIGHT
RECORDS**
Late 1940s (78)

MILTONE
Late 1940s (78)
Label design varies

MILTONE
Late 1940s (78)

MILTONE
Late 1940s (78)

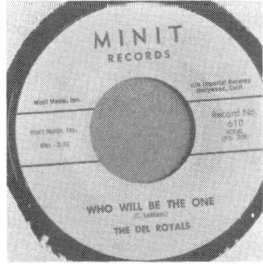

MINIT
Ca. 1960 (45)

MINOR
Late 1950s (45)

MIRACLE
Late 1940s (78)

MIRWOOD
Ca. 1960 (45)

MITCHELL
Mid-1920s (78)

MODE
Late 1950s (45)

**MODERN
HOLLYWOOD**
1950s (78)

MODERN
Mid-1950s (45)

MODERN (MUSIC)
Late 1940s (78)

MODERN (MUSIC)
Late 1940s (78)

MOHAWK
Ca. 1960 (45)

MONARCH RECORD
Ca. 1906 (78)

MONEY
Late 1950s (45)

MONOGRAM
Ca. 1950 (78)

MONTEL
Ca. 1960 (45)

**MONTGOMERY
WARD**
Mid-1930s (78)

**MONTGOMERY
WARD**
Late 1930s (78)

MONUMENT
Early 1960s (45)

MOOD
Mid-1950s (78)

MOTIF
Late 1940s (78)

MOTOWN
Ca. 1960 (45)

MOULDIE FYGGE
Late 1940s (78)
Collectors Series

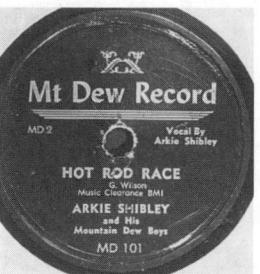

MOUNTAIN DEW
Early 1950s (78)

MOVIN'
Ca. 1960 (45)

MOVIETUNE
Late 1940s (78)

MOXIE
Ca. 1921 (78)

MOZART
Ca. 1918 (78)

MUSE
Early 1920s (78)

MUSIC CITY
Mid-1950s (78)

MUSIC CITY
Late 1950s (45)

MUSIC CITY
Late 1950 (45)

MUSIC CITY
Ca. 1960 (45)

MUSICNOTE
Ca. 1960 (45)

MUSICRAFT
Late 1940s (78)

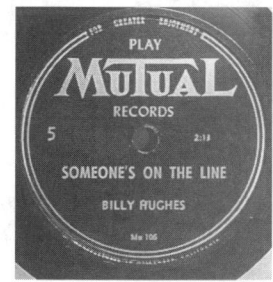

MUTUAL
Ca. 1950 (78)

NRC
Ca. 1958 (45)

NRC
1960 (45)

NADSCO
Early 1920s (78)

NASCO
Late 1950s (78)

NASSAU
Ca. 1908 (78)
Single-sided

NATIONAL
Mid-1920s (78)

NATIONAL
Late 1940s (78)

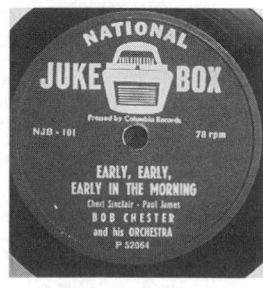

NATIONAL JUKE BOX
Early 1950s (78)
Columbia pressing

NATIONAL MUSIC LOVERS
Mid-1920s (78)

NATION'S FORUM
Ca. 1918 (78)

NATION'S FORUM
Ca. 1920 (78)

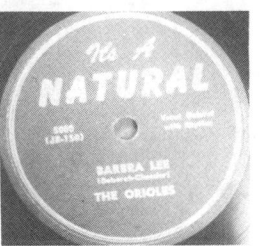

NATURAL
Ca. 1950 (78)

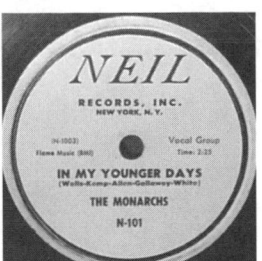

NEIL
Mid-1950s (78)

NEW COMFORT
Mid-1920s (78)

NEW FLEXO
Late 1920s (78)

NEW PHONIC
Ca. 1928 (78)

NEW STAR
Ca. 1960 (45)

NIKE
Late 1950s (45)

NOCTURNE
Ca. 1940 (78)

NORDSKOG
Ca. 1922 (78)

NORDSKOG
Early 1920s (78)

NORDSKOG
Ca. 1951 (78)

NORMAN
Late 1950s (45)

NORTHERN
Late 1950s (45)

NORTH STAR
Mid-1950s (78)

NOR-VA-JAK
Late 1950s (45)

NOTARY
Ca. 1950 (78)

NOTE
Mid-1950s (45)

NUCRAFT
Ca. 1950 (78)

ODEON
Early 1920s (78)

ODEON
Ca. 1930 (78)
American

OKEH
Late Teens (78)

OKEH
Ca. 1920 (78)
Lateral

OKEH
Early 1920s (78)
"Race" Series

OKEH
Mid-1920s (78)

OKEH
Ca. 1926 (78)

OKEH
Mid-1920s (78)
"Race" Series

OKEH
Ca. 1927 (78)

OKEH
Ca. 1930 (78)

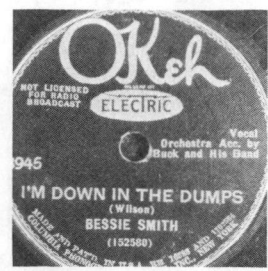

OKEH
Note:8000 Series is "Race"
45000 Series is Hillbilly
Early 1930s (78)

OKEH
Ca. 1931 (78)
Seger Ellis Logo

OKEH
1940-1942 (78)

OKEH
Late 1950s (45)

OKLAHOMA
Late 1950s (45)

OLD SWING-MASTER
Late 1940s (78)

OLD TOWN
Early 1950s (78)

OLD TOWN
Mid-1950s (45)

OLD TOWN
Mid-1950s (78)

OLD TOWN
Mid-1950s (78)

OLD TOWN
Late 1950s (78)

OLD TOWN
Late 1950s (45)

OLD TOWN
Late 1950s (45)

OLIMPIC
Ca. 1960 (45)

OLYMPIC
Early 1920s (78)

ONYX
Late 1950s (45)

ONYX
Late 1950s (45)

OPAL
Ca. 1950 (78)

OPERA
Ca. 1950 (78)

OPERAPHONE
Ca. 1919 (78)

ORBIT
Mid-1950s (45)

ORBIT
H1959 (45)

ORBIT
Ca. 1960 (45)

ORIGINAL
Early 1950s (78)

ORIOLE
Early to Mid-1920s (78)

ORIOLE
Late 1920s (78)
Early 1930s

ORIOLE
Ca. 1960 (45)

OT
Ca. 1950 (78)

OWL
Early 1950s (78)

**OXFORD DISC
RECORD**
Ca. 1905 (78)

**OXFORD DISC
RECORD**
Ca. 1909 (78)

PACEMAKER
Ca. 1950 (78)

PACIFIC
Late 1940s (78)

PAGEANT
Mid-1950s (78)

PAM-NOR
Ca. 1950 (78)

PARADISE
Late 1940s (78)

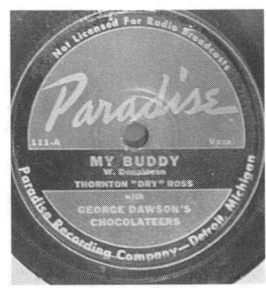

PARADISE
Late 1940s (78)

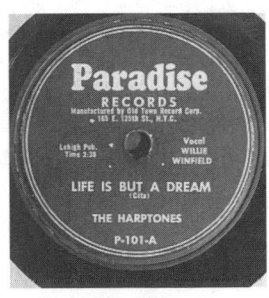

PARADISE
Ca. 1956 (78)

PARAGON
Ca. 1950 (78)

**PARAMOUNT BLACK
SWAN**
Ca. 1923 (78)

PARAMOUNT
Early 1920s (78)

PARAMOUNT
"Race" Series (78)
12-13000 Series
Late 1920s

PARAMOUNT
Hillbilly 3000 Series (78)
Late 1920s

**PARAMOUNT RADIO
RECORDING**
1940s (78)

PARIS
Late 1950s (45)

PARK
Late 1950s (45)

PARKWAY
Ca. 1960 (45)

PARLAY
Ca. 1950 (78)

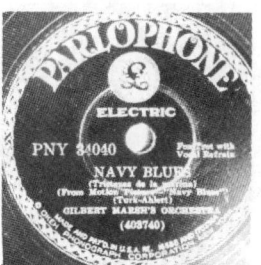

PARLOPHONE
Ca. 1930 (78)

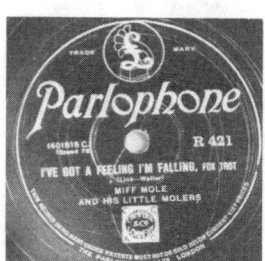

PARLOPHONE
Late 1920s (78)
English

PARROT
Mid-1950s (45)

PARROT
Mid-1950s (78)

PATHÉ
Late Teens to Early 1920s
(78)

PATHÉ
Ca. 1921 (78)

PATHÉ ACTUELLE
Mid to Late 1920s (78)

PATHÉ ACTUELLE
Race Series
Late 1920s (78)

PATSY CLINE
Late 1950s (EP)

PEACOCK
Mid-1950s (78)

PEACOCK
Late 1950s (45)

PEAK
Ca. 1950 (78)

PEARL
Ca. 1950 (78)

PEARL
Late 1950s (45)

PEERLESS
Ca. 1907 (78)
Single-sided

PELICAN
Ca. 1950 (78)

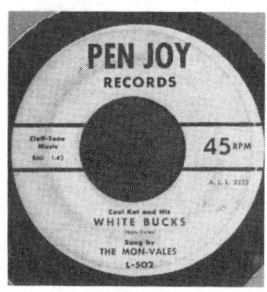

PEN JOY
Late 1950s (45)

PENNINGTON
Ca. 1924 (78)

PENTHOUSE
Late 1950s (45)

PEPPER
Early 1960s (45)

PERFECT
Ca. 1922 (78)

PERFECT
(STAR SERIES)
Mid to Late 1920s (78)

PERFECT
Mid to Late 1920s (78)

PERFECT - PICTURE 65

PERFECT
Late 1920s (78)

PERFECT
Early 1930s (78)

PERFECT
Early 1930s (78)
Race Series

PERFECT
Ca. 1937 (78)

PERFECT
Late 1950s (45)

PERSONAL RECORD
1923-1926 (78)

PERSONAL RECORD
Late 1920s (78)

**PERSONAL
RECORDING**
Ca. 1928 (78)

PERSONALITY
Late 1940s (78)

PERSONALITY
Late 1950s (45)

PETAL
Early 1960s (45)

PETITE
Late 1950s (45)

PHAMOUS
Ca. 1950 (78)

PHANTSIE
Early 1920s (78)

PHILCO
"Hip Pocket"
Ca. 1968 (45)
3-7/8-inch diam.

PHILHARMONIC
Ca. 1940 (78)

PHILLES
Early 1960s (45)

PHILLIPS
Late 1950s (78)

PHILLIPS
Late 1950s (45)

PHILO
Late 1940s (78)

**PHONO-CUT
RECORD**
Ca. 1919 (78)

**PHONOGRAPH
RECORDING CO.**
Ca. 1927 (78)

PIC 1
Ca. 1960 (45)

PICTURE RECORDS
Early 1950s (78)

PICTURE
Late 1950s (45)

PIKE
Ca. 1960 (45)

PILGRIM
Late 1950s (45)

PILGRIM
Mid-1950s (78)

PILGRIM
Late 1950s (78)

PINK
Late 1950s (45)

PLA-BAC
Early 1950s (78)

PLAYTIME RECORDS
Late 1920s (78)
5-inch record

PLUS
Late 1950s (45)

POLK
Ca. 1930 (78)

PONTIAC
Ca. 1960 (45)

POPLAR
Ca. 1960 (45)

PREMIUM
Late 1940s (78)

PREMIUM
Late 1950s (45)

PRESTIGE
Early 1950s (78)

PRESTIGE
Early 1950s (78)

PRESTIGE
Mid-1950s (45)

PRINCESS
Early 1960s (45)

PROCESS
Ca. 1950 (78)

PROFILE
Late 1950s (45)

PUBLIX
Ca. 1930 (78)

PURETONE
Mid-1920s (78)

PURITAN
Ca. 1920 (78)

PURITAN
Early 1920s (78)

PURITAN
Early 1920s (78)

PURITAN
Mid-1920s (78)

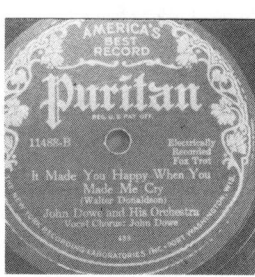

PURITAN
Ca. 1927 (78)

PURITONE
Ca. 1920 (78)

PURITONE
Late 1920s (78)

Q.R.S.
7000 "Race" Series
9000 Series is Hillbilly (78)

Q.R.S.
Ca. 1930 (78)

QUE
Late 1950s (45)

QUEEN
Mid-1940s (78)

QUEEN
Late 1940s (78)

RADIEX
Ca. 1924 (78)

RADIEX
Mid-1920s (78)

RADIEX
Ca. 1928 (78)

RADIO
Ca. 1960 (45)

RADIO ARTIST
Ca. 1950 (78)

RADIO RECORDERS
Late 1930s (78)
Special purpose/Personal

RAINBOW
Early 1920s (78)
Sacred record

RAINBOW
Mid-1920s (78)

RAINBOW
Early 1950s (78)

RAINBOW
Mid-1950s (78)

RAINBOW
Early 1950s (45)

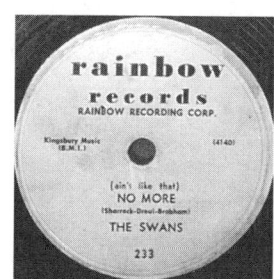

RAINBOW
Early 1950s (78)

RAM RECORDS
Late 1950s (45)

RAMA
Mid-1950s (78)

RAMA
Mid-1950s (45)

RAMA
Rhythm & Blues
Late 1950s (45)

RAVEN
Ca. 1950 (78)

RAYMOND
Ca. 1950 (78)

RAYS
Mid-1950s (45)

RCA VICTOR
Early 1930s (LP)
Program transcription

RCA VICTOR
Ca. 1933 (78)
12-inch picture record

RCA VICTOR
Ca. 1933 (78)
obverse

RCA VICTOR
Jimmie Rodgers (78)
reverse

RCA VICTOR
Ca. 1953 (78) D.J. copy

RCA VICTOR
Early 1950s (45)

RCA VICTOR
Early 1950s (45)

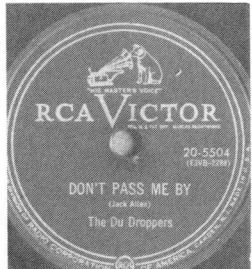

RCA VICTOR
Mid-1950s (78)

RCA VICTOR
Early 1950s (45)
Special purpose EP

RCA VICTOR
Mid-1950s (78)
Marilyn Monroe
promotional record

RCA VICTOR
Mid-1950s (78)
M. Monroe promo-flip side

RCA VICTOR
Mid-1950s (33 1/3)
promotional record

RCA VICTOR
Mid-1950s (33 1/3)
promotion record

RCA VICTOR
Late 1950s (78)

RCA VICTOR
Mid-1950s (45)

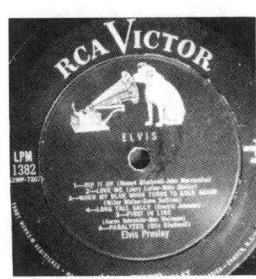

RCA VICTOR
Ca. 1956-59 (LP)

RCA VICTOR
Ca. 1960-1963 (LP)

RCA VICTOR
Late 1950s (33 1/3)
7-inch record

RECORTE
Late 1950s (45)

RED BARN RECORD
Ca. 1950 (78)

RED BIRD
Ca. 1950 (78)

RED RAVEN
Early 1950s (78)

RED ROBIN
Rhythm & Blues
Mid-1950s (45)

RED ROBIN
Mid-1950s (78)

RED TOP
Late 1950s (45)

RED TOP
Late 1950s (45)

REEL RECORDS
Ca. 1950 (78)

REELFOOT
Late 1950s (45)

REGAL
Late 1920s (78)

REGAL
Ca. 1930 (78)

REGAL
Late 1940s (78)

REGENT
Late 1940s (78)

REGIS
Late 1940s (78)

REINA
Ca. 1950 (78)

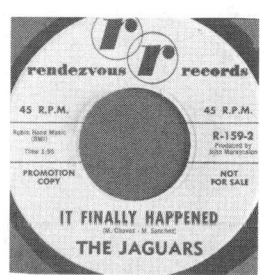

**RENDEZVOUS
RECORDS**
Ca. 1960 (45)

RENNER
Early 1960s (45)

REO
Ca. 1959 (78)
Canadian

REPUBLIC
Ca. 1950 (78)

REPUBLIC
Mid-1950s (45)

REPUBLIC
Ca. 1960 (45)

RESERVE
Late 1950s (45)

RESONA
Early 1920s (78)

RESONA
Ca. 1924 (78)

REV
Late 1950s (45)

REX RECORD
Late Teens (78)

REX
Ca. 1918 (78)

REX
Ca. 1960 (45)

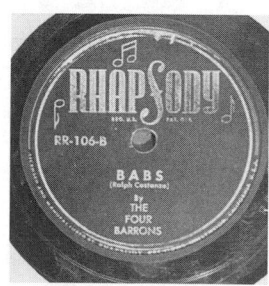

RHAPSODY
Late 1940s (78)

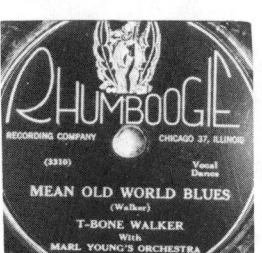

RHUMBOOGIE
Late 1940s (78)

RHYTHM
Early 1950s (78)

RHYTHM
Mid-1950s (45)

RIALTO
Early 1920s (78)

RIC
Rhythm & Blues
Ca. 1960 (45)

RIC
Early 1960s (45)

RICH RECORDS
Ca. 1950 (78)

RICH-R'-TONE
Ca. 1950 (78)

RICH-TONE
Ca. 1922 (78)

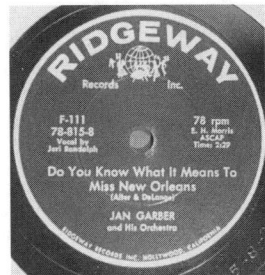

RIDGEWAY
Ca. 1950 (78)

RISHELL
Ca. 1918 (78)

RIVERMONT
Late 1950s (45)

R n B
Late 1950s (45)

ROCKET
Ca. 1950 (78)

ROCKIN'
Mid-1950s (45)

ROME
Ca. 1960 (45)

ROMEO
Late 1920s (78)

ROMEO
Ca. 1930 (78)

ROMEO
Ca. 1932 (78)
"Race" Series

ROMEO
Early 1930s (78)

ROMEO
Ca. 1937 (78)

RON
Late 1950s (78)

RON
Late 1950s (45)

ROOST
Ca. 1950 (78)

ROULETTE
Late 1950s (78)

ROULETTE
Late 1950s (78)

ROULETTE
Late 1950s (45)

ROULETTE
Late 1950s (78)

ROULETTE
Late 1950s (45)

ROULETTE
Ca. 1960 (LP)

ROYAL
Ca. 1922 (78)

ROYAL ROOST
Mid-1950s (45)

ROYAL ROOST
Mid-1950s (78)

ROYALE
Ca. 1940 (78)

ROYALTY
Late 1940s (78)

ROYCROFT
Ca. 1930 (78)

RPM
Early 1950s (78)

RPM
Early 1950s (45)

RPM
Late 1950s (45)

RUDDER RECORDS
Ca. 1950 (78)

RUSHMORE
Ca. 1950 (78)

RUST
Ca. 1960 (45)

SABINA
Ca. 1960 (45)

SABRA
Ca. 1960 (45)

SABRE
Mid-1950s (78)

SABRE
Mid-1950s (45)

SABRINA
Late 1950s (45)

SAGE
Late 1950s (78)

SAGE
Late 1950s (45)

SANDY
Late 1950s (45)

SAPPHIRE
Mid-1950s (45)

SARCO
Late 1940s (78)

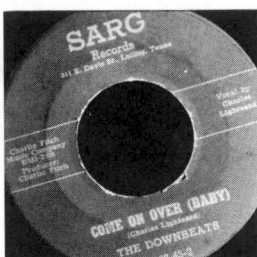
SARG
Late 1950s (45)

SATIN
Ca. 1960 (45)

SAVOY
Ca. 1930 (78)

SAVOY
Late 1940s (78)
Reissue

SAVOY
Late 1940s (78)
"Boogie Blues" label

SAVOY
Rhythm & Blues
Ca. 1948 (78)

SAVOY
Rhythm & Blues
Mid-1950s

SCARLET
Ca. 1960 (45)

SCEPTER
Early 1960s (45)

SCOOP
Ca. 1950 (78)

SCORE
Late 1940s (78)

SCOTTIE
Ca. 1960 (45)

SCOTTY'S
Late 1940s (78)

S D
Late 1940s (78)

S D
Late 1940s (78)

SEE BEE
Early 1930s (78)

SEGER
Ca. 1950 (78)

SELECTIVE
Ca. 1950 (78)

SELMA
Late 1950s (45)

SENSATION
Late 1940s (78)

SESSION
Jazz 1940s (78)

SEVA
Ca. 1950 (78)
Ethnic label

SEVEN-ELEVEN
Mid-1950s (78)

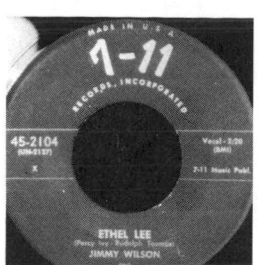

SEVEN-ELEVEN
Mid-1950s (45)

S & G
Ca. 1948 (78)

SHADE
Late 1950s (45)

SHAN-TODD
Ca. 1960 (45)

SHARP
Early 1960s (45)

SHELL
Ca. 1960 (45)

SHO-BIZ
Ca. 1959 (45)

SHOW TIME
Mid-1950s (45)

SHOW TIME
Mid-1950s (78)

SIEGEL COOPER
Ca. 1910 (78)
Single-sided

SIGMA NU
Ca. 1924 (78)

SIGNATURE
Late 1940s (78)

SIGNATURE
Late 1940s (78)

SILHOUETTE
Late 1950s (45)

SILVERTONE
Ca. 1916 (78)

SILVERTONE
Ca. 1916 (78)

SILVERTONE
Ca. 1920 (78)

SILVERTONE
Mid-1920s (78)

SILVERTONE
Ca. 1940 (78)
Columbia pressing

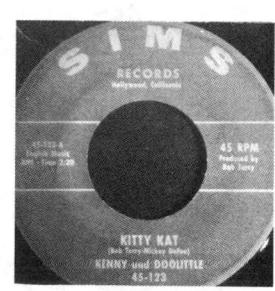

SIMS
Late 1950s (45)

SINGULAR
Late 1950s (45)

SIR
Late 1950s (45)

SITTIN'IN WITH
Late 1940s (78)

SITTIN' IN WITH
Early 1950s (45)

SKYLA
Ca. 1960 (45)

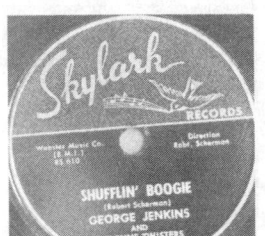

SKYLARK
Ca. 1950 (78)

SKYSTREAK
Ca. 1949 (78)

SKYWAY
Ca. 1950 (78)

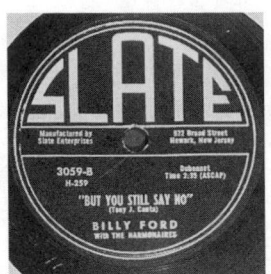

SLATE
Ca. 1950 (78)

SLIM WILLET
Ca. 1956 (78)

SMART
Early 1950s (78)

SMASH
Ca. 1960 (45)

SMOKE
Late 1950s (45)

S M R
Ca. 1950 (78)

SOLO
Ca. 1950 (78)

SONORA
Late 1940s (78)

SOUND
Late 1950 (45)

SOUND TEX
Early 1960s (45)

SPANGLE
Late 1950s (45)

SPAR
Ca. 1960 (45)

SPARK
Mid-1950s (78)

SPARK
Mid-1950s (45)

SPARK
Rhythm & Blues
Mid-1950s (45)

SPARKELL
Late 1950s (45)

SPARTAN
Early 1960s (45)

SPARTON
Ca. 1959 (78)
Canadian

SPECIAL
Ca. 1923 (78)

SPECIAL EDITIONS
Ca. 1940s (78)

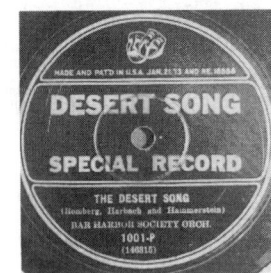

SPECIAL RECORD
Ca. 1927 (78)

SPECIALTY
Ca. 1950 (78)

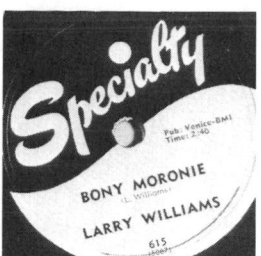

SPECIALTY
Ca. 1950s (78)

SPECIALTY
1950s (45)

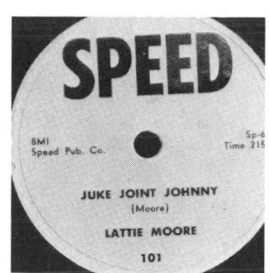

SPEED
Early 1950s (78)

SPEED
Late 1950s (45)

SPINNA
Late 1940s (78)

SPINNING
Late 1950s (45)

SPIRE
Early 1950s (78)

SPOTLIGHT
Late 1950s (45)

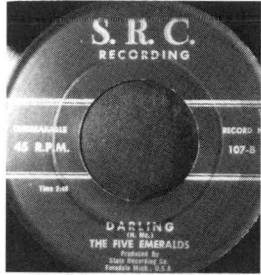

S.R.C.
Late 1950s (45)

STACY
Ca. 1960 (45)

STAFF
Ca. 1947 (78)

STAFF
Early 1950s (45)

STANDARD DISC RECORD
Ca. 1912 (78)

STANDARD DISC RECORD
Ca. 1914 (78)

STANDARD DISC RECORD
Ca. 1915 (78)

STANDARD DISC RECORD
Ca. 1915 (78)

STANDARD DISC RECORD
Ca. 1915 (78)

STAR RECORD
Ca. 1912 (78)

STAR RECORD
Ca. 1914 (78)

STAR X
Late 1950s (45)

STARCK
Mid-1920s (78)

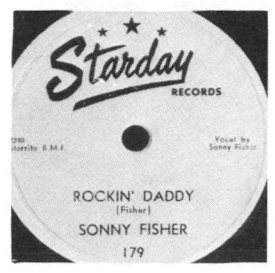

STARDAY
Mid-1950s (78)

STARDAY
Late 1950s (45)

STARDAY
Late 1950s (45)

STARDAY
Early 1960s (45)

STARLIGHT
Ca. 1950 (78)

STARR
Ca. 1921 (78)

STAR GENNETT
Early 1920s (78)

STARRETT
Ca. 1960 (45)

STARTIME
Ca. 1959 (45)

STATES
Mid-1950s (78)

STATES
Mid-1950s (45)

STATUE
Early 1960s (45)

STELLA
Ca. 1950 (78)

STERLING
Ca. 1930 (78)
Canadian

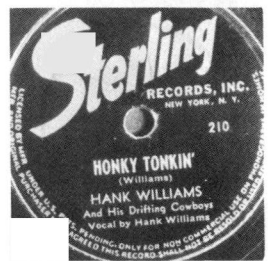

STERLING
Late 1940s (78)

STERLING
Late 1950s (45)

STINSON
1940s (78)

STOMPER TIME
Late 1950s (45)

STORM
Ca. 1960 (45)

STRONG
Ca. 1923 (78)

STYLECRAFT
Ca. 1950 (78)

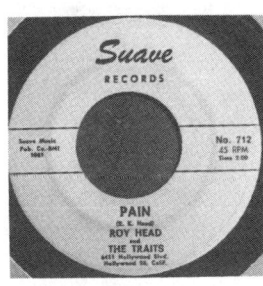

SUAVE
Late 1950s (45)

SUE
Late 1950s (45)

SUEDE
Late 1950s (45)

SUGAR HILL
Mid-1950s (45)

SULLIVAN
Late 1950s (45)

SUMMITT
Late 1950s (45)

SUN RECORD
Ca. 1914 (78)

SUN
Mid-1950s (78)

SUN
Mid-1950s (45)

SUN
Late 1950s (33 1/3)

SUN
Mid-1960s (45)
D.J. copy

SUNBEAM
Ca. 1950 (78)

SUNBEAM
Late 1950s (45)

SUNBIRD RECORDS
Mid-1950s (45)

SUNDOWN
Late 1950s (45)

SUNRISE
Ca. 1929 (78)
Grey Gull product

SUNRISE
Ca. 1933 (78)
RCA Victor product

SUNRISE
Late 1940s (78)

SUNRISE
Late 1940s (78)

SUNSET
Mid-1920s (78)

SUNSET
1940s (78)

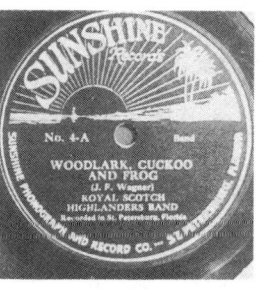

SUNSHINE
Early 1920s (78)

SUNSHINE
Late 1940s (78)

SUPER DISC
Late 1940s (78)

**SUPER
ENTERTAINMENT**
Ca. 1950 (78)

SUPERIOR
Ca. 1928 (78)

SUPERIOR
Ca. 1930 (78)

SUPERIOR
Ca. 1950 (78)

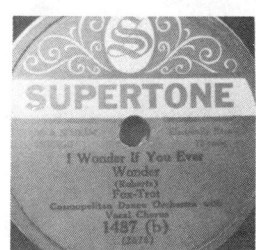

SUPERTONE
Ca. 1925 (78)
Grey Gull product

SUPERTONE
Ca. 1923 (78)

SUPERTONE
Late 1920s (78)

SUPERTONE
Ca. 1927 (78)
Harmony pressing

SUPERTONE
Ca. 1927 (78)

SUPREME
Ca. 1926 (78)
Grey Gull product

SUPREME
Ca. 1950s (78)

SUPREME
Early 1960s (45)

SURE
Late 1950s (45)

SURF
Late 1950s (45)

SWAN
Late 1950s (78)

SWAN
Late 1950s-Early 1960s (45)

SWEET-TONE
Ca. 1950 (78)

SWING
Late 1940s (78)

SWING BEAT
Late 1940s (78)

SWINGIN'
Early 1960s (45)

SWING TIME
Ca. 1950 (78)

SWING TIME
Early 1950s (45)

SYMPHONOLA
Ca. 1919 (78)

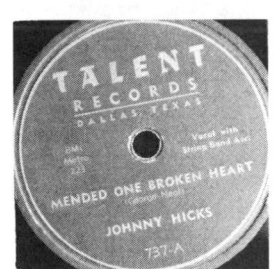

TALENT
Ca. 1950 (78)

TALENT
Early 1960s (45)

TALENT SCOUT
Ca. 1959 (45)

TALENTOON
Ca. 1950 (78)

TALK-O-PHONE
Ca. 1910 (78)
Single-sided

TALLY
Ca. 1960 (45)

TAMLA
1959-60 (45)

TAMLA
Ca. 1960 (45)

TAMPA
Late 1950s (78)

TAMPA
Late 1950s (45)

TANNER
Late 1940s (78)

TARA
Ca. 1959 (45)

TEE GEE
Late 1950s (45)

TEEN
Mid-1950s (78)

TEEN
Mid-1950s (78)

TEENAGE
Mid-1950s (45)

TEEN LIFE
Late 1950s

TELL
Late 1940s (78)

TEMPO
Early 1950s (78)

TENDER
Late 1950s (45)

TENNESSEE
Early 1950s (78)

TENNESSEE
Mid-1950s (78)

TENNESSEE
Mid-1950s (45)

TERP
Mid-1950s (45)

TERRACE
Late 1950s (45)

TETRA
Late 1950s (78)

TETRA
Late 1950s (45)

TEXADISC
Ca. 1951 (78)

TEX-TALENT
Early 1950s (78)

THANKS!
Ca. 1960 (45)

THELMA
Early 1960s (45)

THEME
Ca. 1950 (78)

THE THOMAS RECORD
Ca. 1915 (78)

TIFFANY
Early 1950s (78)

TILT
Early 1960s (45)

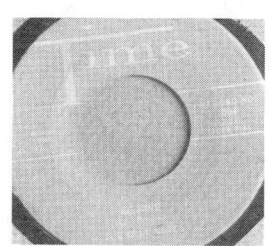
TIME
Late 1950s (45)

TIMELY
Mid-1950s (45)

TIMELY
Early 1950s (78)

TIMELY TUNES
Early 1930s (78)

TIN PAN ALLEY
Mid-1950s (78)

TIN PAN ALLEY
Mid-1950s (45)

TIP TOP
Late 1950s (45)

TITAN
Late 1950s (45)

TNT
Late 1940s (78)

TNT
Early 1950s (78)

TNT
Mid-1950s (45)

TNT
Late 1950s (78)

TNT
Late 1950s (45)

TNT
Late 1950s (45)

TNT
Late 1950s (45)

TONE
Late 1950s (45)

TOP HAT
Late 1940s (78)

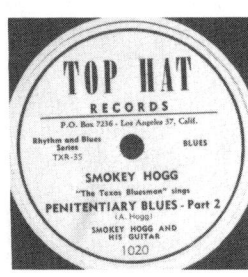

TOP HAT
Ca. 1950 (78)

TOP RANK
Ca. 1960 (45)

TOP TEN
Ca. 1947 (78)

TOP TEN
Early 1960s (45)

TOP TUNE
Ca. 1950 (78)

TOPS
Ca. 1950 (78)

TORCH
Ca. 1950 (78)

TOWER
Late 1940s (78)

TOWN & COUNTRY
Late 1940s (78)

TOWN & COUNTRY
Late 1940s (78)

TREAT
Mid-1950s (78)

TREL
Ca. 1960 (45)

TREMONT
Mid-1920s (78)

TREND
Ca. 1960 (45)

TRESS
Late 1950s (45)

TRI ESS
Early 1960s (45)

TRIANGLE
Early 1920s (78)

TRIDELT
Early 1960s (45)

TRILON
Late 1940s (78)

TRIPLE A
Mid-1950s (78)

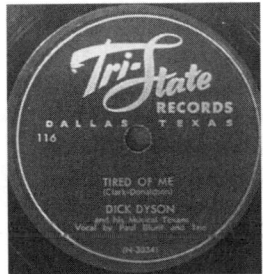

TRI-STATE
Ca. 1950 (78)

TRIUMPH
Ca. 1960 (45)

TROPHY
Late 1950s (45)

TRUMPET
Mid-1950s (78)

TRUMPET
Mid-1950s (45)

TURF
Late 1950s (45)

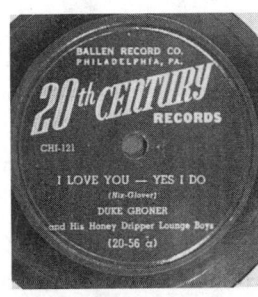

20th CENTURY
Ca. 1950 (78)

20th CENTURY
Mid-1950s (78)

20th CENTURY
Mid-1950s (45)

**TWENTIETH
CENTURY**
Late 1950s (45)

20th FOX
Late 1950s (45)

TWIN STAR
Late 1950s (45)

TWIRL
Ca. 1960 (45)

U.H.C.A.
Late 1930s (78)
Collectors Series

U.S.A.
Early 1960s (45)

ULTRA
Late 1950s (45)

UNIQUE
Early 1950s (78)

UNITED
Ca. 1950 (78)

UNITED
Ca. 1950 (78)

UNITED
Ca. 1951 (78)

UNITED
Mid-1950s (78)

UNITED
Rhythm & Blues
Early 1950s (45)

UNITED
Rhythm & Blues
Mid-1950s (45)

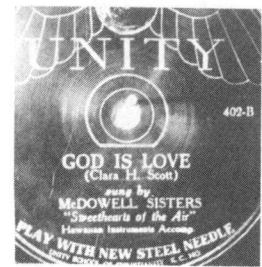
UNITY
Ca. 1925 (78)

UNIVERSAL
Late 1920s (78)

UNIVERSAL ARTIST
Ca. 1960 (45)

UNIVERSAL-FOX
Ca. 1950 (78)

UNIVERSAL ZONOPHONE
Ca. 1903 (78)
Single-sided

UNIVERSITY
Late 1940s (78)

UP-TO-DATE
Ca. 1924 (78)

UPTOWN
Ca. 1950 (78)

URBAN RECORD COMPANY
Ca. 1949 (78)

VADEN
Late 1950s (45)

VADEN
Late 1950s (45)

VALLEY
Late 1950s (45)

VALLEY'S MEADOWLARK
Late 1950s (45)

VALOR
Ca. 1960 (45)

VAN
Late 1950s (45)

VANDAN
Late 1950s (45)

VAN DYKE
Ca. 1930 (78)

VAN-ES
Ca. 1950 (78)

VARIETY
Mid-1920s (78)

VARIETY
Late 1930s (78)

VARSITY
Ca. 1940 (78)

V-DISC
Ca. 1947 (78)
12-inch issued for armed
forces

VEE
Late 1950s (45)

VEE-JAY
Mid-1950s (78)

VEE-JAY
Late 1950s (LP)

VEE-JAY
Early 1960s (45)

VEGA
Ca. 1950 (78)

VEGA
Early 1960s (45)

VELTONE
Late 1950s (45)

VEL-TONE
Mid-1950s (45)

VELVET TONE
Late 1920s (78)

VELVET TONE
Ca. 1932 (78)

VENUS
Late 1950s (45)

VESTA
Late 1950s (45)

VICEROY
Late 1950s (45)

VICTOR
Ca. 1900-1901 (78)
See also: "IMPROVED"

**VICTOR MONARCH
RECORD**
Ca. 1901-1902 (78)
7-inch record

**VICTOR MONARCH
RECORD**
Ca. 1901 (78)

**VICTOR MONARCH
RECORD**
Ca. 1902 (78)

VICTOR RECORD
Ca. 1904-1905 (78)

VICTOR RECORD
Ca. 1905-1908 (78)

VICTOR RECORD
Ca. 1911-1913 (78)

VICTOR
Ca. 1916-1923 (78)

**VICTOR SPECIAL
RECORD**
Ca. 1923 (78)

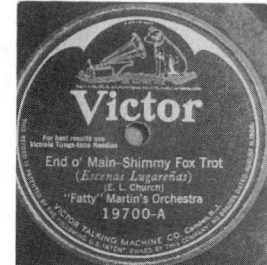

VICTOR
Ca. 1925 (78)

VICTOR
Ca. 1926-1930 (78)

VICTOR
Late 1920s
Special Record

VICTOR
"Hot Dance" V-38000 Series
1929-1930 (78)

VICTOR
V-38500 Series
Ca. 1930 (78)

VICTOR
"PICT-UR-MUSIC"
Ca. 1930 (78)

VICTOR
Ca. 1932 (78)
Canadian

**VICTOR
"SWING CLASSIC"**
Mid-1930s (78)

VICTOR
Late 1930s (78)

VICTOR
1940s (78)
Collectors Reissue Series

VICTORIA
Early 1950s (78)

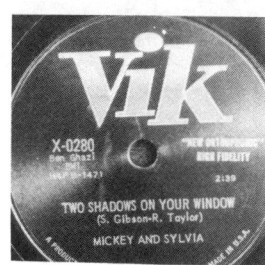

VIK
Late 1950s (78)

VIK
Mid-1950s (45)

VIN
Ca. 1960 (78)

VIN
Ca. 1960 (45)

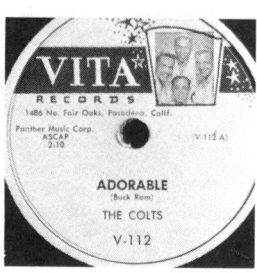

VITA
Rhythm & Blues
Late 1950s (78)

VITA
Late 1950s (45)

VOCALION
Mid-1920s (78)

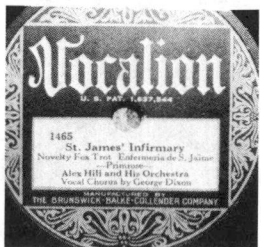

VOCALION
1000 "Race" Series (78)

VOCALION
Early 1930s (78)

VOCALION
Ca. 1934 (78)

VOCALION
Mid-1930s (78)

VOCALION
Late 1930s (78)

VOCALION
Ca. 1937 (78)

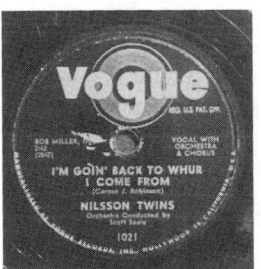

VOGUE
Ca. 1950 (78)

**VOGUE PICTURE
RECORD**
Late 1940s (78)

**VOGUE PICTURE
RECORD**

**VOGUE PICTURE
RECORD**

**VOGUE PICTURE
RECORD**

**VOGUE PICTURE
RECORD**

**VOGUE PICTURE
RECORD**

**VOGUE PICTURE
RECORD**

Pictures vary. This, and following, are representative.

**VOGUE PICTURE
RECORD**

**VOGUE PICTURE
RECORD**

**VOGUE PICTURE
RECORD**

**VOGUE PICTURE
RECORD**

**VOGUE PICTURE
RECORD**

**VOGUE PICTURE
RECORD**

**VOGUE PICTURE
RECORD**

**VOGUE PICTURE
RECORD**

**VOGUE PICTURE
RECORD**

**VOGUE PICTURE
RECORD**

**VOGUE PICTURE
RECORD**

**VOGUE PICTURE
RECORD**

V-TONE
Late 1950s (45)

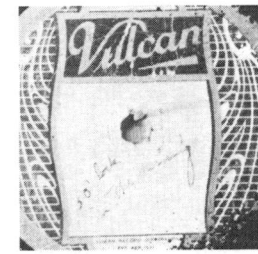

VULCAN
1920s (78)

VULCAN
Late 1950s (45)

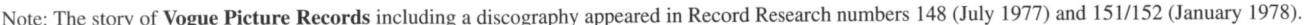

Note: The story of **Vogue Picture Records** including a discography appeared in Record Research numbers 148 (July 1977) and 151/152 (January 1978).

WALDORF
Late 1950s (EP)

WALLIN'S
Ca. 1920 (78)
Scandinavian

WALLIN'S
Early 1920s (78)
Scandinavian

WAR CONN
Early 1960s (45)

WARNER BROS.
Early 1960s (45)

WARRIOR
1959-1960 (45)

WARWICK
Ca. 1959 (78)
Canadian

WASCO
Early 1950s (78)

THE WAX SHOP
Ca. 1950 (78)

WAYSIDE
Late 1950s (45)

WELLS
Late 1950s (45)

WESTERNAIR
Ca. 1950 (78)

WESTPORT
Late 1950s (45)

WHIPPET
Late 1950s (78)

WHIRLIN DISC
Late 1950s (45)

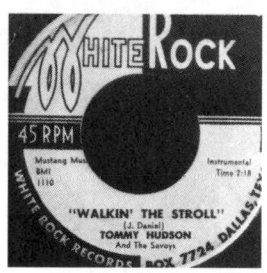

WHITE ROCK
Late 1950s (45)

WIGGS, INC.
Ca. 1950 (78)

WILDCAT
Early 1960s (45)

WINDSOR
Ca. 1950 (78)

WING
Late 1950s (78)

WING
Late 1950s (45)

WINLEY
Late 1950s (45)

WINSTON
Early 1950s (78)

WIZARD
Early 1960s (45)

WOLVERINE
Late 1940s (78)

WONDER
Late 1950s (45)

WOR FEATURE
Ca. 1940 (78)

WORLD RECORD
Ca. 1920 (78)

WORLD RECORD
Ca. 1918 (78)

WORLD RECORDS
Ca. 1950 (78)

WRIGHTMAN
Ca. 1950 (78)

"X"
Mid-1950s (78)

X-TRA
Late 1950s (45)

XYZ
Late 1950s (45)

"Y"
Late 1950s (45)

**YERKES DANCE
RECORDS**
Ca. 1921 (78)

YORK
Ca. 1950 (78)

YOUR COPY
Late 1950s (45)

YUCCA
Ca. 1960 (45)

ZERO
Ca. 1961 (45)

ZODIAC
Early 1950s (78)

ZONOFONO RECORD
1907-1910 (78)

**ZON-O-PHONE
RECORD**
Ca. 1901 (78)
Embossed label

**ZON-O-PHONE
RECORD**
Ca. 1901 (78)
Embossed label

**ZON-O-PHONE
RECORD**
1905-1910 (78)

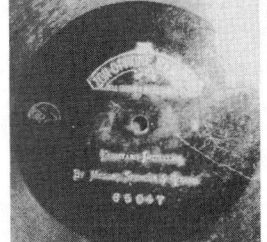
ZON-O-PHONE RECORD
1905-1910 (78)

ZON-O-PHONE RECORD
1910-1912 (78)

ZYNN
Early 1960s (45)

Jazz, Big Bands, Dance Bands, Personality, Pop, Ragtime

Records in this section are generally from the period 1900 to 1950. All records in this section are ten-inch 78 RPM unless otherwise indicated.

IRVING AARONSON & HIS COMMANDERS:

Columbia 2946-D *Pardon My Southern Accent* ....$15.00 - $20.00
  2980-D *Flirtation Walk* ....15.00 - 20.00
  2981-D *Let's Be Thankful*................................15.00 - 20.00
  3037-D *An Evening In June*..........................15.00 - 20.00
  3043-D *Commanderism*....................................20.00 - 30.00
Edison 51685 *Don't Wake Me Up* ....15.00 - 20.00
Victor 20002, 20034, 20059, 20063, 20083, 20094,
  20095, 20100, 20117, 21778, 21786, 21834,
  21867, 21888 ....7.00 - 12.00
Victor 20381 *Everything's Peaches* ....10.00 - 15.00
  20473 *I Never See Maggie Alone* ....10.00 - 15.00
  21260 *Let's Misbehave* ....10.00 - 15.00
  21745 *Let's Do It* ....10.00 - 15.00
Vocalion 2535 *That's How Rhythm Was Born*........15.00 - 20.00
  2536 *The Day You Came Along*.........................15.00 - 20.00
  2570 *You Gotta Be A Football Hero* ....15.00 - 20.00
  2571 *Moonlight Down In Lover's Lane* ....10.00 - 15.00
  25004 *Shadows On The Swanee* ....20.00 - 30.00
  25005 *I've Gotta Get Up And Go To Work* ....20.00 - 30.00

LARRY ABBOTT & HIS ORCHESTRA:

Okeh 41044 *I'm More Than Satisfied* ....50.00 - 80.00

IRWIN ABRAMS & HIS (HOTEL MANAGER/ KNICKERBOCKER GRILL) ORCHESTRA:

Banner, most titles ....5.00 - 8.00
Domino, most titles..5.00 - 8.00
Edison 51625 *Normandy* ....10.00 - 15.00
  51633 *The Co-Ed* ....25.00 - 40.00
  52106 *In An Oriental Garden* ....20.00 - 30.00
  52107 *Are You Happy?* ....20.00 - 30.00
  52114 *Heartaches and Dreams* ....20.00 - 30.00
  52148 *Dream Kisses* ....30.00 - 50.00
  52168 *Moon Of Japan* ....30.00 - 50.00
Okeh 40783 *My Sunday Girl* ....10.00 - 15.00
  40798 *That's My Hap-Hap-Happiness* ....10.00 - 15.00
  40846 *Magnolia* ....15.00 - 25.00
  40864 *I Ain't That Kind Of A Baby* ....10.00 - 15.00
  40869 *It's A Million To One You're In Love* .....10.00 - 15.00
  40880 *Shaking The Blues Away* ....10.00 - 15.00
  40918 *Headin' For Harlem* ....10.00 - 15.00
  40948 *My Heart Stood Still* ....10.00 - 15.00

BERNARD ADDISON & HIS RHYTHM:

Bluebird 6144 *Lovely Liza Lee* ....10.00 - 15.00
  6174 *Toledo Shuffle* ....10.00 - 15.00

ADRIAN & HIS ORCHESTRA/TAP ROOM GANG; ADRIAN'S RAMBLERS:

Brunswick 6786 *Get Goin'* ....10.00 - 15.00
  6877 *Why Don't You Practice What You Preach?*
  ....10.00 - 15.00
  6889 *I Wish I Were Twins*....................................10.00 - 15.00
Columbia 2785-D *Happy As The Day Is Long* ....25.00 - 40.00
Victor 25072 *Weather Man* ....10.00 - 15.00
  25085 *Nagasaki* ....10.00 - 15.00

  25208 *Honeysuckle Rose* ....10.00 - 15.00

ANDREW AIONA'S NOVELTY FOUR:

Columbia 1728-D *Hula Girl*....................................30.00 - 50.00
  1788-D *That Lovin' Hula*.....................................30.00 - 50.00

ALABAMA CREOLE BAND:

Claxtonola 40397 *Choo Choo*..................................20.00 - 30.00

ALABAMA ENTERTAINERS:

Buddy 8009 *Thanks For The Buggy Ride* ....- - -

ALABAMA FUZZY WUZZIES:

Champion 15366 *Fuzzy Wuzzy* ....200.00 - 300.00
  15415 *Congo Stomp* ....250.00 - up

ALABAMA HARMONY BOYS:

Champion 15398 *Chicken Supper Strut*...............250.00 - up
Silvertone 5139 *Sweet Patootie* ....200.00 - 300.00

ALABAMA JAZZ PIRATES:

Bell 1182 *Canned Heat Blues* ....300.00 - up

ALABAMA JUG BAND:

Decca 7000 *My Gal Sal* ....25.00 - 40.00
  7001 *Gulf Coast Blues* ....25.00 - 40.00
  7041 *Somebody Stole My Gal* ....25.00 - 40.00
  7042 *Crazy Blues* ....25.00 - 40.00

ALABAMA RASCALS:

Titles issued contemporaneously on Banner, Melotone, Oriole, Perfect, Romeo: *Dirty Dozen's Cousins; Endurance Stomp; Georgia Grind; Jockey Stomp; Rukus Juice Shuffle; Stomp That Thing* .... 75.00 - 100.00

ALABAMA RED JACKETS:

Champion 15228 *You Can't Cry Over My Shoulder* 15.00 - 20.00
  15229 *I'm Gonna Meet My Sweetie Now* ....15.00 - 20.00

ALABAMA RED PEPPERS:

Titles issued contemporaneously on Cameo, Lincoln, Romeo: *The Drag; Eccentric; A Good Man Is Hard To Find; The New Twister; Red Head Blues; Riverboat Shuffle* ..... 15.00 - 20.00
Additional title: *San* ....10.00 - 15.00

ALABAMA SERENADERS:

Champion 15140 *Alabama Stomp* ....20.00 - 30.00
  15213 *There Ain't No Maybe In My Baby's Eyes*
  ....10.00 - 15.00
  15238 *Underneath The Weeping Willow* ....10.00 - 15.00
  15239 *What Do I Care What Somebody Said?* ..15.00 - 20.00

15271 *South Wind*	15.00 -	20.00
15292 *I'm In Love Again*	10.00 -	15.00
15740 *Louise*	10.00 -	15.00
Herwin 92044 *Congo Stomp*	250.00 -	up

ALABAMA WASHBOARD STOMPERS:

Vocalion 1546 *I Want A Little Girl*	75.00 -	100.00
1587 *Who Stole The Lock?*	75.00 -	100.00
1626 *I Surrender, Dear*	75.00 -	100.00
1630 *Corinne Corinna*	75.00 -	100.00
1635 *I Need Lovin'*	75.00 -	100.00
1684 *Can't We Talk It Over?*	75.00 -	100.00
1689 *If All The World Was Made Of Glass*	75.00 -	100.00
1697 *Pepper Steak*	80.00 -	120.00

ALAMEDA WONDER PLAYERS/ORCHESTRA:

Cardinal 501 *Black Eyed Blues*	15.00 -	25.00
517 *Virginia Blues*	15.00 -	25.00
527 *Lonesome Mammy Blues*	15.00 -	25.00
540 *Stop Your Kidding*	15.00 -	25.00
552 *Yankee Doodle Blues*	15.00 -	25.00
559 *Sugar Blues*	15.00 -	25.00

DON ALBERT & HIS ORCHESTRA:

Vocalion 3401 *True Blue Lou*	20.00 -	30.00
3411 *The Sheik of Araby*	20.00 -	30.00
3423 *On The Sunny Side Of The Street*	20.00 -	30.00
3491 *Liza*	20.00 -	30.00

AL ALBERTS & HIS ORCHESTRA:

Cameo 8280 *You're My Sweetheart*	7.00 -	10.00
8315 *The Jazz Patrol*	7.00 -	10.00
8322 *In A Little Two-By-Four For Two*	8.00 -	12.00
9142 *Building A Nest For Mary*	15.00 -	20.00
9157 *That's My Idea Of Heaven*	7.00 -	10.00
9167 *My Rock-A-Bye Baby*	7.00 -	10.00
9194 *With Someone Like You*	7.00 -	10.00
9213 *Who Ya Gonna Fool*	8.00 -	12.00
9299 *Where The Sweet Forget-Me-Nots Remember*	7.00 -	10.00
Romeo 959 *That's My Idea Of Heaven*	7.00 -	10.00

JACK ALBIN'S ORCHESTRA; JACK ALBIN & HIS HOTEL PENNSYLVANIA MUSIC:

Crown 3002 *You're Driving Me Crazy!*	10.00 -	15.00
3006 *Maybe It's Love*	7.00 -	10.00
3012 *Cheerful Little Earful*	15.00 -	20.00
3013 *You're Lucky To Me*	15.00 -	20.00
3029 *Cryin' Myself To Sleep*	7.00 -	10.00
3046 *You Didn't Have To Tell Me*	30.00 -	50.00
3047 *I Miss A Little Miss*	7.00 -	10.00
3069 *Sweet And Hot*	7.00 -	10.00
3089 *When I Take My Sugar To Tea*	7.00 -	10.00
3091 *I'm Crazy 'Bout My Baby*	7.00 -	10.00
3098 *Smile, Darn Ya, Smile*	7.00 -	10.00
Edison 51811 *Wasn't It Nice?*	30.00 -	50.00
51829 *Hugs And Kisses*	30.00 -	50.00
51831 *The Two Of Us*	25.00 -	40.00
51851 *Cover Me Up With Sunshine*	50.00 -	75.00
51852 *I Found A Million Dollar Baby*	50.00 -	75.00

VAN ALEXANDER & HIS ORCHESTRA:

Bluebird, various titles	5.00 -	10.00
Varsity, various titles	5.00 -	10.00

HENRY ALLEN (JR.) HIS (NEW YORK) ORCHESTRA; HENRY ALLEN-COLEMAN HAWKINS & THEIR ORCHESTRA:

Titles issued contemporaneously on Banner, Melotone, Oriole, Perfect, Romeo: *Aintcha Got Music?; Believe I, Beloved; Dark Clouds; Don't Let Your Love Go Wrong; How's About Tomorrow Night?; I Never Slept A Wink Last Night; It's Written All Over Your Face; I Wish I Were Twins; My Galveston Gal; Pardon My Southern Accent; The River's Takin' Care Of Me; Rug Cutter Swing; Shadows On The Swanee; Smooth Sailing; Stringin' Along On A Shoe String; There's A House In Harlem For Sale; Whose Honey Are You?; Why Don't You Practice What You Preach?; You're Gonna Lose Your Gal* .... 10.00 - 15.00

Victor 23006 *Patrol Wagon Blues*	80.00 -	120.00
23338 *Singing Pretty Songs*	200.00 -	300.00
V38073 *It Should Be You*	75.00 -	100.00
V38080 *Feeling Drowsy*	75.00 -	100.00
V38121 *Dancing Dave*	100.00 -	150.00
V38140 *Sugar Hill Function*	80.00 -	120.00
Vocalion 2956 *Get Rhythm In Your Feet*	10.00 -	15.00
2965 *Rosetta*	10.00 -	15.00
2997 *I Wished On The Moon*	10.00 -	15.00
2998 *Dinah Lou*	10.00 -	15.00
3097 *Red Sails In The Sunset*	10.00 -	15.00
3098 *On Treasure Island*	10.00 -	15.00
3214 *I'll Bet You Tell That To All The Girls*	10.00 -	15.00
3215 *Every Minute Of The Hour*	10.00 -	15.00
3244 *Would You?*	10.00 -	15.00
3245 *Nothing's Blue But The Sky*	10.00 -	15.00
3261 *Take My Heart*	10.00 -	15.00
3262 *You're Not The King*	10.00 -	15.00
3292 *Am I Asking Too Much?*	10.00 -	15.00
3302 *Algiers Stomp*	10.00 -	15.00
3305 *Out Where The Blues Begin*	10.00 -	15.00
3306 *Picture Me Without You*	10.00 -	15.00
3339 *Whatcha Gonna Do When There Ain't No Swing?*	10.00 -	15.00
3340 *Lost In My Dreams*	10.00 -	15.00
3377 *Did You Mean It?*	10.00 -	15.00
3389 *Here's Love In Your Eye*	10.00 -	15.00
3422 *Let's Put Our Heads Together*	10.00 -	15.00
3432 *He Ain't Got Rhythm*	10.00 -	15.00
3490 *There's A Kitchen Up In Heaven*	10.00 -	15.00
3524 *I Was Born To Swing*	10.00 -	15.00
3564 *Sticks And Stones*	10.00 -	15.00
3574 *Meet Me In The Moonlight*	10.00 -	15.00
3594 *The Merry-Go-Round Broke Down*	10.00 -	15.00
3607 *Till The Clock Strikes Three*	10.00 -	15.00
3690 *Can I Forget You?*	10.00 -	10.00
3704 *Have You Ever Been In Love*	10.00 -	15.00

MOON ALLEN & HIS ORCHESTRA:

Champion 15039 *Fallin' Down*	75.00 -	125.00

ALL STAR BAND:

Victor 26144 *The Blues*	7.00 -	10.00

ALL STAR CALIFORNIANS:

Melotone 12000 *Cheerful Little Earful*	20.00 -	30.00
12002 *Never Swat A Fly*	5.00 -	8.00

ALL STAR COLLEGIANS:

Titles on Oriole, Perfect: *Now's The Time To Fall In Love; She's So Nice* .... 8.00 - 12.00

Other titles on Oriole, Perfect .... 5.00 - 8.00

ALL STAR ORCHESTRA:
Victor 21149 *Chloe*..................................7.00 - 10.00
  21212 *My Melancholy Baby* ....7.00 - 10.00
  21326 *I Must Be Dreaming*................................10.00 - 15.00
  21423 *Oh, Baby!* ....10.00 - 15.00
  21605 *I'm More Than Satisfied* ....10.00 - 15.00
  21667 *There's A Rainbow 'Round My Shoulder* ..7.00 - 10.00
  22054 *My Dream Memory*................................7.00 - 10.00
  22073 *Waiting At The End Of The Road* ....7.00 - 10.00
  22104 *Too Wonderful For Words*........................8.00 - 12.00
  22197 *Deep In The Arms Of Love* ....8.00 - 12.00

ALL STAR PLAYERS:
Van Dyke 71732 *There's A Czecho Slovak Waiting For Me*
....8.00 - 12.00

ALL-STAR RHYTHM BOYS:
Titles issued contemporaneously on Clarion, Diva, Velvet Tone:
  Pardon Me, Pretty Baby; Sensation ....15.00 - 30.00

ALMEDA WONDER ORCHESTRA/PLAYERS (See ALAMEDA WONDER ORCH./PLAYERS)

ALOMO GARDEN BAND/JAZZERS:
Buddy 8052 *Spanish Mamma*.....................................50.00 - 75.00
Champion 15132 *St. Louis Hop*...............................15.00 - 20.00
  15133 *Black Bottom* ....15.00 - 20.00

OVIE ALSTON & HIS ORCHESTRA:
Vocalion 4448 *Junk Man's Serenade* ....15.00 - 20.00
  4462 *How Much Do You Mean To Me?* ....15.00 - 20.00
  4500 *Home Cookin' Mama*...............................15.00 - 20.00
  4577 *Spare-Ribs and Spaghetti* ....15.00 - 20.00

DANNY ALTIER & HIS ORCHESTRA:
Vocalion 15740 *My Gal Sal* ....250.00 -   up

THE AMBASSADORS:
Vocalion 14620, 14668, 14686, 14808, 14810, 14823, 14907,
  14916, 14928, ...7.00 - 10.00
  14671 *Upright And Grand* ....20.00 - 30.00
  14851 *Pleasure Mad* ....10.00 - 15.00
  14916 *Gotta Getta Girl* ....10.00 - 15.00
  14933 *The 'Throw-Down' Blues* ....10.00 - 15.00
  15131 *The Promenade Walk* ....7.00 - 10.00
  15156 *Military Mike* ....8.00 - 12.00
  15752 *Me And The Man In The Moon*................10.00 - 15.00
  15793 *You've Never Been Blue* ....10.00 - 15.00

AMERICAN MARIMBAPHONE BAND:
Columbia A2634 *Tishomingo Blues*........................8.00 - 12.00

ALBERT AMMONS (AND HIS RHYTHM KINGS):
Blue Note 2 *Boogie Woogie Stomp* ....10.00 - 15.00
  4 *Chicago In Mind* ....10.00 - 15.00
  21 *Suitcase Blues* ....10.00 - 15.00
Decca 749 *Boogie Woogie Stomp* ....10.00 - 15.00
  975 *Early Mornin' Blues* ....10.00 - 15.00
Solo Art 12000 *Monday Struggle* ....20.00 - 30.00
  12001 *Boogie Woogie* ....20.00 - 30.00
  12003 *St. Louis Blues* ....20.00 - 30.00
Vocalion 4608 *Shout For Joy* ....10.00 - 15.00

AMOS 'N' ANDY (See CORRELL and GOSDEN)

MOREY AMSTERDAM:
Sunset 1140 *Show Me The Way To Go Home* .... -   -   -

EDDIE "ROCHESTER" ANDERSON:
Columbia 35442, 36185 .... 7.00 - 10.00

IVIE ANDERSON & HER BOYS FROM DIXIE:
Variety 591 *All God's Chillun Got Rhythm* .... 10.00 - 15.00

WALT/WALTER ANDERSON & HIS GOLDEN PHEASANT HOODLUMS:
Titles issued contemporaneously on Bell, Challenge, Gennett: *After I've Called You Sweetheart; Alabama Stomp; Melancholy; Mokus; Rain; Sugar Foot Stomp; What'll We Do For Dough?*
.... 50.00 - 80.00

THE ANDREWS SISTERS:
Decca 1496 *Just A Simple Melody*......................... 10.00 - 15.00
  1562 *Bei Mir Bist du Schoen* .... 8.00 - 12.00
  1691, 1703, 1744, 1859, 1875, 1912, 1974, 2016, 2082, 2214,
    2290, 2414 .... 7.00 - 10.00
Decca, most other titles.. 5.00 - 10.00

ANONYMOUS
(Records on which no artist credit, actual or pseudonymous, is given. Descriptions such as "Band," "Orchestra," "Fox Trot with Vocal Chorus," "Baritone," "Banjo Solo with Orchestra," are typical. In most cases, the identity of the artist is unknown. The following have been recognized as collectible. No effort has been made to list test pressings.)
Brunswick "Mood Accompaniment Library" (most dance band selections) .... 7.00 - 10.00
Climax K346 *Ramshackle Rag* ("Band")............... 10.00 - 15.00
Grey Gull 1522 *Loveless Love Blues* .... 10.00 - 15.00
  1589 *What Would I Do Without You*.................. 7.00 - 10.00
  1591 *And Then* .... 7.00 - 10.00
  1598 *Honey* .... 5.00 - 8.00
  1701 *Battleship Kate*....................................... 10.00 - 15.00
  1702 *Jimtown Blues* .... 10.00 - 15.00
  1703 *Let's Get Together* .... 7.00 - 10.00
  1706 *Lead Pipe Blues* .... 10.00 - 15.00
  1710 *Coal Black Blues* .... 30.00 - 50.00
  1718 *Close Fit Blues* .... 40.00 - 60.00
  1724 *Baby, Won't You Please Come Home?*..... 40.00 - 60.00
  7028 *Sure Enough Blues* .... 8.00 - 12.00
  7029 *Mississippi Mud Blues* .... 10.00 - 15.00
  7037 *Jimtown Blues* .... 10.00 - 15.00
La Belle 5077 *Smoky Mokes* .... 10.00 - 15.00
Little Wonder 9 *20th Century Rag* ("Band")
  20 *Back To The Carolina You Love* .... 30.00 - 50.00
(Note: The unidentified baritone on the above is Al Jolson.)
  568 *That Broadway Chicken Walk* ("Banjo solo")
  .... 10.00 - 15.00
  569 *The Smiler* ("Banjo solo")........................... 8.00 - 12.00
Madison 802 *Someone To Love Me* .... 40.00 - 60.00
Okeh 1028 *The Tickle Toe* ("Band")..................... 10.00 - 15.00
Oxford 406 *At A Georgia Camp Meeting* .... 15.00 - 20.00
  686 *Mr. Black Man* .... 15.00 - 20.00
  1038 *Cotton (Southern Breakdown)* .... 15.00 - 20.00
  4117 *Black And White Ragtime Two-Step* .... 15.00 - 20.00
  5534 *Just Noise* .... 15.00 - 20.00
(Note: Above Oxford records are one-sided discs)
Radiex 1502 *Mary Ann* .... 7.00 - 10.00
  1594 *I'm Lost Without You* .... 7.00 - 10.00
  1701 *Battleship Kate*....................................... 10.00 - 15.00
  1706 *Sweat Blues* .... 10.00 - 15.00
  1721 *Oh Gee, There Ain't No Justice* .... 7.00 - 10.00
  7037 *Jimtown Blues* .... 10.00 - 15.00

Silvertone 38644 *Too Much Mustard* ....10.00 - 15.00
    46909 *Pretty Baby* ....10.00 - 15.00
(Note: Above Silvertone records are one-sided)
Victor 4445 *Mr. Black Man* ....15.00 - 20.00
(Note: Above Victor is a one-sided disc)
Victor "Pict-Ur-Music," most dance band selections 7.00 - 12.00
Victor "Pict-Ur-Music" 0294 *Milenberg Joys* .... -   -
    0298 *The New Tulsa Blues* .... -   -

ARCADIAN SERENADERS:
Okeh 40272 *Fidgety Feet* ....50.00 - 75.00
    40378 *San Sue Strut*.......................................50.00 - 75.00
    40440 *Who Can Your Regular Be Blues*............50.00 - 75.00
    40503 *The Co-Ed* ....50.00 - 75.00
    40517 *Angry*..50.00 - 75.00
    40538 *Carry It On Down* ....50.00 - 75.00
    40562 *Yes Sir, Boss*.......................................50.00 - 75.00

ARCADIA PEACOCK ORCHESTRA OF ST. LOUIS:
Okeh 40044 *Dream Boat* ....30.00 - 50.00
    40052 *Ain't You Ashamed?* ....30.00 - 50.00
    40254 *Where's My Sweetie Hiding?*................40.00 - 60.00
    40264 *Ah! Ah! Archie* ....50.00 - 75.00
    40272 *Dog On The Piano* ....50.00 - 75.00
    40372 *Waiting For The Moon* ....40.00 - 60.00
    40440 *Little Boy Blues* ....50.00 - 75.00

HARRY ARCHER & HIS ORCHESTRA:
Brunswick, most issues..5.00 - 10.00

ARDEN-OHMAN & THEIR ORCHESTRA:
Brunswick, most issues...5.00 - 10.00
Victor, most issues...5.00 - 10.00

VICTOR & PHIL ARDEN:
Victor 18867 *I've Got The Wonder Where He Went...Blues*
....10.00 - 15.00
    22608 *Maple Leaf Rag*....................................8.00 - 12.00

ARKANSAS/ARKANSAW TRAVELERS/TRAVELLERS:
Titles issued contemporaneously on Diva, Harmony, Velvet Tone:
  Birmingham Breakdown; Boneyard Shuffle; I Ain't Got Nobody;
  Ja Da; Sensation; Stompin' Fool; Washboard Blues
....15.00 - 20.00
Red Head Blues; That's No Bargain ....35.00 - 50.00
Okeh 40124 *Georgia Blues* ....15.00 - 25.00
    40183 *Any Way The Wind Blows*....................15.00 - 25.00
    40236 *Copenhagen* ....20.00 - 30.00
    40267 *Homebound* ....20.00 - 30.00
    40277 *I'll See You In My Dreams*....................10.00 - 15.00
    40426 *Row, Row, Rosie* ....15.00 - 20.00
    40640 *Breezin' Along With The Breeze*.............15.00 - 20.00
    40674 *Ting-a-ling, The Bells'll Ring* ....35.00 - 50.00
    40700 *Give Me A Ukelele* ....10.00 - 15.00
    40724 *Take In The Sun, Hang Out The Moon* ....15.00 - 20.00
    40727 *Brown Sugar* ....20.00 - 30.00

ARKANSAS TRIO:
Edison 51373 *Boll Weevil Blues* ....20.00 - 30.00

FRED ARMSTRONG & HIS SYNCOPATORS:
Timely Tunes C-1578 *When I Can't Be With You* ..75.00 - 100.00
C-1587 *Sugar Blues* ....75.00 - 100.00

LIL ARMSTRONG & HER DIXIELANDERS/SWING BAND/ORCHESTRA:
Decca 1059 *My Hi-De-Ho Man* ....10.00 - 15.00
    1092 *Brown Gal* ....10.00 - 15.00

1182 *Just For The Thrill* .... 10.00 - 15.00
1272 *I'm Knockin' At The Cabin Door* .... 10.00 - 15.00
1299 *Born To Swing* .... 10.00 - 15.00
1388 *Lindy Hop* .... 10.00 - 15.00
1502 *Let's Call It Love* .... 10.00 - 15.00
1722 *Happy Today, Sad Tomorrow* .... 10.00 - 15.00
1904 *Oriental Swing* .... 10.00 - 15.00
2234 *Harlem On Saturday Night* .... 10.00 - 15.00
2542 *Knock-Kneed Sal* .... 10.00 - 15.00
7739 *Sixth Street* .... 10.00 - 15.00
7803 *Riffin' The Blues* .... 10.00 - 15.00

LOUIS ARMSTRONG & HIS HOT FIVE/SAVOY BALLROOM FIVE/ORCHESTRA/SEBASTIAN NEW COTTON CLUB ORCHESTRA:
Bluebird 5086 *Mahogany Hall Stomp* .... 7.00 - 10.00
    5173 *Hustlin' And Bustlin' For Baby* .... 7.00 - 10.00
    5280 *St. Louis Blues*.. 7.00 - 10.00
    5363 *Laughin' Louie* .... 15.00 - 20.00
    5408 *Dusky Stevedore* .... 7.00 - 10.00
    5409 *Mighty River* .... 7.00 - 10.00
    6501 *Mississippi Basin* .... 7.00 - 10.00
    6590 *Some Sweet Day* .... 7.00 - 10.00
    6644 *That's My Home* .... 7.00 - 10.00
    6771 *High Society* .... 7.00 - 10.00
    6910 *I've Got The World On A String* .... 7.00 - 10.00
    7506 *Sittin' In The Dark* .... 7.00 - 10.00
    7787 *Honey, Do!* .... 7.00 - 10.00
    10225 *Swing, You Cats* .... 7.00 - 10.00
    10236 *That's My Home*..................................... 7.00 - 10.00
(Above titles on Electradisk are worth more; on Sunrise, substantially more)
Columbia 2574-D *Star Dust* .... 15.00 - 20.00
    2606-D *All Of Me*.. 15.00 - 20.00
    2631-D *The New Tiger Rag* .... 15.00 - 20.00
    2646-D *Keepin' Out Of Mischief Now*.............. 15.00 - 20.00
    2688-D *Rockin' Chair*..................................... 15.00 - 20.00
    2709-D *Body And Soul* .... 15.00 - 20.00
    2727-D *After You've Gone* .... 15.00 - 20.00
Decca 579 *Got A Bran' New Suit* .... 10.00 - 15.00
    580 *You Are My Lucky Star* .... 10.00 - 15.00
    622 *Old Man Mose* .... 10.00 - 15.00
    623 *I'm Shooting High* .... 10.00 - 15.00
    648 *Red Sails In The Sunset* .... 10.00 - 15.00
    666 *Thanks A Million* .... 10.00 - 15.00
    672 *Shoe Shine Boy* .... 10.00 - 15.00
    685 *Rhythm Saved The World* .... 10.00 - 15.00
    698 *I'm Putting All My Eggs In One Basket*...... 10.00 - 15.00
    797 *Somebody Stole My Break* .... 10.00 - 15.00
    824 *Mahogany Hall Stomp* .... 10.00 - 15.00
    835 *Lyin' To Myself* .... 10.00 - 15.00
    866 *Swing That Music* .... 10.00 - 15.00
    906 *Dipper Mouth Blues* .... 10.00 - 15.00
    914 *On A Cocoanut Island*............................... 8.00 - 12.00
    949 *Hurdy-Gurdy Man* .... 8.00 - 12.00
    1049 *When Ruben Swings The Cuban* .... 10.00 - 15.00
    1245 *Carry Me Back To Old Virginny* .... 10.00 - 15.00
    1347 *Public Melody Number One*...................... 10.00 - 15.00
    1353 *Cuban Pete* .... 10.00 - 15.00
    1360 *The Old Folks At Home*........................... 10.00 - 15.00
    1369 *Yours And Mine* .... 8.00 - 12.00
    1408 *Alexander's Ragtime Band* .... 8.00 - 12.00
    1495 *In The Shade Of The Old Apple Tree* .... 8.00 - 12.00
    1560 *On The Sunny Side Of The Street*............. 7.00 - 10.00

1635 *Jubilee*	7.00 -	10.00
1636 *Satchel Mouth Swing*	7.00 -	10.00
1653 *The Trumpet Player's Lament*	7.00 -	10.00
1661 *Struttin' With Some Barbecue*	7.00 -	10.00

(Original issues of early Deccas have shaded letters in logo)

Decca, most later numbers	5.00 -	10.00
3011 *Bye and Bye*	8.00 -	12.00
3151 *W.P.A.* (with The Mills Brothers)	10.00 -	15.00
Okeh 8261 *Gut Bucket Blues*	200.00 -	300.00
8299 *Oriental Strut*	200.00 -	300.00
8300 *Heebie Jeebies*	100.00 -	150.00
8318 *Georgia Grind*	200.00 -	300.00
8320 *Cornet Chop Suey*	200.00 -	300.00

(Note: Original issues of early Okeh records have the large, maroon label, product of General Phonograph Corporation. Later issues, and reissues of early issues, are products of Okeh Phonograph Corporation or Columbia Phonograph Corporation, with the Truetone or Electric emblem above the center hole, and are laminated pressings.)

8343 *I'm Gonna Gitcha*	150.00 -	250.00
8357 *Dropping Shucks*	150.00 -	250.00
8379 *Sweet Little Papa*	150.00 -	250.00
8396 *The King Of The Zulus*	150.00 -	250.00
8423 *Big Butter And Egg Man*	150.00 -	250.00
8436 *Jazz Lips*	150.00 -	200.00
8447 *Irish Black Bottom*	150.00 -	200.00
8474 *Wild Man Blues*	150.00 -	200.00
8482 *Willie The Weeper*	125.00 -	175.00
8496 *Keyhole Blues*	125.00 -	175.00
8503 *Potato Head Blues*	125.00 -	175.00
8519 *Weary Blues*	100.00 -	150.00
8535 *Savoy Blues*	80.00 -	120.00
8551 *Got No Blues*	80.00 -	120.00
8566 *Struttin' With Some Barbecue*	80.00 -	120.00
8597 *West End Blues*	80.00 -	120.00
8609 *Sugar Foot Strut*	80.00 -	120.00
8631 *Knee Drops*	80.00 -	120.00
8641 *Squeeze Me*	80.00 -	120.00
8649 *Tight Like This*	75.00 -	100.00
8657 *Save It, Pretty Mama*	60.00 -	100.00
8669 *No-One Else But You*	75.00 -	100.00
8680 *Beau-Koo Jack*	75.00 -	100.00
8690 *Basin Street Blues*	75.00 -	100.00
8703 *Knockin' A Jug*	80.00 -	120.00
8714 *Ain't Misbehavin'*	50.00 -	80.00
8729 *Some Of These Days*	80.00 -	120.00
8756 *Rockin' Chair*	50.00 -	80.00
8774 *Bessie Couldn't Help It*	50.00 -	80.00
8800 *Dinah*	50.00 -	80.00
41078 *Fireworks*	75.00 -	100.00
41157 *Knee Drops*	50.00 -	75.00
41180 *Save It, Pretty Mama*	40.00 -	60.00
41204 *No-One Else But You*	40.00 -	60.00
41241 *Basin Street Blues*	40.00 -	60.00
41276 *Black And Blue*	40.00 -	60.00
41281 *Sweet Savannah Sue*	40.00 -	60.00
41298 *Some Of These Days*	35.00 -	50.00
41350 *After You've Gone*	40.00 -	60.00
41375 *Song Of The Islands*	40.00 -	60.00
41415 *My Sweet*	40.00 -	60.00
41423 *Exactly Like You*	40.00 -	60.00
41442 *I'm A Ding Dong Daddy*	40.00 -	60.00
41448 *Confessin'*	40.00 -	60.00

41454 *Weather Bird*	80.00 -	120.00
41463 *You're Lucky To Me*	40.00 -	60.00
41468 *Body And Soul*	35.00 -	50.00
41478 *You're Drivin' Me Crazy*	35.00 -	50.00
41486 *Shine*	35.00 -	50.00
41497 *Walkin' My Baby Back Home*	35.00 -	50.00
41498 *Blue Again*	35.00 -	50.00
41501 *Them There Eyes*	35.00 -	50.00
41504 *When It's Sleepy Time Down South*	35.00 -	50.00
41530 *Star Dust*	35.00 -	50.00
41534 *Chinatown, My Chinatown*	35.00 -	50.00
41538 *The Lonesome Road*	35.00 -	50.00
41541 *Lazy River*	35.00 -	50.00
41550 *Kickin' The Gong Around*	40.00 -	60.00
41552 *All Of Me*	40.00 -	60.00
41557 *The New Tiger Rag*	35.00 -	50.00
41560 *Keepin' Out Of Mischief Now*	35.00 -	50.00
RCA Victor L-36000 (12-inch "Program Transcription")		
Medley of Armstrong Hits	75.00 -	100.00
Victor 24200 *That's My Home*	15.00 -	20.00
24202 *I Hate To Leave You Now*	15.00 -	20.00
24232 *High Society*	15.00 -	20.00
24233 *I Gotta Right To Sing The Blues*	15.00 -	20.00
24245 *Sittin' In The Dark*	15.00 -	20.00
24257 *Some Sweet Day*	15.00 -	20.00
24320 *St. Louis Blues*	15.00 -	20.00
24321 *Mississippi Basin*	15.00 -	20.00
24334 *There's A Cabin In The Pines*	15.00 -	20.00
24351 *Basin Street Blues*	15.00 -	20.00
24369 *Snowball*	15.00 -	20.00
24425 *Don't Play Me Cheap*	15.00 -	20.00
36084 (12-inch) *Medley Of Armstrong Hits*	30.00 -	50.00
Vocalion 3008 *Basin Street Blues*	8.00 -	12.00
3009 *Tiger Rag*	7.00 -	10.00
3025 *Dallas Blues*	7.00 -	10.00
3026 *The Lonesome Road*	7.00 -	10.00
3039 *Chinatown, My Chinatown*	7.00 -	10.00
3040 *Exactly Like You*	7.00 -	10.00
3055 *Mahogany Hall Stomp*	7.00 -	10.00
3059 *Confessin'*	7.00 -	10.00
3072 *Body And Soul*	7.00 -	10.00
3073 *Georgia On My Mind*	7.00 -	10.00
3085 *Beau Koo Jack*	7.00 -	10.00
3102 *I Ain't Got Nobody*	7.00 -	10.00
3114 *Lazy River*	7.00 -	10.00
3115 *Black And Blue*	7.00 -	10.00
3124 *The New Tiger Rag*	7.00 -	10.00
3125 *Home*	7.00 -	10.00
3135 *All Of Me*	7.00 -	10.00
3136 *Sweet Savannah Sue*	7.00 -	10.00
3137 *Keyhole Blues*	7.00 -	10.00
3148 *Sugar Foot Strut*	7.00 -	10.00
3172 *Wrap Your Troubles In Dreams*	7.00 -	10.00
3180 *You're Lucky To Me*	20.00 -	30.00
3181 *Keepin' Out Of Mischief Now*	7.00 -	10.00
3193 *Gully Low Blues*	7.00 -	10.00
3194 *The Peanut Vendor*	7.00 -	10.00
3202 *When You're Smiling*	7.00 -	10.00
3203 *When It's Sleepy Time Down South*	7.00 -	10.00
3204 *West End Blues*	7.00 -	10.00
3205 *That Rhythm Man*	7.00 -	10.00
3216 *You're Driving Me Crazy*	7.00 -	10.00
3217 *Savoy Blues*	7.00 -	10.00

3237 *Hotter Than That*	7.00 -	10.00
3301 *I'm In The Market For You*	7.00 -	10.00
3303 *Tight Like This*	7.00 -	10.00
3337 *Them There Eyes*	7.00 -	10.00
3370 *Indian Cradle Song*	7.00 -	10.00
3381 *Save It, Pretty Mama*	7.00 -	10.00
3643 *After You've Gone*	7.00 -	10.00

DESI ARNAZ & HIS ORCHESTRA:

Columbia 35216 *South America Way*	5.00 -	10.00
39937 *I Love Lucy*	5.00 -	10.00
Columbia, red label, other issues	5.00 -	8.00
Decca 24713 *Similau*	5.00 -	8.00
28483 (with Andrews Sisters, promo) *Old San Juan*	- -	-
M-G-M 12144 *The Straw Hat Song*	5.00 -	8.00
RCA Victor 20-1865 *Guadalajara*	- -	-
20-2020 *Tia Juana*	4.00 -	7.00
20-2052 *Another Night Like This*	5.00 -	8.00
20-2094 *A Rainy Night In Rio*	5.00 -	8.00
20-2279 *Tabu*	5.00 -	8.00
20-2280 *Babalu*	5.00 -	8.00
20-2281 *Peanut Vendor*	5.00 -	8.00
20-2282 *Siboney/Green Eyes*	5.00 -	8.00
20-2282 *Cuban Pete/Green Eyes*	5.00 -	8.00
20-2499 *I Love To Dance*	7.00 -	10.00
20-2550 *Made For Each Other*	7.00 -	10.00
20-2624 *Siboney*	5.00 -	8.00
20-2827 *In Santiago Chile*	5.00 -	8.00
20-2865 *Cuban Pete*	7.00 -	10.00
20-2866 *Babalu*	5.00 -	8.00
20-2887 *Little Romero*	5.00 -	8.00
20-3070 *You Can In Yucatan*	5.00 -	8.00
20-3113 *Perhaps, Perhaps, Perhaps*	5.00 -	8.00
20-3256 *Cuban Cabby*	7.00 -	10.00
25-1058 *Cuban Pete*	7.00 -	10.00
25-1062 *Guadalajara*	7.00 -	10.00
25-1071 *Carnival In Rio*	7.00 -	10.00

(Many of this artist's records were issued as 45 RPM, EPs, and LPs. See also the **RHYTHM & BLUES, ETC.** section.)

FELIX ARNDT:

Victor 17558 *From Soup To Nuts*	8.00 -	12.00
17608 *Desecration Rag (A Classic Nightmare)*	15.00 -	20.00

GUS ARNHEIM & HIS (AMBASSADOR HOTEL/ COCOANUT GROVE) ORCHESTRA:

Brunswick 6683, 6693, 6729, 6734, 6751, 6765	7.00 -	12.00
7900 *The Image Of You*	10.00 -	15.00
7904 *Exactly Like You*	10.00 -	15.00
7919 *So Rare*	10.00 -	15.00
7922 *High, Wide and Handsome*	10.00 -	15.00
7933 *All You Want To Do Is Dance*	10.00 -	15.00
7937 *On With The Dance*	10.00 -	15.00
Okeh 41037 *If I Can't Have You*	15.00 -	25.00
41057 *Feelin' Good*	15.00 -	25.00
41208 *Glad Rag Doll*	15.00 -	25.00
Victor L-16011 *Medley of Popular Selections*	30.00 -	50.00

(Preceding is long-playing "Program Transcription")

22054 *Lovable And Sweet*	7.00 -	10.00
22384 *Dancing To Save Your Sole*	8.00 -	12.00
22470 *I've Gotta Yen For You*	10.00 -	15.00
22561 *Fool Me Some More*	10.00 -	15.00
22580 *Them There Eyes*	7.00 -	10.00
22618 *I Surrender, Dear*	10.00 -	15.00
22691 *I'm Gonna Get You*	10.00 -	15.00
22700 *One More Time*	10.00 -	15.00
22851 *There's Nothing Too Good For My Baby*	10.00 -	15.00
24061 *Evening*	10.00 -	15.00
24234 *Love Is A Dream*	8.00 -	12.00
24235 *Love In The Moonlight*	8.00 -	12.00

BILLY "PETE" ARTZ & HIS HENRY AND GEORGE ORCHESTRA:

Titles issued contemporaneously on Banner, Conqueror, Oriole, Perfect, and Romeo: *I'm All Dressed Up With A Broken Heart; Never; Parkin' In The Moonlight; There's A Time And Place for Everything* .... 8.00 - 12.00

PAUL ASH & HIS MERRY MAD MUSICAL GANG/ ORCHESTRA:

Brunswick 2482 *Pesticatin' Mamma*	7.00 -	10.00
2629 *Wa Wa Waddle Walk*	7.00 -	10.00
Brunswick, most other issues	5.00 -	8.00
Clarion 5104-C *I Got Rhythm*	15.00 -	20.00
Columbia 707-D *Oh! If I Only Had You*	10.00 -	15.00
828-D *Take In The Sun, Hang Out The Moon*	10.00 -	15.00
1066-D *Ain't That A Grand And Glorious Feeling*	10.00 -	15.00
1349-D *My Pet*	10.00 -	15.00
1531-D *Out Of The Dawn*	10.00 -	15.00
1616-D *Salty*	15.00 -	20.00
2796-D *Shadows On The Swanee*	15.00 -	20.00
2798-D *Louisville Lady*	15.00 -	20.00
Columbia, most other issues	5.00 -	8.00
Harmony 1234-H *I Got Rhythm*	20.00 -	30.00
Variety 505 *Tiger Rag*	10.00 -	15.00
649 *Raggin' The Scale*	7.00 -	10.00

FRED ASTAIRE:

Brunswick 7486 *Cheek To Cheek*	7.00 -	10.00
7608 *Let's Face The Music And Dance*	7.00 -	10.00
7609 *I'm Putting All My Eggs In One Basket*	7.00 -	10.00
7610 *I'd Rather Lead A Band*	7.00 -	10.00
7716 *A Fine Romance*	7.00 -	10.00
7717 *Pick Yourself Up*	7.00 -	10.00
7718 *Never Gonna Dance*	7.00 -	10.00
7855 *Beginner's Luck*	7.00 -	10.00
7856 *Slap That Bass*	7.00 -	10.00
7857 *Let's Call The Whole Thing Off*	7.00 -	10.00
7982 *A Foggy Day*	7.00 -	10.00
7983 *Nice Work If You Can Get It*	7.00 -	10.00
8189 *Change Partners*	7.00 -	10.00
8190 *The Yam Step Explained*	7.00 -	10.00
3164-D *They Can't Take That Away From Me*	15.00 -	20.00
3165-D *They All Laughed*	15.00 -	20.00
3166-D *Shall We Dance?*	15.00 -	20.00
Columbia 35517, 35815, 35852	5.00 -	8.00

THE ASTORITES:

Harmony 201-H *Who Wouldn't*	8.00 -	12.00
228-H *Up and Down The Eight Mile Road*	10.00 -	15.00
251-H *Black Bottom*	8.00 -	12.00
266-H *Gone Again Gal*	8.00 -	12.00
273-H *Just A Little Longer*	7.00 -	10.00
303-H *It Made You Happy When You Made Me Cry*	7.00 -	10.00
305-H *I'd Love To Call You My Sweetheart*	7.00 -	10.00

336-H *I Never See Maggie Alone* ....8.00 - 12.00
438-H *One O'Clock Baby*.................................8.00 - 12.00
528-H *Among My Souvenirs* ....8.00 - 12.00
709-H *Nagasaki* ....8.00 - 12.00

ATLANTA MERRYMAKERS:
Madison 1935 *Black Stomp* ....20.00 - 30.00
   50005 *Sweet Little Sis* ....10.00 - 15.00
   50024 *Sweet Little Sis* ....10.00 - 15.00

ATLANTA SYNCOPATORS:
Grey Gull 1888 *That Wicked Stomp* ....30.00 - 50.00
Madison 50008 *That Wicked Stomp* ....30.00 - 50.00
   50009 *Step On It* ....15.00 - 25.00
   50015 *Lead Pipe Blues* ....15.00 - 25.00
Radiex 5008 *That Wicked Stomp* ....30.00 - 50.00
   5015 *Beale Street Blues* ....15.00 - 25.00
Van Dyke 508 *That Wicked Stomp* ....30.00 - 50.00

ATLANTIC SYNCOPATORS:
Madison 50047 *St. James' Infirmary Blues*.............15.00 - 25.00

FRANK AUBURN & HIS ORCHESTRA:
Clarion 5179-C *I'm Tickled Pink With A Blue-Eyed Baby*
  ....10.00 - 15.00
   5180-C *A Peach of A Pair* ....10.00 - 15.00
   5211-C *I'm So Afraid Of You* ....8.00 - 12.00
   5212-C *Would You Like To Take A Walk?* ....8.00 - 12.00
   5254-C *I Surrender, Dear* ....7.00 - 10.00
   5266-C *Were You Sincere?* ....7.00 - 10.00
   5267-C *Got The Bench, Got The Park*............8.00 - 12.00
   5273-C *Rockin' Chair*.........................15.00 - 20.00
   5277-C *When I Take My Sugar To Tea* ....15.00 - 20.00
   5283-C *I'm Crazy 'Bout My Baby*...............15.00 - 20.00
   5286-C *You'll Be Mine In Apple Blossom Time*...8.00 - 12.00
   5310-C *It Looks Like Love* ....8.00 - 12.00
   5311-C *Think A Little Kindly Of Me* ....8.00 - 12.00
   5335-C *Faithfully Yours* ....8.00 - 12.00
   5340-C *I Found A Million Dollar Baby* ....15.00 - 20.00
   5356-C *Hikin' Down The Highway* ....15.00 - 20.00
   5369-C *Me!* ....15.00 - 20.00
   5450-C *Goodnight, Moon* ....8.00 - 12.00
   5451-C *One Little Quarrel* ....7.00 - 10.00
   5455-C *Between The Devil And The Deep Blue Sea*
  ....15.00 - 20.00
   11001-C *Little Girl*.........................15.00 - 30.00
(Above is a "double track" record)
Harmony 1138-H *Kickin' A Hole In The Sky* ....15.00 - 20.00
   1146-H *Mysterious Mose* ....8.00 - 12.00
   1173-H *Cheer Up* ....8.00 - 12.00
   1182-H *Swinging In A Hammock* ....8.00 - 12.00
   1195-H *Nobody Cares If I'm Blue* ....8.00 - 12.00
   1202-H *Good Evenin'* ....8.00 - 12.00
   1206-H *A Big Bouquet For You* ....8.00 - 12.00
   1234-H *It's A Great Life*.....................20.00 - 30.00
   1240-H *My Ideal*.............................10.00 - 15.00
   1249-H *Cheerful Little Earful* ....15.00 - 20.00
   1269-H *I'm So Afraid Of You* ....10.00 - 15.00
   1284-H *I Surrender, Dear* ....8.00 - 12.00
   1291-H *Got The Bench, Got The Park* ....8.00 - 12.00
   1292-H *Were You Sincere* ....8.00 - 12.00
   1306-H *Rockin' Chair*........................15.00 - 20.00
   1315-H *Think A Little Kindly Of Me* ....8.00 - 12.00
   1327-H *My Cradle Sweetheart* ....8.00 - 12.00
   1331-H *In The Merry Month Of Maybe* ....15.00 - 20.00

   1344-H *Hikin' Down The Highway* ....15.00 - 20.00
   1357-H *Give Me Your Affection, Honey* ....15.00 - 20.00
   1412-H *Between The Devil And The Deep Blue Sea*
  ....15.00 - 20.00
   6001-H *Sunny Skies* ....15.00 - 30.00
(Above is a "double track" record)
Velvet Tone 2333-V *Got The Bench-Got The Park* . 8.00 - 12.00
   2339-V *Rockin' Chair*........................15.00 - 20.00
   2343-V *When I Take My Sugar To Tea* ....15.00 - 20.00
   2349-V *I'm Crazy 'Bout My Baby*...............15.00 - 20.00
   2352-V *You'll Be Mine In Apple Blossom Time* .. 8.00 - 12.00
   2404-V *In The Merry Month of Maybe*............15.00 - 20.00
   2420-V *The Hour Of Parting*...................15.00 - 20.00
   2433-V *Give Me Your Affection, Honey* ....15.00 - 20.00
   2510-V *Goodnight, Moon* ....5.00 - 8.00
   2511-V *One Little Quarrel* ....7.00 - 10.00
   2515-V *Between The Devil And The Deep Blue Sea*
  ....15.00 - 20.00
   10001-V *Sunny Skies* ....15.00 - 30.00
(Above is a "double track" record)

GEORGE AULD & HIS ORCHESTRA:
Varsity 8152, 8159, 8163, 8199, 8212..............7.00 - 10.00

GENE AUSTIN:
Titles issued contemporaneously on Banner, Conqueror, Melotone,
   Oriole, Perfect, Romeo: *Blue Kentucky Moon; Easter Parade;*
   Everything I Have Is Yours; A Faded Summer Love; A Ghost Of
   A Chance; Goodnight, Sweetheart; Guilty; If I Didn't Have You;
   In A Dream; Just A Little Home For The Old Folks; A Little Street
   Where Old Friends Meet; The Lonesome Road; When I Was A
   Boy From The Mountains ....10.00 - 15.00
Titles issued contemporaneously on Banner, Conqueror, Melotone,
   Oriole, Perfect, Romeo: *Build A Little Home; Did You Ever See*
   A Dream Walking?........................10.00 - 20.00
Titles issued contemporaneously on Banner, Conqueror, Melotone,
   Oriole, Perfect, Romeo: *Dear Old Southland; I'm Sorry, Dear;*
   Jail House Blues; Lies ....20.00 - 30.00
Decca 904 *When I'm With You* ....8.00 - 12.00
   926 *I Cried For You*...........................8.00 - 12.00
   1578 *Marie*....................................8.00 - 12.00
   1656 *Dear Old Southland* ....15.00 - 20.00
Decca 1832, 3102, 3939, 4175, 4333, 4354...........7.00 - 10.00
Edison 51611 *Got The Railroad Blues* ....30.00 - 50.00
Hit of the Week L-3 *Now That You're Gone* ....8.00 - 12.00
Victor 19585, 19599, 19625, 19637, 19677 ....8.00 - 15.00
   19656, 19857, 19864, 19899, 19928, 19950,
   19968, 20030, 20044, 20084, 20143, 20371,
   20397, 20411, 20561, 20568, 20569, 20730,
   20964, 20977, 21015, 21098, 21329, 21334,
   21374, 21454, 21545, 21564, 21714, 21779,
   21798, 21833, 21856, 21893, 21915, 21916,
   21952, 22033, 22068....................7.00 - 10.00
   22128 *How Am I To Know?* ....10.00 - 15.00
   22223 *My Fate Is In Your Hands* ....15.00 - 20.00
   22299 *St. James' Infirmary* ....10.00 - 15.00
   22341 *Let Me Sing And I'm Happy* ....10.00 - 15.00
   22416 *Under A Texas Moon* ....10.00 - 15.00
   22451 *Rollin' Down The River* ....10.00 - 15.00
   22490 *For Sweethearts Only* ....10.00 - 15.00
   22518 *Nobody Cares If I'm Blue* ....10.00 - 15.00
   22527 *If I Could Be With You One Hour Tonight*
  ....10.00 - 15.00
   22539 *Alabama Lullaby* ....10.00 - 15.00
   22601 *You're Driving Me Crazy* ....15.00 - 20.00

22635 *When Your Lover Has Gone* ....15.00 - 20.00
22687 *If You Should Ever Need Me* ....15.00 - 20.00
22739 *Without That Gal!* ....15.00 - 20.00
22797 *Star Dust* .... - -
22806 *Love Letters In The Sand* ....15.00 - 20.00
22891 *Mood Indigo* ....20.00 - 30.00
24663 *All I Do Is Dream Of You* ....30.00 - 50.00
24725 *Blue Sky Avenue* ....30.00 - 50.00

HAROLD AUSTIN & HIS NEW YORKERS:
Champion 15980 *Mona* ....15.00 - 20.00
Gennett 7147 *Mona* ....20.00 - 30.00

LOVIE AUSTIN & HER (BLUES) SERENADERS/LOVIE AUSTIN'S SERENADERS:
Paramount 12255 *Steppin' On The Blues* ....200.00 - 300.00
  12277 *Peepin' Blues* ....150.00 - 250.00
  12278 *Charleston Mad* ....150.00 - 250.00
  12283 *Heebie Jeebies* ....150.00 - 250.00
  12300 *Rampart Street Blues* ....150.00 - 250.00
  12313 *Too Sweet For Words* ....150.00 - 250.00
  12361 *Frog Tongue Stop* ....200.00 - 300.00
  12380 *Chicago Mess Around* ....200.00 - 300.00
  12391 *In The Alley Blues* ....200.00 - 300.00

AUSTIN & HIS MUSICAL AMBASSADORS:
Paramount 12359 *Don't Forget To Mess Around When You Do The Charleston* ....80.00 - 120.00

AUSTIN'S SERENADERS:
Broadway 1018 *Jackass Blues* ....150.00 - 200.00

THE AVALONIANS:
Vocalion 15577 *Zulu Wall* ....20.00 - 30.00

CHARLES AVERY:
Paramount 12896 *Dearborn Street Breakdown* .....300.00 - up

JOHN AYRES' ORCHESTRA:
Parlophone PNY-34084 *What's The Use Of Cryin' Baby?* ....75.00 - 100.00
PNY-34085 *When You're Feelin' Blue* ....75.00 - 100.00

BABS & HER BROTHERS:
Decca 505 *Let's Swing It* ....10.00 - 15.00
  518 *Double Trouble* ....10.00 - 15.00
  634 *A Little Bit Independent* ....10.00 - 15.00
  635 *Yankee Doodle Never Went To Town* ....10.00 - 15.00

BABY ARISTOCRATS BAND (See also EDDIE CARLEW):
Gennett 6198 *Darktown Shuffle* ....100.00 - 150.00

BABY ROSE MARIE:
Brunswick 6570 *My Bluebird's Singing The Blues* .20.00 - 30.00
Victor 22960 *Take A Picture Of The Moon* ....50.00 - 80.00
  24196 *In the Dim, Dim Dawning* ....30.00 - 50.00

LES BACKER:
Vocalion 15777 *What a Girl! What a Night!* ....20.00 - 30.00

THE BADGERS:
Broadway 1055 *I Gotta Get Myself Somebody to Love* ....15.00 - 20.00
  1058 *It All Depends On You* ....15.00 - 20.00
  1087 *You Don't Like It-Not Much* ....7.00 - 10.00
  1150 *Back in Your Own Back Yard* ......7.00 - 10.00
  1180 *Just a Little Way From Home* ......7.00 - 10.00
  1261 *He, She and Me* ....7.00 - 10.00

1263 *My Castle in Spain Is a Shack in the Lane* ..7.00 - 10.00
1272 *There's a Four Leaf Clover In My Pocket* ..7.00 - 10.00
1274 *Do Something* ....8.00 - 12.00
1278 *I'm Just a Vagabond Lover* ....7.00 - 10.00
1297 *Miss You* ....7.00 - 10.00
1312 *Orange Blossom Time* ....7.00 - 10.00
1334 *Great Day* ....7.00 - 10.00
1339 *Singin' in the Bathtub* ....7.00 - 10.00
1378 *Just Like In a Story Book* ....7.00 - 10.00
1379 *Exactly Like You* ....7.00 - 10.00
1409 *If I Could Be With You One Hour Tonight* ....10.00 - 15.00
Paramount 20820 *Exactly Like You* ....7.00 - 10.00
Silvertone 3580 *It All Depends On You* ....15.00 - 20.00
  3583 *I Gotta Get Myself Somebody To Love* .....15.00 - 20.00

MOE BAER & HIS WARDMAN PARK ORCHESTRA:
Vocalion 15760 *Susianna* ....40.00 - 60.00

BAILEY'S DIXIE DUDES:
Gennett 5562 *I Want to See My Tennessee* ....15.00 - 20.00
  5577 *I'm Satisfied* ....15.00 - 20.00
  5606 *Go' Long Mule* ....15.00 - 20.00

BAILEY'S LUCKY SEVEN:
Fraternity*(1923 Edition) unnumbered *My Blue and Gold Girl* ....25.00 - 40.00
(*actually a Gennett pressing)
Gennett 3009 *Susie* ....15.00 - 20.00
  3011 *Flag That Train* ....15.00 - 20.00
  3015 *No Wonder* ....5.00 - 8.00
  3072 *Madiera* ....5.00 - 8.00
  3075 *Smile All The While* ....10.00 - 15.00
  3086 *Row Row Rosie* ....10.00 - 15.00
  3088 *Collegiate* ....10.00 - 15.00
  3093 *If I Had A Girl Like You* ....10.00 - 15.00
  3094 *Marguerite* ....10.00 - 15.00
  3114 *Cecilia* ....10.00 - 15.00
  3125 *On A Night Like This* ....10.00 - 15.00
  3135 *Desdemona* ....10.00 - 15.00
  3140 *The Baby Looks Like Me* ....8.00 - 12.00
  3154 *Who Loved You Best?* ....10.00 - 15.00
  3155 *Dream Pal* ....7.00 - 10.00
  3156 *Don't Wake Me Up, Let Me Dream* ....10.00 - 15.00
  3163 *Tomorrow Morning* ....10.00 - 15.00
  3175 *Five Foot Two, Eyes Of Blue* ......15.00 - 20.00
  3191 *Don't Wait Too Long* ....10.00 - 15.00
  3192 *Mother Me, Tennessee* ....10.00 - 15.00
  3198 *Bamboola* ....15.00 - 20.00
  3204 *I Love My Baby* ....15.00 - 20.00
  3216 *Tie Me To Your Apron Strings Again* ....10.00 - 15.00
  3220 *When You're In The Arms Of The One You Love* ....7.00 - 10.00
  3224 *I Wish't I Was In Peoria* ....10.00 - 15.00
  3225 *Kentucky's Way Of Saying "Good Morning"* ....10.00 - 15.00
  3233 *Sweet Child (I'm Wild About You)* ....10.00 - 15.00
  3236 *I Want Somebody To Cheer Me Up* ....20.00 - 30.00
  3241 *Behind The Clouds* ....10.00 - 15.00
  3243 *Dinah* ....10.00 - 15.00
  3249 *Static* ....10.00 - 15.00
  4855 *I Wonder Blues* ....8.00 - 12.00
  4908 *Dancing Fool* ....8.00 - 12.00
  4935 *Hot Lips* ....8.00 - 12.00
  4979 *Carolina In The Morning* ....8.00 - 12.00

5004 *Bees Knees* ....8.00 - 12.00
5016 *Way Down Yonder In New Orleans* ....8.00 - 12.00
5057 *Pay Day Blues* ....8.00 - 12.00
5110 *Snakes Hips* ....8.00 - 10.00
5243 *That Big Blonde Mama* ....8.00 - 12.00
5324 *I'm Goin' South* ....8.00 - 12.00
5349 *Steppin' Out* ....8.00 - 12.00
5357 *The One I Love Belongs To Somebody Else*
....8.00 - 12.00
5363 *Hula Lou* ....8.00 - 12.00
5364 *Mindin' My Business* ....8.00 - 12.00
5407 *Lazy* ....8.00 - 12.00
5424 *What'll I Do?* ....8.00 - 12.00
5432 *It Had To Be You* ....15.00 - 20.00
5433 *After The Storm* ....8.00 - 12.00
5452 *Never Again* ....8.00 - 12.00
5463 *Maytime* ....8.00 - 12.00
5471 *Wait'll You See My Gal* ....8.00 - 12.00
5532 *Go, Emmaline* ....10.00 - 15.00
5540 *Cold Mamas Burn Me Up* ....10.00 - 15.00
5625 *Oh! Mabel* ....15.00 - 20.00
5629 *I'll See You In My Dreams* ....15.00 - 20.00
5637 *Dear One* ....10.00 - 15.00
5645 *Why Couldn't It Be Poor Little Me* ....15.00 - 20.00
5648 *Alabamy Bound* ....15.00 - 20.00
5676 *When I Think Of You* ....10.00 - 15.00
5677 *No Wonder* ....10.00 - 15.00
5710 *Flag That Train* ....15.00 - 20.00
4795, 4815, 4831, 4857, 4868, 4872, 4874, 4887,
4903, 4909, 4910, 4922, 4929, 4933, 4934, 4969,
4975, 4980, 5001, 5005, 5013, 5017, 5022, 5030,
5049, 5076, 5078, 5145, 5153, 5154, 5183, 5186,
5197, 5232, 5241, 5249, 5258, 5264, 5290, 5300,
5301, 5308, 5325, 5344, 5349, 5350 ....5.00 - 10.00

THE BAILEY SWING GROUP:
Juke Box 506 *Eccentric Rag*......................8.00 - 12.00

BUSTER BAILEY & HIS RHYTHM BUSTERS/SEVEN CHOCOLATE DANDIES:
Variety 668 *Dizzy Debutante*.....................15.00 - 20.00
  8333 *The Blue Room*...........................8.00 - 12.00
  8337 *April In Paris*...........................8.00 - 12.00
  8358 *Fable Of A Rose*..........................8.00 - 12.00
  8365 *Eccentric Rag*...........................8.00 - 12.00
Vocalion 2887 *Call Of The Delta*.................30.00 - 50.00
  3846 *Afternoon In Africa*.....................15.00 - 20.00
  4089 *Sloe Jam Fizz*...........................10.00 - 15.00
  4564 *Man With A Horn Goes Berserk*.............10.00 - 15.00
  5510 *Chained To A Dream*......................10.00 - 15.00

JENE BAILEY'S ORCHESTRA:
Gennett 5681 *All Aboard For Heaven*..............30.00 - 50.00

MILDRED BAILEY:
Brunswick 6184 *Wrap Your Troubles In Dreams* ...20.00 - 30.00
  6190 *Blues In My Heart*.......................20.00 - 30.00
  6558 *Is That Religion?* ....15.00 - 20.00
  6587 *Lazy Bones* ....15.00 - 20.00
  6655 *Shouting In The Amen Corner* ....15.00 - 20.00
  6680 *Doin' The Uptown Lowdown* ....15.00 - 20.00
Columbia (most issues) ....7.00 - 10.00
Conqueror (most issues) ....7.00 - 10.00
Decca (most issues) ....5.00 - 10.00

Victor 22874 *Too Late* ....15.00 - 20.00
  22880 *Concentratin'* ....15.00 - 20.00
  22891 *Georgia On My Mind* ....20.00 - 30.00
  22942 *Strangers* ....10.00 - 15.00
  24117 *Rockin' Chair* ....15.00 - 20.00
  24137 *Dear Old Mother Dixie* ....20.00 - 30.00
Vocalion 3056 *I'd Love To Take Orders From You*
....10.00 - 15.00
  3057 *When Day Is Done* ....10.00 - 15.00
  3367 *For Sentimental Reasons* ....15.00 - 20.00
  3378 *More Than You Know* ....10.00 - 15.00
  3449 *My Last Affair* ....10.00 - 15.00
  3456 *You're Laughing At Me* ....10.00 - 15.00
  3508 *Never In A Million Years* ....10.00 - 15.00
  3553 *Rockin' Chair* ....10.00 - 15.00
  3615 *If You Should Ever Leave* ....10.00 - 15.00
  3626 *The Moon Got In My Eyes* ....10.00 - 15.00
  3712 *Bob White* ....10.00 - 15.00
  3758 *Right Or Wrong* ....10.00 - 15.00
  3931 *Thanks For The Memory* ....10.00 - 15.00
  3932 *Lover, Come Back To Me* ....10.00 - 15.00
  4016 *Don't Be That Way* ....10.00 - 15.00
  4036 *At Your Beck And Call* ....10.00 - 15.00
  4083 *I Let a Song Go Out Of My Heart* ....10.00 - 15.00
  4109 *If You Were In My Place* ....10.00 - 15.00
  4139 *Washboard Blues* ....10.00 - 15.00
  4224 *Born To Swing* ....10.00 - 15.00
  4253 *So Help Me* ....10.00 - 15.00
  4282 *Now It Can Be Told* ....10.00 - 15.00
  4345 *Love Is Where You Find It* ....8.00 - 12.00
  4408 *My Reverie* ....8.00 - 12.00
  4432 *Old Folks* ....8.00 - 12.00
  4474 *My Melancholy Baby* ....8.00 - 12.00
  4548 *I Go For That* ....8.00 - 12.00
  4619 *I Cried For You* ....8.00 - 12.00
  4632 *What Shall I Say?* ....8.00 - 12.00
  4708 *'tain't What You Do* ....10.00 - 15.00
  4749 *I Can Read Between The Lines* ....10.00 - 15.00
  4800 *Gulf Coast Blues* ....10.00 - 15.00
  4801 *St. Louis Blues* ....8.00 - 12.00
  4802 *Barrelhouse Music* ....8.00 - 12.00
  4815 *And The Angels Sing* ....10.00 - 15.00
  4845 *Tit Willow* ....10.00 - 15.00
  4939 *It Seems Like Old Times* ....10.00 - 15.00
  4966 *The Little Man Who Wasn't There* ....10.00 - 15.00
  5006 *You're the Moment In My Life* ....10.00 - 15.00
  5086 *A Ghost Of A Chance* ....10.00 - 15.00
  5236 *I've Gone Off The Deep End* ....10.00 - 15.00
  5268 *There'll Be Some Changes Made* ....10.00 - 15.00
  5277 *All The Things You Are* ....10.00 - 15.00

WILLIAM BAILEY:
Banner 1563 *Squeeze Me* ....25.00 - 40.00

MAYNARD BAIRD & HIS ORCHESTRA/SOUTHERN SERENADERS:
Vocalion 1516 *Postage Stomp* ....150.00 - 300.00
  15834 *Sorry*................................150.00 - 300.00

BELLE BAKER:
Brunswick 4550 *If I Had A Talking Picture of You* .8.00 - 12.00
  4558 *I'm Walking With The Moonbeams* ....7.00 - 10.00
  4624 *Love (Your Magic Spell Is Everywhere)* ..10.00 - 15.00
  4714 *Cryin' For The Carolines* ....10.00 - 15.00

4765 *Sing, You Sinners*	10.00 -	15.00
4843 *Cheer Up*	15.00 -	20.00
4962 *Laughing At Life*	10.00 -	15.00
6051 *You're The One I Care For*	10.00 -	15.00
6369 *As Long As Love Lives On*	10.00 -	15.00
Brunswick, most other issues	5.00 -	8.00
Victor 19135 *Jubilee Blues*	7.00 -	10.00
19436 *Hard-Hearted Hannah*	8.00 -	12.00
19609 *Those Panama Mamas*	10.00 -	15.00

GEORGE BAKER:

RCA Victor 17-4003 selections from *Alice In Wonderland* (picture record)	75.00 -	150.00
17-4004 selections from *Alice In Wonderland* (picture record)	75.00 -	150.00

FRANK BAKER'S GROUP:

Tremont 436 *Sweet Papa Joe*	15.00 -	30.00
471 *Hootin' De Hoot*	15.00 -	30.00

SMITH BALLEW & HIS ORCHESTRA:

Banner (most issues)	7.00 -	12.00
Columbia 2320-D *You're Simply Delish*	10.00 -	15.00
2350-D *Nine Little Miles From Ten-Ten-Tennessee*	10.00 -	15.00
2406-D *I Hate Myself (For Falling In Love With You)*	10.00 -	15.00
Melotone (most issues)	7.00 -	12.00
Okeh 41254 *Hittin' The Ceiling*	15.00 -	20.00
41256 *S'posin'*	10.00 -	15.00
41279 *Miss You*	15.00 -	25.00
41282 *Blondy*	15.00 -	20.00
41304 *Can't We Be Friends?*	15.00 -	20.00
41329 *Lady Luck*	15.00 -	20.00
41365 *Funny Dear, What Love Can Do*	15.00 -	20.00
41384 *Sing, You Sinners*	15.00 -	25.00
41385 *We'll Build A Little World Of Our Own*	15.00 -	20.00
41394 *Where The Golden Daffodils Grow*	15.00 -	20.00
41395 *So Sympathetic*	20.00 -	30.00
41429 *You Brought A New Kind Of Love To Me*	20.00 -	30.00
Oriole (most issues)	7.00 -	12.00
Perfect (most titles)	7.00 -	12.00
Romeo (most titles)	7.00 -	12.00
Victor 22147 *Same Old Moon*	15.00 -	20.00

THE BALTIMORE BELLHOPS:

Columbia 2449-D *Hot And Anxious*	20.00 -	30.00

BALTIMORE SOCIETY ORCHESTRA:

Oriole 446 *Oh Say! Can I See You Tonight?*	8.00 -	12.00
569 *Up And At 'Em*	15.00 -	20.00

BANJO BUDDY:

Brunswick 3637 *Oh Doris! Where Do You Live?*	10.00 -	15.00
3865 *Let's Misbehave*	10.00 -	15.00

BANJO IKE & IVORY CHITTISON (See IVORY CHITTISON & BANJO JOE)

BILLY BANKS & HIS ORCHESTRA:

Titles issued contemporaneously on Banner, Oriole, Perfect, Romeo: *Bald-Headed Mama; Bugle Call Rag; Margie; Oh Peter; Spider Crawl; Who's Sorry Now?*	30.00 -	50.00
Victor 23399 *Mighty Sweet*	150.00 -	250.00
24027 *The Scat Song*	50.00 -	80.00
24148 *It Don't Mean A Thing*	50.00 -	80.00

BANNER DANCE ORCHESTRA:

Banner 1229 *Bugle Call Rag*	15.00 -	20.00

FRANK BANTA (& THE AMBASSADORS):

Gennett 4735 *Wild Cherry Rag*	25.00 -	40.00
Victor 19705 *My Sugar*	10.00 -	15.00
19839 *Sweet Man*	8.00 -	12.00
20667 *An Operatic Nightmare*	10.00 -	15.00
Vocalion 14671 *Upright And Grand*	20.00 -	30.00

BARBARY COAST FOUR:

Okeh 40511 *Bugle Blues*	25.00 -	40.00

BARBARY COAST ORCHESTRA:

Decca 501 *Sweet and Slow*	7.00 -	10.00
Personal Record 72-P *Washboard Blues*	75.00 -	100.00
94-P *Weary Blues*	75.00 -	100.00

BARBECUE JOE & HIS HOT DOGS:

Champion 16127 *Up The Country Blues*	200.00 -	300.00
16192 *Shake That Thing*	200.00 -	300.00
40005 *Tin Roof Blues*	30.00 -	50.00
40054 *Shake That Thing*	30.00 -	50.00
Gennett 7320 *Weary Blues*	250.00 -	400.00

BARBECUE PETE:

Champion 15904 *Avenue Strut*	35.00 -	50.00

EDDIE BAREFIELD & HIS QUINTETTE:

Sonora 104 *After Hours*	7.00 -	10.00

ROY BARGY (See also RAMONA):

Victor 18969 *Pianoflagge*	10.00 -	15.00
19320 *Rufenreddy*	10.00 -	15.00
19537 *Jim-Jams*	10.00 -	15.00

BAR HARBOR (SOCIETY) ORCHESTRA:

Banner 1477 *Fascinating Rhythm*	8.00 -	12.00
Harmony 6505-H *Delishious*	15.00 -	20.00
Pathe-Actuelle 036138 *My Best Girl*	8.00 -	12.00
Perfect 14319 *My Best Girl*	8.00 -	12.00
14628 *When The Red, Red, Robin Comes Bob, Bob, Bobbin Along*	8.00 -	12.00
14651 *Tie Me To Your Apron Strings Again*	8.00 -	12.00
14754 *It Made You Happy When You Made Me Cry*	8.00 -	12.00
Puritan 11390 *Insufficient Sweetie*	7.00 -	10.00
11403 *Yes Sir, That's My Baby*	10.00 -	15.00
11417 *Breezin' Along (To Georgia)*	10.00 -	15.00
Silvertone 2498 *If You Knew Susie*	15.00 -	20.00

TOM BARKER & HIS ORCHESTRA:

Parlophone PNY-34084 *Happy Feet*	75.00 -	100.00
PNY-34085 *I Like To Do Things For You*	75.00 -	100.00
PNY-34119 *What's The Use?*	75.00 -	100.00
PNY-34120 *Hittin' The Bottle*	75.00 -	100.00

BILLIE BARNES:

Broadway 5063 *Dearborn Street Breakdown*	150.00 -	250.00

FAYE BARNES:

Paramount 12209 *The Gouge Of Armour Avenue*	40.00 -	70.00

WALTER BARNES & HIS ROYAL CREOLIANS:

Brunswick 4187 *How Long How Long Blues*	50.00 -	80.00
4244 *It's Tight Like That*	100.00 -	150.00
4480 *Birmingham Bertha*	50.00 -	80.00
7072 *Third Rail*	100.00 -	150.00

CHARLIE BARNET & HIS (GLEN ISLAND CASINO) ORCHESTRA:

Titles issued contemporaneously on Banner, Conqueror, Melotone, Oriole, Perfect, Romeo: *Baby, Take a Bow; Buckin' The Wind; Butterfingers; Cross Patch; Emaline; I Lost Another Sweetheart; I'm No Angel; Infatuation; I Want You, I Need You; My First Thrill; The Swing Waltz; This Is Our Last Night Together; Too Good To Be True; What Is Sweeter?* ....10.00 - 15.00

Bluebird 5814 *I'm Keeping Those Keepsakes* ....10.00 - 15.00
　5815 *Nagasaki* ....10.00 - 15.00
　5816 *Growlin'* ....10.00 - 15.00
　6432 *Long Ago And Far Away* ....7.00 - 10.00
　6433 *But Definitely* ....7.00 - 10.00
　6448 *Empty Saddles* ....7.00 - 10.00
　6487 *Always* ....7.00 - 10.00
　6488 *A Star Fell Out Of Heaven* ....7.00 - 10.00
　6504 *Make-Believe Ballroom* ....10.00 - 15.00
　6593 *The Milkman's Matinee* ....7.00 - 10.00
　6594 *It's Love I'm After* ....7.00 - 10.00
　6605 *Did You Mean It?* ....7.00 - 10.00
　6619 *Rainbow On The River* ....7.00 - 10.00
　6967 *A Sailboat In The Moonlight* ....7.00 - 10.00
　6973 *The First Time I Saw You* ....7.00 - 10.00
　6975 *In Your Own Little Way* ....7.00 - 10.00
Bluebird, most higher numbers....................5.00 - 8.00
Capitol 843 *All The Things You Are* ....- - -
Variety 627 *Shame On You*..........................10.00 - 15.00
　633 *Surrealism*..10.00 - 15.00
Vocalion 3835 *Overheard In A Cocktail Lounge* ....10.00 - 15.00

BARREL HOUSE FIVE (ORCHESTRA):

Broadway 5104 *Endurance Stomp* ....150.00 - 200.00
Paramount 12851 *Hot Lovin'*.............................250.00 - up
　12875 *Endurance Stomp*................................200.00 - up
　12942 *Scufflin' Blues* ....250.00 - up
Q.R.S. 7057 *Nobody's Business* ....250.00 - up
　7059 *Hot Lovin'*...250.00 - up

DICK BARRIE & HIS ORCHESTRA:

Vocalion 4193, 4209, 4271, 4285, 4334, 4348,
　4366, 4397, 4409, 4421 ....5.00 - 8.00

BLUE BARRON & HIS ORCHESTRA:

Bluebird 7419, 7429, 7456, 7540, 7542, 7554,
　7605, 7608, 7620, 7709, 7711, 7736, 7856,
　7872, 7886 ....5.00 - 10.00
Bluebird, higher numbers ....5.00 - 8.00
M-G-M, most issues ....5.00 - 8.00
Vocalion 3772 *Yours And Mine*......................8.00 - 12.00

RAYMOND BARROW:

Paramount 12803 *Walking Blues*......................150.00 - 250.00

TED BARTELL & HIS ORCHESTRA:

Harmony 912-H *With A Song In My Heart* ....8.00 - 12.00
　913-H *I Get The Blues When It Rains* ....8.00 - 12.00
　965-H *Now I'm In Love* ....10.00 - 15.00
　973-H *True Blue Lou* ....10.00 - 15.00
(Note: Above titles on Diva, Velvet Tone are similarly valued)

BARTH'S MISSISSIPPIANS/HARRY BARTH'S NOVELTY ORCHESTRA:

Perfect 14329 *That's Georgia* ....7.00 - 10.00
　14383 *I Like Pie, I Like Cake* ....7.00 - 10.00
　14511 *Melancholy Lou* ....8.00 - 12.00
(Above titles, on Pathe-Actuelle, are similarly valued)

ALEX BARTHA & HIS HOTEL TRAYMORE ORCHESTRA:

Victor 24056 *On The Merry-Go-Round*.................20.00 - 30.00
　24059 *Hot Biscuits* ....75.00 - 100.00

SLIM BARTLETT & HIS ORCHESTRA:

Superior 2692 *Asphalt Walk* ....250.00 - up

COUNT BASIE & HIS ORCHESTRA/COUNT BASIE's KANSAS CITY SEVEN:

Columbia 35231 *Riff Interlude* ....8.00 - 12.00
　35338 *Hollywood Jump* ....8.00 - 12.00
　35357 *Ham 'n' Eggs* ....8.00 - 12.00
　35448 *Louisiana*..8.00 - 12.00
　35500 *Somebody Stole My Gal* ....8.00 - 12.00
Columbia 36601, 36647, 36675, 36685, 36709,
　36710, 36711, 36712, 36766, 36795, 36831,
　36845, 36889, 36946, 36990, 37070, 37093........5.00 - 8.00
Conqueror (most issues) ....5.00 - 8.00
Decca 1121 *Pennies From Heaven* ....15.00 - 20.00
　1141 *Honeysuckle Rose* ....15.00 - 20.00
　1228 *The Glory Of Love* ....15.00 - 20.00
　1252 *Exactly Like You* ....15.00 - 20.00
　1363 *One O'Clock Jump* ....10.00 - 15.00
　1379 *Smarty (You Know It All)* ....10.00 - 15.00
　1446 *Good Morning Blues* ....10.00 - 15.00
　1538 *Let Me Dream* ....10.00 - 15.00
　1581 *I Keep Remembering* ....10.00 - 15.00
　1682 *Blues In The Dark* ....10.00 - 15.00
　1728 *Every Tub* ....10.00 - 15.00
　1770 *Don't You Miss Your Baby?* ....10.00 - 15.00
　1880 *Swinging The Blues*...............................7.00 - 10.00
　1965 *Doggin' Around* ....7.00 - 10.00
　2004 *London Bridge Is Falling Down* ....8.00 - 12.00
　2030 *Texas Shuffle*......................................8.00 - 12.00
　2249 *Sing For Your Supper* ....8.00 - 12.00
　2284 *The Blues I Like To Hear* ....8.00 - 12.00
Decca (most other issues) ....5.00 - 10.00
Okeh 5623, 5629, 5732, 5773, 5862, 5884, 5897,
　5922, 5963, 6010, 6047................................7.00 - 10.00
Okeh (most other issues)..............................5.00 - 8.00
Vocalion 4734 *Don't Worry 'Bout Me* ....8.00 - 12.00
　4747 *Rock-A-Bye Basie* ....8.00 - 12.00
　4748 *Taxi War Dance* ....8.00 - 12.00
　4784 *And The Angels Sing* ....8.00 - 12.00
　4860 *Miss Thing*...8.00 - 12.00
　4886 *Twelfth Street Rag* ....7.00 - 10.00
　4967 *You Can Count On Me* ....7.00 - 10.00
　5010 *How Long Blues* ....10.00 - 15.00
　5036 *I Can't Believe That You're In Love With Me*
　..10.00 - 15.00
　5085 *Pound Cake* ....7.00 - 10.00
　5118 *Lester Leaps In* ....10.00 - 15.00
　5169 *Nobody Knows* ....10.00 - 15.00

PHIL BAXTER & HIS ORCHESTRA:

Okeh 40522 *Something Tells Me* ....75.00 - 100.00
　40637 *If I Had You And You Had Me* ....75.00 - 100.00
Victor V-40160 *I Ain't Got No Gal Now*................50.00 - 75.00
V-40204 *Honey Child* ....50.00 - 75.00

JOHNNY BAYERSDORFFER & HIS JAZZOLA NOVELTY ORCHESTRA:

Okeh 40133 *The Waffle Man's Call* ....150.00 - 200.00

BERLYN BAYLOR'S ORCHESTRA:
Champion 16422 *Clarinet Marmalade*.................100.00 - 150.00
    40000 *Riverboat Shuffle* ....25.00 - 40.00
Gennett 6457 *Clarinet Marmalade*.......................150.00 - 200.00

BAY STATE BROADCASTERS:
Van Dyke 81843 *St. James' Infirmary Blues* ....15.00 - 20.00

BEALE STREET FIVE:
Cameo 553 *Who Is The Meanest Gal In Town? Josephine*
....7.00 - 10.00
Lincoln 2219 *Waitin' Around* ....7.00 - 10.00

BEALE STREET SEVEN:
Lincoln 2190 *Sweet Papa Joe*...................................15.00 - 20.00

BEALE STREET WASHBOARD BAND:
Vocalion 1403 *Forty And Tight* ....200.00 - 300.00

IRENE BEASLEY:
Victor 21467 *Choo Choo Train* ....15.00 - 20.00
    21639 *Missin' My Pal*.....................................15.00 - 20.00
    V40092 *Baby's Back Today* ....15.00 - 20.00
    V40125 *Sometimes I Wonder* ....15.00 - 20.00
    V40173 *You'll Come Back To Me Someday*.......15.00 - 20.00

JOSEPHINE BEATTY (ACCOMPANIED BY THE RED ONION JAZZ BABIES):
Buddy 8024 *Early Every Morn*...............................200.00 - 300.00
    8025 *Everybody Loves My Baby*....................200.00 - 300.00
Gennett 3049 *Everybody Loves My Baby* ....150.00 - 250.00
    3044 *Early Every Morn* ....150.00 - 250.00
    5594 *Texas Moaner Blues* ....150.00 - 250.00
Silvertone 4030 *Early Every Morn* ....100.00 - 150.00
    4033 *Texas Moaner Blues* ....100.00 - 150.00

SIDNEY BECHET & HIS NEW ORLEANS FEETWARMERS/ORCHESTRA: SIDNEY BECHET'S BLUE NOTE QUARTET/QUINTET:
Bluebird 7614 *Maple Leaf Rag* ....10.00 - 15.00
    8509 *Sidney's Blues* ....15.00 - 20.00
    10022 *I've Found A New Baby* ....10.00 - 15.00
    10472 *I Want You Tonight* ....10.00 - 15.00
    10623 *Indian Summer*....................................10.00 - 15.00
Blue Note 6 *Summertime* ....10.00 - 15.00
    13 *Lonesome Blues* ....10.00 - 15.00
    502 *Bechet's Steady Rider* ....10.00 - 15.00
Victor 26640, 26663, 26746, 27204, 27240, 27337,
    27386, 27485, 27447, 27574, 27600, 27663,
    27707, 27904 ....7.00 - 12.00
Vocalion 4537 *Jungle Drums* ....15.00 - 20.00
    4575 *What A Dream* ....15.00 - 20.00

NOAH BEERY:
Brunswick 4828 *One Little Drink*.............................15.00 - 20.00

DICK BEESON & HIS ORCHESTRA:
Champion 15054 *Roll 'Em, Girls* ....15.00 - 20.00
    15055 *That Certain Party*..............................15.00 - 20.00
    15059 *Song of the Vagabonds* ....10.00 - 15.00
    15091 *Bye Bye Blackbird* ....8.00 - 12.00
    15093 *Lingering* ....10.00 - 15.00

BIX BEIDERBECKE (& HIS GANG/ORCHESTRA) (See also BIX & HIS RHYTHM JUGGLERS):
Okeh 40916 *In A Mist*...80.00 - 120.00
    40923 *At The Jazz Band Ball* ....80.00 - 120.00

    41001 *Sorry*...80.00 - 120.00
    41030 *Somebody Stole My Gal* ....80.00 - 120.00
    41088 *Ol' Man River* ....80.00 - 120.00
    41173 *Rhythm King* ....80.00 - 120.00
Special Edition 5013-S *Margie*.............................15.00 - 20.00
Victor 23008 *I Don't Mind Walking In The Rain* ... 30.00 - 50.00
    23018 *Deep Down South* ....50.00 - 75.00
    25370 *Deep Down South* ....10.00 - 15.00
Vocalion, most issues...8.00 - 12.00

LEON BELASCO & HIS ORCHESTRA:
Vocalion 7863 *Jammin* ....20.00 - 30.00
    7872 *Wake Up And Live* ....20.00 - 30.00

BELL RECORD BOYS:
Bell 533 *Oh Constantine*..5.00 - 8.00

ANNA BELL:
Q.R.S. 7007 *Hopeless Blues* ....200.00 - 300.00
    7008 *Kitchen Woman Blues* ....200.00 - 300.00
    7009 *Shake It, Black Bottom* ....200.00 - 300.00

GEORGE BELSHAW & HIS KFAB ORCHESTRA:
Brunswick 4365 *Sweet Liza* ....30.00 - 50.00

BENJAMAN'S MANHATTAN ORCHESTRA:
Gennett 5041 *I'm Gonna Get You*...........................25.00 - 40.00

BENNETT'S SWAMPLANDERS:
Columbia 14557-D *Big Ben* ....200.00 - 300.00
    14662-D *Jet Black Blues* ....250.00 - up

PHIL BENNETT & HIS ORCHESTRA:
Broadway 1391 *Rollin' Down The River*................15.00 - 20.00

BEN'S BAD BOYS:
Victor 21971 *Wang Wang Blues* ....15.00 - 25.00

BENSON ORCHESTRA OF CHICAGO:
Victor 18850, 19122, 19130, 19138, 19140, 19235,
    19257, 19317, 19327, 19484 ....7.00 - 12.00
    19361 *Lonely Little Wallflower* ....10.00 - 15.00
    19386 *The Doodle-Um Blues* ....10.00 - 15.00
    19470 *Copenhagen* ....10.00 - 15.00
    19568 *Heart-Broken Strain*...........................10.00 - 15.00
    19688 *Riverboat Shuffle*................................10.00 - 15.00
    19693 *Because Of You The World Is Mine* ....10.00 - 15.00
Victor, most other issues ....5.00 - 8.00

BENNY BENSON'S ORCHESTRA:
Champion 15886 *'Tain't No Sin* ....20.00 - 30.00
    15932 *Honeysuckle Rose* ....20.00 - 30.00

BUNNY BERIGAN & HIS BOYS/ORCHESTRA:
Brunswick 7784 *That Foolish Feeling* ....10.00 - 15.00
    7823 *Who's Afraid Of Love?* ....10.00 - 15.00
    7832 *The Goona Goo* ....10.00 - 15.00
    7847 *Big Boy Blue* ....10.00 - 15.00
    7858 *Dixieland Shuffle* ....15.00 - 20.00
    7949 *I Can't Get Started* ....8.00 - 12.00
Elite 5005 *'tis Autumn* ....8.00 - 12.00
    5006 *The White Cliffs Of Dover* ....8.00 - 12.00
    5019 *Somebody Else Is Taking My Place* ....8.00 - 12.00
    5020 *Skylark* ....8.00 - 12.00
Special Editions 5004 *In A Little Spanish Town* .... 15.00 - 20.00
Victor, most issues ....7.00 - 12.00
Vocalion 3178 *I'd Rather Lead A Band*.................15.00 - 20.00
    3179 *Swing, Mister Charlie* ....15.00 - 20.00

3224 *A Melody From The Sky* ....15.00 - 20.00
3225 *I Can't Get Started*...............................15.00 - 20.00
3253 *But Definitely* ....10.00 - 15.00
3254 *If I Had My Way* ....10.00 - 15.00
15875 *A Tree Was A Tree* ....20.00 - 30.00
15884 *Stormy Weather* ....20.00 - 30.00
15887 *Pettin' In The Park* ....20.00 - 30.00
15891 *Remember My Forgotten Man* ....20.00 - 30.00

AL BERNARD:
Banner 1211 *St. Louis Blues*.......................8.00 - 12.00
Brunswick 2084 *Strut Miss Lizzie* ....8.00 - 12.00
    2107 *Memphis Blues* ....7.00 - 10.00
    2448 *Stavin' Change* ....7.00 - 10.00
    3547 *Beale Street Blues* ....8.00 - 12.00
    3553 *Memphis Blues* ....8.00 - 12.00
Okeh 1235 *Shake, Rattle And Roll* .... -   -   -
    40962 *St. Louis Blues* ....15.00 - 20.00
Regal 9426 *Whoa Tillie Take Your Time*.................7.00 - 10.00

MIKE BERNARD:
Columbia A1266 *Everybody Two-Step* ....20.00 - 30.00
    A1313 *That Peculiar Rag*.........................25.00 - 40.00
    A1386 *Tantalizing Tingles* ....25.00 - 40.00
    A1427 *1915 Rag*..................................25.00 - 40.00
    A2577 *Blaze Away*................................15.00 - 20.00

BEN BERNIE & HIS (HOTEL ROOSEVELT) ORCHESTRA:
Brunswick 3042 *Fallen Arches* ....10.00 - 15.00
    3082 *Bell-Hoppin' Blues* ....10.00 - 15.00
    3126 *Jig Walk* ....10.00 - 15.00
    3145 *Up And At 'Em*...............................15.00 - 20.00
    3171 *No Trouble But You* ....8.00 - 12.00
    3271 *Someone Is Losin' Susan* ....8.00 - 12.00
    3308 *She's Still My Baby* ....8.00 - 12.00
    3411 *He's The Last Word* ....10.00 - 15.00
    3444 *Ain't She Sweet* ....8.00 - 12.00
    3496 *I'm In Love Again* ....8.00 - 12.00
    3528 *Rosy Cheeks* ....8.00 - 12.00
    3656 *There's A Cradle In Caroline* ....10.00 - 15.00
    3771 *The Man I Love* ....8.00 - 12.00
    3774 *Mary* ....8.00 - 12.00
    3808 *Make Believe* ....8.00 - 12.00
    3887 *Borneo*...10.00 - 15.00
    3953 *Because My Baby Don't Mean "Maybe" Now*
    ....10.00 - 15.00
    4020 *When Polly Walks Through The Hollyhocks*
    ....10.00 - 15.00
    4042 *Cannon Ball Rag*..............................15.00 - 20.00
    4058 *Roses Of Yesterday* ....10.00 - 15.00
    4085 *Rhythm King* ....10.00 - 15.00
    4132 *She's Funny That Way* ....8.00 - 12.00
    4142 *Makin' Whoopee* ....10.00 - 15.00
    4168 *Glad Rag Doll* ....8.00 - 12.00
    4204 *Button Up Your Overcoat* ....10.00 - 15.00
    4274 *My Castle In Spain Is A Shack In The Lane*
    ....10.00 - 15.00
    4315 *I've Got A Feeling I'm Falling* ....8.00 - 12.00
    4516 *Bottoms Up* ....10.00 - 15.00
    4767 *You Brought A New Kind Of Love To Me*..10.00 - 15.00
    4899 *Liza Lee* ....10.00 - 15.00
    6165 *This Is The Missus* ....10.00 - 15.00
    20064 (12-inch) *Ol' Man River* ....15.00 - 25.00

Brunswick, most other issues.....................7.00 - 10.00
Columbia 2804-D *Marching Along Together*..........8.00 - 12.00
    2809-D *The Duke Is On A Bat Again*.................15.00 - 20.00
    2820-D *This Is Romance*...........................15.00 - 20.00
    2824-D *Shanghai Lil*...............................15.00 - 20.00
    2836-D *So This Is Susie?*.........................15.00 - 20.00
Decca 874 *Long Ago And Far Away*....................8.00 - 12.00
    877 *Am I Asking Too Much?*......................8.00 - 12.00
    878 *When Did You Leave Heaven?*...............7.00 - 10.00
Okeh 5646, 5889, 5914 ....7.00 - 10.00
Perfect (unnumbered) *Jimmy Walker Medley*
    (souvenir record) .... -   -
Vocalion 4916, 4943, 5072, 5087, 5292, 5331,
    5482, 5615 ....7.00 - 10.00
    14555 *Who's Sorry Now?* ....10.00 - 15.00
    14585 *Henpecked Blues* ....15.00 - 20.00
    14854 *Somebody Loves Me* ....10.00 - 15.00
    14878 *Doodle Doo Doo* ....10.00 - 15.00
    14939 *Mandy* ....10.00 - 15.00
    14940 *Where's My Sweetie Hiding?* ....10.00 - 15.00
    14955 *Oh! Lady Be Good* ....10.00 - 15.00
    14957 *Why Couldn't It Be Poor Little Me?* ......10.00 - 15.00
    15002 *Sweet Georgia Brown* ....10.00 - 15.00
    15027 *Cheatin' On Me* ....10.00 - 15.00
    15037 *If You Knew Susie* ....10.00 - 15.00
    15080 *Collegiate* ....10.00 - 15.00
    15130 *Wait'll It's Moonlight* ....10.00 - 15.00
Vocalion (most others in 14000-15000 series) ....5.00 - 10.00

CHU BERRY & HIS STOMPY STEVEDORES:
Commodore 516, 541, 1502, 1508....................7.00 - 10.00
Variety 532 *Too Marvelous For Words*.................10.00 - 15.00
    587 *Limehouse Blues* ....8.00 - 12.00
    657 *My Secret Love Affair* ....10.00 - 15.00
Vocalion 3793 *Ebb Tide* ....10.00 - 15.00
    3824 *Limehouse Blues* ....8.00 - 12.00

VIC BERTON & HIS ORCHESTRA:
Columbia 3074-D *Devil's Kitchen*..........................20.00 - 30.00
    3092-D *Imitations Of You*..........................20.00 - 30.00
Vocalion 2915 *Dardanella* ....20.00 - 30.00
    2944 *Lonesome And Sorry*...........................20.00 - 30.00
    2964 *A Smile Will Go A Long, Long Way*.........20.00 - 30.00
    2974 *Blue* ....20.00 - 30.00

JIMMY BERTRAND'S WASHBOARD WIZARDS:
Vocalion 1035 *Little Bits* ....80.00 - 120.00
    1060 *47th Street Stomp* ....200.00 - 300.00
    1099 *I'm Goin' Huntin'* ....200.00 - 300.00
    1100 *The Blues Stampede* ....200.00 - 300.00
    1280 *I Won't Give You Some* ....200.00 - 300.00

TOM BERWICK & HIS (RITZ-CARLTON) ORCHESTRA:
Bluebird 5526 *Dames* ....8.00 - 12.00
    5578 *The Memphis Blues* ....10.00 - 15.00
    5579 *Ooh, You Miser You* ....8.00 - 12.00
Electradisk 1900, 1921, 1922, 1925 ....7.00 - 12.00

DON BESTOR & HIS ORCHESTRA:
Bluebird 7239, 7240, 7243 ....7.00 - 10.00
Brunswick 6975, 6981, 6986 ....7.00 - 10.00
Brunswick (most other issues) ....5.00 - 10.00
Victor 19746 *Are You Sorry?* ....8.00 - 12.00
    19751 *Charleston Baby Of Mine* ....7.00 - 10.00

19832 *She's Drivin' Me Wild*	25.00	-	40.00
19988 *Say Mister! Have You Met Rosie's Sister?*	8.00	-	12.00
21080 *Baby Your Mother*	8.00	-	12.00
24253 *Forty-Second Street*	10.00	-	15.00
24503 *Inka Dinka Doo*	10.00	-	15.00
24505 *Armful Of Trouble*	20.00	-	30.00
24556 *What's Good For The Goose*	10.00	-	15.00
24596 *Waitin' At The Gate For Katy*	10.00	-	15.00
24658 *Moon Glow*	10.00	-	15.00
Victor, most other issues	5.00	-	10.00

THE BETTY BOOP GIRL (See MAE QUESTAL; and also DOT DARE, GAY ELLIS, and HELEN KANE, as to whom the name is often appropriate, if not strictly accurate)

BEVERLY SYNCOPATORS:
Paramount 12747 *Sugar* ....200.00 - 300.00

HENRY BIAGINI & HIS ORCHESTRA:
Titles on Banner, Melotone, Oriole, Perfect, and Romeo: *Go Into Your Dance; The Little Things You Used To Do* ..7.00 - 10.00

PAUL BIESE & HIS ORCHESTRA:
Columbia, most issues	5.00	-	8.00
Brunswick, most issues	5.00	-	8.00
Victor 19313 *Never Again*	8.00	-	12.00
19314 *Cinderella Blues*	8.00	-	12.00
19474 *Bye Bye Baby*	10.00	-	15.00

THE BIG ACES:
Okeh 41136 *Cherry* ....50.00 - 75.00

BARNEY BIGARD & HIS ORCHESTRA/ JAZZOPATORS:
Bluebird 10981 *A Lull At Dawn*	8.00	-	12.00
11098 *Ready Eddy*	8.00	-	12.00
11581 *Brown Suede*	8.00	-	12.00
Okeh (most issues)	7.00	-	12.00
Variety 515 *Caravan*	8.00	-	12.00
525 *Frolic Sam*	10.00	-	15.00
564 *Four And One-Half Street*	10.00	-	15.00
596 *Get It Southern Style*	10.00	-	15.00
626 *Sponge Cake And Spinach*	10.00	-	15.00
655 *Jazz a la Carte*	10.00	-	15.00
Vocalion 3809 *Caravan*	8.00	-	12.00
3813 *Clouds In My Heart*	8.00	-	12.00
3820 *Lament For A Lost Love*	8.00	-	12.00
3834 *Moonlght Fiesta*	8.00	-	12.00
3842 *Demi-Tasse*	8.00	-	12.00
3985 *Drummer's Delight*	10.00	-	15.00
4928 *Chew-Chew-Chew*	10.00	-	15.00
5378 *Minuet In Blues*	10.00	-	15.00
5422 *Early Mornin'*	10.00	-	15.00
5595 *Mardi Gras Madness*	10.00	-	15.00

BIG TIME TRIO:
Van Dyke 71811 *Hot Moments* ....20.00 - 30.00

JACK BINNEY & HIS ORCHESTRA:
Parlophone PNY-34096 *Freshman Hop* ....75.00 - 100.00

BIRMINGHAM BLUE BUGLERS:
Gennett 5498 *Dancin' Blues* ....15.00 - 20.00

BIRMINGHAM BLUETETTE:
Herwin 92019 *Old Man Blues* ....250.00 - up

BIRMINGHAM FIVE:
Champion 15008 *Red Hot Henry Brown*	15.00	-	20.00
15015 *Sweet Georgia Brown*	15.00	-	20.00
15018 *Oh Boy! What A Girl*	15.00	-	20.90
15028 *Siberia*	15.00	-	20.00
15046 *I'm Gonna Hang Around My Sugar*	15.00	-	20.00
15047 *No Man's Mama*	15.00	-	20.00
15049 *Melancholy Lou*	15.00	-	20.00
15050 *Everybody's Doin' The Charleston Now*	15.00	-	20.00

BIRMINGHAM JUG BAND:
Okeh 8856 *German Blues*	200.00	-	300.00
8866 *Kickin' Mule Blues*	200.00	-	300.00
8895 *Birmingham Blues*	200.00	-	300.00
8908 *Wild Cat Squall*	200.00	-	300.00

BIRMINGHAM RED JACKETS:
Buddy 8008 *Could I? I Certainly Could* ....- - -

BIRMINGHAM SERENADERS:
Decca 7052 *Black Gal Blues*	30.00	-	50.00
7060 *Milk Cow Blues*	30.00	-	50.00

BIX & HIS RHYTHM JUGGLERS:
Gennett 5654 *Davenport Blues* ....150.00 - 250.00

BLACK BIRDS OF PARADISE:
Black Patti 8053 *Razor Edge*	1000.00	-	up
Gennett 6210 *Tishomingo Blues*	300.00	-	up
6211 *Muddy Water*	300.00	-	up

BLACK DIAMOND ORCHESTRA:
Gennett 6442 *I've Got Somebody New*	20.00	-	30.00
6596 *Egypt*	-	-	-
6726 *How Long Must I Wait For You?*	-	-	-

BLACK DIAMOND SERENADERS:
Pathe 36503 *Toe-To-Toe*	15.00	-	20.00
36511 *Ace In The Hole*	20.00	-	30.00
Perfect 14684 *Sally's Not The Same Old Sally*	15.00	-	20.00
14692 *Ace In The Hole*	20.00	-	30.00

THE BLACK DOMINOES:
Gennett 5263 *Black Sheep Blues*	20.00	-	30.00
5347 *Back O' Town Blues*	20.00	-	30.00

BLACK KIDS OF HARMONY:
Silvertone 3831 *So's Your Old Man* ....10.00 - 20.00

THE BLACK PIRATES:
Broadway 1230 *My Old Girl's My New Girl Now*	15.00	-	25.00
1374 *Some Of These Days*	15.00	-	20.00

BLACK SWAN DANCE ORCHESTRA:
Black Swan 2014 *Pretty Ways*..................................25.00 - 40.00

FRANK BLACK & HIS ORCHESTRA:
Brunswick, most issues......................................5.00 - 10.00

TED BLACK & HIS ORCHESTRA:
Bluebird 5370, 5371, 5375, 5387 ....7.00 - 10.00
Champion 16174 *Makin' Time With You* ....10.00 - 15.00
Melotone 12188 *On The Beach With You* ....7.00 - 10.00
Sunrise 3451 *I Knew You When*.....................30.00 - 50.00
   3452 *Sweet And Simple*........................30.00 - 50.00
   3456 *True*......................................30.00 - 50.00
Victor 22762, 22799, 22807, 22816, 22854, 22857 ..7.00 - 10.00
   24046 *Banking On The Weather*.....................8.00 - 12.00
   24050 *Rain, Rain, Go Away* ....8.00 - 12.00
   24051 *We Were Only Walking In The Moonlight*.8.00 - 12.00

BLAKE'S JAZZONE ORCHESTRA:
Pathe 20430 *The Jazz Dance* ....15.00 - 25.00

EUBIE BLAKE (& HIS ORCHESTRA); EUBIE BLAKE TRIO:
Crown 3086 *When Your Lover Has Gone* ....20.00 - 30.00
   3090 *I'm No Account Any More* ....20.00 - 30.00
   3105 *It Looks Like Love*....................................20.00 - 30.00
   3111 *One More Time* ....20.00 - 30.00
   3130 *Nobody's Sweetheart* ....30.00 - 50.00
   3193 *River Stay 'Way From My Door* ....30.00 - 50.00
   3197 *Sweet Georgia Brown*..............................30.00 - 50.00
Emerson 10434 *Baltimore Buzz* ....30.00 - 50.00
   10450 *Ma* ....20.00 - 30.00
   10519 *Cutie* ....20.00 - 30.00
Pathe 20326 *American Jubilee* ....30.00 - 50.00
   20358 *Sarah From Sahara* ....30.00 - 50.00
Victor 18791 *Baltimore Buzz* ....10.00 - 15.00
   22735 *My Blue Days Blew Over*.........................30.00 - 50.00
   22737 *Thumpin And Bumpin* ....30.00 - 50.00

JACK BLAND & HIS RHYTHMAKERS:
Titles issued contemporaneously on Banner, Melotone, Oriole, Perfect, Romeo: *It's Gonna Be You; A Shine On Your Shoes; Someone Stole Gabriel's Horn; Who Stole The Lock* ....30.00 - 50.00

RUBE BLOOM (& HIS BAYOU BOYS):
Brunswick 3366 *Back Beats* ....75.00 - 100.00
Cameo 1153 *Spring Fever* ....10.00 - 15.00
Columbia 1195-D *Silhouette* ....15.00 - 20.00
Columbia 2103-D *The Man From The South* ....20.00 - 30.00
   2186-D *Bessie Couldn't Help It* ....20.00 - 30.00
   2218-D *On Revival Day*...................................20.00 - 30.00
Harmony 164-H *Soliloquy*....................................10.00 - 15.00
Okeh 40842 *The Doll Dance* ....10.00 - 15.00
   40867 *Spring Fever* ....10.00 - 15.00
   40901 *Silhouette* ....10.00 - 15.00
   40931 *My Blue Heaven* ....10.00 - 15.00
   40988 *Mine-All Mine* ....15.00 - 20.00
   41073 *That Futuristic Rag* ....15.00 - 20.00
   41117 *I Can't Give You Anything But Love* ......10.00 - 15.00
Victor 25060 *On The Green* ....15.00 - 20.00
   25227 *One Finger Joe*.....................................15.00 - 20.00

THE BLU-DISC ORCHESTRA:
Blu-Disc T-1005 *I Want To Be Happy* ....50.00 - 80.00
   T-1006 *It Had To Be You*..................................50.00 - 80.00

THE BLUEBIRDS:
Vocalion 15652 *Let's Misbehave*...........................10.00 - 15.00

BLUE GRASS FOOT WARMERS:
Harmony 206-H *Senorita Mine*.............................30.00 - 50.00
   248-H *Old Folks Shuffle* ....30.00 - 50.00
(Same titles also appear on Diva, Velvet Tone)

BLUE JAY BOYS:
Decca 7224 *Endurance Stomp* ....20.00 - 30.00
   7225 *Some Do And Some Don't*........................20.00 - 30.00
   7240 *My Baby* ....20.00 - 30.00

THE BLUE KITTENS:
Puritan 11433 *In Your Green Hat* ....8.00 - 12.00
   11434 *I Love My Baby* ....8.00 - 12.00
(Above titles also issued on Paramount, similarly valued)

BLUE MOON MELODY BOYS:
Champion 15492 *Louisiana* ....15.00 - 25.00
   15542 *My Blue Ridge Mountain Home*..............12.00 - 16.00
   15553 *If You Want The Rainbow* ....12.00 - 16.00
   15557 *Ten Little Miles From Town* ....15.00 - 20.00
   15575 *Pickin' Cotton* ....15.00 - 20.00

BLUE RHYTHM BAND/BOYS:
Brunswick 6143 *Blue Flame*.................................30.00 - 50.00
   6199 *Snake Hips* ....30.00 - 50.00

BLUE RHYTHM ORCHESTRA:
Pathe-Actuelle 36350 *Santa Claus Blues* ....100.00 - 150.00
   36364 *Keep Your Temper* ....100.00 - 150.00
Perfect 14531 *Santa Claus Blues* ....100.00 - 150.00
   14545 *Keep Your Temper* ....100.00 - 150.00

BLUE RIBBON BOYS:
Titles issued contemporaneously on Banner, Conqueror, Regal, Romeo: *Black And Tan Fantasy; Futuristic Jungleism; Low Down On The Bayou; Poor Minnie The Moocher; Star Dust; Sugar Blues* ....8.00 - 15.00

BLUE RIBBON SYNCOPATORS (OF BUFFALO):
Columbia 14215-D *Memphis Sprawler* ....150.00 - 200.00
   14235-D *Whale Dip* ....150.00 - 200.00
Okeh 40349 *My Gal, My Pal* ....150.00 - 250.00

BLUE ROOM ORCHESTRA:
Broadway 1244 *Glad Rag Doll*..............................8.00 - 12.00
   1245 *My Man* ....8.00 - 12.00
   1246 *Guess Who!* ....7.00 - 10.00
   1268 *Pretty Little Thing* ....8.00 - 12.00
   1270 *A Garden In The Rain* ....5.00 - 8.00
   1306 *Waiting At The End Of The Road* ....8.00 - 12.00

BOB BLUE:
Okeh 41464 *I'll Be Blue, Just Thinking Of You*......15.00 - 20.00

BUD BLUE & HIS ORCHESTRA:
Okeh 41466 *Someone Sang A Sweeter Song To Mary* ....15.00 - 20.0

BUDDY BLUE & HIS TEXANS:
Banner 0501, 0605, 0606, 0697, 0700, 0731, 6438, 6442, 6471, 6479 ....5.00 - 10.00
Banner 0619 *Only A Rose* ....8.00 - 12.00
   0695 *Any Old Place With You* ....8.00 - 12.00
   0732 *Bring Back That Hour Of Love* ....8.00 - 12.00
   6411 *Ol' Man River* ....8.00 - 12.00

6419 *S'posin'*	8.00 -	12.00
6515 *Ev'ry Day Away From You*	8.00 -	12.00
6547 *By The Way (I'm Still In Love With You)*	8.00 -	12.00
Cameo 0295 *Any Old Place With You*	8.00 -	12.00
0332 *Bring Back That Hour of Love*	8.00 -	12.00
Crown 3008 *Body And Soul*	10.00 -	15.00
3014 *Little White Lies*	10.00 -	15.00
3015 *I Still Get A Thrill*	8.00 -	12.00
3021 *I'll Be Blue Just Thinking Of You*	8.00 -	12.00
3033 *Tears*	8.00 -	12.00
3036 *You're The One I Care For*	10.00 -	15.00
3068 *Running Between The Raindrops*	8.00 -	12.00
3108 *Little Joe*	15.00 -	20.00
3132 *Nevertheless*	10.00 -	15.00
3146 *How The Time Can Fly*	8.00 -	12.00
3280 *Somebody Loves You*	8.00 -	12.00
3281 *Let's Have Another Cup Of Coffee*	8.00 -	12.00

THE BLUES CHASERS:

Perfect 14428 *Sweet Georgia Brown*	15.00 -	20.00
14432 *Charleston*	15.00 -	20.00

BLUMENBERG'S ORCHESTRA:

Broadway 1490 *Love Letters In The Sand*	10.00 -	15.00

BLYTHE'S BLUE BOYS:

Champion 15344 *There'll Come A Day*	150.00 -	250.00
15399 *Cootie Stomp*	150.00 -	250.00
15528 *My Baby*	150.00 -	250.00
15551 *Pleasure Mad*	150.00 -	250.00
15570 *Tell Me, Cutie*	150.00 -	250.00
15615 *Endurance Stomp*	150.00 -	250.00
15676 *Oriental Man*	150.00 -	250.00
40023 *Oriental Man*	30.00 -	50.00
40025 *Endurance Stomp*	30.00 -	50.00
40062 *Tack It Down*	30.00 -	50.00
40115 *Tell Me, Cutie*	30.00 -	50.00

BLYTHE'S SINFUL FIVE:

Paramount 12346 *Pump Tillie Pump*	150.00 -	250.00

BLYTHE'S WASHBOARD BAND/RAGAMUFFINS:

Paramount 12368 *Bohunkus Blues*	250.00 -	up
12428 *Ape Man*	250.00 -	up

JAMES/JIMMIE/JIMMY BLYTHE (& BURTON/& HIS RAGAMUFFINS); BLYTHE'S OWLS/WASHBOARD WIZARDS:

Champion 16451 *Bow To Your Papa*	200.00 -	300.00
Gennett 6502 *Dustin' The Keys*	200.00 -	300.00
Paramount 12207 *Chicago Stomp*	150.00 -	200.00
12304 *Jimmie Blues*	150.00 -	200.00
12370 *Mr. Freddie Blues*	150.00 -	200.00
12376 *Messin Around*	150.00 -	250.00
Vocalion 1135 *Weary Way Blues*	200.00 -	300.00
1136 *Have Mercy!*	200.00 -	300.00
1180 *Oriental Man*	200.00 -	300.00
1181 *Alley Rat*	200.00 -	300.00

BOBBY'S REVELERS:

Silvertone 3551 *Heebie Jeebies*	75.00 -	100.00
3552 *Mojo Blues*	75.00 -	100.00

BOGAN'S BIRMINGHAM BUSTERS:

Titles issued contemporaneously on Banner, Melotone, Oriole, Perfect, Romeo: *Everything Is Rhythm Now; She Caught The*

Boat	50.00 -	80.00
Vocalion 03540 *She Caught The Boat*	50.00 -	80.00
03570 *The Sheik Of Araby*	50.00 -	80.00

TOMMY BOHN PENN-SIRENS ORCHESTRA:

Odeon ONY-36047 *You've Got That Thing*	50.00 -	80.00
Okeh 41372 *Amos 'n' Andy*	40.00 -	60.00
41374 *You've Got That Thing*	30.00 -	50.00

PAUL BOLOGNESE & HIS ORCHESTRA:

Globe 8109 *Charleston Choo Choo*	7.00 -	10.00
Grey Gull 1439 *At Sundown*	5.00 -	8.00
Madison 1615 *My Girl Pearl*	7.00 -	10.00

BOLTON AND CIPRIANI'S WESTCHESTER BILTMORE FIVE/ORCHESTRA:

Columbia Personal 87-P *You'll Do It Someday*	75.00 -	100.00
93-P *You'll Do It Someday*	75.00 -	100.00

PETE BONTSEMA & HIS HOTEL TULLER ORCHESTRA OF DETROIT:

Gennett 20016 *Salt Your Sugar*	25.00 -	50.00

CHARLES BOOKER; BOOKER ORCHESTRA/ BOOKER'S JAZZ BAND:

Domino 3474 *The West Texas Blues*	30.00 -	50.00
Gennett 6375 *Salty Dog*	150.00 -	200.00
Okeh 8155 *Pencil Papa Blues*	50.00 -	75.00

BETTY BOOP (See THE BETTY BOOP GIRL)

BOONE'S JUMPING JACKS:

Decca 8590 *I'm For It*	10.00 -	15.00
8644 *Please Be Careful*	10.00 -	15.00

BOOTS AND HIS BUDDIES:

Bluebird 6063 *Rose Room*	15.00 -	25.00
6081 *Riffs*	15.00 -	25.00
6132 *Anytime*	10.00 -	15.00
6301 *Georgia*	15.00 -	25.00
6307 *Coquette*	15.00 -	25.00
6333 *The Vamp*	15.00 -	20.00
6357 *Sweet Girl*	15.00 -	20.00
6862 *Jealous*	15.00 -	20.00
6880 *Haunting Memories*	15.00 -	20.00
6921 *Swanee River Blues*	15.00 -	25.00
6968 *Sleepy Gal*	15.00 -	20.00
7005 *San Antonio Tamales*	15.00 -	20.00
7187 *Blues Of Avalon*	15.00 -	20.00
7217 *The Goo*	15.00 -	20.00
7236 *The Sad*	15.00 -	20.00
7241 *Ain't Misbehavin'*	15.00 -	20.00
7245 *The Happy*	15.00 -	20.00
7269 *The Somebody*	15.00 -	20.00
7556 *Deep South*	15.00 -	20.00
7596 *True Blue Lou*	15.00 -	25.00
7669 *Lonely Moments*	15.00 -	20.00
7944 *A Salute To Harlem*	15.00 -	25.00
10036 *East Commerce Stomp*	15.00 -	20.00
10043 *Sweet Girl*	8.00 -	12.00
10044 *San Antonio Tamales*	8.00 -	12.00
10106 *Boots Stomp*	15.00 -	20.00
10113 *Lonesome Road Stomp*	15.00 -	20.00

BORBEE'S JASS ORCHESTRA:
Columbia A2363 *The Ragtime Volunteers Are Off To War*
....15.00 - 20.00

BOSTON SOCIETY ORCHESTRA:
Oriole 1454 *Glad Rag Doll*..........................8.00 - 12.00

THE BOSTONIANS:
Domino 4216 *My Blackbirds Are Bluebirds Now* ..10.00 - 15.00
Regal 8654 *My Blackbirds Are Bluebirds Now* ....10.00 - 15.00
Vocalion 15275 *So Does Your Old Mandarin* ....10.00 - 15.00
    15298 *I've Found A New Baby* ....15.00 - 20.00
    15344 *Reaching For The Moon* ....7.00 - 10.00
    15474 *No-One But You Knows How To Love* .....7.00 - 10.00
    15488 *Ev'rything's Peaches* ....25.00 - 40.00

THE BOSWELL SISTERS:
Brunswick 6083 *When I Take My Sugar To Tea* ....20.00 - 30.00
    6109 *Shout, Sister, Shout* ....20.00 - 30.00
    6151 *It's The Girl* ....20.00 - 30.00
    6170 *Makin' Faces At The Man In The Moon* ...20.00 - 30.00
    6173 *Heebie Jeebies* ....20.00 - 30.00
    6218 *An Evening In Caroline* ....20.00 - 30.00
    6231 *I Thank You, Mr. Moon* ....15.00 - 20.00
    6257 *Was That The Human Thing To Do?* ....15.00 - 20.00
    6271 *Everybody Loves My Baby* ....15.00 - 20.00
    6291 *There'll Be Some Changes Made* ....15.00 - 20.00
    6302 *Got The South In My Soul* ....15.00 - 20.00
    6335 *Hand Me Down My Walkin' Cane* ....15.00 - 20.00
    6360 *Old Yazoo* ....15.00 - 20.00
    6395 *Down On The Delta* ....15.00 - 20.00
    6418 *Down Among The Sheltering Palms* ....15.00 - 20.00
    6442 *It Don't Mean A Thing (If It Ain't Got That Swing)*
....15.00 - 20.00
    6470 *Louisiana Hayride* ....15.00 - 20.00
    6483 *It's All My Fault* ....15.00 - 20.00
    6545 *Shuffle Off To Buffalo* ....15.00 - 20.00
    6596 *The Gold Diggers' Song* ....15.00 - 20.00
    6625 *Puttin' It On* ....15.00 - 20.00
    6650 *That's How Rhythm Was Born* ....15.00 - 20.00
    6733 *Song of Surrender* ....15.00 - 20.00
    6798 *You Oughta Be In Pictures* ....15.00 - 20.00
    6847 *Crazy People* ....10.00 - 15.00
    6929 *Don't Let Your Love Go Wrong* ....10.00 - 15.00
    6951 *Lonesome Road* ....10.00 - 15.00
    7302 *Rock And Roll* ....10.00 - 15.00
    7348 *The Object Of My Affection* ....10.00 - 15.00
    7412 *Alexander's Ragtime Band* ....8.00 - 12.00
    7454 *Every Little Moment* ....10.00 - 15.00
    7467 *St. Louis Blues* ....10.00 - 15.00
Decca 574 *Cheek To Cheek* ....8.00 - 12.00
    671 *The Music Goes 'Round And Around* ....8.00 - 12.00
    709 *Let Yourself Go* ....8.00 - 12.00
Victor 19639 *Nights When I'm Lonely* ....30.00 - 50.00

CONNIE BOSWELL:
Brunswick 6162 *I'm All Dressed Up With A Broken Heart*
....15.00 - 20.00
    6210 *Time On My Hands* ....15.00 - 20.00
    6223 *You Try Somebody Else* ....15.00 - 20.00
    6267 *I Cried For You* ....15.00 - 20.00
    6297 *My Lips Want Kisses* ....15.00 - 20.00
    6405 *Me Minus You* ....10.00 - 15.00
    6483 *It's All My Fault*..................................10.00 - 15.00

Brunswick 6552, 6592, 6603, 6632, 6640, 6754, 6862,
    6871, 6921, 6962, 7303, 7354, 7363, 7445, 7457 7.00 - 12.00
Decca 747 *The Panic Is On* ....10.00 - 15.00
    794 *You Started Me Dreaming* ....10.00 - 15.00
    829 *I Met My Waterloo* ....8.00 - 12.00
    840 *You Can Call It Swing* ....8.00 - 12.00
Decca (most other issues) ....5.00 - 10.00
Victor 19639 *I'm Gonna Cry*........................30.00 - 50.00

BOURNE & ELLIS:
Columbia 398-D *If You Knew Susie* ....10.00 - 15.00

JIMMY BRACKEN'S TOE TICKLERS:
Titles issued contemporaneously on Banner, Conqueror, Domino,
    Regal: *After You've Gone; Icky Blues; It's So Good; It's Tight
    Like That; Making Friends; Four Or Five Times; Shirt Tail
    Stomp; Tiger Rag; Twelfth Street Rag* ....15.00 - 30.00

**PERRY BRADFORD & HIS GANG/PERRY
BRADFORD'S JAZZ PHOOLS:**
Titles issued contemporaneously on Claxtonola, Harmograph,
    Paramount, Puritan: *Day Break Blues; Fade Away Blues*
....100.00 - 150.00
Additional titles: *Charleston, South Carolina;
    Hoola Boola Dance*........................150.00 - 200.00
Columbia 14142-D *So's Your Old Man*...............100.00 - 150.00
Okeh 8324 *So's Your Old Man*......................150.00 - 200.00
    8416 *Kansas City Blues* ....150.00 - 200.00
    8450 *Lucy Long*......................................150.00 - 200.00
Vocalion 15165 *Lucy Long* ....150.00 - 200.00

WILL BRADLEY AND HIS ORCHESTRA:
Columbia 35333, 35354, 35399, 35414, 35464,
    35470, 35485, 35530, 35542, 35543, 35545,
    35566, 35597, 35607, 35645.....................7.00 - 10.00
Columbia, most others ....5.00 - 8.00
Signature 15048, 15049, 15111, 15134 ....7.00 - 10.00
Vocalion 5130 *Memphis Blues* ....10.00 - 15.00
    5182 *Speaking Of Heaven* ....8.00 - 12.00
    5210 *Fit To Be Tied* ....8.00 - 12.00
    5237 *Mean To Me* ....8.00 - 12.00
    5262 *Swingin' A Dream* ....8.00 - 12.00

TINY BRADSHAW & HIS ORCHESTRA:
Decca 194 *The Sheik Of Araby* ....10.00 - 15.00
    236 *Ol' Man River* ....10.00 - 15.00
    317 *She'll Be Coming 'Round The Mountain* ...10.00 - 15.00
    456 *I Ain't Got Nobody* ....10.00 - 15.00
Manor 1052 *Schoolday Blues* ....8.00 - 12.00
    1082 *Salt Lake City Bounce* ....7.00 - 10.00
    1147 *I Found Out Too Late* ....7.00 - 10.00
Regis 1010 *Straighten Up And Fly Right* ....8.00 - 12.00
    1011 *After You've Gone* ....8.00 - 12.00

**ARDELL/ARDELLA/ARDELLE ("SHELLEY") BRAGG
(& HER TEXAS BLUE BLOWERS):**
Paramount 12398 *Pig Meat Blues*......................150.00 - 200.00
    12410 *Bird Nest Blues* ....150.00 - 200.00
    12429 *That's Alright*.............................150.00 - 200.00
    12458 *Wolf Man*..................................150.00 - 200.00

J.H. BRAGG AND HIS RHYTHM FIVE:
Vocalion 03060 *Ethiopian Stomp* ....40.00 - 60.00
    03174 *Frisky Honey*.............................35.00 - 50.00

BRASHEAR'S CALIFORNIA ORCHESTRA:

Black Swan 2078 *Stuttering* ....30.00 -   50.00
     10074 *Stuttering*...30.00 -   50.00
     10079 *Carolina Shout*..................................40.00 -   70.00

BRUCE BRAY'S ORCHESTRA:

Bell 569 *Sweetheart Of Sigma Chi* ....20.00 -   30.00

LEW BRAY accompanied by SUNNY CLAPP & HIS BAND O'SUNSHINE:

Okeh 41261 *We Can't Use Each Other Any More* ..50.00 -   75.00
     41293 *A Bundle of Southern Sunshine* ....10.00 -   15.00
     41307 *When the Real Thing Comes Your Way* ....7.00 -   10.00
     41334 *Lucky Me-Lovable You* ....15.00 -   20.00

PERLEY BREED'S (SHEPARD COLONIAL) ORCHESTRA:

Gennett 3059 *Honey, I'm In Love With You*............30.00 -   50.00
     5608 *Tell Me, Dreamy Eyes*..............................30.00 -   50.00

LARRY BREESE & HIS ORCHESTRA:

Ammor 100 *I've Found A New Baby* ....10.00 -   15.00
     101 *The Jumpin' Jive* ....10.00 -   15.00
     102 *Auld Lang Syne* ....10.00 -   15.00
     107 *All The Things You Are* ....10.00 -   15.00

FANNY BRICE:

Columbia A1973 *I Don't Know Whether To Do It Or Not*
....15.00 -   20.00
     A2122 *If We Could Only Take Her Word* ....15.00 -   20.00
Victor 21168 *My Man*..10.00 -   15.00
     21211 *Mrs. Cohen At The Beach*....................10.00 -   15.00
     21815 *If You Want The Rainbow* ....7.00 -   10.00
     22310 *When A Woman Loves A Man* ....10.00 -   15.00
     45263 *Second Hand Rose* ....15.00 -   30.00
     45303 *Oh, How I Hate That Fellow Nathan*.......15.00 -   20.00
     45323 *The Sheik of Avenue B* ....15.00 -   20.00

ACE BRIGODE & HIS TEN/FOURTEEN VIRGINIANS:

Cameo 725 *My Sugar* ....10.00 -   15.00
     726 *Wondering* ....7.00 -   10.00
     783 *Close Your Eyes* ....7.00 -   10.00
     785 *Tweedle-Dee, Tweedle-Doo* ....8.00 -   12.00
Columbia 282-D *Alabamy Bound* ....10.00 -   15.00
     341-D *When I Think Of You* ....7.00 -   10.00
     385-D *Sleeping Beauty's Wedding* ....10.00 -   15.00
     398-D *Yes, Sir! That's My Baby*.....................10.00 -   15.00
     401-D *Wait'll It's Moonlight* ....10.00 -   15.00
     426-D *Alone At Last* ....10.00 -   15.00
     477-D *Why Aren't Yez Eatin' More Oranges?* ..10.00 -   15.00
Edison 51496 *Ever-Lovin' Bee* ....15.00 -   20.00
Edison 51511 *Tokio Blues* ....15.00 -   20.00
     51533 *Fooling*...15.00 -   20.00
Okeh 40014 *Oklahoma Indian Jazz* ....15.00 -   20.00
     40152 *Don't Take Your Troubles To Bed* ....15.00 -   20.00
     40180 *Follow The Swallow* ....15.00 -   20.00
     40191 *Dreary Weather* ....7.00 -   10.00
     40223 *Bye, Bye, Baby* ....10.00 -   15.00

(A.) BRILLHARDT'S ORCHESTRA:

Pathe-Actuelle 36430 *The Girl Friend* ....15.00 -   20.00
     36438 *Hello, Aloha! How Are You?* ....10.00 -   15.00
     36450 *State Street Shuffle* ....20.00 -   30.00
Perfect 14611 *The Girlfriend* ....15.00 -   20.00
     14619 *Hello, Aloha! How Are You* ....10.00 -   15.00
     14631 *State Street Shuffle*...............................20.00 -   30.00

MATT BRITT & HIS ORCHESTRA:

Victor 21760 *Goose Creek Stomp*...........................40.00 -   60.00
     22933 *Learning* ....10.00 -   15.00
     22956 *Down The Old Back Road*.....................10.00 -   15.00
     V-40012 *Sadness Will Be Gladness*..................40.00 -   60.00

BROADWAY BELL-HOPS:

Harmony 120-H *But I Do-You Know I Do* ....10.00 -   15.00
     121-H *Wimmin-Aaah!* ....25.00 -   40.00
     147-H *Here Comes Malinda* ....10.00 -   15.00
     159-H *Show That Fellow The Door* ....8.00 -   12.00
     163-H *Honey Bunch* ....8.00 -   12.00
     210-H *I'm Walking Around In Circles*.................7.00 -   10.00
     223-H *Someone Is Losin' Susan* ....8.00 -   12.00
     225-H *In A Little Garden* ....7.00 -   10.00
     241-H *She Knows Her Onions* ....8.00 -   12.00
     243-H *Mary Lou* ....8.00 -   12.00
     253-H *Don't Be Angry With Me* ....7.00 -   10.00
     258-H *I Never Knew What The Moonlight Could Do*
....7.00 -   10.00
     272-H *Hello Bluebird* ....7.00 -   10.00
     279-H *Here Comes Fatima* ....8.00 -   12.00
     288-H *Don't Take That Black Bottom Away* .....10.00 -   15.00
     298-H *I Love The Moonlight*..............................7.00 -   10.00
     327-H *He's The Last Word* ....10.00 -   15.00
     338-H *Collette* ....7.00 -   10.00
     355-H *I Wonder How I Look When I'm Asleep* ...7.00 -   10.00
     365-H *That's My Hap-Hap-Happiness* ....7.00 -   10.00
     390-H *Don't Somebody Want Somebody To Love*7.00 -   10.00
     429-H *Under the Moon* ....7.00 -   10.00
     450-H *I'm In Love Again* ....7.00 -   10.00
     479-H *Someday You'll Say "O.K."* ....7.00 -   10.00
     504-H *There Ain't No Land Like Dixieland To Me*
....80.00 -   120.00
     508-H *Rainbow of Love* ....7.00 -   10.00
     536-H *Where The Cot-Cot-Cotton Grows* ....8.00 -   12.00
     564-H *Let A Smile Be Your Umbrella*.................8.00 -   12.00
     605-H *Coquette* ....7.00 -   10.00
     630-H *Happy-Go-Lucky Lane*............................8.00 -   12.00
     644-H *Get Out And Get Under The Moon*..........8.00 -   12.00
     661-H *Old Man Sunshine*.................................8.00 -   12.00

(Note: Above titles on Diva, Silvertone and Velvet Tone are similarly valued)

BROADWAY BROADCASTERS:

Brunswick 4119 *I Must Have That Man*.................30.00 -   50.00
     4124 *Pompanola* ....8.00 -   12.00
Cameo 498 *Sobbin' Blues* ....10.00 -   15.00
     518 *Blue Grass Blues* ....7.00 -   10.00
     522 *Somebody Stole My Gal* ....7.00 -   10.00
     568 *Waitin' Around* ....7.00 -   10.00
     606 *Any Way The Wind Blows* ....8.00 -   12.00
     632 *I Want To See My Tennessee* ....8.00 -   12.00
     678 *Alabamy Bound* ....7.00 -   10.00
     713 *All Aboard For Heaven*.............................10.00 -   15.00
     727 *Isn't She The Sweetest Thing?* ....8.00 -   12.00
     738 *Oh, How I Miss You Tonight*....................7.00 -   10.00
     740 *Flag That Train* ....7.00 -   10.00
     758 *Who Loved You Best* ....7.00 -   10.00
     774 *Breezing Along (To Georgia)* ....10.00 -   15.00
     775 *Just A Little Drink* ....10.00 -   15.00
     782 *I'm Knee Deep In Daisies* ....10.00 -   15.00
     798 *Want A Little Lovin'* ....8.00 -   12.00
     815 *If I Had A Girl Like You*............................8.00 -   12.00

819 *Five Foot Two, Eyes Of Blue* ....10.00 - 15.00
836 *No Man's Mamma* ....10.00 - 15.00
839 *Spanish Shawl*..10.00 - 15.00
850 *I Love My Baby (My Baby Loves Me)* ....8.00 - 12.00
855 *Sweet Child* ....7.00 - 10.00
883 *Wimmin Aaah!* ....8.00 - 12.00
893 *Let's Talk About My Sweetie* ....8.00 - 12.00
896 *Rhythm Rag* ....10.00 - 15.00
912 *Lonesome And Sorry* ....8.00 - 12.00
937 *Bye Bye Blackbird* ....8.00 - 12.00
938 *I've Found A Round-A-Bout Way To Heaven*
....8.00 - 12.00
939 *Hot Henry* ....8.00 - 12.00
954 *When The Red, Red Robin Comes Bob,*
Bob Bobbin' Along ....8.00 - 12.00
955 *Deep Henderson* ....10.00 - 15.00
973 *Breezin' Along With The Breeze* ....8.00 - 12.00
985 *The Birth of The Blues* ....8.00 - 12.00
993 *How Many Times?* ....7.00 - 10.00
996 *High Fever* ....10.00 - 15.00
997 *Crazy Quilt* ....10.00 - 15.00
999 *Oh! If I Only Had You* ....7.00 - 10.00
1088 *Here Or There As Long As I'm With You*....8.00 - 12.00
1090 *High, High, High Up In The Hills* ....8.00 - 12.00
1149 *St. Louis Blues* ....10.00 - 15.00
1212 *Someday Sweetheart* ....8.00 - 12.00
1218 *Some Day You'll Say "O.K."* ....8.00 - 12.00
1239 *Marvelous* ....7.00 - 10.00
1266 *Collegiana* ....10.00 - 15.00
8143 *Beautiful*..7.00 - 10.00
8163 *She's A Great, Great Girl*...........................8.00 - 12.00
8179 *Lila* ....8.00 - 12.00
8195 *Wob-A-Ly Walk*..8.00 - 12.00
8227 *South Bound*..10.00 - 15.00
8228 *Lots O' Mama* ....10.00 - 15.00
8245 *Ready For The River*...................................8.00 - 12.00
9008 *Adorable Dora* ....8.00 - 12.00
9023 *She's Funny That Way* ....15.00 - 20.00
9036 *Gypsy* ....20.00 - 30.00
9056 *Dream Train* ....7.00 - 10.00
9057 *If I Had You* ....7.00 - 10.00
9084 *I Want To Be Bad*.......................................10.00 - 15.00
9088 *He, She And Me* ....7.00 - 10.00
9130 *Honey*...8.00 - 12.00
9158 *Do Something*...8.00 - 12.00
9209 *Maybe! Who Knows?*...................................10.00 - 15.00
9213 *With A Song In My Heart*.............................8.00 - 12.00
Romeo 625 *Wob-A-Ly Walk*................................8.00 - 12.00
668 *Ready For The River* ....7.00 - 10.00
775 *Come On, Baby!*...15.00 - 20.00
861 *If I Had You* ....7.00 - 10.00
900 *What A Girl! What A Night!* ....10.00 - 15.00
932 *Honey* ....8.00 - 12.00
942 *Down Among The Sugar Cane* ....7.00 - 10.00

BROADWAY DANCE ORCHESTRA:
Broadway 1002 *Thanks For the Buggy Ride* ....7.00 - 10.00
1003 *Whose Who Are You* ....7.00 - 10.00
1015 *Honey Bunch* ....7.00 - 10.00
Edison 51165 *Blue Hoosier Blues* ....15.00 - 20.00
51302 *An Orange Grove In California*...............15.00 - 20.00
51303 *Old Fashioned Love*................................15.00 - 20.00
51412 *Sally Lou*..25.00 - 40.00
51419 *I Wonder What's Become Of Sally* ....25.00 - 40.00
51420 *Eliza* ....20.00 - 30.00
51421 *Doodle-Doo-Doo* ....15.00 - 20.00

BROADWAY MELODY MAKERS:
Broadway 11284 *Wild Papa* ....25.00 - 40.00
Carnival 11404 *My Man Rocks Me* .... 100.00 - 150.00
Puretone 11373 *Sooke Hey Hey*......................30.00 - 50.00
Triangle 11200 *Bees Knees*.............................20.00 - 30.00
    11284 *Two Time Dan*...................................25.00 - 40.00

BROADWAY MUSIC MASTERS:
Grey Gull 1188 *Easy Melody* ....15.00 - 20.00

BROADWAY PICKERS:
Broadway 5069 *Salty Dog* .... 200.00 - 300.00

BROADWAY PLAYERS:
Gennett 5407 *I Must Have Company* ....8.00 - 12.00
Q.R.S. Q-1008 *All Day Long* ....8.00 - 12.00
    Q-1021 *Should I Be Sorry*...........................12.00 - 16.00
    Q-1022 *With You*..12.00 - 16.00

BROADWAY RASTUS:
Paramount 12764 *Rock My Soul* .... 200.00 - 300.00

BROADWAY SEVEN:
Grey Gull 1190 *St. Louis Gal* ....15.00 - 20.00
    1192 *Back O' Town Blues*............................15.00 - 20.00

BROADWAY SYNCOPATERS:
Vocalion 14586 *Louisville Lou*..........................10.00 - 15.00
    14598 *Two-Time Dan* ....10.00 - 15.00
    14670 *House Of David Blues*.........................10.00 - 15.00
    14675 *Sittin' In A Corner* ....10.00 - 15.00
Vocalion, other issues .... 5.00 - 10.00

IRVING BRODSKY & HIS ORCHESTRA:
Harmony 1021-H *If You Believed In Me* ....15.00 - 20.00
    1041-H *The End of the Lonesome Trail*...........15.00 - 20.00

THE BROOKLYNITES:
Perfect 14901 *I'm Walkin' On Air* ....8.00 - 12.00

HARVEY BROOKS' QUALITY FOUR:
Hollywood 1008 *Mistreating Daddy* .... 150.00 - 200.00
    1021 *Nobody's Sweetheart* .... 150.00 - 200.00
    1022 *Down On The Farm* .... 100.00 - 150.00

BROWN-MORRIS ORCHESTRA:
Harmony 521-H *Headin' For Harlem*...................15.00 - 20.00
    528-H *Rose Of Monterey* ....8.00 - 12.00
(Note: Above titles on Diva and Velvet Tone are similarly valued)

BROWN AND TERRY'S JAZZOLA BOYS:
Okeh 8006 *Hesitating Blues* ....50.00 - 75.00
    8014 *All By Myself*..50.00 - 75.00
    8017 *Saxophone Blues* ....50.00 - 75.00
    8018 *Aunt Hagar's Blues*................................50.00 - 75.00
    8021 *Jump Steady Blues* ....50.00 - 75.00

BILL BROWN & HIS BROWNIES:
Brunswick 7003 *Bill Brown Blues* ....50.00 - 75.00
    7142 *Zonky*.. 100.00 - 150.00
Vocalion 1128 *Bill Brown Blues*........................ 100.00 - 150.00

CLEO BROWN:
Decca 409 *Lookie, Lookie, Lookie* ....10.00 - 15.00
    410 *You're A Heavenly Thing* ....10.00 - 15.00
    477 *Pelican Stomp* ....15.00 - 20.00
Decca 486, 512, 632, 718, 795, 846 .... 8.00 - 12.00
Hollywood Hot Shots L-0349 *Who'll Chop Your Suey*
....10.00 - 20.00

FRANK BROWN & HIS TOOTERS:

Parlophone PNY-34154 *Ring Dem Bells*..................75.00 - 100.00

   PNY-34156 *Three Little Words*.........................75.00 - 100.00

HENRY BROWN:

Brunswick 7086 *Stomp 'Em Down To The Bricks*......150.00 - 250.00

Paramount 12825 *Twenty-First Street Stomp* ....200.00 - 300.00

   12934 *Blues Stomp* ....250.00 - up

   12988 *Eastern Chimes Blues* ....250.00 - up

IDA G. BROWN & HER BOYS:

Banner 1343 *Jail House Blues*.............................50.00 - 80.00

Regal 9639 *Kiss Me Sweet*.......................................50.00 - 80.00

JACK BROWN & HIS BOYS:

Champion 15741 *After Thinking It Over* ....10.00 - 15.00

KID BROWN & HIS BLUE BAND:

Black Patti 8049 *Bo-Lita* ....500.00 - up

LES BROWN & HIS (DUKE UNIVERSITY) BLUE DEVILS/ORCHESTRA:

Bluebird 7796, 7812, 7858, 7869 ....5.00 - 10.00

Bluebird (most others) ....5.00 - 8.00

Columbia (red label, most issues) ....4.00 - 8.00

Decca 991 *Swing For Sale*....................................10.00 - 15.00

   1231 *Swamp Fire* ....7.00 - 10.00

   1238 *Rigamorole* ....8.00 - 12.00

   1296 *Ramona* ....8.00 - 12.00

   1323 *Lazy River* ....8.00 - 12.00

   2045 *Mutiny On The Bandstand* ....8.00 - 12.00

   3155 *Comanche War Dance* ....7.00 - 10.00

   3167 *Walkin' And Swingin'* ....7.00 - 10.00

Okeh 6377 *Joltin' Joe DiMaggio* ....8.00 - 12.00

Okeh (most other issues) ....5.00 - 10.00

PETE BROWN & HIS BAND:

Decca 8613 *Mound Bayou* ....10.00 - 15.00

   8625 *Cannon Ball* ....10.00 - 15.00

RUSSELL BROWN & HIS ORCHESTRA:

Parlophone PNY-34088 *Washin' The Blues From My Soul*

....25.00 - 40.00

   PNY-34089 *Washin' The Blues From My Soul*

....25.00 - 40.00

   PNY-34090 *Absence Makes The Heart Grow Fonder*

....15.00 - 25.00

   PNY-34091 *I Remember You From Somewhere* ..30.00 - 50.00

   PNY-34130 *Little Sunshine* ....30.00 - 50.00

   PNY-34133 *When The Organ Played At Twilight*

....15.00 - 20.00

TOM BROWN & HIS MERRY MINSTREL ORCHESTRA:

Okeh 40514 *It's The Blues* ....50.00 - 75.00

   40618 *Goodnight, I'll See You In The Morning*

....100.00 - 150.00

(TED) BROWNAGLE AND HIS ORCHESTRA:

Columbia 1741-D *Helen* ....15.00 - 20.00

Victor 20262 *Arcadia Shuffle* ....50.00 - 80.00

SAM BROWNE & HIS ORCHESTRA:

Superior 2693 *Hard Times Stomp*.........................150.00 - 200.00

BROWNLEE'S ORCHESTRA OF NEW ORLEANS:

Okeh 40337 *Dirty Rag*..150.00 - 200.00

BROX SISTERS:

Brunswick 2268 *Schoolhouse Blues* ....7.00 - 10.00

   2305 *Away Down South* ....7.00 - 10.00

   2330 *Early In The Morning Blues* ....7.00 - 10.00

   2538 *Learn To Do The Strut* ....8.00 - 12.00

Victor 19510 *Red Hot Mama* ....10.00 - 15.00

   19631 *Tokio Blues* ....7.00 - 10.00

Victor, most other issues......................................5.00 - 10.00

ALBERT BRUNIES & HIS HALFWAY HOUSE ORCHESTRA:

Columbia 1959-D *Just Pretending* ....30.00 - 50.00

MERRITT BRUNIES & HIS FRIARS INN ORCHESTRA:

Autograph (unnumbered) *Up Jumped The Devil*..200.00 - 300.00

   610 *Angry*..150.00 - 200.00

   624 *Clarinet Marmalade*.............................200.00 - 300.00

Okeh 40526 *Sugar Foot Stomp* ....100.00 - 150.00

   40576 *I'm As Blue As The Blue Grass of Kentucky*

....75.00 - 100.00

   40579 *Flamin' Mamie* ....75.00 - 100.00

   40593 *Someone's Stolen My Sweet Baby* ....75.00 - 100.00

   40618 *Up Jumped The Devil*............................100.00 - 150.00

JIMMY BRYANT:

Broadway 1337 *Drunk Man's Strut* ....75.00 - 100.00

LAURA BRYANT:

Q.R.S. 7055 *Dentist Chair Blues* ....250.00 - up

WILLIE BRYANT & HIS ORCHESTRA:

Bluebird 6361 *All My Life* ....10.00 - 15.00

   6362 *Moonrise On The Lowlands* ....10.00 - 15.00

   6374 *The Glory Of Love* ....10.00 - 15.00

   6435 *Cross Patch* ....10.00 - 15.00

   6436 *I Like Bananas* ....10.00 - 15.00

   6750 *A Viper's Moan* ....10.00 - 15.00

Decca 1772 *On The Alamo* ....10.00 - 15.00

   1881 *You're Gonna Lose Your Gal* ....10.00 - 15.00

Victor 24847 *Chimes At The Meeting* ....15.00 - 20.00

   24858 *A Viper's Moan* ....15.00 - 20.00

   25038 *Rigamarole* ....15.00 - 20.00

   25045 *Jerry The Junker* ....15.00 - 20.00

   25129 *The Voice Of Old Man River* ....15.00 - 20.00

   25160 *Liza* ....15.00 - 20.00

TIM BRYMN & HIS BLACK DEVIL ORCHESTRA:

Okeh 4310 *Wang Wang Blues* ....20.00 - 30.00

   4339 *Camp Meeting Blues* ....30.00 - 50.00

   8002 *Arkansas Blues*................................30.00 - 50.00

   8003 *Don't Tell Your Monkey Man* ....30.00 - 50.00

   8005 *The Jazz Me Blues*.............................30.00 - 50.00

THE BUBBLING-OVER FIVE:

Okeh 8737 *Get Up Off That Jazzophone* ....150.00 - 250.00

BUCK AND BUBBLES:

Columbia 2873-D *Rhythm For Sale* ....50.00 - 75.00

THE BUCKTOWN BUCKS:

Champion 15441 *Wob-A-Ly Walk* ....15.00 - 25.00

THE BUCKTOWN FIVE:

Gennett 5405 *Mobile Blues*................................150.00 - 200.00

   5418 *Buddy's Habits*................................150.00 - 200.00

   5419 *Steady Roll Blues* ....150.00 - 200.00

   5518 *Hot Mittens*...................................150.00 - 200.00

THE BUFFALODIANS:
Banner 1776 *Baby Face*............................10.00 - 15.00
　1778 *How Many Times?* ....10.00 - 15.00
Columbia 665-D *Deep Henderson* ....20.00 - 30.00
　723-D *Wouldja?*.................................20.00 - 30.00
Domino 3747 *How Many Times?* ....10.00 - 15.00
　3749 *Baby Face* ....10.00 - 15.00
Regal 8087 *Baby Face* ....10.00 - 15.00
　8088 *How Many Times?* ....10.00 - 15.00

CHUCK BULLOCK (& HIS LEVEE LOUNGERS):
Titles selected from this artist's large output, contemporaneously
　issued on Banner, Conqueror, Melotone, Oriole, Perfect, Romeo:
　*Ain't Cha Glad?; And Still No Luck With You; Any Time, Any
　Day, Any Where; Chasing Shadows; Darkness on the Delta;
　Extra! (All About That Gal Of Mine); Here It Is Monday and I've
　Still Got A Dollar; I Can't Get Mississippi Off My Mind; I Know
　You're Lying, But I Love It; I'm Hummin', I'm Whistlin', I'm
　Singin'; Keepin' Out Of Mischief Now; I'm Gonna Sit Right
　Down And Write Myself A Letter; Lazy Bones; Mississippi Basin;
　My Melancholy Baby; My River Home; Sing A New Song; Smoke
　Gets In Your Eyes; Stop The Sun, Stop The Moon; What's Good
　For The Goose; With Plenty Of Money And You; You Oughta Be
　In Pictures; You Rascal, You* ....8.00 - 15.00
Many other titles on the same labels: ....7.00 - 12.00
Additional Titles: *Alcoholic Ward Blues; Frankie and Johnnie; I
　Can't Dance (I Got Ants In My Pants); I Heard; Shine; St. James'
　Infirmary; Swingy Little Thingy*.............15.00 - 25.00
Champion 16089 *I Still Get A Thrill*.........10.00 - 15.00
Conqueror (most issues) ....5.00 - 10.00
Melotone 12531 *Brother, Can You Spare A Dime?* 10.00 - 15.00
Okeh 6013 *Smiles* ....10.00 - 15.00
　6100 *There'll Be Some Changes Made* ....10.00 - 15.00
　6123 *Dolores* ....10.00 - 15.00
　6261 *My Melancholy Baby* ....10.00 - 15.00
Perfect 15641 *Syncopate Your Sins Away* ....10.00 - 15.00
　15695 *Brother, Can You Spare A Dime?* ....10.00 - 15.00
Vocalion 15874 *Darkness On The Delta* ....15.00 - 20.00
　15882 *Going! Going!! Gone!!!*.............15.00 - 20.00
Vocalion (most other issues) ....7.00 - 10.00

BILLY BUNCH & HIS SMOKY RHYTHM:
Bluebird 10305 *Three Little Maids*............8.00 - 12.00

FRANK BUNCH & HIS FUZZY WUZZIES:
Gennett 6278 *Fuzzy Wuzzy* ....300.00 - up
　6293 *Fourth Avenue Stomp* ....400.00 - up

SONNY BURKE AND HIS ORCHESTRA:
Okeh 5139, 5813, 5873, 5955, 5989..........8.00 - 12.00
Vocalion 5356, 5397, 5459......................8.00 - 12.00

JOHNNY BURRIS AND HIS ORCHESTRA:
Gennett 6850 *So Comfy* ....100.00 - 150.00

CHARLIE BURSE (See MEMPHIS JUG BAND)

EARL BURTNETT & HIS (LOS ANGELES BILTMORE/ DRAKE HOTEL) ORCHESTRA:
Brunswick 4104 *Happy* ....8.00 - 12.00
　4679 *Puttin' On The Ritz* ....10.00 - 15.00
　4754 *'Leven-Thirty Saturday Night* ....10.00 - 15.00
　4881 *I Wonder How It Feels* ....15.00 - 20.00
Brunswick (most other issues) ....7.00 - 10.00
Columbia 787-D *Song Of The Wanderer* ......10.00 - 15.00
　825-D *Ricketts* ....10.00 - 15.00

1361-D *Sweet Sue-Just You* ....8.00 - 12.00
2921-D *Waitin' At The Gate For Katy* ....15.00 - 20.00
2922-D *Neighbors* ....10.00 - 15.00

DICK BURTON'S ORCHESTRA:
Bell 572 *Sweet Violets* ....20.00 - 30.00
　573 *I Dream About You* ....15.00 - 20.00
　576 *Down South*................................15.00 - 20.00

BUSSE'S BUZZARDS; HENRY BUSSE & HIS ORCHESTRA:
Columbia 2932-D *Fool That I Am* ....15.00 - 20.00
　2937-D *Hot Lips* ....15.00 - 20.00
Decca, most issues ....5.00 - 8.00
Victor 19727 *Deep Elm*..........................10.00 - 15.00
　19782 *Red Hot Henry Brown*..................8.00 - 12.00
　19934 *The Monkey Doodle-Doo* ....8.00 - 12.00
Victor, most other issues.........................5.00 - 10.00

SAMMY BUTLER & HIS NIGHT OWLS:
Vocalion 03917 *Blue Baby* ....20.00 - 30.00
　03980 *Reefer Man's Dream* ....20.00 - 30.00

WALLACE BUTLER'S HOTEL DE SOTA ORCHESTRA:
Columbia 15018-D *Doo Wacka Doo* ....- -

(EZRA) BUZZINGTON'S RUBE BAND/RUSTIC REVELERS:
Gennett 6575 *Bass Blues* ....150.00 - 250.00
　6816 *Kansas City Kitty* ....100.00 - 150.00
　6894 *Alfalfa*....................................100.00 - 150.00
　21024 *Brown Jug Blues* ....150.00 - 200.00
Iragen 18-29-01 *Brown Jug Blues* ....40.00 - 60.00

HALE BYERS & HIS ORCHESTRA:
Brunswick 3092 *Sea Legs* ....10.00 - 15.00
　3108 *So Does Your Old Mandarin*.............10.00 - 15.00
Vocalion 15370 *Roses*...........................15.00 - 20.00

EMILIO CACERES TRIO:
Victor 25710 *I Got Rhythm* ....10.00 - 15.00
　25719 *Who's Sorry Now?* ....10.00 - 15.00
　26109 *Runnin' Wild* ....10.00 - 15.00

CAFÉ ROYAL BOYS:
Challenge 802 *Hurry Sundown Blues* ....75.00 - 100.00
　804 *Landlady's Footsteps* ....75.00 - 100.00

CAHN-CHAPLIN ORCHESTRA:
Champion 40112 *All My Life* ....10.00 - 15.00
Champion 40113 *Christopher Columbus* ....15.00 - 20.00

LOU CALABRESE & HIS HOT SHOTS:
Gennett 6421 *Lip-Stick* ....100.00 - 150.00

CALIFORNIA BLUE BOYS (See CHARLES HAMP):

CALIFORNIA COLLEGIANS:
Conqueror 7189 *Louder And Funnier*..........10.00 - 15.00

CALIFORNIA MELODIE/MELODY MEN/ SYNCOPATORS:
Bell 433 *That's Annabelle* ....8.00 - 12.00
　442 *Lay Me Down in Carolina* ....10.00 - 15.00
　438 *For My Sweetheart*........................8.00 - 12.00
　442 *Lay Me Down in Carolina* ....10.00 - 15.00
Emerson 3053 *Gettin' Happy All the Time* ....10.00 - 15.00

CALIFORNIA POPPIES:
Sunset 506/507 *What A Wonderful Time* ....400.00 -　　　up

CALIFORNIA RAMBLERS:
This orchestra appeared on a very large number of records during the 1920s and 1930s under its own name and pseudonyms (principally THE GOLDEN GATE ORCHESTRA). The records, even those of general interest to collectors, do not generally command sizable premiums. Following is a selected listing only:

Banner 6048 *Farewell Blues* ....20.00 -　　30.00
　6049 *Delirium* ....20.00 -　　30.00
　6050 *Someday Sweetheart* ....15.00 -　　25.00
Bluebird 6076, 6077, 6078, 6082, 6083, 6145, 6146, 6156, 6173, 6189, 6190, 6238, 6239, 6240 ....8.00 -　　12.00
Broadway 1081 *Magnolia* ....10.00 -　　15.00
Columbia 9-D, 15-D, 39-D, 43-D, 49-D, 67-D, 91-D, 92-D, 103-D, 105-D, 153-D, 218-D, 223-D ....8.00 -　　12.00
　127-D *Shine* ....10.00 -　　15.00
　171-D *Charleston Cabin* ....10.00 -　　15.00
　179-D *Big Boy* ....10.00 -　　15.00
　199-D *Susquehanna Home* ....10.00 -　　15.00
　236-D *Copenhagen* ....15.00 -　　20.00
　268-D *Oh! Mabel* ....10.00 -　　15.00
　278-D *Why Couldn't It Be Poor Little Me?* ....10.00 -　　15.00
　293-D *Oh! Lady, Be Good* ....10.00 -　　15.00
　340-D *Just a Little Drink* ....15.00 -　　20.00
　380-D *Sweet Georgia Brown* ....15.00 -　　20.00
　419-D *I'm Gonna Charleston Back To Charleston*
　　..15.00 -　　20.00
　449-D *Moon Dear* ....8.00 -　　12.00
　522-D *Then I'll Be Happy* ....10.00 -　　15.00
　527-D *Smile a Little Bit* ....10.00 -　　15.00
　610-D *I'd Climb the Highest Mountain* ....10.00 -　　15.00
　638-D *No Foolin'* ....15.00 -　　20.00
　647-D *Give Me Today* ....10.00 -　　15.00
　669-D *Ya Gotta Know How To Love* ....15.00 -　　20.00
　704-D *She Belongs To Me* ....15.00 -　　20.00
　758-D *She Knows Her Onions* ....15.00 -　　20.00
　800-D *Here Comes Fatima* ....15.00 -　　20.00
　834-D *Tell Me Tonight* ....15.00 -　　20.00
　883-D *Stockholm Stomp* ....15.00 -　　20.00
　992-D *Pardon The Glove* ....15.00 -　　20.00
　1038-D *Vo-Do-Do-De-O Blues* ....15.00 -　　20.00
　1148-D *Nothin' Does-Does Like It Used To Do-Do-Do*
　　..15.00 -　　20.00
　1227-D *Make My Cot Where the Cot-Cot-Cotton Grows*
　　..15.00 -　　20.00
　1275-D *Changes* ....15.00 -　　20.00
　1314-D *Singapore Sorrows* ....15.00 -　　20.00
　1411-D *Whisper Sweet And Whisper Low* ....15.00 -　　20.00
　1504-D *Who Wouldn't Be Blue?* ....10.00 -　　15.00
　1574-D *You're Just A Great Big Baby Doll* ......15.00 -　　20.00
　1642-D *The Pay Off* ....20.00 -　　30.00
　2208-D *I'm Needin' You* ....10.00 -　　15.00
　A3979 *That Big Blonde Mamma* ....10.00 -　　15.00
Columbia A3554, A3635, A3956, A3970, A3986, A3994.....................................7.00 -　　12.00
Domino 4011 *Beale Street Blues* ....20.00 -　　30.00
　4014 *Delirium* ....20.00 -　　30.00
　4027 *I Ain't Got Nobody* ....15.00 -　　25.00
Edison 11042 *Chinese Jumble* ....100.00 -　　150.00
　14004 *My Sin* ....50.00 -　　75.00
　14005 *I Get The Blues When It Rains* ....50.00 -　　75.00
　14016 *The Wedding Of The Painted Doll* ....50.00 -　　75.00

　14020 *Wishing And Waiting For Love* ....50.00 -　　75.00
　14034 *Painting The Clouds with Sunshine* ....50.00 -　　75.00
　14045 *Song Of The Blues* ....50.00 -　　75.00
　14055 *Someday You'll Realize You're Wrong* ..50.00 -　　75.00
　14072 *Pretty Little You* ....75.00 -　　100.00
　14083 *Lady Luck* ....100.00 -　　150.00
Edison (thick) 52602 *The Wedding Of The Painted Doll*
　　..50.00 -　　75.00
Edison 52610 *I Get The Blues When It Rains* ....50.00 -　　75.00
　52622 *Painting The Clouds With Sunshine* ......50.00 -　　75.00
　52629 *Tip-Toe Through The Tulips With Me* ....50.00 -　　75.00
　52638 *Song Of The Blues* ....75.00 -　　100.00
(Note: Most of the considerable output of **THE CALIFORNIA RAMBLERS** on Edison was issued as by **THE GOLDEN GATE ORCHESTRA**, qv.)
Puritan 11174 *Bees Knees* ....10.00 -　　15.00
　11222 *Red Head Gal* ....15.00 -　　20.00
Puritan 11103, 11116, 11117 ....7.00 -　　10.00

CALIFORNIA VAGABONDS:
Gennett 6140 *I'm Back In Love Again* ....20.00 -　　30.00
　6170 *S-L-U-E Foot* ....20.00 -　　30.00
　6172 *Yes She Do-No She Don't* ....20.00 -　　30.00
　6426 *Waitin' For Katy* ....20.00 -　　30.00

BOB CALL:
Brunswick 7137 *Thirty-One Blues*......................150.00 -　　200.00

BLANCHE CALLOWAY (& HER JOY BOYS/BAND):
Titles issued contemporaneously on Banner, Melotone, Perfect, Oriole, Romeo: *Catch On; Growlin' Dan; I Need Lovin'; What's A Poor Girl Gonna Do?*...................................15.00 -　　25.00
Okeh 8279 *Lazy Woman's Blues* ....200.00 -　　300.00
Victor 22640 *Casey Jones Blues*..........................25.00 -　　40.00
　22641 *I Need Lovin'*.............................15.00 -　　20.00
　22659 *Loveless Love* ....20.00 -　　30.00
　22661 *Sugar Blues* ....15.00 -　　25.00
　22717 *It's Right Here For You* ....20.00 -　　30.00
　22733 *It Looks Like Susie* ....15.00 -　　25.00
　22736 *Make Me Know It* ....25.00 -　　40.00
　22862 *Last Dollar* ....20.00 -　　30.00
　22866 *I Got What It Takes* ....20.00 -　　30.00
　22896 *Blue Memories* ....20.00 -　　30.00
Vocalion 3112 *Louisiana Liza* ....20.00 -　　30.00
　3113 *Line-A-Jive*...............................20.00 -　　30.00

CAB CALLOWAY & HIS ORCHESTRA:
Titles issued contemporaneously on Banner, Cameo, Conqueror, Domino, Jewel, Melotone, Oriole, Perfect, and Romeo: *Ain't Got No Gal In This Town; Angeline; Beale Street Mama; Between The Devil And The Deep Blue Sea; Black Rhythm; Bugle Call Rag; Dinah; Dixie Doorway; Doin' The Rumba; Eadie Was A Lady; Harlem Holiday; Hot Water; How Come You Do Me Like You Do?; I'm Now Prepared To Tell The World It's You; Is That Religion?; Kickin' The Gong Around; The Man From Harlem; Minnie The Moocher; Nobody's Sweetheart; The Old Man Of The Mountain; Reefer Man; Six Or Seven Times; Some Of These Days; St. James' Infirmary; Strange As It Seems; Swanee Lullaby; This Time It's Love; Trickeration; Wah-Dee-Dah; You Gotta Ho-De-Ho (To Get Along With Me); You Rascal, You*
　　..15.00 -　　20.00

Additional Titles: *Basin Street Blues; Blues In My Heart; Corinne Corinna; Creole Love Song; Down-Hearted Blues; Farewell Blues; I'm Crazy 'Bout My Baby; It Looks Like Susie; The Levee Low Down; Mood Indigo; Somebody Stole My Gal; Stack O'Lee Blues; Stardust; Sweet Georgia Brown; Sweet Jennie Lee; The Viper's Drag; Without Rhythm; Yaller; You Can't Stop Me From Lovin' You; You Dog* ....15.00 - 25.00

A few more titles: *Dixie Vagabond; Happy Feet; My Honey's Lovin' Arms; The Nightmare* ....20.00 - 30.00

Bell (7-inch) 1006 *Minnie The Moocher* ....8.00 - 12.00

Brunswick 6020 *Some Of These Days* ....15.00 - 20.00

    6074 *Minnie The Moocher*...........................15.00 - 20.00

    6105 *Nobody's Sweetheart* ....15.00 - 20.00

    6141 *Black Rhythm*..................................15.00 - 20.00

    6196 *You Rascal, You*..............................15.00 - 20.00

    6209 *Kickin' The Gong Around*..................15.00 - 20.00

    6214 *Trickeration* ....15.00 - 20.00

    6272 *The Scat Song* ....15.00 - 20.00

    6292 *Strictly Cullud Affair*.......................15.00 - 25.00

    6321 *Minnie The Moocher's Wedding Day*........15.00 - 20.00

    6340 *Reefer Man*....................................15.00 - 20.00

    6400 *Old Yazoo*......................................15.00 - 20.00

    6424 *I've Got The World On A String* ....15.00 - 20.00

    6435 *Dixie Doorway*................................15.00 - 20.00

    6450 *My Sunday Gal* ....15.00 - 20.00

    6460 *I Gotta Right To Sing The Blues* ....15.00 - 20.00

    6473 *Gotta Go Places And Do Things* ....15.00 - 20.00

    6511 *Minnie The Moocher*...........................8.00 - 12.00

    6992 *Chinese Rhythm* ....10.00 - 15.00

    7386 *Good Sauce From The Gravy Bowl*..........10.00 - 15.00

    7411 *Moonlight Rhapsody*.........................10.00 - 15.00

    7504 *Nagasaki* ....10.00 - 15.00

    7530 *I Ain't Got Nobody*............................10.00 - 15.00

    7638 *Save Me, Sister*...............................10.00 - 15.00

    7639 *You're The Cure For What Ails Me*...........10.00 - 15.00

    7677 *Love Is The Reason* ....10.00 - 15.00

    7685 *When You're Smiling* ....10.00 - 15.00

    7748 *The Wedding Of Mr. And Mrs. Swing*.......10.00 - 15.00

    7756 *The Hi-De-Ho Miracle Man* ....10.00 - 15.00

Columbia, red label, most issues ....5.00 - 10.00

Conqueror (most 9000 series)....................7.00 - 10.00

Okeh 5950 *Levee Lullaby* ....10.00 - 15.00

    6084 *Bye Bye Blues* ....10.00 - 15.00

    6147 *Special Delivery* ....10.00 - 15.00

    6305 *Take The "A" Train* ....10.00 - 15.00

Okeh, most other issues ....7.00 - 12.00

Variety 501 *That Man Is Here Again* ....10.00 - 15.00

    535 *Don't Know If I'm Comin' Or Goin'*.........10.00 - 15.00

    593 *My Gal Mezzanine* ....10.00 - 15.00

    612 *Manhattan Jam* ....8.00 - 12.00

    643 *She's Tall, She's Tan, She's Terrific* ....10.00 - 15.00

    644 *Mama, I Wanna Make Rhythm* ....10.00 - 15.00

    651 *Hi-De-Ho Romeo* ....10.00 - 15.00

    662 *Savage Rhythm*..............................10.00 - 15.00

Victor 24414 *Harlem Hospitality* ....20.00 - 30.00

    24451 *The Lady With The Fan* ....15.00 - 20.00

    24494 *Little Town Gal*..............................20.00 - 30.00

    24511 *The Scat Song* ....20.00 - 30.00

    24557 *Zaz Zuh Zaz*................................20.00 - 30.00

    24592 *Jitter Bug* ....20.00 - 30.00

    24659 *Margie*.....................................20.00 - 30.00

    24690 *Moon Glow* ....20.00 - 30.00

Vocalion 3787 *I'm Always In The Mood for You* ... 10.00 - 15.00

    3788 *Go South, Young Man* ....10.00 - 15.00

    3789 *Moon At Sea* ....10.00 - 15.00

    3796 *Queen Isabella* ....10.00 - 15.00

    3807 *Swing, Swing, Swing* ....10.00 - 15.00

    3825 *Congo* ....10.00 - 15.00

    3830 *Peckin'* ....8.00 - 12.00

    3896 *Every Day's A Holiday* ....10.00 - 15.00

    3970 *Doing The Reactionary* ....10.00 - 15.00

    3995 *Three Swings And Out* ....10.00 - 15.00

    4019 *Bugle Blues* ....10.00 - 15.00

    4045 *Skrontch* ....10.00 - 15.00

    4100 *Azure* ....10.00 - 15.00

    4144 *Rustle of Swing*.............................10.00 - 15.00

    4400 *The Boogie-Woogie* ....10.00 - 15.00

    4538 *Blue Interlude* ....10.00 - 15.00

Vocalion, most other issues ....8.00 - 12.00

ERMINE CALLOWAY:

Champion 15938 *Ain't'cha?* ....15.00 - 20.00

    15961 *I've Got A New Love Affair*.................15.00 - 20.00

Edison (thin) 14024 *Do Something* ....50.00 - 75.00

Edison 14071 *'s Nice, Like This* ....75.00 - 100.00

Edison (thick) 52519 *Good Little, Bad Little You* .. 50.00 - 80.00

Edison 52567 *I Want To Be Bad* ....50.00 - 80.00

    52570 *Do Something*.................................50.00 - 80.00

    52617 *When We Get Together In The Moonlight*. 50.00 - 80.00

JEAN CALLOWAY'S ORCHESTRA:

Victor 22959 *Sadie, The Shaker* ....15.00 - 20.00

BUDDY CAMPBELL & HIS ORCHESTRA:

Okeh 41503 *Let's Get Friendly* ....15.00 - 20.00

    41507 *When Yuba Plays The Rumba On The Tuba* ....15.00 - 20.00

    41511 *My Sweet Tooth Says 'I Wanna'* ....15.00 - 20.00

    41524 *Little Mary Brown* ....15.00 - 20.00

    41527 *Charlie Cadet*................................15.00 - 20.00

    41532 *Last Dollar* ....15.00 - 20.00

    41540 *I Wonder Who's Under The Moon*..........10.00 - 15.00

    41543 *Bend Down, Sister*............................15.00 - 20.00

    41563 *What A Life* ....15.00 - 20.00

    41564 *Sing A New Song*............................15.00 - 20.00

JOHNNIE CAMPBELL'S ORCHESTRA:

New Flexo 301 *Jimtown Blues* ....150.00 - 200.00

    302 *Somebody Loves Me*........................75.00 - 100.00

    303 *The Only, Only One* ....75.00 - 100.00

    304 *Tin Roof Blues*.............................150.00 - 200.00

    305 *Where's My Sweetie Hiding?*.................75.00 - 100.00

    307 *Charleston Cabin* ....75.00 - 100.00

    308 *No Wonder* ....75.00 - 100.00

THE CAMPUS BOYS:

Banner 6124 *Is She My Girl Friend?* ....8.00 - 12.00

    6127 *Make My Cot Where The Cot-Cot Cotton Grows* ....8.00 - 12.00

    6143 *Mary (What Are You Waiting For?)* ....7.00 - 10.00

    6257 *I Faw Down An' Go Boom* ....8.00 - 12.00

    6262 *Mystic Bengal Bay* ....8.00 - 12.00

    6263 *My Supressed Desire*.......................8.00 - 12.00

    6264 *I'm Wild About Horns On Automobiles* .... 15.00 - 20.00

    6300 *When I'm Walking With My Sweetness*..... 10.00 - 15.00

    6357 *I Used To Love Her In The Moonlight*........7.00 - 10.00

    6425 *Rainbow Man* ....10.00 - 15.00

6439 *Singing In The Rain* ....8.00 - 12.00
6449 *Ain't Misbehavin'* ....8.00 - 12.00
6453 *Where the Sweet Forget-Me-Nots Remember*
....7.00 - 10.00
6483 *Lovable And Sweet*..................................15.00 - 20.00
7051 *Hello! Montreal* ....7.00 - 10.00
7137 *Sweet Lorraine*..15.00 - 20.00
7220 *Here's That Party Now In Person* ....15.00 - 20.00
Banner (most other issues) ....5.00 - 10.00

THE CAMPUS CUT-UPS:
Edison 11049 *Farewell Blues* ....100.00 - 150.00
11050 *Ballin' The Jack*.................................100.00 - 150.00
14044 *Campus Rush* ....80.00 - 120.00
Edison (thick) 52591 *Wabash Blues* ....75.00 - 100.00
52616 *Ballin' The Jack* ....75.00 - 100.00
52649 *I'm The Medicine Man For The Blues*.....80.00 - 120.00

CANADIAN CLUB ORCHESTRA:
Pathe-Actuelle 36367 *Keep Your Skirts Down, Mary Ann*
....8.00 - 12.00
Perfect 14548 *Keep Your Skirts Down, Mary Ann* ....8.00 - 12.00

JOE CANDULLO & HIS (EVERGLADES) ORCHESTRA:
Banner 1780 *Hard-To-Get Gertie* ....10.00 - 15.00
1784 *Deep Henderson* ....15.00 - 20.00
1796 *Black Bottom*..15.00 - 20.00
1800 *Nervous Charlie Stomp*............................15.00 - 20.00
1814 *I Wonder What's Become Of Joe?*.............10.00 - 15.00
1815 *Blowin' Off Steam*....................................10.00 - 15.00
1836 *Tuck In Kentucky And Smile* ....10.00 - 15.00
1839 *St. Louis Blues* ....15.00 - 20.00
1986 *St. Louis Blues* ....20.00 - 30.00
7169 *A Jazz Holiday* ....15.00 - 20.00
7192 *Deep Hollow* ....15.00 - 20.00
7217 *What-Cha-Call 'Em Blues* ....15.00 - 20.00
7218 *When Sweet Susie Goes Stepping By*.........15.00 - 20.00
7220 *Dusky Stevedore* ....15.00 - 20.00
Broadway 1203 *Dusky Stevedore* ....15.00 - 20.00
Buddy 8069 *Black Bottom* ....50.00 - 100.00
8070 *Messin' Around*.......................................50.00 - 100.00
Cameo 1048 *Brown Sugar*................................15.00 - 20.00
1049 *I Still Believe In You* ....15.00 - 20.00
1061 *'Deed I Do* ....15.00 - 20.00
1074 *Everything's Made For Love* ....10.00 - 15.00
1077 *Delilah* ....8.00 - 12.00
1105 *Song Of The Wanderer* ....10.00 - 15.00
Challenge 130 *Cry Baby*...................................7.00 - 10.00
137 *That's Why I Love You*...............................7.00 - 10.00
Domino 3750 *Hard-To-Get Gertie* ....10.00 - 15.00
3751 *Jackass Blues* ....15.00 - 20.00
3768 *Nervous Charlie Stomp* ....15.00 - 20.00
3772 *Messin' Around*.......................................15.00 - 20.00
3808 *St. Louis Blues* ....15.00 - 20.00
3809 *Tuck In Kentucky And Smile* ....10.00 - 15.00
3956 *St. Louis Blues* ....20.00 - 30.00
4167 *A Jazz Holiday* ....15.00 - 20.00
4201 *When Sweet Susie Goes Stepping By*.........15.00 - 20.00
Edison 51826 *Bass Ale Blues* ....75.00 - 100.00
51836 *Scatter Your Smiles*...............................25.00 - 40.00
51848 *The Birth Of The Blues* ....40.00 - 60.00
51852 *Brown Sugar* ....50.00 - 75.00
51912 *Windy City Stomp* ....75.00 - 100.00

Gennett 3316 *The Nightmare* ....20.00 - 30.00
3331 *That's Why I Love You* ....10.00 - 15.00
3351 *Only You And Lonely Me* ....8.00 - 12.00
3352 *Cry Baby* ....8.00 - 12.00
3358 *St. Louis Hop*..20.00 - 30.00
3359 *Messin' Around* ....15.00 - 20.00
3385 *She's Still My Baby* ....10.00 - 15.00
3392 *Don't Be Angry With Me*............................8.00 - 12.00
3402 *Bobadilla* ....8.00 - 12.00
3405 *Tomboy Sue* ....30.00 - 50.00
3406 *Lonely Eyes* ....8.00 - 12.00
6009 *Lonely Eyes* ....15.00 - 25.00
Harmony 150-H *Bass Ale Blues* ....15.00 - 25.00
208-H *18th Street Strut* ....15.00 - 20.00
211-H *She Belongs To Me* ....15.00 - 20.00
235-H *Sadie Green* ....15.00 - 20.00
260-H *Susie's "Feller"* ....15.00 - 20.00
286-H *Blowin' Off Steam* ....15.00 - 20.00
361-H *Yes Flo! (The Gal Who Never Says "No")*
....15.00 - 20.00
397-H *Go Wash An Elephant (If You Wanna Do Something?)*
....10.00 - 15.00
700-H *Out Of The Dawn*...................................8.00 - 12.00
703-H *Imagination* ....10.00 - 12.00
710-H *Remember Me To Mary* ....8.00 - 12.00
888-H *Till We Meet* ....8.00 - 12.00
890-H *You Wanted Someone To Play With* ....8.00 - 12.00
(Note: The above titles on Diva and Velvet Tone are similarly valued)
Herwin 55004 *Messin' Around* ....30.00 - 50.00
Pathe-Actuelle (titles as for Perfect, below)
Perfect 14617 *Reaching For The Moon* ....7.00 - 10.00
14625 *Betty* ....8.00 - 12.00
14642 *I Wish You Were Jealous Of Me* ....8.00 - 12.00
14643 *Jackass Blues* ....15.00 - 20.00
14650 *As Long As I Have You* ....7.00 - 10.00
14667 *Down By The Old Sea Shore*....................8.00 - 12.00
14668 *Crazy Quilt*..15.00 - 20.00
14720 *All Alone Monday* ....7.00 - 10.00
14721 *Stampede* ....15.00 - 20.00
14722 *Oh! How I Love Bulgarians* ....8.00 - 12.00
14750 *Delilah*..8.00 - 12.00
14752 *Everything's Made For Love* ....8.00 - 12.00
14841 *It's A Million To One You're In Love* .....10.00 - 15.00
14844 *Sweet Yvette* ....10.00 - 15.00
14874 *Phantom Blues* ....15.00 - 20.00
(Above also issued on Pathe-Actuelle, similarly valued)
Regal 8087 *Hard-To-Get Gertie* ....10.00 - 15.00
8089 *Jackass Blues* ....15.00 - 20.00
8109 *Nervous Charlie Stomp* ....15.00 - 20.00
8120 *I Wonder What's Become Of Joe* ....10.00 - 15.00
8126 *Blowin' Off Steam* ....15.00 - 20.00
8146 *Tuck In Kentucky And Smile* ....10.00 - 15.00
8150 *St. Louis Blues*...15.00 - 20.00
8310 *St. Louis Blues* ....20.00 - 30.00
8595 *A Jazz Holiday* ....15.00 - 20.00

CANDY AND COCO:
Vocalion 2833 *Kingfish Blues* ....50.00 - 75.00
2849 *China Boy*...50.00 - 75.00

CANNON'S JUG STOMPERS:
Bluebird 1850 *Viola Lee Blues* ....100.00 - 150.00

Bluebird 5030 *Minglewood Blues* ....75.00 - 100.00
    5287 *Big Railroad Blues*.................................75.00 - 100.00
    5389 *Bugle Call Rag*.....................................75.00 - 100.00
    5413 *Goin' To Germany* ....75.00 - 100.00
Sunrise 3117 *Minglewood Blues* ....100.00 - 200.00
    3368 *Big Railroad Blues*...........................100.00 - 200.00
Victor 21267 *Minglewood Blues* ....150.00 - 200.00
    21351 *Springdale Blues*............................150.00 - 200.00
    23262 *Money Never Runs Out*.....................300.00 - up
    23272 *Wolf River Blues* ....300.00 - up
    V38006 *Pig Ankle Strut* ....200.00 - 300.00
    V38515 *Feather Bed*..................................200.00 - 300.00
    V38523 *Viola Lee Blues* ....200.00 - 300.00
    V38539 *Ripley Blues* ....200.00 - 300.00
    V38566 *Hollywood Rag* ....250.00 - up
    V38585 *Goin' To Germany* ....250.00 - up
    V38593 *Last Chance Blues* ....250.00 - up
    V38611 *Walk Right In* ....250.00 - up
    V38629 *Jonestown Blues*............................250.00 - up

EDDIE CANTOR:
Aeolian-Vocalion 1220 *The Modern Maiden's Prayer*
    ....50.00 - 80.00
    1228 *Down In Borneo Isle* ....50.00 - 80.00
    1233 *Dixie Volunteers* ....50.00 - 80.00
Columbia 56-D *If You Do What You Do* ....15.00 - 20.00
    120-D *I'll Have Vanilla* ....10.00 - 15.00
    256-D *Those Panama Mammas* ....10.00 - 15.00
    140-D, 182-D, 196-D, 213-D, 234-D, 277-D,
    283-D..8.00 - 12.00
    364-D *If You Knew Susie* ....10.00 - 15.00
    397-D, 415-D, 457-D......................................8.00 - 12.00
    2723-D *What A Perfect Combination*...........15.00 - 20.00
    A-3624, A-3682, A-3754, A-3784, A-3906,
    A-3934, A-3964..8.00 - 12.00
    35325, 35428 ....7.00 - 10.00
Durium De Luxe K-6 *Ballyhoo* ....10.00 - 15.00
Emerson 1071, 1094, 10102, 10105, 10119, 10134,
    10200, 10212, 10263, 10292, 10301, 10327,
    10349, 10352, 10397 ....8.00 - 12.00
Melotone 13001 *The Man On The Flying Trapeze* ..8.00 - 12.00
    13183 *An Earful Of Music* ....10.00 - 15.00
    13184 *Okay, Toots*....................................10.00 - 15.00
Pathe 22163, 22201, 22260, 22318 ....8.00 - 12.00
Victor 18342 *The Modern Maiden's Prayer* ....10.00 - 15.00
    21831 *Makin' Whoopee* ....10.00 - 15.00
    21982, 22189, 24330 ....7.00 - 12.00

THE CAPTIVATORS (Direction of RED NICHOLS):
Brunswick 4308 *I Used To Love Her In The Moonlight*
    ....15.00 - 20.00
    4321 *Building A Nest For Mary* ....8.00 - 12.00
    4591 *Get Happy*..15.00 - 20.00
Melotone 12005 *Sweet Jennie Lee* ....15.00 - 20.00
    12049 *We're Friends Again*........................15.00 - 20.00

CARDINAL DANCE ORCHESTRA/JAZZ BAND:
Cardinal 503 *I've Got The Wonder Where He Went Blues*
    ....15.00 - 20.00
    504 *My Mammy Knows* ....15.00 - 20.00
    523 *On the Gin-Gin-Ginny Shore*................15.00 - 20.00
    527 *Those Longing For You Blues* ....15.00 - 30.00
    529 *Mary Dear* ....15.00 - 20.00
    556 *Apple Sauce* ....15.00 - 20.00
    558 *Carolina Mammy*................................15.00 - 20.00

    560 *Everything Is K.O. In K.Y.* ....15.00 - 20.00
    563 *Down Among The Sleepy Hills Of Tennessee* 15.00 - 20.00
    565 *Snakes Hips*.......................................15.00 - 20.00
    566 *My Old Ramshackle Shack*...................15.00 - 20.00
    571 *Down By The River* ....15.00 - 20.00
    2033 *Weary Blues* ....15.00 - 20.00

ERNEST CARL'S (DANCE) ORCHESTRA:
Cameo 9055 *You Should Know The Girl Friend* ......8.00 - 12.00
    9057 *The Way I'm Feeling Today*.................8.00 - 12.00
Romeo 861 *The Way I'm Feeling Today* ....8.00 - 12.00
    934 *Redskin* ....7.00 - 10.00
    968 *We Can't Live On Love* ....8.00 - 12.00
    1085 *For I'm In Love* ....7.00 - 10.00

CARLETON TERRACE ORCHESTRA:
Harmony 78-H *Pretty Little Baby*.........................8.00 - 12.00
    86-H *A Cup Of Coffee, A Sandwich, And You* .....7.00 - 10.00
    97-H *Drifting Apart* ....7.00 - 10.00
    100-H *Mysterious Eyes* ....7.00 - 10.00

EDDIE CARLEW'S BABY ARISTOCRATS:
Gennett 6184 *Indiana Mud* ....100.00 - 150.00

BILL CARLSEN & HIS ORCHESTRA:
Broadway 1359 *Milenburg Joys* ....50.00 - 75.00
    1365 *Baby, Won't You Please Come Home?*.....30.00 - 50.00
Paramount 20797 *Clarinet Marmalade* ....50.00 - 75.00

ROY CARLSON'S DANCE ORCHESTRA:
Banner 0504 *Hummin' With Love*.........................7.00 - 10.00
    0516 *I'm Kissing The Ground You Walk On* ....7.00 - 10.00
    0542 *Oh, Molly, My Molly-O*........................7.00 - 10.00
    0559 *Yearning* ....7.00 - 10.00
    0563 *I Can't Blame The Boys For Loving You*....8.00 - 12.00
    0567 *We'll Be Married In June* ....7.00 - 10.00
    0573 *Whenever I Think Of You* ....7.00 - 10.00
    0595 *Rainy Weather Rose* ....10.00 - 15.00
    0625 *Dearest Adorable* ....8.00 - 12.00
    0655 *My Little Dixie Home* ....7.00 - 10.00
    0694 *I'll Keep On Loving You* ....8.00 - 12.00
    0729 *Smile The Blues Away* ....10.00 - 15.00
    0752 *Fascinating You* ....10.00 - 15.00
    0779 *The Princeton Prance* ....8.00 - 12.00
    0780 *Making Believe*.................................7.00 - 10.00
    0801 *I Can't Believe It's True* ....8.00 - 12.00
    6411 *Just Tellin' My Troubles To The Moon* ......8.00 - 12.00
    6417 *After All* ....7.00 - 10.00
    6419 *In Springtime* ....8.00 - 12.00
    6423 *Mama Be Nice* ....7.00 - 10.00
    6437 *Beautiful*...7.00 - 10.00
    6443 *Tomorrow Means To Love, To Me*..............7.00 - 10.00
    6444 *Any Old Night Is A Peach Of A Night*.........7.00 - 10.00
    6468 *Loving You*..7.00 - 10.00
    6471 *Dimples* ....7.00 - 10.00
    6478 *My Baby's Sweet, But Oh How Cross-Eyed* ...7.00 - 10.00
    6497 *That's My Idea* ....7.00 - 10.00
    6503 *Evening Brings Memories Of You*...............7.00 - 10.00
    6504 *Send Love Through The Breeze* ....10.00 - 15.00
    6505 *You're Just An Armful Of Love* ....7.00 - 10.00
    6512 *If I Only Loved You A Little Bit Less* ....7.00 - 10.00
    6513 *When I Found You* ....7.00 - 10.00
    6539 *Now That You Are Mine* ....8.00 - 12.00
    6542 *Sweet Kentucky Sue*...........................8.00 - 12.00
    6552 *Would You Believe Me?* ....7.00 - 10.00

Cameo 0104 *Hummin' With Love* ....7.00 - 10.00
 0116 *I'm Kissing The Ground You Walk On* ....7.00 - 10.00
 0173 *Whenever I Think Of You* ....7.00 - 10.00
 0294 *I'll Keep On Loving You* ....8.00 - 12.00
Oriole 1829 *Whenever I Think Of You* ....7.00 - 10.00
Regal 10113 *Syncopated Jamboree* ....10.00 - 15.00
Romeo 1189 *We'll Be Married In June* ....7.00 - 10.00
 1203 *Just A Lone Hill Billy* ....7.00 - 10.00
 1244 *Dearest Adorable* ....8.00 - 12.00

RUSS CARLSON & HIS ORCHESTRA:
Banner 6410 *Sure Enough Blues* ....8.00 - 12.00
Crown 3136 *Love Is Like That* ....7.00 - 10.00
 3137 *Under Your Window Tonight* ....8.00 - 12.00
 3147 *Minnie The Moocher* ....8.00 - 12.00
 3148 *Toodle-oo, So Long, Goodbye* ....8.00 - 12.00
 3163 *It's The Girl!* ....8.00 - 12.00
 3177 *Me!* ....8.00 - 12.00
 3198 *Now That You're Gone* ....8.00 - 12.00
 3246 *Goodnight, Moon* ....7.00 - 10.00
 3259 *I Thank You, Mr. Moon* ....7.00 - 10.00
 3301 *I Know You're Lying, But I Love It* ....10.00 - 15.00
 3311 *Hello, Gorgeous!* ....10.00 - 15.00
 3315 *Got A Date With An Angel* ....7.00 - 10.00
 3330 *Hummin' To Myself* ....7.00 - 10.00
 3338 *Tom Thumb's Drum* ....7.00 - 10.00
 3345 *Sleep, Come On And Take Me* ....8.00 - 12.00
 3347 *You're Blase* ....7.00 - 10.00
 3351 *My Heart's At Ease* ....7.00 - 10.00
 3353 *Banking On The Weather* ....7.00 - 10.00
 3360 *I Can't Believe It's True* ....8.00 - 12.00
 3367 *Thou Shalt Not* ....8.00 - 12.00
 3373 *Everyone Says "I Love You"* ....8.00 - 12.00

BUD CARLTON'S ORCHESTRA:
Crown (Canadian) 81234 *A Little Kiss Each Morning*
 ....7.00 - 10.00
 81308 *Rainy Weather Rose* ....10.00 - 15.00
 81469 *Syncopated Jamboree* ....10.00 - 15.00

HOAGY CARMICHAEL & HIS ORCHESTRA/PALS; CARMICHAEL'S COLLEGIANS:
Brunswick 8250, 8255 ....7.00 - 10.00
Gennett 6311 *Stardust* ....150.00 - 250.00
 6474 *Walkin' The Dog* ....150.00 - 250.00
Victor L-16009 (long-playing "program transcription") *Dance*
 Medley of Hoagy Carmichael Compositions .....35.00 - 50.00
 22864 *Bessie Couldn't Help It* ....50.00 - 80.00
 23013 *One Night In Havana* ....30.00 - 50.00
 23034 *Lazy River* ....20.00 - 30.00
 24119 *After Twelve O'Clock* ....8.00 - 12.00
 24123 *Mighty River* ....10.00 - 15.00
 24182 *Sing It Way Down Low* ....10.00 - 15.00
 24402 *Lazy Bones* ....15.00 - 20.00
 24484 *Stardust* ....20.00 - 30.00
 24505 *One Morning In May* ....20.00 - 30.00
 24627 *Moon Country* ....15.00 - 25.00
 V-38139 *Barnacle Bill The Sailor* ....75.00 - 100.00

CAROLINA CLUB ORCHESTRA:
Harmony 639-H *Waitin' For Katy* ....15.00 - 20.00
 844-H *Dream Train* ....10.00 - 15.00
 852-H *I'm Marching Home To You* ....10.00 - 15.00
 853-H *Guess Who?* ....10.00 - 15.00
 872-H *My Sugar And Me* ....10.00 - 15.00
(Note: Above titles on Diva and Velvet Tone are similarly valued)

Melotone 12110 *Smile, Darn Ya, Smile* ....10.00 - 15.00
 12177 *Sing A Little Jingle* ....8.00 - 12.00
 12364 *Dixie* ....8.00 - 12.00
 12365 *Business In "Q"* ....15.00 - 20.00
Melotone (most other issues) ....5.00 - 8.00
Okeh 41199 *The Eyes Of Texas* ....10.00 - 15.00
 41218 *Coquette* ....10.00 - 15.00
 41226 *Honey* ....15.00 - 20.00
 41229 *My Castle In Spain Is A Shack In The Lane*
 ....15.00 - 20.00
 41237 *That's You, Baby* ....20.00 - 30.00
 41277 *Do Something* ....20.00 - 30.00
 41309 *Miss Wonderful* ....20.00 - 30.00
 41326 *He's So Unusual* ....30.00 - 50.00
 41332 *The World's Greatest Sweetheart Is You* ...15.00 - 20.00
 41337 *How I'll Miss You* ....15.00 - 20.00
 41356 *Nobody But You* ....20.00 - 30.00
 41358 *Hangin' On The Garden Gate* ....20.00 - 30.00
 41360 *Under A Texas Moon* ....20.00 - 30.00
 41366 *D' Ya Love Me?* ....15.00 - 25.00
 41408 *Can't Yo' Heah Me Callin', Caroline?* ...20.00 - 30.00
 41409 *Allah's Holiday* ....20.00 - 30.00
Pathe-Actuelle 036181 *Bye-Bye Baby* ....15.00 - 20.00
 36370 *Sweet Child* ....8.00 - 12.00
 36371 *Pretty Little Baby* ....8.00 - 12.00
 36381 *I Never Knew How Wonderful You Were* . 7.00 - 10.00
Perfect 14362 *Everybody Loves My Baby* ....15.00 - 20.00
 14378 *Who Takes Care Of The Caretaker's Daughter*
 ....10.00 - 15.00
 14426 *Hurry Back, Old Sweetheart Of Mine* ....7.00 - 10.00
 14551 *Sweet Child* ....10.00 - 15.00
 14552 *Pretty Little Baby* ....8.00 - 12.00
 14562 *I Never Knew How Wonderful You Were* . 7.00 - 10.00

CAROLINA COLLEGIANS:
Banner 6316 *Wedding Bells* ....10.00 - 15.00
 6319 *Before The Rain* ....10.00 - 15.00

CAROLINA COTTON PICKERS:
Vocalion 03527 *Let's Get Together* ....30.00 - 50.00
 03539 *Western Swing* ....30.00 - 50.00
 03580 *Off And On Blues* ....30.00 - 50.00

CAROLINA DANDIES:
Victor 22776 *Come Easy, Go Easy Love* ....50.00 - 80.00

THE CAROLINERS:
Banner 0847 *I'm Happy* ....15.00 - 25.00
Cameo 799 *Bam Bam Bamy Shore* ....8.00 - 12.00
 800 *Melancholy Lou* ....10.00 - 15.00
 818 *I'm Sitting On Top Of The World* ....7.00 - 10.00
 850 *She Was Just A Sailor's Sweetheart* ....8.00 - 12.00
 1056 *I've Got The Girl* ....7.00 - 10.00
 1063 *There Ain't No "Maybe" In My Baby's Eyes*
 ....10.00 - 15.00
 1103 *Lolling Around With Lolly* ....7.00 - 10.00
 8322 *Ev'rything We Like We Like Alike* ....8.00 - 12.00
 8325 *Got The Blue Blues* ....8.00 - 12.00
 8336 *It Goes Like This* ....7.00 - 10.00
 8348 *I Don't Care* ....7.00 - 10.00
 8373 *Blue Shadows* ....7.00 - 10.00
 9012 *Dardanella* ....10.00 - 15.00
 9030 *Where The Shy Little Violets Grow* ....15.00 - 20.00
 9086 *I Can't Keep You Out Of My Dreams* ....7.00 - 10.00
 9099 *Lover, Come Back To Me!* ....7.00 - 10.00

9158 *Your Disposition Is Mine* ....8.00 - 12.00
9299 *That's What Love Did To Me* ....7.00 - 10.00
Domino 4656 *Sweet Jennie Lee* ....15.00 - 25.00
Lincoln 2117 *The House Of David Blues* ....8.00 - 12.00
　2196 *Sobbin' Blues* ....8.00 - 12.00
　2242 *Go 'Long Mule* ....5.00 - 8.00
　2388 *I'm Knee Deep In Daisies* ....7.00 - 10.00
Romeo 457 *I'm Coming, Virginia* ....7.00 - 10.00
　858 *I'm Rolling Around In Sunshine* ....7.00 - 10.00

ROY CARROLL & HIS SANDS POINT ORCHESTRA:

Clarion 5252-C, 5253-C, 5255-C, 5262-C, 5263-C ..7.00 - 12.00
　5321-C *Moonlight Saving Time* ....15.00 - 20.00
　5338-C *Let's Get Friendly* ....10.00 - 15.00
　5343-C *High And Low* ....10.00 - 15.00
　5357-C *I Can't Write The Words* ....15.00 - 20.00
　5393-C *Waitin' For A Call From You* ....8.00 - 12.00
　5420-C *Bend Down, Sister* ....15.00 - 20.00
　5442-C *Chances Are* ....20.00 - 30.00
Harmony 1253-H *Overnight* ....8.00 - 12.00
　1261-H *Little Did I Know* ....8.00 - 12.00
　1271-H *Royal Garden Blues* ....10.00 - 15.00
　1289-H, 1297-H ....8.00 - 12.00
　1322-H *Roll On, Mississippi, Roll On* ....15.00 - 20.00
　1328-H *Love Is Like That* ....8.00 - 12.00
　1329-H *One More Time* ....10.00 - 15.00
　1334-H *Dancing In The Dark* ....10.00 - 15.00
　1345-H *It's The Girl* ....15.00 - 20.00
　1379-H *Waitin' For A Call From You* ....8.00 - 12.00
　1397-H *Bend Down, Sister* ....15.00 - 20.00
　1403-H *Chances Are* ....20.00 - 30.00
Velvet Tone 2328-V, 2329-V, 2506-V, 2507-V,
　2515-V ....7.00 - 12.00
　2387-V *Moonlight Savings Time* ....15.00 - 20.00
　2401-V *Love Is Like That* ....8.00 - 12.00
　2402-V *One More Time* ....10.00 - 15.00
　2407-V *High And Low* ....10.00 - 15.00
　2421-V *I Can't Write the Words* ....15.00 - 20.00
　2457-V *Waitin' For A Call From You* ....8.00 - 12.00
　2480-V *Bend Down, Sister* ....15.00 - 20.00
　2502-V *Chances Are* ....20.00 - 30.00

BUD CARSON & HIS COLLEGIANS:

Champion 15514 *Who Wouldn't Be Blue?* ....15.00 - 20.00
　15535 *My Pet* ....15.00 - 20.00
　15728 *She Only Laughs At Me* ....15.00 - 20.00
　15778 *Now I'm In Love* ....15.00 - 20.00
　15779 *Believe It Or Not* ....15.00 - 20.00
　15802 *'s Been A Long Time In Between Time* ....15.00 - 20.00
　15838 *I Gotta Have You* ....15.00 - 20.00
　15840 *Scotchie* ....15.00 - 25.00
　15843 *If I Were You, I'd Fall In Love With Me* ..15.00 - 20.00
　15887 *The Woman In The Shoe* ....15.00 - 20.00
　15890 *Wake Up Your Feet* ....15.00 - 20.00
　15918 *The Man From The South* ....15.00 - 20.00
　15934 *Puttin On The Ritz* ....15.00 - 20.00
　15954 *You've Got That Thing* ....15.00 - 20.00
　15958 *Amos 'n' Andy* ....15.00 - 25.00
　15976 *Chinnin' And Chattin' With May* ....15.00 - 20.00

ROB CARSON & HIS ORCHESTRA:

Broadway 1295 *Whoopee' In Up* ....10.00 - 15.00

CARTER'S ORCHESTRA:

Brunswick, most issues ....5.00 - 8.00

BENNY CARTER & HIS HARLEMITES/ORCHESTRA:

Bluebird (most issues) ....7.00 - 10.00
Columbia 2898-D *Devil's Holiday* ....40.00 - 60.00
Crown 3321 *Tell All Your Day Dreams To Me* ..... 75.00 - 100.00
Decca 3262, 3294 ....8.00 - 12.00
Okeh 6001 *Joe Turner Blues* ....10.00 - 15.00
　41567 *Blue Lou* ....40.00 - 60.00
　(most other issues) ....7.00 - 12.00
Vocalion 2870 *Everybody Shuffle* ....40.00 - 60.00
　2898 *Shoot The Works* ....40.00 - 60.00
Vocalion 4984 *Plymouth Rock* ....10.00 - 15.00
　5112 *Savoy Stampede* ....10.00 - 15.00
　5224 *Vagabond Dreams* ....10.00 - 15.00
　5294 *Riff Romp* ....10.00 - 15.00
　5399 *Slow Freight* ....10.00 - 15.00
Vocalion (most other issues) ....7.00 - 12.00

FREDDIE CARTER & HIS MAJESTIC BALLROOM ORCHESTRA:

Sunset 1101 *Titina* ....15.00 - 25.00

KING CARTER & HIS ROYAL ORCHESTRA:

Columbia 2439-D *Minnie The Moocher* ....20.00 - 30.00
　2504-D *Blue Rhythm* ....20.00 - 30.00
　2638-D *Low Down On The Bayou* ....20.00 - 30.00

MARGARET CARTER:

Pathe-Actuelle 7511 *I Want Plenty Grease In My Frying Pan*
....50.00 - 75.00
Perfect 111 *I Want Plenty Grease In My Frying Pan*
....50.00 - 75.00

CASA LOMA ORCHESTRA:

Brunswick 6085 *When I Take My Sugar To Tea* .... 10.00 - 15.00
　6092 *White Jazz* ....15.00 - 20.00
　6100 *Alexander's Ragtime Band* ....8.00 - 12.00
　6124 *I Wanna Sing About You* ....10.00 - 15.00
　6150 *Do The New York* ....10.00 - 15.00
　6153 *It's The Girl* ....10.00 - 15.00
　6187 *Blue Kentucky Moon* ....10.00 - 15.00
　6201 *Time On My Hands* ....10.00 - 15.00
　6242 *Maniac's Ball* ....10.00 - 15.00
　6252 *Rain On The Roof* ....10.00 - 15.00
　6256 *One Of Us Was Wrong* ....8.00 - 12.00
　6263 *You're Still In My Heart* ....8.00 - 12.00
　6289 *Smoke Rings* ....8.00 - 12.00
　6311 *Lazy Day* ....8.00 - 12.00
　6318 *All Of A Sudden* ....8.00 - 12.00
　6337 *Indiana* ....8.00 - 12.00
　6397 *After Tonight* ....8.00 - 12.00
　6402 *Mighty River* ....8.00 - 12.00
　6463 *Rhythm Man* ....8.00 - 12.00
　6486 *New Orleans* ....8.00 - 12.00
　6494 *Why Can't This Go On Forever* ....8.00 - 12.00
　6513 *Blue Parade* ....8.00 - 12.00
　6584 *Love Is The Thing* ....8.00 - 12.00
　6588 *Wild Goose Chase* ....8.00 - 12.00
　6602 *The River's Takin' Care Of Me* ....8.00 - 12.00
　6606 *I Love You Truly* ....7.00 - 10.00
　6618 *Mississippi Basin* ....8.00 - 12.00
　6626 *That's How Rhythm Was Born* ....8.00 - 12.00
　6628 *Music From Across The Sea* ....7.00 - 10.00
　6642 *This Is Romance* ....7.00 - 10.00
　6647 *Savage Serenade* ....8.00 - 12.00
　6660 *Sweet Madness* ....8.00 - 12.00

6666 *And So, Goodbye* ....7.00 - 10.00
6679 *Heat Wave*..8.00 - 12.00
6708 *You're Gonna Lose Your Gal* ....7.00 - 10.00
6726 *Dixie Lee* ....7.00 - 10.00
6738 *Shadows Of Love* ....7.00 - 10.00
6764 *That's Love* ....7.00 - 10.00
6775 *A Hundred Years From Today*......................7.00 - 10.00
6791 *Infatuation*..7.00 - 10.00
6800 *Ol' Man River* ....8.00 - 12.00
6858 *This House Is Haunted*................................7.00 - 10.00
6870 *Ridin' Around In The Rain* ....7.00 - 10.00
6886 *Limehouse Blues* ....8.00 - 12.00
6910 *Spellbound* ....7.00 - 10.00
6922 *Milenberg Joys* ....8.00 - 12.00
6927 *Long May We Love* ....7.00 - 10.00
6932 *Jungle Fever* ....8.00 - 12.00
6937 *You Ain't Been Living Right* ....8.00 - 12.00
6945 *Pardon My Southern Accent*........................7.00 - 10.00
6954 *Two Cigarettes In The Dark* ....7.00 - 10.00
6964 *Out In The Cold Again*................................7.00 - 10.00
6983 *How Can You Face Me?*................................7.00 - 10.00
7321 *Nocturne* ....7.00 - 10.00
7325 *Linger Awhile* ....7.00 - 10.00
7427 *Corrine Corrina* ....7.00 - 10.00
7532 *Avalon* ....7.00 - 10.00

(Some of above Brunswicks are as **GLEN GRAY & THE CASA LOMA ORCHESTRA**)

Brunswick 20108 (12-inch) *Washboard Blues*........30.00 - 50.00
Brunswick paper advertising record (unnumbered)
   Limehouse Blues ....75.00 - 100.00
Columbia 2884-D *San Sue Strut*......................10.00 - 15.00
Okeh 41339 *Happy Days Are Here Again* ....20.00 - 30.00
   41373 *Sweeping The Clouds Away* ....20.00 - 30.00
   41374 *Romance* ....30.00 - 50.00
   41403 *China Girl*..20.00 - 30.00
   41476 *Alexander's Ragtime Band* ....15.00 - 25.00
   41477 *Overnight* ....15.00 - 20.00
   41492 *Casa Loma Stomp* ....20.00 - 30.00

CASINO DANCE ORCHESTRA:

Perfect 100 *That Toddlin' Hop* ....10.00 - 20.00
   14884 *The Best Things In Life Are Free*..........10.00 - 15.00
   15075 *Adorable Dora* ....10.00 - 15.00

CASTLE FARMS SERENADERS/ENTERTAINERS:

Titles issued contemporaneously on Broadway, Paramount: *Chili Blues; High On A Hilltop; Ol' Man River; Silver Moon; 'taint So, Honey, 'taint So; Tennessee Lazy*......................15.00 - 25.00

(BIG) SID CATLETT QUARTETTE/SEXTETTE/TRIO/ ORCHESTRA; SID CATLETT'S ALL-STARS:

Delta, Manor, Session..5.00 - 10.00

BOB CAUSER & HIS CORNELLIANS:

Melotone 12848 *Puddin' Head Jones* ....10.00 - 15.00
Perfect 15858 *Puddin' Head Jones* ....10.00 - 15.00

CELESTIN'S ORIGINAL TUXEDO JAZZ ORCHESTRA:

Columbia 636-D *Station Calls*............................50.00 - 75.00
   14200-D *I'm Satisfied You Love Me*..................80.00 - 120.00
   14220-D *Papa's Got The Jim-Jams* ....100.00 - 150.00
   14259-D *As You Like It*....................................100.00 - 150.00
   14323-D *It's Jam Up* ....100.00 - 150.00
   14396-D *The Sweetheart Of T.K.O.*..................100.00 - 150.00

THE CELLAR BOYS:

Vocalion 1503 *Barrel House Stomp* ....200.00 - 300.00

THE CENTRE BOYS:

Lincoln 2388 *Headin' For Baltimore* ....8.00 - 12.00

ROD/RON CHADWICK & HIS ORCHESTRA:

Broadway 1312 *I'm The Medicine Man For The Blues*
   ....8.00 - 12.00
   1321 *Sweetheart, We Need Each Other* ....8.00 - 12.00
   1331 *The Things We Want Most Are Hard To Get*
   ....7.00 - 10.00

CHALLENGE DANCE ORCHESTRA:

Challenge 210 *Don't Sing Aloha When I Go* ....40.00 - 60.00
   804 *Sunshine* ....75.00 - 100.00
   806 *Mary Ann* ....150.00 - 200.00
   809 *Sweetheart*..-   -   -

CHAMPION DANCE KINGS:

Champion 15532 *Old Man Sunshine* ....10.00 - 15.00
   15536 *Just A Night For Meditation* ....10.00 - 15.00
   15657 *Betty* ....8.00 - 12.00
   15804 *The World's Greatest Sweetheart Is You*..8.00 - 12.00
   15817 *Bigger and Better Than Ever* ....8.00 - 12.00
   15819 *Pretty Little You* ....10.00 - 15.00
   15863 *I May Be Wrong* ....8.00 - 12.00
   15865 *My Sweeter Than Sweet* ....8.00 - 12.00

CHAMPION RHYTHM KINGS:

Champion 16387 *Sweet Georgia Brown*................100.00 - 150.00

CHARLIE CHAPLIN CONDUCTING ABE LYMAN'S AMBASSADOR ORCHESTRA:

Brunswick 2912 *Sing A Song*................................15.00 - 20.00

JACK CHAPMAN & HIS (DRAKE HOTEL) ORCHESTRA:

Victor 19775 *Carolina Blues* ....75.00 - 100.00
   19915 *Tie Me To Your Apron Strings Again* ......7.00 - 10.00
Victor, most other issues..4.00 - 8.00

JUANITA STINNETTE CHAPPELLE:

Chappelle & Stinnette 5003 *Cheating* ....100.00 - up
   5004 *Caterpillar Wabble* ....100.00 - up
   5005 *Aching-Hearted Blues* ....100.00 - up
   5006 *Southland* ....100.00 - up
Victor 21062 *Florence*..40.00 - 60.00

CHAPPIE'S HOT DOGS (See JUANITA STINNETTE CHAPPELLE)

THE CHARLESTON CHASERS:

Columbia 446-D *Red Hot Henry Brown*................20.00 - 30.00
   861-D *After You've Gone* ....20.00 - 30.00
   909-D *Davenport Blues* ....15.00 - 20.00
   1076-D *Delirium* ....30.00 - 50.00
   1229-D *Five Pennies* ....15.00 - 20.00
   1335-D *My Melancholy Baby* ....15.00 - 20.00
   1539-D *Farewell Blues* ....15.00 - 25.00
   1891-D *Ain't Misbehavin'* ....15.00 - 20.00
   1925-D *Lovable And Sweet*..............................15.00 - 20.00
   1989-D *Turn On The Heat* ....15.00 - 25.00
   2133-D *Sing, You Sinners* ....15.00 - 25.00
   2219-D *Here Comes Emily Brown* ....20.00 - 30.00
   2309-D *You're Lucky To Me*............................20.00 - 30.00
   2415-D *Basin Street Blues* ....25.00 - 40.00

CHARLESTON COLLEGIATES:
Everybodys 1079 *I'm Gonna Charleston Back to Charleston*
....8.00 - 12.00

CHARLESTON MELODY SYNCOPATORS:
Dandy 5073 *Always Got The Blues* ....15.00 - 30.00

THE CHARLESTON SEVEN:
Edison 51446 *Nashville Nightingale* ....40.00 - 60.00

CHECKER BOX BOYS:
Broadway 1179 *Is It Gonna Be Long* ....7.00 - 10.00
   1209 *It Goes Like This*....................................7.00 - 10.00
   1231 *You're the Cream in My Coffee*....................7.00 - 10.00
   1242 *Don't Be Like That*..................................7.00 - 10.00
   1244 *I's Rather Be Blue Over You*....................7.00 - 10.00
   1251 *Cradle of Love* ....7.00 - 10.00
   1259 *My Mother's Eyes*..................................7.00 - 10.00
   1262 *Outside*..7.00 - 10.00
   1266 *My Kinda Love*......................................7.00 - 10.00
   1272 *Louise*...7.00 - 10.00
   1276 *Breakaway* ....7.00 - 10.00
   1287 *Am I Blue?* ....7.00 - 10.00
   1301 *One Sweet Kiss* ....5.00 - 8.00
   1328 *If I Had a Talking Picture of You* ....7.00 - 10.00
   1382 *Dream Avenue* ....7.00 - 10.00
   1391 *Bye Bye Blues* ....10.00 - 15.00
   1406 *My Baby Just Cares For Me* ....8.00 - 12.00

DICK CHERWIN & HIS ORCHESTRA:
Banner 6497 *Birmingham Bertha*............................7.00 - 10.00
   6511 *I'm The Medicine Man For The Blues*........8.00 - 12.00
   6537 *He's A Good Man To Have Around* ....8.00 - 12.00
   6547 *Georgia Pines* ....10.00 - 15.00
Cameo 8179 *Real Estate Papa* ....7.00 - 10.00
   9184 *Hittin' The Ceiling*.................................7.00 - 10.00
   9208 *I'm Doing What I'm Doing For Love* ....10.00 - 15.00
   9227 *True Blue Lou* ....7.00 - 10.00
Conqueror 7716 *Got The Bench, Got The Park* ....7.00 - 10.00
Romeo 607 *Little Log Cabin Of Dreams*....................5.00 - 8.00
   934 *Swanee Cradle Of Mine*..........................5.00 - 8.00

FRED CHESS & THE MERRYMAKERS:
Supertone 9345 *I Faw Down An' Go Boom* ....8.00 - 12.00
   9381 *My Sugar And Me* ....8.00 - 12.00

BOB CHESTER & HIS ORCHESTRA:
Bluebird (most issues) ....5.00 - 8.00

MAURICE CHEVALIER:
Victor 21918, 22007, 22093, 22285 22294, 22368 ..5.00 - 10.00
   22378, 22405, 22415, 22542, 22549, 22634,
   22723, 22731, 22747, 22941, 22944, 24063,
   24066, 24874, 24882, 24883 ....7.00 - 12.00

CHICAGO BLACK SWANS:
Titles issued contemporaneously on Banner, Melotone, Oriole,
   Perfect, Romeo, Vocalion: *Don't Tear My Clothes No 2; You*
   Drink Too Much..15.00 - 20.00

CHICAGO BLUES DANCE ORCHESTRA:
Columbia A-3923 *Blue Grass Blues*........................20.00 - 30.00

CHICAGO DE LUX ORCHESTRA:
Autograph 585 *Sad-Hearted Blues*.............................. -
Paramount 20341 *St. Louis Blues* ....15.00 - 20.00
Puritan 11341 *St. Louis Blues*................................15.00 - 20.00

THE CHICAGO FOOTWARMERS:
Okeh 8533 *Ballin' The Jack*...............................125.00 - 175.00
   8548 *Oriental Man*......................................150.00 - 200.00
   8599 *Get 'Em Again Blues*...........................150.00 - 200.00
   8613 *Brown Bottom Bess* ....150.00 - 200.00
   8675 *Goin' To Town* ....50.00 - 80.00
   8792 *Sweep 'Em Clean* ....150.00 - 250.00

CHICAGO HOT FIVE:
Victor 23285 *Star Dust* ....75.00 - 100.00
   23300 *Wake 'Em Up* ....80.00 - 130.00
   23326 *Oh! What A Thrill* ....75.00 - 100.00

CHICAGO HOTTENTOTS:
Vocalion 1008 *All Nights Shags* ....150.00 - 200.00

THE CHICAGO LOOPERS:
Pathe-Actuelle 36729 *Three Blind Mice* ....100.00 - 150.00
Perfect 14910 *Clorinda* ....100.00 - 150.00

CHICAGO RHYTHM KINGS:
Bluebird 6371 *Little Sandwich Wagon* ....10.00 - 15.00
   6397 *Sarah Jane* ....7.00 - 10.00
   6412 *Stompin' At The Savoy* ....10.00 - 15.00
   6564 *The Breeze* ....15.00 - 20.00
   6690 *Boston Tea Party* ....10.00 - 15.00
Brunswick 4001 *I've Found A New Baby*................30.00 - 50.00
   80064 *Baby, Won't You Please Come Home* ......7.00 - 10.00
Vocalion 03208 *You Battle Head Beetle Head*.......50.00 - 75.00

THE CHICAGO STOMPERS:
Champion 16297 *Wild Man Stomp* ....250.00 - up
   40013 *Wild Man Stomp*.................................50.00 - 75.00

THE CHICKASAW SYNCOPATORS:
Columbia 14301-D *Memphis Rag* ....150.00 - 250.00

IVORY CHITTISON AND BANJO JOE:
Vocalion 25011 *Unlucky Blues*..............................75.00 - 100.00

THE CHOCOLATE DANDIES:
Columbia 2543-D *Bugle Call Rag* ....40.00 - 60.00
   2875-D *I Never Knew* ....40.00 - 60.00
   35679, 36008, 36009 ....5.00 - 8.00
Okeh 8627 *Paducah* ....50.00 - 80.00
   8668 *Birmingham Break-Down* ....75.00 - 100.00
   41568 *Once Upon A Time* ....75.00 - 100.00
Vocalion 1610 *Loveless Love* ....150.00 - 200.00
   1617 *That's My Stuff*..................................150.00 - 200.00
   1646 *Levee Low Down*................................50.00 - 80.00

CHOO CHOO JAZZERS:
Ajax 17038 *Snuggle Up A Bit*...............................25.00 - 40.00

AXEL CHRISTENSEN:
Broadway 1161 *Syncophonic*................................15.00 - 20.00
   8073 *Axel And The Ducks* ....7.00 - 10.00
   8079 *Axel At The Baseball Game* ....8.00 - 12.00
Christensen (unnumbered) *Teasing The Classics* ....- - -
(The above is a picture label with a caricature of the artist)
Paramount 3086 *Axel At The Baseball Game* ....8.00 - 12.00
   20603 *Walking Blues* ....20.00 - 30.00

BUDDY CHRISTIAN'S CREOLE FIVE/JAZZ RIPPERS:
Okeh 8311 *Sunset Blues*....................................150.00 - 200.00
   8342 *Sugar House Stomp*............................150.00 - 200.00
Pathe-Actuelle 8518 *South Rampart Street Blues*.150.00 - 200.00
Perfect 118 *South Rampart Street Blues*................150.00 - 200.00

LILLIE DELK CHRISTIAN:

Okeh 8317 *Sweet Georgia Brown*	30.00 - 50.00
8356 *Baby O' Mine*	150.00 - 200.00
8475 *Ain't She Sweet?*	100.00 - 150.00
8536 *My Blue Heaven*	75.00 - 100.00
8596 *Too Busy*	75.00 - 100.00
8607 *You're A Real Sweetheart*	75.00 - 100.00
8650 *I Can't Give You Anything But Love*	50.00 - 75.00
8660 *I Must Have That Man*	50.00 - 75.00

TOMMY CHRISTIAN & HIS ORCHESTRA:

Harmony 74-H *Show Me The Way To Go Home*	10.00 - 15.00
264-H *How Could Red Riding Hood?*	8.00 - 12.00
330-H *Sam, The Old Accordion Man*	8.00 - 12.00
333-H *If My Baby Cooks (As Good As She Looks)*	8.00 - 12.00
348-H *'Deed I Do*	8.00 - 12.00
358-H *Proud*	8.00 - 12.00
394-H *Beedle Um Bo*	8.00 - 12.00
427-H *Swamp Blues*	15.00 - 20.00

(Note: Above titles on Diva, Silvertone, and Velvet Tone are similarly valued)

CHUBB-STEINBERG ORCHESTRA (OF CINCINNATI):

Gennett 3058 *Mandy, Make Up Your Mind*	50.00 - 75.00
5663 *Because They All Love You*	40.00 - 60.00
Okeh 40106 *From One Till Two*	75.00 - 100.00
40107 *Blue Evening Blues*	75.00 - 100.00

CINCINNATI JUG BAND:

Paramount 12743 *Newport Blues*	300.00 - up

TED CLAIRE'S SNAPPY BITS BAND:

Gennett 5041 *Four O'Clock Blues*	25.00 - 40.00
5060 *Laughin' Cryin' Blues*	25.00 - 40.00

SUNNY CLAPP & HIS BAND O'SUNSHINE:

Harmony 899-H *Remember I Love You*	8.00 - 12.00
Okeh 41283 *A Bundle of Southern Sunshine*	40.00 - 60.00
Victor 22682 *Treat Me Like A Baby*	15.00 - 20.00
22684 *When My Baby Smiles At Me*	20.00 - 30.00
22777 *Reflections Of You*	15.00 - 20.00
V-40152 *Down On Biscayne Bay*	50.00 - 80.00

CLARINET JOE & HIS HOT FOOTERS:

Harmony 8-H *Rabbit Foot Blues*	20.00 - 30.00

DON CLARK & HIS LOS ANGELES BILTMORE HOTEL ORCHESTRA:

Columbia 824-D *I've Got The Girl!*	20.00 - 30.00
Victor 19622 *Cheatin' On Me*	7.00 - 10.00
19736 *It's Too Good To Be True*	7.00 - 10.00

JIM CLARKE:

Vocalion 1536 *Fat Funny Stomp*	100.00 - 150.00

SONNY CLAY'S PLANTATION/HARTFORD BALLROOM ORCHESTRA; SONNY CLAY & HIS ORCHESTRA:

Sonny Clay 22/23 *When It's Sleepy Time Down South*	- -
Vocalion 1000 *Plantation Blues*	150.00 - 200.00
1050 *California Stomp*	150.00 - 250.00
15078 *Jambled Blues*	100.00 - 150.00
15254 *Chicago Breakdown*	150.00 - 250.00
15641 *Devil's Serenade*	150.00 - 200.00

CLAYTON, JACKSON AND DURANTE:

Columbia 1860-D *So I Ups To Him*	15.00 - 20.00

JOHNNY CLESI'S AREOLIANS:

Gennett 3380 *Ain't I Got Rosie?*	50.00 - 80.00
6033 *Brotherly Love*	100.00 - 150.00
6061 *Ain't I Got Rosie*	- - -
Herschel Gold Seal 2010 *Ain't I Got Rosie?*	50.00 - 100.00

THE CLEVELANDERS:

Banner 0623 *With You*	10.00 - 15.00
Banner 0784 *I Still Get A Thrill*	7.00 - 10.00
Brunswick 3047 *Rhythm Of The Day*	7.00 - 10.00
3279 *She Belongs To Me*	10.00 - 15.00
Brunswick, most other issues	4.00 - 8.00
Cameo 0144 *Sunny Side Up*	5.00 - 8.00
0223 *With You*	10.00 - 15.00
0294 *You Brought A New Kind Of Love To Me*	8.00 - 12.00
0405 *I Don't Mind Walkin' In The Rain*	5.00 - 8.00
Challenge 764 *I Don't Mind Walkin' In The Rain*	5.00 - 8.00
Perfect 15258 *A Year From Today*	7.00 - 10.00
Romeo 1159 *Sunny Side Up*	5.00 - 8.00
1243 *With You*	7.00 - 10.00

CLICQUOT CLUB ESKIMOS (See also HARRY RESER):

Banner 0700 *'Leven Thirty Saturday Night*	7.00 - 10.00
0721 *Ro-Ro-Rolling Along*	7.00 - 10.00
0779 *Hittin' The Bottle*	8.00 - 12.00
Cameo 0172 *You've Got That Thing*	7.00 - 10.00
0358 *Out Of Breath (And Scared To Death Of You)*	8.00 - 12.00
Columbia 795-D *Some Day*	7.00 - 10.00
921-D *My Sunday Girl*	10.00 - 15.00
1060-D *I Wonder Who's With You When I'm Not There*	7.00 - 10.00
1213-D *My One And Only*	7.00 - 10.00
1281-D *Henry's Made A Lady Out Of Lizzie*	10.00 - 15.00
1322-D *Humoreskimo*	8.00 - 12.00
1592-D *Come On, Baby!*	10.00 - 15.00
1625-D *Watching The Clouds Roll By*	8.00 - 12.00
1718-D *In a Little Town Called Home Sweet Home*	10.00 - 15.00
1936-D *Marianne*	10.00 - 15.00
Romeo 1189 *I Want To Be Happy*	7.00 - 10.00
1203 *Hallelujah*	7.00 - 10.00
1374 *Little White Lies*	5.00 - 8.00

CLIFFORD'S LOUISVILLE JUG BAND:

Okeh 8221 *Dancing Blues*	250.00 - up
8238 *Struttin' The Blues*	250.00 - up
8248 *Mammy O' Mine Blues*	250.00 - up
8269 *Get It Fixed Blues*	250.00 - up

CLINE'S COLLEGIANS:
DAL-571/572 *Chicadore Stomp*.............................75.00 - 100.00
(Note: Above is a test pressing.)
Brunswick 4162 *Peruna* ....30.00 - 50.00

TOM CLINES & HIS MUSIC:
Brunswick, most issues...7.00 - 10.00
Diva 2928-G *Sing A Little Love Song*.....................15.00 - 20.00
Diva, most other issues ....5.00 - 10.00
Harmony 928-H *Sing A Little Love Song* ....15.00 - 20.00
Harmony, most other issues.......................................5.00 - 10.00
Velvet Tone 1928-V *Sing A Little Love Song* ....15.00 - 20.00
Velvet Tone, most other issues..................................5.00 - 10.00

LARRY CLINTON AND HIS ORCHESTRA; LARRY CLINTON'S BLUEBIRD ORCHESTRA:
Bluebird, most issues..5.00 - 8.00
Decca, most issues ....5.00 - 8.00
Victor, most issues..5.00 - 8.00

CLOVERDALE COUNTRY CLUB ORCHESTRA:
Okeh 41519 *As Time Goes By* ....15.00 - 20.00
    41520 *Why Dance?* ....10.00 - 15.00
    41523 *Goodnight Sweetheart* ....10.00 - 15.00
    41528 *A Faded Summer Love* ....8.00 - 12.00
    41531 *A Cuban Love Song* ....8.00 - 12.00
    41535 *I Promise You* ....8.00 - 12.00
    41539 *Save The Last Dance for Me* ....8.00 - 12.00
    41542 *All Of Me* ....15.00 - 20.00
    41544 *Goodnight, Moon* ....8.00 - 12.00
    41551 *Chances Are* ....30.00 - 50.00
    41555 *Can't We Talk It Over?* ....8.00 - 12.00
    41564 *Keepin' Out of Mischief Now* ....15.00 - 20.00

CLUB ALABAM' ORCHESTRA:
Domino 354 *Jealous* ....10.00 - 15.00
    355 *You Know Me, Alabam'* ....10.00 - 15.00
    356 *Wait'll You See My Gal* ....15.00 - 20.00
    366 *Hard Hearted Hannah* ....15.00 - 20.00
    368 *Where The Dreamy Wabash Flows* ....10.00 - 15.00
    369 *Red Hot Mama* ....15.00 - 20.00
    370 *The Grass Is Always Greener* ....10.00 - 20.00
    371 *Charley, My Boy* ....10.00 - 15.00
    415 *How Come You Do Me Like You Do?* ....15.00 - 20.00
    426 *One Of These Days* ....15.00 - 20.00

CLUB AMBASSADORS:
Brunswick 4966 *My Daddy Rocks Me* ....75.00 - 100.00
    7096 *Apex Blues* ....75.00 - 100.00

CLUB WIGWAM ORCHESTRA:
Domino 3458 *Alabamy Bound*..................................10.00 - 15.00

JACK COAKLEY'S (FLEXO RECORDING) ORCHESTRA:
Flexo 103 *It Seems To Be Spring* ....30.00 - 50.00
    117 *Wabash Blues*...75.00 - 100.00
    130 *Walkin' My Baby Back Home* ....30.00 - 50.00
    131 *Reaching For The Moon* ....30.00 - 50.00

TOM COAKLEY & HIS (PALACE HOTEL) ORCHESTRA:
Brunswick 6577, 6702 ....5.00 - 8.00
Victor, most issues ....5.00 - 8.00

E.C. COBB & HIS CORN EATERS:
Victor V38023 *Transatlantic Stomp* ....100.00 - 150.00

J.C. JUNIE COBB & HIS GRAINS OF CORN; JUNIE COBB'S HOMETOWN BAND:
Paramount 12382 *East Coast Trot* ....200.00 - 300.00
Vocalion 1204 *Endurance Stomp* ....200.00 - 300.00
    1263 *Shake That Jelly Roll* ....200.00 - 300.00
    1269 *Smoke Shop Drag*...................................200.00 - 300.00
    1449 *Once Or Twice* ....100.00 - 150.00
(Note: Repressings on black and gold or blue and gold labels are
   valued much lower.)

OLIVER COBB (& HIS RHYTHM KINGS):
Brunswick 7107 *Hot Stuff*.....................................100.00 - 150.00
Paramount 13002 *Cornet Pleading Blues*.............200.00 - 300.00

GEORGE M. COHAN:
Victor 60042 *Life's a Funny Proposition, After All* ..15.00 - 20.00
    60043 *You Won't Do Any Business* ....15.00 - 20.00
    60044 *I'm Mighty Glad I'm Living That's All* ..15.00 - 20.00
    60045 *I Want To Hear A Yankee Doodle Tune* .20.00 - 30.00
    60049 *Hey There! May There* ....15.00 - 30.00
    60052 *The Small Town Gal* ....15.00 - 30.00
    70039 *P.S.-Mr. Johnson Sends Regards* ....15.00 - 20.00

EDDIE COLE'S SOLID SWINGERS:
Decca 7210 *Thunder* ....20.00 - 30.00
    7215 *Stomping At The Panama*.........................20.00 - 30.00

KING COLE QUARTET/TRIO; KING COLE'S SWINGSTERS; KING COLE & HIS MUSIC WEAVERS:
Ammor 108 *On The Sunny Side Of The Street* ....- - -
    109 *Black Spider* ....- - -
Davis & Schwegler 108 *Land Of Make-Believe* ....- - -
    110 *Ta-De-Ah*...- - -
    111 *Riffin' At The Barbeque* ....- - -
    113 *I Lost Control Of Myself* ....- - -
    115 *That Please Be Mineable Feeling* ....- - -
    119 *Let's Get Happy* ....- - -
Decca 8520 *This Side Up*..10.00 - 15.00
    8535 *Honeysuckle Rose* ....10.00 - 15.00
    8541 *Early Morning Blues*................................10.00 - 15.00
    8556 *Slow Down* ....10.00 - 15.00
    8571 *Hit The Ramp* ....10.00 - 15.00
    8592 *I Like To Riff* ....10.00 - 15.00
    8604 *Call The Police* ....10.00 - 15.00
    8630 *That Ain't Right*.......................................10.00 - 15.00
Excelsior 104/105 *Pitchin' Up A Boogie* ....- - -
Premier 100 *F.S.T.* ....15.00 - 20.00
Savoy 600 *I Like To Riff* ....8.00 - 12.00
Timely Tunes 1589 *They Satisfy* ....- - -
Varsity 8340 *I Like To Riff*......................................- - -

E.L. COLEMAN:
Okeh 8216 *Steel String Blues* ....50.00 - 75.00

EMIL COLEMAN & HIS ORCHESTRA:
Brunswick 4977 *Overnight* ....7.00 - 10.00
    6006 *I'm Getting Myself Ready For You* ....8.00 - 12.00
    6036 *I've Got Five Dollars* ....7.00 - 10.00
    6037 *Heavenly Night* ....7.00 - 10.00
    6082 *Oh Donna Clara!* ....7.00 - 10.00
Columbia 2831-D *Let 'Em Eat Cake* ....10.00 - 15.00
    2846-D *Smoke Gets In Your Eyes* ....10.00 - 15.00
    2847-D *You're Devastating* ....10.00 - 15.00
    2859-D *What Is There To Say?* ....10.00 - 15.00
    2869-D *The Song Of Surrender* ....10.00 - 15.00
    2877-D *One Morning In May* ....10.00 - 15.00
    2882-D *I Was In The Mood* ....10.00 - 15.00
    2893-D *In A Shelter From A Shower* ....10.00 - 15.00
    2894-D *Wunder Bar* ....10.00 - 15.00
    2930-D *So Help Me* ....10.00 - 15.00
    2933-D *I'm Counting On You* ....10.00 - 15.00
    2960-D *If I Had A Million Dollars* ....10.00 - 15.00
    2961-D *When My Ship Comes In* ....10.00 - 15.00
Vocalion, most issues ....5.00 - 8.00

PAUL COLEMAN & HIS BAND:
Champion 15719 *Kansas City Kitty* ....30.00 - 50.00
    45163 *Bass Blues* ....20.00 - 30.00

COLLEGE SERENADERS:
Champion 15227 *A Tree In The Park* ....100.00 - 150.00

THE COLLEGIANS:
Broadway 1349 *Crying For The Carolines* ....7.00 - 10.00
Pathe-Actuelle 36924 *He Ain't Never Been In College*
....15.00 - 20.00
Perfect 15105 *He Ain't Never Been In College* ....15.00 - 20.00
Victor 19049 *That Red-Head Gal* ....7.00 - 10.00

COLLEGIATE JAZZERS:
Van Dyke 71811 *Singin' In The Bathtub* ....20.00 - 30.00

ARTIE COLLINS & HIS ORCHESTRA:
Broadway 1371 *It Happened In Monterey* ....7.00 - 10.00
    1375 *Red Hot and Blue Rhythm* ....10.00 - 15.00
    1376 *I Never Dreamt You'd Fall In Love With Me* ..7.00 - 10.00

ROY COLLINS' DANCE ORCHESTRA:
Banner 1181 *Maxie Jones (King Of The Saxophones)*...7.00 - 10.00
    1239 *Steamboat Sal* ....7.00 - 10.00
    1270 *Sittin' In A Corner* ....7.00 - 10.00
Challenge 914 *I Love To Ride A Camel* ....7.00 - 10.00
    933 *Papa's Mama's Blue* ....8.00 - 12.00
Domino 430 *My Dream Man* ....15.00 - 20.00
    3446 *Nobody Knows What A Red Head Mama Can Do*
....8.00 - 12.00
Jewel 5145 *Homing Bird (Headin' For Home)* ....15.00 - 20.00
Oriole 433 *My Sweet Louise* ....15.00 - 20.00
    652 *Waffles* ....7.00 - 10.00
    706 *Blowin' Off Steam* ....10.00 - 15.00
    724 *The Birth Of The Blues* ....7.00 - 10.00
    1044 *There's Always Somebody Lookin' For Somebody*
....7.00 - 10.00
    1389 *Just Today* ....7.00 - 10.00
    1459 *"Hoo" Ray, I Want To Play* ....7.00 - 10.00
    1460 *I'd Love To Go Around With You* ....7.00 - 10.00
    1488 *Shake Off The Blues* ....8.00 - 12.00
    1541 *Papa's Mama's Blue* ....8.00 - 12.00

    1549 *Why Didn't You Tell Me?* ....7.00 - 10.00
    1627 *My Rosalie* ....7.00 - 10.00
    1723 *Any Old Time Is Loving Time For Me* ....7.00 - 10.00

COLONIAL CLUB ORCHESTRA:
Brunswick 3244 *My Pal Jerry* ....8.00 - 12.00
    4058 *Where The Shy Little Violets Grow* ....10.00 - 15.00
    4281 *You're The Only One For Me* ....7.00 - 10.00
    4554 *My Man Is On The Make* ....7.00 - 10.00
    4809 *Swanee Shuffle* ....7.00 - 10.00
    4858 *Hittin' The Bottle* ....8.00 - 12.00
Brunswick, most other issues ....5.00 - 8.00

COLUMBIA ARTISTS (See also THE HAPPINESS BOYS):
Columbia (12-inch) 50038-D *Studio Stunts* ....20.00 - 30.00

COLUMBIA NOVELTY ORCHESTRA:
Columbia 131-D *Oh, Baby!* ....8.00 - 12.00

COLUMBIA PHOTO PLAYERS:
Columbia 2105-D *Mona* ....10.00 - 15.00
    2131-D *Sweepin' The Clouds Away* ....10.00 - 15.00
    2149-D *The "Free And Easy"* ....10.00 - 15.00
    2177-D *Leave It That Way* ....10.00 - 15.00
    2187-D *I'm In The Market For You* ....10.00 - 15.00
    2196-D *Dust* ....10.00 - 15.00
Columbia (most other issues) ....7.00 - 10.00

RUSS COLUMBO:
Bluebird 6503 *Time On My Hands* ....7.00 - 10.00
Brunswick 6972 *Too Beautiful For Words* ....10.00 - 15.00
Victor 22801 *I Don't Know Why (I Just Do)* ....8.00 - 12.00
    22802 *Sweet And Lovely* ....8.00 - 12.00
    22826 *Time On My Hands* ....8.00 - 12.00
    22861 *You Try Somebody Else* ....8.00 - 12.00
    22867 *Prisoner Of Love* ....8.00 - 12.00
    22903 *All Of Me* ....10.00 - 15.00
    22909 *Just Friends* ....10.00 - 15.00
    22976 *Auf Widersehen, My Dear* ....10.00 - 15.00
    24045 *Just Another Dream Of You* ....15.00 - 20.00
    24076 *As You Desire Me* ....15.00 - 20.00
    24077 *My Love* ....15.00 - 20.00
    24194 *Street Of Dreams* ....15.00 - 20.00
    24195 *Make Love The Thing* ....15.00 - 20.00

EDDIE CONDON & HIS FOOTWARMERS/ ORCHESTRA:
Brunswick 6743 *Home Cooking* ....10.00 - 15.00
Columbia (red label, most issues) ....5.00 - 8.00
Commodore (most issues) ....7.00 - 10.00
Decca (most issues) ....5.00 - 8.00
Okeh 41142 *I'm Sorry I Made You Cry* ....75.00 - 100.00

ZEZ CONFREY & HIS ORCHESTRA:
Victor 19606 *Charleston Chuckles* ....7.00 - 10.00
Victor, most other issues ....5.00 - 8.00

CONNIE'S INN ORCHESTRA:
Crown 3180 *You Rascal, You* ....40.00 - 60.00
    3194 *Sugar Foot Stomp* ....40.00 - 60.00
    3212 *Milenberg Joys* ....40.00 - 60.00
Melotone 12145 *I'm Crazy 'Bout My Baby* ....25.00 - 40.00
    12216 *The House Of David Blues* ....25.00 - 40.00
    12239 *Sugar Foot Stomp* ....25.00 - 40.00
    12340 *Goodbye Blues* ....25.00 - 40.00
Victor 22698 *Moan, You Moaners* ....15.00 - 25.00
    22721 *Singing The Blues* ....20.00 - 30.00

LOU CONNOR & HIS COLLEGIANS/COLLEGIATES/ORCHESTRA:

Jewel 5000 *I'm Looking Over A Four Leaf Clover* ...7.00 - 10.00
 5189 *Keep Sweeping The Cobwebs Off The Moon*
 ....7.00 - 10.00
Oriole 670 *How Many Times?* ....10.00 - 15.00
 1124 *My Ohio Home* ....7.00 - 10.00
 1126 *Keep Sweeping The Cobwebs Off The Moon*
 ....8.00 - 12.00
 1156 *My Melancholy Baby* ....10.00 - 15.00
 1171 *Where Will I Be?* ....10.00 - 15.00
 1172 *Moten Stomp* ....10.00 - 15.00
 1483 *Four Or Five Times* ....15.00 - 20.00

JEROME CONRAD & HIS ORCHESTRA:

Harmony 693-H *When Eliza Rolls Her Eyes* ....8.00 - 12.00
 694-H *Mississippi Mud* ....8.00 - 12.00
 698-H *Mr. Hoover And Mr. Smith* ....8.00 - 12.00
 703-H *You're Just A Great Big Baby Doll* ....10.00 - 15.00
 738-H *Etiquette Blues* ....8.00 - 12.00
 824-H *Susianna* ....8.00 - 12.00
 842-H *I Faw Down An' Go Boom!* ....8.00 - 12.00
 844-H *Wedding Bells (Are Breaking Up That Old Gang Of Mine)*
 ....10.00 - 15.00
(Note: Above titles on Diva and Velvet Tone are similarly valued.)

CONSOLIDATED CLUB ORCHESTRA:

Pathe-Actuelle 36392 *Static Strut* ....15.00 - 20.00
Perfect 14573 *Static Strut* ....15.00 - 20.00

CONWAY'S BAND:

Okeh 4208 *Ragtime In A Toy Shop* ....15.00 - 20.00
Victor 17628 *Sweetie Dear* ....10.00 - 15.00
 17850 *Ragging The Scale* ....7.00 - 10.00
 17851 *Bon Ton One-Step* ....10.00 - 15.00
 18109 *American Jubilee (A Patriotic Rag)* ....10.00 - 15.00
 35600 *The Evolution of Dixie* (12-inch) ....15.00 - 20.00

JACKIE COOGAN:

Official Boy Scout 4 *How To Spell Boy Scout* ....75.00 - 100.00

COOK & HIS DREAMLAND ORCHESTRA; COOK'S DREAMLAND ORCHESTRA; "DOC" COOK & HIS 14 DOCTORS OF SYNCOPATION:

Columbia 727-D *Spanish Mama* ....80.00 - 120.00
 813-D *High Fever* ....75.00 - 100.00
 862-D *Sidewalk Blues* ....50.00 - 80.00
 1070-D *Willie The Weeper* ....75.00 - 100.00
 1298-D *Alligator Crawl* ....75.00 - 100.00
 1430-D *Hum And Strum* ....75.00 - 100.00
Gennett 5360 *So This Is Venice* ....75.00 - 100.00
 5373 *Moanful Man* ....75.00 - 100.00
 5374 *Scissor Grinder Joe* ....80.00 - 120.00
Silvertone 4044 *Scissor Grinder Joe* ....75.00 - 100.00
 4045 *Moanful Man* ....75.00 - 100.00

COOKIE'S GINGERSNAPS:

Okeh 8369 *High Fever* ....200.00 - 300.00
 8390 *Messin' Around* ....150.00 - 250.00
 40675 *Love Found You For Me* ....200.00 - 300.00

PRESIDENT CALVIN COOLIDGE:

Victor 35835 (12-inch) *Pres. Coolidge Welcomes Colonel Lindbergh* ....15.00 - 20.00

COON-SANDERS (ORIGINAL NIGHTHAWK) ORCHESTRA:

Columbia A3403 *Some Little Bird* ....7.00 - 10.00
Victor 19316 *Night Hawk Blues* ....15.00 - 20.00
 19325 *Oriental Love Dreams* ....7.00 - 10.00
 19357 *There's No-One Just Like You* ....8.00 - 12.00
 19522 *Lazy Waters* ....5.00 - 8.00
 19525 *Moonlight And You* ....8.00 - 12.00
 19600 *Some Of These Days* ....15.00 - 20.00
 19727 *I'm Gonna Charleston Back To Charleston*
 ....10.00 - 15.00
 19728 *Alone At Last* ....8.00 - 12.00
 19745 *Yes Sir! That's My Baby* ....8.00 - 12.00
 19750 *That's All There Is-There Ain't No More* .....10.00 - 15.00
 19754 *Who Wouldn't Love You?* ....10.00 - 15.00
 19804 *Dreaming Of To-morrow* ....8.00 - 12.00
 19852 *I Can't Realize* ....15.00 - 20.00
 19922 *Flamin' Mamie* ....10.00 - 15.00
 19958 *Louise, You Tease* ....25.00 - 35.00
 19979 *Moon Deer* ....7.00 - 10.00
 20003 *Everything's Gonna Be All Right* ....8.00 - 12.00
 20015 *Sittin' Around* ....10.00 - 15.00
 20081 *Deep Henderson* ....10.00 - 15.00
 20390 *Brainstorm* ....10.00 - 15.00
 20408 *I Need Lovin'* ....15.00 - 20.00
 20461 *High Fever* ....40.00 - 60.00
 20785 *I Ain't Got Nobody* ....10.00 - 15.00
 21148 *Is She My Girl Friend?* ....10.00 - 15.00
 21258 *Stay Out Of The South* ....10.00 - 15.00
 21305 *The Wail* ....20.00 - 30.00
 21397 *Hallucinations* ....15.00 - 25.00
 21501 *Oh! You Have No Idea* ....10.00 - 15.00
 21546 *Too Busy!* ....10.00 - 15.00
 21562 *Indian Cradle Song* ....7.00 - 10.00
 21680 *Blazin'* ....15.00 - 20.00
 21803 *What A Girl! What A Night!* .....10.00 - 15.00
 21812 *Here Comes My Ball And Chain* ....15.00 - 20.00
 21891 *Rhythm King* ....10.00 - 15.00
 21895 *Little Orphan Annie* ....10.00 - 15.00
 21939 *Kansas City Kitty* ....10.00 - 15.00
 22077 *And Especially You!* ....15.00 - 20.00
 22089 *The Flippety Flop* ....15.00 - 20.00
 22123 *Gotta Great Big Date With A Little Bitta Girl*
 ....8.00 - 12.00
 22262 *Alone In The Rain* ....7.00 - 10.00
 22278 *Moanin' For You* ....15.00 - 25.00
 22300 *Harlem Madness* ....15.00 - 20.00
 22304 *We Love Us* ....10.00 - 15.00
 22342 *After You've Gone* ....15.00 - 20.00
 22346 *Sweepin' The Clouds Away* ....10.00 - 15.00
 22950 *Let That Be A Lesson To You* .....10.00 - 15.00
 22951 *Sing A New Song* ....10.00 - 15.00
 22969 *Keepin' Out Of Mischief Now* .....20.00 - 30.00
 22972 *I Want To Go Home* ....10.00 - 15.00
 22979 *On Revival Day* ....20.00 - 30.00
 V38083 *Louder And Funnier* ....40.00 - 60.00

AL COOPER & HIS (ORIGINAL) SAVOY SULTANS:

Decca 2526 *Jumpin' At The Savoy* ....7.00 - 10.00
   2608 *Stitches* ....7.00 - 10.00
   2819 *Love Gave Me You* ....7.00 - 10.00
   2930 *Jumpin' The Blues* ....7.00 - 10.00
   3142 *Frenzy* ....7.00 - 10.00
   3274 *Sophisticated Jump* ....7.00 - 10.00
   7499 *Rhythm Doctor Man* ....7.00 - 10.00
   7525 *Gettin' In The Groove* ....7.00 - 10.00
   7549 *Looney* ....7.00 - 10.00
   8540 *Norfolk Ferry* ....7.00 - 10.00
   8545 *Second Balcony Jump* ....7.00 - 10.00
   8598 *Fish For Your Supper* ....7.00 - 10.00
   8615 *'At's In There* ....7.00 - 10.00

ROBERT COOPER:

Bluebird 5459 *West Dallas Drag* ....50.00 - 75.00
   5947 *West Dallas Drag-No. 2* ....50.00 - 75.00

ANDREW COPELAND:

Black Swan 14124 *Buzz Mirandy* ....50.00 - 75.00
Paramount 12139 *Down In Dixieland* ....50.00 - 75.00

PAUL CORNELIUS & HIS ORCHESTRA:

Champion 16282 *Ho Hum!* ....15.00 - 30.00
   16523 *Say It Isn't So* ....30.00 - 50.00
   16534 *Sentimental Gentleman From Georgia*..150.00 - 200.00
   16572 *The Scat Song* ....100.00 - 150.00
   16593 *Bubbling Over With Love* ....30.00 - 50.00
   16727 *Smoke Gets In Your Eyes* ....30.00 - 50.00
   16734 *I'm Still Dreaming Of You* ....100.00 - 150.00
   16746 *Cinderella's Fella* ....50.00 - 75.00
   16749 *Rhymes* ....50.00 - 75.00
   40084 *I've Found A New Baby* ....30.00 - 50.00

CORNELL & HIS ORCHESTRA:

Okeh 41386 *Accordion Joe* ....30.00 - 50.00
   41395 *I Was Made To Love You* ....20.00 - 30.00

FRANK CORNWELL & HIS ORCHESTRA:

Cameo 1056 *Have You Forgotten* ....7.00 - 10.00
Edison 52166 *Dawn* ....30.00 - 50.00
Harmony 320-H *Here Or There* ....7.00 - 10.00
   333-H *Schultz Is Back Again* ....8.00 - 12.00
   341-H *Voom Voom* ....8.00 - 12.00
   378-H *Roses For Remembrance* ....8.00 - 12.00
Silvertone 3302 *Crazy Words-Crazy Tune* ....8.00 - 12.00
(Note: Above titles on Velvet Tone are similarly valued.)

(CHARLES) CORRELL AND (FREEMAN) GOSDEN (AS SAM 'N' HENRY; AMOS 'N' ANDY):

Rexall-(12-inch) *The Lord's Prayer* (explained by Amos)/*Silent Night* (introduced by Correll and Gosden) ....15.00 - 20.00
Top Ten Album #1 *The Amos 'n' Andy Album* (set of four records in album) ....25.00 - 40.00
Victor 20032, 20093, 20375, 20788 ....7.00 - 10.00
Victor 21608 *Presidential Election* ....10.00 - 15.00
   22119 *Is Everybody In Your Family Dumb As You Is?* ....10.00 - 15.00
   22234 *At The Bullfight* ....10.00 - 15.00
   22393 *Check And Double Check* ....15.00 - 20.00

COTTON CLUB ORCHESTRA:

Columbia 287-D *Down And Out Blues* ....75.00 - 100.00
   374-D *Riverboat Shuffle* ....100.00 - 150.00
   14113-D *Everybody Stomp* ....80.00 - 120.00

THE COTTON PICKERS:

Brunswick 2292 *Hot Lips* ....15.00 - 20.00
   2338 *Got To Cool My Doggies Now* ....8.00 - 12.00
   2380 *Great White Way Blues* ....10.00 - 15.00
   2382 *Loose Feet* ....15.00 - 20.00
   2404 *You Tell Her, I Stutter* ....10.00 - 15.00
   2418 *Snakes' Hips* ....10.00 - 15.00
   2436 *Down By The River* ....10.00 - 15.00
   2461 *Duck's Quack* ....10.00 - 15.00
   2486 *Back O' Town Blues* ....10.00 - 20.00
   2490 *Walk, Jenny, Walk* ....10.00 - 15.00
   2507 *Just Hot* ....15.00 - 20.00
   2532 *Do Yo' Dooty, Daddy* ....15.00 - 20.00
   2766 *Jimtown Blues* ....15.00 - 20.00
   2818 *Mishawaka Blues* ....15.00 - 20.00
   2879 *Down And Out Blues* ....15.00 - 20.00
   2937 *Milenberg Joys* ....15.00 - 20.00
   2981 *Stomp Off-Let's Go* ....15.00 - 20.00
   3001 *Fallin' Down* ....15.00 - 20.00
   4325 *Rampart Street Blues* ....15.00 - 20.00
   4404 *Sweet Ida Joy* ....15.00 - 20.00
   4440 *St. Louis Gal* ....15.00 - 20.00
   4446 *Moanin' Low* ....10.00 - 15.00
   4447 *Shoo Shoo Boogie Boo* ....15.00 - 20.00
Cameo 9048 *St. Louis Blues* ....15.00 - 20.00
   9174 *Dirty Dog* ....20.00 - 30.00
   9195 *Tiger Rag* ....20.00 - 30.00
   9207 *Hot Heels* ....15.00 - 20.00
Gennett 6380 *What'll You Do?* ....50.00 - 75.00
   6396 *After Awhile* ....50.00 - 75.00
Lincoln 3077 *Railroad Man* ....15.00 - 20.00
   3201 *Dirty Dog* ....20.00 - 30.00
   3222 *Tiger Rag* ....20.00 - 30.00
   3234 *Some Of These Days* ....15.00 - 20.00
Romeo 852 *Railroad Man* ....15.00 - 20.00
   976 *Dirty Dog* ....20.00 - 30.00
   997 *Tiger Rag* ....20.00 - 30.00
   1009 *Some Of These Days* ....15.00 - 20.00
Vocalion 3263 *Woe Is Me* ....7.00 - 10.00

THE COTTON PICKERS ORCHESTRA:

Madison 1649 *Just Blues* ....8.00 - 12.00
   1653 *Geraldine* ....10.00 - 15.00

WALLIE COULTER & HIS BAND:

Gennett 6369 *Hollywood Shuffle* ....200.00 - 300.00

DEL COURTNEY AND HIS ORCHESTRA:

Vocalion 4850, 4864, 4985, 4992, 5046, 5061, 5088, 5127, 5212, 5279, 5291, 5306, 5332, 5354, 5608, 5616...5.00 - 8.00

LYNN COWAN & HIS BOULEVARD THEATRE ORCHESTRA:

Romeo 358 *Ain't She Sweet?* ....8.00 - 12.00
Romeo, most other issues ....5.00 - 8.00

IDA COX (Accompanied by LOVIE AUSTIN'S BLUES SERENADERS; HER FIVE BLUE SPELLS, et al.):

Paramount 12022 *Come Right In* ....50.00 - 75.00
   12044 *Weary Way Blues* ....80.00 - 120.00
   12045 *Bama Bound Blues* ....50.00 - 75.00
   12053 *Blue Monday Blues* ....50.00 - 75.00
   12056 *Chicago Bound Blues* ....50.00 - 75.00
   12063 *I've Got The Blues For Rampart Street* ..80.00 - 120.00

12064 *Moanin' Groanin' Blues*	100.00	-	150.00
12085 *Worried Mama Blues*	100.00	-	150.00
12086 *Confidential Blues*	100.00	-	150.00
12087 *Mail Man Blues*	100.00	-	150.00
12094 *Down The Road Bound Blues*	50.00	-	75.00
12097 *Mean Papa, Turn Your Key*	100.00	-	150.00
12202 *Chicago Monkey Man Blues*	100.00	-	150.00
12212 *Last Time Blues*	100.00	-	150.00
12220 *Kentucky Man Blues*	125.00	-	175.00
12228 *Cherry Picking Blues*	125.00	-	175.00
12237 *Worried In Mind Blues*	125.00	-	175.00
12251 *Mississippi River Blues*	80.00	-	120.00
12258 *Misery Blues*	80.00	-	120.00
12263 *Georgia Bound Blues*	80.00	-	120.00
12275 *Mister Man*	80.00	-	120.00
12282 *Someday Blues*	100.00	-	150.00
12291 *Black Crepe Blues*	100.00	-	150.00
12298 *Southern Woman's Blues*	100.00	-	150.00
12307 *Lonesome Blues*	100.00	-	150.00
12318 *Coffin Blues*	100.00	-	150.00
12325 *One Time Woman Blues*	100.00	-	150.00
12334 *I Ain't Got Nobody*	100.00	-	150.00
12344 *Trouble Trouble Blues*	100.00	-	150.00
12353 *Night And Day Blues*	100.00	-	150.00
12381 *Don't Blame Me*	150.00	-	250.00
12488 *'Fore Day Creep*	100.00	-	150.00
12502 *Mercy Blues*	100.00	-	150.00
12513 *Pleading Blues*	100.00	-	150.00
12540 *Mojo Hand Blues*	100.00	-	150.00
12556 *Seven Day Blues*	100.00	-	150.00
12582 *Midnight Hour Blues*	100.00	-	150.00
12664 *Bone Orchard Blues*	150.00	-	200.00
12667 *Broadcasting Blues*	150.00	-	200.00
12690 *Fogyism*	150.00	-	200.00
12727 *Separated Blues*	150.00	-	250.00
12965 *Jail House Blues*	200.00	-	300.00
Vocalion 05258 *Pink Slip Blues*	15.00	-	20.00
05298 *Hard Times Blues*	15.00	-	20.00
05336 *Death Letter Blues*	15.00	-	20.00

DICK COY & HIS RACKETEERS:

Champion 15958 *Barnacle Bill, The Sailor*	15.00	-	25.00
15977 *'Leven-Thirty Saturday Night*	15.00	-	25.00
40069 *Barnacle Bill The Sailor*	15.00	-	20.00
Gennett 7175 *'Leven-Thirty Saturday Night*	20.00	-	30.00
Supertone 9692 *Barnacle Bill The Sailor*	15.00	-	20.00

FRANCIS CRAIG & HIS ORCHESTRA:

Bullet (most issues)	5.00	-	8.00
Columbia 495-D *Mighty Lak A Rose*	8.00	-	12.00
567-D *Steady Roll Blues*	30.00	-	50.00
709-D *Hard-To-Get Gertie*	15.00	-	20.00
1266-D *That Florida Low Down*	20.00	-	30.00
1440-D *All Day Long*	10.00	-	15.00
1544-D *Coon-Tail*	15.00	-	20.00

JACK CRAWFORD & HIS BOYS/ORCHESTRA:

Champion 15383 *Down South*	25.00	-	40.00
15384 *The Best Things In Life Are Free*	25.00	-	40.00
15400 *Together We Two*	20.00	-	30.00
15404 *For My Baby*	20.00	-	30.00
15418 *One More Night*	15.00	-	20.00
15422 *Beautiful*	25.00	-	35.00
15439 *Dear On A Night Like This*	15.00	-	20.00
Victor 20847 *Who's That Pretty Baby?*	10.00	-	15.00
20901 *I'd Walk A Million Miles*	8.00	-	12.00

20994 *Baltimore*	15.00	-	20.00
21173 *Kiss And Make Up*	10.00	-	15.00
21217 *Beautiful*	10.00	-	15.00

WILTON CRAWLEY (& HIS ORCHESTRA/THE WASHBOARD RHYTHM KINGS):

Bluebird 5827 *She's Got What I Need*	15.00	-	20.00
Okeh 8479 *Crawley Blues*	50.00	-	80.00
8492 *Geechie River Blues*	50.00	-	80.00
8539 *Love Will Drive Me Crazy*	50.00	-	80.00
8555 *She's Nothing But Nice*	50.00	-	80.00
8589 *I'm Forever Changing Sweetheart*	50.00	-	80.00
8619 *Shadow Of The Blues*	50.00	-	80.00
8718 *My Perfect Thrill*	50.00	-	80.00
Victor 23292 *Big Time Woman*	300.00	-	up
23344 *New Crawley Blues*	300.00	-	up
V-38094 *Snake Hip Dance*	100.00	-	150.00
V-38116 *She's Got What I Need*	150.00	-	200.00
V-38136 *You Oughta See My Gal*	150.00	-	200.00

WILLIE CREAGER & HIS ORCHESTRA/ENTERTAINERS/RHYTHM ACES:

Banner 6226 *Cryin' Blues*	10.00	-	15.00
6263 *Wide Open Gate*	8.00	-	12.00
6285 *Pepper Pot*	10.00	-	15.00
6484 *Sweet Tootsies*	7.00	-	10.00
6501 *Contrary Mary*	7.00	-	10.00
Banner, most other issues	5.00	-	8.00
Gennett 3380 *I Never Knew What The Moonlight Could Do*	50.00	-	80.00
3405 *Hello Bluebird*	30.00	-	50.00
(most other 3000 series)	7.00	-	10.00
5577 *Doodle Doo Doo*	15.00	-	20.00
5663 *Show Me The Way*	40.00	-	60.00
(most other 5000 series)	5.00	-	10.00
6083 *The Doll Dance*	25.00	-	40.00
(most other 6000 series)	7.00	-	12.00
Pathe-Actuelle, most issues	5.00	-	8.00
Perfect, most issues	5.00	-	8.00
Regal, most issues	5.00	-	8.00
Romeo, most issues	5.00	-	8.00

CHAS. CREATH'S JAZZ-O-MANIACS:

Okeh 8201 *Pleasure Mad*	100.00	-	150.00
8210 *King Porter Stomp*	150.00	-	250.00
8217 *My Daddy Rocks Me*	150.00	-	250.00
8257 *Grandpa's Spell*	150.00	-	250.00
8280 *Market Street Stomp*	150.00	-	250.00
8477 *Crazy Quilt*	150.00	-	250.00

CRESCENT CITY RED JACKETS:

Champion 15049 *Paddlin' Madelin' Home*	15.00	-	20.00
15269 *I'm On My Merry Way*	15.00	-	20.00
15270 *Beneath The Stars With You*	10.00	-	15.00

CRESCENT MADISON DANCE ORCHESTRA:
Grey Gull 1590 *Talk About Heaven* ....8.00 - 12.00

BING CROSBY:
Bluebird 7102, 7118 ....7.00 - 10.00
Brunswick 6090 *Out Of Nowhere* ....10.00 - 15.00
    6120 *Were You Sincere?*.............................10.00 - 15.00
    6140 *At Your Command*..............................10.00 - 15.00
    6169 *Star Dust* ....10.00 - 15.00
    6179 *I Apologize* ....10.00 - 15.00
    6200 *Now That You're Gone* ....10.00 - 15.00
    6203 *Goodnight Sweetheart* ....8.00 - 12.00
    6226 *Where The Blue Of The Night*............10.00 - 15.00
    6240 *Can't We Talk It Over?* ....10.00 - 15.00
    6248 *I Found You* ....10.00 - 15.00
    6259 *How Long Will It Last?* ....10.00 - 15.00
    6268 *Love, You Funny Thing* ....10.00 - 15.00
    6276 *Shadows On The Window* ....10.00 - 15.00
    6285 *Paradise* ....10.00 - 15.00
    6306 *Lazy Day* ....10.00 - 15.00
    6320 *Sweet Georgia Brown* ....15.00 - 20.00
    6329 *Cabin In The Cotton* ....10.00 - 15.00
    6351 *Some Of These Days* ....15.00 - 20.00
    6394 *Please* ....10.00 - 15.00
    6406 *Here Lies Love*...............................10.00 - 15.00
    6414 *Brother, Can You Spare A Dime?*.............15.00 - 20.00
    6427 *I'll Follow You* ....10.00 - 15.00
    6454 *Just An Echo In The Valley* ....8.00 - 12.00
    6464 *Street Of Dreams* ....10.00 - 15.00
    6472 *Young And Healthy* ....10.00 - 15.00
    6477 *You're Beautiful Tonight, My Dear* ....10.00 - 15.00
    6480 *Try A Little Tenderness* ....10.00 - 15.00
    6485 *Shine* ....10.00 - 15.00
    6491 *You've Got Me Crying Again* ....10.00 - 15.00
    6525 *Someone Stoled Gabriel's Horn* ....15.00 - 20.00
    6594 *Learn To Croon* ....8.00 - 12.00
    6599 *I've Got To Sing A Torch Song* ....8.00 - 12.00
    6601 *Down The Old Ox Road* ....8.00 - 12.00
    6610 *There's A Cabin In The Pines* ....8.00 - 12.00
    6623 *I Would If I Could But I Can't* ....8.00 - 12.00
    6643 *Black Moonlight*...............................8.00 - 12.00
    6644 *The Day You Came Along* ....10.00 - 15.00
    6663 *Home On The Range*.......................7.00 - 10.00
    6694 *Beautiful Girl* ....7.00 - 10.00
    6695 *Temptation* ....7.00 - 10.00
    6696 *Our Big Love Scene* ....7.00 - 10.00
    6724 *Did You Ever See A Dream Walking?* ....10.00 - 15.00
    6794 *Little Dutch Mill* ....7.00 - 10.00
    6852 *Love Thy Neighbor* ....7.00 - 10.00
    6853 *She Reminds Me Of You* ....7.00 - 10.00
    6854 *One In A Blue Moon* ....7.00 - 10.00
    6936 *Straight From The Shoulder* ....7.00 - 10.00
    6953 *Give Me A Heart To Sing To* ....7.00 - 10.00
(Note: Many of the foregoing titles were issued contemporaneously and/or reissued within several years of initial release on Banner, Brunswick, Conqueror, Melotone, Oriole, Perfect and Romeo.)
Brunswick 20105 (12-inch) *St. Louis Blues* ....15.00 - 20.00
    20109 (12-inch) *Lawd, You Made The Night Too Long*
    ....20.00 - 30.00
Columbia 1773-D *My Kinda Love*..........................15.00 - 25.00
    1851-D *I Kiss Your Hand, Madame* ....15.00 - 20.00
    2001-D *Can't We Be Friends?* ....15.00 - 20.00
Decca 100 *I Love You Truly* ....8.00 - 12.00
    101 *Let Me Call You Sweetheart* ....10.00 - 15.00

    179 *The Very Thought Of You* ....10.00 - 15.00
    245 *Two Cigarettes In The Dark* ....10.00 - 15.00
    309 *With Every Breath I Take*...............10.00 - 15.00
    310 *June In January*.........................10.00 - 15.00
    391 *It's Easy To Remember* ....8.00 - 12.00
    392 *Down By The River* ....8.00 - 12.00
    543 *I Wished On The Moon* ....8.00 - 12.00
    547 *From The Top Of Your Head* ....8.00 - 12.00
    548 *Takes Two To Make A Bargain*.................8.00 - 12.00
    616 *Red Sails In The Sunset* ....5.00 - 8.00
    617 *On Treasure Island*....................5.00 - 8.00
    621 *Adeste Fidelis* ....5.00 - 8.00
    631 *Sailor, Beware*........................7.00 - 10.00
    756 *Lovely Lady* ....7.00 - 10.00
    757 *The Touch Of Your Lips* ....7.00 - 10.00
    791 *Robins And Roses*....................7.00 - 10.00
    806 *I Got Plenty O'Nuttin'* ....8.00 - 12.00
    870 *Empty Saddles* ....7.00 - 10.00
    871 *I Can't Seem To Escape From You*.............8.00 - 12.00
    905 *The House Jack Built For Jill* ....8.00 - 12.00
Decca, most other issues on Blue Label Decca ....4.00 - 7.00
Victor 22701 *Wrap Your Troubles In Dreams* ....10.00 - 15.00
(Note: Recordings on which Bing makes mistakes and curses, such as "Blue Serenade" and "Wrap Your Troubles In Dreams" were widely, although illegally, distributed, and are not valuable rarities as some would assume.)

BOB CROSBY (& HIS BOB CATS/ORCHESTRA):
Coral (most issues) ....5.00 - 8.00
Decca 112 *It's My Night To Howl* ....15.00 - 20.00
    363 *Blue Moon* ....8.00 - 12.00
    472 *Kiss Me Goodnight* ....8.00 - 12.00
    478 *The Dixieland Band* ....8.00 - 12.00
    479 *Beale Street Blues* ....8.00 - 12.00
    502 *And Then Some* ....8.00 - 12.00
    508 *I'm In The Mood For Love*............8.00 - 12.00
    544 *Tender Is The Night* ....7.00 - 10.00
    614 *On Treasure Island* ....7.00 - 10.00
    615 *I Found A Dream* ....7.00 - 10.00
    629 *A Little Bit Independent* ....8.00 - 12.00
    633 *Eeny Meeny Miney Mo*.............8.00 - 12.00
    727 *What's The Name Of That Song?*.................8.00 - 12.00
    728 *I Don't Want To Make History* ....8.00 - 12.00
    753 *Christopher Columbus* ....8.00 - 12.00
    759 *You're Toots To Me* ....8.00 - 12.00
    841 *Big Chief De Soto* ....8.00 - 12.00
    836, 896, 903, 930, 1094, 1170, 1196, 1346, 1370,
      1539, 1552, 1555, 1556, 1566, 1576, 1580,
      1593and most subsequent issues....................7.00 - 10.00

CROSSTOWN RAMBLERS:
Champion 15030 *River Bottom Glide* ....75.00 - 125.00
    15039 *Nellie, Where You Goin'?* ....75.00 - 125.00

FRANK CRUM & HIS ORCHESTRA:
Edison 51474 *Lonely And Blue* ....20.00 - 30.00

CUBAN DANCE PLAYERS:
Challenge 210 *I'll Fly To Hawaii* ....40.00 - 60.00

BERNIE CUMMINS & HIS (BILTMORE/HOTEL NEW YORKER/TOADSTOOL) ORCHESTRA:
Brunswick 3722 *Where The Cot-Cot-Cotton Grows*10.00 - 15.00
    3772 *Lonely Melody* ....8.00 - 12.00
    3916 *Sugar Babe, I'm Leavin'!*..........................10.00 - 15.00

3952 *Out-O'-Town Gal*..........................10.00 - 15.00
3980 *Old Man Sunshine*.........................8.00 - 12.00
4083 *My Blackbirds Are Bluebirds Now* ....10.00 - 15.00
Brunswick, other issues ....7.00 - 10.00
Columbia 2827-D *You've Got Everything*..............10.00 - 15.00
2828-D *I'm Dancin' On A Rainbow*..................10.00 - 15.00
2830-D *That Co-Ed Party* ....10.00 - 15.00
2838-D *In A One-Room Flat* ....10.00 - 15.00
2844-D *I Guess It Had To Be That Way*............12.00 - 16.00
2848-D *Our Big Love Scene* ....15.00 - 20.00
2874-D *Alice From Dallas* ....15.00 - 20.00
Gennett 5395 *Home Folks Blues* ....30.00 - 50.00
5466 *St. Louis Blues* ....30.00 - 50.00
5468 *Jiminy Gee* ....20.00 - 30.00
5546 *Keep On Dancing* ....20.00 - 30.00
5555 *That's Georgia* ....20.00 - 30.00
5641 *Poplar Street Blues* ....30.00 - 50.00
Victor 22088 *Little By Little* ....8.00 - 12.00
22110 *Don't Hang Your Dreams On A Rainbow* .7.00 - 10.00
22295 *Cooking Breakfast For The One I Love*.....8.00 - 12.00
22331 *Lucky Little Devil*...........................8.00 - 12.00
22355 *Minnie The Mermaid* ....8.00 - 12.00
22408 *Tellin' It To The Daisies* ....8.00 - 12.00
22409 *Livin' In The Sunlight-Lovin' In The Moonlight*
....8.00 - 12.00
22525 *In My Heart It's You*........................8.00 - 12.00
24053 *Deep Sea Low Down*.........................15.00 - 20.00
Victor, other issues ....5.00 - 10.00
Vocalion 4181 *Basin Street Blues* ....8.00 - 12.00

JOE CURRAN & HIS ORCHESTRA:
Parlophone PNY-34012 *Thank Your Father* ....25.00 - 40.00
PNY-34018 *Sing (A Happy Little Thing)* ....25.00 - 40.00
PNY-41231 *Louise* ....50.00 - 75.00
PNY-41232 *That's A Plenty* ....50.00 - 75.00
PNY-41254 *Hittin' The Ceilin'* ....30.00 - 50.00
PNY-41282 *Just You-Just Me* ....30.00 - 50.00
PNY-41301 *Love Ain't Nothin' But The Blues*...50.00 - 75.00
PNY-41310 *Sophomore Prom*.........................40.00 - 60.00
PNY-41313 *Turn On The Heat*.........................50.00 - 75.00

(FORD) DABNEY'S BAND/(SYNCOPATED) (NOVELTY) ORCHESTRA:
Aeolian-Vocalion 1204 *The Darktown Strutters' Ball*
....40.00 - 60.00
1218 *That's It*......................................40.00 - 60.00
1243 *Sally Trombone* ....20.00 - 30.00
12017 *Slidin' Sid*...................................30.00 - 50.00
12066 *Swinging Along* ....30.00 - 50.00
12068 *Just Blue* ....15.00 - 20.00
12097 *Indigo Blues*.................................75.00 - 100.00
12101 *Johnny's In Town*............................30.00 - 50.00
12105 *Rainy Day Blues* ....30.00 - 50.00
12119 *Lassus Trombone* ....15.00 - 30.00
12126 *Missouri Blues* ....50.00 - 80.00
12179 *Squealing Pig Blues* ....50.00 - 80.00
12195 *Slow Drag Blues* ....50.00 - 75.00
12211 *Florida Blues*................................50.00 - 75.00
12217 *The Dancing Deacon* ....50.00 - 75.00
12229 *I Ain't Gonna Give Nobody None Of This Jelly-Roll*
....40.00 - 60.00
12245 *Blues My Naughty Sweetie Gives To Me* .40.00 - 60.00
12246 *Camp Meeting Blues*.........................40.00 - 60.00
36002 *Cheer Up, Liza* ....40.00 - 60.00

36202 *I'm Sorry I Made You Cry* ....40.00 - 60.00
36205 *Mr. Sousa's Yankee Band* ....50.00 - 80.00
Banner 1061 *Sweet Man O'mine* ....20.00 - 40.00
Paramount 20120 *Doo Dah Blues* ....20.00 - 40.00
20125 *Bugle Call Blues* ....20.00 - 40.00
Puritan 11125 *Bugle Call Blues* ....20.00 - 40.00
Triangle 11124 *Bugle Call Blues* ....20.00 - 40.00

FRANK DAILEY'S MEADOWBROOKS/ORCHESTRA/ MEADOWBROOK ORCHESTRA:
Bell 345 *Suite Sixteen* ....8.00 - 12.00
349 *Save Your Sorrow* ....8.00 - 12.00
485 *Blue Skies* ....7.00 - 10.00
497 *My Regular Gal* ....10.00 - 15.00
Bell, most other issues ....5.00 - 8.00
Bluebird, most issues ....4.00 - 8.00
Emerson 3117 *Blue Skies* ....7.00 - 10.00
3127 *My Regular Gal*..............................10.00 - 15.00
Emerson, most other issues.........................5.00 - 8.00
Okeh 40774 *There's Everything Nice About You* ....8.00 - 12.00
Variety, most issues ....7.00 - 12.00
Vocalion, most issues................................7.00 - 10.00

DALLAS JAMBOREE JUG BAND (See also CARL DAVIS):
Vocalion 03092 *Dusting The Frets*......................100.00 - 150.00

JACK DALTON & THE 7 BLUE BABIES:
Edison (thin) 14011 *The Whoopee-Hat Brigade* ....50.00 - 80.00
14030 *I'm Cuckoo Again* ....50.00 - 80.00
14047 *My Wife Is On A Diet* ....75.00 - 100.00
14066 *If I Give Up The Saxophone* ....50.00 - 80.00
14081 *Collegiate Sam* ....80.00 - 120.00
52508 *I Love To Bumpity Bump On A Bumpy Road With You*
....50.00 - 80.00
52516 *Where Did You Get That Name* ....40.00 - 60.00
52528 *Outside* ....50.00 - 80.00
52556 *If I Give Up The Saxophone*...................50.00 - 80.00
52583 *She's A Good Girl* ....50.00 - 80.00
52621 *I Don't Work For A Living*......................50.00 - 80.00

THE DANCING CHAMPIONS:
Champion 15183 *Don't Take That Black Bottom Away*
....30.00 - 50.00
15184 *I Still Believe In You* ....10.00 - 15.00
15185 *A Little Music In The Moonlight*............10.00 - 15.00

THE DANCING STEVEDORES:
Silvertone 3054 *Panama* ....20.00 - 30.00
3056 *Stretch It, Boy*................................20.00 - 30.00

PUTNEY DANDRIDGE & HIS ORCHESTRA:
Vocalion 2935 *You're A Heavenly Thing* ....10.00 - 15.00
2982 *Chasing Shadows* ....10.00 - 15.00
3006 *Isn't This A Lovely Day?*.......................10.00 - 15.00
3007 *I'm In The Mood For Love* ....10.00 - 15.00
3024 *Nagasaki* ....10.00 - 15.00
3082 *Double Trouble* ....10.00 - 15.00
3083 *Eeny Meeny Miney Mo*........................10.00 - 15.00
3122 *A Little Bit Independent* ....8.00 - 12.00
3123 *You Took My Breath Away* ....8.00 - 12.00
3189 *Dinner For One, Please James* ....8.00 - 12.00
3190 *Honeysuckle Rose* ....10.00 - 15.00
3252 *It's A Sin To Tell A Lie*.........................10.00 - 15.00
3269 *Ol' Man River* ....10.00 - 15.00

3277 *These Foolish Things* ....8.00 - 12.00
3287 *Mary Had A Little Lamb* ....8.00 - 12.00
3291 *Here Comes Your Pappy* ....8.00 - 12.00
3304 *You Turned The Tables On Me* ....8.00 - 12.00
3315 *It's The Gypsy In Me* ....8.00 - 12.00
3351 *You Do The Darndest Things, Baby* ....8.00 - 12.00
3352 *The Skeleton In The Closet* ....8.00 - 12.00
3399 *I'm In A Dancing Mood* ....8.00 - 12.00
3409 *Gee! But You're Swell* ....8.00 - 12.00

JACK DANFORD AND HIS BEN FRANKLIN HOTEL ORCHESTRA:
Phonograph Recording Co. of San Francisco (unnumbered)
　Alabama Stomp ....100.00 - up

DOT DARE (See also ANNETTE HANSHAW, GAY ELLIS):
Harmony 792-H *I Wanna Be Loved By You* ....15.00 - 20.00
　829-H *I Faw Down An' Go Boom!* ....15.00 - 20.00
(Note: **DOT DARE** and **GAY ELLIS** are pseudonyms for **ANNETTE HANSHAW**. These titles, and others which may be found in the other listings referred to, were issued on Harmony, Diva, and Velvet Tone under one or more of these names.)

DOC DAUGHERTY & HIS ORCHESTRA:
Victor 23040 *She's A Gorgeous Thing!* ....25.00 - 40.00
　V-40111 *Ninety In The Shade* ....50.00 - 75.00
　V-40119 *Baby Girl* ....50.00 - 75.00

DAVE'S HARLEM HIGHLIGHTS:
Timely Tunes 1576 *Rockin' Chair* ....75.00 - 100.00
　1577 *Loveless Love* ....75.00 - 100.00
　1587 *Somebody Stole My Gal* ....75.00 - 100.00
　1588 *St. Louis Blues* ....75.00 - 100.00

CHARLES (COW COW) DAVENPORT; CHARLIE DAVENPORT:
Broadway 5046 *Chimes Blues* ....125.00 - 175.00
Gennett 6829 *Givin' It Away* ....200.00 - 300.00
　6838 *Chimes Blues* ....200.00 - 300.00
　6869 *Atlanta Rag* ....200.00 - 300.00
　6994 *He Don't Mean Me No Harm* ....200.00 - 300.00
Paramount 12439 *Jim Crow Blues* ....200.00 - 300.00
　12452 *Stealin' Blues* ....200.00 - 300.00
Supertone 9517 *Atlanta Rag* ....125.00 - 175.00
Vocalion 1198 *Cow Cow Blues* ....100.00 - 150.00
　1227 *Alabama Mistreater* ....150.00 - 200.00
　1253 *Chimin' The Blues* ....150.00 - 200.00
　1282 *Back In The Alley* ....150.00 - 200.00
　1291 *Texas Shout* ....150.00 - 200.00
　1434 *Mama Don't Allow No Easy Riders* ....150.00 - 200.00

(COW COW) DAVENPORT AND (IVA/IVY) SMITH:
Gennett 7231 *Alabammy Mistreated* ....200.00 - 300.00
　7275 *Now She Gives It Away* ....300.00 - up

Superior 2763 *Alabammy Mistreated* ....200.00 - 300.00
Vocalion 1253 *Alabama Strut* ....150.00 - 200.00

COW COW DAVENPORT AND SAM THEARD:
Vocalion 1408 *That'll Get It* ....150.00 - 200.00

JED DAVENPORT (& HIS BEALE STREET JUG BAND):
Vocalion 1440 *How Long How Long Blues* ....150.00 - 200.00
　1478 *The Dirty Dozen* ....250.00 - up
　1504 *Jug Blues* ....250.00 - up
　1513 *Save Me Some* ....250.00 - up

JACK DAVIDSON & HIS ORCHESTRA:
Champion 15819 *Tip-Toe Thru' The Tulips With Me*
　..10.00 - 15.00

JACK DAVIES & HIS KENTUCKIANS:
Champion 16607 *Sick O' Licks* ....250.00 - up

CARL DAVIS WITH THE DALLAS JAMBOREE JUG BAND:
Vocalion 03132 *Flying Crow Blues* ....100.00 - 150.00

CHARLIE DAVIS AND HIS ORCHESTRA:
Brunswick 4037 *Suppose Nobody Cared* ....10.00 - 15.00
Vocalion 15701 *The Drag* ....50.00 - 75.00
　15702 *Just Like A Melody Out Of The Sky* ....25.00 - 40.00

EDDIE DAVIS & HIS ORCHESTRA:
Grey Gull 1120 *Lonesome Mama Blues* ....10.00 - 15.00
Radiex 1120 *Hot Lips* ....10.00 - 15.00

JASPER DAVIS & HIS ORCHESTRA:
Harmony 944-H *Georgia Gigolo* ....80.00 - 120.00
(Above probably also issued on Diva, Velvet Tone, similarly valued)

JOHNNIE DAVIS & HIS ORCHESTRA:
Decca 256 *Were You Foolin'?* ....8.00 - 12.00
　257 *A Hundred To One It's You* ....8.00 - 12.00
　271 *You Gotta Give Credit To Love* ....10.00 - 15.00
　272 *College Rhythm* ....10.00 - 15.00
　573 *Truckin'* ....7.00 - 10.00
　583 *Everything Is Okey-Dokey* ....7.00 - 10.00

JULIA DAVIS:
Paramount 12248 *Black Hand Blues* ....150.00 - 200.00

MADLYN DAVIS (& HER HOT SHOTS/RED HOT SHAKERS):
Paramount 12498 *Climbing Mountain Blues* ....150.00 - 200.00
　12528 *Hurry Sundown Blues* ....150.00 - 200.00
　12615 *Winter Blues* ....150.00 - 250.00
　12755 *Death Bell Blues* ....150.00 - 250.00

PAUL DAVIS & HIS ORCHESTRA:
Champion 16524 *Underneath The Harlem Moon* ....100.00 - 150.00

RED HOT SHAKIN' DAVIS:
Paramount 12703 *It's Red Hot* ....150.00 - 250.00

WILMER DAVIS:
Vocalion 1034 *Gut Struggle* ....125.00 - 175.00

WALTER DAVISON'S LOUISVILLE LOONS:
Cameo 833 *Knowing You The Way I Do* ....7.00 - 10.00
　834 *My Small Town Gal* ....8.00 - 12.00
Columbia 989-D *South Wind* ....10.00 - 15.00
　1031-D *Give Me a Little Bit O' Sunshine* ....15.00 - 20.00

DOLLY DAWN & HER DAWN PATROL (BOYS):
Bluebird 6170 *Shine* ....8.00 - 12.00
    6171 *Yankee Doodle Never Went To Town* ....8.00 - 12.00
    6216 *Eeny Meeny Miney Mo* ....8.00 - 12.00
Bluebird (most other issues) ....7.00 - 10.00
Okeh 5842 *Hep-Tee-Hootie (Juke Box Jive)* ....7.00 - 10.00
    5977 *How Come?* ....7.00 - 10.00
Variety (most issues) ....8.00 - 12.00
Vocalion 3908 *Bei Mir Bist Du Schoen* ....8.00 - 12.00
Vocalion (most other issues) ....7.00 - 10.00

THE DEAN & HIS KIDS:
Vocalion 3342 *Spreadin' Knowledge Around* ....10.00 - 15.00

EDDIE DEAS AND HIS BOSTON BROWNIES:
Victor 22841 *Jes' Shufflin'* ....30.00 - 50.00
    22844 *Little Mary Brown* ....30.00 - 50.00

DEAUVILLE DOZEN:
Pathe-Actuelle 36338 *Pep* ....10.00 - 15.00
Perfect 14519 *Pep* ....10.00 - 15.00

DEAUVILLE SYNCOPATORS:
Parlophone PNY-34144 *Satan's Holiday* ....25.00 - 40.00
    PNY-34149 *I Got Rhythm* ....20.00 - 30.00
    PNY-34157 *Cheerful Little Earful* ....20.00 - 30.00
    PNY-34172 *Would You Like To Take A Walk?*..40.00 - 60.00
    PNY-34186 *The Last One Left On The Corner*..20.00 - 30.00
    PNY-34199 *Just A Crazy Song*..........................20.00 - 30.00

JOHNNY DE DROIT & HIS NEW ORLEANS JAZZ ORCHESTRA:
Okeh 40090 *The Swing* ....100.00 - 150.00
    40150 *Number Two Blues*..............................100.00 - 150.00
    40192 *Brown Eyes*...50.00 - 80.00
    40240 *Panama* ....150.00 - 200.00
    40285 *Lucky Kentucky* ....75.00 - 100.00

DEEP RIVER ORCHESTRA:
Perfect 14728 *After Hours* ....10.00 - 15.00
    14743 *Piano Tuner's Dream* ....10.00 - 15.00
    14744 *Darby Hicks* ....10.00 - 15.00
    14755 *Tampico* ....15.00 - 20.00
    14756 *Mobile Mud (American Suite #6)* ....10.00 - 15.00
    14774 *Deep River (American Suite #7)* ....20.00 - 30.00
    14815 *Hurry Sundown* ....8.00 - 12.00
    14816 *Peck Horn Blues* ....15.00 - 20.00
    14821 *Harlem Blues* ....15.00 - 20.00
    14825 *Rhapsody In Blue* ....10.00 - 15.00
    14828 *Soliloquy* ....10.00 - 15.00
    14871 *Delirium*...15.00 - 20.00
    14875 *Diane* ....8.00 - 12.00
    14879 *We (My Honey and Me)* ....8.00 - 12.00
    14885 *Wherever You Are* ....8.00 - 12.00
    14886 *Low Down Mississippi* ....10.00 - 15.00
    14901 *'Way Down South In Heaven* ....8.00 - 12.00
    14923 *My Ohio Home* ....8.00 - 12.00
    14930 *Four Walls* ....8.00 - 12.00
    14964 *I'm Riding To Glory* ....10.00 - 15.00
    14980 *Just a Night For Meditation* ....15.00 - 20.00
    15001 *I'm Wingin' Home* ....10.00 - 15.00
    15017 *Blue Grass* ....15.00 - 20.00
    15030 *Jumping Jack* ....8.00 - 12.00
    15037 *One Step To Heaven* ....8.00 - 12.00
    15041 *Ev'rything We Like We Like Alike* ....10.00 - 15.00
    15049 *Flower Of Love* ....7.00 - 10.00

    15063 *In Sweetheart Time* ....8.00 - 12.00
    15071 *Rhythm King* ....10.00 - 15.00
    15075 *Where The Shy Little Violets Grow* ....10.00 - 15.00
    15108 *That's Her Now!* ....7.00 - 10.00
    15119 *I'm Bringing a Red, Red Rose* ....7.00 - 10.00
(Above titles also issued on Pathe-Actuelle, similarly valued)

VOLTAIRE DE FAUT:
Autograph 623 *Wolverine Blues* .... 1000.00 - up

MAUD DE FORREST:
Black Swan 14143 *Roamin' Blues*......................40.00 - 60.00
Paramount 12147 *Roamin' Blues* ....35.00 - 50.00
    12148 *Cruel Papa Blues* ....35.00 - 50.00

BOB DEIKMAN & HIS ORCHESTRA:
Gennett 3087 *Ah-Ha!*..15.00 - 20.00
    3142 *Some Other Bird Whistled A Tune* ....12.00 - 16.00
    3161 *The Camel Walk*....................................30.00 - 50.00
    3196 *Spanish Shawl* ....30.00 - 50.00
    3236 *Shanghai Honeymoon* ....20.00 - 30.00
    6235 *Dew-Dew-Dewy Day* ....40.00 - 60.00
    6248 *Here I Am-Broken Hearted* ....20.00 - 30.00
    6325 *Cobble-Stones* ....20.00 - 30.00
    6339 *Roll Up The Carpets* ....30.00 - 50.00
    6356 *When The Moon Comes Peeping Through*....50.00 - 75.00
    6877 *Me And The Clock* ....20.00 - 30.00

EDDIE DE LANGE AND HIS ORCHESTRA:
Bluebird, most issues ....4.00 - 8.00

DEL DELBRIDGE AND HIS CAPITOL THEATRE ORCHESTRA:
Brunswick 4393 *Do Something* ....10.00 - 15.00

VAUGHN DE LEATH (& HER BUDDIES):
Brunswick 4533 *Chant Of The Jungle* ....15.00 - 20.00
Brunswick (most other issues) ....7.00 - 12.00
Columbia 271-D *Nobody Knows What A Red Head Mama Can Do*
....10.00 - 15.00
Columbia (most other issues) ....7.00 - 12.00
Crown 3200 *Shine On Harvest Moon* ....15.00 - 20.00
Edison (thin) *Mother Goose Parade* ....50.00 - 75.00
    11057 *Oh Susanna* ....50.00 - 75.00
    14002 *I've Got A "Code" In My "Doze"* ....50.00 - 75.00
    14025 *Honey* ....50.00 - 75.00
Edison (thick) 51874 *Hello Bluebird* ....15.00 - 20.00
    51904 *Here Or There* ....15.00 - 20.00
    51948 *Blue Skies* ....20.00 - 30.00
    51966 *Positively-Absolutely* ....15.00 - 20.00
    52016 *Somebody Said* ....20.00 - 30.00
    52018 *I'm In Love Again* ....20.00 - 30.00
    52044 *It's a Million To One You're In Love* .....20.00 - 30.00
    52073 *Baby Feet Go Pitter Patter* ....20.00 - 30.00
    52093 *There's A Cradle In Caroline* ....20.00 - 30.00
    52104 *Here Comes The Showboat* ....25.00 - 40.00
    52120 *Make My Cot Where The Cot-Cot-Cotton Grows*
....25.00 - 40.00
    52129 *Christmas In Other Lands* ....25.00 - 40.00
    52131 *Night Before Christmas* ....25.00 - 40.00
    52159 *What'll You Do?* ....25.00 - 40.00
    52192 *My Blue Heaven* ....25.00 - 40.00
    52212 *There Must Be A Silver Lining* ....25.00 - 40.00
    52222 *I Just Roll Along* ....25.00 - 40.00
    52288 *Happy Go Lucky Lane* ....25.00 - 40.00
    52306 *Tin Pan Parade* ....25.00 - 40.00

52341 *Giggling Gertie*	30.00 -	50.00
52357 *Mother Goose Parade*	30.00 -	50.00
52374 *Is It Gonna Be Long?*	30.00 -	50.00
52388 *I Can't Give You Anything But Love*	50.00 -	75.00
52408 *I Ain't Got Nobody*	50.00 -	75.00
52428 *Ev'rything We Like We Like Alike*	40.00 -	60.00
52446 *Alice In Wonderland*	50.00 -	75.00
52517 *Me And The Man In The Moon*	50.00 -	75.00
52543 *I'm Ka-razy For You*	50.00 -	75.00
52569 *I've Got A Feeling I'm Falling*	50.00 -	75.00
52575 *Some Sweet Day*	50.00 -	75.00
52587 *Honey*	50.00 -	75.00
52614 *Marianna*	50.00 -	75.00
52627 *I'd Fall In Love With Me*	75.00 -	100.00
52651 *Oh Susanna*	75.00 -	125.00
Gennett 3347 *How Many Times?*	10.00 -	15.00
3400 *Here Comes Fatima*	15.00 -	20.00
3412 *Pretty Little Thing*	15.00 -	20.00
6024 *She Said And I Said*	15.00 -	20.00
6046 *The Worst Rose of Summer*	15.00 -	20.00
Herschel Gold Seal 2011 *Here Comes Fatima*	15.00 -	30.00
Okeh 40746 *Gotta Get Myself Somebody To Love*	10.00 -	15.00
40768 *Muddy Water*	10.00 -	15.00
40814 *I'm On My Merry Way*	10.00 -	15.00
40844 *Dew-Dew-Dewy Day*	15.00 -	20.00
40906 *Old Names Of Old Flames*	10.00 -	15.00
41206 *Me And The Man In The Moon*	10.00 -	15.00
Victor (most issues)	7.00 -	10.00

HAL DENMAN AND HIS CAROLINA COTTON PICKERS; DENMAN'S COTTON PICKERS:

Champion 16221 *She Loves Me Just The Same*	15.00 -	20.00
16266 *I Can't Get Enough Of You*	15.00 -	20.00
16274 *When I Take My Sugar To Tea*	15.00 -	20.00
16355 *How's Your Uncle?*	30.00 -	50.00
16397 *Was That The Human Thing To Do*	30.00 -	50.00
16533 *Bugle Call Rag*	30.00 -	50.00
16655 *Sweet And Lovely*	30.00 -	50.00
40069 *Hand Me Down My Walking Cane*	15.00 -	20.00
Superior 2667 *It Looks Like Love*	20.00 -	30.00
2774 *When I Take My Sugar To Tea*	20.00 -	30.00
2768 *How's Your Uncle?*	15.00 -	25.00
2800 *Snuggled On Your Shoulder*	15.00 -	25.00

JACK DENNY & HIS ORCHESTRA:

Brunswick 3884 *Hello, Montreal!*	7.00 -	10.00
Brunswick, most other issues	5.00 -	8.00
Cameo 646 *Easy Goin' Mama*	7.00 -	10.00

DEPPE'S SERENADERS:

Gennett 20012 *Falling*	100.00 -	200.00

LOUIS DEPPE:

Gennett 20021 *Southland*	100.00 -	150.00
20022 *Isabel*	100.00 -	150.00

JESSIE DERRICK (See HARVEY BROOKS' QUALITY FOUR)

THE DETROITERS:

Cameo 8137 *Nothin' To Do (But Worry 'Bout You)*	7.00 -	10.00
8149 *Maybe Yes-Maybe No*	7.00 -	10.00
8195 *Spanish Mamma*	8.00 -	12.00
8368 *Here's That Party Now In Person*	8.00 -	12.00
8371 *I'm Choosin' Black Eyed Susan*	7.00 -	10.00
9012 *Star Dust*	10.00 -	15.00

9204 *Am I Blue?*	8.00 -	12.00
9309 *Any Old Time (Is Loving Time For Me)*	7.00 -	10.00
Romeo 500 *Dream Dream Dream*	5.00 -	8.00
572 *Maybe Yes-Maybe No*	7.00 -	10.00
625 *Spanish Mamma*	8.00 -	12.00
809 *Let's Do It*	8.00 -	12.00
816 *Star Dust*	10.00 -	15.00
973 *From Sunrise To Sunset*	8.00 -	12.00
995 *It's a Funny Feeling*	5.00 -	8.00
1006 *Am I Blue?*	8.00 -	12.00
1100 *Any Old Time (Is Loving Time For Me)*	7.00 -	10.00

DEVINE'S WISCONSIN ROOF ORCHESTRA (See also WISCONSIN ROOF ORCHESTRA):

Broadway 1123 *Black Maria*	50.00 -	75.00
1140 *Tiger Rag*	30.00 -	50.00
1142 *Riverboat Blues*	30.00 -	50.00
Paramount 20582 *Tiger Rag*	40.00 -	60.00
20651 *Farewell Blues*	75.00 -	100.00

FRED DEXTER'S PENNSYLVANIANS:

Gennett 7256 *What's The Use?*	30.00 -	50.00

HARRY DIAL'S BLUSICIANS:

Queen 4164 *I Like What I Like Like I Like It*	20.00 -	30.00
Vocalion 1515 *Don't Give It Away*	150.00 -	250.00
1567 *I Like What I Like Like I Like It*	150.00 -	250.00
1594 *Poison*	200.00 -	300.00

CARROLL DICKERSON's SAVOY ORCHESTRA:

Brunswick 3990 *Missouri Squabble*	50.00 -	80.00

CHARLES DICKSON:

Jewel 5043 *Vo-Do-Do-De-O Blues*	8.00 -	12.00
Oriole 940 *Vo-Do-Do-De-O Blues*	8.00 -	12.00

DICKSON'S HARLEM ORCHESTRA:

Victor 23377 *Jazz Rondo*	75.00 -	100.00

DUKE DIGGS & HIS ORCHESTRA:

Supertone 9487 *Nightmare*	150.00 -	200.00
9653 *After You've Gone*	150.00 -	200.00

DIXIE BANJO BOYS:

Puritan 11476 *Baby Face*	100.00 -	150.00

THE DIXIE BOYS:

Autograph (unnumbered) *Poplar Street Blues*	150.00 -	200.00
Champion 15001 *I'm Gonna Charleston Back To Charleston*	15.00 -	20.00
15021 *My Sweetie Turned Me Down*	10.00 -	15.00
15227 *I've Found A New Baby*	100.00 -	150.00
Rich-Tone 7045 *Haunting Blues*	20.00 -	30.00

DIXIE DAISIES:

Banner 0839 *St. Louis Blues*	15.00 -	20.00
Cameo 291 *Lovin' Sam*	7.00 -	10.00
333 *Farewell Blues*	7.00 -	10.00
345 *Louisville Lou*	7.00 -	10.00
348 *Papa Blues*	7.00 -	10.00
357 *Long Lost Mama*	7.00 -	10.00
392 *Salt Your Sugar*	7.00 -	10.00
414 *I've Got A Song For Sale*	7.00 -	10.00
418 *Oh! Sister Ain't That Hot*	7.00 -	10.00
428 *The House Of David Blues*	7.00 -	10.00
476 *Dancin' Dan*	7.00 -	10.00
630 *Oh Flo!*	7.00 -	10.00

682 *Choo Choo (I Gotta Hurry Home)*	7.00 -	10.00
769 *Fritz Is On the Fritz*	7.00 -	10.00
781 *Headin' For Baltimore*	8.00 -	12.00
783 *Footloose*	7.00 -	10.00
834 *Paddlin' Madelin' Home*	8.00 -	12.00
835 *Clap Hands! Here Comes Charlie*	8.00 -	12.00
986 *Where'd You Get Those Eyes?*	8.00 -	12.00
1044 *Yiddisha Charleston*	7.00 -	10.00
1168 *Stompin' Fool*	15.00 -	20.00
1184 *Bless Her Little Heart*	8.00 -	12.00
1238 *Way Back When*	7.00 -	10.00
1257 *Sorry*	7.00 -	10.00
1267 *I Ain't Got Nobody*	8.00 -	12.00
8105 *Changes*	7.00 -	10.00
8111 *Stay Out Of The South*	10.00 -	15.00
8229 *Brotherly Love*	8.00 -	12.00
8245 *Got Everything (Don't Want Anything But You)*		
	8.00 -	12.00
8279 *Don't Mess Around With Me*	7.00 -	10.00
8297 *Crazy Rhythm*	8.00 -	12.00
8310 *When You're Smiling*	7.00 -	10.00
8316 *Imagination*	7.00 -	10.00
8317 *There's a Rainbow 'Round My Shoulder*	7.00 -	10.00
8325 *Somebody Sweet Is Sweet On Me*	8.00 -	12.00
8334 *Moonlight Madness*	7.00 -	10.00
8339 *Doin' The Raccoon*	7.00 -	10.00
8353 *She's Wonderful*	8.00 -	12.00
9004 *Digga Digga Do*	20.00 -	30.00
9034 *Baby*	15.00 -	25.00
9035 *Bugle Call Rag*	15.00 -	25.00
9043 *A Japanese Dream*	10.00 -	15.00
9047 *I'm Just Wondering Who*	10.00 -	15.00
9085 *There's Something New 'Bout The Old Moon Tonight*		
	10.00 -	15.00
9106 *Kansas City Kitty*	8.00 -	12.00
9127 *Somebody Misses Somebody's Kisses*	7.00 -	10.00
9142 *Eyes of Blue, You're My Waterloo*	15.00 -	20.00
9204 *It Took A Lot Of Blue*	8.00 -	12.00
Lincoln 3033 *'Cause I'm In Love*	15.00 -	25.00
Romeo 264 *High Fever*	8.00 -	12.00
491 *Sorry*	7.00 -	10.00
659 *Peek-A-Boo Eyes*	7.00 -	10.00
668 *Got Everything (Don't Want Anything But You)*		
	7.00 -	10.00
700 *Ya Gonna Be Home Tonight?*	7.00 -	10.00
776 *She's Wonderful*	8.00 -	12.00
887 *There's Something New 'Bout The Old Moon Tonight*		
	10.00 -	15.00
1006 *It Took A Lot Of Blue*	8.00 -	12.00

DIXIE DANCE DEMONS:

Cameo 8162 *Birmingham Break Down*	15.00 -	20.00

THE DIXIE DEVILS:

Van Dyke 71804 *In Harlem's Araby*	15.00 -	20.00
71805 *Miss Golden Brown*	15.00 -	20.00

DIXIE FOUR:

Paramount 12661 *St. Louis Man*	250.00 -	up
12674 *Five O'Clock Stomp*	250.00 -	up

DIXIE JAZZ BAND:

Challenge 628 *The Crawl*	10.00 -	15.00
929 *Dusky Stevedore*	15.00 -	20.00
952 *Missouri Squabble*	10.00 -	15.00

958 *Icky Blues*	15.00 -	20.00
995 *Long Lost Daddy*	8.00 -	12.00
999 *Makin' Friends*	15.00 -	20.00
Conqueror 7189 *Missouri Squabble*	10.00 -	15.00
Jewel 5002 *The Crawl*	10.00 -	15.00
5048 *Black Bottom*	10.00 -	15.00
5067 *Struttin' Jerry*	10.00 -	15.00
5145 *There's A Rickety Rackety Shack*	15.00 -	20.00
5171 *Sorry*	15.00 -	20.00
5199 *Steppin' It Off*	10.00 -	15.00
5263 *Moten Stomp*	10.00 -	15.00
5291 *Know Nothin' Blues*	15.00 -	20.00
5331 *Puttin' On The Dog*	15.00 -	20.00
5335 *Deep Hollow*	15.00 -	20.00
5392 *What-Cha-Call-Em-Blues*	15.00 -	20.00
5405 *Baby's Coming Back*	15.00 -	20.00
5412 *West End Blues*	15.00 -	20.00
5446 *Dixie Drag*	15.00 -	20.00
5488 *Cat's Kittens*	10.00 -	15.00
5521 *Some Of These Days*	10.00 -	15.00
5547 *Icky Blues*	15.00 -	20.00
5565 *Long Lost Daddy*	8.00 -	12.00
5569 *Makin' Friends*	15.00 -	20.00
5575 *Sweet Liza*	15.00 -	20.00
5576 *Pa's Old Hat*	10.00 -	15.00
5677 *My Sweetie Turned Sour On Me*	7.00 -	10.00
5707 *St. Louis Blues*	10.00 -	15.00
5748 *Twelfth Street Rag*	15.00 -	20.00
5685 *It's So Good*	15.00 -	20.00
5729 *The Way He Loves Is Just Too Bad*	15.00 -	20.00
5730 *Broadway Rhythm*	20.00 -	30.00
Oriole 269 *My Lovie Lee*	20.00 -	30.00
271 *How Could You Leave Me Now?*	20.00 -	30.00
291 *Copenhagen*	20.00 -	30.00
315 *Hot Sax*	20.00 -	30.00
347 *West Texas Blues*	20.00 -	30.00
364 *When My Sugar Walks Down The Street*	7.00 -	10.00
413 *Some Of These Days*	20.00 -	30.00
424 *Flag That Train*	15.00 -	20.00
443 *Milenberg Joys*	15.00 -	20.00
445 *Right Or Wrong*	20.00 -	30.00
464 *Red Hot Henry Brown*	20.00 -	30.00
475 *Angry*	10.00 -	15.00
517 *Hot Aire*	15.00 -	20.00
521 *I'm Sitting On Top Of The World*	7.00 -	10.00
530 *Has Been Blues*	15.00 -	20.00
531 *My Charleston Dancing Man*	7.00 -	10.00
565 *Wait Till You See My Baby Do The Charleston*		
	50.00 -	75.00
590 *Say Mister! Have You Met Rosie's Sister?*	8.00 -	12.00
598 *For No Reason*	7.00 -	10.00
601 *I've Got Those Charleston Blues*	7.00 -	10.00
605 *On The Puppy's Tail*	15.00 -	20.00
619 *I'm Gonna Tear Your Playhouse Down*	15.00 -	20.00
625 *Junk Bucket Blues*	15.00 -	20.00
674 *Deep Henderson*	15.00 -	20.00
682 *Jackass Blues*	15.00 -	20.00
685 *Hard-To-Get Gertie*	15.00 -	20.00
688 *Black Bottom*	15.00 -	20.00
691 *Nervous Charlie Stomp*	15.00 -	20.00
705 *I Wonder What's Become Of Joe?*	15.00 -	20.00
717 *Old Folks' Shuffle*	50.00 -	75.00
723 *St. Louis Blues*	15.00 -	20.00

748 *Brown Sugar*	15.00 -	20.00
762 *Stampede*	15.00 -	20.00
776 *Any Day*	15.00 -	20.00
778 *Serenadin' Sarah*	7.00 -	10.00
784 *That Sweet Patootie Of Mine*	8.00 -	12.00
799 *St. Louis Shuffle*	15.00 -	25.00
804 *Stockholm Stomp*	15.00 -	25.00
819 *Indiana Shuffle*	10.00 -	15.00
828 *Coffee Pot Blues*	15.00 -	20.00
829 *The Crawl*	15.00 -	20.00
846 *Ain't She Sweet?*	15.00 -	20.00
880 *I'm In Love Again*	15.00 -	20.00
883 *Rosy Cheeks*	15.00 -	20.00
896 *South Wind*	7.00 -	10.00
909 *Slow River*	7.00 -	10.00
926 *Sugar*	10.00 -	15.00
927 *Some Of These Days*	10.00 -	15.00
952 *Memphis Blues*	20.00 -	30.00
956 *Lighthouse Blues*	10.00 -	15.00
960 *Rarin' To Go*	15.00 -	20.00
963 *My Melancholy Baby*	10.00 -	15.00
977 *Struttin' Jerry*	10.00 -	15.00
984 *Tiger Rag*	15.00 -	20.00
1009 *Someone Who's Fooling Around*	15.00 -	20.00
1022 *Jelly Roll Blues*	20.00 -	30.00
1033 *Hello Miss Liberty!*	7.00 -	10.00
1046 *Washington And Lee Swing*	7.00 -	10.00
1071 *There's A Rickety Rackety Shack*	15.00 -	20.00
1100 *Sorry*	15.00 -	20.00
1122 *Chloe*	5.00 -	8.00
1123 *Steppin' It Off*	10.00 -	15.00
1127 *Once Over Lightly*	10.00 -	15.00
1131 *Candied Sweets*	10.00 -	15.00
1163 *You're Gonna Regret*	5.00 -	8.00
1171 *Where Will I Be?*	10.00 -	15.00
1172 *Moten Stomp*	10.00 -	15.00
1178 *Lila*	10.00 -	15.00
1181 *She's A Great, Great Girl*	10.00 -	15.00
1200 *Tin Ear*	8.00 -	12.00
1226 *Collegiana*	7.00 -	10.00
1230 *Know Nothin' Blues*	15.00 -	20.00
1253 *Persian Rug*	7.00 -	10.00
1256 *Try To Smile*	5.00 -	8.00
1275 *Somebody's Making A Fuss Over Somebody*	8.00 -	12.00
1278 *Puttin' On The Dog*	15.00 -	20.00
1282 *If I Can Ba-Ba-Baby You*	5.00 -	8.00
1287 *A Jazz Holiday*	15.00 -	20.00
1313 *Deep Hollow*	15.00 -	20.00
1339 *When Sweet Susie Goes Steppin' By*	15.00 -	20.00
1343 *What-Cha-Call-'Em Blues*	15.00 -	20.00
1346 *Dusky Stevedore*	15.00 -	20.00
1360 *Baby's Coming Back*	15.00 -	20.00
1363 *High Hattin' Hattie*	15.00 -	20.00
1368 *Easy*	15.00 -	20.00
1371 *Cool Papa*	15.00 -	25.00
1387 *Sunday Afternoon*	15.00 -	20.00
1396 *Dixie Drag*	15.00 -	20.00
1403 *Fraternity Prom*	7.00 -	10.00
1416 *Missouri Squabble*	10.00 -	15.00
1417 *Talkin' To Myself*	7.00 -	10.00
1423 *Happy In The Rain*	7.00 -	10.00
1426 *I Love My Best Girl Best*	7.00 -	10.00
1447 *Wide Open Gate*	7.00 -	10.00
1450 *Mystic Bengal Bay*	7.00 -	10.00
1454 *Cat's Kittens*	8.00 -	12.00
1457 *You Please Me*	7.00 -	10.00
1474 *Pepper Pot*	7.00 -	10.00
1475 *Susianna*	7.00 -	10.00
1476 *She's My Sweet Patootie*	5.00 -	8.00
1481 *Some Of These Days*	10.00 -	15.00
1504 *Geraldine*	10.00 -	15.00
1505 *What Do You Think Of My Baby?*	10.00 -	15.00
1507 *Let's Get Together*	10.00 -	15.00
1515 *Icky Blues*	15.00 -	20.00
1536 *Pa's Old Hat*	8.00 -	12.00
1537 *Makin' Friends*	15.00 -	20.00
1540 *Sweet Liza*	15.00 -	20.00
1576 *Where Has Mammy Gone?*	8.00 -	12.00
1582 *I've Got The San Francisco Blues*	8.00 -	12.00
1611 *Along About Now*	7.00 -	10.00
1612 *Some Of These Days*	10.00 -	15.00
1624 *After You've Gone*	15.00 -	20.00
1638 *Whoopeein' Up*	10.00 -	15.00
1662 *My Sweetie Turned Sour On Me*	7.00 -	10.00
1663 *You're Gonna Regret*	7.00 -	10.00
1668 *It's So Good*	15.00 -	20.00
1690 *St. Louis Blues*	10.00 -	15.00
1726 *The Way He Loves Is Just Too Bad*	15.00 -	20.00
1728 *Broadway Rhythm*	20.00 -	30.00
1730 *Saturday Night Function*	20.00 -	30.00
1768 *Sweet Baby, Tell Me You're My Pretty Baby*	7.00 -	10.00

DIXIE JAZZERS WASHBOARD BAND:

Pathe-Actuelle 7536 *Memphis Shake*	150.00 -	200.00
7539 *Kansas City Shuffle*	150.00 -	200.00
Perfect 136 *Memphis Shake*	150.00 -	200.00
139 *Kansas City Shuffle*	150.00 -	200.00

DIXIE JAZZ HOUNDS:

Domino 306 *Hula Lou*	20.00 -	30.00
308 *Lots O' Mamma*	20.00 -	30.00
328 *31st Street Blues*	20.00 -	30.00
329 *Waitin' Around*	20.00 -	30.00

DIXIELAND JUG BLOWERS:

Victor 20403 *Florida Blues*	75.00 -	100.00
20415 *Memphis Shake*	35.00 -	50.00
20420 *Don't Give All The Lard Away*	75.00 -	100.00
20480 *Carpet Alley*	75.00 -	100.00
20649 *Hen Party Blues*	80.00 -	120.00
20770 *When I Stopped Runnin' I Was At Home*	80.00 -	120.00
20854 *I Never Did Want You*	100.00 -	150.00
20954 *Southern Shout*	100.00 -	150.00
21126 *Garden Of Joy Blues*	100.00 -	150.00
21473 *Banjoreno*	100.00 -	150.00

DIXIELAND SWINGSTERS:

Bluebird 7109, 7160, 7258, 7857, 7882, 7899, 7948	7.00 -	12.00

DIXIELAND THUMPERS:

Paramount 12525 *Weary Way Blues*	500.00 -	up
12595 *Oriental Man*	500.00 -	up

DIXIE MUSIC MAKERS:

Romeo 307 *Messin' Around*	8.00 -	12.00

DIXIE PLAYERS:
Champion 15134 *Looking At The World Through Rose-Colored Glasses* ....8.00 -　12.00

DIXIE RAMBLERS:
Champion 15494 *I'm More Than Satisfied* ....15.00 -　20.00

DIXIE REVELERS:
Sunrise 30009 *Hoppin' 'Round* ....25.00 -　40.00

DIXIE RHYTHM KINGS:
Brunswick 7115 *Congo Love Song*.........................150.00 -　300.00
　7127 *Easy Rider*....................................150.00 -　300.00

DIXIE SERENADERS:
Champion 16341 *When It's Sleepy-Time Down South*
　..150.00 -　200.00
　16365 *St. Louis Blues* ....150.00 -　200.00
　40003 *St. Louis Blues* ....40.00 -　60.00

THE DIXIE STOMPERS:
Harmony 70-H *Spanish Shawl*...............................25.00 -　40.00
　88-H *Get It Fixed*..30.00 -　50.00
　92-H *Chinese Blues* ....30.00 -　50.00
　121-H *I Found A New Baby*.........................25.00 -　40.00
　153-H *Nervous Charlie Stomp*.....................25.00 -　40.00
　166-H *Jackass Blues* ....25.00 -　40.00
　179-H *Hi-Diddle-Diddle*.............................20.00 -　30.00
　197-H *Static Strut* ....20.00 -　30.00
　209-H *Dynamite*...20.00 -　30.00
　283-H *Alabama Stomp*................................20.00 -　30.00
　299-H *Off To Buffalo* ....30.00 -　50.00
　353-H *Ain't She Sweet?* ....15.00 -　25.00
　407-H *The Wang Wang Blues*.....................20.00 -　30.00
　451-H *The St. Louis Blues* ....15.00 -　25.00
　467-H *St. Louis Shuffle* ....25.00 -　40.00
　526-H *Black Maria* ....25.00 -　40.00
　545-H *Goose Pimples* ....25.00 -　40.00
　636-H *Feelin' Good*....................................25.00 -　40.00
　974-H *I'm Feeling Devilish* ....30.00 -　50.00
(Note: Above titles on Diva and Velvet Tone are similarly valued.)

DIXIE TRIO:
Grey Gull 1340 *Poor Papa* ....10.00 -　15.00
　1464 *St. Louis Blues* ....10.00 -　15.00

DIXIE WASHBOARD BAND:
Banner 1696 *Shake That Thing*................................80.00 -　130.00
　1781 *I've Found A New Baby*.................40.00 -　60.00
Columbia 14128-D *Livin' High*...............................80.00 -　120.00
　14141-D *My Own Blues*.........................100.00 -　150.00
　14171-D *King Of The Zulus* ....150.00 -　200.00
　14188-D *Gimmie Blues*...........................150.00 -　200.00
　14239-D *Cushion Foot Stomp* ....100.00 -　150.00
Regal 8093 *Boodle Am* ....40.00 -　60.00

DIXON'S CHICAGO SERENADERS:
Black Patti 8010 *Monte Carlo Joys* ....500.00 -　up

DIXON'S JAZZ DUO/MANIACS:
Paramount 12385 *Headache Blues*...........................100.00 -　150.00
　12405 *Tiger Rag* ....150.00 -　200.00
　12446 *Crazy Quilt*.................................150.00 -　200.00

BOBBY DIXON'S BROADCASTERS:
Hit of the Week 1061 *Mysterious Mose* ....30.00 -　50.00

VANCE DIXON & HIS PENCILS:
Columbia 14608-D *Hot Peanuts*...........................150.00 -　250.00
　14673-D *Who Stole The Lock?* ....150.00 -　250.00
Okeh 8891 *Who Stole The Lock?* ....150.00 -　200.00

DIXON AND CHANNEY:
Paramount 12471 *Sweet Patunia* ....300.00 -　up

JOHNNY DODDS; JOHNNY DODDS' BLACK BOTTOM STOMPERS/ORCHESTRA/TRIO/WASHBOARD BAND; JOHNNY DODDS & HIS CHICAGO BOYS:
Bluebird 8549 *Bucktown Stomp* ....15.00 -　20.00
　10239 *Bull Fiddle Blues* ....8.00 -　12.00
　10241 *My Little Isabel* ....8.00 -　12.00
Brunswick 3567 *Wild Man Blues* ....25.00 -　40.00
　3568 *After You've Gone* ....40.00 -　60.00
　3574 *Clarinet Wobble* ....25.00 -　40.00
　3585 *The New St. Louis Blues* ....25.00 -　40.00
　3696 *When Erastus Plays His Old Kazoo* ....- -　-
　3997 *Joe Turner Blues* ....40.00 -　60.00
　7015 *The New St. Louis Blues* ....40.00 -　60.00
　7016 *San*...40.00 -　60.00
Decca 1676 *Melancholy* ....15.00 -　20.00
　2111 *Wild Man Blues* ....15.00 -　20.00
　7413 *Blues Galore* ....15.00 -　20.00
Victor 21552 *Bull Fiddle Blues* ....80.00 -　120.00
　21554 *Blue Clarinet Stomp* ....80.00 -　120.00
　23396 *Goober Dance* ....400.00 -　up
　V-38004 *Bucktown Stomp*.......................150.00 -　200.00
　V-38038 *Pencil Papa*................................100.00 -　150.00
　V-38541 *My Little Isabel* ....100.00 -　150.00
Vocalion 1128 *Melancholy* ....100.00 -　150.00
　1148 *After You've Gone*...........................100.00 -　150.00
　15632 *Weary Blues* ....500.00 -　up

DODDS AND PARHAM:
Paramount 12471 *Oh Daddy*...................................300.00 -　up
　12483 *19th Street Blues* ....300.00 -　up

CLYDE DOERR AND HIS ORCHESTRA:
Edison 51873 *Son of The Sheik* ....10.00 -　15.00
　51898 *I'm Tellin' The Birds, Tellin' The Bees* .10.00 -　15.00
　51905 *Wouldn't You?* ....20.00 -　30.00
　51988 *Ain't She Sweet?* ....15.00 -　25.00
　51989 *You Can't Cry Over My Shoulder* ....10.00 -　15.00
　52065 *Dew-Dew-Dewy Day* ....15.00 -　20.00
　52297 *Just Across the Street From Heaven* ......15.00 -　20.00
　52304 *The Yale Blues* ....20.00 -　30.00

PAT DOLLOHAN AND HIS ORCHESTRA:
Gennett 6711 *My Supressed Desire* ....30.00 -　50.00
　6784 *True Blue*..30.00 -　50.00

AL DONOHUE AND HIS ORCHESTRA:
Decca 559, 604, 608, 626, 630, 665, 673, 981, 989..7.00 -　10.00

Okeh 5660 *Southern Fried* ....8.00 - 12.00
   5828 *Burning The Midnight Oil* ....8.00 - 12.00
   5888 *I Hear A Rhapsody* ....7.00 - 10.00
   5925 *Ohio Breakaway* ....7.00 - 10.00
Okeh, most other issues ....5.00 - 10.00
Vocalion 4562 *Alexander's Swingin'* ....8.00 - 12.00
   4587 *I Cried For You* ....8.00 - 12.00
   4846 *Cinderella, Stay In My Arms* ....7.00 - 10.00
   4956 *Persian Rug* ....8.00 - 12.00
   4993 *Oh, You Crazy Moon* ....7.00 - 10.00
   5314 *Copenhagen* ....8.00 - 12.00
   5384 *Tuxedo Junction* ....8.00 - 12.00
Vocalion, most other issues ....5.00 - 10.00

CHARLES DORNBERGER & HIS ORCHESTRA:

Harmony 6507-H* *Strangers* ....10.00 - 15.00
(Above is a dual-track "five minute" record, probably also issued on
   Clarion and Velvet Tone)
Victor 19138 *Oh, Sister! Ain't That Hot* ....7.00 - 10.00
   19346 *Nobody's Sweetheart* ....8.00 - 12.00
   19580 *I Can't Stop Babying You* ....10.00 - 15.00
   19633 *Oh! That Sweet In Suite 16* ......15.00 - 20.00
   20647 *Tiger Rag* ....12.00 - 16.00
   22031 *Maybe! Who Knows?* ....8.00 - 12.00
   22215 *Campus Capers* ....8.00 - 12.00
   24198 *Jingle Bells*..............................10.00 - 15.00
   24199 *Old MacDonald Had A Farm* ....10.00 - 15.00
Victor, most other issues............................4.00 - 8.00

D'ORSAY DANCE ORCHESTRA:

Clarion 5394-C *Little Mary Brown*...........................10.00 - 15.00
Clarion 5440-C, 5450-C, 5466-C ....7.00 - 10.00
Harmony 1380-H *Little Mary Brown* ....10.00 - 15.00
Harmony 1409-H, 1419-H.....................................5.00 - 10.00
Velvet Tone 2458-V *Little Mary Brown* ....10.00 - 15.00
Velvet Tone 2510-V, 2526-V ....5.00 - 10.00

THE DORSEY BROTHERS' ORCHESTRA; THE DORSEY BROTHERS AND THEIR ORCHESTRA:

Banner 0566 Congratulations ....10.00 - 15.00
   0571 *Have A Little Faith in Me* ....10.00 - 15.00
   0589 *Beside An Open Fireplace* ....8.00 - 12.00
(Above titles were also issued on Cameo, Conqueror, Domino,
   Jewel, Oriole, Pathe-Actuelle, Perfect, Regal, and Romeo,
   similarly valued)
Brunswick 6409 *I'm Gettin' Sentimental Over You*
   ....10.00 - 15.00
   6537 *Mood Hollywood* ....10.00 - 15.00
   6624 *Old Man Harlem* ....10.00 - 15.00
   6722 *Fidgety* ....10.00 - 15.00
   6938 *Judy* ....10.00 - 15.00
Columbia 2581-D *Ooh! That Kiss* ....15.00 - 20.00
   2589-D *Why Did It Have To Be Me?*.................15.00 - 20.00
Decca 115 *I'm Gettin' Sentimental Over You* ....8.00 - 12.00
   116 *I Can't Dance (I Got Ants In My Pants)* .....10.00 - 15.00
   117 *Dr. Heckle and Mr. Jibe* ....10.00 - 15.00
   118 *Basin Street Blues* ....10.00 - 15.00
Decca 195, 196, 206, 207, 208, 258, 259, 260, 283,
   291, 296, 297, 311, 314, 318, 319, 320, 321, 335,
   340, 348, 357, 358, 367, 368, 370, 371, 469, 476,
   482, 515, 516, 519, 520, 559, 560, 561,
   1503 (12-inch) ....7.00 - 12.00
Okeh 40995 *Mary Ann*.............................20.00 - 30.00
   41007 *The Yale Blues* ....20.00 - 30.00
   41032 *My Melancholy Baby* ....20.00 - 30.00

41050 *Dixie Dawn* ....20.00 - 30.00
41065 *Evening Star* ....15.00 - 25.00
41083 *Was It A Dream* ....8.00 - 12.00
41124 *Out Of The Dawn* ....15.00 - 25.00
41151 *Cross Roads* ....15.00 - 25.00
41158 *She's Funny That Way* ....15.00 - 25.00
41181 *The Spell Of The Blues*.........30.00 - 50.00
41188 *My Kinda Love* ....30.00 - 50.00
41210 *Mean To Me* ....15.00 - 25.00
41220 *I'll Never Ask For More* ....15.00 - 25.00
41272 *Singin' In The Rain* ....15.00 - 25.00
41279 *Maybe-Who Knows?* ....15.00 - 25.00

JIM/JIMMY DORSEY (AND HIS ORCHESTRA):

Brunswick 6352 *Oodles of Noodles*.....................10.00 - 15.00
Decca 570, 571, 602, 607, 655...........................7.00 - 10.00
Decca 762, 764, 768, 776, 782, 808, 873, 901..........5.00 - 8.00
Decca 939 *Rap Tap On Wood* ....7.00 - 10.00
   940 *Swingin' The Jinx Away*............................7.00 - 10.00
Decca 941, 950, 951, 1040, 1086, 1187, 1200, 1203,
   1204, 1256, 1301, 1377, 1378, 1508, 1651, 1652,
   1660, 1671, 1723, 1724, 1745, 1746, 1784, 1799,
   1809, 1834, 1860, 1921, 1939 ....5.00 - 8.00
Decca, most other issues ....4.00 - 8.00
M-G-M, most issues...4.00 - 8.00
Okeh 41245 *Prayin' The Blues*.........................30.00 - 50.00

TOM DORSEY (& HIS NOVELTY ORCHESTRA); TOMMY DORSEY & HIS CLAMBAKE SEVEN/ ORCHESTRA:

Okeh 41178 *It's Right Here For You*...................40.00 - 60.00
   41422 *You Can't Cheat A Cheater* ....30.00 - 50.00
Victor 25144, 25145, 25158, 25159, 25172, 25173,
   25183, 25191, 25201, 25206, 25214, 25216,
   25217, 25220, 25246, 25256, 25284, 25291,
   25292, 25335, 25341, 35349, 25352, 25476,
   25482, 25314, 25320 25363, 25446, 25447,
   25467, 25484, 25496, 25508, 25509, 25513,
   25516, 25519, 25523, 25532, 25534, 25539,
   25544, 25549, 25553, 25556, 25557, 25568,
   25570, 25573, 25577, 25581, 25591, 25596,
   25600, 25603, 25605, 25607, 25610, 25620,
   25623, 25625, 25630, 25635, 25647, 25648,
   25649, 25652, 25657, 25663, 25673, 25676,
   25686, 25692, 25693, 25694, 25695..........7.00 - 12.00
(Note: Foregoing issues, if first pressings, have the "scroll" label.)
Victor 25703, 25741, 25750, 25763, 25768, 25774,
   25780, 25795, 25799, 25803, 25813, 25815,
   25821, 25824, 25828, 25832, 25848, 25856,
   25862, 25866, 25899, 26005, 26016, 26030........7.00 - 10.00
Victor (most other issues) ....5.00 - 8.00
(Victor 26500, 26518, 26525, 26535, 26539, 26555, 26581, 26593,
   26596, 26606, 26609, 26616, 26628 and many subsequent issues
   offer early recordings of Frank Sinatra, which might be of
   somewhat greater interest and value to Sinatra specialists; they
   have little premium value to most collectors)

MIKE DOTY AND HIS ORCHESTRA:

Bluebird 5251 *Puddin' Head Jones* ....8.00 - 12.00
   5252 *Lenox Avenue* ....8.00 - 12.00
   5253 *My Galveston Gal* ....8.00 - 12.00
   5277 *You're My Thrill* ....8.00 - 12.00
(Note: The above titles on Electradisk bring somewhat more; on
   Sunrise, substantially more.)

DOWN HOME SERENADERS:
Champion 15399 *Cootie Crawl* ....150.00 - 250.00

GEORGE DREW & HIS ORCHESTRA:
Superior 2829 *Hard Luck* ....75.00 - 100.00

LEO DREYER AND HIS ORCHESTRA:
Crown 3404 *Fit As A Fiddle* ....10.00 - 15.00
Edison 52466 *Pompanola* ....50.00 - 75.00

EDDIE DROESCH AND HIS ORCHESTRA:
Clarion 5407-C *Last Dollar* ....15.00 - 20.00
Harmony 1388-H *Last Dollar* ....15.00 - 20.00
Velvet Tone 2467-V *Last Dollar* ....15.00 - 20.00

GEORGE DRUCK'S SWEETS BALLROOM ORCHESTRA:
Flexo (unnumbered) *Tiger Rag* ....100.00 - 150.00

DUBIN'S DANDIES:
Banner 0505 *Gettin' Along* ....8.00 - 12.00
0510 *What Do You Care?* ....7.00 - 10.00
0513 *I Wouldn't Care (If You Cared For Me)* ......7.00 - 10.00
0515 *Will You Think Of Me As I Think of You?* ...7.00 - 10.00
0533 *Can You Fry An Egg?* ....7.00 - 10.00
0537 *Can't Stop Caring For You* ....7.00 - 10.00
0557 *Stay in the Sunshine And Smile* ....8.00 - 12.00
0564 *You Know Better Than That* ....7.00 - 12.00
0569 *In Harlem's Araby* ....10.00 - 15.00
0570 *When the Moon Shines Down On Sunshine And Me*
....8.00 - 12.00
0572 *Angel Eyes* ....7.00 - 10.00
0584 *Just A Lone Hillbilly* ....7.00 - 10.00
0590 *Lonely Lady* ....10.00 - 15.00
0619 *One Hour Of Happiness* ....10.00 - 15.00
0623 *She Stole My Heart* ....10.00 - 15.00
0659 *Are You Blue?* ....8.00 - 12.00
0691 *Ain't Life A Load Of Happiness?* ....8.00 - 12.00
0693 *Every Highway, Every By Way (Points My Way Home)*
....7.00 - 10.00
0720 *You And Me And The Baby* ....8.00 - 12.00
0748 *Just a Song About You* ....7.00 - 10.00
0750 *Myrtle (My Little Turtle Dove)* ....15.00 - 20.00
0756 *I've Got My Mind On You* ....7.00 - 10.00
0757 *The Harvard Hop* ....8.00 - 12.00
0784 *Let's Be Sweethearts Now* ....7.00 - 10.00
0802 *The Recipe Song* ....7.00 - 10.00
(Above titles were also issued on Cameo, similarly valued)
6425 *Hoodoo Voodoo Man* ....7.00 - 10.00
6426 *Along About Now* ....7.00 - 10.00
6439 *Sweet Baby* ....8.00 - 12.00
6440 *My Rosalie* ....7.00 - 10.00
6445 *Doesn't That Mean Anything To You?* ....7.00 - 10.00
6447 *Queen Of The Caravan* ....7.00 - 10.00
6449 *Adorable You* ....8.00 - 12.00
6451 *What Will I Do Without You, Sweetheart* ....7.00 - 10.00
6452 *Whoopeein' Up* ....10.00 - 15.00
6468 *Loving You* ....7.00 - 10.00
6470 *Who's Making You Forget Me* ....7.00 - 10.00
6472 *My Sweetie Turned Sour On Me* ....7.00 - 10.00
6473 *Someone Thinks There's No One Like Me* ...7.00 - 10.00
6477 *You're Gonna Regret* ....7.00 - 10.00
6502 *What Am I Now?* ....7.00 - 10.00
6506 *Happy Highways* ....7.00 - 10.00
6507 *In My Wedding Gown* ....7.00 - 10.00
6511 *Whisper Why You Feel Blue* ....8.00 - 12.00

6516 *That's What Love Did To Me* ....7.00 - 10.00
6537 *Any Old Time Is Loving Time For Me* ....8.00 - 12.00
Jewel 6056 *The Recipe Song* ....7.00 - 10.00
Oriole 1786 *Can't Stop Caring For You* ....7.00 - 10.00
Romeo 1133 *Will You Think Of Me As I Think of You* ..7.00 - 10.00
1151 *Can't Stop Caring For You* ....7.00 - 10.00
1398 *Let's Be Sweethearts Now* ....8.00 - 12.00

EDDIE DUCHIN AND HIS (CENTRAL PARK CASINO) ORCHESTRA:
Brunswick 6425, 6431, 6439, 6445, 6458, 6476,
6481, 6488..5.00 - 10.00
8155 *Between The Devil And The Deep Blue Sea*
....7.00 - 10.00
Brunswick, most other issues.................................5.00 - 8.00
Columbia 2625-D *Can't We Talk It Over?* ....8.00 - 12.00
2626-D *By The Fireside* ....8.00 - 12.00
2677-D *You're Blase* ....8.00 - 12.00
2680-D *The Clouds Will Soon Roll By* ....8.00 - 12.00
Columbia, most other issues.................................3.00 - 6.00
Victor 24274, 24275, 24280, 24325, 24326, 24327,
24376, 34277, 24380, 24441, 24447, 24461,
24477, 24479, 24492, 24510, 24512, 14518,
24576...7.00 - 10.00
24579 *As Long As I Live* ....8.00 - 12.00
Victor, most other issues.......................................5.00 - 8.00

ROBERTA DUDLEY:
Nordskog 3007 *Krooked Blues* ....500.00 - up
Sunshine 3001 *Krooked Blues* ....500.00 - up
(Sunshine label is pasted over Nordskog label.)

HERVE DUERSON:
Gennett 7009 *Avenue Strut* ....150.00 - 250.00
7191 *Easy Drag* ....150.00 - 250.00

LOUIS DUMAINE'S JAZZOLA EIGHT:
Victor 20580 *Red Onion Drag* ....150.00 - 250.00
20723 *Pretty Audrey* ....150.00 - 250.00

SONNY DUNHAM AND HIS ORCHESTRA:
Bluebird 11124, 11148, 11200, 11214, 11239,
11253, 11305, 11337, 11504, 11514....................5.00 - 8.00
Varsity 8205, 8227, 8234.......................................5.00 - 8.00
Vogue R-774 *Save Me A Dream* ....35.00 - 50.00
R-775 *Clementine* ....35.00 - 50.00

BLIND WILLIE DUNN; BLIND WILLIE DUNN'S GIN BOTTLE FOUR:
Okey 8633 *Church Street Sobbin' Blues* ....40.00 - 60.00
8689 *Jet Black Blues* ....150.00 - 200.00

JOHNNY DUNN (& HIS BAND/JAZZ BAND); DUNN'S ORIGINAL JAZZ HOUNDS:
Columbia 124-D *Dunn's Cornet Blues* ....25.00 - 40.00
A3541 *Bugle Blues* ....15.00 - 20.00
A3579 *Moanful Blues* ....15.00 - 20.00
A3729 *Four O'Clock Blues* ....15.00 - 20.00
A3839 *Hallelujah Blues* ....15.00 - 20.00
A3878 *Sugar Blues* ....15.00 - 20.00
A3893 *Vamping Sal* ....15.00 - 20.00
13004-D *Jazzin' Babies Blues* ....50.00 - 75.00
14306-D *Buffalo Blues* ....150.00 - 200.00
14358-D *Ham And Eggs* ....150.00 - 200.00
Vocalion 1176 *Original Bugle Blues* ....150.00 - 250.00

JIMMY DURANTE; DURANTE'S JAZZ BAND (See also CLAYTON, JACKSON AND DURANTE):

Brunswick 6774 *Inka Dinka Doo* ....15.00 - 20.00
Columbia 36732 *Inka Dinka Doo* ....7.00 - 10.00
Gennett 9045 *Why Cry Blues*..........................15.00 - 20.00

BURT EARLE with ANGLO-AMERICAN ORCHESTRA:

Pathe 30124 *King Chanticleer*..........................15.00 - 20.00

CHARLIE EATON:

Herwin 93017 *Bucket of Blood*............................100.00 - 150.00

GEORGE ECKHARDT, JR., & HIS (CAFE LAFAYETTE) ORCHESTRA:

Vocalion 15738 *Roses Of Yesterday*.....................10.00 - 20.00
  15796 *Broadway Melody*........................10.00 - 20.00
  15803 *My Sin*.......................................10.00 - 20.00
  15806 *You Were Meant For Me* ....10.00 - 20.00

WILLIE ECKSTEIN:

Okeh 40018 *Maple Leaf Rag*....................................15.00 - 20.00
  40076 *Dizzy Fingers* ....7.00 - 10.00
  40121 *Puttin' On The Dog*.................................15.00 - 20.00

EDDIE'S HOT SHOTS:

Victor V-38046 *That's A Serious Thing* ....80.00 - 120.00

EDDIE AND SUGAR LOU'S HOTEL TYLER ORCHESTRA:

Vocalion 1445 *K.W.K.H. Blues* ....200.00 - 300.00
  1455 *There'll Be Some Changes Made* ....200.00 - 300.00
  1514 *Eddie And Sugar Lou Stomp*....................200.00 - 300.00
  1714 *Sympathetic Blues*.....................................250.00 - 400.00
  1723 *Cruel Mama Blues* ....250.00 - 400.00

EDGEWATER CROWS:

Titles issued contemporaneously on Banner, Melotone, Oriole, Perfect Romeo: *No Bonus Blues; Swinging Rhythm Around*
....50.00 - 100.00

EDDIE EDINBOROUGH & HIS NEW ORLEANS WILDCATS/WASHBOARD BAND:

Columbia 14613-D *Wild Cat's Ball* ....200.00 - up
  14629-D *Brown Baby*...200.00 - up
  14669-D *Do You Call That A Buddy?* ....150.00 - 250.00
Vocalion 1701 *Dream Sweetheart*........................150.00 - 250.00
  1702 *Nobody's Sweetheart* ....150.00 - 250.00

THOMAS A. EDISON: (See also HOLIDAY GREETINGS FROM THE BUNCH AT ORANGE)

Edison (master number) 6540 *"Let Us Not Forget"*75.00 - 100.00

CLIFF EDWARDS:

Titles, issued contemporaneously on Pathe-Actuelle and Perfect: *Clap Hands! Here Comes Charley; Dinah; How Can You Look So Good; I Don't Mind Being All Alone; I Know That You Know; I'm Back In Love Again; I'm Tellin' The Birds, Tellin' The Bees; I Never Knew What the Moonlight Could Do; I Want Somebody To Cheer Me Up; Meadow Lark; One O'Clock Baby; Say! Who Is That Baby Doll?; Side By Side; Since I Found You; Sunday; Sweet Child; That's All There Is; The Whisper Song*
....10.00 - 15.00
Brunswick 6307 *All Of A Sudden* ....8.00 - 12.00
  6319 *Crazy People* ....8.00 - 12.00
Columbia 1471-D *That's My Weakness Now* ....8.00 - 12.00
  1523-D *It Goes Like This* ....8.00 - 12.00
  1551-D *Stack O'Lee* ....8.00 - 12.00
  1639-D *My Old Girl's My New Girl Now* ....8.00 - 12.00
  1705-D *Me And The Man In The Moon* ....8.00 - 12.00

Columbia (most other issues) ....5.00 - 10.00
Pathe-Actuelle (most issues, other than titles above)
....7.00 - 10.00
Perfect (most issues, other than titles above) ....7.00 - 10.00
Vocalion 2578 *Hush My Mouth* ....10.00 - 15.00
  2587 *It's Only A Paper Moon* ....10.00 - 15.00

DAVID EDWARDS & HIS BOYS:

Okeh 41492 *Just A Crazy Song* ....20.00 - 30.00

GUS C. EDWARDS & HIS ORCHESTRA:

Victor 20167 *Crying For The Moon* ....7.00 - 10.00
  20207 *Monte Carlo Joys* ....10.00 - 15.00
  20230 *Alabama Stomp* ....7.00 - 10.00

JOAN EDWARDS WITH THE VOGUE RECORDING ORCHESTRA:

Vogue R-761 *More Than You Know* ....25.00 - 40.00
  R-767 *This Is Always* ....25.00 - 40.00
  R-782 *Maybe You'll Be There* ....25.00 - 40.00

BOB EFFROS:

Brunswick 4620 *Tin Ear*......................................20.00 - 30.00

EL COTA:

Columbia A1118 *Black And White-Ragtime Two-Step*
....10.00 - 15.00
  A1149 *Red Pepper-A Spicy Rag* ....10.00 - 15.00

ROY ELDRIDGE & HIS ORCHESTRA:

Varsity 8084 *It's My Turn Now* ....8.00 - 12.00
  8107 *Pluckin' The Bass* ....8.00 - 12.00
  8144 *Does Your Heart Beat For Me?* ....8.00 - 12.00
  8154 *High Society* ....10.00 - 15.00
Vocalion 3458 *After You've Gone* ....8.00 - 12.00
  3479 *Florida Stomp* ....8.00 - 12.00
  3577 *Heckler's Hop* ....8.00 - 12.00

ELGAR'S CREOLE ORCHESTRA:

Brunswick 3404 *Nightmare* ....75.00 - 100.00
Vocalion 15477 *Cafe Capers* ....100.00 - 150.00
  15478 *Brotherly Love* ....100.00 - 150.00

FRED ELIZALDE'S CINDERELLA ROOF ORCHESTRA:

Hollywood 1012 *Boneyard Shuffle* ....150.00 - 200.00
  1013 *Melancholy Weeps* ....150.00 - 200.00
  1014 *Tonight's My Night With Baby* ....150.00 - 200.00
  1015 *Tickling Julie*..150.00 - 200.00

DUKE ELLINGTON (& HIS ORCHESTRA/COTTON CLUB ORCHESTRA/KENTUCKY CLUB ORCHESTRA/ WASHINGTONIANS):

Blu-Disc T-1004 *Rose Marie* ....60.00 - 100.00
Bluebird 6269, 6280, 6305, 6306, 6335, 6396,
  6415, 6430...7.00 - 12.00
  6450 *Old Man Blues* ....15.00 - 20.00
  6531, 6565, 6614, 6727, 6728, 7182, 10242,
    10243, 10245...7.00 - 10.00
Brunswick 3480 *Birmingham Breakdown* ....15.00 - 25.00
  3987 *Tishomingo Blues*....................................20.00 - 30.00
  4110 *Louisiana*..20.00 - 30.00
  4122 *The Mooche*...15.00 - 25.00
  6093 *Creole Rhapsody*.....................................20.00 - 30.00
Brunswick 6265, 6288, 6317, 6355, 6374, 6404,
  6432, 6516, 6527, 6571, 6600, 6607, 6638, 6646 ... 10.00 - 12.00

Brunswick 6987, 7310, 7440, 7461, 7514, 7526,
7546, 7547, 7625, 7627, 7650, 7667, 7710,
7734, 7752, 7989, 7990, 7994, 8004, 8029,
8044, 8063, 8083, 8093, 8099, 8108, 8131,
8168, 8169, 8174, 8186, 8200, 8204, 8221,
8231, 8256, 8293, 8297, 8306, 8344, 8365,
8380, 8405, 8411 ....8.00 -   12.00
Buddy 8010 *If You Can't Hold The Man You Love* .. 250.00 -   up
    8063 *Animal Crackers* ....150.00 - 200.00
Champion 15105 *(You've Got Those) Wanna Go Back Again Blues*
    ....150.00 - 200.00
    15118 *I'm Just Wild About Animal Crackers* .....75.00 - 100.00
    15120 *Li'l Farina* ....75.00 - 100.00
Columbia 953-D *Hop Head* ....40.00 -   60.00
    1076-D *Down In Our Alley Blues* ....30.00 -   50.00
Columbia (red label, most issues) ....5.00 -   10.00
Gennett 3291 *Wanna Go Back Again Blues* ....200.00 - 300.00
    3342 *Animal Crackers* ....125.00 - 175.00
Master 101 *The New East St.Louis Toodle-Oo* ....10.00 -   15.00
    117 *It's Swell of You* ....8.00 -   12.00
    123 *The New Birmingham Breakdown* ....10.00 -   15.00
    124 *The Lady Who Couldn't Be Kissed* ....8.00 -   12.00
    131 *Azure* ....7.00 -   10.00
Okeh 8521 *Black And Tan Fantasy* ....40.00 -   60.00
    8602 *Diga Diga Doo* ....40.00 -   60.00
    8623 *The Mooche* ....40.00 -   60.00
    8636 *Black Beauty* ....80.00 - 120.00
    8662 *Misty Mornin'* ....50.00 -   75.00
    40955 *Black And Tan Fantasy* ....40.00 -   60.00
    41013 *Jubilee Stomp* ....40.00 -   60.00
    41096 *Doin' The New Low Down* ....40.00 -   60.00
Pathe-Actuelle 7504 *Georgia Grind* ....125.00 - 175.00
    36333 *Trombone Blues* ....100.00 - 150.00
Perfect 104 *Georgia Grind* ....125.00 - 175.00
    14514 *Trombone Blues* ....100.00 - 150.00
Victor L-16006 *Mood Indigo (Plus 2)* ....75.00 - 100.00
Victor L-16007 *East St. Louis Toodle-Oo (Plus 2)* .75.00 - 100.00
(The above two titles are long-playing, 33-1/3 RPM "program
    transcriptions.")

Victor 21137 *Creole Love Call* ....30.00 -   50.00
    21284 *Washington Wobble* ....50.00 -   75.00
    21490 *The Blues I Love To Sing* ....50.00 -   75.00
    21580 *Black Beauty* ....40.00 -   60.00
    21703 *Got Everything But You* ....40.00 -   60.00
    22528 *Three Little Words* ....8.00 -   12.00
    22586 *What Good Am I Without You* ....15.00 -   20.00
    22587 *Mood Indigo* ....15.00 -   20.00
    22603 *Blue Again* ....15.00 -   20.00
    22614 *Keep A Song In Your Soul* ....15.00 -   20.00
    22743 *Limehouse Blues* ....15.00 -   20.00
    22791 *It's Glory* ....15.00 -   25.00
    22800 *The Mystery Song* ....20.00 -   30.00

22938 *Bugle Call Rag* ....30.00 -   50.00
22985 *Blue Bubbles* ....15.00 -   20.00
23016 *Hittin' The Bottle* ....35.00 -   50.00
23017 *You're Lucky To Me* ....25.00 -   40.00
23022 *Jungle Nights In Harlem* ....50.00 -   75.00
23036 *Sam And Delilah* ....25.00 -   35.00
23041 *Shout 'Em, Aunt Tillie* ....30.00 -   50.00
24431 *Rude Interlude* ....20.00 -   30.00
24501 *Daybreak Express* ....15.00 -   20.00 *
24617 *Cocktails For Two* ....10.00 -   15.00
24622 *Ebony Rhapsody* ....10.00 -   15.00
24651 *My Old Flame* ....10.00 -   15.00
24755 *Delta Serenade* ....15.00 -   20.00 *
24861 *Black And Tan Fantasie* ....15.00 -   20.00 *
*extensively reissued; value is for original "scroll" Victor issue.
V 38007 *Bandanna Babies* ....35.00 -   50.00
V 38008 *Diga Diga Doo* ....35.00 -   50.00
V 38034 *The Mooche* ....75.00 - 100.00
V 38035 *Flaming Youth* ....40.00 -   60.00
V 38036 *Saturday Night Function* ....35.00 -   50.00
V 38045 *Japanese Dream* ....25.00 -   40.00
V 38053 *Stevedore Stomp* ....40.00 -   60.00
V 38058 *Saratoga Swing* ....35.00 -   50.00
V 38065 *Hot Feet* ....40.00 -   60.00
V 38079 *Cotton Club Stomp* ....40.00 -   60.00
V 38089 *Swanee Shuffle* ....40.00 -   60.00
V 38092 *The Duke Steps Out* ....40.00 -   60.00
V 38115 *Breakfast Dance* ....35.00 -   50.00
V 38129 *Jazz Lips* ....40.00 -   60.00
V 38130 *I Was Made To Love You* ....50.00 -   75.00
V 38143 *Sweet Jazz O' Mine* ....40.00 -   60.00
Vocalion 1064 *Birmingham Breakdown* ....150.00 - 200.00
    1077 *Immigration Blues* ....200.00 - 300.00
    1086 *New Orleans Low-Down* ....200.00 - 300.00
    1153 *Red Hot Band* ....200.00 - 300.00

FAY ELLIOTT'S NEW YORKERS:
Flexo 1640 *Come Easy Go Easy Love* ....75.00 - 100.00

GAY ELLIS (See also DOT DARE and ANNETTE HANSHAW, the latter being the real name of this artist, whose recordings for Diva, Harmony, and Velvet Tone were issued under all three names.):
Diva 2706-G I *Must Have That Man* ....10.00 -   15.00
Harmony 766-H *My Blackbirds Are Bluebirds Now*
    ....15.00 -   20.00
    785-H *You're The Cream In My Coffee* ....10.00 -   15.00
    832-H *When The World Is At Rest* ....10.00 -   15.00
    859-H *Mean To Me* ....10.00 -   15.00
    981-H *True Blue Lou* ....10.00 -   15.00
    1196-H *Little White Lies* ....10.00 -   15.00
    1273-H *You're The One I Care For* ....15.00 -   20.00
    1324-H *Ho Hum!* ....15.00 -   20.00

SEGER ELLIS; SEGER ELLIS & HIS (CHOIRS OF BRASS) ORCHESTRA:
Ammor 118 *Way Down* ....8.00 -   12.00
Brunswick 6022 *It's A Lonesome Old Town* ....15.00 -   20.00
    6050 *Tie A Little String Around Your Finger* ....10.00 -   15.00
    6076 *One Little Raindrop* ....10.00 -   15.00
    6078 *I've Found What I Wanted In You* ....10.00 -   15.00
    6135 *Nevertheless* ....10.00 -   15.00
Bullet 1011 *Let's Drive Out To Joe's Drive In* ....7.00 -   10.00
    1014 *Little Jack Frost Get Lost* ....7.00 -   10.00

Columbia 2362-D *Cheerful Little Earful*.................15.00 - 20.00
Decca 1275 *Shivery Stomp* ....8.00 - 12.00
   1322 *I Know That You Know*................................8.00 - 12.00
   1350 *Bees Knees* ....8.00 - 12.00
Okeh 5966 *No Jug, No Jazz* ....7.00 - 10.00
   6051 *Mellow Stuff*...7.00 - 10.00
   40970 *Poppin' 'Em Out*...................................30.00 - 50.00
   41024 *I Must Be Dreaming*...........................15.00 - 20.00
   41047 *If I Can't Have You*..............................15.00 - 20.00
   41061 *Sweet Sue-Just You* ....10.00 - 15.00
   41077 *I Can't Give You Anything But Love* ....15.00 - 20.00
   41103 *Out Of The Dawn*..................................15.00 - 20.00
   41127 *Dream House* ....8.00 - 12.00
   41160 *Don't Be Like That*................................15.00 - 20.00
   41165 *Where The Shy Little Violets Grow* ....15.00 - 20.00
   41190 *My Inspiration Is You* ....15.00 - 20.00
   41221 *Louise*...15.00 - 20.00
   41222 *Mean To Me* ....15.00 - 20.00
   41224 *You, Just You* ....15.00 - 20.00
   41225 *Only For You* ....15.00 - 20.00
   41255 *To Be In Love (Espesh'ly With You)*........40.00 - 60.00
   41289 *Nobody But You* ....15.00 - 20.00
   41290 *True Blue Lou* ....40.00 - 60.00
   41291 *Ain't Misbehavin'* ....40.00 - 60.00
   41321 *If I Had A Talking Picture Of You* ....15.00 - 25.00
   41349 *Have A Little Faith In Me* ....15.00 - 20.00
   41396 *Should I?* ....15.00 - 20.00
   41405 *What Is This Thing Called Love?* ....15.00 - 20.00
   41413 *The Moon Is Low* ....15.00 - 20.00
   41417 *Sentimental Blues*..................................35.00 - 50.00
   41424 *Exactly Like You* ....15.00 - 25.00
   41436 *Swinging In A Hammock* ....15.00 - 20.00
   41441 *Confessin'* ....20.00 - 30.00
   41443 *Little White Lies* ....20.00 - 30.00
   41447 *Shivery Stomp* ....40.00 - 60.00
   41452 *If I Could Be With You One Hour Tonight*.. 20.00 - 30.00
   41467 *Sweet Jennie Lee*...................................20.00 - 30.00
   41473 *You're Driving Me Crazy* ....25.00 - 40.00
   41479 *You're The One I Care For* ....20.00 - 30.00
(Later issues on Okeh have a special Seger Ellis picture label.)
Victor 19755 *Prairie Blues*............................10.00 - 15.00
   19952 *Ash Can Blues*.......................................15.00 - 20.00
Vocalion 5534 *Bye Bye Blues* ....7.00 - 10.00
   5966 *When It's Sleepy Time Down South*............7.00 - 10.00
   5721 *Happy Travelin'* ....7.00 - 10.00

ZIGGY ELMAN & HIS ORCHESTRA:
Bluebird, most issues ....5.00 - 10.00
MGM, most issues ....4.00 - 8.00

EMERSON DANCE/SYMPHONY ORCHESTRA; EMERSON MILITARY BAND:
Emerson 1025 *The Alcoholic Blues* (10-inch) ....10.00 - 15.00
   7122 *Honky-Tonk Rag* ....15.00 - 20.00
   7145 *Razzazza Mazzazza* ....15.00 - 20.00
   7161 *Chicken Walk* ....10.00 - 15.00
   7162 *Rooster Rag* ....15.00 - 20.00
   7163 *Saxophone Sobs* ....15.00 - 20.00
   7211 *Shim-Me-Sha-Wabble* ....15.00 - 20.00
   7212 *The Darktown Strutters' Ball*...................8.00 - 12.00
   7224 *Indiana* ....8.00 - 12.00
   7225 *Zamp-A-Zamp Rag* ....15.00 - 20.00
   7265 *Spooky Spooks* ....15.00 - 20.00
   7295 *Yah-De-Dah* ....10.00 - 15.00

   7319 *Indianola* ....10.00 - 15.00
   7322 *The Wild, Wild Women Are Making A Wild Man Of Me*
....10.00 - 15.00
(Note: Above are 7-inch records.)

THE EMPERORS:
Harmony 362-H *Clarinet Marmalade* ....35.00 - 50.00
   383-H *Go, Joe, Go* ....35.00 - 50.00

PEGGY ENGLISH:
Vocalion 15093 *Charleston Baby O' Mine*............. 10.00 - 15.00
   15118 *You Can't Shush Katy* .... 15.00 - 20.00
   15132 *Sweet Man* .... 15.00 - 20.00
   15381 *How Many Times?* .... 15.00 - 20.00
   15504 *High-High-High Up In The Hills* .... 15.00 - 20.00

SHARLIE ENGLISH:
Paramount 12610 *Transom Blues* .... 150.00 - 200.00
   12644 *Broke Woman Blues*............................ 150.00 - 200.00

EQUINOX ORCHESTRA OF PRINCETON, NEW JERSEY:
Personal Record 115-P *China Boy*......................... 75.00 - 100.00

WALLY ERICKSON'S COLISEUM ORCHESTRA:
Gennett 3068 *The Meanest Kind Of Blues*.............. 75.00 - 100.00
   3069 *The Call Of The South*............................ 20.00 - 30.00
Vocalion 15778 *Hard Luck*................................... 75.00 - 100.00

ERWING BROTHERS' ORCHESTRA:
Vocalion 2564 *The Erwing Blues* .... 50.00 - 75.00

ESSEX CLUB ORCHESTRA:
Vocalion 15170 *A Little Bit Bad* .... 8.00 - 12.00
   15221, 15224, 15230, 15423............................. 5.00 - 8.00
   15424 *My Cutey's Due At Two-To-Two Today*
.... 10.00 - 15.00

RUTH ETTING:
Titles issued contemporaneously on Banner, Conqueror, Melotone, Oriole, Perfect, Romeo: *All Of Me; Can't We Talk It Over; Happy-Go-Lucky You; Have You Forgotten?; Hey! Young Fella; How Can I Go On Without You; If I Didn't Have You; I'll Follow You; I'll Never Be The Same; I'll Never Have To Dream Again; It Was So Beautiful; Just One More Chance; Lazy Day; Let Me Call You Sweetheart; Linger A Little While Longer In The Twilight; Love Letters In The Sand, Nevertheless; Some Day We'll Meet Again; Take Me In Your Arms Again; That's What Heaven Means To Me; Try a Little Tenderness; Without That Gal; With Summer Coming On; You've Got Me Crying Again*
.... 10.00 - 20.00
Brunswick 6657 *Close Your Eyes*......................... 10.00 - 15.00
   6671 *What Is Sweeter*.................................... 10.00 - 15.00
   6697 *Build A Little Home* .... 10.00 - 15.00
   6719 *Everything I Have Is Yours* .... 10.00 - 15.00
   6761 *Keep Romance Alive* .... 10.00 - 15.00
   6769 *Smoke Gets In Your Eyes* .... 10.00 - 15.00
   6892 *Easy Come, Easy Go* .... 10.00 - 15.00
   6914 *Were Your Ears Burning?* .... 10.00 - 15.00
   7646 *It's Been So Long* .... 10.00 - 15.00
Columbia 580-D *Let's Talk About My Sweetie*....... 15.00 - 25.00
   633-D *Could I? I Certainly Could* .... 15.00 - 20.00
   644-D *Lonesome And Sorry* .... 15.00 - 20.00
   675-D *What A Man!* .... 15.00 - 20.00
   692-D *I Ain't Got Nobody* .... 10.00 - 15.00
   722-D *Her Beaus Are Only Rainbows* .... 10.00 - 15.00

764-D *Stars* ....10.00 - 15.00
827-D *Thinking Of You* ....10.00 - 15.00
865-D *'Deed I Do* ....10.00 - 15.00
908-D *It All Depends On You* ....10.00 - 15.00
924-D *Hoosier Sweetheart* ....10.00 - 15.00
979-D *Dew-Dew Dewy Day* ....10.00 - 15.00
995-D *After You've Gone* ....8.00 - 12.00
1052-D *Sing Me A Baby Song* ....10.00 - 15.00
1075-D *Swanee Shore* ....10.00 - 15.00
1104-D *You Don't Like It-Not Much!* ....10.00 - 15.00
1113-D *Shaking The Blues Away* ....10.00 - 15.00
1196-D *Together, We Two* ....10.00 - 15.00
1208-D *Blue River* ....10.00 - 15.00
1237-D *The Varsity Drag* ....10.00 - 15.00
1288-D *Back In Your Own Backyard* ....10.00 - 15.00
1312-D *I Ain't Got Nobody* ....10.00 - 15.00
1352-D *Ramona* ....8.00 - 12.00
1393-D *I Must Be Dreaming* ....10.00 - 15.00
1420-D *Because My Baby Don't Mean "Maybe" Now*
....10.00 - 15.00
1454-D *Lonely Little Bluebird* ....8.00 - 12.00
1563-D *Sonny Boy* ....8.00 - 12.00
1595-D *My Blackbirds Are Bluebirds Now* ....8.00 - 12.00
1680-D *Love Me Or Leave Me* ....7.00 - 10.00
1707-D *You're The Cream In My Coffee* ....10.00 - 15.00
1733-D *I'll Get By* ....10.00 - 15.00
1762-D *Button Up Your Overcoat* ....10.00 - 15.00
1801-D *Maybe-Who Knows?* ....10.00 - 15.00
1830-D *Walking Around In A Dream* ....10.00 - 15.00
1883-D *I Want To Meander In The Meadow* .....10.00 - 15.00
1958-D *Ain't Misbehavin'* ....15.00 - 20.00
1998-D *The Right Kind Of Man* ....10.00 - 15.00
2038-D *More Than You Know* ....15.00 - 20.00
2073-D *Crying For The Carolines* ....15.00 - 20.00
2146-D *Ten Cents A Dance* ....8.00 - 12.00
2172-D *Let Me Sing And I'm Happy* ....15.00 - 20.00
2199-D *Exactly Like You* ....15.00 - 20.00
2216-D *Dancing With Tears In My Eyes* ....8.00 - 12.00
2280-D *The Kiss Waltz* ....10.00 - 15.00
2300-D *If I Could Be With You* ....15.00 - 20.00
2307-D *Just A Little Closer* ....15.00 - 20.00
2318-D *Laughing At Life* ....15.00 - 20.00
2377-D *Reaching For The Moon* ....15.00 - 20.00
2398-D *You're The One I Care For* ....15.00 - 20.00
2445-D *Were You Sincere?* ....15.00 - 20.00
2454-D *Out Of Nowhere* ....15.00 - 20.00
2470-D *Moonlight Saving Time* ....15.00 - 20.00
2505-D *I'm Falling In Love* ....15.00 - 20.00
2529-D *Guilty* ....10.00 - 15.00
2557-D *Goodnight, Sweetheart* ....15.00 - 20.00
2580-D *Cuban Love Song* ....15.00 - 20.00
2630-D *When We're Alone* ....15.00 - 20.00
2660-D *The Voice In The Old Village Choir* ......15.00 - 20.00
2681-D *Holding My Honey's Hand* ....15.00 - 20.00
2954-D *Talkin' To Myself* ....20.00 - 30.00
2955-D *Out In The Cold Again* ....20.00 - 30.00
2979-D *A Needle In A Haystack* ....20.00 - 30.00
2985-D *Am I To Blame?* ....20.00 - 30.00
3014-D *March Winds And April Showers* ....20.00 - 30.00
3031-D *It's Easy To Remember* ....20.00 - 30.00
3070-D *I Wished On The Moon* ....20.00 - 30.00
3085-D *Ten Cents A Dance* ....20.00 - 30.00

Decca 1084 *There's Something In The Air* ....8.00 - 12.00
    1107 *Goodnight, My Love* ....8.00 - 12.00
    1212 *It's Swell Of You* ....7.00 - 10.00
    1259 *On A Little Dream Ranch* ....8.00 - 12.00

EUROPE'S SOCIETY ORCHESTRA; LT. JIM EUROPE'S 369th INFANTRY (HELL FIGHTERS) BAND:
Pathe 22081 *Darktown Strutters' Ball* ....15.00 - 20.00
    22082 *Ja Da* ....15.00 - 20.00
    22085 *Memphis Blues* ....15.00 - 25.00
    22086 *Hesitating Blues* ....15.00 - 25.00
    22087 *St. Louis Blues* ....15.00 - 25.00
    22103 *Jazz Baby* ....15.00 - 25.00
    22167 *Clarinet Marmalade* ....15.00 - 25.00
Pathe, most other issues including those by singing groups
....8.00 - 12.00
Victor 17533 *Castle Walk* ....10.00 - 15.00
    35359 *Down Home Rag* (12 inch) ....15.00 - 20.00
    35372 *Castle House Rag* (12 inch) ....15.00 - 20.00

BILLY EVANS' HAPPY FIVE:
Domino 3990 *Vo-Do-Do-De-O Blues* ....10.00 - 15.00
Regal 8353 *Vo-Do-Do-De-O Blues* ....10.00 - 15.00

EDITH EVANS:
Brunswick 4291 *My Kinda Love* ....10.00 - 15.00

ROY EVANS:
Columbia 1380-D, 1697-D, 1934-D ....5.00 - 10.00
Columbia 1449-D *Dusky Stevedore* ....10.00 - 15.00
    1559-D *Syncopated Yodelin' Man* ....10.00 - 15.00
Columbia 2198-D *I Lost My Gal From Memphis* ..10.00 - 15.00
    2257-D *So Sorry* ....10.00 - 15.00
    2338-D *I'm Tickled Pink With A Blue-Eyed Baby*
....10.00 - 15.00
    2469-D *Roll On, Mississippi, Roll On* ....15.00 - 20.00
    15272-D *I Ain't Got Nobody* ....10.00 - 15.00
Crown 3154 *One More Time* ....10.00 - 15.00

EVERETT'S SERENADERS:
Dandy 5118 *I Wonder Where My Baby Is Tonight* ... 8.00 - 12.00

ELIOT EVERETT AND HIS ORCHESTRA:
Victor 22921 *Blue Danube Blues* ....10.00 - 15.00
    24080 *In A Little Blue Canoe With You* ....10.00 - 15.00
    24085 *Little Nell* ....10.00 - 15.00

EVERGLADES ORCHESTRA:
Okeh 40800 *Mine* ....10.00 - 15.00

WILL EZELL:
Paramount 12549 *Barrel House Man* ....200.00 - 300.00
    12688 *Mixed Up Rag* ....200.00 - 300.00
    12729 *Crawlin' Spider Blues* ....150.00 - 200.00
    12753 *Barrel House Woman* ....200.00 - 300.00
    12773 *Bucket Of Blood* ....200.00 - 300.00
    12855 *Pitchin' Boogie* ....300.00 - up
    12914 *Freakish Mistreater Blues* ....300.00 - up

SAMMY FAIN:
Harmony 843-H *Love Me Or Leave Me* ....7.00 - 10.00
    904-H *The Things That Were Made For Love* ... 10.00 - 15.00
    943-H *What A Day!* ....15.00 - 20.00
    961-H *Why Can't You* ....10.00 - 15.00
    993-H *Ain't Misbehavin'* ....10.00 - 15.00
    1014-H *Painting The Clouds With Sunshine* ......8.00 - 12.00
    1078-H *Navy Blues* ....8.00 - 12.00

1114-H *The One I Love Just Can't Be Bothered With Me* ....8.00 - 12.00
1163-H *I'm In The Market For You* ....10.00 - 15.00
1179-H *You Brought A New Kind of Love To Me* ....10.00 - 15.00
1203-H *Confessin'* ....8.00 - 12.00
1250-H *You're Driving Me Crazy* ....8.00 - 12.00
(Above titles, on Diva and Velvet Tone, are similarly valued)

OWEN FALLON AND HIS CALIFORNIANS:
Melotone 12199 *Under Your Window Tonight* ....10.00 - 15.00
12212 *Take It From Me (I'm Takin' To You)* .....10.00 - 15.00
12337 *I Know You're Lying, But I Love It* ....10.00 - 15.00
12409 *Sleep (Come On And Take Me)* ....10.00 - 15.00
Silver Screen 143 *If You Hadn't Gone Away* ....30.00 - 50.00
Sunset 1134 *Lonesome Me* ....15.00 - 25.00
1135 *Darktown Shuffle* ....40.00 - 60.00
1142 *That Certain Party* ....15.00 - 25.00
1152 *I Love My Baby* ....20.00 - 30.00

WILLIE FARMER AND HIS ORCHESTRA:
Bluebird 7024, 7026, 7036, 7170, 7171, 7181, 7183, 7519, 7527, 7685, 7687, 7698, 7722, 7724, 7735, 7795, 7799, 7813 ....7.00 - 12.00

FRANK FARRELL & HIS (GREENWICH VILLAGE INN) ORCHESTRA:
Cameo 1195 *Zulu Wail* ....8.00 - 12.00
1209 *It's A Million To One You're In Love* ....10.00 - 15.00
Cameo, most other issues ....5.00 - 8.00
Harmony 371-H *South Wind* ....7.00 - 10.00
402-H *I'm Back In Love Again* ....7.00 - 10.00
434-H *Gorgeous* ....7.00 - 10.00
462-H *Miss Annabelle Lee* ....10.00 - 15.00
471-H *Are You Happy?* ....7.00 - 10.00
483-H *Shaking The Blues Away* ....10.00 - 15.00
488-H *The Varsity Drag* ....8.00 - 12.00
584-H *Back In Your Own Back Yard* ....8.00 - 12.00
590-H *Singapore Sorrows* ....8.00 - 12.00
(Note: Above titles on Diva and Velvet Tone are similarly valued.)
Lincoln 2658 *Zulu Wail* ....8.00 - 12.00
2674 *It's A Million To One You're In Love* ....10.00 - 15.00
Lincoln, most other issues ....5.00 - 8.00
Romeo 423 *Zulu Wail* ....8.00 - 12.00
437 *It's A Million To One You're In Love* ....10.00 - 15.00
Romeo, most other issues ....5.00 - 8.00

ALICE FAYE:
Titles issued contemporaneously on Banner, Brunswick, Melotone, Oriole, Perfect, Romeo: *According To The Moonlight; I Love To Ride The Horses; I'm Shootin' High; I've Got My Fingers Crossed; My Future Star; Oh, I Didn't Know; Spreadin' Rhythm Around; Yes To You* ....10.00 - 15.00
Brunswick 7821, 7825, 7860, 7876 ....8.00 - 12.00

EARL FEGAN & HIS HOTEL DEL CORONADO ORCHESTRA:
Hollywood 1051 *Who Do You Love* ....8.00 - 12.00

CARL FENTON & HIS ORCHESTRA:
Brunswick 3519 *Delirium* ....8.00 - 12.00
4421 *What A Day!* ....15.00 - 20.00
Brunswick, most other issues ....4.00 - 7.00
QRS Q-1004 *Night Time is Love Time* ....10.00 - 15.00
Q-1005 *Bless Her Little Heart* ....15.00 - 25.00
Q-1018 *Hello Little Sweetheart* ....10.00 - 15.00
Q-1023 *Shake It Down* ....50.00 - 100.00
Q-1026 *Won'tcha* ....10.00 - 15.00

Q-1037 *That's When I Learned To Love You* ... 10.00 - 15.00
Q-1038 *The Moon Is Low* ....10.00 - 15.00
Q-1039 *Sing You Sinners* ....20.00 - 30.00
Q-1046 *The Stein Song* ....10.00 - 15.00
Q-1049 *Exactly Like You* ....10.00 - 15.00
Q-1051 *Whippoorwill* ....10.00 - 15.00
Q-1060 *Without You, Emaline* ....15.00 - 20.00
Supertone 9360 *Mississippi, Here I Am* ....7.00 - 10.00
9378 *That's What I Call Heaven* ....7.00 - 10.00
9480 *I've Made A Habit Of You* ....7.00 - 10.00

JERRY FENWYCK AND HIS ORCHESTRA:
Clarion 5282-C *Little Joe* ....7.00 - 10.00
5305-C *That Little Boy Of Mine* ....7.00 - 10.00
5352-C *How The Time Can Fly* ....8.00 - 12.00
5360-C *Take It From Me* ....10.00 - 15.00
5364-C *Do The New York* ....10.00 - 15.00
5398-C *A Faded Summer Love* ....8.00 - 12.00
5408-C *You Didn't Know The Music* ....8.00 - 12.00
5415-C *Now's The Time To Fall In Love* ....15.00 - 20.00
5420-C *By The Sycamore Tree* ....15.00 - 20.00
5421-C *I Wouldn't Change You For The World* .....10.00 - 15.00
5442-C *All Of Me* ....20.00 - 30.00
11500-C *You Call It Madness* ....10.00 - 15.00
11503-C *Who's Your Little Who-Zis!* ....20.00 - 30.00
(Note: 11503-C is a five-minute record having two cuts of the tune- one instrumental, the other vocal.)
Harmony 1301-H *I'll See You In Kentucky* ....7.00 - 10.00
1314-H *That Little Boy Of Mine* ....7.00 - 10.00
1341-H *How The Time Can Fly* ....8.00 - 12.00
1348-H *Take It From Me* ....10.00 - 15.00
1352-H *Do The New York* ....10.00 - 15.00
1384-H *A Faded Summer Love* ....7.00 - 10.00
1389-H *You Didn't Know The Music* ....8.00 - 12.00
1394-H *Now's The Time To Fall In Love* ....15.00 - 20.00
1397-H *By The Sycamore Tree* ....15.00 - 20.00
1398-H *I Wouldn't Change You For The World* . 7.00 - 10.00
1403-H *All Of Me* ....20.00 - 30.00
6500-H *You Call It Madness* ....10.00 - 15.00
Velvet Tone 2348-V *Little Joe* ....5.00 - 8.00
2371-V *Out Of Nowhere* ....7.00 - 10.00
2373-V *That Little Boy Of Mine* ....5.00 - 8.00
2416-V *How The Time Can Fly* ....8.00 - 12.00
2424-V *Take It From Me* ....10.00 - 15.00
2461-V *Lies* ....7.00 - 10.00
2462-V *A Faded Summer Love* ....7.00 - 10.00
2468-V *You Didn't Know The Music* ....8.00 - 12.00
2475-V *Now's The Time To Fall In Love* ....15.00 - 20.00
2480-V *By The Sycamore Tree* ....15.00 - 20.00
2481-V *I Wouldn't Change You For The World* . 7.00 - 10.00
2502-V *All Of Me* ....20.00 - 30.00
10500-V *When The Rest Of The Crowd Goes Home* ....10.00 - 15.00

ARTHUR FIELDS AND HIS ASSASSINATORS/ NOODLERS/WINDJAMMERS:
Banner 6314 *Let's Get Together* ....10.00 - 15.00
6315 *Geraldine* ....10.00 - 15.00
6317 *What Do You Think Of My Baby* ....10.00 - 15.00
Edison (thin) 14061 *Sophomore Prom* ....50.00 - 80.00
14075 *Piccolo Pete* ....75.00 - 100.00
Edison (thick) 52123 *Is It Possible?* ....40.00 - 60.00
52180 *Look In The Mirror* ....50.00 - 75.00
52264 *She's A Great, Great Girl* ....75.00 - 100.00

52535 *She Only Laughs At Me* ....75.00 - 100.00
52553 *I Faw Down An' Go 'Boom* ....75.00 - 100.00
Grey Gull 1753 *Humpty Dumpty Baby* ....8.00 - 12.00
  1781 *Bluer Than You* ....8.00 - 12.00
  1833 *So Do I* ....8.00 - 12.00
(Note: Other titles by **ARTHUR FIELDS & HIS
  WINDJAMMERS** on Grey Gull, Radiex, Van Dyke, and
  possibly other related labels not yet documented, are similarly
  valued.)

BUDDY FIELDS AND HIS ORCHESTRA:
Romeo 1052, 1053, 1069, 1070, 1084 ....7.00 - 12.00
  1068 *Lovable And Sweet* ....10.00 - 15.00

ERNIE FIELDS & HIS ORCHESTRA:
Vocalion 5073 *Lard Stomp* ....10.00 - 15.00
  5157 *High Jivin'* ....10.00 - 15.00
  5240 *I'm Living In A Great Big Way* ....10.00 - 15.00
  5344 *Blues At Midnight* ....10.00 - 15.00

SHEP FIELDS AND HIS ORCHESTRA/RIPPLING RHYTHM:
Bluebird, most issues ....5.00 - 10.00
Musicraft, most issues ....4.00 - 8.00
Victor, most issues ....4.00 - 8.00
Vogue R-712 *Atlanta, Ga* ....35.00 - 40.00
  R-715 *I Can't Begin To Tell You* ....500.00 - up
  R-764 *Whattaya Gonna Do* ....25.00 - 40.00
  R-765 *What Is Love* ....500.00 - up

LLOYD FINLAY AND HIS ORCHESTRA:
Victor 19643 *You'll Want Me Back Someday* ....20.00 - 30.00
  19644 *Jews-Harp Blues* ....20.00 - 30.00
  19696 *Rope 'Em, Cowboy* ....20.00 - 30.00

BOB FINLEY AND HIS ORCHESTRA:
Cameo 9101 *Doin' The Campus Crawl* ....8.00 - 12.00
  9103 *Nobody's Baby But Mine* ....8.00 - 12.00
  9105 *Audition Blues* ....10.00 - 15.00
Romeo 903 *Doin' The Campus Crawl* ....8.00 - 12.00
  905 *Nobody's Baby But Mine* ....8.00 - 12.00
  907 *Audition Blues* ....10.00 - 15.00
(The foregoing titles might also be found on Lincoln, similarly
  valued)

DOUGLAS FINNELL AND HIS ROYAL STOMPERS:
Brunswick 7123 *Sweet Sweet Mama* ....150.00 - 200.00

ETHEL FINNIE:
Ajax 17015 *Don't You Quit Me, Daddy* ....25.00 - 40.00
  17027 *Hula Blues* ....25.00 - 40.00
Emerson 10846 *Heart-Breakin' Joe* ....35.00 - 50.00

FINZEL'S ARCADIA ORCHESTRA OF DETROIT:
Okeh 4735 *Stop Your Kiddin'* ....8.00 - 12.00
  4743 *I Gave You Up Just Before You Threw Me Down*
    ....8.00 - 12.00
  4758 *Falling* ....7.00 - 10.00
  4759 *Teddy Bear Blues* ....7.00 - 10.00
  4847 *Farewell Blues* ....15.00 - 20.00
  4858 *Morning Will Come* ....7.00 - 10.00
  4859 *Who's Sorry Now?* ....7.00 - 10.00
  4861 *Barney Google* ....7.00 - 10.00
  4985 *Stealing To Virginia* ....7.00 - 10.00
  4999 *Mama Loves Papa, Papa Loves Mama* ....10.00 - 15.00
  40043 *Keep A-Goin'* ....10.00 - 15.00

40053 *Mom-Ma* ....7.00 - 10.00
40069 *The Animal Fair* ....7.00 - 10.00
40148 *Lots O' Mama* ....10.00 - 15.00
40161 *Dicty Blues* ....15.00 - 20.00
40298 *Laff It Off* ....10.00 - 15.00
40301 *Weepin' The Blues* ....15.00 - 20.00
40304 *I Can't Stop Babying You* ....10.00 - 15.00

TED FIORITO AND HIS (EDGEWATER BEACH HOTEL) ORCHESTRA:
Brunswick 6422, 6478, 6479, 6493, 6503, 6505,
  6526, 6555, 6556, 5686, 6598, 6627, 6670, 6705,
  6706, 6736, 6746, 6859, 6860, 6863, 6902, 6919,
  6924, 6928, 7311, 7315, 7327, 7364, 7379, 7380,
  7392, 7399, 7446, 7451, 7452, 7478, 7489 ....7.00 - 10.00
Columbia 1967-D *Then You've Never Been Blue* ... 10.00 - 15.00
Decca 677, 678, 679, 694, 697, 746, 771, 777, 784,
  793, 894, 909, 910, 925, 935, 936, 954, 1176,
  1193, 1257, 1258, 1450, 1452, 1453, 1561,
  1567, 1591 ....7.00 - 10.00
Decca, most other issues ....5.00 - 8.00
Hit of the Week 1104 *My Baby Just Cares For Me* . 8.00 - 12.00
Victor 22252 *Under A Texas Moon* ....8.00 - 12.00
  22262 *Molly* ....7.00 - 10.00
  22300 *There Will Never Be Another Mary* ....15.00 - 20.00
  22301 *Hangin' On The Garden Gate* ....7.00 - 10.00
  22501 *Tomorrow Is Another Day* ....7.00 - 10.00

FREDDIE ("SCHNICKELFRITZ") FISHER & HIS ORCHESTRA:
Decca 1400 *I'm A Ding Dong Daddy* ....8.00 - 12.00
  1501 *When My Baby Smiles At Me* ....8.00 - 12.00
  1537 *Washboard Man* ....8.00 - 12.00
  5330 *My Bonnie Lies Over The Ocean* ....8.00 - 12.00
  5331 *Red Hot Mama* ....8.00 - 12.00
  5335 *Schnickelfritz Waltz* ....8.00 - 12.00
Decca (most other issues) ....5.00 - 10.00
United Artist 326 *Get Away From The Fish Wagon, Gertrude*
  ....8.00 - 12.00

MARK FISHER AND HIS EDGEWATER BEACH HOTEL ORCHESTRA:
Columbia 2749-D *Black-Eyed Susan Brown* ....15.00 - 20.00
  2754-D *Why Can't This Night Go On Forever* ... 8.00 - 12.00

MAX FISHER & HIS (CALIFORNIA) ORCHESTRA:
Columbia 1008-D, 1064-D, 1226-D ....7.00 - 10.00
  1235-D *Is She My Girl Friend?* ....8.00 - 12.00
  1376-D *So Tired* ....7.00 - 10.00

ELLA FITZGERALD & HER SAVOY EIGHT/FAMOUS ORCHESTRA:
Decca 1061 *My Last Affair* ....10.00 - 15.00
  1062 *Organ Grinder's Swing* ....10.00 - 15.00
  1302 *If You Should Ever Leave* ....10.00 - 15.00
  1339 *All Over Nothing At All* ....10.00 - 15.00
  1596 *Bei Mir Bist Du Schoen* ....10.00 - 15.00
  1669 *It's Wonderful* ....8.00 - 12.00
  1806 *This Time It's Real* ....8.00 - 12.00
  1846 *Saving Myself For You* ....8.00 - 12.00
  1967 *If You Only Knew* ....8.00 - 12.00
Decca (most other issues) ....7.00 - 10.00

FIVE BIRMINGHAM BABIES:
Pathe-Actuelle 036129 *Tessie! Stop Teasing Me* ....10.00 - 15.00
036130 *Hard-Hearted Hannah*............................10.00 - 15.00
036142 *Arkansas* ....15.00 - 20.00
036168 *Go, Emmaline* ....15.00 - 20.00
036169 *Copenhagen* ....10.00 - 15.00
36218 *Pickin' On Your Baby* ....15.00 - 20.00
36228 *Down And Out Blues* ....15.00 - 20.00
36235 *You're In Wrong With The Right Baby*....10.00 - 15.00
36236 *Mamie* ....10.00 - 15.00
36266 *Tiger Rag* ....20.00 - 30.00
36274 *I'm Grieving For You* ....15.00 - 20.00
36296 *I Know What It Means* ....15.00 - 20.00
36340 *Dixie Stomp*..15.00 - 20.00
36349 *Indigo Blues* ....15.00 - 20.00
36350 *One Week From Now* ....100.00 - 150.00
36352 *Go Back Where You Stayed Last Night* ...15.00 - 20.00
36379 *What! No Women?*....................................15.00 - 20.00
36432 *What A Man!*..15.00 - 20.00
36451 *She's Not Too Hot, Not Too Cold*............15.00 - 20.00
36454 *Remember The Night* ....10.00 - 15.00
36467 *Some Baby, My Gal* ....15.00 - 20.00
Perfect 14310 *Tessie! Stop Teasing Me* ....10.00 - 15.00
14311 *Hard-Hearted Hannah*............................10.00 - 15.00
14323 *Arkansas* ....15.00 - 20.00
14349 *Go, Emmaline* ....15.00 - 20.00
14350 *Copenhagen* ....10.00 - 15.00
14399 *You Better Keep The Home Fires Burning* . 15.00 - 20.00
14409 *Not Now-Not Yet-But Soon* ....15.00 - 20.00
14416 *You're In Wrong With The Right Baby*....10.00 - 15.00
14417 *What Do We Get From Boston?* ....10.00 - 15.00
14447 *Tiger Rag* ....20.00 - 30.00
14455 *Love Me Daddy Blues*...............................15.00 - 20.00
14477 *As Far As I'm Concerned* ....15.00 - 20.00
14521 *Dixie Stomp*..15.00 - 20.00
14530 *Indigo Blues* ....15.00 - 20.00
14531 *One Week From Now* ....100.00 - 150.00
14533 *Go Back Where You Stayed Last Night* ...15.00 - 20.00
14560 *What! No Women?*....................................15.00 - 20.00
14613 *What A Man!*..15.00 - 20.00
14632 *She's Not Too Hot, Not Too Cold*............15.00 - 20.00
14635 *Remember The Night* ....10.00 - 15.00
14648 *Some Baby, My Gal* ....15.00 - 20.00

FIVE HARMANIACS; FIVE HARMONIACS:
Brunswick 3664 *Carolina Bound* ....20.00 - 30.00
7002 *Sleepy Blues* ....80.00 - 120.00
Edison 51902 *Rippin' It Off* ....100.00 - 150.00
Gennett 6033 *What Did Romie-O-Juliet* ....100.00 - 150.00
Victor 20293 *Coney Island Washboard* ....10.00 - 15.00
20507 *What Makes My Baby Cry?* ....20.00 - 30.00

FIVE HOT CHOCOLATES:
Radiex 952 *Baby Knows How* ....40.00 - 60.00
Van Dyke 71767 *Baby Knows How* ....40.00 - 60.00
71775 *Alabama Shuffle*......................................50.00 - 75.00
71786 *Memphis Stomp*..50.00 - 75.00

FIVE LITTLE CHOCOLATE DANDIES:
Okeh 8627 *Four Or Five Times*................................50.00 - 80.00

FIVE MUSICAL BLACKBIRDS:
Pathe-Actuelle 7508 *18th Street Strut* ....80.00 - 120.00
36404 *Hot Coffee*..75.00 - 100.00
Perfect 108 *18th Street Strut*..................................80.00 - 120.00
14585 *Hot Coffee* ....75.00 - 100.00

FIVE RHYTHM KINGS:
Victor 23269 *Minnie The Moocher* ....40.00 - 60.00

FLEETWOOD ORCHESTRA:
Vocalion 15152, 15222, 15422, 15462, 15466,
15470, 15516... 5.00 - 10.00

JAY C. FLIPPEN (& HIS HOT COMBINATION):
Pathe-Actuelle 32196 *Lucky Day* .... 10.00 - 15.00
32218 *She Knows Her Onions* .... 15.00 - 20.00
32223 *Short And Sweet* .... 15.00 - 20.00
32229 *If I Didn't Know Your Husband*............. 15.00 - 20.00
32260 *South Wind* .... 15.00 - 20.00
32288 *You Don't Like It-Not Much* .... 15.00 - 20.00
32294 *I Ain't Got Nobody* .... 15.00 - 20.00
32313 *Oh! My Operation* .... 15.00 - 20.00
32321 *I Told Them All About You*...................... 15.00 - 20.00
32329 *Let A Smile Be Your Umbrella*............... 15.00 - 20.00
Perfect 12284 *Baby Face* .... 10.00 - 15.00
12295 *How Many Times?* .... 10.00 - 15.00
12297 *How Could Red Riding Hood?* .... 15.00 - 20.00
12302 *For My Sweetheart*................................. 15.00 - 20.00
12308 *Hello Bluebird* .... 15.00 - 20.00
12339 *Sixty Seconds Every Minute* .... 15.00 - 20.00
12367 *Clementine (From New Orleans)*........... 15.00 - 20.00
12373 *An' Furthermore* .... 15.00 - 20.00
12392 *Did You Mean It?*.................................... 15.00 - 20.00
12400 *Is She My Girl Friend?* .... 15.00 - 20.00
12406 *Away Down South In Heaven* .... 15.00 - 20.00

TROY FLOYD & HIS PLAZA HOTEL/SHADOWLAND ORCHESTRA:
Okeh 8571 *Shadowland Blues* .... 150.00 - 200.00
8719 *Dreamland Blues* .... 150.00 - 200.00

BILL FOLEY (See KEYSTONE SERENADERS)

FOOR-ROBINSON CAROLINA CLUB ORCHESTRA:
Okeh 40466 *Collegiate* .... 40.00 - 60.00

LOUIS FORBSTEIN'S ROYAL SYNCOPATORS:
Okeh 40379 *Deep Elm* .... 75.00 - 100.00
40392 *Someday We'll Meet Again*..................... 30.00 - 50.00
40417 *Down And Out Blues*............................... 75.00 - 100.00

FORD AND FORD:
Paramount 12244 *I'm Three Times Seven* .... 150.00 - 250.00

REGINALD FORESYTHE, THE NEW MUSIC OF:
Columbia 3000-D *The Duke Insists* .... 10.00 - 15.00
3012-D *Dodging A Divorcee* .... 30.00 - 50.00
3060-D *Melancholy Clown* .... 30.00 - 50.00
3088-D *St. Louis Blues* .... 15.00 - 20.00

GENE FOSDICK'S HOOSIERS:
Vocalion 14473 *One Night In June* .... 8.00 - 12.00
14496 *'Way Down Yonder In New Orleans*
.... 10.00 - 15.00
14503 *Apple Sauce*.. 8.00 - 12.00
14535 *Farewell Blues* .... 15.00 - 20.00
14585 *Railroad Man* .... 15.00 - 20.00

DEACON FOSTER & HIS BOYS:
Champion 15656 *Black And Blue Rhapsody* .... 150.00 - 200.00

ISA FOSTER & HER AMBASSADORS:
Broadway 1499 *The Cute Little Things You Do* .... 8.00 - 12.00

FOUR ACES AND THE JOKER (See JABBO SMITH)

FOUR HAWAIIAN GUITARS (See also Q.R.S. BOYS):
Q.R.S. 1015 *Singin' In The Bathtub* ....75.00 - 100.00

FOUR INSTRUMENTAL STARS:
Pathe-Actuelle 36664 *I Like What You Like* ....25.00 - 40.00
Perfect 14845 *I Like What You Like* ....25.00 - 40.00

THE FOUR SPADES:
Columbia 14028-D *Squabblin' Blues* ....50.00 - 75.00

LEMUEL FOWLER; FOWLER'S FAVORITES/ WASHBOARD WONDERS:
Columbia A-3959 *Blues Mixture* ....20.00 - 30.00
   14084-D *Chitterlin' Strut* ....80.00 - 120.00
   14096-D *Pig Foot Shuffle* ....80.00 - 120.00
   14101-D *Express Train Blues* ....80.00 - 120.00
   14111-D *Salty Dog* ....80.00 - 120.00
   14155-D *Jelly Roll Blues* ....100.00 - 150.00
   14230-D *Percolatin' Blues* ....100.00 - 150.00

ROY FOX & HIS MONTMARTRE ORCHESTRA:
Vocalion 15770 *Makin' Whoopee!* ....15.00 - 20.00

WILLIAM FRANCIS AND RICHARD SOWELL:
Vocalion 1090 *John Henry Blues* ....100.00 - 150.00

FRANCISCO ORCHESTRA:
Emerson 10587 *Dreary Weary Blues* ....20.00 - 30.00

ARNOLD FRANK & HIS (ROGERS CAFE) ORCHESTRA:
Okeh 40896 *Black Maria*...15.00 - 20.00
   41086 *You're A Real Sweetheart*.................15.00 - 20.00

FRANKIE & HER JAZZ DEVILS:
Pathe-Actuelle 7507 *Those Creeping Sneaking Blues*
....75.00 - 100.00
Perfect 107 *Those Creeping Sneaking Blues* ....75.00 - 100.00

FRANKIE AND JOHNNIE ORCHESTRA:
Bluebird 6470 *Swing Fever* ....15.00 - 20.00
   6499 *Stompin'* ....15.00 - 20.00
   6564 *I'm Looking For Someone To Love* ....15.00 - 20.00
   6760 *Frankie And Johnnie Swing*.................15.00 - 20.00

FRANKIE FRANKO & HIS LOUISIANIANS:
Melotone 12009 *Somebody Stole My Gal* ....100.00 - 150.00

EDDIE FRAZIER AND HIS PLANTATION ORCHESTRA:
Sunset 1100 *Cheatin' On Me*..................................50.00 - 75.00

JAKE FRAZIER:
Ajax 17117 *Jake's Weary Blues* ....50.00 - 75.00

BUD FREEMAN & HIS FAMOUS CHICAGOANS/ (SUMMA CUM LAUDE) ORCHESTRA/TRIO:
Bluebird 10370 *I've Found A New Baby* ....7.00 - 10.00
   10386 *China Boy* ....7.00 - 10.00
Columbia (red label) ....5.00 - 8.00
Commodore 501, 502, 503, 504, 507, 508, 513,
   514, 529 ....7.00 - 10.00
Okeh 41168 *Craze-O-Logy*.....................................75.00 - 100.00

JAY/JERRY FREEMAN AND HIS ORCHESTRA:
Titles issued contemporaneously on Banner, Melotone, Oriole,
   Perfect, Romeo: *Alabama Barbecue; Copper-Colored Gal;*
   Getting Away With Murder; I'm At The Mercy Of Love; Mr.
   Ghost Goes To Town; A Moment In The Dark; My Newest
   Excitement; That's What You Mean To Me ....8.00 - 12.00
Additional titles issued on Banner, Melotone, Oriole, Perfect,
   Romeo: *Sugar Foot Stomp; Night Ride* ....10.00 - 15.00
Bluebird 5231, 5232, 5233...7.00 - 10.00
Variety 511 *Poor Robinson Crusoe* ....10.00 - 15.00

FRENCHY'S STRING BAND:
Columbia 14387-D *Sunshine Special* ....200.00 - up

FRIARS SOCIETY ORCHESTRA:
Gennett 4966 *Farewell Blues* ....40.00 - 60.00
   4967 *Bugle Call Blues* ....40.00 - 60.00
   4968 *Panama* ....50.00 - 75.00
   5009 *Eccentric* ....35.00 - 50.00

AL FRIEDMAN & HIS ORCHESTRA:
Cameo 1149 *Somebody Else* ....10.00 - 15.00
Edison 52102 *I'm Coming Virginia* ....20.00 - 30.00
   52103 *Manhattan Mary* ....20.00 - 30.00
   52128 *My Blue Heaven* ....20.00 - 30.00
   52155 *Rain* ....20.00 - 30.00
   52162 *Blue Baby (Why Are You Blue?)* ....50.00 - 75.00
   52190 *He Loves And She Loves* ....20.00 - 30.00
   52244 *Speedy Boy*.......................................50.00 - 75.00
   52305 *Girl Of My Dreams* ....50.00 - 75.00
   52342 *After I've Called You Sweetheart*.......40.00 - 60.00
   52352 *Evening Shadows* ....25.00 - 40.00
   52365 *Just A Night For Meditation* ....25.00 - 40.00
   52444 *Don't Wait Until Lights Are Low* ....75.00 - 100.00
   52445 *Good Boy* ....40.00 - 60.00
   52484 *Me And The Man In The Moon* ....40.00 - 60.00
   52529 *Guess Who's In Town* ....40.00 - 60.00
   52560 *Broadway Melody* ....50.00 - 75.00
   52565 *Building A Nest For Mary* ....50.00 - 80.00

BEN FRIEDMAN'S PARAMOUNT HOTEL ORCHESTRA:
Timely Tunes 1580 *The One-Man Band*..................20.00 - 30.00
   1583 *Some Of These Days* ....20.00 - 30.00
   1584 *Swamp Ghosts*...................................20.00 - 30.00
   1588 *Roll On Mississippi, Roll On* ....75.00 - 100.00

JOE FRIEDMAN'S MONTE CARLO ORCHESTRA:
Harmony 11-H *Collegiate*..8.00 - 12.00
   19-H *Oh! Boy, What A Girl!* ....15.00 - 20.00
   30-H *Speech!*...8.00 - 12.00
   33-H *What Do I Care? What Do I Care?* ....8.00 - 12.00

FRISCOE:
Emerson 7245 *Peacock Strut* .... - - -

FRISCO FIVE:
Emerson 7481 *A Good Man Is Hard To Find* ....15.00 - 20.00
   7491 *Orange Blossom Rag* ....15.00 - 20.00
   7494 *Laughing Blues* ....15.00 - 20.00
   7507 *That Shanghai Melody* ....15.00 - 20.00
   7517 *Church Street Sobbin' Blues* ....15.00 - 20.00
   7519 *Rainy Day Blues* ....15.00 - 20.00
   7549 *Thunderbolt* ....15.00 - 20.00
(Above are 7-inch records)

FRISCO "JASS" BAND; FRISCO JAZZ BAND:
Edison 50470 *Johnson "Jass" Blues* ....15.00 -   20.00
(Note: Record number on above may be found on record's edge.)
    50950 *That's It* ....15.00 -   20.00
    51081 *Yah-De-Dah* ....15.00 -   20.00

FRISCO SYNCOPATORS:
Cardinal 2072 *Everybody Step* ....10.00 -   15.00
Claxtonola 40244 *Buddy's Habits* ....75.00 - 100.00
    40264 *Arkansas Mule* ....50.00 -   80.00
    40291 *Forgetful Blues* ....50.00 -   80.00
Puritan 11271 *Sweet Henry The Pride Of Tennessee*
    ....20.00 -   30.00
    11291 *Forgetful Blues* ....50.00 -   80.00
    11330 *Back O' Town Blues* ....15.00 -   25.00
Resona 11307 *Sweet Henry The Pride Of Tennessee*
    ....20.00 -   30.00
    11359 *Sioux City Sue* ....15.00 -   25.00
Triangle 11270 *Sittin' In A Corner* ....10.00 -   15.00
    11384 *I Can't Get The One I Want* ....15.00 -   20.00
    11431 *Choo Choo* ....10.00 -   15.00

FRIVOLITY CLUB ORCHESTRA:
Vocalion (most issues) ....7.00 -   12.00

FRANK FROEBA & HIS SWING BAND:
Columbia 3110-D *The Music Goes 'Round And Around*
    ....15.00 -   20.00
    3131-D *Just To Be In Caroline* ....20.00 -   30.00
    3151-D *Organ Grinder's Swing* ....20.00 -   30.00
    3152-D *It All Begins And Ends With You* ....20.00 -   30.00

JANE FROMAN:
Capitol, most issues ....5.00 -   8.00
Decca 180 *My Melancholy Baby* ....15.00 -   20.00
    181 *I Only Have Eyes For You* ....15.00 -   20.00
    710 *Please Believe Me* ....10.00 -   15.00
    725 *If You Love Me* ....10.00 -   15.00
Majestic 1048 *You, So It's You!* ....5.00 -   8.00
    1086 *A Garden In The Rain* ....5.00 -   8.00
V-Disc 668 *Can't Help Lovin' Dat Man* ....10.00 -   15.00
    858 *For Every Man There's A Woman* ....10.00 -   15.00
Victor 12333 *Rhapsody in Blue-Middle Movement* .... -   -
(Note: Records by **JANE FROMAN** on Capitol and Decca were
    issued in LP and 45 RPM formats. See Rhythm & Blues section.)

(CHARLIE) FRY & HIS MILLION DOLLAR PIER ORCHESTRA; FRY'S MILLION DOLLAR PIER ORCHESTRA:
Edison 51406 *Copenhagen* ....15.00 -   20.00
    51416 *Shanghai Shuffle* ....15.00 -   20.00
    51435 *Tessie (Stop Teasing Me)* ....15.00 -   20.00
    51469 *Gotta Getta Girl* ....15.00 -   20.00
    51471 *Dixie Dreams* ....20.00 -   30.00
    51474 *I Can't Stop Babying You* ....20.00 -   30.00
    51503 *No Wonder (That I Love You)* ......15.00 -   20.00
    51574 *Deep Elm* ....15.00 -   20.00
    51599 *Underneath The Yum Yum Tree* ......10.00 -   15.00
    51642 *I'm Knee Deep In Daisies* ....10.00 -   15.00
Pathe-Actuelle 036122 *Where The Dreamy Wabash Flows*
    ....15.00 -   20.00
Pathe-Actuelle, most other issues ....5.00 -   8.00
Perfect 14303 *Where The Dreamy Wabash Flows* ..15.00 -   20.00
Perfect, most other issues ....5.00 -   8.00
Victor 20726 *My Wife's In Europe Today* ....7.00 -   10.00
    21496 *Look What You've Done* ....7.00 -   10.00
    21610 *Happy Days And Lonely Nights* ....7.00 -   10.00

CHARLES FULCHER & HIS ORCHESTRA; FULCHER'S DANCE TRIO:
Columbia 316-D *The Georgia Stomp* ....30.00 -   50.00
    551-D *My Pretty Girl* ....30.00 -   50.00
    726-D *Blue Georgia Moon* ....20.00 -   30.00
    1267-D *After That* ....30.00 -   50.00
    1706-D *Hey! Hey!* ....20.00 -   30.00
    1734-D *Atlanta Gal* ....20.00 -   30.00
Okeh 4889 *The Eskimo Song* ....30.00 -   50.00

BOB FULLER:
Ajax 17088 *Crossword Puzzle Blues* ....30.00 -   50.00
    17091 *Spread Yo' Stuff* ....30.00 -   50.00
    17117 *Growin' Old Blues* ....50.00 -   75.00.
Banner 7151 *Alligator Crawl* ....15.00 -   25.00
Brunswick 7006 *I Ain't Got Nobody* ....30.00 -   50.00
Columbia 14068-D *Black Cat Blues* ....20.00 -   30.00
    14120-D *Grand Opera Blues* ....50.00 -   75.00
Domino 0249 *Here 'tis* ....15.00 -   25.00
Harmony 580-H *Too Bad Jim* ....15.00 -   25.00
    688-H *Ridiculous Blues* ....15.00 -   25.00
(Note: Above titles on Diva and Velvet Tone are similarly valued.)
Regal 8589 *Fireworks* ....15.00 -   25.00

EARL FULLER'S FAMOUS JAZZ BAND/RECTOR NOVELTY ORCHESTRA:
Columbia A2298 *Twelfth Street Rag* ....8.00 -   12.00
    A2523 *Graveyard Blues* ....8.00 -   12.00
Columbia, most other issues ....7.00 -   10.00
Edison 50505 *Jazzbo Jazz One Step* ....15.00 -   20.00
    50521 *I'm Sorry I Made You Cry* ....15.00 -   20.00
    50541 *Jazz De Luxe* ....15.00 -   20.00
Emerson 952 *Jazz De Luxe* ....15.00 -   20.00
Victor 18321 *Slippery Hank* ....10.00 -   15.00
    18369 *Beale Street Blues* ....10.00 -   15.00
    18394 *A Coon Band Contest* ....7.00 -   10.00
    18456 *Fuzzy Wuzzy Rag* ....75.00 - 100.00

SLIM GAILLARD AND HIS FLAT FOOT FLOOGIE BOYS/QUARTETTE/ETC.:
Atomic 215 *Atomic Cocktail* ....8.00 -   12.00
Atomic (other issues) ....7.00 -   10.00
Cadet 201 *Cement Mixer* ....7.00 -   10.00
Clef, M-G-M, Mercury (most issues) ....5.00 -   10.00
Okeh, most issues ....7.00 -   10.00
Queen, most issues ....7.00 -   10.00
Vocalion, most issues ....7.00 -   10.00

ALBERT GALE AND HIS ORCHESTRA:
Vocalion 03514 *Horses And Numbers* ....30.00 -   50.00

GALVESTON SERENADERS:
Champion 15266 *Twin Blues* ....150.00 - 200.00
    15285 *Monte Carlo Joys* ....150.00 - 200.00

JAN GARBER & HIS (GREATER COLUMBIA RECORDING) ORCHESTRA:
Brunswick, most issues ....5.00 -   8.00
Capitol (most issues) ....4.00 -   7.00
Columbia 1306-D *Since My Best Gal Turned Me Down*
    ....15.00 -   20.00
    1334-D *Back In Your Own Back Yard* ......15.00 -   20.00
    1372-D *She's A Great, Great Girl* ....15.00 -   20.00
    1615-D *Louisiana* ....15.00 -   20.00
    1642-D *Tin Ear* ....20.00 -   30.00
    1740-D *Guess Who?* ....8.00 -   12.00
    1823-D *'Way Down Yonder In New Orleans* ....15.00 -   20.00
    2115-D *Puttin' On The Ritz* ....15.00 -   20.00

Columbia, most other issues ....5.00 - 8.00
Decca, most issues ....5.00 - 8.00
Okeh, most issues ....5.00 - 8.00
Victor 19496 *If You Don't Want Me (Stop Doggin' Me 'Round)*
....8.00 - 12.00
    19708 *Cross Words Between Sweetie And Me* .....8.00 - 12.00
    20114 *There's A Blue Ridge In My Heart, Virginia*
....8.00 - 12.00
    20105 *Baby Face* ....7.00 - 10.00
    20322 *How Could Red Riding Hood?* ....20.00 - 30.00
    20336 *There Ain't No "Maybe" In My Baby's Eyes*
....8.00 - 12.00
    20360 *Sweetie Pie*..7.00 - 10.00
    20367 *Steppin' Around* ....10.00 - 15.00
    20676 *Positively-Absolutely* ....10.00 - 15.00
    20754 *What Do I Care What Somebody Said* .....10.00 - 15.00
Victor 24334, 24336, 24337, 24360, 24361, 24363,
    24375, 24411, 24412, 24413, 24438, 24444,
    24446, 24460, 24498, 24502, 24507, 24560,
    24562, 24567, 24629, 24634, 24636, 24644,
    24726, 24727, 24730, 24731, 24809, 24810,
    24814, 24816, 24878, 24880, 24881, 24886,
    25013, 25014, 25017, 25108, 25110, 25112,
    25121 ....7.00 - 12.00
Victor 24885 *Love And A Dime*.........................10.00 - 15.00
Victor, most other issues..................................5.00 - 8.00
Vocalion, most issues ....5.00 - 8.00

LOUIS "KING" GARCIA AND HIS SWING BAND:
Bluebird 6302 *Love Is Like A Cigarette* ....8.00 - 12.00
    6303 *Christopher Columbus*............................8.00 - 12.00
    6357 *Swing, Mr. Charlie* ....15.00 - 20.00
    10043 *Swing, Mr. Charlie* ....8.00 - 12.00

GARDEN DANCING PALACE ORCHESTRA:
Columbia 1501-D *Deep Hollow* ....15.00 - 20.00
    1599-D *When Erastus Plays His Old Kazoo* .....10.00 - 15.00

FRED GARDNER'S TEXAS UNIVERSITY TROUBADOURS:
Okeh 41440 *Papa's Gone*........................80.00 - 120.00
    41458 *No Trumps* ....80.00 - 120.00

JACK GARDNER'S ORCHESTRA:
Okeh 40245 *Ponjola*...............................40.00 - 60.00
    40265 *Too Late Now* ....40.00 - 60.00
    40339 *Who'd A Thunk It?*.........................40.00 - 60.00
    40495 *Hitch Up The Horses* ....40.00 - 60.00
    40501 *Ida, I Do*.....................................50.00 - 80.00
    40518 *Hot Aire* ....50.00 - 80.00
    40555 *Japp-A-Jazz*.................................40.00 - 60.00
    40572 *You'll Never Know The Difference*..........40.00 - 60.00

JUDY GARLAND:
Decca 848 *Stompin' At The Savoy*.................15.00 - 25.00
    1432 *All God's Chillun Got Rhythm*.................15.00 - 20.00
    1463 *You Can't Have Everything* ....15.00 - 20.00
(original issues of foregoing have shaded, or "sunrise" style
letters in Decca)
    1796 *Sleep, My Baby, Sleep*........................8.00 - 12.00
Decca (blue label), most others ....7.00 - 10.00

BLIND LEROY GARNETT:
Paramount 12879 *Louisiana Glide* ....250.00 - up

SID GARRY:
Melotone 12069 *At Last I'm Happy* ....15.00 - 20.00

TOM GATES & HIS ORCHESTRA/TOM GATES ORCHESTRA:
Champion 15305 *The Bucket's Got A Hole In It* .... 80.00 - 130.00
    15307 *Wabash Blues*................................80.00 - 130.00
Gennett 6184 *The Bucket's Got A Hole In It* .... 100.00 - 150.00
    6198 *Wabash Blues* ....100.00 - 150.00

CARL GAY & HIS ORCHESTRA:
Tremont 436 *Limehouse Blues*................................ 10.00 - 15.00

GLORIA GEER:
Banner 1530 *When My Sugar Walks Down The Street*7.00- 10.00
Cameo 761 *Yes Sir, That's My Baby* .... 8.00 - 12.00
    804 *Alone At Last*..................................7.00 - 10.00
    845 *Clap Hands! Here Comes Charlie!*...............7.00 - 10.00
    867 *He Left Her Behind Before* ....7.00 - 10.00
    868 *She's a Girl Who Can't Say No* ....7.00 - 10.00
    945 *After I Say I'm Sorry* ....7.00 - 10.00
    962 *Tonight's My Night With Baby* ....7.00 - 10.00
    963 *Bye Bye Blackbird*.............................7.00 - 10.00
Emerson 10831 *Everybody Loves My Baby* .... 20.00 - 30.00
Regal 8901 *He's So Unusual* .... 8.00 - 12.00

HENRI GENDRON & HIS STRAND ROOF ORCHESTRA; HENRI GENDRON'S AMBASSADORS:
Banner 1490 *Prince Of Wails* .... 40.00 - 60.00
Columbia 2396-D *Little Joe* .... 7.00 - 10.00
    2455-D *With The Help Of The Moon* ....7.00 - 10.00
Domino 3456 *Prince Of Wails* .... 40.00 - 60.00
Edison 51494 *Me Neenyah (My Little One)*........... 15.00 - 20.00
    51570 *Ah-Ha!* ....10.00 - 15.00
Regal 9788 *Prince Of Wails* .... 40.00 - 60.00

GENE & HIS GLORIANS:
Timely Tunes 1575 *Lazy River* .... 20.00 - 30.00
    1579 *Left My Gal In The Mountains*.................20.00 - 30.00
    1581 *Georgia On My Mind*..........................20.00 - 30.00
    1582 *Jig Time*......................................20.00 - 30.00

GENNETT BAND:
Gennett 10015 *Shim-Me-Sha-Wabble*.................... 20.00 - 30.00

AL GENTILE & HIS ORCHESTRA:
Gennett 3379 *Blowin' The Blues Away* .... 40.00 - 60.00
    6055 *A Tree In The Park*...........................30.00 - 50.00

GEORGIA COTTON PICKERS:
Diva 6064-G *Cotton Pickers' Shuffle* .... 60.00 - 100.00
Harmony 1090-H *Cotton Pickers' Shuffle* .... 60.00 - 100.00
    1127-H *Louisiana Bo Bo* ....50.00 - 80.00

GEORGIA JAZZ BAND:
Federal 5162 *Wang Wang Blues* .... 10.00 - 15.00
    5221 *Early In The Morning Blues* ....10.00 - 15.00
Silvertone 3077 *Kansas City Stomps* .... 15.00 - 20.00

GEORGIA JUMPERS:
Columbia 14603-D *California Blues* .... 200.00 - up
    14620-D *The Big Feet Rag* ....200.00 - up

GEORGIA MELODIANS:
Edison 51336 *Wop Blues* .... 20.00 - 30.00
    51338 *Wait'll You See My Gal*.....................20.00 - 30.00
    51346 *Savannah* ....20.00 - 30.00
    51347 *Tea Pot Dome Blues*.........................20.00 - 30.00
    51359 *How You Gonna Keep Kool?* ....20.00 - 30.00
    51378 *Why Did You Do It?*.........................10.00 - 15.00

51394 *Red Hot Mama* ....10.00 - 15.00
51412 *San* ....25.00 - 40.00
51419 *Everybody Loves My Baby*.....................25.00 - 40.00
51420 *Doo Wacka Doo*..................................20.00 - 30.00
51425 *I'm Satisfied Beside That Sweetie O' Mine*
....20.00 - 30.00
51437 *I'm Bound For Tennessee* ....20.00 - 30.00
51438 *My Mammy's Blues* ....50.00 - 80.00
51588 *Give Us The Charleston*........................40.00 - 60.00
51598 *She's Drivin' Me Wild* ....50.00 - 80.00
51678 *Charleston Ball*...................................30.00 - 50.00
51730 *Rhythm Of The Day* ....30.00 - 50.00

THE GEORGIANS:
Cameo 8111 *Without You Sweetheart* ....10.00 - 15.00
Columbia 11-D *Learn To Do The Strut* ....15.00 - 20.00
  23-D *Home Town Blues*........................20.00 - 30.00
  30-D *Shake Your Feet* ....15.00 - 25.00
  40-D *I've Got A Cross-Eyed Papa* ....15.00 - 25.00
  62-D *Dancin' Dan* ....15.00 - 25.00
  70-D *Hula Lou*...................................15.00 - 25.00
  142-D *Savannah* ....10.00 - 15.00
  252-D *Everybody Loves My Baby* ....10.00 - 15.00
  407-D *Charleston Baby O' Mine*................20.00 - 30.00
  523-D *Spanish Shawl*...........................15.00 - 20.00
  634-D *Spring Is Here* ....15.00 - 20.00
  923-D *'Frisco Bay* ....20.00 - 30.00
  A3775 *Chicago (That Toddlin' Town)* ....8.00 - 12.00
  A3804 *'Way Down Yonder In New Orleans*.......15.00 - 20.00
  A3825 *Aggravatin' Papa*........................10.00 - 15.00
  A3857 *You Tell Her-I Stutter* ....10.00 - 15.00
  A3864 *Farewell Blues* ....15.00 - 20.00
  A3902 *Barney Google* ....10.00 - 15.00
  A3907 *Henpecked Blues* ....15.00 - 20.00
  A3987 *Land of Cotton Blues* ....15.00 - 25.00
  A3996 *Mama Goes Where Papa Goes*.........15.00 - 20.00
Harmony 776-H *Glorianna* ....15.00 - 20.00
  1005-H *You Want Lovin' (But I Want Love)* ......10.00 - 15.00
  1008-H *When You're Counting The Stars Alone*..8.00 - 12.00
  1010-H *A Year From Today* ....7.00 - 10.00
  1023-H *Georgia Pines* ....8.00 - 12.00
  1034-H *If I Had A Talking Picture Of You*...........7.00 - 10.00
  1062-H *Can't We Be Friends?* ....15.00 - 20.00
  1063-H *Singin' In The Bathtub*......................15.00 - 20.00
(Note: Above titles issued on Diva and Velvet Tone are similarly valued.)

GEORGIA STRUTTERS:
Harmony 231-H *Georgia Grind* ....25.00 - 40.00
  311-H *Original Black Bottom Dance* ....25.00 - 40.00
  468-H *It's Right Here For You* ....75.00 - 125.00

GEORGIA WASHBOARD STOMPERS:
Bluebird 5027 *Wake 'Em Up* ....20.00 - 30.00
  5088 *Happy As The Day Is Long* ....15.00 - 20.00
  5089 *My Pretty Girl*..............................15.00 - 20.00
  5092 *Bug A-Boo*.................................15.00 - 25.00
  5127 *Dinah* ....15.00 - 20.00
Decca 7002 *Everybody Loves My Baby*..................30.00 - 50.00
  7004 *I Can't Dance (I Got Ants In My Pants)*....30.00 - 50.00
  7005 *Limehouse Blues*...........................30.00 - 50.00
  7006 *After You've Gone*.........................30.00 - 50.00
  7094 *You're An Angel*...........................20.00 - 30.00
  7095 *Lulu's Back In Town*........................20.00 - 30.00
  7096 *Every Little Moment* ....20.00 - 30.00
  7097 *The Lady In Red*...........................20.00 - 30.00

JULIA GERITY & HER PLAYBOYS:
Victor 22812 *A Good Man Is Hard To Find*...........20.00 - 30.00
  22896 *Sittin' On A Rubbish Can*......................20.00 - 30.00

GEORGE GERSHWIN (See also PAUL WHITEMAN & HIS ORCHESTRA):
Columbia 809-D *Clap Yo' Hands* .... 15.00 - 20.00
  812-D *Someone To Watch Over Me* .... 20.00 - 30.00
  50107-D (12 inch) *Preludes No. 1, 2* .... 20.00 - 30.00

TOM GERUN/GERUNOVITCH & HIS (ROOF GARDEN) ORCHESTRA:
Brunswick 4047 *Sincerely I Do* .... 8.00 - 12.00
  4050 *My Gal Sal* .... 15.00 - 20.00
  4115 *I Gotta Tell Someone* .... 8.00 - 12.00
  4190 *I'm Telling You* .... 8.00 - 12.00
  4429 *Am I Blue?* .... 8.00 - 12.00
  4430 *The Boogie Man Is Here* .... 8.00 - 12.00
  4628 *My Love Parade* .... 8.00 - 12.00
  4727 *Sing, You Sinners* .... 8.00 - 12.00
  4755 *Atta Boy* .... 8.00 - 12.00
Brunswick, most other issues................................. 7.00 - 10.00

THE GET-HAPPY BAND:
Columbia 14091-D *Harlem's Araby*.................... 125.00 - 175.00
  14099-D *Puddin' Pappa* .... 100.00 - 150.00

IRENE GIBBONS (& JAZZ BAND); IRENE GIBBONS & CLARENCE WILLIAMS' JAZZ BAND:
Columbia A-3834 *That Da Da Strain* .... 20.00 - 30.00
  A-3922 *My Pillow And Me* .... 20.00 - 30.00
  14296-D *Longing* .... 50.00 - 80.00
  14362-D *I'm Busy And You Can't Come In*..... 150.00 - 200.00

ARTHUR GIBBS & HIS GANG:
Victor 19070 *Beale Street Mama*........................ 8.00 - 12.00
  19165 *Charleston* .... 10.00 - 15.00

CLEO GIBSON:
Okeh 8700 *Nothing But Blues*............................. 100.00 - 150.00

GENE GIFFORD & HIS ORCHESTRA:
Victor 25041 *New Orleans Twist* .... 10.00 - 15.00
  25065 *Squareface* .... 10.00 - 15.00

EMERSON GILL & HIS (BAMBOO GARDEN/CASTLE OF PARIS) ORCHESTRA:
Columbia 1355-D *The Yale Blues* .... 10.00 - 15.00
  1396-D *That's What I Call Keen* .... 15.00 - 20.00
  1408-D *Ready For The River* .... 15.00 - 20.00
  2416-D *I've Got Five Dollars*......................... 8.00 - 12.00
Okeh 40065 *On Saturday Night*........................... 20.00 - 30.00
  40066 *Days Of Yesterday* .... 20.00 - 30.00
  40313 *My Name Will Always Be Chickie* .... 30.00 - 50.00
  40315 *That's My Gal* .... 30.00 - 50.00
  40369 *Birmingham Bound* .... 30.00 - 50.00
  40577 *It Must Be Love* .... 30.00 - 50.00
  40590 *Say It Again* .... 30.00 - 50.00
  40594 *The Rhythm Rag* .... 30.00 - 50.00
  40615 *Lo-Nah* .... 30.00 - 50.00

RAY GILL & HIS MOVIELAND ORCHESTRA:
Silver Screen 162 *Poor Papa* .... 30.00 - 50.00
Sunset 1153 *Poor Papa* .... 20.00 - 30.00
  1160 *Let's Talk About My Sweetie* .... 20.00 - 30.00
  1161 *Tie Me To Your Apron Strings Again* .... 20.00 - 30.00

ART GILLHAM:

Columbia 1116-D *I'd Walk A Million Miles*	8.00	-	12.00
1726-D *Some Sweet Day*	8.00	-	12.00
2265-D *Confessin'*	15.00	-	20.00
2291-D *Good Evenin'*	15.00	-	20.00
2331-D *When They Changed My Name To A Number*	10.00	-	15.00
Columbia (most other issues)	5.00	-	10.00

MAX GILMORE AND HIS BOYS:

Superior 2565 *I'll Sing A Love Song*	15.00	-	20.00

JOSEPH GISH AND HIS ORCHESTRA:

New Flexo 311 *Milenberg Joys*	100.00	-	up

(NATHAN) GLANTZ & HIS ORCHESTRA:

Bell 391 *Spanish Shawl*	7.00	-	10.00
Edison 51336 *I'm Worried Over You*	20.00	-	30.00
Gennett 3011 *Don't Bring Lulu*	15.00	-	20.00
3037 *Will You Remember Me*	7.00	-	10.00
3038 *I Ain't Got Nobody To Love*	-		-
3087 *One Smile*	15.00	-	25.00
3128 *Let's Wander Away*	7.00	-	10.00
Pathe-Actuelle 036138 *Any Way The Wind Blows*	8.00	-	12.00
36497 *Oh! If I Only Had You*	10.00	-	15.00
Perfect 14319 *Any Way The Wind Blows*	8.00	-	12.00
14476 *Charleston Baby Of Mine*	10.00	-	15.00
4678 *Oh! If I Only Had You*	10.00	-	15.00
Puritan 11425 *Five Feet Two, Eyes Of Blue*	8.00	-	12.00
11429 *Sweet Man*	8.00	-	12.00

PERCY GLASCOE:

Columbia 14088-D *Stomp 'Em Down*	50.00	-	75.00

JACK GLASSNER AND HIS COLONIAL INN ORCHESTRA:

Okeh 40559 *Hot Coffee*	8.00	-	12.00
40644 *Tonight's My Night With Baby*	20.00	-	30.00

AL GOERING'S COLLEGIANS:

Banner 1693 *Up And At 'Em*	15.00	-	20.00
7001 *Once Over Lightly*	10.00	-	15.00
7004 *Candied Sweets*	10.00	-	15.00
7005 *Steppin' It Off*	10.00	-	15.00
Domino 3666 *Up And At 'Em*	15.00	-	20.00
Vocalion 15337 *What Was I To Do?*	7.00	-	10.00
15374 *Hard-To-Get Gertie*	10.00	-	15.00
15409 *Baby Face*	7.00	-	10.00
15495 *Hello! Swanee, Hello!*	8.00	-	12.00
15508 *He's The Last Word*	10.00	-	15.00

LOU GOLD & HIS ORCHESTRA/MELODY MEN:

Banner 1544 *Everything Is Hotsy Totsy Now*	20.00	-	30.00
1636 *Roll 'Em Girls*	7.00	-	10.00
1640 *No Man's Mama*	7.00	-	10.00
1660 *What Did I Tell Ya?*	7.00	-	10.00
6209 *When Polly Walks Through The Hollyhocks*	7.00	-	10.00
Cameo 678 *Everybody Loves My Baby*	7.00	-	10.00
713 *Love Light Lane*	7.00	-	10.00
759 *Say Arabella*	7.00	-	10.00
769 *I Miss My Swiss*	7.00	-	10.00
799 *When You See That Aunt Of Mine*	8.00	-	12.00
800 *Let's Wander Away*	10.00	-	15.00
815 *Better Get Acquainted*	7.00	-	10.00
847 *Nobody's Business*	10.00	-	15.00
860 *Keep Your Skirts Down, Mary Ann*	7.00	-	10.00

883 *I'd Rather Be Alone*	8.00	-	12.00
898 *Say Mister! Have You Met Rosie's Sister?*	7.00	-	10.00
1221 *The Varsity Drag*	8.00	-	12.00
1260 *Go Home And Tell Your Mother*	15.00	-	20.00
Cameo, most other issues	5.00	-	8.00
Challenge 253 *Ain't She Sweet?*	8.00	-	12.00
Champion 15798 *Gotta Feeling For You*	8.00	-	12.00
15817 *Bottoms Up*	8.00	-	12.00
15820 *Why Can't You Love That Way*	8.00	-	12.00
15822 *Lovable And Sweet*	8.00	-	12.00
15865 *Painting The Clouds With Sunshine*	8.00	-	12.00
15866 *Chant Of The Jungle*	8.00	-	12.00
15889 *I Love You, Believe Me, I Love You*	7.00	-	10.00
15909 *Lucky Me, Lovable You*	8.00	-	12.00
15933 *I'm On A Diet of Love*	8.00	-	12.00
15935 *Soon*	7.00	-	10.00
15978 *Sweetheart Trail*	7.00	-	10.00
16152 *You're The One I Care For*	7.00	-	10.00
16173 *Wasting My Love On You*	7.00	-	10.00
16175 *I'll Sing A Love Song*	-		-
16198 *Sunlit Skies*	-		-
16219 *Tie A Little String Around Your Finger*	10.00	-	15.00
16220 *What Good Am I Without You?*	-		-
16302 *Naughty Baby*	7.00	-	10.00
16465 *Walking Through A Field Of Daisies*	100.00	-	150.00
16472 *Love Slave*	-		-
Conqueror 7217 *You're The Cream In My Coffee*	7.00	-	10.00
Crown 3060 *Would You Like To Take A Walk?*	7.00	-	10.00
3063 *Walkin' My Baby Back Home*	7.00	-	10.00
3092 *It Must Be True*	7.00	-	10.00
3099 *Out Of Nowhere*	8.00	-	12.00
3109 *Thrill Me*	7.00	-	10.00
3112 *Mary Jane*	7.00	-	10.00
3165 *I'm Just A Dancing Sweetheart*	7.00	-	10.00
3167 *Begging For Love*	7.00	-	10.00
3190 *If I Didn't Have You*	7.00	-	10.00
3192 *In a Dream*	7.00	-	10.00
3211 *Time On My Hands*	7.00	-	10.00
3213 *When The Rest Of The Crowd Goes Home*	-		-
3215 *Where the Blue Of The Night Meets The Gold Of The Day*	7.00	-	10.00
3226 *When It's Sleepy Time Down South*	-		-
3229 *An Ev'ning In Caroline*	7.00	-	10.00
3230 *Old Playmate*	7.00	-	10.00
3241 *All Of Me*	7.00	-	10.00
3242 *Ooh! That Kiss*	7.00	-	10.00
3252 *Delishious*	7.00	-	10.00
3267 *Dancing On The Ceiling*	7.00	-	10.00
3268 *Let That Be A Lesson To You*	7.00	-	10.00
3287 *Put That Sun Back In The Sky*	7.00	-	10.00
Domino 3634 *What Did I Tell Ya?*	7.00	-	10.00
4229 *When Polly Walks Through The Hollyhocks*	7.00	-	10.00
Gennett 6037 *Forgive Me*	-		-
6068 *You Should See My Tootsie*	10.00	-	15.00
6936 *Fascinating You*	10.00	-	15.00
6950 *Liza*	-		-
6983 *Why Can't You Love That Way?*	-		-
6995 *Lovable And Sweet*	15.00	-	20.00
7028 *Painting The Clouds With Sunshine*	-		-
7029 *Shoo Shoo Boogie Boo*	15.00	-	20.00
7074 *I Love You, Believe Me , I Love You*	10.00	-	15.00
7088 *I'm Following You*	8.00	-	12.00
7133 *Soon*	8.00	-	12.00
7135 *I'm On A Diet Of Love*	-		-

Harmony 95-H *Let Me Introduce You To My Rosie* ..7.00 - 10.00
   98-H *Sweet And Low-Down* ....8.00 - 12.00
   616-H *Luscious* ....7.00 - 10.00
   635-H *That's My Mammy* ....7.00 - 10.00
   659-H *Is It Gonna Be Long? (Till You Belong To Me)*
   ....8.00 - 12.00
   660-H *I Can't Give You Anything But Love* ....7.00 - 10.00
   669-H *I Must Be Dreaming* ....8.00 - 12.00
   698-H *Skadatin-Dee* ....8.00 - 12.00
   702-H *If You Want The Rainbow* ....7.00 - 10.00
   732-H *Come On, Baby!* ....7.00 - 10.00
   733-H *Everything We Like We Like Alike* ....7.00 - 10.00
   745-H *My Blackbirds Are Bluebirds Now* ....7.00 - 10.00
   770-H *You're the Cream In My Coffee* ....7.00 - 10.00
   814-H *Buy, Buy For Baby* ....7.00 - 10.00
   822-H *That's Her Now* ....8.00 - 12.00
   851-H *It's Tight Like That* ....15.00 - 20.00
   891-H *In Old Tia Juana* ....7.00 - 10.00
   920-H *Walking With Susie* ....8.00 - 12.00
   933-H *Hittin' The Ceiling* ....8.00 - 12.00
   950-H *He's A Good Man To Have Around* ....8.00 - 12.00
   976-H *Lovable And Sweet* ....7.00 - 10.00
   977-H *Moanin' Low* ....7.00 - 10.00
   1000-H *Hang On To Me* ....7.00 - 10.00
   1001-H *Lonesome Little Doll* ....8.00 - 12.00
   1052-H *Piccolo Pete* ....10.00 - 15.00
(Note: Above titles on Harmony are also found on Diva and Velvet
   Tone, similarly valued.)
Harmony (most other issues) ....5.00 - 8.00
Lincoln 2352 *Who's Loving My Sweetie Now?* ....7.00 - 10.00
Marathon 166 (7-inch) *Go Home And Tell Your Mother*
   ....10.00 - 20.00
   174 (7-inch) *What'll You Do?* ....10.00 - 20.00
Oriole 2007 *Nobody Cares If I'm Blue* ....7.00 - 10.00
Perfect 14381 *The Blues Have Got Me* ....10.00 - 15.00
   14414 *If You Knew Suzie (sic)* ....7.00 - 10.00
   14468 *Speech* ....10.00 - 15.00
   14469 *Let's Wander Away* ....8.00 - 12.00
   14476 *I'm Gonna Charleston Back To Charleston*
   ....10.00 - 15.00.
   14496 *When You See That Aunt Of Mine* ....10.00 - 15.00
   14500 *What Did I Tell You* ....10.00 - 15.00
   14503 *I Wonder Where My Baby Is Tonight?* ......7.00 - 10.00
   14530 *Roll 'Em, Girls* ....15.00 - 20.00.
   14534 *Who* ....8.00 - 12.00
   14542 *Someone's Stolen My Sweet, Sweet Baby* ... 15.00 - 20.00
   14549 *I Wish't I Was In Peoria* ....8.00 - 12.00
   14550 *I Want Someone To Cheer Me Up* ....8.00 - 12.00
   14556 *Sweet And Low Down* ....8.00 - 12.00
   14584 *I've Found A New Baby* ....15.00 - 20.00
   14743 *Thinking Of You* ....10.00 - 15.00
   14744 *Angel Eyes* ....10.00 - 15.00
   14777 *Ain't She Sweet?* ....7.00 - 10.00
   14797 *South Wind* ....7.00 - 10.00
   14821 *Magnolia* ....15.00 - 20.00
   14862 *The Varsity Drag* ....7.00 - 10.00
   14906 *Mary (What Are You Waiting For?)* ....15.00 - 20.00
   14907 *What'll You Do?* ....15.00 - 20.00
   14914 *Who Gives You All Your Kisses?* ....15.00 - 20.00
   14932 *You Gotta Be Good To Me* ....15.00 - 20.00
   14933 *In the Sing Song Sycamore Tree* ....15.00 - 20.00
   14940 *After My Laughter Came Tears* ....8.00 - 12.00
   14942 *Losin' You* ....15.00 - 20.00

Perfect (most other issues) ....5.00 - 8.00
Puritone 1025-S *Come On, Baby* ....8.00 - 12.00
   1032-S *When Summer Is Gone* ....8.00 - 12.00
   1037-S *Buy, Buy For Baby* ....8.00 - 12.00
Regal 10118 *Am I To Blame?* ....7.00 - 10.00
   10153 *Loving You The Way I Do* ....7.00 - 10.00
Regal, most other issues ....5.00 - 8.00
Romeo, most issues ....5.00 - 8.00

BUDDY GOLDEN & HIS MICHIGAN WOLVERINES:
Harmony 855-H *Button Up Your Overcoat* ....8.00 - 12.00
(Note: Above title issued on Diva and Velvet Tone is similarly
   valued.)

ERNIE GOLDEN & HIS (HOTEL MCALPIN) ORCHESTRA:
Banner 0758 *Dirty Hot* ....15.00 - 20.00
   6226 *Doin' The Raccoon* ....10.00 - 15.00
   6227 *Come On, Baby* ....8.00 - 12.00
   6271 *Makin' Whoopee!* ....8.00 - 12.00
   7109 *My Pet* ....10.00 - 15.00
   7244 *My Blackbirds Are Bluebirds Now* ....10.00 - 15.00
Banner (most other issues) ....5.00 - 8.00
Brunswick 2999 *Five Foot Two, Eyes Of Blue* ....7.00 - 10.00
   3302 *I Wonder What's Become Of Joe?* ....8.00 - 12.00
   3359 *Ev'rything's Peaches* ....8.00 - 12.00
Cameo 0358 *Dirty Hot* ....15.00 - 20.00
Champion 16084 *Pick Yourself Up* ....8.00 - 12.00
   16086 *If I Could Be With You (One Hour Tonight)*
   ....8.00 - 12.00
   16107 *My Baby Just Cares For Me* ....8.00 - 12.00
   16661 *Dirty Hot* ....150.00 - 200.00
Columbia 1799-D *She's Got Great Ideas* ....8.00 - 12.00
Domino 4238 *Doin' The Raccoon* ....10.00 - 15.00
Edison 51658 *Sleepy Time Gal* ....20.00 - 30.00
   51944 *Oriental Moonlight* ....35.00 - 50.00
   51977 *Calling* ....15.00 - 20.00
   52109 *The Varsity Drag* ....75.00 - 100.00
   52191 *It's Ray Ray Raining* ....15.00 - 20.00
   52289 *I'm Away From The World When I'm Away From You*
   ....20.00 - 30.00
Gennett 6802 *Mean To Me* ....10.00 - 15.00
   6818 *I'll Tell The World* ....10.00 - 15.00
   6846 *You Were Meant For Me* ....10.00 - 15.00
   6847 *Heigh-Ho, Ev'rybod, Heigh-Ho* ....10.00 - 15.00
   6907 *With a Song In My Heart* ....15.00 - 20.00
   6923 *Don't Hang Your Dreams On A Rainbow* 10.00 - 15.00
   6937 *Tip-Toe Thru' The Tulips With Me* ....15.00 - 20.00
   6981 *By The Way* ....10.00 - 15.00
   6996 *How Am I To Know?* ....10.00 - 15.00
   7027 *You've Made Me Happy Today* ....10.00 - 15.00
   7043 *Little By Little* ....10.00 - 15.00
   7073 *Why Do You Suppose?* ....10.00 - 15.00
   7074 *Can't You Understand?* ....10.00 - 15.00
   7089 *H'lo, Baby* ....15.00 - 20.00
   7102 *Watching My Dreams Go By* ....10.00 - 15.00
   7192 *Without You, Emaline* ....25.00 - 40.00
   7194 *Let Me Sing And I'm Happy* ....10.00 - 15.00
   7212 *On The Sunny Side Of The Street* ....10.00 - 15.00
   7233 *Here Comes Emily Brown* ....15.00 - 20.00
   7256 *Sing (A Happy Little Thing)* ....15.00 - 20.00
   7258 *Pick Yourself Up* ....15.00 - 20.00
   7280 *If I Could Be With You* ....15.00 - 20.00
   7301 *My Baby Just Cares For Me* ....20.00 - 30.00

Harmony 84-H *I Wish't I Was In Peoria* ....8.00 - 12.00
    578-H *Golden Gate*.................8.00 - 12.00
    603-H *Who's Blue Now?* ....8.00 - 12.00
Harmony (most other issues) ....5.00 - 8.00

THE GOLDEN BEARS:
Crown 3485 *The Gold Diggers' Song* ....10.00 - 15.00
    3486 *An Orchid To You* ....7.00 - 10.00
    3498 *My Bluebird's Singing The Blues* ....8.00 - 12.00

GOLDEN GATE (DANCE) ORCHESTRA (See comments on CALIFORNIA RAMBLERS):
Banner 0663 *She's Nobody's Fool* ....8.00 - 12.00
    0664 *If You Were All My Own* ....8.00 - 12.00
    0666 *Wouldn't It Be Wonderful, Baby?* ....8.00 - 12.00
    1409 *I'm Satisfied Beside That Sweetie Of Mine* ..7.00 - 10.00
    1413 *Look-a What I Got Now* ....7.00 - 10.00
    1459 *Nobody Knows What A Red Head Mama Can Do* ....10.00 - 15.00
    1472 *Oh! Mabel* ....10.00 - 15.00
    1474 *Blue Eyed Sally* ....7.00 - 10.00
    1500 *I Ain't Got Nobody To Love* ....7.00 - 10.00
    1502 *My Gal Don't Love Me Anymore* ....10.00 - 15.00
    1566 *Oh Say! Can I See You Tonight* ....10.00 - 15.00
    1568 *Say Arabella* ....10.00 - 15.00
    1569 *I Miss My Swiss* ....7.00 - 10.00
    1623 *She Was Just A Sailor's Sweetheart* ....8.00 - 12.00
    1999 *Magnolia* ....10.00 - 15.00
    6007 *Zulu Wail* ....15.00 - 20.00
    6082 *Jelly Roll Blues* ....20.00 - 30.00
Bell 245 *Saw Mill River Road* ....7.00 - 10.00
    253 *Linger Awhile* ....7.00 - 10.00
    294 *Too Tired* ....7.00 - 10.00
    354 *Oh Say Can I See You Tonight* ....8.00 - 12.00
Broadway 11404 *Manda* ....100.00 - 150.00
Cameo 0266 *Wouldn't It Be Wonderful, Baby* ....8.00 - 12.00
    0269 *She's Nobody's Fool* ....8.00 - 12.00
Domino 3535 *I Miss My Swiss* ....7.00 - 10.00
    3973 *Zulu Wail* ....15.00 - 20.00
    4039 *Jelly Roll Blues* ....15.00 - 20.00
Edison 51387 *Sing A Little Song* ....15.00 - 20.00
    51388 *Lucille* ....15.00 - 20.00
    51443 *Southern Rose* ....20.00 - 30.00
    51491 *Oh! Mabel* ....25.00 - 40.00
    51538 *On The Oregon Trail* ....25.00 - 40.00
    51542 *Charleston* ....50.00 - 75.00
    51551 *Everything Is Hotsy-Totsy Now* ....40.00 - 60.00
    51562 *Cheatin' On Me* ....40.00 - 60.00
    51580 *Collegiate* ....25.00 - 35.00
    51590 *Manhattan* ....30.00 - 50.00
    51591 *Look Who's Here* ....30.00 - 50.00
    51622 *Sweet Man* ....30.00 - 50.00
    51633 *Freshie* ....25.00 - 40.00
    51661 *Five Foot Two, Eyes Of Blue* ....50.00 - 75.00
    51725 *Here Comes Malinda* ....40.00 - 60.00
    51737 *Shake* ....50.00 - 75.00
    51746 *Static Strut* ....50.00 - 75.00
    51762 *Hard-To-Get Gertie* ....40.00 - 60.00
    51768 *I Wonder What's Become Of Joe?* ....40.00 - 60.00
    51797 *To Be With You* ....25.00 - 40.00
    51799 *When The Red Red Robin Comes Bob, Bob Bobbin' Along* ....30.00 - 50.00
    51814 *Looking At The World Thru Rose Colored Glasses* ....30.00 - 50.00

51820 *Up And At 'Em* ....50.00 - 75.00
51822 *How Many Times?* ....40.00 - 60.00
51824 *You Need Someone To Love* ....40.00 - 60.00
51851 *Lay Me Down To Sleep In Carolina* ....50.00 - 75.00
51860 *Pretty Cinderella* ....30.00 - 50.00
51862 *All Alone Monday* ....30.00 - 50.00
51897 *Stockholm Stomp* ....50.00 - 75.00
51960 *Lonely Eyes* ....40.00 - 60.00
51970 *Look At The World And Smile* ....25.00 - 40.00
51975 *Crazy Words-Crazy Tune* ....40.00 - 60.00
52014 *Yes She Do-No She Don't* ....40.00 - 60.00
52043 *Beedle-Um Bo* ....50.00 - 75.00
52075 *Miss Annabelle Lee* ....75.00 - 100.00
52097 *You Don't Like It-Not Much* ....75.00 - 100.00
52101 *Dawning* ....50.00 - 75.00
52105 *Blue River* ....50.00 - 75.00
52109 *Clementine* ....75.00 - 100.00
52162 *Tell Me, Little Daisy* ....50.00 - 75.00
52164 *Make My Cot Where The Cot-Cot-Cotton Grows* ....75.00 - 100.00
52181 *The Pay Off* ....75.00 - 100.00
52206 *Third Rail* ....100.00 - 150.00
52366 *Dream House* ....30.00 - 50.00
52390 *Vaniteaser* ....75.00 - 100.00
52399 *'Cause I Feel Low Down* ....80.00 - 120.00
52416 *Get Out And Get Under The Moon* ....75.00 - 100.00
52437 *There's A Rainbow 'Round My Shoulder* 75.00 - 100.00
52444 *You're The Cream In My Coffee* ....75.00 - 100.00
52477 *Along Came Sweetness* ....50.00 - 75.00
52480 *To Know You Is To Love You* ....40.00 - 60.00
52486 *Glad Rag Doll* ....50.00 - 80.00
52506 *Sweethearts On Parade* ....50.00 - 80.00
52513 *Button Up Your Overcoat* ....80.00 - 120.00
52515 *I Loved You Then* ....50.00 - 80.00
52535 *Guess Who?* ....75.00 - 100.00
52542 *When I'm Walking With My Sweetness* ... 50.00 - 80.00
52547 *A Precious Little Thing Called Love* ....50.00 - 80.00
52550 *My Suppressed Desire* ....50.00 - 80.00
52553 *The One That I Love Loves Me* ....75.00 - 100.00.
52561 *Avalon Town* ....50.00 - 80.00
52562 *Lover Come Back* ....50.00 - 80.00
52568 *That's Living* ....50.00 - 80.00
52580 *Honey* ....50.00 - 80.00
52590 *Huggable, Kissable You* ....50.00 - 80.00
Harmony 719-H *Vaniteaser* ....15.00 - 20.00
    760-H *My Old Girl's My New Girl Now* ....15.00 - 20.00
    778-H *Me And The Man In The Moon* ....15.00 - 20.00
    816-H *My Troubles Are Over* ....15.00 - 20.00
    830-H *Let Me Dream In Your Arms* ....15.00 - 20.00
    839-H *Weary River* ....8.00 - 12.00
    840-H *I'd Rather Be Blue Over You* ....10.00 - 15.00
    872-H *My Sugar And Me* ....10.00 - 15.00
    873-H *An Eyeful Of You* ....10.00 - 15.00
    923-H *I'm Croonin' A Tune About June* ....10.00 - 15.00
    937-H *Wishing And Waiting For Love* ....12.00 - 16.00
    938-H *Am I Blue?* ....8.00 - 12.00
    947-H *Painting The Clouds With Sunshine* ....8.00 - 12.00
    948-H *Am I A Passing Fancy?* ....8.00 - 12.00
    958-H *Song Of The Blues* ....10.00 - 15.00
    959-H *Maybe-Who Knows?* ....10.00 - 15.00
    962-H *Why Can't You* ....10.00 - 15.00
    973-H *The Flippity Flop* ....10.00 - 15.00
    984-H *Just You, Just Me* ....10.00 - 15.00

1015-H *Love Ain't Nothin' But The Blues*..........10.00 - 15.00
1041-H *Blondy*....................................15.00 - 20.00
(Note: Above titles on Harmony also occur on Diva and Velvet
Tone, and are similarly valued.)
Paramount 20349, 20352, 20353, 20380, 20389,
20394, 20395, 20405 ....7.00 - 12.00
Perfect 14275 *Frankie And Johnnie* ....15.00 - 20.00
14302 *Somebody Loves Me* ....10.00 - 15.00
14309 *Ramblin' Blues* ....10.00 - 15.00
14311 *Charley, My Boy* ....10.00 - 15.00
14348 *Nashville Nightingale* ....10.00 - 15.00
14386 *Ain't My Baby Grand* ....10.00 - 15.00
14412 *Isn't She The Sweetest Thing?* ....10.00 - 15.00
14416 *Just A Little Drink* ....10.00 - 15.00
14441 *Dusting The Donkey* ....10.00 - 15.00
14464 *I Wonder Where My Old Gal Is To-night* .. 10.00 - 15.00
14471 *Alone At Last* ....8.00 - 12.00
14481 *Footloose* ....10.00 - 15.00
14485 *Fallin' Down* ....15.00 - 20.00
14488 *Show Me The Way To Go Home* ....10.00 - 15.00
14496 *Make Those Naughty Eyes Behave* ....10.00 - 15.00
14499 *Desdemona* ....10.00 - 15.00
14500 *Red Hot Henry Brown* ....10.00 - 15.00
14542 *I Ain't Got Nobody* ....15.00 - 20.00
14609 *Horses* ....10.00 - 15.00
14611 *The Blue Room* ....15.00 - 20.00
14619 *Am I Wasting My Time On You* ....10.00 - 15.00
14622 *I Wonder What's Become Of Joe?* ....10.00 - 15.00
14633 *Hi-Ho! The Merrio* ....15.00 - 20.00
14644 *Where'd You Get Those Eyes?* ....10.00 - 15.00
14646 *Breezin' Along With The Breeze* ....10.00 - 15.00
14678 *Stayin' Home* ....10.00 - 15.00
14690 *Wha-Cha-Ma-Call It* ....10.00 - 15.00
14691 *Me Too* ....10.00 - 15.00
14721 *Don't Take That Black Bottom Away* .....15.00 - 20.00
14724 *She Belongs To Me* ....10.00 - 15.00
14735 *Brand New Mama* ....10.00 - 15.00
14771 *Crazy Words-Crazy Tune* ....10.00 - 15.00
14773 *I Love The College Girls* ....10.00 - 15.00
14793 *There's Everything Nice About You* ....8.00 - 12.00
14794 *Leave My Baby Alone* ....10.00 - 15.00
14834 *After You're Gone* ....10.00 - 15.00
14837 *Vo-Do-Do-De-O Blues* ....15.00 - 20.00
14874 *Heart Breaking Baby* ....15.00 - 20.00
14888 *Goin' Home Again Blues*....................25.00 - 35.00
14897 *Is She My Girl Friend?* ....10.00 - 15.00
14905 *For My Baby*............................100.00 - 150.00
15084 *Glorianna* ....20.00 - 30.00
(Some of the above titles were also issued on Pathe-Actuelle,
similarly valued)
Perfect (most other issues) ....5.00 - 10.00
Puritan 11285, 11352, 11353, 11380, 11389,
11394, 11395, 11405 ....7.00 - 12.00
Regal 8334 *Zulu Wail* ....15.00 - 20.00
8377 *Someday, Sweetheart* ....15.00 - 20.00
8413 *Jelly Roll Blues* ....15.00 - 20.00
9970 *She Was Just A Sailor's Sweetheart* ....8.00 - 12.00
Triangle 11421 *Tessie, Stop Teasing Me* ....10.00 - 15.00
11462 *The Only, Only One* ....10.00 - 15.00
Velvet Tone 2394-V *I'd Be Lying* ....8.00 - 12.00

GOLDEN GATE SERENADERS:

Gennett 6487 *Oh! Baby* ....10.00 - 15.00
6488 *He's Worth His Weight In Gold*..............15.00 - 20.00

JEAN GOLDKETTE & HIS (BOOK CADILLAC) ORCHESTRA:

Victor 19308 *Where The Lazy Daisies Grow* .... 8.00 - 12.00
19313 *My Sweetheart*............................ 8.00 - 12.00
19317 *Cover Me Up With The Sunshine Of Virginia*
.... 8.00 - 12.00
19327 *Eileen* .... 8.00 - 12.00
19345 *Fox Trot Classique* .... 8.00 - 12.00
19548 *I Want To See My Tennessee* .... 8.00 - 12.00
19600 *It's The Blues (No. 14 Blues)* .... 15.00 - 20.00
19664 *Play Me Slow* .... 10.00 - 15.00
19947 *After I Say I'm Sorry* .... 8.00 - 12.00
19962 *Sorry And Blue* .... 5.00 - 8.00
19965 *Behind The Clouds* .... 7.00 - 10.00
19975 *Drifting Apart*............................ 7.00 - 10.00
20031 *Lonesome And Sorry* .... 7.00 - 10.00
20033 *Roses* .... 7.00 - 10.00
20256 *Don't Be Angry With Me* .... 5.00 - 8.00
20257 *I'd Love To Call You My Sweetheart* .... 5.00 - 8.00
20268 *Just A Bird's-Eye View Of My Old Kentucky Home*
.... 5.00 - 8.00
20270 *Idolizing* .... 8.00 - 12.00
20273 *Sunday*.................................. 8.00 - 12.00
20300 *Just One More Kiss*...................... 7.00 - 10.00
20466 *I'm Looking Over A Four Leaf Clover* ... 10.00 - 15.00
20469 *Proud Of A Baby Like You* .... 50.00 - 75.00
20471 *Hoosier Sweetheart*..................... 10.00 - 15.00
20472 *Look At The World And Smile*.................. 7.00 - 10.00
20491 *A Lane In Spain* .... 7.00 - 10.00
20493 *Sunny Disposish* .... 10.00 - 15.00
20588 *My Pretty Girl* .... 15.00 - 20.00
20675 *I'm Gonna Meet My Sweetie Now* .... 10.00 - 15.00
20926 *Slow River* .... 10.00 - 15.00
20981 *Blue River* .... 8.00 - 12.00
20994 *Clementine* .... 15.00 - 20.00
21150 *Just A Little Kiss From A Little Miss*....... 8.00 - 12.00
21166 *My Ohio Home* .... 7.00 - 10.00
21527 *Rosetta* .... 5.00 - 8.00
21565 *Just Imagine* .... 8.00 - 12.00
21590 *That's Just My Way Of Forgetting You* .... 8.00 - 12.00
21689 *If I Lost You* .... 5.00 - 8.00
21800 *That's What Puts The "Sweet" in Home, Sweet Home*
.... 8.00 - 12.00
21804 *Withered Roses*......................... 7.00 - 10.00
21805 *My Blackbirds Are Bluebirds Now* .... 10.00 - 15.00
21853 *She's Funny That Way* .... 8.00 - 12.00
21871 *Can You Blame Me* .... 5.00 - 8.00.
21889 *Take A Good Look At Mine*.................... 10.00 - 15.00
22027 *Painting The Clouds With Sunshine* .... 7.00 - 10.00
22077 *Birmingham Bertha*...................... 15.00 - 20.00
22123 *An Old Italian Love Song*................... 8.00 - 12.00
25354 *Slow River* .... 10.00 - 15.00
Victor (unnumbered) *In My Merry Oldsmobile* .... 150.00 - up
(Note: Above is a special pressing, designated "special record for
private use only", having the tune rendered as a fox-trot on one
side, as a waltz on the flip side.)

BENNY GOODMAN; BENNY (BENNIE) GOODMAN'S BOYS (WITH JIM AND GLENN); BENNY GOODMAN AND HIS (MUSIC HALL) ORCHESTRA:

Brunswick 3975 *Shirt Tail Stomp* .... 20.00 - 30.00
4013 *Jungle Blues*............................ 30.00 - 50.00
4968 *After A While* .... 50.00 - 80.00
7644 *Bugle Call Rag* .... 8.00 - 12.00

Capitol, most issues ....5.00 - 10.00
Columbia 2542-D *Not That I Care* ....30.00 - 50.00
    2835-D *Ain'tcha Glad?* ....30.00 - 50.00
    2845-D *Dr. Heckle And Mr. Jibe*......................30.00 - 50.00
    2856-D *Your Mother's Son-in-Law* ....40.00 - 60.00
    2867-D *Riffin' The Scotch* ....40.00 - 60.00
    2871-D *Love Me Or Leave Me* ....30.00 - 50.00
    2892-D *Junk Man* ....30.00 - 50.00
    2907-D *Georgia Jubilee* ....30.00 - 50.00
    2923-D *I Ain't Lazy-I'm Just Dreamin'* ....30.00 - 50.00
    2927-D *Breakfast Ball* ....20.00 - 30.00
    2947-D *Take My Word* ....25.00 - 40.00
    2958-D *Bugle Call Rag* ....25.00 - 40.00
    2988-D *Like A Bolt From The Blue* ....20.00 - 30.00
    3003-D *Blue Moon* ....20.00 - 30.00
    3011-D *Music Hall Rag* ....20.00 - 30.00
    3015-D *Night Wind*..20.00 - 30.00
    3018-D *Singing A Happy Song*.....................20.00 - 30.00
    3022-D *Down Home Rag*...............................20.00 - 30.00
(many of the foregoing are pressed of royal blue shellac)
Columbia 35201, 35210, 35211, 35230, 35241,
    35254,35289, 35308, 35313, 35331, 35374,
    35391, 35396, 35420, 35461, 35472, 35487 ....7.00 - 10.00
Columbia, most others on red label ....5.00 - 8.00
Melotone 12023 *He's Not Worth Your Tears*.........20.00 - 30.00
    12024 *Overnight* ....20.00 - 30.00
    12079 *Falling In Love Again*..........................20.00 - 30.00
    12100 *99 Out Of A Hundred Wanna Be Loved* ..20.00 - 30.00
    12120 *We Can Live On Love* ....20.00 - 30.00
    12138 *I Wanna Be Around My Baby All The Time*
    ....20.00 - 30.00
    12149 *It Looks Like Love*................................20.00 - 30.00
    12205 *Slow But Sure*......................................20.00 - 30.00
    12208 *Pardon Me, Pretty Baby* ....20.00 - 30.00
Victor 25009 *Hunkadola* ....15.00 - 20.00
    25011 *Hooray For Love* ....15.00 - 20.00
    25021 *Restless* ....15.00 - 20.00
    25024 *Japanese Sandman*................................8.00 - 12.00
    25081 *Ballad In Blue* ....15.00 - 20.00
    25090 *King Porter* ....8.00 - 12.00
    25115, 25136, 25145 ....7.00 - 12.00
    25193 *No Other One* ....10.00 - 15.00
    25195 *Eeeny Meeny Miney Mo*.....................10.00 - 15.00
    25215, 25245, 25247, 25258 ....7.00 - 12.00
    25263 *Madhouse*..10.00 - 15.00
    25279, 25290, 25316, 25320, 25329, 25333 ....7.00 - 12.00
    25340 *Sing Me A Swing Song*.........................8.00 - 12.00
    25345 *Nobody's Sweetheart* ....7.00 - 10.00
    25350 *House Hop* ....8.00 - 12.00
    25351, 25355, 25363, 25387, 25391, 25398,
    25406, 25411, 25434, 25445 ....7.00 - 10.00
    25461 *Goodnight My Love (vocal Ella Fitzgerald)/Take Another
    Guess (vocal, Ella Fitzgerald)*............................20.00 - 30.00
    25461 *Goodnight My Love (vocal, Frances Hunt)/Tain't No Use*
    ....15.00 - 25.00
    25469 *Did You Mean It?/Tain't No Use*............20.00 - 30.00
    25467, 25473, 25481, 25497 ....5.00 - 10.00
    25486 *Smoke Dreams* ....8.00 - 12.00
    25492 *Swing Low, Sweet Chariot*....................8.00 - 12.00
    25500, 25505, 25510, 25521, 25529, 25531,
    25621, 25627, 25634, 25644, 26660, 25678,
    25683, 25705, 25708, 25711, 25717, 25720,
    25725, 25726, 25727, 25751 ....7.00 - 12.00

(Note: The foregoing, up to number 25683, if original pressings, are
    of the "scroll" label or scroll label "Swing Classic" label.)
    25808 *Pop-Corn Man/oooOO-Oh Boom*......... 250.00 - up
(Note: The rare coupling above should be distinguished from the
    common issue, below, which does not have the song "Pop-Corn
    Man.")
    25808 *Always and Always/oooOO-Oh Boom!*..... 7.00 - 10.00
    25814, 25822, 25827, 25840, 25846, 25867,
    25871, 25878, 25880, 26000, 26021, 26044,
    26060, 26053, 26071, 26082, 26087, 26090,
    26095, 26099, 26107, 26110, 26125, 25130,
    26134, 26139, 26159, 26166, 26170, 26175,
    26187, 26211, 26230, 26240, 26263 .... 7.00 - 10.00
Vocalion 15656 *A Jazz Holiday*........................... 150.00 - 200.00
    15795 *That's A Plenty*.................................... 150.00 - 200.00

LILLIAN GOODNER:
Ajax 17018 *Ramblin' Blues* .... 35.00 - 50.00
    17020 *Chicago Blues* .... 35.00 - 50.00
    17028 *Four-Flushin' Papa* .... 30.00 - 50.00

GOODY AND HIS GOOD TIMERS:
Pathe-Actuelle 36902 *Diga Diga Doo* .... 15.00 - 20.00
    36903 *Stardust* .... 20.00 - 30.00
    36924 *'Cause I'm In Love*................................. 15.00 - 20.00
Perfect 15083 *Diga Diga Doo* .... 15.00 - 20.00
    15084 *Stardust* .... 20.00 - 30.00
    15105 *'Cause I'm In Love*................................. 15.00 - 20.00

THE GOOFUS FIVE (AND THEIR ORCHESTRA):
Okeh 40179 *Them Ramblin' Blues* .... 20.00 - 30.00
    40208 *Go, Emmaline* .... 25.00 - 40.00
    40233 *Go 'Long, Mule*.................................... 25.00 - 40.00
    40244 *Everybody Loves My Baby* .... 25.00 - 40.00
    40261 *Oh! Mabel* .... 20.00 - 30.00
    40292 *Alabamy Bound* .... 25.00 - 40.00
    40314 *Hot Tamale Molly* .... 25.00 - 40.00
    40340 *I Had Someone Else Before I Had You* ... 20.00 - 30.00
    40423 *Yes, Sir! That's My Baby* .... 20.00 - 30.00
    40442 *I'm Gonna Charleston Back To Charleston*
    .... 30.00 - 50.00
    40464 *Loud Speakin' Papa* .... 25.00 - 40.00
    40474 *Sweet Man* .... 20.00 - 30.00
    40500 *Clap Hands! Here Comes Charlie* .... 20.00 - 30.00
    40534 *That Certain Party* .... 20.00 - 30.00
    40624 *I Wonder What's Become Of Joe?* .... 20.00 - 30.00
    40644 *You Gotta Know How To Love* .... 20.00 - 30.00.
    40649 *Where'd You Get Those Eyes*................ 20.00 - 30.00
    40661 *Mary Lou* .... 20.00 - 30.00
    40687 *Crazy Quilt* .... 30.00 - 50.00
    40690 *Heebie Jeebies* .... 20.00 - 30.00
    40739 *I've Got The Girl*................................... 20.00 - 30.00
    40767 *Farewell Blues* .... 30.00 - 50.00
    40809 *Muddy Water*.. 20.00 - 30.00
    40817 *Arkansas Blues* .... 30.00 - 50.00
    40821 *The Whisper Song* .... 20.00 - 30.00
    40841 *Vo-Do-Do-De-O Blues* .... 25.00 - 40.00
    40886 *Clementine* .... 25.00 - 40.00
    40997 *Nothin' Does-Does Like To Used To Do-Do-Do*
    .... 25.00 - 40.00
    41069 *Ready For The River* .... 15.00 - 20.00
    41110 *Right Or Wrong*.................................... 15.00 - 20.00
    41113 *Vaniteaser* .... 20.00 - 30.00
    41138 *My Blackbirds Are Bluebirds Now* .... 20.00 - 30.00

41169 *Sweetheart Of All My Dreams* ....10.00 - 20.00
41177 *Rambling Wreck From Georgia Tech*......15.00 - 20.00
41202 *Caressing You* ....15.00 - 20.00
41220 *Deep Night* ....15.00 - 25.00

EDDIE GORDON'S BAND:
Odeon ONY-36008 *March Of The Hoodlums*.........50.00 - 75.00
ONY-41153 *Wild Oat Joe* ....50.00 - 75.00
ONY-41204 *No One Else But You* ....50.00 - 75.00
ONY-41273 *Birmingham Bertha* ....50.00 - 75.00
Parlophone PNY-41320 *Chant Of The Jungle* ....50.00 - 75.00

GRAY GORDON & HIS TIC-TOC RHYTHM:
Bluebird, most issues ....4.00 - 8.00
Victor, most issues..4.00 - 8.00

HERB(ERT) GORDON & HIS (HOTEL ADELPHIA/TEN EYCK) (WHISPERING) ORCHESTRA:
Brunswick 4064 *Jo-Anne*....................................7.00 - 10.00
4372 *Then We Canoe-dle-oodle Along*.................8.00 - 12.00
Brunswick, most other issues ....4.00 - 8.00

JIMMY GORDON (AND HIS VIP VOP BAND):
Decca 7322, 7334, 7373, 7409, 7474, 7490, 7519,
7536, 7555, 7592, 7611, 7624, 7661, 7702, 7764,
7794 ....7.00 - 12.00

RALPH GORDON & HIS ORCHESTRA:
Victor 26033 *Two Left Feet* ....8.00 - 12.00
26041 *Arabian Nightmare* ....8.00 - 12.00

REX GORDON AND HIS ACES:
Champion 15441 *I Just Roll Along*.........................15.00 - 25.00
15457 *Rain Or Shine* ....15.00 - 20.00
15459 *Ol' Man River* ....20.00 - 30.00
15512 *Dixie Dawn* ....8.00 - 12.00
15515 *You're A Real Sweetheart*....................7.00 - 10.00
15532 *C-O-N-S-T-A-N-T-I-N-O-P-L-E* ....10.00 - 15.00
15533 *Crazy Rhythm* ....8.00 - 12.00
15557 *Just Like A Melody Out Of The Sky*........12.00 - 16.00
15619 *Where the Shy Little Violets Grow*.............8.00 - 12.00
15620 *Once In A Lifetime* ....7.00 - 10.00
15701 *She's Got Great Ideas*..........................40.00 - 60.00
15740 *My Kinda Love*....................................10.00 - 15.00

ROSS GORMAN & HIS (EARL CARROLL) ORCHESTRA/FIRE EATERS/VIRGINIANS; GORMAN'S NOVELTY SYNCOPATORS:
Cameo 1063 *Idolizing* ....10.00 - 15.00
Columbia 435-D, 460-D, 495-D, 563-D, 576-D,
631-D ....7.00 - 12.00
498-D *Rhythm Of The Day* ....15.00 - 20.00
516-D *Sleepy Time Gal*..................................10.00 - 15.00
615-D *No More Worryin'* ....10.00 - 15.00
A2844 *Barkin' Dog* ....10.00 - 15.00
Edison 51876 *Idolizing* ....30.00 - 50.00
51896 *You're Burning Me Up* ....30.00 - 50.00
51905 *The Sphinx* ....20.00 - 30.00
51944 *High, High, High Up In The Hills* ....35.00 - 50.00
Gennett 6057 *She Looks Like Helen Brown* ....25.00 - 40.00
6118 *Phantom Blues* ....40.00 - 60.00
6132 *Pardon The Glove* ....40.00 - 60.00
Harmony 322-H *Sidewalk Blues*..........................15.00 - 20.00
350-H *You're The One For Me* ....8.00 - 12.00
372-H *She Looks Like Helen Brown*................15.00 - 20.00
379-H *Ev'ry Little While* ....7.00 - 10.00

403-H *My Wife's In Europe Today*....................10.00 - 15.00
427-H *Phantom Blues*......................................15.00 - 20.00
(Note: Above titles on Harmony also are found on Diva and Velvet Tone, similarly valued.)

GORMAN'S SUNDODGERS:
Challenge 721 *When Day Is Done* ....10.00 - 15.00
736 *Just Another Day Wasted Away* ....10.00 - 15.00
744 *How Do You Like My Sweetie?* ....8.00 - 12.00
759 *The Sweetheart Of Sigma Chi* ....20.00 - 30.00

GOTHAM CLUB ORCHESTRA:
Silvertone 2400 *Red Hot Mama* ....10.00 - 15.00
2660 *Stockholm Stomp* ....15.00 - 20.00

THE GOTHAM NIGHTINGALES:
Okeh 40291 *Keep Smiling At Trouble* ....8.00 - 12.00
40679 *Bobadilla*..8.00 - 12.00
40686 *She Belongs To Me*................................12.00 - 16.00

THE GOTHAM STOMPERS:
Variety 541 *Did Anyone Ever Tell You*...................10.00 - 15.00
629 *My Honey's Lovin' Arms* ....10.00 - 15.00

TOM/TOMMY GOTT & HIS ORCHESTRA:
Banner 6317 *I Want To Be Bad* ....10.00 - 15.00
Crown 3134, 3166, 3182, 3189 ....7.00 - 10.00

GOWAN'S RHAPSODY MAKERS:
Gennett 3408 *I'll Fly To Hawaii*..........................75.00 - 100.00
6039 *Sunny Hawaii*..80.00 - 120.00

PORTER GRAINGER:
Ajax 17039 *In Harlem's Araby*............................75.00 - 100.00

GRANDVIEW INN ORCHESTRA:
Challenge 362 *Here I Am Broken Hearted* ....10.00 - 15.00
Champion 15342 *Dew-Dew-Dewy Day*..................20.00 - 30.00
15343 *No Wonder I'm Happy* ....25.00 - 35.00
15345 *(Here I Am) Broken Hearted*.................50.00 - 75.00
15401 *Roll Up The Carpets* ....20.00 - 30.00
15421 *Everybody Loves My Girl* ....15.00 - 25.00

GLEN GRAY & HIS CASA LOMA ORCHESTRA (See also THE CASA LOMA ORCHESTRA):
Decca 192 *I'm In Love* ....7.00 - 10.00
193 *You're A Builder-Upper*............................7.00 - 10.00
199 *Chinatown, My Chinatown* ....10.00 - 15.00
200 *Nagasaki* ....10.00 - 15.00
286 *Stompin' Around* ....10.00 - 15.00
287 *Maybe I'm Wrong Again*..........................7.00 - 10.00
298 *Two In A Dream* ....7.00 - 10.00
312 *Blue Moon* ....7.00 - 10.00
334 *You Took Advantage Of Me* ....7.00 - 10.00
339 *In My Country That Means Love* ....7.00 - 10.00
349 *The Night Is Young*..................................7.00 - 10.00
352 *Fare Thee Well, Annabelle* ....7.00 - 10.00
375 *Ain't It Just Too Bad?* ....7.00 - 10.00
379 *Who's Sorry Now?* ....7.00 - 10.00
386 *My Heart Is An Open Book* ....7.00 - 10.00
387 *My Dance* ....7.00 - 10.00
405 *You're Walking In My Sleep* ....7.00 - 10.00
430 *Once Upon A Midnight* ....7.00 - 10.00
463 *Chant Of The Jungle* ....8.00 - 12.00
552 *Without A Word Of Warning* ....7.00 - 10.00
553 *The Devil Is Afraid Of Music* ....7.00 - 10.00
603 *Yankee Doodle Never Went To Town* ....7.00 - 10.00

652 *With All My Heart*..........................7.00 - 10.00
688 *Moonburn* ....7.00 - 10.00
696 *I'd Rather Lead A Band*..................8.00 - 12.00
869 *Bugle Call Rag*...........................8.00 - 12.00
986 *Shades Of Hades* ....8.00 - 12.00
1048 *Jungle Jitters*............................8.00 - 12.00
1126 *You're Laughing At Me* ....7.00 - 10.00
1129 *Swing High, Swing Low* ....7.00 - 10.00
1158 *Too Marvelous For Words*.............7.00 - 10.00
1159 *A Study In Brown* ....7.00 - 10.00
1179 *I'd Be A Fool Again*....................7.00 - 10.00
1180 *Was It Rain?* ....7.00 - 10.00
1211 *Never In A Million Years* ....7.00 - 10.00
1246 *One, Two, Three Little Hours* ....7.00 - 10.00
1312 *Zig-Zag* ....8.00 - 12.00
1368 *Yours And Mine* ....7.00 - 10.00
1396 *Swing Low, Sweet Chariot* ....8.00 - 12.00
1412 *Casa Loma Stomp* ....8.00 - 12.00
1473 *Smoke Rings* ....8.00 - 12.00
Decca 1519, 1520, 1530, 1540, 1541, 1575, 1596,
    1607, 1608, 1634, 1650, 1672, 1679, 1725, 1755,
    1783, 1864, and higher numbers ....5.00 - 10.00
Victor L-16023 *Dardanella* and 2 other tunes ....40.00 - 60.00
(Note: Above is a long-playing "Program Transcription.")
    24222 *Hey! Young Fella* ....8.00 - 12.00
    24224 *Sittin' By The Fire With You*....10.00 - 15.00
    24254 *Black-Eyed Susan Brown*........15.00 - 20.00
    24256 *Casa Loma Stomp* ....10.00 - 15.00

JANE GRAY:
Harmony 300-H, 395-H, 485-H, 513-H, 646-H ....7.00 - 10.00
    464-H *Miss Annabelle Lee*................10.00 - 15.00
(Note: Title also appears on Diva and Velvet Tone.)

KITTY GRAY & HER WAMPUS CATS:
Vocalion 03869 *Swingology* ....20.00 - 30.00
    03992 *I Can't Dance (I Got Ants In My Pants)*..15.00 - 20.00
    04014 *Weeping Willow Swing* ....20.00 - 30.00
    04121 *My Baby's Ways* ....20.00 - 30.00
    04629 *I'm Yours To Command*.............20.00 - 30.00

RUSSELL GRAY & HIS ORCHESTRA:
Okeh 40846 *Ain't That A Grand And Glorious Feeling*
    ....15.00 - 25.00
    40938 *Sugar*...................................75.00 - 100.00

GREAT WESTERN SERENADERS:
Pathe-Actuelle 36403 *Bell Hoppin' Blues* ....15.00 - 20.00

GREEN BROTHERS' NOVELTY BAND/XYLOPHONE ORCHESTRA:
Aeolian-Vocalion 12098 *Ring-Tail Blues* ....10.00 - 15.00
Edison 50926 *Eddie (Steady)* ....10.00 - 15.00
    51274 *You Better Keep Babying Baby* ....10.00 - 15.00
    51321 *New Orleans Wiggle* ....15.00 - 20.00
    51385 *Go, Emmaline* ....10.00 - 15.00
    51425 *Some Other Day*......................20.00 - 30.00
    51437 *Back Where the Daffodils Grow* ......20.00 - 30.00
    51493 *Those Panama Mamas*................15.00 - 20.00
    51497 *Fascinating Rhythm*..................15.00 - 20.00
    51753 *As Long As I Have You* ....10.00 - 15.00
    51913 *Look Up And Smile* ....15.00 - 20.00
    51876 *That's What God Made Mothers For* ......30.00 - 50.00
    52072 *Say It With A Red, Red Rose* ....30.00 - 50.00
    52410 *I Wanna Be Loved By You* ....50.00 - 75.00
Gennett 5122 *That Red-Head Gal* ....8.00 - 12.00
Odeon 20074 *I've Got The Joys* ....7.00 - 10.00

Okeh 4180 *The Blacksmith Rag*.............. 7.00 - 10.00
Pathe 22067 *Tackin' 'Em Down* .... 7.00 - 10.00

GREEN PARROT INN ORCHESTRA:
Champion 15322 *At Sundown*............... 30.00 - 50.00
    15326 *One O'Clock Baby* .... 50.00 - 75.00
    15345 *Is It Possible That She Loves Me* .... 50.00 - 75.00

BOB GREEN'S DANCE ORCHESTRA:
Oriole 722 *Tuck In Kentucky And Smile* .... 10.00 - 15.00
    1126 *A Little West Of West Virginia*................ 7.00 - 10.00
    1134 *Stay Out Of The South*.......................... 7.00 - 10.00
    1313 *Ready For The River* .... 15.00 - 20.00
    1338 *They Don't Come Better Than Betty*.......... 7.00 - 10.00
    1477 *I Must Be Falling In Love* .... 7.00 - 10.00
    1580 *Why Can't It Be Me?*............................ 7.00 - 10.00
    1598 *Sure Enough Blues* .... 8.00 - 12.00
    1613 *Momma Be Nice (Papa Will Be Nice To You)*
    .... 7.00 - 10.00
    1692 *If I Only Loved You A Little Bit Less* .... 7.00 - 10.00
    1700 *When I Found You* .... 7.00 - 10.00

JANE GREEN:
Victor 19215 *Mama Loves Papa* .... 7.00 - 10.00
    19502 *Me and The Boy Friend* .... 7.00 - 10.00
    19604 *Somebody Like You* .... 15.00 - 20.00
    19609 *The Blues Have Got Me* .... 10.00 - 15.00
    19687 *Got No Time* .... 10.00 - 15.00
    19707 *If You Hadn't Gone Away* .... 15.00 - 20.00
    19995 *Honey Bunch* .... 15.00 - 20.00
    20323 *Hard-To-Get Gertie* .... 7.00 - 10.00
    20391 *If I'd Only Believed In You* .... 7.00 - 10.00
    20509 *I'm Gonna Meet My Sweetie Now* .... 8.00 - 12.00
    21114 *My One and Only*................................ 7.00 - 10.00

JOHNNY GREEN AND HIS ORCHESTRA:
Brunswick 6797 *Live and Love Tonight* .... 15.00 - 20.00
    6855 *Easy Come, Easy Go*............................. 15.00 - 20.00
    7441, 7455, 7521, 7522, 7661, 7662, 7716
    .... 5.00 - 10.00
    7487 *Isn't This A Lovely Day?*........................ 7.00 - 10.00
    7497 *Fruitas*... 7.00 - 10.00
Columbia 2940-D *A New Moon Is Over My Shoulder*
    .... 8.00 - 12.00
    2943-D *Two Cigarettes In The Dark* .... 8.00 - 12.00
    2959-D *Were You Foolin'?*............................. 8.00 - 12.00
    2999-D *Because of Once Upon A Time* .... 8.00 - 12.00
    3002-D *Let's Hold Hands* .... 8.00 - 12.00
    3022-D *Lovely To Look At* .... 8.00 - 12.00
    3024-D *Beyond A Shadow Of A Doubt*............... 8.00 - 12.00
    3028-D *Go Into Your Dance* .... 8.00 - 12.00
    3029-D *She's A Latin From Manhattan* .... 8.00 - 12.00
(Note: Many of above Columbia records were pressed of "royal
    blue" shellac.)

RUBY GREEN'S MANHATTAN MADCAPS:
Gennett 6457 *Hot Coffee* .... 150.00 - 200.00
    6629 *Oh Dem Golden Slippers* .... 15.00 - 25.00

GREENWICH VILLAGE ORCHESTRA:

Titles issued contemporaneously on Broadway, Claxtonola, Harmograph, Paramount, Pennington, Puritan, Triangle: *House of David Blues; Ringside Blues* ....40.00 - 60.00

SONNY GREER & THE D'C'NS/HIS MEMPHIS MEN:

Columbia 1868-D *Saturday Night Function* ....15.00 - 20.00
    2833-D *Saturday Night Function* ....10.00 - 15.00

EARL GRESH AND HIS GANGPLANK ORCHESTRA; EARL GRESH'S ORCHESTRA:

Columbia 424-D *Row, Row, Rosie* ....15.00 - 20.00
    469-D *Freshie* ....20.00 - 30.00
    672-D *Ace In The Hole* ....20.00 - 30.00
    693-D *Scatter Your Smiles* ....15.00 - 20.00
    841-D *Ah! Ah! Aw! Aw!* ....15.00 - 20.00
    1031-D *Where the Wild, Wild Flowers Grow* ....15.00 - 20.00
Pathe-Actuelle 36636 *White Ghost Shivers* ....15.00 - 20.00
Perfect 14818 *White Ghost Shivers* ....15.00 - 20.00

JIMMIE GRIER & HIS (COCOANUT GROVE) ORCHESTRA:

Brunswick 6597, 7306, 7307, 7308, 7355, 7381,
    7383, 7505, 7519, 7528, 7619, 7622, 7679, 7683,
    7733, 7760, 7790, 7802, 7887, 7901, 7908 ....7.00 - 12.00
Decca 1474, 1475, 1486, 1497, 1797, 1812, 1813 ....7.00 - 10.00
Victor 22970, 22971 ....7.00 - 10.00
Victor 24174 *Here Lies Love* ....8.00 - 12.00
    24175 *Second-Hand Heart* ....8.00 - 12.00

GORDON GRIMES & HIS ORCHESTRA:

Champion 15290 *Yes She Do-No She Don't* ....15.00 - 20.00
    15293 *I'm Back In Love Again* ....15.00 - 20.00
    15322 *S-L-U-E Foot* ....30.00 - 50.00
    15456 *In The Sing-Song Sycamore Tree* ....20.00 - 30.00
    15495 *Oh! Baby* ....15.00 - 20.00
    15496 *Delores* ....15.00 - 20.00

TOM GRISELLE AND HIS ORCHESTRA:

Gennett 3081 *Stop, You're Tickling Me* ....15.00 - 25.00

FERDIE GROFE AND HIS ORCHESTRA:

Columbia 2851-D *Cinderella's Fella* ....15.00 - 20.00
    2858-D *Inka Dinka Doo* ....15.00 - 20.00

WALTER GROSS:

Bluebird 10795 *A Slight Case Of Ivory* ....8.00 - 12.00
    10937 *Creepy Weepy* ....8.00 - 12.00

ELMER GROSSO AND HIS (MOUNT ROYAL) ORCHESTRA:

Champion 15957 *I'm Climbing Up A Rainbow* ....7.00 - 10.00
    15977 *Sing You Sinners* ....15.00 - 25.00
    16083 *Just A Little Closer* ....10.00 - 15.00
    16128 *Sweet Jennie Lee* ....10.00 - 15.00
    16154 *You're Driving Me Crazy* ....15.00 - 20.00
    16176 *Cheerful Little Earful* ....15.00 - 20.00

Gennett 6520 *Old Man Sunshine* ....20.00 - 30.00
    7119 *As Long As I'm With You* ....25.00 - 40.00
    7148 *Sing, You Sinners* ....25.00 - 40.00

FRANK GUARENTE AND HIS ORCHESTRA:

Harmony 787-H *Sweethearts On Parade* ....7.00 - 10.00
    788-H *My Mother's Eyes* ....7.00 - 10.00
    830-H *When Polly Walks Through The Hollyhocks*
    ....15.00 - 20.00
(Note: Above titles on Diva and Velvet Tone are similarly valued.)

VERA GUILAROFF:

Pathe-Actuelle 21178 *Calico Rag* ....10.00 - 15.00
Perfect 11251 *Calico Rag* ....10.00 - 15.00

THE GULF COAST SEVEN:

Columbia A-3916 *Daybreak Blues* ....30.00 - 50.00
    A-3978 *Memphis, Tennessee* ....30.00 - 50.00
    14107-D *Santa Claus Blues* ....150.00 - 200.00
    14373-D *Daylight Savin' Blues* ....150.00 - 200.00

GULF COAST TRIO:

Buddy 8041 *Grand Opera Blues* ....80.00 - 130.00

JOE GUMIN AND HIS ORCHESTRA:

Broadway 1430 *Tie A Little String Around Your Finger*
    ....10.00 - 15.00
Columbia 2571-D *I'll Think Of You* ....15.00 - 20.00

JIMMIE GUNN AND HIS ORCHESTRA:

Bluebird 6469 *My Blue Heaven* ....15.00 - 20.00
    6500 *I've Found A New Baby* ....15.00 - 20.00
    6508 *Slats Shuffle* ....15.00 - 20.00
    6578 *The Operator Special* ....15.00 - 25.00

MICKEY GUY AND HIS ROSE-TREE CAFE ORCHESTRA; MICKEY GUY'S HOTTENTOTS:

Okeh 40462 *Rose-Tree Strut* ....75.00 - 100.00
    40588 *In Your Green Hat* ....50.00 - 80.00
Pathe-Actuelle 36433 *Rhythm Rag* ....25.00 - 40.00
    36478 *Two-Ton Tessie* ....15.00 - 25.00
Perfect 14614 *Philadelphia* ....25.00 - 40.00
    14659 *Two-Ton Tessie* ....15.00 - 25.00

GUYON'S PARADISE ORCHESTRA:

Okeh 4732, 4737, 4742 ....7.00 - 10.00
    4862 *Louisville Lou* ....10.00 - 15.00
    4866 *I've Got The Ain't Got Nothin' Never Had Nothin' Blues*
    ....7.00 - 10.00
    4883 *I Never Miss The Sunshine* ....7.00 - 10.00
    4999 *Land Of Cotton Blues* ....10.00 - 15.00

BOBBY HACKETT AND HIS ORCHESTRA:

Okeh 4047, 4142, 4499, 4565, 4806, 4877, 5198,
    5375, 5493, 5620...7.00 - 12.00
Vocalion 4047, 4152, 4499, 4565, 4806, 4877,
    5198, 5375, 5493, 5620......................................7.00 - 12.00

(W.G.) HAENSCHEN'S (BANJO) ORCHESTRA SAINT LOUIS:

Personal Record 60781 *Country Club Melody* ....40.00 - 60.00
    M61068 *Honky Tonky* ....50.00 - 80.00
    M6l070 *Maple Leaf Rag* ....50.00 - 80.00
    M61071 *Admiration* ....40.00 - 60.00
(Note: Other records by this band, if they exist, would probably be of equal interest to collectors.)

CASS HAGAN AND HIS (HOTEL MANAGER/PARK CENTRAL HOTEL) ORCHESTRA:

Columbia 966-D *Sometimes I'm Happy* ....8.00 - 12.00
    1033-D *Melancholy Charlie* ....15.00 - 20.00
    1089-D *Havana* ....8.00 - 12.00
    1114-D *The Varsity Drag* ....10.00 - 15.00
    1138-D *Manhattan Mary* ....5.00 - 8.00
    1176-D *My Lady* ....7.00 - 10.00
    1222-D *Dear, On A Night Like This* ....7.00 - 10.00
    1301-D *My Ohio Home* ....8.00 - 12.00
    1334-D *Golden Gate* ....15.00 - 20.00
Edison 51959 *It All Depends On You* ....30.00 - 50.00
    52012 *Lily* ....40.00 - 60.00

HAGER'S BAND (DANCE) ORCHESTRA:

Okeh 4406 *Broncho Trot* ....10.00 - 15.00
Rex 5271 *Rigo(letto) Rag* ....30.00 - 50.00
Zonophone 160 *Dixie Belles* ....15.00 - 30.00

BILL HAID & HIS CUBS/THIEVES OF SLEEP:

Broadway 1187 *Slue Foot* ....15.00 - 20.00
    1188 *I'm Walking Between The Raindrops* ....10.00 - 15.00
    1200 *Blue Grass* ....10.00 - 15.00
    1201 *If You Don't Love Me* ....8.00 - 12.00
    1205 *Pickin' Cotton* ....10.00 - 15.00
    1206 *I Can't Give You Anything But Love* ....8.00 - 12.00
    1207 *That's My Way Of Forgetting You* ....7.00 - 10.00
    1211 *Good Girl* ....7.00 - 10.00
    1217 *A Good Man Is Hard To Find* ....15.00 - 20.00
    1220 *Shake It Down* ....20.00 - 30.00
    1229 *Marie* ....5.00 - 8.00
    1235 *Me And The Man In The Moon* ....8.00 - 12.00
    1237 *Lonesome* ....7.00 - 10.00
Paramount 20628 *Slue Foot* ....15.00 - 20.00
    20630 *I'm Walking Between The Raindrops* ......10.00 - 15.00
    20643 *Jeannine, I Dream Of Lilac Time* ....8.00 - 12.00
    20644 *Hold Everything, Here Comes My Girl* ...10.00 - 15.00
    20646 *Etiquette* ....10.00 - 15.00
    20647 *Crazy Rhythm* ....8.00 - 12.00
    20648 *Blue Shadows* ....7.00 - 10.00
    20652 *Good Girl* ....7.00 - 10.00
    20658 *I Ain't Got Nobody* ....15.00 - 20.00
    20660 *That Old Sweetheart Of Mine* ....5.00 - 8.00
    20661 *Weary Weasel* ....20.00 - 30.00
    20676 *Doin' The Raccoon* ....8.00 - 12.00
    20678 *Lonesome* ....7.00 - 10.00

HAITIAN ORCHESTRA:

Varsity 8360, 8363, 8364, 8399, 8405......................7.00 - 12.00

HALFWAY HOUSE (DANCE) ORCHESTRA:

Columbia 476-D *Maple Leaf Rag* ....35.00 - 50.00
    541-D *New Orleans Shuffle* ....50.00 - 75.00
    681-D *Since You're Gone* ....50.00 - 75.00
    1041-D *Snookum* ....50.00 - 75.00
    1263-D *When I'm Blue* ....50.00 - 75.00
    1542-D *Tell Me Who* ....35.00 - 50.00
Okeh 40318 *Pussy Cat Rag* ....100.00 - 150.00

ADELAIDE HALL:

Brunswick 4031 I *Must Have That Man* ....10.00 - 15.00
    6362 *I'll Never Be The Same* ....10.00 - 15.00
    6376 *Strange As It Seems* ....10.00 - 15.00
    6518 *Baby* ....15.00 - 20.00

ARTHUR HALL with THE ORIGINAL GEORGIA FIVE:

Majestic 1519 *Yes We Have No Bananas* ....15.00 - 20.00
Olympic 1519 *Maggie! Yes Ma'am! Come Right Up Stairs*
....10.00 - 20.00

BOBBY HALL & HIS ORCHESTRA:

Champion 15801 *Just A Little Glimpse Of Paradise* ...15.00 - 20.00

FRED "SUGAR" HALL AND HIS (ROSELAND) ORCHESTRA/SUGAR BABIES; FRED HALL'S JAZZ BAND:

Banner 6264 *Missouri Squabble* ....15.00 - 20.00
    6269 *Louder And Funnier* ....15.00 - 20.00
    7248 *West End Blues* ....20.00 - 30.00
Bell 462 *It Made You Happy When You Made Me Cry*
....7.00 - 10.00
    466 *In A Little White House* ....7.00 - 10.00
Clover 1738 *Precious* ....10.00 - 15.00
Emerson 3007 *Say It Again*................................8.00 - 12.00
    3021 *After I Say I'm Sorry* ....8.00 - 12.00
    3030 *I Found A Round-A-Bout Way To Heaven* . 8.00 - 12.00
    3082 *Here Comes Fatima* ....8.00 - 12.00
    3089 *The Sphinx* ....7.00 - 10.00
    3094 *Tell Me Tonight* ....8.00 - 12.00
    3112 *The Birth Of The Blues* ....8.00 - 12.00
Harmony 19-H *Say Arabella*..............................15.00 - 20.00
Marathon 166 *She's My Baby Now* ....15.00 - 20.00
    210 *Hello Montreal!* ....15.00 - 20.00
    221 *Maybe You're Right* ....15.00 - 20.00
    229 *I'm Trying So Hard To Be Happy* ....15.00 - 20.00
    230 *I Can't Give You Anything But Love*..........15.00 - 20.00
    231 *Tonight's The Night* ....15.00 - 20.00
    232 *You're The Only Girl For Me* ....15.00 - 20.00
    234 *On A Moonlight Night*............................15.00 - 20.00
    235 *Tell Me When* ....15.00 - 20.00
(Note: Above are 7-inch records. Other issues on this scarce label are similarly valued.)
National Music Lovers 1138 *Charleston With Me* ... 8.00 - 12.00
    1147 *Nice And Pretty*....................................8.00 - 12.00
    1159 *Forever With You* ....7.00 - 10.00
    1171 *Take It From Me* ....7.00 - 10.00
    1184 *I'll See You In Kentucky*......................7.00 - 10.00
Okeh 40410 *Look Who's Here!* ....30.00 - 50.00
    40437 *Dallas Blues* ....30.00 - 50.00
    40442 *She's Driving Me Wild* ....30.00 - 50.00.
    40482 *Melancholy Lou* ....30.00 - 50.00
    40496 *I Ain't Got Nobody* ....30.00 - 50.00
    40891 *Is It Possible?*....................................15.00 - 20.00
    40986 *Plenty Of Sunshine* ....15.00 - 20.00
    41008 *It's Balogney* ....15.00 - 20.00
    41026 *Waitin' For Katy* ....15.00 - 20.00
    41055 *Chilly Pom-Pom-Pee* ....15.00 - 20.00
    41112 *Butternut* ....15.00 - 20.00
    41123 *It Goes Like This* ....15.00 - 20.00
    41152 *Come On, Baby* ....15.00 - 20.00
    41183 *She Only Laughs At Me* ....15.00 - 20.00
    41239 *Here's That Party Now In Person* ....20.00 - 30.00
    41269 *It Ain't No Fault Of Mine* ....20.00 - 30.00
    41310 *Sophomore Prom* ....20.00 - 30.00
    41317 *Piccolo Pete* ....20.00 - 30.00
    41369 *Harmonica Harry*................................20.00 - 30.00
    41425 *When I Look To The West* ....20.00 - 30.00
    45450 *Maw And Paw And Me* ....20.00 - 30.00
Regal 8648 *Louder And Funnier* ....15.00 - 20.00
    8655 *West End Blues* ....20.00 - 30.00

GEORGE HALL AND HIS (HOTEL TAFT) ORCHESTRA:

Bluebird 5021 *Have You Ever Been Lonely?* ....8.00 - 12.00
    5022 *I'm Young And Healthy* ....8.00 - 12.00
    5023 *My Dixie Hidee-Hideaway* ....8.00 - 12.00

Bluebird, most other issues ....5.00 - 8.00
Cameo 8300 *Ten Little Miles From Town* ....8.00 - 12.00
Cameo, most other issues ....5.00 - 8.00
Electradisk 1950 *Down A Carolina Lane* ....8.00 - 12.00
     1951 *In the Valley Of The Moon*........................8.00 - 12.00
     1952 *There's A Cabin In The Pines*.....................8.00 - 12.00
     2016 *Under A Blanket Of Blue* ....8.00 - 12.00
     2017 *Remember My Forgotten Man* ....8.00 - 12.00
     2027 *Did My Heart Beat?* ....8.00 - 12.00
Pathe-Actuelle 36608 *Take Your Finger Out Of Your Mouth*
                                                  10.00 - 15.00
     36627 *Positively-Absolutely* ....10.00 - 15.00
     36641 *Just Another Day Wasted Away*..............10.00 - 15.00
Perfect 14789 *Take Your Finger Out Of Your Mouth*
                                                  10.00 - 15.00
     14808 *Positively-Absolutely* ....10.00 - 15.00
     14822 *Just Another Day Wasted Away*..............10.00 - 15.00
Sunrise 3102 *Have You Ever Been Lonely?* ....20.00 - 30.00
     3103 *I'm Young And Healthy* ....20.00 - 30.00
     3182 *Under A Blanket Of Blue* ....20.00 - 30.00
     3183 *Shadow Waltz*...20.00 - 30.00
     3198 *I May Be Dancing With Somebody Else* ....20.00 - 30.00
     3393 *Good Morning, Glory* ....20.00 - 30.00
     3394 *My Blue-Eyed Sue* ....20.00 - 30.00
     3395 *Tired Of It All*...20.00 - 30.00
     3409 *I Was In The Mood* .... - -
Variety, most issues ....7.00 - 10.00
Vocalion, most issues ....7.00 - 10.00

WENDELL HALL:

Bluebird 5291 *Jimmy Had A Nickel* ....7.00 - 10.00
     5332 *New It Ain't Gonna Rain No Mo'* ....7.00 - 10.00
     5410 *My Carolina Home* ....7.00 - 10.00
Brunswick 3086 *Spanish Shawl*...............................8.00 - 12.00
     3330 *She's Still My Baby* ....7.00 - 10.00
     3983 *Hot Feet* ....7.00 - 10.00
Brunswick, most other issues ....5.00 - 8.00
Columbia 942-D *Hot Feet* ....8.00 - 12.00
     1028-D *Headin' Home* ....10.00 - 15.00
Edison 51261 *It Ain't Gonna Rain No Mo'* ....10.00 - 15.00
Electradisk 2162 *Jimmy Had A Nickel* ....7.00 - 10.00
Gennett 5271 *It Ain't Gonna Rain No Mo'* ....7.00 - 10.00
     6084 *Hot Feet* ....10.00 - 15.00
Sunrise 3372 *Where's Elmer?* ....20.00 - 30.00
     3413 *New It Ain't Gonna Rain No Mo'* ....20.00 - 30.00
Victor 19171 *It Ain't Gonna Rain No Mo'* ....5.00 - 8.00
     19226 *Bluebird Blues* ....7.00 - 10.00
     19338 *Whistling The Blues Away* ....7.00 - 10.00
     19886 *It Ain't Gonna Rain No Mo'* ....7.00 - 10.00
     19890 *It Ain't Gonna Rain No Mo' Part 2* ....7.00 - 10.00
Victor, most other issues ....5.00 - 8.00

MAL HALLETT AND HIS ORCHESTRA:

Titles issued contemporaneously on Banner, Conqueror, Melotone,
     Oriole, and Perfect: *An Earful Of Music; Okay, Toots; When My*
     Ship Comes In; Your Head On My Shoulder........7.00 - 10.00
Columbia 917-D *Oh, Lizzie* ....7.00 - 10.00
     967-D *(Does She Love Me) Positively-Absolutely*8.00 - 12.00
     996-D *Ya Gonna Be Home Tonight? (Oh Yeh? Then I'll Be Over)*
                                                  8.00 - 12.00
     1287-D *My New York* ....8.00 - 12.00
     1341-D *The Sunrise* ....7.00 - 10.00
Decca 1163 *Big Boy Blue* ....8.00 - 12.00
     1167, 1281, 1282, 1384 ....7.00 - 10.00
Edison (thin) 14080 *Boomerang*...........................100.00 - 150.00

Harmony 126-H *Whose Who Are You* ....8.00 - 12.00
     147-H *My Bundle Of Love* ....10.00 - 15.00
     16l-H *What Good Is "Good Morning"?* ....8.00 - 12.00
Okeh 40573 *Whose Who Are You* ....10.00 - 15.00
Pathe-Actuelle 36435 *Lonesome And Sorry* ....7.00 - 10.00
     36437 *She's A Corn-fed Indiana Girl* ....8.00 - 12.00
Perfect 14616 *What Good Is "Good Morning"?* ......7.00 - 10.00
     14618 *She's A Corn-fed Indiana Girl* ....8.00 - 12.00
Vocalion 3235 *The Glory Of Love* ....8.00 - 12.00
     3236 *Swing Fever* ....8.00 - 12.00
     3268 *I'm An Old Cowhand* ....7.00 - 10.00
     3278 *The Boston Tea-Party* ....7.00 - 10.00

WILL HALLEY:

Victor 17728 *Ruff Johnson's Harmony Band* ....15.00 - 20.00

HENRY HALSTEAD & HIS ORCHESTRA:

Victor 19406 *Sweet Little You* ....8.00 - 12.00
     19474 *Tessie (Stop Teasing Me)* ....10.00 - 15.00
     19482 *That's My Girl*.......................................10.00 - 15.00
     19498 *China Girl* ....8.00 - 12.00
     19511 *Bull Frog Serenade* ....10.00 - 15.00
     19513 *Frantic* ....15.00 - 20.00
     19514 *Panama* ....20.00 - 30.00
     19575 *Playmates* ....7.00 - 10.00
     19579 *Moonlight And Roses* ....5.00 - 8.00
     20061 *Give Me Today*.....................................15.00 - 20.00
     20062 *Dream Of Love And You* ....7.00 - 10.00
     20688 *Pal of My Lonesome Hours*....................7.00 - 10.00
     20689 *My Idea of Heaven (Is To Be In Love With You)*
                                                  7.00 - 10.00
     20691 *Ain't That Too Bad?*................................10.00 - 15.00
     22000 *One More Moment With You* ....7.00 - 10.00

PAUL HAMILTON AND HIS ORCHESTRA:

Vocalion 2662 *She Reminds Me Of You* ....15.00 - 20.00
     2708 *I've Had My Moments*..............................15.00 - 20.00
     2721 *Easy Come, Easy Go*...............................15.00 - 20.00

FRED HAMM AND HIS ORCHESTRA:

Brunswick 4294 *True Blue Lou* ....7.00 - 10.00
     4689 *We Love Us* ....8.00 - 12.00
Victor 19662 *Bye Bye Blues*...................................7.00 - 10.00
     19672 *Stomp Off, Let's Go*...............................10.00 - 15.00
     19737 *She's Got 'Im* ....7.00 - 10.00
     19915 *Want A Little Lovin'*................................7.00 - 10.00
     20023 *Sugar Foot Stomp* ....10.00 - 15.00

CHARLES W. HAMP (& EARL REYNOLDS):

Columbia 1816-D *Pretty Little Thing* ....10.00 - 15.00
Okeh 41213 *My Kinda Love* ....10.00 - 15.00
     41266 *I'm In Seventh Heaven* ....10.00 - 15.00
     41308 *Sweethearts' Holiday* ....10.00 - 15.00
Sunset 1128 *Red Hot Henry Brown* ....8.00 - 12.00
     1146 *Always* ....7.00 - 10.00
     1154 *I Love My Baby* ....7.00 - 10.00

JOHNNY HAMP'S KENTUCKY SERENADERS;
JOHNNY HAMP AND HIS ORCHESTRA:

Bluebird 6745, 6746, 6748..7.00 - 10.00
Victor 19807 *Nobody But Fanny* ....15.00 - 20.00
     20101 *Black Bottom* ....8.00 - 12.00
     20105 *That's Why I Love You* ....8.00 - 12.00
     20117 *Who Wouldn't* ....8.00 - 12.00
     20207 *Turkish Towel* ....10.00 - 15.00
     20241 *Gone Again Gal* ....8.00 - 12.00

20290 *The Two of Us* ....7.00 - 10.00
20644 *One O'Clock Baby* ....8.00 - 12.00
20759 *Gorgeous* ....7.00 - 10.00
20819 *Is It Possible?* ....7.00 - 10.00
20823 *I Haven't Told Her She Hasn't Told Me* ..8.00 - 12.00
20829 *I'm Afraid You Sing That Song To Someody Else*
....8.00 - 12.00
20900 *Someday You'll Say "O.K."* ......8.00 - 12.00
20923 *Dawning* ....7.00 - 10.00
21323 *Oh Look At That Baby* ....8.00 - 12.00
21511 *C-O-N-S-T-A-N-T-I-N-O-P-L-E* ...8.00 - 12.00
21547, 21804, 21829, 22219, 22650, 22722, 22727, 22795,
22796 ....5.00 - 10.00
22636 *All On Account Of Your Kisses* ...8.00 - 12.00
22730 *On The Beach With You* ....8.00 - 12.00
22999 *Cabin In The Cotton* ....8.00 - 12.00
24000 *Whistle And Blow Your Blues Away* ....8.00 - 12.00
Victor, most other issues........................5.00 - 8.00

LIONEL HAMPTON & HIS ORCHESTRA:
Victor 25527, 25535, 25575, 25586, 25592, 25601,
25658, 25666, 25674, 25682, 25699 ....7.00 - 12.00
Victor, most other issues........................5.00 - 8.00

EPH HANAFORD'S BAND:
Banner 1295 *I'm Goin' South* ....10.00 - 15.00

HOGAN HANCOCK & HIS ORCHESTRA:
Gennett 6354 *Lady Of Havana* ....20.00 - 30.00
6368 *Keep Sweeping The Cobwebs Off The Moon*
....20.00 - 30.00
6413 *So Long* ....30.00 - 50.00

AL HANDLER AND HIS (ALAMO HOTEL CAFE) ORCHESTRA:
Columbia 713-D *Crying For The Moon* ....15.00 - 20.00
833-D *Pretty Lips* ....10.00 - 15.00
866-D *Havin' Lots Of Fun* ....10.00 - 15.00
1047-D *Magnolia* ....10.00 - 15.00
1126-D *That's What I Think Of You* ....8.00 - 12.00

KATHERINE HANDY:
Paramount 12011 *Loveless Love* ....75.00 - 100.00

(W.C.) HANDY'S MEMPHIS BLUES BAND; HANDY'S ORCHESTRA (OF MEMPHIS):
Banner 1036 *St. Louis Blues*....................30.00 - 50.00
1053 *She's A Mean Job* ....20.00 - 30.00
Black Swan 2053 *Yellow Dog Blues* ....50.00 - 75.00
2054 *Muscle Shoals Blues* ....30.00 - 50.00
Columbia A-2417, A-2418, A-2419, A-2420,
A-2421 ....7.00 - 12.00
Lyratone 4211 *Beale Street Blues* ....100.00 - up
4212 *Yellow Dog Blues*.......................100.00 - up
Okeh 4789 *Aunt Hagar's Blues*...................50.00 - 80.00
4880 *Gulf Coast Blues*.......................50.00 - 80.00
4886 *Florida Blues* ....50.00 - 80.00
4896 *Memphis Blues*..........................50.00 - 80.00
8046 *Louisville Blues*.........................50.00 - 80.00
8059 *Down-Hearted Blues* ....75.00 - 100.00
8066 *Mama's Got The Blues* ....50.00 - 80.00
8110 *Darktown Reveille* ....75.00 - 100.00
Paramount 20098 *St. Louis Blues* ....30.00 - 50.00
20012 *She's A Mean Job* ....20.00 - 30.00
Puritan 11098 *St. Louis Blues* ....30.00 - 50.00
11112 *Muscle Shoals Blues* ....20.00 - 30.00
Varsity 8162 *Loveless Love* ....10.00 - 15.00
8163 *St. Louis Blues* ....10.00 - 15.00

(MISS) ANNETTE HANSHAW (AND HER SIZZLIN' SYNCOPATORS):
Titles issued contemporaneously on Banner, Conqueror, Melotone, Oriole, Perfect, and Romeo include: *Don't Blame Me; Give Me Liberty Or Give Me Love; Fit As A Fiddle; I Cover The Waterfront; Love Me Tonight; Moon Song; Say It Isn't So* ....15.00 - 25.00
Clarion 5017-C *I Want A Good Man* ....20.00 - 30.00
5037-C *The Way I Feel Today*.................20.00 - 30.00
5093-C *Yes Indeedy* ....20.00 - 30.00
5101-C *Now I Know* ....20.00 - 30.00
5216-C *Crying To The Moon* ....20.00 - 30.00
5217-C *I'll Lock You In My Arms*.................20.00 - 30.00
5248-C *Walkin' My Baby Back Home* ....20.00 - 30.00
5249-C *Would You Like To Take A Walk?* ....20.00 - 30.00
5327-C *Moonlight Saving Time* ....20.00 - 30.00
5390-C *I Don't Know Why* ....20.00 - 30.00
Columbia 1769-D *Lover, Come Back To Me* ....20.00 - 30.00
1812-D *Big City Blues* ....20.00 - 30.00
Diva 2915-G *The One In The World*.................10.00 - 15.00
2940-G *Am I Blue?* ....10.00 - 15.00
2981-G *True Blue Lou* ....10.00 - 15.00
3012-G *Tip-Toe Thru The Tulips With Me* ....7.00 - 10.00
3066-G *Aren't We All?* ....15.00 - 20.00
3106-G *I'm Following You* ....10.00 - 15.00
3196-G *Nobody Cares If I'm Blue* ....10.00 - 15.00
Harmony 706-H *I Must Have That Man* ....10.00 - 15.00
734-H *High Up On A Hill Top* ....10.00 - 15.00.
1224-H *Body And Soul*........................20.00 - 30.00
1288-H *Walkin' My Baby Back Home* ....20.00 - 30.00
1376-H *Guilty* ....20.00 - 30.00
Okeh 41292 *Moanin' Low* ....30.00 - 50.00
41327 *If I Can't Have You* ....30.00 - 50.00
41351 *I Have To Have You* ....30.00 - 50.00
41370 *When A Woman Loves A Man*.................30.00 - 50.00
41397 *With You*................................30.00 - 50.00
Pathe-Actuelle (see Perfect listing, below)
Perfect 12286 *Black Bottom*.....................15.00 - 20.00
12290 *Falling In Love With You* ....15.00 - 25.00
12292 *Don't Take That Black Bottom Away* .....15.00 - 20.00
12296 *I'm All Alone In A Palace of Stone* ....15.00 - 20.00
12301 *My Baby Knows How* ....15.00 - 20.00
12305 *If I'd Only Believed In You* ....15.00 - 20.00
12309 *Everything's Made For Love* ....15.00 - 20.00
12314 *Here Or There* ....15.00 - 20.00
12319 *He's The Last Word* ....15.00 - 20.00
12323 *Ain't He Sweet?* ....15.00 - 20.00
12329 *Song Of The Wanderer* ....15.00 - 20.00
12334 *My Idea Of Heaven* ....15.00 - 20.00
12338 *Rosy Cheeks* ....15.00 - 20.00
12346 *Aw, Gee! Don't Be That Way Now* ....15.00 - 25.00
12354 *Ain't That A Grand And Glorious Feeling*
....15.00 - 20.00
12362 *Miss Annabelle Lee* ....15.00 - 20.00
12372 *Who's That Knocking At My Door?*........15.00 - 25.00
12388 *Just Another Day Wasted Away*..............20.00 - 30.00
12393 *Thinking Of You* ....15.00 - 25.00
12399 *There Must Be Somebody Else* ....20.00 - 30.00
12411 *When You're With Somebody Else* ....20.00 - 30.00
12419 *I Just Roll Along*........................20.00 - 30.00
12427 *'Cause I Feel Low Down* ....20.00 - 30.00
12437 *Ready For The River* ....20.00 - 30.00
12444 *We Love It* ....20.00 - 30.00
(Foregoing titles were also issued on Pathe-Actuelle, similarly valued)

Velvet Tone 1706-V *I Must Have That Man!* ....10.00 - 15.00
   1734-V *That's Just My Way Of Forgetting You*.10.00 - 15.00
   1766-V *My Blackbirds Are Bluebirds Now* ....15.00 - 20.00
   1785-V *My Inspiration Is You* ....10.00 - 15.00
   1792-V *I Wanna Be Loved By You* ....15.00 - 20.00
   1832-V *In a Great Big Way*........................10.00 - 15.00
   1859-V *Mean To Me* ....10.00 - 15.00
   1910-V *My Sin* ....10.00 - 15.00
   1915-V *The One In The World* ....10.00 - 15.00
   1940-V *Daddy Won't You Please Come Home* ..10.00 - 15.00
   1981-V *Here We Are* ....10.00 - 15.00.
   2012-V *What Wouldn't I Do For That Man* ....10.00 - 15.00
   2066-V *If I Had A Talking Picture Of You* ....8.00 - 12.00
   2106-V *Happy Days Are Here Again* ....10.00 - 15.00
   2155-V *I've Got "It"* ....10.00 - 15.00
   2178-V *My Future Just Passed* ....10.00 - 15.00
   2196-V *Nobody Cares If I'm Blue* ....10.00 - 15.00
   2274-V *Crying To The Moon* ....15.00 - 20.00
   2289-V *Wasting My Love On You* ....15.00 - 20.00
   2314-V *Ever Since Time Began*.....................15.00 - 20.00
   2315-V *Would You Like To Take A Walk* ....15.00 - 20.00
   2393-V *Ho Hum!* ....15.00 - 20.00
   2454-V *Guilty* ....20.00 - 30.00
Vocalion 2635 *Let's Fall In Love* ....30.00 - 50.00

THE HAPPINESS BOYS:

The large recorded legacy of Billy Jones and Ernest Hare, consisting of mostly humorous and novelty songs, and issued on most labels of the 1920s, is beyond the scope of this book. Most of their records are of minimal value. Following are a few examples:

Banner 1772 *My Cutie's Due At Two To Two Today* ....7.00 - 10.00
   1875 *If My Baby Cooks As Good As She Looks* ...7.00 - 10.00
   1953 *I've Never Seen A Straight Banana* ....7.00 - 10.00
   7116 *She's The Sweetheart Of Six Other Guys* ....7.00 - 10.00
Broadway 1063 *I've Never Seen A Straight Banana*.7.00 - 10.00
Brunswick 2654 *The Big Butter And Egg Man* ....8.00 - 12.00
   2888 *If You Knew Susie* ....8.00 - 12.00
Cameo 504 *Does the Spearmint Lose Its Flavor On The Bedpost Over Night?* ....8.00 - 12.00
   707 *In Sweet Onion Time*........................7.00 - 10.00
Columbia 378-D *As A Porcupine Pines For Its Pork* ....8.00 - 12.00
   534-D *I Wish't I Was In Peoria*........................8.00 - 12.00
   50038-D (12-inch) *Studio Stunts* ....20.00 - 30.00
(Note: Jones & Hare "host" various Columbia artists.)
Edison (unnumbered) *Say It To The Ediphone* .... - -
Edison 51155 *Barney Google* ....8.00 - 12.00
   51470 *Laff It Off* ....10.00 - 15.00
   51535 *As a Porcupine Pines For Its Pork* ....10.00 - 15.00
   51555 *Don't Bring Lulu*............................10.00 - 15.00
   51660 *Show Me The Way To Go Home* ....10.00 - -15.00
   51667 *I Wish't I Was In Peoria* ....10.00 - 15.00
   51695 *What! No Women?* ....10.00 - 20.00
   51704 *Wimmin-Aaah!* ....10.00 - -20.00
   51755 *Lunatic's Lullaby* ....10.00 - 20.00
   51802 *Gentlemen Prefer Blondes* ....10.00 - 20.00
   51903 *Short An' Sweet* ....15.00 - 20.00
   51973 *I've Never Seen A Straight Banana* ....15.00 - 20.00
   52028 *You Never Get Nowhere Holding Hands* ...15.00 - 25.00
   52149 *Get 'Em In A Rumble Seat* ....20.00 - 30.00
   52200 *Henry's Made A Lady Out Of Lizzie* ....30.00 - 50.00
   52236 *It's In The Bag* ....15.00 - 25.00
   52333 *Must You Wear A Moustache?* ....20.00 - 30.00
   52367 *Mr. Hoover And Mr. Smith* ....25.00 - 40.00
Harmony 9-H *I Miss My Swiss* ....7.00 - 10.00
   665-H *Gotta Big Date With A Little Girl*............8.00 - 12.00

Puritan 11236 *Barney Google* .... 7.00 - 10.00
Regal 8014 *Tie Me To Your Apron Strings Again* .... 7.00 - 10.00
   9954 *That Certain Party* .... 7.00 - 10.00
Romeo 1169 *Singin' In The Bathtub* .... 7.00 - 10.00
Victor 21797 *Etiquette Blues* .... 8.00 - 12.00
   35953 (12-inch) *Twisting The Dials* .... 15.00 - 20.00

THE HAPPINESS ORCHESTRA:

Gennett 6489 *In The Evening*............................... - -
   6490 *All Day Long* .... - -
   6538 *Sweet Ella May* .... 10.00 - 15.00
   6555 *My Window Of Dreams*........................... 10.00 - 15.00
Silvertone 8060 *Barbara*................................... 8.00 - 12.00
   8075 *Persian Rug* .... 8.00 - 12.00

THE HAPPY COLLEGIANS:

Gennett 3121 *Oh! Lovey, Be Mine* .... 15.00 - 20.00
   3122 *Brown Eyes, Why Are You Blue?* .... 7.00 - 10.00
   3135 *Speech* .... 10.00 - 15.00
   3225 *Sunny* .... 10.00 - 15.00
   3227 *Too Many Parties* .... 10.00 - 15.00

THE HAPPY HARMONISTS:

Gennett 5286 *Home Brew Blues* .... 100.00 - 150.00
   5402 *Ethiopian Nightmare*........................... 100.00 - 150.00
   5518 *Steady Steppin' Papa* .... 150.00 - 200.00

THE HAPPY SIX:

Columbia A2929 *Shake Your Little Shoulder*........... 7.00 - 10.00
   A2949 *Dance-O-Mania* .... 7.00 - 10.00
   A2971 *Goodbye Sunshine, Hello Moon*.............. 7.00 - 10.00
   A3379 *Siam Soo*............................... 10.00 - 15.00
   A3645 *Nobody Lied* .... 7.00 - 10.00
Columbia, most other issues .... 4.00 - 7.00

LIL HARDAWAY'S ORCHESTRA; DIAMOND LIL HARDAWAY & HER GEMS OF RHYTHM:

Vocalion 1252 *Milenberg Joys* .... 200.00 - up
Decca 7241, 7247, 7276, 7293.............................. 8.00 - 12.00

(LATE PRESIDENT) WARREN G. HARDING:

Victor 35718 *Address At Washington/Hoboken* ..... 15.00 - 20.00

GLENN HARDMAN & HIS HAMMOND FIVE:

Columbia 25341, 35263............................... 7.00 - 10.00
Vocalion 4971 *Exactly Like You*............................. 7.00 - 10.00

MARLOW HARDY & HIS ALABAMIANS:

Columbia 2034-D *Song Of The Bayou* .... 40.00 - 60.00

ERNEST HARE (See THE HAPPINESS BOYS)

BOB HARING AND HIS ORCHESTRA; HARING'S HAPPY HARMONIZERS:

Banner 32162 *Ho Hum!* .... 8.00 - 12.00
Brunswick 4545 *Revolutionary Rhythm* .... 7.00 - 10.00
   4608 *Georgia Pines* .... 7.00 - 10.00
   4672 *Do Ya Love Me?*............................ 7.00 - 10.00
Brunswick, most other issues.............................. 5.00 - 8.00
Cameo 797 *Angry* .... 10.00 - 15.00
   824 *Roll 'Em, Girls (Roll Your Own)* .... 10.00 - 15.00
   893 *In The Spring* .... 8.00 - 12.00
   8132 *I Just Roll Along* .... 15.00 - 20.00
   9006 *How About Me?* .... 7.00 - 10.00
   9025 *Me And The Man In The Moon* .... 20.00 - 30.00
   9033 *All By Yourself In The Moonlight* .... 20.00 - 30.00
   9041 *I Faw Down An' Go Boom*................... 8.00 - 12.00
   9105 *Four Or Five Times* .... 10.00 - 15.00

(foregoing titles also appeared on Romeo, similarly valued)

Cameo, most other issues	4.00 -	8.00
Gennett 6115 *Go Wash An Elephant*	15.00 -	20.00
6151 *Zulu Wail*	20.00 -	30.00
Oriole 2222 *When I Take My Sugar To Tea*	8.00 -	12.00
Romeo, most issues	4.00 -	8.00

EARL HARLAN AND HIS ORCHESTRA:

Banner 32806, 32924	7.00 -	12.00
Melotone 12417 *Got The South In My Soul*	10.00 -	15.00
Melotone 12739, 12840, 12867	7.00 -	12.00
Oriole 2798, 2812	7.00 -	12.00
Perfect 15789, 15862	7.00 -	12.00
Romeo 2095, 2171, 2185	7.00 -	12.00

THE HARLEM FOOTWARMERS:

Columbia 14670-D *Sweet Chariot*	100.00 -	150.00
Okeh 8720 *Jungle Jamboree*	60.00 -	100.00
8746 *Syncopated Shuffle*	60.00 -	100.00
8760 *Lazy Duke*	75.00 -	100.00
8836 *Big House Blues*	60.00 -	100.00
8840 *Mood Indigo*	60.00 -	100.00
8869 *Old Man Blues*	60.00 -	100.00

HARLEM HAMFATS:

Decca 7182, 7196, 7205, 7206, 7218, 7229, 7245, 7251, 7266, 7274, 7310, 7362, 7283, 7299, 7312, 7326, 7339, 7351, 7367, 7382, 7395, 7406, 7439, 7454, 7466, 7484, 7530, 7761	7.00 -	12.00
Vocalion 04813, 04828, 04870, 04925, 05136, 05179, 05233, 05287	7.00 -	12.00

HARLEM HARLEY & HIS WASHBOARD BAND:

Decca 7492 *Hold It*	15.00 -	20.00
7505 *Life Goes On And On*	15.00 -	20.00

HARLEM HOT CHOCOLATES:

Hit of the Week 1045 *Sing, You Sinners*	20.00 -	30.00
1046 *St. James Infirmary*	20.00 -	30.00

HARLEM HOT SHOTS:

Titles issued contemporaneously on Banner, Melotone, Oriole, Perfect and Romeo: *Dust Off That Old Pianna; Love Is Just Around The Corner; House Rent Party Day; March Winds And April Showers*	10.00 -	15.00
Bluebird 5481 *Somebody Stole My Gal*	8.00 -	12.00
Electradisk 1931 *St. Louis Blues*	75.00 -	100.00
Oriole 2284 *Black And Tan Fantasy*	15.00 -	20.00

HARLEM HOUSE RENT STOMPERS:

Brunswick 7120 *Gravel Pit Stomp*	150.00 -	200.00

HARLEM STOMPERS:

Decca 7600 *The Monkey Swing*	10.00 -	15.00
7616 *Jammin' In Georgia*	10.00 -	15.00

HARLEM TRIO:

Herwin 93012 *Fuzzy Wuzzy*	200.00 -	300.00
Okeh 8072 *Clarinet Laughing Blues*	75.00 -	100.00
8158 *The Poor Man's Blues*	75.00 -	100.00
8189 *Bass Clarinet Blues*	75.00 -	100.00
40220 *Muddy Water Blues*	75.00 -	100.00

DAVE HARMAN & HIS ORCHESTRA:

Bluebird 5436, 5437, 5438	7.00 -	12.00
Edison 51458 *Prince Of Wails*	15.00 -	20.00
51479 *Hot-Hot-Hottentot*	20.00 -	30.00

51510 *Sob Sister Sadie*	15.00 -	25.00

HARMANIAC FIVE:

Paramount 20476 *Harmaniac Blues*	100.00 -	150.00
Puritan 11476 *Harmaniac Blues*	100.00 -	150.00

HARMOGRAPH DANCE ORCHESTRA:

Harmograph 888 *My Sweetie's Sweeter Than That*	30.00 -	50.00
889 *Forgetful Blues*	50.00 -	75.00

THE HARMONIANS:

Harmony 106-H *Roll 'Em Girls*	15.00 -	20.00
127-H *Say It Again*	8.00 -	12.00
170-H *Lonesome And Sorry*	8.00 -	12.00
185-H *I Wonder What's Become Of Joe?*	8.00 -	12.00
291-H *For My Sweetheart*	8.00 -	12.00
321-H *There Ain't No Maybe In My Baby's Eyes*	8.00 -	12.00
350-H *I'm Looking Over A Four Leaf Clover*	8.00 -	12.00
393-H *Positively-Absolutely*	8.00 -	12.00
413-H *I'll Always Remember You*	8.00 -	12.00
447-H *You Don't Like It-Not Much*	8.00 -	12.00
503-H *Everybody Loves My Girl*	7.00 -	10.00
560-H *Keep Sweeping The Cobwebs Off The Moon*	7.00 -	10.00
596-H *I Just Roll Along*	7.00 -	10.00
638-H *Hello Montreal!*	8.00 -	12.00
667-H *That's My Weakness Now*	10.00 -	15.00
679-H *If You Don't Love Me*	7.00 -	10.00
693-H *I'm Walking Between The Raindrops*	8.00 -	12.00
694-H *Sweet Ella May*	8.00 -	12.00
701-H *Ten Little Miles From Town*	7.00 -	10.00
702-H *Half Way To Heaven*	7.00 -	10.00
716-H *What A Night For Spooning*	7.00 -	10.00
735-H *I'm Sorry Sally*	7.00 -	10.00
749-H *There's A Rainbow 'Round My Shoulder*	7.00 -	10.00
762-H *I Wanna Be Loved By You*	7.00 -	10.00
763-H *Here's That Party Now In Person*	20.00 -	30.00
801-H *Sunny Skies*	7.00 -	10.00
802-H *Along Came Sweetness*	7.00 -	10.00
822-H *Cradle Of Love*	8.00 -	12.00
863-H *Some Sweet Day*	10.00 -	15.00
942-H *Baby-Oh Where Can You Be?*	7.00 -	10.00
962-H *I'm In Seventh Heaven*	10.00 -	15.00
1028-H *Miss Wonderful*	8.00 -	12.00
1308-H *If You Should Ever Need Me*	7.00 -	10.00
1310-H *I'm Crazy 'Bout My Baby*	10.00 -	15.00
1311-H *You'll Be Mine In Apple Blossom Time*	7.00 -	10.00
Harmony, most other issues	4.00 -	8.00

(Above titles are also found on Diva and Velvet Tone, similarly valued)

HARMONICA TIM:

Clarion 5194-C *Harmonica Blues*	50.00 -	80.00
5195-C *Mean Low Blues*	50.00 -	80.00
Velvet Tone 7123-V *Mean Low Blues*	50.00 -	80.00

HARMONY DANCE ORCHESTRA:

Harmony 10-H *Yes, Sir, That's My Baby*	8.00 -	12.00
60-H *Tweedle-Dee Tweedle-Doo*	8.00 -	12.00

HAMTREE HARRINGTON:

Brunswick 2465 *I'm Gone, Dat's All*	10.00 -	15.00
2588 *C.O.D*	10.00 -	15.00

ACE HARRIS & HIS (SUNSET ROYAL) ORCHESTRA:

Coral 65072 *Don't Cry, Little Girl!*	8.00 -	12.00
Hub 3019 *After Hours*	8.00 -	12.00

Vocalion 3864 *Hurly Burly* ....10.00 - 15.00
     3935 *Rhythm 'Bout Town* ....10.00 - 15.00

HELEN HARRIS ACCOMPANIED BY SKILLET DICK & HIS FRYING PANS:
Champion 15881 *Don't Say Goodbye* ....150.00 - 250.00

LILLIAN HARRIS:
Banner 1173 *Four O'Clock Blues* ....30.00 - 50.00
     1212 *Mama's Got The Blues* ....30.00 - 50.00
     1224 *Down-Hearted Blues* ....30.00 - 50.00
Regal 9445 *Sugar Blues*..30.00 - 50.00
     9497 *Baby, Won't You Please Come Home*.......30.00 - 50.00
     9510 *Gulf Coast Blues* ....30.00 - 50.00

MARION HARRIS (WITH ISHAM JONES' ORCHESTRA):
Brunswick 2309 *I'm Just Wild About Harry* ....10.00 - 15.00
     2310 *Sweet Indiana Home* ....10.00 - 15.00
     2329 *Carolina In The Morning* ....10.00 - 15.00
     2361 *Mississippi Choo-Choo* ....10.00 - 15.00
     2395 *St. Louis Blues* ....10.00 - 15.00
     2539 *Nashville Nightingale* ....10.00 - 15.00
     2552 *St. Louis Gal* ....10.00 - 15.00
     2622 *Hey Hey And Hee Hee* ....10.00 - 15.00
     2651 *There'll Be Some Changes Made* ....10.00 - 15.00
     2672 *Go, Emmaline* ....10.00 - 15.00
     2735 *Charleston Charlie* ....10.00 - 15.00
     2784 *Why Couldn't It Be Poor Little Me?*............8.00 - 12.00
     2807 *Does My Sweetie Do-And How!* ....8.00 - 12.00
     4663 *Nobody's Using It Now* ....10.00 - 15.00
     4681 *Nobody's Sweetheart* ....10.00 - 15.00
     4806 *You Do Something To Me* ....10.00 - 15.00
     4812 *Nobody Cares If I'm Blue* ....10.00 - 15.00
     4873 *Humming A Love Song* .... - -
     4873 *Little White Lies* ....10.00 - 20.00
     4972 *He's Not Worth Your Tear* ....10.00 - 20.00
     6016 *He's My Secret Passion* ....5.00 - 20.00
Brunswick, most other issues ....7.00 - 10.00
Columbia A2944 *The St. Louis Blues* ....10.00 - 15.00
     A3474 *Beale Street Blues* ....10.00 - 15.00
Columbia (most other issues) ....7.00 - 10.00
Victor 18152 *My Syncopated Melody Man* ....10.00 - 15.00
     18398 *When I Hear That Jazz Band Play*...........10.00 - 15.00
     19486 *When Alexander Takes His Ragtime Band To France*
     ....10.00 - 15.00
     18535 *A Good Man Is Hard To Find* ....10.00 - 15.00
     18593 *Take Me To The Land Of Jazz* ....10.00 - 15.00
     21116 *The Man I Love* ....8.00 - 12.00
Victor (most other issues) ....5.00 - 10.00

PHIL HARRIS & HIS (COCOANUT GROVE) ORCHESTRA:
Columbia 2761-D *You've Got Me Crying Again* ....15.00 - 20.00
     2766-D *How's About It?*................................15.00 - 20.00
Decca 564 *I'd Love To Take Orders From You* ....8.00 - 12.00
     565 *Now You've Got Me Doing It* ....8.00 - 12.00
Vocalion 3447 *Swing High, Swing Low* ....8.00 - 12.00
     3466 *Swingin' For The King* ....8.00 - 12.00
     3488 *Too Marvelous For Words*........................8.00 - 12.00
     3533 *Jammin'* ....8.00 - 12.00
     3565 *The Darktown Strutters' Ball*....................8.00 - 12.00
     3583 *That's What I Like About The South*............8.00 - 12.00

HARRIS BROTHERS TEXANS:
Brunswick 4644 *Gut Bucket Shuffle* ....50.00 - 75.00
     6047 *The South's Been A Mother To Me* ....50.00 - 75.00
Vocalion 15747 *The Pay-Off* ....75.00 - 125.00

HARRY'S HAPPY FOUR:
Okeh 8229 *Swinging The Swing* ....50.00 - 80.00
     8266 *Western Melody* ....50.00 - 80.00

HARRY'S MELODY MEN:
Broadway 1051 *I Never See Maggie Alone* ....8.00 - 12.00
     1052 *Blue Skies* ....7.00 - 10.00
     1174 *Stayin' Home Nights* ....150.00 - up
     1204 *Someone Left Me Mighty Lonesome* ....7.00 - 10.00
     1208 *My Wonderful You* ....7.00 - 10.00
     1209 *Tennessee Mammy* ....8.00 - 12.00
     1234 *My Arms Are Open For You* ....7.00 - 10.00
     1240 *Happy In The Rain* ....7.00 - 10.00

HARRY'S RECKLESS FIVE:
Broadway 1355 *Wailing Blues*..............................150.00 - 200.00

BOB HARTMAN & HIS ORCHESTRA:
Broadway 1501 *Charley Cadet*..............................10.00 - 15.00

GEORGIA HARVEY:
Black Swan 14119 *Castaway*.................................40.00 - 60.00
     14135 *That Sweet Something, Dear*................40.00 - 60.00
Paramount 12141 *Just Because You're You* ....35.00 - 50.00
     12142 *What Could Be Sweeter, Dear?* ....35.00 - 50.00

GUS HASTON & HIS ORCHESTRA:
Victor 22898 *Kicking The Gong Around* ....30.00 - 50.00

MICHAEL HAUER & HIS ORCHESTRA:
Champion 16085 *You're The Sweetest Girl This Side of Heaven*
     ....10.00 - 15.00
     16405 *Whistle And Blow Your Blues Away* ....20.00 - 30.00
Gennett 7299 *You Darlin'*.....................................15.00 - 20.00

COLEMAN HAWKINS AND HIS ALL-STAR OCTET/ ORCHESTRA/RHYTHM:
Apollo 751, 752, 753 ....5.00 - 10.00
Bluebird 10253, 10477, 10523, 10693, 10770..........5.00 - 8.00
Capitol, most issues ....5.00 - 8.00
Manor 1036 *Step On It* ....7.00 - 10.00
Mercury, most issues ....5.00 - 8.00
Okeh 6284 *Rocky Comfort* ....8.00 - 12.00
     6347 *Serenade To A Sleeping Beauty* ....8.00 - 12.00

ERSKINE HAWKINS AND HIS 'BAMA STATE COLLEGIANS:
Bluebird, most issues ....7.00 - 10.00
RCA Victor, most issues ....4.00 - 8.00
Victor, most issues ....5.00 - 8.00
Vocalion 3280 *I Can't Escape From You*...............10.00 - 15.00
     3289 *It Was A Sad Night In Harlem* ....10.00 - 15.00
     3318 *Big John's Special*................................10.00 - 15.00
     3336 *A Swingy Little Rhythm* ....10.00 - 15.00
     3545 *Uproar Shout* ....10.00 - 15.00
     3567 *Dear Old Southland* ....10.00 - 15.00
     3668 *Red Cap* ....10.00 - 15.00
     3689 *I'll See You In My Dreams* ....10.00 - 15.00
     4007 *Lost In The Shuffle* ....10.00 - 15.00
     4072 *Who's Sorry Now?* ....10.00 - 15.00

BILL HAWLEY:
Victor 21383 *Delores* ....15.00 - 25.00

CLIFFORD HAYES' LOUISVILLE STOMPERS:
Victor 20955 *Blue Guitar Stomp* ....25.00 - 40.00
21489 *Bare-Foot Stomp*....................75.00 - 100.00
21583 *Blue Harmony*......................35.00 - 50.00
21584 *The Petter's Stomp*.................35.00 - 50.00
23346 *Tenor Guitar Fiend*................250.00 - up
23407 *Automobile Blues*..................250.00 - up
V38011 *Clef Club Stomp*..................75.00 - 100.00
V38022 *Old Chord's Stomp*...............150.00 - 250.00
V38514 *Frog Hop*........................150.00 - 250.00
V38529 *You're Ticklin' Me*..............150.00 - 200.00
V38557 *Hey! Am I Blue*..................150.00 - 200.00

EDGAR HAYES AND HIS ORCHESTRA; EDGAR HAYES QUINTET:
Decca 1338 *Caravan* ....8.00 - 12.00
1382 *Satan Takes A Holiday*...............8.00 - 12.00
1416 *Stomping At The Renny*...............8.00 - 12.00
1444 *So Rare* ....10.00 - 15.00
1509 *I Know Now* ....10.00 - 15.00
1527 *Queen Isabella*......................8.00 - 12.00
1665 *Swingin' In The Promised Land* ......10.00 - 15.00
1684 *Blue Skies*.........................10.00 - 15.00
1748 *Fugitive From A Harem*...............7.00 - 10.00
1882 *Star Dust* ....7.00 - 10.00
1940 *Meet The Band* ....8.00 - 12.00
2048 *Shindig* ....8.00 - 12.00
2193 *Help Me* ....8.00 - 12.00

NAP HAYES:
Okeh 45231 *Somethin' Doin'* ....150.00 - 200.00

JOE HAYMES & HIS ORCHESTRA:
Numerous titles on Banner, Conqueror, Melotone, Oriole, Perfect, and Romeo ....7.00 - 10.00
Bluebird 5116 *Louisville Lady*.............8.00 - 12.00
5119 *Modern Melody*.......................8.00 - 12.00
5133 *Limehouse Blues* ....10.00 - 15.00
5178 *I Never Knew* ....8.00 - 12.00
5220 *I Ain't Gonna Grieve No More*........8.00 - 12.00
5916 *Life Is A Song*......................7.00 - 10.00
5918 *My Melancholy Baby* ....10.00 - 15.00
5920 *Honeysuckle Rose* ....10.00 - 15.00
6412 *He's a Curbstone Cutie* ....10.00 - 15.00
(Note: Above titles on Electradisk are valued slightly higher; on Sunrise, substantially higher.)
Columbia 2704-D *Let's Have A Party*.......15.00 - 20.00
2716-D *Ain't Gonna Pay No Toll*..........15.00 - 20.00
2739-D *One-Note Trumpet Player*..........15.00 - 20.00
2781-D *Uncle Joe's Music Store*..........15.00 - 20.00
2784-D *Just Give Me The Girl* ....15.00 - 20.00
(Note: Preceding Columbia records are often pressed of "royal blue" shellac.)
Victor 24038 *It's About Time* ....8.00 - 12.00
24040 *Pray For The Lights To Go Out* ......8.00 - 12.00
24055 *Let's Have A Party*................10.00 - 15.00
24123 *Hot Jazz Pie*......................10.00 - 15.00
24152 *He's The Life Of The Party*........10.00 - 15.00
24154 *Hey, Hey, Hey! Have You Had Your Corn Today?*
....8.00 - 12.00
24353 *Get Cannibal*......................10.00 - 15.00
Vocalion 3307 *That's A Plenty*...........10.00 - 15.00

3335 *Doin' The Suzy-Q*....................8.00 - 12.00
3369 *St. Louis Blues*.....................8.00 - 12.00

CARL HAYNE & HIS ARCADIANS:
Champion 16218 *Smile, Darn Ya', Smile* ....10.00 - 15.00

BILLY HAYS & HIS (CATHAY) ORCHESTRA:
Okeh 41091 *Why? (Do I Love You Like I Do?)* ....7.00 - 10.00
41137 *Doin' The Raccoon* ....8.00 - 12.00
41193 *All By Yourself In The Moonlight* ....7.00 - 10.00
Victor V-40056 *My Sugar And Me* ....15.00 - 20.00
V-40087 *The Bay Rum Song* ....15.00 - 20.00
V-40103 *When Carolina Smiles* ....25.00 - 40.00
V-40113 *I've Got To Have A Mamma Now* ......25.00 - 40.00

LENNIE HAYTON'S BLUE FOUR:
Vocalion 15750 *Old-Fashioned Girl* ....150.00 - 200.00

MONK HAZEL & HIS BIENVILLE ROOF ORCHESTRA:
Brunswick 4181 *High Society*..............35.00 - 50.00
4182 *Git-Wit-It*.........................35.00 - 50.00

LUCILLE HEGAMIN (AND HER BLUE FLAME SYNCOPATORS/JAZZ ARTISTS):
Arto 9045 *The Jazz Me Blues* ....15.00 - 20.00
9053 *Arkansas Blues* ....15.00 - 20.00
9058 *He's My Man* ....15.00 - 20.00
9063 *You'll Want My Love* ....15.00 - 20.00
9068 *Wang-Wang Blues* ....15.00 - 20.00
9069 *Strut, Miss Lizzie* ....15.00 - 25.00
9074 *Getting Old Blues* ....15.00 - 25.00
9105 *Wabash Blues* ....15.00 - 20.00
9119 *Ain't Givin' Nothin' Away* ....15.00 - 20.00
9129 *He May Be Your Man* ....15.00 - 20.00
9169 *You Can Have Him I Don't Want Him Blues*
....15.00 - 20.00
(Above titles also occur on Banner, Bell, Cleartone, Globe, and Hy-Tone, similarly valued)
Banner 1048 *He May Be Your Man* ....15.00 - 25.00
1072 *High Brown Blues* ....20.00 - 30.00
1093 *I've Got To Cool My Doggies Now* ....15.00 - 25.00
(Above titles also occur on Claxtonola, Harmograph, Paramount, and Regal, similarly valued)
Black Swan 2032 *Arkansas Blues*..........25.00 - 40.00
2049 *He May Be Your Man* ....25.00 - 40.00
Cameo 254 *I've Got What It Takes* ....10.00 - 15.00
317 *Syncopatin' Mama* ....10.00 - 15.00
381 *Down Hearted Blues* ....10.00 - 15.00
397 *Sweet Papa Joe* ....10.00 - 15.00
407 *Land Of Cotton Blues* ....10.00 - 15.00
415 *Cold, Cold Winter Blues* ....10.00 - 15.00
433 *St. Louis Gal* ....10.00 - 15.00
494 *Rampart Street Blues* ....10.00 - 15.00
612 *Mama's The Boss* ....10.00 - 15.00
613 *If You'll Come Back* ....10.00 - 15.00
701 *Alabamy Bound* ....10.00 - 15.00
723 *Hot Tamale Molly* ....10.00 - 15.00
Cameo, most other issues ....7.00 - 10.00
Columbia 14164-D *Senorita Mine*..........75.00 - 100.00
Okeh 8941 *Totem Pole* ....50.00 - 80.00

HORACE HEIDT AND HIS MUSICAL KNIGHTS/ ORCHESTRA:
Brunswick, most issues ....5.00 - 8.00
Columbia, most issues ....4.00 - 8.00
Victor 20608 *Hello Cutie!* ....10.00 - 15.00

21310 *Golden Gate*	10.00 -	15.00
21311 *Get 'Em In A Rumble Seat*	10.00 -	15.00
21312 *Every Evening*	7.00 -	10.00
21335, 21568, 21956, 21957, 22195, 22222	7.00 -	10.00

SIG HELLER & HIS ORCHESTRA:
Broadway 1509 *Snuggled On Your Shoulder*	7.00 -	10.00
1513 *Somebody Loves You*	10.00 -	15.00

BUD HELMS & HIS BAND:
Champion 15285 *Pee Wee Blues*	150.00 -	200.00
15364 *Hot Lips*	60.00 -	100.00

BERTHA HENDERSON:
Paramount 12511 *Six Thirty Blues*	150.00 -	200.00
Okeh 8265 *Jamboree Blues*	150.00 -	200.00

CATHERINE HENDERSON:
Diva 6040-G *Keep It To Yourself*	30.00 -	50.00
6050-G *What If We Do?*	30.00 -	50.00
Okeh 8240 *Four Thirty Blues*	50.00 -	80.00
Velvet Tone 7066-V *What If We Do?*	30.00 -	50.00
7076-V *Keep It To Yourself*	30.00 -	50.00

EDMONIA HENDERSON:
Paramount 12084 *Black Man Blues*	80.00 -	120.00
12095 *Brownskin Man*	80.00 -	120.00
12097 *If You Sheik On Your Mama*	100.00 -	150.00
12203 *Hateful Blues*	80.00 -	120.00
12239 *Jelly Roll Blues*	150.00 -	250.00
Vocalion 1015 *Nobody Else Will Do*	200.00 -	300.00
1043 *Dead Man Blues*	200.00 -	300.00

FLETCHER HENDERSON & HIS (CONNIE INN) ORCHESTRA/SAWIN' SIX; F.H. HENDERSON (JR.); HENDERSON'S (CLUB ALABAM'/DANCE) ORCHESTRA/HOT SIX/SIX WONDER BOYS:

Titles issued contemporaneously on Broadway, Claxtonola, Famous, Harmograph, Puritan, and Triangle: *Beale Street Mama; Down Hearted Blues; When You Walked Out Someone Else Walked Right In*	25.00 -	50.00
Ajax 17016 *Bull Blues*	75.00 -	100.00
17017 *Chattanooga*	75.00 -	100.00
17022 *Mistreatin' Daddy*	75.00 -	100.00
17023 *House Rent Ball*	75.00 -	100.00
17029 *Just Blues*	75.00 -	100.00
17030 *I'm Crazy Over You*	75.00 -	100.00
17109 *Everybody Loves My Baby*	150.00 -	200.00
17113 *Alabama Bound*	30.00 -	50.00
17114 *I'll See You In My Dreams*	40.00 -	60.00
17123 *Why Couldn't It Be Poor Little Me?*	80.00 -	120.00
Apex 8218 *Wait'll You See My Gal*	20.00 -	30.00
8300 *Everybody Loves My Baby*	100.00 -	150.00
8309 *Alabamy Bound*	30.00 -	50.00
8311 *I'll See You In My Dreams*	25.00 -	40.00
8316 *Why Couldn't It Be Poor Little Me?*	80.00 -	120.00
Apex (other titles as on Banner, below, similarl valued)		
Banner 1361 *Jiminy Gee*	15.00 -	20.00
1364 *Red Hot Mama*	20.00 -	30.00
1372 *You Know Me Alabam'*	20.00 -	30.00
1373 *Wait'll You See My Gal*	20.00 -	30.00
1375 *Oh Eva!*	20.00 -	30.00
1383 *Hard Hearted Hannah*	15.00 -	25.00
1384 *I Can't Get The One I Want*	15.00 -	20.00
1388 *Where The Dreamy Wabash Flows*	15.00 -	20.00
1445 *How Come You Do Me Like You Do*	20.00 -	30.00

1457 *One Of These Days*	15.00 -	20.00
1470 *I'll See You In My Dreams*	15.00 -	20.00
1471 *Everybody Loves My Baby*	50.00 -	75.00
1475 *My Dream Man*	15.00 -	20.00
1476 *Why Couldn't It Be Poor Little Me?*	40.00 -	60.00
1488 *Alabamy Bound*	25.00 -	40.00
1508 *Swanee Butterfly*	15.00 -	20.00
1639 *Sleepy Time Gal*	10.00 -	15.00
1654 *Then I'll Be Happy*	10.00 -	15.00
(Above titles, on Apex and Regal are similarly valued)		
Black Swan 2022 *My Oriental Rose*	30.00 -	50.00
2026 *The Unknown Blues*	100.00 -	150.00
2034 *Aunt Hagar's Children Blues*	25.00 -	40.00
2076 *Love Days*	30.00 -	50.00
2079 *Blue*	30.00 -	50.00
2116 *Chime Blues*	50.00 -	80.00
10072 *Love Days*	30.00 -	50.00
10075 *Blue*	30.00 -	50.00
10083 *Dumbell*	15.00 -	25.00
Bluebird 5682 *Hocus Pocus*	15.00 -	20.00
6515, 10246	7.00 -	10.00
Brunswick 2592 *War Horse Mama*	20.00 -	30.00
3026 *Let Me Introduce You To My Rosie*	20.00 -	30.00
3406 *Clarinet Marmalade*	20.00 -	30.00
3460 *Stockholm Stomp*	20.00 -	30.00
3521 *Sensation*	10.00 -	15.00
4119 *Hop Off*	30.00 -	50.00
Cameo 9033 *Old Black Joe's Blues*	20.00 -	30.00
9174 *Freeze And Melt*	20.00 -	30.00
9175 *Raisin' The Roof*	20.00 -	30.00
Columbia 126-D *Somebody Stole My Gal*	20.00 -	30.00
164-D *Muscle Shoals Blues*	20.00 -	30.00
202-D *That's Georgia*	20.00 -	30.00
209-D *He's The Hottest Man In Town*	20.00 -	30.00
228-D *Manda*	40.00 -	60.00
249-D *The Meanest Kind Of Blues*	40.00 -	60.00
292-D *Play Me Slow*	40.00 -	60.00
383-D *Money Blues*	40.00 -	60.00
395-D *Sugar Foot Stomp*	25.00 -	40.00
509-D *Carolina Stomp*	40.00 -	60.00
532-D *Pensacola*	30.00 -	50.00
654-D *The Stampede*	35.00 -	50.00
817-D *The Chant*	35.00 -	50.00
854-D *Sweet Thing*	35.00 -	50.00
970-D *Rocky Mountain Blues*	35.00 -	50.00
1002-D *P.D.Q. Blues*	35.00 -	50.00
1059-D *Whiteman Stomp*	35.00 -	50.00
1543-D *King Porter Stomp*	35.00 -	50.00
1913-D *Blazin*	20.00 -	30.00
2329-D *Somebody Loves Me*	20.00 -	30.00
2352-D *Keep A Song In Your Soul*	20.00 -	30.00
2414-D *Sweet And Hot*	20.00 -	30.00
2513-D *Clarinet Marmalade*	20.00 -	30.00
2559-D *Sugar*	20.00 -	30.00
2565-D *Singin' The Blues*	20.00 -	30.00
2586-D *My Gal Sal*	20.00 -	30.00
2615-D *Business in F*	20.00 -	30.00
2732-D *Honeysuckle Rose*	25.00 -	40.00
2825-D *Nagasaki*	20.00 -	30.00
A3951 *Gulf Coast Blues*	20.00 -	30.00
A3995 *Dicty Blues*	20.00 -	30.00

14392-D *Easy Money* ....75.00 - 100.00
Crown 3093 *After You've Gone*............................30.00 - 50.00
  3107 *Tiger Rag* ....30.00 - 50.00
Decca 157 *Limehouse Blues* ....10.00 - 15.00
  158 *Shanghai Shuffle* ....10.00 - 15.00
  213 *Tidal Wave* ....10.00 - 15.00
  214 *Big John's Special* ....10.00 - 15.00
  342 *Rug Cutter's Swing* ....10.00 - 15.00
  555 *Hotter Than 'Ell*....................................10.00 - 15.00
Domino 3475 *Swanee Butterfly* ....10.00 - 15.00
  3999 *Swamp Blues* ....75.00 - 100.00
Edison 51276 *Shake Your Feet* ....25.00 - 40.00
  51277 *Linger Awhile*.....................................15.00 - 25.00
Emerson 10713 *Mamma's Gonna Slow You Down*.30.00 - 50.00
  10714 *Steppin' Out*.......................................30.00 - 50.00
  10744 *Ghost Of The Blues*.............................35.00 - 50.00
Gennett 3285 *When Spring Comes Peeping Through*
  ....50.00 - 80.00
  3286 *Honeybunch* ....50.00 - 80.00
Lincoln 3062 *Old Black Joe's Blues* ....20.00 - 30.00
  3201 *Freeze And Melt*...................................20.00 - 30.00
  3202 *Raisin' The Roof* ....20.00 - 30.00
Paramount 12143 *Chime Blues*............................50.00 - 80.00
  12144 *The Unknown Blues* ....100.00 - 150.00
  12486 *Off To Buffalo* ....75.00 - 100.00
  20367 *Prince Of Wails*..................................75.00 - 100.00
Pathe-Actuelle (titles as on Perfect, following)
Perfect 14208 *Shake Your Feet* ....20.00 - 30.00
  14223 *Old Black Joe's Blues* ....20.00 - 30.00
  14250 *Chicago Blues* ....20.00 - 30.00
  14264 *After The Storm* ....10.00 - 20.00
  14265 *Say Say Sadie* ....20.00 - 30.00
  14271 *Driftwood* ....10.00 - 20.00
  14337 *My Rose Marie* ....15.00 - 25.00
  14338 *Shanghai Shuffle* ....30.00 - 50.00
  14447 *Don't Forget, You'll Regret Day By Day* ... 20.00 - 30.00
(Above titles, on Pathe-Actuelle, are similarly valued)
Puritan 11226 *Don't Think You'll Be Missed*..........20.00 - 30.00
  11251 *My Sweetie Went Away*..........................100.00 - 150.00
  11359 *Prince Of Wails*..................................75.00 - 100.00
  11367 *Prince Of Wails*..................................75.00 - 100.00
Regal 8360 *Off To Buffalo* ....75.00 - 100.00
  8441 *Dear, On A Night Like This* ....10.00 - 15.00
  8442 *There's A Rickety Rackety Shack* ....15.00 - 20.00
  8455 *Sorry* ....15.00 - 20.00
Regal (titles as on Banner, above, are similarly valued)
Romeo 837 *Old Black Joe's Blues* ....20.00 - 30.00
  976 *Freeze And Melt*......................................20.00 - 30.00
  977 *Raisin' The Roof* ....20.00 - 30.00
Victor 20944 *St. Louis Shuffle* ....50.00 - 75.00
  22775 *Malinda's Wedding Day*.........................15.00 - 20.00
  22786 *Oh, It Looks Like Rain* ....15.00 - 20.00

22955 *Strangers* ....15.00 - 20.00
24008 *Poor Old Joe* ....15.00 - 20.00
24699 *Harlem Madness* ....15.00 - 20.00
25339 *Grand Terrace Rhythm* ....10.00 - 15.00
25379 *Jim Town Blues* ....10.00 - 15.00
25298, 25317, 25334, 25373, 25375..............7.00 - 12.00
Vocalion 1065 *Clarinet Marmalade* ....75.00 - 100.00
  1079 *Some Of These Days* ....100.00 - 150.00
  1092 *Fidgety Feet* ....50.00 - 75.00
  2527 *Yeah Man!* ....15.00 - 25.00
  2583 *Queer Notions* ....15.00 - 20.00
  3211 *Christopher Columbus* ....10.00 - 15.00
  3213 *Stealin' Apples* ....10.00 - 15.00
  3485 *Slumming On Park Avenue* ....8.00 - 12.00
  3487 *It's Wearin' Me Down* ....8.00 - 12.00
  3511 *Back In Your Own Backyard* ....10.00 - 15.00
  3534 *Stampede* ....10.00 - 15.00
  3627 *If You Should Ever Leave* ....8.00 - 12.00
  3641 *All God's Children Got Rhythm*...............10.00 - 15.00
  3713 *Worried Over You* ....8.00 - 12.00
  3760 *What's Your Story* ....8.00 - 12.00
  3850 *If It's The Last Thing I Do* ....8.00 - 12.00
  4125 *Sing You Sinners* ....10.00 - 15.00
  4154 *Saving Myself For You* ....8.00 - 12.00
  4167 *There's Rain In My Eyes*........................8.00 - 12.00
  4180 *Moten Stomp* ....10.00 - 15.00
  14636 *Gulf Coast Blues* ....20.00 - 30.00
  14654 *Dicty Blues* ....20.00 - 30.00
  14726 *Charleston Crazy* ....20.00 - 30.00
  14740 *Potomac River Blues* ....20.00 - 30.00
  14759 *Lots O' Mama* ....20.00 - 30.00
  14788 *Chicago Blues* ....20.00 - 30.00
  14800 *Tea Pot Dome Blues*.............................20.00 - 30.00
  14828 *Strutter's Drag* ....20.00 - 30.00
  14838 *Do That Thing* ....20.00 - 30.00
  14880 *A New Kind Of Man* ....20.00 - 30.00
  14892 *Forsaken Blues* ....20.00 - 30.00
  14926 *Copenhagen* ....40.00 - 60.00
  14935 *Shanghai Shuffle* ....50.00 - 80.00
  15030 *Memphis Bound* ....75.00 - 100.00
  15174 *Hay Foot, Straw Foot* ....50.00 - 80.00
  15204 *Dinah*..50.00 - 80.00
  15205 *Let Me Introduce You To My Rosie* ....40.00 - 60.00
  15497 *Clarinet Marmalade*.............................40.00 - 60.00
  15532 *Stockholm Stomp* ....40.00 - 60.00

FRANK HENDERSON & HIS ORCHESTRA:
Vocalion 15323 *Brain Storm* ....60.00 - 100.00

HORACE HENDERSON & HIS ORCHESTRA:
Okeh 5433, 5518, 5579, 5606, 5632, 5748, 5841,
  5900, 5953, 5978, 6026....................................7.00 - 12.00
Vocalion 5433, 5518, 5579, 5606 ....7.00 - 12.00

HENNY HENDRICKSON'S LOUISVILLE SERENADERS:
Timely Tunes C-1585 *I Ain't Got Nobody* ....20.00 - 30.00
  C-1586 *Washington And Lee Swing* ....20.00 - 30.00
Victor 22749 *On The Beach With You*...................20.00 - 30.00
  22750 *Without That Gal!* ....20.00 - 30.00

TAL HENRY AND HIS NORTH CAROLINIANS/ ORCHESTRA:
Bluebird 5364, 5365, 5366......................................7.00 - 10.00
Victor 21404 *Some Little Someone* ....8.00 - 12.00

21471 *Lonesome* ....8.00 - 12.00
21573 *Louise, I Love You* ....8.00 - 12.00
V-40034 *When Shadows Fall* ....20.00 - 30.00
V-40035 *Found My Gal* ....40.00 - 60.00
V-40133 *Shame On You* ....20.00 - 30.00

RAY HERBECK AND HIS MUSIC WITH ROMANCE:
Okeh, most issues ....4.00 - 8.00
Vocalion, most issues ....4.00 - 8.00

JULES HERBUVEAUX AND HIS PALMER HOUSE VICTORIANS:
Brunswick 3360, 3479, 3557, 3606, 3646, 3754,
   3888 ....7.00 - 10.00
Vocalion 15380 *Where'd You Get Those Eyes?* ....8.00 - 12.00
15402 *Mandy* ....8.00 - 12.00
15403 *Someone Is Losin' Susan* ....8.00 - 12.00
15426 *Havin' Lots Of Fun* ....8.00 - 12.00

JOE HERLIHY & HIS ORCHESTRA:
Edison 52059 *Cornfed* ....75.00 - 100.00
52076 *State And Madison* ....75.00 - 100.00
52098 *Bye-Bye, Pretty Baby* ....35.00 - 50.00
52100 *Rolling Around In Roses* ....35.00 - 50.00

WOODY HERMAN & HIS ORCHESTRA:
Columbia, most issues ....5.00 - 8.00
Decca 1056 *The Goose Hangs High* ....10.00 - 15.00
1057 *I Can't Pretend* ....10.00 - 15.00
1064 *Old Fashioned Swing* ....10.00 - 15.00
1079 *Mr. Ghost Goes To Town* ....10.00 - 15.00
1288 *Dupree Blues* ....10.00 - 15.00
1307 *Trouble In Mind* ....10.00 - 15.00
1385 *Stardust On The Moon* ....8.00 - 12.00
1397 *Double Or Nothing* ....8.00 - 12.00
1523, 1535, 1570, 1583, 1801, 1839, 1879, 1900
   ....7.00 - 10.00
Decca, blue label, most other issues ....5.00 - 8.00

MILT HERTH (TRIO):
Decca 911, 1183, 1300, 1344 ....8.00 - 12.00
Decca, blue label, most other issues ....5.00 - 10.00

HERWIN HOT SHOTS:
Herwin 93015 *Salty Dog* ....200.00 - 300.00

EDDIE HEYWOOD/AND HIS JAZZ SIX ORCHESTRA:
Decca, most issues ....5.00 - 10.00
Okeh 8094 *The Mixed Up Blues* ....80.00 - 120.00
8402 *Trombone Moanin' Blues* ....150.00 - 200.00

ART HICKMAN'S ORCHESTRA:
Columbia (most issues) ....4.00 - 8.00
Victor 19399 *G'wan With It* ....7.00 - 10.00
19732 *Ships That Pass In The Night* ....8.00 - 12.00
19734 *This Is The Last Time* ....8.00 - 12.00

BILLY HICKS & HIS SIZZLIN' SIX:
Variety 601 *Fade Out* ....10.00 - 15.00
Vocalion 3804 *Joe The Bomber* ....10.00 - 15.00

RAMONA HICKS:
Bluebird 8173, 8200, 8233 ....8.00 - 12.00

J.C. HIGGINBOTHAM & HIS SIX HICKS; J.C. HIGGINBOTHAM QUINTET:
Okeh 8772 *Higginbotham Blues* ....80.00 - 120.00
Session 10013, 12016 ....7.00 - 10.00

SI HIGGINS & HIS SODBUSTERS:
Harmony 739-H *The Prune Song* ....10.00 - 15.00
(Note: Also issued on Diva and Velvet Tone, similarly valued.)

THE HIGH HATTERS:
Victor 21682 *Some Sweet Someone* ....8.00 - 12.00
21835 *Wipin' The Pan* ....8.00 - 12.00
22041 *Low Down Rhythm* ....7.00 - 10.00
22046 *Daddy, Won't You Please Come Home* ....7.00 - 10.00
22219 *Singin' In The Bathtub* ....7.00 - 10.00
22409 *You Brought A New Kind of Love To Me* .8.00 - 12.00
22703 *There Ought To Be A Moonlight Saving Time*
   ....8.00 - 12.00
22809 *Singin' The Blues* ....10.00 - 15.00
22810 *Sugar* ....10.00 - 15.00
24300 *Two Buck Tim From Timbuctoo* ....8.00 - 12.00
24301 *Easy Rider* ....15.00 - 20.00
24352 *My Handy Man* ....15.00 - 20.00
Victor, most other issues ....5.00 - 10.00

THE HIGH STEPPERS:
Crown 3009 *You're Simply Delish* ....10.00 - 15.00
3031 *When Kentucky Bids The World Good Morning*
   ....7.00 - 10.00
3032 *Baby's Birthday Party* ....7.00 - 10.00
3048 *What Good Am I Without You?* ....7.00 - 10.00
3050 *Say "Hello" To The Folks Back Home* ......7.00 - 10.00
3059 *The King's Horses* ....5.00 - 8.00
3064 *The One-Man Band* ....7.00 - 10.00
3085 *By My Side* ....7.00 - 10.00
3105 *Let's Get Friendly* ....20.00 - 30.00
3133 *I Wanna Sing About You* ....7.00 - 10.00
3136 *Just A Blue-Eyed Blonde* ....7.00 - 10.00
3137 *Little Girl* ....8.00 - 12.00
3148 *Without That Gal!* ....8.00 - 12.00
3161 *Makin' Faces At The Man In The Moon* ....8.00 - 12.00
3179 *There's No Other Girl* ....7.00 - 10.00
3184 *You Can't Stop Me From Loving You* ....10.00 - 15.00
3298 *Lawd, You Made The Night Too Long* ......10.00 - 15.00
3300 *Keepin' Out Of Mischief Now* .....10.00 - 15.00
3314 *Is I In Love? I Is!* ....7.00 - 10.00
3334 *A Great Big Bunch Of You* ....7.00 - 10.00
3337 *In A Shanty In Old Shanty Town* ..7.00 - 10.00
3338 *The Clouds Will Soon Roll By* ......7.00 - 10.00
3345 *Holding My Honey's Hand* ....8.00 - 12.00
3353 *There's Oceans Of Love By The Beautiful Sea*
   ....7.00 - 10.00
3365 *Here's Hoping* ....7.00 - 10.00
3394 *Please* ....10.00 - 15.00

HIGHTOWER'S NIGHT HAWKS:
Black Patti 8045 *Boar Hog Blues* ....750.00 - up

ALEX HILL/AND HIS HOLLYWOOD SEPIANS/ ORCHESTRA:
Vocalion 1270 *Tack Head Blues* ....150.00 - 250.00
1465 *Southbound* ....150.00 - 250.00
1493 *Dyin' With The Blues* ....150.00 - 250.00
2826 *Ain't It Nice?* ....50.00 - 80.00
2848 *Song Of The Plow* ....50.00 - 80.00

JUD HILL'S BLUE DEVILS/CLUB MOROCCO ORCHESTRA:
Champion 15050 *Manhattan* ....15.00 - 20.00
Gennett 3180 *Manhattan* ....8.00 - 12.00

3186 *Evolution Blues* ....15.00 - 20.00
3200 *Military Mike* ....20.00 - 30.00
3211 *Lonesome* ....8.00 - 12.00
3218 *Song Of The Vagabonds* ....20.00 - 30.00

SAM HILL & HIS ORCHESTRA:
Oriole 245 *One Of These Days* ....20.00 - 30.00
290 *My Dream Man* ....15.00 - 20.00
303 *Everybody Loves My Baby* ....50.00 - 75.00
304 *How Come You Do Me Like You Do* ....20.00 - 30.00
341 *I'll See You In My Dreams* ....15.00 - 20.00
347 *Alabamy Bound* ....30.00 - 50.00
348 *Why Couldn't It Be Poor Little Me?* ....30.00 - 50.00
365 *Swanee Butterfly* ....15.00 - 25.00
374 *One Of These Days* ....20.00 - 30.00
410 *The Flapper Wife* ....8.00 - 12.00
437 *Naughty Man* ....50.00 - 75.00

TEDDY HILL & HIS (NBC) ORCHESTRA:
Titles issued contemporaneously on Banner, Conqueror, Melotone, Oriole, Perfect, and Romeo: *Got Me Doin' Things; Here Comes Cookie; When The Robin Sings His Song Again* ....10.00 - 15.00
Bluebird 6897 *The Love Bug Will Bite You* ....8.00 - 12.00
6898 *My Marie* ....8.00 - 12.00
6908 *Big Boy Blue* ....10.00 - 15.00
6941 *China Boy* ....10.00 - 15.00
6943 *A Study In Brown* ....8.00 - 12.00
6954 *I Know Now* ....7.00 - 10.00
6988 *King Porter Stomp* ....10.00 - 20.00
6989 *Blue Rhythm Fantasy* ....10.00 - 20.00
7013 *Yours And Mine* ....10.00 - 15.00
Vocalion 3247 *Blue Rhythm Fantasy* ....15.00 - 20.00
3294 *Uptown Rhapsody* ....15.00 - 20.00

TINY HILL AND HIS ORCHESTRA:
Mercury, most issues ....5.00 - 8.00
Okeh, most issues ....5.00 - 10.00
Vocalion 4957 *Angry* ....8.00 - 12.00
5060 *Doodle Doo Doo* ....8.00 - 12.00
5128 *Mama's Gone, Goodbye* ....8.00 - 12.00
5340 *Skirts* ....8.00 - 12.00
Vocalion, most other issues ....5.00 - 10.00

LLOYD HILLMAN'S 1640 BOYS:
Columbia 40000-D *I Got A Misery* ....- - -

HILL TOP INN ORCHESTRA:
Champion 15031 *Choose Your Pal* ....25.00 - 40.00
15064 *Love Bound* ....15.00 - 25.00
15090 *Talking To The Moon* ....10.00 - 15.00
15091 *Lonesome And Sorry* ....10.00 - 15.00
15203 *Brotherly Love* ....50.00 - 80.00
15270 *Dawn of Tomorrow* ....10.00 - 15.00

RICHARD HIMBER & HIS ESSEX HOUSE/RHYTHMIC PYRAMIDS (RITZ-CARLTON) ORCHESTRA; RICHARD HIMBER'S SEVEN STYLISTS:
Bluebird 5418, 5419, 5421 ....7.00 - 10.00
Victor 24661, 24662, 24670, 24672, 24680, 24745, 24750, 24756, 24757, 24764, 24811, 24823, 24824, 24829, 24868, 24869, 24886, 25036, 25037, 25042, 25049, 25073, 25074, 25077, 25119, 25122, 25124, 25128, 25132, 25161, 25179, 25189, 25235, 25239, 25243, 25293, 25298, 25299, 25365, 25392, 25443, 25457, 25738, 25754, 26101, 26148 ....7.00 - 12.00

Vocalion 2526, 2537, 2538, 2551, 2560, 2572, 2588, 2589, 25008 ....7.00 - 12.00

EARL HINES & HIS ORCHESTRA:
Bluebird 6744 *Blue Nights* ....10.00 - 15.00
7040 *Beau-Koo Jack* ....10.00 - 15.00
7768 *Good Little, Bad Little You* ....10.00 - 15.00
10391 *G. T. Stomp* ....8.00 - 12.00
10555 *Glad Rag Doll* ....10.00 - 15.00
Bluebird (most other issues) ....7.00 - 10.00
Brunswick 6345 *Blue Drag* ....10.00 - 15.00
6379 *Sensational Mood* ....8.00 - 12.00
6403 *Love Me Tonight* ....15.00 - 20.00
6541 *Rosetta* ....8.00 - 12.00
6710 *Bubbling Over* ....10.00 - 15.00
6771 *Harlem Lament* ....10.00 - 15.00
6872 *Blue* ....8.00 - 12.00
6960 *Just To Be In Caroline* ....8.00 - 12.00
Columbia 2800-D *Fifty-Seven Varieties* ....25.00 - 40.00
Decca 182 *That's A Plenty* ....10.00 - 15.00
183 *Cavernism* ....10.00 - 15.00
218 *Maple Leaf Rag* ....10.00 - 15.00
337 *Copenhagen* ....10.00 - 15.00
389 *Rhythm Lullaby* ....8.00 - 12.00
577 *Wolverine Blues* ....10.00 - 15.00
654 *Japanese Sandman* ....8.00 - 12.00
714 *Bubbling Over* ....8.00 - 12.00

Okeh 8653 *Fifty-Seven Varieties* ....80.00 - 120.00
8832 *A Monday Date* ....80.00 - 120.00
41175 *Fifty-Seven Varieties* ....75.00 - 100.00
Q.R.S. 7036 *Off Time Blues* ....250.00 - up
7037 *A Monday Date* ....250.00 - up
7038 *Chimes In Blues* ....250.00 - up
7039 *Panther Rag* ....250.00 - up
Victor 22683 *Sister Kate* ....40.00 - 60.00
22842 *Sweet Ella May* ....75.00 - 100.00
V38042 *Chicago Rhythm* ....50.00 - 75.00
V38043 *Beau-Koo Jack* ....50.00 - 75.00
V38048 *Have You Ever Felt That Way?* ....75.00 - 100.00
V38096 *Grand Piano Blues* ....75.00 - 100.00
Vocalion 3379 *Madhouse* ....15.00 - 20.00
3392 *Swingin' Down* ....15.00 - 20.00
3467 *Rhythm Sundae* ....10.00 - 15.00
3501 *Flany Doodle Swing* ....8.00 - 12.00
3586 *Honeysuckle Rose* ....10.00 - 15.00
4008 *Please Be Kind* ....8.00 - 12.00
4032 *Dominick Swing* ....8.00 - 12.00
4143 *Tippin' At The Terrace* ....8.00 - 12.00
4272 *Jack Climbed A Beanstalk* ....8.00 - 12.00

HITCH'S HAPPY HARMONISTS:
Gennett 3066 *Boneyard Shuffle* ....80.00 - 120.00
5633 *Cataract Rag Blues* ....100.00 - 150.00

LES HITE & HIS ORCHESTRA:
Bluebird 11109 *Board Meetin'* ....8.00 - 12.00
    11210 *That's The Lick* ....8.00 - 12.00
Hit 7001 *Jersey Bounce* ....10.00 - 15.00
    7002 *Idaho* ....10.00 - 15.00
Varsity 8373 *The World Is Waiting For The Sunrise* ....8.00 - 12.00
    8391 *T-Bone Blues* ....8.00 - 12.00
    8396 *That's The Lick* ....8.00 - 12.00

RICHARD HITTER'S BLUE KNIGHTS/CABINEERS:
Everbody's 1062 *Eccentric*.................................150.00 - 200.00
    1063 *Riverboat Shuffle* ....150.00 - 200.00
Gennett 3149 *Stomp Off, Let's Go*.........................100.00 - 150.00

ART HODES; ART HODES' COLUMBIA QUINTET:
Black & White 1 *Snowy Morning Blues* ....8.00 - 12.00
    2 *St. Louis Blues* ....8.00 - 12.00
Jazz Records 1001, 1002, 1003, 1004, 1005, 1009 ...7.00 - 12.00
Solo Art 12005 *South Side Shuffle* ....20.00 - 30.00

JOHNNY HODGES & HIS ORCHESTRA:
Bluebird (most issues) ....5.00 - 10.00
Variety 576 *Foolin' Myself* ....10.00 - 15.00
    586 *A Sailboat In The Moonlight* ....10.00 - 15.00
Vocalion 3948, 4046, 4115, 4213, 4242, 4309, 4335,
    4351, 4386, 4573, 4622, 4710, 4849, 4917, 4941,
    5100, 5170, 5330, 5353, 5533, 5940 ....5.00 - 10.00

HARVEY HOFFMAN & HIS ORCHESTRA:
Champion 15263 *Original Black Bottom Dance* ...150.00 - 200.00
    15266 *All That I Had Is Gone*..........................150.00 - 200.00

HOKUM TRIO:
Titles issued comtemporaneously on Clarion, Diva, and Velvet
    Tone: *He Wouldn't Stop Doing It; I'm Havin' My Fun; You're
    Bound To Look Like A Monkey; You've Had Your Way*
    ....60.00 - 100.00

BILLIE HOLIDAY (& HER ORCHESTRA):
Aladdin 3094 *Be Fair To Me* ....8.00 - 12.00
    3102 *Blue, Turning Grey Over You* ....8.00 - 12.00
Columbia 30229 *Loveless Love* ....10.00 - 15.00
    30235 *Georgia On My Mind* ....10.00 - 15.00
    37586 *Am I Blue?* ....8.00 - 12.00
    38044 *Gloomy Sunday* ....8.00 - 12.00
Commodore 526 *Strange Fruit* ....8.00 - 12.00
    527 I *Gotta Right To Sing The Blues* ....8.00 - 12.00
Conqueror 9097, 9457, 9458 ....8.00 - 12.00
Harmony 1075 *Wherever You Are*..........................10.00 - 15.00
Okeh 3276, 3288, 3333, 3334, 3431, 3440, 3520,
    3543, 3593, 3605, 3701, 3748, 3947, 4029, 4126,
    4151, 4208, 4238, 4396, 4457, 4631, 4786, 4834,
    5021, 5129, 5302, 5377, 5481, 5609, 5719 ....7.00 - 12.00
    5806 *Practice Makes Perfect*............................10.00 - 20.00
    5831 *I'm All For You* ....10.00 - 20.00
    5991 *Time On My Hands* ....10.00 - 20.00
    6064 *St. Louis Blues* ....10.00 - 20.00
    6134 *Let's Do It* ....10.00 - 20.00
    6214 *All Of Me*..10.00 - 20.00
    6270 *Solitude* ....10.00 - 20.00
    6369 *Love Me Or Leave Me* ....10.00 - 15.00
    6451 *Gloomy Sunday*...................................10.00 - 20.00
Vocalion 3276 *Did I Remember?* ....15.00 - 20.00
    3288 *Billie's Blues* ....15.00 - 20.00
    3333 *A Fine Romance*..................................15.00 - 20.00
    3334 *Let's Call A Heart A Heart* ....15.00 - 20.00

    3431 *One Never Knows, Does One?*.................15.00 - 20.00
    3440 *If My Heart Could Only Talk* ....15.00 - 20.00
    3520 *Let's Call The Whole Thing Off*...............15.00 - 20.00
    3543 *Where Is The Sun?* ....15.00 - 20.00
    3593 *Without Your Love* ....15.00 - 20.00
    3605 *A Sailboat In The Moonlight*....................12.00 - 16.00
    3701 *Getting Some Fun Out Of Life* ....15.00 - 20.00
    3748 *He's Funny That Way* ....15.00 - 20.00
    3947 *Now They Call It Swing* ....15.00 - 20.00
    4029 *When A Woman Loves A Man*.................15.00 - 20.00
    4126 *You Go To My Head* ....15.00 - 20.00
    4151 *If I Were You* ....15.00 - 20.00
    4208 *Having Myself A Time* ....15.00 - 20.00
    4238 *I Wish I Had You!* ....15.00 - 20.00
    4396 *I've Got A Date With A Dream* ....12.00 - 16.00
    4457 *The Very Thought Of You* ....12.00 - 16.00
    4631 *Dream Of Life* ....15.00 - 20.00
    4786 *Under A Blue Jungle Moon*......................15.00 - 20.00
    4834 *You're Too Lovely To Last*......................15.00 - 20.00
    5021 *Them There Eyes* ....15.00 - 20.00
    5129 *Swing, Brother Swing*.............................15.00 - 20.00
    5302 *You're Just A No-Account*......................15.00 - 20.00
    5377 *Night And Day*....................................10.00 - 15.00
    5481 *Body And Soul* ....10.00 - 15.00
    5609 *Falling In Love Again* ....10.00 - 15.00
    5719 *Tell Me More*......................................12.00 - 16.00

HOLIDAY GREETINGS FROM THE BUNCH AT ORANGE:
Edison (master number) 10068 "jazzed" by various Edison officers,
    including "Thomas A. Edison himself." Red and green label,
    issued to Edison dealers. ....100.00 - 150.00
(Above was issued in a special sleeve, which, if intact and in nice
    condition, adds to the value of the record)

HOLLYWOOD DANCE ORCHESTRA:
Banner 0503 *Gonna Be a Moon Out Tonight* ....7.00 - 10.00
    0506 *Find A Sweetheart (Who'll Kiss Your Troubles Goodbye)*
    ....7.00 - 10.00
    0509 *Walk On The Sunny Side*.........................7.00 - 10.00
    0517 *Let Me Drown In An Ocean Of Love* ....7.00 - 10.00
    0539 *I'm Following You* ....7.00 - 10.00
    0563 *Hello Baby* ....8.00 - 12.00
    0564 *I Have To Have You* ....7.00 - 10.00
    0573 *I've Got To Have You* ....7.00 - 10.00
    0596 *What Do I Care?*..................................8.00 - 12.00
    0598 *Nobody's Sweetheart* ....15.00 - 20.00
    0632 *Sweetheart*..7.00 - 10.00
    0720 *Kitty From Kansas City* ....8.00 - 12.00
    0730 *I Love You So Much* ....7.00 - 10.00
    0786 *Go Home And Tell Your Mother* ....7.00 - 10.00
(Above titles were also issued on Cameo, similarly valued)
    1429 *Everything You Do*................................7.00 - 10.00
    1727 *What Good Is "Good Morning"?* ....7.00 - 10.00
    1762 *June, The Moon And You* ....7.00 - 10.00
    6007 *Just Another Day Wasted Away* ....15.00 - 20.00
    6052 *Oh! Constantine* ....8.00 - 12.00
    6106 *Let's Make Love In The Moonlight* ....7.00 - 10.00
    6131 *Lonely Melody*.....................................7.00 - 10.00
    6210 *That's What's Good For Me* ....7.00 - 10.00
    6232 *What's The Answer* ....7.00 - 10.00
    6257 *Cat's Kittens*.......................................8.00 - 12.00
    6259 *Just A Little Cuter Than The Rest* ....7.00 - 10.00
    6268 *I'd Love To Go Around With You* ....7.00 - 10.00

6292 *Shake Off The Blues* ....7.00 - 10.00
6326 *My Castle In Spain Is A Shack In The Lane* .....7.00 - 10.00
6348 *Papa's Mama's Blue ('Cause Mama's Papa's Through)*
....8.00 - 12.00
6388 *Ditto* ....7.00 - 10.00
6417 *I'm Doing What I'm Doing For Love* ....7.00 - 10.00
6453 *That's What I Call Love* ....7.00 - 10.00
6455 *Me And That Gal O'mine* ....7.00 - 10.00
6515 *Bashful* ....7.00 - 10.00
6544 *Every Once In A While* ....7.00 - 10.00
6552 *Same Old Moon* ....7.00 - 10.00
7049 *What Good Is The Moon Above?* ....7.00 - 10.00
7076 *Though You Threw Me Down* ....7.00 - 10.00
7136 *A Pretty Girl, A Pretty Tune* ....7.00 - 10.00
7157 *Mississippi Mud* ....15.00 - 20.00
7158 *Bring Back My Lovin' Man* ....7.00 - 10.00
7162 *I'm Sorry And You're Sorry (We're Both Sorry Now)*
....7.00 - 10.00
7213 *Nobody Knows* ....7.00 - 10.00
7241 *They Don't Come Better Than Betty* ....7.00 - 10.00
Cameo, titles as on Banner 0503 through 0786, similarly valued.
Oriole 1770 *Let Me Drown in an Ocean of Love* ......7.00 - 10.00
Perfect 14392 *King Porter Stomp* ....20.00 - 30.00
Regal 8475 *Chloe* ....7.00 - 10.00
Romeo 1402 *Dixianna*...8.00 - 12.00
Silvertone 21512 *Who's That Pretty Baby?* ....7.00 - 10.00

HOLLYWOOD RAMBLERS:
Bell 351 *Charleston*..10.00 - 15.00

HOLLYWOOD SHUFFLERS:
Vocalion 15837 *Low Down Rhythm* ....100.00 - 150.00
15841 *Bigger And Better Than Ever* ....100.00 - 150.00

HOLLYWOOD SYNCOPATORS:
Nordskog 3013 *Pacific Coast Blues* ....50.00 - 75.00

LIBBY HOLMAN:
Brunswick 3798 *The Way He Loves Is Just Too Bad* ...8.00 - 10.00
Brunswick (most other issues) ....5.00 - 10.00

SAXI HOLSWORTH & HIS ORCHESTRA:
Gennett 5508 *Charleston Cabin* ....10.00 - 20.00
5530 *How Come You Do Me Like You Do?* ......10.00 - 20.00

THE HOME TOWNERS:
Titles, issued contemporaneously on Banner, Cameo, Jewel, Oriole, Regal, and Romeo:
College Days; Coming Thru The Sky; Headin' South; There's a Czecho-Slovak That's Waiting For Me; There's No Good Reason Why; What's The Use?; Why Don't You Marry The Girl?; Yes Indeedy! ....10.00 - 20.00
Additional titles: *Let's Get Together; What A Funny World This Would Be; What D'Ya Think Of My Baby?* ....8.00 - 15.00

HONEY SWAMP STOMPERS:
Harmony 856-H *Wipin' The Pan*............................15.00 - 20.00
(Also issued on Diva and Velvet Tone, similarly valued)

CLAUDE HOPKINS AND HIS ORCHESTRA:
Ammor 114, 115, 116..8.00 - 12.00
Brunswick 6750 *Washington Squabble* ....15.00 - 25.00
6864 *My Gal Sal* ....10.00 - 15.00
6891 *I Can't Dance* ....10.00 - 15.00
6916 *Everybody Shuffle* ....10.00 - 15.00

Columbia 2665-D *Mad Moments*............................20.00 - 30.00
2674-D *Mush Mouth* ....20.00 - 30.00
2741-D *California, Here I Come* ....20.00 - 30.00
2747-D *He's A Son Of The South* ....20.00 - 30.00
2880-D *Ain't Misbehavin* ....20.00 - 30.00
2904-D *Marie*..20.00 - 30.00
Decca 184 *King Porter Stomp* ....10.00 - 15.00
185 *Just You, Just Me* ....10.00 - 15.00
270 *Walkin' The Dog* ....10.00 - 15.00
353 *Do You Ever Think Of Me?*........................10.00 - 15.00
374 *Love In Bloom* ....10.00 - 15.00
441 *Chasing All The Blues Away*......................10.00 - 15.00
674 *Monkey Business* ....8.00 - 12.00
1153 *Sunday*..10.00 - 15.00
1286 *Church Street Sobbin' Blues* ....10.00 - 15.00
1316 *My Kinda Love* ....10.00 - 15.00

DE WOLF HOPPER:
Victor 35290 *(12-inch) Casey At The Bat*...............15.00 - 20.00

HORSEY'S HOT FIVE:
Gennett 6722 *Weeping Blues* ....250.00 - up

HOTEL COMMODORE DANCE ORCHESTRA:
Edison 51880 *Nightmare* ....10.00 - 20.00
51895 *Clap Yo' Hands* ....10.00 - 15.00
51899 *In A Little Spanish Town* ....10.00 - 15.00

HOTEL PENNSYLVANIA MUSIC:
Harmony 1082-H *Lucky Little Devil*........................7.00 - 10.00
1086-H *Nobody's Sweetheart* ....7.00 - 10.00
1092-H *Tiger Rag* ....15.00 - 20.00
(Note: Titles also occur on Diva and Velvet Tone, similarly valued. Numerous other titles on these labels, and Clarion, are of minimal interest/value.)

THE HOT AIR MEN:
Columbia 2092-D *Navy Blues* ....20.00 - 30.00
2175-D *Red Hot Chicago*.................................20.00 - 30.00

HOT AND HEAVY:
Pathe-Actuelle 7510 *Memphis Rag*......................100.00 - 150.00
Perfect 110 *Memphis Rag* ....100.00 - 150.00

HOTCHA TRIO:
Bluebird 5296 *Chinatown, My Chinatown* ....15.00 - 20.00
Electradisk 2167 *Dinah* ....15.00 - 20.00
Sunrise S-3377 *Chinatown, My Chinatown* ....40.00 - 60.00

THE HOT DOGS:
Silvertone 3560 *Hot Mustard*................................80.00 - 120.00
3567 *Mojo Blues* ....80.00 - 120.00
3572 *Carolina Shuffle* ....80.00 - 120.00
3574 *Steady Roll* ....100.00 - 150.00

THE HOTSEY TOTSEY BOYS:
Clover 1710 *Steppin' Along* ....15.00 - 25.00

THE HOTSY TOTSY GANG (See also IRVING MILLS):
Brunswick 4014 *Doin' The New Low Down* ....20.00 - 30.00
4044 *Don't Mess Around With Me* ....20.00 - 30.00
4112 *I Couldn't If I Wanted To*.........................15.00 - 20.00
4122 *Since You Went Away*.............................15.00 - 25.00
4200 *Futuristic Rhythm*...................................25.00 - 40.00

THE HOTTENTOTS/HOTENTOTS:
Paramount 12359 *Lots O'Mama*..........................80.00 - 120.00
Supertone 9447 *Chicago Rhythm*.........................50.00 - 80.00

Vocalion 15161 *Down And Out Blues*......................40.00 - 60.00
     15209 *Pensacola*..40.00 - 60.00

THE HOUR OF CHARM ALL GIRL ORCHESTRA:
Vogue R-725 *Alice Blue Gown*......................20.00 - 30.00
     R-726 *Blue Skies* ....20.00 - 30.00
(Note: The above two records comprise Vogue album No. V100 "A Study In Blue.")
Vogue R-733 *Seville* ....20.00 - 30.00

BOB HOWARD & HIS ORCHESTRA:
Decca 343 *Throwin' Stones At The Sun* ....8.00 - 12.00
     347 *It's Unbelievable*................................8.00 - 12.00
     400 *Pardon My Love* ....10.00 - 15.00
     407 *Breakin' The Ice* ....8.00 - 12.00
     439 *I'll Never Change* ....8.00 - 12.00
     460 *A Porter's Love Song*........................7.00 - 10.00
     484 *Corrine Corrina*................................10.00 - 15.00
     504 *If The Moon Turns Green* ....10.00 - 15.00
     513 *In A Little Gypsy Tea Room* ....10.00 - 15.00
     524 *I'm Painting The Town Red* ....10.00 - 15.00
     598 *It's Written In The Stars* ....7.00 - 10.00
     627 *Give Me A Break, Baby* ....7.00 - 10.00
     689 *You Hit The Spot*................................8.00 - 12.00
     720 *Spreadin' Rhythm Around* ....8.00 - 12.00
     722 *Much Too Much*................................8.00 - 12.00
     839 *Let's Not Fall In Love* ....8.00 - 12.00
     862 *Public Weakness No. 1* ....8.00 - 12.00
Decca 917, 927, 983, 1195, 1205, 1293, 1306 and higher numbers
....5.00 - 10.00

GORDON HOWARD & HIS MULTNOMAH CHIEFTAINS:
Gennett 6381 *Wob-A-Ly Walk* ....20.00 - 30.00
     6395 *Golden Gate* ....20.00 - 30.00

PAUL HOWARD'S QUALITY SERENADERS:
Bluebird 5804 *Stuff*..20.00 - 30.00
Victor 22001 *Overnight Blues* ....80.00 - 120.00
     22660 *New Kinda Blues*........................80.00 - 120.00
     23354 *California Swing* ....300.00 - up
     23420 *Gettin' Ready Blues* ....300.00 - up
     V38068 *The Ramble* ....80.00 - 120.00
     V38070 *Charlie's Idea* ....80.00 - 120.00
     V38122 *Quality Shout* ....100.00 - 150.00

HOWELL'S METROPOLITAN SEVEN:
Hollywood (unnumbered) *Slippery Elm* ....20.00 - 30.00

BERT HOWELL:
Paramount 13063 *You're Driving Me Crazy* ....75.00 - 100.00
Victor 21062 *Bye Bye Florence*................................40.00 - 60.00

HUDSON TRIO:
Famous 3024 *Twelfth Street Rag*..............................7.00 - 10.00

HUDSON-DE LANGE ORCHESTRA; WILL HUDSON & HIS ORCHESTRA/SEVEN SWINGSTERS:
Brunswick 7598, 7618, 7656, 7667, 7700, 7708,
     7715, 7727, 7743, 7785, 7795, 7809, 7828, 7991,
     7996, 7998, 8002, 8007, 8016, 8023, 8040, 8049,
     8071, 8077, 8081, 8090, 8113, 8147, 8156, 8164,
     8177, 8191, 8195, 8213, 8222 ....7.00 - 10.00
Master 103, 112, 125, 132, 138 ....7.00 - 12.00

PHIL HUGHES AND HIS HIGH HATTERS:
Clarion 5304-C *Just A Crazy Song* .... 10.00 - 15.00
     5342-C *Treat Me Like A Baby* .... 8.00 - 12.00
     5365-C *It's A Long Time Between Kisses*............ 7.00 - 10.00
Harmony 1313-H *Just A Crazy Song* .... 10.00 - 15.00
     1333-H *Look In The Looking Glass* .... 8.00 - 12.00
     1353-H *It's A Long Time Between Kisses*........... 7.00 - 10.00
Pathe-Actuelle (titles as on Perfect, below)
Perfect 14558 *Thanks For The Buggy Ride* .... 8.00 - 12.00
     14606 *Show That Fellow The Door* .... 8.00 - 12.00
     14624 *Georgianna* .... 8.00 - 12.00
     14643 *Animal Crackers* .... 15.00 - 20.00
     14707 *Meadow Lark* .... 8.00 - 12.00
(Above titles also issued on Pathe-Actuelle, similarly valued)
Velvet Tone 2370-V *Just A Crazy Song* .... 10.00 - 15.00
     2406-V *Treat Me Like A Baby* .... 8.00 - 12.00
     2429-V *It's A Long Time Between Kisses*........... 7.00 - 10.00

CLAIRE HULL & HIS WANDERERS:
Gennett 6356 *Nobody's Sweetheart* .... 50.00 - 75.00

HUNTER'S SERENADERS:
Vocalion 1621 *Sensational Mood* .... 150.00 - 200.00

CHARLEY HUNTER'S ORCHESTRA:
Broadway 5023 *Bottomland* .... 80.00 - 130.00

EDDIE HUNTER:
Victor 19247 *Bootleggers' Ball* .... 15.00 - 20.00

INA RAY HUTTON & HER MELODEARS:
Victor 24692 *How's About Tomorrow Night?*........ 15.00 - 20.00
Vocalion 2801 *Georgia's Gorgeous Gal* .... 15.00 - 20.00
     2816 *Wild Party*....................................... 15.00 - 20.00

JOHN HYMAN'S BAYOU STOMPERS:
Victor 20593 *Alligator Blues* .... 100.00 - 150.00

BERTHA IDAHO:
Columbia 14437-D *Move It On Out Of Here* .... 75.00 - 100.00

IDEAL SERENADERS:
Columbia 1131-D *Dawning* .... 8.00 - 12.00

IMPERIAL DANCE ORCHESTRA:
Banner 0505 *Can't We Be Friends* .... 8.00 - 12.00
     0514 *It's Not A Secret Any More* .... 5.00 - 8.00
     0532 *Lady Luck*....................................... 10.00 - 15.00
     0589 *Ring Around The Moon*........................... 10.00 - 15.00
     0626 *The Stein Song* .... 8.00 - 12.00
     0631 *Sing You Sinners* .... 15.00 - 20.00
     0747 *Because I'm Lonesome* .... 8.00 - 12.00
     0759 *Hear Dem Bells*................................... 8.00 - 12.00
(Foregoing titles also issued on Cameo, similarly valued)
     1943 *The Dixie Vagabond* .... 5.00 - 8.00
     6070 *Strolling In The Sunshine* .... 5.00 - 8.00
     6245 *Let's Do It* .... 5.00 - 8.00
     6379 *Time Will Tell* .... 5.00 - 8.00
     6444 *I Want To Meander In The Meadow* .... 5.00 - 8.00
     6500 *Where Do Holes Go In Doughnuts?* .... 5.00 - 8.00
     7131 *Boo-Hoo-Hoo (What Am I Gonna Do?)* ..... 5.00 - 8.00
     7165 *I Wanna Go Back To Indiana* .... 5.00 - 8.00
     7192 *Ready For The River* .... 15.00 - 20.00
Cameo (titles as on Banner 0505 through 0759, which see)
Domino 4449 *Miss Wonderful* .... 8.00 - 12.00
     4469 *I'm Following You* .... 7.00 - 10.00
     4479 *Hello Baby* .... 8.00 - 12.00

4485 *Try Dancing* ....7.00 - 10.00
4575 *Kitty From Kansas City* ....7.00 - 10.00
4592 *She'll Be Comin 'Round The Mountain* ......8.00 - 12.00
4646 *Just A Little Dance, Mam'selle* ....25.00 - 40.00
4649 *You're Simply Delish* ....15.00 - 25.00
4651 *Son Of The Sun* ....15.00 - 25.00
Jewel 5883 *Sing You Sinners* ....15.00 - 20.00
Oriole 1766 *It's Not A Secret Any More* ....5.00 - 8.00
1883 *Sing You Sinners* ....15.00 - 20.00
1998 *Because I'm Lonesome* ....8.00 - 12.00
Pathe-Actuelle 36299 *Milenburg Joys* ....15.00 - 20.00
Perfect 15258 *I'm Following You!* ....7.00 - 10.00
15264 *Hello Baby* ....8.00 - 12.00
15274 *What Do I Care?* ....8.00 - 12.00
Regal 8041 *Show That Fellow The Door* ....7.00 - 10.00
8893 *Miss Wonderful* ....8.00 - 12.00
8914 *I'm Following You* ....7.00 - 10.00
8924 *Hello Baby* ....8.00 - 12.00
8930 *Try Dancing* ....7.00 - 10.00
8943 *What Do I Care?* ....8.00 - 12.00
Romeo 1246 *Sing You Sinners* ....15.00 - 20.00

IMPERIAL ORCHESTRA:
Bell 534 *Sing Me A Baby Song* ....8.00 - 12.00
564 *Highways Are Happy Ways* ....7.00 - 10.00

INDIANA FIVE (See ORIGINAL INDIANA FIVE)

INDIANA HOTEL BROADCASTERS:
Champion 15110 *Spanish Mamma* ....12.00 - 16.00
15111 *The Nightmare* ....12.00 - 16.00
15119 *That's Why I Love You* ....8.00 - 12.00

INDIANA SYNCOPATERS:
LaBelle 1418 *Bees Knees* ....20.00 - 30.00

THE INK SPOTS:
Decca 817, 883, 1036, 1154, 1236, 1251 ....7.00 - 12.00
Victor 24851 *Your Feet's Too Big* ....30.00 - 50.00
24876 *Swing Gate, Swing* ....30.00 - 50.00

INTERNATIONAL DANCE ORCHESTRA:
Globe 1333 *Lady Lou* ....15.00 - 20.00

INTERNATIONAL NOVELTY ORCHESTRA:
Victor 19457 *Boll Weevil Blues* ....7.00 - 10.00
19509 *Hey! Hey! And Hee! Hee!* ....7.00 - 10.00
19817 *Oh! Boy, What A Girl* ....8.00 - 12.00
19832 *Monkey Biz-ness (Down in Tennessee)* ...25.00 - 40.00

INTERSTATE BLUE JACKETS:
Champion 15037 *The Camel Walk* ....25.00 - 35.00
15040 *Mama, Let Rosie Alone* ....25.00 - 35.00
15053 *Spanish Shawl* ....25.00 - 35.00
15064 *Shanghai Honeymoon* ....15.00 - 25.00
15304 *Indiana Mud* ....80.00 - 130.00

IPANA TROUBADOURS:
Columbia 503-D *Paddlin' Madelin' Home* ....10.00 - 15.00
528-D *Jig Walk* ....10.00 - 15.00
1009-D *Side By Side* ....7.00 - 10.00
1412-D *I'm Ridin To Glory* ....8.00 - 12.00
1463-D *Nagasaki* ....10.00 - 15.00
1586-D *I Can't Make Her Happy* ....10.00 - 15.00
1638-D *Glorianna* ....20.00 - 30.00
1694-D *Rose Of Mandalay* ....25.00 - 40.00
1717-D *Mississippi* ....8.00 - 12.00

1779-D *Wake Up! Chill'un, Wake Up!* ....10.00 - 15.00
1815-D *I Used To Love Her In The Moonlight* ...8.00 - 12.00
1881-D *There Was Nothing Else To Do* ....7.00 - 10.00
1920-D *Hang On To Me* ....8.00 - 12.00
1982-D *True Blue Lou* ....8.00 - 12.00
2006-D *My Sweeter Than Sweet* ....8.00 - 12.00
2117-D *Kickin' A Hole In The Sky* ....10.00 - 15.00
2174-D *Whippoorwill* ....8.00 - 12.00
2220-D *Sing* ....8.00 - 12.00
2317-D *Three Little Words* ....8.00 - 12.00
2368-D *I'm So Afraid Of You* ....8.00 - 12.00
2486-D *On The Beach With You* ....8.00 - 12.00
Columbia (most other issues) ....5.00 - 10.00
Columbia 3585-X *Just A Little Glimpse Of Paradise*
....10.00 - 20.00

(Note: Above is part of a Spanish series issued as by "Trovadores
Ipana," lacking the vocal present in the performance issued for
U.S. market. Other similar issues probably exist, and would
possibly be of interest to collectors.)

KITTY IRVIN:
Gennett 5592 *Copenhagen* .... 150.00 - 200.00

VIC/VICTOR IRWIN & HIS ORCHESTRA:
Titles issued contemporaneously on Banner, Oriole, Perfect, and
Romeo: *I Don't Blame You; Now's The Time To Fall In Love;
She's So Nice; Who's Your Little Who-Zis?* ...... 10.00 - 15.00
Harmony 422-H *Rhapsody In Blue* .... 10.00 - 15.00
487-H *I Can't Believe That You're In Love With Me*
.... 7.00 - 10.00
571-H *Lady Of Havana* .... 7.00 - 10.00
610-H *Danger! Look Out For That Gal* .... 7.00 - 10.00
(Note: Above titles on Diva and Velvet Tone are similarly valued.)

JACK'S FAST-STEPPIN' BELLHOPS:
Champion 15088 *Honey Bunch* .... 50.00 - 80.00
15089 *Here Comes Emaline* .... 15.00 - 20.00
15090 *Horses* .... 10.00 - 15.00
15093 *I'd Rather Be Alone* .... 10.00 - 15.00

JACKSON & HIS SOUTHERN STOMPERS:
Marathon 227 (7-inch record) *Dusky Stevedore* ... 150.00 - 200.00

ALEX JACKSON'S PLANTATION ORCHESTRA:
Gennett 6249 *Jackass Blues* .... 300.00 - up
6296 *Missouri Squabble* .... 250.00 - up

CLIFF JACKSON & HIS CRAZY KATS:
Van Dyke 81839 *Horse Feathers* .... 40.00 - 60.00
81842 *Torrid Rhythm* .... 40.00 - 60.00
(Foregoing titles on Madison, Radiex are similarly valued)

DEWEY JACKSON'S PEACOCK ORCHESTRA:
Vocalion 1039 *Go 'Won To Town* .... 150.00 - 200.00
1040 *She's Cryin' For Me* .... 150.00 - 250.00

DUKE JACKSON'S SERENADERS:
Gennett 6124 *Now Cut Loose* .... 250.00 - up

EARL JACKSON'S MUSICAL CHAMPIONS:
Melotone 12080 *Is That Religion?* .... 20.00 - 30.00
12093 *Rockin' Chair* .... 8.00 - 12.00
12164 *Red Devil* .... 15.00 - 20.00
Perfect 15468 *Star Dust* .... 15.00 - 20.00
15481 *Black And Tan Fantasy* .... 15.00 - 20.00

FRISKY FOOT JACKSON & HIS THUMPERS:
Champion 15696 *Good Time Mama* ....300.00 - up
   15929 *Mississippi Stomp* ....300.00 - up
   40043 *Good Time Mama* ....75.00 - 100.00

LITTLE JOE JACKSON & HIS BOYS:
Bell 1174 *Fourth Avenue Stomp* ....300.00 - up

MARY JACKSON:
Pathe-Actuelle 032013 *All The Time* ....30.00 - 50.00
Perfect 12097 *All The Time* ....30.00 - 50.00

MIKE JACKSON:
Victor 20181 *Just Too Bad* ....25.00 - 35.00
   20482 *Alabama* ....30.00 - 50.00

PRESTON JACKSON & HIS UPTOWN BAND:
Paramount 12400 *Harmony Blues* ....200.00 - 300.00
   12411 *Trombone Man* ....200.00 - 300.00

SLIM JACKSON TRIO:
Cameo 705 *Freakish Blues* ....15.00 - 20.00

SMOKE JACKSON & HIS RED ONIONS:
Champion 15714 *It's Tight Like That* ....80.00 - 120.00
   15905 *Wailin' Blues* ....200.00 - 300.00

JACKSONVILLE HARMONY TRIO:
Victor 20960 *Jacksonville Blues* ....40.00 - 60.00
   21204 *I Wonder* ....50.00 - 80.00

BUD JACOBSON'S JUNGLE KINGS:
Signature 103, 106, 903, 904 ....7.00 - 10.00

JAFFE'S COLLEGIANS:
Okeh 40561 *Sweet And Low Down* ....15.00 - 25.00

JAMAICA JAZZERS:
Okeh 40117 *West Indies Blues* ....100.00 - 150.00

BILLY JAMES' DANCE ORCHESTRA:
Banner 6356 *Pa's Old Hat* ....8.00 - 12.00
Challenge 964 *Dixieanna (The Pride Of The South)* .7.00 - 10.00
Crown 3321 *The Song Doctor* ....75.00 - 100.00
Jewel 5028 *Do A Little Of Everything* ....7.00 - 10.00
   5073 *I'm Her Beau* ....10.00 - 15.00
   5146 *Lonely Melody* ....7.00 - 10.00
Oriole 547, 599, 850, 1284, 1319, 1480, 1512, 1536,
   1548, 1634, 1637, 1721 ....7.00 - 12.00
   271 *Hard Hearted Hannah* ....10.00 - 15.00
   565 *Sweet Child* ....15.00 - 20.00
   829 *Muddy Water* ....15.00 - 20.00
   984 *Blame It On The Black Bottom Craze* ...10.00 - 15.00
   1008 *Swanee's Calling Me* ....15.00 - 20.00
   1250 *Straight Back Home* ....15.00 - 20.00
   1489 *And Then* ....10.00 - 15.00
Oriole, most other issues ....5.00 - 10.00

CORKY JAMES & HIS BLACKBIRDS:
Bell 1182 *Bugahoma Blues* ....300.00 - up

HARRY JAMES & HIS ORCHESTRA; HARRY JAMES & THE BOOGIE WOOGIE TRIO:
Brunswick 8035 *When We're Alone* ....10.00 - 15.00
   8038 *(I Can Dream) Can't I?* ....10.00 - 15.00
   8055 *One O'Clock Jump* ....7.00 - 10.00
   8067 *Texas Chatter* ....7.00 - 10.00
   8136 *Out Of Nowhere* ....7.00 - 10.00

   8178 *Wrap Your Troubles In Dreams* ....5.00 - 8.00
   8318 *Boo-Woo* ....7.00 - 10.00
   8326 *Blame It On My Last Affair* ....5.00 - 8.00
   8327 *Ciribiribin* ....5.00 - 8.00
   8337 *Two O'Clock Jump* ....5.00 - 8.00
   8350 *Home James* ....7.00 - 10.00
   8355 *Got No Time* ....7.00 - 10.00
   8366 *King Porter Stomp* ....7.00 - 10.00
   8395 *I Can't Afford To Dream* ....7.00 - 10.00
   8406 *I Found A New Baby* ....7.00 - 10.00
   8443 *From The Bottom Of My Heart* ....75.00 - 100.00
Columbia 35209 *It's Funny To Everyone But Me* .. 10.00 - 15.00
   35227 *Here Comes The Night* ....10.00 - 15.00
   35242 *My Buddy* ....8.00 - 12.00
   35261 *Who Told You I Cared?* ....8.00 - 12.00
Columbia, most other issues ....4.00 - 7.00
Varsity, most issues ....7.00 - 10.00

JEANETTE JAMES:
Paramount 12451 *What's That Thing?* ....200.00 - 300.00
   12470 *Midnight Stomp* ....200.00 - 300.00

JELLY JAMES & HIS FEWSICIANS:
Gennett 6045 *Georgia Bo Bo* ....150.00 - 200.00

VIN JAMES:
Okeh 40515 *Footloose* ....15.00 - 25.00

ART JARRETT:
Columbia 2672-D *Goodbye Blues* ....20.00 - 30.00
   2691-D *Music, Music Everywhere* ....20.00 - 30.00

HOTSY JARVIS (& HER GANG):
Banner 1848 *The Birth Of The Blues* ....8.00 - 12.00
Domino 3821 *Lucky Day* ....8.00 - 12.00
Oriole 807 *Sunday* ....10.00 - 15.00
Regal 8132 *Breezin' Along With The Breeze* ....8.00 - 12.00
   8159 *Lucky Day* ....8.00 - 12.00

JAUDAS' SOCIETY ORCHESTRA:
Edison 50469 *The Darktown Strutters' Ball* ....15.00 - 20.00
(Note: Record number may be found only on record's edge.)

FRANKIE "HALF-PINT" JAXON (& HIS HOT SHOTS):
Black Patti 8040 *Can't You Wait Till You Get Home*
   ....300.00 - up
   8048 *Willie The Weeper* ....300.00 - up
Decca 7286, 7304, 7345, 7360, 7482, 7523, 7548,
   7619, 7638, 7733, 7742, 7786, 7795, 7806 ....7.00 - 12.00
Gennett 6214 *Can't You Wait Till You Get Home?*
   ....100.00 - 150.00
   6244 *She's Got "It"* ....75.00 - 100.00
Vocalion 1226 *Down At Jasper's Bar-Be-Que* ..... 150.00 - 250.00
   1257 *Fan It* ....80.00 - 120.00
   1285 *Let's Knock A Jug* ....150.00 - 200.00
   1424 *Take It Easy* ....150.00 - 250.00
   1472 *Down Home In Kentucky* ....150.00 - 250.00
   1539 *Jive Man Blues* ....150.00 - 200.00
   1583 *Scuddlin* ....150.00 - 200.00
   2553 *My Baby's Hot* ....30.00 - 50.00
   2603 *Fifteen Cents* ....20.00 - 30.00

JAZZ-BO'S CAROLINA SERENADERS:
Cameo 218 *My Honey's Lovin' Arms* ....8.00 - 12.00
   232 *Hopeless Blues* ....10.00 - 15.00
   257 *Hot Lips* ....7.00 - 10.00

258 *Yankee Doodle Blues* ....7.00 - 10.00
269 *Achin' Hearted Blues* ....7.00 - 10.00

THE JAZZ HARMONISTS/HARMONIZERS:
Claxtonola 40336 *Copenhagen*..................150.00 - 250.00
40339 *Riverboat Shuffle* ....150.00 - 250.00
40375 *Sensation*....................................200.00 - 300.00
Rich-Tone 7014 *How Many Times?* ....8.00 - 12.00
7022 *In My Heart, On My Mind, All Day Long*....8.00 - 12.00
7033 *Pick Me Up And Lay Me Down In Dear Old Dixieland*
....10.00 - 15.00
7037 *Carolina Rolling Stone* ....8.00 - 12.00

THE JAZZ MASTERS (See also ETHEL WATERS):
Black Swan 2109 *Bees Knees*......................20.00 - 30.00

THE JAZZ-O-HARMONISTS:
Edison 51157 *Snakes Hips*.........................15.00 - 20.00
51161 *Funny Feet* ....10.00 - 15.00
51165 *Long-Lost Mama*.............................15.00 - 20.00
51168 *The Cat's Whiskers* ....10.00 - 15.00
51171 *I Ain't Never Had Nobody Crazy Over Me*
....15.00 - 20.00
51172 *Henpecked Blues*...........................15.00 - 20.00
51229 *I've Got the 'Yes We Have No Bananas' Blues*
....10.00 - 15.00
51247 *Darktown Reveille* ....25.00 - 35.00
51302 *I'm Goin' South* ....15.00 - 20.00
51303 *If I Stay Away Too Long From Carolina* .15.00 - 20.00

THE JAZZOPATORS:
Grey Gull 1803 *I Don't Know and Don't Care*.......15.00 - 20.00
1816 *Everybody Dance*.............................15.00 - 20.00
1819 *Blue Ridge Blues*............................15.00 - 20.00
Van Dyke 71747 *Sweet Little Sis*.................8.00 - 12.00

THE JAZZ PILOTS (See also HARRY RESER):
Okeh 40502 *Sleepy Time Gal* ....8.00 - 12.00
40533 *I'm Sitting On Top Of The World* ....10.00 - 15.00
40548 *I Wish't I Was In Peoria* ....10.00 - 15.00
40569 *Thanks For The Buggy Ride* ....10.00 - 15.00
40611 *Gimme A Little Kiss, Will Ya, Huh?* ....8.00 - 12.00
40635 *Yea, Alabama!*..............................8.00 - 12.00
40637 *Hi-Ho, The Merrio* ....75.00 - 100.00
40650 *Hi-Diddle-Diddle* ....8.00 - 12.00
40660 *No Foolin'* ....40.00 - 60.00
40665 *The Judge Cliff Davis Blues* ....10.00 - 15.00
40688 *That's My Girl* ....10.00 - 15.00
40701 *Meadow Lark* ....10.00 - 15.00
40702 *Dancing The Charleston*.....................15.00 - 20.00
40707 *Fire!* ....10.00 - 15.00
40709 *Susie's "Feller"* ....10.00 - 15.00
40719 *How Could Red Riding Hood?* ....10.00 - 15.00
40730 *That's A Good Girl* ....10.00 - 15.00
40741 *Everything's Made For Love* ....8.00 - 12.00
40751 *Since I Found You*..........................15.00 - 20.00
40771 *I've Never Seen A Straight Banana* ....10.00 - 15.00
40809 *Just The Same* ....20.00 - 30.00
40812 *The More We Are Together* ....10.00 - 15.00
40821 *Go Wash An Elephant (If You Wanna Do Something Big)*
....20.00 - 30.00
40908 *Pastafazoola* ....10.00 - 15.00
40914 *Who's That Pretty Baby?*....................10.00 - 15.00
41021 *Hello, Montreal!* ....12.00 - 16.00
41066 *That's My Weakness Now* ....12.00 - 16.00
41219 *Down Among The Sugar Cane* ....12.00 - 16.00

SPEED JEFFRIES & HIS NIGHT OWLS:
Superior 2648 *Georgia Grind*......................250.00 - up
2670 *Kentucky Blues* ....250.00 - up
2728 *Stomp Your Stuff* ....250.00 - up
2738 *Sic 'Em, Tige*..............................250.00 - up
2755 *Tiger Moon* ....250.00 - up
2797 *Richmond Stomp* ....250.00 - up

THE JELLY WHIPPERS:
Herwin 92018 *S.O.B. Blues* ....200.00 - 300.00

FREDDY JENKINS & HIS HARLEM SEVEN:
Bluebird 6129 *Old Fashioned Love* ....8.00 - 12.00
6193 *Swingin' 'Em Down* ....8.00 - 12.00

JACK JENNEY & HIS ORCHESTRA:
Conqueror 9493, 9494 ....5.00 - 10.00
Okeh 5304, 5494 ....7.00 - 10.00
Vocalion 3972, 4130, 4803, 5304, 5407, 5494,
5535, 5545...7.00 - 12.00

JETER-PILLARS CLUB PLANTATION ORCHESTRA:
Vocalion 3715 *Lazy Rhythm* ....20.00 - 30.00
3973 *Make Believe*................................20.00 - 30.00

THE JIM-DANDIES:
Harmony 55-H *Shake That Thing* ....25.00 - 35.00

JIMMIE'S BLUE MELODY BOYS:
Vocalion 1439 *Love Me* ....100.00 - 150.00

JIMMIE'S JOYS:
Golden 1858 *No No Nora* ....200.00 - up
1865 *Bugle Call Rag* ....200.00 - up

AL JOCKERS & HIS ORCHESTRA:
Cameo 847 *The Promenade Walk*.....................10.00 - 15.00

JOE'S HOT BABIES:
Paramount 12783 *Beans And Greens*.................250.00 - up

JOE & HIS RHYTHM ORCHESTRA:
Bluebird 6447 *Confessin'* ....8.00 - 12.00

THE JOHNSON BOYS:
Okeh 8708 *Violin Blues* ....150.00 - 200.00

JOHNSON'S JAZZERS:
Columbia 14247-D *Can I Get It Now?* ....100.00 - 150.00

JOHNSON'S PLANTATION SERENADERS:
Silvertone 5024 *A Blues Serenade* ....50.00 - 75.00

ARNOLD JOHNSON & HIS ORCHESTRA:
Brunswick 3840 *I'm Riding To Glory* ....8.00 - 12.00
3895 *Happy-Go-Lucky Lane* ....8.00 - 12.00
3914 *What's The Reason?* ....7.00 - 10.00
3980 *Georgie Porgie*.............................8.00 - 12.00
4037 *Pickin' Cotton* ....10.00 - 15.00
4080 *That's How I Feel About You*................7.00 - 10.00
4125 *Me And The Man In The Moon* ....8.00 - 12.00
Brunswick, most other issues.......................5.00 - 8.00

BERT JOHNSON:
Brunswick 7136 *Nasty But Nice* ....200.00 - up

BILL JOHNSON'S LOUISIANA JUG BAND:
Brunswick 7067 *Don't Drink It In Here*............150.00 - 200.00

BLANCHE JOHNSON:
Herwin 92016 *Galveston Blues*.....................150.00 - 200.00

BUNK JOHNSON & HIS BAND:
American Music 101......................................7.00 - 10.00
American Music (12 inch) 251, 253, 255 ....7.00 - 10.00
Jazz Information 12, 14 ....7.00 - 10.00
Jazz Man 8, 9, 10 ....7.00 - 10.00
V-Disc (12 inch) 630, 658 ....7.00 - 10.00

CAROLINE JOHNSON:
Buddy 8033 *Mama's Losin' A Mighty Good Chance*
....100.00 - 150.00
   8034 *Ain't Got Nobody To Grind My Coffee*....100.00 - 150.00
Gennett 3307 *Mama's Losin' A Mighty Good Chance*
....80.00 - 120.00
Pathe-Actuelle 7503 *Georgia Grind*.....................100.00 - 150.00
Perfect 103 *Georgia Grind* ....100.00 - 150.00

CHARLIE JOHNSON'S (ORIGINAL) (PARADISE) ORCHESTRA/TEN; CHARLIE JOHNSON & HIS (PARADISE) BAND/ORCHESTRA:
Bluebird 10248 *Walk That Thing* ....15.00 - 20.00
Emerson 10854 *Don't Forget You'll Regret Day By Day*
....75.00 - 100.00
   10856 *Meddlin' With The Blues* ....75.00 - 100.00
Victor 20551 *Paradise Wobble* ....100.00 - 150.00
   20653 *Don't You Leave Me Here* ....100.00 - 150.00
   21247 *You Ain't The One* ....100.00 - 150.00
   21491 *Charleston Is The Best Dance After All*.100.00 - 150.00
   21712 *Walk That Thing* ....100.00 - 150.00
   V-38059 *Hot Bones And Rice* ....100.00 - 150.00

EDDIE JOHNSON'S CRACKERJACKS:
Victor 23329 *The Duck's Yas Yas Yas* ....200.00 - 300.00

FLO JOHNSON & BEALE STREET FIVE:
Cameo 318 *Four O'Clock Blues*..................8.00 - 12.00
   319 *Sugar Blues*.................................7.00 - 10.00

GRAVEYARD JOHNSON & HIS GANG:
Supertone 9369 *Good Times Mama* ....250.00 - up
   9431 *Original Stomp*............................250.00 - up
   9432 *Shake Your Shimmy* ....250.00 - up

HAROLD JOHNSON & HIS BOYS:
Superior 2610 *Hello Beautiful* ....75.00 - 100.00
   2786 *An Evening In Caroline* ....75.00 - 100.00
   2801 *In The Shade Of The Old Apple Tree* ......100.00 - 150.00

HAVEN JOHNSON & HIS ORCHESTRA:
Vocalion 3457 *There Is No Moon* ....15.00 - 20.00

HENRY JOHNSON'S BOYS:
Gennett 6156 *Blue Hawaii*........................200.00 - 300.00
   6168 *Ash Can Stomp*...........................200.00 - 300.00
Herwin 92024 *Hawaiian Harmony Blues*..............200.00 - 300.00

J.C. JOHNSON & HIS FIVE HOT SPARKS:
Q.R.S. 7064 *Red Hot Hottentot* ....250.00 - up

JAMES P. JOHNSON; JAMES P. JOHNSON'S HARMONY EIGHT; JIMMIE JOHNSON'S JAZZ BOYS; JIMMIE/JIMMY JOHNSON & HIS BAND/ORCHESTRA:
Black Swan 2026 *The Harlem Strut* ....100.00 - 150.00
Brunswick 4712 *Crying For The Carolines* ....20.00 - 30.00
   4762 *You've Got To Be Modernistic* ....20.00 - 30.00
Cleartone P-96 *Carolina Shout*....................80.00 - 120.00
Columbia A-3950 *Weeping Blues* ....30.00 - 50.00
   2448-D *Go Harlem*.................................100.00 - 150.00

14204-D *Snowy Morning Blues* ....100.00 - 150.00
14334-D *Chicago Blues* ....150.00 - 200.00
14417-D *Fare Thee Honey Blues* ....150.00 - 200.00
14502-D *I've Found A New Baby*....................150.00 - 200.00
14668-D *A Porter's Love Song*......................250.00 - up
Okeh 4495 *Carolina Shout* ....40.00 - 60.00
   4504 *Dear Old Southland* ....75.00 - 100.00
   4937 *Toddlin'* ....75.00 - 100.00
   8770 *Riffs* ....80.00 - 120.00
Paramount 12144 *The Harlem Strut* ....100.00 - 150.00
Victor 19123 *Bleeding Hearted Blues* ....20.00 - 30.00
   V-38099 *You Don't Understand*....................75.00 - 100.00
Vocalion 4768 *Harlem Woogie*.......................20.00 - 30.00
   4903 *Back Water Blues* ....20.00 - 30.00

JOHNNY JOHNSON & HIS (POST LODGE) ORCHESTRA/STATLER PENNSYLVANIANS:
Most titles, issued contemporaneously on Banner, Conqueror,
   Melotone, Oriole, and Romeo:...........................5.00 - 10.00
Cameo 476 *Climbing Up The Scale*.......................7.00 - 10.00
   477 *WOP Blues*....................................7.00 - 10.00
   553 *My Papa Doesn't Two-Time No Time* ....7.00 - 10.00
Lincoln 2158 *WOP Blues*...............................7.00 - 10.00
Victor 21113 *Thou Swell* ....7.00 - 10.00
   21275 *The Grass Grows Greener* ....5.00 - 8.00
   22468 *On Revival Day* ....8.00 - 12.00
   22493 *What's The Use* ....8.00 - 12.00
   22516 *A Big Bouquet For You* ....8.00 - 12.00
   22525 *Sittin' On A Rainbow* ....8.00 - 12.00
   22564 *I'm A Ding Dong Daddy* ....10.00 - 15.00
Victor, most other issues.................................5.00 - 8.00
Vocalion 2811 *Rock And Roll*...........................8.00 - 12.00
   2847 *Ding Dong Daddy* ....8.00 - 12.00

LEM JOHNSON (& HIS WASHBOARD BAND):
Decca 7820 *Louise Louise* ....10.00 - 15.00
   7895 *Goin' Down Slow* ....10.00 - 15.00

LEROY JOHNSON:
Bluebird 8075 *Syncopated Swing* ....- - -

PETE JOHNSON (AND HIS BLUES TRIO/BOOGIE WOOGIE BOYS):
Blue Note 10, 11, 12 ....7.00 - 12.00
Solo Art 12004 *How Long How Long* ....20.00 - 30.00
   12005 *Pete's Blues*................................20.00 - 30.00
   12006 *B & O Blues* ....20.00 - 30.00
   12010 *Shuffle Boogie* ....20.00 - 30.00
Vocalion 4997 *Cherry Red* ....10.00 - 15.00

ROY JOHNSON'S HAPPY PALS:
Okeh 8723 *Savoy Rhythm* ....150.00 - 200.00

SAM JOHNSON & HIS ORCHESTRA:
Timely Tunes 1580 *I Found A Million Dollar Baby*....20.00 - 30.00

GRACE JOHNSTON:
Melotone 12010 *Sweet Jennie Lee!* ....8.00 - 12.00
   12032 *Them There Eyes* ....8.00 - 12.00
   12065 *Walkin' My Baby Back Home* ....10.00 - 15.00
   12095 *Keep A Song In Your Soul*....................10.00 - 15.00
   12104 *By A Lazy Country Lane* ....10.00 - 15.00
   12151 *I'm Crazy 'Bout My Baby* ....8.00 - 12.00
   12168 *One More Time* ....8.00 - 12.00

MERLE JOHNSTON & HIS CECO COURIERS:
Columbia 1968-D *Where The Sweet Forget-Me-Nots Remember*
....10.00 - 15.00
    2114-D *Watching My Dreams Go By* ....8.00 - 12.00

THE JOLLY THREE:
Vocalion 03955 *Ain't Got A Dime Blues* ....20.00 - 30.00

AL JOLSON:
Brunswick 2567, 2569, 2582, 2595, 2611, 2650,
    2671, 2743, 2763, 3013, 3014, 3183, 3196, 3222,
    3719, 3775, 3867, 3912, 4033, 4400, 4401 ....7.00 - 12.00
Brunswick 4402 *Liza* ....10.00 - 15.00
    4721 *Let Me Sing, And I'm Happy* ....10.00 - 15.00
    4722 *To My Mammy* ....10.00 - 15.00
    6500 *You Are Too Beautiful* ....25.00 - 40.00
    6502 *April Showers*...25.00 - 40.00
Columbia A-1356 *That Little German Band* ....25.00 - 40.00
    A-1374 *Pullman Porter's Parade* ....25.00 - 40.00
    A-1621 *Back To The Carolina You Love* ....15.00 - 20.00
    A-1671 *Sister Susie's Sewing Shirts For Soldiers*
....15.00 - 20.00
Columbia A-1956, A-1976, A-2007, A-2021 ....7.00 - 12.00
Columbia, most other issues ....7.00 - 12.00
Victor 17037 *That Haunting Melody*......................20.00 - 30.00
    17068 *Brass Band Ephram Jones*.......................20.00 - 30.00
    17075 *Snap Your Fingers* ....20.00 - 30.00
    17081 *Ragging The Baby To Sleep*.....................20.00 - 30.00
    17119 *That Lovin' Traumerei*..............................15.00 - 20.00
    17915 *Asleep In The Deep* ....10.00 - 15.00
(Note: See **ANONYMOUS** listing, Little Wonder 20.)

JONES' CHICAGO COSMOPOLITANS (See RICHARD M. JONES)

BILLY JONES & ERNEST HARE (See THE HAPPINESS BOYS)

BOBBY JONES & HIS NEW YORKERS/ORCHESTRA:
Buddy 8001 *Leaky Roof Blues*...........................150.00 - 200.00
Champion 15177 *Blowin' The Blues Away* ....25.00 - 40.00
    15203 *A Blues Serenade* ....50.00 - 80.00
    15294 *St. Louis Blues* ....50.00 - 80.00

CLARENCE M. JONES:
Titles on Autograph (unnumbered) are: *Modulation; Trot Along;*
    Hula Lou; Maybe ....100.00 - 150.00
Okeh 8404 *The Arm Breaker* ....250.00 - up
Paramount 12716 *'mid The Pyramids* ....150.00 - 250.00
    12747 *Hold It Boy Blues*...................................200.00 - 300.00

HANK JONES & HIS GINGER:
Champion 15338 *Neck Bones And Beans*..............200.00 - 300.00
    15437 *Ash Can Stomp*..200.00 - 300.00
    15509 *Down Home Special* ....200.00 - 300.00

HOWARD JONES & HIS ORCHESTRA:
Champion 15553 *One Step To Heaven*...................12.00 - 16.00

ISHAM JONES & HIS ORCHESTRA; ISHAM JONES' JUNIORS:
Brunswick 2423 *Memphis Blues* ....8.00 - 12.00
    2854 *River Boat Shuffle* ....8.00 - 12.00
    2877 *Poplar Street Blues* ....8.00 - 12.00
    2970 *The Original Charleston* ....10.00 - 15.00
    3027 *It's The Blues* ....8.00 - 12.00
    3204 *Three-Thirty Blues* ....8.00 - 12.00

    3695 *The Japanese Sandman* ....7.00 - 10.00
    4826 *Not A Cloud In The Sky* ....10.00 - 15.00
    4868 *Miss Hannah* ....10.00 - 15.00
    4907 *My Baby Just Cares For Me* ....8.00 - 12.00
    4909 *Sweet Jennie Lee!* ....8.00 - 12.00
    4914 *I'll Be Blue, Just Thinking Of You* ....8.00 - 12.00
    4985 *Travelin' All Alone*...................................10.00 - 15.00
    6277 *Keepin' Out Of Mischief Now* ....10.00 - 15.00
    6308 *I Can't Believe It's True* ....8.00 - 12.00
Brunswick, most other issues.................................5.00 - 10.00
Decca 170 *Out Of Space* ....8.00 - 12.00
    220 *You're O. K.* ....8.00 - 12.00
    262 *I've Found A New Baby* ....10.00 - 15.00
    300 *Jimtown Blues* ....10.00 - 15.00
    443 *China Boy*...10.00 - 15.00
    493 *Blue Room* ....10.00 - 15.00
    569 *Dallas Blues* ....10.00 - 15.00
    662 *Rock Your Blues Away* ....8.00 - 12.00
    754 *Stompin' At The Savoy* ....8.00 - 12.00
    770 *I've Had The Blues So Long* ....8.00 - 12.00
    834 *Nola* ....8.00 - 12.00
Decca 168, 169, 171, 219, 261, 327, 338, 605,
    610, 695, 704, 713 ....7.00 - 10.00
Melotone, most issues...7.00 - 10.00
Perfect, most issues ....7.00 - 10.00
Victor 24098 *Music, Music Everywhere* ....10.00 - 15.00
    24099 *Sentimental Gentleman From Georgia* .....8.00 - 12.00
    24209 *Darkness On The Delta*..........................8.00 - 12.00
    24298 *Blue Prelude*..10.00 - 15.00
    24394 *Ain't Cha Glad?* ....10.00 - 15.00
    24409 *Doin' The Uptown Lowdown* ....10.00 - 15.00
    24421 *That Dallas Man* ....10.00 - 15.00
    24496 *Got The Jitters* ....10.00 - 15.00
    24500 *Roll Out Of Bed With A Smile* ....10.00 - 15.00
    24519 *Junk Man* ....10.00 - 15.00
    24606 *I Ain't Lazy, I'm Just Dreaming* ....10.00 - 15.00
    24628 *Don't Let Your Love Go Wrong* ....10.00 - 15.00
    24649 *China Boy* ....15.00 - 20.00
    24695 *Out Of Space* ....15.00 - 20.00
    24701 *The Blue Room* ....15.00 - 20.00
Victor, most other issues..7.00 - 12.00
Vocalion, most issues..7.00 - 10.00

PIGGY JONES & HIS ORCHESTRA:
Gennett 3086 *I Miss My Swiss* ....10.00 - 15.00
    3104 *Does My Sweetie Do-And How!* ....10.00 - 15.00
    3109 *Mighty Blue*...10.00 - 15.00
    3115 *I'm Knee Deep In Daisies* ....8.00 - 12.00

RICHARD M. JONES; RICHARD M. JONES' (THREE) JAZZ MEN/WIZARDS; JONES' CHICAGO COSMOPOLITANS; RICHARD M. JONES & HIS JAZZ WIZARDS:
Bluebird 6569 *Trouble In Mind* ....20.00 - 30.00
Decca 7051 *Blue Reefer Blues* ....20.00 - 30.00
    7064 *Muggin' The Blues* ....20.00 - 30.00
    7115 *Joe Louis Chant* ....20.00 - 30.00
Gennett 5174 *Jazzin' Babies' Blues*......................80.00 - 120.00
Okeh 8260 *29th And Dearborn*............................100.00 - 150.00
    8290 *New Orleans Shags* ....100.00 - 150.00
    8349 *Mushmouth Blues*....................................200.00 - 300.00
    8390 *Baby O' Mine* ....200.00 - 300.00
    8431 *Dusty Bottom Blues* ....150.00 - 250.00
Paramount 12705 *Hot And Ready*.........................250.00 - up

Session 12-006, 12-007 ....8.00 - 12.00
Victor 20812 *Hollywood Shuffle* ....75.00 - 100.00
   20859 *Smoked Meat Blues*....................75.00 - 100.00
   21203 *Boar Hog Blues*..........................75.00 - 100.00
   21345 *African Hunch*.............................80.00 - 120.00
   V38040 *Tickle Britches Blues* ....100.00 - 150.00

SADIE JONES:
Oriole 267 *Jail House Blues* ....50.00 - 80.00

SPIKE JONES & HIS CITY SLICKERS/COUNTRY COUSINS:
Bluebird 11282 *Red Wing* ....10.00 - 15.00
   11364 *Barstool Cowboy From Old Barstow* ......10.00 - 15.00
   11466 *Clink, Clink, Another Drink*......................8.00 - 12.00
   11530 *Little Bo Peep Has Lost Her Jeep*.............8.00 - 12.00
   11560 *Come, Josephine, In My Flying Machine* ..8.00 - 12.00
   11586 *Der Fuehrer's Face (from Disney's "Der Fuehrers Face")*.............5.00 - 8.00
   11586 *Der Fuehrer's Face (from Disney's "Nuttsey Land")*
   ....15.00 - 20.00
   30-0812 *The Sheik of Araby* ....7.00 - 10.00
   30-0818 *Hotcha Cornia* ....7.00 - 10.00
   30-0821 *Behind Those Swinging Doors* ....5.00 - 8.00
Radio Recorders 8692 *Black Magic* ....- - -
   10520 *Cocktails* ....- - -
   10521 *SNAFU* ....- - -
Rainbo (unnumbered) *Happy New Year* (picture record).- - -
RCA Victor 1628, 1654, 1733, 1739, 1740, 1741,
   1762 ....5.00 - 8.00
   1836, 1893, 1894, 1895, 1983, 2023, 2092 ....5.00 - 8.00
   2093, 2118, 2245, 2375, 2507, 2537, 2592 ....5.00 - 8.00
   2861 *By The Beautiful Sea/William Tell Overture*
   ....25.00 - 50.00
   2861 *The Man On The Flying Trapeze/William Tell Overture*
   ....5.00 - 8.00
   2949, 3177, 3338, 3359, 3516, 3620 ....5.00 - 10.00
   3675, 3676, 3677 (comprise set P-277) ....5.00 - 10.00
   3741 *Riders In The Sky* (credit "Spike Jones and his City Slickers" on a single line) ....5.00 - 8.00
   3741 *Riders In The Sky* (credit "Spike Jones" is above "and his City Slickers") ....30.00 - 50.00
   3827, 3912, 3934, 3939, 4011, 4055, 4125 ....7.00 - 10.00
   4546, 4568, 4669 ....7.00 - 10.00
   4728, 4729, 4730, 4731 ....unissued?
   4875, 5015, 5067, 5107, 5239, 5320 ....7.00 - 12.00
   5413 *God Bless Us All*.............................8.00 - 12.00
   5472 *Dragnet* ....8.00 - 12.00
   5497 *Where Did My Snowman Go?* ....7.00 - 10.00
   5742 *I'm In The Mood For Love* ....5.00 - 8.00
   5920 *I Want Eddie Fisher For Christmas* ....8.00 - 12.00
   6064 *Hi Mister!*..................................8.00 - 12.00
RCA Victor D7-CB-416 *All Hail COINegie Tech!* .... - - -
(Note: First pressings of earlier RCA Victor issues are on Victor label. Many of Spike Jones' records were issued as 45 RPM, EPs, and LPs. See **RHYTHM & BLUES, ETC.** section.)

WILLIE JONES & HIS ORCHESTRA:
Gennett 6326 *Michigan Stomp* ....200.00 - 300.00
   6370 *Ragamuffin Stomp* ....200.00 - 300.00

JONES AND COLLINS ASTORIA HOT EIGHT:
Bluebird 8168 *Duet Stomp* ....15.00 - 20.00
   10952 *Damp Weather* ....15.00 - 20.00
Victor V38576 *Astoria Strut*....................150.00 - 250.00

JONES' PARAMOUNT CHARLESTON FOUR:
Paramount 12279 *Old Steady Roll* ....75.00 - 100.00

JONES-SMITH INCORPORATED:
Vocalion 3441 *Shoe-Shine Boy*................................10.00 - 15.00
   3459 *Lady Be Good* ....10.00 - 15.00

JOE JORDAN'S TEN SHARPS AND FLATS:
Banner 1821 *Morocco Blues*..............................75.00 - 100.00
Columbia 14144-D *Senegalese Stomp* ....150.00 - 200.00
Domino 3791 *Morocco Blues* ....75.00 - 100.00
Regal 8129 *Old Folks Shuffle* ....75.00 - 100.00

LOUIS JORDAN & HIS TYMPANY FIVE:
Decca 7556, 7590, 7609, 7623, 7675, 7693, 7705,
   7719, 7723, 7729, 7745, 7777..........................7.00 - 12.00
Decca (blue label, most other issues) ....7.00 - 10.00
Decca (black label, most issues) ....5.00 - 8.00

TAFT JORDAN AND THE MOB:
Titles issued contemporaneously on Banner, Conqueror, Melotone, Oriole, Perfect, and Romeo: *Devil In The Moon; If The Moon Turns Green; Louisiana Fairy Tale; Night Wind* ....7.00 - 12.00

JIMMIE/JIMMY JOY'S (BAKER ST. ANTHONY HOTEL) ORCHESTRA:
Brunswick 3905 *From Monday On* ....8.00 - 12.00
   3959 *I Got Worry* ....8.00 - 12.00
   3960 *Today Is Today*............................8.00 - 12.00
   4640 *Harmonica Harry*...........................8.00 - 12.00
Okeh 40251 *Milenberg Joys* ....75.00 - 100.00
   40329 *Clarinet Marmalade Blues*....................100.00 - 150.00
   40381 *China Girl* ....30.00 - 50.00
   40388 *Riverboat Shuffle* ....80.00 - 120.00
   40420 *Wild Jazz* ....75.00 - 100.00
   40484 *Springtime Is Love Time* ....30.00 - 50.00
   40494 *Fallin' Down* ....75.00 - 100.00
   40504 *Everybody* Stomp ....75.00 - 100.00
   40539 *St. Louis Blues*............................75.00 - 100.00
   40627 *Stomp It, Mr. Kelly* ....80.00 - 130.00

TEDDY JOYCE & HIS PENN STAGE RECORDERS:
Harmony 1009-H *Collegiate Sam*............................10.00 - 15.00
(Note: Also issued on Diva and Velvet Tone.)

THE JUNGLE BAND:
Brunswick 4238 *Tiger Rag* ....20.00 - 30.00
   4309 *Paducah* ....20.00 - 30.00
   4345 *Doin' The Voom Voom* ....25.00 - 35.00
   4450 *Dog Bottom* ....25.00 - 35.00
   4492 *Jungle Jamboree* ....25.00 - 35.00
   4760 *Sweet Mama* ....25.00 - 35.00
   4776 *Maori* ....20.00 - 30.00
   4783 *Double Check Stomp* ....20.00 - 30.00
   4887 *Wall Street Wail* ....25.00 - 35.00
   4936 *St. Louis Blues* ....30.00 - 50.00
   4952 *Runnin' Wild* ....20.00 - 30.00
   6003 *Wang Wang Blues*............................20.00 - 30.00
   6038 *Rockin' In Rhythm* ....15.00 - 20.00

JUNGLE KINGS:
Paramount 12654 *Friars Point Shuffle* ....300.00 - up

JUNGLE TOWN STOMPERS:
Okeh 8686 *Slow As Molasses* ....100.00 - 150.00

ART KAHN (& HIS ORCHESTRA):
Titles issued contemporaneously on Banner, Melotone, Oriole, Perfect, and Romeo: *The Gold-diggers' Song; Pettin' In The Park* ....7.00 - 10.00
Columbia 16-D *Sobbin' Blues* ....15.00 - 20.00
   45-D *Bahama* ....15.00 - 20.00
   104-D *Blue Evening Blues* ....10.00 - 15.00
   221-D *Off And Gone* ....10.00 - 15.00
   310-D *Lucky Kentucky*.....................................10.00 - 15.00
   468-D *Back Home In Illinois* ....8.00 - 12.00
   624-D *Hobo's Prayer* ....15.00 - 25.00
   716-D *Hello Baby* ....10.00 - 15.00
   769-D *Hoodle Dee Doo Doodoo* ....10.00 - 15.00
   830-D *He's The Last Word* ....8.00 - 12.00
Columbia, other issues...5.00 - 8.00
Conqueror 8279 *I'll Be Faithful* ....7.00 - 10.00
Melotone 12090 *I'm Happy When You're Happy* ...15.00 - 20.00
   12415, 12568, 12660, 12692 ....7.00 - 10.00
Okeh 40857 *When Day Is Done* ....15.00 - 20.00
Supertone 9334 *Blue Night*..................................20.00 - 30.00

ROGER WOLFE KAHN & HIS ORCHESTRA:
Brunswick 4374 *Pretty Little Thing* ....10.00 - 15.00
   4479 *Do What You Do*......................................8.00 - 12.00
   4571 *Then You've Never Been Blue* ....8.00 - 12.00
   4699 *Cooking Breakfast For The One I Love*.....10.00 - 15.00
   4742 *Exactly Like You* ....10.00 - 15.00
   4811 *Into My Heart* ....8.00 - 12.00
   4826 *Cheer Up (Good Times Are Comin')*.........10.00 - 15.00
Brunswick 4583, 4600, 4614, 4750 ....5.00 - 10.00
Columbia 2653-D *Lazy Day* ....15.00 - 20.00
   2662-D *There I Go Dreaming Again*..................15.00 - 20.00
   2695-D *You've Got Me In The Palm Of Your Hand* ....15.00 - 20.00
   2697-D *Another Night Alone* ....15.00 - 20.00
   2722-D *It Don't Mean A Thing (If It Ain't Got That Swing)* ....20.00 - 30.00
   2726-D *Fit As A Fiddle*.....................................15.00 - 20.00
Victor 19616 *Hot-Hot-Hottentot* ....8.00 - 12.00
   19808 *Look Who's Here!*...................................8.00 - 12.00
   19845 *I Never Knew* ....8.00 - 12.00
   19851 *You Told Me To Go*.................................10.00 - 15.00
   19860 *Lucky Boy*..8.00 - 12.00
   19866 *Down And Out Blues* ....10.00 - 15.00
   19935 *A Cup of Coffee, A Sandwich And You* ......8.00 - 12.00
   19939 *Looking For A Boy*..................................8.00 - 12.00
   19942 *Baby* ....8.00 - 12.00
   20059 *Somebody's Lonely* ....8.00 - 12.00
   20379 *Wouldn't You?* ....8.00 - 12.00
   20466 *Yankee Rose*...10.00 - 15.00
   20493 *A Little Birdie Told Me So* ....10.00 - 15.00
   20573 *Following You Around* ....7.00 - 10.00
   20634 *Just The Same* ....8.00 - 12.00
   20717 *Where The Wild, Wild Flowers Grow* ....8.00 - 12.00
   21233 *Let A Smile Be Your Umbrella* ....8.00 - 12.00
   21326 *She's A Great, Great Girl*........................10.00 - 15.00
   21368 *Crazy Rhythm*...8.00 - 12.00
   21425 *Give Me The Sunshine* ....8.00 - 12.00
   21507 *Say "Yes" Today*......................................8.00 - 12.00
   21801 *A Room With A View*...............................8.00 - 12.00
Victor, most other issues..5.00 - 10.00

ELMER KAISER & HIS BALLROOM ORCHESTRA:
Autograph (unnumbered) *Monkey Business*............75.00 - 100.00

CHARLES KALEY (& HIS ORCHESTRA):
Columbia 886-D *Muddy Water* ....7.00 - 10.00
   910-D *Alabama Stomp*......................................10.00 - 15.00
   1408-D *My Blue Ridge Mountain Home* ....15.00 - 20.00.
   1541-D *I'm Waiting For Ships That Never Come In* ....7.00 - 10.00

HELEN KANE:
Victor 21557, 21684, 21830, 21863, 21917, 22080 . 7.00 - 12.00
Victor 22192 *Ain't cha?*......................................8.00 - 12.00
   22397 *Thank Your Father* ....8.00 - 12.00
   22407 *Dangerous Nan McGrew* ....8.00 - 12.00
   22475 *My Man Is On The Make* ....8.00 - 12.00
   22520 *Readin' Ritin' Rhythm*.............................8.00 - 12.00

KANSAS CITY FIVE/FOUR/SIX:
Ajax 17072 *Louisville Blues* ....75.00 - 100.00
   17078 *Believe Me, Hot Mama* ....75.00 - 100.00
   17128 *Dark Gal Blues* ....75.00 - 100.00
Commodore (most issues) ....7.00 - 10.00
Pathe-Actuelle 036175 *Get Yourself A Monkey Man* ....50.00 - 80.00
   36355 *Get It Fixed* ....75.00 - 100.00
   36366 *Growin' Old Blues* ....75.00 - 100.00
Perfect 14356 *Get Yourself A Monkey Man* ....50.00 - 80.00
   14377 *Louisville Blues* ....75.00 - 100.00
   14516 *Dark Gal Blues* ....75.00 - 100.00
   14547 *Jake's Weary Blues* ....75.00 - 100.00

KANSAS CITY FRANK (AND HIS FOOTWARMERS):
Brunswick 7062 *Jelly Roll Stomp* ....100.00 - 150.00
Paramount 12898 *Wailing Blues*...........................200.00 - 300.00
   14026 *Blue Slug* ....8.00 - 12.00

KANSAS CITY (TIN ROOF) STOMPERS:
Brunswick 7066 *Aunt Jemima Stomp* ....200.00 - 300.00
   7091 *Shanghai Honeymoon* ....200.00 - 300.00

(BERT) KAPLAN & HIS COLLEGIANS/ORCHESTRA:
Bell 453 *In A Little Spanish Town* ....7.00 - 10.00
   474 *Lonely Eyes* ....7.00 - 10.00
   476 *Do-Do-Do* ....7.00 - 10.00
   489 *I'm Looking Over A Four Leaf Clover* ....7.00 - 10.00
   508 *I'll Just Go Along* ....7.00 - 10.00
Emerson 3078 *How I Love You* ....7.00 - 10.00
   3080 *If I'd Only Believed In You* ....7.00 - 10.00
   3116 *At Sundown* ....7.00 - 10.00
   3136 *Side By Side*..7.00 - 10.00
(Note: Other issues on Bell and Emerson are similarly valued.)

DAVE KAPLAN & HIS ORCHESTRA; KAPLAN'S MELODISTS:
Edison 51713 *Oh! You Lulu Belle* ....10.00 - 15.00
   51899 *Hello Bluebird* ....10.00 - 15.00
   52058 *Sweet Marie* ....30.00 - 50.00
   52091 *It's A Million To One You're In Love* .....20.00 - 30.00
   52106 *Good News* ....20.00 - 30.00
   52108 *Barbara* ....75.00 - 100.00
   52147 *My New York* ....100.00 - 150.00
   52170 *Lady Of Havana* ....15.00 - 20.00
   52234 *Golden Gate* ....20.00 - 30.00
   52304 *You May Be Right-You May Be Wrong*... 20.00 - 30.00
   52595 *Am I A Passing Fancy?*...........................25.00 - 40.00
Edison, most other issues.......................................5.00 - 10.00

GENE KARDOS & HIS ORCHESTRA:

Titles issued contemporaneously on Banner, Conqueror, Melotone, Oriole, Perfect, and Romeo: *Did You Ever See A Dream Walking?; Good Morning, Glory; Many Moons Ago; You're Such A Comfort To Me* ....8.00 - 12.00
Most other titles ....5.00 - 10.00
Victor 22790 *China Boy* ....20.00 - 30.00
   22792 *Waiting For The Moon* ....15.00 - 20.00
   22840 *A Hot Dog, A Blanket, And You*................8.00 - 12.00
   22843 *You've Got To Sell It*................8.00 - 12.00
   22863 *Sweet Violets* ....8.00 - 12.00
   22865 *Now's The Time To Fall In Love* ....10.00 - 15.00
   22897 *Tell Tales* ....8.00 - 12.00
   22899 *Business In "F"* ....10.00 - 15.00
   22918 *Fate Introduced Me To You*......................7.00 - 10.00
   22920 *Alexander's Ragtime Band* ....10.00 - 15.00
   22957 *Sailin' On The Robert E. Lee*................10.00 - 15.00
   22986 *My Extraordinary Gal* ....10.00 - 15.00
   24006 *I Can't Believe That It's You* ....8.00 - 12.00
   24081 *Sing* ....10.00 - 15.00
   24122 *San* ....15.00 - 20.00

ART KARLE & HIS BOYS:

Vocalion 3146 *Moon Over Miami*..........................15.00 - 20.00
   3147 *Lights Out* ....15.00 - 20.00

BETTY KASHMAN:

Okeh 8942 *Hoochee Miss Lou*..................................75.00 - 100.00

ART KASSEL'S IN THE AIR; ART KASSEL & HIS ORCHESTRA:

Bluebird 7669 *Sobbin' Blues* ....15.00 - 20.00
Bluebird, most other issues................5.00 - 8.00
Columbia 2636-D *Sing A New Song* ....10.00 - 15.00
   2643-D *Strangers* ....8.00 - 12.00
   2682-D *Hell's Bells* ....15.00 - 20.00
   2687-D *Rain, Rain, Go Away* ....10.00 - 15.00
   2742-D *Moon Song* ....8.00 - 12.00
   2743-D *Chewing Gum* ....8.00 - 12.00
   2745-D *(Where Will You Be) In 1933?* ....8.00 - 12.00
   2765-D *Chant Of The Swamp*......................20.00 - 30.00
Victor 21884, 21885 ....7.00 - 10.00
Vogue R714 *Doodle Doo Doo* ....20.00 - 30.00
   R723 *Wave To Me My Lady* ....30.00 - 50.00
   R734 *A Little Consideration*................25.00 - 40.00
   R770 *The Wiffenpoof Song* ....20.00 - 30.00
   R771 *Jeannine* ....20.00 - 30.00
   R780 *Touch Me Not*................25.00 - 35.00
   R781 *Sooner Or Later* ....25.00 - 35.00
   R784 *Queen For A Day (rare)**
*A sale in excess of $11,000 has been reported.
   R785 *The Echo Said No*................25.00 - 35.00

AL KATZ AND HIS KITTENS:

Victor 20081 *Ace In The Hole* ....10.00 - 15.00

IRVING KAUFMAN:

Banner 1720 *After I Say I'm Sorry* ....7.00 - 10.00
   1723 *Say It Again* ....7.00 - 10.00
   1756 *Tonight's My Night With Baby*...................7.00 - 10.00
   6015 *Oh! Constantine* ....8.00 - 12.00
(Foregoing titles on Conqueror, Domino, and Regal, similarly valued)
   6323 *St. Louis Blues* ....15.00 - 20.00
   6508 *St. Louis Blues* ....10.00 - 15.00

Challenge 554 *Henry's Made A Lady Out Of Lizzie*. 7.00 - 10.00
Harmony 424-H *Vo-Do-Do-De-O Blues* .... 7.00 - 10.00
   440-H *Who-oo? You-oo, That's Who!* .... 7.00 - 10.00
Okeh 41230 *You Were Meant For Me* .... 10.00 - 15.00
   41412 *Let Me Sing And I'm Happy*................. 10.00 - 15.00
Perfect 12432 *Every Evening* .... 10.00 - 15.00
Q. R. S. 1012 *Blowin' Off Steam* .... 10.00 - 15.00
   1031 *Blue Turning Grey Over You* .... 10.00 - 15.00
Vocalion 14950 *Nobody Knows What A Red Head Mama Can Do* .... 8.00 - 12.00
   15024 *Red Hot Henry Brown*............................. 8.00 - 12.00

JACK KAUFMAN (& THE 7 BLUE BABIES):

Banner 6492 *My Wife Is On A Diet*........................... 8.00 - 12.00
   7142 *Mama's Grown Young, Papa's Grown Old* ...8.00 - 12.00
(Above titles also on Domino and Regal, similarly valued)
Cameo 8115 *I Scream-You Scream-We All Scream For Ice-Cream* .... 8.00 - 12.00
   8145 *I've Got Nothin'-You've Got Nothin'-We Ain't Got Nothin'* .... 8.00 - 12.00
   8197 *When A Blonde Makes Up Her Mind*.......... 8.00 - 12.00
   8272 *Oh! You Have No Idea* .... 8.00 - 12.00
   8273 *That's My Weakness Now* .... 8.00 - 12.00
   8274 *You've Got To Give 'Em Something* .... 8.00 - 12.00
   8311 *I Should Shay Sho!* .... 8.00 - 12.00
   9013 *Oh, Boy! It's A Pleasure* .... 8.00 - 12.00
   9089 *What Good Is A Sandwich (If It Hasn't Any Bread)* .... 8.00 - 12.00
   9100 *I'm Wild About Horns On Automobiles* ..... 8.00 - 12.00
   9210 *He Always Goes Farther Than Father*........ 8.00 - 12.00
(Foregoing titles on Romeo, similarly valued)
Edison 52209 *The Grass Grows Greener* .... 50.00 - 80.00
   52298 *What's The Color Of A Yellow Horse?* ... 50.00 - 80.00
   52323 *Since She Learned To Ride A Horse* .... 50.00 - 80.00
   52364 *That's My Weakness Now* .... 50.00 - 80.00
   52405 *Nagasaki* .... 50.00 - 80.00
Perfect 12450 *She's A Great, Great Girl* .... 8.00 - 12.00

WHITEY KAUFMAN'S ORIGINAL PENNSYLVANIA SERENADERS; WHITEY KAUFMAN & HIS ORCHESTRA:

Victor 19127 *Henpecked Blues*................................. 7.00 - 10.00
   19304 *Charleston Cabin* .... 7.00 - 10.00
   19384 *Come On, Red* .... 7.00 - 10.00
   19638 *Who Takes Care Of The Caretakers Daughter?* .... 8.00 - 12.00
   19673 *My Girl*... 7.00 - 10.00
   19834 *Paddlin' Madelin' Home* .... 10.00 - 15.00
   19996 *Tamiami Trail* .... 7.00 - 10.00
   20125 *Deep River Blues*.................................... 8.00 - 12.00

DOLLY KAY:

Columbia 102-D *Mindin' My Business*................... 10.00 - 15.00
   117-D *Someday, Sweetheart* .... 10.00 - 15.00
   151-D *Hard Hearted Hannah* .... 10.00 - 15.00
   A3534 *Got To Have My Daddy Blues* .... 8.00 - 12.00
   A3644 *Buzz Mirandy* .... 10.00 - 15.00
   A3664 *Lonesome Longin' Blues* .... 10.00 - 15.00
   A3692 *I'm Nobody's Gal* .... 10.00 - 15.00
   A3758 *Hot Lips* .... 8.00 - 12.00
   A3808 *You've Got To See Mama Ev'ry Night*..... 8.00 - 12.00
   A3828 *Seven Or Eleven* .... 8.00 - 12.00
   A3882 *Don't Think You'll Be Missed* .... 8.00 - 12.00
   A3955 *Oh! Sister, Ain't That Hot!*...................... 8.00 - 12.00
   A3980 *The Gold-Digger* .... 10.00 - 15.00

Harmony 268-H *How Could Red Riding Hood?* .... 8.00 - 12.00
Vocalion 15664 *A Good Man Is Hard To Find* .... 50.00 - 80.00

SWING AND SWAY WITH SAMMY KAYE; SAMMY KAYE AND HIS ORCHESTRA:

Titles issued contemporaneously on Banner, Conqueror, Melotone, Oriole, Perfect, and Romeo: *After You; Alibi Baby; Avalon; Cry, Baby, Cry; The Dipsy Doodle; Dreamy Eyes; Good Mornin'; Have You Met Miss Jones?; If I Can Count On You; If You Were Someone Else; Indiana; It Looks Like Rain In Cherry Blossom Lane; Josephine; Moonlight On The Highway; My Buddy, Night and Day; Rosalie; Somebody Loves Me; So You Won't Sing; A Strange Loneliness; Swing Is Here To Stay; True Confession; We'll Ride The Tide Together; What Makes You So Sweet?*
.... 5.00 - 10.00
Victor, most issues .... 4.00 - 8.00
Vocalion, most issues .... 5.00 - 10.00

JOE KAYSER AND HIS NOVELTY ORCHESTRA:
Gennett Personal (unnumbered) *Everybody Step* .... - - -

LLOYD KEATING AND HIS MUSIC/ORCHESTRA:
Clarion 5045-C *I Love You So Much* .... 7.00 - 10.00
5103-C *I'll Be Blue* .... 8.00 - 12.00
5186-C *You're Driving Me Crazy* .... 10.00 - 15.00
5322-C *Wrap Your Troubles In Dreams* .... 10.00 - 15.00
5328-C *Sweet And Hot* .... 10.00 - 15.00
5334-C *Under Your Window Tonight* .... 10.00 - 15.00
5339-C *Sing A Little Jingle* .... 10.00 - 15.00
5350-C *I'm Keepin' Company* .... 10.00 - 15.00
5355-C *Let's Drink A Drink To The Future* ...... 10.00 - 15.00
5362-C *My Sweet Tooth Says I Wanna* .... 10.00 - 15.00
5368-C *There's No Depression In Love* .... 10.00 - 15.00
5379-C *I Apologize* .... 8.00 - 12.00
5386-C *Can't You See* .... 8.00 - 12.00
5407-C *You Try Somebody Else* .... 15.00 - 20.00
11002-C *Love Letters In The Sand* .... 15.00 - 20.00
(Note: 11002-C is a "double track" record, with instrumental and vocal versions of the same title occupying the same playing surface.)
Diva 3052-G *Low Down Rhythm* .... 10.00 - 15.00
3118-G *Sing You Sinners* .... 8.00 - 12.00
Harmony 1052-H *Low Down Rhythm* .... 10.00 - 15.00
1053-H *Turn On The Heat* .... 8.00 - 12.00
1143-H *Strike Up The Band!* .... 8.00 - 12.00
1145-H *Looking At You Across The Breakfast Table*
.... 8.00 - 12.00
1146-H *I'm In The Market For You* .... 8.00 - 12.00
1181-H *I Love You So Much* .... 7.00 - 10.00
1233-H *I'll Be Blue* .... 8.00 - 12.00
1246-H *I'm Tickled Pink With A Blue-Eyed Baby*. 10.00 - 15.00
1251-H *You're Driving Me Crazy!* .... 10.00 - 15.00
1252-H *I Hate Myself* .... 8.00 - 12.00
1274-H *Keep A Song In Your Soul* .... 10.00 - 15.00
1290-H *Sweet And Hot* .... 10.00 - 15.00
1323-H *Wrap Your Troubles In Dreams* ...... 10.00 - 15.00
1326-H *Under Your Window Tonight* .... 10.00 - 15.00
1339-H *I'm Keepin' Company* .... 10.00 - 15.00
1343-H *Let's Drink A Drink To The Future* ...... 10.00 - 15.00
1350-H *My Sweet Tooth Says I Wanna* .... 10.00 - 15.00
1356-H *There's A Time And Place For Everything*
.... 10.00 - 15.00
1367-H *As Time Goes By* .... 10.00 - 15.00
1372-H *Can't You See* .... 8.00 - 12.00

1388-H *You Try Somebody Else* .... 15.00 - 20.00
6501-H *An Evening In Caroline* .... 10.00 - 15.00
6502-H *Ooh! That Kiss* .... 10.00 - 15.00
Velvet Tone 2394-V *Sweet And Hot* .... 10.00 - 15.00
2388-V *Wrap Your Troubles In Dreams* .... 10.00 - 15.00
2398-V *Under Your Window Tonight* .... 10.00 - 15.00
2414-V *I'm Keepin' Company* .... 10.00 - 15.00
2419-V *Let's Drink A Drink To The Future* ...... 10.00 - 15.00
2426-V *My Sweet Tooth Says I Wanna* .... 10.00 - 15.00
2432-V *There's No Depression In Love*
.... 10.00 - 15.00
2443-V *I Apologize* .... 8.00 - 12.00
2450-V *Can't You See* .... 8.00 - 12.00
2467-V *You Try Somebody Else* .... 15.00 - 20.00
10501-V *An Evening In Caroline* .... 10.00 - 15.00
10502-V *Oooh! That Kiss* .... 10.00 - 15.00

EDDIE KELLY'S WASHBOARD BAND:
Bluebird 7127 *Come On 'Round To My House* ...... 25.00 - 35.00
7134 *Corrina, I'm Goin' Away* .... 25.00 - 35.00
7148 *Shim Shaming* .... 15.00 - 20.00
7204 *Blues In The Rain* .... 25.00 - 35.00
7277 *Goin' Back To Alabama* .... 30.00 - 50.00

GEORGE KELLY: (See THE ORIGINAL SIX)

HAL KEMP AND HIS ORCHESTRA (from THE UNIVERSITY OF NORTH CAROLINA):
Brunswick 3486 *Brown Sugar* .... 10.00 - 15.00
3536 *Go, Joe, Go* .... 10.00 - 15.00
3792 *If I Can't Have You* .... 7.00 - 10.00
3841 *Who's Blue Now?* .... 7.00 - 10.00
3863 *She's A Great, Great Girl* .... 7.00 - 10.00
3937 *I Don't Care* .... 8.00 - 12.00
3954 *Oh, Baby!* .... 8.00 - 12.00
4078 *Washington And Lee Swing* .... 10.00 - 15.00
4151 *My Troubles Are Over* .... 7.00 - 10.00
4212 *My Lucky Star* .... 7.00 - 10.00
4307 *That's What I Call Heaven* .... 7.00 - 10.00
4327 *That's You, Baby* .... 7.00 - 10.00
4388 *To Be In Love* .... 7.00 - 10.00
4424 *In The Hush Of The Night* .... 7.00 - 10.00
4580 *I Gotta Have You* .... 8.00 - 12.00
4612 *A Little Kiss Each Morning* .... 8.00 - 12.00
4674 *H'lo Baby* .... 15.00 - 25.00
4676 *Navy Blues* .... 8.00 - 12.00
4805 *Washin' The Blues From My Soul* .... 8.00 - 12.00
4807 *If I Had A Girl Like You* .... 8.00 - 12.00
4988 *Fraternity Blues* .... 10.00 - 15.00
4992 *Them There Eyes* .... 8.00 - 12.00
6055 *Would You Like To Take A Walk?* .... 7.00 - 10.00
6056 *I Want You For Myself* .... 7.00 - 10.00
6071 *Little Joe* .... 7.00 - 10.00
6108 *Moonlight Saving Time* .... 8.00 - 12.00
6110 *Whistles* .... 8.00 - 12.00
6130 *I'm Keepin' Company* .... 8.00 - 12.00
6416, 6419, 6436, 6437, 6452, 6471, 6487, 6492, 6528, 6532, 6568, 6574, 6582, 6583, 6587, 6598, 6605, 6609, 6613, 6616, 6636, 6648, 6656, 6703, 6707, 6790 .... 5.00 - 10.00

6925, 6943, 6947, 6974, 6985, 7315, 7317, 7319,
7322, 7334, 7343, 7351, 7357, 7360, 7369, 7370,
7385, 7388, 7404, 7413, 7429, 7434, 7437, 7458,
7493, 7503, 7509, 7517, 7552, 7553, 7565, 7566,
7578, 7587, 7589, 7600, 7601, 7626, 7630, 7634,
7636, 7668, 7681, 7707, 7711, 7720, 7730, 7745,
7749, 7766, 7769, 7775, 7783, 7812, 7830, 7854,
7865, 7883 ....5.00 - 8.00
Columbia 671-D *Peg Leg Stomp* ....40.00 - 60.00
Victor, most issues...............................5.00 - 10.00

HERMAN KENIN & HIS AMBASSADOR/MULTNOMAH HOTEL ORCHESTRA:
Victor 20725 *Pretty Little Thing*..............8.00 - 12.00
20782 *Some Other Day*.........................7.00 - 10.00
21313 *Persian Rug* ....5.00 - 8.00
21314 *Rose Of Monterey* ....10.00 - 15.00
21336 *When Love Comes Stealing* ....7.00 - 10.00
21568 *There's Somebody New* ....7.00 - 10.00
21980 *After Thinking It Over*.................7.00 - 10.00
21991 *Building A Nest For Mary* ....7.00 - 10.00
22005 *He's A Good Man To Have Around* ....8.00 - 12.00
22006 *There's A Place In The Sun For You* ....7.00 - 10.00
22016 *I'm Doin' What I'm Doin' For Love* .....7.00 - 10.00
22058 *If I Had My Way* ....7.00 - 10.00

FRANK KENNEDY & CO.:
Okeh 4039 *Mutt And Jeff In Mexico* ....7.00 - 10.00
4317 *Mutt and Jeff In A Shooting Gallery*.....7.00 - 10.00

JOE KENNEDY & HIS RHYTHM ORCHESTRA:
Bluebird 6062 *Double Trouble* ....15.00 - 20.00
6080 *Rosetta* ....15.00 - 20.00
6102 *I Never Knew* ....15.00 - 25.00
6233 *Rhythm Is Our Business* ....15.00 - 20.00
6245 *You Can Depend On Me* ....15.00 - 20.00

KEN KENNY & HIS ORCHESTRA:
Champion 40100 *Let Yourself Go* ....10.00 - 15.00
40101 *Misty Islands Of The Highlands* ....10.00 - 15.00
40107 *What's The Name Of That Song?* ....10.00 - 15.00

THE KENTUCKY BLOWERS:
Gennett 5517 *Rambling Blues* ....15.00 - 20.00
5602 *Choo Choo* ....15.00 - 20.00

THE KENTUCKY COLONELS:
Vocalion 14697 *Mama Loves Papa (Papa Loves Mama)* ...8.00 - 12.00
14714 *Learn To Do The Strut* ....10.00 - 15.00
14738 *I'm Goin' South* ....8.00 - 12.00
14748 *If You'll Come Back* ....8.00 - 12.00

KENTUCKY GRASSHOPPERS:
Banner 6295 *Four Or Five Times*...............15.00 - 20.00
6323 *Icky Blues*..............................15.00 - 20.00
6355 *Tiger Rag* ....15.00 - 20.00
6358 *Sweet Liza* ....15.00 - 20.00
6360 *Makin' Friends* ....15.00 - 20.00
Conqueror 7303 *Icky Blues*....................15.00 - 20.00

KENTUCKY HOT HOPPERS:
Pathe-Actuelle 36841 *Red Head Blues*..........15.00 - 20.00
Perfect 15022 *Red Head Blues* ....15.00 - 20.00

KENTUCKY JAZZ BABIES:
Victor V38616 *Old Folks Shake* ....300.00 - up

KENTUCKY JUG BAND:
Vocalion 1564 *Walkin' Cane Stomp*.............200.00 - 300.00

KENTUCKY SERENADERS:
Regal 9134 *Shake It And Break It*.............20.00 - 30.00
9139 *My Sunny Tennessee* ....10.00 - 15.00
9143 *Gypsy Blues*.............................10.00 - 15.00

FREDDIE KEPPARD'S JAZZ CARDINALS:
Paramount 12399 *Stock Yards Strut* ....500.00 - up

CHARLIE KERR'S ORCHESTRA; KERR'S FAMOUS PLAYERS:
Edison 51147 *In A Caravan* ....10.00 - 15.00
51164 *No One Loves You Better Than Your M-A-M-M-Y* ...10.00 - 15.00
51167 *Mad ('Cause You Treat Me This Way)* ..15.00 - 20.00
51194 *Opehelia* ....15.00 - 20.00
Gennett 3219 *What Did I Tell Ya?*.............30.00 - 50.00

FRANK KEYES & HIS ORCHESTRA:
Perfect 15142 *I Get The Blues When It Rains*..........8.00 - 12.00
15358 *Just A Little Dance, Mam'selle*.........25.00 - 40.00

KEYSTONE SERENADERS:
Vocalion 15122 *Ev'rything Is Hotsy Totsy Now* ....10.00 - 15.00
15123 *I'm Knee-Deep In Daisies* ....8.00 - 12.00
15124 *The Co-Ed* ....8.00 - 12.00

KING BRADY'S CLARINET BAND:
Champion 15455 *Lazybone Blues*................200.00 - 300.00
15491 *Embarrassment Blues* ....250.00 - up
Gennett 6393 *Embarrassment Blues*.............300.00 - up

KING DAVID'S JUG BAND:
Okeh 8861 *Georgia Bo Bo*......................200.00 - 300.00
8901 *Sweet Potato Blues*......................200.00 - 300.00
8913 *Rising Sun Blues* ....200.00 - 300.00

KING GEORGE (AND QUEEN MARY) OF ENGLAND:
Victor 19072 *Empire Day Messages* ....7.00 - 10.00
22338 *At the opening of the five-power naval conference* ...7.00 - 10.00

KING MUTT AND HIS TENNESSEE THUMPERS:
Gennett 6796 *Nut House Stomp* ....500.00 - up
6844 *Good Time Mama* ....500.00 - up

CHUCK KING & HIS KENTUCKIANS:
Champion 15456 *Isabella (Tell Your Fella)*...........20.00 - 30.00
15458 *Caroline* ....25.00 - 40.00
15459 *Green River Blues* ....20.00 - 30.00

FRANCES KING:
Okeh 40854 *She's Got It* .... 10.00 - 15.00

HENRY KING AND HIS ORCHESTRA:
Columbia 2941-D, 2945-D, 2949-D, 2950-D,
    2991-D, 2992-D, 2998-D, 3005-D, 3010-D,
    3036-D, 3042-D, 3049-D .... 7.00 - 12.00
Decca, most issues .... 4.00 - 8.00
Victor 24457, 24466, 24478, 24608, 24612,
    24647, 24656 .... 7.00 - 12.00
Vocalion 2550, 2561, 2562, 2573, 2579, 2580 .... 7.00 - 12.00

REX KING & HIS SOVEREIGNS:
Clarion, most issues .... 5.00 - 8.00
Odeon ONY-36204 *African Lament* .... 25.00 - 40.00
Velvet Tone, most issues .... 5.00 - 8.00

ROY KING & HIS ORCHESTRA:
Romeo 369 *Pardon The Glove* .... 15.00 - 20.00

TEMPO KING AND HIS KINGS OF TEMPO:
Titles issued contemporaneously on Banner, Conqueror, Melotone,
    Oriole, Perfect, Romeo, and Vocalion: *Alligator Crawl; All Over*
    Nothing At All; Am I Dreaming?; Don't You Know Or Don't You
    Care?; The Folks Who Live On The Hill; High, Wide And
    Handsome; I Can Always Dream: I'm Gonna Put You In Your
    Place; On With The Dance; The One Rose; Riding On The Old
    Ferris Wheel; You've Got Me Under Your Thumb
    .... 7.00 - 12.00
Bluebird 6335, 6534, 6553, 6560, 6563, 6575, 6637,
    6642, 6643, 6684, 6687, 6688, 6721, 6725, 6758,
    6768, 6770, 6880 .... 7.00 - 12.00
Vocalion 3716, 4073, 4156 .... 7.00 - 12.00

WAYNE KING & HIS ORCHESTRA:
Brunswick, most issues, 6000 series .... 5.00 - 8.00
RCA Victor L-16000 *Home; Save The Last Dance For Me*
    .... 10.00 - 15.00
(Note: Above title is a "Program Transcription," 33-1/3 RPM)
Victor 22240 *Sally* .... 7.00 - 10.00
    22256 *Put A Little Salt On The Bluebird's Tail* ... 7.00 - 10.00
    22278 *Somebody Mighty Like You* .... 15.00 - 25.00
    22642 *Hello, Beautiful!* .... 7.00 - 10.00
    22643 *Dream A Little Dream Of Me* .... 7.00 - 10.00
    22656 *Star Dust* .... 10.00 - 15.00
    22979 *Way Down Between Dem Rows (A Pickin' Dat Cotton)*
    .... 20.00 - 30.00
    24137 *Forbidden Love* .... 20.00 - 30.00
Victor, most other 22000 series, and subsequent issues
    .... 5.00 - 10.00

THE KING'S JESTERS (AND LOUISE):
Bluebird 5149 *After You've Gone* .... 8.00 - 12.00
    5184 *China Boy* .... 8.00 - 12.00
(Note: Above titles on Electradisk are valued somewhat higher; on
    Sunrise, substantially higher.)
Bluebird 6517 *Some Of These Days* .... 8.00 - 12.00
Vogue R-708 *I Surrender, Dear* .... 75.00 - 100.00
    R-716 *Mean To Me* .... 500.00 - up
    R-750 *Who's Got A Tent For Rent* .... 50.00 - 80.00
    R-751 *Humphrey, The Sweet Singing Pig* ...... 75.00 - 100.00
    R-766 *Sepulveda* .... 30.00 - 50.00

KIRBY'S KINGS OF JAZZ:
Bell 589 *Oh! Daisy* .... 20.00 - 30.00
    591 *Green River Blues* .... 20.00 - 30.00

    592 *Isabella (Tell Your Fella)* .... 20.00 - 30.00
    598 *Caroline* .... 20.00 - 30.00

JOHN KIRBY & HIS ONYX CLUB BOYS/ORCHESTRA:
Decca 2216 *Undecided* .... 8.00 - 12.00
    2367 *Pastel Blue* .... 8.00 - 12.00
Okeh 4624, 4653, 4890, 5048, 5187, 5520, 5542,
    5570, 5605, 5632, 5661, 5705, 5761, 5805 .... 7.00 - 12.00
Victor 27568, 27598, 27667, 27712, 27890, 27926   7.00 - 10.00
Vocalion 4624, 4653, 4890, 5048, 5187, 5520,
    5542, 5570 .... 7.00 - 12.00

ANDY KIRK & HIS TWELVE CLOUDS OF JOY:
Brunswick 4653 *Casey Jones Special* .... 50.00 - 75.00
    4694 *Blue Clarinet Stomp* .... 50.00 - 75.00
    4803 *I Lost My Gal From Memphis* .... 40.00 - 60.00
    4863 *Once Or Twice* .... 40.00 - 60.00
    4878 *Snag It* .... 50.00 - 75.00
    4893 *Froggy Bottom* .... 40.00 - 60.00
    4981 *Honey, Just For You* .... 40.00 - 60.00
    6027 *Saturday* .... 35.00 - 50.00
    6129 *Dallas Blues* .... 35.00 - 50.00
Decca 729 *Froggy Bottom* .... 10.00 - 10.00
    744 *All The Jive Is Gone* .... 10.00 - 15.00
    772 *Blue Illusion* .... 10.00 - 15.00
    809 *Walkin' And Swingin'* .... 10.00 - 15.00
    853 *Moten Swing* .... 10.00 - 15.00
    931 *Steppin' Pretty* .... 10.00 - 15.00
    1046 *Bearcat Shuffle* .... 10.00 - 15.00
    1085 *The Lady Who Swings The Band* .... 10.00 - 15.00
    1146 *Fifty-Second Street* .... 10.00 - 15.00
    1208 *Puddin' Head Serenade* .... 10.00 - 15.00
    1261 *In The Groove* .... 10.00 - 15.00
    1303 *Wednesday Night Hop* .... 10.00 - 15.00
    1349 *Skies Are Blue* .... 8.00 - 12.00
    1422 *Better Luck Next Time* .... 8.00 - 12.00
    1477 *With Love In My Heart* .... 8.00 - 12.00
    1531 *Downstream* .... 8.00 - 12.00
    1579 *A Mellow Bit Of Rhythm* .... 8.00 - 12.00
    1606 *The Big Dipper* .... 8.00 - 12.00
    1663 *Poor Butterfly* .... 8.00 - 12.00
Decca (blue label, most other issues) .... 7.00 - 10.00

MANNIE KLEIN/KLINE & HIS ORCHESTRA:
Brunswick 7605 *Ringside Table For Two* .... 10.00 - 15.00
    7606 *Hot Spell* .... 10.00 - 15.00

ORVILLE KNAPP & HIS ORCHESTRA:
Brunswick 7649, 7654, 7671, 7675 .... 7.00 - 10.00
Decca 128 *Blue Sky Avenue* .... 10.00 - 15.00
    224 *Believe Me* .... 8.00 - 12.00
Decca 315, 316, 330, 331, 412, 413, 538, 539, 554 . 5.00 - 10.00

THE KNICKERBOCKERS:
Columbia 450-D *Breezin' Along (To Georgia)* .... 7.00 - 10.00
    549-D *Sweet And Low Down* .... 8.00 - 12.00
    1940-D *Song Of The Blues* .... 8.00 - 12.00
    2003-D *From Now On* .... 8.00 - 12.00
    2067-D *My Man Is On The Make* .... 15.00 - 20.00
    2129-D *Good For You, Bad For Me* .... 10.00 - 15.00
    2502-D *Me!* .... 8.00 - 12.00
Columbia, most other issues .... 5.00 - 8.00

KOLSTER DANCE ORCHESTRA:
Columbia 2072-D *When I Am Housekeeping For You*
    .... 15.00 - 20.00

HOWARD KOPP:

Columbia A2241 *Calico Rag* ....15.00 - 20.00
  A2282 *Night Time In Little Italy* ....10.00 - 15.00
  A2321 *Oh, Johnny! Oh, Johnny!* ....10.00 - 15.00
  A2376 *One Step More* ....10.00 - 10.00

ART KRUEGER & HIS ORCHESTRA:

Broadway 1523 *Sing A New Song* ....8.00 - 12.00

BENNIE KRUEGER & HIS ORCHESTRA:

Brunswick 2105 *Satanic Blues* ....8.00 - 12.00
  2109 *Dangerous Blues* ....8.00 - 12.00
  2419 *Wild Papa* ....8.00 - 12.00
  2445 *Long Lost Mamma* ....7.00 - 10.00
  2563 *Steppin' Out* ....8.00 - 12.00
  2667 *Pleasure Mad* ....7.00 - 10.00
  3060 *Forever And Ever With You* ....8.00 - 12.00
Brunswick, most others, 2000 and 3000 series..........5.00 - 8.00
  6280 *Sing A New Song* ....8.00 - 12.00
Brunswick, most others, 6000 series ....5.00 - 10.00
Columbia 2918-D *Once In A Blue Moon* ....8.00 - 12.00
  2919-D *A Thousand Goodnights* ....8.00 - 12.00
Victor 21903 *That's The Good Old Sunny South* ......7.00 - 10.00

JERRY KRUGER (AND HER ORCHESTRA):

Variety 666 *The Bed Song* ....10.00 - 15.00
Vocalion 3799 *So You Won't Sing* ....10.00 - 15.00
  4927 *Rain, Rain, Go Away* ....10.00 - 15.00

GENE KRUPA AND HIS ORCHESTRA; GENE KRUPA'S SWING BAND:

Brunswick 8123, 8124, 8139, 8161, 8166, 8188,
  8198, 8205, 8211, 8246, 8249, 8253, 8274, 8280,
  8282, 8289, 8296, 8335, 8340, 8346, 8361, 8387,
  8400, 8412, 8448, 8451 ....7.00 - 12.00
Columbia 32505, 35218, 35237, 35262, 35304,
  35324, 35336, 35361, 35366, 35387, 35408,
  35415, 35423, 35429, 35444 ....7.00 - 12.00
Columbia, most higher numbers.........................5.00 - 8.00
Conqueror, most issues ....5.00 - 8.00
Okeh, most issues ....5.00 - 8.00
Victor 25263 *Mutiny In The Parlor* ....8.00 - 12.00
  25276 *Swing Is Here* ....8.00 - 12.00

KXYZ NOVELTY BAND:

Bluebird 5831 *The Sheik Of Araby* ....20.00 - 30.00
  5832 *I Never Knew* ....20.00 - 30.00
  5852 *Bugle Call Rag* ....20.00 - 30.00
  5868 *Indiana* ....20.00 - 30.00

BILLY KYLE & HIS SWING CLUB BAND:

Variety 531 *Big Boy Blue* ....10.00 - 15.00
  574 *Havin' A Ball* ....10.00 - 15.00
  617 *Can I Forget You?* ....10.00 - 15.00
  659 *Girl Of My Dreams* ....10.00 - 15.00
Vocalion 3778 *All You Want To Do Is Dance* ....10.00 - 15.00
  3815 *Margie*...10.00 - 15.00
  3843 *Handle My Heart With Care*................10.00 - 15.00

KAY KYSER AND HIS ORCHESTRA:

Bluebird 5951 *Collegiate Fanny* ....10.00 - 15.00

Brunswick 7449, 7453, 7465, 7470, 7541, 7555,
  7647, 7648, 7682, 7701, 7755, 7759, 7793, 7805,
  7819, 7826, 7836, 7846, 7881, 7891, 8114, 8120,
  8126, 8143, 8149, 8165, 8170, 8181, 8185, 8193,
  8197, 8201, 8209, 8210, 8215, 8222, 8225, 8228,
  8234, 8244, 8258, 8263, 8267, 8279, 8295, 8301,
  8308, 8312, 8317, 8320, 8324, 8328, 8338, 8353,
  8368, 8377, 8381, 8385, 8392, 8415, 8439, 8440,
  8446, 8456..5.00 - 10.00
Columbia, most issues ....5.00 - 8.00
Victor V-40028 *Broken Dreams Of Yesterday* ....20.00 - 30.00
  V-40222 *Rainy Weather* ....35.00 - 50.00
  V-40258 *Collegiate Fanny* ....50.00 - 80.00

LADA'S LOUISIANA LADS/ORCHESTRA:

Emerson 10567 *Early In The Morning Blues* ....15.00 - 20.00
  10570 *Jimbo Jambo* ....15.00 - 20.00
  10587 *Nothing But* ....20.00 - 30.00
  10598 *Farewell Blues* ....25.00 - 40.00
Sunset 1149 *Everybody Stomp* ....80.00 - 120.00
  1151 *Everything's Gonna Be All Right*............30.00 - 50.00

LADD'S BLACK ACES:

Gennett 4762 *Shake It And Break It* ....25.00 - 35.00
  4794 *Gypsy Blues*.......................................25.00 - 35.00
  4806 *Brother Low Down*..............................25.00 - 35.00
  4809 *She's A Mean Job*................................15.00 - 25.00
  4843 *Virginia Blues* ....20.00 - 30.00
  4856 *My Honey's Lovin' Arms* ....20.00 - 30.00
  4869 *Muscle Shoals Blues* ....20.00 - 30.00
  4886 *Hopeless Blues* ....20.00 - 30.00
  4938 *You Can Have Him, I Don't Want Him* ....15.00 - 20.00
  4995 *Yankee Doodle Blues* ....20.00 - 30.00
  5018 *Great White Way Blues* ....20.00 - 30.00
  5023 *Aggravatin' Papa*................................15.00 - 20.00
  5035 *Runnin' Wild* ....15.00 - 20.00
  5060 *Aggravatin' Papa*................................25.00 - 40.00
  5075 *Beale Street Mamma* ....20.00 - 30.00
  5125 *I'm A Harmony Baby* ....20.00 - 30.00
  5127 *Papa Blues* ....20.00 - 30.00
  5142 *Papa, Better Watch Your Step* ....20.00 - 30.00
  5150 *Two-Time Dan* ....20.00 - 30.00
  5164 *I Ain't Never Had Nobody Crazy Over Me*....15.00 - 20.00
  5187 *Bad News Blues*..................................25.00 - 35.00
  5272 *I've Got A Song For Sale* ....20.00 - 30.00
  5366 *Lots O'Mama* ....20.00 - 30.00
  5422 *Unfortunate Blues* ....20.00 - 30.00
  5521 *Any Way The Wind Blows* ....15.00 - 20.00
Superior 2748 *When It's Sleepy Time Down South*... 150.00 - 200.00
  2771 *St. Louis Blues*...................................150.00 - 200.00

TOMMY LADNIER & HIS ORCHESTRA:

Bluebird 10086 *Weary Blues* ....10.00 - 15.00
  10089 *Really The Blues* ....10.00 - 15.00

SLIM LAMAR & HIS SOUTHERNERS; SLIM LAMAR'S ORCHESTRA:

Victor 21710 *Happy*.......................................30.00 - 50.00
  V-40005 *I'm Crazy Over Daisy* ....40.00 - 60.00
  V-40049 *I'm Glad It Was Somebody Else* ....40.00 - 60.00
  V-40093 *Nancy*..50.00 - 80.00
  V-40130 *You Never Did That Before* ....50.00 - 80.00
  V-40146 *Memphis Kick-Up* ....75.00 - 100.00

DOROTHY LAMOUR:
Brunswick 7829, 7838, 7017, 8132, 8154, 8291,
   8304 ....7.00 - 12.00

LAMPE'S ORCHESTRA FROM THE TRIANON BALLROOM; DELL LAMPE & HIS ORCHESTRA:
Autograph (unnumbered) Trianon (A New Dance).50.00 - 100.00
   604 *Prince Of Wails*...............................80.00 - 120.00
   628 *Lady Of The Nile*............................30.00 - 50.00
   629 *Candied Sweets*.............................75.00 - 100.00
Crown 3409 *Street Of Dreams* ....10.00 - 15.00
   3426 *My River Home* ....10.00 - 15.00
   3441 *Darkness On The Delta* ....10.00 - 15.00
Victor 24005 *Spring Is Here Again* ....15.00 - 20.00
   24020 *Scattin' The Skeeter Scoot* ....15.00 - 20.00

MIKE LANDAU & HIS OAKLAND TERRACE ORCHESTRA:
Edison 52538 *Sugar Is Back In Town*.....................40.00 - 60.00

ART LANDRY'S CALL OF THE NORTH ORCHESTRA/ SYNCOPATIN' SIX; ART LANDRY AND HIS ORCHESTRA:
Gennett 5053, 5170, 5222 ....7.00 - 10.00
Gennett 5171 *Rip Saw Blues*........................15.00 - 20.00
   5184 *Choo Choo Blues* ....200.00 - 300.00
   5189 *Some Of These Days* ....15.00 - 20.00
   5255 *Rip Saw Blues* ....15.00 - 20.00
Victor 19398 *Rip Saw Blues* ....10.00 - 15.00
   19488 *It'll Get You*...............................8.00 - 12.00
   19514 *I'm A Lonesome Little Mama* ....20.00 - 30.00
   19843 *Sleepy-Time Gal*.........................7.00 - 10.00
   19850 *Don't Wait Too Long* ....7.00 - 10.00
   19858 *Everybody Stomp* ....10.00 - 15.00
   19866 *Swamp Blues*............................10.00 - 15.00
   20023 *Slippery Elm*..............................10.00 - 15.00
   20142 *Tell Me You Love Me* ....10.00 - 15.00
   20147 *That's Annabelle*........................7.00 - 10.00
   20300 *Song of the Wanderer* ....7.00 - 10.00
   20598 *Who'll Be The One?*....................8.00 - 12.00
   20644 *The Whisper Song* ....8.00 - 12.00
Victor, most other issues..5.00 - 8.00

DUKE LANEY & HIS ORCHESTRA:
Champion 15699 *Some Sweet Day* ....25.00 - 35.00

EDDIE LANG; ED LANG & HIS ORCHESTRA (See also JOE VENUTI):
Brunswick 6254 *Pickin' My Way* ....10.00 - 15.00
Okeh 8696 *Freeze An' Melt*.....................................35.00 - 50.00
   40807 *Eddie's Twister* ....20.00 - 30.00
   40936 *Melody Man's Dream* ....20.00 - 30.00
   40989 *A Little Love, A Little Kiss*.............20.00 - 30.00
   41134 *Add A Little Wiggle* ....20.00 - 30.00
   41253 *Freeze An' Melt* ....30.00 - 50.00
   41344 *Walkin' The Dog*..........................40.00 - 60.00
   41410 *Bugle Call Rag*............................50.00 - 75.00

TEDDY LANG & HIS ORCHESTRA:
Crown 3453 *Forty-Second Street* ....10.00 - 15.00

LANGE-McKAY ORCHESTRA AT CASTLE FARMS:
Gennett 3046 *Leaky Roof Blues* ....50.00 - 75.00
   5584 *Leaky Roof Blues* ....80.00 - 120.00

ART/ARTHUR LANGE & HIS ORCHESTRA:
Cameo 391 *Land Of Cotton Blues* ....7.00 - 10.00
   545 *Limehouse Blues* ....7.00 - 10.00
   557 *Oh Baby!* ....7.00 - 10.00
   916 *Honey Bunch* ....7.00 - 10.00
   917 *I've Got Some Lovin' To Do* ....7.00 - 10.00
Cameo (most other issues) ....4.00 - 8.00

HENRY LANGE; HENRY LANGE & HIS (BAKER HOTEL) ORCHESTRA:
Brunswick 2344 *Rufenreddy*..............................10.00 - 15.00
   4161 *I Want You More* ....15.00 - 20.00
   4478 *China Boy*...................................50.00 - 75.00
Champion 16294 *Moonlight Saving Time* ....35.00 - 50.00
   16332 *Mood Indigo* ....100.00 - 150.00
   16420 *Sweet* ....100.00 - 150.00
   40044 *Mood Indigo* ....25.00 - 40.00
Gennett 6263 *Hot Lips* ....75.00 - 100.00
   20389 *Sweet* ....50.00 - 80.00

FRANCES LANGFORD:
Nasty Man, issued contemporaneously on Banner, Melotone, Oriole,
   Perfect, and Romeo....................................15.00 - 25.00
Bluebird 5016 *Moon Song* ....15.00 - 20.00
Brunswick 7512 *I Feel A Song Coming On* ....15.00 - 20.00
   7513 *I'm In The Mood For Love* ....15.00 - 20.00
Columbia 2696-D *I Can't Believe It's True*............20.00 - 30.00
Decca 663, 775, 783, 893, 902, 939, 940, 1202,
   1440, 1441, 1454, 1464, 1542, 1577, 1760, 1831 7.00 - 12.00
Decca (most other issues) ....5.00 - 10.00
Mercury 5057 *Please Don't Play Number Six Tonight*
   (picture record)...................................50.00 - 100.00
Victor 24191 *When Mother Played The Organ* ......15.00 - 25.00

LANIN'S RED HEADS; LANIN'S SOUTHERN SERENADERS (See SAM LANIN)

HOWARD LANIN'S (ARCADIA/BENJAMIN FRANKLIN HOTEL) ORCHESTRA:
Columbia 333-D, 689-D, 762-D, 804-D, 882-D,
   1029-D ....5.00 - 10.00
Gennett 3320 *Her Beaus Are Only Rainbows* ....10.00 - 15.00
   5167 *I Cried For You*...........................15.00 - 20.00
   5484 *You Know Me, Alabam'* ....8.00 - 12.00
Victor 19711 *On a Night Like This*........................7.00 - 10.00
   19797 *Melancholy Lou* ....10.00 - 15.00

SAM LANIN & HIS ORCHESTRA/FAMOUS PLAYERS (AND SINGERS); LANIN'S RED HEADS; SAM LANIN'S DANCE ORCHESTRA/TROUBADOURS; LANIN'S SOUTHERN SERENADERS; LANIN'S ARCADIANS:
Arto 9097 *Memphis Blues*....................................25.00 - 35.00
(Above also issued on Bell, Hy-Tone, similarly valued)
Banner 0503 *Great Day* ....7.00 - 10.00
   0504 *Without A Song* ....7.00 - 10.00
   0601 *Mona* ....7.00 - 10.00
   0688 *Exactly Like You* ....7.00 - 10.00
(Foregoing titles on Cameo, similarly valued)
   1015 *Shake It And Break It* ....25.00 - 35.00
   1182 *Aunt Hagar's Children Blues*...................15.00 - 20.00
   1500 *When My Sugar Walks Down The Street* ....7.00 - 10.00
Banner 1517, 1518, 1521, 1524, 1538, 1541, 1542,
   1543, 1567, 1570, 1617, 1619, 1620, 1622, 1642,
   1644, 1655, 1659, 1663, 1674 ....7.00 - 10.00
   1676 *Sweet Child* ....8.00 - 12.00

1711 *Could I? I Certainly Could*	8.00 -	12.00
1747 *I'm In Love With You, That's Why*	8.00 -	12.00
Banner 1862, 1883, 6261, 6325, 6328, 6388, 6445	7.00 -	12.00
6452 *What A Day!*	10.00 -	15.00
7031 *Back In Your Own Back Yard*	8.00 -	12.00
7161 *Two Lips (To Kiss My Cares Away)*	8.00 -	12.00
32219 *Little Girl*	7.00 -	10.00
Cameo 871 *That Certain Feeling*	8.00 -	12.00
874 *After I Say I'm Sorry?*	8.00 -	12.00
987 *Baby Face*	7.00 -	10.00
1012 *Just a Bird's Eye View (Of My Old Kentucky Home)*		
	7.00 -	10.00
1044 *Sunday*	7.00 -	10.00
1106 *I Wonder How I Look When I'm Asleep*	7.00 -	10.00
1164 *At Sundown*	7.00 -	10.00
1268 *What'll You Do?*	7.00 -	10.00
8103 *Let A Smile Be Your Umbrella*	7.00 -	10.00
8109 *My Ohio Home*	10.00 -	15.00
8225 *My Pet*	8.00 -	12.00
8227 *Sweet Sue-Just You*	10.00 -	15.00
8228 *Who Wouldn't Be Blue?*	10.00 -	15.00
8234 *I Can't Give You Anything But Love*	7.00 -	10.00
8245 *Ready For The River*	8.00 -	12.00
8247 *That's My Weakness Now*	7.00 -	10.00
8248 *That's Just My Way Of Forgetting You*	7.00 -	10.00
8251 *Old Man Sunshine*	7.00 -	10.00
8258 *Just Like A Melody Out Of The Sky*	7.00 -	10.00
8290 *You Took Advantage Of Me*	7.00 -	10.00
9003 *You're The Cream In My Coffee*	8.00 -	12.00
9103 *Mean To Me*	8.00 -	12.00
9157 *Louise*	7.00 -	10.00
9167 *I Wanna Go Places And Do Things*	8.00 -	12.00
(Above titles, on Lincoln and Romeo are similarly valued)		
Cameo (most of the numerous other issues)	5.00 -	8.00
Challenge 543 *Down Where the Sun Goes Down*	7.00 -	10.00
Champion 15803 *Ain't Misbehavin'*	8.00 -	12.00
15839 *Miss Wonderful*	8.00 -	12.00
15861 *Lady Luck*	8.00 -	12.00
15930 *Happy Days Are Here Again*	10.00 -	15.00
15935 *There's Danger In Your Eyes, Cherie*	7.00 -	10.00
15955 *Gone*	7.00 -	10.00
15975 *The Stein Song*	8.00 -	12.00
15978 *Thank Your Father*	7.00 -	10.00
16039 *Hullabaloo*	15.00 -	20.00
16107 *I'm Yours*	8.00 -	12.00
16128 *Always In All Ways*	10.00 -	15.00
16130 *Something To Remember You By*	8.00 -	12.00
Columbia 279-D *Fascinating Rhythm*	7.00 -	10.00
285-D *I Can't Stop Babying You*	7.00 -	10.00
327-D *King Porter Stomp*	25.00 -	40.00
360-D *Suite 16*	15.00 -	20.00
376-D *Flag That Train*	15.00 -	20.00
396-D *Who Loved You Best?*	8.00 -	12.00
414-D *If I Had a Girl Like You*	8.00 -	12.00
438-D *Cecilia*	7.00 -	10.00
447-D *Desdemona*	8.00 -	12.00
483-D *Five Foot Two, Eyes Of Blue*	10.00 -	15.00
Conqueror 7810 *Little Girl*	7.00 -	10.00
Diva 3083-G *Crying For The Carolines*	8.00 -	12.00
Domino 3536 *If I Had A Girl Like You*	7.00 -	10.00
3626 *I Love My Baby, My Baby Loves Me*	7.00 -	10.00
3628 *Good Mornin'*	7.00 -	10.00
3644 *Sweet Child*	7.00 -	10.00

3647 *I Wish't I Was In Peoria*	7.00 -	10.00
3682 *Let's Talk About My Sweetie*	8.00 -	12.00
Edison 51518 *I Like Pie-I Like Cake*	10.00 -	15.00
Emerson 10439 *Aunt Hagar's Children Blues*	20.00 -	30.00
10496 *Arkansas Blues*	15.00 -	20.00
Federal 5299 *Snakes Hips*	15.00 -	20.00
5362 *Dancin' Dan*	10.00 -	15.00
5363 *Toodle-Oo*	7.00 -	10.00
5371 *Forgetful Blues*	8.00 -	12.00
Harmony 968-H *Don't Hang Your Dreams on a Rainbow*		
	7.00 -	10.00
984-H *Marianne*	10.00 -	15.00
1001-H *Little By Little*	8.00 -	12.00
1018-H *Melancholy*	8.00 -	12.00
1029-H *Campus Capers*	8.00 -	12.00
1036-H *Sophomore Prom*	8.00 -	12.00
1049-H *That Wonderful Something Is Love*	8.00 -	12.00
1065-H *Hoosier Hop*	8.00 -	12.00
1083-H *Crying For The Carolines*	8.00 -	12.00
1084-H *When I Am Housekeeping For You*	15.00 -	20.00
1107-H *Hangin' On The Garden Gate*	8.00 -	12.00
1109-H *Keepin' Myself For You*	8.00 -	12.00
1139-H *The Free And Easy*	8.00 -	12.00
1165-H *Be Careful With Those Eyes*	8.00 -	12.00
1265-H *You're Simply Delish*	8.00 -	12.00
(Above titles on Diva, Velvet Tone, similarly valued)		
Lincoln (titles as on Cameo, similarly valued)		
Odeon ONY-36112 *Seems To Me*	25.00 -	35.00
ONY-36113 *Rollin' Down The River*	25.00 -	35.00
ONY-36189 *Please Don't Talk About Me When I'm Gone*		
	25.00 -	35.00
ONY-36190 *I Surrender, Dear*	25.00 -	35.00
ONY-36195 *The One-Man Band*	25.00 -	35.00
Okeh 40111 *Big Boy*	15.00 -	20.00
40170 *Somebody Loves Me*	10.00 -	15.00
40200 *My Best Girl*	8.00 -	12.00
40219 *I Want To See My Tennessee*	8.00 -	12.00
40707 *Here Comes Fatima*	10.00 -	15.00
40709 *Looking At The World Thru Rose Colored Glasses*		
	10.00 -	15.00
40738 *I Gotta Get Myself Somebody To Love*	10.00 -	15.00
40766 *I'm Looking Over A Four Leaf Clover*	10.00 -	15.00
40810 *Side By Side*	8.00 -	12.00
40833 *She's Got "It"*	8.00 -	12.00
40855 *Sing Me A Baby Song*	10.00 -	15.00
40863 *Just Once Again*	8.00 -	12.00
40933 *There Must Be Somebody Else*	8.00 -	12.00
40937 *My New York*	10.00 -	15.00
40977 *Let A Smile Be Your Umbrella*	10.00 -	15.00
41031 *Sweet Sue, Just You*	10.00 -	15.00
41038 *Get Out And Get Under The Moon*	10.00 -	15.00
41063 *Sorry For Me*	7.00 -	10.00
41097 *Ten Little Miles From Town*	10.00 -	15.00
41121 *Roses Of Yesterday*	8.00 -	12.00
41159 *Sweethearts On Parade*	10.00 -	15.00
41188 *If I Had You*	30.00 -	50.00
41228 *If I'm Crazy Over You*	30.00 -	50.00
41383 *Cooking Breakfast For The One I Love*	25.00 -	35.00
41385 *Mona*	15.00 -	20.00
Pathe-Actuelle 036075 *Unfortunate Blues*	10.00 -	15.00
036184 *Forsaken Blues*	10.00 -	15.00
036202 *Lucky Kentucky*	7.00 -	10.00
036203 *Alabamy Bound*	8.00 -	12.00

036219 *All Aboard For Heaven* ....8.00 - 12.00
036234 *Don't Bring Lulu* ....7.00 - 10.00
36305 *Sweet Man* ....8.00 - 12.00
36342 *I'm Sitting On Top Of The World* ....7.00 - 10.00
36343 *Five Foot Two, Eyes Of Blue* ....10.00 - 15.00
36344 *Say, Who Is That Baby Doll?* ....10.00 - 15.00
36357 *Spanish Shawl* ....10.00 - 15.00
36363 *No Man's Mama* ....10.00 - 15.00
36374 *After I Say I'm Sorry?* ....8.00 - 12.00
36392 *Let's Talk About My Sweetie* ....15.00 - 20.00
36450 *I'd Give A Lot of Love* ....20.00 - 30.00
36454 *That's Why I Love You* ....10.00 - 15.00
36512 *Any Ice Today, Lady?* ....7.00 - 10.00
36545 *Sunday* ....10.00 - 15.00
36547 *My Baby Knows How* ....10.00 - 15.00
36656 *Lucky Lindy* ....15.00 - 20.00
36797 *My Pet* ....8.00 - 12.00
36802 *Sweet Sue, Just You* ....8.00 - 12.00
36804 *Who Wouldn't Be Blue?* ....8.00 - 12.00
Pathe-Actuelle, most other issues ....5.00 - 8.00
Perfect 14256 *Nobody's Sweetheart Now* ....10.00 - 15.00
14283 *I Can't Get The One I Want* ....10.00 - 15.00
14330 *I Want To See My Tennessee* ....10.00 - 15.00
14365 *Forsaken Blues* ....10.00 - 15.00
14383 *Lucky Kentucky* ....7.00 - 10.00
14384 *Alabamy Bound* ....8.00 - 12.00
14400 *All Aboard For Heaven* ....8.00 - 12.00
14415 *Don't Bring Lulu* ....7.00 - 10.00
14486 *Sweet Man* ....8.00 - 12.00
14497 *Paddlin' Madelin' Home* ....8.00 - 12.00
14523 *I'm Sitting On Top Of The World* ....7.00 - 10.00
14524 *Five Foot Two, Eyes Of Blue* ....10.00 - 15.00
14525 *Say, Who Is That Baby Doll?* ....10.00 - 15.00
14538 *Spanish Shawl* ....10.00 - 15.00
14544 *No Man's Mama* ....10.00 - 15.00
14555 *After I Say I'm Sorry?* ....8.00 - 12.00
14573 *Let's Talk About My Sweetie* ....15.00 - 20.00
14631 *I'd Give A Lot Of Love* ....20.00 - 30.00
14635 *That's Why I Love You* ....10.00 - 15.00
14693 *Any Ice Today, Lady?* ....7.00 - 10.00
14726 *Sunday* ....10.00 - 15.00
14728 *My Baby Knows How* ....10.00 - 15.00
14837 *Lucky Lindy* ....15.00 - 20.00
14841 *Bless Her Little Heart* ....10.00 - 15.00
14978 *My Pet* ....7.00 - 10.00
14983 *Sweet Sue, Just You* ....7.00 - 10.00
14985 *Who Wouldn't Be Blue?* ....7.00 - 10.00
15486 *Little Girl* ....7.00 - 10.00
Perfect, most other issues ....5.00 - 8.00
Radio Tono 15491 *Just One More Chance* (picture disc)
....50.00 - 100.00
Paramount 20068 *Aunt Hagar's Children Blues* ....20.00 - 30.00
Puritan 11222 *Aunt Hagar's Blues* ....20.00 - 30.00
Regal 8059 *I'm In Love With You, That's Why* ....7.00 - 10.00
8120 *She's Still My Baby* ....8.00 - 12.00
8413 *The Varsity Drag* ....15.00 - 20.00
8557 *Rag Doll* ....7.00 - 10.00
8598 *You're A Real Sweetheart* ....7.00 - 10.00
8600 *Two Lips* ....7.00 - 10.00
8610 *Down Where The Sun Goes Down* ....7.00 - 10.00
8671 *Me And The Man In The Moon* ....8.00 - 12.00
8701 *Happy Days And Lonely Nights* ....7.00 - 10.00
8745 *He, She And Me* ....7.00 - 10.00

8817 *Wishing And Waiting For Love* ....7.00 - 10.00
8818 *What A Day!* ....7.00 - 10.00
8945 *I'm On A Diet Of Love* ....10.00 - 15.00
9200 *Doo Dah Blues* ....15.00 - 20.00
9486 *Blue Hoosier Blues* ....8.00 - 12.00
9704 *Tessie, Stop Teasing Me* ....8.00 - 12.00
9866 *Marguerite* ....8.00 - 12.00
9900 *Let's Wander Away* ....7.00 - 10.00
9919 *Bam Bam Bamy Shore* ....7.00 - 10.00
9967 *Smile A Little Bit* ....8.00 - 12.00
9970 *I Love My Baby, My Baby Loves Me* ....8.00 - 12.00
9981 *Sweet Child (I'm Wild About You)* ....7.00 - 10.00
Romeo (titles as on Cameo, above, are similarly valued)
1306 *Just Like In A Story Book* ....7.00 - 10.00
1580 *Walkin' My Baby Back Home* ....7.00 - 10.00
Silvertone 2498 *My Sweet Louise* ....15.00 - 20.00
Superior 2576 *When Kentucky Bids The World Good Morning*
....15.00 - 20.00
Supertone 9458 *I'm In Seventh Heaven* ....10.00 - 15.00
9480 *Or What Have You* ....10.00 - 15.00
9550 *Hang On To Me* ....10.00 - 15.00
9576 *Miss Wonderful* ....10.00 - 15.00
9580 *Lady Luck* ....10.00 - 15.00
9744 *Hullabaloo* ....15.00 - 20.00
Triangle 11068 *Shake It And Break It* ....20.00 - 30.00

LA PALINA BROADCASTERS:

Titles, issued contemporaneously on Conqueror, Domino, Pathe-Actuelle, Perfect, and Regal: *I Want To Meander In The Meadow; Little By Little; Piccolo Pete; Singin' In The Rain; Sweetheart, We Need Each Other; Sweetness; When My Dreams Come True* ....8.00 - 15.00

HAL LASKA AND HIS ORCHESTRA:

Parlophone PNY-34034 *Romance* ....20.00 - 30.00
PNY-34038 *Sweeping The Clouds Away* (instrumental)
....75.00 - 100.00
PNY-34039 *Any Time's The Time To Fall In Love* (instrumental)
....75.00 - 100.00
PNY-34040 *Sweeping The Clouds Away* ....40.00 - 60.00
PNY-34041 *Any Time's The Time To Fall In Love*
....40.00 - 60.00
PNY-34064 *When The Little Red Roses Get The Blues*
....30.00 - 50.00
PNY-34070 *Exactly Like You* ....25.00 - 40.00
PNY-34072 *Dust* ....25.00 - 35.00
PNY-34073 *Leave It That Way* ....25.00 - 35.00
PNY-34074 *On The Sunny Side Of The Street* ..25.00 - 35.00
PNY-34162 *Alexander's Ragtime Band* ....25.00 - 35.00
PNY-34164 *Overnight* ....20.00 - 30.00
PNY-34165 *Little Did I Know* ....20.00 - 30.00

HARLAN LATTIMORE & HIS CONNIE'S INN ORCHESTRA:

Columbia 2675-D *Chant Of The Weed* ....35.00 - 50.00
2678-D *Reefer Man* ....35.00 - 50.00

LA VEEDA DANCE ORCHESTRA:

Columbia 1549-D *Strut Yo' Stuff* ....50.00 - 75.00

THELMA LA VIZZO:

Paramount 12206 *Trouble In Mind Blues* ....80.00 - 120.00
12250 *The Stomps* ....150.00 - 250.00

GERTRUDE LAWRENCE:
Columbia 512-D *A Cup Of Coffee, A Sandwich And You*
....15.00 - 20.00
  513-D *Poor Little Rich Girl* ....15.00 - 20.00
  514-D *Russian Blues* ....15.00 - 20.00
Victor 20331 *Someone To Watch Over Me* ....15.00 - 20.00

SARA LAWRENCE:
Oriole 894 *Don't Love Me* ....50.00 - 100.00

DAVE LAWSON'S ORCHESTRA:
Challenge 365 *Me And My Shadow* ....15.00 - 20.00
Champion 15326 *Me And My Shadow* ....50.00 - 75.00

YANK LAWSON'S JAZZ BAND:
Signature ....5.00 - 10.00

LAZY LEVEE LOUNGERS:
Columbia 2243-D *Shout, Sister, Shout* ....50.00 - 80.00

LEE'S BLACK DIAMONDS:
Broadway 1294 *Piggly Wiggly Blues* ....250.00 - up

BARON LEE & THE BLUE RHYTHM BAND:
Titles issued contemporaneously on Banner, Melotone, Oriole,
 Perfect, and Romeo: *Cabin In The Cotton; The Crawl; Doin' The
 Shake; Heatwaves; Jazz Cocktail; Mighty Sweet; Minnie The
 Moocher's Wedding Day; Old Yazoo; Reefer Man; Rhythm
 Spasm; The Scat Song; Sentimental Gentleman From Georgia;
 Smoke Rings; White Lightning; Wild Waves; You Gave Me
 Everything But Love* ....10.00 - 20.00

CHAUNCEY C. LEE:
Okeh 40321 *Banjo Rag*.............................100.00 - 150.00

ELIZA CHRISTMAS LEE:
Gennett 4801 *Arkansas Blues* ....20.00 - 30.00

GEORGE E. LEE & HIS (NOVELTY SINGING) ORCHESTRA:
Brunswick 4684 *Ruff Scufflin'* ....50.00 - 80.00
  7132 *Paseo Strut*..................................80.00 - 120.00
Merrit 2206 *Down Home Syncopated Blues*..........500.00 - up

JULIA LEE:
Brunswick 4761 *He's Tall And Dark And Handsome*
....75.00 - 100.00
Capitol (most issues) ....5.00 -   8.00

MANDY LEE:
Titles issued contemporaneously on Banner, Conqueror, Domino,
 Oriole, and Regal: *Crap Shootin' Poppa, Mama Done Caught
 Your Dice; I Needs Plenty Of Grease In My Frying Pan*
....15.00 - 20.00
Additional titles: *Harlem Blues; Someone's Been Lovin' My Baby*
....20.00 - 30.00
Pathe-Actuelle 7509 *Rounders Blues* ....75.00 - 100.00
Perfect 109 *Wandering Papa Blues* ....75.00 - 100.00

MANDY LEE & LADD'S BLACK ACES (See LADD'S BLACK ACES)

MARGUERITE LEE:
Vocalion 1150 *You Will Always Live In Our Memory*
....150.00 - 200.00

RUTH LEE:
Nordskog 3008 *Maybe Someday* ....300.00 - up
Sunshine 3002 *Maybe Someday* ....300.00 - up
(Note: Sunshine 3002 label is pasted over Nordskog label.)

WINTHROP LEE & HIS ORCHESTRA:
Parlophone PNY-34124 *Loveless Love*..................75.00 - 100.00
  PNY-34125 *Papa's Gone* ....75.00 - 100.00
  PNY-34148 *Daniel's Blues*..................75.00 - 100.00

BOBBIE LEECAN; BOBBIE LEECAN'S NEEDMORE BAND:
Victor 20251 *Black Cat Bone Blues* ....35.00 - 50.00
  20660 *Midnight Susie* ....75.00 - 100.00
  20768 *Blue Harmonica* ....75.00 - 100.00
  20853 *Appaloosa Blues*..................75.00 - 100.00
  20958 *Royal Palm Blues* ....75.00 - 100.00

CHESTER LEIGHTON AND HIS SOPHOMORES:
Clarion 5125-C *Cheerful Little Earful* ....10.00 - 15.00
  5177-C *Someone Sang A Sweeter Song To Mary*......7.00 - 10.00
  5186-C *The Little Things In Life*...................10.00 - 15.00
  5276-C *If You Should Ever Need Me* ....7.00 - 10.00
  5319-C *Star Dust* ....15.00 - 20.00
  5337-C *Love Is Like That* ....8.00 - 12.00
  5351-C *On The Beach With You* ....15.00 - 20.00
  5363-C *The Kiss That You've Forgotten* ....7.00 - 10.00
Harmony 1233-H *A Peach Of A Pair* ....7.00 - 10.00
  1242-H *My Love For You* ....7.00 - 10.00
  1248-H *Satan's Holiday* ....10.00 - 15.00
  1251-H *Someone Sang A Sweeter Song To Mary*.....7.00 - 10.00
  1307-H *When I Take My Sugar To Tea* ....15.00 - 20.00
  1328-H *Love Is Like That* ....7.00 - 10.00
  1340-H *Without That Gal!* ....15.00 - 20.00
  1342-H *Makin' Faces At The Man In The Moon*. 8.00 - 12.00
  1351-H *The Kiss That You've Forgotten* ....7.00 - 10.00
Velvet Tone 2342-V *If You Should Ever Need Me* ... 7.00 - 10.00
  2401-V *Love Is Like That* ....7.00 - 10.00
  2415-V *On The Beach With You*...................15.00 - 20.00
  2417-V *Just One More Chance* ....8.00 - 12.00
  2427-V *The Kiss That You've Forgotten* ....7.00 - 10.00

FRANK LEITHNER & HIS ORCHESTRA:
Banner 6418 *I'm Feathering A Nest* ....10.00 - 15.00
  6422 *With A Song In My Heart*.........................8.00 - 12.00
  6468 *I'm In Seventh Heaven* ....7.00 - 10.00
Conqueror 7366 *With A Song In My Heart*...............8.00 - 12.00
(Foregoing titles also issued on Regal, similarly valued)

HAROLD LEM & HIS ORCHESTRA:
Okeh 41465 *I Got Rhythm* ....20.00 - 30.00

LENOX/LENNOX DANCE ORCHESTRA:
Pathe-Actuelle 36345 *Mammy Chasing Blues* .... 10.00 - 15.00
  36355 *I Love My Baby* ....8.00 - 12.00
Perfect 14394 *Me Neenyah* ....20.00 - 30.00

JAMES I. LENT (WITH ARTHUR PRYOR'S BAND):
Emerson 5122 *The Ragtime Drummer* ....15.00 - 20.00
Victor 17092 *The Ragtime Drummer*.....................10.00 - 15.00

AL LENTZ & HIS (DANCE) ORCHESTRA:
Banner 1812 *Sweet Thing* ....10.00 - 15.00
  1818 *No One But You Knows How To Love* ...... 10.00 - 15.00
  1861 *Gone Again Gal* ....8.00 - 12.00
  1863 *How Could Red Riding Hood?* ....10.00 - 15.00
  1868 *I've Got The Girl* ....10.00 - 15.00
  1889 *'Deed I Do* ....8.00 - 12.00
Columbia 856-D *I Never See Maggie Alone* ....8.00 - 12.00
  867-D *Sam, The Old Accordion Man* ....7.00 - 10.00
  1037-D *Who Was The Lady?* ....7.00 - 10.00

1072-D *Zulu Wail* ....8.00 - 12.00
1134-D *When I Ring Your Front Door Bell* ....8.00 - 12.00
Domino 3793 *Sweet Thing*.................................10.00 - 15.00
Puritan 11481 *How Could Red Riding Hood* ....10.00 - 15.00
11486 *I've Got The Girl* ....10.00 - 15.00
Regal 8130 *Sweet Thing* ....10.00 - 15.00
8146 *Just A Bird's Eye View Of My Old Kentucky Home*
....10.00 - 15.00
8177 *How Could Red Riding Hood?* ....10.00 - 15.00

HARLAN LEONARD & HIS ROCKETS:
Bluebird (most issues) ....7.00 - 10.00

HAROLD LEONARD & HIS RED JACKETS:
Gennett 5137 *China Boy* ....8.00 - 12.00
5138 *The Cat's Whiskers* ....10.00 - 15.00
Okeh 40030 *Forgetful Blues*...........................8.00 - 12.00
40042 *WOP Blues* ....10.00 - 15.00
40083 *Limehouse Blues* ....10.00 - 15.00
40091 *Unfortunate Blues* ....10.00 - 15.00

LEROY'S DALLAS BAND:
Columbia 14402-D *Tampa Shout* ....200.00 - up

LEW LESLIE'S BLACKBIRD'S ORCHESTRA:
Brunswick 4030 *Bandanna Babies*.......................40.00 - 60.00

NATE LESLIE & HIS ORCHESTRA:
Vocalion 3584 *Shake Yo' Bones*.........................20.00 - 30.00

LEVEE LOUNGERS:
Pathe-Actuelle (titles as on Perfect, below)
Perfect 14818 *The Devil Is Afraid Of Music* ....15.00 - 20.00
14860 *Frankie And Johnnie*.............................20.00 - 30.00
14904 *There's A Rickety Rackety Shack*.............10.00 - 15.00
14924 *When You're With Somebody Else* ....10.00 - 15.00
14926 *My Melancholy Baby* ....8.00 - 12.00
14966 *Speedy Boy* ....10.00 - 15.00
14971 *Today Is Today* ....8.00 - 12.00
14973 *Waitin' For Katy* ....10.00 - 15.00
14979 *Get Out And Get Under The Moon* ....10.00 - 15.00
15017 *What's The Reason* ....15.00 - 20.00
15018 *Someone To Admire, Someone To Adore* .8.00 - 12.00
15030 *Crazy Rhythm* ....8.00 - 12.00
15038 *'tain't So, Honey, 'tain't So* ....15.00 - 20.00
15064 *Easy Goin'* ....10.00 - 15.00
15069 *In A Little Hide-away* ....8.00 - 12.00
(Above titles, on Pathe-Actuelle, similarly valued)
Most other issues on Pathe-Actuelle and Perfect labels
....5.00 - 10.00

LEVEE SERENADERS:
Vocalion 1154 *Midnight Mama*...........................150.00 - 250.00

LEVEE SYNCOPATORS:
Titles issued contemporaneously on Gray Gull, Madison, Radiex,
and Van Dyke: *The Rackett; The Harlem Stomp Down*
....25.00 - 40.00

ALFRED LEWIS:
Vocalion 1498 *Friday Moan Blues*.......................80.00 - 120.00

MEADE LUX LEWIS:
Blue Note (most issues) ....7.00 - 12.00
Decca 819 *Yancey Special* ....15.00 - 20.00
Paramount 12896 *Honky Train Blues*....................300.00 - up

Solo Art 12002 *Messin' Around* ....20.00 - 30.00
12003 *Deep Fives* ....20.00 - 30.00
12004 *Closin' Hour Blues* ....25.00 - 40.00
Victor 25541 *Honky Tonk Train Blues* ....15.00 - 20.00
Vocalion 4606 *Boogie Woogie Prayer* ....10.00 - 15.00
4608 *Bear Cat Crawl*.................................10.00 - 15.00

NOAH LEWIS; NOAH LEWIS'S JUG BAND:
Bluebird 5675 *Ticket Agent Blues*......................150.00 - 200.00
Victor 23266 *New Minglewood Blues* ....300.00 - up
23336 *Like I Want To Be* ....300.00 - up
V38581 *Chickasaw Special* ....300.00 - up

SAMMY LEWIS (AND HIS BAMVILLE SYNCOPATORS):
Okeh 8285 *Just Too Late* ....50.00 - 75.00
Vocalion 1029 *Hateful Papa Blues* ....100.00 - 150.00
1030 *Arkansas Shout*................................100.00 - 150.00

TED LEWIS & HIS BAND:
Columbia 1-S *Popular Favorites* (medley) ....5.00 - 8.00
48-D *Unfortunate Blues* ....10.00 - 15.00
122-D *San* ....10.00 - 15.00
170-D *Barnyard Blues* ....15.00 - 20.00
195-D *Eccentric* ....10.00 - 15.00
406-D *I Miss My Swiss* ....8.00 - 12.00
416-D *Angry* ....10.00 - 15.00
439-D *Tin Roof Blues*...............................20.00 - 30.00
478-D *The Camel Walk*...............................8.00 - 12.00
531-D *That Certain Party* ....8.00 - 12.00
543-D *I Wish't I Was In Peoria* ....10.00 - 15.00
585-D *Poor Papa* ....8.00 - 12.00
600-D *I've Found A New Baby* ....10.00 - 15.00
Columbia 52-D, 82-D, 157-D, 227-D, 241-D, 255-D,
274-D, 295-D, 311-D, 504-D, 620-D, 754-D ......7.00 - 10.00
Columbia 667-D *Where'd You Get Those Eyes?*.... 10.00 - 15.00
670-D *Hi-Diddle-Diddle*.............................8.00 - 12.00
697-D *The New St. Louis Blues* ....10.00 - 15.00
770-D *Tiger Rag* ....10.00 - 15.00
826-D *Bugle Call Rag*...............................10.00 - 15.00
922-D *When My Baby Smiles At Me*................10.00 - 15.00
988-D *Fifty Million Frenchmen Can't Be Wrong* 8.00 - 12.00
1017-D *Frankie And Johnny*...........................10.00 - 15.00
1050-D *The Memphis Blues*............................10.00 - 15.00
1084-D *The Darktown Strutters' Ball*...............10.00 - 15.00
1207-D *Is Everybody Happy Now?* ....10.00 - 15.00
Columbia 844-D, 895-D, 1296-D ....7.00 - 10.00
Columbia 1242-D *Away Down South In Heaven*.... 10.00 - 15.00
1313-D *Cobble-Stones* ....10.00 - 15.00
1346-D *Hello, Montreal!* ....10.00 - 15.00
1391-D *Oh Baby!* ....10.00 - 15.00
1428-D *A Good Man Is Hard To Find*.............. 10.00 - 15.00
1485-D *Moonlight Madness* ....8.00 - 12.00
1525-D *A Jazz Holiday* ....10.00 - 15.00
1573-D *Clarinet Marmalade* ....15.00 - 20.00
1656-D *She's Funny That Way* ....10.00 - 15.00
1709-D *Glad Rag Doll*...............................10.00 - 15.00
1789-D *Limehouse Blues* ....10.00 - 15.00
1854-D *Maybe Who Knows?* ....10.00 - 15.00
1882-D *I'm The Medicine Man For The Blues*.. 10.00 - 15.00
1916-D *Lewisada Blues* ....10.00 - 15.00
1957-D *Lonely Troubadour* ....7.00 - 10.00
1999-D *Lady Luck*...................................10.00 - 15.00
2029-D *Farewell Blues* ....15.00 - 25.00

2088-D *Harmonica Harry* ....15.00 - 20.00
2113-D *Aunt Hagar's Blues* ....15.00 - 20.00
2144-D *Singing A Vagabond Song* ....15.00 - 20.00
2181-D *Dinah* ....15.00 - 20.00
2217-D *Sobbin' Blues* ....20.00 - 30.00
2246-D *The World Is Waiting For The Sunrise*..10.00 - 15.00
2311-D *Laughing At Life* ....20.00 - 30.00
2336-D *Somebody Stole My Gal* ....20.00 - 30.00
2378-D *Headin' For Better Times* ....20.00 - 30.00
2408-D *At Last I'm Happy* ....20.00 - 30.00
2428-D *Egyptian Ella*....................................25.00 - 40.00
2452-D *Ho Hum!* ....25.00 - 35.00
2467-D *Dip Your Brush In The Sunshine* ....25.00 - 40.00
2492-D *I'm All Dressed Up With A Broken Heart*
....20.00 - 30.00
2527-D *Royal Garden Blues*............................25.00 - 40.00
2560-D *An Evening In Caroline* ....25.00 - 35.00
2635-D *Somebody Loves You* ....25.00 - 35.00
2652-D *A Shanty In Old Shanty Town*...............20.00 - 30.00
2728-D *Play, Fiddle, Play* ....20.00 - 30.00
2748-D *Buy American!* ....20.00 - 30.00
2753-D *There's A New Day Coming* ....20.00 - 30.00
2758-D *All Aboard For Dreamland, Baby* ....20.00 - 30.00
2774-D *Stormy Weather* ....30.00 - 50.00
2775-D *The Gold-Diggers' Song*.......................25.00 - 35.00
2777-D *In A Garden In Old Kalua* ....20.00 - 30.00
2786-D *Rhythm* ....30.00 - 50.00
2799-D *Here You Come With Love* ....25.00 - 40.00
2807-D *Ten Thousand Years Ago*......................25.00 - 35.00
(Note: most of the foregoing, after number 1656-D were issued with
    the special Ted Lewis picture label, and some earlier issues were
    repressed with this label. Also, many of the later issues, and
    repressings of earlier issues, are pressed of royal blue shellac.)
Columbia A2844 "O" ....10.00 - 15.00
Columbia A2798, A2895, A2908, A2927, A294,
    A2998, A3306, A3329, A3351, A3400, A3411,
    A3421, A3434, A3453, A3473, A3499, A3538,
    A3590, A3647, A3662, A3709, A3730, A3738,
    A3814, A3944, A3957 ....5.00 - 10.00
Columbia A3464 *Home Again Blues* ....8.00 - 10.00
    A3790 *Runnin' Wild* ....8.00 - 12.00
    A3813 *Tiger Rag* ....10.00 - 15.00
    A3879 *Aunt Hagar's Blues* ....10.00 - 15.00
    A3892 *Beale Street Mama* ....8.00 - 12.00
    A3972 *Beale Street Blues* ....10.00 - 15.00
Decca 107 *Jazznocracy*..................................15.00 - 20.00
Decca 106, 239, 240, 241, 242 ....7.00 - 12.00
Decca, most other issues..................................5.00 - 8.00

JOIE LICHTER'S STRAND SYMPHONISTS:
Gennett 5409 *I'm In A Fool's Paradise* ....20.00 - 30.00
    5423 *Patricia Mine* ....20.00 - 30.00
    5427 *Orange Blossom Time*........................20.00 - 30.00
Harmograph 887 *I'm All Broke Out With The Blues*
....30.00 - 50.00
Paramount 20289 *Linger Awhile* ....30.00 - 50.00
    20428 *Spanish Shawl* ....20.00 - 30.00
    20439 *Slippery Elm*..................................20.00 - 30.00
Puritan 11428 *Sandy* ....20.00 - 30.00
    11439 *After I Said I'm Sorry* ....20.00 - 30.00
Silvertone 3502 *Spanish Shawl* ....20.00 - 30.00
    3507 *Slippery Elm*....................................20.00 - 30.00

LIDO VENICE DANCE ORCHESTRA:
Pathe-Actuelle 036110 *San*..............................15.00 - 20.00
    036114 *I Wonder What's Become Of Sally?*........8.00 - 12.00
Perfect 14291 *When Things Go Wrong*.................15.00 - 20.00
    14295 *I Wonder What's Become Of Sally?*..........8.00 - 12.00

(GLEN) LIETZKE'S MIDNIGHT/MIDNITE SERENADERS:
Broadway 1399 *So Beats My Heart For You*............8.00 - 12.00
    1425 *You're The One I Care For*........................8.00 - 12.00

LOUIS LILIENFELD & HIS HOTEL BILTMORE ORCHESTRA:
Edison 52128 *The Calinda*................................20.00 - 30.00.
    52176 *Normandy* ....15.00 - 20.00
    52216 *My Ohio Home* ....20.00 - 30.00
    52237 *Mary Ann* ....35.00 - 50.00
    52241 *Let a Smile Be Your Umbrella* ....50.00 - 75.00
    52272 *Forever And Ever*.............................50.00 - 75.00
    52289 *Ma Belle* ....20.00 - 30.00

LILL'S HOT SHOTS:
Vocalion 1037 *Drop That Sack* ....150.00 - 250.00

DONALD LINDLEY (& HIS BOYS):
Columbia 546-D *Trumpet Blues* ....15.00 - 20.00
    1443-D *Slidin' Around*...............................15.00 - 20.00
Edison 51771 *Hot As A Summer's Day* ....40.00 - 60.00

PETER LING:
Romeo 310 *Usen't You Used To Be My Sweetie?*..12.00 - 16.00

JACK LINX & HIS (BIRMINGHAM) SOCIETY SERENADERS:
Okeh 40188 *Doodle Doo Doo* ....15.00 - 20.00
    40192 *How Come You Do Me Like You Do?* ...50.00 - 80.00
    40365 *Sweet Georgia Brown* ....40.00 - 60.00
    40429 *She's My Sheba, I'm Her Sheik*.............50.00 - 80.00
    40439 *When Eyes Of Blue Are Fooling You* ......50.00 - 80.00
    40458 *Don't You Try To High-Hat Me* ....50.00 - 80.00
    40587 *Nobody's Rose* ....50.00 - 80.00
    40602 *Fallen Arches* ....50.00 - 80.00
    40619 *Tiger Rag* ....75.00 - 100.00
    40803 *Beale Street Blues* ....75.00 - 100.00
    41014 *Pardon The Glove* ....75.00 - 100.00

THE LITTLE ACES:
Okeh 41136 *Four Or Five Times*...........................50.00 - 75.00

THE LITTLE CHOCOLATE DANDIES:
Okeh 8728 *Six Or Seven Times*............................50.00 - 75.00

LITTLE'S COLLEGIANS:
Superior 2817 *Clarinet Marmalade* ....100.00 - 150.00

THE LITTLE RAMBLERS:
Bluebird 6144 *Everything Is Okey Dokey* ....10.00 - 15.00
    6043, 6045, 6077, 6130, 6131, 6189, 6191, 6192,
    6193, 6220, 6232, 6237..............................7.00 - 12.00
Columbia 175-D *Arkansas Blues* ....15.00 - 20.00
    203-D *Hard Hearted Hannah* ....12.00 - 16.00
    217-D *Deep Blue Sea Blues* ....15.00 - 20.00
    248-D *Prince Of Wails* ....15.00 - 20.00
    346-D *Don't Bring Lulu* ....12.00 - 16.00
    403-D *Got No Time* ....15.00 - 25.00
    423-D *Deep Elm* ....15.00 - 25.00
    524-D *In Your Green Hat* ....15.00 - 20.00

535-D *To-Morrow Mornin'* ....15.00 - 25.00
628-D *Here Comes Malinda* ....15.00 - 20.00
679-D *Hot Henry!* ....15.00 - 20.00
719-D *And Then I Forget* ....15.00 - 20.00
1103-D *Swamp Blues* ....15.00 - 20.00

LITTLE JACK LITTLE & HIS ORCHESTRA:
Bluebird 5056, 5065 ....8.00 - 12.00
Columbia 2895-D, 2900-D, 2969-D, 2978-D,
2984-D, 2993-D, 3006-D, 3009-D 3068-D,
3069-D, 3095-D, 3107-D, 3108-D ....8.00 - 12.00

ED LLOYD AND HIS ORCHESTRA (See ED LOYD)

PAUL LOCH & HIS ORCHESTRA:
Parlophone PNY-34059 *I Was Made To Love You* .25.00 - 40.00
PNY-34063 *Accordion Joe* ....30.00 - 50.00
PNY-34065 *Collegiate Love* ....35.00 - 50.00

LOCKE BROTHERS' RHYTHM ORCHESTRA:
Bluebird 6287 *Don't You Tear My Clothes* ....15.00 - 20.00
6288 *Sills Stomp* ....20.00 - 30.00
6297 *Elephant Stomp* ....20.00 - 30.00
6216 *Some Of These Days* ....20.00 - 30.00
6332 *China Boy* ....20.00 - 30.00

LOFNER-HARRIS ST. FRANCIS HOTEL ORCHESTRA:
Victor 22830 *I Got The Ritz From The One I Love* .15.00 - 20.00
22831 *River, Stay 'Way From My Door* ....15.00 - 20.00

GUY LOMBARDO & HIS ROYAL CANADIANS:
Brunswick, most issues, 6000 series ....5.00 - 10.00
Columbia 1395-D *Waitin' For Katy* ....10.00 - 15.00
1451-D *The Cannon Ball* ....15.00 - 20.00
1721-D *Baby* ....8.00 - 12.00
2457-D *Moonlight Saving Time* ....10.00 - 15.00
2578-D *River, Stay 'Way From My Door* ....10.00 - 15.00
Columbia, most other issues ....5.00 - 10.00
Decca 102 *Love In Bloom* ....8.00 - 12.00
103 *Moon Glow* ....8.00 - 12.00
104 *Stars Fell On Alabama* ....8.00 - 12.00
Decca (blue label), most other issues ....5.00 - 8.00
Gennett 5416 *So This Is Venice* ....50.00 - 75.00
5417 *Cotton Picker's Ball* ....75.00 - 100.00
Melotone, most issues ....5.00 - 8.00
Oriole, most issues ....5.00 - 8.00
Perfect, most issues ....5.00 - 8.00
Personal Record 140-P *She'll Come Along* ....20.00 - 30.00
Romeo, most issues ....5.00 - 8.00
Victor, most issues, 25000 series ....5.00 - 10.00

FRED LONGSHAW:
Columbia 14080-D *Chili Pepper* ....75.00 - 100.00

ERNEST LOOMIS' ORCHESTRA:
Victor 20755 *Sweet Someone* ....30.00 - 50.00

VINCENT LOPEZ & HIS (CASA LOPEZ/HOTEL PENNSYLVANIA) ORCHESTRA:
Banner 0557 *Look For The Silver Lining* ....8.00 - 12.00
0569 *'tain't No Sin* ....10.00 - 15.00
Banner, most other issues ....5.00 - 8.00
Bluebird, most issues ....5.00 - 8.00
Brunswick 20065 (12 inch) *St. Louis Blues* ....15.00 - 25.00
20066 (12 inch) *Alexander's Ragtime Band* ....15.00 - 25.00
Brunswick, most other issues ....5.00 - 8.00
Cameo, most issues ....5.00 - 8.00

Domino, most issues ....5.00 - 8.00
Hit-of-the-Week, most issues ....5.00 - 8.00
(Note: Above are one-sided paper records.)
Okeh 4783 *Aggravatin' Papa* ....8.00 - 12.00
4819 *You've Got To See Mama Ev'ry Night* ....8.00 - 12.00
4869 *Blue Hoosier Blues* ....8.00 - 12.00
40009 *Raggedy Ann* ....8.00 - 12.00
40024 *Steppin' Out* ....8.00 - 12.00
40199 *Me And The Boy Friend* ....8.00 - 12.00
40478 *Stomp Off, Let's Go* ....15.00 - 20.00
40516 *Show Me The Way To Go Home* ....10.00 - 15.00
40542 *A Cup Of Coffee, A Sandwich And You* .. 10.00 - 15.00
40552 *Black Horse Stomp* ....15.00 - 25.00
40586 *Rhythm Of The Day* ....15.00 - 20.00
Okeh, most other issues ....5.00 - 10.00
Oriole, most issues ....5.00 - 8.00
Perfect 15262 *Look For The Silver Lining* ....8.00 - 12.00
7-02-12 *Love And Learn* ....7.00 - 10.00
7-04-12 *Music On The Mall* ....7.00 - 10.00
8-01-09 *Ham On Rye* ....7.00 - 10.00
Perfect, most other issues ....5.00 - 8.00
Regal, most issues ....5.00 - 8.00
Romeo, most issues ....5.00 - 8.00
Van Dyke 71785 *If I Had A Talking Picture Of You* ....7.00 - 10.00
71791 *Chant of the Jungle* ....8.00 - 12.00
Vocalion 4129 *Day Dreaming (All Night Long)* ....7.00 - 10.00
4141 *There's Honey On The Moon Tonight* ....7.00 - 10.00

LOS ANGELES BILTMORE HOTEL TRIO:
Okeh 41064 *Clowin' The Frets* ....10.00 - 15.00

LOU & HIS GINGER SNAPS:
Banner 6536 *Broadway Rhythm* ....15.00 - 25.00
6540 *The Way He Loves Is Just Too Bad* ....10.00 - 15.00
Cameo 9319 *Broadway Rhythm* ....15.00 - 25.00
9320 *The Way He Loves Is Just Too Bad* ....10.00 - 15.00

LOUIS' HARLEM STOMPERS:
Columbia 2615-D *Casa Loma Stomp* ....20.00 - 30.00

LOUISIANA FIVE (JAZZ ORCHESTRA):
Columbia A2742 *Yelping Hound Blues* ....7.00 - 10.00
A2949 *Slow And Easy* ....7.00 - 10.00
Columbia, most other issues ....5.00 - 10.00
Edison 50609 *Clarinet Squawk* ....15.00 - 20.00
50622 *Yelping Hound Blues* ....15.00 - 20.00
Emerson 501 (12-inch) *Yelping Hound Blues* ....20.00 - 30.00
Emerson 1026 *Dixie Blues* ....15.00 - 20.00
1076 *Virginia Blues* ....15.00 - 20.00
1083 *Ringtail Blues* ....15.00 - 20.00
9150 *Heart-Sickness Blues* ....15.00 - 20.00
9158 *A Good Man Is Hard To Find* ....15.00 - 20.00
9178 *Rainy Day Blues* ....15.00 - 20.00
9179 *Yama Yama Blues* ....15.00 - 20.00
10116 *Weary Blues* ....10.00 - 15.00
10172 *Weeping Willow Blues* ....10.00 - 15.00
10229 *Sunshine Girl* ....10.00 - 15.00
10241 *Town Topic Rag* ....10.00 - 15.00
(some of above titles are found on Medallion, similarly valued.)
Lyric 4233 *Land Of Creole Girls* ....-- - --
Okeh 1200 *After All* ....7.00 - 10.00
1249 *Laughing Blues* ....7.00 - 10.00

LOUISIANA JOE AND SLIM:
Champion 50063 *Crossin' Beale Street* ....50.00 - 75.00

LOUISIANA MASTER PLAYERS:
Van Dyke 71798 *Just You, Honey* ....20.00 - 30.00

LOUISIANA RHYTHM KINGS:
Brunswick 4706 *Oh, Lady Be Good* ....30.00 - 50.00
    4845 *Swanee* ....30.00 - 50.00
    4908 *Karavan* ....35.00 - 50.00
    4923 *Lazy Daddy* ....35.00 - 50.00
    4938 *Pretty Baby* ....35.00 - 50.00
    4953 *Squeeze Me* ....35.00 - 50.00
Vocalion 15657 *Nobody's Sweetheart*....................35.00 - 50.00
    15710 *I Can't Give You Anything But Love* ....75.00 - 100.00
    15716 *Dusky Stevedore*.............................50.00 - 80.00
    15729 *Skinner's Sock*...............................80.00 - 120.00
    15779 *Futuristic Rhythm* ....150.00 - 200.00
    15784 *That's A Plenty* ....150.00 - 200.00
    15810 *I'm Walking Through Clover*.................150.00 - 200.00
    15815 *Last Cent* ....150.00 - 250.00
    15828 *Ballin' The Jack*.............................150.00 - 250.00
    15833 *Waiting At The End Of The Road* ....100.00 - 150.00
    15841 *Little By Little* ....100.00 - 150.00

LOUISIANA RHYTHMAKERS:
Titles issued contemporaneously on Banner, Melotone, Oriole, Perfect, and Romeo: *Casa Loma Stomp; Clarinet Marmalade; Runnin' Wild; Twelfth Street Rag*..........10.00 - 20.00

LOUISIANA STOMPERS:
Paramount 12550 *Hop Off*...................................150.00 - 200.00

LOUISIANA SUGAR BABES:
Bluebird 10260 *Thou Swell* ....15.00 - 20.00
Victor 21346 *Persian Rug* ....20.00 - 30.00
    21348 *Willow Tree*...................................20.00 - 30.00

LOUISIANA WASHBOARD BAND:
Domino 3671 *Shake That Thing* ....80.00 - 120.00

LOUISVILLE RHYTHM KINGS:
Okeh 41189 *In A Great Big Way*...........................75.00 - 100.00

LOUISVILLE WASHBOARD BAND:
Domino 3755 *Boodle Am* ....50.00 - 75.00
Oriole 650 *Boodle Am* ....40.00 - 60.00
    674 *I've Found A New Baby* ....40.00 - 60.00

BERT LOWN & HIS LOUNGERS/ORCHESTRA/HOTEL BILTMORE ORCHESTRA:
Titles issued contemporaneously on Banner, Cameo, Conqueror, Perfect, Oriole, Regal, and Romeo: *Blue Is The Night; I Love You, Believe Me; I Never Dreamt; Keepin' Myself For You; The One I Love Just Can't Be Bothered With Me; The Perfect Song; Strike Up The Band* ....10.00 - 15.00
Bluebird 5067 *Isn't It Heavenly?* ....8.00 - 12.00
    5068 *I Cover The Waterfront*.....................8.00 - 12.00
    5087 *My Heart's Desire* ....8.00 - 12.00
    5088 *We'll Have A Honeymoon Some Day*........15.00 - 20.00
    5099 *Here You Come With Love* ....15.00 - 20.00
    5100 *Black Panther* ....15.00 - 20.00
(Note: Above titles on Electradisk are valued similarly, or slightly higher; on Sunrise, substantially higher.)
Columbia 2258-D *Bye Bye Blues* ....8.00 - 12.00
    2292-D *Maybe It's Love* ....8.00 - 12.00
Harmony 852-H *Redskin* ....10.00 - 15.00
    853-H *My Castle In Spain Is A Shack In The Lane* ....10.00 - 15.00

    863-H *Tomorrow's Violets* ....10.00 - 15.00
    892-H *Here Comes My Ball And Chain* ....15.00 - 20.00
    920-H *Big City Blues* ....8.00 - 12.00
    974-H *The Jazz Me Blues* ....30.00 - 50.00
    1088-H *Under A Texas Moon* ....10.00 - 15.00
    1111-H *Only A Rose* ....8.00 - 12.00
(Note: Above titles on Diva and Velvet Tone are similarly valued.)
Hit of the Week 1020 *Through* ....10.00 - 15.00
    1021 *Hello, Baby* ....15.00 - 20.00
    1032 *Congratulations* ....8.00 - 12.00
    1090 *Bye Bye Blues* ....7.00 - 10.00
(Note: Above Hit-of-the-Week records are single-sided, paper discs.)
Victor 22582 *You're Simply Delish* ....10.00 - 15.00
    22603 *To Whom It May Concern*....................15.00 - 20.00
    22652 *Please Don't Talk About Me When I'm Gone* ....10.00 - 15.00
    22654 *When I Take My Sugar To Tea* ....10.00 - 15.00
    22810 *Blues In My Heart* ....10.00 - 15.00
    22541, 22568, 22583, 22602, 22612, 22623, 22653, 22689, 22696, 22725, 22738, 22740, 22744, 22754, 22787, 22795, 22804, 22805, 22908, 22927, 24086, 24087, 24116 ....7.00 - 12.00

ED LOYD AND HIS ORCHESTRA:
Banner 6413 *Walking With Susie*.............................7.00 - 10.00
    6421 *To Be In Love*.......................................7.00 - 10.00
Odeon ONY-36060 *The Free And Easy* (instrumental) ....30.00 - 50.00
    ONY-36061 *The Free And Easy* ....25.00 - 30.00
    ONY-36065 *You Brought A New Kind Of Love To Me* ....20.00 - 30.00
    ONY-36080 *Reminiscing* ....20.00 - 40.00
    ONY-36081 *Nobody Cares If I'm Blue* ....20.00 - 30.00
    ONY-36089 *You For Me* ....20.00 - 30.00
    ONY-36090 *Ro-Ro Rolling Along* ....20.00 - 30.00
    ONY-36113 *Just A Little Closer*......................25.00 - 35.00
    ONY-36123 *Hullabaloo* ....20.00 - 30.00
    ONY-36124 *My One Ambition Is You* ....20.00 - 30.00
    ONY-36132 *I'm Doin' That Thing* ....20.00 - 30.00
    ONY-36133 *Don't Tell Her* ....20.00 - 30.00
    ONY-36147 *I'll Still Belong To You* ....20.00 - 30.00
    ONY-36150 *Sweet Jennie Lee* ....20.00 - 30.00
    ONY-36161 *Morning, Noon And Night*............20.00 - 30.00
    ONY-36172 *Fall In Love With Me* ....20.00 - 30.00
    ONY-36176 *Where Have You Been?* ....20.00 - 30.00
    ONY-36177 *He's My Secret Passion* ....20.00 - 30.00
    ONY-36182 *It Must Be True* ....20.00 - 30.00
    ONY-36185 *Sing Song Girl* ....20.00 - 30.00
    ONY-36186 *Hello! Beautiful*...........................20.00 - 30.00
    ONY-36193 *All On Account Of Your Kisses* .....20.00 - 30.00
Okeh 41250 *I Get The Blues When It Rains* ....15.00 - 20.00
    41259 *The One In The World*........................25.00 - 40.00
    41294 *Lovable And Sweet* ....15.00 - 20.00
    41295 *I'm Doing What I'm Doing For Love* .....15.00 - 20.00
    41312 *Wouldn't It Be Wonderful?* ....15.00 - 20.00
    41319 *Lonely Troubadour* ....8.00 - 12.00
    41338 *A Little Kiss Each Morning* ....15.00 - 20.00
    41348 *If You Were The Only Girl In The World* ....12.00 - 16.00
    41353 *What Do I Care?*................................15.00 - 20.00
    41354 *Put A Little Salt On The Bluebird's Tail*. 15.00 - 20.00
    41367 *Singing A Vagabond Song* ....15.00 - 20.00
    41368 *Beside An Open Fireplace* ....10.00 - 15.00
    41392 *The Free And Easy*............................15.00 - 20.00

41407 *You Brought A New Kind Of Love To Me* 15.00 - 20.00
41428 *I'm Needin' You* 15.00 - 20.00
41435 *I've Got My Eye On You* 15.00 - 20.00

NICK LUCAS:
Brunswick 6508 *Teasin' The Frets* 8.00 - 12.00
Brunswick (most other issues) 5.00 - 10.00
MacGregor (10-inch transcriptions, usually pressed of blue shellac) 10.00 - 15.00

LUCKY DEVILS:
Perfect 14806, 14812, 14833, 14857, 14917 7.00 - 12.00

LUCKY TEN ENTERTAINERS:
Domino 3992 *Dew Dew Dewy Day* 7.00 - 10.00
3996 *Sing Me A Baby Song* 8.00 - 12.00
3997 *You Don't Like It-Not Much* 10.00 - 15.00
Regal 8352 *Dew Dew Dewy Day* 7.00 - 10.00
8354 *You Don't Like It- Not Much* 10.00 - 15.00
8355 *Sing Me A Baby Song* 8.00 - 12.00

THE LUMBERJACKS:
Cameo 8352 *Black Beauty* 15.00 - 20.00
8356 *Spanish Dream* 10.00 - 15.00
8368 *Since You Went Away* 8.00 - 12.00
9007 *Oh, Boy! It's A Pleasure* 10.00 - 15.00
9020 *I Found My Sunshine In The Rain* 8.00 - 12.00
9030 *Whoopee Stomp* 15.00 - 20.00
9041 *Blue Little You* 8.00 - 12.00
9045 *Let Me Be Alone With You* 7.00 - 10.00
9084 *I've Never Been Loved By Anyone Like You.* 10.00 - 15.00
9147 *Would You Be Happy?* 7.00 - 10.00
9171 *Will You, Won't You* 8.00 - 12.00
9183 *Crazy Baby* 10.00 - 15.00
9209 *Somebody Loves You* 10.00 - 15.00
(Foregoing titles also issued on Lincoln, Romeo, similarly valued)

GUY LUMPKIN:
QRS 7078 *Decatur Street Rag* 150.00 - 200.00

JIMMIE LUNCEFORD & HIS CHICKASAW SYNCOPATORS/ORCHESTRA:
Bluebird 5330 *Sweet Rhythm* 20.00 - 30.00
5713 *White Heat* 5.00 - 8.00
6133 *Breakfast Ball* 8.00 - 12.00
Columbia (red label), most issues 5.00 - 10.00
Decca 129 *Sophisticated Lady* 10.00 - 15.00
130 *Nana* 10.00 - 15.00
131 *Mood Indigo* 10.00 - 20.00
299 *Solitude* 10.00 - 20.00
369 *Stardust* 8.00 - 12.00
415 *Because You're You* 10.00 - 15.00
453 *Since My Best Gal Turned Me Down* 10.00 - 15.00
503 *Four or Five Times* 10.00 - 15.00
572 *Rhythm In My Nursery Rhymes* 8.00 - 12.00
576 *Thunder* 8.00 - 12.00
628 *Charmaine* 8.00 - 12.00
639 *Bird of Paradise* 8.00 - 12.00
668 *Swanee River* 8.00 - 12.00
682 *I'm Nuts About Screwy Music* 8.00 - 12.00
712 *My Blue Heaven* 8.00 - 12.00
765 *Hittin' The Bottle* 8.00 - 12.00
788 *The Best Things In Life Are Free* 8.00 - 12.00
805 *The Melody Man* 8.00 - 12.00
908 *Organ Grinder's Song* 8.00 - 12.00
915 *Me And The Moon* 8.00 - 12.00

960 *Living From Day To Day* 8.00 - 12.00
980 *Harlem Shout* 10.00 - 15.00
1035 *Running A Temperature* 8.00 - 12.00
1128 *He Ain't Got Rhythm* 8.00 - 12.00
1219 *Muddy Water* 8.00 - 12.00
1229 *Linger Awhile* 8.00 - 12.00
1318 *I'll See You In My Dreams* 8.00 - 12.00
1340 *For Dancers Only* 8.00 - 12.00
1355 *Honey, Keep Your Mind On Me* 8.00 - 12.00
1364 *Ragging The Scale* 8.00 - 12.00
1506 *Hell's Bells* 8.00 - 12.00
1569 *Annie Laurie* 8.00 - 12.00
1617 *Margie* 7.00 - 10.00
1659 *Pigeon Walk* 8.00 - 12.00
1734 *Teasin' Tessie Brown* 8.00 - 12.00
1808 *My Melancholy Baby* 8.00 - 12.00
1927 *Down By The Old Mill Stream* 8.00 - 12.00
Decca (most other issues) 5.00 - 10.00
Okeh (most issues) 7.00 - 10.00
Victor 24522 *Jazznocracy* 15.00 - 25.00
24586 *White Heat* 15.00 - 25.00
24601 *Breakfast Ball* 15.00 - 25.00
24669 *Swingin' Uptown* 15.00 - 25.00
V-38141 *In Dat Mornin'* 100.00 - 150.00
Vocalion 4582, 4595, 4667, 4712, 4754, 4831, 4875,
4979, 5033, 5116, 5156, 5276 7.00 - 12.00

HUNK LUNSFORD & HIS CLARINET:
Champion 15263 *Mississippi Valley Blues* 150.00 - 200.00

JIMMY LUVERTE & HIS SOCIETY TROUBADOURS:
Vocalion 03559 *You Think She Ain't* 20.00 - 30.00
03602 *Music Box Blues* 20.00 - 30.00

ABE LYMAN & HIS CALIFORNIA ORCHESTRA; ABE LYMAN'S SHARPS & FLATS; ABE LYMAN'S CALIFORNIA (AMBASSADOR HOTEL) ORCHESTRA:
Bluebird, most issues 5.00 - 8.00
Brunswick 2481 *Bugle Call Rag* 10.00 - 15.00
2504 *Weary Weasel* 10.00 - 15.00
2563 *Honey Babe* 8.00 - 12.00
2780 *Sally's Got The Blues* 8.00 - 12.00
2980 *Everybody Stomp* 15.00 - 20.00
3069 *Shake That Thing* 10.00 - 15.00
3084 *Too Bad* 8.00 - 12.00
3241 *Ace In The Hole* 8.00 - 12.00
3286 *Havin' Lots Of Fun* 8.00 - 12.00
3316 *New St. Louis Blues* 10.00 - 15.00
3317 *Wistful And Blue* 7.00 - 10.00
3753 *Keep Sweeping The Cobwebs Off The Moon* 8.00 - 12.00
3964 *Weary Weasel* 15.00 - 20.00
3971 *That's My Weakness Now* 8.00 - 12.00
4155 *A Jazz Holiday* 10.00 - 15.00
4912 *Hullabaloo* 10.00 - 15.00
4924 *Never Swat A Fly* 10.00 - 15.00
6314 *Farewell Blues* 10.00 - 15.00
6325 *Milenberg Joys* 10.00 - 15.00
6380 *Riddle Me This* 8.00 - 12.00
6637 *Weary Blues* 8.00 - 12.00
6674 *Doin' The Uptown Lowdown* 8.00 - 12.00
6756 *Jimmy Had A Nickel* 8.00 - 12.00
Brunswick (12-inch) 20063 *"Good News"* medley 15.00 - 20.00
20103 (12-inch) *"The Laugh Parade"* medley 20.00 - 30.00
20122 (12-inch) *"Stormy Weather"* 25.00 - 35.00

Brunswick, most other issues ....7.00 - 10.00
Columbia, most issues ....5.00 - 8.00
Decca 1098, 1104, 1105, 1119, 1120, 1127,
   1130, 1225, 1226, 1235 ....7.00 - 10.00

LYNCH'S RHYTHM ACES:
Challenge 742 *She's My Baby Now* ....10.00 - 15.00
   749 *Oh! Constantine* ....8.00 - 12.00

AL LYNCH & HIS ORCHESTRA:
Banner 6149 *I'm Gonna March With April In May* ..7.00 - 10.00
   6151 *Sweet Mandy*..7.00 - 10.00
   6155 *I'm Just Wondering*..............................7.00 - 10.00
   7032 *I've Got The Blue Grass Blues* ....8.00 - 12.00
   7033 *For My Gal And Me*..............................8.00 - 12.00
   7038 *Oh, How I Love To Look At You*..................7.00 - 10.00
   7077 *Who Says They Don't Care*.......................7.00 - 10.00
   7107 *Light The Way To Somebody's Heart*........10.00 - 15.00
   7109 *Put Your Loving Arms Around Me* ....10.00 - 15.00
   7112 *They Can't Take You Away From Me Now* .7.00 - 10.00
   7130 *What Do I Care*....................................7.00 - 10.00
Broadway 1105 *Washington & Lee Swing* ....7.00 - 10.00
   1106 *Sweetheart of Sigma Chi*........................7.00 - 10.00
   1107 *Baltimore* ....7.00 - 10.00
Challenge 615 *Light The Way To Somebody's Heart*
   ....10.00 - 15.00
   616 *Put Your Loving Arms Around Me* ....10.00 - 15.00

AL LYNN'S MUSIC MASTERS:
Edison 51952 *Indian Butterfly* ....15.00 - 20.00
   52004 *There Ain't No Maybe In My Baby's Eyes*.. 20.00 - 30.00
   52041 *Sometimes I'm Happy* ....25.00 - 40.00
   52086 *Me And My Shadow* ....25.00 - 40.00
   52099 *Marvelous* ....50.00 - 75.00
   52101 *Who Gives You All Your Kisses* ....50.00 - 75.00
   52148 *I'm Telling The World (That I Love You)* 30.00 - 50.00
   52226 *Anything To Make You Happy*..................30.00 - 50.00
   52227 *Symphonic Raps*.................................50.00 - 75.00
   52270 *Whisper Sweet And Whisper Low* ....100.00 - up
   52399 *Lonely Little Bluebird* ....80.00 - 120.00
Jewel 5011 *Would You Care?* ....10.00 - 15.00
Oriole 874 *I'm Crazy For Her* ....7.00 - 10.00
   883 *Take A Little Walk* ....15.00 - 20.00
   900 *Me And My Shadow* ....7.00 - 10.00
   902 *One O'Clock Baby* ....7.00 - 10.00

GLEN LYTE & HIS ORCHESTRA:
Broadway 1459 *When I Take My Sugar To Tea*........8.00 - 12.00
   1475 *Pardon Me, Pretty Baby* ....8.00 - 12.00

JIMMY LYTELL:
Pathe-Actuelle (titles as on Perfect, below)
Perfect 14749 *Old Folks Shuffle* ....25.00 - 40.00
   14765 *Messin' Around*...................................35.00 - 50.00
   14788 *Pardon The Glove* ....35.00 - 50.00
   14846 *Zulu Wail* ....35.00 - 50.00
   14898 *Headin' For Harlem* ....35.00 - 50.00
   14922 *Stockholm Stomp*................................35.00 - 50.00
   14956 *Missouri Squabble* ....35.00 - 50.00
   15005 *Yellow Dog Blues*................................35.00 - 50.00
(Foregoing titles on Pathe-Actuelle are similarly valued)

ART MACE & MAJESTIC EIGHT:
Sunset 1150 *In Your Green Hat*...................... - - -

BABY MACK:
Okeh 8313 *What Kind Of Man Is You?* .... 150.00 - 200.00

CHARLES E. MACK:
Columbia 50061-D (12 inch) *Our Child*................. 15.00 - 20.00

ENRIC MADRIGUERA AND HIS ORCHESTRA:
Columbia 2651-D *My Extraordinary Gal* .... 10.00 - 15.00
   2906-D *I Knew You When* .... 15.00 - 20.00
Columbia, most other "-D" series .... 7.00 - 12.00
Vogue R-760 *So It Goes* .... 25.00 - 40.00
   R-776 *Mujercita*.. 30.00 - 50.00
   R-777 *La Rumbita Tropical* .... 40.00 - 60.00
   R-778 *Guilty Of Love* .... 40.00 - 60.00
   R-779 *A Man, A Moon, And A Maid*............... 40.00 - 60.00

SHERRY MAGEE & HIS DIXIELANDERS:
Okeh 5436 *Satanic Blues* .... 8.00 - 12.00
Vocalion 5281 *Shake It And Break It*........................ 8.00 - 12.00
   5436 *Bluin' The Blues*.................................. 8.00 - 12.00

MAJESTIC BAND:
Majestic 144 (7 inch) *Razzazza Mazzazza* .... 15.00 - 25.00

MAJESTIC DANCE ORCHESTRA:
Banner 0561 *My Way Right Back To Arkansas* .... 7.00 - 10.00
   0590 *The Man From The South* .... 10.00 - 15.00
   0596 *I've Seen My Baby* .... 8.00 - 12.00
   0692 *My Love Parade*.................................. 7.00 - 10.00
   0851 *You're Simply Delish* .... 15.00 - 25.00
(Foregoing titles, also found on Cameo, Jewel, Oriole, Regal, and
   Romeo, similarly valued)
Cameo (titles as on Banner, above, similarly valued)
Challenge 892 *Sweetheart*.. 5.00 - 8.00
Conqueror 7623 *I'll Be Blue (Just Thinking of You)* 7.00 - 10.00
Domino 4449 *Somebody Mighty Like You*............... 7.00 - 10.00
Oriole 928 *Magnolia*.................................... 10.00 - 15.00
   933 *Zulu Wail*.. 10.00 - 15.00
   961 *Dew-Dew-Dewy Day* .... 7.00 - 10.00
   977 *Sing Me A Baby Song*.............................. 10.00 - 15.00
   980 *Delirium* .... 15.00 - 25.00
   990 *Farewell Blues* .... 20.00 - 30.00
   2379 *An Ev'ning In Caroline* .... 7.00 - 10.00
Pathe-Actuelle 37004 *Am I Blue?* .... 8.00 - 12.00
Perfect 14391 *Why Couldn't It Be Poor Little Me?* ....15.00 - 20.00
   15034 *If You Don't Love Me*.............................. 7.00 - 10.00
   15083 *Four Or Five Times* .... 15.00 - 20.00
   15185 *Am I Blue?*...................................... 8.00 - 12.00
   15244 *Somebody Mighty Like You* .... 7.00 - 10.00
Regal 8893 *Somebody Mighty Like You* .... 7.00 - 10.00
   10118 *Always In All Ways* .... 5.00 - 8.00
Romeo 1129 *Somebody Mighty Like You* .... 7.00 - 10.00
   1426 *Always In All Ways* .... 7.00 - 10.00
   1605 *Out Of Nowhere* .... 7.00 - 10.00
Van Dyke 71797 *I Won't Be Satisfied* .... 7.00 - 10.00

MAJOR & HIS ORCHESTRA:
Hollywood 1028 *Blue Evening Blues* .... 200.00 - 300.00

THOMAS MALIN:
Pathe 20376 *Romping Bessie* .... 7.00 - 10.00

FRANKLIN MALVIN:
Emerson 7122 (7 inch) *It's A Peach* .... - -

TERRY MANDEL & HIS ORCHESTRA:
Broadway 1498 *Black And Tan Fantasy*................. 20.00 - 30.00

MANHATTAN DANCE MAKERS:
Columbia 440-D *She's Drivin' Me Wild* ....8.00 - 12.00
Harmony 241-H *She's Still My Baby* ....8.00 - 12.00
   413-H *I'm Gonna Meet My Sweetie Now* ....8.00 - 12.00
   458-H *Dew-Dew-Dewy Day* ....7.00 - 10.00
   462-H *Is It Possible? (That She Loves Me)* ....10.00 - 15.00
   486-H *Dawning* ....7.00 - 10.00
   604-H *Down South* ....7.00 - 10.00
(Note: Above titles on Diva and Velvet Tone are similarly valued.)

MANHATTAN DANCE ORCHESTRA:
National Music Lovers 1099 *I Can't Get The One I Want*
....10.00 - 15.00

MANHATTAN IMPERIAL ORCHESTRA:
Broadway 11312 *Bathing Beauty Blues* ....35.00 - 50.00
Puritan 11229 *Farewell Blues* ....15.00 - 25.00
   11264 *Bathing Beauty Blues* ....35.00 - 50.00
Triangle 11268 *Louisville Lou* ....15.00 - 20.00

MANHATTAN MUSICIANS:
National Music Lovers 1163 *I'll Make You Answer Yes*
....10.00 - 15.00
   1187 *Can You Picture That* ....10.00 - 15.00
National Music Lovers, most other issues ....5.00 - 8.00
New Phonic 1243 *Somebody's Making A Fuss* ....15.00 - 20.00
   1247 *If I Can Ba-Ba-Baby You* ....10.00 - 15.00

MANHATTAN NIGHT CAPS:
Champion 15442 *Down Moonlight Lane* ....10.00 - 15.00
   15495 *Hot Coffee* ....15.00 - 20.00
   15534 *Was It A Dream?* ....8.00 - 12.00
   15536 *Sweet Lorraine* ....10.00 - 15.00

MARION MANN WITH BOB HAGGART'S ORCHESTRA:
Vogue R-731 *You Took Advantage Of Me* ....50.00 - 75.00
   R-758 *Long, Strong And Consecutive* ....25.00 - 40.00

SAM MANNING & HIS COLE JAZZ ORCHESTRA/BLUE HOT SYNCOPATORS:
Columbia 14110-D *Bingo* ....75.00 - 100.00
Okeh 8302 *Keep Your Hand Off That* ....100.00 - 150.00

JOE MANNONE'S HARMONY KINGS; JOE "WINGY" MANNONE & HIS CLUB ROYALE ORCHESTRA; WINGY MANNONE & HIS ORCHESTRA:
Bluebird 6359, 6360, 6375, 6393, 6411, 6472,
   6473, 6483, 6536, 6537, 6549, 6605, 6606,
   6616, 6618, 6804, 6806, 6816, 7002, 7003,
   7014, 7197, 7198, 7214, 7389, 7391, 7395 ....8.00 - 12.00
Bluebird, other issues..7.00 - 10.00
Brunswick 6911 *No Calling Card* ....15.00 - 20.00
   6940 *Send Me* ....15.00 - 20.00
Champion 16153 *Tin Roof Blues* ....200.00 - 300.00
   40055 *Big Butter And Egg Man* ....30.00 - 50.00
Columbia 1044-D *Up The Country Blues* ....150.00 - 250.00
   14282-D *Cat's Head* ....150.00 - 250.00
Okeh 41569 *She's Crying For Me* ....30.00 - 50.00
   41570 *Royal Garden Blues* ....30.00 - 50.00
   41573 *Nickel In The Slot* ....30.00 - 50.00
Special Edition 5011-S *Never Had No Lovin'* ....15.00 - 20.00
Vocalion 2913 *I Believe In Miracles* ....10.00 - 15.00
   2914 *Fare Thee Well, Annabelle* ....10.00 - 15.00
   2933 *You're An Angel* ....10.00 - 15.00
   2934 *Let's Spill The Beans* ....10.00 - 15.00
   2963 *Black Coffee* ....10.00 - 15.00

   2972 *Lulu's Back In Town* ....10.00 - 15.00
   2989 *Love And Kisses* ....10.00 - 15.00
   2990 *Let's Swing It* ....10.00 - 15.00
   3023 *From The Top Of Your Head* ....10.00 - 15.00
   3058 *I'm Gonna Sit Right Down And Write Myself A Letter*
....10.00 - 15.00
   3070 *You Are My Lucky Star* ....10.00 - 15.00
   3071 *I've Got A Note* ....10.00 - 15.00
   3134 *The Music Goes 'Round and 'Round* ....10.00 - 15.00
   3135 *I've Got My Fingers Crossed* ....10.00 - 15.00
   3158 *The Broken Record* ....10.00 - 15.00
   3159 *Old Man Mose* ....10.00 - 15.00
   3171 *Nickel In The Slot* ....8.00 - 12.00
   3191 *Is It True What They Say About Dixie?* ....10.00 - 15.00
   3192 *Shoe-Shine Boy* ....10.00 - 15.00
   15728 *Fare Thee Well* ....150.00 - 250.00
   15797 *Isn't There A Little Love?* ....150.00 - 250.00

ANDY MANSFIELD & HIS BAND:
Champion 15438 *Third Rail* ....50.00 - 80.00

EDDIE MAPP:
   Q.R.S. 7078 *Riding The Blues* ....150.00 - 200.00

MARATHON DANCE ORCHESTRA:
Marathon 165 *When We're Together* ....10.00 - 15.00
   222 *They All Stare At My Girl* ....15.00 - 20.00
   229 *I'm Trying So Hard To Be Happy* ....15.00 - 20.00
(Note: Above Marathon records are 7-inch discs.)

HARVEY MARBURGER & HIS ORCHESTRA:
Harmony 165-H *Don't Let Me Stand In Your Way* .. 8.00 - 12.00

MARDI GRAS SEXTETTE:
Gennett 4843 *You've Had Your Day* ....20.00 - 30.00
   4871 *Rosy Posy* ....10.00 - 15.00

PAUL MARES & HIS FRIARS SOCIETY ORCHESTRA:
Okeh 41574 *Nagasaki* ....35.00 - 50.00
   41575 *Reincarnation* ....35.00 - 50.00

THE MARIGOLD ENTERTAINERS:
Vocalion 15800 *Jealous* ....40.00 - 60.00

THE MARINERS:
Okeh 41433 *Happy Feet* ....15.00 - 20.00
   41449 *I Don't Mind Walkin' In The Rain* ....15.00 - 20.00

MARK STRAND THEATRE ORCHESTRA:
Columbia 443-D *Who Wouldn't Love You?* ....7.00 - 10.00

MIKE MARKEL & HIS ORCHESTRA; MARKEL'S ORCHESTRA; MARKELS' ORCHESTRA; MARKEL'S SOCIETY ORCHESTRA:
Brunswick 3091 *Flamin' Mamie* ....10.00 - 15.00
   3189 *Lulu Belle* ....7.00 - 10.00
   3218 *Hello, Aloha! How Are You?* ....7.00 - 10.00
   3263 *Precious* ....7.00 - 10.00
Columbia 372-D *Little Peach* ....7.00 - 10.00
   385-D *Don't Bother Me* ....10.00 - 15.00
   475-D *Nobody But Fanny* ....8.00 - 12.00
   617-D *Black Horse Stomp* ....30.00 - 50.00
Edison 51752 *Tonight's My Night With Baby* ....25.00 - 40.00
   51764 *Her Beaus Are Only Rainbows* ....10.00 - 15.00
   51794 *That's Why I Love You* ....10.00 - 15.00
   51800 *Baby Face* ....25.00 - 40.00
   51842 *Don't Be Angry With Me* ....10.00 - 15.00
   51971 *Wistful And Blue* ....10.00 - 15.00

Okeh 4580 *Lonesome Mama Blues* ....10.00 - 15.00
    4610 *Black Eyed Blues* ....10.00 - 15.00
    4641 *My Honey's Lovin' Arms* ....10.00 - 15.00
    4656 *Blued Eyed Blues* ....10.00 - 15.00
    4777 *That Barkin' Dog* ....10.00 - 15.00
    4902 *Waitin' For The Evenin' Mail* ....7.00 - 10.00
    4967 *Stavin' Change*...............................10.00 - 15.00
    40045 *31st Street Blues* ....15.00 - 20.00
    40161 *Africa* ....15.00 - 20.00
    40625 *Deep Henderson* ....15.00 - 20.00
    40686 *For My Sweetheart* ....12.00 - 16.00
    40724 *Hello, Swanee, Hello!* ....15.00 - 20.00
    40760 *Wistful And Blue* ....15.00 - 20.00

GERALD MARKS AND HIS ORCHESTRA:
Columbia 1432-D *If I Can't Have You*...................10.00 - 15.00

EARL MARLOW AND HIS ORCHESTRA:
Parlophone PNY-34018 *Wrapped In A Red, Red Rose*
....25.00 - 40.00
    PNY-34019 *Put A Little Salt On The Bluebird's Tail*
....20.00 - 30.00
    PNY-34022 *What Do I Care?* ....20.00 - 30.00
    PNY-34025 *There's Danger In Your Eyes, Cherie*
....20.00 - 30.00
    PNY-34026 *Singing a Vagabond Song* ....20.00 - 30.00
    PNY-34058 *Living In The Sunlight, Loving In The Moonlight*
....25.00 - 35.00
    PNY-34059 *You Brought A New Kind Of Love To Me*
....25.00 - 40.00
    PNY-34074 *Nobody Cares If I'm Blue*.............25.00 - 35.00
    PNY-34075 *Mysterious Mose*................25.00 - 35.00
    PNY-34082 *I'm Needin' You*.................25.00 - 35.00
    PNY-34083 *Ro-Ro-Rolling Along* ....25.00 - 35.00
    PNY-34105 *This Love* ....15.00 - 25.00
    PNY-34106 *I've Got My Eye On You*.................20.00 - 30.00
    PNY-34115 *Dixiana* ....20.00 - 30.00
    PNY-34116 *My One Ambition Is You* ....20.00 - 30.00
    PNY-34124 *I'm Doing That Thing*.....................75.00 - 100.00
    PNY-34125 *A Big Bouquet For You* ....75.00 - 100.00
    PNY-34126 *Don't Tell Her* ....50.00 - 75.00
    PNY-34139 *I Am The Words*.................15.00 - 25.00
    PNY-34140 *I Still Belong To You* ....15.00 - 25.00
    PNY-34142 *Sweet Jennie Lee* ....20.00 - 30.00
    PNY-34143 *Roamin' Thru The Roses* ....20.00 - 30.00
    PNY-34167 *Reaching For The Moon*.................15.00 - 25.00
    PNY-34168 *Fall In Love With Me*.....................15.00 - 25.00
    PNY-34169 *He's My Secret Passion*.................15.00 - 25.00
    PNY-34170 *Lady, Play Your Mandolin*.................15.00 - 25.00
    PNY-34174 *It Must Be True*.................25.00 - 40.00
    PNY-34176 *Hello! Beautiful* ....25.00 - 35.00
    PNY-34177 *Walkin' My Baby Back Home* ....25.00 - 35.00
    PNY-34178 *Sing Song Girl* ....25.00 - 35.00
    PNY-34179 *Wabash Moon*..................15.00 - 25.00
    PNY-34184 *All On Account Of Your Kisses* ......30.00 - 40.00

RUDY MARLOW AND HIS ORCHESTRA:
Harmony 988-H *How Am I To Know?* ....10.00 - 15.00
    1062-H *Dixie Jamboree*.........................15.00 - 20.00
    1063-H *He's So Unusual* ....15.00 - 20.00
    1088-H *Do Ya Love Me?* ....10.00 - 15.00
    1119-H *Thank Your Father* ....7.00 - 10.00
    1137-H *Get Happy*...............................10.00 - 15.00

    1162-H *Dark Night* ....7.00 - 10.00
    1232-H *Three Little Words* ....7.00 - 10.00
(Note: Some of above also issued on Diva and Velvet Tone are
    similarly valued.)

JOE MARSALA & HIS DELTA FOUR; JOE MARSALA'S CHICAGOANS:
General 1717 *Salty Mama Blues* ....10.00 - 15.00
    3001 *Reunion In Harlem* ....10.00 - 15.00
Variety 565 *Wolverine Blues* ....10.00 - 15.00
Vocalion 4116 *Jim Jam Stomp* ....10.00 - 15.00
    4168 *Mighty Like The Blues* ....10.00 - 15.00

GILBERT MARSH & HIS ORCHESTRA:
Parlophone PNY-34038 *Navy Blues* ....75.00 - 100.00
    PNY-34039 *Lucky Little Devil*..........................75.00 - 100.00
    PNY-34040 *Navy Blues* ....40.00 - 60.00
    PNY-34041 *Lucky Little Devil*..........................40.00 - 60.00

TED MARSHALL & HIS BOYS:
Champion 15001 *Headin' For Home* ....15.00 - 20.00

DEAN MARTIN:
Apollo 1088 *Oh Marie*..25.00 - 35.00
    1116 *Santa Lucia* ....25.00 - 35.00
Capitol 57-549 *Three Wishes* ....8.00 - 12.00
    57-691 *Just For Fun* ....8.00 - 12.00
    57-726 *That Lucky Old Sun* ....8.00 - 12.00
    937 *Rain* ....8.00 - 12.00
    948 *Muskrat Ramble* ....5.00 - 10.00
    981 *Choo'n Gum* ....5.00 - 10.00
    1002 *I Still Get A Thrill* ....5.00 - 10.00
    1028 *Baby, Obey Me* ....5.00 - 8.00
    1052 *Happy Feet* ....5.00 - 8.00
    1139 *Wham! Bam! Thank You, Ma'am!* ....5.00 - 10.00
    1682 *I'll Always Love You* ....- - -
    2071 *I Passed Your House Tonight* ....8.00 - 12.00
    2165 *You Belong To Me* ....8.00 - 12.00
    2378 *Little Did We Know* ....8.00 - 12.00
    2555 *If I Could Sing Like Bing* ....- - -
    3787 *Promise Her Anything*...............10.00 - 15.00
    3841 *Good Mornin', Life* ....15.00 - 30.00
    3894 *Return To Me* ....15.00 - 30.00
    15249 *The Money Song* (with Jerry Lewis) ....10.00 - 15.00
    15329 *Once In Love With Amy* ....8.00 - 12.00
    15349 *You Was* (with Peggy Lee)........................8.00 - 12.00
    15351 *Absence Makes The Heart Grow Fonder*.. 8.00 - 12.00
    15395 *Have A Little Sympathy*...............8.00 - 12.00
Capitol, most other issues ....4.00 - 8.00
Diamond 2035 *All Of Me* ....30.00 - 50.00
    2036 *The Sweetheart of Sigma Chi*...................30.00 - 50.00
Embassy 124 *One Foot In Heaven* ....30.00 - 50.00
(Note: Many of Dean Martin's records were issued in 45 RPM, EP,
    and LP formats; see **RHYTHM & BLUES, ETC.** section of this
    book.)

FATTY MARTIN'S ORCHESTRA:
Victor 19700 *Jimtown Blues* ....50.00 - 80.00

FREDDIE MARTIN & HIS ORCHESTRA:
Bluebird, most issues ....5.00 - 8.00
Brunswick 6407 *A Rainy Day*................................8.00 - 12.00
    6408 *Someday We'll Meet Again* ....8.00 - 12.00
Brunswick, most other issues ....5.00 - 10.00
Columbia 2703-D *Goodbye To Love* ....8.00 - 12.00
    2708-D *Three On A Match* ....8.00 - 12.00
    2770-D *We're Together Again* ....8.00 - 12.00

MARY MARTIN:
Brunswick 8282 *My Heart Belongs To Daddy* .... 7.00 - 10.00
Decca (most issues) .... 5.00 - 8.00
V-Disc 542 (12-inch) *Wait Till The Sun Shines, Nellie*
.... 10.00 - 15.00

SARA MARTIN'S JUG BAND:
Okeh 8188 *Blue Devil Blues* .... 150.00 - 200.00

JELLY ROLL MARTON & HIS ORCHESTRA:
"Muddy Water Blues" issued contemporaneously on Famous 3245,
     Harmograph 834, National 12251, Paramount 12050 and 20251,
     and Puritan 11251 .... 100.00 - 150.00

FRANK MARVIN (See also COUNTRY-WESTERN listing):
Brunswick 400 *Frankie And Johnny* .... 8.00 - 12.00
     4949 *You're Simply Delish* .... 10.00 - 15.00

JOHNNY MARVIN (See also COUNTRY-WESTERN listing):
Columbia 2655-D *Medley* .... 8.00 - 12.00
     15750-D *Seven Come Eleven* .... 10.00 - 15.00
Columbia, most other issues .... 5.00 - 8.00
Edison 51709 *The Memphis Blues* .... 15.00 - 20.00
Melotone 12610 *I'm Playing With Fire* .... 8.00 - 12.00
Victor 20386 *12th Street Rag* .... 7.00 - 10.00
     20714 *Side By Side* .... 7.00 - 10.00
     20731 *Magnolia* .... 8.00 - 12.00
     20832 *It's A Million To One You're In Love* ...... 8.00 - 12.00
     21376 *Angel* .... 10.00 - 15.00
     21427 *Golden Gate* .... 9.00 - 12.00
     21435 *My Pet* .... 10.00 - 15.00
     21509 *Oh! You Have No Idea* .... 7.00 - 10.00
     21650 *Crazy Rhythm* .... 7.00 - 10.00

ALBERT MASON'S ORCHESTRA:
Parlophone PNY-34069 *Girl Trouble* .... 20.00 - 30.00
     PNY-34104 *Rollin' Down The River* .... 20.00 - 30.00
     PNY-34105 *Seems To Me* .... 15.00 - 25.00
     PNY-34114 *I Wonder How It Feels* .... 20.00 - 30.00
     PNY-34174 *Keep a Song In Your Soul* .... 25.00 - 40.00
     PNY-34185 *The One Man Band* .... 20.00 - 30.00
     PNY-34187 *Got The Bench-Got The Park* .... 35.00 - 50.00

JERRY MASON'S CALIFORNIANS:
Harmony 795-H *Don't Hold Everything* .... 20.00 - 30.00
     965-H *Ain't Misbehavin'* .... 10.00 - 15.00
     1242-H *Can This Be Love?* .... 7.00 - 10.00

MASON-DIXON ORCHESTRA:
Columbia 1861-D *What A Day!* .... 25.00 - 35.00

MASTER MELODY MAKERS:
National Music Lovers 1133 *Then I'll Be Happy* .... 10.00 - 15.00
     1161 *Keep Your Kisses* .... 7.00 - 10.00
     1164 *This Is My Lucky Day* .... 7.00 - 10.00
     1169 *Bird's Eye View Of My Old Kentucky Home*
.... 7.00 - 10.00
     1178 *Baby Face* .... 10.00 - 15.00
New Phonic 1245 *Get Out And Get Under The Moon*
.... 10.00 - 15.00
     1249 *My Pet* .... 10.00 - 15.00

FRANKIE MASTERS & HIS ORCHESTRA:
Victor 21102 *I'm Walkin' On Air* .... 8.00 - 12.00
     21217 *Everywhere You Go* .... 10.00 - 15.00

     21565 *My Darling* .... 8.00 - 12.00
     21602 *Is It Gonna Be Long (Till You Belong To Me?)*
.... 7.00 - 10.00
Okeh, most issues .... 5.00 - 8.00
Vocalion, most issues .... 5.00 - 8.00
Vogue R-724 *Everybody Knew But Me* .... 75.00 - 100.00
     R-735 *Welcome To My Dreams* .... 50.00 - 75.00
     R-772 *All By Myself* .... 25.00 - 35.00

FRANK MATER (See also RUDY VALLEE):
Diva 2759-G *Doin' The Raccoon* .... 10.00 - 15.00
Harmony 759-H *Doin' The Raccoon* .... 10.00 - 15.00
     808-H *Let's Do It* .... 15.00 - 20.00
     811-H *The Song I Love* .... 10.00 - 15.00
     825-H *Makin' Whoopee* .... 15.00 - 20.00
     834-H *Caressing You* .... 8.00 - 12.00

CHARLES A. MATSON'S CREOLE SERENADERS; MATSON'S LUCKY SEVEN:
Edison 51222 *Tain't Nobody's Business If I Do* ..... 35.00 - 50.00
     51224 *I Just Want A Daddy* .... 35.00 - 50.00
Lawdy, Lawdy Blues issued contemporaneously on Claxtonola,
     Paramount, and Puritan .... 100.00 - 150.00

LIEUTENANT MATT & HIS ORCHESTRA/ RHAPSODISTS:
Gennett 6064 *You're The One For Me* .... 10.00 - 15.00
Perfect 14649 *Hoodle Dee Doo Dee Doodoo* .... 7.00 - 10.00

EMMETT MATTHEWS & HIS ORCHESTRA:
Vocalion 3226 *I'll Stand By* .... 10.00 - 15.00
     3228 *Take A Good Look At Mine* .... 10.00 - 15.00
     3371 *Bojangles Of Harlem* .... 10.00 - 15.00
     3332 *You Came To My Rescue* .... 10.00 - 15.00

GEORGE MATTHEWS & THE CAROLINA NIGHT HAWKS:
Gennett 6183 *Oh Miss Hannah!* .... 100.00 - 150.00

NORRIDGE MAYHAMS & HIS BARBECUE BOYS:
Sloppy Drunk Woman and *Wrap Your Troubles In Dreams* issued
     contemporaneously on Banner, Melotone, Oriole, Perfect, and
     Romeo .... 15.00 - 20.00
Vocalion 03429 *Ash Haulin' Blues* .... 15.00 - 20.00
     03465 *If I Had My Way* .... 15.00 - 20.00
     03498 *Sloppy Drunk Woman* .... 15.00 - 20.00

TED MAYS AND HIS BAND:
Bluebird 7193 *Gee, It Must Be Love* .... 15.00 - 20.00
     7237 *Married Man Blues* .... 15.00 - 20.00

THE McALPINEERS:
Edison 52237 *One More Night* .... 35.00 - 50.00
     52239 *Persian Rug* .... 35.00 - 50.00
     52266 *Rhapsody In Rhythm* .... 80.00 - 120.00
     52371 *I'm On The Crest Of A Wave* .... 50.00 - 80.00
     52385 *Memories Of France* .... 15.00 - 25.00
     52411 *High Up On A Hill-Top* .... 50.00 - 80.00

GEORGE McCLENNON; GEORGE McCLENNON'S JAZZ BAND/DEVILS:
Okeh 8143 *Dark Alley Blues* .... 150.00 - 200.00
     8150 *New Orleans Wiggle* .... 150.00 - 200.00
     8236 *Home Alone Blues* .... 150.00 - 200.00
     8314 *Cut Throat Blues* .... 80.00 - 130.00
     8329 *While You're Sneakin' Out* .... 100.00 - 150.00
     8337 *Everybody But Me* .... 100.00 - 150.00

8397 *Pig Foot Blues*	100.00 -	150.00
8406 *Disaster*	150.00 -	250.00

CLYDE McCOY & HIS (DRAKE HOTEL) ORCHESTRA:

Columbia 2389-D *Sugar Blues*	10.00 -	15.00
2453-D *It Looks Like Love*	8.00 -	12.00
2466-D *Black And Tan Fantasy*	15.00 -	20.00
2531-D *I Found A New Baby*	15.00 -	20.00
2597-D *Creole Love Call*	15.00 -	20.00
2794-D *Smoke Rings*	12.00 -	16.00
2801-D *Some Of These Days*	12.00 -	16.00
2808-D *Nobody's Sweetheart*	15.00 -	20.00
2865-D *Palooka*	10.00 -	15.00
2866-D *Little Women*	10.00 -	15.00
2874-D *Business on the Q. T.*	15.00 -	20.00
Decca 381 *Sugar Blues*	7.00 -	10.00
382 *Japanese Sandman*	8.00 -	12.00
422 *China Boy*	8.00 -	12.00
461 *There'll Be Some Changes Made*	8.00 -	12.00
509 *Twelfth Street Rag*	8.00 -	12.00
566 *Dry Ice*	8.00 -	12.00
620 *Basin Street Blues*	7.00 -	10.00
681 *Maple Leaf Rag*	7.00 -	10.00
758 *Ridin' To Glory On A Trumpet*	7.00 -	10.00
833 *Roseland Stomp*	7.00 -	10.00
1109 *The "Gonna Goo"*	7.00 -	10.00
1152 *Black And Tan Fantasy*	7.00 -	10.00
1230 *Doodle Doo Doo*	7.00 -	10.00
1297 *Doo Wacka Doo*	7.00 -	10.00
Decca, most other issues	5.00 -	8.00
Vogue R-707 *Sugar Blues*	15.00 -	25.00
R-722 *Tear It Down*	25.00 -	40.00
R-752 *There's Good Blues Tonight*	20.00 -	30.00
R-753 *Way Down Yonder In New Orleans*	25.00 -	35.00

RANDOLPH McCURTAIN'S COLLEGE RAMBLERS:

Okeh Ramblers' 1 *Low Down Brown*	75.00 -	100.00

EARL McDONALD'S ORIGINAL LOUISVILLE JUG BAND:

Columbia 14206-D *Under the Chicken Tree*	200.00 -	300.00
14226-D *Rocking Chair Blues*	200.00 -	300.00
14255-D *She's In The Graveyard Now*	200.00 -	300.00
14371-D *Casey Bill*	200.00 -	300.00

DICK McDONOUGH & HIS ORCHESTRA:

Titles issued contemporaneously on Banner, Melotone, Oriole, Perfect, and Romeo: *Afterglow; All God's Chillun Got Rhythm; The Big Apple; Dardanella; Dear Old Southland; The Gonna Goo; He Ain't Got Rhythm; I'm in a Dancing Mood; It Ain't Right; Love, What Are You Doing To My Heart; The Mood That I'm In; Now Or Never; When The Moon Hangs High; With Thee I Swing; You and I Know* .... 7.00 - 12.00

ABE McDOW & HIS BAND SOUTHERN/ORCHESTRA:

Broadway 1481 *I Idolize My Baby's Eyes*	15.00 -	25.00
1482 *Minnie The Moocher*	15.00 -	25.00

COLE McELROY'S SPANISH BALLROOM ORCHESTRA:

Columbia 1677-D *Ida! Sweet As Apple Cider*	15.00 -	20.00
Columbia, most other issues	5.00 -	10.00
Victor 22837, 22850	5.00 -	8.00

EDWIN J. McENELLY'S ORCHESTRA:

Victor 19851 *Spanish Shawl*	10.00 -	15.00

20379 *Tuck In Kentucky and Smile!*	8.00 -	12.00
20589 *My Sunday Girl*	8.00 -	12.00
21154 *What Are We Waiting For?*	7.00 -	10.00
21773 *Take Your Tomorrow (And Give Me Today)*	7.00 -	10.00
Victor, most other issues	5.00 -	8.00

HOWARD McGHEE:

Dial 1005, 1007, 1010, 1011, 1027	7.00 -	12.00

BOB McGOWAN & HIS ORCHESTRA:

Gennett 6709 *Me And The Man In The Moon*	20.00 -	30.00
6754 *As Long As We're In Love*	15.00 -	30.00

JIMMY McHUGH'S BOSTONIANS:

Harmony 763-H *I Don't Care*	20.00 -	30.00
795-H *Baby*	20.00 -	30.00
823-H *Let's Sit And Talk About You*	30.00 -	50.00
836-H *The Whoopee Stomp*	30.00 -	50.00

(Note: Above titles on Diva and Velvet Tone are similarly valued.)

MARION McKAY & HIS ORCHESTRA:

Gennett 5615 *Doo Wacka Doo*	10.00 -	15.00
6294 *My Blue Heaven*	15.00 -	20.00

BUD McKEE & HIS GANG:

Champion 15238 *Ain't She Sweet?*	10.00 -	15.00
15239 *You Should See My Tootsie*	15.00 -	20.00

RED McKENZIE; McKENZIE'S CANDY KIDS; RED McKENZIE & HIS MUSIC BOX/RHYTHM KINGS; RED McKENZIE WITH THE SPIRITS OF RHYTHM:

Titles issued contemporaneously on Banner, Melotone, Oriole, Perfect, and Romeo: *Georgianna; Farewell My Love* .... 10.00 - 15.00

Columbia 2556-D *Just Friends*	10.00 -	15.00
2587-D *I'm Sorry, Dear*	10.00 -	15.00
2620-D *Can't We Talk It Over?*	10.00 -	15.00
2645-D *Dream Sweetheart*	10.00 -	15.00
Decca 186 *From Monday On*	10.00 -	15.00
243 *It's All Forgotten Now*	8.00 -	12.00
302 *As Long As I Live*	10.00 -	15.00
507 *Let's Swing It*	10.00 -	15.00
521 *Double Trouble*	10.00 -	15.00
587 *Every Now And Then*	10.00 -	15.00
609 *Georgia Rockin' Chair*	10.00 -	15.00
667 *I'm Building Up To An Awful Letdown*	8.00 -	12.00
721 *Don't Count Your Kisses (Before You're Kissed)*	8.00 -	12.00
734 *When Love Has Gone*	8.00 -	12.00
790 *I Can't Get Started With You*	8.00 -	12.00
Okeh 40893 *There'll Be Some Changes Made*	50.00 -	75.00
41071 *From Monday On*	60.00 -	100.00
Variety 520 *Sweet Lorraine*	8.00 -	12.00
589 *I Cried For You*	10.00 -	15.00
Vocalion 2534 *It's The Talk Of The Town*	10.00 -	15.00
3875 *Farewell, My Love*	8.00 -	12.00
3898 *You're Out Of This World*	8.00 -	12.00
14977 *Panama*	25.00 -	35.00
14978 *Stretch It, Boy*	35.00 -	50.00
15088 *The Morning After Blues*	35.00 -	50.00
15166 *Hot Honey*	35.00 -	50.00
15539 *Nervous Puppies*	15.00 -	25.00

McKENZIE & CONDON'S CHICAGOANS:

Okeh 40971 *Nobody's Sweetheart*	50.00 -	80.00
41011 *China Boy*	50.00 -	80.00

RAY McKINLEY'S JAZZ BAND:
Decca 1019, 1020 ....8.00 - 12.00

McKINNEY'S COTTON PICKERS:
Victor 21583 *Four Or Five Times* ....35.00 - 50.00
    21611 *Milenberg Joys*...........................25.00 - 40.00
    21730 *Cherry* ....30.00 - 50.00
    22511 *Hullabaloo* ....20.00 - 30.00
    22628 *She's My Secret Passion*.......................12.00 - 16.00
    22640 *Talk To Me*..............................25.00 - 40.00
    22683 *I Want Your Love* ....40.00 - 60.00
    22736 *Wherever There's A Will, Baby* ....25.00 - 40.00
    22811 *Wrap Your Troubles In Dreams* ....15.00 - 20.00
    22932 *Rocky Road* ....50.00 - 75.00
    23000 *Okay, Baby*..............................25.00 - 40.00
    23012 *Just A Shade Corn* ....40.00 - 60.00
    23020 *Never Swat A Fly* ....20.00 - 30.00
    23024 *I Miss A Little Miss* ....20.00 - 30.00
    23031 *Hello!* ....30.00 - 50.00
    23035 *To Whom It May Concern*...................25.00 - 35.00
    V38000 *Nobody's Sweetheart* ....25.00 - 35.00
    V38013 *It's Tight Like That* ....25.00 - 35.00
    V38025 *Put It There* ....25.00 - 35.00
    V38051 *Do Something*........................25.00 - 35.00
    V38052 *Sellin' That Stuff* ....25.00 - 35.00
    V38061 *I've Found a New Baby* ....30.00 - 50.00
    V38097 *Plain Dirt*.............................40.00 - 60.00
    V38102 *Miss Hannah* ....40.00 - 60.00
    V38112 *Travelin' All Alone*...................40.00 - 60.00
    V38118 *Zonky*..................................25.00 - 35.00
    V38133 *I'd Love It*.............................40.00 - 60.00
    V38142 *I'll Make Fun For You* ....50.00 - 75.00

McLAUGHLIN'S MELODIANS:
Pathe-Actuelle (titles as on Perfect, below)
Perfect 14696 *Play, Gypsies, Dance, Gypsies*...........5.00 - 8.00
    14698 *I Never Knew What The Moonlight Could Do*
    ....7.00 - 10.00
    14699 *Someone Is Losin' Susan* ....15.00 - 20.00
    14705 *Broken-Hearted Sue*................10.00 - 15.00
(Foregoing titles on Pathe-Actuelle are similarly valued)

CONNIE McLEAN & HIS RHYTHM ORCHESTRA; CONNIE McLEANS RHYTHM BOYS:
Bluebird 6474, 6482, 6485 ....8.00 - 12.00
Decca 7175, 7176, 7189 ....8.00 - 12.00

GEORGE McMURPHEY & HIS ORCHESTRA:
Columbia 1498-D *Allah's Holiday*...........................10.00 - 15.00
    1526-D *Trumpet Sobs* ....10.00 - 15.00

McMURRAY'S CALIFORNIA THUMPERS:
Gennett 4904 *Haunting Blues*...................20.00 - 30.00
    4943 *Oogie Oogie Wa Wa* ....15.00 - 20.00

JIMMY McPARTLAND'S SQUIRRELS:
Hot Record Society 1003, 1004.................7.00 - 12.00

JAY McSHANN (AND HIS ORCHESTRA/QUARTET):
Decca 8559 *Hootie Blues* ....10.00 - 15.00
    8570 *Swingmatism* ....10.00 - 15.00
    8583 *Hold 'Em Hootie* ....10.00 - 15.00
    4387, 4418, 8595, 8607, 8623, 8635 ....7.00 - 12.00
Mercury 8002, 8014, 8018, 8020, 8026, 8032,
    8041, 8049, 8283 ....7.00 - 12.00
Supreme 1540 *McShann's Bounce* ....8.00 - 12.00

THE MELODY FOUR:
Victor 23289 *I'm Crazy 'Bout My Baby*.................75.00 - 100.00

MELODY KINGS DANCE ORCHESTRA:
His Master's Voice (Canadian) 216450 *Limehouse Blues*
....10.00 - 15.00

MELODY MEN:
Challenge 757 *So Tired* ....10.00 - 15.00

THE MELODY SHEIKS (See also SAM LANIN):
Okeh 40279 *Tokio Blues*.........................15.00 - 20.00
    40303 *Why Couldn't It Be Poor Little Me* ....15.00 - 20.00
    40326 *Sob Sister Sadie*........................15.00 - 20.00
    40341 *All Aboard For Heaven* ....15.00 - 20.00
    40357 *If You Knew Susie* ....15.00 - 20.00
    40358 *Isn't She The Sweetest Thing?* ....15.00 - 20.00
    40369 *Let Me Linger Longer In Your Arms*.......30.00 - 50.00
    40387 *Steppin' In Society* ....12.00 - 16.00
    40412 *Ukelele Lady* ....8.00 - 12.00
    40438 *Indian Nights*..........................8.00 - 12.00
    40451 *Marguerite* ....12.00 - 16.00
    40472 *Brown Eyes, Why Are You Blue?* ....12.00 - 16.00
    40484 *Mighty Blue* ....30.00 - 50.00
    40529 *Tomorrow Morning*....................15.00 - 20.00
    40550 *Pretty Little Baby* ....15.00 - 20.00
    40560 *Behind The Clouds* ....12.00 - 16.00
    40580 *So Does Your Old Mandarin* ....12.00 - 16.00
    40590 *Let's Talk About My Sweetie*...................30.00 - 50.00
    40603 *The Blue Room*........................12.00 - 16.00
    40632 *Roses Remind Me Of You*........................12.00 - 16.00
    40649 *Baby Face* ....20.00 - 30.00
    40651 *Barcelona*...............................8.00 - 12.00

JAMES MELTON:
Brunswick 20115 (12-inch) *Make Believe*..............10.00 - 15.00
Columbia 2065-D, 2084-D ....7.00 - 10.00

MEMPHIS BELL-HOPS:
Challenge 134 *Li'l Farina* ....50.00 - 80.00
    135 *Animal Crackers* ....50.00 - 80.00

MEMPHIS DADDY & HIS BOYS:
Silvertone 5023 *Georgia Bo Bo* ....80.00 - 130.00

MEMPHIS FIVE (See ORIGINAL MEMPHIS FIVE)

MEMPHIS HOT SHOTS:
I'm So In Love With You issued contemporaneously on
    Clarion 5391-C, Harmony 1377-H, and Velvet Tone
    2455-V ....50.00 - 80.00
Shout, Sister, Shout issued contemporaneously on Clarion
    5381-C, Harmony 1368-H, and Velvet Tone 2445-V
    ....50.00 - 80.00

MEMPHIS JAZZERS:
Titles, issued contemporaneously on Grey Gull, Radiex, Supreme:
    Miss Golden Brown; In Harlem's Araby..........15.00 - 20.00
Sunrise 33024 *Close Fit Blues* ....40.00 - 60.00
Van Dyke 1803 *I Don't Know And I Don't Care* ..15.00 - 20.00
    7801 *Close Fit Blues* ....40.00 - 60.00
    71739 *Just Blues* ....7.00 - 10.00
    71749 *Stomp Along* ....10.00 - 15.00
    71751 *Wow Wow Blues* ....10.00 - 15.00

ACTUELLE
Early 1920s (78)

ACE
Late 1950s
Picture sleeve for 45 RPM record

AEOLIAN-VOCALION
Late teens (78) "Splatter" record
(colors of WWI allies' flags)

AMERICAN RECORD COMPANY
Ca. 1915 (78) (single-sided)

AMERICAN RECORD CORPORATION
Ca. 1931 (33-1/3 rpm)
for theatre use; same tune each side)

AMERICAN RECORD MFG.
Ca. 1920
Official Boy Scout Record

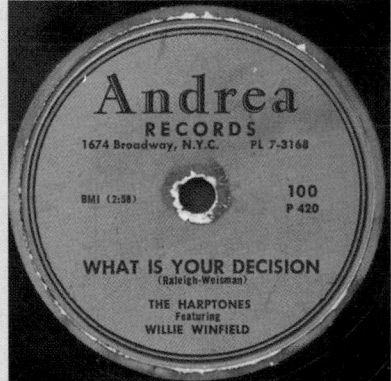

ANDREA
Mid-1950s (78)

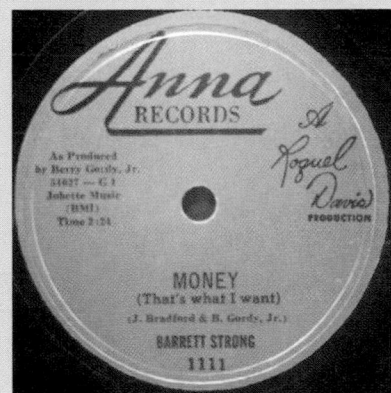

ANNA
Ca. 1959-1960
One of the last 78s issued in U.S.

APEX (Canadian)
Early 1920s (78)
Canadian pressing using U.S. recording

APOLLO (red vinyl)
Mid-1950s (45)

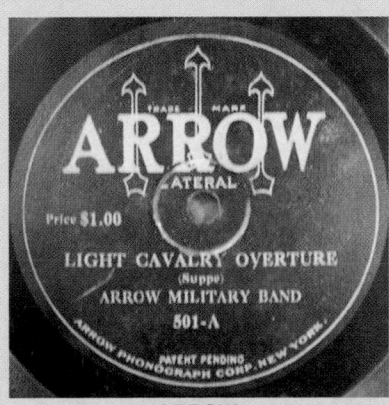

ARROW
Ca. 1920 (78)

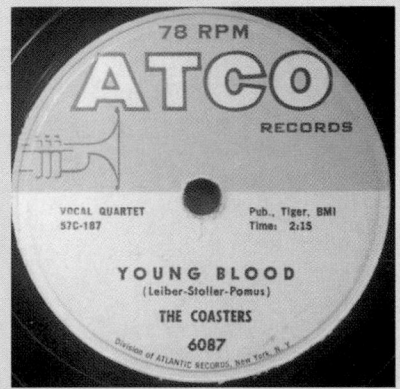

ATCO
Late 1950s (78)

ATCO
Ca. 1963
Picture sleeve for Beatles' 45 RPM record

ATLANTIC
Ca. 1960
Cover of LP (33-1/3 rpm)

ATLAS
Mid-1950s (78)

AURORA (Canadian)
Ca. 1933 (78) Pressed in Canada, using
U.S. recordings

AUTOGRAPH
Mid-1920s (78)

AUTOGRAPH
Ca. 1924 (78)

BELL
Early 1920s (78)

BELVEDERE
Early 1920s (78)

BERNARDO
Late 1920s (78)

BINGOLA (small record)
Late-1920s (78) (in sleeve)

BLACK PATTI
Ca. 1927 (78)
Scarce, sought-after "race" label

BLACK SWAN
Ca. 1921 (78)
Early "race" label

BLUEBIRD
Ca. 1933
(78) Scarce, early version of the label

BLUEBIRD
Ca. 1935
(78) Usually-seen "buff" label

BLUE BONNET
Ca. 1948 (78)
Scarce blues issue on Dallas label

BROADWAY
Early 1920s (78)

BUDDY
Ca. 1925 (78)
Scarce Gennett-related label

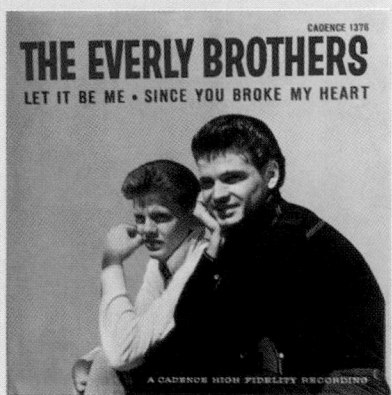

CADENCE
Ca. 1958
Picture sleeve for (45) record

CAPITOL (picture disc)
Ca. 1947 (78) Promotional

CAPITOL (picture disc)
Ca. 1947 (78)
Promotional (flip side)

CAPITOL
Ca. 1965
33-1/3 (miniature LP)

CAPITOL
Mid-1950s jacket of EP

CARDINAL
Ca. 1923 (78)
Gennett-affiliated label

CARLTON (Canadian)
Late 1950s (78)
Canadian issue using U.S. recordings

CARLTON
Late 1950s
Picture sleeve for 45 RPM record

CARNIVAL
Early 1920s (78)

CHAMPION
Ca. 1927 (78)

CHANCE
Mid-1950s (45)

CHAPPELLE AND STINNETTE
Ca. 1922 (78)
Scarce, early "race" label

CHAUTAUQUA
Ca. 1922 (78) (rare label)
the one shown is only known issue

CHECKER
Mid-1950s (45)

CHESS (red vinyl)
Early 1950s (45)

CLAXTONOLA
Ca. 1923 (78)

CLOVER
Ca. 1926 (78)

COLUMBIA ("flag" label)
Ca. 1923 (78)

COLUMBIA
Ca. 1916 (78)
Red Cross fund-raising issue

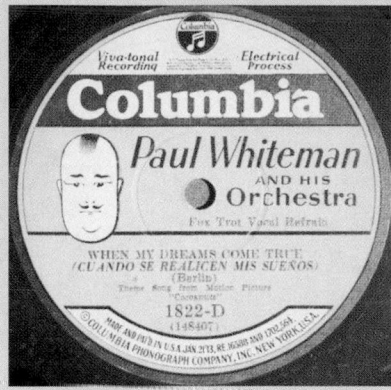

COLUMBIA ("potato-head" label)
Ca. 1929 (78)
Paul Whiteman's special label

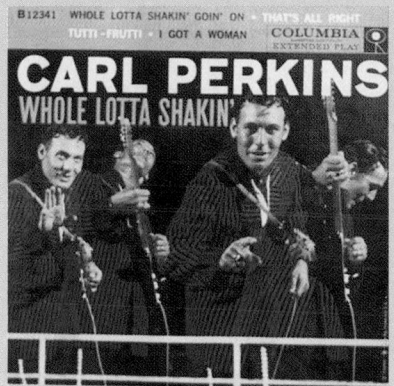

COLUMBIA
Ca. 1959 jacket of EP

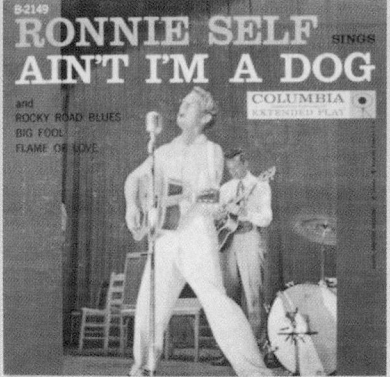

COLUMBIA
Late 1950s jacket of EP

CONNORIZED
Ca. 1922 (78)

CONQUEROR
Late 1930s (78)
Sought-after Robert Johnson issue

D
Late 1950s (45)
Original issue of Big Bopper's hit

DANDY
Ca. 1924 (78)
Scarce Emerson-related label

DECCA
Mid-1950s jacket of Bill Haley; EP

DOMESTIC
Ca. 1918 (78)
Pressed of blue shellac

DOMINO
Early 1920s (78)

EDISON
Ca. 1924 (78)
One of just a few blues issues on Edison

EDISON (special record in sleeve)
Ca. 1924 (78)
"Holiday Greetings" from the Bunch at Orange

198 🎵

EDISON (special record)
Ca. 1924 (78)
"Holiday Greetings" has voice of T. Edison

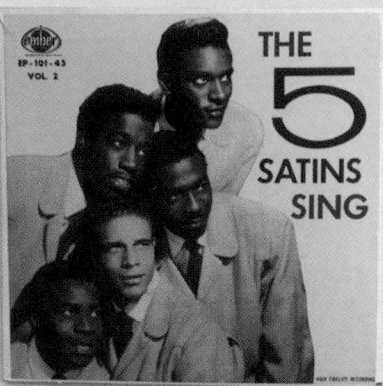
EMBER
Late 1950s
Jacket for 5 Satins EP

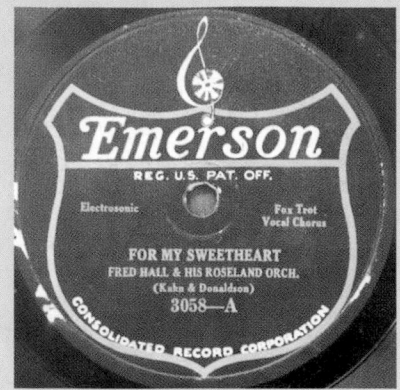
EMERSON
Ca. 1926 (78)
Emerson 3000 series

END
Late 1950s
Jacket for Flamingos LP

EKKO
Ca. 1956 (78)

ELECTRIC RECORDING LABORATORIES
Mid-1920s (78)
Personal record by and for Rudy Vallee

EMERSON
Ca. 1918 (78)
(7-inch record)

FEDERAL
Mid-1950s (45) "gold-top" label

FLEXO (green plastic)
Ca. 1930 (78)
Small, flexible record

FLEXO (pink plastic)
Ca. 1930 (78)
Small, flexible record (obverse)

FLEXO (pink plastic)
Ca. 1930 (78)
Small, flexible (flip side)

GEE
Mid-1950s (45)
Sought-after record by THE COINS

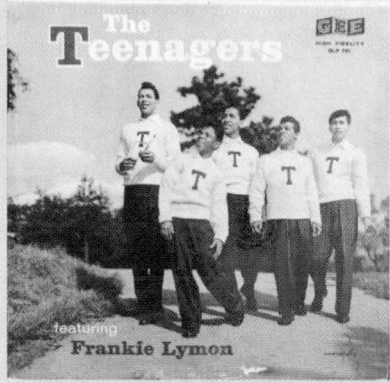

GEE
Late 1950s
Jacket for LP by The Teenagers

GEM
Early 1950s (78)

GENNETT (special "Fraternity" disc)
Ca. 1923 (78)
Gennett personal record

GENNETT (personal record)
Ca. 1924 (78)
Special record by MIAMI LUCKY SEVEN

GENNETT "New Electrobeam"
Ca. 1930 (78) blues record

GLOBE
Ca. 1921 (78)

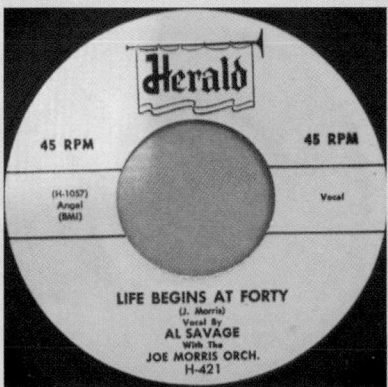

GREY GULL
Ca. 1927 (78)

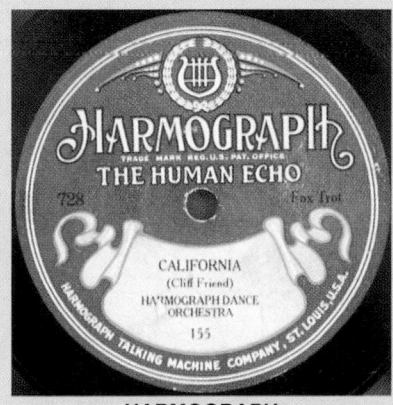

HARMOGRAPH
Ca. 1922 (78) St. Louis label

HARMOGRAPH
Ca. 1923-1924 (78)
Paramount-related St. Louis label

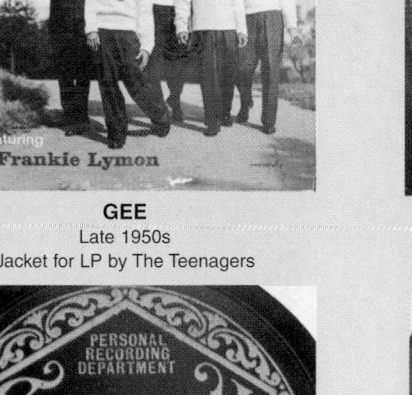

HERALD (red vinyl)
Mid-1950s (45)

HIT OF THE WEEK
Ca. 1930 (78)
One-sided paper record

HOMESTEAD
Ca. 1930 (78)

IMPERIAL (one-sided)
Ca. 1908 (78)

IMPERIAL
Late 1950s
Jacket for Fats Domino EP

INTERNATIONAL RECORD
(one-sided)
Ca. 1907 (78)

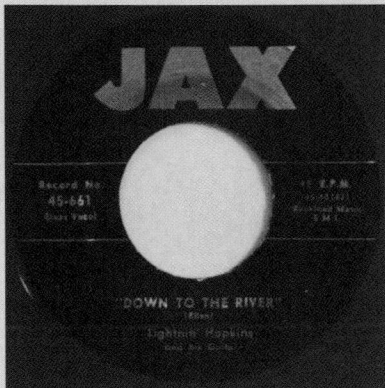

JAX (red vinyl)
Early 1950s (45)
(Blues record)

JEWEL
Early-1920s (78)
Grey-Gull affiliated "Jewel" label

J.O.B. RECORDS
Ca. 1950 (78)
Chicago "race" label

JUBILEE
Early 1950s (78)

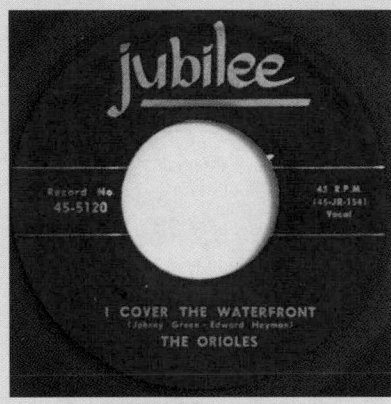

JUBILEE (red vinyl)
Early 1950s (45)
Sought-after ORIOLES recording

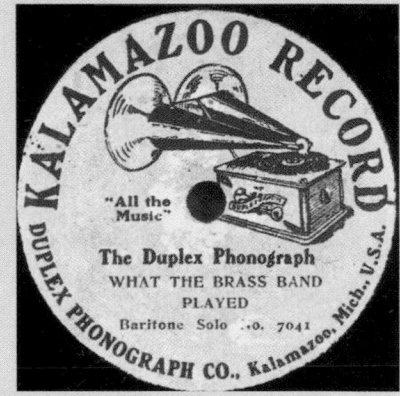

KALAMAZOO RECORD
(one-sided)
Ca. 1908 (78)

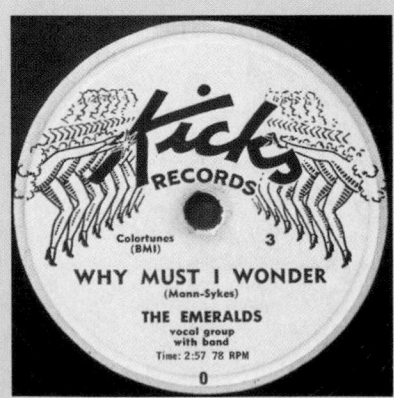

KICKS
Mid-1950s (78)

KING
Mid-1950s
Jacket for DOMINOES LP

LEEDS (one-sided)
Ca. 1906 (78)
Embossed, foil label

MEMPHIS JUG BAND:

Bluebird 5040 *Oh Ambulance Man*	75.00 -	100.00
5430 *Kansas City Blues*	25.00 -	40.00
5675 *Stonewall Blues*	150.00 -	200.00
Okeh 8955 *Jazzbo Stomp*	150.00 -	250.00
8956 *Boodle Bum Bum*	150.00 -	250.00
8958 *Gator Wobble*	150.00 -	250.00
8960 *Mary Anna Cut Off*	150.00 -	250.00
8963 *My Love Is Cold*	150.00 -	250.00
8966 *Jug Band Quartette*	150.00 -	250.00

Victor 20552 *Sun Brimmers*	80.00 -	130.00
20576 *Newport News*	80.00 -	130.00
20781 *Sunshine Blues*	100.00 -	150.00
20809 *Memphis Boy*	100.00 -	150.00
21066 *Beale Street Mess Around*	100.00 -	150.00
21185 *State of Tennessee Blues*	50.00 -	80.00
21278 *Coal Oil Blues*	125.00 -	175.00
21412 *Bob Lee Junior Blues*	100.00 -	150.00
21524 *Snitchin' Gambler Blues*	80.00 -	130.00
21657 *Evergreen Money Blues*	150.00 -	200.00
21740 *Sugar Pudding*	150.00 -	200.00
23251 *Fourth Street Mess Around*	200.00 -	300.00
23347 *Taking Your Place*	300.00 -	up
23421 *Meningitis Blues*	300.00 -	up
V38015 *On The Road Again*	200.00 -	300.00
V38504 *Whitewash Station Blues*	200.00 -	300.00
V38537 *Jug Band Waltz*	200.00 -	300.00
V38551 *I Can't Stand It*	200.00 -	300.00
V38558 *K.C. Moan*	200.00 -	300.00
V38578 *Feed Your Friend With A Long-Handled Spoon*	200.00 -	300.00
V38586 *Tired Of Your Driving Me*	200.00 -	300.00
V38599 *Bumble Bee Blues*	200.00 -	300.00
V38605 *Cave Man Blues*	200.00 -	300.00
V38620 *Cocaine Habit Blues*	200.00 -	300.00
Vocalion 03050 *Little Green Slippers*	150.00 -	200.00
03081 *My Love Is Cold*	150.00 -	200.00
03175 *Take Your Fingers Off It*	150.00 -	250.00
03182 *Boodle Bum Bum*	150.00 -	200.00

MEMPHIS MELODY BOYS:

Buddy 8005 *Washboard Blues*	80.00 -	120.00
8068 *On The Riviera*	30.00 -	50.00
Challenge 143 *I'd Rather Be Alone*	10.00 -	15.00

MEMPHIS MELODY MEN:

Superior 2502 *Night Time Is Love Time*	15.00 -	20.00
2503 *I've Got Somebody New*	20.00 -	30.00
2724 *Minnie The Moocher*	100.00 -	150.00
2737 *New Moten Stomp*	100.00 -	150.00

MEMPHIS MELODY PLAYERS:

Challenge 233 *Song Of The Wanderer*	10.00 -	15.00
234 *A Blues Serenade*	40.00 -	70.00
237 *Indian Butterfly*	8.00 -	12.00

MEMPHIS NIGHT HAWKS:

Vocalion 1736 *Sweet Feet*	150.00 -	200.00
1744 *Biscuit Roller*	150.00 -	200.00
2593 *Shanghai Honeymoon*	150.00 -	200.00

MEMPHIS SHEIKS:

Victor 23256 *He's In The Jailhouse Now*	200.00 -	300.00

MEMPHIS STOMPERS:

Electradisk 1930 *Somebody Stole My Gal*	75.00 -	100.00
Victor 21270 *Kansas City Blues*	50.00 -	75.00
21641 *Memphis Stomp*	50.00 -	75.00
21709 *Yea Alabama*	20.00 -	30.00
23371 *Stompin' Away*	150.00 -	200.00

THE MEMPHIS STRUTTERS:

Champion 15415 *Canned Heat Blues*	250.00 -	up

MENDELLO'S DANCE ORCHESTRA:

Banner 6205 *Baby's Coming Back*	15.00 -	25.00
6206 *Cool Papa*	15.00 -	25.00
6213 *High Hattin' Hattie*	15.00 -	25.00
6214 *Dixie Drag*	15.00 -	25.00
7246 *Easy*	15.00 -	20.00
7248 *Sunday Afternoon*	20.00 -	30.00

JOHNNY MERCER:

Decca 142 *The Bathtub Ran Over Again*	10.00 -	15.00

BENNY MEROFF AND HIS ORCHESTRA:

Brunswick 4709 *The Talk Of The Town*	8.00 -	12.00
Columbia 3065-D *Aristocrat Of Harlem*	15.00 -	20.00
3072-D *Yankee In Havana*	15.00 -	20.00
Okeh 40847 *There's A Trick In Pickin' A Chick-Chick-Chicken*	10.00 -	15.00
40912 *Just An Hour Of Love*	80.00 -	120.00
40967 *When You're With Somebody Else*	10.00 -	15.00
41079 *Too Busy!*	10.00 -	15.00
41171 *Smiling Skies*	75.00 -	100.00

ROY MERRITT & HIS ORCHESTRA:

Champion 15637 *Me And The Man In The Moon*	15.00 -	25.00

CYRIL MERRIVALE & HIS ORCHESTRA; CYRIL MERRIVALE'S ORCHESTRA:

Parlophone PNY-34016 *I'm Following You*	20.00 -	30.00
PNY-34020 *I'm Following You*	20.00 -	30.00
PNY-34024 *Cryin' For The Carolines*	25.00 -	40.00
PNY-34025 *Have A Little Faith In Me*	20.00 -	30.00
PNY-34045 *Montana Call*	35.00 -	50.00
PNY-34046 *The Moon Is Low*	35.00 -	50.00
PNY-34047 *Montana Call*	20.00 -	30.00
PNY-34048 *The Moon Is Low*	20.00 -	30.00
PNY-34049 *'Leven-thirty Saturday Night*	30.00 -	50.00
PNY-34053 *It Must Be You*	20.00 -	30.00
PNY-34056 *It Must Be You*	20.00 -	30.00
PNY-34086 *Sharing*	20.00 -	30.00
PNY-34087 *Sharing*	20.00 -	30.00
PNY-34088 *The Song Without A Name*	25.00 -	40.00
PNY-34089 *The Song Without A Name*	25.00 -	40.00
PNY-34092 *Lo Lo*	25.00 -	35.00

(Note: Duplication of titles is due to the issuance of vocal and non-vocal takes.)

THE MERRY COLLEGIANS:

Van Dyke 71775 *Bottom's Up* (sic)	50.00 -	75.00

71786 *Shoo-Shoo-Boogie-Boo* ....50.00 - 75.00
71791 *Tennessee Tess Among The Hills*..............8.00 - 12.00
81852 *You've Got That Thing*.............................10.00 - 15.00

THE MERRY SPARKLERS:
Edison 51346 *You Are Too Sweet For A Dream* .....20.00 - 30.00
51347 *When Dreams Come True*........................20.00 - 30.00

METOMKIN INN ORCHESTRA:
Champion 15419 *Keep Sweepin' The Cobwebs Off The Moon*
....15.00 - 25.00
15421 *You Can Tell Her Anything Under The Sun*
....15.00 - 25.00
15458 *So Long* ....25.00 - 40.00

METROPOLITAN DANCE PLAYERS:
Harlem's Araby, issued contemporaneously on Globe, Grey Gull,
Nadsco, and Radiex ....8.00 - 12.00

METROPOLITAN ORCHESTRA:
Berliner, titles as below, and others.........................35.00 - up
Monarch 1023 *Creole Belles* ....20.00 - 40.00
Victor 251 *A Bunch O' Blackberries*......................20.00 - 40.00
271 *Smoky Mokes* ....25.00 - 50.00
289 *Who Dat Say Chicken In Dis Crowd?* ....25.00 - 50.00
872 *Rag Time Society* ....25.00 - 50.00
(Note: Above turn-of-the-century recordings are single-sided discs.
Berliners and Victor 872 are 7-inch discs, or approximately that
diameter. Berliners have embossed, crudely executed labels.
Some of above recordings have spoken introductions.)

(TED) METZGER'S CAMPUS/NIGHT OWLS/ ORCHESTRA:
Champion 16439 *It's That Rhythm*......................100.00 - 150.00
16459 *Give A Thought To Love* ....- - -
16471 *I Keep Remembering*...................................- - -
Superior 2629 *When Dreams Come True* ....15.00 - 20.00
2646 *It's That Rhythm* ....20.00 - 30.00

KEN MEYERS:
Regal 8183 *Stampede* ....15.00 - 20.00

TOMMY MEYERS & HIS GANG:
Gennett 6783 *Things Look Wonderful Now*..............15.00 - 20.00

VIC MEYERS AND HIS ORCHESTRA; VIC MEYERS' MUSIC:
Brunswick 2501 *Shake It And Break It*....................15.00 - 20.00
2630 *Springtime Rag* ....15.00 - 20.00
2664 *Weary Blues* ....10.00 - 15.00
2685 *Burmalone*...7.00 - 10.00
2733 *Mean Looks* ....8.00 - 12.00
2774 *The Only, Only One For Me* ....7.00 - 10.00
2800 *Shimmy*...8.00 - 12.00
Columbia 1168-D *Now That You're Gone* ....10.00 - 15.00
1456-D *Bow Down To Washington* ....7.00 - 10.00
1516-D *Estrellita* ....5.00 - 8.00
1530-D *Nobody's Sweetheart*................................8.00 - 12.00
1678-D *Could I Cry?* ....7.00 - 10.00
2026-D *Congratulations* ....8.00 - 12.00
2120-D *Rose Room* ....10.00 - 15.00
Vocalion 15056 *Three O'Clock Blues*....................35.00 - 50.00

MEZZ MEZZROW AND HIS ORCHESTRA/SWING BAND; MEZZROW-LADNIER QUINTET:
Bluebird 6319 *The Panic Is On* ....8.00 - 12.00
6320 *Lost* ....8.00 - 12.00

6321 *I'se A-Muggin'* ....8.00 - 12.00
10085, 10087, 10088, 10090................................. 7.00 - 12.00
Brunswick 6778 *Swingin' With Mezz* .... 10.00 - 15.00
7551 *Dissonance*... 10.00 - 15.00
Victor 25019 *Sendin' The Vipers*........................... 10.00 - 15.00
25202 *Old Fashioned Love* .... 10.00 - 15.00
25612 *Hot Club Stomp*... 10.00 - 15.00
25636 *Blues In Disguise* .... 10.00 - 15.00

MIAMI GARDEN ORCHESTRA:
Silvertone 5027 *She Looks Like Helen Brown*........ 15.00 - 20.00

MIAMI LUCKY SEVEN:
Gennett (personal) unnumbered *I Wonder Blues*.... 25.00 - 40.00
Gennett 3165 *Fallin' Down* .... 15.00 - 25.00
3174 *Slippery Elm*... 15.00 - 25.00
5473 *Red Hot Mama* .... 15.00 - 25.00
5585 *Boll Weevil Blues* .... 15.00 - 25.00

MIAMI ROYAL PALM ORCHESTRA:
Cameo 8136 *There Must Be A Silver Lining* .... 8.00 - 12.00
8137 *Back In Your Own Back Yard* .... 7.00 - 10.00
8139 *My Blue Ridge Mountain Home* .... 8.00 - 12.00
8162 *Why Do I Love You?* .... 15.00 - 20.00
8180 *Can't Help Lovin' Dat Man* .... 8.00 - 12.00
8186 *Ol' Man River* .... 8.00 - 12.00
8236 *Get Out And Get Under The Moon*............... 7.00 - 10.00
(Foregoing titles on Lincoln, Romeo are similarly valued)

MIAMI SOCIETY ORCHESTRA:
Jewel 5011 *Side By Side* .... 10.00 - 15.00

ERNEST MICHALL (CLARINET BAND); ERNEST MICHALL & HIS NEW ORLEANS BOYS:
Black Patti 8046 *Sidewalk Blues*........................... 750.00 - up
Superior 372 *Embarrassment Blues* .... 300.00 - up

MICHIGAN MELODY MAKERS:
Pennington 1453 *Indian Love Call* .... 20.00 - 30.00
1455 *Dixie Dreams* .... 30.00 - 50.00

MICKEY MOUSE & THE TURTLE (See also WILLIAMS' WASHBOARD BAND):
Bluebird 5202 *Move Turtle* .... 75.00 - 100.00

THE MIDNIGHT AIREDALES:
Columbia 1981-D *Swanee Shuffle* .... 20.00 - 30.00

THE MIDNIGHT RAMBLERS:
Broadway 1114 *Together, We Two*.......................... 7.00 - 10.00
1121 *Make My Cot Where the Cot-Cot-Cotton Grows*
.... 7.00 - 10.00
1122 *Is She My Girl Friend?* .... 7.00 - 10.00
1175 *Too Busy* .... 7.00 - 10.00
1179 *Just Like A Melody Out Of The Sky* .... 7.00 - 10.00
1242 *I Faw Down An' Go Boom*........................... 7.00 - 10.00
1259 *That's What I Call Heaven* .... 7.00 - 10.00
1263 *I'm Wild About Horns On Automobiles* ...... 7.00 - 10.00
1264 *Kansas City Kitty* .... 7.00 - 10.00
1271 *Honey* .... 7.00 - 10.00
1275 *When My Dreams Come True* .... 7.00 - 10.00
1276 *That's You, Baby* .... 7.00 - 10.00
1281 *My Sin* .... 7.00 - 10.00
1302 *Ain't Misbehavin'*.. 7.00 - 10.00
1310 *Lovable And Sweet* .... 8.00 - 12.00

THE MIDNIGHT ROUNDERS:
Vocalion 1218 *Shake Your Shimmy* .... 200.00 - up
1237 *Bull Fiddle Rag* .... 150.00 - 250.00

THE MIDNIGHT SERENADERS:
Broadway 1216 *Tin Roof Blues* ....50.00 - 75.00
Paramount 20657 *Tin Roof Blues* ....50.00 - 75.00

THE MIDWAY DANCE ORCHESTRA:
Columbia 33-D *The Black Sheep Blues* ....35.00 - 50.00
    51-D *Cotton Pickers' Ball* ....35.00 - 50.00

MIDWAY GARDEN ORCHESTRA:
Claxtonola 40272 *Black Sheep Blues* ....150.00 - 250.00
    40273 *Lots O' Mama* ....50.00 - 80.00
Harmograph 863 *Black Sheep Blues* ....150.00 - 250.00
    864 *Sobbin' Blues* ....50.00 - 80.00
Paramount 20272 *Black Sheep Blues* ....150.00 - 250.00
    20273 *Sobbin' Blues* ....50.00 - 80.00
Puritan 11273 *Lots O' Mama* ....50.00 - 80.00
Triangle 11311 *Sobbin' Blues* ....50.00 - 80.00

EDDIE MILES & HIS FLORENTINE ORCHESTRA:
Gennett 6200 *One O'Clock Baby* ....50.00 - 80.00
    6247 *Is It Possible?* ....50.00 - 80.00

BUBBER MILEY & HIS MILEAGE MAKERS:
Victor 23010 *The Penalty Of Love* ....35.00 - 50.00
    V38138 *I Lost My Gal From Memphis*.............40.00 - 60.00
    V38146 *Black Maria* ....75.00 - 100.00

EMMETT MILLER (accompanied by HIS GEORGIA CRACKERS):
Bluebird 6550 *I Ain't Got Nobody* ....8.00 - 12.00
    6577 *Anytime* ....8.00 - 12.00
Okeh 40239 *Anytime* ....30.00 - 50.00
    40465 *Lovesick Blues* ....30.00 - 50.00
    40545 *I Never Had The Blues* ....30.00 - 50.00
    41062 *I Ain't Got Nobody* ....15.00 - 25.00
    41095 *Anytime* ....15.00 - 25.00
    41135 *Take Your Tomorrow* ....20.00 - 30.00
    41182 *You're The Cream In My Coffee*...........20.00 - 30.00
    41205 *The Lion Tamers* ....30.00 - 50.00
    41280 *Right Or Wrong* ....20.00 - 30.00
    41305 *Lovin' Sam* ....20.00 - 30.00
    41342 *Sweet Mama* ....25.00 - 40.00
    41377 *The Pickaninnies' Paradise*..................25.00 - 40.00
    41438 *God's River Blues* ....25.00 - 40.00

FLASH MILLER & HIS ORCHESTRA:
Gennett 3178 *I'm Sitting On Top Of The World* .....10.00 - 15.00
    3180 *Paddlin' Madelin' Home* ....8.00 - 12.00
    3186 *Whoopee!* ....15.00 - 20.00

GLENN MILLER AND HIS ORCHESTRA:
Bluebird, most issues ....5.00 - 10.00
Brunswick 7915 *I Got Rhythm* ....10.00 - 15.00
    7923 *Sleepy Time Gal* ....10.00 - 15.00
    8034 *My Fine Feathered Friend* ....10.00 - 15.00
    8041 *Sweet Stranger* ....10.00 - 15.00
    8062 *Doin' The Jive* ....10.00 - 15.00
    8152 *Don't Wake Up My Heart* ....10.00 - 15.00
    8173 *Dippermouth Blues* ....10.00 - 15.00
Columbia 3052-D *A Blues Serenade* ....50.00 - 80.00
    3058-D *Solo Hop* ....50.00 - 80.00
Decca 1239 *How Am I To Know* ....10.00 - 15.00
    1284 *Wistful And Blue* ....10.00 - 15.00
    1342 *I'm Sitting On Top Of The World* ....8.00 - 12.00
Decca, most other issues..5.00 - 8.00
Victor, most issues ....5.00 - 8.00
Vocalion (titles as on Brunswick, similarly valued)

JOHNNIE MILLER'S NEW ORLEANS FROLICKERS:
Columbia 1546-D *Dipper Mouth Blues* ....50.00 - 75.00

RAY MILLER & HIS ORCHESTRA:
Brunswick 2546 *I'm Goin' South* ....8.00 - 12.00
    2573 *Nine O'Clock Sal* ....8.00 - 12.00
    2606 *Come On Red* ....8.00 - 12.00
    2607 *You Can Take Me Away From Dixie* ....8.00 - 12.00
    2613 *Lots O' Mama* ....10.00 - 15.00
    2632 *Mama's Gone, Good Bye* ....10.00 - 15.00
    2643 *I Can't Get The One I Want* ....7.00 - 10.00
    2681 *Red Hot Mama* ....10.00 - 15.00
    2724 *Doodle-Doo-Doo* ....7.00 - 10.00
    2753 *Me And The Boy Friend* ....7.00 - 10.00
    2778 *Nobody Knows What A Red Head Mama Can Do*
    ....8.00 - 12.00
    2823 *That's My Girl*..8.00 - 12.00
    2830 *Tessie (Stop Teasing Me)* ....7.00 - 10.00
    2855 *Red Hot Henry Brown* ....10.00 - 15.00
    2898 *Phoebe Snow* ....8.00 - 12.00
    2935 *Ya! Ya! Alma* ....7.00 - 10.00
    2989 *Spanish Shawl* ....7.00 - 10.00
    3132 *Stomp Your Stuff* ....8.00 - 12.00
    3133 *Oh! Oh! Oh! What A Night!* ....10.00 - 15.00
    3328 *Mercy Percy* ....10.00 - 15.00
    3676 *Blue Baby* ....8.00 - 12.00
    3677 *I Ain't Got Nobody*.................................8.00 - 12.00
    3828 *My Honey's Lovin' Arms* ....10.00 - 15.00
    3829 *Is She My Girl Friend?* ....10.00 - 15.00
    4077 *Anything You Say* ....8.00 - 12.00
    4131 *Rose Of Mandalay* ....8.00 - 12.00
    4194 *Mississippi, Here I Am* ....10.00 - 15.00
    4223 *In A Great Big Way* ....10.00 - 15.00
    4224 *That's A Plenty* ....15.00 - 20.00
    4233 *Cradle Of Love* ....15.00 - 20.00
    4258 *He, She And Me* ....8.00 - 12.00
    4425 *You Want Lovin' (But I Want Love)*............8.00 - 12.00
    4669 *Blue Butterfly* ....7.00 - 10.00
    4682 *That's Where You Come In* ....8.00 - 12.00
    4687 *Hoosier Hop* ....10.00 - 15.00
    4692 *Harlem Madness* ....15.00 - 20.00
Brunswick, most other issues....................................5.00 - 8.00
Columbia A3563 *Doo-Dah Blues* ....10.00 - 15.00
    A3926 *Blue Hoosier Blues* ....10.00 - 15.00
Columbia, most other issues ....5.00 - 8.00

LUCKY MILLINDER WITH MILLS BLUE RHYTHM BAND; MILLS BLUE RHYTHM BAND; LUCKY MILLINDER & IIIS ORCHESTRA:
Bluebird 5688 *The Growl* ....20.00 - 30.00
Brunswick 6156 *Moanin'* ....30.00 - 50.00
    6199 *Snake Hips* ....20.00 - 30.00
    6229 *Savage Rhythm* ....20.00 - 30.00
Columbia 2963-D *Let's Have A Jubilee* ....20.00 - 30.00
    2994-D *Keep The Rhythm Going* ....20.00 - 30.00
    3020-D *Back Beats* ....20.00 - 30.00
    3038-D *African Lullaby* ....20.00 - 30.00
    3071-D *Harlem Heat* ....20.00 - 30.00
    3078-D *Truckin'* ....15.00 - 25.00
    3083-D *Dinah Lou* ....20.00 - 30.00
    3087-D *Congo Caravan* ....12.00 - 16.00
    3111-D *Yes! Yes!*...15.00 - 25.00
    3134-D *Everything Is Still Okay* ....15.00 - 25.00
    3135-D *Red Rhythm* ....20.00 - 30.00

3147-D *Merry-Go-Round* ....15.00 - 25.00
3148-D *In A Sentimental Mood* ....15.00 - 25.00
3156-D *Balloonacy*...20.00 - 30.00
3157-D *Showboat Shuffle* ....20.00 - 30.00
3158-D *Algiers Stomp*.......................................15.00 - 25.00
3162-D *Big John's Special* ....15.00 - 25.00
Decca (most issues) ....5.00 - 10.00
King (most issues) ....5.00 - 10.00
Variety 503 *Jungle Madness* ....12.00 - 16.00
546 *Rhythm Jam*...12.00 - 16.00
604 *The Lucky Swing*.......................................12.00 - 16.00
624 *Camp Meeting Jamboree* ....12.00 - 16.00
634 *Jammin' For The Jack-Pot* ....12.00 - 16.00
Victor 22763 *Heebie Jeebies* ....20.00 - 30.00
22800 *Moanin'* ....20.00 - 30.00
24442 *Harlem After Midnight* ....20.00 - 30.00
24482 *Break It Down*..20.00 - 30.00
Vocalion 3808 *Blue Rhythm Fantasy* ....12.00 - 16.00
3817 *Rhythm Jam* ....12.00 - 16.00

THE MILLS BROTHERS:
Brunswick 6197 *Tiger Rag* ....10.00 - 15.00
6225 *Baby, Won't You Please Come Home* ....10.00 - 15.00
6269 *How'm I Doin', Hey-Hey* ....10.00 - 20.00
6278 *Rockin' Chair* ....10.00 - 15.00
6305, 6330, 6357, 6430, 6785, 6913 ....7.00 - 12.00
6517 *Doin' The New Low-Down* ....15.00 - 20.00
6519 *Diga Diga Doo* ....15.00 - 20.00
6894 *Swing It, Sister*..10.00 - 15.00
Decca 165, 166, 167, 176, 228, 380, 402, 497, 1148 7.00 - 12.00
Decca (most other issues) ....5.00 - 10.00
(Note: In the February 1979 issue of *Goldmine's* Record Swapper, an advertiser offered "up to $950.00 for a Mills Brothers 78 on the Gennett label cut in 1928. Titles unknown." The existence of any Gennett issues by The Mills Brothers has never been verified.)

MILLS CAVALCADE ORCHESTRA:
Columbia 3066-D *Lovely Liza Lee* ....15.00 - 25.00

(PAUL)MILLS' MERRY MAKERS:
Titles issued contemporaneously on Cameo, Lincoln, and Romeo: *Bad Girl; Distortion; I'm Rollin' In Love; I'm Talking About My Wonderful Gal; Moanin' Low; You Oughta Know* ....7.00 - 12.00
Additional titles: *In A Great Big Way; The Junior-Senior Prom; My Honey's Lovin' Arms* ....10.00 - 20.00
Another title: *Milwaukee Walk* ....20.00 - 30.00
Harmony 1099-H *When You're Smiling*..............20.00 - 30.00
1104-H *St. James Infirmary*.............................20.00 - 30.00
(Note: Above two titles on Diva and Velvet Tone are similarly valued.)
Pathe-Actuelle 36961 *Honey* ....8.00 - 12.00
37027 *Moanin' Low*...7.00 - 10.00
Perfect 15142 *Honey*..8.00 - 12.00
15208 *Moanin' Low*...7.00 - 10.00
Velvet Tone 7121-V *Farewell Blues* ....40.00 - 60.00

MILLS MUSICAL CLOWNS:
Pathe-Actuelle (titles as on Perfect, following)
Perfect 15096 *Whoopee Stomp* ....40.00 - 60.00
15111 *Railroad Man*..20.00 - 30.00
15125 *Futuristic Rhythm* ....20.00 - 30.00
15136 *Sweetest Melody* ....10.00 - 15.00
15155 *Wipin' The Pan* ....15.00 - 25.00
(foregoing titles on Pathe-Actuelle are similarly valued)

MILLS SWINGPHONIC ORCHESTRA:
Master 119 *Lullaby To A Lamp Post* ....10.00 - 15.00
126 *Merry Widow On A Spree* ....10.00 - 15.00

MILLS' TEN BLACK BERRIES:
Titles issued contemporaneously on Clarion, Diva, and Velvet Tone: *Black And Tan Fantasy; Double Check Stomp; East St. Louis Toodle-oo; Hot and Bothered; The Mooche; Sweet Mama* ....40.00 - 60.00

FLOYD MILLS & HIS MARYLANDERS:
Champion 16423 *Chicago Rhythm* ....80.00 - 120.00
Gennett 6909 *Hard Luck*...................................80.00 - 120.00

IRVING MILLS & HIS HOTSY TOTSY GANG/ MODERNISTS/ORCHESTRA: (See also HOTSY TOTSY GANG)
Brunswick 4482 *Sweet Savannah Sue* ....20.00 - 30.00
4498 *Some Fun* ....20.00 - 30.00
4559 *Harvey*..15.00 - 25.00
4587 *Star Dust* ....15.00 - 25.00
4641 *Manhattan Rag*...15.00 - 25.00
4674 *My Little Honey And Me* ....15.00 - 25.00
4838 *Railroad Man* ....20.00 - 30.00
4920 *Barbaric* ....20.00 - 30.00
4983 *Deep Harlem*..80.00 - 120.00
4998 *What A Night!* ....30.00 - 50.00
5013 *High And Dry* ....20.00 - 30.00
Lincoln 3209 *In The Moonlight* ....7.00 - 10.00
Victor 22669 *So Sweet* ....7.00 - 10.00
V-38105 *At The Prom* ....75.00 - 100.00

WARREN MILLS & HIS BLUES SERENADERS:
Victor 35962 (12 inch) *St. Louis Blues*..................35.00 - 50.00

MISSISSIPPI MAULERS:
Columbia 1545-D *My Angeline* ....20.00 - 30.00

MISSISSIPPI MUSIC MAKERS:
Title issued contemporaneously on Cameo, Lincoln, and Romeo: *If You Want The Rainbow (You Must Have The Rain)* ....10.00 - 15.00

MISSISSIPPI TRIO:
Van Dyke 77039 *Coal Black Blues*........................15.00 - 20.00

THE MISSOURIANS:
Victor V-38067 *Market Street Stomp* ....80.00 - 120.00
V-38071 *Ozark Mountain Blues* ....80.00 - 120.00
V-38084 *Scotty Blues*..100.00 - 150.00
V-38103 *Vine Street Drag* ....100.00 - 150.00
V-38120 *Stoppin' The Traffic* ....125.00 - 175.00
V-38145 *Two Hundred Squabble* ....125.00 - 175.00

MISSOURI DANCE ORCHESTRA; MISSOURI JAZZ BAND:
Banner 0518 *I'm Gonna Count My Sheep* ....7.00 - 10.00
1399 *San*..8.00 - 12.00
1409 *Any Way The Wind Blows* ....7.00 - 10.00
1456 *How I Love That Girl*................................15.00 - 20.00
1457 *Where's My Sweetie Hiding?* ....15.00 - 20.00
1564 *Save Your Sorrow (For Tomorrow)*............7.00 - 10.00
1621 *Stomp Off, Let's Go*................................15.00 - 20.00
1624 *Sweet Man* ....15.00 - 20.00
1644 *I'm Gonna Charleston Back To Charleston* ....7.00 - 10.00
1657 *(How She Loves Me Is) Nobody's Business* .....8.00 - 12.00
1662 *Spanish Shawl* ....8.00 - 12.00

1674 *Keep Your Skirts Down, Mary Ann*...............8.00 - 12.00
1728 *I've Got The Charleston Blues* ....7.00 - 10.00
1733 *Show That Fellow The Door*.......................7.00 - 10.00
1764 *Waffles* ....7.00 - 10.00
1795 *She Belongs To Me* ....7.00 - 10.00
1797 *Out In The New Mown Hay* ....7.00 - 10.00
1819 *The Captivating Rhythm* ....7.00 - 10.00
1842 *Susie, My Susie, Why Don't You Marry Me*.....7.00 - 10.00
1846 *Sadie Green (The Vamp of New Orleans)* .10.00 - 15.00
1863 *My Baby Knows How*................................10.00 - 15.00
1864 *I Love Her* ....7.00 - 10.00
1904 *How Could Red Riding Hood?* ....8.00 - 12.00
1999 *How I Hate That Desert Song*...................10.00 - 15.00
6030 *Miss Annabelle Lee*................................7.00 - 10.00
6031 *Twelfth Street Rag*................................15.00 - 20.00
6099 *Who's Got The Blues For You Now*............7.00 - 10.00
6100 *That's When A Feller Needs A Sweetheart*..7.00 - 10.00
6129 *Homing Bird (Headin' For Home)*............15.00 - 20.00
6202 *I Could Stand A Lot Of Lovin' From You*....8.00 - 12.00
6209 *Don't Send Your Wifey To The Country* ......7.00 - 10.00
6238 *I Love My Best Girl Best*.........................7.00 - 10.00
6262 *Mystic Bengal Bay*................................8.00 - 12.00
6267 *Lily Lou* ....7.00 - 10.00
6271 *"Hoo" Ray, I Want To Play* ....8.00 - 12.00
7052 *Do I Get It? (I'll Say I Do)* ....7.00 - 10.00
7054 *My Little Sunshine* ....7.00 - 10.00
7077 *You Can't Blame Me For That* ....7.00 - 10.00
7106 *Know Nothin' Blues*................................15.00 - 20.00
7140 *Straight Back Home* ....15.00 - 20.00
7157 *Puttin' On The Dog* ....15.00 - 20.00
7160 *If I Can't Ba-Ba-Baby You* ....7.00 - 10.00
7193 *Raggedy Maggie* ....7.00 - 10.00
7199 *Oh! How She Could Shake Her Tambourine*...7.00 - 10.00
7212 *See My Tennessee* ....7.00 - 10.00
7221 *I Love To Ride A Camel* ....7.00 - 10.00
7239 *Tennessee Mammy* ....7.00 - 10.00
Challenge 543 *Oh! How She Could Shake Her Tambourine*
....7.00 - 10.00
900 *If I Can Ba-Ba-Baby You* ....7.00 - 10.00
Conqueror 7110 *Ready For The River*...................10.00 - 15.00
7487 *The Man From The South* ....15.00 - 20.00
Domino 3507 *Ah-Ha!* ....8.00 - 12.00
3592 *Stomp Off, Let's Go* ....15.00 - 20.00
3594 *Sweet Man* ....15.00 - 20.00
3605 *Angry* ....7.00 - 10.00
3696 *I've Got Those Charleston Blues*................7.00 - 10.00
4011 *Tiger Rag* ....20.00 - 30.00
4184 *Ready For The River*..............................10.00 - 15.00
4497 *Nobody's Sweetheart* ....15.00 - 20.00
Oriole 518 *Fallin' Down* ....10.00 - 15.00
521 *When A Blonde Makes Up Her Mind To Do You Good*
....8.00 - 12.00
528 *Then I'll Be Happy*.................................10.00 - 15.00
536 *Sleepy Time Gal*....................................10.00 - 15.00
Perfect 15273 *Nobody's Sweetheart*.....................15.00 - 20.00
15283 *Sing, You Sinners* ....10.00 - 15.00
Regal 8361 *Bye-Bye Pretty Baby*........................7.00 - 10.00
8478 *My Ohio Home* ....7.00 - 10.00
8480 *Keep Sweeping The Cobwebs Off The Moon*...7.00 - 10.00
8942 *Nobody's Sweetheart* ....15.00 - 20.00
8959 *Sing You Sinners* ....10.00 - 15.00
9504 *Long Lost Mama* ....8.00 - 12.00
9514 *My Sweetie Went Away*...........................8.00 - 12.00

9925 *Stomp Off, Let's Go*.....................................15.00 - 20.00
9970 *My Charleston Dancing Man*.....................8.00 - 12.00
9985 *Dinah*...7.00 - 10.00

EDDIE MITCHELL & HIS ORCHESTRA:
Gennett 5612 *Pleasure Mad* ....40.00 - 60.00

THE MODERNISTS:
Titles issued contemporaneously on Banner, Conqueror, Melotone,
     Oriole, Perfect, and Romeo: *Solitude; I'm Getting Sentimental
     Over You* ....15.00 - 20.00

MIFF MOLE'S (LITTLE) MOLERS; MIFF MOLE:
Brunswick 7842 *How Could You?* ....10.00 - 15.00
Okeh 40758 *Alexander's Ragtime Band* ....40.00 - 60.00
     40784 *The Darktown Strutters' Ball*................40.00 - 60.00
     40848 *Hurricane* ....40.00 - 60.00
     40890 *Imagination* ....40.00 - 60.00
     40932 *My Gal Sal* ....40.00 - 60.00
     40984 *The New Twister* ....35.00 - 50.00
     41098 *Crazy Rhythm*................................35.00 - 50.00
     41153 *Wild Oat Joe* ....35.00 - 50.00
     41232 *That's A Plenty*...............................35.00 - 50.00
     41273 *Birmingham Bertha*..........................35.00 - 50.00
     41371 *Navy Blues* ....40.00 - 60.00
     41445 *After You've Gone* ....50.00 - 75.00
Parlophone (English) R-647 *You Made Me Love You*
     ....40.00 - 60.00
Premium 852, 853 ....5.00 - 8.00
Vocalion 3468 *Love And Learn* ....10.00 - 15.00

TOOTS MONDELLO; TOOTS MONDELLO & HIS ORCHESTRA:
Brunswick 8031 *Thanks For The Memory* ....7.00 - 10.00
     8061 *You're In Love With Love* ....7.00 - 10.00
     8094 *Let Me Day Dream*...............................7.00 - 10.00
     8105 *At Sundown* ....5.00 - 10.00
Royal 1817 *Burnin' Sticks* ....8.00 - 12.00
     1823 *Shades Of Jade* ....8.00 - 12.00
Varsity 8110 *Sweet Lorraine* ....7.00 - 10.00
     8118 *St. Louis Gal*......................................7.00 - 10.00

J. NEAL MONTGOMERY & HIS ORCHESTRA:
Okeh 8682 *Atlanta Low-Down* ....100.00 - 150.00

JACK MONTROSE & HIS ORCHESTRA:
Q.R.S. Q-1022 *I'm So Tired Of It All* ....12.00 - 16.00
     Q-1027 *Valparaiso* ....20.00 - 30.00
Q-1038 *When I Met My Sunshine* ....10.00 - 15.00

HENRY MOON & GEORGE THOMAS:
Herwin 92025 *Neck Bones And Beans*.................250.00 - up

ART MOONEY & HIS ORCHESTRA:
*Vogue R-711 *Seems Like Old Times*....................50.00 - up
     *R-713 *I've Been Working On The Railroad* ...35.00 - up
     R-730 *Piper's Junction* ....35.00 - 50.00
     *R-732 *In The Moonmist* ....25.00 - 40.00
(*Note: These occur with different record numbers on each side, e.g.
     713/732. Some of these combinations are very scarce, and are
     valued more highly than the foregoing by Vogue record
     collectors.)

THE MOONLIGHT REVELERS:
Grey Gull 1767 *Baby Knows How*........................40.00 - 60.00
     1775 *Alabama Shuffle*................................50.00 - 75.00
     1786 *Memphis Stomp*................................50.00 - 75.00

MOONLIGHT SERENADERS:
Bell 383 *Hot Stuff Blues* ....10.00 -   15.00

GRANT MOORE & HIS NEW ORLEANS BLACK DEVILS:
Vocalion 1622 *Original Dixieland One-Step* ....250.00 -   up

SAM MOORE:
Gennett 4747 *Laughing Rag* ....15.00 -   20.00
Okeh 4412 *Chain Gang Blues* ....15.00 -   20.00
   4423 *Wang-Wang Blues* ....15.00 -   20.00
Victor 18849 *Laughing Rag* ....8.00 -   12.00

WEBSTER MOORE & HIS HIGH HATTERS:
Harmony 1197-H *I Wonder How It Feels* ....10.00 -   15.00
Velvet Tone 2197-V *I Wonder How It Feels* ....10.00 -   15.00

FATE MORABLE'S SOCIETY SYNCOPATORS:
Okeh 40113 *Frankie And Johnny* ....150.00 -   200.00

MORAN AND MACK:
Columbia 935-D, 1094-D, 1198-D ....7.00 -   12.00
Columbia 1350-D *Two Black Crows, Part 7/8* ....10.00 -   15.00
   1560-D *Two Black Crows In Jail* ....10.00 -   15.00
   1652-D *Two Black Crows In Hades* ....15.00 -   20.00
   1929-D *Foolishments* ....15.00 -   20.00
Columbia Personal 170330 *Two Black Crows In The AEF*
....40.00 -   60.00
(Note: Above is a one-sided record made for Bobbs-Merrill Co.)

CHAUNCEY MOREHOUSE & HIS SWING SIX/ ORCHESTRA:
Brunswick 8122 *Plastered In Paris* ....7.00 -   10.00
   8142 *Oriental Nocturne* ....7.00 -   10.00
Variety 608 *Blues In B Flat* ....10.00 -   15.00
   638 *My Gal Sal* ....8.00 -   12.00

BETTY MORGAN:
Pathe-Actuelle 32241 *I Meet Her In The Moonlight* .8.00 -   12.00
   32256 *There's Everything Nice About You* ....15.00 -   20.00
Perfect 12320 *You Went Away Too Far And Stayed Away Too Long*
....8.00 -   12.00
   12335 *There's Everything Nice About You* ....15.00 -   20.00

BUDDY MORGAN & HIS VETERANS:
Columbia 2182-D *Some Other Girl In Some Other Port*
....8.00 -   12.00

RUSS MORGAN AND HIS ORCHESTRA; MUSIC IN THE RUSS MORGAN MANNER:
Brunswick, most issues................................5.00 -   8.00
Columbia 3050-D *Tidal Wave* ....15.00 -   20.00
   3064-D *In A Little Gypsy Tearoom* ....7.00 -   10.00
   3067-D *Sliphorn Sam* ....15.00 -   20.00
Decca, most issues ....4.00 -   7.00
Odeon ONY-36094 *Washin' The Blues From My Soul*
   (instrumental) ....20.00 -   30.00
   ONY-36095 *Washin' The Blues From My Soul* .....15.00 -   25.00
   ONY-36097 *I Remember You From Somewhere* ...15.00 -   20.00
   ONY-36140 *When The Organ Played At Twilight*
....15.00 -   20.00

SAM MORGAN'S JAZZ BAND:
Columbia 14213-D *Sing On* ....200.00 -   300.00
   14258-D *Steppin' On The Gas* ....200.00 -   300.00
   14267-D *Down By The Riverside* ....200.00 -   300.00
   14351-D *Short Dress Gal* ....200.00 -   300.00
   14539-D *Over In The Glory Land* ....200.00 -   300.00

JOE MORRIS & HIS ORCHESTRA:
Champion 15717 *Button Up Your Overcoat* ....10.00 -   15.00
   15719 *Lover Come Back To Me* ....30.00 -   50.00
   15738 *I've Got A Feeling I'm Falling* ....10.00 -   15.00
   15741 *What A Day!* ....10.00 -   15.00
   15758 *Singin' In The Rain* ....8.00 -   12.00
   15777 *I'm In Seventh Heaven* ....8.00 -   12.00
   15780 *Am I Blue?* ....15.00 -   20.00
   15804 *Where the Sweet Forget-Me-Nots Remember*
....8.00 -   12.00
   15842 *Hang On To Me* ....8.00 -   12.00

THOMAS MORRIS & HIS ORCHESTRA/SEVEN HOT BABIES; THOMAS MORRIS PAST JAZZ MASTERS:
Okeh 4867 *Lonesome Journey Blues* ....80.00 -   120.00
   4940 *Those Blues* ....80.00 -   120.00
   8055 *Original Charleston Strut* ....80.00 -   120.00
   8075 *Just Blues, That's All* ....80.00 -   120.00
Victor 20179 *Ham Gravy* ....25.00 -   40.00
   20180 *Georgia Grind* ....25.00 -   40.00
   20316 *Who's Dis Heah Stranger?* ....50.00 -   75.00
   20330 *P.D.Q. Blues* ....35.00 -   50.00
   20364 *The Mess* ....35.00 -   50.00
   20483 *The Chinch* ....40.00 -   60.00

HERB MORRISON & CHARLES NEHLSEN OF W.L.S.:
Issued contemporaneously on Melotone, Perfect: *The Crash Of The Hindenberg* ....10.00 -   15.00

MORSE AND FRANKEL:
Pathe 20430 *Jazzin' Around* ....15.00 -   25.00

(MISS) LEE MORSE (& HER BLUE GRASS BOYS/ SOUTHERN SERENADERS):
Bluebird 5052 *Pettin' In The Park* ....8.00 -   12.00
Columbia 1063-D *What Do I Care What Somebody Said?*
....8.00 -   12.00
   1922-D *Sweetness* ....10.00 -   15.00
   2136-D *'tain't No Sin* ....12.00 -   16.00
   2165-D *Sing, You Sinners* ....12.00 -   16.00
   2333-D *Loving You The Way I Do* ....12.00 -   16.00
   2348-D *He's My Secret Passion* ....12.00 -   16.00
   2417-D *I've Got Five Dollars* ....15.00 -   20.00
   2497-D *It's The Girl!* ....15.00 -   20.00
Columbia, most other issues ....5.00 -   10.00
Pathe-Actuelle (titles as on Perfect, below)
Perfect 11586 *Blue Soldier Blues* ....8.00 -   12.00
   11590 *What-Cha-Call-'Em Blues* ....8.00 -   12.00
   11591 *Sweet Man* ....8.00 -   12.00
   11592 *Oh Boy! What A Girl* ....8.00 -   12.00
   11595 *Want A Little Lovin'* ....8.00 -   12.00
   11602 *I Love My Baby (My Baby Loves Me)* ....8.00 -   12.00
   11608 *Tentin' Down In Tennessee* ....8.00 -   12.00
   11616 *Could I? I Certainly Could* ....8.00 -   12.00
   11621 *Hoodle Dee Doo Dee Doodoo* ....8.00 -   12.00
   11628 *He's Still My Baby* ....8.00 -   12.00
   11635 *The Little White House (In Honeymoon Lane)*
....7.00 -   10.00
   11636 *The Jersey Walk* ....8.00 -   12.00
   11639 *Ain't That Too Bad?* ....8.00 -   12.00
   14722 *Bolshevik* ....8.00 -   12.00
   14726 *Look Up And Smile* ....10.00 -   15.00
   14727 *Ev'rything's Peaches (For Peaches And Me)*
....10.00 -   15.00
   14737 *Tuck In Kentucky (And Smile)* ....10.00 -   15.00

Perfect, most other issues ....5.00 - 10.00
(Foregoing titles, on Pathe-Actuelle, similarly valued)

BENNY MORTON & HIS ORCHESTRA:
Columbia 2902-D *Get Goin'* ....30.00 - 40.00
   2924-D *Taylor Made* ....30.00 - 40.00

FERD (JELLY ROLL) MORTON: FRED (JELLY ROLL) MORTON; JELLY ROLL MORTON'S INCOMPARABLES/JAZZ BAND/JAZZ KIDS/KINGS OF JAZZ/STEAMBOAT FOUR/STOMPS KINGS/TRIO; JELLY ROLL MORTON & HIS ORCHESTRA RED HOT PEPPERS:
Autograph 606 *Fish Tail Blues* ....1500.00 - up
   607 *Weary Blues* ....1500.00 - up
   623 *Wolverine Blues* ....1500.00 - up
Broadway 11397 *Mr. Jelly Lord*.................200.00 - 300.00
Buddy 8015 *Bucktown Blues* ....150.00 - 300.00
Carnival 11397 *Mr. Jelly Roll* ....200.00 - 300.00
Champion 15105 *Mr. Jelly Lord* ....150.00 - 200.00
Gennett 3043 *Tia Juana*............................100.00 - 150.00
   3259 *Mr. Jelly Lord* ....150.00 - 250.00
   5218 *Grandpa's Spells* ....125.00 - 175.00
   5289 *Wolverine Blues* ....125.00 - 175.00
   5323 *The Pearls* ....75.00 - 125.00
   5486 *New Orleans (Blues) Joys*.........125.00 - 175.00
   5515 *Tom Cat Blues*............................100.00 - 150.00
   5552 *Big Foot Ham* ....100.00 - 150.00
   5590 *Stratford Hunch* ....125.00 - 175.00
   5632 *Tia Juana* ....100.00 - 150.00
Mitchell 11397 *Mr. Jelly Lord*...................200.00 - 300.00
Okeh 8105 *London Blues*............................400.00 - up
Oriole 1007 *The Pearls* ....75.00 - 100.00
Paramount 12216 *Mamanita*......................200.00 - 300.00
   14032 *Froggie Moore*.............................8.00 - 12.00
   20332 *Mr. Jelly Lord* ....200.00 - 300.00

Puritan 11332 *Mr. Jelly Lord*....................200.00 - 300.00
   11397 *Mr. Jelly Lord* ....200.00 - 300.00
   12216 *Mamanita*................................200.00 - 300.00
Rialto (unnumbered) *London Blues*........2,000.00 - up
Silvertone 4028 *Mamanita* ....75.00 - 100.00
   4036 *Stratford Hunch* ....75.00 - 125.00

4038 *Big Foot Ham* ....75.00 - 100.00
4040 *Tom Cat Blues*...........................75.00 - 100.00
4041 *Perfect Rag*...............................75.00 - 125.00
Triangle 11397 *Mr. Jelly Lord* ....200.00 - 300.00
Victor 20221 *Black Bottom Stomp*...........25.00 - 40.00
   20252 *Sidewalk Blues* ....25.00 - 40.00
   20296 *Steamboat Stomp*.......................80.00 - 120.00
   20405 *Someday Sweetheart* ....75.00 - 100.00
   20415 *Doctor Jazz* ....35.00 - 50.00
   20431 *Cannon Ball Blues* ....80.00 - 120.00
   20772 *Hyena Stomp* ....80.00 - 120.00
   20948 *Beale Street Blues* ....80.00 - 120.00
   21064 *Wolverine Blues* ....40.00 - 60.00
   21345 *Jungle Blues* ....80.00 - 120.00
   21658 *Shoe Shiner's Drag* ....35.00 - 50.00
   22681 *Blue Blood Blues* ....75.00 - 100.00
   23004 *Mushmouth Shuffle* ....100.00 - 150.00
   23019 *Fickle Fay Creep* ....100.00 - 150.00
   23307 *Gambling Jack* ....300.00 - up
   23321 *Oil Well* ....300.00 - up
   23334 *Low Gravy*.................................300.00 - up
   23351 *Strokin' Away*............................300.00 - up
   23424 *Primrose Stomp*.........................400.00 - up
   23429 *Load Of Coal*............................400.00 - up
   V38010 *Kansas City Stomps*..................50.00 - 80.00
   V38024 *Georgia Swing* ....40.00 - 60.00
   V38055 *Deep Creek*.............................75.00 - 100.00
   V38075 *Burnin' The Iceberg* ....100.00 - 150.00
   V38078 *New Orleans Bump* ....80.00 - 120.00
   V38093 *Courthouse Bump*.....................100.00 - 150.00
   V38108 *Turtle Twist* ....100.00 - 150.00
   V38113 *Down My Way*.........................150.00 - 200.00
   V38125 *Ponchatrain*............................150.00 - 200.00
   V38135 *Little Lawrence* ....150.00 - 200.00
   V38527 *Freakish* ....150.00 - 250.00
   V38601 *My Little Dixie Home*.................150.00 - 250.00
   V38627 *Pep* ....200.00 - 300.00
Vocalion 1019 *Fat Meat And Greens* ....80.00 - 120.00
   1020 *The Pearls* ....75.00 - 100.00

TOM MORTON'S ORCHESTRA; TOMMY MORTON'S GRANGERS:
Harmony 930-H *Birmingham Bertha* ....15.00 - 20.00
   937-H *Broadway Baby Dolls*............................12.00 - 16.00
(Note: Above titles also issued on Diva and Velvet Tone.)
Pathe-Actuelle 36544 *How Could Red Riding Hood?*
....10.00 - 15.00
   36548 *Baby Mine* ....10.00 - 15.00
   36549 *When I Kissed You I Kissed The Blues Goodbye*
....8.00 - 12.00
Perfect 14725 *How Could Red Riding Hood?* ....10.00 - 15.00
   14729 *Baby Mine* ....10.00 - 15.00
   14730 *When I Kissed You I Kissed The Blues Goodbye*
....8.00 - 12.00

CURTIS MOSBY & HIS DIXIELAND BLUE BLOWERS:
Columbia 1191-D *Weary Stomp* ....80.00 - 120.00
   1192-D *Tiger Stomp*..80.00 - 120.00
   1442-D *Blue Blowers Blues* ....80.00 - 120.00
   40001-D *Between You And Me* ....100.00 - 150.00

MIKE MOSIELLO'S RADIO STARS:
Van Dyke 909 *Meanest Kind Of Blues* ....25.00 - 40.00
   914 *Two Red Lips* ....8.00 - 12.00
Van Dyke (other issues) ....5.00 - 10.00

JOSEPH MOSKOWITZ:
Victor 17978 *Operatic Rag* ....15.00 - 20.00

SID MOSLEY'S BLUE BOYS:
Supertone 9686 *Asphalt Walk*................100.00 - 150.00

SNUB MOSELY AND HIS BAND/ORCHESTRA:
Coral 65020 *Swampland* ....8.00 - 12.00
Decca 7728, 7768, 8586, 8614, 8626, 8636 ....8.00 - 12.00
Sonora, most issues.................................5.00 - 10.00
Super Disc 1060 *Boston Baked Boogie* ....7.00 - 10.00

BENNIE MOTEN'S KANSAS CITY ORCHESTRA;
BUSTER MOTEN-BENNIE MOTEN:
Bluebird 5078 *The Only Girl I Ever Loved* ....15.00 - 20.00
 5585 *Milenberg Joys*..........................8.00 - 12.00
 6032 *Moten Swing* ....8.00 - 12.00
 6204 *Moten Stomp* ....8.00 - 12.00
 6218 *New Orleans* ....8.00 - 12.00
 6304 *Terrific Stomp* ....8.00 - 12.00
 6431 *It's Hard To Laugh Or Smile* ....10.00 - 15.00
 6638 *Mary Lee* ....8.00 - 12.00
 6709 *New Moten Stomp* ....8.00 - 12.00
 6710 *New Vine Street Blues*.................10.00 - 15.00
 6711 *Now That I Need You* ....15.00 - 20.00
 6719 *The Count*............................10.00 - 15.00
 6851 *Sweetheart Of Yesterday*................8.00 - 12.00
 7938 *Moten's Blues* ....8.00 - 12.00
Okeh 8100 *Elephant's Wobble* ....150.00 - 200.00
 8184 *Goofy Dust* ....150.00 - 200.00
 8194 *South* ....150.00 - 200.00
 8213 *Baby Dear* ....150.00 - 200.00
 8242 *18th Street Strut* ....100.00 - 150.00
 8255 *South Street Blues* ....125.00 - 175.00
 8277 *Kater Street Rag* ....150.00 - 200.00
Victor 20406 *Thick Lip Stomp* ....50.00 - 80.00
 20422 *Missouri Wobble* ....50.00 - 80.00
 20485 *Kansas City Shuffle*..................40.00 - 60.00
 20811 *White Lightnin' Blues* ....50.00 - 80.00
 20855 *Dear Heart*...........................40.00 - 60.00
 20946 *12th Street Rag* ....50.00 - 80.00
 20955 *Moten Stomp* ....25.00 - 40.00
 21199 *Ding Dong Blues*......................50.00 - 80.00
 21584 *The New Tulsa Blues* ....35.00 - 50.00
 21693 *Kansas City Breakdown*................40.00 - 60.00
 21739 *Justrite* ....40.00 - 60.00
 22660 *As Long As I Love You* ....80.00 - 120.00
 22680 *Ya Got Love* ....40.00 - 60.00
 22734 *When I'm Alone* ....50.00 - 80.00
 22793 *That Too, Do* ....50.00 - 80.00
 22958 *Oh! Eddie*............................75.00 - 100.00
 23007 *New Vine Street Blues*................80.00 - 120.00
 23023 *Liza Lee* ....80.00 - 120.00
 23028 *Somebody Stole My Gal*................30.00 - 50.00
 23030 *Bouncin' Round* ....80.00 - 120.00
 23037 *Rumba Negro* ....35.00 - 50.00
 23342 *Small Black* ....250.00 - up
 23357 *The Jones Law Blues* ....250.00 - up
 23378 *The Only Girl I Ever Loved* ....250.00 - up
 23384 *Moten Swing* ....250.00 - up
 23391 *The Count*............................300.00 - up
 23393 *Prince Of Wails* ....300.00 - up
 23429 *Professor Hot Stuff* ....400.00 - up
 24216 *Lafayette* ....50.00 - 75.00

 24381 *Milenberg Joys*......................100.00 - 150.00
 24893 *South* ....10.00 - 15.00
 V38012 *Slow Motion* ....75.00 - 100.00
 V38021 *South*.............................50.00 - 75.00
 V38037 *Tough Breaks* ....40.00 - 60.00
 V38048 *Sad Man Blues* ....75.00 - 100.00
 V38072 *Moten's Blues* ....50.00 - 80.00
 V38081 *Terrific Stomp* ....50.00 - 80.00
 V38091 *Kansas City Squabble* ....75.00 - 100.00
 V38104 *Rite Tite* ....50.00 - 80.00
 V38114 *Mary Lee* ....50.00 - 80.00
 V38123 *It Won't Be Long* ....75.00 - 100.00
 V38132 *When Life Seems So Blue* ....75.00 - 100.00
 V38144 *Boot It*............................75.00 - 100.00

MOUND CITY BLUE BLOWERS:
Bluebird 6270 *Hello, Lola* ....7.00 - 10.00
 6456 *One Hour* ....7.00 - 10.00
Brunswick 2581 *Arkansaw Blues* ....15.00 - 20.00
 2602 *Red Hot!* ....15.00 - 20.00
 2648 *Barb Wire Blues* ....15.00 - 20.00
 2804 *Deep Second Street Blues* ....15.00 - 20.00
 2849 *Gettin' Told* ....15.00 - 20.00
 2908 *Wigwam Blues*........................15.00 - 20.00
 3484 *Nervous Puppies* ....15.00 - 25.00
Champion 40059 *Thanks A Million*..............10.00 - 15.00
 40060 *Red Sails In The Sunset*............10.00 - 15.00
 40073 *Eeeney Meeney Miney Mo* ....10.00 - 15.00
 40076 *I'm Shootin' High* ....10.00 - 15.00
 40081 *The Broken Record* ....10.00 - 15.00
 40082 *Rhythm In My Nursery Rhymes*........10.00 - 15.00
 40091 *Mama Don't Allow It* ....10.00 - 15.00
 40098 *You Hit The Spot* ....10.00 - 15.00
 40090 *Wah-Hoo!*...........................10.00 - 15.00
 40103 *High Society* ....10.00 - 15.00
Columbia 1946-D *Indiana* ....25.00 - 35.00
Okeh 41515 *Georgia On My Mind* ....60.00 - 100.00
 41526 *You Rascal, You* ....60.00 - 100.00
Victor V38087 *Tailspin Blues* ....50.00 - 80.00
 V38100 *Hello, Lola* ....50.00 - 80.00
Vocalion 2957 *What's The Reason*.............15.00 - 20.00
 2973 *Indiana*............................15.00 - 20.00

KEN "GOOF" MOYER; KEN MOYER'S NOVELTY TRIO:
Banner 0620 *Idol Of My Eyes* ....10.00 - 15.00
Banner 1872 *Stampede*........................15.00 - 20.00
 1891 *Mellophone Stomp* ....15.00 - 20.00
(Foregoing titles on Domino, Regal are similarly valued)
Pathe-Actuelle 36511 *Mellophone Stomp* ....20.00 - 30.00
 36528 *Idol Of My Eyes* ....10.00 - 15.00
Perfect 14692 *Mellophone Stomp* ....20.00 - 30.00
 14709 *Idol Of My Eyes* ....10.00 - 15.00

JIMMY MUNDY AND HIS ORCHESTRA/SWING CLUB SEVEN:
Variety 598 *Ain't Misbehavin'* ....10.00 -   15.00
Varsity 8136 *A Lover Is Blue*.............................8.00 -   12.00
   8148 *Sunday Special*...............................8.00 -   12.00

RONNIE MUNRO & HIS ORCHESTRA:
Bluebird 7245 *Ten Pretty Girls* ....15.00 -   20.00

LARRY MURPHY & HIS ORCHESTRA:
Cameo 1146 *That's My Hap-Hap-Happiness* ....10.00 -   15.00
   1169 *You Know I Love You* ....7.00 -   10.00

LYLE "SPUD" MURPHY AND HIS ORCHESTRA:
Bluebird 10151, 10157, 10539, 10875 ....5.00 -   10.00
Decca 1853, 2040, 2109 ....5.00 -   10.00

BILLY MURRAY (& HIS MERRY MELODY MEN/& THE SEVEN BLUE BABIES):
Edison 52448 *Doin' The Raccoon* ....50.00 -   80.00
   52454 *Don't Do That To The Poor Puss Cat* .....40.00 -   60.00
   52518 *Ever Since The Movies Learned To Talk*.50.00 -   80.00
   52559 *She's Got Great Ideas!* ....50.00 -   80.00
   52609 *In Old Tia Juana* ....40.00 -   60.00
   52611 *If I'm Wrong, Sue Me* ....40.00 -   60.00
Harmony 784-H *Ever Since The Movies Learned To Talk*
   ....10.00 -   15.00
Victor 16144 *American Ragtime* ....10.00 -   15.00
   17584 *This Is The Life* ....10.00 -   15.00
   17620 *Fido Is A Hot Dog Now* ....10.00 -   15.00
Zon-o-phone 260 *Hiram Green Good Bye* ....10.00 -   15.00
   392 *Don't Be What You Ain't* ....10.00 -   15.00
   415 *Keep On The Sunny Side*.............................10.00 -   15.00
   419 *Nothing Like That In Our Family* ....10.00 -   15.00

GLADYS MURRAY:
Banner 1464 *Big Bad Bill Is Sweet William Now*....15.00 -   20.00
   1479 *Nobody Knows What A Red Head Mama Can Do*
   ....15.00 -   20.00
Regal 9760 *Everybody Loves My Baby* ....15.00 -   20.00
   9782 *I'm Done Done Done With You* ....15.00 -   20.00

MUSICAL COMEDY ORCHESTRA:
Harmony 686-H *I'm On The Crest Of A Wave*..........8.00 -   12.00
   699-H *Watch My Baby Walk* ....8.00 -   12.00
(Note: Above titles on Diva and Velvet Tone are similarly valued.)

THE MUSICAL COMRADES:
Tremont 468, 490, 491 ....7.00 -   12.00
Tremont 0515 *Copenhagen* ....10.00 -   20.00
   0526 *Nobody Knows What A Red Head Mama Can Do*
   ....10.00 -   20.00
   0537 *Cheatin' On Me* ....10.00 -   20.00
   0544 *If You Knew Susie* ....10.00 -   20.00

THE MUSICAL MANIACS:
Vocalion 3655 *Somebody Stole My Gal* ....10.00 -   15.00
   3691 *Down By The Old Mill Stream* ....10.00 -   15.00

MUSICAL STEVEDORES:
Columbia 14406-D *Happy Rhythm* ....100.00 -   150.00

MUSICAL TRIO:
Madison 1920 *Beale Street Blues* ....8.00 -   12.00

THE MUSICAL VOYAGERS:
Parlophone PNY-34152 *Can This Be Love?* ....25.00 -   35.00
   PNY-34153 *Fine And Dandy*.............................25.00 -   35.00

THE MUSIC MASTERS:
Broadway 1470 *Wrap Your Troubles In Dreams* ... 10.00 -   15.00
   1471 *Little Girl* ....10.00 -   15.00
   1476 *Without That Gal*......................................15.00 -   20.00
Brunswick, most issues .... 5.00 -   8.00

MUSTANG BAND OF SOUTHERN METHODIST UNIVERSITY:
Decca 705 *Peruna*...10.00 -   15.00
   706 *Limehouse Blues* ....10.00 -   15.00

VICK MYERS' ATLANTA MELODY ARTISTS/MELODY ORCHESTRA:
Cameo 576 *Africa* .... 8.00 -   12.00
Okeh 40281 *Blue-Eyed Sally* ....50.00 -   75.00
   40364 *Flag That Train* ....50.00 -   75.00
   40386 *Sweet Man Blues* ....50.00 -   75.00
   40434 *Nantucket Nan*.......................................50.00 -   75.00
   40614 *I'd Rather Be Alone* ....50.00 -   80.00

PHIL NAPOLEON & HIS EMPERORS OF RHYTHM/ ORCHESTRA/WHISPERING RHYTHM; NAPOLEON'S EMPERORS:
Edison 51908 *Tiger Rag* ....100.00 -   150.00
   51960 *It Made You Happy When You Made Me Cry*
   ....40.00 -   60.00
   51962 *The Cat*..75.00 -   100.00
   51996 *Underneath The Weeping Willow* ....40.00 -   60.00
   51997 *La Lo La* ....40.00 -   60.00
   52021 *Clarinet Marmalade*...............................100.00 -   150.00
   52147 *Five Pennies* ....100.00 -   150.00
Variety 656 *Blue Bayou* ....10.00 -   15.00
   669 *Swing Patrol* ....10.00 -   15.00
Victor 20605 *Go, Joe, Go* ....12.00 -   16.00
   20647 *Clarinet Marmalade* ....12.00 -   16.00
   V38057 *Mean To Me* ....25.00 -   40.00
   V38069 *You Can't Cheat A Cheater* ....25.00 -   40.00
Vocalion 3792 *Love Me* ....10.00 -   15.00
   3800 *That's A Plenty* ....10.00 -   15.00

WILLIAM NAPPI & HIS ORCHESTRA:
Columbia 1042-D *I'll Dream Of You* ....30.00 -   50.00
   1262-D *If You Just Knew* ....30.00 -   50.00

SAM NASH & HIS ORCHESTRA:
Parlophone PNY-34098 *Can I Help It?* ....20.00 -   30.00
   PNY-34099 *I Love You So Much* ....20.00 -   30.00
   PNY-34187 *I've Found What I Wanted In You* ...... 35.00 -   50.00
   PNY-34197 *I'm Crazy 'Bout My Baby* ....35.00 -   50.00

NASHVILLE JAZZERS:
Title issued contemporaneously on Madison, Van Dyke: *St. Louis Blues*... 15.00 -   20.00

NATIONAL MUSIC LOVERS DANCE ORCHESTRA:
National Music Lovers 1097 *Charley, My Boy* .... 8.00 -   12.00
   1132 *Charleston Your Blues Away* .... 7.00 -   10.00
   1152 *Stepping Along* ....15.00 -   20.00
   1155 *Desert Blues* ....10.00 -   15.00
   1156 *Dancing The Blues* .... 8.00 -   12.00
   1163 *Black Bottom* ....10.00 -   15.00
   1186 *Brown Pepper* ....15.00 -   20.00
   1199 *I'm Looking Over A Four Leaf Clover* ...... 8.00 -   12.00

NAYLOR'S SEVEN ACES/OLIVER NAYLOR'S ORCHESTRA:

Gennett 5375 *Hugo (I Go Where You Go)*	20.00 -	30.00
5376 *She Wouldn't Do (What I Asked Her To)*	20.00 -	30.00
5386 *So I Took The Fifty Thousand Dollars*	20.00 -	30.00
5392 *31st Street Blues*	75.00 -	100.00
5393 *Ringleberg Blues*	50.00 -	80.00
5432 *Twilight Rose*	15.00 -	20.00
5470 *Say, Say, Sadie*	20.00 -	30.00
5638 *Susquehanna Home*	20.00 -	30.00
5643 *Bye Bye Baby*	20.00 -	30.00
Victor 19688 *Sweet Georgia Brown*	10.00 -	15.00

NOBBY NEALE & AL LYONS:

Paramount 12775 *Go To It*	80.00 -	120.00

ARNETT NELSON & HIS HOT FOUR:

Titles issued contemporaneously on Banner, Conqueror, Melotone, Oriole, Perfect, and Romeo: *Oh! Red; You Waited Too Long* ....15.00 - 20.00

CHUCK NELSON & HIS BOYS:

Champion 40016 *West End Blues*	25.00 -	40.00

(D.C.) NELSON'S PARAMOUNT SERENADERS:

Paramount 12494 *Phillips Street Stomp*	150.00 -	250.00
12543 New Orleans Breakdown	150.00 -	250.00

DAVE NELSON & THE KING'S MEN:

Victor 22639 *I Ain't Got Nobody*	75.00 -	100.00
23039 *Some Of These Days*	80.00 -	120.00

JEWELL NELSON:

Columbia 14390-D *Beating Me Blues*	75.00 -	100.00

OZZIE NELSON & HIS ORCHESTRA:

Bluebird 6875, 6965, 6974, 7256, 7502, 7517, 7726, 7814	7.00 -	12.00
Bluebird, most other issues	5.00 -	10.00
Brunswick 4897, 4922, 4979, 6018	7.00 -	12.00
6060 *Dream A Little Dream Of Me*	10.00 -	15.00
6131, 6155, 6186, 6228, 6313, 6347, 6372, 6373, 6410, 6413, 6443, 6447, 6547, 6551	7.00 -	12.00
6861 *Dr. Heckle And Mr. Jibe*	8.00 -	12.00
7523 *Tiger Rag*	8.00 -	12.00
7651 *Streamline Strut*	8.00 -	12.00
7659 *Stompin' At The Savoy*	8.00 -	12.00
Brunswick, most other issues	5.00 -	10.00
Vocalion 2547, 2558, 2559, 2581, 2582, 2600, 2601, 2625, 2636, 2642	7.00 -	12.00

RUBY NEWMAN AND HIS ORCHESTRA:

Brunswick 7632, 7633	7.00 -	10.00
Decca, most issues	4.00 -	8.00
Victor 22931 *Can't We Talk It Over?*	8.00 -	12.00
22934 *Winnie The Wailer*	8.00 -	12.00
24042, 24043, 24048, 24072, 24073, 24074, 24894, 25005	7.00 -	12.00
25327, 25328, 25337, 25344	7.00 -	10.00
25401 *Make-Believe Ballroom*	10.00 -	15.00
25402, 25405, 25468, 25543, 25546, 26470	5.00 -	10.00

NEW ORLEANS BLACK BIRDS:

Bluebird 6611 *Red Head*	10.00 -	15.00
7881 *Playing The Blues*	10.00 -	15.00
Victor V38026 *Baby*	35.00 -	50.00
V38027 *Playing The Blues*	35.00 -	50.00

NEW ORLEANS BLUE FIVE:

Victor 20316 *The King Of The Zulus*	50.00 -	75.00
20364 *My Baby Doesn't Squawk*	50.00 -	75.00
20653 *South Rampart Street Blues*	100.00 -	150.00

NEW ORLEANS BLUES BAND:

Varsity 6029 *Big Blues*	15.00 -	20.00

NEW ORLEANS BOOTBLACKS:

Columbia 14337-D *Flat Foot*	200.00 -	300.00
14465-D *Mixed Salad*	200.00 -	300.00

NEW ORLEANS FEETWARMERS:

Victor 23358 *Lay Your Racket*	200.00 -	300.00
23360 *Maple Leaf Rag*	100.00 -	150.00
24150 *I've Found A New Baby*	80.00 -	120.00

NEW ORLEANS FIVE:

Romeo 371 *Memphis Blues*	15.00 -	20.00

NEW ORLEANS JAZZ BAND:

Apex 8429 *Camel Walk*	15.00 -	25.00
Banner 1318 *Tin Roof Blues*	20.00 -	30.00
1445 *Copenhagen*	20.00 -	30.00
1544 *Some Of These Days*	20.00 -	30.00
1556 *My Sweet Louise*	15.00 -	20.00
1618 *The Camel Walk*	15.00 -	20.00
1624 *Melancholy Lou*	15.00 -	20.00
Domino 335 *It Had To Be You*	20.00 -	30.00
338 *Limehouse Blues*	20.00 -	30.00
387 *How Could You Leave Me Now?*	20.00 -	30.00
389 *I'm Gonna Get Acquainted In A Quaint Old Fashioned Town*	20.00 -	30.00
403 *Alabamy Stay At Home*	20.00 -	30.00
3439 *Hot Sax*	20.00 -	30.00
3509 *Some Of These Days*	15.00 -	20.00
3524 *My Sweet Louise*	15.00 -	20.00
3590 *The Camel Walk*	15.00 -	20.00
3594 *Melancholy Lou*	15.00 -	20.00
Okeh 1155 *Ja Da*	15.00 -	20.00
1156 *Ole Miss*	15.00 -	20.00
Regal 9615 *Tin Roof Blues*	20.00 -	30.00
9739 *Copenhagen*	20.00 -	30.00
9839 *Some Of These Days*	20.00 -	30.00
9852 *My Sweet Louise*	15.00 -	20.00
9920 *Melancholy Lou*	15.00 -	20.00
9923 *The Camel Walk*	15.00 -	20.00

NEW ORLEANS LUCKY SEVEN:

Okeh 8544 *Goose Pimples*	100.00 -	150.00

NEW ORLEANS OWLS:

Columbia 489-D *Stomp Off, Let's Go*	50.00 -	80.00
605-D *The Owls' Hoot*	40.00 -	60.00
688-D *West End Romp*	40.00 -	60.00
823-D *Blowin' Off Steam*	50.00 -	80.00
862-D *White Ghost Shivers*	50.00 -	80.00
943-D *Eccentric*	50.00 -	80.00
1045-D *Dynamite*	50.00 -	80.00
1158-D *Meat On The Table*	75.00 -	100.00
1261-D *Goose Pimples*	75.00 -	100.00
1547-D *That's A Plenty*	75.00 -	100.00

NEW ORLEANS PEPSTERS:

Van Dyke 7038 *Close Fit Blues*	40.00 -	60.00
81836 *The Harlem Stomp Down*	25.00 -	40.00
81843 *The Rackett*	25.00 -	40.00

NEW ORLEANS RAMBLERS:

Melotone 12133 *No Wonder I'm Blue* ....20.00 - 30.00
  12230 *That's The Kind Of Man For Me* ....20.00 - 30.00

NEW ORLEANS RHYTHM KINGS (FORMERLY FRIARS SOCIETY ORCHESTRA):

Bluebird 10956 *She's Cryin' For Me* ....10.00 - 15.00
Buddy 8001 *Tin Roof Blues* ....150.00 - 200.00
  8002 *Angry* ....150.00 - 200.00
  8003 *Weary Blues* ....150.00 - 200.00
  8004 *Clarinet Marmalade* ....150.00 - 200.00
Decca 161 *San Antonio Shout* ....10.00 - 15.00
  162 *Panama* ....10.00 - 15.00
  229 *Original Dixieland One-Step* ....10.00 - 15.00
  388 *Dust Off That Old Piano* ....8.00 - 12.00
  401 *Baby Brown* ....10.00 - 15.00
  464 *Sensation* ....10.00 - 15.00
Gennett 3076 *Milenberg Joys* ....100.00 - 150.00
  5102 *Wolverine Blues* ....80.00 - 130.00
  5104 *Maple Leaf Rag* ....80.00 - 130.00
  5105 *That's A Plenty* ....50.00 - 80.00
  5106 *Da Da Strain* ....80.00 - 120.00
  5217 *Milenberg Joys* ....80.00 - 130.00
  5219 *Sobbin' Blues* ....80.00 - 130.00
  5220 *Mr. Jelly Lord* ....150.00 - 200.00
  5221 *London Blues* ....150.00 - 200.00
Savoy 500 *Up The Country Blues* ....250.00 - up
Victor 19645 *She's Cryin' For Me* ....75.00 - 100.00

NEW ORLEANS STRUTTERS:

Champion 15398 *Fourth Avenue Stomp* ....250.00 - up

NEW ORLEANS WANDERERS:

Columbia 698-D *Perdido Street Blues* ....125.00 - 175.00
  735-D *Papa Dip* ....100.00 - 150.00

NEW ORLEANS WILD CATS WITH TAP DANCING JOE:

  14662-D *Baby Mine* ....250.00 - up
  14668-D *Wild Cat Stomp* ....250.00 - up

NEWPORT SOCIETY ORCHESTRA:

Banner 1655 *Headin' For Louisville* ....8.00 - 12.00
(Above also issued on Domino and Regal, similarly valued)
Harmony 659-H *Hiding In The Corner Of Your Smile*
....8.00 - 12.00
(Note: Above issued on Diva and Velvet Tone similarly valued.)

NEWPORT SYNCOPATORS:

Van Dyke 81850 *Ring Around The Moon* ....20.00 - 30.00
  81851 *Because I'm Lonesome* ....20.00 - 30.00
  81852 *She's Just The Baby For Me* ....10.00 - 15.00
  81854 *Desert Blues* ....20.00 - 30.00
  81879 *The Terror* ....40.00 - 60.00

NEW SYNCO BAND; NEW SYNCO JAZZ BAND (See also SYNCO JAZZ BAND):

Pathe-Actuelle 036190 *Big Bad Bill Is Sweet William Now*
....10.00 - 15.00
  036200 *The Blues Have Got Me* ....10.00 - 15.00
(Other titles as on Perfect, following)
Perfect 14087 *Whoa, Tillie, Take Your Time* ....15.00 - 20.00
  14104 *Liza* ....15.00 - 20.00
  14178 *House Of David Blues* ....15.00 - 20.00
  14197 *Land Of Cotton Blues* ....15.00 - 20.00
  14242 *Red Hot!* ....15.00 - 20.00

  14315 *West Indies Blues* ....15.00 - 20.00
  14582 *Say Mister! Have You Met Rosie's Sister?*
....10.00 - 15.00
  14584 *Bell Hoppin' Blues* ....15.00 - 20.00
(Foregoing titles on Pathe-Actuelle are similarly valued)

FRANK NEWTON & HIS (CAFE SOCIETY ORCHESTRA/UPTOWN SERENADERS); FRANK NEWTON QUINTET:

Bluebird 10176 *The World Is Waiting For The Sunrise*
....10.00 - 15.00
  10186 *Minor Jive* ....10.00 - 15.00
  10216 *Who?* ....10.00 - 15.00
Blue Note 14 *After Hour Blues* ....10.00 - 15.00
  501 *Daybreak Blues* ....10.00 - 15.00
Variety 518 *You Showed Me The Way* ....12.00 - 16.00
  550 *'Cause My Baby Says It's So* ....12.00 - 16.00
  571 *I Found A New Baby* ....12.00 - 16.00
  616 *Where Or When* ....12.00 - 16.00
  647 *Who's Sorry Now?* ....12.00 - 16.00
Vocalion 3777 *Easy Living* ....12.00 - 16.00
  3811 *You Showed Me The Way* ....12.00 - 16.00
  3839 *The Onyx Hop* ....12.00 - 16.00
  4821 *Tab's Blues* ....10.00 - 15.00
  4851 *Jam Fever* ....10.00 - 15.00
  5410 *Parallel Fifths* ....10.00 - 15.00

LLOYD NEWTON & HIS VARSITY 11:

Crown 3012 I *Got Rhythm* ....15.00 - 20.00
  3013 *Sweet Jennie Lee* ....15.00 - 20.00
  3017 *St. Louis Blues* ....50.00 - 75.00

THE NEWTOWN PIPPINS:

Gennett 6413 *Isabella (Tell Your Fella)* ....30.00 - 50.00
  6741 *Caroline* ....30.00 - 50.00

THE NEW YORKERS:

Brunswick 6164 *Parkin' In The Moonlight* ....20.00 - 30.00
Gennett 6172 *Close To Your Heart* ....20.00 - 30.00
  6395 *What Do You Say?* ....20.00 - 30.00
Q.R.S. Q-1002 *Go Get 'Em Caroline* ....20.00 - 30.00
  Q-1003 *Under A Texas Moon* ....15.00 - 20.00
  Q-1020 *Happy Days Are Here Again* ....15.00 - 20.00
  Q-1027 *Kicking A Hole In The Sky* ....20.00 - 30.00
  Q-1037 *If I Were King* ....10.00 - 15.00
  Q-1053 *Let Me Sing And I'm Happy* ....20.00 - 30.00

NEW YORK MILITARY BAND:

Edison 50514 *Creole Belles; Soldiers In The Park* 15.00 - 20.00
  50636 *At A Georgia Camp Meeting* ....15.00 - 20.00

NEW YORK SYNCOPATORS:

Odeon ONY-36148 *It's A Great Life* ....25.00 - 35.00
  ONY-36149 *When Kentucky Bids The World "Good Morning"*
....25.00 - 35.00
  ONY-36152 *Satan's Holiday* ....25.00 - 40.00
  ONY-36157 *I'll Be Blue, Just Thinking Of You* 25.00 - 35.00
  ONY-36158 *I Got Rhythm* ....25.00 - 35.00
  ONY-36159 *Ukelele Moon* ....20.00 - 30.00
  ONY-36165 *Cheerful Little Earful* ....20.00 - 30.00
  ONY-36189 *I'm So In Love With You* ....25.00 - 50.00
  ONY-36190 *I Can't Realize You Love Me* ....25.00 - 50.00
  ONY-36194 *The King's Horses* ....20.00 - 30.00
  ONY-36206 *Dream A Little Dream Of Me* ....20.00 - 30.00
  ONY-36208 *Just A Crazy Song* ....20.00 - 30.00

Okeh 40757 *There Ain't No Maybe In My Baby's Eyes* ....15.00 - 20.00
    40860 *Bless Her Little Heart* ....15.00 - 20.00
    40965 *Mary* ....15.00 - 20.00
    41003 *I've Been Looking For A Girl Like You* ...12.00 - 16.00
    41202 *Dream Train* ....15.00 - 20.00
    41264 *The One That I Love Loves Me* ....15.00 - 20.00
Parlophone PNY-34155 *I'm Tickled Pink With A Blue-Eyed Baby* ....25.00 - 40.00

BOB NICHOLS & HIS ORCHESTRA:
Champion 15820 *The Flippity Flop* ....8.00 - 12.00
    15822 *Waiting At The End Of The Road* ....8.00 - 12.00

NICK NICHOLS & HIS ORCHESTRA:
Grey Gull 1820 *Breakin' A Leg* ....20.00 - 30.00

RAY NICHOLS & HIS FOUR TOWERS ORCHESTRA:
Bluebird 5902 *Who's Sorry Now?* ....10.00 - 15.00
    5904 *Restless* ....10.00 - 15.00
    6013 *Black Coffee* ....8.00 - 12.00
Bluebird, other issues ....5.00 - 10.00
Harmony 909-H *I've Got A Feeling I'm Falling* .....10.00 - 15.00
(Note: Above on Diva and Velvet Tone is similarly valued.)

RED NICHOLS & HIS FIVE PENNIES/ORCHESTRA/CAPTIVATORS; RED NICHOLS' STOMPERS; LORING NICHOLS & HIS ORCHESTRA; RED NICHOLS & HIS WORLD-FAMOUS PENNIES:
American Record Corporation E-654* *Yaaka Hula Hickey Dula* .... - -
*("For Theatre-Use Only," this 33 1/3 RPM record has the same tune on each side. Other similar issues probably exist.)
Bluebird 5547 *Rockin' In Rhythm* ....10.00 - 15.00
    5548 *Rollin' Home* ....7.00 - 10.00
    5549 *The Prize Waltz* ....7.00 - 10.00
    5552 *Straight From The Shoulder* ....7.00 - 10.00
    5553 *Runnin' Wild* ....8.00 - 12.00
    5583 *Old White's Whiskers* ....7.00 - 10.00
Bluebird 10179, 10190, 10200, 10328, 10332, 10360, 10408, 10451, 10522, 10593, 10683 ....5.00 - 10.00
Brunswick 3407 *Washboard Blues* ....15.00 - 25.00
    3477 *Buddy's Habits* ....15.00 - 25.00
    3490 *Back Beats* ....15.00 - 25.00
    3550 *Alabama Stomp* ....15.00 - 25.00
    3597 *Mean Dog Blues* ....15.00 - 25.00
    3626 *Feelin' No Pain* ....15.00 - 20.00
    3627 *Riverboat Shuffle* ....15.00 - 20.00
    3850 *Whispering* ....20.00 - 30.00
    3854 *Avalon* ....20.00 - 30.00
    3855 *Five Pennies* ....20.00 - 30.00
    3955 *There'll Come A Time* ....20.00 - 30.00
    3961 *Panama* ....20.00 - 30.00
    3989 *Original Dixieland One-Step* ....20.00 - 30.00
    3991 *I'm Marching Home To You* ....20.00 - 30.00
    4243 *Who's Sorry Now?* ....20.00 - 30.00
    4286 *Roses Of Picardy* ....20.00 - 30.00
    4363 *Chinatown, My Chinatown* ....20.00 - 30.00
    4373 *Indiana* ....20.00 - 30.00
    4456 *Alice Blue Gown* ....25.00 - 35.00
    4500 *The New Yorkers* ....20.00 - 30.00
    4510 *Can't We Be Friends?* ....20.00 - 30.00
    4651 *They Didn't Believe Me* ....20.00 - 30.00
    4695 *Strike Up The Band* ....20.00 - 30.00
    4701 *Sometimes I'm Happy* ....20.00 - 30.00

    4724 *I Want To Be Happy* ....25.00 - 35.00
    4778 *Rose Of Washington Square* ....25.00 - 35.00
    4790 *Smiles* ....25.00 - 35.00
    4839 *After You've Gone* ....30.00 - 40.00
    4844 (Canadian issue) *Five Pennies* (plays "My Gal Sal," which was not issued on U.S. Brunswick) ....100.00 - up
    4877 *China Boy* ....30.00 - 40.00
    4885 *The Sheik Of Araby* ....30.00 - 50.00
    4925 *Carolina In The Morning* ....30.00 - 50.00
    4944 *Sweet Georgia Brown* ....30.00 - 50.00
    4957 *I Got Rhythm* ....25.00 - 35.00
    4982 *Yours And Mine* ....25.00 - 35.00
    5014 *Building A Nest For Mary* ....10.00 - 15.00
    6012 *My Honey's Lovin' Arms* ....20.00 - 30.00
    6014 *Blue Again* ....20.00 - 30.00
    6026 *On Revival Day* ....30.00 - 50.00
    6029 *Sweet And Hot* ....25.00 - 35.00
    6035 *The Peanut Vendor* ....25.00 - 35.00
    6058 *Bugaboo* ....20.00 - 30.00
    6068 *Keep A Song In Your Soul* ....30.00 - 40.00
    6070 *Were You Sincere?* ....20.00 - 30.00
    6118 *Love Is Like That* ....20.00 - 30.00
    6133 *You Rascal, You* ....25.00 - 35.00
    6138 *Little Girl* ....15.00 - 20.00
    6149 *Moan, You Moaners* ....25.00 - 35.00
    6160 *Fan It* ....25.00 - 35.00
    6164 *How The Time Can Fly* ....20.00 - 30.00
    6191 *Singin' The Blues* ....20.00 - 30.00
    6198 *Honolulu Blues* ....20.00 - 30.00
    6219 *Junk Man Blues* ....20.00 - 30.00
    6234 *Haunting Blues* ....20.00 - 30.00
    6241 *Twenty-One Years* ....20.00 - 30.00
    6266 *Clarinet Marmalade* ....20.00 - 30.00
    6312 *Goofus* ....15.00 - 20.00
    6348 *Our Home Town Mountain Band* ....15.00 - 20.00
    6451 *Love, Nuts And Noodles* ....15.00 - 20.00
    6461 *Everybody Loves My Baby* ....15.00 - 20.00
    6534 *Dinah Lou* ....15.00 - 20.00
    6767 *Slow And Easy* ....15.00 - 20.00
Brunswick 6681, 6711, 6718, 6753, 6814, 6815, 6816, 6817, 6818, 6819, 6820, 6821, 6822, 6823, 6824, 6825, 6826, 6827, 6828, 6829, 6830, 6831, 6832, 6833, 6834, 6835, 6836, 6837, 6838, 6839, 6840, 6841, 6842, 6843, 6844, 6845 ....8.00 - 12.00
    7358 *Dardanella* ....10.00 - 15.00
    7460 *Three Little Words* ....10.00 - 15.00
Brunswick 20062 (12 inch) *Poor Butterfly* ....25.00 - 40.00
    20070 (12 inch) *Dear Old Southland* ....25.00 - 40.00
    20091 (12 inch) *Some Of These Days* ....25.00 - 40.00
    20092 (12 inch) *It Had To Be You* ....25.00 - 40.00
    20107 (12 inch) *California Medley* ....25.00 - 40.00
    20110 (12 inch) *New Orleans Medley* ....25.00 - 40.00
Capitol, most issues ....5.00 - 10.00
Okeh 5648, 5676 ....7.00 - 10.00
University 507 *Perfidia* ....5.00 - 8.00
Variety 502 *They All Laughed* ....8.00 - 12.00
    524 *Wake Up And Live* ....8.00 - 12.00
    545 *Troublesome Trumpet* ....8.00 - 12.00
    595 *Humoresque* ....10.00 - 15.00
    655 *Twilight In Turkey* ....10.00 - 15.00
Victor 21056 *Sugar* ....15.00 - 20.00
    21560 *Five Pennies* ....20.00 - 30.00

Vocalion 3816 *Love's Old Sweet Song*......................8.00 - 12.00
   3827 *Humoresque*.................................10.00 - 15.00
   3833 *Cream Puff*...................................10.00 - 15.00
   15498 *Washboard Blues*....................35.00 - 50.00
   15566 *Alabama Stomp*......................35.00 - 50.00
   15536 *Back Beats* ....35.00 - 50.00

NICK NICHOLSON & HIS BAND:
Champion 15699 *True Blue*......................25.00 - 35.00

NIGHT CLUB ORCHESTRA:
Harmony 102-H *Flamin' Mamie* ....7.00 - 10.00
   256-H *Hum Your Troubles Away* ....7.00 - 10.00
   266-H *I'll Fly To Hawaii* ....8.00 - 12.00
   302-H *Hello, Swanee, Hello!* ....7.00 - 10.00
   308-H *Where Do You Work-a, John?*....7.00 - 10.00
   345-H *Cock-A-Doodle, I'm Off My Noodle*..........7.00 - 10.00
   349-H *Pretty Lips* ....7.00 - 10.00
   473-H *I'm Gonna Dance With the Guy Wot Brung Me*
   ....7.00 - 10.00
   573-H *Is Everybody Happy Now* ....7.00 - 10.00
   610-H *I Found A Horseshoe* ....7.00 - 10.00
   624-H *Hey! Hey! Hazel* ....8.00 - 12.00
(Note: Above on Diva and Velvet Tone are similarly valued.)
Vocalion 15278 *Blinky Moon Bay* ....8.00 - 12.00
Vocalion (most other issues) ....5.00 - 8.00

THE NIGHT OWLS:
Silvertone 3549 *Pump Tille* ....75.00 - 125.00

TOM NILES & HIS ORCHESTRA:
Parlophone PNY-34032 *The Perfect Song* ....40.00 - 60.00
   PNY-34033 *Amos 'n' Andy* ....40.00 - 60.00

NIXON'S ROYAL FLUSH ORCHESTRA:
Bell 590 *Egypt* ....- - -
   593 *Night Time Is Love Time* ....- - -
   594 *How Long Must I Wait For You?* ...- - -
   595 *I've Got Somebody Now* ....15.00 - 25.00
   617 *Ping Sing*.....................................- - -

RAY NOBLE & HIS ORCHESTRA:
Brunswick 8098 *Crazy Rhythm* ....8.00 - 12.00
   8180 *Alexander's Ragtime Band* ....8.00 - 12.00
Brunswick, most other issues ....5.00 - 8.00
Columbia, most issues ....4.00 - 8.00
Victor 24879 *Down By The River*............10.00 - 15.00
   25070 *Let's Swing It*........................10.00 - 15.00
   25082 *St. Louis Blues* ....10.00 - 15.00
   25223 *Bugle Call Rag* ....10.00 - 15.00
Victor 24865, 24891, 25040, 25094, 25104, 25105,
   25187, 25190, 25200, 25209, 25240, 25241,
   25277, 25282, 25336, 25346, 25422, 25428,
   25448, 25459, 25504, 25507 ....7.00 - 12.00

JIMMIE NOONE'S APEX CLUB ORCHESTRA; JIMMY NOONE & HIS ORCHESTRA; JIMMY NOONE TRIO:
Bluebird 8609 *They Got My Number Now* ....15.00 - 20.00
   8649 *Then You're Drunk* ....15.00 - 20.00
Brunswick 6174 *I Need Lovin'* ....30.00 - 50.00
   6192 *River, Stay 'Way From My Door*...............30.00 - 50.00
Decca 1584 *I Know That You Know* ....10.00 - 15.00
   1621 *Four Or Five Times* ....10.00 - 15.00
   1730 *I'm Walkin' This Town* ....10.00 - 15.00
   7553 *Sweet Lorraine* ....10.00 - 15.00
Vocalion 1184 *I Know That You Know* ....50.00 - 75.00
   1185 *Four Or Five Times* ....40.00 - 60.00

1188 *Ready For The River* ....75.00 - 100.00
1207 *Apex Blues* ....75.00 - 100.00
1215 *Oh, Sister! Ain't That Hot?* ....80.00 - 120.00
1229 *A Monday Date* ....75.00 - 100.00
1238 *It's Tight Like That*.................................75.00 - 100.00
1240 *She's Funny That Way* ....80.00 - 120.00
1267 *Chicago Rhythm*.....................................80.00 - 120.00
1272 *Love Me Or Leave Me*............................80.00 - 120.00
1296 *Birmingham Bertha* ....80.00 - 120.00
1415 *True Blue Lou* ....80.00 - 120.00
1416 *Satisfied*...80.00 - 120.00
1436 *He's A Good Man To Have Around*.........80.00 - 130.00
1466 *Cryin' For The Carolines* ....80.00 - 130.00
1471 *Should I?* ....80.00 - 130.00
1490 *Deep Trouble* ....100.00 - 150.00
1497 *When You're Smiling* ....80.00 - 120.00
1506 *On Revival Day* ....80.00 - 120.00
1518 *Virginia Lee* ....80.00 - 120.00
1531 *Little White Lies* ....75.00 - 100.00
1554 *Three Little Words* ....75.00 - 100.00
1580 *Trav'lin' All Alone* ....80.00 - 130.00
1584 *You Rascal, You* ....75.00 - 100.00
2619 *Inka Dinka Doo* ....75.00 - 100.00
2620 *Delta Bound* ....75.00 - 100.00
2779 *Apex Blues*...75.00 - 100.00
2862 *Liza* ....50.00 - 80.00
2888 *Shine* ....50.00 - 80.00
2907 *It's Easy To Remember* ....50.00 - 80.00
2908 *Lullaby Of Broadway* ....50.00 - 80.00
15819 *Ain't Misbehavin'*..................................100.00 - 150.00
15823 *Anything You Want* ....100.00 - 150.00

NORTHWEST MELODY BOYS:
Champion 15362 *After I've Called You Sweetheart* .....40.00 - 60.00
   15363 *Sugar Foot Strut*................................75.00 - 100.00
   15364 *Melancholy*..60.00 - 100.00
   15365 *Rain* ....30.00 - 50.00
Gennett 6278 *Sugar Foot Strut* ....300.00 - up

RED NORVO; RED NORVO & HIS SWING SEXTETTE/SEPTET/OCTET/ORCHESTRA:
Brunswick 6562 *Hole In The Wall*.......................15.00 - 20.00
   6906 *In A Mist*..15.00 - 20.00
   7732, 7744, 7761, 7767, 7813, 7815, 7868, 7928,
   7932, 7970, 7975, 8068, 8069, 8085, 8088, 8089,
   8103, 8135, 8145, 8171, 8182, 8194, 8202, 8227,
   8230, 8240, 8288 ....7.00 - 12.00
Columbia 2927-D *Tomboy*....................................20.00 - 30.00
   3026-D *The Night Is Blue* ....20.00 - 30.00
   3059-D *Old Fashioned Love*..........................20.00 - 30.00
   3079-D *Bughouse*...2.00 - 30.00
(Many of foregoing are pressed of royal blue shellac)
Decca 670, 691, 779..7.00 - 12.00
Vocalion 4083, 4109, 4282, 4345, 4432, 4548, 4632,
   4648, 4698, 4738, 4785, 4818, 4833, 4953, 5009 7.00 - 12.00

FRANK NOVAK & HIS COLLEGIANS/ORCHESTRA:
Crown 3016 *Betty Co-Ed* ....30.00 - 50.00
   3018 *Washington And Lee Swing* ....10.00 - 15.00
Crown 3150, 3152, 3168, 3368, 3372, 3409 ....7.00 - 12.00
Van Dyke 81878 *Just Like In A Story Book* ....7.00 - 10.00
   81879 *I'm In The Market For You* ....40.00 - 60.00
(See the third section of this book for the cornball/rustic recordings
  of **FRANK NOVAK & HIS ROOTIN' TOOTIN' BOYS**)

NOVELTY BLUE BOYS:
Van Dyke 7023 *John Henry Blues* ....10.00 - 15.00
   7026 *Deep River Blues* ....10.00 - 15.00

NOVELTY FIVE:
Aeolian-Vocalion 12117 *Bluin' The Blues* ....25.00 - 40.00
   12124 *Shake, Rattle And Roll* ....20.00 - 30.00
   12135 *Lonesome Road Blues* ....20.00 - 30.00
   12148 *St. Louis Blues* ....25.00 - 40.00
Vocalion 14047 *Railroad Blues* ....15.00 - 20.00
   14061 *Barking Dog* ....20.00 - 30.00

SAM NOWLIN:
Champion 16828 *So What* ....150.00 - 200.00

JACK OAKIE:
Titles issued contemporaneously on Banner, Melotone, Oriole,
   Perfect, and Romeo: *Miss Brown To You; Why Dream*
   ....10.00 - 15.00
Melotone 13236 *College Rhythm* ....10.00 - 15.00

JIMMIE/JIMMY O'BRYANT'S (FAMOUS ORIGINAL) WASHBOARD BAND:
Paramount 12246 *Red Hot Mama*.........................150.00 - 200.00
   12260 *Skoodlum Blues*...................................150.00 - 200.00
   12265 *Brand New Charleston* ....150.00 - 200.00
   12277 *Georgia Breakdown*..............................150.00 - 250.00
   12287 *Clarinet Getaway*..................................150.00 - 250.00
   12288 *Blue Eyed Sally*...................................150.00 - 200.00
   12294 *Steppin' On The Gas*.............................150.00 - 250.00
   12297 *The Joys* ....150.00 - 250.00
   12308 *Down To The Bricks* ....150.00 - 250.00
   12312 *Charleston Fever* ....150.00 - 250.00
   12321 *Milenberg Joys*....................................150.00 - 250.00
   12329 *Thirty-Eight And Two* ....150.00 - 250.00
   12339 *Chicago Skiffle*....................................150.00 - 250.00
   12346 *Shake That Thing* ....150.00 - 250.00
   20400 *Alabamy Bound*....................................150.00 - 250.00

JACK ODIN & HIS ORCHESTRA:
Broadway 1415 *You're Driving Me Crazy*................8.00 - 12.00
   1432 *Fall In Love With Me*.................................7.00 - 10.00

HUSK O'HARE'S SUPER ORCHESTRA OF CHICAGO; HUSK O'HARE'S WOLVERINES:
Cardinal 512 *Tiger Rag* ....40.00 - 60.00
Gennett 4850 *Tiger Rag*..40.00 - 60.00
   5009 *San* ....35.00 - 50.00
Vocalion 15646 *Milenberg Joys*...........................200.00 - 300.00

OKEH MELODIANS:
Okeh 40876 *The Varsity Drag*...............................15.00 - 20.00
   40898 *There Ain't No Land Like Dixieland To Me*
   ....15.00 - 20.00
   40905 *When The Morning Glories Wake Up In The Morning*
   ....12.00 - 16.00
   40941 *How Long Has This Been Going On?* .....10.00 - 15.00
   40960 *I Fell Head Over Heels In Love*...............10.00 - 15.00
   40978 *Oh, Gee! Oh Joy!*...................................10.00 - 15.00
   41002 *I Just Roll Along (Havin' My Ups And Downs)*
   ....15.00 - 20.00
   41017 *Rain Or Shine* ....10.00 - 15.00

OKEH MELODY STARS:
Okeh 8382 *Look Out, Mr. Jazz* ....250.00 - up

OKEH SYNCOPATORS:
Okeh 4694 *I Wish I Could Shimmy Like My Sister Kate*
   ....10.00 - 15.00
   40072 *Nobody's Sweetheart* ....15.00 - 20.00
   40100 *Savannah (The Georgianna Blues)*.........15.00 - 20.00
   40258 *Doo Wacka Doo* ....50.00 - 80.00
   40267 *There'll Be Some Changes Made* ....20.00 - 30.00
   40303 *Nuthin's Gonna Stop Me Now* ....15.00 - 20.00
   40316 *Birmingham Papa* ....15.00 - 20.00
   40493 *Footloose*..15.00 - 20.00
   40614 *Jig Walk* ....50.00 - 80.00
   40641 *Black Bottom*..15.00 - 20.00
   40642 *Just A Little Dance*................................15.00 - 20.00

OLD SOUTHERN JUG BAND:
Silvertone 3061 *Hatchet Head Blues*...................100.00 - 150.00
Vocalion 14958 *Hatchet Head Blues*....................100.00 - 150.00

ANNA OLIVER & YOUNG'S CREOLE JAZZ BAND:
Paramount 12060 *What's The Use Of Lovin'* ......200.00 - 300.00

EARL OLIVER'S JAZZ BABIES:
Edison 51698 *The Village Blacksmith Owns The Village Now*
   ....15.00 - 20.00
   51724 *Jig Walk* ....25.00 - 40.00
   51745 *Show That Fellow The Door* ....15.00 - 20.00
   51760 *Hi-Ho! The Merrio* ....15.00 - 20.00
   51762 *Lulu Lou* ....40.00 - 60.00
   51776 *She's A Corn-Fed Indiana Girl*...............15.00 - 20.00
   51877 *Fire! (An "Alarming" Novelty)* ....15.00 - 20.00
   51900 *Where Do You Work-a, John?* ....15.00 - 20.00
   51929 *I Love The College Girls*........................20.00 - 30.00

JOE "KING" OLIVER; KING OLIVER'S (CREOLE) JAZZ BAND; KING OLIVER & HIS DIXIE SYNCOPATORS:
Autograph 617 *King Porter* ....2000.00 - up
Bluebird 5466 *St. James Infirmary* ....8.00 - 12.00
   6546 *Call Of The Freaks*..................................10.00 - 15.00
   6778 *Boogie Woogie* ....10.00 - 15.00
   7242 *What You Want Me To Do?* ....10.00 - 15.00
   10707 *Shake It And Break It* ....10.00 - 15.00
Brunswick 3398 *Showboat Shuffle* ....30.00 - 50.00
   3741 *Farewell Blues* ....30.00 - 50.00
   4028 *Four Or Five Times* ....30.00 - 50.00

   4469 *I'm Watching The Clock* ....40.00 - 60.00
   6053 *Papa De Da Da*.......................................50.00 - 75.00
   6065 *I'm Crazy 'Bout My Baby* ....50.00 - 75.00
Claxtonola 40292 *Riverside Blues* ....250.00 - up
Columbia 13003-D *Chattanooga Stomp* ....80.00 - 120.00
   14003-D *Camp Meeting Blues*.........................80.00 - 120.00
Gennett 3076 *Sugar Foot Stomp* ....100.00 - 150.00
   5132 *Weather Bird Rag* ....200.00 - 300.00
   5133 *Canal Street Blues*.................................200.00 - 300.00

5134 *Mandy Lee Blues*	250.00 -	up
5135 *Froggie Moore*	250.00 -	up
5184 *Snake Rag*	200.00 -	300.00
5274 *Krooked Blues*	300.00 -	up
5275 *Zulus Ball* (Extremely Rare)	5000.00 -	up
Harmograph 890 *Mabel's Dream*	250.00 -	up
Okeh 4906 *Sobbin' Blues*	100.00 -	150.00
4918 *Dipper Mouth Blues*	150.00 -	200.00
4933 *Snake Rag*	100.00 -	150.00
4975 *Jazzin' Babies' Blues*	150.00 -	250.00
8148 *Room Rent Blues*	300.00 -	up
8235 *Mabel's Dream*	300.00 -	up
40000 *Buddy's Habits*	150.00 -	200.00
40034 *Riverside Blues*	150.00 -	200.00
Paramount 12088 *The Southern Stomps*	250.00 -	up
20292 *Mabel's Dream*	250.00 -	up
Puritan 11292 *Mabel's Dream*	250.00 -	up
Victor 22298 *When You're Smiling*	15.00 -	20.00
22681 *Olga*	75.00 -	100.00
23001 *Struggle Buggy*	75.00 -	100.00
23009 *Shake It And Break It*	100.00 -	150.00
23011 *You Were Only Passing Time With Me*	50.00 -	75.00
23029 *I Can't Stop Loving You*	100.00 -	150.00
23388 *New Orleans Shout*	300.00 -	up
V38034 *West End Blues*	75.00 -	100.00
V38039 *Call Of The Freaks*	75.00 -	100.00
V38049 *My Good Man Sam*	75.00 -	100.00
V38090 *Too Late*	100.00 -	150.00
V38101 *Sweet Like This*	100.00 -	150.00
V38109 *Frankie And Johnny*	50.00 -	80.00
V38124 *I Must Have It*	100.00 -	150.00
V38134 *Boogie Woogie*	100.00 -	150.00
V38137 *Edna*	100.00 -	150.00
V38521 *Freakish Light Blues*	200.00 -	300.00
Vocalion 1007 *Too Bad*	150.00 -	200.00
1014 *Jackass Blues*	75.00 -	100.00

1033 *Sugar Foot Stomp*	75.00 -	100.00
1049 *Tack Annie*	200.00 -	300.00
1059 *Dead Man Blues*	50.00 -	75.00
1112 *Willie The Weeper*	150.00 -	200.00
1113 *Doctor Jazz*	1000.00 -	up
1114 *Showboat Shuffle*	150.00 -	200.00
1152 *Farewell Blues*	150.00 -	150.00
1189 *West End Blues*	150.00 -	200.00
1190 *Sweet Emmaline*	200.00 -	300.00
1225 *Speakeasy Blues*	150.00 -	250.00
15394 *Deep Henderson*	100.00 -	150.00
15493 *Dead Man Blues*	50.00 -	75.00
15503 *Snag It*	75.00 -	100.00

GEORGE OLSEN & HIS MUSIC:

Columbia 2790-D *Let's Make Up*	8.00 -	12.00
2791-D *The Last Round-Up*	8.00 -	12.00
2803-D *Bless Your Heart*	8.00 -	12.00
2810-D *Savage Serenade*	10.00 -	15.00
2811-D *It's Only A Paper Moon*	10.00 -	15.00
2837-D *There's A Home In Wyomin'*	8.00 -	12.00
2842-D *Everything I Have Is Yours*	8.00 -	12.00
2843-D *Sing A Low-Down Tune*	8.00 -	12.00
2848-D *Roll Out Of Bed With A Smile*	15.00 -	20.00
2857-D *Surprise*	8.00 -	12.00
2860-D *The Colonel From Kentucky*	8.00 -	12.00
2872-D *I'm Weaving Rainbows*	8.00 -	12.00
2878-D *This Little Piggie Went To Market*	8.00 -	12.00
2881-D *Wagon Wheels*	8.00 -	12.00
2891-D *Old Man Jingle*	8.00 -	12.00
(Preceding Columbia records are often pressed of royal blue shellac.)		
Decca 1785, 1786, 1824	5.00 -	8.00
Victor 19374, 19375, 19405, 19419, 19457, 19507	7.00 -	10.00
19509 *Sax-O-Phun*	7.00 -	10.00
19573 *Why Couldn't It Be Poor Little Me?*	10.00 -	15.00
19580 *Nobody Knows What A Red Head Mama Can Do*	10.00 -	15.00
19610 *Everybody Loves My Baby*	10.00 -	15.00
19633 *Those Panama Mamas*	15.00 -	20.00
19710 *Say Arabella*	10.00 -	15.00
19715 *Save Your Sorrow For Tomorrow*	10.00 -	15.00
19761 *Hot Aire*	10.00 -	15.00
19817 *Lonesome Me*	8.00 -	12.00
19834 *Just A Little Thing Called Rhythm*	10.00 -	15.00
19852 *A Little Bit Bad*	15.00 -	20.00
19977 *Horses*	7.00 -	10.00
20024 *Too Bad*	8.00 -	12.00
20029 *The Girl Friend*	7.00 -	10.00
20101, 20105, 20112, 20116	7.00 -	10.00
20322 *I'm Tellin', The Birds Tellin' The Bees*	20.00 -	30.00
20327, 20337, 20352, 20359	7.00 -	10.00
20367 *I'm Tellin', The Birds Tellin' The Bees*	10.00 -	15.00
20394 *Thinking of You*	8.00 -	12.00
20425 *Sam, The Old Accordion Man*	10.00 -	15.00
22279, 22430, 22935, 22937, 22947, 22967, 22968, 22994, 22998, 24002, 24069, 24070, 24090, 24124, 24125, 24138, 24139, 24165, 24166, 24179, 24220, 24221, 24222, 24229	7.00 -	12.00
Victor, most other issues	5.00 -	8.00

OLE OLSEN AND HIS ORCHESTRA:

Pathe-Actuelle 36488 *Sadie Green*	15.00 -	20.00
36510 *Take Your Time*	10.00 -	15.00
Perfect 14669 *Snag It*	15.00 -	20.00
14691 *Take Your Time*	10.00 -	15.00

OLYMPIC DANCE ORCHESTRA:

Olympic 1421 *Aggravatin' Papa*	10.00 -	20.00
1429 *Wonderful One*	7.00 -	10.00
Supreme 1334 *Someone Waits For Me*	10.00 -	15.00

ZELMA O'NEAL:

Brunswick 3864 *Can't Help Lovin' Dat Man*	7.00 -	10.00
4207 *Button Up Your Overcoat*	8.00 -	12.00
4322 *I'm Ka-Razy For You*	7.00 -	10.00
4330 *Do Something*	7.00 -	10.00
4476 *I've Made A Habit Of You*	7.00 -	10.00

D. ONIVAS & HIS ORCHESTRA:

Pathe-Actuelle 036196 *Louisville Blues*	75.00 -	100.00

ORESTE & HIS QUEENSLAND ORCHESTRA:

Edison 51857 *Ev'rything's Peaches*	25.00	-	40.00
51885 *Thinking Of You*	15.00	-	25.00
51886 *Hello! Swanee Hello*	25.00	-	40.00
51920 *Yankee Rose*	15.00	-	25.00
51983 *I'm Looking Over A Four-Leaf Clover*	25.00	-	40.00
51988 *Coronado Nights*	15.00	-	25.00
52017 *High Hat Harry*	35.00	-	50.00
52057 *Rosa Lee*	25.00	-	35.00
52058 *She's Got It*	30.00	-	50.00
52102 *Sailin' On*	20.00	-	30.00
52103 *Moonlit Waters*	20.00	-	30.00
52167 *I'm Walkin' On Air*	75.00	-	100.00
52169 *When The Morning Glories Wake Up*	50.00	-	80.00
52214 *Danger! (Look Out For That Gal)*	35.00	-	50.00
52272 *Borneo*	50.00	-	75.00
52273 *Lila*	75.00	-	100.00
52383 *Ten Little Miles From Town*	50.00	-	75.00
52466 *Cross Roads*	50.00	-	75.00
52560 *Where The Shy Little Violets Grow*	50.00	-	75.00
52592 *Me And The Clock (Tick-I-Ty Tock And You)*	50.00	-	75.00

ORIGINAL ATLANTA FOOTWARMERS:

Bell 585 *Hot Licks*	50.00	-	100.00

ORIGINAL CRESCENT CITY JAZZERS:

Okeh 40101 *Sensation Rag*	150.00	-	200.00

ORIGINAL DIXIELAND FIVE:

Victor 25502 *Original Dixieland One-Step*	7.00	-	10.00
25524 *Tiger Rag*	7.00	-	10.00
25525 *Clarinet Marmalade*	7.00	-	10.00

ORIGINAL DIXIELAND JAZZ BAND:

Aeolian-Vocalion 1205 *Barnyard Blues*	80.00	-	130.00
1206 *Ostrich Walk*	80.00	-	130.00
1242 *Reisenweber Rag*	80.00	-	130.00
12097 *Oriental Jazz*	75.00	-	100.00
Bluebird 7442, 7444, 7454	7.00	-	10.00
Columbia A2297 *Indiana*	20.00	-	30.00
Okeh 4738 *Toddlin' Blues*	50.00	-	75.00
4841 *Tiger Rag*	50.00	-	75.00
Victor 18255 *Livery Stable Blues*	15.00	-	20.00
18457 *At The Jazz Band Ball*	15.00	-	20.00
18472 *Skeleton Jangle*	15.00	-	20.00
18483 *Sensation Rag*	15.00	-	20.00
18513 *Clarinet Marmalade Blues*	15.00	-	20.00
18564 *Lazy Daddy*	15.00	-	20.00
18717 *Palesteena*	5.00	-	8.00
18722 *Broadway Rose*	7.00	-	10.00
18729 *Home Again Blues*	7.00	-	10.00
18772 *Jazz Me Blues*	15.00	-	20.00
18798 *Royal Garden Blues*	15.00	-	20.00
18850 *Bow Wow Blues*	8.00	-	12.00
Vocalion 3084 *I Live For Love*	8.00	-	12.00
3099 *You Stayed Away Too Long*	8.00	-	12.00

ORIGINAL DIXIE RAG PICKERS:

Title, issued contemporaneously on Grey Gull, Mitchell, and

Radiex: *My Own Blues*	15.00	-	20.00

ORIGINAL GEORGIA FIVE (See also ARTHUR HALL):

Olympic 1434 *Down Among The Sleepy Hills Of Ten-Ten-Tennessee*	20.00	-	30.00
1445 *Oh, Sister! Ain't That Hot*	20.00	-	30.00

ORIGINAL INDIANA FIVE:

Banner 1931 *Indiana Shuffle*	15.00	-	20.00
6006 *Some Of These Days*	10.00	-	15.00
6008 *Sugar*	15.00	-	20.00
6023 *Struttin' Jerry*	10.00	-	15.00
6028 *The Lighthouse Blues*	15.00	-	20.00
6031 *Rarin' To Go*	15.00	-	20.00
6032 *My Melancholy Baby*	10.00	-	15.00
7027 *My Melancholy Baby*	10.00	-	15.00
7057 *Where Will I Be?*	10.00	-	15.00
7084 *Moten Stomp*	10.00	-	15.00
7137 *Somebody's Making A Fuss Over Somebody*	15.00	-	20.00
Bell 456 *My Baby Knows How*	20.00	-	30.00
463 *Brown Sugar*	20.00	-	30.00
490 *St. Louis Blues*	30.00	-	50.00
547 *Low-Down Sawed-Off Blues*	40.00	-	60.00
Cameo 924 *Pensacola*	15.00	-	20.00
1138 *Memphis Blues*	15.00	-	20.00
8154 *Nobody's Sweetheart*	15.00	-	20.00
Clover 1755 *Jackass Blues*	25.00	-	40.00
Conqueror 7143 *Moten Stomp*	10.00	-	15.00
Diva (titles as on Harmony, below)			
Domino 3901 *Indiana Shuffle*	15.00	-	20.00
3971 *Some Of These Days*	10.00	-	15.00
3995 *My Melancholy Baby*	10.00	-	15.00
3997 *Struttin' Jerry*	10.00	-	15.00
3998 *The Lighthouse Blues*	15.00	-	20.00
4165 *Moten Stomp*	10.00	-	15.00
Emerson 3069 *Can You Picture That?*	20.00	-	30.00
3070 *Gettin' The Blues*	20.00	-	30.00
3079 *My Baby Knows How*	20.00	-	30.00
3088 *There Ain't No Maybe In My Baby's Eyes*	20.00	-	30.00
3119 *St. Louis Blues*	30.00	-	50.00
3131 *Memphis Blues*	30.00	-	50.00
Gennett 3059 *Sweet Georgia Brown*	30.00	-	50.00
3060 *Everything Is Hotsy Totsy Now*	15.00	-	25.00
3083 *Say, Arabella*	20.00	-	30.00
3093 *Two Tired Eyes*	10.00	-	15.00
3106 *Croonin' A Tune*	10.00	-	15.00
3112 *Red Hot Henry Brown*	15.00	-	20.00
3121 *Oh! Boy, What A Girl*	15.00	-	20.00
3148 *I'm Goin' Out If Lizzie Comes In*	15.00	-	20.00
3150 *Siberia*	15.00	-	20.00
3153 *Pretty Puppy*	10.00	-	15.00
3165 *Melancholy Lou*	15.00	-	25.00
3166 *I'm Gonna Hang Around My Sugar*	15.00	-	20.00
3181 *Everybody Stomp*	15.00	-	20.00
3182 *Everybody's Doin' The Charleston Now*	50.00	-	75.00
3183 *No Man's Mama*	15.00	-	20.00
3218 *Pensacola*	20.00	-	30.00
3230 *Fallen Arches*	15.00	-	20.00
Harmony 47-H *Everybody Stomp*	15.00	-	25.00
58-H *Everybody's Doin' The Charleston Now*	15.00	-	25.00
101-H *I'd Rather Be Alone*	15.00	-	20.00
134-H *Running After You*	15.00	-	20.00
179-H *So Is Your Old Lady*	20.00	-	30.00
217-H *Spanish Mamma*	15.00	-	20.00
245-H *I'd Leave Ten Men Like Yours To Love One Man Like Mine*	15.00	-	25.00
267-H *Florida Low-Down*	15.00	-	25.00
327-H *Delilah*	10.00	-	15.00
387-H *Stockholm Stomp*	15.00	-	25.00

432-H *Play It, Red* ....15.00 - 25.00
459-H *Struttin' Jerry* ....15.00 - 20.00
501-H *Someday, Sweetheart* ....15.00 - 20.00
510-H *Clementine* ....15.00 - 20.00
632-H *Junk Man's Dream* ....15.00 - 20.00
(Foregoing titles also issued on Diva and Velvet Tone, similarly
valued)
Lincoln 2499 *Hard-To-Get Gertie* ....15.00 - 20.00
  2808 *Nobody's Sweetheart* ....15.00 - 20.00
National Music Lovers 1191 *Cow Bell Blues* ....15.00 - 20.00
Okeh 40456 *Indiana Stomp* ....20.00 - 30.00
  40599 *Hard-To-Get Gertie* ....20.00 - 30.00
Olympic 1443 *Two-Time Dan* ....25.00 - 35.00
  1444 *Bebe* ....25.00 - 35.00
Pathe-Actuelle 021070 *Stavin' Change* ....20.00 - 30.00
  036019 *Tin Roof Blues* ....20.00 - 30.00
  036044 *Jubilee Blues* ....20.00 - 30.00
  36377 *I'd Rather Be Alone* ....8.00 - 12.00
  36379 *Lo-Nah* ....15.00 - 20.00
  36420 *Sittin' Around* ....15.00 - 20.00
  36428 *Hard-To-Get Gertie* ....10.00 - 15.00
Perfect 14173 *Mean, Mean Mama* ....20.00 - 30.00
  14200 *St. Louis Gal* ....20.00 - 30.00
  14225 *Back O'*Town Blues* ....20.00 - 30.00
  14558 *I'd Rather Be Alone* ....8.00 - 12.00
  14560 *Lo-Nah* ....15.00 - 20.00
  14601 *Too Bad* ....15.00 - 20.00
  14609 *Hard-To-Get Gertie* ....10.00 - 15.00
Regal 8248 *Coffee Pot Blues* ....15.00 - 20.00
  8337 *Some Of These Days* ....10.00 - 15.00
  8354 *Struttin' Jerry* ....10.00 - 15.00
  8356 *My Melancholy Baby* ....10.00 - 15.00
  8358 *The Lighthouse Blues* ....15.00 - 20.00
  8592 *Moten Stomp* ....10.00 - 15.00
Silvertone 4002 *I'm Goin' Out If Lizzie Comes In* .15.00 - 20.00
  21509 *Struttin' Jerry* ....10.00 - 15.00
Velvet Tone (titles as on Harmony, above)

ORIGINAL INDIANA SYNCOPATORS:
Olympic 1439 *Louisville Lou* ....25.00 - 40.00

ORIGINAL JAZZ HOUNDS:
Columbia 14086-D *Fo-Day Blues* ....80.00 - 120.00
  14094-D *Slow Down* ....80.00 - 120.00
  14124-D *Cannon Ball Blues* ....80.00 - 120.00
  14207-D *Lucy Long* ....100.00 - 150.00

ORIGINAL LOUISIANA FIVE:
Titles issued contemporaneously on Puritan, Triangle: *The Hoodoo
  Man; Louisiana Toddle; San; Too Tired* ....20.00 - 30.00

ORIGINAL MEMPHIS FIVE:
This band recorded a large number of records, which appeared on
  almost every label, under its own name and pseudonyms (such as
  THE COTTON PICKERS on Brunswick, q.v.). The following
  listing is not exhaustive. Any not listed are probably not of
  exceptional value.
Arto 9149 *Cuddle Up Blues* ....20.00 - 30.00
  9153 *Pacific Coast Blues* ....20.00 - 30.00
  9168 *Chicago* ....10.00 - 15.00
  9177 *Indigo Blues* ....20.00 - 30.00
  9185 *The Wicked Dirty Fives* ....20.00 - 30.00
  9192 *Railroad Man* ....20.00 - 30.00
  9199 *Hot 'N' Cold* ....20.00 - 30.00
  9204 *Papa Blues* ....20.00 - 30.00
  9210 *Harmony Blues* ....20.00 - 30.00

Banner 1062 *Don't Pan Me* ....15.00 - 20.00
  1068 *Lonesome Mama Blues* ....10.00 - 15.00
  1082 *Buzz Mirandy* ....15.00 - 20.00
  1104 *Wish I Could Shimmy Like My Sister Kate* ....10.00 - 15.00
  1110 *Struttin' At The Strutters' Ball* ....10.00 - 15.00
  1132 *Stop Your Kidding* ....15.00 - 20.00
  1143 *Runnin' Wild* ....15.00 - 20.00
  1178 *Papa Blues* ....15.00 - 20.00
  1193 *Shufflin' Mose* ....15.00 - 20.00
  1254 *Sad News Blues* ....15.00 - 20.00
  1282 *Oh Sister Ain't That Hot* ....15.00 - 20.00
  1292 *Dancin' Dan* ....15.00 - 20.00
  1296 *Your Mama's Gonna Slow You Down* ......15.00 - 20.00
  1309 *That Bran' New Gal O' Mine* ....15.00 - 25.00
  1322 *Maybe She'll Write Me, Maybe She'll Phone Me*
  ....15.00 - 25.00
  1336 *31st Street Blues* ....15.00 - 20.00
  1346 *Forgetful Blues* ....15.00 - 20.00
  1360 *Big Boy!* ....15.00 - 20.00
  1373 *Sioux City Sue* ....20.00 - 30.00
  1375 *A Man Never Knows When A Woman's Gonna Change Her
    Mind* ....20.00 - 30.00
(Foregoing titles were also issued on Regal, similarly valued)
Bell P-140 *My Honey's Lovin' Arms* ....20.00 - 30.00
  P-149 *Lonesome Mamma Blues* ....20.00 - 30.00
  P-153 *Pacific Coast Blues* ....20.00 - 30.00
  P-168 *Got To Cool My Doggies Now* ....10.00 - 15.00
  P-177 *That Da Da Strain* ....20.00 - 30.00
  P-185 *Stop Your Kiddin'* ....20.00 - 30.00
  P-192 *Great White Way Blues* ....20.00 - 30.00
  P-199 *Hot 'N' Cold* ....20.00 - 30.00
  P-204 *Sweet Mama, Please Come Back To Me* ......20.00 - 30.00
  P-210 *Farewell Blues* ....20.00 - 30.00
  P-216 *Laughin' Cryin' Blues* ....20.00 - 30.00
  P-228 *You've Got To See Mama Ev'ry Night* .... 10.00 - 15.00
  P-262 *Steppin' Out* ....10.00 - 15.00
Brunswick 3039 *Chinese Blues* ....15.00 - 20.00
  3630 *Lovey Lee* ....15.00 - 20.00
Cameo 478 *Sweet Papa Joe* ....15.00 - 20.00
  481 *Hootin' De Hoot* ....15.00 - 20.00
Chautauqua 11138 *Deedle-Deedle-Dum* ....100.00 - up
Claxtonola 40139 *Buzz Mirandy* ....15.00 - 20.00
  40161 *Struttin' At The Strutters' Ball* ....15.00 - 20.00
  40192 *Four O'Clock Blues* ....20.00 - 30.00
  40281 *St. Louis Gal* ....20.00 - 30.00
Clover 1527 *The Meanest Blues* ....20.00 - 30.00
Columbia 7-D *Walk, Jenny, Walk!* ....8.00 - 12.00
  37-D *More* ....8.00 - 12.00
  50-D *St. Louis Gal* ....10.00 - 15.00
  74-D *Since Ma Is Playing Mah Jongg* ....15.00 - 20.00
  155-D *Red Hot Mamma* ....15.00 - 20.00
  186-D *Sioux City Sue* ....15.00 - 20.00
  308-D *Doo Wacka Doo* ....10.00 - 15.00
  480-D *Indiana Stomp* ....20.00 - 30.00
  502-D *'tain't Cold* ....20.00 - 30.00
  2577-D *St. Louis Gal* ....20.00 - 30.00
  2588-D *Anything* ....20.00 - 30.00
  A3924 *Pickles* ....10.00 - 15.00
Edison 51204 *Shufflin' Mose* ....25.00 - 40.00
  51246 *The Jelly-Roll Blues* ....30.00 - 50.00
Emerson 10557 *Stop Your Kiddin'* ....15.00 - 20.00
  10558 *Bees Knees* ....15.00 - 20.00
  10723 *I've Got A Cross-Eyed Papa* ....15.00 - 20.00

10725 *Lots O' Mama*	15.00 -	25.00
10740 *Sioux City Sue*	15.00 -	25.00
10741 *31st Street Blues*	20.00 -	30.00
10782 *Red Hot Mama*	15.00 -	20.00
10783 *You Know Me, Alabam'*	15.00 -	20.00
10815 *The Meanest Blues*	15.00 -	25.00
10820 *Take Me*	15.00 -	20.00
Famous 3125 *Lonesome Mama Blues*	15.00 -	20.00
3132 *Buzz Mirandy*	15.00 -	20.00
3136 *I'm Going Away To Wear You Off My Mind*		
	15.00 -	20.00
3186 *Haunting Blues*	15.00 -	20.00
Globe 1246 *No One Knows What It's All About*	15.00 -	20.00
7013 *Four O'Clock Blues*	20.00 -	30.00
Grey Gull 1140 *I Wish I Could Shimmy Like My Sister Kate*		
	10.00 -	15.00
1153 *Four O'Clock Blues*	15.00 -	20.00
1184 *Sad News Blues*	15.00 -	20.00
1188 *That Teasin' Squeezin' Man O' Mine*	15.00 -	20.00
1200 *Mindin' My Business*	10.00 -	15.00
1206 *My Papa Doesn't Two Time No Time*	10.00 -	20.00
1226 *Red Hot Mamma*	15.00 -	20.00
1246 *No-One Knows What It's All About*	10.00 -	20.00
1247 *The Meanest Blues*	15.00 -	25.00
Harmograph 951 *Superstitious Blues*	25.00 -	35.00
975 *The Meanest Blues*	25.00 -	35.00
992 *Mama's Boy*	25.00 -	35.00
Nordskog 3013 *Pacific Coast Blues*	35.00 -	50.00
Oriole 127 *That Teasin' Squeezin' Man O' Mine*	10.00 -	15.00
173 *Mindin' My Business*	10.00 -	15.00
Paramount 20131 *Those Longing For You Blues*	15.00 -	25.00
20139 *Buzz Mirandy*	15.00 -	20.00
20142 *Don't Pan Me When I'm Gone*	20.00 -	30.00
20161 *Struttin' At The Strutters Ball*	15.00 -	20.00
20192 *Haunting Blues*	20.00 -	30.00
Pathe-Actuelle 11471 *Nothin'*	35.00 -	50.00
Pathe-Actuelle (other titles as on Perfect, following)		
Perfect 14067 *He May Be Your Man But He Comes To See Me*		
	10.00 -	15.00
14081 *Railroad Man*	15.00 -	20.00
14087 *Four O'Clock Blues*	15.00 -	20.00
14104 *Farewell Blues*	15.00 -	20.00
14105 *That Eccentric Rag*	15.00 -	20.00
14121 *That Red Head Gal*	12.00 -	16.00
14129 *Papa Blues*	15.00 -	20.00
14132 *Memphis Glide*	8.00 -	12.00
14138 *Henpecked Blues*	15.00 -	20.00
14150 *Shufflin' Mose*	12.00 -	16.00
14155 *Struttin' Jim*	15.00 -	20.00
14224 *Snuggle Up A Bit*	12.00 -	16.00
14242 *Just Hot!*	15.00 -	20.00
14253 *Sioux City Sue*	12.00 -	16.00
14275 *Shine*	15.00 -	20.00
14276 *Oh Baby*	15.00 -	20.00
14298 *Africa*	15.00 -	20.00
14315 *I'm Going Back To Those Who Won't Go Back On Me*		
	15.00 -	20.00
14322 *Somebody Stole My Gal*	15.00 -	20.00
14323 *The Meanest Blues*	15.00 -	20.00
14349 *Mama's Boy*	15.00 -	20.00
14539 *Nobody's Rose*	20.00 -	30.00
14565 *Thrown Down Blues*	30.00 -	50.00
14594 *Bass Ale Blues*	25.00 -	40.00

14603 *Indiana Stomp*	20.00 -	30.00
14746 *One Sweet Letter From You*	20.00 -	30.00
14757 *Go, Joe, Go*	25.00 -	40.00
14804 *What Do I Care What Somebody Said*	15.00 -	25.00
(Foregoing titles also issued on Pathe-Actuelle, similarly valued)		
Puritan 11131 *Lonesome Mama Blues*	15.00 -	20.00
11139 *Deedle-Deedle-Dum*	15.00 -	20.00
11161 *I Wish I Could Shimmy Like My Sister Kate*		
	12.00 -	16.00
11209 *Four O'Clock Blues*	20.00 -	30.00
Radiex (titles issued on Grey Gull are also found on Radiex, similarly valued)		
Regal 9628 *31st Street Blues*	15.00 -	20.00
9656 *Big Boy*	15.00 -	20.00
(Other titles as on Banner, above, are similarly valued)		
Victor 19052 *Who's Sorry Now?*	15.00 -	20.00
19170 *Tin Roof Blues*	15.00 -	20.00
19480 *Meanest Blues*	15.00 -	20.00
19594 *Throw Down Blues*	15.00 -	20.00
19805 *Military Mike*	15.00 -	20.00
20039 *Static Strut*	15.00 -	20.00
Vocalion 14461 *Stop Your Kidding*	15.00 -	20.00
14506 *Four O'Clock Blues*	15.00 -	20.00
14527 *Loose Feet*	15.00 -	20.00
15623 *Lovey Lee*	40.00 -	60.00
15712 *My Angeline*	150.00 -	200.00
15761 *Fireworks*	150.00 -	200.00
15805 *Memphis Blues*	150.00 -	200.00
15810 *Kansas City Kitty*	150.00 -	200.00

ORIGINAL MEMPHIS MELODY BOYS:

Cardinal 562 *Wonderful Dream*	20.00 -	30.00
Champion 15005 *Made A Monkey Out Of Me*	20.00 -	30.00
Gennett 3097 *Made A Monkey Out Of Me*	20.00 -	30.00
5123 *Wonderful Dream*	25.00 -	35.00
5157 *Blue Grass Blues*	30.00 -	50.00

ORIGINAL MIDNIGHT RAMBLERS ORCHESTRA:

Autograph (unnumbered) *Midnight Ramblers Stomps Owl Strut*		
	250.00 -	up

ORIGINAL NEW ORLEANS RHYTHM KINGS:

Okeh 40327 *Golden Leaf Strut*	150.00 -	200.00
40422 *Baby*	150.00 -	200.00

ORIGINAL ST. LOUIS CRACKERJACKS:

Decca 7235 *Swing Jackson*	10.00 -	15.00
7236 *Crackerjack Stomp*	10.00 -	15.00
7248 *Echo In The Dark*	10.00 -	15.00
7265 *Chasing The Blues Away*	10.00 -	15.00

THE ORIGINAL SIX:

Okeh 4546 *She's A Mean Job*	15.00 -	20.00
4655 *Jump Steady Blues*	15.00 -	20.00
4694 *The Broadway Strut*	10.00 -	15.00
4778 *Way Down Yonder In New Orleans*	10.00 -	15.00
4847 *Mad ('Cause You Treat Me This Way)*	15.00 -	20.00

ORIGINAL TAMPA FIVE:

Dandy 5154 *My Own Blues*	15.00 -	20.00
5248 *Heebie Jeebies*	20.00 -	30.00

ORIGINAL TUXEDO JAZZ ORCHESTRA:

Okeh 8198 *Black Rag*	200.00 -	300.00
8215 *Original Tuxedo Rag*	200.00 -	300.00

THE ORIGINAL WOLVERINES:

Brunswick 3707 Shim-Me-Sha-Wabble	25.00	-	35.00
3708 Royal Garden Blues	100.00	-	up
4000 Royal Garden Blues	25.00	-	35.00
Vocalion 15635 Royal Garden Blues	50.00	-	75.00
15708 Limehouse Blues	100.00	-	150.00
15732 There's a Rainbow 'Round My Shoulder	35.00	-	50.00
15751 Sweethearts On Parade	35.00	-	50.00
15766 If I Had You	100.00	-	150.00
15768 I'll Never Ask For More	150.00	-	200.00
15784 He, She and Me	150.00	-	200.00
15795 Some Sweet Day	35.00	-	50.00

ORIGINAL YELLOW JACKETS:

Vocalion 03504 Business After Midnight	20.00	-	30.00
03549 Swingin' At The Chat 'n' Chew	20.00	-	30.00
03591 Cross Street Swing	20.00	-	30.00

ORIOLE (DANCE) ORCHESTRA; ORIOLE (TERRACE) ORCHESTRA:

Brunswick 2389 Bees Knees	8.00	-	12.00
2398 Honolulu Blues	7.00	-	10.00
2466 Shim-Me-Sha-Wabble	8.00	-	12.00
2560 Sobbin' Blues	8.00	-	12.00
2616 Eccentric Rag	8.00	-	12.00
2633 You'll Never Get To Heaven With Those Eyes	7.00	-	10.00
2637 I Need Some Pettin'	7.00	-	10.00
2741 Mandy, Make Up Your Mind	7.00	-	10.00
2752 Copenhagen	8.00	-	12.00
2832 Off And Gone	8.00	-	12.00
Brunswick, most other issues	5.00	-	8.00
Oriole 272 Alabamy Stay At Home	20.00	-	30.00
374 Those Panama Mamas	20.00	-	30.00
777 Tell 'Em Nothing	8.00	-	12.00
1394 Me And The Man In The Moon	7.00	-	10.00
1612 I'm Doing What I'm Doing For Love	8.00	-	12.00
Oriole, most other issues	4.00	-	8.00

ORIOLE SERENADERS:

Champion 15271 Ask Me Another	15.00	-	20.00

ORPHEUM MELODY MASTERS:

Bell 298 San	10.00	-	15.00
310 Copenhagen	10.00	-	15.00

HAROLD ORTLI & HIS OHIO STATE COLLEGIANS:

Okeh 40332 My Daddy Rocks Me	100.00	-	150.00

ORY'S SUNSHINE ORCHESTRA:

Sunshine 3003 Ory's Creole Trombone	300.00	-	up

(Above occurs with label pasted over another)

GEORGE OSBORN & HIS ORCHESTRA:

Gennett 6215 Brainstorm	100.00	-	150.00

WILL OSBORNE & HIS ORCHESTRA:

Banner, most issues	4.00	-	8.00
Columbia 3080-D That's What You Think	10.00	-	15.00
3081-D I Wish I Were Aladdin	8.00	-	12.00
Columbia, most other issues	4.00	-	8.00
Conqueror, most issues	4.00	-	8.00
Decca, most issues	4.00	-	8.00
Melotone 12099 Hello! Beautiful	10.00	-	15.00
12189 Star Dust	8.00	-	12.00
Melotone, most other issues	5.00	-	10.00

Oriole, most issues	5.00	-	8.00
Perfect, most issues	5.00	-	8.00
Romeo, most issues	5.00	-	8.00

OSCAR'S CHICAGO SWINGERS:

Decca 7186 I Wonder Who's Boogiein' My Woogie	10.00	-	15.00
7201 Try Some Of That	10.00	-	15.00

VESS L. OSSMAN; OSSMAN'S BANJO ORCHESTRA; OSSMAN-DUDLEY TRIO:

Columbia A218 The Buffalo Rag	15.00	-	20.00
A220 Chicken Chowder	15.00	-	20.00
A224 Florida Rag	15.00	-	20.00
A228 Maple Leaf Rag	15.00	-	20.00
A787 Moose March	15.00	-	20.00
A937 St. Louis Tickle	15.00	-	20.00
A972 The Smiler Rag	15.00	-	20.00
A2321 He's Just Like You	10.00	-	15.00
290 Hunky Dory (one-sided disc)	15.00	-	20.00
461 A Coon Band Contest (one-sided disc)	15.00	-	20.00
464 Hot Corn (one-sided disc)	20.00	-	30.00
465 Creole Belles (one-sided disc)	20.00	-	30.00
469 Rusty Rags Medley (one-sided disc)	20.00	-	30.00
723 Whistling Rufus (one-sided disc)	15.00	-	20.00
1540 Hiawatha (one-sided disc)	15.00	-	20.00
3360 The Buffalo Rag (one-sided disc)	15.00	-	20.00
3591 Chicken Chowder (one-sided disc)	15.00	-	20.00
Silvertone 3626 Maple Leaf Rag (one-sided disc)	15.00	-	20.00
Victor 149 Whistling Rufus (one-sided disc)	15.00	-	20.00
150 An Ethiopian Mardi Gras (one-sided disc)	20.00	-	30.00
153 A Bunch Of Rags (one-sided disc)	20.00	-	30.00
154 A Coon Band Contest (one-sided disc)	15.00	-	20.00
1291 Creole Belles (one-sided disc)	20.00	-	30.00
1660 Harmony Moze (one-sided disc)	20.00	-	30.00
1664 Old Plunk's New Coon Medley (one-sided disc)	20.00	-	30.00
2616 Keep Off The Grass (one-sided disc)	15.00	-	20.00
3042 A Coon Band Contest (one-sided disc)	15.00	-	20.00
3043 An Ethiopian Mardi Gras (one-sided disc)	20.00	-	30.00
3050 A Bunch Of Rags (one-sided disc)	20.00	-	30.00
4628 The Buffalo Rag (one-sided disc)	15.00	-	20.00
16092 St. Louis Tickle	8.00	-	12.00
16127 Persian Lamb Rag	10.00	-	15.00
16779 Buffalo Rag	10.00	-	15.00

(Note: Foregoing are only representative of the early ragtime recordings of banjoist Vess L. Ossman. Many of the titles were issued on affiliated and antecedent labels, some of which are of far greater interest and value than most of the records above. Most notable are recordings on the primitive Berliner discs, and some of the other companies' small-sized (usually 7-inch) records. Also, a given tune may have been recorded at several sessions, with the various "takes" being issued with the same catalog number; no attempt to distinguish between these performances is made here. Finally, some recordings were issued anonymously, e.g. Little Wonder 569, in the ANONYMOUS listing.)

GLEN OSWALD'S SERENADERS:

Victor 19733 Bucktown Blues	50.00	-	80.00
19410, 19611, 19809	5.00	-	10.00

RED OWENS & HIS GANG:

Champion 15759 Chicago Rhythm	50.00	-	75.00

THE OXFORD RHYTHM MAKERS:

Parlophone PNY-34045 Puttin' On The Ritz	35.00	-	50.00
PNY-34046 With You	35.00	-	50.00

HAROLD OXLEY AND HIS POST LODGE ORCHESTRA:

Okeh 40134 *Step, Henrietta*	8.00 -	12.00
40180 *I Don't Know Why*	15.00 -	20.00

PACIFIC COAST PLAYERS:

Radiex 1326 *Jazzing Around*	8.00 -	12.00

HOT LIPS PAGE (& HIS BAND); HOT LIPS PAGE TRIO:

Bluebird 7567, 7568, 7583, 7680, 7682, 7684, 8634, 8660, 8981	7.00 -	12.00
Columbia 30130, 30159, 30192, 30204, 30220	7.00 -	12.00
Decca 7433, 7451, 7699, 7714, 7757, 8531	7.00 -	12.00

WALTER PAGE'S BLUE DEVILS:

Vocalion 1463 *Blue Devil Blues*	300.00 -	up

PALACE DANCE ORCHESTRA:

Broadway 1330 *Same Old Moon*	7.00 -	10.00
1349 *I'm Following You*	7.00 -	10.00

PALACE GARDEN ORCHESTRA:

Pathe-Actuelle 036206 *Cuddles And Kisses*	8.00 -	12.00
036231 *Isn't She The Sweetest Thing?*	10.00 -	15.00
036235 *Just A Little Drink*	10.00 -	15.00
036241 *Montmartre Rose*	7.00 -	10.00
036272 *Sonya (Yup! Alay Yup!)*	7.00 -	10.00
36314 *Peaceful Valley*	7.00 -	10.00
36341 *Forever*	7.00 -	10.00
36438 *Am I Wasting My Time On You?*	10.00 -	15.00
36441 *I Wonder What's Become Of Joe?*	10.00 -	15.00
36452 *Hi-Ho! The Merrio*	15.00 -	20.00
36463 *Where'd You Get Those Eyes?*	10.00 -	15.00
36467 *Here I Am*	15.00 -	20.00
36612 *I'll Just Go Along*	10.00 -	15.00
36653 *After You've Gone*	10.00 -	15.00
Perfect 14387 *Cuddles And Kisses*	8.00 -	12.00
14648 *Here I Am*	15.00 -	20.00

PALLEDO ORCHESTRA OF ST. LOUIS:

Okeh 40521 *What-Cha-Call-'Em Blues*	100.00 -	150.00

CHARLIE PALLOY & HIS ORCHESTRA:

Crown 3389 *You're Telling Me*	10.00 -	15.00
3392 *Brother, Can You Spare A Dime?*	10.00 -	15.00
3410 *What A Perfect Combination*	10.00 -	15.00
3512 *Pettin' In The Park*	10.00 -	15.00

GLADYS PALMER:

Decca 7106 *I'm Livin' In A Great Big Way*	15.00 -	20.00
7017 *Get Behind Me, Satan*	15.00 -	20.00

PALMER HOUSE VICTORIANS (See JULES HERBUVEAUX):

PALMETTO NIGHT CLUB ORCHESTRA:

Champion 15308 *Darktown Shuffle*	80.00 -	130.00

PALOOKA WASHBOARD BAND:

Decca 7378 *We Gonna Move*	15.00 -	20.00
7398 *You Done Tore Your Pants With Me*	15.00 -	20.00

LOUIS PANICO & HIS ORCHESTRA:

Brunswick 4736 *Wabash Blues*	20.00 -	30.00
Decca 159 *Wabash Blues*	10.00 -	15.00

PAPALIA & HIS ORCHESTRA:

Okeh 40347 *Cross-Word Mama, You're Puzzling Me*	100.00 -	150.00

PARADISE CLUB ORCHESTRA:

Conqueror 7189 *It Goes Like This (That Funny Melody)*	8.00 -	12.00
7209 *Glorianna*	8.00 -	12.00

THE PARAMOUNTEERS:

Publix 2008-P *I Have To Have You*	10.00 -	15.00

PARAMOUNT PICKERS:

Paramount 12779 *Salty Dog*	300.00 -	up

TONY PARENTI; ANTHONY PARENTI & HIS FAMOUS MELODY BOYS; (TONY) PARENTI'S LIBERTY SYNCOPATORS/NEW ORLEANIANS:

Title issued contemporaneously on Banner, Cameo, Jewel, Oriole, and Romeo: *Old Man Rhythm*	15.00 -	25.00
Brunswick 4148 *Gumbo*	30.00 -	40.00
Columbia 545-D *Midnight Papa*	75.00 -	100.00
836-D *Up Jumped The Devil*	75.00 -	100.00
1264-D *African Echoes*	75.00 -	100.00
1548-D *In The Dungeon*	75.00 -	100.00
Okeh 40308 *That's A Plenty*	75.00 -	100.00
Victor 19647 *Creole Blues*	75.00 -	100.00
19697 *Dizzy Lizzy*	75.00 -	100.00
19698 *Be Yourself*	75.00 -	100.00

PARHAM'S BLACK PATTI BAND:

Black Patti 8038 *Um Ta Da Da Da*	200.00 -	up

TINY PARHAM & HIS "FORTY" FIVE; TINY PARHAM & HIS MUSICIANS:

Bluebird 5146 *Black Cat Moan*	15.00 -	20.00
6031 *Subway Sobs*	15.00 -	20.00
6570 *Washboard Wiggles*	15.00 -	20.00
7005 *Blue Island Blues*	15.00 -	20.00
8130 *Stuttering Blues*	15.00 -	20.00
10044 *Blue Island Blues*	8.00 -	12.00
Paramount 12586 *Jim Jackson's Kansas City Blues*	250.00 -	up
Victor 21553 *Cuckoo Blues*	80.00 -	130.00
21659 *Snake Eyes*	80.00 -	130.00
22778 *Sud Buster's Dream*	80.00 -	130.00
22842 *Rock Bottom*	75.00 -	100.00
23027 *Blue Moon Blues*	150.00 -	200.00
23386 *Nervous Tension*	300.00 -	up
23410 *Steel String Blues*	300.00 -	up
23426 *Golden Lily*	300.00 -	up
23432 *My Dreams*	300.00 -	up
V38009 *Jogo Rhythm*	80.00 -	130.00
V38041 *Subway Sobs*	50.00 -	75.00
V38047 *Blue Melody Blues*	50.00 -	75.00
V38054 *Voodoo*	80.00 -	130.00
V38060 *Stompin' On Down*	80.00 -	130.00
V38076 *Echo Blues*	80.00 -	130.00
V38082 *Jungle Crawl*	80.00 -	130.00
V38111 *Dixieland Doin's*	80.00 -	120.00
V38126 *Fat Man Blues*	100.00 -	150.00

CHARLIE PARKER QUINTET (& OTHER COMBINATIONS):

Dial 1002, 1006, 1007, 1012, 1013, 1015, 1058	7.00 -	12.00

DON PARKER & HIS ORCHESTRA/WESTERN MELODY BOYS:

Pathe-Actuelle 020824 *Yankee Doodle Blues* ....10.00 - 15.00
   020934 *Snakes Hips* ....10.00 - 15.00
   021031 *Wild Papa* ....15.00 - 20.00
   036002 *Learn To Do The Strut* ....10.00 - 15.00
(Note: Above titles on Perfect are similarly valued.)

ED PARKER & HIS ORCHESTRA:

Okeh 41537 *Potatoes Are Cheaper, Tomatoes Are Cheaper*
....15.00 - 20.00

PARK LANE ORCHESTRA:

Brunswick 3487 *It's A Happy Old World After All* ..8.00 - 12.00
   3513 *You Can't Cry Over My Shoulder* ....10.00 - 15.00
Brunswick, most other issues ....5.00 - 10.00

ISABELLE PATRICOLA:

Vocalion 14623 *Oh! Sister, Ain't That Hot?* ....10.00 - 15.00
   14669 *Mamma's Gonna Slow You Down* ....10.00 - 15.00
   14886 *No-One Knows What It's All About* ....10.00 - 15.00
Vocalion, other issues ....7.00 - 10.00

PAUL'S NOVELTY ORCHESTRA:

Champion 16041 *Give Yourself A Pat On The Back* .8.00 - 12.00
   16062 *Nobody Cares If I'm Blue* ....10.00 - 15.00
   16082 *Sing Something Simple* ....10.00 - 15.00
   16106 *Looking For The Lovelight In The Dark* ....8.00 - 12.00
   16132 *Loving You The Way I Do* ....10.00 - 15.00
   16151 *I Got Rhythm* ....15.00 - 20.00
   16178 *Headin' For Better Times* ....15.00 - 20.00
   40016 *I Got Rhythm* ....25.00 - 40.00

LES PAUL TRIO:

Capitol, most issues ....4.00 - 8.00
Mercury 5103 *My Extraordinary Gal* ....8.00 - 12.00
   5133 *Suspicion* ....8.00 - 12.00
   5137 *Nobody But You* ....8.00 - 12.00
Okeh 6027 *Swanee River* ....15.00 - 20.00
Vocalion 5447 *Out Of Nowhere* ....15.00 - 20.00

ART PAYNE & HIS ORCHESTRA:

Gennett 5063 *Some Winter Night* ....10.00 - 15.00
   5064 *Jingle Bells* ....15.00 - 20.00
   5631 *Oh Maud* ....35.00 - 50.00
   6007 *Susie's Feller* ....20.00 - 30.00
   6644 *Igloo Stomp* ....75.00 - 100.00
   6694 *Jo-Anne* ....75.00 - 100.00

RAY PEARL AND HIS ORCHESTRA:

Vocalion 3408, 3420, 3522, 3536....................7.00 - 10.00

HAROLD PEARY (THE GREAT GILDERSLEEVE):

Capitol Album CD-11 (four records: Capitol 40017,
   40018, 40019, 40020, in album) "Stories for Children Told
   in His Own Way by The Great Gildersleeve" ...20.00 - 30.00
Album CD-33 (four records: Capitol 10058, 10059, 10060, 10061,
   in album) "Stories for Children Told in His Own Way by The
   Great Gildersleeve" Vol. II ....20.00 - 30.00

PELHAM INN SOCIETY ORCHESTRA:

Banner 7082 *I'm Riding To Glory (With A Glorious Girl)*
....7.00 - 10.00
Conqueror 7142 *Get Out And Get Under The Moon*.7.00 - 10.00
Domino 4134 *I'm Riding To Glory (With A Glorious Girl)*
....7.00 - 10.00

PAUL PENDARVIS AND HIS ORCHESTRA:

Columbia 2973-D *The Object Of My Affection* ...... 10.00 - 15.00
   2974-D *A Little Angel Told Me So*................ 10.00 - 15.00
   3025-D *It's Easy To Remember* .... 10.00 - 15.00
   3032-D *I'm In Love All Over Again* .... 10.00 - 15.00
   3082-D *Accent On Youth* .... 10.00 - 15.00
   3091-D *Thanks A Million*............................ 10.00 - 15.00
(Note: Many of foregoing are pressed of "royal blue" shellac.)

ANDY PENDLETON:

Okeh 8625 *Sweet Emmaline* .... 50.00 - 75.00
Victor 23389 *Thinking Of You* .... 100.00 - 150.00

TWIN-SIX GUITAR JACK PENEWELL:

Autograph 608 *Penewell Blues* .... 20.00 - 30.00

PENNINGTON ORCHESTRA:

Pennington 1384 *I Can't Get The One I Want*........ 20.00 - 30.00
Triangle 11424 *Adoring You*............................... 7.00 - 10.00

THE PENNSYLVANIA DANCE ORCHESTRA:

Marathon 228 (7 inch) *It's The Last Time* .... 15.00 - 20.00
   231 (7 inch) *Old Man Sunshine* .... 15.00 - 20.00

PENNSYLVANIA DANCE SYNCOPATORS:

Marathon 174 (7 inch) *She's Everybody's Girl But Mine*
.... 10.00 - 20.00

PENNSYLVANIA SYNCOPATORS:

Bell 439 *Black Bottom* .... 10.00 - 15.00
   451 *Don't Take That Black Bottom Away*.......... 10.00 - 15.00
Clover 1747 *Black Bottom* .... 10.00 - 15.00
Emerson 3022 *Tentin' Down In Tennessee* .... 10.00 - 15.00
   3027 *Let's Talk About My Sweetie* .... 10.00 - 15.00
   3032 *Steppin' Along* .... 10.00 - 15.00
   3059 *I Never Knew What The Moonlight Could Do*
.... 8.00 - 12.00
   3060 *Black Bottom* .... 10.00 - 15.00
   3072 *I'm On My Way Home* .... 7.00 - 10.00
   3077 *Take It From Me* .... 7.00 - 10.00
   10773 *I Can't Get The One I Want* .... 15.00 - 20.00
   10868 *My Sweet Louise* .... 15.00 - 20.00

JACK PENNY & HIS ORCHESTRA:

Champion 15457 *Nothin' On My Mind* .... 15.00 - 20.00
   15474 *Lauretta* .... 8.00 - 12.00
   15493 *Afraid Of You* .... 8.00 - 12.00
   15496 *Back In Your Own Backyard*................... 15.00 - 20.00
   15575 *Here's That Party Now In Person* .... 15.00 - 20.00

ALBERTA PERKINS:

Ajax 17125 *Levee Man* .... 40.00 - 60.00
Harmograph 983 *Sweet Mandy* .... 35.00 - 50.00

GERTRUDE PERKINS:

Columbia 14313-D *Gold Daddy Blues* .... 100.00 - 150.00

RED PERKINS & HIS DIXIE RAMBLERS:

Champion 16288 *Hard Times Stomp* .... 150.00 - 200.00
   16439 *Old Man Blues* .... 100.00 - 150.00
   16661 *My Baby Knows How*........................... 150.00 - 200.00

SLIM PERKINS:

Banner 1515 *Freakish Blues* .... 15.00 - 25.00
   1533 *Spread Yo' Stuff* .... 15.00 - 20.00

CLIFF PERRINE & HIS ORCHESTRA:

Champion 15999 *Mysterious Mose* .... 80.00 - 120.00
Gennett 7214 *I Lost My Gal From Memphis* .... 100.00 - 150.00

PERRY & HIS STOMP BAND:
Black Patti 8037 *Ash Can Stomp* ....1000.00 -   up

PERRY'S HOT DOGS:
Banner 1615 *There Ain't No Flies On Auntie* ....8.00 -   12.00
     1617 *Tweedle Dee, Tweedle Doo* ....7.00 -   10.00
     1618 *Milenberg Joys*.....................................15.00 -   20.00
     1641 *Has Been Blues* ....10.00 -   15.00
     1692 *Flamin' Mamie* ....8.00 -   12.00
     1714 *Say Mister! Have You Met Rosie's Sister?* ..8.00 -   12.00
Regal 9917 *Show Me The Way To Go Home* ....8.00 -   12.00
     9919 *Tweedle Dee, Tweedle Doo* ....7.00 -   10.00
     9920 *Milenberg Joys* ....15.00 -   20.00
     9945 *Has Been Blues* ....10.00 -   15.00
     9965 *Steppin' Fool* ....10.00 -   15.00
     9967 *Nobody's Business* ....8.00 -   12.00

PERRY'S ORCHESTRA:
Paramount 20431 *Headin' For Louisville* ....15.00 -   25.00
Puritan 11431 *That Certain Party* ....15.00 -   25.00

HERMAN PERRY & HIS BANJO:
Black Patti 8037 *Muddy Water* ....1000.00 -   up

SAM PERRY'S RUBE BAND:
Supertone 9039 *Bass Blues*................................100.00 -   150.00

TEDDY PETERS:
Vocalion 1006 *Georgia Man* ....200.00 -   300.00

JACK PETTIS AND HIS BAND/PETS:
Banner 1907 *Stockholm Stomp* ....15.00 -   25.00
     1908 *St. Louis Shuffle* ....15.00 -   25.00
     1911 *He's The Last Word* ....15.00 -   20.00
     1927 *It All Depends On You* ....15.00 -   20.00
     1929 *I Gotta Get Myself Somebody To Love* ......15.00 -   20.00
     1940 *I'm Back In Love Again* ....15.00 -   20.00
     1942 *That's My Hap-Hap-Happiness*.................15.00 -   25.00
(Foregoing titles also on Domino and Regal, similarly valued)
Domino 4080 *Candied Sweets*..............................10.00 -   15.00
     4094 *Once Over Lightly*..............................10.00 -   15.00
Okeh 41410 *Bag O' Blues*....................................50.00 -   75.00
     41411 *Freshman Hop*................................50.00 -   75.00
Puritan 11506 *Ain't She Sweet?* ....20.00 -   30.00
Regal (titles as on Banner, above, similarly valued)
Regal 8463 *Candied Sweets*...................................10.00 -   15.00
     8483 *Steppin' It Off* ....10.00 -   15.00
Victor 21559 *Doin' The New Low Down* ....20.00 -   30.00
     21793 *Freshman Hop* ....20.00 -   30.00
     V-38105 *Bugle Call Blues* ....75.00 -   100.00
Vocalion 15703 *Hot Heels* ....150.00 -   200.00
     15761 *Broadway Stomp*.............................150.00 -   200.00

PHILLIPS' LOUISVILLE JUG BAND:
Brunswick 7187 *Smackin' The Sax* ....150.00 -   250.00
     7194 *Tiger Rag* ....150.00 -   200.00
     7207 *Soldier Boy Blues*................................150.00 -   250.00

SIDNEY PHILLIPS & HIS ORCHESTRA:
Brunswick 8133, 8187, 8332 ....5.00 -   10.00
Variety 654 *Annie Laurie* ....7.00 -   10.00
Vocalion 3934 *Message From Mars* ....7.00 -   10.00

THE PICCADILLY PLAYERS (& SINGERS/&THE RADIO GIRL):
Edison (thin) 14023 *Susianna*................................50.00 -   80.00
     14032 *The One In The World* ....40.00 -   60.00

     14034 *Hittin' The Ceiling* ....50.00 -   75.00
     14035 *Someday Soon* ....50.00 -   75.00
     14036 *Maybe-Who Knows?* ....50.00 -   75.00
     14038 *You Ought To See My New Baby* ....40.00 -   60.00
     14056 *Tip Toe Thru The Tulips With Me* ....50.00 -   80.00
     14088 *Wanting You (unissued?)* ....-   -   -
Edison (thick) 52167 *Someday, Sweetheart*.......75.00 -   100.00
     52169 *She Don't Wanna* ....50.00 -   80.00
     52198 *What'll You Do?* ....50.00 -   80.00
     52215 *Rose Room* ....40.00 -   60.00
     52232 *Feelin' Good* ....50.00 -   80.00
     52273 *That's What I Call Keen* ....75.00 -   100.00
     52280 *My One And Only*................................50.00 -   80.00
     52327 *You're Just A Great Big Baby Doll*.........50.00 -   80.00
     52363 *If You Don't Love Me*..........................50.00 -   80.00
     52391 *Take Your Tomorrow* ....50.00 -   80.00
     52442 *I'm Sorry, Sally* ....40.00 -   60.00
     52478 *Easy Goin'* ....50.00 -   80.00
     52527 *Susanna* ....50.00 -   80.00
     52545 *You Were Meant For Me*......................40.00 -   60.00
     52562 *My Lucky Star* ....50.00 -   80.00
     52565 *I'm Thirsty For Kisses, Hungry For Love*
     ....50.00 -   80.00
     52574 *On With The Dance!* ....50.00 -   80.00
     52590 *I've Made A Habit Of You* ....50.00 -   80.00
     52613 *Walking With Susie* ....50.00 -   80.00
     52635 *You Ought To See My New Baby* ....50.00 -   80.00

WALTER PICHON:
Victor V38544 *Yo Yo* ....50.00 -   75.00

THE PICKENS SISTERS (AND THEIR ORCHESTRA):
Victor 22929 *Goodnight, Moon* ....10.00 -   15.00
     22965 *Somebody Loves You*..........................10.00 -   15.00
     22975 *Lawd, You Made The Night Too Long* ....10.00 -   15.00
     24025 *Sweet Georgia Brown* ....15.00 -   20.00
     24180 *Back In The Old Sunday School* ....10.00 -   15.00
     24190 *Sentimental Gentleman From Georgia* ... 15.00 -   20.00
     24355 *China Boy*..15.00 -   25.00
     24468 *Did You Ever See A Dream Walking?* ....15.00 -   20.00
     24471 *Many Moons Ago* ....10.00 -   15.00
     24625 *The Beat O' My Heart*...........................10.00 -   15.00
     24630 *Riptide* ....10.00 -   15.00
     24751 *Happiness Ahead* ....10.00 -   15.00
     24753 *The Thief of Bagdad* ....10.00 -   15.00
     24815 *Love Is Just Around The Corner*............10.00 -   15.00

PICKETT-PARHAM APOLLO SYNCOPATORS:
Paramount 12441 *Mojo Strut* ....400.00 -   up

CHARLES PIERCE & HIS ORCHESTRA:
Broadway 1174 *Nobody's Sweetheart* ....150.00 -   up
Paramount 12619 *China Boy* ....250.00 -   up
     12640 *Jazz Me Blues*................................250.00 -   up
     20616 *Nobody's Sweetheart* ....250.00 -   up

PIERROT SYNCOPATORS:
Crown (Canadian) 81008 *Somebody's Making A Fuss Over*
     Somebody ....10.00 -   15.00
     81020 *Dixie Drag* ....15.00 -   25.00
     81109 *The Rainbow Man* ....8.00 -   12.00
     81161 *Piccolo Pete* ....8.00 -   12.00

PINKIE'S BIRMINGHAM FIVE:
Gennett 3208 *Carolina Stomp* ....80.00 -   120.00

PIRON'S NEW ORLEANS ORCHESTRA:
Columbia 99-D *Ghost Of The Blues* ....30.00 - 50.00
　　14007-D *Sud Bustin' Blues* ....30.00 - 50.00
Okeh 40021 *Bouncing Around* ....60.00 - 100.00
　　40189 *Lou'siana Swing* ....100.00 - 150.00
Victor 19233 *New Orleans Wiggle* ....10.00 - 15.00
　　19255 *West Indies Blues* ....10.00 - 15.00
　　19646 *Red Man Blues* ....40.00 - 60.00

THE PLANTATION SERENADES:
Champion 15386 *Missouri Squabble* ....150.00 - 200.00
　　15402 *I Call You Sugar* ....150.00 - 200.00
Silvertone 5138 *Jackass Blues* ....125.00 - 175.00
　　5502 *I Call You Sugar* ....125.00 - 175.00

PLETCHER'S ELI PROM TROTTERS:
Q.R.S. Q-1055 *That's Where You're Wrong* ....75.00 - 100.00

STEW PLETCHER & HIS ORCHESTRA:
Bluebird 6343 *You Never Looked So Beautiful* ....10.00 - 15.00
　　6344 *I Don't Want To Make History* ....10.00 - 15.00
　　6345 *I Hope Gabriel Likes My Music* ....10.00 - 15.00

THE PODS OF PEPPER:
Columbia 14590-D *You've Had Your Way* ....150.00 - 200.00
　　14664-D *I Was A Good Loser Until I Lost You* ... 150.00 - 200.00

POLLA'S CLOVER GARDENS ORCHESTRA:
Edison 51456 *Travelling Blues (An Indigo Wail)* ....15.00 - 20.00
　　51554 *The Time Will Come* ....10.00 - 15.00
　　51575 *Isn't She The Sweetest Thing?* ....15.00 - 20.00
　　51586 *Save Your Sorrow (For Tomorrow)* ....15.00 - 20.00
　　51613 *The Promenade Walk* ....15.00 - 20.00
Edison, most other issues ....7.00 - 10.00

BEN POLLACK & HIS CALIFORNIANS (PARK CENTRAL) ORCHESTRA/PICK-A-RIB BOYS; BEN POLLACK'S ORCHESTRA:
Titles issued contemporaneously on Banner, Cameo, Conqueror,
　　Domino, Jewel, Oriole, Perfect, Regal, and Romeo: *Fall In Love
　　With Me; I'm A Ding Dong Daddy; I've Got Five Dollars; Rollin'
　　Down The River; Sing-Song Girl; Sweet and Hot; There's A Wah
　　Wah Girl In Agua Caliente; You Didn't Have To Tell Me*
　　...15.00 - 20.00
Another title: *If I Could Be With You (One Hour Tonight)*
　　...8.00 - 12.00
Brunswick 7747, 7751, 7764 ....8.00 - 12.00
Columbia 2870-D *Got The Jitters* ....20.00 - 30.00
　　2879-D *Deep Jungle* ....20.00 - 30.00
　　2886-D *Goin' To Heaven On A Mule* ....15.00 - 20.00
　　2901-D *Dancing In The Moonlight* ....15.00 - 20.00
　　2905-D *Here Goes* ....15.00 - 20.00
　　2906-D *The Voodoo* ....15.00 - 20.00
　　2910-D *Alone On The Range* ....15.00 - 20.00
　　2929-D *Sleepy Head* ....15.00 - 20.00
　　2931-D *Freckle Face, You're Beautiful* ....15.00 - 20.00
Decca 1424, 1435, 1458, 1465, 1476, 1488,
　　1517, 1546 ....7.00 - 10.00
Hit of the Week 1026 *I'm Following You* ....15.00 - 20.00
　　1027 *Cryin' For The Carolines* ....15.00 - 20.00
(Note: Above are single-sided cardboard records.)
Variety 504 *Deep Elm* ....10.00 - 15.00
　　556 *Peckin'* ....10.00 - 15.00
Victor 20394 *When I First Met Mary* ....8.00 - 12.00
　　20408 *Deed I Do* ....15.00 - 20.00
　　20425 *He's The Last Word* ....10.00 - 15.00

　　20461 *You're The One For Me* ....40.00 - 60.00
　　21184 *Memphis Blues* ....20.00 - 30.00
　　21437 *Singapore Sorrows* ....15.00 - 20.00
　　21743 *Buy, Buy For Baby* ....10.00 - 15.00
　　21827 *Sentimental Baby* ....15.00 - 20.00
　　21858 *Futuristic Rhythm* ....15.00 - 20.00
　　21941 *Louise* ....10.00 - 15.00
　　21944 *On With The Dance!* ....12.00 - 16.00
　　22071 *In The Hush Of The Night* ....12.00 - 16.00
　　22074 *Bashful Baby* ....15.00 - 20.00
　　22089 *True Blue Lou* ....15.00 - 20.00
　　22101 *Sweetheart, We Need Each Other* ....10.00 - 15.00
　　22106 *Where The Sweet Forget-Me-Nots Remember*
　　...10.00 - 15.00
　　22147 *Song of The Blues* ....15.00 - 20.00
　　22158 *You've Made Me Happy Today* ....10.00 - 15.00
　　22252 *I'd Like To Be A Gypsy* ....8.00 - 12.00
　　22267 *Keep Your Undershirt On* ....15.00 - 20.00
　　24284 *Two Tickets To Georgia* ....15.00 - 20.00
Vocalion 3769 *The Moon Is Grinning At Me* ....10.00 - 15.00
　　3819 *In A Sentimental Mood* ....10.00 - 15.00

HARRY POLLOCK'S BLUE DIAMONDS/CLUB MAURICE DIAMONDS; HARRY POLLOCK'S ORCHESTRA:
Edison 51933 *How'd Ya Like To Meet Me In The Moonlight?*
　　...15.00 - 20.00
　　51934 *Where's That Rainbow?* ....15.00 - 20.00
Gennett 3377 *Alabama Stomp* ....25.00 - 40.00
　　6026 *There Ain't No Maybe In My Baby's Eyes* ....50.00 - 80.00
　　6067 *You Can't Cry Over My Shoulder* ....15.00 - 20.00
　　6069 *Underneath The Weeping Willow* ....15.00 - 20.00
　　6083 *What Do I Care What Somebody Said?* .... 25.00 - 40.00
　　6159 *I'm In Love Again* ....20.00 - 30.00
　　6383 *There Ain't No Sweet Man That's Worth The Salt Of My
　　　　Tears* ....25.00 - 40.00

THE PONCE SISTERS:
Edison 51646 *My Sweetie Turned Me Down* ....10.00 - 15.00
　　51816 *Put Your Arms Where They Belong* ....10.00 - 15.00
　　52285 *In The Evening* ....20.00 - 30.00
　　52318 *I'd Rather Cry Over You* ....20.00 - 30.00

BOB POPE AND HIS (HOTEL CHARLOTTE) ORCHESTRA:
Titles issued contemporaneously on Banner, Melotone, Oriole,
　　Perfect, and Romeo: *Always; Blue Skies; Nero; Rockin' Chair;
　　Whoa Babe!* ....10.00 - 15.00
Bluebird 6283 *Early Bird* ....10.00 - 15.00
　　6284 *Moon Rose* ....8.00 - 12.00
　　6285 *Breakin' In A Pair Of Shoes* ....8.00 - 12.00
　　6286 *Shoe-Shine Boy* ....8.00 - 12.00
　　6299 *That Never-To-Be Forgotten Night* ....8.00 - 12.00
　　6300 *Stop That Dog* ....10.00 - 15.00
　　6452 *Big Chief De Sota* ....8.00 - 12.00
　　6453 *On Your Toes* ....8.00 - 12.00
　　6454 *Let's Sing Again* ....8.00 - 12.00
　　6471 *Swamp Fire* ....10.00 - 15.00
　　6502 *On The Alamo* ....10.00 - 15.00
　　6508 *Madhouse* ....15.00 - 20.00

PORTER'S BLUE DEVILS:
Gennett 5210 *Original Charleston Strut* ....20.00 - 30.00
　　5249 *Steamboat Sal* ....15.00 - 20.00
　　5251 *Somebody's Wrong* ....10.00 - 15.00

5281 *Mama Loves Papa (Papa Loves Mama)* ...10.00 - 15.00
5282 *Walk, Jenny, Walk*..................................10.00 - 15.00
5305 *When It's Night Time In Italy* ....10.00 - 15.00

COLE PORTER:
Victor 24766, 24825, 24843, 24859 ....8.00 - 12.00

DICK PORTER & HIS ORCHESTRA:
Vocalion 3355 *Sweet Thing* ....10.00 - 15.00
3469 *There's No Two Ways About It*..................10.00 - 15.00
3478 *Poor Robinson Crusoe*..............................10.00 - 15.00

KING PORTER & HIS ORCHESTRA:
Champion 15305 *Oh Miss Hannah!* ....80.00 - 130.00

PORTLAND ROSEBUDS:
Gennett 6079 *Beedle-Um-Bo* ....20.00 - 30.00

PORT OF HARLEM JASSMEN/SEVEN:
Blue Note 3 *Rocking The Blues* ....10.00 - 15.00
6 *Pounding Heart Blues*....................................10.00 - 15.00
7 *Blues For Tommy*..10.00 - 15.00
14 *Port Of Harlem Blues* ....10.00 - 15.00

POWELL'S JAZZ MONARCHS:
Okeh 8333 *Laughing Blues* ....250.00 - up

DICK POWELL:
Brunswick 4884 *June Kisses* ....15.00 - 20.00
6667 *Honeymoon Hotel* ....8.00 - 12.00
6685 *Lonely Lane* ....8.00 - 12.00
6979 *Happiness Ahead* ....8.00 - 12.00
7328 *Mr. & Mrs. Is The Name*............................8.00 - 12.00
7374 *Lullaby Of Broadway*................................8.00 - 12.00
7407 *I'm Goin' Shoppin' With You* ....8.00 - 12.00
7468 *Lonely Gondolier*......................................8.00 - 12.00
7469 *Lulu's Back In Town*..................................10.00 - 15.00
Conqueror 8183 *Pettin' In The Park* ....10.00 - 15.00
8184 *The Gold Diggers' Song* ....10.00 - 15.00
Decca, most issues ....5.00 - 10.00
Perfect 12919 *The Gold Diggers' Song*..................10.00 - 15.00
12920 *Pettin' In The Park* ....10.00 - 15.00
Romeo 2084 *I've Got To Sing A Torch Song* ....10.00 - 15.00
Vocalion 15647 *Is She My Girl Friend?* ....30.00 - 50.00
15648 *There's No End To My Love For You*......30.00 - 50.00
15674 *Mary Ann* ....30.00 - 50.00
15675 *Coquette* ....30.00 - 50.00
15686 *There Must Be A Silver Lining*................30.00 - 50.00
15699 *Was It A Dream?* ....30.00 - 50.00
15700 *If You Don't Love Me* ....30.00 - 50.00

MEL POWELL & HIS ORCHESTRA:
Commodore 543, 544 ....7.00 - 10.00

TEDDY POWELL AND HIS ORCHESTRA:
Bluebird, most issues ....5.00 - 10.00
Decca, most issues ....5.00 - 10.00

TOMMY POWELL AND HIS HI-DE-HO BOYS:
Decca 7231 *The Cat Is High*................................15.00 - 20.00

WALTER POWELL & HIS ORCHESTRA:
Vocalion 4612 *Devil's Holiday* ....15.00 - 20.00

OLLIE POWERS' HARMONY SYNCOPATORS/ ORCHESTRA:
Claxtonola 40263 *Play That Thing*......................250.00 - up
Harmograph 851 *Play That Thing* ....150.00 - up

Paramount 12059 *Jazzbo Jenkins* ....250.00 - up
20263 *Play That Thing* ....250.00 - up
Puritan 11263 *Play That Thing* ....150.00 - up

ANDY PREER & THE COTTON CLUB ORCHESTRA:
Gennett 6056 *I've Found A New Baby*..................250.00 - up

EVELYN PREER:
Banner 1824 *Breezin' Along With The Breeze*..........8.00 - 12.00
1873 *Sadie Green (The Vamp Of New Orleans)* 10.00 - 15.00
1895 *Sunday*... 10.00 - 15.00
1972 *Muddy Water* .... 10.00 - 15.00
6016 *One Sweet Letter From You* .... 8.00 - 12.00
6036 *Magnolia* .... 8.00 - 12.00
(Foregoing titles are also found on Domino and Regal, similarly valued)
Domino 3864 *Cock-A-Doodle, I'm Off My Noodle* .....10.00 - 15.00
Victor 20306 *Make Me Know It*............................50.00 - 75.00

SAMMY PRICE AND HIS FOUR QUARTERS/TEXAS BLUSICIANS:
Brunswick 7136 *Blue Rhythm Stomp*....................200.00 - up
Decca 7732, 7781, 7820, 7836, 7850, 7877, 8505,
8515, 8547, 8557, 8566, 8575, 8601, 8624, 8649 7.00 - 12.00

VIC PRICE AND HIS ORCHESTRA:
Gennett 6411 *When*..25.00 - 40.00
6440 *I'm More Than Satisfied* .... 30.00 - 50.00
6475 *Back In Your Own Backyard*....................25.00 - 40.00
6612 *Here's That Party Now In Person* .... 25.00 - 40.00
Herwin 8046 *Everywhere You Go* .... 20.00 - 30.00
8049 *Back In Your Own Backyard*....................25.00 - 40.00
8052 *Mary Ann* ....25.00 - 40.00
Supertone 9003 *Back In Your Own Backyard* .... 20.00 - 30.00
9006 *Speedy Boy*..15.00 - 20.00
9043 *Here's That Party Now In Person* ....20.00 - 30.00

LOUIS PRIMA & HIS NEW ORLEANS GANG:
Brunswick 7320 *I Still Want You*.......................... 10.00 - 15.00
7335 *Star Dust* .... 10.00 - 15.00
7376 *House Rent Party Day* .... 10.00 - 15.00
7394 *Sing It 'Way Down Low* .... 10.00 - 15.00
7419 *I'm Livin' In A Great Big Way*..................10.00 - 15.00
7431 *Swing Me With Rhythm* .... 10.00 - 15.00
7524 *Jamaica Shout* .... 10.00 - 15.00
Brunswick 7448, 7456, 7471, 7479, 7499, 7531,
7586, 7596, 7628, 7657, 7666, 7680, 7709, 7740 7.00 - 12.00
Decca 1618, 1674, 1871, 1953, 2242, 2279,
2660, 2749.. 7.00 - 12.00
Hit, most issues .... 5.00 - 10.00
Majestic, most issues .... 5.00 - 10.00
Varsity 8245, 8247.. 7.00 - 12.00
Vocalion 3376, 3388, 3509, 3628, 3921 .... 7.00 - 12.00
Vocalion 3376 *Pennies From Heaven* .... 7.00 - 10.00
3657 *Tin Roof Blues*...................................... 10.00 - 15.00

ALBERTA PRIME:
Blu-Disc T-1007 *Parlor Social De Luxe* .... 500.00 - up

PRINCE'S (MILITARY) BAND/ORCHESTRA:
Columbia A139 *St. Louis Tickle* .... 15.00 - 20.00
A711 *Black And White Rag* .... 15.00 - 20.00
A854 *Temptation Rag* .... 15.00 - 20.00
A901 *Porcupine Rag*...................................... 15.00 - 20.00
A972 *Tickled To Death* .... 15.00 - 20.00
A1031 *Red Pepper-A Spicy Rag* .... 10.00 - 15.00
A1038 *High Society* .... 15.00 - 20.00

A1107 *Ramshackle Rag*......15.00 - 20.00
A1140 *Black Diamond Rag* ......15.00 - 20.00
A1149 *The Gaby Glide*......10.00 - 15.00
A1164 *Cabaret Rag* ......15.00 - 20.00
A1292 *Another Rag* ......10.00 - 15.00
A1307 *Too Much Mustard*......10.00 - 15.00
A2327 *Beale Street* ......10.00 - 15.00
A2347 *Everybody's Jazzin' It*......10.00 - 15.00
A2370 *Mr. Jazz Himself* ......10.00 - 15.00
A2499 *Rigoletto Rag* ......10.00 - 15.00
A2825 *Miss Trombone (A Slippery Rag)*......10.00 - 15.00
A5582 *That's A Plenty* (12 inch) ......10.00 - 15.00
A5591 *Memphis Blues* (12 inch) ......10.00 - 15.00
A5772 *St. Louis Blues* (12 inch) ......15.00 - 20.00
A5938 *Inner Circle Toddle* (12 inch) ......15.00 - 20.00
A5983 *New Orleans Jazz* (12 inch) ......15.00 - 20.00
Columbia, most other issues ......4.00 - 7.00
(Note: Many of the above titles appear anonymously on affiliated labels, such as Climax and Oxford.)

PRINCETON TRIANGLE CLUB DANCE ORCHESTRA:
Columbia Personal (170615/170614) *Make Time* ...50.00 - 75.00
(Note: The vocalist "J.M. Stewart" on the flip side is actor Jimmy Stewart.)

PRINCETON TRIANGLE CLUB JAZZ BAND:
Personal Record 30-P *Join The Navy* ......50.00 - 75.00
31-P *Pirate Gold*......50.00 - 75.00
59-P *I'll Build An Igloo For You* ......50.00 - 75.00
63-P *Broke Again*......50.00 - 75.00
84-P *Twilight* ......30.00 - 50.00
85-P *Pretty Please* ......30.00 - 50.00
100-P *Rhythmic Refrain*......75.00 - 100.00
114-P *You Know Who*......75.00 - 100.00

CLARENCE PROFIT TRIO:
Brunswick 8341 *Tea For Two* ......8.00 - 12.00
Columbia 35378 *Body And Soul*......8.00 - 12.00
Decca 8503 *Hot And Bothered* ......8.00 - 12.00
8527 *Dark Eyes*......8.00 - 12.00

ALBERTA PRYME (See ALBERTA PRIME)

ARTHUR PRYOR'S BAND:
Victor 5607 *A Georgia Sunset-Cakewalk*......20.00 - 30.00
Victor 16021 *Artful Artie*......15.00 - 20.00
16043 *That Rag*......15.00 - 20.00
16073 *Southern Beauties Rag*......15.00 - 20.00
16079 *A Coon Band Contest*......8.00 - 12.00
16155 *A Southern Belle* ......15.00 - 20.00
16306 *White Wash Man*......15.00 - 20.00
16444 *The African 400 (An Educated Rag)*......15.00 - 20.00
16482 *Dill Pickles Rag* ......10.00 - 15.00
16511 *Temptation Rag*......15.00 - 20.00
16668 *Mr. Black Man*......15.00 - 20.00
16796 *Georgia Sunset-Cakewalk* ......15.00 - 20.00
16816 *Razzazza Mazzazza* ......10.00 - 15.00
16818 *Sweetmeats-Ragtime March* ......15.00 - 20.00
16819 *Dixie* ......10.00 - 15.00
16821 *The King Of Rags* (a two step oddity) ......15.00 - 20.00
16834 *A Rhinewine Rag*......15.00 - 20.00
16883 *Canhanibalmo Rag*......15.00 - 20.00
17044 *Surprise Medley*......10.00 - 15.00
17063 *Oh, You Beautiful Doll-Two-Step* ......10.00 - 15.00
17111 *Grizzly Bear Turkey Trot* ......10.00 - 15.00
17138 *Red Rose Rag* ......15.00 - 20.00
17223 *Frozen Bill-Cakewalk* ......15.00 - 20.00
35040 *Razzazza Mazzazza* (12 inch)......10.00 - 15.00
35098 *Tobasco-A Rag Waltz* (12 inch) ......15.00 - 20.00
*(Note: Some of the above titles were issued earlier on the single-sided Victor records of 2000, 4000, 5000 series. Since some of these were issued anonymously ("Band," "Dance Orchestra"), and others have not been verified, an authoritative listing is not attempted. Generally, as 'original issues' and examples of turn-of-the-century recordings, they are of greater interest and value than most of the records listed above. This is especially true of those issued in 7-inch and 8-inch sizes.)

PURPLE PIRATES ORCHESTRA (WILLIAMS COLLEGE):
W (unnumbered) *Tiger Rag* ......200.00 - up

JACK PURVIS; JACK PURVIS & HIS ORCHESTRA:
Odeon ONY-36093 *When You're Feelin' Blue* ......80.00 - 120.00
Okeh 8782 *Down Georgia Way* ......75.00 - 100.00
8808 *Dismal Dan* ......75.00 - 100.00
41404 *Copyin' Louis* ......75.00 - 100.00

Q.R.S. BOYS (See also FOUR HAWAIIAN GUITARS):
Q.R.S. 7062 *Wiggle Yo Toes* ......150.00 - 200.00
7067 *Dad Blame Blues* ......150.00 - 250.00

FRANKIE QUARTELL & HIS LITTLE CLUB ORCHESTRA/MELODY BOYS:
Brunswick 4183 *Sweet Baby*......35.00 - 50.00
Okeh 40257 *Heart Broken Strain* ......30.00 - 50.00
40258 *Prince Of Wails*......50.00 - 80.00

QUEEN CITY BLOWERS:
Champion 15030 *Stomp Off, Let's Go* ......75.00 - 125.00

QUEEN CITY BOYS:
Champion 15015 *Stop, You're Ticklin' Me* ......15.00 - 20.00

MAE QUESTAL ("THE BETTY BOOP GIRL"):
Decca 346 *On The Good Ship Lollipop* ......10.00 - 15.00
447 *The Choc'late Soldier Man*......10.00 - 15.00
540 *Animal Crackers In My Soup* ......10.00 - 15.00
653 *The Wedding Of Jack And Jill* ......10.00 - 15.00
680 *The Broken Record* ......10.00 - 15.00
769 *At The Codfish Ball* ......10.00 - 15.00
832 *You've Gotta Eat Your Spinach, Baby* ......10.00 - 15.00
876 *Medley: Songs From Shirley Temple Films*......15.00 - 20.00
1544 *I Want You For Christmas* ......10.00 - 15.00
2974 *You'd Be Surprised* ......10.00 - 15.00
Victor 24261 *Sweet Betty (Don't Take My Boop-Oop-A-Doop Away)* ......35.00 - 50.00

SNOOZER QUINN:
Wiggs 2100 *Snoozer's Telephone Blues* ......10.00 - 15.00

QUINTONES:
Vocalion 4928 *Chew-Chew-Chew (Your Bubble Gum)* ......15.00 - 20.00
5172 *When My Sugar Walks Down The Street* ..15.00 - 20.00
5409 *Midnight Jamboree* ......15.00 - 20.00
5509 *Sly Mongoose* ......15.00 - 20.00
5596 *Harmony In Harlem* ......15.00 - 20.00

HARRY RADERMAN'S (BILTMORE CASCADE ROOF/ JAZZ) ORCHESTRA; ORCHESTRA; RADERMAN'S RED HOTTERS/ROYSTERS (See also THE RED HOTTERS):

Everybody's 1067 *Seminola* ....8.00 - 12.00
   1068 *Oh Say, Can I See You Tonight?* ....8.00 - 12.00
Harmony 22-H *Sweet Man* ....8.00 - 12.00
   25-H *Want A Little Lovin'* ....10.00 - 15.00
   45-H *Hugo, I Go Where You Go* ....8.00 - 12.00
   48-H *I Ain't Got Nobody* ....8.00 - 12.00
Lyric 4218 *Railroad Blues*.....................................20.00 - 30.00
Moxie (unnumbered) *Moxie* ....20.00 - 30.00
("A Gennett record made for the Moxie Co." for advertising purposes)
Okeh 4477 *Muscle Shoals Blues*............................10.00 - 15.00
   4885 *Tin Roof Blues* ....15.00 - 20.00
   4923 *Pay Day Blues* ....15.00 - 20.00
   40610 *Horses* ....10.00 - 15.00
   40652 *The Birth Of The Blues* ....10.00 - 15.00
   40663 *Bye Bye Blackbird* ....10.00 - 15.00
   40700 *I'm Gonna Park Myself In Your Arms* ....10.00 - 15.00
   40712 *Cross Your Heart* ....8.00 - 12.00
   40736 *Sunday* ....10.00 - 15.00
   40771 *I Wonder How I Look When I'm Asleep* .10.00 - 15.00
   40773 *Hoosier Sweetheart* ....10.00 - 15.00
   40829 *Hallelujah!* ....10.00 - 15.00
Paramount 20263 *Bleeding Hearted Blues*............250.00 - up

LOU RADERMAN & HIS PELHAM HEATH INN ORCHESTRA:

Banner 7133 *Georgie Porgie*...................................8.00 - 12.00
   7135 *Get Out And Get Under The Moon*.............8.00 - 12.00
Harmony 607-H *Ol' Man River* ....15.00 - 20.00
   611-H *Oh Gee!-Oh Joy!* ....10.00 - 15.00
(Note: Above two titles on Diva and Velvet Tone are similarly valued.)
"Show Boat" Special Record 1086-P *Why Do I Love You?*
....10.00 - 15.00

RADIO ALL STAR NOVELTY ORCHESTRA:

Brunswick 4755 *Mysterious Mose*............................8.00 - 12.00

THE RADIO GIRL (See VAUGHN DE LEATH)

THE RADIOLITES:

Columbia 1432-D *Sweet Lorraine* ....10.00 - 15.00
   2540-D *I Don't Know Why*..............................10.00 - 15.00

RADIO RASCALS (ORCHESTRA):

Bluebird 5249 *Down On The Farm*.........................10.00 - 15.00
Sunrise 3332 *Down On The Farm* ....50.00 - 80.00
Victor 22989 *Dixie* ....10.00 - 15.00
   24007 *Song Of The Fiddlers*...........................10.00 - 15.00

KARL RADLACH & HIS ORCHESTRA:

Titles issued contemporaneously on Banner, Broadway, Cameo, Oriole, and Perfect: *Absence Makes The Heart Grow Fonder; Around The Corner; Be Careful With Those Eyes; Cheer Up (Good Times Are Comin'); Dust; Give Yourself A Pat On The Back; Hand Me Down My Walking Cane; Mysterious Mose; Telling It To The Daisies* ....7.00 - 12.00

BILL RAGEN'S VAGABONDS:

Champion 15442 *Danger! Look Out For That Gal*.10.00 - 15.00

IKE RAGON & HIS ORCHESTRA:

Vocalion 03513 *Maple Leaf Rag* ....25.00 - 35.00
   03547 *Truckin' On The Old Camp Ground*.......25.00 - 40.00

RAG PICKERS:

Autograph (unnumbered) *Suite 16*......................150.00 - 250.00

RAINBOW DANCE ORCHESTRA:

Romeo 366 *St. Louis Blues* ....15.00 - 20.00

RAINBOW SERENADERS:

Gennett 3008 *Isn't She The Sweetest Thing?* ....15.00 - 20.00

MA RAINEY (AND HER GEORGIA BAND):

Paramount 12080 *Last Minute Blues* ....80.00 - 120.00
   12081 *Bad Luck Blues* ....80.00 - 120.00
   12082 *Walking Blues* ....80.00 - 120.00
   12083 *Southern Blues* ....80.00 - 120.00
   12098 *Dream Blues* ....75.00 - 100.00
   12200 *Ma Rainey's Mystery Record*...............100.00 - 150.00
   12215 *Lucky Rock Blues* ....100.00 - 150.00
   12222 *Farewell Daddy Blues*.........................75.00 - 100.00
   12227 *South Bound Blues* ....80.00 - 130.00
   12238 *Jelly Bean Blues* ....150.00 - 250.00
   12242 *Toad Frog Blues* ....150.00 - 200.00
   12252 *See See Rider Blues* ....150.00 - 250.00
   12257 *Cell Bound Blues* ....100.00 - 150.00
   12284 *Explaining The Blues* ....100.00 - 150.00
   12290 *Louisiana Hoo Doo Blues* ....100.00 - 150.00
   12295 *Stormy Sea Blues* ....100.00 - 150.00
   12303 *Night Time Blues* ....100.00 - 150.00
   12311 *Rough And Tumble Blues* ....100.00 - 150.00
   12332 *Slave To The Blues* ....100.00 - 150.00
   12338 *Chain Gang Blues* ....100.00 - 150.00
   12352 *Seeking Blues* ....100.00 - 150.00
   12357 *Stack O' Lee Blues* ....100.00 - 150.00
   12364 *Broken Hearted Blues* ....100.00 - 150.00
   12374 *Titanic Man Blues* ....100.00 - 150.00
   12384 *Sissy Blues*...100.00 - 150.00
   12395 *Down In The Basement* ....100.00 - 150.00
   12419 *Grievin' Hearted Blues* ....100.00 - 150.00
   12438 *Don't Fish In My Sea*...........................100.00 - 150.00
   12455 *Morning Hour Blues* ....100.00 - 150.00
   12508 *Misery Blues*......................................150.00 - 200.00
   12526 *Gone Daddy Blues* ....150.00 - 200.00
   12548 *Big Boy Blues* ....150.00 - 200.00
   12566 *Oh Papa Blues* ....150.00 - 200.00
   12590 *Georgia Cakewalk* ....100.00 - 150.00
   12603 *Moonshine Blues* ....100.00 - 150.00
   12612 *Ice Bag Papa*.....................................150.00 - 250.00
   12647 *Blues The World Forgot*......................100.00 - 150.00
   12668 *Prove It On Me Blues* ....150.00 - 250.00
   12687 *Victim Of The Blues* ....200.00 - 300.00
   12706 *Traveling Blues* ....200.00 - 300.00
   12718 *Big Feeling Blues* ....100.00 - 150.00
   12735 *Tough Luck Blues* ....150.00 - 250.00
   12760 *Sleep Talking Blues* ....100.00 - 150.00
   12804 *Log Camp Blues* ....150.00 - 250.00
   12902 *Runaway Blues* ....150.00 - 250.00
   12926 *Sweet Rough Man* ....150.00 - 250.00
   12963 *Daddy Goodbye Blues*..........................150.00 - 250.00

THE RAMBLERS:

Romeo 266 *She Knows Her Onions*........................10.00 - 15.00
   273 *Precious* ....8.00 - 12.00
   315 *Lonely Eyes* ....7.00 - 10.00
   437 *Arkansas Blues* ....10.00 - 15.00

RAMONA AND HER GANG/GRAND PIANO:
(Note: Some of the following are credited **ROY BARGY & RAMONA**.)
Victor 24260 *A Penny For Your Thoughts* ....10.00 - 15.00
 24268 *What Have We Got To Lose?* ....10.00 - 15.00
 24303 *I've Got To Sing A Torch Song* ....10.00 - 15.00
 24310 *Was My Face Red?* ....10.00 - 15.00
 24316 *Raisin' The Rent* ....10.00 - 15.00
 24389 *You Excite Me!* ....10.00 - 15.00
 24408 *Ah! The Moon Is Here* ....10.00 - 15.00
 24440 *I'm No Angel* ....10.00 - 15.00
 24445 *Not For All The Rice In China* ....10.00 - 15.00
 25138 *Every Now And Then* ....10.00 - 15.00
 25156 *Barrel-House Music* ....10.00 - 15.00

RAMPART STREET WASHBOARD BAND:
Titles issued contemporaneously on Banner, Conqueror, Oriole, Perfect, and Romeo: *Forty and Tight, Piggly Wiggly*
....80.00 - 130.00

CLARK RANDALL & HIS ORCHESTRA:
Brunswick 7415 *Troublesome Trumpet* ....8.00 - 12.00
 7436 *Drifting Tide* ....8.00 - 12.00
 7466 *Jitter Bug* ....8.00 - 12.00

DUKE RANDALL & HIS BOYS:
Champion 15491 *Squeeze Me* ....250.00 - up

SLATZ RANDALL & HIS ORCHESTRA:
Brunswick 4331 *Bessie Couldn't Help It* ....10.00 - 15.00
 4562 *Blame It On The Moon* ....10.00 - 15.00
 4568 *Let's Don't 'n' Say We Did* ....10.00 - 15.00
 4779 *I'm A Ding Dong Daddy* (From Dumas) ..10.00 - 15.00
 6304 *Hello! Gorgeous* ....10.00 - 15.00

AMANDA RANDOLPH & HER ORCHESTRA:
Bluebird 6615, 6616, 6617, 6619 ....7.00 - 12.00

TED/TEDDY RAPH & HIS ORCHESTRA:
Columbia 2440-D *When I Take My Sugar To Tea* ....7.00 - 10.00
 2450-D *Dream A Little Dream Of Me* ....7.00 - 10.00
 2482-D *Wrap Your Troubles In Dreams* ....7.00 - 10.00

JIMMY RASCHEL & HIS ORCHESTRA:
Champion 16534 *It Don't Mean A Thing* ....150.00 - 200.00

REB'S LEGION CLUB FORTY FIVES:
Hollywood (unnumbered) *Steppin' High* ....250.00 - up

RECTORS' JAZZ BAND:
Arto 9003 *Bluin' The Blues* ....10.00 - 15.00

RED & HIS BIG TEN:
Victor 23026 *That's Where The South Begins* ....25.00 - 40.00
 23033 *At Last I'm Happy* ....25.00 - 40.00

RED AND MIFF'S STOMPERS:
Edison 51854 *Alabama Stomp* ....200.00 - 300.00
 51878 *Black Bottom Stomp* ....200.00 - 300.00
Victor 20778 *Delirium* ....15.00 - 25.00
 21183 *Feelin' No Pain* ....15.00 - 25.00
 21397 *Slippin' Around* ....15.00 - 25.00

THE RED CAPS:
Okeh 4838 *Snakes Hips* ....10.00 - 15.00
Victor 23382 *Niagara Falls* ....150.00 - 250.00

THE RED DEVILS:
Title issued contemporaneously on Banner, Oriole, and Romeo:
 Ballin The Jack ....75.00 - 100.00
Columbia 14586-D *Tiger Rag* ....150.00 - 200.00

THE RED HEADS:
Melotone 12443 *Feelin' No Pain* ....7.00 - 10.00
 12495 *Bugaboo* ....5.00 - 8.00
Oriole 2555 *Nobody's Sweetheart* ....7.00 - 10.00
 2574 *Bugaboo* ....5.00 - 8.00
Pathe-Actuelle 11347 *Get A Load Of This* ....40.00 - 60.00
 36347 *Nervous Charlie* ....30.00 - 50.00
 36384 *Fallen Arches* ....30.00 - 50.00
 36387 *Poor Papa* ....15.00 - 25.00
 36419 *'tain't Cold* ....30.00 - 50.00
 36458 *Dynamite* ....25.00 - 35.00
 36492 *Wild And Foolish* ....30.00 - 50.00
 36527 *Alabama Stomp* ....25.00 - 35.00
 36536 *The Hurricane* ....25.00 - 35.00
 36557 *Heebie Jeebies* ....25.00 - 35.00
 36576 *That's No Bargain* ....25.00 - 40.00
 36583 *Tell Me Tonight* ....20.00 - 30.00
 36593 *You Should See My Tootsie* ....20.00 - 30.00
 36701 *A Good Man Is Hard To Find* ....30.00 - 50.00
 36707 *Nothin' Does-Does Like It Used To Do-Do-Do*
....25.00 - 35.00
Perfect 14528 *Headin' For Louisville* ....30.00 - 50.00
 14565 *Fallen Arches* ....30.00 - 50.00
 14568 *Poor Papa* ....15.00 - 25.00
 14600 *Hangover* ....30.00 - 50.00
 14639 *Hi-Diddle-Diddle* ....25.00 - 35.00
 14673 *Wild And Foolish* ....30.00 - 50.00
 14708 *Brown Sugar* ....25.00 - 35.00
 14717 *The Hurricane* ....25.00 - 35.00
 14738 *Black Bottom Stomp* ....25.00 - 35.00
 14757 *That's No Bargain* ....25.00 - 40.00
 14764 *Here Or There* ....20.00 - 30.00
 14774 *You Should See My Tootsie* ....20.00 - 30.00
 14882 *Baltimore* ....30.00 - 50.00
 14888 *Nothin' Does-Does Like It Used To Do-Do-Do*
....25.00 - 35.00

RED HOT DOGS:
Banner 6057 *Blame It On The Black Bottom Craze* .....15.00 - 20.00
 6069 *Swanee's Calling Me* ....15.00 - 20.00

RED HOT SYNCOPATORS (See also ORIGINAL INDIANA FIVE):
Bell 445 *Jackass Blues* ....20.00 - 30.00

THE RED HOTTERS (See also HARRY RADERMAN):
Okeh 40360 *What Is The Use?* ....10.00 - 15.00
 40380 *Ev'rything Is Hotsy Totsy Now* ....10.00 - 15.00
 40382 *The Flapper Wife* ....8.00 - 12.00
 40426 *Alone At Last* ....15.00 - 20.00
 40443 *Pango Pango Maid* ....10.00 - 15.00
 40474 *Oh Lovey, Be Mine* ....20.00 - 30.00
 40523 *Roll 'Em, Girls* ....10.00 - 15.00
 40534 *Then I'll Be Happy* ....20.00 - 30.00
 40543 *What Did I Tell Ya?* ....10.00 - 15.00
 40560 *When You See That Aunt Of Mine* ....12.00 - 16.00
 40570 *Love Bound* ....12.00 - 16.00
Silvertone 3526 *St. Louis Blues* ....15.00 - 20.00
 3527 *Gin Houn' Blues* ....15.00 - 20.00
 3560 *Third Alley Breakdown* ....75.00 - 100.00

DON REDMAN & HIS ORCHESTRA:

Titles issued contemporaneously on Banner, Conqueror, Melotone, Oriole, Perfect, and Romeo: *A Little Bit Later On; Bugle Call Rag; I Gotcha; Lazy Weather; Moonrise On The Lowlands; Too Bad; We Don't Know From Nothin'; Who Wants To Sing My Love Song?* ....10.00 - 15.00

Bluebird 10061 *Down Home Rag* ....10.00 - 15.00
    10071 *Milenberg Joys* ....10.00 - 15.00
    10081 *'Deed I Do* ....8.00 - 12.00
    10095 *Auld Lang Syne* ....8.00 - 12.00
    10615 *You Ain't Nowhere* ....8.00 - 12.00
    10765 *Shim-Me-Sha-Wabble* ....10.00 - 15.00
Brunswick 6211 *Chant Of The Weed* ....15.00 - 20.00
    6233 *I Heard* ....15.00 - 20.00
    6273 *How'm I Doin'?* ....15.00 - 20.00
    6344 *It's A Great World After All* ....10.00 - 15.00
    6354 *Tea For Two* ....10.00 - 15.00
    6368 *Hot And Anxious* ....10.00 - 15.00
    6401 *Ain't I The Lucky One?* ....10.00 - 15.00
    6412 *Two-Time Man* ....10.00 - 15.00
    6429 *Nagasaki* ....10.00 - 15.00
    6520 *Doin' The New Low-Down* ....10.00 - 15.00
    6523 *How Ya Feelin?* ....10.00 - 15.00
    6560 *Sophisticated Lady* ....10.00 - 15.00
    6585 *I Won't Tell* ....10.00 - 15.00
    6622 *Lazy Bones* ....10.00 - 15.00
    6684 *I Found A New Way To Go* ....10.00 - 15.00
    6745 *Got The Jitters* ....10.00 - 15.00
    6935 *Lonely Cabin* ....10.00 - 15.00
Variety 580 *On The Sunny Side Of The Street* ....10.00 - 15.00
    605 *Stormy Weather* ....10.00 - 15.00
    635 *The Man On The Flying Trapeze* ....10.00 - 15.00
Victor 26206 *Jump Session* ....8.00 - 12.00
    26258 *Igloo* ....8.00 - 12.00
    26266 *Ain't I Good To You?* ....8.00 - 12.00
Vocalion 3354 *Bugle Call Rag* ....10.00 - 15.00
    3359 *We Don't Know From Nothin'* ....10.00 - 15.00
    3823 *Exactly Like You* ....10.00 - 15.00
    3829 *Sweet Sue* ....10.00 - 15.00
    3836 *The Man On The Flying Trapeze* ....10.00 - 15.00

RED ONION JAZZ BABIES:

Gennett 5607 *Terrible Blues* ....125.00 - 175.00
    5627 *Cake Walking Babies* ....125.00 - 175.00
Silvertone 4029 *Cake Walking Babies* ....100.00 - 150.00
    4032 *Santa Claus Blues* ....100.00 - 150.00
    5024 *Brotherly Love* ....50.00 - 75.00

REUBEN/RUBEN "RIVER" REEVES & HIS RIVER BOYS/TRIBUTARIES:

Vocalion 1292 *River Blues* ....150.00 - 250.00
    1297 *Bugle Call Blues* ....150.00 - 250.00
    1407 *Moanin' Low* ....200.00 - 300.00
    1411 *Texas Special Blues* ....200.00 - 300.00
    2638 *Screws, Nuts And Bolts* ....75.00 - 100.00
    2723 *Zuddan* ....50.00 - 80.00
    15836 *Head Low* ....150.00 - 250.00
    15839 *Shoo Shoo Boogie Boo* ....150.00 - 250.00

REILLY-FARLEY AND THEIR ONYX CLUB BOYS (See RILEY-FARLEY)

LEO REISMAN AND HIS ORCHESTRA:

Brunswick (most issues) ....5.00 - 10.00

Columbia 517-D *A Cup Of Coffee, A Sandwich And You* ....10.00 - 15.00
    701-D, 776-D, 973-D, 1467-D, 1561-D, 1682-D ....8.00 - 12.00
Victor L-16005 *Music From The Cat And The Fiddle* ....20.00 - 30.00
    L-16026, L-16028 ....15.00 - 25.00
(Note: Above are long-playing "Program Transcriptions.")
    22306 *Puttin' On The Ritz* ....10.00 - 15.00
    22398 *Happy Feet* ....7.00 - 10.00
    22398, 22433, 22459, 22537, 22538, 22546, 22605, 22606, 22647, 22668, 22670, 22696, 22746, 22755, 22757, 22794, 22798, 22839, 22849 ....7.00 - 12.00
    22836 *White Heat* ....10.00 - 15.00
    22851 *Bend Down, Sister* ....10.00 - 15.00
    22869, 22870, 22904, 22912, 22913, 22914, 22915, 22927, 22954, 22961, 24029, 24044, 24047, 24126, 24131, 24132, 24156 ....7.00 - 12.00
    24011 *If It Ain't Love* ....10.00 - 15.00
    24048 *Got The South In My Soul* ....10.00 - 15.00
    24156 *Brother, Can You Spare A Dime?* ....10.00 - 15.00
    24157 *A Rainy Day* ....10.00 - 15.00
    24192, 24193, 24259, 24262, 24269, 24312 ....7.00 - 12.00
    24315 *Happy Is The Day Is Long* ....10.00 - 15.00
    24358 *Smoke Rings* ....10.00 - 15.00
    24398, 24399, 24407 ....7.00 - 12.00
    24418 *Easter Parade* ....10.00 - 15.00
    24419 *Savage Serenade* ....10.00 - 15.00
    24428 *Not For All The Rice In China* ....10.00 - 15.00
    24429, 24448 ....7.00 - 12.00
Victor (most subsequent issues) ....5.00 - 8.00
Victor 39002 (picture disc) Noel Coward's Songs from "Bittersweet" ....100.00 - 150.00

HENRY "KID" RENA'S JAZZ BAND:

Delta 800, 801, 802, 803, 804, 805, 806, 807 ....8.00 - 12.00

JACQUES RENARD AND HIS ORCHESTRA:

Brunswick 4918 *Lucky Seven* ....8.00 - 12.00
    4919 *Can This Be Love?* ....8.00 - 12.00
    4939 *Three Little Words* ....8.00 - 12.00
    4940 *Readin', 'Ritin', Rhythm* ....8.00 - 12.00
    6205 *As Time Goes By* ....15.00 - 20.00
    6205 *As Time Goes By* (green label reissue) ....7.00 - 10.00
Brunswick, most other issues ....5.00 - 10.00
Columbia 3086-D, 3090-D ....8.00 - 12.00
Victor 20728 *Just Call On Me* ....8.00 - 12.00
    20981 *When The Morning Glories Wake Up in the Morning* ....8.00 - 12.00
Vocalion 2524, 2525, 2549, 2557 ....7.00 - 12.00

RENDEZVOUS DANCE ORCHESTRA:

Puritan 11244 *Buddy's Habits* ....50.00 - 75.00

DUNK RENDLEMAN & THE ALABAMIANS; RENDLEMAN'S DANCE ORCHESTRA:

Gennett 6233 *Hot Heels* ....50.00 - 80.00
    6322 *Mean Dog Blues* ....300.00 - up
Silvertone 5052 *Hot Heels* ....40.00 - 70.00
    25052 *Me And My Shadow* ....40.00 - 70.00

HARRY RESER'S JUMPING JACKS/ROUNDERS/ SYNCOPATORS; HARRY RESER AND HIS ORCHESTRA (See also THE CLICQUOT CLUB ESKIMOS; THE JAZZ PILOTS):

Banner 6052 *I Ain't That Kind Of A Baby*.................8.00 - 12.00
Brunswick 2308 *Pickin's*...10.00 - 15.00
Columbia 454-D, 510-D, 594-D, 604-D, 678-D,
  708-D, 725-D, 774-D, 803-D, 853-D, 857-D,
  907-D, 981-D, 1087-D ....7.00 - 12.00
  1109-D *Shaking The Blues Away* ....10.00 - 15.00
  1244-D *I Scream-You Scream-We All Scream For Ice Cream*
  ....10.00 - 15.00
  1378-D *Crazy Rhythm* ....10.00 - 15.00
  1524-D *What A Night For Spooning* ....10.00 - 15.00
  1696-D *Don't Be Like That* ....10.00 - 15.00
  1761-D *Kansas City Kitty*............................10.00 - 15.00
  1806-D *I Got A "Code" In My" "Doze"* ....10.00 - 15.00
  1835-D *Here Comes The Show Boat*.............10.00 - 15.00
  1884-D *The Whoopee Hat Brigade* ....10.00 - 15.00
  1973-D *Piccolo Pete*...................................10.00 - 15.00
  2818-D *I Want To Ring Bells* ....8.00 - 12.00
  2833-D *When You Were The Girl On The Scooter*
  ....10.00 - 15.00
  2840-D *My Galveston Gal*...........................10.00 - 15.00
Columbia, most other issues ....5.00 - 8.00
Edison 14032 *I'm Still Caring*.........................40.00 - 60.00
  52034 *Hello Cutie*......................................25.00 - 40.00
  52184 *Highways Are Happy Ways* ....40.00 - 60.00
  52282 *Hey! Hey! Hazel* ....40.00 - 60.00
  52525 *That's The Good Old Sunny South* ....50.00 - 80.00
Gennett 3009 *When You Do What You Do* ....15.00 - 20.00
Okeh 4452 *Everybody Step*................................7.00 - 10.00
  41489 *Little Joe*..15.00 - 20.00
Variety 510 *Top Of The Town* ....8.00 - 12.00
  588 *Hook And Ladder 31*............................8.00 - 12.00

FRANKIE REYNOLDS AND HIS ORCHESTRA:

Bluebird 7137 *Chicken On The Apple*.................7.00 - 10.00
  7241 *Lady, Be Good* ....15.00 - 20.00

LEW REYNOLDS FLEXO RECORDING ORCHESTRA:

Flexo 123 *At Last I'm Happy* ....35.00 - 50.00
  124 *You're Driving Me Crazy* ....35.00 - 50.00
  125 *To Whom It May Concern*......................35.00 - 50.00
  128 *What A Fool I've Been* ....35.00 - 50.00
  133 *Casey Jones* ....35.00 - 50.00
  134 *I Surrender Dear*..................................35.00 - 50.00
  138 *Ho Hum!* ....35.00 - 50.00

LYST REYNOLDS' LOGOLA ORCHESTRA:

Gennett 6235 *What Do We Do On A Dew-Dew Dewy Day*
....40.00 - 60.00
  6263 *Barbara*..75.00 - 100.00

ROSS REYNOLDS & HIS PALAIS GARDENS ORCHESTRA:

Gennett 3046 *Creole* ....50.00 - 75.00
  5611 *Creole* ....50.00 - 75.00

THE RHYTHM ACES:

Brunswick 4244 *Jazz Battle*..............................100.00 - 150.00
  7120 *I Got The Stinger* ....150.00 - 200.00

THE RHYTHMAKERS:

Titles issued contemporaneously on Banner, Melotone, and Oriole: *I Would Do Anything For You; Mean Old Bed Bug Blues; Yellow Dog Blues; Yes, Suh!*......................25.00 - 40.00

THE RHYTHM KINGS:

Victor 23276 *One More Time* ....75.00 - 100.00
  23279 *You Rascal, You* ....75.00 - 100.00
  23283 *Please Tell Me*...................................75.00 - 100.00

THE RHYTHM MAKERS:

Vocalion 15763 *Wabash Blues* ....200.00 - up

THE RHYTHM WRECKERS:

Vocalion 3341 *Sugar Blues* ....10.00 - 15.00
  3390 *Wabash Blues*....................................10.00 - 15.00
  3523 *Twelfth Street Rag* ....10.00 - 15.00
  3566 *St. Louis Blues* ....10.00 - 15.00
  3608 *September In The Rain* ....10.00 - 15.00
  3642 *Desert Blues* ....10.00 - 15.00
  3670 *Blue Yodel No. 3* ....10.00 - 15.00

RIALTO DANCE ORCHESTRA:

Domino 416 *Copenhagen* ....20.00 - 30.00

FRED/FREDDIE RICH AND HIS (LA PALINA/RADIO/ TIMES SQUARE) ORCHESTRA:

Banner 0508 *Sweetheart, We Need Each Other* ....8.00 - 12.00
  0804 *I've Got A Yen For You*...........................10.00 - 15.00
  0806 *Good Evenin'*.......................................8.00 - 12.00
  0835 *Sing Something Simple*..........................10.00 - 15.00
(Foregoing titles on Cameo are similarly valued)
  6360 *I Get The Blues When It Rains*.................15.00 - 20.00
  6477 *Sweetness* ....7.00 - 10.00
  6503 *Little By Little* ....7.00 - 10.00
  6508 *Piccolo Pete* ....10.00 - 15.00
  6512 *Wouldn't It Be Wonderful?* ....7.00 - 10.00
Cameo 872 *Shake That Thing* ....15.00 - 20.00
  938 *Betty* ....7.00 - 10.00
  1019 *I Can't Get Over A Girl Like You* ....7.00 - 10.00
  9194 *Kids Again*..7.00 - 10.00
  9203 *Now I'm In Love* ....20.00 - 30.00
  9229 *Sweetness* ....7.00 - 10.00
  9233 *Piccolo Pete* ....8.00 - 12.00
  9265 *Little By Little* ....7.00 - 10.00
  9300 *Singin' In The Rain* ....8.00 - 12.00
  9320 *How Am I To Know* ....10.00 - 15.00
Columbia 1740-D *Wedding Bells* ....8.00 - 12.00
  1838-D *Singin' In The Rain*...........................8.00 - 12.00
  1893-D *Don't Hang Your Dreams On A Rainbow*...8.00 - 12.00
  1924-D *Wishing And Waiting For Love* ....8.00 - 12.00
  1965-D *Revolutionary Rhythm* ....10.00 - 15.00
  1979-D *I Don't Want Your Kisses* ....8.00 - 12.00
  2043-D *Dixie Jamboree* ....15.00 - 20.00
  2132-D *Strike Up The Band!* ....10.00 - 15.00
  2299-D *Sing Something Simple* ....10.00 - 15.00
  2328-D *I Got Rhythm*...................................15.00 - 20.00
  2387-D *Tie A Little String Around Your Finger* .....15.00 - 20.00
  2484-D *Pardon Me Pretty Baby* ....10.00 - 15.00
  2536-D *As Time Goes By*...............................15.00 - 20.00
  2534-D, 2751-D, 2752-D, 2868-D, 2872-D
  ....7.00 - 12.00
  3613-X *Don't Hang Your Dreams On A Rainbow*
  ....10.00 - 20.00

(Note: No. 3613-X is part of a Spanish series having green labels and utilizing instrumental versions of songs which, for U.S. market, have vocal choruses. See Columbia 1893-D.)

Gennett 3384 *Don't Forget*	50.00 -	80.00
6001 *Don't Take That Black Bottom Away*	20.00 -	30.00
6007 *A Little Music In The Moonlight*	20.00 -	30.00
6015 *I Love To Baby You*	15.00 -	20.00
6016 *Sweeter Than You*	15.00 -	20.00
6133 *I'm On My Merry Way*	20.00 -	30.00
6151 *Ask Me Another*	20.00 -	30.00
6159 *I Adore You*	20.00 -	30.00
Harmony 37-H *You Told Me To Go*	10.00 -	15.00
38-H *Feelin' Kind O' Blue*	8.00 -	12.00
57-H *I Would Be Where I Am If You Hadn't Gone Away*	10.00 -	15.00
64-H *I'm Sitting On Top Of The World*	10.00 -	15.00
84-H *The Monkey Doodle-Doo*	8.00 -	12.00
90-H *Someone's Stolen My Sweet, Sweet Baby*	8.00 -	12.00
119-H *Bell Hoppin' Blues*	15.00 -	20.00
136-H *Could I? I Certainly Could*	10.00 -	15.00
Hit of the Week J-4 *Little Girl*	10.00 -	15.00
K-1 *It's The Girl*	10.00 -	15.00

(Foregoing are single-sided cardboard records)

Okeh 41482 *Would You Like To Take A Walk?*	15.00 -	20.00
41484 *Please Don't Talk About Me When I'm Gone*	15.00 -	20.00
41489 *When I Take My Sugar To Tea*	15.00 -	20.00

Pathe-Actuelle (titles as on Perfect, following)

Perfect 14570 *Drifting And Dreaming*	8.00 -	12.00
14575 *A Little Bit Bad*	15.00 -	20.00
14582 *Chinky Butterfly*	10.00 -	15.00
14606 *Honey Bunch*	8.00 -	12.00
14633 *Up And At 'Em*	15.00 -	20.00

(Foregoing titles on Pathe-Actuelle are similarly valued)

Regal 8761 *I Get The Blues When It Rains*	7.00 -	10.00
10113 *I've Got A Yen For You*	10.00 -	15.00
Romeo 968 *When My Dreams Come True*	8.00 -	12.00
1109 *Singin' In The Rain*	8.00 -	12.00
Vocalion 5420 *How High The Moon*	7.00 -	10.00
5507 *I'm Forever Blowing Bubbles*	7.00 -	10.00

CHUCK RICHARDS:

Vocalion 2877 *Blue Interlude*	15.00 -	20.00

PETE RICHARDS & HIS ORCHESTRA:

Champion 15402 *Bugs*	150.00 -	200.00
15455 *Michigan Stomp*	200.00 -	300.00

VINCENT RICHARDS & HIS ORCHESTRA:

Cameo 9024, 9040, 9045, 9072, 9082, 9086, 9093, 9101, 9138, 9161, 9184, 9199, 9212, 9249, 9272	7.00 -	12.00
Romeo 828, 844, 849, 876, 884, 888, 895, 903, 940, 963, 986, 1001, 1014, 1051, 1074	7.00 -	12.00

DICK RICHARDSON & HIS BAND/ORCHESTRA:

Parlophone PNY-34091 *Dancing With Tears In My Eyes*	30.00 -	50.00
PNY-34092 *Promises*	25.00 -	35.00
PNY-34129 *Out Of Breath*	50.00 -	75.00
PNY-34130 *I Am Only Human After All*	30.00 -	50.00

INEZ RICHARDSON:

Black Swan 2023 *My June Love*	40.00 -	70.00

BUD RICHIE & HIS BOYS:

Champion 16109 *Slappin' The Bass*	75.00 -	100.00
40010 *Rockin' Chair*	25.00 -	40.00

HARRY RICHMAN:

Banner 1510 *No Hot Water*	20.00 -	30.00
Brunswick 4677 *Puttin' On The Ritz*	8.00 -	12.00
Brunswick, most other issues	7.00 -	12.00
Columbia 2701-D *I Love A Parade*	10.00 -	15.00
2965-D *When Love Comes Swinging Along*	15.00 -	20.00
2995-D *June In January*	15.00 -	20.00
3017-D *According To The Moonlight*	15.00 -	20.00
Decca 700 *Let's Go*	15.00 -	20.00
701 *There'll Be No South*	15.00 -	20.00
Vocalion 15457 *Susie's "Feller"*	10.00 -	15.00
15511 *Blue Skies*	10.00 -	15.00
15540 *Moonbeam, Kiss Her For Me*	10.00 -	15.00
15560 *Rosy Cheeks*	10.00 -	15.00
15725 *Out Of The Dawn*	15.00 -	25.00

BOB RICKETT'S BAND:

Gennett 5156 *Mean Mean Mama*	30.00 -	50.00

THE RIFFERS:

Columbia 14677-D *Rhapsody In Love*	100.00 -	150.00

MIKE RILEY, EDDIE FARLEY & THEIR ONYX CLUB BOYS:

Decca 578 *The Music Goes 'Round And 'Round*	8.00 -	12.00
619 *I Never Knew*	10.00 -	15.00
641 *Blue Clarinet Stomp*	10.00 -	15.00
683, 684, 994, 1031, 1041, 1263, 1271, 1655, 1662	7.00 -	12.00

JUSTIN RING & HIS OKEH ORCHESTRA:

Okeh 40869 *Miss Annabelle Lee*	15.00 -	25.00
40919 *Together, We Two*	10.00 -	15.00
40945 *Away Down South In Heaven*	10.00 -	15.00
40972 *My Ohio Home*	10.00 -	15.00
40991 *There Must Be A Silver Lining*	10.00 -	15.00
41295 *True Blue Lou*	15.00 -	20.00

JOHNNY RINGER'S ROSEMONT ORCHESTRA:

Gennett 6183 *Buffalo Rhythm*	100.00 -	150.00
6199 *Swamp Blues*	125.00 -	175.00
6264 *Moonlit Waters*	75.00 -	100.00
6280 *The Varsity Drag*	75.00 -	100.00

ARTHUR RIVER'S NOVELTY ORCHESTRA:

Clarion 5422-C *Red-Headed Baby*	15.00 -	20.00
5443-C *Yes, Indeedy (She Do)*	15.00 -	20.00

VINCENT RIZZO AND HIS HOTEL SYLVANIA ORCHESTRA OF PHILADELPHIA:

Okeh 40130, 40135, 40291, 40356, 40609	7.00 -	12.00
40725 *Clap Yo' Hands*	10.00 -	15.00

ROANE'S PENNSYLVANIANS:

Victor 22919 *Chinatown, My Chinatown*	15.00 -	20.00
22922 *Between The Devil And The Deep Blue Sea*	10.00 -	15.00
24036 *Goodbye Blues*	10.00 -	15.00

EVERETT ROBBINS & HIS SYNCOPATING ROBBINS:

Autograph (unnumbered) You Didn't Want Me When I Wanted You	-	-

JOSEPH ROBECHAUX & HIS NEW ORLEANS RHYTHM BOYS:

Vocalion 2539 *King Kong Stomp*	30.00 -	50.00
2540 *Lazy Bones*	25.00 -	40.00

2545 *Jig Music*	25.00 -	40.00
2575 *Ring Dem Bells*	25.00 -	40.00
2592 *Shake It And Break It*	30.00 -	50.00
2610 *Why Should I Cry For You?*	25.00 -	40.00
2646 *Zola*	30.00 -	50.00
2796 *Foot Scuffle*	30.00 -	50.00
2827 *Every Tub*	30.00 -	50.00
2881 *Just Like A Falling Star*	25.00 -	40.00

ORLANDO ROBERSON:
Variety 513 *Just A Quiet Evening* ......10.00 - 15.00

CLIFF ROBERTS' (DANCE) ORCHESTRA:
Cameo 9020 *That's How I Feel About You, Sweetheart*
........8.00 - 12.00
9032 *The Sun Is At My Window* ......15.00 - 25.00
9127, 9138, 9145, 9165, 9193, 9200, 9201, 9260,
9263, 9303 ....7.00 - 12.00
Regal 10117 *Rough House Rosie* ......10.00 - 15.00
Romeo 836 *The Sun Is At My Window* ......15.00 - 25.00
824, 929, 940, 947, 967, 995, 1002, 1003, 1062,
1065, 1111 ....7.00 - 12.00

GLENN ROBERTS & HIS ORCHESTRA:
Champion 15476 *Happy Go Lucky Lane* ......15.00 - 20.00
15478 *Speedy Boy* ......15.00 - 20.00

(HAROLD) ROBERTS' GOLDEN STATE ORCHESTRA OF HOLLYWOOD:
Hollywood 1019 *Old Timers' Waltz* ......10.00 - 15.00
Sunset 1110 *Ah-Ha!* ......15.00 - 20.00

DICK ROBERTSON (& HIS ORCHESTRA):
Brunswick 4367 *Some Sweet Day* ......15.00 - 20.00
Champion 40077 *Moon Over Miami* ......10.00 - 15.00
40078 *With All My Heart* ......10.00 - 15.00
40087 *Lights Out* ......10.00 - 15.00
40088 *Alone* ......8.00 - 12.00
40092 *But Where Are You?* ......8.00 - 12.00
40093 *I'd Rather Lead A Band* ......8.00 - 12.00
40104 *Welcome Stranger* ......8.00 - 12.00
40105 *Is It True What They Say About Dixie?* ......8.00 - 12.00
40106 *The Touch Of Your Lips* ......8.00 - 12.00
40111 *Robins And Roses* ......8.00 - 12.00
40116 *The Glory Of Love* ......8.00 - 12.00
40117 *She Shall Have Music* ......8.00 - 12.00
40118 *On The Beach At Bali Bali* ......8.00 - 12.00
Crown 3211, 3213, 3427, 3428, 3438, 3440, 3491 ...7.00 - 12.00
Decca 1125, 1131, 1169, 1181, 1209, 1215, 1260,
1283, 1334, 1335, 1367, 1374, 1407, 1415, 1436,
1487,1498, 1511, 1512, 1536, 1585, 1599, 1601,
1619, 1620 ....7.00 - 10.00
Decca, most other issues (blue label) ......5.00 - 8.00
Edison 52194 *I Must Be Dreaming* ......15.00 - 25.00
52379 *Ten Little Miles From Town* ......20.00 - 30.00
52473 *She's Funny That Way* ......25.00 - 40.00
52521 *The Song I Love* ......25.00 - 40.00
52551 *If I Had You* ......25.00 - 40.00
Melotone 12082 *Would You like To Take A Walk?* ...8.00 - 12.00
12162 *Moonlight Saving Time* ......8.00 - 12.00
12163 *I Wanna Sing About You* ......8.00 - 12.00
12408 *Holding My Honey's Hand* ......8.00 - 12.00
12417 *West Bound Freight* ......10.00 - 15.00
12418 *Bull Fiddle Blues* ......10.00 - 15.00

ROBINSON'S KNIGHTS OF REST:
Champion 16607 *Mean Baby Blues* ......250.00 - up

BILL ROBINSON:
Brunswick 4535 *Doin' The New Low Down* ......10.00 - 15.00
6134 *Keep A Song In Your Soul* ......15.00 - 20.00
6520 *Doin' The New Low Down* ......10.00 - 15.00

BOB ROBINSON & HIS BOB CATS; BOB ROBINSON TRIO:
Titles, issued contemporaneously on Banner, Melotone, Oriole,
Perfect, Romeo, and Vocalion: *Crying For Love; Heart-Breaking Blues* ......15.00 - 25.00
Bluebird 6929 *She's A Mellow Thing* ......15.00 - 20.00
7898 *Down In The Alley* ......15.00 - 20.00

ELZADIE ROBINSON:
Paramount 12417 *Barrel House Man* ......100.00 - 150.00
12420 *Houston Bound* ......150.00 - 250.00
12469 *Baltimore Blues* ......125.00 - 175.00
12509 *Whiskey Blues* ......125.00 - 175.00
12544 *Tick-Tock Blues* ......125.00 - 175.00
12573 *St. Louis Cyclone Blues* ......150.00 - 200.00
12627 *Love Crazy Blues* ......150.00 - 200.00
12635 *Elzadie's Policy Blues* ......200.00 - 300.00
12676 *Mad Blues* ......150.00 - 200.00
12689 *Wicked Daddy* ......125.00 - 175.00
12701 *Arkansas Mill Blues* ......125.00 - 175.00
12724 *Rowdy Man Blues* ......125.00 - 175.00
12745 *Unsatisfied Blues* ......125.00 - 175.00
12768 *Cheatin' Daddy* ......125.00 - 175.00
12795 *My Pullman Porter Man* ......125.00 - 175.00
12900 *Driving Me South* ......150.00 - 200.00

("BANJO") IKEY ROBINSON & HIS (BULL FIDDLE) BAND/WINDY CITY FIVE:
Brunswick 4963 *Got Butter On It* ......200.00 - up
4964 *Rock Me Mama* ......150.00 - 250.00
7052 *Rock Pile Blues* ......150.00 - 250.00
7057 *Got Butter On It* ......200.00 - up
7059 *Rock Me Mama* ......150.00 - 200.00
7068 *Without A Dime* ......150.00 - 250.00
Champion 40011 *Swing It* ......20.00 - 30.00
50073 *Sunshine* ......20.00 - 30.00
Decca 7430 *Scrunch-Lo* ......20.00 - 30.00
7650 *Sunshine* ......20.00 - 30.00

ROB ROBINSON (AND MEADE LUX LEWIS):
Paramount 13028 *I Got Some Of That* ......200.00 - 300.00
13030 *Don't Put That Thing* ......200.00 - 300.00
13064 *I Don't Want It Now* ......200.00 - 300.00

CARSON ROBISON'S KANSAS CITY JACKRABBITS/ MADCAPS; THE CARSON ROBISON ORCHESTRA:
Edison (thin) 14085 *Nonsense* (possibly unissued) ... - - -
Okeh 41389 *Nothin'* ......25.00 - 40.00
Victor V-38074 *Nonsense* ......40.00 - 60.00

WILLARD ROBISON (& HIS ORCHESTRA); WILLARD ROBISON'S DEEP RIVER FOUR:
Autograph 600 *The Rhythm Rag* ......200.00 - up
601 *Out Of The South* ......200.00 - up
603 *Peaceful Valley* ......200.00 - up
Columbia 1818-D *Head Low* ......15.00 - 20.00
Pathe-Actuelle (titles as on Perfect, following)
Perfect 12280 *Deep River Blues* ......15.00 - 20.00
12285 *The Devil Is Afraid Of Music* ......15.00 - 20.00

12287 *Why Do Ya Roll Those Eyes?*	10.00 -	15.00
12294 *Hugs And Kisses*	10.00 -	15.00
12303 *Harlem Blues*	15.00 -	20.00
12307 *Truthful Parson Brown*	15.00 -	20.00
12311 *Clap Yo' Hands*	10.00 -	15.00
12318 *That G-String Melody*	15.00 -	20.00
12322 *Yellow Dog Blues*	15.00 -	25.00
12337 *Muddy Water*	15.00 -	20.00
12341 *Beale Street Blues*	20.00 -	30.00
12353 *Lazy Weather*	15.00 -	20.00
12412 *In The Sing Song Sycamore Tree*	20.00 -	30.00
12428 *'tain't So, Honey, 'tain't So*	20.00 -	30.00
Perfect 14727 *Just A Little Longer*	10.00 -	15.00
14729 *Hello Bluebird*	8.00 -	12.00
14747 *Take In The Sun, Hang Out The Moon*	8.00 -	12.00
14756 *There Ain't No "Maybe" In My Baby's Eyes*	10.00 -	15.00
14803 *Rosy Cheeks*	10.00 -	15.00
14805 *The More We Are Together*	8.00 -	12.00
14807 *Where The Wild, Wild Flowers Grow*	8.00 -	12.00
14811 *At Sundown*	8.00 -	12.00
14812 *Hallelujah*	8.00 -	12.00
14813 *Just Like A Butterfly*	8.00 -	12.00
14814 *You Know I Love You*	8.00 -	12.00
14815 *Just The Same*	8.00 -	12.00
14819 *Lazy Weather*	8.00 -	12.00
14827 *I'm Coming, Virginia*	10.00 -	15.00
14834 *Dew-Dew-Dewy Day*	10.00 -	15.00
14836 *Flaperette*	8.00 -	12.00
14844 *No Wonder I'm Happy*	10.00 -	15.00
14849 *Blue River*	10.00 -	15.00
14850 *Bye Bye Pretty Baby*	10.00 -	15.00
14852 *Havana*	10.00 -	15.00
14859 *Fallen Leaf*	8.00 -	12.00
14873 *Manhattan Mary*	8.00 -	12.00
14875 *My Blue Heaven*	8.00 -	12.00
14878 *There's A Cradle In Caroline*	8.00 -	12.00
14883 *Together (We Two)*	8.00 -	12.00
14891 *Make My Cot Where The Cot-Cot-Cotton Grows*	10.00 -	15.00
14895 *Go Home And Tell Your Mother*	8.00 -	12.00
14903 *Cobblestones*	8.00 -	12.00
14905 *I'm More Than Satisfied*	100.00 -	150.00

14907 *Lovely Lady*	15.00 -	20.00
14908 *I Fell Head Over Heels In Love*	8.00 -	12.00
14925 *Thou Swell*	15.00 -	20.00
14931 *Who's Blue Now*	8.00 -	12.00
14934 *Everywhere You Go*	8.00 -	12.00
14938 *There Must Be A Silver Lining*	8.00 -	12.00
14940 *My Blue Ridge Mountain Home*	8.00 -	12.00
14942 *I Just Roll Along*	15.00 -	20.00
14946 *I Can't Help Lovin' Dat Man*	10.00 -	15.00

14952 *Luscious*	8.00 -	12.00
14953 *So Tired*	8.00 -	12.00
14963 *I Love My Old Fashioned Man*	20.00 -	30.00
14972 *Rag Doll*	8.00 -	12.00
14977 *Japanese Sandman*	15.00 -	20.00
(Foregoing titles on Pathe-Actuelle are similarly valued)		
Supertone 36753 *Everywhere You Go*	8.00 -	12.00

TOM ROCK & HIS ORCHESTRA:

Odeon ONY-36157 *I'll Be Blue, Just Thinking Of You*	25.00 -	35.00
ONY-36158 *A Peach Of A Pair*	25.00 -	35.00
ONY-36159 *My Love For You*	20.00 -	30.00
ONY-36164 *The Little Things In Life*	25.00 -	35.00
ONY-36179 *Would You Like To Take A Walk?*	25.00 -	35.00

ROCKY MOUNTAIN TRIO:

Gennett 3002 *Freakish Blues*	25.00 -	35.00
3184 *Grand Opera Blues*	35.00 -	50.00
3288 *Blowin' Off Steam*	35.00 -	50.00

GENE RODEMICH & HIS ORCHESTRA:

Brunswick 2480 *St. Louis Tickle*	10.00 -	15.00
2599 *Tenth Interval Rag*	10.00 -	15.00
2389, 2398, 2455, 2474, 2527, 2558, 2616, 2731, 2760, 2843, 2892, 3073	7.00 -	12.00
Brunswick (most other issues)	5.00 -	8.00

IKE RODGERS (& HIS BIDDLE STREET BOYS):

Broadway 5081 *It Hurts So Good*	150.00 -	200.00
Brunswick 7086 *Malt Can Blues*	150.00 -	250.00
Paramount 12816 *It Hurts So Good*	200.00 -	300.00

GIL RODIN & HIS ORCHESTRA; GIL RODIN'S BOYS:

Titles issued contemporaneously on Banner, Conqueror, Melotone, Oriole, Perfect, and Romeo: *Love's Serenade; Restless; Right About Face; What's The Reason*	8.00 -	12.00
Another title, on Banner, Conqueror, Domino, and Regal: *It's So Good*	15.00 -	20.00
Crown 3016 *If I Could Be With You One Hour Tonight*	30.00 -	50.00
3017 *Beale Street Blues*	50.00 -	75.00
3045 *Ninety-Nine Out Of A Hundred Wanna Be Loved*	20.00 -	30.00
3046 *Hello, Beautiful*	30.00 -	50.00

BUDDY ROGERS (AND HIS CALIFORNIA CAVLIERS); CHARLES "BUDDY" ROGERS:

Columbia 2143-D *Sweepin' The Clouds Away*	15.00 -	20.00
2183-D *My Future Just Passed*	15.00 -	20.00
Victor 24001 *You Fascinate Me*	10.00 -	15.00
24015 *In My Hideaway*	10.00 -	15.00
24031 *I Beg Your Pardon, Madamoiselle*	10.00 -	15.00
24049 *Please Handle With Care*	10.00 -	15.00

GINGER ROGERS:

Bluebird 7981 *I Used To Be Color Blind*	10.00 -	15.00
Decca 638 *Eeny, Meeny, Miney Mo*	8.00 -	12.00
DA-376 (set of three 12-inch records: Decca 29142, 29143, 29144) *Alice In Wonderland* (in album)	25.00 -	40.00

MACK ROGERS & HIS GUNTER HOTEL ORCHESTRA:

Bluebird 5603 *Casa Loma Stomp*	15.00 -	20.00
5635 *Here Comes The Show Boat*	15.00 -	20.00
5601, 5829, 5830	7.00 -	10.00

RODNEY ROGERS RED PEPPERS:
Brunswick 3744 *Milenberg Joys* ....7.00 -   10.00

WILL ROGERS:
Victor 45347 *A New Slant On War* ....12.00 -   16.00
  45369 *Will Rogers Nominates Henry Ford For President*
  ....15.00 -   20.00
  45374 *Will Rogers Talks To The Bankers* ....15.00 -   20.00

B.A. ROLFE & HIS LUCKY STRIKE DANCE/PALAIS D'OR ORCHESTRA:
Edison 10008 (24-minute Long-Playing) *The Merry Widow*
  selections, etc. ....50.00 - 100.00
Edison 14003 *Fioretta* ....40.00 -   60.00
  14006 *Mean To Me* ....50.00 -   75.00
  14012 *Am I Blue?* ....50.00 -   75.00
  14020 *Spanish Doll* ....50.00 -   75.00
  14033 *The Flippity Flop* ....50.00 -   75.00
  14048 *Why Can't You?* ....50.00 -   75.00
  14049 *Do What You Do!* ....50.00 -   75.00
  14050 *Little Pal* ....50.00 -   75.00
  14055 *Singin' In The Rain* ....50.00 -   75.00
  14059 *Wouldn't It Be Wonderful?* ...50.00 -   75.00
  14068 *Won't You Give In?* ....50.00 -   75.00
  14069 *Lonely Troubadour* ....50.00 -   75.00
  14079 *Here Am I* (possibly unissued) .....-   -   -
  14082 *Without A Song* (possibly unissued) ......-   -   -
  14084 *Sympathy* (possibly unissued) .....-   -   -
(Note: Foregoing are the "thin", "Needle Type Electric" Edison
  records.)
  51750 *What Good Is Good Morning?* ....12.00 -   16.00
  51757 *Bye Bye Blackbird* ....12.00 -   16.00
  51761 *Blue Bonnet-You Make Me Feel Blue* ......12.00 -   16.00
  51772 *Roses Remind Me Of You* ....12.00 -   16.00
  51782 *Only You And Lonely Me* ....12.00 -   16.00
  51790 *Crazy Quilt* ....15.00 -   20.00
  51797 *Wondering Why* ....25.00 -   40.00
  51799 *Barcelona* ....30.00 -   50.00
  51810 *And Then I Forget* ....12.00 -   16.00
  51814 *Ain't We Carryin' On?* ....30.00 -   50.00
  51817 *The One I'm Looking For* .....12.00 -   16.00
  51821 *Oo-gle Oo-gle-Ee* ....12.00 -   16.00
  51828 *Trudy* ....12.00 -   16.00
  51829 *Who Are You Vamping Tonight?* ....30.00 -   50.00
  51840 *Zoubeeda* ....12.00 -   16.00
  51848 *Why Do Ya Roll Those Eyes?* ....40.00 -   60.00
  51866 *Chinese Moon* ....12.00 -   16.00
  51872 *Stars (Are The Windows Of Heaven)* ....12.00 -   16.00
  51888 *No One But You Knows How To Love* .....15.00 -   20.00
  51890 *My Baby's Back* ....25.00 -   40.00
  51925 *One Alone* ....12.00 -   16.00
  51954 *It's O.K., Katy, With Me* ....12.00 -   16.00
  51972 *You're The One For Me* ....12.00 -   16.00
  52002 *There's Everything Nice About You* ......15.00 -   25.00
  52013 *Some Other Day* ....15.00 -   25.00
  52015 *Oh! Isabella* ....15.00 -   25.00
  52037 *Buffalo Rhythm* ....50.00 -   75.00
  52047 *Sax Appeal* ....20.00 -   30.00
  52049 *Magnolia* ....25.00 -   35.00
  52057 *Gonna Get A Girl* ....25.00 -   35.00
  52059 *S-L-U-E-F-O-O-T* ....75.00 - 100.00
  52094 *It Was Only A Sun Shower* ......20.00 -   30.00
  52105 *A Siren Dream* ....50.00 -   75.00
  52107 *Just A Memory* ....20.00 -   30.00

  52124 *Wherever You Are* ....20.00 -   30.00
  52130 *Playground In The Sky* ....20.00 -   30.00
  52132 *Down South* ....20.00 -   30.00
  52155 *Among My Souvenirs* ....20.00 -   30.00
  52166 *Singapore Sorrows* ....30.00 -   50.00
  52168 *When The Robert E. Lee Comes To Town* ...30.00 -   50.00
  52202 *Maybe I'll Baby You* ....20.00 -   30.00
  52210 *My Heart Stood Still* ....25.00 -   35.00
  52223 *Can't Help Lovin' Dat Man* ....25.00 -   35.00
  52239 *My Blue Ridge Mountain Home* ....35.00 -   50.00
  52244 *Louisiana Bo Bo* ....50.00 -   75.00
  52261 *What'll I Do If The Mississippi Goes Dry?*
  ....35.00 -   50.00
  52268 *Hiding In The Corner Of Your Smile* ......35.00 -   50.00
  52295 *St. Louis Blues* ....50.00 -   75.00
  52300 *She Didn't Say "Yes", She Didn't Say "No"*
  ....35.00 -   50.00
  52319 *Deep Hollow* ....50.00 -   75.00
  52321 *Tomorrow* ....75.00 - 100.00
  52326 *When Sweet Susie Goes Steppin' By* ......40.00 -   60.00
  52342 *Georgie Porgie* ....40.00 -   60.00
  52343 *That's My Weakness Now* ....40.00 -   60.00
  52353 *No Parking* ....40.00 -   60.00
  52366 *Pell Street Bells* ....30.00 -   50.00
  52402 *It Must Be Love* ....50.00 -   75.00
  52424 *Where Were You-Where Was I?* ....40.00 -   60.00
  52445 *Woman Disputed* ....40.00 -   60.00
  52455 *Blue Night* ....40.00 -   60.00
  52462 *A Room With A View* ....50.00 -   75.00
  52474 *Makin' Whoopee* ....50.00 -   75.00
  52480 *A Love Tale of Alsace-Lorraine* ....40.00 -   60.00
  52505 *Let's Do It* ....50.00 -   80.00
  52515 *I'll Get By* ....50.00 -   80.00
  52531 *If I Had You* ....50.00 -   80.00
  52548 *Hello Sweetie* ....40.00 -   60.00
  52584 *Mean To Me* ....50.00 -   80.00
  52597 *Spanish Doll* ....40.00 -   60.00
  52604 *Birmingham Bertha* ....75.00 - 100.00
  52626 *Singin' In The Rain* ....75.00 - 100.00
  52640 *Liza (All The Clouds'll Roll Away)* ....50.00 -   80.00
  52645 *Why Can't You?* ....75.00 - 100.00

THE ROLLICKERS:
Edison 52158 *I Scream-You Scream- We All Scream For Ice Cream*
  ....25.00 -   40.00
  52183 *Wait A Little Longer, Love Bird* ....15.00 -   20.00
  52188 *Ev'rybody Loves My Girl* ....15.00 -   20.00
  52213 *Auf Widerseh'n* ....20.00 -   30.00
  52246 *Oh! Miss Hannah* ....20.00 -   30.00
  52279 *Southern Skies* ....20.00 -   30.00
  52331 *Ready For The River* ....25.00 -   35.00
  52358 *Ol' Man River* ....25.00 -   40.00
  52397 *Pickin' Cotton* ....25.00 -   35.00
  52494 *Comin' Home* ....25.00 -   35.00
  52522 *Out-O'-Town Gal* ....25.00 -   40.00
  52544 *Yo Te Amo* ....25.00 -   40.00
  52600 *Lonely Little Cinderella* ....40.00 -   60.00

ADRIAN ROLLINI & HIS ORCHESTRA/QUINTET/TRIO:
Titles issued contemporaneously on Banner, Conqueror, Melotone, Oriole, Perfect, and Romeo: *Ah! But Is It Love?; And So, Goodbye; Beloved; By A Waterfall; Coffee In The Morning And Kisses In The Night; Dream On; Got The Jitters; Have You Ever Been Lonely?; Hustlin' And Bustlin' For Baby; If I Had*

Somebody To Love; I Gotta Get Up And Go To Work; I'll Be Faithful; I Raised My Hat; Ol' Pappy; On The Wrong Side Of The Fence; Savage Serenade; Sittin' On A Backyard Fence; Sittin' On A Log; Song Of Surrender; Sweet Madness; Who Walks In When I Walk Out?; You Must Believe Me; You've Got Everything; You've Got Me Cryin' Again ....15.00 - 20.00
Decca 265 *Sugar* ....15.00 - 20.00
   359 *Davenport Blues* ....15.00 - 20.00
   787 *Tap Room Swing* ....8.00 - 12.00
   807 *Swing Low* ....8.00 - 12.00
   1132 *Vibrollini* ....10.00 - 15.00
   1157 *Rebound* ....10.00 - 15.00
   1638 *Bei Mir Bist Du Schoen* ....8.00 - 12.00
   1639 *Josephine* ....8.00 - 12.00
   1654 *True Confession* ....8.00 - 12.00
   1973 *Singin' The Blues* ....8.00 - 12.00
Master 114 *Slap That Bass* ....12.00 - 16.00
Okeh 5200 *Moonglow* ....8.00 - 12.00
   5376 *Diga Diga Doo* ....8.00 - 12.00
   5435 *Dark Eyes* ....8.00 - 12.00
   5582 *Honky Tonk Train Blues* ....8.00 - 12.00
   5621 *Dardanella* ....8.00 - 12.00
   5979 *Isle Of Capri* ....5.00 - 12.00
Vocalion 2672 *A Thousand Goodnights* ....15.00 - 25.00
   2673 *Waitin' At The Gate For Katy* ....15.00 - 25.00
   2675 *A Hundred Years From Today* ....15.00 - 25.00
   4212 *Small Fry* ....8.00 - 12.00
   4257 *On The Bumpy Road To Love* ....8.00 - 12.00
   5200 *Pavanne* ....8.00 - 12.00
   5376 *Diga Diga Doo* ....8.00 - 12.00
   5435 *Estrellita* ....8.00 - 12.00
WOR Feature 1006 *Hesitation Blues* ....15.00 - 20.00

TODD ROLLINS AND HIS ORCHESTRA:
Titles issued contemporaneously on Banner, Melotone, Oriole, Perfect, and Romeo: *The Boogie Man; Christmas Night In Harlem; Fare Thee Well To Harlem; Get Goin'; Jimmy Had A Nickel; Jungle Fever; Junk Man; Moon Country; Take A Lesson From The Lark* ....10.00 - 15.00
Romeo 2222 *Let's Go Places And Do Things* ....15.00 - 20.00

ROMANCE OF HARMONY ORCHESTRA:
Gennett 20068 *Blue Evening Blues* ....35.00 - 50.00

PHIL ROMANO AND HIS ORCHESTRA:
Victor 19803 *I'm Goin' Out If Lizzie Comes In* ......10.00 - 15.00

MICKEY ROONEY:
MacGregor 10/11 *Let The Sunshine In/Flower Vase* - - -

THEODORE ROOSEVELT:
Victor 31872 *The Liberty Of The People* (12 inch, one-sided) ....15.00 - 30.00
   35249 (12-inch) *Abyssinian Treatment* ....15.00 - 30.00
   35250 (12-inch) *The Farmer And The Business Man* ....15.00 - 30.00

DAVID ROSE & HIS ORCHESTRA:
Bluebird 5708 *Jig-Saw Rhythm* ....15.00 - 20.00

VINCENT ROSE & HIS ORCHESTRA:
Titles issued contemporaneously on Banner, Conqueror, Melotone, Oriole, Perfect, and Romeo: *Learning; Stars Fell On Alabama* ....15.00 - 25.00
Additional titles: *My Dog Loves Your Dog; Nasty Man; Without That Gal* ....10.00 - 15.00

Victor 19379 *String Beans* ....8.00 - 12.00
   19398 *Helen Gone* ....10.00 - 15.00
   19511 *Sadie (You Are The Lady For Me)* ....10.00 - 15.00
   19513 *Montmartre* ....15.00 - 20.00
   19515 *Since You've Been Gone* ....8.00 - 12.00

ROSELAND DANCE ORCHESTRA:
Ajax 17119 *Where's My Sweetie Hiding?* ....10.00 - 20.00
Banner 6129 *There's A Rickety Rackety Shack* ......15.00 - 20.00
   6154 *Sorry* ....15.00 - 20.00
Domino 3441 *Araby* ....10.00 - 15.00
   3445 *I'll See You In My Dreams* ....10.00 - 15.00
   3492 *All Aboard For Heaven* ....7.00 - 10.00

TIMME ROSENKRANTZ & HIS BARRELHOUSE BARONS:
Victor 25876, 25883 ....7.00 - 12.00

HARRY ROSENTHAL & HIS ORCHESTRA:
Columbia 2982-D *Say When* ....20.00 - 30.00
   2986-D *You're The Top* ....20.00 - 30.00
   3016-D *The Hunkadola* ....10.00 - 15.00
   3019-D *My Heart Is An Open Book* ....8.00 - 12.00

ROSE ROOM ORCHESTRA:
Titles, issued contemporaneously on Banner, Conqueror, Domino, and Regal: *Get Yourself A Sweetie and Kiss Your Troubles Away; Glad Rag Doll; Glorianna; How About Me?; I'm In Love With Someone; It Must Be Love; I've Got A Feeling I'm Falling; My Inspiration Is You; My Lucky Star; My Man; She's Got Great Ideas; Sweetheart's Holiday (sic); Waiting At The End Of The Road* ....7.00 - 12.00
Banner 6205 *Glorianna* ....15.00 - 25.00
   6206 *It Must Be Love* ....15.00 - 25.00
Domino 4290 *I Want To Be Bad* ....10.00 - 15.00
Regal 8767 *Pretty Little Thing* ....8.00 - 12.00

ARTHUR ROSS AND HIS WESTERNERS:
Harmony 701-H *Moonlight Madness* ....7.00 - 10.00
   709-H *Jo-Anne* ....8.00 - 12.00
   723-H *Take Your Tomorrow* ....10.00 - 15.00
   748-H *Where The Shy Little Violets Grow* ....8.00 - 12.00
   777-H *Won't You Tell Me, Hon* ....8.00 - 12.00
   793-H *A Room With A View* ....7.00 - 10.00
   874-H *The One That I Love Loves Me* ......8.00 - 12.00
   891-H *My Sin* ....7.00 - 10.00
   892-H *She's My Girl (Oh! What A Diff'rence That Makes)* ....15.00 - 20.00
   913-H *Do Something* ....8.00 - 12.00
   926-H *Alabamy Snow* ....8.00 - 12.00
(Note: Above titles also issued on Diva, Puritone, and Velvet Tone.)

ROSS DE LUXE SYNCOPATORS:
Victor 20952 *Mary Bell* ....75.00 - 100.00
   20961 *Skad-O-Lee* ....75.00 - 100.00
   21077 *Monia* ....75.00 - 100.00
   21537 *Believe Me, Dear* ....75.00 - 100.00

THE ROUNDERS:
Titles, issued contemporaneously on Conqueror, Domino, Regal: *Ain't Misbehavin'; Broadway Melody; Down Among The Sugar Cane; I'm On The Crest Of A Wave; Lovable And Sweet; Too Busy; When My Dreams Come True; Where The Shy Little Violets Grow* ....7.00 - 12.00
Another title: *Rainbow Man* ....10.00 - 15.00

THE ROVING ROMEOS:
Romeo 291 *If My Baby Cooks (As Good As She Looks)*
....8.00 - 12.00

ROYAL DANCE ORCHESTRA:
Broadway 1297 *I Want To Meander In The Meadow*....7.00 - 10.00
    1467 *Just A Blue-Eyed Blonde* ....8.00 - 12.00

ROYAL RHYTHM BOYS:
Decca 2830 *In A Shanty In Old Shanty Town* ....10.00 - 15.00
    7759 *Blue Skies* ....10.00 - 15.00

ROYAL TROUBADOURS:
Gennett 3231, 3232, 3257, 3278, 3281, 3287,
    3346, 3388, 3390 ....7.00 - 12.00
Gennett 3340 *When The Red, Red Robin Comes Bob-Bob-Bobbin'*
    Along ....10.00 - 15.00
    3341 *Unexpected Papa* ....10.00 - 15.00
    3359 *Nothing Else Matters But Love* ....15.00 - 20.00
Harmony 420-H, 465-H, 477-H, 494-H, 498-H ....7.00 - 10.00
(Note: Titles on Harmony may also be found on Diva and Velvet
    Tone, similarly valued.)

RUTH ROYE:
Columbia 63-D *Big-Hearted Bennie* ....10.00 - 15.00
    A3714 *I'm Askin' Ye Ain't It The Truth* ....10.00 - 15.00
    A3881 *Hotsy Totsy Town* ....10.00 - 15.00

DAVE RUBINOFF:
Perfect 14483 *Fiddlin' The Fiddle* ....12.00 - 16.00
    14502 *Strad' Blues* ....12.00 - 16.00
    14518 *Feelin' Kind Of Blue*...............................12.00 - 16.00
(Note: Above titles on Pathe-Actuelle are similarly valued.)

RUSSELL'S ROVING REVELERS:
Champion 15701 *Alfalfa* ....40.00 - 60.00

BUD RUSSELL & HIS BAND:
Champion 15909 *H'lo Baby* ....8.00 - 12.00

LUIS RUSSELL & HIS BURNING EIGHT/ORCHESTRA; (LUIS) RUSSELL'S HEEBIE JEEBIE STOMPERS/HOT SIX:
Titles issued contemporaneously on Banner, Melotone, Oriole,
    Perfect, and Romeo: *At The Darktown Strutters' Ball; Ghost Of*
    The Freaks; Hokus Pocus; My Blue Heaven; Ol' Man River,
    Primitive ....25.00 - 40.00
Melotone 12000 *I Got Rhythm* ....20.00 - 30.00
Okeh 8424 *Plantation Joys* ....250.00 - up
    8454 *Sweet Mumtaz* ....200.00 - 300.00
    8656 *The Call Of The Freaks* ....50.00 - 75.00
    8734 *Jersey Lightnin'* ....50.00 - 75.00
    8760 *Savoy Shout* ....75.00 - 100.00
    8766 *Feelin' The Spirit* ....50.00 - 75.00
    8780 *Saratoga Shout*......................................50.00 - 75.00
    8811 *Louisiana Swing*.....................................60.00 - 100.00
    8830 *Muggin' Lightly* ....60.00 - 100.00
    8849 *High Tension* ....60.00 - 100.00
Victor 22789 *Goin' To Town* ....40.00 - 70.00
    22793 *You Rascal, You* ....50.00 - 80.00
    22815 *Freakish Blues* ....50.00 - 80.00
Vocalion 1010 *29th And Dearborn* ....150.00 - 250.00
    1579 *Saratoga Drag* ....250.00 - up

PEE WEE RUSSELL's RHYTHMAKERS:
Hot Rhythm Society 17, 1000, 1001 ....7.00 - 12.00

RED RUSSELL'S RHYTHM:
Superior 2719 *Mood Indigo* ....100.00 - 150.00

TED RUSSELL & HIS ORCHESTRA:
Champion 40040 *I Wished On The Moon*..............10.00 - 15.00
    40041 *In The Middle Of A Kiss*........................10.00 - 15.00
    40042 *Rhythm Is Our Business* ....10.00 - 15.00
    40056 *Santa Claus Is Comin' To Town* ....10.00 - 15.00
    40057 *You Are My Lucky Star* ....10.00 - 15.00
    40066 *Here's To Romance* ....10.00 - 15.00
    40071 *I Found A Dream* ....10.00 - 15.00
    40072 *You Took My Breath Away* ....10.00 - 15.00
    40079 *I Fell Like A Feather In My Breeze* ....10.00 - 15.00
    40089 *Dinner For One, Please James* ....10.00 - 15.00
    40109 *Melody From The Sky* ....10.00 - 15.00
    40110 *Knick-Knacks On The Mantel* ....10.00 - 15.00

DAN RUSSO & HIS ORIOLE ORCHESTRA; DAN RUSSO & HIS ORIOLES:
Brunswick 4490 *I'm The Medicine Man For The Blues*
....10.00 - 15.00
    4622 *My Little Honey And Me* ....10.00 - 15.00
    4708 *'tain't No Sin* ....10.00 - 15.00
Columbia 2641-D *I'm A Ding Dong Daddy* ....15.00 - 20.00
    2647-D *Old MacDonald Had A Farm* ....15.00 - 20.00

RUSSO & FIORITO'S ORIOLE ORCHESTRA:
Victor 19917 *That Certain Party*............................8.00 - 12.00
    19924 *I Wish't I Was In Peoria* ....8.00 - 12.00
    19989 *Let's Talk About My Sweetie*...................10.00 - 15.00
    20015 *Nothing Else To Do But Sit Around And Think About You*
....10.00 - 15.00
    20046 *Sweet Southern Breeze* ....7.00 - 10.00

ST. LOUIS LEVEE BAND:
Okeh 8404 *Soap Suds* ....250.00 - up

ST. LOUIS RHYTHM KINGS:
Columbia 349-D *Papa De Da Da*..........................50.00 - 75.00

ST. LOUIS SYNCOPATORS:
Majestic 1431 *Way Down Yonder In New Orleans* 25.00 - 40.00
Olympic 1436 *Long Lost Mama* ....25.00 - 40.00
    1437 *The Snakes' Hips* ....25.00 - 40.00

HARRY SALTER & HIS ORCHESTRA:
Titles issued contemporaneously on Cameo, Lincoln, and Romeo:
    Sing Me A Song; Goodness Gracious Gracie; I Ain't Got Nothing
    For Nobody But You; I'm Just A Vagabond Lover; Poor People;
    We Were In The Moonlight ....5.00 - 10.00.

SAM 'N' HENRY (See CORRELL and GOSDEN)

EDGAR SAMPSON & HIS ORCHESTRA:
Vocalion 4942 *Pick Your Own Lick*......................10.00 - 15.00

JOSEPH SAMUELS' JAZZ BAND/ORCHESTRA; SAMUELS' JAZZ BAND:
Banner 1203 *That Red Head Gal* ....8.00 - 12.00
    1214 *I Ain't Never Had Nobody Crazy Over Me*. 8.00 - 12.00
Mastertone 1056 *Loose Feet* ....15.00 - 20.00
Odeon 20028 *Hey Paw!* ....10.00 - 15.00
    20087 *Dangerous Blues* ....10.00 - 15.00
Okeh 4122, 4124, 4166, 4167, 4220, 4233, 4252,
    4255, 4260, 4460, 4474 ....7.00 - 12.00
    4250 *Home Again Blues*..................................15.00 - 20.00
    4282 *Tropical Blues* ....10.00 - 15.00

4302 *I'm Nobody's Baby* ....8.00 - 12.00
4370 *Pullman Porter Blues* ....10.00 - 15.00
4453 *Mysterious Blues* ....10.00 - 15.00
4477 *I've Got My Habits On* ....10.00 - 15.00
4573 *13 I'm So Unlucky 13* ....15.00 - 25.00
4609 *Boo Hoo Hoo* ....10.00 - 15.00
4663 *Houston Blues* ....15.00 - 20.00
Perfect 14371 *Big Bad Bill Is Sweet William Now* .10.00 - 15.00

FRANKIE SANDERS & HIS ORCHESTRA:
Broadway 1455 *When I Take My Sugar To Tea* .... - - -

JOE SANDERS (AND HIS ORCHESTRA):
Decca 658, 659, 676, 692, 843, 850, 952, 955, 956 ...7.00 - 12.00
Victor 24033 *Intangibility* ....10.00 - 15.00

RED SANDERS AND HIS ORCHESTRA:
Gennett 3147 *What Could Be Sweeter Than You?* ....8.00 - 12.00
3148 *On The Bam Bam Bamy Shore* ....15.00 - 20.00
3166 *When You See That Aunt Of Mine* ....15.00 - 20.00
3178 *Show Me The Way To Go Home* ....10.00 - 15.00

JIMMY SAUTER'S NIGHT OWLS:
Gennett 6755 *Avalon Town* ....15.00 - 20.00
6769 *Glad Rag Doll* ....15.00 - 20.00

HELEN SAVAGE:
Brunswick 4536 *It's Bad For Your Soul* ....80.00 - 120.00

SAVANNAH NIGHT HAWKS:
Champion 15641 *Nightmare* ....150.00 - 250.00

SAVANNAH SIX:
Harmony 56-H *Hot Aire* ....20.00 - 30.00
58-H *Jacksonville Gal* ....15.00 - 25.00

SAVANNAH SYNCOPATORS:
Brunswick 3245 *Deep Henderson* ....25.00 - 40.00
3361 *Sugar Foot Stomp* ....25.00 - 40.00
3373 *Wa Wa Wa* ....20.00 - 30.00
6046 *Who's Blue?* ....40.00 - 60.00
6176 *Radio Rhythm* ....25.00 - 40.00
7124 *My Melancholy Baby* ....75.00 - 100.00

JAN SAVITT & HIS TOP HATTERS:
Bluebird 7281, 7283, 7295, 7490, 7493, 7504, 7593,
7595, 7607, 7666, 7670, 7679, 7733, 7737, 7748,
7783, 7786, 7797, 10005, 10013, 10018 ....7.00 - 10.00
Decca, blue label, most issues ....5.00 - 10.00
Variety 506 *How Could You?* ....8.00 - 12.00
542 *Supposing* ....8.00 - 12.00
585 *Cross Country Hop* ....8.00 - 12.00
Victor, most issues ....5.00 - 10.00

SAVOY BEARCATS:
Victor 20182 *Senegalese Stomp* ....50.00 - 75.00
20307 *Bearcat Stomp* ....50.00 - 75.00
20406 *Stampede* ....50.00 - 75.00

THE SCARE CROW:
Gennett 7209 *Traveling Blues* ....250.00 - up
7229 *Easy Creeping Mama* ....300.00 - up
7275 *The Scare Crow Ball* ....300.00 - up
(See the second section of this book for additional recordings by
THE SCARE CROW)

REX SCHEPP:
Autograph 630 *Russian Rag* ....50.00 - 100.00

ELMER SCHOEBEL & HIS FRIARS SOCIETY ORCHESTRA:
Brunswick 4652 *Copenhagen* ....30.00 - 50.00

ADRIAN SCHUBERT AND HIS (DANCE/SALON) ORCHESTRA:
Banner 0804 *Syncopated Jamboree* ....10.00 - 15.00
Crown 3086 *I'm The Last One Left on the Corner* 20.00 - 30.00
3129 *Moonlight Saving Time* ....10.00 - 15.00
3181 *This Is The Missus* ....10.00 - 15.00
3484 *I've Got To Sing A Torch Song* ....10.00 - 15.00
3004, 3007, 3011, 3034, 3052, 3062, 3066, 3087,
3088, 3110, 3135, 3151, 3164, 3178, 3191, 3206,
3207, 3225, 3226, 3245, 3257, 3258, 3269, 3274,
3282, 3303, 3316, 3318, 3335, 3348, 3350, 3359
3364, 3388, 3408, 3411, 3439, 3483, 3493, 3496,
3508 ....7.00 - 12.00
Domino 4606 *When Love Comes In The Moonlight*. 7.00 - 10.00
4609 *Living A Life Of Dreams* ....8.00 - 12.00

BERNIE SCHULTZ & HIS CRESCENT ORCHESTRA:
Gennett 6216 *Sweet Violets* ....30.00 - 50.00
6234 *Hold Everything* ....30.00 - 50.00
6235 *Show Me That Kind Of A Girl* ....40.00 - 60.00

ARTHUR SCHUTT (& HIS ORCHESTRA):
Harmony 860-H *Rambling In Rhythm* ....15.00 - 20.00
(Note: Above title on Diva or Velvet Tone is similarly valued.)
Okeh 41243 *Piano Puzzle* ....15.00 - 20.00
41345 *Take Everything But You* ....15.00 - 20.00
41346 *My Fate Is In Your Hands* ....15.00 - 20.00
41359 *Cryin' For The Carolines* ....15.00 - 25.00
41360 *I'm Following You!* ....20.00 - 30.00
41391 *The Moon Is Low* ....15.00 - 20.00
41392 *It Must Be You* ....15.00 - 20.00
41400 *'Leven-Thirty Saturday Night* ....25.00 - 40.00

BLUE SCOTT & HIS BLUE BOYS:
Bluebird 6520 *I Can Dish It- Can You Take It?* ....15.00 - 20.00
6557 *You Can't Lose* ....15.00 - 20.00

CECIL SCOTT & HIS BRIGHT BOYS/ORCHESTRA:
Victor V38098 *In A Corner* ....100.00 - 150.00
V38117 *Bright Boy Blues* ....100.00 - 150.00

LEONARD SCOTT:
Vocalion 03311 *She's Got Something Good*...........15.00 - 20.00

LLOYD SCOTT & HIS ORCHESTRA:
Victor 20495 *Happy Hour Blues* ....75.00 - 100.00
21491 *Harlem Shuffle* ....100.00 - 150.00

THE SCRANTON SIRENS ORCHESTRA:
Okeh 40297 *Why Should I Believe In You?* ....100.00 - 150.00
40329 *Common Street Blues* ....100.00 - 150.00

SEARCY TRIO:
Okeh 8360 *Kansas Avenue Blues*..........................80.00 - 120.00

SEATTLE HARMONY KINGS:
Victor 19772 *Darktown Shuffle* ....10.00 - 15.00
20133 *How Many Times?* ....10.00 - 15.00
20142 *Breezin' Along With The Breeze* ....10.00 - 15.00

GENE SEDRIC & HIS HONEY BEARS:
Vocalion 4552 *Choo Choo* ....12.00 - 16.00
4576 *The Joint Is Jumpin'* ....12.00 - 16.00

BLOSSOM SEELEY:

Columbia 114-D *Don't Mind The Rain* ....8.00 - 12.00
   136-D *Bringin' Home The Bacon* ....8.00 - 12.00
   304-D *Everybody Loves My Baby* ....7.00 - 10.00
   386-D *Yes Sir, That's My Baby* ....5.00 - 8.00
   613-D *Spanish Shawl* ....7.00 - 10.00

RAY SEELEY & HIS ORCHESTRA:

Odeon ONY-36106 *I Love You So Much* ....20.00 - 30.00
   ONY-36107 *Can I Help It?* ....20.00 - 30.00
   ONY-36192 *I Found What I Wanted In You* ......25.00 - 40.00
   ONY-36203 *I'm Crazy 'Bout My Baby* ....25.00 - 40.00

EMIL SEIDEL & HIS ORCHESTRA:

Gennett 6295 *The Best Things In Life Are Free* ......80.00 - 120.00
   6309 *Down South* ....40.00 - 60.00
   6324 *Together, We Two* ....25.00 - 35.00
   6327 *For My Baby* ....25.00 - 35.00
   6340 *One More Night* ....20.00 - 30.00
   6355 *Counting The Days* ....20.00 - 30.00
   6367 *Beautiful* ....25.00 - 35.00

BEN SELVIN & HIS ORCHESTRA:

Banner 1586 *Loud Speakin' Papa* ....10.00 - 15.00
Banner 1583, 1597, 1635 ....7.00 - 10.00
Brunswick 3172 *Betty* ....8.00 - 12.00
   3213 *Hoodle-Dee-Doo-Dee-Doo-Doo* ....8.00 - 12.00
Brunswick, most other issues ....5.00 - 10.00
Columbia 1274-D, 1285-D, 1321-D, 1399-D,
  1426-D, 1538-D, 1605-D, 1635-D, 1693-D,
  1702-D, 1751-D, 1800-D, 1831-D, 1900-D,
  1937-D, 1956-D, 1964-D, 2014-D, 2024-D,
  2077-D ....7.00 - 12.00
Columbia 2096-D *'tain't No Sin* ....8.00 - 12.00
   2116-D *Happy Days Are Here Again* ....8.00 - 12.00
   2150-D *Let Me Sing And I'm Happy* ....8.00 - 12.00
   2255-D *It's Easy To Fall In Love* ....8.00 - 12.00
   2287-D *Dixiana* ....8.00 - 12.00
   2323-D *My Man From Caroline* ....15.00 - 20.00
   2356-D *Cheerful Little Earful* ....15.00 - 20.00
   2366-D *Yours And Mine* ....15.00 - 20.00
   2381-D *Would You Like To Take A Walk?* ....10.00 - 15.00
   2400-D *99 Out Of A Hundred Wanna Be Loved* ... 10.00 - 15.00
   2421-D *Smile, Darn Ya, Smile* ....15.00 - 20.00
   2426-D *Lean To Croon* ....10.00 - 15.00
   2463-D *Now You're In My Arms* ....10.00 - 15.00
   2487-D *Let's Drink A Drink To The Future* ....10.00 - 15.00
   2491-D *Sing Another Chorus, Please* ....15.00 - 20.00
   2499-D *Hikin' Down The Highway* ....15.00 - 20.00
   2501-D *My Sweet Tooth Says "I Wanna"* ....15.00 - 20.00
   2515-D *This Is The Missus* ....15.00 - 20.00
   2554-D *Little Mary Brown* ....15.00 - 20.00
   2575-D *Bend Down, Sister* ....15.00 - 20.00

   2661-D *Crazy People* ....15.00 - 20.00
   2669-D *Cabin In The Cotton* ....15.00 - 20.00
   2731-D *Young And Healthy* ....15.00 - 20.00
   2789-D *Morning, Noon And Night* ....15.00 - 20.00
   2844-D *My Dancing Lady* ....12.00 - 16.00
   12126-F *Happy Days Are Here Again* (instrumental)
   ....20.00 - 30.00
(Note: Above is green label ethnic series.)
Columbia 18000-D *"Hot Cha"* medley ....20.00 - 30.00
(Note: Above is a "longer playing" record.)
Vocalion 14671 *Corn On The Cob* ....20.00 - 30.00
   14851 *San* ....10.00 - 15.00
   14853 *Red Hot Mama* ....10.00 - 15.00
   14871 *Susquehanna Home* ....10.00 - 15.00
   15029 *Suite 16* ....10.00 - 15.00
   15038 *Charleston* ....10.00 - 15.00
   15083 *Let's Wander Away* ....10.00 - 15.00
   15110 *Brown Eyes, Why Are You Blue?* ....10.00 - 15.00
   15154 *Sleepy Time Gal* ....10.00 - 15.00

SEMINOLE SYNCOPATORS:

Okeh 40228 *Blue Grass Blues* .... 100.00 - 150.00

BOYD SENTER (& HIS SENTERPEDES/ZOBO-KA-ZOOS):

Titles on Autograph (unnumbered): *Bucktown Blues; Gertie; Laugh; Mobile Blues; Mr. Jelly Lord; Omaha Blues; Powder Rag*
   ....80.00 - 130.00
Banner 0620 *Hobo's Prayer* ....10.00 - 15.00
   0621 *St. Louis Blues* ....12.00 - 16.00
   0622 *Beef Stew* ....10.00 - 15.00
(Foregoing titles on Cameo are similarly valued)
   1633 *Fat Mama Blues* ....15.00 - 20.00
Broadway 1337 *Mobile Blues* ....75.00 - 100.00
Cameo (titles as on Banner, above)
Clarion 5054-C *I Ain't Got Nobody* ....12.00 - 16.00
   5112-C *The New St. Louis Blues* ....12.00 - 16.00
   5181-C *Beale Street Blues* ....12.00 - 16.00
Diva 6034-G *I Ain't Got Nobody* ....10.00 - 15.00
   6044-G *Original Stack O'Lee Blues* ....10.00 - 15.00
Domino 3604 *Fat Mama Blues* ....15.00 - 20.00
Okeh 40755 *Bad Habits* ....12.00 - 16.00
   40777 *Clarinet Tickle* ....12.00 - 16.00
   40819 *Someday, Sweetheart* ....15.00 - 25.00
   40836 *Beale Street Blues* ....15.00 - 20.00
   40861 *Sigh And Cry Blues* ....15.00 - 20.00
   40888 *Hot Lips* ....15.00 - 20.00
   40949 *Wabash Blues* ....15.00 - 20.00
   41018 *I Wish I Could Shimmy Like My Sister Kate*
   ....15.00 - 20.00
   41059 *Somebody's Wrong* ....15.00 - 25.00
   41115 *Down-Hearted Blues* ....15.00 - 20.00
   41163 *Prickly Heat* ....15.00 - 20.00

Pathe-Actuelle (titles as on Perfect, following)

Perfect 14437 *Slippery Elm*	10.00 -	15.00
14451 *Gertie*	8.00 -	12.00
14466 *Bucktown Blues*	15.00 -	20.00
14501 *Milenberg Joys*	15.00 -	20.00
14517 *Shake Your Dogs*	15.00 -	30.00
14532 *I'm Taking My Own Sweet Time*	15.00 -	20.00
14540 *You're The One And Only*	15.00 -	20.00
14578 *St. Louis Blues*	10.00 -	15.00
14605 *Poison*	15.00 -	30.00
14664 *Hobo's Prayer*	10.00 -	15.00
14674 *Steamboat Stomp*	15.00 -	30.00
14709 *Beef Stew*	10.00 -	15.00

(Foregoing titles on Pathe-Actuelle are similarly valued)

Puritan 11341 *Mobile Blues*	10.00 -	15.00
Regal 9937 *Fat Mama Blues*	15.00 -	20.00
Velvet Tone 7060-V *I Ain't Got Nobody*	10.00 -	15.00
7070-V *Down-Hearted Blues*	10.00 -	15.00
7118-V *Beale Street Blues*	10.00 -	15.00
7120-V *I Wish I Could Shimmy Like My Sister Kate*	15.00 -	20.00
7121-V *Hot Lips*	40.00 -	60.00
Victor 21864 *Wabash Blues*	20.00 -	30.00
21912 *Shine*	15.00 -	20.00
22010 *I'm In The Jailhouse Now*	15.00 -	20.00
22303 *Copenhagen*	20.00 -	30.00
22464 *No One*	20.00 -	30.00
22812 *Waterloo*	20.00 -	30.00
23032 *Smiles*	40.00 -	60.00

THE SEPIA SERENADERS:

Bluebird 5770 *Ridiculous Blues*	20.00 -	30.00
5782 *Breakin' The Ice*	20.00 -	30.00
5803 *Alligator Crawl*	20.00 -	30.00

THE SEVEN ACES (See WARNER'S SEVEN ACES)

THE 7 BLUE BABIES (See also JACK DALTON, JACK KAUFMAN, BILLY MURRAY):

Edison 14016 *Heigh Ho! Ev'rybody, Heigh Ho!*	50.00 -	75.00
52495 *That's Her Now!*	80.00 -	120.00
52602 *Heigh Ho! Ev'rybody, Heigh Ho!*	50.00 -	75.00

SEVEN BROWN BABIES:

Ajax 17009 *Do Doodle Oom*	50.00 -	75.00
17011 *Dicty Blues*	50.00 -	75.00

THE SEVEN CHAMPIONS:

Champion 15009 *Collegiate*	8.00 -	12.00
15013 *Cecilia*	8.00 -	12.00
15016 *Susie*	10.00 -	15.00
15020 *Desdemona*	10.00 -	15.00
15031 *Dream Pal*	25.00 -	40.00
15032 *Who Loved You Best?*	15.00 -	20.00
15040 *Tomorrow Mornin'*	25.00 -	35.00
15047 *Don't Wake Me Up*	15.00 -	20.00
15052 *I Wonder Where My Baby Is Tonight*	10.00 -	15.00
15055 *Then I'll Be Happy*	15.00 -	20.00
15060 *Tie Me To Your Apron Strings Again*	10.00 -	15.00
15062 *I Wish't I Was In Peoria*	10.00 -	15.00
15065 *I Love My Baby*	10.00 -	15.00
15066 *Static*	10.00 -	15.00

THE SEVEN GALLON JUG BAND:

Columbia 2087-D *Wipe 'Em Off*	80.00 -	120.00

THE SEVEN HOT AIR MEN:

Columbia 1850-D *Gotta Feelin' For You*	20.00 -	30.00

SEVEN LITTLE CLOUDS OF JOY:

Brunswick 7180 *You Rascal, You*	75.00 -	100.00

SEVEN LITTLE POLAR BEARS:

Titles, issued contemporaneously on Cameo, Lincoln, and Romeo: *Any Ice To-Day, Lady?; The Cat And The Dog; Clicquot; Don't Take That Black Bottom Away; Fiddle-Dee-Dee-Dee; Gigolo; Got No Time To Feel Lonesome; Hello Montreal; Hello! Swanee-Hello!; Hi-Diddle-Diddle; Hi-Ho! The Merrio; Horses; How Could Red Riding Hood?; If I Didn't Know Your Husband; If My Bab Cooks (As Good As She Looks); I Love Her!; I'm Just Wild About Animal Crackers; It's O. K. Katy With Me; I Walked Back From The Buggy Ride; Me Too; My Girl Has Eye Trouble; Oh! You Have No Idea; Our Bungalow Of Dreams; Out In The New Mown Hay; She Said And I Said; Show That Fellow The Door; Since She Learned To Ride A Horse; Someone Is Losin' Susan; That's My Girl; Where Do You Work-a, John?; You Never Get Nowehere Holding Hands; You Should See My Tootsie*

	7.00 -	12.00
Another title: *Mississippi Mud*	15.00 -	20.00

SEVEN MISSING LINKS:

Perfect 14480 *Angry*	15.00 -	20.00

SEVEN WILD MEN:

Harmony 193-H *The Lunatic's Lullaby*	10.00 -	15.00

HATCH SEWARD:

Broadway 5063 *Honky Train Blues*	150.00 -	250.00

THE SHADYSIDE SERENADERS:

Van Dyke 81833 *Cryin' For The Carolines*	8.00 -	12.00

THE SHAMROCK JAZZERS:

Champion 15032 *Patricia My Own*	15.00 -	20.00

TERRY SHAND AND HIS ORCHESTRA:

Decca, blue label, most issues	7.00 -	10.00
Vocalion 4113, 4131	7.00 -	12.00

SHARKEY'S NEW ORLEANS BOYS/SHARKS OF RHYTHM:

Decca 1014 *Everybody Loves My Baby*	10.00 -	15.00
Vocalion 3353 *Mudhole Blues*	10.00 -	15.00
3380 *High Society*	10.00 -	15.00
3400 *When You're Smiling*	10.00 -	15.00
3410 *Blowin Off Steam*	10.00 -	15.00
3450 *Big Boy Blue*	10.00 -	15.00
3470 *Swing Like A Rusty Gate*	10.00 -	15.00

FRED SHARP'S DIXIE PLAYERS/ROYAL CUBANS:

Champion 15183 *I'll Fly To Hawaii*	30.00 -	50.00
15216 *I'm Looking Over A Four-Leaf Clover*	80.00 -	120.00

CHARLIE SHAVERS QUINTET:

Vogue 754 *She's Funny That Way*	30.00 -	50.00
755 *Serenade To A Pair Of Nylons*	30.00 -	50.00
756 *If I Had You*	50.00 -	100.00

ART(IE) SHAW & HIS NEW MUSIC/ORCHESTRA/STRINGS:

Bluebird 7746, 7759, 7772, 7875, 7889, 7952, 10001, 10054, 10055, 10075, 10079, 10091, 10125, 10126, 10127, 10128, 10134, 10141, 10148, 10178, 10188, 10195, 10202, 10215,

10307, 10319, 10320, 10324, 10334, 10345,
10347, 10385, 10406, 10412, 10430, 10446,
10468, 10482, 10492 ....5.00 - 10.00
Brunswick 7688, 7698, 7721, 7735, 7741, 7750,
7771, 7778, 7787, 7794, 7806, 7827, 7835, 7841,
7852, 7895, 7899, 7907, 7914, 7934, 7936, 7942,
7947, 7952, 7965, 7971, 7976, 7986, 8010, 8019,
8050, 8054 ....7.00 - 12.00
Musicraft, most issues ....5.00 -   8.00
Victor, most issues ....5.00 -   8.00

FRANK SHAW:
Brunswick 4100 *A Night At Coffee Dan's* ....10.00 - 15.00

JOEL SHAW & HIS ORCHESTRA:
Crown 3244 *Who's Your Little Who-Zis?* ....10.00 - 15.00
   3271 *Business In F* ....10.00 - 15.00
   3273 *Barnacle Bill, The Sailor* ....10.00 - 15.00
   3285 *Some Of These Days* ....10.00 - 15.00
   3298 *If It Ain't Love* ....10.00 - 15.00
   3300 *Sing A New Song* ....10.00 - 15.00
   3302 *Goofus* ....8.00 - 12.00
   3304 *Business In Q* ....10.00 - 15.00
   3306 *Minnie The Moocher* ....15.00 - 20.00
   3311 *Whistle And Blow Your Blues Away* ....10.00 - 15.00
   3312 *The Call Of The Freaks* ....15.00 - 20.00
   3319 *Dinah* ....10.00 - 15.00
   3332 *Minnie The Moocher's Wedding Day* ....10.00 - 15.00
   3333 *How'm I Doin'?* ....10.00 - 15.00
   3349 *Why Don't You Get Lost?* ....8.00 - 12.00
   3352 *That's A Plenty* ....15.00 - 20.00
   3362 *Basin Street Blues* ....15.00 - 20.00
   3381 *Sing (It's Good For Ya)* ....8.00 - 12.00
   3382 *Margie* ....15.00 - 20.00
   3383 *Tiger Rag* ....15.00 - 20.00
   3413 *White Zombie* ....15.00 - 20.00
   3414 *Jazz Pie* ....15.00 - 20.00
   3423 *Reefer Man* ....15.00 - 20.00
   3442 *The Old Kitchen Kettle* ....7.00 - 10.00
   3444 *Original Dixieland One Step* ....15.00 - 20.00
   3451 *Indiana* ....10.00 - 15.00

MILT SHAW & HIS DETROITERS:
Crown 3002 *What's The Use Of Living Without Love*
   ....10.00 - 15.00
   3005 *My Baby Just Cares For Me* ....10.00 - 15.00
Columbia 1811-D *Walking With Susie* ....10.00 - 15.00
Melotone, most issues ....5.00 - 10.00
Okeh 41158 *Where The Shy Little Violets Grow* .....15.00 - 25.00
   41172 *On The Alamo* ....10.00 - 15.00
   41196 *A Precious Little Thing Called Love* ....15.00 - 20.00
Vocalion 15665 *Golden Gate* ....30.00 - 40.00
   15666 *Borneo* ....30.00 - 40.00
   15697 *That's My Weakness Now* ....25.00 - 40.00

TED SHAWNE & HIS ORCHESTRA:
Odeon ONY-41276 *Ain't Misbehavin'* ....50.00 - 75.00
Parlophone PNY-34027 *Rockin' Chair* ....30.00 - 50.00
   PNY-34032 *Song Of The Islands* ....40.00 - 60.00
   PNY-34033 *Blue, Turning Grey Over You* ....40.00 - 60.00
   PNY-34126 *I Ain't Got Nobody* ....50.00 - 75.00
   PNY-34129 *I'm In The Market For You* ....50.00 - 75.00
   PNY-34131 *I'm A Ding Dong Daddy* ....30.00 - 50.00
   PNY-34172 *The Peanut Vendor* ....40.00 - 60.00
   PNY-34173 *Sweethearts On Parade* ....40.00 - 60.00

HARRY "FREDDIE" SHAYNE:
Champion 50061 *Lonesome Man Blues* ....40.00 - 70.00
Decca 7663 *Lonesome Man Blues* ....25.00 - 35.00

BERT SHEFTER & HIS ORCHESTRA/RHYTHM OCTET:
Decca 2525, 2584, 2653 ....7.00 - 12.00
Victor 25614, 25622, 25632 ....7.00 - 12.00

OLLIE SHEPARD:
Decca (most issues) ....7.00 - 12.00
Okeh (most issues) ....7.00 - 12.00

SHERIDAN ENTERTAINERS:
Titles, issued contemporaneously on Banner, Broadway, Challenge:
   Baltimore; Blue Baby; Sing Me A Baby Song; Sweetheart Of
   Sigma Chi; Washington And Lee Swing; What Do We Do On A
   Dew-Dew-Dewy Day; You Don't Like It- Not Much
   ....7.00 - 12.00

KARL SHERMAN & HIS ORCHESTRA:
Superior 2502 *If I Could Be With You (One Hour To-Night)*
   ....15.00 - 20.00
   2503 *Go Home And Tell Your Mother* ....20.00 - 30.00

SHERMAN CLUB ORCHESTRA:
Challenge 712 *Me And My Shadow* ....8.00 - 12.00
   715 *Muddy Waters* ....100.00 - 150.00

SHERMAN'S GLOBE TROTTERS:
Bell 615 *Louisiana* ....15.00 - 25.00
Silvertone 8071 *Louisiana* ....15.00 - 25.00

SHERMAN SUNDODGERS/SUNDOWNERS:
Herwin 8059 *Happy-Go-Lucky Lane* ....30.00 - 50.00
Silvertone 8057 *Happy-Go-Lucky Lane* ....15.00 - 20.00

JACK SHILKRET & HIS ORCHESTRA:
Titles issued contemporaneously on Banner, Melotone, Oriole, and
   Perfect: *Another Perfect Night Is Ending; Dream Awhile; Gee!*
   But You're Swell; Hey, Babe, Hey!; Hidden Valley; I Can't
   Escape From You; Never Should Have Told You; One
   Hamburger For Madame; San Francisco; Shoe Shine Boy; So
   Divine; There's Always A Happy Ending; There's A Small Hotel;
   Twinkle, Twinkle, Little Star ....7.00 - 10.00
Bluebird 5884, 5885, 5886, 5986, 5987, 5988, 6013 .....7.00 - 10.00
Brunswick 7602, 7603 ....7.00 - 10.00
Victor 19394, 19818, 19931 ....7.00 - 12.00
   19922 *Roll 'Em, Girls* ....10.00 - 15.00

NAT SHILKRET & THE VICTOR ORCHESTRA:
RCA Victor L-16004 *Don't Ask Me Why; Fate* .....15.00 - 20.00
(Note: Above is a 33-1/3 RPM "Program Transcription".)
RCA Victor 39001 (12-inch picture record) selections from *"Music In The Air"* ....80.00 - 130.00
Victor 20469 *I Love You But I Don't Know Why* ...50.00 - 75.00
   20471 *What Does It Matter?* ....10.00 - 15.00
   20508 *Ain't She Sweet?* ....10.00 - 15.00
   20634 *Fifty Million Frenchmen Can't Be Wrong* .....8.00 - 12.00
   20675 *Me And My Shadow* ....10.00 - 15.00
   20882 *Baby's Blue* ....8.00 - 12.00
   20926 *Zulu Wail* ....10.00 - 15.00
   21080 *Nothin'* ....8.00 - 12.00
   21497 *That's My Weakness Now* ....8.00 - 12.00
   21515 *When Sweet Susie Goes Steppin' By* ....8.00 - 12.00
   21603 *Moonlight Madness* ....8.00 - 12.00
   21729 *Here's That Party Now In Person* ......10.00 - 15.00

21818 *I Want A Daddy To Cuddle Me*.................. 8.00 - 12.00
21853 *Dream Train* ....8.00 - 12.00
21859 *I Want To Be Bad*.................................. 8.00 - 12.00
21913 *There Is A Happy Land* ....8.00 - 12.00
21996 *Susianna* ....8.00 - 12.00
22055 *I'm The Medicine Man For The Blues* ....10.00 - 15.00
22106 *You Made Me Love You-Why Did You?* .10.00 - 15.00
22109 *Bottoms Up* ....8.00 - 12.00
22258 *When I'm Looking At You*.........................8.00 - 12.00
22306 *Singing A Vagabond Song* ....10.00 - 15.00
22408 *Whippoorwill* ....8.00 - 12.00
22472 *Dixiana* ....8.00 - 12.00

ALBERT E. SHORT & HIS TIVOLI SYNCOPATORS:
Vocalion 14554 *Wolverine Blues* ....10.00 - 15.00
14600 *Long Lost Mama* ....15.00 - 20.00
14658 *Bugle Call Rag* ....10.00 - 15.00

SHREVEPORT SIZZLERS:
Okeh 8918 *Zonky* ....50.00 - 75.00
41561 *You've Got To Be Modernistic* ....50.00 - 75.00

AL SIEGEL & HIS ORCHESTRA:
Titles issued contemporaneously on Broadway, Claxtonola, Harmograph, Paramount, Pennington, and Puritan: *Blue Grass Blues; So Long To You And The Blues; Sooke Hey Hey* ....75.00 - 100.00
Paramount 20301 *You've Got Ways I'm Crazy About* ....150.00 - 200.00

SIGLER'S BIRMINGHAM MERRYMAKERS:
Okeh 40280 *Mama's Gone Goodbye* ....75.00 - 100.00
40310 *I Love Her* ....50.00 - 80.00

FRANK SIGNORELLI AND HIS ORCHESTRA:
Pathe-Actuelle 36518 *She's Still My Baby* ....15.00 - 20.00
36523 *Don't Be Angry With Me* ....10.00 - 15.00
36535 *St. Louis Hop* ....20.00 - 30.00
Perfect 14699 *She's Still My Baby*.....................15.00 - 20.00
14704 *Don't Be Angry With Me* ....10.00 - 15.00
14716 *A Blues Serenade* ....20.00 - 30.00

SILENT JOE & HIS BOYS:
Champion 15051 *Cooler Hot* ....15.00 - 20.00
15052 *Give Me Your Heart* ....10.00 - 15.00
15053 *Any Blues (Is Good Enough For Me)* .....25.00 - 35.00

DAVID H. SILVERMAN & HIS ORCHESTRA:
Victor 19195, 19237 ....7.00 - 12.00

SILVER SLIPPER ORCHESTRA:
Challenge 801 *A Little Bit Closer*..........................150.00 - 200.00
806 *There'll Come A Day* ....150.00 - 200.00

JOHNNY SILVESTER AND HIS ORCHESTRA (See JOHNNY SYLVESTER)

OMER SIMEON:
Brunswick 7109 *Beau-Koo Jack* ....125.00 - 175.00

LESTER SIMMONS & HIS ORCHESTRA:
Champion 15475 *I've Got Somebody Now*..............20.00 - 30.00

GINNY SIMMS:
Okeh 5990 *I'm Out Of Style* ....8.00 - 12.00
6087 *You Danced With Dynamite* ....8.00 - 12.00

HOWARD SIMMS:
Harmograph 841 *Pensacola Joe* ....50.00 - 75.00

JOS SIMPKINS & HIS RUBE BAND:
Champion 15581 *Bass Blues* ....100.00 - 150.00

ARTHUR SIMS & HIS CREOLE ROOF ORCHESTRA:
Okeh 8373 *Soapstick Blues* ....200.00 - 300.00
40675 *As Long As I Have You* ....200.00 - 300.00

THE SINGING BOYS & THEIR NOVELTY ORCHESTRA:
Harmony 928-H *My Kinda Love*.............................15.00 - 20.00
1087-H *You'll Recognize My Baby*....................15.00 - 25.00
(Note: Above titles on Diva and Velvet Tone are similarly valued.)

SIOUX CITY SIX (FEATURING BIX/MIFF MOOL):
Gennett 5569 *Flock O' Blues*...............................250.00 - up

NOBLE SISSLE; (NOBLE) SISSEL/SISSLE & (EUBIE) BLAKE; NOBLE SISSLE & HIS (INTERNATIONAL) ORCHESTRA/SIZZLIN' SYNCOPATORS SWINGSTERS:
Brunswick 6073 *Got The Bench, Got The Park*...... 20.00 - 30.00
6111 *Roll On, Mississippi, Roll On* .... 25.00 - 35.00
6129 *Basement Blues* .... 35.00 - 50.00
Decca 153 *Under The Creole Moon* .... 15.00 - 20.00
154 *Loveless Love* .... 15.00 - 20.00
766 *I Wonder Who Made Rhythm* .... 10.00 - 15.00
778 *That's What Love Did To Me* .... 15.00 - 20.00
847 *I Take To You* .... 15.00 - 20.00
2129 *Blackstick* .... 10.00 - 15.00
7429 *Viper Mad* .... 10.00 - 15.00
Edison 50754 *Crazy Blues* .... 40.00 - 60.00
51572 *Broken Busted Blues* .... 30.00 - 50.00
Emerson 10296 *Broadway Blues* .... 15.00 - 20.00
10326 *Crazy Blues* .... 15.00 - 20.00
10357 *Boll Weevil Blues* .... 15.00 - 20.00
10365 *Low Down Blues* .... 20.00 - 30.00
10367 *Royal Garden Blues* .... 15.00 - 20.00
10385 *Baltimore Buzz* .... 15.00 - 20.00
10396 *Oriental Blues* .... 15.00 - 20.00
10443 *Arkansas Blues* .... 20.00 - 30.00
10484 *I'm A Doggone Struttin' Fool* .... 15.00 - 20.00
Okeh 40776 *'Deed I Do* .... 25.00 - 40.00
40824 *Slow River* .... 25.00 - 40.00
40859 *Sometimes I'm Happy* .... 25.00 - 40.00
40877 *Broken Hearted* .... 20.00 - 30.00
40882 *Give Me A Night In June*........................ 20.00 - 30.00
40917 *Pickaninny Shoes* .... 25.00 - 40.00
Paramount 12002 *Bandana Days*........................ 35.00 - 50.00
12007 *Crazy Blues* .... 35.00 - 50.00
Pathe 20210 *Mammy's Little Choc'late Cullud Chile* .... 20.00 - 30.00
20226 *Goodnight, Angeline* .... 15.00 - 20.00
20233 *Stay In Your Own Back Yard* .... 15.00 - 20.00
20267 *There It Goes Again* .... 15.00 - 20.00
20280 *That's The Kind Of A Baby For Me*........ 15.00 - 20.00
20295 *Mandy Lou* .... 15.00 - 20.00
20470 *Affectionate Dan* .... 15.00 - 20.00
22284 *I'm Just Simply Full Of Jazz* .... 15.00 - 20.00
22357 *Melodious Jazz* .... 15.00 - 20.00
22394 *Mammy's Little Sugar Plum* .... 15.00 - 20.00
Variety 552 *I'm Just Wild About Harry*............... 15.00 - 20.00
648 *Characteristic Blues* .... 15.00 - 20.00

Victor 19086 *Down-Hearted Blues* ....15.00 - 20.00
  19253 *Old Fashioned Love* ....15.00 - 20.00
  19494 *Manda* ....20.00 - 30.00
Vocalion 3840 *Characteristic Blues*........................15.00 - 20.00

KENN SISSON & HIS ORCHESTRA:
Brunswick 3502 *Hello Cutie* ....8.00 - 12.00
  3595 *Bamboola* ....8.00 - 12.00
  3703 *It Was Only A Sun Shower* ....8.00 - 12.00
Brunswick, other issues ....5.00 - 10.00

SIX BLACK DIAMONDS:
Banner 1217, 1227, 1385, 1842, 6093, 6104, 6167,
  6289, 6291, 6298, 6318, 6324, 6352, 6382, 6383,
  6384, 6392, 7008 ....7.00 - 12.00
  1181 *Farewell Blues* ....10.00 - 15.00
  1265 *Sobbin' Blues* ....10.00 - 15.00
  1318 *Mindin' My Business* ....20.00 - 30.00
  1322 *Lots O' Mamma* ....15.00 - 25.00
  1336 *Waitin' Around* ....15.00 - 20.00
  1346 *My Papa Doesn't Two-Time No Time* ....15.00 - 20.00
  1349 *Nobody's Sweetheart* ....10.00 - 15.00
  1428 *Dixie Flyer Sam* ....15.00 - 20.00
  1456 *Those Panama Mamas* ....15.00 - 20.00
  1540 *Sweet Georgia Brown*.................................15.00 - 20.00
  1656 *Steppin' Fool* ....10.00 - 15.00
  1662 *My Charleston Dancing Man* ....10.00 - 15.00
  6076 *I Can't Fool Around With Someone Who's Foolin'*
  ....15.00 - 20.00
  6300 *Some Of These Days* ....10.00 - 15.00
  6418 *Some Of These Days* ....10.00 - 15.00
Domino 392 *Any Way The Wind Blows*....................7.00 - 10.00
(Domino, other titles as on Banner, above, similarly valued)
Oriole 497 *Melancholy Lou* ....15.00 - 20.00
  518 *I'm Gonna Charleston Back To Charleston* ..8.00 - 12.00
Regal 8006 *Flamin' Mamie* ....8.00 - 12.00
  8022 *Say Mister! Have You Met Rosie's Sister?* ..8.00 - 12.00
  8150 *Here Comes Fatima* ....15.00 - 20.00
  9458 *Farewell Blues* ....10.00 - 15.00
  9503 *Beale Street Mama* ....8.00 - 12.00
  9553 *Sobbin' Blues* ....10.00 - 15.00
  9612 *Lots O' Mama* ....10.00 - 15.00
  9628 *Waitin' Around* ....15.00 - 20.00
  9643 *Josephine (Who's The Meanest Gal In Town)*
  ....15.00 - 20.00
  9646 *My Papa Doesn't Two-Time No Time* ....10.00 - 15.00
  9706 *Any Way The Wind Blows* ....7.00 - 10.00
  9725 *Dixie Flyer Sam* ....15.00 - 20.00
  9835 *Charleston* ....15.00 - 25.00
  9981 *Charleston Baby* ....8.00 - 12.00

SIX BROWN BROTHERS:
Victor 17677 *That Moaning Saxophone Rag* ....8.00 - 12.00
  17834 *Down Home Rag*.......................................10.00 - 15.00
  18097 *Bull Frog Blues*..8.00 - 12.00
  18140 *Walkin' The Dog*..8.00 - 12.00
  18310 *For Me And My Gal*...................................8.00 - 12.00
  18376 *The Darktown Strutters' Ball*....................7.00 - 10.00
  18385 *Smiles And Chuckles*................................8.00 - 12.00

THE SIX HAYSEEDS:
Vocalion 15239 *Wimmin, Aah!*................................10.00 - 15.00
  15240 *The Wind Blew Through His Whiskers*......8.00 - 12.00
  15244 *Charleston Ball*..8.00 - 12.00
  15301 *Horses* ....10.00 - 15.00

15358 *Spring Is Here* ....10.00 - 15.00
15428 *Any Ice To-Day, Lady?* ....10.00 - 15.00
15487 *Fire!* ....15.00 - 20.00
15500 *Where Do You Work-a, John?* ....10.00 - 15.00
15508 *Cock-A-Doodle, I'm Off My Noodle* ....10.00 - 15.00
15514 *I Love The College Girls*........................10.00 - 15.00
15520 *Crazy Words - Crazy Tune*.....................10.00 - 15.00
15552 *I Wonder How I Look When I'm Asleep* . 10.00 - 15.00
15563 *You Never Get Nowhere Holding Hands* 10.00 - 15.00
15564 *The More We Are Together*.....................10.00 - 10.00
15580 *There's A Trick In Pickin' A Chick-Chick-Chicken*
....10.00 - 15.00
15596 *She's Got "It"* ....10.00 - 15.00
15609 *She's Just What The Doctor Ordered* ..... 10.00 - 15.00

THE SIX HOTTENTOTS:
Titles, issued contemporaneously on Banner, Domino, Regal:
  *Hurricane; I'm In Love Again; Melancholy Charlie; The
  Memphis Blues; Rosy Cheeks; Sometimes I'm Happy*
....15.00 - 30.00

SIX JOLLY JESTERS:
Vocalion 1449 *Oklahoma Stomp* ....100.00 - 150.00
(Note: Reissues of above, on black and gold, or blue and gold label
  are valued much lower.)
  15843 *Six Or Seven Times* ....250.00 - up

SIX JUMPING JACKS:
Brunswick 3031 *Wimmin-Aaah!*.............................10.00 - 15.00
  3064 *Charleston Ball* ....8.00 - 12.00
  3094 *Thanks For The Buggy Ride* ....8.00 - 12.00
  3095 *Masculine Women! Feminine Men!* ....10.00 - 15.00
  3109 *I'm Gonna Let The Bumble Bee Be*.............8.00 - 12.00
  3131 *Say Mister! Have You Met Rosie's Sister?* ....10.00 - 15.00
  3169 *Rah-Rah-Rah*...10.00 - 15.00
  3216 *I'm Just Wild About Animal Crackers* ......10.00 - 15.00
  3252 *Out In The New Mown Hay* ....10.00 - 15.00
  3254 *How Could Red Riding Hood?* ....10.00 - 15.00
  3374 *If You Can't Land 'Er On The Old Veranda*
....10.00 - 15.00
  3412 *The Coat And Pants Do All The Work* ......10.00 - 15.00
  3434 *I Love The College Girls*.............................10.00 - 15.00
  3511 *I Wonder How I Look When I'm Asleep* ...10.00 - 15.00
  3524 *The More We Are Together*........................10.00 - 15.00
  3582 *Positively-Absolutely*..................................10.00 - 15.00
  3603 *She's Got "It"* ....10.00 - 15.00
  3623 *I'm Gonna Dance Wit De Guy Wot Brung Me*
....10.00 - 15.00
  3650 *Pastafazoola*..10.00 - 15.00
  3699 *Here Comes The Show Boat* ....10.00 - 15.00
  3726 *Fair Co-Ed*...10.00 - 15.00
  3782 *Henry's Made A Lady Out Of Lizzie*.........15.00 - 20.00
  3856 *Get 'Em In A Rumble Seat* ....10.00 - 15.00
  3876 *Hey! Hey! Hazel*..10.00 - 15.00
  3917 *He Ain't Never Been In College*................10.00 - 15.00
  3923 *They Landed Over Here From Over There* ....10.00 - 15.00
  3930 *I Love That Girl* ....10.00 - 15.00
  3940 *Etiquette Blues* ....10.00 - 15.00
  4011 *Nagasaki* ....10.00 - 15.00
  4073 *The Prune Song* ....10.00 - 15.00
  4196 *I Faw Down An' Go Boom!* ....10.00 - 15.00
  4219 *Olaf (You Ought-a Hear Olaf Laff)* ....10.00 - 15.00
  4220 *Outside* ....10.00 - 15.00
  4351 *She's Got Great Ideas* ....15.00 - 20.00

4457 *The Whoopee Hat Brigade*..........................10.00 - 15.00
4498 *He's A Big, Big Man From The South*.......20.00 - 30.00
4589 *My Wife Is On A Diet*...............................12.00 - 16.00
4590 *It's Unanimous Now* ....12.00 - 16.00
4759 *Send For Our Free Booklet* ....12.00 - 16.00
4946 *Football Freddy*......................................12.00 - 16.00
4948 *It's A Great Life* ....12.00 - 16.00
6007 *Twenty Swedes Ran Through The Weeds* ..12.00 - 16.00
6081 *Egyptian Ella* ....15.00 - 20.00
6137 *When Yuba Plays The Rumba On The Tuba*
....15.00 - 20.00

SIX MEN AND A GIRL:
Varsity 8193 *Tea For Two*..............................8.00 - 12.00
8190 *Zonky*.......................................8.00 - 12.00

THE SIZZLERS:
Edison 52463 *Diga Diga Doo* ....75.00 - 100.00

CHARLEY SKEETE'S ORCHESTRA:
Edison 51775 *Deep Henderson* ....150.00 - 200.00

DUDE SKILES & HIS VINE STREET BOYS:
Variety 516 *My Girl* ....10.00 - 15.00
584 *Farewell Blues* ....10.00 - 15.00

SKILLET DICK & HIS FRYING PANS:
Champion 15883 *Asphalt Walk* ....150.00 - 250.00
15996 *Rock And Gravel*.................150.00 - 250.00

SLEMER'S COLLEGIANS; EDDIE SLEMER & HIS ORCHESTRA:
Champion 15780 *Birmingham Bertha*.................... 15.00 - 20.00
Gennett 6922 *Freeze Out*........................... 30.00 - 50.00

SLIM & HIS HOT BOYS:
Victor V38044 *That's A Plenty* .... 80.00 - 120.00

SLIM AND SLAM:
Vocalion 3981, 4021, 4110, 4163, 4225, 4346,
4461, 4521, 4594 ....8.00 - 12.00

ROY SMECK & ART KAHN:
Columbia 1127-D *The Ghost Of The Banjo* .... 10.00 - 15.00

FATS SMITH & HIS RHYTHM KINGS:
Vocalion 03528 *If I Had You In My Arms*...............20.00 - 30.00

FRED SMITH & HIS SOCIETY ORCHESTRA:
Black Swan 2052, 2114, 2119 ....8.00 - 15.00

HARL SMITH AND HIS ORCHESTRA:
Pathe-Actuelle 036158 *Rose Marie* ....15.00 - 20.00
Perfect 14339 *Bring Back Those Rock-A-Bye Baby Days*
....15.00 - 20.00

JABBO SMITH & HIS RHYTHM ACES (See also THE RHYTHM ACES):
Brunswick 7058 *Little Willie Blues* ....100.00 - 150.00
7061 *Take Your Time*....................................100.00 - 150.00
7065 *Let's Get Together* ....100.00 - 150.00
7069 *Michigander Blues*................................100.00 - 150.00
7071 *Ace Of Rhythm* ....100.00 - 150.00
7078 *Decatur Street Tutti* ....100.00 - 150.00
7087 *Lina Blues* ....100.00 - 150.00
7101 *Tanguay Blues* ....100.00 - 150.00
7111 *Band Box Stomp*...................................100.00 - 150.00
Decca 1712, 1980 ....7.00 - 12.00

JOE SMITH'S MARTHA LEE CLUB ORCHESTRA:
Okeh 40322 *Don't Bother Me*................................. 20.00 - 30.00

KATE SMITH:
Brunswick 6496 *Twenty Million People* .... 8.00 - 12.00
6497 *Moon Song* .... 8.00 - 12.00
Clarion 5015-C *Don't Let Me Hold You, Baby Mine* ...10.00 - 15.00
5038-C *You'll Be Coming Back To Me*.............. 10.00 - 15.00
5074-C *You'll Never Know, Sweetheart* .... 10.00 - 15.00
5123-C *Held By The Spell Of The Moon* .... 10.00 - 15.00
5124-C *Morning, Noon And Night*..................... 10.00 - 15.00
5227-C *You Don't Want Me Any More*.............. 10.00 - 15.00
5228-C *Grievin* .... 10.00 - 15.00
5278-C *Dinah Lee From Tennessee* .... 10.00 - 15.00
5279-C *Now's The Time* .... 10.00 - 15.00
(Note: Above titles, on Velvet Tone, are similarly valued.)
Columbia 810-D *Jersey Walk* .... 8.00 - 12.00
911-D *One Sweet Letter From You*.................... 20.00 - 30.00
1132-D *Clementine (From New Orleans)*............ 8.00 - 12.00
1348-D *In The Evening* .... 8.00 - 12.00
2516-D *When The Moon Comes Over The Mountain*
.... 8.00 - 12.00
2539-D *I Don't Know Why (I Just Do)*.............. 10.00 - 15.00
2563-D *Tell Me With A Love Song* .... 10.00 - 15.00
2605-D *Twenty-One Years*................................ 10.00 - 15.00
2624-D *Snuggled On Your Shoulder* .... 10.00 - 15.00
Decca 276, 277, 288... 7.00 - 12.00
Harmony 970-H *He's A Good Man To Have Around*
.... 10.00 - 15.00
999-H *Moanin' Low*.. 10.00 - 15.00
1050-H *I May Be Wrong, But I Think You're Wonderful*
.... 10.00 - 15.00
1069-H *Chant Of The Jungle* .... 10.00 - 15.00
1170-H *Dancing With Tears In My Eyes*............. 7.00 - 10.00
1191-H *Swingin' In A Hammock* .... 10.00 - 15.00
1216-H *Maybe It's Love* .... 10.00 - 15.00
1235-H *I Got Rhythm*... 10.00 - 15.00
1280-H *Overnight* .... 10.00 - 15.00
1303-H *Wabash Moon* .... 10.00 - 15.00
1347-H *Makin' Faces At The Man In The Moon* ....10.00 - 15.00
1371-H *Shine On, Harvest Moon*........................ 8.00 - 12.00
(Note: Above titles, on Diva or Velvet Tone, are similarly valued.)
Velvet Tone 2465-V *Goodnight, Sweetheart*............ 8.00 - 12.00
2483-V *All Of Me*... 10.00 - 15.00
2512-V *Between The Devil And The Deep Blue Sea*
.... 10.00 - 15.00

LEROY SMITH & HIS ORCHESTRA:
Blu-Disc T-1001 *Stop And Listen* .... 100.00 - 200.00
Everybody's 1020 *Harlem's Araby* .... 75.00 - 100.00
1027 *Dixie Dreams* .... 75.00 - 100.00
Victor 21328 *St. Louis Blues* .... 35.00 - 50.00
21472 *St. Louis Blues*...................................... 20.00 - 30.00

LLOYD SMITH'S GUT-BUCKETEERS:
Vocalion 1560 *Wake Up, Sinners* .... 200.00 - 300.00
1573 *That's My Stuff*....................................... 200.00 - 300.00

SAMMY SMITH'S STOMPERS:
Clarion 5417-C *Blues In My Heart* .... 20.00 - 30.00
Velvet Tone 2477-V *Blues In My Heart*................... 20.00 - 30.00

STUFF SMITH & HIS ORCHESTRA: ONYX CLUB BOYS:
Decca 1279, 1287 .... 8.00 - 12.00
Varsity 8063, 8081, 8242, 8251 .... 8.00 - 12.00
Vocalion 3169, 3170, 3200, 3201, 3234, 3270,
3300, 3316 .... 8.00 - 12.00

TED SMITH'S RHYTHM ACES:

Champion 16321 *Minnie The Moocher* ....100.00 - 150.00
    16332 *Boogie Woogie* ....100.00 - 150.00
    16420 *New Moten Stomp* ....100.00 - 150.00
    40006 *Jig Time* ....35.00 - 50.00

WILLIE "THE LION" SMITH (& HIS ORCHESTRA); WILLIE SMITH (THE LION) & HIS CUBS:

Commodore 518, 519, 521, 522, 523, 524, 525 ....7.00 - 12.00
Decca 1291 *The Swampland Is Calling Me* ....15.00 - 20.00
    1308 *More Than That* ....15.00 - 20.00
    1366 *Knock Wood* ....10.00 - 15.00
    1380 *Get Acquainted With Yourself* ....10.00 - 15.00
    1503 *Achin' Hearted Blues* ....10.00 - 15.00
    1957 *I've Got To Think It Over* ....10.00 - 15.00
    7073 *There's Gonna Be The Devil To Pay* ....15.00 - 25.00
    7074 *Streamline Gal* ....15.00 - 20.00
    7086 *Sittin' At The Table* ....15.00 - 20.00
    7090 *Swing, Brother, Swing* ....15.00 - 20.00
General 1712 *Peace On You* ....10.00 - 15.00
    1713 *Rushin'* ....10.00 - 15.00

MARVIN SMOLEV & HIS SYNCOPATORS:

Titles, issued contemporaneously on Grey Gull, and Radiex: *Apart From You; Because I'm Lonesome; Desert Blues; No-One But Betty Brown; Ring Around The Moon; She's Just The Baby For Me; Soubrette; The Terror; We'll Be Married In June*
.... 20.00 - 30.00

SMYTH & WEST ORCHESTRA:

Broadway 1486 *I Need Lovin'* ....8.00 - 12.00

JACK SNEED AND HIS SNEEZERS:

Decca 7522 *Big Joe Louis* ....10.00 - 15.00
    7566 *Sly Mangoose* ....8.00 - 12.00
    7621 *Paul Revere* ....8.00 - 12.00

HARRY SNODGRASS:

Brunswick 2852 *Blue Evening Blues* ....7.00 - 10.00
    3239 *Maple Leaf Rag* ....7.00 - 10.00

SNOOKS & HIS MEMPHIS RAMBLERS/STOMPERS; SNOOKS & HIS PARAMOUNT THEATRE ORCHESTRA:

Titles, issued contemporaneously on Banner, Oriole, Perfect, and Romeo: *One More Time; That's My Desire; Under Your Window Tonight* ....8.00 - 12.00
Melotone 12203, 12210, 12245, 12259 ....8.00 - 12.00
Victor 22629 *I'm Happy When You're Happy* ....12.00 - 16.00
    22662 *Smile, Darn Ya, Smile* ....15.00 - 20.00
    22684 *Bon Soir* ....20.00 - 30.00
    22704 *You Don't Need Glasses* ....12.00 - 16.00
    22720 *Dip Your Brush In The Sunshine* ....13.00 - 20.00
    22737 *I'm Blue, But Nobody Cares* ....30.00 - 50.00
    22779 *Sweet Georgia Brown* ....15.00 - 25.00
    22813 *Kissable Baby* ....12.00 - 16.00
    22815 *Japanese Sandman* ....50.00 - 80.00
    22895 *Nothin' To Do But Love* ....15.00 - 20.00
    22988 *'Neath The Silvery Moon* ....7.00 - 10.00
    23038 *Hello, Beautiful!* ....25.00 - 40.00

BOB SNYDER & HIS ORCHESTRA:

Vocalion 2660 *My Dog Loves Your Dog* ....10.00 - 15.00
    2661 *Nasty Man* ....10.00 - 15.00
    2707 *Love Thy Neighbor* ....10.00 - 15.00

JOE SODJA'S SWINGTETTE:

Variety 609 *Limehouse Blues* .... 10.00 - 15.00

HARRY SOSNIK & HIS (EDGEWATER BEACH HOTEL) ORCHESTRA:

Decca (most issues) .... 4.00 - 8.00
Nocturne 3135 **Swinging The Jingle* .... 15.00 - 30.00
*(Note: Actually, a Pepsi-Cola commercial!)
Victor 24481, 24488, 24570, 24572, 24623, 24626 ....7.00 - 10.00

JACKIE SOUDERS AND HIS ORCHESTRA:

Columbia 837-D *Every Little Thing* .... 10.00 - 15.00
    906-D *Maybe Sometime* .... 10.00 - 15.00
    785-D, 958-D, 1216-D .... 5.00 - 10.00

SOUSA'S BAND:

RCA Victor L-16027 *Stars And Stripes Forever; Golden Jubilee*
.... 10.00 - 15.00
(Foregoing is a 33-1/3 RPM "Program Transcription")
Victor 312 *A Coon Band Contest* (one-sided disc) 20.00 - 30.00
    315 *At A Georgia Camp Meeting* (one-sided disc)20.00- 30.00
    316 *A Hot Time In The Old Town Tonight* (one-sided disc)
.... 20.00 - 30.00
    361 *Whistling Rufus* (one-sided disc) .... 20.00 - 30.00
    362 *Who Dat Say Chicken In Dis Crowd* (one-sided)
.... 20.00 - 30.00
    1182 *Creole Belles* (one-sided disc) .... 15.00 - 25.00
    1223 *Trombone Sneeze* (one-sided disc)........... 20.00 - 30.00
    1417 *The Passing Of Rag Time* (one-sided disc)20.00 - 30.00
    2443 *Hiawatha* (one-sided disc) .... 20.00 - 30.00
    4538 *Silence And Fun - A Rag Time Oddity* (one-sided)
.... 25.00 - 40.00
    16402 *At A Georgia Camp Meeting*................... 10.00 - 15.00
    17252 *Creole Belles* .... 10.00 - 15.00
(Note: Some of the above titles were issued on the small, primitive Berliner records; these are of greater interest and value than the foregoing. Also of premium value are those of the above Victor records issued as 7-inch records, and/or with label variations (e.g., Monarch, Victor Monarch, Improved), which are the earliest products of the Victor Talking Machine Company.)

EDDIE SOUTH & HIS ALABAMIANS/ORCHESTRA:

Victor 21151 *By The Waters Of Minnetonka*............ 8.00 - 12.00
    21155 *The Voice Of The Southland* .... 8.00 - 12.00
    21605 *That's What I Call Keen* .... 10.00 - 15.00
    24324 *Old Man Harlem* .... 30.00 - 50.00
    24343 *Gotta Go!* .... 30.00 - 50.00
    24383 *Nagasaki* .... 30.00 - 50.00

SOUTHAMPTON SOCIETY ORCHESTRA:

Pathe-Actuelle (titles as on Perfect, following)
Perfect 14395 *Poplar Street Blues* .... 30.00 - 50.00
    14433 *Cross Words Between My Sweetie And Me*8.00 - 12.00
    14434 *Ev'rything Is Hotsy Totsy Now* .... 10.00 - 15.00
    14445 *Flag That Train* .... 10.00 - 15.00
    14450 *Flapper Wife* .... 8.00 - 12.00
    14457 *Oh Say! Can I See You Tonight* .... 10.00 - 15.00
    14472 *Cecilia* .... 8.00 - 12.00
    14482 *Loud Speakin' Papa* .... 10.00 - 15.00
    14493 *Mighty Blue* .... 8.00 - 12.00
    14824 *I'm In Love Again* .... 15.00 - 20.00
(Foregoing titles on Pathe-Actuelle are similarly valued)

THE SOUTHERNERS:

Gennett 3061 *Craving* .... 30.00 - 50.00
    3198 *Clap Hands! Here Comes Charley* .... 15.00 - 20.00

3199 *Rhythm Of The Day* ....15.00 - 20.00
3204 *That Certain Party*......................15.00 - 20.00
3212 *Someone's Stolen My Sweet Sweet Baby*...15.00 - 20.00
3265 *My Bundle Of Love* ....15.00 - 20.00
3266 *But I Do-You Know I Do* ....15.00 - 20.00

THE SOUTHERN FIVE:
LaBelle 1410 *I Wish I Could Shimmy Like My Sister Kate*
....15.00 - 20.00
Melody 1410 *I Wish I Could Shimmy Like My Sister Kate*
....15.00 - 20.00

SOUTHERN MELODY ARTISTS:
Okeh 41216 *When The World Is At Rest* ....15.00 - 20.00

SOUTHERN MELODY SERENADERS:
Marathon 221 *Oh! You Have No Idea* ....15.00 - 20.00
222 *I'm Afraid Of You* ....15.00 - 20.00
(Note: Above are 7-inch records)

SOUTHERN MELODY SYNCOPATORS:
Marathon 229 *I'm On The Crest of a Wave*.............15.00 - 20.00
232 *Sonny Boy* ....10.00 - 20.00
234 *High Up On A Hill Top*................................10.00 - 20.00
235 *Roses Of Yesterday* ....10.00 - 20.00
(Note: Above are 7-inch records.)

SOUTHERN ORCHESTRA:
Victor 707 *West Indies Rhythm* ....10.00 - 15.00

SOUTHERN RHYTHM MASTERS:
Van Dyke 81891 *Sweetheart It's You*.......................10.00 - 15.00

THE SOUTHERN SERENADERS:
Bluebird 7367 *Goin' To Town*.................................10.00 - 15.00
Cameo 310 *Runnin' Wild*..8.00 - 12.00
Harmony 4-H *I Miss My Swiss* ....15.00 - 20.00
5-H *Alone At Last*.....................................15.00 - 20.00
Okeh 41456 *Body And Soul* ....15.00 - 20.00
Regal 9164 *Lonesome Lovesick Blues*....................15.00 - 20.00
9191 *Satanic Blues*...................................15.00 - 20.00
Silvertone 2320 *Oh Sister! Ain't That Hot?* ....15.00 - 20.00
2770 *I've Found A New Baby*.............................35.00 - 50.00

SOUTHLAND SIX:
Vocalion 14476 *Runnin' Wild* ....10.00 - 15.00

SOUTHLAND SYNCOPATORS:
Vocalion 15544 *Brown Sugar* ....10.00 - 15.00

SOUTH SHORE MELODY BOYS:
Champion 15036 *Oh Maud* ....25.00 - 35.00
15037 *You Can't Make A Woman Change Her Mind*
....25.00 - 35.00
15068 *Lantern Of Love*..............................8.00 - 12.00
15638 *Jo-Anne* ....80.00 - 120.00
15639 *Blue Night* ....80.00 - 120.00

SOUTH STREET RAMBLERS:
Q.R.S. 7019 *Endurance Stomp* ....200.00 - 300.00

SOUTH STREET TRIO:
Victor 20402 *Need More Blues*...............................75.00 - 100.00
21135 *Dallas Blues*..............................100.00 - 150.00
21249 *Suitcase Breakdown*..................100.00 - 150.00
V-38509 *South Street Stomp*..............100.00 - 150.00

BUD SPAIGHT'S HARMONY KINGS:
Broadway 1389 *Don't Lose It*...............................100.00 - 150.00

ROY SPANGLER:
Rex 5024 *Cannon Ball Rag* ....100.00 - 150.00
5026 *Red Onion Rag* ....100.00 - 150.00
5342 *Red Onion Rag* ....100.00 - 150.00
(Foregoing titles on Keen-O-Phone, similarly valued)

MUGGSY SPANIER & HIS RAGTIME BAND:
Bluebird 10384, 10417, 10506, 10518, 10532,
10682, 10719, 10766..............................7.00 - 12.00

SPARTON SYNCOPATORS:
Okeh 41331 *Sweetheart, We Need Each Other* ...... 10.00 - 15.00
41345 *I'll Still Go On Wanting You*...................15.00 - 20.00
Parlophone PNY-34071 *My Mad Moment*.............. 15.00 - 20.00
PNY-34072 *Mia Cara (My Dear)*.........................25.00 - 35.00

PAUL SPECHT & HIS ORCHESTRA; SPECHT'S SOCIETY SERENADERS:
Titles, issued contemporaneously on Clarion, Harmony, and Velvet
Tone: *Keepin' Out Of Mischief Now; Sing A New Song; What A Life* ....10.00 - 15.00
Additional titles, issued on Banner, Paramount, Puritan, and
Triangle: *Hot Lips; You Can Have Him, I Don't Want Him Blues*
....15.00 - 25.00
Columbia 554-D, 577-D, 619-D, 819-D, 853-D,
880-D, 902-D, 1064-D, 1117-D, 1708-D, 1766-D,
1807-D, 1890-D, 1943-D, 2056-D, 2482-D ....7.00 - 12.00
627-D *Static Strut* ....15.00 - 20.00
997-D *She Looks Like Helen Brown* ....10.00 - 15.00
1186-D *Roll Up The Carpets* ....10.00 - 15.00
1273-D *Let A Smile Be Your Umbrella*..............10.00 - 15.00
1307-D *St. Louis Shuffle* ....15.00 - 20.00
1333-D *Not Too Good - Not Too Bad*...............10.00 - 15.00
1836-D *Hittin' The Ceiling* ....10.00 - 15.00
2106-D *Keepin' Myself For You*.......................10.00 - 15.00
2472-D *Falling In Love* ....10.00 - 15.00
A3817 *When You And I Were Young Maggie Blues*
....8.00 - 12.00
Columbia (most other issues)..............................5.00 - 8.00
Mastertone 1030 *Hot Lips* ....20.00 - 30.00

MIKE SPECIALE/SPECIAL & HIS (CARLTON TERRACE) ORCHESTRA:
Cameo 854 *Charleston Baby of Mine* ....8.00 - 12.00
Cameo 51573 *Row, Row, Rosie!* ....20.00 - 30.00
51603 *I Can't See The Beautiful Sea* ....15.00 - 20.00
51612 *When The Dear Old Summer Goes*.........15.00 - 20.00
51614 *Alone At Last*....................................15.00 - 20.00
51635 *When You See That Aunt Of Mine* ....10.00 - 15.00
51673 *A Cup Of Coffee, A Sandwich And You* .10.00 - 15.00
51687 *What Did I Tell Ya?* ....10.00 - 15.00
51688 *As Long As We're In Love* ....10.00 - 15.00
51706 *Tentin' Down In Tennessee* ....15.00 - 20.00
51715 *Behind The Clouds* ....10.00 - 15.00
51751 *The Blue Room* ....15.00 - 20.00
51773 *I'd Give A Lot Of Love* ....15.00 - 20.00
52498 *My Inspiration Is You*...........................30.00 - 40.00
Perfect 14375 *There'll Be Some Changes Made* ......7.00 - 10.00
14405 *Breakin' The Leg*................................10.00 - 15.00
14456 *Row, Row, Rosie* ....8.00 - 12.00
14489 *Breezin' Along* ....10.00 - 15.00
14491 *Want A Little Lovin'* ....10.00 - 15.00
14494 *Walking The Rails* ....10.00 - 15.00
14497 *I'm Knee Deep In Daisies* ....8.00 - 12.00
14505 *Let's Make Believe* ....7.00 - 10.00

14506 *Bam Bam Bamy Shore*	8.00 -	12.00
14526 *Mammy Chasing Blues*	10.00 -	15.00
14536 *I Love My Baby (My Baby Loves Me)*	8.00 -	12.00
14568 *Tentin' Down In Tennessee*	15.00 -	25.00
14569 *Dinah*	10.00 -	15.00
14575 *Ev'rything's Gonna Be All Right*	15.00 -	20.00
14579 *Let's Do It*	8.00 -	12.00
14581 *But I Do -You Know I Do*	10.00 -	15.00
14590 *Could I? I Certainly Could*	8.00 -	12.00
14897 *Highways Are Happy Ways*	10.00 -	15.00
14931 *He Loves And She Loves*	8.00 -	12.00
Perfect, most other issues	5.00 -	10.00

SPENCER TRIO:

Decca 1873 *John Henry*	10.00 -	15.00
1941 *Baby, Won't You Please Come Home*	10.00 -	15.00

HERBERT SPENCER AND HIS ORCHESTRA:

Banner 7032 *Why Do I Love You?*	8.00 -	12.00
7050 *Tin Ear*	10.00 -	15.00
7054 *I Still Love You*	7.00 -	10.00
7055 *She's A Great, Great Girl*	8.00 -	12.00
7057 *Lila*	10.00 -	15.00
7106 *Collegiana*	15.00 -	20.00
7107 *Last Night I Dreamed You Kissed Me*	10.00 -	15.00
7140 *Persian Rug*	15.00 -	20.00
Conqueror 7017 *Rose Room*	10.00 -	15.00
7127 *Persian Rug*	7.00 -	10.00
Domino 4119 *She's A Great, Great Girl*	10.00 -	15.00
Regal 8516 *Lila*	10.00 -	15.00

WALLY SPENCER'S GEORGIANS/HOOSIERS:

15088 *What Happened To Rose (Might Happen To You)*	50.00 -	80.00
15089 *Moonlight And Roses Blues*	15.00 -	20.00
15090 *Horses*	10.00 -	15.00
15093 *I'd Rather Be Alone*	10.00 -	15.00
15304 *Buffalo Rhythm*	80.00 -	130.00
15307 *Rubber Heels*	80.00 -	130.00
15308 *Swamp Blues*	80.00 -	130.00
15362 *Who's That Knockin' At My Door?*	40.00 -	60.00
15363 *The Varsity Drag*	75.00 -	100.00
15366 *Gold Digger*	150.00 -	250.00

SPIKE'S SEVEN PODS OF PEPPER ORCHESTRA:

Nordskog 3009 *Ory's Creole Trombone*	300.00 -	up

REB SPIKES MAJORS AND MINORS:

Columbia 1193-D *My Mammy's Blues*	75.00 -	100.00

PHILIP/PHIL SPITALNY & HIS MUSIC/ORCHESTRA (See also THE HOUR OF CHARM ALL GIRL ORCHESTRA):

Brunswick 4917 *Maybe It's Love*	8.00 -	12.00
Edison 14035 *I Want To Meander In The Meadow*	50.00 -	75.00
14048 *So Sentimental*	50.00 -	75.00
14050 *Same Old Moon*	50.00 -	75.00
14058 *Waiting At The End Of The Road*	50.00 -	75.00
14062 *Just You, Just Me*	50.00 -	75.00
14069 *I May Be Wrong*	50.00 -	75.00
14076 *Bottoms Up*	50.00 -	75.00
14086 *If I Can't Have You*	50.00 -	75.00
(Foregoing are thin, "needle type electric" Edisons)		
52568 *An Eyeful Of You*	50.00 -	80.00
52577 *To Be In Love*	40.00 -	60.00
52589 *Here We Are*	40.00 -	60.00

52605 *When My Dreams Come True*	40.00 -	60.00
52622 *I Want To Meander In The Meadow*	50.00 -	75.00
52637 *So Sentimental*	50.00 -	75.00
Hit of the Week 1096 *Medley Of Canadian Songs* (promotional)	15.00 -	20.00
1100 *Medley Of Northwestern University Songs* (souvenir record)	15.00 -	20.00
Hit of the Week 1053, 1063, 1070, 1076, 1077, 1082, 1086, 1094, 1097, 1132	4.00 -	8.00
Hit of the Week F-3-4 *Lullaby Of The Leaves; Betty Boop*	10.00 -	15.00
Hit of the Week (most other letter-number series)	5.00 -	8.00
(foregoing are single-sided cardboard records)		
Victor 19361 *Worryin' Blues*	10.00 -	15.00
19593 *Don't Bother Me*	8.00 -	12.00
20108 *Jackass Blues*	10.00 -	15.00
20115 *Hello Baby*	7.00 -	10.00
20475 *Rippin' It Off*	10.00 -	15.00
22346 *Any Time's The Time To Fall In Love*	10.00 -	15.00

DICK STABILE AND HIS ORCHESTRA:

Bluebird 7388 *In The Shade Of The Old Apple Tree*	7.00 -	10.00
Decca 716 *Just Because*	10.00 -	15.00
977 *Ja Da*	10.00 -	15.00
Vocalion 3368 *Riffin' At The Ritz*	10.00 -	15.00

JESS STACY (& HIS ORCHESTRA):

Commodore 506, 507, 529, 1503	7.00 -	12.00
Varsity 8064, 8076, 8121, 8132, 8140	7.00 -	12.00

BILL STAFFON & HIS ORCHESTRA:

Bluebird 6048, 6049, 6082, 6115, 6175	7.00 -	12.00

JESSE STAFFORD & HIS (PALACE HOTEL) ORCHESTRA:

Brunswick 4032, 4048, 4070, 4129, 4198, 4250, 4525, 4526, 4527, 4548, 4549, 4629, 4630, 4822, 4823, 4824, 6126, 6171	7.00 -	12.00

MARY STAFFORD AND HER JAZZ BAND:

Columbia A-3365 *Royal Garden Blues*	10.00 -	15.00
A3390 *Down Where They Play The Blues*	10.00 -	15.00
A3418 *Strut Miss Lizzie*	10.00 -	15.00
A3426 *Wild Weeping Blues*	15.00 -	20.00
A3493 *Blind Man Blues*	15.00 -	20.00
A3511 *Monday Morning Blues*	15.00 -	20.00
Pathe Actuelle 7502 *Take Your Finger Off It*	75.00 -	100.00
Perfect 102 -*Take Your Finger Off It*	75.00 -	100.00

AILEEN STANLEY:

Edison 51207 *On The Isle Of Wicky Woo*	15.00 -	20.00
Okeh 4326 *I've Got The Traveling Choo Choo Blues*	10.00 -	15.00
4358 *It Takes A Good Man To Do That*	10.00 -	15.00
4415 *'tain't Nothin' Else But Jazz*	10.00 -	15.00
Okeh, most other issues	7.00 -	10.00
Victor 19373 *Nobody's Sweetheart*	7.00 -	10.00
19486 *Everybody Loves My Baby*	8.00 -	12.00
19863 *No Man's Mama*	8.00 -	12.00
20056 *I Wonder What's Become of Joe?*	8.00 -	12.00
22469 *Swingin' In A Hammock*	10.00 -	15.00
22524 *Wasn't It Nice?*	10.00 -	15.00
Victor, most other issues	5.00 -	8.00

STAN STANLEY & HIS ORCHESTRA:
Champion 16083 *Little White Lies* .... 10.00 - 15.00
    16084 *I Remember You From Somewhere* ....8.00 - 12.00
Gennett 7255 *You Brought A New Kind Of Love To Me*
    ....15.00 - 20.00
    7278 *Little White Lies* ....15.00 - 20.00

AL STARITA & HIS SOCIETY ORCHESTRA:
Cleartone L-3049 *Wang Wang Blues* ....10.00 - 15.00
(Note: Above title on Grey Gull, Jewel is similarly valued; other
    titles are of minimal value.)

HENRY STARR:
Columbia 40003-D *Ploddin' Along* .... -   -   -
Flexo 148 *Mr. Froggie* ....150.00 -   up

STATE STREET RAMBLERS:
Champion 16247 *Tiger Moan* ....250.00 -   up
    16279 *Georgia Grind* ....300.00 -   up
    16320 *Kentucky Blues*.....................................300.00 -   up
    16350 *Richmond Stomp* ....300.00 -   up
    16464 *Careless Love* ....300.00 -   up
    40007 *Barrel House Stomp*.............................30.00 - 50.00
    40009 *Georgia Grind* ....30.00 - 50.00
    40070 *Sic 'Em Tige*...30.00 - 50.00
    40086 *Careless Love*..30.00 - 50.00
Gennett 6232 *Cootie Stomp* ....200.00 -   up
    6249 *There'll Come A Day* ....300.00 -   up
    6454 *My Baby* ....300.00 -   up
    6485 *Shanghai Honeymoon*..............................300.00 -   up
    6552 *Endurance Stomp* ....300.00 -   up
    6569 *Brown-Skin Mama* ....300.00 -   up
    6589 *Tuxedo Stomp*..300.00 -   up
    6641 *Yearning And Blue* ....300.00 -   up
    6692 *Oriental Man* ....400.00 -   up
Savoy 503 *Tiger Moan* ....300.00 -   up
    504 *Wild Man Stomp* .... -   -

STATE STREET SWINGERS:
Vocalion 03284 *Chicago Rhythm*..........................15.00 - 20.00
    03319 *Whippin' That Jelly*................................15.00 - 20.00
    03347 *You Waited Too Long* ....15.00 - 20.00
    03364 *Swing Cat Swing*...................................15.00 - 20.00
    03395 *Rattlesnakin' Daddy* ....15.00 - 20.00
    03462 *You Drink Too Much* ....15.00 - 20.00
    03572 *You Can't Do That To Me* ....20.00 - 30.00

STEAMBOAT JOE & HIS LAFFEN' CLARINET:
Black Patti 8020 *Texas Shuffle* ....300.00 -   up
Gennett 6103 *Mississippi Valley Blues*..................100.00 - 150.00

BLUE STEELE & HIS ORCHESTRA:
Bluebird 5867 *Sugar Babe, I'm Leavin'!* ....7.00 - 10.00
Victor 20971 *Sugar Babe, I'm Leavin'!* ....10.00 - 15.00
    21183 *Betty Jean* ....15.00 - 25.00
    21262 *Washington And Lee Swing* ....15.00 - 20.00
    21355 *Be My Baby*..15.00 - 20.00
    21400 *Because You Are My Dream Girl* ....10.00 - 15.00
    21530 *Beyond The Sunset*..................................10.00 - 15.00
    22436 *You Darlin'* ....10.00 - 15.00
    23002 *Searching* ....20.00 - 30.00
    23014 *Shooin' Flies*..35.00 - 50.00
    23501 *Worries On My Mind*..............................20.00 - 30.00
    V-40140 *Coronado (Brings Memories Of You)* .15.00 - 20.00
    V-40161 *Tennessee Memories*...........................15.00 - 20.00
    V-40182 *Are You Lonesome?* ....50.00 - 75.00
    V-40288 *How Can You Forget?*........................20.00 - 30.00

JOE STEELE & HIS ORCHESTRA:
Victor V-38066 *Coal - Yard Shuffle* ....150.00 - 200.00

BILLY STENNETT'S CAROLINA STOMPERS:
Broadway 1193 *Down Where The Sun Goes Down* .....25.00 - 35.00
    1194 *Buffalo Rhythm*.......................................50.00 - 75.00

LEITH STEVENS AND HIS SATURDAY NIGHT SWING CLUB ORCHESTRA:
Vocalon 4210, 4350 ....7.00 - 12.00

CARLYLE STEVENSON'S BON TON/EL PATIO ORCHESTRA:
Hollywood 1024 *Eccentric* ....75.00 - 100.00
Silver Screen 143 *Thanks For The Buggy Ride* .....30.00 - 50.00
Sunset 1114 *Charleston* ....15.00 - 20.00
    1117 *Milenburg Joys*..50.00 - 75.00
    1119 *Cecilia* ....8.00 - 12.00
    1120 *Collegiate* ....8.00 - 12.00
    1121 *I'm Tired Of Everything But You* ....10.00 - 15.00
    1134 *Remember* ....15.00 - 25.00
    1136 *Sleepy Time Gal* ....15.00 - 20.00

REX STEWART & HIS FIFTY-SECOND STREET STOMPERS/ORCHESTRA; REX STEWART'S BIG SEVEN:
Bluebird 10946, 11057, 11258 ....7.00 - 12.00
Hot Record Society 2004 *Diga Diga Doo* ....10.00 - 15.00
    2005 *Bugle Call Rag* ....10.00 - 15.00
Okeh 3831, 3844, 5448, 5510 ....7.00 - 12.00
Variety 517, 618, 664 ....7.00 - 12.00
Vocalion 2880 *Stingaree* ....20.00 - 30.00
    3831 *Tea And Trumpets* ....8.00 - 12.00
    3844 *Sugar Hill Shim-Sham* ....7.00 - 10.00
    5448 *Fat Stuff Serenade*...................................8.00 - 12.00
    5510 *San Juan Hill*..10.00 - 15.00

SAMMY STEWART & HIS ORCHESTRA; SAMMY STEWART'S TEN KNIGHTS OF SYNCOPATION:
Paramount 20340 *My Man Rocks Me* ....100.00 - 150.00
    20359 *Copenhagen* ....75.00 - 100.00
Puritan 11340 *My Man Rocks Me* ....100.00 - 150.00
    11359 *Copenhagen* ....75.00 - 100.00
Vocalion 15724 *'Cause I Feel Low Down*............100.00 - 150.00
    15734 *Crazy Rhythm*.......................................100.00 - 150.00

JACK STILLMAN'S ORCHESTRA; ORIOLES/ORIOLE ORCHESTRA; STILLMAN CLUB ORCHESTRA:

Bell 368 *Sweet Georgia Brown* ....10.00 - 15.00
 382 *I Wish't I Was In Peoria* ....8.00 - 12.00
 457 *Gone Again Gal* ....8.00 - 12.00
 477 *High-High-High Up In The Hills*...........8.00 - 12.00
Broadway 1001 *Say It Again* ....8.00 - 12.00
 1013 *Blue Bonnet* ....8.00 - 12.00
Challenge 362 *Go Away And Don't Come Back* .....10.00 - 15.00
Champion 15975 *Once Upon A Time* ....8.00 - 12.00
Cameo 51471 *Nobody Knows What A Red-Head Mamma Can Do*
 ....20.00 - 30.00
 51538 *Little Peach*........................25.00 - 40.00
 51768 *Valentine* ....40.00 - 60.00
Emerson 3082 *Gone Again Gal* ....8.00 - 12.00
 3103 *High-High-High Up In The Hills*........8.00 - 12.00
 3106 *My Little Bunch Of Happiness* ....8.00 - 12.00
Gennett 3183 *Cooler Hot* ....15.00 - 20.00
 3226 *Go Away And Don't Come Back* ....8.00 - 12.00
 3227 *Charleston Of The Evening* ....10.00 - 15.00
 3233 *Where Were You Then?* ....10.00 - 15.00
 3244 *Lantern Of Love* ....8.00 - 12.00
 3407 *Faustine* ....8.00 - 12.00
Oriole 494 *Any Blues* ....10.00 - 15.00
 499 *Mr. Cooler Hot* ....10.00 - 15.00
Paramount 20423 *I Wonder Where My Baby Is Tonight*
 ....10.00 - 15.00
 20427 *Clap Hands, Here Comes Charley* ......10.00 - 15.00
 20455 *Blue Bonnet (You Make Me Feel Blue)* .....8.00 - 12.00
Pathe-Actuelle (titles as on Perfect, following)
Perfect 14485 *Mr. Cooler Hot* ....15.00 - 20.00
 14486 *Charleston Of The Evening* ....8.00 - 12.00
 14508 *Hip! Hip!*...........................8.00 - 12.00
 14510 *Go Away And Don't Come Back* ....8.00 - 12.00
 14549 *I Found You, I Want You* ....8.00 - 12.00
 14551 *What A Bird- What A Girl* ....10.00 - 15.00
 14622 *Blue Bonnet*.........................10.00 - 15.00
 14624 *Tonight's My Night With Baby* ....8.00 - 12.00
 14646 *Come On And Do Your Red Hot Business*10.00 - 15.00
 14654 *Nothing But Love* ....10.00 - 15.00
 14655 *Twilight And You* ....10.00 - 15.00
(Foregoing titles also issued on Pathe-Actuelle, similarly valued)
Puritan 11424 *Dream Pal* ....8.00 - 12.00
 11427 *Roll 'Em, Girls* ....10.00 - 15.00
 11429 *If I Had A Girl Like You* ....8.00 - 12.00
 11443 *Say It Again* ....8.00 - 12.00
 11446 *Oh, You Lulu Belle*..................8.00 - 12.00

BERT STOCK & HIS ORCHESTRA:

Gennett 7059 *Honeysuckle Rose* ....35.00 - 50.00
 7075 *'tain't No Sin*.......................35.00 - 50.00
 7213 *Get Happy* ....20.00 - 30.00

OCIE STOCKARD & THE WANDERERS:

Bluebird 7208 *Ain't Nobody Truck Like You* ....15.00 - 20.00
 7296 *One Of Us Was Wrong* ....15.00 - 20.00
 7459 *Same Thing All The Time*.............15.00 - 20.00
 7570 *There'll Be Some Changes Made* ....15.00 - 20.00
 7652 *Black And Blue* ....15.00 - 20.00
 7716 *Just Blues*...........................15.00 - 20.00
 8021 *Wabash Blues*.........................15.00 - 20.00

THE STOMPIN' SIX:

Sunset 1098 *Jimtown Blues* ....300.00 - up
 1099 *Down And Out Blues*...................300.00 - up

THE STOMP SIX:

Autograph 626 *Everybody Loves My Baby*...........500.00 - up

EDDIE STONE & HIS ORCHESTRA:

Vocalion 3555, 3576, 3585, 3703, 3750,
 3984, 3996, 4101.............................7.00 - 12.00

JESSE STONE & HIS BLUES SERENADERS/ ORCHESTRA:

Okeh 8471 *Boot To Boot*.....................150.00 - 200.00
Variety 521 *Wind Storm*......................15.00 - 20.00

CHARLEY STRAIGHT & HIS ORCHESTRA:

Brunswick 3136 *What A Man!*..................10.00 - 15.00
 3224 *Hobo's Prayer*........................10.00 - 15.00
 3076, 3203, 3324, 3516, 3797, 3900 ....7.00 - 10.00
 3899 *That's What I Call Keen* ....8.00 - 12.00
 3945 *Too Busy*.............................10.00 - 15.00
 4026 *Do You, Don't You?* ....10.00 - 15.00
Harmograph 862 *Easy Melody*..................50.00 - 75.00
Paramount 20244 *Buddy's Habits* ....50.00 - 75.00
 20264 *Arkansas Mule* ....50.00 - 75.00
 20266 *That Old Gang Of Mine* ....10.00 - 15.00
 20270 *Tweet Tweet* ....10.00 - 15.00
 20271 *Sweet Henry* ....50.00 - 75.00

STRAND ROOF ORCHESTRA:

Domino 3456 *Prince Of Wails*.................40.00 - 60.00

ELLIS STRATAKOS & HIS HOTEL JUNG ORCHESTRA:

Vocalion 15792 *Weary River*.................200.00 - up

STRAUN'S PULLMAN PORTERS:

Gennett 3005 *Casey Jones* ....10.00 - 15.00

HAL STUART & HIS GANG:

Bell 602 *Hot Coffee* ....15.00 - 20.00
Champion 15680 *Avalon Town*..................8.00 - 12.00

JOE SULLIVAN:

Columbia 2876-D *Gin Mill Blues* ....25.00 - 40.00
 2925-D *Onyx Bringdown* ....35.00 - 50.00
Commodore 538, 540...........................7.00 - 10.00
Decca 600 *Little Rock Getaway* ....10.00 - 15.00
Okeh 5496, 5531, 5647 ....7.00 - 10.00
Vocalion 5496, 5531, 5556 ....7.00 - 12.00

MAXINE SULLIVAN:

Victor 25802, 25810, 25894, 25895, 26124, 26132 .7.00 - 12.00
Vocalion 3654, 3679, 3848, 3885, 3993, 4015, 4068 7.00 - 12.00

SUNNY AND THE D'C'NS:

Blu-Disc T-1003 *Oh-How I Love My Darling!* .... 500.00 - up

SUNSET DANCE ORCHESTRA:

Champion 15038 *High Society* ....40.00 - 60.00

SUNSET SYNCOPATORS:

Sunset 1050 *Copenhagen*......................35.00 - 50.00

THE SUNSHINE BOYS:

Columbia 1834-D, 2303-D, 2489-D ....7.00 - 12.00

SUPER SYNCOPATORS:

Autograph (unnumbered) *Jimtown Blues* ....200.00 - up
 625 *South Bound* ....200.00 - up

SUPERIOR DANCE KINGS:

Superior 2801 *Sweet Georgia Brown* ....100.00 - 150.00

THE SWANEE SWINGERS:
Decca 1022 *Slappin' The Bass* ....10.00 - 15.00

WILBUR (C.) SWEATMAN'S ORIGINAL JAZZ BAND/ ORCHESTRA ; WILBUR SWEATMAN'S BROWNIES; WILBUR SWEATMAN (& HIS ACME SYNCOPATORS/ JAZZ BAND/ORCHESTRA):
Columbia A2611, A2645, A2663, A2682, A2707,
   A2721, A2752, A2768, A2775, A2818, A2994 ...7.00 - 12.00
Cameo 51438 *Battleship Kate* ....50.00 - 80.00
Emerson 5163 (6 inch) *Down Home Rag* ....20.00 - 30.00
   7161 (7 inch) *Down Home Rag* ....20.00 - 30.00
Gennett 5584 *Battleship Kate* ....80.00 - 120.00
Pathe 20145 *Dancing An American Rag* ....25.00 - 40.00
   20147 *Boogie Rag* ....25.00 - 40.00
   20167 *Joe Turner Blues* ....25.00 - 40.00
Victor 23254 *Got 'Em Blues*............................150.00 - 200.00
   V-38597 *Sweat Blues* ....125.00 - 175.00
Vocalion 2945 *Battleship Kate* ....25.00 - 35.00
   2983 *The Hooking Cow Blues* ....25.00 - 35.00

SAMMY SWIFT'S JAZZ BAND:
Black Swan 2042 *Blue Danube Blues* ....25.00 - 40.00
   2082 *The Carolina Shout*.....................................40.00 - 60.00
   2113 *That Red-Head Gal*......................................25.00 - 35.00
   2117 *Way Down Yonder In New Orleans*...........25.00 - 35.00
   10078 *The Carolina Shout*....................................40.00 - 60.00

JOHN(NY) SYLVESTER & HIS ORCHESTRA/ PLAYMATES:
Gennett 3384 *No-One But You (Knows How To Love)*
   ....50.00 - 80.00
   6026 *A Blues Serenade* ....50.00 - 80.00
   6027 *Song Of The Wanderer* ....20.00 - 30.00
   6056 *Indiana Butterfly*......................................250.00 - up
   6061 *No-One But You*...50.00 - 80.00
   6095 *Mine* ....20.00 - 30.00
   6099 *St. Louis Blues* ....50.00 - 80.00
Herschel Gold Seal 2010 *No-One But You*..............75.00 - 100.00
Pathe-Actuelle 036086 *Sweet Man Joe* ....15.00 - 25.00
   036154 *I Wanna Jazz Some More* ....15.00 - 25.00
   036211 *King Porter Stomp* ....20.00 - 30.00
   36331 *I'm Goin' Out If Lizzie Comes In* ....10.00 - 15.00
   36354 *I Would Rather Be Alone In The South*....10.00 - 15.00
   36502 *Looking At The World Thru' Rose Colored Glasses*
   ....8.00 - 12.00
   36555 *Idolizing* ....8.00 - 12.00
   36556 *I've Got The Girl* ....10.00 - 15.00
   36599 *What's The Use?*...10.00 - 15.00
Perfect 14267 *Clearing House Blues*......................15.00 - 25.00
   14335 *Temperamental Papa* ....15.00 - 25.00
   14512 *I'm Goin' Out If Lizzie Comes In* ....10.00 - 15.00
   14535 *1 Would Rather Be Alone In The South*...10.00 - 15.00
   14683 *Looking At The World Thru' Rose Colored Glasses*
   ....8.00 - 12.00
   14736 *Idolizing* ....8.00 - 12.00
   14737 *I've Got The Girl* ....10.00 - 15.00
   14780 *What's The Use*...10.00 - 15.00

SYNCO JAZZ BAND (See also NEW SYNCO JAZZ BAND):
Pathe 20499 *Sweet Mamma (Papa's Getting Mad)*...8.00 - 12.00
   22099 *Slim Trombone*..8.00 - 12.00
   22117 *Alcoholic Blues* ....8.00 - 12.00
   22122 *At The Jazz Band Ball* ....10.00 - 20.00
   22207 *Old Joe Blues*..10.00 - 15.00

Pathe-Actuelle 020558 *Satanic Blues* ....10.00 - 15.00
   020565 *Mysterious Blues*......................................10.00 - 15.00
   020699 *Carolina Blues* ....10.00 - 15.00
Perfect 14013 *Carolina Blues* ....10.00 - 15.00
   14022 *State Street Blues* ....10.00 - 15.00
   14027 *Haunting Blues* ....10.00 - 15.00

SYNCO JAZZERS:
Madison 5059 *Boop Oop A Doop* ....10.00 - 15.00
   50009 *Necking Nellie Home* ....15.00 - 25.00

THE SYNCOPATING FIVE:
Gennett (unnumbered) *Lips* ....20.00 - 30.00

THE SYNCOPATING SEVEN:
Gennett (unnumbered) *Toot-Toot Tootsie* ....100.00 - 150.00
   (unnumbered) *Strutting At The Strutters' Ball*. 100.00 - 150.00

WILLIAM HOWARD TAFT:
Victor 16143 *Our Army And Navy*......................10.00 - 20.00
   35255 *A Protective Tariff* (12 inch) ....10.00 - 20.00
   35256 *Who Are The People* (12 inch)...............10.00 - 20.00

BOB TAMMS & HIS ORCHESTRA:
Broadway 1372 *Blue Is The Night* ....7.00 - 10.00
   1373 *Strike Up The Band* ....8.00 - 12.00
   1374 *Sweeping The Clouds Away* ....15.00 - 20.00
   1509 *Every Time My Heart Beats* ....8.00 - 12.00

TAMPA BLUE JAZZ BAND:
Okeh 4397 *Get Hot* ....10.00 - 15.00
   4405 *Bad Land Blues* ....10.00 - 15.00
   4425 *I've Got The Joys* ....10.00 - 15.00
   4453 *The Missing Link*..10.00 - 15.00
   4461 *Brother Low Down*.......................................10.00 - 15.00
   4485 *Torrid Dora* ....10.00 - 15.00
   4499 *Down Home Blues*.......................................10.00 - 20.00
   4522 *Atta Baby*..10.00 - 15.00
   4544 *Hurry Back Home* ....10.00 - 20.00
   4573 *Dying With The Blues* ....15.00 - 25.00
   4595 *The West Texas Blues*...................................15.00 - 20.00
   4663 *Hot Lips* ....15.00 - 20.00
   4671 *Haunting Blues*...10.00 - 15.00
   4773 *Four O'Clock Blues* ....15.00 - 20.00
   4777 *At The Weeping Widow's Ball* ....10.00 - 15.00
   4791 *The Cootie Crawl*...15.00 - 20.00
   4803 *Sunny Jim* ....10.00 - 15.00
   4816 *Railroad Man* ....15.00 - 20.00
   4826 *Maxie Jones* ....10.00 - 20.00

FRANK TANNER'S RHYTHM KINGS:
Bluebird 6667 *You Don't Love Me* ....10.00 - 15.00
   6686 *Wrappin' It Up* ....10.00 - 15.00
   6690 *Sailor Man Rhythm* ....10.00 - 15.00
   6719 *Death In B Flat* ....10.00 - 15.00
   6750 *Texas Teaser* ....10.00 - 15.00

CARROLL C. TATE:
Victor 21061 *You Live On In Memory*...................30.00 - 50.00

ERSKINE TATE'S VENDOME ORCHESTRA:
Okeh 4907 *Chinaman Blues* ....200.00 - 300.00
Vocalion 1027 *Static Strut* ....200.00 - 300.00
   15372 *Static Strut*..200.00 - 300.00

ART TATUM (& HIS BAND/SWINGSTERS):
Brunswick 6543 *St. Louis Blues* ....15.00 - 20.00
   6553 *Tea For Two*...15.00 - 20.00

Decca 155 *Moon Glow* ....10.00 - 15.00
  156 *Cocktails For Two* ....10.00 - 15.00
  306 *Star Dust* ....10.00 - 15.00
  468 *The Shout* ....10.00 - 15.00
  741 *When A Woman Loves A Man* ....10.00 - 15.00
  1197 *Body And Soul*...10.00 - 15.00
  1198 *With Plenty Of Money And You* ....10.00 - 15.00
  1373 *(I Would Do) Anything For You* ....8.00 - 12.00
  1603 *Stormy Weather* ....8.00 - 12.00
(foregoing have shaded letters in DECCA)
  2052, 2456 ....7.00 - 10.00
  8526 *Battery Bounce*..10.00 - 15.00
  8536 *Stompin' At The Savoy*..................................10.00 - 15.00
  8563 *Corrine Corrina*..10.00 - 15.00
  8577 *Rock Me, Mama* ....10.00 - 15.00

JACKIE TAYLOR & HIS ORCHESTRA:
Victor 22500 *We're On The Highway To Heaven*...10.00 - 15.00

JASPER TAYLOR & HIS ORIGINAL WASHBOARD BAND/STATE STREET BOYS:
Paramount 12409 *Stomp Time Blues* ....250.00 - up
Vocalion 1196 *Jasper Taylor Blues* ....250.00 - up

RAY/ROY TAYLOR & HIS (SINGING) ORCHESTRA:
Champion 15323 *Sweetheart Of Sigma Chi* ....60.00 - 100.00
  15324 *Sweet Violets*...20.00 - 30.00
  15342 *Somebody And Me* ....20.00 - 30.00
  15343 *Show Me That Kind Of A Girl* ....25.00 - 35.00
Superior 356 *Sweet Violets* ....50.00 - 100.00
  359 *Show Me That Kind Of A Girl* ....50.00 - 100.00

TAYLOR'S DIXIE SERENADERS:
Victor 23277 *Everybody Loves My Baby* ....200.00 - 300.00

JACK TEAGARDEN (& HIS CHICAGOANS/ ORCHESTRA):
Brunswick 6716 *A Hundred Years From Today* .....10.00 - 15.00
  6741 *Blue River* ....10.00 - 15.00
  6780 *Ol' Pappy* ....10.00 - 15.00
  6993 *Stars Fell On Alabama* ....10.00 - 15.00
  7652 *Junk Man* ....8.00 - 12.00
Columbia 2558-D *You Rascal, You* ....25.00 - 40.00
  2802-D *Shake Your Hips* ....25.00 - 40.00
  2913-D *Plantation Moods* ....25.00 - 40.00
  35206, 35215, 35224, 35233, 35245, 35252,
  35297, 35323 ....7.00 - 12.00
Crown 3051 *Rockin' Chair*......................................50.00 - 75.00
Decca, most issues ....7.00 - 10.00
Hot Record Society 2006, 2007.................................7.00 - 12.00
Perfect 15361 *You're Simply Delish*.......................15.00 - 25.00
  15363 *Son Of The Sun* ....15.00 - 25.00
Varsity, most issues ....7.00 - 12.00

TED & HIS GANG:
Radiex 1531 *Forgetting You*....................................10.00 - 15.00
(Note: Above also issued on Grey Gull)

THE TEMPO KINGS:
Pathe-Actuelle 36385 *Rhythm Of The Day*.............12.00 - 16.00
Perfect 14566 *Rhythm Of The Day* ....12.00 - 16.00

TEN BLACK BERRIES:
Titles, issued contemporaneously on Banner, Cameo, Challenge, Conqueror, Domino, Jewel, Oriole, Perfect, Regal, and Romeo:

Jungle Blues; Rent Party Blues; St. James' Infirmary; When You're Smiling ....15.00 - 20.00
Banner 0839 *Tiger Rag* ....15.00 - 20.00
Jewel 6089 *Tiger Rag* ....15.00 - 20.00
Oriole 2089 *St. Louis Blues* ....15.00 - 20.00
Regal 10145 *St. Louis Blues* ....15.00 - 20.00
  1453 *Tiger Rag* ....15.00 - 20.00

TEN BLACK DIAMONDS:
Title issued contemporaneously on Banner, Cameo, and Romeo:
  Freshman Hop ....15.00 - 25.00
Banner 6539 *Look What You've Done To Me*..........8.00 - 12.00
  6542 *That's Why I'm Jealous Of You* ....8.00 - 12.00

TEN FRESHMEN:
Pathe-Actuelle 37054 *A Bag O' Blues* ....20.00 - 30.00
Perfect 15150 *My Kinda Love* ....8.00 - 12.00
  15235 *A Bag O' Blues*...20.00 - 30.00
Perfect, most other issues ....7.00 - 10.00

TENNESSEE CHOCOLATE DROPS:
Vocalion 1517 *Vine Street Drag*..........................100.00 - 150.00

TENNESSEE HAPPY BOYS:
Cameo 51575 *Sweet Georgia Brown* ....15.00 - 20.00
  51613 *Wait'll It's Moonlight* ....15.00 - 20.00
  51703 *Birdie*...15.00 - 20.00
  51736 *Tie Me To Your Apron Strings Again* ....15.00 - 20.00
Cameo (most other issues) ....8.00 - 12.00

TENNESSEE MUSIC MEN:
Clarion 5389-C *Georgia On My Mind* ....35.00 - 50.00
  5392-C *You Rascal You* ....35.00 - 50.00
  5446-C *Loveless Love* ....20.00 - 30.00
  5461-C *Bugle Call Rag* ....35.00 - 50.00
  5467-C *Choo Choo* ....20.00 - 30.00
  5469-C *Baby Won't You Please Come Home*....50.00 - 75.00
  5474-C *Shim-Me-Sha- Wabble* ....25.00 - 35.00
Harmony 1375-H *Georgia On My Mind*..................35.00 - 50.00
  1378-H *You Rascal You* ....35.00 - 50.00
  1406-H *Loveless Love*..20.00 - 30.00
  1415-H *Bugle Call Rag* ....35.00 - 50.00
  1420-H *Choo Choo* ....20.00 - 30.00
  1422-H *Baby, Won't You Please Come Home*...50.00 - 75.00
  1427-H *Shim-Me-Sha-Wabble* ....25.00 - 35.00
Velvet Tone 2453-V *Georgia On My Mind*............35.00 - 50.00
  2456-V *You Rascal You* ....35.00 - 50.00
  2506-V *Loveless Love* ....20.00 - 30.00
  2521-V *Bugle Call Rag* ....35.00 - 50.00
  2527-V *Choo Choo* ....20.00 - 30.00
  2529-V *Baby, Won't You Please Come Home* ..50.00 - 75.00
  2534-V *Shim-Me-Sha-Wabble* ....25.00 - 35.00

TENNESSEE TEN:
Gennett 3285 *What Happened To Rose (Might Happen To You)*
....50.00 - 80.00
   3286 *Here Comes Emaline* ....50.00 - 80.00
Victor 19073, 19094, 19105, 19109, 19130 ....7.00 - 12.00

THE TENNESSEE TOOTERS:
Vocalion 14952 *Prince Of Wails*..................20.00 - 30.00
  14967 *Hot-Hot-Hottentot*......................20.00 - 30.00
  14985 *Everybody Loves My Baby*.............20.00 - 30.00
  15004 *Red Hot Henry Brown* ....20.00 - 30.00
  15022 *Jimtown Blues* ....20.00 - 30.00
  15068 *Milenberg Joys*..........................20.00 - 30.00
  15086 *Charleston*...............................15.00 - 20.00
  15109 *Deep Elm*.................................25.00 - 35.00
  15135 *I Ain't Got Nobody*.....................25.00 - 35.00
  15169 *Hot Aire* ....25.00 - 35.00
  15201 *Fallin' Down*.............................15.00 - 20.00
  15388 *Hobo's Prayer* ....35.00 - 50.00
  15487 *Crazy Quilt*..............................15.00 - 20.00
  15488 *You're Burnin' Me Up* ....25.00 - 40.00

TENNESSEE TRIO:
Vocalion 5472 *Knox County Stomp*...............100.00 - 150.00

MAX TERR & HIS ORCHESTRA:
Pathe-Actuelle 036175 *Have A Little Fun*.......50.00 - 80.00
  036197 *How Do You Do* ....10.00 - 15.00
Perfect 14356 *Have A Little Fun* ....50.00 - 80.00
  14378 *How Do You Do* ....10.00 - 15.00
  14464 *My Dawg*...............................10.00 - 15.00
  14468 *Fascinatin' Baby*.......................10.00 - 15.00
  14469 *When You Do What You Do*.........8.00 - 12.00
  14475 *Charleston Bound* ....10.00 - 15.00
  14478 *Farewell* ....8.00 - 12.00
  14576 *Pensacola* ....12.00 - 16.00

BOB TERRY & HIS ORCHESTRA:
Champion 40093 *My Heart And I* ....10.00 - 15.00
  40094 *It's Been So Long*......................10.00 - 15.00

THELMA TERRY & HER PLAY BOYS:
Columbia 1390-D *Voice Of The Southland*.........10.00 - 15.00
  1532-D *Starlight And Tulips*..................8.00 - 12.00
  1588-D *Dusky Stevedore* ....15.00 - 20.00
  1706-D *Mama's Gone, Goodbye*............20.00 - 30.00

FRANK TESCHEMACHER (See CHICAGO RHYTHM KINGS)

THE TEXANS:
Okeh 40892 *Barbara* ....8.00 - 12.00
  40914 *Everybody Loves My Girl* ....10.00 - 15.00
  40938 *Did You Mean It?* ....75.00 - 100.00

TEXAS BLUES DESTROYERS:
Ajax 17065 *Lenox Avenue Shuffle*..............50.00 - 75.00
Pathe-Actuelle 036160 *Lenox Avenue Shuffle*........50.00 - 75.00
Perfect 14314 *Lenox Avenue Shuffle* ....50.00 - 75.00
Vocalion 14913 *Lenox Avenue Shuffle*..........50.00 - 75.00

TEXAS TODDLERS:
Varsity 5081 *Keepin' Out Of Mischief Now*............7.00 - 10.00

THEM BIRMINGHAM NIGHT OWLS:
Champion 15338 *Sugar!*........................200.00 - 300.00

HENRY THIES AND HIS (CASTLE FARM/HOTEL SINTON) ORCHESTRA:
Gennett 3118 *Angry* ....20.00 - 30.00
  3142 *Spanish Melody* ....12.00 - 16.00
Victor 21890 *Sweet Liza* ....15.00 - 20.00
  21462 *When You're Smiling* ....8.00 - 12.00
  22460 *June Kisses* ....10.00 - 15.00
  22461 *Sharing* ....10.00 - 15.00
  22476 *Here Comes Emily Brown*............15.00 - 20.00

THOMAS' DEVILS:
Brunswick 7064 *Boot It, Boy* ....200.00 - up

THOMAS' MUSCLE SHOALS DEVILS:
Okeh 8225 *Wash Woman Blues* ....150.00 - 250.00

EDDIE THOMAS' COLLEGIANS:
Columbia 1154-D *Sugar* ....10.00 - 15.00

GEORGE THOMAS & HIS BOYS:
Champion 15434 *Blue Hawaii* ....125.00 - 175.00

HARRY THOMAS:
Victor 18229 *A Classical Spasm*...............15.00 - 25.00

HERSAL THOMAS:
Okeh 8227 *Suitcase Blues*.....................100.00 - 150.00

HOCIEL THOMAS:
Buddy 8020 *I Must Have It*....................100.00 - 150.00
  8021 *Worried Down With The Blues* ....100.00 - 150.00
Gennett 3004 *I Can't Feel Frisky Without My Liquor*
....75.00 - 100.00
  3006 *I Must Have It* ....50.00 - 75.00
Okeh 8222 *Fish Tail Dance* ....75.00 - 100.00
  8258 *Adam And Eve Got The Blues* ....150.00 - 250.00
  8289 *Gambler's Dream* ....150.00 - 250.00
  8297 *Deep Water Blues* ....150.00 - 250.00
  8326 *Sunshine Baby* ....150.00 - 250.00
  8346 *Listen To Ma* ....150.00 - 250.00

HOWARD THOMAS & HIS ORCHESTRA:
Champion 15840 *Piccolo Pete*.................15.00 - 25.00
  15980 *That's All I Want In Life* ....15.00 - 20.00
  16380 *Business In F*..........................100.00 - 150.00
  16387 *In The Shade Of The Old Apple Tree*....100.00 - 150.00
  16554 *New Orleans* ....- - -
  16656 *Rose Of Washington Square* ....100.00 - 150.00
  16776 *Moonglow* ....- - -
  16785 *White Heat* ....- - -
  16787 *I Ain't Lazy, I'm Just Dreaming* ....- - -
  16813 *Emaline* ....- - -
  40080 *Business In F* ....30.00 - 50.00
  Gennett 6611 *My Darling* ....- - -
6998 *Piccolo Pete* ....25.00 - 40.00
  7195 *Since You've Gone Away* ....20.00 - 30.00

MILLARD G. THOMAS (& HIS CHICAGO NOVELTY ORCHESTRA):
Ajax 17045 *Lazy Drag*.........................80.00 - 120.00
  17052 *More* ....80.00 - 120.00
  17053 *Hard Luck Blues* ....80.00 - 120.00
  17056 *Worryin' Blues*........................80.00 - 120.00
  17074 *Blue Ivories* ....150.00 - 200.00

JOHNNY THOMPSON:
Columbia 14285-D *Back In Your Own Backyard*...20.00 - 30.00

KAY THOMPSON AND THE BOYS/HER ORCHESTRA:
Brunswick 7560, 7564 ....8.00 -   12.00
Victor 25564, 25582 ....8.00 -   12.00

CLAUDE THORNHILL AND HIS ORCHESTRA:
Brunswick 7951, 7957 ....8.00 -   12.00
Columbia, most issues ....5.00 -   10.00
Harmony 1038 *Lullaby Of The Rain* ....7.00 -   10.00
Okeh 6124, 6168, 6178, 6202, 6234............7.00 -   10.00
V-Disc (12-inch) 612 *Stealin' Apples*........10.00 -   15.00
Vocalion 3595 *Gone With The Wind* ....8.00 -   12.00
    3616 *Stop! You're Breaking My Heart* ....8.00 -   12.00

THE THREE BARBERS:
Pathe-Actuelle 36414 *Down Town Rag* ....30.00 -   50.00
Perfect 14565 *Down Town Rag* ....30.00 -   50.00

THREE BLACK DIAMONDS:
Lincoln 2331 *Freakish Blues* ....15.00 -   20.00

THREE BLUES CHASERS:
Okeh 8595 *Nothin' But Blues* ....50.00 -   75.00

THE THREE BOSWELL SISTERS:
Okeh 41444 *Heebie Jeebies*.........................30.00 -   50.00
    41470 *Gee, But I'd Like To Make You Happy*....30.00 -   50.00

THE THREE DEUCES:
Commodore 537, 539 ....7.00 -   12.00

THREE HAPPY DARKIES:
Silvertone 3057 *Freakish Blues* ....15.00 -   20.00

THREE HOT ESKIMOS:
Pathe-Actuele 036298 *Black Cat Blues* ....20.00 -   30.00
Perfect 14479 *Black Cat Blues* ....20.00 -   30.00

THE THREE JACKS:
Okeh 41102 *Spanish Shawl* ....15.00 -   20.00

THREE JOLLY MINERS:
Vocalion 1003 *Pig Alley Stomp*...................40.00 -   60.00
    1004 *Chicago Back Step* ....40.00 -   60.00
    15009 *Freakish Blues* ....15.00 -   20.00
    15051 *Black Cat Blues*...........................15.00 -   20.00
    15087 *Lake George Blues* ....30.00 -   50.00
    15111 *Plain Old Blues* ....30.00 -   50.00
    15141 *Texas Shuffle* ....25.00 -   40.00
    15164 *House Party Stomp* ....25.00 -   40.00
    15269 *Pig Alley Stomp*...........................35.00 -   50.00
    15271 *Chicago Back Step* ....35.00 -   50.00

THE THREE KEYS:
Brunswick 6388 *Jig Time* ....15.00 -   20.00
    6411 *Nagasaki* ....15.00 -   20.00
    6423 *Wah-Dee-Dah*.................................15.00 -   20.00
    6522 *That Doggone Dog Of Mine* ....15.00 -   20.00
    6567 *Rasputin* ....15.00 -   20.00
Columbia 2706-D *Mood Indigo*....................20.00 -   30.00
Vocalion 2523 *Heebie Jeebies*......................20.00 -   30.00
    2569 *I Found A New Baby* ....20.00 -   30.00
    2730 *Someone Stole Gabriel's Horn* ....15.00 -   20.00
    2732 *Fit As A Fiddle* ....15.00 -   20.00
    2744 *Basin Street Blues*...........................15.00 -   20.00
    2755 *(I Would Do) Anything For You* ....15.00 -   20.00
    2765 *Oh! By Jingo* ....15.00 -   20.00

THREE MONKEY CHASERS:
Harmony 23-H *Corn Bread Wiggle*...............20.00 -   30.00
    50-H *Uncle Remus Stomp* ....25.00 -   35.00

THE THREE PEPPERS:
Decca 2239, 2557, 2609, 2751, 3342, 8508..............8.00 -   12.00
Variety 523 *Alexander's Ragtime Band*................10.00 -   15.00
    590 *The Duck's Yas Yas*.........................10.00 -   15.00
    630 *Serenade In The Night* ....10.00 -   15.00
    650 *Swingin' At The Cotton Club* ....10.00 -   15.00
Vocalion 3803 *Swing Out Uncle Wilson* ....10.00 -   15.00
    3805 *The Midnight Ride Of Paul Revere* ....10.00 -   15.00

THREE'S A CROWD:
Bluebird 10014, 10051, 10160...................... 7.00 -   10.00

THE THREE T'S:
Victor 25273 *I'se A Muggin'* .... 15.00 -   20.00

THREE-FIFTEEN & HIS SQUARES:
Vocalion 03515 *Three Fifteen Blues* ....30.00 -   50.00
    03560 *Mollie Mae Blues* ....30.00 -   50.00

LE ROY TIBBS & HIS CONNIE'S INN ORCHESTRA:
Columbia 14309-D *One O'Clock Blues*................100.00 -   150.00

THE TICKLE TOE TEN:
Okeh 40325 *Yearning* .... 8.00 -   12.00
    40414 *Just A Little Drink* .... 10.00 -   15.00
    40428 *The Promenade Walk* .... 10.00 -   15.00

TIM TIMOTHY & HIS FRIVOLITY CLUB ORCHESTRA:
Cameo 1276, 1279 .... 7.00 -   10.00
Cameo 52311 *My Pet*................................ 40.00 -   60.00

KLIEN TINDULL'S PARAMOUNT SERENADERS:
Paramount 12377 *Down On The Amazon* .... 250.00 -   up

THE TIN PAN PARADERS:
Gennett 6456 *My Pet*................................ 20.00 -   30.00
    6488 *Mama's Grown Young, Papa's Grown Old*15.00 -   20.00
    6504 *Who Wouldn't Be Blue*............................ 15.00 -   20.00
    6520 *When Sweet Susie Goes Steppin' By*......... 20.00 -   30.00
    6849 *She Only Laughs At Me*........................ 20.00 -   30.00
    6921 *Believe It Or Not* .... 20.00 -   30.00
    6965 *If I Were You I'd Fall In Love With Me* .... 20.00 -   30.00
    6967 *I'm Finding The Long Way Home* .... 15.00 -   20.00
    6998 *Scotchie* .... 25.00 -   40.00
    7012 *Clowning* .... 20.00 -   30.00
    7072 *Wake Up Your Feet* .... 20.00 -   30.00
    7119 *Kickin' A Hole In The Sky* .... 25.00 -   40.00
    7132 *Harmonica Harry*.............................. 30.00 -   50.00
    7146 *You've Got That Thing* .... 25.00 -   40.00
    7148 *Puttin' On The Ritz* .... 25.00 -   40.00
    7174 *Chinnin' And Chattin' With May*............ 30.00 -   50.00
    7192 *The Free And Easy* .... 25.00 -   40.00
Silvertone 8067 *My Pet*.............................. 15.00 -   20.00
Supertone 9333 *My Scandinavian Gal*.................. 15.00 -   20.00
    9416 *She Only Laughs At Me*....................... 15.00 -   20.00
    9464 *Now I'm In Love*.............................. 15.00 -   20.00
    9477 *I Lift Up My Finger And I Say "Tweet Tweet"*
    .... 15.00 -   20.00
    9544 *I Gotta Have You* .... 15.00 -   20.00
    9616 *The Man From The South* .... 20.00 -   30.00
    9620 *Just Can't Be Bothered With Me* .... 15.00 -   20.00
    9634 *The Free And Easy*............................ 15.00 -   20.00
    9692 *Chinnin' And Chattin' With May* .... 15.00 -   20.00

TINSLEY'S WASHBOARD BAND:
Victor 24405 *Shoutin' In The Amen Corner* .... 50.00 -   75.00

BEN TOBIER & HIS CALIFORNIA CYCLONES:
Champion 16465 *Hot And Heavy* ....100.00 - 150.00
Superior 2571 *Hot And Heavy* ....100.00 - 150.00

TOBIN'S MIDNIGHT SERENADERS:
Okeh 40297 *I'm Afraid To Care For You* ....100.00 - 150.00

SKEETS TOLBERT AND HIS GENTLEMEN OF SWING:
Decca 7570, 7591, 7630, 7653, 7669, 7717, 7722,
7751, 7791, 8506, 8516, 8528, 8534, 8565, 8579,
8589, 8608, 8617, 8631, 8641 ....7.00 - 12.00

TOM AND JERRY:
Champion 15507 *Dustin' The Keys* ....150.00 - 250.00

PINKY TOMLIN:
Brunswick 7377, 7378, 7502, 7525, 7594, 7653,
7731, 7811, 7849, 7897 ....7.00 - 12.00

TOMMY "RED" TOMPKINS & HIS ORCHESTRA:
Variety 543, 610 ....7.00 - 12.00
Vocalion 3271, 3293 ....7.00 - 12.00

TRACY-BROWN'S ORCHESTRA:
Columbia 1344-D *Chloe (Song Of The Swamp)*........8.00 - 12.00
1405-D *Sh-h! Here Comes My Sugar* ....10.00 - 15.00
1541-D *Joline* ....7.00 - 10.00

TRAM, BIX & EDDIE:
Okeh 40871 *For No Reason At All In C* ....80.00 - 120.00

TRAM, BIX & LANG:
Okeh 40916 *Wringin' And Twistin'* ....80.00 - 120.00

THE TRAVELERS:
Melotone 12113 *Sweet And Hot* ....8.00 - 12.00
12148 *I've Got A Sweet Somebody* ....8.00 - 12.00
12227 *I Apologize* ....6.00 - 10.00
12230 *I Can't Get Mississippi Off My Mind* ......20.00 - 30.00
Okeh 41259 *Am I Blue* ....25.00 - 40.00
41260 *Breakaway* ....25.00 - 40.00
41471 *Fine And Dandy* ....25.00 - 40.00

VINCENT TRAVERS AND HIS (HOTEL WALTON) ORCHESTRA:
Titles issued contemporaneously on Banner, Melotone, Oriole,
Perfect, Romeo, and Vocalion: *Love Is Good For Anything That
Ails You; Was It Rain?* ....8.00 - 12.00
Electradisk, any issues ....7.00 - 12.00
Sunrise, any issues ....20.00 - 30.00

PHILIP TRAVERSI & HIS ORCHESTRA:
Radio Tono 15482 *Tamales Calientes*.....................50.00 - 100.00
(Note: Above is a picture record)

TRAVIS-CARLTON ORCHESTRA:
Gennett 3096 *Alone At Last* ....10.00 - 15.00
3099 *Headin' For Home*....................................15.00 - 25.00
3216 *Somebody's Eyes* ....10.00 - 15.00

THE TRAYMORE ORCHESTRA:
Vocalion 15555 *Soliloquy* ....50.00 - 75.00
15556 *Black And Tan Fantasy*............................50.00 - 75.00

PAUL TREMAINE AND HIS ARISTOCRATS/ ORCHESTRA:
Bluebird 5049 *Stormy Weather* ....8.00 - 12.00
5050 *It's Sunday Down In Caroline* ....8.00 - 12.00
5053 *She'll Be Comin' 'Round The Mountain* ....8.00 - 12.00
(Foregoing titles on Electradisk are valued similarly; on Sunrise,
substantially higher)

Columbia 2130-D *Hand Me Down My Walkin' Cane* ...8.00 - 12.00
2200-D *Rockin' Chair*......................................10.00 - 15.00
2229-D *Steamboat Bill*....................................10.00 - 15.00
2302-D *Gospel Train* ....10.00 - 15.00
2462-D *I Wanna Sing About You*.....................10.00 - 15.00
2510-D *I Can't Get Mississippi Off My Mind* ... 10.00 - 15.00
Victor V-40176 *Four-Four Rhythm*......................35.00 - 50.00
V-40230 *Sarah Lee* ....20.00 - 30.00

GEORGE H. TREMER:
Champion 15372 *Some Of These Days*.................125.00 - 175.00
15436 *Spirit Of '49 Rag* ....150.00 - 250.00
Decca 7137 *Spirit of '49 Rag* ....10.00 - 15.00
Gennett 6242 *Spirit Of '49 Rag* ....250.00 - up

ALPHONSE TRENT & HIS ORCHESTRA:
Champion 15956 *St. James Infirmary* ....200.00 - up
16587 *I've Found A New Baby* ....250.00 - up
Gennett 6664 *Louder and Funnier* ....250.00 - up
6710 *Nightmare* ....250.00 - up
7161 *After You've Gone* ....300.00 - up

JO TRENT AND THE D'C'NS:
Blu-Disc T-1003 *Deacon Jazz* ....500.00 - up

TRIANGLE HARMONY BOYS:
Gennett 6275 *Sweet Patootie* ....300.00 - up
6322 *Canned Heat Blues* ....300.00 - up
Superior 372 *Chicken Supper Strut* ....300.00 - up

BARNEY TRIMBLE & HIS OKLAHOMANS:
Harmony 781-H *Are We Downhearted? No!*............ 8.00 - 12.00
926-H *Honey*...8.00 - 12.00
948-H *I'm Featuring A Nest* ....8.00 - 12.00
958-H *Where The Sweet Forget-Me-Nots Remember*
....10.00 - 15.00
987-H *Bashful Baby*.......................................10.00 - 15.00
1093-H *Blue, Turning Grey Over You* .... 8.00 - 12.00
(Note: Above titles, on Diva and Velvet Tone, are similarly valued.)

TRI-STATE DANCE RAMBLERS:
Champion 15094 *But I Do- You Know I Do* ....12.00 - 16.00

TROMBONE RED AND HIS BLUE SIX:
Columbia 14612-D *Greasy Plate Stomp*...............200.00 - 300.00

CHARLIE TROUTT'S MELODY ARTISTS:
Columbia 1030-D *Transportation Blues* ....10.00 - 15.00
1265-D *Transportation Blues, Parts 3/4* ....15.00 - 20.00
Okeh 40589 *Mountain City Blues*..........................75.00 - 100.00
40627 *Sweet Child (I'm Wild About You)*..........80.00 - 130.00

THE TROY HARMONISTS:
Pathe-Actuelle 7508 *Great Scott*...........................80.00 - 120.00
Perfect 108 *Great Scott*.......................................80.00 - 120.00

FRANKIE TRUMBAUER & HIS ORCHESTRA; FRANKIE TRUMBAUER'S AUGMENTED ORCHESTRA:
Brunswick 6146 *Crazy Quilt* ....20.00 - 30.00
6159 *Honeysuckle Rose* ....20.00 - 30.00
6763 *Juba Dance* ....10.00 - 15.00
6788 *Emaline* ....10.00 - 15.00
6912 *China Boy*..10.00 - 15.00
6997 *In A Mist* ....10.00 - 15.00
7613 *Breakin' In A Pair Of Shoes* ....8.00 - 12.00
7629 *Announcer's Blues* ....8.00 - 12.00

7663 *'s Wonderful*	8.00 -	12.00
7665 *Ain't Misbehavin'*	8.00 -	12.00
7687 *Diga Diga Doo*	8.00 -	12.00
Columbia 2710-D *Business In Q*	15.00 -	25.00
2729-D *The Newest St. Louis Blues*	15.00 -	25.00
2879-D *Bass Drum Dan*	15.00 -	25.00
18002-D *Sizzling One-Step Medley*	20.00 -	30.00
Okeh 40772 *Singin' The Blues*	35.00 -	50.00
40822 *Ostrich Walk*	75.00 -	100.00
40843 *I'm Coming Virginia*	75.00 -	100.00
40871 *Trumbology*	80.00 -	120.00
40879 *Blue River*	50.00 -	80.00
40903 *Three Blind Mice*	75.00 -	100.00
40926 *Humpty Dumpty*	75.00 -	100.00
40966 *A Good Man Is Hard To Find*	75.00 -	100.00
40979 *There'll Come A Time*	50.00 -	80.00
41019 *Lila*	50.00 -	80.00
41039 *My Pet*	50.00 -	80.00
41044 *Jubilee*	50.00 -	80.00
41100 *Dusky Stevedore*	50.00 -	80.00
41128 *High Up On A Hill Top*	50.00 -	80.00
41145 *Take Your Tomorrow*	50.00 -	80.00
41209 *Futuristic Rhythm*	50.00 -	80.00
41231 *Louise*	50.00 -	80.00
41252 *Nobody But You*	35.00 -	50.00
41268 *Shivery Stomp*	35.00 -	50.00
41286 *Baby, Won't You Please Come Home?*	50.00 -	80.00
41301 *How Am I To Know?*	30.00 -	50.00
41313 *Turn On The Heat*	30.00 -	50.00
41326 *My Sweeter Than Sweet*	30.00 -	50.00
41330 *What Wouldn't I Do For That Man?*	30.00 -	50.00
41421 *Happy Feet*	30.00 -	50.00
41431 *Deep Harlem*	30.00 -	50.00
41437 *What's The Use?*	30.00 -	50.00
41450 *Choo Choo*	30.00 -	50.00
Varsity, most issues	7.00 -	12.00
Victor 24812 *Blue Moon*	15.00 -	20.00
24834 *Troubled*	15.00 -	20.00

TRUMP'S AMBASSADOR BELL HOPS ORCHESTRA:

Okeh 1 *What A Man*	- -	-

GEORGE TUCKER & HIS NOVELTY BAND:

Champion 15638 *Doin' The New Low Down*	80.00 -	120.00
15639 *Spiked Beer*	80.00 -	120.00

ORRIN TUCKER AND HIS ORCHESTRA:

Columbia, most issues	4.00 -	8.00
Vocalion, most issues	5.00 -	8.00

SOPHIE TUCKER:

Aeolian-Vocalion 12099 *Everybody Shimmies Now*	50.00 -	80.00
Arto 9065 *Don't You Throw Me Down*	- -	-
Columbia 826-D *Some Of These Days*	10.00 -	15.00
Okeh 4565 *High Brown Blues*	20.00 -	30.00
4590 *Jig Walk*	15.00 -	20.00
4617, 4817, 4818, 4837, 4839, 40054	8.00 -	15.00
40068 *I've Got A Cross-Eyed Papa*	20.00 -	30.00
40129 *Hula Lou*	15.00 -	25.00
40813 *One Sweet Letter From You*	20.00 -	30.00
40837 *After You've Gone*	20.00 -	30.00
40895 *There's A Cradle In Caroline*	10.00 -	15.00
40921 *There'll Be Some Changes Made*	15.00 -	25.00
41010 *The Man I Love*	15.00 -	20.00
41058 *'Cause I Feel Low Down*	15.00 -	20.00
41249 *I Ain't Takin' Orders From No-One*	15.00 -	20.00

Victor 21993, 21994, 21995	8.00 -	12.00
Victor 22049 *Some Of These Days*	15.00 -	20.00

TOMMY TUCKER & HIS CALIFORNIANS/ ORCHESTRA; TOMMY TUCKER TIME:

Columbia *(most issues)*	4.00 -	8.00
Crown 3470 *Low Down Upon The Harlem River*	10.00 -	15.00
3497 *Blue Prelude*	10.00 -	15.00
3471, 3477, 3478, 3479, 3499	7.00 -	10.00
Okeh (most issues)	4.00 -	8.00
Varsity 8070 *Blue Prelude*	8.00 -	12.00
Vocalion (most issues)	5.00 -	8.00

EDDIE TULLER & HIS REDONDO PAVILION ORCHESTRA:

Hollywood 1067 *Charleston Charley*	- -	-

AL TURK'S (PRINCESS) ORCHESTRA:

Okeh 8362 *Snag It*	150.00 -	200.00
8377 *Mean Man*	125.00 -	175.00
40648 *I'm Just Wild About Animal Crackers*	30.00 -	50.00
40653 *Snag It*	150.00 -	200.00
40660 *Shanghai Honeymoon*	40.00 -	60.00
Olympic 1461 *Copenhagen*	150.00 -	up
1464 *Down Romany Way*	- -	-
1463 *King Porter Stomp*	150.00 -	up

JOE TURNER AND HIS MEMPHIS MEN:

Columbia 1813-D *Freeze And Melt*	15.00 -	25.00

LLOYD TURNER AND HIS (VILLA VENICE) ORCHESTRA:

Okeh 40648 *Blue Bonnet, You Make Me Blue*	30.00 -	50.00
40658 *Let's Forget*	10.00 -	15.00
40674 *My Mama's In Town*	35.00 -	50.00

TUXEDO ORCHESTRA:

Vocalion 15486 *Take In The Sun, Hang Out The Moon*	10.00 -	15.00
15555 *Doll Dance*	50.00 -	75.00
15556 *Delirium*	50.00 -	75.00
Vocalion, most other issues	7.00 -	12.00

TUXEDO SYNCOPATORS:

Titles, issued contemporaneously on Globe, and Madison, Radiex, and Van Dyke: *Horse Feathers; Torrid Rhythm; Zoolithique*

	40.00 -	60.00

TWIN CITIES DANCE ORCHESTRA:

Challenge 257 *I'm Looking Over A Four-Leaf Clover*	75.00 -	100.00

TWIN CITY BELL HOPS:

Champion 15174 *No-One But You (Knows How To Love)*	50.00 -	80.00

TWO BLACK CROWS (See MORAN & MACK)

UKELELE IKE (See CLIFF EDWARDS)

SUGAR UNDERWOOD:

Victor 21538 *Dew Drop Alley Stomp*	80.00 -	120.00

UNITED STATES MARINE BAND:

Victor 16792 *Maple Leaf Rag*	15.00 -	20.00
35880 *Crazy Bone Rag* (12 inch)	15.00 -	25.00

(Note: Earlier issues, on the primitive Berliner discs, are scarcer and considerably more valuable than the foregoing.)

U. S. NAVAL ACADEMY BAND/TEN:

Okeh 40447 *Navy Girl* ....30.00 - 50.00
    40454 *My Dream Ship* ....30.00 - 50.00
    40463 *Anchors Aweigh* ....30.00 - 50.00
    40490 *Seminole* ....30.00 - 50.00
(Above have a special navy blue label with two anchors)

UNITED STATES NAVAL RESERVE BAND:

Columbia *A2627 A Slippery Place A Comic Rag* ....10.00 - 15.00

UNIVERSAL DANCE ORCHESTRA:

Madison 1620 *Pepper Blues* ....15.00 - 25.00

UNIVERSAL SEXTETTE:

Lincoln 2417 *Milenberg Joys* ....10.00 - 15.00

UNIVERSITY BOYS:

Oriole 1069, 1152, 1175, 1183, 1254, 1260, 1261,
    1446, 1627, 1692 ....7.00 - 12.00
    1668 *Lovable And Sweet* ....10.00 - 15.00

UNIVERSITY DANCE ORCHESTRA:

Globe 8109 *Black Bottom Slide* ....8.00 - 12.00

UNIVERSITY EIGHT:

Lincoln 2543 *Ya Gotta Know How To Love* ....10.00 - 15.00
    2566 *She Knows Her Onions* ....10.00 - 15.00
    2606 *Crazy Words-Crazy Tune* ....10.00 - 15.00
    2626 *Ain't She Sweet?* ....10.00 - 15.00
    2674 *Arkansas Blues* ....10.00 - 15.00

UNIVERSITY ORCHESTRA:

Gennett 6815 *Button Up Your Overcoat* ....15.00 - 25.00
    6862 *I've Got A Feeling I'm Failing* ....15.00 - 20.00
    6892 *Singin' In The Rain* ....15.00 - 20.00
    6907 *That's You, Baby!* ....15.00 - 20.00
    6920 *I'm In Seventh Heaven* ....15.00 - 25.00
    6980 *Hang On To Me* ....15.00 - 25.00
    7011 *Miss Wonderful* ....20.00 - 30.00
    7042 *Lady Luck* ....15.00 - 20.00
    7089 *Why?* ....15.00 - 20.00
    7117 *Happy Days Are Here Again* ....20.00 - 30.00
    7234 *Swingin' In A Hammock* ....20.00 - 30.00
    7257 *Hullabaloo* ....25.00 - 35.00

UNIVERSITY SEXTETTE:

Lincoln 2093, 2105, 2116, 2127, 2130, 2142, 2154,
    2166, 2167, 2168, 2176, 2208, 2216, 2219, 2229,
    2231, 2238, 2241, 2242, 2245, 2250, 2256, 2264,
    2270, 2276, 2279, 2288, 2302, 2306, 2307, 2311,
    2315, 2330, 2339, 2343, 2441, 2463, 2598, 2864,
    2865 ....7.00 - 12.00
    2268 *Copenhagen* ....10.00 - 15.00
    2290 *Oh! Mabel* ....10.00 - 15.00
    2328 *Nobody Knows What A Red Head Mama Can Do*
    ....10.00 - 15.00
    2337 *Cheatin' On Me* ....10.00 - 15.00
    2340 *Sweet Georgia Brown* ....10.00 - 15.00
    2352 *If You Knew Susie* ....10.00 - 15.00
    2355 *Charleston* ....15.00 - 20.00
    2371 *Yes, Sir! That's My Baby* ....10.00 - 15.00
    2380 *Oh, Say! Can I See You Tonight?* ....10.00 - 15.00
    2382 *I Want To See A Little More Of What I Saw In Arkansas*
    ....10.00 - 15.00
    2387 *Tryin' To Keep Away From You* ....10.00 - 15.00
    2403 *Sweet Man* ....10.00 - 15.00

2435 *Show Me The Way To Go Home* ....10.00 - 15.00
2517 *What A Man!* ....10.00 - 15.00
2557 *Static Strut* ....15.00 - 20.00
2578 *Lay Me Down To Sleep In Carolina* ....10.00 - 15.00
2697 *Vo-Do-Do-De-O Blues* ....10.00 - 15.00
2745 *Is She My Girl Friend?* ....10.00 - 15.00
2795 *Farewell Blues* ....15.00 - 20.00
2809 *Steamboat Bill* ....15.00 - 20.00
3260 *What Do We Get From Boston?* ....8.00 - 12.00

UNIVERSITY SIX:

Harmony 36-H *The Camel Walk* ....10.00 - 15.00
    37-H *Desdemona* ....10.00 - 15.00
    71-H *Smile A Little Bit* ....10.00 - 15.00
    73-H *In Your Green Hat* ....10.00 - 15.00
    106-H *Fallin' Down* ....15.00 - 20.00
    134-H *Dustin' The Donkey* ....15.00 - 20.00
    155-H *Georgianna* ....8.00 - 12.00
    160-H *Sittin' Around* ....15.00 - 20.00
    209-H *Ace In The Hole* ....20.00 - 30.00
    224-H *Tiger Rag* ....15.00 - 25.00
    230-H *I Ain't Got Nobody* ....15.00 - 20.00
    245-H *St. Louis Hop* ....15.00 - 25.00
    262-H *That's A Good Girl* ....10.00 - 15.00
    296-H *My Baby Knows How* ....10.00 - 15.00
    316-H *It Takes A Good Woman* ....15.00 - 20.00
    367-H *The Cat* ....15.00 - 20.00
    382-H *It's Ok Katy With Me* ....15.00 - 20.00
    399-H *Rosy Cheeks* ....10.00 - 15.00
    414-H *Beale Street Blues* ....15.00 - 20.00
    425-H *Yes She Do-No She Don't* ....12.00 - 16.00
    433-H *Lazy Weather* ....10.00 - 15.00
    444-H *Bless Her Little Heart* ....10.00 - 15.00
    466-H *Swanee Shore* ....8.00 - 12.00
    474-H *Pastafazoola* ....8.00 - 12.00
    489-H *Oh, Doris! Where Do You Live* ....15.00 - 20.00
    510-H *Zulu Wail* ....15.00 - 20.00
    529-H *Manhattan Mary* ....8.00 - 12.00
    534-H *Is She My Girl Friend?* ....8.00 - 12.00
    551-H *Changes* ....8.00 - 12.00
    557-H *Tell Me, Little Daisy* ....5.00 - 8.00
    565-H *Mine-All Mine* ....10.00 - 15.00
    570-H *Under The Clover Moon* ....5.00 - 8.00
    581-H *Let A Smile Be Your Umbrella* ....10.00 - 15.00
    591-H *What Do You Say?* ....12.00 - 16.00
    617-H *Stay Out Of The South* ....12.00 - 16.00
    619-H *Speedy Boy* ....12.00 - 16.00
    652-H *Chilly-Pom-Pom-Pee* ....8.00 - 12.00
    653-H *C-O-N-S-T-A-N-T-I-N-O-P-L-E* ....8.00 - 12.00
(Note: Above titles, issued also on Diva and Velvet Tone, are of
    equal value and interest.)

THE VAGABONDS:

Cameo 896 *What! No Women?* ....10.00 - 15.00
Gennett 3099 *I'm Gonna Charleston Back To Charleston*
    ....15.00 - 25.00
Gennett 3100, 3128, 5288, 5291, 5362, 5448, 5485,
    5501, 5502, 5504, 5529, 5539, 5540, 5568, 5576,
    5630...7.00 - 12.00
    3137 *Sweet Man* ....10.00 - 15.00
    3282 *(Could I?) I Certainly Could!* ....10.00 - 15.00
    3283 *If I Knew I'd Find You* ....10.00 - 15.00
    3361 *The Birth Of The Blues* ....10.00 - 15.00

3362 *Looking At The World Thru' Rose-Colored Glasses*
....10.00 - 15.00
5447 *Shine* ....10.00 - 15.00
5602 *Back Where The Daffodils Grow* ....15.00 - 20.00.
Gennett 6398 *You Gotta Be Good To Me* ....15.00 - 20.00

SYD VALENTINE & HIS PATENT LEATHER KIDS:
Gennett 7026 *Patent Leather Stomp* ....300.00 - up
7071 *Asphalt Walk*...300.00 - up

RUDOLPH VALENTINO:
Special Record (unnumbered) *Kashmiri Song* ....35.00 - 50.00

RUDY VALLEE AND HIS CONNECTICUT YANKEES:
Titles, issued contemporaneously on Banner, Conqueror, Melotone, Oriole, Perfect, and Romeo: *All's Fair In Love And War; Bojangles Of Harlem; Call Of The Prairie; The Coronation Waltz; Dream Time; Empty Saddles; A Fine Romance; The Glory Of Love; I'm On A Wild Goose Chase; I Was Saying To The Moon; Rhythm On The Range; Seventh Heaven; She Shall Have Music; Speaking Of The Weather; That's Southern Hospitality; These Foolish Things; Turn Off The Moon; Us On A Bus; The Waltz In Swing Time; The Way You Look Tonight; The Whiffenpoof Song; Who Loves You?; Would You?*
....7.00 - 12.00
Bluebird 5097 *On The Air* ....10.00 - 15.00
5098 *Thank Heaven For You* ....10.00 - 15.00
5114 *Lazy Bones* ....10.00 - 15.00
5115 *Don't Blame Me*.......................................10.00 - 15.00
5118 *To Be Or Not To Be In Love* ....10.00 - 15.00
5132 *Three Wishes*..10.00 - 15.00
5171 *Honeymoon Hotel* ....15.00 - 20.00
5172 *Shanghai Lil* ....7.00 - 10.00
5175 *Shame On You*...10.00 - 15.00
5177 *Nagasuki* ....10.00 - 15.00
5182 *Happy Boy-Happy Girl*...............................10.00 - 15.00
(Note: Above titles, on Electradisk are worth somewhat more; on Sunrise, substantially more.)
7067, 7069, 7078, 7120, 7135, 7140, 7226, 7238,
7331, 7342, 7368, 7543, 7645, 7649, 7667 .....5.00 - 10.00
Clarion 5086-C *Sweetheart Of All My Dreams* ....10.00 - 15.00
Columbia 2700-D *Maori* ....15.00 - 25.00
2702-D *Strange Interlude* ....15.00 - 25.00
2714-D *Say It Isn't So*.....................................15.00 - 25.00
2715-D *Me Minus You* ....15.00 - 25.00
2724-D *Please* ....20.00 - 30.00
2725-D *Brother, Can You Spare A Dime?* ....20.00 - 30.00
2730-D *Till Tomorrow*......................................15.00 - 25.00
2733-D *The Language Of Love* ....15.00 - 25.00
2737-D *I'm Playing With Fire*............................15.00 - 25.00
2738-D *A Jug Of Wine, A Loaf Of Bread* ....15.00 - 25.00
2744-D *Hey! Young Fella*..................................15.00 - 25.00
2746-D *Pretending You Care* ....15.00 - 25.00
2756-D *Meet Me In the Gloaming* ....15.00 - 25.00
2764-D *Old Man Harlem*...................................15.00 - 25.00
2771-D *I Lay Me Down To Sleep* ....15.00 - 25.00
2773-D *I've Got To Sing A Torch Song*...............15.00 - 25.00
(Note: Many of foregoing are pressed of royal blue shellac.)
Diva 2825-G *Makin' Whoopee* ....15.00 - 20.00
2834-G *Marie* ....8.00 - 12.00
2857-G *Outside*..10.00 - 15.00
2881-G *Lover, Come Back To Me!* ....8.00 - 12.00
3087-G *The Land of Going To Be* ....15.00 - 25.00

Harmony 724-H *Right Out Of Heaven* ....10.00 - 15.00
728-H *Salaaming The Rajah*..............................10.00 - 15.00
811-H *The Song I Love* ....8.00 - 12.00
834-H *Marie* ....8.00 - 12.00
881-H *Lover, Come Back To Me!* ....8.00 - 12.00
1087-H *The Land Of Going To Be* ....15.00 - 25.00
1247-H *You'll Do It Someday, So Why Not Now?*
....20.00 - 30.00
(Note: See also FRANK MATER, a pseudonym used on some of the above recordings on affiliated labels, and other titles.)
Hit of the Week A-3-4 *Home* ....8.00 - 12.00
B-1-2 *By The Sycamore Tree* ....8.00 - 12.00
C-1-2 *Was That The Human Thing To Do?* ....8.00 - 12.00
C-3-4 *The Wooden Soldier And The China Doll* . 8.00 - 12.00
D-2-3 *By The Fireside; Lovable* ....8.00 - 12.00
M-4-5 *A Faded Summer Love* ....8.00 - 12.00
MM-4-5 *You Try Somebody Else*........................8.00 - 12.00
(Note: Above are one-sided cardboard records, which may have a picture of Rudy Vallee on the non-playing side.)
Personal* 6168 *Valse Vanite* ....20.00 - 30.00
(* Single-sided, product of Electric Recording Laboratories, New York City)
Velvet Tone 1759-V *Bye And Bye Sweetheart* ....8.00 - 12.00
1808-V *Let's Do It*..10.00 - 15.00
1834-V *Marie* ....8.00 - 12.00
1857-V *Outside* ....10.00 - 15.00
1905-V *Bye And Bye Sweetheart* ....8.00 - 12.00
2087-V *The Land of Going To Be* ....15.00 - 25.00
(Note: See Diva and Harmony listing, above; and also FRANK MATER, a pseudonym for Rudy Vallee.)
Victor 21868, 21869, 21880, 21924, 21963, 21967,
21983, 21998, 22029, 22034, 22062, 22084,
22090, 22118, 22136, 22193. 22196, 22227,
22261, 22284, 22321, 22361, 22412, 22419,
22435, 22445, 22473, 22489, 22506, 22545,
22560, 22572, 22574, 22585, 22595, 22611,
22615, 22672, 22679, 22742, 22751, 22752,
22774, 22784 ....7.00 - 12.00
22773 *As Time Goes By* ....15.00 - 20.00
22783 *This Is The Missus*.................................10.00 - 15.00
24458 *My Dancing Lady*..................................10.00 - 15.00
24459 *Flying Down To Rio*...............................10.00 - 15.00
24475 *Puddin' Head Jones* ....10.00 - 15.00
24476 *What Is There To Say?*............................10.00 - 15.00
24554 *Goin' To Heaven On A Mule* ....10.00 - 15.00
24558 *Carolina* ....10.00 - 15.00
24580 *You Oughta Be In Pictures* ....10.00 - 15.00
24581 *Nasty Man* ....10.00 - 15.00
24642 *The Sweetest Music This Side Of Heaven* .....10.00 - 15.00
24646 *So Help Me* ....10.00 - 15.00
24697 *Panama* ....10.00 - 15.00
24702 *Somewhere In Your Heart* ....10.00 - 15.00
24721 *The Drunkard Song* ....8.00 - 12.00
24722 *Out In The Cold Again* ....10.00 - 15.00
24723 *P.S. I Love You*.....................................10.00 - 15.00
24739 *The Tattooed Lady* ....8.00 - 12.00
(Note: Copies of Victor 24739 having white labels with simulated handwriting in red are not particularly scarce).
24827 *Sweet Music* ....10.00 - 15.00
24833 *Fare Thee Well, Annabelle* ....10.00 - 15.00
24838 *On The Good Ship Lollipop* ....10.00 - 15.00
24895 *You Opened My Eyes* ....10.00 - 15.00
24899 *Seein' Is Believin'* ....10.00 - 15.00
25089 *His Majesty The Baby* ....10.00 - 15.00

25092 *The Gentleman Obviously Doesn't Believe* .... 8.00 - 12.00
25109 *Plain Old Me*...8.00 - 12.00
25231, 25233, 25234, 25260, 25267, 25313,
    25835, 25836 ....7.00 - 10.00
27823, 27841, 27842, 27843, 27844 ....5.00 - 8.00

VALLEY INN ORCHESTRA:
Claxtonola 40421 *Because They All Love You* ....50.00 - 80.00

VAN'S COLLEGIANS; VAN & HIS HALF MOON HOTEL ORCHESTRA:
Gennett 6397 *Rainy Day Pal* ....15.00 - 20.00
    6455 *In My Bouquet Of Memories*....................15.00 - 20.00
    6472 *Louisiana* ....20.00 - 30.00
    6473 *I'm Tired Of Making Believe* ....10.00 - 15.00
    6556 *If You Want The Rainbow* ....15.00 - 25.00
    6594 *Pickin' Cotton*...15.00 - 20.00
    6629 *My Blue Ridge Mountain Home* ....15.00 - 25.00
Pathe-Actuelle (titles as on Perfect, following)
Perfect 14603 *Jig Walk* ....20.00 - 30.00
    14613 *Whose Who Are You* ....15.00 - 20.00
    14654 *You Gotta Know How To Love* ....10.00 - 15.00
    14655 *Oh Boy! How It Was Raining* ....10.00 - 15.00
    14740 *Sweet Thing*..10.00 - 15.00
    14860 *Cornfed* ....20.00 - 30.00
    14918 *Without You, Sweetheart*......................10.00 - 15.00
    14976 *Happy-Go-Lucky Lane*...........................10.00 - 15.00
(foregoing titles on Pathe-Actuelle are similarly valued)

FRED VAN EPS/VAN EPPS; VAN EPS TRIO/BANJO ORCHESTRA; VAN EPS-BANTA DANCE ORCHESTRA:
Columbia A1063 *Pearl Of The Harem* ....15.00 - 20.00
    A1118 *The White Wash Man* ....10.00 - 15.00
    A1294 *Whipped Cream* ....10.00 - 15.00
    A1417 *Junk Man Rag* ....15.00 - 20.00
    A1593 *Thanks For The Lobster*.......................10.00 - 15.00
    A1594 *Some Baby*..10.00 - 15.00
    A1629 *Soup To Nuts* ....10.00 - 15.00
    A2034 *Hill And Dale* ....10.00 - 15.00
    A5613 *As You Please* (12 inch)......................15.00 - 20.00
    A5618 *Old Folks Rag* (12 inch)......................15.00 - 20.00
Cameo 51324 *Ragtime Oriole* ....20.00 - 30.00
    51480 *Dancing On The House Top* ....20.00 - 30.00
    51514 *A Ragtime Episode*...............................20.00 - 30.00
    51604 *The New Gaiety*....................................20.00 - 30.00
D & R 3810 *The White Wash Man* ....10.00 - 15.00
Emerson 10206 *Palm Beach Rag* ....10.00 - 15.00
Okeh 1140 *Below Deck Rag* ....15.00 - 20.00
Pathe 20087 *Teasin' The Cat*.............................8.00 - 12.00
    20094 *Down Home Rag* ....15.00 - 20.00
    20328 *Stockyard Blues* ....15.00 - 20.00
    29030 *Florida Rag*..15.00 - 20.00
    29081 *The Smiler Rag* ....15.00 - 20.00
    29082 *The White Wash Man*............................15.00 - 20.00
    29083 *A Rag Time Episode*.............................15.00 - 20.00
Perfect 11160 *Grace And Beauty* ....8.00 - 12.00
Phono-Cut 5052 *The Smiler*.............................20.00 - 30.00
Victor 16667 *A Bunch Of Rags* ....8.00 - 12.00
    16845 *A Ragtime Episode*...............................10.00 - 15.00
    16934 *Rag Pickings* ....10.00 - 15.00
    16969 *Pearl Of The Harem* ....10.00 - 15.00
    17033 *Red Pepper-A Spicy Rag*.....................8.00 - 12.00
    17168 *Black Diamond Rag* ....10.00 - 15.00
    17308 *Florida Rag*..10.00 - 15.00

    17369 *Frolic Of The Coons* ....8.00 - 12.00
    17575 *The Smiler-A Joplin Rag* ....10.00 - 15.00
    17601 *Notoriety Rag* ....10.00 - 15.00
    17677 *Original Fox Trot*....................................8.00 - 12.00
    18085 *Ragging The Scale* ....8.00 - 12.00
    18226 *Teasin' The Cat*.....................................8.00 - 12.00
    18376 *Razzberries-One-Step* ....7.00 - 10.00
    35400 *Old Folks Rag* (12 inch)......................10.00 - 15.00
Zonophone 5828 *Chatterbox Rag* ....20.00 - 30.00

PAUL VAN LOAN AND HIS ORCHESTRA:
Cameo 798, 820, 848, 853 ....7.00 - 12.00

VARSITY EIGHT:
Titles, issued contemporaneously on Cameo, Lincoln, and Romeo:
    Sorority Stomp; Dance Your Blues Away .... 10.00 - 15.00
Titles, issued contemporaneously on Banner, Conqueror, Domino, Jewel, Oriole, Perfect, Regal, and Romeo: *Fraternity Blues; Never Swat A Fly; One Pair Of Pants At A Time; Sweetheart Of My Student Days; Toodle-Oo; When Kentucky Bids The World 'Good Morning!; Who's Calling You Sweetheart Tonight?*
    ....7.00 - 12.00
Cameo 400, 420, 426, 444, 445, 454, 456, 480, 505, 507, 516, 559, 567, 571, 574, 577, 580, 588, 593, 602, 605, 606, 617, 620, 632, 633, 640, 641, 680, 694, 695, 732, 753, 780, 835, 1077, 8321, 8324, 9003, 9233, 9272...7.00 - 12.00
    498 *Mean Blues*..10.00 - 15.00
    556 *San*...10.00 - 15.00
    622 *Copenhagen* ....10.00 - 15.00
    635 *Those Panama Mamas* ....10.00 - 15.00
    646 *Oh, Mabel!* ....10.00 - 15.00
    711 *He's The Kind Of Man You Like* ....10.00 - 15.00
    714 *Don't Bring Lulu* ....10.00 - 15.00
    724 *If You Knew Susie* ....10.00 - 15.00
    725 *Cheatin' On Me*..10.00 - 15.00
    730 *Sweet Georgia Brown* ....10.00 - 15.00
    741 *Charleston*..15.00 - 20.00
    750 *Yes, Sir! That's My Baby* ....10.00 - 15.00
    772 *Oh, Say! Can I See You Tonight?* ....10.00 - 15.00
    774 *Row Row Rosie!* ....10.00 - 15.00
    782 *Fallin' Down*..10.00 - 15.00
    797 *Sweet Man* ....10.00 - 15.00
    817 *Milenberg Joys* ....10.00 - 15.00
    824 *I'm Gonna Hang Around My Sugar*............10.00 - 15.00
    832 *Show Me The Way To Go Home* ....10.00 - 15.00
    837 *She Doesn't* ....10.00 - 15.00
    870 *T.N.T.* ....15.00 - 20.00
    925 *What A Man!* ....10.00 - 15.00
    975 *Static Strut*...15.00 - 20.00
    986 *I'd Give A Lot Of Love* ....10.00 - 15.00
    1016 *Lay Me Down To Sleep In Carolina* ....10.00 - 15.00
    1017 *Precious* ....10.00 - 15.00
    1020 *She Knows Her Onions* ....10.00 - 15.00
    1040 *Susie's Feller* ....10.00 - 15.00
    1049 *My Baby Knows How* ....15.00 - 20.00
    1110 *Crazy Words-Crazy Tune*........................10.00 - 15.00
    1114 *Ain't She Sweet?* ....10.00 - 15.00
    1209 *Arkansas Blues* ....10.00 - 15.00
    1232 *Vo-Do-Do-De-O Blues*...............................10.00 - 15.00
    1245 *Clementine* ....15.00 - 20.00
    1266 *Steamboat Bill*..15.00 - 20.00
    1280 *Is She My Girl Friend?* ....10.00 - 15.00
    8141 *Farewell Blues* ....15.00 - 20.00

9007 *Glorianna* ....10.00 - 15.00
9208 *Dance Your Blues Away* ....10.00 - 15.00
Lincoln 2697 *Vo-Do-Do-Dee-O Blues* ....10.00 - 15.00
2710 *Clementine* ....10.00 - 15.00
Perfect 15473 *Popeye (The Sailor Man)* ....10.00 - 15.00
Romeo 900 *Sorority Stomp*..............................15.00 - 20.00
1035 *What Do We Get From Boston?* ....8.00 - 12.00
1068 *Send Love Through The Breeze* ....10.00 - 15.00

VARSITY SEVEN:
Varsity 8135 *Scratch My Back* ....10.00 - 15.00
8147 *It's Tight Like That* ....10.00 - 15.00
8173 *How Long, How Long Blues* ....10.00 - 15.00
8179 *Shake It And Break It* ....10.00 - 15.00

JOE VENUTI (& HIS NEW YORKERS/ORCHESTRA); JOE VENUTI'S BLUE FOUR; JOE VENUTI & HIS BLUE FIVE; JOE VENUTI-EDDIE LANG BLUE FIVE; JOE VENUTI-EDDIE LANG & THEIR ALLSTAR ORCHESTRA; JOE VENUTI & RUSS MORGAN:
Titles, issued contemporaneously on Banner, Conqueror, Melotone, Oriole, Perfect, and Romeo: *Alice In Wonderland; Build A Little House; Cheese And Crackers; Cinderella's Fella; Doin' The Up Town Lowdown; Easter Parade; Everything I Have Is Yours; Heat Wave; I Want To Ring Bells; Moon Glow; My Dancing Lady, No More Love; One Minute To One; You Must Have Taken My Heart; You're My Past, Present And Future* ..7.00 - 12.00
Bluebird 5293 *Fiddlesticks*......................................10.00 - 15.00
(Note: This title, on Electradisk, valued slightly higher; on Sunrise, substantially higher.)
5520 *Everybody Shuffle* ....10.00 - 15.00
10280 *Doin' Things* ....7.00 - 10.00
Columbia 914-D *Stringin' The Blues* ....20.00 - 30.00
2488-D *Little Girl*..20.00 - 30.00
2535-D *There's No Other Girl* ....15.00 - 20.00
2589-D *The Wolf Wobble* ....15.00 - 20.00
2765-D *Raggin' The Scale*..................................20.00 - 30.00
2782-D *Vibraphonia* ....15.00 - 25.00
2783-D *Isn't It Heavenly?* ....15.00 - 20.00
2834-D *Doin' The Uptown Lowdown*..................15.00 - 20.00
3103-D *Eeny Meeny Miney Mo* ....15.00 - 20.00
3104-D *Stop, Look And Listen* ....15.00 - 20.00
3105-D *Red Velvet* ....15.00 - 20.00
Decca 624 *Nothing But Notes* ....10.00 - 15.00
625 *Tap Room Blues* ....10.00 - 15.00
669 *Vibraphonia No. 2* ....10.00 - 15.00
Melotone 12277 *Farewell Blues* ....25.00 - 40.00
12294 *Beale Street Blues* ....25.00 - 40.00
Okeh 40762 *Wild Cat* ....30.00 - 40.00
40825 *Doin' Things* ....20.00 - 30.00
40853 *Kickin' The Cat* ....20.00 - 30.00
40897 *A Mug Of Ale* ....20.00 - 30.00
40947 *Penn Beach Blues* ....30.00 - 40.00
41025 *The Wild Dog*..30.00 - 40.00
41051 *Tain't So, Honey, Tain't So* ....25.00 - 40.00
41056 *Because My Baby Don't Mean "Maybe" Now*
....25.00 - 40.00
41076 *The Man From The South* ....25.00 - 40.00
41087 *Pickin' Cotton* ....25.00 - 40.00
41133 *I Must Have That Man* ....25.00 - 40.00
41144 *The Blue Room* ....30.00 - 50.00
41192 *Weary River* ....25.00 - 40.00
41251 *My Honey's Lovin' Arms* ....30.00 - 50.00
41263 *I'm In Seventh Heaven* ....25.00 - 40.00

41320 *Chant Of The Jungle* ....25.00 - 40.00
41361 *Apple Blossoms* ....30.00 - 40.00
41427 *Promises* ....25.00 - 40.00
41432 *Raggin' The Scale* ....25.00 - 40.00
41451 *Out Of Breath* ....25.00 - 40.00
41469 *I've Found A New Baby* ....30.00 - 50.00
41506 *Pardon Me, Pretty Baby* ....25.00 - 40.00
41586 *Fiddlesticks* ....25.00 - 40.00
Victor 21561 *Doin' Things* ....15.00 - 20.00
23015 *My Man From Caroline* ....30.00 - 50.00
23018 *Wasting My Love On You* ....50.00 - 75.00
23021 *The Wild Dog* ....40.00 - 60.00
23039 *Gettin' Hot* ....80.00 - 120.00
Vocalion 15858 *Farewell Blues*.............................50.00 - 75.00
15864 *Beale Street Blues* ....50.00 - 75.00

VICKSBURG BLOWERS:
Gennett 6089 *Monte Carlo Joys* ....300.00 - up

VICKSBURG TEN:
Champion 15477 *Clarinet Marmalade* ....100.00 - 150.00

VICTOR MILITARY BAND:
Victor 17006 *Slippery Place Rag*...........................10.00 - 15.00
17044 *Ragtime Violin* ....10.00 - 15.00
17362 *Melinda's Wedding Day-Medley One-Step*
....10.00 - 15.00
17489 *The Junk Man Rag* ....10.00 - 15.00
17508 *Stomp Dance* ....15.00 - 20.00
17585 *Swanee Ripples Rag* ....15.00 - 20.00
17619 *Rag-a-Muffin Rag-One-Step* ....10.00 - 15.00
17764 *Blame It On The Blues* ....10.00 - 15.00
18163 *Kansas City Blues* ....10.00 - 15.00
18203 *Brown Skin* ....10.00 - 15.00
18252 *Spooky Spooks One-Step*........................10.00 - 15.00
35405 *Balling The Jack* (12 inch).......................10.00 - 15.00
35429 *Music Box Rag* (12 inch).........................10.00 - 15.00
35431 *Midnight Whirl Rag-One Step* (12 inch). 10.00 - 15.00
35533 *Bugle Call Rag*..10.00 - 15.00

VICTOR ORCHESTRA:
Victor 16350 *Black And White Rag* ....10.00 - 15.00
16472 *Wild Cherries Rag*...................................10.00 - 15.00
16515 *The Cakewalk In The Sky* ....15.00 - 20.00
17063 *The Gaby Glide* ....8.00 - 12.00
35088 *The Cakewalk In The Sky* (12 inch) ....15.00 - 20.00

JOHN VINCENT'S CALIFORNIANS:
Conqueror 7108, 7209, 7233, 7235, 7245, 7321, 7322, 7354, 7357, 7369, 7401, 7440...................7.00 - 12.00

THE VIRGINIA CREEPERS:
Pathe-Actuelle 36403 *I've Found A New Baby* ......15.00 - 20.00

THE VIRGINIANS:
Victor 18881, 18895, 19021, 19032, 19135, 19140, 19175, 19189, 19269, 19334, 19419, 20837, 21219, 21228..7.00 - 12.00
21680 *Low Down* ....15.00 - 20.00
Victor, most other issues...5.00 - 8.00

VOCALION MILITARY BAND:
Aeolian-Vocalion 12000 *America And Star Spangled Banner-Patriotic Medley*..75.00 - 100.00
(Note: Above is pressed of red, white and blue shellac; its value is due to its novelty and striking appearance.)

THE VOLUNTEER FIREMEN:
Brunswick 3025, 3041, 3045, 3077 ....8.00 - 12.00

DON VOORHEES & HIS (EARL CARROLL VANITIES) ORCHESTRA:
Broadway 1015 *Painting The Clouds With Sunshine*
....25.00 - 40.00
(foregoing is a 7-inch, single-sided cardboard record)
Cameo 1134 *Pardon The Glove* ....15.00 - 20.00
Columbia 765-D *Hugs And Kisses* ....10.00 - 15.00
   835-D *The Riff Song* ....10.00 - 15.00
   881-D *Muddy Water* ....10.00 - 15.00
   954-D *Dancing The Devil Away* ....10.00 - 15.00
   990-D *The Same Old Moon* ....10.00 - 15.00
   1078-D *Fantasy on St. Louis Blues* ....10.00 - 15.00
   1123-D *Baby's Blue* ....10.00 - 15.00
   1124-D *Highways Are Happy Ways* ....10.00 - 15.00
   1126-D *Rain*...8.00 - 12.00
   1129-D *My Blue Heaven* ....8.00 - 12.00
   1180-D *Clementine*..15.00 - 20.00
   1284-D *Ol' Man River*..15.00 - 20.00
Edison 51855 *Just One More Kiss*............................20.00 - 30.00
   51888 *Somebody's Eyes* ....15.00 - 20.00
   51890 *Sunday*..25.00 - 40.00
   51919 *Blue Skies* ....25.00 - 35.00
   51927 *Muddy Water* ....25.00 - 40.00
   51962 *Pardon The Glove*....................................75.00 - 100.00
   51963 *Never Without You*...................................25.00 - 40.00
   51997 *I'll Always Remember You*........................40.00 - 60.00
   51999 *Dancing The Devil Away* ....50.00 - 75.00
   52024 *Room For Two* ....20.00 - 30.00
   52070 *Show Me That Kind Of A Girl* ....30.00 - 50.00
   52072 *Oh! Doris, Where Do You Live?*..............30.00 - 50.00
Hit of the Week 1019 *Tip-Toe Through The Tulips With Me*
   (Demonstration Record) ....20.00 - 30.00
   1091, 1154 ....7.00 - 10.00
Perfect 14748 *Some Day* ....10.00 - 15.00
   14775 *Who Do You Love?* ....10.00 - 15.00
(foregoing titles on Pathe-Actuelle are similarly valued)

WABASH TRIO:
Titles, issued contemporaneously on Grey Gull, and Radiex: *Coal Black Blues; Hoppin' Round; Lone Western Blues*
....15.00 - 30.00
Additional titles: *Beale Street Blues; Hard Times Blues; Yellow Dog Blues* ....10.00 - 15.00

(JIMMY) WADE'S CLUB ALABAM/MOULIN ROUGE/ MOULIN ROUGE ORCHESTRA; JIMMY WADE & HIS DIXIELANDERS:
Black Patti 8019 *Original Black Bottom Dance*....500.00 - up
Gennett 6105 *Original Black Bottom Dance*.........250.00 - up
Harmograph 893 *Mobile Blues*..............................150.00 - 250.00
Paramount 20295 *Someday Sweetheart*.................150.00 - 250.00
Puritan 11295 *Someday Sweetheart*.......................150.00 - 250.00
   11363 *You've Got Ways I'm Crazy About*........150.00 - 200.00
Vocalion 1236 *Mississippi Wobble* ....250.00 - up

SOL S. WAGNER & HIS ORCHESTRA:
Gennett 5311 *My Sweet Girl*....................................50.00 - 75.00
   5313 *Oklahoma Indian Jazz* ....50.00 - 75.00
   5323 *Dream Daddy* ....75.00 - 125.00
Okeh 40827 *South Wind* ....35.00 - 50.00
   40838 *You Don't Like It- Not Much!* ....25.00 - 40.00
   40973 *Countin' The Days*...................................25.00 - 40.00

HERMAN WALDMAN AND HIS ORCHESTRA:
Bluebird 5437, 5439, 5478 ....7.00 - 12.00
Brunswick 4649 *Marbles*...20.00 - 30.00
   6181 *Lazy River* ....15.00 - 20.00

ESTHER WALKER:
Brunswick 3008 *What Did I Tell Ya?* ....8.00 - 12.00
   3215 *Hard-To-Get Gertie* ....10.00 - 15.00
Brunswick (most other issues) ....5.00 - 8.00

JOHNNY WALKER & HIS ORCHESTRA/ROLLICKERS:
Columbia 2247-D *Kitty From Kansas City* ....10.00 - 15.00
   2380-D *Personally, I Love You*.........................8.00 - 12.00
   2404-D *Walkin' My Baby Back Home*..............15.00 - 20.00

JACK WALKUP & HIS MELODY BOYS/ORCHESTRA:
Champion 16108 *I Like A Little Girl Like That* ......10.00 - 15.00
Champion 16133 *Three Little Words*.......................10.00 - 15.00
   16262 *Spread A Little Sunshine* ....10.00 - 15.00
   16576 *You've Got Me Loving You* ....- - -
   16197 *That Lindy Hop* ....- - -
   16831 *P. S. - I Love You* ....30.00 - 50.00
   16832 *Out In The Cold Again* ....30.00 - 50.00
Gennett 7300 *Along The Highway Of Love* ....15.00 - 25.00

TED WALLACE & HIS ORCHESTRA/SWING SWING MUSIC/CAMPUS BOYS:
Titles, issued contemporaneously on Banner, Conqueror, Domino, and Regal: *All By Yourself In The Moonlight; I'll Get By; She's Funny That Way; There's A Rainbow 'Round My Shoulder*
....7.00 - 12.00
Bluebird 6251, 6252, 6253, 6254.............................4.00 - 8.00
Columbia 1756-D *The One That I Love Loves Me* .10.00 - 15.00
   1833-D *I've Got A Feeling I'm Falling* ....10.00 - 15.00
   1970-D *Bigger And Better Than Ever* ....10.00 - 15.00
   2046-D *Lucky Me-Lovable You* ....10.00 - 15.00
   2140-D *Get Happy* ....10.00 - 15.00
   2236-D *Here Comes The Sun* ....10.00 - 15.00
   2254-D *Little White Lies* ....10.00 - 15.00
   2301-D *Sweet Jennie Lee!* ....10.00 - 15.00
Columbia, most other issues ....7.00 - 10.00
Okeh 40749 *When I First Met Mary*.......................15.00 - 20.00
   40751 *Usen't You Used To Be My Sweetie?*......15.00 - 20.00
   40760 *Ain't She Sweet?* ....15.00 - 20.00
   40778 *The Cat*..15.00 - 25.00
   40850 *Love And Kisses* ....15.00 - 20.00
   40915 *Zulu Wail*..30.00 - 50.00
   40961 *Changes*..20.00 - 30.00
   41002 *What Do You Say?* ....15.00 - 20.00
   41014 *Buffalo Rhythm*.......................................75.00 - 100.00

TRIXIE WALLACE:
Claxtonola 40393 *Copenhagen*..............................150.00 - 200.00

THOMAS ("FATS") WALLER (WITH MORRIS'S HOT BABIES); FATS WALLER & HIS BUDDIES/RHYTHM:
Bluebird *(Most issues)* ....7.00 - 12.00
Columbia 14593-D *I'm Crazy 'Bout My Baby* .....100.00 - 150.00
Okeh 4757 *Birmingham Blues* ....100.00 - 150.00
Victor 20357 *St. Louis Blues* ....10.00 - 15.00
   20470 *Soothin' Syrup Stomp*.............................30.00 - 50.00
   20492 *Rusty Pail*...30.00 - 50.00
   20655 *Stompin' The Bug*...................................30.00 - 50.00
   20776 *Savannah Blues*......................................75.00 - 100.00
   20890 *Beale Street Blues* ....75.00 - 100.00
   21127 *I Ain't Got Nobody*..................................75.00 - 100.00

21202 *He's Gone Away* ....75.00 - 100.00
21358 *The Digah's Stomp* ....75.00 - 100.00
21525 *Hog Maw Stomp* ....50.00 - 75.00
22092 *Love Me Or Leave Me* ....8.00 - 12.00
22108 *Sweet Savannah Sue* ....10.00 - 15.00
22371 *St. Louis Blues* ....10.00 - 15.00
23260 *That's All* ....100.00 - 150.00
23331 *Sugar* ....75.00 - 100.00
24830 *African Ripples* ....15.00 - 20.00
25015 *Viper's Drag* ....15.00 - 20.00
Victor 24641, 24648, 24708, 24714, 24737, 24738,
     24742, 24801, 24808, 24826, 24846, 24853,
     24863, 24867, 24888, 24889, 24892, 24898,
     25026, 25037, 25039, 25044, 25063, 25078,
     25087, 25116, 25120, 25123, 25131, 25140,
     25175, 25194, 25196, 25211, 25222, 25253,
     25255, 25266, 25281, 25295, 25296, 25315,
     25342, 25348, 25353, 25359, 25374, 25388,
     25394, 25409, 25415, 25430, 25471, 25478,
     25483, 25489, 25490, 25491, 25498, 26499,
     25515, 25530, 25536, 25537, 25550, 25551,
     25554, 25563, 25565, 25571, 25579, 25580,
     25604, 25608, 25618, 25631, 25652, 25671,
     25672, 25679, 25681, 25684, 25689, 25712,
     25749, 25762, 25806, 25812, 25817, 25830,
     25834, 25847, 25891, 25898, 26002, 26045 ....7.00 - 12.00
V38050 *Harlem Fuss*....................................75.00 - 100.00
V38086 *Lookin' Good But Feelin' Bad*..............75.00 - 100.00
V38110 *When I'm Alone* ....75.00 - 100.00
V38119 *Ridin' But Walkin.*............................75.00 - 100.00
V38508 *Numb Fumblin'* ....75.00 - 100.00
V38554 *Valentine Stomp* ....100.00 - 150.00
V38568 *Turn On The Heat* ....80.00 - 120.00
V38613 *Smashing Thirds* ....75.00 - 100.00

EDDIE WALTERS:
Columbia 1763-D, 1969-D ....8.00 - 12.00
     2035-D *Singin' In The Bathtub*...........................10.00 - 15.00
     2137-D *'Leven-Thirty Saturday Night*................10.00 - 15.00
     2232-D *It Must Be Love*................................10.00 - 15.00
     2290-D *(Since They're All Playing) Miniature Golf*
     ....10.00 - 15.00

THE WANDERERS:
Bluebird 5834 *A Good Man Is Hard To Find*..........15.00 - 20.00
     5869 *I Ain't Got Nobody*....................................15.00 - 20.00
     5887 *Tiger Rag* ....15.00 - 20.00
     5921 *Thousand Miles*....................................8.00 - 12.00
     5994 *Footwarmer* ....15.00 - 20.00
Cameo 1133 *My Sunday Girl* ....7.00 - 10.00

BILLY WARD:
Oriole 4472 *Squeeze Me* ....20.00 - 30.00

JOE WARD'S SWANEE CLUB ORCHESTRA:
Titles, issued contemporaneously on Cameo, Lincoln and Romeo:
     Scorchin'; Traffic Jam..20.00 - 30.00

WARING'S PENNSYLVANIANS:
Victor L-16016, L-16018 (Program Transcriptions:
     Long Playing 33 1/3 RPM)........................15.00 - 25.00
     19189, 19254, 19257, 19303, 19346, 19377,
     19492, 19533 ....7.00 - 12.00
     19610 *When My Sugar Walks Down The Street*
     ....10.00 - 15.00

19768 *Syncopation Sal* .... 10.00 - 15.00
20003, 20083, 20598, 21323, 21715, 21836, 21888
     ....7.00 - 12.00
21508 *Stack O'Lee Blues* .... 10.00 - 15.00
22266 *Hello Baby* .... 10.00 - 15.00
22272 *Crying For The Carolines* .... 10.00 - 15.00
22325 *Red-Hot Chicago* .... 10.00 - 15.00
22326 *Good For You, Bad For Me* .... 10.00 - 15.00
22470 *It Seems To Be Spring* .... 10.00 - 15.00
22936 *Let's Have Another Cup O'Coffee* .... 10.00 - 15.00
22978 *How Am I Doin'?* .... 15.00 - 20.00
24030 *I Heard* .... 15.00 - 20.00
24051 *Holding My Honey's Hand* .... 10.00 - 15.00
24062 *Old Yazoo* .... 10.00 - 15.00
24168 *Fit As A Fiddle* .... 10.00 - 15.00
24179 *More Beautiful Than Ever* .... 8.00 - 12.00
24181 *Here It Is Monday And I've Still Got A Dollar*
     .... 10.00 - 15.00
24214 *You're Getting To Be A Habit With Me* .. 10.00 - 15.00
Victor, most other issues.......................... 5.00 - 10.00

BUD WARNER & HIS RED CAPS:
Bell 1174 *Down Home Special* .... 300.00 - up

WARNER'S SEVEN ACES:
Columbia 305-D *Cheatin' On Me*...................... 10.00 - 15.00
     336-D *The Blues Have Got Me* .... 15.00 - 25.00
     491-D *Go Get 'Em, Caroline* .... 20.00 - 30.00
     605-D *Breakin' The Leg* .... 40.00 - 60.00
     656-D *So Is Your Old Lady*............................ 15.00 - 20.00
     816-D *Don't Take That Black Bottom Away* ..... 10.00 - 15.00
     863-D *Who'll Be The One?*............................ 10.00 - 15.00
     1001-D *There's Everything Nice About You* .... 8.00 - 12.00
     1046-D *That's My Hap-Hap-Happiness*............ 10.00 - 15.00
Okeh 4888 *In A Tent* .... 10.00 - 15.00
     4911 *Dream Girl of P.K.A.* .... 15.00 - 20.00
     4924 *Mean Eyes* .... 15.00 - 20.00
     40080 *Ace Of Spades* .... 15.00 - 25.00
     40198 *Bessie Couldn't Help It* .... 15.00 - 25.00
     40201 *Love Time*..................................... 15.00 - 20.00

WASHBOARD RHYTHM BAND:
Columbia 14680-D *Going, Going, Gone* .... 100.00 - 150.00

WASHBOARD RHYTHM BOYS/KINGS:
Titles, issued contemporaneously on Banner, Melotone, Oriole,
     Perfect, and Romeo: *Dog And Cat; I Cover The Waterfront;*
     Lazybones; Learn To Croon; Mississippi Basin; Old Man Blues;
     St. Louis Blues; Some Of These Days .... 20.00 - 30.00
Bluebird 5389 *Sloppy Drunk Blues* .... 75.00 - 100.00
     6157 *Arlena*... 20.00 - 30.00
     6186 *Street Walkin' Blues*................................ 20.00 - 30.00
     6278 *Hot Nuts* .... 20.00 - 30.00
     8155 *Street Walkin' Blues* .... 10.00 - 15.00
Victor 22719 *A Porter's Love Song To A Chambermaid*
     .... 40.00 - 60.00
     22814 *Shoot 'Em* .... 75.00 - 100.00
     22958 *Pepper Steak* .... 75.00 - 100.00
     23301 *Georgia On My Mind*......................... 100.00 - 150.00
     23303 *Boola Boo*.................................... 150.00 - 200.00
     23323 *If You Don't Love Me* .... 100.00 - 150.00
     23337 *All This World Is Made Of Glass* .... 150.00 - 200.00
     23348 *My Silent Love*................................ 100.00 - 150.00
     23357 *Depression Stomp* .... 150.00 - 250.00
     23364 *Say It Isn't So* .... 150.00 - 200.00

23367 *Ash Man Crawl* ....150.00 - 200.00
23368 *The Boy In The Boat* ....150.00 - 200.00
23373 *How Deep Is The Ocean?* ....125.00 - 175.00
23375 *A Nickel For A Pickel* ....150.00 - 200.00
23380 *Sloppy Drunk Blues* ....150.00 - 250.00
23403 *Nobody's Sweetheart* ....150.00 - 250.00
23405 *Sophisticated Lady* ....150.00 - 200.00
23408 *Bug-A-Boo* ....150.00 - 250.00
23413 *Move Turtle* ....150.00 - 250.00
23415 *Hard Corn* ....150.00 - 250.00
24059 *Tiger Rag* ....75.00 - 100.00
24065 *Hummin' To Myself* ....75.00 - 100.00
Vocalion 1724 *Sentimental Gentleman From Georgia*
....75.00 - 100.00
1725 *The Scat Song* ....80.00 - 120.00
1729 *Syncopate Your Sins Away* ....80.00 - 120.00
1730 *Oh! You Sweet Thing* ....80.00 - 120.00
1731 *Angeline* ....80.00 - 120.00
1732 *Blue Drag* ....80.00 - 120.00
1733 *Old Yazoo* ....80.00 - 120.00
1734 *Spider Crawl* ....80.00 - 120.00

WASHBOARD SERENADERS:

Victor V-38127 *Kazoo Moan* ....150.00 - 200.00
V-38610 *Teddy's Blues* ....150.00 - 200.00

WASHBOARD TRIO:

Paramount 12682 *Washboard Rag* ....250.00 - up
Radiex 1485 *Yellow Dog Blues* .... - - -

WASHBOARD WONDERS:

Silvertone 3548 *Shake That Thing* ....100.00 - 150.00
3549 *Skoodlum Blues* ....100.00 - 150.00

BENNIE WASHINGTON'S SIX ACES:

Okeh 8269 *Compton Ave. Blues* ....250.00 - up

BUCK WASHINGTON:

Columbia 2925-D *Old Fashioned Love* ...35.00 - 50.00

STEVE WASHINGTON & HIS ORCHESTRA:

Vocalion 2598 *Sing A Little Low-Down Tune* ....20.00 - 30.00
2607 *Blue River* ....20.00 - 30.00

THE WASHINGTONIANS:

Titles issued contemporaneously on Cameo, Lincoln, and Romeo:
East St. Louis Toodle-Oo; Hot And Bothered; Hottentot; Jubilee Stomp; The Mooche; Move Over; Saratoga Swing; Take It Easy; Who Said "It's Tight Like That"? ....15.00 - 30.00
Additional titles, issued contemporaneously on Cameo, Lincoln, and Romeo: *It's Tight Like That; Mississippi, Here I Am*
....10.00 - 15.00
Blu-Disc T-1002 *Choo Choo* ....500.00 - up
Brunswick 3526 *Black And Tan Fantasy* ....15.00 - 20.00
4009 *Black Beauty* ....20.00 - 30.00
4044 *Jubilee Stomp* ....20.00 - 30.00
Diva 2577-G *Bugle Call Rag* ....35.00 - 50.00
2601-G *Stack O'Lee Blues* ....35.00 - 50.00
Harmony 577-H *Bugle Call Rag* ....35.00 - 50.00
601-H *Stack O'Lee Blues* ....35.00 - 50.00
Pathe-Actuelle 36333 *Trombone Blues* ....100.00 - 150.00
Pennington 1437 *Rainy Nights* ....100.00 - 150.00
Perfect 14514 *Trombone Blues* ....100.00 - 150.00
Puritan 11437 *Rainy Nights* ....100.00 - 150.00
Triangle 11437 *Rainy Nights* ....100.00 - 150.00
Velvet Tone 1577-V *Bugle Call Rag* .....35.00 - 50.00
1601-V *Stack O'Lee Blues* ....35.00 - 50.00

Vocalion 15704 *Take It Easy* ....75.00 - 100.00
15710 *Jubilee Stomp* ....75.00 - 100.00

ETHEL WATERS: ETHEL WATERS' JAZZ MASTERS:

Black Swan 2010 *Down Home Blues* ....30.00 - 50.00
2021 *There'll Be Some Changes Made* ....30.00 - 50.00
2035 *Royal Garden Blues* ....40.00 - 60.00
2037 *Bugle Blues* ....40.00 - 60.00
2038 *Dyin' With The Blues* ....40.00 - 60.00
2074 *Struggle* ....40.00 - 60.00
2077 *Tiger Rag* ....50.00 - 80.00
10077 *Struggle* ....40.00 - 60.00
10073 *Tiger Rag* ....50.00 - 80.00
14117 *Jazzin' Babies Blues* ....50.00 - 80.00
14120 *Georgia Blues* ....50.00 - 80.00
14128 *At The New Jump Steady Ball* ...50.00 - 80.00
14145 *Brown Baby* ....50.00 - 80.00
14146 *Memphis Man* ....50.00 - 80.00
14148 *Long-Lost Mama* ....50.00 - 80.00
14151 *Lost Out Blues* ....50.00 - 80.00
14154 *Ethel Sings 'Em* ....50.00 - 80.00
14155 *All The Time* ....50.00 - 80.00
Brunswick 6517 *I Can't Give You Anything But Love*
....8.00 - 12.00
6521 *St. Louis Blues* ....10.00 - 15.00
6564 *Stormy Weather* ....8.00 - 12.00
6617 *Shadows On The Swanee* ....10.00 - 15.00
6885 *You've Seen Harlem At Its Best* ....10.00 - 15.00
Cardinal 2036 *The New York Glide* ....50.00 - 80.00
Columbia 379-D *Sweet Georgia Brown* ....10.00 - 15.00
433-D *Sympathetic Dan* ....10.00 - 15.00
472-D *Pickaninny Blues* ....10.00 - 15.00
487-D *Sweet Man* ....10.00 - 15.00
561-D *I've Found A New Baby* ....15.00 - 25.00
1837-D *Birmingham Bertha* ....10.00 - 15.00
1871-D *True Blue Lou* ....10.00 - 15.00
1905-D *Shoo Shoo Boogie Boo* ....15.00 - 20.00
1933-D *Trav'lin All Alone* ....15.00 - 20.00
2184-D *Porgy* ....10.00 - 15.00
2222-D *My Kind Of Man* ....15.00 - 20.00
2288-D *You're Lucky To Me* ....10.00 - 15.00
2346-D *I Got Rhythm* ....10.00 - 15.00
2409-D *When Your Lover Has Gone* ....20.00 - 30.00
2481-D *Without That Gal* ....20.00 - 30.00
2511-D *River, Stay 'Way From My Door* ....15.00 - 20.00
2826-D *Harlem On My Mind* ....30.00 - 50.00
2853-D *A Hundred Years From Today* ....25.00 - 40.00
14093-D *Down Home Blues* ....15.00 - 20.00
14112-D *Maybe Not At All* ....15.00 - 20.00
14116-D *No Man's Mama* ....10.00 - 15.00
14125-D *Bring Your Greenbacks* ....15.00 - 20.00
14132-D *Throw Dirt In Your Face* .....15.00 - 20.00
14134-D *I Wonder What's Become Of Joe?* ......15.00 - 20.00
14146-D *You'll Want Me Back* ....15.00 - 20.00
14153-D *Heebie Jeebies* ....15.00 - 20.00
14162-D *Take What You Want* ....15.00 - 20.00
14170-D *I'm Coming, Virginia* ....15.00 - 20.00
14182-D *Jersey Walk* ....15.00 - 20.00
14199-D *Satisfyin' Papa* ....15.00 - 20.00
14214-D *Take Your Black Bottom Outside* ....15.00 - 20.00
14229-D *Smile!* ....20.00 - 30.00
14264-D *Someday, Sweetheart* ....15.00 - 20.00
14297-D *I'm Saving It All For You* .....15.00 - 25.00
14353-D *My Handy Man* ....10.00 - 15.00

14365-D *West End Blues* ....15.00 - 20.00
14380-D *Do What You Did Last Night* ....25.00 - 40.00
14411-D *Lonesome Swallow* ....35.00 - 50.00
14458-D *Long Lean Lanky Mama* ....25.00 - 40.00
14565-D *Georgia Blues* ....50.00 - 75.00
Decca 140, 141, 234 ....7.00 - 12.00
Liberty Music Shop 188 *Thief In The Night* ....10.00 - 15.00
310 *Taking A Chance On Love* ....7.00 - 10.00
311 *Cabin In The Sky* ....7.00 - 10.00

Paramount 12169 *Down Home Blues* ....30.00 - 50.00
12170 *There'll Be Some Changes Made* ....30.00 - 50.00
12171 *Royal Garden Blues* ....30.00 - 50.00
12173 *Bugle Blues* ....30.00 - 50.00
12174 *Dying With The Blues* ....30.00 - 50.00
12175 *Jazzin' Babies Blues* ....50.00 - 80.00
12176 *At The New Jump Steady Ball* ....50.00 - 80.00
12177 *Georgia Blues* ....50.00 - 80.00
12178 *Brown Baby* ....50.00 - 80.00
12179 *Memphis Man* ....50.00 - 80.00
12180 *Long-Last Mama* ....50.00 - 80.00
12181 *Lost Out Blues* ....50.00 - 80.00
12182 *Ethel Sings 'Em* ....50.00 - 80.00
12189 *Tell 'Em 'Bout Me* ....50.00 - 80.00
12230 *Black Spatch Blues* ....150.00 - 250.00
12313 *Craving Blues* ....150.00 - 250.00
Vocalion 14680 *Pleasure Mad* ....20.00 - 30.00

WATSON'S PULLMAN PORTERS:
Gennett 6353 *Barbecue Blues* ....250.00 - up
6378 *Down Home Special* ....250.00 - up

EL WATSON:
Victor 20951 *Narrow Gauge Blues* ....25.00 - 40.00
21440 *El Watson's Fox Chase* ....25.00 - 40.00
21585 *Bay Rum Blues* ....30.00 - 50.00

LU WATTERS' YERBA BUENA JAZZ BAND:
Jazz Man 1, 2, 3, 4, 5, 6, 7, 13, 14, 15, 17 ....8.00 - 12.00
Mercury 11026, 11065, 11090.............................7.00 - 10.00
West Coast 101, 103, 104, 111, 152 ....7.00 - 10.00

CHICK WEBB & HIS LITTLE CHICKS/ORCHESTRA;
CHICK WEBB'S SAVOY ORCHESTRA:
Brunswick 6156 *Blues In My Heart* ....30.00 - 50.00
Columbia 2875-D *On The Sunny Side Of The Street*
....40.00 - 60.00
2883-D *If Dreams Come True* ....30.00 - 40.00
2920-D *Imagination*..30.00 - 40.00
2926-D *Stompin' At The Savoy*.........................30.00 - 40.00
Decca 172 *Blue Minor* ....15.00 - 20.00
173 *That Rhythm Man* ....15.00 - 20.00
Decca 483, 494, 588, 640, 785, 830, 831, 995, 1032,
1065, 1087, 1114, 1115, 1123, 1213, 1220, 1273,
1513, 1521, 1586, 1681, 1716, 1759 ....7.00 - 12.00
Okeh 41571 *If It Ain't Love* ....25.00 - 40.00
41572 *Blue Minor* ....30.00 - 50.00

Vocalion 1607 *Heebie Jeebies* ....150.00 - 200.00
3100 *If It Ain't Love* ....10.00 - 15.00
3101 *True* ....10.00 - 15.00
3246 *Stompin' At The Savoy* ....8.00 - 12.00

MALCOLM WEBB & HIS GANG:
Champion 15420 *Friday Night* ....75.00 - 100.00

CARL WEBSTER'S YALE COLLEGIANS:
Okeh 41393 *Puttin' On The Ritz*............................40.00 - 60.00
Personal Record 139-P *If I'm Without You* ....60.00 - 100.00

JULIAN WEBSTER AND HIS BAY STATE ACES:
Cameo 52061 *Just Once Again* ....25.00 - 40.00

ANSON WEEKS AND HIS (HOTEL MARK HOPKINS) ORCHESTRA:
Brunswick 6524, 6526, 6569, 6575, 6604, 6619,
6639, 6661, 6665, 6727, 6730, 6772, 6795, 6944,
6946, 6965, 6969, 6983, 6989, 6990, 6997, 7349,
7350, 7477, 7510, 7515, 7518..........................7.00 - 12.00
Brunswick 20120 *"Strike Me Pink"* medley ....15.00 - 20.00
(Note: Brunswick 20120 is a 12 inch record.)
Columbia 1409-D *Wob-A-Ly Walk* ....10.00 - 15.00
1915-D *Someday Soon* ....10.00 - 15.00
Columbia 2211-D *Ro-Ro-Rollin' Along* ....10.00 - 15.00
40004-D *Susianna*..15.00 - 25.00
Decca 1134, 1139, 1140.....................................7.00 - 10.00

TED WEEMS & HIS ORCHESTRA:
Bluebird 5130 *Trouble In Paradise* ....8.00 - 12.00
5131 *Heartaches* ....8.00 - 12.00
5148 *If I Had Somebody To Love* ....8.00 - 12.00
5235 *In A One-Room Flat* ....8.00 - 12.00
5236 *Doin' The Uptown Lowdown* ....10.00 - 15.00
5239 *Why Am I Happy?* ....8.00 - 12.00
5288 *The Boulevard Of Broken Dreams*..............8.00 - 12.00
5289 *The Music Man* ....10.00 - 15.00
5290 *The Rooftop Serenade* ....8.00 - 12.00
5292 *I Guess It Had To Be That Way* ....8.00 - 12.00
(foregoing titles on Electradisk are of slightly higher value; on
Sunrise, substantially higher)
Columbia 2956-D *Ten Yards To Go* ....15.00 - 20.00
2957-D *Blue Sky Avenue* ....15.00 - 20.00
2975-D *I'm Growing Fonder Of You*.................15.00 - 20.00
2976-D *Winter Wonderland*...............................15.00 - 20.00
Decca 820 *You Can't Pull The Wool Over My Eyes*.....10.00 - 15.00
822 *Lazy Weather* ....10.00 - 15.00
Decca 895, 921, 958, 959, 969 ....7.00 - 12.00
Decca (blue label) most other issues.......................5.00 - 10.00
Electradisk (same titles as Bluebirds, slightly higher values)
Sunrise (same titles as Bluebird, much higher values)
Victor L-16025 Long-Playing "Program Transcription"
....25.00 - 35.00
Victor 19258, 19287, 19344, 19377, 19496, 19722,
19804, 19930, 19938, 20033, 20120, 20196,
20206, 20230, 20234, 20829, 20846, 20901,
20910, 21105, 21364, 21511, 21670, 21767,
21773, 21809, 22032, 22137, 22138, 22157,
22215..7.00 - 12.00
20133 *Oh! If I Only Had You*............................10.00 - 15.00
20475 *She Belongs To Me*................................10.00 - 15.00
21173 *Everybody Loves My Girl* ....10.00 - 15.00
21729 *Come On, Baby!* ....10.00 - 15.00
22037 *Piccolo Pete* ....10.00 - 15.00
22038 *What A Day!* ....10.00 - 15.00

22238 *The Man From The South* ....10.00 - 15.00
22304 *Talk Of The Town* ....10.00 - 15.00
22406 *Collegiate Love* ....10.00 - 15.00
22411 *Slappin' The Bass* ....10.00 - 15.00
22426 *Washing Dishes With My Sweetie*............10.00 - 15.00
22499 *My Baby Just Cares For Me* ....10.00 - 15.00
22515 *I Still Get A Thrill* ....10.00 - 15.00
22564 *The One-Man Band*................................10.00 - 15.00
22637 *Walkin' My Baby Back Home* ....10.00 - 15.00
22644 *Egyptian Ella* ....10.00 - 15.00
22646 *Little Joe* ....10.00 - 15.00
22656 *My Favorite Band* ....10.00 - 15.00
22822 *Oh! Monah* ....10.00 - 15.00
22829 *Nobody's Baby Is Somebody's Baby Now*.10.00 - 15.00
22838 *I'm For You A Hundred Percent* ....10.00 - 15.00
22877 *One Of Us Was Wrong* ....10.00 - 15.00
22881 *She's So Nice* ....10.00 - 15.00
24053 *Play That Hot Guitar* ....15.00 - 20.00
24219 *At The Baby Parade* ....10.00 - 15.00
24227 *When The Morning Rolls Around*...........10.00 - 15.00
24265 *Juggling A Jigsaw* ....10.00 - 15.00
24266 *I Like Mountain Music*..........................10.00 - 15.00
24302 *Panhandle Pete* ....15.00 - 20.00
24308 *Hats Off, Here Comes A Lady* ....10.00 - 15.00

GENE WEIMER & HIS PEPPERS:
Champion 15422 *Clementine* ....30.00 - 40.00

LEW WEINER'S GOLD AND BLACK ACES:
Gennett 6540 *Louisiana Bo Bo* ....30.00 - 50.00

LAWRENCE WELK & HIS ORCHESTRA:
Broadway 1462 *Smile, Darn Ya, Smile* ....15.00 - 25.00
1481 *This Is The Missus* ....15.00 - 25.00
Gennett 6697 *Doin' The New Low Down*..............100.00 - 150.00
6712 *Spiked Beer* ....100.00 - 150.00
20341 *Shanghai Honeymoon* ....100.00 - 150.00

DICKEY WELLS' SHIM SHAMMERS: DICKIE WELLS' ORCHESTRA:
Columbia 2829-D *Baby, Are You Satisfied?* ....50.00 - 80.00
Signature, most issues...7.00 - 10.00

PETE WENDLING:
Cameo 1021 *Someone Is Losin' Susan* ....12.00 - 16.00
1064 *Mary Lou* ....10.00 - 15.00
Okeh 4868 *Papa Blues* ....15.00 - 25.00
4984 *Page Paderewski* ....15.00 - 25.00

MAE WEST:
Brunswick 6495 *Easy Rider* ....15.00 - 20.00
6675 *I'm No Angel*......................................15.00 - 20.00
6676 *They Call Me Sister Honky-Tonk*..............15.00 - 20.00

THEADOR WEST:
Ajax 17118 *Hot Jelly Blues* ....50.00 - 80.00
17129 *Blues, Just Blues* ....50.00 - 80.00
17136 *Devilish Blues* ....50.00 - 100.00

JACK WESTBROOK & HIS ORCHESTRA:
Champion 16324 *Helen* ....15.00 - 20.00
Superior 2571 *I Got Rhythm* ....100.00 - 150.00

THE WESTERNERS:
Harmony 297-H *Take In The Sun, Hang Out The Moon*
....8.00 - 12.00
358-H *There's Everything Nice About You* ....8.00 - 12.00

366-H *My Regular Gal* ....8.00 - 12.00
447-H *I Ain't That Kind Of A Baby* ....8.00 - 12.00
547-H *Away Down South In Heaven* ....5.00 - 8.00
611-H *She's A Great, Great Girl* ....10.00 - 15.00
638-H *Sweet Sue-Just You* ....8.00 - 12.00
651-H *The Pay-Off*..10.00 - 15.00
(Note: Above Titles, on Diva and Velvet Tone, are similarly valued.)

FRANK WESTPHAL & HIS ORCHESTRA:
Columbia 17-D *All Wrong* ....10.00 - 15.00
22-D *Oh! Sister, Ain't That Hot?*......................10.00 - 15.00
32-D *Forgetful Blues* ....10.00 - 15.00
A3571 *She's A Mean Job* ....8.00 - 12.00
A3693 *State Street Blues* ....8.00 - 12.00
A3743 *Choo Choo Blues* ....8.00 - 12.00
A3872 *Bugle Call Rag* ....10.00 - 15.00
A3911 *Wolverine Blues* ....10.00 - 15.00
A3929 *Off Again-On Again Blues* ....10.00 - 15.00
Columbia, most other issues ....5.00 - 10.00

WE THREE:
Pathe-Actuelle 36464 *Trumpet Sobs*......................30.00 - 50.00
36492 *Plenty Off Center* ....30.00 - 50.00
Perfect 14645 *Trumpet Sobs* ....30.00 - 50.00
14673 *Plenty Off Center* ....30.00 - 50.00

WHISTLER & HIS JUG BAND:
Gennett 5554 *Chicago Flip*................................200.00 - 300.00
5614 *Jail House Blues* ....200.00 - 300.00
Okeh 8469 *Low Down Blues*...............................250.00 - up
8816 *Pig Meat Blues* ....200.00 - 300.00
Victor 23305 *Hold That Tiger* ....250.00 - up

BETSY WHITE:
Q.R.S. Q-1035 *Calamity Jane* ....10.00 - 15.00

BOB WHITE'S DIXIE TRIO:
Puritan 11400 *Alabamy Bound* ....150.00 - 250.00

HAL WHITE'S SYNCOPATORS:
Domino 3444 *Everybody Loves My Baby*
(instrumental)...50.00 - 75.00
3444 *Everybody Loves My Baby* (vocal chorus)....125.00 - 175.00

HAROLD WHITE & HIS ORCHESTRA:
Romeo 1833, 1891 ....8.00 - 12.00

STEVE WHITE'S DANCELAND ORCHESTRA:
Hollywood (unnumbered) *Slippery Elm* ....30.00 - 50.00
Sunset 1132 *Then I'll Be Happy* ....30.00 - 50.00
1137 *Paddlin' Madelin Home*..........................10.00 - 15.00

TED WHITE'S COLLEGIANS:
Jewel 5073 *Miss Annabelle Lee* ....10.00 - 15.00
5410 *My Blackbirds Are Bluebirds Now* ....10.00 - 15.00
5461 *Doin' The Raccoon* ....8.00 - 12.00
Oriole 797, 821, 875, 954, 962, 989, 1157, 1160,
1203, 1257, 1262, 1277, 1281, 1304, 1392, 1398,
1449, 1613, 1634, 1664, 1694 ....7.00 - 12.00
Oriole 828 *Crazy Words- Crazy Tune* ....15.00 - 20.00
931 *Hurricane* ....15.00 - 20.00
960 *12th Street Rag*.......................................15.00 - 20.00
1152 *For My Gal And Me* ....10.00 - 15.00
1231 *Light The Way To Somebody's Heart* ......10.00 - 15.00
1359 *My Blackbirds Are Bluebirds Now* ....10.00 - 15.00
1489 *Good-Little-Bad-Little You* ....10.00 - 15.00
1503 *Wedding Bells* ....10.00 - 15.00
1544 *Shirt Tail Stomp* ....15.00 - 20.00

WILLY WHITE:
Perfect 11175 *Try And Play It* ....10.00 - 15.00

PAUL WHITEMAN & HIS (CONCERT) ORCHESTRA:
Columbia 1401-D, 1448-D, 1553-D, 1558-D, 1630-D, 2224-D,
2263-D ....7.00 - 12.00
Columbia 1402-D *Get Out And Get Under The Moon*
....12.00 - 16.00
  1441-D *Because My Baby Don't Mean "Maybe" Now*
....15.00 - 20.00
  1444-D *That's My Weakness Now* ....15.00 - 20.00
  1464-D *Pickin' Cotton* ....10.00 - 15.00
  1465-D *I'm On The Crest Of A Wave* ....15.00 - 20.00
  1478-D *Felix The Cat* ....30.00 - 50.00
  1491-D *Georgie Porgie* ....20.00 - 30.00
  1496-D *I'd Rather Cry Over You* ....15.00 - 20.00
  1505-D *Out O' Town Gal* ....20.00 - 30.00
  1683-D *Makin' Whoopee* ....12.00 - 16.00
  1701-D *Let's Do It* ....12.00 - 16.00
  1723-D *How About Me?* ....12.00 - 16.00
  1736-D *Button Up Your Overcoat* ....15.00 - 20.00
  1755-D *Coquette* ....10.00 - 15.00
  1771-D *Louise* ....12.00 - 16.00
  1822-D *When My Dreams Come True* ....15.00 - 20.00
  1845-D *Your Mother And Mine* ....10.00 - 15.00
  1862-D *S'posin'* ....12.00 - 16.00
  1877-D *I'm In Seventh Heaven* ....15.00 - 20.00
  1945-D *China Boy* ....15.00 - 20.00
  1974-D *Waiting At The End Of The Road* ....15.00 - 20.00
  1993-D *When You're Counting The Stars Alone* .....12.00 - 16.00
  2010-D *If I Had A Talking Picture Of You* ....12.00 - 16.00
  2023-D *Great Day* ....12.00 - 16.00
  2047-D *Should I?* ....10.00 - 15.00
  2098-D *After You've Gone* ....15.00 - 20.00
  2163-D *Song Of The Dawn* ....12.00 - 16.00
  2164-D *A Bench In The Park* ....12.00 - 16.00
  2170-D *I Like To Do Things For You* ....12.00 - 16.00
  2171-D *You Brought A New Kind Of Love To Me*
....12.00 - 16.00
  2277-D *The New Tiger Rag* ....12.00 - 16.00
  2289-D *A Big Bouquet For You* ....10.00 - 15.00
  2297-D *Body And Soul* ....10.00 - 15.00
  2491-D *Choo Choo* ....15.00 - 20.00
  50068-D *My Melancholy Baby* (12 inch) ....30.00 - 50.00
  50103-D *Sweet Sue* (12 inch) ....25.00 - 40.00
Victor L-16001 *George White's Scandals Medley* ..25.00 - 40.00
  L-16002 *I'm Sorry Dear* plus 2 more tunes........30.00 - 50.00
  L-16017 *Willow, Weep For Me* plus 2 more tunes
....30.00 - 50.00
(Note: Above are long-playing "Program Transcriptions".)
  19345, 19381, 19720, 19773, 19785, 19920, 19934
....7.00 - 12.00
  19671 *Charleston* ....15.00 - 20.00
Victor, most other issues in the 19000 series ....5.00 - 8.00
  20017 *Tentin' Down In Tennessee* ....8.00 - 12.00
  20019 *No Foolin'* ....8.00 - 12.00
  20092 *St. Louis Blues* ....10.00 - 15.00
  20177 *When The Red, Red Robin Comes Bob, Bob, Bobbin'*
    Along...8.00 - 12.00
  20418 *Wistful And Blue* ....8.00 - 12.00
  20508 *Muddy Water* ....10.00 - 15.00
  20627 *Side By Side* ....10.00 - 15.00
  20679 *Magnolia*...10.00 - 15.00
  20751 *I'm Coming, Virginia*..............................10.00 - 15.00
  20883 *It Won't Be Long Now* ....8.00 - 12.00

Victor (most others in 20000 series) ....5.00 - 10.00
  21103 *Changes*...15.00 - 20.00
  21119 *Whiteman Stomp* ....10.00 - 15.00
  21214 *Lonely Melody*...10.00 - 15.00
  21218 *Ol' Man River* ....10.00 - 15.00
  21228 *Smile* ....8.00 - 12.00
  21240 *Back In Your Own Backyard*..................15.00 - 20.00
  21274 *From Monday On* ....15.00 - 20.00
  21301 *Coquette* ....10.00 - 15.00
  21338 *When* ....10.00 - 15.00
  21365 *When You're With Somebody Else*..........20.00 - 30.00
  21388 *My Angel* ....8.00 - 12.00
  21389 *My Pet* ....12.00 - 16.00
  21398 *You Took Advantage Of Me* ....12.00 - 16.00
  21438 *Louisiana*...12.00 - 16.00
  21453 *It Was The Dawn of Love*.......................15.00 - 20.00
  21464 *Sugar* ....15.00 - 20.00
  22883 *'Leven Pounds Of Heaven* ....10.00 - 15.00
  22984 *Lawd, You Made The Night Too Long* ....10.00 - 15.00
  24078 *San* ....20.00 - 30.00
  24105 *Love Nest*..20.00 - 30.00
  24140 *You're Telling Me* ....10.00 - 15.00
  24400 *It's Only A Paper Moon* ....15.00 - 20.00
  24403 *Shanghai Lil* ....10.00 - 15.00
  24571 *Fare-Thee-Well To Harlem*....................10.00 - 15.00
  24615 *Christmas Night In Harlem* ....10.00 - 15.00
  24668 *G Blues* ....15.00 - 20.00
  24704 *Pardon My Southern Accent* ....10.00 - 15.00
  24852 *Serenade For A Wealthy Widow* ....10.00 - 15.00
  24885 *Itchols* ....10.00 - 15.00
  25086 *Dodging A Divorcee* ....10.00 - 15.00
  25088 *And Then Some* ....10.00 - 15.00
  25091 *I'm In Ihe Mood For Love* ....10.00 - 15.00
  25113 *The Duke Insists* ....10.00 - 15.00
  25150 *Sugar Plum*...10.00 - 15.00
  25192, 25238, 25319, 25404, 25675, 26415.........7.00 - 12.00
  25366 *Mississippi Mud* ....8.00 - 12.00
  25367 *San*..8.00 - 12.00
  25368 *From Monday On*....................................8.00 - 12.00
  25369 *Louisiana*..8.00 - 12.00
  25370 *Changes*..8.00 - 12.00
(Note: *25366 through 25370 were issued as a set.)
  27685 *Loveable* ....8.00 - 12.00
  27686 *Forget-Me-Not* ....8.00 - 12.00
  27687 *Dancing Shadows*....................................8.00 - 12.00
  27688 *From Monday On*....................................8.00 - 12.00
  27689 *Back In Your Own Back Yard* ....8.00 - 12.00
(Note: *27685 through 27689 were issued as a set.)
  L-35001 *Grand Canyon Suite* ....25.00 - 40.00
  L-35002 *Grand Canyon Suite* ....25.00 - 40.00
  35822 (12-inch) *Rhapsody In Blue* ....15.00 - 20.00
  35877 (12-inch) *Washboard Blues* ....15.00 - 20.00
  35934 (12-inch) *Metropolis* ....15.00 - 20.00
  35828, 35859, 35883, 35912, 35933 (12-inch)....8.00 - 12.00
  *39000 *A Night With Paul Whiteman At The Biltmore*
....100.00 - 200.00
  *39003 *Let 'Em Eat Cake*-Program................100.00 - 150.00
(Note: *12-inch picture records, in the style of the more familiar
  Vogue issues.)
  55225 *Rhapsody In Blue* (12 inch)...................20.00 - 30.00
  *67-2000 *A Night With Paul Whiteman At The Biltmore*
....100.00 - 200.00

PAUL WHITEMAN'S RHYTHM BOYS:

Columbia 1455-D *Wa Da Da*	10.00 -	15.00
1629-D *Rhythm King*	10.00 -	15.00
1819-D *Louise*	10.00 -	15.00
2223-D *A Bench In The Park*	10.00 -	15.00
Victor 20783 *Mississippi Mud, etc.*	8.00 -	12.00
21302 *From Monday On*	10.00 -	15.00
24095 *Bahama Mamas*	10.00 -	15.00
24190 *Jig Time*	15.00 -	20.00
24240 *Mississippi Mud, etc.*	10.00 -	15.00
24349 *From Monday On*	10.00 -	15.00

WHITE WAY DANCE ORCHESTRA:

Supreme 1325 *Fool Me Nice*	8.00 -	12.00

(Note: Above title on Grey Gull, Radiex is similarly valued.)

WHITEWAY JAZZ BAND:

Paramount 20014 *Tiger Rag*	25.00 -	40.00

WHITE WAY PLAYERS:

Van Dyke 71797 *My Sweeter Than Sweet*	7.00 -	10.00
71816 *Ev'rybody Dance*	15.00 -	20.00
71819 *Blue Ridge Blues*	15.00 -	20.00

JACK WHITNEY AND HIS ORCHESTRA:

Titles, issued contemporaneously on Clarion, Harmony, and Velvet Tone: *So Sure of You; You Forgot Your Gloves*	8.00 -	12.00
Clarion 5270-C *Please Don't Talk About Me When I'm Gone*	10.00 -	15.00
Parlophone PNY-34194 *If You Should Ever Need Me*	20.00 -	30.00

THE WHOOPEE MAKERS:

Titles, issued contemporaneously on Banner, Jewel, Oriole, Regal, and Romeo: *Rockin' Chair; Them There Eyes*	15.00 -	25.00
Titles, issued contemporaneously on Cameo, Lincoln, and Romeo: *Hottentot; Misty Mornin'; Saturday Night Function*	15.00 -	30.00
Banner 0859 *Humpty Dumpty Baby*	20.00 -	30.00
6548 *Saturday Night Function*	20.00 -	30.00
Columbia 14367-D *Sister Kate*	35.00 -	50.00
Conqueror 7428 *Flaming Youth*	20.00 -	30.00
Domino 4428 *Flaming Youth*	20.00 -	30.00
Pathe-Actuelle (titles as on Perfect, following)		
Perfect 14962 *East St. Louis Toodle-Oo*	50.00 -	75.00
14968 *Take It Easy*	50.00 -	75.00
15080 *Move Over*	40.00 -	60.00
15096 *Hot And Bothered*	40.00 -	60.00
15104 *Misty Mornin'*	40.00 -	60.00
15126 *Bugle Call Rag*	15.00 -	20.00
15194 *Tiger Rag*	15.00 -	20.00
15217 *Twelfth Street Rag*	15.00 -	20.00
15223 *The Sorority Stomp*	20.00 -	30.00
15240 *Doin' The Voom Voom*	20.00 -	30.00
(foregoing titles on Pathe-Actuelle are similarly valued)		
15376 *Happy Feet*	20.00 -	30.00
15418 *Them There Eyes*	15.00 -	25.00
15507 *Slow But Sure*	8.00 -	12.00
Regal 8874 *Flaming Youth*	20.00 -	30.00
10173 *Humpty Dumpty Baby*	20.00 -	30.00
Vocalion 15763 *Dardanella*	200.00 -	up
15768 *I've Never Been Loved By Anyone Like You*	150.00 -	200.00
15769 *Freshman Hop*	150.00 -	200.00

ZACH WHYTE'S CHOCOLATE BEAU BRUMMELS:

Gennett 6781 *Mandy*	250.00 -	up
6798 *It's Tight Like That*	250.00 -	up
7086 *Good Feelin' Blues*	300.00 -	up

BUS WIDMER & HIS ORCHESTRA:

Champion 16129 *I'm Doin' That Thing*	10.00 -	15.00

HERB WIEDOEFT & HIS (CINDERELLA ROOF) ORCHESTRA:

Brunswick 2542, 2627, 2647, 2660, 2730, 2751, 2781, 2795, 2893, 2916, 2982, 3810, 3811	7.00 -	12.00
Brunswick 3812 *Golden Gate*	10.00 -	15.00
3813 *Sad Moments*	10.00 -	15.00
3814 *Trianon*	10.00 -	15.00

S. D. WILBER:

Clover 1673 *Get It Now*	15.00 -	20.00

LEE WILEY:

Decca 132 *Careless Love*	10.00 -	15.00
322 *Hands Across The Table*	10.00 -	15.00
Gala 1, 2, 3, 4	7.00 -	12.00
Libery Music Shop 281, 282, 283, 284, 294, 295, 296, 297	7.00 -	12.00

WILLIAMS' COTTON CLUB ORCHESTRA:

Victor 24039 *Charlie Two-Step*	30.00 -	50.00
24083 *Red Blues*	50.00 -	75.00

WILLIAMS' PURPLE KNIGHTS:

Victor 22625 *Dinah*	15.00 -	25.00

WILLIAMS' WASHBOARD BAND:

Bluebird 5183 *I Want To Ring Bells*	75.00 -	100.00
5204 *Hard Corn*	75.00 -	100.00
5230 *Shoutin' In The Amen Corner*	75.00 -	100.00

(Note: Above titles on Sunrise are worth more.)

WILLLAMS & MOORE:

Q.R.S. 7016 *Block And Tackle Blues*	200.00 -	300.00

BILL WILLIAMS & HIS GANG:

Champion 15011 *Doo Wacka Doo*	8.00 -	12.00
15215 *Make Me Know It*	75.00 -	100.00
15216 *Georgia Bo Bo*	80.00 -	120.00
15226 *She Looks Like Helen Brown*	15.00 -	25.00
15253 *Zulu Wail*	15.00 -	25.00
15268 *Go Wash An Elephant (If You Want To Do Something Big)*	15.00 -	20.00
Silvertone 3099 *I'm Sitting On Top Of The World*	8.00 -	12.00

CLARENCE WILLIAMS (& HIS WASHBOARD BAND/ ORCHESTRA); CLARENCE WILLIAMS' BLUE FIVE/ JAZZ KINGS/JUG BAND/NOVELTY BAND/ ORCHESTRA/ STOMPERS/TRIO/WASHBOARD FOUR/ WASHBOARD FIVE:

Titles, issued contemporaneously on Banner, Domino, Jewel, Oriole, Perfect, Regal, and Romeo: *Baby, Won't You Please Come Home?; Hot Lovin'; Papa-De-Da-Da; Shout, Sister, Shout!*	35.00 -	50.00
Bluebird 6918 *More Than That*	10.00 -	15.00
6919 *Jammin'*	10.00 -	15.00
6932 *Wanted*	10.00 -	15.00
Broadway 1347 *Long, Deep And Wide*	150.00 -	200.00
1348 *Squeeze Me*	150.00 -	200.00
5067 *Saturday Night Jag*	150.00 -	300.00

Brunswick 3580 *Slow River*..20.00 - 30.00
    3664 *Baltimore* ....20.00 - 30.00
    7000 *Cushion Foot Stomp* ....35.00 - 50.00
    7017 *Baltimore* ....20.00 - 30.00
Columbia 1735-D *Have You Ever Felt That Way?* .35.00 - 50.00
    2806-D *High Society*...50.00 - 80.00
    2829-D *Chizzlin' Sam*...50.00 - 80.00
    2863-D *Organ Grinder Blues*.............................50.00 - 80.00
    14193-D *Candy Lips*..75.00 - 100.00
    14241-D *Shootin' The Pistol* ....50.00 - 75.00
    14244-D *I'm Goin' Back To Bottomland* ....75.00 - 100.00
    14287-D *Dreaming The Hours Away* ....75.00 - 100.00
    14314-D *Any Time* ....75.00 - 100.00
    14326-D *Red River Blues* ....80.00 - 120.00
    14341-D *Farm Hand Papa* ....80.00 - 120.00
    14348-D *Walk That Broad* ....80.00 - 120.00
    14422-D *Mountain City Blues* ....75.00 - 100.00
    14434-D *In Our Cottage Of Love* ....75.00 - 100.00
    14447-D *Whoop It Up* ....75.00 - 100.00
    14460-D *Freeze Out* ....75.00 - 100.00
    14468-D *Railroad Rhythm* ....75.00 - 100.00
    14488-D *Zonky* ....75.00 - 100.00
    14555-D *High Society Blues*..............................80.00 - 120.00
    14666-D *Baby, Won't You Please Come Home?*
....100.00 - 150.00
Okeh 4893 *Mixing The Blues* ....75.00 - 100.00
    4925 *Wild Cat Blues* ....100.00 - 150.00
    4966 *Achin' Hearted Blues* ....125.00 - 175.00
    4975 *New Orleans Hop Scop Blues* ....150.00 - 250.00
    4993 *Old Fashioned Love*................................100.00 - 150.00
    8020 *Pullman Porter Blues* ....50.00 - 75.00
    8021 *Roumania*...50.00 - 75.00
    8027 *Brown Skin (Who You For)*......................35.00 - 50.00
    8029 *The Dance They Call The Georgia Hunch* .....35.00 - 50.00
    8171 *Texas Moaner Blues* ....150.00 - 250.00
    8181 *Everybody Loves My Baby*......................75.00 - 100.00
    8204 *Temptation Blues* ....50.00 - 75.00
    8215 *Papa De-Da-Da*..200.00 - 300.00
    8245 *Coal Cart Blues* ....100.00 - 150.00
    8254 *Santa Claus Blues* ....150.00 - 250.00
    8267 *Get It Fixed* ....80.00 - 120.00
    8272 *Livin' High Sometimes*............................150.00 - 200.00
    8286 *I've Found A New Baby* ....100.00 - 150.00
    8440 *Candy Lips* ....75.00 - 100.00
    8443 *Senegalese Stomp*....................................100.00 - 150.00
    8462 *Cushion Foot Stomp* ....50.00 - 80.00
    8465 *Black Snake Blues*....................................50.00 - 80.00
    8510 *Close Fit Blues* ....50.00 - 80.00
    8525 *Yama Yama Blues* ....50.00 - 80.00
    8572 *Log Cabin Blues* ....50.00 - 80.00
    8584 *Red River Blues* ....80.00 - 120.00
    8592 *Lazy Mama* ....80.00 - 120.00
    8604 *Wildflower Rag* ....75.00 - 100.00
    8617 *Organ Grinder Blues* ....75.00 - 100.00
    8629 *Walk That Broad*......................................50.00 - 80.00
    8645 *In The Bottle Blues* ....100.00 - 150.00
    8663 *Freeze Out* ....50.00 - 80.00
    8672 *Steamboat Days* ....75.00 - 100.00
    8706 *High Society* ....50.00 - 80.00
    8738 *I've Got What It Takes* ....50.00 - 80.00
    8752 *You Don't Understand*..............................50.00 - 80.00
    8763 *I've Found A New Baby* ....75.00 - 100.00
    8790 *Worn Out Blues*..75.00 - 100.00

    8798 *He Wouldn't Stop Doin' It* ....80.00 - 120.00
    8806 *You Rascal, You* ....75.00 - 100.00
    8821 *Shout, Sister, Shout!* ....75.00 - 100.00
    8826 *Kansas City Man Blues* ....80.00 - 120.00
    8842 *Papa De-Da-Da*..80.00 - 120.00
    40006 *Shreveport* ....100.00 - 150.00
    40172 *My Own Blues* ....75.00 - 100.00
    40260 *Mandy, Make Up Your Mind* ....75.00 - 100.00
    40321 *Cake-Walking Babies From Home* ....100.00 - 150.00
    40541 *Dinah*..50.00 - 80.00
    40598 *What's The Matter Now?* ....40.00 - 60.00
    41565 *Mister, Will You Serenade?* ....50.00 - 80.00
Paramount 12435 *Shut Your Mouth* ....100.00 - 150.00
    12517 *Bottomland*..100.00 - 150.00
    12587 *Jingles* ....100.00 - 150.00
    12839 *Midnight Stomp* ....250.00 - up
    12870 *Pane In The Glass* ....250.00 - up
    12884 *Speakeasy* ....150.00 - 250.00
    12885 *Squeeze Me*...150.00 - 250.00
Q.R.S. 7004 *Speakeasy* ....150.00 - 250.00
    7005 *Squeeze Me* ....150.00 - 250.00
    7033 *Midnight Stomp* ....250.00 - up
    7034 *Bozo* ....250.00 - up
    7040 *I'm Through* ....250.00 - up
    7044 *Sister Kate* ....200.00 - 300.00
Victor V-38063 *Lazy Mama* ....50.00 - 80.00
    V-38524 *Too Low* ....100.00 - 150.00
    V-38630 *I'm Not Worryin'* ....100.00 - 150.00
Vocalion 1088 *Cushion Foot Stomp* ....30.00 - 50.00
    1130 *Baltimore*...30.00 - 50.00
    2541 *Breeze*...10.00 - 15.00
    2563 *The Right Key But The Wrong Keyhole* ....15.00 - 20.00
    2584 *Chocolate Avenue* ....15.00 - 25.00
    2602 *Harlem Rhythm Dance*............................20.00 - 30.00
    2616 *Swaller-Tail Coat* ....12.00 - 16.00
    2629 *Jimmy Had A Nickel* ....12.00 - 16.00
    2630 *How Can I Get It?* ....12.00 - 16.00
    2654 *New Orleans Hop Scop Blues* ....15.00 - 25.00
    2674 *As Long As I Live* ....12.00 - 16.00
    2676 *St. Louis Blues* ....15.00 - 25.00
    2689 *I Can't Dance, I Got Ants In My Pants*.....15.00 - 20.00
    2718 *Pretty Baby, Is It Yes Or No?*....................12.00 - 16.00
    2736 *After Tonight* ....12.00 - 16.00
    2759 *Let's Have A Showdown* ....15.00 - 20.00
    2778 *Bimbo* ....15.00 - 20.00
    2788 *Trouble* ....20.00 - 30.00
    2805 *Ain't Gonna Give You None Of My Jelly Roll*
....15.00 - 20.00
    2838 *Big Fat Mama* ....15.00 - 20.00
    2854 *Chizzlin' Sam* ....15.00 - 20.00
    2871 *Organ Grinder Blues* ....15.00 - 20.00
    2889 *Tell The Truth* ....10.00 - 15.00
    2899 *I Saw Stars* ....10.00 - 15.00
    2909 *Jungle Crawl* ....15.00 - 20.00
    2927 *Milk Cow Blues* ....15.00 - 20.00
    2938 *Black Gal* ....15.00 - 20.00
    2958 *I Can See You All Over The Place* ....12.00 - 16.00
    2991 *Yama Yama Blues* ....12.00 - 16.00
    3195 *This Is My Sunday Off*..............................12.00 - 16.00
    03350 *Mississippi Basin* ....20.00 - 30.00
    25009 *Black-Eyed Susan Brown* ....20.00 - 30.00
    25010 *High Society* ....25.00 - 40.00

COOTIE WILLIAMS & HIS ORCHESTRA/RUG CUTTERS:
Okeh 5618, 5690, 6224, 6336, 6370 ....7.00 - 12.00
Variety 527 *Downtown Uproar* ....10.00 - 15.00
    555 *Diga Diga Doo* ....10.00 - 15.00
Vocalion 3814 *Blue Reverie* ....10.00 - 15.00
    3818 *Diga Diga Doo* ....10.00 - 15.00
    3890 *I Can't Give You Anything But Love* ....10.00 - 15.00
    3922 *Pigeons And Peppers* ....10.00 - 15.00
Vocalion 3960, 4061, 4086, 4324, 4425, 4574, 4646,
    4726, 4958, 5411, 5618, 5690 ....7.00 - 12.00

DOUGLAS WILLIAMS (FOUR) (& HIS ORCHESTRA):
Victor 21269 *Roadhouse Stomp* ....15.00 - 20.00
    21413 *Far Away Texas Blues* ....40.00 - 60.00
    21695 *Kind Daddy* ....40.00 - 60.00
    23264 *Darktown Jubilee* ....150.00 - 250.00
    23303 *Thrill Me* ....150.00 - 200.00
    23337 *Clarinet Jiggles* ....150.00 - 200.00
    23362 *Memphis Gal* ....150.00 - 250.00
    23387 *Leaving Blues* ....150.00 - 250.00
    V-38031 *Riverside Stomp* ....50.00 - 80.00
    V-38518 *Neal's Blues* ....100.00 - 150.00
    V-38550 *P-Wee Strut* ....150.00 - 200.00
    V-38623 *Louisiana Hop* ....150.00 - 200.00

FESS WILLIAMS & HIS JOY BOYS:
Vocalion 15690 *Dixie Stomp* ....80.00 - 120.00

FESS WILLIAMS & HIS ROYAL FLUSH (SAVOY) ORCHESTRA:
Brunswick 3532 *Variety Stomp* ....20.00 - 30.00
    3589 *Alligator Crawl* ....20.00 - 30.00
    3596 *Razor Edge* ....20.00 - 30.00
Champion 15118 *Ya Gotta Know How To Love* .....75.00 - 100.00
    15120 *It's Breaking My Heart* ....75.00 - 100.00
Diva 2189-G *My Mama's In Town* ....35.00 - 50.00
Gennett 3182 *Green River Blues* ....50.00 - 75.00
    3210 *Caroline* ....50.00 - 75.00
    3259 *Wimmin-Aah!* ....150.00 - 250.00
    3336 *Ya Gotta Know How To Love* ....50.00 - 75.00
Harmony 189-H *My Mama's In Town* ....35.00 - 50.00
Okeh 8322 *Make Me Know It* ....75.00 - 100.00
Velvet Tone 1189-V *My Mama's In Town* ....35.00 - 50.00
Victor 22864 *Hot Mama* ....50.00 - 80.00
    23003 *Everything's O. K. With Me* ....50.00 - 80.00
    23005 *Dinah* ....50.00 - 80.00
    23025 *She's Still Dizzy* ....100.00 - 150.00
    24153 *Playing My Saxophone* ....50.00 - 80.00
    V-38056 *Here 'tis* ....50.00 - 80.00
    V-38062 *Betsy Brown* ....50.00 - 80.00
    V-38064 *A Few Riffs* ....50.00 - 80.00
    V-38065 *Sweet Savannah Sue* ....50.00 - 80.00
    V-38077 *Hot Town* ....75.00 - 100.00
    V-38095 *Buttons* ....75.00 - 100.00
    V-38106 *Slide, Mr. Jelly* ....75.00 - 100.00
    V-38128 *Big Shot* ....75.00 - 100.00
    V-38131 *I'm Feelin' Devilish* ....50.00 - 80.00
Vocalion 1054 *Heebie Jeebies* ....30.00 - 40.00
    1058 *High Fever* ....100.00 - 150.00
    1085 *White Ghost Shivers* ....100.00 - 150.00
    1087 *Gambler's Blues* ....100.00 - 150.00
    1117 *Ozark Blues* ....35.00 - 50.00
    15492 *High Fever* ....100.00 - 150.00
    15550 *Variety Stomp* ....35.00 - 50.00

FRANCES WILLIAMS:
Brunswick 4499 *It's Unanimous Now* ....10.00 - 15.00

HOD WILLIAMS AND HIS ORCHESTRA:
Bluebird 7104, 7119, 7141...7.00 - 10.00

JOHN WILLIAMS & HIS MEMPHIS STOMPERS:
Black Patti 8009 *Peewee Blues* ....600.00 - up
Vocalion 1453 *Lotta Sax Appeal* ....250.00 - up

JOHN WILLIAMS' SYNCO JAZZERS:
Paramount 12457 *Goose Grease* ....300.00 - up

(DRUMMER MAN) JOHNNY WILLIAMS & HIS BOYS/ SWING SEXTETTE:
Variety 594 *Where's My Sweetie Hiding?* ....8.00 - 12.00
    638 *I'll Build A Stairway To Paradise* ....8.00 - 12.00
Vocalion 3826, 3827, 5077, 5213 ....7.00 - 12.00

LEONA WILLIAMS & HER DIXIE BAND:
Columbia A-3565 *Cruel Daddy Blues* ....10.00 - 15.00
    A-3599 *Achin' Hearted Blues* ....10.00 - 15.00
    A-3642 *Got To Cool My Doggies Now* ....8.00 - 12.00
    A-3696 *Sugar Blues* ....10.00 - 15.00
    A-3713 *I Wish I Could Shimmy Like My Sister Kate*
    ....8.00 - 12.00
    A-3736 *Mexican Blues* ....10.00 - 15.00
    A-3815 *Bring It With You When You Come* ......10.00 - 15.00
    A-3835 *If Your Man Is Like My Man*.................10.00 - 15.00

MARY LOU WILLIAMS:
Brunswick 7178 *Night Life* ....125.00 - 175.00
Decca 781 *Mary's Special* ....10.00 - 15.00
    1021 *Isabelle* ....10.00 - 15.00
    1155 *Clean Pickin'* ....10.00 - 15.00
Decca 2796, 2797, 18122..7.00 - 12.00

MIDGE WILLIAMS & HER JAZZ JESTERS:
Variety 519 *Walkin' The Dog* ....8.00 - 12.00
    566 *Let's Begin Again*....................................8.00 - 12.00
    620 *That Old Feeling* ....10.00 - 15.00
    670 *The One Rose (That's Left In My Heart)* ....10.00 - 15.00
Vocalion 3779 *I Know Now* ....10.00 - 15.00
    3801 *An Old Flame Never Dies* ....10.00 - 15.00
    3812 *Walkin' The Dog* ....8.00 - 12.00
    3821 *I'm Getting Sentimental Over You* ....8.00 - 12.00
    3838 *I Was Born To Swing* ....10.00 - 15.00
    3865 *Fortune Tellin' Man* ....10.00 - 15.00
    3900 *Singin' The Blues* ....10.00 - 15.00
    3961 *Goodnight, Angel* ....10.00 - 15.00
    4026 *Love Is Like Whiskey*............................10.00 - 15.00
    4177 *In Any Language* ....10.00 - 15.00
    4192 *Don't Wake Up My Heart* ....8.00 - 12.00

RALPH WILLIAMS & HIS ORCHESTRA:
Victor 19504, 19528, 19957 ....7.00 - 12.00
    19573 *Wait Till You See Me With My Baby*.......10.00 - 15.00
    19775 *Cocaine Dance* ....75.00 - 100.00
    19958 *I Could Fall In Love With Someone Like You*
    ....25.00 - 35.00

SAMMY WILLIAMS (& HIS THREE NATURALS):
Autograph (unnumbered) *House Of David Blues* ...75.00 - 100.00
    Mandy, Make Up Your Mind ....75.00 - 100.00
Vocalion 4197, 4229, 4243, 4259 ....7.00 - 12.00

SID/SIDNEY WILLIAMS:

Champion 15372 *Mississippi Shivers*	125.00 -	175.00
Gennett 6353 *Mississippi Shivers*	250.00 -	up
Vocalion 15691 *My Pet*	35.00 -	50.00

SPEED WILLIAMS' ORCHESTRA:

Superior 2818 *Tin Roof Blues*	250.00 -	up

TE ROY WILLIAMS & HIS ORCHESTRA:

Titles, issued contemporaneously on Diva, Harmony, and Velvet-Tone: *Lindberg Hop; Oh Malinda* .... 50.00 - 80.00

WILLIAMSON'S BEALE STREET FROLIC ORCHESTRA:

Victor 20555 *Memphis Scrontch*	100.00 -	150.00
21410 *Scandinavian Stomp*	100.00 -	150.00

VIRGINIA WILLRICH & HER TEXAS RANGERS:

Okeh 41328 *Same Old Moon*	75.00 -	100.00

WILSHIRE DANCE ORCHESTRA:

Sunset 1059 *My Best Girl*	15.00 -	20.00
1088 *Charleston Charley*	15.00 -	20.00

WILSON'S T.O.B.A. BAND:

Paramount 12408 *Steady Roll*	200.00 -	300.00

CHICKEN WILSON AND SKEETER HINTON:

Q.R.S. 7051 *Myrtle Avenue Stomp*	200.00 -	300.00
7052 *House Snake Blues*	150.00 -	250.00

DUKE WILSON & HIS TEN BLACK BERRIES:

Titles, issued contemporaneously on Banner, Domino, Melotone, Oriole, Perfect, and Romeo: *Beale Street Blues; Goodbye Blues; House of David Blues; How'm I Doin' (Hey Hey); Mary's Idea; Once Or Twice* .... 20.00 - 30.00

Perfect 15632 *Bull Fiddle Blues*	10.00 -	15.00
Royal 91358 *(Canadian) Beale Street Blues*	75.00 -	up

EDITH WILSON (& HER/JOHNNY DUNN'S JAZZ BAND/HOUNDS):

Brunswick 4685 *Black And Blue*	50.00 -	80.00
Columbia A3479 *Vampin' Liza Jane*	15.00 -	20.00
A3506 *Old Time Blues*	15.00 -	25.00
A3537 *The West Texas Blues*	15.00 -	25.00
A3558 *Birmingham Blues*	15.00 -	20.00
A3634 *Mammy, I'm Thinking Of You*	10.00 -	15.00
A3653 *He May Be Your Man (But He Comes To See Me Sometimes)*	10.00 -	15.00
A3674 *Lonesome Mama Blues*	10.00 -	15.00
A3746 *Evil Blues*	15.00 -	20.00
A3787 *He Used To Be Your Man But He's My Man Now*	10.00 -	15.00
14008-D *Daddy, Change Your Mind*	40.00 -	60.00
14027-D *Muscle Shoals Blues*	20.00 -	30.00
14054-D *Double Crossin' Papa*	35.00 -	50.00
14066-D *There'll Be Some Changes Made*	35.00 -	50.00
Diva 6025-G *I Don't Know And I Don't Care Blues*	35.00 -	50.00
Velvet Tone 7051-V *Daddy, Change Your Mind*	35.00 -	50.00
Victor V-38624 *I'll Get Even With You*	150.00 -	200.00

GARLAND WILSON:

Okeh 41556 *Rockin' Chair*	35.00 -	50.00

GEORGE WILSON AND JIMMY HINTON:

Paramount 12843 *Chicken Wilson Blues*	150.00 -	250.00
Q.R.S. 7060 *Frog Eye Stomp*	200.00 -	300.00

LENA WILSON:

Ajax 17014 *Down South Blues*	30.00 -	50.00
17025 *He Wasn't Born In Araby*	30.00 -	50.00
Black Swan 14129 *The Wicked Fives' Blues*	50.00 -	75.00
Brunswick 2464 *Chirpin' The Blues*	15.00 -	20.00
2590 *Four-Flushin' Papa*	20.00 -	30.00
Clarion 5036-C *Chiropractor Blues*	35.00 -	50.00
Columbia A3915 *Memphis, Tennessee*	25.00 -	40.00
14618-D *My Man O'War*	150.00 -	200.00
Diva 6038-G *Baby, It Upsets Me So*	35.00 -	50.00
6045-G *Chiropractor Blues*	35.00 -	50.00
Emerson 10745 *I Don't Love Nobody*	15.00 -	25.00
Harmograph 2543 *Deceitful Blues*	50.00 -	80.00
Paramount 12029 *Deceitful Blues*	50.00 -	80.00
12042 *Memphis, Tennessee*	50.00 -	80.00
12044 *Memphis, Tennessee*	15.00 -	25.00
Pathe-Actuelle 020910 *Memphis, Tennessee*	15.00 -	20.00
032015 *Mistreatin' Daddy*	15.00 -	20.00
Perfect 12044 *Memphis, Tennessee*	15.00 -	20.00
12094 *Mistreatin' Daddy*	15.00 -	20.00
Silvertone 3009 *I Need You To Drive My Blues Away*	15.00 -	20.00
3010 *Afternoon Blues*	40.00 -	60.00
Velvet Tone 7064-V *I'm A Stationary Mama*	35.00 -	50.00
7071-V *Chiropractor Blues*	35.00 -	50.00
Victor 19085 *Triflin' Blues*	7.00 -	10.00
Vocalion 14631 *Your Time Now*	15.00 -	25.00
14651 *Afternoon Blues*	50.00 -	75.00

ROY WILSON & HIS GEORGIA CRACKERS:

Melotone 12026 *Swamp Blues*	50.00 -	80.00

TEDDY WILSON (& HIS ORCHESTRA) TEDDY WILSON QUARTET:

Brunswick 7498 *What A Little Moonlight Can Do*	15.00 -	20.00
7501 *Miss Brown To You*	15.00 -	20.00
7511 *It's Too Hot For Words*	15.00 -	20.00
7520 *I'm Painting The Town Red*	15.00 -	20.00
7543 *Every Now And Then*	10.00 -	15.00
7550 *Yankee Doodle Never Went To Town*	15.00 -	20.00
7554 *Eeny Meeny Miney Moe*	15.00 -	20.00
7577 *These 'N' That 'N' Those*	15.00 -	20.00
7581 *Spreadin' Rhythm Around*	15.00 -	20.00
7612 *Life Begins When You're In Love*	15.00 -	20.00
7702 *Guess Who*	15.00 -	20.00
7729 *I Cried For You*	12.00 -	16.00
7762 *The Way You Look Tonight*	12.00 -	16.00
7768 *With Thee I Swing*	12.00 -	16.00
7781 *I Can't Give You Anything But Love*	12.00 -	16.00
7789 *Pennies From Heaven*	12.00 -	16.00
7824 *He Ain't Got Rhythm*	15.00 -	20.00
7840 *My Last Affair*	15.00 -	20.00
7844 *The Mood That I'm In*	15.00 -	20.00
7859 *I Must Have That Man!*	15.00 -	20.00
7867 *Carelessly*	15.00 -	20.00
7877 *Moanin' Low*	15.00 -	20.00
7903 *I'll Get By*	12.00 -	16.00
7911 *Foolin' Myself*	12.00 -	16.00
7917 *Yours And Mine*	15.00 -	20.00
7926 *I'll Never Be The Same*	15.00 -	20.00
8008 *My Man*	12.00 -	16.00
8015 *Nice Work If You Can Get It*	15.00 -	20.00
8053 *If Dreams Come True*	15.00 -	20.00
8070 *When You're Smiling*	12.00 -	16.00

8259 *Everybody's Laughing* ....15.00 - 20.00
8265 *I'll Never Fail You* ....15.00 - 20.00
8270 *They Say* ....12.00 - 16.00
8281 *Hello, My Darling* ....15.00 - 20.00
8283 *You're So Desirable* ....15.00 - 20.00
8314 *What Shall I Say?* ....15.00 - 20.00
8319 *More Than You Know* ....12.00 - 16.00
7563, 7522, 7572, 7599, 7640, 7663, 7684, 7699,
7702, 7729, 7736, 7797, 7816, 7840, 7844, 7884,
7893, 7940, 7943, 7954, 7960, 7964, 7973, 8025,
8112, 8116, 8141, 8153, 8199, 8207, 8438, 8455
....8.00 - 12.00
Columbia 35207, 35220, 35232, 35298, 35354,
35372, 35711, 35737 ....7.00 - 12.00

WOODROW WILSON:
Victor 35251 *Woodrow Wilson On The Third Party* (12-inch)
....15.00 - 20.00
35252 *Democratic Principles* (12-inch) ....15.00 - 20.00
35253 *The Tariff* ....15.00 - 20.00

DALE WIMBROW (THE DEL-MAR-VA SONGSTER) & HIS RUBEVILLE TUNERS:
Columbia 821-D *Country Bred And Chicken Fed* ...10.00 - 15.00
1200-D *Oshkosh* ....10.00 - 15.00
Edison 51894 *So Long North (I'm Headin' South)* .20.00 - 30.00
52292 *Oshkosh* ....30.00 - 50.00
Q.R.S. Q-1009 *Crying For The Carolines* ....10.00 - 15.00
Q-1019 *The Preacher And The Bear* ....10.00 - 15.00
Q-1056 *Sing You Sinners* ....10.00 - 15.00

WINDY RHYTHM KINGS:
Paramount 12770 *Piggly Wiggly Blues* ....300.00 - up

WINEGAR'S PENN. BOYS:
Edison 52097 *Shaking The Blues Away* ....75.00 - 100.00
52099 *Ooh! Maybe It's You* ....50.00 - 75.00
52221 *Since My Best Gal Turned Me Down** ....50.00 - 75.00
52224 *Stay Out Of The South* ....40.00 - 60.00
52241 *Since My Best Gal Turned Me Down* ......50.00 - 75.00
52255 *Say So!* ....30.00 - 50.00
52305 *My Gal Sal* ....50.00 - 75.00
52321 *Ida! Sweet As Apple Cider* ....75.00 - 100.00
52381 *Imagination* ....40.00 - 60.00
52596 *Dream Mother* ....50.00 - 75.00
(Note: *All copies seen of 52221 play same song both sides, although flip side is labeled A Good Man Is Hard To Find.)

JACK WINN'S/WYNN'S DALLAS DANDIES:
Melotone 12008 *Lovey Lee* ....12.00 - 16.00
12027 *Wild Man Blues* ....15.00 - 20.00
12051 *Loved One* ....150.00 - 200.00
12064 *Melancholy* ....15.00 - 20.00
Vocalion 15860 *Loved One* ....150.00 - 200.00

GUS WINSON & HIS ORCHESTRA:
Broadway 1476 *It's The Girl* ....15.00 - 20.00.

CHIC WINTERS' (HOTEL GRAMATIN) ORCHESTRA:
Gennett 3294 *Spring Is Here* ....10.00 - 15.00
3314 *Will You Be True?* ....7.00 - 10.00
3320 *No More Worryin'* ....10.00 - 15.00
3340 *Faded Cherry Blossom* ....10.00 - 15.00
Hudson 11423 *Nashville Nightingale* ....10.00 - 20.00
Triangle 11423 *Nashville Nightingale* ....10.00 - 15.00

JULIE WINTZ AND HIS (HOFBRAU/MAYFLOWER) ORCHESTRA: JULIE WINTZ AND GEORGE ZIMMER'S JERSEY COLLEGIANS:
Harmony 436-H *Vo-Do-Do-De-O Blues* ....10.00 - 15.00
438-H *Magnolia* ....8.00 - 12.00
899-H *Perfume Of Roses* ....7.00 - 10.00
1040-H *H'lo Baby* ....7.00 - 10.00
1044-H *Till Your Happiness Happens Along* ......8.00 - 12.00
1051-H *I Gotta Have You* ....8.00 - 12.00
1092-H *The Man From The South* ....15.00 - 20.00
1104-H *Harmonica Harry* ....20.00 - 30.00
1169-H *After You've Gone* ....10.00 - 15.00
(foregoing titles on Diva and Velvet Tone are similarly valued)
Pathe-Actuelle 36451 *Deep Henderson* ....15.00 - 20.00
36460 *Spanish Mamma* ....15.00 - 20.00
Perfect 14632 *Deep Henderson* ....15.00 - 20.00
14641 *Spanish Mamma* ....15.00 - 20.00

BILL WIRGES & HIS ORCHESTRA; WILLIAM F. WIRGES & HIS ORCHESTRA:
Brunswick (most issues) ....5.00 - 8.00
Perfect 14404 *Cheatin' On Me* ....7.00 - 10.00
14440 *Yes Sir, That's My Baby* ....8.00 - 12.00
14443 *Pango Pango Maid* ....10.00 - 15.00
14474 *So's Your Old Man* ....10.00 - 15.00
14475 *I Want A Lovable Baby* ....10.00 - 15.00
14533 *Shake That Thing* ....15.00 - 20.00
14762 *Where's That Rainbow?* ....8.00 - 12.00
(Note: Above titles, on Pathe-Actuelle, are similarly valued.)

WISCONSIN ROOF ORCHESTRA: (See also DEVINE'S WISCONSIN ROOF ORCHESTRA)
Broadway 1043 *She's Still My Baby* ....10.00 - 15.00
1063 *There's Everything Nice About You* ....8.00 - 12.00
1087 *Shanghai Honeymoon* ....10.00 - 15.00
1142 *Riverboat Blues* ....30.00 - 50.00
1177 *Wob-A-Ly Walk* ....10.00 - 15.00
1178 *Whispering* ....8.00 - 12.00
1180 *When You're Smiling* ....8.00 - 12.00
1210 *Farewell Blues* ....75.00 - 100.00
1249 *Dream Train* ....8.00 - 12.00
1268 *There's A Place In The Sun For You* ....7.00 - 10.00
Paramount 12599 *Tiger Rag* ....40.00 - 60.00
12686 *Farewell Blues* ....75.00 - 100.00
20561 *Who's That Knockin' At My Door?* ....15.00 - 20.00
20583 *Singapore Sorrows* ....20.00 - 30.00
20619 *Wob-A-Ly Walk* ....15.00 - 20.00
20621 *Whispering* ....8.00 - 12.00
20622 *When You're Smiling* ....8.00 - 12.00

WISCONSIN U SKYROCKETS:
Paramount 12641 *Slow Beef* ....300.00 - up
12642 *Postage Stomp* ....300.00 - up

W M C A BROADCASTERS:
Harmony 283-H *All Alone Monday* ....20.00 - 30.00
336-H *I Love The College Girls* ....8.00 - 12.00

WOLVERINE ORCHESTRA; THE WOLVERINES (See also THE ORIGINAL WOLVERINES):
Brunswick 3332 *Crazy Quilt* ....15.00 - 20.00
Gennett 5408 *Jazz Me Blues* ....150.00 - 250.00
5453 *Copenhagen* ....150.00 - 250.00
5454 *Riverboat Shuffle* ....150.00 - 200.00
5542 *Lazy Daddy* ....150.00 - 250.00

5565 *Tia Juana* ....150.00 - 250.00
5620 *Prince Of Wails*..........................75.00 - 125.00
20062 *Royal Garden Blues* ....200.00 - up

WOODING'S GRAND CENTRAL RED CAPS:
Victor 22718 *I Can't Get Enough Of You* ....40.00 - 60.00

BABE WOODS & HIS PALS:
Champion 15468 *Let's Misbehave* ....50.00 - 75.00

ALLISTER WYLIE & HIS CORONADO HOTEL ORCHESTRA:
Brunswick 4143 *Come On, Baby!* ....15.00 - 25.00

(ALBERT) WYNN'S (AND HIS) GUT BUCKET FIVE/ CREOLE JAZZ BAND:
Okeh 8350 *When*....................................200.00 - 300.00
Vocalion 1218 *Crying My Blues Away*..................200.00 - up
    1220 *Parkway Stomp* ....250.00 - up
    1252 *She's Crying For Me* ....200.00 - up

JACK WYNN'S DALLAS DANDIES (See JACK WINN'S DALLAS DANDIES)

ALBERT WYNNE (See ALBERT WYNN)

BILLY WYNNE & HIS GREENWICH VILLAGE INN ORCHESTRA:
Edison 51432, 51452, 51488, 51501, 51519 ....8.00 - 12.00
Edison 51503 *The Only Only One For Me* ....15.00 - 20.00
    51549 *Lenore* ....20.00 - 30.00
    51566 *Pango Pango Maid* ....20.00 - 30.00
    51573 *Say, Arabella*.............................20.00 - 30.00
    51578 *Nantucket Nan* ....10.00 - 15.00
    51580 *Steppin' In Society* ....25.00 - 35.00
    51603 *Cecilia*....................................15.00 - 20.00
    51606 *Charleston Baby O'Mine* ....20.00 - 30.00
    51715 *Everything's Gonna Be All Right* ....10.00 - 15.00
Harmony 33-H *The Co-Ed*...........................8.00 - 12.00
    34-H *Let's Wander Away*.........................8.00 - 12.00
    54-H *Why Aren't Yez Eatin' More Oranges?*.......8.00 - 12.00
    57-H *Five Foot Two, Eyes Of Blue*................10.00 - 15.00
    135-H *Sweet Southern Breeze* ....8.00 - 12.00
    163-H *I'm In Love With You, That's Why* ....8.00 - 12.00
Pathe-Actuelle 36431 *Dorothy* ....8.00 - 12.00
    36460 *If You Can't Hold The Man You Love* .....15.00 - 20.00
Perfect 14612 *No Foolin'* ....8.00 - 12.00
    14641 *If You Can't Hold The Man You Love* .....15.00 - 20.00

THE YACHT CLUB BOYS:
Brunswick, most issues ....5.00 - 10.00
Columbia 2887-D *We Own A Salon* ....20.00 - 30.00
    2908-D *The Great American Tourist*.................20.00 - 30.00

YALE COLLEGIANS:
Edison 52108 *You'll Do It Someday*....................75.00 - 100.00
Okeh 41474 *Blue Again*................................50.00 - 80.00

JIMMY YANCEY:
Bluebird 8630 *Death Letter Blues* ....15.00 - 20.00
Session 10001, 10003, 10005 ....8.00 - 12.00
Solo Art 12008 *The Fives* ....35.00 - 50.00
Vocalion 05464 *East St. Louis Blues*..................15.00 - 20.00
    05490 *Bear Trap Blues* ....15.00 - 20.00

THE YANKEE SIX:
Okeh 40335 *Oh! Those Eyes* ....75.00 - 100.00
    40348 *Jimtown Blues*.............................75.00 - 100.00

THE YANKEE TEN (DANCE) ORCHESTRA:
Oriole 684 *Baby Face* ....10.00 - 15.00
    846 *Ain't She Sweet?* ....15.00 - 20.00
    933 *Sometimes I'm Happy* ....15.00 - 20.00
    1455 *Makin' Whoopee* ....10.00 - 15.00
    1726 *Look What You've Done To Me* ....10.00 - 15.00

DUKE YELLMAN AND HIS ORCHESTRA; DUKE YELLMAN'S PARODY CLUB PALS:
Edison 51927 *Song Of The Wanderer* ....25.00 - 40.00
    52051 *Zulu Wail*.................................20.00 - 30.00
    52076 *The Light House Blues* ....75.00 - 100.00
    52098 *All My Life*...............................35.00 - 50.00
    52100 *Roam On My Little Gypsy Sweetheart* .... 35.00 - 50.00
    52225 *Missouri Squabble* ....50.00 - 75.00
    52227 *I'm More Than Satisfied* ....50.00 - 75.00
    52328 *Fireworks* ....40.00 - 60.00
    52353 *Louisiana*.................................40.00 - 60.00
    52381 *Blue Shadows* ....40.00 - 60.00
    52416 *Do You? Don't You Love Me?* ....75.00 - 100.00
    52419 *Loving You Like I Do* ....35.00 - 50.00
    52470 *If You Want The Rainbow* ....40.00 - 60.00

YERKES' JAZARIMBA ORCHESTRA; YERKES' MARIMBAPHONE ORCHESTRA; YERKES' NOVELTY FIVE; YERKES' SAXOPHONE SEXTET; YERKES' SOUTHERN FIVE:
Aeolian-Vocalion 14047 *Railroad Blues*................15.00 - 20.00
Columbia A2634 *Hear Dem Bells* ....8.00 - 12.00
    A2720 *Bevo Blues* ....10.00 - 15.00
    A2929 *Railroad Blues*............................8.00 - 12.00
    A6166 *Sensation* (12 inch)........................15.00 - 20.00
Gennett 9089 *Squealing Pig Blues* ....- - -
Lyric 4207 *Missouri Blues* ....15.00 - 20.00
Vocalion 14071 *Syncopated Dream* ....10.00 - 15.00
    14272 *Arkansas Blues* ....10.00 - 15.00
Yerkes Dance Records 3101 *I Love You*.................15.00 - 20.00

YOUNG'S CREOLE JAZZ BAND:
Claxtonola 40272 *Tin Roof Blues* ....150.00 - 250.00
Harmograph 863 *Tin Roof Blues*........................150.00 - 250.00
Paramount 12060 *Every Saturday Night*...............200.00 - 300.00
    12088 *Dearborn Street Blues*.....................250.00 - up
    20272 *Tin Roof Blues*............................150.00 - 250.00
Puritan 11272 *Tin Roof Blues* ....150.00 - 250.00

CLARENCE YOUNG'S HARMONY SYNCOPATORS:
Harmograph 874 *Jazzbo Jenkins*..........................250.00 - up

MARGARET YOUNG:
Brunswick 2253, 2265, 2284, 2297, 2319, 2346,
    2359, 2371, 2386, 2413, 2442, 2459, 2475, 2514,
    2537, 2553, 2583, 2596, 2621, 2652, 2673, 2687,
    2736 ....7.00 - 12.00
    2806 *Nobody Knows What A Red-Head Mama Can Do*
    ....10.00 - 15.00
    2939 *Red Hot Henry Brown* ....10.00 - 15.00

PATSY YOUNG (See also DOT DARE, ANNETTE HANSHAW):
Harmony 878-H *I Want To Be Bad*......................15.00 - 20.00
Publix 1057-P *I Think You'll Like It* ....15.00 - 20.00
Velvet Tone 1792-V *Is There Anything Wrong In That?*
....15.00 - 20.00
    1829-V *Don't Be Like That*.......................15.00 - 20.00

VICTOR YOUNG & HIS ORCHESTRA:
Brunswick 6128 *Sing A Little Jingle* ....15.00 - 20.00
  6554 *Two Tickets To Georgia*.....................10.00 - 15.00
  6747 *This Little Piggie Went To Market*.......10.00 - 15.00
  20106 (12 inch) *Face The Music* ....15.00 - 25.00
Decca 278 *When Love Comes Swingin' Along* ....10.00 - 15.00
  279 *Mr. And Mrs. Is The Name* ....8.00 - 12.00
  280 *You're Nothin' But A Nothin'* ....8.00 - 12.00
Decca, most other issues............................5.00 - 8.00

BARNEY ZEEMAN'S KENTUCKY CARDINALS:
Gennett 3299 *I'd Rather Be Alone*...................10.00 - 15.00
  3360 *Horses* ....10.00 - 15.00

ZENITH KNIGHTS:
Q.R.S. Q-1007 *My Blue Ridge Mountain Home* .....12.00 - 16.00
  Q-1020 *Eyes Of Blue* ....15.00 - 20.00

  Q-1021 *Congratulations* ....12.00 - 16.00
  Q-1025 *Get Yourself A Sweetie*...............15.00 - 20.00
  Q-1039 *Keep On The Sunny Side*..............20.00 - 30.00
  Q-1045 *We'll Be Married In June* ....10.00 - 15.00

ZON-O-PHONE ORCHESTRA:
Zon-o-phone 5285 *Noodles-Rag-Time Two-Step* ... 15.00 - 25.00
  5320 *Persian Lamb Rag*........................15.00 - 25.00

BOB ZURKE & HIS DELTA RHYTHM BAND:
Victor, most issues ....5.00 - 10.00

ZUTTY & HIS BAND:
Decca 431 *Look Over Yonder* ....8.00 - 12.00
  432 *Clarinet Marmalade*......................8.00 - 12.00
  465 *Royal Garden Blues* ....8.00 - 12.00

Blues; Rhythm & Blues

1920s to early 1950s

All records in this section are 78 RPM unless otherwise stated. An asterisk (*) after price indicates that the record is known or likely to exist in 45 RPM form, with the same label and catalog number. The price of such 45 RPM records is often substantially higher than the 78 RPM counterpart. Some issues are listed in this section (78 RPM) and in the 45 RPM (fourth) section.

(PEG LEG) BEN ABNEY:
Bluebird 6496 *Dirty Double Crosser* ....30.00 - 50.00
   6628 *I'm Rattlesnakin' Daddy*...........................30.00 - 50.00
   8121 *'Way Down In Town* ....30.00 - 50.00

WOODROW ADAMS & THE THREE B'S:
Checker 757 *Pretty Baby Blues* ....40.00 - 70.00 *

KATHERINE ADKINS:
Okeh 8363 *Individual Blues* ....30.00 - 50.00

GARFIELD AKERS:
Vocalion 1442 *Cottonfield Blues*...........................150.00 - 250.00
   1481 *Dough Roller Blues*.................................150.00 - 250.00

ALABAMA FOUR:
Victor 21136 *Queen Street Rag* ....30.00 - 50.00

ALABAMA JIM (AND GEORGE):
Gennett 6905 *Crossin' Beale Street* ....150.00 - 200.00
   6918 *All Over You* ....150.00 - 200.00
   6949 *Deep Blue Sea*.....................................150.00 - 200.00

ALABAMA SAM:
Titles issued contemporaneously on Banner, Conqueror, Melotone, Oriole, Perfect, and Romeo: *Red Cross Blues; You Gonna Need Me* ....50.00 - 75.00

ALABAMA SHIEKS:
Victor 23261 *Sittin' On Top Of The World* ....200.00 - 300.00
   23265 *Travelin' Railroad Man Blues* ....200.00 - 300.00

ALABAMA SLIM:
Savoy 5553 *Boar Hog Blues*..................................40.00 - 60.00

MOZELLE ALDERSON (AND BLIND JAMES BECK):
Black Patti 8003 *Mozelle Blues* ....500.00 - up

   8004 *Room Rent Blues*....................................500.00 - up
   8029 *Tall Man Blues*.....................................500.00 - up
Brunswick 7159 *Tight In Chicago*.........................100.00 - 150.00

ALEXANDER BROTHERS:
Champion 16493 *Limehouse Blues* ....150.00 - 300.00
   16497 *Tiger Rag* ....150.00 - 300.00
   16499 *St. Louis Blues* ....150.00 - 300.00

LITTLE DAVID ALEXANDER:
Ebony 1005 *Dupree Blues* ....30.00 - 50.00

HILDA ALEXANDER:
Brunswick 7069 *He's Tight Like This* ....100.00 - 150.00

JOE ALEXANDER & THE CUBANS:
Ballad 1008 *Oh Maria* ....50.00 - 80.00 *

ORA ALEXANDER:
Columbia 14626-D *Sweetest Daddy In Town* ....100.00 - 150.00
   14646-D *Ugly Man Blues* ....100.00 - 150.00
   14651-D *Rider Needs A Fast Horse* ....100.00 - 150.00

TEXAS ALEXANDER:
Freedom 1538 *Crossroads* ....50.00 - 80.00
Okeh 8498 *Section Gang Blues* ....50.00 - 80.00
   8511 *Corn-Bread Blues* ....50.00 - 80.00
   8526 *Farm Hand Blues* ....50.00 - 80.00
   8542 *Sabine River Blues* ....50.00 - 80.00
   8563 *Bell Cow-Blues*....................................50.00 - 80.00
   8578 *Death Bed Blues* ....50.00 - 80.00
   8591 *Deep Blue Sea Blues*..............................50.00 - 80.00
   8603 *West Texas Blues*..................................50.00 - 80.00
   8624 *Sittin' On A Log* ....50.00 - 80.00
   8640 *Blue Devil Blues* ....55.00 - 80.00
   8658 *'Frisco Train Blues* ....100.00 - 150.00
   8673 *Tell Me Woman Blues* ....100.00 - 150.00
   8688 *St. Louis Fair Blues*..............................75.00 - 100.00
   8705 *Gold Tooth Blues* ....75.00 - 100.00
   8731 *Awful Moaning Blues* ....75.00 - 100.00
   8745 *Double Crossing Blues* ....75.00 - 100.00
   8751 *Peaceful Blues*.....................................75.00 - 100.00
   8764 *Broken Yo Yo*......................................75.00 - 100.00
   8771 *Texas Special* ....75.00 - 100.00
   8785 *Thirty Day Blues* ....75.00 - 100.00
   8801 *Yellow Girl Blues* ....100.00 - 150.00
   8813 *She's So Far*......................................100.00 - 150.00
   8823 *Last Stage Blues* ....100.00 - 150.00
   8835 *Days Is Lonesome* ....100.00 - 150.00
   8890 *Seen Better Days* ....100.00 - 150.00
Vocalion 02743 *Blues In My Mind* ....100.00 - 150.00
   02764 *Prairie Dog Hole Blues* ....100.00 - 150.00
   02772 *Worried Blues*...................................100.00 - 150.00
   02856 *Justice Blues*....................................100.00 - 150.00
   02876 *Lonesome Valley Blues*........................100.00 - 150.00
   02894 *Katy Crossing Blues*...........................100.00 - 150.00
   02912 *Deceitful Blues* ....100.00 - 150.00

MAY ALIX (& HER HARMOGRAPH JAZZ BOYS):
Famous 3193 *Come On Home* ....40.00 - 60.00
   3237 *Loveless Love* ....40.00 - 60.00
Harmograph 791 *Aggravatin' Papa*.......................40.00 - 60.00
   801 *Chirping The Blues* ....20.00 - 30.00
   816 *You Shall Reap Just What You Sow* ....20.00 - 30.00
   873 *Experience Blues*..................................100.00 - 150.00
Paramount 20243 *Loveless Love* ....40.00 - 60.00
Puritan 11199 *Come On Home* ....30.00 - 50.00
   11243 *Loveless Love* ....25.00 - 40.00

GEORGE ALLISON & WILLIE WHITE:
Paramount 12960 *How I Feel My Love* ....150.00 - 200.00

TESSIE AMES:
Silvertone 3565 *Rider Blues* ....50.00 - 80.00
   3576 *High Yellow Blues*.................................100.00 - 150.00
   3577 *Ada Jane's Blues*....................................50.00 - 80.00

AMOS:
Bluebird 5780 *Mean Mistreatin' Woman* ....15.00 - 20.00
   5862 *Muddy Water Blues*...................................15.00 - 20.00

IRA AMOS:
Modern 817 *Blue And Disgusted* ....20.00 - 30.00
Octave 23-20 *I'm Lonesome* ....25.00 - 40.00

BLIND JOE AMOS:
Vocalion 1116 *C & O Blues* ....200.00 - 400.00

CURTIS AMY:
Gold Star 618 *Sleepin' Blues* ....20.00 - 30.00

"TALKING" BILLY ANDERSON:
Columbia 14216-D *Adam And Eve*.......................20.00 - 30.00
   14274-D *Cow Cow Blues*.................................35.00 - 50.00

JELLY ROLL ANDERSON:
Gennett 6135 *Free Woman Blues* ....150.00 - 200.00
   6181 *Good Time Blues*....................................250.00 - 400.00
   6226 *Salt Tear Blues*......................................300.00 - 500.00
Herwin 92014 *Salt Tear Blues*.............................200.00 - 300.00
   92020 *Free Woman Blues*..............................200.00 - 300.00

JIMMIE ANDERSON:
Broadway 5111 *Ko Ko Mo Blues* ....250.00 - 400.00

LOUISE ANDERSON:
Gennett 6242 *Papa, You're Too Slow* ....75.00 - 100.00

MAYBELLE ANDERSON:
Supertone 9429 *Moanful Wailin' Blues*................150.00 - 200.00

MISSOURI ANDERSON:
Vocalion 1041 *Somebody Else's Blues*....................75.00 - 125.00

PINK ANDERSON & DOOLEY SIMMS:
Columbia 14336-D *Gonna Tip Out Tonight*............75.00 - 100.00
   14400-D *CC & O Blues*...................................75.00 - 100.00

ED ANDREWS:
Okeh 8137 *Barrel House Blues* ....75.00 - 100.00

MOSE ANDREWS:
Decca 7338 *Ten Pound Hammer* ....15.00 - 25.00

ANDY BOY:
Bluebird 6858 *House Raid Blues*...........................15.00 - 25.00
   6893 *Jive Blues*..15.00 - 25.00
   6940 *Yellow Gal Blues*..................................15.00 - 25.00
   7075 *Evil Blues*..15.00 - 25.00

ROOSEVELT ANTRIM:
Bluebird 7149 *Complaint To Make* ....30.00 - 50.00
   7475 *Station Boy Blues*..................................30.00 - 50.00

ARCHIBALD:
Colony 105 *Crescent City Bounce*...........................15.00 - 20.00
Imperial 5068 *Stack A Lee* ....20.00 - 30.00
   5082 *Ballin' With Archie* ....15.00 - 20.00
   5089 *Frantic Chick* ....15.00 - 20.00
   5101 *My Gal* ....15.00 - 20.00
   5212 *Early Morning Blues* ....15.00 - 20.00 *

ARKANSAS SHORTY:
Bluebird 6545 *Greyhound Bus*.............................20.00 - 30.00
   6571 *Double Crossing Buddy* ....20.00 - 30.00
   6983 *Blue As A Fool Can Be* ....20.00 - 30.00

MAY ARMSTRONG:
Brunswick 7010 *Joe Boy Blues*.............................100.00 - 150.00
Vocalion 1129 *Joe Boy Blues* ....100.00 - 150.00

RICHARD ARMSTRONG:
Randy's 104 *Gene Nobel's Boogie* ....- - -

SHELLEY ARMSTRONG:
Champion 50008 *How Long, How Long Blues* ......20.00 - 30.00
   50024 *Chain Gang Bound* ....20.00 - 30.00
   50028 *B & O Blues* ....20.00 - 30.00
   50029 *D. B. A. Blues*......................................20.00 - 30.00

KOKOMO ARNOLD:
Decca 7026 *Milk Cow Blues* ....75.00 - 100.00
   7044 *Back To The Woods* ....80.00 - 120.00
   7050 *Sissy Man Blues* ....80.00 - 120.00
   7059 *Milk Cow Blues-No. 2* ....75.00 - 100.00
   7069 *Chain Gang Blues* ....75.00 - 100.00
   7070 *How Long, How Long Blues* ....75.00 - 100.00
   7083 *Feels So Good* ....75.00 - 100.00
   7092 *Slop Jar Blues* ....75.00 - 100.00
   7103 *Tonic Head Blues* ....75.00 - 100.00
   7116 *Milk Cow Blues-No. 3* ....60.00 - 100.00
   7133 *Monday Morning Blues*...........................60.00 - 100.00
   7139 *Southern Railroad Blues* ....60.00 - 100.00
   7147 *Policy Wheel Blues* ....50.00 - 80.00
   7156 *Back Door Blues* ....50.00 - 80.00
   7163 *Milk Cow Blues-No. 4* ....50.00 - 80.00
   7165 *Desert Blues* ....50.00 - 80.00
   7172 *Sundown Blues* ....50.00 - 80.00
   7181 *Stop Look And Listen* ....50.00 - 80.00
   7198 *Model 'T' Woman Blues* ....50.00 - 80.00
   7212 *Bull Headed Woman Blues* ....50.00 - 80.00
   7242 *Coffin Blues* ....50.00 - 80.00
   7261 *Lonesome Road Blues* ....50.00 - 80.00
   7267 *Salty Dog*...40.00 - 60.00
   7275 *Fool Man Blues* ....40.00 - 60.00
   7285 *Laugh And Grin Blues* ....40.00 - 60.00
   7306 *Long And Tall* ....40.00 - 60.00
   7319 *Black Mattie* ....40.00 - 60.00
   7347 *Red Beans And Rice* ....30.00 - 50.00
   7361 *Big Ship Blues* ....30.00 - 50.00
   7390 *Back On The Job* ....30.00 - 50.00
   7417 *Head Cuttin' Blues* ....30.00 - 50.00
   7431 *Neck Bone Blues* ....25.00 - 40.00
   7449 *Rocky Road Blues* ....25.00 - 40.00
   7464 *Kid Man Blues*.......................................25.00 - 40.00
   7485 *Something's Hot*......................................25.00 - 40.00
   7510 *Midnight Blues* ....25.00 - 40.00
   7540 *Bad Luck Blues* ....25.00 - 40.00
   48000 *Milk Cow Blues* ....8.00 - 12.00

JOE (MR. GOOGLE EYES) AUGUST:
Domino 350 *Rock My Soul* ....20.00 - 30.00
   352 *Bad Nerves* ....20.00 - 30.00
Duke 117 *Play The Game* ....10.00 - 15.00 *
Lee 209 *My Old Love* ....15.00 - 20.00
Okeh 6820 *No Wine No Women* ....10.00 - 15.00

MILDRED AUSTIN:
Champion 15530 *Sing That Song With Feeling* ......75.00 - 100.00

BABY BONNIE:
Buddy 8021 *I Got Your Water On* ....150.00 - 200.00
   8023 *Home, Sweet Home Blues* ....100.00 - 200.00
Gennett 3041 *Longing Blues* ....50.00 - 80.00
   5593 *I Got Your Water On*..............................50.00 - 80.00
   5616 *Backbiting Moan*....................................50.00 - 80.00
   5644 *Longing Blues*.......................................75.00 - 100.00
Silvertone 4027 *Home, Sweet Home Blues*.............40.00 - 60.00
   4031 *Backbiting Moan*...................................50.00 - 80.00
   4034 *I Got Your Water On*..............................40.00 - 60.00

BABY BOY:
Sampson 633 *Taxi Driver* ....50.00 - 75.00

BABY DOO:
Decca 7763 *The Death Of Walter Barnes* ....15.00 - 20.00
   7773 *I'm Gonna Walk Your Dog* ....15.00 - 20.00

BABY FACE & SUNNYLAND TRIO:
J.O.B. 1002 *Pet Rabbit* ....80.00 - 120.00

(VOCALIST) BABY FACE (LEROY) (TRIO):
Chess 1447 *Take A Little Walk With Me* ....100.00 - 150.00
J.O.B. 100 *Take A Little Walk With Me*................150.00 - 250.00
Parkway 104 *Boll Weevil*....................................150.00 - 250.00
   501 *Rollin' And Tumblin'* ....150.00 - 250.00
Savoy 1122 *Red Headed Woman* ....30.00 - 50.00

THE BACK PORCH BOYS:
Apollo 392 *Big Hip Mama* ....50.00 - 100.00
   406 *Sweet Woman Blues*................................50.00 - 100.00

DE FORD BAILEY:
Bluebird 5147 *Ice Water Blues*.................................8.00 - 12.00
Brunswick 146 *Pan-American Blues*......................20.00 - 30.00
   147 *Muscle Shoals Blues* ....30.00 - 50.00
   148 *Alcoholic Blues* ....30.00 - 50.00
   149 *Fox Chase* ....20.00 - 30.00
   434 *Up Country Blues* ....20.00 - 30.00
Victor 23336 *John Henry* ....150.00 - 300.00
   23831 *John Henry*...150.00 - 300.00
   V38014 *Ice Water Blues* ....100.00 - 150.00

KID BAILEY:
Brunswick 7114 *Rowdy Blues* ....150.00 - 300.00

MAX (BLUES) BAILEY:
Bullet 306 *Delinquency Blues* ....15.00 - 20.00
   310 *Coming Home Blues* ....15.00 - 20.00
Coral 65060 *Sorry Girl Blues* ....15.00 - 20.00

RED MIKE BAILEY:
Pararmount 13077 *Neck Bone Blues*.....................300.00 - up

HOUSTON BAINES:
Blues & Rhythm 7001 *Going Home*........................50.00 - 100.00

BLIND BOBBY BAKER:
Pathe-Actuelle 7533 *Macon Georgia Cut-Out* ....80.00 - 120.00
Perfect 133 *Macon Georgia Cut-Out* ....80.00 - 120.00

C.B. BAKER:
Sittin' In With 625 *Skin To Skin* ....20.00 - 30.00

DOROTHY BAKER:
Decca 7080 *Steady Grinding Blues* ....75.00 - 100.00

KATHERINE BAKER:
Gennett 6125 *I Helped You, Sick Man* ....150.00 - 200.00
   6157 *Chicago Fire Blues* ....150.00 - 200.00
   6194 *Wild Woman Blues* ....150.00 - 200.00
   6228 *Money; Woman Blues* ....150.00 - 200.00
   6321 *Mistreated Blues* ....150.00 - 200.00
Herwin 92017 *My Man Left Me Blues* ....150.00 - 250.00
   92022 *Chicago Fire Blues* ....150.00 - 250.00
   92037 *Daddy Sunshine Blues* ....150.00 - 250.00
   92038 *Wild Woman Blues* ....150.00 - 250.00
   92039 *Mistreated Blues* ....150.00 - 250.00

VIOLA BAKER:
Okeh 8141 *Sweet Man Blues* ....40.00 - 60.00

WILLIE BAKER:
De Luxe 6023 *Goin' Back Home Today* ....20.00 - 30.00 *
Gennett 6751 *Weak-Minded Blues*........................200.00 - 400.00
   6766 *No No Blues* ....200.00 - 400.00
   6812 *Bad Luck Moan* ....200.00 - 400.00
   6846 *Crooked Woman Blues* ....200.00 - 400.00
Rockin' 527 *Goin' Back Home Today* ....20.00 - 30.00 *

BANJO JOE:
Paramount 12571 *Poor Boy, Long Ways From Home*
  ....150.00 - 300.00
   12588 *Jonestown Blues*...................................150.00 - 300.00
   12604 *Jazz Gypsy Blues*.................................150.00 - 300.00

BARBECUE BOB:
Columbia 14205-D *Barbecue Blues* ....20.00 - 30.00
   14222-D *Mississippi Heavy Water Blues* ....25.00 - 50.00
   14246-D *Honey You Don't Know My Mind* ......25.00 - 50.00
   14257-D *Brown-Skin Gal* ....25.00 - 50.00
   14268-D *It Won't Be Long Now* ....40.00 - 60.00
   14280-D *Crooked Woman Blues* ....40.00 - 60.00
   14299-D *Thinkin' Funny Blues*........................40.00 - 60.00
   14316-D *Goin' Up The Country* ....40.00 - 60.00
   14331-D *Waycross Georgia Blues*....................50.00 - 80.00
   14350-D *My Mistake Blues* ....50.00 - 80.00
   14372-D *Blind Pig Blues* ....50.00 - 80.00
   14383-D *Cold Wave Blues* ....75.00 - 100.00
   14412-D *Dollar Down Blues* ....75.00 - 100.00
   14424-D *It's Just Too Bad* ....75.00 - 100.00
   14436-D *It's A Funny Little Thing*...................75.00 - 100.00
   14449-D *Good Time Rounder*..........................75.00 - 100.00
   14461-D *Bad Time Blues* ....75.00 - 100.00
   14479-D *Yo Yo Blues* ....75.00 - 100.00
   14507-D *Me And My Whiskey* ....75.00 - 100.00
   14523-D *Yo Yo Blues No. 2* ....75.00 - 100.00
   14546-D *Telling It To You* ....75.00 - 100.00
   14588-D *The Spider And The Fly* ....80.00 - 120.00
   14573-D *California Blues* ....80.00 - 120.00
   14581-D *Jambooger Blues* ....100.00 - 150.00
   14591-D *Atlanta Moan* ....100.00 - 150.00
   14614 -D *It Just Won't Quit*...........................100.00 - 150.00

JOHN HENRY BARBEE:
Vocalion 04417 *Six Weeks Old Blues* ....20.00 - 30.00

BAREFOOT BILL (FROM ALABAMA):
Columbia 14481-D *Big Rock Jail* ....150.00 - 300.00
   14510-D *My Crime Blues* ....150.00 - 300.00
   14526-D *Squabblin' Blues* ....150.00 - 300.00
   14561-D *One More Time* ....150.00 - 300.00

WILEY BARNER:
Gennett 6261 *My Gal Treats Me Mean* ....150.00 - 200.00

FAE BARNES:
Black Swan 12153 *I Just Want A Daddy* ....30.00 - 50.00
Paramount 12099 *Good-Bye Blues* ....25.00 - 40.00
   12136 *I Just Want A Daddy* ....25.00 - 40.00

WILLIE BARNES:
Champion 15378 *My Gal Treats Me Mean* ....80.00 - 120.00
Silvertone 5121 *My Gal Treats Me Mean* ....150.00 - 200.00

MARTHA BARR:
Broadway 5017 *Memphis Earthquake* ....50.00 - 75.00

BARRELL HOUSE ANNIE:
Vocalion 03542 *Must Get Mine In Front* ....20.00 - 30.00

BARREL HOUSE BUCK:
Decca 7013 *Lamp Post Blues* ....50.00 - 100.00
   7030 *Mercy Mercy Blues* ....50.00 - 75.00

BARRELHOUSE FRANKIE:
Paramount 13019 *Smother Me Blues* ....150.00 - 250.00

BARRELHOUSE SAMMY (THE COUNTRY BOY):
Atlantic 891 *Kill It Kid* ....75.00 - 100.00

VIOLA BARTLETTE:
Paramount 12322 *Tennessee Blues* ....100.00 - 150.00
   12345 *Quit Knocking On My Door* ....100.00 - 150.00
   12351 *Anna Mina Forty And St. Louis Shorty* ..100.00 - 150.00
   12363 *Out Bound Train Blues* ....100.00 - 150.00
   12369 *Sunday Morning Blues* ....150.00 - 200.00

SLIM BARTON (& EDDIE MAPP) (& MOORE):
Paramount 13114 *Fourth Avenue Blues* ....100.00 - 150.00
Q.R.S. 7081 *It's Tight Like That* ....100.00 - 150.00
   7088 *I'm Hot Like That* ....100.00 - 150.00
   7089 *Fourth Avenue Blues* ....100.00 - 150.00

TIPPY BARTON:
Vocalion 1742 *High Brown Cheater* ....75.00 - 100.00

BAT THE HUMMING BIRD:
Varsity 6068 *Humming Blues* ....30.00 - 50.00

DEACON L. J. BATES:
Paramount 12585 *He Arose From The Dead* ....80.00 - 130.00

WILL BATTS:
Vocalion 02531 *Country Woman* ....100.00 - 150.00
   02542 *Cadillac Baby* ....100.00 - 150.00

A. & J. ANDREW AND JIM BAXTER:
Victor 20962 *K. C. Railroad Blues* ....125.00 - 175.00
   21475 *The Moore Girl* ....150.00 - 200.00
   23394 *Done Wrong Blues* ....250.00 - 400.00
   23404 *Operator Blues* ....250.00 - 400.00
   V38002 *Georgia Stomp* ....200.00 - 300.00
   V38603 *It Tickles Me* ....200.00 - 300.00

HELEN BAXTER:
Banner 1920 *I Wants A Real Man* ....20.00 - 30.00
   1958 *Scrubbin' Blues* ....20.00 - 30.00
Columbia A3922 *You Got Ev'rything A Sweet Mama Needs But Me*
....20.00 - 30.00
Domino 3892 *I Wants A Real Man* ....20.00 - 30.00
   3929 *Scrubbin' Blues* ....20.00 - 30.00
Regal 8238 *I Wants A Real Man* ....20.00 - 30.00
   8283 *Scrubbin' Blues* ....20.00 - 30.00

BEALE STREET ROUNDERS:
Vocalion 1555 *I'm Sittin' On Top Of The World* . 150.00 - 300.00

BEALE STREET SHEIKS:
Paramount 12518 *It's A Good Thing* .... 150.00 - 300.00
   12531 *Half Cup Of Tea* .... 150.00 - 300.00
   12552 *Blues In 'D'* .... 150.00 - 300.00
   12576 *Beale Town Bound* .... 150.00 - 300.00
   12591 *Jazzin' The Blues* .... 150.00 - 300.00
   12758 *Rockin' On The Hill Blues* .... 150.00 - 300.00
   12774 *Hunting Blues* .... 150.00 - 300.00
   12894 *Fillin' In Blues* .... 150.00 - 300.00

LOTTIE BEAMAN:
Brunswick 7147 *Going Away Blues* .... 75.00 - 100.00
Paramount 12201 *Honey Blues* .... 25.00 - 35.00
   12235 *Regular Man Blues* .... 40.00 - 60.00
   12254 *Sugar Daddy Blues* .... 40.00 - 60.00

HELEN BEASLEY:
Brunswick 7077 *Tia Juana Blues* .... 35.00 - 50.00

WALTER BEASLEY:
Okeh 8540 *Georgia Skin* .... 15.00 - 20.00
   8564 *Sore Feet Blues* .... 15.00 - 20.00

CHARLES/ELDER CHARLIE BECK:
Bluebird 8244 *Changes* .... 15.00 - 20.00
   8271 *You Can't Hurry God* .... 15.00 - 20.00
   8317 *Dry Bones* .... 15.00 - 20.00
   8337 *Talk On Talkers* .... 15.00 - 20.00
Chart 624 *Rock And Roll Sermon* .... 20.00 - 30.00
Decca 7320 *If I Have To Run* .... 20.00 - 30.00
   7344 *I'm A Stranger* .... 15.00 - 20.00
   7372 *Love, Oh Love Divine* .... 15.00 - 20.00
   7418 *That's The Way I Do* .... 15.00 - 20.00
Okeh 8907 *When The World's On Fire* .... 75.00 - 100.00

JOHNNY BECK (THE BLIND BOY):
Sittin' In With 531 *Locked In Jail Blues* .... 50.00 - 75.00

SON BECKY:
Vocalion 03942 *Sunrise Blues* .... 50.00 - 75.00
   03967 *Sweet Woman Blues* .... 50.00 - 75.00
   04081 *Cryin' Shame Blues* .... 50.00 - 75.00

WILLIE BEE:
Vocalion 03907 *Ramblin' Mind Blues* .... 15.00 - 20.00

BROTHER BELL:
Blues & Rhythm 7002 *If You Feel Froggish* .... 30.00 - 50.00

ED BELL:
Columbia 14595-D *She's A Fool Gal* .... 100.00 - 150.00
Paramount 12524 *Ham Bone Blues* .... 100.00 - 150.00
   12546 *Mean Conductor Blues* .... 100.00 - 150.00

BABY BENBOW:
Okeh 8098 *Down Home Gal* .... 20.00 - 30.00

ELOISE BENNETT:
Black Patti 8006 *Sting Me, Mr. Strange Man* .... 300.00 - up
Gennett 6147 *I Can't Be Satisfied With One* .... 100.00 - 150.00
Paramount 12412 *Effervescent Daddy* .... 30.00 - 50.00

WILL BENNETT:
Vocalion 1464 *Railroad Bill* .... 150.00 - 200.00

GLADYS BENTLEY:
Okeh 8610 *Ground Hog Blues* .... 15.00 - 20.00

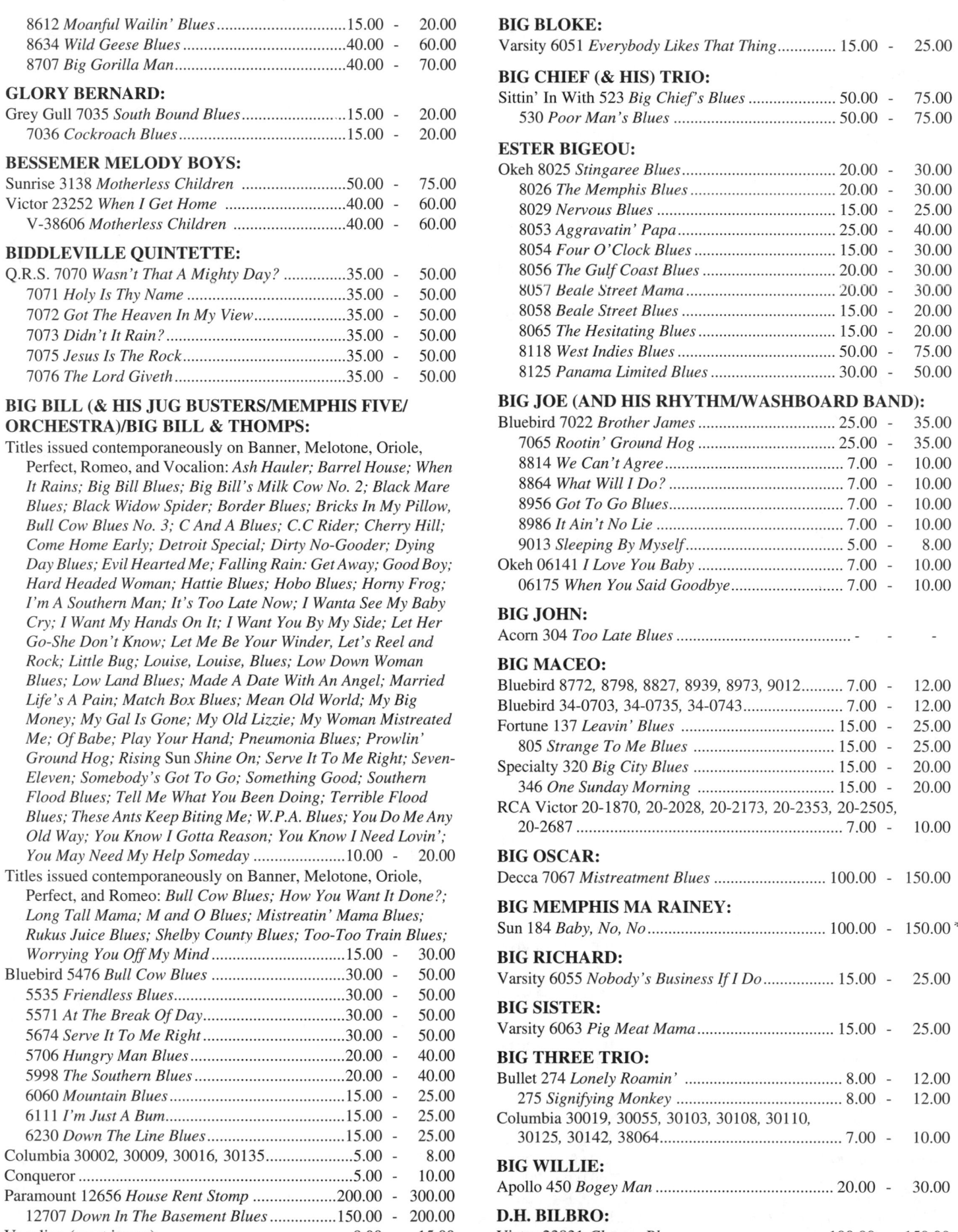

8612 *Moanful Wailin' Blues* ....15.00 - 20.00
8634 *Wild Geese Blues* ....40.00 - 60.00
8707 *Big Gorilla Man* ....40.00 - 70.00

GLORY BERNARD:
Grey Gull 7035 *South Bound Blues* ....15.00 - 20.00
  7036 *Cockroach Blues* ....15.00 - 20.00

BESSEMER MELODY BOYS:
Sunrise 3138 *Motherless Children* ....50.00 - 75.00
Victor 23252 *When I Get Home* ....40.00 - 60.00
  V-38606 *Motherless Children* ....40.00 - 60.00

BIDDLEVILLE QUINTETTE:
Q.R.S. 7070 *Wasn't That A Mighty Day?* ....35.00 - 50.00
  7071 *Holy Is Thy Name* ....35.00 - 50.00
  7072 *Got The Heaven In My View*....................35.00 - 50.00
  7073 *Didn't It Rain?*..35.00 - 50.00
  7075 *Jesus Is The Rock*....................................35.00 - 50.00
  7076 *The Lord Giveth* ....35.00 - 50.00

BIG BILL (& HIS JUG BUSTERS/MEMPHIS FIVE/ ORCHESTRA)/BIG BILL & THOMPS:
Titles issued contemporaneously on Banner, Melotone, Oriole, Perfect, Romeo, and Vocalion: *Ash Hauler; Barrel House; When It Rains; Big Bill Blues; Big Bill's Milk Cow No. 2; Black Mare Blues; Black Widow Spider; Border Blues; Bricks In My Pillow, Bull Cow Blues No. 3; C And A Blues; C.C Rider; Cherry Hill; Come Home Early; Detroit Special; Dirty No-Gooder; Dying Day Blues; Evil Hearted Me; Falling Rain: Get Away; Good Boy; Hard Headed Woman; Hattie Blues; Hobo Blues; Horny Frog; I'm A Southern Man; It's Too Late Now; I Wanta See My Baby Cry; I Want My Hands On It; I Want You By My Side; Let Her Go-She Don't Know; Let Me Be Your Winder, Let's Reel and Rock; Little Bug; Louise, Louise, Blues; Low Down Woman Blues; Low Land Blues; Made A Date With An Angel; Married Life's A Pain; Match Box Blues; Mean Old World; My Big Money; My Gal Is Gone; My Old Lizzie; My Woman Mistreated Me; Of Babe; Play Your Hand; Pneumonia Blues; Prowlin' Ground Hog; Rising Sun Shine On; Serve It To Me Right; Seven-Eleven; Somebody's Got To Go; Something Good; Southern Flood Blues; Tell Me What You Been Doing; Terrible Flood Blues; These Ants Keep Biting Me; W.P.A. Blues; You Do Me Any Old Way; You Know I Gotta Reason; You Know I Need Lovin'; You May Need My Help Someday* ....10.00 - 20.00
Titles issued contemporaneously on Banner, Melotone, Oriole, Perfect, and Romeo: *Bull Cow Blues; How You Want It Done?; Long Tall Mama; M and O Blues; Mistreatin' Mama Blues; Rukus Juice Blues; Shelby County Blues; Too-Too Train Blues; Worrying You Off My Mind* ....15.00 - 30.00
Bluebird 5476 *Bull Cow Blues* ....30.00 - 50.00
  5535 *Friendless Blues*..30.00 - 50.00
  5571 *At The Break Of Day*...................................30.00 - 50.00
  5674 *Serve It To Me Right* ....30.00 - 50.00
  5706 *Hungry Man Blues* ....20.00 - 40.00
  5998 *The Southern Blues* ....20.00 - 40.00
  6060 *Mountain Blues* ....15.00 - 25.00
  6111 *I'm Just A Bum*...15.00 - 25.00
  6230 *Down The Line Blues*...................................15.00 - 25.00
Columbia 30002, 30009, 30016, 30135....................5.00 - 8.00
Conqueror ....5.00 - 10.00
Paramount 12656 *House Rent Stomp* ....200.00 - 300.00
  12707 *Down In The Basement Blues* ....150.00 - 200.00
Vocalion (most issues)...8.00 - 15.00

BIG BLOKE:
Varsity 6051 *Everybody Likes That Thing*..............15.00 - 25.00

BIG CHIEF (& HIS) TRIO:
Sittin' In With 523 *Big Chief's Blues* ....50.00 - 75.00
  530 *Poor Man's Blues* ....50.00 - 75.00

ESTER BIGEOU:
Okeh 8025 *Stingaree Blues*....................................20.00 - 30.00
  8026 *The Memphis Blues* ....20.00 - 30.00
  8029 *Nervous Blues* ....15.00 - 25.00
  8053 *Aggravatin' Papa*..25.00 - 40.00
  8054 *Four O'Clock Blues* ....15.00 - 30.00
  8056 *The Gulf Coast Blues* ....20.00 - 30.00
  8057 *Beale Street Mama* ....20.00 - 30.00
  8058 *Beale Street Blues* ....15.00 - 20.00
  8065 *The Hesitating Blues* ....15.00 - 20.00
  8118 *West Indies Blues* ....50.00 - 75.00
  8125 *Panama Limited Blues* ....30.00 - 50.00

BIG JOE (AND HIS RHYTHM/WASHBOARD BAND):
Bluebird 7022 *Brother James* ....25.00 - 35.00
  7065 *Rootin' Ground Hog* ....25.00 - 35.00
  8814 *We Can't Agree*..7.00 - 10.00
  8864 *What Will I Do?* ....7.00 - 10.00
  8956 *Got To Go Blues* ....7.00 - 10.00
  8986 *It Ain't No Lie* ....7.00 - 10.00
  9013 *Sleeping By Myself*.....................................5.00 - 8.00
Okeh 06141 *I Love You Baby* ....7.00 - 10.00
  06175 *When You Said Goodbye*.........................7.00 - 10.00

BIG JOHN:
Acorn 304 *Too Late Blues* ....- - -

BIG MACEO:
Bluebird 8772, 8798, 8827, 8939, 8973, 9012..........7.00 - 12.00
Bluebird 34-0703, 34-0735, 34-0743.......................7.00 - 12.00
Fortune 137 *Leavin' Blues* ....15.00 - 25.00
  805 *Strange To Me Blues* ....15.00 - 25.00
Specialty 320 *Big City Blues* ....15.00 - 20.00
  346 *One Sunday Morning* ....15.00 - 20.00
RCA Victor 20-1870, 20-2028, 20-2173, 20-2353, 20-2505, 20-2687 ....7.00 - 10.00

BIG OSCAR:
Decca 7067 *Mistreatment Blues* ....100.00 - 150.00

BIG MEMPHIS MA RAINEY:
Sun 184 *Baby, No, No*...100.00 - 150.00 *

BIG RICHARD:
Varsity 6055 *Nobody's Business If I Do*.................15.00 - 25.00

BIG SISTER:
Varsity 6063 *Pig Meat Mama*.................................15.00 - 25.00

BIG THREE TRIO:
Bullet 274 *Lonely Roamin'* ....8.00 - 12.00
  275 *Signifying Monkey* ....8.00 - 12.00
Columbia 30019, 30055, 30103, 30108, 30110, 30125, 30142, 38064...7.00 - 10.00

BIG WILLIE:
Apollo 450 *Bogey Man* ....20.00 - 30.00

D.H. BILBRO:
Victor 23831 *Chester Blues* ....100.00 - 150.00

BILL AND SLIM:
Champion 16015 *Papa's Gettin' Hot* ....150.00 - 200.00

BILLY & JESSE:
Brunswick 7099 *Put Your Mind On It* ....75.00 - 100.00

BILLY BIRD:
Columbia 14381-D *Mill Man Blues* ....100.00 - 150.00
 14418-D *Alabama Blues* ....100.00 - 150.00

BIRMINGHAM QUARTET:
Columbia 14154-D, 14190-D, 14224-D,
 14263-D, 14311-D, 14567-D..........................10.00 - 20.00

BIRMINGHAM SAM:
Savoy 5558 *Landing Blues* ....10.00 - 15.00

BLACK ACE:
Decca 7281 *Trifling Woman*..............................20.00 - 30.00
 7340 *Whiskey And Woman* ....20.00 - 30.00
 7387 *Christmas Time Blues*........................20.00 - 30.00

BLACK BOY SHINE:
Vocalion 03417 *Sugarland Blues* ....30.00 - 50.00
 03454 *Crazy Woman Blues*..........................30.00 - 50.00
 03484 *Back Home Blues* ....30.00 - 50.00
 03551 *Wrong Doing Woman Blues* ....30.00 - 50.00
 03613 *Grey With Worry Blues*......................30.00 - 50.00
 03624 *Bed And Breakfast Blues* ....30.00 - 50.00
 03687 *Business Woman Blues* ....30.00 - 50.00
 03757 *Coal Woman Blues* ....30.00 - 50.00
 04003 *Hobo Blues*..................................30.00 - 50.00
(Note: First four titles issued contemporaneously on Banner,
 Melotone, Oriole, Perfect, and Romeo: ....30.00 - 50.00)

BLACK DIAMOND:
Jaxyson 50 *Lonesome Blues* ....20.00 - 30.00

BLACK IVORY KING:
Decca 7307 *The Flying Crow* ....30.00 - 50.00
 7355 *Match Box Blues*..............................30.00 - 50.00

BLACK SPIDER DUMPLIN':
Bluebird 6972 *John D. Blues*............................25.00 - 40.00
 6995 *Sold It To The Devil*........................25.00 - 40.00
 7011 *Death Of The Gambler* ....20.00 - 30.00

FRANKIE BLACK:
Champion 50000 *Wayback Blues* ....25.00 - 50.00
 50036 *Bad Liquor Blues*............................25.00 - 50.00
 50049 *Alley Sally Blues*...........................25.00 - 50.00

LEWIS BLACK:
Columbia 14291-D *Gravel Camp Blues*....................80.00 - 120.00
 14429-D *Rock Island Blues* ....100.00 - 150.00

MAMIE BLACKBURN:
Herwin 92015 *Bird Nest Blues* ....100.00 - 150.00

FRANCIS/SCRAPPER BLACKWELL:
Bluebird 5914 *A Blues*..................................100.00 - 150.00
Champion 15973 *Springtime Blues* ....150.00 - 200.00
 16361 *Back Door Blues*.............................150.00 - 200.00
 16370 *Rambling Blues*..............................150.00 - 200.00
 16452 *Down South Blues*............................150.00 - 200.00
Gennett 7158 *Springtime Blues* ....200.00 - 300.00
Vocalion 1192 *Kokomo Blues* ....150.00 - 200.00
 1213 *Trouble Blues*................................150.00 - 200.00
 1276 *Non-Skid Tread*...............................150.00 - 200.00
 1417 *Mr. Scrapper's Blues*.........................150.00 - 200.00
 02752 *Morning Mail Blues*..........................100.00 - 150.00

WILLIE "61" BLACKWELL:
Bluebird 8810 *Noiseless Motor Blues* ....15.00 - 20.00
 8845 *Bald Eagle Blues* ....15.00 - 20.00
 8876 *Machine Gun Blues* ....15.00 - 20.00
 8921 *Four O'Clock Flower Blues* ....15.00 - 20.00

SUNNY BLAIR:
Meteor 5006 *Please Send My Baby Back* ....50.00 - 80.00 *
RPM 354 *Five Foot Three Blues* ....30.00 - 50.00 *

BLAZER BOY (See JAMES (BLAZER BOY) LOCKS) THE BLENDERS:
Decca 27403 *I'm Afraid The Masquerade Is Over* ... 8.00 - 12.00
 27587 *All I Gotta Do Is Think Of You* ....8.00 - 12.00
 28092 *I'd Be A Fool Again* ....8.00 - 12.00
 28241 *Never In A Million Years* ....8.00 - 12.00
 48156 *Honeysuckle Rose* ....30.00 - 50.00
 48158 *Count Every Star*..............................30.00 - 50.00
M-G-M 11488 *I Don't Miss You Any More*...........10.00 - 15.00
 11531 *Isn't It A Shame*..............................10.00 - 15.00
National 9092 *I Can Dream Can't I* ....10.00 - 20.00

BLIND ARTHUR:
Paramount 12892 *Blind Arthur's Breakdown* .... 200.00 - 300.00

BLIND BLAKE:
Paramount 12387 *Early Morning Blues* ....75.00 - 125.00
 12413 *Skeedle Loo Doo Blues* ....75.00 - 125.00
 12431 *Too Tight* ....75.00 - 125.00
 12442 *Tampa Bound* ....75.00 - 125.00
 12464 *Buck-Town Blues* ....75.00 - 125.00
 12479 *One Time Blues* ....75.00 - 125.00
 12497 *Bad Feeling Blues* ....75.00 - 125.00
 12565 *Southern Rag* ....75.00 - 125.00
 12583 *Hard Road Blues* ....75.00 - 125.00
 12597 *Wabash Rag* ....75.00 - 125.00
 12606 *Brownskin Mama Blues* ....75.00 - 125.00
 12634 *CC Pill Blues*.................................150.00 - 200.00
 12643 *Tootie Blues* ....100.00 - 150.00
 12657 *Detroit Bound Blues*..........................100.00 - 150.00
 12673 *Hot Potatoes*..................................150.00 - 300.00
 12681 *South Bound Rag*...............................150.00 - 200.00
 12695 *Low Down Loving Gal* ....100.00 - 150.00
 12710 *Back Door Slam Blues* ....100.00 - 150.00
 12723 *No Dough Blues*................................100.00 - 150.00
 12737 *Search Warrant Blues* ....100.00 - 150.00
 12754 *Notoriety Woman Blues* ....150.00 - 200.00
 12767 *Ramblin' Mama Blues*..........................150.00 - 200.00
 12794 *Hookworm Blues*................................150.00 - 200.00
 12810 *Poker Woman Blues*.............................150.00 - 200.00
 12824 *Georgia Bound*.................................100.00 - 200.00
 12863 *Fightin' The Jug*..............................200.00 - 300.00
 12867 *Third Degree Blues* ....150.00 - 200.00
 12888 *Police Dog Blues* ....150.00 - 200.00
 12904 *Ice Man Blues* ....150.00 - 200.00
 12918 *Cold Love Blues* ....150.00 - 200.00
 12964 *Keep It Home* ....150.00 - 200.00
 12994 *Hard Pushing Papa*.............................150.00 - 200.00
 13016 *Ain't Gonna Do That No More* ....150.00 - 200.00
 13035 *Playing Policy Blues* ....150.00 - 200.00
 13103 *Rope Stretchin' Blues*........................200.00 - 300.00
 13115 *Dissatisfied Blues* ....200.00 - 300.00
 13123 *Night And Day Blues*..........................250.00 - 400.00
 13137 *Depression's Gone From Me Blues*......200.00 - 400.00

BLIND GARY:
Titles issued contemporaneously on Banner, Melotone, Oriole, Perfect, and Romeo: *Cross And Evil Woman Blues; I'm Throwin' Up My Hand* ....30.00 - 50.00
(other religious/gospel titles are similarly valued)

BLIND MACK:
Vocalion 03167 *Rootin' Ground Hog Blues* ....75.00 - 100.00

BLIND NORRIS:
Decca 7290 *Sundown Blues* ....40.00 - 70.00

BLIND PERCY & HIS BLIND BAND:
Paramount 12584 *Coal River Blues* ....150.00 - 300.00

BLIND SAMMIE:
Columbia 14484-D *Travelin' Blues* ....250.00 - up
    14551-D *Razor Ball* ....250.00 - up
    14632-D *Broke Down Engine Blues* ....250.00 - up
    14657-D *Atlanta Strut* ....250.00 - up

BLIND WILLIE (& PARTNER):
Regal 3260 *How About You* ....100.00 - 150.00
    3272 *It's My Desire* ....100.00 - 150.00
Vocalion 02568 *Weary Hearted Blues* ....150.00 - 300.00
    02577 *Death Cell Blues* ....150.00 - 300.00
    02595 *Warm It Up To Me* ....150.00 - 300.00
    02622 *It's A Good Little Thing* ....150.00 - 300.00
    02623 *Lord Have Mercy If You Please* ....150.00 - 300.00
    02668 *My Baby's Gone* ....150.00 - 300.00

BLUE BELLE:
Okeh 8483 *High Water Blues* ....50.00 - 75.00
    8538 *Sneakin' Lizard Blues* ....40.00 - 60.00
    8553 *Dead Sea Blues* ....40.00 - 60.00
    8588 *Ghost Creepin' Blues* ....40.00 - 60.00
    8659 *Good Feelin' Blues* ....40.00 - 60.00
    8704 *Death Valley Moan* ....50.00 - 75.00

BLUE BILL:
Bluebird 6795 *More Blues* ....30.00 - 50.00

BLUE BOY:
Varsity 6052 *Back-Biter Blues* ....10.00 - 15.00
    6059 *Electric Chair* ....10.00 - 15.00

BLUE HARMONY BOYS:
Paramount 12889 *Take It Out Too Deep* ....100.00 - 150.00
    12901 *Sweet Miss Stella Blues* ....100.00 - 150.00
    12976 *Ragged But Right* ....100.00 - 150.00

THE BLUEJACKS:
Dot 1000 *Late Hour Blues* ....10.00 - 15.00

BLUES BIRDHEAD:
Okeh 8824 *Harmonica Blues* ....75.00 - 100.00

BLUE SMITTY & HIS STRING MEN:
Chess 1522 *Sad Story* ....20.00 - 30.00

THE BLUES KING:
Solo 10-0003 *Me And My Baby* ....50.00 - 80.00

THE BLUES MAN:
Specialty 501 *Baby's Blues* .... -

THE BLUES ROCKERS:
Aristocrat 407 *Trouble In My Home* ....30.00 - 50.00
    413 *Blues Rockers' Bop* ....30.00 - 50.00
Chess 1483 *My Mama's Baby Child* ....20.00 - 30.00

LOUIS BLUIE AND TED BOGAN:
Bluebird 5490 *I'm Through With You* ....150.00 - 200.00
    5593 *Ted's Stomp* ....150.00 - 200.00

CALVIN BOAZ WITH MARVIN JOHNSON & HIS ORCHESTRA:
G & G 1029 *Saffronia Bee* ....10.00 - 15.00

LUCILLE BOGAN:
Brunswick 7051 *New Way Blues* ....80.00 - 120.00
    7083 *Coffee Grindin' Blues* ....75.00 - 100.00
    7145 *My Georgia Blues* ....75.00 - 100.00
    7163 *Dirty Treatin' Blues* ....75.00 - 100.00
    7186 *Black Angel Blues* ....75.00 - 100.00
    7193 *Crawlin' Lizard Blues* ....75.00 - 100.00
    7210 *Alley Boogie* ....75.00 - 100.00
Okeh 8071 *Chirpin' The Blues* ....20.00 - 30.00
    8074 *Lonesome Daddy Blues* ....20.00 - 30.00
Okeh 8079 *Pawn Shop Blues* ....30.00 - 50.00
Paramount 12459 *Sweet Petunia* ....60.00 - 100.00
    12504 *Kind Stella Blues* ....80.00 - 120.00
    12514 *Doggone Wicked Blues* ....80.00 - 120.00
    12560 *War Time Man Blues* ....80.00 - 120.00
    12577 *Cravin' Whiskey Blues* ....80.00 - 120.00

HOUSTON BOINES:
RPM 364 *Monkey Motion* ....30.00 - 60.00 *

LELA BOLDEN:
Okeh 8139 *Southern Woman Blues* ....50.00 - 80.00

ZU ZU BOLLIN:
Torch 6910 *Headlight Blues* ....20.00 - 30.00
    6912 *Stavin' Chain* ....20.00 - 30.00

PILLIE BOLLING (AND BAREFOOT BILL):
Columbia 14544-D *I Don't Like That* ....100.00 - 150.00
    14654-D *Brown Skin Woman* ....100.00 - 150.00

HATTIE BOLTEN:
Vocalion 04470 *Down Home Shake* ....15.00 - 20.00

BROTHER SON BONDS; BROWNSVILLE SON BONDS; SON BONDS/BOND:
Bluebird 8927 *80 Highway Blues* ....20.00 - 30.00
    8950 *Come Back Home, Little Girl* ....20.00 - 30.00
Champion 50064 *Weary Worried Blues* ....75.00 - 100.00
Decca 7022 *All Night Long* ....75.00 - 100.00
    7024 *In My Father's House* ....60.00 - 100.00
    7039 *Ain't That News?* ....60.00 - 100.00
    7558 *Old Bachelor Blues* ....25.00 - 40.00

THE BOOGIE MAN:
Acorn 308 *Do The Boogie* ....10.00 - 15.00

CHARLEY BOOKER:
Blues & Rhythm 7003 *Rabbit Blues* ....50.00 - 75.00
Modern 878 *Moonrise Blues* ....30.00 - 50.00

CONNIE MAC/MACK BOOKER:
Freedom 1520 *Come Back Baby* ....15.00 - 20.00

JOHN LEE BOOKER (See also: JOHN LEE HOOKER):
Chance 1108 *Miss Lorraine* ....20.00 - 30.00
    1110 *Graveyard Blues* ....20.00 - 30.00
    1122 *609 Boogie* ....20.00 - 30.00
De Luxe 6004 *Lovin' Guitar Man* ....10.00 - 15.00
    6032 *Stuttering Blues* ....10.00 - 15.00
    6046 *Real Real Gone* ....10.00 - 15.00
Rockin' 525 *Pouring Down Rain* ....15.00 - 25.00

ALONZO BOONE:
Supertone 9428 *Kansas City Blues*.....................250.00 - 400.00

CALVIN BOSTICK & HIS TRIO:
Chess 1444 *All Of My Life*.....................................10.00 - 15.00
   1451 *Fleetwood Blues*...................................10.00 - 15.00
Chess 1530, 1571...5.00 - 10.00 *

EDDIE BOYD (& HIS CHESS MEN); LITTLE EDDIE BOYD (& HIS BOOGIE BAND):
Chess 1523 *Cool Kind Treatment*.......................10.00 - 15.00 *
Chess 1533, 1541, 1552, 1561.............................8.00 - 12.00 *
J.O.B. 1005 *I'm Pleading* ....10.00 - 15.00 *
   1007 *Five Long Years* ....10.00 - 15.00 *
RCA Victor (most issues) ....5.00 - 8.00 *

ERNIE BOYD:
Regal 3305 *I Gotta Find My Baby*.........................15.00 - 20.00

GEORGIA BOYD:
Bluebird 5573 *I'm Sorry Blues* ....75.00 - 100.00

RAYMOND BOYD:
Okeh 8528 *Unkind Mama*.......................................30.00 - 50.00

ROBERT BOYD:
Wasco 201 *East St. Louis Baby* ....75.00 - 100.00 *

CALVIN BOZE:
Aladdin 3055 *Safronia B* ....8.00 - 12.00
   3072 *Stinkin' From Drinkin'* ....8.00 - 12.00
   3086 *Slippin' And Slidin'* ....8.00 - 12.00
   3100 *I've Got News For You* ....8.00 - 12.00
   3110 *Fish Tail*..8.00 - 12.00 *
   3122 *Hey Lawdy, Miss Claudie* ....8.00 - 12.00 *

ISHMAN BRACEY/BRACY (& HIS NEW ORLEANS NEHI BOYS):
Paramount 12941 *Jake Liquor Blues*.................200.00 - 400.00
   12970 *Suitcase Full Of Blues* ....200.00 - 400.00
   13038 *Pay Me No Mind* ....200.00 - 400.00
Victor 21349 *Saturday Blues*.............................150.00 - 250.00
   21691 *Trouble-Hearted Blues* ....150.00 - 250.00
   V38560 *The Four Day Blues*............................150.00 - 300.00

MISSISSIPPI BRACY:
Okeh 8867 *Cherry Ball*......................................200.00 - 300.00
   8904 *I'll Overcome Someday*............................200.00 - 300.00

AUNTIE MARY BRADFORD:
Paramount 12617 *Loafing Blues*............................75.00 - 100.00

MARY H. BRADFORD:
Okeh 8102 *Chattanooga Blues*...........................100.00 - 150.00
   8123 *Waco Texas Blues* ....100.00 - 150.00

WALTER BRADFORD:
Sun 176 *Dreary Nights* ....500.00 - up
(Note: The issuance of the above record has not been verified.)

BIG CHARLEY BRADIX:
Aristocrat 418 *Wee Wee Hours*...........................100.00 - 150.00
Blue Bonnet 153 *Dollar Diggin' Woman*..............100.00 - 150.00
Colonial 108 *Boogie Like You Wanna*....................50.00 - 80.00

MARIE BRADLEY:
Paramount 12456 *Down Home Moan*...................100.00 - 150.00
   12466 *Stormy Hailing Blues*............................100.00 - 150.00

TOMMIE BRADLEY (& JAMES COLE):
Champion 16149 *Adam And Eve*...........................300.00 - up
   16308 *When You're Down And Out* ....400.00 - up

   16339 *Four Day Blues* ....400.00 - up
   16696 *Window Pane Blues* ....200.00 - 300.00
   16782 *Where Have You Been So Long?* ....500.00 - up
   50050 *Adam And Eve*..80.00 - 130.00

VELMA BRADLEY:
Broadway 5075 *Gypsy Glass Blues* ....50.00 - 75.00

JEAN BRADY:
Okeh 06254 *My Mellow Man*..................................10.00 - 15.00

DOBBY BRAGG (AND CHARLIE MCFADDEN):
Paramount 12827 *Fire Detective Blues* ....200.00 - 300.00
   13004 *We Can Sell That Thing* ....200.00 - 300.00
   13044 *Little Snow Blues*...................................200.00 - 300.00
   13083 *Don't Look Strange At Me* ....200.00 - 300.00
   13093 *You Got That Thing*...............................200.00 - 300.00

FRANK BRASSWELL:
Titles issued contemporaneously on Banner, Oriole, Perfect, and
   Romeo: *Mountain Girl Blues; Western Blues* ... 50.00 - 75.00

JACKIE BRENSTON & HIS DELTA CATS:
Chess 1458 *Rocket '88*...20.00 - 30.00 *
   1469 *My Real Gone Rocket*...............................20.00 - 30.00
   1472 *Juiced* ....15.00 - 25.00
   1496 *Leo The Louse* ....15.00 - 20.00
   1532 *Starvation*..15.00 - 20.00
(Note: Copies of above pressed of colored plastic bring substantially
   more.)

EVELYN BRICKEY:
Okeh 8256 *Down In The Valley Blues* ....40.00 - 60.00

GRACE BRIM:
J.O.B. 117 *Hospitality Blues*...............................100.00 - 150.00

JOHN BRIM (& HIS COMBO/GARY KINGS/ STOMPERS); JOHN BRIM TRIO:
Checker 769 *Rattlesnake*.......................................50.00 - 100.00 *
Chess 1588 *That Ain't Right* ....50.00 - 100.00 *
   1624 *You Got Me Where You Want Me*............50.00 - 75.00 *
Fortune 801 *Strange Man* ....50.00 - 80.00
J.O.B. 110 *Trouble In The Morning* ....100.00 - 200.00
Parrot 799 *Gary Stomp*...75.00 - 100.00 *
Random 201 *Dark Clouds* ....50.00 - 80.00

MRS. JOHN BRIM:
Random 202 *Going Down The Line* ....50.00 - 80.00

FLORENCE BRISTOL:
Up-To-Date 2019 *How Come You Do Me Like You Do?*
....300.00 - 500.00

DUSTY BROOKS:
Sun 182 *Heaven On Fire* ....150.00 - 200.00 *

EMORY BROOKS:
Champion 15416 *The Worried Man Blues* ....150.00 - 200.00

JUNIOR BROOKS:
RPM 343 *Lone Town Blues* ....75.00 - 100.00 *

BIG BILL BROOMSLEY:
Paramount 13084 *Station Blues*.............................300.00 - 500.00

BIG BILL BROONZY (& HIS FAT FOUR):
Mercury 8122, 8126, 8139, 8160, 8261, 8271, 8284.7.00 - 12.00

BROTHER BELL (See BELL)

BROTHER BLUES & THE BACK ROOM BOYS:
Abbey 3015 *Day Break* ....15.00 - 25.00

BROTHER GEORGE & HIS SANCTIFIED SINGERS:
Conqueror 9361 *I Feel Like Shoutin'* ....10.00 - 15.00
Okeh 05671 *No Stranger Now* ....10.00 - 15.00
    05729 *Precious Lord* ....10.00 - 15.00
    05893 *Talkin' With Jesus* ....10.00 - 15.00
    06019 *Jesus Touched Me* ....10.00 - 15.00
Vocalion 05261 *I Feel Like Shoutin'* ....15.00 - 20.00
    05465 *Twelve Gates To The City* ....15.00 - 20.00

ADA BROWN:
Okeh 8101 *Evil Mama Blues* ....100.00 - 150.00
    8123 *Ill-Natured Blues* ....100.00 - 150.00
    8694 *Down Home Dance*................................20.00 - 30.00
Vocalion 1009 *Panama Limited Blues* ....100.00 - 150.00

ALBERTA BROWN:
Columbia 14321-D *Lonely Blues*...........................100.00 - 150.00

BESSIE BROWN:
Banner 1833 *What's The Matter Now?* ....10.00 - 15.00
    1859 *Nobody But My Baby Is Getting My Love* .10.00 - 15.00
Brunswick 3922 *Blue Ridge* ....20.00 - 30.00
    4346 *The Blues Singer From Alabam'* ....25.00 - 40.00
    4409 *He Just Don't Appeal To Me* ....25.00 - 40.00
Domino 3781 *How Could I Be Blue?* ....10.00 - 15.00
    3829 *Nobody But My Baby Is Getting My Love* .10.00 - 15.00
Regal 8143 *What's The Matter Now?* ....10.00 - 15.00
    8171 *St. Louis Blues* ....10.00 - 15.00
Vocalion 1182 *Arkansas Blues*.............................35.00 - 50.00
    15688 *Can't Help Lovin' Dat Man*....................50.00 - 75.00

BILL BROWN:
Varsity 6064 *Goin' Away And Leavin' My Baby* ....15.00 - 25.00

CHARLES BROWN:
Aladdin (most issues) ....5.00 - 10.00 *
Swing Time 238 *Lost In The Night*..........................10.00 - 15.00
    259 *Be Fair With Me* ....10.00 - 15.00
    271 *Moonrise* ....10.00 - 15.00

CHOCOLATE BROWN:
Paramount 12944 *Itching Heel* ....150.00 - 200.00
    12798 *Cherry Hill Blues*..................................150.00 - 200.00

DANIEL BROWN:
Paramount 12663 *Now Is The Needy Time*............150.00 - 200.00

DEMUS BROWN:
Conqueror 7263 *On an Island All By Myself* ....100.00 - 150.00

DUDLEY BROWN:
Supertone 9524 *Western Traveler Blues* ....100.00 - 150.00

ELIZA BROWN:
Columbia 14466-D *Get On Out Of Here* ....50.00 - 75.00
    14471-D *Peddlin' Man* ....50.00 - 75.00
    14478-D *Take A Little Bit* ....50.00 - 75.00

FLOSSIE (AND DUKE) BROWN:
Champion 15814 *Shake It Daddy* ....80.00 - 120.00
    15858 *Pig Meat Mama*....................................80.00 - 120.00

FREDDIE BROWN:
Paramount 12910 *Whip It To A Jelly* ....80.00 - 120.00

GABRIEL BROWN:
Beacon 5021 *Boogie Woogie Guitar* ....10.00 - 15.00
Coral 65019 *I Can't Last Long* ....15.00 - 20.00
Joe Davis 5003, 5004, 5006, 5008, 5015, 5016, 5017,
    5020, 5021, 5025, 5026, 5027, 5028.................10.00 - 15.00
Gennett 5003 *You Ain't No Good* ....10.00 - 15.00
    5004 *Going My Way* ....10.00 - 15.00
Jay-Dee 779 *Hold Me Baby* ....15.00 - 20.00
M-G-M 11407 *Cold Mama* ....10.00 - 20.00

GATEMOUTH BROWN:
Aladdin 198 *Gatemouth Boogie* ....10.00 - 20.00
    199 *Guitar In My Hands* ....10.00 - 20.00
Peacock 1500 *Mercy On Me* ....15.00 - 20.00
    1501 *Ditch Diggin' Daddy* ....15.00 - 20.00
    1504 *My Time's Expensive* ....15.00 - 20.00
    1505 *Boogie Rambler* ....15.00 - 20.00
    1508 *I've Been Mistreated* ....15.00 - 20.00
    1561 *Win With Me Baby* ....10.00 - 20.00
    1568 *I Live My Life* ....10.00 - 20.00
    1575 *Pale Dry Boogie* ....15.00 - 20.00
    1576 *She Winked Her Eye* ....10.00 - 20.00
    1586 *Too Late Baby* ....10.00 - 20.00
    1600 *Just Got Lucky* ....10.00 - 20.00
    1607 *Dirty Work At The Crossroads* ....10.00 - 20.00
Peacock (higher numbers).....................................7.00 - 12.00 *

"HI" HENRY BROWN:
Vocalion 1692 *Skin Man Blues*..............................200.00 - 300.00
    1715 *Hospital Blues*..200.00 - 300.00
    1728 *Titanic Blues* ....200.00 - 300.00

ELDER J.C. BROWN:
Herwin 93004 *Where Shall I Be?* ....150.00 - 200.00

JAMES "WIDEMOUTH" BROWN - HIS GUITAR & ORCHESTRA:
Jax 306 *Boogie Woogie Night Hawk* ....10.00 - 15.00 *

JOE BROWN:
Okeh 8491 *Cotton Patch Blues*.............................50.00 - 75.00

TEXAS JOHNNY BROWN:
Atlantic 876 *There Go The Blues*...........................75.00 - 100.00

JUDSON BROWN:
Brunswick 7220 *You Don't Know My Mind Blues*100.00 - 150.00

KITTY BROWN:
Banner 1436 *Family Skeleton Blues* ....15.00 - 20.00
    1437 *I Wanna Jazz Some More*........................15.00 - 20.00
    1452 *Keep On Going* ....15.00 - 20.00
Okeh 8052 *Evil Blues*..25.00 - 40.00
    8053 *Mean Eyes* ....25.00 - 40.00
Paramount 12223 *Keep On Going* ....40.00 - 70.00
Regal 9734 *One Of These Days* ....15.00 - 20.00

LEE BROWN:
Chicago 104 *Bobby Town Boogie* ....15.00 - 25.00
Decca 7386 *Pitchin' Boogie* ....15.00 - 20.00
   7504 *Carpenter Man Blues* ....15.00 - 20.00
Decca 7575, 7587 ....7.00 - 12.00
Decca 7615 *Forsaken Blues* ....10.00 - 15.00
   7626 *Low Down Feelin'* ....8.00 - 12.00
   7654 *Lock And Key Blues* ....10.00 - 15.00
   7686 *My Driving Wheel* ....10.00 - 15.00
Decca 7697, 7710, 7726, 7744, 7775, 7790 ....7.00 - 12.00
King 4157 *New Little Girl* ....20.00 - 30.00
Queen 4157 *Brownie's Boogie* ....20.00 - 30.00

LIL & WILL BROWN:
Black Patti 8007 *Moanful Mama* ....400.00 - up
   8008 *Three Card Monte Blues* ....400.00 - up

LOTTIE BROWN:
Supertone 9286 *Wayward Girl Blues* ....150.00 - 200.00
   9289 *Don't Speak To Me* ....150.00 - 200.00
   9367 *Goin' Away Blues* ....150.00 - 200.00
   9429 *Blue World Blues* ....150.00 - 250.00

LOVER BOY BROWN:
Regent 1007 *Just The Blues* ....10.00 - 15.00

LUCILLE BROWN:
Superior 2552 *Pay With Money* ....150.00 - 300.00
   2633 *Can't Get Enough* ....150.00 - 300.00

OLIVER BROWN:
Bluebird 6042 *I Ain't Got Nobody* ....15.00 - 20.00

ORA BROWN:
Paramount 12481 *Jinx Blues* ....80.00 - 120.00
   12500 *Jailhouse Moan* ....80.00 - 120.00

PINEY BROWN:
Apollo 402 *Gloomy Monday Blues* ....20.00 - 30.00
   418 *That's Right Baby* ....20.00 - 30.00
   423 *Lovin' Gal Blues* ....20.00 - 30.00

RICHARD "RABBIT" BROWN:
Victor 20578 *James Alley Blues* ....150.00 - 200.00
   21475 *Never Let the Same Bee Sting You Twice*
....150.00 - 200.00
   35840 (12 inch) *Sinking Of The Titanic* ....150.00 - 250.00

ROY BROWN:
De Luxe 1098, 1128, 1166, 3154, 3189, 3198, 3212,
   3226, 3300, 3301, 3302, 3304, 3308, 3312, 3319 .....7.00 - 12.00
Gold Star 636 *Deep Sea Diver* ....20.00 - 30.00
King (most issues) ....7.00 - 10.00 *
Miltone (cartoon labels) ....8.00 - 12.00

SAMMY BROWN:
Gennett 6337 *Barrel House Blues* ....200.00 - 300.00

SKEET BROWN:
Vocalion 1205 *Skeet Skat Blues* ....75.00 - 100.00

WILLIE BROWN:
Champion 50023 *M And O Blues* ....100.00 - 150.00
Paramount 13090 *M And O Blues* ....500.00 - 1000.00
   13099 *Kicking In My Sleep Blues* ....500.00 - 1000.00

YODELING KID BROWN:
Vocalion 1205 *Policy Blues* ....75.00 - 100.00

THE BROWN DOTS (See DEEK WATSON)

ALTA BROWNE:
Gennett 3308 *Couldn't Hear Nobody Pray* ....20.00 - 30.00
   3318 *Nobody Knows Da Trouble I See* ....20.00 - 30.00

BRYANT'S JUBLIEE QUARTET/QUINTETTE:
Gennett 6608 *Who Stole The Lock Off The Hen House Door?*
....50.00 - 75.00
Q.R.S. 7018 *When The World's On Fire* ....50.00 - 75.00
   7020 *Do You Call That Religion?* ....50.00 - 75.00

BEULAH BRYANT:
M-G-M 11427 *Fat Man Blues* ....7.00 - 10.00
   11509 *He's Got Plenty On The Ball* ....7.00 - 10.00

GLADYS BRYANT:
Harmograph 818 *Beale Street Mama* ....30.00 - 50.00
   2539 *Triflin' Blues* ....20.00 - 30.00
   2540 *Laughin' Cryin' Blues* ....20.00 - 30.00
Paramount 12026 *Laughin' Cryin' Blues* ....20.00 - 30.00
   12027 *Triflin' Blues* ....20.00 - 30.00
   12031 *Beale Street Mama* ....30.00 - 50.00

ELDER RICHARD BRYANT ('S SANCTIFIED SINGERS):
Okeh 8559 *Come Over Here* ....100.00 - 150.00
   8579 *How Much I Owe For Love Divine* ....100.00 - 150.00
Victor 21357 *The Master Come And Called To Me*
....100.00 - 150.00
   21694 *A Wild Man In Town* ....100.00 - 150.00
   V38507 *Everybody Was There* ....100.00 - 150.00

JOHN BULLARD (QUARTET):
De Luxe 6019 *Spoiled Hambone Blues* ....25.00 - 40.00 *
   6035 *Mary Lou* ....25.00 - 40.00 *
Index 300 *Callin' The Blues* ....30.00 - 50.00

BULL CITY RED:
Titles issued contemporaneously on Banner, Melotone, Oriole, Perfect, and Romeo: *Black Woman And Poison Blues; I Won't Be Dogged Around; Now I'm Taking To You; Mississippi River; Pick And Shovel Blues; Richmond Blues* ....30.00 - 50.00

BUMBLE BEE SLIM (& HIS THREE SHARKS):
Titles issued contemporaneously on Banner, Melotone, Oriole, Perfect, and Romeo: *Big Six; Bumble Bee's New Muddy Water; Goodbye; I'm Having So Much Trouble; I'm Needing Someone; My Big Moments; Rising River Blues; Rough Treatment; She Never; 12 O' Clock Midnight; 12 O'Clock Southern Train; Woman For Every Man* ....25.00 - 40.00
Bluebird 5563 *Sad And Lonesome* ....20.00 - 30.00
   6521 *Everybody's Fishing* ....50.00 - 80.00
   6559 *Guilty Woman Blues* ....10.00 - 15.00
   6586 *Muddy Water Blues* ....10.00 - 15.00
   6612 *Mean Bad Man Blues* ....10.00 - 15.00
   6635 *Bye Bye Baby Blues* ....10.00 - 15.00
   6649 *Squalling Panther Blues* ....10.00 - 15.00
   6834 *Sad And Lonesome* ....25.00 - 40.00
Decca 7021 *Cruel Hearted Woman Blues* ....50.00 - 75.00
   7031 *Ain't It A Crying Shame?* ....50.00 - 75.00
   7045 *The Longest Day You Live* ....50.00 - 75.00
   7053 *Bleeding Heart Blues* ....50.00 - 75.00
   7054 *Let's Pitch A Boogie Woogie* ....50.00 - 75.00
   7071 *My Black Gal Blues* ....30.00 - 50.00
   7079 *Mean Bloody Murder Blues* ....30.00 - 50.00
   7089 *Good Evening Blues* ....20.00 - 30.00

7098 *The Death Of Leroy Carr*	20.00 -	30.00
7101 *Sail On Sail On Blues*	20.00 -	30.00
7121 *I'll Take You Back*	20.00 -	30.00
7126 *Smoky Mountain Blues*	20.00 -	30.00
7127 *My Old Pal Blues*	20.00 -	30.00
7138 *Happy Life Blues*	20.00 -	30.00
7145 *Some Old Rainy Days*	20.00 -	30.00
7162 *Deep Bass Blues*	20.00 -	30.00
7170 *No Good Woman*	15.00 -	25.00
7208 *Honest Confession*	15.00 -	20.00
7214 *Funny Feelin'*	15.00 -	20.00
7220 *Upside Down*	15.00 -	20.00
7232 *Ease Me Down*	15.00 -	20.00
7239 *Christmas and No Santa Claus*	15.00 -	20.00
7249 *Buggie Bed*	15.00 -	20.00
7273 *Letter Writing*	15.00 -	20.00
7300 *Blue Expression Blues*	15.00 -	20.00
7343 *Past and Gone*	10.00 -	15.00
7371 *True Blue*	10.00 -	15.00
7423 *Please Baby*	10.00 -	15.00
7440 *If I Could Speak My Mind*	10.00 -	15.00
Fidelity 3004 *Ida Red*	20.00 -	30.00
Paramount 13102 *Yo Yo String Blues*	200.00 -	300.00
13109 *Chain Gang Bound*	200.00 -	300.00
13132 *Honey Bee Blues*	200.00 -	300.00
Vocalion 1691 *Piney Woods Working Man*	75.00 -	100.00
1719 *Greasy Greens*	75.00 -	100.00
1720 *B And O Blues*	75.00 -	100.00
02713 *Busy Devil*	75.00 -	100.00
02728 *Baby So Long*	75.00 -	100.00
02742 *East St. Louis Blues*	75.00 -	100.00
02773 *Wrecked Life Blues*	75.00 -	100.00
02809 *Helping Hand Blues*	75.00 -	100.00
02829 *Rough Road Blues*	75.00 -	100.00
02865 *Cold-Blooded Murder*	75.00 -	100.00
02885 *Burned Down Mill*	75.00 -	100.00
02903 *Running Bad Luck Blues*	75.00 -	100.00
02930 *Blues Before Daylight*	75.00 -	100.00
02970 *Way Down In Georgia*	75.00 -	100.00
03005 *Lemon Squeezing Blues*	75.00 -	100.00
03037 *I Keep On Drinking*	75.00 -	100.00
03054 *When The Sun Goes Down*	75.00 -	100.00
03090 *Big 80 Blues*	50.00 -	80.00
03130 *Sometimes Blues*	50.00 -	80.00
03165 *Cold Blooded Murder No. 2*	40.00 -	60.00
03197 *When Somebody Loses*	40.00 -	60.00
03209 *Can't You Trust Me No More?*	40.00 -	60.00
03221 *Dumb Tricks Blues*	40.00 -	60.00
03242 *Back In Jail Again*	40.00 -	60.00
03267 *Wet Clothes Blues*	30.00 -	50.00
03298 *Any Time At Night*	30.00 -	50.00
03328 *Hard Rocks In My Bed*	25.00 -	40.00
03384 *Meet Me At The Landing*	25.00 -	40.00
03418 *Slave Man Blues*	25.00 -	40.00
03446 *Fast Life Blues*	25.00 -	40.00
03473 *12 O'Clock Midnight*	25.00 -	40.00
03506 *She Never*	25.00 -	40.00
03550 *Big Six*	25.00 -	40.00
03582 *Woman For Every Man*	25.00 -	40.00
03611 *Good Bye*	25.00 -	40.00
03637 *Rough Treatment*	25.00 -	40.00
03698 *Just Yesterday*	25.00 -	40.00
03767 *The Old Life I'm Living*	25.00 -	40.00
03870 *When Your Deal Goes Down*	25.00 -	40.00
03929 *Rock Hearted Woman*	25.00 -	40.00
04042 *If I Make It Over*	25.00 -	40.00
04661 *Where Was You Last Night?*	25.00 -	40.00

ALLEN BUNN:

Apollo 436 *She'll Be Sorry*	15.00 -	20.00
439 *I Got You Covered*	15.00 -	20.00
442 *Wine*	10.00 -	15.00
447 *My Flight*	10.00 -	15.00

TEDDY BUNN (& SPENCER WILLIAMS):

Selective 105 *Irritatin' Blues*	10.00 -	15.00
Victor 23253 *Tampa Twirl*	150.00 -	250.00
V38592 *Pattin' Dat Cat*	150.00 -	250.00
V38602 *Goose And Gander*	150.00 -	250.00
V38617 *Blow it Up*	150.00 -	250.00

PINETOP BURKS:

Titles issued contemporaneously on Banner, Melotone, Oriole, Perfect, Romeo, and Vocalion: *Mountain Jack Blues; Shake The Shack* .... 40.00 - 60.00

Vocalion 03979 *Jack Of All Trades Blues*	40.00 -	60.00
04107 *Fannie Mae Blues*	40.00 -	60.00

HATTIE BURLESON:

Brunswick 7042 *Superstitious Blues*	150.00 -	200.00
7054 *Bye Bye Baby*	150.00 -	200.00
Paramount 13050 *Clearin' House Blues*	100.00 -	150.00
13138 *Dead Lover Blues*	200.00 -	300.00

DAN BURLEY:

Circle 1020 *South Side Shake*	10.00 -	20.00
1021 *Big Cat, Little Cat*	10.00 -	20.00
1022 *Shotgun House Rag*	10.00 -	20.00

EDDIE BURNS:

De Luxe 6024 *Dealing With The Devil*	50.00 -	75.00

(CHARLIE) BURSE (& HIS MEMPHIS MUD-CATS); CHARLIE BURSE WITH THE MEMPHIS JUG BAND; BURSE & SHADE; BURSE & STEPHEN:

Champion 16481 *I Got Good Taters*	400.00 -	up
16599 *Fishing In The Dark*	400.00 -	up
16654 *Tapping That Thing*	400.00 -	up
Conqueror 9355 *It Makes No Difference Now*	10.00 -	15.00
9356 *Magic Spell Blues*	10.00 -	15.00
Okeh 8959 *Bottle It Up And Go*	150.00 -	200.00
Vocalion 03080 *Bottle It Up And Go*	100.00 -	150.00
05017 *Beale Street Holiday*	15.00 -	25.00
05070 *Memphis Highway Stomp*	15.00 -	20.00
05123 *Magic Spell Blues*	15.00 -	20.00
05192 *Scared To Death*	20.00 -	30.00
05299 *Good Potatoes On The Hill*	15.00 -	25.00
05393 *Too Much Beef*	15.00 -	25.00
05551 *Dawn Of Day Blues*	15.00 -	25.00

CLARA BURSTON:

Champion 16125 *Try That Man O'Mine*	150.00 -	300.00
16216 *Pay With Money*	150.00 -	300.00
16756 *Good And Hot*	250.00 -	up
Gennett 7319 *Pay With Money*	250.00 -	up
Paramount 12881 *Georgia Man Blues*	200.00 -	300.00
13003 *C.P. Blues*	150.00 -	200.00
13045 *Ginger Snappin'*	150.00 -	200.00

BUDDY (BUDDY) BURTON:
Gennett 6453 *Silvery Moon* ....100.00 - 150.00
   6471 *It's No-One But You*......................100.00 - 150.00
Paramount 12625 *Ham-Fatchet Blues*...................150.00 - 300.00

W.H. BURTON-MARCUS MOMAN - (CLIFF) MOORE:
Paramount 12787 *St. Louis Blues* ....100.00 - 150.00
   12789 *Roll That Jelly*................................100.00 - 150.00

FRANK BUSBY:
Decca 7295 *Prisoner Bound* ....10.00 - 15.00

MARY BUTLER:
Brunswick 7046 *Bungalow Blues*.........................150.00 - 200.00
   7049 *Mad Dog Blues* ....150.00 - 200.00

SAM BUTLER:
Vocalion 1056 *Heaven Is My View* ....100.00 - 150.00
   1057 *Poor Boy Blues* ....100.00 - 150.00

TRIXIE BUTLER:
Bluebird 6392 *Take It Easy Greasy*......................10.00 - 15.00
   6429 *You Got The Right Key* ....15.00 - 25.00

BUTTERBEANS AND SUSIE:
Okeh 8147, 8180...15.00 - 20.00
   8163 *Construction Gang*............................75.00 - 125.00
   8182 *Kiss Me Sweet*...................................75.00 - 125.00
   8192, 8199, 8202, 8209, 8219, 8224, 8233, 8241,
   8303, 8307, 8319, 8323, 8335 ....15.00 - 30.00
   8355 *He Likes It Slow* ....75.00 - 100.00
   8392, 8399, 8432, 8520 ....15.00 - 30.00
   8502 *I Wanna Hot Dog For My Roll* ....50.00 - 75.00
   8556 *Gonna Make You Sorry* ....50.00 - 75.00
   8598, 8614, 8670, 8687, 8701 ....20.00 - 30.00
   8769 *Ain't Gonna Do That No More*..............50.00 - 75.00
   8833 *Times Is Hard* ....50.00 - 75.00
   8893 *Broke Down Mama* ....75.00 - 100.00
   8911 *Radio Papa* ....75.00 - 100.00
   8950 *Papa Ain't No Santa Claus*....................75.00 - 100.00

JOHN BYRD:
Paramount 12997 *Billy Goat Blues*.......................150.00 - 300.00

JOSEPHINE BYRD:
Columbia 14349-D *Mosquito Blues* ....30.00 - 60.00

ROLAND BYRD:
Atlantic 947 *Hey Little Girl* ....20.00 - 30.00

ROY ("BALD HEAD") BYRD; ROY BYRD & HIS BLUES JUMPERS:
Atlantic 897 *She Walks Right In* ....30.00 - 50.00
Federal 12061 *K.C. Blues* ....20.00 - 30.00 *
   12073 *Rockin' With Fes*................................20.00 - 30.00 *
Mercury 8175 *Bald Head* ....10.00 - 20.00
   8184 *Oh Well* ....10.00 - 20.00

BOBBY (BOBBIE) CADILLAC:
Columbia 14413-D *Carbolic Acid Blues*...............150.00 - 200.00
   14505-D *Easin' In* ....150.00 - 200.00
   14604-D *I Can't Stand That* ....150.00 - 200.00

ROBERT CAFFREY:
Chess 1470 *Ida Bee* ....30.00 - 50.00

PERRY CAIN:
Gold Star 632 *All The Way From Texas*..................15.00 - 25.00

JOE CALICOTT:
Brunswick 7166 *Fare Thee Well Blues*.................250.00 - 500.00

BOB CALL:
Brunswick 7137 *31 Blues* ....150.00 - 200.00
Coral 65009 *Talkin' Baby Blues* ....30.00 - 50.00

BOB CAMP (& HIS BUDDIES/THE NIGHTHAWKS):
Decca 48112 *My Little Rose* ....10.00 - 15.00
   48118 *Between You and Me* ....10.00 - 15.00
Essex 714 *Pitch A Boogie* ....15.00 - 30.00
Southern 121 *Gonna Pitch A Boogie Woogie* ....20.00 - 30.00
   130 *Without Your Love* ....20.00 - 30.00

BOB CAMPBELL:
Vocalion 02798 *Starvation Farm Blues* ....150.00 - 250.00
   02830 *Shotgun Blues*.................................150.00 - 250.00

CARL CAMPBELL (WITH HAYES 4 KINGS):
Freedom 1521 *Ooh Wee Baby* ....20.00 - 30.00
Peacock 1538 *Early Morning Blues*......................15.00 - 20.00

CHARLIE CAMPBELL & HIS RED PEPPERS:
Vocalion 03571 *Pepper Sauce Mama*................... 150.00 - 200.00

GENE CAMPBELL:
Brunswick 7139 *Bended Knee Blues* ....80.00 - 120.00
   7154 *Western Plain Blues* ....80.00 - 120.00
   7161 *Freight Train Yodeling Blues*.................80.00 - 120.00
   7170 *Wandering Blues* ....80.00 - 120.00
   7177 *Wash And Iron Woman Blues* ....80.00 - 120.00
   7184 *Lazy Woman Blues* ....80.00 - 120.00
   7197 *Wedding Day Blues* ....80.00 - 120.00
   7206 *Face To Face Blues* ....80.00 - 120.00
   7214 *Doggone Mean Blues*.........................80.00 - 120.00
   7225 *Crooked Woman Blues*.....................100.00 - 150.00
   7226 *Turned Out Blues* ....100.00 - 150.00
   7227 *Married Life Blues* ....100.00 - 150.00

CANNON & WOODS:
Brunswick 7138 *Fourth And Beale*......................150.00 - 250.00

THE CAP-TANS:
Dot 1018 *With All My Love* ....10.00 - 15.00

CAROLINA PEANUT BOYS:
Victor 23267 *Got A Letter From My Baby* ....200.00 - 300.00
   23274 *You Got Me Rollin'* ....200.00 - 300.00
   23319 *Spider's Nest Blues* ....250.00 - 400.00

CAROLINA SLIM:
Acorn 319 *Pleading Blues* ....15.00 - 20.00
   323 *Worry You Off My Mind* ....15.00 - 20.00
   324 *Rag Mama* ....15.00 - 20.00
   3015 *Mama's Boogie* ....15.00 - 20.00
Sharp 2002 *Blues Go Away From Me* ....20.00 - 30.00

CAROLINA WASHBOARD TRIO:
Varsity 6036 *That Thing Blues* ....20.00 - 30.00

DORA CARR; DORA CARR-CHAS. DAVENPORT:
Okeh 8130 *You Might Pizen Me* ....40.00 - 60.00
   8244 *Good Woman's Blues*........................40.00 - 60.00
   8250 *Cow Cow Blues*.................................75.00 - 100.00
   8284 *Fifth Street Blues*...............................50.00 - 75.00

GUNTER LEE CARR:
Decca 48167 *Goodnight Irene* ....10.00 - 15.00
   48170 *We're Gonna Rock* ....10.00 - 15.00

LEROY CARR (AND/WITH SCRAPPER BLACKWELL):

Bluebird 5877 *Ain't It A Shame* ....50.00 - 80.00
   5915 *Big Four Blues* ....60.00 - 100.00
   5946 *Just A Rag* ....60.00 - 100.00
   5963 *Going Back Home* ....60.00 - 100.00
   7970 *Big Four Blues* ....25.00 - 40.00
Vocalion 1191 *My Own Lonesome Blues* ....30.00 - 50.00
   1200 *Tennessee Blues* ....100.00 - 150.00
   1214 *Low Down Dirty Blues* ....75.00 - 100.00
   1232 *Truthful Blues* ....80.00 - 120.00
   1241 *Prison Bound Blues* ....75.00 - 100.00
   1259 *How About Me?* ....75.00 - 100.00
   1261 *Tired Of Your Low Down Ways* ....75.00 - 100.00
   1279 *You Don't Mean Me No Good* ....75.00 - 100.00
   1290 *Straight Alky Blues* ....150.00 - 200.00
   1400 *Naptown Blues* ....150.00 - 200.00
   1405 *Wrong Man Blues* ....150.00 - 200.00
   1412 *Gambler's Blues* ....150.00 - 200.00
   1423 *Gettin' All Wet* ....150.00 - 200.00
   1432 *Prison Cell Blues* ....150.00 - 200.00
   1435 *Love Hides All Faults* ....150.00 - 200.00
   1454 *The Dirty Dozen* ....150.00 - 200.00
   1460 *I'm Going Back To Tennessee* ....150.00 - 200.00
   1473 *Rainy Day Blues* ....150.00 - 200.00
   1483 *That's Tellin' 'Em* ....150.00 - 200.00
   1499 *Blue With The Blues* ....150.00 - 200.00
   1519 *I Know That I'll Be Blue* ....150.00 - 200.00
   1527 *Memphis Town* ....150.00 - 200.00
   1541 *Sloppy Drunk Blues* ....100.00 - 150.00
   1561 *Papa Wants A Cookie* ....150.00 - 200.00
   1574 *Jail Cell Blues* ....150.00 - 200.00
   1585 *Big House Blues* ....150.00 - 200.00
   1593 *Papa's On The House Top* ....150.00 - 200.00
   1605 *Low Down Dog Blues* ....150.00 - 200.00
   1624 *Let's Disagree* ....150.00 - 200.00
   1636 *Papa's Got Your Water On* ....150.00 - 200.00
   1651 *What More Can I Do?* ....150.00 - 200.00
   1693 *The Depression Blues* ....150.00 - 200.00
   1703 *Midnight Hour Blues* ....150.00 - 200.00
   1709 *I Keep The Blues* ....150.00 - 200.00
   1716 *Quittin' Papa* ....150.00 - 200.00
   02657 *Blues Before Sunrise* ....60.00 - 100.00
   02681 *Blues She Gave Me* ....100.00 - 150.00
   02741 *Hurry Down Sunshine* ....100.00 - 150.00
   02751 *Court Room Blues* ....100.00 - 150.00
   02762 *Shady Lane Blues* ....60.00 - 100.00
   02791 *Barrel House Woman* ....75.00 - 100.00
   02820 *I Believe I'll Make A Change* ....100.00 - 150.00
   02875 *Longing For My Sugar* ....100.00 - 150.00
   02893 *Cruel Woman Blues* ....100.00 - 150.00
   02922 *Stormy Weather Blues* ....100.00 - 150.00
   02950 *My Woman's Gone Wrong* ....100.00 - 150.00
   02969 *Bo Bo Stomp* ....75.00 - 100.00
   02986 *George Street Blues* ....100.00 - 150.00
   03034 *Tight Time Blues* ....100.00 - 150.00
   03067 *Black Wagon Blues* ....100.00 - 150.00
   03107 *Muddy Water* ....80.00 - 120.00
   03157 *My Good For Nothin' Gal* ....75.00 - 100.00
Vocalion 03233 *Blue Night Blues* ....75.00 - 100.00
   03296 *Good Woman Blues* ....75.00 - 100.00
   03349 *Big Four Blues* ....75.00 - 100.00

ALICE CARTER:

Okeh 8070 *Midnight Blues* ....20.00 - 40.00
   8076 *Bleeding Hearted Blues* ....20.00 - 40.00

ALICE LESLIE CARTER:

Titles issued contemporaneously on Arto, Bell, and Globe: *The Also-Ran Blues; Aunt Hagar's Blues; Cry Baby Blues; Dangerous Blues; Decatur Street Blues; Down Home Blues; Got To Have My Daddy Blues; I Want Some Lovin' Blues; You'll Think Of Me Blues* .... 15.00 - 30.00

BO CARTER (& WALTER JACOBS):

Bluebird 5489 *Bo Carter Special* ....30.00 - 50.00
   5536 *Howlin' Tom Cat Blues* ....30.00 - 50.00
   5594 *Pin In Your Cushion* ....30.00 - 50.00
   5629 *Beans* ....30.00 - 50.00
   5704 *Nobody's Business* ....30.00 - 50.00
   5825 *Backache Blues* ....30.00 - 50.00
   5861 *Old Shoe Blues* ....30.00 - 50.00
   5912 *Mashing That Thing* ....30.00 - 50.00
   5997 *Skin Ball Blues* ....25.00 - 35.00
   6024 *Blue Runner Blues* ....20.00 - 30.00
   6058 *Please Warm My Weiner* ....20.00 - 30.00
   6124 *When You Left* ....20.00 - 30.00
   6295 *Cigarette Blues* ....20.00 - 30.00
   6315 *Ride My Mule* ....20.00 - 30.00
   6363 *Rolling Blues* ....20.00 - 30.00
   6407 *It's Too Wet* ....15.00 - 25.00
   6444 *Fat Mouth Blues* ....15.00 - 25.00
   6529 *T Baby Blues* ....50.00 - 80.00
   6589 *I Get The Blues* ....75.00 - 100.00
   6659 *Doubled Up In A Knot* ....15.00 - 25.00
   6695 *Sue Cow* ....15.00 - 20.00
   6735 *Worried G Blues* ....15.00 - 30.00
   7073 *Got To Work Somewhere* ....15.00 - 30.00
   7213 *The Ins And Outs Of My Girl* ....15.00 - 30.00
   7927 *Shake 'Em On Down* ....15.00 - 30.00
   7952 *Lucille, Lucille* ....15.00 - 30.00
   7968 *Shoo That Chicken* ....15.00 - 30.00
   8045 *Let's Get Drunk Again* ....15.00 - 20.00
   8078 *World In A Jug* ....15.00 - 20.00
   8093 *Old Devil* ....15.00 - 20.00
   8122 *Whiskey Blues* ....15.00 - 20.00
   8147 *Santa Claus* ....15.00 - 20.00
   8159 *Trouble In Blues* ....15.00 - 20.00
   8397 *The County Farm Blues* ....15.00 - 20.00
   8423 *Lock The Lock* ....15.00 - 20.00
   8459 *Baby Ruth* ....15.00 - 20.00
   8495 *Policy Blues* ....15.00 - 20.00
   8514 *My Little Mind* ....15.00 - 20.00
   8555 *Honey* ....15.00 - 20.00
Columbia 14661-D *Pussy Cat Blues* ....80.00 - 120.00
   14671-D *New Auto Blues* ....80.00 - 120.00
Okeh 8852 *I'm An Old Bumble Bee* ....80.00 - 120.00
   8858 *Times Is Tight Like That* ....80.00 - 120.00
   8870 *Mean Feeling Blues* ....80.00 - 120.00
   8887 *Pin In Your Cushion* ....80.00 - 120.00
   8888 *Loveless Love* ....80.00 - 120.00
   8889 *Howling Tom Cat Blues* ....80.00 - 120.00
   8897 *Ants In My Pants* ....80.00 - 120.00
   8906 *Blue Runner Blues* ....80.00 - 120.00
   8923 *What Kind Of Scent Is This?* ....80.00 - 120.00
   8930 *Last Go Round* ....80.00 - 120.00
   8935 *I Want You To Know* ....80.00 - 120.00
   8952 *Baby, How Can It Be?* ....80.00 - 120.00
Vocalion 03091 *Pussy Cat Blues* ....50.00 - 75.00
   03259 *Ants In My Pants* ....40.00 - 60.00

BUNNY CARTER:
Conqueror 7266 *Midnight Special Blues* ....100.00 - 150.00

CHARLIE CARTER:
Broadway 5076 *Long Gone Lost John* ....35.00 - 50.00

EDDIE CARTER QUARTET:
M-G-M 11405 *Don't Turn Your Back On Me* ....10.00 - 15.00

GEORGE CARTER:
Paramount 12750 *Hot Jelly Roll Blues* ....150.00 - 200.00
  12769 *Weeping Willow Woman* ....150.00 - 200.00

GOREY/GORY CARTER (AND/WITH HIS GUITAR & ROCKIN' RHYTHM ORCHESTRA/HEPCATS):
Coral 65058 *I've Got News For You* ....10.00 - 15.00
  65064 *I'm Your Boogie Man* ....10.00 - 15.00
Freedom 1502 *Sweet Ole Woman's Blues* ....15.00 - 20.00
  1506 *Back Home Blues* ....10.00 - 15.00
  1511 *How Can You Love Me* ....10.00 - 15.00
  1518 *She's Just Old Fashioned* ....10.00 - 15.00
  1522 *She's My Best Bet* ....10.00 - 15.00
  1525 *Workin' With My Baby* ....10.00 - 15.00
  1536 *Come On Let's Boogie* ....10.00 - 15.00
Modern 819 *Seven Days* ....10.00 - 15.00
Sittin' In With 556 *Let's Rock* ....10.00 - 15.00
  572 *Jumpin' At Jeff's* ....10.00 - 15.00

HARRY CARTER:
Bluebird 6009 *Letter From Texas* ....30.00 - 50.00
  6095 *Hoo Doo Blues* ....30.00 - 50.00
  6210 *Deep Blues Ocean Blues* ....30.00 - 50.00

JOSEPHINE CARTER:
Okeh 8012 *The Jim Jam Blues* ....25.00 - 40.00
  8015 *The Darned Blues* ....25.00 - 40.00

LEROY CARTER:
Vocalion 03120 *Black Widow Spider* ....150.00 - 200.00

NELSON CARTER & HIS GUITAR:
Sittin' In With 557 *My Baby Left Me* ....10.00 - 15.00

"SPIDER" CARTER:
Brunswick 7181 *Dry Spell Blues* ....80.00 - 120.00
  7188 *Don't Leave Me Blues* ....100.00 - 150.00

CASEY BILL (AND THE BROWN BOMBERS OF SWING):
Bluebird 6212 *Long-Eared Mule* ....30.00 - 50.00
  6243 *My Stove Won't Work* ....30.00 - 50.00
  6262 *Howlin' Dog Blues* ....30.00 - 50.00
  6356 *Somebody's Got To Go* ....30.00 - 50.00
  6390 *Let Me Be Your Butcher* ....30.00 - 50.00
  6465 *I'm A Stranger In Your Town* ....30.00 - 50.00
  6519 *Casey Blues* ....30.00 - 50.00
  8004 *You Gotta Do Your Duty* ....30.00 - 50.00
  8060 *Midnight Blues* ....30.00 - 50.00
Vocalion 03186 *W.P.A. Blues* ....30.00 - 50.00
  03220 *Rood Water Blues* ....30.00 - 50.00
  03250 *Keyhole Blues* ....30.00 - 50.00
  03274 *Big Bill Blues* ....30.00 - 50.00
  03330 *Back Door Blues* ....30.00 - 50.00
  03373 *Gonna Take My Time* ....30.00 - 50.00
  03407 *Talkin' To Myself* ....30.00 - 50.00
  03437 *Streamline Woman* ....30.00 - 50.00
  03464 *Big Katy Adam* ....30.00 - 50.00
  03496 *Jinx Blues* ....30.00 - 50.00

  03529 *Round And Round* ....30.00 - 50.00
  03561 *I've Been Tricked* ....30.00 - 50.00
  03592 *No Good Woman* ....30.00 - 50.00
  03859 *Sales Lady* ....30.00 - 50.00
  03860 *New Round And Round* ....30.00 - 50.00
  03930 *Rooster Blues* ....30.00 - 50.00
  04001 *Go Ahead, Buddy* ....30.00 - 50.00
  04066 *Red Hot Blues* ....30.00 - 50.00
  04138 *Spider Blues* ....30.00 - 50.00

THE CATS & THE FIDDLE:
Bluebird 10484 *Thursday Evening Swing* ....8.00 - 12.00
  10547 *Till The Day I Die* ....8.00 - 12.00
Gotham 197 *Start Talking, Baby* ....8.00 - 12.00

CHARLIE CHAPMAN:
Broadway 5079 *Moanin' The Blues* ....300.00 - up
  5091 *Back To The Wood Blues* ....300.00 - up
  5108 *She's Got Good Stuff* ....300.00 - up

HENRY CHARLES:
Broadway 5094 *Henry Charles Blues* ....100.00 - 150.00

RAY CHARLES (TRIO):
Swing Beat 171 *I Love You, I Love You* ....15.00 - 25.00
  211 *Alone In This City* ....15.00 - 25.00
  212 *Rockin' Chair Blues* ....15.00 - 25.00
  213 *If I Give You My Love* ....15.00 - 25.00
Swing Time (numbers as above, similarly valued)
  215 *I've Had My Fun* ....15.00 - 20.00
  216 *Ain't That Fine* ....15.00 - 20.00
  228 *Late In The Evening Blues* ....15.00 - 20.00
  229 *I'll Do Anything But Work* ....15.00 - 20.00
  249 *All To Myself* ....10.00 - 15.00
  250 *Lonely Boy* ....10.00 - 15.00
  274 *Kiss Me Baby* ....10.00 - 15.00
  297 *Hey Now* ....10.00 - 15.00
  300 *Guitar Blues* ....10.00 - 15.00
  326 *Misery In My Heart* ....10.00 - 15.00

THE CHARLESTON BLUES TRIO:
Champion 15734 *Lighthouse Blues* ....100.00 - 150.00
  15755 *Runnin' Wild* ....125.00 - 175.00

CHATMAN BROTHERS:
Bluebird 6657 *Stir In Now* ....30.00 - 50.00
  6682 *Hold It At The Bottom* ....30.00 - 50.00
  6717 *NW Me Just Before Day* ....30.00 - 50.00
  7167 *Radio Blues* ....30.00 - 50.00
  8139 *Jumping Out Blues* ....30.00 - 50.00

ANDY CHATMAN:
Brunswick 7185 *Shakin' The Jelly* ....80.00 - 120.00

BO CHATMAN:
Brunswick 7048 *Good Old Turnip Greens* ....150.00 - 200.00

PETER CHATMAN:
Okeh 05799 *Last Pair Of Shoes Blues* ....15.00 - 20.00
  05845 *Miss Ora Lee Blues* ....15.00 - 20.00
  05908 *The Jive Blues* ....15.00 - 20.00

CHATMAN & McCOY:
Supertone 2212 *Corrine Corrina* ....25.00 - 40.00

HARRY CHATMON:
Vocalion 03143 *Black Ants Blues* ....75.00 - 100.00

CHICAGO FIVE:
Bluebird 6543 *I'm A Gamblin' Man*........................10.00 - 15.00

THE CHICAGO SHEIKS:
Superior 2798 *Beedle Um Bum*..............................150.00 - 250.00

CHICAGO SUNNY BOY:
Meteor 5004 *Western Union Man* ....50.00 - 100.00 *

VIRGIL CHILDERS:
Bluebird 7441 *Somebody Stole My Jane* ....20.00 - 30.00
   7464 *Red River Blues*...............................20.00 - 30.00
   7487 *Travelin' Man* ....20.00 - 30.00

BUDDY CHILES:
Gold Star 660 *Jet Black Woman* ....50.00 - 80.00

ANNA LEE CHISHOLM:
Paramount 12213 *Georgia Sam Blues*.....................50.00 - 80.00

THE CHORDS:
Gem 211 *In The Woods* ....30.00 - 50.00

BUDDY CHRISTIAN'S FOUR CRY-BABIES:
Okeh 8332 *Nina Lee* ....30.00 - 50.00

BLIND CLYDE CHURCH:
Victor 23271 *Number Nine Blues*..........................150.00 - 250.00

DOT CLARK:
Supertone 9288 *Papa, You're Too Slow*.................... -   -   -

ETHEL CLARK:
Silvertone 3521 *Black Man Blues*...........................75.00 - 100.00
   3523 *Jelly Roll Blues* ....100.00 - 150.00

LONNIE CLARK:
Paramount 12871 *Broke Down Engine*..................150.00 - 200.00

GEORGE CLARKE:
Bluebird 7485 *Prisoner Blues* ....30.00 - 50.00

DOCTOR CLAYTON:
Bluebird 8901, 8938, 9003, 9021, 34-0702 ....8.00 - 12.00
RCA Victor 20-1995, 20-2153, 20-2323 ....5.00 - 10.00

JESSE CLAYTON:
Vocalion 1598 *Neckbone Blues* ....80.00 - 120.00

PETER J. CLAYTON:
Bluebird 6071 *Peter's Blues*...................................25.00 - 40.00
   6096 *Yo Yo Jive* ....50.00 - 80.00

THE CLEFS:
Chess 1521 *We Three* ....30.00 - 50.00

PETER CLEIGHTON:
Conqueror 9447 *Roaming Gambler*.........................10.00 - 15.00
   9948 *Back Door Man Blues*.....................10.00 - 15.00
Okeh 06375 *Love Is Gone* ....10.00 - 15.00
   06398 *Slick Man Blues* ....10.00 - 15.00
   06464 *Streamline Love* ....10.00 - 15.00
   06514 *Something Going On Wrong*...........10.00 - 15.00

ALBERT CLEMENS:
Bluebird 5930 *Policy Blues* ....75.00 - 100.00

BIG BOY CLEVELAND:
Gennett 6108 *Quill Blues*.....................................150.00 - 250.00

KAISER CLIFTON:
Victor 23278 *Cash Money Blues* ....400.00 - up
   V38600 *Teach Me Right From Wrong* ......400.00 - up

JAMES COLE; JAMES COLE'S WASHBOARD BAND/FOUR:
Champion 16150 *Sweet Lizzie* ....300.00 - up
   16308 *I Love My Mary*.............................400.00 - up
   16718 *Mistreated The Only Friend You Had* ..500.00 - up
   40047 *Runnin' Wild* ....75.00 - 100.00

KID COLE:
Vocalion 1186 *Sixth Street Moan* ....100.00 - 150.00
   1187 *Hard Hearted Mama Blues* ....100.00 - 150.00

LUCY COLE:
Champion 15549 *Empty Bed Blues*........................75.00 - 100.00

WALTER COLE:
Champion 16104 *Everybody Got Somebody* ....200.00 - 300.00
Gennett 7318 *Everybody Got Somebody* ....250.00 - 400.00

BOB COLEMAN:
Paramount 12731 *Cincinnati Underworld Moan* .250.00 - 400.00
   12791 *Sing Song Blues*...................................150.00 - 200.00

ELLEN COLEMAN:
Edison 51200 *Cruel Back Bitin' Blues* ....30.00 - 50.00
   51242 *She Walked Right Up And Took*.............30.00 - 50.00

JAYBIRD COLEMAN:
Black Patti 8055 *Boll Weevil* ....1000.00 - up
Columbia 14534-D *Man Trouble Blues*................200.00 - 300.00
Gennett 6226 *Mill Log Blues* ....300.00 - 500.00
   6245 *Man Trouble Blues*.........................250.00 - 400.00
   6276 *No More Good Water*.....................250.00 - 400.00

LONNIE COLEMAN:
Columbia 14440-D *Old Rock Island Blues*.............80.00 - 120.00

WALTER COLEMAN:
Decca 7157 *Smack That Thing*...............................30.00 - 50.00
   7168 *I'm Going To Cincinnati* ....30.00 - 50.00

THE COLEMAN BROTHERS:
Manor 100 *It's My Desire* ....20.00 - 30.00
   101 *We'll Understand* ....20.00 - 30.00
   1055 *New What A Time* ....20.00 - 30.00

THE COLEMANS:
Regal 3297 *You Know I Love You Baby* ....20.00 - 30.00
   3208 *If You Should Need Me* ....20.00 - 30.00

CHASEY COLLINS:
Bluebird 6187 *Atlanta Town* ....50.00 - 80.00
   6261 *Walking Blues* ....60.00 - 100.00

SAM COLLINS:
Black Patti 8025 *The Jail House Blues* ....500.00 - up
   8026 *Yellow Dog Blues* ....400.00 - up
Gennett 6146 *Yellow Dog Blues* ....200.00 - 300.00
   6167 *The Jail House Blues* ....200.00 - 300.00
   6181 *Devil In The Lion's Den*.......................200.00 - 300.00
   6260 *Dark Cloudy Blues* ....250.00 - 400.00
   6291 *Lead Me All The Way* ....250.00 - 400.00
   6307 *Midnight Special Blues* ....250.00 - 400.00
   6379 *Hesitation Blues* ....250.00 - 400.00
Herwin 92043 *Riverside Blues*...............................250.00 - 400.00
Superior 330 *Midnight Special Blues* ....250.00 - 400.00
   350 *Hesitation Blues* ....250.00 - 400.00
   369 *Dark Cloudy Blues* ....250.00 - 400.00

BIG TOM COLLINS:
King 4483 *Heartache Blues*....................................15.00 - 20.00 *
   4568 *Watchin' My Stuff* ....15.00 - 20.00 *

VIE COLLINS:
Silvertone 3518 *Nobody Knows* ....35.00 - 50.00
   3519 *Who'll Drive My Blues Away* ....35.00 - 50.00
   3538 *Confessin' Blues* ....35.00 - 50.00
   3539 *Reckless Don't Care Mama Blues* ....35.00 - 50.00
   3540 *Midnight Special* ....40.00 - 60.00

CONNIE'S/CONNEY'S COMBO (WITH L.C. WILLIAMS):
Freedom 1508 *Ugly Mae* ....10.00 - 15.00
   1510 *That's Alright* ....10.00 - 15.00

BEN CONWAY:
Herwin 93014 *Sing Song Blues* ....150.00 - 250.00

ANN COOK:
Victor 20579 *Mamma Cookie* ....100.00 - 150.00

DONALD COOKS (& HIS BAND):
Jade 202 *Dolphin Street Stomp* ....15.00 - 20.00

SILVER COOKS WITH THE GONDOLIERS:
Peacock 1510 *Mr. Ticket Agent* ....20.00 - 30.00

RATTLESNAKE COOPER:
Talent 804 *Rattlesnake Blues* ....80.00 - 120.00

MARTHA COPELAND:
Columbia 14161-D *Black Snake Blues* ....15.00 - 20.00
   14189-D *Fortune Teller Blues* ....20.00 - 30.00
   14196-D *The Black Snake Moan* ....15.00 - 25.00
   14208-D *Sorrow Valley Blues* ....20.00 - 30.00
   14227-D *Dyin' Crap-Shooter's Blues* ....20.00 - 30.00
   14237-D *Skeleton Key Blues* ....20.00 - 30.00
   14248-D *Hobo Bill* ....20.00 - 30.00
   14262-D *Good Time Mama Blues* ....20.00 - 30.00
   14281-D *Second-Hand Daddy* ....20.00 - 30.00
   14310-D *Wylie Avenue Blues* ....25.00 - 50.00
   14327-D *I Can't Give You Anything But Love* ..20.00 - 30.00
Columbia 14352-D *Desert Blues* ....60.00 - 100.00
   14377-D *Mama's Well Has Done Gone Dry* ......50.00 - 75.00
Okeh 8091 *The Penetrating Blues* ....15.00 - 20.00
   8112 *The Pawn Shop Blues* ....15.00 - 20.00
Victor 20548 *Hard-Headed Mama* ....40.00 - 70.00
   20769 *Stole My Man Blues* ....40.00 - 70.00

COTTON TOP MOUNTAIN SANCTIFIED SINGER:
Brunswick 7100 *Give Me That Old Time Religion* .....100.00 - 150.00
   7119 *She's Coming Round The Mountain* ....100.00 - 150.00

JAMES COTTON:
Sun 199 *Straighten Up Baby* ....100.00 - 150.00 *
   206 *Cotton Crop Blues* ....100.00 - 150.00 *

SYLVESTER COTTON:
Modern 655 *Ugly Woman Blues* ....20.00 - 30.00
Sensation 7000 *Ugly Woman Blues* ....25.00 - 50.00

LITTLE WILLIE COTTON:
Swing Time 319 *Gonna Shake It Up And Go* ....30.00 - 50.00

DIPPER BOY COUNCIL:
Titles issued contemporaneously on Banner, Conqueror, Melotone, Oriole, Perfect, and Romeo: *I'm Grievin' And I'm Worryin'; Poor And Ain't Got A Dime; Runaway Man Blues; Working Man Blues*
   ....50.00 - 80.00

COUNTRY JIM:
Imperial 5062 *Rainy Morning Blues* ....15.00 - 25.00

   5073 *Old River Blues* ....15.00 - 25.00
   5091 *Good Looking Mama* ....10.00 - 15.00
   5095 *Philippine Blues* ....10.00 - 15.00

COUNTRY PAUL:
King 4517 *Your Picture Done Faded* ....30.00 - 50.00 *
   4532 *One More Time* ....30.00 - 50.00 *
   4560 *Black Cat Trail* ....15.00 - 30.00 *
   4573 *Side Walk Boogie* ....15.00 - 30.00 *

(MISS) COUNTRY SLIM:
Hollywood 1005 *What Wrong Have I Done* ....40.00 - 80.00 *

COUSIN JOE (with EARL BOSTIC'S SEXTETTE):
Gotham 500 *Fly Hen Blues* ....10.00 - 15.00
Decca 48045 *Box Car Shorty* ....15.00 - 20.00
Savoy 5527 *Weddin' Day Blues* ....10.00 - 15.00
Signature 1013 *Come Down Baby* ....10.00 - 15.00

BLIND/BOGUS BEN COVINGTON:
Brunswick 7121 *Boodle-De-Bum Bum* ....75.00 - 100.00
Paramount 12693 *Adam And Eve In The Garden* . 100.00 - 150.00

BOB CRANE:
Herwin 93018 *Ghost Woman Blues* ....150.00 - 200.00

MAY CRANE:
Oriole 949 *Anything That Happens Just Pleases Me*
   ....50.00 - 75.00
   976 *Black Snake Blues* ....50.00 - 75.00

JAMES CRAWFORD:
Gennett 6536 *Flood And Thunder* ....75.00 - 100.00

ROSETTA CRAWFORD:
Decca 7567 *Stop It Joe* ....15.00 - 20.00
   7584 *I'm Tired of Fattenin' Frogs For Snakes* .. 15.00 - 20.00
Okeh 8096 *Down On The Levee Blues* ....80.00 - 120.00
Pathe-Actuelle 7505 *Misery* ....50.00 - 80.00
Perfect 105 *Misery* ....50.00 - 80.00

PEE WEE CRAYTON:
Aladdin 3112 *Day Break* ....7.00 - 10.00 *
Imperial 5288, 5297, 5321, 5338, 5345 ....7.00 - 10.00 *
   5353 *Yours Truly* ....10.00 - 15.00 *
Modern 624, 643, 658, 675, 707, 719, 732, 742, 763,
   774, 796, 816, 892...7.00 - 12.00
Post 2007 *I Must Go On* ....8.00 - 12.00 *
Vee Jay 214, 252, 266 ....5.00 - 8.00 *

JOHNNIE CRINER (See ROY MILTON)

KATIE CRIPPEN:
Black Swan 2003 *Blind Man's Blues* ....30.00 - 50.00
   2018 *That's My Cup Blues* ....30.00 - 50.00
Same Titles on Claxtonola, Paramount, Puritan ..... 25.00 - 40.00

DAVID CROSS:
Brunswick 7079 *Then My Gal's In Town* ....80.00 - 120.00

SCAT MAN CROTHERS:
Intro 6016 *Free Samples* ....10.00 - 15.00
   6017 *King Berman's Stomp* ....10.00 - 15.00
Orchid 1 *Shuffleboard Blues* ....20.00 - 30.00

(ARTHUR) "BIG BOY" CRUDUP:
Bluebird 8858 *Death Valley Blues* ....20.00 - 30.00
   8896 *Black Pony Blues* ....20.00 - 30.00
   9019 *Raised To My Hand* ....10.00 - 15.00
   34-0704 *Mean Old Frisco Blues* ....10.00 - 15.00

34-0717 *My Mamma Don't Allow Me* ....10.00 - 15.00
34-0725 *Rock Me Mama*...............................8.00 - 12.00
34-0738 *Cool Disposition*.............................8.00 - 12.00
34-0746 *She's Gone*...................................8.00 - 12.00
RCA Victor 20-1949 *Ethel Mae* ....7.00 - 10.00
20-2105 *I Want My Lovin'* ....7.00 - 10.00
20-2205 *That's All Right* ....15.00 - 30.00
20-2387 *That's Your Red Wagon* ....7.00 - 10.00
20-2565 *Train Fare Blues* ....7.00 - 10.00
20-2757 *Dirty Road Blues* ....7.00 - 10.00
20-2989 *Boy Friend Blues* ....7.00 - 10.00
20-3140 *Just Like A Spider* ....7.00 - 10.00
20 3261 *Chicago Blues*................................7.00 - 10.00
20-4367 *Love Me Mama* ....7.00 - 10.00
20-4572 *Goin' Back To Georgia* ....7.00 - 10.00
20-4753 *Late In The Evening* ....7.00 - 10.00
20-4933 *Second Man Blues* ....7.00 - 10.00
20-5070 *Lookin' For My Baby* ....7.00 - 10.00
20-5167 *Nelvina*...7.00 - 10.00
20-5563 *The War Is Over* ....7.00 - 10.00
22-0007 *Gonna Be Some Changes Made* ....7.00 - 10.00
22-0029 *Crudup's Vicksburg Blues* ....7.00 - 10.00
22-0048 *Hoodoo Lady Blues* ....7.00 - 10.00
22-0061 *Come Back Baby* ....7.00 - 10.00
22-0074 *Dust My Broom* ....7.00 - 10.00
22-0092 *Mean Old Santa-Fe* ....7.00 - 10.00
22-0100 *Lonesome World To Me* ....7.00 - 10.00
22-0105 *She's Just Like Caldonia* ....7.00 - 10.00
22-0117 *Nobody Wants Me* ....7.00 - 10.00
22-0126 *Roberta Blues* ....7.00 - 10.00
22-0141 *Too Much Competition* ....7.00 - 10.00

(Note: 45 RPM issues have catalog number prefixes 47 or 50 instead of 20 or 22; catalog numbers may also be different in some cases. See 45 RPM section.)

PERCY LEE CRUDUP:

Checker 754 *Tears In My Eyes* ....40.00 - 70.00

DENNIS CRUMPTON & ROBERT SUMMERS:

Titles issued contemporaneously on Banner, Melotone, Oriole, Perfect, and Romeo: *Everybody Ought To Pray Sometime; Go I'll Send Thee*..30.00 - 50.00

THE CRYSTALS:

Rockin' 518 *Don't You Go* ....60.00 - 100.00 *

BEN CURRY:

Champion 50019 *You Rascal You* ....75.00 - 100.00
Paramount 13118 *Fat Mouth Blues* ....200.00 - 300.00
13122 *Hot Dog* ....200.00 - 300.00
13140 *The New Dirty Dozen*...............200.00 - 300.00

ELDER CURRY:

Okeh 8857 *Memphis Flu* ....75.00 - 100.00
8879 *Hard Times* ....75.00 - 100.00
8892 *None Good But One*....................75.00 - 100.00
8910 *Prove All Things* ....75.00 - 100.00

DADDY STOVEPIPE (AND MISSISSIPPI SARAH):

Bluebird 5913 *The Spasm* ....100.00 - 150.00
6023 *35 Depression* ....100.00 - 150.00
Claxtonola 40335 *Sundown Blues* ....150.00 - 200.00
Gennett 5459 *Stove Pipe Blues* ....150.00 - 200.00

DUSKY DAILEY:

Titles issued contemporaneously on Banner, Melotone, Oriole, Perfect, Romeo, and Vocalion: *Flying Crow Blues; I Want You, I Need You; I Would Do Anything For You; Screamin' And Hollerin' Blues*..................................30.00 - 50.00
Vocalion 04963 *Miss Georgia Blues* ....15.00 - 25.00
04977 *Can Cutter Blues*......................15.00 - 20.00
05044 *Lost Lovin' Blues* ....15.00 - 20.00
05110 *Misunderstandin' Man*................15.00 - 20.00

FLORA DALE:

Domino 360 *Jail House Blues* ....25.00 - 40.00
3504 *Everything My Sweetie Does (Pleases Me)* ....20.00 - 30.00

SALLY DALE:

Domino 3452 *A Good Man Is Hard To Find*..........20.00 - 30.00
3453 *Blind Man Blues* ....20.00 - 30.00

DALLAS RED:

Selective 112 *Cold Blooded Blues* ....10.00 - 15.00

DALLAS STRING BAND (WITH COLEY JONES):

Columbia 14290-D *Dallas Red*................150.00 - 200.00
14389-D *Hokum Blues* ....150.00 - 200.00
14410-D *Chasin' Rainbows* ....150.00 - 200.00
14574-D *Sugar Blues*..........................150.00 - 200.00

LEROY DALLAS:

Sittin' In With 522 *Jump Little Children* ....20.00 - 30.00
526 *Good Morning Blues*.....................20.00 - 30.00
537 *Your Sweet Man's Blues* ....20.00 - 30.00

JULIUS DANIELS (AND TORRENCE):

Victor 20499 *I'm Gonna Tell God How You Doin'* ....100.00 - 150.00
20658 *Ninety-Nine Year Blues*..............100.00 - 150.00
21065 *Richmond Blues* ....100.00 - 150.00
21359 *Can't Put The Bridle On That Mule* .....100.00 - 150.00

BLIND (BLUES) DARBY:

Decca 7328 *Heart Trouble Blues*............30.00 - 50.00
7816 *Spike Driver* ....25.00 - 40.00
Vocalion 02953 *I'm Gonna Wreck Your Vee Eight* ......80.00 - 120.00
02988 *Pokino Blues* ....80.00 - 120.00
03177 *Sweet Memories Blues* ....75.00 - 100.00

TEDDY DARBY:

Paramount 12828 *My Laona Blues* ....200.00 - 400.00
12907 *What Am I To Do?* ....300.00 - up
Victor 23311 *Deceiving Blues* ....250.00 - up

"DOC" DASHER:

Columbia 14106-D *West Palm Beach Blues* ....30.00 - 50.00

COW COW DAVENPORT & IVY SMITH:

Gennett 7231 *Alabammy Mistreated* ....200.00 - 300.00

GENEVIEVE DAVIS:

Victor 20648 *I've Got Something* ....150.00 - 200.00

GEORGE DAVIS:

Decca 7756 *Radio Brown Blues* ....15.00 - 20.00
7799 *Fast Asleep Blues* ....15.00 - 20.00

HENRYETTE DAVIS:

Okeh 8371 *Another Sweet Daddy* ....50.00 - 80.00
8395 *Mail Box Blues* ....50.00 - 80.00

BLIND JOHN(NY) DAVIS (TRIO):

M-G-M 10574 *No Mail Today*................15.00 - 20.00
10738 *My Love*.................................15.00 - 20.00

10919 *Telegram To My Baby* ....15.00 - 20.00
10976 *The Day Will Come* ....7.00 - 10.00
Vocalion 04079 *Jersey Cow Blues* ....20.00 - 30.00
04189 *Alley Woman Blues* ....20.00 - 30.00
04580 *Anna Lou Breakdowm* ....20.00 - 30.00

MARTHA DAVIS:
Decca 48174 *Kitchen Blues* ....10.00 - 20.00 *

SONNY BOY DAVIS:
Talent 802 *I Don't Live Here No More* ....75.00 - 100.00

WALTER DAVIS:
Bluebird 5031 *M. & O. Blues* ....100.00 - 150.00
5038 *Blue Sea Blues* ....100.00 - 150.00
5077 *Howling Wind Blues* ....100.00 - 150.00
5094 *Hijack Blues* ....100.00 - 150.00
5129 *Worried Man Blues* ....100.00 - 150.00
5143 *Red Cross Blues* ....100.00 - 150.00
5192 *Moonlight Blues* ....100.00 - 150.00
5228 *Evil Woman* ....100.00 - 150.00
5305 *Red Cross Blues-No. 2* ....80.00 - 120.00
5324 *You Don't Smell Right* ....80.00 - 120.00
5361 *What's The Use Of Worryin'?* ....80.00 - 120.00
5390 *Oil Field Blues* ....80.00 - 120.00
5411 *Stormy Weather Blues-No. 2* ....100.00 - 150.00
(Note: Above titles on Sunrise label are valued more highly.)
5879 *Sloppy Drunk Again* ....50.00 - 75.00
5931 *Sweet Sixteen* ....50.00 - 75.00
5965 *Minute Man Blues* ....50.00 - 75.00
5982 *Sad And Lonesome Blues* ....50.00 - 75.00
6040 *Dentist Blues* ....40.00 - 60.00
6059 *I Can Tell By The Way You Smell* ....40.00 - 60.00
6074 *Pearly May* ....40.00 - 60.00
6125 *Santa Claus* ....75.00 - 100.00
6167 *Moonlight Is My Spread* ....25.00 - 40.00
6201 *Katy Blues* ....25.00 - 40.00
6228 *Blues At Midnight* ....25.00 - 40.00
6236 *Sweet Sixteen* ....15.00 - 20.00
6354 *Carpenter Man* ....25.00 - 40.00
6410 *Fallin' Rain* ....20.00 - 30.00
6468 *Jacksonville* ....20.00 - 30.00
6498 *Think You Need A Shot* ....20.00 - 30.00
6971 *Nightmare Blues* ....20.00 - 30.00
6996 *Good Gal* ....20.00 - 30.00
7021 *Fifth Avenue Blues* ....20.00 - 30.00
7064 *Angel Child* ....20.00 - 30.00
7292 *Guiding Rod* ....20.00 - 30.00
7329 *Holiday Blues* ....20.00 - 30.00
7375 *Big Jack Engine Blues* ....20.00 - 30.00
7512 *Walking The Avenue* ....15.00 - 20.00
7551 *Easy Goin' Mama* ....15.00 - 20.00
7589 *Million-Dollar* ....15.00 - 20.00
7643 *Candy Man* ....15.00 - 20.00
7663 *Friendless Blues* ....15.00 - 20.00
7693 *13 Highway* ....15.00 - 20.00
7745 *Call Me Anytime* ....15.00 - 20.00
7792 *Love Will Kill You* ....15.00 - 20.00
7836 *Homesick* ....15.00 - 20.00
7978 *Cuttin' Off My Days* ....15.00 - 20.00
8002 *Early This Mornin'* ....15.00 - 20.00
8026 *Smoky Mountain* ....15.00 - 20.00
8058 *Mercy Blues* ....15.00 - 20.00
8107 *Troubled And Weary* ....15.00 - 20.00
8227 *Corinne* ....15.00 - 20.00

8261 *Big Four Blues* ....15.00 - 20.00
8282 *Green And Lucky* ....15.00 - 20.00
8312 *Bachelor Blues* ....15.00 - 20.00
8343 *Froggy Bottom* ....15.00 - 20.00
8367 *Doctor Blues* ....15.00 - 20.00
8393 *Sundown Blues* ....15.00 - 20.00
8434 *Jungle Blues* ....15.00 - 20.00
8470 *Western Land* ....15.00 - 20.00
8510 *Come Back Baby* ....10.00 - 20.00
8534 *The Way I Love You* ....10.00 - 20.00
8574 *Four Foot Eleven* ....10.00 - 20.00
8600 *Can't See Your Face* ....10.00 - 20.00
8664 *Just Thinking* ....10.00 - 20.00
8694 *Soon Forgotten* ....10.00 - 20.00
8737 *Friends Must Part* ....10.00 - 20.00
8773 *The Only Woman* ....10.00 - 20.00
8802 *All My Money Gone* ....10.00 - 20.00
8833 *I'll Be Back After A While* ....8.00 - 12.00
8860 *You Keep On Crying* ....8.00 - 12.00
8926 *Teasin' Brown Skin* ....8.00 - 12.00
8961 *Frisco Blues* ....15.00 - 20.00
8998 *Hello Baby* ....8.00 - 12.00
9027 *Goodbye* ....8.00 - 12.00
Bullet 305 *Move Back To The Woods* ....15.00 - 20.00
311 *I Would Hate To Hate You* ....15.00 - 20.00
321 *Santa Claus Blues* ....15.00 - 20.00
326 *Stop That Train In Harlem* ....15.00 - 20.00
328 *Come On Baby* ....15.00 - 20.00
341 *I Just Can't Help It* ....15.00 - 20.00
342 *Going Back To Texas* ....15.00 - 20.00
Montgomery Ward
(many titles same as Bluebird, above) ....10.00 - 15.00
Victor 20-1999 *New B & O Blues* ....8.00 - 12.00
20-2156 *My Friends Don't Know Me* ....8.00 - 12.00
20-2335 *Just One More Time* ....8.00 - 12.00
20-2487 *It's Been So Long* ....8.00 - 12.00
20-5012 *Tears Came Rolling Down* ....8.00 - 12.00
20-5168 *So Long Baby* ....8.00 - 12.00
Victor 23250 *Blue Sea Blues* ....250.00 - 400.00
23282 *What Made Me Love You So?* ....250.00 - 400.00
23291 *Railroad Man Blues* ....200.00 - 300.00
23302 *Mr. Davis Blues- No. 2* ....200.00 - 300.00
23308 *Howling Wind Blues* ....200.00 - 300.00
23315 *Strange Land Blues* ....200.00 - 300.00
23325 *Lonesome Hill Blues* ....250.00 - 400.00
23333 *Worried Man Blues* ....250.00 - 400.00
23343 *Hijack Blues* ....250.00 - 400.00
23355 *South-West Missouri Blues* ....200.00 - 300.00
23414 *Night Creepin'* ....250.00 - 400.00
23418 *L & N Blues* ....250.00 - 400.00
23423 *Red Cross Blues* ....250.00 - 400.00
V-38618 *Mr. Davis' Blues* ....250.00 - 400.00

BLIND WILLIE DAVIS:
Paramount 12658 *When The Saints Go Marching In*
....150.00 - 200.00
12726 *Your Enemy Cannot Harm You* ....150.00 - 200.00
12979 *I Believe I'll Go Back Home* ....200.00 - 300.00

RUTH DAY:
Columbia 14642-D *Painful Blues* ....150.00 - 250.00

TEXAS BILL DAY (& BILLIKEN JOHNSON):
Columbia 14494-D *Goin' Back To My Baby* ....100.00 - 150.00
14514-D *Elm Street Blues* ....100.00 - 150.00
14587-D *Good Mornin' Blues* ....100.00 - 150.00

WILL DAY:
Columbia 14318-D *Sunrise Blues* ....100.00 - 150.00

JOE DEAN:
Vocalion 1544 *Mexico Bound Blues*.......................75.00 - 100.00

JAMES/JIMMY DE BERRY (& HIS MEMPHIS PLAYBOYS):
Okeh 05800 *Spider Bite Blues* ....20.00 - 30.00
Sun 185 *Take A Little Chance* ....100.00 - 150.00 *
Vocalion 05084 *You Can Go* ....20.00 - 30.00
  05247 *Insane Jealous Blues*...........................20.00 - 30.00
  05349 *You Played A Trick On Me* ....20.00 - 30.00

MERCY DEE:
Bayou 003 *Please Understand* ....15.00 - 20.00
  013 *Happy Bachelor* ....10.00 - 15.00
Colony 102 *Straight And Narrow* ....10.00 - 15.00
  107 *Old Fashioned Ways* ....10.00 - 15.00
  111 *Birdbrain Baby* ....10.00 - 15.00
Imperial 5104 *Empty Life* ....10.00 - 15.00
  5110 *Big Foot Country* ....10.00 - 15.00
  5118 *Bought Love* ....10.00 - 15.00
  5127 *Pay Off* ....10.00 - 15.00
Specialty 458 *One Room Country Shack*...................8.00 - 12.00 *
  466 *Rent Man Blues* ....8.00 - 12.00 *
  481 *Dark Muddy Bottom* ....8.00 - 12.00 *
Spire 11-001 *Lonesome Cabin Blues*.......................15.00 - 25.00
  11-002 *Travelin' Alone Blues* ....15.00 - 25.00

MATTIE DELANEY:
Vocalion 1480 *Tallahatchie River Blues* ....250.00 - 500.00

TOM DELANEY:
Columbia 14082-D *Georgia Stockade Blues*...........15.00 - 20.00
  14122-D *Bow Legged Mama* ....15.00 - 20.00

THE DELLS:
Vee Jay 134 *Tell The World* ....20.00 - 40.00

DELTA BOYS:
Bluebird 8852 *Black Gal Swing* ....30.00 - 50.00
  8891 *When The Saints Go Marching In* ....30.00 - 50.00
  8915 *Get Up And Go* ....30.00 - 50.00

DELTA JOE:
Chance 1115 *Four O'Clock Blues* ....75.00 - 100.00

DELTA JOHN:
Regent 1001 *Goin' Mad Blues* ....15.00 - 20.00

DELTA RHYTHM BOYS:
Atlantic 889, 899, 900, 905, 1023 ....8.00 - 12.00
Decca 8514, 8522, 8530, 8542 ....8.00 - 12.00

DESCRIPTIVE NOVELTY: (See BLIND LEMON JEFFERSON)

DETROIT COUNT:
JVB 75830 *Hastings Street Opera* ....80.00 - 130.00
  75831 *Hastings St. Woogie Man* ....75.00 - 100.00
King 4264 *Hastings Street Opera*...........................25.00 - 50.00
  4265 *I'm Crazy About You* ....25.00 - 40.00
  4279 *Little Tillie Willie*...........................25.00 - 40.00

THE DEVIL'S DADDY-IN-LAW:
Conqueror 9204 *Lookin' For My Baby* ....20.00 - 30.00
Vocalion 04643 *Lookin' For My Baby*.......................25.00 - 40.00

PEARL DICKSON:
Columbia 14286-D *Little Rock Blues* ....100.00 - 150.00

PERE DICKSON:
Victor 23335 *Red Hot Papa*..........................150.00 - 250.00

TOM DICKSON:
Okeh 8570 *Worry Blues*..........................100.00 - 150.00
  8590 *Death Cell Blues* ....100.00 - 150.00

DIRTY RED:
Aladdin 194 *Home Last Night* ....15.00 - 20.00
  207 *Hotel Boogie* ....15.00 - 20.00

FLOYD DIXON (TRIO) (WITH JOHNNY MOOR'S THREE BLAZERS):
Aladdin 3069, 3073, 3074, 3075, 3078, 3082, 3083,
  3084, 3101, 3111, 3135, 3144, 3151, 3166, 3196,
  3230..........................5.00 - 10.00
Modern 653, 664, 700, 724, 725, 744, 761, 776, 797..5.00 - 8.00
Supreme 1528, 1535, 1546, 1547 ....7.00 - 10.00
Swing Time 261, 287 ....7.00 - 10.00

MARY DIXON:
Columbia 14415-D *Daddy You Got Ev'rything*......50.00 - 80.00
  14442-D *All Around Mama* ....50.00 - 80.00
  14459-D *Black Dog Blues* ....50.00 - 80.00
  14532-D *Unhappy Blues*.................75.00 - 100.00
Vocalion 1199 *Dusky Stevedore* ....75.00 - 100.00

PERRY DIXON:
Columbia 14522-D *Back To Georgia Blues* ....150.00 - 250.00

DOCTOR CLAYTON'S BUDDY:
RCA Victor 20-2733, 20-2954, 20-3085, 20-3255...7.00 - 10.00

DR. HEPCAT (See L. DURST)

FATS DOMINO:
Imperial 5058 *The Fat Man* ....40.00 - 70.00
  5065 *Boogie Woogie Baby*...........................40.00 - 70.00
  5077 *Hide Away Blues* ....40.00 - 70.00
  5085 *Brand New Baby* ....40.00 - 70.00
  5099 *Every Night About This Time* ....40.00 - 70.00
  5114 *What's The Matter Baby* ....30.00 - 50.00
  5123 *Don't You Lie To Me*...........................30.00 - 50.00
  5138 *No, No Baby* ....20.00 - 30.00
  5145 *Rockin' Chair* ....20.00 - 30.00
  5167 *I'll Be Gone* ....15.00 - 25.00
(subsequent issues, which occur as 45 RPM records as well as 78
  RPM, are listed in the fourth section of this book)

BLIND JOE DONNELL:
Broadway 5089 *There's A Hand Writing On the Wall*
..........................200.00 - 400.00

MATTIE DORSEY:
Paramount 12521 *Mattie Blues* ....75.00 - 100.00
  12554 *Stingaree Blues* ....75.00 - 100.00

THOMAS A.DORSEY (THE GOSPEL SINGER/AND THE GOSPEL SINGERS):
Vocalion 1710 *How About You* ....100.00 - 150.00
  02729 *Singing In My Soul* ....100.00 - 150.00
  04646 *If You See My Savior* ....20.00 - 30.00

BIG BILL DOTSON & HIS GUITAR:
Blues & Rhythm 7004 *Dark Old World* ....50.00 - 75.00

DAISY DOUGLAS:
Columbia 14175-D *Down-Hearted Blues*...............50.00 - 80.00

K.C. DOUGLAS:
Down Town 2004 *Mercury Boogie* ....40.00 - 70.00

DOWN HOME BOYS:
Bluebird 6331 *You Do It*...30.00 - 50.00
Victor V38567 *It's All Gone Now* ....250.00 - 400.00

DOWN HOME TRIO:
Down Town 2017 *Down Town Shuffle*....................30.00 - 50.00

DOWN SOUTH BOYS:
Varsity 6009 *The New Stop And Listen Blues* ....20.00 - 30.00
     6019 *Down On My Bended Knees*......................20.00 - 30.00

LITTLE BUDDY DOYLE:
Vocalion 05111 *Grief Will Kill You* ....150.00 - 200.00
     05246 *Sweet Man Blues*.................................150.00 - 200.00
     05771 *Renewed Love Blues* ....150.00 - 200.00

THE DOZIER BOYS:
Aristocrat 3002 *Big Time Baby*.............................15.00 - 30.00

ARIZONA DRANES:
Okeh 8352 *John Said He Saw A Number* ....50.00 - 75.00
     8353 *It's All Right Now* ....50.00 - 75.00
     8380 *In That Day*..50.00 - 75.00
     8419 *I'm Going Home On The Morning Train* ..50.00 - 80.00
     8438 *I'm Glad My Lord Saved Me* ....50.00 - 80.00
     8600 *I Shall Wear A Crown*...............................50.00 - 80.00
     8646 *Don't You Want To Go?* ....50.00 - 80.00

DRIFTIN' SLIM/SMITH:
Modern 849 *My Little Machine* ....30.00 - 50.00
RPM 370 *Good Morning Baby*................................30.00 - 50.00 *

SLIM DUCKETT & PIG NORWOOD:
Okey 8871 *You Gotta Stand Judgement For Yourself*
     ....150.00 - 200.00
     8899 *When The Saints Go Marching In* ....150.00 - 200.00

SIDEWHEEL SALLIE/SALLY DUFFIE:
Paramount 12519 *King Papa Blues* ....80.00 - 120.00
     12545 *Bunker Hill Blues*...................................80.00 - 120.00
     12581 *Kid Man Blues* ....80.00 - 120.00

BERNICE DUKE:
Broadway 5037 *Sawmill Blues* ....80.00 - 120.00
     5038 *Back Door Blues* ....80.00 - 120.00
     5088 *Arkansas Mill Blues*..................................80.00 - 120.00

DUKE BAYOU & HIS MYSTIC 6:
Apollo 440 *Rub A Little Boogie*.............................20.00 - 30.00

WILLIE DUKES:
Champion 16126 *Snake Hip Twirl* ....100.00 - 200.00
     16745 *Sweet Poplar Bluff Blues* ....300.00 - up
     50055 *Snake Hip Twirl* ....30.00 - 50.00

ANDREW DUNHAM:
Sensation 23 *Hattie Mae*..30.00 - 50.00

FRED DUNN & HIS BARRELHOUSE RHYTHM:
Signature 1026 *Fred's Boogie Woogie* ....10.00 - 15.00
     1027 *The Morning After* ....10.00 - 15.00
     32010 *Railroad Blues* ....10.00 - 15.00

CHAMPION JACK DUPREE; JACK DUPREE & HIS (COUNTRY BLUES) BAND/TRIO/QUARTET:
Alert 421 *Highway 51*..15.00 - 20.00
Apollo 407 *Chittlins And Rice* ....10.00 - 15.00
     413 *Mean Mistreatin' Mama*..............................10.00 - 15.00

     421 *Old Women Blues*...........................8.00 - 12.00
     426 *Deacon's Party* ....8.00 - 12.00
     428 *Just Plain Tired*...............................8.00 - 12.00
Celebrity 2012 *Big Legged Mama* ....10.00 - 15.00
Continental 6064 *I Think You Need A Shot* ....10.00 - 15.00
     6065 *Let's Have a Ball* ....10.00 - 15.00
     6066 *Mean Old Frisco* ....10.00 - 15.00
Derby 783 *Thursday Night Party*...........................- -
Joe Davis 5100 *She Makes Good Jelly* ....10.00 - 15.00
     5101 *Johnson Street Boogie Woogie* ......10.00 - 15.00
     5102 *F. D. R. Blues*..................................10.00 - 15.00
     5103 *County Jail Special* ....10.00 - 15.00
     5104 *Black Wolf* ....10.00 - 15.00
     5105 *Walkin' By Myself* ....10.00 - 15.00
     5106 *Forget It Mama* ....10.00 - 15.00
     5107 *Santa Claus Blues* ....10.00 - 15.00
     5108 *Wet Deck Mama* ....10.00 - 15.00
Lenox 505 *Bus Station Blues* ....- -
Okeh 05656 *Chain Gang Blues* ....15.00 - 20.00
     05713 *Cabbage Greens* ....15.00 - 20.00
     05769 *Gamblin' Man Blues* ....15.00 - 20.00
     05823 *Angola Blues* ....15.00 - 20.00
     06068 *That's All Right* ....15.00 - 20.00
     06104 *Dupree Shake Dance* ....15.00 - 20.00
     06152 *My Cabin Inn* ....15.00 - 20.00
     06197 *Weed Head Woman* ....15.00 - 20.00
     06597 *Heavy Heart Blues* ....15.00 - 20.00
     06642 *Black Cow Blues* ....15.00 - 20.00
Solo 10-014 *Once I Had A Girl* ....20.00 - 30.00
(Other records by this artist, found also or only in 45 RPM format, are listed in the fourth section of this book)

LAVADA DURST (DR. HEPCAT):
Peacock 1509 *Hattie Green* ....100.00 - 200.00
Uptown 201 *Hattie Green*....................................150.00 - 300.00

JIMMY EAGER & HIS TRIO:
Sabre 100 *Please Mr. Doctor*................................20.00 - 30.00 *

AMOS EASTON (& HIS ORCHESTRA):
Specialty 410 *Strange Angel* ....10.00 - 15.00
Vocalion 1694 *M and O Blues*..............................80.00 - 120.00

THE EBONAIRES:
M-G-M 10361 *Come In Mr. Blues* ....- -

THE EBONY MOODS:
Theron 108 *I've Got News For You*.......................30.00 - 50.00

EBONY THREE:
Decca 7503 *Mississippi Moan* ....15.00 - 20.00
     7527 *Swing Low Sweet Chariot* ....15.00 - 20.00

THE ECHOES:
Rockin' 523 *Please Say You're Mine* ....50.00 - 80.00

EDDIE AND OSCAR:
Victor 23324 *Flying Crow Blues* ....500.00 - up

EDDY TEDDY:
Brunswick 7223 *Alcohol Mama*............................150.00 - 200.00

EDDIE EDINBOROUGH:
Columbia 14669-D *Do You Call That A Buddy?* . 150.00 - 200.00

BERNICE EDWARDS (BLACK BOY SHINE & HOWLING SMITH):
Paramount 12620 *Southbound Blues* ....100.00 - 150.00
     12633 *Long Tall Mama*...................................100.00 - 150.00

12653 *Sunshine Blues* ....100.00 - 150.00
12713 *Jack Of All Trades* ....100.00 - 150.00
12741 *Born To Die Blues* ....100.00 - 150.00
12766 *Hard Hustlin' Blues* ....100.00 - 150.00
Vocalion 03036 *Bantam Rooster Blues* ....100.00 - 150.00
03168 *Hot Mattress Stomp* ....100.00 - 150.00

BIG BOY EDWARDS:

Titles issued contemporaneously on Banner, Melotone, Oriole,
   Perfect, Romeo, and Vocalion: *It Was No Dream; Louise*
   ....25.00 -   40.00
Vocalion 02866 *Who Did You Give My Barbecue To?*
   ....30.00 -   40.00
   02932 *Hoodoo Blues*............................30.00 -   40.00
   03079 *Dancing The Blues Away*.................30.00 -   40.00

CARRIE EDWARDS:

Columbia 14652-D *Dirty Mistreater* ....75.00 - 100.00
Okeh 8938 *Hard Time Blues* ....50.00 -   75.00

FLO EDWARDS:

Gennett 6107 *Indian Brown Blues*...............80.00 - 120.00

FRANK EDWARDS:

Okeh 06393 *Terraplane Blues*...................20.00 -   30.00
   06493 *Sweet Man Blues* ....20.00 -   30.00

HONEYBOY EDWARDS:

Artist 102 *Build A Cave* ....30.00 -   50.00

J. D. EDWARDS:

Imperial 5245 *Hobo* ....20.00 -   30.00 *

PIANO KID EDWARDS:

Paramount 13051 *Piano Kid Special*............150.00 - 250.00
   13086 *Hard Luck Gamblin' Man* ....150.00 - 300.00

(BIG BOY) TEDDY EDWARDS; BIG TEDDY BOY EDWARDS:

Bluebird 5628 *Who Did You Give My Barbecue To?*
   ....75.00 - 100.00
   5813 *Love Will Provide For Me* ....75.00 - 100.00
   5826 *Louise*..................................75.00 - 100.00
Decca 7184 *Louisiana* ....75.00 - 100.00
Melotone 12037 *Them Things* ....100.00 - 150.00
   12097 *Lovin' Blues*..........................100.00 - 150.00
Polk 9008 *Lovin' Blues*........................100.00 - 200.00
   9009 *Them Things*............................100.00 - 200.00
Vocalion 02698 *Lovin' Blues* ....150.00 - 200.00

TENDERFOOT EDWARDS:

Paramount 12873 *Seven Sister Blues*............200.00 - 300.00
   12952 *Up On The Hill Blues* ....200.00 - 300.00

WILLIE EGANS:

Mambo 106 *Sad Sad Feeling*.......................7.00 -   10.00 *

W.C. ELKINS & HIS DEXTRA SINGERS:

Q.R.S. 7045 *Climbing Up The Mountain* ....30.00 -   60.00
   7046 *Oh, Mother, Don't You Weep* ....30.00 -   60.00
   7047 *Roll, Roll Chariot*.....................30.00 -   60.00
   7063 *Eloi*...................................30.00 -   60.00
   7066 *Ride On, Moses* ....30.00 -   60.00
   7068 *A Wheel In A Wheel* ....30.00 -   60.00

BIG BOY ELLIS & HIS RHYTHM:

Lenox 521 *Dices Dices*..........................50.00 -   80.00

PERLINE ELLISON:

Decca 7910 *Razor Totin' Mama* ....8.00 -   12.00
   48064 *Razor Totin' Mama* ....8.00 -   12.00

THE EL TONES:

Chief 800 *I Won't Be Your Fool* ....40.00 -   60.00 *

BILLY (THE KID) EMERSON:

Sun 195 *No Teasin' Around*......................50.00 -   80.00 *
   214 *Move Baby Move*...........................30.00 -   50.00 *
219 *Red Hot* ....30.00 -   50.00 *
   233 *Something For Nothing* ....20.00 -   30.00 *
(The above, in 45 RPM format, and other recordings by this artist are
   listed in the fourth section of this book)

JACK ERBY:

Columbia 14570-D *Hot Peter* ....35.00 -   50.00

JOHN ERBY:

Columbia 14151-D *Lonesome Jimmy Blues* ....35.00 -   50.00

LEROY ERVIN:

Gold Star 628 *Rock Island Blues* ....30.00 -   50.00
Swing 415 *Rock Island Blues* ....30.00 -   50.00

(SLEEPY) JOHN ESTES; JOHN ESTES & JAMES RACHEL:

Bluebird 7677 *Diving Duck Blues* ....30.00 -   50.00
   7849 *The Girl I Love, She Got Long Curly Hair* 30.00 -   50.00
   8871 *Little Laura Blues* ....20.00 -   30.00
   8950 *Working Man Blues*.......................20.00 -   30.00
Champion 50001 *Stop That Thing* ....20.00 -   30.00
   50048 *Drop Down Mama*.........................20.00 -   30.00
   50068 *Someday Baby Blues* ....20.00 -   30.00
Decca 7279 *Someday Baby Blues* ....20.00 -   30.00
   7289 *Married Woman Blues* ....20.00 -   30.00
   7325 *Down South Blues* ....15.00 -   20.00
7342 *Vernita Blues* ....15.00 -   20.00
   7354 *Hobo Jungle Blues* ....15.00 -   20.00
   7365 *Need More Blues* ....15.00 -   20.00
   7414 *Government Money* ....15.00 -   20.00
   7442 *Floating Bridge* ....12.00 -   16.00
   7473 *Brownsville Blues* ....15.00 -   20.00
   7491 *Liquor Store Blues* ....15.00 -   20.00
   7516 *Easin' Back To Tennessee* ....15.00 -   20.00
   7561 *Everybody Oughta Make A Change*..........15.00 -   20.00
   7766 *Drop Down*...............................15.00 -   20.00
   7789 *Mailman Blues*...........................15.00 -   20.00
   7814 *Jailhouse Blues* ....15.00 -   20.00
Victor 23318 *Expressman Blues* ....400.00 -   up
   23397 *Stack O'Dollars* ....400.00 -   up
   V38549 *Diving Duck Blues* ....400.00 -   up
   V38582 *Black Mattie Blues* ....400.00 -   up
   V38595 *T-Bone Steak Blues* ....400.00 -   up
   V38614 *Milk Cow Blues* ....400.00 -   up
   V38628 *Poor John Blues* ....400.00 -   up

CHARLOTTE EVANS:

Domino 3453 *I'm Done, Done, Done With You* .....20.00 -   30.00

JOE EVANS:

Titles issued contemporaneously on Oriole, Perfect, and Romeo:
   Boogity Woogity; Down In Black Bottom; Early Some Morning
   Blues; Georgia Rose; Mill Man Blues; New Huntsville Jail; Oh
   You Son Of A Gun; Shook It This Morning Blues 75.00 - 125.00
Gennett 6259 *Little Son Of A Gun* ....150.00 - 300.00

EVANS AND MCCLAIN:

Titles, issued contemporaneously on Banner, Oriole, Perfect, and
   Romeo: *So Sorry Dear; Sourwood Mountain*.... 75.00 - 125.00

DOROTHY EVERETTS:
Columbia 14444-D *Macon Blues* ....50.00 - 80.00

LOTTIE EVERSON (& HER BUDDY):
Champion 15591 *Lost Lover Blues* ....125.00 - 175.00
  15636 *Blue World Blues* ....125.00 - 175.00
  15755 *Wayward Girl Blues* ....125.00 - 175.00

EXCELSIOR (NORFOLK) QUARTETTE:
Black Swan 2060 *Jelly Roll Blues* ....25.00 - 40.00
Gennett 4881 *Kitchen Mechanic Blues* ....20.00 - 30.00
Okeh 4481 *Kitchen Mechanic Blues* ....20.00 - 30.00
  8033 *Roll Them Bones* ....20.00 - 30.00
  8035 *Down By The Old Mill Stream* ....15.00 - 25.00
  8038 *Goodbye, My Coney Island Baby* ....15.00 - 25.00
Paramount 12131 *Coney Island Babe* ....20.00 - 30.00

FAMOUS HOKUM BOYS:
Titles issued contemporaneously on Banner, Homestead, Jewel, Oriole, Perfect, and Romeo: *Ain't Going There No More; Black Cat Rag; Come On In; Come On Mama; Eagle Riding Papa; Guitar Rag; It's All Used Up; Nancy Jane; Papa's Getting Hot; Pat That Bread; Pie-Eating Strut; Pig Meat Strut; Saturday Night Rub; Somebody's Been Using That Thing; That Stuff I Got; That's The Way She Likes It; You Can't Get Enough Of That Stuff; You Do It* ....50.00 - 100.00

Perfect 155 *Do That Thing* ....150.00 - 200.00
  161 *Rollin' Mill* ....150.00 - 200.00

THE FAT MAN:
J.O.B. 103 *You've Got To Stop This Mess* ....50.00 - 80.00

FEATHERS AND FROGS:
Paramount 12812 *How You Get That Way* ....150.00 - 200.00

BEN FERGUSON:
Victor 23297 *Please Don't Holler, Mama* ....400.00 - up

TROY FERGUSON:
Columbia 14483-D *College Blues* ....75.00 - 100.00
  14644-D *You Better Keep It At Home* ....75.00 - 100.00

ALFRED FIELDS:
Okeh 06020 *Quit Your Jivin'* ....10.00 - 15.00
  06129 *Mighty Blue* ....10.00 - 15.00
Vocalion 05018 *In My Prime* ....15.00 - 20.00
  05727 *Step Pepper Stepper* ....10.00 - 20.00

FINE ART(S) TRIO (SIPPIN AT THE PIANO):
Fine Art 203 *Caught In The Web Of Sin* ....10.00 - 15.00
  204 *Here I Go Where The Morning Glories Grow*
....10.00 - 15.00

THE FIVE BREEZES:
Bluebird 8590 *Sweet Louise* ....20.00 - 30.00
  8614 *My Buddy Blues* ....20.00 - 30.00
  8679 *Swingin' The Blues* ....20.00 - 30.00
  8710 *Just A Jitterbug* ....20.00 - 30.00

FIVE JINKS:
Bluebird 6857 *I'm Moaning All Day For You* ....15.00 - 20.00
  6905 *Cushion Foot* ....15.00 - 20.00
  6951 *There Goes My Headache* ....15.00 - 20.00

FIVE ROCQUETTES:
Decca 7848 *Dearie* ....10.00 - 15.00

FIVE SCAMPS:
Columbia (most issues) ....7.00 - 10.00

THE FIVE SHARPS:
JubiLee 5104 *Stormy Weather/Sleepy Cowboy* (Almost legendary among Rhythm & Blues collectors, this record was reportedly sold at auction for over $3,800.00. Only two or three copies are known, despite the seemingly inordinate publicity given this record over the years)...Rare

THE FLAMINGOS:
Parrot 811 *I Really Don't Want To Know* ....100.00 - 200.00 *

NAPOLEON FLETCHER:
Bluebird 5383 *She Showed It All* ....150.00 - 200.00
Sunrise 3464 *She Showed It All* ....150.00 - 250.00

NELLIE FLORENCE:
Columbia 14342-D *Jacksonville Blues* ....80.00 - 130.00

THE FLORIDA KID:
Bluebird 8589 *Hitler Blues* ....10.00 - 15.00
  8625 *Lazy Mule Blues* ....10.00 - 15.00
  8680 *Back Log Blues* ....10.00 - 15.00
  8743 *That's All Right Baby* ....10.00 - 15.00

ELL-ZEE FLOYD:
Brunswick 7181 *Snow Bound And Blues* ....80.00 - 120.00

FLYIN' LINDBURG:
Decca 7066 *No Good Woman Blues* ....50.00 - 75.00

A.C. FOREHAND:
Victor 20547 *Mother's Prayer*...............................75.00 - 100.00

BLIND MAMIE FOREHAND:
Victor 20574 *Honey In The Rock*...........................75.00 - 100.00

FOREST CITY JOE:
Aristocrat 3101 *Memory of Sonny Boy* ....75.00 - 100.00

DESSA FOSTER & HOWLING SMITH:
Melotone 12117 *Tell It To The Judge* ....35.00 - 50.00

EVELYN FOSTER:
Champion 15569 *Park No More Mama Blues* ......150.00 - 200.00
  15590 *Beating Blues* ....150.00 - 250.00

JIM FOSTER:
Champion 15301 *Riverside Blues* ....175.00 - 250.00
  15320 *The Jail House Blues* ....175.00 - 250.00
  15359 *Pork Chop Blues* ....200.00 - 300.00

15397 *Dark Cloudy Blues*..................................175.00 - 250.00
15453 *It Won't Be Long*..................................200.00 - 300.00
15472 *Hesitation Blues*..................................200.00 - 300.00
Silvertone 5127 *Yellow Dog Blues* ....175.00 - 250.00
5131 *Do That Thing*..................................175.00 - 250.00
5172 *I Want To Be Like Jesus In My Heart*......200.00 - 300.00
Superior 330 *Pork Chop Blues* ....200.00 - up
350 *Devil In The Lions Den*......................200.00 - up
369 *Dark Cloudy Blues*..............................200.00 - up

LEROY FOSTER & MUDDY WATERS:
Aristocrat 1234 *Locked Out Boogie* ....75.00 - 100.00

NAT FOSTER:
M-G-M 11445 *Lonely Soldier Blues* ....8.00 - 12.00

RUDY FOSTER:
Paramount 12981 *Corn Trimmer Blues* ....150.00 - 200.00

FOSTER & HARRIS:
Paramount 12709 *The Alley Crap Game* ....200.00 - 300.00

THE FOUR BELLS:
Gem 220 *My Tree* ....30.00 - 60.00

FOUR BLACKAMOORS (See also MABEL ROBINSON):
Decca 7850 *Break It Up Charlie* ....8.00 - 12.00
8512 *Romance In The Dark* ....8.00 - 12.00

THE FOUR BLUEJACKETS:
Mercury 8017 *Baby Baby Please Come Home*..........8.00 - 12.00

THE FOUR BLUES:
De Luxe 1002 *The Things You Want Most Of All* ...10.00 - 15.00
1004 *Blues Can Jump* ....10.00 - 15.00

4 DEEP TONES:
Coral 65061 *Just In Case You Change Your Mind*..20.00 - 30.00
65062 *The Night You Said Goodbye*....................20.00 - 30.00

THE FOUR DOTS:
Dot 1043 *My Dear* ....10.00 - 15.00

THE FOUR FLAMES:
Fidelity 3001 *Tabarin* ....20.00 - 30.00
Specialty 423 *Later* ....20.00 - 30.00

FOUR HARMONY KINGS:
Black Swan 2016 *Ain't It A Shame*....................15.00 - 20.00

THE FOUR JACKS:
Allen 21000 *I Challenge Your Kiss* ....20.00 - 40.00
21001 *Careless Love*..............................20.00 - 40.00

FOUR PODS OF PEPPER:
Brunswick 7103 *Ain't Got No Mama Now*.............30.00 - 50.00

THE FOUR ROCKETS:
Aladdin 3007 *Travelin' Light* ....15.00 - 25.00

FOUR SHADES OF RHYTHM:
Chance 1126 *So There* ....20.00 - 40.00 *
Old Swing-Master 13 *My Blue Walk* ....20.00 - 30.00
33 *Don't Blame Me* ....20.00 - 30.00

THE FOUR SHARPS:
Atlantic 875 *Don't Ask Me Why* ....25.00 - 40.00

THE FOUR SOUTHERNERS:
Decca 7291 *Dan The Back Door Man*..................10.00 - 15.00

FOUR SOUTHERN SINGERS:
Bluebird 8392 *Old Man Harlem*.........................15.00 - 25.00

Victor 24262 *Mammy Lou* ....20.00 - 30.00
24328 *Hamebone Am Sweet* ....20.00 - 30.00

THE FOUR TONES:
A-1 Records 1001 *Do, Do Baby* ....- - -

T. J. FOWLER:
National 9072 *Red Hot Blues* ....8.00 - 12.00
9075 *T J Boogie* ....8.00 - 12.00

JOHN D. FOX:
Gennett 6352 *The Worried Man Blues* ....200.00 - 300.00
Superior 389 *The Worried Man Blues* ....200.00 - up

ELI FRAMER:
Victor 23409 *Framer's Blues* ....400.00 - up

FRANKIE AND CLARA:
Paramount 13010 *Frankie And Clara*..................100.00 - 150.00

BUCK FRANKLIN:
Victor 23310 *Crooked World Blues*......................400.00 - up

EMERY FRANKLIN:
Cava-Tone 251 *Lonesome Day* ....15.00 - 25.00

TINY FRANKLIN:
Gennett 5345 *Shorty George Blues*.......................40.00 - 60.00
5346 *Up The Country Blues*......................40.00 - 60.00
Silvertone 4049 *Houston Blues*..........................40.00 - 60.00
4050 *Shorty George Blues* ....40.00 - 60.00

BEULAH FRAZIER:
Essex 905 *Salt Lake City Blues* ....25.00 - 40.00

CALVIN FRAZIER:
Alben 106 *Sweet Lucy (Drinking Woman)* ....30.00 - 50.00
New Song 120 *I Need Love*...............................30.00 - 50.00
121 *Rock House* ....30.00 - 50.00

FREEZONE:
Paramount 12803 *Indian Squaw Blues* ....150.00 - 250.00

JOE (PAPOOSE) FRITZ:
Modern 750 *Wrong Doing Woman* ....10.00 - 15.00
Peacock 1606 *Real Fine Girl*..............................10.00 - 15.00
1640 *If I Didn't Love You So* ....10.00 - 15.00 *
Sittin' In With 559 *Please Get Off My Mind* ....10.00 - 15.00
574 *I'm So Sorry* ....10.00 - 15.00
584 *Cool Cool Baby Blues* ....10.00 - 15.00
591 *Lady Bear Boogie* ....10.00 - 15.00
602 *Please, My Darling* ....10.00 - 15.00

BLIND BOY FULLER:
Titles issued contemporancously on Banner, Conqueror, Melotone, Oriole, Perfect, Romeo, and Vocalion: *Ain't It A Crying Shame?; Babe, You Got To Do Better; Baby, I Don't Have To Worry; Baby You Gotta Change Your Mind; Big Red Blues; Black And Tan; Boots And Shoes; Careless Love; Cat Man Blues; Death Valley; Evil Hearted Woman; Homesick And Lonesome Blues; Hungry Calf Blues; If You Don't Give Me What I Want; I'm A Rattlesnakin' Daddy, I'm Climbin' On Top Of The Hill, I'm Going To Move; Let Me Squeeze Your Lemon; Log Cabin Blues; Looking For My Woman; Mama Let Me Lay It On You; Mamie; Mistreater, You're Going To Be Sorry; Mojo Hidin' Woman; My Baby Don't Mean Me No Good; My Best Gal Gonna Leave Me; My Brownskin Sugar Plum; New Louise; Louise Blues; New Oh Red, Rag, Mama Rag; Shaggy Like A Bear; She's Funny That*

Way; Somebody's Been Playing With That Thing; Snake Woman Blues; Stealing Bo-Hog; Sweet Honey Hole; Throw You Yas Yas Back In Jail; Tom Cat Blues; Truckin' My Blues Away, Truckin' My Blues Away-No. 2; Untrue Blues; Walking My Troubles Away; When You Gal Picks Up And Leaves; Wires All Down; Worried And Evil Man Blues .... 15.00 - 30.00

Columbia (red label, issues of foregoing titles)
.... 7.00 - 10.00

Conqueror 9038, 9075, 9076, 9157, 9158, 9171,
9202, 9280, 9281, 9310, 9311, 9344, 9373, 9374,
9376, 9377, 9580, 9757, 9758 .... 7.00 - 12.00

Decca 7330 *If You See My Pigmeat* .... 20.00 - 30.00
    7878 *Bulldog Blues* .... 15.00 - 20.00
    7892 *Stingy Mama* .... 15.00 - 20.00
    7899 *Working Man Blues* .... 15.00 - 20.00
    7903 *Put You Back In The Jail* .... 15.00 - 20.00
Okeh 05657 *Thousand Woman Blues* .... 10.00 - 15.00
    05712 *Bye Bye Baby* .... 10.00 - 15.00
    05756 *Lost Lover Blues* .... 10.00 - 15.00
    05785 *Night Rambling Woman* .... 10.00 - 15.00
    05933 *Bus Rider Blues* .... 10.00 - 15.00
    06231 *Good Feeling Blues* .... 10.00 - 20.00
    06437 *Piccolo Rag* .... 10.00 - 20.00
Vocalion 04054 *Ten O'Clock Peeper* .... 15.00 - 20.00
    04106 *Mean and No Good Woman* .... 15.00 - 20.00
    04137 *Meat Shakin' Woman* .... 15.00 - 20.00
    04175 *Painful Hearted Man* .... 15.00 - 20.00
    04237 *Funny Feeling Blues* .... 15.00 - 20.00
    04343 *Shake That Shimmy* .... 15.00 - 20.00
    04391 *Bull Dog Blues* .... 15.00 - 20.00
    04456 *Break Of Day Blues* .... 15.00 - 20.00
    04519 *What's That Smells Like Fish* .... 10.00 - 20.00
    04557 *Flyin' Airplane Blues* .... 10.00 - 15.00
    04603 *She's A Truckin' Little Baby* .... 10.00 - 15.00
    04675 *Blacksnakin' Jiver* .... 15.00 - 20.00
    04732 *Heart Ease Blues* .... 15.00 - 20.00
    04782 *Too Many Women Blues* .... 10.00 - 15.00
    04843 *Steel Hearted Woman* .... 15.00 - 20.00
    04897 *Big House Bound* .... 15.00 - 20.00
    05030 *I Want Some Of Your Pie* .... 8.00 - 12.00
    05083 *Baby Quit Your Low Down Ways* .... 8.00 - 12.00
    05150 *It Doesn't Matter Baby* .... 8.00 - 12.00
    05218 *Jivin' Big Bill Blues* .... 10.00 - 15.00
    05273 *I'm A Stranger Here* .... 10.00 - 15.00
    05324 *Black Bottom Blues* .... 10.00 - 15.00
    05476 *Step It Up And Go* .... 10.00 - 15.00
    05527 *Crooked Woman Blues* .... 10.00 - 15.00
    05540 *Three Ball Blues* .... 10.00 - 15.00
    05575 *Shake It, Baby* .... 8.00 - 12.00

ROCKY FULLER:
Checker 753 *Soon One Morning* .... 80.00 - 120.00

LOWELL FULSON/FULSOM (WITH GUITAR/ ORCHESTRA):
Aladdin 3088 *Double Trouble Blues* .... 8.00 - 12.00
    3104 *Stormin' And Rainin'* .... 8.00 - 12.00
Big Town 1068 *You're Going To Miss Me When I'm Gone*
.... 8.00 - 12.00
    1070 *Miss Katie Lee Blues* .... 8.00 - 12.00
    1071 *Rambling Blues* .... 8.00 - 12.00
    1072 *San Francisco Blues* .... 8.00 - 12.00
    1074 *Trouble Blues* .... 8.00 - 12.00
    1077 *Black Widow Spider Blues* .... 8.00 - 12.00

Colonial 122 *Goodbye, Goodbye* .... 10.00 - 15.00
Down Beat 116, 118, 119, 120, 121 .... 8.00 - 12.00
Down Town 2002 *Three O'Clock Blues* .... 10.00 - 15.00
    2021 *I'm Prison Bound* .... 10.00 - 15.00
Gilt Edge 5041 *Katie Lee Blues* .... 8.00 - 12.00
    5043 *Mercury Boogie* .... 15.00 - 20.00
    5050 *Bad Luck And Trouble* .... 8.00 - 12.00
RPM 305 *Some Old Lonesome Day* .... 8.00 - 12.00
Scotty's 101 *Scotty's Blues* .... 8.00 - 12.00
SwingTime 110, 111, 112, 113, 114, 115, 116, 117,
119, 120, 121, 122, 123, 133, 134, 167, 196, 197,
201, 202, 203, 219, 220, 226, 227, 230, 231, 237,
242, 243, 272, 295, 301, 308, 315, 320, 325, 330,
335, 338 .... 7.00 - 12.00
Trilon 185, 186, 192, 193 .... 7.00 - 12.00

BOB GADDY & HIS ALLEY CATS:
Jackson 2303 *Bicycle Boogie* .... 10.00 - 15.00
Jax 308 *Little Girl's Boogie* .... 10.00 - 15.00*

(LITTLE) BILL GAITHER (LEROY'S BUDDY):
Decca 7141 *Georgia Woman Stomp* .... 10.00 - 15.00
    7625 *I Got Your Water On* .... 8.00 - 12.00
Okeh 05655 *Money Kills Love* .... 10.00 - 15.00
    05714 *Georgia Barrel House* .... 10.00 - 15.00
    05770 *The Life of Leroy Carr* .... 10.00 - 15.00
    05824 *Love Trifling Blues* .... 10.00 - 15.00
    06044 *1941 Blues* .... 10.00 - 15.00
    06092 *Uncle Sam Called The Roll* .... 10.00 - 15.00
    06128 *I Got So Many Women* .... 10.00 - 15.00
    06164 *Moonshine By The Keg* .... 10.00 - 15.00
    06208 *I Can Drink Muddy Water* .... 10.00 - 15.00
    06561 *Worried Life Blues* .... 10.00 - 15.00
    06659 *Please Baby* .... 10.00 - 15.00

(PVT.) CECIL GANT (& HIS TRIO):
Bullet 250, 255, 256, 257, 264, 265, 272, 280, 289,
299, 300, 313, 320 .... 7.00 - 12.00
Decca 48171, 48185, 48190, 48200, 48212,
48231, 48249 .... 7.00 - 12.00
4 Star 1176, 1284, 1339, 1377, 1452, 1526,
1561, 1584, 1606 .... 7.00 - 10.00
Gilt Edge 500 *Cecil Boogie* (cardboard picture record)
.... 50.00 - 80.00
    501, 502, 503, 504, 505, 506, 508, 509, 510, 511,
512, 513, 514, 515, 516, 517, 518, 519, 525, 534 7.00 - 10.00

HATTIE GARLAND:
Black Patti 8005 *Strange Woman's Dream* .... 400.00 - up

CLARENCE ("BON TON") GARLOW (& HIS GUITAR/ ORCHESTRA):
Aladdin 3179 *New Bon Ton Roula* .... 10.00 - 15.00
    3225 *I'm Hurt* .... 10.00 - 15.00*
Feature 1000 *New Bon Ton Roula* .... 20.00 - 30.00
Lyric 100 *Louisiana Blues* .... 20.00 - 30.00
    101 *Wrong Doing Woman* .... 20.00 - 30.00
Macy's 5001 *She's So Fine* .... 20.00 - 30.00
    5002 *Bon Ton Roula* .... 20.00 - 30.00

(Other records by this artist, in 45 RPM format, are listed in the fourth section of this book)

CORA GARNER:
Columbia 14659-D *Wouldn't Stop Doing It* ....40.00 - 60.00

BOB GEDDINS (& HIS CAVALIERS):
Cavatone 5 *Thinkin' And Thinkin'* ....8.00 - 12.00
103 *I'm A Stranger* ....8.00 - 12.00
Trilon 1058 *Irma Jean* ....10.00 - 15.00

GEORGIA BILL:
Okeh 8924 *Georgia Rag* ....200.00 - 300.00
8936 *Stomp Down Rider* ....200.00 - 300.00

THE GEORGIA BROWNS:
Titles issued contemporaneously on Banner, Melotone, Oriole,
Perfect and Romeo: *Decatur Street 81; It Must Have Been Her;
Tampa Strut; Who Stole De Lock?* ....50.00 - 80.00

GEORGIA COTTON PICKERS:
Columbia 14577-D *Diddle-Da-Diddle* ....150.00 - 200.00
14594-D *She Looks So Good* ....150.00 - 200.00

GEORGIA PINE BOY:
Champion 50009 *One In A Hundred* ....30.00 - 50.00
50041 *Look Who's Coming Down The Road* .....30.00 - 50.00
50057 *What's The Matter With You* ....30.00 - 50.00
Decca 7828 *Look Who's Coming Down The Road* ......20.00 - 30.00

GEORGIA SLIM:
Titles issued contemporaneously on Banner, Melotone, Oriole,
Perfect, Romeo: *Evil Hearted Woman; I've Been Mistreated;
New Root Man Blues; Ocean Wide Blues; Separatin' Blues;
Sweet Woman Blues* ....80.00 - 120.00

GEORGIA TOM:
Titles issued contemporaneously on Banner, Jewel, Melotone,
Oriole, Perfect, and Romeo: *Don't Leave Me Here; Don't Mean
To Mistreat You; The Duck's Yas Yas Yas; Mama's Leaving
Town; My Texas Blues; Pig Meat Strut; Six Shooter Blues; You
Got Me In This Mess* ....75.00 - 100.00
Champion 16237 *Been Mistreated Blues* ....250.00 - up
16360 *Don't Leave Me Blues* ....300.00 - up
Decca 7362 *Levee Bound Blues* ....10.00 - 15.00
Gennett 6919 *My Texas Blues* ....150.00 - 200.00
6933 *Suicide Blues* ....150.00 - 200.00
7008 *Pig Meat Blues* ....150.00 - 200.00
7041 *Rollin Mill Stomp* ....150.00 - 200.00
7130 *Six Shooter Blues* ....150.00 - 300.00
7190 *Dark Hour Blues* ....150.00 - 300.00
Supertone 9506 *My Texas Blues* ....100.00 - 150.00
9507 *Pig Meat Blues* ....100.00 - 150.00
9508 *Eagle Ridin' Papa* ....100.00 - 150.00
9512 *Rollin' Mill Stomp* ....100.00 - 150.00
9647 *Second-Hand Woman Blues* ....100.00 - 150.00
Vocalion 1216 *Grievin' Me Blues* ....30.00 - 50.00
1246 *Lonesome Man Blues* ....75.00 - 100.00
1282 *If You Want Me To Love You* ....75.00 - 100.00
1685 *Don't Leave Me Here* ....80.00 - 120.00

GEORGIA TOM & JANE LUCAS:
Champion 16171 *Terrible Operation Blues* ....150.00 - 200.00
16215 *What's That I Smell* ....150.00 - 200.00
16289 *Double Trouble Blues* ....150.00 - 200.00
50015 *Terrible Operation Blues* ....40.00 - 60.00
50042 *What's That I Smell* ....40.00 - 60.00
Decca 7259 *Terrible Operation Blues* ....20.00 - 30.00

GEORGIA TOM & HANNAH MAY:
Titles, issued contemporaneously on Oriole (8033, 8034, 8041),
Perfect (169, 170, 171), and Romeo (5033, 5034, 5041): *Come On
Mama; It's Been So Long; Rent Man Blues; Terrible Operation
Blues; What's That I Smell* .... 50.00 - 100.00
Same Titles on Banner, Melotone; and on Oriole Perfect, Romeo
(different numbers than above): .... 50.00 - 100.00

GEORGIA TOM & TAMPA RED (AND FRANKIE JAXON) (THE BLACK HILL BILLIES):
Vocalion 1246 *Long Ago Blues* .... 75.00 - 100.00
1286 *Pat That Bread* .... 100.00 - 150.00
1450 *Kunjine Baby* .... 150.00 - 200.00

CLIFFORD GIBSON:
Bluebird 5110 *Jive Me Blues* .... 100.00 - 150.00
Paramount 12866 *Tired Of Being Mistreated* .... 200.00 - 300.00
12923 *Stop Your Rambling* .... 200.00 - 300.00
Q.R.S. 7079 *Tired Of Being Mistreated* .... 200.00 - 300.00
7082 *No No Blues* .... 200.00 - 300.00
7083 *Stop Your Rambling* .... 200.00 - 300.00
7087 *Whiskey Moan Blues* .... 200.00 - 300.00
7090 *Morgan Street Blues* .... 200.00 - 350.00
Sunrise 3193 *Jive Me Blues* .... 100.00 - 200.00
Victor 23255 *Old Timer Rider* .... 250.00 - up
23290 *Railroad Man Blues* .... 300.00 - up
V38562 *Ice And Snow Blues* .... 200.00 - 300.00
V38572 *Don't Put That Thing On Me* .... 200.00 - 300.00
V38577 *Levee Camp Moan* .... 200.00 - 300.00
V38590 *Bad Luck Dice* .... 200.00 - 300.00
V38612 *Society Blues* .... 200.00 - 300.00

BILL/JAZZ GILLUM (& HIS JAZZ BOYS):
Bluebird 5565 *Early In The Morning* .... 20.00 - 30.00
6409 *Jockey Blues* .... 10.00 - 15.00
6445 *Sarah Jane* .... 10.00 - 15.00
Bluebird 7253, 7341, 7524, 7563, 7615, 7718,
7769, 7821 .... 8.00 - 12.00
7986, 8027, 8016, 8189, 8221, 8257, 8287, 8505,
8529, 8739, 8778, 8816, 8846, 8872 .... 8.00 - 12.00
8943, 8975, 9004, 9034, 9042, 34-0707,
34-0709, 34-0730, 34-0741, 34-0747 .... 7.00 - 10.00
RCA Victor (most issues) .... 7.00 - 10.00
(For other recordings by this artist in 45 RPM format, see the fourth
section of this book)

BOYD GILMORE:
Modern 860 *Ramblin' On My Mind* .... 15.00 - 20.00 *
872 *Take A Little Walk With Me* .... 15.00 - 20.00 *

GENE GILMORE:
Decca 7671 *Brown Skin Woman* .... 10.00 - 15.00
7763 *The Natchez Fire* .... 15.00 - 20.00
7773 *She Got Something There* .... 15.00 - 20.00

THE GIRL FRIEND:
Varsity 6045 *Good And Hot* .... 20.00 - 30.00

GITFIDDLE JIM:
Victor 23268 *Paddlin' Blues* .... 400.00 - up

RUBY GLAZE & HOT SHOT WILLIE:
Bluebird 5362 *Rollin' Mama Blues* .... 100.00 - 150.00
5391 *Lonesome Day Blues* .... 100.00 - 150.00
6007 *Rollin' Mama Blues* .... 50.00 - 75.00
Sunrise 3443 *Rollin' Mama Blues* .... 150.00 - 300.00
Victor 23328 *Rollin' Mama Blues* .... 500.00 - up
23353 *Lonesome Day Blues* .... 500.00 - up

EMERY GLEN:

Columbia 14283-D *Two Ways To Texas* ....75.00 - 100.00
    14472-D *Back Door Blues*.................................75.00 - 100.00

LILLIAN GLINN:

Columbia 14275-D *Doggin' Me Blues* ....75.00 - 100.00
    14300-D *Come Home Daddy*...........................75.00 - 100.00
    14315-D *Shake It Down*..................................75.00 - 100.00
    14330-D *Best Friend Blues* ....75.00 - 100.00
    14360-D *Lost Letter Blues* ....75.00 - 100.00
    14421-D *Atlanta Blues* ....80.00 - 120.00
    14433-D *Black Man Blues* ....80.00 - 120.00
    14493-D *Don't Leave Me Daddy* ....80.00 - 120.00
    14519-D *Shreveport Blues* ....100.00 - 150.00
    14559-D *I Love That Thing* ....100.00 - 150.00
    14617-D *Cannon Ball Blues*.........................100.00 - 150.00

MAE GLOVER (AND JAMES PARKER):

Champion 16238 *My Man Blues* ....100.00 - 150.00
    16244 *Two Timin' Mama*.................................100.00 - 150.00
    16268 *Hoboken Prison Blues* ....100.00 - 150.00

    16351 *Grasshopper Papa* ....150.00 - 200.00
    16408 *North Wind Blues*................................150.00 - 200.00
Gennett 6948 *Pig Meat Mama*.............................150.00 - 250.00
    6964 *Shake It Daddy*......................................150.00 - 250.00

CRY BABY GODFREY:

Okeh 8064 *Sweet Baby, Goodbye!* ....50.00 - 75.00

GOLDEN LEAF QUARTET/QUARTETTE:

Brunswick 7032 *Alabama Camp Meetin'*................50.00 - 75.00
    7050 *I Wouldn't Mind Dying* ....25.00 - 40.00
    7150 *Central Georgia Blues*...............................75.00 - 100.00
    7169 *Let Me Ride*...75.00 - 100.00
    7176 *Shake My Righteous Hand*..........................30.00 - 50.00
    7221 *I Sing Because I'm Happy* ....30.00 - 50.00
    7228 *Let God Use You*..30.00 - 50.00

GOLDRUSH:

Jaxyson 6 *All My Money Is Gone* ....20.00 - 30.00

FANNIE MAE GOOSBY:

Brunswick 7029 *Dirty Moaner Blues* ....75.00 - 100.00
    7030 *Fortune Teller Blues* ....75.00 - 100.00
Okeh 8079 *Grievous Blues* ....30.00 - 50.00
    8095 *I've Got the Blues, That's All* ....25.00 - 40.00
    8121 *All Alone Blues* ....25.00 - 40.00
    8128 *Goosby Blues* ....25.00 - 40.00

JAMES/JIMMIE GORDON (See also THE MISSISSIPPI MUDDER):

Bluebird 5661 *Neck Bone Blues* ....75.00 - 100.00
Champion 50075 *Graveyard Blues* ....30.00 - 50.00
Decca 7007 *Bed Springs Blues* ....50.00 - 75.00
    7099 *Bed Springs Blues No. 2* ....30.00 - 50.00

Decca 7230 *She Sells Good Meat* ....15.00 - 20.00
    7250 *I'd Rather Drink Muddy Water* ....15.00 - 20.00
    7264 *Jacksonville* ....15.00 - 20.00
    7268 *Think You Need a Shot* ....15.00 - 20.00
    7282 *Drunken Woman Blues* ....15.00 - 20.00
    7301 *Graveyard Blues* ....10.00 - 15.00
    7322 *Good As I Been To You* ....10.00 - 15.00
    7334 *Drive Me Away Blues* ....10.00 - 15.00
Decca (most higher numbers) ....7.00 - 12.00

ROSCOE GORDON:

Chess 1487 *Booted*.. 15.00 - 20.00 *
Duke 109 *Too Many Women* .... 15.00 - 20.00 *
Flip 227 *Weeping Blues* .... 40.00 - 60.00 *
RPM 322 *Roscoe's Boogie* .... 15.00 - 20.00
    324 *Ouch, Pretty Baby*................................... 15.00 - 20.00 *
    336 *Dime A Dozen* .... 15.00 - 20.00 *
    350 *No More Doggin'* .... 10.00 - 15.00 *
    365 *Two Kinds Of Women* .... 10.00 - 15.00 *
Sun 227 *Weeping Blues* .... 75.00 - 100.00 *
(For other recordings by Roscoe Gordon, in 45 RPM format, see the
    fourth section of this book)

SLIM GORDON:

Vocalion 1743 *Leg Iron Blues* .... 75.00 - 100.00

STOMP GORDON:

Decca 48287 *Fat Mama Blues* .... 8.00 - 12.00 *
    48289 *Oooh Yes!* .... 8.00 - 12.00 *
Mercury 70233 *Sloppy Daddy Blues* .... 7.00 - 10.00 *

GEORGIA GORHAM:

Black Swan 2017 *Broadway Blues* .... 30.00 - 50.00

GOSPEL CAMP MEETING SINGERS:

Vocalion 1283 *Come And Go To That Land* .... 80.00 - 120.00

GOSPEL MINNIE:

Decca 7063 *Let Me Ride* .... 40.00 - 70.00

EMMA GOVER:

Pathe-Actuelle 021006, 021060, 021061 .... 10.00 - 15.00
Perfect 12065, 12073, 12074 .... 10.00 - 15.00

JACK GOWDLOCK:

Victor 23419 *Rollin' Dough Blues* .... 300.00 - up

RUBY GOWDY:

Champion 15569 *Moanful Wailin' Blues* .... 150.00 - 200.00
    15613 *Florida Flood Blues* .... 200.00 - 300.00
    15635 *Breath And Britches Blues* .... 200.00 - 300.00
Gennett 6570 *Moanful Wailin' Blues* .... 250.00 - 400.00
    6708 *Florida Flood Blues* .... 300.00 - 500.00

GRAND CENTRAL RED CAP QUARTET:

Columbia 14621-D *My Little Dixie Home* .... 50.00 - 80.00

(COOT) GRANT AND (KID WESLEY)/(SOCKS/SOX) WILSON:

Titles issued contemporaneously on Banner, Melotone, Oriole,
    Perfect, and Romeo: *Do It Again; Water Trough Blues*
    .... 50.00 - 75.00
Cameo 9015 *Ducks* .... 30.00 - 50.00
Columbia 14637-D *You Can't Do That To Me*..... 100.00 - 150.00
    14649-D *Deceiving Man Blues* .... 100.00 - 150.00
Decca 7500 *Uncle Joe*... 10.00 - 15.00
Lincoln 3044 *Ducks* .... 30.00 - 50.00
Okeh 8944 *Do Your Duty* .... 50.00 - 80.00
Paramount 12272 *Rock, Aunt Dinah, Rock*........... 75.00 - 100.00
    12317 *Come On Coot Do That Thing* .... 100.00 - 150.00

12324 *You Dirty Mistreater*..............................100.00 - 150.00
12337 *Find Me At The Greasy Spoon*..............100.00 - 150.00
12379 *Scoop It*...100.00 - 150.00
12831 *Big Trunk Blues* ....75.00 - 100.00
12833 *Uncle Joe* ....75.00 - 100.00
Pathe-Actuelle 7540 *Mama Didn't Do It*................25.00 - 50.00
Perfect 140 *Mama Didn't Do It* ....25.00 - 50.00
Q.R.S. 7065 *Uncle Joe* ....100.00 - 150.00
7085 *Big Trunk Blues* ....100.00 - 150.00
7092 *Take It Right Back* ....100.00 - 150.00
Romeo 819 *Ducks*..30.00 - 50.00
03121 *Do Your Duty*.....................................25.00 - 40.00

LEE GRAVES:
Mercury 8214, 8222.......................................7.00 - 10.00

(BLIND) ROOSEVELT GRAVES AND (HIS) BROTHER:
Paramount 12820 *Guitar Boogie* ....300.00 - up
12859 *Bustin' The Jug* ....300.00 - up
12891 *Staggerin' Blues*..300.00 - up
12913 *Happy Sunshine* ....300.00 - up
12961 *St. Louis Rambler Blues*........................300.00 - up
12974 *When I Lay My Burdens Down*..............300.00 - up

BETTY GRAY:
Titles issued contemporaneously on Cameo, Lincoln, and Romeo:
Loud And Wrong; Mean Old Bed Bug Blues......15.00 - 20.00

CHRISTINA GRAY:
Okeh 8757 *The Reverend Is My Man* ....75.00 - 100.00

GENEVA GRAY:
Okeh 8449 *Fortune Teller Blues* ....40.00 - 60.00

THE GREAT GATES:
Aladdin 3310 *Jump Jump Jump* ....8.00 - 12.00 *
Selective 103 *Late After Hours* ....10.00 - 20.00
108 *Race-Track Blues* ....10.00 - 20.00

BOY GREEN:
Regis 120 *A and B Blues* ....30.00 - 50.00

L.M./LEE/LEOTHUS GREEN:
Bluebird 7353 *My Best Friend* ....20.00 - 30.00
Decca 7016 *Memphis Fives* ....75.00 - 100.00
7032 *Doctorin' Fool Blues* ....50.00 - 75.00
7062 *Round The World Blues* ....40.00 - 60.00
7346 *The Way I Feel* ....20.00 - 30.00
7368 *Sealskin Black Woman*...........................20.00 - 30.00
7437 *Country Gal Blues* ....20.00 - 30.00
Gennett 6934 *Pork Chop Stomp* ....200.00 - 300.00
Paramount 12865 *Five Minute Blues*....................150.00 - 200.00
Vocalion 1401 *Railroad Blues*............................100.00 - 150.00
1422 *The Way I Feel Blues* ....100.00 - 150.00
1441 *Little Eddie Jones* ....100.00 - 150.00
1467 *Dud-Low Joe*...100.00 - 150.00
1485 *Death Bell Blues* ....100.00 - 150.00
1501 *Bootleggin -My Jelly* ....100.00 - 150.00
1510 *Wash Day And No Soap* ....100.00 - 150.00
1533 *Gambling Man Blues* ....100.00 - 150.00
1562 *Pork Chop Blues* ....100.00 - 150.00
1566 *Train Number 14* ....100.00 - 150.00
1648 *Five Minute Blues* ....100.00 - 150.00

L.C. GREEN:
Dot 1103 *When The Sun Is Shining* ....30.00 - 50.00
1128 *Little School Girl* ....30.00 - 50.00
1147 *Little Machine* ....30.00 - 50.00
Von 42 *Going Down To The River Blues*..............50.00 - 80.00

LIL GREEN:
Atlantic 951 *Every Time* ....10.00 - 15.00 *
Bluebird (most issues).....................................7.00 - 10.00

PORK CHOP GREEN:
Gennett 7116 *She Walks Like A Maltese Cat*........250.00 - 400.00

R. GREEN & TURNER:
J & M Fullbright 123 *Central Avenue Blues* ....30.00 - 50.00

ROSA GREEN:
Oriole 263 *Barrel House Blues*..............................15.00 - 25.00
281 *The Basement Blues* ....20.00 - 30.00

RUDY GREEN (TRIO):
Bullet 260 *Evil Man Blues* ....15.00 - 20.00
261 *No Good Woman Blues* ....15.00 - 20.00
266 *Florida Blues* ....15.00 - 20.00
Chance 1146 *The Letter* ....15.00 - 20.00 *

RUTH GREEN:
Okeh 8140 *Sad And Lonely Blues*..........................30.00 - 50.00

SADIE GREEN:
Oriole 716 *Ain't Much Good In The Best Of Men Now Days*
....15.00 - 20.00
746 *St. Louis Blues*..15.00 - 20.00
771 *Nobody But My Baby Is Getting My Love* .. 15.00 - 20.00
Pathe-Actuelle 7524 *Alley Man (Haul My Ashes)* .. 40.00 - 60.00
Perfect 124 *Don't Wear Your Welcome Out*...........40.00 - 60.00

SLIM GREEN:
Murray 501 *Tricky Woman Blues* ....30.00 - 50.00

GRIFFIN BROTHERS:
Dot 1094 *It'd Surprise You* ....10.00 - 15.00
1095 *I've Got a New Love* ....10.00 - 15.00
1104 *Stormy Night* ....10.00 - 15.00
1108 *Ace in the Hole* ....10.00 - 15.00
1117 *Slow And Mellow* ....10.00 - 15.00
1145 *My Baby's Done Me Wrong*.....................10.00 - 15.00
1152 *Fare Thee Well Pretty Baby*.....................10.00 - 15.00
1171 *Move It On Over* ....10.00 - 15.00

BUDDY GRIFFIN:
1193 *Oh What a Smile Can Do*...........................7.00 - 10.00

FLOYD GRIFFIN:
Supertone 9521 *Ocean Wave Blues* ....125.00 - 175.00
9522 *You Broke My Heart Baby* ....125.00 - 175.00
9523 *Back-Biter Blues* ....125.00 - 175.00
9525 *Easy Papa* ....125.00 - 175.00

MARIE GRIFFIN:
Paramount 13015 *Blue And Disgusted* ....150.00 - 200.00

TOMMY GRIFFIN:
Bluebird 6696 *I'm Gonna Try That Meat*..............25.00 - 40.00
6734 *Young Heifer Blues* ....25.00 - 40.00
6756 *Dream Book Blues* ....25.00 - 40.00
6793 *On My Way Blues*...................................25.00 - 40.00
6834 *Dying Sinner Blues-Part 2* ....25.00 - 40.00
6872 *Mistreatin' Papa* ....25.00 - 40.00
Bluebird 7179 *Hey Hey Blues*..............................15.00 - 20.00
7194 *Young Heifer Blues* ....15.00 - 20.00
Vocalion 1479 *Bell Tolling Blues* ....100.00 - 150.00
1507 *Mistreatment Blues* ....100.00 - 150.00

MARIE GRINTER:
Buddy 8023 *Morning Dove Blues*........................150.00 - 200.00

Gennett 3004 *Morning Dove Blues* ....75.00 - 100.00
    6551 *Road House Blues*.....................................200.00 - 300.00
    6738 *St. Louis Man*......................................250.00 - 400.00
Okeh 8384 *East And West Blues* ....75.00 - 100.00
Supertone 9304 *Road House Blues*....................150.00 - 250.00
    9530 *Charleston Blues*..............................100.00 - 150.00

JIMMY GRISSOM:
Miltone 212 (cartoon label) *I'll Miss You* ....10.00 - 15.00

BLIND ARTHUR GROOM & BRO.:
Paramount 12874 *Telephone To Glory*..................200.00 - 300.00

THE GROOVY FIVE:
Groovy 103 *Wrong Love Blues*................................15.00 - 20.00

THE GROOVY TRIO:
Groovy 101 *Too Late Baby*.....................................15.00 - 20.00

HELEN GROSS:
Ajax 17036 *Haunted House Blues*..........................30.00 - 50.00
    17037 *Hard Luck Blues* ....30.00 - 50.00
    17042 *I Wanna Jazz Some More* ....30.00 - 50.00
    17046 *Rockin' Chair Blues*.................................30.00 - 50.00
    17049 *What'll I Do?* ....30.00 - 50.00
    17050 *Strange Man*..30.00 - 50.00
    17051 *My Man Ain't Yo' Man* ....30.00 - 50.00
    17060 *Ticket Agent, Ease Your Window Down*..30.00 - 50.00
    17062 *Chicago Monkey Man Blues*....................35.00 - 50.00
    17071 *Neglected Blues* ....35.00 - 50.00
    17077 *If You Can't Ride Slow And Easy* ....35.00 - 50.00
    17082 *Conjure Man Blues* ....35.00 - 50.00
    17086 *Bitter Feelin' Blues* ....35.00 - 50.00
    17090 *Last Journey Blues*....................................35.00 - 50.00
    17133 *Workin' Woman's Blues* ....40.00 - 70.00

CREOLE GEORGE GUESNON:
Bluebird 6706 *Goodbye Good Luck To You*............25.00 - 40.00
Decca 7740 *Iberville And Franklin* ....10.00 - 15.00
    7792 *Black Woman Blues* ....10.00 - 15.00

GUITAR GABLE:
Excello 2082 *Life Problem* ....10.00 - 15.00 *
    2094 *Irene* ....7.00 - 10.00 *
    2140 *Have Mercy On Me* ....8.00 - 12.00 *

GUITAR RED:
Excello 2085 *Chili Pot*.. 7.00 - 10.00 *

GUITAR SLIM: (See also: EDDIE JONES)
Titles issued contemporaneously on Banner, Melotone, Oriole,
    Perfect, and Romeo: *Ain't It A Shame?, Katie May-Katie May*
    ....50.00 - 100.00
Imperial 5278 *Cryin' In the Mornin'* ....8.00 - 12.00 *
    5310 *Standin' At The Station* ....8.00 - 12.00 *
Specialty 482, 490, 527, 536, 542, 551, 557, 569 .....7.00 - 10.00 *

GULF COAST QUARTET:
Columbia 14012-D *Alabama Blues* ....20.00 - 30.00

ARTHUR GUNTER:
Excello 2047 *Baby Let's Play House* ....10.00 - 15.00 *
    2053 *She's Mine All Mine* ....7.00 - 10.00 *
    2058 *No Happy Home* ....10.00 - 15.00 *
    2073 *Trouble With My Baby* ....10.00 - 15.00 *
    2084 *Hear My Plea Baby* ....10.00 - 15.00 *
    2125 *Baby Can't You See* ....5.00 - 10.00 *
(Subsequent issues, usually/only found in 45 RPM format, are listed
    in the fourth section of this book)

ELDER J.J. HADLEY:
Paramount 12799 *Prayer Of Death* .... 600.00 - up

JAMES HALL:
Vocalion 04231 *My Jivin' Woman*......................... 15.00 - 20.00
    04316 *Street Walkin' Woman* .... 15.00 - 20.00

HALLELUJAH JOE (& CONGREGATION):
Decca 7047 *If I Be Lifted Up* .... 30.00 - 50.00
    7118 *The Great Love* .... 30.00 - 50.00
    7302 *Twenty Minutes In Hell* .... 15.00 - 30.00
    7802 *Highway 61* .... 15.00 - 30.00

HAM GRAVY:
Conqueror 9168 *Who Pumped the Wind in My Doughnut*
.... 10.00 - 15.00
Vocalion 03275 *Mama Don't Allow-No.1* .... 15.00 - 20.00
    03375 *Mama Don't Allow No. 2* .... 15.00 - 20.00

"BEANS" HAMBONE & EL MORROW:
Victor 23280 *Beans*... 300.00 - up

GEORGE HAMILTON:
Champion 15726 *Atlanta Rag*............................... 150.00 - 200.00
    15756 *Givin' It Away* .... 150.00 - 200.00

HAMMIE AND SON:
Decca 7040 *Tennessee Worried Blues* .... 75.00 - 100.00

STICK HORSE HAMMOND:
Gotham 504 *Truck 'em On Down* .... 75.00 - 100.00
J.O.B. 100 *Gambling Man* .... 150.00 - 200.00
    105 *Highway 51* .... 100.00 - 150.00
Royalty 906 *Too Late Baby* .... 80.00 - 120.00

R.T. HANEN:
Victor 23288 *Happy Days Blues*........................... 400.00 - up

GEORGE HANNAH:
Paramount 12786 *The Snitches Blues* .... 150.00 - 200.00
    12788 *Gutter Man Blues*.................................. 150.00 - 200.00
    13024 *Freakish Man Blues* .... 200.00 - 300.00
    13048 *Alley Rat Blues*...................................... 200.00 - 300.00
Vocalion 1047 *Hurry Home Blues*........................ 75.00 - 125.00

LANE HARDIN:
Bluebird 6242 *Hard Time Blues* .... 25.00 - 40.00

BERNARD HARDISON:
Tennessee 111 *Hey Little Girl* .... 10.00 - 15.00

LUCIUS HARDY:
Paramount 12598 *Jelly Bean Man* .... 60.00 - 100.00

MATTIE HARDY:
Conqueror 9203 *Striped Ape Blues*........................ 10.00 - 20.00
Vocalion 04660 *Striped Ape Blues* .... 15.00 - 25.00

TRILBY HARGENS:
Herwin 92012 *Goofer Dust Blues* ....150.00 - 250.00

HARLEM DUDES:
Broadway 5035 *Beedle Um Bum* ....50.00 - 80.00

HARLEM STARS:
E & W 100 *All Right Baby* ....50.00 - 80.00

JOSIE HARLEY:
Paramount 12025 *2 A. M. Blues* ....25.00 - 40.00

HARMONICA FRANK:
Chess 1475 *Swamp Root*.....................................100.00 - 150.00
   1494 *Howlin' Tomcat* ....150.00 - 300.00
Sun 205 *The Great Medical Menagerist* ....150.00 - 200.00 *

HARMONY HOUNDS:
Columbia 14119-D *Done Got De Blues* ....25.00 - 40.00

HARRIS & HARRIS:
Victor 21285 *That Same Cat* ....80.00 - 120.00
   V38594 *Teasing Brown* ....400.00 - up

ALFONCY HARRIS:
Vocalion 02902 *All Alone Blues* ....80.00 - 120.00
   02971 *No Good Guy* ....80.00 - 120.00
   02996 *Absent Freight Train Blues*.....................80.00 - 120.00

BOB HARRIS; LITTLE BOBBY HARRIS:
Derby 770 *Drinkin' Little Woman* ....15.00 - 20.00
   773 *Doggin' Blues* ....15.00 - 20.00
Jackson 2301 *Friendly Advice* ....10.00 - 15.00
Par 1304 *Heavyweight Mama* ....15.00 - 20.00

CLARENCE HARRIS:
Bluebird 8138 *Try My Whiskey Blues* ....25.00 - 40.00

ERLINE (ROCK & ROLL) HARRIS:
De Luxe 3220 *Rock And Roll Blues* ....15.00 - 20.00
Regal 3233 *Jump And Shout* ....15.00 - 20.00

FRED HARRIS & HIS BAND:
New Song 101 *Sad Man Blues* ....10.00 - 20.00

HELEN HARRIS:
Champion 15510 *You Just Can't Keep A Good Woman Down*
   ....100.00 - 150.00
   15529 *Butcher Shop Blues* ....100.00 - 150.00

JAMES HARRIS:
Broadway 5061 *Forty-Four Blues*..........................150.00 - 200.00

JOHN HARRIS:
Victor 23284 *Howling Wolf Blues*.........................400.00 - up

MAE HARRIS:
Domino 361 *Plug Ugly* ....15.00 - 25.00
   362 *'Tain't A Doggone Thing But The Blues* ....15.00 - 25.00
   413 *The Basement Blues* ....20.00 - 30.00

MAGNOLIA HARRIS AND HOWLING SMITH:
Melotone 12077 *Mama's Quittin' And Leavin'*.......75.00 - 100.00
Vocalion 1602 *Mama's Quittin' And Leavin'* ....75.00 - 100.00

MARY HARRIS:
Champion 50045 *Happy New Year Blues* ....30.00 - 50.00
Decca 7804 *No Christmas Blues* ....20.00 - 30.00

MAXINE HARRIS:
Champion 15490 *Satisfied Blues* ....100.00 - 150.00

OTIS HARRIS:
Columbia 14428-D *Waking Blues* ....75.00 - 100.00

PEARL HARRIS:
Olympic 1515 *Four O'Clock Blues* ....30.00 - 50.00

PEPPERMINT HARRIS:
Aladdin 3097 *I Got Loaded* ....10.00 - 15.00 *
   3107 *Have Another Drink And Talk To Me* ....7.00 - 10.00
   3108 *P. H. Blues*...7.00 - 10.00
   3130 *Maggie's Boogie* ....7.00 - 10.00
   3141 *Hey Little Schoolgirl* ....7.00 - 10.00
   3147 *There's a Dead Cat On The Line* ....10.00 - 15.00
   3154 *I Sure Do Miss My Baby* ....7.00 - 10.00
   3177 *Goodbye Blues* ....7.00 - 10.00
   3183 *Wet Rag* ....7.00 - 10.00
   3206 *Three Sheets In The Wind* ....8.00 - 12.00 *
(Above, in 45 RPM format, bring substantially more; see also the
   fourth section of this book)
Cash 1003 *Cadillac Funeral* ....10.00 - 15.00 *
Modern 936 *Black Cat Bone* ....8.00 - 12.00 *
Money 214 *Cadillac Funeral* ....10.00 - 15.00 *
Sittin' In With 543 *Raining In My Heart* ....15.00 - 20.00
   554 *This Is Goodbye Baby* ....15.00 - 20.00
   568 *Texarkana Blues* ....15.00 - 20.00
   576 *Hey Sweet Thing* ....15.00 - 20.00
   578 *Reckless Lover* ....15.00 - 20.00
   587 *I'm Telling You People* ....10.00 - 20.00
   597 *The Blues Pick On Me* ....10.00 - 20.00
   612 *I Always End Up Blue* ....10.00 - 20.00
   623 *I Wake Up Screaming* ....10.00 - 20.00
   638 *I'm Going Crazy Baby* ....10.00 - 20.00
   650 *Got a Big Fine Baby* ....10.00 - 20.00

RODNEY HARRIS:
Imperial 5084 *Blow Your Top* ....10.00 - 15.00

WILLIAM HARRIS:
Gennett 6306 *I'm Leavin' Town* ....400.00 - 800.00
   6661 *Bull Frog Blues* ....400.00 - 800.00
   6677 *Kitchen Range Blues* ....400.00 - 800.00
   6693 *Leavin' Here Blues* ....400.00 - 800.00
   6707 *Kansas City Blues* ....400.00 - 800.00
   6737 *I'm A Roamin' Gambler*.............................500.00 - 1000.00
   6752 *Electric Chair Blues*..................................500.00 - 1000.00
   6904 *Nothin' Right Blues*...................................500.00 - 1000.00

(BLIND) WILLIE HARRIS:
Brunswick 7092 *West Side Blues*...........................80.00 - 120.00
   7149 *Lonesome Midnight Dream*.......................80.00 - 120.00
Vocalion 1273 *Where He Leads Me I Will Follow* ....100.00 - 150.00

WYNONIE HARRIS:
Aladdin 171 *Mr. Blues Jumped the Rabbit* ....10.00 - 15.00
Apollo 360 *Young Man's Blues* ....10.00 - 15.00
   361 *Baby Love* ....10.00 - 15.00
   362 *Wynonie's Blues* ....10.00 - 15.00
   363 *She's Gone With the Wind* ....10.00 - 15.00
   372 *Playful Baby* ....10.00 - 15.00
   378 *Everybody's Boogie* ....10.00 - 15.00
   381 *Young and Wild* ....10.00 - 15.00
   387 *Rebecca's Blues* ....10.00 - 15.00
Bullet 251 *Dig This Boogie* ....30.00 - 50.00
   252 *Drinkin' By Myself* ....30.00 - 50.00
Hamp-Tone 1001 *Good Morning Corrine* ....10.00 - 15.00
King (most issues) ....7.00 - 12.00 *

Philo 103 *Around The Clock* ....10.00 - 15.00
(For other records by Wynone Harris in 45 RPM format, see the
   fourth section of this book*)*

SMOKEY/SMOKY HARRISON:
Paramount 12920 *Hop Head Blues*........................150.00 - 200.00
   12936 *St. Peter's Blues*......................................150.00 - 200.00
   12984 *Mail Coach Blues* ....150.00 - 200.00

HATTIE HART:
Victor 23273 *You Wouldn't, Would You, Papa?* ...400.00 - up
Vocalion 02821 *Coldest Stuff In Town*..................150.00 - 300.00
   02855 *I'm Missing That Thing* ....150.00 - 300.00

HARUM SCARUMS:
Broadway 5097 *I'm The Lonesome One* ....100.00 - 150.00
Crown 3324 *I'm The Lonesome One* ....100.00 - 150.00
   3358 *Where Did You Stay Last Night?* ....100.00 - 150.00
Paramount 13054 *Alabama Scratch* ....200.00 - 300.00
   13104 *Come On In*...200.00 - 300.00

CLEO HARVES WITH LIGHTNING GUITAR:
Okla Tornado 105 *Skinny Woman Boogie*..............15.00 - 20.00

WILLIE HATCHER:
Bluebird 8003 *They're Mean To Me* ....20.00 - 30.00

BERT (SNAKE-ROOT) HATTON:
Vocalion 1101 *Down In Black Bottom* ....75.00 - 100.00

BUDDY BOY HAWKINS:
Paramount 12475 *Number Three Blues* ....100.00 - 150.00
   12489 *Jailhouse Fire Blues* ....100.00 - 150.00
   12539 *Awful Fix Blues*...100.00 - 150.00
   12558 *Yellow Woman Blues* ....100.00 - 150.00

JALACY HAWKINS:
Timely 1004 *Baptize Me In Wine* ....15.00 - 20.00

ROY HAWKINS:
Down Town 2018 *Christmas Blues* ....15.00 - 20.00
   2020 *It's Too Late To Change* ....15.00 - 20.00
   2024 *I Don't Know Why* ....15.00 - 20.00
   2025 *Quarter To One* ....15.00 - 20.00
   2026 *Easy Going Magic* ....15.00 - 20.00
Modern 693 *Strange Land* ....10.00 - 15.00
   705 *It's Too Late To Change* ....10.00 - 15.00
   720 *Mistreatin' Baby* ....10.00 - 15.00
   752 *Where You Been* ....10.00 - 15.00
   765 *Wine Drinkin' Woman* ....10.00 - 15.00
   777 *Just a Poor Boy* ....10.00 - 15.00
   794 *Blues All Around Me* ....10.00 - 15.00
   812 *I'm Never Satisfied* ....10.00 - 15.00
   826 *The Thrill Is Gone* ....10.00 - 15.00
   842 *I Walk Alone* ....10.00 - 15.00
   853 *You're A Free Little Girl* ....8.00 - 12.00 *
   859 *Highway 59* ....8.00 - 12.00 *
   869 *Doin' All Right* ....8.00 - 12.00 *
(See also listings for Roy Hawkins in the fourth section of this book)

WALTER HAWKINS:
Paramount 12802 *Voice Throwin' Blues* ....150.00 - 200.00
   12814 *A Rag Blues*...150.00 - 200.00

BILL HAYES & HIS BAND/ORCHESTRA:
Jade 211 *I'm Just Another Fool*...............................15.00 - 20.00
Sittin' In With 551 *Highway 75* ....15.00 - 20.00
   560 *South Texas Blues* ....15.00 - 20.00

DADDY MOON HAYES & HIS BOYS:
Gennett 6122 *Gang of Brown Skin Women* ....250.00 - 400.00
Champion 15283 *Two Little Tommie Blues*..........200.00 - 300.00

HENRY HAYES & HIS BAND:
Gold Star 633 *Bowlegged Angeline* ....25.00 - 40.00
Swing 414 *Bowlegged Angeline* ....25.00 - 40.00

BLIND ROGER HAYS:
Brunswick 7047 *On My Way To Heaven*.............. 150.00 - 200.00

EDDIE HEAD:
Columbia 14548-D *Down On Me* ....75.00 - 100.00
   14589-D *Within My Mind* ....75.00 - 100.00

JOHNNIE HEAD:
Paramount 12628 *Fare Thee Blues*......................100.00 - 150.00

LUCILLE HEGAMIN:
Okeh 8941 *Totem Pole* ....40.00 - 60.00
(Most of this artist's records have accompaniments of jazz interest,
   and are referenced in the first section of this book)

(BIG) BERTHA HENDERSON:
Chance 1143 *Rock, Daddy, Rock* ....10.00 - 15.00 *
Paramount 12645 *So Sorry Blues* ....150.00 - 200.00
   12655 *Lead Hearted Blues*..................................150.00 - 200.00
   12697 *Leavin' Gal Blues* ....150.00 - 200.00

DUKE HENDERSON:
Apollo 373 *Lottery Blues* ....15.00 - 20.00
   384 *Woman's Blues* ....15.00 - 20.00
   400 *H. D. Blues* ....15.00 - 20.00
Imperial 5109 *Ten Days Of Agony* ....10.00 - 20.00
Modern 632 *Trouble In Mind* ....15.00 - 20.00
Specialty 442 *Lucy Brown* ....10.00 - 15.00 *
United Artists 505 *San Quentin Quail* ....10.00 - 20.00

KATHERINE HENDERSON:
Broadway 5034 *West End Blues* ....150.00 - 200.00
Paramount 12840 *If You Like Me*..........................200.00 - 300.00
Q.R.S. 7024 *West End Blues*...................................150.00 - 200.00
   7032 *Lonesome Lovesick Blues* ....200.00 - 300.00
   7041 *If You Like Me*..200.00 - 300.00
   7054 *What Can You Do Without Me?*..............200.00 - 300.00

LEROY HENDERSON:
Vocalion 02979 *Good Scuffler Blues*......................75.00 - 100.00
   03020 *Deep Sea Diver* ....75.00 - 100.00

ROSA HENDERSON:
Ajax 17021 *When You Walked Out*........................30.00 - 40.00
   17049 *I Can't Get The One I Want*.....................30.00 - 50.00
   17055 *Strut Yo Puddy* ....30.00 - 50.00
   17060 *Hard Hearted Hannah* ....30.00 - 50.00
   17069 *Memphis Bound* ....30.00 - 50.00
   17081 *Twelfth Street Blues* ....30.00 - 50.00
   17116 *It Takes A Two-Time Papa*.......................30.00 - 50.00
Banner 1534 *Everything My Sweetie Does (Pleases Me)*
   ....10.00 - 20.00
Brunswick 2589 *I'm A Good Gal* ....20.00 - 30.00
   2612 *Clearing House Blues* ....20.00 - 30.00
Columbia A-3958 *I Need You*................................10.00 - 15.00
   14130-D *Let's Talk About My Sweetie* ....30.00 - 50.00
   14152-D *He's My Man* ....30.00 - 50.00
   14627-D *Doggone Blues* ....150.00 - 200.00
Edison 51476 *Undertakers Blues*..........................200.00 - 300.00
   51478 *Don't Advertise Your Man* ....250.00 - 400.00

Emerson 10747 *West Indies Blues* ....15.00 - 20.00
    10763 *Four-Flushin' Papa* ....25.00 - 40.00
Marathon 045 (7 inch) *Shake It Down* ....100.00 - 150.00
Pathe-Actuelle 7519 *Git Goin'* ....20.00 - 30.00
    7522 *Slow Up Papa* ....20.00 - 30.00
    7529 *Black Snake Moan* ....50.00 - 75.00
    7534 *I'm Saving It All For You* ....50.00 - 75.00
    7535 *Dyin' Crap Shooters Blues* ....35.00 - 50.00
    7538 *Police Blues* ....35.00 - 50.00
    032021 *Every Day Blues* ....20.00 - 30.00
Perfect 119 *Some Day You'll Come Back To Me* ....20.00 - 30.00
    122 *Hock Shop Blues* ....20.00 - 30.00
    129 *Fortune Teller Blues* ....50.00 - 75.00
    134 *Gay Cattin' Daddy* ....50.00 - 75.00
    135 *Dyin' Crap Shooters Blues* ....35.00 - 50.00
    138 *Police Blues* ....35.00 - 50.00
Regal 9831 *Everything My Sweetie Does (Pleases Me)*
    ....10.00 - 15.00
Victor 19084 *I'm Broke Fooling With You* ....10.00 - 15.00
    19124 *Midnight Blues* ....20.00 - 30.00
    19157 *Struttin' Blues* ....15.00 - 20.00
Vocalion 1011 *Fulton Street Blues* ....200.00 - up
    1021 *Chicago Policeman Blues* ....80.00 - 120.00
    1025 *Daddy, Come Back* ....80.00 - 120.00
    1026 *Hock Shop Blues* ....200.00 - up
    1038 *Rough House Blues* ....80.00 - 120.00
    1177 *Get It Fixed* ....100.00 - 150.00
    14635 *Down South Blues* ....15.00 - 20.00
    14652 *So Long To You And The Blues* ....15.00 - 20.00
    14682 *Every Woman's Blues* ....15.00 - 20.00
    14708 *I Want My Sweet Daddy Now* ....15.00 - 20.00
    14770 *Do Right Blues* ....20.00 - 30.00
    14795 *My Papa Doesn't Two-Time No Time* .....15.00 - 20.00
    14825 *Barbadoes Blues* ....20.00 - 30.00
    14831 *Barrel House Blues* ....15.00 - 25.00
    14832 *Chicago Monkey Man Blues* ....15.00 - 25.00
    14995 *Penitentiary Bound Blues* ....40.00 - 80.00
    15011 *Low Down Daddy* ....50.00 - 75.00
    15044 *Get It Fixed* ....75.00 - 100.00
    15215 *And I Don't Mean If* ....50.00 - 80.00

CURTIS HENRY:
Bluebird 6845 *G-Man Blues* ....25.00 - 40.00
    6888 *The Worried Blues* ....25.00 - 40.00

HOUND HEAD HENRY:
Vocalion 1208 *Freight Train Special* ....150.00 - 200.00
    1209 *Hound Head Blues* ....150.00 - 200.00
    1210 *Laughin' Blues* ....150.00 - 200.00
    1288 *My Silver Dollar Mama* ....150.00 - 200.00

LENA HENRY:
Silvertone 3015 *Sinful Blues* ....15.00 - 20.00
    3017 *Low Down Despondent Blues* ....15.00 - 20.00
    3020 *Freight Train Blues* ....15.00 - 20.00
Vocalion 14873 *Consolation Blues* ....15.00 - 25.00
    14902 *Family Skeleton Blues* ....25.00 - 40.00
    14910 *Ghost Walkin' Blues* ....20.00 - 30.00

ROBERT HENRY:
King 4624 *Miss Anna B* ....40.00 - 70.00 *
    4646 *Old Battle Ax* ....40.00 - 70.00 *

"SLOPPY" HENRY:
Okeh 8178 *Tom Cat Rag* ....100.00 - 150.00
    8305 *Traveling Blues* ....75.00 - 100.00
    8334 *Goose-Pecked Man* ....75.00 - 100.00
    8368 *Foggy Morning Blues* ....75.00 - 100.00
    8630 *Canned Heat Blues* ....150.00 - 200.00
    8683 *Hobo Blues* ....100.00 - 150.00
    8805 *Say I Do It* ....100.00 - 150.00
    8845 *Royal Palm Special Blues* ....100.00 - 150.00

LAURA HENTON:
Brunswick 7129 *I Can Tell The World About This* .80.00 - 120.00
    7144 *Plenty Good Room In My Father's Kingdom*
    ....80.00 - 120.00
Columbia 14388-D *He's Coming Soon* ....75.00 - 100.00

CLARA HERRING:
Gennett 6591 *Beating Blues* ....200.00 - 300.00

EDNA HICKS:
Ajax 17006 *Just Thinkin'* ....40.00 - 60.00
    17008 *Mistreatin' Daddy* ....25.00 - 40.00
    17012 *Kind Lovin' Blues* ....25.00 - 40.00
Brunswick 2463 *Gulf Coast Blues* ....10.00 - 15.00
Columbia 14001-D *No Name Blues* ....15.00 - 20.00
Gennett 5195 *Bleeding Hearted Blues* ....15.00 - 25.00
    5234 *Tin Roof Blues* ....25.00 - 40.00
Paramount 12023 *Hard Luck Blues* ....30.00 - 50.00
    12024 *Mistreatin' Daddy* ....25.00 - 40.00
    12069 *Uncle Sam Blues* ....30.00 - 50.00
    12089 *Cemetery Blues* ....30.00 - 50.00
    12090 *Where Can That Somebody Be?* ....30.00 - 50.00
    12204 *Down On The Levee Blues* ....100.00 - 150.00
Victor 19083 *I'm Goin' Away* ....8.00 - 12.00
Vocalion 14650 *You've Got Everything* ....25.00 - 40.00
    14659 *Wicked Dirty Fives* ....15.00 - 25.00

MINNIE HICKS:
Broadway 5099 *Sweet Rider* ....150.00 - 250.00
Melotone 12549 *Jim Jam Blues* ....100.00 - 150.00

ROBERT HICKS:
Columbia 14231-D *When The Saints Go Marching In*
    ....100.00 - 150.00

ROBERT AND CHARLIE HICKS:
Columbia 14531-D *Darktown Gamblin'* ....150.00 - 200.00

BILLY HIGGINS:
Ajax 17125 *Levee Blues* ....40.00 - 60.00
    17135 *Ain't Trustin' Nobody No More* ....40.00 - 60.00
Regal 9749 *Sweet Mandy* ....10.00 - 15.00

CHUCK HIGGINS & HIS MELLOTONES:
Hollywood 399 *Song Of Love* ....20.00 - 30.00

BERTHA "CHIPPIE" HILL:
Okeh 8273 *Low Land Blues* ....150.00 - 300.00
    8312 *Trouble In Mind* ....100.00 - 150.00
    8339 *Lonesome, All Alone And Blue* ....150.00 - 200.00
    8367 *Panama Limited Blues* ....150.00 - 200.00
    8420 *Pratt City Blues* ....150.00 - 200.00
    8437 *Mess, Katie, Mess* ....150.00 - 200.00
    8453 *Lovesick Blues* ....150.00 - 200.00
    8473 *Do Dirty Blues* ....150.00 - 200.00
Vocalion 1224 *Weary Money Blues* ....100.00 - 150.00
    1248 *Hangman Blues* ....150.00 - 300.00
    1264 *Hard Time Blues* ....100.00 - 150.00
    1406 *Pratt City Blues* ....100.00 - 150.00

CHARLIE HILL:
Gennett 6904 *Papa Charlie Hill Blues* ....500.00 - 1000.00

CHIPPIE HILL (See BERTHA "CHIPPIE" HILL)

HENRY HILL:
Federal 12030 *Wandering Blues* ....15.00 -   20.00
    12037 *Hold Me Baby* ....15.00 -   20.00
    12044 *If You Love Me* ....15.00 -   20.00
    12083 *My Baby's Back Home* ....10.00 -   15.00 *

KING SOLOMON HILL:
Champion 50022 *Tell Me Baby* ....100.00 - 150.00
Crown 3325 *Whoopee Blues*................................100.00 - 150.00
Paramount 13116 *Whoopee Blues* ....250.00 - 400.00
    13125 *My Buddy Blind Papa Lemon* ....250.00 - 500.00
    13129 *The Gone Dead Train* ....250.00 - 400.00

ROBERT HILL:
Bluebird 6680 *It Is So Good* ....30.00 -   50.00
    6706 *Pal, How I Miss You Tonight*....................30.00 -   50.00
    6716 *Just Smilin'* ....30.00 -   50.00
    6741 *Tell Me What's Wrong With You* ....30.00 -   50.00
    6776 *Lumber-Yard Blues*..................................30.00 -   50.00
    6795 *G Blues* ....30.00 -   50.00
    6963 *You Gonna Look Like A Monkey* ....15.00 -   25.00

RAYMOND HILL:
Sun 204 *Bourbon Street Jump* ....150.00 - 200.00 *

SAM HILL FROM LOUISVILLE:
Brunswick 7195 *Near The End*...............................100.00 - 150.00
    7216 *Things 'Bout Coming My Way*.................100.00 - 150.00

SAMMY HILL:
Victor V38588 *Needin' My Woman Blues* ....250.00 - 400.00

OTIS HINTON:
Timely 1003 *Walkin' Down Hill* ....20.00 -   40.00

MATTIE HITE:
Bell 263 *An Awful Moanin' Blues* ....15.00 -   25.00
    273 *Do Right Blues*..15.00 -   25.00
Columbia 14503-D *Texas Twist* ....75.00 - 100.00

NELLIE HITE:
Bell 256 *Oh Daddy Blues* ....15.00 -   20.00

CHA CHA HOGAN:
Talent 810 *My Walking Baby* ....40.00 -   60.00

WALTER HOGAN:
Herwin 93011 *The Duck's Yas Yas* ....150.00 - 250.00

ANDREW HOGG:
Crown 122 *Dark Clouds*.......................................10.00 -   15.00
Decca 7303 *Family Trouble Blues* ....25.00 -   40.00
Exclusive 89 *He Knows How Much We Can Bear*..15.00 -   25.00

JOHN HOGG:
Mercury 8230 *Got A Mean Woman* ....10.00 -   15.00
Octive 705 *Black Snake Blues* ....-   -
    706 *West Texas Blues*...-   -

SMOKEY/SMOKY HOGG:
Bullet 285 *Hard Times*...15.00 -   20.00
Colony 103 *In This World Alone* ....15.00 -   20.00
Fidelity 3007 *Crawdad* ....10.00 -   15.00
Imperial 5106 *Worryin' Blues* ....10.00 -   15.00
    5111 *Great Big Mama* ....10.00 -   15.00
Independent 300 *Misery Blues* ....15.00 -   25.00
Jade 210 *Comin' Out Blues* ....10.00 -   15.00
    212 *I Have Often Wondered* ....10.00 -   15.00
Macy's 5003 *You Gotta Go* ....15.00 -   20.00
    5008 *Change Your Ways* ....15.00 -   20.00
Mercury 8228 *She's Always On My Mind* ....10.00 -   15.00
    8235 *Dirty Mistreater* ....10.00 -   15.00
Modern 532 *Country Gal* ....15.00 -   20.00
    556 *Unemployment Blues* ....15.00 -   20.00
    563 *Anytime Is The Right Time* ....15.00 -   20.00
    574 *Long Tall Mama* ....15.00 -   20.00
    596 *Jivin' Little Woman* ....15.00 -   20.00
    606 *Oh Woman! Oh Woman!* ....15.00 -   20.00
    615 *My Baby's Worryin' Me* ....10.00 -   20.00
    630 *My Christmas Baby* ....10.00 -   15.00
    667 *Who's Heah* ....10.00 -   15.00
    704 *Suitcase Blues* ....10.00 -   15.00
    735 *Everybody's Got A Racket* ....10.00 -   15.00
    758 *You're Gonna Look Like A Monkey* ....10.00 -   15.00
    770 *Classification Blues* ....10.00 -   15.00
    783 *Possum Hunt* ....10.00 -   15.00
    802 *Smokey's In Town* ....10.00 -   15.00
    815 *High Priced Meat* ....10.00 -   15.00
    833 *Country Gal* ....10.00 -   15.00
    844 *Patrol Wagon Blues* ....10.00 -   15.00
    884 *Highway 51* ....8.00 -   12.00 *
    896 *Too Late Old Man* ....8.00 -   12.00 *
    924 *Can't Do Nothin'* ....8.00 -   12.00 *
Ray's 33 *Penitentiary Blues*.................................15.00 -   25.00 *
    35 *I Used To Be Rich* ....15.00 -   25.00
Sittin' In With 555 *You Won't Stay Home* ....10.00 -   15.00
    565 *I Love You Baby* ....10.00 -   15.00
    615 *She's The Girl I Need* ....10.00 -   15.00
    632 *I'm Leaving* ....10.00 -   15.00
Specialty 321 *Nobody Treats Me Right* ....15.00 -   20.00
    334 *Evil Mind Blues* ....15.00 -   20.00
    342 *Goin' Back To Texas* ....10.00 -   15.00
    356 *Low Down Women Blues* ....10.00 -   15.00
    369 *You Better Watch Yourself* ....10.00 -   15.00
Top Hat 1023 *Baby Shake Your Leg*.....................10.00 -   15.00 *
(For other records by Smokey Hogg in 45 RPM format, see the
    fourth section of this book)

**THE HOKUM BOYS (WITH PIANO & GUITAR); THE
HOKUM BOYS AND JANE LUCAS:**
Broadway 5060 *It's All Worn Out* ....100.00 - 150.00
    5078 *Cut That Out* ....75.00 - 100.00
Brunswick 7070 *You Ain't Livin' Right*................100.00 - 150.00
Champion 16081 *Pig Meat Strut* ....200.00 - 300.00
    16237 *Hip Shakin' Strut*.................................250.00 -   up
    16360 *Hokum Stomp* ....300.00 -   up
Okeh 8747 *Gin Mill Blues* ....150.00 - 200.00
    8788 *That's My Business* ....150.00 - 200.00

Paramount 12714 *Selling That Stuff*	125.00	-	175.00
12746 *Pat-A-Foot Blues*	150.00	-	300.00
12777 *Better Cut That Out*	150.00	-	250.00
12778 *Selling That Stuff*	200.00	-	300.00
12796 *It's All Worn Out*	150.00	-	200.00
12811 *Hokum Blues*	150.00	-	200.00
12821 *Ain't Goin' That Way*	150.00	-	250.00
12858 *Went To His Head*	150.00	-	250.00
12882 *I Was Afraid Of That*	200.00	-	300.00
12897 *Let Me Have It*	200.00	-	300.00
12919 *Gambler's Blues-No. 2*	200.00	-	300.00
12935 *The Folks Down Stairs*	200.00	-	300.00
Savoy 502 *Hip Shakin' Strut*	300.00	-	up

Vocalion 03156 *Caught Us Doing It*	15.00	-	25.00
03232 *Keep Your Mind On It*	15.00	-	25.00
03265 *Nancy Jane*	20.00	-	30.00
03386 *Every Man For Himself*	20.00	-	30.00
03406 *Something Good*	20.00	-	30.00
03463 *Georgia Mule*	20.00	-	30.00
03516 *Just Diddling Around*	20.00	-	30.00
03572 *You Got Your Ribs Out Of Pawn*	20.00	-	30.00

ROSA HOLLEY:
| Vocalion 1179 *Lookin' For The Blues* | 125.00 | - | 175.00 |

TONY HOLLINS:
Okeh 06351 *Crawlin' King Snake*	20.00	-	30.00
06523 *Traveling Man Blues*	20.00	-	30.00
06605 *Big Time Woman*	20.00	-	30.00

THE HOLLYWOOD FOUR FLAMES:
| Recorded In Hollywood 164 *I'll Always Be A Fool* | 15.00 | - | 25.00 |
| 165 *Young Girl* | 15.00 | - | 25.00 |

HOLLYWOOD'S FOUR BLAZERS:
| Excelsior 110 *The Big Leg Mama's Fine* | 15.00 | - | 20.00 |

HAPPY HOLMES:
| Victor 21075 *Solid Ground* | 30.00 | - | 50.00 |

SONNY BOY HOLMES:
| Recorded in Hollywood 223 *Walking And Crying Blues* | 25.00 | - | 40.00 |
| 225 *I Got Them Blues* | 25.00 | - | 40.00 |

SPEEDY HOLMES:
| Supertone 9364 *Mister Mary Blues* | 100.00 | - | 150.00 |

WINSTON HOLMES AND CHARLIE TURNER:
| Paramount 12798 *Rounders Lament* | 150.00 | - | 200.00 |
| 12815 *Skinner* | 150.00 | - | 200.00 |

WRIGHT HOLMES:
Gotham 508 *Drove Home Blues*	50.00	-	80.00
511 *Quinsella*	50.00	-	80.00
Miltone 5221 *Alley Special*	75.00	-	100.00

THE HOME WRECKERS:
| Bluebird 5341 *Home Wreckin' Blues* | 150.00 | - | 250.00 |
| Sunrise 3422 *Fence Breakin' Blues* | 200.00 | - | up |

THE HONEY DRIPPER (ROOSEVELT SYKES):
Decca 7160 *She Left Me Cold In Hand*	20.00	-	30.00
7164 *The Honey Dripper*	30.00	-	50.00
7173 *D. B. A. Blues*	20.00	-	30.00
7188 *The Cannon Ball*	30.00	-	50.00
7197 *Sugar Hill Blues*	20.00	-	30.00
7252 *Driving Wheel Blues*	20.00	-	30.00
7324 *Little And Low*	15.00	-	20.00
7352 *Monte Carlo Blues*	15.00	-	20.00
7381 *Love Lease Blues*	15.00	-	20.00
7401 *Hospital, Heaven Or Hell*	15.00	-	20.00
7411 *Night Gown Blues*	15.00	-	20.00
7432 *Drunken Gambler*	15.00	-	20.00
Decca (most subsequent issues)	8.00	-	12.00

EARL HOOKER:
| King 4600 *Race Track* | 15.00 | - | 20.00 * |
| Rockin' 519 *On The Hook* | 10.00 | - | 15.00 |

JOHN LEE HOOKER:
Chart 609 *Wobbling Baby*	8.00	-	12.00 *
614 *Misbelieving Baby*	10.00	-	15.00 *
Chess 1462 *Mad Man Blues*	30.00	-	50.00
1467 *Ramblin' By Myself*	25.00	-	40.00
1482 *Ground Hog Blues*	25.00	-	40.00
1505 *High Priced Woman*	20.00	-	30.00 *
1513 *Walkin' The Boogie*	20.00	-	30.00 *
JVB 30 *Boogie Rambler*	50.00	-	100.00
Modern 627 *Boogie Chillen*	30.00	-	50.00
663 *Hobo Blues*	15.00	-	20.00
688 *Whistlin' And Moanin' Blues*	15.00	-	20.00
714 *Crawling Kingsnake*	15.00	-	20.00
730 *Howlin' Wolf*	15.00	-	20.00
746 *No Friend Around*	15.00	-	20.00
767 *Give Me Your Phone Number*	15.00	-	20.00
790 *One More Time*	15.00	-	20.00
814 *Queen Bee*	15.00	-	20.00
829 *Women In My Life*	15.00	-	20.00
835 *How Can You Do It*	10.00	-	20.00
847 *Turn Over A New Leaf*	10.00	-	20.00
862 *Rock Me Mama*	10.00	-	15.00
876 *It Hurts Me So*	10.00	-	15.00
886 *Key To The Highway*	10.00	-	15.00 *
Modern 897, 901, 908, 916, 923, 931, 935, 942, 948, 958, 966, 978	7.00	-	12.00 *
Regal 3295 *Boogie Chillen No. 2*	20.00	-	30.00
3304 *Notoriety Woman*	20.00	-	30.00
Sensation 21 *Burnin' Hell*	25.00	-	40.00
26 *Canal Street Blues*	20.00	-	30.00
30 *Goin' On Highway #51*	20.00	-	30.00
33 *Decoration Day Blues*	25.00	-	40.00
34 *Miss Eloise*	25.00	-	40.00

(For other recordings by John Lee Hooker, see the fourth section of this book)

LIGHTNIN' HOPKINS:
Aladdin 165 *West Coast Blues*	30.00	-	50.00
167 *Katie Mae Blues*	30.00	-	50.00
168 *Feel So Bad*	30.00	-	50.00
204 *Thinkin' And Worryin'*	30.00	-	50.00
209 *Down Now Baby*	30.00	-	50.00

3005 *Short Haired Woman*	30.00	-	50.00
3015 *Picture On The Wall*	15.00	-	20.00
3028 *Nightmare Blues*	15.00	-	20.00
3035 *Morning Blues*	15.00	-	20.00
3052 *Baby Child*	15.00	-	20.00
3063 *Rollin' Blues*	15.00	-	20.00
3077 *Moonrise Blues*	15.00	-	30.00
3096 *Abilene*	15.00	-	25.00
3117 *Daddy Will Be Home One Day*	15.00	-	20.00
3262 *So Long*	8.00	-	12.00 *
Gold Star 613 *Ida Mae*	40.00	-	60.00
616 *Mercy*	40.00	-	60.00
624 *Appetite Blues*	30.00	-	50.00
634 *Lightning Blues*	20.00	-	30.00
637 *No Mail Blues*	20.00	-	30.00
640 *Tim Moore's Farm*	20.00	-	30.00
641 *Treat Me Kind*	25.00	-	50.00
646 *Death Bells*	25.00	-	50.00
652 *Airplane Blues*	20.00	-	30.00
656 *Unsuccessful Blues*	20.00	-	30.00
662 *Jail House Blues*	30.00	-	50.00
664 *Unkind Blues*	20.00	-	30.00
665 *European Blues*	25.00	-	40.00
666 *Automobile Blues*	20.00	-	30.00
669 *Old Woman Blues*	20.00	-	30.00
671 *Henny Penny Blues*	75.00	-	100.00
673 *Grievance Blues*	25.00	-	50.00
3131 *Short Haired Woman*	20.00	-	30.00
Harlem 2324 *Mad Man's Boogie*	10.00	-	20.00 *
2336 *Untrue*	10.00	-	20.00 *
Jax 315 *No Good Woman*	15.00	-	20.00 *
318 *Automobile*	15.00	-	20.00 *
321 *I'm Begging You*	15.00	-	20.00 *
635 *Coffee Blues*	10.00	-	15.00
642 *Tap Dance Boogie*	10.00	-	15.00
649 *New Worried Life Blues*	10.00	-	15.00
660 *I've Been A Bad Man*	10.00	-	15.00
661 *Down To The River*	10.00	-	15.00
Mercury 8252 *Everybody's Down On Me*	10.00	-	20.00
8274 *Sad News From Korea*	10.00	-	15.00
8293 *Gone With The Wind*	10.00	-	15.00
70081 *Ain't It A Shame*	10.00	-	15.00
70191 *My Mama Told Me*	10.00	-	15.00
Modern 529 *Short Haired Woman*	10.00	-	15.00
543 *Shining Moon*	10.00	-	15.00
552 *What Can It Be*	10.00	-	15.00
568 *Appetite Blues*	10.00	-	15.00
594 *Walking Blues*	10.00	-	15.00
621 *No Mail Blues*	10.00	-	15.00
673 *Tim Moore's Farm*	10.00	-	15.00
RPM 337 *Bad Luck And Trouble*	15.00	-	20.00 *
346 *Jake Head Boogie*	15.00	-	20.00 *
351 *Last Affair*	15.00	-	20.00 *
359 *One Kind Favor*	15.00	-	20.00 *
378 *Another Fool In Town*	10.00	-	20.00 *
388 *Black Cat*	10.00	-	20.00 *
398 *Santa Fe Blues*	10.00	-	15.00 *
Score 4002 *Whiskey Head Woman*	15.00	-	20.00
Sittin' In With 599 *Praying Ground Blues*	15.00	-	20.00
611 *Long Way From Texas*	15.00	-	20.00
621 *New York Boogie*	15.00	-	20.00
635 *Coffee Blues*	15.00	-	20.00
642 *Tap Dance Boogie*	15.00	-	20.00

644 *T Model Blues*	15.00	-	20.00
647 *Bald Headed Woman*	15.00	-	20.00
649 *New Worried Life Blues*	15.00	-	20.00
652 *Papa Bones Boogie*	15.00	-	20.00
658 *Freight Train Blues*	15.00	-	20.00
660 *Mad Blues*	15.00	-	20.00
661 *Down To The River*	15.00	-	20.00
TNT 8002 *Lightning Jump*	25.00	-	40.00 *
8008 *Moanin' Blues*	25.00	-	40.00 *

(See the fourth section of this book for additional recordings by
    Lightnin' Hopkins)

J.D. HORTON:
Bullet 350 *Cadillac Blues*	75.00	-	100.00

SHAKEY/WALTER HORTON:
Chess 1529 *Walter's Boogie*	30.00	-	60.00 *
Cobra 5002 *Need My Baby*	25.00	-	40.00 *

SON HOUSE:
Paramount 12990 *Dry Spell Blues*	400.00	-	800.00
13013 *Preachin' The Blues*	400.00	-	800.00
13042 *My Black Mama*	400.00	-	800.00
13096 *Clarksdale Moan*	500.00	-	1000.00

EMERSON HOUSTON:
Bluebird 5791 *Hard Luck Blues*	75.00	-	100.00

LAWYER HOUSTON:
Atlantic 916 *Dallas Be Bop Blues*	50.00	-	100.00

SOLDIER BOY HOUSTON:
Atlantic 971 *Western Rider Blues*	50.00	-	100.00

JANE HOWARD:
Jewel 5188 *Peepin' Jim Blues*	15.00	-	20.00
Oriole 1059 *Kissin' Mule Blues*	15.00	-	20.00

JOHN HENRY HOWARD:
Gennett 3117 *I've Started For The Kingdom*	25.00	-	40.00
3124 *Black Snake*	25.00	-	40.00

JOHNNY HOWARD:
De Luxe 6044 *Hastings Street Jump*	50.00	-	80.00 *

ROSETTA HOWARD:
Decca 7370, 7392, 7410, 7447, 7459, 7515, 7531, 7551, 7618, 7627, 7640, 7658, 7687, 7801	7.00	-	12.00

WHISTLING BOB HOWE & FRANKIE GRIGGS:
Decca 7085 *The Hottest Stuff In Town*	20.00	-	30.00

PEG LEG HOWELL (& HIS GANG); PEG LEG HOWELL & EDDIE ANTHONY/JIM HILL:
Columbia 14177-D *New Prison Blues*	100.00	-	150.00
14194-D *Coal Man Blues*	100.00	-	150.00
14210-D *New Jelly Roll Blues*	100.00	-	150.00
14238-D *Sadie Lee Blues*	100.00	-	150.00
14270-D *Hobo Blues*	100.00	-	150.00
14298-D *Peg Leg Stomp*	100.00	-	150.00
14320-D *Rock And Gravel Blues*	100.00	-	150.00
14356-D *Fairy Blues*	100.00	-	150.00
14382-D *Turkey Buzzard Blues*	100.00	-	200.00
14426-D *Monkey Man Blues*	100.00	-	200.00
14438-D *Rolling Mill Blues*	100.00	-	200.00
14456-D *Turtle Dove Blues*	100.00	-	200.00
14473-D *Skin Game Blues*	100.00	-	200.00
14535-D *Ball And Chain Blues*	150.00	-	250.00

HOWLIN' WOLF:

Chess 1479 *Moanin' At Midnight*	30.00 -	50.00
1497 *Howlin' Wolf Boogie*	30.00 -	50.00
1510 *Mr. Highway Man*	20.00 -	30.00 *
1515 *Saddle My Pony*	30.00 -	50.00 *
1528 *My Last Affair*	20.00 -	30.00 *
1557 *All Night Boogie*	15.00 -	20.00 *
1566 *No Place To Go*	15.00 -	20.00 *
RPM 333 *Morning At Midnight*	25.00 -	40.00 *
340 *Crying At Daybreak*	20.00 -	30.00 *
347 *My Baby Stole Off*	20.00 -	30.00 *

(See the fourth section of this book for additional Howlin' Wolf recordings in 45 RPM format)

ED "FATS" HUDSON:

Champion 16414 *Fats' Hard Luck Blues*	150.00 -	300.00

HATTIE HUDSON:

Columbia 14279-D *Black Hand Blues*	50.00 -	75.00

LUTHER HUFF:

Trumpet 132 *1951 Blues*	40.00 -	70.00
141 *Bull Dog Blues*	40.00 -	70.00

WILLIE B. HUFF:

Big Town 105 *Operator 209*	15.00 -	20.00

PEE WEE HUGHES & THE DELTA DUO:

De Luxe 3228 *Santa Fe Blues*	30.00 -	50.00

PAPA HARVEY HULL & THE DOWN HOME BOYS/& LONG "CLEVE" REED (See LONG "CLEVE" REED)

HELEN HUMES:

Okeh 8467 *A Worried Woman's Blues*	75.00 -	100.00
8529 *Alligator Blues*	50.00 -	75.00
8545 *If Papa Has Outside Lovin'*	50.00 -	75.00
8674 *Garlic Blues*	50.00 -	75.00
8825 *Race Horse Blues*	50.00 -	75.00

D.A. HUNT:

Sun 183 *Lonesome Ol' Jail*	100.00 -	150.00

HUNTER BROTHERS:

Superior 2836 *Stove Pipe Stomp*	250.00 -	up

ALBERTA HUNTER:

Black Swan 2008 *Bring Back The Joys*	40.00 -	60.00
2019 *Someday Sweetheart*	40.00 -	60.00
Bluebird 8485 *I Won't Let You Down*	15.00 -	20.00
8539 *My Castle's Rockin'*	15.00 -	20.00
Columbia 14450-D *My Particular Man*	75.00 -	100.00
Decca 7633, 7644, 7727	7.00 -	12.00
Okeh 8268 *Your Jelly Roll Is Good*	100.00 -	150.00
8278 *Everybody Does It Now*	100.00 -	150.00
8294 *I'm Hard To Satisfy*	80.00 -	120.00
8315 *Empty Cellar Blues*	100.00 -	150.00
8365 *You For Me, Me For You*	50.00 -	75.00
8383 *Everybody Mess Around*	100.00 -	150.00
8393 *Wasn't It Nice?*	75.00 -	100.00
8409 *Don't Forget To Mess Around*	100.00 -	150.00
Paramount 12001 *Daddy Blues*	40.00 -	60.00
12005 *Down Hearted Blues*	40.00 -	60.00
12006 *Jazzin' Baby Blues*	40.00 -	60.00
12007 *Lonesome Monday Morning Blues*	40.00 -	60.00
12008 *You Can't Have It All*	40.00 -	60.00
12010 *After All These Years*	40.00 -	60.00
12012 *Someday Sweetheart*	30.00 -	50.00
12013 *Aggravatin' Papa*	30.00 -	50.00
12014 *Bring Back The Joys*	30.00 -	50.00
12016 *'Tain't Nobody's Bizness*	25.00 -	40.00
12017 *Chirping The Blues*	25.00 -	40.00
12018 *Bring It With You When You Come*	30.00 -	50.00
12019 *Loveless Love*	30.00 -	50.00
12020 *Vamping Brown*	30.00 -	50.00
12021 *Bleeding Hearted Blues*	30.00 -	50.00
12036 *Michigan Water Blues*	30.00 -	50.00
12043 *Mistreated Blues*	60.00 -	100.00
12049 *Stingaree Blues*	60.00 -	100.00
12065 *Experience Blues*	100.00 -	150.00
12066 *Miss Anna Brown*	100.00 -	150.00
12093 *Old-Fashioned Love*	30.00 -	50.00
Victor 20497 *I'll Forgive You 'Cause I Love You*	30.00 -	50.00
20651 *My Old Daddy's Got A Brand New*	30.00 -	50.00
20771 *Sugar*	60.00 -	100.00
21539 *I'm Going To See My Ma*	80.00 -	120.00

IVORY JOE HUNTER:

M-G-M 10578 *I Almost Lost My Mind*	10.00 -	15.00
10963 *Time Has Passed*	8.00 -	12.00
11459 *If You See My Baby*	8.00 -	12.00
Pacific (Most Issues)	7.00 -	12.00

(See also the fourth section of this book for other recordings by Ivory Joe Hunter)

LOST JOHN HUNTER & THE BLIND BATS:

4 Star 1492 *Cool Down Mama*	15.00 -	20.00
1511 *Boogie For Me Baby*	15.00 -	20.00

LEE HUNTER:

Gold Star 651 *Lee's Boogie*	25.00 -	40.00

PATSY HUNTER:

Vocalion 02799 *Daddy, What You Done To Me*	50.00 -	75.00

SLIM HUNTER:

Superior 2560 *How You Want It Done?*	150.00 -	250.00
2604 *The Banker's Blues*	150.00 -	250.00
Superior 2808 *Mistreatin' Mama*	250.00 -	up
2837 *Big Bill Blues*	250.00 -	up

HUNTER & JENKINS:

Vocalion 02613 *Meat Cuttin' Blues*	30.00 -	50.00

(Note: Above is gold label; blue label, and black and gold label reissues exist.)

02799 *Whippin' The Wolf*	50.00 -	75.00

MISSISSIPPI JOHN HURT:

Okeh 8560 *Nobody's Dirty Business*	150.00 -	200.00
8654 *Stack O' Lee Blues*	150.00 -	200.00
8666 *Blessed Be The Name*	150.00 -	200.00
8692 *Spike Driver Blues*	150.00 -	200.00
8724 *Louis Collins*	150.00 -	200.00
8759 *Avalon Blues*	150.00 -	200.00

J. B. HUTTO:

Chance 1165 *Dim Lights*	40.00 -	70.00 *

HATTIE HYDE:

Victor 23374 *Special Question Blues*	200.00 -	300.00

IMPERIALS:

Great Lakes 1201 *Life Of Ease*	30.00 -	50.00 *
1212 *You'll Never Walk Alone*	50.00 -	100.00
Savoy 1104 *My Darling*	50.00 -	80.00

J. B. & HIS BAYOU BOYS (See J. B. LENORE)

J. B. & HIS HAWKS:
Chance 1155 *Combination Boogie* ....40.00 - 60.00 *
    1160 *Pet Cream Man* ....50.00 - 75.00 *

J. D. & HIS JIVING FIVE:
Elko 1024 *Lonesome Road* ....15.00 - 20.00

JACKIE BOY & LITTLE WALTER:
Sun 174 *Sellin' My Whiskey* (possibly unissued) .... -   -   -

JACK O'DIAMONDS:
Paramount 12786 *The Duck's Yas Yas* ....150.00 - 200.00
    12791 *Smiling Blues* ....150.00 - 200.00

JACKSON BLUE BOYS:
Columbia 14397-D *Sweet Alberta* ....150.00 - 200.00

BESSIE JACKSON:
Titles issued contemporaneously on Banner, Melotone, Oriole,
    Perfect, and Romeo: *Alley Boogie; R.B. Woman Blues; Baking
    Powder Blues; Barbecue Bess; Black Angel Blues; Boogan Ways
    Blues; Changed Way Blues; Down In Boogie Alley; Drinking
    Blues; Forty-Two Hundred Blues; Groceries On The Shelf;
    House Top Blues; I Hate That Train Called The M & O; Jump
    Steady Daddy; Lonesome Midnight Blues; Man Stealer Blues;
    Mean Twister; My Baby Came Back; My Man Is Boogan Me;
    New Muscle Shoals Blues; Pig Iron Sally; Reckless Woman; Red
    Cross Man; Roll And Rattler; Seaboard Blues; Shave 'Em Dry;
    Skin Game Blues; Sloppy Drunk Blues; Stew Meat Blues;
    Superstitious Blues; That's What My Baby Likes; Tired As I Can
    Be; Tricks Ain't Walkin' No More; Troubled Mind; Walkin'
    Blues; You Got To Die Someday* ....40.00 - 70.00

BO WEAVIL JACKSON:
Paramount 12389 *Pistol Blues* ....100.00 - 150.00
    12390 *When The Saints Come Marching Home*....100.00 - 150.00
    12423 *Who Do You Moan?* ....100.00 - 150.00

(PAPA) CHARLIE JACKSON (AND BLIND BLAKE):
Okeh 8954 *Skoodle Um Skoo* ....50.00 - 75.00
    8957 *If I Got What You Want* ....50.00 - 75.00
Paramount 12219 *Papa's Lawdy Lawdy Blues* ....20.00 - 35.00
    12236 *Salty Dog Blues*..20.00 - 35.00
    12259 *The Cat's Got The Measles*....................20.00 - 35.00
    12264 *Coffee Pot Blues* ....20.00 - 35.00
    12281 *Shake That Thing* ....30.00 - 40.00
    12289 *Drop That Sack* ....30.00 - 40.00
    12296 *Take Me Back Blues*................................30.00 - 40.00
    12305 *Mama, Don't You Think I Know?*............30.00 - 40.00
    12320 *Maxwell Street Blues* ....30.00 - 40.00
    12335 *Texas Blues*...30.00 - 50.00
    12348 *Jackson's Blues*......................................30.00 - 50.00
    12358 *Butter And Egg Man Blues* ....30.00 - 50.00
    12366 *The Judge Cliff Davis Blues* ....30.00 - 50.00
    12375 *Up The Way Bound* ....30.00 - 50.00
    12383 *Bad Luck Woman Blues* ....30.00 - 50.00
    12422 *Fat Mouth Blues* ....30.00 - 50.00
    12461 *Coal Man Blues* ....30.00 - 50.00
    12501 *Skoodle Um Skoo* ....30.00 - 50.00
    12553 *Baby Don't You Be So Mean* ....30.00 - 50.00
    12574 *Bright Eyes*...30.00 - 50.00
    12602 *Long Gone Lost John*................................30.00 - 50.00
    12660 *Ash Tray Blues*.......................................40.00 - 60.00
    12675 *I Like To Love My Baby*............................40.00 - 60.00
    12700 *Lexington Kentucky Blues*........................40.00 - 60.00

    12721 *Corn Liquor Blues*..................................40.00 - 60.00
    12736 *Don't Break Down On Me* ....50.00 - 75.00
    12765 *We Can't Buy It No More* ....75.00 - 100.00
    12797 *Tailor Made Lover* ....75.00 - 100.00
    12853 *Forgotten Blues*......................................75.00 - 100.00
    12905 *I'll Be Gone Babe*.................................75.00 - 100.00
    12911 *Papa Charlie And Blind Blake Talk About It*
    ....150.00 - 200.00
    12956 *Self Experience*....................................100.00 - 150.00

DEACON JACKSON:
Herwin 93031 *All I Want Is That Pure Religion*... 150.00 - 200.00

FRANKIE JACKSON:
Okeh 8359 *Hannah Fell In Love With My Piano* ... 75.00 - 100.00

GEORGE JACKSON & BESSIE JONES:
Superior 2555 *I'm Long Gone* ....500.00 -   up

HANDY JACKSON:
Sun 177 *Got My Application Baby* ....150.00 - 300.00

JIM JACKSON:
Victor 21236 *My Monday Woman Blues* ....75.00 - 100.00
    21268 *Bootlegging Blues* ....75.00 - 100.00
    21387 *Old Dog Blue* ....75.00 - 100.00
    21671 *I'm Gonna Move To Louisiana* ....80.00 - 120.00
    V-38003 *This Mornin' She Was Gone*.............100.00 - 150.00
    V-38505 *What A Time* ....100.00 - 150.00
    V-38517 *Traveling Man* ....100.00 - 150.00
    V-38525 *Going 'Round The Mountain* ....100.00 - 150.00
Vocalion 1144 *Jim Jackson's Kansas City Blues-Part 1/2*
    ....40.00 - 60.00
    1145 *Mobile Central Blues* ....75.00 - 100.00
    1146 *He's In The Jailhouse Now* ....75.00 - 100.00
    1155 *Jim Jackson's Kansas City Blues-Part 3/4* 50.00 - 80.00
    1164 *I'm A Bad Bad Man* ....100.00 - 150.00
    1284 *Hey Mama, It's Nice Like That* ....100.00 - 150.00
    1295 *Foot Achin' Blues* ....100.00 - 150.00
    1413 *Ain't You Sorry Mama?* ....100.00 - 150.00
    1428 *Jim Jackson's Jamboree* ....150.00 - 200.00
    1477 *Hesitation Blues* ....150.00 - 200.00

LILLIAN JACKSON:
Supertone 9281 *I'm All Broke Out With The Blues* 75.00 - 100.00
    9287 *Sing That Song With Feeling* ....75.00 - 100.00
    9294 *Cow Cow Blues*......................................75.00 - 100.00

LIL'/LITTLE SON JACKSON:
Gold Star 638 *Roberta Blues* ....20.00 - 30.00
    642 *Ground Hog Blues* ....20.00 - 30.00
    653 *No Money, No Love*..................................20.00 - 30.00
    663 *Cairo Blues* ....20.00 - 30.00
    668 *Gambling Blues*.......................................20.00 - 30.00
Imperial 5100 *Ticket Agent Blues* ....15.00 - 20.00
    5108 *Tough Luck Blues*..................................15.00 - 20.00
    5113 *Rockin' And Rollin'* ....15.00 - 20.00
    5119 *Rocky Road* ....15.00 - 20.00
    5125 *Young Woman Blues* ....15.00 - 20.00
    5131 *Time Changes Things* ....15.00 - 20.00
    5137 *Restless Blues* ....15.00 - 20.00
    5144 *Red Light* ....15.00 - 20.00
    5156 *Everybody's Blues* ....10.00 - 15.00
    5165 *Upstairs Boogie* ....10.00 - 15.00
    5175 *My Little Girl* ....10.00 - 15.00
    5192 *Travelin' Alone* ....8.00 - 12.00
    5204 *Journey Back Home* ....10.00 - 15.00

5218 *Sad Letter Blues*	10.00 - 15.00
5229 *Lonely Blues*	10.00 - 15.00
5237 *All Alone*	10.00 - 15.00
5248 *Movin' To The Country*	10.00 - 15.00
5259 *Little Girl*	10.00 - 15.00
5267 *Doctor, Doctor*	10.00 - 15.00 *
Imperial (subsequent issues)	7.00 - 10.00 *
Modern 840 *Talkin' Boogie*	15.00 - 20.00
Sittin' In With 643 *Gambling Blues*	15.00 - 20.00

(See the fourth section of this book for additional recordings by **LIL' SON JACKSON** in 45 RPM format)

LULU JACKSON:
Vocalion 1193 *Careless Love Blues*	50.00 - 75.00
1206 *After You've Had Your Way*	50.00 - 75.00
1242 *Lost Lover Blues*	50.00 - 75.00
1276 *Little Rosewood Casket*	50.00 - 75.00

MONROE "MOE" JACKSON:
| Mercury 8127 *Move It On Over* | 15.00 - 20.00 |

ODIS JACKSON:
| Fechi 90 *Pretty Baby* | 15.00 - 20.00 |

PORKCHOP JACKSON:
| Supertone 9510 *Lonesome Man Blues* | 150.00 - 300.00 |
| 9516 *Washboard Rub* | 150.00 - 200.00 |

SADIE JACKSON:
| Columbia 14181-D *Original Black Bottom Dance* | 50.00 - 80.00 |

VIOLET JACKSON:
| Gennett 6090 *Blue And All By Myself* | 100.00 - 150.00 |

(BLIND/NEW ORLEANS) WILLIE JACKSON (& BROTHER):
Broadway 5050 *Telephone To Glory*	150.00 - 200.00
Columbia 14136-D *Willie Jackson's Blues*	50.00 - 75.00
14156-D *Bad, Bad Mama*	50.00 - 75.00
14165-D *Who'll Chop Your Suey When I'm Gone*	50.00 - 75.00
14184-D *Numbers On The Brain*	50.00 - 75.00
14218-D *Railroad Man Blues*	50.00 - 75.00
14284-D *Kansas City Blues*	75.00 - 100.00
14432-D *Corn And Bunion Blues*	75.00 - 100.00
Crown 3326 *Telephone To Glory*	75.00 - 100.00
Herwin 92035 *Telephone To Glory*	150.00 - 250.00
93005 *Rock Of Ages*	100.00 - 150.00

WALTER JACOBS (& THE CARTER BROTHERS):
Bluebird 6673 *Rats Been On My Cheese*	25.00 - 40.00
Montgomery Ward 7064 *How Did It Happen*	20.00 - 30.00
Okeh 45436 *The Sheik Waltz*	150.00 - 250.00
45468 *Sheiks Special*	150.00 - 250.00
45482 *Mississippi Low Down*	150.00 - 250.00

ELMER JAMES:
| Trumpet 186 *Gonna Find My Baby* | 20.00 - 30.00 * |

ELMO/ELMORE JAMES (& HIS BROOMDUSTERS):
Checker 777 *Country Boogie*	30.00 - 50.00 *
Flair 1011 *Hawaiian Boogie*	20.00 - 30.00 *
1014 *Make A Little Love*	25.00 - 40.00 *
Meteor 5000 *I Believe*	40.00 - 60.00 *
5003 *Sinful Woman*	40.00 - 60.00 *
Trumpet 146 *Dust My Broom*	30.00 - 50.00

(See the fourth section of this book for additional **ELMORE JAMES** recordings in 45 RPM format)

FRANK JAMES:
Champion 16798 *Mistreated Blues*	300.00 - up
16809 *Frank's Lonesome Blues*	300.00 - up
50017 *Forsaken Blues*	75.00 - 100.00
50018 *Snake Hip Blues*	75.00 - 100.00

JESSE JAMES:
| Decca 7213 *Southern Casey Jones* | 30.00 - 50.00 |
| Sittin' In With 569 *Forgive Me Blues* | 20.00 - 30.00 |

MADELYN JAMES:
| Brunswick 7155 *Stinging Snake Blues* | 150.00 - 200.00 |

PAULINE JAMES:
| Gennett 6147 *You Used To Be Sugar Blues* | 100.00 - 150.00 |

SADIE JAMES:
| Victor 20575 *Mama, Fold Your Hands* | 50.00 - 75.00 |

SKIP JAMES:
Paramount 13065 *Cherry Ball Blues*	600.00 - up
13066 *22-20 Blues*	750.00 - up
13072 *Illinois Blues*	750.00 - up

13085 *How Long "Buck"*	750.00 - up
13088 *Devil Got My Woman*	750.00 - up
13098 *Special Rider Blues*	750.00 - up
13106 *Hard Luck Child*	750.00 - up
13108 *Be Ready When He Comes*	750.00 - up
13111 *Drunken Spree*	750.00 - up

SPRINGBACK JAMES:
Titles issued contemporaneously on Banner, Melotone, Oriole, Perfect, Romeo, and Vocalion: *Hard Driving Mama; Hellish Ways*	50.00 - 80.00
Bluebird 6777 *See For Yourself*	40.00 - 60.00
6824 *New Red Cross Blues*	40.00 - 60.00
7116 *Poor Coal Passer*	35.00 - 50.00
Champion 50076 *Lonesome Love Blues*	75.00 - 100.00
Decca 7091 *Rusty Can Blues*	75.00 - 100.00
7119 *Stingaree Mama Blues*	75.00 - 100.00

SUNNY JAMES:
| Down Town 2010 *Excuse Me Baby* | 40.00 - 60.00 |

ULYSSES JAMES:
| Cava-Tone 250 *Poor Boy* | 15.00 - 20.00 |

W. LAWRENCE JAMES:
| Paramount 12450 *Oh Cap'n* | 40.00 - 60.00 |

JAMMIN' JIM:
| Savoy 1106 *Shake Boogie* | 7.00 - 10.00 |

JAZZBO TOMMY & HIS LOWLANDERS:
| Titles issued contemporaneously on Banner, Melotone, Oriole, Perfect, and Romeo: *Blaze Face Cow; You Don't Mean Me No Good* | 75.00 - 100.00 |

GEORGE JEFFERSON:
Bluebird 7926 *Honey Bee* ....15.00 - 25.00
Champion 15452 *Why Should I Grieve After You've Gone*
....100.00 - 150.00
   15472 *When A Man Is Treated Like A Dog* ......200.00 - 300.00

BLIND LEMON JEFFERSON:
Okeh 8455 *Black Snake Moon* ....150.00 - 200.00
Paramount 12347 *Booster Blues* ....100.00 - 150.00
  12354 *Got The Blues* ....80.00 - 130.00
  12367 *Black Horse Blues* ....100.00 - 150.00
  12373 *Jack O' Diamond Blues* ....100.00 - 150.00
  12394 *Beggin' Back* ....100.00 - 150.00
  12407 *Stocking Feet Blues* ....80.00 - 120.00
  12425 *Wartime Blues* ....150.00 - 200.00
  12443 *Bad Luck Blues* ....150.00 - 200.00
  12454 *Rabbit Foot Blues* ....150.00 - 200.00
  12474 *Match Box Blues* ....150.00 - 200.00
  12487 *Teddy Bear Blues* ....150.00 - 200.00
  12493 *Weary Dog Blues* ....150.00 - 200.00
  12510 *Right Of Way Blues* ....150.00 - 200.00
  12541 *Rambler Blues* ....150.00 - 200.00
  12551 *Chinch Bug Blues* ....150.00 - 200.00
  12578 *Gone Dead On You Blues* ....150.00 - 200.00
  12593 *Lonesome House Blues* ....150.00 - 200.00
  12608 *'Lectric Chair Blues* ....150.00 - 200.00
  12622 *Prison Cell Blues* ....150.00 - 200.00
  12631 *Mean Jumper Blues* ....150.00 - 200.00
  12639 *Lemon's Cannon Ball Moan* ....150.00 - 200.00
  *12650 *Piney Woods Mama Blues* ....150.00 - 200.00
  12666 *Blind Lemon's Penitentiary Blues* ....150.00 - 250.00
  12679 *Lock Step Blues* ....150.00 - 200.00
  12685 *How Long, How Long* ....200.00 - 300.00
  12692 *Happy New Year Blues* ....150.00 - 250.00
  12712 *Maltese Cat Blues* ....150.00 - 250.00
  12728 *Competition Bed Blues* ....150.00 - 250.00
  12739 *Eagle Eyed Mama* ....150.00 - 250.00
  12756 *Tin Cup Blues* ....150.00 - 250.00
  12771 *Oil Well Blues* ....150.00 - 250.00
  12801 *Peach Orchard Mama* ....150.00 - 250.00
  12852 *Long Distance Moan* ....150.00 - 250.00
  12872 *Bed Springs Blues* ....150.00 - 250.00
  12880 *Pneumonia Blues* ....150.00 - 250.00
  **12886 *Hometown Skiffle* ....125.00 - 175.00
  12899 *Mosquito Moan* ....150.00 - 250.00
  12921 *Cat Man Blues* ....200.00 - 300.00
  12933 *The Cheaters Spell* ....300.00 - 500.00
  12946 *Empty House Blues* ....200.00 - 300.00

(*Note: Paramount 12650 is designated "Blind Lemon Jefferson's Birthday Record; and bears a portrait of the artist.)
(**Note: Paramount 12886 is designated "Descriptive Novelty," performed by several artists. Since Blind Lemon Jefferson's name appears first, it is included in his output.)

JELLY BELLY & SLIM SEWARD:
Apollo 412 *Sorry Woman Blues* ....50.00 - 75.00

JENKINS AND JENKINS:
Columbia 14040-D *Hen Pecked Man* ....30.00 - 50.00
  14100-D *Sister, It's Too Bad* ....30.00 - 50.00
Gennett 3335 *Miserable Blues* ....30.00 - 50.00

HAZEKIAH JENKINS:
Columbia 14585-D *The Panic Is On* ....50.00 - 80.00

ROBERT JENKINS:
Parkway 103 *Steelin' Boogie* ....30.00 - 50.00

JIM JAM:
Varsity 6044 *Diamond Ring Blues* ....25.00 - 40.00
  6054 *Window Pane Blues* ....30.00 - 50.00

JOE JOE:
Varsity 6032 *Humming Blues* ....15.00 - 20.00

JIMMY & WALTER:
Sun 180 *Before Long* ....150.00 - 200.00

JOHNSON AND JACKSON:
Champion 15835 *Everybody Likes That Thing* ....75.00 - 100.00

JOHNSON AND SMITH:
Champion 16411 *Brown Skin Shuffle* ....150.00 - 300.00

JOHNSON-NELSON-PORKCHOP:
Okeh 8577 *In The Mornin'* ....75.00 - 100.00

ALEC JOHNSON (& HIS BAND):
Columbia 14378-D *Mysterious Coon* ....200.00 - 300.00
  14416-D *Next Week Sometime* ....200.00 - 300.00
  14446-D *Sundown Blues* ....200.00 - 300.00

BABE JOHNSON:
Silvertone 3562 *Worried 'Bout Him Blues* ....75.00 - 100.00

BESSIE JOHNSON; BESSIE JOHNSON'S SANCTIFIED SINGERS:
Okeh 8725 *No Room At The Hotel* ....50.00 - 75.00
  8765 *The Whole World In His Hand* ....50.00 - 75.00

BIG BILL JOHNSON:
Champion 16081 *Saturday Night Rub* ....150.00 - 250.00
  16172 *That Won't Do* ....150.00 - 250.00
  16327 *The Banker's Blues* ....200.00 - 300.00
  16396 *Big Bill Blues* ....200.00 - 300.00
  16426 *Mr. Conductor Man* ....250.00 - 400.00
  50060 *Big Bill Blues* ....50.00 - 75.00
  50069 *Too Too Train Blues* ....50.00 - 75.00
Gennett 7210 *Skoodle Do Do* ....200.00 - 300.00
  7230 *I Can't Be Satisfied* ....200.00 - 300.00

BILLIKEN/BILLIKIN JOHNSON & FRED ADAMS/ WITH NEAL ROBERTS:
Columbia 14293-D *Sun Beam Blues* ....80.00 - 120.00
  14405-D *Wild Jack Blues* ....80.00 - 120.00

BUD JOHNSON:
Champion 15614 *Kitchen Range Blues* ....300.00 - 500.00
  15675 *Hot Time Blues* ....300.00 - 500.00

BUSTER JOHNSON:
Champion 16718 *Undertaker Blues* ....500.00 - up

CONRAD JOHNSON:
Gold Star 622 *Howling On Dowling* ....10.00 - 20.00

EASY PAPA JOHNSON:
Melotone 12048 *Drinkin' Woman Blues* ....100.00 - 150.00
  12086 *Cotton Seed Blues* ....100.00 - 150.00
Polk 9010 *No Good Woman Blues* ....100.00 - 200.00
  9011 *Drinkin' Woman Blues* ....100.00 - 200.00
Vocalion 02669 *No Good Woman Blues* ....100.00 - 150.00
  02697 *Papa Sweetback Blues* ....100.00 - 150.00

EDDIE JOHNSON & HIS ORCHESTRA:
Colony 101 *Juice Head* ....10.00 - 20.00

Imperial 5120 *Corn Licker Blues* ....10.00 - 20.00
   5126 *Mr. Juice Head* ....10.00 - 20.00

EDITH (NORTH) JOHNSON:
Okeh 8748 *Heart Aching Blues* ....150.00 - 200.00
Paramount 12823 *Honey Dripper Blues*...............150.00 - 250.00
   12864 *Can't Make Another Day*......................150.00 - 250.00
   12915 *Honey Dripper Blues No. 2* ....150.00 - 250.00
   12939 *Eight Hour Woman* ....150.00 - 250.00
   13032 *Whispering To My Man* ....150.00 - 250.00
Q.R.S. 7048 *You Ain't No Good Blues*.................150.00 - 200.00

EDNA JOHNSON:
Gennett 5367 *I'm Drifting From You Blues* ....40.00 - 70.00

ELIZABETH JOHNSON:
Okeh 8593 *Empty Bed Blues* ....150.00 - 200.00
   8789 *Be My Kid Blues* ....100.00 - 150.00

ELNORA JOHNSON:
Black Patti 8033 *Freakish Papa* ....250.00 - up
   8039 *Red Cap Porter Blues* ....250.00 - up

ELVIRA JOHNSON:
Gennett 3337 *Numbers On The Brain* ....75.00 - 100.00
Champion 15126 *Numbers On The Brain* ....75.00 - 100.00
   15127 *How Could I Be Blue* ....75.00 - 100.00

FANNIE JOHNSON:
Cameo 1066 *I'm Savin' It All For You*...................15.00 - 25.00
   1144 *Slow Up Papa* ....15.00 - 25.00
   1158 *Black Snake Blues* ....15.00 - 25.00
Romeo 416 *Back Water Blues* ....15.00 - 25.00
   453 *Dyin' Crap-Shooter's Blues* ....15.00 - 25.00

FRANK JOHNSON:
Herwin 92038 *Trouble 'Bout My Soul*...................150.00 - 250.00

GLADYS JOHNSON:
Variety 5033 *I'm Savin' It All For You* ....15.00 - 20.00
   5048 *Slow Up Papa* ....15.00 - 20.00
   5085 *Black Snake Blues*...................................15.00 - 20.00

HARRY "SLICK" JOHNSON:
Peacock 1560 *My Baby's Coming Home*.................15.00 - 20.00

JAMES "STEADYROLL" JOHNSON:
Okeh 8287 *Newport Blues* ....30.00 - 50.00

JAMES (STUMP) JOHNSON & HIS PIANO (See also STUMP JOHNSON):
Paramount 12842 *The Duck's Yas-Yas-Yas* ....75.00 - 100.00
Q.R.S. 7049 *The Snitchers Blues*.............................50.00 - 80.00
   7050 *My Babe Blues* ....150.00 - 200.00

JELLY ROLL JOHNSON:
Champion 15281 *Free Woman Blues* ....200.00 - 300.00
Silvertone 5121 *Free Woman Blues* ....150.00 - 200.00

JESSE JOHNSON:
Paramount 12829 *I Wish I Had Died in Egyptland*
   ....300.00 - up

JULIA JOHNSON:
Gennett 6519 *Hard Headed Daddy* ....75.00 - 100.00

KI KI JOHNSON:
Q.R.S. 7001 *Lone Grave*......................................150.00 - 200.00
   7003 *Lady, Your Clock Ain't Right*................150.00 - 200.00

LEM JOHNSON:
Cincinnati 3501 *Esskay Blues* ....15.00 - 20.00

M-G-M 11467 *It Takes Money, Honey* ....7.00 - 10.00
   11532 *Eatin' And Sleepin' Blues* ....7.00 - 10.00

LEROY "COUNTRY" JOHNSON:
Freedom 1509 *Loghouse On The Hill*....................15.00 - 20.00
Okeh 6813 *Unlucky Blues* ....8.00 - 12.00

LIL JOHNSON:
Bluebird 6112 *Keep On Knocking* ....15.00 - 20.00
Champion 50002 *Get 'Em From The Peanut Man*.15.00 - 20.00
   50052 *Snake Man Blues*...................................20.00 - 30.00
Vocalion 1299 *Never Let Your Left Hand Know* ..100.00 - 150.00
   1410 *House Rend Scuffle* ....100.00 - 150.00
   03199 *Press My Button* ....10.00 - 15.00
   03241 *Get 'Em From The Peanut Man (The New Hot Nuts)*
   ....10.00 - 15.00
   03251 *My Stove's In Good Condition*...............15.00 - 20.00
   03266 *Two Timin' Man*.....................................10.00 - 15.00
   03299 *Murder In The First Degree* ....15.00 - 20.00
   03312 *Hottest Gal In Town*...............................15.00 - 20.00
   03331 *Ramblin' Man Blues* ....15.00 - 20.00
   03374 *Black And Evil Blues*..............................15.00 - 20.00
   03397 *Crazy About My Rider* ....15.00 - 20.00
   03428 *New Shave 'Em Dry* ....15.00 - 20.00
   03455 *River Hip Papa* ....15.00 - 20.00
   03483 *You Can't Bet On Love* ....15.00 - 20.00
   03530 *I'm A Sales Lady* ....15.00 - 20.00
   03562 *Meat Balls* ....15.00 - 20.00
   03600 *Goofer Dust Swing* ....15.00 - 20.00
   03604 *Joe Louis Fight* ....15.00 - 20.00
   03604 *Winner Joe (The Knock Out King)*..........15.00 - 20.00
   03666 *Mellow Stuff* ....15.00 - 20.00
   03710 *Broken-Hearted Blues*............................15.00 - 20.00
   03941 *When Your Troubles Are Like Mine*........10.00 - 15.00
   03978 *Ain't That A Shame?* ....10.00 - 15.00
   04067 *Snake In The Grass* ....10.00 - 15.00
Titles issued contemporaneously on Banner, Melotone, Oriole,
   Perfect, and Romeo: *Get 'Em From The Peanut Man; If You Can
   Dish It; I'm Bettin' On You; Press My Button; Take It Easy,
   Greasy; That Bonus Done Gone Through* ....8.00 - 15.00

LONNIE JOHNSON (& BLIND WILLIE DUNN)/& CLARENCE & SPENCER WILLIAMS:
Aladdin 197 *How Could You* ....15.00 - 20.00
   3029 *Blues For Lonnie* ....15.00 - 20.00
   3047 *You Know I Do* ....15.00 - 20.00
Bluebird 8322 *She's My Mary* ....15.00 - 20.00
   8338 *The Loveless Blues* ....10.00 - 15.00
   8363 *Why Women Go Wrong* ....10.00 - 15.00
   8387 *Trust Your Husband* ....10.00 - 15.00
   8530 *Don't Be No Fool* ....10.00 - 15.00
   8564 *I'm Just Dumb* ....10.00 - 15.00
   8684 *She Ain't Right* ....10.00 - 15.00
   8748 *Lazy Woman Blues* ....10.00 - 15.00
   8779 *Chicago Blues* ....10.00 - 15.00
   8804 *Crowing Rooster* ....10.00 - 15.00
   8980 *The Last Call* ....10.00 - 15.00
   9006 *He's A Jelly-Roll Baker* ....10.00 - 15.00
   9022 *Heart Of Iron* ....10.00 - 15.00
   34-0708 *Rambler's Blues* ....8.00 - 12.00
   34-0714 *Lonesome Road* ....8.00 - 12.00
   34-0732 *Some Day Baby* ....8.00 - 12.00
   34-0742 *My Love Is Down* ....8.00 - 12.00
Columbia 14667-D *Home Wreckers Blues* ....50.00 - 75.00
   14674-D *Unselfish Love* ....50.00 - 75.00

Decca 7388 *Hard Times Ain't Gone Nowhere*	10.00	-	15.00
7397 *Flood Water Blues*	10.00	-	15.00
7427 *Swing Out Rhythm*	8.00	-	12.00
7445 *Man Killing Broad*	10.00	-	15.00
7461 *New Falling Rain Blues*	10.00	-	15.00
7487 *Friendless And Blue*	10.00	-	15.00
7509 *Mr. Johnson Swing*	10.00	-	15.00
7537 *Blue Ghost Blues*	10.00	-	15.00
48078 *It Ain't What You Usta Be*	8.00	-	12.00
Disc 5060 *Tell Me Why*	10.00	-	15.00
5061 *My Last Love*	10.00	-	15.00
5062 *Keep What You Got*	10.00	-	15.00
5063 *Rocks In My Bed*	10.00	-	15.00
5064 *Drifting Along Blues*	10.00	-	15.00
5065 *Blues In My Soul*	10.00	-	15.00
King (most issues)	7.00	-	12.00 *
Okeh 8253 *Mr Johnson's Blues*	50.00	-	80.00
8282 *Love Story Blues*	50.00	-	80.00
8291 *Bed Of Sand*	50.00	-	80.00
8309 *Lonesome Jail Blues*	50.00	-	80.00
8340 *A Good Happy Home*	40.00	-	60.00
8358 *Good Old Wagon*	40.00	-	60.00
8376 *Baby Please Tell Me*	40.00	-	60.00
8391 *Oh! Doctor, The Blues*	40.00	-	60.00
8411 *Lonnie's Got The Blues*	40.00	-	60.00
8417 *Johnson Trio Stomp*	40.00	-	60.00
8435 *Ball And Chain Blues*	40.00	-	60.00
8451 *You Drove A Good Man Away*	40.00	-	60.00
8466 *South Bound Water*	40.00	-	60.00
8484 *Treat 'Em Right*	40.00	-	60.00
8497 *Roaming Rambler Blues*	35.00	-	50.00
8505 *Fickle Mamma Blues*	35.00	-	50.00
8512 *St. Louis Cyclone Blues*	35.00	-	50.00
8524 *Tin Can Alley Blues*	35.00	-	50.00
8537 *Kansas City Blues*	35.00	-	50.00
8557 *Life Saver Blues*	35.00	-	50.00
8558 *Playing With The Strings*	50.00	-	75.00
8574 *Crowing Rooster Blues*	35.00	-	50.00
8575 *Blues In G*	50.00	-	75.00
8586 *Bed Bug Blues No. 2*	35.00	-	50.00
8601 *Wrong Woman Blues*	35.00	-	50.00
8618 *Broken Levee Blues*	35.00	-	50.00
8635 *Careless Love*	35.00	-	50.00
8637 *Two Tone Stomp*	40.00	-	60.00
8664 *It Feels So Good Part 1/2*	15.00	-	20.00
8691 *Death Is On Your Track*	35.00	-	50.00
8695 *Bull Frog Moan*	50.00	-	75.00
8697 *It Feels So Good-Part 3/4*	15.00	-	30.00
8709 *Mr. Johnson's Blues-No. 2*	35.00	-	50.00
8722 *From Now On Make Your Whoopee At Home*			
	35.00	-	50.00
8754 *Sundown Blues*	40.00	-	60.00
8762 *Wipe It Off*	60.00	-	100.00
8768 *She's Making Whoopee In Hell Tonight*	50.00	-	75.00
8775 *The Dirty Dozen*	50.00	-	75.00
8786 *Headed For Southland*	50.00	-	75.00
8796 *Don't Drive Me From Your Door*	50.00	-	75.00
8802 *The Bull Frog And The Toad*	50.00	-	75.00
8812 *Keep It To Yourself*	60.00	-	100.00
8822 *Deep Sea Blues*	50.00	-	75.00
8831 *No More Troubles Now*	50.00	-	75.00
8846 *Let All Married Women Alone*	50.00	-	75.00
8875 *Just A Roaming Man*	50.00	-	75.00
8886 *I Just Can't Stand These Blues*	50.00	-	75.00
8898 *Beautiful But Dumb*	50.00	-	75.00
8909 *I Have To Do My Time*	50.00	-	75.00
8916 *The Best Jockey In Town*	50.00	-	75.00
8926 *Sleepy Water Blues*	50.00	-	75.00
8937 *Sam You're Just A Rat*	50.00	-	75.00
8946 *Racketeers Blues*	50.00	-	75.00
40695 *Nile Of Genago*	50.00	-	75.00
Paradise 110 *Tomorrow Night*	15.00	-	20.00
123 *Lonesome Day Blues*	15.00	-	20.00

(See also the fourth section of this book for additional recordings by Lonnie Johnson in 45 RPM format)

LOUISE JOHNSON:

Paramount 12992 *All Night Long Blues*	200.00	-	300.00
13008 *On The Wall*	200.00	-	300.00

LUELLA JOHNSON:

Domino 438 *Who Calls You Sweet Mama Now*	20.00	-	30.00

MARGARET JOHNSON:

Okeh 8107 *E Flat Blues*	150.00	-	200.00
8162 *Absent Minded Blues*	100.00	-	150.00
8185 *Changeable Daddy Of Mine*	150.00	-	250.00
8193 *Who'll Chop Your Suey When I'm Gone?*			
	100.00	-	150.00
8220 *Nobody's Blues But Mine*	40.00	-	60.00
8230 *I'm A Good Hearted Mama*	75.00	-	100.00
8405 *Mama Papa Dan't Wanna Come Back Home*			
	50.00	-	75.00
8418 *Heavy Burden Blues*	50.00	-	75.00
8506 *Stinging Bee Blues*	50.00	-	75.00
Victor 20178 *My Man's Done Done Me Dirty*	35.00	-	50.00
20333 *Graysom Street Blues*	35.00	-	50.00
20652 *Good Woman Blues*	80.00	-	120.00
20982 *Dead Drunk Blues*	80.00	-	120.00

MARTHA JOHNSON:

Superior 2753 *Goin' Away Blues*	150.00	-	250.00

MARY JOHNSON:

Brunswick 7081 *Western Union Blues*	100.00	-	150.00
7093 *Muddy Creek Blues*	100.00	-	150.00
7153 *Dawn Of Day Blues*	100.00	-	150.00
7160 *Death Cell Blues*	100.00	-	150.00
7175 *Morning Sun Blues*	75.00	-	100.00
Champion 16570 *Mary Johnson Blues*	300.00	-	up
50062 *Mary Johnson Blues*	50.00	-	100.00
Decca 7012 *Those Black Man Blues*	100.00	-	150.00
7014 *Black Gal Blues*	75.00	-	100.00
7305 *Delmar Avenue*	40.00	-	70.00
Paramount 12931 *Dream Daddy Blues*	150.00	-	300.00
12996 *Barrel House Flat Blues*	150.00	-	300.00

"MEAT HEAD" JOHNSON:

Gotham 514 *Mean Black Snake*	15.00	-	25.00

MERLINE JOHNSON:

Bluebird 6985 *He Roars Like A Lion*	20.00	-	30.00
7032 *My Baby Left Me*	20.00	-	30.00
7166 *Pallet On The Floor*	20.00	-	30.00

PORKCHOP JOHNSON:

Champion 15796 *Pork Chop Stomp*	150.00	-	250.00

RAY JOHNSON:

Mercury 70203 *House Of Blues*	10.00	-	15.00
70231 *Smilin' Blues*	10.00	-	15.00

RED JOHNSON:
Mercury 70141 *West Coast Blues* ....10.00 - 15.00
   70194 *Mama Does The Boogie* ....10.00 - 15.00

ROBERT JOHNSON:
Titles, issued contemporaneously on Banner, Conqueror, Melotone, Oriole, Perfect, Romeo, and Vocalion: *Come On In My Kitchen; Cross Road Blues; Dead Shrimp Blues; From Four Until Late; Hell Hound On My Trail; I Believe I'll Dust My Broom; I'm A Steady Rollin' Man; Kind Hearted Woman Blues; Last Fair Deal Gone Down; Malted Milk; Milkcow's Calf Blues; Ramblin' On My Mind; Stones In My Passway; Terraplane Blues; They're Red Hot; 32-20 Blues* ....800.00 -   up *
Vocalion 03601 *Sweet Home Chicago* ....800.00 -   up
   04002 *Honeymoon Blues* ....1000.00 -   up
   04108 *Me And The Devil Blues* ....1200.00 -   up
   04630 *Love In Vain*...1200.00 -   up
* Several of the above titles occur on Conqueror, which being slightly later issues, are valued somewhat lower.

ROCKHEART JOHNSON:
RCA Victor 20-4967 *Rockheart's Blues* ....15.00 - 20.00 *
   20-5136 *Black Spider* ....15.00 - 20.00 *

RUTH JOHNSON:
Paramount 13060 *Rockin' Chair* ....75.00 - 100.00

SAM (SUITCASE) JOHNSON:
Sittin' In With 608 *Sam's Boogie* ....20.00 - 30.00

SARA JOHNSON:
Banner 1882 *Papa If You Can't Do Better*.............15.00 - 20.00
Domino 3852 *Papa If You Can't Do Better* ....15.00 - 20.00
Regal 8196 *Papa If You Can't Do Better* ....15.00 - 20.00

SHERMAN JOHNSON (& HIS CLOUDS OF JOY):
Nashboro 507 *Back Alley Boogie* ....15.00 - 20.00
Trumpet 189 *Pretty Baby Blues* ....15.00 - 20.00
   190 *Lost In Korea* ....15.00 - 20.00

SLIM JOHNSON:
Gennett 6570 *If Mama Has Outside Lovin'* ....250.00 - 400.00

SONNY BOY JOHNSON & HIS BLUE BLAZERS:
Murray 505 *Come And Go With Me* ....50.00 - 80.00
   507 *Swimming Pool Blues* ....50.00 - 80.00

STOVEPIPE JOHNSON:
Vocaltion 1203 *Devilish Blues* ....150.00 - 200.00
   1211 *I Ain't Got Nobody*.................................150.00 - 200.00

STUMP JOHNSON (See also JAMES "STUMP" JOHNSON):
Bluebird 5159 *Don't Give My Lard Away*.............200.00 - 300.00
   5247 *Money Johnson* ....200.00 - 300.00
Paramount 12862 *Kind Babe Blues* ....150.00 - 200.00
   12906 *Soaking Wet Blues* ....150.00 - 200.00
   12938 *You Buzzard You*....................................150.00 - 200.00

Sunrise 3240 *Steady Grindin'* ....200.00 - 300.00
   3330 *Money Johnson* ....200.00 - 300.00
Victor 23327 *Barrel Of Whiskey Blues*................250.00 -   up

T.C. JOHNSON & "BLUE COAT" TOM NELSON:
Okeh 8838 *J.C. Johnson's Blues* ....100.00 - 150.00

TILLIE JOHNSON:
Gennett 6438 *Chicago Man Blues* ....100.00 - 150.00
   6471 *My Baby* ....100.00 - 150.00

TOMMY JOHNSON:
Paramount 12950 *Alcohol And Jake Blues* ....1500.00 -   up
   12975 *Slidin' Delta* ....1500.00 -   up
   13000 *Black Mare Blues* ....1500.00 -   up
Victor 21279 *Big Road Blues* ....1000.00 -   up
   21409 *Bye-Bye Blues* ....1000.00 -   up
   V38535 *Canned Heat Blues*............................1500.00 -   up

BLIND WILLIE JOHNSON:
Columbia 14276-D *Jesus Make Up My Dying Bed* 150.00 - 200.00
   14303-D *Nobody's Fault But Mine*.................150.00 - 200.00
   14343-D *Mother's Children Have A Hard Time*
   ....150.00 - 200.00
   14391-D *Jesus Is Coming Soon* ....150.00 - 200.00
   14425-D *Keep Your Lamp Trimmed And Burning*
   ....150.00 - 200.00
   14490-D *Let Your Light Shine On* ....150.00 - 200.00
   14504-D *You'll Need Somebody On Your Bond* 150.00 - 200.00
   14520-D *God Moves On The Water* ....150.00 - 250.00
   14530-D *John The Revelator* ....150.00 - 250.00
   14537-D *The Rain Don't Fall On Me*..............150.00 - 250.00
   14545-D *When The War Was On*.....................150.00 - 250.00
   14556-D *Can't Nobody Hide From God* ....150.00 - 250.00
   14582-D *The Soul Of A Man* ....150.00 - 250.00
   14597-D *Go With Me To That Land*...............150.00 - 250.00
   14624-D *Take Your Stand*................................150.00 - 250.00

JOLLY JIVERS:
Vocalion 02532 *Whatcha Gonna Do?* ....150.00 - 200.00
   25015 *Hungry Man's Scuffle* ....150.00 - 200.00

JOLLY JUG BAND:
Varsity 6037 *Tappin' That Thing* ....20.00 - 30.00

JOLLY TWO:
Vocalion 25014 *Frisco Blues*..................................150.00 - 200.00
   25018 *Guitar Stomp* ....150.00 - 200.00

ALBERTA JONES (TRIO) AND HER RED PEPPERS:
Buddy 8024 *Sud Bustin' Blues* ....100.00 - 150.00
   8025 *Home Alone Blues*....................................100.00 - 150.00
   8033 *It Must Be Hard* ....100.00 - 150.00
   8034 *Take Your Fingers Off It* ....100.00 - 150.00
Champion 16216 *Bring It Back Daddy*..................150.00 - 300.00
Gennett 3144 *Home Alone Blues* ....40.00 - 60.00
   3306 *Take Your Finger Off It*..........................60.00 - 90.00
   3403 *Lucky Number Blues* ....100.00 - 150.00
   6424 *Dying Blues* ....75.00 - 100.00
   6439 *Shake A Little Bit* ....100.00 - 150.00
   6535 *My Slow and Easy Man*..........................150.00 - 200.00
   6642 *Wild Geese Blues* ....150.00 - 250.00
   7252 *On Revival Day* ....150.00 - 250.00
   7274 *I Lost My Man* ....150.00 - 250.00
Herwin 92001 *Lucky Number Blues* ....150.00 - 200.00
Silvertone 4052 *Home Alone Blues* ....35.00 - 50.00
   5025 *Lucky Number Blues* ....50.00 - 80.00

ALBINIA JONES:
National 9012 *Evil Gal Blues* ....10.00 - 15.00
   9013 *Salty Papa Blues* ....10.00 - 15.00

ANNA JONES:
Harmograph 859 *Trixie Blues*...........................75.00 - 100.00
Paramount 12043 *You Can't Do What My Last Man Did*
   ....50.00 - 75.00
   12052 *Trixie Blues*..50.00 - 75.00

BESSIE JONES:
Superior 2633 *Stop Bitin' Other Women In The Back*
   ....150.00 - 300.00
Supertone 9474 *I Ain't Givin' Nobody None*.........100.00 - 150.00
   9509 *Pig Meat Mama* ....125.00 - 175.00

"BO" JONES:
Vocalion 1452 *Leavenworth Prison Blues* ....100.00 - 150.00

CLINT JONES:
Columbia 14322-D *Right Or Wrong* ....20.00 - 30.00
Okeh 8587 *Blue Valley Blues* ....30.00 - 50.00

COLEY JONES:
Columbia 14288-D *Traveling Man* ....100.00 - 150.00
   14489-D *Drunkard's Special*............................100.00 - 150.00

CURTIS JONES:
Bluebird 7387 *Good Old Easy Street* ....15.00 - 20.00
   7452 *Schoolmate Blues* ....15.00 - 20.00
   8412 *Gold Digger Blues* ....10.00 - 20.00
   8455 *Solid Jive* ....10.00 - 20.00
Conqueror 9030 *You Got Good Business* ....10.00 - 15.00
   9031 *My Baby's Getting Buggish* ....10.00 - 15.00
   9032 *Let Me Be Your Playmate* ....10.00 - 15.00
   9077 *Lonesome Bedroom Blues No. 2* ....10.00 - 15.00
   9161 *War Broke Out In Hell* ....10.00 - 15.00
   9196 *Blues In the Alley* ....10.00 - 15.00
   9273 *Love I'm Without A Shelter* ....10.00 - 15.00
   9279 *Little Girl, Little Girl* ....10.00 - 15.00
   9358 *Private Talk Blues* ....10.00 - 15.00
   9768 *Moonlight Lover Blues* ....8.00 - 12.00
   9944 *Dream Land Blues* ....8.00 - 12.00
   9945 *Tin Pan Alley* ....7.00 - 10.00
   9946 *Glamor And Glory Blues* ....7.00 - 10.00
Okeh 05744 *Blue And Lonesome* ....15.00 - 20.00
   05834 *Heart Breaking Blues* ....15.00 - 20.00
   05907 *Day And Night Blues* ....10.00 - 15.00
   05947 *Treat Me Like I Treat You* ....10.00 - 15.00
   05996 *Down Town Blues* ....10.00 - 15.00
   06069 *Love Valley Blues* ....10.00 - 15.00
   06105 *Itty Bitty Jitter Bug* ....10.00 - 15.00
   06140 *Low Down Worried Blues* ....10.00 - 15.00
   06186 *Too Many Blues* ....10.00 - 15.00
   06428 *Her Love Will Get It* ....8.00 - 12.00
   06494 *Tin Pan Alley* ....8.00 - 12.00
   06615 *Bed Side Blues* ....8.00 - 12.00
Parrot 782 *Cool Playing Blues* ....15.00 - 20.00 *
Vocalion 03756 *Lonesome Bedroom Blues* ....15.00 - 20.00
   03953 *Blues And Trouble* ....15.00 - 20.00
   03990 *Highway 51 Blues* ....15.00 - 20.00
   04027 *It's A Low Down Dirty Shame* ....15.00 - 20.00
   04080 *Reckless Life Blues* ....15.00 - 20.00
   04120 *Bull And Cow Blues* ....15.00 - 20.00
   04162 *Palace Blues* ....15.00 - 25.00
   04249 *Alley Bound Blues* ....15.00 - 25.00

   04330 *Loving Blues* ....15.00 - 25.00
   04392 *Good Whiskey* ....15.00 - 25.00
   04430 *Hot Dog Man* ....15.00 - 20.00
   04520 *Reefer Hound Blues* ....15.00 - 20.00
   04570 *Night Life Blues* ....15.00 - 20.00
   04617 *I'm Losing My Mind Over You* ....15.00 - 20.00
   04693 *Roll Me Mama* ....15.00 - 20.00
   04761 *Hattie Mae Blues* ....15.00 - 20.00
   04798 *Down In The Gutter* ....15.00 - 20.00
   04857 *Blues In The Basement* ....15.00 - 20.00
   04950 *I Like The Way You Do* ....15.00 - 20.00
   05003 *I'm In The Mood For You* ....15.00 - 20.00
   05071 *Heavy Hip Mama* ....15.00 - 20.00

EDDIE (GUITAR SLIM) JONES (& HIS PLAYBOYS) (See also GUITAR SLIM):
Imperial 5134 *Bad Luck Is On Me* ....20.00 - 30.00
Jim Bullet 603 *Feelin' Sad* ....20.00 - 30.00

ELIJAH JONES:
Bluebird 7526 *E Stuff Stomp*.................................30.00 - 50.00
   7565 *Big Boat* ....30.00 - 50.00
   7616 *Katy Fly*...30.00 - 50.00
   7655 *Lonesome Man* ....30.00 - 50.00

ELSIE JONES WITH SMILIN' JOE:
Flip 1003 *Old Man's Sweetheart* .... - - -

FLOYD JONES (& HIS TRIO) (WITH SNOOKY & MOODY):
Chess 1498 *Dark Road* ....50.00 - 80.00
   1527 *Early Morning*..30.00 - 50.00 *
J.O.B. 1001 *Big World*...80.00 - 130.00
   1013 *On The Road Again*.................................75.00 - 100.00 *
Old Swingmaster 22 *Stockyard Blues*..................100.00 - 150.00
Vee Jay 111 *Schooldays On My Mind* ....40.00 - 60.00 *
   126 *Any Old Lonesome Day* ....40.00 - 60.00 *

FRANKIE JONES:
Vocalion 04206 *My Lincoln*...................................15.00 - 20.00
   04266 *Jockey Blues*..15.00 - 20.00

REV. (GEORGE) JONES (& CONGREGATION):
Champion 15816 *The Heavenly Airplane* ....75.00 - 100.00
Gennett 6979 *The Heavenly Airplane* ....80.00 - 120.00
Supertone 9518 *The Heavenly Airplane* ....75.00 - 100.00

JAKE JONES:
Brunswick 7130 *Monkeyin' Around* ....150.00 - 200.00

JOSEPHINE JONES:
Ajax 17094 *Just One Word Of Consolation* ....30.00 - 50.00

JULIA JONES:
Champion 15265 *Save My Jelly*..............................50.00 - 75.00
Gennett 5177 *That Thing Called Love*...................15.00 - 20.00
   5233 *Deceitful Blues*..15.00 - 20.00
Starr 9407 *That Thing Called Love*........................15.00 - 20.00

LITTLE HAT JONES:
Okeh 8712 *Two String Blues* ....100.00 - 150.00
   8735 *Corpus Blues* ....100.00 - 150.00
   8794 *Little Hat Blues* ....100.00 - 150.00
   8815 *Kentucky Blues* ....100.00 - 150.00
   8829 *Cherry Street Blues* ....100.00 - 150.00

LOUELLA JONES (& JAZZ CASPER):
Banner 1451 *Sweet Mandy* ....15.00 - 20.00
   1467 *Who Calls You Sweet Mama Now*............15.00 - 20.00
Harmograph 983 *Sweet Mandy* ....30.00 - 50.00

MAGGIE JONES:
Columbia 14044-D *Jealous Mamma Blues* ....15.00 -   20.00
    14047-D *Western Union Blues* ....20.00 -   30.00
    14050-D *Poor House Blues* ....30.00 -   50.00
    14055-D *Screamin' The Blues* ....30.00 -   50.00
    14059-D *If I Lose Let Me Lose* ....30.00 -   50.00
    14063-D *Anybody Here Want To Try My Cabbage?*
    ....30.00 -   50.00
    14070-D *Suicide Blues* ....20.00 -   30.00
    14074-D *Cheatin' On Me* ....30.00 -   50.00
    14081-D *Go Get 'Em Caroline* ....20.00 -   30.00
    14092-D *Undertaker's Blues* ....25.00 -   40.00
    14102-D *Single Woman's Blues* ....30.00 -   50.00
    14114-D *South Street Blues* ....30.00 -   50.00
    14127-D *I'm A Back-Bitin' Mama* ....30.00 -   50.00
14139-D *I'm Leaving You* ....40.00 -   60.00
    14167-D *He Belongs To Me* ....25.00 -   40.00
    14243-D *The Man I Love Is Oh So Good* ....40.00 -   60.00
Pathe-Actuelle 021062 *You Can't Do What My Last Man Did*
....15.00 -   20.00
Perfect 12075 *You Can't Do What My Last Man Did*
....15.00 -   20.00

MARY JONES:
Gennett 6860 *You Lied About That Woman* ....20.00 -   30.00

ELDER OTIS JONES:
Bluebird 6466 *Repentance* ....30.00 -   50.00
    6626 *I Am The Vine* ....30.00 -   50.00
    7720 *O Lord, I'm Your Child* ....30.00 -   50.00

SONNY JONES:
Vocalion 05056 *Dough Roller* ....30.00 -   50.00
    05124 *I'm Pretty Good At It* ....30.00 -   50.00

WILLIE (DOC) JONES:
Peacock 1540 *Do You Want To Roll* ....15.00 -   20.00
Supertone 9366 *Sweet Petunia Blues* ....80.00 -   120.00
    9427 *No No Blues* ....80.00 -   120.00
    9434 *Crooked Woman Blues* ....80.00 -   120.00
    9435 *Rag Baby* ....80.00 -   120.00
Vocalion 1194 *Willie's Weary Blues* ....100.00 -   150.00

CHARLIE/CHARLEY JORDAN/JORDON:
Decca 7015 *Rolling Moon Blues* ....150.00 -   200.00
    7065 *Tight Time Blues* ....150.00 -   200.00
    7130 *Christmas Christmas Blues* ....100.00 -   150.00
Victor 23304 *Working Man Blues* ....500.00 -   up
    23372 *Greyhound Blues* ....500.00 -   up
Vocalion 1511 *Big Four Blues* ....200.00 -   300.00
    1528 *Raidin' Squad Blues* ....200.00 -   300.00
    1543 *Just A Spoonful* ....200.00 -   300.00
    1551 *Running Mad Blues* ....200.00 -   300.00
    1557 *Dollar Bill Blues* ....200.00 -   300.00
    1568 *Tough Times Blues* ....200.00 -   300.00
    1611 *You Run And Tell Your Daddy* ....200.00 -   300.00
    1627 *Starvation Blues* ....200.00 -   300.00
    1645 *Tight Haired Mama Blues* ....200.00 -   300.00
    1657 *Hungry Blues* ....150.00 -   250.00
    1666 *Silver Dollar Blues* ....150.00 -   250.00
    1696 *Stir It Up* ....200.00 -   300.00
    1707 *Cherry Wine Woman* ....200.00 -   300.00
    1717 *Honey Sucker Blues* ....200.00 -   300.00
    02763 *Bottle Passing Blues* ....200.00 -   300.00

JENNIE JORDAN:
Champion 15267 *Blue And All By Myself* ....75.00 -   100.00

JIMMY JORDAN:
Columbia 14622-D *Jelly Killed Old Sam* ....75.00 -   100.00
    14647-D *She's Dangerous With That Thing*......75.00 -   100.00
    14655-D *There Is No Justice* ....75.00 -   100.00

LUKE JORDAN:
Victor 20957 *Traveling Coon* ....100.00 -   150.00
    21076 *Cocaine Blues* ....100.00 -   150.00
    23400 *If I Call You Mama* ....300.00 -   up
    V38564 *My Gal's Done Quit Me* ....200.00 -   300.00

CHARLEY JORDON (See CHARLIE/CHARLEY JORDAN)

JUBILEE GOSPEL TEAM:
Paramount 12835 *Dry Bones In The Valley*...........30.00 -   50.00
    12836 *Station Will Be Changed* ....50.00 -   75.00
    12837 *I Know The Lord Has Laid His Hands On Me*
    ....50.00 -   75.00
    12838 *I Have Crossed The Separating Line* ......50.00 -   75.00
    13113 *Jesus Is Mine* ....50.00 -   75.00
Q.R.S. 7013 *Dry Bones In The Valley* ....50.00 -   75.00
    7014 *Station Will Be Changed* ....50.00 -   75.00
    7015 *Oh Lord, Remember Me* ....50.00 -   75.00
7026 *I Know The Lord Has Laid His Hands On Me*50.00 -   75.00
7027 *I Have Crossed The Separating Line* ....50.00 -   75.00
7053 *I'm 'Termined To Pray Right On* ....50.00 -   75.00
7058 *When The Train Comes Along* ....50.00 -   75.00

THE JUMPING JACKS:
Lloyds 101 *Why Oh Why* ....30.00 -   60.00

JUNIOR BLUES:
RPM 320 *Whiskey Head Woman* ....40.00 -   60.00

KANSAS CITY BLUES STRUMMERS:
Vocalion 1048 *String Band Blues* ....200.00 -   300.00

KANSAS CITY KITTY:
Bluebird 5726 *Christmas Morning Blues* ....50.00 -   75.00
    5756 *Leave My Man Alone* ....50.00 -   75.00
Vocalion 1508 *You Got That Stuff* ....150.00 -   250.00
    1534 *Room Rent Blues* ....150.00 -   300.00
    1545 *Fish House Blues* ....150.00 -   300.00
    1565 *Killing Floor Blues* ....150.00 -   300.00
    1575 *Who's Been Here Since I Been Gone?*....150.00 -   300.00
    1600 *Root Man Blues* ....150.00 -   300.00
    1613 *Knife Man Blues* ....150.00 -   300.00
    1632 *Scronchin'* ....150.00 -   300.00
    1642 *That Thing's A Mess* ....150.00 -   300.00

KANSAS JOE (& MEMPHIS MINNIE):
Bluebird 6260 *Something Gonna Happen To You*..20.00 -   30.00
Columbia 14439-D *When The Levee Breaks* ....150.00 -   200.00
    14455-D *Goin' Back To Texas* ....150.00 -   200.00
    14542-D *I Want That* ....150.00 -   200.00
Vocalion 1500 *What Fault You Find Of Me?* ....150.00 -   200.00
    1523 *Can I Do It For You?* ....150.00 -   200.00
    1535 *Cherry Ball Blues* ....150.00 -   200.00
    1550 *North Memphis Blues* ....150.00 -   200.00
    1570 *Botherin' That Thing* ....150.00 -   200.00
    1576 *She Wouldn't Give Me None* ....150.00 -   200.00
    1612 *Pile Drivin' Blues* ....150.00 -   200.00
    1631 *I Called You This Morning* ....150.00 -   200.00
    1643 *Preachers Blue* ....150.00 -   200.00
    1653 *Somebody's Got To Help You* ....150.00 -   200.00
    1660 *Pickin' The Blues* ....150.00 -   250.00

1668 *My Wash Women's Gone* ....150.00 - 200.00
1677 *I'm Fixed For You* ....150.00 - 200.00
1686 *Joliet Bound* ....150.00 - 200.00
1688 *You Stole My Cake* ....150.00 - 200.00
1705 *Dresser Drawer Blues* ....150.00 - 250.00
1718 *You Know You Done Me Wrong* .... 150.00 - 200.00

KANSAS KATIE:
Bluebird 8944 *Deep Sea Diver* ....15.00 - 20.00
8999 *He's My Man* ....15.00 - 20.00

KEGHOUSE:
Okeh 8583 *Keghouse Blues* ....100.00 - 150.00
Vocalion 1239 *Canned Heat Blues* ....150.00 - 300.00

JACK KELLY (& HIS SOUTH MEMPHIS JUG BAND):
Titles, issued contemporaneously on Banner, Conqueror, Melotone, Oriole, Perfect, and Romeo: *Believe I'll Go Back Home; Cold Iron Bed; Highway No. 61 Blues; Highway No. 61 Blues No. 2; Ko-Ko Mo Blues; President Blues; Red Ripe Tomatoes; R.F.C. Blues* ....100.00 - 150.00
Vocalion 05031 *Diamond Buyer Blues* ....75.00 - 100.00
05193 *Neck Bone Blues* ....75.00 - 100.00
05312 *Men Fooler Blues* ....75.00 - 100.00

SAM KELLY & HIS HARMONICA:
Von 43 *Ramblin' Around Blues* ....50.00 - 80.00

WILLIE KELLY:
Victor 23259 *Kelly's Special* ....300.00 - 500.00
23263 *Side Door Blues* ....300.00 - 500.00
23270 *Big Time Woman* ....300.00 - 500.00
23286 *Don't Squeeze Me Too Tight* ....300.00 - 500.00
23299 *Nasty But It's Clean* ....300.00 - 500.00
23320 *Hard Luck Man Blues* ....300.00 - 500.00
23416 *Sad And Lonely Day* ....300.00 - up
V38608 *Kelly's 44 Blues* ....250.00 - 300.00
V38619 *32-20 Blues* ....250.00 - 400.00

ROBERT KELTON & HIS TRIO:
Aladdin 3054 *Muddy Shoes* .... - - -
3187 *Don't Care What You Say* .... - - -

TINY KENNEDY:
Trumpet 187 *Strange Kind Of Feeling* ....8.00 - 12.00 *
188 *Blues Disease* ....8.00 - 12.00 *

HERB KENNEY & THE ROCKETS:
M-G-M 11332 *You Never Heard A Word I Said* ....10.00 - 15.00 *

KID AND COOT:
Columbia 14363-D *Keyhole Blues* ....50.00 - 80.00

KID COLEY:
Bluebird 5248 *Clair And Pearley Blues* ....150.00 - 200.00
Sunrise 3331 *Clair And Pearly Blues* ....150.00 - 250.00
Victor 23293 *Tricks Ain't Walkin' No More* ....400.00 - up
23369 *Freight Train Blues* ....500.00 - up

KID STORMY WEATHER:
Vocalion 03145 *Short Hair Blues* ....100.00 - 150.00

LENA (AND SYLVESTER) KIMBROUGH:
Meritt 2201 *Cabbage Head Blues* ....300.00 - 500.00

LOTTIE KIMBROUGH (AND WINSTON HOLMES):
Gennett 6607 *Wayward Girl Blues* ....150.00 - 250.00
6624 *Rolling Log Blues* ....150.00 - 250.00
6660 *Blue World Blues* ....150.00 - 250.00

SYLVESTER KIMBROUGH:
Brunswick 7135 *Garbage Can Blues* ....150.00 - 200.00

KING GENE:
Blues & Rhythm 7005 *Train Time Boogie* ....10.00 - 15.00

KING TUT:
Sittin' In With 542 *Inquisitive Man* ....15.00 - 20.00
550 *You've Been Fiddling Around* ....15.00 - 20.00

B. B. ("BLUES BOY") KING:
Bullet 309 *Miss Martha King* ....50.00 - 75.00
315 *Got The Blues* ....50.00 - 75.00
RPM 304 *Mistreated Woman* ....30.00 - 50.00
311 *Other Night Blues* ....30.00 - 50.00
318 *My Baby's Gone* ....30.00 - 50.00
323 *She's Dynamite* ....25.00 - 40.00 *
330 *Hard Working Woman* ....25.00 - 40.00 *
339 *Three O'Clock Blues* ....25.00 - 30.00 *
RPM 348, 355, 360, 363, 374, 380, 386, 391, 395, 403, 408, 411, 412, 416, 421. 425, 430 .... 7.00 - 12.00 *
(See the fourth section of this book for additional recordings by B. B. King)

JEWEL KING:
Imperial 5055 *Don't Marry Too Soon* ....10.00 - 15.00
5061 *Broke My Mother's Rule* ....10.00 - 15.00
5076 *Keep Your Big Mouth Shut* ....10.00 - 15.00
5087 *Low Down Feeling* ....10.00 - 15.00

JULIUS KING:
Tennessee 123 *I Want A Slice Of Your Pudding* ..... 20.00 - 30.00

RICHARD KING & HIS ORCHESTRA:
Khoury's 800 *Ride, Daddy, Ride* ....15.00 - 20.00

WEE WILLIE KIRK:
Bullet 340 *Your Love Was So Nice And Warm* .... - - -

(LITTLE) EDDIE KIRKLAND:
King 4659 *No Shoes* ....20.00 - 30.00 *
4680 *Mistreated Woman* ....20.00 - 30.00 *
RPM 367 *That's All Right* ....30.00 - 50.00 *

LILLIE MAE KIRKMAN:
Vocalion 04951 *Hop Head Blues* ....15.00 - 20.00
04991 *When You Leave Me Honey* ....15.00 - 20.00

JESSIE KNIGHT:
Checker 797 *Nothing But Money* ....10.00 - 15.00 *

KNITES OF RHYTHM:
Bluebird 8882 *Chattanooga Choo Choo* ....10.00 - 15.00

BIG BOY KNOX:
Bluebird 6904 *Texas Blues* ....20.00 - 30.00
6952 *Blue Man Blues* ....20.00 - 30.00

CHARLIE KYLE:
Victor 21707 *Kyle's Worried Blues* ....200.00 - 300.00
V38625 *Walking Blues* ....250.00 - up

RUBE LACY:
Paramount 12629 *Mississippi Jail House Groan* .. 100.00 - 150.00

RUTH LADSON & THREE SHADOWS:
Okeh 06667 *Kicking My Man Around* ....8.00 - 12.00

JUSTINE LAMAR:
Decca 7238 *Always Mine* ....8.00 - 12.00

ERNEST LANE:
Blues & Rhythm 700 *What's Wrong Baby* ....15.00 - 25.00

WILLIE LANE:
Talent 805 *Prowlin' Ground Hog* ....75.00 - 100.00
    806 *Black Cat Rag* ....75.00 - 100.00

THE LARKS:
Apollo 427 *Eyesight To The Blind* ....30.00 - 50.00
    429 *Hey Little Girl* ....30.00 - 50.00
    437 *Lucy Brown* ....30.00 - 50.00
(See the fourth section of this book for additional recordings by The Larks in 45 RPM format)

SOPHISTICATED JIMMY LA RUE:
Champion 50070 *Money Truckin' Blues* ....15.00 - 20.00
    50071 *Two Old Maids In A Folding Bed Blues* ..40.00 - 60.00

LOUIS LASKY:
Vocalion 02955 *Teasin' Brown Blues* ....100.00 - 150.00

LAUGHING CHARLEY:
Columbia 14272-D *Chain Gang Trouble* ....100.00 - 150.00

LAZY BILL & HIS BLUE RHYTHMS:
Chance 1148 *I Had A Dream* ....30.00 - 50.00 *

LAZY SLIM JIM:
Savoy 868 *Sugaree* ....15.00 - 20.00

(HUDDIE) LEADBELLY:
Titles issued contemporaneously on Banner, Melotone, Oriole, Perfect, and Romeo: *Becky Deem, She Was A Gamblin' Gal; Four Day Worry Blues; Honey, I'm All Out And Down; New Black Snake Moan; Packin' Trunk Blues; Pig Meat Papa*
    ....50.00 - 100.00
Asch (most issues) ....7.00 - 10.00
Bluebird 8550 *Sail On, Little Girl Sail On* ....15.00 - 25.00
    8559 *T.B. Blues* ....15.00 - 25.00
    8570 *Easy Rider* ....15.00 - 25.00
    8709 *Roberta* ....15.00 - 25.00
    8750 *New York City* ....15.00 - 25.00
    8791 *Leaving Blues* ....15.00 - 25.00
Disc 3001, 3002, 3003 ....7.00 - 10.00
Musicraft (most issues) ....7.00 - 12.00
Stinson (most issues) ....7.00 - 10.00

HUDDIE LEDBETTER WITH THE GOLDEN GATE QUARTET:
Victor 27266, 27267, 27268 ....5.00 - 10.00

BERTHA LEE:
Vocalion 02650 *Mind Reader Blues* ....250.00 - 500.00

BESSIE LEE:
Silvertone 3525 *He Likes It Slow* ....50.00 - 80.00
    3534 *Sorrowful Blues* ....50.00 - 80.00

CAROLINE LEE:
Oriole 353 *Thunderstorm Blues* ....15.00 - 20.00
    698 *What's The Matter Now?* ....15.00 - 20.00

ELIZA CHRISTMAS LEE:
Gennett 4801 *Arkansas Blues* ....15.00 - 20.00

EMMA DELL LEE & TRIO:
Khoury's 900 *No Good Daddy* ....15.00 - 20.00

JERRY LEE:
Herwin 93011 *The Snitches Blues* ....150.00 - 250.00
    93014 *Smiling Blues* ....150.00 - 250.00

JOHN LEE:
Federal 12054 *Down At The Depot* ....30.00 - 50.00
    12089 *Blind's Blues* ....30.00 - 50.00
Gotham 515 *Mean Old Train* ....15.00 - 25.00
J.O.B. 114 *Rhythm Rockin' Boogie* ....80.00 - 120.00

JOHNNY LEE:
DeLuxe 6009 *I Came To See You Baby* ....15.00 - 20.00

LEONARD LEE:
Lamp 8001 *When The Sun Goes Down* ....15.00 - 20.00

MAE BELLE LEE & GEORGE RAMSEY:
Paramount 13069 *Bumble Bee No. 2* ....150.00 - 300.00

RUSSELL LEE & DAISY WRIGHT:
Okeh 8263 *Vampire Brown* ....25.00 - 40.00

THELMA LEE - B. SMITH:
Victor 21413 *One Hour Tonight* ....40.00 - 60.00

TOMMY LEE:
Delta 403 *Highway 80 Blues* ....30.00 - 50.00

VERDI LEE (& CHARLEY JORDAN):
Decca 7130 *Christmas Tree Blues* ....100.00 - 150.00
    7142 *Get It If You Can* ....100.00 - 150.00

J. B. LENOIR/LENORE (& HIS BAYOU BOYS/COMBO):
Chess 1449 *My Baby Told Me* ....30.00 - 50.00
    1463 *Deep In Debt Blues* ....30.00 - 50.00
J.O.B. 112 *Let's Roll* ....30.00 - 50.00
    1008 *The Mountain* ....15.00 - 20.00 *
    1012 *The Mojo* ....15.00 - 20.00 *
    1016 *I'll Die Trying* ....20.00 - 30.00 *
    1102 *Play A Little While* ....15.00 - 25.00 *
Parrot 802 *Eisenhower Blues/I'm In Korea* ....30.00 - 50.00 *
    802 *Tax Paying Blues/I'm In Korea* ....15.00 - 20.00 *
    809 *Mama Talk To Your Daughter* ....15.00 - 20.00 *
    814 *What Have I Done* ....20.00 - 30.00 *
    821 *I Lost My Baby* ....20.00 - 30.00 *
(See the fourth section of this book for additional J. B. Lenore recordings in 45 RPM format)

LEROY'S BUDDY:
Decca 7179 *Naptown Stomp* ....15.00 - 20.00
    7180 *Strange Woman* ....15.00 - 20.00
    7194 *Which One I Love The Best* ....15.00 - 20.00
    7202 *Bad Luck Child* ....15.00 - 20.00
    7223 *Stoney Lonesome* ....15.00 - 20.00
    7233 *Just The Wrong Man* ....15.00 - 20.00
    7246 *Gravel In My Bread* ....15.00 - 20.00
    7258 *Tired Of Your Line Of Jive* ....15.00 - 20.00
    7271 *Curbstone Blues* ....15.00 - 20.00
    7298 *Evil Hearted Me* ....15.00 - 20.00
    7308 *Too Many Women* ....15.00 - 20.00
    7335 *You're A Mean Mistreater* ....10.00 - 20.00
    7356 *New Bad Luck Child* ....10.00 - 20.00
    7374 *Sunrise Blues* ....10.00 - 20.00
    7394 *Jiving Man Blues* ....10.00 - 20.00
    7404 *New Evil Hearted Blues* ....10.00 - 15.00
    7420 *Blake Street Blues* ....10.00 - 15.00
    7434 *Rocky Mountain Blues* ....10.00 - 15.00
    7460 *Won't You Tell Me Baby* ....10.00 - 15.00
Decca (most higher numbers) ....7.00 - 12.00

LEVEE JOE:
Conqueror 8658 *Flood Water Blues* ....15.00 - 20.00

ARCHIE LEWIS:
Champion 16677 *Miss Handy Hanks* ....200.00 - 300.00

BUDDY LEWIS:
Swing Time 312 *You've Got Good Business*...........30.00 - 50.00

EMMA LEWIS:
Victor 19158 *I Don't Let No One Man Worry Me* .15.00 - 20.00

ERNEST LEWIS:
Parrot 791 *West Coast Blues*................................50.00 - 80.00 *

FURRY LEWIS:
Victor 21664 *Kassie Jones* ....300.00 - 500.00
　23345 *Cannon Ball Blues* ....500.00 - up
　V38506 *Judge Harsh Blues* ....300.00 - 600.00
　V38519 *Mistreatin' Mama* ....300.00 - 600.00
Vocalion 1111 *Rock Island Blues* ....200.00 - 400.00
　1115 *Mr. Furry's Blues* ....200.00 - 400.00
　1116 *Sweet Papa Moan* ....200.00 - 400.00
　1132 *Good Looking Girl Blues* ....200.00 - 300.00
　1133 *Big Chief Blues* ....200.00 - 300.00
　1134 *Mean Old Bedbug Blues* ....200.00 - 300.00
　1474 *John Henry*...200.00 - 400.00
　1547 *Creeper's Blues* ....250.00 - 400.00

IDA LEWIS:
Silvertone 3556 *Tennessee Blues*..........................75.00 - 100.00

JOHNNY LEWIS ORCHESTRA:
Rockin' 517 *She's Taking All My Money*................30.00 - 50.00 *

KATE LEWIS:
Broadway 5016 *Mercy Blues*.................................50.00 - 75.00

PETE (GUITAR) LEWIS:
Federal 12056 *Louisiana Hop* ....10.00 - 15.00 *
　12076 *Harmonica Boogie*..................................10.00 - 15.00 *
　12103 *Scratchin' Boogie*...................................10.00 - 15.00 *
　12112 *The Blast* ....10.00 - 15.00 *

RAY LEWIS (& THE FOUR BARS):
Imperial 5136 *Jealous Blues*...............................15.00 - 20.00 *
　5154 *I Can't Go Home* ....15.00 - 20.00 *

SAMMIE LEWIS:
Gennett 5147 *Cootie Crawl*....................................- - -

SAMMY LEWIS:
Sun 218 *I Feel So Worried* ....50.00 - 75.00 *

LEWIS BRONZEVILLE FIVE:
Bluebird 8433 *Cotton Blossom Blues*......................15.00 - 20.00
　8445 *Natchez Mississippi Blues*.........................15.00 - 20.00
　8460 *Low Down Gal Blues* ....15.00 - 20.00
　8480 *It Can Happen To You* ....15.00 - 20.00
Montgomery Ward 8898 *Laughing At Life* ....15.00 - 20.00
　8899 *Linda Brown* ....15.00 - 20.00
　8900 *Mississippi Fire Blues*...............................15.00 - 20.00

PAPA LIGHTFOOT:
Aladdin 3171 *P. L. Blues*....................................50.00 - 75.00 *
　3304 *Jumpin' With Jarvis*.................................30.00 - 50.00 *
Imperial 5289 *Mean Old Train*.............................30.00 - 50.00 *

PRESTON LILLARD:
Champion 15416 *Barrel House Blues* ....150.00 - 200.00
　15436 *The Jockey Blues*...................................150.00 - 250.00

LILLIE MAE:
Columbia 14600-D *Buggy Jail House Blues* ....75.00 - 100.00
Okeh 8920 *Mama Don't Want It* ....80.00 - 120.00

CHARLEY/CHARLIE LINCOLN:
Columbia 14305-D *Jealous Hearted Blues* ....125.00 - 175.00
　14332-D *Ugly Papa* ....125.00 - 175.00
　14420-D *Gamblin' Charley* ....150.00 - 200.00
　14475-D *Country Breakdown* ....150.00 - 200.00
　14550-D *Mama Don't Rush Me*..........................150.00 - 200.00

JOE LINTHECOME:
Gennett 7131 *Humming Blues* ....100.00 - 150.00

VIRGINIA LISTON:
Okeh 8092 *Bed Time Blues*.................................25.00 - 40.00
　8115 *Sally Long Blues* ....25.00 - 40.00
　8122 *Shreveport Blues* ....25.00 - 40.00
　8126 *You Can Have It* ....25.00 - 40.00
　8134 *House Rent Stomp* ....25.00 - 40.00
　8138 *I Don't Love Nobody*.................................25.00 - 40.00
　8151 *Don't Agitate Me Blues*.............................25.00 - 40.00
　8160 *Mississippi Blues*.....................................25.00 - 40.00
　8173 *You've Got The Right Key, But The Wrong Keyhole*
　...100.00 - 150.00
　8175 *Weeping Willow Blues* ....15.00 - 20.00
　8187 *Early In The Morning* ....100.00 - 150.00
　8196 *Night Latch Key Blues*..............................30.00 - 50.00
　8218 *You Can Dip Your Bread In My Gravy, But You Can't Have None Of My Chops* ....60.00 - 100.00
　8223 *Black Sheep Blues* ....40.00 - 60.00
　8234 *I'm Sick Of Fattening Frogs For Snakes* .. 40.00 - 60.00
　8247 *Make Me A Pallet*....................................50.00 - 80.00
Vocalion 1031 *Titanic Blues*...............................100.00 - 150.00
　1032 *Rolls-Royce Papa*....................................100.00 - 150.00

LITTLE BILL:
Bluebird 6972 *You Can't Love Me And Someone Else Too*
　...25.00 - 40.00

LITTLE BROTHER:
Bluebird 6658 *Chinese Man Blues* ....30.00 - 50.00
　6697 *Louisiana Blues-Part 2* ....30.00 - 50.00
　6733 *Crescent City Blues* ....30.00 - 50.00
　6766 *Tantalizing Blues* ....30.00 - 50.00
　6811 *Santa Fe Blues* ....30.00 - 50.00
　6825 *Never Go Wrong Blues* ....30.00 - 50.00
　6894 *Farish Street Jive* ....30.00 - 50.00
　6916 *Out West Blues* ....30.00 - 50.00
　7178 *West Texas Blues*......................................30.00 - 50.00
　7277 *Sorrowful Blues* ....30.00 - 50.00
　7806 *Misled Blues*..30.00 - 50.00
　10177 *Farish Street Jive* ....20.00 - 30.00
　10953 *Crescent City*..15.00 - 25.00
Montgomery Ward 7111 *Louisiana Blues*..............15.00 - 20.00
　7112 *Tantalizing Blues* ....15.00 - 20.00

LITTLE DAVID:
Decca 7211 *Standing By A Lamp Post*..................25.00 - 40.00
　7270 *Ramblin' Mind Blues* ....25.00 - 40.00
Regal 3271 *Shackles' Round My Body* ....40.00 - 60.00
RPM 371 *Crying Blues* ....20.00 - 30.00 *

LITTLE EDDIE:
Bullet 348 *My Baby Left Me* ....- - -

LITTLE ESTHER:
Decca 28804 *If You Want Me* ....10.00 - 15.00 *
Savoy 750 *Just Can't Get Free*.............................10.00 - 15.00
　759 *Deceivin' Blues* ....10.00 - 15.00
(See the fourth section of this book for additional Little Esther recordings in 45 RPM format)

LITTLE FOUR:
Southern 122 *Don't Forget To Be True*...................10.00 -   20.00

LITTLE HUDSON & HIS RED DEVIL TRIO:
J.O.B. 1015 *Rough Treatment* ....40.00 -   70.00 *

LITTLE JIMMY:
Acorn 301 *Rock That Boogie*.................................15.00 -   20.00

LITTLE JOHNNY:
Aristocrat 405 *Shelby County Blues* ....100.00 - 150.00

LITTLE JUNIOR'S BLUE FLAMES:
Sun 187 *Feelin' Good*...................................50.00 -   75.00 *
    192 *Mystery Train*......................................50.00 -   75.00 *

LITTLE MILTON:
Delta 403 *Little Milton's Boogie* ....50.00 -   75.00
Sun 194 *Beggin' My Baby* ....50.00 -   75.00
    200 *Alone And Blue* ....75.00 - 100.00 *
    220 *Looking For My Baby*................................75.00 - 125.00 *

LITTLE MISS CORNSHUCKS:
Aladdin 3034 *Keep Your Hand On Your Heart*........8.00 -   12.00
    3126 *Waiting In Vain*......................................8.00 -   12.00
Miltone (cartoon label) 243 *In The Rain* ....15.00 -   20.00

LITTLE MR. MIDNIGHT:
Regal 3287 *Four O'Clock Blues*................................ -   -   -

LITTLE PAPA JOE:
Blue Lake 116 *Looking For My Baby* ....15.00 -   30.00 *

LITTLE PORK CHOPS:
DRC Danceland 403 *Wayne County Ramblin' Blues*.......-   -   -

LITTLE SISTER:
Varsity 6050 *My Back To The Wall*........................15.00 -   20.00

LITTLE SON JOE:
Okeh 06707 *Black Rat Swing* ....7.00 -   10.00
Vocalion 04707 *Diggin' My Potatoes* ....15.00 -   20.00
    04776 *A.B.C. Blues*......................................15.00 -   20.00
    04978 *My Black Buffalo* ....15.00 -   20.00
    05004 *Key To The World*................................15.00 -   20.00

LITTLE T-BONE:
Miltone 5223 *Christmas Blues* ....30.00 -   50.00

LITTLE WALTER (TRIO) (& HIS JUKES/NIGHT CAPS):
Chance 1116 *I Just Keep Loving Her*.....................50.00 -   75.00
Checker 758 *Juke*...25.00 -   40.00
    764 *Mean Old World*.....................................15.00 -   25.00 *
    767 *Tonight With A Fool* ....10.00 -   15.00 *
    770 *Off The Wall* ....10.00 -   15.00 *
    780 *Quarter To Twelve* ....10.00 -   15.00 *
    786 *Lights Out*..10.00 -   15.00 *
    793 *Oh Baby*...10.00 -   15.00 *
    799 *Blue Light*..10.00 -   15.00 *
    805 *Mellow Down Easy* ....10.00 -   15.00 *
    811 *Thunder Bird*.......................................10.00 -   15.00 *
    817 *Roller Coaster* ....10.00 -   15.00 *
    825 *Too Late* ....10.00 -   15.00 *
    833 *It Ain't Right* ....8.00 -   12.00 *
    838 *Flying Saucer*.......................................8.00 -   12.00 *
    845 *Just A Feeling* ....8.00 -   12.00 *
    852 *Take Me Back* ....8.00 -   12.00 *
    859 *Nobody But You* ....8.00 -   12.00 *
    867 *Boom Boom Out Goes The Lights* ....8.00 -   12.00 *
    890 *The Toddle* ....8.00 -   12.00 *
(Subsequent issues on Checker, normally found in 45 RPM format,
    are listed in the fourth section of this book)

Ora Nelle 711 *I Just Keep Loving Her*......................-   -   -
Regal 3296 *Muskadine Blues* ....300.00 -   up

LITTLE WILLIE LITTLEFIELD:
Eddie's 1202 *Little Willie's Boogie* ....20.00 -   30.00
    1205 *Chicago Bound*.....................................20.00 -   30.00
    1212 *Boogie Woogie Playgirl* ....20.00 -   30.00
Freedom 1502 *Littlefield Boogie* ....15.00 -   20.00
Modern 686 *Midnight Whistle* ....10.00 -   15.00
    709 *Drinkin' Hadacol* ....10.00 -   15.00
    716 *Come On Baby* ....10.00 -   15.00
    726 *The Moon Is Risin'* ....10.00 -   15.00
    729 *Rockin' Chair Mama* ....10.00 -   15.00
    747 *Tell Me Baby* ....10.00 -   15.00
    754 *Cheerful Baby* ....10.00 -   15.00
    775 *Hit The Road* ....10.00 -   15.00
    781 *Ain't A Better Story Told*..........................10.00 -   15.00
    785 *Come On Baby* ....8.00 -   12.00
    801 *Once Was Lucky* ....8.00 -   12.00
    837 *Mean Mean Woman* ....8.00 -   12.00
    854 *Life Of Trouble*......................................8.00 -   12.00
(See the fourth section of this book for additional recordings by
    Little Willie Littlefield)

**JESSE LOCKETT & HIS ORCHESTRA (See also WILL
ROWLAND):**
Gulf 3000 *Blacker The Berry*................................15.00 -   20.00

JAMES (BLAZER BOY) LOCKS:
Imperial 5199 *Mornin' Train*................................25.00 -   40.00 *
    5244 *Waiting For My Baby*..............................15.00 -   20.00 *
Regal 3231 *Blazer Boy Blues*...............................30.00 -   50.00

ROBERT LOCKWOOD:
Bluebird 8820 *Take A Little Walk With Me* ....15.00 -   20.00
    8877 *Black Spider Blues* ....15.00 -   20.00

ROBERT LOCKWOOD, JR./ROBERT JR. LOCKWOOD:
J.O.B. 1107 *Sweet Woman From Maine* ....40.00 -   60.00 *
Mercury 8260 *Dust My Broom* ....20.00 -   30.00

CRIPPLE CLARENCE LOFTON:
Titles issued contemporaneously on Banner, Conqueror, Melotone,
    Oriole, and Perfect: *Brown Skin Girls; You Done Tore Your
    Playhouse Down* ....80.00 - 130.00
Session 10-002 *The Fives* ....10.00 -   15.00
    10-006 *Early Blues* ....10.00 -   15.00
    10-014 *Policy Blues* ....10.00 -   15.00
    12-005 *Streamline Train* ....10.00 -   20.00
Solo Art 12003 *Streamline Train*...........................25.00 -   40.00
    12009 *Pine Top's Boogie Woogie*......................25.00 -   40.00
Vocalion 02951 *Monkey Man Blues* ....150.00 - 200.00

POOR BOY LOFTON:
Decca 7010 *Poor Boy Blues*...............................100.00 - 150.00
    7049 *Rainy Day Blues* ....75.00 - 100.00
    7076 *Jake Leg Blues* ....75.00 - 100.00

WILLIE LOFTON TRIO:
Bluebird 6229 *Beer Garden Blues* ....20.00 -   30.00

RAY LOGAN:
Paramount 12310 *Lost John Blues* ....100.00 - 150.00

CLARENCE LONDON:
Fidelity 3009 *One Rainy Morning* ....20.00 -   30.00

JOHNNY LONDON:
Sun 175 *Flat Tire*...500.00 -   up

LOTTIE AND WINSTON:
Superior 2717 *Wayward Girl Blues* ....150.00 - 300.00

JOE HILL LOUIS:
Checker 763 *Dorothy May*...................50.00 - 100.00 *
Columbia 30182 *Railroad Blues* ....50.00 - 100.00
   30221 *Joe's Jump* ....50.00 - 100.00
Modern 795 *Heartache Baby*...............50.00 - 80.00
   813 *Boogie In The Park*................50.00 - 80.00
   822 *Walking Talkin' Blues*............50.00 - 80.00
   828 *Eyesight To The Blind*...........50.00 - 80.00
   839 *Gotta Go Baby*.....................30.00 - 50.00 *
   856 *Peace Of Mind* ....30.00 - 50.00 *
Phillips 9002 *Boogie In The Park*.........500.00 - up
Sun 178 *We All Gotta Go Sometime* ......500.00 - up

LESLIE LOUIS:
Rockin' 509 *Riding Home* ....15.00 - 25.00

LOUISIANA JOE & SLIM:
Champion 50063 *Crossin' Beale Street* ...50.00 - 75.00

LOUISIANA JOHNNY:
Vocalion 02980 *Policy Blues*..............40.00 - 70.00
   03497 *Whiskey Head Woman* ....30.00 - 50.00

BILLY "RED" LOVE:
Chess 1508 *Drop Top* ....20.00 - 30.00 *

HOT SHOT LOVE:
Sun 196 *Wolf Call Boogie* ....150.00 - 200.00 *

WILLIE LOVE & HIS THREE ACES; WILLIE LOVE'S THREE ACES:
Trumpet 137 *Take It Easy Baby* ....15.00 - 25.00
   147 *My Own Boogie* ....15.00 - 25.00
   172, 173, 174, 175, 209 ....8.00 - 12.00 *

LOVIN' SAM (FROM DOWN IN 'BAM); LOVIN' SAM & BURNS CAMPBELL ORCHESTRA/HIS SWING RASCALS:
Bluebird 7514 *You Turned Your Back On Me*.........10.00 - 15.00
   7629 *Big Time Rose* ....10.00 - 15.00
   7916 *That's Chicago's South Side*....10.00 - 15.00
Brunswick 7073 *She's Givin' It Away*......50.00 - 80.00
   7075 *What You Gonna Do?* ....50.00 - 80.00
   7090 *Get Your Mind On It* ....50.00 - 80.00
   7094 *I Ain't No Ice Man* ....50.00 - 80.00
   7098 *You Rascal You*..................40.00 - 70.00
   7117 *Huggin' And Kissin' Gwine On*...50.00 - 80.00
   7131 *Get It In Front*................50.00 - 80.00
   7167 *You Rascal You-No. 2* ....50.00 - 80.00
   7183 *Ugly Child*......................75.00 - 100.00
   7198 *Three Sixes*.....................75.00 - 100.00
   7218 *That New Kinda Stuff*............100.00 - 150.00
Vocalion 03686 *Spo-Dee-O-Dee* ....15.00 - 25.00

FLORENCE LOWERY:
Vocalion 1106 *Poor Girl Blues* ....75.00 - 100.00
   1107 *Thirty Day Blues* ....75.00 - 100.00

JANE LUCAS (& GEORGIA TOM):
Champion 16215 *Fix It*...................150.00 - 200.00
   50042 *Fix It*........................40.00 - 60.00
Vocalion 03314 *I Can't Last Long* ....15.00 - 20.00
   03346 *Mr. Freddie Blues*..............15.00 - 20.00

LONNIE LYONS (COMBO); LONNIE LYONS, HIS PIANO & ORCHESTRA:
Freedom 1504 *Lonely Heart Blues* ....10.00 - 15.00
   1507 *Far Away Blues* ....10.00 - 15.00
   1512 *Neat And Sweet* ....10.00 - 15.00
   1519 *Helpless* ....10.00 - 15.00
   1523 *Sneaky Joe*......................10.00 - 15.00
Sittin' In With 566 *I Need Romance* ......10.00 - 15.00

SMILING SMOKEY LYNN:
Peacock 1555 *Unfaithful Woman*...........10.00 - 15.00
   1579 *Leave My Girl Alone* ....10.00 - 15.00
Specialty 323 *State Street Boogie* ....10.00 - 15.00

ALURA MACK:
Gennett 6767 *Old Fashioned Blues* ....150.00 - 200.00
   6797 *My Kitchen Man*..................150.00 - 200.00
   6813 *West End Blues*..................150.00 - 200.00
   6876 *Loose Like That*.................150.00 - 200.00
   6890 *Beef Blood Blues*................150.00 - 200.00
   6964 *The Long Lost Blues*.............150.00 - 250.00
   7273 *Monkey Blues*....................150.00 - 200.00
   7295 *Everybody's Man Is Mine* ....150.00 - 200.00

BILLY AND MARY MACK:
Okeh 8195 *My Heart Breakin' Gal*..........80.00 - 120.00
   8274 *Fetch It When You Come* ....50.00 - 75.00
   8296 *You Don't Want Much* ....50.00 - 75.00
   8339 *Oh! Me Oh! My Blues*.............150.00 - 200.00

IDA MAY MACK:
Victor 21690 *Mr. Moore Blues* ....80.00 - 120.00
   V-38030 *Elm Street Blues*.............150.00 - 200.00
   V-38532 *Wrong Doin' Daddy* ....150.00 - 250.00

RED MACK:
Atlas 117 *Black Man's Blues*..............10.00 - 15.00

MACK AND MACK:
Bluebird 6894 *You Gotta Quit Your Low Down Ways* ...30.00 - 50.00
   7908 *Black* ....20.00 - 30.00

MACON ED (AND TAMPA JOE):
Okeh 8676 *Worrying Blues*................100.00 - 150.00
   8855 *Try That Thing* ....100.00 - 150.00
   8877 *Tickle Britches* ....100.00 - 150.00
   8896 *Mean Florida Blues* ....100.00 - 150.00

SIDNEY MAIDEN:
Imperial 5189 *Honey Bee Blues*............50.00 - 75.00

THE MAJORS:
Derby 763 *At Last* ....20.00 - 30.00
   779 *Laughing On The Outside* ....20.00 - 30.00

HELENA MANLEY:
Okeh 8111 *Loving Blues*..................25.00 - 40.00

LEOLA MANNING:
Vocalion 1446 *He Fans Me* ....75.00 - 100.00
   1492 *The Arcade Building Moan*........75.00 - 100.00
   1529 *Laying In The Graveyard*.........75.00 - 100.00

MARSHALL BROTHERS:
Savoy 825 *Who Will Be The Fool*...........30.00 - 50.00
   828 *Just Because*....................30.00 - 50.00
   833 *Why Make A Fool Out Of Me* ....30.00 - 50.00

MARTIN AND ROBERT:
Brunswick 7007 *Dollar Blues* ....80.00 - 120.00
Vocalion 1127 *South Street Blues* ....150.00 - 200.00

ARETHA MARTIN:
Champion 15340 *Lost Man Blues*.............150.00 - 200.00
   15360 *Tea-Rollin' Blues* ....150.00 - 200.00
Silvertone 5129 *Lost Man Blues* ....150.00 - 200.00

CARL MARTIN:
Bluebird 5745 *Kid Man Blues* ....50.00 - 80.00
   6139 *Old Time Blues* ....30.00 - 50.00
Champion 50074 *High Water Flood Blues* ....30.00 - 50.00
Decca 7114 *Let's Have A New Deal*.....................30.00 - 50.00
Okeh 8961 *Badly Mistreated Man*.....................75.00 - 100.00
Vocalion 03003 *Badly Mistreated Man*..................40.00 - 60.00
   03047 *Good Morning, Judge* ....40.00 - 60.00
   03496 *That New Kind Of Stuff*...........................30.00 - 50.00

DAISY MARTIN:
Banner 1262 *Feelin' Blue* ....15.00 - 20.00
Gennett 4712 *Spread Yo' Stuff* ....15.00 - 20.00
Okeh 8001 *I Won't Be Back 'Til You Change Your Ways*
   ....30.00 - 50.00
   8008 *Everybodys Man Is My Man* ....30.00 - 50.00
   8009 *I Didn't Start In To Love You* ....20.00 - 30.00
   8010 *Sweet Daddy* ....20.00 - 30.00
   8013 *Nightmare Blues* ....20.00 - 30.00
   8027 *If You Don't Want Me Please Don't Dog Me 'Round*
   ....20.00 - 30.00
Regal 9548 *Feelin' Blue* ....15.00 - 20.00

DOLLY MARTIN:
Decca 7080 *All Men Blues*....................75.00 - 100.00

BLIND GEORGE MARTIN:
Broadway 5040 *Worried Blues*...............100.00 - 150.00
   5053 *Southern Rag* ....100.00 - 150.00
   5080 *Hookworm Blues*...................100.00 - 150.00
   5084 *Goodbye Mama Moan* ....150.00 - 200.00

OLLIS MARTIN:
Gennett 6306 *Police And High Sheriff Come Ridin' Down*
   ....400.00 - 800.00

SARA MARTIN:
Okeh 4904, 8041 8058, 8060, 8062, 8063, 8065,
   8078, 8083, 8084, 8085, 8086, 8087, 8088, 8093,
   8097, 8104, 8117, 8136, 8146, 8161, 8172, 8191,
   8226, 8249, ...10.00 - 20.00
   8043 *'Tain't Nobodys Biz-ness If I Do* ....15.00 - 20.00
   8045 *Last Go Round Blues* ....15.00 - 20.00
   8061 *Come Home Papa Blues* ....50.00 - 75.00
   8064 *Laughin' Cryin' Blues* ....50.00 - 75.00
   8067 *Yodeling Blues* ....30.00 - 50.00
   8082 *Hesitation Blues*........................30.00 - 50.00
   8090 *Blind Man Blues* ....80.00 - 120.00
   8099 *Graveyard Dream Blues* ....80.00 - 120.00
   8108 *Squabbling Blues* ....80.00 - 120.00
   8154 *He's Never Gonna Throw Me Down* ....75.00 - 100.00
   8166 *Jug Band Blues* ....100.00 - 150.00
   8176 *I Got The Crying Blues* ....100.00 - 150.00
   8211 *I Ain't Got No Man* ....100.00 - 150.00
   8203 *Things Done Got Too Much* ....75.00 - 100.00
   8214 *Strange Lovin' Blues*.....................50.00 - 75.00
   8231 *Papa, Papa Blues*....................100.00 - 150.00
   8237 *Daddy, Ease This Pain Of Mine* ....50.00 - 75.00

   8262 *Alabamy Bound*........................75.00 - 100.00
   8270 *I'm Gonna Hoodoo You* ....75.00 - 100.00
   8283 *Down At The Razor Ball* ....100.00 - 150.00
   8292 *Forget Me Not Blues* ....100.00 - 150.00
   8304 *Give Me Just A Little Of Your Time*........100.00 - 150.00
   8308 *That Dance Called Messin' Around* ....50.00 - 75.00
   8325 *Careless Man Blues* ....100.00 - 150.00
   8336 *What's The Matter Now?* ....100.00 - 150.00
   8354 *Don't Never Figure* ....50.00 - 75.00
   8374 *Some Sweet Day* ....150.00 - 200.00
   8394 *Look Out Mr Jazz* ....50.00 - 75.00
   8412 *Shipwrecked Blues* ....50.00 - 75.00
   8427 *Georgia Stockade Blues* ....80.00 - 120.00
   8442 *The Prisoner's Blues* ....100.00 - 150.00
   8461 *Cushion Foot Stomp* ....75.00 - 100.00
   8513 *Orn'ry Blues*..............................25.00 - 40.00
Paramount 12841 *Death Sting Me Blues* ....200.00 - 300.00
QRS 7035 *Hole In The Wall* ....200.00 - 300.00
   7042 *Death Sting Me Blues* ....200.00 - 300.00
   7043 *Kitchen Man Blues*....................200.00 - 300.00

MARY AND MACK:
Bluebird 6894 *You Gotta Quit Your Low Down Ways*
   ....25.00 - 40.00
   7908 *Black* ....30.00 - 40.00

THE MASKED MARVEL:
Paramount 12805 *Mississippi Bo Weavil Blues*.... 600.00 - up

MINNIE MATHES:
Vocalion 04431 *Ball Game Blues*..........................15.00 - 20.00

EMMETT MATHEWS:
Paramount 13087 *Upside Down* ....150.00 - 200.00

LENA MATLOCK:
Champion 16170 *Stop Bitin' Other Women In The Back*
   ....100.00 - 150.00

MAE MATTHEWS:
Gennett 6438 *Dirty Woman Blues* ....100.00 - 150.00
   6439 *Satisfied Blues* ....100.00 - 150.00

CLAUDE MAXWELL:
Sterling 3006 *Bad Woman Blues* ....10.00 - 15.00

HANNAH MAY & THE STATE STREET FOUR:
Titles issued contemporaneously on Banner, Oriole, Perfect, and Romeo:
   Pussy Cat Blues; What You Call That? ....75.00 - 100.00
Vocalion 03313 *Kansas City Hill* ....15.00 - 20.00

TINY MAYBERRY:
Decca 7496 *Oh That Nasty Man* ....10.00 - 15.00
   7520 *Mayberry Blues* ....10.00 - 15.00
   7593 *Mailman Blues* ....10.00 - 15.00

ETHEL MAYES:
Harmograph 781 *Sugar Blues* ....20.00 - 30.00
   842 *Goin' Down To The Levee* ....100.00 - 150.00
   2544 *Gulf Coast Blues* ....20.00 - 30.00

BERT (M.) MAYS:
Paramount 12614 *Mama's Man Blues* ....100.00 - 150.00
   12632 *Midnight Rambler's Blues* ....100.00 - 150.00
Vocalion 1223 *Michigan River Blues* ....100.00 - 150.00

BUCK MacFARLAND:
Paramount 12982 *St. Louis Fire Blues* ....100.00 - 150.00

PALMER McABEE:
Victor 21352 *McAbee's Railroad Piece* ....30.00 - 50.00

CONNIE McBOOKER:
Eddie's 1928 *Short Baby Boogie* ....50.00 - 80.00

JAMES McCAIN:
Chicago 103 *Good Mr. Roosevelt* ....30.00 - 50.00

ARTHUR McCLAIN (AND JOE EVANS):
Titles, issued contemporaneously on Banner, Oriole, Perfect, and
  Romeo: *Cream And Sugar Blues; Old Hen Cackle*
  ....100.00 - 150.00

ERNEST McCLAY & HIS TRIO:
Murray 506 *Big Timing Woman* ....25.00 - 50.00

TOMMY McCLENNAN:
Bluebird 8347 *You Can Mistreat Me Here* ....10.00 - 15.00
  8373 *Bottle It Up And Go* ....7.00 - 10.00
  8408 *Cotton Patch Blues* ....10.00 - 15.00
  8444 *Brown Skin Girl* ....10.00 - 15.00
  8499 *New Highway No. 51* ....10.00 - 15.00
  8545 *My Babys Doggin' Me* ....10.00 - 15.00
  8605 *My Little Girl* ....10.00 - 15.00
  8669 *My Baby's Gone* ....10.00 - 15.00
  8689 *Katy Mae Blues* ....10.00 - 15.00
  8704, 8725, 8853, 8897, 8957, 9005, 9015,
  9037, 34-0706, 34-0716..7.00 - 12.00

LILI McCLINTOCK:
Columbia 14575-D *Furniture Man* ....50.00 - 75.00
  14602-D *Sow Good Seeds* ....50.00 - 75.00

MATTHEW McCLURE:
Champion 16514 *True Love Blues* ....300.00 - up

McCOY AND JOHNSON:
Bluebird 5385 *I Never Told A Lie*..........................100.00 - 150.00
Sunrise 3466 *Don't Want No Woman*.......................100.00 - 200.00
Victor 23313 *I Never Told A Lie* ....300.00 - up
  23352 *Georgia Skin* ....400.00 - up

ANN SORTER McCOY:
Southern 100 *Tell It To The O. P. A.* ....10.00 - 20.00

("PAPA") CHARLES/CHARLIE McCOY (AND BO CARTER/BO CHATMAN/WITH CHATMAN'S MISSISSIPPI HOT FOOTERS):
Brunswick 7080 *Corrine Corrina* ....100.00 - 150.00
Brunswick 7118 *It Ain't No Good* ....150.00 - 200.00
  7141 *Last Time Blues*......................................150.00 - 250.00
  7156 *Your Valves Need Grinding* ....150.00 - 250.00
  7165 *Glad Hand Blues*......................................150.00 - 250.00
Okeh 8853 *Mississippi I'm Longing For You*........150.00 - 250.00
  8863 *It Is So Good-Part 1*.................................150.00 - 250.00
  8873 *You Gonna Need Me* ....150.00 - 250.00
  8881 *It Is So Good-Part 2*.................................150.00 - 250.00
Vocalion 1683 *Boogie Woogie* ....150.00 - 250.00
  1712 *Too Long*...150.00 - 200.00
  1726 *Bottle It Up* ....150.00 - 200.00
  02687 *It Ain't No Good* ....50.00 - 80.00

ROBERT/LEE McCOY:
Bluebird 6995 *Prowling Night Hawk* ....25.00 - 40.00
  7045 *Lonesome World* ....25.00 - 40.00
  7090 *G-Man*..25.00 - 40.00
  7115 *Tough Luck* ....25.00 - 40.00
  7303 *Mean Black Cat* ....25.00 - 40.00

7386 *Take It Easy Baby* ....25.00 - 40.00
7416 *My Friend Has Forsaken Me* ....25.00 - 40.00
7440 *CNA* ....25.00 - 40.00

VIOLA/VIOLET McCOY:
Ajax 17010 *Lonesome Daddy Blues* ....25.00 - 40.00
  17066 *Keep On Going* ....30.00 - 50.00
  17069 *I Don't Want Nobody* ....30.00 - 50.00
Banner 1357 *Buzzin' Around* ....10.00 - 15.00
  1371 *You Don't Know My Mind* ....10.00 - 15.00
  1394 *Clearing House Blues* ....10.00 - 15.00
Brunswick 2591 *If Your Good Man Quits You* ....20.00 - 30.00
  2625* *It Makes No Difference Now*....................... -   -
(*supposedly unissued, but copies do exist)
Cameo 1097 *Some Day You'll Come Back To Me*.. 15.00 - 25.00
  1189 *Back Water Blues*....................................15.00 - 25.00
  1225 *Dyin' Crap Shooter's Blues* ....15.00 - 25.00
Columbia 14395-D *I Want A Good Man* ....50.00 - 75.00
Edison 51478 *Memphis Bound* ....250.00 - 400.00
Gennett 5108 *Laughin' Cryin' Blues* ....20.00 - 30.00
  5128 *Triflin' Blues* ....25.00 - 40.00
  5151 *Gulf Coast Blues* ....25.00 - 40.00
  5162 *Chirpin' The Blues* ....20.00 - 30.00
  5175 *Long Lost Mama* ....20.00 - 30.00
Regal 9653, 9667, 9690 ....10.00 - 15.00
Vocalion 1002 *South Street Blues* ....50.00 - 75.00
  14632 *Sad And Lonely Blues* ....15.00 - 20.00
  14633 *Bleeding Hearted Blues* ....15.00 - 20.00
  14653 *'Bama Bound Blues* ....15.00 - 20.00
  14689 *Mistreatin' Daddy* ....15.00 - 20.00
  14801 *West Indies Blues* ....40.00 - 60.00
  14818 *Mamma, Mamma* ....15.00 - 25.00
  14912 *Keep On Going* ....30.00 - 50.00
  15245 *Stomp Your Blues Away* ....75.00 - 100.00
  15268 *South Street Blues* ....50.00 - 75.00

WILLIAM McCOY:
Columbia 14302-D *Mama Blues* ....25.00 - 40.00
  14393-D *How Long Baby* ....50.00 - 75.00
  14453-D *Central Tracks Blues* ....50.00 - 75.00
  15269-D *Mama Blues* ....25.00 - 40.00

JIMMY McCRACKLIN (& HIS BLUES BLASTERS/ ORCHESTRA):
Aladdin 3089 *Bad Luck And Trouble* ....8.00 - 12.00
Cava-Tone 251 *Jimmy's Blues*.............................15.00 - 20.00
Courtney 123 *You Had Your Chance* ....10.00 - 15.00
Down Town 2023 *Bad Condition Blues* ....15.00 - 20.00
  2027 *Low Down Mood*....................................15.00 - 20.00
Excelsior 182 *You Deceived Me* ....15.00 - 20.00
Globe 102 *Miss Mattie Left Me* ....20.00 - 30.00
  104 *Highway 101* ....20.00 - 30.00
  109 *Street Loafn' Woman* ....20.00 - 30.00
J & M Fullbright 123 *Special For You* ....15.00 - 20.00
  124 *Rock And Rye* ....15.00 - 20.00
Modern 722 *Beer Drinking Woman* ....10.00 - 15.00
  728 *Deceiving Blues* ....10.00 - 15.00
  741 *Gotta Cut Out* ....10.00 - 15.00
  762 *Rockin' All Day* ....10.00 - 15.00
  806 *Blues Blaster Shuffle* ....10.00 - 15.00
Old Swing-Master 24 *South Side Mood* ....15.00 - 20.00
  25 *When I'm Gone* ....15.00 - 20.00
Peacock 1605 *She's Gone* ....7.00 - 10.00
  1615 *Share And Share Alike* ....7.00 - 10.00*
  1639 *My Story* ....7.00 - 10.00*

RPM 317 *Your Heart Ain't Right* ....15.00 - 20.00
Swing Time 260 *Looking For A Woman* ....10.00 - 15.00
    264 *True Love Blues* ....10.00 - 15.00
    270 *Rockin' Man* ....10.00 - 15.00
    285 *That's Life* ....10.00 - 15.00
    286 *Blues For The People* ....10.00 - 15.00
    291 *House Rockin' Blues* ....10.00 - 15.00
Trilon 197 *Rock And Rye* ....15.00 - 20.00
    231 *Big Foot Mama* ....15.00 - 20.00
    244 *South Side Mood* ....15.00 - 20.00
    245 *Listen Woman* ....15.00 - 20.00
(See the fourth section of this book for additional Jimmy McCracklin recordings in 45 RPM format)

JAMES McCRAVY:
Columbia 14641-D *Shove It Up It There* ....80.00 - 120.00

ROBERT McCULLUM:
Aristocrat 413 *Jackson Town Woman* ....75.00 - 100.00

HATTIE McDANIEL(S):
Merritt 2202 *Brown-Skin Baby Doll* ....250.00 - up
Okeh 8434 *Boo Hoo Blues* ....150.00 - 200.00
    8569 *I Thought I'd Do It* ....75.00 - 100.00
Paramount 12751 *Dentist Chair Blues* ....150.00 - 200.00
    12790 *That New Love Maker Of Mine* ....150.00 - 200.00

WILLARD McDANIEL:
Specialty 415, 424 ....7.00 - 10.00

KATHERINE McDAVID:
Okeh 8295 *Underground Blues* ....50.00 - 75.00

HELEN McDONALD:
Gennett 5193 *Squawkin' My Blues* ....25.00 - 40.00

TEE McDONALD:
Decca 7018 *Beef Man Blues* ....75.00 - 100.00

TECUMSEH McDOWELL:
Bluebird 5286 *My Man Blues* ....100.00 - 150.00
Sunrise 3367 *So Called Friend* ....100.00 - 200.00

BLACK PATCH McFADDEN:
Paramount 13021 *Whiskey Head Man* ....250.00 - 400.00

CHARLES/CHARLIE McFADDEN; "SPECKS" CHARLIE McFADDEN:
Bluebird 5160 *Piggly Wiggly Blues* ....100.00 - 150.00
    5203 *Times Are So Tight* ....150.00 - 200.00
    5325 *Last Journey Blues* ....100.00 - 150.00
    5384 *Lonesome Ghost Blues* ....100.00 - 150.00
Decca 7317 *People, People* ....25.00 - 40.00
Okeh 8894 *Don't Bite That Thing* ....100.00 - 150.00
Paramount 12928 *Groceries On The Shelf* ....200.00 - 300.00
    13076 *Groceries On The Shelf No. 2* ....250.00 - 400.00
Sunrise 3241 *People, People* ....100.00 - 200.00
    3284 *Friendless Man* ....150.00 - 300.00
    3406 *Low Down Rounders Blues* ....100.00 - 200.00
Victor 23420 *Lonesome Ghost Blues* ....400.00 - up

BROWNIE McGHEE (& SONNY TERRY/& HIS JOOK BLOCK BUSTERS):
Alert 400 *Key To The Highway* ....15.00 - 20.00
    401 *Mean Ole Frisco* ....15.00 - 20.00
    402 *Rock Me Mama* ....15.00 - 20.00
    403 *Worried Life Blues* ....15.00 - 20.00
    404 *Night Time Is The Right Time* ....15.00 - 20.00
    405 *Going Down Slow* ....15.00 - 20.00

    406 *Bad Blood* ....15.00 - 20.00
    407 *Strange Woman* ....15.00 - 20.00
    408 *Greyhound Bus* ....15.00 - 20.00
    409 *Evil But Kindhearted* ....15.00 - 20.00
    410 *Brownie Blues* ....15.00 - 20.00
    411 *My Mary Blues* ....15.00 - 20.00
    412 *Best Jelly Roll In Town* ....15.00 - 20.00
    413 *Baseball Boogie* ....15.00 - 20.00
    420 *How Can I Love You* ....15.00 - 20.00
Conqueror 9563, 9564, 9566, 9765, 9766, 9937,
  9938, 9939, 9940 ....7.00 - 10.00
Derby 776 *Sleepless Nights* ....10.00 - 15.00
    783 *All Night Party* ....10.00 - 15.00
Disc 6057 *Lonesome Blues* ....10.00 - 15.00
    6058 *Pawnshop Blues* ....10.00 - 15.00
    6059 *The Way I Feel* ....10.00 - 15.00
    6088 *Telegram Blues* ....15.00 - 20.00
Harlem 2323 *Worrying Over You* ....10.00 - 20.00 *
    2329 *My Confession* ....10.00 - 20.00 *
Jax 304 *Key To The Highway* ....10.00 - 15.00 *
    307 *Brownie's Blues* ....10.00 - 15.00 *
    310 *Dissatisfied Woman* ....10.00 - 15.00 *
    312 *Cherry Red* ....10.00 - 15.00 *
    322 *New Bad Blood* ....10.00 - 15.00 *
Savoy 704 *Wholesale And Retail* ....15.00 - 20.00
    714 *Good Roller Blues* ....15.00 - 20.00
    747 *Brownie's New Worried Life Blues* ....15.00 - 20.00
    760 *Feed Me Baby* ....15.00 - 20.00
    778 *My Consolation* ....15.00 - 20.00
    826 *That's The Stuff* ....10.00 - 15.00
    835 *Diamond Ring* ....15.00 - 20.00
    844 *Bottom Blues* ....10.00 - 15.00
    872 *Tell Me Baby* ....10.00 - 15.00 *
    899 *Sweet Baby Blues* ....10.00 - 15.00
    5533 *Knockabout Blues* ....15.00 - 20.00
    5534 *Woman Lover Blues* ....15.00 - 20.00
    5538 *Country Boy Boogie* ....15.00 - 25.00
    5541 *Auto Mechanic Blues* ....15.00 - 25.00
    5548 *Mabelle* ....15.00 - 20.00
    5550 *Hard Bed Blues* ....15.00 - 20.00
    5551 *Married Women Blues* ....15.00 - 20.00
    5557 *I Was Fooled* ....15.00 - 20.00
    5559 *Wrong Man Blues* ....15.00 - 20.00
    5561 *Good Thing Gone* ....15.00 - 20.00
    5565 *Poor Boy Blues* ....15.00 - 20.00
Sittin' In With 302 *A Letter To Lightnin' Hopkins* 15.00 - 20.00
    517 *My Bulldog Blues* ....15.00 - 20.00
Okeh 05785 *Picking My Tomatoes* ....8.00 - 12.00
    05812 *My Barkin' Bulldog Blues* ....10.00 - 20.00
    05881 *Not Guilty Blues* ....10.00 - 20.00
    05933 *Me And My Dog Blues* ....10.00 - 15.00
    06007 *Back Door Stranger* ....10.00 - 20.00
    06056 *Born For Bad Luck* ....10.00 - 20.00
    06265 *The Death Of Blind Boy Fuller* ....10.00 - 20.00
    06329 *Dealin With The Devil* ....10.00 - 20.00
    06419 *Double Trouble* ....10.00 - 20.00
    06437 *Key To My Door* ....10.00 - 15.00
    06472 *Barbecue Any Old Time* ....10.00 - 15.00
    06524 *I'm A Black Woman's Man* ....10.00 - 15.00
    06579 *Back Home Blues* ....10.00 - 15.00
    06698 *Step It Up And Go #2* ....10.00 - 15.00
(See the fourth section of this book for additional recordings by Brownie McGhee)

STICKS McGHEE (& HIS BUDDIES):

Atlantic 873 *Drinkin' Wine Spo-Dee-O-Dee*	15.00 -	30.00
881 *Lonesome Road Blues*	15.00 -	20.00
898 *Drank Up All That Wine*	15.00 -	20.00
909 *My Baby's Coming Back*	15.00 -	20.00
912 *She's Gone*	15.00 -	20.00
926 *House Warmin' Boogie*	15.00 -	20.00
937 *Blue Barrelhouse*	15.00 -	20.00
955 *Wee Wee Hours*	15.00 -	20.00
991 *New Found Love*	10.00 -	15.00 *
Decca 48104 *Drinkin' Wine Spo-Dee-O-Dee*	15.00 -	25.00
Essex 709 *My Little Rose*	15.00 -	20.00
Harlem 1018 *Drinkin' Wine Spo-Dee-O-Dee*	30.00 -	50.00
King 4610, 4628, 4672, 4700, 4783, 4800	7.00 -	12.00 *

(See the fourth section of this book for additional recordings by Sticks McGee in 45 RPM format)

ELDERS McINTORSH & EDWARD; LONNIE McINTORSH:

Okeh 8647 *The 1927 Flood*	50.00 -	100.00
8671 *Take A Stand*	50.00 -	100.00
8698 *Since I Laid My Burden Down*	50.00 -	100.00
Victor 21271 *The Lion And The Tribes Of Judah*	75.00 -	100.00
21411 *Arise And Shine*	75.00 -	100.00

ARTHUR/ART McKAY:

Decca 7068 *Central Limited Blues*	50.00 -	75.00
7364 *She Squeezed My Lemon*	25.00 -	40.00

McKENZIE AND CRUMP:

Paramount 12857 *That's A Married Man's Weakness*	75.00 -	100.00

BILLIE McKENZIE:

Vocalion 03385 *Romeo And Juliet*	15.00 -	20.00

WILLIE MAE McKENZIE:

Vocalion 03507 *Oh, Babe*	15.00 -	20.00
03552 *I'm Getting Even With You*	15.00 -	20.00
03562 *Little Red Wagon*	15.00 -	20.00

BILL McKINLEY:

Titles issued contemporaneously on Banner, Melotone, Oriole, Perfect, and Romeo: *I Went To The Gypsy; She Keeps On Kickin'* ....25.00 - 40.00

(DAVID) PETE McKINLEY:

Fidelity 3008 *Black Snake Blues*	20.00 -	30.00
Gotham 505 *Shreveport Blues*	20.00 -	30.00

SADIE McKINNEY:

Victor 20565 *Rock Away*	75.00 -	100.00

JIMMY McLAIN:

Vocalion 04444 *Tailor Made Blues*	15.00 -	20.00

CAB McMILLAN & HIS FADEAWAYS:

Macy's 5011 *I'm Young And Able*	15.00 -	20.00

DENNIS McMILLON:

Regal 3232 *Poor Little Angel*	30.00 -	50.00
3257 *I Woke Up One Morning*	30.00 -	50.00

FRED McMULLEN (AND RUTH WILLIS):

Titles issued contemporaneously on Banner, Melotone, Oriole, Perfect, and Romeo: *De Kalb Chain Blues; Just Can't Stand It; Poor Stranger Blues; Rolling Mama; Wait And Listen* ....50.00 - 75.00

BIG JAY McNEELY:

Imperial 5115 *All That Wine Is Gone*	15.00 -	25.00 *
5130 *Sad Story*	15.00 -	25.00
5164 *Let's Do It*	10.00 -	20.00
5169 *Tall Brown Woman*	15.00 -	20.00
5170 *Deacon Rides Again*	10.00 -	15.00 *
5176 *Jay Walk*	10.00 -	15.00 *

BLACK BOTTOM McPHAIL:

Vocalion 1690 *Mix That Thing*	150.00 -	200.00
1721 *Down In Black Bottom*	150.00 -	200.00
04220 *New Whiskey Man*	20.00 -	30.00
04317 *Don't Go Down In Black Bottom*	20.00 -	30.00

OZIE (DAYBREAK) McPHERSON:

Paramount 12327 *You Gotta Know How*	75.00 -	125.00
12350 *Standing On The Corner Blues*	75.00 -	125.00
12355 *Nobody Rolls Their Jelly Roll Like Mine*	50.00 -	80.00
12362 *I Want My Loving*	50.00 -	80.00

BLIND WILLIE McTELL; BLIND WILLIE & KATE McTELL:

Decca 7078 *Ticket Agent Blues*	150.00 -	200.00
7093 *Dying Gambler*	150.00 -	200.00
7117 *Hillbilly Willie's Blues*	100.00 -	150.00
7140 *We Got To Meet Death One Day*	100.00 -	150.00
7810 *Cold Winter Day*	50.00 -	75.00
Regal 3272 *It's My Desire*	50.00 -	80.00
Victor 21124 *Mr. McTell Got The Blues*	250.00 -	up
21474 *Writin' Paper Blues*	250.00 -	up
V38001 *Three Women Blues*	400.00 -	up
V38032 *Dark Night Blues*	400.00 -	up
V38580 *Drive Away Blues*	500.00 -	up

THE MELLO MOODS:

Red Robin 104 *I Couldn't Sleep A Wink Last Night*	100.00 -	200.00

MEMPHIS EDDIE:

RPM 301 *Velma Lee*	10.00 -	15.00
308 *Mercy Blues*	10.00 -	15.00
310 *Highway 61*	10.00 -	15.00
315 *Real Fine Girl*	10.00 -	15.00

MEMPHIS JIM/JIMMY:

RCA Victor 20-1887, 20-2278	7.00 -	10.00
Superior 2560 *Don't Leave Me Blues*	150.00 -	250.00

MEMPHIS JOE:

Vocalion 1277 *Plenty Gals Blues*	150.00 -	200.00

MEMPHIS MINNIE & KANSAS JOE (& HER JUG BAND/ & HER COMBO/WITH LITTLE JOE & HIS BAND):

Titles issued contemporaneously on Banner, Melotone, Oriole, Perfect, and Romeo: *Bumble Bee; Bumble Bee No. 2; Fishin' Blues; I'm Talkin' 'Bout You; Kind Treatment Blues; Outdoor Blues; Where Is My Good Man* ....50.00 - 100.00

Bluebird 6187 *When The Sun Goes Down*	50.00 -	80.00
6199 *Doctor, Doctor Blues*	30.00 -	50.00
6202 *Hustlin' Woman Blues*	75.00 -	100.00
Checker 771 *Me And My Chauffeur*	20.00 -	30.00 *
Columbia (red label, most issues)	7.00 -	10.00
Conqueror 9025, 9026, 9162, 9198, 9275, 9282, 9372, 9763, 9764, 9934, 9935, 9936	8.00 -	12.00
Decca 7019 *Chickasaw Train Blues*	100.00 -	150.00
7023 *Hole In The Wall*	100.00 -	150.00
7037 *Keep It To Yourself*	100.00 -	150.00
7038 *You Got To Move*	100.00 -	150.00

7048 *You Can't Give It Away*	75.00 -	100.00
7084 *Sylvester And His Mule Blues*	75.00 -	100.00
7102 *Down In New Orleans*	60.00 -	100.00
7125 *Jockey Man Blues*	60.00 -	100.00
7146 *Squat It*	50.00 -	80.00
J.O.B. 1101 *Kissing In The Dark*	25.00 -	50.00 *
Okeh 05670, 05728, 05811, 06288, 06410,		
06505, 06224, 06707	7.00 -	12.00
Okeh 8948 *My Butcher Man*	100.00 -	150.00
Regal 3259 *Kidman Blues*	30.00 -	50.00
Vocalion 1476 *Bumble Bee*	100.00 -	150.00
1512 *I'm Gonna Bake My Biscuits*	150.00 -	200.00
1556 *Bumble Bee-No. 2*	100.00 -	150.00
1576 *She Wouldn't Give Me None*	150.00 -	200.00
1588 *Frankie Jean*	150.00 -	200.00
1601 *Garage Fire Blues*	200.00 -	300.00
1603 *Good Girl Blues*	100.00 -	150.00
1618 *New Dirty Dozen*	150.00 -	200.00
1631 *Plymouth Rock Blues*	150.00 -	200.00
1638 *Dirt Dauber Blues*	150.00 -	200.00
1653 *Tricks Ain't Walkin' No More*	150.00 -	200.00
1658 *Soo Cow Soo*	150.00 -	200.00
1673 *Don't Bother It*	150.00 -	200.00
Vocalion 1678 *Crazy Cryin' Blues*	150.00 -	200.00
1682 *Minnie Minnie Bumble Bee*	150.00 -	200.00
1688 *Socket Blues*	150.00 -	250.00
1698 *Outdoor Blues*	100.00 -	150.00
1711 *Fishin' Blues*	100.00 -	150.00
1718 *Jailhouse Trouble Blues*	150.00 -	200.00
02711 *Stinging Snake Blues*	100.00 -	150.00
03046 *Joe Louis Strut*	30.00 -	50.00
03144 *Biting Bug Blues*	30.00 -	50.00
03187 *Ain't Nobody Home But Me*	30.00 -	50.00
03222 *Ice Man (Come On Up)*	30.00 -	50.00
03258 *I'm A Gamblin' Woman*	30.00 -	50.00
03285 *If You See My Rooster (Please Run Him Home)*		
	20.00 -	30.00
03398 *Dragging My Heart Around*	20.00 -	30.00
03436 *I Don't Want You No More*	20.00 -	30.00
03474 *It's Hard To Be Mistreated*	20.00 -	30.00
03541 *Ball And Chain Blues*	20.00 -	30.00
03581 *Black Cat Blues*	15.00 -	20.00
03612 *Down In The Alley*	15.00 -	20.00
03651 *Keep On Sailing*	15.00 -	20.00
03697 *No Need You Doggin' Me*	15.00 -	20.00
03768 *Living The Best I Can*	15.00 -	20.00
03894 *My Baby Don't Want Me No More*	15.00 -	20.00
03966 *Walking And Crying Blues*	15.00 -	20.00
04250 *I've Been Treated Wrong*	15.00 -	20.00
04295 *Good Biscuits*	15.00 -	20.00
04356 *Keep On Walking*	15.00 -	20.00
04506 *I'd Rather See Him Dead*	15.00 -	20.00
04694 *Good Soppin'*	15.00 -	20.00
04797 *Bad Outside Friends*	15.00 -	20.00
04858 *Call The Fire Wagon*	15.00 -	20.00
04898 *Don't Lead My Baby Wrong*	15.00 -	20.00
05004 *Poor And Wandering Woman Blues*	15.00 -	20.00

MEMPHIS MOSE:

Brunswick 7102 *Pig Meat Papa*	150.00 -	200.00
7134 *Blue Moanin' Blues*	150.00 -	200.00
7143 *Billie The Grinder*	150.00 -	200.00

MEMPHIS SAM AND JOHN:

Gennett 6987 *It's Just All Right*	100.00 -	150.00

MEMPHIS SLIM (& HIS/THE HOUSE ROCKERS; & HIS SOLID BAND):

Bluebird 8584 *Beer Drinking Woman*	15.00 -	25.00
8615 *Empty Room Blues*	15.00 -	25.00
8645 *Shelby County Blues*	15.00 -	25.00
8749 *Two Of A Kind*	15.00 -	20.00
8784 *Me Myself, And I*	15.00 -	20.00
8834 *Whiskey Store Blues*	15.00 -	20.00
8903 *Old Taylor*	15.00 -	20.00
8945 *Whiskey And Gin Blues*	15.00 -	20.00
8974 *Caught The Old Coon At Last*	15.00 -	20.00
9028 *Lend Me Your Love*	15.00 -	20.00
Chess 1491 *Walking Alone*	20.00 -	30.00
Federal 12007, 12015, 12021, 12033	8.00 -	12.00
Hy-Tone 10 *Mistake In Life*	10.00 -	15.00
17 *Slim's Boogie*	10.00 -	15.00
19 *Cheatin' Around*	10.00 -	15.00
King 4284, 4312, 4324, 4327	7.00 -	10.00
Master 1010, 1020, 1030	7.00 -	10.00
Mercury 8251, 8266, 8281, 70063	5.00 -	10.00
Miracle 102, 103, 110, 111, 125, 132, 145, 153	7.00 -	10.00
Old Swingmaster 1010 *Country Girl*	10.00 -	20.00
Peacock 1517 *Mean Little Woman*	8.00 -	12.00
1602 *Sittin' And Thinkin'*	8.00 -	12.00
Premium 850, 860, 867, 873, 878, 903	7.00 -	10.00

(See the fourth section of this book for additional recordings by Memphis Slim in 45 RPM and LP formats)

SARA MESSON:

Oriole 325 *Nobody Knows The Way I Feel*	15.00 -	30.00

ANNA MEYERS:

Davega 5067 *That Da Da Strain*	15.00 -	20.00
Pathe-Actuelle 020870 *That Da Da Strain*	10.00 -	15.00
020877 *Evil Minded Blues*	10.00 -	15.00
Perfect 12031 *That Da Da Strain*	10.00 -	15.00
12038 *Last Go Round Blues*	10.00 -	20.00

HAZEL MEYERS:

Ajax 17007 *Love Ain't Blind No More*	20.00 -	40.00
17019 *Mississippi Blues*	20.00 -	40.00
17026 *Heart Breakin' Joe*	30.00 -	50.00
17039 *Papa Don't Ask Mama Where She Was*	40.00 -	60.00
17040 *I'm Every Man's Mama*	25.00 -	40.00
17047 *War Horse Mama*	30.00 -	50.00
17048 *Hateful Blues*	30.00 -	50.00
17054 *Lonesome For That Man Of Mine*	30.00 -	50.00
17077 *Lost My Sweetie Blues*	35.00 -	50.00
17082 *He Used To Be Mine*	35.00 -	50.00
Banner 1358 *Plug Ugly*	10.00 -	15.00
Bell P-255 *Down Hearted Blues*	15.00 -	25.00
Emerson 10748 *Don't Know And Don't Care Blues*	20.00 -	30.00
Harmograph 925 *'Tain't A Doggone Thing But The Blues*		
	15.00 -	20.00
967 *Pipe Dream Blues*	20.00 -	30.00
Okeh 8364 *Blackville After Dark*	150.00 -	200.00
Pathe-Actuelle 032053 *Pipe Dream Blues*	20.00 -	30.00
Perfect 12132 *Pipe Dream Blues*	20.00 -	30.00
Regal 9654 *Plug Ugly*	10.00 -	15.00
Silvertone 3011 *Graveyard Dream Blues*	15.00 -	20.00
3012 *Maybe Someday*	25.00 -	40.00
Vocalion 14688 *Graveyard Dream Blues*	15.00 -	25.00

14709 *Awful Moanin' Blues* ....25.00 - 40.00
14725 *Mason-Dixon Blues* ....25.00 - 40.00
14861 *Maybe Someday* ....40.00 - 60.00

MIDNIGHT RAMBLERS:
Vocalion 03395 *Out With The Wrong Woman* ....15.00 - 25.00
03517 *Down In The Alley* ....15.00 - 30.00

AMOS MILBURN:
Aladdin 159, 160, 161, 173, 174 ....7.00 - 12.00
Aladdin (higher numbers).................................5.00 - 10.00
(See the fourth section of this book for additional Amos Milburn
    recordings in 45 RPM and LP format)

JOSIE MILES (accompanied by THE CHOO CHOO JAZZERS):
Ajax 17057 *Lovin' Henry Blues* ....30.00 - 50.00
17066 *Believe Me Hot Mama* ....30.00 - 50.00
17070 *South Bound Blues* ....30.00 - 50.00
17076 *Sweet Man Joe* ....30.00 - 50.00
17080 *A To Z Blues*..35.00 - 50.00
17083 *Picnic Time* ....35.00 - 50.00
17087 *Cross Word Papa*..................................35.00 - 50.00
17090 *I'm A Cabaret Nightingale* ....35.00 - 50.00
17092 *It Ain't Gonna Rain No Mo* ....25.00 - 40.00
17127 *At The Cake Walk Steppers Ball*..............50.00 - 80.00
17134 *Give Me Just A Little Bit Of Love* ....50.00 - 80.00
Banner 1498 *Bitter Feelin' Blues* ....20.00 - 30.00
1499 *Let's Agree To Disagree* ....20.00 - 30.00
1516 *Ghost Walkin' Blues* ....20.00 - 30.00
1534 *Low Down Daddy Blues* ....20.00 - 30.00
Black Swan 14121 *When You're Crazy Over Daddy*
....30.00 - 50.00
14130 *If You Want To Keep Your Daddy Home*.40.00 - 60.00
14133 *When I Dream Of Old Tennessee Blues* ..40.00 - 60.00
14136 *Four O'Clock Blues*...............................40.00 - 60.00
14139 *Low Down 'Bama Blues* ....40.00 - 60.00
Domino 3468 *Bitter Feelin' Blues*.........................20.00 - 30.00
3469 *Let's Agree To Disagree* ....20.00 - 30.00
3485 *Ghost Walkin' Blues* ....20.00 - 30.00
3504 *Low Down Daddy Blues* ....20.00 - 30.00
Edison 51476 *Sweet Man Joe* ....200.00 - 300.00
51477 *Temper'mental Papa*............................250.00 - 400.00
Gennett 5261 *Kansas City Man Blues* ....20.00 - 30.00
5292 *Graveyard Dream Blues* ....25.00 - 40.00
5307 *I Want My Sweet Daddy Now* ....20.00 - 30.00
5339 *Awful Moanin' Blues* ....20.00 - 30.00
5359 *War Horse Mamma*.................................20.00 - 30.00
5391 *31st Street Blues* ....20.00 - 30.00
Paramount 12156 *When You're Crazy Over Daddy* .....20.00 - 30.00
12157 *If You Want To Keep Your Daddy Home*.30.00 - 50.00
12158 *When I Dream Of Old Tennessee Blues* ..30.00 - 50.00
12159 *Four O'Clock Blues*...............................30.00 - 50.00
12160 *Low Down 'Bama Blues* ....30.00 - 50.00
Regal 9796 *Let's Agree To Disagree*.....................20.00 - 30.00
9797 *Bitter Feelin' Blues*.................................20.00 - 30.00
9810 *Can't Be Trusted Blues* ....20.00 - 30.00
9831 *Low Down Daddy Blues* ....20.00 - 30.00
Silvertone 4043 *Pipe Dream Blues* ....15.00 - 20.00
4048 *War Horse Mamma* ....15.00 - 20.00
4051 *Awful Moanin' Blues* ....15.00 - 20.00

LIZZIE MILES; LIZZIE MILES & THE MELROSE STOMPERS:
Titles issued contemporaneously on Banner, Conqueror, Domino,
    and Regal: *Banjo Papa; If You Can't Control Your Man;
    Lonesome Ghost Blues; Mean Old Bed Bug Blues; Police Blues;
    Second Hand Daddy; Shake It Down; Shootin' Star Blues; When
    You Get Tired Of Your New Sweetie* ....20.00 - 30.00
Bluebird 5064 *Electrician Blues* ....75.00 - 100.00
6152 *My Man O'War* ....15.00 - 25.00
Brunswick 2462 *My Pillow And Me* ....15.00 - 20.00
Columbia A-3897 *Haitian Blues* ....15.00 - 20.00
A-3920 *Triflin' Man* ....15.00 - 20.00
14335-D *My Diff-rent Kind O' Man* ....150.00 - 200.00
Emerson 10586 *Aggravatin' Papa*........................20.00 - 30.00
10603 *Tell Me Gypsy* ....15.00 - 25.00
10613 *Your Time Now* ....15.00 - 25.00
Okeh 8031 *Muscle Shoals Blues* ....30.00 - 50.00
8032 *State Street Blues* ....30.00 - 50.00
8037 *Wicked Blues* ....25.00 - 40.00
8039 *Lonesome Monday Morning Blues* ....25.00 - 40.00
8040 *Hot Lips* ....30.00 - 50.00
8048 *Sweet Smellin' Mama* ....30.00 - 50.00
8049 *The Trixie Blues* ....30.00 - 50.00
8050 *Black Bottom Blues* ....30.00 - 50.00
8052 *The Yellow Dog Blues* ....25.00 - 40.00
8456 *Slow Up Papa* ....50.00 - 80.00
Sunrise 3149 *My Man O'War* ....100.00 - 200.00
Victor 19083 *You're Always Messin' 'Round With My Man*
....8.00 - 12.00
19124 *Cotton Belt Blues* ....20.00 - 30.00
19158 *Keep Yourself Together Sweet Papa* ....15.00 - 20.00
Victor 23281 *My Man O' War*...........................250.00 - up
23298 *Electrician Blues*.................................500.00 - up
23306 *Done Throwed The Key Away*...............250.00 - up
V38607 *Good Time Papa* ....75.00 - 100.00
V38571 *I Hate A Man Like You* ....150.00 - 250.00
Vocalion 05165 *That's All Right Daddy*................10.00 - 15.00
05260 *Mellow Rhythm* ....10.00 - 15.00
05325 *He's Red Hot To Me* ....10.00 - 15.00
05392 *Twenty Grand Blues*.............................10.00 - 15.00

MILLER AND RODGERS:
Gennett 6782 *Everybody's Been Using That Thing*
....150.00 - 300.00
Paramount 12778 *I Would If I Could* ....200.00 - 300.00

AL MILLER (& HIS MARKET STREET BOYS/SWING STOMPERS); AL MILLER'S STRING BAND:
Black Patti 8047 *Someday Sweetheart*..................500.00 - up
8049 *Saturday Night Hymn*.............................500.00 - up
Brunswick 7063 *I Would If I Could* ....80.00 - 130.00
7084 *It Ain't Killed Nobody Yet*......................100.00 - 150.00
7088 *I Found Your Key Hole* ....100.00 - 150.00
7097 *It Must Be Good* ....100.00 - 150.00
7105 *Thirty First And State*............................100.00 - 150.00
7140 *That Stuff You Sell* ....100.00 - 150.00
7143 *Gimme A Li'l Taste* ....150.00 - 200.00
7212 *That Stuff Ain't No Good* ....75.00 - 125.00
Champion 50067 *Truckin' Old Fool*....................30.00 - 50.00
50072 *Ain't That A Mess?*..............................25.00 - 40.00
Decca 7830 *Juicy Mouth Shorty* ....15.00 - 20.00
Gennett 6875 *Mister Mary Blues*......................150.00 - 250.00

EDDIE MILLER:
Titles issued contemporaneously on Banner, Melotone, Oriole,
  Perfect, and Romeo: *I'd Rather Drink Muddy Water; Whoopie*
  ....50.00 - 75.00
Brunswick 7133 *Freight Train Blues* ....100.00 - 150.00
  7213 *School Day Blues* ....100.00 - 150.00

JIM MILLER:
Vocalion 1735 *Bye Bye Mama* ....75.00 - 100.00
  1737 *Joker Man Blues* ....100.00 - 150.00
  1741 *Hard Times Blues* ....75.00 - 100.00

LILLIAN MILLER:
Gennett 6486 *Butcher Shop Blues* ....100.00 - 150.00
  6518 *Dead Drunk Blues*..100.00 - 150.00
Okeh 8381 *Kitchen Blues* ....75.00 - 100.00

LUELLA MILLER (& HER DAGO HILL STRUTTERS):
Vocalion 1044 *Dago Hill Blues*...........................100.00 - 150.00
  1080 *Down In The Alley* ....75.00 - 100.00
  1081 *Rattle Snake Groan* ....75.00 - 100.00
  1102 *Carrier Pigeon Blues* ....100.00 - 150.00
  1103 *Jackson's Blues*..100.00 - 150.00
  1104 *Smiling Rose Blues* ....100.00 - 150.00
  1105 *North Wind Blues* ....100.00 - 150.00
  1147 *Tornado Groan* ....150.00 - 200.00
  1151 *Tombstone Blues* ....150.00 - 200.00
  1202 *'Frisco Blues*..150.00 - 200.00
  1234 *Chicago Blues*..150.00 - 200.00

MAE BELLE MILLER:
Broadway 5041 *Trouble Everywhere Blues* ....150.00 - 200.00
Paramount 12985 *Long Tall Man Blues* ....150.00 - 300.00

SODARISA/SODARISSA MILLER:
Paramount 12231 *Hot Springs Water Blues* ....50.00 - 80.00
  12243 *Don't Dog Me 'Round* ....75.00 - 125.00
  12261 *Broadway Daddy Blues* ....75.00 - 125.00
  12276 *Be Yourself*...75.00 - 100.00
  12293 *Nobody Knows* ....75.00 - 100.00
  12306 *Midnight Special*......................................75.00 - 100.00
Victor 20404 *Lonesome Room Blues*......................60.00 - 100.00

JOSIE MILLS:
Emerson 10874 *Low Down Daddy Blues* ....15.00 - 25.00

LILLIAN MILLS (See: LILLIAN MILLER)

MAUDE MILLS:
Titles issued contemporaneously on Banner, Domino, and Regal:
  Anything That Happens Just Pleases Me; Black Snake Blues
  ....50.00 - 75.00
Banner 6067 *Golden Brown Blues* ....30.00 - 50.00
Emerson 10624 *Triflin' Blues*..................................30.00 - 50.00
Pathe-Actuelle 7526 *Somebody's Been Loving My Baby*
  ....40.00 - 60.00
Perfect 126 *Somebody's Been Loving My Baby* ......40.00 - 60.00

VIOLET MILLS:
Domino 425 *Mad Mama's Blues*..............................20.00 - 30.00
  437 *Worried Blues* ....20.00 - 30.00
  438 *Don't Forget, You'll Regret*..........................20.00 - 30.00

ROY MILTON & HIS BAND/SOLID SENDERS:
Roy Milton 11 *Blues In My Heart* ....10.00 - 20.00
  18 *Wee Baby Brother Blues* ....10.00 - 20.00
  105 *R. M. Blues* ....10.00 - 20.00
  201 *Little Boy Blues* ....10.00 - 20.00

IRENE MIMS:
Vocalion 1183 *Dirty Blues*......................................50.00 - 75.00

MISS FRANKIE:
Titles issued contemporaneously on Banner, Domino, and Regal:
  Kissin' Mule Blues; Peepin' Jim Blues..............10.00 - 20.00
Titles issued contemporaneously on Grey Gull, Radiex: *I Can't Be
  Worried Long; I Need A Good Man Bad* ....15.00 - 30.00

MISSISSIPPI BLACKSNAKES:
Brunswick 7196 *It's So Nice And Warm* ....150.00 - 250.00
  7202 *Five Pound Ax Blues*..............................150.00 - 250.00
  7215 *Easy Going Woman Blues*......................150.00 - 250.00
  7222 *Bye Bye Baby Blues* ....150.00 - 250.00

MISSISSIPPI HOT FOOTERS:
Melotone 12303 *It Ain't No Good* ....75.00 - 100.00

MISSISSIPPI JOOK BAND:
Titles issued contemporaneously on Banner, Melotone, Oriole,
  Perfect, and Romeo: *Barbecue Bust; Dangerous Woman; Hittin'
  The Bottle Stomp; Skippy Whippy*.....................80.00 - 120.00

MISSISSIPPI MATILDA:
Bluebird 6812 *Hard Working Woman* ....25.00 - 40.00
  7908 *A. & V Blues*...20.00 - 30.00

THE MISSISSIPPI MOANER:
Vocalion 03166 *Mississippi Moan*....................... 100.00 - 200.00

THE MISSISSIPPI MUDDER: (See also: JIMMIE GORDON)
Decca 7008 *Someday I'll Be In The Clay* ....60.00 - 100.00
  7009 *Meat Cutter Blues* ....60.00 - 100.00
  7020 *Mean Mistreatin' Blues* ....50.00 - 75.00
  7036 *Candy Man Blues* ....50.00 - 75.00
  7046 *Bye Bye Baby Blues* ....50.00 - 75.00
  7087 *Going Back Home Blues* ....50.00 - 75.00
  7207 *Sweet Jelly Rollin'*.....................................20.00 - 30.00
  7822 *Evil Devil Woman Blues* ....20.00 - 30.00

MISSISSIPPI MUD MASHERS:
Bluebird 5845 *Bring It On Home To Grandma* ......20.00 - 30.00
  5988 *Take My Seat And Sit Down*.....................20.00 - 30.00
  7316 *Tiger Rag* ....15.00 - 20.00

MISSISSIPPI MUD STEPPERS:
Okeh 45504 *Jackson Stomp* .... 150.00 - 200.00
  45519 *Vicksburg Stomp* .... 150.00 - 200.00
  45532 *Farewell Waltz*.................................... 150.00 - 200.00

MISSISSIPPI SARAH (& DADDY STOVEPIPE):
Vocalion 1662 *Greenville Strut* .... 150.00 - 250.00
  1667 *Do You Love Him?* .... 150.00 - 250.00
  1670 *Jail Cell Blues* .... 150.00 - 300.00
  1676 *Jake Leg Blues* .... 150.00 - 300.00

MISSISSIPPI SHEIKS (WITH BO CARTER):
Bluebird 5452 *Pop Skull Blues* .... 60.00 - 100.00
  5453 *Sales Tax* .... 60.00 - 100.00
  5474 *Hitting The Numbers* .... 60.00 - 100.00
  5516 *I Am The Devil* .... 60.00 - 100.00
  5564 *Blues On My Mind* .... 60.00 - 100.00
  5618 *She's Got Something Crazy* .... 60.00 - 100.00
  5659 *Somebody's Got To Help Me* .... 60.00 - 100.00
  5847 *Do Right Blues* .... 50.00 - 75.00
  5881 *I Can't Go Wrong* .... 50.00 - 75.00
  5949 *Lean To One Woman* .... 50.00 - 75.00
  6006 *Dead Wagon Blues*................................... 50.00 - 75.00

Champion 50003 *Tell Me To Do Right*....................50.00 - 100.00
  50004 *Please Baby* ....50.00 - 100.00
  50007 *Don't Wake It Up*..50.00 - 100.00
  50013 *New Shake That Thing* ....50.00 - 100.00
  50021 *The New Stop And Listen Blues* ....50.00 - 100.00
  50030 *Shooting High Dice*......................................50.00 - 100.00
Columbia 14660-D *The World Is Going Wrong*....200.00 - 300.00
  14672-D *Kind Treatment* ....200.00 - 300.00
Okeh 8773 *Wintertime Blues* ....100.00 - 150.00
  8784 *Sitting On Top Of The World* ....75.00 - 100.00
  8807 *Driving That Thing* ....80.00 - 120.00
  8810 *Back To Mississippi* ....150.00 - 200.00
  8820 *Bootleggers' Blues*..150.00 - 200.00
  8834 *Jail Bird Love Song* ....150.00 - 200.00
  8843 *River Bottom Blues* ....150.00 - 200.00
  8854 *Sitting On Top Of The World-No. 2*.........125.00 - 175.00
  8859 *Unhappy Blues*..150.00 - 200.00
  8876 *Church Bell Blues* ....150.00 - 200.00
  8885 *She Ain't No Good* ....150.00 - 200.00
  8905 *Ram Rod Blues* ....150.00 - 200.00
  8922 *Please Baby* ....150.00 - 200.00
  8927 *Bed Spring Poker* ....150.00 - 200.00
  8933 *She's A Bad Girl* ....150.00 - 200.00
  8939 *Jake Leg Blues* ....150.00 - 200.00
  8947 *Kitty Cat Blues* ....150.00 - 200.00
  8951 *Shake Hands And Tell Me Goodbye* ....150.00 - 200.00
  8953 *Too Long* ....150.00 - 200.00
Paramount 13134 *The New Stop And Listen Blues*
  ....250.00 - up
  13142 *Shooting High Dice*....................................300.00 - up
  13143 *New Shake That Thing* ....300.00 - up
  13152 *Don't Wake It Up*..300.00 - up
  13152 *Please Baby* ....300.00 - up
  13156 *Tell Me To Do Right* ....300.00 - up

MISSISSIPPI TRIO:
Supertone 9528 *Doin' That Thing* ....125.00 - 175.00

BILLY MITCHELL:
Bluebird 6358 *Two Old Maids* ....20.00 - 30.00
  6391 *Looking For A Cherry* ....20.00 - 30.00
  6651 *I Never See Maggie Alone* ....20.00 - 30.00

WALTER MITCHELL:
JVB 75827 *Pet Milk Blues*..................................100.00 - 200.00

MONARCH JAZZ QUARTET:
Okeh 8736 *Four Or Five Times*............................30.00 - 50.00
  8761 *I Ain't Got Nobody*......................................30.00 - 50.00
  8931 *Pleading Blues* ....40.00 - 60.00

MONKEY JOE (& HIS MUSIC GRINDERS):
Bluebird 6061 *Sweet Petunia Stomp*......................30.00 - 50.00
  6114 *Monkey Joe Got The Blues* ....30.00 - 50.00
Conqueror 9163 *Taxes On My Pole* ....10.00 - 20.00
  9286 *B. V. D. Blues* ....10.00 - 20.00
Okeh 05685 *We Can't Get Along* ....15.00 - 20.00
  06153 *McComb City Blues* ....15.00 - 20.00
Vocalion 04161 *O. K. With Me Baby* ....20.00 - 30.00
  04219 *Hair Parted In The Middle* ....20.00 - 30.00
  04294 *Some Sweet Day*..20.00 - 30.00
  04416 *Preach, Pray And Moan* ....15.00 - 20.00
  04471 *Rabbit Foot Blues* ....15.00 - 20.00
  04618 *New York Central* ....15.00 - 20.00
  04814 *Tailor Made Woman* ....15.00 - 20.00
  04871 *Good Business No. 2* ....15.00 - 20.00
  04926 *Wise To The Jive* ....15.00 - 20.00

  04978 *Mobile And K.C. Line* ....15.00 - 20.00
  05166 *Carry My Business On* ....15.00 - 20.00
  05274 *That Same Cat*..15.00 - 20.00
  05348 *Mountain Baby Blues* ....15.00 - 20.00

ALEX MONROE:
Bell 1190 *The Worried Man Blues* ....250.00 - 300.00

"E." MONTGOMERY:
Melotone 12548 *Louisiana Blues* ....100.00 - 200.00
Vocalion 02706 *Louisiana Blues* ....100.00 - 200.00

LITTLE BROTHER MONTGOMERY:
Bluebird 6072 *Vicksburg Blues No. 2* ....35.00 - 50.00
  6140 *Pleading Blues* ....35.00 - 50.00
  7970 *Vicksburg Blues No. 2* ....25.00 - 40.00
Century 4009 *Long Time* ....10.00 - 15.00
  4010 *Swingin' With Lee* ....10.00 - 15.00
Paramount 13006 *Vicksburg Blues* ....400.00 - up

SAM MONTGOMERY ("KING OF SPADES"):
Titles issued contemporaneously on Banner, Melotone, Oriole,
   Perfect, and Romeo: *Baby Please Don't Go; Blue Devil Blues;*
   Honey Dripper; I'm Through With You; King Of Knave; King Of
   Knave No. 2.; Low In Mind Blues; Mercy Mercy Blues
   ....75.00 - 100.00

JULIA MOODY:
Titles issued contemporaneously on Banner and Regal: *Don't*
   Forget, You'll Regret; Mad Mama's Blues; Worried Blues
   ....15.00 - 30.00
Black Swan 14122 *The Cootie Crawl*......................50.00 - 75.00
  14140 *Starvin' For Love* ....50.00 - 75.00
  14144 *Good Man Sam* ....50.00 - 75.00
Columbia 14087-D *Strivin' Blues*............................30.00 - 50.00
  14103-D *Midnight Dan* ....60.00 - 100.00
  14121-D *That Chicago Wiggle* ....60.00 - 100.00
Paramount 12153 *That Cootie Crawl* ....50.00 - 75.00
  12154 *Starvin' For Love* ....50.00 - 75.00
  12155 *Good Man Sam* ....50.00 - 75.00

ETTA MOONEY:
Black Swan 14118 *Early Every Morn* ....50.00 - 75.00
  14134 *Cootie For Your Tootie* ....50.00 - 75.00
Paramount 12151 *Early Every Morn* ....50.00 - 75.00
  12152 *Cootie For Your Tootie* ....50.00 - 75.00

(WHISTLIN') ALEX (ANDER) MOORE:
Columbia 14496-D *West Texas Woman* ....150.00 - 200.00
  14518-D *Ice Pick Blues* ....150.00 - 200.00
  14596-D *Blue Bloomer Blues* ....150.00 - 200.00
Decca 7288 *Blue Bloomer Blues*............................30.00 - 50.00
  7552 *Hard Hearted Woman* ....30.00 - 50.00
RPM 326 *Neglected Woman* ....30.00 - 50.00

ALICE MOORE:
Decca 7028 *Riverside Blues*....................................75.00 - 100.00
  7056 *Lonesome Woman Blues* ....75.00 - 100.00
  7109 *Just Sitting Here Wondering* ....30.00 - 50.00
  7132 *Blue Black And Evil Blues* ....30.00 - 50.00
  7153 *Daddy Calling Mama* ....30.00 - 50.00
  7190 *Grass Cutter Blues* ....30.00 - 50.00
  7227 *Money Tree Man* ....30.00 - 50.00
  7253 *I'm Going Fishing Too*................................30.00 - 50.00
  7293 *New Blue Black And Evil Blues* ....15.00 - 20.00
  7327 *Midnight Creepers* ....15.00 - 20.00
  7369 *Don't Deny Me Baby* ....15.00 - 20.00

7380 *Doggin' Man Blues*.....................................15.00 - 20.00
7393 *Push Cart Pusher*.......................................15.00 - 20.00
Paramount 12819 *Black And Evil Blues* ....200.00 - 300.00
12868 *My Man Blues* ....200.00 - 300.00
12947 *Serving Time Blues* ....200.00 - 300.00
12973 *Have Mercy Blues*......................................200.00 - 300.00
13107 *Lonesome Dream Blues* ....200.00 - 300.00

ARAH "BABY" MOORE:
Victor 20553 *Drop Down Blues* ....75.00 - 100.00

BILL MOORE:
Paramount 12613 *Barbershop Rag*......................150.00 - 250.00
12636 *Ragtime Millionaire*................................150.00 - 250.00
12648 *One Way Gal*..150.00 - 250.00

JAZZ BABY MOORE:
Vocalion 1045 *Morning Prayer* ....50.00 - 75.00

(KID) PRINCE MOORE:
Titles issued contemporaneously on Banner, Melotone, Oriole, Perfect, and Romeo: *Bug Juice Blues; Church Bells; Honey Dripping Papa; Sign Of Judgment* ....50.00 - 75.00
Decca 7475 *Single Man Blues* ....25.00 - 40.00
7514 *Ford V-8 Blues*..25.00 - 40.00
7539 *That's Lovin' Me*...25.00 - 40.00

MONETTE MOORE:
Ajax 17124 *Memphis Blues* ....30.00 - 50.00
Columbia 14105-D *Get It Fixed* ....50.00 - 80.00
Decca 7161 *Rhythm Shop Swing* ....15.00 - 20.00
Paramount 12015 *Sugar Blues*................................25.00 - 40.00
12028 *I Just Want A Daddy*.................................25.00 - 40.00
12030 *Gulf Coast Blues*.......................................25.00 - 40.00
12046 *I'll Go To My Grave With The Blues*.....100.00 - 150.00
12067 *Muddy Water Blues*....................................25.00 - 40.00
12210 *Friendless Blues*...30.00 - 50.00
Victor 20356 *If You Don't Like Potatoes* ....50.00 - 75.00
20484 *Moaning Sinner Blues* ....50.00 - 75.00
Vocalion 14903 *I Wanna Jazz Some More*..............25.00 - 40.00
14911 *Death Letter Blues* ....25.00 - 40.00

PHILIP MOORE & COMPANY:
Brunswick 7018 *One Thin Dime* ....50.00 - 75.00
Vocalion 1169 *Loaded Dice* ....50.00 - 75.00

ROSIE MAE MOORE:
Victor 21280 *Staggering Blues*...............................75.00 - 100.00
21408 *School Girl Blues*......................................75.00 - 100.00

WILLIAM MOORE:
Paramount 12761 *Raggin' The Blues* ....200.00 - 300.00

EDDIE MORGAN:
Bluebird 5757 *Rock House Blues* ....40.00 - 60.00

CLARA MORRIS:
Bluebird 8700 *I Stagger In My Sleep* ....15.00 - 20.00
8767 *Poker Playing Daddy*..................................15.00 - 20.00

MOSBY AND SYKES:
Champion 16513 *Mosby Stomp* ....300.00 - up

TOMMY MOSLEY:
Two Mikes 602 *I'm Still A Fool* ....15.00 - 20.00

BUDDY MOSS:
Titles issued contemporaneously on Banner, Conqueror*, Melotone, Oriole, Perfect, and Romeo: *Bachelors' Blues; Back To My Used-To-Be; Best Gal; B & O Blues No. 2; Broke Down Engine; Bye Bye Mama; Can't Use You No More; Cold Country Blues; Daddy Don't Care; Dough Rolling Papa; Evil Hearted Papa; Going To Your Funeral In A Vee-Eight Ford; Gravy Server; Hard Road Blues; Hard Times Blues; Insane Blues; Jealous Hearted Man; Jinx Man Blues; Love Me Baby, Love Me; Married Man's Blues; Misery Man Blues; Mistreated Boy; My Baby Wont's Pay Me No Mind; New Lovin' Blues; Oh Lordy Mama; Oh Lordy Mama No. 2; Prowlin' Gambler Blues; Prowling Woman; Red River Blues; Restless Night Blues; See What You Done Done; Shake It All Night Long; Sleepless Night; Somebody Keeps Calling Me; Someday Baby; Some Lonesome Day; Stinging Bull Nettle; Stop Hanging Around; T.B.'s Killing Me; Too Doggone Jealous; Travelin' Blues; Tricks Ain't Walking No More; Undertaker Blues; Unkind Woman; When I'm Dead And Gone; When The Hearse Rolls Me From My Door; Worrysome Woman; You Got To Give Me Some Of It; Your Hard Head Will Bring You Sorrow Some Day* ....50.00 - 75.00
(*Some of the Conqueror issues are worth less, being reissues)
Columbia (red label) ....7.00 - 10.00
Okeh 06473 *Joy Rag* ....15.00 - 20.00
06515 *You Need A Woman* ....10.00 - 20.00
06679 *Little Angel Blues* ....15.00 - 20.00

TEDDY MOSS:
Gennett 6993 *Texas Dream Blues*......................150.00 - 200.00
7010 *You Broke My Heart Baby* ....150.00 - 200.00
7055 *Ocean Wave Blues* ....150.00 - 200.00
7084 *Back-Biter Blues* ....150.00 - 200.00
7158 *Rocky Luck Blues* ....200.00 - 300.00

MR. FREDDIE:
Bluebird 5995 *4A Highway*................................60.00 - 100.00
6025 *Your Good Man Is Gone* ....60.00 - 100.00
6261 *Let's Go Riding* ....60.00 - 100.00

MR. GOOGLE EYES (See JOE AUGUST)

MUDDY WATERS:
Aristocrat 406 *Screamin' And Cryin'* ....80.00 - 130.00
412 *Rollin' And Tumblin'* ....50.00 - 75.00
1302 *Little Anna Mae*..80.00 - 130.00
1304 *She Ain't Nowhere* ....50.00 - 80.00
1305 *I Feel Like Going Home*............................50.00 - 80.00
1306 *Train Fare Home* ....50.00 - 80.00
1307 *Mean Red Spider* ....80.00 - 130.00
1310 *Muddy Jumps One* ....80.00 - 130.00
1311 *Little Geneva*..80.00 - 130.00
Chess 1426 *Rollin' Stone* ....50.00 - 75.00
1434 *You're Gonna Need My Help I Said* ....50.00 - 75.00
1441 *Louisiana Blues*..50.00 - 75.00
1452 *Long Distance Call* ....50.00 - 75.00
1468 *Honey Bee* ....50.00 - 75.00
1480 *My Fault* ....40.00 - 60.00
1490 *Early Morning Blues* ....40.00 - 60.00
1509 *All Night Long* ....25.00 - 40.00
1514 *Please Have Mercy* ....25.00 - 40.00
1526 *Gone To Main Street* ....20.00 - 30.00 *
1537 *Sad, Sad Day*..20.00 - 30.00 *
(See the fourth section of this book for additional recordings by Muddy Waters in 45 RPM and LP formats)

MUMBLES:
Modern 809 *Little Boy Blue*.................................50.00 - 75.00
RPM 338 *Black Gal*.......................................50.00 - 75.00 *

GLADYS MURRAY:
Banner 1464 *Everybody Loves My Baby*.................20.00 - 30.00
    1479 *Nobody Knows What A Red Head Mama Can Do*
....20.00 - 30.00
Regal 9760 *Everybody Loves My Baby*....................20.00 - 30.00
    9779 *Nobody Knows What A Red Head Mama Can Do*
....20.00 - 30.00

THE MUSKATEERS:
Roxy 801 *Deep In My Heart*.............................50.00 - 100.00
Swing Time 331 *Deep In My Heart*......................50.00 - 100.00

MABEL NANCE:
Silvertone 3547 *The Stomps*.........................100.00 - 150.00

(CHARLIE) DAD NELSON (& HIS GUITAR):
Paramount 12401 *Red River Blues*.....................100.00 - 150.00
    12430 *Mississippi Strut*..........................100.00 - 150.00
    12467 *Traveling Daddy*............................100.00 - 150.00
    12492 *Cleveland Stomp*............................100.00 - 150.00

PEPPERMINT NELSON:
Gold Star 626 *Peppermint Boogie*......................50.00 - 80.00

RED NELSON:
Bluebird 7265 *Relief Blues*...........................20.00 - 30.00
    7918 *Black Gal Stomp*...............................20.00 - 30.00
    7960 *Working Man Blues*...........................20.00 - 30.00
Decca 7136 *Grand Trunk Blues*........................40.00 - 60.00
    7154 *Detroit Special*...............................40.00 - 60.00
    7155 *Sweetest Thing Born*.........................50.00 - 75.00
    7171 *Streamline Train*.............................50.00 - 75.00
    7185 *Enpty Bed Blues*..............................25.00 - 40.00
    7256 *Gambling Man*................................25.00 - 40.00
    7263 *Gravel In My Bed*.............................25.00 - 40.00
Vocalion 03001 *Six Cold Feet In The Ground*........40.00 - 60.00

ROMEO NELSON:
Vocalion 1447 *Head Rag Hop*.........................150.00 - 250.00
    1494 *Dyin' Rider Blues*...........................150.00 - 200.00

SONNY BOY NELSON:
Bluebird 6672 *Street Walkin'*........................30.00 - 50.00
    6718 *Lovin' Blues*.................................30.00 - 50.00
    7091 *Low Down*....................................30.00 - 50.00
    7849 *Long Tall Woman*.............................30.00 - 50.00

"BLUE COAT" TOM NELSON:
Okeh 8838 *Blue Coat Blues*..........................100.00 - 150.00

BLIND (GUSSIE) NESBIT/NESBITT:
Columbia 14576-D *Pure Religion*......................50.00 - 75.00
Decca 7113 *He's The Joy Of My Salvation*............30.00 - 50.00
    7131 *Motherless Children*.........................30.00 - 50.00

SCOTTIE NESBITT:
Bluebird 7125 *Sundown Blues*.........................10.00 - 15.00
    7155 *Troubled And Blue*...........................10.00 - 15.00

HAMBONE WILLIE NEWBERN:
Okeh 8679 *Roll And Tumble Blues*....................150.00 - 200.00
    8693 *My Down In Arkansas*.........................150.00 - 200.00
    8740 *She Could Toddle-Oo*.........................150.00 - 200.00

JACK NEWMAN:
Vocalion 04265 *Blackberry Wine*......................15.00 - 20.00
    04344 *New Prison Blues*............................15.00 - 20.00

NEW ORLEANS NEHI BOYS:
Paramount 12980 *Mobile Stomp*........................250.00 - up

MANNY NICHOLS:
FCB 125 *Walkin' Talkin' Blues*.......................100.00 - 150.00
Imperial 5162 *No One To Love Me*.....................50.00 - 75.00
    5173 *Worried Life Blues*...........................50.00 - 75.00

NICK NICHOLS:
Columbia 2071-D *Frankie And Johnny*.................30.00 - 50.00
    14512-D *Riverside Blues*...........................80.00 - 120.00

FREDDIE "REDD" NICHOLSON:
Brunswick 7152 *Dirty No Gooder*......................100.00 - 150.00
    7204 *Freddie's Got The Blues*.....................100.00 - 150.00
    7220 *Tee Roller's Rub*.............................100.00 - 150.00

"BOZO" NICKERSON:
Vocalion 1487 *What's The Matter Now? Part 1/2* . 80.00 - 120.00
    1525 *Bozo's Blues*................................100.00 - 150.00
    1604 *What's The Matter Now? Part 3/4*..........100.00 - 150.00

CHARLIE NICKERSON:
Victor 23310 *Going Back To Memphis*................400.00 - up

NIC NACS:
RPM 316 *You Didn't Want My Love*.....................30.00 - 60.00

THE NIGHTHAWKS:
Aristocrat 413 *Jackson Town Gal*......................80.00 - 120.00
    2301 *Black Angel Blues*...........................80.00 - 120.00

ROBERT NIGHTHAWK (& HIS NIGHTHAWKS BAND):
Chess 1484 *Return Mail Blues*........................25.00 - 40.00
States 131 *Maggie Campbell*..........................30.00 - 50.00 *
United 102 *Kansas City Blues*........................50.00 - 75.00
    105 *Take It Easy Baby*.............................50.00 - 75.00

BILLY NIGHTINGALE (See BILL REESE)

WILLIE NIX (& HIS COMBO):
Chance 1163 *Nervous Wreck*...........................30.00 - 50.00 *
Checker 756 *Truckin' Little Woman*...................20.00 - 30.00
RPM 327 *Lonesome Bedroom Blues*.....................25.00 - 40.00 *
Sabre 104 *All By Myself*.............................30.00 - 50.00 *
Sun 179 *Baker Shop Boogie*..........................150.00 - 300.00

ELMORE NIXON:
Mercury 70061 *Playboy Blues*.........................10.00 - 15.00
Peacock 1537 *Alabama Blues*..........................10.00 - 15.00
    1572 *A Hep Cat's Advice*..........................10.00 - 15.00
Savoy 878 *Forgive Me Baby*...........................10.00 - 15.00
    889 *Sad And Blue*.................................10.00 - 15.00
    1105 *If You'll Be My Love*.........................10.00 - 15.00
Sittin' In With 546 *Foolish Love*....................15.00 - 20.00
    580 *I'm Moving Out*...............................15.00 - 20.00
    601 *Shout and Rock*...............................15.00 - 20.00

GEORGE NOBLE:
Titles issued contemporaneously on Banner, Melotone, Oriole,
    Perfect, and Romeo: *If You Lose Your Good Gal; Don't Mess
    With Mine; The Seminole Blues*......................150.00 - 200.00
Vocalion 02905 *New Milk Cow Blues*...................150.00 - 200.00
    02923 *Bed Spring Blues*...........................150.00 - 200.00
    02954 *On My Death Bed*............................150.00 - 200.00

HATTIE NOEL:
MGM 10275 *Put Some Glue On That Mule*..........10.00 - 15.00
    10355 *High Livin' Papa*...........................10.00 - 15.00
    10752 *Evil Daddy Blues*...........................10.00 - 15.00

DIXIE NOLAN-JOHNNY HARDGE:
Victor V38556 *Worried Love* ....150.00 - 200.00

NORA AND DELLE:
Decca 7852 *Army Camp Blues* ....10.00 - 15.00
   7858 *Keep A Knockin'* ....10.00 - 15.00

NORFOLK JAZZ QUARTET:
Decca 7333 *Tell That Broad*.......................10.00 - 15.00
   7349 *Just Dream Of You*............................10.00 - 15.00
   7383 *What's The Matter Now?*...................10.00 - 15.00
   7443 *Suntan Baby Brown* ....10.00 - 15.00
Okeh 4318 *Jelly Roll Blues*.......................20.00 - 30.00
   4345 *Monday Morning Blues* ....20.00 - 30.00
   4366 *Preacher Man Blues* ....20.00 - 30.00
   4380 *Big Fat Mamma* ....20.00 - 30.00
   4391 *Going Home Blues* ....20.00 - 30.00
   8007 *Strut Miss Lizzie*.........................20.00 - 30.00
   8019 *Honey, Bless Your Heart* ....20.00 - 30.00
   8022 *Wang Wang Blues* ....20.00 - 30.00
   8028 *I Could Learn To Love You* ....20.00 - 30.00
Paramount 12032 *Ain't It A Shame?* ....25.00 - 40.00
   12054 *Sad Blues* ....25.00 - 40.00
   12055 *Dixie Blues* ....25.00 - 40.00
   12218 *Jelly Roll's First Cousin* ....40.00 - 60.00
   12453 *Louisiana Bo Bo* ....40.00 - 60.00
   12844 *Please Give Me Some Of That* ....50.00 - 75.00

BEN NORSINGLE:
Brunswick 7041 *Rover's Blues*...............150.00 - 200.00
   7043 *Black Cat Blues*............................150.00 - 200.00

HATTIE NORTH:
Vocalion 1433 *Honey Dripper Blues* ......100.00 - 150.00

NUGRAPE TWINS:
Columbia 14187-D *I Got Your Ice Cold Nugrape*...30.00 - 50.00
   14251-D *The Road Is Rough And Rocky* ....30.00 - 50.00

THE NU-TONES:
Hollywood Star 798 *Believe* ....50.00 - 80.00

OAK CLIFF T-BONE:
Columbia 14506-D *Trinity River Blues* ....150.00 - 200.00

JIMMIE/JIMMY ODEN:
Bluebird 5260 *My Dream Blues* ....100.00 - 150.00
Champion 16540 *I Have Made Up My Mind* ....200.00 - 300.00
   16613 *Patrol Wagon Blues* ....250.00 - up
   50044 *Patrol Wagon Blues* ....50.00 - 80.00
Sunrise 3343 *Warning Spirit Blues*.........100.00 - 200.00

OLD MAN ODEN:
Decca 7017 *Six Feet In The Ground*.......75.00 - 100.00
   7412 *Silk Worm Blues*...........................30.00 - 50.00
   7545 *Thick And Thin*.............................30.00 - 50.00

OLD CED ODOM:
Decca 7241 *Hotter Than Fire* ....10.00 - 15.00
   7247 *Break 'Er Down*.............................10.00 - 15.00
   7276 *Fore Day In The Morning*..............10.00 - 15.00

OLD MAN MOSE:
Regent 1046 *Matchbox Blues* ....- - -

OLD PAL SMOKE SHOP FOUR:
Vocalion 1046 *Black Cat Blues*.............150.00 - 250.00

OLD SOUTH QUARTETTE:
Broadway 5031 *Pussy Cat Rag* ....100.00 - 150.00

QRS 7006 *Pussy Cat Rag* ....100.00 - 150.00
   7025 *No Hiding Place Down Here* ....100.00 - 150.00
   7029 *Watermelon Party* ....100.00 - 150.00

ONE ARM SLIM:
Bluebird 7806 *Howling Man Blues*........................30.00 - 50.00
Vocalion 04676 *Crap Shootin' Blues* ....15.00 - 20.00

ONE STRING SAM:
J.V.B. 40 *I Need A Hundred Dollars* ....50.00 - 80.00

ORIGINAL LOUISIANA ENTERTAINERS:
Champion 15264 *The France Blues* ....200.00 - 300.00

THE ORIOLES:
Jubilee 5000 *Barbra Lee* ....20.00 - 30.00
   5001 *Dare To Dream* ....40.00 - 70.00
   5002 *It Seems So Long Ago* ....20.00 - 30.00
   5005 *Tell Me So* ....20.00 - 30.00
   5008 *I Challenge Your Kiss* ....20.00 - 30.00
Jubilee 5009 *A Kiss And A Rose* ....25.00 - 40.00
   5018 *Will You Still Be The One In My Heart*.....25.00 - 50.00
   5026 *Moonlight* ....25.00 - 50.00
   5028 *You're Gone* ....25.00 - 50.00
   5031 *I'd Rather Have You Under The Moon*.....30.00 - 60.00
   5037 *I Need You So*.............................40.00 - 70.00
   5055 *Pal Of Mine* ....40.00 - 60.00
   5057 *Would I Love You* ....20.00 - 40.00
Natural 5000 *Barbra Lee* ....20.00 - 30.00
(Note: See also the **RHYTHM & BLUES, ETC.** section for other records by The Orioles)

JOHN OSCAR (TRIO):
Brunswick 7080 *In The Gutter* ....100.00 - 150.00
   7104 *Mama Don't Allow No Easy Riders Here*. 80.00 - 120.00
   7203 *Whoopee Mama Blues*........................100.00 - 150.00
Decca 7029 *Got To Be Worried Now*....................50.00 - 80.00
Supertone 2212 *In The Gutter* ....25.00 - 40.00
Vocalion 02701 *In The Gutter* ....50.00 - 80.00

DUKE OWENS & BUD WILSON:
Gennett 6366 *When A Man Is Treated Like A Dog*
   ....150.00 - 250.00
   6423 *It's Hot-Let It Alone* ....150.00 - 250.00

"BIG BOY" GEORGE OWENS:
Gennett 6006 *Kentucky Blues* ....100.00 - 150.00

MARSHALL OWENS:
Paramount 13117 *Texas Blues* ....500.00 - 1000.00
   13131 *Texas Blues-Part 2* ....500.00 - 1000.00

WILLIE "SCARE CROW" OWENS:
Brunswick 7213 *Cut It Out* ....100.00 - 150.00

STAR PAGE:
Paramount 12684 *Georgia Blues* ....80.00 - 120.00

DUKE PAIGE:
Juke Box 520 *Two Faced Woman Blues*.................10.00 - 15.00

SYLVESTER PALMER:
Columbia 14492-D *Lonesome Man Blues* ....50.00 - 75.00
   14524-D *Broke Man Blues*................................50.00 - 75.00

FRANK PALMES:
Paramount 12893 *Troubled 'Bout My Soul* ....150.00 - 300.00

PALMETTO JAZZ QUARTET:
Okeh 8011 *My Jazz Gal* ....20.00 - 30.00
   8016 *Sweet Mamma (Papa's Getting Mad)*.......20.00 - 30.00

8023 *Baseball Blues* ....20.00 - 30.00
8028 *"U" Need Some Loving* ....20.00 - 30.00
8034 *Norfolk Religion*................................20.00 - 30.00

PAPA CHARLIE'S BOYS:
Bluebird 6408 *Let My Peaches Be*...................25.00 - 40.00
6602 *Gypsy Woman Blues* ....25.00 - 40.00

PAPA EGG SHELL:
Brunswick 7082 *I'm Goin' Up In The Country* .....100.00 - 150.00
7095 *Whole Soul Blues* ....100.00 - 150.00

PAPA FREDDIE:
Okeh 8422 *Muddy Water Blues* ....150.00 - 200.00

PAPA TOO SWEET:
Okeh 8651 *Big Fat Mama* ....75.00 - 100.00

EVA PARKER:
Victor 20414 *You Got Yourself Another Woman* ....15.00 - 30.00
V-38020 *Careless Love* ....15.00 - 30.00

LITTLE JUNIOR PARKER & HIS BLUE FLAMES:
Modern 864 *You're My Angel* ....15.00 - 20.00

MONISTER PARKER:
Nucraft 100 *Black Snake Blues*..........................50.00 - 75.00

SHORTY BOB PARKER:
Decca 7470 *Death Of Slim Green* ....25.00 - 40.00
7488 *Tired Of Being Drug Around*....................25.00 - 40.00
7526 *Rain And Snow*..25.00 - 40.00

SONNY PARKER:
Columbia 30154 *Tossin' And Turnin'* ....7.00 - 10.00

GENE PARRISH:
RPM 302 *Gone Awhile Blues* ....15.00 - 25.00
307 *You're Worrying Me* ....15.00 - 25.00

TURNER PARRISH:
Champion 16509 *Four Day Blues* ....200.00 - 300.00
16629 *Graveyard Blues* ....200.00 - 300.00
16645 *Trenches*..200.00 - 300.00
50027 *Graveyard Blues* ....50.00 - 75.00
50046 *Fives*..35.00 - 50.00

LILA PATTERSON:
Broadway 5005 *Grievin' Hearted Blues* ....100.00 - 150.00
5010 *Don't Fish In My Sea*............................100.00 - 150.00
5018 *Dead Drunk Blues*..................................100.00 - 150.00

PATTON AND LEE:
Vocalion 02904 *Troubled 'Bout My Mother* ....250.00 - 500.00

CHARLEY PATTON:
Paramount 12792 *Banty Rooster Blues* ....800.00 - up
12854 *It Won't Be Long*................................800.00 - up
12869 *A Spoonful Blues*..................................800.00 - up
12877 *Pea Vine Blues*....................................800.00 - up
12883 *Lord I'm Discouraged* ....800.00 - up

12909 *High Water Everywhere*........................800.00 - up
12924 *Rattlesnake Blues* ....800.00 - up
12943 *Magnolia Blues* ....800.00 - up
12953 *Mean Black Moan* ....800.00 - up
12972 *Green River Blues* ....800.00 - up
12986 *I Shall Not Be Moved* ....800.00 - up
12998 *Hammer Blues*.......................................800.00 - up
13014 *Moon Going Down*...............................800.00 - up
13031 *Some Happy Day*..................................800.00 - up
13040 *Devil Sent The Rain* ....800.00 - up
13070 *Dry Well Blues* ....800.00 - up
13080 *Some Summer Day* ....1000.00 - up
13110 *Frankie And Albert* ....1000.00 - up
13133 *Joe Kirby*..1000.00 - up
Vocalion 02651 *Poor Me*..................................300.00 - 600.00
02680 *High Sheriff Blues* ....300.00 - 600.00
02782 *Love My Stuff* ....300.00 - 600.00
02931 *Revenue Man Blues* ....300.00 - 600.00

RUBY PAUL:
Paramount 12592 *Red Letter Blues*........................75.00 - 100.00

PHIL PAVEY:
Okeh 45308 *Bronco Bustin' Blues* ....50.00 - 80.00
45355 *Utah Mormon Blues* ....50.00 - 80.00

GUILFORD (PEACHTREE) PAYNE:
Okeh 8103 *Peachtree Man Blues*...........................40.00 - 60.00

PEANUT THE KIDNAPPER:
Titles issued contemporaneously on Banner, Conqueror, Melotone,
Oriole, Perfect, and Romeo: *Eighth Avenue Blues; Silver Spade
Blues; Suicide Blues; Swagger Woman Blues* ... 50.00 - 100.00

ALICE PEARSON:
Paramount 12507 *Memphis Earthquake* ....50.00 - 75.00
12523 *Greyhound Blues*...................................50.00 - 75.00
12547 *Black Sow Blues* ....50.00 - 75.00

BILL PEARSON:
Brunswick 7053 *Detroit Blues*...............................75.00 - 100.00

DAVID PEARSON:
Okeh 8847 *Friendless Blues* ....80.00 - 120.00

MEMPHIS EDDIE PEE:
Globe 103 *Mistreated All The Time* ....10.00 - 15.00
108 *My House Fell Down* ....10.00 - 15.00

ROBERT PEEPLES:
Paramount 12995 *Fat Greasy Baby*.....................150.00 - 300.00
13033 *Mama's Boy* ....150.00 - 300.00

PEETIE'S BOY:
Decca 7767 *Gonna Keep It For My Daddy* ....15.00 - 20.00
7819 *Friar's Point Blues* ....15.00 - 20.00

PEETIE WHEATSTRAW'S BUDDY:
Hy-Tone 38 *Miss Irene* ....30.00 - 50.00

MORRIS PEJOE:
Checker 766 *Gonna Buy Me A Telephone* ....15.00 - 20.00 *

BOB PERKINS TRIO:
Planet 108 *Boogie Woogie Bowl*.................................... -

CORA PERKINS:
Okeh 8348 *Today Blues* ....50.00 - 75.00

DOLLY PERKINS:
Emerson 10761 *My Doggone Lazy Man*.................15.00 - 20.00

CHARLES "SPECK" PERTUM:
Brunswick 7128 *Broken Down Blues* ....100.00 - 150.00
7146 *Gambler's Blues* ....100.00 - 150.00

PETE AND REPEAT:
Brunswick 7055 *Hymn-Singing Bill* ....50.00 - 75.00
7104 *Toodle-Oodle-Oo* ....80.00 - 120.00

CHARLEY PETERS:
Herwin 92036 *Lord I'm Discouraged* ....200.00 - 300.00

ARTHUR PETTIES/PETTIS:
Brunswick 7182 *Good Boy Blues* ....100.00 - 200.00
7209 *Quarrelin' Mama Blues* ....150.00 - 200.00
Victor 21282 *Two Time Blues* ....100.00 - 150.00

LEOLA B. PETTIGREW:
Columbia 14625-D *Boop-Poop-A-Doop* ....150.00 - 200.00

ROBERT PETWAY:
Bluebird 8726 *Rockin' Chair Blues* ....10.00 - 15.00
8756 *Sleepy Woman Blues* ....10.00 - 15.00
8786 *My Little Girl* ....10.00 - 15.00
8838 *Catfish Blues* ....10.00 - 15.00
8987 *Boogie Woogie Woman* ....7.00 - 10.00
9008 *My Baby Left Me* ....10.00 - 15.00

WASHINGTON PHILLIPS:
Columbia 14277-D *Lift Him Up That's All* ....75.00 - 100.00
14333-D *Denomination Blues* ....75.00 - 100.00
14369-D *Paul And Silas In Jail* ....75.00 - 100.00
14404-D *Jesus Is My Friend* ....75.00 - 100.00
14448-D *Train Your Child* ....75.00 - 100.00
14511-D *I've Got The Key To The Kingdom* ....100.00 - 150.00
14566-D *The Church Needs Good Deacons* ....100.00 - 150.00

PIANO RED:
RCA Victor, most issues.................................7.00 - 10.00
(See the fourth section of this book for additional Piano Red recordings in 45 RPM and LPs formats)

PICANINNY/PICKANINNY JUG BAND:
Champion 16615 *Bottle It Up and Go* ....400.00 - up

WALTER/FATS PICHON:
DeLuxe 3069 *Pinetop's Boogie* ....10.00 - 15.00
3072 *Cherry* ....10.00 - 15.00
Raynac 1101 *Fat And Greasy* ....10.00 - 15.00

CHARLIE PICKETT:
Decca 7707 *Down The Highway* ....20.00 - 30.00
7762 *Trembling Blues* ....20.00 - 30.00

DAN PICKETT:
Gotham 201 *Laughing Rag* ....30.00 - 50.00
510 *Early One Morning* ....30.00 - 50.00
512 *Chicago Blues* ....30.00 - 50.00
516 *Lemon Man* ....30.00 - 50.00
542 *Baby How Long* ....30.00 - 50.00

PIG 'N' WHISTLE BAND:
Regal 3277 *Talking To You Mama* ....50.00 - 100.00

PIGMEAT PETE (AND CATJUICE CHARLIE):
Columbia 14452-D *Can You Do That To Me?* ....80.00 - 120.00
14463-D *Do It Right* ....80.00 - 120.00
14485-D *My Friend John* ....80.00 - 120.00
14513-D *Our Family Doctor* ....100.00 - 150.00
14563-D *In Kentucky* ....100.00 - 150.00
14588-D *Hard Times* ....100.00 - 150.00

14598-D *Honey You Done Gone Too Far* .... 150.00 - 200.00
14640-D *Rockin' Chair Mary* ....150.00 - 250.00

PIGMEAT TERRY:
Champion 50043 *Black Sheep Blues* .... 25.00 - 40.00
Decca 7829 *Moaning The Blues* .... 25.00 - 40.00

PINETOP:
Bluebird 6041 *Workhouse Blues* .... 75.00 - 100.00
6125 *Every Day I Have The Blues* .... 75.00 - 100.00
6202 *Got The Blues About My Baby* .... 75.00 - 100.00

PINETOP AND LINDBERG:
Bluebird 10177 *East Chicago Blues* .... 20.00 - 30.00
Victor 23330 *East Chicago Blues* .... 300.00 - up
23359 *Louisiana Bound* .... 300.00 - up

PINETOP SLIM:
Colonial 106 *Applejack Boogie* .... 75.00 - 100.00

PINEWOOD TOM (& HIS BLUES HOUNDS):
Titles issued contemporaneously on Banner, Conqueror, Melotone, Oriole, Perfect, and Romeo: *Badly Mistreated Man; Bed Springs Blues; Black Gal; Black Man; Broad Players Blues; Cherry Picker; D.B.A. Blues; Did You Read That Letter?; Evil Man Blues; Friendless City Blues; Gone Dry Blues; Gone Mother Blues; Good Gal; Greenville Sheik; Homeless And Hungry Blues; Mean Mistreater Mama; Milk Cow Blues; New D.B.A. Blues; New Mean Mistreater Blues; New Milk Cow Blues; No More Ball And Chain; Pigmeat And Whiskey Blues; Prodigal Son; She's Alright With Me; Silicosis Is Killin' Me; Sissy Man; Stormy Weather No. 1; Talking About My Time; Tweet Tweet Mama Blues; Welfare Blues; When The Sun Goes Down* .... 40.00 - 60.00

JAMES PLATT:
Champion 15860 *Sympathizin' Blues* .... 150.00 - 200.00
15880 *Easy Papa* .... 150.00 - 200.00
15927 *Back-Biter Blues* .... 150.00 - 200.00
16059 *Texas Dream Blues* .... 200.00 - 300.00

FRANK PLUITT:
Bluebird 5383 *Found A Note On My Door* .... 150.00 - 200.00
Sunrise 3464 *Found A Note On My Door* .... 150.00 - 250.00
Victor 23428 *Meningitis Blues* .... 400.00 - up

POOR BILL:
Varsity 6020 *A Hundred Women* .... 15.00 - 20.00

POOR CHARLIE:
Vocalion 03652 *My Little Machine* .... 15.00 - 20.00

POOR JAB:
Champion 16483 *Poor Jab Blues* .... 400.00 - up
16630 *Get It From Behind* .... 400.00 - up
16654 *Come Along Little Children* .... 400.00 - up

POOR JIM (WITH DAN JACKSON):
Titles issued contemporaneously on Banner, Conqueror, Melotone, Oriole, Perfect, and Romeo: *Blue And Worried Woman; Squeaky Work Bench Blues; Stack O' Dollars Blues; Sugar Farm Blues* .... 75.00 - 100.00

JENNY POPE:
Vocalion 1438 *Whiskey Drinkin' Blues* .... 150.00 - 250.00
1489 *Mr. Postman Blues* .... 150.00 - 250.00
1522 *Bull Frog Blues* .... 150.00 - 200.00

FLOSSIE PORTER:
Champion 15101 *Ain't Got Nobody To Grind My Coffee*
....75.00 - 100.00
   15102 *Mama's Losin' A Mighty Good Chance* ..75.00 - 100.00

SCHOOLBOY PORTER:
Chance 1114 *Rollin' Along*.....................................15.00 - 30.00

SONNY PORTER:
Columbia 14366-D *Deck Hand Blues* ....75.00 - 100.00

NETTIE POTTER:
Banner 1483 *A Good Man Is Hard To Find*...........20.00 - 30.00
   1484 *Blind Man Blues* ....20.00 - 30.00
Pathe-Actuelle 032122 *Nobody Knows The Way I Feel*
....25.00 - 40.00
   032124 *Meat Man Blues*....................................25.00 - 40.00
Regal 9764 *Who Calls You Sweet Mama Now?* ......20.00 - 30.00
   9781 *Blind Man Blues* ....20.00 - 30.00
   9782 *A Good Man Is Hard To Find*...................20.00 - 30.00

LOUIS POWELL:
Vocalion 04040 *Mushmouth Blues* ....15.00 - 20.00

JULIA/JULIUS POWERS:
Harmograph 827 *Weary Way Blues*........................80.00 - 120.00
   829 *'Bama Bound Blues* ....25.00 - 40.00
   847 *Any Woman's Blues* ....25.00 - 40.00
   858 *Chicago Bound Blues* ....25.00 - 40.00
   872 *Chattanooga Blues* ....80.00 - 120.00
   883 *Moanin' Groanin' Blues* ....80.00 - 120.00
   897 *Mama Doo Shee Blues*...............................80.00 - 120.00

BUD PRESTON'S STRING BAND:
Champion 15509 *Those Next Mornin' Blues*.........200.00 - 300.00

JIMMY PRESTON:
Derby 751 *Rock With It Baby* ....10.00 - 15.00
Gotham 170 *Number Blues* ....10.00 - 15.00
   180 *Hold Me, Baby* ....10.00 - 15.00

L. C. PRIGETT:
Victor 20953 *Sure As You Take A Woman From Somebody Else*
....50.00 - 75.00
   21359 *Frogtown Blues*.......................................100.00 - 150.00

WES PRINCE & HIS RHYTHM PRINCES:
Excelsior 167 *Doghouse Blues* ....10.00 - 20.00
   170 *Pop Fly Blues* ....10.00 - 20.00

HELEN PROCTOR:
Decca 7666 *Cheatin' On Me* ....15.00 - 20.00
   7703 *Let's Call It A Day*....................................15.00 - 20.00

SNOOKY PRYOR:
J.O.B. 101 *Boogy Fool* ....100.00 - 150.00
   115 *Going Back On The Road*..........................80.00 - 120.00
Parrot 807 *Crosstown Blues*....................................40.00 - 70.00 *

PULLMAN PORTERS OUARTETTE:
Paramount 12580 *Every Time I Feel The Spirit* ....50.00 - 100.00
   12607 *Pullman Passenger Train* ....75.00 - 100.00

JOE PULLEM/PULLUM (& HIS ORCHESTRA/ROBERT COOPER):
Bluebird 5459 *Black Gal What Makes Your Head So Hard?*
....50.00 - 75.00
   5534 *Cows, See That Train Comin'*....................30.00 - 50.00
   5592 *Black Gal What Makes Your Head So Hard No. 2*
....30.00 - 50.00
   5661 *McKinney Street Stomp*.............................75.00 - 100.00

   5844 *Mississippi Flood Blues* ....40.00 - 60.00
   5859 *Careful Drivin' Mama* ....50.00 - 75.00
   5898 *Rack It Back And Tell It Right* ....50.00 - 75.00
   5947 *Black Gal No. 4*...50.00 - 75.00
   6071 *Joe Louis Is The Man* ....25.00 - 40.00
   6093 *Bad Break Blues* ....15.00 - 25.00
   6123 *I Can't Control Myself*...............................15.00 - 25.00
   6185 *Ice Man Blues* ....15.00 - 25.00
   6276 *Hard Working Man Blues* ....15.00 - 25.00
   6298 *Telephone Blues* ....15.00 - 25.00
   6314 *Swing Them Blues* ....15.00 - 20.00
   6372 *Woman Trouble Blues*................................15.00 - 20.00
   6426 *Hattie Green*...15.00 - 20.00
Montgomery Ward 4833 *I Believe In You* ....15.00 - 20.00
   4986 *Traveling Blues*..15.00 - 20.00
Swing Time 267 *My Woman*....................................30.00 - 50.00

DOUG QUATTLEBAUM:
Gotham 519 *Lizzie Lou* ....40.00 - 60.00

SIS QUANDER:
Pathe-Actuelle 7528 *Mama Is Waiting For You*.....20.00 - 30.00
   7530 *Black Snake Blues* ....20.00 - 30.00
Perfect 128 *Mama Is Waiting For You* ....20.00 - 30.00
   130 *Black Snake Blues* ....20.00 - 30.00

RUFUS AND BEN QUILLIAN (WITH JAMES McCRAVY):
Columbia 14560-D *Keep It Clean* ....80.00 - 120.00
   14584-D *Working It Slow* ....80.00 - 120.00
   14616-D *It's Dirty But Good* ....80.00 - 120.00
   14639-D *Workin' It Fast*....................................100.00 - 150.00

THE QUINTONES:
Jordan 1601 *Just A Little Loving* ....30.00 - 50.00

YANK RACHELL (AND DAN SMITH):
Bluebird 7525 *Rachell Blues* ....25.00 - 40.00
   7602 *Lake Michigan Blues*..................................25.00 - 40.00
   7694 *It's All Over*...20.00 - 30.00
   7731 *Texas Tommy* ....20.00 - 30.00
Bluebird 8732 *38 Pistol Blues* ....15.00 - 20.00
   8768 *Biscuit Baking Woman* ....15.00 - 20.00
   8796 *Insurance Man Blues* ....15.00 - 20.00
   8840 *Army Man Blues*..15.00 - 20.00
   8951 *Yellow Yam Blues*......................................15.00 - 20.00
   8993 *Rainy Day Blues*..15.00 - 20.00
   9033 *Peach Tree Blues* ....10.00 - 15.00
   34-0715 *Katy Lee Blues*.....................................10.00 - 15.00
RCA Victor 20-2955 *38 Pistol Blues*......................8.00 - 12.00
Vocalion 02649 *Gravel Road Woman* ....75.00 - 100.00

THE RADARS:
Abbey 3025 *I Need You All The Time* ....30.00 - 50.00
Rhythm & Blues - *Too Bad* ....- - -

CARL RAFFERTY:
Bluebird 5429 *Mr. Carl's Blues*.............................100.00 - 150.00

RAILROAD BILL:
Melotone 12373 *M And O Blues*..............................75.00 - 100.00

BIG MEMPHIS MA RAINEY (See Big....)

RAMBLIN' BOB:
Bluebird 7987 *Big Apple Blues*...............................20.00 - 30.00
   8020 *Ol' Mose*..20.00 - 30.00

8059 *Good Gamblin'* ....20.00 - 30.00
8067 *Freight Train Blues*...........................20.00 - 30.00

GEORGE RAMSEY (AND MAE BELLE LEE):
Paramount 13067 *Times Done Get Hard*..............150.00 - 300.00
13068 *Bumble Bee No. 1* ....150.00 - 300.00
13071 *Perfect Mess Blues* ....150.00 - 300.00

JACK RANGER:
Okeh 8795 *Thieving Blues*.............................75.00 - 100.00
8847 *Lonesome Grave Blues* ....80.00 - 120.00

RUBY RANKIN (AND GEORGE HAMILTON):
Champion 15736 *Shadow Blues* ....150.00 - 200.00
15756 *Mistreated Mama Blues*......150.00 - 200.00
15857 *Got Jelly On My Mind* ....150.00 - 200.00
15902 *Doin' That Thing* ....150.00 - 200.00
16057 *Southern High Water Blues* ....150.00 - 200.00

HERMAN RAY:
Decca 48105 *Trouble Blues* ....10.00 - 15.00
48107 *Working Man* ....10.00 - 15.00

RED AND HIS WASHBOARD BAND:
Vocalion 03965 *Prowling Groundhog No. 2*...........20.00 - 30.00

THE RED DEVIL:
Vocalion 03954 *Huntsman Blues* ....15.00 - 25.00

IRENE REDFIELD:
MGM 11408 *Whalin' Away* ....7.00 - 10.00
11489 *Shakin' The Blues Away* ....7.00 - 10.00

(RED HOT) OLD MOSE:
Paramount 12605 *Shrimp Man* ....250.00 - up

RED ONION JOE AND HIS UKE THUMPERS:
Champion 15928 *Humming Blues* ....75.00 - 125.00

JIMMY REED:
Chance 1142 *High And Lonesome*.....................20.00 - 30.00 *
Vee Jay 100 *High And Lonesome* ....15.00 - 20.00 *
105 *Jimmy's Boogie*.................................15.00 - 20.00 *
119 *Boogie In The Dark* ....10.00 - 15.00 *
132 *I'm Gonna Ruin You* ....8.00 - 12.00 *
Vee Jay 153, 168, 186, 203, 226, 237.....................7.00 - 10.00 *
(See the fourth section of this book for additional recordings by
Jimmy Reed in 45 RPM and LP formats)

LONG "CLEVE" REED & THE DOWN-HOME BOYS/ LITTLE HARVEY HULL:
Black Patti 8001 *Hey! Lawdy Mama - The France Blues*
....600.00 - up
8002 *Don't You Leave Me Here* ......600.00 - up
8030 *Mama You Don't Know How*................600.00 - up

SADIE REED:
Champion 15435 *Fall Or Summer Blues*...............100.00 - 150.00

WILLIE REED:
Columbia 14407-D *Dreaming Blues* ....80.00 - 120.00
Vocalion 03093 *All Worn Out And Dry Blues*.........80.00 - 120.00

BILL REESE (& HIS RHYTHM/QUINTET & THE CORONETS):
Sterling 902 *Baby Keep Moving* .... - - -
903 *Don't Deprive Me* ....30.00 - 50.00 *

SLIM REESE:
Sittin' In With 581 *Got The World In A Jug* ....20.00 - 30.00

BLIND JOE REYNOLDS:
Broadway 5106 *Outside Woman Blues*.................200.00 - 400.00
Paramount 12927 *Nehi Blues* ....300.00 - 500.00
12983 *Cold Woman Blues* ....300.00 - 500.00

TEDDY REYNOLDS:
Sittin' In With 558 *Why Baby Why* ....10.00 - 15.00
571 *Walkin' The Floor Baby* ....10.00 - 15.00
586 *My Heart's Full Of Misery* ....15.00 - 20.00
594 *Too Late To Change* ....10.00 - 15.00
613 *Suicide Blues* ....10.00 - 15.00

BLIND WILLIE REYNOLDS:
Victor 23258 *Third Street Woman Blues* .... 300.00 - up

MACK RIIINEIIART & BROWNIE STUBBLEFIELD:
Titles issued contemporaneously on Banner, Melotone, Oriole,
Perfect, and Romeo: *Blues After Sundown; Broke And Hungry;
Clay County Blues; Dirty No Gooder; I Can't Take It Any More;
If I Leave Here Running; Lonesome House Blues; Lost Woman
Blues; Open Back Door Blues; T.P.N. Moaner; Up-town Blues;
You Don't Know My Mind* ....50.00 - 100.00

WALTER RHODES:
Columbia 14289-D *The Crowing Rooster* .... 80.00 - 120.00

THE RHYTHMASTERS:
Bennett 401 *Until Now*.................................... - - -

RHYTHM WILLIE (& HIS GANG):
Okeh 05856 *Bedroom Stomp* .... 15.00 - 20.00
05960 *Boarding House Blues* .... 15.00 - 20.00
Premium 866 *Wailin' Willie* .... 15.00 - 20.00

ROBERT RICHARD:
JVB 75828 *Cadillac Woman* .... 80.00 - 130.00
King 4274 *Wigwam Woman* .... 50.00 - 80.00 *

SETH RICHARD:
Columbia 14325-D *Lonely Seth Blues* .... 100.00 - 150.00

UNCLE CHARLIE RICHARDS:
Pathe-Actuelle 7521 *Levee Blues*........................... 60.00 - 100.00
7527 *Sore Bunion Blues* .... 60.00 - 100.00
Perfect 121 *Levee Blues* .... 60.00 - 100.00
127 *Sore Bunion Blues* .... 60.00 - 100.00

"MOOCH" RICHARDSON:
Okeh 8554 *T And T Blues* .... 75.00 - 100.00
8576 *Big Kate Adams Blues* .... 75.00 - 100.00
8611 *Helena Blues* .... 75.00 - 100.00

RICHMOND STARLIGHT (JAZZ) QUARTET:
QRS 7028 *Gone Jazz Crazy*................................. 50.00 - 80.00
7056 *Oh, You Better Mind* .... 50.00 - 80.00

ETHEL RIDLEY:
Ajax 17126 *Get It Fixed*...................................... 40.00 - 60.00
17131 *He Was A Good Man* .... 40.00 - 60.00
Columbia A-3941 *Here's Your Opportunity Blues*
.... 15.00 - 20.00
A-3965 *Alabama Bound Blues* .... 15.00 - 20.00
Victor 19111 *Memphis Tennessee* .... 30.00 - 50.00

WILLIE (BOODLE IT) RIGHT:
Okeh 05959 *Down South Blues* .... 15.00 - 20.00
06008 *Sunny Land Blues* .... 15.00 - 20.00
06057 *West Texas Blues*................................. 15.00 - 20.00

ISSIE RINGGOLD:
Columbia 14509-D *He's A Good Meat Cutter* .... 50.00 - 75.00

SALLY RITZ:
Banner 1394 *Barrel House Blues* ....15.00 - 20.00
    1437 *The Basement Blues* ....15.00 - 20.00
    1452 *Deep River Blues* ....15.00 - 20.00

THE RIVALS:
Apollo 1166 *Don't Say You're Sorry Again*............30.00 - 50.00

HUBERT ROBERSON & HIS ORCHESTRA:
Eddie's 1211 *Lonely Traveler* ....15.00 - 20.00

BENNY ROBERTS & HIS MADCATS:
Columbia 30194 *Hotbox Mama* ....10.00 - 15.00

GIP ROBERTS:
JVB 29 *Sandman* ....30.00 - 50.00 *

HELEN ROBERTS:
Silvertone 3570 *Lonely Blues* ....80.00 - 120.00

SISTER MINNIE PEARL ROBERTS:
Brunswick 7179 *You Make Your Troubles So Hard*
    ....50.00 - 80.00

SALLY ROBERTS:
Okeh 8485 *Gonna Ramble Blues*............................40.00 - 60.00
    8500 *Black Hearse Blues*....................................40.00 - 60.00

SNITCHER ROBERTS:
Okeh 8750 *Low Moaning Blues* ....100.00 - 150.00
    8781 *Snitcher's Blues* ....100.00 - 150.00

THE ROBINS:
Aladdin 3031 *Come Back Baby*..............................20.00 - 30.00
Modern 807 *Rockin'*...................................... - - -
Savoy (most issues) ....7.00 - 12.00
Score 4010 *Around About Midnight* ....20.00 - 30.00

ROBINSON BROTHERS:
Black & White 107 *Come Back To Me Baby* ....15.00 - 20.00
    108 *L. C. Boogie* ....15.00 - 20.00

ROBINSON & MACK:
Okeh 8259 *I Beg To Be Excused* ....60.00 - 100.00
    8298 *It's All The Same To Me* ....60.00 - 100.00
    8321 *Booze*...60.00 - 100.00

ALEXANDER ROBINSON:
Paramount 12649 *My Baby*....................................150.00 - 250.00

FAT MAN ROBINSON QUINTET:
Motif 2001 *Lavender Coffin* ....20.00 - 30.00
Regent 1005 *Bye Bye Roberta* ....15.00 - 20.00

HUBERT ROBINSON (& HIS YARDBIRDS):
Jade 206 *Hard Lovin' Daddy*..................................10.00 - 15.00
Macy's 5005 *Boogie The Joint* ....15.00 - 20.00
    5007 *Old Woman Boogie* ....15.00 - 20.00
    5010 *Room And Board Boogie* ....15.00 - 20.00
    5015 *High Class Woman* ....15.00 - 20.00

JAMES "BAT" ROBINSON:
Champion 16236 *Bat's Own Blues*.........................150.00 - 200.00
    16745 *Humming Blues*.......................................300.00 - up

MABEL ROBINSON:
Decca 8568 *Search Your Heart and See* ....10.00 - 15.00
    8580 *You Don't Know My Mind*.........................10.00 - 15.00
    8601 *Me And My Chauffeur* ....10.00 - 15.00

MUSHMOUTH ROBINSON:
Black & White 105 *Boogie Boo Blues* ....8.00 - 12.00
Chief 700 *Hey Pretty Mama* ....20.00 - 30.00
    701 *Take It Out In The Alley*..............................20.00 - 30.00

NETTIE ROBINSON:
Pathe-Actuelle 7523 *I've Got The Right Man Now*
    ....40.00 - 60.00
Perfect 123 *I've Got The Right Man Now*..............40.00 - 60.00

JIMMY ROGERS (& HIS TRIO/ROCKING FOUR):
Chess 1435 *That's All Right* ....50.00 - 75.00
    1442 *Going Away Baby* ....50.00 - 75.00
    1453 *She Loves Another Man* ....20.00 - 30.00
    1476 *Chance To Love* ....30.00 - 50.00
    1506 *Back Door Friend* ....15.00 - 20.00
    1519 *Out On the Road* ....15.00 - 20.00
    1543 *Act Like You Love Me* ....10.00 - 15.00 *
    1574 *Chicago Bound* ....20.00 - 30.00 *
    1616 *Blues All Day Long* ....15.00 - 20.00 *
    1643 *Walking By Myself* ....10.00 - 20.00 *
    1659 *I Can't Believe* ....10.00 - 15.00 *
    1687 *What Have I Done* ....10.00 - 15.00 *
    1721 *Rock This House* ....15.00 - 20.00 *

MAE ROGERS:
Champion 16530 *My Time Blues* ....250.00 - up

MAY ROGERS:
Champion 15590 *Road House Blues* ....150.00 - 250.00

WALTER ROLAND:
Titles issued contemporaneously on Banner, Conqueror, Melotone,
    Oriole, Perfect, and Romeo: *Back Door Blues; Bad Dream Blues:*
    Big Mama; Club Meeting Blues; Cold Blooded Murder,
    Collector Man Blues; C.W.A. Blues; Dices' Blues; Early This
    Morning; Early In The Morning No. 2; Every Morning Blues; 45
    Pistol Blues; House Lady Blues; Last Year Blues; Man, Man,
    Man; Money Taker Woman; O.B.O. Blues; Overall Blues;
    Penniless Blues; Red Cross Blues No. 2; Sail On Little Girl No.
    2; Schoolboy Blues; Screw Worm; Slavin' Blues; S.O.L. Blues;
    Talkin' Low Blues; T Model Blues; Worn Out Man Blues; You
    Gonna Want Me ....50.00 - 75.00

MAMIE ROMER:
Oriole 325 *A Good Man Is Hard To Find*..............15.00 - 30.00

BAYLESS ROSE:
Champion 16037 *Black Dog Blues* ....100.00 - 150.00
    16772 *Frisco Blues* ....250.00 - up
Gennett 7250 *Black Dog Blues* ....150.00 - 200.00

LUCY ROSE:
Champion 15471 *Papa, You're Too Slow*...............75.00 - 100.00

BERTHA ROSS:
Gennett 6227 *My Jelly Blues* ....200.00 - 300.00
    6243 *Lost Man Blues* ....200.00 - 300.00
Superior 331 *Tea Rollin' Blues*............................250.00 - up

DOCTOR/DR. ROSS (& HIS JUMP & JIVE BOYS):
Chess 1504 *Dr. Ross Boogie*..................................75.00 - 100.00
Sun 193 *Chicago Breakdown*..................................80.00 - 130.00 *
    212 *The Boogie Disease*...................................100.00 - 200.00 *

DOLLY ROSS:
Brunswick 7005 *Hootin' Owl Blues* ....50.00 - 75.00
Vocalion 1166 *Hootin' Owl Blues* ....50.00 - 75.00

LOUISE ROSS:
Columbia 14118-D *No Home Blues* ....30.00 - 50.00

LUCY ROSS:
Champion 15715 *West End Blues*..........................100.00 - 150.00
    15754 *Loose Like That*......................................100.00 - 150.00
    15775 *Cotton Belt Blues* ....80.00 - 130.00

OLLIE ROSS:
Brunswick 7045 *Ox Meat Blues* ....150.00 - 200.00

TED ROSS:
Champion 15859 *Mother-In-Law Blues* ....150.00 - 200.00
15882 *Clickety-Clack Blues*..............................150.00 - 200.00

WILL ROWLAND & HIS BAND (Vocal, JESSE LOCKETT):
Gold Star 650 *Cold Blooded Woman* ....15.00 - 20.00
657 *Don't Lose Your Mind* ....15.00 - 20.00

LAURA RUCKER:
Paramount 13030 *I'm The Lonesome One*............200.00 - 300.00
13075 *Little Joe* ....150.00 - 200.00
13138 *Fancy Tricks* ....200.00 - 300.00

OLLIE RUPERT:
Victor 20577 *Ain't Goin' To Be Your Low Down Dog*
....200.00 - 300.00

LILLIAN RUSH:
Champion 15510 *Do What You Did Last Night* ....100.00 - 150.00
15529 *There's Been Some Changes Made* ....100.00 - 150.00

BLIND TIM RUSSELL:
Herwin 93008 *I've Crossed The Separation Line* .300.00 - 500.00

GEORGE "HAMBONE" RUTHERS:
Champion 15795 *Street Walkin' Blues* ....100.00 - 150.00

ST. LOUIS BESSIE:
Vocalion 1559 *Sugar Man Blues* ....150.00 - 200.00
1615 *Meat Cutter Blues* ....150.00 - 200.00

ST. LOUIS JIMMY:
Apollo 420 *Chicago Woman Blues*............................20.00 - 30.00
Aristocrat 7001 *Florida Hurricane* ....75.00 - 100.00
Bluebird 8889 *Going Down Slow* ....20.00 - 30.00
8933 *Lost Ball Blues*...20.00 - 30.00
9016 *Can't Stand Your Evil Ways* ....15.00 - 20.00
9040 *St. Louis Woman Blues* ....15.00 - 20.00
34-0718 *Back On My Feet Again* ....10.00 - 15.00
34-0727 *Strange Woman Blues* ....10.00 - 15.00
Bullet 270 *Going Down Slow* ....15.00 - 20.00
278 *Sittin' And Thinkin'*......................................15.00 - 20.00
291 *Mr. Brown Boogie* ....15.00 - 20.00
Herald 407 *Hard Luck Boogie* ....20.00 - 30.00 *
J.O.B. 101 *Mother's Day*..50.00 - 100.00
Mercury 8137 *Shame On You Baby*.......................15.00 - 20.00
Miracle 134 *Biscuit Roller*......................................10.00 - 15.00
Parrot 823 *Going Down Slow* ....15.00 - 20.00 *
RCA Victor 20-2650 *Dog House Blues*....................5.00 - 8.00

ST. LOUIS JOHNNY:
Champion 50071 *Sister Kelly Blues* ....40.00 - 60.00

ST. LOUIS RED MIKE:
Bluebird 7744 *Red Mike Blues* ....20.00 - 30.00
7781 *Wash My Hands Nice And Clean*................20.00 - 30.00
7896 *Gamblin' Man Blues*..................................20.00 - 30.00

SALLY SAD:
Varsity 6033 *Don't Say Goodbye* ....15.00 - 20.00
6040 *Gin House Blues* ....15.00 - 20.00
6058 *Mistreated Mamma Blues* ....15.00 - 20.00
6066 *Gypsy Woman Blues* ....15.00 - 20.00

SALTY DOG SAM:
Titles issued contemporaneously on Banner, Melotone, Oriole, Perfect, and Romeo: *Graveyard Digger's Blues; I'm Still Sitting On Top Of The World; Lonesome Road Blues; New Salty Dog; Signifying Blues; Slow Mama Slow* .... 100.00 - 200.00

SAM AND OSCAR:
Brunswick 7208 *You Can't Get That Stuff No More*
.... 75.00 - 125.00
7212 *I Done Caught That Rascal Now* .... 75.00 - 125.00

SAMMY SAMPSON:
Titles issued contemporaneously on Banner, Oriole, Perfect, and Romeo: *I Got The Blues For My Baby; Meanest Kind Of Blues; Police Station Blues; State Street Woman; Tadpole Blues; They Can't Do That* .... 75.00 - 100.00

CLARENCE SAMUELS:
Aristocrat 1001 *Boogie Woogie Blues* .... 15.00 - 20.00
DeLuxe 3219 *Stompin' At The Jubilee* .... 10.00 - 15.00
Freedom 1533 *Lost My Head* .... 10.00 - 15.00
1541 *She Walk, She Walk, She Walk* .... 10.00 - 15.00
1544 *Somebody Gotta Go* .... 10.00 - 15.00
Swing Time 131 *Household Troubles* .... 15.00 - 20.00
149 *Deep Sea Diver* .... 15.00 - 20.00

BESSIE SANDERS (& HER DIXIE DUDES):
Champion 15101 *It Must Be Hard*......................... 75.00 - 100.00
15102 *Take Your Fingers Off It* .... 75.00 - 100.00
15106 *Home Alone Blues*.................................. 40.00 - 60.00
15180 *Lucky Number Blues* .... 80.00 - 120.00
15471 *Shake A Little Bit* .... 75.00 - 100.00
15490 *Dying Blues* .... 100.00 - 150.00
15550 *Where Have All The Black Men Gone?* 100.00 - 150.00
15613 *Wild Geese Blues* .... 200.00 - 300.00
15635 *Red Beans And Rice* .... 200.00 - 300.00
16058 *I Lost My Man*....................................... 150.00 - 200.00

GERTRUDE SAUNDERS:
Okeh 8004 *Daddy, Won't You Please Come Home* .....25.00 - 40.00
Victor 19159 *Potomac River Blues* .... 15.00 - 20.00
Vocalion 1131 *Don't Let Your Love Come Down* .. 40.00 - 60.00

THE SCARCE CROW:
Varsity 6024 *Shake My Tree* .... 20.00 - 30.00

THE SCARE CROW:
Champion 16014 *Easy Creeping Mama* .... 150.00 - 200.00
16036 *Traveling Blues* .... 150.00 - 200.00
16103 *Ornery Blues* .... 150.00 - 200.00
16194 *That Black Bottom Dance* .... 150.00 - 200.00

BEVERLY SCOTT & HIS TRIO:
Murray 503 *Shaking The Boogie* .... 10.00 - 20.00

EFFIE SCOTT:
Vocalion 1461 *Sunshine Special*........................... 150.00 - 200.00

LANNIE SCOTT TRIO:
Savoy 614 *Lannie's Boogie Woogie* .... 30.00 - 50.00

LULU SCOTT:
Bluebird 7706 *Baby Can I Holler* .... 15.00 - 20.00

MAE SCOTT:
Paramount 12048 *Squawkin' The Blues* .... 35.00 - 50.00

ROOSEVELT SCOTT:
Vocalion 05137 *Do You Call That Right?* .... 15.00 - 20.00
05206 *Brownskin Woman Swing* .... 15.00 - 20.00
05371 *Tender Foot Blues* .... 15.00 - 20.00

05415 *Look Up And Down* ....15.00 - 20.00
05502 *Doctor Bill Blues* ....15.00 - 20.00
05550 *Down In The Gutter* ....15.00 - 20.00

SONNY SCOTT:
Vocalion 02533 *No Good Biddie* ....50.00 - 80.00
02586 *Black Horse Blues* ....75.00 - 100.00
02614 *Fire Wood Man* ....75.00 - 100.00
25012 *Noal Mountain Blues* ....75.00 - 100.00
25013 *Working Man's Moan* ....75.00 - 100.00
25016 *Naked Man Blues* ....75.00 - 100.00
25017 *Red Rooster Blues* ....75.00 - 100.00

IRENE SCRUGGS:
Champion 16102 *Borrowed Love* ....150.00 - 200.00
16148 *My Back To The Wall* ....150.00 - 200.00
16756 *The Voice Of The Blues* ....150.00 - 250.00
Gennett 7296 *You've Got What I Want* ....150.00 - 200.00
Okeh 8142 *Why He Left Me I Don't Know* ....30.00 - 50.00
8156 *My Daddy's Calling Me* ....30.00 - 50.00
8476 *Lonesome Valley Blues* ....50.00 - 75.00
Paramount 13023 *Good Meat Grinder* ....200.00 - 300.00
13046 *Back To The Wall* ....200.00 - 300.00
13121 *You've Got What I Want* ....1000.00 - up
Vocalion 1017 *Home Town Blues* ....200.00 - 300.00

CHARLIE SEGAR:
Decca 7027 *Southern Hospitality* ....50.00 - 75.00
7075 *Cow Cow Blues* ....40.00 - 60.00
Vocalion 05441 *Key To The Highway* ....15.00 - 25.00
05539 *Lonesome Graveyard Blues* ....15.00 - 25.00

JOHNNY SELLERS:
Chance 1120 *Rock Me In The Cradle* ....20.00 - 30.00
1123 *Mighty Lonesome* ....20.00 - 30.00
1138 *Mirror Blues* ....20.00 - 30.00 *

HOWARD SERATT:
St. Francis 100 *Make Room In The Lifeboat For Me*
...........................250.00 - up
Sun 198 *Troublesome Waters* ....150.00 - 200.00

THE SERENADERS:
Colony 100 *My Last Affair* ....30.00 - 50.00
Coral 60720 *It's Funny* ....25.00 - 50.00
65093 *Misery* ....25.00 - 50.00
J.V.B. 2001 *Tomorrow Night* ....80.00 - 120.00

TOMMY SETTLERS & HIS BLUE MOANER:
Paramount 13049 *Low Down Blues Moan* ....150.00 - 250.00
13056 *Big Bed Bug* ....150.00 - 250.00
13120 *Blowing The Bugle Blues* ....200.00 - 300.00

TOMMY SETTLES WITH EZIEKIEL LOWE & LEE BUNKLEY:
Titles issued contemporaneously on Banner, Melotone, Oriole,
Perfect, and Romeo: *Don't Want You No More; Pearlie Mae Blues* ....100.00 - 150.00

SEVEN MELODY MEN:
Aristocrat 901 *Rockin' Lord* ....- - -

SLIM SEWARD (& FAT BOY HAYES):
MGM 10306 *Christmas Time Blues* ....30.00 - 50.00
10770 *Railroad Blues* ....30.00 - 50.00

GEORGE SEYMOUR:
Herwin 93016 *Southland Blues* ....100.00 - 150.00

WILL SHADE:
Champion 16599 *She Done Sold It Out* ....400.00 - up
16630 *Get It From The Front* ....400.00 - up
Victor 21725 *Better Leave That Stuff Alone* ....250.00 - 500.00

THE SHADOWS:
Decca 28765 *Stay* ....8.00 - 12.00
Lee 200 *I've Been A Fool* ....8.00 - 12.00
202 *You Are Closer To My Heart* ....10.00 - 15.00
207 *Don't Blame My Dreams* ....10.00 - 15.00
Sittin' In With 583 *Jitterbug Special* ....15.00 - 20.00
590 *Don't Be Late* ....15.00 - 20.00
627 *It's Too Bad* ....15.00 - 20.00

THE SHARPS:
Two Mikes 101 *Love Me My Darling* ....50.00 - 100.00

ALLEN SHAW:
Vocalion 02844 *Moanin' The Blues* ....150.00 - 300.00

THE SHA-WEEZ:
Aladdin 3170 *No One To Love Me* ....50.00 - 100.00 *

THE SHEPPARDS:
Theron 112 *Love* ....50.00 - 100.00

JOHNNY SHINES:
J.O.B. 116 *Cool Driver* ....80.00 - 130.00
1010 *Brutal Hearted Woman* ....80.00 - 130.00

SHOE SHINE JOHNNY:
Chess 1443 *Joliet Blues* ....75.00 - 100.00

JAYDEE SHORT:
Paramount 13040 *Drafted Mama* ....400.00 - up
13043 *Telephone Arguin' Blues* ....400.00 - up
13091 *Flaggin' It To Georgia* ....500.00 - up

JELLY JAW SHORT:
Vocalion 1704 *Snake Doctor Blues* ....150.00 - 300.00
1708 *Let Me Mash That Thing* ....150.00 - 300.00

SHORTY GEORGE:
Brunswick 7106 *Jones Law Blues* ....150.00 - 200.00

SHREVEPORT HOME WRECKERS:
Victor 23275 *Home Wreckin' Blues* ....500.00 - up

SHUFFLIN' SAM & HIS RHYTHM:
Vocalion 03329 *Good Liquor* ....15.00 - 20.00

BILL SIMPSON:
Lin 100 *Jelly Roll Man* ....7.00 - 10.00

COLETHA SIMPSON:
Brunswick 7089 *Riverside Blues* ....75.00 - 100.00
7112 *Black Man Blues* ....75.00 - 100.00

FRANKIE LEE SIMS:
Blue Bonnet 147 *Home Again Blues* ....150.00 - 200.00
148 *Single Man Blues* ....150.00 - 200.00

HENRY SIMS:
Paramount 12912 *Farrell Blues* ....600.00 - up
12940 *Be True Be True Blues* ....600.00 - up

JOE SIMS AND CLARENCE WILLIAMS:
Paramount 12435 *Shut Your Mouth* ....100.00 - 150.00

SKOODLE DUM DOO AND SHEFFIELD:
Manor 1056 *West Kinney Street Blues* ....50.00 - 80.00
Regis 107 *Gas Ration Blues* ....50.00 - 80.00

SLEEPY JOE & HIS WASHBOARD BAND:
Savoy 753 *Amen Blues* ....30.00 - 50.00

SLOKE & IKE:
Decca 7315 *Chocolate Candy Bars* ....20.00 - 30.00
    7375 *Slocum Blues* ....20.00 - 30.00

SLUEFOOT JOE:
QRS 7080 *House Top Blues* ....150.00 - 300.00
    7084 *Grab It And Run*...150.00 - 300.00
    7086 *Shouting Baby Blues* ....150.00 - 300.00
    7091 *Rocky Road Moan*.....................................150.00 - 300.00

SMITH AND HARPER:
Titles issued contemporaneously on Banner, Melotone, Oriole, Perfect, and Romeo: *Insurance Policy Blues; Poor Girl*
....50.00 - 80.00

ANNIE SMITH:
Harmograph 896 *Moonshine Blues* ....80.00 - 120.00

BESSIE SMITH:
Columbia A-3844 *Down Hearted Blues*..................20.00 - 30.00
    A-3877 *Beale Street Mamma*..............................20.00 - 30.00
    A-3888 *Oh Daddy Blues*.....................................15.00 - 25.00
    A-3898 *'Tain't Nobody's Business If I Do* ....15.00 - 25.00
    A-3900 *Mama's Got The Blues* ....20.00 - 30.00
    A-3936 *Bleeding Hearted Blues* ....20.00 - 30.00
    A-3939 *Lady Luck Blues* ....20.00 - 30.00
    A-3942 *Nobody In Town Can Bake A Sweet Jelly Roll Like Mine*
....20.00 - 30.00
    A-4001 *Graveyard Dream Blues*.........................20.00 - 30.00
    13000-D *My Sweetie Went Away*.......................20.00 - 30.00
    13001-D *Any Woman's Blues*.............................20.00 - 30.00
    13005-D *Sam Jones Blues* ....20.00 - 30.00
    13007-D *Far Away Blues* ....20.00 - 30.00
    14000-D *Chicago Bound Blues* ....25.00 - 40.00
    14005-D *Frosty Mornin' Blues* ....25.00 - 40.00
    14010-D *Eavesdropper's Blues*...........................30.00 - 50.00
    14018-D *Moonshine Blues* ....20.00 - 30.00
    14020-D *Sorrowful Blues* ....20.00 - 30.00
    14023-D *Hateful Blues* ....25.00 - 40.00
    14025-D *Pinchbacks-Take 'Em Away*................20.00 - 30.00
    14031-D *Mountain Top Blues* ....30.00 - 50.00
    14032-D *House Rent Blues*..................................30.00 - 50.00
    14037-D *Rainy Weather Blues* ....30.00 - 50.00
    14042-D *Weeping Willow Blues*..........................30.00 - 50.00
    14051-D *Dying Gambler's Blues*.........................30.00 - 50.00
    14052-D *Sinful Blues* ....25.00 - 40.00
    14056-D *Sobbin' Hearted Blues* ....50.00 - 80.00
    14064-D *Cold In Hand Blues* ....50.00 - 80.00
    14075-D *Soft Pedal Blues*....................................80.00 - 120.00
    14079-D *You've Been A Good Old Wagon* ....80.00 - 120.00
    14083-D *Careless Love* ....100.00 - 150.00
    14090-D *Nashville Woman's Blues* ....100.00 - 150.00
    14095-D *J. C. Holmes Blues*..............................100.00 - 150.00
    14098-D *Nobody's Blues But Mine* ....75.00 - 100.00
    14109-D *New Gulf Coast Blues*..........................75.00 - 100.00
    14115-D *Red Mountain Blues* ....75.00 - 100.00
    14123-D *Lonesome Desert Blues* ....75.00 - 100.00
    14129-D *What's The Matter Now?*.......................75.00 - 100.00
    14133-D *Jazzbo Brown From Memphis Town* ...75.00 - 100.00
    14137-D *Hard Driving Papa* ....75.00 - 100.00
    14147-D *Baby Doll* ....75.00 - 100.00
    14158-D *Lost Your Head Blues* ....75.00 - 100.00
    14172-D *One And Two Blue*................................75.00 - 100.00

    14179-D *Young Woman's Blues* ....75.00 - 100.00
    14195-D *Back Water Blues*..............................100.00 - 150.00
    14197-D *After You've Gone*..............................100.00 - 150.00
    14209-D *Them's Graveyard Words* ....100.00 - 150.00
    14219-D *Alexander's Ragtime Band* ....100.00 - 150.00
    14232-D *Trombone Cholly* ....100.00 - 150.00
    14250-D *Mean Old Bed Bug Blues*..................100.00 - 150.00
    14260-D *Sweet Mistreater* ....100.00 - 150.00
    14273-D *Foolish Man Blues* ....100.00 - 150.00
    14292-D *Thinking Blues* ....100.00 - 150.00
    14304-D *Pickpocket Blues* ....100.00 - 150.00
    14312-D *Empty Bed Blues* ....30.00 - 50.00
    14324-D *Spider Man Blues* ....100.00 - 150.00
    14338-D *Standin' In The Rain Blues* ....100.00 - 150.00
    14354-D *Devil's Gonna Git You* ....100.00 - 150.00
    14375-D *Washwoman's Blues* ....100.00 - 150.00
    14384-D *Slow And Easy Man* ....100.00 - 150.00
    14399-D *You Ought To Be Ashamed* ....100.00 - 150.00
    14427-D *I'm Wild About That Thing* ....30.00 - 50.00
    14435-D *I've Got What It Takes* ....100.00 - 150.00
    14451-D *Take It Right Back* ....100.00 - 150.00
    14464-D *He's Got Me Goin'* ....150.00 - 200.00
    14476-D *Wasted Life Blues* ....150.00 - 200.00
    14487-D *You Don't Understand* ....150.00 - 200.00
    14516-D *Keep It To Yourself* ....150.00 - 200.00
    14527-D *Blue Spirit Blues* ....150.00 - 200.00
    14538-D *Moan, You Moaners* ....150.00 - 200.00
    14554-D *Hustlin' Dan* ....150.00 - 200.00
    14569-D *Hot Springs Blues* ....150.00 - 250.00
    14611-D *In The House Blues* ....200.00 - 300.00
    14634-D *Safety Mama* ....200.00 - 300.00
    14663-D *Shipwreck Blues* ....200.00 - 300.00
Okeh 8945 *Do Your Duty* ....60.00 - 100.00
    8949 *Gimme A Pigfoot*.......................................60.00 - 100.00

BESSIE MAE SMITH (& WESLEY WALLACE):
Paramount 12922 *St. Louis Daddy*.........................150.00 - 200.00

BUSTER SMITH:
Torch 6900 *Boogie Daddy* ....15.00 - 25.00

CLARA SMITH:
Black Patti 8034 *Sand Raisin' Blues* ....300.00 - up
    8035 *Clara Blues* ....300.00 - up
Columbia 12-D *Kansas City Man Blues*.................25.00 - 40.00
    A-3943 *Every Woman's Blues* ....15.00 - 20.00
    A-3961 *Kind Lovin' Blues* ....15.00 - 20.00
    A-3966 *All Night Blues*......................................15.00 - 20.00
    A-3991 *Irresistible Blues* ....20.00 - 30.00
    A-4000 *Awful Moanin' Blues* ....15.00 - 20.00
Columbia 13002-D *Don't Never Tell Nobody* ....20.00 - 30.00
    14006-D *It Won't Be Long Now* ....30.00 - 50.00
    14009-D *31st. Street Blues* ....40.00 - 60.00
    14013-D *I'm Gonna Tear Your Playhouse Down*
....25.00 - 40.00
    14016-D *My Doggone Lazy Man*........................25.00 - 40.00
    14019-D *The Clearing House Blues* ....20.00 - 30.00
    14021-D *Cold Weather Papa*..............................20.00 - 30.00
    14022-D *Mean Papa, Turn In Your Key*............20.00 - 30.00
    14026-D *Don't Advertise Your Man*..................20.00 - 30.00
    14034-D *Deep Blues Sea Blues* ....25.00 - 40.00
    14039-D *Basement Blues* ....25.00 - 40.00
    14041-D *Blues* ....30.00 - 50.00
    14045-D *Blues* ....30.00 - 50.00
    14049-D *San Francisco Blues* ....30.00 - 50.00
    14053-D *Steel Drivin' Sam* ....25.00 - 40.00

14058-D *Nobody Knows The Way I Feel Dis Mornin'*
....50.00 -   75.00
14062-D *Broken Busted Blues*.........................50.00 -   75.00
14069-D *When I Steps Out* ....25.00 -   40.00
14073-D *Courthouse Blues*...........................100.00 - 150.00
14077-D *Shipwrecked Blues*.........................100.00 - 150.00
14085-D *Different Way Blues*.........................75.00 - 100.00
14097-D *Kitchen Mechanic Blues* ....75.00 - 100.00
14098-D *My Man Blues*...................................75.00 - 100.00
14104-D *Alley Rat Blues* ....75.00 - 100.00
14108-D *The Market Street Blues* ....75.00 - 100.00
14117-D *I'm Tired Of Bein' Good* ....75.00 - 100.00
14126-D *Disappointed Blues*...........................75.00 - 100.00
14138-D *Rock Church, Rock* ....75.00 - 100.00
14143-D *Salty Dog* ....75.00 - 100.00
14150-D *Whip It To A Jelly* ....50.00 -   80.00
14160-D *Separation Blues*...............................50.00 -   80.00
14183-D *Get On Board* ....50.00 -   80.00
14192-D *Cheatin' Daddy* ....75.00 - 100.00
14202-D *Percolatin' Blues* ....50.00 -   80.00
14223-D *Black Woman's Blues* ....50.00 -   80.00
14240-D *Black Cat Moan* ....50.00 -   80.00
14256-D *Troublesome Blues* ....50.00 -   80.00
14294-D *Race Track Blues* ....75.00 - 100.00
14319-D *It's All Coming Home To You* ....75.00 - 100.00
14344-D *Steamboat Man Blues* ....80.00 - 120.00
14368-D *Ain't Got Nobody To Grind My Coffee* ....80.00 - 120.00
14398-D *It's Tight Like That* ....80.00 - 120.00
14409-D *Empty House Blues* ....80.00 - 120.00
14419-D *Got My Mind On That Thing* ....80.00 - 120.00
14462-D *Papa I Don't Need You Now* ....100.00 - 150.00
14536-D *Where Is My Man?* ....150.00 - 200.00
14553-D *Don't Fool Around On Me* ....100.00 - 150.00
14568-D *You're Getting Old On Your Job*.......150.00 - 200.00
14580-D *Woman To Woman* ....100.00 - 150.00
14592-D *Good Times*..100.00 - 150.00
14619-D *Ol' Sam Tages* ....150.00 - 200.00
14633-D *You Dirty Dog*...................................150.00 - 200.00
14645-D *Street Department Papa* ....150.00 - 200.00
14653-D *So Long Jim* ....150.00 - 200.00

CLEMENTINE SMITH:

Banner 1483 *I'm Done Done Done With You* ....20.00 -   30.00
    1484 *Nobody Knows The Way I Feel This Morning*
....20.00 -   30.00
Pathe-Actuelle 032067 *Hard Luck Blues* ....25.00 -   40.00
Perfect 12146 *Hard Luck Blues*......................25.00 -   40.00
Regal 9779 *Nobody Knows What A Red Head Mama Can Do*
....20.00 -   30.00
    9781 *Nobody Knows The Way I Feel This Morning*
....20.00 -   30.00

EITHEL SMITH:

Champion 16613 *Jelly Roll Mill*...........................250.00 -   up

ELIZABETH SMITH:

Victor 20297 *No Sooner Blues* ....30.00 -   50.00
    20334 *When My Wants Run Out*........................50.00 -   75.00
    21539 *Police Done Tore My Playhouse Down*...80.00 - 120.00

FLOSSIE SMITH & THE RED HOT TWINS:

Superior 2603 *Hokum Stomp* ....150.00 - 250.00
    2699 *That's The Way She Likes It* ....150.00 - 250.00

"FUNNY PAPER" SMITH:

Vocalion 1558 *Howling Wolf Blues-No.1/2* ....150.00 - 200.00
    1590 *Good Coffee Blues* ....150.00 - 200.00

    1614 *Howling Wolf Blues-No. 3/4* ....150.00 - 200.00
    1633 *Corn Whiskey Blues* ....150.00 - 200.00
    1641 *Seven Sisters Blues-Part 1/2* ....150.00 - 200.00
    1655 *Hungry Wolf*...150.00 - 200.00
    1664 *Forty-Five Blues* ....150.00 - 200.00
    1674 *Fool's Blues* ....150.00 - 200.00
    1679 *County Jail Blues* ....150.00 - 200.00

GRACE SMITH:

National 9046 *Competition Blues* ....15.00 -   20.00
    9051 *What's On The Rail For The Lizard* ....15.00 -   20.00

GUY SMITH:

Paramount 12806 *Southland Blues* ....100.00 - 150.00

HAZEL SMITH:

Okeh 8620 *West End Blues*...................................150.00 - 300.00

HENRY SMITH:

Dot 1220 *Good Rocking Mama* ....20.00 -   30.00 *
Fortune 802 *Dog Me Blues* ....30.00 -   50.00

HORACE SMITH:

Gennett 7025 *Mother-In-Law Blues* ....150.00 - 250.00
    7056 *Clickety-Clack Blues*.............................150.00 - 250.00
Superior 2604 *Mother-In-Law Blues* ....150.00 - 250.00

IKE SMITH'S CHICAGO BOYS:

Champion 50040 *Fighting Joe Louis*.....................20.00 -   30.00

IVA/IVY SMITH (AND CHARLIE DAVENPORT/AND HER BUDDIES):

Champion 16080 *Milkman Blues*..........................150.00 - 250.00
Gennett 6829 *Shadow Blues* ....200.00 - 300.00
    6861 *Gin House Blues* ....150.00 - 200.00
    6875 *Mistreated Mama Blues* ....150.00 - 300.00
    7024 *Wringin' And Twistin' Papa* ....150.00 - 200.00
    7040 *Doin' That Thing*...................................150.00 - 200.00
    7101 *Cheating Only Blues* ....150.00 - 200.00
    7231 *That's The Kind Of Girl I'm Looking For*
....200.00 - 300.00
    7251 *Milkman Blues* ....200.00 - 300.00
Paramount 12436 *Rising Sun Blues* ....150.00 - 200.00
    12447 *Sad And Blue*.......................................150.00 - 200.00
    12472 *Barrel House Mojo* ....150.00 - 200.00
    12496 *Ninety-Nine Years Blues* ....150.00 - 200.00
Supertone 9509 *Shadow Blues*..............................125.00 - 175.00
    9515 *No Good Man Blues*..............................125.00 - 175.00
    9527 *Wingin' And Twistin' Papa*...................125.00 - 175.00
    9531 *Mistreated Mama Blues* ....125.00 - 175.00
    9533 *Southern High Waters Blues*..................125.00 - 175.00

JANE SMITH:

Silvertone 3559 *Blue Monday Blues*......................50.00 -   75.00
    3563 *Kentucky Blues*......................................50.00 -   75.00

JULIA SMITH:

Oriole 771 *Crap Shootin' Papa, Mama Done Caught Your Dice*
....15.00 -   20.00
    772 *I Needs Plenty Of Grease In My Frying Pan*
....15.00 -   20.00
    816 *Harlem Blues* ....15.00 -   20.00

LAURA SMITH:

Title issued contemporaneously on Banner, Domino, and Regal:
    Don't You Leave Me Here ....20.00 -   30.00
Okeh 8157 *Texas Moaner Blues* ....100.00 - 150.00
    8169 *Two-Faced Woman Blues* ....100.00 - 150.00
    8179 *Gravier Street Blues* ....100.00 - 150.00

8186 *I'm Gonna Get Myself A Real Man* ....100.00 - 150.00

8246 *Disgusted Blues* ....100.00 - 150.00

8252 *Face To Face* ....50.00 - 80.00

8316 *I'll Get Even With You* ....100.00 - 150.00

8331 *Them Has Been Blues* ....50.00 - 75.00

8366 *Cool Can Blues* ....80.00 - 120.00

8445 *Hateful Blues* ....75.00 - 100.00

Pathe-Actuelle 7520 *When A Gator Hollers* ....50.00 - 75.00

7525 *I'm Gonna Kill Myself* ....50.00 - 75.00

Perfect 120 *When A Gator Hollers* ....50.00 - 75.00

125 *I'm Gonna Kill Myself* ....50.00 - 75.00

Victor 20775 *Lonesome Refugee* ....40.00 - 60.00

20945 *Red River Blues*..40.00 - 60.00

MAMIE SMITH (& HER JAZZ BAND/HOUNDS); MAMIE SMITH'S JAZZ HOUNDS:

Ajax 17058 *Good Time Ball* ....40.00 - 60.00

17063 *Remorseful Blues* ....40.00 - 60.00

17068 *What You Need Is Me* ....40.00 - 60.00

Okeh 4113 *That Thing Called Love*.........................20.00 - 30.00

4169 *Crazy Blues* ....15.00 - 20.00

4194 *Fare Thee Honey Blues* ....15.00 - 25.00

4228 *If You Don't Want Me Blues* ....25.00 - 40.00

4253 *Don't Care Blues* ....25.00 - 40.00

4254 *Royal Garden Blues* ....30.00 - 50.00

4295 *Jazzbo Ball* ....25.00 - 40.00

4296 *That Thing Called Love* ....25.00 - 40.00

4305 *You Can't Keep A Good Man Down*..........30.00 - 50.00

4351 *Dangerous Blues* ....30.00 - 50.00

4416 *Sax-O-Phoney Blues* ....30.00 - 50.00

4427 *Mamma Whip! Mamma Spank!* ....25.00 - 40.00

4445 *The Wang Wang Blues* ....30.00 - 50.00

4446 *Down Home Blues* ....30.00 - 50.00

4471 *Weepin'* ....30.00 - 50.00

4511 *Sweet Man O' Mine* ....30.00 - 50.00

4542 *Oh, Joe (Please Don't Go)* ....30.00 - 50.00

4578 *Doo-Dah Blues* ....30.00 - 50.00

4600 *A-Wearin' Away The Blues*........................30.00 - 50.00

4623 *I Want A Jazzy Kiss* ....30.00 - 50.00

4630 *Lonesome Mama Blues* ....30.00 - 50.00

4631 *Mean Daddy Blues* ....30.00 - 50.00

4658 *Alabama Blues* ....30.00 - 50.00

4670 *Got To Cool My Doggies Now*..................25.00 - 40.00

4689 *That Da Da Strain* ....40.00 - 60.00

4752 *I Ain't Gonna Give Nobody None O' This Jelly Roll*

....30.00 - 50.00

4767 *The Darktown Flappers Ball* ....40.00 - 60.00

4781 *I'm Gonna Get You* ....25.00 - 40.00

4856 *Mean Man*..30.00 - 50.00

4926 *Kansas City Man Blues* ....75.00 - 100.00

4935 *Good Looking Papa* ....25.00 - 40.00

4960 *Mistreatin' Daddy Blues*...........................25.00 - 40.00

8024 *Rambling Blues* ....40.00 - 60.00

8030 *Carolina Blues* ....40.00 - 60.00

8036 *Strut Your Material*..................................40.00 - 60.00

8072 *Those Longing For You Blues* ....40.00 - 60.00

8864 *Don't Advertise Your Man*........................80.00 - 120.00

8915 *Golfing Papa*...80.00 - 120.00

40019 *Do It, Mr. So And So* ....25.00 - 40.00

Victor 20210 *Goin' Crazy With The Blues*.............30.00 - 50.00

20233 *Sweet Virginia Blues*...............................40.00 - 60.00

MANDY SMITH:

Jewel 5138 *Mean Old Bedbug Blues* ....15.00 - 20.00

5188 *When You Get Tired Of Your New Sweetie* ...15.00 - 20.00

5207 *Shootin' Star Blues* ....15.00 - 20.00

5230 *Lonesome Ghost Blues* ....15.00 - 20.00

5254 *Second Hand Daddy* ....15.00 - 20.00

5309 *Your Worries Ain't Like Mine* ....15.00 - 20.00

Oriole 1059 *Mean Old Bedbug Blues* ....15.00 - 20.00

1118 *You Can't Have It Unless I Give It To You*

....15.00 - 20.00

1147 *Don't Let Your Love Come Down* ....15.00 - 20.00

1170 *If You Can't Control Your Man* ....15.00 - 20.00

1197 *A Good Man Is Hard To Find* ....15.00 - 25.00

1249 *Shake It Down* ....15.00 - 25.00

PINE TOP SMITH:

Vocalion 1245 *Pine Top's Boogie Woogie* ....150.00 - 200.00

1256 *Big Boy They Can't Do That*..................150.00 - 200.00

1266 *I'm Sober Now* ....150.00 - 200.00

1298 *Jump Steady Blues* ....150.00 - 200.00

ROBERT SMITH:

Independent 301 *Freeway Boogie*.........................15.00 - 20.00

RUBY SMITH:

Bluebird 7654 *Dream Man Blues* ....15.00 - 20.00

7794 *Flyin' Mosquito Blues* ....15.00 - 20.00

7864 *Hard Up Blues* ....15.00 - 20.00

Decca 7869 *Black Gal* ....15.00 - 20.00

7875 *Thinking Blues* ....15.00 - 20.00

Vocalion 04903 *Back Water Blues* ....15.00 - 20.00

SIX CYLINDER SMITH:

Paramount 12968 *Pennsylvania Woman Blues*.....200.00 - 300.00

SPARK PLUG SMITH:

Titles issued contemporaneously on Banner, Melotone, Oriole, Perfect, and Romeo: *Deserted Man Blues; In A Shanty In Old Shanty Town; Make It Tight; Mama's Doughnut; Motherless Boy; New Blues Heaven; Stopped Clock Blues; Sweet Evening Breeze; Vampire Woman; You Put That Thing On Me*

....50.00 - 75.00

SUSIE SMITH:

Ajax 17064 *House Rent Blues* ....30.00 - 50.00

17073 *Salt Water Blues*......................................30.00 - 50.00

17075 *Bullet Wound Blues*.................................30.00 - 50.00

17079 *The Bye Bye Blues*...................................30.00 - 50.00

17081 *Meat Man Pete* ....30.00 - 50.00

17086 *Nobody Knows The Way I Feel Dis Mornin'*

....30.00 - 50.00

17089 *Sore Bunion Blues*...................................30.00 - 50.00

17093 *Scandal Blues*..30.00 - 50.00

17095 *How Can I Miss You* ....30.00 - 50.00

17127 *Texas Special Blues*.................................50.00 - 80.00

17132 *Undertaker's Blues*..................................30.00 - 50.00

17134 *Crepe Hanger Blues*.................................50.00 - 80.00

THUNDER SMITH (AND ROCKIE):

Aladdin 166 *Little Mama Boogie*...........................40.00 - 60.00

Down Town 2011 *Thunder's Unfinished Boogie* ...50.00 - 75.00

2012 *New Worried Life Blues* ....50.00 - 75.00

2013 *Low Down Dirty Ways* ....50.00 - 75.00

Gold Star 615 *Cruel Hearted Woman*....................50.00 - 75.00

644 *Santa Fe Blues* ....50.00 - 75.00

TRIXIE SMITH:

Black Swan 2039 *Trixie's Blues* ....40.00 - 60.00

2044 *Long Lost Weary Blues* ....40.00 - 60.00

14114 *Pensacola Blues* ....40.00 - 60.00

14127 *My Man Rocks Me* ....50.00 - 75.00

14132 *I'm Through With You* ....50.00 - 75.00
14138 *I'm Gonna Get You* ....50.00 - 75.00
14142 *Log Cabin Blues* ....50.00 - 75.00
14149 *Triflin' Blues* ....40.00 - 60.00
Decca 7469 *Trixie Blues* ....15.00 - 20.00
7489 *My Unusual Man* ....15.00 - 20.00
7528 *Jack, I'm Mellow* ....15.00 - 20.00
7617 *No Good Man* ....15.00 - 20.00
Paramount 12161 *Trixie's Blues*......................35.00 - 50.00
12162 *Long Lost Weary Blues*.........................35.00 - 50.00
12163 *Pensacola Blues*..................................35.00 - 50.00
12164 *My Man Rocks Me* ....40.00 - 60.00
12165 *I'm Through With You* ....40.00 - 60.00
12166 *I'm Gonna Get You* ....40.00 - 60.00
12167 *Log Cabin Blues* ....40.00 - 60.00
12168 *Triflin' Blues* ....35.00 - 50.00
12208 *Sorrowful Blues* ....75.00 - 100.00
12211 *Freight Train Blues*..............................75.00 - 100.00
12232 *Praying Blues*.....................................75.00 - 100.00
12245 *Choo Choo Blues*.................................75.00 - 100.00
12256 *Mining Camp Blues* ....100.00 - 150.00
12262 *Railroad Blues*....................................100.00 - 150.00
12330 *Love Me Like You Used To Do* ....100.00 - 150.00
12336 *Black Bottom Hop*................................100.00 - 150.00

WALTER (TANG) SMITH:
J-B 606 *High Tone Mama* ....20.00 - 30.00

WILLIAM & VERSEY SMITH:
Paramount 12505 *When That Great Ship Went Down*
....75.00 - 100.00
12516 *I Believe I'll Go Back Home* ....75.00 - 100.00

WILLIE (LONG TIME) SMITH:
Columbia 30097 *No Special Rider Here* ....8.00 - 12.00
30104 *My Buddy Doctor Clayton* ....8.00 - 12.00
30140 *Flying Cloud Boogie*.................................8.00 - 12.00

SMITH & LEE:
Victor V-38607 *One Hour Tonight* ....75.00 - 100.00

SMOKEHOUSE CHARLEY:
Champion 15794 *My Texas Blues* ....100.00 - 150.00
15815 *Pig Meat Blues*..................................100.00 - 150.00
15834 *Broke Man's Blues*..............................100.00 - 150.00
15903 *Rollin' Mill Stomp*...............................100.00 - 150.00
15950 *Six Shooter Blues*...............................150.00 - 200.00
15994 *Second Hand Love*...............................150.00 - 200.00
16682 *Levee Bound Blues*..............................300.00 - up
50014 *Gee, But It's Hard*..............................50.00 - 75.00

SMOKEY JOE:
Flip 502 *Split Personality* ....40.00 - 60.00 *
Sun 228 *Split Personality* ....75.00 - 100.00 *

SNOOKY AND MOODY: (See also SNOOKY PRYOR)
Old Swing-Master 18 *Calling Up My Baby Blues*...75.00 - 100.00
Planet 101 *Telephone Blues*...................................100.00 - 150.00

EDDIE SNOW:
Sun 226 *Ain't That Right* ....75.00 - 100.00 *

HATTIE SNOW:
Gennett 7039 *Don't Say Goodbye* ....250.00 - up
7070 *Make That Gravel Fly*...............................250.00 - up
7115 *Two Train Blues*.....................................250.00 - up

Q. ROSCOE SNOWDEN:
Okeh 8119 *Misery Blues*................................40.00 - 60.00

SONNY BOY & LONNIE:
Continental 6050 *Quincy Avenue Boogie* ....15.00 - 20.00
6052 *Talking Boogie* ....15.00 - 20.00
6053 *Big Moose Blues* ....15.00 - 20.00
6054 *I'll Water You Every Day* ....15.00 - 20.00

SONNY BOY & SAM:
Continenal 6055 *Mama Blues* ....15.00 - 20.00

ANN SORTIER:
Decca 7819 *Never Leave Me* ....15.00 - 20.00

SOUTH CAROLINA QUARTETTE:
QRS 7012 *Paul And Silas*..............................30.00 - 50.00
7061 *I'm A Pilgrim* ....30.00 - 50.00

SOUTHERN BLUES SINGERS:
Gennett 6828 *Lighthouse Blues* ....125.00 - 175.00
6845 *Runnin' Wild* ....125.00 - 175.00

SOUTHERN JUBILEE QUARTET:
Black Patti 8036 *Listen To The Lambs* ....150.00 - 250.00

SOUTH MEMPHIS JUG BAND:
Vocalion 02585 *Doctor Medicine*.........................100.00 - 150.00

SOUTHERN (NEGRO) QUARTETTE:
Columbia A-3444 *I'm Wild About Moonshine* ....10.00 - 20.00
A-3450 *I Ain't Givin' Nothin' Away*..................10.00 - 20.00
A-3489 *He Took It Away From Me* ....10.00 - 20.00
14038-D *Hampton Road Blues* ....25.00 - 40.00
14043-D *Moanin' Croanin' Blues* ....25.00 - 40.00
14048-D *My Man Rocks Me (With One Steady Roll)*
....25.00 - 40.00

SOUTHERN SANCTIFIED SINGERS:
Brunswick 7074 *Soon We'll Gather At The River* .. 75.00 - 100.00

SOUTHERN UNIVERSITY QUARTET:
Bluebird 5846 *All Over The World*........................15.00 - 20.00
5932 *I'm Tired Of Living In The Country*..........15.00 - 20.00
6142 *I'm Troubled In Mind*.............................15.00 - 20.00

CHARLIE SPAND:
Okeh 05699 *Rock And Rye*.............................30.00 - 50.00
05757 *Gold Tooth Mama* ....30.00 - 50.00
05894 *Big Alley Rat Blues* ....30.00 - 50.00
05946 *Gone Mother Blues* ....30.00 - 50.00
Paramount 12790 *Soon This Morning* ....500.00 - up
12817 *Back To The Woods Blues*....................500.00 - up
12856 *Moanin' The Blues*..............................500.00 - up
12887 *In The Barrel Blues*............................500.00 - up
12917 *Mississippi Blues*...............................500.00 - up
12930 *Room Rent Blues*...............................500.00 - up
13005 *She's Got Good Stuff*..........................500.00 - up
13022 *Mistreatment Blues*............................500.00 - up
13047 *Thirsty Woman Blues*..........................500.00 - up
13101 *Georgia Mule Blues* ....500.00 - up
13112 *Hard Times Blues*..............................500.00 - up

THE SPANIELS:
Chance 1141 *Baby It's You*...................................25.00 - 50.00 *
(Note: Many of this group's records were issued as 45 RPM See also
the **RHYTHM & BLUES, ETC.** section.)

SPARKLING FOUR QUARTETTE:
QRS 7011 *Keep On To Galilee* ....25.00 - 40.00

SPARKS BROTHERS:
Bluebird 5193 *61 Highway*.................................200.00 - 300.00
   5247 *Chicago's Too Much For Me* ....200.00 - 300.00
Sunrise 3273 *Down On The Levee*.....................200.00 - 400.00
   3330 *Chicago's Too Much For Me* ....200.00 - 400.00

MILTON SPARKS:
Bluebird 6096 *Grinder Blues*.............................50.00 - 80.00
   6126 *I Wake Up In The Morning* ....50.00 - 80.00
   6521 *Ina Blues* ....50.00 - 80.00
   6529 *Erie Train Blues*.................................50.00 - 80.00

HENRY SPAULDING:
Brunswick 7085 *Cairo Blues*..............................75.00 - 125.00

BLOSSOM SPEARS:
Champion 15267 *Indian Brown Blues*...............75.00 - 100.00

SPECKLED RED (TRIO):
Bluebird 7985 *St. Louis Stomp* ....20.00 - 30.00
   8012 *Try Me One More Time* ....20.00 - 30.00
   8036 *You Got To Fix It*................................20.00 - 30.00
   8069 *Welfare Blues*....................................20.00 - 30.00
   8113 *Down On The Levee*............................20.00 - 30.00
Brunswick 7116 *The Dirty Dozen* ....150.00 - 200.00
   7137 *House Dance Blues*...........................150.00 - 200.00
   7151 *The Dirty Dozen-Part No. 2*..............150.00 - 200.00
   7164 *Speckled Red's Blues* ....150.00 - 200.00
   7200 *We Got To Get That Thing Fixed* ....150.00 - 200.00

MAMIE SPENCER:
Oriole 795 *Scrubbin' Blues* ....20.00 - 30.00

BIG BOY SPIRES & HIS TRIO:
Chance 1137 *About To Lose My Mind* ....40.00 - 70.00
Checker 752 *One Of These Days*.............................15.00 - 20.00

SWEET PEASE SPIVEY & HER/DOT SCOTT'S RHYTHM DUKES:
Decca 7204 *Grievin' Me*....................................15.00 - 20.00
   7237 *410 Blues* ....15.00 - 20.00

(ORIGINAL) VICTORIA SPIVEY (AND CHICAGO FOUR/DOT SCOTT'S RHYTHM DUKES/HER HALLELUJAH BOYS):
Bluebird 8619 *Blood Hound Blues* ....20.00 - 30.00
Decca 7203 *Black Snake Swing* ....15.00 - 20.00
   7222 *T. B.'s Got Me Blues*................................15.00 - 20.00
Okeh 8338 *No More Jelly Bean Blues*....................50.00 - 75.00
   8351 *Dirty Woman's Blues* ....50.00 - 75.00
   8370 *Hoodoo Man Blues* ....40.00 - 60.00
   8389 *Humored And Petted Blues*....................80.00 - 120.00
   8401 *Big Houston Blues* ....50.00 - 80.00
   8410 *Santa Fe Blues* ....50.00 - 80.00
   8464 *Idle Hour Blues* ....50.00 - 80.00
   8481 *The Alligator Pond Went Dry* ....50.00 - 80.00
   8494 *TR Blues*..50.00 - 80.00
   8517 *Garter Snake Blues* ....40.00 - 60.00
   8531 *Blood Thirsty Blues* ....40.00 - 60.00
   8550 *Red Lantern Blues* ....40.00 - 60.00
   8565 *Your Worries Ain't Like Mine*..................40.00 - 60.00
   8581 *Murder In The First Degree* ....40.00 - 60.00
   8615 *Organ Grinder Blues* ....100.00 - 150.00
   8626 *New Black Snake Blues, Part 1/2* ....30.00 - 50.00
   8634 *Mosquito, Fly And Flea* ....50.00 - 80.00
   8652 *Furniture Man Blues-Part 1/2*................25.00 - 40.00
   8713 *How Do You Do It That Way?*................100.00 - 150.00

8733 *You Done Lost Your Good Thing Now Part 1/2*
....30.00 - 50.00
   8744 *Toothache Blues-Part 1/2* ....35.00 - 50.00
Victor 23349 *Haulin' Water Blues* ....200.00 - 300.00
   V38546 *Telephoning The Blues*....................150.00 - 200.00
   V38570 *Dirty T. B. Blues*..............................150.00 - 200.00
   V38584 *New York Blues* ....75.00 - 100.00
   V38598 *Haunted By The Blues* ....75.00 - 100.00
   V38609 *You've Gotta Have What It Takes*......100.00 - 150.00
Vocalion 1606 *Nebraska Blues*.........................150.00 - 200.00
   1640 *Low Down Man Blues* ....150.00 - 200.00
   03243 *Toothache Blues-Part 1/2* ....8.00 - 12.00
   03260 *Furniture Man Blues-Part 1/2* ....8.00 - 12.00
   03366 *I Ain't Gonna Let You See My Santa Claus*
....15.00 - 20.00
   03405 *Detroit Moan*.....................................15.00 - 20.00
   03505 *One Hour Mama*.................................15.00 - 20.00
   03639 *Good Cabbage* ....15.00 - 20.00

"MR. FREDDIE" SPRUELL:
Paramount 12665 *Tom Cat Blues* ....150.00 - 250.00

STABLE BOY SAM:
Vocalion 1739 *Mama's Doughnut*......................50.00 - 75.00

STATE STREET BOYS:
Okeh 8962 *Don't Tear My Clothes*....................75.00 - 100.00
   8964 *Crazy About You* ....80.00 - 120.00
   8965 *Sweet To Mama*...................................80.00 - 120.00
Vocalion 03002 *She Caught The Train* ....30.00 - 50.00
   03004 *Crazy About You* ....40.00 - 60.00
   03049 *Sweet To Mama*.................................40.00 - 60.00
   03131 *Mobile And Western Line*.....................75.00 - 100.00

STEAMBOAT BILL & HIS GUITAR:
Champion 15674 *No No Blues*...........................150.00 - 200.00
   15694 *Weak-Minded Blues* ....150.00 - 200.00
   15716 *Bad Luck Moan* ....150.00 - 200.00
   15735 *Rag Baby*..150.00 - 200.00

STEELE AND JOHNSON:
Champion 16395 *Selling That Stuff* ....150.00 - 250.00

VOL STEVENS:
Victor 21356 *Vol Stevens Blues*.........................150.00 - 300.00

DAN STEWART:
Vocalion 1536 *New Orleans Blues* ....100.00 - 150.00

MAE STEWART:
Silvertone 3518 *I Was Born A Brownskin* ....75.00 - 100.00
   3520 *You Ain't Foolin' Me* ....75.00 - 100.00
   3541 *Going To The Nation* ....50.00 - 75.00

PRISCILLA STEWART:
Paramount 12205 *True Blues*.............................75.00 - 100.00
   12224 *Mecca Flat Blues* ....75.00 - 100.00
   12240 Delta *Bottom Blues* ....100.00 - 150.00
   12253 *The Woman Ain't Born* ....150.00 - 200.00
   12286 *Priscilla Blues* ....75.00 - 100.00
   12299 *Going To The Nation* ....50.00 - 80.00
   12360 *It Must Be Hard* ....75.00 - 100.00
   12402 *Biscuit Roller* ....100.00 - 150.00
   12463 *Lonesome Hour Blues* ....100.00 - 150.00
   12465 *P.D.Q. Blues* ....100.00 - 150.00
   12740 *A Little Bit Closer* ....100.00 - 150.00

ARBEE STIDHAM:
Abco 100 *I'll Always Remember* ....10.00 -   15.00 *
  107 *When I Find My Baby* ....10.00 -   15.00 *
Checker 751 *Mr. Commissioner* ....15.00 -   20.00
  778 *I Don't Play* ....10.00 -   15.00 *
RCA Victor (most issues) ....7.00 -   12.00
Sittin' In With 596 *Nothing Seems Right* ....10.00 -   15.00
  606 *I've Got News For You Baby* ....10.00 -   15.00
  617 *Bad Dreams Blues* ....10.00 -   15.00
(See the fourth section of this book for additional recordings by
  Arbee Stidham in 45 RPM format)

FRANK STOKES:
Victor 21272 *Downtown Blues* ....150.00 -   250.00
  21672 *Mistreatin' Blues* ....150.00 -   250.00
  21738 *Stomp That Thing* ....150.00 -   250.00
  23341 *I'm Going Away Blues* ....400.00 -   up
  23411 *Frank Stokes' Dream* ....400.00 -   up
  V38500 *'Tain't Nobody's Business If I Do* ......200.00 -   300.00
  V38512 *I Got Mine* ....200.00 -   300.00
  V38531 *Take Me Back* ....200.00 -   300.00
  V38548 *South Memphis Blues* ....300.00 -   up
  V38589 *Right Now Blues* ....300.00 -   up

JOE STONE:
Bluebird 5169 *Back Door Blues* ....150.00 -   200.00
Sunrise 3250 *It's Hard Time* ....150.00 -   300.00

LUTHER STONEHAM:
Mercury 8275 *Sittin' And Wonderin'* ....20.00 -   30.00

STOVEPIPE NO. 1 (AND DAVID CROCKETT):
Columbia 201-D *Turkey In The Straw* ....75.00 -   100.00
  15011-D *Lonesome John* ....100.00 -   150.00
Okeh 8514 *Court Street Blues* ....150.00 -   200.00
  8543 *Bed Slats* ....150.00 -   200.00

FREEMAN STOWERS:
Gennett 6814 *Railroad Blues* ....100.00 -   150.00
  6830 *Texas Wildcat Chase* ....100.00 -   150.00
Supertone 9396 *Sunrise On The Farm* ....50.00 -   80.00

MARY STRAINE:
Black Swan 14115 *Ain't Got Nothing Blues* ....40.00 -   60.00
  14123 *Last Go Round Blues* ....40.00 -   60.00
  14150 *Chirpin' The Blues* ....30.00 -   50.00
Paramount 12132 *Ain't Got Nothing Blues* ....35.00 -   50.00
  12149 *Last Go Round Blues* ....35.00 -   50.00
  12150 *Chirpin' The Blues* ....25.00 -   40.00

JIMMY STRANGE:
Victor 23317 *No Limit Blues* ....400.00 -   up

JOHNNIE STRAUSS:
Decca 7035 *Old Market Street Blues* ....50.00 -   80.00
  7081 *Hard Working Woman* ....50.00 -   80.00

STREAMLINE MAE:
Okeh 06045 *Romance In The Dark* ....15.00 -   20.00
  06093 *School Boy Blues* ....15.00 -   20.00

SUGAR CANE JOHNNY:
Bluebird 5948 *Who Pumped The Wind In The Doughnuts?*
  ....100.00 -   150.00

THE SUGARMAN:
Sittin' In With 609 *Which Woman Do I Love* ....20.00 -   30.00

ANNIE SUMMERFORD:
Okeh 8174 *'Fo Day Blues* ....80.00 -   120.00

SUNNY BOY & HIS PALS:
Champion 15283 *Don't You Leave Me Here* ....200.00 -   300.00
Gennett 6106 *France Blues* ....250.00 -   400.00

SUNNY JIM AND WHISTLIN' JOE:
Champion 15361 *Black Snake Blues* ....250.00 -   400.00

SUNNYLAND SLIM & HIS SUNNY (LAND) BOYS/TRIO;
SUNNYLAND SLIM & MUDDY WATERS (COMBO);
SUNNYLAND TRIO:
Apollo 416 *Bad Times* ....30.00 -   50.00
Aristocrat 1301 *Fly Right, Little Girl* ....75.00 -   100.00
  1304 *She Ain't Nowhere* ....75.00 -   100.00
Blue Lake 105 *Going Back To Memphis* ....30.00 -   50.00 *
  107 *Shake It Baby* ....30.00 -   50.00 *
Club 51 106 *Sad And Lonesome* ....40.00 -   60.00 *
Cobra 5006 *Highway 61* ....30.00 -   50.00 *
Ebony 1009 *Shake It Baby* ....- -   -
Hytone 32 *Jivin' Boogie* ....30.00 -   50.00
  33 *My Heavy Load* ....30.00 -   50.00
  33 *Miss Bessie Mae* ....30.00 -   50.00
  37 *I've Done You Wrong* ....30.00 -   50.00
J.O.B. 102 *Down Home Child* ....100.00 -   150.00
  1003 *Mary Lee* ....80.00 -   120.00
  1105 *Shake It Baby* ....50.00 -   80.00
  1108 *Four Day Bounce* ....50.00 -   80.00
Mercury 8132 *Mud Kicking Woman* ....30.00 -   50.00
  8264 *Gin Drinkin' Baby* ....30.00 -   50.00
  8277 *Brown Skinned Woman* ....30.00 -   50.00
Regal 3327 *Orphan Boy Blues* ....50.00 -   75.00
Sunny 101 *Back To Korea Blues* ....- -   -
Tempo Tone 1001 *Hard Times* ....50.00 -   100.00
  1002 *Blue Baby* ....50.00 -   100.00

THE SWALLOWS:
King 4458, 4466, 4501, 4515, 4521, 4612, 4632....20.00 -   30.00 *
*The foregoing records are sometimes found in the 45 RPM format.
  45s are generally more valuable than their 78 RPM counterparts.
  See the **RHYTHM & BLUES, ETC.** section for additional
  additional recordings in 45 RPM format.

SWAN AND LEE:
Okeh 8732 *Fishy Little Thing* ....50.00 -   75.00

SWEET PAPA STOVEPIPE:
Paramount 12404 *Mama's Angel Child* ....150.00 -   200.00

SWEET PAPA TADPOLE:
Vocalion 1592 *Have You Ever Been Worried In Mind*
  ....150.00 -   200.00
  1680 *Black Spider Blues* ....150.00 -   200.00
  1687 *Your Baby Can't Get Enough* ....150.00 -   200.00

SWEET PEA(S):
Bluebird 7224 *Cold In Hand* ....20.00 -   30.00
  8114 *Blood Drippin' Blues* ....20.00 -   30.00
  8146 *Disgusted Blues* ....20.00 -   30.00
Victor 23361 *Day Breakin' Blues* ....250.00 -   400.00
  V38565 *Heart-Breakin' Blues* ....200.00 -   300.00

SYKES AND JOHNSON:
Champion 16558 *Steady Grinding* ....250.00 -   up

ISABEL SYKES:
Bluebird 5170 *Don't Rush Yourself* ....100.00 -   150.00
Sunrise 3251 *Don't Rush Yourself* ....100.00 -   200.00

ROOSEVELT SYKES:

Black & White 100 *This Tavern Boogie*...................10.00 - 15.00
Bluebird 5323 *New 44 Blues* ....100.00 - 150.00
   5342 *Working Dollar Blues* ....100.00 - 150.00
   34-0721 *I Wonder* ....10.00 - 15.00
   34-0729 *Jivin' The Jive* ....10.00 - 15.00
Bullet 319 *Candy Man Blues* ....15.00 - 20.00
Champion 16586 *Highway 61 Blues* ....300.00 - up
   50012 *Highway 61 Blues* ....50.00 - 75.00
Columbia *(red label, most issues)* ....7.00 - 10.00
Conqueror 9941, 9942, 9943 ....7.00 - 10.00
Decca 7011 *Ethel Mae Blues* ....80.00 - 120.00
   7280 *Mister Sykes Blues* ....20.00 - 30.00
   7586 *Have You Seen Ida B* ....15.00 - 20.00
   7597 *Love Will Wear You Down* ....15.00 - 20.00
   48124 *44 Blues* ....10.00 - 15.00
Okeh 06219 *Just Hanging Around* ....10.00 - 15.00
   06387 *Roll On Blues* ....10.00 - 15.00
   06455 *Skin and Bones Blues* ....10.00 - 15.00
   06542 *Third Degree Blues* ....10.00 - 15.00
   06709 *Sugar Babe Blues* ....10.00 - 15.00
   8702 *Boot That Thing* ....80.00 - 120.00
   8727 *The Way I Feel Blues* ....100.00 - 150.00
   8742 *Henry Ford Blues* ....100.00 - 150.00
   8749 *Skeet And Garret* ....100.00 - 150.00
   8776 *Roosevelt's Blues* ....100.00 - 150.00
   8787 *Poor Boy Blues* ....100.00 - 150.00
   8819 *Bury That Thing* ....100.00 - 150.00
RCA Victor *(most issues)*.................................7.00 - 10.00
Regal 3269 *Rock It*...15.00 - 20.00
   3286 *Drivin' Wheel*......................................15.00 - 20.00
   3306 *Mailbox Blues* ....15.00 - 20.00
   3324 *Green Onion Top* ....15.00 - 20.00
Sunrise 3404 *New 44 Blues* ....100.00 - 200.00
   3423 *Devil's Island Gin Blues* ....100.00 - 200.00
United 101 *Fine And Brown* ....10.00 - 15.00
   120 *Raining In My Heart* ....10.00 - 15.00
   129 *Walkin' This Boogie* ....10.00 - 15.00 *
   139 *Four O'Clock Blues* ....8.00 - 12.00 *
   152 *Come Back Baby* ....8.00 - 12.00 *
(See the fourth section of this book for additional **ROOSEVELT SYKES** recordings in 45 RPM format)

HANNAH SYLVESTER:

Emerson 10625 *Midnight Blues*............................30.00 - 50.00
Famous 3237 *Farewell Blues* ....40.00 - 60.00
Majestic 1520 *Papa, Better Watch Your Step* ....30.00 - 50.00
   1521 *Long Lost Mamma* ....30.00 - 50.00
Olympic 1520 *Papa, Better Watch Your Step* ....25.00 - 40.00
   1521 *You Gotta See Mamma Ev'ry Night* ....25.00 - 40.00
Paramount 12033 *Midnight Blues* ....40.00 - 60.00
   12034 *The Wicked Fives* ....40.00 - 60.00
   20243 *Farewell Blues* ....40.00 - 60.00
Pathe-Actuelle 032007 *Down South Blues* ....25.00 - 40.00
Perfect 12086 *I Want My Sweet Daddy* ....25.00 - 40.00
Puritan 11243 *Farewell Blues* ....40.00 - 60.00

BLIND JOE/JOEL TAGGART (& BERTHA/EMMA/ JAMES TAGGART):

Decca 7033 *I Wonder Will My Mother Be On That Train?*
   ....100.00 - 150.00
   7034 *I Ain't No Sinner Now*............................100.00 - 150.00
Paramount 12611 *Been Listening All The Day*......300.00 - 500.00
   12717 *I've Crossed The Separation Line* ....300.00 - 500.00

   12744 *Mother's Love* ....300.00 - 500.00
   12780 *Scandalous And A Shame* ....300.00 - 500.00
   13020 *Wonder Will My Troubles Then Be Over*
   ....300.00 - 500.00
   13059 *Pressin' Up That Shiny Way* ....300.00 - 500.00
   13081 *Satan Your Kingdom Must Come Down*.....300.00 - 500.00
   13094 *I Ain't No Sinner Now* ....300.00 - 500.00
Vocalion 1061 *Take Your Burden To The Lord*.... 150.00 - 300.00
   1062 *I Will Not Be Removed* ....150.00 - 300.00
   1063 *I'll Be Satisfied*....................................150.00 - 300.00
   1070 *Keep On The Firing Line* ....150.00 - 300.00
   1123 *The Storm Is Passing Over* ....150.00 - 300.00

TALLAHASSEE TIGHT:

Titles issued contemporaneously on Banner, Conqueror, Domino, Melotone, Oriole, Perfect, and Romeo: *Black Gal; Black Snake Blues; Coast Line Blues; Homesick Blues; Jealous Man; Lonesome And Worried Blues; Quincey Wimmems; Ramblin' Mind Blues; Screaming Woman; Tallahassee Women*
   ....60.00 - 100.00

TAMPA JOE (See MACON ED)

TAMPA KID:

Decca 7278 *Keep On Trying* ....30.00 - 50.00

TAMPA RED, "THE GUITAR WIZARD"; TAMPA RED'S HOKUM JUG BAND; TAMPA RED & THE CHICAGO FIVE/HOKUM JUG BAND:

Titles issued contemporaneously on Banner, Melotone, Oriole, Perfect, and Romeo: *Dead Cats On The Line; Georgia Hound Blues; How Long How Long Blues; Mama Don't Allow No Easy Riders Here; New Strangers Blues; Reckless Man Blues; You Rascal You* ....60.00 - 100.00
Bluebird 5450 *I'll Find My Way* ....35.00 - 50.00
   5515 *I'll Kill Your Soul*...................................40.00 - 60.00
   5546 *Mean Mistreater Blues*............................40.00 - 60.00
   5572 *Somebody's Been Using That Thing* ....40.00 - 60.00
   5617 *Kingfish Blues* ....50.00 - 75.00
   5673 *I'm Just Crazy Bout You* ....50.00 - 75.00
   5723 *Witchin' Hour Blues* ....40.00 - 60.00
   5744 *Worried Devil Blues*................................40.00 - 60.00
   5779 *Happy Jack*..40.00 - 60.00
   5812 *Stockyard Fire* ....40.00 - 60.00
   5878 *Shake It Up A Little* ....40.00 - 60.00
   5929 *Don't Dog Your Woman* ....40.00 - 60.00
   5981 *Worthy Of You*.....................................50.00 - 80.00
   6037 *My Baby Said Yes*.................................30.00 - 50.00
   6059 *Keep On Dealin'* ....40.00 - 60.00
   6126 *Rowdy Woman Blues*.............................50.00 - 80.00
   6166 *You Missed A Good Man* ....20.00 - 30.00
   6211 *Drinkin' My Blues Away* ....20.00 - 30.00
   6241 *Waiting Blues* ....20.00 - 30.00
   6353 *Let's Get Drunk And Truck* ....8.00 - 12.00
Bluebird 6388 *She Don't Know My Mind*.............25.00 - 40.00
   6425 *Nutty And Buggy Blues* ....20.00 - 30.00
   6443 *When You Were A Gal Of Seven* ....8.00 - 12.00
   6498 *She Don't Know My Mind-Part 2* ....20.00 - 30.00
   6532 *All Night Long* ....8.00 - 12.00
   6578 *That's The Way I Do* ....15.00 - 25.00
   6620 *You Stole My Heart* ....10.00 - 15.00
   6681 *Blue And Evil Blues* ....15.00 - 20.00
   6755 *Stop Truckin' And Suzi-Q* ....10.00 - 15.00
   6787 *If It Wasn't For You* ....10.00 - 15.00
   6825 *Someday I'm Bound To Win* ....30.00 - 50.00
   6832 *Cheatin' On Me*....................................10.00 - 15.00

6968 *You Got To Learn To Do It* .... 15.00 - 20.00
6990 *I See You Can't Take It* .... 10.00 - 15.00
7010 *My Gal Is Gone* .... 20.00 - 30.00
7058 *I Give My Love To You* .... 10.00 - 15.00
7091 *When Love Comes In* .... 30.00 - 50.00
7115 *Taking It And Make My Get Away* .... 25.00 - 40.00
7225 *Harlem Swing* .... 10.00 - 15.00
7236 *I'm Gonna Get High* .... 15.00 - 20.00
7269 *Oh Babe, Oh Baby* .... 15.00 - 20.00
7276 *Wrong Idea* .... 20.00 - 30.00
7315 *Deceitful Friend Blues* .... 20.00 - 30.00
7364 *Whoopee Mama* .... 20.00 - 30.00
7499 *The Most Of Us Do* .... 10.00 - 15.00
7538 *We Gonna Get High Together* .... 10.00 - 15.00
7591 *A Lie In My Heart* .... 10.00 - 15.00
7642 *Grouchy Hearted Woman* .... 15.00 - 20.00
7675 *Got To Leave My Woman* .... 15.00 - 20.00
7743 *Rock It In Rhythm* .... 10.00 - 15.00
7793 *Sweetest Gal In Town* .... 10.00 - 15.00
7822 *When I Had A Good Woman* .... 20.00 - 30.00
7879 *Crazy With The Blues* .... 20.00 - 30.00
7976 *Checkin' Up On You* .... 10.00 - 15.00
8011 *Mr. Rhythm Man* .... 10.00 - 15.00
8046 *Blues For My Baby* .... 15.00 - 20.00
8086 *Hellish Old Feeling* .... 15.00 - 20.00
8179 *Please Don't Throw Me Down* .... 15.00 - 20.00
8205 *Poor Old Gal Blues* .... 15.00 - 20.00
8238 *No Good Woman Blues* .... 15.00 - 20.00
8266 *Booze Head Woman* .... 15.00 - 20.00
8291 *Sad Letter Blues* .... 15.00 - 20.00
8327 *Sweet Mellow Woman Blues* .... 15.00 - 20.00
8353 *Ready For Rhythm* .... 15.00 - 20.00
8368 *I Got A Big Surprise For You* .... 15.00 - 20.00
8407 *Dangerous Woman Blues* .... 15.00 - 25.00
8454 *I Don't Care No More* .... 15.00 - 20.00
8475 *You Say We're Through* .... 10.00 - 15.00
8575 *Baby Take A Chance With Me* .... 10.00 - 15.00
8635 *It Hurts Me Too* .... 10.00 - 15.00
8654 *Anna Lou Blues* .... 8.00 - 12.00
8715 *I Want To Swing* .... 15.00 - 20.00
8744 *This Ain't No Place For Me* .... 15.00 - 20.00
8780 *Hard Road Blues* .... 15.00 - 20.00
8821 *Noonday Hour Blues* .... 15.00 - 20.00
8890, 8919, 8962, 8991, 9009, 9024, 34-0700,
     34-0711, 34-0724, 34-0731, 34-0740 .... 7.00 - 12.00
Paramount 12685 *Through Train Blues* .... 200.00 - 300.00
RCA Victor (most issues) .... 7.00 - 12.00
Victor (most issues) .... 7.00 - 12.00
Vocalion 1216 *It's Tight Like That* .... 35.00 - 50.00
   1228 *It's Tight Like That* .... 50.00 - 80.00
   1237 *You Can't Come In* .... 150.00 - 250.00
   1244 *It's Tight Like That-No. 2* .... 150.00 - 200.00
   1251 *Jelly Whippin' Blues* .... 150.00 - 200.00
   1254 *Down In The Alley* .... 150.00 - 250.00
   1258 *It's Tight Like That* .... 150.00 - 200.00
   1268 *Juicy Lemon Blues* .... 150.00 - 200.00
   1274 *Boot It Boy* .... 150.00 - 250.00
   1277 *The Duck Yas-Yas-Yas* .... 150.00 - 200.00
   1281 *Mess, Katie, Mess* .... 150.00 - 250.00
   1294 *It's So Nice* .... 150.00 - 200.00
   1404 *Prison Bound Blues* .... 150.00 - 250.00
   1409 *Givin' It Away* .... 150.00 - 200.00
   1418 *Strange Woman Blues* .... 150.00 - 200.00

1420 *Come On, Mama, Do That Dance* .... 150.00 - 250.00
1426 *You Better Tighten Up On It* .... 150.00 - 200.00
1429 *Strewin' Your Mess* .... 150.00 - 200.00
1430 *Saturday Night Scrontch* .... 150.00 - 200.00
1450 *Corrine Corrina* .... 150.00 - 200.00
1456 *That Stuff You Sell* .... 150.00 - 200.00
1469 *Mrs. Baker's Blues* .... 150.00 - 250.00
1484 *Moanin' Heart Blues* .... 150.00 - 250.00
1491 *Dying Mercy Blues* .... 150.00 - 250.00
1496 *Corrine Corrina-No. 2* .... 125.00 - 175.00
1521 *You Rascal You* .... 75.00 - 100.00
1538 *The Dirty Dozen-No. 2* .... 100.00 - 150.00
1540 *You Rascal You* .... 150.00 - 200.00
1571 *Poor Old Bachelor Blues* .... 150.00 - 200.00
1572 *Dying Mercy Blues* .... 150.00 - 250.00
1577 *It's My Time Blues* .... 150.00 - 250.00
1596 *Jinx Doctor Blues* .... 150.00 - 250.00
1608 *Bear Cat's Kitten* .... 150.00 - 250.00
1619 *Boogie Woogie Dance* .... 150.00 - 250.00
1623 *Cryin' Shame Blues* .... 150.00 - 250.00
1628 *They Call It Boogie Woogie* .... 150.00 - 250.00
1637 *Cotton Seed Blues* .... 150.00 - 250.00
1654 *Georgia Hound Blues* .... 75.00 - 100.00
1656 *Depression Blues* .... 150.00 - 250.00
1661 *Stop And Listen Blues* .... 150.00 - 250.00
1671 *Please Mister Blues* .... 150.00 - 250.00
1685 *Dead Cats On The Line* .... 80.00 - 120.00
1699 *No Matter How She Done It* .... 150.00 - 250.00
1700 *Turpentine Blues* .... 150.00 - 250.00
1706 *Reckless Man Blues* .... 80.00 - 120.00
02720 *That Stuff Is Here* .... 80.00 - 120.00
02753 *Black Angel Blues* .... 100.00 - 150.00
02774 *Denver Blues* .... 150.00 - 200.00

(See also the fourth section of this book for additional Tampa Red
   recordings in 45 RPM format)

FRANK TANNEHILL:

Titles issued contemporaneously on Banner, Melotone, Oriole,
   Perfect, Romeo, and Vocalion: *I.G.N Blues; Steel Mill Blues*
   .... 35.00 - 50.00
Bluebird 7945 *Warehouse Blues* .... 20.00 - 30.00
   8028 *Door Bell Blues* .... 20.00 - 30.00
   8762 *Lillie Mae* .... 15.00 - 20.00
   8803 *Sweet Jelly Roll* .... 15.00 - 20.00

SAM TARPLEY:

Champion 16327 *Try Some Of That* .... 200.00 - 300.00
   16782 *That Stuff* .... 500.00 - up
Superior 2584 *Try Some Of That* .... 150.00 - 250.00

SLIM TARPLEY:

Paramount 13062 *Alabama Hustler* .... 150.00 - 250.00

TARTER AND GAY:

Victor V38017 *Brownie Blues* .... 150.00 - 200.00

TASKIANA FOUR:

- 20852 *Dixie Bo-Bo* .... 20.00 - 30.00

HATTIE TATE:

Supertone 9288 *There's Been Some Changes Made* .. - - -

ROSE TATE:

Champion 15302 *My Man Left Me Blues* .... 125.00 - 175.00
   15319 *Wild Woman Blues* .... 125.00 - 175.00
   15417 *Money Woman Blues* .... 125.00 - 175.00
Silvertone 5133 *My Man Left Me Blues* .... 125.00 - 175.00
   5168 *Mistreated Blues* .... 125.00 - 175.00

TAYLOR'S WEATHERBIRDS:
Victor 23309 *Coal Camp Blues* ....300.00 -   up

TAYLOR AND ANDERSON:
Champion 15951 *Corrine Corrina* ....150.00 - 250.00
 50016 *You Rascal, You* ....50.00 -   75.00
Supertone 9646 *You Rascal, You* ....150.00 - 250.00

CHARLES/CHARLEY TAYLOR:
Paramount 12949 *Where My Shoes At?* ....300.00 -   up
 12967 *Heavy Suitcase Blues* ....300.00 -   up
 13121 *C. P. Railroad Blues* ....1000.00 -   up

EDNA TAYLOR:
Paramount 12057 *Good Man Blues* ....80.00 - 120.00

ETHEL TAYLOR:
Supertone 9285 *Empty Bed Blues* ....75.00 - 100.00

EVA TAYLOR (& HER BOY FRIENDS):
Titles issued contemporaneously on Banner, Melotone, Oriole,
 Perfect, and Romeo: *Crazy Blues; The Stuff Is Here And It's
 Mellow* ....20.00 -   30.00
Black Swan 2103 *New Moon* ....30.00 -   50.00
Edison 14046 *West End Blues* ....150.00 - 200.00
 52646 *West End Blues* ....150.00 - 200.00
Okeh 3055 (12 inch) *Farewell Blues* ....150.00 - 200.00
 4740 *Baby, Won't You Please Come Home* ....20.00 -   30.00
 4805 *Down Hearted Blues* ....25.00 -   40.00
 4927 *Oh! Daddy Blues* ....100.00 - 150.00
 8047 *You Missed A Good Woman When You Picked All Over Me*
 ....20.00 -   30.00
 8049 *12th Street Rag* ....30.00 -   50.00
 8050 *You Can Have My Man* ....30.00 -   50.00
 8051 *My Pillow And Me* ....20.00 -   30.00
 8067 *Yodeling Blues* ....30.00 -   50.00
 8068 *You'll Never Have No Luck By Quittin' Me* 30.00 -   50.00
 8069 *Church Street Sobbin' Blues* ....25.00 -   40.00
 8073 *Barefoot Blues* ....80.00 - 120.00
 8089 *Original Charleston Strut* ....80.00 - 120.00
 8114 *Old Fashioned Love* ....75.00 - 100.00
 8129 *Jazzin' Babies Blues* ....80.00 - 120.00
 8145 *Ghost Of The Blues* ....75.00 - 100.00
 8183 *Terrible Blues* ....75.00 - 100.00
 8228 *Get Off My Money Blues* ....75.00 - 100.00
 8342 *You Can't Shush Katie (The Gabbiest Gal In Town)*
 ....150.00 - 200.00
 8407 *Morocco Blues* ....75.00 - 100.00
 8414 *Scatter Your Smiles* ....75.00 - 100.00
 8444 *I Wish You Would* ....100.00 - 150.00
 8463 *Red Hot Flo* ....80.00 - 120.00
 8518 *May We Meet Again* ....30.00 -   50.00
 8585 *Chloe* ....50.00 -   80.00
 8665 *Happy Days And Lonely Nights* ....50.00 -   80.00
 40330 *Pickin' On Your Baby* ....80.00 - 120.00
 40655 *Senorita Mine* ....30.00 -   50.00
 40671 *When The Red, Red Robin Comes Bob, Bob*
 ....30.00 -   50.00
 40715 *Candy Lips* ....75.00 - 100.00
Victor V38575 *Don't You Understand* ....150.00 - 200.00

BLIND JEREMIAH TAYLOR:
Herwin 93027 *Mother's Love* ....300.00 - 500.00

LOUELLA TAYLOR:
Domino 3452 *Nobody Knows The Way I Feel This Mornin'*
 ....20.00 -   30.00

MONTANA TAYLOR (& THE JAZOO BOYS):
Circle 1008 *In The Bottom* ....10.00 -   15.00
 1009 *Low Down Boogie* ....10.00 -   15.00
 1010 *Sweet Sue* ....10.00 -   15.00
 1015 *Montana's Blues* ....10.00 -   15.00
Vocalion 1275 *Whoop And Holler Stomp* ....150.00 - 200.00
 1419 *Detroit Rocks* ....150.00 - 200.00

SALLIE TAYLOR:
Supertone 9365 *Seven Men Blues* ....90.00 - 130.00
 9392 *West End Blues* ....90.00 - 130.00
 9426 *Old Fashioned Blues* ....90.00 - 130.00
 9440 *Loose Like That* ....90.00 - 130.00
 9514 *Cotton Belt Blues* ....100.00 - 150.00
 9530 *The Long Lost Blues* ....100.00 - 150.00

WALTER TAYLOR:
Champion 15972 *Yo-Yo Blues* ....200.00 - 300.00
 15995 *Diamond Ring Blues* ....200.00 - 300.00
 16059 *Broadcasting Blues* ....200.00 - 300.00
Gennett 7144 *Corrine Corrina* ....200.00 - 300.00
 7157 *Broadcasting Blues* ....250.00 - 400.00
 7171 *Deal Rag* ....250.00 - 400.00
 7189 *It Ain't No Good* ....250.00 - 400.00
Supertone 9681 *Yo-Yo Blues* ....200.00 - 300.00
 9682 *Thirty-Eight And Plus* ....200.00 - 300.00

"BIG ROAD" WEBSTER TAYLOR:
Vocalion 1271 *Sunny Southern Blues* ....80.00 - 120.00

YACK TAYLOR:
Decca 7836 *My Mellow Man* ....8.00 -   12.00
 7850 *You're Gonna Go Your Way* ....8.00 -   12.00
 7855 *Chicago Bound Blues* ....8.00 -   12.00
 7864 *My Nightmare Jockey* ....8.00 -   12.00

T. C. I. SECTION CREW:
Paramount 12478 *Section Gang Song* ....50.00 -   80.00

TEARDROPS:
Sampson 634 *Come Back To Me* ....40.00 -   70.00

JOHNNIE/JOHNNY TEMPLE:
Bluebird 8913 *Sundown Blues* ....20.00 -   30.00
 8968 *Big Woman Blues* ....10.00 -   15.00
Decca 7244 *Louise Louise Blues* ....20.00 -   30.00
 7316 *Peepin' Through The Keyhole* ....15.00 -   20.00
 7337 *So Lonely And Blue* ....15.00 -   20.00
 7385 *Hoodoo Women* ....10.00 -   15.00
 7416 *Snapping Cat* ....10.00 -   15.00
 7444 *Mean Baby Blues* ....10.00 -   15.00
 7456 *County Jail Blues* ....10.00 -   15.00
 7495 *Fare You Well* ....10.00 -   15.00
 7532 *Stavin' Chain* ....10.00 -   15.00
 7547 *Big Leg Woman* ....10.00 -   15.00
 7564 *Mississippi Woman's Blues* ....10.00 -   15.00
 7573 *What A Fool I've Been* ....10.00 -   15.00
 7583 *Grinding Mill* ....10.00 -   15.00
 7599 *If I Could Holler* ....10.00 -   15.00
 7632 *The Sun Goes Down In Blood* ....10.00 -   15.00
 7643 *Down In Mississippi* ....10.00 -   15.00
 7660 *Streamline Blues* ....10.00 -   15.00
 7678 *Cherry Ball* ....10.00 -   15.00
 7735 *Good Woman Blues* ....10.00 -   15.00
 7750 *Skin And Bones Woman* ....10.00 -   15.00
 7772 *Lovin' Woman Blues* ....10.00 -   15.00
 7782 *Roomin' House Blues* ....10.00 -   15.00

7800 *Fix It Up And Go*	10.00	-	15.00
7817 *Bow Leg Woman*	10.00	-	15.00
7825 *Corrine Corrina*	10.00	-	15.00
King 4151 *I Believe I'll Go Downtown*	8.00	-	12.00
Miracle 156 *Sit Right On It*	10.00	-	15.00
Vocalion 02987 *Jacksonville Blues*	50.00	-	80.00
03068 *Big Boat Whistle*	50.00	-	80.00

TENNESSEE SHAKERS:
Brunswick 7199 *Grind So Fine* ....150.00 - 250.00

NAT TERRY:
Imperial 5150 *Take It Easy* ....20.00 - 30.00

SONNY ("HOOTIN") TERRY (& HIS BUCKSHOT FIVE/ NIGHT OWLS):

Capitol 931, 15237, 40003, 40043, 40061, 40097, 40121	7.00	-	10.00
Columbia (red label)	7.00	-	10.00
Conqueror 9382 *Harmonica Blues*	10.00	-	15.00
Gotham 517 *Four O'Clock Blues*	10.00	-	15.00
518 *Lonesome Room*	10.00	-	15.00
Gramercy 1004/1005 *Hootin' Blues*	10.00	-	15.00
Harlem 2327 *Dangerous Woman*	10.00	-	15.00 *
Jackson 2302 *Harmonica Train*	10.00	-	15.00
Jax 305 *I Don't Worry*	10.00	-	15.00 *
Okeh 05453 *Harmonica Blues*	15.00	-	20.00
05538 *Harmonica Stomp*	15.00	-	20.00
05684 *Blowing The Blues*	15.00	-	20.00
Red Robin 110 *Harmonica Hop*	15.00	-	20.00 *

TEXAS RED & JIMMY:
Viceroy 3333 *Black Snake Blues* ....20.00 - 30.00 *

TEXAS SLIM:

King 4283 *Black Man Blues*	10.00	-	15.00
4315 *The Numbers*	10.00	-	15.00
4323 *Nightmare Blues*	10.00	-	15.00
4329 *Heart Trouble Blues*	10.00	-	15.00
4334 *Wandering Blues*	10.00	-	15.00
4366 *Don't You Remember Me*	10.00	-	15.00
4377 *Moaning Blues*	10.00	-	15.00

TEXAS TOMMY:
Brunswick 7044 *Jail Break Blues* ....50.00 - 80.00
Varsity 6035 *Ridin' Papa* ....15.00 - 20.00
6039 *Broke And Hungry* ....15.00 - 20.00

(SISTER) ROSETTA THARPE:

Decca 2243 *The Lonesome Road*	15.00	-	20.00
2328 *God Don't Like It*	10.00	-	15.00
2503 *That's All*	15.00	-	20.00
2558 *This Train*	10.00	-	15.00
3254 *Beams Of Heaven*	10.00	-	15.00
8538 *End Of My Journey*	10.00	-	15.00
8548 *Stand By Me*	10.00	-	15.00
8594 *Just a Closer Walk With Thee*	10.00	-	15.00
8610 *Nobody's Fault But Mine*	10.00	-	15.00
8634 *Pure Religion*	10.00	-	15.00
8639 *All Over This World*	10.00	-	15.00
8657 *I Want To Live So God Can Use Me*	10.00	-	15.00
Decca (most other issues)	7.00	-	10.00

SAM THEARD ("LOVIN" SAM FROM DOWN IN 'BAM) (See also LOVIN' SAM):
Decca 7025 *That Rhythm Gal* ....30.00 - 50.00
7146 *Till I Die* ....50.00 - 80.00

3rd WARD SIR-CATS:
Humming Bird 5001 *Rocket 88* ....20.00 - 30.00

AL "FATS" THOMAS:
Checker 759 *Dog Days* ....10.00 - 15.00

ANDREW THOMAS:
Swing With The Stars 1038 *Chicago Blues*......40.00 - 60.00

ANDY THOMAS:
Gold Star 645 *My Baby Quit Me Blues* ....40.00 - 60.00
659 *Walking And Crying* ....40.00 - 60.00

BESSIE THOMAS:
Supertone 9282 *Harbor Blues* ....100.00 - 150.00

BUD THOMAS:
Supertone 9511 *Street Walkin' Blues* ....100.00 - 150.00

EARL THOMAS:
Decca 7195 *Sugar Girl Blues* ....20.00 - 30.00
7221 *Rent Day Blues* ....20.00 - 30.00

ELVIE THOMAS:
Paramount 12977 *Motherless Child Blues*.......300.00 - 600.00

F. T. THOMAS:
Gennett 6963 *Street Walkin' Blues* ....150.00 - 200.00

GEORGE THOMAS:
Paramount 12826 *Fast Stuff Blues* ....150.00 - 250.00

HENRY THOMAS:

Bluebird 5343 *My Sweet Candy*	100.00	-	150.00
5411 *Sick With The Blues*	100.00	-	150.00
Sunrise 3424 *She's Got What I Want*	100.00	-	200.00
Vocalion 1094 *John Henry*	100.00	-	150.00
1137 *Red River Blues*	100.00	-	150.00
1138 *The Little Red Caboose*	100.00	-	150.00
1139 *Woodhouse Blues*	100.00	-	150.00
1140 *Jonah In The Wilderness*	100.00	-	150.00
1141 *Run, Mollie, Run*	100.00	-	150.00
1197 *Texas Easy Street Blues*	100.00	-	150.00
1230 *Bull Doze Blues*	100.00	-	150.00
1249 *Texas Worried Blues*	100.00	-	150.00
1286 *Arkansas*	100.00	-	150.00
1443 *Don't Leave Me Here*	150.00	-	200.00
1468 *Lovin' Babe*	150.00	-	200.00

JESSE THOMAS; JESSE (BABYFACE) THOMAS:

Club (unnumbered) *You Are My Dreams*	30.00	-	50.00
Club (unnumbered) *I Wonder Why*	30.00	-	50.00
Freedom 1513 *Guess I'll Walk Alone*	15.00	-	20.00
Hollywood 1072 *Cool Kind Lover*	7.00	-	10.00 *
Miltone 232 *Same Old Stuff*	20.00	-	30.00
233 *Mountain Key Blues*	20.00	-	30.00
Modern 710 *Texas Blues*	10.00	-	15.00
Specialty 419 *When You Say I Love You*	7.00	-	10.00
Swing Time 240 *I Can't Stay Here*	15.00	-	20.00
241 *Now's The Time*	15.00	-	20.00
Victor 23381 *Down In Texas Blues*	250.00	-	400.00
V-38555 *Blue Goose Blues*	200.00	-	300.00

JOSEPHINE THOMAS:
Pathe-Actuelle 032122 *Memphis Bound*.........25.00 - 40.00
Perfect 12201 *Memphis Bound* ....25.00 - 40.00

L. J. THOMAS:
Chess 1493 *Sam's Drag* ....10.00 - 15.00

LILLETTE THOMAS & HER BOYS:
Sterling 100 *Lillette's Boogie* ....10.00 - 15.00

RAMBLIN'/RAMBLING THOMAS:
Paramount 12609 *Back Gnawing Blues* ....100.00 - 150.00
  12616 *Sawmill Moan* ....100.00 - 150.00
  12637 *Lock And Key Blues* ....100.00 - 150.00
  12670 *No Baby Blues* ....100.00 - 150.00
  12708 *Ramblin' Man* ....100.00 - 150.00
  12752 *Good Time Blues* ....100.00 - 150.00
Victor 23332 *Ground Hog Blues* ....250.00 - up
  23365 *Ground Hog Blues No. 2* ....250.00 - up

ROLLIE THOMAS:
Conqueror 7264 *Early Mornin' Blues* ....300.00 - 600.00

RUFUS THOMAS:
Chess 1466 *Night Walkin' Blues* ....20.00 - 30.00
  1492 *No More Doggin' Around* ....20.00 - 30.00
  1517 *Juanita* ....15.00 - 25.00 *
Sun 181 *Walkin' In The Rain* ....30.00 - 50.00 *
  188 *Tiger Man* ....30.00 - 50.00 *
Talent 807 *I'm So Worried* ....50.00 - 80.00

SIPPIE THOMAS:
Victor V-38502 *I'm A Mighty Tight Woman* ....300.00 - up

WASHINGTON THOMAS:
Champion 15489 *Time Enough* ....75.00 - 100.00
  15511 *Silvery Moon* ....75.00 - 100.00

JIM THOMPKINS:
Brunswick 7200 *Bedside Blues* ....150.00 - 200.00

EDWARD THOMPSON:
Paramount 13018 *West Virginia Blues* ....200.00 - 300.00

EVELYN THOMPSON:
Vocalion 1075 *Someday, Sweetheart* ....40.00 - 60.00
  1083 *After You've Gone* ....40.00 - 60.00
  1084 *One More Kiss* ....40.00 - 60.00
  15529 *One More Kiss* ....35.00 - 50.00
  15548 *One Sweet Letter From You* ....35.00 - 50.00

MARGARET THORNTON:
Black Patti 8041 *Jockey Blues* ....400.00 - up

WILLIE MAE (BIG MAMA) THORNTON:
Peacock 1612 *Hound Dog* ....20.00 - 30.00 *
Peacock (most other issues) ....7.00 - 12.00 *
(See the fourth section of this book for other Willie Mae Thornton
  recordings in 45 RPM format)

THREE BITS OF RHYTHM:
Modern 118 *That's The Boogie* ....10.00 - 15.00

THE THRILLERS:
Big Town 109 *The Drunkard* ....10.00 - 15.00 *

BUD THURSTON:
Champion 15489 *My Senorita* ....75.00 - 100.00

ANDREW/ANDY TIBBS (& THE DOZIER BOYS):
Aristocrat 1103 *Married Man Blues* ....15.00 - 20.00
  1104 *Going Down Fast* ....15.00 - 20.00
  1105 *In A Traveling Mood* ....30.00 - 50.00
  1107 *How Long* ....15.00 - 20.00

SLIM TINSLEY:
Globe 117 *606 Blues* ....10.00 - 15.00
  118 *Big Shot Mama* ....10.00 - 15.00

JAMES TISDOM:
Universal-Fox 100 *Last Affair Blues* ....30.00 - 50.00
  101 *Throw This Dog A Bone* ....30.00 - 50.00
  102 *Overhaul Blues* ....30.00 - 50.00

KINGFISH BILL TOMLIN:
Paramount 13034 *Hot Box* ....150.00 - 200.00
  13057 *Dupree Blues* ....150.00 - 200.00

TOMMY AND JIMMY:
Superior 2555 *Where You Been So Long?* ....500.00 - up

THE TOO BAD BOYS:
Paramount 12861 *Ballin' The Jack* ....80.00 - 120.00

TOO TIGHT HENRY:
Brunswick 7189 *Squinch Owl Moan* ....200.00 - 300.00
Columbia 14374-D *Charleston Contest* ....100.00 - 150.00

GEORGE TOREY:
Titles issued contemporaneously on Banner, Melotone, Oriole,
  Perfect, and Romeo: *Lonesome Man Blues; Married Woman
  Blues* ....75.00 - 100.00

JIM TOWEL:
Brunswick 7060 *Buckwheat Cakes* ....75.00 - 100.00

HENRY TOWNSEND:
Bluebird 5966 *She's Got A Mean Disposition* ....100.00 - 150.00
  6589 *She's Got A Mean Disposition* ....75.00 - 100.00
  7453 *Lose Your Man* ....30.00 - 50.00
  7474 *A Ramblin' Mind* ....30.00 - 50.00
Columbia 14491-D *Mistreated Blues* ....150.00 - 300.00
  14529-D *Henry's Worry Blues* ....150.00 - 300.00
Paramount 13097 *Doctor, Oh Doctor* ....500.00 - up

JESSE TOWNSEND:
Victor 23322 *No Home Blues* ....400.00 - up

SAM TOWNSEND:
Brunswick 7116 *Curbstone Blues* ....250.00 - 400.00
Columbia 14571-D *I'm Missing That* ....100.00 - 150.00

TRIANGLE QUARTETTE:
Broadway 5071 *She Done Quit Me Blues* ....75.00 - 100.00
Paramount 12781 *She Done Quit Me Blues* ....80.00 - 120.00

RICH TRICE:
Decca 7701 *Come On Baby* ....15.00 - 25.00

WELLY TRICE:
Decca 7358 *Come On In Here Mama* ....15.00 - 25.00

DOROTHA TROWBRIDGE:
Bluebird 5431 *Bad Luck Blues* ....100.00 - 150.00

TUB JUG WASHBOARD BAND:
Paramount 12671 *Tub-Jug Rag* ....250.00 - up

BESSIE TUCKER:
Bluebird 5128 *Bogey Man Blues* ....80.00 - 130.00
Sunrise 3208 *Bogey Man Blues* ....100.00 - 150.00
Victor 21692 *Black Name Moan* ....80.00 - 120.00
  21708 *The Dummy* ....80.00 - 120.00
  23385 *Bogey Man Blues* ....300.00 - up
  23392 *T. B. Moan* ....300.00 - up
  V38018 *Fryin' Pan Skillet Blues* ....150.00 - 250.00
  V38526 *Bessie's Moan* ....200.00 - 300.00
  V38538 *Old Black Mary* ....200.00 - 300.00
  V38542 *Katy Blues* ....200.00 - 300.00

ANNIE TURNER:
Bluebird 6707 *Black Pony Blues* ....50.00 - 75.00
 6788 *Workhouse Blues* ....50.00 - 75.00
 7156 *Hard On You* ....30.00 - 50.00

BABY FACE TURNER:
Modern 882 *Gonna Let You Go*......................30.00 - 50.00 *

BEE TURNER:
Paramount 13017 *Rough Treatin' Daddy*.............250.00 - up

CHARLIE TURNER AND WINSTON HOLMES:
Paramount 12793 *The Death Of Holmes Mule*......150.00 - 200.00
 12815 *Kansas City Dog Walk* ....150.00 - 200.00

IKE TURNER:
Chess 1459 *I'm Lonesome Baby*..............................15.00 - 20.00

(BIG) JOE TURNER (& THE ALL STARS/PETE JOHNSON):
Atlantic 939 *Chains Of Love* ....15.00 - 25.00
 949 *The Chill Is On* ....15.00 - 25.00
 960 *Sweet Sixteen* ....10.00 - 20.00 *
 970 *Don't You Cry* ....10.00 - 15.00 *
 982 *Still In Love* ....10.00 - 15.00 *
Bayou 015 *Blues Jump The Rabbit*......................15.00 - 20.00
Coral 65004 *Blues On Central Avenue*.................15.00 - 20.00
Decca 4093 *Rocks In My Bed* ....15.00 - 20.00
 7824 *Doggin' The Dog* ....15.00 - 20.00
 7827 *Jumpin' Down Blues*............................15.00 - 20.00
 7856 *Somebody's Got To Go* ....10.00 - 15.00
 7868 *Nobody In Mind* ....10.00 - 15.00
 7885 *Blues In The Night* ....10.00 - 15.00
 7889 *Sun Risin' Blues*................................10.00 - 15.00
Excelsior (most issues) ....7.00 - 12.00
Freedom 1531 *Still In The Dark* ....15.00 - 20.00
MGM 10274 *Mardi Gras Boogie* ....10.00 - 15.00
 10321 *Messin' Around* ....10.00 - 15.00
 10397 *Rainy Weather Blues* ....10.00 - 15.00
 10719 *Moody Baby* ....10.00 - 15.00
National 9010 *S. K. Blues* ....10.00 - 15.00
 9011 *Watch That Jive* ....10.00 - 15.00
 9099 *It's A Low Down Dirty Shame* ....10.00 - 15.00
 9100 *Ooh Wee Baby Blues* ....10.00 - 15.00
 9106 *Still In The Dark* ....10.00 - 15.00
RPM 331 *Roll 'Em Boys* ....15.00 - 25.00 *
 345 *Playful Baby* ....15.00 - 20.00 *
Vocalion 4607 *Goin' Away Blues*......................15.00 - 20.00
(Note: See also the **RHYTHM & BLUES, ETC.** section for other records by Joe Turner.)

LAVINIA TURNER:
Pathe-Actuelle 020544 *How Many Times?* ....15.00 - 25.00
 020572 *Sweet Man O'Mine* ....15.00 - 25.00
 020627 *If I Were Your Daddy* ....20.00 - 30.00
 020705 *You Never Miss A Good Thing Until It's Gone*
 ....30.00 - 50.00
 020878 *When The Rain Turns Into Snow* ....20.00 - 30.00
Perfect 12005 *Watch Me Go*..........................30.00 - 50.00
 12032 *Can't Get Lovin' Blues* ....15.00 - 25.00
 12033 *A-Wearin' Away The Blues* ....15.00 - 25.00
 12034 *He Took It Away From Me* ....20.00 - 30.00
 12039 *Who'll Drive Your Blues Away* ....20.00 - 30.00

PETE TURNER:
Haven 3001 *Little Man Blues* ....10.00 - 15.00

SMILEY TURNER:
Mercury 8153 *My Soul* ....8.00 - 12.00
 8161 *Lonely Boy Blues*................................8.00 - 12.00

BLIND SQUIRE TURNER:
Bluebird 5307 *She Thinks She's Slick*..................100.00 - 150.00
 5412 *Low Mellow*.....................................100.00 - 150.00
 5491 *Pitty Pat Blues*.................................100.00 - 150.00
Sunrise 3388 *She Thinks She's Slick*...................100.00 - 200.00

JOHN D. TWITTY:
Titles issued contemporaneously on Banner, Melotone, Oriole, Perfect, Romeo, and Vocalion: *A Gang Of Trouble; Walking Blues*..30.00 - 50.00

TWO BOYS FROM SAVANNAH:
Supertone 9485 *It's Just All Right* ....75.00 - 100.00
 9529 *Messed Up Blues*.................................100.00 - 150.00

THE TWO CHARLIES:
Titles issued contemporaneously on Banner, Melotone, Oriole, Perfect, and Romeo: *Don't Put Your Dirty Hands On Me; Got Your Water On; I Couldn't Stay Here; Pork Chops Blues*
 ....75.00 - 125.00

THE TWO OF SPADES:
Columbia 14072-D *Meddlin' With The Blues* ....50.00 - 75.00

TWO POOR BOYS:
Titles issued contemporaneously on Banner, Oriole, Perfect, and Romeo: *John Henry Blues; Sitting On Top Of The World; Take A Look At That Baby; Two White Horses In A Line*
 ....75.00 - 125.00

TYUS & TYUS:
Columbia 14638-D *Dad's Ole Mule*....................100.00 - 150.00

CHARLES (& EFFIE) TYUS:
Okeh 8133 *Omaha Blues* ....30.00 - 50.00
 8149 *I Want To Go Back To The Farm*.............30.00 - 50.00
 8200 *Cuddle Up Closer, It's Winter Time* ....40.00 - 60.00
 8330 *Good Old Bygone Days* ....40.00 - 60.00
 8459 *Alibi-ing Papa*..................................75.00 - 100.00

UMBRIAN GLEE CLUB:
Vocalion 1012 *Swing Along*............................20.00 - 30.00
 1013 *Rain Song* ....20.00 - 30.00

UNCLE SKIPPER:
Decca 7353 *Cutting My ABC's* ....30.00 - 50.00
 7455 *Look What Shape I'm In* ....30.00 - 50.00

LOUISE VANT:
Okeh 8264 *Show Me The Way To Go Home* ....75.00 - 100.00
 8275 *I'm Tired Of Everything But You* ....75.00 - 100.00
 8281 *Just A Little Bit Bad* ....80.00 - 120.00
 8293 *Do Right Blues* ....80.00 - 120.00
 8310 *Pensacola Blues* ....80.00 - 120.00
 8341 *Daddy, Don't You Try To Pull That Two Time Thing On Me*
 ....50.00 - 80.00

VARIETEERS:
MGM 10888 *I'll Try To Forget* ....20.00 - 30.00 *

VARIETY FOUR:
Brunswick 7025 *Miss Annabelle Lee* ....25.00 - 50.00

CALLIE VASSAR:
Gennett 5172 *All Night Blues* ....50.00 - 75.00
 5173 *Original Stomps* ....50.00 - 75.00

EDITH VAUGHAN:
Oriole 298 *Mad Mama's Blues* ....20.00 - 30.00
   311 *Broken Busted Can't Be Trusted Blues* ....20.00 - 30.00

THE VELVETONES:
Columbia 30224 *I'm Disillusioned* .... - - -

JOHN P. VIGAL:
Black Swan 14115 *Fowler Twist* ....40.00 - 60.00
Paramount 12132 *Fowler Twist* ....35.00 - 50.00

WALTER VINCENT:
Brunswick 7126 *Your Friends Gonna Use It Too* .150.00 - 200.00
   7141 *Overtime Blues*...............................150.00 - 250.00
   7190 *Mississippi Yodelin' Blues* ....150.00 - 250.00
Decca 7169 *Losin' Blues* ....50.00 - 75.00
   7178 *The Wrong Man* ....50.00 - 75.00

WALTER VINCSON:
Bluebird 8828 *Every Dog Must Have His Day* ....20.00 - 30.00
   8908 *Gulf Coast Boy*..............................20.00 - 30.00
   8963 *Rosa Lee Blues* ....20.00 - 30.00

OTTO VIRGIAL:
Bluebird 6213 *Bad Notion Blues* ....15.00 - 25.00
   6279 *Seven Year Itch* ....15.00 - 25.00

THE VIRGINIA FOUR:
Decca 7662 *Dig My Jelly Roll* ....15.00 - 20.00
   7808 *Queen Street Rag* ....15.00 - 20.00

THE VOCALEERS:
Red Robin 130 *Shim Sham Shimmy*............................ - - -
(Note: The existence of this record has not been verified. It is known
   that labels for such issue were printed. Offers of hundreds of
   dollars have been made. Note that the title was issued on Red
   Robin 130 by Champion Jack Dupree, and a simple printing error
   may be all that's involved.)

JOSEPH VON BATTLE:
JVB 75828 *Looking For My Woman*.......................80.00 - 130.00

UNCLE BUD WALKER:
Okeh 8828 *Stand Up Suitcase Blues* ....75.00 - 100.00

JAMES WALKER:
Silvertone 3553 *Lost John Blues* ....75.00 - 100.00

MONROE WALKER:
Columbia 14549-D *High Powered Mama* ....80.00 - 120.00

PRETTY BOY WALKER:
Vocalion 1713 *The Break I'm Gettin'* ....75.00 - 100.00

T-BONE WALKER:
Black & White 110, 111, 115, 121, 122, 123, 125,
   126, 127 ....7.00 - 12.00
Capitol 10033 *Mean Old World* ....10.00 - 15.00
Capitol (most other issues) ....5.00 - 10.00
Comet 50, 51, 52, 53..7.00 - 12.00
Imperial 5071 *Strollin' With Bones* ....10.00 - 15.00
   5081 *The Hustle Is On* ....10.00 - 15.00
   5086 *You Don't Love Me* ....10.00 - 15.00
   5094 *Evil Hearted Woman* ....10.00 - 15.00
   5103 *Too Lazy* ....10.00 - 15.00
   5116 *No Reason* ....10.00 - 15.00
Imperial (most other issues)...........................7.00 - 12.00 *
Mercury 8016 *My Baby Left Me* ....7.00 - 10.00
Old Swing-Master 11 *She Is Going To Ruin Me* .....20.00 - 30.00
Rhumbboogie 4000 *Sail On Boogie* ....10.00 - 15.00
   4002 *T-Bone Boogie* ....10.00 - 15.00

4003 *Mean Old World Blues* ....10.00 - 15.00
(Note: See also the **RHYTHM & BLUES, ETC.** section for other
   records by T-bone Walker.)

WILLIAM WALKER:
Gennet 7100 *I'll Remember You* ....35.00 - 50.00

WILLIE WALKER:
Columbia 14578-D *South Carolina Rag*................80.00 - 120.00

FRANCES WALLACE:
Brunswick 7076 *Low Down Man Blues*.................75.00 - 100.00

INEZ WALLACE:
Black Swan 14137 *Radio Blues* ....20.00 - 30.00
   14144 *Come Back Dear* ....30.00 - 50.00
   14147 *Kissin' Daddy* ....30.00 - 50.00
Paramount 12145 *Radio Blues* ....25.00 - 40.00
   12146 *Kissin' Daddy*.............................. - - -
   12155 *Come Back Dear* ....25.00 - 40.00

MINNIE WALLACE:
Bluebird 5144 *Dirty Butter* ....100.00 - 150.00
Sunrise 3225 *Dirty Butter* ....100.00 - 200.00
Victor V38547 *Dirty Butter*..........................400.00 - up
Vocalion 03106 *Field Mouse Stomp*....................150.00 - 200.00
   03154 *Let's All Do That Thing* ....150.00 - 200.00

SIPPIE WALLACE:
Mercury 2010 *Bedroom Blues* .... - - -
Okeh 8106 *Up The Country Blues* ....50.00 - 75.00
   8144 *Underworld Blues* ....40.00 - 60.00
   8159 *Stranger's Blues*.........................40.00 - 60.00
   8168 *Mama's Gone, Goodbye* ....40.00 - 60.00
   8177 *Sud Bustin' Blues* ....80.00 - 120.00
   8190 *Let My Man Alone Blues* ....75.00 - 100.00
   8197 *Off And On Blues* ....100.00 - 150.00
   8205 *Every Dog IIas His Day*........................150.00 - 200.00
   8206 *Devil Dance Blues*...........................150.00 - 200.00
   8212 *Trouble Everywhere I Roam* ....100.00 - 150.00
   8232 *Section Hand Blues* ....100.00 - 150.00
   8243 *Murder's Gonna Be My Crime* ....75.00 - 100.00
   8251 *The Man I Love* ....75.00 - 100.00
   8276 *Advice Blues*..............................75.00 - 100.00
   8288 *I'm Leaving You* ....50.00 - 75.00
   8301 *A Jealous Woman Like Me*....................150.00 - 200.00
   8328 *Jack O' Diamonds Blues* ....150.00 - 200.00
   8345 *The Mail Train Blues* ....150.00 - 200.00
Okeh 8381 *I Must Have It* ....75.00 - 100.00
   8439 *Bedroom Blues* ....100.00 - 150.00
   8470 *Lazy Man Blues*...........................150.00 - 200.00
   8499 *Dead Drunk Blues* ....150.00 - 200.00

WESLEY WALLACE:
Paramount 12958 *Fanny Lee Blues* ....150.00 - 200.00

PEGGY WALLER AND GEORGE RAMSEY:
Paramount 13037 *Blacksnake Wiggle*...................150.00 - 250.00

CHARLOTTE WALSH:
Silvertone 3567 *Cool Daddy Blues*........................50.00 - 75.00

WALTER & BYRD:
Paramount 12945 *Wasn't It Sad About Lemon* .....200.00 - 300.00

LORRAINE WALTON:
Bluebird 7577 *Whiskey Blues* ....15.00 - 20.00
   7630 *Freight Train Blues*.........................15.00 - 20.00
Vocalion 03989 *If You're A Viper* ....15.00 - 20.00

SQUARE WALTON:
RCA Victor 20-5493 *Pepper Head Woman* ....10.00 - 15.00 *
    20-5584 *Bad Hangover* ....10.00 - 15.00 *

AMY WARD:
Silvertone 3566 *Uptown Daddy*..............................60.00 - 100.00
    3568 *Riverside Blues* ....60.00 - 100.00
    3573 *Nobody Knows* ....60.00 - 100.00

ROOSEVELT WARDELL:
Rockin' 508 *Lost My Woman* ....15.00 - 25.00

EDDIE WARE & HIS BAND:
Chess 1461 *Wandering Lover* ....15.00 - 20.00
    1507 *Jealous Woman* ....10.00 - 15.00 *
States 130 *That's The Stuff I Like* ....15.00 - 20.00 *

REV. I. B. WARE:
Vocalion 1235 *You Better Quit Drinking Shine* ....100.00 - 150.00

OZIE WARE:
Titles issued contemporaneously on Cameo, Lincoln, Pathe-
    Actuelle, Perfect, and Romeo: *He Just Don't Appeal To Me; Hit*
    Me In The Nose Blues ....50.00 - 75.00
Victor 21777 *I Done Caught You Blues* ....150.00 - 300.00

PETER WARFIELD:
Miltone 5249 *Morning Train Blues* ....30.00 - 50.00

BABY BOY WARREN (& HIS BUDDY):
Blue Lake 106 *Mattie Mae* ....30.00 - 50.00 *
Drummond 3002 *Baby Boy Blues*...........................75.00 - 100.00
    3003 *Stop Breakin' Down*..............................75.00 - 100.00 *
Federal 12008 *Forgive Me Darling* ....20.00 - 30.00
Gotham 507 *My Special Friend Blues*.....................30.00 - 50.00
JVB 26 *Hello Stranger* ....80.00 - 130.00
Staff 706 *My Special Friend Blues* ....80.00 - 120.00
    707 *Lonesome Cabin Blues* ....80.00 - 120.00
    709 *Forgive Me Darling*................................80.00 - 120.00

WASHBOARD PETE:
Savoy 5556 *Christmas Blues* ....30.00 - 50.00

WASHBOARD SAM (& HIS WASHBOARD BAND); WASHBOARD SAM'S BAND:
Bluebird 5983 *Ocean Blues* ....75.00 - 100.00
    6355 *You Done Tore Your Playhouse Down*......15.00 - 25.00
    6518 *Give Me Lovin'* ....15.00 - 25.00
    6556 *Cherry Hill Blues* ....15.00 - 25.00
    6765 *Razor Cuttin' Man* ....15.00 - 25.00
    6794 *Out With The Wrong Woman*..................15.00 - 25.00
    6870 *Big Woman*..15.00 - 25.00
    6970 *Easy Ridin' Mama* ....15.00 - 20.00
    7001 *We Gonna Move* ....15.00 - 20.00
    7048 *I Drink Good Whiskey* ....15.00 - 20.00
    7096 *Lowland Blues* ....15.00 - 20.00
    7148 *Out With The Wrong Woman*..................15.00 - 20.00
    7179 *I Love All My Women* ....15.00 - 20.00
    7194 *You Done Tore Your Playhouse Down*......15.00 - 20.00
    7291 *Washboard's Barrel House Song* ....8.00 - 12.00
    7328 *Beer Garden Blues*...................................8.00 - 12.00
    7365 *Gonna Be Some Walkin' Done* ....8.00 - 12.00
    7403 *Second Story Man* ....10.00 - 15.00
    7440 *Want To Woogie Some More* ....25.00 - 40.00
    7501 *Don't Leave Me Here* ....15.00 - 20.00
    7526 *Down At The Old Village Store* ....20.00 - 30.00
    7552 *My Woman's A Sender* ....15.00 - 20.00
    7601 *Phantom Black Snake* ....15.00 - 20.00

    7655 *The Gal I Love* ....20.00 - 30.00
    7664 *Yellow, Black And Brown* ....15.00 - 20.00
    7732 *Serve It Right*..15.00 - 20.00
    7780 *Sophisticated Mama*................................15.00 - 20.00
    7834 *Policy Writer's Blues* ....15.00 - 20.00
    7866 *Jumpin' Rooster* ....15.00 - 20.00
    7906 *Bucket's Got A Hole In It* ....15.00 - 20.00
    7977 *Walkin' In My Sleep* ....15.00 - 20.00
    7993 *Warehouse Blues*.....................................15.00 - 20.00
    8018 *Gonna Kill My Baby* ....15.00 - 20.00
    8044 *Rack 'Em Back* ....15.00 - 20.00
    8076 *Suspicious Blues*.....................................15.00 - 20.00
    8184 *That Will Get It* ....15.00 - 20.00
    8211 *Diggin' My Potatoes* ....10.00 - 20.00
    8243 *Good Old Easy Street*.............................15.00 - 20.00
    8270 *This Time Is My Time* ....15.00 - 20.00
    8323 *Has My Gal Been By Here?* ....15.00 - 20.00
    8342 *Jersey Cow Blues* ....15.00 - 20.00
    8358 *So Early In The Morning* ....15.00 - 20.00
    8377 *Beauty Spot* ....15.00 - 20.00
    8424 *Going Back To Arkansas* ....10.00 - 15.00
    8450 *How Can I Play Fair?* ....10.00 - 15.00
    8469 *Louise* ....10.00 - 15.00
    8500 *Beale Street Sheik* ....10.00 - 15.00
    8525 *Chiselin' Blues* ....10.00 - 15.00
    8540 *Greyhound Bus* ....10.00 - 15.00
    8554 *Diggin' My Potatoes No. 2* ....10.00 - 15.00
    8569 *Good Luck Blues* ....10.00 - 15.00
    8599 *Just Got To Hold You* ....10.00 - 15.00
    8644 *Good Time Tonight* ....10.00 - 15.00
    8675 *She's a Bad Luck Woman* ....10.00 - 15.00
    8699 *Come On Back* ....10.00 - 15.00
Bluebird 8727, 8761, 8792, 8815, 8844, 8878, 8909,
    8937, 8967, 8997, 9007, 9018, 9039, 34-0705,
    34-0710 .... 7.00 - 12.00
Chess 1545 *Diggin' My Potatoes* ....20.00 - 30.00 *
Montgomery Ward 7050 *Don't 'Low* ....10.00 - 15.00
    7062 *Razor Cuttin' Man* ....10.00 - 15.00
    7497 *Towboat Blues*..10.00 - 15.00
    7498 *Barbecue* ....10.00 - 15.00
    7499 *Want To Woogie Some More* ....10.00 - 15.00
    7500 *Down At The Old Village Store* ....15.00 - 20.00
    7588, 7790, 7759, 7760, 7761, 8801, 8804......... 7.00 - 12.00
RCA Victor .... 7.00 - 10.00
Vocalion 02937 *Don't Tear My Clothes*.................15.00 - 20.00
    03365 *Mixed Up Blues*..................................15.00 - 20.00
Titles issued contemporaneously on Banner, Conqueror, Melotone,
    Oriole, Perfect, and Romeo: *Don't Tear My Clothes; I'm A*
    Prowlin' Groundhog......................................15.00 - 20.00

WASHBOARD WALTER (& HIS BAND):
Paramount 12954 *Narrow Face Blues* .... 250.00 - up
    12991 *Disconnected Mama*............................ 250.00 - up
    13100 *Wuffin' Blues*...................................... 250.00 - up

WASHBOARD WILLIE & HIS SUPER SUDS OF RHYTHM:
JVB 59 *Cherry Red Blues* .... 50.00 - 80.00
    70 *Washboard Blues* .... 50.00 - 80.00

ALBERTA WASHBURN (AND PAPA HALL):
Superior 2668 *Skeeter Blues* .... 200.00 - 300.00
    2739 *Pig Meat Mama*.................................... 200.00 - 300.00
    2783 *Forty-Four Blues* .... 200.00 - 300.00
    2826 *Hoboken Prison Blues*........................... 200.00 - 300.00

BOOKER T. WASHINGTON:
Bluebird 8352 *Just Want To Think* ....20.00 - 30.00
    8378 *Cotton Club Blues*...............................20.00 - 30.00
    8413 *Cozy Corner Blues*.............................20.00 - 30.00
    8449 *Wrapped Up In Bad Luck* ....20.00 - 30.00

D. C. WASHINGTON:
Gold Star 661 *Happy Home Blues* ....40.00 - 60.00

ELIZABETH WASHINGTON:
Bluebird 5229 *Riot Call Blues* ....150.00 - 200.00
Sunrise 3312 *You Put That Thing On Me* ....150.00 - 250.00
Victor 23425 *Mistreated Blues* ....500.00 - up

ISABELLE WASHINGTON:
Black Swan 14141 *That's Why I'm Loving You* ......40.00 - 60.00
Paramount 12135 *I Want To* ....35.00 - 50.00

LIZZIE WASHINGTON:
Black Patti 8054 *Mexico Blues* ....500.00 - up
Champion 15282 *Skeleton Key Blues* ....100.00 - 150.00
    15303 *East Coast Blues* ....100.00 - 150.00
    15319 *Sport Model Mamma Blues* ....125.00 - 175.00
Gennett 6126 *Working Man Blues*..........................150.00 - 200.00
    6134 *Skeleton Key Blues* ....150.00 - 200.00
    6195 *Fall Or Summer Blues* ....150.00 - 200.00
    6321 *Brick Flat Blues* ....150.00 - 200.00
    6408 *Lord Have Mercy Blues* ....150.00 - 200.00
Herwin 92013 *East Coast Blues* ....150.00 - 200.00
    92021 *My Low Down Brown* ....150.00 - 200.00
    92039 *Lord Have Mercy Blues* ....150.00 - 250.00
    92040 *Mexico Blues* ....150.00 - 250.00
    92041 *Brick Flat Blues* ....150.00 - 200.00
    92042 *Ease Away Blues*...............................200.00 - 300.00
Vocalion 1459 *Whiskey Head Blues*.......................100.00 - 150.00

LOUIS WASHINGTON:
Vocalion 02634 *Run, Sinner, Run* ....75.00 - 100.00
    02658 *Standin' On A Rock* ....75.00 - 100.00

WALTER (COWBOY) WASHINGTON:
Bluebird 6917 *Ice Pick Mama* ....20.00 - 30.00
    7314 *I Need You Blues*.............................20.00 - 30.00

CROWN PRINCE WATERFORD:
Aladdin 534 *The Prince Strikes Back* ....15.00 - 20.00
    535 *Washboard Blues* ....15.00 - 20.00
    3009 *Washboard Blues* ....15.00 - 20.00
Capitol 40074, 40103, 40132, 40137.....................7.00 - 10.00
Hy-Tone 20 *Girl Friend Blues* ....15.00 - 20.00
King 4310, 4374, 4393 ....7.00 - 10.00
Torch 6911 *Eatin' Watermelon* ....15.00 - 20.00

KITTY WATERS:
Pathe-Actuelle 7531 *Back Water Blues*...................30.00 - 50.00
    7537 *Loud And Wrong*...............................30.00 - 50.00
Perfect 131 *Back Water Blues*............................30.00 - 50.00
    137 *Loud And Wrong*.................................30.00 - 50.00

KATIE WATKINS:
Viceroy 3333 *Trying To Get You Off My Mind* ....20.00 - 30.00 *

VIOLA WATKINS:
Jubilee 5007 *Jelly And Bread* ....10.00 - 15.00
MGM 10232 *Now I Know* ....10.00 - 15.00
    10344 *Hey Mama* ....10.00 - 15.00

DEEK WATSON & THE BROWN DOTS:
Manor (most issues)...7.00 - 12.00

YOUNG JOHN WATSON:
Federal 12120 *Highway 60* ....10.00 - 15.00 *
    12131 *Motor Head Baby* ....10.00 - 15.00 *
    12143 *Walkin' To My Baby* ....10.00 - 15.00 *
    12157 *What's Going On* ....10.00 - 15.00 *
    12175 *Space Guitar* ....10.00 - 15.00 *

MOJO WATSON:
Atlas 1080 *All Alone* ....25.00 - 40.00

KENNY WATT'S HOT FIVE:
Savoy 645 *Shame On You* ....10.00 - 20.00

JAMES WAYNE/WAYNES:
Aladdin 3234 *Crying in Vain* ....8.00 - 12.00 *
Imperial 5151 *Home Town Blues* ....10.00 - 15.00
    5160 *Bad Weather Blues* ....10.00 - 15.00
    5166 *Vacant Pillow Blues* ....10.00 - 15.00
    5258 *Sweet Little Woman* ....8.00 - 12.00 *
Sittin' In With 573 *Gypsy Blues* ....10.00 - 15.00
    588 *Love Me Blues* ....10.00 - 15.00
    607 *Junco Partner* ....10.00 - 20.00
    622 *Please Baby Please* ....10.00 - 15.00
    639 *Money Blues* ....10.00 - 15.00

WEAVER AND BEASLEY:
Okeh 8530 *Bottleneck Blues* ....100.00 - 150.00

CURLEY WEAVER (& HIS GUITAR/& EDDIE MAPP/& CLARENCE MOORE/& RUTH WILLIS):
Titles issued contemporaneously on Banner, Melotone, Oriole, Perfect, and Romeo: *Birmingham Gambler; Black Woman; City Cell Blues; Early Morning Blues; Leg Iron Blues; No No Blues; Some Cold Rainy Day; Tippin' Tom* ....50.00 - 100.00
Champion 50065 *Two-Faced Woman* ....60.00 - 100.00
    50077 *Fried Pie Blues* ....60.00 - 100.00
Columbia 14386-D *No No Blues* ....100.00 - 150.00
Decca 7077 *Early Morning Blues*.........................60.00 - 100.00
    7664 *Oh Lawdy Mama* ....20.00 - 30.00
    7906 *Sometime Mama* ....20.00 - 30.00
Okeh 8928 *Baby Boogie Woogie* ....100.00 - 150.00
QRS 7077 *Dirty Deal Blues*...............................150.00 - 200.00
Sittin' In With 547 *My Baby's Gone* ....40.00 - 60.00
    646 *Some Rainy Day*...............................30.00 - 50.00

SYLVESTER WEAVER:
Okeh 8109 *Guitar Rag* ....80.00 - 120.00
    8152 *Smoketown Strut*.............................80.00 - 120.00
    8207 *Weaver's Blues*..............................80.00 - 120.00
    8460 *True Love Blues* ....60.00 - 100.00
    8480 *Guitar Rag* ....80.00 - 120.00
    8504 *Penitentiary Bound Blues* ....60.00 - 100.00
    8522 *What Makes A Man Blue?*......................60.00 - 100.00
    8534 *Black Spider Blues* ....60.00 - 100.00
    8549 *Rock Pile Blues* ....60.00 - 100.00
    8608 *Polecat Blues* ....60.00 - 100.00

BOOGIE BILL WEBB:
Imperial 5257 *Bad Dog*...................................20.00 - 30.00 *

TINY WEBB TRIO:
Globe 108 *G. I. Blues*...................................10.00 - 15.00

MARGARET WEBSTER:
Diva 6040-G *How Can I Get It*............................30.00 - 50.00
Velvet Tone 7066-V *How Can I Get It* ....30.00 - 50.00
    7076-V *Wipe 'Em Off* ....30.00 - 50.00

BARREL HOUSE WELCH:
Paramount 12759 *Dying Pickpocket Blues*............150.00 - 300.00

KANSAS CITY BILL WELDON:
Vocalion 03078 *Race Horse Filly Blues* ....75.00 - 100.00
  03198 *Doctor's Blues* ....75.00 - 100.00

WILL WELDON:
Victor 21134 *Turpentine Blues*.............................150.00 - 300.00

JUNIOR WELLS:
States 122 *Eagle Rock* ....50.00 - 80.00 *
  134 *Junior's Wail* ....40.00 - 60.00 *
  139 *'Bout The Break Of Day* ....25.00 - 40.00 *
(See the fourth section of this book for additional Junior Wells recordings in 45 RPM format)

TUDIE WELLS:
Pathe-Actuelle 032006 *Uncle Sam Blues* ....20.00 - 30.00
Perfect 12085 *Uncle Sam Blues*...............................20.00 - 30.00

NOLAN WELSH:
Okeh 8372 *St. Peter Blues* ....150.00 - 250.00
  8425 *Bouncing Blues* ....80.00 - 120.00

CHARLEY WEST:
Bluebird 7033 *Poor Boy Blues* ....20.00 - 30.00
  8085 *Rollin' Stone Blues* ....20.00 - 30.00

WESTERN KID:
Gennett 7210 *Mountain Girl Blues*.........................200.00 - 300.00
  7230 *Western Blues* ....200.00 - 300.00

PERRY WESTON:
Vocalion 03699 *Border Blues* ....20.00 - 30.00

WEST TEXAS SLIM:
Flame 1007 *Little Mae Bell* ....75.00 - 100.00

LITTLE DAVID WHEATON:
Capitol 40009 *I Just Couldn't Help It* ....15.00 - 20.00
  40034 *Too Long Blues* ....15.00 - 20.00
  40139 *It Just Ain't For Me* ....15.00 - 20.00

PEETIE WHEATSTRAW:
Titles issued contemporaneously on Banner, Conqueror, Melotone, Oriole, Perfect, Romeo, and Vocalion: *Froggie Blues; Good Whiskey Blues; Kidnappers Blues; The Last Dime; Letter Writing Blues; Long Lonesome Drive; Mistreated Love Blues; Remember And Forget Blues* ....20.00 - 30.00
Bluebird 5451 *Devil's Son-In-Law* ....50.00 - 75.00
  5626 *Ice And Snow Blues* ....50.00 - 75.00
Conqueror 8850 *The Last Dime* ....15.00 - 20.00
  8858 *More Good Whiskey Blues* ....15.00 - 20.00
  9027 *Blues At My Door* ....15.00 - 20.00
  9028 *King of Spades* ....15.00 - 20.00
  9201 *Police Station Blues* ....15.00 - 20.00
  9277 *Ain't It A Pity And A Shame?* ....15.00 - 20.00
  9767 *Hi-De-Ho Woman Blues* ....15.00 - 20.00
Decca 7007 *Doin' The Best I Can* ....50.00 - 75.00
  7018 *Throw Me In The Alley* ....75.00 - 100.00
  7061 *Good Home Blues* ....60.00 - 100.00
  7082 *Numbers Blues* ....60.00 - 100.00
  7111 *Whiskey Head Blues* ....30.00 - 50.00
  7123 *Good Hustler Blues*....................................30.00 - 50.00
  7129 *Santa Claus Blues* ....30.00 - 50.00
  7144 *King Spider Blues* ....30.00 - 50.00
  7159 *Coon Can Shorty*..30.00 - 50.00
  7167 *Deep Sea Love* ....30.00 - 50.00

7177 *Poor Millionaire Blues* .... 25.00 -		40.00
7187 *Meat Cutter Blues* .... 25.00 -		40.00
7200 *Low Down Rascal* .... 30.00 -		50.00
7228 *Country Fool Blues* .... 25.00 -		40.00
7243 *False Hearted Woman* .... 25.00 -		40.00
7257 *I Don't Want No Pretty-Faced Woman* .... 25.00 -		40.00
7272 *Beggar Man Blues*..................................... 25.00 -		40.00
7292 *Crapshooter's Blues*................................. 15.00 -		20.00
7311 *Working On The Project* .... 15.00 -		20.00
7348 *Crazy With The Blues*............................... 15.00 -		20.00
7379 *New Working On The Project*................... 15.00 -		20.00
7391 *Give Me Black Or Brown*.......................... 15.00 -		20.00
7403 *Sick Bed Blues*.. 15.00 -		20.00
7422 *Devilment Blues* .... 15.00 -		20.00
7441 *Cake Alley* .... 15.00 -		20.00
7453 *Hard Headed Black Gal* .... 15.00 -		20.00
7465 *Banana Man* .... 15.00 -		20.00
7479 *Shack Bully Stomp* .... 15.00 -		20.00
7498 *Saturday Night Blues* .... 15.00 -		20.00
7529 *Sugar Mama* .... 15.00 -		20.00
7544 *Hot Springs Blues* .... 15.00 -		20.00
7568 *Black Horse Blues* .... 15.00 -		20.00
7578 *Sinking Sun Blues* .... 15.00 -		20.00
7589 *Possum Den Blues* .... 15.00 -		20.00
7605 *One To Twelve* .... 15.00 -		20.00
7641 *Easy Way Blues* .... 15.00 -		20.00
7657 *Beer Tavern* .... 15.00 -		20.00
7676 *Love Bug Blues* .... 15.00 -		20.00
7692 *Confidence Man* .... 15.00 -		20.00
7738 *Big Money Blues* .... 10.00 -		15.00
7753 *Big Apple Blues* .... 10.00 -		15.00
7778 *Machine Gun Blues* .... 15.00 -		20.00
7788 *Suicide Blues* .... 10.00 -		15.00
7798 *Jaybird Blues* .... 10.00 -		15.00
7815 *Gangster's Blues* .... 10.00 -		15.00
7823 *No 'Count Woman* .... 10.00 -		15.00
7837 *I Don't Feel Sleepy* .... 10.00 -		20.00
7844 *Love Me With Attention* .... 10.00 -		20.00
7857 *Seeing Is Believing* .... 10.00 -		20.00
7879 *The Good Lawd's Children* .... 10.00 -		20.00
7886 *Hearse Man Blues* .... 10.00 -		15.00
7894 *Pawn Broker Blues* .... 10.00 -		20.00
7901 *Old Organ Blues* .... 10.00 -		20.00
7904 *Southern Girl Blues*.................................. 20.00 -		30.00
Vocalion 1552 *Tennessee Peaches Blues* .... 150.00 -		200.00
1569 *School Days* .... 150.00 -		200.00
1597 *Strange Man Blues* .... 150.00 -		200.00
1620 *Mama's Advice*.. 150.00 -		200.00
1649 *Ain't It A Pity And A Shame*.................... 100.00 -		150.00
1672 *C And A Blues* .... 100.00 -		150.00
1722 *Police Station Blues* .... 100.00 -		150.00
1727 *Can't See Blues* .... 100.00 -		150.00
02712 *The Last Dime* .... 75.00 -		100.00
02783 *Back Door Blues* .... 100.00 -		150.00
02810 *C And A Train Blues* .... 75.00 -		100.00
02843 *Keyhole Blues*... 75.00 -		100.00
02942 *Blues At My Door*.................................... 50.00 -		80.00
02978 *Good Whiskey Blues*................................ 50.00 -		80.00
03035 *Up The Road Blues* .... 50.00 -		80.00
03066 *King Of Spades* .... 50.00 -		80.00
03119 *Sorrow Hearted Blues*............................. 50.00 -		80.00
03155 *Johnnie Blues* .... 75.00 -		100.00
03185 *True Blue Woman* .... 30.00 -		50.00

03231 *Jungle Man Blues* ....30.00 - 50.00
03249 *Froggie Blues*.........................30.00 - 50.00
03273 *Mistreated Love Blues* ....20.00 - 30.00
03348 *Block And Tackle* ....20.00 - 30.00
03396 *Sweet Home Blues*..................20.00 - 30.00
03444 *Cut Out Blues* ....30.00 - 50.00
04443 *Don't Feel Welcome Blues* ......20.00 - 30.00
04487 *Police Station Blues* ....20.00 - 30.00
04592 *Sleepless Nights Blues* ....20.00 - 30.00
04733 *Ain't It A Pity And A Shame?* ....20.00 - 30.00
04912 *Can't See Blues* ....20.00 - 30.00

LULU WHIDBY:
Black Swan 2005 *Home Again Blues* ....50.00 - 75.00
Home Again Blues also issued contemporaneously on Claxtonola,
  Paramount, and Puritan.........................50.00 - 75.00

WHISTLIN' PETE AND DADDY STOVEPIPE:
Gennett 6212 *Black Snake Blues* ....400.00 - up

WHISTLIN' RUFUS:
Bluebird 5306 *Sweet Jelly Rollin'* ....75.00 - 125.00
  5360 *Sweet Thing*............................75.00 - 125.00
Sunrise 3387 *Tired Of Sleeping By Myself At Night*
  ....100.00 - 200.00
  3441 *Mama I Hope You're Satisfied* ....100.00 - 200.00

BOB WHITE:
Bluebird 8595 *I'm The Woogie Man* ....30.00 - 50.00

BUKKA WHITE:
Conqueror 9072 *Shake 'Em On Down*.....................20.00 - 30.00
Okeh 05625 *Good Gin Blues* ....20.00 - 30.00
  05683 *District Attorney Blues* ....20.00 - 30.00
  05743 *Sleepy Man Blues*....................20.00 - 30.00
Vocalion 03711 *Shake 'Em On Down* ....30.00 - 50.00
  05489 *High Fever Blues* ....25.00 - 40.00
  05526 *Strange Place Blues*..................25.00 - 40.00
  05588 *Black Train Blues* ....25.00 - 40.00

CLARA WHITE (accompanied by SAM HILL/HARRY SIMS):
Oriole 263 *Clearing House Blues*...........15.00 - 25.00
  264 *Buzzin' Around* ....15.00 - 25.00
  265 *You Don't Know My Mind*............15.00 - 25.00

FLORENCE WHITE:
Victor 20584 *Cold Rocks Was My Pillow* ....50.00 - 80.00

GEORGIA WHITE:
Decca 7072 *Your Worries Ain't Like Mine*..............20.00 - 30.00
  7100 *Dupree Blues* ....20.00 - 30.00
  7122 *Honey Dripper Blues* ....15.00 - 25.00
  7135 *Easy Rider Blues* ....15.00 - 25.00
  7143 *Your Worries Ain't Like Mine No. 2* ....15.00 - 20.00
  7149 *If You Can't Get Five, Take Two* ....15.00 - 20.00
  7152 *Tell Me Baby*............................10.00 - 15.00
  7166 *Can't Read, Can't Write* ....15.00 - 20.00
  7174 *Rattlesnakin' Daddy* ....10.00 - 15.00
  7183 *New Hot Nuts (Get 'Em From The Peanut Man)*
  ....10.00 - 15.00
  7192 *Trouble In Mind* ....10.00 - 15.00
  7199 *I Just Want Your Stingaree* ....10.00 - 15.00
  7209 *Pigmeat Blues* ....10.00 - 15.00
  7216 *No Second Hand Woman*............10.00 - 15.00
  7254 *Your Hellish Ways* ....10.00 - 15.00
  7269 *Sinking Sun Blues* ....10.00 - 15.00

7277 *You Don't Know My Mind* ....10.00 - 15.00
7287 *Little Red Wagon*............................10.00 - 15.00
7309 *Toothache Blues* ....10.00 - 15.00
7323 *When My Love Comes Down* ....8.00 - 12.00
7332 *New Trouble In Mind* ....8.00 - 12.00
7357 *Biscuit Roller* ....7.00 - 10.00
7377 *Georgia Man* ....8.00 - 12.00
7389 *Red Cap Porter* ....8.00 - 12.00
7405 *All Night Blues* ....8.00 - 12.00
7419 *Strewin' Your Mess* ....7.00 - 10.00
7436 *The Stuff Is Here* ....7.00 - 10.00
7450 *Almost Afraid To Love* ....7.00 - 10.00
7477 *Too Much Trouble* ....7.00 - 10.00
7521 *Trouble In Mind Swing* ....7.00 - 10.00
7534 *Dead Man's Blues* ....8.00 - 12.00
7562 *My Worried Mind Blues* ....8.00 - 12.00
7596 *Married Woman Blues* ....8.00 - 12.00
7608 *Fire In The Mountain*......................8.00 - 12.00
7620 *Beggin' My Daddy* ....8.00 - 12.00
7631 *Hydrant Love* ....8.00 - 12.00
7652 *Do It Again* ....8.00 - 12.00
7672 *I'm Doing What My Heart Says Do* ....7.00 - 10.00
7689 *Furniture Man* ....7.00 - 10.00
7741 *Jazzin' Babies Blues* ....10.00 - 15.00
7754 *Sensation Blues* ....10.00 - 15.00
7783 *Papa Pleaser* ....10.00 - 15.00
7807 *Worried Head Blues* ....7.00 - 10.00
7841 *Come Around To My House* ....7.00 - 10.00
7853 *Territory Blues* ....7.00 - 10.00
7866 *Mail Plane Blues* ....7.00 - 10.00

GLADYS WHITE:
Oriole 746 *I'm Saving It All For You*.....................15.00 - 20.00
  772 *Papa, If You Can't Do Better*....................15.00 - 20.00

GRACE WHITE:
Silvertone 3542 *Friendless Blues* ....20.00 - 30.00

JANE WHITE:
Domino 425 *Keep On Going* ....20.00 - 30.00

JOSH/JOSHUA WHITE:
Titles issued contemporaneously on Banner, Conqueror, Melotone,
  Oriole, Perfect, and Romeo: *Baby, Won't You Doodle-Doo Doo;
  Bad Depression Blues; Big House Blues; Black And Evil Blues;
  Blood Red River; Can't Help But Crying Sometimes; Crying
  Blues; Death's Coming Back After You; Double Crossing
  Women; Downhearted Man Blues; Down On Me; Four And
  Twenty Elders; Got A Key To The Kingdom; High Brown
  Cheater; How About You?; Howlin' Wolf Blues; I Don't Intend
  To Die In Egyptland; I Got A Home In That Rock; Jesus Gonna
  Make Up My Dying Bed; Lay Some Flowers On My Grave; Lazy
  Black Snake Blues; Little Brother Blues; Lord, I Want To Die
  Easy; Motherless Children; My Father Is A Husbandman; My
  Soul Is Gonna Live With God; On My Way; Paul And Silas Bound
  In Jail; Pickin' Low Cotton; Pure Religion Hallilu; So Sweet, So
  Sweet; That Suits Me; There's A Man Going Round Taking
  Names; Things About Coming My Way; This Heart Of Mine;
  While The Blood Runs Warm In Your Veins; You Sinner You*
  ....30.00 - 60.00
Blue Note 23 *Milk Cow Blues* ....15.00 - 20.00
Conqueror 9959 *Gotta Go* ....15.00 - 20.00
  9960 *Eve's Apple Tree* ....15.00 - 20.00

WASHINGTON WHITE/WHITE & HAIRISTON:
Victor 23295 *The Panama Limited* ....300.00 - up
  V38615 *Promise True And Grand* ....200.00 - 300.00

ELSIE WHITMAN:
Paramount 12172 *Sweet Daddy It's You I Love* ......35.00 - 50.00

ESSIE WHITMAN:
Black Swan 2036 *If You Don't Believe I Love You* .40.00 - 60.00

MARGARET WHITMIRE:
Brunswick 7024 *Tain't A Cow In Texas* ....50.00 - 75.00
Vocalion 1173 *Tain't A Cow In Texas* ....50.00 - 75.00

(JAMES) "BOODLE IT" WIGGINS:
Paramount 12662 *Evil Woman Blues* ....150.00 - 250.00
   12860 *Forty-Four Blues* ....150.00 - 250.00
   12878 *Weary Heart Blues* ....150.00 - 250.00
   12916 *Gotta Shave 'Em Dry* ....150.00 - 250.00

BILL WILBER:
Champion 50053 *Greyhound Blues* ....50.00 - 80.00

WILEY AND WILEY:
Brunswick 7022 *The Dixie Drug Store Down On* ...75.00 - 100.00
Columbia 14610-D *Irene's Bakershop Blues* ....75.00 - 100.00
   14630-D *Jumpin' Judy Blues* ....50.00 - 80.00
Okeh 8385 *Dear Old Companion* ....40.00 - 60.00
Vocalion 1171 *The Dixie Drug Store Down On* ......75.00 - 100.00

ARNOLD WILEY:
Apollo 391 *Wiley's Boogie* ....15.00 - 25.00
Brunswick 7113 *Windy City* ....75.00 - 100.00
Paramount 12955 *Jumping Blues* ....150.00 - 200.00

DOC WILEY (TRIO):
Bullet 323 *Play Your Hand* ....15.00 - 25.00
King 4241 *Big Four Boogie* ....15.00 - 20.00
Sensation 24 *Wild Cat Boogie* ....15.00 - 30.00

GEESHIE WILEY:
Paramount 12951 *Skinny Leg Blues* ....150.00 - 200.00
   13074 *Pick Poor Robin Clean* ....150.00 - 200.00

ROBERT WILKINS:
Brunswick 7125 *Falling Down Blues* ....200.00 - 300.00
   7158 *Get Away Blues* ....200.00 - 300.00
   7168 *Police Sergeant Blues* ....200.00 - 300.00
   7205 *Long Train Blues* ....200.00 - 300.00
Victor 21741 *Rolling Stone* ....200.00 - 300.00
   23379 *Jail House Blues* ....300.00 - up

TIM WILKINS:
Vocalion 03176 *Black Rat Blues* ....150.00 - 200.00
   03223 *Dirty Deal Blues* ....150.00 - 200.00

B. WILLIAMS:
Top Tunes 101 *Mortgaged Love* ....15.00 - 20.00

BESSIE WILLIAMS:
Domino 361 *Mama's Gone, Goodbye* ....15.00 - 25.00
   362 *How Come You Do Me Like You Do* ....15.00 - 25.00
   363 *You Don't Know My Mind* ....15.00 - 25.00
   364 *Clearing House Blues* ....15.00 - 25.00
   412 *I Wanna Jazz Some More* ....20.00 - 30.00
   413 *Family Skeleton Blues* ....20.00 - 30.00
   424 *Deep River Blues* ....20.00 - 30.00

BILL WILLIAMS (& SAMMY SAMPSON):
Titles issued contemporaneously on Banner, Oriole, Perfect, and
   Romeo: *Mr. Conductor Man; No Good Buddy* ..75.00 - 100.00

BILYE WILLIAMS:
Acorn 310 *Disgusted Blues* ....10.00 - 15.00

BLIND BOY WILLIAMS:
Sittin' In With 538 *Just Drifting* ....15.00 - 20.00

BOODLE IT WILLIAMS:
Broadway 5086 *Evil Woman Blues* ....150.00 - 200.00

BROTHER WILLIAMS' AND HIS-MEMPHIS SANCTIFIED SINGERS:
Vocalion 1482 *He's Got The Whole World In His Hands*
....100.00 - 150.00

EDDIE WILLIAMS & THE BROWN BUDDIES:
Selective 121 *Unfaithful Woman* ....8.00 - 12.00
Supreme 1528, 1535, 1542, 1546, 1547, 1548 ....7.00 - 12.00

ELLIS WILLIAMS:
Columbia 14482-D *Smokey Blues* ....100.00 - 150.00

ELSIE WILLIAMS:
Decca 7399 *Bind It Back* ....10.00 - 15.00

GEORGE ("BULLET") WILLIAMS:
Broadway 5085 *Frisco Leaving Birmingham* ....100.00 - 150.00
Paramount 12651 *The Escaped Convict* ....150.00 - 200.00
   12680 *Touch Me Light Mama* ....150.00 - 200.00

GEORGE WILLIAMS (AND BESSIE BROWN):
Columbia A-3974 *Satisfied Blues* ....15.00 - 25.00
   13006-D *If Mama Quits Papa, What Will Papa Do?*
....15.00 - 25.00
   14002-D *A Woman Gets Tired Of One Man All Of The Time*
....15.00 - 25.00
   14011-D *You Ain't Quittin' Me Without Two Weeks' Notice*
....15.00 - 25.00
   14015-D *I Won't Stand No Leavin' Now* ....15.00 - 25.00
   14017-D *You Need Some Lovin'* ....15.00 - 25.00
   14030-D *Hard Headed Gal* ....20.00 - 30.00
   14033-D *If You Hit My Dog I'll Kick Your Cat*. 25.00 - 40.00
   14046-D *I Can Do What You Do* ....40.00 - 60.00
   14049-D *Chain Gang Blues* ....30.00 - 50.00
   14065-D *Bald-Headed Mama Blues* ....30.00 - 50.00
   14071-D *Cheatin' Blues* ....50.00 - 80.00
   14078-D *Oh! Dark Gal* ....35.00 - 50.00
   14135-D *Hit Me But Don't Quit Me* ....40.00 - 60.00
   14148-D *West Virginia Blues* ....50.00 - 80.00
   14201-D *West Virginia Blues* ....40.00 - 60.00
   14543-D *Yodelin' The Blues Away* ....75.00 - 100.00
Diva 6027-G *You Ain't Quittin' Me Without Two Weeks' Notice*
....15.00 - 20.00
Velvet Tone 7053-V *It Takes A Brownskin Man To Make A High*
   Yellow Blue ....15.00 - 20.00

GUSSIE WILLIAMS:
Okeh 8934 *It's Too Slippery* ....50.00 - 75.00

HENRY WILLIAMS AND EDDIE ANTHONY:
Columbia 14328-D *Georgia Crawl* ....150.00 - 200.00

"JABO" WILLIAMS:
Paramount 13127 *Ko Ko Mo Blues* ....600.00 - up
   13130 *Fat Mama Blues* ....600.00 - up
   13136 *House Lady Blues* ....600.00 - up
   13141 *Pratt City Blues* ....600.00 - up

(BIG) JOE WILLIAMS (& HIS 9-STRING GUITAR); JOE WILLIAMS' WASHBOARD BLUES SINGERS:
Bluebird 5900 *Little Leg Woman* ....50.00 - 80.00
   5930 *Providence Help The Poor People* ....75.00 - 100.00
   5948 *My Grey Pony* ....100.00 - 150.00

5996 *40 Highway Blues*	40.00 -	60.00
6200 *Wild Cow Blues*	30.00 -	50.00
6231 *Worried Man Blues*	30.00 -	50.00
7719 *Get Your Head Trimmed Down*	25.00 -	40.00
7770 *Peach Orchard Mama*	25.00 -	40.00
8738 *Crawlin' King Snake*	20.00 -	30.00
8774 *I'm Getting Wild About Her*	20.00 -	30.00
8969 *Please Don't Go*	20.00 -	30.00
9025 *Highway 49*	15.00 -	20.00
34-0739 *Vitamin A*	15.00 -	20.00
Bullet 337 *Jivin' Woman*	25.00 -	40.00
Chicago 103 *His Spirit Lives On*	30.00 -	50.00
Columbia 30099 *Wild Cow Moan*	10.00 -	15.00
30107 *Stack Of Dollars*	10.00 -	15.00
30119 *House Lady Blues*	10.00 -	15.00
30129 *King Biscuit Stomp*	15.00 -	20.00
30191 *I'm A Highway Man*	15.00 -	20.00
37945 *Baby Please Don't Go*	10.00 -	15.00
38055 *Mellow Apples*	10.00 -	15.00
38190 *House Lady Blues*	10.00 -	15.00
Trumpet 151 *Delta Blues*	30.00 -	50.00
169 *Overhauling Blues*	30.00 -	50.00
171 *She Left Me A Mule*	30.00 -	50.00
Vocalion 1457 *Mr. Devil Blues*	250.00 -	up

JOHNNY WILLIAMS:

Gotham 506 *Wandering Blues*	15.00 -	25.00
509 *Questionnaire Blues*	20.00 -	30.00
513 *My Daddy Was A Jockey*	20.00 -	30.00
Staff 704 *Highway Blues*	25.00 -	40.00
710 *Wandering Blues*	25.00 -	40.00
717 *I Got Lucky*	50.00 -	100.00
718 *Prison Bound*	20.00 -	30.00
Swing Time 225 *I Got Lucky*	50.00 -	100.00
266 *Prison Bound*	20.00 -	30.00

L. C. WILLIAMS (with J. C. CONNEY'S COMBO); L. C. (LIGHTNIN' JR.) WILLIAMS:

Bayou 008 *All Through My Dreams*	15.00 -	20.00
Dot 1052 *You Never Miss The Water*	15.00 -	20.00
Freedom 1501 *Why Don't You Come Back*	15.00 -	20.00
1517 *Ethel Mae*	15.00 -	20.00
1524 *Louisiana Boogie*	15.00 -	20.00
1529 *All Through My Dreams*	20.00 -	30.00
Gold Star 614 *Trying, Trying*	30.00 -	50.00
623 *Hole In The Wall*	30.00 -	50.00
Imperial 5195 *Mean And Evil Blues*	10.00 -	20.00
Jax 640 *Baby Child*	20.00 -	30.00
648 *Fannie Mae*	20.00 -	30.00
Mercury 8276 *Don't Want No Woman*	15.00 -	20.00
Sittin' In With 640 *So Sorry*	25.00 -	40.00
648 *Fannie Mae*	25.00 -	40.00

LESTER WILLIAMS:

Macy's 5000 *Winter Time Blues*	15.00 -	20.00
5004 *All I Need Is You*	15.00 -	20.00
5006 *Dowling Street Hop*	15.00 -	20.00
5009 *Mary Lou*	15.00 -	25.00
5016 *The Folks Around The Corner*	15.00 -	25.00
Specialty 422 *I Can't Lose With the Stuff I Use*	10.00 -	15.00
431 *Tryin' To Forget*	10.00 -	15.00
437 *Sweet Lovin' Daddy*	10.00 -	15.00
450 *Brand New Baby*	10.00 -	15.00

LIGHTNIN' JR. WILLIAMS:

Gold Star 648 *Black Woman*	25.00 -	40.00

(PAPA) LONNIE WILLIAMS (& GEORGE HOLMES):

Champion 15695 *Somebody's Been Using That Thing*	150.00 -	200.00
Sittin' In With 567 *New Road Blues*	30.00 -	50.00
93 *Wavin' Sea Blues*	30.00 -	50.00

LULU WILLIAMS:

Titles issued contemporaneously on Banner, Oriole, Perfect, and Romeo: *Careless Love Blues; You're Going To Leave The Old Home, Jim* .... 35.00 - 50.00

MAMIE WILLIAMS:

Silvertone 5134 *Ease Away Blues*	100.00 -	150.00

RABBITS FOOT WILLIAMS:

Black Patti 8052 *Mistreatin' Mama*	1000.00 -	up
Champion 15339 *Mill Log Blues*	250.00 -	up
5379 *Man Trouble Blues*	250.00 -	up
Silvertone 5172 *I'm Gonna Cross The River*	200.00 -	300.00

SONNY BOY WILLIAMS:

Decca 7888, 7898, 8513, 8532, 8643, 8651	7.00 -	12.00

SUNNY WILLIAMS TRIO:

Super Disc 1030 *The Boogie Man*	20.00 -	30.00
058 *You'll Never Cry Again*	20.00 -	30.00

SUSAN WILLIAMS:

Lincoln 2612 *Someday You'll Come Back To Me*	15.00 -	25.00
651 *Black Water Blues*	15.00 -	25.00
690 *Gay-Cattin' Daddy*	15.00 -	25.00

TRIXIE WILLIAMS:

Gennett 6107 *Save My Jelly*	80.00 -	120.00

JAMES WILLIAMSON & HIS TRIO:

Chance 1121 *Lonesome Ole Train*	50.00 -	100.00
1131 *Homesick*	50.00 -	100.00

SONNY BOY WILLIAMSON:

Ace 511 *Boppin' With Sonny*	7.00 -	10.00 *
Bluebird 7012 *Skinny Woman*	20.00 -	30.00
7059 *Sugar Mama Blues*	20.00 -	30.00
7098 *Blue Bird Blues*	20.00 -	30.00
7302 *Early In The Morning*	20.00 -	30.00
7352 *Suzanna Blues*	20.00 -	30.00
7404 *Frigidaire Blues*	20.00 -	30.00
7428 *Collector Man Blues*	20.00 -	30.00
7500 *Sunny Land*	15.00 -	20.00
7536 *You Can Lead Me*	20.00 -	30.00
7576 *Miss Louisa Blues*	20.00 -	30.00
7603 *Beauty Parlor*	20.00 -	30.00
7665 *Decoration Blues*	20.00 -	30.00
7707 *Honey Bee Blues*	20.00 -	30.00
7756 *You Give An Account*	20.00 -	30.00
7805 *Deep Down In The Ground*	20.00 -	30.00
7847 *Shannon Street Blues*	20.00 -	30.00
7979 *Low Down Ways*	15.00 -	20.00
7995 *Susie-Q*	15.00 -	20.00
8010 *Number Five Blues*	15.00 -	20.00
8034 *Insurance Man Blues*	15.00 -	20.00
8094 *Christmas Morning Blues*	15.00 -	20.00
8237 *Good For Nothing Blues*	15.00 -	20.00
8265 *Bad Luck Blues*	15.00 -	20.00
8307 *Doggin' My Love Around*	15.00 -	20.00

8333 *T. B. Blues*.................................15.00 - 20.00
8357 *Good Gal Blues*...........................15.00 - 20.00
8383 *New Jail House Blues* ....15.00 - 20.00
8403 *Joe Louis And John Henry Blues*........15.00 - 20.00
8439 *Miss Ida Lee*..............................15.00 - 20.00
8474 *Honey Bee Blues*.........................15.00 - 20.00
8580 *War Time Blues*...........................10.00 - 20.00
8610 *Welfare Store Blues* ....10.00 - 20.00
8674 *My Little Machine*........................10.00 - 20.00
8731 *Western Union Man*.......................10.00 - 20.00
8766 *Big Apple Blues*..........................10.00 - 20.00
8797 *Mattie Mae Blues*.........................10.00 - 20.00
8822 *Sloppy Drunk Blues* ....10.00 - 20.00
8866 *Million Years Blues*......................10.00 - 20.00
8914 *She Was A Dreamer*......................10.00 - 20.00
8955 *Drink On, Little Girl* ....10.00 - 20.00
8992 *My Black Name Blues* ....10.00 - 15.00
9031 *Ground Hog Blues*........................10.00 - 15.00
Bluebird 34-0701 *She Don't Love Me That Way*.....10.00 - 15.00
34-0713 *Love Me,Baby* ....10.00 - 15.00
34-0722 *Win The War Blues* ....10.00 - 20.00
34-0736 *Miss Stella Brown Blues* ....10.00 - 15.00
34-0744 *Sonny Boy's Jump* ....10.00 - 15.00
Checker 824 *All My Love In Vain* ....8.00 - 12.00 *
834 *Let Me Explain* ....8.00 - 12.00 *
847 *The Key To Your Door* ....8.00 - 12.00 *
864 *Fattening Frogs For Snakes* ....8.00 - 12.00 *
883 *Born Blind* ....8.00 - 12.00 *
RCA Victor (most issues)....................7.00 - 12.00
Trumpet 129 *Eyesight To The Blind*.......30.00 - 50.00
139 *Do It If You Wanna* ....30.00 - 50.00
140 *Stop Crying*..................................30.00 - 50.00
144 *West Memphis Blues*........................25.00 - 40.00
145 *Pontiac Blues*................................30.00 - 50.00
166 *Nine Below Zero* ....20.00 - 30.00 *
167 *Too Close Together* ....20.00 - 30.00 *
168 *Mr. Down Child* ....20.00 - 30.00 *
212 *Cat Hop* ....10.00 - 15.00 *
215 *Getting' Out Of Town* ....10.00 - 15.00 *
228 *Empty Bedroom* ....10.00 - 15.00 *
(See the fourth section of this book for additional Sonny Boy
Williamson recordings in 45 RPM format)

WILLIE MAE:
Vocalion 03404 *I'd Rather Drink Muddy Water*.....15.00 - 25.00

LITTLE SON WILLIS:
Swing Time 304 *Bad Luck And Trouble* ....50.00 - 80.00 *
305 *Harlem Blues* ....50.00 - 80.00
306 *Nothing But The Blues*....................50.00 - 80.00
341 *Roll Me Over Slow*........................50.00 - 80.00 *

MAC WILLIS:
Elko 254 *Pretty Woman*.......................30.00 - 50.00

MARY WILLIS:
Okeh 8921 *Rough Alley Blues* ....150.00 - 250.00
8932 *Merciful Blues*.............................150.00 - 250.00

MILTON WILLIS COMBO:
Lucky 75001 *Little Joe's Boogie*............10.00 - 15.00

**RALPH ('BAMA) WILLIS (& HIS ALABAMA TRIO);
RALPH WILLIS' COUNTRY BOYS:**
Abbey 3002 *Cool That Thing* ....50.00 - 80.00

Jubilee 5034 *Somebody Is Got To Go* ....40.00 - 60.00
5044 *Every Day I Weep And Moan* ....40.00 - 60.00
5078 *Income Tax Blues* ....40.00 - 60.00
King 4611 *Why'd You Do It* ....50.00 - 75.00 *
4631 *Door Bell Blues* ....40.00 - 70.00 *
Prestige 923 *Cold Chills* ....- -
Regis 118 *Worried Blues* ....50.00 - 75.00
Signature 32012 *Shake That Thing* ....- -
32016 *Church Bells* ....- -
20th Century 20-09 *So Many Days* ....- -
20-11 *New Goin' Down Slow* ....- -
20-12 *Steel Mill Bles* ....- -

RUTH WILLIS:
Titles issued contemporaneously on Banner, Melotone, Oriole,
Perfect, and Romeo: *I'm Still Sloppy Drunk; Man Of My Own*
....40.00 - 60.00

TURNER WILLIS:
Trilon 1058 *Re-Enlistment Blues* ....10.00 - 15.00

JIMMY WILSON (& HIS ALL STARS):
Aladdin 3087 *Honey Bee* ....10.00 - 15.00
3140 *Mistake In Life* ....10.00 - 15.00
3169 *Lemon Squeezer* ....10.00 - 15.00
3241 *It's Time To Change* ....8.00 - 12.00 *
Cavatone 252 *Mistake In Life* ....15.00 - 20.00
(See the fourth section of this book for additional Jimmy Wilson
recordings in 45 RPM format)

**LEOLA WILSON WITH WESLEY WILSON AND COOT
GRANT:**
Columbia 14669-D *I Can't Get Enough*...............150.00 - 250.00
14675-D *Dirty Spoon Blues* ....150.00 - 200.00

LEOLA B. WILSON:
Paramount 12392 *Ashley St. Blues*.....................150.00 - 250.00
12403 *Dishrag Blues*.....................................125.00 - 175.00
12426 *Wilson Dam*..150.00 - 300.00
12444 *Down The Country*...............................150.00 - 300.00

WILSON & REED:
Champion 15264 *Hey! Lawdy Mama-The France Blues*
....200.00 - 300.00

EDNA WINSTON:
Victor 20407 *Peepin' Jim* ....50.00 - 75.00
20424 *Pail In My Hand*...................................50.00 - 75.00
20654 *Joogie Blues*.......................................50.00 - 75.00
20857 *Rent Man Blues*....................................50.00 - 75.00

BIG BOY WOODS:
Bell 1173 *The Jail House Blues*...........................200.00 - 300.00
1180 *Do That Thing* ....200.00 - 300.00
1181 *Dark Cloudy Blues* ....200.00 - 300.00

BUDDY WOODS:
Vocalion 03906 *Muscat Hill Blues* ....20.00 - 30.00
04604 *Jam Session Blues* ....20.00 - 30.00
04745 *Low Life Blues*....................................20.00 - 30.00

EVA WOODS:
Silvertone 3522 *You Gotta Know How* ....75.00 - 100.00
3557 *He's My Man*..75.00 - 100.00

OSCAR WOODS:
Decca 7219 *Lone Wolf Blues* ....30.00 - 50.00
7904 *Evil Hearted Woman Blues* ....20.00 - 30.00

EMMA WRIGHT:
Columbia 14413-D *Lonesome Trail Blues* ....150.00 - 200.00

BIG JIM WYNN:
Million 2004 *I'm The Boss* ....10.00 - 15.00

THE YAS YAS GIRL:
Titles issued contemporaneously on Banner, Conqueror, Melotone, Oriole, Perfect, Romeo, and Vocalion: *Blues Everywhere; Crime Don't Pay; Got A Man In The 'Bama Mines; Grandma And Grandpa; I'd Rather Drink Muddy Water-No. 2; I Drink Good Whiskey; Jackass For Sale; New Drinking My Blues Away; Patrol Wagon Blues; Sold It To The Devil; Working On The Project; You Got To Pay*......................................10.00 - 20.00
Columbia (red label, most issues) ....7.00 - 10.00
Conqueror 9079 *Don't You Leave Me Here* ....10.00 - 15.00
   9147 *Don't You Make Me High*..........................10.00 - 15.00
   9205 *Breakin' 'Em Down Tonight*......................10.00 - 15.00
   9375 *Want To Woogie Some More* ....8.00 - 12.00
   9449 *You're A Pain In The Neck To Me*..............8.00 - 12.00
   9451 *I'll Try To Forget*....................................8.00 - 12.00
   9601 *I Won't Sell My Love* ....8.00 - 12.00
   9949 *Good Old Easy Street* ....8.00 - 12.00
   9950 *Milk Man Blues*.....................................8.00 - 12.00
Okeh 05870 *Worried Heart Blues* ....10.00 - 15.00
   05932 *You Know It Ain't Right*....................10.00 - 15.00
   05984 *Got The Blues For My Baby* ....10.00 - 15.00
   06032 *Evil Old Nightmare*..............................10.00 - 15.00
   06340 *Blues Before Daybreak*..........................10.00 - 15.00
   06446 *Good Old Easy Street* ....10.00 - 15.00
   06570 *Froggy Bottom* ....10.00 - 15.00
Vocalion 04013 *He May Be Your Man*...................15.00 - 25.00
   04094 *Love Shows Weakness*..........................15.00 - 20.00
   04150 *About My Time To Check* ....15.00 - 20.00
   04188 *Jelly Bean Blues*...................................15.00 - 20.00
   04331 *You Can't Shoot Your Pistol*.................10.00 - 15.00
   04455 *Don't You Make Me High* ....10.00 - 15.00
   04545 *Whiskey Fool*..10.00 - 15.00
   04719 *Reckless Life Blues*.................................10.00 - 15.00
   04775 *Grieving Heart Blues* ....10.00 - 15.00
   04830 *Easy Towing Mama*.................................10.00 - 15.00
   04885 *Got A Mind To Ramble* ....10.00 - 15.00
   05105 *Fine And Mellow* ....10.00 - 15.00
   05180 *I'd Rather Be Drunk*................................8.00 - 12.00
   05219 *I Need You By My Side*.........................10.00 - 15.00
   05286 *I Got To Have It Daddy* ....8.00 - 12.00
   05337 *I'll Try To Forget*...................................8.00 - 12.00
   05382 *Mama's Bad Luck Child* ....10.00 - 15.00
   05501 *You Don't Know My Mind* ....8.00 - 12.00
   05576 *Stop And Listen* ....10.00 - 15.00
   05614 *Black Gypsy Blues*..................................10.00 - 15.00

BLIND RICHARD YATES:
Black Patti 8021 *Sore Bunion Blues* ....300.00 - up
Champion 15264 *I'm Gonna Moan My Blues Away*
  ....200.00 - 300.00
   15281 *Sore Bunion Blues*.................................200.00 - 300.00
Gennett 6104 *Sore Bunion Blues* ....50.00 - 80.00

BILLE YOUNG:
Victor 23339 *You Done Played Out Blues*............300.00 - up

JOHNNY YOUNG:
Ora Nelle 712 *Worried Man Blues* ....80.00 - 120.00

MAN YOUNG:
Old Swing Master 19 *Let Me Ride Your Mule*........60.00 - 100.00
Planet 104 *Let Me Ride Your Mule* ....80.00 - 120.00

THE ZA ZU GIRL:
Titles issued contemporaneously on Banner, Melotone, Oriole, Perfect, Romeo, and Vocalion: *He Left Me; My Righteous Man*
  ....15.00 - 20.00

COUNTRY/WESTERN; OLD TIME SINGING; STRING BANDS; ETC.

1920s to early 1950s-78 RPM

All records in this section are 78 RPM.

Note: * after listing means that the record may exist also in 45 RPM form.

ABIGAIL and BUDDY:
Imperial 8054 *Hang Out A Sign* ....5.00 - 8.00
   8057 *If You Were Only Mine* ....5.00 - 8.00

ROY ACUFF & HIS CRAZY TENNESSEANS/SMOKY MOUNTAIN BOYS:
Titles issued contemporaneously on Banner, Conqueror, Melotone, Oriole, Perfect, and Romeo: *All Night Long; Charmin' Betsy; 'Gonna Have A Big Time Tonight; Gonna Raise A Ruckus Tonight; Great Speckle Bird; Great Speckle Bird No. 2; My Gal Sal; My Mountain Home Sweet Home; New Greenback Dollar; Red Lips; Sailing Along; She No Longer Belongs To Me; Steamboat Whistle Blues; Steel Guitar Blues; Steel Guitar Chimes; Tell Mother I'll Be There; Trouble Trouble; Yes Sir, That's My Baby; You're The Only Star (In My Blue Heaven); You've Gotta See Mama Every Night* ....5.00 - 8.00
Conqueror 9123, 9170, 9255, 9257, 9324, 9404, 9432
....4.00 - 7.00
Vocalion 03255, 04252, 04374, 04376, 04466, 04505, 04531, 04590, 04657, 04730, 04795, 04867, 04909, 04915, 05041 ....5.00 - 10.00

CHARLIE ADAMS & THE LONE STAR PLAYBOYS:
Decca 28397, 46335, 46358, 46373, 46391 ....5.00 - 10.00*
Imperial 8100, 8113...8.00 - 12.00

CLARENCE ADAMS:
Challenge 229, 232 ....5.00 - 8.00

AIKEN COUNTRY STRING BAND:
Okeh 45143 *Carolina Stompdown*............................50.00 - 75.00
   45219 *Charleston Rag* ....50.00 - 75.00
   45294 *Harrisburg Itch* ....50.00 - 75.00

AKINS BIRMINGHAM BOYS:
Columbia 15348-D *I Walked And Walked*...............20.00 - 30.00

ALABAMA FOUR:
Broadway 8209 *Looking This Way*.........................20.00 - 30.00

ALEXANDER & MILLER:
Supertone 9398 *Medley* ....5.00 - 8.00

WELDON ALLARD:
Imperial 8117 *Too Late You Say* ....7.00 - 10.00

ALLEGHENY HIGHLANDERS:
Brunswick 324, 325 ....8.00 - 12.00

ALLEN BROTHERS:
Bluebird 5001 *Fruit Jar Blues*...............................5.00 - 8.00
   5104 *Tiple Blues* ....15.00 - 20.00
   5165 *Shake It, Ida, Shake It* ....15.00 - 20.00
   5224 *Reckless Night Blues*..................................10.00 - 15.00
   5317 *Slide, Daddy, Slide*.....................................10.00 - 15.00

   5380 *New Chattanooga Blues*...........................10.00 - 15.00
   5403 *Browns Ferry Blues* ....5.00 - 8.00
   5448 *No Low Down Hanging Around* ....7.00 - 10.00
   5470 *Chattanooga Mama* ....10.00 - 15.00
   5533 *It Can't Be Done* ....10.00 - 15.00
   5668 *Shanghai Rooster Blues* ....10.00 - 15.00
   5700 *Roll Down The Line* ....10.00 - 15.00
   5701 *Glorious Night Blues*.................................10.00 - 15.00
   5702 *When You Leave, You'll Leave Me Sad* ....10.00 - 15.00
   5772 *Skipping And Flying*..................................10.00 - 15.00

Bluebird 6148, 6149, 6195...5.00 - 10.00
Columbia 15175-D *Salty Dog Blues*.......................75.00 - 100.00
   15270-D *Ain't That Skippin?* ....75.00 - 100.00
Victor 23507 *Price Of Cotton Blues* ....40.00 - 60.00
   23514 *New Salty Dog*...25.00 - 40.00
   23536 *No Low Down Hanging Around* ....25.00 - 40.00
   23551 *Roll Down The Line* ....30.00 - 50.00
   23567 *Chattanooga Mama* ....40.00 - 60.00
   23578 *Pile Drivin' Papa*......................................40.00 - 60.00
   23590 *Slide, Daddy, Slide* ....40.00 - 60.00
   23607 *Mother-In-Law Blues* ....40.00 - 60.00
   23623 *Unlucky Man* ....40.00 - 60.00
   23631 *Moonshine Bill* ....40.00 - 60.00
   23662 *It Can't Be Done* ....40.00 - 60.00
   23678 *Maybe Next Week Some Time No. 2* ....40.00 - 60.00
   23692 *Window Shade Blues*.................................60.00 - 80.00
   23707 *Glorious Night Blues*.................................80.00 - 120.00
   23756 *Rough Neck Blues*....................................50.00 - 75.00
   23773 *Slipping Clutch Blues*................................75.00 - 100.00
   23786 *Red Hot Rambling Dan* ....75.00 - 100.00
   23805 *Warm Knees Blues* ....80.00 - 120.00
   23817 *Midnight Mama*..80.00 - 120.00
   V40003 *Frisco Blues* ....30.00 - 50.00
   V40210 *Prisoner's Dream* ....30.00 - 50.00
   V40266 *Skipping And Flying* ....30.00 - 50.00
   V40276 *Enforcement Blues* ....35.00 - 50.00
   V40303 *Jake Walk Blues* ....35.00 - 50.00
   V40326 *Shanghai Rooster Blues* ....40.00 - 60.00
Vocalion 02817 *Red Pajama Sal* ....50.00 - 80.00
   02818 *Salty Dog Blues*.......................................15.00 - 20.00
   02841 *Midnight Mama*.......................................50.00 - 80.00
   02853 *Daddy Park Your Car* ....40.00 - 60.00
   02874 *The Prisoner's Dream*...............................40.00 - 60.00
   02890 *New Deal Blues*..40.00 - 60.00
   02891 *Tiple Blues* ....30.00 - 50.00
   02939 *Allen Brothers' Rag* ....30.00 - 50.00

CLAY ALLEN:
Decca 46324, 46360 ....5.00 - 8.00 *

LEE ALLEN & AUSTIN:
Columbia 14266-D *Chattanooga Blues*...............80.00 - 120.00

JULES ALLEN (THE SINGING COWBOY):
Victor 21470 *Jack O' Diamonds* ....5.00 - 8.00
   21627 *Home On The Range* ....5.00 - 8.00
   23598 *Sweetie Dear*...............................20.00 - 30.00
   23757 *The Cow Trail To Mexico* ....25.00 - 40.00
   23834 *The Dying Cowboy* ....25.00 - 40.00
   V40022 *Zebra Dun* ....8.00 - 12.00
   V40068 *The Texas Cowboy* ....10.00 - 15.00
   V40118 *Two Fragments* ....10.00 - 15.00
   V40167 *Chisholm Trail*...........................10.00 - 15.00
   V40178 *The Cowboy's Dream* ....15.00 - 20.00
   V40263 *Punchin' The Dough*......................15.00 - 20.00

SHELLEY LEE ALLEY & HIS ALLEY CATS:
Globe 112 *Low Down Blues* ....7.00 - 10.00
Vocalion 03891, 03939, 03975, 04145, 04201,
  04276, 04371, 04451, 04600, 04670, 04728,
  04793, 04879, 04986, 05053 ....5.00 - 10.00

THE ALLEY BOYS OF ABBEVILLE:
Vocalion 05167 *Jolie Petite Blond* ....- - -
   05168 *Abbeville Breakdown* ....- - -
   05423 *Tu Ma Quite Seul* ....- - -
   05424 *What's The Use?*........................- - -

ALLISON'S SACRED HARP SINGERS:
Gennett 6499 *Sweet Canaan*.....................15.00 - 20.00
   6583 *Weeping Pilgrim* ....15.00 - 20.00

LEROY ANDERSON (THE RED HEADED BRIER HOPPER):
Champion 45024 *The Pine Tree On The Hill* ....10.00 - 15.00
   45045 *The Fatal Derby Day* ....10.00 - 15.00
   45055 *A Mother's Wayward Son* ....10.00 - 15.00
   45059 *Gambling On The Sabbath* ....10.00 - 15.00

LES "CARROT TOP" ANDERSON:
Cormac 1107 *Queen Of The Saddle* ....15.00 - 20.00
   1108 *He's Just A Hobo* ....15.00 - 20.00
Decca 46250, 46259, 46303, 46326, 46352 ....5.00 - 10.00 *

ANGLIN BROTHERS/TWINS:
Vocalion 02963, 04078, 04579, 04692, 04774,
  04896 ....7.00 - 12.00

JUDY ANN AND ZEKE WITH PETE:
Okeh 45576 *Me And My Still*...................10.00 - 15.00
   45578 *Mississippi Waters* ....10.00 - 15.00

APPALACHIAN VAGABOND:
Vocalion 5450 *The Peddler And His Wife*.............20.00 - 30.00

CAPTAIN APPLEBLOSSOM:
Okeh 45373 *Time Table Blues*..................5.00 - 10.00
   45416 *The Book Of Etiquette*.................5.00 - 10.00

ARKANSAS BAREFOOT BOYS:
Okeh 45217 *Eighth Of January*...............30.00 - 50.00

ARKANSAS CHARLIE:
Vocalion 5270 *Goodbye Old Paint*................10.00 - 15.00
   5292 *The Texas Trail* ....10.00 - 15.00
   5298 *He Was A Travelin' Man* ....10.00 - 15.00
   5355 *The Poor Fish* ....10.00 - 15.00

   5367 *We All Grow In Time* ....10.00 - 15.00
   5384 *Old Zip Coon*...........................10.00 - 15.00
   5401 *The Sheriff And The Robber*.............10.00 - 15.00

ARKANSAS WOODCHOPPER:
Champion 45058 *Frankie And Johnny* ....7.00 - 10.00
   45192 *Old And Only In The Way* ....7.00 - 10.00
Columbia 15463-D *The Dying Cowboy* ....10.00 - 15.00
Gennett 7036 *In The Jailhouse Now* ....15.00 - 20.00
   7065 *Home On The Range* ....15.00 - 20.00
   7095 *Zeb Tuney's Gal* ....15.00 - 20.00
   7126 *Take Me Back To Colorado* ....15.00 - 20.00
   7154 *Old And Only In The Way* ....15.00 - 20.00
   7184 *A Hard Luck Guy* ....20.00 - 30.00
   7264 *The Little Green Valley* ....20.00 - 30.00
Supertone 9569 *Barney McCoy* ....10.00 - 15.00
   9570 *In The Jailhouse Now*..................10.00 - 15.00
   9571 *The Cowboy's Dream* ....10.00 - 15.00
   9628 *If Brother Jack Were Here* ....10.00 - 15.00
   9639 *Prisoner At The Bar* ....10.00 - 15.00
   9643 *The Little Green Valley* ....10.00 - 15.00
   9664 *A Hard Luck Guy* ....15.00 - 20.00
   9665 *Write Me A Song About Father*...........15.00 - 20.00

ARMSTRONG'S PLAYERS (See also NICHOLSON'S PLAYERS):
Supertone 9644 *Medley*..........................5.00 - 8.00
   9661 *Sweet Bunch Of Daisies* ....5.00 - 8.00
   9733 *Muskakatuck Waltz* ....7.00 - 10.00

ARMSTRONG & ASHLEY:
Paramount 3291 *No More Dying* ....50.00 - 75.00

ARMSTRONG & JACOBS:
Supertone 9661 *Let Me Call You Sweetheart* ....5.00 - 10.00

GENE ARNOLD:
Victor 23777, 23780, 23785, 23818, 23827, 23839 . 7.00 - 12.00

ARTHUR & REXROAT:
Vocalion 5323 *I Tickled Her Under The Chin*........25.00 - 50.00
   5335 *The White Rose* ....25.00 - 50.00

CHARLINE ARTHUR:
Bullet 707 *I've Got The Boogie Blues* ....7.00 - 10.00

EMRY ARTHUR (& HENRY ARTHUR & THE CUMBERLAND SINGERS/ & DELLA HATFIELD):
Paramount 3221 *The Broken Wedding*....................35.00 - 50.00
   3222 *The Bluefield Murder* ....35.00 - 50.00
   3237 *She Lied To Me* ....35.00 - 50.00
   3243 *Blood Stained Dress* ....35.00 - 50.00
   3249 *Jennie My Own True Love* ....35.00 - 50.00
   3251 *Sunshine And Shadows* ....35.00 - 50.00
   3289 *The Married Man* ....35.00 - 50.00
   3290 *Short Life Of Trouble* ....35.00 - 50.00
   3295 *She Lied To Me* ....35.00 - 50.00
   3298 *Careless Love* ....35.00 - 50.00
   3301 *I Tickled Her Under The Chin* ....35.00 - 50.00
Vocalion 5225 *In The Heart Of The City That Has No Heart*
   ....30.00 - 50.00
   5228 *Where Gates Swing Outward Never* ....30.00 - 50.00
   5229 *Let That Liar Alone* ....30.00 - 50.00
   5230 *Nobody's Business* ....30.00 - 50.00
   5234 *Wandering Gypsy Girl* ....30.00 - 50.00
   5249 *The Rich Man And Joseph Smith* ....30.00 - 50.00
   5264 *Train Whistle Blues* ....30.00 - 50.00
   5288 *My Girl-She's A Lulu* ....30.00 - 50.00

5340 *Frankie Baker*	40.00 -	60.00
5351 *Prison Bound Blues*	40.00 -	60.00
5354 *My Mother-In-Law*	40.00 -	60.00
5358 *The Blind Boy*	40.00 -	60.00
5385 *The Bootleggers Song*	40.00 -	60.00
5396 *Remember The Old Folks Back Home*	40.00 -	60.00

ASHFORD QUARTET:
Brunswick 393, 402, 456	5.00 -	10.00

ASHLEY'S MELODY MAKERS/MEN:
Victor 23661 *I Never Felt So Blue*	50.00 -	75.00
23767 *Come Back Lottie*	50.00 -	75.00
V40158 *Bath House Blues*	25.00 -	40.00
V40199 *Sweetest Flower Waltz*	25.00 -	40.00
V40300 *Somewhere In Arkansas*	25.00 -	40.00

ASHLEY & FOSTER:
Vocalion 02554 *Greenback Dollar*	7.00 -	10.00
02611 *Sideline Blues*	30.00 -	50.00
02647 *Frankie Silvers*	30.00 -	50.00
02666 *Faded Roses*	30.00 -	50.00
02750 *One Dark And Stormy Night*	30.00 -	50.00
02780 *Baby, All Night Long*	30.00 -	50.00
02789 *Ain't No Use To High Hat Me*	30.00 -	50.00
02900 *My North Carolina Home*	30.00 -	50.00

CLARENCE ASHLEY:
Columbia 15489-D *Dark Holler Blues*	40.00 -	60.00
15522-D *Little Sadie*	40.00 -	60.00
15654-D *Old John Hardy*	50.00 -	80.00

CLYDE ASHLEY:
Superior 2558 *Down In Arkansas*	15.00 -	25.00
2605 *The Ramblin' Railroad Boy*	15.00 -	25.00
2636 *The Hand Car Yodel*	15.00 -	25.00
2676 *High Silk Hat And Gold Top Walking Cane*	15.00 -	25.00
2711 *The Bootlegger's Plea*	15.00 -	25.00
2723 *Leaving Town Blues*	15.00 -	25.00
Superior 2751 *My Alabama Home*	15.00 -	25.00
2778 *Alimony; Woman*	15.00 -	25.00
2833 *In 1992*	15.00 -	25.00

THOMAS C./TOM ASHLEY:
Conqueror 8103 *The Fiddlers Contest*	7.00 -	10.00
Gennett 6404 *Four Night's Experience*	30.00 -	50.00
Romeo 5113 *Haunted Road Blues*	15.00 -	20.00

ASPARAGUS JOE:
Champion 15688 *Hand Me Down My Walking Cane*	7.00 -	10.00
15709 *Asleep At The Switch*	7.00 -	10.00
15752 *Boston Burglar*	7.00 -	10.00
15970 *Waiting For The Railroad Train*	7.00 -	10.00
16012 *Nutty Song*	6.00 -	10.00
16071 *The Lightning Express*	10.00 -	15.00
16118 *The Roving Gambler*	10.00 -	15.00

BOB ATCHER & BONNIE BLUE EYES:
Vocalion 04882, 04898, 05001, 05069	4.00 -	8.00

CHESTER/CHET ATKINS (& THE ALL-STAR HILLBILLIES):
Bullet 617 *Guitar Blues*	15.00 -	25.00
RCA Victor (most issues)	4.00 -	7.00

(Note: See also the **RHYTHM & BLUES, ETC.** section for other records by Chet Atkins.)

AUGUSTA TRIO:
Champion 15729 *Down Yonder*	15.00 -	20.00
15768 *Back Up And Push*	15.00 -	20.00
45159 *Whistlin' Rufus*	10.00 -	15.00

AUSTIN AND LEE ALLEN (See ALLEN)

GENE AUTRY (& JIMMY LONG); GENE AUTRY TRIO:

Titles issued contemporaneously on Banner, Conqueror, Melotone, Oriole, Perfect, and Romeo: *Always Dreaming Of You; Atlanta Bound; Bear Cat Papa Blues; Birmingham Daddy; Blue Days; Cowboy's Yodel; The Crime I Didn't Do; Dallas County Jail Blues; The Death Of Jimmie Rodgers; Don't Take Me Back To The Chain Gang; Do Right Daddy Blues; Eleven Months In Leavenworth; A Gangster's Warning; He's In The Jail House Now No. 2; High Steppin' Mama Blues; I'll Always Be A Rambler; Jailhouse Blues; Methodist Pie; Missouri I'm Calling; My Alabama Home; My Cross-Eyed Girl; Night Time; Pistol Packin' Papa; Rheumatism Blues; T.B. Blues; That's How I Got My Start; True Blue Bill; Uncle Noah's Ark; Wild Cat Mama Blues; The Yodeling Hobo* .... 10.00 - 15.00

Additional titles issued contemporaneously on Banner, Conqueror, Melotone, Oriole, Perfect, and Romeo: *After 21 Years; Alone With My Sorrows; Angel Baby; The Answer To Nobody's Darling; The Answer To Red River Valley, The Answer To 21 Years; At The Old Barn Dance; Back To Old Smokey Mountain; Beautiful Texas; The Convict's Dream; Cowboy's Heaven; Don't Waste Your Tears On Me; Dust Pan Blues; The End Of The Trail; Good Luck Old Pal; Gosh! I Miss You All The Time; Guns And Guitars; Have You Found Someone Else; A Hill Billy Wedding In June; Hold On Little Dogies; If I Could Bring Back My Buddy; I Hate To Say Goodbye To The Prairie; I'll Be Thinking Of You Little Girl; I'll Be True While You're Gone; I'll Go Riding Down That Texas Trail; I'm Always Dreaming Of You; It's Roundup Time In Reno; The Last Round Up; Little Farm Home; Little Ranch House On The Circle B; Louisiana Moon; Memories Of That Silver Haired Daddy Of Mine; Mexicali Rose; Mississippi Valley Blues; Moonlight And Skies; My Carolina Mountain Rose; My Old Pal Of Yesterday; My Old Saddle Pal; Nobody's Darling But Mine; Old Buckaroo Goodbye; The Old Covered Wagon; The Old Folks Back Home; Old Missouri Moon; Ole Faithful; The One Rose; Rhythm Of The Range; Ridin' The Range; Sail Along Silv'ry Moon; Seven More Days; Silver Haired Daddy Of Mine; Some Day In Wyomin'; The Stump Of The Old Pine Tree; Texas Plains; That Old Feather Bed On The Farm; That Ramshackle Shack; That's Why I'm Nobody Darling; There's A Gold Mine In The Sky; There's A Little Old Lady In Waiting; There's An Empty Cot In The Bunkhouse Tonight; Tumbling Tumleweeds; Watching The Clouds Roll By; Way Out West In Texas; When The Golden Leaves Are Falling; When It's Springtime In The Rockies; When Jimmie Rodgers Said Goodbye; When The Tumbleweeds Come Tumbling Down Again; Why Don't You Come Back To Me; With A Song In My Heart; The Yellow Rose Of Texas; You're The Only Star* .... 5.00 - 10.00

Titles issued contemporaneously on Clarion, Diva, and Velvet Tone:
Blue Yodel No. 5; Dust Pan Blues; Hobo Yodel; Left My Gal In The Mountains ....15.00 - 25.00
California Blues; Cowboy Yodel; Daddy And Home; Frankie And Johnny; A Gangster's Warning; I'll Be Thinking Of You Little Girl; Lullaby Yodel; My Alabama Home; My Rough And Rowdy Ways; No One To Call Me Darling; Pictures Of My Mother; Slue Foot Lue; Stay Away From My Chicken House; That's How I Got My Start; That's Why I Left The Mountains; True Blue Bill; Waiting For A Train; Why Don't You Come Back To Me ....20.00 - 30.00

Champion 16030 *I'll Be Thinking Of You Little Girl* ....30.00 - 50.00
　16050 *In The Shadow Of The Pine* ....30.00 - 50.00
　16073 *Hobo Bill's Last Ride*............................30.00 - 50.00
　16096 *Hobo Yodel* ....30.00 - 50.00
　16119 *Dust Pan Blues* ....30.00 - 50.00
　16166 *High Powered Mama*............................30.00 - 50.00
　16210 *Mean Mama Blues*................................30.00 - 50.00
　16230 *Any Old Time* ....30.00 - 50.00
　16245 *Blue Days*..30.00 - 50.00
　16275 *T. B. Blues*..40.00 - 60.00
　16328 *True Blue Bill*..50.00 - 75.00
　16372 *Dad In The Hills* ....50.00 - 75.00
　16485 *That's How I Got My Start* ....50.00 - 75.00
　45025 *Pistol Packin' Papa* ....15.00 - 20.00
　45027 *Bear Cat Papa Blues*............................15.00 - 20.00
　45060 *Dad In The Hills* ....15.00 - 20.00
　45071 *In The Shadow Of The Pine* ....15.00 - 20.00
　45073 *T. B. Blues*..15.00 - 20.00
　45156 *Money Ain't No Use Anyway*..................8.00 - 12.00
　45172 *Yodeling Hobo* ....10.00 - 15.00
　45183 *I'll Always Be A Rambler* ....15.00 - 25.00
Columbia (red label, most issues)............................3.00 - 5.00
Decca 5426, 5464, 5488, 5501, 5517, 5527 ....5.00 - 10.00
Gennett 7243 *Cowboy Yodel* ....100.00 - 150.00
　7265 *In The Shadow Of The Pine* ....100.00 - 150.00
　7290 *Hobo Bill's Last Ride* ....100.00 - 150.00
　7310 *Train Whistle Blues*...............................150.00 - 200.00
Q.R.S. 1044 *Living In The Mountains* ....300.00 - 500.00
　1047 *Blue Yodel No. 6* ....400.00 - 600.00
　1048 *That's Why I Left The Mountains* ....400.00 - 600.00
Superior 2561 *The Girl I Left Behind* ....150.00 - 200.00
　2596 *Dad In The Hills* ....100.00 - 150.00
　2637 *Pistol Packin' Papa* ....100.00 - 150.00
　2660 *Mean Mama Blues* ....100.00 - 150.00
　2681 *That's How I Got My Start* ....100.00 - 150.00
　2710 *Blue Days* ....100.00 - 150.00
　2732 *Money Ain't No Use Anyway*.................100.00 - 150.00
　2769 *Hobo Bill's Last Ride*.............................100.00 - 150.00
Supertone 9702 *Hobo Bill's Last Ride* ....35.00 - 50.00
　9704 *They Cut Down The Old Pine Tree*.........35.00 - 50.00
　9705 *Whisper Your Mother's Name* ....35.00 - 50.00
　9706 *Train Whistle Blues*................................35.00 - 50.00
Victor 23530 *Bear Cat Papa* ....80.00 - 120.00
　23548 *Do Right Daddy* ....80.00 - 120.00
　23561 *There's A Good Gal In The Mountains* ...75.00 - 100.00
　23589 *High Steppin' Mama*.............................80.00 - 120.00
　23617 *She's A Low Down Mamma* ....80.00 - 120.00
　23630 *Rheumatism Blues*...............................80.00 - 120.00
　23642 *Wild Cat Mama*....................................80.00 - 120.00
　23673 *I'm Always Dreaming Of You*................80.00 - 120.00
　23707 *Black Bottom Blues* ....80.00 - 120.00

　23720 *Kentucky Lullaby* ....80.00 - 120.00
　23725 *The Gangster's Warning*........................80.00 - 120.00
　23726 *Back To Old Smoky Mountain* ....80.00 - 120.00
　23783 *Cowboy's Heaven* ....100.00 - 150.00
　23792 *Louisiana Moon* ....100.00 - 150.00
　23810 *Your Voice Is Calling*...........................100.00 - 150.00
　V40200 *My Alabama Home* ....80.00 - 120.00
Vocalion 02991, 03007, 03070, 03097, 03101,
　03138, 03229, 03262, 03291, 03317, 03358,
　03448 ....7.00 - 10.00
Vocalion 04091, 04146, 04172, 04246, 04262,
　04267, 04274, 04340, 04375, 04415...................5.00 - 10.00

HARVEY AYERS (See GROVER RANN)

GREEN BAILEY:
Gennett 6702 *The Santa Barbara Earthquake*........ 25.00 - 40.00
　6732 *If I Die A Railroad Man* .... 25.00 - 40.00

MR. & MRS. BAKER:
Victor 20863 *The Newmarket Wreck* .... 15.00 - 20.00

BUDDY BAKER:
Victor 21549 *Box Car Blues* .... 10.00 - 15.00
　V40017 *Matrimonial Intentions* .... 15.00 - 20.00

CHARLES BAKER (THE WYOMING COWBOY):
Champion 16614 *Just Plain Folks* .... 20.00 - 30.00
Champion 45044, 45052...7.00 - 10.00

ELDON BAKER'S BROWN COUNTY REVELERS:
Vocalion 04217 *Lost John* ....7.00 - 10.00
　04279 *I Will Meet You* ....7.00 - 10.00
　04355 *Happy Cowboy*..5.00 - 8.00
　04441 *Dear Old Dixieland*...................................5.00 - 8.00

LUKE BALDWIN:
Champion 15792 *Hungry Hash House Blues* .... 10.00 - 15.00
　15811 *Daddy And Home* .... 10.00 - 15.00
　15853 *California Blues* .... 10.00 - 15.00
　15877 *Alabama Blues* .... 10.00 - 15.00
　15945 *I Love The Jailer's Daughter* .... 10.00 - 15.00
　16009 *The Yodeling Cowboy* .... 15.00 - 20.00
　16075 *The Handcar Yodel* .... 15.00 - 20.00
　16142 *It Won't Happen Again* .... 15.00 - 20.00
　16162 *Don't Ever Marry A Widow* .... 15.00 - 20.00
　16186 *The Bootlegger's Plea* .... 15.00 - 20.00
　16232 *The Ramblin' Railroad Boy* .... 15.00 - 20.00
　16254 *When The Roses Bloom In Dixie*............. 15.00 - 20.00
　16313 *Leaving Town Blues*............................... 15.00 - 25.00
　16317 *Alimony Woman* .... 15.00 - 25.00
　16343 *Travelin' Blues*....................................... 15.00 - 25.00
　16443 *In 1992* .... 15.00 - 25.00

BENTLEY BALL:
Columbia A-3084 *The Gallows Tree* .... 8.00 - 12.00

ERNEST R. BALL:
Hollywood (unnumbered) *West of the Great Divide* ..- - -

WOLFE BALLARD (& CLAUDE SAMUELS):
Broadway; Paramount..4.00 - 8.00
Herwin 75545 *I Want A Pardon For Daddy*........... 15.00 - 20.00

JOHN BALTZELL ("CHAMPION OLD TIME FIDDLER"):
Banner 2151 *Turkey In The Straw* .... 7.00 - 10.00
　2159 *Sailor's Hornpipe*......................................7.00 - 10.00
Conqueror 7741 *The Girl I Left Behind* .... 5.00 - 8.00

Edison 51236, 51354, 51548, 51995, 52022 ....7.00 - 10.00
Edison 52281 *Emmett Quadrille* ....10.00 - 15.00
   52294 *Arkansas Traveler*.................................10.00 - 15.00
   52313 *Flowers Of Edinburgh Hornpipe*............10.00 - 15.00
   52370 *Soldier's Joy Hornpipe* ....10.00 - 15.00
   52395 *My Highland Fling* ....10.00 - 15.00
   52425 *Starlight Waltz* ....15.00 - 20.00
   52450 *S. J. Rafferty Reel* ....15.00 - 20.00
Paramount 3015 *Turkey In The Straw* ....7.00 - 10.00
   3017 *Sailor's Hornpipe* ....7.00 - 10.00

BANG BOYS:
Vocalion 03372 *When Lulu's Gone*.................25.00 - 40.00

BANJO JOE (See also WILLARD HODGIN):
Columbia 15238-D *Engineer Joe* ....20.00 - 30.00

EMMETT BANKSTON & RED HENDERSON:
Okeh 45292 *Six Nights Drunk* ....25.00 - 40.00

GLEN BARBER:
Hallmark 1110 *Styles And Ways Of The World*.........7.00 - 10.00 *
Stampede 104 *Ring Around The Moon*....................7.00 - 10.00 *

JOHNNY BARFIELD (& HOYT BRYANT, ACC. BY BERT LAYNE & GEORGIA SERENADERS):
Bluebird (most issues) ....4.00 - 8.00
Bullet 620 *Doin' The Boogie Woogie*......................8.00 - 12.00
Champion 16406 *Back To My Georgia Home* ....50.00 - 75.00
   16415 *Highway Hobo* ....50.00 - 75.00

JERRY BARLOW:
Lyric 703 *Just Thinking Of You*...............................10.00 - 15.00
O.T. 103 *Louisiana Baby*..10.00 - 15.00

(YODELING) FRANKIE BARNES:
Champion 16366 *Hokey Pokey*...............................7.00 - 10.00
Superior 2746 *Nervy Bum*......................................15.00 - 20.00

H. M. BARNES & HIS BLUE RIDGE RAMBLERS:
Brunswick 310 *Who Broke The Lock On The Hen House Door?*
....8.00 - 12.00
   313 *Old Joe Clark*...8.00 - 12.00
   327 *Goin' Down The Road Feelin' Bad*.............15.00 - 20.00
   361 *Our Director March* ....15.00 - 20.00
   397 *Mandolin Rag* ....15.00 - 20.00
   463 *Honolulu Stomp* ....20.00 - 30.00

THE BARNSTORMERS:
Silverton 5401 *Party Quadrille* ....7.00 - 10.00

BARNYARD STEVE:
Okeh 45366 *Out On The Farm* ....7.00 - 10.00

BARTLETT'S BOOSTERS:
Paramount 3245 *The Bumble Bee*...........................10.00 - 15.00

JOHN BARTON:
Broadway 8051, 8052...5.00 - 8.00

KENNETH BARTON (See KENNETH BORTON)

DR. HUMPHREY BATE & HIS POSSUM HUNTERS:
Brunswick 232 *Goin' Up Town* ....20.00 - 30.00
   239 *Billy In The Low Ground* ....20.00 - 30.00
   243 *Bill Pickle Rag* ....20.00 - 30.00
   271 *Old Joe*...20.00 - 30.00
   275 *Greenback Dollar Bill* ....20.00 - 30.00
Vocalion 5238 *Ham Beats All Meat* ....40.00 - 60.00

RAY BATTS:
Bullet 754 *Bear Cat Daddy*................................15.00 - 20.00

BAXTER FAMILY TRIO:
Superior 2557 *I Am Coming Home* ....15.00 - 20.00

JOHNNY BAXTER:
Superior 2811 *I Want My Rib* ....20.00 - 30.00

MUMFORD BEAN & HIS ITAWAMBIANS:
Okeh 45303 *Flow Rain Waltz* ....50.00 - 75.00

JOHNNIE/ JOHNNY BEE:
Talent 744 *Hang-Over Blues* ....8.00 - 12.00
   748 *Warm Red Wine* ....8.00 - 12.00

JERRY BEHRENS:
Okeh 45535 *Drifting In Along* ....15.00 - 25.00
   45564 *Nobody's Business* ....15.00 - 25.00

DICK BELL:
Challenge 425 *Shut Up In Cool Creek Mine*.............5.00 - 8.00

LEE BELL & THE TEXAS PIONEERS:
Imperial 8021 *Sad And Weary* ....8.00 - 12.00
   8031 *Bring A Little Sunshine* ....8.00 - 12.00

BENTLEY BOYS:
Columbia 15565-D *Henhouse Blues*.....................30.00 - 50.00

JEAN BERTRAND & THE LOUISIANA PLAYBOYS:
Imperial 8043 *Vos Yeux Blues* ....- - -

BEVERLY HILL BILLIES (See also GLEN RICE):
Brunswick 421 *Red River Valley* ....5.00 - 8.00
   441 *My Pretty Quadroon* ....5.00 - 8.00
   455 *Mellow Mountain Moon* ....5.00 - 8.00
   462 *Peek A Boo* ....5.00 - 8.00
   506 *Wonder Valley*...5.00 - 8.00
   514 *Strawberry Roan* ....5.00 - 8.00
   519 *Prairie Skies*..5.00 - 8.00

BIG JEFF & THE RADIO PLAYBOYS:
Dot 1004 *Juke Box Boogie*...................................10.00 - 15.00
   1058 *Step It Up And Go* ....10.00 - 15.00
   1064 *Fast Women, Slow Horses And Wine*..........8.00 - 12.00
   1088 *Move On Baby*..8.00 - 12.00
World Records 1520 *Poppin' Bubble Gum* ....5.00 - 8.00 *

BUD & JOE BILLINGS; BUD BILLINGS TRIO:
Victor 23500, 23534, 23539, 23556, 23706,
   23709, 23715...7.00 - 15.00
Victor 23725 *I Wonder If He's Singing* ....80.00 - 120.00
Victor 23740, 23744, 23784 ....10.00 - 15.00
Victor V40082, V40267, V40299, V40322............5.00 - 10.00

DOUG BINE & HIS DIXIE RAMBLERS:
Bluebird 6677, 6705, 6789, 6847, 8133...................5.00 - 10.00

BINKLEY BROTHERS' DIXIE CLODHOPPERS:
Victor 21758 *All Go Hungry Hash House* ....30.00 - 50.00
   V40048 *Give Me Back My Fifteen Cents* ....35.00 - 50.00
   V40129 *When I Had But Fifty Cents* ....35.00 - 50.00

BIRD'S KENTUCKY CORN CRACKERS:
Victor 23608 *Ship That's Sailing High*...................75.00 - 100.00

CONNIE BIRD:
Gennett 6929 *Little Mamie* ....30.00 - 50.00

ELMER BIRD'S HAPPY FOUR/STRING BAND:
Champion 16421 *Kentucky Stomp* ....80.00 - 120.00
   45168 *Kentucky Stomp*...................................40.00 - 60.00

Gennett 7064 *Kentucky Stomp* ....80.00 - 120.00
    7182 *Muscle Shoals Blues* ....80.00 - 120.00
Superior 2598 *Sleepy Creek* ....80.00 - 120.00

LOUIS BIRD:
Vocalion 5428 *It's Funny What Whiskey Will Do* ...20.00 - 30.00

NAT BIRD & TOM COLLINS:
Brunswick 376 *Hornpipe Medley* ....10.00 - 15.00

L. O. BIRKHEAD & R. M. LANE:
Columbia 15757-D *Robinson County* ....75.00 - 100.00

JASPER BISBEE:
Edison 51381, 51382 ....5.00 - 10.00

BILLY BISHOP:
Champion 15331 *Medley Of Old Favorites* ....4.00 - 7.00
Gennett 6203 *Medley Of Old Favorites* ....5.00 - 8.00
Supertone 9171 *Medley Of Old Favorites* ....4.00 - 7.00

LESTER PETE BIVINS:
Bluebird 6886, 6950 ....5.00 - 8.00

BLACK BROTHERS:
Okeh 45244, 45253, 45270, 45296, 45312, 45336,
    45345, 45374, 45487, 45493, 45572 ....5.00 - 10.00

JIMMY BLACK:
Okeh 45275, 45298 ....5.00 - 10.00

DAD BLACKARD'S MOONSHINERS:
Victor 21130 *Sandy River Belle* ....30.00 - 50.00

CHARLEY BLAKE:
Supertone 9476 *Daddy And Home* ....10.00 - 15.00
    9489 *Back Home In Tennessee* ....10.00 - 15.00
    9534 *California Blues* ....10.00 - 15.00
    9540 *Go 'Long Mule No. 2* ....10.00 - 15.00
    9556 *She'll Be Coming 'Round The Mountain* ...10.00 - 15.00
    9559 *Jackson County* ....10.00 - 15.00
    9600 *Alabama Blues* ....10.00 - 15.00
    9641 *I Love The Jailer's Daughter* ....10.00 - 15.00
    9714 *My Old Log Cabin Home* ....10.00 - 15.00
    9722 *The Yodeling Cowboy* ....10.00 - 15.00
    9724 *My Rough And Rowdy Ways* ....10.00 - 15.00

CURLEY BLAKE: (See CHARLEY BLAKE)

GUY BLAKEMAN & HIS BLUE GRASS SERENADERS:
Chess 1525 *I Ain't Gonna Give Nobody None Of My Jelly Roll*
....7.00 - 10.00 *

BLALOCK & YATES:
Columbia 15576-D *Pride Of The Ball* ....25.00 - 40.00

DAN BLANCHARD:
Champion 15526 *The West Plains Explosion* ....7.00 - 10.00
    15578 *Just A Little West Of West Virginia* ....7.00 - 10.00

BLANKENSHIP FAMILY:
Victor 23583 *Jack And Mae* ....40.00 - 60.00

FRANK BLEVINS' TAR HEEL RATTLERS:
Columbia 15210-D *Old Aunt Betsy* ....100.00 - 150.00
    15280-D *Nine Pound Hammer* ....100.00 - 150.00
    15765-D *I've Got No Honey Babe Now* ....150.00 - 250.00
Velvet Tone 7101-V *Old Aunt Betsy* ....100.00 - 150.00
    7103-V *Fly Around My Pretty Little Miss* ......100.00 - 150.00

RUBYE BLEVINS:
Bluebird 5404, 5973 ....5.00 - 10.00

BLIND ANDY (See also ANDREW JENKINS):
Okeh 40393 *Floyd Collins In The Sand Cave* ....5.00 - 8.00
    45007 *The Little Newsboy* ....5.00 - 8.00
    45043 *Charming Billy* ....5.00 - 8.00
    45197 *Little Marian Parker* ....5.00 - 8.00
    45319 *The Alabama Flood* ....7.00 - 10.00
    45343 *Tragedy On Daytona Beach* ....8.00 - 12.00
    45347 *Ramblin' Yodel Sam* ....8.00 - 12.00
    45454 *Stop And Look For The Train* ....10.00 - 15.00
Okeh (special) unnumbered (master #403814) *"Hello World Song"*
....- -

BLUE BOYS:
Okeh 45314 *Memphis Stomp* ....75.00 - 100.00

BLUE RIDGE CORNSHUCKERS:
Victor 20835 *Old Time Corn Shuckin'* ....20.00 - 30.00

BLUE RIDGE DUO (GENE AUSTIN & GEORGE RENEAU):
Edison 51422 *Little Brown Jug* ....8.00 - 12.00
    51498 *Life's Railway To Heaven* ....8.00 - 12.00
    51502 *Turkey In The Straw* ....8.00 - 12.00
    51515 *Blue Ridge Blues* ....8.00 - 12.00

BLUE RIDGE HIGHBALLERS (LED BY CHARLEY LA PRADE, FIDDLER):
Columbia 15070-D *Under The Double Eagle* ....15.00 - 25.00
    15081-D *Fourteen Days In Georgia* ....15.00 - 25.00
    15089-D *Round Town Girls* ....15.00 - 25.00
    15096-D *Going Down To Lynchburg Town* .....15.00 - 25.00
    15132-D *Darned* ....15.00 - 25.00
    15168-D *Soldier's Joy* ....15.00 - 25.00
Paramount 3077 *I'm Tired Of Living Here Alone* ...15.00 - 25.00
    3083 *Red Wing* ....15.00 - 25.00

BLUE RIDGE HILLBILLIES:
Bluebird 6541, 6609, 6786, 7070 ....5.00 - 8.00

BLUE RIDGE MOUNTAINEER:
Edison 51832 *The Sinking Of The Titanic* ....15.00 - 20.00

BLUE RIDGE MOUNTAINEERS:
Gennett 6870 *Old Flannigan* ....25.00 - 40.00

BLUE RIDGE MOUNTAIN ENTERTAINERS:
Conqueror 7942 *Goodnight Waltz* ....7.00 - 10.00

BLUE RIDGE MOUNTAIN GIRLS:
Champion 16701 *The First Whippoorwill Song* .....30.00 - 50.00
    16715 *Woman's Answer To 21 Years* ....30.00 - 50.00
    16743 *She Came Rolling Down The Mountain* ...30.00 - 50.00
    16752 *New Answer To 21 Years* ....30.00 - 50.00
    16763 *My Heart Is Where The Mohawk Flows* .30.00 - 50.00
    16778 *When It's Prayer Meetin' Time In The Hollow*
....30.00 - 50.00
    16795 *Memories Of That Silver Haired Daddy* .30.00 - 50.00
Champion 45077, 45083, 45090, 45100, 45198 ....7.00 - 10.00

BLUE RIDGE MOUNTAIN SINGERS:
Columbia 15550-D *Lorena* ....20.00 - 30.00
    15580-D *Give My Love To Nell* ....20.00 - 30.00
    15647-D *The Engineer's Last Run* ....20.00 - 30.00
    15678-D *Mansion Of Aching Hearts* ....20.00 - 30.00

BLUE RIDGE PLAYBOYS:
Vocalion 03425, 03526, 03558, 03765 ....5.00 - 10.00

BLUE SKY BOYS TRIO:
Bluebird 6480, 6538, 6567, 6621, 6669, 6714, 6764,
  6808, 6854, 6901, 7113, 7132, 7173, 7311, 7348,
  7411, 7472, 7550, 7661, 7755, 7803, 7878, 7933,
  7984 ....5.00 - 10.00
Bluebird (higher numbers)........................4.00 - 8.00
Montgomery Ward.....................................4.00 - 8.00

BUD BLUE:
Okeh 45254 *A Blind Mother's Prayer* ....7.00 - 10.00

BOA'S PINE CABIN BOYS:
Vocalion 02594 *Hurry, Johnny, Hurry*.................20.00 - 30.00

BOB & MONTE:
Vocalion 5279 *The Utah Trail*................................4.00 - 6.00
  5343 *Old Virginia Lullaby*..............................5.00 - 8.00
  5373 *Back To Hawaii And You*.........................5.00 - 8.00
  5387 *From The Heart Of The West* ....5.00 - 8.00

(LOY) BODINE (& HOWARD KEESEE):
Champion 16305 *I Still Got Ninety-Nine*.................50.00 - 75.00
  16391 *Where The Old Red River Flows* ....50.00 - 75.00
Superior 2608 *Wabash Cannon Ball* ....50.00 - 75.00
  2809 *A Gangster's Warning* ....50.00 - 75.00

"DOCK" BOGGS:
Brunswick 118 *Down South Blues* ....35.00 - 50.00
  131 *Country Blues* ....35.00 - 50.00
  132 *Danville Girl*...35.00 - 50.00
  133 *Hard Luck Blues* ....35.00 - 50.00
Vocalion 5144 *Hard Luck Blues*............................40.00 - 60.00

CAP. M. J. BONNER (THE TEXAS FIDDLER):
Victor 19699 *Medley-Yearling's In The Canebreak etc.*
  ....10.00 - 20.00

BOONE COUNTY ENTERTAINERS:
Supertone 9163 *Arkansas Traveler* ....5.00 - 8.00
  9177 *Fiddlin' Bootleggers*................................10.00 - 15.00
  9181 *The Blind Man And His Child* ....7.00 - 10.00
  9182 *Something Wrong With My Gal*...............7.00 - 10.00
  9492 *Virginia Bootleggers*................................7.00 - 10.00

CLAUDE BOONE (& WALTER HURDT):
Bluebird 7817 *The Poor Widow* ....5.00 - 8.00
  7008 *The Hobo Blues*......................................5.00 - 8.00

REV. EDWARD (& MRS.) BOONE (& MISS OLIVE BOONE):
Gennett 6903 *Will David Play His Harp*.................20.00 - 30.00
  7208 *Springing Up Within My Soul*.................25.00 - 40.00
  7225 *Flowers On The Open Grave*...................25.00 - 40.00
  7248 *Salvation Is For All*...............................25.00 - 40.00
  7321 *A Mansion There For Me* ....35.00 - 50.00
  7322 *The Book That Mother Gave Me* ....35.00 - 50.00
  7323 *Dying On Calvary*...................................35.00 - 50.00

JIMMY BOONE:
Superior 2638 *The Brakeman's Reply* ....20.00 - 30.00
  2661 *Crazy Blues*..20.00 - 30.00
  2698 *Box Car Blues*..20.00 - 30.00
  2742 *The Fatal Run* ....20.00 - 30.00
  2775 *Hobo Jack's Last Ride* ....20.00 - 30.00
  2831 *The Cowboy Song* ....20.00 - 30.00

BOOTS & HIS BUDDIES:
Talent 709 *Poor Little Joe*.....................................7.00 - 10.00

BENNY BORG (THE SINGING SOLDIER):
Columbia 15148-D *I Want A Pardon For Daddy*.....5.00 - 8.00
  15183-D *Pictures From Life's Other Side*...........5.00 - 8.00

GODFREY BORTON:
Bell 1186 *Don't Forget Me, Little Darling* ....5.00 - 8.00
  1187 *Two Little Orphans* ....5.00 - 8.00

KENNETH BORTON:
Challenge 331 *That's What The Old Bachelor's Made Of*
  ....5.00 - 8.00

LEO BOSWELL (& DEWEY BOSWELL):
Columbia 15290-D *The Fatal Rose Of Red* ....7.00 - 10.00
  15469-D *Memory That Time Cannot Erase*.........8.00 - 12.00

(MR. & MRS.) CHRIS BOUCHILLON:
Columbia 15120-D *Talking Blues* ....8.00 - 12.00
  15151-D *Born In Hard Luck* ....8.00 - 12.00
  15178-D *Let It Alone* ....10.00 - 15.00
  15213-D *Christ Visits The Barber Shop* ....10.00 - 15.00
  15244-D *You Look Awful Good To Me*..............10.00 - 15.00
  15262-D *New Talking Blues* ....10.00 - 15.00
  15289-D *I've Been Married Three Times* ....10.00 - 15.00
  15317-D *Oyster Stew* ....15.00 - 20.00
  15345-D *Adam And Eve*...................................15.00 - 20.00
  15373-D *Speed Maniac*....................................15.00 - 20.00
  15508-D *Girls Of Today* ....15.00 - 20.00

BOWERS & LEWIS:
Superior 2659 *Put On Your Old Gray Bonnet* ....15.00 - 25.00

EARL BOWERS:
Superior 2526 *I Tickled Her Under The Chin*........15.00 - 25.00
  2607 *The Contented Hobo* ....15.00 - 25.00

BOWMAN SISTERS:
Columbia 15473-D *My Old Kentucky Home* ....7.00 - 10.00
  15621-D *Old Lonesome Blues* ....15.00 - 20.00

CHARLIE BOWMAN & HIS BROTHERS:
Columbia 15357-D *Gonna Raise The Ruckus Tonight*
  ....20.00 - 30.00
  15387-D *The Moonshiner And His Money* ....20.00 - 30.00
Vocalion 5118 *Hickman Rag* ....30.00 - 50.00
  15377 *Hickman Rag*...30.00 - 50.00

DONNIE BOWSHIER:
King 1219 *We'll Never Part* ....- - -

AARON BOYD:
Champion 15652 *The Santa Barbara Earthquake*.. 12.00 - 18.00

BILL BOYD & HIS COWBOY RAMBLERS:
Bluebird 5608, 5667, 5740, 5788, 5945, 6109, 6119,
  6161, 6177, 6235, 6308, 6323, 6328, 6346, 6351,
  6384, 6420, 6486, 6492, 6523, 6599, 6670, 6694,
  6715, 6731, 6772, 6807, 6889, 6959, 7004, 7006,
  7053, 7088, 7128, 7189, 7260, 7299, 7345, 7437,
  7507, 7521, 7531, 7573, 7624, 7662, 7691, 7739,
  7754, 7788, 7867, 7880, 7910, 7921, 7940, 7971,
  7989, 8081...5.00 - 10.00

JOHN BOYD AND HIS SOUTHERNERS:
Vocalion 03661 *Doin' The Raccoon*.........................7.00 - 10.00

BOYS FROM WILDCAT HOLLOW:
Champion 15633 *The Fiddlin' Bootleggers* ....10.00 - 15.00
  45010 *The Fiddlin' Bootleggers* ....5.00 - 8.00

VERGEL BOZMAN & CIRCLE C BOYS:
O.T. 112 *Troubles, Troubles*..................................8.00 - 12.00

BRANCH & COLEMAN:
Okeh 45556 *My Free Wheelin' Baby* ....30.00 - 50.00
    45561 *Telegraph Shack* ....30.00 - 50.00
    45568 *Since My Darling Went Away*.................30.00 - 50.00

ERNEST BRANCH:
Champion 16286 *Lulu Love*....................................30.00 - 50.00

HOMER BRIARHOPPER:
Bluebird 6903 *If You Ever Had The Blues* ....20.00 - 30.00

BRIER HOPPER (BROTHERS) (See also RED HEADED BRIER HOPPER):
Champion 16648 *Answer To Ninety-Nine Years* .....30.00 - 50.00
    16692 *Bring Back My Blue-Eyed Boy* ....30.00 - 50.00
    16708 *Lorena*..50.00 - 75.00
Champion 45032, 45066..8.00 - 12.00

BILLY BRIGGS:
Imperial 8102, 8104, 8111.......................................7.00 - 12.00

BRITT BROTHERS; BRITT & FORD; ELTON BRITT:
Titles issued contemporaneously on Banner, Melotone, Oriole, Perfect, and Romeo: *Alpine Milkman Yodel; Answer To Ninety-Nine Years; Chime Bells; Dear Old Daddy; Good Night, Little Girl Of My Dreams; In The Hills Of Pennsylvania; I Was Born In The Mountains; My Mother's Tears; Old Fashioned Dipper; There's A Home In Wyoming; When It's Harvest Time In Old New England; When You Played The Old Church Organ; The Wrong Man And The Wrong Woman*...................5.00 - 10.00

MAYNARD BRITTON:
Champion 16543 *The Drunkard's Hell* ....50.00 - 75.00
    45051 *The Drunkard's Hell*................................15.00 - 20.00
Superior 2563 *I Don't Want No Woman*.................50.00 - 75.00
    2524 *Always Blue, Lonesome Too* ....50.00 - 75.00

BROCK SISTERS:
Paramount 3163 *Bring Me Back My Darling* ....20.00 - 30.00

BROCK & DUDLEY:
Columbia 15645-D *I'll Remember You Love* ....15.00 - 20.00

BILLY BROOKS:
Columbia 15614-D *Freight Train Blues*..................25.00 - 50.00

BOB BROOKS:
Columbia 15676-D *Wandering Lamb* ....8.00 - 12.00
    15689-D *Red River Valley*...................................8.00 - 12.00

CHARLIE (C. S.) BROOKS (& CHARLIE TURNER):
Columbia 15733-D *My Mammy's Cabin*.................15.00 - 20.00
    15756-D *Will You Love Me When I'm Old*.........15.00 - 20.00

(RICHARD) BROOKS (& REUBEN PUCKETT):
Brunswick 273 *Long Gone* ....10.00 - 15.00
    281 *She's More To Be Pitied Than Censured* ....10.00 - 15.00
    301 *The Longest Way Home* ....10.00 - 15.00
    317 *All In, Down And Out* ....10.00 - 15.00
Victor 20541 *Something's Going To Happen* ....10.00 - 15.00
    20542 *Hello Central, Give Me Heaven* ....10.00 - 15.00

BROWN'S MUSICAL BROWNIES: (See MILTON BROWN)

BROWN'S HAPPY FOUR:
Champion 16549 *Bootlegger's Dream*...................25.00 - 40.00

BROWN & BUNCH:
Supertone 9375 *Let Her Go, I'll Meet Her* ....8.00 - 12.00
    9443 *My Carolina Home* ....8.00 - 12.00

BROWN, GRAY & DILLY:
Vocalion 5432 *A Fiddlers Tryout In Georgia*.........75.00 - 100.00

HERSAL/HERSHAL/HERSCHEL BROWN & HIS BOYS/ HAPPY FIVE/WASHBOARD BAND; HERSCHEL BROWN & L. K. SENTELL:
Okeh 45247 *New Talking Blues*..............................25.00 - 40.00
    45250 *Home Brew Party*....................................35.00 - 50.00
    45286 *I Wish That Gal Was Mine*....................35.00 - 50.00
    45337 *New Talking Blues No. 2*.......................35.00 - 50.00
    45354 *Alabama Breakdown*................................50.00 - 75.00
    45484 *Spanish Rag* ....50.00 - 75.00
    45494 *County Fair* ....50.00 - 75.00
Victor 21403 *Down Yonder* ....20.00 - 30.00
    V-40070 *Shanghai Rag*......................................50.00 - 75.00

JIMMY BROWN:
Champion 16812 *Keep A Light In Your Window Tonight*
....30.00 - 50.00
    45074 *Keep A Light In Your Window Tonight*.....8.00 - 12.00

(MILTON) BROWN'S (MUSICAL) BROWNIES:
Bluebird 5444 *Oh You Pretty Woman* ....8.00 - 12.00
(Note: Some copies issued as by **FORT WORTH BOYS**.)
    5484, 5558, 5610, 5654, 5690, 5715, 5775, 5808 7.00 - 12.00
Decca (most issues)..5.00 - 8.00

OSCAR BROWN:
Champion 15523 *You're A Little Too Small* ....10.00 - 15.00

STUBBY BROWN:
Imperial 8063 *Night On The Prairie*........................5.00 - 8.00

THOMAS BROWN:
Brunswick 593 *On The Plains Of Texas*...................7.00 - 10.00

BILL BRUNER:
Okeh 45400 *My Pal Of Yesterday*..........................20.00 - 30.00
    45438 *He's In The Jailhouse Now* ....20.00 - 30.00
    45643 *A Gal Like You* ....25.00 - 40.00
    45497 *My Old Home Town Girl* ....25.00 - 40.00

(HOYT) "SLIM" BRYANT (& HIS RIVERSIDERS):
Champion 16407 *Peach Picking Time In Georgia* .50.00 - 75.00
Crown 3384 *Wreck Of The Old 97*..........................15.00 - 20.00
Superior 2812 *The Rabbit Hunt* ....50.00 - 75.00

BUCKEYE BOYS:
Champion 16168 *Duck Foot Sue* ....7.00 - 10.00
    45160, 45200..3.00 - 6.00
Superior 2616 *That Old Fashioned Phonograph*....15.00 - 20.00

BUCK MOUNTAIN BAND:
Okeh 45428 *Don't Let The Blues Get You Down* ...50.00 - 75.00

ALVIN BUNCH:
Supertone 9180 *Only A Miner Killed In The Ground* .....8.00 - 12.00

CARL BUNCH:
Bell 1186 *True And Trembling Brakeman*................8.00 - 12.00

SAM BUNCH:
Supertone 9372 *My Sarah Jane* ....7.00 - 10.00

JACK & JIM BURBANK:
Superior 2741 *Try Not To Forget* ....15.00 - 20.00
    2761 *On The Banks Of The Brandywine*...........15.00 - 20.00
    2825 *Oh Mary Don't You Weep*.......................15.00 - 20.00

JACK BURDETTE & BERT MOSS:
Superior 2696 *That Old Tiger Rag* ....75.00 - 125.00

BURKE BROTHERS:
Victor V40294 *Lonesome And Lonely*......................15.00 - 20.00

(FIDDLIN') JIM BURKE (& JESSE COAT):
Champion 15396 *Cripple Creek*................................5.00 - 8.00
    15449 *Waynesburgh* ....7.00 - 10.00
    15500 *Billy In The Low Ground* ....7.00 - 10.00
    15564 *Smoky Row* ....8.00 - 12.00
    15603 *Brick Yard Joe* ....8.00 - 12.00
    15668 *Shoot That Turkey Buzzard*....................8.00 - 12.00
    15690 *Knoxville Rag*..10.00 - 15.00
    15749 *Jack's Creek Waltz* ....8.00 - 12.00
    15788 *The Devil In Georgia* ....7.00 - 10.00
    15783 *Johnny Inchin' Along*................................7.00 - 10.00
    15921 *Sally Gooden*..7.00 - 10.00
    16027 *Rye Straw*..10.00 - 15.00
    16208 *The Drunken Man's Dream*....................10.00 - 15.00
Silvertone 8179 *And The Cat Came Back* ....6.00 - 10.00
    8185 *Arkansas Traveler*......................................6.00 - 10.00
Supertone 9164 *Buck Creek Gal*.............................6.00 - 10.00
    9165 *And The Cat Came Back*............................6.00 - 10.00
    9168 *Cripple Creek*..6.00 - 10.00
    9169 *Dance With The Girl With The Hole* ....6.00 - 10.00
    9172 *Arkansas Traveler*......................................6.00 - 10.00
    9173 *Brick Yard Joe*...6.00 - 10.00
    9176 *Billy In The Low Ground* ....6.00 - 10.00
    9260 *Knoxville Girl* ....8.00 - 12.00
    9311 *Run Smoke Run* ....7.00 - 10.00
    9355 *New Money* ....7.00 - 10.00
    9390 *The Devil In Georgia* ....7.00 - 10.00
    9650 *Chicken Reel* ....7.00 - 10.00

PETE BURKE TRIO:
Humming Bird 1007 *Super Boogie Woogie* ....- - -

ABNER BURKHARDT:
Champion 15261, 15279, 15356, 15669....................5.00 - 8.00

BURNETT BROTHERS:
Victor 23727 *Old Shoes A-Draggin'* ....15.00 - 20.00
    23730 *Countin' Cross Ties* ....15.00 - 20.00
    23745 *Rockin' Chair*...15.00 - 20.00

BURNETTE & MILLER:
Superior 2764 *Twenty-One Years*............................15.00 - 20.00

BURNETT & RUTHERFORD:
Columbia 15113-D *Pearl Bryan*..............................10.00 - 15.00
    15122-D *Lost John* ....8.00 - 12.00
    15133-D *A Short Life Of Trouble* ....8.00 - 12.00
    15187-D *My Sweetheart In Tennessee* ....8.00 - 12.00
    15209-D *Ladies On A Steamboat* ....8.00 - 12.00
    15204-D *Curley Headed Woman*........................12.00 - 15.00
    15314-D *All Night Long Blues* ....15.00 - 20.00

BURNETTE & RUTTLEDGE:
Columbia 15567-D *Blackberry Blossoms* ....10.00 - 15.00

SMILIE BURNETTE:
Titles issued contemporaneously on Banner, Melotone, Oriole, Perfect, and Romeo include: *He Was A Traveling Man; Mama Don't Like Music; Matilda Higgins; Peg Leg Jack*
....10.00 - 15.00

DAPHNE BURNS:
Paramount 3032 *Weeping Willow Tree*...................10.00 - 15.00

RUBEN BURNS:
Champion 15376 *The Burglar Man* ....10.00 - 15.00
Gennett 6222 *The Burglar Man* ....20.00 - 30.00

(JOHN) BURTON (& BODINE):
Superior 2522 *I Don't Want You Mama* ....50.00 - 75.00
    2573 *Memphis Special Blues* ....50.00 - 75.00
    2618 *Little Old Home Down In New Orleans*.... 50.00 - 75.00
    2672 *Treasure Untold* ....50.00 - 75.00
    2810 *Pal Of My Sunny Days* ....50.00 - 75.00
    2823 *The Longest Train I Ever Saw* ....75.00 - 100.00

RUSSELL & LOUIS BURTON:
Champion 16454 *Down In Tennessee*....................35.00 - 50.00
Superior 2703 *The Old Corn Mill* ....50.00 - 75.00

BUSTER & JACK:
Montgomery Ward 4084 *Guitar Duet Blues*...........15.00 - 20.00
Victor 23257 *Guitar Duet Blues* ....75.00 - 100.00

DWIGHT BUTCHER:
Champion 45187 *Broken Hearted Cowboy* ....10.00 - 15.00
Victor 23772 *Lonesome Cowboy* ....25.00 - 50.00
    23794 *By A Little Bayou* ....25.00 - 50.00
    23802 *Alarm Clock Blues* ....40.00 - 60.00
    23810 *Your Voice Is Calling*........................... 100.00 - 150.00
    23819 *Pistol Pete* ....30.00 - 60.00
    23826 *My Rambling Days Are Over*.................30.00 - 60.00

ALBERT CAIN:
Okeh 45557 *Pickin' On The Old Guitar*................. 30.00 - 50.00
    45567 *Runnin' Wild* ....30.00 - 50.00

CALDWELL BROTHERS:
Supertone 9343 *Somebody's Waiting For Me* ....7.00 - 10.00

CALDWELL & BUNCH:
Superior 2791 *My Bones Is Gonna Rise Again*....... 20.00 - 30.00

BOB CALEN:
Okeh 45372 *Carolina Rolling Stone* ....10.00 - 15.00

HANK CALDWELL & THE SADDLE KINGS:
D'Oro 103 *Alibi* ....- - -

SAM CALDWELL:
Supertone 9185 *The Prisoner's Lament* ....7.00 - 10.00

CALLAHAN BROTHERS; HOMER CALLAHAN; WALTER CALLAHAN:
Titles, issued contemporaneously on Banner, Conqueror, Melotone, Oriole, Perfect, and Romeo *include: Asheville Blues; Brown's Ferry Blues; Cowboy Jack; Days Are Blue; Don't You Remember The Time; Going To Heaven On My Own Expense; Gonna Quit Drinkin' When I Die; Gonna Quit My Rowdy Ways; Green Back Dollar; I Don't Want To Hear Your Name; Katie Dear; Little Poplar Log House On The Hill; Lonesome And Wear Blues; Maple On The Hill; Mean Mama; New Birmingham Jail No. 3; North Carolina Moon; Once I Had A Darling Mother; Rattle Snake Daddy, Rounder's Luck; St. Louis Blues; She's Killing Me; She's My Curley Headed Baby No. 2; T.B. Blues No. 2; True Lover* .... 5.00 - 10.00
Vocalion 02973 *Take The News To Mother* .... 10.00 - 15.00
    03108 *Just One Year*..10.00 - 15.00
    03171 *Freight Train Blues*................................10.00 - 15.00
    03335 *She's My Curley Headed Baby No. 3*...... 10.00 - 15.00
    04358, 04359, 04360, 04361, 04362, 04363........ 5.00 - 10.00

CALOWAY'S WEST VIRGINIA MOUNTAINEERS:
Gennett 6546 *The Corn Shuckers' Frolic* ....20.00 - 30.00

AARON CAMPBELL'S MOUNTAINEERS:
Champion 16689 *The Flying Trapeze* ....10.00 - 15.00
   16740 *Mother's Knee* ....10.00 - 15.00
   16751 *Daisies Won't Tell* ....15.00 - 20.00
   45008,45038,45086 ....4.00 - 8.00

ORAN CAMPBELL:
Champion 15429, 15502 ....5.00 - 8.00

HARMON CANADA:
Gennett 6961 *My Little Home In Tennessee* ....20.00 - 30.00
   6972 *Born In Hard Luck* ....20.00 - 30.00

WARREN CAPLINGER & CUMBERLAND MOUNTAIN ENTERTAINERS/THE DIXIE HARMONIZERS:
Brunswick 224 *Nobody's Business* ....20.00 - 30.00
   241 *Big Ball In Town* ....20.00 - 30.00
Gennett 6915 *The Music Man* ....75.00 - 100.00
Vocalion 5222 *Chicken Reel* ....35.00 - 50.00
   5237 *When The Redeemed Are Gathered In* ....35.00 - 50.00
   5240 *Jerusalem Mourn* ....35.00 - 50.00

KEN CARD:
Champion 45148 *The Last Flight Of Wiley Post* ....8.00 - 12.00

CARLISLE BROTHERS:
Titles issued contemporaneously on Banner, Melotone, Oriole, Perfect, and Romeo include: *The Little Dobie Shack; Looking For Tomorrow; Ramshackled Shack On The Hill; Sunshine And Daisies* ....5.00 - 10.00
Bluebird (most issues) ....5.00 - 10.00

(SMILING) BILL CARLISLE:
Bluebird 6478, 6568, 6600, 6608, 6775, 6938, 7019, 7087, 7153, 7414, 7613 ....5.00 - 10.00
Melotone 7-02-64 *House Cat Mama* ....8.00 - 12.00
(Note: Also issued on Banner, Oriole, Perfect, Romeo)
Vocalion 02520 *Rattle Snake Daddy* ....20.00 - 30.00
   02946 *I'm Gonna Kill Myself* ....20.00 - 30.00

CLIFF/CLIFFORD CARLISLE:
Titles issued contemporaneously on Banner, Conqueror, Melotone, Oriole, Perfect, Romeo include: *Birmingham Jail No. 2, Blue Eyes; Chicken Roost Blues; Desert Blues; Don't Marry The Wrong Woman; Fussin' Mama; Gamblin' Dan; Going Back To Alabama; Hen Pecked Man; I Don't Mind; I'm Glad I'm A Hobo; Just A Lonely Hobo; Louisiana Blues; My Two Time Mama; On The Banks of The Rio Grande; Shanghai Rooster Yodel; Wreck Of No. 52; Written Letter* ....8.00 - 12.00
Additional titles: *The Bunch Of Cactus On The Wall; Casey County Jail; Childhood Dreams; Dang My Rowdy Soul; Dream A Little Dream Of Me; Georgia Moon; Goodbye Old Pal; Lonely Valley; Lonesome For Caroline; Longing For You; Memories That Haunt Me; Memories That Make Me Cry; On The Prairie; Seven Years With The Wrong Woman; When It's Roundup Time In Texas; Where Romance Calls; Won't Somebody Pal With Me* ....7.00 - 10.00
Bluebird 6350 *Rambling Yodeler* ....7.00 - 10.00
   6405 *A Stretch Of 28 Years* ....7.00 - 10.00
   6439 *Cowboy Johnny's Last Ride* ....7.00 - 10.00
   6458 *You'll Miss Me When I'm Gone* ....7.00 - 10.00
   6493 *When I Feel Froggie, I'm Gonna Hop* ......7.00 - 10.00
   6524 *Wigglin' Mama* ....7.00 - 10.00
   6540, 6631, 6647 ....5.00 - 10.00

6754, 6791, 6830, 6855, 6980, 7031, 7094, 7147, 7290, 7702, 7717, 7740, 7790, 7817, 8199, 8228 ......5.00 - 8.00
Champion 15969 *Memphis Yodel* ....15.00 - 20.00
   15992 *Desert Blues* ....15.00 - 20.00
   16028 *Virginia Blues* ....15.00 - 20.00
Champion *I'm Lonely And Blue* ....15.00 - 20.00
   16140 *Crazy Blues* ....15.00 - 20.00
   16165 *No Daddy Blues* ....15.00 - 20.00
   16212 *Box Car Blues* ....20.00 - 30.00
   16239 *High Steppin' Mama* ....20.00 - 30.00
   16270 *Hobo Jack's Last Ride* ....20.00 - 30.00
   16329 *Nobody Wants Me* ....20.00 - 30.00
   16419 *Memories That Haunt Me* ....25.00 - 50.00
   16434 *She's Waiting For Me* ....25.00 - 50.00
   16447 *The Fatal Run* ....25.00 - 50.00
   45029, 45042, 45132, 45134, 45139, 45140, 45147, 45155, 45162, 45179, 45186 ....7.00 - 12.00
Gennett 7153 *Down In The Jailhouse On My Knees* ....25.00 - 40.00
   7187 *Desert Blues* ....25.00 - 40.00
   7206 *Memphis Yodel* ....25.00 - 50.00
   7244 *Virginia Blues* ....30.00 - 60.00
   7288 *I'm Lonely And Blue* ....30.00 - 60.00

CAROLINA BUDDIES:
Columbia 15537-D *The Murder Of The Lawson Family* ....15.00 - 20.00
   15641-D *The Story That The Crow Told Me* .....15.00 - 20.00
   15652-D *Otto Wood The Bandit* ....15.00 - 20.00
   15663-D *Work Don't Bother Me* ....15.00 - 20.00
   15770-D *Mistreated Blues* ....30.00 - 50.00

CAROLINA MANDOLINE BAND:
Okeh 45191 *Georgia Camp Meeting* ....50.00 - 80.00

CAROLINA NIGHT HAWKS:
Columbia 15256-D *Governor Al Smith For President-* ...... - -

CAROLINA RAMBLERS STRING BAND:
Melotone 13047 *Chinese Breakdown* ....7.00 - 10.00

CAROLINA TAR HEELS:
Victor 20544 *I'm Going To Georgia* ....15.00 - 20.00
   20545 *Bring Me A Leaf From The Sea* ....10.00 - 15.00
   20931 *I Love My Mountain Home* ....15.00 - 20.00
   20941 *Bulldog Down In Sunny Tennessee* ....15.00 - 20.00
   21193 *My Mamma Scolds Me* ....40.00 - 60.00
   23516 *Farm Girl Blues* ....40.00 - 60.00
   23546 *The Hen House Door Is Locked* ....40.00 - 60.00
   23611 *Got The Farm Land Blues* ....50.00 - 75.00
   23671 *Nobody Cares If I'm Blue* ....75.00 - 100.00
   23682 *Times Ain't Like They Used To Be* ....75.00 - 100.00
   V40007 *Peg And Awl* ....40.00 - 60.00
   V40024 *Roll On, Boys* ....40.00 - 60.00
   V40053 *I Don't Like The Blues No More* ....40.00 - 60.00
   V40077 *Rude And Rambling Man* ....40.00 - 60.00
   V40100 *My Home's Across The Blue Ridge Mountains* ....40.00 - 60.00
   V40128 *Somebody's Tall And Handsome* ....40.00 - 60.00
   V40177 *The Old Gray Goose* ....40.00 - 60.00
   V40219 *I'll Be Washed* ....40.00 - 60.00

CAROLINA TWINS:
Victor 21363 *Off To War I'm Going* ....25.00 - 40.00
   21575 *One Dark And Rainy Night* ....25.00 - 40.00

23502 *Since My Baby's Gone Away*	25.00 -	40.00
V40044 *When You Go A-Courtin'*	25.00 -	40.00
V40098 *Mr. Brown, Here I Come*	25.00 -	40.00
V40123 *New Orleans Is The Town I Like Best*	25.00 -	40.00
V40243 *Change In Business All Around*	25.00 -	40.00
V40310 *Southern Jack*	30.00 -	50.00

BOYDEN CARPENTER:
Champion 16519 *The Hobos' Convention* ....15.00 - 25.00

JOHN CARPENTER:
Bell 1178 *Sourwood Mountain* ....5.00 - 8.00

CARROLL COUNTY RAMBLERS:
Vocalion 5433 *Georgia Wobble Blues* ....50.00 - 75.00

CARSON BROTHERS & SMITH/SPRINKLE:
Okeh 45013, 45023...8.00 - 12.00
    45398 *The Highway Man*................................10.00 - 15.00

BERT CARSON:
Superior 2520 *My Red Haired Lady* ....15.00 - 20.00

FIDDLIN' JOHN CARSON (& HIS VIRGINIA REELERS/ with MOONSHINE KATE):

Bluebird 5401 *New Comin' Round The Mountain*	10.00 -	15.00
5447 *Stockade Blues*	10.00 -	15.00
5483 *The Storm That Struck Miami*	10.00 -	15.00
5560, 5652, 5742, 5787, 5959, 6022, 6247	5.00 -	10.00
Montgomery Ward 4848, 4849, 4851, 4852	4.00 -	7.00
Okeh 4890 *The Little Old Log Cabin In The Lane*	10.00 -	15.00

(Note: The existence of an unnumbered issue of the above record, of which 500 copies were supposedly pressed, has not been confirmed.)

4994 *Papa's Billy Goat*	10.00 -	15.00
7003 (12-inch) *Sugar In The Gourd*	40.00 -	60.00
7004 (12-inch) *John Henry Blues*	40.00 -	60.00
7006 (12-inch) *The Baggage Coach Ahead*	40.00 -	60.00
7008 (12-inch) *The Lightning Express*	40.00 -	60.00
40020 *Billy In The Low Ground*	8.00 -	15.00
40038 *Casey Jones*	8.00 -	15.00
40050 *Tom Watson Special*	8.00 -	15.00
40071 *The Kickin' Mule*	8.00 -	15.00
40095 *Dixie Boll Weevil*	8.00 -	15.00
40108 *Arkansas Traveler*	8.00 -	15.00
40181 *Ode And In The Way*	10.00 -	15.00
40196 *I'm Nine Hundred Miles From Home*	10.00 -	15.00
40204 *Alabama Gal*	10.00 -	15.00
40230 *Turkey In The Straw*	10.00 -	15.00
40238 *Nancy Rowland*	10.00 -	15.00
40263 *Old Dan Tucker*	10.00 -	15.00
40306 *Steamboat Bill*	10.00 -	15.00
40343 *My North Georgia Home*	10.00 -	15.00
40363 *Charming Betsy*	10.00 -	15.00
40411 *The Honest Farmer*	10.00 -	15.00
40419 *The Boston Burglar*	10.00 -	15.00
40444 *Bully Of The Town*	10.00 -	15.00
40446 *Little Mary Phagan*	10.00 -	15.00
45001 *Run Along Home With Lindy*	10.00 -	15.00
45011 *Soldier's Joy*	10.00 -	15.00
45018 *Hell Broke Loose In Georgia*	10.00 -	15.00
45028 *The Grave Of Little Mary Phagan*	10.00 -	15.00
45032 *The Drunkard's Hiccoughs*	10.00 -	15.00
45035 *Liberty*	10.00 -	15.00
45040 *Georgia Wagner*	10.00 -	15.00
45045 *Everybody Works But Father*	10.00 -	15.00

45049 *Good-Bye Liza Jane*	10.00 -	15.00
45056 *The Bachelor's Hall*	10.00 -	15.00
45068 *Fire In The Mountain*	10.00 -	15.00
45077 *Long Way To Tipperary*	10.00 -	15.00
45096 *Don't Let Your Deal Go Down*	10.00 -	15.00
45122 *Cotton-Eyed Joe*	10.00 -	15.00
45139 *Swanee River*	10.00 -	15.00
45159 *Hell Bound For Alabama*	10.00 -	15.00
45167 *Turkey In The Hay*	10.00 -	15.00
45176 *Engineer On The Mogull*	10.00 -	15.00
45186 *Quit That Ticklin' Me*	10.00 -	15.00
45198 *Old Joe Clark*	10.00 -	15.00
45214 *Going Down To Cripple Creek*	15.00 -	20.00
45249 *Ain't No Bugs On Me*	15.00 -	20.00
45273 *Old And In The Way*	15.00 -	20.00
45290 *John Makes Good Licker*	15.00 -	20.00
45301 *Be Kind To A Man When He's Down*	20.00 -	30.00
45321 *Going To The County Fair*	20.00 -	30.00
45338 *Hawk And Buzzard*	20.00 -	30.00
45353 *My Ford Sedan*	25.00 -	40.00
45369 *John Makes Good Licker, Part 3/4*	20.00 -	30.00
45384 *You'll Never Miss Your Mother, No. 2*	25.00 -	40.00
45402 *Times Are Not Like They Used To Be*	30.00 -	50.00
45415 *Corn Licker And Barbecue, Part 1/2*	30.00 -	50.00
45434 *Sunny Tennessee*	40.00 -	60.00
45440 *Kate's Snuff Box*	40.00 -	60.00
45445 *The Raccoon And The Possum*	40.00 -	60.00
45448 *Who's The Best Fiddler?*	40.00 -	60.00
45458 *John In The Army*	40.00 -	60.00
45471 *The Last Old Dollar Is Gone*	50.00 -	75.00
45488 *On The Banks Of Old Tennessee*	50.00 -	75.00
45498 *The Dominicker Duck*	50.00 -	75.00
45513 *My Home In Dixie-Land*	50.00 -	75.00
45542 *Take The Train To Charlotte*	50.00 -	75.00
45555 *I Intend To Heaven My Home*	50.00 -	75.00
45569 *Didn't He Ramble*	50.00 -	75.00

ROSA LEE CARSON:
Okeh 45005 *The Drinker's Child* ....10.00 - 15.00

CARTER BROTHERS (& SON):

Okeh 45202 *Saddle Up The Grey,*	15.00 -	25.00
45289 *Give The Fiddler A Drum*	15.00 -	25.00
Vocalion 5295 *Give Me A Chaw Tobacco*	50.00 -	75.00
5297 *Jenny On The Railroad*	50.00 -	75.00

CARTER FAMILY:
Titles issued contemporaneously on Banner, Conqueror, Melotone, Oriole, Perfect, and Romeo: *Broken Hearted Lover, By The Touch Of Her Hand; Cannon Ball Blues; Can The Circle Be Unbroken; East Virginia Blues No. 2; The Fate Of Dewey Lee; Gathering Flowers On The Hillside; Glory To The Lamb; God Gave Noah The Rainbow Sign; He Took A White Rose From Her Hair; I'm Thinking Tonight Of My Blue Eyes; Keep On The Sunny Side; Kissing Is A Crime, Let's Be Lovers Again; Little Darling Pal Of Mine; On The Rocks Where Moses Stood; River Of Jordan; Worried Man Blues* ....8.00 - 12.00

Bluebird 5006 *Keep On The Sunny Side*	8.00 -	12.00
5058 *Where We'll Never Grow Old*	8.00 -	12.00
5096 *Meet Me By The Moonlight Alone*	8.00 -	12.00
5122 *When The Springtime Comes Again*	8.00 -	12.00
5161 *Will The Roses Bloom In Heaven?*	8.00 -	12.00
5185 *Amber Tresses*	8.00 -	12.00
5243 *Mid The Green Fields Of Virginia*	8.00 -	12.00
5272 *God Gave Noah The Rainbow Sign*	8.00 -	12.00

5301 *My Clinch Mountain Home*	8.00 -	12.00
5356 *Wildwood Flower*	7.00 -	10.00
5406 *Anchored In Love*	7.00 -	10.00
5468 *Sow 'Em On The Mountain*	7.00 -	10.00
5529 *I'll Be All Smiles Tonight*	7.00 -	10.00
5543 *A Distant Land To Roam*	7.00 -	10.00
5586 *Darling Daisies*	7.00 -	10.00
5650 *The East Virginia Blues*	7.00 -	10.00
5716 *I'm Working On A Building*	7.00 -	10.00
5771 *One Little Word*	7.00 -	10.00
5817 *I'll Aggravate Your Soul*	7.00 -	10.00
5856 *Longing For Old Virginia*	7.00 -	10.00
5908 *My Heart's Tonight In Texas*	7.00 -	10.00
5911 *I'll Be Home Some Day*	7.00 -	10.00
5924 *Little Moses*	7.00 -	10.00
5927 *Lulu Wall*	7.00 -	10.00
5956 *The Mountains Of Tennessee*	7.00 -	10.00
5961 *On A Hill Lone And Gray*	7.00 -	10.00
5974 *Sailor Boy*	7.00 -	10.00
5990 *Kitty Waltz*	7.00 -	10.00
5993 *The Church In The Wildwood*	7.00 -	10.00
6000 *Lonesome For You*	7.00 -	10.00
6020 *Worried Man Blues*	7.00 -	10.00
6033 *Diamonds In The Rough*	7.00 -	10.00
6036 *Carter's Blues*	7.00 -	10.00
6053 *When I'm Gone*	7.00 -	10.00
6055 *Where Shall I Be?*	7.00 -	10.00
6106 *Two Sweethearts*	7.00 -	10.00
6117 *Lonesome Valley*	7.00 -	10.00
6176 *Fond Affection*	7.00 -	10.00
6223 *Engine One-Forty-Three*	7.00 -	10.00
6257 *I Never Loved But One*	7.00 -	10.00
6271 *Little Log Cabin By The Sea*	7.00 -	10.00
6762 *The Carter Family & Jimmie Rodgers In Texas*	10.00 -	15.00
8350 *Wabash Cannon Ball*	7.00 -	10.00
8868 *Dark And Stormy Weather*	7.00 -	10.00
Decca 5240 *My Dixie Darling*	7.00 -	10.00
5241 *My Native Home*	7.00 -	10.00
5242 *No Depression*	7.00 -	10.00
5254 *Just Another Broken Heart*	7.00 -	10.00
5263 *My Honey Lou*	7.00 -	10.00
5283 *You've Been A Friend To Me*	7.00 -	10.00
5304 *Bonnie Blue Eyes*	7.00 -	10.00
5318 *Sweet Heaven In My View*	7.00 -	10.00
5359 *In The Shadow Of The Pines*	7.00 -	10.00
5386 *The Last Move For Me*	7.00 -	10.00
5411 *The Only Girl*	7.00 -	10.00
5430 *Lover's Lane*	7.00 -	10.00
5447 *He Never Came Back*	7.00 -	10.00
5452 *Honey In The Rock*	7.00 -	10.00
5467 *Jim Blake's Message*	7.00 -	10.00
5479 *Hello Stranger*	7.00 -	10.00
5494 *Lord I'm In Your Care*	7.00 -	10.00
5518 *Broken Down Tramp*	7.00 -	10.00
5532 *Goodbye To The Plains*	7.00 -	10.00
5565 *Stern Old Bachelor*	7.00 -	10.00
5579 *Happy In The Prison*	7.00 -	10.00
5596 *Coal Miner's Blues*	7.00 -	10.00
5612 *Who's That Knockin' On My Window*	7.00 -	10.00
5632 *Little Joe*	7.00 -	10.00
5649 *Bring Back My Boy*	7.00 -	10.00
5662 *Cuban Soldiers*	7.00 -	10.00

5677 *Farewell Nellie*	7.00 -	10.00
5692 *You Are My Flower*	7.00 -	10.00
5702 *Charlie And Nellie*	7.00 -	10.00
5722 *Reckless Motorman*	7.00 -	10.00
Montgomery Ward (Many titles, same as on Bluebird and Victor, valued approximately the same as Bluebird issues)	5.00 -	10.00
Victor 20877 *The Poor Orphan Child*	10.00 -	15.00
20937 *Storms Are On The Ocean*	10.00 -	15.00
21074 *Little Log Cabin By The Sea*	10.00 -	15.00
21434 *Keep On The Sunny Side*	10.00 -	15.00
21517 *Chewing Gum*	10.00 -	15.00
21638 *Will You Miss Me When I'm Gone?*	10.00 -	15.00
23513 *On The Rock*	25.00 -	40.00
23523 *Where Shall I Be?*	25.00 -	40.00
23541 *Lonesome Valley*	25.00 -	40.00
23554 *There's Someone A Waiting For Me*	30.00 -	50.00
23569 *Can't Feel At Home*	30.00 -	50.00
23574 *Jimmie Rodgers Visits The Carter Family*	30.00 -	50.00
23585 *Sow 'Em On The Mountain*	30.00 -	50.00
23599 *My Old Cottage Home*	40.00 -	60.00
23618 *Let The Church Roll On*	40.00 -	60.00
23626 *Weary Prodigal Son*	40.00 -	60.00
23641 *Dying Soldier*	40.00 -	60.00
23656 *I Have Never Loved But One*	40.00 -	60.00
23672 *Where We'll Never Grow Old*	40.00 -	60.00
23686 *'Mid The Green Fields Of Virginia*	50.00 -	75.00
23701 *Amber Tresses*	50.00 -	75.00
23716 *Carter's Blues*	50.00 -	75.00
23731 *Wabash Cannon Ball*	75.00 -	100.00
23748 *Will The Roses Bloom In Heaven?*	75.00 -	100.00
23761 *Sweet As The Flowers In May Time*	75.00 -	100.00
23776 *The Church In The Wildwood*	75.00 -	100.00
23791 *Two Sweet Hearts*	75.00 -	100.00
23807 *I Wouldn't Mind Dying*	80.00 -	120.00
23821 *Gold Watch And Chain*	80.00 -	120.00
23835 *I Loved You Better Than I Know*	100.00 -	150.00
23845 *On The Sea Of Galilee*	100.00 -	150.00
V40000 *Wildwood Flower*	15.00 -	25.00
V40036 *I Have No One*	15.00 -	25.00
V40058 *Foggy Mountain Top*	20.00 -	30.00
V40089 *Engine One-Forty-Three*	20.00 -	30.00
V40110 *Little Moses*	20.00 -	30.00
V0126 *Sweet Fern*	20.00 -	30.00
V0150 *Diamonds In The Rough*	20.00 -	30.00
V40190 *Bring Back My Blue-Eyed Boy*	25.00 -	40.00
V40207 *The Homestead On The Farm*	30.00 -	50.00
V40229 *When The Roses Bloom In Dixieland*	30.00 -	50.00
V40255 *Western Hobo*	30.00 -	50.00
V40277 *Lover's Farewell*	30.00 -	50.00
V40293 *When The World's On Fire*	30.00 -	50.00
V40317 *Worried Man Blues*	40.00 -	60.00
V40328 *Don't Forget This Song*	50.00 -	75.00

(Note: The prices quoted herein are for records in excellent condition. It is particularly appropriate to restate this here, because many of the foregoing records are plentiful in worn condition, and are usually found in that state. Worn copies are worth nominal sums at most, and are probably unsaleable at any price.)

Vocalion 02990 *Broken Hearted Lover*	20.00 -	30.00
03027 *Can The Circle Be Unbroken*	15.00 -	20.00
03112 *Lonesome Valley*	15.00 -	20.00
03160 *The Storms Are On The Ocean*	15.00 -	20.00
04390 *Don't Forget Me Little Darling*	15.00 -	20.00

(BUSTER) CARTER & (PRESTON) YOUNG:
Columbia 15690-D *I'll Roll In My Sweet Baby's Arms*
....50.00 - 75.00
   15702-D *It Won't Hurt No More* ....50.00 - 75.00
   15758-D *Bill Morgan And His Gal* ....50.00 - 75.00

FLOYD CARTER:
Oriole 8847 *Flemington Kidnap Trial* ....7.00 - 10.00

WILF CARTER:
Bluebird 5536, 5545, 5871, 6009, 6107, 6208, 6380,
   6814, 6826, 6827 ....5.00 - 10.00
Bluebird (lower numbers/Canadian issues) ....5.00 - 10.00
Bluebird (higher numbers)..3.00 - 6.00

CARTWRIGHT BROTHERS:
Columbia 15220-D *Kelly Waltz*...............................5.00 - 10.00
   15346-D *On The Old Chisholm Trail*..................8.00 - 12.00
   15410-D *Utah Carroll* ....8.00 - 12.00
   15677-D *Over The Waves* ....15.00 - 20.00
Victor V40147 *San Antonio*....................................10.00 - 15.00
   V40198 *The Dying Ranger* ....10.00 - 15.00
   V40247 *The Wandering Cowboy*........................15.00 - 20.00

CARVER BOYS:
Broadway 8151 *Wang Wang Harmonica Blues* ......80.00 - 120.00
Paramount 3182 *No One To Welcome Me Home* ....75.00 - 100.00
   3198 *The Brave Engineer* ....75.00 - 100.00
   3199 *Tim Brook* ....75.00 - 100.00
   3233 *Simpson County* ....75.00 - 100.00
   12822 *Sisco Harmonica Blues*...........................80.00 - 120.00

CASEY'S OLD TIME FIDDLERS:
Victor 23560 *Casey's Old Time Waltz* ....30.00 - 50.00

CLAUDE CASEY (& THE PINE STATE PLAYBOYS):
Bluebird 7863, 7883 ....5.00 - 8.00

ELRY CASH:
Columbia 15399-D *My Old New Hampshire Home* 10.00 - 15.00
   15457-D *Then My Love Began To Wane*............10.00 - 15.00

CASS COUNTY BOYS:
Bluebird 8006, 8824 ....5.00 - 10.00

BILLY CASTEEL WITH SILVER SAGE BUCKAROOS:
Hot Wax 1614 *Hollywood Mama* ....7.00 - 10.00
   1615 *Trifling On Me* ....7.00 - 10.00

THOMPSON CATES:
Paramount 3103 *Curse Of An Aching Heart* ....15.00 - 20.00

CAULEY FAMILY:
Melotone 13113 *New River Train* ....8.00 - 12.00
   13114 *Duplin County Blues*................................8.00 - 12.00
(Note: Probably also issued on Banner, Oriole, Perfect, Romeo)

ROLAND CAULEY & LAKE HOWARD:
Melotone 6-04-54 *Grey Eagle* ....8.00 - 12.00
(Note: Also issued on Perfect)

(JACK) CAWLEY'S (OKLAHOMA) RIDGE RUNNERS:
Victor 23521 *White River Stomp* ....50.00 - 80.00
   23540 *Cross Tie Blues* ....75.00 - 100.00
   23570 *The Vine-Covered Cottage* ....75.00 - 125.00
   V40175 *Ft. Worth Rag* ....75.00 - 100.00
   V40254 *Oklahoma Waltz*....................................75.00 - 100.00

CEDAR CREEK SHEIK:
Bluebird 6467 *Don't Use That Stuff*........................10.00 - 20.00
   6528 *She's Totin' Something Good* ....15.00 - 25.00

   6587 *What A Pity* ....15.00 - 25.00
   6634 *Don't Credit My Stuff*...............................15.00 - 25.00
   6939 *Ford V-8*..15.00 - 25.00

CEDAR CREST SINGERS (See also WILLIAM REXROAT):
Vocalion 5294 *Dying For Someone To Love Me*.... 25.00 - 40.00

DICK CHAFFIN:
Hoosier 402 *Little Old Band Of Gold* .... - - -

LEON CHAPPELEAR (THE LONE STAR COWBOY):
Champion 16497 *Little Joe The Wrangler*.............. 30.00 - 50.00
   45068 *Little Joe The Wrangler* .... 10.00 - 15.00
   45167 *Trifling Mama Blues* .... 10.00 - 15.00

CHARLESTON ENTERTAINERS:
Supertone 9718 *Wait Till The Sun Shines Nellie* ...... 5.00 - 8.00

CHEZZ CHASE:
Paramount 3178 *Log Cabin Blues* .... 5.00 - 8.00

CHENOWETH'S CORNFIELD SYMPHONY ORCHESTRA:
Okeh 45025 *Arkansaw Wampus Cat* .... 40.00 - 60.00

CHEROKEE RAMBLERS:
Decca 5402 *Back Up And Push* .... 5.00 - 8.00

TED CHESNUT:
Gennett 6480 *The Letter From Home* .... 20.00 - 30.00
   6513 *The Death Of J. B. Marcum* .... 20.00 - 30.00
   6603 *Bring Back My Boy* .... 20.00 - 30.00
   6638 *The Drunkard's Doom* .... 20.00 - 30.00
   6673 *Only A Tramp*.. 20.00 - 30.00

CHIEF SHUNATONA, DOUG MATAGUE, AND SNOOKUM:
Columbia 15781-D *Cowboy Tom's Roundup* .... 75.00 - 125.00

CHILDERS & WHITE:
Okeh 45208 *Red River Valley*................................. 7.00 - 10.00
   45213 *Don't Grieve Your Mother* .... 7.00 - 10.00

BILL CHILDERS:
Okeh 45203 *Bury Me Not On The Lone Prairie* .... 7.00 - 10.00

(MR. & MRS.) W. C. CHILDERS:
Champion 16467 *Strawberry Roan* .... 15.00 - 20.00
   45103, 45166.. 4.00 - 7.00
Gennett 6931 *The Grand Roundup* .... 15.00 - 20.00
   6943 *Over The Hills To The Poor House* .... 15.00 - 20.00
   6973 *Our Mother's Always Waiting* .... 15.00 - 20.00
   7021 *Workin' Habits* .... 15.00 - 20.00
   7066 *Crepe On The Little Cabin Door* .... 15.00 - 20.00
   7113 *I'll Smoke My Long Stemmed Pipe* .... 20.00 - 30.00
   7223 *Two Little Girls In Blue* .... 20.00 - 30.00
   7292 *The Prison Warden's Secret* .... 20.00 - 30.00
Paramount 3181 *Amber Tresses Tied In Blue* .... 15.00 - 20.00

LEW CHILDRE:
Champion 16011 *Moonshine Blues* .... 30.00 - 50.00
Gennett 7183 *Moonshine Blues* .... 40.00 - 60.00
   7312 *The Old Grey Mare* .... 40.00 - 60.00

BILL CHITWOOD (& GEORGIA MOUNTAINEERS/BUD LANDRESS):
Brunswick 2884 *Furniture Man* .... 5.00 - 8.00
Okeh 45100 *Fourth Of July At The County Fair* .... 10.00 - 15.00
   45110 *Smiling Watermelon* .... 10.00 - 15.00

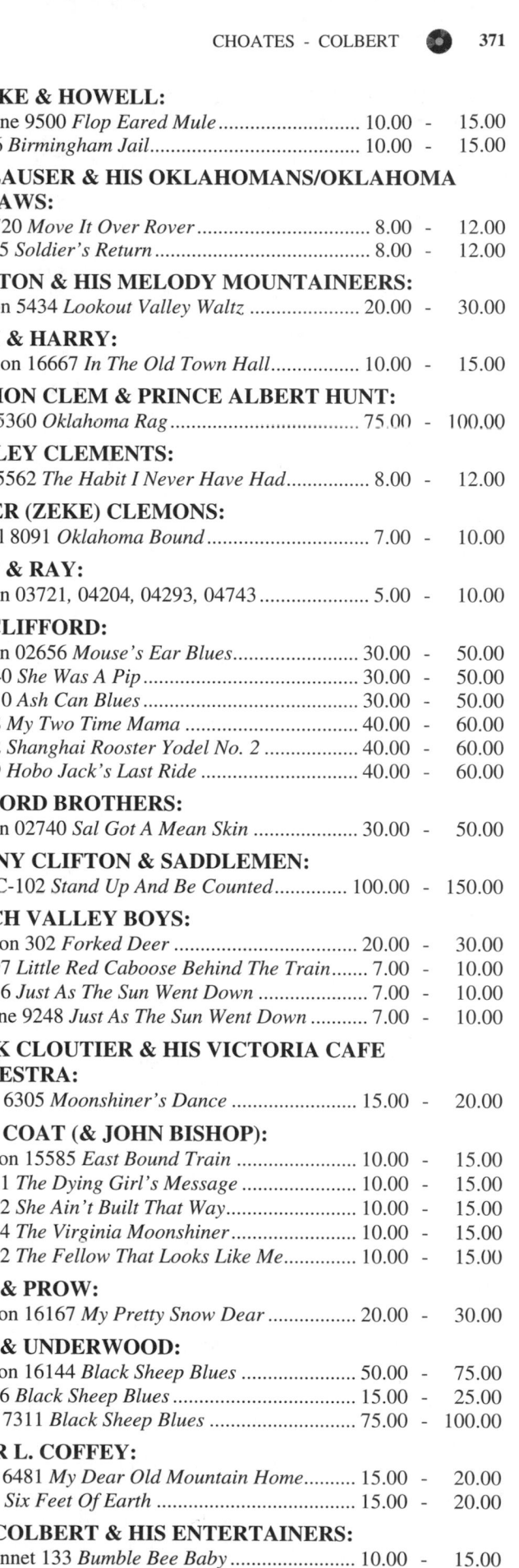

45131 *Preacher Blues*...10.00 - 15.00
45162 *Kitty Hill* ....10.00 - 15.00
45236 *Bill Wishes He Was Single Again* ....10.00 - 15.00
Silvertone 3048 *Howdy Bill* ....7.00 - 10.00
3049 *Over The Sea* ....7.00 - 10.00
3050 *Hen Cackle* ....7.00 - 10.00

HARRY CHOATES:
Allied 103, 104 ....8.00 - 12.00
Cajun Classics 1007/1010 *Hackberry Hop*.............10.00 - 15.00
Gold Star 1314, 1319, 1326, 1330, 1333, 1335, 1336,
　1343, 1380, 1385, 1388 ....7.00 - 12.00
Macy's 124, 134, 141, 147, 158 ....8.00 - 12.00

BEN CHRISTIAN & HIS TEXAS COWBOYS:
Four Star 1270 *Moonlight Island*.........................7.00 - 10.00
Melody 501 *You Played The Game And Lost*...........8.00 - 12.00
502 *Moonlight Island*...................................8.00 - 12.00

HOMER CHRISTOPHER (& RANEY VAN WINK/& WIFE):
Okeh 45041 *Southern Railroad* ....7.00 - 10.00
45097 *Red Wing* ....5.00 - 8.00
45117 *Going Slow* ....7.00 - 10.00
45138 *Hilo March* ....7.00 - 10.00
45147 *Home Town Rag* ....7.00 - 10.00
45195 *Old Fashioned Waltz* ....7.00 - 10.00
45277 *March In "D"* ....7.00 - 10.00
Victor 20656 *Lost Mamma Blues* ....8 00 - 12.00
21128 *Going Slow* ....5.00 - 8.00

CHUCK WAGON GANG:
Banner, Conqueror, Melotone, Oriole, Perfect, Romeo (various
　titles) ....5.00 - 10.00
Vocalion 02938, 03028, 03224, 03434, 03472,
　04105, 04342 ....5.00 - 10.00

CHUMBLER'S BREAKDOWN GANG:
Q.R.S. 9016 *May I Sleep In Your Barn Tonight?* ....75.00 - 100.00

CHUMBLER FAMILY:
Columbia 15481-D *Jacobs Ladder*.......................15.00 - 20.00
15513-D *I'm Going Home To My Wife* ....20.00 - 30.00

GENE CLARDY & STAN CLEMENTS:
Vocalion 5418 *Black Mustache* ....10.00 - 15.00
5462 *Sleeping Time Waltz* ....10.00 - 15.00

CLARK BROTHERS (See JOHN CLARK)

DUKE CLARK:
Champion 16470 *Make A Change In Business*........50.00 - 80.00
16565 *Thirty Minutes Behind The Time* ....50.00 - 80.00
16624 *11:29 Blues* ....75.00 - 100.00
Superior 2687 *The Wreck Of The F. F. & V.* ....50.00 - 100.00

FRANK CLARK:
Champion 15946 *Sad And Lonely Blues* ....15.00 - 25.00

JOHN CLARK:
Champion 15565 *The Prisoner's Lament*...................8.00 - 12.00
15586 *Falling By The Wayside* ....8.00 - 12.00

LUTHER B. CLARK (Acc. by BLUE RIDGE HIGHBALLERS):
Columbia 15069-D *Bright Sherman Valley*.............10.00 - 15.00
15096-D *Wish To Lord I Had Never Been Born* 10.00 - 15.00

THEO. & GUS CLARK:
Okeh 45339 *Wimbush Rag* ....40.00 - 60.00

CLARKE & HOWELL:
Supertone 9500 *Flop Eared Mule* ....10.00 - 15.00
9536 *Birmingham Jail*....................................10.00 - 15.00

AL CLAUSER & HIS OKLAHOMANS/OKLAHOMA OUTLAWS:
Bullet 720 *Move It Over Rover* ....8.00 - 12.00
Gulf 105 *Soldier's Return* ....8.00 - 12.00

CLAYTON & HIS MELODY MOUNTAINEERS:
Vocalion 5434 *Lookout Valley Waltz* ....20.00 - 30.00

CLEM & HARRY:
Champion 16667 *In The Old Town Hall*................10.00 - 15.00

HARMON CLEM & PRINCE ALBERT HUNT:
Okeh 45360 *Oklahoma Rag* ....75.00 - 100.00

STANLEY CLEMENTS:
Okeh 45562 *The Habit I Never Have Had*...............8.00 - 12.00

HOMER (ZEKE) CLEMONS:
Imperial 8091 *Oklahoma Bound* ....7.00 - 10.00

CLIFF & RAY:
Vocalion 03721, 04204, 04293, 04743 ....5.00 - 10.00

BOB CLIFFORD:
Vocalion 02656 *Mouse's Ear Blues*......................30.00 - 50.00
02740 *She Was A Pip* ....30.00 - 50.00
02910 *Ash Can Blues* ....30.00 - 50.00
5488 *My Two Time Mama* ....40.00 - 60.00
5492 *Shanghai Rooster Yodel No. 2* ....40.00 - 60.00
5499 *Hobo Jack's Last Ride* ....40.00 - 60.00

CLIFFORD BROTHERS:
Vocalion 02740 *Sal Got A Mean Skin* ....30.00 - 50.00

JOHNNY CLIFTON & SADDLEMEN:
Center C-102 *Stand Up And Be Counted*..............100.00 - 150.00

CLINCH VALLEY BOYS:
Champion 302 *Forked Deer* ....20.00 - 30.00
15297 *Little Red Caboose Behind The Train*.......7.00 - 10.00
15316 *Just As The Sun Went Down* ....7.00 - 10.00
Supertone 9248 *Just As The Sun Went Down* ....7.00 - 10.00

FRANK CLOUTIER & HIS VICTORIA CAFE ORCHESTRA:
Gennett 6305 *Moonshiner's Dance* ....15.00 - 20.00

JESSE COAT (& JOHN BISHOP):
Champion 15585 *East Bound Train* ....10.00 - 15.00
15611 *The Dying Girl's Message* ....10.00 - 15.00
15712 *She Ain't Built That Way*........................10.00 - 15.00
15854 *The Virginia Moonshiner* ....10.00 - 15.00
15922 *The Fellow That Looks Like Me*..............10.00 - 15.00

COBB & PROW:
Champion 16167 *My Pretty Snow Dear* ....20.00 - 30.00

COBB & UNDERWOOD:
Champion 16144 *Black Sheep Blues* ....50.00 - 75.00
45146 *Black Sheep Blues* ....15.00 - 25.00
Gennett 7311 *Black Sheep Blues* ....75.00 - 100.00

OSCAR L. COFFEY:
Gennett 6481 *My Dear Old Mountain Home*..........15.00 - 20.00
6496 *Six Feet Of Earth* ....15.00 - 20.00

TINY COLBERT & HIS ENTERTAINERS:
Blue Bonnet 133 *Bumble Bee Baby* ....10.00 - 15.00
150 *Our Own Sweet Baby Boy*........................7.00 - 10.00
Colonial 109 *Stand In Line And Take Your Turn* .....5.00 - 10.00

JAMES COLE STRING BAND:
Vocalion 5226 *I Got A GaL*..................50.00 - 75.00

JIM COLE'S (TENNESSEE) MOUNTAINEERS:
Crown 3102 *I'm Pining For The Pines And Caroline*
....15.00 - 20.00
   3122 *Rocky Mountain Sal*..................15.00 - 20.00
   3142 *Down In The Valley*....................15.00 - 20.00
   3158 *Old Folks' Dance Medley*............15.00 - 20.00
Paramount 3279 *Rocky Mountain Sal*..............25.00 - 40.00

REX COLE'S MOUNTAINEERS:
Melotone 12055 *Wilderness*......................5.00 - 8.00

BERNICE COLEMAN acc. by WEST VIRGINIA RAMBLERS:
Champion 16456 *The Ring My Mother Wore*..........30.00 - 50.00

DUTCH COLEMAN:
Vocalion 5391 *New Ground Blues*............40.00 - 60.00
   5408 *The Clayton Case*......................40.00 - 60.00
   5467 *Gonna Raise Some Bacon At Home*..........40.00 - 60.00

BIFF COLLIE:
Macy's 126 *I Want A Gal (To Cook For Me)*..........15.00 - 20.00

BILL COLLINS:
Victor 20673 *When The Moon Shines*.......................7.00 - 10.00

POP COLLINS & HIS BOYS:
Edison 52426 *The Train That Never Arrived*..........10.00 - 15.00
   52507 *Pappy's Buried On The Hill*...................10.00 - 15.00

UNCLE TOM COLLINS:
Okeh 45119 *Four Sons Of A Gun*..........10.00 - 15.00
   45132 *Little Brown Jug*........................10.00 - 15.00
   45140 *Chicken You Can't Roost Too High For Me*
....10.00 - 15.00

COLT BROTHERS:
Melotone 12106 Eleven More Months & Ten More Days
....5.00 - 8.00
   12314 *Eleven More Months Part 3/4*..............5.00 - 8.00
   12333 *That Goes On For Days And Days*...........5.00 - 8.00
   12348 *Hang It On The Hen House*..............5.00 - 8.00
   12449 *In 1992*..........................5.00 - 8.00
   12458 *Our Home Town Mountain Band*.............5.00 - 8.00
   12483 *Somethin' I Et*........................5.00 - 8.00
   12506 *After The Old Barn Dance*.........5.00 - 8.00
   12601 *The Last Words I Said*................5.00 - 8.00
(Note: Above probably issued contemporaneously on Banner, Oriole, Perfect, Romeo.)

FIDDLIN' COLVIN:
Victor V40271 *Old Lady Blues* ....30.00 - 50.00

HITER COLVIN:
Victor 23815 *Indian War Woop*.............75.00 - 100.00
   V40239 *Rabbit Up The Gum Stump*...................30.00 - 50.00

PETER J. CONLON:
Okeh 45030 *Barn Dance*.............................8.00 - 12.00

CARL CONNER:
Columbia 15076-D *The Story Of Gerald Chapman*..8.00 - 12.00

FRED COOK:
Imperial 8079 *Hitch Hikers Blues*............... - - -

HERB COOK:
Columbia 15729-D *Arkansas Sweetheart*................10.00 - 15.00
   15778-D *Just A Little Happiness*........................10.00 - 15.00

JAMES COOK'S OLD TIME FIDDLERS:
Vocalion 5265 *Medley Of Old Fiddler's Favorites* 15.00 - 20.00

JOE COOK:
Bluebird 5135 *Got That Old Fashioned Love*......... 10.00 - 15.00
   6884 *Sweet Little Girl In Blue*............5.00 - 8.00
   7362 *Nobody Knows My Name*............5.00 - 8.00

COON CREEK GIRLS (See also AUNT JOY HARPER):
Vocalion 04278, 04413, 04504, 04659.............5.00 - 10.00

COON HOLLOW BOYS:
Champion 15748 *Coon Hollow Boys At The Still*...10.00 - 15.00

WALTER COON (& HIS IDY BOYS):
Gennett 7002 *Huskin' Bee*.....................20.00 - 30.00
   7005 *The Boys Best Friend*................20.00 - 30.00
   7079 *Polly Wolly Doodle*.................20.00 - 30.00
   7097 *Fly Away Birdie To Heaven*.......................25.00 - 40.00

CORN COB CRUSHERS:
Champion 16373 *Dill Pickle Rag*..........50.00 - 80.00
   16449 *Lonesome Road Blues*................50.00 - 80.00
   45178 *Lonesome Road Blues*...............15.00 - 20.00

ARTHUR CORNWALL & JOHN GIBSON:
Champion 16429 *Walking The Highway*...............50.00 - 75.00

COUCH & WILKS RAMBLERS:
Bluebird 7552 *Fourteen Days In Georgia*................7.00 - 10.00

COURVILLE & McGEE:
Vocalion 5315 *Courville & McGee Waltz*..............50.00 - 80.00

COX & HENSON:
Champion 16694 *National Blues*............75.00 - 100.00

(BILL) COX & (CLIFF) HOBBS:
Titles issued contemporaneously on Banner, Conqueror, Melotone, Oriole, Perfect, and Romeo include: *Alimony Woman; Barefoot Boy With Boots On; Best Friend I Ever Had; Blue Eyed Sally; Blue Ridge Mountain Blues; Bring Back The Sunshine And Roses; Brown Eyes; Brown's Ferry Blues; The Clouds Gwine Roll Away; The Democratic Donkey; Down In Dixie Land, East Cairo Street Blues; The Fate Of Will Rogers And Wiley Post; Fiddling Soldier; The Ganster's Yodel; Hard Luck Blues; I Get Those Drunken Blues; I Long For Your Love Each Day; Lay My Head Beneath The Rose; Long Chain Charlie Blues; Married Life Blues; Midnight Special; My Gamblin' Days; New Mama, N. R. A. Blues; Ramblin' Hobo; Sally Let Your Bangs Hang Down; Sweethearts And Kisses; Sweet Kentucky Lou; The Trial Of Bruno Hauptmann; When The Women Get In Power; Where The Red Roses Grow; Will And Wiley's Last Flight*...7.00 - 12.00
Champion 45007, 45021, 45092, 45106,
   45141, 45157.......................8.00 - 12.00
Gennett 6928 *California Blues*..............25.00 - 40.00
   6946 *Daddy And Home*..................25.00 - 40.00
   6974 *Hungry Hash House Blues*...................30.00 - 50.00
   7004 *When We Meet On That Beautiful Shore*..30.00 - 50.00
   7037 *Back Home In Tennessee*.........30.00 - 50.00
   7052 *When We Sing Of Home*.................30.00 - 50.00
   7080 *Alabama Blues*.........................40.00 - 60.00
   7155 *I Love The Jailer's Daughter*...................40.00 - 60.00
   7226 *My Rough And Rowdy Ways*...................40.00 - 60.00
   7266 *The Hand Car Yodel*.................40.00 - 60.00
Vocalion 03043, 03161, 03253, 03380..........7.00 - 12.00
   04077, 04148, 04235, 04341, 04454, 04641,
   04811, 04869, 05055......................5.00 - 10.00

RICHARD COX (& HIS NATIONAL FIDDLERS):

Champion 16475 *Sleeping Lulu* ....40.00 - 60.00
16563 *East Tennessee Blues* ....40.00 - 60.00
16693 *Chewing Chawin' Gum* ....75.00 - 100.00
Champion 45040 *It Ain't No Good* ....20.00 - 30.00

GENE CRABB:

Richtone 353 *Truck Stop Lucy* .... - - -

RILEY CRABTREE:

(Star) Talent 719, 724, 756, 761 ....5.00 - 10.00

EDWARD L. CRAIN (THE TEXAS COWBOY):

Columbia 15710-D *Bandit Cole Younger* ....50.00 - 80.00
Crown 3238 *Twenty-One Years* ....10.00 - 15.00
3239 *Little Joe The Wrangler* ....10.00 - 15.00
3250 *Cowboy's Home Sweet Home* ....10.00 - 15.00
3275 *The Old Chisholm Trail* ....10.00 - 15.00

CRAMER BROTHERS:

Broadway 8058 *Love Always Has Its Way* ....15.00 - 20.00
8059 *Sara Jane* ....15.00 - 20.00
8060 *In The Good Old Summertime* ....15.00 - 20.00
8071 *On Top Of Old Smoky* ....15.00 - 20.00
8180 *Simpson County* ....20.00 - 30.00

(BOB) CRANFORD & (ERNEST) THOMPSON (with THE RED FOX CHASERS):

Champion 16243 *That Sweetie Of Mine* ....30.00 - 50.00
16261 *Otto Wood* ....30.00 - 50.00
16490 *Sweet Fern* ....30.00 - 50.00
16676 *Katy Cline* ....50.00 - 75.00
16768 *Two Babes In The Woods* ....50.00 - 75.00
45061, 45097 ....10.00 - 15.00
Gennett 6636 *Stolen Love* ....40.00 - 60.00
6672 *Something Wrong With My Gal* ....40.00 - 60.00
6901 *Little Sweetheart Pal Of Mine* ....40.00 - 60.00
6945 *Devilish Mary* ....40.00 - 60.00
6959 *How I Love My Mabel* ....40.00 - 60.00

AL CRAVER (& CHARLIE WELLS):

Columbia 15031-D, 15034-D, 15044-D, 15046-D,
15049-D, 15053-D, 15056-D, 15060-D, 15065-D,
15086-D, 15098-D, 15109-D, 15121-D, 15126-D,
15135-D, 15146-D, 15169-D, 15192-D, 15218-D,
15223-D, 15251-D, 15256-D ....5.00 - 10.00
15449-D, 15512-D, 15530-D, 15546-D, 15561-D,
15585-D ....7.00 - 12.00

ALVIN CRAWFORD:

Superior 2528 *I Sit Broken Hearted* ....20.00 - 30.00

CRAZY HILL BILLIES BAND:

Okeh 45575 *Danced All Night With A Bottle In My Hand*
....25.00 - 40.00
45579 *Going Down The Road Feeling Bad* ....25.00 - 40.00

CROCKER & CANNON:

Challenge 423 *Two Faithful Lovers* ....5.00 - 8.00

CROCKETT FAMILY MOUNTAINEERS; CROCKETT'S KENTUCKY MOUNTAINEERS:

Brunswick 290 *Hard Cider Song* ....15.00 - 20.00
291 *Medley* ....15.00 - 20.00
353 *Bonaparte's Retreat* ....15.00 - 20.00
394 *After The Ball* ....15.00 - 20.00
Crown 3074 *Lightnin' Express* ....20.00 - 30.00
3075 *Buffalo Gals Medley* ....20.00 - 30.00

3121 *Sweet Betsy From Pike* ....20.00 - 30.00
3172 *Cripple Creek* ....20.00 - 30.00
3188 *Skip To My Lou* ....20.00 - 30.00
Paramount 3277 *Granny's Old Arm Chair* ....50.00 - 75.00
3302 *Roving Gambler* ....50.00 - 75.00
3303 *Take Me Back To Old Kentucky* ....50.00 - 75.00

JOHNNY (& ALBERT) CROCKETT (& CROCKETT'S KENTUCKY MOUNTAINEERS):

Brunswick 372 *Fresno Blues* ....15.00 - 20.00
Crown 3101 *I Was Born About 10,000 Years Ago* . 15.00 - 20.00
Paramount 3278 *The Blind Man's Lament* ....50.00 - 75.00
Specialty 702 *Just A Minute* ....7.00 - 10.00

BALLARD CROSS:

Vocalion 5359 *My Poodle Dog* ....15.00 - 25.00
5377 *The Wabash Cannon Ball* ....15.00 - 25.00
5402 *Down Where The Swanee River Flows* .....15.00 - 25.00

BOB CROSS & HIS TROUBADOURS:

Personality 321/322 *Black Mountain Rag* ....10.00 - 15.00
323/324 *Combination Rag* ....10.00 - 15.00

(HUGH) CROSS (& McCARTT/BOB NICHOLS/RILEY PUCKETT):

Columbia 15143-D *Sweet Rosie O'Grady* ....5.00 - 8.00
15182-D *I'm Going Away From The Cotton Fields*
....5.00 - 8.00
15206-D *Red River Valley* ....5.00 - 8.00
15231-D *The Mansion Of Aching Hearts* ....5.00 - 8.00
15266-D *Where The Morning Glories Grow* ....5.00 - 8.00
15337-D *Clover Blossoms* ....8.00 - 12.00
15365-D *Never No More Blues* ....15.00 - 20.00
15421-D *Go Feather Your Nest* ....15.00 - 20.00
15439-D *Wabash Cannon Ball* ....15.00 - 20.00
15455-D *Gonna Raise A Ruckus Tonight* ....15.00 - 20.00
15458-D *Pretty Little Blue-Eyed Sally* ....10.00 - 15.00
15478-D *Smiles* ....10.00 - 15.00
15480-D *I Left My Gal In The Mountains* ....10.00 - 15.00
15482-D *Kickapoo Medicine Show* ....15.00 - 20.00
15613-D *My Little Home In Tennessee* ....20.00 - 30.00

CROWDER BROTHERS:

Titles issued contemporaneously on Banner, Conqueror, Melotone, Oriole, Perfect, and Romeo include: *Blonde Headed Baby; Depot Blues; Dying In Ashville Jail; Got No Use For Women; Lonesome Lost Gal Blues; New Maple On The Hill; The Sailing Ship*
....10.00 - 15.00
Vocalion 03030 *Got No Use For Women* ....10.00 - 15.00

(PAUL) CRUTCHFIELD (& CLOTWORTHY):

Okeh 45261 *Death's River* ....10.00 - 15.00
45266 *Uncle Hiram's Trip To The City* ....10.00 - 15.00

CRUTHERS BROTHERS:

Okeh 45307 *Carolina Moon* ....7.00 - 10.00

CRYSEL BOYS with ALLEN BULLARD:

Titles issued contemporaneously on Banner, Melotone, Oriole, Perfect, and Romeo: *Crazy Blues; My Gal Kate*
....10.00 - 15.00

CRYSTAL SPRINGS RAMBLERS:

Vocalion 03646 *Fort Worth Stomp* ....8.00 - 12.00
03707 *Tell Me Pretty Mama* ....8.00 - 12.00
03856 *Down in Arkansas* ....8.00 - 12.00

CUMBERLAND RIDGE RUNNERS:
Conqueror 8310 *I'm Here To Get My Baby Out Of Jail*
....5.00 - 8.00
Melotone 12981 *Roundin' Up The Yearlings*............5.00 - 8.00
Perfect 12993 *Roundin' Up The Yearlings*................5.00 - 8.00

CUMBERLAND STRING BAND:
Superior 2536 *Wink The Other Eye* ....20.00 - 30.00

DAVE CUTRELL:
Okeh 45057 *Pistol Pete's Midnight Special*............15.00 - 20.00

DA COSTA WOLTZ'S SOUTHERN BROADCASTERS (featuring FRANK JENKINS/PRICE GOODSON):
Gennett 6187 *Lost Train Blues* ....30.00 - 50.00
6220 *John Brown's Dream*................................30.00 - 50.00
6223 *Roving Cowboy* ....30.00 - 50.00
6240 *Evening Star Waltz* ....30.00 - 50.00

VERNON DALHART:
(Note: This artist recorded for almost every label during the 1920's. Most of his records command minimal premiums. The selective listing following represents only a tiny fraction of his recorded output.)
Black Patti 8027 *The Mississippi Flood* ....100.00 - 150.00
8028 *Barbara Allen* ....100.00 - 150.00
Buddy 8011 *The Engineer's Child* ....50.00 - 75.00
8012 *The Freight Wreck At Altoona* ....50.00 - 75.00
8037 *The Great Titanic*...................................50.00 - 75.00
Edison (thin) 11002 *The West Plains Explosion* .....50.00 - 80.00
20001 *Eleven Cent Cotton* ....50.00 - 80.00
20003 *Big Rock Candy Mountain*......................50.00 - 80.00
20010 *Dixie Way*..100.00 - 150.00
Edison (thick) 51459 *The Prisoner's Song*...............8.00 - 12.00
51541 *Doin' The Best I Can* ....10.00 - 15.00
51557 *In The Baggage Coach Ahead* ....8.00 - 12.00
51584 *Rovin' Gambler* ....10.00 - 15.00
51597 *New River Train*....................................10.00 - 15.00
51605 *The Sneeze Song* ....10.00 - 15.00
51607 *The Little Rosewood Casket*....................10.00 - 15.00
51608 *The Boston Burglar*...............................10.00 - 15.00
51609 *The John T. Scopes Trial* ....10.00 - 20.00
51610 *After The Ball*......................................10.00 - 15.00
51611 *Casey Jones* ....15.00 - 20.00
51620 *Wreck Of The 1256*...............................10.00 - 15.00
51621 *Jesse James* ....10.00 - 15.00
51637 *Stone Mountain Memorial* ....10.00 - 15.00
51643 *The Convict And The Rose*......................10.00 - 15.00
51649 *The Letter Edged In Black* ....10.00 - 15.00
51656 *Zeb Turner's Gal* ....10.00 - 15.00
51669 *Behind These Gray Walls* ....10.00 - 15.00
51670 *Unknown Soldier's Grave*......................10.00 - 15.00
51693 *Frank Dupre* ....10.00 - 15.00
51714 *Floyd Collins Waltz* ....10.00 - 20.00
51718 *Freight Wreck At Altoona*......................10.00 - 20.00
51729 *Sydney Allen* ....10.00 - 20.00
51735 *Lightning Express* ....10.00 - 20.00
51749 *The Drunkard's Lone Child*....................10.00 - 20.00
51807 *Just A Melody* ....10.00 - 20.00
51827 *There's A New Star In Heaven To-Night*.15.00 - 20.00
51856 *Billy Richardson's Last Ride* ....15.00 - 20.00
51883 *The Dying Girl's Message* ....15.00 - 20.00
51901 *Can I Sleep In Your Barn Tonight, Mister?*
....15.00 - 20.00
51949 *Don't Let The Deal Go Down*..................15.00 - 20.00

51974 *Pretty Little Dear* ....15.00 - 20.00
52020 *Kennie Wagner's Surrender* ....15.00 - 25.00
52029 *Lucky Lindy*.....................................15.00 - 25.00
52077 *My Horses Ain't Hungry*......................20.00 - 30.00
52088 *The Mississippi Flood* ....15.00 - 25.00
52095 *My Blue Ridge Mountain Home* ....15.00 - 25.00
52118 *Puttin' On The Style*...........................15.00 - 25.00
52134 *Sing On, Brother, Sing!*......................15.00 - 25.00
52144 *Where The Coosa River Flows* ....15.00 - 25.00
52174 *My Carolina Home* ....15.00 - 25.00
52229 *A Memory That Time Cannot Erase* ....15.00 - 25.00
52248 *You Can't Blame Me For That*................15.00 - 30.00
52307 *The Death of Floyd Bennett* ....20.00 - 30.00
52335 *The West Plains Explosion*....................20.00 - 30.00
52423 *The Old Bureau Drawer* ....25.00 - 50.00
52434 *Ohio River Blues* ....20.00 - 30.00
52457 *Eleven Cent Cotton* ....25.00 - 40.00
52472 *The Bum Song No. 2*..........................25.00 - 40.00
52487 *Ninety And Nine* ....30.00 - 50.00
52533 *Low Bridge, Everybody Down* ....30.00 - 50.00
52558 *Lucky Lindy's Lucky Day* ....40.00 - 60.00
52566 *Alabama Flood*.................................30.00 - 50.00
52599 *Ain't Gonna Grieve My Mind* ....50.00 - 80.00
52628 *Dixie Way*...50.00 - 100.00
Herschel Gold Seal 2005 *The Miami Storm*............50.00 - 75.00
2018 *Just A Melody*....................................50.00 - 75.00
Herwin 75501 *Blue Ridge Mountain Blues*............25.00 - 50.00
75505 *The Prisoner's Song*...........................25.00 - 50.00
75506 *The New River Train* ....25.00 - 50.00
75507 *Jesse James* ....25.00 - 50.00
75516 *Behind These Gray Walls*....................25.00 - 50.00
75517 *The Life Of Tom Watson* ....25.00 - 50.00
75531 *Papa's Billy Goat*..............................25.00 - 50.00
75540 *The Wreck Of The Royal Palm*..............25.00 - 50.00
75546 *The Mississippi Flood* ....25.00 - 50.00

(TOMMY) DANDURAND & THE BARN DANCE FIDDLERS/HIS BARN DANCE GANG OF WLS/HIS GANG:
Gennett 6273 *Buffalo Gal* ....15.00 - 20.00
6351 *McLeod's Reel* ....15.00 - 20.00
Supertone 9156 *Big Town Fling* ....6.00 - 10.00
9157 *Buffalo Girl*..6.00 - 10.00
9158 *Haste To The Wedding* ....6.00 - 10.00
9159 *McLeod's Reel* ....6.00 - 10.00
9160 *The Irish Washerwoman* ....6.00 - 10.00
9162 *Devil's Dream*.....................................6.00 - 10.00

(TOM) DARBY AND (JIMMIE) TARLTON:
Columbia 15197-D *Birmingham Town*..................15.00 - 20.00
15212-D *Birmingham Jail* ....10.00 - 15.00
15254-D *After The Ball*................................20.00 - 30.00
15293-D *The Irish Police*.............................20.00 - 30.00
15319-D *Mexican Rag* ....20.00 - 30.00
15330-D *Heavy Hearted Blues* ....20.00 - 30.00
15360-D *The Rainbow Division* ....20.00 - 30.00
15375-D *Birmingham Jail No. 2*....................20.00 - 30.00
15388-D *If You Ever Learn To Love Me* ....20.00 - 30.00
15403-D *Down In The Old Cherry Orchard* .....25.00 - 40.00
15419-D *Slow Wicked Blues* ....25.00 - 40.00
15436-D *Sweet Sarah Blues* ....30.00 - 50.00
15452-D *Black Jack Moonshine* ....30.00 - 50.00
15477-D *All Bound Down In Texas* ....30.00 - 50.00
15492-D *Little Bessie*...................................30.00 - 50.00

15511-D *Freight Train Ramble* ....30.00 - 50.00
15528-D *Jack And May* ....30.00 - 50.00
15552-D *Faithless Husband* ....30.00 - 50.00
15572-D *My Little Blue Heaven* ....30.00 - 50.00
15591-D *The Maple On The Hill* ....30.00 - 50.00
15611-D *Hard Time Blues* ....50.00 - 75.00
15624-D *Beggar Joe* ....50.00 - 75.00
15674-D *The Black Sheep* ....50.00 - 75.00
15684-D *Gamblin' Jim* ....50.00 - 75.00
15701-D *Rising Sun Blues* ....50.00 - 75.00
15715-D *Going Back To My Texas Home* ....75.00 - 100.00

MOUNTAIN DEW DARE:
Okeh 45170 *Don't Love A Smiling Sweetheart* ....10.00 - 15.00

CHUCK DARLING:
Bluebird 5285 *Harmonica Rag* ....7.00 - 10.00
Victor V40330 *Blowin' The Blues* ....25.00 - 40.00

DAVE AND HOWARD:
Victor 23566 *Bay Rum Blues* ....50.00 - 75.00
 23577 *Serves 'Em Fine* ....50.00 - 75.00

CARL DAVENPORT & HIS GANG:
Vocalion 5371 *Broken Hearted Lover* ....15.00 - 20.00
 5394 *Double Eagle March* ....15.00 - 20.00

EMMETT DAVENPORT:
Supertone 9178 *The Dingy Miner's Cabin* ....8.00 - 12.00
 9179 *The Dying Girl's Message* ....8.00 - 12.00
 9388 *She Ain't Built That Way* ....8.00 - 12.00
 9539 *The Virginia Moonshiner* ....8.00 - 12.00
 9642 *Johnny The Drunkard* ....8.00 - 12.00
 9774 *An Old Fashioned Picture Of Mother* ....8.00 - 12.00

HOMER DAVENPORT & THE YOUNG BROTHERS:
Silvertone 4009 *Down In Tennessee Blues* ....8.00 - 12.00

DAVIS & NELSON:
Paramount 3186 *I Shall Not Be Moved* ....20.00 - 30.00
 3187 *I Don't Bother Work* ....20.00 - 30.00
 3188 *I Don't Want Your Greenback Dollar* ....20.00 - 30.00
 3227 *Charming Betsy* ....25.00 - 50.00
Q.R.S. 9014 *I Don't Want Your Greenback Dollar* 30.00 - 50.00
 9018 *I Don't Bother Work* ....30.00 - 50.00

DAVIS, STOKES & LAYNE:
Gennett 6548 *Way Down In Alabam'* ....30.00 - 50.00

DAVIS TRIO:
Paramount 3238 *Sleepy Hollow* ....20.00 - 30.00

C. W./CHARLIE DAVIS:
Aurora 36-107 *When The Flowers Bloom In The Springtime*
....30.00 - 50.00
Gennett 6637 *Sweet Bunch Of Daisies* ....20.00 - 40.00
Timely Tunes 1559 *Down In A Southern Town* ....25.00 - 50.00

CLAUDE DAVIS (TRIO) (& BOB NICHOLS):
Brunswick 503 *Over In The Hills Of California* ....5.00 - 8.00
Columbia 15397-D *We Were Pals Together* ....5.00 - 8.00
 15466-D *Underneath The Southern Moon* ....5.00 - 8.00
 15740-D *Standing By The Highway* ....8.00 - 12.00

EVA DAVIS:
Columbia 129-D *Wild Bill Jones* ....7.00 - 10.00

JEWELL DAVIS:
Okeh 45152 *Thinking Of The Days I've Done Wrong*
....7.00 - 10.00

JIMMIE DAVIS:
Bluebird 5005 *She's A Hum-Dum Dinger* ....20.00 - 30.00
 5156 *The Keyhole In The Door* ....30.00 - 50.00
 5187 *I Wonder If She's Blue* ....10.00 - 15.00
 5359 *I Want Her Tailor-Made* ....30.00 - 50.00
 5394 *Beautiful Texas* ....8.00 - 12.00
 5425 *Alimony Blues* ....40.00 - 60.00
 5496 *Arabella Blues* ....25.00 - 40.00
 5570 *Easy Rider Blues* ....25.00 - 40.00
 5635 *Triflin' Mama Blues* ....25.00 - 40.00
 5697 *I'll Get Mine Bye And Bye* ....25.00 - 40.00
 5699 *Red Nightgown Blues* ....50.00 - 75.00
 5751 *Sewing Machine Blues* ....25.00 - 40.00
 5806 *I'll Be Happy Today* ....25.00 - 40.00
 5965 *Minute Man, Part 1/2* ....25.00 - 40.00
 6040 *Dentist Blues* ....25.00 - 40.00
 6167 *Moonlight* ....20.00 - 30.00
 6236 *Sweet Sixteen* ....15.00 - 20.00
 6249 *The Davis Limited* ....15.00 - 20.00
 6272 *Organ Grinder Blues* ....15.00 - 20.00
 6437 *Yo Yo Mama* ....15.00 - 20.00
 7071 *My Dixie Sweetheart* ....15.00 - 20.00
Decca (most issues)..4.00 - 8.00
Victor 23517 *Arabella Blues* ....50.00 - 75.00
 23525 *In Arkansas* ....50.00 - 75.00
 23544 *Penitentiary Blues* ....50.00 - 75.00
 23559 *Before You Say Farewell* ....50.00 - 75.00
 23573 *Pea Pickin' Papa* ....50.00 - 75.00
 23587 *She's A Hum-Dinger* ....50.00 - 75.00
 23601 *The Davis Limited* ....50.00 - 75.00
 23620 *Market House Blues* ....75.00 - 100.00
 23628 *Wild And Reckless John* ....75.00 - 100.00
 23648 *Lonely Hobo* ....75.00 - 100.00
 23659 *Red Nightgown Blues* ....100.00 - 150.00
 23674 *Davis' Salty Dog* ....100.00 - 150.00
 23688 *1982 Blues* ....100.00 - 150.00
 23703 *High Behind Blues* ....100.00 - 150.00
 23718 *Cowboy's Home Sweet Home* ....100.00 - 150.00
 23746 *Shotgun Wedding* ....100.00 - 150.00
 23749 *Bury Me In Old Kentucky* ....100.00 - 150.00
 23752 *Hold 'Er Newt* ....75.00 - 100.00
 23763 *Organ Grinder Blues* ....100.00 - 150.00
 23778 *The Gambler's Return* ....100.00 - 150.00
 23793 *Yo Yo Mama* ....100.00 - 150.00
 V40154 *The Barroom Message* ....75.00 - 100.00
 V40215 *Out Of Town Blues* ....75.00 - 100.00
 V40286 *Doggone That Train* ....75.00 - 100.00
 V40302 *My Louisiana Girl* ....75.00 - 100.00
 V40332 *Settling Down For Life* ....75.00 - 100.00

LINK DAVIS:
Imperial 8004 *My Pretty Blonde* ....8.00 - 12.00
 8008 *Tired Of Being Lonesome* ....8.00 - 12.00
 8009 *I'm Waiting For You* ....8.00 - 12.00
 8018 *Rice And Gravy Blues* ....8.00 - 12.00
 8025 *You Loved Me Too Late* ....8.00 - 12.00
 8030 *You Low Down Conceited Dog* ....8.00 - 12.00
(Note: See also the **RHYTHM & BLUES, ETC.**, section for 45
 RPM records by Link Davis)

STAN DAVIS:
Okeh 45401 *The Body In The Bag* ....10.00 - 15.00

DAVE DAWSON'S STRING BAND:
Superior 2517 *Over The Waves* ....30.00 - 50.00
 2575 *Grey Eagle* ....30.00 - 50.00

DECKERS:

Paramount 3281 *When It's Night Time In Nevada*	10.00 -	20.00
3323 *That Little Boy Of Mine*	10.00 -	20.00

DANNY DEDMAN/DEDMON & THE RHYTHM RAMBLERS:

Imperial 8019 *Too Many Blue Eyes*	8.00 -	12.00
8023 *It's Time To Say Goodbye*	8.00 -	12.00
8045 *Drinkin' Beer All Night*	8.00 -	12.00
8058 *You Can't Henpeck Me*	8.00 -	12.00
8061 *That Lonesome Old Moon*	8.00 -	12.00
8065 *Gin Drinkin' Mama*	8.00 -	12.00
8068 *Mama-In-Law Troubles*	8.00 -	12.00
8099 *Lanes Budded With Roses*	7.00 -	10.00

TED DE LEON & HIS RAMBLERS:

Imperial 8024 *I Was A Stranger*	8.00 -	12.00
8035 *I Get Lonesome*	8.00 -	12.00

ROSCOE & SAM DELLINGER:

Bluebird 6852 *The Ohio River Floods*	5.00 -	10.00
6868 *Tellin' The Stars*	5.00 -	10.00

DELMORE BROTHERS:

Bluebird 5299 *Lonesome Yodel Blues*	15.00 -	20.00
5338 *The Frozen Girl*	15.00 -	20.00
5358 *I'm Leaving You*	15.00 -	20.00
5403 *Browns Ferry Blues*	5.00 -	8.00
5467 *Ramblin' Minded Blues*	8.00 -	12.00
5531 *Blue Railroad Train*	8.00 -	12.00
5589 *Smoky Mountain Bill*	8.00 -	12.00
5653 *I'm Mississippi Bound*	8.00 -	12.00
5741 *Lonesome Jailhouse Blues*	8.00 -	12.00
5857 *Hey! Hey! I'm Memphis Bound*	8.00 -	12.00
5893 *Brown's Ferry Blues, Part 2*	8.00 -	12.00
5925 *Lorena, The Slave*	7.00 -	10.00
5957 *I Long To See My Mother*	7.00 -	10.00
6002 *I Got The Kansas City Blues*	7.00 -	10.00
6019 *The Fugitive's Lament*	7.00 -	10.00
6034 *Alabama Lullaby*	7.00 -	10.00
6312 *The Nashville Blues*	7.00 -	10.00
6349 *I'm Worried Now*	7.00 -	10.00
6386 *Lonesome Yodel Blues No.2*	7.00 -	10.00
6401 *Carry Me Back To Alabama*	7.00 -	10.00
6522 *The Lover's Warning*	7.00 -	10.00
6841 *Southern Moon*	7.00 -	10.00
6915 *No Drunkard Can Enter There*	7.00 -	10.00
6949 *False Hearted Girl*	7.00 -	10.00
6998 *No One*	7.00 -	10.00
7029 *Don't Forget Me, Darling*	7.00 -	10.00
7129 *Singing My Troubles Away*	7.00 -	10.00
7192 *They Say It Is Sinful To Flirt*	7.00 -	10.00
7262 *The Budded Rose*	7.00 -	10.00
7300 *Weary Lonesome Blues*	7.00 -	10.00
7337 *Lead Me*	7.00 -	10.00
7383 *The Farmers Girl*	7.00 -	10.00
7436 *Goodbye Booze*	7.00 -	10.00
7496 *'Cause I Don't Mean To Cry*	5.00 -	10.00
7560 *Big Ball In Texas*	5.00 -	10.00
7672 *Wonderful There*	5.00 -	10.00
7741 *Brother, Take Warning*	5.00 -	10.00
7778 *Alcatraz Island Blues*	5.00 -	10.00
7913 *Leavin' On That Train*	5.00 -	10.00
7957 *Where Is My Sailor Boy?*	5.00 -	10.00
7991 *The Cannon Ball*	5.00 -	10.00

8031 *Fifteen Miles From Birmingham*	5.00 -	10.00
8052 *Home On The River*	5.00 -	10.00
8177 *Baby, You're Throwing Me Down*	5.00 -	10.00
8204 *Wabash Blues*	5.00 -	10.00
8215 *I Loved You Better Than You Knew*	5.00 -	10.00
8230 *Gambler's Yodel*	5.00 -	10.00
8247 *Nothing But The Blues*	5.00 -	10.00
8264 *I'm Alabama Bound*	5.00 -	10.00
8290 *A Better Range Is Home*	5.00 -	10.00
8404 *Scatterbrain Mama*	5.00 -	10.00
8418 *Back To Birmingham*	5.00 -	10.00
8451 *Over The Hills*	5.00 -	10.00
8488 *The Eastern Gate*	5.00 -	10.00
8557 *Rainin' On The Mountain*	5.00 -	10.00
8613 *Storms Are On The Ocean*	5.00 -	10.00
8637 *Heart Of Sorrow*	5.00 -	10.00
8687 *That Yodelin' Gal, Miss Julie*	5.00 -	10.00

(Note: Some of above titles were also issued on Montgomery Ward label.)

Columbia 15724-D *Got The Kansas City Blues*	75.00 -	125.00
Decca 5878, 5890, 5897, 5907, 5925, 5970, 6000, 6051, 6080	5.00 -	8.00
King 509, 514, 518, 525, 527, 533	4.00 -	8.00

MORGAN DENMON:

Okeh 45075 *Naomi Wise*	8.00 -	12.00
45105 *I've Still Got Ninety-Nine*	10.00 -	15.00
45306 *The Two Drummers*	10.00 -	15.00
45327 *The Drunkard's Dream*	10.00 -	15.00

DICK DEVALL:

Timely Tunes 1563 *Out On The Lone Star Cow Trail*	25.00 -	40.00

CHARLES M. (BUDDY) DE WITTE (THE SINGING MOONSHINER/MOUNTAINEER; THE VAGABOND YODELER):

Champion 16371 *Vagabond Yodel*	40.00 -	60.00
16444 *Vagabond Yodel No. 2*	40.00 -	60.00
16658 *My Kentucky Cabin*	50.00 -	80.00
16680 *Rose Of Mother's Day*	50.00 -	80.00
16759 *The Girl I Met In Bluefield*	75.00 -	100.00
16825 *The Sad, Sad Story*	75.00 -	100.00

AL DEXTER & HIS TROOPERS:

Vocalion 03435 *New Jellyroll Blues*	7.00 -	10.00
03569, 03719, 03927, 03988	5.00 -	10.00
04174, 04277, 04327, 04405, 04988, 05042	5.00 -	8.00

DEZURIK SISTERS:

Vocalion 04616, 04704, 04781	5.00 -	8.00

DICKSON & CARROLL:

Superior 2523 *Advice To Husband Seekers*	15.00 -	20.00

BOB DICKSON:

Victor 23633, 23679	7.00 -	12.00

M. S. DILLEHAY:

Victor V40155 *Mother-In-Law*	20.00 -	30.00

JOHN DILLESHAW & THE STRING MARVEL:

Okeh 45328 *Cotton Patch Rag*	75.00 -	100.00

(SEVEN FOOT) DILLEY (See DILLY)

JOHN DILLINGSHAW:

Vocalion 5459 *Farmer's Blues*	50.00 -	75.00

DILLY, LINDSEY, LINDSEY, GRAY & BROWN; DILLY, TUCKER, LEE, STOKES & MELVIN; (SEVEN FOOT) DILLY & HIS DILL PICKLES:

Brunswick 489 *A Bootlegger's Joint In Atlanta* ......30.00 - 50.00
   575 *Kenesaw Mountain Rag* ......30.00 - 50.00
Vocalion 5419 *Square Dance Fight On Bald Top Mountain*
   ....50.00 - 75.00
   5421 *Bust Down Stomp* ......50.00 - 75.00
   5436 *Georgia Bust Down* ......50.00 - 75.00
   5446 *Lye Soap* ......50.00 - 75.00
   5454 *A Georgia Barbecue At Stone Mountain* ...50.00 - 75.00

DIX & WILSON:
Bluebird 5397, 5472 ......5.00 - 10.00

DIXIE CRACKERS:
Paramount 3151 *The Old Bell Cow* ......20.00 - 30.00

DIXIE HARMONIZERS:
Gennett 6872 *Gonna Raise A Ruckus Tonight* ......25.00 - 40.00

DIXIE MOUNTAINEERS:
Edison 52057 *Hop Light Ladies* ......15.00 - 20.00

DIXIE STRING BAND:
Paramount 3164 *Atlanta Special* ......25.00 - 40.00
   3166 *Show Me The Way To Go Home* ......20.00 - 30.00

DIXIELAND SWINGSTERS:
Bluebird 7857, 7882, 7899, 7948 ......5.00 - 8.00

DIXIE RAMBLERS: (See also DOUG BINE)
Bluebird 6118, 6179, 6248, 6352, 6442 ......5.00 - 10.00

DIXIE REELERS:
Bluebird 6461, 6713, 6738, 6831 ......5.00 - 80.00

DIXIE STRING BAND:
Columbia 15273-D *Dixie Waltz* ......15.00 - 30.00
Silvertone 3516 *Soldier's Joy* ......7.00 - 10.00

DIXON'S CLOD HOPPERS:
Melotone 12007 *Steamboat Bill* ......5.00 - 8.00
   12052 *Wreck On The Southern Old 97* ......5.00 - 8.00

DIXON BROTHERS:
Bluebird 6327 *Intoxicated Rat* ......5.00 - 10.00
   6441 *Weave Room Blues* ......5.00 - 10.00
   6462 *Answer To Maple On The Hill* ......5.00 - 10.00
   6582 *My Girl In Sunny Tennessee* ......5.00 - 10.00
   6630, 6691, 6809, 6867, 6979, 7020, 7263, 7449,
   7674, 7767, 7801 ......4.00 - 8.00

DIXON TRIO:
Victor 23790 *Carolina Lullaby* ......10.00 - 20.00

BOB DIXON:
Victor 23752 *There Ain't No Man In The Moon* ......75.00 - 100.00
   23764 *Old Bill Smith* ......10.00 - 15.00
   23787 *What Are We Gonna Use For Money* ......10.00 - 15.00

JOHNNY DODDS:
Okeh 45417 *The Railroad Boomer* ......75.00 - 100.00
   45462 *No One To Call Me Darling* ......75.00 - 100.00
   45472 *Slu Foot Lue* ......75.00 - 100.00
   45560 *Cowboy Yodel* ......75.00 - 100.00

DONALDSON QUARTET:
Victor 23788 *Hannah From Panama* ......7.00 - 10.00

DONALDSON TRIO:
Bluebird 5003, 5035, 5060, 5134, 5166, 5221 ......4.00 - 8.00

LOUIE DONALDSON & HOKE RICE:
Gennett 6885 *The Gang's All Here* ......40.00 - 60.00

BUSTER DOSS & HIS ARKANSAS PLAYBOYS:
Talent 734 *Playboy Boogie* ......10.00 - 15.00

EVAN DOUGLAS & NATE SMITH:
Champion 15651 *If I Could Only Blot Out The Past*
   ......10.00 - 15.00
   15711 *If I Only Had A Home* ......10.00 - 15.00

THE DOWN HOMERS: (See also WOWO DOWN HOMERS)
Vogue 736 *Out Where The West Winds Blow* ......40.00 - 70.00

DOYLE BROS:
TNT 113 *T. N. T. Baby* ...... - - -

FRANK DUDGEON:
Champion 16532 *Atlanta Bound* ......50.00 - 75.00
   16575 *Sweet Betsy From Pike* ......50.00 - 75.00
   16580 *The Crime I Didn't Do* ......50.00 - 75.00
   16602 *Birmingham Jail No. 2* ......50.00 - 75.00

FRANK DUNBAR:
Superior 2538 *Nobody's Darling On Earth* ......15.00 - 20.00

DUNCAN BOYS:
Supertone 9676 *Kentucky Stomp* ......20.00 - 30.00

DUNCAN SISTERS:
Columbia 15745-D *Dusty Roads* ......10.00 - 15.00

UNCLE ECK DUNFORD:
Victor 20880 *The Whip-Poor-Will Song* ......10.00 - 15.00
   20938 *Barney McCoy* ......8.00 - 12.00
   21131 *My First Bicycle Ride* ......15.00 - 20.00
   21244 *The Taffy-Pulling Party* ......15.00 - 20.00
   21578 *Sweat Summer Has Gone Away* ......10.00 - 15.00
   V40060 *Old Shoes And Leggin's* ......20.00 - 30.00

BARNEY DUNROE:
Champion 15523 *Six Feet Of Earth* ......10.00 - 15.00

DUPREE'S ROME BOYS:
Okeh 45320 *Wedding Bells Waltz* ......50.00 - 80.00
   45356 *Cat Rag-Breakdown* ......50.00 - 80.00

BILLY DYAR:
Hoosier 201 *Driftwood on the River* ...... - - -

DYE'S SACRED HARP SINGERS:
Gennett 6889 *Amazing Grace* ......20.00 - 30.00

DYKES' MAGIC CITY TRIO:
Brunswick 120 *Cotton-Eyed Joe* ......20.00 - 30.00
   125 *Ida Red* ......20.00 - 30.00
   127 *Poor Ellen Smith* ......20.00 - 30.00
   128 *Hook And Line* ......20.00 - 30.00
   129 *Huckleberry Blues* ......20.00 - 30.00
   130 *Far Beyond The Blue Sky* ......20.00 - 30.00
Vocalion 5143 *Frankie* ......35.00 - 50.00
   5181 *Callahan's Reel* ......35.00 - 50.00

DICK DYSON (& HIS MUSICAL TEXANS):
Blue Bonnet 118 *Salty Dog Blues* ......8.00 - 12.00
   126 *Waited Too Long Blues* ......7.00 - 10.00
Tri-State 113 *Hell's Fire* ...... - - -

EARL & BELL:
Vocalion 15014 *On The Oregon Trail* ....5.00 - 8.00

EAST TEXAS SERENADERS:
Brunswick 282 *Acorn Stomp* ....8.00 - 12.00
    298 *Deacon Jones* ....10.00 - 15.00
    379 *Three-In-One Two Step* ....10.00 - 15.00
    429 *McKinney Waltz* ....10.00 - 15.00
    453 *Babe* ....15.00 - 20.00
    538 *Ozark Rag* ....15.00 - 20.00
    562 *Mineola Rag* ....15.00 - 20.00
Columbia 15229-D *Combination Rag* ....15.00 - 20.00

GARNER ECKLER & ROLAND GAINES (YODELING TWINS):
Champion 45043 *Moonlight And Skies* ....5.00 - 8.00
    45087 *Mountain Rangers Lullaby* ....5.00 - 8.00

GEORGE EDGIN'S CORN DODGERS:
Columbia 15754-D *My Ozark Mountain Home* ......50.00 - 80.00

DAVE EDWARDS & HIS ALABAMA BOYS:
Decca 5470, 5478, 5493, 5507, 5522, 5536, 5564 ....5.00 - 10.00

HAROLD EDWARDS:
Champion 15702 *Who Cares What You Have Been* ..7.00 - 10.00

ELK CREEK TRIO:
Champion 15584 *Silvery Bell* ....5.00 - 8.00

ELKINS' STRINGED STEPPERS:
Okeh 45079 *Speed* ....50.00 - 75.00

RAY ELKINS:
Champion 15831 *The Boy's Best Friend* ....8.00 - 12.00

ELLIOTT (& MITCHELL):
Victor 23646 *When It's Springtime In The Blue Ridge Mountains*
    ....15.00 - 20.00
    23652 *When The Oriole Sings Again* ....15.00 - 20.00

ELM CITY QUARTET:
Champion 16827 *The Tree Song* ....8.00 - 12.00

ELMER & JUD:
Broadway 8052 *Turkey In The Straw* ....5.00 - 8.00
Conqueror 7332 *Turkey In The Straw* ....5.00 - 8.00
Oriole 1414 *Turkey In The Straw* ....5.00 - 8.00

EMMY LOU:
Hoosier 301 *Rocky Road Blues* .... - -

EVANS' OLD TIMERS:
Champion 16512 *Honeysuckle Time* ....100.00 - 150.00
    16531 *The Old Elm Tree* ....100.00 - 150.00
    16709 *No Low Down Hanging Around* ....150.00 - 300.00

CLYDE EVANS BAND:
Columbia 15597-D *How I Got My Gal* ....20.00 - 30.00

DEACON EVANS & HIS TEXANS:
Imperial 8038 *When You Smile* ....7.00 - 10.00

JOHN B. EVANS:
Brunswick 237 *Three Night's Experience* ....10.00 - 15.00
    276 *The Last Mile Of The Way* ....10.00 - 15.00
Supertone 2051 *Mother's Grave* ....10.00 - 15.00

CLAY EVERHEART & THE NORTH CAROLINA COOPER BOYS:
Columbia 15737-D *Standing By A Window* ....75.00 - 100.00

BOB FAGAN:
Challenge 839 *She Was A Moonshiner's Daughter* ..7.00 - 10.00

JIMMIE FAIR:
Kentucky 532 *I'll Walk Alone* ....4.00 - 7.00
    533 *Just A Little Lovin'* ....4.00 - 7.00
    538 *Anytime* ....4.00 - 7.00

J. D. FARLEY:
Victor V40269 *Bill Was A Texas Lad* ....25.00 - 35.00

FARM HANDS:
Paramount 3294 *The Old Hayloft Waltz* ....20.00 - 30.00

HARVEY FARR:
Supertone 9320 *The Santa Barbara Earthquake* ......8.00 - 12.00
    9372 *The Fate Of Ellen Smith* ....8.00 - 12.00

FAY & THE JAYWALKERS:
Paramount 3100 *My Baby Don't Love Me* ....20.00 - 30.00
    3156 *Longing For Home* ....20.00 - 30.00

BOB FERGUSON (& HIS SCALAWAGGERS):
Columbia 15297-D, 15433-D, 15476-D, 15529-D,
    15553-D, 15616-D, 15664-D ....4.00 - 8.00
    15677-D *The Strawberry Roan* ....8.00 - 12.00
    15704-D, 15727-D, 15732-D, 15739-D, 15759-D,
    15782-D ....4.00 - 8.00
Victor 23697, 23704, 23715 ....10.00 - 15.00

JOHN FERGUSON:
Challenge 158 *Wild Bill Jones* ....10.00 - 15.00
    159 *Railroad Daddy* ....10.00 - 15.00
    324 *Wild Bill Jones* ....10.00 - 15.00
    325 *Frankie's Gamblin' Man* ....8.00 - 12.00
Supertone 9259 *Down Where The Swanee River Flows*
    ....6.00 - 10.00

FIDDLER JOE & HIS BOYS:
Okeh 45042 *Turkey In The Straw* ....10.00 - 15.00

FLANNERY SISTERS:
Decca 5000, 5256, 5284 ....5.00 - 8.00

ALAN FLATT & HIS BAND:
Jamboree 508 *It's All Over Now* ....5.00 - 8.00
    511 *I'm Movin' On* ....5.00 - 8.00

FLEMING & TOWNSEND:
Bluebird 5002, 5106, 5186. 5256, 5378, 5426, 5470,
    5497, 5566, 5634, 5694, 5695, 5696, 5821, 5874 .....7.00 - 10.00
Decca 5419, 5427, 5445, 5463, 5487, 5516 ....5.00 - 8.00
Melotone 13231 *She's Just That Kind* ....8.00 - 12.00
(Note: Probably issued also on Banner, Oriole, Perfect, Romeo.)
Victor 23509 *She's Always On My Mind* ....20.00 - 30.00
    23520 *I'll Tell You About Women* ....20.00 - 30.00
    23543 *Gonna Quit Drinkin'* ....20.00 - 30.00
    23557 *Ramblin' Boy* ....20.00 - 30.00
    23563 *I'm Leavin' This Town* ....20.00 - 30.00
    23575 *Sweet Daddy From Tennessee* ....20.00 - 30.00
    23594 *How Can You Be Mean To Me* ....20.00 - 30.00
    23604 *Come And Drift With Me* ....20.00 - 30.00
    23625 *I Feel So Blue* ....20.00 - 30.00
    23635 *Blowin' The Blues* ....35.00 - 50.00
    23666 *First Time In Jail* ....35.00 - 50.00
    23676 *Yes, I Got Mine* ....35.00 - 50.00
    23694 *Bad Reputations* ....40.00 - 60.00
    23710 *That Lonesome Train* ....50.00 - 75.00
    23758 *Blues Have Gone* ....50.00 - 75.00

23771 *When It's Hottest Down South*..................50.00 - 75.00
23789 *Picture On My Dresser*.........................50.00 - 75.00
23793 *Do-Do-Daddling Thing* ....50.00 - 75.00
23814 *Right Always Wins* ....75.00 - 100.00
23829 *Gambler's Advice* ....75.00 - 100.00
V40297 *She's Just That Kind* ....30.00 - 50.00
V40321 *I'm Blue And Lonesome* ....35.00 - 50.00

FLETCHER & FOSTER:
Champion 16121 *Travelin' North* ....50.00 - 80.00
Victor V40232 *Charlotte Hot Step* ....50.00 - 80.00

OTTO & JIM FLETCHER:
Superior 2669 *True And Trembling Brakeman* ....35.00 - 50.00
   2726 *When The Cactus Is In Bloom* ....35.00 - 50.00
   2749 *Columbus Stockade Blues* ....35.00 - 50.00
   2777 *The Chicken Roost Blues* ....35.00 - 50.00

TEX FLETCHER (& JOE ROGERS); TEX FLETCHER'S LONELY COWBOYS:
Decca 5300, 5302, 5320, 5332, 5391, 5403, 5441,
   5460, 5489, 5500, 5520 ....4.00 - 8.00

TIM FLORA & RUFUS LINGO:
Okeh 45311 *Stuttering Billy* ....10.00 - 15.00

FLOYD COUNTY RAMBLERS:
Victor 23759 *Barn Dance*............................50.00 - 75.00
   V40307 *Sunny Tennessee* ....25.00 - 40.00
   V40331 *Aunt Dinah's Quilting Party*.................30.00 - 50.00

ELZIE FLOYD & LEO BOSWELL:
Columbia 15150-D *Nellie Dare*......................7.00 - 10.00
   15167-D *The Two Orphans* ....7.00 - 10.00

DAVID FOLEY:
Challenge 393 *I'll Never Be Yours* ....8.00 - 12.00
   394 *Poor Little Joe* ....8.00 - 12.00
   397 *Train No. 45*.................................8.00 - 12.00

(RAMBLING) RED FOLEY (Acc. by THE CUMBERLAND RIDGE RUNNERS):
Titles issued contemporaneously on Banner, Melotone, Oriole, Perfect, and Romeo: *Blonde Headed Girl; The Dying Rustler; Echoes of My Plantation Home; I Got The Freight Train Blues; Just One Little Kiss; The Lone Cowboy; Seven Long Years; Single Life Is Good Enough For Me*.................7.00 - 12.00

FORD & GRACE:
Okeh 45157 *Kiss Me Cindy*.........................10.00 - 15.00
   45237 *Hide Away*................................10.00 - 15.00

JACK FORD:
Chess 4858 *That's All You Gotta Do*.............5.00 - 8.00

OSCAR FORD:
Columbia 15437-D *Henry Ford's Model A*..........10.00 - 15.00
   15554-D *Me And My Gal* ....10.00 - 15.00
   15599-D *The Farmer's Dream*..................15.00 - 20.00

15634-D *Georgia Is My Home* ....15.00 - 25.00
15673-D *Little Nan* ....15.00 - 25.00

FORT WORTH BOYS (See MILTON BROWN)

FORT WORTH DOUGHBOYS:
Bluebird 5257 *Nancy Jane*............................40.00 - 60.00
Montgomery Ward 4416 *Nancy Jane* ....15.00 - 30.00
Victor 23653 *Nancy Jane*...............................100.00 - 150.00

JOE FOSS & HIS HUNGRY SANDLAPPERS:
Columbia 15268-D *Oh! How She Lied* ....20.00 - 40.00

(J. D.) FOSTER (& J. D. JAMES); FOSTER & (T. S.) YOUNG; JOHN FOSTER:
Champion 16733 *My Boyhood Happy Days*..........20.00 - 30.00
   16753 *Some Day I'll Wander Back Again* ....20.00 - 30.00
   45037, 45102................................7.00 - 10.00
Gennett 6434 *When I Was Single, My Pockets Would Jingle*
   ....20.00 - 30.00
   6791 *My Sarah Jane* ....20.00 - 30.00

OWEN FOSTER:
Victor 20934 *Wilkes County Blues* ....25.00 - 40.00

SALLY FOSTER & THE TRAVELERS:
Decca 5229, 5308, 5333, 5352, 5387...................4.00 - 8.00

FOUR BUZZ SAWS:
Vocalion 5471 *The Tree Song*.......................7.00 - 10.00

FOUR PICKLED PEPPERS:
Bluebird ....4.00 - 8.00

FOUR VIRGINIANS:
Okeh 45163 *Two Little Lads* ....15.00 - 20.00
   45181 *Swing Your Partner*.....................15.00 - 20.00

FOX CHASERS:
Okeh 45477 *Red Wing* ....15.00 - 25.00
   45496 *Forked Deer*............................15.00 - 25.00

FOX & DAVIS:
Supertone 9406 *Monroe County Quickstep* ....10.00 - 15.00

CODY FOX & HIS YELLOW JACKETS:
Vocalion 03493 *I Only Want A Buddy*................5.00 - 8.00

CURLEY FOX:
Decca 5169 *Tennessee Roll*..........................8.00 - 12.00
   5185 *Yum Yum Blues* ....8.00 - 12.00
   5213 *Listen To The Mockingbird*...............8.00 - 12.00

GLEN FOX & JOE WILSON:
Vocalion 5490 *My Dixie Home*.......................5.00 - 8.00
   5495 *The Old Covered Bridge* ....5.00 - 8.00
   5496 *The Roundup In The Spring* ....5.00 - 8.00

OSCAR FOX:
Supertone 9325 *My Dear Old Mountain Home* ....7.00 - 10.00

DUEL FRADY:
Victor 20930 *Leavenworth* ....7.00 - 10.00

LEE FRAZIER:
Champion 16626 *The Ice Man Blues* ....50.00 - 80.00

FREDERICK & MASON:
Victor 20965 *Missouri Waltz* ....5.00 - 8.00

FREED & MOORE:
Vocalion 14865 *Harmonica Blues*...................7.00 - 10.00
   14917 *Banjo Blues* ....7.00 - 10.00
   15116 *Plantation Medley* ....7.00 - 10.00

FREEMAN & ASHCRAFT:
Columbia 15442-D *Alabama Rag* ....40.00 - 60.00

FREENY'S BARN DANCE BAND:
Okeh 45508 *Don't You Remember The Time* ....50.00 - 75.00
    45524 *The Leake County Two Step* ....50.00 - 75.00
    45533 *Mississippi Square Dance*........................50.00 - 75.00

THE FRONTIERSMEN:
Bullet 708 *Honky Tonk Hop* ....5.00 - 8.00

FRUIT JAR GUZZLERS:
Paramount 3095 *Sourwood Mountain* ....35.00 - 50.00
    3099 *Black Sheep Of The Family* ....35.00 - 50.00
    3106 *Yes, I'm Free*..35.00 - 50.00
    3113 *Kentucky Bootlegger*................................35.00 - 50.00
    3116 *Cripple Creek*..35.00 - 50.00
    3121 *Steel Driving Man* ....35.00 - 50.00
    3148 *Old Joe Clark*..25.00 - 50.00

JEP FULLER:
Vocalion 5074, 15125...4.00 - 7.00

CLARENCE (& CLAUDE) GANUS:
Vocalion 5272 *Memories Of Floyd Collins*.............15.00 - 20.00
    5284 *Down In Indiana*......................................15.00 - 20.00
    5312 *Just The Thought Of Mother*....................15.00 - 20.00
    5385 *I Love Nobody But You* ....15.00 - 20.00
    5386 *Sleeping At The Foot Of The Bed* ....15.00 - 20.00
    5396 *The Dying Soldier* ....15.00 - 20.00
    5409 *Take A Tater And Wait* ....15.00 - 20.00
    5417 *I'm Going Away*.......................................15.00 - 20.00
    5452 *Won't The Angels Let Mama Come* ....15.00 - 20.00

GARDNER & DAVID:
Diva 6010-G *John Hardy* ....5.00 - 8.00

BLIND UNCLE GASPARD:
Vocalion 5320 *Marksville Blues*...................75.00 - 125.00
    5333 *Natchitocheo*...............................75.00 - 125.00

AUBREY GASS:
Capitol 1427 *K. C Boogie*.....................................8.00 - 12.00
Gold Star 1318 *Delivery Man Blues* ....8.00 - 12.00

JOHNNIE GATES:
Columbia 15573-D *Saw Mill Blues No. 1* ....10.00 - 15.00
    15661-D *Saw Mill Blues No. 2* ....10.00 - 15.00

GATWOOD SQUARE DANCE BAND:
Columbia 15363-D *Third Party*..............................15.00 - 20.00

RED GAY & JACK WELLMAN:
Brunswick 523 *Flat Wheel Train Blues*...................15.00 - 20.00

WHIT GAYDON:
Victor V40315 *Tennessee Coon Hunt* ....20.00 - 30.00

NORMAN GAYLE:
Champion 15447 *Train No. 45* ....10.00 - 15.00
    15465 *She's Mine All Mine*...............................10.00 - 15.00
    15501 *Sally Gooden*...10.00 - 15.00

GEORGE'S HOT SHOTS:
Victor 23729 *We Do It Just The Same*.....................10.00 - 15.00

GEORGIA CRACKERS:
Okeh 45098 *Diamond Joe* ....25.00 - 40.00
    45111 *Georgia Black Bottom* ....15.00 - 25.00
    45192 *Stockade Blues* ....25.00 - 40.00

GEORGIA MELODY BOYS:
Broadway 8119 *Cabin Home* ....7.00 - 10.00

GEORGIA ORGAN GRINDERS:
Columbia 15394-D *Back Up And Push* ....25.00 - 40.00
    15415-D *Charming Betsy* ....25.00 - 40.00
    15445-D *Georgia Man*......................................30.00 - 50.00

GEORGIA POT LICKERS:
Brunswick 595 *Up Jumped The Rabbit* ....15.00 - 20.00

GEORGIA SERENADERS:
Supertone 9473 *Gonna Raise A Ruckus Tonight* ....10.00 - 15.00

GEORGIA WILDCATS:
Victor 23640 *She's Waiting For Me* ....30.00 - 50.00

GEORGIA YELLOW HAMMERS:
Victor 20549 *Fourth Of July*................................8.00 - 12.00
    20550 *Pass Around The Bottle* ....7.00 - 10.00
    20928 *Mary, Don't You Weep* ....10.00 - 15.00
    20943 *My Carolina Girl* ....7.00 - 10.00
    21073 *Tennessee Coon* ....15.00 - 20.00
    21195 *G Rag* ....20.00 - 30.00
    21362 *The Song Of The Doodle Bug* ....20.00 - 30.00
    21486 *The Old Rock Jail*..................................20.00 - 30.00
    21626 *Moonshine Hollow Band*......................20.00 - 30.00
    23542 *No One To Welcome Me* ....50.00 - 75.00
    23547 *Child Hood Days*....................................50.00 - 75.00
    23683 *Peaches Down In Georgia* ....75.00 - 100.00
    V40004 *Warhorse Game* ....30.00 - 50.00
    V40069 *The Sale Of Simon Slick* ....30.00 - 50.00
    V40091 *Kiss Me Quick* ....25.00 - 35.00
    V40138 *Big Ball In Memphis* ....30.00 - 50.00

FRANK GERARD-HOWARD DIXON-MUTT EVANS:
Bluebird 7895 *Honey, Baby Mine*...........................7.00 - 10.00

GIBBS BROTHERS & CLYDE DAVIS:
Vocalion 5447 *I Love My Toodlum-Doo* ....25.00 - 40.00
    5464 *Strolling Home With Jenny* ....25.00 - 40.00

HUGH GIBBS STRING BAND:
Paramount 3001 *I'm Goin' Crazy*..........................25.00 - 40.00
    3002 *Almost Persuaded* ....25.00 - 40.00
    3003 *Chicken Feed* ....25.00 - 40.00
    3004 *In The Good Old Summertime* ....25.00 - 40.00

GRINNELL GIGGERS (See GRINNELL):

CECIL GILL (YODELING COUNTRY BOY):
Silver Star 100, 101...5.00 - 10.00

GIRLS OF THE GOLDEN WEST:
Bluebird 5155, 5167, 5189, 5226, 5288, 5318, 5382,
    5394, 5427, 5718, 5719, 5737, 5732, 6004, 6054,
    6163, 6164, 6178, 6255..............................5.00 - 10.00
Victor 23857 *The Cowgirl's Dream* ....35.00 - 50.00
Vocalion 04022, 04053, 04103, 04147, 04234,
    04292, 04373..5.00 - 8.00

SHORTY GODWIN:
Columbia 15411-D *Turnip Greens* ....8.00 - 12.00

GOLDEN MELODY BOYS:
Paramount 3068 *The Cross Eyed Butcher* ....5.00 - 8.00
    3074 *Would You Ever Think Of Me* ....5.00 - 8.00
    3081 *Cabin Home* ....5.00 - 8.00
    3087 *Way Down In Arkansas*............................5.00 - 8.00
    3107 *Freak Melody* ....10.00 - 15.00

3124 *Jack And May* ....10.00 - 15.00
3137 *When The Lilac Blooms* ....10.00 - 15.00
3153 *Uncle Ebner & Ebner At The Rehearsal* ...10.00 - 15.00
3169 *Guitar Rag* ....12.00 - 15.00

DAN GOLDEN:
Champion 15525 *Good Old Turip Greens* ....10.00 - 15.00

GOOD'S BOX WHITTLERS:
Vocalion 5352 *Election Day In Kentucky* ....10.00 - 15.00

HERALD GOODMAN & HIS TENNESSEE VALLEY BOYS:
Bluebird 7868, 7935, 7999, 8033 ....5.00 - 10.00

PRICE GOODSON:
Gennett 6154 *Lonesome Road Blues* ....40.00 - 60.00

GOOSE CREEK GULLY JUMPERS:
Superior 2639 *Let Me Call You Sweetheart* ....15.00 - 20.00
2738 *Medley*..................................15.00 - 20.00

ALEX GORDON:
Conqueror 7269 *A Message From Home Sweet Home*
....10.00 - 15.00
7270 *The Burial Of Wild Bill* ....10.00 - 15.00

TOMMY GORDON & HIS CORN HUSKERS:
Superior 2614 *Halfway To Arkansas* ....30.00 - 60.00
2712 *Wild Hog In The Woods*...................30.00 - 60.00

TED GOSSETT'S BAND:
Champion 16116 *Fox Chase* ....15.00 - 25.00
16310 *Bow Legged Irishman* ....20.00 - 30.00
Gennett 7308 *Fox Chase* ....30.00 - 50.00

GRADY FAMILY:
Columbia 15633-D *Carolina's Best* ....10.00 - 15.00

GRAHAM BROTHERS:
Victor 23654 *Ninety-Nine Years*...............10.00 - 15.00
23664 *Gene, The Fighting Marine* ....10.00 - 15.00
23668 *Spring's Tornado* ....10.00 - 15.00
23670 *Don't Hang Me* ....10.00 - 15.00
23690 *Bobby Boy*.............................15.00 - 20.00

HENRY GRAHAM:
Bell 1167 *The Marion Parker Murder* ....7.00 - 10.00
1177 *The Sinking Of The Submarine S-4*.........7.00 - 10.00

GRANT BROTHERS & THEIR MUSIC:
Columbia 15322-D *Tell It To Me* ....15.00 - 20.00
15460-D *Goodbye My Honey, I'm Gone* ....15.00 - 20.00

GRANT TRIO:
Victor 23667 *Under The Old Umbrella*...........8.00 - 12.00
23743 *Say A Prayer For Baby*..................8.00 - 12.00

GRAPEVINE COON HUNTERS:
Brunswick 584 *The Broan Waltz* ....15.00 - 20.00

GRAVES & TANNER:
Vocalion 5342 *The Bum's Rush* ....15.00 - 20.00

GRAY & NELSON:
Supertone 9309 *Mandolin Rag* ....8.00 - 12.00
9377 *Farewell Waltz*..........................8.00 - 12.00
9397 *Martha Campbell* ....8.00 - 12.00
9670 *Waltz The Hall* ....8.00 - 12.00

A. A. GRAY & SEVEN FOOT DILLY:
Vocalion 5430 *Streak O' Lean-Streak O' Fat*.........50.00 - 75.00
5458 *The Old Ark's A 'Moving*................50.00 - 75.00

"MOMMIE" GRAY/OWEN GRAY/OTTO GRAY'S (OKLAHOMA) COWBOY BAND:
Champion 16027 *It Can't Be Done* ....20.00 - 30.00
Gennett 6376 *It Can't Be Done*...................25.00 - 40.00
6387 *In The Baggage Coach Ahead* ....25.00 - 40.00
6405 *The Drunkard's Lone Child* ....25.00 - 40.00
7222 *Down Where The Swanee River Flows*.....50.00 - 75.00
Superior 2550 *It Can't Be Done* ....30.00 - 50.00
Vocalion 5250 *It Can't Be Done*.................40.00 - 60.00
5267 *Tom Cat Blues* ....50.00 - 75.00
5301 *Be Home Early Tonight, My Dear* ....50.00 - 75.00
5327 *The Terrible Marriage* ....50.00 - 75.00
5337 *Midnight Special* ....50.00 - 75.00
5479 *Who Stole The Lock* ....50.00 - 75.00

(G. B.) GRAYSON & (HENRY) WHITTER (See also WHITTER & GRAYSON):
Bluebird 5498, 7072..............................5.00 - 10.00
Gennett 6304 *Nobody's Darling* ....30.00 - 50.00
Victor 21139 *Don't Go Out Tonight My Darling* ... 15.00 - 20.00
21189 *Train Forty-Five* ....15.00 - 20.00
21625 *Rose Conley* ....25.00 - 40.00
23565 *Going Down The Lee Highvay*...............40.00 - 60.00
V40038 *Joking Henry* ....15.00 - 20.00
V40063 *Red And Green Signal Lights* ....15.00 - 25.00
V40268 *I Have Lost You Darling* ....20.00 - 30.00
V40324 *I've Always Been A Rambler*..............25.00 - 40.00

GREAT GAP ENTERTAINERS:
Broadway 8137 *Barn Dance On The Mountain* .....10.00 - 15.00
8140 *Pussy Cat Rag*..........................10.00 - 15.00
8200 *O Wasn't I Getting Away* ....10.00 - 15.00

GREEN'S STRING BAND:
Champion 16115 *Zenda Waltz*...................15.00 - 20.00
16249 *Gray Eagle* ....15.00 - 20.00
16489 *Rickett's Hornpipe* ....20.00 - 30.00
Gennett 7307 *Glide Waltz*.....................25.00 - 40.00

GREEN & RUSSELL:
Supertone 9377 *Goodnight Waltz* ....10.00 - 15.00

UNCLE GEORGE GREEN & HIS BOYS:
Champion 15828 *Louisiana Hop* ....8.00 - 12.00
15896 *Polly Wolly Doodle* ....8.00 - 12.00

JERRY GREEN:
Specialty 712 *Naggin' Women And Braggin' Men*... 8.00 - 12.00
714 *Are You Goin' My Way?* ....8.00 - 12.00

AMOS GREENE:
Supertone 9651 *Down In The Jailhouse On My Knees*
....12.00 - 18.00
9671 *Memphis Yodel*..........................12.00 - 18.00
9707 *I'm Lonely And Blue* ....12.00 - 18.00
9708 *Yodeling Them Blues Away*................12.00 - 18.00
9709 *Just A Lonely Hobo* ....12.00 - 18.00

CLARENCE GREENE (& THE WISE BROTHERS):
Columbia 15311-D *Fond Affection*.................20.00 - 30.00
15461-D *Johnson City Blues* ....30.00 - 50.00
15580-D *Pride Of The Ball*....................30.00 - 50.00
Victor V40141 *Little Bunch Of Roses* ....25.00 - 40.00

LEM GREEN:
Okeh 45418 *Eleven More Months & Ten More Days*
....8.00 - 12.00

PROFESSOR & MRS. GREER:
Paramount 3195 *Black Jack Davy* ....25.00 - 40.00
   3236 *Sweet William And Fair Ellen* ....25.00 - 40.00

BOBBY GREGORY:
Okeh 45350 *The Runaway Boys* ....10.00 - 15.00
   45473 *Hoopee Scoopee*..................................10.00 - 15.00
   45500 *Little Pal Of Mine* ....10.00 - 15.00

WALLACE GREY:
Champion 15832 *Little Mamie* ....8.00 - 12.00

REX GRIFFIN:
Decca 5088, 5089, 5118, 5147, 5202, 5227, 5250,
   5269, 5294, 5383, 5395 ....5.00 - 10.00

TAYLOR GRIGGS' MELODY MAKERS (See TAYLOR'S MELODY MAKERS)

GRINNELL GIGGERS:
Bluebird 5284 *Ruth's Rag* ....20.00 - 30.00
Victor 23511 *Duck Shoes Rag* ....50.00 - 80.00
   23632 *Cotton Picker's Rag* ....75.00 - 100.00
   23675 *Plow Boy Hop* ....75.00 - 100.00
   V40275 *Giggers Waltz* ....50.00 - 80.00

DEWEY GROOM & HIS TEXAS LONGHORNS:
Imperial 8073 *Butane Blues*...............................5.00 - 8.00
   8078 *Stop, Look and Listen* ....5.00 - 8.00

BILL GRUBBS & HIS OKLAHOMA RAMBLERS:
Blue Bonnet 101 *My Gal Alice* ....7.00 - 10.00
   105 *I'm Gonna Wake Up In Waco*......................7.00 - 10.00

GUNBOAT BILLY & THE SPARROW:
Crown 3077 *Eleven More Months And Ten More Days*
....7.00 - 10.00
Paramount 3273 *Eleven More Months And Ten More Days*
....7.00 - 10.00
Victor 23698 *I'm Glad I'm A Bum* ....10.00 - 15.00
   23714 *Four Stone Walls* ....10.00 - 15.00
   24024 *Oh Lord The Life Of A Hobo* ....7.00 - 10.00

HARDROCK GUNTER & THE PEBBLES:
Bama 104 *Birmingham Bounce* ....8.00 - 12.00
   202 *Lonesome Blues* ....10.00 - 15.00
M-G-M 11520 *Naptown, Indiana* ....7.00 - 10.00
M-G-M 11596 *Sunday Angel* ....7.00 - 10.00

(E. E.) HACK'S STRING BAND:
Champion 16292 *Kentucky Plow Boy's March*.......30.00 - 50.00
   45149 *Wink The Other Eye* ....10.00 - 15.00
Columbia 15418-D *Too Tight Rag* ....20.00 - 30.00
   15466-D *Black Lake Waltz* ....20.00 - 30.00

HACKBERRY RAMBLERS:
Bluebird 2002 *Bring It Down To The Jailhouse, Honey*
....8.00 - 12.00
   2003 *Jolie Blonde* ....8.00 - 12.00
   2005 *Vinton High Society* ....8.00 - 12.00
   2010 *Rambling* ....8.00 - 12.00
   2013 *Cajun Crawl*..8.00 - 12.00
   2017 *Rice City Stomp* ....8.00 - 12.00
   2019 *Dobie Shack* ....8.00 - 12.00
   2021, 2066, 6069, 6110, 6120, 6136, 6181,
   6289, 6368 ....8.00 - 12.00

RED HADLEY'S WRANGLERS:
Meteor 5017 *Brother, That's All* ....7.00 - 10.00

EWEN HAIL:
Brunswick 141 *Cowboy's Lament* ....5.00 - 8.00
   433 *Cowboy's Lament*..5.00 - 8.00
Vocalion 5146 *Cowboy's Lament* ....7.00 - 10.00

THERON HALE & DAUGHTERS:
Victor V40019 *Turkey Gobbler* ....30.00 - 50.00
   V40046 *Jolly Blacksmith* ....30.00 - 50.00

TRAVIS B. HALE (& E. J. DERRY, JR.):
Victor 20796 *Oh Bury Me Out On The Prairie* ....5.00 - 8.00
   20866 *Long Gone*..7.00 - 10.00

AMBROSE HALEY'S OZARK RAMBLERS:
Vocalion 03590 *It Looks Like Rain In Cherry Blossom Lane*
....7.00 - 10.00
   03648 *How's Your Folks & My Folks* ....7.00 - 10.00
   03709 *I Can't Lose That Longing For You*..........7.00 - 10.00

HALL BROTHERS:
Bluebird 6843 *Little Mohee* ....5.00 - 8.00
   6925 *Whistle, Honey, Whistle* ....7.00 - 10.00
   7103 *Little Girl, You've Done Me Wrong*...........7.00 - 10.00
   7363 *Spartanburg Jail* ....7.00 - 10.00
   7462 *Alcatraz Prisoner* ....7.00 - 10.00
   7728 *The Wrong Road* ....7.00 - 10.00
   7801 *Hitch-Hike Blues* ....7.00 - 10.00
Clarion 5183-C *That Goes On For Days And Days* . 7.00 - 10.00

HALL TRIO:
Victor 23782 *The Answer To 21 Years* ....10.00 - 15.00
   23797 *It Makes No Difference* ....10.00 - 15.00
   23799 *I'm Twisting Loops In Pretzels* ....10.00 - 15.00
   23836 *Absolutely Free* ....10.00 - 15.00
   23838 *Shepherd Of The Air* ....10.00 - 15.00

ROY HALL (& HIS BLUE RIDGE ENTERTAINERS):
Bluebird 8561 *New San Antonio Rose* ....5.00 - 8.00
   8656 *Don't Let Your Sweet Love Die* ....5.00 - 8.00
   8863 *Polecat Blues* ....5.00 - 8.00
   8959 *I Wonder Where You Are Tonight*...............5.00 - 8.00
Bullet 704 *Mule Boogie* ....5.00 - 8.00
   712 *Ain't You Afraid* ....5.00 - 8.00
Vocalion 04627 *Good For Nothing Gal* ....5.00 - 10.00
   04717 *Lonesome Dove* ....5.00 - 10.00
   04771 *Where The Roses Never Fade* ....5.00 - 10.00
   04842 *Come Back Little Pal* ....5.00 - 10.00

HALTON BROTHERS:
Champion 16628 *Hook And Line* ....50.00 - 75.00

STUART HAMBLEN (COWBOY JOE) (& HIS COVERED WAGON JUBILEE):
Bluebird 5242 *Boy In Blue*...............................10.00 - 15.00
Decca 5001, 5077, 5109, 5145..............................8.00 - 12.00
Victor 23685 *My Brown-Eyed Texas Rose* ....30.00 - 50.00
   V40109 *Boy In Blue* ....30.00 - 50.00
   V40242 *Wrong Keyhole* ....30.00 - 50.00
   V40306 *Standin' On The Pier In The Rain* ....30.00 - 50.00
Victor V40311 *Sailor's Farewell* ....30.00 - 50.00
   V40319 *Drifting Back To Dixie* ....30.00 - 50.00

PAUL HAMBLIN:
Victor V40260 *Strawberry Roan* ....10.00 - 15.00
   V40280 *Prairie Maiden* ....10.00 - 15.00

WYZEE HAMILTON (Acc. by HAMILTON HARMONIANS):
Gennett 6272 *Old Sefus Brown*.......................15.00 - 25.00

HAMLIN QUARTETTE:
Herwin 75572 *Darling Nellie Gray*......................15.00 - 25.00

JOHN HAMMOND:
Champion 15356 *Drunken Hiccoughs*......................8.00 - 12.00
Gennett 6256 *Little Birdie* ....15.00 - 20.00
Supertone 9249 *Little Birdie*..............................7.00 - 10.00

SID HAMPTON (THE YODELIN' MAN FROM DIXIE LAND):
Columbia 15555-D *Kicking Mule* ....8.00 - 12.00
   15583-D *The Hills Of Tennessee*........................8.00 - 12.00

WILLIAM HANSON:
Okeh 45506 *Stop And Listen Blues* ....30.00 - 50.00
   45523 *Gambling On The Sabbath* ....30.00 - 50.00

HAPPY HOLLOW HOODLUMS:
Decca 5098 *Down Home Rag* ....7.00 - 10.00

HAPPY HAYSEEDS:
Victor 23722 *Ladies' Quadrille* ....15.00 - 25.00
   23774 *Cottonwood Reel*.....................................15.00 - 25.00

HAPPY JACK:
Columbia 15720-D *I'm Only Suggesting This*...........7.00 - 10.00

HAPPY VALLEY FAMILY:
Vocalion 04251 *Lily Of The Valley* ....5.00 - 8.00
   04296 *My Clinch Mountain Home* ....5.00 - 8.00
   04484 *Going Down To The Valley* ....5.00 - 8.00
(Note: Above titles and others were also issued on Banner, Melotone, Oriole, Perfect, and Romeo.)

TEX HARDIN:
Champion 16552 *The Trail To California*...............15.00 - 20.00

BILLY HARDISON (See TENNESSEE DRIFTERS)

HARKINS & MORAN:
Broadway 8055 *Hand Me Down My Walking Cane* .8.00 - 12.00
   8056 *Bully Of The Town*......................................8.00 - 12.00
   8064 *Lazy Tennessee* ....10.00 - 15.00
   8081 *Land Where We'll Never Grow Old* ....10.00 - 15.00
   8114 *John Henry*..10.00 - 15.00
   8115 *The Gambler's Dying Words* ....10.00 - 15.00
   8117 *In The Sweet Bye And Bye* ....10.00 - 15.00
   8157 *Kitty Wells*..10.00 - 15.00

HARKINS & OWENS:
Broadway 8214 *A Mother's Plea* ....8.00 - 12.00

HARKINS & PERRY:
Broadway 8129 *Life's Railway To Heaven* ....8.00 - 12.00

(SID) HARKREADER & (GRADY) MOORE; HARKREADER & (BLYTHE) POTEET:
Paramount 3022 *Bully Of The Town*.......................10.00 - 15.00
   3023 *John Henry*...10.00 - 15.00
   3024 *There's A Little Rosewood Casket*............10.00 - 15.00
   3025 *The Gambler's Dying Words* ....10.00 - 15.00
   3033 *Mockingbird Breakdown* ....25.00 - 40.00
   3035 *Only As Far As The Gate* ....10.00 - 15.00
   3043 *Kitty Wells*...10.00 - 15.00
   3044 *Bits Of Blues* ....25.00 - 40.00
   3052 *Land Where We'll Never Grow Old* ....10.00 - 15.00
   3054 *It Looks To Me Like A Big Night Tonight* . 25.00 - 40.00
   3061 *The Old Rugged Cross* ....10.00 - 15.00
   3063 *Lazy Tennessee*..25.00 - 40.00
   3094 *Life's Railway To Heaven* ....10.00 - 15.00
   3104 *Take Me Back To Carolina Home* ....15.00 - 20.00
   3112 *Sweet Bird* ....15.00 - 20.00
   3118 *Wang Wang Blues* ....25.00 - 40.00
   3141 *Red River Valley* ....15.00 - 20.00
   3183 *On The Bowery* ....15.00 - 20.00
   3296 *Land Where We'll Never Grow Old*..........10.00 - 15.00
Vocalion 5063 *Never River Train* ....15.00 - 20.00
   5066 *Oh, Where Is My Boy Tonight* ....15.00 - 20.00
   5082 *Struttin' Round* ....15.00 - 20.00
   5114 *Dark Eyes* ....15.00 - 20.00
   14887 *Soldier's Joy*..15.00 - 20.00
   15035 *New River Train* ....15.00 - 20.00
   15075 *The Dying Girl's Message* ....15.00 - 20.00
   15193 *Struttin' Round* ....15.00 - 20.00
   15366 *Dark Eyes* ....15.00 - 20.00

HARMONICA BILL:
Champion 16393 *The Prisoner's Radio* ....25.00 - 40.00
   16399 *Answer To The Gypsy's Warning* ....25.00 - 40.00
   16425 *Georgia The Dear Old State I Love* ....25.00 - 40.00

HARMONICA JIM:
Superior 2789 *The Prisoner's Radio* ....30.00 - 50.00
   2806 *Great Grandad And Grandma* ....30.00 - 50.00

RICHARD HAROLD:
Columbia 15426-D *Sweet Bird* ....8.00 - 12.00
   15586-D *The Battleship Maine* ....8.00 - 12.00

HARPER BROTHERS:
Brunswick 469 *Dreamy Rocky Mountain Moon*.......5.00 - 8.00
   505 *Blue Pacific Moonlight* ....5.00 - 8.00

HARPER FAMILY TRIO:
Supertone 9645, 9649, 9656, 9729 ....4.00 - 7.00

HARPER & HALL:
Superior 2678 *Down The Lane To Home Sweet Home*
   ....15.00 - 20.00
   2799 *Life's Railway To Heaven*........................15.00 - 20.00

HARPER & PAGE:
Supertone 9314 *Sweet William* ....7.00 - 10.00

HARPER & TURNER:
Supertone 9262, 9266, 9316, 9353, 9391, 9658 ....4.00 - 8.00
   9640 *Sweet Adeline At The Still* ....5.00 - 10.00
   9656 *There's A Vacant Chair At Home Sweet Home*
   ....5.00 - 10.00
   9678 *No Never Alone* ....5.00 - 10.00
   9725 *I Surrender All* ....5.00 - 10.00
   9726 *Beautiful Garden of Prayer* ....5.00 - 10.00

DIXIE HARPER & HER BLUEBONNET BRATS:
Royalty P-31 *Sweeter Than The Flowers*................8.00 - 12.00
   P-38/39 *Lovesick Blues* ....8.00 - 12.00

AUNT IDY HARPER & THE COON CREEK GIRLS:
Vocalion 04203, 04354 ....7.00 - 10.00

JACK HARPER:
Vocalion 5494 *The Tramp's Last Ride* ....7.00 - 10.00

OSCAR HARPER'S TEXAS STRING BAND:
Okeh 45227 *Bouquet Waltz* ....30.00 - 50.00
Vocalion 5403 *Sally Johnson* ....30.00 - 50.00

OSCAR & DOC HARPER:

Okeh 45397 *Beaumont Rag* ....35.00 - 50.00
   45420 *Terrell Texas Blues* ....40.00 - 60.00
   45485 *Bitter Creek*................................40.00 - 60.00

ROY HARPER & EARL SHIRKEY (See also SHIRKEY & HARPER):

Columbia 15429-D *Bootlegger's Dream*.................25.00 - 40.00
   15467-D *Cowboy's Lullaby*..............................25.00 - 40.00

KELLY HARRELL (& HENRY NORTON):

Okeh 40486 *Wild Bill Jones* ....8.00 - 12.00
Victor 19596 *New River Train* ....5.00 - 8.00
   20103 *My Horses Ain't Hungry*.....................5.00 - 8.00
   20171 *Rovin' Gambler* ....5.00 - 8.00
   20242 *Butcher's Boy*..............................5.00 - 8.00
   20527 *Bright Sherman Valley*......................5.00 - 8.00
   20535 *Bye And Bye You Will Forget* ....5.00 - 8.00
   20657 *I'm Nobody's Darling On Earth*..............5.00 - 8.00
   20797 *Charles Giteau*.............................6.00 - 10.00
   20867 *I Love My Sweetheart The Best* ....6.00 - 10.00
   20935 *Row Us Over The Tide*.......................8.00 - 12.00
   21069 *For Seven Long Years*.......................8.00 - 12.00
   21520 *My Wife, She Has Gone* ....8.00 - 12.00
   23741 *I Heard Somebody Call* ....20.00 - 30.00
   V40047 *Oh, My Pretty Monkey*....................20.00 - 30.00
   V40095 *She Just Kept Kissing On*.................20.00 - 30.00

EARL HARRIS:

Okeh 45566 *Gene, The Fighting Marine*..................5.00 - 8.00

GEORGE HARRIS:

Columbia 15543-D *That's The Blue Heaven For Me*
....10.00 - 15.00

J. D. HARRIS:

Okeh 45024 *Cackling Hen*...........................15.00 - 20.00

SIM HARRIS:

Oriole 916 *Pass Around The Bottle* ....7.00 - 10.00
   946 *The Fatal Wedding* ....7.00 - 10.00
   947 *Bully Of The Town* ....7.00 - 10.00

HAPPY BUD HARRISON:

Vocalion 5344 *Mail Man Blues*............................20.00 - 30.00
   5350 *I'm Glad I'm Free*............................20.00 - 30.00
   5370 *Ball And Chain Blues*.........................20.00 - 30.00
   5405 *Mama Don't Allow No Easy Riders*...........20.00 - 30.00

HART BROTHERS:

Paramount 3162 *The Miner's Prayer* ....10.00 - 15.00
   3176 *The Empty Cradle* ....10.00 - 15.00
   3262 *Lamp Lighting Time In The Valley* ....10.00 - 15.00
   3265 *The Prodigal Son* ....10.00 - 15.00

HART & CATES:

Okeh 45499 *In The Valley Of Broken Hearts*..........15.00 - 20.00

HART & OGLE:

Broadway 8299 *Two Locks of Hair*.........................20.00 - 30.00
   8303 *Seeing Nellie Home*.........................20.00 - 30.00
Paramount 3297 *They Cut Down The Old Pine Tree*
....20.00 - 30.00

HARTMAN'S HEARTBREAKERS; DICK HARTMAN'S TENNESSEE RAMBLERS:

Bluebird 5796, 5797, 5837, 5875, 5876, 5891, 5909,
   5962, 5992, 6003, 6089, 6105, 6122, 6135, 6162,
   6180, 6207, 6226, 6227, 6274, 6481, 6494, 6516,
   6542, 6566, 6622, 6656.............................5.00 - 10.00

BOB HARTSELL:

Bluebird 7439 *Rambling Freight Train Yodel* ....7.00 - 10.00
   7473 *Rock Me To Sleep In My Rocky Mountain Home*
....7.00 - 10.00

(ROY) HARVEY (& COLEMAN/LEONARD HOKE COPELAND/BOB HOKE/JESS JOHNSON/HIS NORTH CAROLINA RAMBLERS/POSEY RORER):

Brunswick 223 *There'll Come A Time*....................10.00 - 15.00
   234 *I'll Be There Mary Dear* ....10.00 - 15.00
   250 *The Bluefield Murder*.............................10.00 - 15.00
   268 *Budded Roses*....................................10.00 - 15.00
Champion 16187 *No Room For A Tramp*..................30.00 - 50.00
   16213 *When The Bees Are In The Hives*...........30.00 - 50.00
   16255 *Railroad Blues*..............................50.00 - 75.00
   16281 *Gambling Blues*.............................50.00 - 75.00
   16312 *Called To The Foreign Fields*..................50.00 - 75.00
   16331 *You're Bound To Look Like A Monkey*... 50.00 - 75.00
   16662 *The Great Reaping Day* ....50.00 - 75.00
   16781 *Jefferson Street Rag* ....80.00 - 120.00
   45011, 45035, 45117................................10.00 - 20.00
Columbia 15155-D *Daisies Won't Tell*...................10.00 - 15.00
   15514-D *Beckley Rag* ....30.00 - 50.00
   15582-D *Lonesome Weary Blues*...................30.00 - 50.00
   15637-D *Greasy Wagon* ....75.00 - 100.00
   15714-D *Dark Eyes*...............................75.00 - 100.00
Gennett 6303 *The Old Clay Pipe* ....20.00 - 30.00
   6350 *We Will Outshine The Sun* ....15.00 - 25.00
Vocalion 5243 *Sweet Refrain*............................35.00 - 50.00

OVERTON HATFIELD:

Columbia 15687-D *A Gangster's Warning* ....100.00 - 150.00

HAUULEA ENTERTAINERS:

Okeh 45461 *Twelfth Street Rag* ....20.00 - 30.00
   45490 *Railroad Blues* ....20.00 - 30.00

HAWAIIAN PALS:

Victor 23588 *It's Awful What Whiskey Will Do* ..... 25.00 - 40.00

BUDDY HAWK & HIS BUDDIES:

Atlantic 7074 *Painting The Big Town* ....- - -

HAWKINS & PUCKETT:

Bluebird 5691 *Down In The Valley* ....10.00 - 15.00

UNCLE BEN HAWKINS (& HIS BOYS):

Challenge 244 *The Poor Tramp Has To Live* ....7.00 - 10.00
Champion 15248 *Round Town Gals* ....7.00 - 10.00
Silvertone 5001 *The Poor Tramp Has To Live* ....7.00 - 10.00
   5003 *Long Eared Mule* ....7.00 - 10.00
Supertone 9255 *When The Roses Bloom Again*........7.00 - 10.00
   9400 *The New River Train*........................7.00 - 10.00

UNCLE BILLY HAWKINS:

Champion 15084 *Turkey In The Straw* ....5.00 - 8.00

UNCLE JIM HAWKINS:

Challenge 101 *Hell Broke Loose In Georgia*............5.00 - 8.00
   109 *Turkey In The Straw*..........................5.00 - 8.00
   111 *Dixie*..5.00 - 8.00

112 *Billy In The Low Ground* ....5.00 - 8.00
301 *Arkansas Traveler* ....5.00 - 8.00
304 *Hell Broke Loose In Georgia* ....5.00 - 8.00
Champion 15098 *Seneca Square Dance* ....7.00 - 10.00

TED HAWKINS' MOUNTAINEERS:
Columbia 15752-D *Roamin' Jack* ....50.00 - 75.00

HAYES & JENKINS:
Superior 2537 *I Played On My Spanish Guitar* ....25.00 - 35.00

DEWEY HAYES (THE CAROLINA TROUBADOUR):
Columbia 15753-D *Bring Back The One I Love* .....25.00 - 40.00

ED HAYES:
Okeh 45025 *Big White Rooster And The Little Brown Hen*
....15.00 - 20.00

SELMA & DEWEY HAYES:
Victor 23629 *Broken Heart* ....15.00 - 20.00

HAYWOOD COUNTY RAMBLERS:
Victor 23779 *Buncombe Chain Gang* ....75.00 - 100.00

EDDIE HAZLEWOOD:
Imperial 8056 *Way Way Down In San Antone* ....7.00 - 10.00
8062 *A Package Of Lies Tied In Blue* ....7.00 - 10.00
Intro 6019 *Truck Drivin' Woman* ....5.00 - 8.00
6028 *I'll Pay You No Never Mind* ....5.00 - 8.00
6039 *A Rag, A Bone, A Hank Of Hair* ....5.00 - 8.00
6050 *I've Got A Bad Case Of The Blues* ....5.00 - 8.00

JIMMY HEAP & THE MELODY MASTERS:
Imperial 8064 *That's My Baby* ....8.00 - 12.00
8066 *Snakes in My Boots* ....8.00 - 12.00
8069 *A Broken Pane In The Window of My Heart* ...8.00 - 12.00
8074 *Mean Old Blues* ....8.00 - 12.00
8077 *Love For Sale* ....8.00 - 12.00
8089 *Ethyl In My Gas Tank (No Gal In My Arms)* .....8.00 - 12.00
8090 *The Woods Are Full Of Them* ....8.00 - 12.00
8098 *Don't Steal My Dreams* ....7.00 - 10.00
8103 *Butter Ball Bounce* ....7.00 - 10.00
8122 *More Than Friends* ....7.00 - 10.00
8129 *That's That* ....7.00 - 10.00
8133 *My Angel Isn't On My Christmas Tree* ....8.00 - 12.00

BILL HELMS & HIS UPSON COUNTY BAND:
Victor 21649 *Georgia Blues* ....20.00 - 30.00
V40079 *Alabama Jubilee* ....25.00 - 50.00

BILL HELMS & RILEY PUCKETT:
Columbia 15774-D *Lost Love* ....75.00 - 125.00

ERNEST HELTON:
Okeh 45010 *Royal Clog* ....15.00 - 20.00

HENDERSON BROTHERS:
Vocalion 03128 *The Grave Beneath The Pines* ....8.00 - 12.00

RED HENDERSON:
Okeh 45283 *Auto Ride Through Alabama* ....8.00 - 12.00

(FISHER) HENDLEY (& HIS ARISTOCRATIC PIGS/ CAROLINA TAR HEELS/& SMALL):
Bluebird 6555 *Another Man's Wife* ....7.00 - 10.00
Okeh 45012 *Let Your Shack Burn Down* ....40.00 - 60.00
Victor 23528 *Shuffle Feet, Shuffle* ....75.00 - 100.00
Vocalion 02530 *Greasy Possum* ....30.00 - 50.00
02543 *Answer To Big Rock Candy Mountain* .....30.00 - 50.00
02612 *Going Down Town* ....25.00 - 40.00

02679 *Hook And Line* ....25.00 - 40.00
04516, 04556, 04658, 04718, 04780, 04881,
04937, 05016 ....4.00 - 7.00

(CHIEF) HENRY'S STRING BAND:
Victor V40195 *Cherokee Rag* ....40.00 - 60.00
V40225 *Choctaw Waltz* ....40.00 - 60.00
V40281 *Indian Tom Tom* ....40.00 - 60.00

HENSLEY, TAYLOR & WALKER:
Vocalion 02639 *It's Hard To Make Gertie* ....30.00 - 50.00
02640 *Scottdale Stomp* ....30.00 - 50.00
02678 *Match Box Blues* ....30.00 - 50.00

HERMAN BROTHERS:
Broadway 8165 *Turkey In The Straw* ....5.00 - 8.00

HERNANDEZ BROTHERS:
Victor V40081 *When You And I Were Young, Maggie*
....5.00 - 10.00

ZEB HERRELSON & M. B. PADGETT:
Okeh 45078 *Soldier's Joy* ....10.00 - 15.00

BENNIE HESS (& HIS NATION'S PLAY BOYS):
Opera 102 *I'm Not Gonna Fool With You* ....10.00 - 15.00
104 *Drink Drink Drink* ....10.00 - 15.00
1013 *Bennie Hess Boogie* ....10.00 - 15.00
1015 *Novelty Yodel No. 1* ....8.00 - 12.00
1018 *To Be Loved* ....8.00 - 12.00
1019 *Texas Stars* ....8.00 - 12.00

HICKORY NUTS:
Okeh 45169 *The Louisville Burglar* ....10.00 - 15.00
45220 *There'll Be No Liars There* ....10.00 - 15.00

HI-FLYERS:
Vocalion 03684, 03964, 04011, 04093, 04589, 04671,
04703, 05000, 05054 ....5.00 - 8.00

LEN & JOE HIGGINS:
Columbia 15243-D *Kentucky Wedding Chimes* ....8.00 - 12.00
15354-D *Slippery Elm Tree* ....10.00 - 15.00

HIGHLANDERS:
Paramount 3171 *Flop-Eared Mule* ....30.00 - 50.00
3184 *Richmond Square* ....30.00 - 50.00
3200 *Tennessee Blues* ....30.00 - 50.00

HIGH NEIGHBOR BOYS:
Vocalion 04555, 04691, 04773, 04895 ....4.00 - 7.00

LUKE HIGHNIGHT & HIS OZARK STRUTTERS:
Vocalion 5325 *There's No Hell In Georgia* ....50.00 - 80.00
5339 *Fort Smith Breakdown* ....50.00 - 80.00

HILL'S VIRGINIA MOUNTAINEERS:
Supertone 9170 *Forked Deer* ....5.00 - 10.00

BOB HILL:
Victor 23718 *He Was A Good Man* ....30.00 - 40.00

EZRA HILL & HENRY JOHNSON:
Champion 15750 *Birmingham Jail* ....20.00 - 30.00

FRANK HILL:
Supertone 9319 *Lonely Village Churchyard* ....6.00 - 10.00
9612 *I'll Not Forget You Daddy* ....6.00 - 10.00

LUCKY HILL with THE ROLLING STONES:
TNT 109 *Life Of Love* ....8.00 - 12.00

JESS HILLARD (See JESS HILLIARD)

HILLBILLIES:

Vocalion 5016 *East Tennessee Blues*	7.00 -	10.00
5017 *Blue Eyed Girl*	7.00 -	10.00
5018 *Kitty Wells*	7.00 -	10.00
5019 *Sally Ann*	7.00 -	10.00
5020 *Cluck, Old Hen*	7.00 -	10.00
5021 *Texas Gals*	7.00 -	10.00
5022 *Sourwood Mountain*	7.00 -	10.00
5023 *Buck-Eyed Rabbits*	7.00 -	10.00
5024 *Cumberland Gap*	7.00 -	10.00
5025 *Bristol Tennessee Blues*	7.00 -	10.00
5115 *Cripple Creek*	7.00 -	10.00
5116 *Mississippi Sawyer*	7.00 -	10.00
5117 *Old Joe Clark*	7.00 -	10.00
5173 *Hear Dem Bells*	7.00 -	10.00
5178 *Sweet Bunch Of Daisies*	7.00 -	10.00
5179 *Black-Eyed Susie*	7.00 -	10.00
5182 *Baby, Your Time Ain't Long*	7.00 -	10.00
5183 *Wasn't She A Dandy*	7.00 -	10.00
Vocalion 5186 *Darling Nellie Gray*	7.00 -	10.00
15367 *Cripple Creek*	7.00 -	10.00
15368 *Mississippi Sawyer*	7.00 -	10.00
15369 *Old Joe Clark*	7.00 -	10.00

HARRY HILLIARD:

Champion 16337 *Blue Yodel No. 9*	60.00 -	90.00
Superior 2663 *The Mystery Of No. 5*	75.00 -	100.00

JESS HILLIARD (& HIS ACES/WEST VIRGINIA HILLBILLIES):

Champion 16333 *Cackling Hen*	50.00 -	75.00
16347 *Pea Pickin Papa*	50.00 -	75.00
16368 *Penitentiary Blues*	50.00 -	75.00
16398 *Ninety-Nine Years*	50.00 -	75.00
16525 *Red Night Gown Blues*	50.00 -	75.00
16564 *Mississippi Moon*	50.00 -	75.00
16571 *The Barnyard Stomp*	50.00 -	75.00
16617 *99 Years Blues*	50.00 -	75.00
16638 *Hell Up Flat Rock*	50.00 -	75.00
16640 *Tall Mamma Blues*	50.00 -	75.00
16651 *Austin Breakdown*	50.00 -	75.00
16670 *Dixie Rag*	50.00 -	75.00
Champion 45001, 45003, 45026, 45047, 45091, 45095	10.00 -	20.00
Superior 2695 *The Ramblers Blues*	80.00 -	120.00

HINSON, PITTS & COLEY:

Bluebird 7438 *Whoa, Mule, Whoa*	5.00 -	8.00

W. A. HINTON:

Victor 23555 *Leather Breeches*	75.00 -	100.00

HOBBS BROTHER:

Conqueror 7332 *Patty On The Turnpike*	4.00 -	7.00
Paramount 3219 *Devils Dream*	7.00 -	10.00
3220 *Patty On The Turnpike*	7.00 -	10.00
3224 *Hell Among The Yearlings*	7.00 -	10.00
Q. R. S. 9003 *Turkey In The Straw*	20.00 -	30.00

GEORGE HOBSON:

Silvertone 3045 *The Lighting Express*	5.00 -	8.00
3047 *The Baggage Coach Ahead*	5.00 -	8.00

WILLARD HODGIN (BANJO JOE):

Edison 52204 *Courtin' The Widow*	15.00 -	20.00

52243 *Girl That Lived On Polecat Creek*	15.00 -	20.00
52278 *Judge Done Me Wrong*	15.00 -	20.00
52332 *Ugly Gals Got Something Hard To Beat*	15.00 -	20.00
Victor 21485 *Don't Get One Woman*	15.00 -	20.00

ADOLPH HOFNER & HIS TEXANS:

Bluebird 7597, 7641, 7701, 7752, 7833, 7900, 7931, 7955, 7988, 8071	5.00 -	10.00
Imperial 8010 *Alamo Schottische*	5.00 -	8.00
8012 *Prune Waltz*	5.00 -	8.00
8015 *Kelley Waltz*	7.00 -	10.00
8016 *White Christmas*	8.00 -	12.00
8020 *Julida Polka*	7.00 -	10.00
8022 *Texas Is My Home*	7.00 -	10.00
8027 *Shiner Song*	7.00 -	10.00
8028 *Longhorn Stomp*	7.00 -	10.00
8033 *Rose of The Alamo*	7.00 -	10.00
8037 *The Blue Bonnet Polka*	7.00 -	10.00
8041 *Forgive Me*	7.00 -	10.00

GEORGE HOLDEN:

Challenge 385 *The Marion Parker Murder*	7.00 -	10.00
392 *The Preacher And The Bear*	7.00 -	10.00

HOLMES & TAYLOR:

Superior 2713 *The Pretty Quadroon*	15.00 -	20.00

GEORGE HOLMES:

Superior 2525 *A Mother's Plea*	15.00 -	20.00

SALTY HOLMES:

Bluebird 5303 *I Want My Mama*	8.00 -	12.00

HOME TOWN BOYS:

Columbia 15736-D *Still Got Ninety-Nine*	25.00 -	40.00
15762-D *Home Town Rag*	25.00 -	40.00

HONEYBOY & SASSAFRAS:

Brunswick 417 *The Lighthouse Song*	7.00 -	10.00
509 *The Chicken Sermon*	8.00 -	12.00
585 *Some Family*	8.00 -	12.00

HONOLULU STROLLERS:

Okeh 45226 *Ole Oaken Bucket*	8.00 -	12.00
45239 *Mighty Lak' A Rose*	8.00 -	12.00
Victor 23600 *Don't Say No*	20.00 -	30.00

HOOSIER HOT SHOTS:

This largely corn-ball group, which became popular in the 1930s, still seems to have a following. So, popular demand has resulted in this expanded listing, notwithstanding the minimal value of most of the records. A case can be made for putting this listing in the first section of this book, based on the group's pseudo-rusticity, and its great popularity beyond the rural market. But, many of the records were issued in the folk series of various labels; they'll remain with their country cousins in this section.

Titles issued contemporaneously* on Banner, Conqueror, Melotone, Oriole, Perfect, Romeo, and Vocalion:

After You've Gone	5.00 -	10.00
Ain't She Sweet	5.00 -	10.00
Alexander's Ragtime Band	5.00 -	10.00
At The Darktown Strutters' Ball	5.00 -	10.00
Back In Indiana	5.00 -	10.00
The Band Played On	5.00 -	10.00
Black Eyed Susan Brown	5.00 -	10.00
Bow Wow Blues	5.00 -	10.00
Breezin' Along With The Breeze	5.00 -	10.00

Bye Bye Blues	5.00 -	10.00
The Coat And Pants Do All The Work	5.00 -	10.00
Diga Diga Do	5.00 -	10.00
Don't Change Horses	5.00 -	10.00
Down Home Rag	5.00 -	10.00
Down In The Valley	5.00 -	10.00
Everybody Stomp	5.00 -	10.00
Farmer Gray	5.00 -	10.00
Ferdinand The Bull	5.00 -	10.00
Four Thousand Years Ago	5.00 -	10.00
Goofus	5.00 -	10.00
Ha-Cha-Nan (The Daughter Of San)	5.00 -	10.00
Hold 'Er Eb'ner	5.00 -	10.00
Hoosier Stomp	5.00 -	10.00
Hot Lips	5.00 -	10.00
How Ya Gonna Keep 'Em Down On The Farm	5.00 -	10.00
I Can't Give You Anything But Love	5.00 -	10.00
I Like Bananas, Because They Have No Bones	5.00 -	10.00
I Like Mountain Music	5.00 -	10.00
I Wish I Could Shimmy Like My Sister Kate	5.00 -	10.00
I'm Just Wild About Harry	5.00 -	10.00
I've Got A Bimbo Down On The Bamboo Isle	5.00 -	10.00
Ida! (Sweet As Apple Cider)	5.00 -	10.00
Is It True What They Say About Dixie?	5.00 -	10.00
Man With The Whiskers	5.00 -	10.00
Margie	5.00 -	10.00
Meet Me By The Ice House Lizzie	5.00 -	10.00
The Merry-Go-Roundup	5.00 -	10.00
Milenberg Joys	5.00 -	10.00
Moving Day in Jungle Town	5.00 -	10.00
My Wife Is On A Diet	5.00 -	10.00
Nobody's Sweetheart	5.00 -	10.00
Oh You Beautiful Doll	5.00 -	10.00
Pick That Bass	5.00 -	10.00
Put On Your Old Red Flannels	5.00 -	10.00
Red Hot Fannie	5.00 -	10.00
San	5.00 -	10.00
Shake Your Dogs	5.00 -	10.00
Sheik Of Araby	5.00 -	10.00
Shirley	5.00 -	10.00
Some Of These Days	5.00 -	10.00
St. Louis Blues	5.00 -	10.00
Start The Day Right	5.00 -	10.00
Sweet Sue-Just You	5.00 -	10.00
Take Me Out To The Ball Game	5.00 -	10.00
That's What I Learned In College	5.00 -	10.00
Them Hill-Billies Are Mountain-Williams Now	5.00 -	10.00
There'll Be Some Changes Made	5.00 -	10.00
This Is The Chorus	5.00 -	10.00
Tiger Rag	5.00 -	10.00
Toot, Toot, Tootsie, Goo'bye	5.00 -	10.00
Wabash Blues	5.00 -	10.00
Wah-Hoo!	5.00 -	10.00
Way Down In Arkansaw	5.00 -	10.00
What Is So Rare	5.00 -	10.00
When Paw Was Courtin' Maw	5.00 -	10.00
When You Wore A Tulip	5.00 -	10.00
Where Has My Little Dog Gone!	5.00 -	10.00
Where You Going Honey	5.00 -	10.00
Whistlin' Joe From Kokomo	5.00 -	10.00
Yes She Do-No She Don't	5.00 -	10.00
You're Driving Me Crazy	5.00 -	10.00

(Note: * Strictly speaking, some of the foregoing might be regarded as more "original," e.g. issues on the Melotone 13000 series. These might bring slightly more. Some recordings, issued several years later on Decca, Okeh and Vocalion are not necessarily more common; some are harder to find than some of the group's earlier big sellers that appeared on several labels and remained in print for years.)

AL HOPKINS & HIS BUCKLE BUSTERS:

Brunswick 103 *Round Town Gals*	10.00 -	15.00
104 *Bristol Tennessee Blues*	10.00 -	15.00
105 *Sally Ann*	10.00 -	15.00
106 *Governor Alf Taylor's Fox Chase*	10.00 -	15.00
174 *Sweet Bunch Of Daisies*	5.00 -	8.00
175 *Black Eyed Susie*	5.00 -	8.00
176 *Down The Meadow Lane*	5.00 -	8.00
177 *The Nine Pound Hammer*	5.00 -	8.00
179 *Johnson Boys*	5.00 -	8.00
180 *Echoes Of The Chimes*	5.00 -	8.00
181 *Hear Dem Bells*	5.00 -	8.00
182 *Bug In The Taters*	5.00 -	8.00
183 *Baby Your Time Ain't Long*	8.00 -	12.00
184 *Down To The Club*	5.00 -	8.00
185 *Sleep Baby Sleep*	5.00 -	8.00
186 *Ride That Mule*	5.00 -	8.00
187 *Wasn't She A Dandy?*	5.00 -	8.00
189 *Hear Dem Bells*	5.00 -	8.00
295 *Old Dan Tucker*	8.00 -	12.00
318 *Carolina Moonshiner*	8.00 -	12.00
321 *Polka Medley*	8.00 -	12.00
335 *Wild Hoss*	8.00 -	12.00

ANDY HOPKINS:

Supertone 9490 *Put Me Off At Buffalo*	8.00 -	12.00
9601 *Crepe On The Little Cabin Door*	8.00 -	12.00
9655 *I'll Smoke My Long Stemmed Pipe*	8.00 -	12.00
9713 *The Prison Wardens Secret*	8.00 -	12.00

DOC HOPKINS:

Broadway 8306 *Sugar Babe*	20.00 -	30.00
8337 *Methodist Pie*	20.00 -	30.00

DAN HORNSBY (NOVELTY) ORCH./QUARTETTE/ (LION'S DEN) TRIO:

Columbia 15276-D *On Mobile Bay*	5.00 -	8.00
15321-D *The Shelby Disaster*	7.00 -	10.00
15381-D *She Was Bred In Old Kentucky*	7.00 -	10.00
15444-D *Hinky Dinky Dee*	7.00 -	10.00
15578-D *I'm Sorry I Made You Cry*	7.00 -	10.00
15628-D *The Lunatics Lullaby*	8.00 -	12.00
15769-D *Dear Old Girl*	15.00 -	20.00
15771-D *Three Blind Mice*	15.00 -	20.00

JOHNNY HORTON:

Abbott 100 *Candy Jones*	15.00 -	20.00 *
101 *Happy Millionaire*	15.00 -	20.00 *
102 *Plaid And Calico*	15.00 -	20.00 *
103 *Birds And Butterflies*	15.00 -	20.00 *
104 *In My Home In Shelby County*	15.00 -	20.00 *
105 *Shadows On The Bayou*	15.00 -	20.00 *
106 *Smokey Joes Barbeque*	15.00 -	20.00 *
107 *It's A Long Rocky Road*	15.00 -	20.00 *
108 *Betty Lorraine*	15.00 -	20.00 *
109 *Rhythm In My Baby's Walk*	15.00 -	20.00 *
Cormac 1193 *Plaid And Calico*	20.00 -	30.00
1197 *Birds And Butterflies*	20.00 -	30.00

(Note: See also **RHYTHM & BLUES, ETC.**, section for other records by Johnny Horton.)

WILLIAM B. HOUCHENS:
Gennett 5240 *Turkey In The Straw* ....7.00 - 10.00

KENNETH HOUCHINS (& SLIM COX):
Champion 16473 *Fancy Nancy* ....35.00 - 50.00
    16484 *Do Right Daddy Blues* ....40.00 - 60.00
    16501 *Tennessee Blues* ....40.00 - 60.00
    16553 *The Wanderer's Warning* ....40.00 - 60.00
    16584 *The Yodeling Drifter* ....40.00 - 60.00
    16603 *Mean Old Ball And Chain Blues* ....40.00 - 60.00
    16619 *Bay Rum Blues* ....40.00 - 60.00
    16636 *I'm Just A Yodeling Rambler* ....40.00 - 60.00
    16637 *The Old Missouri Moon* ....40.00 - 60.00
    16650 *Back To Old Smoky Mountain* ....40.00 - 60.00
    16669 *Behind These Grey Walls* ....40.00 - 60.00
    16679 *Homesick For Heaven* ....40.00 - 60.00
    16695 *Our Old Family Album* ....40.00 - 60.00
    16755 *Louisiana Moon* ....50.00 - 75.00
    16775 *My Little Ozark Mountain Home* ....50.00 - 75.00
    16787 *Blue Ridge Lullaby* ....50.00 - 75.00
    16793 *When Jimmie Rodgers Said Goodbye* ......50.00 - 75.00
    16807 *The Gangster's Brother* ....50.00 - 75.00
    45028 *Cowboys Meditation* ....8.00 - 12.00
    45030 *Blue Ridge Lullaby* ....8.00 - 12.00
    45049 *Louisiana Moon* ....8.00 - 12.00
    45054 *The End Of Memory Lane* ....8.00 - 12.00
    45062 *When Jimmie Rodgers Said Goodbye* ......15.00 - 20.00
    45078 *Back To Old Smoky Mountain* ....8.00 - 12.00

LAKE HOWARD:
Titles issued contemporaneously on Banner, Melotone, Oriole,
    Perfect, Romeo: *Chewing Chewing Gum; Don't Let Our Deal Go*
    Down; Forsaken Love; Get Your Head In Here; I Have No One
    To Leave Me; It's None Of Your Business; Little Annie; Love Me
    Darling; Love Me; Lover's Farewell; New Chattanooga Mama;
    *Streamlined Mama; Within My Father's House.*10.00 - 20.00

J. H. HOWELL'S CAROLINA HILLBILLIES:
Bluebird 7162 *Lost John* ....8.00 - 12.00
    7409 *The Burning Of Cleveland School* ....8.00 - 12.00
    8219 *Mollie Married a Travelin Man* ....8.00 - 12.00

UNCLE STEVE HUBBARD (& HIS BOYS):
Gennett 6088 *Big Town Fling* ....10.00 - 15.00
    6101 *Two Step Quadrille* ....10.00 - 15.00
    6121 *Devil's Dream* ....10.00 - 15.00
    6436 *Over The Ocean Waves* ....10.00 - 15.00
Supertone 9161 *Soldiers Joy* ....7.00 - 10.00

HUGH & SHUG'S RADIO PALS:
Decca 5406, 5407, 5428, 5431, 5451, 5466, 5506,
    5534 ....5.00 - 10.00

DAN HUGHEY:
Champion 15428 *The Fatal Wedding* ....7.00 - 10.00
    15466 *Froggie Went A-Courtin* ....7.00 - 10.00
    15502 *Sweet Kitty Wells* ....7.00 - 10.00
    15631 *An Old Camp Meeting* ....7.00 - 10.00
    15687 *Four Thousand Years Ago* ....7.00 - 10.00
    15710 *The Red River Valley* ....7.00 - 10.00
    15731 *The Little Mohee* ....7.00 - 10.00
    15771 *Will The Angels Play Their Harps For Me* ......8.00 - 12.00
    15851 *Cindy* ....8.00 - 12.00
    15876 *After The Ball* ....8.00 - 12.00
    15923 *Old Number Three* ....10.00 - 15.00
    16029 *Charlie Brooks* ....10.00 - 15.00

HUMPHRIES BROTHERS:
Okeh 45464 *Black And White Rag* ....40.00 - 60.00
    45478 *After The Ball* ....40.00 - 60.00
    45489 *Ragged Ann Rag* ....40.00 - 60.00
    45501 *What Made The Wild Cat Wild* ....40.00 - 60.00

PRINCE ALBERT HUNT'S TEXAS RAMBLERS:
Okeh 45230 *Blues In A Bottle* ....80.00 - 120.00
    45375 *Wake Up Jacob* ....80.00 - 120.00
    45446 *Houston Slide* ....80.00 - 120.00

DAVE HUNT:
Champion 15565 *Katy Lee* ....10.00 - 15.00
    15610 *Wake Up In The Morning* ....10.00 - 15.00

WALTER HURDT & HIS BOYS/SINGING COWBOYS:
Bluebird 7915 *My Skinny Sarah Jane* ....5.00 - 8.00
    7959 *I've Always Loved My Old Guitar* ....5.00 - 8.00

ZACK HURT:
Okeh 45212 *Gamblers Lament* ....7.00 - 10.00

HUTCHENS BROTHERS:
Champion 15464 *Praise The Lord, It's So* ....7.00 - 10.00
    15485 *I'm On The Sunny Side* ....7.00 - 10.00
    15567 *Climbing Up The Golden Stairs* ....7.00 - 10.00
    15588 *I'm Free Again* ....7.00 - 10.00
    15632 *I Feel Like Traveling On* ....7.00 - 10.00
    15671 *I Wants My Lulu* ....7.00 - 10.00
    15693 *Why Not Tonight* ....8.00 - 12.00
    15753 *At The Battle Front* ....8.00 - 12.00
    15900 *No Never Alone* ....8.00 - 12.00
    15944 *Old Kentucky Dew* ....8.00 - 12.00
    15971 *Life's Railway To Heaven* ....8.00 - 12.00
    16101 *I Surrender All* ....8.00 - 12.00
    16122 *Down The Lane To Home Sweet Home* .. 10.00 - 15.00

JOHN HUTCHENS:
Champion 15414 *The Preacher And The Bear* ....7.00 - 10.00
    15427 *The Sinking Of The Submarine S-4* ....7.00 - 10.00
    15467 *The Wreck Of The Virginian Train* ....7.00 - 10.00
    15483 *The Volunteer Organist* ....7.00 - 10.00
    15503 *I Got Mine* ....7.00 - 10.00
    15549 *He Included Me* ....7.00 - 10.00
    15550 *The Vestris Disaster* ....10.00 - 15.00
    15751 *Hard Luck Jim* ....10.00 - 15.00

FRANK HUTCHISON (& SHERMAN LAWSON):
Okeh 45064 *Worried Blues* ....30.00 - 50.00
    45083 *The West Virginia Rag* ....30.00 - 50.00
    45089 *The C & O Excursion Train* ....30.00 - 50.00
    45093 *The Wild Horse* ....30.00 - 50.00
    45106 *Stackalee* ....30.00 - 50.00
    45114 *Worried Blues* ....30.00 - 50.00
    45121 *Logan County Blues* ....30.00 - 50.00
    45144 *All Night Long* ....30.00 - 50.00
    45258 *The Miners Blues* ....30.00 - 50.00
    45274 *Hutchisons Rag* ....30.00 - 50.00
    45313 *The Burglar Man* ....30.00 - 50.00
    45361 *Johnny And Jane* ....30.00 - 50.00
    45378 *Cannon Ball Blues* ....40.00 - 60.00
    45425 *Railroad Bill* ....40.00 - 60.00
    45452 *Hell Bound Train* ....40.00 - 60.00
    45570 *Cumberland Gap* ....50.00 - 75.00
Velvet-Tone 7107-V *Worried Blues* ....25.00 - 40.00

H. K. HUTCHISON:
Gennett 6464 *Good Old Turnip Greens* ....20.00 - 30.00

JERRY IRBY (& THE TEXAS RANCHERS):
Cireco 101 *Almost Every Time* ....8.00 - 12.00
Globe 113 *Nails In My Coffin*...................................8.00 - 12.00
    114 *Steel Guitar Special* ....8.00 - 12.00
    115 *Don't You Weep* ....8.00 - 12.00
    120 *Super Boogie Woogie* ....8.00 - 12.00
Gulf 103 *Nails In My Coffin* ....10.00 - 15.00
Humming Bird 1001 *After Today* ....8.00 - 12.00
Imperial 8003 *Texas Gal Polka* ....8.00 - 12.00
    8005 *Ball And Chain* ....8.00 - 12.00
    8006 *Don't Lie My Darlin'* ....8.00 - 12.00
    8007 *Too Many Women* ....8.00 - 12.00
    8011 *Uptown Swing* ....8.00 - 12.00
    8013 *Super Boogie Woogie.* ....8.00 - 12.00
    8014 *My Gal From Tennessee* ....8.00 - 12.00
    8017 *Mama Don't Allow* ....10.00 - 15.00
M-G-M 10117, 10151, 10188, 10253, 10284,
    10345,10396, 10475 ....7.00 - 10.00
M-G-M 10580 *Mama Don't Allow It* ....8.00 - 12.00
M-G-M 10595, 10771, 10809, 11109 ....7.00 - 10.00

HARVEY IRWIN:
Okeh 45014 *The Blind Child* ....10.00 - 15.00
    45052 *Sunny Tennessee* ....10.00 - 15.00

WALLIE & TEX ISABELL:
Eddie's 1219 *Sugar Cain Gal*.............................15.00 - 20.00

JACK & BILL:
Okeh 45368 *The Lonesome Road* ....10.00 - 15.00

JACK HARMONICA PLAYERS:
Vocalion 5353 *Mouth Harp Blues* ....20.00 - 30.00

JACK & TONY:
Okeh 45421 *Since I Gave My Heart To You* ....10.00 - 15.00
    45422 *The Burial Of The Miners Child*..............10.00 - 15.00

JACKSON COUNTY BARN OWLS:
Champion 16031 *Bake That Chicken Pie* ....20.00 - 30.00

JACKSON COUNTY RAMBLERS:
Champion 16284 *Carolina Girl*...........................25.00 - 50.00

JACK JACKSON:
Columbia 15497-D *I'm Just A Black Sheep* ....10.00 - 15.00
    15662-D *Flat Tire Blues* ....15.00 - 20.00

AUNT MOLLY JACKSON:
Columbia 15731-D *Kentucky Miner's Wife* ....15.00 - 20.00

JACOBY BROS.:
TNT 1002 *There's No Use To Go Wrong* ....10.00 - 15.00
    1004 *Cannonball* ....10.00 - 15.00
    1009 *Bicycle Wreck* ....8.00 - 12.00

BEN JARRELL (Acc. by DA COSTA WOLTZ'S SOUTHERN BROADCASTERS):
Gennett 6143 *Merry Girl* ....20.00 - 30.00
    6164 *I Know My Name Is Written There* ....20.00 - 30.00
    6176 *When You Ask A Girl To Leave Her Happy Home*
    ....20.00 - 30.00

JARVIS & JUSTICE:
Brunswick 333 *Guian Valley Waltz*.....................8.00 - 12.00
    358 *Muskrat Rag* ....10.00 - 15.00

(BLIND ANDREW) JENKINS (& FRANK HICKS/ CARSON ROBINSON/WHITWORTH):
Okeh 45232 *On The Banks Of The Old Omaha*........5.00 - 8.00
    45234 *In The Baggage Coach Ahead* ....5.00 - 8.00
    45246 *Silver Threads Among The Gold* ....5.00 - 8.00
    45264 *My Dixie Home* ....5.00 - 8.00
    45331 *I'll Be All Smiles Tonight* ....5.00 - 8.00
    45443 *Don't Stop Praying* ....5.00 - 8.00
    45481 *The Little Flower Girl* ....6.00 - 10.00

FRANK JENKINS (& HIS PILOT MOUNTAINEERS):
Gennett 6165 *Home Sweet Home*........................15.00 - 20.00
    7034 *Sunny Home In Dixie* ....20.00 - 30.00

"GOOBY" JENKINS:
Okeh 45069 *Fiddlin' Bill* ....15.00 - 20.00
    45082 *The Prisoners Dream* ....15.00 - 20.00
    45088 *Georgia Girl* ....15.00 - 20.00
    45115 *Hopeful Walter Booth* ....15.00 - 20.00

OSCAR JENKINS' MOUNTAINEERS:
Broadway 8249 *Burial of Wild Bill* ....15.00 - 25.00
Paramount 3240 *The Railway Flagman's Sweetheart*
    ....15.00 - 25.00

JENNINGS BROS.:
Champion 15148 *Cripple Creek* ....5.00 - 8.00

HERB JENNINGS:
Champion 15198 *The Death Of John Henry* ....7.00 - 10.00
    15209 *The Roving Gambler* ....7.00 - 10.00

JESSE'S STRING FIVE:
Bluebird 6443 *River Blues* ....7.00 - 10.00

JO AND ALMA:
Vocalion 04173 *When The Bees Are In The Hive* .....5.00 - 8.00
    04248 *Little Moses* ....5.00 - 8.00
    04313 *Lorena* ....5.00 - 8.00

JOHNNY & SLIM:
Superior 2752 *Back To My Georgia Home*.............25.00 - 40.00

WHITEY JOHNS:
Challenge 852 *The Farm Relief Song* ....5.00 - 8.00
    895 *The Prisoners Rosary*..................................5.00 - 8.00
Paramount 3190 *The Little Old Sod Shanty* ....7.00 - 10.00

JOHNSON BROTHERS:
Victor 20661 *Down In Happy Valley*......................8.00 - 12.00
    20662 *Sweet Nellie Brown* ....8.00 - 12.00
    20891 *The Soldiers Poor Little Boy* ....8.00 - 12.00
    20940 *Careless Love*..8.00 - 12.00
    21243 *Two Brothers Are We* ....8.00 - 12.00
    21532 *Old Timer From Caroliner* ....10.00 - 15.00
    21646 *The Crime Of The D'Autremount Brothers*
    ....12.00 - 16.00

JOHNSON & HARVEY:
Champion 16449 *Birdie* ....50.00 - 80.00

EARL JOHNSON (& HIS CLODHOPPERS/DIXIE ENTERTAINERS):
Okeh 45092 *Ain't Nobody's Business*...................25.00 - 50.00
    45101 *John Henry Blues* ....25.00 - 50.00
    45112 *Shortenin' Bread* ....20.00 - 30.00
    45123 *Johnson's Old Grey Mule* ....25.00 - 50.00
    45129 *I'm Satisfied* ....25.00 - 50.00
    45156 *Twinkle Little Star*...................................40.00 - 60.00

45171 *Johnnie Get Your Gun*	40.00 -	60.00
45183 *They Don't Roost Too High For Me*	40.00 -	60.00
45209 *Red Hot Breakdown*	50.00 -	75.00
45223 *Mississippi Jubilee*	50.00 -	75.00
45269 *Wire Grass Drag*	50.00 -	75.00
45300 *G Rag*	50.00 -	75.00
45383 *All Night Long*	50.00 -	75.00
45406 *Poor Little Joe*	50.00 -	75.00
45412 *Bringing In The Sheaves*	50.00 -	75.00
45528 *Take Me Back To My Old Mountain Home*	50.00 -	75.00
45545 *There's No Place Like Home*	50.00 -	75.00
45559 *Way Down In Georgia*	50.00 -	75.00
Victor 23638 *I Lost My Gal*	75.00 -	100.00
V40212 *Fiddlin Rufus*	50.00 -	75.00
V40304 *Green Mountain Polka*	50.00 -	75.00

EDWARD JOHNSON:
Champion 15048 *Sand Cave*	4.00 -	7.00

GENE JOHNSON:
Timely Tunes 1550 *TB Blues*	50.00 -	75.00
1551 *Jimmie The Kid*	50.00 -	75.00
1552 *Do Right Daddy Blues*	75.00 -	100.00

HENRY JOHNSON:
Champion 15732 *When The Snowflakes Fall Again*	20.00 -	30.00

JAMES JOHNSON:
Columbia 15453-D *Papa Please Buy Me An Airship*	10.00 -	15.00

JESS JOHNSON (& ROY HARVEY):
Champion 16255 *The Dying Brakeman*	35.00 -	50.00
16780 *By A Cottage In The Twilight*	50.00 -	75.00

JIMMIE/JIMMY JOHNSON'S STRING BAND:
Champion 16389 *Washington Quadrille*	100.00 -	150.00
16430 *Ching Chow*	100.00 -	150.00
16506 *Bury Me On The Prairie*	100.00 -	150.00
16516 *Drink More Cider*	100.00 -	150.00
16541 *Old Blind Dog*	150.00 -	200.00
16559 *Jennie Baker*	150.00 -	200.00
Superior 2821 *Step Lively*	150.00 -	200.00

JULIAN JOHNSON & LEON HYATT:
Bluebird 7510 *T. B. Killed My Daddy*	10.00 -	15.00

PAUL (AND CHARLES) JOHNSON:
Gennett 7313 *Wild Cat Hollow*	50.00 -	75.00
Superior 2612 *Wild Cat Hollow*	50.00 -	100.00

SMILIN' TUBBY JOHNSON:
Champion 15247 *I'm A Stern Old Bachelor*	5.00 -	8.00
15260 *Whoa, Mule, Whoa*	5.00 -	8.00
15278 *Oh, Suzanna*	5.00 -	8.00
15298 *Little Brown Jug*	5.00 -	8.00
15430 *Oh, Dem Golden Slippers*	5.00 -	8.00

JONES BROTHERS:
Melotone 12017 *The Memory That Time Cannot Erase*	5.00 -	8.00
12179 *The Little Green Valley*	5.00 -	8.00

BUDDY JONES:
Decca 5345, 5372, 5414, 5476, 5490, 5521, 5538, 5539	5.00 -	10.00

CARL JONES:
Okeh 45516 *The Wild Man Of Borneo*	20.00 -	30.00
45540 *My Tennessee Girl*	20.00 -	30.00

COLON JONES & RILEY PUCKETT:
Columbia 15774-D *That Saxophone Waltz*	50.00 -	75.00

DEMPSEY JONES:
Champion 16356 *The Cross-Eyed Butcher*	15.00 -	25.00
16416 *Jack And May*	20.00 -	30.00
16697 *Cabin Home*	50.00 -	75.00

FLOYD JONES:
Paramount 3029 *My Dream Of The Big Parade*	10.00 -	15.00
3030 *Someone Is Waiting Your Light*	10.00 -	15.00

GENE JONES:
Gold Star 1382 *Stop, Look And Listen*	7.00 -	10.00

GRANDPA JONES:
King 502, 508, 513, 517, 524	4.00 -	8.00

HIRAM JONES:
Homestead 16492 *Sailor's Hornpipe*	15.00 -	20.00

ROY JONES:
Columbia 15428-D *Southern Yodel Blues*	20.00 -	30.00

JORDAN BROTHERS:
Bluebird 7123 *Answer To Birmingham Jail*	8.00 -	12.00
7235 *Goin' Back Home*	8.00 -	12.00

JORDAN & RUPERT:
Supertone 9494 *It Won't Be Long Till My Grave Is Made*	7.00 -	10.00

JERRY JORDAN:
Supertone 9407 *The Cat's Got The Measles And The Whooping Cough*	8.00 -	12.00
9454 *The Baldheaded End Of A Broom*	8.00 -	12.00

JUDY & JEN, ACCOMP. BY THE HILLTOPPERS:
Vogue 744 *Flat River, Missouri*	30.00 -	50.00

JUERLING & JUSTIS:
Supertone 9099 *Grasshopper Polka*	7.00 -	10.00

DICK JUSTICE:
Brunswick 336 *Brown Skin Blues*	10.00 -	15.00
367 *Henry Lee*	15.00 -	20.00
395 *Cocaine*	15.00 -	20.00

BOB KACKLEY (& BEN WEAVER):
Okeh 45531 *The Strawberry Roan*	10.00 -	15.00

KARL (DAVIS) & HARTY (TAYLOR):
Banner, Conqueror, Melotone, Perfect, Oriole, Romeo	5.00 -	10.00

ALFRED G. KARNES:
Victor 20840 *Where We'll Never Grow Old*	5.00 -	8.00
20933 *To The Work*	5.00 -	8.00
V40076 *Days Of My Childhood Plays*	15.00 -	20.00
V40327 *Called To The Foreign Field*	15.00 -	20.00

BUELL KAZEE (& SOOKIE HOBBS):
Brunswick 144 *John Hardy*	15.00 -	20.00
145 *Rock Island*	15.00 -	20.00
154 *East Virginia*	15.00 -	20.00
155 *The Ship That's Sailing High*	15.00 -	20.00
156 *The Little Mohee*	10.00 -	15.00
157 *The Old Maid*	10.00 -	15.00
206 *The Faded Coat Of Blue*	15.00 -	20.00

210 *Red Wing* ....8.00 - 12.00
211 *The Orphan Girl* ....8.00 - 12.00
212 *The Cowboy's Farewell* ....8.00 - 12.00
213 *The Butcher's Boy* ....15.00 - 20.00
215 *Little Bessie* ....15.00 - 20.00
216 *In The Shadow Of The Pines* ....15.00 - 20.00
217 *Poor Boys Long Ways From Home* ....15.00 - 20.00
218 *Gambling Blues* ....15.00 - 20.00
330 *The Hobo's Last Ride* ....15.00 - 20.00
338 *A Mountain Boy Makes His First Record* ....15.00 - 25.00
351 *The Blind Man* ....15.00 - 25.00
436 *The Little Mohee* ....10.00 - 15.00
437 *The Old Maid* ....10.00 - 15.00
481 *The Cowboy Trail* ....15.00 - 20.00
Vocalion 5221 *In The Shadow Of The Pines* ....15.00 - 20.00
 5231 *Little Bessie* ....15.00 - 20.00

HANK KEENE (& HIS CONNECTICUT HILLBILLIES):
Bluebird 5241, 5254, 5339, 6035 ....5.00 - 8.00
Brunswick 516 *The Run Away Boy* ....7.00 - 10.00

(HOWARD) KEESE/KEESEE (& LOY BODINE):
Champion 16097 *Indiana Pal Of Mine* ....25.00 - 40.00
 16260 *The Mystery Of Number 5* ....30.00 - 50.00
 16374 *The Longest Train I Ever Saw* ....30.00 - 50.00
 16446 *Pal Of My Sunny Days* ....30.00 - 50.00
Gennett 7082 *Blue Yodel No. 5* ....25.00 - 40.00
 7113 *My Dear Old Sunny South By The Sea* ......25.00 - 40.00
 7166 *Memphis Special Blues* ....40.00 - 60.00
 7315 *A Sailor's Plea* ....40.00 - 60.00

KELLY BROTHERS:
Decca 5027 *Precious One* ....8.00 - 12.00
Victor 23822 *After You've Gone* ....15.00 - 20.00
 23828 *Floating Down A River* ....15.00 - 20.00
 23833 *Always Remember* ....15.00 - 20.00
 23853 *Stormy Hawaiian Weather* ....20.00 - 30.00

BUD KELLY:
Paramount 3303 *Skip To My Lou* ....20.00 - 30.00

R. D. KELLY & JULIUS DUNN:
Okeh 45510 *Moonlight On The Colorado* ....15.00 - 25.00
 45543 *Harem Scarem* ....15.00 - 25.00

REX KELLY:
Paramount 3319 *Down By The Railroad Track* ....25.00 - 40.00

TOBY KELLY & HIS RHYTHM MAKERS:
Imperial 8026 *Kinda Late To Be Sorry* ....8.00 - 12.00
 8036 *Jeep Blues* ....8.00 - 12.00

KEN, CHUCK & JIM:
Champion 16579 *I Like Mountain Music* ....15.00 - 25.00
 16672 *Cattlesburg* ....25.00 - 40.00
 45131 *Home On The Range* ....7.00 - 10.00

KENTUCKY GIRLS:
Columbia 15364-D *Old And Only In The Way* ....10.00 - 15.00

KENTUCKY MOUNTAIN BOYS:
Supertone 2026 *The Two Orphans* ....5.00 - 8.00
 2260 *Many Happy Returns Of The Day* ....5.00 - 8.00

KENTUCKY RAMBLERS:
Paramount 3283 *With My Mother Dead And Gone* .25.00 - 35.00
 3284 *The Prisoner's Sweetheart* ....25.00 - 35.00
 3285 *The Unfortunate Brakeman* ....25.00 - 35.00
 3300 *Some Mother's Boy* ....25.00 - 35.00

KENTUCKY SERENADERS:
Champion 15770 *Gonna Raise A Ruckus Tonight* .. 10.00 - 15.00

KENTUCKY STRING TICKLERS:
Champion 16577 *Stove Pipe Blues* ....50.00 - 75.00
 16581 *Georgia Bust Down* ....50.00 - 75.00
 16681 *Leaving Here Blues* ....75.00 - 100.00
 45014 *Leaving Here Blues* ....15.00 - 20.00

KENTUCKY THOROBREDS:
Paramount 3010 *I Love You Best Of All* ....15.00 - 20.00
 3011 *Mother's Advice* ....15.00 - 20.00
 3014 *This World Is Not My Home* ....15.00 - 20.00
 3036 *The Preacher And The Bear* ....15.00 - 20.00
 3059 *Till We Meet Again* ....15.00 - 20.00
 3071 *I've Waited Long For You* ....15.00 - 20.00
 3080 *I'll Not Marry At All* ....15.00 - 20.00

KESSINGER BROTHERS:
Brunswick 220 *Wednesday Night Waltz* ....7.00 - 10.00
 235 *Turkey In The Straw* ....7.00 - 10.00
 238 *Garfield March* ....8.00 - 12.00
 247 *Arkansas Traveler* ....7.00 - 10.00
 256 *Devil's Dream* ....7.00 - 10.00
 267 *Sixteen Days In Georgia* ....7.00 - 10.00
 308 *Sourwood Mountain* ....7.00 - 10.00
 309 *Mississippi Sawyer* ....10.00 - 15.00
 315 *Dill Pickle* ....10.00 - 15.00
 323 *Old Jake Gillespie* ....10.00 - 15.00
 331 *Wild Goose Chase* ....10.00 - 15.00
 344 *Black Hawk Waltz* ....10.00 - 15.00
 352 *Midnight Serenade Waltz* ....10.00 - 15.00
 364 *Durang Hornpipe* ....10.00 - 15.00
 396 *Chinky Pin* ....10.00 - 15.00
 411 *Sopping The Gravy* ....10.00 - 15.00
 458 *Rat Cheese Under The Hill* ....10.00 - 15.00
 468 *Little Brown Jug* ....8.00 - 12.00
 480 *Chicken Reel* ....10.00 - 15.00
 484 *Mary Jane Waltz* ....10.00 - 15.00
 518 *Dixie* ....10.00 - 15.00
 521 *Liza Jane* ....10.00 - 15.00
 540 *Ragtime Annie* ....15.00 - 20.00
 554 *Shoo, Fly* ....15.00 - 20.00
 563 *Steamboat Bill* ....15.00 - 20.00
 567 *Mexican Waltz* ....15.00 - 20.00
 580 *Little Betty Brown* ....15.00 - 20.00
 592 *Regal March* ....15.00 - 20.00
Vocalion 02565 *Brownstown Girl* ....35.00 - 50.00
 02566 *Kanawha County Rag* ....35.00 - 50.00
 5248 *Patty On The Turnpike* ....25.00 - 40.00
 5481 *Hot Foot* ....40.00 - 60.00

KIDOODLERS:
Vocalion 03717, 03866, 03925, 03974, 04063,
 04133, 04202, 04260, 04338, 04404, 04503,
 04907, 04960 ....4.00 - 8.00

B. F. KINCAID (THE BRIER HOPPER OF WFIW):
Gennett 7309 *Lane County Bachelor* .... 25.00 - 40.00

BRADLEY KINCAID:
Titles issued contemporaneously on Banner, Conqueror, Melotone, Oriole, Perfect, Romeo, and Vocalion: *After The Ball; Bury Me Out On The Prairie; The Fatal Derby Day; The Fatal Wedding; For Sale, A Baby; Gooseberry Pie; The Innocent Prisoner; I Wish I Had Someone To Love Me; The Lightning Express;*

A Picture From Life's Other Side; Red River Valley;
Somewhere Somebody's Waiting For You; Sourwood Mountain;
The True And Trembling Brakeman; Two Little Girls In Blue
....7.00 - 12.00
Bluebird 5179 *Long Long Ago* ....7.00 - 10.00
  5201 *The Old Wooden Bucket* ....7.00 - 10.00
  5255 *House Carpenter*.....................................8.00 - 12.00
  5321 *Sweet Betsy From Pike* ....7.00 - 10.00
  5377 *The Death Of Jimmie Rodgers*...................10.00 - 15.00
  5423 *Mrs. Jimmie Rodgers Lament* ....10.00 - 15.00
  5486 *The Life Of Jimmie Rodgers* ....10.00 - 15.00
  5569 *The Ship That Never Returned* ....5.00 - 8.00
  5895 *The Letter Edged In Black* ....5.00 - 8.00
  5971 *In The Hills Of Kentucky* ....5.00 - 8.00
  8410 *Zeh Turney's Gal* ....5.00 - 8.00
  8478 *Mammy's Precious Baby* ....5.00 - 8.00
  8501 *The Blind Girl* ....5.00 - 8.00
Brunswick 403 *Give My Love To Neil*....................7.00 - 10.00
  420 *Methodist Pie* ....7.00 - 10.00
  464 *Cindy*..7.00 - 10.00
  485 *Old Coon Dog* ....7.00 - 10.00
Bullet 615 *Ain't We Crazy*..................................8.00 - 12.00
Champion 45039 *On Top Of Old Smoky* ....5.00 - 8.00
  45057 *Four Thousand Years Ago* ....5.00 - 8.00
  45098 *Wreck On The C & O Road* ....5.00 - 8.00
  45130 *Angels In Heaven Know I Love You* ....5.00 - 8.00
Decca 5025 *Ain't We Crazy* ....8.00 - 12.00
  5026 *The Old Wooden Rocker* ....8.00 - 12.00
  5048 *The Cowboy's Dream* ....8.00 - 12.00
Gennett 6363 *The Fatal Wedding* ....15.00 - 25.00
  6417 *Methodist Pie* ....15.00 - 25.00
  6462 *The Swapping Song*..................................15.00 - 25.00
  6620 *The Cuckoo Is A Pretty Bird* ....15.00 - 25.00
  6761 *Four Thousand Tears Ago* ....15.00 - 25.00
  6823 *Pearl Bryan* ....15.00 - 25.00
  6856 *The Little Mohee* ....15.00 - 25.00
  6900 *Angels In Heaven Know I Love You* ....20.00 - 30.00
  6944 *Let That Mule Go Aunk! Aunk!*...................20.00 - 30.00
  6958 *Charlie Brooks* ....20.00 - 30.00
  7020 *Old Number Three* ....20.00 - 30.00
  7053 *On Top Of Old Smoky* ....20.00 - 30.00
  7081 *After The Ball*..20.00 - 30.00
  7112 *Cindy*...20.00 - 30.00
Superior 366 *Sourwood Mountain.* ....25.00 - 50.00
  2656 *Four Thousand Years Ago* ....20.00 - 30.00
  2770 *On Top Of Old Smoky*...............................20.00 - 30.00
  2788 *Old Number Three* ....20.00 - 30.00
Supertone 9208 *Bury Me On The Prairie* ....7.00 - 10.00
  9209 *Froggie Went A-Courting* ....8.00 - 12.00
  9210 *Methodist Pie* ....8.00 - 12.00
  9211 *The Fatal Wedding* ....8.00 - 12.00
  9212 *Two Sisters* ....8.00 - 12.00
  9350 *Give My Love To Nell* ....8.00 - 12.00
  9362 *Four Thousand Years Ago* ....8.00 - 12.00
  9402 *The Little Mohee* ....8.00 - 12.00
  9403 *The Red River Valley* ....8.00 - 12.00
  9404 *Pearl Bryan* ....8.00 - 12.00
  9452 *Angels In Heaven Know I Love You* ....8.00 - 12.00
  9471 *Happy Days Long Ago*...............................8.00 - 12.00
  9505 *Old Number Three* ....8.00 - 12.00
  9565 *The Blind Girl* ....10.00 - 15.00
  9566 *On Top Of Old Smoky* ....10.00 - 15.00
  9648 *After The Ball*..10.00 - 15.00
  9666 *Pretty Little Pink* ....10.00 - 15.00

CHICKIE KING:
Speed 108 *Lov-ie Lov-ie* ....- - -

MARTIN KING:
Superior 2530 *We Parted By The Riverside*............ 15.00 - 20.00
  2574 *Lane County Bachelor* .... 15.00 - 20.00

RANDY KING:
TNT 108 *Tied And Bound*..- - -

KIRBY & PHILLIPS:
Bluebird 6367, 7056... 4.00 - 6.00

FRED KIRBY:
Bluebird 6325 *In The Shade Of The Pine* .... 5.00 - 8.00
  6419 *I'm A Gold Diggin' Papa*........................... 5.00 - 8.00
  6597 *My Heavenly Sweetheart*.......................... 5.00 - 8.00
Bluebird 6763, 7009, 7164, 7190, 7261, 7310......... 4.00 - 7.00

FRED KIRBY (& DON WHITE/CLIFF CARLISLE):
Bluebird 6540 *My Old Saddle Horse Is Missing* ...... 5.00 - 8.00

ROCKY KIRKLAND:
J-B 1503 *Candy Baby* ....- - -

BERT KNOWLES:
Okeh 45427 *Blue Undertaker's Blues No. 2*........... 20.00 - 30.00

VANCE KNOWLES & RED LAY:
Bluebird 6585 *A Thousand Miles From Texas* .... 5.00 - 8.00

DON KUTTER:
Challenge 326 *Two Little Orphans* .... 7.00 - 10.00
  327 *That Bad Man Stackalee* .... 8.00 - 12.00

PIERRE LA DIEU:
Columbia 15278-D *The Shanty-Man's Life* .... 20.00 - 30.00

SLIM LAKE:
Superior 2819 *Peach Picking Time In Georgia* ...... 75.00 - 100.00

BELLA LAM & HIS GREENE COUNTY SINGERS:
Okeh 45126, 45136, 45145, 45177, 45228, 45407,
  45456.. 8.00 - 12.00

LAMBERT & HILLPOT:
Paramount 3013 *My Carolina Home* .... 5.00 - 8.00

G. E. LANCASTER:
Superior 2538 *Tennessee Yodel* .... 25.00 - 40.00

LEE LANDERS:
Champion 15727 *Blue Yodel No. 3*........................ 10.00 - 15.00
  15767 *Lullaby Yodel* .... 10.00 - 15.00

UNCLE BUD LANDRESS:
Victor 21036 *Candy Pulling Time* .... 8.00 - 12.00
  21354 *Coon Hunting In Moonshine Hollow*........ 8.00 - 12.00
  23606 *The Daddy Song* .... 10.00 - 15.00
  V40252 *Rubber Doll Rag* .... 10.00 - 15.00

DUKE LANE:
Supertone 9425 *Blue Yodel No. 4* .... 8.00 - 12.00
  9496 *Waiting For A Train* .... 8.00 - 12.00

LAND & MILES:
Supertone 9314 *The Old New Hampshire Village* .... 7.00 - 10.00

(FIDDLIN') BOB LARKAN/LARKIN (FAMILY/HIS MUSIC MAKERS):
Okeh 45205 *Kansas City Reel* .... 25.00 - 50.00
  45229 *Beautiful Belle*....................................... 25.00 - 50.00
  45349 *The Woman Wears No Clothes At All* ..... 25.00 - 50.00

Vocalion 5277 *Saturday Night Waltz* ....25.00 - 50.00
    5313 *McLeod's Reel* ....25.00 - 50.00
    5329 *Arkansas Waltz* ....25.00 - 50.00

CHARLIE LAWMAN:
Crown 3144 *There Must Be A Bright Tomorrow* ......5.00 - 8.00
Paramount 3304 *There Must Be A Bright Tomorrow* 7.00 - 10.00

JIMMIE LAWSON:
Victor 20477 *Tennessee Blues* ....10.00 - 15.00

ZORA LAYMAN:
Decca 5033, 5034 ....5.00 - 10.00

BERT LAYNE (& HIS GEORGIA SERENADERS/ MELODY BOYS):
Brunswick 502 *Nights Of Gladness* ....10.00 - 15.00
    582 *I Ain't Got No Sweetheart* ....10.00 - 15.00
Champion 16346 *The Rabbit Hunt* ....20.00 - 30.00

BENNIE LEADERS:
Freedom 5012 *Boots Don't Leave Me* ....8.00 - 12.00
    5020 *I'll Be Jumped Up And Down* ....8.00 - 12.00
    5029 *Naggin' Woman* ....8.00 - 12.00
Nucraft 105 *Clean Town Blues* ....10.00 - 15.00
Ok'ed 1050 *Hey Miss Fannie* ....8.00 - 12.00

LEAKE COUNTY REVELERS:
Columbia 15149-D *Johnson Gal* ....15.00 - 20.00
    15189-D *Wednesday Night Waltz* ....5.00 - 8.00
    15205-D *The Old Hat* ....8.00 - 12.00
    15227-D *My Bonnie Lies Over The Ocean* ....8.00 - 12.00
    15264-D *Merry Widow Waltz* ....8.00 - 12.00
    15292-D *They Go Wild Over Me* ....10.00 - 15.00
    15318-D *Crow Black Chicken* ....15.00 - 20.00
    15353-D *Rockin' Yodel* ....15.00 - 20.00
    15380-D *Bring Me A Bottle* ....15.00 - 20.00
    15409-D *Georgia Camp Meeting* ....15.00 - 20.00
    15427-D *Memories Waltz* ....10.00 - 15.00
    15441-D *Dry Town Blues* ....15.00 - 20.00
    15470-D *Saturday Night Breakdown* ....15.00 - 20.00
    15501-D *Beautiful Bells* ....15.00 - 20.00
    15520-D *Leake County Blues* ....15.00 - 20.00
    15569-D *Mississippi Moon* ....15.00 - 20.00
    15625-D *Birds In The Brook* ....15.00 - 20.00
    15648-D *When It's Springtime In The Rockies* ..10.00 - 15.00
    15668-D *Mississippi Breakdown* ....25.00 - 40.00
    15691-D *Texas Fair* ....25.00 - 40.00
    15767-D *Lazy Kate* ....30.00 - 50.00
    15776-D *Listen To The Mockingbird* ....30.00 - 50.00

LEATHERMAN SISTERS:
Bluebird 6490, 6590 ....4.00 - 7.00

STEVE LEDFORD & HIS MOUNTAINERS:
Bluebird 7626, 7742 ....5.00 - 8.00

LEE BROTHERS TRIO:
Brunswick 501 *Cotton Mills Blues* ....20.00 - 30.00

A. LEE, B. BROWN, P. MELVIN, H. RICE, P. LINDSEY & JUDGE LEE:
Brunswick 419 *A Bootlegger's Joint In Atlanta* ......15.00 - 20.00

NANCY LEE & THE HILLTOPPERS:
Vogue 744 *Don't Tetch It* ....30.00 - 50.00

WOODY LEFTWICH & ROY LILLY:
Champion 16345 *Lonesome Road Blues* ....40.00 - 60.00

MALCOLM LEGETTE:
Columbia 15424-D *Song Of The Tramp* ....7.00 - 10.00

LEON'S LONE STAR COWBOYS:
Champion 45151 *Mistreated Blues* ....8.00 - 12.00
    45152 *Sweet Sue* ....8.00 - 12.00
    45165 *Weary Blues* ....8.00 - 12.00
    45169 *Bugle Call Rag* ....8.00 - 12.00
    45174 *Dinah* ....8.00 - 12.00
    45185 *White River Stomp* ....8.00 - 12.00
    45195 *Just Forget* ....8.00 - 12.00
    45196 *Milenburg Joys* ....8.00 - 12.00
Decca 5280, 5288, 5289, 5301, 5323, 5328, 5340,
    5361, 5377, 5388, 5396, 5511, 5530 ....5.00 - 10.00

JOE (& MARY) LESTER (& DICK MOSS):
Superior 2606 *My Old Cottage Home* ....20.00 - 30.00
    2632 *That Silver Haired Daddy Of Mine* ....20.00 - 30.00
    2654 *Missouri Is Calling* ....20.00 - 30.00
    2675 *Yodel Your Troubles Away* ....25.00 - 40.00
    2683 *Down And Out Blues* ....25.00 - 40.00
    2702 *By The Ozark Trail* ....25.00 - 40.00

LEWIS BROTHERS:
Victor V40172 *Sally Johnson* ....20.00 - 30.00
    V40187 *When Summer Comes Again* ....20.00 - 30.00

ARCHIE LEWIS:
Champion 16677 *Miss Handy Hanks* ....25.00 - 40.00

TEXAS JIM LEWIS & LONE STAR COWBOYS:
Vocalion 03754, 03915, 03977 ....5.00 - 8.00

LIGHT CRUST DOUGHBOYS:
Okeh (most issues) ....5.00 - 8.00
Vocalion 02992 *My Pretty Quadroon* ....8.00 - 12.00
    03017 *El Rancho Grande* ....8.00 - 12.00
Vocalion 03065, 03141, 03239, 03610, 03660,
    03867, 03926, 04158, 04216, 04261, 04326,
    04403, 04468, 04559, 04560, 04638, 04701,
    04702, 04770, 04825, 04921, 04965, 04973,
    04974, 05039 ....5.00 - 10.00

ADD LINDSAY:
Victor 21401 *Whoa Mule* ....15.00 - 20.00

RED LINDSEY:
Talent 711 *Penitentiary Blues* ....10.00 - 15.00

W. A. LINDSEY & ALVIN CONDER:
Okeh 45346 *Good Old Turnip Greens* ....15.00 - 20.00

LITTLE JIMMIE: (See ASHER SIZEMORE)

TOBE LITTLE:
Okeh 40460, 40479, 45090 ....7.00 - 12.00

DOCTOR LLOYD & HOWARD MAXEY:
Okeh 45150 *Western Union* ....30.00 - 50.00

RUSTY LOCKE:
TNT 1012 *Milk Cow Blues* ....8.00 - 12.00

HANK LOCKLIN:
Gold Star 1341 *Rio Grande Waltz* ....15.00 - 20.00
Royalty 603 *Please Come Back And Stay* ....15.00 - 20.00
    604 *You've Been Talking In Your Sleep* ....15.00 - 20.00

GEORGE E. LOGAN ("PETE THE HIRED MAN"):
Champion 45036 *By The Ozark Trail* ....7.00 - 10.00

LOGAN COUNTY TRIO:
Challenge 302 *The Buckin' Mule* ....5.00 - 8.00
   325 *Hand Me Down My Walking Cane* ....5.00 - 8.00

LOG CABIN BOYS:
Banner 32903 *Ole Bill Jackson Brown* ....5.00 - 8.00
Decca 5035, 5036, 5103, 5110 ....15.00 - 20.00

LONESOME COWBOY:
Champion 16767 *Memphis Gal* ....50.00 - 75.00
   45080 *Memphis Gal* ....10.00 - 15.00
Perfect 12591 *I'm Just A Black Sheep* ....5.00 - 8.00
Superior 2652 *The Yodeling Cowboy* ....50.00 - 75.00

LONESOME COWGIRL:
Champion 16767 *Lonesome Cowboy* ....50.00 - 75.00
Superior 2631 *Livin' In The Mountains*..................20.00 - 30.00
   2652 *My Mother Was A Lady*....................50.00 - 75.00

LONESOME LUKE (& HIS FARM BOYS):
Champion 16229 *Dogs In The Ash Can* ....20.00 - 30.00
   16269 *Beaver Valley Breakdown*........................20.00 - 30.00

LONESOME PINE TWINS:
Banner 6041 *A Picture From Life's Other Side* ....4.00 - 7.00

LONE STAR COWBOYS:
Bluebird 5283 *Who Wouldn't Be Lonely?* ....7.00 - 10.00
   6001 *Deep Elm Blues*...7.00 - 10.00
   6052 *Just Because*...5.00 - 10.00
Victor 23846 *Deep Elm Blues* ....25.00 - 40.00
   23850 *Wonderful Child*....................................25.00 - 40.00

LONE STAR RANGERS:
Broadway 8141 *The Prison Warden's Secret*............7.00 - 10.00
   8142 *The Train That Never Arrived* ....7.00 - 10.00
   8144 *Farm Relief Song* ....7.00 - 10.00
   8150 *Eleven More Months And Ten More Days* ..7.00 - 10.00
   3202 *The Train That Never Arrived* ....7.00 - 10.00
   3208 *Farm Relief Song* ....7.00 - 10.00
   3218 *Eleven More Months And Ten More Days* ..7.00 - 10.00
Regal 8973 *Eleven More Months And Ten More Days*
   ....5.00 - 8.00

LONG BROTHERS:
Victor 23622 *Cross-Eyed Gal That Lived Upon The Hill*
   ....50.00 - 80.00
   23637 *Missouri Is Calling* ....50.00 - 80.00

BEVERLY & JIM/JIMMIE/ JIMMY LONG:
Bluebird 5139, 5188 ....5.00 - 10.00
Champion 16659 *Two Little Orphans* ....20.00 - 30.00

CLAY LONG & HIS LONG HORNS:
Vocalion 04602, 04731, 04812.................................7.00 - 10.00

JIMMIE/JIMMY LONG (& BEVERLY LONG/CLIFF KEISER):
Champion 16099 *Missouri I'm Calling You*............10.00 - 15.00
   16117 *That's Why I Left The Mountains* ....10.00 - 15.00
   16164 *My Alabama Home* ....15.00 - 20.00
   16190 *My Old Pal Of Yesterday*........................10.00 - 15.00
   16214 *Listen To The Voice* ....10.00 - 15.00
   16233 *Yodel Your Troubles Away* ....15.00 - 20.00
   16280 *Have You Found Somebody Else To Love*
   ....15.00 - 20.00
   16296 *Down And Out Blues* ....20.00 - 30.00
   16311 *Let's Get Together*....................................20.00 - 30.00
   16632 *The Answer To 21 Years* ....25.00 - 40.00
   16641 *Hang It In The Hen House*......................30.00 - 50.00

   16663 *The Old Folks Back Home* ....30.00 - 50.00
   16671 *My California Mountain Rose* ....30.00 - 50.00
Champion 45022, 45023, 45084, 45089 ....5.00 - 10.00
Gennett 7287 *Blue Pining For You* ....30.00 - 50.00
   7314 *Missouri Is Calling* ....30.00 - 50.00
Victor 23705 *Doggone Blues* ....50.00 - 75.00
   23724 *Down And Out*..50.00 - 75.00
   23824 *Alone With My Sorrows* ....75.00 - 100.00

LOOKOUT MOUNTAIN BOYS:
Paramount 3164 *Down In Atlanta*...........................20.00 - 30.00
   3264 *Down In Atlanta* ....20.00 - 30.00

LOOKOUT MOUNTAIN REVELERS:
Paramount 3105 *Barn Dance On The Mountain* ....15.00 - 20.00
   3111 *Pussy Cat Rag* ....15.00 - 20.00
   3123 *Dreaming Of Mother*.................................10.00 - 15.00
   3143 *Bury Me Beneath The Willow* ....10.00 - 15.00

LOUISIANA LOU:
Bluebird 5424 *Sinful To Flirt* ....15.00 - 20.00
   5484 *A Package Of Love Letters* ....15.00 - 20.00
   5636 *With A Banjo On My Knee*......................15.00 - 20.00
   5749 *Go 'Long Mule* ....15.00 - 20.00
Victor 23858 *Go 'Long Mule*..................................50.00 - 80.00

LOUISIANA ROUNDERS:
Decca 5483, 5495..5.00 - 10.00

LOUISIANA STROLLERS:
Champion 45199 *Strollers Waltz*............................7.00 - 10.00

(DADDY) JOHN LOVE:
Bluebird 6294 *My Little Red Ford*..........................15.00 - 20.00
   6491 *Cotton Mill Blues* ....15.00 - 20.00
   6583 *Blue Days* ....15.00 - 20.00
   6624 *Railroad Blues* ....15.00 - 20.00
   6675 *Over The Hills In Carolina* ....15.00 - 20.00

RAMBLIN' RED LOWERY:
Vocalion 02631 *Ramblin' Red's Memphis Yodel No. 1*
   ....30.00 - 50.00
   02641 *Take Me Back To Tennessee* ....25.00 - 50.00
   02665 *Ramblin' Red's Memphis Yodel*.............25.00 - 50.00

LUKE THE DRIFTER: (See HANK WILLIAMS)

LULLABY LARKERS:
Champion 16257 *Shine On Harvest Moon* ....20.00 - 30.00
   16295 *The True And Trembling Brakeman* ....20.00 - 30.00
   16322 *When The Cactus Is In Bloom*................20.00 - 30.00
   16364 *The Chicken Roost Blues* ....25.00 - 40.00
   16417 *My Lonely Boyhood Days* ....25.00 - 40.00
Champion 45132, 45186 ....8.00 - 12.00

LULU BELLE & SCOTTY:
Vocalion 04690, 04772, 04841, 04910, 04962 ....5.00 - 8.00
Vogue 718 *Some Sunday Morning*..........................30.00 - 50.00
   719 *I Get A Kick Out Of Corn* ....30.00 - 50.00
   720 *Time Will Tell*..40.00 - 60.00

BASCOM LAMAR LUNSFORD:
Brunswick 219 *Mountain Dew* ....8.00 - 12.00
   227 *Lost John Dean* ....8.00 - 12.00
   228 *Darby's Ram* ....8.00 - 12.00
   229 *Lulu Wall* ....8.00 - 12.00
Brunswick 230 *Kidder Cole* ....8.00 - 12.00
   231 *Dry Bones* ....8.00 - 12.00
   314 *Dry Bones* ....8.00 - 12.00

Columbia 15595-D *Speaking The Truth*...................8.00 - 12.00
Okeh 40155 *Jesse James* ....10.00 - 15.00
   45008 *Fate Of Santa Barbara* ....10.00 - 15.00
Vocalion 5246 *Lost John Dean* ....10.00 - 15.00
   5252 *Little Turtle Dove*.............................10.00 - 15.00

TED LUNSFORD:
Champion 16287 *The Hobo's Return* ....20.00 - 30.00

FRANK LUTHER:
This artist recorded for many labels in the 1920s and 1930s. Most of his records are of minimal value or interest to the collector. Following are a few exceptions.

Broadway 8102 *Memphis Yodel* ....7.00 - 10.00
Columbia 15588 D *Oklahoma Charley*..............7.00 - 10.00
   15768-D *Carry Me Back To The Mountains* ......10.00 - 15.00
Edison (thick)...10.00 - 20.00
Edison (thin) 20008 *Peg Leg Jack* ....30.00 - 60.00
Edison (thin) most others............................20.00 - 30.00
RCA Victor 226 (7-inch picture record)
   Dance Of The Bogey Man......................25.00 - 50.00
Timely Tunes 1558 *Divorce Blues* ....10.00 - 15.00
Victor 23737 *Sweetest Of All My Dreams* ....10.00 - 15.00
Vocalion 5227, 5278.....................................5.00 - 10.00

"MAC" (AND HIS HAYWIRE ORCHESTRA) (See also "RADIO MAC"):
Victor 21343, 21420, 21421, 21487, 21704, 21761 ..5.00 - 10.00
   V40016 *Trail To Mexico* ....10.00 - 15.00

W. W. MacBETH:
Brunswick 373 *Southern Melodies* ....5.00 - 8.00
   443 *Red Wing*...5.00 - 8.00
   571 *Darling Nellie Gray* ....5.00 - 8.00

BOB MacGIMSEY:
Victor 23562 *Religion Ain't Nothin' To Play With* ...8.00 - 12.00
   23584 *Bob's Medley* ....8.00 - 12.00
   23612 *Southern Melodies* ....8.00 - 12.00

MACK BROTHERS:
Decca 5073, 5086, 5125 ....5.00 - 10.00

BILL MACK:
Imperial 8114 *Crazy Baby Boogie*....................8.00 - 12.00
   8151 *Big Bad Daddy*.................................8.00 - 12.00
   8174 *Play My Boogie*................................8.00 - 12.00
   8192 *Forever I'll Wait For You*....................8.00 - 12.00

MACON QUARTETTE:
Columbia 15211-D *Uncle Joe* ....8.00 - 12.00

UNCLE DAVE MACON; MACON & (SID) HARKREADER; UNCLE DAVE MACON & KIRK/SAM McGEE; UNCLE DAVE MACON & HIS FRUIT JAR DRINKERS:
Bluebird 5842 *One More River To Cross*.............20.00 - 30.00
   5873 *I'll Tickle Nancy* ....20.00 - 30.00
   5926 *Just One Way To The Pearly Gates*..........20.00 - 30.00
   7174 *From Jerusalem To Jericho*.....................15.00 - 20.00
   7234 *Travelin' Down The Road* ....15.00 - 20.00
   7350 *Bum Hotel* ....15.00 - 20.00
   7385 *Fame Apart From God's Approval*............15.00 - 20.00
   7549 *She's Got The Money Too* ....15.00 - 20.00
   7779 *Peek-A-Boo* ....15.00 - 20.00
   7951 *Country Ham And Red Gravy* ....15.00 - 20.00
   8279 *Working For My Lord* ....15.00 - 20.00
   8325 *Railroadin' And Gamblin'* ....15.00 - 20.00

   8341 *Beautiful Love* ....15.00 - 20.00
   8379 *Johnny Grey* ....15.00 - 20.00
   8422 *They're After Me* ....15.00 - 20.00
Brunswick 112 *On The Dixie Bee Line*...............15.00 - 20.00
   114 *The Cross Eyed Butcher & The Cackling Hen*
   ....15.00 - 20.00
   263 *Governor Al Smith* ....20.00 - 30.00
   266 *Worthy Of Estimation* ....20.00 - 30.00
   292 *I'm The Child To Fight* ....20.00 - 30.00
   329 *From Earth To Heaven* ....20.00 - 30.00
   340 *Uncle Dave's Travels-Part 1* ....20.00 - 30.00
   349 *Uncle Dave's Travels-Part 2* ....20.00 - 30.00
   355 *Uncle Dave's Travels-Part 3* ....20.00 - 30.00
   362 *Uncle Dave's Travels-Part 4* ....20.00 - 30.00
   425 *Coming 'Round The Mountains* ....20.00 - 30.00
Champion 16805 *When The Train Comes Along* . 100.00 - 150.00
   16822 *Don't Get Weary Children* ....100.00 - 150.00
   45048 *Don't Get Weary Children* ....15.00 - 25.00
   45105 *When The Train Comes Along* ....15.00 - 25.00
Decca 5369 *Don't Get Weary Children* ....10.00 - 15.00
   5373 *Thank God For Everything* ....10.00 - 15.00
Montgomery Ward 4819 *One More River To Cross*.....10.00 - 15.00
   7347 *The Bum Hotel* ....10.00 - 15.00
   7348 *Honest Confession Is Good For The Soul*. 10.00 - 15.00
   7349 *From Jerusalem To Jericho* ....10.00 - 15.00
   7350 *Two-In-One Chewing Gum* ....10.00 - 15.00
   7884 *She's Got The Money Too* ....10.00 - 15.00
   7885 *Johnny Grey*.....................................10.00 - 15.00
   8029 *Don't Get Weary Children* ....10.00 - 15.00
Okeh 45507 *Tennessee Red Fox Chase* ....75.00 - 125.00
   45522 *Mysteries Of The World* ....75.00 - 125.00
   45552 *She's Got The Money Too* ....75.00 - 125.00

Vocalion 5001 *Deliverance Will Come* ....20.00 - 30.00
   5002 *Arcade Blues* ....20.00 - 30.00
   5003 *The Old Man's Drunk Again*....................20.00 - 30.00
   5004 *Something's Always Sure To Tickle Me* ....20.00 - 30.00
   5005 *Sourwood Mountain Medley* ....20.00 - 30.00
   5006 *Sassy Sam*.......................................20.00 - 30.00
   5007 *My Girl's A High Born Lady* ....20.00 - 30.00
   5008 *Them Two Gals Of Mine* ....20.00 - 30.00
   5009 *I Ain't Got Long To Stay* ....20.00 - 30.00
   5010 *Sho' Fly, Don't Bother Me*....................20.00 - 30.00
   5011 *Uncle Ned*.......................................20.00 - 30.00
   5012 *Diamond In The Rough* ....20.00 - 30.00
   5013 *Tossing The Baby So High* ....20.00 - 30.00
   5014 *Never Make Love-No More* ....20.00 - 30.00
   5040 *(She Was Always) Chewing Gum*..............20.00 - 30.00
   5041 *Papa's Billie Goat*.............................20.00 - 30.00
   5042 *Down By The River*............................20.00 - 30.00
   5043 *The Fox Chase* ....20.00 - 30.00
   5046 *Jonah And The Whale* ....20.00 - 30.00
   5047 *Soldier's Joy*...................................20.00 - 30.00

5051 *All I've Got's Gone*	20.00	-	30.00
5060 *Run, Nigger, Run*	20.00	-	30.00
5061 *Old Dan Tucker*	20.00	-	30.00
5062 *The Girl I Left Behind Me*	20.00	-	30.00
5065 *Southern Whistling Coon*	20.00	-	30.00
5066 *Oh, Where Is My Boy Tonight*	20.00	-	30.00
5067 *All-Go-Hungry Hash House*	20.00	-	30.00
5070 *Save My Mother's Picture From The Sale*	20.00	-	30.00
5071 *Muskrat Medley*	20.00	-	30.00
5075 *Down By The Old Mill Stream*	20.00	-	30.00
5081 *Arkansas Travelers*	20.00	-	30.00
5082 *Struttin' 'Round*	20.00	-	30.00
5095 *I've Got The Mourning Blues*	20.00	-	30.00
5096 *On The Dixie Bee Line*	20.00	-	30.00
5097 *Way Down The Old Plank Road*	20.00	-	30.00
5098 *He Won The Heart Of My Sarah Jane*	20.00	-	30.00
5099 *Whoop 'Em Up Cindy*	20.00	-	30.00
5100 *Poor Sinners, Fare You Well*	20.00	-	30.00
5104 *Old Ties*	20.00	-	30.00
5109 *I Tickled Nancy*	20.00	-	30.00
5148 *Bake That Chicken Pie*	25.00	-	40.00
5149 *In The Shade Of The Old Apple Tree*	25.00	-	40.00
5151 *Carve That Possum*	25.00	-	40.00
5152 *Rockabout My Sara Jane*	25.00	-	40.00
5153 *Tell Her To Come Back Home*	25.00	-	40.00
5154 *Walk, Tom Wilson, Walk*	25.00	-	40.00
5155 *Sail Away, Ladies*	25.00	-	40.00
5156 *Sleepy Lou*	25.00	-	40.00
5157 *I's Gwine Back To Dixie*	25.00	-	40.00
5159 *Poor Old Dad*	25.00	-	40.00
5161 *The Mockingbird Song Medley*	25.00	-	40.00
5163 *When Ruebin Comes To Town*	25.00	-	40.00
5164 *Backwater Blues*	25.00	-	40.00
5165 *Go Along Mule*	25.00	-	40.00
5172 *More Like Your Dad Every Day*	25.00	-	40.00
5261 *The New Ford Car*	25.00	-	40.00
5316 *Jesus, Lover Of My Soul*	25.00	-	40.00
5341 *Farm Relief*	25.00	-	40.00
5356 *The Life And Death Of Jesse James*	25.00	-	40.00
5374 *We Need A Change In Business All Around*	25.00	-	40.00
5380 *Susie Lee*	25.00	-	40.00
5397 *Put Me In My Little Bed*	25.00	-	40.00
14847 *(She Was Always) Chewing Gum*	20.00	-	30.00
14848 *Keep My Skillet Good And Greasy*	20.00	-	30.00
14849 *Down By The River*	20.00	-	30.00
14850 *Old Maid's Last Hope (A Burglar Song)*	20.00	-	30.00
14864 *Jonah And The Whale*	20.00	-	30.00
14904 *All I've Got's Gone*	20.00	-	30.00
15032 *Run, Nigger, Run*	20.00	-	30.00
15033 *Old Dan Tucker*	20.00	-	30.00
15034 *Down In Arkansas*	20.00	-	30.00
15063 *Watermelon Smilin' On The Vine*	20.00	-	30.00
15076 *All-Go-Hungry Hash House*	20.00	-	30.00
15100 *Save My Mother's Picture From The Sale*	20.00	-	30.00
15101 *Muskrat Medley*	20.00	-	30.00
15143 *Down By The Old Mill Stream*	20.00	-	30.00
15192 *Arkansas Travelers*	20.00	-	30.00
15319 *I've Got The Mourning Blues*	20.00	-	30.00
15320 *On The Dixie Bee Line*	20.00	-	30.00
15321 *Rise When The Rooster Crows*	20.00	-	30.00
15322 *He Won The Heart Of My Sarah Jane*	20.00	-	30.00
15323 *Whoop 'Em Up Cindy*	20.00	-	30.00
15324 *Poor Sinners, Fare You Well*	20.00	-	30.00
15325 *Old Ties*	20.00	-	30.00
15341 *I Tickled Nancy.*	20.00	-	30.00
15439 *Uncle Dave's Beloved Solo*	20.00	-	30.00
15441 *In The Good Old Summer Time*	20.00	-	30.00
15442 *Something's Always Sure To Tickle Me*	20.00	-	30.00
15443 *Sourwood Mountain Medley*	20.00	-	30.00
15444 *Sassy Sam*	20.00	-	30.00
15445 *My Girl's A High Born Lady*	20.00	-	30.00
15446 *Them Two Girls Of Mine*	20.00	-	30.00
15447 *We Are Up Against It Now*	20.00	-	30.00
15448 *Sho' Fly Don't Bother Me*	20.00	-	30.00
15450 *Uncle Ned*	20.00	-	30.00
15451 *Hold On To The Sleigh*	20.00	-	30.00
15452 *Kissin' On The Sly*	20.00	-	30.00
15453 *Never Make Love No More*	20.00	-	30.00

(Note: The prices quoted herein are for records in excellent condition. It is particularly appropriate to restate this here, because many of the foregoing records are plentiful in worn condition, and are usually found in that state. Worn copies are worth nominal sums at most, and are probably unsaleable at any price.)

MADDOX BROS. & ROSE:

4-Star 1184 *Midnight Train*	5.00	-	8.00
1185 *Milk Cow Blues*	5.00	-	8.00

MADDUX FAMILY:

Decca 5393 *Stone Rag*	4.00	-	7.00

MADISONVILLE STRING BAND:

Champion 16452 *B Flat Rag*	20.00	-	30.00
16503 *Next To Your Mother, Who Do You Love*	20.00	-	30.00
45005 *B Flat Rag*	7.00	-	10.00
Decca 5437 *B Flat Rag*	5.00	-	8.00
Superior 2756 *B Flat Rag*	25.00	-	40.00

MAGNOLIA TRIO:

Okeh 45505 *My Carolina Sweetheart*	10.00	-	15.00
45521 *'Neath The Old Pine Tree At Twilight*	10.00	-	15.00

JACK MAHONEY:

Columbia 15685-D *The Convict And The Bird*	15.00	-	20.00
15712-D *The Convict's Return*	15.00	-	20.00

J. E. MAINER (& HIS MOUNTAINEERS); WADE MAINER & SONS; WADE MAINER & ZEKE MORRIS; WADE MAINER & SON OF THE MOUNTAINEERS; MAINER'S MOUNTAINEERS; MAINER'S SMILIN' RANGERS:

Bluebird 6065 *Maple On The Hill*	5.00	-	8.00
6088 *This World Is Not My Home*	7.00	-	10.00
6090 *Broken Hearted Blues*	7.00	-	10.00
6104 *Let Her Go, God Bless Her*	7.00	-	10.00
6160 *The City On The Hill*	7.00	-	10.00
6194 *Write A Letter To Mother*	7.00	-	10.00
6222 *Longest Train*	7.00	-	10.00
6290 *Fatal Wreck Of The Bus*	7.00	-	10.00
6293 *Maple On The Hill-Part 2*	7.00	-	10.00
6324 *Satisfied*	7.00	-	10.00
6347 *A Leaf From The Sea*	7.00	-	10.00
6383 *Just As The Sun Went Down*	7.00	-	10.00
6385 *When I Reach My Home Eternal*	7.00	-	10.00
6424 *New Lost Train Blues*	7.00	-	10.00
6440 *Behind The Parlor Door*	7.00	-	10.00
6460 *Nobody's Darling On Earth*	7.00	-	10.00

6479 *The Old And Faded Picture* ....7.00 - 10.00
6489 *Cradle Days* ....7.00 - 10.00
6539 *Got A Home In That Rock* ....7.00 - 10.00
6551 *Come Back To Your Dobie Shack* ....7.00 - 10.00
6584 *Watermelon On The Vine* ....7.00 - 10.00
6596 *Shake Hands With Mother* ....7.00 - 10.00
6624 *What Makes Him Do It?* ....7.00 - 10.00
6629 *John Henry Was A Little Boy* ....7.00 - 10.00
6653 *Cowboy's Pony In Heaven* ....7.00 - 10.00
6675 *Budded Roses* ....7.00 - 10.00
6704 *Been Foolin' Me Baby* ....7.00 - 10.00
6738 *Won't Be Worried Long* ....7.00 - 10.00
6752 *Hop Along Peter* ....7.00 - 10.00
6784 *Just One Way To The Pearly Gates* ....7.00 - 10.00
6792 *Seven And A Half* ....7.00 - 10.00
6840 *Little Birdie* ....7.00 - 10.00
6890 *Always Born A Gambler* ....7.00 - 10.00
6936 *In The Land Beyond The Blue* ....7.00 - 10.00
6993 *Little Rosebuds* ....7.00 - 10.00
7114 *Answer To Two Little Rosebuds* ....7.00 - 10.00
7151 *Answer To Greenback Dollar* ....7.00 - 10.00
7165 *I'm Not Turning Backward* ....7.00 - 10.00
7201 *Little Maggie* ....7.00 - 10.00
7222 *In The Little Village Churchyard* ....7.00 - 10.00
7249 *Wild Bill Jones* ....7.00 - 10.00
7274 *Memory Lane* ....5.00 - 10.00
7289 *Kiss Me Cindy* ....5.00 - 10.00
7298 *Riding On Train 45* ....5.00 - 10.00
7349 *Don't Go Out* ....5.00 - 10.00
7384 *What Are You Goin' To Do, Brother?* ....5.00 - 8.00
7412 *Lamp Lightin' Time In Heaven* ....5.00 - 8.00
7424 *All My Friends* ....5.00 - 8.00
7471 *If I Lose, Let Me Lose* ....5.00 - 8.00
7483 *Don't Get Too Deep In Love* ....5.00 - 8.00
7523 *Floating Down The Stream Of Time* ....5.00 - 8.00
7561 *I Won't Be Worried* ....5.00 - 8.00
7586 *Your Best Friend Is Always Near* ....5.00 - 8.00
7587 *Mountain Sweetheart* ....5.00 - 8.00
7659 *I Once Loved A Young Man* ....5.00 - 8.00
7730 *Just Over In Glory Land* ....5.00 - 8.00
7753 *Where Romance Calls* ....5.00 - 8.00
7845 *Mitchell Blues* ....5.00 - 8.00
7965 *Great Reaping Day* ....5.00 - 8.00
7965 *More Good Women Gone Wrong* ....5.00 - 8.00
8042 *Sparkling Blue Eyes* ....5.00 - 8.00
Bluebird (higher numbers)..................................4.00 - 7.00
King ....3.00 - 5.00

JACK MAJOR:

Brunswick 252 *Tennessee Mountain Girl* ....10.00 - 15.00
Columbia 15362-D *My Kentucky Mountain*
Sweetheart...20.00 - 30.00

BLIND JOE MANGUM & FRED SHRIBER:

Okeh 40018 *Bacon And Cabbage*...........................15.00 - 20.00

MAPLE CITY FOUR:

Supertone 9193 *Roll Dem Bones* ....5.00 - 8.00

MARKHAM BROS.:

Challenge 399 *I Am Resolved* ....5.00 - 8.00
400 *Constantly Abiding* ....5.00 - 8.00
401 *I'm On The Sunny Side* ....7.00 - 10.00

ANDY MARLOW:

Champion 15875 *My Little Lady* ....15.00 - 20.00
15899 *Blue Yodel No. 5* ....15.00 - 20.00

MARLOW AND YOUNG:

Champion 15691 *Let Her Go, I'll Meet Her*.............7.00 - 10.00
15732 *My Carolina Home* ....20.00 - 30.00
15750 *Six Months Ain't Long* ....20.00 - 30.00

CHARLIE MARSHALL:

Vocalion 03045 *The Old Hitchin' Rail* ....10.00 - 15.00

MARTIN BROTHERS:

Paramount 3194 *The Marion Massacre*...................30.00 - 50.00
3217 *Whistling Rufus* ....30.00 - 50.00
3248 *Don't Marry A Man If He Drinks* ....30.00 - 50.00

MARTIN MELODY BOYS:

Columbia 15413-D *The Donald Rag* ....25.00 - 40.00

(ASA) MARTIN & (JAMES) ROBERTS; MARTIN & ROSE; MARTIN & HOBBS:

Titles issued contemporaneously on Banner, Conqueror, Melotone, Oriole, Perfect, and Romeo: *Aged Mother; Bronco Bill; Budded Roses; Bury Me 'Neath The Weeping Willow; Careless Love; The Contented Hobo; Crawdad Song; Darling Nellie Gray; Down On The Farm; The Dying Cowboy; The East Bound Train; Give My Love To Nellie, Jack; Good Bye Bett; Hang Down Your Head And Cry; Hot Corn; I Tickled Her Under The Chin; The Knoxville Girl; A Letter From Home Sweet Home; Lillie Dale; The Little Old Jailhouse; Little Shack Around The Corner; Low Down Hanging Around; Message Of A Broken Heart; My Blue Eyed Boy; My Dixie Home; My Lover On The Deep Blue Sea; My Old Homestead By The Sea; My Rocky Mountain Queen; Ninety-Nine Years; The Pine Tree On The Hill; Prisoner No. 999; The Roundup In The Spring; The Rovin' Moonshiner; Rycove Cyclone; Shadows And Dreams; She Ain't Built That Way; The Ship That Never Returned; Sunny Tennessee; Sweet Florine; There's A Little Box Of Pine On The 7:29; There's No Place Like Home; There's Someone Waiting For You; The Wandering Hobo; When It's Lamp Lighting Time In The Valley; When The Roses Bloom In Dixie; Where's My Sweetie Now*
.... 8.00 - 15.00
Champion 16049 *An Old Fashioned Picture Of Mother*
.... 15.00 - 30.00
16272 *Mind Your Own Business*........................ 15.00 - 30.00
16299 *The Contented Hobo* .... 15.00 - 30.00
16520 *Hot Corn* .... 50.00 - 80.00
16529 *Prisoner No. 999* .... 50.00 - 80.00
16536 *Wild Cat Rag* .... 75.00 - 100.00
16539 *The Little Old Jailhouse* .... 75.00 - 100.00
16557 *The Roving Moonshiner* .... 75.00 - 100.00
16568 *I Must See My Mother* .... 75.00 - 100.00
16589 *I'm On My Way Back Home* .... 75.00 - 100.00
16597 *Shadows And Dreams* .... 75.00 - 100.00
16610 *Wolf County Blues*.................................. 80.00 - 120.00
16611 *Gamblin' Cowboy* .... 80.00 - 120.00
16627 *Cakewalk Papa* .... 80.00 - 120.00
16769 *It's Funny When You Feel That Way* .... 100.00 - 150.00
45034 *Bronco Bill* .... 10.00 - 15.00
45065 *Hot Corn* .... 10.00 - 15.00
45067 *My Cabin Home Among The Hills* .... 10.00 - 15.00
45129 *She Ain't Built That Way*........................ 10.00 - 15.00
45133 *Red River Valley Rose* .... 10.00 - 15.00
45142 *Take Those Lips Away* .... 10.00 - 15.00
45175 *The Dying Girls Message*........................ 10.00 - 15.00
45176 *Prisoner No. 999* .... 10.00 - 15.00
Decca 5444 *Take Those Lips Away*........................ 5.00 - 8.00

Gennett 6531 *The Dingy Miner's Cabin* ....50.00 - 80.00
  6601 *The Old New Hampshire Valley* ....50.00 - 80.00
  6621 *The Dying Girls Message* ....50.00 - 80.00
  6762 *Bad Companions*......................................50.00 - 80.00
  6808 *She Ain't Built That Way* ....50.00 - 80.00
  6975 *The Virginia Moonshiner*.........................75.00 - 100.00
  7050 *Gwine Down To Town* ....75.00 - 100.00
  7068 *Down On The Farm*...................................75.00 - 100.00
  7207 *Johnny The Drunkard* ....80.00 - 120.00
  7242 *Put On Your Old Gray Bonnet*..................80.00 - 120.00
Vocalion 04529, 04569, 04673, 04759, 04827,
  04894 ....4.00 - 8.00

BUSTER MARTIN'S BRONCO BUSTERS:
Groovy 701 *Herbie's Steel Guitar Polka* ....10.00 - 15.00

CLYDE MARTIN & HIS HOOSIER RANGERS:
Champion 16409 *Shuber's Hoe Down* ....25.00 - 40.00

DAN MARTIN:
Superior 2824 *The Cross-Eyed Butcher* ....10.00 - 20.00

JOHN MARTIN:
Superior 2626 *Railroad Blues* ....20.00 - 30.00
  2658 *The Hobos Pal* ....20.00 - 30.00
  2701 *The Wreck Of The C & O Sportsman* ....20.00 - 30.00

JOHNNY MARTIN:
Supertone 9721 *Sweet Wimmin'* ....25.00 - 40.00

MARVIN FAMILY:
Columbia 15474-D *Yodeling Them Blues Away* .....15.00 - 20.00

MARVIN'S STRING BAND:
Supertone 9738 *Fox Chase*....................................7.00 - 10.00

FRANKIE MARVIN (& HIS GUITAR & JIMMIE SMITH):
Following is a selective listing from the large number of records,
  mostly of minimal value, by the artist:
Crown 3125, 3204 ....5.00 - 8.00
Edison (thin) 11006 *Away Out On The Mountain* ...30.00 - 50.00
  20002 *Ben Dewberry's Final Run* ....30.00 - 50.00
  20011 *Oklahoma, Land Of The Sunny West*.......... - -
(Note: 20011 was not officially issued, but copies have been
  reported.)
Edison (thick) 52436 *In The Jailhouse Now*............10.00 - 20.00
  52451 *Barber's Blues* ....10.00 - 20.00
  52460 *Walking Down The Railroad Track*.........10.00 - 20.00
  52490 *Poor Man's Blues* ....10.00 - 20.00
  52523 *Riding On The Elevated Railroad*............15.00 - 20.00
  52576 *The Two Gun Cowboy* ....15.00 - 20.00
  52607 *A High Silk Hat And A Walking Cane* .....15.00 - 20.00
  52650 *Blue Yodel No. 4* ....20.00 - 30.00
Paramount 3275 *T. B. Blues* ....10.00 - 15.00
  3276 *The Gangster's Warning*...........................10.00 - 15.00
Timely Tunes 1553 *She's Just That Kind*................15.00 - 20.00
  1554 *She's Always On My Mind*........................15.00 - 20.00
  1555 *I'm Blue And Lonesome*...........................15.00 - 20.00
Victor 23553 *Old Man Duff*...................................10.00 - 15.00
  23561 *When It's Night Time In Nevada* ....75.00 - 100.00

JOHNNY MARVIN:
(Note: Most of the records by this artist are of little value or interest
  as country/western music.)
Victor 23691 *I'm Gonna Yodel My Way To Heaven*......10.00 - 15.00
  23708 *Seven Come Eleven*.................................10.00 - 20.00
  23728 *Go Along Bum*..10.00 - 20.00

MASSEY FAMILY:
Vocalion 02993 *Sweet Mama Tree Top Tall* .... 8.00 - 12.00

LOUISE MASSEY:
Okeh (most issues)... 4.00 - 7.00
Vocalion 04221 *Nobody To Love* .... 5.00 - 8.00

JACK MATHIS:
Columbia 15344-D *Your Mother Still Prays For You*
.... 8.00 - 12.00
  15450-D *Charming Bessie Lee* .... 8.00 - 12.00

JOHNNY MATHIS:
Talent 738 *Tell Me Why*...................................... 8.00 - 12.00

JIMMIE MATTOX:
Gennett 7227 *Goodbye Mama* .... 35.00 - 50.00

BILLIE MAXWELL (THE COWGIRL SINGER):
Victor V40148 *Billy Venero* .... 8.00 - 12.00
  V40188 *The Cowboy's Wife* .... 10.00 - 15.00
  V40241 *Haunted Hunted* .... 10.00 - 15.00

KEN MAYNARD:
Columbia 2310-D *The Cowboy's Lament*............... 75.00 - 100.00

DAVID McCARN:
Victor 23506 *Poor Man, Rich Man* .... 50.00 - 80.00
  23532 *Hobo Life* .... 50.00 - 80.00
  23555 *Gastonia Gallop*................................... 75.00 - 100.00
  V40274 *Cotton Mill Colic* .... 50.00 - 80.00

McCARTT BROTHERS & PATTERSON:
Columbia 15454-D *Green Valley Waltz* .... 5.00 - 8.00

McCLAIN & HARPOLD:
Gennett 7224 *Bake That Chicken Pie* .... 20.00 - 30.00
Supertone 9716 *Bake That Chicken Pie*................. 15.00 - 20.00

McCLENDON BROTHERS:
Bluebird 6961 *My Little Mountain Lady* .... 5.00 - 8.00
  7339 *Free As I Can Be*....................................... 8.00 - 12.00
  7832 *Corns On My Feet*...................................... 5.00 - 8.00

HARRY McCLINTOCK (See "RADIO MAC" AND "MAC"):

McCLUNG BROTHERS (& CLEVE CHAFFIN):
Brunswick 134 *Birdie* .... 8.00 - 12.00
  135 *Chicken* .... 8.00 - 12.00
  136 *It's A Long, Long Way To Tipperary*............ 8.00 - 12.00
Paramount 3161 *Alabama Jubilee* .... 15.00 - 20.00
  3179 *Rock House Gamblers*............................... 15.00 - 20.00

(SMILIN') ED McCONNELL:
Bluebird 5075, 5105, 5140, 5200, 5275.................... 4.00 - 8.00
Champion 16209 *The Hell Bound Train*................ 10.00 - 15.00
  16263 *Leave It There* .... 10.00 - 15.00
  45137 *The Devil Song* .... 5.00 - 10.00
Victor 23808 *Tiny Toys* .... 10.00 - 15.00
  23812 *The Royal Telephone* .... 10.00 - 15.00
  23823 *Life's Railway To Heaven* .... 10.00 - 15.00
  23825 *Where Is My Boy Tonight* .... 10.00 - 15.00
  23844 *The Old Rugged Cross* .... 10.00 - 15.00
  23848 *Leave It There* .... 10.00 - 15.00

EARL McCOY (& JESSIE BROCK/ALFRED MENG & CLEM GARNER):
Columbia 15499-D *Cotton Mill Girl* .... 40.00 - 60.00
  15604-D *Off To War* .... 40.00 - 60.00
  15622-D *Forty Percent* .... 40.00 - 60.00

HAL McCOY:

Imperial 8052 *Mountain Rhythm*	7.00 -	10.00
8053 *Don't Pretend*	7.00 -	10.00
8059 *My Pecos Rose*	7.00 -	10.00
8060 *My Pinto Kicked Me In The Pants*	7.00 -	10.00

FRANK & JAMES McCRAVY:

Brunswick 192, 193, 194, 424, 444, 452, 465, 467, 504, 515, 528, 535, 566, 572, 589	4.00 -	8.00
Columbia 15617-D *No More Dying*	8.00 -	12.00
15764-D *I Love You In The Same Old Way*	10.00 -	15.00
Okeh 45128, 45135, 45433, 45435, 45447, 45457, 45466	5.00 -	10.00
Victor (most issues)	5.00 -	10.00
Vocalion 5193, 5194, 5195, 5255, 5293	5.00 -	10.00

LEWIS/LOUIS McDANIEL (& GID SMITH):

Timely Tunes 1560 *One More Kiss Before I Go*	30.00 -	50.00
Victor 23505 *I've Loved You So True*	30.00 -	50.00
V40287 *We'll Talk About One Another*	30.00 -	50.00

McDONALD BROTHERS:

Vocalion 5406 *Poor Little Joe*	10.00 -	15.00

(LESTER) McFARLAND & (BOB) GARDNER:

Brunswick 107, 108, 109, 110, 111, 116, 160, 163, 164, 167, 168, 169, 170, 171, 190, 195, 199, 200, 201, 202, 203, 286, 293, 305, 307, 311, 316, 322, 326, 332, 334, 339, 350, 356, 366, 398, 409, 426, 432, 438, 439, 451, 454, 461, 466, 475, 479, 483, 492, 499, 520, 524, 525, 527, 537, 541, 548, 551, 553, 561, 568, 570, 578, 586, 588, 594, 596	5.00 -	10.00
Vocalion 5026, 5027, 5028, 5120, 5121, 5122, 5123, 5124, 5125, 5126, 5127, 5128, 5129, 5130, 5174, 5177, 5184, 5187, 5191, 5192, 5259, 5285, 5307, 5322, 5364, 5369, 5381, 5392	5.00 -	10.00

(Note: Other records by this duo usually command similar premiums.)

J. D. McFARLANE & DAUGHTER:

Okeh 45027 *Devil In The Wood Pile*	15.00 -	25.00

ALPHUS McFAYDEN:

Victor 21128 *Medley*	5.00 -	8.00

DENNIS McGEE:

Vocalion 5334 *Allen And Tassone*	15.00 -	25.00
5348 *Myself*	15.00 -	25.00

SAM (& KIRK) McGEE; KIRK & SAM McGEE; KIRK McGEE (& BLYTHE POTEET):

Champion 16804 *Brown's Ferry Blues*	75.00 -	100.00
45033 *Brown's Ferry Blues*	10.00 -	15.00
Decca 5348 *Brown's Ferry Blues*	10.00 -	15.00
Gennett 6704 *If I Only Had A Home*	30.00 -	50.00
6731 *If I Could Hear My Mother Pray Again*	30.00 -	50.00
6778 *Only A Step To The Grave*	30.00 -	50.00
6960 *My Wife Left Me*	30.00 -	50.00
7022 *Kickin' Mule*	30.00 -	50.00
Vocalion 5094 *The Franklin Blues*	20.00 -	30.00
5101 *Knoxville Blues*	20.00 -	30.00
5150 *Salty Dog Blues*	20.00 -	30.00
5166 *Charming Bill*	20.00 -	30.00
5167 *Old Master's Runaway*	20.00 -	30.00
5169 *Salt Lake City Blues*	20.00 -	30.00
5254 *Easy Rider*	20.00 -	30.00
5310 *The Ship Without A Sail*	20.00 -	30.00
15318 *Buck Dancer's Choice*	20.00 -	30.00
15326 *Knoxville Blues*	20.00 -	30.00

McGHEE & COGER:

Gennett 6703 *The Vestris Disaster*	15.00 -	25.00
6795 *He Included Me*	15.00 -	25.00
6932 *Calling The Prodigal*	15.00 -	25.00

(JOHN) McGHEE & (FRANK) WELLING (See also WELLING & McGHEE):

Brunswick 222 *He Abides*	7.00 -	10.00
251 *I Would Not Be Denied*	7.00 -	10.00
258 *Dwelling In Beulah Land*	7.00 -	10.00
272 *I Am Coming Home*	7.00 -	10.00
Champion 16479 *My Burdens Rolled Away*	15.00 -	20.00
16542 *He Abides*	15.00 -	20.00
Gennett 6334 *I've Been Redeemed*	15.00 -	20.00
6389 *Praise The Lord, It's So*	15.00 -	20.00
6435 *I Am Resolved*	15.00 -	20.00
6533 *I'm Free Again*	15.00 -	20.00
6657 *Get A Transfer*	15.00 -	20.00
6671 *I Wants My Lulu*	15.00 -	25.00
6690 *Why Not Tonight*	15.00 -	25.00
6749 *At The Battle Front*	15.00 -	25.00
6874 *I Have To Tell The Story*	15.00 -	25.00
7083 *Beautiful Garden Of Prayer*	15.00 -	25.00
7114 *No Never Alone*	20.00 -	30.00
7128 *Old Kentucky Dew*	20.00 -	30.00
7143 *He'll Understand*	20.00 -	30.00
7156 *Life's Railway To Heaven*	20.00 -	30.00
7185 *Where Is My Mamma*	20.00 -	30.00
7228 *Sweeping Through The Gates*	20.00 -	30.00
7247 *I'm Drifting Back To Dreamland*	20.00 -	30.00
7294 *I Surrender All*	20.00 -	30.00
7316 *I'm Forever Blowing Bubbles*	30.00 -	50.00
Paramount 3234 *The Prisoners Child*	20.00 -	30.00
Superior 323 *He Keeps Me Singing*	30.00 -	50.00
345 *I Am Resolved*	30.00 -	50.00
Supertone 9626 *Down The Lane To Home Sweet Home*	7.00 -	10.00
Vocalion 5251 *The Lily Of The Valley*	15.00 -	20.00

JOHN McGHEE:

Gennett 6362 *The Sinking Of Submarine S-4*	7.00 -	10.00
6103 *The Preacher And The Bear*	10.00 -	15.00
6149 *Aged Mother*	10.00 -	15.00
6450 *The Volunteer Organist*	10.00 -	15.00
6479 *Bill Bailey, Ain't That A Shame*	10.00 -	15.00
6546 *Hard Luck Jim*	10.00 -	15.00
6587 *The Hatfield-McCoy Feud*	15.00 -	25.00
6960 *Life Ain't Worth Living When You're Broke*	25.00 -	35.00
7096 *The Great Airplane Crash*	20.00 -	30.00
7168 *You're As Welcome As The Flowers In May*	20.00 -	30.00
Superior 325 *The Preacher And The Bear*	30.00 -	50.00
344 *The Marian Parker Murder*	30.00 -	50.00
367 *The Sinking Of Submarine S-4*	30.00 -	50.00

KIRK McGHEE/SAM McGHEE (See McGEE)

MERLE McGINNIS:

Gennett 6990 *Highway Blues*	30.00 -	50.00

McGINTY'S OKLAHOMA COWBOY BAND:
Champion 15446 *It Can't Be Done* ....8.00 - 12.00
   15482 *Adam And Eve*.........................8.00 - 12.00
Okeh 45057 *The Cowboy's Dream*..........................10.00 - 15.00

LEON McGUIRE:
Vocalion 5393 *When The Blue Eyes Meet The Brown*
....7.00 - 10.00

McKINNEY BROTHERS:
Champion 16830 *Old Uncle Joe*...............................20.00 - 30.00

McLAUGHLIN'S (OLD TIME) MELODY MAKERS:
Victor 21286 *Dill Pickles Rag*..........................8.00 - 12.00
   V40117 *Whistlin' Rufus*.........................10.00 - 15.00
Vocalion 5296 *Mississippi Shadows* ....10.00 - 15.00
   5330 *Hilarious Zeb* ....10.00 - 15.00

McMANN & ROBERTS:
Supertone 9318 *If I Could Hear My Mother Pray Again*
....7.00 - 10.00

(CLAYTON) McMICHEN'S MELODY MEN; McMICHEN LAYNE STRING ORCHESTRA; CLAYTON McMICHEN & DAN HORNSBY/RILEY PUCKETT; CLAYTON McMICHEN & HIS GEORGIA WILDCATS/HARMONY BOYS/HOME TOWN BAND:
Columbia 15111-D *Sweet Bunch Of Daisies*.............7.00 - 10.00
   15130-D *House Of David Blues* ....8.00 - 12.00
   *15140-D *A Fiddlers Convention In Georgia* ......7.00 - 10.00
   15190-D *St. Louis Blues* ....10.00 - 15.00
   *15201-D *A Corn Licker Still In Georgia* ....7.00 - 10.00
   15202-D *The Missouri Waltz*................................8.00 - 12.00
   15224-D *Fifty Years Ago* ....10.00 - 15.00
   15247-D *Silver Threads Among The Gold* ....7.00 - 10.00
   15253-D *The Original Arkansas Traveler*..........10.00 - 15.00
   *15258-D *A Corn Licker Still In Georgia* ....7.00 - 10.00
   15288-D *Home Sweet Home*................................7.00 - 10.00
   15310-D *Ain't She Sweet* ....10.00 - 15.00
   15333-D *The Blind Child's Prayer*....................10.00 - 15.00
   15340-D *Lonesome Mama Blues*........................15.00 - 20.00
   15356-D *Down The Ozark Trail*........................15.00 - 20.00
   *15366-D *Corn Licker Still, Part 5/6* ....8.00 - 12.00
   15391-D *When You're Far From The Ones Who Love You*
....10.00 - 15.00
   *15432-D *Corn Licker Still, Part 7/8* ....10.00 - 15.00
   15464-D *The Dying Hobo* ....15.00 - 20.00
   *15503-D *A Night In A Blind Tiger*....................15.00 - 20.00
   15521-D *McMichen's Reel*.................................15.00 - 20.00
   *15531-D *Corn Licker Still, Part 9/10* ....15.00 - 20.00
   15540-D *Honolulu Moon*...................................15.00 - 20.00
   *15549-D *Taking The Census* ....15.00 - 20.00
   *15598-D *Jeremiah Hopkins' Store At Sand Mountain*
....15.00 - 20.00
   *15618-D *Corn Licker Still, Part 11/12* ....20.00 - 30.00
   *15632-D *Prohibition-Yes Or No*......................20.00 - 30.00
   *15667-D *Fiddler's Convention, Part 3/4*..........20.00 - 30.00
   15686-D *The Arkansas Sheik*.............................30.00 - 50.00
   *15700-D *A Bee Hunt On Hell For Sartin Creek*
....30.00 - 50.00
   *15703-D *Corn Licker Still, Part 13/14* ....40.00 - 60.00
   15723-D *Yum Yum Blues* ....75.00 - 100.00
   15775-D *Wild Cat Rag* ....80.00 - 120.00

(Note: *These "descriptive novelty" records credit several or more artists on the labels; since McMichen's name appears first, all are included in this listing.)
Crown 3384 *Singing An Old Hymn* ....20.00 - 30.00
   3385 *Georgia Wildcat Breakdown* ....20.00 - 30.00
   3386 *Way Down In Caroline* ....20.00 - 30.00
   3397 *Arkansas Traveler* ....15.00 - 20.00
   3416 *Old Joe Clarke* ....15.00 - 20.00
   3419 *When The Bloom Is On The Sage* ....15.00 - 20.00
   3432 *Countin' Cross Ties* ....20.00 - 30.00
Decca 5418, 5424, 5436, 5448, 5491.......................5.00 - 8.00
Okeh 45022 *Alabama Jubilee*................................15.00 - 25.00
   45034 *Bully Of The Town* ....15.00 - 20.00
   45330 *Ain't She Sweet?* ....20.00 - 30.00

WHITEY McPHERSON:
Vocalion 03883 *Little Lady* ....7.00 - 10.00
   03937 *Brakeman Blues* ....7.00 - 10.00
   04245 *Blue Ridge Mountain Blues* ....7.00 - 10.00
   04339 *Am I Blue*...7.00 - 10.00

ODDIE McWINDERS:
Crown 3398 *Down In Old Kentucky*......................20.00 - 30.00

GRACE MEANS:
Supertone 9244 *Your Mother Still Prays For You*.... 5.00 - 8.00

"THE MEDICINE SHOW" (See EMMETT MILLER)

DAVID MEEK & HIS BOYS:
Champion 15376 *Old Sefus Brown*..........................7.00 - 10.00

DICK MEEKS:
Supertone 9306 *Poor, But A Gentleman Still* ....8.00 - 12.00

MELTON & MINTER/WAGGONER:
Columbia 15423-D *In The Hills Of Old Kentucky*.... 7.00 - 10.00
Vocalion 5435 *Let Me Call You Sweetheart*.............7.00 - 10.00

MEMPHIS BOB:
Columbia 15735-D *Little Marion McLean* ....7.00 - 10.00

MERIDIAN HUSTLERS:
Paramount 3173 *Queen City Square Dance* ....25.00 - 40.00

MERT'S HOMETOWN SERENADERS:
Vocalion 5338 *We Gotta Look Into This* ....7.00 - 10.00

ARTHUR MILES:
Victor V40156 *The Lonely Cowboy* ....8.00 - 12.00

PAUL MILES & THE RED FOX CHASERS:
Gennett 6461 *Under The Double Eagle*..................20.00 - 30.00
   6516 *The Arkansas Traveler* ....20.00 - 30.00
   6547 *Weeping Willow Tree* ....20.00 - 30.00
   6568 *Mississippi Sawyer*.................................20.00 - 30.00
   6866 *The Red Fox-Makin' Licker, Part 1/2*.......20.00 - 30.00
   6912 *The Red Fox-Makin' Licker, Part 3/4*.......20.00 - 30.00
   6930 *Virginia Bootleggers* ....20.00 - 30.00

MILLER'S BULL FROG ENTERTAINERS:
Okeh 45348, 45358, 45386.....................................7.00 - 10.00

MILLER & BURNETT:
Champion 15963 *Missouri Joe* ....7.00 - 10.00
   15985 *Long White Robe* ....7.00 - 10.00
Gennett 7164 *Missouri Joe* ....10.00 - 15.00
   7220 *Twenty-One Years* ....10.00 - 15.00
Okeh 45442, 45541...5.00 - 10.00

BOB MILLER (& HIS HINKY DINKERS/TRIO); CHARLOTTE MILLER & HINKY DINKERS:

Brunswick 404, 428, 4431	5.00 -	10.00
Champion 16008 *The Ohio Prison Fire*	10.00 -	15.00
7239 *Five Cent Glass Of Beer*	10.00 -	15.00
Okeh 45475 *Little Cotton Mill Girl*	10.00 -	15.00
45497 *Nebuchudneezer*	10.00 -	15.00
Victor 23693 *Twenty-One Years, Part 2*	8.00 -	12.00
23712 *Happy Warrior*	8.00 -	12.00
23719 *The Rich Man And The Poor Man*	8.00 -	12.00
23733 *Prisoner No. 999*	8.00 -	12.00
23742 *Duck Foot Sue*	8.00 -	12.00
23747 *What Does The Deep Sea Say?*	10.00 -	15.00
23768 *Beatrice Snipes*	10.00 -	15.00
23775 *Don't Forget Me*	10.00 -	15.00

DAVID MILLER:

Champion 15298 *Don't Forget Me, Little Darling*	8.00 -	12.00
15317 *The Lonesome Valley*	5.00 -	8.00
15334 *The Bad Man Stackalee*	5.00 -	8.00
Gennett 6175 *The Lonesome Valley*	15.00 -	20.00
6188 *The Bad Man Stackalee*	15.00 -	20.00
6333 *Sweet Floetta*	15.00 -	20.00
6349 *A Little Child Shall Lead Them*	15.00 -	20.00
6388 *Give My Love To Nellie, Jack*	15.00 -	20.00
Superior 324 *Sweet Floetta*	25.00 -	50.00
368 *Give My Love To Nellie, Jack*	12.00 -	18.00
384 *No Little Orphans*	25.00 -	50.00
Supertone 9258 *Two Little Orphans*	12.00 -	18.00

EMMETT MILLER:

Okeh 45380 *The Medicine Show, Act 1/2*	8.00 -	12.00
45391 *The Medicine Show, Act 3/4*	8.00 -	12.00
45413 *The Medicine Show, Act 5/6*	10.00 -	15.00

(Note: Although the labels of the above "descriptive novelty" records credit several artists, they are listed here, since Emmett Miller's name appears first.)

Okeh 45546 *Sam's New Job*	15.00 -	20.00

(Note: Other records by Emmett Miller are listed in the jazz and dance bands section.)

JOHN MILLER:

Superior 2839 *Highway Hobo*	15.00 -	25.00

STANLEY MILLER:

Champion 15297 *Be Kind To A Man When He Is Down*	15.00 -	20.00
15315 *Lost Train Blues*	25.00 -	40.00

OWEN MILLS & FRANK WELLING (& McGHEE):

Paramount 3155 *A Mother's Plea*	8.00 -	12.00
3158 *Don't Forget Me Darling*	10.00 -	15.00
3159 *It's Hard To Be Shut Up In Prison*	10.00 -	15.00

MILNER & CURTIS WITH THE MAGNOLIA RAMBLERS:

Vocalion 5426 *Northeast Texas*	50.00 -	75.00

BILLY MILTON & ONE MAN BAND:

Gennett 6318 *Dill Pickles*	20.00 -	30.00

FLOYD MING'S PEP STEPPERS:

Victor 21294 *Indian War Whoop*	30.00 -	50.00
21534 *Tupelo Blues*	40.00 -	60.00

MISSISSIPPI 'POSSUM HUNTERS:

Victor 23595 *Mississippi Breakdown*	75.00 -	100.00

MITCHELL FAMILY TRIO:

Superior 2641 *Picture On The Wall*	10.00 -	20.00
2657 *The Old Rugged Cross*	10.00 -	20.00
2700 *Hide Me*	10.00 -	20.00
2776 *There Is Power In The Blood*	10.00 -	20.00

MOATSVILLE STRING TICKLERS:

Columbia 15491-D *Moatsville Blues*	20.00 -	30.00

MODERN MOUNTAINEERS:

Bluebird 6911, 6976, 6997, 7047, 7247, 7323, 7423, 7470, 7671, 8558	5.00 -	10.00

MONROE BROTHERS:

Bluebird 6309 *This World Is Not My Home*	8.00 -	12.00
6363 *What Is Home Without Love?*	8.00 -	12.00
6422 *My Long Journey Home*	8.00 -	12.00
6477 *God Holds The Future In His Hands*	8.00 -	12.00
6512 *Six Months Ain't Long*	8.00 -	12.00
6552 *Just A Song Of Old Kentucky*	8.00 -	12.00
6607 *On Some Foggy Mountain Top*	8.00 -	12.00
6645 *New River Train*	8.00 -	12.00
6676 *The Old Crossroad*	8.00 -	12.00
6729 *My Savior's Train*	8.00 -	12.00
6762 *Where Is My Sailor Boy*	10.00 -	15.00
6773 *Roll In My Sweet Baby's Arms*	6.00 -	10.00
6820 *Will The Circle Be Unbroken*	6.00 -	10.00
6829 *Forgotten Soldier Boy*	6.00 -	10.00
6866 *I Am Ready To Go*	6.00 -	10.00
6912 *What Would The Profit Be?*	6.00 -	10.00
6960 *Katy Cline*	6.00 -	10.00
7007 *I Am Going That*	6.00 -	10.00
7055 *Do You Call That Religion*	6.00 -	10.00
7093 *Weeping Willow Tree*	6.00 -	10.00
7122 *What Would You Give In Exchange?*	6.00 -	10.00
7145 *On My Way To Glory*	6.00 -	10.00
7191 *Let Us Be Lovers*	6.00 -	10.00
7273 *My Last Moving Day*	6.00 -	10.00
7326 *Sinner, You Better Get Ready*	6.00 -	10.00
7385 *On The Banks Of The Ohio*	8.00 -	12.00
7425 *I've Still Got Ninety-Nine*	5.00 -	8.00
7460 *On My Way Back Home*	5.00 -	8.00
7508 *Goodbye, Maggie*	5.00 -	8.00
7562 *A Beautiful Life*	5.00 -	8.00
7598 *Rollin' On*	5.00 -	8.00
Montgomery Ward (some titles as above)	4.00 -	8.00

MONROE COUNTY BOTTLE TIPPERS:

Gennett 6585 *The Fiddlin' Bootleggers*	30.00 -	50.00

BILL MONROE & THE BLUE GRASS BOYS:

Bluebird 8568 *Mule Skinner Blues*	8.00 -	12.00
8611 *No Letter In The Mail*	7.00 -	10.00
8692 *Dog House Blues*	5.00 -	8.00
8813 *Tennessee Blues*	7.00 -	10.00
8861 *Blue Yodel No. 7*	7.00 -	10.00
Columbia (red label)	4.00 -	7.00

CHARLIE MONROE'S BOYS:

Bluebird 7862 *Great Speckled Bird*	5.00 -	8.00
7922 *Farther Along*	5.00 -	8.00
7949 *You're Gonna Miss Me*	5.00 -	8.00
7990 *When The World's On Fire*	5.00 -	8.00
8050 *Guided By Love*	5.00 -	8.00
8118 *Joy Bells In My Soul*	5.00 -	8.00

MONTANA SLIM (See also WILF CARTER):
Bluebird 6515 *Midnight, The Unconquered Outlaw* .5.00 - 8.00
   6814 *Prairie Sunset* ....5.00 - 8.00
   6826 *Round-Up Time In Heaven* ....5.00 - 8.00
   6827 *Yodeling Cowgirl* ....5.00 - 8.00
   7618 *By The Grave Of Nobody's Darling* ....5.00 - 8.00
Bluebird 8150, 8202, 8241, 8313, 8329, 8361, 8374,
   8425, 8441, 8456, 8472, 8517, 8531, 8566, 8696,
   8875, 8924, 8983 ....4.00 - 7.00

PATSY MONTANA (with THE PRAIRIE RAMBLERS):
Titles issued contemporaneously on Banner, Conqueror, Melotone,
   Oriole, Perfect, and Romeo: *Blazin' The Trail; A Cowboy
   Honeymoon; Give Me A Home In Montana; Gold Coast Express;
   I Wanna Be A Cowboy's Sweetheart; Lone Star; Pride Of The
   Prairie; Ridin' The Sunset Trail; Sweetheart Of The Saddle;
   Swingtime Cowgirl; With A Banjo On My Knee* ..5.00 - 8.00
Victor 23760 *I Love My Daddy Too* ....40.00 - 60.00
Vocalion 03010, 03135, 03268, 03292,
   03377, 03422 ....5.00 - 8.00
Vocalion 04023, 04076, 04135, 04247, 04291, 04469,
   04482, 04518, 04568, 04689, 04742, 05081 ....4.00 - 7.00
Vogue 721 *When I Gets To Where I'm Going* ....30.00 - 50.00

PHIL MONTGOMERY:
Superior 2542 *That Old Covered Bridge* ....15.00 - 20.00

OKLAHOMA ED MOODY with THE SIX WESTERNERS:
Black & White 10004 *Sitting Alone on My Doorstep* ......5.00 - 8.00
(Note: Other issues, similarly valued.)

TOMMY MOONEY (WITH BOBBY MOONEY) & HIS AUTOMOBILE BABIES:
Floto 78001 *Bingo Boogie* .... - - -
   78003 *Rose Covered Garden* .... - - -

MOONSHINE DAVE:
Champion 15789 *Biscuit Jim* ....10.00 - 15.00

MOONSHINE HARRY:
Supertone 9553 *Son Of A Gun* ....10.00 - 15.00

MOONSHINE KATE (& HER PALS):
Okeh 45444 *Texas Blues* ....50.00 - 80.00
   45515 *Texas Bound* ....50.00 - 80.00
   45547 *The Poor Girl's Story* ....50.00 - 80.00
   45555 *My Man's A Jolly Railroad Man* ....50.00 - 80.00

MOONSHINERS:
Victor V40223 *Fulton County* ....25.00 - 40.00
   V40284 *Midnight Waltz* ....25.00 - 40.00

MOORE, BURNETTE & RUTHERFORD:
Gennett 6706 *Cumberland Gap* ....15.00 - 20.00

MOORE & FREED (See also FREED & MOORE):
Vocalion 5131 *Harmonica Blues* ....8.00 - 12.00
   5132 *Plantation Medley* ....8.00 - 12.00

MOORE & GREENE:
Champion 16357 *Cincinnati Rag* ....25.00 - 40.00

MOORE & SMECK:
Vocalion 5133 *Dear Old Pal Of Mine* ....7.00 - 10.00

BYRD MOORE (& HIS HOT SHOTS):
Champion 16498 *Oh Take Me Back* ....75.00 - 100.00
Columbia 15496-D *Careless Love* ....50.00 - 75.00
   15536-D *Frankie Silvers* ....50.00 - 75.00

Gennett 6549 *Hobo's Paradise* ....35.00 - 50.00
   6586 *Mama Toot Your Whistle* ....40.00 - 60.00
   6686 *Back Water Blues* ....40.00 - 60.00
   6763 *Snatch 'Em Back Blues* ....40.00 - 60.00
   6841 *When The Snowflakes Fall Again* ....40.00 - 60.00
   6991 *Mama Don't Allow No Low Down Hanging Round*
   ....75.00 - 100.00

JOHN MOORE:
Broadway 8188 *Columbus Prison Fire* ....8.00 - 12.00

LATTIE MOORE:
Speed 101 *Juke Joint Johnny* ....10.00 - 20.00 *

O. MOORE:
Challenge 422 *The Drunkard's Doom* ....7.00 - 10.00

SAM MOORE & HORACE DAVIS:
Vocalion 14430 *Annie Laurie* ....8.00 - 12.00

PEG MORELAND:
Victor 21548 *The Prisoner At The Bar* ....7.00 - 10.00
   21653 *Going Back To Dixie* ....7.00 - 10.00
   21724 *Maple In The Lane* ....7.00 - 10.00
   23510 *I Got Mine* ....15.00 - 20.00
   23539 *In Berry Picking Time* ....10.00 - 15.00
   23593 *Cowboy Jack* ....10.00 - 15.00
   V40008 *Stay In The Wagon Yard* ....7.00 - 10.00
   V40101 *He Never Came Back* ....10.00 - 15.00
   V40137 *You're Gonna Miss Me* ....10.00 - 15.00
   V40209 *When I Had But Fifty Cents* ....10.00 - 15.00
   V40272 *Make Me A Cowboy Again* ....10.00 - 15.00
   V40296 *In The Town Where I Was Born* ....10.00 - 15.00

EVERETT MORGAN:
Champion 16616 *Texas Home* ....25.00 - 40.00

MORRIS BROTHERS:
Bluebird 7903 *The Story Of Charlie Lawson* ....8.00 - 12.00
   7967 *Let Me Be Your Salty Dog* ....8.00 - 12.00

FRANK MORRIS:
Paramount 3070 *Old Brown Pants* ....7.00 - 10.00

WALTER MORRIS:
Columbia 15079-D *Crazy Coon* ....10.00 - 15.00
   15101-D *The Railroad Tramp* ....8.00 - 12.00
   15115-D *Sweet Marie* ....7.00 - 10.00
   15186-D *In The Time Of Long Ago* ....7.00 - 10.00

ZEKE MORRIS:
Bluebird 7362 *Garden Of Prayer* ....7.00 - 10.00

MORRISON BROTHERS BAND:
Victor V40323 *Dry And Dusty* ....30.00 - 50.00

MORTON, BOND & WILLIAMS:
Champion 15653 *Cumberland Gap* ....10.00 - 15.00

MORTON & CRANE:
Supertone 9497 *Budded Roses* ....8.00 - 12.00
   9535 *Put My Little Shoes Away* ....8.00 - 12.00

JACK MOSER & HIS OKLAHOMA CAVALIERS:
Bluebird 6728, 6751...5.00 - 10.00

(BERT) MOSS & (JOE) LONG:
Superior 2539 *My Trouble Blues* ....50.00 - 80.00
   2559 *Jake Leg Blues* ....50.00 - 80.00
   2838 *Pig Ankle* ....100.00 - 150.00

OTIS MOTE (& TOM):
Okeh 45389 *Tight Like That* ....15.00 - 20.00
   45429 *Home In The Rock* ....10.00 - 15.00

BILL MOUNCE:
Bluebird (most issues) ....5.00 - 8.00

MURPHY BROTHERS:
Champion 16455 *When Katie Comes Down To The Gate*
....20.00 - 30.00

CHARLES NABELL:
Okeh 40252 *The Great Round Up* ....10.00 - 15.00
   45021 *After The War Is Over* ....10.00 - 15.00
   45031 *The Hills Of Old Kentucky* ....10.00 - 15.00
   45039 *The Scopes Trial* ....10.00 - 15.00

NANCE FAMILY (& CLARENCE DOOLEY/with THE TRAPHILL TWINS):
Brunswick 542 *The Lawson Murder* ....10.00 - 15.00
   565 *Sweet Freedom*..........................10.00 - 15.00
Champion 16316 *A Mother's Advice* ....10.00 - 15.00
   16330 *I'm On My Way To Heaven* ....10.00 - 15.00
   16369 *Somebody's Knocking At Your Door* ......10.00 - 15.00

NARMOUR & SMITH:
Bluebird 5615 *New Carroll County Blues No. 2* .....20.00 - 30.00
   5616 *Sweet Milk And Peaches* ....20.00 - 30.00
   5637 *Someone I Love* ....20.00 - 30.00
   5669 *Gallop To Georgia*......................20.00 - 30.00
   5720 *New Carroll County Blues No. 2* ....20.00 - 30.00
   5754 *Rose Waltz* ....20.00 - 30.00
   5810 *New Charleston No. 3* ....20.00 - 30.00
   6234 *New Charleston No. 2* ....15.00 - 20.00
Okeh 45242 *The Sunny Waltz*....................25.00 - 35.00
   45263 *Whistling Coon* ....25.00 - 35.00
   45276 *Little Star* ....25.00 - 35.00
   45317 *Carroll County Blues* ....15.00 - 20.00
   45329 *Someone I Love* ....25.00 - 35.00
   45344 *Gallop To Georgia-Breakdown* ....35.00 - 50.00
   45377 *Charleston No. 2* ....35.00 - 50.00
   45390 *Dry Gin Rag*...........................35.00 - 50.00
   45414 *Avalon Blues* ....40.00 - 60.00
   45424 *Sweet Milk And Peaches - Breakdown* ....40.00 - 60.00
   45459 *Charleston No. 3* ....40.00 - 60.00
   45469 *Jake Leg Rag*..........................50.00 - 80.00
   45480 *Where The Southern Crosses The Dog*....50.00 - 80.00
   45492 *Texas Breakdown*.....................75.00 - 100.00
   45536 *Tequila Hop Blues* ....75.00 - 100.00
   45548 *Limber Neck Blues* ....75.00 - 100.00

LEN NASH (& HIS COUNTRY BOYS):
Brunswick 354 *On The Road To California*..............8.00 - 12.00
   387 *The Ozark Trail*.........................8.00 - 12.00
   440 *Goin' Down To Town* ....8.00 - 12.00
Supertone 2069 *The Trail To Mexico* ....8.00 - 12.00

BUCK NATION (& RAY WHITLEY):
Decca 5065, 5066, 5075, 5081, 5105, 5114, 5124, 5172
....5.00 - 10.00

NATIONAL BARN DANCE ORCHESTRA:
Bluebird 5212, 5213, 5214, 5215, 5216, 5217 ....5.00 - 8.00

AMOS NEAL:
Champion 15692 *She'll Be Coming 'Round The Mountain*
....8.00 - 12.00

FIDDLIN' DAVE NEAL:
Challenge 102 *Seneca Square Dance* ....5.00 - 8.00
   103 *Sandy Land*..........................5.00 - 8.00
   301 *Seneca Square Dance* ....5.00 - 8.00

DAVID NEAL:
Supertone 9184 *Good Old Turnip Greens* ....8.00 - 12.00

RUSH NEAL & WANDA NEAL:
Okeh 45124 *The Two Orphans* ....7.00 - 10.00

FIDDLIN' FRANK NELSON:
Challenge 303 *Cripple Creek*....................5.00 - 8.00

NELSTONE'S HAWAIIANS:
Victor V40273 *Mobile County Blues*....................10.00 - 15.00

NETTLE BROS. STRING BAND:
Bluebird (most issues)..........................5.00 - 10.00

BILL NETTLES (& HIS DIXIE BLUE BOYS):
Bullet 637 *High Falutin' Mama* ....7.00 - 10.00
Imperial 8032 *Ain't No Tellin' What A Woman Will Do*
....8.00 - 12.00
   8039 *Somebody's Darling*.................8.00 - 12.00
Vocalion 03634 *My Cross-Eyed Nancy Jane* ....7.00 - 10.00
   03662 *No Daddy Blues* ....7.00 - 10.00
Vocalion 03694, 03903, 03952, 04012, 04075,
   04615, 04655, 04757.....................5.00 - 10.00

JIM NEW:
Timely Tunes 1564 *Wreck Of The Six Wheeler* ......20.00 - 30.00

NEW ARKANSAS TRAVELERS:
Victor 21288 *Handy Man* ....10.00 - 15.00

ELMO NEWCOMER:
Cro Mart 101 *Cotton Eyed Joe* ....8.00 - 12.00

NEW DIXIE DEMONS:
Decca 5140, 5141, 5148, 5163, 5171, 5253, 5257, 5259,
   5264, 5271, 5277, 5292, 5314, 5343, 5362, 5363, 5392
....5.00 - 10.00

THE NEWMAN BROTHERS (HANK & SLIM):
Vocalion 02807 *Mississippi River Blues* ....- - -
   02808 *How Beautiful Heaven Must Be* ....- - -
   02840 *Dear Old Mother*.................- - -
   02852 *Good Old Country Town*................- - -

CHARLIE NEWMAN (& BUD NEWMAN):
Okeh 45072 *Sweet Bunch Of Daisies* ....5.00 - 8.00
   45095 *Pretty Little Dear* ....5.00 - 8.00
   45116 *Susie Ann*............................7.00 - 10.00
   45184 *Blue Ridge Mountain Blues* ....8.00 - 12.00
   45200 *My Blue Ridge Mountain Queen*............8.00 - 12.00
   45431 *The Old Traveling Man*............8.00 - 12.00

FRED NEWMAN:
Paramount 3177 *San Antonio*.................10.00 - 15.00
   3267 *San Antonio*........................10.00 - 15.00

ROY NEWMAN & HIS BOYS:
Vocalion 02883 *Chicken Reel* ....8.00 - 12.00
   02906 *Messin' Around* ....8.00 - 12.00
   02994 *Garbage Man Blues* ....8.00 - 12.00
   03000 *Barn Dance Rag*....................8.00 - 12.00
   03103 *Slow and Easy* ....8.00 - 12.00
   03117 *Corrine Corrina* ....8.00 - 12.00
   03151 *How Many Times?* ....8.00 - 12.00
   03183 *Dinah*..............................7.00 - 10.00
   03212 *Birmingham Jail*....................7.00 - 12.00

03240 *12th Street Rag* ....7.00 - 10.00
03272 *Shine On Harvest Moon*..................7.00 - 10.00
03371 *Hot Dog Stomp* ....7.00 - 10.00
Vocalion 03598, 03752, 03878, 03938, 03963, 04025,
04578, 04639, 04740, 04792, 04866, 04959, 05014,
05066 ....5.00 - 10.00

NEWTON COUNTY HILLBILLIES:
Okeh 45520 *Happy Hour Breakdown* ....35.00 - 50.00
45544 *Nine O'Clock Breakdown* ....35.00 - 50.00
45549 *Going To The Wedding To Get Some Cake*
....35.00 - 50.00

NICHOLS BROTHERS:
Victor 23582 *She's Killing Me* ....75.00 - 100.00
23596 *Dear Old Tennessee*...................50.00 - 80.00

BOB NICHOLS (& HUGH CROSS/RILEY PUCKETT):
Columbia 15114-D, 15136-D, 15161-D.................7.00 - 10.00
Columbia 15198-D *Let The Rest Of The World Go By*
....8.00 - 12.00
15216-D *In The Shade Of The Old Apple Tree* ....8.00 - 12.00
15304-D *The Trail Of The Lonesome Pine*..........8.00 - 12.00
15350-D *Dear Old Dixieland* ....10.00 - 15.00
15480-D *Corrine Corrina*...................20.00 - 30.00
15556-D *Smoky Mountain Home*......................20.00 - 30.00
15590-D *The Killing Of Tom Slaughter* ....20.00 - 30.00
15698-D *When It's Peach Pickin' Time In Georgia*
....30.00 - 50.00

JOE & BOB NICHOLS:
Crown 3399 *Smoky Mountain Home* ....7.00 - 10.00
3419 *Red Wing*.....................................10.00 - 15.00
3447 *Blue Hills Of Virginia* ....7.00 - 10.00

SAM NICHOLS:
M-G-M 10015,10038, 10061, 10134, 10189, 10292,
10320, 10440,10579 ....7.00 - 12.00

SLUMBER NICHOLS:
Imperial 8040 *Cocaine Blues*....................8.00 - 12.00

NICHOLSON'S PLAYERS:
Champion 15942 *Muskakatuck Waltz* ....8.00 - 12.00
16007 *Sweet Bunch Of Daisies*.....................8.00 - 12.00
16137 *My Honey*..................................10.00 - 15.00
45193 *Let Me Call You Sweetheart* ....5.00 - 8.00
Gennett 7125 *Muskakatuck Waltz* ....10.00 - 15.00
7151 *Sweet Bunch Of Daisies*...................10.00 - 15.00
7241 *Let Me Call You Sweetheart* ....12.00 - 18.00

NITE OWLS:
Vocalion 03621, 03675, 03706, 03879, 03905, 03951,
03987, 04064, 04118, 04159, 04233, 04312, 04372,
04452, 04517, 04626, 04715, 04794, 04853, 04935...7.00 - 10.00

HOYLE/HOYAL NIX & HIS WEST TEXAS COWBOYS:
Talent 709 *A Big Ball's In Cowtown* ....8.00 - 12.00

EDDIE NOACK:
Gold Star 1352 *Triflin' Mama Blues* ....10.00 - 15.00

FLORA NOLES:
Okeh 45037 *Little Mohee* ....7.00 - 10.00

FATE NORRIS (& HIS PLAYBOYS/& THE TANNER BOYS):
Columbia 15124-D *New Dixie*.......................15.00 - 20.00
15332-D *A Day At The County Fair*...................10.00 - 15.00
15435-D *Johnnie Get Your Gun* ....20.00 - 30.00

(Note: The label of Columbia 15332-D credits several artists, but
since Fate Norris' name appears first, the record is listed here.)

LAND NORRIS:
Okeh 40096 *Groundhog* ....15.00 - 20.00
45006 *Ida Red*...10.00 - 15.00
45017 *Pat That Butter Down* ....15.00 - 20.00
45033 *Charming Betsy*...........................15.00 - 20.00
45047 *The Old Grey Mare* ....15.00 - 20.00
45058 *Getting Into Trouble* ....15.00 - 25.00

LYMON NORRIS:
Champion 16431 *In A Lonely Jail* ....30.00 - 50.00
45070 *In A Lonely Jail*.................................15.00 - 20.00

NORTH CAROLINA COOPER BOYS:
Okeh 45174 *Red Rose Of Texas*............................15.00 - 20.00

NORTH CAROLINA FOX CHASERS:
Supertone 9322 *Mountain Sweetheart* ....10.00 - 15.00

NORTH CAROLINA HAWAIIANS:
Okeh 45248 *Soldier's Joy*.........................7.00 - 10.00
45297 *Bully Of The Town* ....7.00 - 10.00
45405 *Chinese Breakdown* ....20.00 - 30.00

NORTH CAROLINA RAMBLERS (& ROY HARVEY) (See also ROY HARVEY):
Columbia 15106-D *Flyin' Clouds* ....20.00 - 30.00
15127-D *Rag Time Annie*............................20.00 - 30.00
15279-D *Mountain Reel*..............................20.00 - 30.00
Gennett 6288 *Poor Little Joe* ....40.00 - 60.00
Paramount 3064 *Take Back The Ring* ....20.00 - 30.00
3065 *Give My Love To Nell* ....20.00 - 30.00
3072 *Blue Eyes* ....20.00 - 30.00
3079 *Bill Mason* ....20.00 - 30.00
3136 *Sweet Sunny South* ....30.00 - 50.00

NORTH CAROLINA RIDGE RUNNERS:
Columbia 15650-D *Nobody's Darling*...................30.00 - 50.00

NORTH GEORGIA FOUR:
Paramount 3135 *I Can, I Do, I Will* ....30.00 - 50.00
3149 *Amazing Grace*.....................................30.00 - 50.00
3174 *She Was A Lulu* ....30.00 - 50.00

NORTHLANDERS:
Vocalion 5274 *Over The Waves*................................8.00 - 12.00

FRANK NOVAK & HIS ROOTIN' TOOTIN' BOYS:
Vocalion 03525, 03557, 03588, 03658, 03877, 03913,
03936, 03962, 03998, 04052, 04117, 04171, 04232,
04290, 04370, 04467, 04567, 04744, 04777........7.00 - 12.00

SLIM OAKDALE:
Crown 3433 *Lonesome Road Blues* ....10.00 - 15.00
3461 *No Hard Times* ....10.00 - 15.00
3476 *Roll Along Kentucky Moon* ....10.00 - 15.00
3503 *Cowboy's Heaven* ....10.00 - 15.00
3516 *When Jimmie Rodgers Said Goodbye* ....15.00 - 20.00

JESSE OAKLEY:
Supertone 9243 *Aged Mother* ....8.00 - 12.00
9256 *I Got Mine* ....5.00 - 8.00
9257 *Sinking Of The Submarine S-4* ....5.00 - 8.00
9674 *You're As Welcome As The Flowers In May*5.00 - 8.00

OAK MOUNTAIN FOUR:
Champion 15874 *Medley* ....7.00 - 10.00

CHARLIE OAKS:

Vocalion 5068 *The John T. Scopes Trial* .... 7.00 - 10.00
　　5069 *Little Mary Phagan* .... 7.00 - 10.00
　　5072 *Poor Little Joe* .... 7.00 - 10.00
　　5073 *The Kaiser And Uncle Sam* .... 7.00 - 10.00
　　5076 *The Fatal Wedding* .... 7.00 - 10.00
　　5105 *The Old Cottage Home* .... 7.00 - 10.00
　　5110 *Darling Nellie Gray* .... 7.00 - 10.00
　　5111 *Ginger Blues* .... 8.00 - 12.00
　　5112 *Home Of The Soul* .... 8.00 - 12.00
　　15094 *The John T. Scopes Trial* .... 8.00 - 12.00
　　15099 *Little Mary Phagan* .... 8.00 - 12.00
　　15103 *Poor Little Joe* .... 8.00 - 12.00
　　15104 *The Kaiser And Uncle Sam* .... 8.00 - 12.00
　　15144 *The Fatal Wedding* .... 8.00 - 12.00
　　15195 *Moonshine* .... 8.00 - 12.00
　　15342 *Boll Weevil* .... 8.00 - 12.00
　　15343 *Darling Nellie Gray* .... 8.00 - 12.00
　　15344 *Ginger Blues* .... 8.00 - 12.00
　　15345 *Home Of The Soul* .... 8.00 - 12.00
　　15346 *The Old Cottage Home* .... 8.00 - 12.00

W. LEE O'DANIEL & HILLBILLY BOYS/THE LIGHT CRUST DOUGHBOYS:

Vocalion 02604 *In The Fall Of '29* .... 15.00 - 25.00
　　02605 *Memories Of Jimmy Rodgers* .... 15.00 - 25.00
　　02621 *Beautiful Texas* .... 8.00 - 12.00
　　02633 *Doughboy Rag* .... 10.00 - 15.00
　　02695 *Please Come Back To Me* .... 10.00 - 15.00
　　02726 *My Brown-Eyed Texas Rose* .... 8.00 - 12.00
　　02727 *Kelly Waltz* .... 8.00 - 12.00
　　02769 *Alamo Waltz* .... 10.00 - 15.00
　　02832 *When It's Roundup Time In Heaven* ..... 8.00 - 12.00
　　02842 *Saturday Night Rag* .... 20.00 - 30.00
　　02863 *The Governor's Ball* .... 8.00 - 12.00
　　02892 *Bill Cheatum* .... 10.00 - 15.00
　　02929 *That City for Shut-Ins* .... 10.00 - 15.00
　　02975 *Old Joe Clark* .... 8.00 - 12.00
　　03127 *I Never Knew* .... 8.00 - 12.00
　　03162 *Mother's Crazy Quilt* .... 8.00 - 12.00
　　03196 *Peach Pickin' Time In Georgia* .... 8.00 - 12.00
　　03412 *Everybody Kiss Your Partner* .... 7.00 - 10.00
　　03538 *Keep A Light In Your Window Tonight* .... 7.00 - 10.00
　　03568 *Back To Old Smoky Mountain* .... 7.00 - 10.00
　　03674 *When You Hear Me Call* .... 7.00 - 10.00
Vocalion 03753, 03902, 03950, 03986, 04049, 04102,
04185, 04244, 04311, 04353, 04388, 04440, 04542,
04588, 04656, 04727, 04778, 04852 .... 5.00 - 10.00

CHESTER ODOM & HIS WESTERN RHYTHM BOYS:

Blue Bonnet 128 *You've Done Broke My Heart* ..... 10.00 - 15.00
　　144 *That's All* .... 10.00 - 15.00
Royalty 301 *Don't Rob Another Man's Castle* .... 10.00 - 15.00
　　329 *Rag Time Annie* .... 10.00 - 15.00

OKLAHOMA WRANGLERS (with THE WILLIS BROTHERS):

Sterling 202 *I Can't Go On This Way* .... 10.00 - 15.00
Sterling 203 *Farther And Farther Apart* .... 10.00 - 15.00

OLD KING COLE:

Edison 52401 *Etiquette Blues* .... 15.00 - 20.00

OLIVER & ALLEN:

Bluebird 7124, 7175, 7327, 7402 .... 7.00 - 12.00

OWENS BROTHERS:

Columbia 15416-D *If You Don't Like My Ford Coupe, Don't You Cadillac Me* .... 15.00 - 20.00
Victor V-40283 *Right Upon The Firing Line* .... 15.00 - 20.00
　　V-40309 *Harvest Field* .... 15.00 - 20.00

E. B. OWENS:

Columbia 15414-D *Sweet Carlyle* .... 15.00 - 20.00

TEX OWENS:

Decca 5015, 5187 .... 5.00 - 10.00

TOM OWENS' WLS BARN DANCE TRIO:

Challenge 104, 105, 106, 107, 306 .... 5.00 - 10.00
Silvertone 3104 *Kings Head* .... 5.00 - 10.00
　　3105 *Buffalo Girls* .... 5.00 - 10.00
　　3106 *Buckwheat Batter* .... 5.00 - 10.00
　　3107 *McLeod's Reel* .... 5.00 - 10.00

OZARKERS:

Okeh 45573 *There's More Pretty Girls Than One* . 20.00 - 30.00

OZARK RAMBLER:

Paramount 585 *Abdul Abul Abul Amir* .... 30.00 - 40.00
　　3322 *The Wreck Of The 1262* .... 30.00 - 40.00

OZARK WARBLERS:

Paramount 3127 *Memories Of Floyd Collins* .... 15.00 - 20.00

JACK PADGETT:

Talent 729 *Boogie Woogie Gal* .... 10.00 - 15.00

BUTTERBALL PAIGE:

Bullet 695 *I'm Too Old To Boogie Anymore* .... 10.00 - 15.00

BILL PALMER (TRIO):

Bluebird 1824 *Free Wheelin' Hobo* .... 15.00 - 20.00
　　1825 *Duck Foot Sue* .... 15.00 - 20.00
Bluebird 5009, 5010, 5012, 5013, 5034 .... 7.00 - 12.00
Electradisk 1938 *Duck Foot Sue* .... 8.00 - 12.00
Victor 23723 *In The Hills Of Arkansas* .... 20.00 - 30.00

PAPPY, ZEKE, EZRA & ELTON:

Decca 5097, 5126, 5153 .... 7.00 - 12.00

GEO. R. PARISEAU'S ORCHESTRA:

Champion 15987 *Moonshiner's Serenade* .... 15.00 - 20.00
　　16802 *Falling Leaf* .... 30.00 - 50.00
　　45009 *Falling Leaf* .... 10.00 - 15.00
Gennett 6899 *Waggoner's Hornpipe* .... 20.00 - 30.00
　　7033 *Fisher's Hornpipe* .... 20.00 - 30.00
　　7203 *Moonshiner's Serenade* .... 25.00 - 40.00

CHARLIE PARKER (& MACK WOOLBRIGHT):

Columbia 15154-D *Rabbit Chase* .... 15.00 - 20.00
　　15236-D *Ticklish Reuben* .... 15.00 - 20.00
　　15694-D *Will, The Weaver* .... 25.00 - 40.00

CHUBBY PARKER (& HIS OLD TIME BANJO):

Champion 15393 *Uncle Ned* .... 5.00 - 8.00
　　16143 *I'm A Stern Old Bachelor* .... 8.00 - 12.00
　　16163 *The Old Wooden Rocker* .... 8.00 - 12.00
　　16211 *Get Away, Old Maids, Get Away* .... 10.00 - 15.00
Columbia 15296-D *Down On The Farm* .... 15.00 - 20.00
Gennett 6077 *Nickety Nackety Now Now Now* ...... 10.00 - 15.00
　　6097 *I'm A Stern Old Bachelor* .... 10.00 - 15.00
　　6120 *Little Brown Jug* .... 10.00 - 15.00
　　6287 *Uncle Ned* .... 10.00 - 15.00
　　6319 *My Little Old Sod Shanty* .... 10.00 - 15.00
　　6374 *A Rovin' Little Darky* .... 10.00 - 15.00

Melotone 12524 *Get Away, Old Maids* ....8.00 - 12.00
    12525 *Walking The Last Mile* ....8.00 - 12.00
    12526 *Many Times I've Wondered* ....8.00 - 12.00
    12653 *Bringing In The Sheaves* ....8.00 - 12.00
Silvertone 5011 *Whoa, Mule, Whoa* ....5.00 - 8.00
    5013 *Little Brown Jug* ....5.00 - 8.00
Supertone 9187 *Darling Nellie Gray* ....5.00 - 8.00
    9188 *Whoa, Mule, Whoa* ....5.00 - 8.00
    9190 *Oh, Dem Golden Slippers* ....5.00 - 8.00
    9191 *Oh, Susanna* ....5.00 - 8.00
    9192 *Uncle Ned* ....5.00 - 8.00
    9723 *In Kansas* ....5.00 - 8.00
    9731 *You'll Hear The Bell In The Morning*..........5.00 - 8.00
    9732 *Grandfather's Clock* ....5.00 - 8.00

DAN PARKER & BILL PARKER:
Crown 3248 *They Cut Down The Old Pine Tree*.....10.00 - 15.00
    3265 *That Silver Haired Daddy Of Mine* ....10.00 - 15.00
    3266 *Fifty Years Repentin'* ....10.00 - 15.00
    3279 *Carry Me Back To The Mountains* ....10.00 - 15.00
    3291 *Ninety-Nine Years* ....10.00 - 15.00

SILVIA PARKER-THE HAPPY BUCKEYE:
Champion 45094 *Old Bill Mosher's Ford*.................7.00 - 10.00

(DICK) PARMAN (OF KENTUCKY); PARMAN & SMITH:
Champion 16010 *I Love You Best Of All*..................20.00 - 30.00
    16055 *The Trail Of The Lonesome Pine*.............20.00 - 30.00
    16300 *In The Hills Of Old Kentucky* ....40.00 - 60.00
    45189 *I Love You Best Of All* ....15.00 - 20.00
Gennett 6718 *She'll Be Coming Around The Mountain*
    ....40.00 - 60.00
    6747 *Many Trouble Blues*................................40.00 - 60.00
    6792 *Seven Long Years Of Trouble* ....40.00 - 60.00
    7127 *Are You From Dixie* ....40.00 - 60.00
    7204 *I Love You Best Of All* ....50.00 - 80.00
Paramount 3138 *We've Been Chums For Fifty Years*
    ....50.00 - 80.00
    3261 *Old Covered Bridge* ....50.00 - 80.00

V. D. PARMAN & SNYDER:
Okeh 45302 *Blue Bell*..15.00 - 20.00

FIDDLIN' IKE PATE:
Champion 15085 *Medley*..5.00 - 8.00

FIDDLIN' JIM PATE:
Victor V-40170 *Texas Farewell* ....20.00 - 30.00

LUTHER PATRICK:
Gennett 6448 *Cornbread* ....20.00 - 30.00

COLONEL JOHN A. PATTEE:
Columbia 231-D *Old Money Must Quadrille*..........10.00 - 15.00

PATTERSON'S PIEDMONT LOG ROLLERS:
Victor 20936 *I'll Never Get Drunk Anymore* ....25.00 - 40.00
    21132 *Sweet Sunny South* ....20.00 - 30.00
    21187 *My Sweetheart Is Shy*............................20.00 - 30.00
    35874 (12-inch) *Poor Little Joe* ....40.00 - 60.00

PATTERSON & CAPLINGER:
Gennett 7003 *The Black Sheep* ....30.00 - 50.00

PATT PATTERSON (& LOIS DEXTER):
Romeo 5022 *A Home On The Range* ....5.00 - 8.00
    5031 *The Cowboy's Love Song*........................5.00 - 8.00

RED PATTERSON'S PIEDMONT LOG ROLLERS: (See PATTERSON'S PIEDMONT LOG ROLLERS)

SAM PATTERSON TRIO:
Edison 51644 *Old MacDonald Had A Farm* ....15.00 - 20.00
    52085 *Pictures From Life's Other Side* ....15.00 - 20.00

PAUL & JOHN:
Okeh 45280 *Band Rehearsal For Old Settler's Union*
    ....10.00 - 15.00

EZRA PAULETTE & THE BEVERLY HILLBILLIES:
Titles issued contemporaneously on Banner, Melotone, Oriole, Perfect, and Romeo: *The Old Arapahoe Trail; On The Texas Prairie; The Prisoner's Song; Rosalie; When The Wild Flowers Are In Bloom* ....7.00 - 10.00
Conqueror 8954, 8955, 8956, 9011 ....5.00 - 8.00
Vocalion 03164, 03263, 03882, 04104 ....7.00 - 10.00

LEON PAYNE:
Bullet 649, 670, 671, 679..7.00 - 10.00

PECK'S MALE QUARTET:
Q.R.S. 9029 *There Is Power In The Blood* ....20.00 - 30.00
    9030 *The Home Over There*..............................20.00 - 30.00

BERT PECK:
Brunswick 522 *Over The Hills To The Poorhouse*...8.00 - 12.00

FRED PENDLETON & HIS MELODY BOYS:
Champion 16457 *Come Take A Trip In My Airship*......20.00 - 30.00

JACK PENEWELL:
Paramount 3130 *When Irish Eyes Are Smiling* ....5.00 - 8.00
    3131 *Last Night I Was Dreaming* ....5.00 - 8.00

BESS PENNINGTON:
Vocalion 5423 *Jake And May* ....15.00 - 20.00

(OLD) HANK PENNY (& HIS RADIO COWBOYS):
Columbia 15766-D *My Blue Ridge Mountain Bride* .....75.00 - 100.00
King 507, 512, 519, 521, 528, 534...........................4.00 - 8.00
Okeh (most issues)...4.00 - 8.00
Vocalion 04543, 04640, 04741, 04826, 04922,
    05067...5.00 - 10.00

PERRY COUNTY MUSIC MAKERS:
Vocalion 5425 *Madaline*.......................................20.00 - 30.00
    5443 *Got A Buddy I Must See* ....20.00 - 30.00

PETE THE HIRED MAN (GEORGE E. LOGAN):
Champion 45004 *Will The Roses Bloom In Heaven*. 7.00 - 10.00

PETERSON'S HOBO ORCHESTRA:
Victor 20677 *Submarine Waltz*..............................5.00 - 8.00

W. C./WALTER PETERSON:
Champion 45000, 45018..3.00 - 5.00
Gennett 6078 *Medley* ....7.00 - 10.00
    6102 *Over The Waves* ....7.00 - 10.00
    6221 *Medley*..7.00 - 10.00
    6274 *One-Two-Three-Four*...............................7.00 - 10.00
    6406 *Marching Through Georgia*....................8.00 - 12.00
    6463 *Where The River Shannon Flows*.............8.00 - 12.00
    6674 *Medley*..8.00 - 12.00
Superior 349 *Over The Waves* ....10.00 - 15.00
Supertone 9194 *Lazy Old Man* ....5.00 - 8.00
    9195 *Bummelpetrus* ....5.00 - 8.00
    9196 *Medley Of Old Timers*...............................5.00 - 8.00
    9197 *Medley*..5.00 - 8.00

9198 *Over The Waves* ....5.00 - 8.00
9199 *One-Two-Three-Four* ....5.00 - 8.00
9200 *Medley* ....5.00 - 8.00
9201 *Marching Through Georgia* ....5.00 - 8.00

NORMAN PHELPS' VIRGINIA ROUNDERS:
Decca 5191, 5192, 5193, 5204, 5212, 5224, 5225,
5237, 5245, 5252, 5268, 5307 ....5.00 - 10.00

WILLIE PHELPS:
Decca 5223 *The Terrible Tupelo Storm* ....7.00 - 10.00

PHILYAW BROTHERS:
Vocalion 02974, 02997, 03011, 03111, 03379,
03419, 04065, 04119, 04186, 04218, 04314 ....5.00 - 10.00

PICKARD FAMILY:
Banner 6283 *Down In Arkansas* ....5.00 - 8.00
Broadway 8179 *Thompson's Old Gray Mare* ....5.00 - 8.00
Brunswick 348 *Down In Arkansas* ....7.00 - 10.00
363 *Buffalo Gals* ....7.00 - 10.00
385 *Get Me Out Of This Birmingham Jail*............7.00 - 10.00
Conqueror 7251 *Down In Arkansas* ....5.00 - 8.00
Oriole 1502 *Rabbit In The Pea Patch*....................5.00 - 8.00
Paramount 3213 *Rabbit In The Pea Patch* ....5.00 - 8.00
3214 *Down In Arkansas*............................5.00 - 8.00
3218 *On The Dummy Line* ....7.00 - 10.00
3231 *Thompson's Old Gray Mare* ....5.00 - 8.00
Q.R.S. 9022 *Down In Arkansas* ....10.00 - 20.00
9006 *Thompson's Old Gray Mare* ....10.00 - 20.00

OBED PICKARD:
Columbia 15141-D *Kitty Wells*..................................8.00 - 12.00
15246-D *The Old Gray Horse* ....8.00 - 12.00

JACK PICKELL:
Columbia 15117-D *Don't You Love Your Daddy Too*
....10.00 - 15.00

WILL PICKETT:
Bell 1169 *It Can't Be Done* ....10.00 - 15.00

PIEDMONT MELODY BOYS:
Victor 23660 *Tell Him Now* ....40.00 - 60.00

JOHNNY PIEMONTE:
Gennett 6348 *Over The Waves* ....7.00 - 12.00

PIE PLANT PETE:
Champion 16770 *Medley Of Old Familiar Tunes* ...12.00 - 16.00
Champion 45015, 45063, 45064, 45093..................5.00 - 10.00
Decca 5014, 5030 ....5.00 - 8.00
Gennett 6748 *Boston Burglar* ....10.00 - 15.00
6776 *Ben Tucker Reel* ....10.00 - 15.00
6810 *Asleep At The Switch* ....10.00 - 15.00
7167 *Waiting For The Railroad Train*..............10.00 - 15.00
7205 *Nutty Song* ....10.00 - 15.00
7289 *The Lightning Express* ....15.00 - 20.00
Melotone 13277 *Stay On The Farm* ....5.00 - 8.00
13278 *Do You Hear The Goldfish Sing?* ....5.00 - 8.00
6-06-52 *Prairie Moon*...............................5.00 - 8.00
(Note: Above titles and others were also issued on Banner, Oriole, Perfect, Romeo.)
Process 1014 *I'm Gonna Ride That Train* .... - -
Supertone 9351 *Boston Burglar* ....5.00 - 8.00
9363 *The Letter That Never Came*.................6.00 - 10.00
9405 *Ben Tucker Reel* ....6.00 - 10.00
9652 *Nutty Song* ....6.00 - 10.00

9667 *Medley Of Old Familiar Tunes* ....6.00 - 10.00
9668 *O' Jailer Bring Back That Key* ....6.00 - 10.00
9669 *Sand Will Do It*...................................6.00 - 10.00
9701 *The Lightning Express* ....8.00 - 12.00
9712 *Good Old Turnip Greens* ....8.00 - 12.00
9717 *Little Brown Jug* ....7.00 - 10.00

JACK PIERCE'S OKLAHOMA (COW) BOYS:
Bluebird 6610, 6632, 6646, 6785, 6822....................5.00 - 8.00

WEBB PIERCE:
4 Star ....5.00 - 8.00
Pacemaker 1015 *In The Jailhouse* ....10.00 - 15.00

PINE KNOB SERENADERS:
Superior 2556 *Apple Cider* ....50.00 - 75.00

PINE MOUNTAIN BOYS:
Victor 23582 *She Wouldn't Be Still* ....75.00 - 100.00
23592 *Wild Woman Blues* ....75.00 - 100.00
23605 *Apron String Blues* ....75.00 - 100.00

PINE MOUNTAIN RAMBLERS:
Champion 15610 *Ramblin' Reckless Hobo* ....10.00 - 15.00

PINE RIDGE BOYS:
Bluebird 8360 *The Convict And The Rose* ....7.00 - 10.00
8671 *Railroad Boomer*...............................7.00 - 10.00
8940 *Lonesome For You* ....7.00 - 10.00

PINE STATE PLAYBOYS (See also CLAUDE CASEY):
Bluebird 7451, 7535, 7704....................................5.00 - 8.00

PIPERS GAP RAMBLERS:
Okeh 45185 *I Ain't Nobody's Darling*....................20.00 - 30.00

JACK PITTS & HIS CRYSTAL MOUNTAINEERS:
Imperial 8001 *Engine Boogie* ....- - -
8002 *Talkin' Blues* ....- - -
8034 *Happy's Talking Blues* ....- - -
8042 *Way Down In Arkansas*.........................- - -

PLAINSMEN & RUFUS HALL:
Broadway 8183 *Bill Mason* ....15.00 - 25.00

PLANTATION BOYS:
Bluebird 6678, 6981...5.00 - 10.00

PLEASANT FAMILY:
Broadway 8148 *Rabbit In The Pea Patch*.................5.00 - 8.00
8149 *Down In Arkansas*.............................5.00 - 8.00
8150 *On The Dummy Line* ....7.00 - 10.00

PLYMOUTH VERMONT OLD TIME BARN DANCE ORCHESTRA:
Okeh 45073 *Portland Fancy*.................................15.00 - 20.00

POHLMANN & HATHAWAY:
Supertone 9139 *Throw Out The Life Line*................. - -

DOUG POINDEXTER:
Sun 202 *Now She Cares No More* ....50.00 - 100.00 *

TALMADGE POLLARD:
Bluebird 7176 *Mind Your Own Business*.................7.00 - 10.00

CHARLIE POOLE (& ROY HARVEY/& THE NORTH CAROLINA RAMBLERS):
Columbia 15038-D *Don't Let Your Deal Go Down Blues*
....10.00 - 15.00
15043-D *The Girl I Left In Sunny Tennessee*.......8.00 - 12.00
15099-D *White House Blues* ....8.00 - 12.00

15116-D *There'll Come A Time* ....8.00 - 12.00
15138-D *Goodbye Booze* ....10.00 - 15.00
15160-D *The Highwayman* ....10.00 - 15.00
15179-D *Falling By The Wayside* ....10.00 - 15.00
15193-D *You Ain't Talkin' To Me* ....10.00 - 15.00
15215-D *If You Lose I Don't Care* ....10.00 - 15.00
15286-D *Ramblin' Blues* ....15.00 - 20.00
15307-D *I Cannot Call Her Mother* ....15.00 - 20.00
15342-D *Jealous Mary* ....15.00 - 20.00
15385-D *Hangman, Hangman, Slack The Rope*.20.00 - 30.00
15407-D *Bill Mason* ....20.00 - 30.00
15425-D *Sweet Sunny South* ....20.00 - 30.00
15456-D *The Wayward Boy* ....20.00 - 30.00
15509-D *The Baltimore Fire* ....25.00 - 40.00
15519-D *Sweet Sixteen* ....25.00 - 40.00
15545-D *If The River Was Whiskey* ....30.00 - 50.00
15584-D *A Young Boy Left His Home One Day*.30.00 - 50.00
15601-D *Look Before You Leap* ....30.00 - 50.00
15615-D *Southern Medley* ....30.00 - 50.00
15636-D *Just Keep Waiting Till The Good Time Comes*
....30.00 - 50.00
15672-D *Took My Gal A-Walkin'* ....50.00 - 75.00
15688-D *Milwaukee Blues* ....50.00 - 75.00
15711-D *Write A Letter To My Mother* ....50.00 - 75.00

POPE'S ARKANSAS MOUNTAINEERS:
Victor 21295 *Hog Eye* ....15.00 - 20.00
  21469 *Cotton-Eyed Joe* ....20.00 - 30.00
  21577 *Jaw Bone* ....20.00 - 30.00

POPLIN-WOODS TENNESSEE STRING BAND:
Victor V40080 *Are You From Dixie?* ....20.00 - 30.00

ARCHIE PORTER & HIS HAPPY BUCKEYES:
Champion 16729 *Log Cabin Call* ....50.00 - 75.00

POTTER & JAMES:
Supertone 9541 *Down On The Farm* ....8.00 - 12.00

POWDER RIVER JACK & KITTY LEE:
Victor 23527 *Tying A Knot In The Devil's Tail* ......40.00 - 60.00

JACK & JOHNNIE POWELL:
Victor 23568 *By The Old Garden Gate* ....30.00 - 50.00
  V40259 *You Ain't Talking To Me* ....15.00 - 20.00

FIDDLIN' POWERS (& FAMILY):
Edison 51662 *Old Joe Clark* ....10.00 - 15.00
  51789 *Sourwood Mountains* ....15.00 - 20.00
  52083 *Cluck Old Hen* ....15.00 - 20.00
Okeh 45154 *Old Virginia Reel* ....10.00 - 15.00
  45268 *Did You Ever See The Devil, Uncle Joe?* 15.00 - 20.00
Victor 19448 *Sourwood Mountains* ....5.00 - 8.00
  19449 *Cripple Creek* ....5.00 - 8.00

PRAIRIE RAMBLERS:
Titles issued contemporaneously on Banner, Conqueror, Melotone, Oriole, Perfect, and Romeo: *Deep Elem Blues; Gonna Have A Feast Here Tonight; I'm Looking For The Bully Of The Town; Isle Of Capri; Jim's Windy Mule; Jug Rag; Just Come On In; The Lady In Red; Mistook In The Woman I Love; Nobody's Darling But Mine; On Treasure Island; The Oregon Trail; Put On An Old Pair Of Boots; Snowflakes; Swingin' Down The Old Orchard Lane; Truckin'; Uncle Oph's Got The Coon; When I Grow Too Old To Dream; Woman's Answer To Nobody's Dream*
....5.00 - 10.00

Bluebird 5302 *Blue River* ....25.00 - 50.00
  5320 *Go Easy Blues* ....25.00 - 40.00
  5322 *Gonna Have A Feast Here Tonight* ....25.00 - 40.00
  5395 *Next Year* ....20.00 - 30.00
Okeh 05851, 05878, 06053, 06102, 06230, 06243,
  and others ....4.00 - 8.00
Victor 23856 *Go Easy Blues* ....75.00 - 100.00
  23859 *Kentucky Blues* ....75.00 - 100.00
Vocalion 03061 *Maple On The Hill, Part 2* ....10.00 - 15.00
  03085 *You Look Pretty In An Evening Gown* .... 10.00 - 15.00
  03100 *This World Is Not My Home* ....10.00 - 15.00
  03115 *Jesus Hold My Hand* ....10.00 - 15.00
Vocalion 03332, 03422, 03469, 04039, 04092,
  04134, 04427, 04601, 04672, 04796, 04868,
  04899, 04936, 05002, 05081 ....5.00 - 10.00

PRAIRIE SERENADERS:
Champion 45164 *The Lonely Cowboy* ....7.00 - 10.00
  45190 *I'm The Last Of The Texas Rangers* ....7.00 - 10.00

CHARLIE PRESCOTT:
Challenge 335 *The Dixie Cowboy* ....20.00 - 30.00

RAY PRICE:
Bullet 701 *Jealous Lies* ....40.00 - 60.00

WILLIAM PRICE:
Challenge 332 *Little Birdie* ....5.00 - 8.00

RICHARD PRINE & HIS ALL STARS:
Ayo 108 *Are You Happy* ....7.00 - 10.00
  115 *I Loved And Lost* ....7.00 - 10.00

B. L./SUNSHINE PRITCHARD:
Gennett 6902 *Son Of A Gun* ....35.00 - 50.00
Paramount 3320 *Stone Mountain Wobble* ....35.00 - 50.00

HOLLAND PUCKETT:
Gennett 6144 *Weeping Willow Tree* ....10.00 - 15.00
  6163 *A Mother's Advice* ....10.00 - 15.00
  6189 *Drunken Hiccoughs* ....10.00 - 15.00
  6206 *He Lives On High* ....10.00 - 15.00
  6271 *The Dying Cowboy* ....10.00 - 15.00
  6433 *Come And Kiss Me Baby Darling* ....10.00 - 15.00
  6532 *The Maple On The Hill* ....10.00 - 15.00
  6720 *Little Bessie* ....10.00 - 15.00
Silvertone 25065 *The Dying Cowboy* ....10.00 - 15.00
Supertone 9324 *Little Bessie* ....10.00 - 15.00

RILEY PUCKETT (& TED HAWKINS/RED JONES/ CLAYTON McMICHEN):
Bluebird 5432 *The Old Spinning Wheel* ....10.00 - 20.00
  5471 *K. C. Railroad* ....10.00 - 20.00
  5473 *Texas Hop* ....10.00 - 20.00
  5514 *Kimball Blues* ....10.00 - 20.00
  5532 *Careless Love* ....10.00 - 20.00
  5587 *I'm Gettin' Ready To Go* ....10.00 - 20.00
  5607 *Renfro Valley Home* ....10.00 - 20.00
  5656 *Tokio Rag* ....10.00 - 20.00
  5666 *Lost Love* ....10.00 - 20.00
  5691 *Down In The Valley* ....10.00 - 20.00
  5738 *Puckett Blues* ....10.00 - 20.00
  5786 *Four Day Blues* ....10.00 - 20.00
  5818 *Chain Gang Blues* ....10.00 - 20.00
  6064 *Roll Back The Carpet* ....10.00 - 15.00
  6067 *Don't Let Your Deal Go Down* ....7.00 - 10.00
  6103 *Nobody's Business* ....7.00 - 10.00

6134 *Curly Headed Baby*......................................7.00 - 10.00
6196 *Blue Ridge Mountain Blues* ....7.00 - 10.00
6291 *When I Grow Too Old To Dream* ....7.00 - 10.00
6313 *Ol' Faithful* ....7.00 - 10.00
6348 *Back To My Home In The Smoky Mountains*
....7.00 - 10.00
6404 *My Old Mule* ....7.00 - 10.00
7303 *Carolina Sunshine Girl* ....7.00 - 10.00
7717 *Old Maid's Brown Ferry* ....7.00 - 10.00
Columbia 107-D *Rock All Your Babies To Sleep* ......8.00 - 12.00
110-D *Hen Cackle* ....8.00 - 12.00
113-D *Casey Jones* ....8.00 - 12.00
119-D *Black-Eyed Alabama Gal* ....8.00 - 12.00
150-D *Johnson's Old Gray Mule* ....8.00 - 12.00
240-D *Just As The Sun Went Down* ....7.00 - 10.00
254-D *Blue Ridge Mountain Blues* ....10.00 - 15.00
405-D *Let Me Call You Sweetheart* ....8.00 - 12.00
15003-D *Swanee River* ....15.00 - 20.00
15015-D *Burglar Man* ....15.00 - 20.00
15033-D *Jesse James* ....10.00 - 15.00
15035-D *Just Break The News To Mother* ....10.00 - 15.00
15036-D *I Wish I Was Single Again* ....10.00 - 15.00
15045-D *Long Tongue Woman* ....10.00 - 15.00
15050-D *The Orphan Girl* ....10.00 - 15.00
15055-D *When I'm Gone You'll Soon Forget* ....10.00 - 15.00
15058-D *Down By The Old Mill Stream* ....8.00 - 12.00
15063-D *You'd Be Surprised* ....10.00 - 15.00
15068-D *Hello Central Give Me Heaven* ....10.00 - 15.00
15073-D *Wait Till The Sun Shines Nellie* ....7.00 - 10.00
15074-D *Bully Of The Town* ....7.00 - 10.00
15078-D *Everybody Works But Father* ....7.00 - 10.00
15088-D *Sauerkraut* ....7.00 - 10.00
15095-D *My Carolina Home* ....7.00 - 10.00
15102-D *Ida Red* ....7.00 - 10.00
15125-D *Put My Little Shoes Away* ....7.00 - 10.00
15139-D *Down In Arkansas* ....8.00 - 12.00
15163-D *Fuzzy Rag* ....10.00 - 15.00
15171-D *Little Log Cabin In The Lane* ....7.00 - 10.00
15185-D *Alabama Gal* ....10.00 - 15.00
15196-D *My Poodle Dog* ....10.00 - 15.00
15198-D *That Old Irish Mother Of Mine* ....7.00 - 10.00
15226-D *Red Wing* ....7.00 - 10.00
15232-D *Little Brown Jug* ....7.00 - 10.00
15250-D *All Bound 'Round With The Mason-Dixon Line*
....10.00 - 15.00
15261-D *Blue Yodel* ....10.00 - 15.00
15277-D *Little Maumee* ....10.00 - 15.00
15295-D *Slim Gal* ....10.00 - 15.00
15324-D *The Moonshiner's Dream* ....15.00 - 20.00
15358-D *Bill Johnson* ....15.00 - 20.00
15374-D *I'm Going To Georgia* ....15.00 - 20.00
15392-D *Don't Try It For It Can't Be Done* ......15.00 - 20.00
15393-D *Carolina Moon* ....15.00 - 20.00
15408-D *Waiting For A Train* ....20.00 - 30.00
15448-D *McKinley*..20.00 - 30.00
15505-D *Frankie And Johnny* ....20.00 - 30.00
15563-D *Dark Town Strutters Ball* ....20.00 - 30.00
15605-D *Waitin' For The Evenin' Mail* ....25.00 - 40.00
15631-D *Somewhere In Old Wyoming* ....25.00 - 40.00
15656-D *The Cat Came Back* ....25.00 - 40.00
15708-D *There's A Hard Time Coming* ....30.00 - 50.00
15719-D *All Bound Down In Prison* ....30.00 - 50.00
15747-D *East Bound Train* ....50.00 - 80.00

Decca 5438 *There's More Pretty Girls Than One* ....7.00 - 10.00
5442 *Short Life Of Trouble* ....7.00 - 10.00
5455 *Altoona Freight Wreck*..............................7.00 - 10.00
5472 *Gulf Coast Blues* ....7.00 - 10.00
5523 *Somebody's Waiting For You* ....5.00 - 8.00
5540 *Moonlight On The Colorado*......................5.00 - 8.00

SI PUCKETT:
Supertone 9186 *The Maple On The Hill* ....7.00 - 10.00
9254 *The Bright Sherman Valley* ....7.00 - 10.00

PETE PYLE:
Bluebird 8581, 8711..5.00 - 8.00
Bullet 602 *Talking The Blues*.............................7.00 - 10.00

QUADRILLERS:
Paramount 3008 *Drunk Man Blues*.....................15.00 - 20.00
3009 *Cumberland Blues*....................................15.00 - 20.00

FRANK QUINN:
Okeh 45030 *Pop Goes The Weasel* ....10.00 - 15.00

RADIO MAC:
Victor 23510 *Home Spun Gal* ....15.00 - 20.00
23586 *He Sure Can Play A Harmoniky* ....15.00 - 20.00
23690 *Last Old Dollar* ....15.00 - 20.00
23704 *Sweet Betsy From Pike* ....10.00 - 15.00
23829 *Bald Top Mountain* ....30.00 - 50.00
V40101 *Ain't We Crazy* ....10.00 - 15.00
V40264 *Roamin'* ....10.00 - 15.00

JAMES RAGAN & OLIVER BECK:
Challenge 390 *Please Papa Come Home* ....8.00 - 12.00
401 *Walking On The Streets Of Glory* ....7.00 - 10.00

RAGGEDY ANN'S MELODY MAKERS:
Okeh 45235 *Zenda Waltz*.................................8.00 - 12.00

RAILROAD BOYS:
Superior 2684 *By A Cottage In The Twilight*.........15.00 - 20.00
2779 *You're Bound To Look Like A Monkey* .....20.00 - 30.00

RAINEY OLD TIME BAND:
Columbia 15675-D *Engineer Frank Hawk*.............50.00 - 75.00

RALEY BROTHERS:
Bluebird 7062 *Chicken Roost Blues* ....7.00 - 10.00

RAMBLING DUET:
Bluebird 7131, 7233, 7450, 7484, 7534, 7574.........5.00 - 10.00

RAMBLING KID & PROFESSOR:
Melotone 7-07-54 *Little Home In Tennessee*.........10.00 - 15.00

RAMBLING RAMBLERS:
Vocalion 04628, 04758, 04949 ....5.00 - 10.00

RANCH BOYS:
Decca 5016, 5017, 5040, 5045, 5046, 5061, 5074,
5113, 5128, 5167, 5319, 5341, 5354....................5.00 - 10.00

RAND & FOSTER:
Supertone 9326 *The Vestris Disaster*....................8.00 - 12.00
9373 *Only A Step To The Grave* ....8.00 - 12.00

GROVER RANN & HIS LOOKOUT MOUNTAINEERS:
Columbia 15638-D *Don't Stay After Ten* ....40.00 - 60.00

OLE RASMUSSEN & HIS NEBRASKA CORNHUSKERS:
Crystal 223 *Chill In My Heart* ....10.00 - 20.00
224 *Nebraska Moon*...10.00 - 20.00

RAY BROTHERS:

Bluebird 5789 *Winona Rag* ....20.00 - 30.00
Victor 21508 *Got The Jake Leg Too*......................50.00 - 80.00
   23552 *Mississippi Echoes*........................50.00 - 80.00
   23713 *Winona Rag* ....75.00 - 100.00
   V40291 *Jake Leg Wobble* ....50.00 - 80.00
   V40313 *Choctaw County Rag* ....50.00 - 80.00

AULTON RAY/RAYL:

Champion 15332 *Maxwell Girl* ....10.00 - 15.00
Gennett 6129 *True And Trembling Brakeman*.........20.00 - 30.00
   6177 *The Dixie Cowboy*........................20.00 - 30.00
   6205 *Maxwell Girl*............................25.00 - 40.00
Herwin 75550 *Maxwell Girl*......................20.00 - 30.00
   75552 *True And Trembling Brakeman* ....15.00 - 30.00
Silvertone 8150 *The Dixie Cowboy*...............10.00 - 20.00
Superior 385 *The Dixie Cowboy*..................25.00 - 40.00
Supertone 9250 *The Maxwell Girl*................10.00 - 20.00

REAVES' WHITE COUNTY RAMBLERS:

Vocalion 5218 *Ten Cent Piece* ....100.00 - 200.00
   5219 *Rattler Tree'd A Possum*..................100.00 - 200.00
   5224 *Down In Arkansas*.........................100.00 - 200.00
   5247 *Drunkard's Hiccups*.......................100.00 - 200.00
   5260 *Arkansas Pullet*..........................100.00 - 200.00

RECORD BOYS:

Vocalion 5136 *Harmonica Jim*.....................8.00 - 12.00

RECTOR TRIO:

Columbia 15658-D *Skyland Rag* ....15.00 - 20.00

RED BRUSH ROWDIES/SINGERS:

Paramount 3122 *The Hatfield-McCoy Feud*............30.00 - 50.00
   3140 *The Third Of July*........................30.00 - 50.00
   3143 *Beyond The Starry Plain*..................30.00 - 50.00
   3150 *Midnight Serenade*........................30.00 - 50.00

RED HEADED BRIER HOPPER (LEROY ANDERSON):

Champion 16578 *Gooseberry Pie* ....30.00 - 50.00
   16668 *Three Wishes*............................30.00 - 50.00
   16678 *The Fatal Derby Day*.....................40.00 - 60.00
   16708 *Is There No Chance For Me Tonight, Love*
   ....40.00 - 60.00
   16797 *The Wrong Man And The Wrong Woman*50.00 - 75.00
   16811 *A Mother's Wayward Son*..................50.00 - 75.00
   16820 *Gambling On The Sabbath* ....50.00 - 75.00

RED HEADED FIDDLERS:

Brunswick 285 *Texas Quickstep*..................15.00 - 20.00
   388 *Rag Time Annie*...........................15.00 - 20.00
   460 *The Fatal Wedding* ....15.00 - 20.00
   470 *Cheat 'Em*................................15.00 - 20.00
   526 *The Steeley Rag*...........................15.00 - 20.00

RED MOUNTAIN TRIO:

Columbia 15260-D *The Wang Wang Blues*............10.00 - 15.00
   15369-D *Dixie* ....10.00 - 15.00
   15462-D *Carolina Sunshine* ....15.00 - 20.00

RED RIVER COON HUNTERS:

Superior 2647 *The Wreck Of The West Bound Airliner*
   ....20.00 - 30.00
   2754 *By And By You Will Forgive Me*............20.00 - 30.00

RED & SON RAYMOND:

Champion 16797 *Mother's Beautiful Hands*..........15.00 - 20.00

REED CHILDREN:

Columbia 15525-D *I'll Be All Smiles Tonight*.........7.00 - 10.00

ALFRED & ORVILLE REED:

Victor 23550 *Beware* ....75.00 - 100.00
   23650 *Old Fashioned Cottage* ....80.00 - 120.00

BLIND ALFRED REED:

Victor 20836 *The Wreck Of The Virginia*..............25.00 - 40.00
   20939 *You Must Unload* ....25.00 - 40.00
   21191 *Explosion In The Fairmount Mines* ....30.00 - 50.00
   21360 *Why Do You Bob Your Hair, Girls?* ....20.00 - 30.00
   21533 *The Fate Of Chris Lively And Wife* ....35.00 - 50.00
   V40196 *Woman's Been After Man Ever Since* .. 40.00 - 60.00
   V40236 *Money Cravin' Folks* ....40.00 - 60.00
   V40290 *Black And Blue Blues* ....50.00 - 75.00

L. K. REEDER:

Okeh 45026 *Falling Leaf*..........................5.00 - 8.00

JACK REEDY & HIS WALKER MOUNTAIN STRING BAND:

Brunswick 221 *Chinese Breakdown* ....20.00 - 30.00

JIMMY REESE:

Supertone 9613 *Blue Yodel No. 5* ....10.00 - 15.00
   9627 *You And My Old Guitar* ....10.00 - 15.00

REEVES & MOODY:

Victor 20540 *Down Where The Watermelon Grows*10.00 - 15.00
   20929 *Rock All Our Babies To Sleep*................. 8.00 - 12.00
   21188 *Sweet Evelina*..........................10.00 - 15.00

GOEBEL REEVES (THE TEXAS DRIFTER):

Titles issued contemporaneously on Banner, Conqueror, Melotone,
   Oriole, Perfect, and Romeo: *The Bar None Ranch; Big Rock
   Candy Mountain; The Cowboy's Dizzy Sweetheart; It's True I'm
   Just A Convict; Reckless Tex From Texas; The Wandering Boy;
   Where The Mississippi Washes* ....7.00 - 12.00
Brunswick 539 *Station H.O.B.O.* ....10.00 - 15.00
Champion 16139 *The Hobo's Grave* ....15.00 - 20.00
   16189 *Station H.O.B.O.* ....15.00 - 20.00
   16234 *The Drifter* ....15.00 - 20.00
   45181 *The Drifter's Buddy* ....5.00 - 8.00
   45194 *I Learned About Women From Her* ....5.00 - 8.00
Conqueror 8442 *Cold And Hungry* ....7.00 - 10.00
   8443 *The Bar None Ranch* ....7.00 - 10.00
Okeh 45365 *The Drifter* ....10.00 - 15.00
   45381 *The Tramp's Mother* ....15.00 - 20.00
   45408 *Blue Undertaker's Blues* ....15.00 - 20.00
   45449 *The Texas Drifter's Warning* ....15.00 - 20.00
   45491 *In The Land Of Never Was*....................15.00 - 20.00

JIM REEVES:

Macy's 115 *Teardrops Of Regret* ....40.00 - 60.00
   132 *I've Never Been So Blue* ....40.00 - 60.00

WALTER REGAN:

Superior 2524 *Just As Your Mother Was* ....15.00 - 25.00
   2585 *Moundsville Prisoner*....................25.00 - 40.00

DICK REINHART:

Brunswick 386 *Rambling Lover* ....10.00 - 15.00

GEORGE RENEAU ("THE BLIND MUSICIAN OF THE SMOKEY MOUNTAINS"):

Vocalion 5029 *Lonesome Road Blues* ....6.00 - 10.00
   5030 *Life's Railway To Heaven* ....6.00 - 10.00
   5031 *Little Brown Jug*........................6.00 - 10.00

5032 *Arkansas Traveler*	6.00 -	10.00
5033 *Here, Rattler, Here*	6.00 -	10.00
5034 *Blue Ridge Blues*	6.00 -	10.00
5049 *Red Wing*	6.00 -	10.00
5050 *C & O Wreck*	6.00 -	10.00
5052 *The Baggage Coach Ahead*	6.00 -	10.00
5054 *The New Market Wreck*	6.00 -	10.00
5055 *I've Got The Railroad Blues*	6.00 -	10.00
5056 *The Prisoner's Song*	6.00 -	10.00
5057 *Little Rosewood Casket*	6.00 -	10.00
5058 *Wild Bill Jones*	6.00 -	10.00
5059 *Wild And Reckless Hobos*	6.00 -	10.00
5064 *My Redeemer*	6.00 -	10.00
5077 *Rovin' Gambler*	6.00 -	10.00
5078 *Gambling On The Sabbath Day*	6.00 -	10.00
5079 *Bad Companions*	6.00 -	10.00
5080 *The Hand Of Fate*	6.00 -	10.00
5083 *Railroad Lover*	6.00 -	10.00
5106 *Old Man On The Hill*	6.00 -	10.00
5107 *Old Rugged Cross*	6.00 -	10.00
5108 *Two Orphans*	6.00 -	10.00
14809 *Lonesome Road Blues*	6.00 -	10.00
14811 *Life's Railway To Heaven*	6.00 -	10.00
14812 *Little Brown Jug*	6.00 -	10.00
14813 *Arkansas Traveler*	6.00 -	10.00
14814 *Here, Rattler, Here*	8.00 -	12.00
14815 *Blue Ridge Blues*	8.00 -	12.00
14896 *Red Wing*	6.00 -	10.00
14897 *C & W Wreck*	8.00 -	12.00
14918 *The Baggage Coach Ahead*	6.00 -	10.00
14930 *The New Market Wreck*	8.00 -	12.00
14946 *I've Got The Railroad Blues*	8.00 -	12.00
14991 *The Prisoner's Song*	6.00 -	10.00
14997 *The Little Rosewood Casket*	6.00 -	10.00
14998 *Wild Bill Jones*	8.00 -	12.00
14999 *Wild And Reckless Hobos*	8.00 -	12.00
15046 *My Redeemer*	7.00 -	10.00
15148 *Rovin' Gambler*	7.00 -	10.00
15149 *Gambling On The Sabbath Day*	7.00 -	10.00
15150 *Bad Companions*	7.00 -	10.00
15182 *The Hand Of Fate*	7.00 -	10.00
15194 *Railroad Lover*	7.00 -	10.00
15347 *Old Man On The Hill*	7.00 -	10.00
15348 *The Old Rugged Cross*	7.00 -	10.00
15349 *Two Orphans*	7.00 -	10.00
15366 *On Top Of Old Smoky*	15.00 -	20.00

RENFRO VALLEY BOYS:

Paramount 3311 *Twenty-One Years*	15.00 -	20.00
3315 *My Renfro Valley Home*	15.00 -	20.00
3316 *The Yellow Rose Of Texas*	15.00 -	20.00
3321 *Loreena*	25.00 -	40.00

JIMMIE REVARD & THE OKLAHOMA PLAYBOYS:

Bluebird 6654, 6679, 6712, 6739, 6753, 6774, 6823, 6842, 6877, 6935, 6992, 7028, 7061, 7085, 7172, 7199, 7248, 7309, 7370, 7371, 7481, 7520, 7559, 7610, 7727, 7776, 7911, 7939, 7964	5.00 -	8.00
Bluebird (higher numbers)	4.00 -	7.00
Everstate 1011 *Holdin' The Sack*	7.00 -	10.00

WILLIAM REXROAT (& HIS CEDAR CREST SINGERS):

Vocalion 5290 *Fading Away*	15.00 -	25.00
5323 *Build Me A Bungalow*	15.00 -	25.00
5345 *We Shall Wear A Crown*	15.00 -	25.00

REYNOLDS & ROBINSON:

Superior 2653 *Rocky Mountain Rose*	- -	-

RALPH REYNOLDS & HIS DUDE RANCH WRANGLERS:

Globe 127, 128	5.00 -	10.00

RICE BROTHERS' GANG:

Decca (most issues)	5.00 -	10.00

RICE, DAVIS & THOMAS:

Paramount 3309 *Circus Day Rag*	25.00 -	40.00
Q.R.S. 9019 *Circus Day Rag*	35.00 -	50.00

EDD RICE:

Vocalion 5220 *Cricket On The Hearth*	10.00 -	15.00

GLEN RICE & HIS BEVERLY HILLBILLIES: (See also BEVERLY HILLBILLIES)

Brunswick 506 *My Old Iowa Home*	5.00 -	8.00
519 *Prairie Skies*	5.00 -	8.00
597 *Swiss Yodel*	5.00 -	8.00
598 *The Big Corral*	5.00 -	8.00
599 *Ridge Runnin' Roan*	5.00 -	8.00
600 *Cowboy Joe*	5.00 -	8.00

HOKE RICE & HIS HOKY POKY BOYS/SOUTHERN BAND/STRING BAND; HOKE RICE & HARRY STARK:

Brunswick 416 *Georgia Jubilee*	15.00 -	20.00
473 *Wabash Blues*	15.00 -	20.00
482 *Georgia Gal*	15.00 -	20.00
552 *Floating Down To Cotton Town*	10.00 -	15.00
Gennett 6839 *Waiting For A Train*	25.00 -	40.00
6855 *Blue Yodel No. 4*	25.00 -	40.00
7067 *Unexplained Blues*	25.00 -	40.00
Paramount 3212 *I'm Lonely And Blue*	25.00 -	40.00
3229 *Chinese Breakdown*	25.00 -	40.00
3239 *Down In A Southern Town*	25.00 -	40.00
3308 *Macon Georgia Breakdown*	30.00 -	50.00
Q.R.S. 9012 *Waiting For A Train*	35.00 -	50.00
9015 *Down In A Southern Town*	35.00 -	50.00
9022 *Way Down South By The Sea*	35.00 -	50.00

RENUS RICH & CARL BRADSHAW:

Columbia 15341-D *Sleep, Baby, Sleep*	7.00 -	10.00

FRED RICHARDS:

Columbia 15483-D *Danville Blues*	8.00 -	12.00

LUCKY RICHARDS & HIS RAMBLERS:

Imperial 8044 *Puppy Lovin' Women*	- -	-

RALPH RICHARDSON:

Okeh 45267 *Little Dog Yodel*	5.00 -	8.00

RIDGEL'S FOUNTAIN CITIANS:

Vocalion 5363 *Be Ready*	50.00 -	75.00
5389 *Little Bonnie*	50.00 -	75.00
5427 *Baby, Call Your Dog Off*	50.00 -	75.00
5455 *The Bald Headed End Of The Broom*	50.00 -	75.00

RILEY'S MOUNTAINEERS:

Supertone 9677 *Sunny Home In Dixie*	7.00 -	10.00

GEORGE RILEY:

Perfect 12653 *The Texas Drifter's Warning*	7.00 -	10.00

(Note: Probably also issued on Melotone, Oriole, Romeo.)

TEX RITTER:

Titles issued contemporaneously on Banner, Conqueror, Melotone, Oriole, Perfect, Romeo, and Vocalion: *A-Ridin' Old Paint; Every Day In The Saddle; Goodbye Old Paint; Rye Whiskey, Rye Whiskey* ....10.00 - 15.00
Champion 45153 *Nobody's Darling But Mine* ....10.00 - 15.00
   45154 *The Oregon Trail* ....10.00 - 15.00
   45191 *Bill The Bar Fly* ....10.00 - 15.00
   45197 *Answer To Nobody's Darling But Mine* ..10.00 - 15.00
   45198 *The Hills Of Old Wyomin'* ....10.00 - 15.00
Decca 5076 *Lady Killin' Cowboy* ....15.00 - 20.00
   5112 *Thirty-Three Years In Prison* ....15.00 - 20.00
   5305 *Bill The Bar Fly* ....8.00 - 12.00
   5306 *Jailhouse Lament* ....8.00 - 12.00
   5315 *High, Wide And Handsome* ....7.00 - 10.00
   5389 *Down The Colorado Trail* ....7.00 - 10.00
   5405 *I'm Hittin' The Trail (For Home)* ....7.00 - 10.00
Decca, 5639, 5648, 5922 ....5.00 - 10.00
Montgomery Ward 8020, 8032................................8.00 - 12.00

RIVERSIDE RAMBLERS:

Bluebird 6926, 7063, 7202, 7251, 7846, 7942, 7974........5.00 - 10.00

ROANE COUNTY RAMBLERS:

Columbia 15328-D *Home Town Blues* ....30.00 - 50.00
   15377-D *Tennessee Waltz*...............................30.00 - 50.00
   15398-D *Roane County Rag* ....30.00 - 50.00
   15438-D *McCarroll's Breakdown* ....40.00 - 60.00
   15498-D *Johnson City Rag* ....40.00 - 60.00
   15570-D *Alabama Trot*...................................50.00 - 80.00

ROANOKE JUG BAND:

Okeh 45393 *Home Brew Rag* ....75.00 - 125.00
   45423 *Stone Mountain Rag* ....75.00 - 125.00

GEORGE ROARK:

Columbia 15383-D *I Ain't A Bit Drunk*.................8.00 - 12.00

SHORTBUCKLE ROARK & FAMILY:

Victor V40023 *My Mother's Hands* ....15.00 - 20.00

FIDDLIN' DOC ROBERTS (TRIO):

Titles issued contemporaneously on Banner, Conqueror, Melotone, Oriole, Perfect, and Romeo: *Blue Grass Rag; Carroll County Blues; Charleston No. 1; Coal Tipple Blues; Cumberland Blues; Did You Ever See The Devil, Uncle Joe?; Down Yonder; Farewell Waltz; A Good Man Is Waiting For You; I Don't Love Nobody; In The Shadow Of The Pines; Ninety-Nine Years; Over The Waves; Pickin' And Playin'; Ragtime Chicken Joe; Sally Ann; Shortenin' Bread; Turkey In The Straw; The Waggoner; 'Way Down South; Wednesday Night Waltz*.........7.00 - 12.00
Challenge 501 *All I've Got Is Done Gone* ....8.00 - 12.00
Champion 45099, 45135, 45136................................5.00 - 10.00
Gennett 3152 *Martha Campbell* ....10.00 - 15.00
   3162 *All I've Got Is Done Gone* ....10.00 - 15.00
   3235 *Billy In The Low Ground* ....10.00 - 15.00
   6025 *In The Shadow Of The Pine* ....12.00 - 16.00
   6257 *Waynesburgh* ....12.00 - 16.00
   6336 *Old Buzzard* ....12.00 - 16.00
   6390 *Billy In The Low Ground* ....10.00 - 15.00
   6495 *Old Zip Coon & Medley Of Reels*.............15.00 - 20.00
   6588 *My Old Coon Dog*...................................15.00 - 20.00
   6635 *Brickyard Joe*..15.00 - 20.00
   6689 *Shippin' Sport* ....15.00 - 20.00
   6717 *Farewell Waltz*......................................15.00 - 20.00
   6750 *Mandolin Rag* ....15.00 - 20.00
   6775 *Shoot That Turkey Buzzard* ....15.00 - 20.00
   6826 *Who's Been Here Since I Been Gone*........15.00 - 20.00
   6942 *The Devil In Georgia* ....15.00 - 25.00
   7017 *Jack's Creek Waltz*..................................15.00 - 25.00
   7049 *Johnny Inchin' Along* ....15.00 - 25.00
   7094 *My Baby Don't Love Me* ....20.00 - 30.00
   7110 *Hawk's Got A Chicken* ....20.00 - 30.00
   7221 *Rye Straw* ....20.00 - 30.00
Superior 348 *And The Cat Came Back* ....50.00 - 75.00
   386 *Billy In The Low Ground* ....50.00 - 75.00
   2762 *Sally Gooden* ....25.00 - 35.00
Supertone 9252 *In The Shadow Of The Pine* ....7.00 - 10.00
   9397 *Martha Campbell* ....7.00 - 10.00

JAMES ROBERTS:

Titles issued contemporaneously on Banner, Conqueror, Melotone, Oriole, Perfect, and Romeo: *The Crepe On The Cabin Door; Down And Out Blues; Duval County Blues; May I Sleep In Your Barn Tonight, Mister?; String Bean Mama* ....8.00 - 12.00

A. C. (ECK) ROBERTSON (& DR. J. B. CRANFILL/& FAMILY):

Victor 18956 *Arkansas Traveler*..............................5.00 - 8.00
   19149 *Turkey In The Straw* ....5.00 - 8.00
   19372 *Sally Johnson* ....5.00 - 8.00
   V40145 *Texas Wagoner*...................................10.00 - 15.00
   V40166 *The Island Unknown* ....10.00 - 15.00
   V40205 *Great Big Taters*..................................10.00 - 15.00
   V40298 *Amarillo Waltz* ....15.00 - 20.00
   V40334 *Brown Kelly Waltz* ....15.00 - 20.00

TEXAS JIM ROBERTSON:

Bluebird 8186, 8606, 8706..................................3.00 - 6.00

MELVIN ROBINETTE & BYRD MOORE:

Gennett 6841 *Birmingham Jail* ....100.00 - 150.00
   6884 *Flop Eared Mule* ....100.00 - 150.00
   6957 *That Old Tiger Rag* ....100.00 - 150.00
   7068 *Goodbye Sweetheart* ....100.00 - 150.00

CARSON ROBISON (& VERNON DALHART/FRANK LUTHER/THE PIONEERS):

(Note: This artist recorded seemingly countless records for many labels from the 1920s to the 1950s. Most of his records are of minimal value and interest to collectors of country music. A few selected exceptions are listed following and also see the Jazz and the Rockabilly/Rock & Roll, etc., sections!)
Columbia 15548-D, 15627-D, 15644-D, 15768-D... 5.00 - 10.00
Columbia 15773-D *Old Familiar Tunes*.................10.00 - 15.00
   15779-D *Missouri Valley*..................................10.00 - 15.00
Okeh 45537 *So I Joined The Navy*..........................8.00 - 12.00
Superior 2546 *When The Sun Goes Down Again* ... 15.00 - 25.00
   2580 *Cross-Eyed Sue* ....15.00 - 25.00

ROCKY MOUNTAIN RANGERS:

Bluebird 6907, 6908..4.00 - 7.00

HUGH RODEN (& ROY ROGERS/HIS TEXAS NIGHTHAWKS):

Okeh 45430 *Deep Sea Waltz*................................30.00 - 50.00
   45465 *Tulsa Waltz*...30.00 - 50.00
   45540 *Hogs In The Potato Patch* ....30.00 - 50.00

RODEO TRIO:

Victor V40136 *Arkansas Traveler* ....5.00 - 8.00
   V40186 *Medley*..5.00 - 8.00

ART RODGERS (See TEXAS TOPHANDS):

JESSIE RODGERS:

Bluebird 5443 *The Ramblers' Yodel*	7.00 -	10.00
5499 *Way Down In Mississippi*	7.00 -	10.00
5632 *Roughneck Blues*	7.00 -	10.00
5839 *Rattlesnake Daddy*	7.00 -	10.00
5853 *Headin' Home*	7.00 -	10.00
5910 *An Old Rugged Road*	7.00 -	10.00
5942 *Leave Me Alone*	25.00 -	40.00
5958 *Lonely Days In Texas*	7.00 -	10.00
6066 *Hummin' To My Honey*	7.00 -	10.00
6087 *Window Shopping Mama*	7.00 -	10.00
6116 *When I Was A Boy*	7.00 -	10.00
6143 *Jessie's Talking Blues*	7.00 -	10.00
6196 *Give Your Love*	7.00 -	10.00
6256 *When The Texas Moon Is Shining*	5.00 -	8.00
6311 *Little Prairie Town*	5.00 -	8.00
6364 *San Antonio Blues*	5.00 -	8.00
6402 *Tell You About A Gal Named Sal*	5.00 -	8.00
6924 *Troubled In Mind And Blues*	5.00 -	8.00
7018 *Just One Little Kiss*	5.00 -	8.00
7042 *Back In Jail Again*	5.00 -	8.00
7209 *I'm A Roaming Cowboy*	5.00 -	8.00

JIMMIE RODGERS:

Bluebird 5000 *Moonlight And Skies*	7.00 -	10.00
5037 *Gambling Bar Room Blues*	10.00 -	15.00
5057 *Happy Till She Met You*	10.00 -	15.00
5061 *You've Got Me Crying Again*	10.00 -	15.00
5076 *Prairie Lullaby*	10.00 -	15.00
5080 *Mother, Queen Of My Heart*	10.00 -	15.00
5081 *Down The Old Road To Home*	10.00 -	15.00
5082 *Roll Along, Kentucky Moon*	10.00 -	15.00
5083 *My Time Ain't Long*	10.00 -	15.00
5084 *What's It*	10.00 -	15.00
5085 *Blue Yodel*	7.00 -	10.00
5136 *Mississippi Moon*	8.00 -	12.00
5163 *Waiting For A Train*	7.00 -	10.00
5199 *When It's Harvest Time*	10.00 -	15.00
5223 *In The Jailhouse Now*	6.00 -	10.00
5281 *Jimmie Rodgers' Last Blue Yodel*	20.00 -	30.00
5393 *My Blue-Eyed Jane*	10.00 -	15.00
5482 *Ben Dewberry's Final Run*	6.00 -	10.00
5556 *Yodeling Ranger*	6.00 -	10.00
5609 *My Old Pal*	6.00 -	10.00
5739 *I'm Lonesome Too*	8.00 -	12.00
5784 *In The Hills Of Tennessee*	8.00 -	12.00
5838 *Treasures Untold*	5.00 -	8.00
5892 *Why Did You Give Me Your Love*	10.00 -	15.00
5942 *My Good Gal's Gone*	25.00 -	40.00
5991 *Daddy And Home*	5.00 -	8.00
6198 *Old Love Letters*	15.00 -	20.00
6225 *Sleep, Baby, Sleep*	5.00 -	8.00
6246 *The Sailor's Plea*	5.00 -	8.00
6275 *Mule Skinner Blues*	15.00 -	20.00
6698 *Why There's A Tear In My Eye*	15.00 -	25.00
6762 *The Carter Family & Jimmie Rodgers In Texas*	10.00 -	15.00
6810 *I've Only Loved Three Women*	10.00 -	15.00

(Note: First pressings of above are "buff" Bluebird label; subsequent pressings with blue label are worth less.)

7280 *Yodeling My Way Back Home*	10.00 -	15.00
7600 *Take Me Back Again*	10.00 -	15.00

Montgomery Ward (many titles as on Bluebird)	7.00 -	10.00
4209 *Blue Yodel No. 9*	15.00 -	20.00
5014 *My Good Gal's Gone Blues*	15.00 -	20.00
Victor 20864 *Soldier's Sweetheart*	15.00 -	20.00
21142 *Away Out On The Mountain*	15.00 -	20.00
21245 *Ben Dewberry's Final Run*	15.00 -	20.00
21291 *Blue Yodel No. 2*	15.00 -	20.00
21433 *Treasures Untold*	15.00 -	20.00
21531 *Blue Yodel No. 3*	15.00 -	20.00
21574 *Dear Old Sunny South By The Sea*	15.00 -	20.00

21636 *Memphis Yodel*	15.00 -	20.00
21757 *Daddy And Home*	15.00 -	20.00
22072 *Blue Yodel No. 5*	15.00 -	25.00
22143 *Frankie And Johnny*	15.00 -	25.00
22220 *My Rough And Rowdy Ways*	20.00 -	30.00
22271 *Blue Yodel No. 6*	20.00 -	30.00
22319 *The Drunkard's Child*	20.00 -	30.00
22379 *Train Whistle Blues*	20.00 -	30.00
22421 *Hobo Bill's Last Ride*	20.00 -	30.00
22488 *Any Old Time*	20.00 -	30.00
22523 *High Powered Mama*	20.00 -	30.00
22554 *Pistol Packin' Papa*	20.00 -	30.00
23503 *Blue Yodel No. 8*	25.00 -	40.00
23518 *Nobody Knows But Me*	25.00 -	40.00
23535 *T.B. Blues*	30.00 -	50.00
23549 *Jimmie, The Kid*	30.00 -	50.00
23564 *I'm Lonesome, Too*	30.00 -	50.00
23574 *Moonlight And Skies*	30.00 -	50.00
23580 *Blue Yodel No. 9*	50.00 -	80.00
23609 *What's It*	50.00 -	80.00
23621 *Rodgers Puzzle Record*	50.00 -	80.00
23636 *Gambling Polka Dot Blues*	50.00 -	80.00
23651 *Roll Along Kentucky Moon*	50.00 -	80.00
23669 *My Time Ain't Long*	50.00 -	80.00
23681 *Home Call*	50.00 -	80.00
23696 *Blue Yodel No. 10*	50.00 -	80.00
23711 *Hobo's Meditation*	50.00 -	80.00
23721 *Mother, The Queen Of My Heart*	50.00 -	80.00
23736 *Miss The Mississippi And You*	75.00 -	100.00
23751 *Whippin' That Old T.B.*	75.00 -	100.00
23766 *Gambling Bar Room Blues*	75.00 -	100.00
23781 *Peach Pickin' Time In Georgia*	75.00 -	100.00
23796 *Blue Yodel No. 11*	80.00 -	120.00
23811 *The Southern Cannon Ball*	100.00 -	150.00
23816 *Mississippi Delta Blues*	100.00 -	150.00
23830 *The Yodeling Ranger*	100.00 -	150.00
23840 *Old Love Letters*	125.00 -	175.00
24456 *Blue Yodel No. 12*	75.00 -	100.00
V40014 *Blue Yodel No. 4*	10.00 -	15.00
V40054 *The Sailor's Plea*	10.00 -	15.00
V40072 *My Little Lady*	15.00 -	20.00
V40096 *My Carolina Sunshine Girl*	10.00 -	15.00

(Note: The prices quoted herein are for records in excellent condition. It is particularly appropriate to restate this here, because many of the foregoing records are plentiful in worn condition, and are usually found in that state. Worn copies are worth nominal sums at most, and are probably unsaleable at any price.)

18-6000 (picture record) *Blue Yodel No. 12* .....300.00 -   up

MRS. JIMMIE RODGERS:
Bluebird 6698 *We Miss Him When The Evening Shadows Fall*
....10.00 -   15.00
7339 *My Rainbow Trail* ....10.00 -   15.00

ROE BROTHERS (& MORRELL):
Columbia 15156-D *The Ship That Never Returned*.10.00 -   15.00
15199-D *Goin' Down The Road Feelin' Bad*.....10.00 -   15.00

ERNEST ROGERS:
Victor 20502 *Willie, The Chimney Sweeper* ....5.00 -   8.00
20672 *The Flight of "Lucky" Lindberg* ....10.00 -   15.00
20798 *Steamboat Bill* ....8.00 -   12.00
20870 *My Red-Haired Lady* ....8.00 -   12.00
21361 *Mythological Blues* ....8.00 -   12.00

ROY ROGERS:
Vocalion 04050 *When A Cowboy Sings A Song* ....8.00 -   12.00
04051 *Listen To The Rhythm Of The Range* ....8.00 -   12.00
04091 *Hi-Yo Silver* ....8.00 -   12.00
04263 *I'm A Lonely Ranger* ....8.00 -   12.00
04389 *When The Sun Is Setting On The Prairie*...8.00 -   12.00
04453 *Colorado Sunset*.......................................8.00 -   12.00
04544 *Born To The Saddle* ....8.00 -   12.00
04840 *Somebody's Smile* ....8.00 -   12.00
04923 *Headin' For Texas And Home* ....8.00 -   12.00
04961 *Let Me Build A Cabin* ....8.00 -   12.00

ROLLING STONES:
Victor V40316 *Down By The Old Rio Grande*........15.00 -   20.00

POSEY RORER & THE NORTH CAROLINA RAMBLERS:
Edison (thin) 11009 *A Wild And Reckless Hobo* .... -   -   -
20005 *As We Sat Beneath The Maple On The Hill*......- -   -
(Note: The above two discs were never officially released, but copies have gotten out.)
Edison (thick) 52414 *As We Sat Beneath The Maple On The Hill*
....50.00 -   75.00

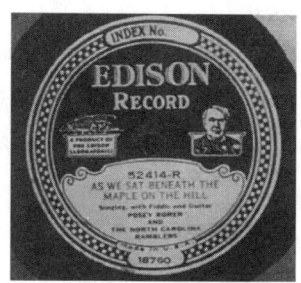

ROSE FAMILY:
Bluebird 5004, 5036, 5074 ....4.00 -   7.00

JACK ROSE:
Okeh 45370 *Jack And Babe Blues* ....10.00 -   15.00

ROSS' RHYTHM RASCALS:
Decca 5344, 5384, 5399, 5410, 5446, 5480,
5512, 5528.. 5.00 -   10.00

RED ROWE (& THE RIDGE RUNNERS):
Imperial 8048 *Two Sides To Every Story* ....5.00 -   8.00
8049 *Lock The Door and Shut The Window* ....5.00 -   8.00
8050 *Little Rock Lou* ....5.00 -   8.00
8051 *Finders Keepers* ....5.00 -   8.00
8055 *A Million Memories* ....5.00 -   8.00
Intro 6043 *Waste Paper Doll* ....5.00 -   8.00

CARTER ROWLAND & SON:
Vocalion 5349 *Cotton-Eyed Joe* .... 20.00 -   30.00

GEORGE RUNNELS:
Champion 15394 *Write A Letter To My Mother* ..... 15.00 -   25.00

FLOYD RUSSELL:
Supertone 9167 *Coal Creek March* .... 7.00 -   10.00

JIMMY RUSSELL & THE MUSICAL RANGERS:
Imperial 8046 *The Weaker Sex* ....- -   -

RUSTIC REVELERS:
Decca 5059 *Dixie Get Together* .... 7.00 -   10.00
5062 *Chicken Reel* .... 7.00 -   10.00
5063 *Fiddlin' Away*.. 7.00 -   10.00

RUTHERFORD & BURNETT/FOSTER/MOORE:
Brunswick 490 *Six Months Ain't Long* .... 25.00 -   40.00
581 *My Boyhood Happy Days* .... 25.00 -   40.00
Gennett 6688 *Under The Pale Moonlight* .... 75.00 -   100.00
6746 *Let Her Go, I'll Meet Her* .... 75.00 -   100.00
6760 *Good Night Waltz*....................................... 80.00 -   120.00
6807 *Six Months Ain't Long* .... 80.00 -   120.00
6873 *My Carolina Home* .... 80.00 -   120.00
6913 *Taylor's Quickstep* .... 80.00 -   120.00
6976 *Richmond Blues* .... 80.00 -   120.00
Superior 2640 *My Carolina Home*......................... 80.00 -   120.00

J. P./JOE RYAN:
Champion 16342 *It Just Suits Me* .... 25.00 -   40.00
Gennett 7006 *Bed Bug Groan*................................ 30.00 -   50.00
7140 *Worried Daddy Blues*................................. 30.00 -   50.00
Supertone 9542 *Sad And Lonely Blues* .... 15.00 -   20.00

SADDLE TRAMPS:
Vocalion 03609, 03649, 03940, 04037 .... 5.00 -   8.00

SALEM HIGHBALLERS:
Okeh 45455 *Going On To Town* .... 20.00 -   30.00

CURLEY SANDERS:
Talent 749 *Last On Your List*................................. 7.00 -   10.00

DILLIARD SANDERS:
Supertone 9247 *I'll Never Be Yours* .... 8.00 -   12.00

IRENE SANDERS (Acc. by AARON CAMPBELL'S MOUNTAINEERS):
Champion 16719 *Fond Affection* .... 40.00 -   60.00
45056 *Fond Affection*.. 10.00 -   15.00

LITTLE TOMMIE SANDS:
Freedom 5022 *Syrup Soppin' Blues*........................ 7.00 -   10.00

SANDY CREEK WOOD CHOPPERS:
Supertone 9543 *Huskin' Bee*.................................. 7.00 -   10.00
9680 *Polly Wolly Doodle* .... 7.00 -   10.00

SANFORD & McCONNELL:
Victor 23765 *Over The Bar* ....10.00 -   15.00

SAXTON BROTHERS:
Superior 2537 *Going-A-Courtin'* ....25.00 -   35.00

JIMMIE SCOTT:
Star Talent 781 *Rocky Road* ....7.00 -   10.00

RAMBLIN' TOMMY SCOTT:
Macy's 130 *Smoky Mountain Sunset* ....8.00 -   12.00

SCOTT COUNTY TRIO:
Supertone 9308 *Silvery Bell*.....................................5.00 -   8.00

SCOTTSDALE STRING BAND:
Okeh 45074 *Aunt Hager's Blues* ....15.00 -   20.00
    45103 *Chinese Breakdown* ....10.00 -   15.00
    45118 *Stone Mountain Wobble*.......................10.00 -   15.00
    45142 *Carolina Glide* ....10.00 -   15.00
    45158 *Hiawatha Breakdown* ....10.00 -   15.00
    45173 *Scottdale Stomp* ....10.00 -   15.00
    45188 *Down Yonder* ....10.00 -   15.00
    45201 *Goin' Crazy Blues*.................................15.00 -   20.00
    45256 *Share 'Em* ....15.00 -   20.00
    45279 *Silver Bell*...15.00 -   20.00
    45341 *Coughdrop Blues* ....20.00 -   30.00
    45352 *The Moonshiner's Waltz*.........................20.00 -   30.00
    45379 *Honolulu Moon* ....20.00 -   30.00
    45509 *Japanese Breakdown* ....25.00 -   40.00
    45527 *Charleston Wobble* ....35.00 -   50.00

SCOTTY THE DRIFTER:
Decca 5296 *Gooseberry Pie* ....7.00 -   10.00

LISTON SCROGGINS:
Brunswick 378 *Goodbye To Friends And Home* ....8.00 -   12.00

JOHN SEAGLE--LEONARD STOKES:
Victor 22060 *Life's Railway To Heaven* ....7.00 -   10.00
    22289 *Will There Be Any Stars*............................7.00 -   10.00

(UNCLE) JIM SEANY:
Challenge 324 *The Poor Tramp Has To Live* ....7.00 -   10.00
    398 *The Poor Tramp Has To Live* ....7.00 -   10.00
Champion 15222 *Kenney Wagner's Surrender* ....8.00 -   12.00
    15233 *Sweet Bunch Of Violets*.............................8.00 -   12.00

JILSON SETTERS:
Victor 21353 *The Wild Wagoner* ....10.00 -   15.00
    21407 *Forked Deer*...8.00 -   12.00
    21635 *Way Up On Clinch Mountain* ....10.00 -   15.00
    V40025 *Wild Horse Of Stoney Point*..................15.00 -   20.00
    V40127 *Black-Eyed Susie*................................10.00 -   15.00

BILL SHAFER:
Vocalion 5413 *Kicking Mule* ....10.00 -   15.00

"TED" SHARP, HINMAN & SHARP:
Champion 16712 *Hell Among The Yearlings* ....30.00 -   50.00
    16739 *Where's My Other Foot* ....30.00 -   50.00
    16766 *Goin' On Up To Town* ....30.00 -   50.00
Champion 45002, 45012, 45182..............................10.00 -   15.00

BERT/BURT SHAW:
Superior 2733 *Pea Pickin' Papa*...........................75.00 - 100.00
    2760 *Doggone Them Blues*................................80.00 - 120.00
    2805 *Ninety-Nine Years* ....75.00 - 100.00

MIKE SHAW & HIS ALABAMA ENTERTAINERS:
Okeh 45518 *Tennessee River Bottom Blues* ....35.00 -   50.00
    45529 *Going Crazy* ....35.00 -   50.00

SHELOR FAMILY:
Victor 20865 *Big Bend Gal*.................................. 8.00 -   12.00

SHELTON BROTHERS (BOB & JOE):
Decca 5079, 5087, 5099, 5100, 5135, 5137, 5161,
    5170, 5173, 5177, 5180, 5184, 5187, 5190, 5198,
    5219, 5244, 5261, 5339, 5353, 5367, 5381, 5397,
    5409, 5422, 5440, 5456, 5471, 5475, 5484, 5496,
    5508, 5519, 5533.. 5.00 -   10.00

B. F. SHELTON:
Victor V40107 *Cold Penitentiary Blues* .... 30.00 -   50.00

BILL SHEPARD (Acc. by SHEPARD BROS. & ED WEBB):
Champion 16383 *Aunt Jane Blues* .... 50.00 -   75.00

ARKEY SHIBLEY:
Gilt-Edge 5021, 5030... 5.00 -   10.00

UNCLE JOE SHIPPEE:
Pathe 21164 *Old Time Fiddler*................................ 7.00 -   10.00
Perfect 11237 *Old Time Fiddler* .... 7.00 -   10.00

EARL SHIRKEY & ROY HARPER:
    15376-D *Poor Little Joe* .... 25.00 -   40.00
    15490-D *My Yodeling Sweetheart* .... 30.00 -   50.00
    15535-D *The Virginian Strike of '23* .... 30.00 -   50.00
    15642-D *We Have Moonshine In The West Virginia Hills*
    .... 50.00 -   75.00

CHESLEY SHIRLEY (THE TEXAS RAMBLER):
Champion 16826 *The Last Great Roundup* .... 25.00 -   40.00
    45075 *Only Flirting* .... 8.00 -   12.00

SHORE'S SOUTHERN TRIO:
Gennett 6842 *Whistling Rufus* .... 25.00 -   40.00
    6927 *Goin' Crazy*... 25.00 -   40.00

BILL SHORES & MELVIN DUPREE:
Columbia 15506-D *West Texas Breakdown* .... 25.00 -   40.00

SHORT BROTHERS:
Okeh 45206 *Whistling Coon* .... 10.00 -   15.00

SHORT CREEK TRIO:
Gennett 6272 *Hand Me Down My Walking Cane*... 10.00 -   15.00
    6364 *The Buckin' Mule* .... 10.00 -   15.00

CHIEF SHUNATONA, ET AL: (See CHIEF)

CONNIE SIDES:
Columbia 15009-D *In The Shadow Of The Pine* ...... 8.00 -   12.00

BILL SIMMON (S' COWBOYS):
Victor 23533 *The Cowboy's Plea* .... 15.00 -   20.00
    23603 *Rocky Mountain Blues* .... 15.00 -   20.00

MATT SIMMONS & FRANK MILLER:
Okeh 45148 *That Little Old Hut* ....8.00 - 12.00

OLIVER SIMS:
Columbia 15103-D *Lost John* ....10.00 - 15.00

ALLEN SISSON:
Edison 51522 *Farewell Ducktown-Reel* ....8.00 - 12.00
   51559 *Walking Water* ....8.00 - 12.00
   51690 *Katy Hill-Reel* ....8.00 - 12.00
   51720 *Gray Eagle-Reel* ....8.00 - 12.00

ASHER SIZEMORE (& LITTLE JIMMY):
Bluebird 5445 *Goodbye To Jimmie Rodgers* ....30.00 - 50.00
   5495 *Cowboy Jim* ....25.00 - 40.00
   5568 *Shake Hands With Mother* ....25.00 - 40.00
   5717 *My West Virginia Home* ....25.00 - 40.00
   5774 *Memories Of Kentucky* ....25.00 - 40.00
   6021 *I Dreamed I Searched* ....25.00 - 40.00

BILL SKIDMORE:
Columbia 15761-D *Behind The Big White House* ...10.00 - 15.00

BOB SKILES (4 OLD TUNERS):
Okeh 45211 *Rye Waltz* ....5.00 - 10.00
   45225 *Casey Jones* ....5.00 - 10.00
   45243 *Wagner* ....5.00 - 8.00

JIMMIE SKINNER:
Radio Artist 246, 250, 251, 253 ....5.00 - 8.00

SKYLAND SCOTTY:
Bluebird 5357 *Great Grandad* ....20.00 - 30.00
   5906 *Two Little Frogs* ....20.00 - 30.00

BOB SKYLES & HIS SKYROCKETS:
Bluebird (most issues) ....5.00 - 8.00

SLOAN & THREADGILL:
Brunswick 284 *Clover Blossoms* ....8.00 - 12.00
   299 *When The Harvest Is Shining* ....8.00 - 12.00

LESTER SMALLWOOD:
Victor V40181 *Cotton Mill Girl* ....20.00 - 30.00

(DR.) SMITH'S (CHAMPION) HOSS HAIR PULLERS:
Victor 21711 *Going Down The River* ....30.00 - 50.00
   V40059 *Save My Mother's Picture From The Sale*
   ....30.00 - 50.00
   V40124 *Just Give Me The Leavings* ....40.00 - 60.00

SMITH'S GARAGE FIDDLE BAND:
Vocalion 5268 *Beaumont Rag* ....25.00 - 40.00
   5287 *Done Gone* ....25.00 - 40.00
   5306 *Dill Pickle Rag* ....25.00 - 40.00
   5336 *Miss Lola* ....25.00 - 40.00
   5375 *Tom & Jerry* ....25.00 - 40.00

SMITH & WOODLIEFF:
Gennett 6809 *The Old Schoolhouse Playground* .....30.00 - 50.00
   6840 *I Ain't Gonna Grieve My Lord Anymore* ...30.00 - 50.00
   6858 *I'd Rather Be With Rosy Nell* ....30.00 - 50.00

ARTHUR SMITH (TRIO) (& HIS DIXIE LINERS):
Bluebird 5896 *Blackberry Blossom* ....7.00 - 10.00
   6322 *Chittlin' Cookin' Time* ....7.00 - 10.00
   6369 *Cheatham County Breakdown* ....7.00 - 10.00
   6442 *Fiddler's Blues* ....7.00 - 10.00
   6514 *Take Me Back To Tennessee* ....7.00 - 10.00
   6844 *Florida Blues* ....7.00 - 10.00

   6869 *Never Alone* ....7.00 - 10.00
   6913 *The Girl I Love Don't Pay Me No Mind* .....7.00 - 10.00
   6927 *Sugar Tree Stomp* ....7.00 - 10.00
   6994 *It's Hard To Please Your Mind* ....7.00 - 10.00
   7043 *Walking In My Sleep* ....7.00 - 10.00
   7146 *Lonesome For You* ....5.00 - 8.00
   7203 *Beautiful Memories* ....5.00 - 8.00
   7221 *Across The Blue Ridge Mountains* ....5.00 - 8.00
   7325 *Nellie's Blue Eyes* ....5.00 - 8.00
   7351 *Cheatham County Breakdown No. 2* ....7.00 - 10.00
   7437 *Answer To More Pretty Girls Than One* .....7.00 - 10.00
   7498 *Henpecked Husband Blues* ....7.00 - 10.00
   7511 *Smith's Breakdown* ....7.00 - 10.00
   7547 *Her Little Brown Hand* ....7.00 - 10.00
   7651 *Lost Love* ....7.00 - 10.00
   7893 *The Gypsy's Warning* ....7.00 - 10.00
   7943 *Why Should I Wonder?* ....7.00 - 10.00
   7982 *Give Me Old Time Music* ....7.00 - 10.00
Bluebird (higher numbers) ....5.00 - 8.00

BLAINE & CAL SMITH:
Vocalion 04705, 04855, 04976 ....5.00 - 10.00

CHARLES B. SMITH:
Columbia 15755-D *Walkin' Georgia Rose* ....15.00 - 20.00

HANK SMITH:
Vocalion 5318 *Eleven Cent Cotton And Forty Cent Meat*
....10.00 - 15.00

HARRY SMITH:
Okeh 45260 *The Death Of Floyd Collins* ....10.00 - 15.00

TRAVELIN' J. SMITH:
Columbia 15547-D *So I Joined The Navy* ....7.00 - 10.00

JIMMIE SMITH:
Timely Tunes 1556 *She's A Low Down Mama* ......75.00 - 100.00
   1557 *There's A Good Gal In The Mountains* .....75.00 - 100.00

JOE SMITH (THE COLORADO COWBOY):
Bluebird 5522 *John Dillinger* ....8.00 - 12.00
   5530 *Pining For The Pines In Caroline* ....5.00 - 8.00
   5651 *That Silver-Haired Mother* ....5.00 - 8.00
Champion 15808 *The Talkin' Blues* ....10.00 - 15.00
   45173 *Born In Hard Luck* ....7.00 - 10.00

KID SMITH'S FAMILY:
Victor 23576 *Little Bessie* ....40.00 - 60.00
Vocalion 03414 *I'm Not Angry With You Darling* ...8.00 - 12.00
   03415 *Mississippi Freight Train Blues* ....10.00 - 15.00
   03443 *Ten Is Served And Ten To Serve* ....10.00 - 15.00

MARSHALL SMITH:
Columbia 15080-D *Jonah And The Whale* ....7.00 - 10.00

(MERRITT) SMITH & (KEITH) POOSER:
Okeh 45318 *Carolina Moon* ....5.00 - 8.00
   45326 *Softly And Tenderly* ....5.00 - 8.00
   45362 *The Lonesome Road* ....5.00 - 8.00
   45474 *Death Is Only A Dream* ....5.00 - 8.00

MERRITT SMITH & LEO BOSWELL:
Champion 16335 *On The Banks Of The Brandywine* .....7.00 - 10.00
   16344 *Oh Mary Don't You Weep* ....7.00 - 10.00
   16433 *Daisies Never Tell* ....7.00 - 10.00
Columbia 15748-D *Try Not To Forget* ....8.00 - 12.00

R. B. SMITH & S. J. ALLGOOD:
Okeh 45010 *American And Spanish Fandango*.......10.00 - 15.00

SLIM SMITH:
Crown 3118 *Bread Line Blues*...................................15.00 - 20.00
Victor 23526 *Bread Line Blues* ....30.00 - 50.00
Vocalion 05082 *Sad And Alone* ....8.00 - 12.00

WALTER SMITH:
Gennett 6825 *The Cat's Got The Measles, The Dogs Got The
    Whoopin' Cough* ....15.00 - 20.00

SMOKY MOUNTAIN BOYS:
Gennett 6871 *The Smoky Mountain Boys At The Still*
    ....25.00 - 40.00

SMOKY MOUNTAIN FIDDLER TRIO:
Bluebird 6387 *Bonaparte's Retreat*...........................5.00 - 8.00

SMOKY MOUNTAIN RAMBLERS:
Vocalion 5422 *San Antonio* ....30.00 - 50.00
    5437 *Bear Mountain Rag*.................................30.00 - 50.00
    5451 *Born In Tennessee*.................................30.00 - 50.00

SMYTH'S COUNTY RAMBLERS:
Victor V40144 *Way Down In Alabama*..................50.00 - 75.00

(LEO) SOILEAU & LAFLEUR/(MOISE) ROBIN:
Decca 5101, 5102, 5116, 5117, 5133, 5157, 5182,
    5210, 5215, 5236, 5262, 5279, 5299, 5326 ....5.00 - 10.00
Paramount 12808 *Easy Rider* ....75.00 - 100.00
Victor 21769 *Basile* ....15.00 - 25.00
    21770 *The Criminal*.......................................15.00 - 25.00
    22183 *Penitentiary Waltz* ....15.00 - 25.00
    22207 *Grosse Mama*.......................................15.00 - 25.00

SOLOMON & HUGHES:
Victor V40244 *Ragtime Annie*...............................10.00 - 15.00

SONS OF THE PIONEERS:
Decca 5013 *Ridin' Home*..10.00 - 15.00
    5047 *Moonlight On The Prairie* ....10.00 - 15.00
Decca 5082, 5083, 5168, 5178, 5218, 5232, 5243,
    5247, 5248, 5275, 5358 ....5.00 - 10.00
Vocalion 03399 *Power In The Blood* ....8.00 - 12.00
    03880 *Open Range Ahead* ....8.00 - 12.00
    03881 *Smilin' Through* ....7.00 - 10.00
    03916 *I Love You, Nelly*................................7.00 - 10.00
    04136 *Billie The Kid* ....7.00 - 10.00
    04187 *Hear Dem Bells*...................................7.00 - 10.00
    04264 *Cajon Stomp*.......................................7.00 - 10.00
    04328 *Send Him Home To Me* ....7.00 - 10.00

SOUTHERN KENTUCKY MOUNTAINEERS:
Supertone 9310 *Cumberland Gap* ....8.00 - 12.00

SOUTHERN MOONLIGHT ENTERTAINERS:
Vocalion 5372 *My Blue Ridge Mountain Queen* .....15.00 - 20.00
    5388 *My Carolina Girl* ....15.00 - 20.00
    5407 *Buckin' Mule*..15.00 - 20.00
    5440 *Then I'll Move To Town* ....15.00 - 20.00
    5460 *Lost John*..15.00 - 20.00

SOUTH GEORGIA HIGHBALLERS:
Okeh 45155 *Bibb County Grind* ....40.00 - 60.00

SPANGLE & PEARSON:
Okeh 45287 *Patrick County Blues* ....50.00 - 80.00

SPOONEY FIVE:
Columbia 15234-D *Chinese Rag* ....15.00 - 20.00

CARL T. SPRAGUE:
Aurora 418 *Cowboy Love Song* ....20.00 - 30.00
Bluebird 6258 *The Prisoner's Meditation* ....7.00 - 10.00
Victor 19747 *Bad Companions*................................5.00 - 8.00
    20067 *Cowboy Love Song* ....5.00 - 8.00
    20122 *The Cowboy's Dream* ....5.00 - 8.00
    20534 *The Boston Burglar* ....7.00 - 10.00
    20932 *The Last Great Roundup* ....7.00 - 10.00
    21194 *Utah Carroll* ....8.00 - 12.00
    21402 *Cowman's Prayer* ....8.00 - 12.00
    V40066 *Here's To The Texas Ranger* ....10.00 - 15.00
    V40197 *The Last Longhorn* ....10.00 - 15.00
    V40246 *The Wayward Daughter* ....10.00 - 15.00

FRED STANLEY:
Columbia 15559-D *The Tie That Binds* ....8.00 - 12.00

JOHN STANLEY'S ORCHESTRA:
Superior 2691 *Moonshiner's Serenade*...................25.00 - 40.00

ROBA STANLEY & WILLIAM PATTERSON:
Okeh 40213 *Devilish Mary*....................................10.00 - 15.00
    45036 *Old Maid Blues* ....10.00 - 15.00

STANTON'S JOY BOYS:
Superior 2671 *Huskin' Bee* ....35.00 - 50.00

FRANK STANTON:
Superior 2521 *Creole Girl* ....35.00 - 50.00
    2544 *Poor Old Dad*..35.00 - 50.00

STAPLETON BROTHERS:
Columbia 15284-D *In A Cool Shady Nook*...............8.00 - 12.00
Victor 23591 *Won't You Take Me Back Again* ....20.00 - 30.00

GENE STEELE:
Vocalion 05068 *Here's Your Opportunity*................8.00 - 12.00
    05135 *Rio Grande Moon* ....8.00 - 12.00
    05204 *Freight Train Blues*..............................8.00 - 12.00

JOE STEEN:
Bluebird 5567 *I'll Love Ya Till The Cows Come Home*
    ....5.00 - 8.00
Champion 16258 *Railroad Jack* ....10.00 - 15.00
Victor 23634 *Crazy Engineer* ....20.00 - 30.00

UNCLE "BUNT" STEPHENS;
Columbia 15071-D *Louisburg Blues* ....10.00 - 15.00
    15085-D *Left In The Dark Blues*.......................10.00 - 15.00

STEVE'S HOT SHOTS:
Victor 23699 *Sour Apple Cider* ....30.00 - 50.00
    V40308 *The Press* ....20.00 - 30.00

OTIS STEWART:
Supertone 9242 *Adam And Eve*..............................8.00 - 12.00

CHARLES LEWIS STINE:
Columbia 15027-D *The Wreck On The C & O* ....7.00 - 10.00

STOKES, MILLER, McKINNEY, MARTIN, WILLIAMS & BROWN:
Brunswick 422 *The Great Hatfield-McCoy Feud, Part 1/2*
    ....15.00 - 20.00
    423 *The Great Hatfield-McCoy Feud, Part 3/4* .15.00 - 20.00

LEONARD STOKES:
Bluebird 7349 *Will You Miss Me When I'm Gone* ....7.00 - 10.00
    7401 *There's A Green Hill Far Away*.................5.00 - 8.00
Electradisk 1920 *He's Too Far Gone* ....8.00 - 12.00

LOWE STOKES & HIS NORTH GEORGIANS/POT LUCKERS; LOWE STOKES & RILEY PUCKETT/MIKE WHITTEN:

Brunswick 491 *Prohibition Is A Failure*	20.00	-	30.00
549 *Four Cent Cotton*	20.00	-	30.00
Columbia 15241-D *Home Brew Rag*	25.00	-	40.00
15369-D *Wave That Frame*	25.00	-	40.00
15486-D *Take Me Back To Georgia*	30.00	-	50.00
15557-D *Left All Alone Again Blues*	30.00	-	50.00
15620-D *Everybody's Doing It*	40.00	-	60.00
15660-D *Bone Dry Blues*	50.00	-	75.00
15693-D *Sailing On The Robert E. Lee*	50.00	-	75.00

JIMMY STONE:

Imperial 8137 *Midnight Boogie*	7.00	-	10.00

STONEMAN FAMILY:

Victor V40030 *Broken-Hearted Lover*	12.00	-	16.00
V40116 *Going Up The Mountain After Liquor*	15.00	-	20.00
V40206 *Too Late*	15.00	-	20.00

MR. & MRS. ERNEST V. STONEMAN & HIS DIXIE MOUNTAINEERS/GRAYSON COUNTY BOYS; ERNEST V. STONEMAN (TRIO) (& FIDDLER JOE):

Banner 1993 *Hand Me Down My Walking Cane*	5.00	-	8.00
2157 *Pass Around The Bottle*	5.00	-	8.00
2158 *It's Sinful To Flirt*	5.00	-	8.00
Broadway 8054 *Pass Around The Bottle*	5.00	-	8.00
8055 *Hand Me Down My Walking Cane*	5.00	-	8.00
Challenge 151 *Katy Cline*	5.00	-	8.00
152 *Barney McCoy*	5.00	-	8.00
153 *Silver Bell*	5.00	-	8.00
309 *Barney McCoy*	5.00	-	8.00
312 *May I Sleep In Your Barn Tonight Mister*	5.00	-	8.00
665 *Pass Around The Bottle*	5.00	-	8.00
Conqueror 7064 *Pass Around The Bottle*	5.00	-	8.00
7755 *Bully Of The Town*	5.00	-	8.00
Domino 0187 *The Old Hickory Cane*	5.00	-	8.00
3964 *Hand Me Down My Walking Cane*	5.00	-	8.00
3984 *The Fatal Wedding*	5.00	-	8.00
3985 *Pass Around The Bottle*	5.00	-	8.00
Edison (thin) 20004 *He Is Coming After Me*	-	-	-
(Note: Not supposed to have been issued, but copies did get out.)			
Edison (thick) 51788 *Bad Companions*	20.00	-	30.00
51864 *Watermelon Hanging On The Vine*	20.00	-	30.00
51869 *Wild Bill Jones*	20.00	-	30.00
51909 *Bury Me Beneath The Weeping Willow Tree*	20.00	-	30.00
51935 *Once I Had A Fortune*	20.00	-	30.00
51938 *Hand Me Down My Walking Cane*	20.00	-	30.00
51951 *Bully Of The Town*	20.00	-	30.00
51994 *Kitty Wells*	20.00	-	30.00
52026 *The Fate Of Talmadge Osborne*	20.00	-	30.00
52077 *The Orphan Girl*	20.00	-	30.00
52290 *When The Redeemed Are Gathered In*	20.00	-	30.00
52299 *Unlucky Road To Washington*	25.00	-	40.00
52312 *Down On The Banks Of The Ohio*	25.00	-	40.00
52350 *All Go Hungry Hash House*	25.00	-	40.00
52369 *The Old Maid And The Burglar*	25.00	-	40.00
52386 *It's Sinful To Flirt*	25.00	-	40.00
52461 *The Prisoner's Lament*	30.00	-	50.00
52479 *He Is Coming After Me*	30.00	-	50.00
52489 *All I've Got's Gone*	30.00	-	50.00

Gennett 3368 *May I Sleep In Your Barn Tonight Mister?*	8.00	-	12.00
3369 *Pretty Snow Deer*	8.00	-	12.00
3381 *Barney McCoy*	8.00	-	12.00
6044 *Kenney Wagner's Surrender*	15.00	-	20.00
6052 *Long Eared Mule*	15.00	-	20.00
6065 *Sweet Bunch Of Violets*	15.00	-	20.00
Herwin 75528 *Barney McCoy*	15.00	-	20.00
75529 *Silver Bell*	15.00	-	20.00
75530 *Pretty Snow Deer*	15.00	-	20.00
75535 *The Poor Tramp Has To Live*	15.00	-	20.00
75541 *Sweet Bunch Of Violets*	15.00	-	20.00
Homestead 16490 *Pass Around The Bottle*	15.00	-	20.00
16498 *The Fatal Wedding*	15.00	-	20.00
16500 *Bully Of The Town*	15.00	-	20.00
Okeh 7011 (12 inch) *John Hardy*	35.00	-	50.00
40288 *The Titanic*	15.00	-	20.00
40312 *Freckled Face Mary Jane*	15.00	-	20.00
40384 *Dying Girl's Farewell*	15.00	-	20.00
40405 *The Long Eared Mule*	15.00	-	20.00
40408 *The Lightning Express*	15.00	-	20.00
40430 *Uncle Sam And The Kaiser*	15.00	-	20.00
45009 *All I've Got's Gone*	15.00	-	20.00
45015 *The Fancy Ball*	15.00	-	20.00
45036 *The Kicking Mule*	15.00	-	20.00
45044 *Asleep At The Switch*	15.00	-	20.00
45048 *In The Shadow Of The Pine*	15.00	-	20.00
45051 *The Religious Critic*	15.00	-	20.00
45054 *The Texas Ranger*	15.00	-	20.00
45059 *The Old Hickory Cane*	15.00	-	20.00
45060 *My Pretty Snow Dear*	15.00	-	20.00
45062 *The All Go Hungry Hash House*	15.00	-	20.00
45065 *Katie Cline*	15.00	-	20.00
45084 *The Fatal Wedding*	15.00	-	20.00
45094 *Lonesome Road Blues*	15.00	-	20.00
45125 *The Mountaineer's Courtship*	15.00	-	20.00
Paramount 3021 *Pass Around The Bottle*	5.00	-	8.00
Pathe-Actuelle 32271 *The Old Hickory Cane*	5.00	-	8.00
32278 *The Fatal Wedding*	5.00	-	8.00
32279 *Bully Of The Town*	5.00	-	8.00
Perfect 12350 *Sinful To Flirt*	5.00	-	8.00
12357 *Pass Around The Bottle*	5.00	-	8.00
12358 *Bully Of The Town*	5.00	-	8.00
Regal 8324 *Hand Me Down My Walking Cane*	5.00	-	8.00
8346 *Sinful To Flirt*	5.00	-	8.00
8347 *The Fatal Wedding*	5.00	-	8.00
8369 *The Old Hickory Cane*	5.00	-	8.00
Romeo 597 *Bully Of The Town*	5.00	-	8.00
600 *Sinful To Flirt*	5.00	-	8.00
Silvertone 5004 *Sweet Bunch Of Violets*	7.00	-	10.00
Supertone 9255 *The Poor Tramp Has To Live*	7.00	-	10.00
Victor 20223 *In The Golden Bye And Bye*	7.00	-	10.00
20224 *Hallelujah Side*	7.00	-	10.00
20235 *The Little Old Log Cabin In The Lane*	7.00	-	10.00
20237 *All Go Hungry Hash House*	7.00	-	10.00
20294 *Sugar In The Gourd*	7.00	-	10.00
20302 *Old Joe Clark*	7.00	-	10.00
20531 *Going Down The Valley*	8.00	-	12.00
20532 *The Great Reaping Day*	8.00	-	12.00
20533 *I'll Be Satisfied*	8.00	-	12.00
20540 *Peekaboo*	8.00	-	12.00
20671 *The Story Of The Mighty Mississippi*	8.00	-	12.00
20672 *The Fate Of Talmadge Osborne*	8.00	-	12.00

20799 *The Old Hickory Cane* ....8.00 - 12.00
20844 *Are You Washed In The Blood?* ....10.00 - 15.00
20880 *The Mountaineer's Courtship* ....10.00 - 15.00
21071 *I Am Resolved* ....10.00 - 15.00
21129 *The Dying Girl's Farewell* ....10.00 - 15.00
21186 *I Know My Name Is There* ....10.00 - 15.00
21264 *Possum Trot School Exhibition* ....12.00 - 18.00
21518 *Serenade In The Mountains* ....12.00 - 18.00
21648 *The Raging Sea, How It Roars* ....12.00 - 18.00
V40078 *There's A Light Lit Up In Galilee* ....15.00 - 20.00
Vocalion 02632 *Texas Ranger* ....10.00 - 15.00
02655 *Nine Pound Hammer* ....15.00 - 20.00
02901 *All I Got's Gone* ....15.00 - 20.00

WILLIE STONEMAN:
Gennett 6565 *Katy Lee* ....15.00 - 25.00

STONE MOUNTAIN BOYS:
Supertone 9456 *Makin' Licker In North Carolina* ..10.00 - 15.00

STONE MOUNTAIN ENTERTAINERS:
Broadway 8159 *Red Wing* ....5.00 - 8.00

STONE MOUNTAIN TRIO:
Brunswick 543 *Maple Leaf Waltz* ....10.00 - 15.00
Vocalion 5457 *Stone Mountain Waltz* ....10.00 - 15.00

SMOKEY STOVER:
Specialty 715 *What A Shame* .... - - -

DICK STRATTON & THE NITE OWLS:
Tennessee 795 *Pistol Boogie* .... - - -

HARLEY STRATTON:
Superior 2588 *The Red River Valley* ....15.00 - 20.00

STRIPLING BROTHERS:
Decca 5018, 5019, 5041, 5049, 5069, 5207, 5246,
5267, 5291, 5313, 5417 ....7.00 - 12.00
Melotone 12173 *Moonlight Waltz* ....8.00 - 12.00
12181 *Big Footed Nigger In The Sandy Lot* ....8.00 - 12.00
Vocalion 02738 *June Rose Waltz* ....30.00 - 50.00
02739 *Coal Mine Blues* ....30.00 - 50.00
02761 *Kennedy Rag* ....30.00 - 50.00
02770 *Wolves Howling* ....30.00 - 50.00
5321 *The Lost Child* ....20.00 - 30.00
5365 *Railroad Bum* ....20.00 - 30.00
5366 *Red River Waltz* ....20.00 - 30.00
5382 *New Born Blues* ....20.00 - 30.00
5395 *Dance All Night With A Bottle In My Hand*
........................20.00 - 30.00
5412 *Wolves Howling* ....25.00 - 40.00
5441 *Lost John* ....25.00 - 40.00
5453 *Coal Mine Blues* ....25.00 - 40.00
5468 *Midnight Waltz* ....25.00 - 40.00

UNCLE "AM" STUART:
Vocalion 5035 *Cumberland Gap* ....8.00 - 12.00
5036 *Sourwood Mountain* ....8.00 - 12.00
5037 *Leather Breeches* ....8.00 - 12.00
5038 *Billie In The Low Ground* ....8.00 - 12.00
5039 *Forked Deer* ....8.00 - 12.00
5048 *Dixie* ....8.00 - 12.00
5053 *George Boker* ....8.00 - 12.00
14839 *Cumberland Gap* ....8.00 - 12.00
14840 *Sourwood Mountain* ....8.00 - 12.00
14841 *Leather Breeches* ....8.00 - 12.00
14843 *Billie In The Low Ground* ....8.00 - 12.00

14846 *Forked Deer* .... 8.00 - 12.00
14888 *Dixie* .... 8.00 - 12.00
14919 *George Boker* .... 8.00 - 12.00

SUE & RAWHIDE (Acc. by THE CRAZY HILLBILLIES BAND):
Okeh 45577 *Falling Leaf* .... 30.00 - 50.00

SWAMP ROOTERS:
Brunswick 556 *Swamp Cat Rag* .... 15.00 - 20.00

SWEET BROTHERS:
Gennett 6620 *I Got A Bulldog* .... 20.00 - 30.00
6655 *Falling By The Wayside* .... 20.00 - 30.00

HERBERT SWEET:
Gennett 6567 *The Prisoner's Lament* .... 15.00 - 20.00

SWEET VIOLET BOYS:
Vocalion 03110, 03218, 03219, 03256, 03281,
03327, 03402, 03587, 03663, 03766, 04010,
04428, 04528, 04714, 04756 .... 5.00 - 10.00

SWIFT JEWEL COWBOYS:
Okeh (most issues) .... 4.00 - 8.00
Vocalion 05052 *Memphis Oomph* .... 5.00 - 8.00
05133 *Chuck Wagon Swing* .... 5.00 - 8.00
05188 *Memphis Blues* .... 5.00 - 8.00
05243 *Kansas City Blues* .... 5.00 - 8.00
05309 *Dill Pickle Rag* .... 5.00 - 8.00
05369 *My Untrue Cowgirl* .... 5.00 - 8.00
05449 *Rose Room* .... 5.00 - 8.00
05499 *Bug Scuffle* .... 5.00 - 8.00
05598 *Look Down That Railroad Line* .... 5.00 - 8.00

SWING BILLIES:
Bluebird 7121, 7143, 7161, 7338 .... 5.00 - 8.00

CHARLES ROSS TAGGART:
Edison 51001 *A Country Fiddler At Home* .... 7.00 - 10.00
51048 *A Country Fiddler At The Telephone* .... 7.00 - 10.00
51448 *Sister Sorrowful* .... 10.00 - 15.00
Victor 18036 *Old Country Fiddler At The Party* ...... 5.00 - 8.00

ARTHUR TANNER & HIS CORNSHUCKERS/& RILEY PUCKETT:
Columbia 15145-D *Knoxville Girl* .... 10.00 - 15.00
15180-D *Two Little Children* .... 10.00 - 15.00
15352-D *Sleep On Blue Eyes* .... 10.00 - 15.00
15479-D *Dr. Ginger Blue* .... 30.00 - 50.00
15577-D *Gather The Flowers* .... 30.00 - 50.00
Paramount 3159 *Devilish Mary* .... 20.00 - 30.00
3160 *The Lightning Express Train* .... 20.00 - 30.00
3161 *The Little Old Log Cabin In The Lane* ...... 20.00 - 30.00
3162 *The Knoxville Girl* .... 20.00 - 30.00
3163 *When I Was Single My Pockets Would Jingle Jingle*
.... 20.00 - 30.00
Silvertone 3514 *The Burglar Man* .... 15.00 - 20.00
3515 *The Knoxville Girl* .... 15.00 - 20.00

GID TANNER & HIS GEORGIA BOYS/SKILLET LICKERS; GID TANNER & FATE NORRIS/RILEY PUCKETT; TANNER, McMICHEN, PUCKETT, STOKES & NORRIS:
Bluebird 5433 *Mississippi Sawyer* .... 10.00 - 15.00
5434 *Cumberland Gap On A Buckin' Mule* .... 10.00 - 15.00
5435 *Skillet Licker Breakdown* .... 10.00 - 15.00
5446 *Prosperity And Politics* .... 10.00 - 15.00

5488 *Ida Red* ....10.00 - 15.00
5559 *Practice Night With The Skillet Lickers* .....10.00 - 15.00
5562 *Down Yonder* ....7.00 - 10.00
5591 *Cotton Patch* ....10.00 - 15.00
5633 *Hinkey-Dinkey-Dee* ....10.00 - 15.00
5657 *Tanner's Rag* ....10.00 - 15.00
5658 *Soldier's Joy* ....7.00 - 10.00
5665 *On Tanner's Farm* ....10.00 - 15.00
5748 *Three Nights Drunk* ....10.00 - 15.00
5805 *I Ain't No Better Now* ....10.00 - 15.00
Columbia 119-D *Black-Eyed Susie* ....8.00 - 12.00
15010-D *Don't Grieve Your Mother* ....10.00 - 15.00
15017-D *Fox Chase* ....10.00 - 15.00
15019-D *Georgia Railroad* ....10.00 - 15.00
15059-D *Just Gimme The Leavings* ....10.00 - 15.00
15084-D *Turkey In The Straw* ....7.00 - 10.00
15091-D *Hand Me Down My Walking Cane* ....7.00 - 10.00
15104-D *Alabama Jubilee* ....10.00 - 15.00
15105-D *Goodbye, Booze* ....10.00 - 15.00
15108-D *Old Joe Clark* ....10.00 - 15.00
15123-D *Shortening Bread* ....10.00 - 15.00
15134-D *I Got Mine* ....10.00 - 15.00
15142-D *John Henry* ....10.00 - 15.00
15158-D *Dixie* ....10.00 - 15.00
15165-D *Football Rag* ....15.00 - 20.00
15170-D *The Old Gray Mare* ....10.00 - 15.00
15188-D *The Darktown Strutters Ball* ....10.00 - 15.00
15200-D *She'll Be Coming 'Round The Mountain*
....10.00 - 15.00
15204-D *Big Ball In Town* ....10.00 - 15.00
15217-D *Please Do Not Get Offended* ....10.00 - 15.00
15221-D *Uncle Bud* ....10.00 - 15.00
15237-D *Casey Jones* ....10.00 - 15.00
15249-D *Bile Them Cabbage Down* ....10.00 - 15.00
15267-D *Slow Buck* ....10.00 - 15.00
15283-D *Cotton-Eyed Joe* ....10.00 - 15.00
*15298-D *Possum Hunt On Stump Mountain* ....10.00 - 15.00
15303-D *Cumberland Gap* ....8.00 - 12.00
15315-D *Settin' In The Chimney Jamb* ....8.00 - 12.00
15334-D *Liberty* ....10.00 - 15.00
15382-D *Old Dan Tucker* ....10.00 - 15.00
15404-D *Cotton Baggin'* ....15.00 - 20.00
15420-D *Mississippi Sawyer* ....15.00 - 20.00
15447-D *The Rovin' Gambler* ....15.00 - 20.00
*15468-D *Hog Killing Day* ....15.00 - 20.00
15472-D *Flatwoods* ....15.00 - 20.00
15485-D *Cripple Creek* ....15.00 - 20.00
15516-D *Hell's Broke Loose In Georgia* ....20.00 - 30.00
15562-D *Sal's Gone To The Cider Mill* ....20.00 - 30.00
15589-D *Devilish Mary* ....20.00 - 30.00
15612-D *Sugar In The Gourd* ....20.00 - 30.00
15623-D *New Arkansas Traveler* ....20.00 - 30.00
15640-D *Bully Of The Town No. 2* ....25.00 - 40.00
15665-D *Don't You Cry My Honey* ....25.00 - 40.00
15682-D *Ricketts Hornpipe* ....25.00 - 40.00
15695-D *Giddup Napoleon* ....30.00 - 50.00
15709-D *Fly Around My Pretty Little Miss* ....30.00 - 50.00
15716-D *You've Got To Stop Drinking 'Shine* ...30.00 - 50.00
15730-D *Miss McLeod's Reel* ....30.00 - 50.00
15746-D *Four Cent Cotton* ....40.00 - 60.00
15777-D *McMichen's Breakdown* ....50.00 - 80.00

*(Note: These "descriptive novelty" records credit several artists on the labels; since Tanner's name appears first, they are listed here.)

LUCY TANNER & THE SKILLET LICKERS:
Columbia 15538-D *Rock That Cradle Lucy* .... 20.00 - 30.00

JIMMIE TARLTON (& DARBY); LOUISE J. TARLTON:
Columbia 15629-D *New Birmingham Jail* .... 50.00 - 75.00
   15651-D *Moonshine Blues* .... 75.00 - 100.00
   15763-D *By The Old Oaken Bucket* .... 80.00 - 120.00
Montgomery Ward 4335 *Once I Had A Fortune* .... 10.00 - 15.00
Victor 23665 *Dixie Jail* .... 100.00 - 150.00
   23680 *13 Years In Kilby Prison* .... 100.00 - 150.00
   23700 *Ooze Up To Me* .... 100.00 - 150.00

TATE BROTHERS & (RHODA) HICKS:
Champion 15965 *Medley* .... 10.00 - 15.00
Gennett 7165 *Medley* .... 15.00 - 20.00

TAYLOR'S KENTUCKY BOYS:
Gennett 6130 *Forked Deer* .... 25.00 - 40.00

TAYLOR'S (LOUISIANA) MELODY MAKERS:
Victor 21768 *Big Ball Uptown* .... 15.00 - 20.00
   23613 *'Mid The Shamrock Of Shannon* .... 20.00 - 30.00
   V40261 *On The Bridge At Midnight* .... 20.00 - 30.00

TAYLOR & BUNCH:
Supertone 9352 *Six Months Ain't Long* .... 8.00 - 12.00

TAYLOR and DAVIS:
Vocalion 03056 *I'm Here To Get My Baby Out of Jail*
.... 7.00 - 10.00

TAYLOR-GRIGGS LOUISIANA MELODY MAKERS:
Victor V40083 *Ione* .... 20.00 - 30.00
   V40184 *The Yodeler's Serenade* .... 20.00 - 30.00

TAYLOR, MOORE & BURNETT:
Gennett 6760 *Knoxville Rag* .... 25.00 - 40.00

JIM TAYLOR & BILL SHELBY:
Champion 15730 *It's Sad To Leave You Sweetheart*
.... 10.00 - 15.00
   15772 *The Bald-Headed End Of A Broom* .... 10.00 - 15.00
   15812 *I Ain't Gonna Grieve My Lord Anymore* 10.00 - 15.00
   15855 *The Old Schoolhouse Playground* .... 10.00 - 15.00
   45072 *It's Sad To Leave You Sweetheart* .... 7.00 - 10.00

UNCLE FRANK TEMPLETON:
Bell 1172 *Over The Waves* .... 7.00 - 10.00

TENNESSEE DRIFTERS:
Dot 1001 *Boogie Beat Rag* .... 8.00 - 12.00
   1002 *Mean Ol' Boogie* .... 8.00 - 12.00

TENNESSEE FIDDLERS:
Timely Tunes 1562 *Cottonwood Reel* .... 15.00 - 20.00

TENNESSEE RAMBLERS:
Brunswick 255 *Arkansas Traveler* .... 8.00 - 12.00
   252 *Medley Of Mountain Songs* .... 10.00 - 15.00
   257 *A Fiddlers Contest* .... 10.00 - 15.00
Vocalion 5362 *Give The Fiddler A Dram* .... 20.00 - 30.00
   5398 *In My Dear Old Sunny South* .... 20.00 - 30.00

TENNESSEE TRAVELERS:
Champion 15300 *Forked Deer* .... 15.00 - 25.00

TENNEVA RAMBLERS:
Victor 20861 *The Longest Train* .... 10.00 - 15.00
   21141 *Miss Liza, Poor Gal* .... 15.00 - 20.00
   21289 *The Curtains Of Night* .... 15.00 - 20.00
   21406 *Seven Long Years In Prison* .... 15.00 - 20.00
   21645 *I'm Goin' To Georgia* .... 15.00 - 20.00

JACK TETER:
Paramount 3235 *Silver Threads Among The Gold* ..10.00 - 15.00

NORWOOD TEW:
Bluebird 6553 *Sailorman Blues* ....10.00 - 15.00
   6892 *My Old Crippled Daddy* ....10.00 - 15.00
Bluebird 7288, 7618, 7791, 7950 ....7.00 - 10.00

TEXAS COWBOY BAND:
Supertone 9673 *New Harmony Waltz* ....8.00 - 12.00

TEXAS DRIFTER (See also GOEBEL REEVES):
Decca 5020 *The Yodeling Teacher* ....8.00 - 12.00
   5021 *Cowboy's Lullaby* ....8.00 - 12.00
Melotone 12016 *The Texas Drifter* ....7.00 - 10.00
   12047 *The Oklahoma Kid* ....7.00 - 10.00
   12186 *Bright Sherman Valley* ....7.00 - 10.00
   12214 *Little Joe, The Wrangler* ....7.00 - 10.00
   12232 *Mother-In-Law Blues* ....7.00 - 10.00
   12242 *The Tramp's Mother* ....7.00 - 10.00
   12290 *John Law And The Hobo* ....8.00 - 12.00
   12302 *The Cowboy's Secret* ....8.00 - 12.00
Vocalion 5484 *The Drifter* ....10.00 - 15.00

TEXAS NIGHT HAWKS:
Okeh 45363 *Possum Rag* ....25.00 - 40.00

TEXAS RANGER:
Superior 2774 *Eleven Cent Cotton-Forty Cent Meat*
   ....35.00 - 50.00
   2792 *All Aboard For Blanket Bay* ....35.00 - 50.00
Supertone S-2055 *The Brakeman's Blues* ....7.00 - 10.00

TEXAS RANGERS:
Decca 5022, 5107, 5139, 5183 ....5.00 - 10.00

TEXAS RHYTHM BOYS:
Royalty 600 *Benzedrine Blues* ....10.00 - 15.00

TEXAS TOP HANDS:
Everstate 101 *Bandera Waltz* ....8.00 - 12.00
   112 *Bear Creek Hop* ....8.00 - 12.00
   128 *Low-Down Lonely Blues* ....8.00 - 12.00
Savoy 3011 *Ida Red* ....7.00 - 10.00

GEORGE THOMAS & HIS BOYS/MUSIC:
Champion 15262 *Big Town Fling* ....5.00 - 8.00
   15280 *Larry O'Gaff* ....5.00 - 8.00
   15354 *Haste To The Wedding* ....5.00 - 8.00
   15410 *Leather Breeches* ....5.00 - 8.00
   15434 *Blue Hawaii* ....5.00 - 8.00

GRAYSON THOMAS & WILL LOTTY:
Champion 15395 *Nobody's Darling* ....15.00 - 20.00

THOMPSON, CRANFORD & MILES:
Gennett 6602 *The Blind Man And His Child* ....20.00 - 30.00

THOMPSON & MILES WITH THE RED FOX CHASERS:
Gennett 6914 *Put My Little Shoes Away* ....25.00 - 40.00
   6930 *The Girl I Loved In Sunny Tennessee* ....30.00 - 50.00

BUD THOMPSON:
Crown 3418 *Five Cent Cotton* ....8.00 - 12.00
   3430 *I'm A Fugitive From A Chain Gang* ....8.00 - 12.00
   3489 *The Lie He Wrote Home* ....8.00 - 12.00
   3502 *When The White Azaleas Start Blooming* ....8.00 - 12.00

ERNEST THOMPSON:
Columbia 130-D *Are You From Dixie* ....8.00 - 12.00
   145-D *Lightning Express* ....8.00 - 12.00
   147-D *Little Brown Jug* ....8.00 - 12.00
   153-D *Life's Railway To Heaven* ....8.00 - 12.00
   189-D *Mississippi Sawyer* ....8.00 - 12.00
   190-D *Red Wing* ....8.00 - 12.00
   216-D *In The Baggage Coach Ahead* ....7.00 - 10.00
   15001-D *Weeping Willow Tree* ....15.00 - 20.00
   15002-D *Silly Bill* ....15.00 - 20.00
   15006-D *Whistlin' Rufus* ....15.00 - 20.00
   15007-D *The Old Time Religion* ....15.00 - 20.00

ERNEST E. THOMPSON:
Gennett 7139 *Medley* ....20.00 - 30.00

FLOYD THOMPSON & HIS HOMETOWNERS:
Vocalion 5233 *Sidewalks Of New York* ....10.00 - 15.00
   5236 *Little Brown Jug* ....10.00 - 15.00
   5242 *Oh My Darling Clementine* ....10.00 - 15.00
   5253 *The Trail Of The Lonesome Pine* ....10.00 - 15.00
   5258 *Billy Boy* ....10.00 - 15.00
   5266 *I Wonder How She Did It* ....10.00 - 15.00
   5300 *When The Sunset Turns The Ocean Blue To Gold*
   ....10.00 - 15.00
   5317 *Mountains Of Virginia* ....10.00 - 15.00
   5331 *Red Wing* ....10.00 - 15.00

GEORGIA THOMPSON:
Columbia 15532-D *Cross-Eyed Sue* ....7.00 - 10.00

HANK THOMPSON (& HIS BRAZOS VALLEY BOYS):
Blue Bonnet 107 *My Starry-Eyed Texas Gal* ....10.00 - 15.00
   123 *California Women* ....8.00 - 12.00
Globe 124 *Whoa Sailor!* ....7.00 - 12.00

HUGH THOMPSON:
Crystal 385 *Naggin' Wife* ....- - -

UNCLE JIMMY THOMPSON:
Columbia 15118-D *Billy Wilson* ....10.00 - 15.00
Vocalion 5456 *Lynchburg* ....20.00 - 30.00

THREE 'BACCER TAGS:
Victor 23571 *Ain't Gonna Do It* ....25.00 - 40.00

THREE GEORGIA CRACKERS:
Columbia 15630-D *I've Been Hoodooed* ....10.00 - 15.00
   15653-D *Hannah-My Love* ....10.00 - 15.00

THREE HOWARD BOYS:
Challenge 110 *Down In Tennessee Blues* ....8.00 - 12.00
   304 *Down In Tennessee Blues* ....8.00 - 12.00

THREE KENTUCKY SERENADERS:
Supertone 9246 *Pearl Bryant* ....8.00 - 12.00
   9251 *Please, Papa, Come Home* ....8.00 - 12.00
   9269 *We Will Outshine The Sun* ....8.00 - 12.00

THREE MUSKETEERS:
Bluebird 8129 *Chattanooga Mama* ....5.00 - 8.00

THREE OLD CRONIES:
Vocalion 5134 *Turkey In The Straw* ....7.00 - 10.00
   15305 *Turkey In The Straw* ....7.00 - 10.00

THREE STRIPPED GEARS:
Okeh 45553 *Depression Blues* ....75.00 - 100.00
   45571 *Alabama Blues* ....75.00 - 100.00

THREE TOBACCO TAGS:
Bluebird 6668, 6730, 6853, 6902, 6948, 6999, 7044,
7130, 7163, 7211, 7250, 7312, 7361, 7400, 7448,
7482, 7533, 7692, 7715, 7777, 7877, 7912, 7973 ....7.00 - 10.00
Champion 16480 *The Teacher's Hair Was Red* ......40.00 - 60.00
    16674 *Reno Blues* ....50.00 - 80.00

THREE TWEEDY BOYS/BROTHERS:
Champion 15486 *The Bully Of The Town* ....7.00 - 10.00
    15548 *Sugar In The Gourd* ....7.00 - 10.00
    15689 *Ida Red* ....7.00 - 10.00

THREE VIRGINIANS:
Okeh 45451 *June Tenth Blues* ....30.00 - 50.00

THREE WILLIAMSONS:
Bluebird 7819 *Fiddlers Blues* ....7.00 - 10.00

TOBACCO TAGS:
Bluebird 8396, 8420 ....7.00 - 10.00

TOM & CHUCK:
Victor V40305 *White River Road* ....15.00 - 25.00

TOM & ROY:
Bluebird 5073, 5138, 5198, 5245 ....5.00 - 8.00
Victor 23800 *Grandfather's Clock* ....10.00 - 15.00
    23804 *In My Old Cabin Home* ....10.00 - 15.00
    23813 *Chant Of The Jungle* ....10.00 - 15.00

TOMMIE & WILLIE:
Champion 16034 *By The Old Oak Tree* ....8.00 - 12.00
    16231 *I'm The Last One Left On The Corner* .....10.00 - 15.00
    16240 *By My Side* ....10.00 - 15.00
    16259 *My Canary Has Circles Under His Eyes* .10.00 - 15.00
    16276 *Rocky Mountain Rose* ....10.00 - 15.00
    16301 *When It's Night Time In Nevada* ....10.00 - 15.00
    16314 *If You Can't Sing, Whistle* ....10.00 - 15.00
    16432 *There's A Little Box Of Pine On The 7:29*
    ....10.00 - 15.00
Champion 45006, 45180 ....5.00 - 10.00
Gennett 7246 *By The Old Oak Tree* ....10.00 - 20.00

JED THOMPKINS:
Harmony 5096-H *Life's Railway To Heaven* ....5.00 - 8.00
    5099-H *Mississippi Sawyer* ....5.00 - 8.00
    5101-H *Coon Crap Game* ....5.00 - 8.00
Velvet Tone 7034-V *Mississippi Sawyer* ....5.00 - 8.00

JACK TOOMBS:
Excello 2033 *Two Cheaters In Love* ....5.00 - 10.00
    2041 *My Imagination* ....5.00 - 10.00
Speed 111 *Pin Ball Fever* ....10.00 - 15.00

WELBY TOOMEY:
Gennett 6005 *Roving Gambler* ....12.00 - 16.00
    6025 *Little Brown Jug* ....12.00 - 16.00
Silvertone 8151 *Roving Gambler* ....7.00 - 10.00
Supertone 9245 *Little Brown Jug* ....7.00 - 10.00
    9252 *Roving Gambler* ....7.00 - 10.00

GEORGE TOON & THE TENNESSEE DRIFTERS (See also TENNESSEE DRIFTERS):
Dot 1008 *That There Gal O' Mine* ....8.00 - 12.00

MITCHELL TOROK:
FBC 102 *Nacogdoches County Line* ....15.00 - 20.00
    115 *Piney Woods Boogie* ....15.00 - 20.00

TRAVELERS:
Decca 5453, 5461 ....5.00 - 8.00

CARL TRIMBLE:
Champion 16717 *Down On The Old Plantation* ..... 20.00 - 30.00
    45050 *In A Lonely Little Cottage* ....7.00 - 10.00

ERNEST TUBB:
Bluebird 6693 *The Passing Of Jimmie Rodgers* ... 100.00 - 150.00
    7000 *Since That Black Cat Crossed My Path* .. 100.00 - 150.00
    8899 *Mean Old Bed Bug Blues* .... 80.00 - 120.00
    8966 *My Mother Is Lonely* .... 75.00 - 100.00
Decca 5825, 5846, 5900, 5910, 5920, 5938, 5958,
5976, 5993, 6007, 6023, 6040 ....5.00 - 10.00

TUNE WRANGLERS:
Bluebird 6310, 6326, 6365, 6403, 6421, 6438, 6513,
6554, 6655, 6692, 6703, 6828, 6856, 6900, 6947,
6962, 6982, 7030, 7076, 7089, 7200, 7272, 7336,
7413, 7571, 7612, 7673, 7703, 7766, 7830, 7867,
7947, 7966, 7972, 7992, 8014 ....5.00 - 10.00

BUCK TURNER:
Title issued contemporaneously on Banner, Melotone, Oriole,
    Perfect, and Romeo: *Sing Sing Blues* ....8.00 - 12.00

CAL TURNER:
Champion 15524 *The Rowan County Feud* .... 10.00 - 15.00
    15544 *The Death Of J. B. Marcum* .... 10.00 - 15.00
    15587 *Only A Tramp* .... 10.00 - 15.00
    15630 *By The Silvery Rio Grande* .... 10.00 - 15.00

DAVE TURNER:
Supertone 9318 *She'll Be Comin 'Round The Mountain*
    ....7.00 - 10.00
    9319 *That Old Covered Bridge* ....7.00 - 10.00
    9374 *Many Troubles Blues* ....8.00 - 12.00
    9560 *We've Been Chums For Fifty Years* ....8.00 - 12.00

HOBO JACK TURNER:
(Note: Various recordings issued on Diva, Harmony and Velvet
    Tone under this name are of little interest or value.)

JACK TURNER:
Gennett 7305 *Honey Stay In Your Own Backyard* .. 20.00 - 30.00

LEMUEL TURNER:
Victor 21292 *'Way Down Yonder Blues* .... 20.00 - 30.00
    V40052 *Jake Bottle Blues* .... 20.00 - 30.00

BILL TUTTLE:
Columbia 15697-D *Gamblin' Bill Driv' On* .... 10.00 - 15.00

FRANK TUTTLE:
Velvet Tone 2148-V *The Prison Fire* .... 5.00 - 8.00

TWEEDY BROTHERS (See also THREE TWEEDY BOYS/BROTHERS):
Champion 16048 *Home Brew Rag* .... 15.00 - 20.00
Gennett 6447 *The Bully Of The Town* .... 8.00 - 12.00
    6483 *Sugar In The Gourd* .... 8.00 - 12.00
    6529 *Shortnin' Bread* .... 8.00 - 12.00
    6604 *Buckwheat Batter* .... 8.00 - 12.00
    6734 *Dixie* .... 8.00 - 12.00
    7240 *Home Brew Rag* .... 15.00 - 25.00
Superior 2784 *Home Brew Rag* .... 20.00 - 30.00
Supertone 9166 *Ida Red* .... 8.00 - 12.00
    9174 *Shortnin' Bread* .... 8.00 - 12.00

UNCLE BUD & HIS PLOWBOYS:
Oriole 8170 *Five Cent Cotton*.....................5.00 -   8.00

CHAS. UNDERWOOD (Acc. by HACK'S STRING BAND):
Champion 16144 *Black Snake Moan*.......................30.00 -   50.00
  16362 *I Want My Rib*.......................30.00 -   50.00

MARION UNDERWOOD (& SAM HARRIS):
Gennett 6155 *A Picture From Life's Other Side* .....20.00 -   30.00
  6177 *Just As The Sun Went Down* ....20.00 -   30.00
  6240 *Coal Creek March* ....35.00 -   50.00

UNIVERSAL COWBOYS (See also DICK REINHART):
Vocalion 04987 *Steel Guitar Honky Tonk*.................5.00 -   8.00
  05040 *Little Rubber Dolly* ....5.00 -   8.00
  05107 *Cow Town Swing* ....5.00 -   8.00
  05189 *Night Spot Blues* ....5.00 -   8.00

VAGABONDS:
Bluebird 5072, 5103, 5124, 5137, 5197, 5282, 5297,
  5300, 5315, 5335, 5381, 5402, 5588, 6184 ....5.00 -   12.00
Victor 23801 *In The Sleepy Hills Of Tennessee* ......20.00 -   30.00
  23809 *The Old Rugged Cross*...........................20.00 -   30.00
  23820 *Ninety-Nine Years* ....20.00 -   30.00
  23849 *My Pretty Quadroon* ....20.00 -   30.00
  23855 *In The Valley Of Yesterday*.....................20.00 -   30.00

VAGABOND YODELER:
Superior 2793 *No More To Ride The Rails* ....40.00 -   60.00

VAL & PETE:
Okeh 45224 *Yodel Blues*........................5.00 -   8.00

VANCE'S TENNESSEE BREAKDOWNERS:
Okeh 45151 *Tennessee Breakdown* ....30.00 -   50.00

VASS FAMILY:
Decca 5425 *Jimmy Randall* ....5.00 -   10.00
  5432 *Deep Blue Sea*........................5.00 -   10.00

BILLY VEST:
Titles issued on Banner, Conqueror, Melotone, Oriole, Perfect, and
  Romeo: *Big City Jail, Dear Old Texas*.................6.00 -   10.00
Columbia 15669-D *She'll Never Find Another Daddy Like Me*
  ....10.00 -   15.00
  15692-D *Billy's Blue Yodel* ....10.00 -   15.00

VIRGINIA DANDIES:
Crown 3145 *God's Getting Worried* ....15.00 -   20.00
Paramount 3305 *Mid The Green Fields Of Virginia*
  ....20.00 -   30.00

VIRGINIA MOUNTAIN BOOMERS:
Gennett 6567 *Ramblin' Reckless Hobo* ....20.00 -   30.00
  6687 *Cousin Sally Brown* ....20.00 -   30.00
Supertone 9305 *Rambling Reckless Hobo*...............15.00 -   20.00
  9406 *East Tennessee Polka* ....15.00 -   20.00

VIRGINIA POSSUM TAMERS:
Champion 15484 *The Wreck On The Mountain Road*
  ....10.00 -   15.00
  15522 *Turkey In The Straw*........................10.00 -   15.00
  15566 *Weeping Willow Tree*........................10.00 -   15.00
  15609 *The Blind Man And His Child* ....10.00 -   15.00
  15672 *Something Wrong With My Gal*..............10.00 -   15.00
  15769 *The Virginia Possum Tamers Makin' Licker*
  ....12.00 -   18.00

  15790 *Virginia Bootleggers*.....................12.00 -   18.00
  15809 *The Virginia Possum Tamers Makin' Licker Part 3/4*
  ....12.00 -   18.00
  15925 *Put My Little Shoes Away* ....10.00 -   15.00
  45079 *Virginia Bootleggers* ....7.00 -   10.00

VIRGINIA RAMBLERS:
Timely Tunes 1561 *Rag Time Annie* ....15.00 -   25.00

WILD BILL WADE:
Okeh 45550 *Weeping Daddy Blues* ....15.00 -   20.00

GEORGE WADE & CAROLINIANS:
Bluebird 7904 *Long And Bony*........................7.00 -   10.00
Columbia 15515-D *When We Go A-Courtin'* ....10.00 -   15.00

JIMMY WAKELY:
Capitol (most issues)........................4.00 -   8.00
Sterling 213 *Cool Water* ....10.00 -   15.00
Sterling 214 *I've Got Nuggets In My Pocket* ....10.00 -   15.00

GEORGE WALBURN'S FOOT-SCORCHERS; GEORGE WALBURN & EMMETT HETHCOX:
Columbia 15721-D *Dixie Flyer* ....75.00 -   100.00
Okeh 45024 *Lee County Blues* ....30.00 -   50.00
  45066 *Home Brew* ....30.00 -   50.00
  45178 *Kansas City Railroad Blues* ....30.00 -   50.00
  45305 *Decatur Street Rag*........................40.00 -   60.00

WALKER'S CORBIN RAMBLERS:
Vocalion 02468 *Nobody's Business*........................20.00 -   30.00
  02667 *Ned Went A-Fishin'* ....20.00 -   30.00
  02678 *The Dying Tramp*...............................30.00 -   50.00
  02719 *I Had A Dream*...............................20.00 -   30.00
  02771 *Dark Town Strutters Ball* ....20.00 -   30.00
  02790 *Stone Mountain Toddle* ....20.00 -   30.00

DAVE WALKER:
Superior 2688 *Someone Owns A Cottage* ....15.00 -   20.00

FRANCIS/FRANKIE WALLACE:
(Note: Most records issued under these names-pseudonyms for
  Frank Marvin-are of minimal value.)
Edison 52356 *Away Out On The Mountain* ....15.00 -   20.00
  52387 *Drowsy Moonlight* ....10.00 -   20.00
Paramount 3180 *Yodeling Them Blues Away* ....8.00 -   12.00
  3190 *Mississippi Moonshine* ....8.00 -   12.00
  3203 *I'm Riding The Blinds On A Train Headed West*
  ....10.00 -   15.00
  3209 *I Don't Work For A Living*.........................5.00 -   8.00
  3211 *Blue Yodel No. 5* ....7.00 -   10.00
  3272 *Jimmie Rodger's Blue Yodel* ....5.00 -   8.00
Supertone 9082 *Blue Yodel No. 2* ....5.00 -   8.00

JERRY WALLACE:
Superior 2577 *Waiting For The Railroad Train* .....15.00 -   20.00
  2643 *O Jailer Bring Back That Key*...................15.00 -   20.00
  2677 *Hand Me Down My Walking Cane* ....15.00 -   20.00

"DOCK" WALSH:
Columbia 15047-D *The East Bound Train* ....10.00 -   15.00
  15057-D *The Educated Man* ....10.00 -   15.00
  15075-D *We Courted In The Rain* ....8.00 -   12.00
  15094-D *In The Pines* ....10.00 -   15.00
  15105-D *Traveling Man* ....10.00 -   15.00
Victor V40237 *Bathe In The Beautiful Pool*......30.00 -   50.00
  V40325 *We're Just Plain Folks* ....30.00 -   50.00

WALTER FAMILY:
Champion 16595 *Too Young To Get Married* ....150.00 - 200.00
   16622 *Flying Cloud Waltz* ....150.00 - 200.00
   16643 *Patty On The Turnpike* ....150.00 - 200.00
   16653 *Shaker Ben* ....150.00 - 200.00

WANNER & JENKINS/WHITE:
Champion 16306 *The Pretty Quadroon* ....20.00 - 30.00
   16348 *The Little Old Church In The Valley* ....20.00 - 30.00
Columbia 15728-D *A Sweetheart's Promise* ....20.00 - 30.00
Superior 2734 *That Little Boy Of Mine* ....15.00 - 25.00

ENOS WANNER:
Champion 15791 *Over The Hills To The Poorhouse* 8.00 - 12.00
   15810 *Don't Grieve Your Mother* ....8.00 - 12.00
   15830 *Put Me Off At Buffalo* ....8.00 - 12.00
   15898 *Crepe On The Little Cabin Door* ....8.00 - 12.00
   16052 *The Prison Warden's Secret* ....10.00 - 15.00
   16098 *Two Little Girls In Blue* ....10.00 - 15.00
Superior 2722 *Strawberry Roan* ....20.00 - 30.00

A. E. WARD & HIS PLOW BOYS:
Columbia 15734-D *Going To Leave Old Arkansas* .75.00 - 100.00

CROCKETT WARD & HIS BOYS:
Okeh 45179 *Deadheads And Suckers* ....35.00 - 50.00
   45304 *Ain't That Trouble In Mind?* ....35.00 - 50.00

PRESTON WARD:
Kentucky 540, 541 ....3.00 - 6.00

TOMMY WARD:
Superior 2689 *Mississippi River Blues* ....40.00 - 60.00

PAUL WARMACK & HIS GULLY JUMPERS:
Victor V40009 *Robertson County* ....30.00 - 50.00
   V40067 *Little Red Caboose Behind The Train* ...25.00 - 40.00

HANK WARNER:
Banner 5-11-61 *The Death Of Hughey P. Long* ....7.00 - 10.00
(Note: Probably also issued on Melotone, Oriole, Perfect, and Romeo.)

YODELIN' JIMMY WARNER:
Champion 15562 *Blue Yodel No. 2* ....7.00 - 10.00

WASHBOARD WONDERS:
Bluebird 6455 *You Gotta Eat Your Spinach, Baby* ....6.00 - 10.00
   6463 *All Quiet On The Old Front Porch* ....6.00 - 10.00
   6464 *It Ain't Right* ....6.00 - 10.00
   6495 *Feather Your Nest* ....6.00 - 10.00
   6526 *Meet Me At The Ice House* ....6.00 - 10.00
   6648 *Apple Tree* ....6.00 - 10.00
   6671 *Roll Your Own* ....6.00 - 10.00
   6737 *You're Everything Sweet* ....6.00 - 10.00
   6761 *Breeze* ....4.00 - 6.00

W. L. "RUSTIC" WATERS:
Columbia 15705-D *Sweet Nora Shannon* ....8.00 - 12.00

WATKINS BAND:
Victor 21405 *Gideon* ....7.00 - 10.00

DR. CLAUDE WATSON & L. W. McCREIGHTON:
Okeh 45020 *Chicken Reel* ....20.00 - 30.00
   45034 *Ballin' The Jack And Nigger Blues* ....20.00 - 30.00

GEORGE P. WATSON:
Edison 51530 *Love's A Magic Spell* ....5.00 - 8.00
   51691 *Medley Of J. K. Emmett's Yodel Songs* .....5.00 - 8.00
Victor 20190, 20247 ....3.00 - 5.00

HARVEY WATSON:
Challenge 328 *Drunken Hiccoughs* ....8.00 - 12.00
   329 *Bright Sherman Valley* ....8.00 - 12.00
   330 *Weeping Willow Tree* ....8.00 - 12.00
Champion 15299 *A Mother's Advice* ....7.00 - 10.00
   15333 *He Lives On High* ....7.00 - 10.00
   15334 *Weeping Willow Tree* ....8.00 - 12.00
   15356 *Drunken Hiccoughs* ....8.00 - 12.00
   15428 *The Dying Cowboy* ....7.00 - 10.00
Supertone 9243 *Weeping Willow Tree* ....8.00 - 12.00
   9263 *He Lives On High* ....7.00 - 10.00

LUIS WATSON:
Supertone 9167 *Home Sweet Home* ....7.00 - 10.00
   9175 *Wandering Boy* ....7.00 - 10.00

TOM WATSON:
Silvertone 3262 *Georgia Railroad* ....7.00 - 10.00

WATTS & WILSON:
Paramount 3006 *The Sporting Cowboy* ....100.00 - 150.00
   3007 *The Night Express* ....100.00 - 150.00
   3019 *The Chain Gang Special* ....100.00 - 150.00

OLD POP WATTS:
Phamous 701 *Kissin' And Huggin'* ....- - -

WILMER WATTS & THE LONELY EAGLES:
Broadway 8248 *Knockin' Down Casey Jones* ......100.00 - 150.00
Paramount 3210 *Knockin' Down Casey Jones* .....100.00 - 150.00
   3232 *Charles Gitaw* ....100.00 - 150.00
   3242 *Banjo Sam* ....100.00 - 150.00
   3247 *She's A Hard Boiled Rose* ....100.00 - 150.00
   3254 *Cotton Mill Blues* ....100.00 - 150.00
   3271 *Banjo Sam* ....100.00 - 150.00
   3282 *Sleepy Desert* ....75.00 - 100.00
   3299 *Bonnie Bess* ....75.00 - 100.00

WEAVER BROTHERS:
Columbia 15487-D *Prison Sorrows* ....10.00 - 15.00

WEAVER & WIGGINS:
Broadway 8112 *The Sporting Cowboy* ....75.00 - 100.00
   8113 *The Night Express* ....75.00 - 100.00
   8114 *The Chain Gang Special* ....75.00 - 100.00

J. D. WEAVER:
Okeh 45016 *Arkansas Traveler* ....8.00 - 12.00

WEBER & BROOKS:
Superior 2740 *The Utah Trail* ....20.00 - 30.00

DAN WEBER:
Superior 2527 *Fair Florella* ....25.00 - 40.00
   2582 *Worried Daddy Blues* ....35.00 - 50.00

SAM WEBER:
Superior 2822 *My Ozark Mountain Home* ....30.00 - 50.00

WEEMS STRING BAND:
Columbia 15300-D *Greenback Dollar* ....20.00 - 30.00

WELLING TRIO:
Champion 16035 *Will The Circle Be Unbroken* .....10.00 - 15.00
   16054 *Wait Till The Sun Shines Nellie* ....10.00 - 15.00
   16078 *Hallelujah All The Way* ....10.00 - 15.00
   16120 *School Days* ....10.00 - 15.00
Champion 45123, 45171 ....5.00 - 10.00
Gennett 7291 *Tie Me To Your Apron Strings Again* 15.00 - 25.00

LYRIC
Ca. 1918 (78)

MANDEL
Early 1920s (78)
Scarce Chicago label

MELODICS
Early 1920s (78)
(7-inch record)

MELOTONE
Ca. 1937 (78)
Sought-after blues record by GEORGE NOBLE

MERITT
Ca. 1927 (78)
Rare Kansas City label

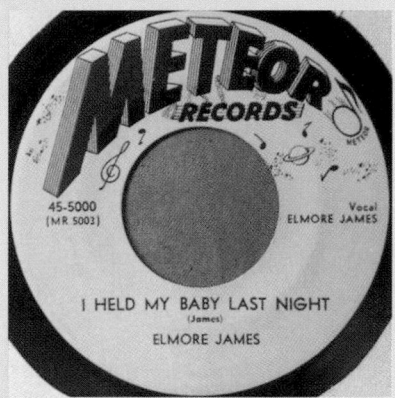

METEOR
Mid-1950s (45)
Sought-after blues record by
ELMORE JAMES

M-G-M
Late 1950s
Jacket for Hank Williams EP

M-G-M
Ca. 1960
Picture sleeve for Connie Francis (45) record

MONUMENT
Late 1950s
Picture sleeve for Roy Orbison (45) record

MOXIE
Ca. 1921 (78)
Exploitation record for soft drink

MOZART
Ca. 1917 (78)
St. Louis label

OKEH
Ca. 1924 (78)
Rare jazz record

OKEH ("Truetone")
Ca. 1926 (78)
Scarce jazz record

OKEH (special purpose record)
Ca. 1925 (78)
Fund-raiser for Naval Relief Fund

OLD SWING-MASTER
Ca. 1950 (78)
Blues on Chicago label

OLD TOWN
Early 1950s (78)
Sought-after vocal group record

OLD TOWN
Mid-1950s (78)

OLYMPIC
Ca. 1923 (78)

OPERATOR
Ca. 1942 (78)
Patriotic issue by jukebox operators

ORIOLE
Ca. 1928 (78)

OXFORD (one-sided)
Ca. 1914 (78)

PARROT
Early 1950s (78)
Blues record by Curtis Jones

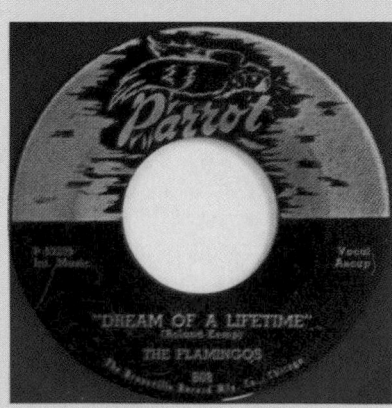

PARROT (red vinyl)
Early 1950s (45)
Sought-after vocal group record

PATHE ACTUELLE (English label)
Ca. 1926 (78)
English label, but issued many U.S. records

PENNINGTON
Ca. 1924 (78)
Early Duke Ellington on this scarce label

PERFECT
Mid-1920c (78)
Label often used orange shellac

PHILLIPS INTERNATIONAL
Mid-1950s (78)
Memphis Sun-related label

PURETONE
Ca. 1924 (78)

PURITAN
Ca. 1923 (78)
Scarce jazz record

Q.R.S.
Ca. 1930 (78)
Scarce label

RAINBOW
Early 1950s (78)
Sought-after vocal group

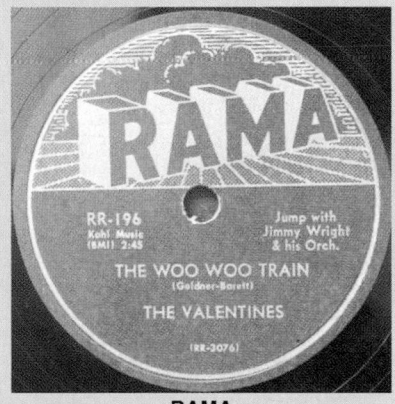

RAMA
Mid-1950s (78)
Rhythm & blues label

RADIEX
Ca. 1928 (78)

RCA VICTOR (picture record)
Ca. 1933 (78) (12-inch)
Tabloid version of show

RCA VICTOR (picture record) (flip side)
Ca. 1933 (78) (12-inch)
Tabloid version of show

RCA VICTOR (picture record)
Ca. 1933 (78) (12-inch)
"Music In The Air"

RCA VICTOR (picture record) (flip side)
Ca. 1933 (78) (12-inch)
"Music In The Air" cast members

RCA VICTOR (picture record)
Ca. 1933 (78) (10-inch)
Jimmie Rodgers picture disc

RCA VICTOR (picture record) (flip side)
Ca. 1933 (78) (10-inch)
Rodgers' records listed

RCA VICTOR (Whiteman picture disc)
Ca. 1933 (78) (12-inch)
"A Night with Paul Whiteman"

RCA VICTOR
(Whiteman pic. disc, flip side)
Ca. 1933 (78) (12-inch)

RCA VICTOR
Ca. 1957 Jacket for Elvis Presley's
"Perfect for Parties" EP

RCA VICTOR
Ca. 1957 Picture sleeve for Elvis' 45RPM
"All Shook Up"

RED ROBIN
Mid-1950s (78)
Rhythm & blues label

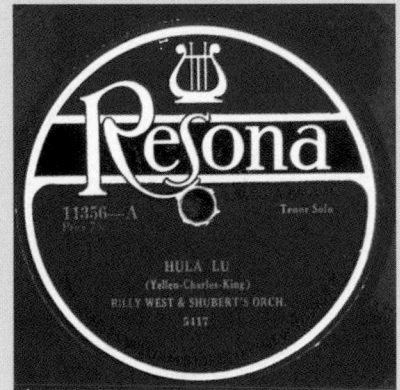

RESONA
Ca. 1923 (78)

RISHELL
Ca. 1918 (78)

ROSS STORES
Ca. 1924 (78)

ROYAL ROOST
Mid-1950s (78)

ROYALTY
Ca. 1950 (78)

ROYCROFT
Ca. 1930 (78)

SAVOY
Ca. 1930 (78)
Rare Gennett-related label

SCOTTIE
Ca. 1959 (45)

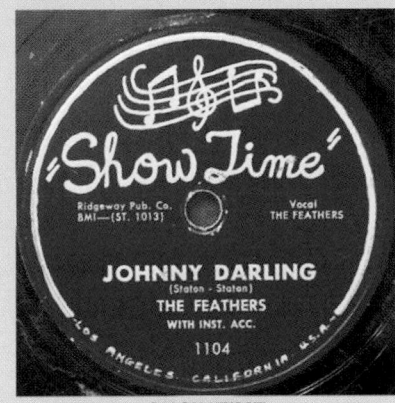

SHOW TIME
Mid-1950s (78)

SILVER SCREEN
Mid-1920s (78) (California label)

SILVERTONE (one-sided)
Ca. 1917 (78)

SILVERTONE (one-sided)
Ca. 1916 (78)

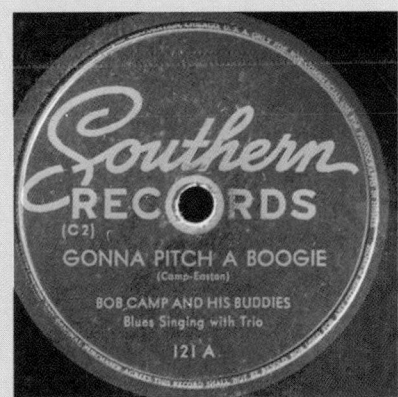

SOUTHERN
Ca. 1950 (78)

STARR
Ca. 1916 (78)
Gennett-related label

STATES
Mid-1950s (78)
Rhythm & blues label

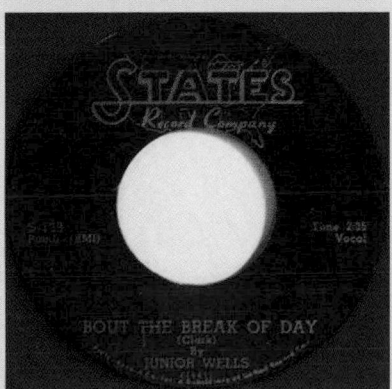

STATES (red vinyl)
Early 1950s (45)
Sought-after blues by Junior Wells

SUN (sample record)
Early 1950s (78)

SUN
Early 1950s
(78) scarce early issue by Handy Jackson

SUN
Ca. 1955 (78)
Sought-after Elvis Presley record

SUNRISE
Ca. 1930 (78)
Grey Gull-affiliated label

SUNRISE
Ca. 1933 (78)
Scarce RCA Victor-affiliated label

SUPREME
Ca. 1926 (78)
Grey Gull-affiliated label

SWAN
Ca. 1961
Jacket for Freddy Cannon LP

SWAN
Ca. 1964
Picture sleeve for Beatles (45) record

SYMPHONOLA
Ca. 1919 (78) (9-inch record)

TALENT
Ca. 1950 (78)
Dallas, Texas label

TIMELY
Early 1950s (78)

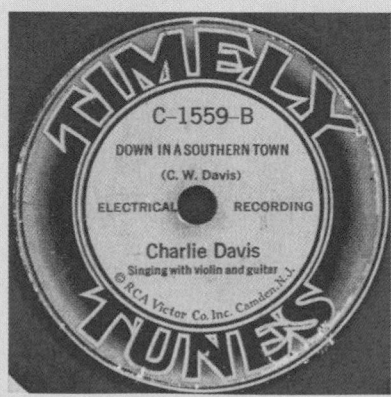

TIMELY TUNES
Ca. 1931 (78)
RCA Victor product

HANK WILLIAMS:

(Note: Some issues on MGM label are credited as by Luke The Drifter.)

MGM 10033, 10073, 10124, 10171, 10212,
10226, 10271 ....7.00 -   12.00
MGM 10328, 10352, 10832 ....5.00 -   10.00
MGM 10401, 10434, 10461, 10506, 10560, 10609,
10645, 10696, 10760, 10813, 10904, 10961,
11000, 11054, 11100, 11160, 11202, 11283,
11318, 11366, 11416 ....5.00 -   10.00
MGM 11479, 11533, 11574, 11628, 11707,
11768, 11861 ....7.00 -   12.00
MGM 11975 *Message To My Mother* ....8.00 -   12.00
  12029 *Alone And Forsaken* ....8.00 -   12.00
  12077 *Someday You'll Call My Name* ....8.00 -   12.00
  12127 *Thank God* ....8.00 -   12.00
  12185 *Thy Burdens Are Greater Than Mine* ....8.00 -   12.00
  12244 *I Wish I Had A Nickel* ....10.00 -   15.00

(Note: Early issues, to about 10401, designated "Metrolite," are later pressings; little difference in premium between the "original" and subsequent pressings exist.)

Sterling 201 *Never Again (Will I Knock On Your Door)*
....100.00 -   150.00
  204 *Wealth Won't Save Your Soul* ....100.00 -   150.00
  208 *I Don't Care (If Tomorrow Never Comes)* 100.00 -   150.00
  210 *Pan American* ....75.00 -   100.00

(Note: Many of Hank Williams' records were issued as 45 RPM, EPs, and LPs. See also the **RHYTHM & BLUES, ETC.** section.)

MARC WILLIAMS:

Brunswick 240 *Willie The Weeper* ....8.00 -   12.00
  244 *The Cowboy's Dream* ....7.00 -   10.00
  269 *Jesse James* ....8.00 -   12.00
  304 *Sam Bass* ....8.00 -   12.00
  377 *The Cowboy's Last Wish* ....8.00 -   12.00
  430 *Cowboy Jack* ....8.00 -   12.00
  497 *The Dying Ranger* ....8.00 -   12.00
  544 *Cole Younger* ....8.00 -   12.00
  564 *The Boys In Blue* ....8.00 -   12.00
Decca 5010 *Roy Bean* ....10.00 -   15.00
  5011 *Sioux Indians* ....10.00 -   15.00
  5012 *Old Montana* ....10.00 -   15.00
  5106 *Old Chism Trail* ....5.00 -   8.00
  5196 *When They Changed My Name To A Number*
....5.00 -   8.00
  5216 *My Blue Heaven* ....5.00 -   8.00
  5327 *William And Mary* ....5.00 -   8.00
Supertone 2051 *The Crepe Upon The Little Cabin Door*
....8.00 -   12.00

MARVIN WILLIAMS (THE SUNSHINE YODELER):

Okeh 45467 *Can't Sleep In Your Barn Tonight, Mister*
....8.00 -   12.00
  45483 *Back Where The Blue Bonnets Grow* ....8.00 -   12.00

ZEKE WILLIAMS:

Vocalion 03755 *Breeze* ....5.00 -   8.00
  03892 *The Cowboy's Dream* ....5.00 -   8.00
  03635 *Westward Ho* ....5.00 -   8.00
  04000 *One More Ride* ....5.00 -   8.00

WILLIAMSON BROTHERS & CURRY:

Okeh 45108 *Cumberland Gap* ....50.00 -   75.00
  45127 *Gonna Die With My Hammer In My Hand*
....50.00 -   75.00
  45146 *Lonesome Road Blues* ....50.00 -   75.00

BOB WILLS & SLEEPY JOHNSON:

Titles issued on Banner, Melotone, Oriole, Perfect, and Romeo (all numbered 6-11-58): *Harmony; Smith's Reel* ..... 30.00 -   50.00

BOB WILLS & HIS TEXAS PLAYBOYS:

The Antones 501 *Have I Stayed Away Too Long?* .. 10.00 -   15.00
(Note: Above is limited issue for Bob Wills Fan Club. There are others, of like value and interest.)
Columbia (most issues)...4.00 -   7.00
MGM (most issues)..5.00 -   8.00
Okeh (most issues)...5.00 -   8.00
Vocalion 03076 *St. Louis Blues* ....10.00 -   15.00
  03086 *Mexicali Rose* ....10.00 -   15.00
  03096 *Osage Stomp* ....10.00 -   15.00
  03139 *Black And Blue Rag* ....10.00 -   15.00
  03173 *Wang Wang Blues* ....10.00 -   15.00
  03206 *I Ain't Got Nobody* ....8.00 -   12.00
  03230 *Blue River* ....8.00 -   12.00
  03264 *Never No More Blues* ....8.00 -   12.00
  03295 *Oklahoma Rag* ....8.00 -   12.00
  03343 *Trouble In Mind* ....7.00 -   10.00
  03344 *Basin Street Blues* ....7.00 -   10.00
  03361 *Fan It* ....7.00 -   10.00
  03394 *Steel Guitar Rag* ....7.00 -   10.00
  03424 *She's Killing Me* ....7.00 -   10.00
  03451 *Right Or Wrong* ....7.00 -   10.00
  03492 *Mean Mama Blues* ....7.00 -   10.00
  03537 *Too Busy*...7.00 -   10.00
  03578 *Swing Blues No. 2* ....7.00 -   10.00
  03597 *Bleeding Hearted Blues* ....7.00 -   10.00
  03614 *White Heat* ....7.00 -   10.00
  03659 *Rosetta*..7.00 -   10.00
  03693 *The New St. Louis Blues*...........................7.00 -   10.00
  03924 *Maiden's Prayer* ....6.00 -   10.00
  03977 *Sunbonnet Sue* ....6.00 -   10.00
  04132 *Black Rider*...6.00 -   10.00
  04184 *Empty Bed Blues* ....6.00 -   10.00
  04275 *Gambling Polka Dot Blues* ....6.00 -   10.00
  04325 *Tulsa Stomp*...5.00 -   8.00
  04387 *Loveless Love* ....5.00 -   8.00
  04439 *Moonlight And Roses* ....5.00 -   8.00
  04515 *Oh, Lady Be Good*....................................5.00 -   8.00
  04566 *That's What I Like 'Bout The South*..........5.00 -   8.00
  04625 *Whoa, Babe* ....5.00 -   8.00
Vocalion 04755, 04839, 04934, 04999, 05079,
05161, 05228, 05282..5.00 -   10.00

JOHNNIE LEE WILLS:

Bullet 696, 700, 710, 711, 717, 721, 724, 726,
737, 741, 743...5.00 -   10.00

FRANK WILSON & HIS BLUE RIDGE MOUNTAIN TRIO:

Columbia 15372-D *Katy-Did Waltz*........................15.00 -   20.00

JIMMIE WILSON'S CATFISH STRING BAND; JIMMIE WILSON:

Okeh 45019 *Let Me Call You Sweetheart* ....15.00 -   20.00
  45029 *Over The Waves* ....15.00 -   20.00
Victor V40163 *Catfish Whiskers* ....10.00 -   15.00
  V40216 *Catfish Medley March*............................15.00 -   20.00
  V40240 *Polecat Creek* ....20.00 -   30.00

TOMMY WILSON:

Vocalion 5262 *The Sinking Of The Vestris* ....8.00 -   12.00

JUSTIN WINFIELD:
Gennett 6619 *The New River Train* ....25.00 - 40.00
   6733 *Say, Darling, Say* ....25.00 - 40.00

WING'S ROCKY MOUNTAIN RAMBLERS:
Champion 16808 *Jackson County Rag* ....50.00 - 75.00
   16819 *Whiskers*...50.00 - 75.00
   45019 *Ragged Ann*...15.00 - 20.00

F. WINGATE:
Supertone 9121 *Sleep, Baby, Sleep* ....5.00 - 8.00
   9122 *Emmett's Cuckoo Song* ....5.00 - 8.00

WISE STRING BAND:
Vocalion 5360 *Yellow Dog Blues* ....50.00 - 80.00

HASKELL WOLFBERGER:
Vocalion 5390 *My Little Girl* ....10.00 - 15.00

WONDER STATE HARMONISTS:
Vocalion 5275 *Turnip Greens* ....8.00 - 12.00
   5291 *On The Wing*..8.00 - 12.00
   5346 *My Castle On The Nile* ....8.00 - 12.00

SMOKY WOOD & HIS WOOD CHIPS:
Bluebird 7660, 7729 ....5.00 - 10.00

JACK WOODCLIFF:
Paramount 3280 *I Wonder If She Cares To See Me Now*
....20.00 - 30.00

JAKE WOODFIELD:
Crown 3103 *There's A Mother Old And Gray Who Needs Me Now*
....10.00 - 15.00

WOODIE BROTHERS:
Victor 23579 *Like Likker Better Than Me* ....40.00 - 60.00

EPPHRIAM WOODIE & THE HENPECKED HUSBANDS:
Columbia 15564-D *Last Gold Dollar*.........................8.00 - 12.00

NORMAN WOODLIEFF:
Gennett 6824 *Brace Up And Be A Man*....................25.00 - 40.00

FRANK WOODS:
Okeh *Canadian Husking Bee/Money Musk*.................. - -

LAWRENCE WOODS:
Champion 16517 *The Cyclone Of Rycove* ....40.00 - 60.00

SHEB WOOLEY (& THE CALUMET INDIANS):
Blue Bonnet 124 *Lazy Mazy* ....15.00 - 25.00
   125 *Peeping Through The Keyhole* ....15.00 - 25.00
   126 *Your Papa Ain't Steppin' Anymore* ....15.00 - 25.00
Bullet 603 *Oklahoma Honky Tonk Gal* ....10.00 - 15.00
MGM 10304, 10363, 10436, 10697, 10960, 11059,
   11180, 11308, 11272 ....7.00 - 10.00

KYLE WOOTEN:
Okeh 45511 *Lumber Camp Blues*..........................30.00 - 50.00
   45526 *Choking Blues* ....30.00 - 50.00

WORKMAN, RAMSEY & WOLFE:
Gennett 6659 *The South Salon Quadrille* ....20.00 - 30.00

W O W O DOWN HOMERS (See also THE DOWN HOMERS):
Vogue 786 *Boogie Woogie Yodel* ....50.00 - 75.00

WRIGHT & McNEW (THE HOOSIER HAWAIIANS):
Champion 16336 *The Utah Trail*...............................15.00 - 20.00

CECIL "ROWDY" WRIGHT:
Flexo 8-964-1 *The Strawberry Roan* ....15.00 - 25.00
(Note: Above is a small, flexible record, pressed of green plastic.)

EARL WRIGHT (Acc. by THE ARKANSAS CORN DODGERS):
Champion 16382 *My Ozark Mountain Home* ....25.00 - 40.00

WYATT & BRANDON:
Columbia 15523-D *Evalina* ....15.00 - 20.00

WYOMING COWBOY (CHARLES BAKER):
Champion 16724 *Utah Carroll* ....20.00 - 30.00
   16737 *Curly Joe* ....25.00 - 40.00
Champion 45044, 45052 ....7.00 - 10.00

SKEETS YANEY:
Town & Country 504, 506 ....7.00 - 10.00
MGM (most issues) ....5.00 - 8.00

IRA & EUGENE YATES:
Columbia 15581-D *Sarah Jane* ....30.00 - 50.00

JIMMY YATES' BOLL WEEVILS:
Victor 21723 *Smiles* ....20.00 - 30.00
   V40065 *Bloody War* ....25.00 - 40.00

YELLOW JACKETS:
Champion 16070 *Heel And Toe Polka*....................10.00 - 15.00
   16161 *Medley* ....10.00 - 15.00
Gennett 7262 *Medley* ....10.00 - 15.00
Vocalion 03914 *Swinging Rhythm*...........................5.00 - 8.00
   03976 *Willie Blow Your Blower* ....5.00 - 8.00
   04038 *Columbus Stockade Blues* ....5.00 - 8.00

YODELING TWINS (GARNER ECKLER & ROLAND GAINES):
Champion 16723 *Mountain Rangers Lullaby*.........20.00 - 30.00
   16747 *Moonlight And Skies* ....20.00 - 30.00

YORK BROTHERS:
Bullet 618 *Hamtramck Mama* ....10.00 - 15.00

YOUNG BROTHERS TENNESSEE BAND:
Columbia 15219-D *Are You From Dixie?* ....15.00 - 20.00

BUDDY YOUNG'S KENTUCKIANS:
Superior 2519 *Fire On The Mountain* ....30.00 - 50.00
   2655 *Eighth Of January*.....................................30.00 - 50.00
   2731 *Rocky Mountain Goat* ....30.00 - 50.00

CLARENCE YOUNG:
Champion 15550 *The Lonely Village Churchyard* . 10.00 - 15.00
   15582 *Yodelin' Daddy Blues* ....10.00 - 15.00
   15924 *Little Pal*...10.00 - 15.00
   15991 *That's A Plenty*...10.00 - 15.00

JACKSON YOUNG:
Champion 15318 *Take Me Back To The Sweet Sunny South*
....8.00 - 12.00
   15333 *I Know My Name Is There* ....7.00 - 10.00

JESS YOUNG'S TENNESSEE BAND:
Columbia 15338-D *Fiddle Up* ....15.00 - 20.00
   15400-D *Sweet Bunch Of Daisies* ....15.00 - 20.00
   15431-D *Lovin' Henry* ....15.00 - 20.00
   15493-D *Old Weary Blues* ....20.00 - 30.00

EDDIE YOUNGER & HIS MOUNTAINEERS:
Clarion (most issues)..5.00 - 10.00
Velvet Tone (most issues) ....5.00 - 8.00

ZACK & GLENN:
Okeh 45212 *The Gambler's Lament*........................5.00 - 8.00
   45240 *Love's Old Sweet Song*...............................5.00 - 8.00

ZORA & THE HOMETOWNERS:
Decca 5459, 5460...5.00 - 10.00

RHYTHM & BLUES; ROCK & ROLL; ROCKABILLY; BLUES; ETC.

1950s through early 1960s

All records in this section are 45 RPM unless otherwise indicated. Albums and Extended-Play records are denoted by (LP) or (EP) between the name of the label and the record/catalog number. LPs and EPs must be in their original jackets. LPs and EPs lacking jackets or having damaged or defaced jackets are worth substantially less than the prices listed (and may, in fact, be virtually unsaleable).

Collectors of 1950s records are particularly fussy about labels. The color, logo, style of type, or sheen may distinguish first from subsequent pressings or bootlegs. An effort has been made, where repressings involving label variations are notorious, to designate the label color (or other determinant) of the original pressing. For in-depth coverage of this topic respecting vocal group records, see Lou Silvani's *Collecting Rare Records*, and Jeff Kreiter's *Group Collector's Record Price Guide*, which are noted in the Bibliography. Also, the presence of writing, stickers, tears, or other damage to labels detracts from desirability and value more so than with earlier 78 RPM records.

Although most of the records listed in this section are 45 RPM, EPs, and LPs, selected 78 RPM records are listed. These are the 78 RPM counterparts (having the same label and catalog/record number) of big-selling 45 RPM hits, usually rock and roll, of the late 1950s. Such records, common and of minimal value as 45s (and usually not listed herein), are often scarcer as 78s. By the late 1950s, the process of phasing out 78s in favor of 45s had nearly concluded. The major companies discontinued 78s in 1957-1958; some smaller labels continued to produce 78s as late as 1960. In other countries, 78s continued to be made even later. These are not dealt with in this book, which lists U.S. pressings only. Canadian pressings, which often conform in label and number to records listed, are worth less. The market for these "late 78s," originally fueled by the demand of jukebox owners, has grown greatly in recent years, and prices have increased sharply.

While the "late 78s" are usually worth more than their 45 RPM counterparts, the opposite is generally true of records from the early to mid 1950s. During this period, 45s, being relatively new, had not yet supplanted 78s, and were often issued in smaller quantities than 78s. This is particularly true of Rhythm and Blues, Blues, and Country records, whose purchasers were among the last to retire their old 78s and record players in favor of the new format. Thus, for most of the records listed in this section, a 78 RPM copy is worth less (often much less, in the case of valuable records) than its 45 RPM counterpart.

Readers will note the presence of incomplete listings, which lack label, catalog/record number, title, or price. These records are deemed worthy of inclusion notwithstanding missing information, due to their having appeared in want lists or auction lists of knowledgeable collectors and dealers. It is expected that collectors will supply some of the missing information, or in some cases will advise the deletion of records, in time for a seventh edition of this book.

THE ACADEMICS:
Ancho 101 *Too Good To Be True* .... 50.00 - 80.00
    103 *Darla, My Darling* .... 50.00 - 80.00

THE ACCENTS:
Brunswick 55100 *Wiggle Wiggle* .... 5.00 - 8.00
    55100 *Wiggle Wiggle* (78 rpm) .... 15.00 - 20.00
    55123 *Ching A Ling* .... 8.00 - 12.00

JOHNNY ACE:
Duke (EP) 80 *Memorial Album;* (EP) 81 .... 30.00 - 40.00
    (LP) DLP-70 (10 inch) *"Memorial Album for Johnny Ace"*
    .... 80.00 - 120.00
    (LP) DLP 71 *Memorial Album* .... 50.00 - 75.00
    102 *My Song* .... 15.00 - 20.00
    107 *Cross My Heart* .... 15.00 - 20.00
    112 *The Clock* .... 10.00 - 15.00
    118 *Saving My Love For You* .... 10.00 - 15.00
    128 *Please Forgive Me* .... 8.00 - 12.00
    136 *Pledging My Love* .... 8.00 - 12.00
    144 *Anymore* .... 5.00 - 8.00
    148 *So Lonely* .... 5.00 - 8.00
Flair 1015 *Midnight Hours Journey* .... 15.00 - 20.00

SONNY ACE:
TNT 153 *If My Teardrops Could Talk* .... 35.00 - 50.00

JOHNNY ACEY:
Fling 728 *I Go Into Orbit* .... 8.00 - 12.00

ACORNS:
Unart 2006, 2015 .... 8.00 - 12.00

ROY ACUFF:
Capitol (LP) T-617 .... 10.00 - 15.00
Columbia (LP) 9004 (10 inch) *Songs Of The Smoky Mountains*
    .... 20.00 - 30.00
    (LP) 9010 (10 inch) *Old Time Barn Dance* .... 20.00 - 30.00
Harmony (LP) 7082 *Great Speckled Bird* .... 10.00 - 15.00
MGM (LP) 3707 *Favorite Hymns* .... 10.00 - 15.00

ART ADAMS:
Cherry 1005 *Rock Crazy Baby* .... 75.00 - 100.00
    1019 *Dancing Doll* .... 60.00 - 100.00

ARTHUR K. ADAMS:
Jetstar 102 *Beetle Bust Out* .... - - -

BILLY ADAMS (& THE ROCK-A-TEERS):
Decca 30724 *Baby I'm Bugged* .... 8.00 - 12.00
Dot 15689 *You Heard Me Knocking* .... 10.00 - 15.00
Nau-Voo 805 *That's My Baby* .... 30.00 - 50.00

CHARLIE ADAMS:
Columbia 21239, 21355 .... 7.00 - 10.00
    21445 *Pistol Packin' Mama has Laid Her Pistol Down*
    .... 8.00 - 12.00
    21524 *Black Land Blues* .... 8.00 - 12.00
Decca 46335, 46358, 46373 .... 7.00 - 10.00

FAYE ADAMS:
Herald 416 *Shake A Hand* .... 7.00 - 10.00
    416 *Shake A Hand* (red plastic) .... 20.00 - 30.00
    419 *I'll Be True* .... 5.00 - 8.00
    423 *Say A Prayer* .... 5.00 - 8.00
    429 *Crazy Mixed up World* .... 5.00 - 8.00

434 *Ain't Gonna Tell* ....5.00 - 8.00
439 *Love Ain't Nothin' To Play With* ....5.00 - 8.00
Herald 444, 450, 457, 462, 470, 480, 489, 512 ....4.00 - 7.00
Warwick (LP) 2031 *Shake A Hand* ....80.00 - 120.00

JO JO ADAMS:
Chance 1127 *Didn't I Tell You* ....30.00 - 50.00

WOODROW ADAMS (& THE BOOGIE BLUES BLASTERS/THE THREE B'S):
Checker 757 *Pretty Baby Blues* ....40.00 - 70.00
Meteor 5018 *Wine Head Woman* (red label) ....50.00 - 80.00

ADELPHIS:
Rim 2022 *Shine Again* ....10.00 - 15.00

THE ADMIRALS:
King 4772 *Left With A Broken Heart* ....50.00 - 80.00
4782 *Close Your Eyes* ....50.00 - 80.00

ADMIRAL TONES:
Felsted 8563 *Rocksville, Pa* ....10.00 - 15.00

THE ADMIRATIONS:
Mercury 71521 *The Bells of Rosa Rita* ....10.00 - 15.00
71823 *To The Aisle* ....40.00 - 60.00

THE ADVENTURERS:
Columbia 42227 *Rock And Roll Uprising* ....15.00 - 25.00

RAY AGEE:
Spark 119 *Another Fool Sings The Blues* ....15.00 - 20.00

AGGIE DUKES:
Aladdin 3364 *Swing Low Sweet Cadillac* ....- - -

JIM AKINS:
Marlo 1517 *Floating On A Cloud* ....5.00 - 8.00

AL & THE ECHOES:
Echo 103 *Baby Remember Me* ....10.00 - 15.00

THE ALADDINS:
Aladdin 3275 *Cry Cry Baby* ....50.00 - 80.00
3298 *I Had Dream Last Night* ....40.00 - 60.00
3314 *All Of My Life* ....50.00 - 80.00
Witch 109 *Please Love Me* ....10.00 - 15.00
111 *Simple Simon* ....10.00 - 15.00

STEVE ALAIMO & THE RED COATS:
Lifetime 6112 *The Girl Can't Help It* ....7.00 - 10.00
Marlin 6064 *I Want You To Love Me* ....10.00 - 15.00
6067 *She's My Baby* ....10.00 - 15.00

DENNI ALAN:
Academy 434 *Turn-About Date* ....15.00 - 20.00

MEL ALBERT:
Apollo 530 *Sugar Plum* ....8.00 - 12.00

JOE ALEXANDER & THE CUBANS:
Ballad 1008 *Oh Maria* ....75.00 - 150.00

MAX ALEXANDER:
Caprock 116 *Rock, Rock, Rock Everybody* ....20.00 - 30.00

ANNIE ALFORD:
Groove 0172 *It's Heavenly* ....15.00 - 20.00

THE ALGERS:
Northern 3730 *Heavenly Father* ....15.00 - 20.00

BILL(Y) ALLEN (& THE BACK BEATS):
Eldorado 505 *Oo-Wee-Baby* ....7.00 - 10.00
Imperial 5500 *Please Give Me Something* ....20.00 - 30.00

CHARLIE ALLEN:
Portrait 107 *Wheelin' And Dealin'* ....7.00 - 10.00

CONNIE ALLEN:
King 4528 *Rocket 69* ....15.00 - 20.00

DANNY ALLEN:
Valley 101 *Teenage Blues* ....8.00 - 12.00

DEAN ALLEN:
Argo 5272 *Ooh-Ooh Baby Baby* ....10.00 - 15.00

HAROLD ALLEN:
Mar Vel 1200 *Honky Tonkin Women* ....15.00 - 20.00
1201 *If You Were Mine Again* ....15.00 - 20.00

IRA ALLEN:
Mav-Rick 105 *Nursery Rock* ....50.00 - 75.00

LITTLE JOE ALLEN & THE OFF BEATS:
M-C-M 411 *'Cause I Love You* ....50.00 - 100.00

LEE ALLEN:
Ember (LP) ELP 200 *Walkin' With Mr Lee* ....50.00 - 75.00

MILTON ALLEN:
RCA Victor 6994 *Just Look, Don't Touch* ....10.00 - 15.00
7116 *Don't Bug Me Baby* ....10.00 - 15.00
Robin 61824 *Anything Goes* ....25.00 - 40.00

RAY ALLEN:
Blast (LP) 6004 *Tribute To Six* ....25.00 - 40.00

REX ALLEN:
Decca (LP) 8402 *Under Western Skies* ....10.00 - 15.00
30674 *Knock Knock Rattle* ....8.00 - 12.00

RONNIE ALLEN:
San 208 *Juvenile Delinquent* ....15.00 - 20.00
209 *High School Love* ....15.00 - 20.00
300 *Gonna Get My Baby* ....15.00 - 20.00

TONY ALLEN (& THE CHAMPS/TWILIGHTERS/ WONDERS) (See also THE CHIMES):
Bethlehem 3002 *Just Like Before* ....5.00 - 8.00
Crown (LP) CLP 5231 *Rock And Roll with* ....25.00 - 50.00
Dig 109 *I Found An Angel* ....15.00 - 20.00
Jamie 1119 *Looking For My Baby* ....7.00 - 10.00
Kent 356 *Everybody's Somebody's Fool* ....15.00 - 20.00
364 *Dreamin'* ....10.00 - 20.00
Specialty 560 *Nite Owl* ....10.00 - 15.00
Ultra 104 *It Hurts Me So* ....5.00 - 8.00

JOE ALLISON:
Dot 15714 *Baby Doll* ....10.00 - 15.00

"ALL STAR ROCK & ROLL REVUE:"
King (LP) 513 (various artists) ....50.00 - 75.00

"ALL TIME COUNTRY & HILLBILLY FAVORITES:"
Capitol *(LP)* 9103, 9107, (10 inch) ....15.00 - 20.00

"ALL TIME COUNTRY & WESTERN HITS:"
King (LP) 537 ....15.00 - 20.00

HERSCHEL ALMOND:
Ace 558 *Let's Get It On* ....15.00 - 20.00

LUCKY JOE ALMOND:
Trumpet 199 *Rock Me* ....10.00 - 15.00
221 *Gonna Roll And Rock* ....10.00 - 15.00

HENRY ALSTON:
Skyline 551 *Once In A Beautiful Lifetime* ....7.00 - 10.00

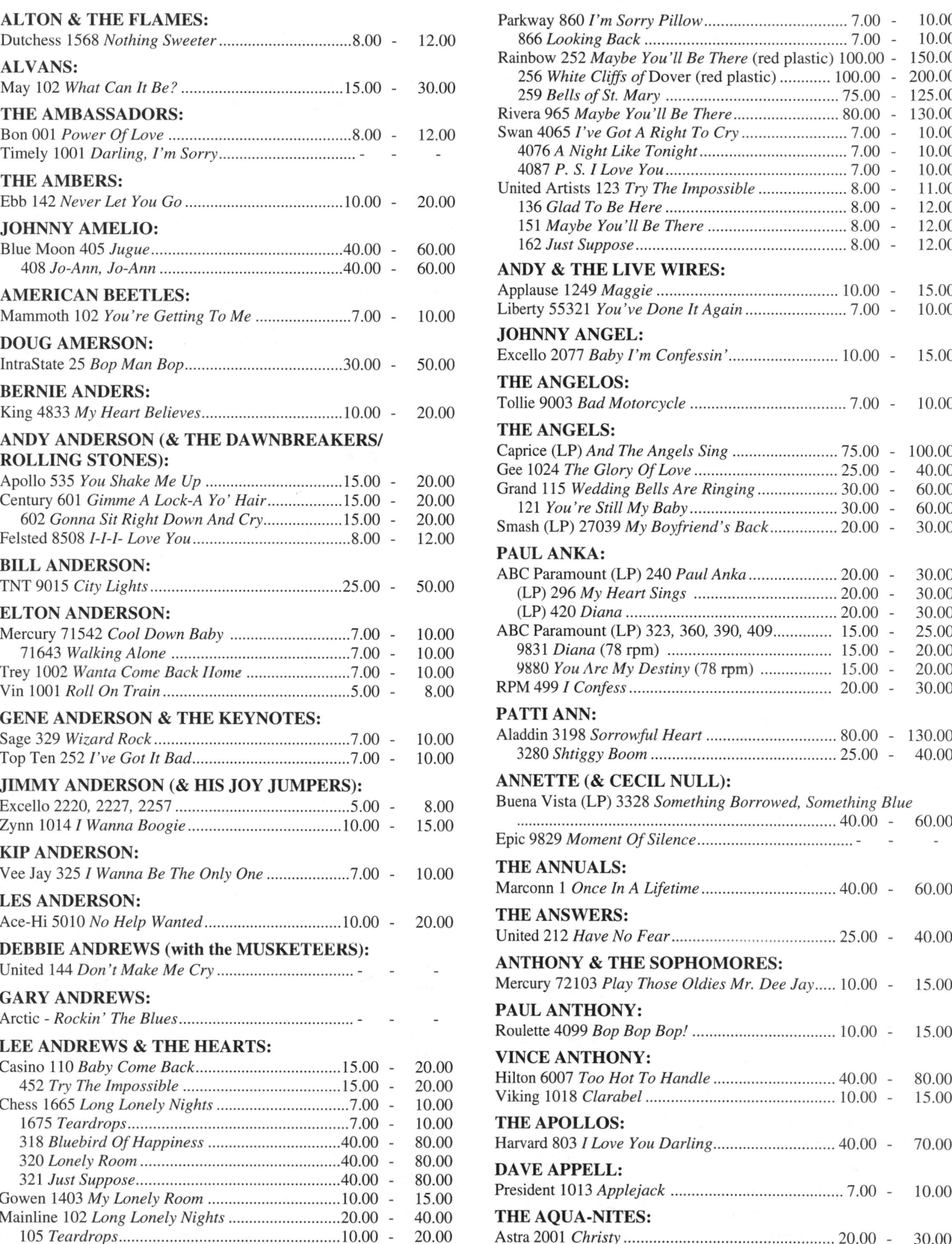

ALTON & THE FLAMES:
Dutchess 1568 *Nothing Sweeter* ....8.00 - 12.00

ALVANS:
May 102 *What Can It Be?* ....15.00 - 30.00

THE AMBASSADORS:
Bon 001 *Power Of Love* ....8.00 - 12.00
Timely 1001 *Darling, I'm Sorry* .... - - -

THE AMBERS:
Ebb 142 *Never Let You Go* ....10.00 - 20.00

JOHNNY AMELIO:
Blue Moon 405 *Jugue* ....40.00 - 60.00
 408 *Jo-Ann, Jo-Ann* ....40.00 - 60.00

AMERICAN BEETLES:
Mammoth 102 *You're Getting To Me* ....7.00 - 10.00

DOUG AMERSON:
IntraState 25 *Bop Man Bop* ....30.00 - 50.00

BERNIE ANDERS:
King 4833 *My Heart Believes* ....10.00 - 20.00

ANDY ANDERSON (& THE DAWNBREAKERS/ ROLLING STONES):
Apollo 535 *You Shake Me Up* ....15.00 - 20.00
Century 601 *Gimme A Lock-A Yo' Hair* ....15.00 - 20.00
 602 *Gonna Sit Right Down And Cry* ....15.00 - 20.00
Felsted 8508 *I-I-I- Love You* ....8.00 - 12.00

BILL ANDERSON:
TNT 9015 *City Lights* ....25.00 - 50.00

ELTON ANDERSON:
Mercury 71542 *Cool Down Baby* ....7.00 - 10.00
 71643 *Walking Alone* ....7.00 - 10.00
Trey 1002 *Wanta Come Back Home* ....7.00 - 10.00
Vin 1001 *Roll On Train* ....5.00 - 8.00

GENE ANDERSON & THE KEYNOTES:
Sage 329 *Wizard Rock* ....7.00 - 10.00
Top Ten 252 *I've Got It Bad* ....7.00 - 10.00

JIMMY ANDERSON (& HIS JOY JUMPERS):
Excello 2220, 2227, 2257 ....5.00 - 8.00
Zynn 1014 *I Wanna Boogie* ....10.00 - 15.00

KIP ANDERSON:
Vee Jay 325 *I Wanna Be The Only One* ....7.00 - 10.00

LES ANDERSON:
Ace-Hi 5010 *No Help Wanted* ....10.00 - 20.00

DEBBIE ANDREWS (with the MUSKETEERS):
United 144 *Don't Make Me Cry* .... - - -

GARY ANDREWS:
Arctic - *Rockin' The Blues* .... - - -

LEE ANDREWS & THE HEARTS:
Casino 110 *Baby Come Back* ....15.00 - 20.00
 452 *Try The Impossible* ....15.00 - 20.00
Chess 1665 *Long Lonely Nights* ....7.00 - 10.00
 1675 *Teardrops* ....7.00 - 10.00
 318 *Bluebird Of Happiness* ....40.00 - 80.00
 320 *Lonely Room* ....40.00 - 80.00
 321 *Just Suppose* ....40.00 - 80.00
Gowen 1403 *My Lonely Room* ....10.00 - 15.00
Mainline 102 *Long Lonely Nights* ....20.00 - 40.00
 105 *Teardrops* ....10.00 - 20.00

Parkway 860 *I'm Sorry Pillow* ....7.00 - 10.00
 866 *Looking Back* ....7.00 - 10.00
Rainbow 252 *Maybe You'll Be There* (red plastic) 100.00 - 150.00
 256 *White Cliffs of* Dover (red plastic) .... 100.00 - 200.00
 259 *Bells of St. Mary* ....75.00 - 125.00
Rivera 965 *Maybe You'll Be There* ....80.00 - 130.00
Swan 4065 *I've Got A Right To Cry* ....7.00 - 10.00
 4076 *A Night Like Tonight* ....7.00 - 10.00
 4087 *P. S. I Love You* ....7.00 - 10.00
United Artists 123 *Try The Impossible* ....8.00 - 11.00
 136 *Glad To Be Here* ....8.00 - 12.00
 151 *Maybe You'll Be There* ....8.00 - 12.00
 162 *Just Suppose* ....8.00 - 12.00

ANDY & THE LIVE WIRES:
Applause 1249 *Maggie* ....10.00 - 15.00
Liberty 55321 *You've Done It Again* ....7.00 - 10.00

JOHNNY ANGEL:
Excello 2077 *Baby I'm Confessin'* ....10.00 - 15.00

THE ANGELOS:
Tollie 9003 *Bad Motorcycle* ....7.00 - 10.00

THE ANGELS:
Caprice (LP) *And The Angels Sing* ....75.00 - 100.00
Gee 1024 *The Glory Of Love* ....25.00 - 40.00
Grand 115 *Wedding Bells Are Ringing* ....30.00 - 60.00
 121 *You're Still My Baby* ....30.00 - 60.00
Smash (LP) 27039 *My Boyfriend's Back* ....20.00 - 30.00

PAUL ANKA:
ABC Paramount (LP) 240 *Paul Anka* ....20.00 - 30.00
 (LP) 296 *My Heart Sings* ....20.00 - 30.00
 (LP) 420 *Diana* ....20.00 - 30.00
ABC Paramount (LP) 323, 360, 390, 409 .... 15.00 - 25.00
 9831 *Diana* (78 rpm) ....15.00 - 20.00
 9880 *You Are My Destiny* (78 rpm) ....15.00 - 20.00
RPM 499 *I Confess* ....20.00 - 30.00

PATTI ANN:
Aladdin 3198 *Sorrowful Heart* ....80.00 - 130.00
 3280 *Shtiggy Boom* ....25.00 - 40.00

ANNETTE (& CECIL NULL):
Buena Vista (LP) 3328 *Something Borrowed, Something Blue*
...........................40.00 - 60.00
Epic 9829 *Moment Of Silence* .... - - -

THE ANNUALS:
Marconn 1 *Once In A Lifetime* ....40.00 - 60.00

THE ANSWERS:
United 212 *Have No Fear* ....25.00 - 40.00

ANTHONY & THE SOPHOMORES:
Mercury 72103 *Play Those Oldies Mr. Dee Jay* ..... 10.00 - 15.00

PAUL ANTHONY:
Roulette 4099 *Bop Bop Bop!* ....10.00 - 15.00

VINCE ANTHONY:
Hilton 6007 *Too Hot To Handle* ....40.00 - 80.00
Viking 1018 *Clarabel* ....10.00 - 15.00

THE APOLLOS:
Harvard 803 *I Love You Darling* ....40.00 - 70.00

DAVE APPELL:
President 1013 *Applejack* ....7.00 - 10.00

THE AQUA-NITES:
Astra 2001 *Christy* ....20.00 - 30.00

2003 *Carioca* ....15.00 - 20.00

THE AQUATONES:
Fargo 1001 *You*..................................5.00 - 8.00
1002 *So Fine* ....7.00 - 10.00
1003 *Our First Kiss* ....7.00 - 10.00
1005 *My One Desire*.........................8.00 - 12.00
1015 *Every Time* ....7.00 - 10.00
1016 *Crazy For You* ....7.00 - 10.00
1022 *My Treasure* ....7.00 - 10.00
Fargo (LP) FLP 3001 *"The Aquatones Sing"* ....100.00 - 150.00

THE ARABIANS:
Carrie 1516 *My One Possession* ....50.00 - 80.00
JAM 3738 *Heaven Sent You* ....75.00 - 100.00
Magnificent 102 *My Heart Beats Over* ....100.00 - up
114 *Teardrops In The Night* ....50.00 - 80.00
Teek 4824 *Condition Your Heart* ....40.00 - 70.00
Twin Star 1018 *Heaven Sent You* ....15.00 - 20.00

ARCHIBALD:
Imperial 5212 *Great Big Eyes* ....30.00 - 50.00
5358 *Stack-A-Lee*................................20.00 - 30.00

ARIST-O-KATS:
Vita 168 *I Don't See Me In Your Eyes* ....15.00 - 30.00

SMOKEY ARMEN
Peek-A-Boo 102 *Baby What Am I Gonna Do* ....15.00 - 20.00

DON ARMSTRONG:
Don Ray 5962 *Betty Jo* ....20.00 - 40.00

DESI ARNAZ & HIS ORCHESTRA:
Columbia 39937 *I Love Lucy*...................10.00 - 15.00
Decca 28483 *Old San Juan*........................ - - -
MGM 12144 *The Straw Hat Song* ....5.00 - 10.00
RCA Victor (EP) EPB-3096 *Babalu* (two-record set)
..................................20.00 - 30.00
(LP) LPM-3096 *Babalu* ....20.00 - 30.00
EPB-3096 (EP) *Babalu*........................10.00 - 20.00
(Note: See also the **DANCE BANDS**, etc. section for earlier
(78 rpm) records by Desi Arnaz.)

BILLY BOY ARNOLD:
Cool 103 *Hello Stranger*........................10.00 - 20.00

EDDY ARNOLD:
Camden (LP) 471, 563.........................7.00 - 10.00
RCA Victor (LP) 1111 *Wanderin'* ....20.00 - 30.00
1223 *All-Time Favorites* ....15.00 - 20.00
1224 *Anytime* ....15.00 - 20.00
1225 *Chapel On The Hill*....................20.00 - 30.00
1293 *A Dozen Hits* ....10.00 - 15.00
1377 *A Little On The Lonely Side*.......15.00 - 20.00
1484 *When They Were Young* ....15.00 - 20.00
(LP) 3027 (10 inch) *Country Classics* ....30.00 - 40.00
3031 (10 inch) *All-Time Hits* ....20.00 - 30.00
3117 (10 inch) *Eddy Arnold* ....20.00 - 30.00
3230 (10 inch) *An American Institution* ....20.00 - 30.00
3249 (10 inch) *When It's Round-up* Time *In Heaven*
..................................20.00 - 30.00
Tops (LP) 1612 *Cowboy Songs Of The West*............8.00 - 12.00

JACK ARNOLD & THE CHALECOS:
Wildcat W-00018 *Pistol Packing Mama* ....10.00 - 15.00

JAMES ARP:
Vellez 1515 *Let It Rock* ....10.00 - 15.00

THE ARROGANTS:
Lute 6226 *Canadian Sunset*........................15.00 - 25.00

THE ARROWS:
Flash 132 *Annie Mae* ....15.00 - 20.00
Hugo 11172 *No Other Arms* ....10.00 - 15.00

RICHIE ARTHUR:
Platter *Walkin' Down A Lonesome Road*.................7.00 - 10.00

THE ARTISTICS:
S & G 302 *One Way*.............................50.00 - 80.00

LITTLE JOE ARTWOOD:
Kingsport 105 *Cue Ball Blues*..................10.00 - 15.00

THE ASCOTS:
Ace 650 *Perfect Love* ....10.00 - 15.00
J & S 1628/1629 *What Love Can Do*...............15.00 - 20.00

JOHN ASHLEY:
Dot 15775 *Born To Rock* ....10.00 - 15.00

ASTRONAUTS:
Palladium 610 *Come Along Baby* ....30.00 - 40.00

BOB ATCHER:
Columbia (LP) 9006 (10 inch) *Early American Folksongs*
..................................15.00 - 20.00
(LP) 9013 (10 inch) *Songs Of The Saddle* ....15.00 - 20.00
Tiffany 1309 *High And Dry*....................10.00 - 15.00

CHUCK ATHA:
Fox 1169 *Just Me And My Baby* ....15.00 - 20.00

CHET ATKINS:
RCA Victor (LP) 1090 *Session*.............20.00 - 30.00
1197 *In Three Dimensions* ....20.00 - 30.00
1236 *Stringin' Along*.........................20.00 - 30.00
1383 *Finger-Style Guitar*....................20.00 - 30.00
1544 *At Home* ....15.00 - 20.00
1577 *Hi-Fi In Focus*..........................15.00 - 20.00
(LP) 3079 (10 inch) *Galloping Guitar*...............30.00 - 50.00
3163 (10 inch) *Stringin' Along* ....30.00 - 50.00

DAVE ATKINS AND HIS OFFBEATS:
Back Beat 511 *Shake-Kum-Down*............8.00 - 12.00

THE ATLANTICS:
Linda 107 *Remember The Night* ....25.00 - 50.00

AUDREY:
Plus 104 *Dear Elvis* ....10.00 - 15.00

LITTLE AUGIE AUSTIN (& THE CHROMATICS):
Brunswick 55080 *My Heart Let Me Be Free*..........15.00 - 25.00
Pontiac 101 *I Thank My Lucky Star*.........8.00 - 12.00

BILLY AUSTIN & THE HEARTS:
Apollo 444 *Angel Baby*.........................200.00 - up

DON AUSTIN & THE SENSATIONAL DELLOS:
Mida 106 *So Shy* ....15.00 - 20.00
109 *So Don't Go* ....20.00 - 30.00

GENE AUTRY:
Columbia (LP) 9001 (10 inch) *Western Classics* ...20.00 - 30.00
(LP) 9002 (10 inch) *Western Classics, Vol. 2*....20.00 - 30.00
(Note: See also the **COUNTRY/WESTERN, ETC.** section for
other (78 rpm) records by Gene Autry.)

GEORGE AVAK:
Cinatone 501 *Lindy Lou*.........................8.00 - 12.00

FRANKIE AVALON:
Chancellor 1011 *De De Dinah* (78 rpm) ....25.00 - 50.00
(LP) 5001 *Frankie Avalon* ....15.00 - 20.00
(LP) 5002 *Young Frankie Avalon* ....15.00 - 20.00

(LP) 5004, 5009, 5011 ....10.00 - 15.00
(LP) 5022, 5027, 5031, 5032 ....10.00 - 15.00

THE AVALONS:
Casino 108 *You Do Something To Me* ....80.00 - 130.00
Grove 0141 *Chains Around My Heart*...................50.00 - 80.00
    0174 *It's Funny But It's True* ....50.00 - 80.00
NPC 302 *Begin The Beguine* ....10.00 - 15.00
Unart 2007 *Heart's Desire* ....50.00 - 80.00

THE AVONS:
Groove 0039 *Whatever Happened To Our Love* ....7.00 - 10.00
Hull 717 (black label) *Our Love Will Never End* ....40.00 - 70.00
    717 (orange label) *Our Love Will Never End* .....10.00 - 20.00
    722 *Baby* ....20.00 - 30.00
    726 *You Are So Close To Me* ....30.00 - 50.00
    728 *What Will I Do* ....30.00 - 50.00
    731 *What Love Can Do*.........................15.00 - 25.00
    744 *Whisper (Softly)* ....20.00 - 30.00
    754 *A Girl To Call My Own* ....25.00 - 40.00
    (LP) HLP *The Avons*........................200.00 - 300.00

BABY DEE:
MGM 1179 *Hold The Light for Me* ....7.00 - 10.00

THE BACHELORS:
Aladdin 3210 *Can't Help Lovin' You* ....200.00 - up
Earl 101 *Delores* ....40.00 - 80.00
    102 *Tell Me Now*.................................100.00 - 150.00

GAR BACON:
Baton 248 *There's Gonna Be Rocking Tonight* ....5.00 - 8.00

SHORTY BACON:
Ozark 1237 *Fire Of Love* ....7.00 - 10.00

DAVID BAILEY:
Banner 60204 *Rocky Road Blues* ....15.00 - 20.00

JACK BAILEY & THE NATURALS:
Ford 105 *Oh What Love Is* ....30.00 - 40.00

LITTLE MARIE BAILEY:
Excello 2007 *Brownskin Woman Blues* ....50.00 - 100.00
    2016 *My Baby's Blues* ....50.00 - 100.00

MORRIS BAILEY:
Bailey 500 *Calendar Hanging On The Wall* ....8.00 - 12.00

WILLIE BAILEY:
Loadstone 1616 *If You Were Blue* ....8.00 - 12.00

BILL BAKER:
Vim 515 *Thank Heaven* ....- - -

BOB BAKER:
Veeda 4006 *Turned On The Ice* ....- - -

CHARLIE BAKER:
Liberty 55226 *You Crack Me Up* ....10.00 - 15.00
Mun Rab 106 *You Crack Me Up* ....30.00 - 50.00

DONNY BAKER:
Rainbow 219 *Drinking Wine Spo-Dee-O-Dee* ....15.00 - 20.00

KENNY BAKER:
Orbit 541 *I'm Gonna Love You* ....7.00 - 10.00

LAVERNE BAKER:
Atlantic (EP) 566, 588, 617 ....30.00 - 50.00
    1004, 1030, 1047 ....5.00 - 10.00
    (LP) 1281 *Sings Bessie Smith* ....50.00 - 80.00
    (LP) 8007 *Laverne Baker* ....50.00 - 100.00
    (LP) 8030 *Blues Ballads* ....50.00 - 100.00

(LP) 8036 *Precious Memories* ....40.00 - 70.00
(LP) 8071 *See See Rider* ....25.00 - 40.00
King 4556 *Trying* ....15.00 - 25.00

MICKEY BAKER:
Atlantic (LP) 8035 *The Wildest Guitar*...................75.00 - 100.00

RONNIE BAKER & THE DELTONES:
Laurie 3128 *My Story*...............................5.00 - 8.00

WILLIE BAKER:
DeLuxe 6023 *Before She Leaves Town* ....30.00 - 50.00
Rockin' 527 *Before She Leaves Town* ....40.00 - 70.00

EARL BALL:
Pathenon 101 *Party Of One* ....7.00 - 10.00

THE BALLADS:
Franwil 5028 *Before You Fall In Love* ....15.00 - 20.00
Ron-Cris 1003 *Somehow*...............................25.00 - 40.00
Veltone 1738 *I Hope I Never Fall In Love* ....25.00 - 40.00

FRANK BALLARD:
Phillips Int. (LP) 198 *"Rhythm-Blues Party"* ....100.00 - up

HANK BALLARD (& THE MIDNIGHTERS) (See also THE MIDNIGHTERS):
Federal (EP) 333, 435, 451 ....100.00 - 150.00
King (LP) 541 *Their Greatest Juke Box Hits*........150.00 - 200.00
    (LP) 581 *Hank Ballard & The Midnighters*.....150.00 - 200.00
    (LP) 618, 674 ....50.00 - 100.00
    (LP) 700, 748, 759, 781, 793 ....50.00 - 80.00
    5171 *The Twist* ....7.00 - 10.00
    5195 *Kansas City* ....7.00 - 10.00
    5215 *Sugaree* ....10.00 - 15.00
    5275, 5312, 5341, 5459...........................5.00 - 10.00

JERRY BALLARD:
Skippy 120 *Pinch Me*...............................5.00 - 8.00

THE BALTINEERS:
Teenage 1000 *Moments Like This*...........................25.00 - 50.00
    1002 *Tears In My Eyes* ....50.00 - 80.00

JAMES BANISTER & HIS COMBO:
States 141 *Gold Digger*...........................25.00 - 40.00

DICK BANKS:
Liberty 55145 *Dirty Dog* ....15.00 - 20.00

MACK BANKS:
Fame 580 *Be Boppin' Daddy* ....150.00 - 200.00

OTIS BANKS:
Bow 304 *She's My Baby* ....7.00 - 10.00

THE BANNERS:
MGM 12810 *My Own True Love*...........................8.00 - 12.00
    12862 *Fortune Teller* ....8.00 - 12.00

DON BARBER & THE DUKES:
Personality 3505 *Henrietta* ....7.00 - 10.00

GLENN BARBER:
D 1098 *Go Home Letter*...............................10.00 - 15.00
Pic 1143 *I Created A Monster* ....10.00 - 15.00
Starday 166 *Ice Water*...............................30.00 - 50.00
    196 *Poor Man's Baby* ....20.00 - 30.00
    249 *Shadow My Baby*.........................25.00 - 50.00

PHIL BARCLAY & THE SLIDERS:
Doke 101 *Young Long John*...........................20.00 - 30.00
    102 *I Love 'Em All* ....20.00 - 30.00

BOBBY BARE:
Fraternity 861 *That's Where I Want To Be*.................5.00 -   8.00

BARKER BROS:
Decca 30811 *Lovin' Honey* ....10.00 -   15.00
Kent 302 *Hey Little Mama* ....15.00 -   20.00

DELBERT BARKER:
King 4951 *No Good Robin Hood* ....20.00 -   30.00

AL BARKLE:
Frantic 108 *Muscle Beach* ....10.00 -   15.00
M&M 4041 *Jumpin' From Six To Six* ....30.00 -   50.00

DEAN BARLOW (featured with THE CRICKETS, which also see):
Jay-Dee 799, 803 ....5.00 -   10.00

DEAN BARLOW & THE MONTEREYS:
Onyx 513 *Dearest One* ....25.00 -   40.00

JUKE BOY BARNER:
Irma 111 *Well Baby* ....25.00 -   50.00

BENNY BARNES:
D 1052 *Happy Little Blue Bird* ....7.00 -   10.00
Starday 401 *You Gotta Pay*.....................................15.00 -   20.00

DAVID BARNES:
San 302 *Lovin' On My Mind* ....15.00 -   25.00

JIMMY BARNES & THE GIBRALTARS:
Gibraltar 102 *Be Careful With My Love* ....5.00 -   8.00

THE BARONS:
Decca (EP) ED-2400 ....30.00 -   50.00
    29293 *Forget About Me*.......................................25.00 -   40.00
    48323 *A Year And A Day*....................................50.00 -   80.00
Imperial 5343 *Eternally Yours*.................................40.00 -   70.00
    5359 *I Know I Was Wrong*...................................20.00 -   30.00
    5370 *Searching For You*.......................................50.00 -   80.00
    5383 *So Long My Darling* ....25.00 -   40.00
    5397 *Once In A Lifetime*......................................25.00 -   40.00
Spartan 400 *I've Been Hurt* ....7.00 -   10.00

CHUCK BARR & THE ROCKABILLIES:
Elsan 100 *Susie Or Mary Lou*.................................15.00 -   20.00

HAROLD BARRAGE (See HAROLD BURRAGE)

THE BARRETT SINGERS:
Reserve 124 *Lonesome Road*....................................10.00 -   15.00

HUGH BARRETT:
Lucky Four 1015 *Devil's Love* ....15.00 -   20.00

RICHARD BARRETT:
Seville 104 *Dream On* ....7.00 -   10.00

BILLY BARRIX:
Chess 1662 *Cool Off Baby*.....................................300.00 -   600.00

LONNIE BARRON:
Sage 230 *Teenage Queen*..10.00 -   15.00

DAVE BARRY & SARA BERNER:
RPM 469 *Out Of This World With Flying Saucers* ...5.00 -   8.00

JAY BARRY:
ABC Paramount 10226 *Love Spell* ....7.00 -   10.00

JEFF BARRY:
RCA Victor 7477 *It's Called Rock And Roll*.............7.00 -   10.00
    7797 *Lonely Lips*..7.00 -   10.00
    7821 *All You Need Is A Quarter* ....7.00 -   10.00

JOE BARRY:
Jin 144, 152...5.00 -   8.00

TEDDY BART:
Felsted 8514 *Headin' For A Weddin'* .... -   -

DAVE BARTHOLOMEW:
Bayou 005 *Country Gal* ....20.00 -   30.00
Imperial 5322 *Another Mule* ....7.00 -   10.00
    (LP) 9162 *Fats Domino Presents* ....20.00 -   30.00
    (LP) 9217 *New Orleans House Party* ....20.00 -   30.00
King 4523 *Lawdy Lawdy Lord* ....30.00 -   50.00

BART BARTON:
E & M 1651 *Ain't I'm A Mess* ....20.00 -   30.00

BILLY (BOY) BARTON:
Gulf Reef 1001 *Monkey Business* ....8.00 -   12.00
King 1478 *Do You Love Me*.....................................8.00 -   12.00
Radio 117 *Doorway To Heaven*................................8.00 -   12.00
Sims 176 *Even Steven* ....8.00 -   12.00
Vidor 1007 *Crazy Lover* ....8.00 -   12.00

DICK BARTON & THE REBELS:
Anthem 61712 *I Get The Blues* ....20.00 -   30.00

OTTO BASH with THE RHYTHM ROCKERS:
Hidus 2008 *My Babe*...8.00 -   12.00
RCA Victor 6585 *The Elvis Blues* ....8.00 -   12.00
RCA Victor (most other issues).................................4.00 -   7.00

NORVEN BASKERVILLE & THE ADMIRATIONS:
X-tra 100 *Gonna Find My Pretty Baby*...................20.00 -   30.00

TONY BASSETT:
Orchid 873 *Rocking Little Mama*............................15.00 -   20.00

"BATTLE OF THE BLUES":
King (LP) 607 *Vol. 1 Roy Brown, Wynonie Harris, Eddie Vinson*
....80.00 -   120.00
    (LP) 627 *Vol. 2*...80.00 -   120.00
    (LP) 634 *Vol. 3 Eddie Vinson, Jimmy Witherspoon*
....100.00 -   150.00
    (LP) 668 *Vol. 4*..150.00 -   250.00

RAY BATTS:
Bullet *Wild Man Boogie*.. -   -
Excello 2028 *Stealin' Sugar* ....25.00 -   40.00

DAVE BAUCOM:
Giant 1101 *That'll Be The Day* ....10.00 -   15.00

ALLEN BAUM:
Red Robin 124 *My Kinda Woman* ....75.00 -   100.00

RONNIE BAXTER:
Mark-X 8001 *It's Magic* ....10.00 -   15.00

THE BAY BOPS:
Coral 61975 *Joanie* ....7.00 -   10.00

BILL BEACH:
King 4940 *Peg Pants* ....25.00 -   35.00

RUFUS BEACHAM:
Chart 617 *Don't Say You Love Me*.........................10.00 -   15.00
    627 *I Can't Believe* ....10.00 -   15.00

THE BEACH BOYS:
Candix 301 *Surfin'*...75.00 -   100.00
    301 (same, but bears notation: "Dist. by ERA
        RECORD SALES, INC.") ....50.00 -   75.00
    331 *Surfin'* ....50.00 -   75.00

Capitol (Custom) *KFWB Promotional Souvenir Spirit Of America* ....40.00 - 60.00

SXA-1981 (7 inch, for juke boxes) *Surfer Girl* ..30.00 - 40.00

DU 2269 (7 inch, for juke boxes) *The Beach Boys Today* ....30.00 - 40.00

PRO 2937 (Courtesy Of Downtown Salt Lake City Stores) *Salt Lake City*..75.00 - 100.00

(EP) *PRO* 2993 *Barbara Ann + 3* ....40.00 - 60.00

4880 *Ten Little Indians* ....5.00 - 8.00

(Note: Picture Sleeves for Cap. 4880 are scarce.)

Capitol *(EP)* 5267 *4 by the Beach Boys*............30.00 - 50.00

"X" 301 *Surfin'* ....80.00 - 120.00

DEAN BEARD (WITH THE CREW CATS/FOX FOUR SEVENS):

Atlantic 1137 *Rakin' And Scrapin'*...........................8.00 - 12.00

1137 *Rakin' And Scrapin'* (78 rpm) ....10.00 - 20.00

1162 *Party Party* ....8.00 - 12.00

1182 *Hold Me Close* ....8.00 - 12.00

Challenge 59033 *Egad Charlie Brown*....................5.00 - 8.00

59048 *Little Lover* ....5.00 - 8.00

Edmoral 1011 *Rakin' And Scrapin'*........................15.00 - 25.00

Fox 405 *Red Rover* ....15.00 - 20.00

408 *Sing Sing Sing* ....15.00 - 20.00

Sangelo *1Party Party* ....15.00 - 20.00

JIMMY BEASLEY:

Crown (LP) *CLP* 5014 *The Fabulous*......................25.00 - 50.00

GOOD ROCKIN' (SAM) BEASLEY (See also KID KING'S COMBO):

Excello 2011 *Happy Go Lucky* ....50.00 - 75.00

2051 *Now Listen Baby* ....30.00 - 50.00

THE BEATLES:

Atco (LP) 169 *Ain't She Sweet* (MONO) ....30.00 - 50.00

(LP) 169 *Ain't She Sweet* (STEREO) ....50.00 - 75.00

(LP) 169 (DJ) *Ain't She Sweet*...........................100.00 - 150.00

6302 *Sweet Georgia Brown* ....7.00 - 10.00

6302 (DJ) *Sweet Georgia Brown* ....30.00 - 40.00

6308 *Ain't She Sweet* ....7.00 - 10.00

6308 (DJ) *Ain't She Sweet* ....30.00 - 40.00

(Note: Picture sleeve to Atco 6308 is very scarce; originals have sold for over $75.00)

Capitol SXA 2047 (7 inch, 33 1/3 RPM) *Meet The Beatles* ....30.00 - 50.00

2056 (DJ) *Hello Goodbye* ....20.00 - 30.00

SXA 2080 (7 inch, 33 1/3 RPM) *Beatles Second Album* ....30.00 - 50.00

SXAS 2108 (7 inch, 33 1/3 RPM) *Something New* .40.00 - 60.00

(EP) EAP-2121 *Four By The Beatles* ....50.00 - 75.00

2138 (DJ) *Lady Madonna* ....20.00 - 30.00

(LP) ST-2553 *Yesterday and Today* (STEREO, with "first state" "Butcher" cover: Beatles are sitting among doll parts and pieces of raw meat. Withdrawn shortly after issue, and replaced with a more tasteful depiction of the Beatles gathered around a trunk. Prices as high as $5,000.00 have been quoted for this issue.)..................1,000.00 - up

(LP) ST-2553 (same as foregoing, but with new cover pasted over "butcher" cover, traces of which are visible*) ....250.00 - up

(LP) T-2553 (MONO, with "first state" "butcher" cover. Prices as high as $1,500.00 have been seen for this issue) ....300.00 - up(LP)

T-2553 (same as foregoing, but new cover pasted over "butcher" cover, traces of which are visible*) ....150.00 - up

(Note: *beware of "peeled" paste-overs being offered as "first state" issues)

2637 (DJ) *KFW Beatles*....................................100.00 - 200.00

(Note: Picture sleeve for above is valuable)

5150 *Can't Buy Me Love (picture sleeve is quite scarce-record is of minimal value)*

(EP) EPR 5365 *Four By The Beatles* ....75.00 - 100.00

5810 (DJ) *Penny Lane* ....50.00 - 100.00

5964 (DJ) *All You Need Is Love*..........................50.00 - 100.00

(Note: Certain Capitol reissues, including some of fairly recent vintage, are valued far more highly than original issues)

Clarion (LP) 601 *The Amazing Beatles And Other Great English Group Sounds*.........................25.00 - 35.00

MGM 13213 *My Bonnie* ....7.00 - 10.00

13213 *(DJ) My Bonnie* ....30.00 - 50.00

13227 *Why* ....10.00 - 15.00

13227 (DJ) *Why* ....30.00 - 50.00

(Note: Picture sleeve for MGM 13227 is scarce)

Radio Pulsebeat (LP) *The American Tour With Ed Rudy* ....20.00 - 30.00

#Swan 4152 *(white label, red printing, without legend "Don't Drop Out") She Loves You*..50.00 - 80.00

4152 *(white label, red printing, with legend "Don't Drop Out") She Loves You*......................................30.00 - 40.00

4152 *(DJ) She Loves You*....................................75.00 - 100.00

Tollie 9008 *(DJ) Love Me Do* ....30.00 - 50.00

#Tollie (most other issues)....................................5.00 - 15.00

United Artists (LP) UAL-336 *A Hard Day's Night* (MONO) ....100.00 - up

#*Vee Jay* 498 *Please Please Me* ....200.00 - 400.00

498 (DJ) *Please Please Me* ....250.00 - 500.00

(Note: Some issues of Vee Jay 498 have the group's name as by THE BEATTLES)

522 *From Me To You* ....150.00 - 300.00

522 (DJ) *From Me To You* ....150.00 - 300.00

581 *Please Please Me* (purple label) ....80.00 - 120.00

581 *Please Please Me* (white label)..................50.00 - 100.00

581 (DJ) *Please Please Me* ....80.00 - 120.00

(Note: Picture sleeve for Vee Jay 581 is very scarce)

587 *Do You Want To Know A Secret* ....15.00 - 20.00

587 (DJ) *Do You Want To Know A Secret*.........75.00 - 100.00

(Note: Picture sleeve for Vee Jay 587 is scarce)

(EP) 1-903 *Souvenir Of Their Visit To America* 20.00 - 30.00

Vee Jay (LP) DX-30 *Beatles Vs. The Four Seasons* ....100.00 - 200.00

#Vee Jay (LP) LP-1062 *Introducing The Beatles* (Mono, black label, reverse of jacket depicts "other fine albums of significant interest").......................250.00 - up

#(LP) LP-1062 *Introducing The Beatles* (MONO, black label, reverse of jacket is blank) ....100.00 - up

#(LP) LPS-1062 *Introducing The Beatles* (STEREO, black label, reverse of jacket has ads for other albums)......500.00 - up

#(LP) LPS-1062 *Introducing The Beatles* (STEREO, black label, reverse of jacket is blank) ....200.00 - up

#*(LP) LP-1085 The Beatles And Frank Ifield On Stage* (MONO, picture of Beatles on cover; not to be confused with nominally-valued version having drawing of an old man on cover) ....200.00 - up

#*(LP) LPS-1085 The Beatles And Frank Ifield On Stage* (STEREO, picture of Beatles on cover) ....500.00 - up

(LP) LPS-1092 *Songs, Pictures And Stories Of The Fabulous Beatles* (STEREO)..200.00 - up

(**Note:** Prices far in excess of those listed above have been quoted for most of these top-drawer Beatles collectibles, with an occasional "still-sealed" copy being valued at as much as ten times the foregoing estimates. Whether such lofty figures are ever actually realized is not known. Also, how does the purchaser of a "still sealed" album satisfy himself that the appropriate LP is actually contained by the jacket?)

(**#Note:** These records (and others) occur with seemingly minute variations in label and/or covers, which may affect prices drastically. One interesting variation of Vee Jay 498 has the group designated as "THE BEATTLES.")

IMPORTANT: The generally applicable caveat concerning bootlegs and reissues deserves particular emphasis in the case of the Beatles' records. Also note that in many instances picture sleeves are worth far more than the record. Mentioned above are some of the most sought-after sleeves, but there are others which, although of lesser scarcity and value, are desirable (even where the record, unlisted here, is of nominal value). Finally, where a record listed is a promotional copy ("DJ" after record number), it should not be inferred that the regular issue is of comparable value; the regular issue, unless it is also listed, is common and of little value.

Those interested in pursuing the intricacies of Beatle records (and peripheral collectibles) should consult one of the books dealing with same, such as *The Official Price Guide to Memorabilia of Elvis Presley and The Beatles*, by Osborne, Cox, and Lindsay.

THE BEATNICKS:
Key-Lock 913 *Blue Angel* ....100.00 - up

E. C. BEATTY:
Colonial 7009 *Little Blue Eyes* ....5.00 - 8.00

THE BEAU-JIVES:
Shepherd 2202 *I'll Never Be The Same* ....15.00 - 20.00

THE BEAU-MARKS:
Rust 5035 *School Is Out* ....5.00 - 8.00
Shad 5017 *Clap Your Hands* ....5.00 - 8.00
   5021 *'Cause We're In Love* ....7.00 - 10.00
Time 1032 *Rockin' Blues* ....7.00 - 10.00

STAN BEAVER:
Petal 1012 *I Got A Rocket In My Pocket* ....5.00 - 8.00

THE BEAVERS:
Coral 65018 *If You See Tears In My Eyes* ....75.00 - 100.00
   65026 *I'd Rather Be Wrong Than Blue* ....75.00 - 100.00

THE BEES:
Finch 7322 *Tough Enough* ....10.00 - 15.00
Imperial 5314 *Toy Bell* ....75.00 - 100.00
   5320 *I Want To Be Loved* ....150.00 - up

THE BEL-AIRES/BELAIRES:
Flip 303 *This Paradise* ....20.00 - 30.00
Raft 604 *Are You My Girl* ....100.00 - up

CARL BELEW:
Decca 30947 *Cool Gator Shoes* ....10.00 - 15.00
Sowder 248 *I'm Long Gone* ....80.00 - 120.00

BILL BELL & THE FOUR UNKNOWNS:
Mida 112 *Little Bitty Girl* ....15.00 - 20.00

CARL BELL & THE NOVAIRS:
Laurie 3014 *Birth Of The Beat* ....10.00 - 15.00

DWAIN BELL:
Summit 110 *Rock & Roll On A Saturday Night* ....100.00 - 150.00

EDDIE/EDDY BELL:
Belaire 956 *He's A Square* ....75.00 - 125.00
Coed 512 *Countin' The Days* ....5.00 - 8.00
Mercury 71677 *The Masked Man* ....7.00 - 10.00

FREDDIE BELL & THE BELL BOYS:
Mercury (LP) 20289 *Rock And Roll* ....20.00 - 30.00
   71105 *Rockin' Is My Business* ....5.00 - 8.00
Teen 101 *Hound Dog* (78 rpm) ....10.00 - 15.00

JOHNNY BELL:
Brunswick 55142 *Flip Flop And Fly* ....15.00 - 20.00

LEE BELL:
RCA Victor 5148 *Beatin' Out The Boogie* ....7.00 - 10.00

TOMMY BELL:
Zil 9001 *Swamp Gal* ....25.00 - 40.00

THE BEL-LARKS:
Ransom 5001 *1 Million And One Dreams* ....50.00 - 80.00

THE BELL NOTES:
Madison 141 *Real Wild Child* ....5.00 - 10.00
Time (EP) 100 *I've Had It* ....75.00 - 100.00
   1013 *Betty Dear* ....7.00 - 10.00

THE BELLS:
Rama 166 *What Can I Tell Her Now* ....200.00 - up

THE BELLTONES:
Grand (blue) 102 *Estelle* (red plastic) ....300.00 - up

TONY BELLUS:
NRC (LP) LPA 8 *Robbin The Cradle* ....75.00 - 100.00

THE BELMONTS:
Mohawk 106 *Santa Margarita* ....10.00 - 15.00
Sabrina 500 *Tell Me Why* ....10.00 - 15.00
   501 *Searching For A New Love* ....10.00 - 15.00
   502 *I Need Someone* ....10.00 - 15.00
   503 *I Confess* ....10.00 - 15.00
   506 *Come On Little Angel* ....7.00 - 10.00
   507 *Diddle-Dee-Dum* ....8.00 - 12.00
   509 *Ann Marie* ....8.00 - 12.00
   513 *Let's Call It A Day* ....8.00 - 12.00
   517 *Walk On By* ....10.00 - 15.00
   519 *C'mon Everybody* ....10.00 - 15.00
   521 *Summertime* ....20.00 - 30.00
   (LP) 5001 *Carnival Of Hits* ....40.00 - 60.00

THE BELTONES:
Hull 721 *I Talk To My Echo* ....15.00 - 20.00
Jell 188 *I Want To Be Loved* ....15.00 - 20.00

THE BELVEDERES:
Baton 214 *Come To Me Baby* ....15.00 - 20.00
   217 *Pepper Hot Baby* ....10.00 - 15.00
JOPZ 1771 *Buona Sera* ....- -
Lucky Four 1003 *Wage Assignment Blues* ....15.00 - 20.00
Trend 30-009 *Let's Get Married* ....10.00 - 15.00

JESSE BELVIN (See also THREE DOTS & A DASH):
Cash 1056 *Beware* ....25.00 - 50.00
J.R.M. 003/004 *Going Away Baby* ....7.00 - 10.00
Modern 1005 *Goodnight My Love* ....7.00 - 10.00
RCA Victor (LP) 2089 ....20.00 - 30.00
   (LP) 2105 *Mr. Easy* ....20.00 - 30.00
Specialty 550 *Gone* ....10.00 - 15.00
   559 *Where's My Girl* ....7.00 - 10.00

ARNOLD BENNETT:
Sharp 110 *Wahoo* ....7.00 - 10.00

BARBARA BENNETT:
Swade 101 *Big Daddy Rabbit* .... -   -   -

BOYD BENNETT (& HIS ROCKETS):
King (EP) 383 *Rock And Roll* ....80.00 - 120.00
  (LP) 532 *Boyd Bennett* ....150.00 - 200.00
  (LP) 594 *Boyd Bennett "17 All-Time Hits"* .....150.00 - 200.00
  1413 *I've Had Enough* ....7.00 - 10.00
  1432 *You Upset Me Baby* ....7.00 - 10.00
  1275 *Tennessee Rock And Roll* ....10.00 - 15.00
  1494 *My Boy Flat Top* ....4.00 - 7.00
  4903 *Blue Suede Shoes* ....7.00 - 10.00
  4985 *Rockin' Up A Storm* ....8.00 - 12.00
  5094 *Put The Chain On The Door* ....7.00 - 10.00
  5115 *Move* ....10.00 - 15.00
Mercury 71479 *Boogie Bear* ....5.00 - 8.00

CLIFF BENNETT:
Capitol 4621 *You Got What I Like* ....20.00 - 30.00

CHUCK BENNETT:
Bonnie 101 *I Went To Your House* ....8.00 - 12.00

JOE BENSON:
DeLuxe 6146 *Rock And Roll Jungle* ....7.00 - 10.00

BROOK BENTON (& THE SANDMEN):
Camden (LP) 564 ....8.00 - 12.00
Epic (LP) LN-3573 *At His Best* ....20.00 - 30.00
Mercury (LP) 20421 *It's Just A Matter Of Time* .....20.00 - 30.00
  (LP) 20464 *Endlessly* ....20.00 - 30.00
  (LP) 20565 *So Many Ways* ....15.00 - 20.00
Okeh 7058 *Ooh* ....10.00 - 15.00
Vik 0311 *A Million Miles From Nowhere* ....7.00 - 10.00

BUSTER BENTON:
Melloway 20668 *Hole In My Head* ....7.00 - 10.00

MERV BENTON:
MarVel 401 *Twenty Hole In My Head* ....20.00 - 30.00

WALT BENTON (& THE SNAPPERS):
Scottie 1321 *Summer School Blues* ....15.00 - 20.00
20th Fox 143 *Big Wheel* ....15.00 - 20.00

SHIRLEY BERGERON:
Lanor 510 *French Rocking Boogie* ....10.00 - 15.00

ROD BERNARD (& THE TWISTERS):
Argo 5327 *Pardon Mr. Gordon* ....7.00 - 10.00
  5327 *Pardon Mr. Gordon* (78 rpm) ....10.00 - 15.00
  5338 *My Life Is A Mystery* ....7.00 - 10.00
Jin 105 *Pardon Mr. Gordon* ....12.00 - 16.00
  (LP) 1007 *Rod Bernard* ....20.00 - 30.00
Mercury 71654 *Dance Fool Dance* ....7.00 - 10.00
Mercury (most other issues) ....5.00 - 8.00

THE BERRY CUPS:
Khoury's 710 *Delores Darlin'* ....8.00 - 12.00

THE BERRY KIDS:
MGM 12379 *Go, Go, Go, Right Into Town* ....15.00 - 20.00
  12496 *You're My Teen Age Baby* ....15.00 - 20.00

CHUCK BERRY:
Chess (LP) 1426 *After School Session* ....50.00 - 80.00
  (LP) 1432 *One Dozen Berrys* ....50.00 - 80.00
  (LP) 1435 *Chuck Berry Is On Top* ....50.00 - 80.00
  (LP) 1448 *Rockin' At The Hops* ....50.00 - 80.00
(Note: LPs must have black labels with silver printing.)
Chess 1604 *Maybelline* (silver top label) ....15.00 - 20.00
  1604 *Maybelline* (78 rpm) ....15.00 - 25.00

1610 *Thirty Days* ....8.00 - 12.00
1610 *Thirty Days* (78 rpm) ....10.00 - 15.00
1615 *No Money Down* ....8.00 - 12.00
1615 *No Money Down* (78 rpm) ....15.00 - 20.00
1626 *Roll Over Beethoven* ....8.00 - 12.00
1626 *Roll Over Beethoven* (78 rpm) ....30.00 - 50.00
1635 *Brown Eyed Handsome Man* ....7.00 - 10.00
1635 *Brown Eyed Handsome Man* (78 rpm) ....20.00 - 30.00
1645 *You Can't Catch Me* ....5.00 - 8.00
1645 *You Can't Catch Me* (78 rpm) ....20.00 - 30.00
1653 *School Day* ....5.00 - 8.00
1653 *School Day* (78 rpm) ....20.00 - 30.00
1664 *Oh Baby* ....5.00 - 8.00
1664 *Oh Baby* (78 rpm) ....20.00 - 30.00
(Note: Foregoing have "silver top" labels)
1671 *Rock & Roll Music* ....7.00 - 10.00
1671 *Rock & Roll Music* (78 rpm) ....30.00 - 50.00
1683 *Reelin' And Rockin'* ....7.00 - 10.00
1683 *Reelin' And Rockin'* (78 rpm) ....30.00 - 50.00
1691 *Johnny B. Goode* ....7.00 - 10.00
1691 *Johnny B. Goode* (78 rpm) ....50.00 - 80.00
1697 *Vacation Time* ....7.00 - 10.00
1697 *Vacation Time* (78 rpm) ....20.00 - 30.00
1700 *Carol* ....8.00 - 12.00
1700 *Carol* (78 rpm) ....40.00 - 60.00
1709 *Sweet Little Rock And Roller* ....10.00 - 15.00
1709 *Sweet Little Rock And Roller* (78 rpm) ....50.00 - 80.00
1714 *Run Rudolph Run* ....15.00 - 20.00
1714 *Run Rudolph Run* (78 rpm) ....50.00 - 80.00
1716 *That's My Desire* ....7.00 - 10.00
1716 *That's My Desire* (78 rpm) ....40.00 - 60.00
1722 *Little Queenie* ....7.00 - 10.00
1722 *Little Queenie* (78 rpm) ....75.00 - 100.00
1729 *Back In The U.S.A.* ....7.00 - 10.00
1729 *Back In The U.S.A.* (78 rpm) ....75.00 - 100.00
1737 *Childhood Sweetheart* ....7.00 - 10.00
1737 *Childhood Sweetheart* (78 rpm) ....50.00 - 80.00
1747 *Let It Rock* ....7.00 - 10.00
1747 *Let It Rock* (78 rpm) ....80.00 - 120.00
Chess (most issues, higher numbers) ....4.00 - 7.00
  (EP) 5118 *After School Session* ....40.00 - 60.00
  (EP) 5119 *Rock & Roll Music* ....50.00 - 80.00
  (EP) 5121 *Sweet Little Sixteen* ....50.00 - 80.00
  (EP) 5126 *Sweet Little Rock and Roller* ....75.00 - 100.00
  (EP) 5124 *Pickin' Berries* ....40.00 - 60.00

DOROTHY BERRY:
Planetary 101 *Ain't That Love* ....7.00 - 10.00

LOU BERRY & THE BELL RAVES:
Dreem 1001 *What A Dolly* ....50.00 - 75.00
20th Fox 169 *What A Dolly* ....15.00 - 25.00

MIKE BERRY & THE OUTLAWS:
Coral 62341 *Tribute To Buddy Holly* ....10.00 - 15.00
  62357 *Don't You Think It's Time* ....8.00 - 12.00
  62483 *Gonna Fall In Love* ....8.00 - 12.00

RED BERRY & THE BELL RAVES (See LOU BERRY)

RICHARD BERRY (& THE DREAMERS/PHARAOHS):
Crown (LP) 5371 *Richard Berry & The Dreamers* ......40.00 - 60.00
Flair 1016 *I'm Still In Love With You* ....20.00 - 30.00
  1055 *What You Do To Me* ....15.00 - 20.00
  1058 *Baby Darling* ....15.00 - 20.00
  1064 *Please Tell Me* ....10.00 - 15.00
  1068 *God Gave Me You* ....10.00 - 15.00
Flip 318 *Take The Key* ....10.00 - 15.00
  321 *Louie Louie* ....10.00 - 20.00

327 *Rock Rock Rock* ....8.00 - 12.00
331 *You're The Girl*...8.00 - 12.00
336 *Heaven On Wheels*...7.00 - 10.00
Flip (other issues) ....5.00 - 10.00
RPM 448 *Rockin' Man* ....15.00 - 20.00
452 *I Am Bewildered* ....10.00 - 15.00
465 *Angel Of My Life*..8.00 - 12.00
476 *Wait For Me*..8.00 - 12.00

THE BEST OF RHYTHM AND BLUES:
Jubilee (LP) 1014...50.00 - 100.00

THE BEST VOCAL GROUPS IN RHYTHM & BLUES:
Dootone (LP) 204 ....80.00 - 120.00

STAN BEVERLY & THE HOLLYWOOD SAXONS:
Entra 1214 *Diamonds* ....25.00 - 50.00

BIG BILL:
Chess 1546 *Little City Woman* ....50.00 - 80.00

BIG BOPPER (See also JAPE RICHARDSON):
D1008 *Chantilly Lace*...20.00 - 30.00
Mercury (LP) MG-20402 *Chantilly Lace* (black & silver label)
....100.00 - 150.00
(LP) MG-20402 *Chantilly Lace* (red label)........20.00 - 30.00
71343 *Chantilly Lace*...5.00 - 8.00
71343 *Chantilly Lace* (78 rpm) ....100.00 - up
71375 *Big Bopper's Wedding*..............................5.00 - 8.00
71416 *Walking Through My Dreams* ....10.00 - 15.00
71451 *It's The Truth, Ruth*................................10.00 - 15.00
71482 *The Clock* ....10.00 - 15.00

BIG CONNIE:
Groove 0142 *Mumbles Blues*..............................10.00 - 15.00

BIG DADDY:
Gee (LP) 704 *Big Daddy's Blues*.................................- - -

BIG ED & HIS COMBO:
Checker 790 *Biscuit Baking Mama* ....100.00 - 150.00

THE BIG FIVE:
Shad 5019 *Blue Eyes* ....8.00 - 12.00

BIG FOUR:
Moon 306 *Outa Tune*...10.00 - 15.00

BIG MAC:
Tri-Mac 501 *Someday You're Gonna Sing The Blues*
....10.00 - 15.00

BIG MACEO (with TAMPA RED):
Groove 5001 *Worried Life Blues* ....10.00 - 15.00
RCA Victor 50-0002 (orange plastic) *If You Ever*
Change Your Ways ....35.00 - 50.00

BIG MAYBELLE:
Okeh 7060 *Whole Lotta Shakin' Goin On* ....15.00 - 20.00
(LP) 14005 *Big Maybelle Sings*........................50.00 - 80.00
Savoy (LP) 14011 *Blues, Candy And Big Maybelle*.......50.00 - 80.00

BIG WALTER (& HIS COMBO/THE THUNDERBIRDS):
Global 409 *Watusie Freeze*..................................5.00 - 8.00
Goldband 1080 *Crazy Dream* ....10.00 - 15.00
Myrl 406 *Feelin' A Little Worried*...........................5.00 - 8.00
Peacock 1661 *Gamblin' Woman* ....7.00 - 10.00
States 145 *Hard Hearted Woman* ....30.00 - 50.00
Teardrop 3130 *Get To Gitten'* ....5.00 - 8.00
TNT 8005 *Calling Margie*....................................20.00 - 30.00
8006 *Oh No, No Blues* ....20.00 - 30.00

DICK BILLS:
Crest 1089 *Rockin' And Rollin'* ....15.00 - 20.00

BILLY & LILLIE (& THE THUNDERBIRDS):
ABC Paramount 10421 *Love Me Sincerely* ....15.00 - 25.00
10489 *Carry Me 'Cross The Threshhold* ....15.00 - 25.00
Casino 105 *La Dee Dah*......................................5.00 - 8.00
Swan 4002 *La Dee Dah* (78 rpm) ....20.00 - 30.00

BILLY BOY:
Vee Jay 146 *I Was Fooled* ....10.00 - 15.00
171 *I Ain't Got You* ....8.00 - 12.00
192 *Here's My Picture*..8.00 - 12.00
238, 260...7.00 - 10.00

BILLY GUITAR & HIS NIGHTHAWKS:
Decca 30634 *Here Comes The Night*....................10.00 - 15.00

BILLY THE KID:
Kapp 261 *Apron Strings*.....................................10.00 - 15.00

LONG MAN BINDER:
United 194 *I'm A Lover* ....30.00 - 50.00

BING BONGS:
Dragon 10205 *Ding-A-Ling-A-Ling-Ding-Dong* .... 25.00 - 50.00

JIMMY BINKLEY:
Chance 1134 *Hey Hey Sugar Ray* ....50.00 - 80.00

BIP AND BOP:
Aladdin 3287 *Ding Dong Ding* ....7.00 - 10.00

LARRY BIRDSONG:
Excello 2064, 2076 ....7.00 - 10.00

THE BISHOPS:
Bridges 1105 *The Wedding* ....25.00 - 50.00

JOE BLACKWELL (See THE INDIVIDUALS)

OTIS BLACKWELL:
Davis (LP) 109 *Singin' The Blues* ....75.00 - 100.00
455 *Daddy Rollin' Stone* ....10.00 - 15.00
Jay-Dee 784 *Daddy Rollin' Stone* ....15.00 - 20.00
787 *Bartender, Fill It Up Again*............................8.00 - 12.00
791 *On That Power Line* ....8.00 - 12.00
792 *I'm Standing At The Doorway* ....8.00 - 12.00
794 *Ain't Got No Time* ....8.00 - 12.00
798 *Go Away Mr. Blues* ....8.00 - 12.00
802 *You Move Me Baby* ....7.00 - 10.00
808 *Let The Daddy Hold You*...............................10.00 - 15.00
Jubilee 5095 *Paint A Sky For Me* ....- - -

THE BLACKWELLS:
GB 125 *Here's The Question*................................15.00 - 20.00

EMERY BLADES:
Arvis 110 *I Feel Like a Million* ....15.00 - 20.00

TOMMY BLAKE:
Buddy 107 *Cool It (Baby)*...................................100.00 - 150.00
RCA Victor 6925 *Freedom*...................................5.00 - 8.00
Sun 278 *Flat Foot Sam* ....15.00 - 20.00
300 *I Dig You Baby*...100.00 - 150.00

CLIFF BLAKELEY:
Starday 352 *High Steppin'* ....30.00 - 50.00
369 *Get Off My Toes* ....30.00 - 50.00

CORNELL BLAKELY:
Fulton 2453 *Don't Touch The Moon* ....20.00 - 30.00

JIMMY BLAKELEY:
Starday 299 *Crazy Blues* ....30.00 - 50.00

WELLINGTON BLAKELY:
Vee Jay 104 *Sailor Joe* ....30.00 - 50.00

JACKIE BLANCHARD W/THE ROCKING IMPALAS:
Mida 111 *The King O'Hearts* ....15.00 - 20.00

BILLY BLAND:
Old Town 1016 *The Fat Man* ....7.00 - 10.00

BOBBY BLUE BLAND:
Crown (LP) 5258 *Two In Blues* ....20.00 - 30.00
Duke (LP) 74 *Two Steps From The Blues* ....20.00 - 30.00
   (LP) 77 *Call On Me* ....20.00 - 30.00
   (LP) 78 *Ain't Nothing You Can Do* ....20.00 - 30.00
(Note: Above LPs are MONO issues)
Duke 105 *I.O.U. Blues* ....30.00 - 50.00
   115 *Army Blues* ....20.00 - 30.00
Duke 141, 153, 170, 182, 185 ....5.00 - 10.00

GLENN BLAND:
Sarg 159 *Mean Gene* ....15.00 - 20.00
   164 *When My Baby Passes By* ....20.00 - 30.00

BLANKENSHIP BROTHERS:
Skyline 106 *That's Why I'm Blue* ....50.00 - 75.00

THE BLASERS:
United 191 *She Needs To Be Loved* ....10.00 - 15.00

JULES BLATTNER:
Bobbin 105 *Rock And Roll Blues* ....25.00 - 40.00
K-Ark 609 *Lonesome* ....10.00 - 15.00
Norman 509 *Slip 'N Slide* ....5.00 - 8.00

BLAZER BOY (See also JAMES LOCKS):
Imperial 5199 *Mornin' Train* ....150.00 - 300.00
   5244 *Waiting For My Baby* ....60.00 - 100.00

STEVE BLEDSOE:
Scope 8266 *Cool Steppin' Baby* ....20.00 - 30.00
Superstar 712 *That's All Right* ....8.00 - 12.00
Witch 102 *Dumb Dumb Bunny* ....10.00 - 15.00

THE BLENDAIRS:
Tin Pan Alley 252 *My Love Is Just For You* ......50.00 - 80.00

THE BLENDERS:
Aladdin 3449 *Soda Shop* ....200.00 - up
Class 236 *Little Rose* ....30.00 - 60.00
Decca 31284 *Tell Me What's On Your Mind* ......10.00 - 15.00
   48156 *Honeysuckle Rose* ....- - -
   48158 *Count Every Star* ....- - -
(Note: *The existence of foregoing in 45 RPM format has not been verified; 78s are known, for which see **RHYTHM & BLUES, ETC.** section.)
   48183 *What About Tonight* ....75.00 - 125.00
   48244 *My Heart Will Never Forget* ....75.00 - 125.00
Jay-Dee 780 *You'll Never Be Mine Again* ....50.00 - 80.00
Paradise 111 *I Won't Tell The World* ....15.00 - 20.00
Smash 2005 *Desert Sands* ....15.00 - 25.00
(Note: See also the **RHYTHM & BLUES, ETC.** section for other (78 rpm) records by this group.)

THE BLENDS:
Casa Grande 5000 *A Thousand Miles Away* ....10.00 - 15.00
   5037 *Someone To Care* ....8.00 - 12.00
Talent 110 *Tell Me* ....10.00 - 20.00

THE BLENDTONES:
MGM 12782 *Lilly* ....7.00 - 10.00
Success 101 *Dear Diary* ....5.00 - 8.00
   105 *Come On Home* ....5.00 - 8.00

MARV BLIHOVE:
Lindy 113 *Cigarettes And Coffee Blues* ....15.00 - 25.00

THE BLOCKBUSTERS:
Aladdin 3319 *Why Baby Why* ....10.00 - 15.00

JAY BLUE:
Imperial 5587 *Get Off My Back* ....20.00 - 30.00

THE BLUE ANGELS:
Edsel 781 *Deserie* ....15.00 - 30.00

THE BLUE BELLES:
Atlantic 987 *The Story Of A Fool* ....25.00 - 40.00

BLUE CHARLIE:
Nasco 6002 *I'm Gonna Kill That Hen* ....15.00 - 25.00

THE BLUE CHIPS:
DeLuxe 6100 *Appointment With Love* ....50.00 - 80.00
Groove 0006 *Promise* ....5.00 - 8.00

THE BLUE DIAMONDS:
Savoy 1134 *No Money* ....15.00 - 20.00

THE BLUE DOTS:
Ace 526 *Please Don't Tell 'Em* ....10.00 - 15.00
De Luxe 6052 *You've Got To Live For Yourself* ....20.00 - 30.00
   6055 *Street Of Sorrow* ....25.00 - 40.00
   6061 *Save All Your Love For Me* ....25.00 - 40.00
   6067 *Hold Me Tight* ....20.00 - 30.00
NRC 504 *All You Gotta Do* ....50.00 - 100.00

BLUE FLAMES (See LITTLE JUNIOR):

THE BLUE JAYS:
Blue Jay 102 *Write Me A Letter* ....50.00 - 80.00
Checker 782 *White Cliffs Of Dover* ....200.00 - up
Milestone 2008 *Lover's Island* ....5.00 - 8.00
   2010 *Let's Make Love* ....5.00 - 8.00
   2014 *Venus My Love* ....20.00 - 30.00
Roulette 4169 *Barbara* ....5.00 - 8.00

THE BLUE NOTES:
Josie 800 *If You Love Me* ....25.00 - 40.00
   823 *The Retribution Blues* ....20.00 - 30.00
Lost 104 *She Is Mine* ....100.00 - 150.00
Port 70021 *If You Love Me* ....8.00 - 12.00
TNT 150 *Darling Of Mine* ....20.00 - 30.00
20th Century 1213 *Pucker Your Lips* ......5.00 - 8.00
Value 213 *My Hero* ....15.00 - 25.00

"THE BLUES":
Argo (LP) 4026 ....35.00 - 50.00

THE BLUES KINGS:
K-Dee 1000 *Blues Stay Away From Me* ......8.00 - 12.00

THE BLUES ROCKERS:
Excello 2062 *Calling All Cows* ....10.00 - 15.00

BLUES SLIM:
Five-Four 5435 *Drivin' Me, Baby* ....7.00 - 10.00

THE BLUES TOPPERS:
Duke 172 *Sleeping In An Ocean Of Tears* ......15.00 - 20.00

THE BLUE TONES:
King 5088 *Shake Shake* ....15.00 - 20.00

TOOTER BOATMAN:
Twinkle 501 *More And More* ....100.00 - 150.00

HARMON BOAZEMAN:
Sarg 145 *No Love In You* ....35.00 - 50.00

BOB AND LUCILLE:
Ditto 121 *Eenie Meenie Miney Moe* ....100.00 - 150.00
   126 *What's The Password* ....30.00 - 50.00
Imperial 5631 *Eenie Meenie Miney Moe* ....15.00 - 30.00

BOB AND RAY:
Nasco 6023 *Shorty Shorty* ....8.00 - 12.00
   6029 *Sweet Nancy* ....8.00 - 12.00

BOB & THE ROCKABILLIES:
Blue Chip 011 *Your Kind Of Love* ....15.00 - 20.00

BOB AND SHERI:
Safari 101 *The Surfer Moon* ....500.00 - up
(Note: DJ; white label; regular issue; blue label. Caution: Bootlegs
   exist of this early **BEACH BOYS** related disc.)

BOB & SHIRLEY:
Band Box 225 *Your True Love* ....7.00 - 10.00

THE BOBBETTES:
Atlantic 1144 *Mr. Lee* (78 rpm) ....10.00 - 15.00

BOB-B-SOXX & THE BLUE JEANS:
Philles (LP) 4002 *Zip-A-Dee-Doo-Dah* ....100.00 - 150.00

BOBBY & THE CONSOLES:
Diamond 141 *Nita I Deed You So* ....20.00 - 30.00

BOBBY & THE ORBITS:
Seeco 6067 *Felicia* ....7.00 - 10.00

BOBBY SUE & HER FREELOADERS:
Harlem 2335 *Relief Check* ....15.00 - 20.00

BILL BODAFORD & THE ROCKETS:
Back Beat 507 *Little Girl* ....15.00 - 20.00

THE BON-AIRES:
Dootone 325 *It's Xmas Time* ....100.00 - 150.00
King 4975 *Stop The World* ....7.00 - 10.00

DAVE BOND:
Khoury's 723 *Tell Me* ....20.00 - 30.00

EDDIE BOND (& HIS STOMPERS):
Coral 62200 *Little Black Book* ....15.00 - 20.00
D 1016 *The Blues Got Me* ....15.00 - 20.00
Diplomat 8566 *The Monkey And The Baboon* ....15.00 - 20.00
Ekko 1015 *Talkin' Off The Wall* ....50.00 - 75.00
   1016 *Love Makes A Fool* ....30.00 - 40.00
Memphis 115 *Here Comes The Train* ....20.00 - 30.00
Mercury 70826 *Rockin' Daddy* ....15.00 - 20.00
   70882 *Slip Slip Slippin' In* ....15.00 - 20.00
   70941 *Boppin' Bonnie* ....15.00 - 25.00
   71067 *You're Part Of Me* ....10.00 - 15.00
   71153 *Hershey Bar* ....10.00 - 15.00
   71237 *Backslidin'* ....10.00 - 15.00
Phillips (LP) 1980 *Sings Greatest Country Gospel Hits*
....50.00 - 100.00
Stomper Time 1156 *You'll Never Be A Stranger* ....10.00 - 15.00

JOHNNY BOND:
Columbia 21521 *The Little Rock Roll* ....7.00 - 10.00
Republic 2005 *Hot Rod Lincoln* ....5.00 - 8.00
   2008 *The Way A Star Is Born* ....8.00 - 12.00
   2010 *Side Car Cycle* ....8.00 - 12.00
   2022 *Sadie Was A Lady* ....7.00 - 10.00

LUTHER BOND & HIS EMERALDS:
Federal 12279 *He Loves You Baby* ....15.00 - 20.00
   12368 *Old Mother Nature* ....10.00 - 15.00

Savoy 1124 *What If You* ....15.00 - 20.00
   1131 *Starlight, Starbright* ....15.00 - 20.00
   1159 *It's Written In The Stars* ....15.00 - 25.00

GARY U. S. BONDS: (See U. S. BONDS)

LEE BONDS:
Decca 29338 *I'm Lookin' For Some Lovin'* ....5.00 - 8.00
Tennessee 804 *Oh-Huh Honey* ....10.00 - 15.00
   826 *Wild Cattin' Woman* ....10.00 - 15.00

U.S. BONDS:
Legrand (LP) 3001 *Dance Till Quarter To Three*... 50.00 - 80.00
   (LP) 3002 *Twist Up Calypso* ....40.00 - 60.00

JOHNNY BONI:
Black-Crest 108 *Ruby Baby* ....10.00 - 15.00

SKEETER BONN:
RCA Victor 5814 *Honey Baby* ....5.00 - 10.00

JUKE BOY BONNER:
Goldband 1102 *Call Me Juke Boy* ....15.00 - 20.00

THE BONNEVILLES:
Barry 104 *Lorraine* ....8.00 - 12.00
Munich 103 *Lorraine* ....75.00 - 100.00

BOOGALOO:
Crest 1030 *Cops And Robbers* (red plastic) ....15.00 - 20.00

BOOGIE JAKE:
Chess 1746 *Bad Luck And Trouble* ....10.00 - 15.00
Instant 3314 *Early Morning Blues* ....8.00 - 12.00

BOOGIE KINGS:
Pic 1 133 *Let It Be Me* ....10.00 - 15.00

JOHN LEE BOOKER:
De Luxe 6004 *Blue Monday* ....20.00 - 30.00
   6032 *Pouring Down Rain* ....15.00 - 20.00
   6046 *Real Real Gone* ....15.00 - 20.00
Rockin' 525 *Pouring Down Rain* ....35.00 - 50.00

CONNIE BOOKS:
Citation 5001 *Black Magic And Witchcraft* ....7.00 - 10.00

PAT BOONE:
Dot (LP) 3050, *Pat* ....10.00 - 15.00
Republic 7049, 7062, 7084 ....5.00 - 8.00

THE BOP-CHORDS:
Holiday 2601 *Castle In The Sky* ....25.00 - 40.00
   2603 *When I Woke Up This Morning* ....25.00 - 50.00
   2608 *Baby* ....50.00 - 100.00

"BOPPIN" (With THE ORIOLES, THE MARYLANDERS, et. al.):
Jubilee (LP) 1118 ....50.00 - 80.00

BOSSTONES:
Boss 501 *Mope-Itty Mope* ....10.00 - 15.00
V-Tone 208 *Mope-Itty Mope* ....5.00 - 8.00

BOBBY BOSTON:
Starwin 7001 *Lazy Daisy* ....10.00 - 20.00

BOSWELL, JO ANN (See THE EL TONES)

RICK BOUNTY:
Bow 6144 *It Will Be Me* ....8.00 - 12.00

BILL BOWEN & THE ROCKETS:
Meteor 5033 *Have Myself A Ball* ....40.00 - 60.00

JIMMY BOWEN:
Blue Moon 402 *I'm Stickin' With You* ....50.00 - 75.00
Roulette 4001, 4010 ....4.00 - 7.00
   4010 *I'm Stickin' With You* (78 rpm) ....10.00 - 15.00
   4010 *Warm Up To Me Baby* (78 rpm) ....10.00 - 15.00
   4023 *It's Shameful* ....4.00 - 7.00
   4023 *It's Shameful* (78 rpm) ....10.00 - 15.00
   (LP) 25004 *Jimmy Bowen* ....30.00 - 50.00
Triple-D 797 *I'm Stickin' With You* ....100.00 - 150.00

CHUCK BOWERS:
Decca 30356 *Til My Baby Comes Home* ....7.00 - 10.00

DOUG BOWLES:
Tune 206 *Cadillac Baby* ....25.00 - 50.00

CECIL BOWMAN:
D 1048 *Man-A-Waitin'* ....7.00 - 10.00
Saturday 336 *Blues Around My Door* ....15.00 - 20.00

JANE BOWMAN:
Sapien 1005 *Mad Mama* ....10.00 - 20.00

DONNIE BOWSER:
Era 3029 *Stone Heart* ....8.00 - 12.00
Sage 265 *I Love You Baby* ....15.00 - 20.00
   276 *Got The Best Of Me* ....15.00 - 20.00

LITTLE DONNIE BOWSHIER:
Dess 7002 *Rock And Roll Joys* ....50.00 - 80.00

DAVID BOX:
Joed 717 *Do The Best I Can* ....15.00 - 20.00

EDDIE BOYD:
Bea & Baby 101, 107, 108 ....8.00 - 12.00
Chess 1523 *Cool Kind Treatment* ....20.00 - 30.00
   1533 *The Tickler* ....15.00 - 20.00
   1541, 1552, 1561, 1573, 1576, 1582, 1595,
   1606, 1621, 1634 ....8.00 - 12.00
   1660, 1674 ....7.00 - 10.00
Herald 406 *I'm Goin' Downtown* ....30.00 - 50.00
J.O.B. 1005 *I'm Pleading* ....50.00 - 80.00
   1007 *Five Long Years* ....30.00 - 50.00
   1009 *I'm Pleading* ....50.00 - 75.00
   1114 *I Love You* ....50.00 - 80.00
Oriole 1316/1317 *Five Long Years* ....10.00 - 15.00

JIMMY BOYD:
Columbia 21571 *Shakin' Down The Mississippi* ....7.00 - 10.00

ROBERT BOYD:
Wasco 201 *Boyd's Bounce* ....150.00 - 300.00

THE BOYFRIENDS:
Kapp 569 *Oh Lana* ....15.00 - 25.00

HELEN BOZEMAN:
Sandy 1011 *Sugar Baby* ....15.00 - 20.00

TOMMY BRADEN:
United 177 *Do The Do* ....25.00 - 40.00

ROCKIN' BRADLEY:
Fire 1007 *Look Out* ....20.00 - 30.00

JACK BRADSHAW:
Mar Vel 750 *Don't Tease Me* ....10.00 - 15.00
   752 *Naughty Girls* ....10.00 - 15.00

JIMMY BRADSHAW:
McBrad 1000 *When School's Out* ....7.00 - 10.00

TINY BRADSHAW:
King (LP) 501 *Selections* ....100.00 - 150.00
   4427 *Walk That Mess* ....30.00 - 60.00
   4497 *Train Kept-A-Rollin'* ....15.00 - 20.00

DOUG BRAGG:
Coral 61716 *Barbed Wire Love* ....10.00 - 15.00
D 1018 *If I Find My Dream Girl* ....15.00 - 30.00
   1045 *Calling Me Back* ....10.00 - 15.00
Dixie 2002 *Lovin' On My Mind* ....20.00 - 30.00
   - *Pretty Little Thing* ....15.00 - 20.00

JOHNNY BRAGG & THE MARIGOLDS:
Excello 2078 *Foolish Me* ....20.00 - 30.00
   2091 *Juke Box Rock 'n' Roll* ....20.00 - 30.00

RONNIE BRANAM:
Pep 117 *Puppy Dog Love* ....80.00 - 120.00

BOBBY BRANT:
East West 124 *Piano Nellie* ....15.00 - 20.00
White Rock 1114 *Piano Nellie* ....50.00 - 80.00

NICKY BRAZZELL:
Sparr - *Betty Joe* ....- -

JIMMY BREEDLOVE:
Atco 6094 *That's My Baby* ....7.00 - 10.00
Diamond 144 *Jealous Fool* ....7.00 - 10.00

JACKIE BRENSTON:
Chess 1458 *Rocket 88* ....300.00 - up
   1469 *In My Real Gone Rocket* ....100.00 - 150.00
   1472 *Juiced* ....100.00 - 150.00
   1496 *Hi-Ho Baby* ....75.00 - 100.00
   1532 *Blues Got Me Again* ....30.00 - 60.00
(Note: *These are rarely found as first-pressings in 45 RPM format;
   beware of bootlegs and later pressings)
Federal 12283 *Gonna Wait for My Chance* ....15.00 - 30.00
   12291 *The Mistreater* ....15.00 - 30.00

FRANKIE BRENT (& THE COUNTS):
Calvert 201 *No Rock 'n' Rollin' Here* ....15.00 - 20.00
Strand 25014 *No Rock 'n' Rollin' Here* ....10.00 - 15.00
Vik 0322 *Cold As Ice* ....10.00 - 15.00

RONNIE BRENT:
Colt 45 101 *Shirley Ann* ....15.00 - 20.00

BRENTWOODS:
Dore 559 *Midnight Star* ....10.00 - 20.00

ROBIN HOOD BRIANS:
Fraternity 803 *Dis A Itty Bit* ....30.00 - 50.00

JOHN BRIM:
Checker 769 *Rattlesnake* ....75.00 - 100.00
Chess 1588 *That Ain't Right* ....50.00 - 75.00
   1624 *You Got Me Where You Want Me* ....30.00 - 50.00
Parrot 799 *Gary Stomp* ....75.00 - 100.00
(Note: See also Blues, etc. section for 78 RPM records by **JOHN
   BRIM**)

JAY BRINKLEY:
Kliff 101 *Guitar Smoke* ....30.00 - 40.00

LARRY BRINKLEY:
Magic - *Right String But The Wrong Yo Yo* ....- -
Westwood - *Jackson Dog* ....- -

DARRYL BRITT:
Blue 1199 *Lover Lover* ....10.00 - 15.00

ELTON BRITT:
ABC Paramount (LP) 293 *Wandering Cowboy*.......15.00 - 25.00
　　(LP) 322 *Beyond The Sunset*....................15.00 - 25.00
RCA Victor (LP) 1288 *Yodel Songs* ....20.00 - 30.00

BOBBY BROOKES:
RCA Victor 7238 *You'd Better Move* ....7.00 - 10.00

BROOKLYN BOYS:
Ferris 902 *Every Night*....................................8.00 - 12.00

CHUCK BROOKS:
Dub 2844 *Spinning My Wheels*.........................15.00 - 25.00

ELOISE BROOKS (See THE DREAMERS)

LEON BROOKS & THE TWILIGHTERS:
Cholly 712 *Money Talks* ....150.00 - 300.00

LILLIAN BROOKS (& THE MOROCCOS):
King 4934 *For Only You* ....15.00 - 20.00
　　4956 *Sweet Sweet William* ....10.00 - 15.00

LOUIS BROOKS (& HIS HI-TOPPERS):
Excello 2042, 2056, 2063, 2100, 2119 ....7.00 - 10.00
　　2141, 2159 ....5.00 - 8.00

SONNY BROOKS & THE SAVOYS:
Tip Top 1007 *Here I Am*...............................50.00 - 80.00
　　1008 *Sweetheart Darling* ....50.00 - 80.00

BIG BILL BROONZY(& WASHBOARD SAM):
Chess (LP) 1468 *...and Washboard Sam* ....40.00 - 70.00
Columbia (LP) 111 *Big Bill's Blues* ....15.00 - 20.00
EmArcy (LP) 20634 (10 inches) *Folk Blues* ....40.00 - 60.00
Folkways (LP) 2326 *Sings Country Blues* ....15.00 - 20.00
　　(LP) 3586 *Songs And Story* ....15.00 - 20.00
Mercury (LP) 36137 *Blues* ....40.00 - 60.00
Period (LP) 1114 (10 inches) *Sings* ....50.00 - 80.00

THE BROTHERS:
Argo 5318 *Deep Sleep* ....7.00 - 10.00

BILLY BROWN:
Columbia 41029 *Did We Have A Party*..................10.00 - 15.00
　　41100 *Meet Me In The Alley, Sally*.................10.00 - 15.00
　　41297 *Flip Out*.......................................10.00 - 15.00
　　41380 *Run 'Em Off* ....8.00 - 12.00
Republic 2007 *Lost Weekend*...........................8.00 - 12.00

BOBBY BROWN & THE CURIOS:
Vaden 100 *Down At Big Mary's Place*...................30.00 - 50.00

BUSTER BROWN:
Fire (LP) 102 *The New King Of The Blues*..............80.00 - 130.00
　　1008 *Fannie Mae* (78 rpm) ....150.00 - 300.00
(This is one of the last 78 RPM records to be issued, and as such, is
　　much sought-after. Rumors of prices far in excess of those quoted
　　here remain unconfirmed.)

CHARLES BROWN:
Ace 561 *Educated Fool* ....7.00 - 10.00
Aladdin (LP) 702 (10 inches) *Mood Music* (pressed of red vinyl)
　　...200.00 - 300.00
　　(LP) 702 (10 inches) *Mood Music* (black vinyl)....150.00 - 200.00
　　(LP) 809 (12 inches) *Mood Music* ....150.00 - 250.00
　　3091 *The Message* ....20.00 - 30.00
　　3092 *Seven Long Days*................................20.00 - 30.00
　　3116 *Hard Times* ....15.00 - 20.00
　　3120 *My Last Affair* ....15.00 - 20.00
　　3138 *Without Your Love* ....15.00 - 20.00
　　3157 *Rollin' Like A Pebble In The Sand* ....15.00 - 20.00
　　3163 *Moonrise* ....15.00 - 20.00

　　3176 *Rising Sun* ....15.00 - 20.00
　　3191 *Lonesome Feeling* ....15.00 - 20.00
　　3200 *All My Life* ....15.00 - 20.00
　　3209 *Cryin' And Driftin' Blues*.......................15.00 - 20.00
　　3220 *Everybody's Got Troubles* ....15.00 - 20.00
　　3235 *Crying Mercy* ....15.00 - 20.00
　　3254 *My Silent Love*..................................15.00 - 25.00
　　3284, 3290, 3316, 3339, 3342, 3348..................10.00 - 15.00
(Note: Aladdin numbers prior to 3091 may be found as 45 RPM
　　records, but they are scarce, and would command prices higher
　　than earliest issues listed above. Aladdin 78 RPM records by
　　Charles Brown are usually valued at $5.00 to $10.00.)
Hollywood 1006 *Pleading For Your Love*............ 10.00 - 20.00
　　1021 *Merry Christmas Baby*....................... 8.00 - 12.00
Imperial (LP) 9257 *The Best Of The Blues* .... 50.00 - 80.00
King (LP) 775 *...Sings Christmas Songs* .... 40.00 - 60.00
Score (LP) 4011 *Drifting Blues* .... 100.00 - 150.00

CHARLIE BROWN & HIS CISCO KIDS:
Rose 101 *Mean, Mean Mama* .... 30.00 - 50.00
　　102 *Have You Heard The Gossip*..................... 30.00 - 50.00

DANNY BROWN:
Earth 702 *Standing On The Corner* .... 7.00 - 10.00

DUSTY BROWN:
Bandera 2503 *Please Don't Go* .... 8.00 - 12.00
Parrot 820 *Yes She's Gone* .... 50.00 - 80.00

EARL "GOOD ROCKING" BROWN:
Checker 802 *Shake Your Shimmy* .... 15.00 - 25.00
Kappa 207 *Turn Back The Time* .... 15.00 - 20.00

GATEMOUTH BROWN (See also Blues 78 RPM section):
Cue 1050 *Leftover Blues* .... 10.00 - 20.00
Peacock 1617 *Boogie Uproar* .... 15.00 - 20.00
　　1619 *Please Tell Me Baby* .... 15.00 - 20.00
　　1633 *Midnight Hour* .... 15.00 - 20.00
　　1637 *Depression Blues* .... 10.00 - 15.00
　　1653 *Gate's Salty Blues* .... 10.00 - 15.00
　　1662 *September Song*.............................. 8.00 - 12.00

GENE BROWN:
Gene Brown 28 *Big Door* .... 15.00 - 20.00
Dot 15709 *Big Door* .... 10.00 - 15.00

GUY BROWN with RED CAMPI & HIS BAND:
Echo 5002 *How Long Will It Be* .... 25.00 - 50.00

HYLO BROWN:
Capitol (LP) 1168 .... 25.00 - 40.00

J.T. BROWN:
Meteor 5016 *Dumb Woman Blues* .... 30.00 - 40.00

JAMES BROWN (& THE FAMOUS FLAMES):
King (LP) 610 *Please, Please, Please* .... 50.00 - 100.00
　　(LP) 635 *Try Me*................................... 50.00 - 100.00
　　(LP) 743 *The Amazing James Brown*................ 25.00 - 40.00
　　(LP) 826 *Live At The Apollo* .... 40.00 - 60.00

JIM EDWARD & THE BROWNS:
RCA Victor (LP) 1438................................. 15.00 - 25.00
　　(LP) 2144 *Sweet Sounds* .... 15.00 - 25.00
　　(LP) 2174 *Town & Country* .... 15.00 - 25.00

JIMMY BROWN:
Capitol 3255 *It's Over* .... 10.00 - 15.00

MARCUS BROWN:
Khoury's 734 *Lover Lee* .... 10.00 - 15.00

MILTON BROWN & HIS BROWNIES:
Decca (LP) 5561 (10 inches) *Dance-O-Rama*.........30.00 -   50.00

NAPPY BROWN:
Savoy most issues ....5.00 -   8.00
 (LP) 14002 *Nappy Brown Sings* ....25.00 -   50.00
 (LP) 14025 *The Right Time* ....20.00 -   30.00

PRISCILLA BROWN:
Abner 1018 *A Rockin' Good Way* ....10.00 -   15.00

ROY BROWN (See also "Battle Of The Blues"):
Home of the Blues 107 *Don't Break My Heart* ....7.00 -   10.00
 110 *Rocking All The Time*....................................7.00 -   10.00
 115 *Sugar Baby*...7.00 -   10.00
Imperial 5422, 5427, 5439 ....7.00 -   10.00
 5510 *Hip Shakin' Baby*......................................15.00 -   20.00
King (EP) 254 *Blues Boogie* ....100.00 -   200.00
 4602 *Travelin' Man*..15.00 -   20.00
 4609 *Money Can't Buy Love* ....15.00 -   20.00
 4627 *Gamblin' Man*..15.00 -   20.00
 4637 *Old Age Boogie*...15.00 -   20.00
 4669 *Caldonia's Wedding Day*............................15.00 -   20.00
 4704, 4715, 4731, 4761, 4834 ....10.00 -   15.00
King (higher numbers)...7.00 -   10.00

RUTH BROWN:
Atlantic (EP) 535 *Ruth Brown Sings* ....50.00 -   100.00
 919 *Teardrops From My Eyes* ....25.00 -   40.00
 941 *I Know* ....15.00 -   20.00
 973 *Have A Good Time*.......................................15.00 -   20.00
 978 *Three Letters* ....10.00 -   15.00
 1005, 1023, 1027, 1036, 1044 ....8.00 -   12.00
 (LP) 1308 *Late Date With*..................................40.00 -   60.00
 (LP) 8004 *Ruth Brown*.......................................40.00 -   60.00
 (LP) 8026 *Miss Rhythm* ....40.00 -   60.00
 (LP) 8080 *The Best Of Ruth Brown* ....15.00 -   20.00
(Note: Above must be original MONO issues)
King (LP) 115 (10 inches) reported; existence not verified
....300.00 -   up

(LITTLE) TOMMY BROWN:
Imperial 5476 *Rock Away My Blues* ....10.00 -   15.00
 5533 *Just For You*..10.00 -   15.00
King 4658 *How Much Do You Think I Can Stand* ..20.00 -   30.00
United 183 *Southern Women* ....25.00 -   50.00
 183 *Southern Women* (red plastic).....................50.00 -   80.00

WALTER BROWN:
Zip 4686 *Alley Cat*..30.00 -   40.00

(LITTLE) WILLIE BROWN:
Chart 1485 *Things Ain't Like They Use To Be* ....10.00 -   15.00
Do-Ra-Me 1404 *Cut It Out* ....10.00 -   15.00
Suntan 1112 *Going Back To The Country*...............10.00 -   15.00
Topic 223 *Do It Like That* ....10.00 -   15.00

WINI BROWN & HER BOYFRIENDS:
Mercury 5870 *Here In My Heart*...........................20.00 -   30.00
 8270 *Heaven Knows Why* ....25.00 -   50.00

DORIS BROWNE:
Gotham 290 *Please Believe Me* ....15.00 -   20.00
 296 *Until The End Of Time*..................................15.00 -   20.00
 298 *My Cherie* ....15.00 -   20.00
 303 *When The Moon Is High* ....15.00 -   20.00

CLAUDE BROWNELL:
Arcade 178 *Twist And Yodel*...................................-   -   -

BILL BROWNING:
Island 3 *One Day A Month*....................................8.00 -   12.00
 10 *Lay Me Low* ....8.00 -   12.00
Lucky 0001 *I'll Pay You Back* ....20.00 -   40.00
Starday 432 *Don't Push Don't Shove* ....10.00 -   15.00

EDWIN BRUCE:
Sun 276 *Rock Boppin' Baby* ....10.00 -   20.00
 292 *Sweet Woman* ....15.00 -   20.00

GEORGE BRUCE:
Web 1070 *Rock & Rollin' Roller Coaster Ride* ....8.00 -   12.00

JAMES BRUCE & THE DEL CATOS:
Palos 1203 *Brand New Baby*.................................20.00 -   30.00

FRANK BRUNSON:
Groove 0173 *Charmaine*...7.00 -   10.00

BILLY BRYAN:
Blaze 351 *Cradle Of Your Arms* ....7.00 -   10.00
Everest 19420 *All Summer Long* ....5.00 -   8.00
Festival 25002 *Please, Come Back Baby*..................5.00 -   8.00

DAVE BRYAN:
Speck 103 *Let's Make It Real* ....15.00 -   20.00

WES BRYAN:
Clock 1013 *Honey Baby* ....10.00 -   15.00
Roulette 4289 *I Guess I'll Never Know* ....7.00 -   10.00
United Artist 102 *Tiny Spaceman* ....7.00 -   10.00
 122 *Wait For Me Baby*...7.00 -   10.00

GENE BUA:
ABC Paramount 9928 *Well Honey* ....7.00 -   10.00
Warner Bros. 5037 *Once Upon A Time* ....7.00 -   10.00

THE BUCCANEERS:
Rama 21 *The Stars Will Remember* ....200.00 -   up
 24 *In The Mission Of St. Augustine* ....200.00 -   up
Southern 101 *Fine Brown Frame* ....200.00 -   up

BUCHANAN & ANCELL:
Flying Saucer 501 *The Creature* ....8.00 -   12.00

BUCHANAN & GOODMAN:
Luniverse 100 *Flying Saucer* ....5.00 -   8.00
 101 *Back To Earth* ....5.00 -   8.00
 102 *Buchanan & Goodman On Trial*....................5.00 -   8.00
 103 *The Mystery*..7.00 -   10.00
 105 *Flying Saucer The 2nd* ....7.00 -   10.00
 107 *Santa & The Satellite* ....7.00 -   10.00
 108 *The Flying Saucer Goes West* ....7.00 -   10.00
(Note: 78 RPM issues of above are worth more)
Radioactive 101 *Flying Saucer* ....15.00 -   20.00

BUCHANAN & GREENFIELD:
Novel 711 *The Invasion* ....7.00 -   10.00

WES BUCHANAN:
Pep 114 *Give Some Love My Way* ....40.00 -   60.00

ART BUCHANON:
Dixie 823 *Queen From Bowling Green* ....150.00 -   200.00

GARY BUCK:
Petal 1011 *Savin' All My Love For You*.....................7.00 -   10.00

PETER BUCK:
Drew-Blan 1005 *That's Enough* ....10.00 -   15.00

THE BUCKEYES:
De Luxe 6110 *Since I Fell For You* ....50.00 -   80.00
 6126 *Dottie Baby* ....75.00 -   125.00

BUCKY & THE PREMIERES:
Nu-Phi 701 *Cruisin'* ....20.00 - 30.00

THE BUDDIES:
Glory 230 *I Stole Your Heart*.........................75.00 - 125.00

JOHN BULLARD:
De Luxe 6019 *Spoiled Hambone Blues* ....40.00 - 70.00

NORMAN BULLOCK:
M & J 1-2 *Moanin' The Blues* ....20.00 - 30.00
    1108 *Lies, Lies, Lies* ....20.00 - 30.00

BUNCH OF GOODIES:
Chess (LP) 1441 ....25.00 - 50.00

ALLEN BUNN:
Red Robin 124 *Too Much Competition* ....75.00 - 100.00

BILLY BUNN & HIS BUDDIES:
RCA Victor 4483 *I Need A Shoulder To Cry On* ....50.00 - 80.00
    4657 *That's When Your Heartaches Begin* ....50.00 - 80.00

RAY BURDEN:
Adonis 112 *A Hot Rodder's Dream*.........................20.00 - 30.00
Cullman 6403 *That Kind Of Carrying On* ....20.00 - 30.00

DAVE BURGESS:
Challenge 1018 *Maybelle* ....7.00 - 10.00
    59027 *I Don't Want To Know* ....7.00 - 10.00
    59032 *Lovey Dovey Baby* ....7.00 - 10.00
Challenge 59037 *Lula* ....5.00 - 8.00
    59045 *Everlovin'* ....5.00 - 8.00

SONNY BURGESS:
Phillips 3551 *Sadie's Back In Town* ....8.00 - 12.00
Razorback 136 *Odessa* ....10.00 - 15.00
Sun 247 *Red Headed Woman* ....25.00 - 40.00
    263 *Ain't Got A Thing*.....................................40.00 - 60.00
    285 *My Bucket's Got A Hole In It* ....30.00 - 50.00
    304 *Thunderbird* ....30.00 - 50.00

JIM BURGETT:
GO 6565 *Pick-up-A-Coupla' Records*....................15.00 - 20.00
Oro 1502 *Live It Up*..15.00 - 20.00

TOMMY BURK & THE COUNTS: (See also THE COUNTS)
Rich Rose 1001 *Ding-A-Ling* ....10.00 - 15.00
    1003 *You Took My Heart*....................................7.00 - 10.00

BUDDY BURKE:
Bullseye 1002 *That Big Old Moon* ....15.00 - 20.00

EDDIE BURKE:
D 1063 *Rock Mop* ....7.00 - 10.00

JIMMY BURKE & THE SEQUINS:
Fortune 537 *Forbidden Love* ....30.00 - 50.00

SOLOMON BURKE:
Kenwood (LP) 498 *Solomon Burke* ....30.00 - 50.00

THE BURNETTE BROTHERS:
Imperial 5509 *Warm Love* ....20.00 - 30.00

DORSEY BURNETTE:
Abbott 190 *At A Distance* ....7.00 - 10.00
Cee-Jam 16 *Bertha Lou* ....10.00 - 15.00
Imperial 5668 *Way In The Middle Of The Night* .....10.00 - 15.00
    5561, 5597 ....7.00 - 10.00

JOHNNY BURNETTE (& THE ROCK 'N' ROLL TRIO);
JOHNNY BURNETTE TRIO:
Coral (LP) 57080 *Johnny Burnette & The Rock 'N' Roll Trio*
....250.00 - 500.00
    61651 *Tear It Up* ....25.00 - 50.00
    61675 *Midnight Train* ....20.00 - 30.00
    61719 *The Train Kept A-Rollin'* ....20.00 - 30.00
    61758 *Lonesome Train* ....20.00 - 30.00
    61829 *Eager Beaver Baby* ....30.00 - 50.00
    61869 *Drinkin' Wine Spo-Dee-O-Dee* ....30.00 - 50.00
    61918 *If You Want It Enough*.............................30.00 - 50.00
    62190 *Midnight Train* ....15.00 - 20.00
Freedom 44001 *I'm Restless* ....8.00 - 12.00
    44011 *Me And The Bear* ....8.00 - 12.00
    44017 *Sweet Baby Doll* ....10.00 - 15.00
Liberty (EP) 1011 *"Hits"* ....50.00 - 75.00
Liberty (LPs) 3179, 3183, 3190, 3206, 7183,
    7190, 7197, 7206...20.00 - 30.00

LINDA BURNETTE:
Perry 5 *Rattle Bones Rock*......................................15.00 - 25.00

MAC BURNEY & THE FOUR JACKS:
Aladdin 3274 *Tired Of Your Sexy Ways* (blue label) .....50.00 - 80.00
Hollywood 1058 *Walking And Crying*....................50.00 - 80.00

EDDIE BURNS:
Chess 1672 *Treat Me Like I Treat You* ....8.00 - 12.00
De Luxe 6024 *Dealing With The Devil*..................20.00 - 30.00
Harvey 111, 115, 118..7.00 - 10.00
JVB 82 *Treat Me Like I Treat You*.........................50.00 - 80.00

JACKIE BURNS:
Del-Fi 4102 *Hey Then There Now* ....7.00 - 10.00

SONNY BURNS:
Starday 114 *Blue, Blue Rain* ....10.00 - 15.00
    118 *Too Hot To Handle* ....15.00 - 30.00
    131, 152, 175, 189...5.00 - 10.00
    209 *A Real Cool Cat* ....30.00 - 50.00
    223, 254...5.00 - 10.00

HAROLD BURRAGE:
Cobra 5004 *One More Dance* ....8.00 - 12.00
    5012 *Messed Up*..8.00 - 12.00
    5018 *Satisfied* ....8.00 - 12.00
    5022 *She Knocks Me Out* ....8.00 - 12.00
    5026 *Betty Jean*...8.00 - 12.00
Decca 48175 *I Need My Baby* ....30.00 - 50.00
States 144 *You're Gonna Cry* ....20.00 - 30.00

BOB BURTON:
Mar-Vel 953 *Tired Of Rocking* ....20.00 - 30.00

DAVE BURTON:
RCA Victor 6535 *Rock And Roll Ruby*.....................7.00 - 10.00

BUZZ/WAYNE BUSBY:
Empire 506 *Goin' Back To Dixie*............................8.00 - 12.00
    507 *Don't Leave Me Alone* ....8.00 - 12.00

EDDIE BUSH:
Jaxon 503 *Little Darling* ....30.00 - 40.00

BOB BUSTER:
Darsa 129 *Swamp Hop*..5.00 - 10.00

THE BUTANES:
Enrica 1007 *That's My Desire* ....7.00 - 10.00

SAM BUTERA & THE WITNESSES:
Capitol 4014 *Bim Bam* ....10.00 - 15.00

CLIFF BUTLER & THE DOVES:
States 123 *When You Love*................................75.00 - 100.00
　　148 *Jealous Hearted Woman*....................40.00 - 60.00

JERRY BUTLER & THE IMPRESSIONS:
Abner 1013, 1017, 1023 ....5.00 - 8.00
　　1013 *For Your Precious Love* (78 rpm) ....15.00 - 20.00
Falcon 1013 *For Your Precious Love*.....................10.00 - 15.00
Vee Jay 280 *For Your Precious Love* (Rare)........500.00 - up

BOBBY BYRD & THE BIRDS:
Cash 1031 *Let's Live Together As One* ....15.00 - 20.00

ROBERT BYRD:
Jamie 1039 *Bippin' And Boppin'*..............................8.00 - 12.00
Spark 501 *Bippin' And Boppin'*...............................15.00 - 20.00

ROY BYRD:
Federal 12061 *Curly Haired Baby*...................30.00 - 50.00
　　12073 *Rockin' With Fes*.............................30.00 - 50.00

JERRY BYRNE:
Specialty 635 *Lights Out* ....8.00 - 12.00

EDD BYRNES:
Warner Bros. (LP) 1309 *Kookie* ....20.00 - 30.00

JIMMIE BYRON:
Teen 113 *Sidewalk Rock*....................................8.00 - 12.00

WILLIE C.:
Ruler 5000 *Slow Down Baby* ....5.00 - 8.00

THE CABINEERS:
Prestige 904 *Each Time* ....150.00 - 200.00
917 *Baby Mine*.. - - -

FREDDIE CADDELL:
Ardent 12-001 *At The Rockhouse* ....15.00 - 20.00

THE CADETS;
Crown (LP) 5015 *Rockin' n' Rollin'* ....40.00 - 70.00
　　(LP) 5370 *The Cadets*.................................30.00 - 60.00
　　(LP) CST 370 *The Cadets*...........................20.00 - 30.00
Jan Lar 102 *Car Crash* ....25.00 - 40.00
Modern 956 *Don't Be Angry* ....10.00 - 15.00
　　960 *Rollin' Stone* ....10.00 - 15.00
　　963 *I Cried*..8.00 - 12.00
　　969 *Annie Met Henry* ....10.00 - 15.00
　　971 *Do You Wanna Rock*...........................25.00 - 40.00
　　985 *Church Bells May Ring*........................15.00 - 20.00
　　994 *Stranded In The Jungle*.........................7.00 - 10.00
　　1000 *I Got Loaded* ....8.00 - 12.00
　　1006 *Fools Rush In* ....7.00 - 10.00
　　1012 *Heaven Help Me* ....7.00 - 10.00
　　1017 *You Belong To Me* ....10.00 - 15.00
　　1019 *Pretty Evey*.......................................10.00 - 20.00
　　1024 *Hands Across The Table* ....10.00 - 15.00
　　1026 *Baby Ya Know*...................................10.00 - 15.00

THE CADILLACS:
Capitol 4825 *White Gardenia*........................10.00 - 15.00
Josie 759 *Carelessly* .... - - -
　　765 *Gloria*..75.00 - 100.00
　　769 *Wishing Well* ....75.00 - 100.00
　　773 *Sympathy*...30.00 - 60.00
　　778 *Down The Road* ....30.00 - 60.00
　　785 *Speedo* ....7.00 - 10.00
　　785 *Speedo* (78 rpm) ....10.00 - 15.00
　　792 *Zoom* ....7.00 - 10.00
　　792 *Zoom* (78 rpm) ....10.00 - 15.00
　　798, 805, 812, 820, 821, 846, 866 ....7.00 - 15.00

*Jubilee (LP) 1045 *The Fabulous Cadillacs* ....100.00 - 125.00
　*(LP) 1089 *The Crazy Cadillacs* ....75.00 - 100.00
　*(LP) 1117 *The Cadillacs Meet The Orioles*.....40.00 - 60.00
　(LP) 5009 *Twisting With The Cadillacs*............10.00 - 15.00
(Note: *original issues have blue labels)
Mercury 71738 *I'm Willing* ....25.00 - 40.00

CAESER & THE ROMANS:
Hi-Note 602 *Your True Love* ....10.00 - 15.00

AUBREY CAGLE:
Glee 1001 *Come Along Little Girl* ....30.00 - 50.00
　　1013 *Bop 'N' Stroll*..30.00 - 50.00
　　- *Be Bop Blues*..30.00 - 50.00
House Of Sound 504 *Real Cool*..............................30.00 - 50.00

ANDY CALDWELL:
Liberty 55142 *She's So Fine* ....10.00 - 15.00

JOE CALDWELL:
Esta 1001 *Rowdy Mae*..20.00 - 30.00

THE CALENDARS:
Coed 564 *I'm Gonna Laugh At You* ....75.00 - 100.00
Swingin' 649 *One-Week Romance* ....5.00 - 8.00

THE CALIFORNIANS:
Federal 12231 *My Angel* ....50.00 - 100.00

MIKE CALLAHAN:
Protone 204 *I Can't Help It* ....15.00 - 20.00

BOB CALLAWAY:
Big Red 102 *Tick Tock*..30.00 - 40.00
U B C 1013 *Wake Up Little Boy Blue*....................30.00 - 40.00

DUDLEY CALLICUT & THE "GO" BOYS:
"DC" 0412 *Get Ready Baby*....................................20.00 - 30.00

BABY CALLOWAY:
Bay-Tone 106 *Midnight Blues* ....8.00 - 12.00

THE CALVAES:
Checker 928 *So Bad*..8.00 - 12.00
Cobra 5003 *Fine Girl* ....100.00 - 150.00
　　5014 *Lonely Lonely Village* ....75.00 - 125.00

THE CALVANES:
Deck 579 *Dreamworld*..25.00 - 40.00
Dootone (EP) 205 ....50.00 - 100.00
　　380 *Florabelle*..25.00 - 50.00

THE CALVEYS:
Comma 445 *The Wind* ....20.00 - 30.00

THE CAMELOTS:
Aanko 1001 *Your Way*...20.00 - 30.00
　　1004 *My Imagination*..20.00 - 30.00
Ember 1108 *Searchin' For My Baby* ....7.00 - 10.00

THE CAMEOS:
Dean 504 *Lost Lover*..25.00 - 40.00

THE CAMERONS:
Felsted 8638 *Guardian Angel* ....8.00 - 12.00

DAVID CAMPANELLA & THE DELLCHORDS:
Kane 5593 *Over The Rainbow* ....15.00 - 25.00

CECIL CAMPBELL:
MGM 12245 *Dixieland Rock*...................................10.00 - 20.00
　　12482 *Rock & Roll Fever* ....20.00 - 30.00

DICK CAMPBELL:
Great 4703 *She's My Girl* ....7.00 - 10.00

GLEN CAMPBELL:
Capitol 5441 *Guess I'm Dumb* ....7.00 - 10.00
Capitol (most other issues) ....3.00 - 5.00
Crest 1087 *Turn Around Look At Me* ....7.00 - 10.00
    1096 *The Miracle Of Love*.............................7.00 - 10.00

JO ANN CAMPBELL:
End (LP) 306 *I'm Nobody's Baby* ....80.00 - 130.00
Gone 5014 *Wait A Minute* ....7.00 - 10.00
    5021 *Rock And Roll Love* ....7.00 - 10.00
    5027 *Whatsa Matter With You* ....7.00 - 10.00
    5037 *I'm Nobody's Baby Now* ....7.00 - 10.00
    5049 *Happy New Year Baby*...........................7.00 - 10.00
    5055 *Nervous* ....7.00 - 10.00
    5068 *I Ain't Got No Steady Date* ....7.00 - 10.00

LOUIS CAMPBELL:
Excello 2035 *The Natural Facts*......................30.00 - 50.00

RAY CAMPI:
Colpix 166 *French Fries* ....8.00 - 12.00
D 1047 *The Ballad Of Donna And Peggy Sue*........10.00 - 15.00
Domino 700 *My Screamin' Mimie* ....20.00 - 30.00
Dot 15617 *It Ain't Me*..................................20.00 - 30.00
TNT 145 *Catapillar*....................................100.00 - 150.00

CAMP MEETING CHOIR:
Mercury (LP) 25084 (10 inch) *Negro Spirituals* .....30.00 - 40.00

THE CAMPS:
Parkway 974 *The Ballad Of Batman* ....5.00 - 8.00

CARL CANIDA:
Creole 1740 *Party Date*...............................80.00 - 130.00

FREDDY CANNON:
Swan (LP) 502 *The Explosive Freddy Cannon* ....40.00 - 60.00
    (LP) 504 *Freddy Cannon Sings Happy Shades Of Blue*
    ....40.00 - 60.00
    (LP) 505 *Solid Gold Hits* ....20.00 - 30.00
    (LP) 506 *Twistin' All Night Long* ....20.00 - 30.00
    (LP) 507 *Palisades Park*.............................30.00 - 50.00
    (LP) 511 *Freddy Cannon Steps Out* ....30.00 - 50.00

JACKIE CANNON:
Chan 103 *Proof Of Your Love* ....10.00 - 15.00

THE CANUCKS with RAY PARK:
Diadon 60-116 *Rock Around The Barn* ....15.00 - 20.00

JERRY CAPEHART:
Cash 1021 *Walking Stick Boogie*...................12.00 - 16.00

THE CAPERS:
Vee Jay 297 *Miss You My Dear* ....20.00 - 30.00

THE CAPISTRANOS:
Duke 179 *Now Darling*..................................15.00 - 25.00

THE CAPITOLS:
Cindy 3002 *Rose-Marie*...............................75.00 - 100.00
Gateway 721 *Day By Day*............................50.00 - 100.00
Pet 807 *Angel Of Love* ....75.00 - 100.00

THE CAPRIS:
Gotham 7304 *God Only Knows* ....50.00 - 80.00
    7306 *It Was Moonglow* ....50.00 - 80.00
    7308 *It's A Miracle* ....75.00 - 100.00
Lifetime 1001/1002 *Oh, My Darling*.......................20.00 - 30.00
Old Town 1094 *There's A Moon Out Tonight*...........7.00 - 10.00
    1099 *Some People Think* ....8.00 - 12.00
    1103 *Tears In My Eyes*................................10.00 - 15.00
    1107 *Girl In My Dreams*.............................10.00 - 15.00

Planet 1010 *There's A Moon Out Tonight* .... 150.00 - 250.00
20th Century 1201 *My Weakness*.................... 10.00 - 15.00

THE CAPS:
White Star 102 *Daddy Dean* .... 5.00 - 8.00

CAPTAIN & TENILLE:
Butter-Castle 001 *The Way I Want To Touch You* ...... - - -

THE CAP-TANS:
Anna 1122 *I'm Afraid* .... 20.00 - 30.00
Dot 15114 *With All My Love* .... 40.00 - 60.00

BOBBY & TERRY CARAWAY & THE RO-CATS:
Crest 1065 *Ballin' Keen*................................. 15.00 - 20.00

JIM CARAWAY & THE JUMPIN' JACKS:
Deb 1001 *You Know* .... 10.00 - 15.00

LEONARD CARBO:
Vee Jay 291 *Pigtails And Blue Jeans*....................... 8.00 - 12.00

THE CARDELLS:
Middle Tone 011 *Helen* .... 100.00 - 150.00

JACK CARDELL:
Rama 227 *Rock-A-Billy Yodler* .... 8.00 - 12.00

THE CARDINALS:
Atlantic 938 *Shouldn't I Know* .... - - -
    952 *I'll Always Love You* .... 100.00 - 200.00
    958 *Wheel Of Fortune*................................. 100.00 - 200.00
    972 *She Rocks* .... 75.00 - 100.00
    995 *You Are My Only Love* .... 75.00 - 100.00
    1025 *Under A Blanket Of Blues*........................ 50.00 - 100.00
    1054 *The Door Is Still Open* .... 30.00 - 50.00
    1067 *Come Back My Love* .... 30.00 - 50.00
    1079 *Lovely Girl* .... 30.00 - 50.00
(Note: Above are yellow label; following are red label)
    1090 *Off Shore* .... 20.00 - 30.00
    1103 *The End Of The Story* .... 25.00 - 40.00
    1126 *One Love* .... 20.00 - 30.00
Rose 835 *Why Don't You Write Me?* .... 80.00 - 130.00

THE CARIANS:
Magenta 04 *Only A Dream* .... 15.00 - 20.00

THE CARIBBEANS:
20th Fox 112 *Keep Her By My Side*........................ 10.00 - 15.00

STEVE CARL:
Meteor 5046 *Curfew* .... 40.00 - 60.00

CARLISLE BROTHERS:
King (LP) 643 *Fresh From The Country* .... 25.00 - 50.00

THE CARLISLES:
Mercury 70351 *Shake A Leg* .... 7.00 - 10.00

"CARL, LEFTY AND MARTY":
Columbia (LP) 2544 (10 inches)............................ 50.00 - 80.00

CARLO:
Laurie 3151 *Baby Doll*................................. 10.00 - 20.00
    3157 *Little Orphan Girl* .... 10.00 - 20.00
    3175 *The Story Of Love* .... 10.00 - 20.00
    3227 *Ring-A-Ling*................................. 10.00 - 20.00

CARLOS BROS.:
Zen 106 *I Realize* .... 7.00 - 10.00

CARL CARLTON:
Lando 8527 *I Love Only You* .... 10.00 - 15.00

THE CARNATIONS:
Lescay 3002 *Long Tall Girl*..............................40.00 - 60.00
Music City 736 *You Gave Peace Of Mind*..............25.00 - 40.00
Savoy 1172 *The Angels Sent You To Me* ....20.00 - 30.00

PAUL CARNES:
P.R.C. 4417 *I'm A Mean, Mean Daddy*..................15.00 - 25.00

CAROLINA SLIM:
Sharp (LP) 2002 *Blues From The Cotton Fields* ...100.00 - 150.00

THE CAROLS:
Lamp 2001 *My Search Is Over*...............................20.00 - 30.00
Savoy 896 *Fifty Million Women* ....30.00 - 50.00

THE CAROUSELS:
Gone 5118 *If You Want To* ....20.00 - 30.00
Jaguar 3029 *Rendezvous* ....20.00 - 30.00

STEVE CARPENTER:
San Dee 1004 *The Big Hit* .... - - -

THE CARPETS:
Federal 12257 *Why Do I* ....50.00 - 80.00
　　12269 *Lonely Me* ....40.00 - 70.00

CATHY CARR:
Fraternity 734 *Ivory Tower* (78 rpm) ....10.00 - 15.00
　　(LP) 1005 *Ivory Tower* ....30.00 - 50.00

GUNTER LEE CARR:
Decca 48170 *We're Gonna Rock* ....30.00 - 50.00

CARRIBIANS:
Brooks 2000 *Wonderland* ....300.00 - up

CURTIS CARRINGTON:
Fury 1018 *I'm Gonna Catch You*...........................5.00 - 8.00

THE CARROLL BROS.:
Camco 140 *Red Hot* ....10.00 - 15.00

BILL(Y) CARROLL:
Dixie 2010 *I Feel So Good* ....50.00 - 80.00
Fascination 2000 *Big Green Car* (also issued as by Jimmy Carroll)
....20.00 - 30.00

CHUCK CARROLL:
Happy Heart 133 *Mean Ole Blues* .... - - -

EARL CARROLL & THE ORIGINAL CADILLACS:
Josie 829 *Buzz-Buzz-Buzz* ....5.00 - 8.00

JIMMY CARROLL:
Fascination 2000 *Big Green Car* (also issued as by Billy Carroll)
....20.00 - 30.00

JOHNNY CARROLL (& HIS HOT ROCKS):
Decca 29940 *Rock 'N' Roll Baby* ....20.00 - 30.00
　　29941 *Wild Wild Women* ....20.00 - 30.00
　　30013 *Hot Rock* ....20.00 - 30.00
Phillips 3520 *That's The Way I Love*.....................15.00 - 20.00
WA 112 *Trudy* ....10.00 - 15.00
Warner Bros. 5042 *Bandstand Doll*........................10.00 - 15.00

WAYNE CARROLL:
King 5123 *Chicken Out* ....10.00 - 15.00
　　5134 *Rockin' Chair Mama* ....10.00 - 15.00
　　5146 *He Cheated* ....7.00 - 10.00

DON CARSON:
Crest 1051 *Three Carburetors*................................7.00 - 10.00

THE CARTER KIDS:
Gambler 1638 *Gotta Rock* ....8.00 - 12.00

THE CARTER RAYS:
Gone 5006 *My Secret Love* ....50.00 - 80.00
Jubilee 5142 *Goodnight, Sweetheart, Goodnight* ... 10.00 - 15.00
Mala 433 *Bless You* ....10.00 - 15.00

BILL CARTER:
Ozark 1234 *Cool Tom Cat* ....30.00 - 50.00
Tally 111 *I Wanna Feel Good*................................20.00 - 30.00

BOB CARTER:
Den 11229 *The Fortunate Few* ....7.00 - 10.00

DEAN CARTER:
Milky Way 0111 *Jailhouse Rock* .... - - -

HARRY CARTER:
Mar-Vel 1300 *Jump Baby Jump* ....20.00 - 30.00
　　1301 *You Made Me Love You Baby* ....20.00 - 30.00

JOHNNY CARTER:
Kim 105 *Hey Mama* ....10.00 - 20.00

PHIL CARTER:
Challenge 59020 *Amazon* ....10.00 - 15.00

WILF CARTER:
Camden (LP) 527 *Montana Slim* ....20.00 - 30.00

RIC CARTEY & JIVA TONES:
ABC Paramount 10415 *Something In My Eye*........10.00 - 15.00
NRC 503 *Scratchin' On My Screen*.......................75.00 - 100.00
RCA Victor 6751 *Ooh Eee* ....20.00 - 30.00
　　6828 *Heart Throb* ....15.00 - 20.00
　　6920 *Let Me Tell You About Love*.....................15.00 - 20.00
　　7011 *My Babe* ....20.00 - 30.00

CASANOVA & THE CHANTS:
Sapphire 2254 *Geraldine* ....20.00 - 30.00

CASANOVA, JR.:
Port 7001 *Sally Mae* ....15.00 - 20.00

TONY CASANOVA:
American International 532 *Diary Of A High School Bride*
....8.00 - 12.00
Crest 1053 *Yea! Yea! Come Another Day*...............15.00 - 20.00
Dore 535 *Boogie Woogie Feeling* ....15.00 - 20.00

THE CASANOVAS:
Apollo 471 *That's All*..50.00 - 80.00
　　474 *Hush-A-Mecca* ....50.00 - 80.00
　　477 *Please Be My Love*...................................75.00 - 100.00
　　483 *My Baby's Love*.......................................50.00 - 80.00
　　519 *Please Be Mine* ....50.00 - 100.00
　　523 *You Are My Queen* ....50.00 - 100.00
Planet 1027 *In My Land Of Dreams* ....80.00 - 130.00

THE CASCADES:
Renee 105 *Pains In My Heart* ....8.00 - 12.00
Valiant (LP) 405 *Rhythm Of The Rain*..................40.00 - 70.00

AL CASEY:
Dot 15563 *Guitar Man*..8.00 - 12.00
Highland 1002 *Teenage Blues* ....15.00 - 20.00
Liberty 55117 *She Gotta Shake* ....8.00 - 12.00

EDDIE CASH:
Peak 1001 *Doin' All Right* ....25.00 - 40.00

JOHNNY CASH:
Sun (EP) 111 *Sings Hank Williams* ....40.00 - 60.00
　　(EP) 112 *Country Boy*.....................................40.00 - 60.00
　　221 *Hey Porter* ....25.00 - 40.00
　　232 *Folsom Prison Blues* ....10.00 - 15.00

232 *Folsom Prison Blues* (78 rpm)	20.00	-	40.00
241 *I Walk The Line*	8.00	-	12.00
241 *I Walk The Line* (78 rpm)	15.00	-	20.00
258 *Train Of Love*	7.00	-	10.00
258 *Train Of Love* (78 rpm)	15.00	-	20.00
266 *Next In Line*	7.00	-	10.00
266 *Next In Line* (78 rpm)	15.00	-	20.00
279 *Home Of The Blues*	7.00	-	10.00
279 *Home Of The Blues* (78 rpm)	15.00	-	20.00
283 *Big River*	8.00	-	12.00
283 *Big River* (78 rpm)	30.00	-	50.00
295 *Guess Things Happen That Way*	7.00	-	10.00
295 *Guess Things Happen That Way* (78 rpm)	25.00	-	40.00
302 *The Ways Of A Woman In Love*	7.00	-	10.00
302 *The Ways Of A Woman In Love* (78 rpm)	30.00	-	50.00
309 *It's Just About Time*	7.00	-	10.00
309 *It's Just About Time* (78 rpm)	40.00	-	70.00
316 *Luther Played The Boogie*	7.00	-	10.00
316 *Luther Played The Boogie* (78 rpm)	50.00	-	100.00
Sun (most subsequent issues)	5.00		8.00
(LP) 1240 *Greatest!*	50.00	-	80.00
(LP) 1270 *All Aboard The Blue Train*	50.00	-	80.00
(LP) 1275 *The Original Sun Sound Of*	20.00	-	30.00

THE CASHMERES:

Herald 474 *Little Dream Girl*	20.00	-	30.00
Josie 894 *Where Have You Been*	5.00	-	8.00
Laurie 3088 *Singing Waters*	5.00	-	8.00
Mercury 70501 *My Sentimental Heart*	10.00	-	15.00
70617 *Don't Let It Happen Again*	15.00	-	20.00
70679 *There's A Rumor*	15.00	-	20.00

THE CASINOS:

Fraternity (LP) 1019	50.00	-	100.00

THE CASLONS:

Amy 836 *For All We Know*	7.00	-	10.00
Seeco 6078 *Anniversary Of Love*	10.00	-	15.00

TOMMY CASSELL:

Cassell 58-1/2 *Go Ahead On*	20.00	-	30.00

THE CASTALEERS:

Donna 1349 *That's Why I Cry*	10.00	-	15.00
Felsted 8504 *Come Back*	10.00	-	15.00
8512 *Lonely Boy*	15.00	-	20.00
8585 *You're My Dream*	15.00	-	20.00

(GEORGE CASTELLE &) THE CASTELLES:

Atco 6069 *Hey Baby, Baby*	10.00	-	15.00
Grand 101 *My Girl Awaits Me* (blue label)	50.00	-	80.00
103 *This Silver Ring*	50.00	-	80.00
105 *Do You Remember*	50.00	-	80.00
109 *Over A Cup Of Coffee*	80.00	-	120.00
114 *Marcella*	80.00	-	120.00
118 *Over The Rainbow*	50.00	-	80.00
122 *Heavenly Father*	80.00	-	120.00

(Note: Original Grand issues have no address on label)

JOE(Y) CASTLE (& DADDY-O'S):

Headline 1008 *Rock And Roll Daddy-O*	30.00	-	50.00
RCA Victor 7283 *That Ain't Nothin' But Right*	10.00	-	15.00

THE CASTLE-TONES:

Rift 502 *Goodnight*	15.00	-	20.00
504 *We Met At A Dance*	15.00	-	20.00

JIMMY CASTOR & THE JUNIORS:

Wing 90078 *I Know The Meaning Of Love*	8.00	-	12.00

THE CASTROES/CASTROS (See also: LARRY SMITH):

Grand 2002 *Dearest Darling*	50.00	-	80.00
Lasso 501 *Lucky Me*	150.00	-	up
502 *In My Dreams*	200.00	-	up

CASUAL-AIRES:

Brunswick 55064 *Thunderbird*	10.00	-	15.00

THE CASUALS (See also THE ORIGINAL CASUALS):

Dot 15557 *My Love Song For You*	7.00	-	10.00

THE CASUALTEENS:

Felsted 8529 *Need You So*	7.00	-	10.00

THE CASUAL THREE:

Luniverse 109 *The Invisible Thing*	10.00	-	15.00

THE CASUALTONES:

Success 102 *Summer School*	-	-	-

VINNY CATALANO:

Hammer 6312 *Please Mr. Jukebox Man*	10.00	-	15.00

THE CATALINAS:

Back Beat 513 *Speechless*	20.00	-	30.00
Glory 285 *With Your Girl-Yeah!*	8.00	-	12.00
Little 812 *Castle Of Love*	50.00	-	80.00

RONNIE CATES:

Terrace 7501 *Long Time*	20.00	-	30.00
7508 *For My Very Own*	20.00	-	30.00

CATHY JEAN & THE ROOMMATES:

Valmor (LP) 789 *At The Hop!*	100.00	-	up
(LP) *Great Oldies*	100.00	-	up

(Note: cover variations exist)

THE CATS:

Federal 12238 *After I Gave You My Heart*	20.00	-	30.00
12248 *You're So Nice*	15.00	-	20.00

THE CATS & THE FIDDLE:

RCA Victor 50-0077 *I Miss You So*	20.00	-	30.00

JOHNNY CAVALIER:

Hi Class 105 *Knock Off The Rock*	15.00	-	25.00

JIM CAVALLO:

Sunnyside 3105 *Don't Move Me No More*	20.00	-	30.00

JIMMY CAVELLO & HOUSE ROCKERS:

Coral 61689 *Soda Shoppe Rock*	15.00	-	20.00
61728 *Rock, Rock, Rock*	20.00	-	30.00
61787 *Ooh Wee*	20.00	-	30.00
61868 *Yo-Yo Baby*	10.00	-	15.00
61919 *Cherry Pie*	10.00	-	15.00

JOHN W. CAVES:

Mem'ry Lane 102 *Rocket To The Moon*	-	-	-

PHIL CAY:

Hart 1001 *Meet Me In The Barnyard*	10.00	-	15.00

THE CELLOS:

Apollo 510 *You Took My Love*	15.00	-	20.00
515 *Under Your Spell*	10.00	-	15.00
516 *The Be-Bop Mouse*	15.00	-	20.00
524 *I Beg For Your Love*	40.00	-	70.00

THE CELTICS:

Al Jacks 2 *Can You Remember?*	300.00	-	up
War Conn 2216 *Darlene Darling*	75.00	-	100.00

THE CENTURIES:

Life 501 *In This Whole World*	20.00	-	30.00

THE CENTURY'S:
Fortune 533 *Take My Hand* ....40.00 - 70.00

ERNIE CHAFFIN:
Hickory 1024 *I Can't Lose The Blues* ....5.00 - 8.00
Sun 262 *Feelin' Low* ....8.00 - 12.00
   275 *Laughin' and Jokin'* ....10.00 - 15.00

THE CHALETS:
Dart 1026 *Who's Laughing? Who's Crying?* .... - - -
Tru-Lite 1001 *Who's Laughing? Who's Crying?* ...20.00 - 30.00

THE CHALONS:
Dice 89 *Oh You*.....................................75.00 - 100.00

THE CHAMBERLAIN BROS:
Columbia 41227 *Baby Walked Out* ....10.00 - 15.00

EDDIE CHAMBLEE:
United 160, 181 ....8.00 - 12.00

HOLLIS CHAMPION:
Stripe 501 *Long Gone Lonesome Blues*..................... - - -

JOHNNY CHAMPION:
Natural Sound 2004 *Beer Drinking Daddy* ....5.00 - 8.00

THE CHAMPIONS:
Ace 541 *I'm So Blue* ....10.00 - 15.00
Chart 602 *Annie Met Henry*...................10.00 - 15.00
   611 *Mexico Bound* ....15.00 - 25.00
   620 *Pay Me Some Attention*.................15.00 - 25.00
   631 *Come On* ....15.00 - 20.00

THE CHAMPS:
Challenge (LP) 601 *Go Champs Go* ....40.00 - 60.00
   (LP) 601 (same, but pressed of blue vinyl).......100.00 - up
   1016 *Tequila* (78 rpm) ....15.00 - 20.00
   59007 *El Rancho Rock* (78 rpm) ....15.00 - 20.00

THE CHANCELLORS:
Eastwood 120 *Judy*...............................20.00 - 40.00
   XYZ 104 *I'm Coming Home* ....8.00 - 12.00
   105 *Seaport At Sunset*.........................7.00 - 10.00

THE CHANCES:
Roulette 4549 *What Would You Say*...............15.00 - 20.00

THE CHANCETEERS:
Chess 1636 *Night Beat*...........................10.00 - 15.00

THE CHANDELIERS:
Angel Tone 521 *Blueberry Sweet*.............15.00 - 20.00
DuWell 102 *Once More*..........................10.00 - 15.00

ELAINE CHANDLER:
4 Star 1700 *Tiptoin' Thru The Teepee* .... - - -

HOWARD CHANDLER:
Wampus 100 *Wampus Cat*....................100.00 - 150.00
(Note: Beware of 1970s re-pressings)

LEE CHANDLER:
Band Box 224 *Tree-Top* ....10.00 - 15.00
   242 *That's The Way Of Love* ....10.00 - 15.00
   250 *Sweet Dreams* ....10.00 - 15.00

WAYLAND CHANDLER:
4 Star 1716 *Little Lover* ....8.00 - 12.00

THE CHANELS:
Deb 500 *The Reason*...............................8.00 - 12.00

CLISTON CHANIER (See also CLIFTON CHENIER):
Post 2010 *Rockin' The Bop*....................15.00 - 20.00
   2016 *Rockin' Hop* ....15.00 - 20.00

BRUCE CHANNEL:
Le Cam 953 *Hey! Baby*...........................20.00 - 30.00
Manco 1035 *Run, Romance, Run*...........10.00 - 15.00
Teen Ager 601 *Run, Romance, Run*.........7.00 - 10.00

THE CHANNELS:
Fire 1001 *The Girl Next Door*................10.00 - 15.00
Fury 1021 *Bye Bye Baby*.......................10.00 - 15.00
Gone 5012 *That's My Desire*..................10.00 - 15.00
   5019 *Altar Of Love*..............................10.00 - 20.00
Groove 0061 *You Can Count On Me*.........5.00 - 8.00
Port 70014 *The Closer You Are*................5.00 - 10.00
   70017 *The Gleam In Your Eye*...............5.00 - 10.00
   70022 *Flames In My Heart*....................5.00 - 10.00
   70023 *I Really Love*.............................5.00 - 10.00
Whirlin Disc 100 *The Closer You Are*.......7.00 - 10.00
   102 *The Gleam In Your Eyes*...............15.00 - 25.00
   107 *I Really Love You*.........................20.00 - 30.00
   109 *Flames In My Heart*......................10.00 - 20.00

CHANTAYS:
Dot (LP) 3516 *Pipeline* (MONO) ....20.00 - 30.00
   (LP) 3771 *Two Sides of...* (MONO) ....20.00 - 30.00
   (LP) 25516 *Pipeline* (STEREO) ....30.00 - 40.00
   (LP) 25571 *Two Sides of...* (STEREO) ......20.00 - 30.00
Downey 104 *Pipeline*..............................7.00 - 10.00
   108 *Monsoon*.......................................7.00 - 10.00
   (LP) 1002 *Pipeline* ....75.00 - 100.00

THE CHANTECLAIRS:
Dot 1227 *Baby Please*.............................8.00 - 12.00

THE CHANTELS:
Carlton (LP) 144 *On Tour* ....15.00 - 30.00
End (EP) 201 *I Love You So* ....75.00 - 100.00
   (EP) 202 *"C'est Si Bon"*.......................75.00 - 100.00
   (LP) 301 *We Are The Chantels* (group photo)........100.00 - 150.00
   (LP) 301 *The Chantels* (juke box) ....30.00 - 50.00
   (LP) 312 *There's Our Song Again* ....30.00 - 50.00
   1001 *He's Gone* (black label) ....10.00 - 15.00
   1005 *Maybe* (black label)...................10.00 - 15.00
   1005 *Maybe* (78 rpm) ....20.00 - 30.00
   1015 *Every Night* ....7.00 - 10.00
   1015 *Every Night* (78 rpm) ....10.00 - 15.00
   1020 *I Love You So* ....7.00 - 10.00
   1020 *I Love You So* (78 rpm) ....10.00 - 15.00
Ludix 101 *Eternally* ....8.00 - 12.00
Verve 10435 *It's Just Me*.........................5.00 - 8.00

THE CHANTERS:
Combo 78 *Why*.....................................60.00 - 100.00
   92 *I Love You* ....50.00 - 80.00
De Luxe 6162 *My My Darling*................20.00 - 30.00
   6166 *Stars In The Skies*......................20.00 - 30.00
   6172 *Angel Darling*............................20.00 - 40.00
   6177 *Over The Rainbow* ....20.00 - 30.00
   6191 *I Make This Pledge (To You)* ....8.00 - 12.00
   6194 *At My Door* ....8.00 - 12.00
   6200 *No No No*....................................8.00 - 12.00
Kem 2740 *Lonesome Me*........................15.00 - 20.00
RPM 415 *Tell Me, Thrill Me*..................75.00 - 100.00

THE CHANTICLEERS:
Lyric 103 *To Keep Your Love* ....15.00 - 20.00

THE CHANTONES:
TNT 167 *Dear Diary* ....25.00 - 40.00

THE CHANTS:
Cameo 277 *Come Go With Me* ....7.00 - 10.00

MGM 13008 *Respectable* ....7.00 - 10.00
Nite Owl 40 *Heaven And Paradise* ....50.00 - 80.00
Tru Eko 3567 *Respectable* ....10.00 - 15.00

JEAN CHAPEL:
RCA Victor 6892 *Oo-Ba La Baby*.....................10.00 - 15.00
Sun 244 *I Won't Be Rockin' Tonight* ....20.00 - 30.00

THE CHAPERONES:
Josie 885 *Shining Star* ....7.00 - 10.00

PAUL CHAPLAIN:
Harper 100 *Nicotine*...............................7.00 - 10.00

GENE CHAPMAN:
Westport 145 *Don't Come Cryin'* ....10.00 - 15.00

THE CHAPPARALS:
Rebel 108 *Sweet Lies* ....75.00 - 150.00

LEON CHAPPEL:
Capitol 1954 *Booger Blues* ....8.00 - 12.00
   2065 *True Detective* ....8.00 - 12.00
   2167 *Automatic Mama*..............................8.00 - 12.00
   2526 *I'm Getting Mighty Tired*.....................5.00 - 8.00
   2611 *New Do Right Daddy* ....5.00 - 8.00

BILL CHAPPELL:
Yucca 121 *Lovey Dove* ....10.00 - 15.00
   156 *Down On The Farm Boogie* ....- - -

THE CHAPTERS:
Republic 7038 *Goodbye My Love*.........................80.00 - 130.00

THE CHARADES:
Ava 154 *Please Be My Love Tonight* ....8.00 - 12.00

THE CHARGERS:
RCA Victor 7417 *Here In My Heart* ....8.00 - 12.00

THE CHARIOTEERS:
Columbia (LP) CL 6014 (10 inches) *Sweet And Low*
....75.00 - 100.00
Columbia (most issues) ....7.00 - 10.00
Harmony (LP) 7089...50.00 - 80.00
Keystone 1416 *I'm The World's Biggest Fool* ....20.00 - 30.00
Josie 787 *I've Got My Heart On My Sleeve* ....20.00 - 30.00
MGM 12569 *The Candles* ....20.00 - 30.00

CHARIOTS:
Time 1006 *Gloria* ....25.00 - 40.00

ANDY CHARLES & THE BLUE KINGS:
D 1061 *Baby Don't Go*...20.00 - 30.00

BOBBY CHARLES:
Chess 1609 *Later Alligator*.....................................15.00 - 20.00
   1617 *Why Did You Leave* ....15.00 - 20.00
   1628 *Take It Easy Greasy*..........................15.00 - 20.00
   1638 *No Use Knocking* ....10.00 - 15.00
   1647 *Why Can't You, Honey* ....8.00 - 12.00
   1658 *No More* ....8.00 - 12.00
   1670 *One-Eyed Jack* ....7.00 - 10.00

RAY CHARLES:
ABC Paramount (LP) 385 *"...& Betty Carter"* ....50.00 - 75.00
ABC Paramount (most issues)................................3.00 - 6.00
Atlantic 976 *The Midnight Hour* (yellow label)......30.00 - 50.00
   984 *The Sun's Gonna Shine Again* (yellow label)
....30.00 - 50.00
   999 *Mess Around* (yellow label)....................25.00 - 50.00
   1154 *Swanee River Rock* (78 rpm) ....15.00 - 25.00
   (LP) 1289 *At Newport*...............................15.00 - 20.00

(LP) 1312 *Genius*.....................................15.00 - 20.00
(LP) 1369 *The Genius After Hours* ....15.00 - 20.00
2006 *Rockhouse* (78 rpm) ....20.00 - 30.00
2031 *What'd I Say* (78 rpm) ....75.00 - 100.00
2043 *I'm Movin' On* (78 rpm) ....75.00 - 100.00
(LP) 8006 *Ray Charles* (black label) ....30.00 - 50.00
(LP) 8025 *Yes Indeed!* (black label) ....30.00 - 50.00
(LP) 8029 *What'd I Say* ....15.00 - 20.00

CHARLIE BOP TRIO:
Capitol 4100 *Mr. Big Feet* ....8.00 - 12.00

THE CHARMERS:
Aladdin 3341 *He's Gone*...............................10.00 - 15.00
Allison 921 *Come Back To My Heart* ....10.00 - 15.00
Central 1002 *The Beating Of My Heart*...............150.00 - 300.00
   1006 *Tony, My Darling*............................200.00 - up
JAF 108 *Little Fool* ....5.00 - 8.00
Laurie 3142 *My Kind Of Love*.........................8.00 - 12.00
Sure Play 104 *Lesson From The Stars* ....75.00 - 125.00
Timely 1009 *I Was Wrong*.............................150.00 - 200.00 *
   1011 *The Church On The Hill* ....- - *
(Note:*existence of 45 RPM copies not verified)

THE CHARMS (See also OTIS WILLIAMS):
Chart 608 *Love's Our Inspiration*...........................15.00 - 20.00
   613 *I Offer You*..................................15.00 - 25.00
   623 *I'll Be True* ....20.00 - 30.00
De Luxe (EP) 357 *Hits By The Charms*..................80.00 - 130.00
   (EP) 364 ....80.00 - 130.00
   6000 *Heaven Only Knows* ....80.00 - 130.00
   6014 *Happy Are We* ....50.00 - 80.00
   6034 *Please Believe Me* ....50.00 - 80.00
   6050 *Quiet Please* ....40.00 - 60.00
   6056 *My Baby Dearest Darling* ....50.00 - 80.00
   6062 *Hearts Of Stone* ....10.00 - 15.00
   6065 *Two Hearts* ....8.00 - 12.00
   6072 *Crazy, Crazy Love* ....10.00 - 15.00
   6076 *Ling Ting Tong* ....8.00 - 12.00
   6080 *Ko Ko Mo* ....8.00 - 12.00
   6082 *Whadaya Want?* ....5.00 - 10.00
   6087 *When We Get Together* ....5.00 - 10.00
   6089 *One Fine Day* ....8.00 - 12.00
Rockin' 516 *Heaven Only Knows*.........................80.00 - 130.00

THE CHARTERS:
Alva 1001 *I Lost You* ....30.00 - 50.00
Merry-Go-Round 103 *Lost In A Dream*.................20.00 - 30.00

THE CHARTS:
Everlast 5001 *Deserie* ....10.00 - 15.00
   5002 *Why Do You Cry* ....20.00 - 30.00
   5006 *You're The Reason* ....15.00 - 20.00
   5008 *All Because Of Love* ....15.00 - 20.00
   5010 *My Diane*...................................15.00 - 25.00
   5026 *Deserie* ....7.00 - 10.00
Guyden 2021 *For The Birds* ....10.00 - 15.00

JODY CHASTAIN:
Kay 1002 *Jody's Beat* ....15.00 - 25.00

THE CHATEAUS:
Coral 62364 *Honest I Will* ....10.00 - 15.00
Warner Bros. 5043, 5071 ....8.00 - 12.00

CHRISTINE CHATMAN:
Million 2002 *Wino's Lament* ....7.00 - 10.00

EARL CHATMAN:
Fortune 844 *Take Two Steps Back* ....10.00 - 15.00

THE CHAVIS BROTHERS:
Ascot 2177 *Humpty Dumpty* ....7.00 - 10.00
Clock 1025 *I Love You* ....10.00 - 15.00

BOOZOO CHAVIS:
Folk Star 1197 *Paper In My Shoe* ....15.00 - 20.00
   1201 *Forty One Days* ....15.00 - 20.00
Goldband 1161 *Hamburgers And Popcorn* ....8.00 - 12.00
Imperial 5374 *Boozoo Stomp* ....25.00 - 50.00

CHUBBY CHECKER:
Parkway 804 *The Class* (78 rpm) ....100.00 - up
(Note: the existence of this record in 78 RPM form has not been
   confirmed.)
   965 *You Just Don't Know* ....15.00 - 30.00

THE CHECKER DOTS:
Peacock 1688 *Alpha Omega* ....8.00 - 12.00

THE CHECKERS:
Federal 12375 *White Cliffs Of Dover* ....10.00 - 15.00
King 4558 *Flame In My Heart* ....125.00 - 175.00
   4581 *Night's Curtain* ....150.00 - 300.00
   4596 *My Prayer Tonight* ....125.00 - 175.00
   4626 *Ghost Of My Baby* ....100.00 - 150.00
   4673 *I Promise You* ....100.00 - 150.00
   4675 *White Cliffs Of Dover* ....30.00 - 60.00
(Note: First pressings of early King issues should not have the
   designation "High Fidelity" and should have the suffixes "A" or
   "AA" after the catalog numbers. Records pressed of colored
   plastic can bring substantially higher prices.)
   4710 *House With No Windows* ....20.00 - 30.00
   4719 *Over The Rainbow* ....20.00 - 30.00
   4751 *Mama's Daughter* ....20.00 - 30.00
   4764 *Trying To Hold My Gal* ....20.00 - 30.00
   5156 *Heaven Only Knows* ....15.00 - 20.00
   5199 *Teardrops Are Falling* ....5.00 - 8.00
Skyla 1120 *Blue Saturday* ....7.00 - 10.00

CHELMARS:
Select 712 *Confess* ....5.00 - 8.00

BIG CHENIER & HIS NIGHT OWLS/THE R. B. ORCHESTRA:
Goldband 1051 *Let Me Hold Your Hand* ....15.00 - 20.00
   1131 *The Dog And His Puppies* ....10.00 - 15.00

CLIFTON CHENIER (See also CLISTON CHANIER):
Argo 5262 *The Big Wheel* ....7.00 - 10.00
Bayou 707 *Black Gal* ....30.00 - 50.00
   710 *Louisiana Rock* ....30.00 - 50.00
Checker 939 *Bayou Drive* ....7.00 - 10.00
Elko 920 *Louisiana Stomp* ....30.00 - 50.00
Imperial 5352 *Louisiana Stomp* ....25.00 - 40.00
Specialty 552, 556, 568 ....7.00 - 10.00
Zynn 506 *Goodbye Baby* ....10.00 - 15.00
   1004 *Worried Life Blues* ....10.00 - 15.00
   1011 *Rockin' Accordion* ....10.00 - 15.00

THE CHEROKEES:
Grand 106 *Rainbow Of Love* ....80.00 - 120.00
   110 *Please Tell Me So* ....100.00 - 150.00
Peacock 1656 *Is She Real* ....20.00 - 30.00
United Artists 367 *My Heavenly Angel* ....20.00 - 30.00

FRANKIE CHER-VALI:
Dot 15674 *My First Impression Of You* ....15.00 - 25.00

THE CHESTERFIELDS:
Chess 1559 *I'm In Heaven* ....150.00 - 300.00

THE CHESTERS:
Apollo 521 *The Fires Burn No More* ....25.00 - 40.00

THE CHESTNUTS:
Aladdin 3444 *This Is My Love* ....30.00 - 50.00
Davis 447 *Love Is True* ....25.00 - 40.00
   452 *Forever I Vow* ....30.00 - 50.00
Mercury 70489 *Don't Go* ....20.00 - 30.00

JAY CHEVALIER:
Pel 201 *Billy Cannon* ....20.00 - 30.00

THE CHEVELLES:
Infinity 1007 *I'm Sorry* ....10.00 - 15.00
Vita 127 *Valley Of Love* ....25.00 - 40.00

THE CHEV-RONS (See also LEE WARD):
Gait 100 *The Defense Rest* ....20.00 - 30.00

CHICK & THE HOT RODS:
King 5537 *Jimmy Caught The Dickens* ....7.00 - 10.00

THE CHIFFONS:
Laurie (LP) 2018 *He's So Fine* ....50.00 - 80.00
   (LP) 2036 *Sweet Talkin' Guy* ....50.00 - 80.00

BUDDY CHILDRESS:
Dub 2838 *My Lovin' Arms* ....10.00 - 15.00

THE CHIMES:
Flair 1051 *My Heart's Crying For You* ....100.00 - 150.00
House Of Beauty 3 *Tears From An Angel's Eyes* ... 10.00 - 15.00
Royal Roost 577 *A Fool Was I* (45 RPM) ....- - -
(Note: existence in 45 RPM format unverified)
   577 *A Fool Was I* (78 rpm) ....100.00 - 150.00
Specialty 555 *Zindy Lou* ....15.00 - 20.00
   570, 574 ....10.00 - 20.00

THE CHIPPENDALES:
Andie 5013 *What A Night* ....7.00 - 10.00
Rust 5023 *The Day Will Come* ....7.00 - 10.00

THE CHIPS:
Josie 803 *Rubber Biscuit* ....15.00 - 20.00

CHOCOLATEERS:
Parrot 781 *Bartender Blues* ....150.00 - 200.00

THE CHORALS:
Decca 29914 *In My Dream* ....20.00 - 30.00

THE CHORDCATS:
Cat 109 *Zippity-Zum* ....8.00 - 12.00
   112 *A Girl To Love* ....10.00 - 15.00

THE CHORDELLS:
Jaro 77005 *At Last* ....10.00 - 15.00
Onyx 504 *Here's A Heart For You* ....100.00 - 200.00

THE CHORDS:
Casino 451 *Tears In Your Eyes* ....7.00 - 10.00
Cat 104 *Sh-Boom* ....7.00 - 10.00
   109 *Zippity-Zum* ....8.00 - 12.00
Metro 20015 *Elephant Walk* ....8.00 - 12.00

"A CHRISTMAS GIFT FOR YOU":
Philles (LP) 4005 (various artists) ....75.00 - 100.00

JOHN CHRISTMON:
Excello 2031 *My Baby's Gone* ....50.00 - 100.00

THE CHROMATICS (See also LITTLE AUGIE AUSTIN):
Million 2010 *Here In The Darkness* ....20.00 - 30.00

CHUCK & BILL:
Brunswick 55011 *Watch Your Step* ....15.00 - 20.00
    55034 *Wanna Move A Little Closer*...................15.00 - 20.00

CHUCK & GENE:
R-Dell 113 *Curfew*...15.00 - 20.00

THE CHUCKLES:
West Side 1019 *On The Street Where You Live* ....8.00 - 12.00

CHUCK WAGON GANG:
Columbia (LP) 922 *Sacred Songs*......................20.00 - 30.00
    (LP) 9022 *(10 inches)* ....25.00 - 40.00

EUGENE CHURCH:
Class 235, 254...5.00 - 8.00
    235 *Pretty Girls Everywhere* (78 rpm) ....15.00 - 30.00
    254 *Miami* (78 rpm) ....20.00 - 30.00

THE CINCINNATIANS:
Brunswick 84032 *Lord Let Me Walk With Thee* ....40.00 - 70.00
Emerald 16116 *Magic Genie* ....5.00 - 8.00

CINDY & SANDY:
Tailspin 102 *Make Believe Baby* .... - - -

THE CINERAMAS:
Rhapsody 71964 *Crying For You* ....10.00 - 15.00

PETE CIOLINO:
Recorte 401 *Daddy Joe*.......................................15.00 - 20.00

CIRCLE C BAND:
Melco 105 *Ramshackled Shack* .... - - -

JIMMY CLANTON:
Ace 546 *Just A Dream* (78 rpm) ....30.00 - 50.00
    668 *Heart Hotel* ....7.00 - 10.00
    (LP) 1001 *Just A Dream* ....40.00 - 60.00
    (LP) 1007 *Jimmy's Happy* ....40.00 - 60.00
    (LP) 1008 *Jimmy's Blue* ....40.00 - 60.00
    (LP) 1011 *My Best To You*...........................20.00 - 40.00
    (LP) 1014 *Teenage Millionaire* ....30.00 - 50.00
    (LP) 1026 *Venus In Blue Jeans* ....30.00 - 50.00

THE CLAREMONTS:
Apollo 517 *Angel Of Romance* ....15.00 - 25.00

CHARLES CLARK:
Artistic 1500 *Row Your Boat* ....10.00 - 15.00

CLAUDINE CLARK:
Chancellor (LP) 5029 *Party Lights* ....50.00 - 80.00

DEE CLARK:
Falcon 1002, 1005 ....5.00 - 8.00
    1009 *Oh Little Girl* ....15.00 - 20.00
Vee Jay (LP) 1037 *Hold On...It's Dee Clark* ....30.00 - 50.00

FRED CLARK:
Federal 12136 *Ground Hog Snooper*......................50.00 - 80.00

LEONARD CLARK & LAND OF SKY BOYS:
Klub 3108 *Come To Your Tommy Now*...................10.00 - 15.00

RAY CLARK & THE DEMONS:
Crystal 01 *Little Betty Twist* ....20.00 - 30.00

SANFORD CLARK:
Dot 15534, 15556 ....5.00 - 8.00
    15738 *Modern Romance*...............................30.00 - 60.00
Jamie 1107 *Sing 'Em Some Blues*........................7.00 - 10.00
    1120 *Bad Luck* ....7.00 - 10.00
MCI 1003 *The Fool* ....15.00 - 20.00
Project - *Tennessee Walk*.................................... - - -

THE CLASSICS:
Class 219 *If Only The Sky Was A Mirror*................ 15.00 - 20.00
Crest 1063 *Let Me Dream*................................. 10.00 - 15.00
Dart 1015 *Cinderella* .... 15.00 - 20.00
    1024 *Life Is But A Dream, Sweetheart*............... 50.00 - 100.00
    1032 *Angela Angela*.................................... 10.00 - 15.00
Mercury 71829 *Life Is But A Dream, Sweetheart*..... 8.00 - 12.00
Musicnote 118, 1116.. 7.00 - 10.00
Promo 1010 *Blue Moon* .... 7.00 - 10.00
Steamline 1028 *Life's But A Dream* .... 8.00 - 12.00

THE CLASSICS IV:
Algonquin 1651 *True Story* .... 50.00 - 80.00
Twist 1004 *Heavenly Bliss* ....- - -

THE CLASSMATES:
Marquee 102 *Pretty Little Pet*................................. 10.00 - 15.00

JERRY CLATON:
Up Town Rhythm 301 *Date Bait* ....- - -

CHRIS CLAY:
Veltone 106 *Shot Rod Lincoln* ....- - -

JOE CLAY:
Vik 0211 *Duck Tail*.. 20.00 - 30.00
    0218 *Cracker Jack* .... 40.00 - 60.00

DOCTOR CLAYTON:
Groove 5006 *Honey Stealin' Blues*........................ 15.00 - 20.00

DOUG CLAYTON:
Pure Gold *Sally Ann*..- - -

JOHNNY CLAYTON:
Dixie 838 *Never Again*.. 20.00 - 30.00

CLEAR WATERS:
Atomic H-03 *Boogie Woogie Baby*........................ 25.00 - 40.00

EDDIE CLEARY:
Kawana 102 *Think It Over Baby*............................ 30.00 - 50.00

THE CLEFS:
Peacock 1643 *I'll Be Waiting*................................ 30.00 - 50.00

THE CLEFTONES:
Gee (LP) 705 *Heart And Soul* .... 75.00 - 100.00
    (LP) 707 *For Sentimental Reasons* .... 75.00 - 100.00
    1000 *You, Baby, You*................................... 10.00 - 15.00
    1000 *You, Baby, You* (78 rpm) .... 15.00 - 25.00
    1011 *Little Girl Of Mine* .... 8.00 - 12.00
    1016 *Neki-Hokey*.. 7.00 - 10.00
    1016 *Neki-Hokey* (78 rpm) .... 15.00 - 25.00
    1064, 1067.. 5.00 - 10.00
Old Town 1011 *The Masquerade Is Over* .... 300.00 - up

HENRY CLEMENT:
Spot 1000 *Late Hour Blues* .... 10.00 - 15.00
Zynn 1006 *I'll Be Waiting* .... 8.00 - 12.00

JACK CLEMENT:
Sun 291 *Ten Years* .... 8.00 - 12.00
    311 *The Black Haired Man* .... 7.00 - 10.00

RUSS CLEMENTS:
Shore Bird 1011 *Lonesome Old World* .... 8.00 - 12.00

CLEO & THE CRYSTALIERS:
Cindy 3003 *Please Be My Guy* .... 80.00 - 130.00

THE CLICKS:
Josie 789 *Come Back To Me* .... 40.00 - 70.00

BENNY CLIFF TRIO:

Drift 1441 *Shake-Em Up Rock* ....150.00 - 200.00

THE CLIMBERS:

J & S 1652 *My Darlin' Dear* ....300.00 - up

1658 *I Love You* ....300.00 - up

CECIL CLINE:

Blue Hen 612 *Do Drop In* ....15.00 - 20.00

PATSY CLINE:

Coral 61523 *Turn The Cards Slowly* ....8.00 - 12.00

61583 *Come On In* ....8.00 - 12.00

(EP) 81159 *Songs By Patsy Cline* ....50.00 - 80.00

(LP) 4202 *Patsy Cline Showcase* ....40.00 - 70.00

Decca (LP) 4282 *Sentimentally Yours* ....30.00 - 50.00

(EP) DXSB 7176 *The Patsy Cline Story* (7 inch) (STEREO)

....25.00 - 50.00

(LP) 8611 *Patsy Cline* ....30.00 - 50.00

29963 *Stop, Look And Listen* ....7.00 - 10.00

30221 *Walkin' After Midnight* ....7.00 - 10.00

30221 *Walkin' After Midnight* (78 rpm) ....15.00 - 25.00

Decca (most other issues) ....5.00 - 8.00

Everest 2011 *Hungry For Love* ....8.00 - 12.00

2020 *Walking After Midnight* ....10.00 - 15.00

2031 *Just Out Of Reach* ....8.00 - 12.00

2039 *I've Loved And Lost Again* ....7.00 - 10.00

2045 *In Care Of The Blues* ....7.00 - 10.00

2052 *Got A Lot Of Rhythm (In My Soul)* ....7.00 - 10.00

2060 *Crazy Dream* ....7.00 - 10.00

20005 *I Can't Forget* ....8.00 - 12.00

Everest (LP) ST-90070 *Patsy Cline's Golden Hits* (STEREO)

....40.00 - 60.00

Patsy Cline 1 *A Church, A Courtroom, Then Goodbye*

....15.00 - 20.00

2 *Turn The Cards Slowly* ....15.00 - 20.00

(EP) 11 *Come On In* + 3 ....20.00 - 30.00

(EP) 14 *A Poor Man's Roses* + 3 ....20.00 - 30.00

(EP) 16 *Try Again* + 3 ....20.00 - 30.00

(EP) 21 *Three Cigarettes* + 3 ....20.00 - 30.00

LOY CLINGMAN:

Dot 15567 *I'm Low, Low, Low* ....8.00 - 12.00

Liberty Bell 9012 *I'm Low, Low, Low* ....15.00 - 20.00

THE CLINTONIAN CUBS:

My Brothers 7 *She's Just My Size* ....400.00 - up

THE CLIPS:

Calvert 105 *Let Me Get Close To You Baby* ....50.00 - 80.00

THE CLIQUES:

Modern 987 *The Girl In My Dreams* ....15.00 - 25.00

995 *My Desire* ....15.00 - 25.00

THE CLOUDS:

Cobra 5001 *I Do* ....300.00 - up

Round 1008 *Darling, I Love You* ....30.00 - 50.00

THE CLOVERS:

Atlantic (EP) 504 *One Mint Julep* ....100.00 - 150.00

(EP) 537 *Good Lovin'* ....100.00 - 150.00

(EP) 590 *The Clovers* ....100.00 - 150.00

934 *Don't You Know I Love You* ....100.00 - 200.00

944 *Fool Fool Fool* ....100.00 - 150.00

963 *One Mint Julep* ....50.00 - 80.00

969 *Ting-A-Ling* ....50.00 - 80.00

977 *I Played The Fool* ....50.00 - 80.00

989 *Crawlin'* ....40.00 - 60.00

1000 *Good Lovin'* ....15.00 - 25.00

1001 *The Feeling Is So Good* ....15.00 - 25.00

1022 *Lovey Dovey* ....15.00 - 25.00

1035 *Your Cash Ain't Nothin' But Trash* ....15.00 - 20.00

1046 *I Confess* ....15.00 - 20.00

1052 *Blue Velvet* ....15.00 - 20.00

1060 *Love Bug* ....15.00 - 20.00

1073 *Nip Sip* ....15.00 - 20.00

1083 *Devil Or Angel* ....15.00 - 20.00

(Note: Above are yellow label.)

1094 *Love Love Love* ....15.00 - 20.00

1107 *From The Bottom Of My Heart* ....15.00 - 20.00

1118 *A Lonely Fool* ....15.00 - 20.00

1129 *Here Comes Romance* ....15.00 - 25.00

1139 *So Young* ....15.00 - 20.00

1152 *There's No Tomorrow* ....15.00 - 20.00

1175 *Wishing For Your Love* ....15.00 - 25.00

(LP) 1248 *The Clovers* (black label) ....100.00 - 200.00

(LP) 8009 *The Clovers* (black label) ....100.00 - 150.00

(LP) 8034 *Clovers' Dance Party* ....50.00 - 80.00

Popular (LP) 1001 *The Clovers In Clover* ....50.00 - 100.00

Rainbow 122 *When You Came Back To Me* (78 rpm) - - -

United Artists 174 *That Old Black Magic* (78 rpm) 50.00 - 80.00

180 *Love Potion Number Nine* (78 rpm) (existence of this has not been verified) ....- - -

United Artists (most issues, 45 RPM) ....5.00 - 10.00

(LP) UAS-609 *Love Potion Number Nine* (STEREO)

....75.00 - 100.00

(LP) 3033 *The Clovers In Clover* (MONO) ....40.00 - 60.00

(LP) 3099 *Love Potion Number Nine* (MONO) 50.00 - 75.00

THE CLUSTERS:

Epic 9330 *Forecast Of Our Love* ....- - -

Tee Gee 102 *Pardon My Heart* ....20.00 - 30.00

THE C-NOTES:

ARC 4447 *We Were Meant For Each Other* ....15.00 - 25.00

Everlast 5005 *On Your Mark* ....8.00 - 12.00

THE COASTERS:

Atco (LP) 101 *The Coasters* ....40.00 - 60.00

(LP) 111 *The Coasters' Greatest Hits* ....20.00 - 30.00

(LP) 123 *One By One* ....30.00 - 60.00

(LP) 135 *Coast Along With The Coasters* ....25.00 - 40.00

6064 *Turtle Dovin'* (maroon label) ....10.00 - 15.00

6073 *Brazil* (maroon label) ....10.00 - 15.00

6087 *Searchin'* (maroon label) ....10.00 - 15.00

(higher numbers, yellow label) ....5.00 - 10.00

6098 *My Baby Comes To Me* ....7.00 - 10.00

6104 *What Is The Secret Of Your Success?* ....7.00 - 10.00

6111 *Gee, Golly* (78 rpm) ....25.00 - 50.00

6116 *Yakety Yak* (78 rpm) ....30.00 - 50.00

6126 *The Shadow Knows* (78 rpm) ....15.00 - 25.00

6132 *Charlie Brown* (78 rpm) ....40.00 - 60.00

6146 *Poison Ivy* (78 rpm) ....50.00 - 80.00

(EP) 4501 *Rock & Roll With* ....40.00 - 60.00

(EP) 4502 *Keep Rockin' With The Coasters* ....40.00 - 60.00

(EP) 4506 *The Coasters* ....40.00 - 60.00

(EP) 4507 *The Coasters' Top Hits* ....30.00 - 50.00

THE COBRAS:

Modern 964 *Sindy (or "Cindy")* ....40.00 - 60.00

WILLIE COBBS:

C & F 300/301 *Five Long Years* ....7.00 - 10.00

J.O.B. 1127 *Come On Home* ....50.00 - 80.00

KIMBALL COBURN:

Hi 2010 *Please, Please* ....7.00 - 10.00

THE COCHRAN BROTHERS:
Cash 1021 *Walkin' Stick Boogie*..............................40.00 - 60.00
Ekko 1003 *Two Blue Singing Stars* ....50.00 - 75.00
   1005 *Guilty Conscience* ....50.00 - 75.00
   3001 *Fool's Paradise* ....75.00 - 100.00

EDDIE COCHRAN:
Crest 1026 *Skinny Jim* ....75.00 - 100.00
Liberty (EP) 3061 *Singin' To My Baby* ....75.00 - 100.00
   (LP) 3061 *Singin' To My Baby*.....................100.00 - 150.00
   (LP) 3172 *Eddie Cochran*............................50.00 - 75.00
   (LP) 3220 *Never To Be Forgotten* ....50.00 - 75.00
   55056 *Sittin' In The Balcony* ....7.00 - 10.00
   55056 *Sittin' In The Balcony* (78 rpm) ....40.00 - 60.00
   55070 *Mean When I'm Mad* ....10.00 - 15.00
   55070 (picture sleeve for this record is scarce and of value)
   .... - -
   50087 *Drive In Show* ....10.00 - 15.00
   55112 *Twenty Flight Rock* ....20.00 - 30.00
   55123 *Jeannie, Jeannie, Jeannie* ....10.00 - 15.00
   55138 *Pretty Girl*....................................10.00 - 15.00
   55144 *Summertime Blues* ....7.00 - 10.00
   55166 *C'mon Everybody* ....8.00 - 12.00
   55177 *Teenage Heaven* ....10.00 - 15.00
   55203 *Somethin' Else* ....10.00 - 15.00
   55217 *Little Angel*..................................10.00 - 15.00
   55242 *Cut Across Shorty* ....10.00 - 15.00
   55278 *Sweetie Pie*..................................10.00 - 15.00

JACK(IE) (LEE) COCHRAN:
ABC Paramount 9930 *Buy A Car*.....................20.00 - 30.00
Decca 30206 *Mama Don't You Think I Know*.........30.00 - 50.00
Jaguar 3031 *Georgia Lee Brown* ....30.00 - 50.00
Sims 107 *Hip Shakin' Mama* ....100.00 - 150.00
Spry 120 *Pity Me* ....40.00 - 60.00
Viv 988 *Buy A Car* ....20.00 - 30.00

WAYNE COCHRAN:
Gala 117 *Last Kiss* ....8.00 - 12.00
Scottie 1303 *My Little Girl* ....10.00 - 15.00

JIMMY COE (& HIS GAY CATS OF RHYTHM):
States 129 *Raid On The After Hour Joint* (red plastic)
   ....50.00 - 80.00
   155 *The Jet*..30.00 - 50.00

THE CO-EDS:
Dwain 802 *With All My Heart*.........................10.00 - 15.00
Old Town 1027 *Love You Baby All The Time* ....30.00 - 50.00
   1033 *I Love An Angel* ....30.00 - 50.00
Swing 101 *Mark My Words*............................7.00 - 10.00

THE COGNACS:
Roulette 4340 *Heaven Only Knows*....................10.00 - 15.00

THE COINS:
Gee 10 *Can't Get No Place With You* ....400.00 - up

COKE JINGLES (with THE SHIRELLES, THE FOUR SEASONS, JAN & DEAN, and ROY ORBISON):
   ....20.00 - 30.00

AL COKER with THE COKER FAMILY:
Decca 30053 *Don't Go Baby*...........................10.00 - 15.00

ALVADEAN COKER:
Abbott 176 *We're Gonna Bop* ....10.00 - 15.00

ANN COLE (& THE SUBURBANS):
Baton 232, 237...5.00 - 10.00
Baton 240 *My First And Last Romance*................10.00 - 15.00

BOBBY COLE:
Westland 1490 *Never Fear, I'm Here*.....................10.00 - 15.00

DON COLE:
Coed 548 *Squad Car*....................................10.00 - 15.00
Guyden 2059 *Lie Detector Machine*.......................8.00 - 12.00
Kent 305 *Sweet Lovin' Honey*...........................30.00 - 50.00
RPM 502 *Snake-Eyed Mama*............................30.00 - 50.00

JOHNNY COLE:
Dore 605 *Jenny Lou And Susie May* ....- - -

LEE COLE:
Mist 1010 *Cool Baby* ....30.00 - 50.00

LES COLE with THE ECHOES:
D 1010 *Bee Boppin' Daddy* ....50.00 - 80.00

SONNY COLE:
Excell 124 *Robinson Crusoe Bop* ....40.00 - 60.00

HONEY COLEMAN:
Combo 3 *Daddy Why Did You Leave Me* ....15.00 - 20.00

HOOKS COLEMAN:
Excello 2193 *Teen-Age Baby*.............................10.00 - 15.00

RAY COLEMAN:
Arcade 147 *Jukebox Rock & Roll* ....30.00 - 50.00

COLLAY & THE SATELLITES:
Sho-Biz 102 *Little Girl Next Door*.........................10.00 - 15.00

THE COLLEGIANS:
Winley 224 *Zoom, Zoom, Zoom* ....10.00 - 15.00
   261 *Oh, I Need Your Love*.........................10.00 - 15.00
   263 *Right Around The Corner* ....10.00 - 15.00
   (LP) 6004 *Sing Along With The Collegians*.....100.00 - 150.00
X-Tra 108 *Let's Go For A Ride* ....100.00 - 200.00

GUS COLLETTI:
Tin Pan Alley - *Sample Kiss*..............................- - -

BIFF COLLIE:
Starday 178 *Lonely* ....15.00 - 25.00
   203 *Look On The Good Side* ....15.00 - 20.00
   230 *Empty Kisses* ....10.00 - 15.00
   251 *All Of A Sudden*..............................10.00 - 15.00

THE COLLINS KIDS:
Columbia 21470 *Beetle Bug Bop* ....10.00 - 15.00
   21514 *The Rockaway Rock* ....7.00 - 10.00
   21543 *I'm In My Teens* ....10.00 - 15.00
   21560 *Rock And Roll Polka* ....7.00 - 10.00
   40824 *Move A Little Closer* ....8.00 - 12.00
   40921 *Hop, Skip And Jump* ....8.00 - 12.00
   41012 *Party* ....15.00 - 20.00
   41087 *Mama Worries* ....10.00 - 15.00
   41149 *Mercy* ....15.00 - 20.00
   41225 *Rock Boppin' Baby* ....15.00 - 20.00
   41329 *Sugar Plum*................................8.00 - 12.00

AL COLLINS:
Ace 500 *I Got The Blues For You*.........................75.00 - 100.00

EDDIE COLLINS:
Fernwood 104 *Patience Baby* ....15.00 - 20.00

LORRIE & LARRY COLLINS (See THE COLLINS KIDS)

MARTY COLLINS:
Ammons 6083 *I'm Gonna Walk* ....10.00 - 15.00
Renner 227 *She's Fine* ....15.00 - 20.00

TOMMY COLLINS:
Capitol (LP) T-776 *Words And Music Country Style*
....20.00 - 40.00
   (LP) 1196 *This Is* ....15.00 - 20.00

THE COLONAIRS:
Ember 1017 *Can't Stand To Lose You* ....20.00 - 30.00
Tru-Lite 127 *Do-Pop-Si*.......................................15.00 - 25.00

THE COLTS:
Vita 112 *Adorable*..10.00 - 15.00
   121 *Sweet Sixteen* ....15.00 - 20.00
   130 *Never, No More* ....15.00 - 20.00

CHUCK COMER:
Vaden - *Shall We Dance/Little More Lovin'* .... -   -

THE COMIC BOOKS:
Dynamic Sound 2005 *The First Time In My Life* ....10.00 - 15.00

THE COMMODORES:
Dot 15372 *Uranium* ....10.00 - 15.00
RPM 488 *Hello Baby*...15.00 - 20.00

AMOS COMO:
Starday 257 *Hole In The Wall* ....80.00 - 130.00

THE COMPANIONS:
Arlen 722 *These Foolish Things* ....10.00 - 15.00
Brooks 100 *I Didn't Know* ....20.00 - 30.00
Federal 12397 *Why, Oh, Why Baby* ....15.00 - 20.00
Gina 722 *It's Too Late* ....7.00 - 10.00

THE COMPOSERS:
Era 3118 *I Had A Dream* ....10.00 - 15.00

BOBBY COMSTOCK & THE COUNTS:
Mohawk 124 *Everyday Blues* ....10.00 - 15.00
Triumph 602 *Jealous Fool*....................................7.00 - 10.00

THE CONCORDS:
Ember 1007 *I'll Always Say Please* ....15.00 - 25.00
Epic 9697 *Should I Cry*..20.00 - 30.00
Grammercy 304 *Cross My Heart* ....30.00 - 50.00
Harlem 2328 *Monticello* ....400.00 - up
Herald 576 *Marlene* ....10.00 - 15.00
   578 *Cold And Frosty Morning*.........................10.00 - 15.00

TONY CONN:
Decca 30813 *Like Wow* ....20.00 - 30.00
   30865 *You Pretty Thing* .... -   -

THE CONNOTATIONS:
Technicord 1000 *Before I Go* ....25.00 - 40.00

CONNY & THE BELLHOPS:
R 505 *Shot Road* ....10.00 - 15.00
R 511 *Fafine/Are You Ashamed* ....10.00 - 15.00

THE CONQUERORS:
Lupine 108 *Bill Is My Boyfriend* ....20.00 - 30.00

THE CONSTELLATIONS:
Groove 0140 *Come Sit By Me* ....15.00 - 20.00

THE CONTINENTAL 5:
Nu Kat (unnumbered) *Perdelia* ....10.00 - 20.00
   105/104 *My Lonely Friend* ....20.00 - 30.00

THE CONTINENTALS:
Hunter 3503 *It Doesn't Matter* ....100.00 - 150.00
Port 70018 *Fine Fine Frame* ....10.00 - 15.00
Rama 190 *You're An Angel (blue label)*.................150.00 - 250.00
Whirlin' Disc 101 *Dear Lord* ....30.00 - 50.00
   105 *Picture Of Love* ....30.00 - 50.00

THE CONTOURS:
Gordy (LP) 901 *Do You Love Me* ....100.00 - 150.00
Motown 1012 *Funny*...100.00 - 150.00

DALE COOK:
Specialty 596 *Forever* ....7.00 - 10.00

L. C. COOKE:
Checker 903, 925 ....7.00 - 10.00

SAM COOKE:
Keen (LP) 2001, 2003, 2004 ....25.00 - 50.00
   4-4002 *Desire Me* (78 rpm) ....8.00 - 12.00
   4-4009 *Lonely Island* (78 rpm) ....8.00 - 12.00
   44013 *You Send Me* (78 rpm) ....20.00 - 30.00
RCA Victor (EP) 437 *Another Saturday Night*.......30.00 - 50.00
Specialty 619 *Forever*..5.00 - 10.00
   627 *I Don't Want To Cry* ....5.00 - 10.00

COOKIE & THE CUPCAKES:
Khoury's 703 *Mathilda* ....20.00 - 30.00
Lyric 1008 *All My Lovin'* ....10.00 - 20.00

THE COOKIES:
Josie 822 *King Of Hearts*.....................................8.00 - 12.00

THE COOLBREEZERS:
ABC Paramount 9865 *You Know I Go For You* .....30.00 - 50.00
Bale 100 *The Greatest Love Of All* ....15.00 - 20.00
   102 *Let Christmas Ring* ....50.00 - 80.00

EDDIE COOLEY & THE DIMPLES:
Roost 621 *Priscilla* (78 rpm) ....15.00 - 20.00

SPADE COOLEY:
Columbia (LP) 9007 (10 inch) *Sagebrush Swing* ...20.00 - 30.00

DOLLY COOPER:
Dot 15495 *Big Rock Inn*......................................8.00 - 12.00
Ebb 109 *Wild Love* ....10.00 - 15.00
Modern 977 *Teenage Prayer* ....8.00 - 12.00

LITTLE COOPER & THE DRIFTERS:
Stevens 105 *Evening Train* ....10.00 - 15.00

COWBOY COPAS:
Starday 501, 528, 542, 641 ....5.00 - 10.00

JOHNNY COPELAND:
Mercury 71280 *Rock 'n' Roll Lilly* ....15.00 - 20.00

KEN COPELAND:
Dot 15686 *Where The Rio De Rosa Flows* ....10.00 - 15.00
Lin 5017 *Fanny Brown* ....15.00 - 20.00

THE COPESETICS:
Premium 409 *Collegian* ....30.00 - 50.00

PAT CORDELL & THE CRESCENTS/ELEGANTS:
Club 1011 *Darling Come Back*..............................150.00 - 200.00
Michele 503 *Darling Come Back*...........................15.00 - 25.00
Victory 1001 *Darling Come Back* ....10.00 - 15.00

RITCHIE CORDELL:
Rori 707 *Tick Tock*..20.00 - 30.00

THE CORDELLS:
Bullseye 1017 *Believe In Me* ....30.00 - 50.00

THE CORDIALS:
Felsted 8653 *Once In A Lifetime*...........................10.00 - 15.00
Reveille 106 *Eternal Love* ....50.00 - 80.00
Seven Arts 707 *Dawn Is Almost Here* ....25.00 - 40.00
Whip 276 *My Heart's Desire* ....50.00 - 80.00

HENRY CORDING:
Columbia 40762 *Hiccough Rock* ....15.00 - 25.00

THE CORDONS:
Rowe 010 *Is She The One* ....50.00 - 80.00

THE CORONETS:
Chess 1549 *Nadine* ....40.00 - 70.00
   1549 *Nadine* (red plastic)...............................150.00 - up
   1553 *It Would Be Heavenly* ....100.00 - 150.00
   1553 *It Would Be Heavenly* (red plastic)..........300.00 - up
Groove 0114 *I Love You More* ....40.00 - 60.00
   0116 *Hush* ....40.00 - 60.00

THE CORSAIRS:
Hytone 110 *Goodbye Darling* ....400.00 - up
Tuff 1808 *Smoky Places* ....7.00 - 10.00

THE CORVAIRS:
Clock 1037 *Love Her So* ....30.00 - 50.00

THE CORVELLS:
ABC Paramount 10324 *Take My Love* ....30.00 - 50.00
Blast 203 *The Bells* ....80.00 - 130.00
Lido 509 *We Made A Vow* ....30.00 - 50.00
Tip Top 509 *We Made A Vow* ....10.00 - 15.00

THE CORVETS:
ABC Paramount 9891 *String Band Hop*...................8.00 - 12.00
Sure 1003 *I'm Pleadin'*..8.00 - 12.00

THE COSMIC RAYS:
Saturn 222 *Somebody's In Love* ....200.00 - up
   401 *Dreaming* ....100.00 - 150.00

NED COSTNER:
Hamilton 50030 *Jeopardy* ....7.00 - 10.00

ERNEST COTTON:
J.O.B. 1120 *Going Back To Memphis* ....150.00 - 250.00

JAMES COTTON:
Loma 2042 *Laying In The Weeds* ....7.00 - 10.00
Sun 199 *Straighten Up Baby* ....150.00 - 250.00
   206 *Cotton Crop Blues* ....150.00 - 250.00

JERRY COULSTON & THE JADES:
Christy 131 *Bon-Bon Baby* ....8.00 - 12.00

COUNTRY BOY EDDIE:
Reed 1031 *Hang In There*..50.00 - 80.00

THE COUNTRY DUDES (with CLAY ALLAN):
Azalea 121 *Have A Ball*...15.00 - 30.00

THE COUNTRY G-JS:
Valley - *Go, Girl, Go*.................................. - - -

THE COUNTS:
Dot 1188 *Darling Dear* ....15.00 - 20.00
   1199 *Baby Don't You Know* ....15.00 - 20.00
   1210 *My Dear, My Darling* ....15.00 - 20.00
   1226 *Waitin' Around For You* ....15.00 - 20.00
   1235 *Wailin' Little Mama*.................................15.00 - 20.00
   1243 *From This Day On* ....15.00 - 25.00
   1265 *I Need You Tonight* ....15.00 - 20.00
   1275 *To Our Love* ....15.00 - 20.00
Nat 100 *You'll Feel It Too* ....8.00 - 12.00
   101 *True Love's Gone* ....8.00 - 12.00
Note 20000 *I Guess I Brought It All On Myself* ......30.00 - 50.00
Smash 1821 *Stormy Weather*...................................8.00 - 12.00
Sun-Set 502 *Touch Me*..10.00 - 15.00

FRED COUPLAND (See BLUE TONES):

KEITH COURVALE:
Dot 15844 *Steel Worker Blues* ....15.00 - 20.00

COUSIN LEROY:
Ember 1016 *Highway 41* ....25.00 - 40.00
   1023 *Up The River* ....20.00 - 30.00
Groove 0123 *Catfish* ....15.00 - 25.00
Herald 546 *Waitin' At The Station*.........................15.00 - 20.00

DON COVAY:
Columbia 42197 *Now That I Need You* ....20.00 - 30.00

BUDDY COVELLE:
Coral 62181 *Lorraine* ....75.00 - 100.00

RICKY COYNE:
Event 4298 *Little Darlene*.......................................15.00 - 20.00

C-QUINS/C-QUINNS:
Chess 1815 *My Only Love* ....7.00 - 10.00
Ditto 501 *You've Been Crying* ....8.00 - 12.00

RILEY CRABTREE:
Ekko 1019 *Don't Turn Away From Me* ....8.00 - 12.00

BILL(Y) "CRASH" CRADDOCK:
Colonial 721 *Birddoggin'* ....15.00 - 25.00
   41316 *I Miss You So Much* ....7.00 - 10.00
   41367 *Blabbermouth*..7.00 - 10.00
   41470 *Boom Boom Baby*.................................7.00 - 10.00
   41536 *I Want That* ....7.00 - 10.00
   41619, 41677...5.00 - 8.00
Date 1007 *Ah, Poor Little Baby* ....7.00 - 10.00

JIMMY CRAIG:
Imperial 5592 *Oh! Little Girl!* ....15.00 - 20.00
Prism 1002 *Rocka Socka Hop* ....15.00 - 20.00

PEE WEE CRAIG:
Choice 1000 *Rambling Man* ....10.00 - 15.00

JIMMY CRAIN:
Spangle 2009 *Shig-A-Shag* ....10.00 - 15.00
Vincent 5047/5048 *Why Worry*...............................15.00 - 25.00

BLACKIE CRAWFORD:
Coral 64118, 64128, 64161.......................................5.00 - 8.00

FRED CRAWFORD:
Starday 170 *You Gotta Wait* ....30.00 - 50.00
   199 *Can't Live with 'Em* ....25.00 - 40.00
   243 *Rock Candy Rock* ....25.00 - 40.00

SUGAR BOY CRAWFORD:
Imperial 5424, 5468 ....7.00 - 10.00

JACKIE CRAY:
Limelight 3001 *Maybelle* ....15.00 - 20.00

PEE WEE CRAYTON:
Crown (LP) 5175 *Pee Wee Crayton* ....25.00 - 40.00
Fox 102 *Look Up And Live* ....10.00 - 15.00
Imperial 5288 *Every Dog Has His Day* ....20.00 - 30.00
   5297 *Hurry Hurry*...15.00 - 25.00
   5321 *I Need Your Love* ....10.00 - 15.00
   5338 *I Got News For You* ....10.00 - 15.00
   5345 *Eyes Full Of Tears* ....10.00 - 15.00
   5353 *Be Faithful* ....10.00 - 15.00
Post 2007 *Don't Go* ....15.00 - 20.00
Recorded in Hollywood 408 *Pappy's Blues* ....15.00 - 20.00
   426 *I'm Your Prisoner* ....15.00 - 20.00

Vee Jay 214 *The Telephone Is Ringing* ....8.00 - 12.00
    252 *I Don't Care*...8.00 - 12.00
    266 *Fiddle De Dee*...800 - 12.00

THE CREATIONS:
Jamie 1197 *The Bells* ....10.00 - 15.00
Lido 501 *You Are My Darling* ....75.00 - 100.00
Meridian 6283, 7552 *The Wedding* ....10.00 - 15.00
Patti-Jo 1703 *You'll Always Be Mine* ....80.00 - 130.00
Penny 9022 *We're In Love* ....20.00 - 30.00
Radiant 103 *Don't Listen To What Others Say* ....8.00 - 12.00
Take Ten 1501 *Lady Luck* ....7.00 - 10.00
Tip Top 400 *Mommy and Daddy*....................40.00 - 60.00

THE CREATORS:
Dootone 463 *I've Had You* ....15.00 - 25.00
Dore 635 *Too Far To Turn Around* ....15.00 - 20.00
Epic 9605 *Crazy Love*....................................15.00 - 20.00
Hi-Q 5021 *Wear My Ring*................................15.00 - 20.00
Philips 40058 *Boy He's Got It* ....7.00 - 10.00
    40083 *I'll Stay Home* ....15.00 - 30.00
Tee Kay 110 *I'll Never Have To Do It Again*..........15.00 - 20.00
Time 1038 *Do You Remember* ....7.00 - 10.00

THE CRESCENDOS:
Atlantic 2014 *I'll Be Seeing You* ....7.00 - 10.00
Nasco 6005 *Oh Julie*......................................7.00 - 10.00
    6005 *Oh Julie* (78 rpm) ....20.00 - 30.00
6009 *Crazy Hop* ....8.00 - 12.00
    6021 *Rainy Sunday* ....8.00 - 12.00
Scarlet 4007 *Strange Love* ....10.00 - 15.00
TAP 7027 *Oh Julie* ....5.00 - 8.00

THE CRESCENTS:
Arlen 743 *Smoke Gets In Your Eyes*.................7.00 - 10.00
De Lite 524 *Smoke Gets In Your Eyes*..............7.00 - 10.00
Dot 16447 *When You Wish Upon A Star* ....5.00 - 8.00
Hamilton 50033 *When You Wish Upon A Star*........10.00 - 15.00
Joyce 102 *Everybody Knew But Me* ....50.00 - 80.00

THE CRESCHENDOS:
Gone 5100 *My Heart's Desire*..........................10.00 - 15.00
Music City 831 *My Heart's Desire* ....80.00 - 120.00
    839 *Teenage Prayer*...................................80.00 - 120.00

THE CRESTS:
Coed (EP) 101 *The Angels Listened In*.............80.00 - 120.00
    501 *Pretty Little Angel*..............................20.00 - 30.00
    506 *Sixteen Candles* ....5.00 - 8.00
    509 *Six Nights A Week*...............................5.00 - 8.00
    511 *Flower Of Love* ....7.00 - 10.00
    515 *The Angels Listened In*........................7.00 - 10.00
    421 *A Year Ago Tonight* ....7.00 - 10.00
    525 *Step By Step* ....7.00 - 10.00
    531 *Trouble In Paradise* ....7.00 - 10.00
    535 *Journey Of Love* ....7.00 - 10.00
    537 *Isn't It Amazing*...................................7.00 - 10.00
    543 *Good Golly Miss Molly*.........................7.00 - 10.00
    561 *Little Miracles*.....................................7.00 - 10.00
*(Note: 78 RPM pressings may exist of THE CRESTS' Coed
   records; these would be of value. Canadian 78 RPM pressings
   have been seen.)
Coed (LP) 901 *The Crests Sing All Biggies*.............75.00 - 100.00
   (LP) 904 *The Best Of The Crests* (MONO)........50.00 - 75.00
   (LP) LPS-904 *The Best Of The Crests* (STEREO) (existence not
      confirmed) ....200.00 - up
Coral 62403 *You Blew Out The Candles* ....10.00 - 15.00
Joyce 103 *Sweetest One*..................................40.00 - 70.00
    105 *No One To Love* ....40.00 - 70.00
Selma 311 *Guilty* ....10.00 - 15.00

THE CREW CUTS:
Mercury (LP) 20144 *Rock And Roll Bash* ....20.00 - 30.00

THE CRICKETS (featuring DEAN BARLOW):
Beacon 104 *Be Faithful* ....20.00 - 30.00
Davis (EP) 211 *The Crickets*...........................150.00 - 250.00
    459 *I'm Going To Live My Life Alone* ....20.00 - 30.00
Jay Dee 777 *Dreams And Wishes* ....50.00 - 80.00
    781 *Fine As Wine* ....40.00 - 60.00
    785 *Your Love* ....30.00 - 50.00
    786 *Just You* ....30.00 - 50.00
    789 *Are You Looking For A Sweetheart?* ....30.00 - 50.00
    795 *I'm Going To Live My Life Alone* ....30.00 - 50.00
MGM 11428 *You're Mine* ....40.00 - 60.00
11507 *For You I Have Eyes* ....50.00 - 80.00

THE CRICKETS (with BUDDY HOLLY):
Brunswick (LP) 54038 *The Chirping Crickets* .....100.00 - 150.00
    55009 *That'll Be The Day*...............................10.00 - 15.00
    55009 *That'll Be The Day* (78 rpm) ....50.00 - 80.00
    55035 *Oh Boy!* ....8.00 - 12.00
    55035 *Oh Boy!* (78 rpm) ....50.00 - 80.00
    55053 *Maybe Baby* ....8.00 - 12.00
    55053 *Maybe Baby* (78 rpm) ....75.00 - 100.00
    55072 *Think It Over* ....10.00 - 15.00
    55072 *Think It Over* (78 rpm) ....80.00 - 120.00
    55094 *It's So Easy* ....15.00 - 20.00
    55094 *It's So Easy* (78 rpm) ....80.00 - 120.00
Brunswick (EP) 71036 *The Chirping Crickets* ....75.00 - 100.00
   (EP) 71038 *The Sound Of The Crickets* ....75.00 - 100.00
Coral (LP) 57320 *In Style With The Crickets* ....75.00 - 100.00
    62198 *More Than I Can Say*...........................10.00 - 15.00
    62238 *Don't Cha Know* ....10.00 - 15.00
(EP) 81192 *The Crickets* ....50.00 - 75.00
(Note: Promotional copies of above may be of substantially greater
   interest and value.)

THE CRITERIONS:
Cecilia 1208 *I Remain Truly Yours*........................10.00 - 15.00
Laurie 3305 *I Remain Truly Yours*..........................8.00 - 12.00

HOWARD CROCKET:
Solar 500 *Seven Cards From Now*........................15.00 - 20.00

G. DAVY CROCKETT:
Checker 1121 *Look Out Mabel* ....7.00 - 10.00
Chief 7010 *Look Out Mabel* ....20.00 - 30.00
U.S.A. 816 *Look Out Mabel* ....8.00 - 12.00

CLIFF CROFFORD:
Tally 104 *Ain't Nothin' Happenin' to Me*...............10.00 - 15.00
    109 *Teenage Years* ....10.00 - 15.00
    113 *Love Conquers All*..................................5.00 - 10.00

GEORGE CROMWELL:
Brunswick 55131 *Washed Up*...............................10.00 - 15.00

JERRY CRONIN:
Flame 113 *A-Rock-A Me Baby*...............................10.00 - 15.00

DILLAR CROOM & THE CROOM BROTHERS:
Vee Jay 283 *It's You Love*....................................30.00 - 50.00

HAROLD CROSBY & THE PINE TREE BOYS:
Lorida 3/4 *The Bastille Blues* ....20.00 - 30.00

HANK CROW:
Southwest 204 *Crazy 'Bout You* ....15.00 - 25.00

BOBBY CROWN & THE KAPERS:
Felco 102 *One Way Ticket* ....15.00 - 20.00

THE CROWNS (See also ARTHUR LEE MAYE & THE CROWNS):

Old Town 1171 *Possibility* ....10.00 - 15.00
R n B 6901 *I'll Forget About You* ....15.00 - 20.00

THE CROWS:

Gee 1 *Perfidia* ....300.00 - up
Rama 3 *Seven Lonely Days*.........................300.00 - 600.00
    5 *Gee* (red plastic)............................75.00 - 100.00
    5 *Gee* (black plastic).........................20.00 - 40.00
    10 *Heartbreaker*..............................100.00 - 150.00
    29 *Untrue*...50.00 - 80.00
    30 *Miss You*.....................................75.00 - 100.00
    50 *Sweet Sue*....................................75.00 - 100.00
Tico 1082 *Mambo Shevitz* ....50.00 - 80.00

(ARTHUR) "BIG BOY" CRUDUP:

Ace 503 *My Baby Boogies All The Time* ....30.00 - 50.00
Fire (LP) 103 *Mean Old Frisco* ....150.00 - 200.00
    1502, 1503 ....7.00 - 10.00
Groove 0011 *I Love My Baby*............................20.00 - 30.00
    0026 *She's Got No Hair* ....20.00 - 30.00
    5005 *Rock Me Mama* ....15.00 - 20.00
RCA Victor 5070 *Pearly Lee* ....25.00 - 35.00
    5167 *Keep On Drinkin'* ....25.00 - 35.00
    5563 *My Wife And Women* ....25.00 - 35.00
    50-0000 *That's All Right* ....50.00 - 80.00
    50-0001 *Katie May* ....30.00 - 50.00
    50-0013 *Crudup's Vicksburg Blues*...........30.00 - 50.00
    50-0032 *Hoodoo Lady Blues* ....30.00 - 50.00
    50-0046 *Mercy Blues*............................30.00 - 50.00
(Note: RCA Victor 50-0000 - 50-0046, inclusive, are made of vivid orange plastic.)
RCA Victor 50-0074 *Dust My Broom* ....25.00 - 40.00
    50-0092 *Mean Old Santa Fe*.....................25.00 - 40.00
    50-0100 *Lonesome World To Me* ....25.00 - 40.00
    50-0101 *She's Just Like Caldonia* ....25.00 - 40.00
    50-0117 *Nobody Wants Me* ....25.00 - 40.00
    50-0126 *Roberta Blues* ....25.00 - 40.00
    50-0141 *Too Much Competition* ....25.00 - 40.00

THE CRUISERS:

Finch 353 *The Moon Is Yours*...........................20.00 - 30.00
V-Tone 207 *If I Knew* ....15.00 - 20.00
    213 *Cryin' Over You*..............................10.00 - 15.00
Zebra 119 *Foolish Me* ....80.00 - 130.00

AL CRUM:

Glenn 3800 *Turn 'Em Up* ....7.00 - 10.00

SIMON CRUM:

Capitol (LP) 1880 *The Unpredictable Simon Crum* ....20.00 - 30.00
    3460 *Bop Cat Bop*................................7.00 - 10.00
    4073 *Stand Up, Sit Down, Shut Your Mouth* ....5.00 - 8.00

MANNY CRUSE & THE SOUNDS QUARTETTE:

Dart 127 *Any Time, Any Place*..........................8.00 - 12.00

THE CRYSTALIERS:

Johnson 103 *Don't Cry*...................................300.00 - up

THE CRYSTALS:

Aladdin 3355 *I Do Believe* ....25.00 - 40.00
Cub 9064 *Watching You* ....15.00 - 20.00
De Luxe 6013 *My Dear* ....250.00 - up
    6037 *Have Faith In Me* ....250.00 - up
    6077 *God Only Knows* ....75.00 - 100.00
Felsted 8566 *Blind Date* ....7.00 - 10.00
Luna 5001 *Come To Me Darling* ....30.00 - 50.00
Metro 20026 *That's Where I Belong* ....8.00 - 12.00

Philles 100 *Oh Yeah, Maybe Baby*..........................7.00 - 10.00
    103 *Uptown* ....7.00 - 10.00
    (LP) 4001 *He's A Rebel* (blue label).........75.00 - 100.00
    (LP) 90722 *Twist Uptown* (STEREO) ....rare
Specialty 657 *Love You So*...................................10.00 - 15.00

CRYSTAL TONES: (See also BILLY JAMES & CRYSTAL TONES)

M.Z. 007 *A Girl I Love* ....50.00 - 80.00
    008 *Debra Lee* ....50.00 - 80.00

THE CUBANS:

Flash 133 *Tell Me* ....30.00 - 50.00

THE CUBS:

Savoy 1502 *Why Did You Make Me Cry* ....10.00 - 15.00

THE CUES:

Capitol 3245 *Oh My Darling* ....8.00 - 12.00
    3310 *You're On My Mind* ....8.00 - 12.00
    3483 *Crackerjack* ....8.00 - 12.00

THE CUFF LINKS:

Dootone 409 *Guided Missiles* ....25.00 - 40.00
    413 *How You Lied*...................................15.00 - 20.00
    422 *It's Too Late Now*..............................25.00 - 40.00
Gait 543 *Only One Love*.....................................40.00 - 70.00

THE CUFFLINX:

Dootone 433 *So Tough*..10.00 - 15.00
    434 *A Fool's Fortune* ....10.00 - 15.00
    438 *Lawful Wedding* ....10.00 - 15.00

BRUCE CULVER:

M.M.I. 1235 *Square Record* ....10.00 - 15.00

THE CUPIDS:

Aanko 1002 *For You*...40.00 - 80.00
Aladdin 3404 *Lillie Mae* ....15.00 - 20.00
Decca 30279 *The Answer To Your Prayer*.............10.00 - 15.00
KC 115 *Brenda* ....5.00 - 8.00
Music Note 120 *Lorraine* ....7.00 - 10.00

PAT CUPP:

Crown (LP) 5364 *Pat Cupp and Ray Smith*............50.00 - 75.00
RPM 461 *Do Me No Wrong*................................30.00 - 50.00
    473 *Long Gone Daddy* ....30.00 - 50.00
    - *That's My Girl* .... - - -

CURLEY JIM (MORRISON):

Mida 100 *Rock 'N' Roll Itch* ....50.00 - 80.00
    108 *Sloppy Sloppy Suzie* ....40.00 - 60.00

EARL CURRY:

Post 2001 *Somebody Stole My Girl* ....20.00 - 30.00
    2011 *Hobo*...20.00 - 30.00
R&B 1304 *Late Rising Moon* ....50.00 - 100.00
    1313 *Try And Get Me*..............................30.00 - 60.00
RPM 402 *One Whole Year Baby* ....15.00 - 20.00

JAMES CURRY:

Flash 110 *My Promise* ....8.00 - 12.00

C. C. CURTIS:

Audicon 109 *Aunt Minnie* ....5.00 - 8.00

DON CURTIS:

Kliff 104 *Rough Tough Man* ....30.00 - 50.00

EDDIE CURTIS:

Dot 15505 *You're Much Too Pretty For Me*............5.00 - 8.00

EDDIE "TEX" CURTIS:
Gee 9 *Shake, Pretty Baby, Shake* ....75.00 - 100.00

KING CURTIS:
Atco (LP) 33-102 *Have Tenor Sax* ....30.00 - 60.00

MAC CURTIS:
King 4927 *If I Had Me A Woman* ....25.00 - 40.00
 4949 *Grandaddy's Rockin'* ....30.00 - 50.00
 4965 *You Ain't Treatin' Me Right* ....25.00 - 40.00
 4995 *That Ain't Nothin' But Right* ....25.00 - 40.00
 5059 *Say So* ....15.00 - 20.00
 5107 *What You Want* ....15.00 - 20.00
 5121 *Little Miss Linda* ....10.00 - 15.00
Shalimar 103 *Come On Back* ....5.00 - 8.00

SONNY CURTIS:
Dot 15754 *Laughing Stock* ....10.00 - 15.00
 15799 *Willa May Jones* ....10.00 - 15.00

THE CYCLONES (See also BILL TAYLOR & THE CYCLONES):
Flip 324 *My Dear* ....15.00 - 20.00
Trophy 503 *Aftermath* ....7.00 - 10.00

JOHNNY CYMBAL:
Kapp (LP) 3324 *Mr. Bass Man* ....20.00 - 30.00

THE CYMBALS:
Amazon 709 *One Step Too Far* ....7.00 - 10.00

BUDDY CYPRESS:
Flash 118 *I'm In Love With You* ....7.00 - 10.00

CZARS OF RHYTHM:
De'Voice 782 *Please Don't Leave Me* .....40.00 - 70.00

DADDY CLEANHEAD:
Specialty 541 *Back Home* ....10.00 - 15.00

DICK D'AGOSTIN:
Accent 1046 *I'm Your Daddy-O* ....10.00 - 15.00
Dot 15773 *Nancy Lynne* ....10.00 - 15.00
 15867 *Night Walk* ....7.00 - 10.00
Liberty 55218 *It's You* ....7.00 - 10.00

DICK DALE & THE DEL-TONES:
Deltone (LP) 1001 *Surfer's Choice* ....80.00 - 120.00
 5012 *Ooh-Whee-Marie* ....15.00 - 20.00
 5014 *Jessie Pearl* ....20.00 - 30.00
 5019 *Eight Till Midnight* ....7.00 - 10.00
 5020 *Surf Beat* ....5.00 - 8.00

JIMMIE DALE:
Drew-Blan 1003 *Emma Lee* ....8.00 - 12.00

KENNY DALE:
Picture 310 *Cincy Lee* ....7.00 - 10.00

LARRY DALE (& THE KING NOTES):
Atlantic 2133 *Drinkin' Wine Spo-Dee-O-Dee*...........5.00 - 8.00
Elbridge 12763 *Crying Over You* ....10.00 - 15.00
Herald 463 *No Tellin'* ....10.00 - 15.00

THE DALES:
Onyx 509 *If You Are Meant To Be* ....15.00 - 20.00

JIMMY DALEY & THE DING-A-LINGS:
Decca (EP) 2431, 2432, 2480 ....15.00 - 20.00
 (LP) 8429 *Rock, Pretty Baby* ....30.00 - 40.00
 30163 *Rock, Pretty Baby* ....7.00 - 10.00

CHUCK DALLAS:
K-C 102 *Come On Let's Go* ....7.00 - 10.00

JACKIE DALLAS:
Fawn 6002 *Lorraine* ....15.00 - 20.00

CHUCK DALLIS:
Glenn 2201 *Come On Let's Go*................15.00 - 20.00
 2203 *Good Show, But No Go* ....15.00 - 20.00
Mar-Vel 2204 *Joni Kaye*.....................15.00 - 20.00

BIG LLOYD DALTON:
Yucca 135 *Jenny* ....7.00 - 10.00

DURWOOD DALY:
Caprock 108 *That's The Way It Goes* ....7.00 - 10.00

TERRY DALY:
Caprock 122 *You Don't Bug Me* ....50.00 - 100.00

JOE D'AMBRA & THE EMBERS:
Mercury 71725 *Please Come Home* ....7.00 - 10.00

DONNA DAMERON:
Dart 113 *Bopper 486609*......................15.00 - 25.00

"DANCE THE ROCK & ROLL":
Atlantic (LP) 8013 (various artists) ....30.00 - 60.00

"DANCE TUNES FROM THE VAULT":
Chess (LP) 1476 (various artists)............40.00 - 60.00

THE DANDERLIERS:
B & F 1344 *Chop Chop Boom* ....7.00 - 10.00
States 147 *My Autumn Love*..................30.00 - 50.00
 147 *My Autumn Love* (red plastic) ...300.00 - up
 150 *My Loving Partner* ....50.00 - 80.00
 152 *May God Be With You* ....75.00 - 100.00
 160 *My Love*...............................50.00 - 80.00

DANDEVILLES:
Guyden 2014 *There's A Reason*...............10.00 - 15.00

THE DANDIES:
Peach 121 *Red Light* ....15.00 - 20.00

DANDLEERS (misspelling, see DANLEERS)

EDDIE DANIELS:
Ebb 108 *Whoa-Whoa Baby*.................15.00 - 20.00

JEFF DANIELS:
Astro 108 *Foxy Dan*..........................15.00 - 20.00
Big B 555 *Uh Uh Uh* ....15.00 - 20.00
Big Howdy 777 *Switch Blade Sam* ....20.00 - 30.00
Caravan - *Go Daddyo (?)*.................... - -
Meladee 117 *Daddy-O Rock*.................40.00 - 60.00

THE DANLEERS:
Amp-3 1005 *One Summer Night*...............8.00 - 12.00
 2115 *One Summer Night* (credited as by "The Dandleers")
....20.00 - 40.00
Epic 9367 *If You Don't Care* ....10.00 - 15.00
 9421 *Little Lover*..........................20.00 - 30.00
Everest 19412 *Foolish* ....15.00 - 20.00
Le Mans 008 *I'm Sorry* ....8.00 - 12.00
Mercury 71322 *One Summer Night* ....5.00 - 10.00
 71322 *One Summer Night* (78 rpm)...............100.00 - up
(Note: Existence in 78 RPM format unverified.)
Mercury 71356 *I Really Love You* ....7.00 - 10.00
 71401 *A Picture of You* ....8.00 - 12.00
 71441 *I Can't Sleep* ....10.00 - 15.00
Smash 1872 *If* ....7.00 - 10.00
 1895 *The Angels Sent You*................8.00 - 12.00

DANNY & THE JUNIORS:
ABC Paramount (EP) 11 *At The Hop* ....100.00 - 200.00
 9871 *At The Hop* ....7.00 - 10.00

9871 *At The Hop* (78 rpm)................................30.00 - 50.00
9888 *Rock & Roll Is Here To Stay*.......................8.00 - 12.00
9888 *Rock & Roll Is Here To Stay* (78 rpm) ....100.00 - 150.00
ABC Paramount (most other issues)....................5.00 - 10.00
Guyden 2076 *Now And Then*................................5.00 - 8.00
Singular 711 *At The Hop*.................................100.00 - 200.00

DANNY & THE MEMORIES:
Valiant 705 *Can't Help Lovin' That Girl Of Mine* ..10.00 - 15.00
    6049 *Don't Go* ....15.00 - 20.00

DANNY BOY (& HIS BLUE GUITAR):
Dot 16140 *Send Me Some Lovin'* ....10.00 - 15.00
Kent 300 *Don't Go Pretty Baby*..........................15.00 - 20.00
Tifco 824 *Wild Women* ....20.00 - 30.00

CHARLES BUD DANTE:
Decca (LP) 8430 *Holiday In The Golden West* ....15.00 - 20.00

DANTE & THE EVERGREENS:
Madison (LP) 1002 *Dante & The Evergreens*.........75.00 - 100.00

TONY DANTE:
Frankie 15 *Rock-A-Ree* ....7.00 - 10.00

THE DAPPERS:
Epic 9423 *My Love Is Real* ....10.00 - 15.00
Groove 0156 *Unwanted Love* ....30.00 - 50.00
Peacock 1651 *Come Back To Me* ....30.00 - 50.00
Rainbow 373 *Bop Bop Bu*......................................10.00 - 20.00
Star-X 505 *We're In Love* ....20.00 - 30.00

THE DAPS:
Marterry 5249 *Down And Out* ....8.00 - 12.00

BOBBY DARIN (& THE JAYBIRDS):
Atco (LP) 102 *Bobby Darin* ....15.00 - 20.00
    (LP) 104 *That's All* ....15.00 - 20.00
    (LP) 115 *This Is Bobby Darin* ....15.00 - 20.00
    (EP) 4508 *This Is Darin*....................................20.00 - 30.00
    6117 *Splish Splash* (78 rpm)................................30.00 - 50.00
    6127 *Queen Of The Hop* (78 rpm) ....15.00 - 20.00
    6133 *Plain Jane* (78 rpm) ....25.00 - 40.00
Decca 29983 *Rock Island Line* ....8.00 - 12.00
    29922 *Silly Willie* ....8.00 - 12.00
    30031 *Hear Them Bells* ....8.00 - 12.00
    30225 *Dealer In Dreams* ....8.00 - 12.00

DENVER DARLING:
Audio Lab (LP) 107..20.00 - 30.00

JOHNNY DARLING:
De Luxe 6167 *Baseball Baby* .... - - -

DARNELL & THE DREAMS:
West Side 1030 *I Had A Love*.................................10.00 - 15.00

DON DARNELL:
Brunswick 55144 *In My Own Little Way* ....8.00 - 12.00

DARREL & THE OXFORDS:
Roulette 4174 *Picture In My Wallet* ....8.00 - 12.00

JAMES DARREN:
Colpix (LP) 406 *Album No. 1* ....20.00 - 30.00
    (LP) 418 *Sings The Movies*................................15.00 - 20.00
    (LP) 424 *Sings For All Sizes*...............................15.00 - 20.00
    (LP) 428 *Love Among The Young*.......................15.00 - 20.00

THE DARTS:
Apt 25023 *On My Mind*..8.00 - 12.00
Dot 15752 *Sweet Little Baby* ....7.00 - 10.00

CHUCK DARTY:
Chart 642 *My Steady Girl* .... 15.00 - 20.00
Rama 229 *My Steady Girl*.................................. 8.00 - 12.00

FRANKIE DASH:
Cool 106 *Rock Rhythm Roll* .... 50.00 - 80.00

DAVE & THE STEREOS:
Pennant 1001 *Roamin' Romeo* .... 8.00 - 12.00

DAVEY & THE DOO RAYS:
Guyden 2002 *It's The Beat* .... 8.00 - 12.00

BOB DAVIES & THE RHYTHM JESTERS:
Rama 224 *Never Anymore* .... 7.00 - 10.00

AL DAVIS:
Manco 1052 *Ricky Tic*................................ 10.00 - 15.00
1067 *Go Baby Go*.. 10.00 - 15.00

BO DAVIS:
Crest 1027 *Let's Coast Awhile* .... 20.00 - 30.00

BOB DAVIS:
Bandera 2505 *I Was Wrong* .... 5.00 - 8.00

DALE DAVIS & THE TOMCATS:
Stardale 100/101 *Gotta Rock* .... 20.00 - 30.00
    104/105 *Why'd You Leave Me Blues* .... 20.00 - 30.00
    701/702 *Bearcat Mama*.............................. 20.00 - 30.00

EDDIE DAVIS:
Fable - *Tick Tock Rock*............................... - - -

EMMETT/EMMIT DAVIS:
Fling 721 *One Last Chance* .... 7.00 - 10.00
M and B 101 *How About It Baby*............................ 7.00 - 10.00

EUNICE DAVIS:
De Luxe 6068 *24 Hours A Day*............................ 8.00 - 12.00
Grand 130 *Let's Have A Party* .... 10.00 - 15.00

GENE DAVIS:
Challenge 59091 *The Facts Of Life* .... 7.00 - 10.00
King 5076 *Who'll Dry My Tears* .... 7.00 - 10.00
R-Dell 107 *Curfew*.. 15.00 - 20.00

HAL DAVIS:
Dynamite 1010 *I Don't Love Nobody* .... 30.00 - 60.00

HANK DAVIS:
Stacy 919 *One Way Track*.................................... 8.00 - 12.00

HARLEY DAVIS:
Cindy 3011 *Calling All Cats*................................. 15.00 - 20.00

"HAPPY JACK" DAVIS with PIANO SLIM & THE STEREO-TONES:
Lluvia 5052 *Ten Cents Stew* .... 5.00 - 8.00

JAN DAVIS:
Guild 1900 *She Told Me* .... 30.00 - 60.00

JIMMIE DAVIS:
Decca (LP) 5500 (10 inches) .... 20.00 - 30.00
    (LP) 8896 *You Are My Sunshine*...................... 15.00 - 20.00

JUDGE DAVIS:
Flash 120 *Sawmill Section* .... 7.00 - 10.00

KEN DAVIS:
Pfau 3057 *Bundle Of Lovin'* .... - - -
Star-Light 1006 *Shook Shake* .... 20.00 - 30.00

KING DAVIS:
Hollywood 422 *Waggin' Your Tail*........................ 10.00 - 15.00

LARRY DAVIS:
Duke 192, 313, 328....................................5.00 - 10.00

LARRY & DIXIE DAVIS:
Kangaroo 13 *Gonna Live It Up* ....10.00 - 15.00
    15 *Shark Bait* ....8.00 - 12.00

LENNY DAVIS:
Do-Ra-Me 1413 *Satan's Got You* ....7.00 - 10.00

LINK DAVIS:
Al's 1503 *Johnny Be Good* .... - - -
All Star 7171 *Bon Ton Rula*....................4.00 - 7.00
Nucraft 2026 *Grasshopper Rock* ....7.00 - 10.00
Okeh 7046 *Mama Say No* ....10.00 - 15.00
    18048 *Crawfish Crawl*...................8.00 - 12.00
Sarg 136 *Cockroach* ....15.00 - 30.00
Starday 235 *Sixteen Chicks*....................20.00 - 30.00
    242 *Grasshopper Rock* ....20.00 - 30.00
    255 *Don't Big Shot Me* ....30.00 - 50.00
    275 *Bayou Buffalo* ....20.00 - 30.00
    293 *Slippin' And Slidin' Sometimes* ....30.00 - 50.00

LITTLE SAM DAVIS:
De Luxe 6025 *Goin' To New Orleans* ....50.00 - 80.00
Rockin' 512 1958 *Blues*....................75.00 - 100.00
    519 *Goin' To New Orleans* ....75.00 - 100.00

ROCKY DAVIS:
Blue Sky 102 *Hot Rod Baby* ....50.00 - 100.00

JIMMIE DAVISON:
Target 861 *Froggie Went A-Courtin'* ....7.00 - 10.00

THE DAWNBREAKERS:
Century 600 *Deep In The Heart Of Texas* .... - - -

THE DAWNS:
Catalina 1000 *Trav'lin'*....................75.00 - 100.00
Climax 104 *Why Did You Let Me Love You* ....15.00 - 20.00
Lawn 241 *Like To See You In That Mood* ....15.00 - 20.00

JIMMY DAWSON (THE DIXIE DRIFTER):
K-Ark 774 *Mean Woman Blues*...................15.00 - 20.00
Rustic 1926 *Money Talks* ....8.00 - 12.00

RONNIE DAWSON:
Rockin' Records 1 *Rockin' Bones* ....100.00 - 150.00
Swan 4047 *Hazel* ....7.00 - 10.00
    4054 *Summer's Comin'* ....7.00 - 10.00

BING DAY:
Apex 7761 *Poor Stagger Lee* ....20.00 - 30.00
Federal 12320 *Ponytail Partner* ....20.00 - 30.00
Mercury 71446 *I Can't Help It* ....10.00 - 15.00
    71494 *How Do I Do It* ....10.00 - 15.00

BOBBY DAY:
Clas 211 *Little Bitty Pretty One* (78 rpm)................15.00 - 25.00
    229 *Rockin' Robin* (78 rpm) ....40.00 - 70.00
    (LP) 5002 *Rockin' With Robin* ....100.00 - 200.00

DAVE DAY:
Fee Bee 212 *Blue Moon Baby* ....30.00 - 50.00
    215 *Deep In My Heart* ....15.00 - 20.00

DAVE DIDDLE DAY:
Mercury 71114 *Blue Moon Baby*...................15.00 - 25.00

JACK DAY:
Arcade 155 *Rattle Bone Boogie*...................25.00 - 40.00

MARGIE DAY:
Cat 118 *Ho Ho* ....7.00 - 10.00

THE DAYBREAKERS:
Aladdin 3434 *I Wonder Why*...................25.00 - 40.00

THE DAYLIGHTERS:
Astra 1001 *This Heart Of Mine* ....5.00 - 8.00
Bea & Baby 103 *You're Breaking My Heart*............8.00 - 12.00
Dot 16326 *On What A Way To Be Loved*...............8.00 - 12.00
Tip Top 2002 *Baby I Love You* ....10.00 - 15.00

THE DAZZLERS:
Lee - *Gee Whiz*....................... - -

DEACON & THE ROCK AND ROLLERS:
Nau-Voo 804 *Rockin' On The Moon* ....50.00 - 100.00

AL DEAN & HIS ALL STARS:
Warrior 506 *Fragile Heart*...................40.00 - 60.00

BOB/BOBBY DEAN:
Arcade 195 *Hot Rod Daddy* ....15.00 - 20.00
Chess 1673 *Just Go Wild Over Rock And Roll* ....15.00 - 25.00
    1710 *I'm Ready* ....15.00 - 20.00
Profile 4006 *It's A Fad, Ma* ....10.00 - 15.00

CHARLES DEAN & RONDELLS:
Benton 102 *Train Whistle Boogie* ....20.00 - 30.00

EDDIE DEAN:
Design (LP) 89 *Tribute To Hank Williams* ....10.00 - 15.00
Sage 226 *Rock & Roll Cowboy* ....10.00 - 15.00

FRANK DEAN:
Trend 30-008 *Bubblin'*...................7.00 - 10.00

JERRY DEAN:
Creole 1002 *Walkin' In My Sleep* ....15.00 - 20.00

LENNY DEAN & THE ROCKIN' CHAIRS (See ROCKIN' CHAIRS):

WALLY DEANE:
Arctic 103 *Saddle Up A Satellite* ....10.00 - 15.00
Globe 238 *Cool Cool Daddy*...................15.00 - 20.00
    - *Rockin' With Rosie* .... - -

THE DEANS:
Mohawk 126 *It's You*...................15.00 - 20.00

FRANK DEATON & HIS MAD LADS:
Alta 2000 *Framed* ....15.00 - 20.00
Bally 1042 *Just A Little Bit More* ....15.00 - 20.00

JIMMY DEBERRY:
Sun 185 *Take A Little Chance* ....200.00 - 300.00

THE DE'BONAIRS:
Ping 1001 *Say A Prayer For Me* ....75.00 - 100.00

THE DEBONAIRES:
Combo 129 *As Other Lovers Are* ....200.00 - 300.00
Dore 592 *Every Once In Awhile* ....10.00 - 15.00

DECKERS:
Yeadon 1041 *Sincerely with All My Heart* .... - -

BUD DECKLEMAN & THE DAYDREAMERS:
Meteor 5014 *Daydreamin'*...................20.00 - 30.00

THE DECOYS:
Aanko 1005 *I Want Only You* ....75.00 - 100.00

THE DEDICATIONS:
C & A 506 *Shining Star* ....15.00 - 20.00
Card 2001 *Why Don't You Write Me* ....10.00 - 15.00
Ramarca 602 *Someone To Love* ....7.00 - 10.00

DEE & PATTY:
D 1020 *Sweet Lovin' Baby* ....30.00 - 50.00
Mercury 71252 *Our First Date*................................8.00 - 12.00

FERN DEE:
Ember 1035 *You'll Never Know* ....7.00 - 10.00

FRANKIE DEE with CARTER RAYS:
RCA Victor 7276 *Shake It Up Baby* ....15.00 - 20.00

FRANKIE DEE with THE MASTERTONES:
Future 1001 *I Made A Boo Boo* ....15.00 - 20.00

JACKIE DEE:
Liberty 55148 *Buddy* ....10.00 - 15.00

JIMMY DEE (& THE OFFBEATS):
Ace 627 *Wanda*..15.00 - 20.00
Dot 15664 *Henrietta* ....8.00 - 12.00
   15721 *You're Late, Miss Kate* ....15.00 - 20.00
Scope 103 *I Ain't Givin' Up Nothin'* ....15.00 - 20.00
TNT 148 *Henrietta* ....15.00 - 20.00
   152 *You're Late, Miss Kate* ....20.00 - 30.00
   161 *Rick Tick Tock*.....................................75.00 - 100.00

JOE DEE:
Clix 811 *Satan's Angel* .... - - -

JOHNNY DEE:
Colonial 430 *Sittin' In The Balcony* ....7.00 - 10.00
   430 *Sittin' In The Balcony* (78 rpm)..........15.00 - 20.00
   433 *Teenage Queen* ....7.00 - 10.00
   433 *Teenage Queen* (78 rpm) ....15.00 - 20.00
Dot 15699 *Somebody Sweet*..............................7.00 - 10.00

LYNN DEE & THE STATICS: (See also: THE PAGANS)
Mantis 101 *A Sunday Kind Of Love* ....20.00 - 30.00

MERCY DEE:
Flair 1073 *Romp And Stomp Blues* ....15.00 - 20.00
   1077 *Come Back Maybelline* ....15.00 - 20.00
   1078 *Stubborn Woman* ....15.00 - 20.00
Rhythm 1774 *Trailing My Baby* ....15.00 - 20.00
Specialty 458 *One Room Country Shack*............10.00 - 15.00
   466 *Rent Man Blues*.................................10.00 - 15.00
   481 *Dark Muddy Bottom* ....10.00 - 15.00

RONNIE DEE:
Back Beat 522 *Action Packed*............................8.00 - 12.00

TONY DEE (See THE PAGEANTS)

THE DEE CALS:
Co-Ed 1960 *Stars In The Blue What Shall I Do* ......10.00 - 15.00
Mayhams 1960 *Stars In The Blue What Shall I Do*.10.00 - 15.00

THE DEEJAYS/DEE-JAYS:
Sonata 1100 *You Took Your Love From Me* ....80.00 - 120.00
SRC - *Love Me Baby* ....75.00 - 100.00

THE DEEP RIVER BOYS:
Camden (LP) 303 *Presenting The Deep River Boys*........30.00 - 50.00
   (EP) 341 *Deep River Boys* ....30.00 - 50.00
Jay-Dee 788 *Truthfully* ....15.00 - 20.00
Que (LP) 104 *Midnight Magic* ....100.00 - 150.00
RCA Victor 47-5268 *The Biggest Fool* ....10.00 - 15.00
Vik 0205 *All My Love Belongs To You* ....7.00 - 10.00
   0224 *How Dear Can It Be* ....7.00 - 10.00
   (LP) LXA-1019 ....100.00 - 150.00
Waldorf (LP) 108 (10 inch) *Spiritual And Jubilees*
   ....30.00 - 50.00
   (LP) 120 (10 inch) *Spirituals* ....30.00 - 50.00

THE DEE-VINES:
Lano 2001 *I Believe* ....15.00 - 20.00

THE DEFENDERS:
Parkway 926 *I Laughed So Hard* ....10.00 - 15.00

THE DELACARDOS:
Elgey 1001 *Letter To A School Girl* ....15.00 - 20.00
Shell 308 *Dream Girl* ....10.00 - 15.00
   311 *Loved Is The Greatest Thing* ....10.00 - 15.00

THE DEL-AIRS:
Delsey 302 *Mam Ma Marie* ....7.00 - 10.00
M.B.S. 001 *While Walking* ....10.00 - 15.00

THE DELATONES:
TNT 9027 *Little Jeanie* ....75.00 - 100.00

THE DEL-CHORDS:
Impala 215 *Everybody's Gotta Lose Someday* ....8.00 - 12.00

THE DELCOS:
Ebony 01 *These Three Little Words*......................30.00 - 50.00
Showcase 2501 *Arabia* ....10.00 - 15.00

THE DELEGATES:
Vee Jay 212 *The Convention* ....10.00 - 15.00
   243 *Mother's Son* ....10.00 - 15.00

DEL-FI ALBUM SAMPLER:
Del-Fi (unnumbered) (Valens, et al.) ....50.00 - 100.00

THE DELICATES:
Unart 2017 *Black And White Thunderbird* ....7.00 - 10.00

WAILIN' BILL DELL:
O.J. 1003 *You Gotta Be Loose* ....30.00 - 50.00

DANNY DELL:
Rockin' 160 *Froggy Went A-Courtin'* ....40.00 - 60.00
World Pacific 824 *Froggy Went A-Courtin'* ....15.00 - 20.00

DICKY DELL (See THE BING BONGS)

DON DELL & THE UPSTARTS:
East Coast 105 *A Special Love*............................20.00 - 30.00

JIMMY DELL:
RCA Victor 7194 *Cool It Baby*............................8.00 - 12.00
   7355 *I've Got A Dollar* ....7.00 - 10.00

TONY DELL:
King 5766 *My Girl* ....7.00 - 10.00

THE DEL LARKS:
East-West 116 *Remember The Night* ....15.00 - 25.00

THE DEL LOURDS:
Solar 1001 *All Alone* ....10.00 - 15.00
   1003 *Gloria*..10.00 - 15.00

THE DELLS:
Vee Jay 134 *Tell The World* (red plastic) ....300.00 - 600.00
   134 *Tell The World* ....100.00 - 150.00
   166 *Dreams Of Contentment* ....40.00 - 70.00
   204 *Oh What A Night*..............................15.00 - 25.00
   230 *Movin' On* ....15.00 - 25.00
   236 *Why Do You Have To Go*...................15.00 - 25.00
   251 *A Distant Love*.................................20.00 - 30.00
   258 *Pain In My Heart* ....15.00 - 25.00
   274 *The Springer*....................................10.00 - 15.00
   292 *I'm Calling*......................................15.00 - 20.00
   300 *My Best Girl*....................................30.00 - 50.00
   (LP) 1010 *Oh What A Night* (black label) ....30.00 - 50.00
   (LP) 1010 (same, but maroon label) ....100.00 - 150.00

THE DELLTONES/DELL TONES:

Baton 212 *Don't Be Long* ....10.00 - 15.00
　　223 *My Special Love* ....15.00 - 25.00
Dayhill 1002 *Hey Little Girl*..............................20.00 - 30.00
Rainbow 244 *I'm Not In Love With You*.................30.00 - 50.00

THE DELL-VIKINGS (See THE DEL VIKINGS)

THE DELLWOODS:

Big Top 3137 *Don't Put Onions On Hamburgers*.....8.00 - 12.00

THE DELMONICOS:

Aku 6318 *You Can Call*..10.00 - 15.00
Musictone 6122 *The World's Biggest Fool* ....8.00 - 12.00

THE DELMORE BROTHERS:

King (LP) 589 *Sixteen Favorites* ....25.00 - 50.00

ALTON DELMORE:

Linco 1315 *Good Times In Memphis*.....................10.00 - 15.00

THE DEL-PRADOS:

Lucky Four 1021 *Oh Baby* ....20.00 - 30.00

THE DEL RAYS:

Carousel 213 *Girl In My Heart*............................40.00 - 60.00
Cord 1001 *Our Love Is True*...............................200.00 - up
Future 7209 *When We're Alone* ....10.00 - 15.00
Moon 110 *Have A Heart*.....................................40.00 - 80.00

THE DEL RIOS/DEL-RIOS:

Meteor 5038 *Alone On A Rainy Night* ....50.00 - 80.00
Neptune 108 *I'm Crying* ....10.00 - 15.00
Stax 125 *Just Across The Street* ....15.00 - 20.00

THE DEL ROYALS:

Minit 610 *Who Will Be The One*..........................700 - 10.00

THE DEL-SATINS:

Laurie 3132 *Teardrops Follow Me*...........................800 - 12.00

THE DELTAIRS:

Ivy 101 *Lullaby Of The Bells* (yellow label) ....50.00 - 80.00
　　105 *Standing At The Altar* ....15.00 - 30.00

THE DELTA RHYTHM BOYS:

Camden (LP) 313 *The Delta Rhythm Boys*..............50.00 - 75.00
Decca 29273, 29329 ....7.00 - 10.00
Elektra (LP) 138 *The Delta Rhythm Boys Sing* ....15.00 - 20.00
Jubilee (LP) 1022 *The Delta Rhythm Boys In Sweden*
　　...30.00 - 40.00
Mercury (LP) 25153 (10 inches).............................30.00 - 50.00
RCA Victor (LP) 3085 (10 inches) *Dry Bones*........30.00 - 50.00
2828, 5094, 5217 ....7.00 - 10.00

THE DEL-TONES/DELTONES:

Oro-Ann 1001 *Best Wishes*................................15.00 - 20.00
Vee Jay 288 *I'm Coming Home* ....- - -

DEL VETTS:

End 1106 *Repeat After Me*.................................8.00 - 12.00

THE DEL VICTORS:

Hi-Q 5028 *Acting Up*..15.00 - 20.00
　　5028 *Baby Sitter I Love You* ....8.00 - 12.00
(Hi-Q 5028 was issued with different titles)

THE DEL VIKINGS (THE DELL VIKINGS):

ABC Paramount 10208 *Bring Back Your Heart*.......10.00 - 15.00
　　10248 *I Hear Bells*.......................................15.00 - 20.00
　　10278 *Kiss Me* ....8.00 - 12.00
　　10341 *Confession Of Love*..............................10.00 - 15.00
　　10385 *An Angel Up In Heaven*.........................20.00 - 30.00
Alpine 66 *The Sun* ....15.00 - 20.00
Crown (LP) 5368 *The Del Vikings & The Sonnets*...30.00 - 60.00

Dot (LP) 1003 *The Best Of The Del Vikings*...........50.00 - 75.00
　　(EP) 1058 *Come Go With Us* ....100.00 - 150.00
　　(LP) 3695 *Come Go With Me* ....80.00 - 130.00
Dot 15538 *Come Go With Me* ....5.00 - 8.00
　　15538 *Come Go With Me* (78 rpm) ....20.00 - 30.00
　　15636 *When I Come Home* ....5.00 - 8.00
Fee Bee 205 *Come Go With Me* ....50.00 - 100.00
　　206 *Down In Bermuda* ....8.00 - 12.00
　　210 *When I Come Home* ....30.00 - 60.00
　　214 *Whispering Bells* ....40.00 - 70.00
　　218 *You Say You Love Me* ....40.00 - 70.00
　　221 *Woke Up This Morning* ....40.00 - 70.00
　　227 *Tell Me* ....5.00 - 8.00
　　902 *True Love* ....15.00 - 20.00
Luniverse 106 *Somewhere Over The Rainbow* ....30.00 - 50.00
　　(LP) 1000 *Come Go With The Del Vikings* (has eight songs)
　　...150.00 - 200.00
Mercury (EP) 3362 *They Sing-They Swing*............50.00 - 100.00
　　(EP) 35 *The Del Vikings* ....40.00 - 80.00
　　(LP) 20314 *They Sing-They Swing* ....50.00 - 75.00
　　(LP) 20353 *Swinging Singing Record Session*... 50.00 - 80.00
　　71132 *Cool Shake* (78 rpm) ....15.00 - 20.00
　　71241 *Your Book Of Love* ....8.00 - 12.00
　　71345 *You Cheated* ....8.00 - 12.00

JERRY DEMAR:

Ford 501 *Cross-Eyed Alley Cat* ....50.00 - 75.00

THE DEMENS:

Teenage 1006 *You Broke My Heart*.......................50.00 - 75.00
　　1008 *The Greatest Of Them All* ....80.00 - 130.00

THE DEMENSIONS:

Coral 62293 *As Time Goes By* ....8.00 - 12.00
　　62323 *Your Cheatin' Heart* ....8.00 - 12.00
　　62359 *Fly Me To The Moon*.............................7.00 - 10.00
　　62392 *A Little White Gardenia* ....7.00 - 10.00
　　(LP) 757430 *My Foolish Heart*........................75.00 - 100.00
Mohawk 116 *Over The Rainbow* ....10.00 - 15.00
　　120 *Zing! Went The Strings Of My Heart*...........8.00 - 12.00
　　123 *Theresa*..15.00 - 20.00

THE DEMILLES:

Laurie 3230 *Donna Lee*.....................................8.00 - 12.00

THE DE MIRES:

Lunar 519 *Wheels Of Love*..................................8.00 - 12.00

THE DEMOLYRS:

U.W.R. 900 *Rain*..- - -

LITTLE JIMMY DEMPSEY:

Fox - *Bop Hop*..- - -
　　- *Bouncing Back* ....- - -

GALEN DENNY:

Liberty 55164 *What Ya Gonna Do* ....8.00 - 12.00

DENNIS & THE EXPLORERS:

Coral 62295 *Remember*......................................8.00 - 12.00

THE DENOTATIONS:

Lawn 253 *Lone Stranger* ....30.00 - 50.00

LEE DENSON:

Kent 306 *High School Bop* ....20.00 - 30.00
Vik 0251 *Heart Of A Fool* ....20.00 - 30.00
　　0281 *New Shoes* ....15.00 - 20.00

BOB(BY) DENTON:

Dot 15743 *Skinny Minnie*...................................7.00 - 10.00
　　15833 *Twenty-Four Hour Night* ....5.00 - 8.00

Judd 1011 *Sweet And Innocent* ....5.00 - 8.00
    1013 *I'll Always Be Yours* ....5.00 - 8.00

RAY DE PAUL:
ABC Paramount 9903 *Ready To Rip* ....10.00 - 15.00

THE DERBYS:
Mercury 71437 *Night After Night* ....20.00 - 30.00

TOMMY DEREK:
Flag 120 *Meet Me At The Hop* ....20.00 - 30.00

ARNIE DERKSEN:
Decca 30906 *She Wanna Rock* ....10.00 - 15.00

THE DERRINGERS:
Capitol 4532 *Sheree* ....7.00 - 10.00

SUGARPIE DE SANTO:
Checker (most issues) ....4.00 - 8.00
    (LP) 2979 *Sugar Pie* ....30.00 - 50.00

THE DESIRES:
Hull 730 *Let It Please Be You* ....25.00 - 40.00
    733 *Rendezvous With You* ....20.00 - 30.00
Smash 1763 *There I Go Again* ....7.00 - 10.00
20th Fox 195 *I Don't Know Why* ....5.00 - 8.00

THE DESTINATIONS:
Fortune 864 *Valley Of Tears* ....50.00 - 80.00

DETROIT JUNIOR:
Bea & Baby 111 *Money Tree* ....15.00 - 20.00
CJ 636 *Zig Zag* ....8.00 - 12.00
    637 *Can't Take It* ....8.00 - 12.00
Foxy 002 *Christmas Day* ....7.00 - 10.00
USA 807, 814 ....5.00 - 8.00

DEUCES OF RHYTHM & THE TEMPOS TOPPERS (Lead, LITTLE RICHARD):
Peacock 1616 *Ain't That Good News* ....40.00 - 60.00

THE DE VILLES:
Aladdin 3423 *Kiss Me Again And Again* ....15.00 - 25.00
Arrawak 201 *I Do Believe* ....10.00 - 15.00

JAY DE VORE:
Bodark 004 *Doggone Mean* ....10.00 - 20.00

THE DEVOTIONS:
Cub 9020 *Silly Milly* ....7.00 - 10.00
Delta 1001 *Rip Van Winkle* ....50.00 - 80.00

AL DEXTER:
Columbia (LP) 9005 (10 inches) *Songs Of The Southwest*
....15.00 - 20.00
Ekko 1020 *Pistol Packin' Mama* ....10.00 - 15.00

THE DIABLOS (See NOLAN STRONG & THE DIABLOS):

THE DIADEMS:
Star 514 *Why Don't You Believe Me* ....10.00 - 15.00

THE DIALS:
Hilltop 219 *No Hard Feelings* ....25.00 - 40.00
    2009 *School Bells Are Ringing* ....80.00 - 130.00
    2010 *Wondering About Your Love* ....75.00 - 100.00

THE DIALTONES:
Goldisc 3005 *Till I Heard It From You* ....8.00 - 12.00
Lawn 203 *So Young* ....10.00 - 15.00

THE DIAMONDS:
Atlantic 981 *A Beggar For Your Kisses* ....150.00 - 200.00
    1003 *Two Loves Have I* (yellow label) ....100.00 - 150.00
    1017 *Cherry* (yellow label) ....80.00 - 130.00

Mercury (LP) 20309 *The Diamonds* ....50.00 - 75.00
    (LP) 20368 *The Diamonds Meet Pete Rugolo* ...40.00 - 60.00
    70835, 70934, 71021, 71060 (maroon label).......5.00 - 8.00
    70835 *The Church Bells May Ring* (78 rpm).......7.00 - 10.00
    70934 *Ka-Ding Dong* (78 rpm).........................7.00 - 10.00
    71021 *A Thousand Miles Away* (78 rpm) ....7.00 - 10.00
    71060 *Little Darlin'* (78 rpm) ....10.00 - 15.00
    71128 *Words Of Love* (78 rpm) ....7.00 - 10.00
    71165 *Zip Zip* (78 rpm)...................................7.00 - 10.00
    71242 *The Stroll* (78 rpm)..............................25.00 - 40.00
Wing (LP) 12178 *Pop Hits* ....30.00 - 40.00

THE DIATONES:
Bandera 2509 *Ruby Has Gone* ....15.00 - 20.00

(LITTLE) JIMMY DICKENS:
Columbia (LP) 1047 *Raisin' The Dickens* ....20.00 - 30.00
    (LP) 1545 *Big Songs By Little Jimmy Dickens* ..20.00 - 30.00
    21206 *Rock Me* ....8.00 - 12.00
    41173 *(I Got) A Hole In My Pocket* ....7.00 - 10.00

DUKE DICKSON & THE JIVIN 5:
Global - *Walkin' Shoes* ....- - -

BO DIDDLEY:
Checker 814, *Bo Diddley* ....10.00 - 15.00
    819, 827, 832, 842, 850, 860........................7.00 - 10.00
    878, 896, 921, 936, 942, 951, 1045 ....7.00 - 10.00
    878 *Say! (Boss Man)* (78 rpm)......................15.00 - 20.00
    896 *Hush Your Mouth* (78 rpm).....................15.00 - 20.00
    924 *Crackin' Up* (78 rpm) ....20.00 - 30.00
    931 *Say Man* (78 rpm) ....20.00 - 30.00
Chess (LP) 1431 *Bo Diddley* (black label).............50.00 - 100.00
    (LP) 2974 *Have Guitar Will Travel* ....50.00 - 80.00
    (EP) 5125 *Bo Diddley* ....75.00 - 125.00

ELROY DIETZEL:
Bo-Kay 101 *Teenage Ball* ....50.00 - 80.00
    103 *Rock-N-Bones* ....50.00 - 80.00

THE DIKES:
Federal 12249 *Light Me Up* ....25.00 - 40.00

DANNY DILL:
ABC Paramount 9681 *My Girl And His Girl* ....10.00 - 15.00
    9734 *I'm Hungry For Your Lovin'* ....15.00 - 20.00
Cub 9045 *He's Biding His Time* ....8.00 - 12.00

ARTIE DILLON:
Kandy Kane - *In My Teens* ....- - -

ZIG DILLON:
"R" 501 *On Down The Line* ....15.00 - 20.00
    512 *Bird Song Boogie* ....15.00 - 20.00

THE DING DONGS:
Brunswick 50073 *Early In The Morning* ....15.00 - 30.00

MARK DINNING:
MGM (LP) 3838 *Teen Angel* ....25.00 - 40.00

ANDY DIO:
Gone 5038 *Daisy Belle* ....10.00 - 15.00
Johnson 114 *You Are My Sunshine* ....12.00 - 18.00
Thor 104 *Rough And Bold* ....15.00 - 20.00

DION and/with THE BELMONTS/DIPLOMATS:
Laurie (EP) 302 *Where Or When* ....40.00 - 60.00
    (LP) 1002 *Presenting Dion & The Belmonts* ....40.00 - 60.00
    (LP) 2002 *Presenting* (stereo).......................200.00 - 400.00
    3013 *I Wonder Why* ....5.00 - 10.00
    3015 *I Can't Go On (Rosalie)* ....5.00 - 10.00

3021 *Don't Pity Me* ....5.00 - 10.00
  3103 *My Dream* ....10.00 - 15.00
Laurie (other issues) ....5.00 - 8.00
Mohawk 107 *We Went Away* ....25.00 - 40.00

DION & THE TIMBERLANES:
Mohawk 105 *The Chosen Few* ....10.00 - 15.00
Jubilee 5294 *The Chosen Few* ....7.00 - 10.00

THE DIPPERS:
Epic 9453 *Such A Fool Was I* ....10.00 - 20.00

THE DISCIPLES:
Fortune 573 *I Found Out/12th Street* ....7.00 - 10.00

THE DISTANTS:
Northern 3732 *Come On* ....50.00 - 75.00
Warwick 546 *Always* ....8.00 - 12.00

DIXIE BLUES BOYS:
Flair 1072 *My Baby Left Town* ....15.00 - 20.00

THE DIXIELANDERS:
Do-Ra-Me 1412 *Uncle John's Bongos* ....7.00 - 10.00

BILLY DIXON & THE TOPICS:
Topix 6002 *I Am All Alone* ....10.00 - 20.00
  6008 *Lost Lullaby* ....10.00 - 20.00

FLOYD DIXON:
Aladdin 3101 *Time And Place* ....20.00 - 30.00
  3121 *Bad Neighborhood* ....20.00 - 30.00
  3135 *Wine Wine Wine* ....20.00 - 30.00
  3144 *Red Cherries* ....20.00 - 30.00
  3151 *Come Back Baby* ....20.00 - 30.00
  3166 *Broken Hearted Traveler* ....15.00 - 20.00
  3196 *Married Woman* ....15.00 - 20.00
(earlier issues on Aladdin found as 78 rpm records)
Cash 1057 *Oh Baby* ....5.00 - 8.00
Cat 106 *Moonshine* ....7.00 - 10.00
  114 *Hey Bartender* ....7.00 - 10.00
Checker 857 *Alarm Clock Blues* ....7.00 - 10.00
Ebb 105 *Ooh Little Girl* ....7.00 - 10.00
Kent 311 *Change Your Mind* ....8.00 - 12.00
Specialty 468 *Hard Living Alone* ....8.00 - 12.00
  477 *Hole In The Wall* ....8.00 - 12.00
  486 *Nose Trouble* ....8.00 - 12.00
Swingin' 626 *Tight Skirts* ....5.00 - 8.00

HELENE DIXON:
Vik 0212 *Roll Over Beethoven* ....15.00 - 20.00

WALTER DIXON:
Erwin 212 *Goodbye She's Gone* ....100.00 - 150.00

WEBB DIXON:
Astro 101 *Rock Awhile* ....20.00 - 30.00

WILLIE DIXON:
Checker 822, 828, 851 ....7.00 - 10.00
Prestige (LP) 1003 *Blues* ....50.00 - 100.00

CARL DOBKINS, JR.:
Decca (LP) 8938 *Carl Dobkins, Jr.* ....30.00 - 50.00

LEROY DOBSON:
Ludwig 1006 *I Wanna Make Love* ....7.00 - 10.00

CHUCK DOCKERY:
Dearborn - *Rock While We Ride* ....- - -

THE DODGERS:
Aladdin 3259 *You Make Me Happy* ....25.00 - 40.00
  3271 *Drip Drop* ....50.00 - 80.00

BILL DOGGETT:
King 4950 *Honky Tonk* (78 rpm) ....10.00 - 15.00
King (most other issues) ....4.00 - 7.00

RAY DOGGETT:
Decca 30295 *It Hurts The One Who Loves You* ....8.00 - 12.00
Ken-Lee 101 *Beach Party* ....8.00 - 12.00
Kix 102 *Love Is Made Of This* ....7.00 - 10.00
Pearl 716 *No Doubt About It* ....15.00 - 20.00
Spade 1928 *Go Go Heart* ....20.00 - 30.00
  1932 *It Hurts The One Who Loves You* ....15.00 - 20.00
TNT 159 *Whirlpool Of Love* ....15.00 - 20.00

ANDY DOLL:
AD 101 *Hey Ba Ba Re Bop* ....7.00 - 10.00
Dot 1120 *Looped* ....10.00 - 15.00
Starday 345 *You Can't Stop Me From Dreaming* ... 10.00 - 15.00

THE DOLLS:
Teenage 1010 *Just Before You Leave* ....150.00 - 300.00

THE DOLPHINS:
Empress 102 *Rainbow's End* ....8.00 - 12.00
Shad 5020 *I Found True Love* ....10.00 - 20.00

FATS DOMINO:
Imperial (EP) 127 *Fats Domino* ....20.00 - 30.00
 (EP) 138, 139, 140 *Rockin' & Rollin' With Fats Domino*
                ....20.00 - 30.00
 (EP) 141, 142, 143 *Rock And Rollin'* ....20.00 - 30.00
 (EP) 144, 145, 146 *This Is Fats Domino* ....20.00 - 30.00
 (EP) 147 *Here Comes Fats* ....20.00 - 30.00
 (EP) 148, 149, 150 *Here Stands Fats Domino*... 15.00 - 20.00
 (EP) 151 *Cookin' With Fats* ....15.00 - 20.00
 (EP) 152 *Rockin' With Fats* ....15.00 - 20.00
5180 *Reeling And Rocking* ....30.00 - 50.00
5197 *Poor Poor Me* ....30.00 - 50.00
5209 *How Long* ....30.00 - 50.00
5209 *How Long* (red plastic) ....80.00 - 130.00
5220 *Cheatin'* ....30.00 - 50.00
5220 *Cheatin'* (red plastic) ....80.00 - 130.00
5231 *Going To The River* ....30.00 - 50.00
5231 *Going To The River* (red plastic) ....80.00 - 130.00
5240 *Please Don't Leave Me* ....25.00 - 40.00
5251 *Rose Marie* ....20.00 - 30.00
5262 *Somethings' Wrong* ....20.00 - 30.00
5272 *Little School Girl* ....20.00 - 30.00
5283 *Baby Please* ....20.00 - 30.00
5301 *I Lived My Life* ....20.00 - 30.00
5313 *Love Me* ....15.00 - 20.00
5323 *Thinking Of You* ....15.00 - 20.00
5348 *Ain't It A Shame* ....8.00 - 12.00
5357, 5369, 5375 ....7.00 - 10.00
5586, 5396 ....5.00 - 10.00
5407, 5417, 5428, 5442, 5454, 5477, 5492, 5515,
5526, 5537, 5553 ....5.00 - 8.00
5407, 5417, 5428, 5442, 5454, 5477 (78 rpm) .. 10.00 - 20.00
5492 *Don't You Know I Love You* (78 rpm) ....8.00 - 12.00
5515 *Sick And Tired* (78 rpm) ....10.00 - 15.00
5526 *Little Mary* (78 rpm) ....10.00 - 15.00
5537 *Young School Girl* (78 rpm) ....15.00 - 20.00
5553 *Whole Lotta Lovin'* (78 rpm) ....20.00 - 30.00
5569 *Telling Lies* (78 rpm) ....15.00 - 20.00
(LP) 9004 *Rockin' And Rollin With Fats Domino*
                ....50.00 - 80.00
(LP) 9000 *Rock And Rollin'* ....50.00 - 80.00
(LP) 9028 *This Is Fats Domino* ....30.00 - 50.00
(LP) 9038 *Here Stands Fats Domino* ....25.00 - 40.00

(LP) 9040 *This Is Fats* ....25.00 - 40.00
(LP) 9055 *The Fabulous Mr. Domino* ....20.00 - 30.00
(LP) 9062 *Fats Domino Swings*....................20.00 - 30.00
(LP) 9065 *Let's Play Fats Domino*...................20.00 - 30.00
(LP) 9103 *Fats Domino Sings*....................20.00 - 30.00
(LP) 9138 *A Lot Of Dominoes* ....15.00 - 30.00
(Note: LPs are all MONO. Early issues have maroon labels; later issues and reissues of early issues have multi-colored labels.)

THE DOMINOES (See also BILLY WARD)

Federal 12001 *Do Something for Me* ....100.00 - 150.00
   12010 *Harbor Lights* ....150.00 - 300.00
   12022 *Sixty Minute Man* ....50.00 - 80.00
   12039 *Weeping Willow Blues* ....80.00 - 130.00
   12059 *That's What You're Doing To Me* ....80.00 - 130.00
   12068 *Have Mercy Baby* ....75.00 - 100.00
   12072 *Love Love Love* ....75.00 - 100.00
   12105 *I'll Be Satisfied* ....75.00 - 100.00
   12106 *Yours Forever* ....50.00 - 80.00
   12114 *The Bells* ....50.00 - 80.00
   12129 *These Foolish Things Remind Me Of You* ......40.00 - 80.00
(Note: Above have "gold top" labels. Also, above are usually found as 78 rpm records, which are valued at just a fraction of above prices.)

CHARLIE DONALD:

ABC Paramount 9820 *Bop With Me, Baby* ....8.00 - 12.00

THE DON CLAIRS:

Amp-3 1001 *I Lost My Job* ....10.00 - 15.00

DON & DEWEY:

Rush 1002 *Soul Motion* ....5.00 - 8.00
Shade 1000 *My Heart Is Crying* ....10.00 - 20.00
Specialty 599 *Jungle Hop* ....5.00 - 8.00
   631 *Justine* ....5.00 - 8.00
Spot 101 *Fiddlin' The Blues* ....10.00 - 15.00

DON & HIS ROSES:

Dot 15755 *Right Now* ....15.00 - 25.00
   15874 *Leave Those Cats Alone*........................15.00 - 25.00

DON, DICK & JIMMY:

Dot (LP) 3152 ....50.00 - 100.00

THE DON JUANS (See also LITTLE EDDIE):

Fortune 824 *Going Down To Tia Juana* ....15.00 - 20.00
Jaguar 3020 *Kickin' My Hound Around* .... - - -
Onezy 101 *Dolores* ....100.00 - 150.00

JOHNNY DONN:

Crest 1058 *What Happened Last Night* ....8.00 - 12.00

LARRY DONN:

Vaden 113 *Honey-Bun*..30.00 - 50.00

VIC DONNA (See THE PARAKEETS)

RAL DONNER:

Crown (LP) 5335 *Ral Donner & Ray Smith & Bobby Dale*
....15.00 - 20.00
Gone (LP) 2002 *Takin' Care Of Business* ....100.00 - 150.00
   5102 *Girl Of My Best Friend*..........................10.00 - 15.00
   5114 *I Didn't Figure On Him* ....5.00 - 8.00
   5121 *She's Everything* ....7.00 - 10.00
   5125 *To Love Someone* ....7.00 - 10.00
   5129 *Loveless Life* ....7.00 - 10.00
Gone 5133 *To Love*..7.00 - 10.00
Red Bird 10-057 *Love Isn't Like That* ....15.00 - 20.00
Reprise 20 192 *Beyond The Heartbreak*....................8.00 - 12.00
Scottie 1310 *Tell Me Why* ....15.00 - 25.00

THE DONTELS:

Beltone 2040 *Lover's Reunion* ....50.00 - 80.00

GEORGE DOOLEY:

Chan 104 *Train Ride* ....7.00 - 10.00

THE DOOTONES:

Dootone 366 *Teller Of Fortunes* ....50.00 - 80.00
   470 *Strange Love Affair* ....15.00 - 20.00
   471 *Down The Road*.....................................15.00 - 20.00

LEE DORSEY:

Fury (LP) 1002 *Ya Ya* ....75.00 - 100.00

MEL DORSEY (& CHUCK WAYNE):

Black Jack 103 *Little Lil* ....10.00 - 15.00
Orbit 106 *Ain't Gonna Take It No More* ....15.00 - 20.00

SLIM DORTCH:

Eugenia 1001 *Big Boy Rock*.................................75.00 - 100.00

BOB DOSS:

Lynn 505 *I've Got You*..10.00 - 15.00
Starday 265 *Somebody's Knocking* ....30.00 - 50.00

BUSTER DOSS:

Wizard 1640 *Messing Around*.................................7.00 - 10.00

THE DOTS:

Caddy 101 *I Confess* ....20.00 - 30.00
   111 *Good Luck To You* ....20.00 - 30.00

JIMMY DOTSON (& THE BLUES BOYS):

Rocko 5161 *Need Your Love* ....10.00 - 15.00
Zynn 511 *Looking For My Baby*..............................10.00 - 15.00

BIG BOB DOUGHERTY:

KCM 3701 *Dizzy Miss Lizzie*................................. - - -
Westport 137 *Movin'* ....15.00 - 20.00
   139 *Teen-Age Flip* ....15.00 - 20.00

DAVEY DOUGLAS:

Ditto 110 *Shivers*..25.00 - 40.00
Liberty 55165 *Party Crashin'*................................15.00 - 20.00

DICK DOUGLAS:

Northway 1005 *Rocket Ride* ....10.00 - 15.00

GLENN DOUGLAS:

Decca (LP) 8748 *Heartbreak*.................................40.00 - 60.00
   29815 *Let It Roll* ....8.00 - 12.00
   30119 *Used Up Love*......................................8.00 - 12.00
   30311 *I Can Love Enough* ....7.00 - 10.00
   30602 *You Sure Look Lonesome* ....7.00 - 10.00

K. C. DOUGLAS:

Cook (LP) 5002...30.00 - 40.00

MEL DOUGLAS:

San 1506 *Cadillac Boogie* ....30.00 - 50.00

SHERI LEE DOUGLAS:

Maverick 601 *Chime Bells*....................................10.00 - 15.00

SHY GUY DOUGLAS: (See also: LITTLE SHY GUY)

Excello 2008 *Detroit Arrow*..................................75.00 - 100.00
   2024 *I'm Your Country Man*...........................50.00 - 80.00
   2032 *No Place Like Home* ....50.00 - 80.00

TONY DOUGLAS:

D 1005 *Baby When The Sun Goes Down*................10.00 - 15.00

JERRY DOVE & HIS STRING BUSTERS:

TNT 122, 144, 162, 173 ....7.00 - 10.00
   141 *Pink Bow Tie* ....50.00 - 80.00

LARRY DOWD (& THE ROCK-A-TONES):

Damion 6532 *Tell Me No Lies* .... 7.00 - 10.00
Spinning 6004 *Why Oh Why* .... 10.00 - 15.00
   6009 *Pink Cadillac* .... 15.00 - 20.00

THE DOWLANDS:

Tollie 9002 *All My Loving* .... - - -

THE DOWNBEATS (See also O.S. GRANT; SONNY WOODS):

Gee 1019 *My Girl* .... 75.00 - 100.00
Sarg 168 *Darling Of Mine* .... 15.00 - 20.00
   173 *I Need Your Love* .... 15.00 - 20.00
   186 *I Couldn't See* .... 10.00 - 15.00
   197 *I Just Can't Understand* .... 10.00 - 15.00

("BIG") AL DOWNING:

Carlton 489 *Miss Lucy* .... 10.00 - 15.00
   507 *It Must Be Love* .... 10.00 - 15.00
Challenge 59006 *Down On The Farm* .... 7.00 - 10.00
Columbia 43185 *Georgia Slop* .... 5.00 - 8.00
V-Tone 215 *Please Come Home* .... 5.00 - 8.00
   220 *Words Of Love* .... 5.00 - 8.00
   230 *There'll Come A Time* .... 5.00 - 8.00
White Rock 1111 *Down On The Farm* .... 50.00 - 80.00
   1113 *Miss Lucy* .... 40.00 - 60.00

WAYNE DOWNING:

Big J 164 *Rattlesnake Daddy* .... - - -

THE DOZIER BOYS:

Fraternity 767 *Early Morning Blues* .... 7.00 - 10.00
United 143 *I Keep Thinking Of You* .... 20.00 - 30.00
   143 *Linger Awhile* (red plastic) .... 50.00 - 80.00
   163 *Cold Cold Rain* .... 30.00 - 60.00
   163 *Cold Cold Rain* (red plastic) .... 75.00 - 100.00

RUSTY DRAPER:

Mercury 70921 *Pink Cadillac* .... 7.00 - 10.00
Mercury (most other issues) .... 4.00 - 7.00

THE DREAMERS (See also RICHARD BERRY):

Aladdin 3303 *Charles My Darling* .... 75.00 - 100.00
Cousins 1005 *Because Of You* .... 25.00 - 40.00
Flair 1052 *At Last* .... 15.00 - 20.00
Flip 319 *Since You've Been Gone* .... 8.00 - 12.00
Goldisc 3015 *Teenage Vows Of Love* .... 7.00 - 10.00
Grand 131 *Tears In My Eyes* .... 75.00 - 100.00
Mercury 70019 *Please Don't Love Me* .... 20.00 - 30.00
Rollin 1001 *No Man Is An Island* .... 75.00 - 100.00

THE DREAM KINGS:

Checker 858 *MTYLTT* .... 25.00 - 40.00

THE DREAM LOVERS:

Len 1006 *Take It From A Fool* .... 80.00 - 130.00

THE DREAMLOVERS:

Casino 1308 *Together* .... 7.00 - 10.00
Columbia 42842 *Pretty Little Girl* .... 10.00 - 15.00
End 1114 *If I Should Lose You* .... 10.00 - 15.00
Heritage 102 *When We Get Married* .... 8.00 - 12.00
   104 *Welcome Home* .... 8.00 - 12.00
   107 *Zoom Zoom Zoom* .... 8.00 - 12.00
V-Tone 211 *Annabelle Lee* .... 7.00 - 10.00
   229 *May I Kiss The Bride* .... 7.00 - 10.00

THE DREAMS:

Savoy 1130 *Darlene* .... 25.00 - 50.00
   1140 *Under The Willow* .... 25.00 - 50.00
   1157 *I'll Be Faithful* .... 15.00 - 20.00

THE DREAMTONES:

Astra 551 *A Lover's Answer* .... 10.00 - 15.00
Express 501 *Praying For A Miracle* .... 20.00 - 30.00
Klik 8505 *Love In The Afternoon* .... 80.00 - 130.00
Mercury 71222 *Was I Dreaming* .... 7.00 - 10.00

THE DRIFTERS (featuring CLYDE McPHATTER):

Atlantic (EP) 534 *The Drifters Featuring Clyde McPhatter*
.... 75.00 - 100.00
   1006 *Money Honey* .... 10.00 - 15.00
   1019 *Such A Night* .... 10.00 - 15.00
   1029 *Honey Love* .... 10.00 - 15.00
   1043 *Bip Bam* .... 10.00 - 15.00
   1048 *White Christmas* .... 10.00 - 15.00
   1055 *Gone* .... 10.00 - 15.00
   1070 *Hot Ziggety* .... 10.00 - 15.00
(Note: above are yellow label)
   2025 *There Goes My Baby* (78 rpm) .... 25.00 - 40.00
   (LP) 8003 *Clyde McPhatter & The Drifters* ..... 75.00 - 100.00
   (LP) 8013 *The Good Life With The Drifters* ...... 75.00 - 100.00
   (LP) 8022 *Rockin' And Driftin'* .... 75.00 - 100.00
(Note: above are black label.)
   (LP) 8059 *Save The Last Dance for Me* .... 25.00 - 40.00
Crown 108 *The World Is Changing* .... 100.00 - 150.00

DRIFTING CHARLES:

Lanor 515 *Drifting Cloud* .... 8.00 - 12.00

DRINK SMALL & HIS GUITAR:

Sharp 101 *Cold Cold Rain* .... 10.00 - 15.00

THE DRIVERS:

Alton 252 *Doe Doe* .... 7.00 - 10.00
De Luxe 6094 *Smooth, Slow And Easy* .... 25.00 - 40.00
   6104 *My Lonely Prayer* .... 30.00 - 60.00
   6117 *Dangerous Lips* .... 30.00 - 60.00
Drive 101 *No One For Me* .... - - -
RCA Victor 7023 *Blue Moon* .... 8.00 - 12.00

THE DUALS:

Arc 4446 *Nearest To My Heart* .... 10.00 - 15.00

THE DUBS:

ABC Paramount 10056 *No One* .... 15.00 - 20.00
   10100 *Don't Laugh At Me* .... 15.00 - 20.00
Gone 5002 *I Found Out* .... 15.00 - 20.00
   5011 *Could This Be Magic* .... 10.00 - 15.00
   5011 *Could This Be Magic* (78 rpm) .... 20.00 - 30.00
   5020 *Beside My Love* .... 8.00 - 12.00
   5034 *Be Sure (My Love)* .... 8.00 - 12.00
   5046 *Chapel Of Dreams* .... 10.00 - 15.00
Josie (LP) 4001 *The Dubs Meet The Shells* .... 75.00 - 100.00
Mark-X 8008 *Be Sure My Love* .... 7.00 - 10.00

THE DUDADS:

De Luxe 6083 *I Heard You Call Me Dear* .... 25.00 - 40.00

DAVE DUDLEY:

King 4933 *Rock & Roll Nursery Rhyme* .... 8.00 - 12.00

THE DU DROPPERS:

Groove 0001 *Laughing Blues* .... 15.00 - 20.00
   0013 *Just Whisper* .... 30.00 - 50.00
   0036 *Boot 'Em Up* .... 15.00 - 20.00
   0104 *Talk That Talk* .... 15.00 - 20.00
   0120 *You're Mine Already* .... 15.00 - 20.00
   (LP) *Du Droppin'* .... 150.00 - 250.00
RCA Victor 5321 *I Found Out* .... 10.00 - 15.00
   5425 *Whatever You're Doing* .... 10.00 - 15.00
   5543 *The Note In The Bottle* .... 10.00 - 15.00

Red Robin 108 *Can't Do Sixty No More* ....40.00 - 60.00
    108 *Can't Do Sixty No More* (red plastic) ....150.00 - 250.00
    116 *Come On And Love Me Baby* ....40.00 - 60.00

ARLIE DUFF:
Decca 29987 *Alligator Come Across* ....10.00 - 15.00
Starday 104 *You All Come* ....10.00 - 15.00
    132 *Let Me Be Your Salty Dog* ....10.00 - 15.00
    176 *Fifteen Cents A Sop* ....10.00 - 15.00
    302 *You've Done It Again* ....7.00 - 10.00

TAM DUFFILL:
Groove 58-0004 *Cooly Dooly* ....8.00 - 12.00

EDDIE DUGOSH:
Award 116 *One Mile* ....8.00 - 12.00
Sarg 135 *Strange Kinda Feeling* ....30.00 - 50.00

DUKE & NULL (See DENVER DUKE & JEFFREY NULL)

BILLY DUKE & HIS DUKES:
Casino 138 *Fun Lovin' Woman* ....7.00 - 10.00
Teen 110 *I Know I Was Wrong* ....7.00 - 10.00

DENVER DUKE & JEFFREY NULL:
Blue Hen 214 *Hank Williams That Alabama Boy* ...10.00 - 15.00
Guitar 100 *Blue Blue Blue* ....15.00 - 20.00
Mercury 70970 *Rock And Roll Blues* ....8.00 - 12.00
    71065 *A Million Tears* ....5.00 - 8.00
Starday 446 *I'll Say I Do* ....7.00 - 10.00
    479 *I'm Gonna Get You* ....7.00 - 10.00

ROY DUKE:
Decca 29962 *Behave, Be Quiet, Or Be Gone* ....15.00 - 20.00
    30095 *Honky Tonk Queen* ....15.00 - 20.00
    30325 *I Mean, I'm Mean* ....15.00 - 20.00

DUKE OF EARL (*GENE CHANDLER*):
Vee Jay (LP) 1040 *Duke Of Earl* ....80.00 - 120.00

THE DUKES:
Imperial 5401 *Teardrop Eyes* ....40.00 - 80.00
    5415 *Baby Please* ....10.00 - 15.00
    5480 *Loving You* ....10.00 - 15.00
Specialty 543 *Oh Kay* ....15.00 - 20.00

THE DU MAURIERS:
Fury 1011 *All Night Long* ....15.00 - 20.00

TERRY DUNAVAN & THE EARTHQUAKES:
Fanfare 727 *Earthquake Boogie* ....30.00 - 60.00

SHELTON DUNAWAY:
Lync 1010 *Shake 'Em Up* ....7.00 - 10.00

BILL DUNCAN:
D B C 1232 *Whirlin' Twerlin' Rock* ....40.00 - 60.00

DON DUNCAN:
Venture 111 *Somethin' Special* ....20.00 - 30.00

DUSTY DUNCAN:
San Joaquin 100 *Milk Cow Blues* ....20.00 - 30.00

HERBIE DUNCAN:
Mar-Vel 1400 *Hot Lips Baby* ....30.00 - 50.00
    1402 *That's All* ....10.00 - 15.00

TOMMY DUNCAN & BILL WOODS:
Fire 101 *Crazy Mixed Up Kid* ....30.00 - 60.00

THE DUNDEES:
Space 201 *Evil One* ....40.00 - 70.00

BILL DUNIVEN:
Vaden 306 *Knocking On The Backside (Of Your Heart)*
....30.00 - 40.00

GENE DUNLAP:
- Made In The Shade .... - -

JOHN DUNN:
Spar 720 *If A Woman Answers* .... 8.00 - 12.00

WEBSTER DUNN, JR.:
Dunmar 101 *Go Go Baby* .... 40.00 - 60.00

THE DUPONTS:
Roulette 4060 *Half Past Nothing* .... 8.00 - 12.00
Royal Roost 627 *Somebody* .... 10.00 - 15.00
Winley 212 *Must Be Falling In Love* .... 10.00 - 20.00

CHAMPION JACK DUPREE; JACK DUPREE (& MR. BEAR):
Atlantic (LP) 8019 *Blues From The Gutter* .... 100.00 - 150.00
    (LP) 8045 *Natural & Soulful Blues* .... 50.00 - 80.00
    (LP) 8056 *Champion Of The Blues* .... 50.00 - 80.00
Groove 0171 *Lonely Road Blues* .... 10.00 - 15.00
King (LP) 735 *Champion Jack Dupree Sings The Blues*
.... 50.00 - 80.00
    4633 *Tongue Tied Blues* .... 15.00 - 20.00
    4651 *Please Tell Me Baby* .... 15.00 - 20.00
    4695 *Walkin' Upside Your Head* .... 15.00 - 20.00
    4706 *Hard Feeling* .... 10.00 - 15.00
    4779 *Two Below Zero* .... 10.00 - 15.00
    4792 *Harelip Blues* .... 10.00 - 15.00
Okeh (LP) 12103 *Cabbage Greens* .... 50.00 - 80.00
Red Robin 109 *Stumblin' Block Blues* .... 30.00 - 50.00
    112 *Highway Blues* .... 30.00 - 50.00
    130 *Shim Sham Shimmy* .... 20.00 - 30.00
Vik 0260, 0279, 0304 .... 7.00 - 10.00

THE DUPREES:
Coed 569 *You Belong To Me* .... 7.00 - 10.00
    571 *My Own True Love* .... 7.00 - 10.00
    574 *I Wish You Could Believe Me* .... 7.00 - 10.00
    576, 580, 584, 585, 587, 591, 593, 595, 596 .... 5.00 - 8.00
    (LP) 905 *You Belong To Me* .... 80.00 - 130.00
    (LP) 906 *Have You Heard* .... 80.00 - 130.00
Heritage 804 *My Special Angel* .... 7.00 - 10.00
    805 *Goodnight My Love* .... 7.00 - 10.00
    808 *My Love, My Love* .... 7.00 - 10.00
    811 *Two Different Worlds* .... 7.00 - 10.00
    826 *Have You Heard* .... 7.00 - 10.00

NELDA DUPRY:
United 157 *Riding With The Blues* .... 40.00 - 60.00

TOMMY DURDEN:
Holiday 777 *A-Weepin' And A Wailin'* .... 20.00 - 30.00

PAUL DURHAM:
Sand Spur 15302 *She Lied* .... 10.00 - 20.00

THE DUSTERS:
ARC 3000 *Give Me Time* .... 40.00 - 70.00
Cuspid 5003 *She's Mine* .... - -

HUELYN DUVALL:
Challenge 1012 *Comin' Or Goin'* .... 10.00 - 15.00
    59002 *Hum-Dinger* .... 10.00 - 15.00
    59014 *Three Months To Kill* .... 10.00 - 15.00
    59025 *Friday Night On A Dollar Bill* .... 10.00 - 15.00
    52069 *Pucker Paint* .... 7.00 - 10.00
Starfire 500 *It's No Wonder* .... 7.00 - 10.00
Twinkle - *Beautiful Dreamer* .... - -

THE DUVALS (See also PHIL JOHNSON):

Boss 2117 *Cotton*..10.00 - 15.00
Gee 1003 *Guide Me* ....20.00 - 30.00
Rainbow 335 *You Came To Me* ....25.00 - 40.00

THE DWELLERS:

Conrose 101 *Lonely Guy* ....50.00 - 80.00
Howard 503 *Tell Me Why* ....50.00 - 80.00
Oasis 101 *Oh Sweetie* ....30.00 - 50.00

CONNIE DYCUS:

Mercury 71376 *Rock-A-Bye Baby Rock* ....- - -

JERRY DYKE & THE VENDELLS:

Saturn - *Mean Woman Blues* ....- - -

BOB DYLAN:

Columbia (LP) CL-1986 *The Freewheelin' Bob Dylan* (MONO), red
    label, containing, as cut 3, side 1, *Let Me Die In My Footsteps*
    ....200.00 - up
    42656 *Corrina Corrina*.....................................100.00 - up
    42856 *Blowin' In The Wind*.............................100.00 - up
(Note: Prices on above are very speculative. Promotional copies of
    other 45s have premium value.)

THE DYNAMICS:

ARC 4450 *Enchanted Love* ....15.00 - 20.00
Capri 104 *No One But You* ....75.00 - 100.00
Cindy 3005 *Gone Is My Love* ....25.00 - 40.00
Dynamic 504 *The Girl I Met* ....- - -
    1001 *Darling*..25.00 - 40.00
    1002 *Delsinia*...15.00 - 20.00
Emjay 1928 *This Love Of Ours* ....20.00 - 30.00
Herald 569 *Betty My Own*...20.00 - 30.00
Impala 501 *Moonlight*...20.00 - 30.00
LiBan 1006 *If I Give My Heart To You* ....10.00 - 15.00
Reprise 20183 *So Fine* ....7.00 - 10.00
Seeco 6008 *Moonlight* ....8.00 - 12.00

CLAY EAGER:

Karl 560 *TV Boogie Blues Style* ....15.00 - 20.00

JOHNNY EAGER (& HIS TRIO):

Design 818 *The Howl* ....10.00 - 15.00
Sabre 100 *Please Mr. Doctor* ....40.00 - 70.00

THE EAGLES:

Mercury 70391 *Please, Please* ....8.00 - 12.00
    70464 *Such A Fool*...8.00 - 12.00
70524 *I Told Myself*...8.00 - 12.00

FORD EAGLIN:

Imperial 5671, 5692, 5736, 5765, 5802, 5823, 5857,
    5866, 5890, 5946 ....5.00 - 10.00

THE EARLS:

ABC Paramount 11109 *It's Been A Long Time Comin'*
    ....15.00 - 20.00
Gem 221 *Believe Me, My Love* ....400.00 - up
Old Town (LP) 104 *Remember Me Baby* ....100.00 - 150.00
    1130 *Remember Then* ....10.00 - 15.00
    1133 *Never*..8.00 - 12.00
    1145 *Cry Cry Cry* ....8.00 - 12.00
    1149 *I Believe* ....8.00 - 12.00
    1169 *Ask Anybody* ....10.00 - 15.00
    1182 *Remember Me Baby* ....10.00 - 15.00
Rome 101 *Life Is But A Dream*................................30.00 - 50.00
    102 *Lookin' For My Baby*...............................10.00 - 15.00
    112 *Little Boy And Girl* ....8.00 - 12.00
    115 *Whoever You Are* ....8.00 - 12.00
    5117 *My Heart's Desire* ....10.00 - 15.00

JACK EARLS & THE JIMBOS:

Sun 240 *Slow Down* ....25.00 - 50.00

THE EARTHQUAKES:

Fortune 534 *Darling Be Mine* ....20.00 - 30.00
    538 *This Is Really Real* ....20.00 - 30.00

EDDIE EAY:

Echo 5911 *Dancin' Girl*..75.00 - 100.00

THE EBBTIDES (See also DAVID FORD):

Duane 1022 *Star Of Love*...300.00 - up
Jan Lar 101 *Love Doctor*..80.00 - 130.00
Marco 105 *Little Miss Blue* ....15.00 - 25.00
Recorte 405 *Puppy Love* ....15.00 - 20.00
Teen 121 *What is Your Name, Dear?* ....400.00 - up

THE EBBTONES/EBB-TONES:

Crest 1016 *I Want You Only* ....15.00 - 20.00
    1024 *Baby* ....10.00 - 15.00
Ebb 100 *I've Got A Feeling* ....30.00 - 50.00
Port 70026 *Rockin' On The Range* ....7.00 - 10.00

THE EBONAIRES:

Aladdin 3211 *Three O'Clock In The Morning*........80.00 - 130.00
    3212 *Lawd, Lawd, Lawd*................................80.00 - 130.00
Hollywood 1046 *Love For Christmas* ....50.00 - 80.00
    1062 *Let's Kiss And Say Hello Again* ....50.00 - 80.00
Lena 1001 *Love Call* ....30.00 - 50.00
Money 220 *The Very Best Luck In The World*........10.00 - 15.00

THE EBONIERS:

Port 70013 *Hand In Hand*...15.00 - 20.00

THE EBON-KNIGHTS:

Stepheny (LP) 4001 *First Date With* ....- - -

THE ECHOES:

Andex 22102 *Dee-Dee-Di Oh*...................................10.00 - 15.00
Ascot 2188 *I Love Candy*...8.00 - 12.00
Combo 128 *My Little Honey*.....................................75.00 - 100.00
Felsted 8614 *Angel Of Love* ....15.00 - 20.00
Gee 1028 *Ding Dong* ....20.00 - 30.00
Hi Tide 106 *Angel Of Love* ....80.00 - 130.00
Seg-Way 103, 106...4.00 - 8.00
Specialty 601 *Over The Rainbow* ....10.00 - 15.00
SRG 101 *Baby Blue* ....20.00 - 40.00

ECHOMORES:

Rocket 1041 *Little Chick* ....- - -

THE ECHOTONES:

Dart 1009 *So In Love* ....7.00 - 10.00

THE ECHO VALLEY BOYS:

Island - *Wash Machine Boogie* ....100.00 - 150.00

DUANE EDDY:

Jamie (EP) 100, 301, 302, 304 ....15.00 - 20.00
    1104 *Rebel-'Rouser* (78 rpm) ....15.00 - 25.00

CORKY EDMINSTER:

Raynor 10820 *Chili Dippin' Baby* ....- - -

THE EDSELS:

Capitol 4675 *If Your Pillow Could Talk* ....5.00 - 8.00
Dub 2843 *Lama Rama Ding Dong* ....20.00 - 40.00
    2843 *Rama Lama Ding Dong* ....10.00 - 15.00
Ember 1078 *Three Precious Words* ....7.00 - 10.00
Roulette 4151 *Do You Love Me* ....10.00 - 15.00
Tammy 1010 *What Brought Us Together*.................10.00 - 15.00
    1014 *Three Precious Words*.............................10.00 - 15.00
    1023 *The Girl I Love* ....8.00 - 12.00

1031 *Another Lonely Night*......................................8.00 - 12.00
Twin 700 *Rama Lama Ding Dong*...........................8.00 - 12.00

CHUCK EDWARDS (& THE FIVE CROWNS/& HIS GUITAR):
Alanna 557 *If I Were King*...........................10.00 - 15.00
Duke 159 *If You Love Me*.............................15.00 - 20.00
   163 *I'm Wondering*................................15.00 - 20.00
   174 *Morning Train*................................15.00 - 20.00

EDDIE ALVIS EDWARDS:
- *Real Gone Baby*...................................... - - -

GWEN EDWARDS & THE CO-EDS (See CO-EDS)

JIMMY EDWARDS:
Mercury 71209 *Love Bug Crawl*...........................8.00 - 12.00
   71209 Same, but 78 RPM..............................20.00 - 30.00

JOHNNY EDWARDS & THE WHITE CAPS:
Northland 7002 *Rock 'N' Roll Saddles*..................... - - -

TIBBY EDWARDS:
Mercury 70591 *Flip Flop And Fly*...........................8.00 - 12.00
Starday 278 *Fool That I Was*................................10.00 - 15.00

TOMMY EDWARDS:
MGM (EP) 1003 *It's All In The Game*...................25.00 - 40.00

CHARLES EDWINS:
Duke 124 *I Got Loose*......................................8.00 - 12.00

WILLIE EGAN/EGANS; LITTLE WILLIE EGANS:
Dash 55001 *Rock & Roll Fever*...............................30.00 - 50.00
Mambo 102 *What A Shame*...................................15.00 - 20.00
   11 *Come On*.....................................15.00 - 20.00
Spry 107 *Treat Me Right*...................................15.00 - 20.00
Vita 125 *Wear Your Black Dress*..........................10.00 - 15.00

COZY EGGLESTON:
States 133 *Big Heavy*.......................................15.00 - 20.00

THE EGYPTIAN KINGS:
Nanc 1120 *Give Me Your Love*...............................10.00 - 15.00

BOB EHRET:
Aladdin 3377 *Stop The Clock*...............................30.00 - 50.00

DONNIE ELBERT:
DeLuxe 6125, 6143, 6148, 6156, 6161, 6164, 6168 .5.00 - 10.00
King (LP) 629 *The Sensational Donnie Elbert*......100.00 - 150.00

THE EL CAPRIS:
Bullseye 102 *Oh, But She Did*................................20.00 - 30.00
Fee Bee 216 *Your Star*.......................................75.00 - 100.00
Hi-Q 5006 *Girl Of Mine*.....................................15.00 - 20.00
Paris 525 *They're Always Laughin' At Me*.............10.00 - 15.00

THE ELCHORDS, Featuring DUTCH SAUNDERS:
Good 544 *Peppermint Stick*.................................20.00 - 30.00

THE EL DARADOS (See also THE EL DORADOS):

THE ELDAROS:
Vesta 102 *Please Surrender*...................................80.00 - 130.00

EDDIE ELDER:
Vita 176 *With A Tear In My Heart*.........................10.00 - 15.00

THE EL DOMINGOES:
Kappa Rex 206 *Evening Bells*.............................150.00 - 200.00

THE EL DOMINGOS:
Chelsea 1009 *Lucky Me, I'm In Love*.....................50.00 - 80.00

THE EL DORADOS (See also HAZEL McCOLLUM):
Vee Jay 115 *My Loving Baby*..............................75.00 - 100.00
   115 *My Loving Baby* (red plastic)...................200.00 - up
   127 *One More Chance*...............................50.00 - 80.00
   147 *At My Front Door*..............................10.00 - 15.00
   165 *I'll Be Forever Loving You*....................10.00 - 15.00
   180 *Rock 'N' Roll's For Me*........................15.00 - 20.00
   197 *Chop Ling Soon*................................20.00 - 30.00
   211 *Bim Bam Boom*................................20.00 - 30.00
   250 *Tears On My Pillow*............................20.00 - 30.00
   263 *Boom Diddle Boom*............................20.00 - 30.00
   302 *Lights Are Low*................................25.00 - 40.00
Vee Jay (LP) 1001 *Crazy Little Mama* (maroon label)
....100.00 - 150.00
   (LP) 1001 Same, but black label......................20.00 - 30.00

BILLY ELDRIDGE:
Unart 2011 *Let's Go Baby*..................................20.00 - 30.00
Vulco 1580 *It's Over*...................................... - - -

ELECTRAS:
Infinity 012 *You Lied*.....................................10.00 - 15.00

THE ELEGANTS:
ABC Paramount 10219 *Tiny Cloud*........................10.00 - 15.00
Apt 25005 *Little Star* (rainbow label)...................15.00 - 20.00
   25005 *Little Star* (black label).....................8.00 - 12.00
   25005 *Little Star* (78 rpm)........................75.00 - 100.00
   25017 *Please Believe Me*..........................10.00 - 15.00
   25029 *True Love Affair*...........................10.00 - 15.00
Hull 732 *Little Boy Blue*..................................15.00 - 25.00
Photo 2662 *A Dream Can Come True*...................10.00 - 15.00

LES ELGART & HIS ORCHESTRA:
Columbia 40180 *Bandstand Boogie*.......................15.00 - 20.00

JOHNNY ELGIN:
Roulette 7005 *Sittin' At Home With The Blues*..........7.00 - 10.00

THE ELGINS:
Congress 214 *Ritha Mae*....................................7.00 - 10.00
MGM 12670 *A Picture Of You*.............................20.00 - 30.00
Titan 1724 *My Illness*.....................................25.00 - 40.00

THE ELITES:
Chief 7040 *The Blues*......................................10.00 - 15.00

THE ELLIS BROTHERS:
ABC Paramount 9954 *Sneaky Alligator*..................5.00 - 8.00

LORRAINE ELLIS (See THE CROWS)

REX ELLIS:
Rivermont 1160 .... - - -

RAY ELLSWORTH:
Ellsworth 101 *Rock 'N' Roll Show*.......................10.00 - 15.00
   101/102 *I Wanna Hold You Baby*...................10.00 - 15.00

SUNNIE ELMO & THE MINOR CHORDS:
Flick 009 *Let Me*...10.00 - 15.00

JOHNNY ELMORE:
Jar 105 *War Chant Boogie*.................................10.00 - 15.00

THE EL POLLOS:
Neptune 1001 *Why Treat Me This Way*..................50.00 - 80.00
Studio 999 *High School Dance*...........................100.00 - 150.00

THE EL RAYS:
Checker 794 *Darling I Know*..............................300.00 - up
M & M 104 *Till The End Of Time*.........................10.00 - 15.00

THE EL REYES/EL REYS:
Jade 501 *Mr. Moonglow* ....100.00 - 150.00
Josie 801 *Blue Moon*..................................10.00 - 15.00

ELROY & THE EXCITEMENTS:
Alanna 189 *No One Knows* ....50.00 - 80.00

EL TEMPOS:
Vee Jay 580 *My Love Goes Deep Within* ....10.00 - 15.00

THE EL TONES:
Chief 800 *I Won't Be Your Fool*....................150.00 - 200.00
Cub 9011 *Like Mattie* ....8.00 - 12.00

THE EL TORROS:
Duke 175 *Dance With Me* ....10.00 - 15.00
  333 *You May Say Yes* ....10.00 - 15.00
Fraternity 811 *All The Tears Is Gone* ....20.00 - 30.00

THE EL VENOS:
Groove 0170 *Geraldine* ....20.00 - 30.00
Vik 0305 *My Heart Beats Faster*......................20.00 - 30.00

BOBBY ELVIN:
Drexel 910 *I'm Gonna Tell It* ....10.00 - 15.00
  914 *Think A While* ....10.00 - 15.00

EMANON 4:
Flash 106 *Oh That Girl*.............................30.00 - 50.00

THE EMANONS:
ABC Paramount 9913 *We Teenagers* ....10.00 - 15.00
Gee 1005 *Change Of Time* ....200.00 - 300.00
G.G.S. 443 *You Know I Miss You*.........................100.00 - 150.00
Winley 226 *We Teenagers* ....10.00 - 15.00

THE EMBERS:
Columbia 40287 *Sweet Lips* ....20.00 - 30.00
Dot 16101 *Couldn't Wait Any Longer*....................10.00 - 15.00
Ember 101 *Paradise Hill*..........................100.00 - 150.00
Empress 101 *Solitaire*...............................10.00 - 15.00
  104 *I Was Too Careful*..........................10.00 - 15.00
  107 *Abigail*.....................................10.00 - 15.00
  108 *What A Surprise* ....10.00 - 15.00
Herald 410 *Paradise Hill* (black label).................75.00 - 100.00
  410 *Paradise Hill* (red vinyl)...........100.00 - 150.00

THE EMBRACEABLES:
Sandy 1025 *From Someone Who Loves You* ....30.00 - 50.00

TED EMBRY:
Ac'cent 1057 *New Shoes* ....10.00 - 15.00

THE EMCEES:
Cimarron 4044 *Wine, Wine, Wine* ....15.00 - 25.00

THE EMERALDS (See also LUTHER BOND):
ABC Paramount 9889 *The One I Adore* ....8.00 - 12.00
Allied 10002 *Why Must I Wonder* ....10.00 - 15.00
Bobbin 107 *That's The Way It's Got To Be* ....30.00 - 50.00
  121 *Lover's Cry* ....30.00 - 50.00
Rex 1004 *All The Time* ....10.00 - 15.00
  1013 *I Kneel At Your Throne*......................8.00 - 12.00
Showboat 1501 *Gold Will Never Do* ....7.00 - 10.00

THE EMERALS:
Triple X 100 *Please Don't Crush My Dreams* ......100.00 - 150.00

BILLY (THE KID) EMERSON:
Sun 195 *No Teasin' Around* ....75.00 - 100.00
  214 *Move, Baby, Move* ....30.00 - 50.00
  219 *Red Hot* ....30.00 - 50.00
  233 *Something For Nothing*.......................20.00 - 30.00

Vee Jay 175 *Don't Start Me To Lyin'* ....20.00 - 30.00
  219 *Every Woman I Know* ....10.00 - 15.00
  247 *The Pleasure Is All Mine* ....10.00 - 15.00

THE EMERSONS:
Newport 7004 *Joannie Joannie* .... 10.00 - 15.00

THE EMJAYS:
Greenwich 411 *This Is My Love* .... 7.00 - 10.00

THE EMOTIONS:
Card 600 *Silvery Moon* .... 30.00 - 50.00
Fury 1010 *Candlelight* .... 20.00 - 30.00
Laurie 3167 *Starlit Night* .... 15.00 - 20.00
20th Century Fox 430 *A Story Untold* .... 8.00 - 12.00

THE EMPERORS:
Haven 511 *Come Back, Come Back*..................... 150.00 - 300.00

THE EMPIRES:
Amp-3 132 *If I'm A Fool* .... 20.00 - 30.00
Calico 121 *Definition Of Love* .... 10.00 - 15.00
Candi 1026 *Love You So Bad*....................... 15.00 - 20.00
Chavis 1026 *Love You So Bad* .... 8.00 - 12.00
Epic 9527 *Time And A Place* .... 7.00 - 10.00
Harlem 2325 *Corn Whiskey* .... 80.00 - 130.00
  2333 *Magic Mirror* .... 80.00 - 130.00
Whirlin' Disc 104 *Whispering Heart*................ 20.00 - 30.00
Wing 90023 *Shirley* .... 15.00 - 20.00
  90050 *By The Riverside* .... 10.00 - 15.00
  90080 *My First Discovery* .... 10.00 - 15.00

THE ENCHANTERS:
Bamboo 513 *Touch Of Love* .... 7.00 - 10.00
Coral 61756 *True Love Gone* .... 10.00 - 15.00
  61832 *There Goes* .... 8.00 - 12.00 *
  61916 *Bottle It Up And Go* .... 15.00 - 20.00
  62373 *The Day* .... 8.00 - 12.00
Epsom 1003 *I Need Your Love* .... 100.00 - 150.00
J.J. & M. 1562 *Oh Rosemarie* .... 30.00 - 50.00
Jubilee 5072 *How Could You* .... 100.00 - 150.00
  5080 *I've Lost* .... 100.00 - 200.00
Mercer 922 *True Love Gone* .... 150.00 - 300.00
Musitron 1071/1072 *I Lied To My Heart*............... 10.00 - 15.00
Orbit 532 *Touch Of Love* .... 10.00 - 15.00
Sharp 105 *We Make Mistakes* .... 10.00 - 15.00
Stardust 102 *Spellbound By The Moon* .... 300.00 - up
Vargo 10 *You Worry Me* .... 7.00 - 10.00
(Note: *A longer version is of higher value.)

THE ENCHANTMENTS:
Gone 5130 *Come On Home* .... 10.00 - 15.00
Romac 1001 *Lonely Heart* .... 20.00 - 30.00
Roulette 4751 *Come On Home* .... 7.00 - 10.00

THE ENCHORDS:
Laurie 3089 *I Need You Baby* .... 15.00 - 20.00

THE ENCORES:
Bow 302 *Barbara* .... 10.00 - 15.00
Checker 760 *When I Look At You* .... 500.00 - up
Look 105 *Time Is Moving On* .... 40.00 - 70.00
Ronnex 1003 *Time Is Moving On* .... 15.00 - 25.00

THE ENDORSERS:
Moon 109 *Crying (Over You)* .... 300.00 - up

SCOTT ENGEL:
Orbit 506 *Good For Nothin'* .... 7.00 - 10.00
  545 *Comin' Home* .... 5.00 - 8.00
Orbit (other issues).............................. 4.00 - 7.00

BENNY ENGLAND:
Zenith 103 *Eloping* ....10.00 - 15.00

HANK ENGLAND:
Process 148 *Truck Driving Buddy* ....8.00 - 12.00

JERRY ENGLER & THE 4 EKKOS:
Brunswick 55037 *Sputnik* ....10.00 - 15.00

THE ENSENADAS:
Tar X 1005 *On And On* ....80.00 - 130.00

ENSENATORS:
Tar-X 1001 *Just Like Before* ....100.00 - 150.00

EPICS:
Lifetime 1004 *Lonely* ....15.00 - 25.00

AL EPP:
Wildcat 0018 *Breaking My Heart* ....8.00 - 12.00

DON EPPERSON:
Excell - *You're Gone Again* .... - - -

EARL EPPS:
Minor 103 *Be Bop Blues* ....75.00 - 100.00

ERIK & THE VIKINGS:
Karate 5031 *Heaven And Paradise* ....7.00 - 10.00

ERLENE & HER GIRLFRIENDS:
Old Town 1150 *My Dada Say* ....8.00 - 12.00

THE ERMINES (See CORNELL GUNTER)

FRANKIE ERVIN with JOHNNY MOORE'S THREE BLAZERS:
Blaze 103 *Hot Rod* ....10.00 - 15.00
Hollywood 1031 *Johnny Ace's Last Letter* ....10.00 - 15.00

ODIE ERVIN:
Big Town 111 *Note Pinned To My Bed* ....20.00 - 30.00

BILL ERWIN & THE FOUR JACKS:
Fairlane 21020 *High School Days* ....10.00 - 15.00
Pel 501 *Too Young To Be Blue* ....10.00 - 15.00
   601 *I've Waited Long Enough* ....10.00 - 15.00

THE ESCORTS:
Coral 62302 *Seven Wonders Of The World* ....20.00 - 30.00
   62317 *As I Love You* ....20.00 - 30.00
   62336 *Somewhere* ....20.00 - 30.00
Judd 1014 *My First Year* ....7.00 - 10.00
Premium 407 *Sorry* ....75.00 - 100.00
RCA Victor 6834 *Bad Boy* ....8.00 - 12.00
Scarlet 4005 *I Will Be Home Again* ....8.00 - 12.00

THE ESCOS:
Esta 100 *I'm So Lonesome For You* ....100.00 - 150.00
Federal 12380 *Diamonds and Pearls* ....10.00 - 20.00

ESQUERITA:
Capitol (LP) 1186 *Esquerita* ....150.00 - 200.00
   (EP) 1186 *Esquerita* ....100.00 - 200.00
   4007 *Oh Baby* ....20.00 - 30.00
   4058 *Rockin' The Joint* ....20.00 - 30.00
   4145 *Laid Off* ....20.00 - 30.00

THE ESQUIRE BOYS:
Guyden 705 *Rock-A-Beatin' Boogie* ....10.00 - 15.00
   705 *Rock-A-Beatin' Boogie* (78 rpm) ....15.00 - 20.00

THE ESQUIRES:
Hi-Po 1003 *Only The Angels Know* ....400.00 - up
Meridian 6283 *Mission Bells* ....25.00 - 40.00

THE ESSEX:
Roulette (LP) 25235 *A Walkin' Miracle* ....30.00 - 50.00

SIDNEY ESTER & THE DREAMERS:
Dangold 2001 *Let Me Walk With You*......................10.00 - 15.00

THE ETERNALS:
Hollywood 68 *Rockin' In The Jungle* ....15.00 - 20.00
   70 *Babalu's Wedding Day* ....15.00 - 20.00

ETTA & HARVEY:
Chess 1760, 1771 ....5.00 - 8.00

ROY ETZEL:
Time 1029 *Jenny, Oh Jenny*......................... - - -

BILLY EUSTIS:
"R" 506 *I'm Sorry You're Gone* .... - - -

BARBARA EVANS:
Carlton 490 *I Could Cry* ....20.00 - 30.00

JIMMY EVANS (& THE JESTERS):
Caveman 502 *The Joint's Really Jumpin'* ....150.00 - 200.00
Clearmont 492 *The Joint's Really Jumpin'*.............50.00 - 75.00
River 500 *Fooled Again*...10.00 - 15.00
Shimmy 1054 *Messy Bessy*...................................10.00 - 15.00

LARRY EVANS:
Fabor 4008 *Henpecked* ....10.00 - 15.00
   4009 *Junco Returns* ....10.00 - 15.00

MARK EVANS:
Tab 101 *It's Love* ....10.00 - 15.00

MARTY EVANS:
Coral 62192 *Poor Me*..8.00 - 12.00

PAUL EVANS:
Guaranteed (LP) 1000 *Fabulous Teens* ....50.00 - 80.00

RUSTY EVANS:
Brunswick 55103 *(Let The Midnight Special)*
   Shine Its Light On Me ....7.00 - 10.00

THE EVENTUALS:
Okeh 7142 *Just The Things That You Do* ....10.00 - 15.00

BETTY EVERETT:
CJ 611 *Please Come Back* ....7.00 - 10.00

BRACEY EVERETT:
Atlantic 2013 *The Lover's Curse* ....8.00 - 12.00

VINCE EVERETT:
ABC Paramount 10313 *Such A Night*....................10.00 - 15.00
   10360 *Ain't Gonna Be Your Low Down Dog* ....10.00 - 15.00
   10472 *Baby Let's Play House*..........................10.00 - 15.00
   10624 *Big Brother*..7.00 - 10.00
Jam 1067 *Love Me* ....8.00 - 12.00
Royalty 505 *I'm Snowed* ....10.00 - 15.00
Town 1964 *Buttercup* ....8.00 - 12.00

THE EVERGREENS:
Chart 605 *Very Truly Yours* ....40.00 - 70.00

THE EVERLY BROTHERS:
Cadence (EP) 104 *The Everly Brothers, Vol. 1*.......20.00 - 40.00
   (EP) 105 *The Everly Brothers, Vol. 2* ....20.00 - 40.00
   (EP) 107 *The Everly Brothers, Vol. 3* ....20.00 - 40.00
   (EP) 108 *Songs Our Daddy Taught Us, Vol. 1* ..15.00 - 30.00
   (EP) 109 *Songs Our Daddy Taught Us, Vol. 2* ..15.00 - 30.00
   (EP) 110 *Songs Our Daddy Taught Us, Vol. 3* ..15.00 - 30.00
   (EP) 111, 118, 121, 131 ....15.00 - 25.00
   (EP) 333 *Rockin' With The Everly Brothers*......30.00 - 50.00

(most issues, 45 rpm) ....5.00 - 8.00
1315 *Bye Bye Love* (78 rpm) ....20.00 - 30.00
1337 *Wake Up Little Susie* (78 rpm)..............20.00 - 30.00
1342 *This Little Girl Of Mine* (78 rpm)............20.00 - 30.00
1348 *Claudette* (78 rpm) ....20.00 - 30.00
1350 *Bird Dog* (78 rpm) ....25.00 - 40.00
1355 *Problems* (78 rpm) ....30.00 - 50.00
1364 *Poor Jenny* (78 rpm) ....75.00 - 100.00
(LP) 3003 *Everly Brothers*........................25.00 - 40.00
(LP) 3016 *Songs Our Daddy Taught Us*............,25.00 - 40.00
(LP) 3025 *Everly Brothers Best*...................15.00 - 20.00
(LP) 3040 *The Fabulous Style Of* ....15.00 - 20.00
(LP) 3059 *Folk Songs* ....20.00 - 30.00
(LP) 3062 *15 Everly Hits* ....10.00 - 15.00
Columbia 21496 *Keep A-Loving Me* ....100.00 - 150.00
Warner Brothers (LP) PRO-134 *It's Everly Time* (promotional
   sampler, 10-inch LP) ....80.00 - 130.00
Warner Bros. (EP) 550 ....25.00 - 40.00

"EVERYBODY DIGS THE BOSS RECORD HOP":
Winley (LP) 6001 *Paragons, Jesters, Et Al* ....60.00 - 100.00

THE EXCELLENTS:
Blast 205 *You Baby You* ....15.00 - 20.00
　207 *I Hear A Rhapsody*...........................15.00 - 20.00
Mermaid 106 *Love No One But You* ....50.00 - 80.00

THE EXCELS:
Central 2601 *Baby Doll* ....20.00 - 30.00

THE EXCITERS:
United Artists (LP) 326 *Tell Him* ....25.00 - 40.00

THE EXCLUSIVES:
K&C 102 *It's Over* ....50.00 - 80.00

THE EXECS:
Fargo 1055 *Walking In The Rain* ....75.00 - 100.00

THE EXPLORERS:
Coral 62175 *Don't Be A Fool* ....10.00 - 20.00

THE EXTENSIONS:
Success 109 *I Want To Know* ....7.00 - 10.00

THE EXTREMES:
Everlast 5013 *Let's Elope* ....30.00 - 50.00
Paro 733 *The Bells* ....80.00 - 130.00

DENNY EZBA (& THE GOLDENS):
Renner 213 *Mary Diane* ....15.00 - 20.00
　217 *Come Home Baby* ....15.00 - 20.00
　225 *Dirty Dirty Feeling* ....20.00 - 30.00
　228 *Lover Boy* ....15.00 - 20.00
　234 *Jailbird*...................................15.00 - 20.00
　236 *Love Me* ....15.00 - 20.00
　238 *C. C. City* ....15.00 - 20.00
　242 *It's My Way* ....15.00 - 20.00
　244 *Susie-O* ....15.00 - 20.00
　245 *Little Girl* ....10.00 - 15.00
　246 *Just You And Me* ....10.00 - 15.00
　250 *Please Just Say So* ....10.00 - 15.00

EZRA & THE IVIES:
United Artists 165 *Comic Book Crazy*..............20.00 - 30.00

SHELLEY FABARES:
Colpix (LP) 431 *The Things We Did Last Summer* .25.00 - 40.00

FABIAN:
Chancellor (EP) 5003 *Hold That Tiger* ....30.00 - 50.00
　(LP) 5003 *Hold That Tiger* ....30.00 - 40.00

(LP) 5005 *Fabulous Fabian*..............15.00 - 25.00
(LP) 5009 *Fabian & Avalon-The Hit Makers* ....20.00 - 30.00
(LP) 5012 *Good Old Summertime* ....20.00 - 30.00
(LP) 5019 *Rockin' Hot* ....30.00 - 40.00
(LP) 5024 *16 Fabulous Hits* ....15.00 - 20.00

THE FABULAIRES:
Chelsea 0103 *Wedding Song*......................7.00 - 10.00
East West 103 *While Walking* ....15.00 - 20.00
Main-Line 103 *While Walking* ....40.00 - 70.00

THE FABULONS:
Benson 100 *Connie* ....8.00 - 12.00
Ember 1069 *Give Me Back My Ring*................8.00 - 12.00

THE FABULOUS EGYPTIANS:
Cindy - *End Of Time* ....5.00 - 8.00

THE FABULOUS ENCHANTERS:
Fine Arts 1007 *Why Are You Crying* ....10.00 - 15.00

THE FABULOUS FABULIERS:
Angletone 539 *She Is The Girl For Me*...........15.00 - 20.00

THE FABULOUS FIVE FLAMES:
Time 1023 *No More Tears*........................10.00 - 15.00

THE FABULOUS FLAMES:
Bay-Tone 102 *I Need You Dear*...................15.00 - 20.00
　105 *I'm So All Alone*..........................15.00 - 20.00
Harlem 114 *So Long My Darling*..................20.00 - 30.00
Rex 3000 *My Joan* ....20.00 - 30.00

THE FABULOUS FOUR:
Brass 311 *Now You Cry* ....7.00 - 10.00
Chancellor 1078 *Why Do Fools Fall In Love* ....15.00 - 20.00
　1085 *Betty Ann* ....15.00 - 20.00
Melic 4114 *Welcome Me Home* ....15.00 - 20.00

THE FABULOUS GARDENIAS:
Liz 1004 *It's You You You* ....10.00 - 15.00

THE FABULOUS IDOLS:
Kenco 5011 *Baby* ....- - -

THE FABULOUS PEARL DEVINES:
Alco 631 *So Lonely* ....80.00 - 120.00

THE FABULOUS PEARLS:
Dooto 448 *My Heart's Desire*....................20.00 - 30.00

THE FABULOUS PLAYBOYS:
Apollo 760 *Tears, Tears, Tears* ....7.00 - 10.00

THE FABULOUS SILVER TONES:
West Coast 452 *Wee Wee Hours* ....15.00 - 20.00

THE FABULOUS THREE:
Hale 501 *Cross Every Mountain* ....20.00 - 30.00

THE FABULOUS TWILIGHTS:
Fortune 542 *My Little Darling* ....8.00 - 12.00

THE FABULOUS WINDS:
Celestial 111 *Rock & Roll Radio* ....8.00 - 12.00

TOMMY FACENDA:
Legrande 1001 *High School U.S.A.* ....10.00 - 15.00
Nasco 6018 *Little Baby*.........................10.00 - 15.00

DICK FAGAN & THE SCORES:
Sarg 160 *Nothing Really Shakes Me* ....20.00 - 30.00

TOMMY FAILE:
Lawn 104 *That's All Right* ....15.00 - 20.00
Silver Star 1001 *Long Gone* ....15.00 - 20.00

WERLY FAIRBURN:
Capitol 2770 *Good Deal Lucille* ....7.00 - 10.00
    2844 *Nothin' But Lovin'* ....7.00 - 10.00
    2963 *I Feel Like Cryin'* ....7.00 - 10.00
    3101 *Spiteful Heart* ....5.00 - 8.00
Columbia 21432 *I Guess I'm Crazy* ....7.00 - 10.00
    21483 *Stay Close To Me* ....7.00 - 10.00
    21528 *Everybody's Rockin'* ....10.00 - 15.00
Savoy 1503 *All The Time* ....10.00 - 15.00
    1509 *Speak To Me Baby* ....10.00 - 15.00
    1521 *Telephone Baby* ....10.00 - 15.00

JOHNNY FAIRE:
Fable 601 *You Gotta Walk The Line* ....10.00 - 15.00
Surf 5019 *Bertha Lou* ....15.00 - 20.00
    5024 *Betcha I Getcha* ....15.00 - 20.00

THE FAIRLANES:
Argo 5357 *Comin' After You* ....7.00 - 10.00
Continental 1001 *Writing This Letter* ....75.00 - 100.00
Lucky Seven 102 *Seventeen Steps* ....20.00 - 30.00
Radiant 101 *Baby, Baby* ....75.00 - 100.00

THE FALCONS:
Anna 1110 *This Heart Of Mine* ....15.00 - 25.00
Cash 1002 *I Miss You Darling* ....100.00 - 150.00
Chess 1743 *Just For Your Love* ....10.00 - 15.00
Falcon 1006 *Now That It's Over* ....30.00 - 50.00
Flick 001 *You're So Fine* ....40.00 - 70.00
    008 *You Must Know I Love You* ....20.00 - 30.00
Flip 301 *Stay Mine* ....75.00 - 100.00
    302 *You Are The Only One* ....75.00 - 100.00
Kudo 661 *This Heart Of Mine* ....80.00 - 120.00
Lu Pine 103 *I Found A Love* ....10.00 - 15.00
    124 *Lonely Nights* ....8.00 - 12.00
Mercury 70940 *Baby That's It* ....15.00 - 20.00
Quality 1721 *My Only Love* ....10.00 - 15.00
Savoy 893 *You're The Beating Of My Heart* ....100.00 - 200.00
Silhouette 521 *Can This Be Christmas* ....15.00 - 20.00
Unart 2013 *You're So Fine* ....7.00 - 10.00
    2013 *You're So Fine* (78 rpm) ....100.00 - 150.00
    2022 *You're Mine* ....10.00 - 15.00
United Artists (EP) 10010 *The Falcons* ....200.00 - 300.00

THE FALLEN ANGELS:
Tollie 9049 *Up On The Mountain* ....10.00 - 15.00

JOHNNY FALLIN:
Capitol 4216 *Party Kiss* ....10.00 - 15.00
    4283 *Wild Streak* ....10.00 - 15.00

THE FAMOUS HEARTS:
Guyden 2073 *Aisle Of Love* ....75.00 - 100.00

JAY FANNING:
Acme 2032 *It's Love* ....10.00 - 15.00
    2033 *Baby, Baby* ....8.00 - 12.00
    2035 *Church Bells* ....8.00 - 12.00

THE FANTASTICS:
Copa 8005 *That One* ....7.00 - 10.00
RCA Victor 7572 *There Goes My Love* ....8.00 - 12.00
    7664 *This Is My Wedding Day* ....8.00 - 12.00

THE FANTASYS:
Guyden 2029 *No One But You* ....20.00 - 30.00

JIM FARADAY:
Decca 30698 *T. L. C.* ....7.00 - 10.00

WAYNE FARMER & THE TEEN-BEATS:
Dodge 802 *Yeah! Yeah! My Baby* ....15.00 - 20.00

THE FARMER BOYS:
Capitol 3077 *You're A Humdinger* ....10.00 - 15.00
    3162 *Lend A Helping Hand* ....8.00 - 12.00
    3246 *It Pays To Advertise* ....8.00 - 12.00
    3322 *Flip Flop* ....8.00 - 12.00
    3476 *My Baby Done Left Me* ....8.00 - 12.00
    3569 *Cool Down Mame* ....10.00 - 15.00
    3732 *Flash Crash And Thunder* ....10.00 - 20.00

LITTLE JOEY FARR:
Band Box 286 *Big White Cadillac* ....10.00 - 15.00

LUCIEN FARRAR & THE LIFESAVERS:
Jupiter 1 *Didn't You Know* ....75.00 - 100.00
    2 *Tomorrow Night* ....75.00 - 100.00

BILLY FARRELL:
Imperial 7001 *Slippin' And Slidin'* ....10.00 - 15.00

MICKEY FARRELL & THE DYNAMICS:
Bethlehem 3080 *I'm Calling On You* ....10.00 - 15.00

THE FASCINATIONS:
Sure 106 *Midnight* ....20.00 - 30.00

THE FASCINATORS:
Blue Lake 112 *Can't Stop* ....200.00 - 400.00
Capitol 4053 *Chapel Bells* ....30.00 - 50.00
    4137 *Come To Paradise* ....30.00 - 50.00
    4247 *Oh Rosemarie* ....50.00 - 80.00
King 5119 *Tee Vee* ....20.00 - 30.00
Your Copy 1135 *The Bells Of My Heart* ....200.00 - 400.00
    1136 *Don't Give It Away* ....200.00 - 400.00

THE FASHIONS:
V-Tone 202 *I'm Dreaming Of You* ....10.00 - 20.00

LLOYD FATMAN:
Okeh 7073 *Where You Been* ....10.00 - 15.00
    7083 *Miss Mushmouth* ....10.00 - 15.00

JOHNNY FAY:
Dani 1539 *Sweet Linda Brown* ....30.00 - 50.00

THE FEATHERS:
Aladdin 3267 *Johnny Darling* ....75.00 - 100.00
    3277 *I Need A Girl* ....80.00 - 130.00
Hollywood 1051 *Dear One* ....300.00 - up
Show Time 1103 *Desert Winds* ....75.00 - 100.00
    1104 *Johnny Darling* ....75.00 - 100.00
    1105 *Why Don't You Write Me* ....50.00 - 80.00
    1106 *Love Only You* ....50.00 - 80.00

CHARLIE FEATHERS:
Flip 503 *I've Been Deceived* ....200.00 - 300.00
Holiday Inn 114 *Deep Elm Blues* ....15.00 - 20.00
Kay 1001 *Why Don't You* ....30.00 - 50.00
King 4971 *Everybody's Lovin' My Baby* ....75.00 - 100.00
    4997 *Bottle To The Baby* ....80.00 - 120.00
    5022 *Nobody's Woman* ....50.00 - 80.00
    5043 *When You Come Around* ....50.00 - 80.00
Memphis 103 *Wild Wild Party* ....30.00 - 50.00
Meteor 5032 *Tongue-Tied Jill* ....200.00 - 300.00
Sun 231 *Defrost Your Heart* ....300.00 - 500.00
    503 *I've Been Deceived* ....250.00 - 400.00

THE FEDERALS:
De Luxe 6112 *Come Go With Me* ....20.00 - 30.00
Fury 1009 *Dear Lorraine* ....30.00 - 50.00

DON FEGER:
Ebony 102 *Date On The Corner*........................30.00 - 50.00
    103 *Lookout Baby* ....30.00 - 50.00

TERRY FELL:
"X" 0114 *Mississippi River Shuffle* ....7.00 - 10.00
    0149 *I'm Hot To Trot* ....7.00 - 10.00

DERRELL FELTS:
Dixie 2008 *Playmates*..................................... -   -
Okeh 7118 *Lookie Lookie Lookie* ....15.00 - 20.00

NARVEL FELTS:
Mercury 71140 *Kiss-A-Me Baby* ....10.00 - 15.00
    71190 *Lonesome Feeling* ....7.00 - 10.00
    71275 *Rocket Ride Stroll* ....7.00 - 10.00
    71347 *Vadalou* ....10.00 - 15.00
Pink 701 *Cutie Baby* ....15.00 - 20.00

FREDDY FENDER:
Agro 5375 *A Man Can Cry*........................5.00 -   8.00
Duncan 1000 *Mean Woman* ....15.00 - 20.00
    1001 *Wasted Days & Wasted Nights* ....15.00 - 20.00
    1002 *Wild Side Of Life* ....10.00 - 15.00
    1004 *Little Mama*..............................10.00 - 15.00
Imperial 5659, 5670 ....7.00 - 10.00
Norco 102, 104, 108 ....7.00 - 10.00
    103 *Going Out With The Tide* ....8.00 - 12.00
    107 *Bony Moronie* ....15.00 - 20.00

THE FENDERMEN:
Soma (LP) 1240 *Mule Skinner Blues*....................150.00 - 200.00

FENDERS:
QQ 245 *Honky Tonk Hardwood Floor* .... -   -   -

FENTION & THE CASTLE ROCKERS:
Duke 190 *The Freeze* ....7.00 - 10.00

H BOMB FERGUSON & HIS MAD LADS:
Arc 9001 *Little Tiger* .... -   -
Savoy 830 *Good Lovin'* ....20.00 - 30.00

RUDY FERGUSON:
Deluxe 6028 *Everybody's Blues* ....15.00 - 20.00
    6040 *Cool Competition*......................10.00 - 15.00
    6079 *You've Been Away Too Long* .....8.00 - 12.00
Prestige 798 *Cool Goofin'* ....10.00 - 15.00
    859 *Oh Baby* .... -   -

TROY FERGUSON:
Flame 101 *At The Jamboree* ....7.00 - 10.00

MIKE FERNANDEZ:
Raymond's 755 *A-Bomb Bop* ....40.00 - 60.00

AL FERRIER (& HIS BOPPIN' BILLIES):
Excello 2105 *Hey Baby* ....20.00 - 30.00
Goldband 1031 *No No Baby* ....30.00 - 50.00
    1035 *It's Too Late Now* ....20.00 - 30.00
    1072 *Let's Go Boppin' Tonight* ....40.00 - 60.00
Rocko 502 *Kiss Me Baby*...........................8.00 - 12.00
Zynn 510 *Chisholm Trail Rock*...................8.00 - 12.00
    1013 *Blues Stop Knockin'*....................8.00 - 12.00

FERRIS & THE WHEELS:
Bambi 801 *Chop, Chop* ....8.00 - 12.00
United Artists 458 *Moments Like This* ...20.00 - 30.00

THE FIDELITY'S:
Baton 252 *The Things I Love* ....8.00 - 12.00
    256 *Memories Of You* ....8.00 - 12.00
    261 *My Greatest Thrill* ....8.00 - 12.00
Sir 271, 276..5.00 -   8.00

THE FIELD BROS.:
Carlton 475 *Time And Time Again*..........10.00 - 15.00

THE FIESTAS:
Old Town 1062 *So Fine* ....8.00 - 12.00
    1062 *So Fine (78 rpm)*.......................75.00 - 100.00
    1067 *I'm Your Slave* ....8.00 - 12.00
    1069 *Our Anniversary* ....8.00 - 12.00
    1074 *Good News* ....8.00 - 12.00
    1080 *Dollar Bill* ....8.00 - 12.00
    1090 *You Could Be My Girlfriend* ......8.00 - 12.00
    1104 *Look At That Girl* ....8.00 - 12.00
    1111 *She's Mine* ....15.00 - 20.00
    1122 *Broken Heart* ....8.00 - 12.00
    1127 *Look At That Girl* ....8.00 - 12.00
    1134 *The Gypsy Said* ....8.00 - 12.00
    1140 *The Party's Over* ....8.00 - 12.00
    1148 *Foolish Dreamer* ....8.00 - 12.00
    1166 *All That's Good* ....8.00 - 12.00
    1178 *Anna* ....8.00 - 12.00
    1187 *Love Is Strange* ....8.00 - 12.00
    1189 *Ain't She Sweet* ....8.00 - 12.00
Vigor 712 *So Fine*.. -   -

HERBIE FIELDS:
Parrot 806 *Mr. Jump* ....10.00 - 20.00

LINCOLN FIG & THE DATES:
Worthy 1006 *Kiss Me Tenderly* ....50.00 - 80.00

LEE FINN & RHYTHM MEN:
Rose 4946 *Lonesome Road* ....5.00 - 10.00
Westport 141 *High Class Feelin'* ....15.00 - 20.00

THE FIREBALLS:
Top Rank (EP) 1000 *Bulldog, + 3* ....75.00 - 100.00

BRIEN FISHER:
Spangle 2001 *Fingertips* ....8.00 - 12.00
United Artists 115 *It's Up To You* ....8.00 - 12.00

SONNY FISHER:
Starday 179 *Rockin' Daddy* ....50.00 - 80.00
    190 *Sneaky Pete* ....75.00 - 100.00
    207 *Rockin' & Rollin'* ....80.00 - 120.00
    244 *Pink And Black*...........................75.00 - 100.00

TOMMY FISHER:
B&D 1314 *Rock & Roll Robin Hood* ....15.00 - 20.00

THE FI-TONES:
Angle Tone 525 *You'll Be The Last* ....25.00 - 40.00
    530 *It Wasn't A Lie* ....15.00 - 20.00
    536 *Deep In My Heart* ....15.00 - 25.00
Atlas 1050 *Foolish Dreams* ....75.00 - 100.00
    1051 *It Wasn't A Lie* ....50.00 - 80.00
    1052 *I'll Call To You* ....50.00 - 80.00
    1055 *I Belong To You* ....50.00 - 80.00
O Gee 1003/1004 *I Love You Judy* ....8.00 - 12.00
Old Town 1042 *My Faith* ....80.00 - 130.00
Stroll 101 *Sweet Lovin' Maryann* ....10.00 - 15.00

FIVE ARROWS:
Parrot 816 *Pretty Little Thing* ....75.00 - 100.00

THE FIVE BARS:
Money 224 *Stormy Weather* ....20.00 - 30.00

FIVE BELLS:
Clock 1017 *It's You* ....15.00 - 20.00

THE FIVE BILLS:
Brunswick 84002 *Can't Wait For Tomorrow* ....75.00 - 100.00

THE FIVE BLUE NOTES:
Onda 108 *My Special Prayer*.................................15.00 - 20.00
Sabre 103 *My Gal Is Gone*...................................150.00 - 250.00
    108 *The Beat Of Our Hearts*..........................200.00 - 300.00

FIVE BOPS:
Hamilton 50023 *Unforgotten Love* ....10.00 - 15.00

THE FIVE BUDDS:
Rama 1 *I Was Such A Fool* ....400.00 - up
    2 *I Guess It's All Over Now* ....400.00 - up

FIVE CAMPBELLS:
Music City 794 *Morrine* ....100.00 - 150.00

THE FIVE CHANCES:
Blue Lake 115 *All I Want* ....300.00 - 500.00
Chance 1157 *I May Be Small*...............................300.00 - 500.00
Federal 12303 *My Days Are Blue* ....50.00 - 80.00
States 156 *Gloria* ....100.00 - 150.00
    156 *Gloria* (red plastic) ....300.00 - 500.00

THE 5 CHANELS:
Deb 500 *The Reason* ....10.00 - 15.00

THE FIVE CHORDS:
Cuca 1031 *Red Wine*...20.00 - 30.00
Jamie 1110 *Love Is Like Music*...........................20.00 - 30.00

THE FIVE CLASSICS:
A 317 *Come On Baby*..8.00 - 12.00
Arc 4454 *My Imagination* ....15.00 - 20.00
Pova 6142 *Love Me* ....10.00 - 15.00

THE FIVE CROWNS:
Alanna 576 *If I Were King* ....8.00 - 12.00
Caravan 15609 *I Can't Pretend* ....10.00 - 15.00
Gee 1001 *God Bless You* ....100.00 - 150.00
Old Town 790 *You Could Be My Love* ....300.00 - up
    792 *Lullaby Of The Bells* (78 rpm) ....75.00 - 100.00
Rainbow 179 *A Star*..150.00 - 300.00
    179 *A Star* (red plastic) ....300.00 - up
    184 *Who Can Be True* (78 rpm) ....75.00 - 100.00
    202 *Keep It A Secret* (red plastic) ....250.00 - 400.00
    206 *Alone Again* (78 rpm) ....100.00 - 150.00
Riviera 990 *You Came To Me* ....300.00 - up
Transworld 717 *I Can't Pretend* ....50.00 - 80.00

THE FIVE CRYSTALS:
Delco 827 *Path Of Broken Hearts* ....100.00 - 150.00
Kane 25592 *Hey Landlord*....................................10.00 - 15.00
Music City 821 *Path Of Broken Hearts* ....80.00 - 130.00

FIVE CRYSTELS (See FIVE CRYSTALS)

THE FIVE C'S:
United 172 *Tell Me* ....50.00 - 80.00
    172 *Tell Me* (red plastic)................................100.00 - 200.00
    180 *My Heart's Got The Blues* ....75.00 - 100.00
    180 *My Heart's Got The Blues* (red plastic).....150.00 - 300.00

THE FIVE DAPPS:
Brax 207/208 *You're So Unfaithful* ....75.00 - 100.00

THE FIVE DEBONAIRES:
Herald 509 *Whispering Blues* ....25.00 - 40.00

THE FIVE DELIGHTS:
Abel 228 *That Love Affair* ....75.00 - 100.00
Newport 7002 *There'll Be No Goodbye* ....20.00 - 30.00

THE FIVE DIAMONDS:
Treat 501 *Ten Commandments Of Love*...............200.00 - 300.00

THE FIVE DIPPS:
Original 1005 *Teach Me Tonight* ....50.00 - 80.00

FIVE DISCS:
Calo 202 *My Baby Loves Me* ....20.00 - 40.00
Cheer 1000 *That Was The Time*............................15.00 - 20.00
Dwain 803 *Roses*...100.00 - 150.00
    6072 *Roses* ....150.00 - 250.00
Emge 1004 *I Remember* ....80.00 - 130.00
Vik 0327 *I Remember* ....10.00 - 15.00
Yale 244 *Come On Baby*......................................75.00 - 100.00

FIVE DOLLARS:
Fortune 821 *Harmony Of Love* ....30.00 - 50.00
    826 *So Strange* ....25.00 - 40.00
    830 *I Will Wait* ....20.00 - 30.00
    833 *You Fool* ....20.00 - 30.00
    845 *Yellow Moon* ....20.00 - 30.00
    854 *That's The Way It Goes*............................15.00 - 20.00

THE FIVE DOTS:
Dot 1204 *The Other Night* ....50.00 - 80.00
Note 1003 *I Just Love The Things She Do*.............30.00 - 50.00

FIVE DREAMS:
Mercury 71150 *You Are My Only Love* ....15.00 - 20.00

FIVE ECHOES/ECHOS:
Sabre 102 *Lonely Mood* (red plastic) ....400.00 - up
    105 *So Lonesome* ....150.00 - 250.00
Vee Jay 129 *I Really Do* ....200.00 - 300.00
    156 *Fool's Prayer* ....200.00 - 300.00

FIVE EMBERS:
Gem 224 *Please Come Home* ....200.00 - 300.00

FIVE EMERALDS:
S.R.C. 106 *I'll Beg* ....100.00 - 200.00
    107 *Darling* ....150.00 - 300.00

FIVE ENCORES:
Rama 180 *Double Date*...15.00 - 20.00
    185 *Readin,' Ritin,' 'Rithmetic & Rock 'N' Roll* ......15.00 - 20.00

THE FIVE FLEETS:
Felsted 8513 *Oh What A Feeling* ....15.00 - 20.00

FIVE FORTUNES:
Ransom 103 *You Are My Love*.............................75.00 - 100.00
    - *Time Out for Love*..50.00 - 75.00

FIVE HEARTS:
Arcade 107 *Unbelievable*......................................15.00 - 30.00
Flair 1026 *The Fine One* ....75.00 - 100.00
Music City 833 *Tremble* ....100.00 - 150.00

FIVE J'S:
Fulton 2454 *My Darling* ....40.00 - 70.00

THE FIVE JADES:
Duke 188 *Without Your Love*................................25.00 - 40.00
Your Choice 908 *My Reverie*................................8.00 - 12.00

FIVE JETS:
DeLuxe 6018 *I Am In Love* ....50.00 - 80.00
    6053 *I'm Stuck* ....30.00 - 50.00
    6058 *Tell Me You're Mine* ....30.00 - 50.00
    6064 *Crazy Chicken* ....25.00 - 40.00
    6071 *Please Love Me Baby*.............................25.00 - 40.00
Fortune 833 *I'm Wanderin'*..................................30.00 - 50.00

THE FIVE KEYS:

Aladdin (LP) 806 *Best Of The Five Keys* (blue label)

....400.00 -   up

    3099 *The Glory Of Love* ....300.00 -   up

    3113 *It's Christmas*...........................300.00 -   up

    3118 *Yes, Sir, That's My Baby*.........250.00 -   up

    3127 *Red Sails In The Sunset*..........400.00 -   up

    3131 *Mistakes* ....400.00 -   up

    3136 *I Hadn't Any One Till You* ....400.00 -   up

    3158 *I Cried For You*.....................300.00 -   up

    3167 *Can't Keep From Crying* ....300.00 -   up

    3186 *I'll Always Be In Love With You*..............300.00 -   up

    3190 *These Foolish Things* ....300.00 -   up

    3204 *Teardrops In Your Eyes* ....300.00 -   up

    3214 *My Saddest Hour* ....300.00 -   up

    3228 *Love My Loving* ....250.00 - 400.00

    3245 *Deep In My Heart* ....150.00 - 300.00

    3263 *Why, Oh Why* ....100.00 - 150.00

    3312 *Story Of Love* ....100.00 - 150.00

(Note: Above are to have blue labels; maroon label issues are worth somewhat less.)

Capitol (EP) 572 *The Five Keys* ....50.00 - 75.00

    (EP) 828 *The Five Keys On Stage* ......30.00 - 50.00

    (LP) 828 *The Five Keys On Stage* ......75.00 - 100.00 *

(* Note: Cover variations exist of this LP.)

    (LP) 1769 *The Fantastic Five Keys* ....75.00 - 150.00

    3318 *You Broke The Rules*...............7.00 - 10.00

Capitol (45 RPM-others) ....5.00 - 10.00

King (LP) 688 *The Five Keys* ....150.00 - 200.00

    (LP) 692 *Rhythm & Blues Hits-Past & Present*

....100.00 - 150.00

King (45 RPM) ....5.00 - 10.00

Score (LP) 4003 *On The Town With The Five Keys*

....100.00 - 150.00

THE FIVE KIDS:

Maxwell 101 *Carolyn* ....80.00 - 120.00

THE FIVE KINGS:

Columbia 43060 *Light Bulb*.................20.00 - 30.00

Yvette 101 *Here Comes My Baby* ....10.00 - 15.00

FIVE KNIGHTS:

Bumps 1504 *Dark Was The Night* ....8.00 - 12.00

Specialty 675 *Miracle* ....10.00 - 15.00

FIVE LETTERS:

Ivy 102 *Hold My Baby*.....................100.00 - 150.00

THE FIVE LYRICS:

Music City 799 *I'm Traveling Light* .....300.00 -   up

THE FIVE MASKS:

Jan 101 *Forever And A Day*..................10.00 - 15.00

THE FIVE MASTERS:

Bumble Bee 502 *We Are Like One* ....15.00 - 20.00

FIVE NOTES:

Chess 1614 *Show Me The Way*...............30.00 - 50.00

Jen-D - *You Are So Beautiful*...............150.00 - 200.00

Josie 784 *You Are So Beautiful*..............20.00 - 30.00

Specialty 461 *Thrill Me Baby* ....100.00 - 200.00

FIVE OWLS:

Vulcan 303 *Pleading To You* ....150.00 - 300.00

FIVE PEARLS:

Aladdin 3265 *Please Let Me Know* ....50.00 - 80.00

FIVE PENNIES:

Savoy 1182 *Let It Rain* ....10.00 - 15.00

    1190 *My Heart Trembles* ....10.00 - 15.00

THE FIVE PLAYBOYS:

Dot 15605 *Pages Of My Scrapbook*.........8.00 - 12.00

Fee Bee 213 *Pages Of My Scrapbook* .....25.00 - 40.00

    232 *Angel Mine* ....25.00 - 40.00

Mercury 71289 *Why Be A Fool*..............7.00 - 10.00

FIVE QUAILS:

Harvey 114 *Get To School On Time* ....8.00 - 12.00

Mercury 71154 *Jungle Baby* ....10.00 - 20.00

THE FIVE RAMBLERS:

Lummtone 111 *I Want You To Know* ....20.00 - 30.00

FIVE REASONS:

Cub 9006 *Three O'Clock Rock* ....15.00 - 20.00

FIVE ROVERS:

Music City 798 *Down To The Sea* ....30.00 - 50.00

FIVE ROYALES:

Apollo 441 *Courage To Love* (red plastic) ....75.00 - 100.00

    441 *Courage To Love* (black plastic).................25.00 - 40.00

    443 *Take All Of Me* ....20.00 - 30.00

    446 *Crazy, Crazy, Crazy* ....15.00 - 25.00

    488 *I Want To Thank You* ....15.00 - 25.00

    449 *All Righty* ....15.00 - 25.00

    452 *I Do* ....15.00 - 25.00

    454 *Cry Some More* ....15.00 - 25.00

    458 *Let Me Come Back Home* ....20.00 - 30.00

    467 *With All Your Heart* ....20.00 - 30.00

(Note: The foregoing, if pressed of red vinyl, command substantially higher prices.)

    (LP) 488 *The Rockin' 5 Royales* ....300.00 - 500.00

Home Of The Blues 112, 232,234 ....5.00 - 10.00

King (LP) 580 *Dedicated To You* ....100.00 - 150.00

    (LP) 616 *Sing For You* ....100.00 - 150.00

    (LP) 678 *Five Royales* ....80.00 - 120.00

    4770 *Every Dog Has His Day* ....10.00 - 15.00

    4785 *How I Wonder* ....10.00 - 15.00

    4830 *Someone Made You For Me*.........8.00 - 12.00

King (others) ....5.00 - 10.00

FIVE SATINS:

Chancellor 1110 *Raining In My Heart*......8.00 - 12.00

Cub 9071 *Your Memory* ....10.00 - 15.00

    9077 *These Foolish Things* ....10.00 - 15.00

    9090 *Can I Come Over Tonight* ....8.00 - 12.00

Ember (EP) 101 *To The Aisle* ....50.00 - 80.00

    (EP) 102 *Our Anniversary* ....50.00 - 80.00

Ember (EP) 104 *In The Still Of The Night* ....50.00 - 80.00

    (LP) 101 *The Five Satins Sing* ....150.00 - 200.00

    (LP) 401 *Five Satins Encore* ....75.00 - 100.00

    1005 *In The Still Of The Nite* ....5.00 - 8.00

    1005 *In The Still Of The Nite* (78 rpm) ....30.00 - 50.00

    1014 *Our Love Is Forever*................10.00 - 15.00

    1019 *To The Aisle* ....8.00 - 12.00

    1019 *To The Aisle* (78 rpm) ....20.00 - 30.00

    1025 *Our Anniversary* ....10.00 - 15.00

    1028 *A Million To One* ....10.00 - 15.00

    1038 *A Night To Remember* ....10.00 - 15.00

    1056 *Shadows* ....10.00 - 15.00

    1061 *I'll Be Seeing You*..................10.00 - 15.00

    1070 *Wishing Ring* ....10.00 - 15.00

First 104 *When Your Love Comes Along* ....10.00 - 15.00

Musictone 1108 *Just To Be Near You*......7.00 - 10.00

Standord 100 *All Mine* ....75.00 - 125.00
   200 *In The Still Of The Nite* ....150.00 - 200.00

FIVE SCALDERS:
Drummond 3000 *If Only You Were Mine* ....100.00 - 200.00
   3001 *Willow Blues* ....150.00 - 300.00
Sugar Hill 7-3000 *If Only You Were Mine* ....200.00 - 400.00

FIVE SCAMPS:
Okeh 7049 *With All My Heart* ....50.00 - 80.00

THE FIVE SECRETS:
Decca 30350 *See You Next Year* ....20.00 - 30.00

FIVE SHADES:
Ember 1074 *Lonely Boy* ....10.00 - 15.00

FIVE SHARPS:
Jubilee 5104 *Stormy Weather* ....- - -
(Note: Unknown in 45 RPM format. See Blues, etc. section for
   listing and comments on 78 RPM issue.)
Jubilee 5478 *Stormy Weather* ....10.00 - 15.00
(Note: This is a later rendition by a different group, and should not
   be confused with the legendary recording, above.)

FIVE SHILLINGS:
Decca 30722 *Letter To An Angel* ....20.00 - 30.00

THE FIVE SOUNDS:
Baritone 0940 *Good Time Baby* ....10.00 - 15.00

THE FIVE SPOTS:
Future 2201 *Get With It* ....20.00 - 30.00
Soma 1147 *Mr. Fortune* ....10.00 - 15.00

FIVE STARS:
Blues Boy Kingdom 106 *So Lonely Baby* ....15.00 - 25.00
Columbia 42056 *Baby, Baby* ....10.00 - 15.00
Dot 15579 *Atom Bomb Baby* ....8.00 - 12.00
Hunt 318 *Dreaming* ....8.00 - 12.00
Show Time 1102 *Walkin' And Talkin'* ....75.00 - 100.00
Treat 505 *We Danced In The Moonlight* ....200.00 - 400.00

FIVE STRINGS (See also SID KING):
Columbia 21361 *I Like It* ....7.00 - 10.00
   21403 *Drinking Wine Spoli Oli* ....15.00 - 20.00

FIVE SWANS:
Music City 795 *Little Girl Of My Dreams* ....100.00 - 150.00

FIVE THRILLS:
Parot 796 *My Baby's Gone* ....300.00 - up
   800 *Gloria* ....300.00 - up
   800 *Gloria* (red vinyl) ....500.00 - up

FIVE TINOS:
Sun 222 *Sitting By My Window* ....250.00 - up

FIVE TROJANS:
Edison International 410 *I Hear Those Bells* ....20.00 - 30.00
   412 *Little Doll* ....20.00 - 30.00
Tender 516 *Don't Ask Me To Be Lonely* ....75.00 - 100.00

FIVE VETS:
Allstar 713 *Right Now* ....75.00 - 100.00

FIVE WILLOWS:
Allen 1000 *My Dear Dearest Darling* ....80.00 - 130.00
   1002 *Dolores* ....150.00 - 250.00
   1003 *White Cliffs Of Dover* ....150.00 - 300.00
Herald 433 *Lay Your Head On My Shoulder* ....40.00 - 60.00
   442 *Look Me In The Eyes* ....50.00 - 75.00
Pee Dee 290 *Love Bells* ....300.00 - up

FIVE WINGS (See also BILLY NELSON):
King 4778 *Johnny Has Gone* ....50.00 - 80.00
   4781 *Teardrops Are Falling* ....75.00 - 100.00

BILL FLAGG:
MGM 12637 *Doin' My Time* ....20.00 - 30.00
Tetra 4445 *Go Cat Go* ....20.00 - 30.00
   4448 *Guitar Rock* ....20.00 - 30.00

SONNY FLAHERTY:
Huron 22004 *Teenage War Chant* ....8.00 - 12.00
Spangle 2011 *My Baby's Casual* ....10.00 - 15.00

FLAIRS (See also SHIRLEY GUNTER; FATSO THEUS):
ABC Paramount 9698 *In Self Defense* ....8.00 - 12.00
   9740 *Steppin' Out* ....10.00 - 15.00
Crown (LP) 5356 *The Flairs* ....50.00 - 80.00
Epic 9447 *Shake Shake Sherry* ....7.00 - 10.00
Flair 1012 *I Had A Love* ....50.00 - 80.00
   1019 *You Should Care For Me* ....50.00 - 80.00
   1028 *Love Me Girl* ....50.00 - 80.00
   1044 *This Is The Night For Love* ....50.00 - 80.00
Palms 726 *Roll Over Beethoven* ....- - -

FLAMES:
Aladdin 3198 *Sorrowful Heart* ....80.00 - 120.00
Fransil 14 *Dreams And Memories* ....80.00 - 130.00
G.M. 101 *Darling Jane* ....7.00 - 10.00
7-11 2106 *Keep On Smiling* ....80.00 - 130.00
   2107 *Together* ....150.00 - 250.00

THE FLAMINGOS:
Chance 1133 *If I Can't Have You* ....250.00 - 500.00
   1133 *If I Can't Have You* (red plastic) ....400.00 - up
   1140 *That's My Desire* ....200.00 - 300.00
   1140 *That's My Desire* (red plastic) ....400.00 - up
   1145 *Golden Teardrops* ....150.00 - 300.00
   1145 *Golden Teardrops* (red plastic) ....400.00 - 800.00
   1149 *Plan For Love* ....300.00 - 500.00
   1154 *Listen To My Plea* ....300.00 - 500.00
   1162 *Blues In A Letter* ....400.00 - 600.00
Checker 815 *That's My Baby* ....20.00 - 30.00
   821 *Please* ....20.00 - 30.00
   830 *I'll Be Home* ....20.00 - 30.00
   837 *Get With It* ....15.00 - 25.00
   846 *The Vow* ....15.00 - 25.00
   853 *Would I Be Crying* ....20.00 - 30.00
   915 *Dream Of A Lifetime* ....15.00 - 20.00
Chess (LP) 1433 *The Flamingos* (black label) ......150.00 - 200.00
Decca 30335 *Ladder Of Love* ....10.00 - 15.00
   30454 *My Faith In You* ....10.00 - 15.00
   30880 *Ever Since I Met Lucy* ....8.00 - 12.00
   30948 *Jerri-Lee* ....8.00 - 12.00
End (EP) 205 *Goodnight Sweetheart* ....75.00 - 100.00
   (LP) 205 *Flamingos* ....80.00 - 130.00
   (LP) 304 *Flamingo Serenade* ....75.00 - 100.00
   (LP) STLP 304 *Serenade* (STEREO) ....100.00 - 150.00
   (LP) 307 *Flamingo Favorites* ....40.00 - 70.00
   (LP) 316 *Sound Of The Flamingos* ....50.00 - 75.00
   1046 *Goodnight Sweetheart* ....10.00 - 15.00
   1068 *Besame Mucho* ....10.00 - 15.00
Parrot 808 *Dream Of A Lifetime* ....80.00 - 130.00
   808 *Dream Of A Lifetime* (red plastic) ....200.00 - 400.00
   811 *I Really Don't Want To Know* ....1000.00 - up
   812 *I'm Yours* ....100.00 - 150.00
   812 *I'm Yours* (red plastic) ....200.00 - 400.00
Vee Jay 384 *Golden Teardrops* ....10.00 - 15.00
   (LP) 1052 *Flamingos Meet The Moonglows* .....50.00 - 80.00

THE FLANNELS:
Tampa 121 *So Shy* ....10.00 - 15.00

FLARES:
Felsted 8604 *Loving You* ....8.00 - 12.00
    8607 *Jump And Bump* ....8.00 - 12.00
Press 2803 *Make It Be Me* ....8.00 - 12.00

FLATT & SCRUGGS:
Columbia (LP) 1019 *Foggy Mountain Jamboree*....15.00 - 20.00
Mercury (LP) 20358 *Country Music* ....15.00 - 20.00

THE FLEETWOODS:
Dolton 2001 *Mr. Blue* ....15.00 - 20.00

GEORGE FLEMING:
Fleming 501 *I'm Gonna Tell On You/The Shake*........ -   -   -

KING FLEMING QUINTETTE:
Blue Lake 104 *William's Blues* ....30.00 - 50.00

WADE FLEMONS:
Vee Jay 295 *My Baby Likes to Rock*.........................7.00 - 10.00
Vee Jay (most other issues) ....5.00 - 8.00
    (LP) 1011 *Wade Flemons* ....30.00 - 50.00

THE FLINTS:
Heart 100 *Why Did You Go* ....75.00 - 100.00

THE FLIPPERS:
Flip 305 *My Aching Heart* ....50.00 - 80.00

BILL "BUTTERBALL" FLIPPO:
Lou-Jay 105 *I Just Broke Up With My Baby* ....50.00 - 80.00

FLIPS:
Sapphire 152 *Why Should I* ....20.00 - 30.00

FLORESCENTS:
Bethlehem 3079 *Being In Love* ....15.00 - 20.00

THE FLORIDIANS:
ABC Paramount 10185 *The Luck Old Sun* ....10.00 - 15.00

PHIL FLOWERS:
Domino 501 *Whole Lotta Woman* ....8.00 - 12.00
Hollywood 1070 *I'm A Lover Man*.......................8.00 - 12.00
Sway 903 *No More Tossin' And Turnin'* ....8.00 - 12.00
Wing 2100 *No Kissin' At The Hop* ....10.00 - 15.00

BILL FLOYD:
Topic 8034 *I'll Huff And I'll Puff* ....8.00 - 12.00

HARMONICA FRANK FLOYD:
F & L 100 *Rock A Little Baby* ....200.00 - 300.00

MERDELL FLOYD:
Erwin 100 *Juke Box Mama*..........................100.00 - 150.00

FLUORESCENTS:
Hanover 4520 *The Facts Of Love* ....10.00 - 15.00

THE FLYERS:
Atco 6088 *My Only Desire* ....30.00 - 50.00

RED FOLEY:
Decca (LP) 5303 (10 inches) *Souvenir* ....20.00 - 30.00
    (LP) 5338 (10 inches) *Lift Up Your Voice*...........15.00 - 20.00
    (LP) 8296 *Souvenir Album* ....15.00 - 20.00
    (LP) 8396 *Beyond The Sunset* ....15.00 - 20.00
    (LP) 8298 *And Ernest Tubb* ....20.00 - 30.00
    (LP) 8767, 8806, 8847, 8903 ....10.00 - 15.00
    29517 *Plantation Boogie* ....7.00 - 10.00

"FOLK FESTIVAL OF THE BLUES":
Argo (LP) 4031 (various artists).........................50.00 - 80.00

EDDIE FONTAINE:
Argo 5309 *Nothin' Shakin'* ....8.00 - 12.00
Chancellor 1018 *Goodness, It's Gladys*...............7.00 - 10.00
Decca 30042, 30108.........................5.00 - 8.00
    30256 *Homesick Blues* ....7.00 - 10.00
    30446 *Honky Tonk Man* ....7.00 - 10.00
Jalo 102 *It Ain't Gonna Happen No More* ....10.00 - 15.00
Sunbeam 105 *Nothin' Shakin'* ....10.00 - 15.00
    112 *Nobody Else Can Handle This Job* ....7.00 - 10.00
Vik 0193 *Here 'Tis* ....7.00 - 10.00

FRANK FONTAINE:
MGM 12129 *Everybody Rock*...............................20.00 - 30.00

BUBBA FORD:
MCM 202 *Wiggling Blond*.........................50.00 - 75.00

DAVID FORD & THE EBBTIDES:
Specialty 588 *My Confession*...............................15.00 - 20.00

EARLSON FORD:
Mercury 71108 *Ain't Nothin' Shakin'* ....15.00 - 20.00

TENNESSEE ERNIE FORD:
Capitol (LP) 888 *Ol' Rockin' 'Em* ....20.00 - 30.00
    3262 *Sixteen Tons* (78 rpm) ....10.00 - 15.00
(unnumbered) Special Commemorative Pressing celebrating artist's
    20th anniversary (1949-1969) with Capitol Records. *Sixteen
    Tons/I've Got The Milk Man In The Mornin' Blues* (78 rpm)
    ....15.00 - 20.00

FRANKIE FORD:
Ace (EP) 105 *The Best Of*...............................20.00 - 30.00
    554 *Sea Cruise* 7.00 -10.00
    554 *Sea Cruise* (78 rpm) ....100.00 - up
    (LP) 1005 *On A Sea Cruise With Frankie Ford*........75.00 - 100.00

JIMMIE FORD:
Stylo 2102 *You're Gonna Be Sorry* ....8.00 - 12.00
    2105 *We Belong Together*...............................8.00 - 12.00

EARL FOREST/FORREST:
Duke 108 *Whoopin' And Hollerin'* ....30.00 - 50.00
    113 *53* ....20.00 - 30.00
    121 *Out On A Party* ....20.00 - 30.00
    131 *Oh Ooh Wee*.........................15.00 - 20.00
Meteor 5005 *I Wronged A Woman* ....50.00 - 80.00

FORTES:
Current 103 *Waiting For My Baby* ....10.00 - 15.00

JESSIE FORTUNE:
U.S.A. 738, 747.........................5.00 - 8.00

JOHNNY FORTUNE:
Park Avenue 130 *Dragster* ....-   -   -

FORTUNES:
Checker 818 *Believe In Me* ....20.00 - 30.00
Decca 30541 *Tarnished Angel* ....15.00 - 20.00
    30688 *How Clever Of You* ....15.00 - 20.00
DRA 320 *Running Away From Love* ....75.00 - 100.00
Top Rank 2019 *Steady Vows* ....10.00 - 15.00

THE FORTUNE TELLERS:
Sheryl 340 *Just A Little Bit Of Your Love*.................8.00 - 12.00

THE FOSTER BROS.:
Hi Mi 3005 *Never Again*...............................8.00 - 12.00
Profile 4004 *Trust In Me* ....5.00 - 10.00

CELL FOSTER & THE AUDIOS:
Time 1 *Why Did You Do It To Me?* ....10.00 - 15.00
Ultra 105 *Honest I Do* ....100.00 - 150.00

EDDIE FOSTER:
Lyons 100 *You're The One* ....30.00 - 50.00

JERRY FOSTER & HIS BAND:
Back Beat 520 *What Would I Do*...............................8.00 - 12.00

LITTLE WILLIE FOSTER:
Blue Lake 113 *Falling Rain Blues*........................150.00 - 200.00
Cobra 5011 *Crying The Blues*...............................75.00 - 100.00
Parrot 813 *Falling Rain Blues* ....150.00 - 200.00

FOUR ARCS:
Boulevard 102 *Life Of Ease*...................................100.00 - 150.00

THE FOUR BARS:
Cadillac 2006 *What's On Your Mind*.......................50.00 - 80.00
Dayco 101 *What's On Your Mind* ....15.00 - 25.00
Josie 762 *Grief By Day, Grief By Night* ....50.00 - 80.00
   768 *I'll Give My Heart To You* ....25.00 - 40.00
   783 *Why Treat Me This Way* ....25.00 - 40.00
Republic 7101 *When Did You Leave Heaven*........100.00 - 150.00
Shelley 180 *What's On Your Mind*...........................7.00 - 10.00

THE FOUR BEATS:
Tuxedo 914 *Love Leads A Fool*................................50.00 - 80.00

FOUR BLAZES:
United 114 *Mood Indigo*..10.00 - 20.00
   125 *Night Train*...10.00 - 20.00
   127 *Stop Boogie Woogie*.................................10.00 - 20.00
   146 *Not Any More Tears*.................................10.00 - 20.00
   158 *Ella Louise* ....10.00 - 15.00
   168 *My Great Love Affair*..............................10.00 - 15.00
(Note: All of above exist as red vinyl pressings, which command substantially higher prices.)

FOUR BROTHERS & A COUSIN:
Jaguar 3003 *Trust In Me* ....50.00 - 80.00

FOUR BUDDIES/4 BUDDIES:
Club 51 103 *You Mean Everything To Me* ....80.00 - 120.00
   104 *I Need You So*...80.00 - 120.00
   105 *Look Out* ....75.00 - 100.00
   105 *Look Out* (red plastic) ....200.00 - 400.00
Savoy 769 *I Will Wait*..80.00 - 120.00
   779 *Sweet Slumber*...80.00 - 120.00
   789 *My Summer's Gone*..................................80.00 - 120.00
   817 *Heart And Soul* ....75.00 - 100.00
   823 *Simply Say Goodbye* ....- - -
   845 *You're Part Of Me* ....40.00 - 70.00
   866 *What's The Matter With Me* ....40.00 - 70.00
   888 *My Mother's Eyes* ....40.00 - 70.00
   891 *I'd Climb The Highest Mountain*.............40.00 - 70.00

FOUR CHICKADEES:
Checker 849 *Teenage Blues*....................................10.00 - 15.00

FOUR CLIPPERS:
Fox 960/961 *Rain* ....75.00 - 100.00

FOUR COUSINS:
20th Century 75020 *Time And Time Again* ....15.00 - 25.00

THE FOUR CRUISERS:
Chess 1547 *On Account Of You*...............................50.00 - 80.00

THE FOUR DADDY-O'S:
Logan 3108 *I Don't Want To Say Goodbye*.............10.00 - 15.00

FOUR DATES:
Chancellor 1014 *Eloise* ....5.00 - 8.00
   1019 *I Say Babe*...5.00 - 8.00
   1027 *Feel Good* ....5.00 - 8.00

FOUR DEUCES:
Music City 790 *W-P-L-J* (maroon label) ....20.00 - 30.00
(Note: Above is found with various flip sides, and pressed of colored plastic.)
   796 *Down It Went* ....20.00 - 30.00

FOUR DOTS:
Bullseye 103 *Rita* ....50.00 - 80.00
   104 *Peace Of Mind* ....40.00 - 60.00
Castle 2006 *Strange As It Seems*..........................100.00 - 150.00
Freedom 44002 *It's Heaven*....................................10.00 - 15.00
   44005 *Pleading For Your Love*......................10.00 - 15.00

THE 4 DUKES:
Duke 116 *Crying In The Chapel* ....200.00 - 300.00

THE FOUR ELDORADOS:
Academy 8138 *A Lonely Boy*...............................150.00 - 300.00

FOUR EPICS:
Heritage 109 *When The Music Ends* ....30.00 - 50.00
Laurie 3155 *Again*..10.00 - 15.00
   3183 *Dance, Jo-Ann*......................................8.00 - 12.00

FOUR FELLOWS:
Ad Lib 208 *That's Why I Pray*...............................7.00 - 10.00
Derby 862 *I Tried*..50.00 - 80.00
Glory 231 *I Know Love* ....15.00 - 20.00
   234 *Soldier Boy* ....7.00 - 10.00
   236 *In The Rain* ....10.00 - 15.00
   238 *Fallen Angel* ....10.00 - 15.00
   244 *I Sit In My Window* ....10.00 - 15.00
   248 *You Don't Know Me*.................................10.00 - 15.00
   250 *Give Me Back My Broken Heart*..............15.00 - 20.00
Pop 0208 *That's Why I Pray* ....10.00 - 15.00

FOUR FLICKERS:
Lee 1002 *Is There A Way*.......................................8.00 - 12.00

FOUR GENTS:
Park 113 *On Bended Knee* ....100.00 - 150.00

FOUR GUYS:
Stride 5001 *Tear Drops From My Eyes* ....10.00 - 15.00

FOUR HAVEN KNIGHTS:
Atlas 1066 *In My Lonely Room*..............................50.00 - 80.00
   1092 *Why Go On Pretending* ....50.00 - 80.00
Josie 824 *In My Lonely Room* ....15.00 - 20.00

FOUR HORSEMEN:
United Artists 134 *My Heartbeat*..............................- - -

FOUR IMPERIALS:
Chant 101 *Teen Age Fool* ....10.00 - 15.00
Dial 101 *Valley Of Tears* ....50.00 - 80.00
Dot 15737 *Lazy Bonnie*..8.00 - 12.00
Lorelei 4444 *Lazy Bonnie* ....20.00 - 30.00
Twirl 2005 *Seven Lonely Days* ....10.00 - 15.00

4/FOUR J'S:
Impra 1267/1268 *Class Ring* ....7.00 - 10.00
Jamie 1267 *Here Am I-Broken Hearted*..................8.00 - 12.00
   1274 *By Love Possessed* ....8.00 - 12.00
United Artists 125 *Rock & Roll Age* ....10.00 - 15.00

FOUR JACKS:
Federal 12075 *You Met A Fool* ....80.00 - 120.00
   12087 *I'll Be Home Again* ....75.00 - 100.00
   12093 *Never Again* ....75.00 - 100.00
Rebel 1313 *I Can't Forget* ....10.00 - 15.00

FOUR JOKERS:
Diamond 3004 *Transfusion* ....10.00 - 15.00
Sue 703 *Written In The Stars* ....15.00 - 30.00

FOUR KINGS:
Fortune 517 *Doo-Li-Op* ....20.00 - 30.00
   811 *You Don't Mean Me Right* ....80.00 - 130.00
Stomper Time 1160 *Tell It To Me Baby* ....150.00 - 200.00
   1163 *Walkin' Alone* ....150.00 - 200.00

FOUR KNIGHTS:
Capitol (LP) 346 (10 inch) *Spotlight Songs* ....50.00 - 75.00
  (LP) 346 *Spotlight Songs* ....50.00 - 75.00
Capitol (most issues) ....5.00 - 10.00
Coral (LP) 57221 ....75.00 - 100.00
  62045 *Foolish Tears* ....7.00 - 10.00

FOUR LOVERS:
Epic 9255 *Pucker Up* ....60.00 - 100.00
RCA (EP) 869 *The Four Lovers* ....80.00 - 120.00
  (EP) 871 *Joyride* ....80.00 - 120.00
  (LP) 1317 *Joy Ride* ....150.00 - 200.00
  6518 *The Girl In My Dreams* ....8.00 - 12.00
  6519 *Honey Love* ....8.00 - 12.00
  6646 *Lovey Dovey* ....10.00 - 15.00
  6648 *Never Never* ....10.00 - 15.00
  6812 *Shake A Hand* ....10.00 - 15.00
  Night Train (unissued?) .... - -

RAY FOURNIA & ROCKING RELS:
Diamond Disk 101 *Settle Down* ....20.00 - 40.00

FOUR NOTES:
Blue Key 1001 *I Didn't Mean To Be So Mean* ....80.00 - 130.00

FOUR OF A KIND:
Melba 110 *Dedicated To You* ....10.00 - 15.00

FOUR PAGES:
Plateau 101 *Autograph Book* ....7.00 - 10.00

FOUR PALS:
Roulette 4127 *Yours To Possess* ....10.00 - 15.00
Royal Roost 610 *If I Can't Have The One I Love* ...15.00 - 25.00
  616 *No One Ever Loved Me* ....15.00 - 25.00

FOUR PEARLS:
Dolton 26 *Look At Me* ....40.00 - 70.00

FOUR PENNIES:
Brunswick 55304 *You Have No Time To Lose* ....8.00 - 12.00
  55324 *'Tis The Season* ....15.00 - 20.00

THE 4/FOUR PHARAOHS/PHAROAHS:
Paradise 109 *Give Me Your Love* ....20.00 - 30.00
Ranson 100 *Pray for Me* ....20.00 - 30.00
  101 *Give Me Your Love* ....15.00 - 20.00

FOUR PIPS AND A POP:
Mercedes 5001 *Teenage Rock* ....25.00 - 40.00

FOUR PLAID THROATS:
Mercury 70143 *My Inspiration* ....150.00 - 300.00

THE FOUR PLAYBOYS:
Souvenir 1002 *Stay With Me* .... - -

FOUR SEASONS:
Gone 5122 *Bermuda* ....15.00 - 20.00
Vee Jay 576 *Peanuts* ....10.00 - 15.00
  (EP) 901 *Special Gift from Vee Jay* ....20.00 - 30.00

THE FOUR SENSATIONS:
Rainbow 157 *Heaven Knows Why* ....20.00 - 30.00

FOUR SHADES OF RHYTHM:
Chance 1126 *So There* ....100.00 - 200.00

THE FOUR SHOTS:
Cadillac 159 *Get Off My Fence Hortense* ....50.00 - 80.00

THE FOUR SONICS:
Sport 110 *It Takes Two* ....10.00 - 15.00

FOUR SONS:
Linco 1316 *Little Rock* ....15.00 - 25.00

FOUR SOUNDS:
Tuff 1 *The Ring* ....15.00 - 20.00

FOUR SPEEDS:
De Luxe 6070 *I Need You Baby* ....25.00 - 40.00

THE FOUR SPORTSMEN:
Sunnybrook 1 *Surrender* ....8.00 - 12.00

THE FOUR STARS:
Kay Y 66781 *My Sentimental Heart* ....80.00 - 130.00

FOUR TEENS:
Challenge 59021 *Go Little Go Cat* ....15.00 - 20.00

THE FOUR TEMPTATIONS:
ABC Paramount 9920 *Cathy* ....10.00 - 15.00

THE FOUR TONES:
Sun 182 *Heaven On Fire* .... - -

FOUR TOPS:
Chess 1623 *Could It Be You* ....30.00 - 50.00
Riverside (LP) 217 *Jazz Impressions* ....100.00 - up
  4534 *Where You Are* ....20.00 - 30.00

FOUR TROYS:
Freedom 40013 *In The Moonlight* ....15.00 - 20.00

FOUR TUNES:
Jubilee (LP) 1039 *12 by 4* ....80.00 - 120.00
  5128, 5132, 5135, 5152, 5165, 5174, 5183, 5200,
    5212, 5218, 5232, 5239, 5245, 5455, 5276 ......5.00 - 10.00
RCA Victor 3967 *Cool Water* ....7.00 - 10.00
  4102 *Wishing You Were Here Tonight* ....8.00 - 12.00
  4307 *Early In The Morning* ....8.00 - 12.00
  4427 *Tell Me Why* ....8.00 - 12.00
  4489 *Come What May* ....8.00 - 12.00
  4663 *I Wonder* ....8.00 - 12.00
  4828 *They Don't Understand* ....8.00 - 12.00
  4968 *Let's Give Love Another Chance* ......8.00 - 12.00
  5532 *Water Boy* ....7.00 - 10.00
  50-0008 *Careless Love* ....25.00 - 40.00
  50-0016 *My Last Affair* ....25.00 - 40.00
  50-0042 *The Lonesome Road* ....25.00 - 40.00
(Note: Above three are orange plastic.)
  50-0085 *Old Fashioned Love* ....10.00 - 15.00
  50-0131 *May That Day Never Come* ....10.00 - 15.00

THE FOUR UNIQUES:
Adam 9002 *Lookin' For A Girl* ....20.00 - 30.00
  9004 *She's The Only Girl* ....30.00 - 60.00
Deer 3002 *Good Luck Charm* ....40.00 - 70.00

THE FOUR VAGABONDS:
Lloyds 102 *P. S. I Love You* ....80.00 - 130.00

FOUR VANNS:
Vik 0246 *So Young And So Pretty* ....5.00 - 8.00

THE FOUR VOICES:
Mr. Peacock 106 *Lovely One* .... - -

BUCK FOWLER:
Echo 5001 *She's Just That Kind* ....75.00 - 100.00

JIMMY FOWLER:
Dart 118 *Let's Rock & Roll* .... -   -   -

T. J. FOWLER:
States 132 *The Queen* ....15.00 - 20.00

THE FOX:
RPM 420 *The Dream*................20.00 - 30.00

EUGENE FOX:
Checker 792 *Sinner's Dream*..............75.00 - 100.00

NORMAN FOX & THE ROB-ROYS:
Back Beat 501 *Tell Me Why* ....10.00 - 15.00
   508 *My Dearest One*..........................15.00 - 20.00
Capitol 4128 *Pizza Pie*........................75.00 - 100.00

ORVILLE FOX:
Ellis 101 *Don't Do Me This Way*..............15.00 - 20.00

CAROL FRAN:
Excello 2118 *Emmitt Lee*..............8.00 - 12.00
   2133 *I Quit My Knockin'* ....7.00 - 10.00
   2156 *Emmitt Lee's Come Back* ....7.00 - 10.00

STEVE FRANCE:
Renown 110 *Dream Boy*................10.00 - 15.00

FRANKIE & JOHNNY:
Liberty 55271 *My First Love* ....5.00 - 8.00

JOE FRANKLIN:
Renown 113 *Who Put The Pep In The Punch* ....15.00 - 20.00

JAY FRANKS:
RPM 357 *Fish Tail* ....10.00 - 15.00

TILLMAN FRANKS:
Gotham 6412 *High Tone Poppa*..............15.00 - 20.00
Pacemaker 1101 *Hayride Boogie* ....15.00 - 20.00

CALVIN FRAZIER:
Checker 908 *Track Down* ....10.00 - 15.00
JVB 86 *Have Blues Must Travel* ....75.00 - 100.00
Savoy 858 *Little Baby Child*..............20.00 - 40.00

RAY FRAZIER & THE MOONRAYS:
Excell 111 *Days*..............10.00 - 15.00
   112 *All My Love*..............10.00 - 15.00

STAN FREBERG:
Capitol (EP) 495 *Any Requests?*..............15.00 - 25.00
   (LP) 777 *Child's Garden Of Freberg*..............15.00 - 20.00
   (LP) 1242 *With Original Cast* ....15.00 - 20.00
   2125, 2279, 2596, 2929 ....4.00 - 8.00

DOTTY FREDERICK:
20th Fox 115 *Just Wait* ....7.00 - 10.00

ALAN FREED:
Brunswick (LP) 54043 *The Alan Freed Rock & Roll Show*
..............40.00 - 60.00
Coral (LP) 57063 *Rock & Roll Dance Party*..............30.00 - 50.00
   (LP) 57115 *R & R Dance Party-Vol. 2*..............30.00 - 50.00
   (LP) 57177 *TV Record Hop*..............25.00 - 40.00
   (LP) 57213 *Rock Around The Block*..............25.00 - 40.00
   61626 *Right Now, Right Now* ....8.00 - 12.00
   61714 *Rock 'N' Roll Boogie* ....8.00 - 12.00

BO FREEMAN:
Purl 901 *The Girl For Me* ....50.00 - 80.00

BOBBY FREEMAN:
Jubilee (LP) 1086 *Do You Wanna Dance* ....30.00 - 50.00

ERNIE FREEMAN:
Imperial 5474 *Raunchy* (78 rpm)..............10.00 - 15.00
   5486 *The Tuttle* (78 rpm) ....7.00 - 10.00

DON FRENCH:
Lancer 104 *Lonely Saturday Night* ....8.00 - 12.00
   105 *Little Blond Girl*..............8.00 - 12.00

EDDIE FRIEND & THE EMPIRES:
Colpix 112 *Tears In My Eyes*..............40.00 - 70.00

HAL FRITZ & HIS PLAYBOYS:
Soma 1089 *Three Bad Habits* ....30.00 - 40.00

LEFTY FRIZZELL:
Columbia (LP) 9019 *Sings Jimmy Rodgers Songs* .20.00 - 30.00
   (LP) 9021 *Listen To Lefty* ....20.00 - 30.00

JANE FROMAN:
Capitol (LP) H-354 *Yours Alone* (10 inches)..........20.00 - 30.00
   (most issues)..............5.00 - 10.00
Decca (LP) 6021 *Souvenir Album* (10 inch LP) .....20.00 - 30.00

FRANK FROST:
Jewel 765, 771, 778 ....5.00 - 10.00
Phillips Int. (LP) 197 *Hey Boss Man* ....100.00 - 150.00

BOBBY FULLER:
Exeter 124 *I Fought The Law* ....40.00 - 80.00
Mustang (LP) 901 *I Fought The Law* ....50.00 - 80.00
   (LP) MS-901 *I Fought The Law* (STEREO)......75.00 - 150.00
Yucca 140 *You're In Love* ....8.00 - 12.00
   144 *My Heart Jumped*..............7.00 - 10.00

JERRY FULLER:
Challenge 59085 *Anna From Louisiana* ....5.00 - 8.00
LIN 5011 *Blue Memories*..............8.00 - 12.00
   5012 *Teenage Love* ....8.00 - 12.00
   5015 *A Certain Smile* ....8.00 - 12.00
   5016 *The Door Is Open*..............8.00 - 12.00
   5019 *Lipstick And Rouge* ....10.00 - 15.00

JESSE FULLER:
Cavalier (LP) 5006 (10 inches) *Frisco Bound*........50.00 - 75.00
   (LP) 6009 *Frisco Bound* ....60.00 - 100.00

JOHNNIE/JOHNNY FULLER:
Aladdin 3278 *Johnny Ace's Last Letter*..............15.00 - 25.00
Flair 1054 *Hard Times* ....20.00 - 30.00
Hollywood 1043 *Train, Train Blues*..............15.00 - 20.00
   1057 *Mean Old World* ....10.00 - 15.00
   1063 *Roughest Place In Town* ....10.00 - 15.00
   1077 *Too Late To Change*..............10.00 - 15.00
   1084 *I Can't Succeed* ....10.00 - 15.00
Imperial 5395 *Restless* ....10.00 - 15.00
Irma 110 *First Stage Of The Blues* ....25.00 - 40.00
Money 206 *These Young Girls* ....7.00 - 10.00
Rhythm 1767 *Fool's Paradise* ....20.00 - 30.00
   1773 *Train, Train Blues* ....20.00 - 30.00
   1777 *Lovin' Lovin' Man* ....15.00 - 25.00
   1779 *Mean Old World* ....15.00 - 25.00
   1782 *Johnny Ace's Last Letter*..............15.00 - 20.00
Specialty 655 *Haunted House* ....7.00 - 10.00

ROCKY FULLER:
Checker 753 *Soon One Morning**.............. -   -   -
(*the existence of this record in 45 rpm format is not verified)

LOWELL FULSOM/FULSON:

Aladdin 3217 *Chuck With The Boys* ....15.00 - 20.00
    3233 *You've Got To Reap* ....15.00 - 20.00
Checker 804 *Reconsider Baby* ....8.00 - 12.00
    812 *Check Yourself* ....8.00 - 12.00
    820 *Lonely Hours* ....8.00 - 12.00
    829 *Trouble Trouble* ....8.00 - 12.00
    841, 854, 865, 882 ....5.00 - 10.00
    937, 952, 959, 972, 992, 1027, 1046 ....5.00 - 10.00
Hollywood 1022 *Lonesome Christmas* ....8.00 - 12.00
    1029 *Guitar Shuffle* ....10.00 - 15.00
    1103 *Guitar Shuffle* ....7.00 - 10.00
Kent (LP) 5016 *Lowell Fulsom* ....20.00 - 40.00
    (LP) 5020 *Lowell Fulsom* ....20.00 - 40.00
Parrot 787 *I've Been Mistreated* ....40.00 - 60.00
Swing Time 289 *Best Wishes* ....30.00 - 50.00
    295 *Guitar Shuffle* ....30.00 - 50.00
    301 *The Highway Is My Home* ....30.00 - 50.00
    308 *Black Widow Spider* ....30.00 - 50.00
    315 *Raggedy Daddy Blues* ....30.00 - 50.00
    320 *Good Party Shuffle* ....25.00 - 50.00
    325 *Upstairs* ....20.00 - 40.00
    330 *I Love My Baby* ....20.00 - 40.00
    335 *Cash Box Boogie* ....20.00 - 40.00
    338 *Juke Box Shuffle* ....20.00 - 40.00
(earlier numbers than Swing Time issues above are scarce, and would
    be valued more highly)

SONNY FULTON:

Chelsea 533 *Honest I Do* ....10.00 - 15.00
Hit 1133/1144 *Pardon Me Baby (Did I Hear You Right)*
Lash 1127 *A Lovely Relationship* ....10.00 - 15.00

FURNESS BROTHERS:

Melmar 114 *Only Fate* ....8.00 - 12.00
    116 *Please Don't Call Me Fool* ....8.00 - 12.00

THE FUTURE TONES:

Tress 1/2 *I Know* ....150.00 - up

GUITAR GABLE:

Excello 2082 *Congo Mambo* ....7.00 - 10.00
    2094 *Irene* ....5.00 - 8.00
    2122 *Gumbo Mambo* ....7.00 - 10.00
    2140 *Have Mercy On Me* ....7.00 - 10.00
    2153 *Please Operator* ....7.00 - 10.00

GADABOUTS:

Wing 90008 *Two Things I Have* ....5.00 - 8.00

BOB GADDY (& HIS ALLEY CATS/KEYS):

Harlem 2330 *Slow Down Baby* ....50.00 - 80.00
Jax 308 *Little Girl's Boogie* ....50.00 - 80.00
(Note: Above, pressed of red vinyl, command higher prices.)
Old Town 1031, 1039, 1050, 1057, 1064, 1070,
    1077, 1085 ....5.00 - 10.00

GAIL TONES:

Decca 30726 *Lover Boy* ....8.00 - 12.00

EDDIE GAINES & HIS ROCKIN' FIVE:

Summit 101 *Be Bop Battlin' Ball* ....200.00 - 300.00
    104 *Out Of The Shadows* ....- - -

FATS GAINES:

Authentic 403 *It's Tragic* ....8.00 - 12.00
Big Town 108 *Home Work Blues* ....10.00 - 15.00

ROY GAINES:

De Luxe 6119 *Gainesville* ....7.00 - 10.00
    6132 *You're Right I'm Left* ....7.00 - 10.00

Groove 0146 *Right Now Baby* ....10.00 - 15.00
RCA Victor 7243 *Skippy Is A Sissy* ....10.00 - 20.00

THE GAINORS:

Cameo 151 *The Secret* ....50.00 - 80.00
    156 *You Must Be An Angel* ....50.00 - 80.00
Mercury 71466 *A Message With Flowers* ....8.00 - 12.00
    71569 *Please Consider* ....10.00 - 15.00
    71630 *Nothing Means More* ....8.00 - 12.00

GENE GAITHER:

Astro 232 *Cute Little Chicky* ....- - -

GALAXIES:

Carthay 103 *A Lover's Prayer* ....150.00 - 300.00
Richie 458 *Dear Someone* ....30.00 - 50.00

BARBARA GALE & THE LARKS:

Lloyds 111 *When You're Near* ....40.00 - 60.00

GALES:

J.O.B. 3001 *Darling Patricia* ....200.00 - 300.00
JVB 34 *My Eyes Keep Me In Trouble* ....400.00 - up
    35 *Darling Patricia* ....400.00 - up

JAMES GALLAGHER:

Decca 29984 *Crazy Chicken* ....8.00 - 12.00

JAY GALLAGHER:

Dixie 2023 *Steady Flame* ....20.00 - 30.00

THE GALLAHADS:

Beechwood 3000 *Keeper Of Dreams* ....40.00 - 70.00
Del-Fi 4137 *Lonely Guy* ....7.00 - 10.00
    4148 *Be Fair* ....10.00 - 15.00
Donna 1322 *Lonely Guy* ....10.00 - 20.00
Jubilee 5252 *The Fool* ....7.00 - 10.00
Nite Owl 20 *Gone* ....15.00 - 20.00
Rendezvous 153 *Gone* ....10.00 - 15.00
Sea Crest 65005 *My Offering* ....10.00 - 15.00
Starla 15 *Keeper Of Dreams* ....10.00 - 15.00

BOB GALLION:

MGM 12195 *My Square Dancin' Mamma* ......15.00 - 20.00

KEN GALLOWAY:

Honey 362 *Bayou Lou* ....30.00 - 50.00

CECIL GANT:

King (LP) 671 *The Voice That Has Never Been Copied*
    ....80.00 - 130.00
Sound (LP) 601 *The Incomparable Cecil Gant* ......50.00 - 80.00

DAVE GARDNER:

OJ 1002 *White Silver Sands* (78 rpm) ....10.00 - 15.00

BILL GARLAND:

Pam 201 *Lonesome Guitar* ....10.00 - 15.00

CLARENCE (BON TON) GARLOW:

Aladdin 3179 *New Bon Ton Roula* ....50.00 - 80.00
    3325 *I'm Hurt* ....20.00 - 30.00
Feature 3005 *I Called You Up Daddy* ....25.00 - 40.00
Flair 1021 *Crawfishin'* ....20.00 - 30.00
Folk Star 1130 *Made Me Cry* ....50.00 - 80.00
    1199 *No, No Baby* ....30.00 - 50.00
Goldband 1043 *Sundown* ....15.00 - 20.00
    1065 *Bon Ton Roule* ....15.00 - 20.00

BILLY GARNER:

Mojo 2171 *Little Schoolgirl* ....5.00 - 8.00

GABBY GARNER:

Erald 2052 *Smokin' Heart* ....20.00 - 30.00

JOHNNY GARNER:
Imperial 5536 *Kiss Me Sweet* ....15.00 - 20.00
　　5548 *Didi Didi* ....15.00 - 20.00

JIM GARNETT:
Manco 1029 *I Could Be Had* ....7.00 - 10.00

BOBBY GARRETT:
E & M 1602 *Short Skirts* ....8.00 - 12.00

ROBERT GARRETT:
Excello 2216 *Quit My Drinkin'* ....7.00 - 10.00

GLEN GARRISON (& THE NOTE KINGS):
Crest 1047 *Lovin' Lorene* ....20.00 - 30.00
Lode 106 *Pony Tail Girl* ....15.00 - 20.00

JIMMY GARTIN:
Hi-Q 5014 *Gonna Ride That Satellite* ....8.00 - 12.00

GASSERS:
Cash 1035 *Tell Me* ....10.00 - 15.00
Encino 1011 *Dody Mighty* ....10.00 - 15.00

DAVE/DAVID GATES (& THE ACCENTS):
Del-Fi 4206 *You Had It Comin' To You* ....7.00 - 10.00
East West 123 *Swingin' Baby Doll* ....10.00 - 15.00
Mala 413 *What's This I Hear?* ....10.00 - 15.00
　　418 *The Happiest Man Alive* ....5.00 - 8.00
　　427 *Teardrops In My Heart* ....5.00 - 8.00
Robbins 1008 *Lovin' At Night* ....10.00 - 15.00

THE GATORVETTES:
Bocaldun 1001 *If It's Tonight* ....15.00 - 20.00
Thunder 1001 *If It's Tonight* ....50.00 - 80.00

DEE DEE GAUDET:
Dodge 805 *Where's The Law* ....8.00 - 12.00

TONY GAVIN:
Sims 165 *It's Never Seven Or Eleven* ....7.00 - 10.00

BOBBY GAY & THE SPARKLETONES:
Mida 104 *You're Nice* ....7.00 - 10.00

MARVIN GAYE:
Tamla (LP) 221 *The Soulful Moods of...* ....80.00 - 120.00
　　(LP) 239 *That Stubborn Kinda' Fellow* ....75.00 - 100.00
Tamla (most other LPs) ....10.00 - 20.00

GAY KNIGHTS:
Pet 801 *Angel* ....30.00 - 50.00

GAY LARKS:
Music City 792 *Tell Me Darling* ....50.00 - 80.00
　　793 *Lil Dream Girl* ....50.00 - 80.00
　　809 *Church On The Hill* ....80.00 - 130.00
　　812 *Somewhere In This World* ....20.00 - 30.00
　　819 *Ivy League Clothes* ....10.00 - 15.00

THE GAYLES:
ABC Paramount 9707 *You Fool* ....5.00 - 8.00

BILLY GAYLES:
Federal 12265 *I'm Tore Up* ....15.00 - 20.00
　　12272 *Take Your Fine Frame Home* ....15.00 - 20.00
　　12282 *Do Right Baby* ....10.00 - 15.00
　　12287 *Just One More Time* ....10.00 - 20.00

GAY NOTES:
Drexel 905 *For Only A Moment* ....80.00 - 120.00
Post 2006 *Hear My Plea* ....20.00 - 30.00
Zynn 504 *Plea Of Love* ....15.00 - 25.00

THE GAY POPPERS:
Fire 1026 *I Want To Know* ....10.00 - 15.00
Savoy 1573 *I Need Your Love* ....7.00 - 10.00

THE GAY TUNES:
Dome 502 *Don't Go* ....80.00 - 130.00
Joyce 101 *I Love You* ....40.00 - 60.00
Timely 1002 *Thrill Of Romance* ....100.00 - 150.00

THE GAZELLES:
Gotham 315 *Honest* ....40.00 - 60.00

THE G-CLEFS:
Ditto 503 *Ka-Ding Dong* ....15.00 - 20.00
Paris 502 *Symbol Of Love* ....10.00 - 15.00
　　506 *Zing Zang Zoo* ....10.00 - 15.00
Pilgrim 715 *Ka-Ding-Dong* ....7.00 - 10.00
　　715 *Ka-Ding-Dong* (78 rpm) ....20.00 - 30.00
　　720 *'Cause You're Mine* ....7.00 - 10.00
Terrace 7500 *I Understand (Just How You Feel)* ...10.00 - 15.00
　　7503 *A Girl Has To Know* ....10.00 - 15.00
　　7507 *Make Up Your Mind* ....10.00 - 15.00
　　7510 *Sitting In The Moonlight* ....10.00 - 15.00
　　7514 *All My Trials* ....10.00 - 15.00

THE GEMS:
Drexel 901 *Talk About The Weather* ....75.00 - 100.00
　　901 *Talk About The Weather* (red plastic) ....150.00 - 250.00
　　903 *I Thought You'd Care* ....150.00 - 200.00
　　904 *You're Tired Of Love* ....150.00 - 200.00
　　909 *The Darkest Night* ....150.00 - 200.00
　　915 *Till The Day I Die* ....150.00 - 200.00
Recorte 407 *Please Change Your Mind* ....30.00 - 50.00

GENE & EUNICE:
Aladdin 3276 *Ko Ko Mo* ....10.00 - 15.00
　　3282 *This Is My Story* ....10.00 - 15.00
　　3292 *Flim Flam* ....10.00 - 15.00
　　3305 *I Gotta Go Home* ....10.00 - 15.00
　　3315 *I'll Never Believe In You* ....8.00 - 12.00
　　3321 *Let's Get Together* ....8.00 - 12.00
　　3351 *Bom Bom Lulu* ....8.00 - 12.00
　　3374 *The Vow* ....10.00 - 15.00
　　3376 *Don't Treat Me This Way* ....10.00 - 15.00
　　3414 *I Mean Love* ....10.00 - 15.00
Combo 64 *Ko Ko Mo* ....15.00 - 20.00
Score (LP) 4018 *Rock & Roll Sock Hop* ....150.00 - 250.00

GENIES:
Hollywood 69 *No More Knockin'* ....8.00 - 12.00
Shad 5002 *Who's That Knocking* ....15.00 - 30.00

SONNY GENO:
Rip 130 *Rumble Rock* ....8.00 - 12.00

J. C. GENT:
Marlo 1501 *Bad Gal Blues* ....7.00 - 10.00

GENTLEMEN:
Apollo 464 *Tired Of You* ....20.00 - 30.00
　　470 *Baby Don't Go* ....20.00 - 30.00

THE GENTONES:
Casino 52261 *Counting Stars* ....50.00 - 80.00

BILL GENTRY:
Universal Artist 1001 *Baby What' Ya Say* ....20.00 - 30.00

GEORGE & EARL:
Dixie - *Done Gone* ....20.00 - 30.00
Mercury 70605 *Got Anything Good?* ....7.00 - 10.00
　　70632 *Goin' Steady* ....10.00 - 15.00

70683 *Don't Don't Don't* ....8.00 - 12.00
70852 *Done Gone* ....10.00 - 15.00

BARBARA GEORGE:
A.F.O. (LP) 5001 *I Know* ....40.00 - 60.00

LEE GEORGE:
Wonder 100 *The Little Moon Men* ....30.00 - 50.00

LLOYD GEORGE:
Imperial 5837 *Lucy Lee* ....7.00 - 10.00
Post 1006 *Come On Train* ....8.00 - 12.00

THE GEORGETTES:
Ebb 125 *Love Like A Fool* ....7.00 - 10.00

RAY GERDSEN:
- *Bye Bye Baby* .... - - -

ETHAN GIANT:
Mark 141 *Laughing Stock* ....30.00 - 50.00

GEORGIA GIBBS:
RCA Victor 7098 *Great Balls Of Fire* ....7.00 - 10.00

DADDYO GIBSON:
Checker 848 *Night Train* ....7.00 - 10.00

DON GIBSON:
MGM 12393 *I'm Gonna Fool Everybody* ....8.00 - 12.00
  12494 *I Ain't A-Studyin' You Baby* ....8.00 - 12.00
RCA Victor (LP) 1743 *Lonesome Me* ....15.00 - 20.00
  (LP) 1918, 2038 ....10.00 - 15.00
  48-0424 *Carolina Breakdown* ....10.00 - 15.00
(Note: Above is made of translucent green plastic.)

GRANDDADDY GIBSON:
Bobbin 124 *I Don't Want No Woman* ....20.00 - 30.00
  127 *The Monkey Likes To Boogie* ....20.00 - 30.00

JOE D. GIBSON:
Tetra 4450 *Good Morning Captain* ....10.00 - 15.00

STEVE GIBSON & THE RED CAPS:
Jay Dee 796 *It Hurts Me But I Like It* ....10.00 - 15.00
Mercury (LP) 25116 (10 inches) ....40.00 - 80.00
RCA Victor (most issues) ....5.00 - 8.00
Rose 5534 *I Miss You So* ....7.00 - 10.00

RONNIE GILL:
Rip 108 *Geraldine* ....15.00 - 30.00

DARLENE GILLESPIE:
Disneyland (LP) 3010 *Darlene Of The Teens* ....30.00 - 50.00

MICKEY GILLEY:
Astro (LP) 101 *Lonely Wine* ....150.00 - 200.00
  102 *Down The Line* ....10.00 - 15.00
  103 *Is It Wrong* ....10.00 - 15.00
  104 *Susie-Q* ....15.00 - 20.00
  106 *Lotta Lovin'* ....15.00 - 20.00
  110 *A Certain Smile* ....15.00 - 20.00
  112 *Little Egypt* ....15.00 - 20.00
  5002 *Don't Throw A Good Love Away* ....10.00 - 15.00
  10003 *She Called Me Baby* ....10.00 - 15.00
Daryl 101 *What Have I Done* ....7.00 - 10.00
Dot 15706 *Call Me Shorty* ....30.00 - 40.00
Eric 7021 *Whole Lot Of Twistin' Goin On* ....7.00 - 10.00
Khoury's 712 *Drive-In Movie* ....50.00 - 80.00
Lynn 503 *Your Selfish Pride* ....10.00 - 15.00
  508 *My Baby's Been Cheating Again* ....10.00 - 15.00
  512 *Slippin' And Slidin'* ....15.00 - 20.00
  515 *My Babe* ....15.00 - 20.00

Minor 106 *Ooh Wee Baby* ....150.00 - 300.00
Potomac 901 *No Greater Love* ....8.00 - 12.00
Princess 4004 *Drive In Movie* ....10.00 - 15.00
  4006 *Caught In The Middle* ....10.00 - 15.00
  4011 *I'll Keep On Dreaming* ....10.00 - 15.00
  4015 *World Of My Own* ....15.00 - 20.00
Sabra 518 *Valley Of Tears* ....10.00 - 15.00
San 1513 *I Ain't No Bo Diddley* ....15.00 - 20.00
Supreme 101 *Now That I Have You* ....10.00 - 15.00
  - *No One Will Ever Know* .... - - -

EARL GILLIAM:
Ivory 343 *Just You And I* ....8.00 - 12.00
Sarg 128 *Nobody' Blues* ....20.00 - 30.00
  133 *Wrong Doing Woman* ....20.00 - 30.00

JAZZ GILLUM:
Groove 5002 *Key To The Highway* ....10.00 - 15.00
RCA Victor 50-0004 *Signifying Woman* ....30.00 - 50.00
  50-0017 *Look What You Are Today* ....30.00 - 50.00
  50-0035 *A Lie Is Dangerous* ....30.00 - 50.00
(Note: Above are made of orange plastic.)

GIL GILROY:
Moon 3 *Laura Lee* ....50.00 - 80.00

GINO & THE DELLS:
Golden Crest 567 *Altar Of Dreams* .... - - -

LOU GIORDANO:
Brunswick 55115 *Stay Close To Me* ....50.00 - 100.00

BYRON/WILD CHILD GIPSON:
Hit 2001 *Uncle John* ....15.00 - 25.00
Laurie 3108 *Uncle John* ....8.00 - 12.00

THE GLADIOLAS:
Excello 2101 *Little Darlin'* ....15.00 - 20.00
  2120 *I Wanta Know* ....20.00 - 30.00

GLAD RAGS:
Excello 2121 *My China Doll* ....15.00 - 30.00

CHARLES GLASS:
Magnet 7011 *Screamin' And Dyin'* ....15.00 - 25.00

BILLY GLASSER:
Ozark 1236 *I Left The Dance* ....15.00 - 20.00

DICK GLASSER:
Argo 5279 *Crazy Love* (ship logo) ....8.00 - 12.00
  5283 *Go Along Baby* ....8.00 - 12.00
Columbia 41472 *Crazy Alligator* ....8.00 - 12.00

CLIFF GLEAVES:
Summer 501 *Love Is My Business* ....10.00 - 15.00

DARRELL GLENN:
NRC 004 *Congratulations To Me* ....7.00 - 10.00
  006 *Mr.Moonlight* ....7.00 - 10.00
Valley 105 *Crying In The Chapel* ....7.00 - 10.00
  109 *Only A Pastime* ....7.00 - 10.00

GLEN GLENN:
Dore 523 *Goofin' Around* ....15.00 - 20.00
Era 1061 *Everybody's Movin'* ....15.00 - 25.00
  1074 *One Cup Of Coffee* ....15.00 - 20.00

LLOYD GLENN:
Aladdin 3237 *Tipsy* ....8.00 - 12.00
  3268 *Nite Flite* ....7.00 - 10.00
  (most other issues) ....5.00 - 8.00
  (LP) 808 *Chica-Boo* (red vinyl) ....150.00 - 300.00

THE GLENNS:
Rendezvous 118 *In The Chapel* ....10.00 - 15.00

GLITTERS:
Rubaiyat 413 *You Don't Know* ....8.00 - 12.00

THE GLORYTONES:
Epic 9243 *Was That The Right Thing To Do* ....10.00 - 15.00

THE G NOTES:
Tender 510 *Ronnie* ....8.00 - 12.00

GO BOYS (See also DUDLEY CALLICUTT):
"DC" 0418 *Flippin'* ....20.00 - 30.00

THE GO-CARTS:
Hope 1003 *Rockin' Liza* .... - - -

JACKIE GOETROE:
Rhythm 111 *Raised on Rock And Roll* ....100.00 - 200.00
Vortex 102 *Lobo Jones* ....30.00 - 50.00

"GO, JOHNNY, GO" (Soundtrack):
(Note: With Chuck Berry, Eddie Cochran, Jimmy Clanton, The
Cadillacs, Richie Valens, et al. No designation of issuing record
company.) ....200.00 - up

GOLDEN GATE QUARTET:
Camden (LP) 308 ....25.00 - 50.00
Columbia (LP) 6102 (10 inches) ....40.00 - 70.00
Harmony (LP) 7018 *That Golden Chariot* ....30.00 - 50.00
Mercury 5385 *Didn't That Man Believe* ....7.00 - 10.00
(LP) 25063 (10 inches) *Look Up!* ....75.00 - 100.00

GOLDEN RODS:
Vee Jay 307 *Wish I Was Back In School* ....75.00 - 100.00

THE GOLDENS (See also DENNY EZBA):
Big Star 101 *Don't Leave Me Like This* ....15.00 - 20.00

THE GOLDENTONES:
Beacon 560 *The Meaning Of Love* ....30.00 - 50.00
Hush 102 *Ocean Of Tears* ....8.00 - 12.00
Jay-Dee 806 *The Meaning Of Love* ....40.00 - 70.00
Lifetime 1004 *Stand By Me* ....15.00 - 25.00
Rainbow 351 *She's Funny That Way* ....30.00 - 50.00
Samson 107 *Crying The Blues* ....20.00 - 30.00

THE GOLDTONES:
Y-R-S 1001 *I'm So Lonely* ....50.00 - 80.00

GOOD JELLY BESS:
Hermitage 775 *Come And Get It* ....7.00 - 10.00

DICKIE GOODMAN:
Mark-X 8009 *The Touchables* ....5.00 - 8.00
8010 *The Touchables In Brooklyn* ....5.00 - 8.00
Rori (LP) 3301 *The Many Heads Of Dickie Goodman*
....50.00 - 100.00
701 *Santa And The Touchables* ....7.00 - 10.00

GOOD ROCKIN' BOB:
Goldband 1067 *Take It Easy Katy* ....15.00 - 20.00

GOOD ROCKIN' SAMMY T.:
Junior 500 *Good Rockin' Mama* ....40.00 - 70.00

HAL GOODSON:
Solo 108 *Who's Gonna Be The Next One Honey* ....10.00 - 15.00

BILL GOODWIN:
Band Box 287 *Revenuer Man* ....10.00 - 15.00
293 *Those Same Old Things* ....10.00 - 15.00
309 *Heartaches* ....10.00 - 15.00
Star - *Teenage Blues* .... - - -

THE GOOFERS:
Coral 61383 *Flip Flop And Fly* ....10.00 - 15.00
61650 *Tennessee Rock And Roll* ....10.00 - 15.00
61664 *I'm Gonna Rock & Roll Till I Die* ....10.00 - 15.00

CURTIS GORDON:
Mercury 70861 *Draggin'* ....8.00 - 12.00
71037 *So Tired Of Crying* ....7.00 - 10.00
71097 *Out To Win Your Heart* ....7.00 - 10.00
71121 *Sixteen* ....10.00 - 15.00
71183 *Please Baby Please* ....10.00 - 15.00
RCA Victor 5356 *Rompin' And Stompin'* ....8.00 - 12.00

MIKE GORDON & THE EL TEMPOS:
Cat 101 *Why Don't You Do Right?* ....5.00 - 8.00

ROSCO/ROSCOE GORDON:
Chess 1487 *Booted* ....100.00 - 150.00
Duke 109 *Too Many Women* ....30.00 - 50.00
114 *Ain't No Use* ....25.00 - 40.00
Flip 227 *Weeping Blues* ....100.00 - 150.00
237 *The Chicken* ....15.00 - 20.00
RPM 324 *Ouch! Pretty Baby* ....150.00 - up
336 *Dime A Dozen* ....50.00 - 80.00
350 *No More Doggin'* ....30.00 - 50.00
365 *Two Kinds Of Women* ....30.00 - 50.00
369 *Dream Baby* ....20.00 - 30.00
373 *Blues For My Baby* ....15.00 - 20.00
379 *I'm In Love* ....10.00 - 15.00
384 *We're All Loaded* ....10.00 - 15.00
Sun 227 *Weeping Blues* ....100.00 - 150.00

SONNY GORDON & THE ANGELS:
Grand 115 *Wedding Bells Are Ringing In My Ear* 100.00 - 150.00

STOMP GORDON:
Chess 1601 *The Grind* ....8.00 - 12.00
Decca 48287 *Fat Mama Blues* ....10.00 - 15.00
48289 *Oooh Yes!* ....10.00 - 15.00
Savoy 1504 *Ride Superman Ride* ....5.00 - 10.00

CHARLIE GORE:
Audio Lab (LP) 1526 *Country Gentleman* ....50.00 - 75.00

JOHNNY GOSEY & THE NIGHTHAWKS:
MOA 1001 *Fools Will Take Chances* ....30.00 - 50.00

THE GOTHICS:
Dynamic 101 *Marilyn* ....80.00 - 130.00

SAMMY GOWANS:
United Artists 114 *Rockin' By Myself* ....30.00 - 50.00

CHARLIE GRACIE:
Cadillac - *No Sin In Rhythm* .... - - -
141 *Boogie Boogie Blues* ....15.00 - 20.00
144 *Rockin' An' Rollin'* ....20.00 - 30.00
Cameo 105 *Butterfly* (78 rpm) ....10.00 - 15.00
111 *Wanderin' Eyes* (78 rpm) ....10.00 - 15.00
111, 118, 127 ....5.00 - 8.00
Town & Country 5033 *My Baby Loves Me* ....15.00 - 20.00
5035 *Wildwood Boogie* ....15.00 - 20.00
20th Century 5033 *My Baby Loves Me* ....15.00 - 20.00
5035 *Wildwood Boogie* ....15.00 - 20.00

THE GRADUATES:
Lawn 208 *Care* ....10.00 - 15.00
Shan Todd 0055 *Ballad Of A Boy And Girl* ....15.00 - 20.00

LOU GRAHAM:
Coral 61931 *Wee Willie Brown* ....8.00 - 12.00

BILLY GRAMMER:
Monument (LP) 40000 *Travelin' On*......................50.00 -　80.00

CASEY GRAMS:
Count 101 *Count Down* ....25.00 -　40.00

GERRY GRANAHAN:
Sunbeam 102 *No Chemise Please* ....7.00 -　10.00
Sunbeam 108 *Baby Wait*...............................7.00 -　10.00

O. S. GRANT AND THE DOWNBEATS (See also DOWNBEATS):
Sarg 200 *You Did Me Wrong*........................10.00 -　15.00

JUNIOR GRAVELY:
Velatone 796 *Take My Hands*...........................5.00 -　8.00

ARVELLA GRAY:
Gray 13, 14, 100 ....5.00 -　8.00

BILLY GRAY:
Decca 29800 *Tennessee Toddy* ....8.00 -　12.00

CLAUDE GRAY:
Minor 109 *Barricade* ....20.00 -　30.00

PHIL GRAY & The GO BOYS:
Robbins 1002 *Somebody's Got My Baby* ....15.00 -　25.00

RUDY GRAY:
Capitol 2946, 3044, 3149 ....5.00 -　10.00

RUDY GRAYZELL:
Abbott 145, 147, 157 ....7.00 -　10.00
Award 130 *You'll Be Mine* ....10.00 -　15.00
Mercury 71138 *Let's Get Wild* ....15.00 -　20.00
Starday 229 *The Moon Is Up* ....25.00 -　40.00
　　241 *Duck Tail* ....30.00 -　50.00
　　270 *Jig-Ga-Lee-Ga* ....30.00 -　50.00
　　321 *Let's Get Wild* ....50.00 -　80.00
Sun 290 *Judy*..25.00 -　40.00

"THE GREATEST ROCK & ROLL":
Atlantic (LP) 8001 (various artists) ....30.00 -　50.00

"THE GREATEST WESTERN HITS":
Columbia (LP) 1257, 1408 ....10.00 -　20.00

BOBBY GREEN:
Oak 4429/4430 *Little Heart Attacks* ....50.00 -　80.00

GEORGE GREEN:
Chance 1135 *Brand New Rockin' Chair* ....30.00 -　60.00

LIL GREEN:
Groove 5004 *Why Don't You Do Right* ....7.00 -　10.00

RUDY GREEN:
Chance 1139 *Love Is A Pain*........................40.00 -　70.00
　　1146 *The Letter* ....40.00 -　70.00
　　1151 *Meet Me Baby*...............................40.00 -　70.00
Excello 2074 *Cool Lovin' Mama*...............30.00 -　50.00
　　2090 *Teeny Weeny Baby* ....20.00 -　30.00

(GUITAR) SLIM GREEN:
Canton 1789 *Shake 'Em Up*...........................8.00 -　12.00
Dig 142 *My Woman Done Quit Me* ....7.00 -　10.00
Geenote 907 *Rock The Nation* ....8.00 -　12.00

VERNON GREEN & THE MEDALLIONS:
Dooto 446 *Magic Mountain*..........................15.00 -　20.00
Dootone 407 *Did You Have Fun?* ....20.00 -　30.00

RUDY GREENE (& THE 4 BUDDIES) (See also THE FOUR BUDDIES):
Club 51 103 *You Mean Everything To Me*.............. 80.00 -　120.00
Ember 1012 *Juicy Fruit* .... 20.00 -　30.00

LIL GREENWOOD (& THE FOUR JACKS):
Federal 12082 *Monday Morning Blues*................... 80.00 -　120.00
　　12093 *Grandpa Can Boogie Too* .... 80.00 -　120.00
　　12158 *I'll Go* .... 25.00 -　50.00

(BIG) JOHN GREER (& HIS RHYTHM ROCKERS):
Groove 0119 *Come Back Maybelline* .... 7.00 -　10.00
RCA Victor 4484 *Strong Red Whiskey* .... 10.00 -　15.00
　　5375 *Rhythm In The Breeze* .... 8.00 -　12.00
　　50-0007 *Drinkin' Wine, Spo-Dee-O-Dee* .... 25.00 -　50.00
　　50-0029 *I Found A Dream* .... 20.00 -　30.00
　　50-0051 *Rockin' Jenny Jones* .... 20.00 -　30.00
　　50-0096 *Cheatin'* .... 20.00 -　30.00
(Note: Above are orange plastic.)
　　50-0108, 50-0113, 50-10125, 50-0137 .... 8.00 -　12.00

CHUCK GREY & THE PANICS:
Fable 616 *Push The Panic Button* .... 15.00 -　25.00

BUCK GRIFFIN:
Holiday Inn 109 *Pretty Lou* .... 10.00 -　15.00
Lin 1005 *It Don't Make No Never Mind*............... 20.00 -　30.000
　　1007 *Rollin' Tears* .... 8.00 -　12.00
　　1008 *Going Home, All Alone* .... 8.00 -　12.00
　　1014 *Next To Mine*.................................. 8.00 -　12.00
　　1015 *Ballin' And Squallin'* .... 30.00 -　50.00
　　1016 *Cochise*... 7.00 -　10.00
　　1018 *Neither Do I* .... 7.00 -　10.00
Metro 20007 *The Party* .... 10.00 -　15.00
MGM 12284 *Stutterin' Papa* .... 30.00 -　50.00
　　12439 *Bow My Back* .... 25.00 -　40.00
　　12597 *Jessie Lee* .... 20.00 -　30.00

CURLEY GRIFFIN:
Atomic 303 *You Gotta Play Fair*....................... 30.00 -　50.00
　　305 *Got Rockin' On My Mind* .... 50.00 -　80.00

GRIFFINS:
Mercury 70558 *I Swear By All The Stars Above* .... 25.00 -　50.00
　　70650 *Scheming* .... 25.00 -　50.00
　　70913 *My Baby's Gone*............................ 20.00 -　30.00
Wing 90067 *Forever More* .... 25.00 -　40.00

JOE GRIFFITH & HIS TEENAGE REBELS:
Reelfoot 1250 *Crazy Sack*.......................... 15.00 -　30.00

PEGGY GRIFFITH:
Now 1008 *Rockin' The Blues*............................... - 　- 　-

SANDRA GRIMES:
Red Robin 129 *You Didn't Give Me A Chance* ...... 10.00 -　20.00

TINY GRIMES:
Red Robin 123 *Juicy Fruit*................................. 15.00 -　20.00

MARLON GRISHAM:
Cover 5982 *Ain't That A Dilly* .... 100.00 -　150.00

BIG BOY GROVES:
Money 217 *Traffic Ticket*............................ 10.00 -　15.00
Spark 114 *I Gotta New Car* .... 15.00 -　20.00
Vita 120 *You Can't Beat The Horses*.................. 8.00 -　12.00

CARL GROVES:
Musicale 116 *Canteen Baby* .... - 　- 　-
MAV 468 *Let's Rock Tonight*................................ 40.00 -　60.00

DON GUESS:
Brunswick 55101 *Shirl-Lee* ....10.00 - 15.00

DANNY GUGLIELMI:
Encino 1001 *Hotrod* .... - - -

THE GUIDES:
Guyden 2023 *You Must Try* ....15.00 - 20.00

GUITAR DAVE:
Central 291 *Zoro* ....5.00 - 8.00

GUITAR FRANK:
Bridges 2203/2204 *Wild Track* ....15.00 - 20.00

GUITAR JR.:
Goldband 1058 *I Got It Made* ....15.00 - 20.00
    1076 *Now You Know* ....8.00 - 12.00
Mercury 71602 *Knocks Me Out* ....8.00 - 12.00

GUITAR SHORTY (with BOB TATE & HIS ORCHESTRA):
Cobra 5017 *Irma Lee* ....30.00 - 50.00
Pull 301 *Hard Life* ....10.00 - 15.00
    302 *How Long Can It Last* ....10.00 - 15.00

GUITAR SLIM: (See also EDDIE JONES)
Atco 6072 *Down Through The Years* ....7.00 - 10.00
    6097 *If I Should Lose You* ....7.00 - 10.00
    6108 *I Won't Mind At All* ....7.00 - 10.00
    6120 *If I Had My Life To Live Over* ....7.00 - 10.00
Diamond 204 *Broke And Lonely* ....10.00 - 15.00
Imperial 5278 *Cryin' In The Morning'* ....20.00 - 30.00
    5310 *Standin' At The Station* ....15.00 - 20.00
Specialty 482 *The Things That I Used To Do* ....10.00 - 15.00
    490 *The Story Of My Life* ....10.00 - 15.00
    527 *Later For You Baby* ....8.00 - 12.00
    536 *Sufferin' Mind* ....8.00 - 12.00
    542 *Stand By Me* ....8.00 - 12.00
    551 *You're Gonna Miss Me* ....8.00 - 12.00
    557 *Think It Over* ....7.00 - 10.00
    569 *You Gave Me Nothin' But The Blues* ....7.00 - 10.00
    (LP) 2120 *Things That I Used to Do* ....80.00 - 130.00

THE GUM DROPS:
King 1496 *Don't Take It So Hard* ....15.00 - 20.00
    4913 *I Wonder And Wonder* ....15.00 - 20.00
    4963 *Chapel Of Hearts* ....15.00 - 20.00

ARTHUR GUNTER:
Excello 2047 *Baby Let's Play House* ....30.00 - 50.00
    2053 *She's Mine All Mine* ....20.00 - 30.00
    2058 *Honey Babe* ....30.00 - 50.00
    2073 *Baby You Better Listen* ....25.00 - 40.00
    2084 *Love Has Got Me* ....25.00 - 40.00
    2125 *Baby Can't You See* ....15.00 - 20.00
    2137 *We're Gonna Shake* ....15.00 - 20.00
    2147 *Don't Leave Me Now* ....15.00 - 20.00
    2164 *I Want Her Back* ....15.00 - 20.00
    2191 *Mind Your Own Business Babe* ....15.00 - 20.00
    2201 *My Heart's Always Lonesome* ....15.00 - 20.00
    2204 *Working For My Baby* ....15.00 - 20.00
    (LP) 8017 *Black And Blues* ....75.00 - 100.00

CORNELL GUNTER (& THE ERMINES):
Eagle 301 *I Want You Madly* ....8.00 - 12.00
Liberty 55096 *If We Should Meet Again* ....5.00 - 10.00
Loma 701 *True Love* ....30.00 - 50.00
    703 *You Broke My Heart* ....50.00 - 80.00
    704 *Keep Me Alive* ....50.00 - 80.00
    705 *I'm Sad* ....50.00 - 80.00

HARDROCK GUNTER:
D 1112 *Traveling* ....8.00 - 12.00
Decca 46300 *Boogie Woogie On Saturday Night* ... 15.00 - 20.00
    46350 *I've Done Gone Hog Wild* ....15.00 - 20.00
    46363 *Sixty Minute Man* ....15.00 - 20.00
    46367 *Dixieland Boogie* ....10.00 - 15.00
King 1505 *I'll Give 'Em Rhythm* ....10.00 - 15.00
Sun 201 *Gonna Dance All Night* ....100.00 - 200.00

SHIRLEY GUNTER (& THE FLAIRS/QUEENS):
Flair 1020 *Since I Fell For You* ....10.00 - 15.00
    1027 *Strange Romance* ....10.00 - 15.00
    1050 *Oop Shoop* ....10.00 - 15.00
    1060 *You're Mine* ....15.00 - 25.00
    1065 *What Difference Does It Make* ....10.00 - 15.00
    1070 *That's The Way I Like It* ....10.00 - 15.00
    1076 *How Can I Tell You* ....20.00 - 30.00
Modern 989 *Headin' Home* ....10.00 - 15.00
Tender (unnumbered) *Crazy Little Baby* ....5.00 - 10.00

BUDDY GUY (& HIS BAND):
Artistic 1501, 1503 ....7.00 - 10.00
Chess 1735, 1759, 1784, 1812, 1838, 1878 ....5.00 - 8.00

BROWLEY GUY (See THE SKYSCRAPERS)

THE GUYTONES:
De Luxe 6144 *You Won't Let Me Go* ....20.00 - 30.00
    6152 *She's Mine* ....20.00 - 30.00
    6159 *This Is Love* ....20.00 - 30.00
    6169 *Tell Me (How Was I To Know)* ....20.00 - 30.00

GYPSIES:
Atlas 1073 *Why* ....25.00 - 40.00
Groove 0137 *Rockin' Pretty Baby* ....8.00 - 12.00

WAYNE HAAS:
Choice 5607 *Betty Ann* ....15.00 - 20.00

VELINE HACKERT:
Brunswick 55151 *Show Me How* ....8.00 - 12.00

JIM HADLEY:
Buddy 117 *Midnight Train* ....25.00 - 40.00

SAMMY HAGAN:
Capitol 3772 *Out Of Your Heart* ....10.00 - 15.00
    3818 *Don't Cry* ....10.00 - 15.00
    3885 *Tail-Light* ....10.00 - 15.00

DON HAGAR:
Oak 0357 *Be Bop Boogie* ....30.00 - 50.00
    0358 *Little Liza Jane Bop* ....20.00 - 40.00

JAY HAGGARD:
Daja 503 *Tom Cat* ....15.00 - 20.00

MERLE HAGGARD (& BONNIE OWENS):
Tally 155 *Sing A Sad Song* ....10.00 - 15.00
    178 *Sam Hill* ....8.00 - 12.00
    179 *Please Mr. D. J.* ....8.00 - 12.00
    181 *Just Between The Two Of Us* ....8.00 - 12.00

JIMMY HAGGETT:
Caprock 107 *All I Have Is Love* ....10.00 - 15.00
Meteor 5043 *Gonna Shut Off Baby* ....75.00 - 100.00
Sun 236 *They Call Our Love A Sin* ....200.00 - 300.00
Vaden 116 *Don't Let Me Go* ....15.00 - 20.00

RONNIE HAIG:
ABC Paramount 9912 *Traveler Of Love* ....10.00 - 15.00
Note 10010 *Don't You Hear Me Calling Baby* ....10.00 - 15.00
    10014 *Rocking With Rhythm And Blues* ....10.00 - 15.00

BROTHER WILL HAIRSTON:
J-V-B 44 *The Alabama Bus* ....50.00 - 100.00

REX HALE:
Rhythm 303 *Down At The Big Mama's House* .... -   -   -

BILL HALEY AND/WITH (HIS/THE COMETS/ SADDLEMEN):
APT 25087 *Tongue-Tied Tony* ....8.00 - 12.00
Atlantic 727 *I'm Gonna Dry Ev'ry Tear With A Kiss* (78 RPM)
....100.00 - 150.00
Cowboy 1202 *Candy Kisses* (78 RPM) ....100.00 - 150.00
   1203 *Yodel Your Blues Away* (78 RPM)...........100.00 - 150.00
   1204 *Behind The 8-Ball* (78 RPM) ....100.00 - 150.00
   1700 *Four Leaf Clover Blues* (78 RPM) ....100.00 - 150.00
   1701 *My Palomino And I* (78 RPM)..................100.00 - 150.00
   1705 *Four Leaf Clover Blues* (78 RPM) ....100.00 - 150.00
Decca (EP) 2168 *Shake, Rattle And Roll*................25.00 - 40.00
   (EP) 2209 *Dim, Dim The Lights* ....25.00 - 40.00
   (EP) 2322 *Rock 'N' Roll* ....25.00 - 40.00
   (EP) 2398, 2399, 2400 *He Digs Rock 'N' Roll*...20.00 - 30.00
   (EP) 2416, 2417, 2418 *Rock 'N' Roll Stage Show*
   ....20.00 - 30.00
   (EP) 2532 *Rockin' The Oldies* ....20.00 - 30.00
   (EP) 2564 *Rockin' Around The World*................20.00 - 30.00
   (EP) 2615, 2616 *Rockin' The Joint*....................25.00 - 40.00
   (EP) 2670 *Bill Haley & His Comets* ....25.00 - 40.00
   (EP) 2671 *Top Teen Hits* ....20.00 - 30.00
   (LP) 5560 (10 inch) *Shake, Rattle And Roll* .....100.00 - 150.00
   (LP) 8225 *Rock Around The Clock*.....................75.00 - 100.00
   (LP) 8315 *He Digs Rock 'N' Roll* ....40.00 - 60.00
   (LP) 8345 *Rock 'N' Roll Stage Show* ....40.00 - 60.00
   (LP) 8569 *Rockin' The Oldies* ....40.00 - 60.00
   (LP) 8655 *Let's Have A Party* ....40.00 - 60.00
   (LP) 8692 *Rockin' Around The World*................40.00 - 60.00
   (LP) 8775 *Rockin' The Joint*...............................40.00 - 60.00
Decca 29124 *Rock Around The Clock* (black label)..8.00 - 12.00
   29124 *Rock Around The Clock* (DJ copy) ....25.00 - 40.00
Decca (most other issues) ....5.00 - 10.00
Essex (EP) 102 *Bill Haley's Dance Party* ....100.00 - 150.00
   (EP) 117, 118 *Rock With Bill Haley And The Comets*
   ....100.00 - 150.00
   (LP) 202 *Rock With Bill Haley And The Comets*
   ....150.00 - 200.00
   303 *Rock The Joint*..25.00 - 40.00
   305 *Rocking Chair On The Moon*........................20.00 - 30.00
   310 *Real Rock Drive* ....15.00 - 20.00
   321 *Crazy Man Crazy* ....20.00 - 30.00
   327 *Fractured* ....20.00 - 30.00
   332 *Live It Up* ....15.00 - 25.00
   340 *I'll Be True*..20.00 - 30.00
   348 *Straight Jacket* ....25.00 - 50.00
   374 *Sundown Boogie* ....25.00 - 50.00
   381 *Rocket 88* ....25.00 - 50.00
   399 *Rock The Joint*...15.00 - 25.00
Gone 5116 *War Paint* ....10.00 - 15.00
Holiday 105 *Rocket 88*.......................................100.00 - 200.00
   108 *Green Tree Boogie*....................................100.00 - 200.00
   110 *Pretty Baby* ....100.00 - 200.00
   111 *A Year Ago This Christmas* ....100.00 - 200.00
   113 *Jukebox Cannonball* ....100.00 - 200.00
Keystone 5101 *Deal Me A Hand* (78 RPM) ....150.00 - up
   5102 *I'm Not To Blame* (78 RPM)......................150.00 - up
Radioactive 45 *Rock The Joint* .... -   -   -
   46 *Rock-A-Beatin' Boogie* .... -   -   -
   50 *Crazy Man Crazy* .... -   -   -

Somerset (LP) 4600 *Rock With Bill Haley And The Comets*
....20.00 - 40.00
Transworld (LP) 202.. -   -   -
   318 *Rocket 88*..30.00 - 50.00
   718 *Yes Indeed* ....20.00 - 30.00
Warner Bros. (LP) 1378 *Comets*............................40.00 - 60.00
   5145 *Candy Kisses* ....8.00 - 12.00
   5154 *Chick Safari* ....7.00 - 10.00
   5171 *So Right Tonight* ....7.00 - 10.00
   5228 *Flip, Flop And Fly*.......................................7.00 - 10.00

HALL BROTHERS:
Arc 4444 *My White Convertible* ....15.00 - 20.00

BOBBY HALL & THE KINGS:
Harlem 2322 *Fire In My Heart* (red plastic).........300.00 - up
   2322 *Fire In My Heart* (black plastic) ....80.00 - 130.00
Jax 314 *Why? Oh, Why?* (red plastic) ....150.00 - 200.00
   316 *You Made Me Cry* ....75.00 - 100.00
   320 *Sunday Kind Of Love* ....75.00 - 100.00

FOX HALL:
Limelight 3003 *Do The Rock And Roll*....................8.00 - 12.00

FREDDIE HALL (& THE NIGHT ROCKERS):
Abco 103 *Playin' Hard to Get* ....40.00 - 70.00
Chance 1159 *Knock Me Out* ....50.00 - 80.00
C.J. 601 *She's An Upsetter* (blue label) ....20.00 - 30.00
   610 *Love And Affection* (red label) ....20.00 - 30.00

LARRY HALL:
Strand (LP) 1005 *Sandy* ....40.00 - 70.00

ROY HALL (& HIS JUMPING CATS); ROY HALL'S ALLEY CATS:
Decca 29696 *Whole Lotta Shakin'* ....20.00 - 30.00
   29786 *See You Later, Alligator*...........................20.00 - 30.00
   29820 *Blue Suede Shoes* ....20.00 - 30.00
   30060 *Three Alley Cats*......................................20.00 - 30.00
Fortune *Goin' Down The Road Feelin' Bad*.............. -   -
Hi-Q 5045 *Three Alley Cats* ....15.00 - 25.00
   5050 *Go Go, Little Queenie* ....15.00 - 25.00
Pierce - *One Monkey Can't Stop The Show*.............. -   -   -

SONNY HALL:
D 1035 *The Day You Walked Away* ....15.00 - 25.00

ROY HALLAWAY:
CM 12964 *I Received Your Letter* ....7.00 - 10.00

THE HALLIQUINS:
Juanita 102 *Confession Of Love*...........................300.00 - up

JOHNNY HALO:
Angeltone 538 *Little Annie* ....8.00 - 12.00

THE HALOS:
7 Arts 709 *Copy Cat* ....5.00 - 8.00
Warwick (LP) 2046 *The Halos* ....80.00 - 120.00

KENNY HAMBER:
Spar 101 *Tears In My Eyes* ....20.00 - 30.00
Zenette 101 *Tears In My Eyes* ....30.00 - 50.00

STUART HAMBLEN:
Coral (LP) 57254 *Remember Me* ....20.00 - 30.00
Harmony (LP) 7009 *Hymns* ....15.00 - 25.00
RCA Victor (LP) 1253 *It Is No Secret* ....20.00 - 30.00
   (LP) 1436 *Grand Old Hymns* ....15.00 - 20.00

GEORGE HAMILTON IV:
ABC Paramount (LP) 220, 251 ....15.00 - 20.00
   9765 *If You Don't Know* (78 RPM) ....10.00 - 15.00
Colonial 420 *If You Don't Know* ....10.00 - 15.00

MACK HAMILTON:
Feature 1087 *I'm A Honky-Tonk Daddy* ....20.00 - 30.00

WALTER HAMILTON:
Fortune 849 *Sherry Blues* ....10.00 - 15.00

JACK HAMMER & PACERS:
Milestone 2001 *Black Widow Spider Woman* ....20.00 - 30.00

CURLEY HAMNER:
Fling 720 *Piano Tuner*.........................40.00 - 60.00

JOHN HAMPTON:
United 210 *Honey Hush*.........................30.00 - 50.00

PAUL HAMPTON:
Columbia 41037 *Play It Cool* ....10.00 - 15.00
   41145 *Slam Bam Thank Ya Ma'm* ....10.00 - 15.00

WAYNE HANDY (& THE MELODY MASTERS):
Renown 102 *Say Yeah* ....5.00 - 8.00
   104 *Betcha' Didn't Know* ....7.00 - 10.00
Trend 30-006 *Betcha' Didn't Know* ....5.00 - 8.00
   30-015 *I Think You Oughta Look Again*...........5.00 - 8.00

HANK & THE ELECTRAS:
Dauphin 106 *Get Lost Baby*.....................10.00 - 15.00

MIKE HANKS & THE CONTOURS:
Brax 22 *Can I Be Your Lover Boy* ....50.00 - 80.00

TYE TONGUE HANLEY:
JVB 88 *I'll Try To Understand*.................50.00 - 100.00

RUDY HANSEN:
Decca (most issues) ....4.00 - 7.00
Rudy Hansen 1226 *Saturday Jump*.................10.00 - 15.00

KIRK HANSERD WITH BILL CARRIGAN'S TOP BOP BAND:
Dot 1281 *My Heart's Broke Baby* ....8.00 - 12.00

HAPPY TEENS:
Paradise 114 *One More Kiss*.....................10.00 - 15.00

DOUG HARDEN & THE DESERT SONS:
Liberty Bell 9006 *Dig That Ford*................15.00 - 20.00

BOBBY HARDIN:
Westwood 202 *I'm Loving You Baby* ....30.00 - 50.00

JIM HARDIN:
Volcano 100 *High Stepping Woman*.................25.00 - 40.00

PETE HARDIN:
Peach 748 *Baby Be My Chickadee* ....30.00 - 50.00

BERNARD HARDISON:
Republic 7111 *Too Much*.........................15.00 - 20.00

HARDROCK & THE RHYTHM ROCKERS:
Emperor 112 *Whoo! I Mean Whee!!* ....40.00 - 70.00

BILL HARDY:
Rita 1001 *Rockin At The Zoo*....................20.00 - 30.00

JOHNNIE HARGETT:
Cherry 1016 *Rock The Town Tonight* ....25.00 - 50.00

RON HARGRAVE:
M-G-M 12422 *Latch On*...........................20.00 - 30.00

FREDDIE HARKEY:
Hillcrest 1805 *Marooned On An Island*............8.00 - 12.00

BILLY HARLAN:
Brunswick 55066 *I Wanna Bop* ....20.00 - 30.00

BOB HARMON:
Decca 29872 *Kentucky Home Boogie* ....8.00 - 12.00

HARMONAIRES:
Holiday 2602 *Lorraine* (black label) ....30.00 - 60.00

HARMONICA FATS:
DArcel 5000, 5003................................5.00 - 8.00
Star-A-Fire 100 *Tore Up* ....15.00 - 20.00

HARMONICA FRANK:
F & L 100 *Rock A Little Baby*..................100.00 - 150.00
Sun 205 *Rockin' Chair Daddy* ....200.00 - 300.00

HARMONICA JOE:
Skymac 1008 *Look Here Mama*.....................7.00 - 10.00

HARMONICA KID:
Nucraft 114 *Martha Lee*.........................15.00 - 20.00
   2022 *Jole Blon* ....15.00 - 20.00

HARMONICA KING:
Lapel 103 *Hot Rolls* ....20.00 - 30.00

HARMONICA SLIM:
Aladdin 3317 *Lonely Hours*......................10.00 - 15.00
Cenco 1001 *I'll Take Love* ....7.00 - 10.00
Spry 103 *Going Back Home*.......................10.00 - 15.00
Vita 138 *You Better Believe It*.................7.00 - 10.00
   146 *Drop Anchor* ....7.00 - 10.00

THE HARMONY BROTHERS:
Bobbin 109 *Baby, Tonight* ....30.00 - 50.00
   116 *Saturday Night Bop*...................30.00 - 50.00

HARMONY GRITS:
End 1051 *I Could Have Told You* ....15.00 - 25.00
   1063 *Gee* ....8.00 - 12.00

HAROLD & THE CASUALS:
Scotty 628 *Darling Do You Love Me*...............75.00 - 100.00

BEN HARPER & THE CINCO'S:
Skylark 112 *Union Station Blues*................10.00 - 15.00
Talent 106 *Drive Way Blues* ....7.00 - 10.00

BIG BUD HARPER WITH O. S. GRANT & THE DOWNBEATS:
Harlem 117 *Never Let Me Go* ....15.00 - 20.00

SONNY HARPER:
Ball 1011 *Lonely Stranger* ....5.00 - 8.00

SLIM HARPO:
Excello 2113 *I'm A King Bee*....................15.00 - 20.00
   2138 *Strange Love* ....10.00 - 15.00
   2162, 2171, 2184, 2194.....................8.00 - 12.00
   (LP) 8003 *Raining In My Heart*............50.00 - 80.00
   (LP) 8005 *Baby Scratch My Back*...........50.00 - 80.00

THE HARPTONES:
Andrea 100 *What is Your Decision* (rope-like lines on label)
....15.00 - 25.00
Bruce 101 *A Sunday Kind Of Love* (maroon label). 30.00 - 50.00
   102 *The Laugh's On You* ....25.00 - 40.00
   104 *I Depended On You*....................25.00 - 40.00
   109 *Forever Mine* ....20.00 - 30.00
   113 *Since I Fell For You* ....15.00 - 20.00
   123 *Loving A Girl Like You* ....20.00 - 30.00
   128 *I Almost Lost My Mind*................20.00 - 30.00
   (EP) 201 *The Sensational*....................rare
Companion 103 *Foolish Me*.......................30.00 - 50.00
Cub 9097 *Your Love Is A Good Love* ....8.00 - 12.00

Essex 364 *Honey Love* ....20.00 - 30.00
Gee 1045 *Cry Like I Cried*..............................15.00 - 20.00
KT 201 *I Gotta Have Your Love*........................15.00 - 20.00
Paradise 101 *Life Is But A Dream* (maroon label)...30.00 - 50.00
 103 *My Success (It All Depends On You)*..........30.00 - 50.00
Rama 203 *Three Wishes* ....20.00 - 30.00
 214 *On Sunday Afternoon*..........................20.00 - 30.00
 221 *The Shrine Of St. Cecilia* ....20.00 - 30.00
Raven 8001 *Mambo Boogie*............................7.00 - 10.00
Tip Top 401 *My Memories Of You* ....25.00 - 40.00
Warwick 500 *I Remember* ....8.00 - 12.00
 512 *Love Me Completely* ....8.00 - 12.00
 551 *No Greater Miracle* ....8.00 - 12.00

HANK HARRAL:
Cap Rock 100 *Fabulous Oklahoma*........................5.00 - 8.00
 102 *The D. J. Blues*................................15.00 - 20.00
 104 *Tank Town Boogie* ....20.00 - 30.00
 114 *Oklahoma Land* ....5.00 - 8.00

BILL HARRIS:
Eagle 1002 *Danny Boy* ....15.00 - 20.00

GENEE HARRIS:
ABC Paramount 9900 *Bye Bye Elvis*....................10.00 - 15.00

GEORGIA HARRIS & THE HYTONES:
Hy-Tone 121 *Let Me Hold Your Hand* ....50.00 - 100.00

JOHNNY RAY HARRIS:
Ray's 100 *Cajun Weekend*..............................- - -

PEPPERMINT HARRIS:
Aladdin 3097 *I Got Loaded* ....30.00 - 50.00
 3107 *Have Another Drink And Talk To Me* ....- - -
 3108 *P. H. Blues* ....- - -
 3130 *Maggie's Boogie* ....- - -
 3141 *There's A Dead Cat On The Line* ....- - -
 3154 *Hey Little Schoolgirl* ....- - -
 3177 *Wasted Love* ....- - -
 3183 *Don't Leave Me Alone* ....- - -
 3206 *Three Sheets In The Wind* ....20.00 - 30.00
(Unpriced Aladdin records exist in 78 RPM format, valued at $7.00 - $15.00; existence of 45s has not been verified, but values would be substantially higher than for 78s)
Dart 103 *You Got Me Wonderin'* ....7.00 - 10.00
Duke 319 *Angel Child* ....5.00 - 8.00
Money 214 *Cadillac Funeral* ....10.00 - 15.00
"X" 0142 *Need Your Lovin'* ....10.00 - 15.00

RAY HARRIS:
Sun 254 *Come On Little Mama* ....30.00 - 50.00
 272 *Greenback Dollar* ....40.00 - 60.00

THURSTON HARRIS:
Aladdin 3398 *Little Bitty Pretty One* (78 RPM).......15.00 - 25.00
 3415, 3428 ....7.00 - 10.00

WILLARD HARRIS:
Ekko 2001 *Talking Off The Wall* ....50.00 - 80.00

WYNONIE HARRIS (See also BATTLE OF THE BLUES and PARTY AFTER HOURS):
Atco 6081 *Destination Love* ....7.00 - 10.00
King (EP) 260 *Good Rockin' Tonight* ....200.00 - 300.00
 4210 *Good Rockin' Tonight*.........................50.00 - 100.00
 4461 *Blood Shot Eyes* ....25.00 - 40.00
 4485 *Loving Machine* ....25.00 - 40.00
 4526 *Keep On Churnin'*...............................20.00 - 30.00
King 4555 *Night Train*................................20.00 - 30.00
 4592 *Greyhound* ....20.00 - 30.00

 4620 *Wasn't That Good?* ....20.00 - 30.00
 4635 *The Deacon Doesn't Like It* ....20.00 - 30.00
(Note: First pressings of early KING issues should not have the designation "High Fidelity" and should have the suffixes "A" or "AA" after the catalog numbers. Records pressed of colored plastic can bring substantially higher prices.)
King 4662 *Tremblin'*.................................15.00 - 20.00
 4685 *Quiet Whiskey* ....15.00 - 20.00
 4716 *Shake That Thing* ....15.00 - 20.00
 4763 *Christina* ....10.00 - 20.00
 4774 *Git To Gettin' Baby* ....10.00 - 20.00
 4789 *Fishtail Blues* ....10.00 - 20.00
 4814 *Drinkin' Sherry Wine* ....10.00 - 20.00
 4826 *Wine, Wine, Sweet Wine* ....10.00 - 20.00
 4839 *I Don't Know Where To Go* ....10.00 - 20.00
 4852 *Good Morning Judge* ....10.00 - 20.00
 5050 *Big Ole Country Fool*..........................10.00 - 15.00
 5073 *A Tale Of Woe* ....10.00 - 15.00

DANNY & AUDREY HARRISON:
Event 4273 *Rock-A-Billy Boogie* ....15.00 - 25.00

JOHNNY HARRISON:
Starday 373 *I Don't Want A Sweetheart*...................- - -

LEE HARRISON (Backed by THE KOUNTS):
Pearl 717 *So Unimportant*.....................................20.00 - 30.00

WILBERT HARRISON:
De Luxe 6002 *The Letter* ....20.00 - 30.00
 6031 *Gin And Coconut Milk* ....15.00 - 20.00
Fury 1023 *Kansas City* (78 RPM) ....80.00 - 130.00
 1028 *"1960"* (78 RPM) ....30.00 - 50.00
Rockin' 526 *The Letter* ....15.00 - 20.00
Savoy 1149 *Women And Whiskey*........................5.00 - 8.00
 1164 *Florida Special*................................5.00 - 8.00
 1198, 1517, 1531, 1571............................4.00 - 8.00
Sphere (LP) 7000 *Kansas City*...........................25.00 - 40.00

CHUCK HARROD:
Champion 1013 *They Wanna Fight* ....- - -

BILLY & DON HART:
Roulette 4133 *Rock-A-Bop-A-Lina* ....10.00 - 15.00

CASEY HART:
Choice 14 *Blues For My Baby* ....8.00 - 12.00

FREDDIE HART:
Columbia (LP) 1792 *The Spirited Freddie Hart*..... 30.00 - 50.00
 21512, 21550, 41005..............................7.00 - 10.00

LARRY HART:
Goldband 1070 *I'm Just A Mender* ....10.00 - 15.00
Okeh 7077 *Looka Looka* ....10.00 - 15.00

HARVEY (& THE MOONGLOWS):
Chess 1705 *Ten Commandments Of Love* ....7.00 - 10.00
 1705 *Ten Commandments Of Love* (78 RPM) ......- - -
 1713 *I Want Somebody* ....7.00 - 10.00
 1725 *Twelve Months Of The Year*.....................7.00 - 10.00
 1738 *Mama Loocie* ....7.00 - 10.00
 1749 *Blue Skies* ....7.00 - 10.00
 1781 *The First Time* ....7.00 - 10.00

HARVEY SISTERS:
Newtime 5128 *Kiss Of Love* ....15.00 - 30.00

WAYNE HASS (See HAAS)

MARC HAVEN:
Villa Yore 201 *Janice*.......................................- - -

SHIRLEY HAVEN & THE FOUR JACKS:
Federal 12092 *Troubles Of My Own* ....50.00 - 80.00

"HAVING A BALL":
End (LP) 302 (The Chantels, The Dubs, et al) ....50.00 - 100.00

HAWK:
Phillips 3559 *In The Mood* ....15.00 - 20.00

HAWKETTES:
Chess 1591 *Your Time's Up* ....15.00 - 20.00

DALE HAWKINS:
Checker 843 *See You Soon Baboon* ....15.00 - 20.00
   863 *Susie-Q* (78 RPM)....................................30.00 - 50.00
   863 *Susie-Q*...10.00 - 15.00
   876 *Baby, Baby*...15.00 - 20.00
   876 *Baby, Baby* (78 RPM)..............................40.00 - 60.00
   892 *Tornado*..15.00 - 20.00
   900 *Cross-Ties* ....15.00 - 20.00
   906 *My Babe* (78 RPM) ....50.00 - 80.00
   906 *My Babe* ....15.00 - 20.00
   913 *Someday One Day*...................................15.00 - 20.00
   916 *Class Cutter (Yeah Yeah)*........................15.00 - 20.00
   923 *Ain't That Lovin' You Baby* ....15.00 - 20.00
   929 *Our Turn* ....15.00 - 20.00
   934 *Liza Jane*...15.00 - 20.00
   940 *Hot Dog* ....15.00 - 20.00
   944 *Every Little Girl* ....20.00 - 30.00
   962 *Linda* ....15.00 - 20.00
   970 *I Want To Love You* ....15.00 - 20.00
   (LP) 1429 *Oh! Suzy-Q* (black label, yellow cover)
   ....150.00 - 200.00
Tilt 781 *Money Honey* ....5.00 - 8.00

HAWKSHAW HAWKINS:
King (LP) 587, 592..25.00 - 50.00

SCREAMIN' JAY HAWKINS:
Apollo 506 *Please Try To Understand* ....15.00 - 20.00
   528 *Baptize Me in Wine* ....15.00 - 20.00
Epic (LP) 3448 *At Home With Screamin' Jay*........100.00 - 150.00
Okeh 7072 *I Put a Spell On You* ....7.00 - 10.00
   7084 *You Made Me Love You* ....7.00 - 10.00
   7101 *Alligator Wine* ....8.00 - 12.00
Phillips 40645 *Constipation Blues* ....8.00 - 12.00
Wing 90005 *Well I Tried* ....10.00 - 15.00

RONNIE HAWKINS (& THE HAWKS):
Roulette 4154 *Forty Days*......................................7.00 - 10.00
   4209 *Love Me Like You Can*...........................8.00 - 12.00
   4228 *Lonely Hours* ....8.00 - 12.00
Roulette 4231, 4249, 4267, 4311, 4483, 4502..........5.00 - 10.00
Roulette (LP) 25078 *Ronnie Hawkins* ....50.00 - 80.00
   (LP) 25102 *Mr. Dynamo*................................50.00 - 80.00

ROY HAWKINS:
Rhythm 120 *I Hate To Be Alone*............................15.00 - 20.00
RPM 440 *Is It Too Late* ....20.00 - 30.00

HAWKS:
Imperial 5266 *Candy Girl*.....................................50.00 - 80.00
   5292 *It Ain't That Way* ....25.00 - 40.00
   5306 *Nobody But You* ....25.00 - 40.00
   5317 *That's What You Are* ....20.00 - 30.00
Modern 990 *It's All Over*......................................50.00 - 80.00
Post 2004 *These Blues* ....50.00 - 80.00

MICKEY HAWKS (with MOON MULLINS & HIS NIGHT RAIDERS):
Profile 4002 *Bip Bop Boom*...................................15.00 - 20.00

   4007 *Hidi Hidi Hidi* ....10.00 - 15.00
   4010 *Screamin' Mimi Jeanie* ....10.00 - 15.00

RUDY HAYDEN:
Aragon 279 *Want Me A Woman* ....10.00 - 15.00

WILLIE HAYDEN:
Dooto (LP) 293 *Blame It On The Blues*.................80.00 - 120.00

RON HAYDOCK:
Cha Cha 701 *Be-Bop-A-Jean* ....50.00 - 100.00

JIMMY HAYES:
Happy Hearts 141 *Tom Cat Boogie* ....10.00 - 15.00

LINDA HAYES (& THE PLATTERS):
Hollywood 244 *Yes I Know* ....15.00 - 30.00
   246 *Big City* ....- - -
   1003 *Yours For The Asking* ....10.00 - 15.00
   1009 *No Next Time* ....10.00 - 15.00
   1016 *Play It Right* ....10.00 - 15.00
   1019 *Non Cooperation* ....10.00 - 15.00
   1027 *Change Of Heart*...................................10.00 - 15.00
   1031 *Why, Johnny, Why*.................................10.00 - 15.00
King 4752 *My Name Ain't Annie*...........................30.00 - 50.00
   4773 *Please Have Mercy* ....30.00 - 50.00

DON HEAD:
Dub 2840 *Goin' Strong*..10.00 - 15.00

ROY HEAD & THE TRAITS (See also THE TRAITS):
Suave 712 *Teen-Age Letter*..................................10.00 - 15.00
TNT (LP) 101 *Roy Head And The Traits*...............100.00 - 150.00

WILLIE HEADEN & THE FIVE BIRDS:
Authentic 410 *Let Me Cry* ....10.00 - 15.00

JIMMY HEAP:
Capitol 3156 *Sebbin Come Elebbin* ....7.00 - 10.00
Fame 502 *Little Jewel* ....10.00 - 15.00

ABE HEAPE:
Rose 116 *Short Fellow Blues* ....15.00 - 25.00

BUDDY HEARD & HIS COMBO:
Red Top 501 *Let's Rock With Me* ....20.00 - 30.00

HEARTBEATS; HEART BEATS:
Gee 1043 *When I Found You* ....10.00 - 15.00
   1047 *After New Year's Eve* ....10.00 - 15.00
   1061 *People Are Talking* ....10.00 - 15.00
   1062 *Hurry Home Baby* ....8.00 - 12.00
Guyden 2011 *One Million Tears* ....15.00 - 20.00
Hull 711 *Crazy For You* (pink label) ....20.00 - 30.00
   713 *Darling How Long* ....20.00 - 30.00
   716 *People Are Talking* ....20.00 - 30.00
   720 *A Thousand Miles Away*...........................25.00 - 40.00
Network 71200 *Tormented* ....30.00 - 50.00
Rama 216 *A Thousand Miles Away* ....8.00 - 12.00
(Note: *Label variations exist; some bring higher prices.)
   216 *A Thousand Miles Away* (78 RPM) ....20.00 - 30.00
   222 *Wedding Bells* ....10.00 - 15.00
   231 *Everybody's Somebody's Fool* ....10.00 - 15.00
Roulette 4054 *Down On My Knees*........................10.00 - 15.00
   4091 *One Day Next Year* ....8.00 - 12.00
   4194 *Crazy For You*.......................................8.00 - 12.00
   (LP) 25017 *A Thousand Miles Away* ....80.00 - 120.00

HEARTBREAKERS:
Linda 114 *Please Answer*......................................5.00 - 8.00
RCA Victor 4327 *Heartbreaker* ....75.00 - 100.00
   4508 *You're So Necessary To Me* ....75.00 - 100.00

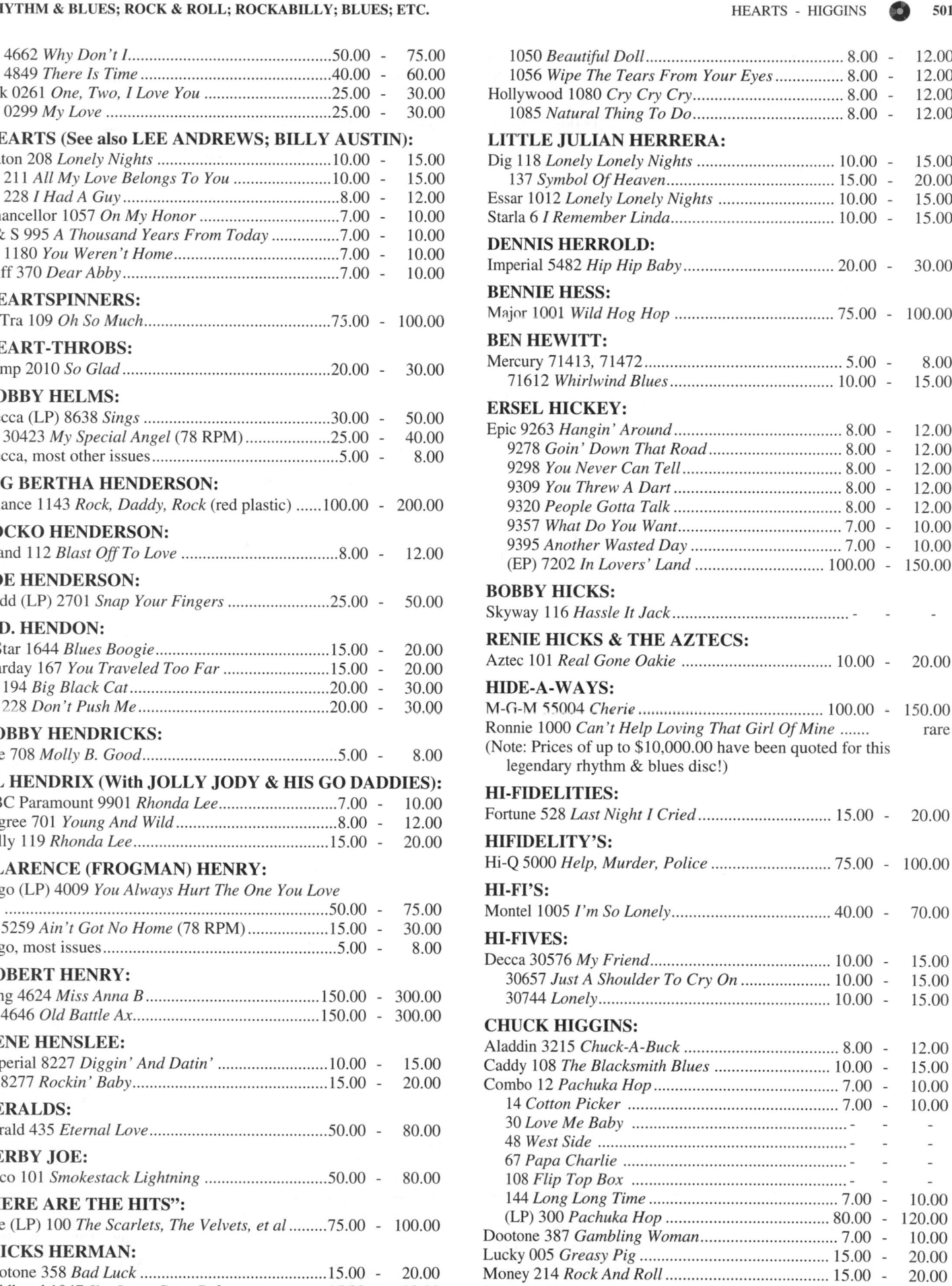

4662 *Why Don't I* ....50.00 - 75.00
4849 *There Is Time* ....40.00 - 60.00
Vik 0261 *One, Two, I Love You* ....25.00 - 30.00
0299 *My Love* ....25.00 - 30.00

HEARTS (See also LEE ANDREWS; BILLY AUSTIN):
Baton 208 *Lonely Nights* ....10.00 - 15.00
211 *All My Love Belongs To You* ....10.00 - 15.00
228 *I Had A Guy* ....8.00 - 12.00
Chancellor 1057 *On My Honor* ....7.00 - 10.00
J & S 995 *A Thousand Years From Today* ....7.00 - 10.00
1180 *You Weren't Home* ....7.00 - 10.00
Tuff 370 *Dear Abby* ....7.00 - 10.00

HEARTSPINNERS:
X-Tra 109 *Oh So Much* ....75.00 - 100.00

HEART-THROBS:
Lamp 2010 *So Glad* ....20.00 - 30.00

BOBBY HELMS:
Decca (LP) 8638 *Sings* ....30.00 - 50.00
30423 *My Special Angel* (78 RPM) ....25.00 - 40.00
Decca, most other issues ....5.00 - 8.00

BIG BERTHA HENDERSON:
Chance 1143 *Rock, Daddy, Rock* (red plastic) ......100.00 - 200.00

JOCKO HENDERSON:
Wand 112 *Blast Off To Love* ....8.00 - 12.00

JOE HENDERSON:
Todd (LP) 2701 *Snap Your Fingers* ....25.00 - 50.00

R.D. HENDON:
4 Star 1644 *Blues Boogie* ....15.00 - 20.00
Starday 167 *You Traveled Too Far* ....15.00 - 20.00
194 *Big Black Cat* ....20.00 - 30.00
228 *Don't Push Me* ....20.00 - 30.00

BOBBY HENDRICKS:
Sue 708 *Molly B. Good* ....5.00 - 8.00

AL HENDRIX (With JOLLY JODY & HIS GO DADDIES):
ABC Paramount 9901 *Rhonda Lee* ....7.00 - 10.00
Lagree 701 *Young And Wild* ....8.00 - 12.00
Tally 119 *Rhonda Lee* ....15.00 - 20.00

CLARENCE (FROGMAN) HENRY:
Argo (LP) 4009 *You Always Hurt The One You Love*
....50.00 - 75.00
5259 *Ain't Got No Home* (78 RPM) ....15.00 - 30.00
Argo, most issues ....5.00 - 8.00

ROBERT HENRY:
King 4624 *Miss Anna B* ....150.00 - 300.00
4646 *Old Battle Ax* ....150.00 - 300.00

GENE HENSLEE:
Imperial 8227 *Diggin' And Datin'* ....10.00 - 15.00
8277 *Rockin' Baby* ....15.00 - 20.00

HERALDS:
Herald 435 *Eternal Love* ....50.00 - 80.00

HERBY JOE:
Abco 101 *Smokestack Lightning* ....50.00 - 80.00

"HERE ARE THE HITS":
Fire (LP) 100 *The Scarlets, The Velvets, et al* ....75.00 - 100.00

STICKS HERMAN:
Dootone 358 *Bad Luck* ....15.00 - 20.00
Goldband 1047 *I'm Long Gone Baby* ....15.00 - 20.00

1050 *Beautiful Doll* ....8.00 - 12.00
1056 *Wipe The Tears From Your Eyes* ....8.00 - 12.00
Hollywood 1080 *Cry Cry Cry* ....8.00 - 12.00
1085 *Natural Thing To Do* ....8.00 - 12.00

LITTLE JULIAN HERRERA:
Dig 118 *Lonely Lonely Nights* ....10.00 - 15.00
137 *Symbol Of Heaven* ....15.00 - 20.00
Essar 1012 *Lonely Lonely Nights* ....10.00 - 15.00
Starla 6 *I Remember Linda* ....10.00 - 15.00

DENNIS HERROLD:
Imperial 5482 *Hip Hip Baby* ....20.00 - 30.00

BENNIE HESS:
Major 1001 *Wild Hog Hop* ....75.00 - 100.00

BEN HEWITT:
Mercury 71413, 71472 ....5.00 - 8.00
71612 *Whirlwind Blues* ....10.00 - 15.00

ERSEL HICKEY:
Epic 9263 *Hangin' Around* ....8.00 - 12.00
9278 *Goin' Down That Road* ....8.00 - 12.00
9298 *You Never Can Tell* ....8.00 - 12.00
9309 *You Threw A Dart* ....8.00 - 12.00
9320 *People Gotta Talk* ....8.00 - 12.00
9357 *What Do You Want* ....7.00 - 10.00
9395 *Another Wasted Day* ....7.00 - 10.00
(EP) 7202 *In Lovers' Land* ....100.00 - 150.00

BOBBY HICKS:
Skyway 116 *Hassle It Jack* .... -   -   -

RENIE HICKS & THE AZTECS:
Aztec 101 *Real Gone Oakie* ....10.00 - 20.00

HIDE-A-WAYS:
M-G-M 55004 *Cherie* ....100.00 - 150.00
Ronnie 1000 *Can't Help Loving That Girl Of Mine* .... rare
(Note: Prices of up to $10,000.00 have been quoted for this
legendary rhythm & blues disc!)

HI-FIDELITIES:
Fortune 528 *Last Night I Cried* ....15.00 - 20.00

HIFIDELITY'S:
Hi-Q 5000 *Help, Murder, Police* ....75.00 - 100.00

HI-FI'S:
Montel 1005 *I'm So Lonely* ....40.00 - 70.00

HI-FIVES:
Decca 30576 *My Friend* ....10.00 - 15.00
30657 *Just A Shoulder To Cry On* ....10.00 - 15.00
30744 *Lonely* ....10.00 - 15.00

CHUCK HIGGINS:
Aladdin 3215 *Chuck-A-Buck* ....8.00 - 12.00
Caddy 108 *The Blacksmith Blues* ....10.00 - 15.00
Combo 12 *Pachuka Hop* ....7.00 - 10.00
14 *Cotton Picker* ....7.00 - 10.00
30 *Love Me Baby* .... -   -   -
48 *West Side* .... -   -   -
67 *Papa Charlie* .... -   -   -
108 *Flip Top Box* .... -   -   -
144 *Long Long Time* ....7.00 - 10.00
(LP) 300 *Pachuka Hop* ....80.00 - 120.00
Dootone 387 *Gambling Woman* ....7.00 - 10.00
Lucky 005 *Greasy Pig* ....15.00 - 20.00
Money 214 *Rock And Roll* ....15.00 - 20.00
Specialty 532 *Broke* ....7.00 - 10.00

THE HIGHLANDERS:
Ray's 36 *Sunday Kind Of Love* ....80.00 - 120.00

DONNA HIGHTOWER:
RPM 432 *Love Me Again* ....15.00 - 20.00
   481 *I Ain't Gonna Tell* ....10.00 - 15.00

WILLIE HIGHTOWER:
Fury 5002 *If I Had A Hammer* ....5.00 - 8.00

"HIGHWAY OF BLUES":
Audio Lab (LP) 1520 *(Brownie McGhee, John Lee Hooker)*
....75.00 - 125.00

THE HI-LITERS:
Mercury 71342 *Dance Me To Death* ....5.00 - 8.00

HILITES/HI-LITES:
Okeh 7046 *I Found A Love* ....75.00 - 100.00
Omen 4 *One By One* ....40.00 - 70.00

FARRIS HILL & FRIENDS/THE MADISON BROTHERS:
Cool 501 *Sexy Ways* ....10.00 - 15.00
V-Tone 231 *Did We Go Steady Too Soon* ....15.00 - 20.00

HARVEY HILL, JR.:
SRC 104 *Boogie Woogie Woman* ....30.00 - 50.00

HENRY HILL:
Federal 12030 *Sunday Morning Blues* ....100.00 - 150.00
   12037 *Hold Me Baby* ....75.00 - 100.00
   12044 *If You Love Me* ....75.00 - 100.00
   12053 *My Baby Is Back Home* ....75.00 - 100.00

J.C. HILL:
Argo 5311 *Only True Love* ....10.00 - 15.00

JAYCEE HILL:
Epic 9185 *Romp Stompin' Boogie* ....15.00 - 20.00
   9193 *Crash-Out* ....10.00 - 15.00

JOEL HILL:
Trans Amer. 519 *Little Lover* ....15.00 - 25.00

RAYMOND HILL:
Sun 204 *The Snuggle* ....200.00 - 300.00

"HILLBILLY JAMBORIEE":
Starday (LP) 101 *(various artists)* ....40.00 - 60.00

CLAYTON HILLIS:
Linco 1319 *Rock City Rock* ....10.00 - 15.00

JOE HINTON:
Back Beat 519 *Ladder Of Prayer* ....7.00 - 10.00

OTIS HINTON:
Timely 1003 *Walkin' Downhill* ....50.00 - 75.00

THE HI-TENSIONS:
Audio *201 The Clock* ....50.00 - 80.00
K & G 101 *So Far Away* ....15.00 - 20.00
Milestone 2018 *Ebbing Of The Tide* ....20.00 - 30.00

THE HI TIMERS:
Sonic 1502 *You're Everything* ....80.00 - 130.00

THE HI-TONES:
Fonsca 201 *Just For You* ....10.00 - 15.00
Seg-Way 105 *Sure As The Flowers* ....80.00 - 120.00

CURTIS HOBECK:
Lu 508 *China Rock* ....25.00 - 40.00

GARY HODGE:
Dolton 7 *Not For Love Or Money* ....7.00 - 10.00

RALPH HODGES:
Whispering Pines 61 *Honey Talk* ....10.00 - 15.00

BASH HOFNER:
Sarg 138 *Rockin' And A-Boppin'* ....- -

CARL HOGAN (See THE MIRACLES):

SILAS HOGAN:
Excello 2221, 2231, 2241, 2251, 2255, 2266,
   2270, 2271 ....5.00 - 10.00

SMOKEY/SMOKY HOGG:
Combo 4 *Bottle Up And Go* ....20.00 - 30.00
   9 *My Woman* ....20.00 - 30.00
Crown (LP) 5226 *Smokey Hogg Sings The Blues* ...30.00 - 60.00
Ebb 127 *Good Mornin' Baby* ....7.00 - 10.00
Federal 12109 *Keep A-Walkin'* ....30.00 - 50.00
   12117 *Your Little Wagon* ....30.00 - 50.00
   12127 *Gone, Gone, Gone* ....30.00 - 50.00
Imperial 5269 *Tear Me Down* ....30.00 - 50.00
   5290 *Train Whistle* ....30.00 - 50.00
Meteor 5021 *Dark Clouds* ....30.00 - 50.00
Modern 924 *Can't Do Nothin'* ....15.00 - 20.00
Ray's 33 *Penitentiary Blues* ....30.00 - 60.00
Show Time 1101 *No More Whiskey* ....30.00 - 50.00

ROY HOGSED:
Capitol 1529 *Shuffleboard Shuffle* ....7.00 - 10.00
   1635 *Cocaine Blues* ....7.00 - 10.00
   1854 *The Snake Dance Boogie* ....7.00 - 10.00
   1987 *Mean Mean Woman* ....7.00 - 10.00

RON HOLDEN & THE THUNDERBIRDS:
Donna 1315 *My Babe* ....7.00 - 10.00
Nite Owl 10 *My Babe* ....50.00 - 80.00

JAY HOLIDAY & THE GIANTS:
CMI 1001 *I'm Gonna Be A Wheel Someday* ....- -

THE HOLIDAYS:
Melba 112 *The Robin* ....30.00 - 50.00
Nix 537 *One Little Kiss* ....10.00 - 20.00
Robbee 103 *Miss You* ....15.00 - 20.00
Specialty 533 *Irene* ....25.00 - 40.00

EDDIE HOLLAND:
Mercury 71290 *Little Miss Ruby* ....8.00 - 12.00
Motown (LP) 604 *Eddie Holland* ....40.00 - 60.00
Tamla 102 *It Moves Me* ....80.00 - 120.00

THE HOLLIDAYS:
Prep 136 *I'm Not Ashamed* ....10.00 - 15.00

HOLLIES:
Imperial (LP) 9265 *Here I Go Again* ....75.00 - 100.00

TONY HOLLINS:
Decca 48300 *Fishin' Blues* ....75.00 - 125.00

THE HOLLY TWINS:
Liberty 55048 *I Want Elvis For Christmas* ....10.00 - 15.00

BUDDY HOLLY:
Coral (LP) 57210 *Buddy Holly* (maroon label) ....75.00 - 100.00
   (LP) 57279 *The Buddy Holly Story* ....50.00 - 80.00
   (LP) 57326 *The Buddy Holly Story, Vol. 2* ....50.00 - 80.00
   (LP) 57426 *Reminiscing* ....40.00 - 70.00
   (LP) 57463 *Holly In The Hills* ....40.00 - 70.00
(Note: Blue-label promotional copies of foregoing LPs are worth
   substantially more.)
Coral 61852 *Words Of Love* ....40.00 - 60.00
   61885 *Peggy Sue* (78 RPM) ....50.00 - 100.00

61885 *Peggy Sue*	8.00 -	12.00
61947 *Listen To Me*	10.00 -	20.00
61947 *Listen To Me* (78 RPM)	80.00 -	130.00
61985 *Rave On*	10.00 -	20.00
62006 *Early In The Morning*	10.00 -	20.00
62051 *Well, All Right*	10.00 -	20.00
62074 *It Doesn't Matter Anymore*	10.00 -	20.00
62134 *Peggy Sue Got Married*	15.00 -	25.00
62210 *True Love Ways*	15.00 -	25.00
62283 *You're So Square*	20.00 -	30.00

(Note: DJ copies of above are of substantially higher values.)

62329 *Reminiscing*	15.00 -	20.00
62352 *True Love Ways*	15.00 -	20.00
62369 *Brown-Eyed Handsome Man*	15.00 -	20.00
62390 *Rock Around With Ollie Vee*	20.00 -	30.00
62407 *Maybe Baby*	20.00 -	30.00
62448 *Slippin' And Slidin'*	25.00 -	40.00
62554 *Rave On*	10.00 -	20.00

65000 *series* (most issues, including DJ copies - which, indeed, may be more common than

commercial issues)	8.00 -	15.00
(EP) 81169 *Listen To Me*	50.00 -	80.00
(EP) 81182 *The Buddy Holly Story*	50.00 -	80.00
(EP) 81191 *Peggy Sue Got Married*	50.00 -	100.00
(EP) 81193 *Brown-Eyed Handsome Man*	50.00 -	100.00
Decca (EP) 2575 *That'll Be The Day*	250.00 -	400.00
(LP) 8707 *That'll Be The Day* (black label)	150.00 -	300.00
(LP) 8707 *That'll Be The Day* (multi-colored label)	50.00 -	100.00
29854 *Love Me*	50.00 -	80.00
30166 *Modern Don Juan*	50.00 -	80.00
30434 *That'll Be The Day*	50.00 -	80.00
30543 *Love Me*	40.00 -	70.00
30650 *Ting A Ling*	30.00 -	60.00

(Note: DJ copies of above are more highly valued.)

Vocalion (LP) 73811 *The Great Buddy Holly*	50.00 -	80.00

HOLLYWOOD ARGYLES:

Lute (LP) 9001 *The Hollywood Argyles*	75.00 -	100.00

HOLLYWOOD ARTIST-O-KATS:

Recorded in Hollywood 406 *I'll Be Home Again*	100.00 -	150.00

HOLLYWOOD FLAMES:

Atco 6155 *If I Thought You Needed Me*	7.00 -	10.00
6164 *Ball and Chain*	8.00 -	12.00
6171 *Devil Or Angel*	8.00 -	12.00
Chess 1787 *Gee*	7.00 -	10.00
Decca 29285 *Peggy*	30.00 -	50.00
48331 *I Know*	50.00 -	75.00
Ebb 119 *Buzz-Buzz-Buzz*	8.00 -	12.00
119 *Buzz-Buzz-Buzz* (78 RPM)	15.00 -	30.00
131 *Give Me Back My Heart*	10.00 -	15.00
144 *Strollin' On The Beach*	10.00 -	15.00
146 *Chains Of Love*	10.00 -	15.00
149 *A Star Fell*	10.00 -	15.00
153 *I'll Be Seeing You*	10.00 -	15.00
158 *So Good*	10.00 -	15.00
162 *Now That You're Gone*	10.00 -	15.00
163 *In The Dark*	10.00 -	15.00
Goldie 1101 *Believe In Me*	5.00 -	8.00
Lucky 001 *One Night With A Fool*	100.00 -	150.00
006 *Peggy*	100.00 -	150.00
009 *I Know*	80.00 -	130.00
Money 202 *Fare Thee Well* (red label)	40.00 -	60.00
Swing Time 345 *Let's Talk It Over*	75.00 -	100.00

THE HOLLYWOOD PLAYBOYS:

Sure 105 *Ding Dong School Is Out*	10.00 -	15.00

THE HOLLYWOOD SAXONS:

Elf 101 *Every Day's A Holiday*	8.00 -	12.00
103 *It's You*	8.00 -	12.00
Hareco 102 *Every Day's A Holiday*	- -	-
Swingin' 631 *Every Day's A Holiday*	8.00 -	12.00
651 *It's You*	8.00 -	12.00
20th Century Fox 312 *Every Day's A Holiday*	10.00 -	15.00

TOMMY HOLMES:

Cherry 112 *Wa-Chic-Ka-Noka*	20.00 -	30.00

DAVEY HOLT & THE HUBCAPS:

United Artist 110 *You Move Me*	- -	-

JIM HOLT:

Gulfstream 1064 *Oh! My Linda*	10.00 -	15.00

COUNTRY HOMES:

De Luxe 6036 *Come On And Put Me In The Alley*	40.00 -	60.00
6048 *It Can't Be*	40.00 -	60.00

HOME SICK JAMES:

Atomic H *Johnnie Mae*	- -	-
Colt 632 *Set A Date*	7.00 -	10.00
U.S.A. 746 *Crossroads*	7.00 -	10.00

THE HONEY BEARS:

Spark 104 *It's A Miracle*	40.00 -	60.00
111 *I Shall Not Fail*	40.00 -	60.00

THE HONEY BEES:

Bee 1101 *Kiss Me My Love*	100.00 -	150.00
Imperial 5400 *Endless*	8.00 -	12.00
5416 *What's To Become Of Me*	8.00 -	12.00

HONEYBOY:

Specialty 476 *Bloodstains On The Wall*	20.00 -	30.00

GLEN HONEYCUTT:

Fernwood 142 *Campus Love*	10.00 -	15.00
Sun 264 *I'll Be Around*	15.00 -	20.00

THE HONEY-DOS:

Sue 746 *Someone*	8.00 -	12.00

HONEYS:

Capitol 4952 *Shoot The Curls*	30.00 -	50.00
5034 *Pray For Surf*	40.00 -	60.00
5093 *The One You Can't Have*	40.00 -	60.00
Warner Bros. 5430 *He's A Doll*	25.00 -	40.00

THE HONORABLES:

Honor 100 *Castle In The Sky*	10.00 -	15.00

EARL HOOKER (& HIS ROADMASTERS):

Age 29101, 29106, 29111, 29114	5.00 -	10.00
Bea & Baby 106 *Dynamite*	10.00 -	15.00
Chief 7016 *Blues In D Natural*	10.00 -	15.00
CJ 613 *Do The Chicken*	7.00 -	10.00
King 4600 *Race Track*	20.00 -	30.00
Rockin' 519 *Sweet Angel*	30.00 -	50.00

JOHN LEE HOOKER:

Atco (LP) 151 *Don't Turn Me From Your Door*	80.00 -	120.00
Chart 609 *Wobbling Baby*	20.00 -	30.00
614 *Misbelieving Baby*	20.00 -	30.00
Chess (LP) 1438 *House Of The Blues* (black label)	100.00 -	150.00
(LP) 1454 *Plays And Sings The Blues*	50.00 -	80.00
1505 *High Priced Woman*	100.00 -	150.00
1513 *Walkin' The Boogie*	100.00 -	150.00

(Note: Earlier issues, usually found in 78 RPM format, would command prices at least as high as the above, as 45 RPM records.)

1562 *It's All My Fault*	20.00 -	30.00
Crown (LP) 5157 *The Blues*	30.00 -	50.00
(LP) 5232 *John Lee Hooker Sings The Blues*	25.00 -	40.00
(LP) 5295 *Folk Blues*	25.00 -	40.00
King (LP) 727 *John Lee Hooker Sings The Blues*	80.00 -	120.00
Modern 835 *I'm In The Mood* (black label)	20.00 -	30.00
897 *It's Been A Long Time Baby*	10.00 -	15.00
901 *Ride Till I Die*	10.00 -	15.00
916 *Too Much Boogie*	10.00 -	15.00
923 *Down Child*	10.00 -	15.00
935 *Let's Talk It Over*	10.00 -	15.00
Modern 942, 948, 958, 966	8.00 -	12.00
Riverside (LP) 12-838 *Folk Blues*	30.00 -	60.00
Specialty 528 *I'm Mad*	8.00 -	12.00
Vee Jay 164, 188, 205, 233, 255, 265, 293	8.00 -	12.00
Vee Jay 308, 319, 331, 349, 366	7.00 -	10.00
Vee Jay (LP) 1007 *I'm John Lee Hooker* (maroon label)	50.00 -	80.00
(LP) 1023 *Travelin'*	30.00 -	60.00
(LP) 1033 *The Folk Lore Of John Lee Hooker*	30.00 -	60.00

JESS HOOPER:

Cherry - *All Messed Up*	-	-
Meteor 5025 *All Messed Up*	200.00 -	300.00

EDDIE HOPE & THE MANISH BOYS:

Marlin 804 *Lost Child*	50.00 -	100.00

HOPELESS HOMER:

Goldband 1040 *New Way Of Rockin'*	15.00 -	20.00

FORD HOPKINS:

Apex 7757 *Ya Fine, Fine, Fine*	15.00 -	20.00

JERRY HOPKINS:

Starday 182 *Mamma's Baby*	30.00 -	50.00

LIGHTNIN'/LIGHTNING HOPKINS:

Bluesville (LP) 1019 *Lightnin'*	25.00 -	50.00
(LP) 1057 *Walkin' This Road By Myself*	25.00 -	50.00
Candid (LP) 8010 *In New York (MONO)*	25.00 -	40.00
Chart 636 *Mussy Haired Woman*	20.00 -	30.00
Crown (LP) 5224 *Sings The Blues*	25.00 -	40.00
Decca 48306 *Happy New Year*	10.00 -	20.00
48312 *Highway Blues*	20.00 -	30.00
48321 *Bad Things On My Mind*	20.00 -	30.00
Fire (LP) 104 *Mojo Hand*	75.00 -	125.00
Harlem 2324 *Mad Man's Boogie*	50.00 -	80.00
Herald 425 *Lightnin's Boogie*	20.00 -	30.00
428 *Lightnin's Special*	20.00 -	30.00
436 *Sick Feeling Blues*	20.00 -	30.00
443 *Early-Mornin' Boogie*	15.00 -	20.00
449 *They Wonder Who I Am*	15.00 -	20.00
456 *Don't Need No Job*	10.00 -	15.00
465 *Blues For My Cookie*	10.00 -	15.00
571 *Hopkins Sky Hop*	10.00 -	15.00
476 *Grandma's Boogie*	10.00 -	15.00
483 *That's All Right Baby*	10.00 -	15.00
490 *Shine On Moon*	10.00 -	15.00
497 *Remember Me*	10.00 -	15.00
Herald, higher numbers	7.00 -	10.00
(LP) 1012 *And The Blues*	100.00 -	200.00
Imperial (LP) 9180 *On Stage*	50.00 -	80.00
(LP) 9186 *Lightning Hopkins Sings The Blues*	50.00 -	80.00
(LP) 9211 *Lightnin' Hopkins And The Blues*	50.00 -	80.00
Jax 315 *No Good Woman*	50.00 -	80.00

318 *Organ Blues*	50.00 -	80.00
321 *Contrary Mary*	50.00 -	80.00

(Note: Above, if pressed of red vinyl, bring substantially higher prices.)

Lightning 104 *Grieving Blues*	100.00 -	200.00
Prestige (most issues)	5.00 -	8.00
RPM 337 *Bad Luck And Troubles*	100.00 -	150.00
346 *Lonesome Dog Blues*	80.00 -	130.00
351 *Don't Keep My Baby Long*	50.00 -	80.00
359 *One Kind Favor*	40.00 -	80.00
378 *Another Fool In Town*	25.00 -	50.00
388 *Mistreated Blues*	25.00 -	50.00
398 *Some Day Baby*	20.00 -	40.00
Score (LP) 4022 *Lightnin' Hopkins Strums The Blues*	150.00 -	300.00
TNT 8002 *Lightnin's Jump*	50.00 -	80.00
8003 *Leavin' Blues*	50.00 -	80.00
Tradition (LP) 1035 *Country Blues*	25.00 -	40.00
(LP) 1040 *Autobiography In Blues*	25.00 -	40.00

(Note: See also the Blues, etc. section for 78 RPM records by Lightnin' Hopkins.)

LYMAN HOPKINS & THE CHESTNUTS:

Standard 100 *Who Knows Better Than I*	50.00 -	80.00

BIG JACK HORNER:

Trel 1001 *If I Can*	15.00 -	20.00

THE HORNETS:

Flash 125 *Crying Over You*	30.00 -	50.00
States 127 *I Can't Believe*	400.00 -	up
127 *I Can't Believe* (red plastic)	600.00 -	up

BILL HORTON (See THE DAWNS; THE SILHOUETTES)

JOHNNY HORTON:

Columbia (EP) B-2130 *Honky Tonk Man*	50.00 -	75.00
Columbia 21504, 21538, 40813, 40919, 40986, 41210	5.00 -	10.00
Columbia 41043 *Lover's Rock*	8.00 -	12.00
41110 *Honky Tonk Hardwood Floor*	10.00 -	15.00
Dot (LP) 3221 *Johnny Horton*	40.00 -	60.00
Mercury 6418 *This Won't Be The First Time*	15.00 -	20.00
(LP) 20478 *The Fantastic Johnny Horton*	40.00 -	70.00
70100 *Tennessee Jive*	15.00 -	20.00
70156 *S.S. Lure-Line*	15.00 -	20.00
70198 *Red Lips And Warm Red Wine*	15.00 -	20.00
70227 *The Love Of A Girl*	15.00 -	20.00
70325 *Move Down The Line*	15.00 -	20.00
70462 *No True Love*	10.00 -	15.00
70636 *Ridin' The Sunshine Special*	10.00 -	15.00
Sesac (EP) 26 *Free 'N' Easy Songs*	30.00 -	50.00
(LP) 1201/2 *Sings Free And Easy*	100.00 -	150.00

(Note: See also the **COUNTRY/WESTERN**, etc. section for other (78 RPM) records by Johnny Horton.)

SHAKEY (WALTER) HORTON:

Argo (LP) 4037 *The Soul Of Blues Harmonica*	75.00 -	100.00
Chess 1529 *Walter's Boogie*	100.00 -	150.00
Cobra 5002 *Have A Good Time*	50.00 -	80.00

THE HOT-TODDYS:

Corsican 0056 *Shakin' And Stompin'*	-	-
Shan-Todd 0056 *Shakin' And Stompin'*	10.00 -	15.00

DAVID HOUSTON:

RCA Victor 6917 *Hackin' Around*	7.00 -	10.00

(MIGHTY) JOE HOUSTON:

Bayou 004 *Sabre Jet*	15.00 -	20.00
012 *Pig Tails*	15.00 -	20.00
017 *Landslide*	15.00 -	20.00

Cash 1013 *Walking Home* ....8.00 - 12.00
　　1018 *Troubles And Worries*.........................8.00 - 12.00
Combo 116 *Rock That Boogie* ....7.00 - 10.00
Crown (LP) 400 *Rockin' At The Drive-In* ....50.00 - 75.00
　　(LP) 5006 *Rocks And Rolls All Night Long* ....30.00 - 50.00
Dooto 439 *Shindig* ....8.00 - 12.00
Imperial 5201 *Earthquake* ....15.00 - 30.00
　　5213 *Atom Bomb*...............................15.00 - 30.00
Lucky 004 *Go, Joe, Go*...........................15.00 - 20.00
Money 203 *All Night Long* ....7.00 - 10.00
RPM 426 *Shtiggy Boom*...........................10.00 - 15.00
　　427 *Riverside Rock* ....10.00 - 15.00

JOHNNY HOUSTON & THE CAPITALS:
East-West 100 *But It's Too Late*........................7.00 - 10.00

CAMILLE HOWARD:
Specialty 433 *Old Baldy Boogie* ....10.00 - 20.00

CHUCK HOWARD:
ESV 1017 *Don't Let It Bother You*.........................7.00 - 10.00
Port 70002 *Crazy, Crazy Baby* ....8.00 - 12.00

JOHNNY HOWARD:
De Luxe 6044 *Hastings Street Jump* ....80.00 - 130.00

VAN HOWARD:
ABC Paramount 9736 *I Found A New Love* ....7.00 - 10.00
Hi-Q 3756 *Truck Driving Jack* ....7.00 - 10.00
Imperial 8202 *Lonesome And Blue* ....10.00 - 15.00
　　8213 *Maybe Baby* ....10.00 - 15.00

HOWIE & THE SAPPHIRES:
Okeh 7112 *More Than The Day Before* ....10.00 - 15.00

HOWLIN' WOLF:
Chess (LP) 1434 *Moanin' In The Moonlight* (black label)
　　..100.00 - 150.00
　　(LP) 1469 *Howlin' Wolf* ....80.00 - 130.00
　　(LP) 1502 *The Real Folk Blues* ....30.00 - 50.00
　　1510 *Mr. Highway Man*...........................100.00 - 150.00
　　1528 *My Last Affair* ....80.00 - 120.00
　　1557 *All Night Boogie* ....30.00 - 50.00
　　1566 *Rockin' Daddy* ....30.00 - 50.00
　　1575 *Baby How Long* ....15.00 - 25.00
　　1584 *Forty-Four* ....15.00 - 25.00
　　1593 *Who Will Be Next*...........................15.00 - 25.00
　　1607 *Come To Me Baby* ....15.00 - 25.00
　　1618 *Smoke Stack Lightning* ....10.00 - 15.00
　　1632 *So Glad* ....8.00 - 12.00
　　1648 *My Life* ....8.00 - 12.00
　　1668 *Somebody In My Home* ....8.00 - 12.00
　　1679 *Sitting On Top Of The World*................8.00 - 12.00
Chess 1695, 1712, 1726, 1735, 1744, 1750, 1762,
　　1777, 1793, 1804, 1813, 1823, 1870, 1890, 1911 ....5.00 - 10.00
RPM 333 *Morning At Midnight*............................150.00 - 200.00
　　340 *Crying At Daybreak*...........................100.00 - 200.00
　　347 *My Baby Stole Off*............................80.00 - 120.00
(Note: See also the **BLUES, ETC.** section for other (78 RPM)
　　records by Howlin' Wolf.)

ORANGIE RAY HUBBARD:
Dixie 662 *Sweet Love* .... -　-　-
Lucky 0007 *Look What I Found*...........................30.00 - 50.00

JACK HUDDLE:
Kapp 207 *Starlight*.................................20.00 - 30.00
Petsey 1002 *Believe Me* ....40.00 - 60.00

JOE HUDGINS:
Robbins 1005 *Where'd You Stay Last Night* ....20.00 - 30.00

JOHNNY HUDSON & THE RIPTIDES:
Challenge 59062 *Let's Run Away* ....7.00 - 10.00

RAY HUDSON:
Dixie (unnumbered) *Mine For One Night* ....50.00 - 80.00

TOMMY HUDSON:
D 1073 *Band Stand Stomp* ....10.00 - 15.00
White Rock 1110 *Rock-It*..............................15.00 - 20.00

HUDSON VALLEY BOYS:
Sessions 807 *Stop! I Like It*................................15.00 - 20.00

JIMMY HUFF:
RPM 366 *She's My Baby* ....80.00 - 120.00
　　390 *Big City Bound*................................50.00 - 80.00

WILLIE HUFF:
Big Town 105 *Operator 209*...................................50.00 - 80.00
Rhythm 1770 *Beggar Man Blues*......................50.00 - 80.00

DONNIE HUFFMAN:
Taurus 3542 *Pink Cadillac And A Red-Headed Girl*..... 20.00 - 30.00

PAUL HUFFMAN & THE REBEL COMBO:
Winston 1015 *She's Mine* ....20.00 - 30.00

JOE HUGHES:
Kangaroo 105/106 *Make Me Dance Little Ant* .... 15.00 - 20.00

WALLY HUGHES:
Ember 1024 *Convertible Car*..............................15.00 - 20.00
　　1024 *Convertible Car* (78 RPM) ....20.00 - 30.00

T.K. HULIN:
L.K. 1001 *Many Nights*...........................15.00 - 25.00

DENNIS HUNT & THE HUNTERS:
Say 11 *A Story Untold*................................30.00 - 50.00

SLIM HUNT:
Excello 2055 *Welcome Home Baby* ....50.00 - 75.00

FLUFFY HUNTER & JESSIE POWELL'S ORCHESTRA:
Federal 12056 *Love's A Fortune*........................50.00 - 100.00
　　12161 *Climb The Wall* ....20.00 - 30.00
　　12172 *Leave It To Me* ....20.00 - 30.00

IVORY JOE HUNTER:
Atlantic 1049, 1066, 1086, 1095............................ 5.00 - 10.00
　　(LP) 8008 *Rock And Roll* (black label) .... 75.00 - 100.00
　　(LP) 8015 *Ivory Joe Hunter Sings The Old & The New*
　　..30.00 - 50.00
King (LP) 605 16 *Of His Greatest Hits* .... 50.00 - 80.00
M-G-M (EP) 1376, 1377, 1378............................. 20.00 - 30.00
M-G-M (LP) 3488 *I Get That Lonesome Feeling*... 75.00 - 100.00

LONG JOHN HUNTER:
Yucca 132 *Paso Rock* .... 7.00 - 10.00
　　138 *Ole Rattler*.. 7.00 - 10.00

TV HUNTER & THE VOICE MASTERS (See VOICE MASTERS):

HURRICANES:
King 4817 *Poor Little Dancing Girl*......................25.00 - 40.00
　　4867 *Maybe It's All For The Best*....................25.00 - 40.00
　　4898 *Raining In My Heart* ....30.00 - 50.00
　　4926 *Your Promise To Me* ....30.00 - 50.00
　　4947 *Dear Mother*....................................30.00 - 50.00
　　5018 *Fallen Angel* ....30.00 - 50.00
　　5042 *Priceless* ....30.00 - 50.00

HUSKIES:
Klik 205 *Sorry*..20.00 - 30.00

FERLIN HUSKY:
Capitol (LP) 718 *Ferlin Husky* ....15.00 - 20.00
(LP) 880 *Boulevard Of Broken Dreams* ....15.00 - 20.00
(LP) 976 *Sittin' On A Rainbow*..........................15.00 - 20.00
(LP) 1204 *Born To Lose* ....15.00 - 20.00
(LP) 1280 *Ferlin's Favorites* ....10.00 - 15.00
3310 *Slow Down, Brother*..............................7.00 - 10.00

THE HY-TONES:
Hy-Tone 120 *I'm A Fool* ....25.00 - 40.00

IDEALS:
Cool 108 *Do I Have The Right* ....75.00 - 100.00
Decca 30720 *My Girl*....................................7.00 - 10.00
30800 *Don't Be A Baby, Baby*.......................7.00 - 10.00
Paso 6401 *Together* ....7.00 - 10.00
6402 *Magic* ....8.00 - 12.00

I DIG ROCK AND ROLL:
Score (LP) 4002 (various artists)..............100.00 - 200.00

THE IDOLS:
Dot 16210 *Why Must I Cry* ....10.00 - 15.00

THE ILLUSIONS:
Ember 1071 *Can't We Fall In Love*....................15.00 - 25.00
Little Debbi 105 *The Story Of My Life* ....75.00 - 100.00
Mali 404 *Lonely Soldier* ....15.00 - 20.00
Sheraton 104 *Hey Boy* ....7.00 - 10.00

THE IMAGINATIONS:
Dual 507 *Guardian Angel*..............................10.00 - 15.00
Music Makers 103 *The Search Is Over* ....15.00 - 20.00
108 *Guardian Angel* ....15.00 - 20.00

THE IMPALAS:
Cub (LP) 8003 *Sorry (I Ran All The Way Home)*....80.00 - 120.00
9022 *I Ran All The Way Home* ....8.00 - 12.00
Echo 6018 *Betty Jean* ....80.00 - 130.00

IMPERIALS:
Buzzy 1 *My Darling* ....10.00 - 15.00
End 1027 *Tears On My Pillow*
(no LITTLE ANTHONY credit) ....25.00 - 50.00
1091 *Traveling Stranger*................................10.00 - 15.00
Great Lakes 1201 *Life Of Ease* ....100.00 - 150.00

IMPLACABLES:
Kain 1004 *My Foolish Pride* ....80.00 - 130.00

IMPRESSIONS (See also JERRY BUTLER):
Abner 1017 *Come Back My Love* ....15.00 - 20.00
1017 *Come Back My Love* (78 RPM)................15.00 - 20.00
1023 *The Gift Of Love* ....15.00 - 20.00
1034 *A New Love* ....15.00 - 20.00
Bandera 2504 *Listen To Me* ....15.00 - 25.00
Swirl 107 *I Need Your Love*...................... - - -
Vee Jay (LP) 1075 *For Your Precious Love* ....50.00 - 100.00

IMPRESSORS:
Cub 9010 *Do You Love Her*.............................20.00 - 30.00
Onyx 514 *Is It Too Late* ....30.00 - 50.00

THE INDIGOS:
Cornel 3001 *Servant Of Love* ....50.00 - 80.00

INDIVIDUALS:
Chase 1300 *Pillow Wet With Tears* ....100.00 - 150.00
Music City 838 *Beverly My Darling* ....150.00 - 250.00
Show Time 595 *Met Her At A Dance*................15.00 - 20.00
598 *Dear One* ....15.00 - 20.00
Sparrow 101 *I've Been Hurt* ....50.00 - 80.00

THE INFATUATORS:
Destiny 504 *Where Are You*.........................75.00 - 100.00
Vee Jay 395 *Found My Love*................................10.00 - 15.00

INFLAMMABLE DAN & THE IGNITERS:
Wine 09 *High Flying Wine* ....10.00 - 15.00

BENNY INGRAM:
Bandera 1302 *Jello Sal* ....10.00 - 15.00

THE INK SPOTS:
Decca, most issues ....4.00 - 8.00
Fabulous 1003 *A Man* ....10.00 - 20.00
King (LP) 535 *Something Old, Something New* .....75.00 - 100.00
(LP) 642 *Songs That Will Live Forever*.............50.00 - 80.00
1297 *Ebb Tide* ....15.00 - 20.00
1304 *Changing Partners* ....15.00 - 20.00
1336 *Melody Of Love* ....15.00 - 20.00
1378 *Yesterdays* ....15.00 - 20.00
1425 *When You Come To the End Of The Day* .15.00 - 20.00
1429 *There Is Something Missing*....................15.00 - 20.00
1512 *Keep It Movin'* ....15.00 - 20.00
4670 *Here In My Lonely Room* ....15.00 - 20.00
4857 *I'll Walk A Country Mile* ....15.00 - 20.00
Waldorf (LP) 144 (10 inch) ....40.00 - 60.00

AUTRY INMAN:
Decca 29936 *Be Bop Baby*....................................10.00 - 15.00

JIMMY INMAN & IMPOLLOS:
Aladdin 3426 *You Never Realized* ....15.00 - 20.00

THE INSPIRATIONS:
Al-Brite 1651 *Angel In Disguise*..........................15.00 - 20.00
Apollo 494 *Raindrops*..40.00 - 60.00
Gone 5097 *Angel In Disguise* ....10.00 - 15.00
Jamie 1034 *Dry Your Eyes*...................................30.00 - 50.00
1212 *Dry Your Eyes* ....8.00 - 12.00
Lamp 2019 *Don't Cry* ....20.00 - 30.00
Rondack 9787 *Ring Those Bells* ....20.00 - 30.00
Sparkle 102 *Angel In Disguise*............................25.00 - 40.00
Sultan 1 *The Feeling Of Her Kiss* ....15.00 - 20.00

THE INSPIRATORS:
Old Town 1053 *Oh What A Feeling* ....50.00 - 80.00
Treat 502 *If Loving You Is Wrong*......................100.00 - 150.00

INTENTIONS:
Jamie 1253 *Summertime Angel*............................150.00 - 250.00
Kent 455 *My Love She's Gone* ....20.00 - 30.00
Melron 5014 *Wonderful Girl* ....20.00 - 30.00

INTERIORS:
Worthy 1008 *Darling Little Angel*........................20.00 - 30.00
1009 *Echoes*...15.00 - 20.00

THE INTERVALS:
Ad 104 *I Still Love That Man* ....15.00 - 20.00
25019 *I Still Love That Man* ....8.00 - 12.00
Class 304 *Here's That Rainy Day*........................30.00 - 50.00

THE INVICTAS:
Pix 1101 *Lest You Forget* ....80.00 - 130.00
TPE 8223 *I Took A Chance* ....75.00 - 100.00

THE INVICTORS:
Bee 1117 *I Don't Wanna Go*................................80.00 - 130.00
TPE 8221 *That's All Right*...................................150.00 - 200.00

INVINCIBLES:
Chess 1727 *Mr. Moonglow* ....10.00 - 15.00

JERRY IRBY:

Daffan 106 *Call For Me Darling*	15.00 -	20.00
108 *Clickety Clack*	20.00 -	30.00
111 *That's Too Bad*	15.00 -	25.00
Jer-Ray 222 *Chantilly Lace*	20.00 -	30.00

THE IRIDESCENTS/IRRIDESCENTS:

Hudson 8102 *Three Coins In The Fountain*	20.00 -	30.00
Ultrasonic 109 *The Angels Sang*	200.00 -	up

CURTIS IRVIN (See THE SPARKS)

ROBERT A. IRVINE:

Presto 525 *Fastest Short In Town*	- -	-

LONNIE IRVING:

Starday 486 *Pinball Machine*	7.00 -	10.00

JIMMY ISLE:

Roulette 4065 *Goin' Wild*	7.00 -	10.00

ISLEY BROTHERS:

Cindy 3009 *Don't Be Jealous*	25.00 -	40.00
Gone 5048 *My Love*	10.00 -	15.00
RCA Victor (LP) 2156 *Shout!*	25.00 -	40.00
Teenage 1004 *Angels Cried*	30.00 -	50.00

IVAN:

Coral 62017 *Real Wild Child*	15.00 -	20.00
62081 *Frankie Frankenstein*	25.00 -	40.00
65607 *Real Wild Child*	10.00 -	15.00

JIMMY IVES:

Comet 2141 *My Fumbling Heart*	5.00 -	8.00

THE IVIES:

Brunswick 55112 *Sunshine*	8.00 -	12.00
Roulette 4183 *Voodoo*	8.00 -	12.00

THE IVORIES:

Jaguar 3019 *Alone*	50.00 -	80.00
3023 *Alone*	40.00 -	60.00
Mercury 71239 *Me And You*	15.00 -	20.00

THE IVORYTONES:

Unidap 448 *Move It Over*	8.00 -	12.00

SONNY JOE IVY:

Jewel 738 *Ruby And The Gambler*	5.00 -	8.00

THE IVY LEAGUERS:

Dot 15677 *Ring Chimes*	8.00 -	12.00
Nau-Voo 803 *Told By The Stars*	50.00 -	80.00
Porter 1003 *The Story*	10.00 -	15.00

IVY THREE:

Shell 302 *Nine Out Of Ten*	7.00 -	10.00
306 *Bagoo*	7.00 -	10.00
720 *Yogi*	5.00 -	8.00
723 *Alone In The Chapel*	10.00 -	15.00

IVY TONES:

Red-Top 105 *Oo Wee Baby* (blue label)	25.00 -	40.00

J.B. & HIS BAYOU BOYS:

J.O.B. 1008 *The Mountain*	80.00 -	120.00

J.B. & HIS HAWKS:

Chance 1155 *Combination Boogie*	150.00 -	250.00
1160 *Pet Cream Man*	200.00 -	300.00

JACK & JILL:

Caddy 110 *Party Time*	10.00 -	15.00
Imperial 5464 *Record Hop*	10.00 -	15.00

JACKIE & STARLITES:

Fire & Fury 1000 *They Laughed At Me*	75.00 -	100.00
Fury 1057 *I Found Out Too Late*	10.00 -	15.00
Mascot 128 *For All We Know*	10.00 -	20.00
131 *Walking From School*	20.00 -	30.00

JACKPOT OF HITS:

Apollo (LP) 490	50.00 -	80.00

JACKS:

Crown (LP) 372 *The Jacks*	40.00 -	70.00
(LP) 5021 *Jumpin' With The Jacks*	40.00 -	70.00
RPM 428 *Why Don't You Write Me*	20.00 -	30.00
433 *Since My Baby's Been Gone*	15.00 -	25.00
444 *This Empty Heart*	10.00 -	15.00
454 *So Wrong*	10.00 -	15.00
458 *Why Did I Fall In Love*	10.00 -	15.00
467 *Let's Make Up*	15.00 -	20.00

JACKSON BROTHERS:

Atlantic 1034 *Love Me*	10.00 -	15.00
RCA Victor 5005 *We're Gonna Rock This Joint*	10.00 -	15.00
5446 *Flat Foot Boogie*	10.00 -	15.00

BOBBY JACKSON:

Brunswick 55026 *Deep Elm Blues*	8.00 -	12.00

BULL MOOSE JACKSON:

Audio Lab (LP) 1524 *Bull Moose Jackson*	100.00 -	150.00
Encino 1004 *Watch My Signals*	7.00 -	10.00
King (EP) 211 *Sings His All Time Hits*	80.00 -	120.00
(EP) 261	80.00 -	120.00
King 4181 *Sneaky Pete*	30.00 -	50.00
4189 *I Want A Bowlegged Woman*	30.00 -	50.00
4524 *Nosey Joe*	25.00 -	40.00
4580 *Big Ten-Inch Record*	25.00 -	40.00

(Note: First pressings of early KING issues should not have the designation "High Fidelity", and should have the suffixes "A" or "AA" after the record/catalog numbers. Records pressed of colored plastic can bring substantially higher prices.)

CLEVE JACKSON & HIS HOUND DOGS:

Herald 6000 *Hound Dog*	50.00 -	80.00

CORDELL JACKSON:

Moon 6407 *Rock and Roll Christmas*	20.00 -	30.00

EDDIE JACKSON:

Fortune 186 *Rock 'N' Roll Baby*	10.00 -	15.00

HANDY JACKSON:

Sun 177 *Got My Application Baby*	400.00 -	up

(existence in 45 RPM format reported, but not verified)

LEE JACKSON:

Cobra 5007 *Fishin' In My Pond*	30.00 -	50.00
Keyhole 115 *Please Baby*	10.00 -	15.00

LIL/LITTLE SON JACKSON (& HIS ROCK & ROLLERS):

Imperial 5156 *Travelin' Woman*	75.00 -	100.00
5165 *Upstairs Boogie*	75.00 -	100.00
5175 *My Little Girl*	75.00 -	100.00
5192 *Travelin' Alone*	75.00 -	100.00
5204 *Journey Back Home*	75.00 -	100.00
5218 *Black And Brown*	75.00 -	100.00
5229 *Lonely Blues*	75.00 -	100.00
5237 *Spending Money Blues*	75.00 -	100.00
5248 *Confession*	75.00 -	100.00
5259 *Dirty Work*	50.00 -	80.00
5267 *Thrill Me Baby*	50.00 -	80.00

5276 *Piggly Wiggly*..............................50.00 - 80.00
5286 *Blues By The Hour*.........................50.00 - 80.00
5300 *Let Me Down Easy*...........................30.00 - 50.00
5312 *How Long*.......................................30.00 - 50.00
5319 *My Younger Days* ....30.00 - 50.00
5339 *Sugar Mama*.....................................25.00 - 40.00
5963 *Prison Bound* ....7.00 - 10.00
(earlier Imperial issues are usually found in 78 RPM format, and
    earliest issues exist only as 78s; see Blues, etc., section)
  (LP) 9142 *Rockin' & Rollin'* ....100.00 - 150.00
Post 2014 *Lonely Blues*..............................40.00 - 60.00

SAMMY JACKSON:
Arvee 5095 *Ladies' Man* ....8.00 - 12.00

WANDA JACKSON:
Capitol (LP) 1041 *Wanda Jackson* ....50.00 - 80.00
  (LP) 1384 *Rockin' With Wanda*...........100.00 - 150.00
  (LP) 1511 *There's A Party Goin' On* ....80.00 - 120.00
Capitol (LP) ST-1511 *There's A Party Goin' On* (STEREO)
  ....100.00 - 150.00
  (LP) 1776 *Wonderful Wanda*..................25.00 - 40.00
Capitol 3485 *I Gotta Know* ....8.00 - 12.00
  3575 *Hot Dog That Made Him Mad*......7.00 - 10.00
  3637 *Baby Loves Him* ....10.00 - 15.00
  3683 *Let Me Explain* ....10.00 - 15.00
  3764 *Cool Love* ....10.00 - 15.00
  3843 *Fujiyama Mama* ....15.00 - 20.00
  3941 *Honey Bop* ....10.00 - 15.00
  4026 *Mean Mean Man* ....15.00 - 20.00
  4081 *Rock Your Baby* ....15.00 - 20.00
  4142 *Savin' My Love* ....10.00 - 15.00
  4207 *You're The One For Me* ....15.00 - 20.00
  4286 *I'd Rather Have You* ....10.00 - 15.00
  4354 *My Destiny* ....10.00 - 15.00
  4397 *Let's Have A Party*....................15.00 - 20.00
  4469 *Mean Mean Man* ....10.00 - 15.00
  4520 *Riot In Cell Block #9*.................10.00 - 15.00
  4553 *Right Or Wrong* ....7.00 - 10.00
  4635 *I'd Be Ashamed*..........................7.00 - 10.00
  4681 *I Don't Wanta Go* ....7.00 - 10.00
Capitol, most other issues ....4.00 - 8.00
(Note: 78 RPM issues of above numbers are worth somewhat more.)
Decca 29253, 29514, 29627, 30153 ....5.00 - 10.00

THE JAC-O-LACS:
Tampa 103 *Cindy Lou* ....15.00 - 20.00

JIM JACONO & THE J'S:
Kay-Y 66783 *Take My Money*..................30.00 - 50.00

ILLINOIS JACQUET & LESTER YOUNG:
Aladdin (LP) 701 *Battle Of The Saxes* (10 inch)...100.00 - 200.00

RUSSELL JACQUET:
Network 71200 *Tormented* ....50.00 - 80.00

THE JADES:
Ching (LP) 69 *So Tough!*............................... - -
Christy 110 *Oh Why*..................................80.00 - 130.00
  113 *Don't Be A Fool* ....75.00 - 100.00
  114 *Look For A Lie* ....80.00 - 130.00
Nau-Voo 807 *Walking All Alone* ....50.00 - 80.00
Time 1002 *So Blue* ....10.00 - 15.00

THE JAGUARS:
Aardell 0003 *I Wanted You*.......................30.00 - 50.00
  0006 *You Don't Believe Me*................30.00 - 50.00
Ebb 129 *Hold Me Tonight* ....20.00 - 30.00
Original Sound 06 *Thinking Of You* ....15.00 - 25.00

R-Dell 11 *The Way You Look Tonight* ....30.00 - 50.00
  11 (same, but red plastic) ....100.00 - 150.00
Rendezvous 159 *It Finally Happened*..................10.00 - 15.00

"JAMBOREE!":
(Note: Complete score of musical, with Jimmy Bowen, Fats
    Domino, Buddy Knox, Jerry Lee Lewis, et al.)
....200.00 - up
(Note: The price of this rare album is conjectural; a copy was offered
    at auction with a minimum bid of several hundred dollars.)

BILL JAMES:
Mun Rab 104 *School's Out* ....15.00 - 20.00

BILLY JAMES & THE CRYSTALTONES:
M.Z. 111 *Meant For Me* ....80.00 - 120.00

BOBBIE JAMES & 4 BUDDIES:
Club 51 104 *I Need You So* ....80.00 - 130.00

DANIEL JAMES:
Allstar 7163 *Rock Moon Rock* ....50.00 - 100.00

DWIGHT JAMES:
Spindletop 111 *Walkin' Out*....................................20.00 - 30.00

ELMER JAMES:
Trumpet 186 *Gonna Find My Baby* ....30.00 - 50.00

ELMORE JAMES (& HIS BROOMDUSTERS):
Ace 508 *Dust My Broom*..40.00 - 70.00
Checker 777 *Country Boogie* ....150.00 - 250.00
Chess 1756 *I Can't Hold Out*..................................10.00 - 15.00
Chief 7001 *The Twelve Year Old Boy*....................15.00 - 20.00
  7004 *It Hurts Me Too* ....15.00 - 20.00
  7006 *Cry For Me Baby* ....15.00 - 20.00
  7020 *Knocking At Your Door* ....10.00 - 15.00
Crown (LP) 5168 *Blues After Hours* ....75.00 - 100.00
Enjoy 2015, 2020 ....5.00 - 10.00
Fire 504 *Shake Your Moneymaker* ....10.00 - 15.00
  1011 *Bobby's Rock* ....10.00 - 15.00
  1016 *The Sky Is Crying* ....10.00 - 15.00
  1024 *Rollin' And Tumblin'* ....10.00 - 15.00
  1031 *Fine Little Mama* ....10.00 - 15.00
  1503 *Anna Lee* ....10.00 - 15.00
  2020 *Pickin' The Blues* ....10.00 - 15.00
Flair 1011 *Early In The Morning* ....100.00 - 150.00
  1014 *Make A Little Love* ....100.00 - 150.00
  1022 *Please Find My Baby* ....100.00 - 150.00
  1031 *Hand In Hand* ....100.00 - 150.00
  1039 *1839 Blues*...75.00 - 100.00
  1048 *Dark And Dreary* ....80.00 - 130.00
  1057 *Sunny Land* ....50.00 - 80.00
  1062 *Late Hours At Midnight* ....50.00 - 80.00
  1069 *Happy Home* ....50.00 - 80.00
  1074 *Dust My Blues* ....50.00 - 80.00
  1079 *Blues Before Sunrise* ....50.00 - 80.00
Kent (LP) 5022 *Original Folk Blues* ....50.00 - 50.00
Meteor 5000 *I Believe* ....100.00 - 150.00
  5003 *Sinful Woman*...100.00 - 150.00
Sphere Sound (LP) 7002 *The Sky Is Crying* ....30.00 - 50.00
  (LP) 7008 *I Need You* ....30.00 - 50.00
Trumpet 146 *Dust My Broom* ....50.00 - 80.00
Vee Jay 249 *Coming Home* ....15.00 - 20.00
  259 *It Hurts Me Too* ....15.00 - 20.00
  269 *Cry For Me Baby* ....15.00 - 20.00

ETTA JAMES (& THE PEACHES):
Argo (LP) 4003 *At Last*..50.00 - 75.00
Modern 947 *Roll With Me Henry*............................10.00 - 15.00
  957 *Hey Henry* ....7.00 - 10.00

962 *Good Rockin' Daddy* ....7.00 - 10.00
972 *W-O-M-A-N* ....7.00 - 10.00
Modern 984, 988, 998, 1007, 1016, 1022.................5.00 - 10.00

JESSIE JAMES:
Kent 314 *Red Hot Rockin' Blues* ....30.00 - 50.00

LEON JAMES:
Bumble Bee 501 *Baby Let's Rock* ....50.00 - 80.00

MCKINLEY JAMES:
Tomahawk 737 *Ain't Gonna Pick No Cotton*..........30.00 - 50.00

SONNY JAMES:
Capitol (LP) 779 *Southern Gentleman* ....15.00 - 25.00
    (LP) 867 *Sonny* ....15.00 - 20.00
    (LP) 988 *Honey* ....15.00 - 20.00
    (LP) 1178 *This Is Sonny James* ....15.00 - 20.00
    3602 *Young Love* (78 RPM) ....15.00 - 20.00
    3674 *First Date, First Kiss, First Love* (78 RPM)
    ....10.00 - 15.00
    3840 *Uh-Huh-Mm* (78 RPM).........................10.00 - 15.00

TOMMY JAMES (& THE SHONDELLS):
La Louisianne (LP) 109 *The Shondells At The Saturday Hop*
    ....40.00 - 60.00
Red Fox 110 *Hanky Panky* .... -   -   -
Snap 102 *Hanky Panky* ....15.00 - 20.00

JAN AND ARNIE:
Arwin 108 *Jennie Lee* (78 RPM)......................40.00 - 60.00
Arwin 108 *Jennie Lee* ....10.00 - 15.00
    111 *Gas Money* ....10.00 - 15.00
    113 *I Love Linda* ....10.00 - 15.00
Dore 522 *Baby Talk* (DJ)............................ -   -   -
(Note: Most copies of Dore 522 are by **JAN & DEAN**; see that artist listing.)
Dot (EP) 1097 *Jan & Arnie* ....100.00 - 150.00

JAN & DEAN:
Challenge 9111 *Those Words* ....15.00 - 20.00
Dore (LP) 101 *Jan & Dean* ....100.00 - 150.00
    522 *Baby Talk* ....8.00 - 12.00
    531 *There's A Girl* ....8.00 - 12.00
    539 *Clementine* ....8.00 - 12.00
    548 *Cindy* ....8.00 - 12.00
    555 *We Go Together* ....8.00 - 12.00
    576 *Gee* ....8.00 - 12.00
    610 *Julie* ....8.00 - 12.00
J&D 401 *California Lullaby*.........................15.00 - 20.00
    402 *Like A Summer Rain* ....15.00 - 20.00
Jan & Dean 10 *Hawaii*...............................20.00 - 30.00
    11 *Fan Tan* ....20.00 - 30.00
Liberty 55522 *She's Still Talking Baby Talk*........10.00 - 15.00
Liberty, most other issues...........................5.00 - 8.00
Magic Lamp 401 *Summertime* ....10.00 - 15.00
Warner Bros. 7219 *Laurel And Hardy* ....10.00 - 15.00

JAN & THE RADIANTS:
Clock 1028 *Now Is The Hour* ....10.00 - 15.00
Queen 24007 *Is It True* ....8.00 - 12.00
Vim 507 *Heart And Soul* ....10.00 - 15.00

JOHNNY JANIS:
ABC Paramount 9800 *I Played The Field*..............7.00 - 10.00
    9840 *Later Baby* ....7.00 - 10.00
Coral 61552 *Move It Or Lose It*.....................7.00 - 10.00

DANNY JANNSEN:
Stepheny 1841 *Mirror On The Wall* ....15.00 - 20.00

JOHNNY JANO:
Excello 2099 *Havin' A Whole Lot Of Fun*.............20.00 - 30.00
Hollywood 1087 *Mabel's Gone* ....20.00 - 30.00

THE JARMELS:
Laurie 3083, 3124 ....5.00 - 8.00

FELTON JARVIS:
M-G-M 12982 *Goin' Downtown* ....7.00 - 10.00

BILL JASON:
Topsy 1001 *This Must Be The Place* ....8.00 - 12.00

BOBBY JAY:
Imperial 5590 *Sweet Little Stranger* ....10.00 - 15.00

DALE JAY:
Raven 001 *Shakin' All Over*.........................7.00 - 10.00

JOHNNY JAY:
Mercury 71232 *Sugar Doll* ....8.00 - 12.00
    71232 *Sugar Doll* (78 RPM)......................20.00 - 30.00
Play 1006 *That's What I Like About Love* ....10.00 - 15.00

P. JAY & THE HAYSTACKERS:
Oak 1202/1203 *High School Rock 'N' Roll*............20.00 - 30.00

THE JAYES (Featuring BILL CURTISS):
Arc 4443 *Panic Stricken* ....10.00 - 15.00

JAYHAWKS:
Aladdin 3379 *Johnny's House Party* ....30.00 - 50.00
    3393 *Everyone Should Know* ....30.00 - 50.00
Eastman 792 *Start The Fire* ....25.00 - 40.00
Flash 105 *Counting My Teardrops* ....50.00 - 80.00
    109 *Stranded In The Jungle* ....10.00 - 15.00
    111 *Love Train* ....15.00 - 20.00

THE JAYNETTS:
Tuff (LP) 13 *Sally Go 'Round The Roses* ....50.00 - 80.00

JAYTONES:
Brunswick 55087 *Gasoline* ....20.00 - 30.00
Cub 9057 *My Only Love* ....20.00 - 30.00
Timely 1003 *The Bells* ....75.00 - 100.00

JAZZBOMBERS:
Tattler 1001 *Bad Boy* .... -   -   -

ALICE JEAN (See MONDELLOS)

CATHY JEAN & ROOMMATES (See CATHY...)

JEANIE & HER BOY FRIENDS:
Warwick 508 *It's Me Knocking* ....15.00 - 25.00

JIMMY JEFFERS & THE JOKERS:
Da-Mor 9220 *Raining Teardrops* ....10.00 - 15.00
Fraternity 837 *Teardrops From My Eyes*..............8.00 - 12.00

EDDIE JEFFERSON:
Checker 855 *Billie's Bounce* ....7.00 - 10.00

WALLY JEFFEREY:
Do-Ra-Me 1402 *Oh Yeah* ....100.00 - 150.00

BOBBY JENKINS:
Hamilton 50001 *White Shorts And A Red Tee Shirt*
    ....10.00 - 15.00

BO BO JENKINS:
Boxer 202 *Tell Me Who* ....50.00 - 80.00
Chess 1565 *Democrat Blues* ....80.00 - 120.00
Duchess 101 *Tell Me Who* ....15.00 - 30.00
Fortune 838 *Ten Below Zero*.........................50.00 - 80.00

GUS JENKINS/JINKINS:
Flash 116, 123, 126, 128, 130, 131 ....5.00 - 10.00

BABY BOY JENNINGS & THE SATELLITES:
Savoy 1589 *Little Girl* ....7.00 - 10.00

WAYLON JENNINGS:
Brunswick 55130 *Jole Blon* ....75.00 - 100.00
Ramco 1989 *My Baby Walks All Over Me* ....10.00 - 15.00
Trend '63 106 *The Stage* ....15.00 - 20.00

CURT JENSEN:
Pet 804 *Just For You* ....25.00 - 40.00

PATTI JEROME:
Central 1005 *Trav'lin' Light* ....8.00 - 12.00

RALPH JEROME:
K.P. 1007 *Rockhouse* ....15.00 - 25.00

JERRY & DEMAR:
Ford 501 *Cross-Eyed Alley Cat* ....30.00 - 40.00

JESSE & BUZZY:
Savoy 1556 *Without Your Love* ....7.00 - 10.00

JESSE & MARVIN:
Specialty 447 *Dream Girl* (red vinyl).............30.00 - 50.00

JESSIE & THE SEQUINS:
Profile 4008 *Hold My Hand* ....10.00 - 15.00

THE JESTERS:
Winley 218 *So Strange* ....15.00 - 20.00
    221 *Please Let Me Love You* ....15.00 - 20.00
    225 *The Plea* ....10.00 - 15.00
    242 *The Wind* ....10.00 - 15.00
    248 *That's How It Goes* ....10.00 - 15.00
    252 *Come Let Me Show You* ....15.00 - 20.00
Winley (LP) 6003 *War!*
    (with **THE PARAGONS**) ....50.00 - 100.00

THE JETS:
Aladdin 3247 *I'll Hide My Tears*.................300.00 - up
Gee 1020 *Heaven Above Me*....................250.00 - up
    7-11 2101 *Volcano*............................100.00 - 150.00

THE JET TONES:
Chess 1723 *Kansas City* ....8.00 - 12.00

JEWEL & EDDIE:
Silver 1004 *Opportunity* ....7.00 - 10.00
    1008 *Sixteen Tons* ....7.00 - 10.00

JEWELS:
Imperial 5351 *Hearts Can Be Broken* ....20.00 - 30.00
    5362 *Please Return*...........................15.00 - 25.00
    5377 *How*......................................15.00 - 20.00
    5387 *My Baby* ....15.00 - 20.00
R & B 1301 *Hearts Of Stone* ....20.00 - 40.00
    1303 *A Fool In Paradise*....................50.00 - 75.00
Rama 10 *Heartbreaker* ....200.00 - up
(Note: Above also issued as by The Crows.)
RPM 474 *She's A Flirt* ....15.00 - 20.00

THE JIANTS:
Claudra 112 *Tornado* ....20.00 - 30.00

JILL & RAY:
Le Cam 929 *Hey Paula*...........................20.00 - 30.00

JIM BOB & HANK MIZELL (See HANK MIZELL)

JIMMY & DUANE:
Preston 212 *Soda Fountain Girl* ....50.00 - 75.00

JIMMY & JOHNNY (& THE JADES):
Chess 4863 *Love Me* ....20.00 - 30.00
D1004 *I Can't Find The Door Knob*.........15.00 - 20.00
    1089 *My Little Baby* ....7.00 - 10.00
Decca 29772 *Sweet Singing Daddy* ....10.00 - 15.00
    30061 *Sweet Love On My Mind* ....20.00 - 30.00
TNT 184 *Don't Call Me, I'll Call You* ....15.00 - 20.00

JIMMY & WALTER:
Sun 180 *Before Long* ....200.00 - up

GUS JINKINS (See GUS JENKINS)

THE JIVE-A-TONES/JIV-A-TONES:
Felsted 8506 *Flirty Gertie*.........................10.00 - 15.00
Fox 1 *Flirty Gertie* ....20.00 - 30.00
Fraternity 823 *The Wild Bird* ....5.00 - 8.00

JIVE BOMBERS:
Savoy 1508 *Bad Boy*..............................8.00 - 12.00
Savoy 1513, 1515, 1535............................5.00 - 10.00

THE JIVE FIVE:
Beltone 1006 *My True Story* ....10.00 - 15.00
    1014 *Never, Never* ....10.00 - 15.00
Lana 105 *My True Story*..........................8.00 - 12.00

JIVERS:
Aladdin 3329 *Cherie* ....50.00 - 75.00
    3347 *Ray Pearl* ....50.00 - 75.00

JIVETONES:
Apt 25020 *Geraldine* ....10.00 - 15.00

JIVIN' GENE:
Jin 109 *Going Out With The Tide* ....15.00 - 20.00
Mercury 71485 *Breaking Up Is Hard To Do* ....7.00 - 10.00
    71561 *Go On Go On* ....7.00 - 10.00
    71680 *Going Out With The Tide* ....7.00 - 10.00
    71751 *Poor Me* ....7.00 - 10.00
    71802 *Don't Pretend* ....7.00 - 10.00

JODIMARS:
Capitol 3285, 3360, 3436, 3512..................5.00 - 8.00

JOEY & THE LEXINGTONS:
Dunes 2029 *Bobbie* ....15.00 - 20.00

LITTLE WILLIE JOHN:
King (LP) 564 *Fever* ....50.00 - 100.00
    (LP) 596 *Talk To Me* ....50.00 - 100.00
    (LP) 603 *Mister Little Willie John* ....40.00 - 80.00
King 4935 *Fever* (78 RPM) ....10.00 - 20.00
    5108 *Talk To Me Talk To Me* (78 RPM)...........15.00 - 30.00
King, most other issues ....5.00 - 8.00
Prize 6900 *Jingle Bells* ....30.00 - 50.00

JOHNNIE & JOE:
ABC Paramount 10117 *Why Do You Hurt Me So* ....7.00 - 10.00
Chess 1654 *Over The Mountain, Across The Sea*.....8.00 - 12.00
J & S 1630 *Warm Soft And Lovely*............8.00 - 12.00
    1631 *False Love Has To Go* ....8.00 - 12.00
    1659 *There Goes My Heart* ....8.00 - 12.00
    1664 *Over The Mountain, Across The Sea* ....20.00 - 30.00
    1677 *I Was So Lonely* ....8.00 - 12.00

JOHNNY & JOE:
Gone 5024 *Who Do You Love*..................10.00 - 15.00

JOHNNY & THE HURRICANES:
Big Top (LP) 1302 *The Big Sound Of* ....40.00 - 60.00
Warwick (EP) 700 *Johnny & The Hurricanes*........50.00 - 80.00
    (LP) 2007 *Johnny & The Hurricanes* ....30.00 - 50.00
    (LP) 2010 *Stormsville* ....30.00 - 50.00

JOHNNY & THE JAMMERS:
Dart 131 *School Day Blues* ....30.00 - 50.00

JOHNNY & THE JOKERS:
Harvard 804 *Do-Re-Mi Rock* ....15.00 - 20.00

JOHNNIE & JONIE:
Challenge 59001 *Kee-Ro-Ryin'* ....8.00 - 12.00
    59041 *Tijuana Jail* ....7.00 - 10.00

AL JOHNSON:
Ric 956 *You Done Me Wrong* ....7.00 - 10.00

BILL JOHNSON:
- *My Hot Rod Car* .... - - -

BROWNIE JOHNSON:
Lynn 101 *One More Kiss* ....20.00 - 30.00

BUBBER JOHNSON:
King (LP) 569 *Come Home* ....50.00 - 80.00
King 4793 *Drop Me a Line* ....10.00 - 15.00
    4822 *Come Home* ....8.00 - 12.00
    4939 *My Lonely Heart* ....8.00 - 12.00
    4988 *Confidential* ....8.00 - 12.00
    5014 *Too Many Hearts* ....8.00 - 12.00
King, most other issues...............................5.00 - 8.00

BUDD JOHNSON ORCHESTRA & VOICES FIVE
(See VOICES FIVE)

BUDDY JOHNSON:
Mercury (LP) 20209 *Rock 'N' Roll* ....20.00 - 30.00

CLIFF JOHNSON:
Columbia 40865 *Go 'Way Hound Dog* ....15.00 - 20.00

CURTIS JOHNSON:
Event 4268 *Baby, Baby*................................15.00 - 20.00

DEE JOHNSON:
Dixie 2022 *Back To School* ....15.00 - 25.00

DON JOHNSON:
Dot 15812 *I'm Hypnotized* ....8.00 - 12.00

GLENN JOHNSON:
Oak 0360 *I'm Gonna Leave You* ....30.00 - 50.00

HOYT JOHNSON:
Erwin 555 *Eenie Meenie Miney Moe*...................100.00 - 150.00
Satellite 110 *I Just Can't Learn*...............40.00 - 70.00

JIMMY JOHNSON:
Class 237 *Cool Cool School* ....10.00 - 15.00
Viv 3001 *Cat Daddy*...................................15.00 - 20.00

JOE D. JOHNSON:
Acme 47 *Rattlesnake Daddy* ....40.00 - 70.00

KAY JOHNSON:
Pamela 203 *Stagger Lee* ....8.00 - 12.00

LONNIE JOHNSON:
King (EP) 267 *Tomorrow Night* ....80.00 - 120.00
    (LP) 395-520 *Lonesome Road* (10 inch LP).....250.00 - 500.00
    (LP) 520 *Lonesome Road* ....100.00 - 200.00
    4201 *Tomorrow Night*.......................20.00 - 30.00
    4212 *Working Man's Blues* ....20.00 - 30.00
    4225 *I Want My Baby* ....20.00 - 30.00
    4245 *Pleasing You* ....20.00 - 30.00
    4261 *I Know It's Love*.......................20.00 - 30.00
    4263 *So Tired*....................................20.00 - 30.00
    4278 *You're Mine You*.......................20.00 - 30.00
    4297 *I Found A Dream*......................20.00 - 30.00

King 4317, 4336, 4346, 4388, 4411, 4423, 4450,
    4459, 4473, 4492, 4510, 4553...........................10.00 - 15.00
(Note: First pressings of early KING issues should not have the
    designation "High Fidelity" and should have the suffixes "A" or
    "AA" after the catalog numbers. Records pressed of colored
    plastic can bring substantially higher prices.)
King, most other issues.............................7.00 - 12.00
Rama 9 *My Woman Is Gone* ....25.00 - 40.00
    14 *Will You Remember*......................20.00 - 30.00
    19 *It's Been So Long* ....20.00 - 30.00
    20 *This Love Of Mine*........................20.00 - 30.00

MARV JOHNSON:
Kudo 663 *Once Upon A Time* ....50.00 - 80.00
Tamla 101 *Come To Me*............................40.00 - 60.00
United Artists (EP) 100...............................50.00 - 80.00
    (LP) 3081 *Marvelous* ....20.00 - 30.00

NEAL JOHNSON:
Specialty 688 *True To You Baby* ....5.00 - 8.00

PHIL JOHNSON & THE DUVALS:
Club 1013 *Yes I Do* ....50.00 - 75.00
Kelit 7033 *I Lie To My Heart* ....50.00 - 75.00
    7034 *Wee Small Hours*......................50.00 - 75.00

RAY JOHNSON:
Demon 1502 *A Yellow Mellow Hardtop* ....10.00 - 15.00

RICK JOHNSON:
Comet 104 *Me And My Baby* ....8.00 - 12.00

ROCKHEART JOHNSON:
RCA Victor 5136 *Black Spider*..............................30.00 - 50.00

STAN JOHNSON:
Ruby 550 *Baby, Baby Doll* ....10.00 - 15.00

THE JOKERS:
Grace 510 *Little Mama* ....20.00 - 30.00
Lin 5027 *Dogfight*.....................................8.00 - 12.00

JOLLY JACKS:
Dasher 501 *Ugly Face*...............................10.00 - 15.00

JONES BOYS (See also JIMMY JONES):
S-G 5007 *The Song Is Ended* ....10.00 - 15.00

ALEX SNOOK JONES:
Blue Boy 1001 *Mean Old Greyhound* ....8.00 - 12.00

ANN JONES:
Audio Lab (LP) 1521 *...And Her American
Sweethearts* ....30.00 - 50.00

CORKY JONES:
Pep 107 *Hot Dog*......................................80.00 - 120.00

CURTIS JONES:
Parrot 782 *Cool Playing Blues*..................50.00 - 100.00

DAVEY JONES:
Apt 25013 *Come On And Love Me* ....10.00 - 15.00
    25064 *I'm In Pain* ....5.00 - 8.00
Dade 1835 *Baby Please Love Me* ....10.00 - 15.00

DEAN JONES:
M-G-M 12620 *Meet Me In The Study Hall*...........10.00 - 15.00

DOTTIE JONES:
TNT 139 *Honey Honey*............................... - - -

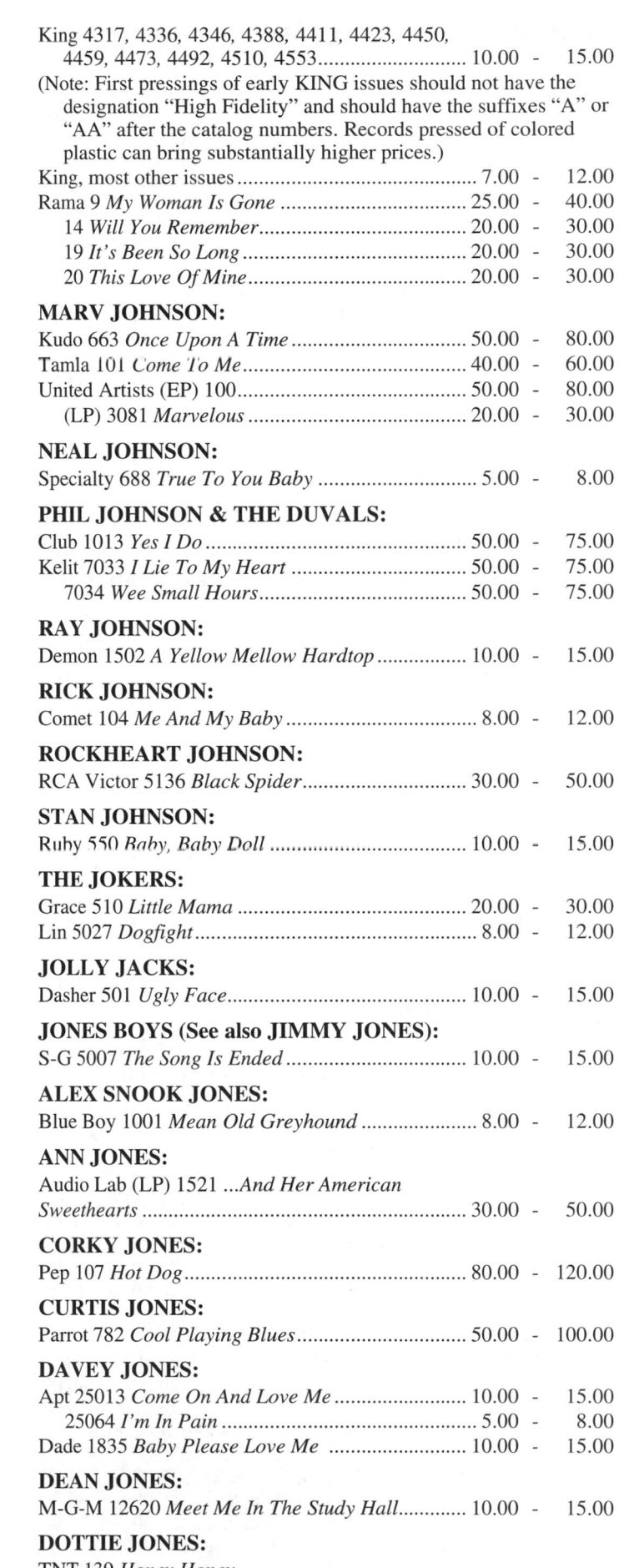

EDDIE JONES (See GUITAR SLIM)

FLOYD JONES:

Chess 1527 *Early Morning* ....100.00 - 200.00
J.O.B. 1013 *On The Road Again* ....150.00 - 300.00
Vee Jay 111 *Ain't Times Hard*.....................150.00 - 300.00
   126 *Floyd's Blues* ....150.00 - 200.00

GEORGE JONES:

Mercury (LP) 20306 *Sings*................................20.00 - 30.00
   (LP) 20477 *Sings* ....20.00 - 30.00
   (LP) 20596 *Salutes Hank Williams*...........20.00 - 30.00
Starday (LP) SLP-101 *Grand Ole Opry's New Star* ... 75.00 - 150.00
   (LP) 125 *The Crown Prince Of Country Music*..30.00 - 50.00
   130 *No Money In This Deal*........................15.00 - 20.00
   202 *Why Baby Why*....................................10.00 - 15.00
   216 *Still Hurtin'* ....10.00 - 15.00
Starday 234, 247, 256, 264, 279 ....7.00 - 12.00

GRANDPA JONES:

King (LP) 554 *Greatest Hits*...........................15.00 - 20.00
   (LP) 625 *Strictly Country Tunes*................15.00 - 20.00

HERMAN JONES:

Gaynote 105 *I'll Be True* ....30.00 - 50.00

JIMMY JONES (& THE JONES BOYS/PRETENDERS/ SAVOYS):

Arrow 717 *Heaven In Your Eyes* ....50.00 - 80.00
Epic 9339 *Whenever You Need Me* ....15.00 - 20.00
Holiday 2610 *Tonight* ....50.00 - 80.00
M-G-M (LP) 3847 *Good Timin'* ....50.00 - 75.00
   (LP) SE-3847 *Good Timin'* (STEREO)..............75.00 - 100.00
Rama 207 *Lover*...40.00 - 70.00
   210 *Lover*...30.00 - 50.00
Roulette 4232 *Plain Old Love* ....10.00 - 20.00
Savoy 1586 *Please Say You're Mine*...............10.00 - 20.00

LITTLE JOHNNY JONES (With THE CHICAGO HOUND DOGS):

Atlantic 1045 *Hoy Hoy*....................................20.00 - 30.00
Flair 1010 *I May Be Wrong* ....20.00 - 30.00

RICKEY JONES:

Herald 498 *Hate To Say Goodbye* ....15.00 - 30.00

LITTLE SONNY JONES:

Imperial 5275 *I Got Booted* ....30.00 - 50.00

SPIKE JONES & HIS CITY SLICKERS/COUNTRY COUSINS/NEW BAND:

(Note: See also the DANCE BANDS, etc. section for earlier
   (78 RPM) records by Spike Jones.)
Kapp 314 *I Want The South To Win The War For Christmas*
   .... -   -
Liberty (LP) 3140 *Omnibust A Hi-Fi Spiketacular* .40.00 - 60.00
   (LP) 3154 *60 Years of Music America Hates Best*
   ....20.00 - 30.00
   (LP) 3338 *Washington Square*..................10.00 - 20.00
   (LP) 3349 *Spike Jones' New Band* ....15.00 - 30.00
   (LP) 3370 *My Man*....................................20.00 - 40.00
   (LP) 3401 *The New Band Of Spike Jones Plays Hank Williams*
   Hits..20.00 - 40.00
   (LP) 7140 *Omnibust* (STEREO)................15.00 - 30.00
   (LP) 7154 (STEREO) *60 Years Of Music America Hates Best*
   ....20.00 - 30.00
   (LP) 7338 (STEREO) *Washington Square*.........10.00 - 20.00
   (LP) 7349 (STEREO) *Spike Jones' New Band*...15.00 - 30.00
   (LP) 7370 (STEREO) *My Man*....................20.00 - 40.00
   (LP) 7401 (STEREO) *...Plays Hank Williams Hits*
   ....20.00 - 40.00

RCA Victor (EP) 18 *Christmas Fun With* ....15.00 - 20.00
   (EP) 143 *The Nutcracker Suite* ....10.00 - 15.00
   (EP) 277 *...Plays The Charleston*.....................15.00 - 25.00
   (EP) 288 *...Favorites*..10.00 - 15.00
   (EP) 415 *...Kids The Classics*...........................15.00 - 25.00
   (EP) 440 *...Murders Carmen*............................20.00 - 30.00
   (EP) 456 *...Country Cousins* ....20.00 - 30.00
   (EP) 3054 (2-record set) *Bottoms Up*................15.00 - 25.00
   (EP) 5058 *Spike Jones* ....10.00 - 15.00
   (EP) 5080 *The Man On The Flying Trapeze*......15.00 - 20.00
   (EP) 599-9049 *Come Josephine... Fiddle Faddle* .... 30.00 - 50.00
   (LP) 18 (10 inch) *...Plays The Charleston* ....30.00 - 50.00
   (LP) 2224 *Thank You, Music Lovers!* ....20.00 - 30.00
   (LP) 3054 (10 inch) *Bottoms Up*........................30.00 - 50.00
   (LP) 3128 (10 inch) *...Murders Carmen And Kids*
   The Classics ....30.00 - 50.00
RCA Victor 2795, 2796, 2797 ....5.00 - 8.00
(Note: Above comprises the set WP-143, "The Nutcracker Suite".)
   2894 *Ya Wanna Buy A Bunny?* ....7.00 - 10.00
   2963 *My Two Front Teeth*...............................7.00 - 10.00
   2992 *Dance Of The Hours* ....5.00 - 8.00
   3126 *Wild Bill Hiccup*....................................7.00 - 10.00
RCA Victor 3198, 3199, 3200 ....7.00 - 10.00
(Note: Above comprises the set "Spike Jones Plays The
   Charleston".)
RCA Victor 3287, 3288, 3289 ....4.00 - 7.00
(Note: Above comprises the set WP-288, "Spike Jones Favorites".)
   3741 *Chinese Mule Train*................................5.00 - 10.00
   3827 *I Know A Secret*.....................................5.00 - 10.00
   3912 *Yes! We Have No Bananas* ....5.00 - 10.00
   3934 *Rudolph The Red-Nosed Reindeer* ....5.00 - 10.00
   3939 *Baby Buggy Boogie*...............................5.00 - 10.00
RCA Victor 4011, 4055, 4125, 4209, 4315 ....4.00 - 8.00
RCA Victor 4546 *Deep Purple* ....5.00 - 10.00
   4568 *Down South*..5.00 - 10.00
   4669 *Stop Your Gamblin'* ....5.00 - 10.00
(Note: First pressings of foregoing have blue-green label; later
   pressings and following have black label.)
   4875 *Hot Lips* ....5.00 - 10.00
   5015 *Barnyard Christmas*...............................5.00 - 10.00
   5067 *I Saw Mommy Kissing Santa Claus* ....5.00 - 10.00
   5107 *I Went To Your Wedding* ....5.00 - 8.00
   5239 *The Boys In The Back Room* ....5.00 - 8.00
   5320 *Three Little Fishies* ....5.00 - 10.00
   5413 *God Bless Us All* ....10.00 - 15.00
   5472 *Dragnet* ....8.00 - 12.00
   5497 *Where Did My Snowman Go?*...................8.00 - 12.00
   5742 *I'm In The Mood For Love*......................5.00 - 8.00
   5920 *I Want Eddie Fisher For Christmas*...........8.00 - 12.00
   6064 *This Song Is For The Birds* ....8.00 - 12.00
Verve 1003 *I'm Popeye The Sailor Man* ....-   -
   2026 *My Birthday Comes On Christmas* ....15.00 - 20.00
   (EP) 2003 *Spike Spoofs The Pops #1* ....30.00 - 50.00
   (EP) 5023 *...Presents A Christmas Spectacular, Vol. 1*
   ....20.00 - 30.00
   (EP) 5024 *...Presents A Christmas Spectacular, Vol. 2*
   ....25.00 - 40.00
   (EP) 5025 *...Presents A Christmas Spectacular, Vol. 3*
   ....25.00 - 40.00
   (EP) 5026 *...Presents A Christmas Spectacular, Vol. 4*
   ....25.00 - 40.00
   (EP) 5056 *Dinner Music For People Who Aren't Very Hungry,*
   Vol. 1 ....30.00 - 50.00
   (EP) 5057 *Dinner Music For People Who Aren't Very Hungry,*
   Vol. 2...30.00 - 50.00
   (LP) 2021 *...Presents A Christmas Spectacular* 50.00 - 75.00

(LP) 4005 *Dinner Music For People Who Aren't Very Hungry*
....50.00 -   80.00
Warner Brothers (LP) WB-1332 *Spike Jones In Hi-Fi* (gray label)
....30.00 -   60.00
(LP) WS-1332 *Spike Jones In Stereo* (gold label)
....50.00 -   80.00
5116 *Monster Movie Ball* ....   -   -

(Note: Spike Jones recorded a number of songs which were issued for children, in albums or sets, such as those in RCA Victor's "Little Nipper" series. Although children's records are outside the present scope of this book, it should be noted that Spike Jones' children records are collectible, and might be of value to Spike Jones collectors and children's records collectors.)

THUMPER JONES:
Starday 240 *Rock It*................................75.00 - 125.00

WILL JONES & THE CADETS (See THE CADETS)

JONESY'S COMBO:
Combo 79 *Ting, Ting Boom Scat*..................10.00 -   15.00

JORDAN & THE FASCINATIONS:
Carol 4116 *Once Upon A Time*....................15.00 -   20.00

JORDAN BROTHERS:
Jamie 1112, 1125, 1133, 1169, 1205 ....7.00 -   10.00

JOHNNY JORDAN:
Jolt 332 *Sweet Sweet Sweet*......................10.00 -   15.00

LOUIS JORDAN:
Aladdin 3223 *Whiskey Do Your Stuff*............15.00 -   20.00
3227 *Ooh Wee!* ....15.00 -   20.00
3243 *A Dollar Down*................................15.00 -   20.00
3246 *Messy Bessie* ....15.00 -   20.00
3249 *Louis' Blues* ....15.00 -   20.00
3264 *Yeah, Yeah, Baby*...........................15.00 -   20.00
3270 *The Dripper* ....15.00 -   20.00
3279 *Time Is A-Passin'* ....10.00 -   15.00
3295 *Gotta Go* ....10.00 -   15.00
Decca (LP) 8551 *Let The Good Times Roll*............75.00 - 100.00
Decca, most issues ....5.00 -   10.00
Score (LP) 4007 *Go Blow Your Horn*.................150.00 - 300.00
Wing (LP) 12126 *Somebody Up There Digs Me*.....50.00 -   80.00

BENNIE JOY:
Antler 4011 *Crash The Party* ....20.00 -   30.00
Disc Jockey 41 *Crash The Party* ....20.00 -   30.00
Dixie 2001 *Spin The Bottle* ....100.00 - 150.00
Ram 1107 *Itty Bitty Everything* ....25.00 -   40.00
Tri-Dec 8668 *Spin The Bottle* ....100.00 - 200.00

THE JOYETTES:
Onyx 502 *Story Of Love* ....20.00 -   40.00

JOYLARKS:
Snag 107 *Betty My Love* ....150.00 - 300.00

JOYTONES:
Rama 191 *All My Love Belongs To You* ....15.00 -   20.00
202 *Is This Really The End?* ....20.00 -   30.00
215 *My Foolish Heart* ....150.00 - 200.00

JUBALAIRES:
Capitol 821 *Blue Ribbon Gal*....................8.00 -   12.00
845 *The Old Piano Roll Blues* ....8.00 -   12.00

JUDY & JOYCE:
Dot 15729 *He's The One* ....10.00 -   15.00

DON JULIAN & THE MEADOWLARKS:
Dooto (EP) 203 ....100.00 - 150.00

Dootone 359 *Heaven And Paradise*..........................25.00 -   40.00
367 *Always And Always* ....25.00 -   40.00
372 *This Must Be Paradise* ....25.00 -   40.00
394 *Please Love A Fool* ....25.00 -   40.00
405 *I'm A Believer* ....25.00 -   40.00
(Above are red label)
Magnum 716 *Lie* ....8.00 -   12.00

JOHNNY JUMPER:
Vance - *Walking Talking/Worried Over You*............. -   -   -

JUMPING JACKS/JUMPIN' JACKS:
Bruce 115 *Embraceable You*................................150.00 - 300.00
Decca 29973 *You'll Wonder Where The Yellow Went*
....8.00 -   12.00

JUMPIN JAGUARS:
Decca 29938 *Shut The Door Baby*........................... -   -   -

JUMPINTONES:
Raven 8004 *I Wonder*......................................10.00 -   15.00
8005 *That Angel Is You* ....10.00 -   15.00

BILL JUSTIS:
Phillips 3519 *Raunchy* (78 RPM) ....20.00 -   30.00

KADAKS (See KODAKS)

THE KALIN TWINS:
Decca (EP) 2623 *When* ....25.00 -   50.00
(LP) 8812 *The Kalin Twins* ....25.00 -   50.00
30642 *When* (78 RPM) ....40.00 -   60.00

THE KAPPAS:
Wonder 112 *Sweet Juanita* ....25.00 -   40.00

SAX KARI & THE QUAILTONES:
Josie 779 *Tears Of Love*...................................50.00 -   80.00

KASANDREA With THE MIDNIGHT RIDERS:
Sahara 101 *My Conscience Is Bothering Me* ....10.00 -   15.00

THE KASHMIRS:
Wonder 104 *Heaven Only Knows*.........................100.00 - 150.00

STEVE KASS & THE LOVELARKS:
Class 10X *Darling, My Love* ....50.00 -   80.00

ANNE KAYE:
Gee 1015 *Every Fortune Teller Tells Me*..................8.00 -   12.00

ERNIE K-DOE:
Minit (LP) 00002 *Mother-In-Law*...........................30.00 -   50.00

RAMSEY KEARNEY:
Jaxon 501 *Rock The Bop* ....100.00 - 150.00

BILLY KEEN & THE TRADEWINDS:
Lesley 1922 *Don't Call Me*.................................15.00 -   20.00

THE KELLY FOUR:
Silver 1001 *Strollin' Guitar* ....8.00 -   12.00
1006 *So, Fine, Be Mine!* ....8.00 -   12.00

JIMMY KELLY:
Cobra 5028 *Little Chickie* ....25.00 -   40.00

LEON KELLY & THE RHYTHM ROCKETS:
Space 795 *You Put My Heart In Orbit* ....40.00 -   60.00

PAT KELLY & THE SHAMROCKS:
Chic 1009 *The Stranger Dressed In Black*............10.00 -   20.00
Jubilee 5315 *Hey Doll Baby/Cloud* 13...............10.00 -   15.00

TINY KENNEDY:
Capitol 840 *Sister Flat Top* ....15.00 -   20.00

KENNY and DOOLITTLE:
Sims 123 *Kitty Kat* ....20.00 - 30.00

KENNY & THE CADETS:
Randy 422 *Barbie* (pink label with blue type).......200.00 - up
422 *Barbie* (multi-colored vinyl) ....300.00 - up

KENNY AND THE KASUALS:
Mark (LP) 5000 *The Impact Sound Of Kenny And The Kasuals*
.... - - -

KENNY & MOE (THE BLUE BOYS):
De Luxe 6101 *Can't Help Myself* ....10.00 - 20.00
6122 *I'm All Alone* ....10.00 - 20.00
6134 *I Sing This Song* ....10.00 - 20.00
6139 *Yes I Will* ....10.00 - 20.00
6154 *Double Talk Baby* ....10.00 - 20.00

FRANK & RAY KENNY:
PL 13 *If You Love Me* ....20.00 - 30.00

HERB KENNY & THE COMETS:
Federal 12083 *Only You* ....40.00 - 70.00

BOBBY KENT & THE KENTONES:
Bay State 82159 *Don't Go 'Way* ....10.00 - 15.00

THE KENTS:
Argo 5299 *With All My Heart And Soul* ....10.00 - 15.00
Dome 501 *I Love You So* ....50.00 - 75.00

CHRIS KEVIN:
Colt 45 103 *Haunted House* .... - - -

KEYNOTES:
Apollo 478 *Suddenly* ....40.00 - 60.00
484 *I Don't Know* ....20.00 - 30.00
493 *Wish You Were Here* ....50.00 - 75.00
498 *Now I Know* ....30.00 - 50.00
503 *In The Evening* ....30.00 - 50.00
513 *Now I Know* ....25.00 - 40.00

THE KEYSTONERS:
Epic 9187 *The Magic Kiss* ....15.00 - 20.00
G & M 102 *I'd Write About The Blues* ....50.00 - 80.00
Okeh 7210 *The Magic Kiss* ....8.00 - 12.00
Riff 202 *TV Gal* ....50.00 - 80.00

THE KEYTONES:
Chess 1821 *Lover Of Mine* ....75.00 - 100.00
Old Town 1041 *Seven Wonders Of The World* ....50.00 - 80.00
Pop 111 *Carelessly* ....10.00 - 15.00

BILLY (THE) KIDD:
Jane 107 *Crazy Guitar* ....15.00 - 20.00

KIDDS:
Imperial 5335 *Are You Forgetting Me* ....150.00 - 300.00
Post 2003 *You Broke My Heart* ....150.00 - 200.00

KIDS FROM TEXAS:
Blue Star 1613 *Shoot The Moon* ....10.00 - 15.00
Hanover 4500 *Long Legged Linda* ....10.00 - 20.00

MERLE KILGORE:
D 1042 *I Take A Trip To The Moon* ....10.00 - 15.00
Imperial 5379 *Teenagers Holiday* ....15.00 - 20.00
5409 *Ernie* ....15.00 - 20.00
5555 *Hang Doll* ....10.00 - 15.00
8300 *Funny Feelin'* ....10.00 - 15.00
Starday 469, 497 ....5.00 - 10.00

BILLY J. KILLEN:
Meridian 1510 *Georgia Boy* ....15.00 - 20.00

ALBERT KING:
Bobbin 114 *Ooh-ee Baby* ....10.00 - 15.00
119 *The Time Has Come* ....10.00 - 15.00
126 *Blues At Sunrise* ....10.00 - 15.00
129 *I Walked All Night Long* ....10.00 - 15.00
135 *I Get Evil* ....15.00 - 20.00
141 *I'll Do Anything You Say* ....10.00 - 15.00
143 *Old Blue Ribbon* ....10.00 - 15.00
Coun-Tree 1006 *C.O.D.* ....7.00 - 10.00
King (LP) 852 *The Big Blues* ....50.00 - 80.00
5575, 5588, 5751 ....7.00 - 10.00
Parrot 798 *Back Luck Blues* ....100.00 - 150.00

B.B. (BLUES BOY) KING:
Crown (LP) 5020 *Singin' The Blues* ....25.00 - 50.00
(LP) 5063 *The Blues* ....25.00 - 50.00
(LP) 5115 *B.B. King Wails* ....25.00 - 50.00
(LP) 5119 *B.B. King Sings Spirituals* ....25.00 - 50.00
(LP) 5143 *The Great B.B. King* ....20.00 - 30.00
(LP) 5167 *King Of The Blues* ....20.00 - 30.00
(LP) 5188 *My Kind Of Blues* ....20.00 - 30.00
Kent 301, 307, 315, 317, 319, 321, 327, 329, 330,
333, 346, 350, 351, 353, 358, 360, 362, 363 ....5.00 - 10.00
RPM 323 *She's Dynamite* ....150.00 - 300.00
330 *Hard Working Woman* ....100.00 - 150.00
339 *Three O'Clock Blues* ....80.00 - 130.00
(Note: The existence of numbers lower than above in 45 RPM format
   has not been verified. 78 RPM counterparts are minimally valued;
   see the BLUES, etc. section.)
348 *Fine Lookin' Woman* ....25.00 - 40.00
355 *Shake It Up And Go* ....20.00 - 30.00
360 *Gotta Find My Baby* ....15.00 - 20.00
363 *You Know I Love You* ....15.00 - 20.00
374 *Boogie Woogie Woman* ....15.00 - 20.00
380 *Woke Up This Morning* ....15.00 - 20.00
386 *Highway Bound* ....15.00 - 20.00
RPM 391, 395, 403, 408, 411, 412, 416, 421,
425, 430, 435, 437, 451 ....7.00 - 10.00
RPM 457, 459, 468, 479, 486, 490, 492, 494,
498, 501 ....5.00 - 10.00

CAROLE KING:
ABC Paramount 9921 *Goin' Wild* ....20.00 - 30.00
9986 *Baby Sittin'* ....25.00 - 40.00
Alpine 57 *Oh, Neil* ....30.00 - 60.00
Companion 2000 *Nobody's Perfect* ....25.00 - 40.00
Dimension 1009 *He's A Bad Boy* ....10.00 - 15.00
RCA Victor 7560 *Queen Of The Beach* ....20.00 - 30.00

EARL KING:
Ace 509 *Baby You Can Get Your Gun* ....10.00 - 15.00
514 *My Love Is Strong* ....10.00 - 15.00
Specialty 531 *No One But Me* ....10.00 - 15.00

EDDIE KING:
J.O.B. 1122 *Shakin' Inside* ....80.00 - 120.00

FREDDY KING:
El-Bee 157 *Country Boy* ....30.00 - 60.00
Federal 12384, 12401, 12415, 12428, 12432,
12443, 12450 ....7.00 - 10.00
King (LP) 762 *Freddy King Sings* ....30.00 - 50.00
(LP) 773 *Let's Hide Away & Dance Away* ....25.00 - 50.00
(LP) 821 *Bossa Nova & The Blues* ....20.00 - 40.00

JACK KING:
4-Star 1725 *I Just Learned to Rock* ....20.00 - 30.00

JIMMY KING:
Herald 535 *Knocking On Your Door* ....10.00 - 15.00

KID KING'S COMBO:
Excello 2009 *Banana Split* ....15.00 - 20.00
    2018 *The Brass Rail* ....15.00 - 20.00
    2025 *Chocolate Sundae* ....10.00 - 15.00
    2037 *Memories In Melody* ....15.00 - 20.00
    2046 *Strollin' Time* ....15.00 - 20.00
    2109 *Are You Sure* ....15.00 - 20.00

PEE WEE KING & HIS BAND:
RCA Victor (LP) 1237 *Swing West* ....30.00 - 50.00
    (LP) 3028 (10 inch) ....40.00 - 60.00
    (LP) 3071 (10 inch) *Pee Wee King's Western Hits*
    ....40.00 - 60.00
    (LP) 3109 (10 inch) *Waltzes* ....40.00 - 60.00
    (LP) 3280 (10 inch) *Swing West* ....40.00 - 60.00
    6450 *Blue Suede Shoes* ....10.00 - 15.00

RANDY KING:
TNT 9009 *Be Boppin' Baby/Whispering Wind* ....40.00 - 60.00

RAY KING:
Karl 222 *A Date At Eight* ....75.00 - 100.00

SID KING (& HIS FIVE STRINGS) (See also FIVE STRINGS):
Columbia 21361 *I Like It* ....8.00 - 12.00
    21449 *Sag, Drag And Fall* ....15.00 - 20.00
    21489 *Purr, Kitty, Purr* ....15.00 - 20.00
    21505 *Blue Suede Shoes* ....15.00 - 25.00
    21564 *Good Rockin' Baby* ....15.00 - 25.00
    40680 *Oobie Doobie* ....15.00 - 25.00
    40833 *When My Baby Left Me* ....10.00 - 15.00
    41019 *I've Got The Blues* ....10.00 - 15.00

SLEEPY KING:
Awake 852 *Rock Rock* ....7.00 - 10.00

WILLIE KING With IKE TURNER'S BAND:
Vita 123 *Peg Leg Woman* ....10.00 - 15.00

THE KING BEES (With LLOYD PRICE'S ORCHESTRA):
Flip 323 *Puppy Love* ....50.00 - 80.00
KRC 302 *Can't You Understand* ....10.00 - 15.00
Noble 715 *Tender Love* ....200.00 - 300.00

KING CHARLES:
Folk Star 1131 *Bop Cat Stomp* ....30.00 - 50.00

KING CROONERS/KROONERS:
Hart 1002 *Lonely Nights* ....100.00 - 150.00
Excello 2168 *Now That She's Gone* ....25.00 - 40.00
    2187 *School Daze* ....25.00 - 40.00

KING PERRY:
Excelsior 600 *Big Fat Mama* ....20.00 - 30.00

KING TOPPERS:
Josie 811 *Walkin' And Talkin' The Blues* ....20.00 - 30.00

KING VICTOR:
Madison 110 *Boppin' Bobbie Jean* ....10.00 - 15.00

THE KINGLETS (with LEROY THOMAS):
Bobbin 104 *Pretty Please* ....25.00 - 40.00
Calvert 101 *Six Days A Week* ....30.00 - 50.00

THE KINGS (See also BOBBY HALL):
Baton 245 *Long, Lonely Nights* ....15.00 - 20.00
Epic 9370 *I Want To Know* ....7.00 - 10.00

Gone 5013 *Don't Go* ....75.00 - 100.00
Gotham 316 *God Made You Mine* ....30.00 - 50.00
Jalo 203 *Angel* ....30.00 - 50.00
Jay Wing 5805 *Surrender* ....25.00 - 40.00
Specialty 497 *What Can I Do* ....25.00 - 40.00

THE KINGS MEN/KINGSMEN:
Arnold 2106 *Goodnight Sweetheart* ....50.00 - 80.00
Club-51 108 *Don't Say You're Sorry* ....200.00 - 300.00
Neil 102 *One Foolish Mistake* ....15.00 - 20.00

KINKS:
Cameo 308 *Long Tall Sally* ....50.00 - 75.00
    345 *Long Tall Sally* ....25.00 - 40.00
    348 *You Still Want Me* ....75.00 - 100.00

MARY KINNEY:
Andex 4031 *Bobby My Love* ....8.00 - 12.00

DAVE KIRK:
Hi-Q 5024 *Lonely Blue Nights* ....10.00 - 15.00

EDDIE KIRKLAND:
King 4680 *I Mistreated A Woman* ....50.00 - 80.00

JIMMY KIRKLAND (with STAN GETZ & THE TOM CATS):
Fox 918/919 *Come On Baby* ....20.00 - 30.00
Teen Life 918/919 *Come On Baby* ....30.00 - 50.00

REX KLINGENSMITH:
Process 103 *Old Country Music* ....10.00 - 15.00

KLIKS/KLIXS:
Music City 817 *It's All Over* ....100.00 - 150.00
    823 *Elaine* ....150.00 - 200.00

TOMMY KNACKIN:
Cascade - *Worry Worry Worry* ....10.00 - 20.00

THE KNICKERBOCKERS:
It's A Natural 3000 *You Must Know* ....150.00 - 250.00

BAKER KNIGHT (& THE KNIGHTMARES):
Coral 62132 *Takin' A Chance* ....10.00 - 15.00
    62160 *Tag Along Blues* ....10.00 - 15.00
Decca 30135 *Bring My Cadillac Back* ......10.00 - 15.00
    30213 *Reelin' And Rockin'* ....10.00 - 20.00
    30426 *Love-A Love-A Love-A* ....10.00 - 15.00
Kit 900 *Bring My Cadillac Back* ....20.00 - 30.00

GLADYS KNIGHT & THE PIPS:
Fury (LP) 1003 *Letter Full Of Tears* ....80.00 - 120.00

JESSIE KNIGHT:
Checker 797 *Nothing But Money* ....20.00 - 30.00

JOHNNY KNIGHT:
Morocco 1005 *Rock And Roll Guitar* ....30.00 - 50.00

MARIE KNIGHT:
Diamond 136 *I Was Born Again* ....10.00 - 15.00
    149 *The Nearness Of You* ....10.00 - 15.00
    171 *Make Yourself At Home* ....10.00 - 15.00
Mercury 70969 *Look At Me* ....10.00 - 15.00
    71055 *Am I Reaching For The Moon* ......10.00 - 15.00
Wing 90069 *Tell Me Why* ....10.00 - 15.00

SONNY KNIGHT:
Dot 15507 *Confidential* (78 RPM) ....15.00 - 30.00
Eastman 787 *Lipstick Kisses* ....5.00 - 10.00
    791 *Barbara* ....5.00 - 10.00
Go Go 711 *Teenage Party* ....- -
Starla 10 *Once In A While* ....7.00 - 10.00
Vita 137 *Confidential* ....10.00 - 15.00

SUNNY KNIGHT:
Dot 15542 *Worthless And Lowdown* ....10.00 - 15.00

KNOCKOUTS:
Shad 5013 *Darling Lorraine* ....10.00 - 20.00

BUDDY KNOX (with THE (RHYTHM) ORCHIDS):
Blue Moon 402 *Party Doll* ....50.00 - 75.00
Liberty (LP) 3251 *Golden Hits*..............................20.00 - 30.00
Roulette (EP) 1-301 *Party Doll* ....40.00 - 70.00
Roulette 4002, 4009, 4018, 4042, 4082..................5.00 - 8.00
   4002 *Party Doll* (78 RPM) ....20.00 - 30.00
   4009 *Rock Your Little Baby To Sleep* (78 RPM).......10.00 - 15.00
   4018 *Hula Love* (78 RPM) ....10.00 - 15.00
   4042 *Swingin' Daddy* (78 RPM) ....15.00 - 20.00
   4082 *C'mon Baby* (78 RPM) ....15.00 - 20.00
   (LP) 25003 *Buddy Knox* ....40.00 - 70.00
   (LP) 25048 *Buddy Knox And Jimmy Bowen*.......50.00 - 75.00
Ruff 1001 *Jo Ann*..5.00 - 10.00
Triple-D 797 *Party Doll* ....100.00 - 150.00

KODAKS:
Fury 1007 *Teenagers Dream* ....20.00 - 40.00
   1015 *Make Believe World*...............................15.00 - 20.00
   1019 *My Baby And Me* ....25.00 - 40.00
   1020 *Guardian Angel* ....25.00 - 40.00
J & S 1683 *Don't Want No Teasing* ....20.00 - 30.00
   1684 *Look Up To The Sky*................................20.00 - 30.00
Sphere Sound (LP) 7005 *The Kodaks Vs. The Starlites*
   ....50.00 - 75.00

KODOKS (See KODAKS)

FREDDY KOENIG:
Lori 9548 *Hey Clarice!*...15.00 - 20.00
Valerie 225 *Hey Clarice!* ....10.00 - 15.00

THE KO KOS:
Combo 141 *The First Day Of School* ....40.00 - 70.00

KOOL GENTS:
Bethlehem 3061 *Picture On The Wall*....................15.00 - 20.00
Vee Jay 173 *This Is The Night*...............................40.00 - 70.00
   207 *I Just Can't Help Myself*...........................40.00 - 70.00

THE KOOL TOPPERS:
Beverly 702 *'Cause I Love You So* ....150.00 - 250.00

PAUL KOSTY:
Fleet *Don't Rock, Let's Roll* .... -   -   -

KUF-LINX:
Challenge 1013 *So Tough*.....................................10.00 - 15.00
   59004 *Eyeballin* ....10.00 - 15.00
   59015 *All That's Good*....................................10.00 - 15.00

SLEEPY LA BEEF/LA BEFF:
Crescent 102 *Turn Me Loose* ....50.00 - 80.00
Dixie (EP) 530 *Ballad Of A Teenage Queen* (other cuts on this EP
   are by other artists; issued without cardboard cover?)
   ....75.00 - 100.00
Gulf 62760 *Can't Get You Off My Mind* ....20.00 - 30.00
Mercury 71112 *I'm Through* ....25.00 - 40.00
   71179 *All The Time*..20.00 - 30.00
Starday 292 *I'm Through*......................................75.00 - 100.00

TOMMY LA BEFF:
Wayside 1654 *Tore Up* ....100.00 - 150.00

LABRADORS:
Chief 7009 *When Someone Loves You* ....80.00 - 120.00

LENNY LACOUR:
Academy *Rockin' Rosalie*......................................15.00 - 20.00

LADDERS:
Holiday 2611 *Counting The Stars*..........................50.00 - 80.00
Vest 826 *My Love Is Gone*.....................................20.00 - 30.00

THE LADDINS:
Angie 1003 *Push, Shake, Kick And Shout* ....10.00 - 15.00
Butane 779 *Dream Baby*..5.00 - 8.00
Central 2602 *Now You're Gone* (black label).........50.00 - 80.00
Grey Cliff 721 *Light A Candle* ....7.00 - 10.00
Groove 64-5 *That's What You Do To Me* ....7.00 - 10.00
Theatre 111 *There Once Was A Time* ....10.00 - 15.00

LA DELL SISTERS:
Mercury 70888 *Rockin' Robert*..............................10.00 - 15.00

KENNY LAINE & HIS BULL DOGS:
- Columbus Stockade Blues .... -   -   -

TOMMY LAM:
Nabor 103 *Speed Limit*...20.00 - 30.00

TONY LA MAR:
Duco 5001 *Come Out Tonight* ....30.00 - 50.00

GENE LAMARR:
Flame 1102 *Just A Stranger*..................................20.00 - 30.00
Spry 113 *Moon Eyes* ....75.00 - 100.00

RUDY LAMBERT (See THE MONDELLOS)

JIMMY LAMBERTH:
Meteor 5044 *Latch On To Your Baby*.....................50.00 - 100.00

TONY & JACKIE LAMIE:
Sunset 706 *Wore To A Frazzell* ....50.00 - 100.00

BILLY LAMONT:
Okeh 7125 *Country Boy*..15.00 - 20.00
   7131 *I'm Gonna Try*.......................................8.00 - 12.00

TOMMY LAMPKIN:
Ebb 110 *Three Minus One* ....8.00 - 12.00
Imperial 5361 *Eternal Love* ....25.00 - 40.00

LAMPLIGHTERS:
Federal 12149 *Part Of Me* ....40.00 - 60.00
   12152 *Give Me*...40.00 - 60.00
   12166 *I Can't Stand It*....................................40.00 - 60.00
   12176 *Tell Me You Care* ....30.00 - 50.00
   12182 *Salty Dog* ....30.00 - 50.00
   12192 *Five Minutes Longer* ....30.00 - 50.00
   12197 *Yum Yum* ....30.00 - 50.00
   12206 *Believe In Me* ....25.00 - 40.00
   12212 *Love Rock And Thrill* ....25.00 - 40.00
   12242 *Hug A Little, Kiss A Little* ....30.00 - 50.00
   12255 *You Were Sent Down From Heaven* ....30.00 - 50.00
   12261 *Everything's All Right*............................30.00 - 50.00

MAJOR LANCE:
Okeh (LP) 12105 *Monkey Time* ....30.00 - 60.00

JERRY LANDIS:
Amy 815 *The Lone Teen Ranger* ....15.00 - 20.00

BUDDY LANDON:
Hollywood 1052 *Foxy*...10.00 - 15.00
Jaguar 3026 *Raunchy Little Baby*..........................15.00 - 20.00
   3028 *A Bolt Of Lightning* ....15.00 - 20.00

LANE BROTHERS:
Leader 804 *Two Dozen And A Half* ....10.00 - 15.00
RCA Victor 6900 *Uh Huh Honey*.....................10.00 - 15.00
   7107 *Don't Tempt Me Baby*..........................8.00 - 12.00
   7220 *Boppin' In A Sack* ....8.00 - 12.00

HARRY LANE:
RA-Q 602 *Gettin' Ready For Love* ....10.00 - 15.00

JIMMY LANE & THE SUGARTONES:
Time 6602 *Let Your Conscience Be Your Guide* .....25.00 - 40.00

MORRIS LANE:
Red Robin 101 *Ghost Town*........................20.00 - 30.00

RALPH LANE & THE WHITEY FOUR:
Cowtown 811 *You Gotta Show Me*.........................30.00 - 50.00

LANES:
Gee 1023 *Open Up Your Heart* ....20.00 - 30.00

CURLEY LANGLEY:
Arcadia *110 Rockin' & Rollin'* ....20.00 - 30.00
   111 *She Wasn't Always Your Girl* ....15.00 - 20.00

DON LANIER:
Roulette 4021 *Pony Tail Girl* ....8.00 - 12.00

LOUISIANA LANNIS:
Snowcap 1125 *Tongue Twister Boogie* ....30.00 - 50.00

THE LAPELS:
Dot 16129 *Sneakin' Around* ....8.00 - 12.00
Melker 10 *Sneakin' Around* ....15.00 - 20.00

LARADOS:
Fox 962/963 *Now The Parting Begins*.....................75.00 - 100.00

THE LA-RELLS:
Robbee 109 *Please Be Fair* ....10.00 - 15.00

THE LARGOS:
Dot 16292 *I Wonder Why* ....8.00 - 12.00
Starmaker 1002 *I Wonder Why*...............................20.00 - 30.00

THE LARKS:
Apollo 427 *Eyesight To The Blind*...........................- - -
   429 *Hey Little Girl*..- - -
(Note: the foregoing, and Apollo 437, following, are not known to
   exist in 45 RPM format; 78 RPM records are listed in the
   BLUES, ETC. section)
Apollo 430 *I Don't Believe In Tomorrow*..............300.00 - 600.00
   435 *My Lost Love*.....................................300.00 - 600.00
   437 *Lucy Brown*.......................................- - -
   475 *No Mama No*......................................75.00 - 100.00
   1180 *Hopefully Yours* ....500.00 - 1000.00
   1184 *My Reverie* ....750.00 - 1500.00
   1190 *In My Lonely Room*..............................600.00 - 1000.00
   1194 *I Live True To You*.................................600.00 - 1000.00
(Note: Last four made of red-orange plastic.)
Cross Fire 74-50 *Life Is Sweeter Now* ....10.00 - 15.00
Guyden 2098 *I Want Her To Love Me*.......................8.00 - 12.00
   2103 *Life Is Sweeter Now* ....7.00 - 10.00
Jett 3001 *Love Me True* ....10.00 - 15.00
Lloyd's 108 *Maggie*................................50.00 - 100.00
   110 *If It's A Crime* ....75.00 - 100.00
   111 *When You're Near* ....75.00 - 100.00
   112 *The World Is Waiting*.............................100.00 - 150.00
   114 *Forget It* ....50.00 - 100.00
Sheryl 334 *It's Unbelievable* ....8.00 - 12.00
   338 *There Is A Girl* ....10.00 - 15.00
Violet 1050 *I Want Her To Love Me* ....10.00 - 15.00

THE LARKTONES:
ABC Paramount 9909 *The Letter* ....8.00 - 12.00
Riki 140 *Why Are You Tearing Us Apart* ....20.00 - 30.00

PAT LA ROCCA:
Bella 4284 *Rowena* ....15.00 - 20.00

LARRY & THE STANDARDS:
Laurie 3119 *My Lucky Night*...................................10.00 - 15.00

ROC LA RUE & 3 PALS:
Rama 226 *Teenage Blues*.....................................30.00 - 50.00

ROGER LARUE & HIS PALS:
Holland 7421 *I Don't Care If The Sun Don't Shine*.......20.00 - 40.00

THE LATONS:
Port 70030 *So In Love* ....15.00 - 20.00

THE LAURELS (See also BOBBY RELF):
Combo 66 *Fine Fine Baby* ....80.00 - 120.00
Spring 1112 *Baby Talk*..30.00 - 50.00
"X" 0143 *Truly, Truly*..50.00 - 80.00

ROD LAUREN:
RCA Victor (LP) 2176 *I'm Rod Lauren* ....15.00 - 20.00

THE LAVENDERS:
CR 1003 *Angel* ....20.00 - 30.00
Lake 706 *The Bells* ....8.00 - 12.00

CHARLES LAVERNE:
Mark 117 *Hudson River Blues* ....10.00 - 15.00

DALE LAVON:
Cavalier - *The Rockin' Chair Roll* ....10.00 - 15.00

ART LAW:
Gulfstream 1050 *Big Train* ....20.00 - 30.00
   1051 *Kitty Kat Rock* ....25.00 - 40.00

MIKE LAWING & DISSONAIRES:
Altair 101 *One Love*..20.00 - 30.00

BILL LAWRENCE:
B.I. 207 *Hey Baby* ....30.00 - 40.00
Freedom 44004 *Hey Baby*......................................10.00 - 15.00

SYD LAWRENCE:
Cosmic 1001 *The Answer To Flying Saucer*.............7.00 - 10.00

BOBBY LAWSON:
Kyser 2122 *Burning Sensation* ....15.00 - 20.00
M.R.C. 600 *Baby Don't Be That Way* ....30.00 - 50.00

LAZY BILL & HIS BLUE RHYTHMS:
Chance 1148 *She Got Me Walkin'* ....150.00 - 250.00

LAZY LESTER:
Excello 2095 *Lester's Stomp* ....10.00 - 15.00
   2107 *They Call Me Lazy* ....10.00 - 15.00
   2129 *Tell Me Pretty Baby* ....10.00 - 15.00
Excello 2143, 2155, 2166, 2182, 2197 ....5.00 - 10.00
   2206, 2219, 2230, 2235, 2243, 2274, 2277..........5.00 - 8.00
   (LP) 8006 *True Blues* ....50.00 - 80.00

LILLIAN LEACH (See THE MELLOWS)

LEADBELLY:
Allegro (LP) 4027 (10 inch) *Sinful Songs*...............30.00 - 50.00
Capitol (LP) 369 (10 inch) *Leadbelly* ....40.00 - 60.00
Folkways (LP) 4, 14, 24, 43 *(10 inch)* ....10.00 - 20.00
   (LP) 241, 242 *Last Session* ....10.00 - 20.00
Stinson (LP) 17 (10 inch) *Memorial* ....15.00 - 20.00
   (LP) 19 (10 inch) *Memorial Vol. 2* ....15.00 - 20.00
   (LP) 39 (10 inch) *Plays Parties* ....15.00 - 20.00

(LP) 41 (10 inch) *Plays Parties, Vol. 2* ....15.00 - 20.00
(LP) 48 (10 inch) *Memorial, Vol. 3* ....15.00 - 20.00
(LP) 51 (10 inch) *Memorial, Vol. 4* ....15.00 - 20.00

LEADERS:
Glory 235 *Stormy Weather* ....10.00 - 15.00
239 *Dearest Beloved Darling* ....20.00 - 30.00
243 *Can't Help Loving That Girl Of Mine* ....10.00 - 15.00

LEE & THE LEOPARDS:
Fortune 867 *What About Me* ....15.00 - 30.00
Gordy 7002 *Come Into My Palace* ....20.00 - 40.00
Laurie 3197 *Come Into My Palace* ....8.00 - 12.00

(LITTLE) BRENDA LEE:
Decca 30050 *Bigelow 6-2000* ....8.00 - 12.00
30107 *Christy Christmas* ....7.00 - 10.00
30198 *One Step At A Time* ....7.00 - 10.00
30333 *Dynamite* ....5.00 - 8.00
30333 *Dynamite* (78 RPM) ....10.00 - 15.00
30411 *Ain't That Love* ....5.00 - 8.00
30535 *Rock The Bop* ....5.00 - 8.00
30673 *Ring-A My Phone* ....5.00 - 8.00
(most other issues) ....4.00 - 8.00

BOB LEE:
Skyla 1117 *You Mostest Girl* ....10.00 - 15.00

BOOKER LEE, JR.:
Federal 12321 *Rockin' Blues* ....20.00 - 30.00

BUDDY LEE:
Brunswick 55228 *Ain't That Right* ....8.00 - 12.00

DICKIE LEE (& THE COLLEGIATES):
Sun 280 *Good Lovin'* ....15.00 - 20.00
297 *Fool Fool Fool* ....25.00 - 40.00
Tampa 131 *Stay True Baby* ....15.00 - 20.00

FLOYD LEE:
Enterprise 1233 *Go Boy* ....15.00 - 20.00

HARRY LEE:
Igloo 101 *Rockin' On A Reindeer* ....75.00 - 100.00
Raynard 2005 *Greedy Lips* .... - -
Vin 1007 *You Don't Know* ....10.00 - 15.00

JESSIE LEE With THE RHYTHMAIRES:
Mida 110 *Lonely Broken Heart* ....15.00 - 25.00

JIMMY LEE:
Bandera 2506 *Chicago Jump* ....10.00 - 15.00

JIMMY LEE AND JOHNNY MATHIS (See also JIMMY & JOHNNY):
Chess 4865 *Love Me* ....30.00 - 40.00

JOE LEE & HIS SEXTET With SCOTTY & BILL:
Fernwood 108 *Ethel Mae* ....25.00 - 40.00

JOHN LEE:
Federal 12089 *Baby's Blues* ....40.00 - 70.00

JOHNNY LEE:
De Luxe 6009 *I'm A Boogie Man* ....30.00 - 50.00

JULIA LEE:
Capitol (LP) H-288 (10 inch) *Party Time* ....50.00 - 75.00
(LP) T-288 *Party Time* ....50.00 - 75.00

LEONARD LEE:
Lamp 8001 *Tryin' To Fool Me* ....20.00 - 30.00

LONESOME LEE:
Bandera 2501 *Lonely Travelin'* ....15.00 - 20.00

MABEL LEE:
Hull 712 *He's My Guy* ....15.00 - 30.00

MYRON LEE (& CADDIES):
Hep 2146 *Aw C'mon, Baby* ....15.00 - 25.00
Jaro 77037 *From Now On* ....10.00 - 15.00
Nor-Va-Jak 1326 *Blue, Lawdy Blues* ....20.00 - 30.00

NANCY LEE:
Acme 711 *So They Say* ....15.00 - 20.00

ROOSEVELT LEE:
Excello 2022 *Lazy Pete* ....75.00 - 100.00

TOMMY LEE:
Delta 403 *Highway 80 Blues* ....50.00 - 75.00

WALLY LEE WITH THE STORMS:
Sundown 122 *I Never Felt This Way* ....20.00 - 30.00

LEFT HAND CHARLIE:
Folk Star 1131 *But You Thrill Me* ....30.00 - 50.00

HANK LE GAULT:
Stardale 703/704 *I Knew* ....40.00 - 60.00

LEGENDS:
Capitol (LP) 1925 *Legends Let Loose* ....30.00 - 50.00
Falco 305 *Well Darling* ....100.00 - 150.00
Hull 727 *The Legend Of Love* ....30.00 - 50.00
Melba 109 *The Eyes Of An Angel* ....30.00 - 50.00
Peacock 1694 *Goodbye Jesse* ....15.00 - 20.00

PRICE LEGGS:
Glen Dell 101 *Jailbird Blues* ....10.00 - 15.00

GARY LEMEL:
Rev 3520 *Rockin' In The Halls* ....7.00 - 10.00

J.B. LENOIR/LENORE (& HIS COMBO):
Checker 844 *If I Give My Love To You* ....8.00 - 12.00
856 *Don't Touch My Head* ....8.00 - 12.00
874 *Five Years* ....8.00 - 12.00
901 *She Don't Know* ....8.00 - 12.00
J.O.B. 1008 *The Mountain* ....30.00 - 50.00
1012 *The Mojo* ....40.00 - 70.00
1016 *I Want My Baby* (red plastic) ....100.00 - 150.00
1102 *Play A Little While* ....75.00 - 100.00
Parrot 802 *I'm In Korea/Eisenhower Blues* ....50.00 - 80.00
802 *I'm In Korea/Tax Paying Blues* ....75.00 - 100.00
(Note: Parrot 802 was issued with two different couplings.)
809 *Mama, Talk To Your Daughter* ....50.00 - 80.00
814 *What Have I Done* ....50.00 - 80.00
821 *I Lost My Baby* ....50.00 - 80.00
Shad 5012 *Lou Ella* ....10.00 - 15.00
Vee Jay 352 *Do What I Say* ....8.00 - 12.00

LEON & CARLOS:
Liberty Tone 108 *Rock Everybody* ....60.00 - 100.00

LESLIE BROTHERS:
Columbia 40651 *Ready Ruby Rock & Roll* .... - -

BOBBY LESTER & THE MOONGLOWS/MOONLIGHTERS:
Checker 806 *Shoo Doo-Be Doo* ....30.00 - 50.00
813 *Hug And A Kiss* ....20.00 - 30.00
921 *Lonely Hearts* ....15.00 - 20.00
Chess 1811 *Blue Velvet* ....15.00 - 20.00
(LP) 1471 *The Best Of Bobby Lester & The Moonglows* (black label) ....80.00 - 120.00

JOHN LESTER & MELLOQUEENS:
C & M 500 *Getting Nearer*..7.00 - 10.00

BOBBY LEWIS:
Beltone (LP) *Tossin' And Turnin'* ....30.00 - 50.00
Chess 1518 *Mumbles Blues* ....50.00 - 75.00
Mercury 71245 *Mumbles Blues* ....8.00 - 12.00
Spotlight 394 *Mumbles Blues* ....8.00 - 12.00

GENE LEWIS:
Josie 819 *Too Young To Settle Down* ....7.00 - 10.00
R-Dell 103 *Crazy Legs* ....10.00 - 15.00

JACK LEWIS:
Crest 1018 *Glendora*...15.00 - 20.00
    1028 *Dilly Dally Sally Baby* ....10.00 - 15.00
    1033 *I.O.U.* ....10.00 - 15.00
Imperial 5880 *Mop Top* ....7.00 - 10.00

JERRY LEE LEWIS:
Sun (EP) 107, 108, 109, 110...................................50.00 - 100.00
    259 *Crazy Arms* ....15.00 - 20.00
    259 *Crazy Arms* (78 RPM) ....20.00 - 30.00
    267 *Whole Lot Of Shakin' Going On*..................10.00 - 15.00
    267 *Whole Lot Of Shakin' Going On* (78 RPM).20.00 - 30.00
    281 *Great Balls Of Fire*....................................7.00 - 10.00
    281 *Great Balls Of Fire* (78 RPM).....................50.00 - 80.00
    288 *Breathless* ....8.00 - 12.00
    288 *Breathless* (78 RPM) ....30.00 - 50.00
    296 *High School Confidential* ....8.00 - 12.00
    296 *High School Confidential* (78 RPM) ....75.00 - 100.00
    303 *Break-Up*..7.00 - 10.00
    303 *Break-Up* (78 RPM) ....50.00 - 80.00
Sun, most other 45 RPM issues ....5.00 - 10.00
    312 *I'll Sail My Ship Alone* (78 RPM)................. - -   -
    317 *Lovin' Up A Storm* (78 RPM)....................... - -   -
(Note: existence of Sun 317 in 78 RPM format is not verified.)
    (LP) 1230 *Jerry Lee Lewis* ....50.00 - 100.00
    (LP) 1265 *Jerry Lee's Greatest* ....40.00 - 60.00
(Note: promotional copies of Sun 45s, having white labels and Jerry
    Lee's picture stamped thereon, exist; their value is conjectural.)

JIMMY LEWIS:
Ment 02 *I Love You* .... -   -   -

JOHNNY LEWIS:
Rockin' 517 *She's Taking All My Money* ....100.00 - 150.00

PAUL LEWIS: (See THE SWANS)

PETE (GUITAR) LEWIS:
Federal 12066 *Louisiana Hop* ....50.00 - 80.00
    12076 *Harmonica Boogie*...................................50.00 - 80.00
    12103 *Scratchin' Boogie* ....50.00 - 80.00
    12112 *The Blast* ....50.00 - 80.00
Peacock 1624 *Goin' Crazy* ....20.00 - 30.00

SAMMY LEWIS & WILLIE JOHNSON:
Sun 218 *I Feel So Worried* ....50.00 - 80.00

SIDNEY JO LEWIS:
Island 6 *Boppin' To Grandfather's Clock* ....30.00 - 50.00

SMILEY LEWIS:
Imperial 5194 *Bells Are Ringing* ....30.00 - 50.00
    5208 *It's So Peaceful* ....30.00 - 40.00
    5234 *Play Girl* ....20.00 - 30.00
    5241 *Caldonia's Party*.......................................20.00 - 30.00
    5252 *It's Music* ....20.00 - 30.00
    5268 *Down The Road* ....20.00 - 30.00
    5279 *I Love You For Sentimental Reasons*.........15.00 - 20.00

    5296 *Can't Stop Loving You* ....15.00 - 20.00
    5316 *Too Many Drivers* ....10.00 - 15.00
    5325 *Jailbird* ....10.00 - 15.00
    5349 *Real Gone Lover* ....10.00 - 15.00
    5356 *I Hear You Knocking* ....7.00 - 10.00
    5372 *Queen Of Hearts* ....7.00 - 10.00
    5380, 5389, 5404, 5418, 5531, 5478, 5531..........5.00 - 10.00
(Note: Numbers lower than 5194 are usually found as 78 RPM
    records, with values of $15.00 to $20.00; 45 RPM issues of these
    lower numbers are valued at $50.00 to $100.00 and more, with
    even higher premiums for those pressed of colored vinyl.)
    (LP) 9141 *I Hear You Knocking* ....150.00 - 200.00
Okeh 7146 *Tore Up* ....15.00 - 20.00

TOMMY LEWIS:
Cenco 115 *Angel* ....5.00 - 10.00

WALLY LEWIS:
Dot 15763 *I'm With You* ....10.00 - 15.00
Liberty 55211 *Lover Boy* ....10.00 - 15.00
Tally 117 *Kathleen*...15.00 - 20.00

RAY LIBERTO:
Dot 15848 *Wicked Wicked Woman*.........................10.00 - 15.00
TNT 156 *Wicked Wicked Woman* ....20.00 - 30.00
    172 *I Want You To Love Me Tonight* ....20.00 - 30.00

LICK, SLICK & SLIDE:
Savoy 1150 *I Got Drunk* ....20.00 - 30.00

LIFEGUARDS:
ABC Paramount 10021 *Teenage Tango* ....7.00 - 10.00
Casa Blanca 5535 *Everybody Outta The Pool* ....10.00 - 15.00

JIMMY LIGGINS:
Specialty 427 *Low Down Blues* ....20.00 - 30.00
    434 *Dark Hour Blues* ....20.00 - 30.00
    470 *Drunk* ....15.00 - 20.00
    520 *I Can't Stop It*...10.00 - 15.00
    521 *Cadillac Boogie* ....10.00 - 15.00
(Note: 45 RPM records with numbers lower than 427 would
    command $30.00 - $50.00 or more; these are usually found as 78
    RPM records, valued at $5.00 to $10.00. Any of above, or earlier
    issues, pressed of red vinyl, command substantial premiums over
    prices stated.)

JOE LIGGINS:
Mercury (LP) 20731 *The Honeydripper* ....40.00 - 60.00
Specialty 338 *The Honeydripper* ....30.00 - 50.00
    430 *Dripper's Boogie* ....20.00 - 30.00
    465 *Farewell Blues* ....10.00 - 15.00
    484 *Come Back Home*..10.00 - 15.00
    492 *A Bird In Hand* ....10.00 - 15.00
    529 *Whiskey, Women & Loaded Dice*..................8.00 - 12.00
(Note: Numbers lower than 430 are usually found as 78 RPM
    records, valued at $5.00 to $10.00. Any of these earlier issues in
    45 RPM form would bring $30.00 to $50.00; substantially more,
    if pressed of red vinyl.)

LIGHTCRUST DOUGHBOYS:
Audio Lab (LP) 1525 ....50.00 - 100.00

LIGHTNIN' JR. & THE EMPIRES:
Haralem 2334 *Ragged And Hungry*.........................50.00 - 75.00

LIGHTNIN' LEON:
Rita 106 *Repossession Blues* ....8.00 - 12.00

LIGHTNIN' SLIM:
Ace 505 *Bad Feeling Blues*.....................................20.00 - 30.00
Excello 2066 *Lightnin' Blues* ....25.00 - 40.00

2075 *Sugar Plum* ....15.00 - 20.00
2080 *Goin' Home* ....15.00 - 20.00
2096 *Bad Luck And Trouble* ....10.00 - 15.00
2106, 2116, 2131, 2142, 2150, 2160, 2169, 2173,
      2179, 2186, 2195 ....5.00 - 10.00
(higher numbers).............................5.00 - 8.00
(LP) 8000 *Rooster Blues*....................50.00 - 80.00
(LP) 8004 *Bell Ringer*.......................50.00 - 80.00
Feature 3006 *Rock Me Mama* ....50.00 - 80.00
    3008 *New Orleans Bound*...............50.00 - 80.00
    3012 *Ethel Mae* ....30.00 - 50.00

BOBBY LILE:
4 Star (EP) 22 *Money Talks, etc.* ....10.00 - 15.00
    1713 *Keep It Confidential* ....10.00 - 15.00
    1723 *Book Worm* ....10.00 - 15.00
    1734 *All The Time* ....10.00 - 15.00

LONNIE LILLIE:
Marathon 5003 *Truck Driver's Special* ....75.00 - 100.00

THE LIMELIGHTERS:
Gilco 213 *This Lonely Boy* ....80.00 - 130.00
Joz 795 *Cabin Hideaway* ....20.00 - 30.00

X. LINCOLN:
Hermitage 779 *Take Me Home Naomi* .... - - -

THE LINCOLNS (QUINTETTE):
Aljon 113 *I Cried*....................150.00 - 250.00
Angle Tone 522 *Dream of Romance* ....75.00 - 100.00
Atlas 1100 *Don't Let Me Shed Any More Tears*......50.00 - 80.00
Bud 113 *Sometime Somewhere*....................10.00 - 15.00
Mercury 71553 *Can't You Go For Me* ....8.00 - 12.00

KATHY LINDEN:
Felsted (LP) 7501 *That Certain Boy*.........................35.00 - 50.00
    8510 *Billy* (78 RPM)...........................15.00 - 20.00

THE LINN TWINS:
Blue Feather 277 *Rockin' Out The Blues* .... - - -

THE LINTONS:
Erica 005 *Lost Love* ....10.00 - 15.00

THE LIONS:
Rendezvous 116 *Two Timing Lover* .... - - -

RICKY LISI:
Roulette 4511 *The River* ....7.00 - 10.00

"LISTEN TO OUR STORY":
Brunswick (LP) 59001 (10 inch) (various artists) ...25.00 - 40.00

LITTLE AL:
Excello 2098 *Little Lean Woman* ....10.00 - 15.00
    2128 *Easy Ridin' Buggy* ....10.00 - 15.00

LITTLE ANTHONY & THE DUPONTS/IMPERIALS:
End 1027 *Tears On My Pillow* ....7.00 - 10.00
    1027 *Tears On My Pillow* (78 RPM) ....30.00 - 50.00
Savoy 1552 *You* ....10.00 - 20.00

LITTLE BEATS:
Mercury 71155 *Someone For Me* ....20.00 - 30.00

LITTLE BOPPERS:
Glendale 1001 *Chattanooga Drummer Man* ....10.00 - 15.00

LITTLE BUDDY:
N R C 010 *Let's Make Love* ....10.00 - 15.00

LITTLE BUTCH & THE VELLS:
Angletone 535 *Over The Rainbow* ....20.00 - 30.00

LITTLE CAESAR (& THE ROMANS):
Big Town 106 *Big Eyes* .... 10.00 - 15.00
    110 *Wonder Why I'm Leaving* .... 10.00 - 15.00
Del-Fi (LP) 1218 *Memories Of These Oldies But Goodies*
                        50.00 - 80.00
Hollywood 234 *Long Time Baby* .... 10.00 - 15.00

LITTLE CAMERON:
Stylo 2106 *K.C. Dog* .... 10.00 - 20.00

LITTLE CLYDIE & THE TEENS:
RPM 462 *A Casual Look* .... 30.00 - 50.00

THE LITTLE COOLBREEZES:
Ebony 1014 *Downstairs*...................... 100.00 - 200.00
    1015 *Won't You Come In*...................... 100.00 - 200.00

LITTLE DANNY:
Sharp 112 *Mind On Loving* .... 7.00 - 10.00

LITTLE DENNY & THE TORKAYS:
Perry 1 *Rock And Roll Blues*...................... 20.00 - 30.00
    2 *She's Everybody's Darling* .... 15.00 - 25.00

LITTLE DOUG (See also DOUG SAHM):
Sarg 113 *Rollin', Rollin'* .... 40.00 - 70.00

LITTLE EDDIE & THE DON JUANS:
Fortune 836 *This Is A Miracle* .... 20.00 - 30.00

LITTLE ESTHER (& THE DOMINOES/With LITTLE WILLIE/With BOBBY NUNN/& THE ROBINS):
Decca 48305 *Stop Crying* .... 30.00 - 60.00
Federal 12016 *The Deacon Moves In* .... 100.00 - 200.00
    12023 *I'm a Bad Bad Girl* .... 100.00 - 200.00
    12042 *Cryin And Singing' The Blues*............ 50.00 - 100.00
    12055 *Ring A Ding Doo*...................... 50.00 - 100.00
    12063 *The Storm* .... 50.00 - 100.00
    12065 *Better Beware* .... 50.00 - 100.00
    12079 *Aged and Mellow* .... 50.00 - 80.00
    12090 *Ramblin' Blues* .... 50.00 - 80.00
    12100 *Saturday Night Daddy* .... 50.00 - 80.00
    12108 *Last Laugh Blues* .... 50.00 - 80.00
    12115 *Hollerin' And Screamin'* .... 40.00 - 80.00
    12122 *You Took My Love Too Fast* .... 40.00 - 80.00
    12126 *Hound Dog* .... 50.00 - 100.00
    12142 *Cherry Wine* .... 40.00 - 80.00
King (LP) 622 *"Melody Lane"* .... 300.00 - 600.00
Savoy 731 *Double Crossing Blues* .... 20.00 - 30.00

LITTLE HUDSON'S RED DEVIL TRIO:
J.O.B. 1015 *Rough Treatment*...................... 150.00 - 300.00

LITTLE IKE With JIMMY BECK ORCH:
Champion 1011 *She Can Rock* .... 20.00 - 30.00

LITTLE JAN & THE RADIANTS:
Goldisc 15 *If You Love Me*...................... 10.00 - 15.00

LITTLE JOE:
Epic (EP) 7198 *"The Thriller"* .... 50.00 - 100.00
House Of Sound 500 *Keep Your Arms Around Me* 30.00 - 40.00
20th Century 1214 *One More Time* .... 15.00 - 25.00

LITTLE JOE BLUE:
Movin' 132 *Dirty Work Going On*...................... 10.00 - 15.00

LITTLE JUNE & THE JANUARYS:
Profile 4009 *Oh My Love* .... 30.00 - 50.00
Salem 188 *Hello*...................... 150.00 - 250.00

LITTLE JUNIOR'S BLUE FLAMES:
Sun 187 *Feelin' Good* .... 50.00 - 100.00
    192 *Mystery Train* .... 50.00 - 100.00

LITTLE LARRY:
Success 103 *Loretta* ......8.00 - 12.00

LITTLE LINDA:
Coral 62279 *Hey Little Lover* ......10.00 - 15.00

LITTLE LUTHER:
Apt 25060 *Ever Lovin' Baby* ......8.00 - 12.00
Criss Cross 110 *Steppin' High* ......8.00 - 12.00

LITTLE MAC/MACK:
Bea & Baby 109 *Don't Come Back* ......15.00 - 20.00
    118 *I'm Your Fool* ......15.00 - 20.00
C.J. 606 *My Walking Blues* (blue label) ......15.00 - 20.00
Checker 991 *I'm Happy Now* ......7.00 - 10.00
Jay Bird 4001 *You Mistreated Me* ......10.00 - 15.00

LITTLE MILTON:
Bobbin 101 *I'm A Lonely Man* ......15.00 - 20.00
    103 *Long Distance Operator* ......15.00 - 20.00
    112 *Strange Dreams* ......15.00 - 20.00
    117 *Same Old Blues* ......10.00 - 20.00
    120 *My Baby Pleases Me* ......10.00 - 20.00
    125 *Hey Girl* ......10.00 - 20.00
    128 *Cross My Heart* ......10.00 - 20.00
Checker (LP) 2995 *We're Gonna Make It* ......30.00 - 50.00
Checker (most issues) ......5.00 - 10.00
Delta 403 *Little Milton's Boogie* ...... - -
Meteor 5040 *Let's Boogie Baby* (black label) ......50.00 - 80.00
Sun 194 *Beggin' My Baby* ......75.00 - 100.00
    200 *Alone And Blue* ......100.00 - 200.00
    220 *Looking For My Baby* ......100.00 - 150.00

LITTLE MOJO:
Indigo 139 *Mojo Theme* ......5.00 - 10.00
Norman 505 *You Ain't The One* ......7.00 - 10.00

LITTLE NAT:
Pik 1 *Do This, Do That* ......10.00 - 15.00

LITTLE NATE & THE CHRYSLERS:
Johnson 318 *Someone Up There* ......30.00 - 50.00

LITTLE NORMAN:
Decca 30353 *Drag Strip Baby* ......7.00 - 10.00

LITTLE PAPA JOE:
Blue Lake 116 *Easy Lovin'* ......80.00 - 130.00

LITTLE RICHARD:
Camden (LP) 420 *Little Richard* ......50.00 - 75.00
  (EP) 446 *Little Richard Rocks* ......80.00 - 120.00
Peacock 1658 *Little Richard's Boogie* ......30.00 - 50.00
    1673 *Maybe I'm Right* ......30.00 - 50.00
RCA Victor 4392 *Taxi Blues* ......50.00 - 80.00
    4582 *Get Rich Quick* ......50.00 - 80.00
    4772 *Ain't Nothin' Happenin'* ......50.00 - 80.00
    5025 *Please Have Mercy On Me* ......50.00 - 80.00
Specialty (EP) 100 *"Here's Little Richard"* ......100.00 - 150.00
  (EP) 400, 401, 402 *Here's Little Richard* ......40.00 - 70.00
  (EP) 403, 404, 405 *Little Richard* ......40.00 - 70.00
    561 *Tutti-Frutti* ......15.00 - 20.00
    561 *Tutti-Frutti* (78 RPM) ......15.00 - 25.00
    572 *Long Tall Sally* ......15.00 - 20.00
    572 *Long Tall Sally* (78 RPM) ......15.00 - 25.00
    584 *Heeby-Jeebies* ......10.00 - 15.00
    584 *Heeby-Jeebies* (78 RPM) ......15.00 - 25.00
    591 *All Around The World* ......10.00 - 15.00
    591 *All Around The World* (78 RPM) ......15.00 - 25.00
    598 *Lucille* ......10.00 - 15.00
    598 *Lucille* (78 RPM) ......15.00 - 25.00
    606 *Jenny, Jenny* ......8.00 - 12.00
    606 *Jenny, Jenny* (78 RPM) ......20.00 - 30.00
    611 *Keep A Knockin'* ......8.00 - 12.00
    611 *Keep A Knockin'* (78 RPM) ......20.00 - 30.00
    624 *Good Golly, Miss Molly* ......8.00 - 12.00
    624 *Good Golly, Miss Molly* (78 RPM) ......30.00 - 50.00
    633, 652, 660 ......7.00 - 10.00
    633 *True, Fine Mama* (78 RPM) ......10.00 - 20.00
    652 *She Knows How To Rock* (78 RPM) ......20.00 - 30.00
    660 *Wonderin'* (78 RPM) ......20.00 - 30.00
  (LP) 2100 *Here's Little Richard* ......50.00 - 100.00
  (LP) 2103 *Little Richard* ......50.00 - 100.00
  (LP) 2114 *The Fabulous Little Richard* ......50.00 - 80.00

LITTLE SAMMY:
Shade 1002 *Can You Love Me* ......20.00 - 30.00

LITTLE SHY GUY:
Calvert 107 *Let's Rock & Roll* ......40.00 - 60.00

LITTLE SONNY:
Duke 186 *Hear My Woman Calling* ......8.00 - 12.00
J-V-B. 5001 *I'll Love You Baby* ......50.00 - 100.00

LITTLE STAN:
Decca 30638 *Block Party Rock* ...... - -

LITTLE TEMPLE & HIS "88":
Specialty 475 *I Ate The Wrong Part* ......20.00 - 40.00

LITTLE VICTOR (& THE VISTAS):
Rendezvous 183 *No More* ......10.00 - 15.00
Richland 2907 *Papa Lou And Gran* ......20.00 - 30.00

LITTLE WALKING' WILLIE:
Jaguar 3012 *Clayhouse Blues* ......40.00 - 60.00

LITTLE WALTER (& HIS JUKES/NIGHT CAPS):
Checker 758 *Juke* ......50.00 - 100.00
    764 *Mean Old World* ......50.00 - 80.00
    767 *Tonight With A Fool* ......40.00 - 60.00
    770 *Off The Wall* ......30.00 - 50.00
    780 *Quarter To Twelve* ......30.00 - 50.00
    786 *Lights Out* ......20.00 - 30.00
    793 *Rocker* ......20.00 - 30.00
    799 *Blue Light* ......15.00 - 25.00
    805 *Mellow Down Easy* ......15.00 - 25.00
    811 *Thunder Bird* ......15.00 - 25.00
    817 *Roller Coaster* ......15.00 - 25.00
(Note: Any of the foregoing, pressed of red vinyl, bring substantially more.)
    825 *Too Late* ......10.00 - 15.00
    833 *It Ain't Right* ......10.00 - 15.00
    838 *One More Chance With You* ......10.00 - 15.00
    845 *Just A Feeling* ......10.00 - 15.00
    852 *Take Me Back* ......10.00 - 15.00
    859 *Nobody But You* ......10.00 - 15.00
    867, 890, 904, 930, 939, 955, 968, 986, 1043,
        1081, 1117 ......7.00 - 12.00
Chess (LP) 1428 *The Best Of Little Walter*
(black label) ......75.00 - 100.00

LITTLE WALTER, JR.:
Lapel 101 *Don't Know* ......15.00 - 20.00

LEE ROY LITTLE:
Cee Jay 578 *Your Evil Thoughts* ......7.00 - 10.00

LITTLE WILLIE JOHN (See JOHN)

LITTLE WILLIE LITTLEFIELD:
Argyle 1013 *Ruby Ruby* ......10.00 - 15.00
Bullseye 1005 *Ruby Ruby* ......15.00 - 25.00

Federal 12101 *Sticking On You Baby* ....30.00 - 50.00
    12110 *K.C. Loving* ....30.00 - 50.00
    12137 *My Best Wishes And Regards* ....30.00 - 50.00
    12148 *Miss K.C.'s Fine* ....25.00 - 40.00
    12163 *Don't Take My Heart Little Girl*..........20.00 - 30.00
    12174 *Goofy Dust Blues* ....20.00 - 30.00
    12221 *Jim Wilson's Boogie* ....20.00 - 30.00
Rhythm 107 *Baby Shame*............................20.00 - 30.00
    108 *Ruby Ruby*................................30.00 - 50.00
Rhythm 115 *I Need A Pay Day*......................15.00 - 25.00
    124 *Theresa* ....15.00 - 25.00
    130 *I Wanna Love You*.........................15.00 - 25.00

BUBBA LITTRELL:
Manco 1037 *Ain't That Cool* ....15.00 - 20.00

JIMMY LLOYD:
Roulette 4062 *I Got A Rocket In My Pocket*.........15.00 - 20.00
    7001 *Where The Rio De Rosa Flows*.............15.00 - 25.00

ROBERT JR. LOCKWOOD:
J.O.B. 1107 *Sweet Woman From Maine*...............100.00 - 200.00

WILLIE LOFTIN & THE DISCORDS:
Smoke 101 *Bad Habit*..............................10.00 - 15.00

WILLIE LOGAN & THE PLAIDS:
Jerry-O 103 *You Conquered Me* ....15.00 - 20.00

LOGICS:
Everlast 5015 *One Love* ....10.00 - 15.00

JIMMIE LOGSDON:
Decca 28913 *Papaya Mama* ....7.00 - 10.00
    29337 *I'm Goin' Back To Tennessee*............7.00 - 10.00
Dot 1274 *Midnight Blues* ....10.00 - 15.00

BOBBY LOLLAR:
Benton 101/102 *Bad Bad Boy*.......................80.00 - 120.00

BOBBY LONERO:
Liberty 55180 *Little Bit* ....10.00 - 15.00

LONESOME DRIFTER:
K 5812 *Eager Boy* ....200.00 - 300.00
RAM 1738 *Honey Do You Love Me*....................10.00 - 15.00

LONESOME LEE (See LEE)

LONESOME SUNDOWN:
Excello 2092 *Lost Without Love*...................20.00 - 30.00
    2101 *My Home Is A Prison*.....................20.00 - 30.00
    2117 *Don't Say A Word* ....15.00 - 20.00
    2132 *I'm A Mo-Jo Man* ....15.00 - 20.00
    2145 *I Stood By* ....15.00 - 20.00
    2154 *No Use To Worry* ....15.00 - 20.00
    2163 *If You See My Baby* ....15.00 - 20.00
    2174 *Learn To Treat Me Better* ....10.00 - 15.00
    2202, 2213, 2236, 2242, 2249, 2254, 2259, 2264
    ....7.00 - 12.00

BUDDY LONG:
Demon 1517 *It's Nothin' To Me*....................8.00 - 12.00

CURTIS LONG (& THE RHYTHM ROCKERS):
Linco 609 *Hootchy Cootchy* ....40.00 - 60.00
Stardale 55800/55801 *Goin' Out Of Town*...........30.00 - 50.00

LONG HAIRS:
Memphis 110 *Go- Go- Go* ....30.00 - 50.00

LONG JOHN:
Duke 122 *Crazy Girl*..............................30.00 - 50.00

LONG TALL LESTER:
Duke 197 *Working Man*.............................8.00 - 12.00

LONG TALL MARVIN:
Modern 993 *Have Mercy Miss Percy* ....10.00 - 15.00

LONNIE & THE CARROLLONS/CRISIS:
Mohawk 108 *Chapel Of Tears*.......................20.00 - 30.00
Universal 103 *Bells In The Chapel* ....30.00 - 60.00

LONNIE THE CAT:
RPM 410 *I Ain't Drunk*............................20.00 - 30.00

LORD LUTHER:
Imperial 5596 *A Thinkin' Man's Girl* ....7.00 - 10.00

BOBBY LORD:
Columbia 21339 *No More, No More, No More*.........15.00 - 20.00
21498 *Pie Peachie Pie Pie*........................10.00 - 15.00
    21539 *Everybody's Rockin' But Me* ....10.00 - 15.00
    40666 *Beautiful Baby*.........................8.00 - 12.00
    40819 *Your Sweet Love*........................8.00 - 12.00
    40927 *High Voltage*...........................8.00 - 12.00
    41030 *Am I A Fool*............................7.00 - 10.00
    41155 *Fire Of Love*...........................7.00 - 10.00
    41288 *When I've Learned* ....7.00 - 10.00
    41352 *Party Pooper*...........................8.00 - 12.00
Harmony (LP) 7322 *The Best Of* ....75.00 - 100.00

DICK LORY:
Columbia 41224 *Wild Blooded Woman*................15.00 - 20.00
    41276 *Crazy Little Daisy* ....10.00 - 15.00
Dot 15496 *Cool It Baby*...........................15.00 - 20.00

LOU & GINNY:
Hep 2141 *Do I Do Right*...........................- - -

JOHN D. LOUDERMILK:
Columbia 41165 *Susie's House* ....15.00 - 20.00
    41209 *Yo Yo* ....10.00 - 15.00
RCA Victor 8308 *Rhythm And Blues*.................8.00 - 12.00

BOBBY LOUIS:
Capitol 4224 *Adult Western* ....20.00 - 30.00
    4272 *Call Of Love*...........................10.00 - 15.00

JOE HILL LOUIS:
Big Town 401 *Bad Woman Blues* ....100.00 - 200.00
Checker 763 *Dorothy May*..........................200.00 - 300.00
Modern 839 *Big Legged Woman* ....80.00 - 130.00
    856 *Peace Of Mind*...........................80.00 - 130.00

LESLIE LOUIS:
Rockin' 519 *Ridin' Home* ....75.00 - 100.00

TOMMY LOUIS (& THE RHYTHM ROCKERS/With MARSHALL & THE VERSATILES):
Muriel 1001 *The Hurt Is On* ....15.00 - 25.00
    1002/1003 *Wail Baby Wail* ....15.00 - 25.00

LOUISIANA RED:
Roulette (LP) 25200 *The Low Down Back Porch Blues*
    ....50.00 - 80.00

THE LOUVIN BROTHERS:
Capitol (LP) 769 *Tragic Songs Of Life* ....20.00 - 30.00
    (LP) 825 *Nearer My God To Thee* ....20.00 - 30.00
    (LP) 910 *Ira & Charlie*......................20.00 - 30.00

THE LOVE BROTHERS:
By Love 843 *Baby I'll Never Let You Go*...........75.00 - 100.00

BILLY LOVE:
Chess 1508 *Drop Top* ....30.00 - 50.00
    1516 *My Teddy Bear Baby*.....................30.00 - 50.00

HOT SHOT LOVE:
Sun 196 *Wolf Call Boogie* ....200.00 - 400.00

WILLIE LOVE & HIS THREE ACES:
Trumpet 172 *Fallin' Rain* ....20.00 - 30.00
 173 *Vanity Dresser Boogie* ....15.00 - 20.00
 174 *Shady Lane Blues*...15.00 - 20.00
 175 *V-8 Ford*...10.00 - 15.00
 209 *Way Back* ....15.00 - 20.00

THE LOVE LARKS:
Mason's 3-070 *Diddle-Le-Bom* ....400.00 -   up

LOVE LETTERS:
Acme 714 *Walking The Streets Alone* ....150.00 - 200.00

LOVE NOTES:
Holiday 2605 *United*...30.00 - 50.00
 2608 *If I Could Make You Mine* ....30.00 - 50.00
Imperial 5254 *Surrender Your Heart* ....150.00 - 200.00
Premium 611 *A Love Like Yours* ....10.00 - 15.00
Rainbow 266 *I'm Sorry*..50.00 - 80.00
Riviera 970 *I'm Sorry*...250.00 - 400.00
 975 *Since I Fell For You*...................................300.00 -   up
Wilshire 200 *Our Songs Of Love* ....10.00 - 15.00

THE LOVERS:
Decca 29862 *Don't Touch Me* ....15.00 - 25.00
Keller 101 *Strange As It Seems* ....80.00 - 130.00
Lamp 2005 *Darling It's Wonderful* ....10.00 - 15.00
 2013 *Let's Elope* ....15.00 - 20.00

THE LOVE TONES:
Plus 108 *Talk To An Angel* ....150.00 - 200.00
Squalor 1313 *I Love Nadine* ....40.00 - 70.00

BUDDY LOWE:
Crest 1049 *Ummmm-Kiss Me Goodnight* ....15.00 - 20.00

JIM LOWE:
Dot (LP) 3051 *Songs They Sing Behind The Green Door*
 ....25.00 - 40.00
 (LP) 3114 *Wicked Women* ....25.00 - 40.00
 15456 *Blue Suede Shoes*..................................10.00 - 15.00

FRANKIE LOWERY:
Khoury's 716 *Kansas City Train* ....20.00 - 30.00

JAY B. LOYD:
ABC Paramount 9922 *You're Just My Kind*............15.00 - 20.00
Hi 2017 *I'm So Lonely* ....10.00 - 15.00

JIM LUCAS:
Republic 7123 *Tutti Frutti* ....20.00 - 30.00

LUKE THE DRIFTER (See HANK WILLIAMS)

ROBIN LUKE:
Bertram International 206 *Susie Darlin'* ....25.00 - 40.00
 208 *My Girl*..15.00 - 20.00
 210 *You Can't Stop Me From Dreamin'* ....20.00 - 30.00
 212 *Five Minutes More* ....15.00 - 20.00
Dot (EP) 1092 *Susie Darlin'*.................................50.00 - 80.00
 15781 *Susie Darlin'* (78 RPM)............................30.00 - 50.00
 15829 *Chica Chicka Honey* ....10.00 - 15.00
 15899 *Strollin' Blues* ....10.00 - 15.00
 15959 *Who's Gonna Hold Your Hand*................10.00 - 15.00

BOB LUMAN:
Capitol 2972 *I Know My Baby Cares* ....7.00 - 10.00
Imperial 5705 *Red Cadillac And A Black Moustache*
 ....10.00 - 15.00
 8311 *Red Cadillac And A Black Moustache*........20.00 - 30.00

 8315 *Make Up Your Mind*..................................15.00 - 20.00
(Note: Above two are maroon label; black label later pressings
 command smaller premiums.)
Warner Brothers (LP) 139 *Let's Think About Livin'*
 ....25.00 - 40.00

LUMBERJACKS:
Hollywood 1040 *Lonely Blues*....................................-   -   -

BOBBY LUMPKIN:
Felco 102 *One Way Ticket* ....75.00 - 100.00

KENNY LUND & THE ROLLER COASTERS:
Holiday Inn 105 *Rip It Up Potato Chip* ....8.00 - 12.00

NELLIE LUTCHER:
Capitol (LP) H-232 (10 inch) *Real Gone*...............40.00 - 70.00
 (LP) T-232 *Real Gone* ....50.00 - 80.00
Epic (LP) 1108 (10 inch) *Whee! Nellie* ....50.00 - 80.00
Liberty (LP) 3014 *Our New Nellie* ....50.00 - 80.00

LY-DELLS:
Master 111 *Genie Of The Lamp* ....30.00 - 50.00
 251 *Wizard Love* ....10.00 - 15.00
Pam 103 *Talking To Myself* ....40.00 - 60.00
Parkway 897 *Talking To Myself* ....10.00 - 15.00

**FRANKIE LYMON (& THE TEENAGERS) (See also
TEENAGERS):**
Gee (EP) 601 *The Teenagers Go Rockin'* ....50.00 - 80.00
 (LP) 701 *The Teenagers Featuring Frankie Lymon*
 ....60.00 - 100.00
 1018 *I Promise To Remember*............................. 5.00 - 8.00
 1018 *I Promise To Remember* (78 RPM) .... 8.00 - 12.00
 1022 *The ABC's Of Love* .... 4.00 - 7.00
 1022 *The ABC's Of Love* (78 RPM) .... 8.00 - 12.00
 1026 *I'm Not A Juvenile Delinquent*................... 4.00 - 70.00
 1026 *I'm Not A Juvenile Delinquent* (78 RPM). 10.00 - 15.00
Gee 1032, 1036, 1039 .... 5.00 - 8.00
Gee 1032 *Paper Castles* (78 RPM) .... 7.00 - 10.00
 1036 *Out In The Cold Again* (78 RPM)............. 7.00 - 10.00
 1039 *Goody Goody* (78 RPM) .... 8.00 - 12.00
Roulette (EP) *At The London Palladium* ....20.00 - 30.00
 (LP) 25013 *Frankie Lymon At The London Palladium*
 ....25.00 - 50.00
 25036 *Rock & Roll* ....30.00 - 60.00

LEWIS LYMON & THE TEENCHORDS:
End 1003 *Too Young*..25.00 - 40.00
 1007 *I Found Out Why*......................................20.00 - 30.00
Fury 1000 *I'm So Happy* ....20.00 - 230.00
 1003 *Honey Honey* ....30.00 - 50.00
 1006 *I'm Not Too Young To Fall In Love* ....30.00 - 50.00
Juanita 101 *Dance Girl* ....20.00 - 30.00

DEBBIE LYNN:
Flight Seven 10001 *Fujiyama Mama*.....................10.00 - 15.00

JERRY LYNN:
D 1041 *Bugger Burns* ....10.00 - 15.00

KATHY LYNN & HER PLAYBOYS:
Swan 4193 *I Got A Guy* ....20.00 - 30.00

LORELEI LYNN:
Award 128 Rock *A Bop* ....15.00 - 20.00

LORETTA LYNN:
Zero 107 *I'm A Honky Tonk Girl* ....50.00 - 80.00
 110 *Heartaches Meet Mr. Blues* ....50.00 - 80.00
 112 *The Darkest Day* ....50.00 - 80.00

RONNIE LYNN:
Spangle 2006 *Burning Eyes* ....15.00 - 20.00

JOE LYONS & THE ARROWS:
Hollywood 1065 *Honey Chile* ....50.00 - 80.00

LYRES:
J & G 101 *Ship Of Love*.. - - -
(Note: Existence of above in 45 RPM format has not been verified.)

THE LYRICS: (See also IKE PERRY)
Coral 62322 *Oh, Please Love Me* ....15.00 - 20.00
Fernwood 129 *Let's Be Sweethearts Again* ....100.00 - 150.00
Goldwax 101 *Darling* ....7.00 - 10.00
Harlem 101 *Oh, Please Love Me* ....75.00 - 100.00
   104 *The Beating Of My Heart* ....75.00 - 100.00
Hy-Tone 111 *I'm In Love* ....400.00 - up
Mama 3614 *Come Back To Me Darling*.................15.00 - 20.00
Mid South 1500 *Crying Over You* ....10.00 - 15.00
Rhythm 127 *Every Night* ....500.00 - up
Vee Jay 285 *Come On Home* ....50.00 - 80.00
Wildcat 0028 *Oh, Please Love Me* ....15.00 - 25.00

WILLIE MABON (& HIS COMBO):
Chess (LP) 1439 *Willie Mabon*................................50.00 - 80.00
   1531 *Worry Blues* ....15.00 - 25.00
   1538 *Night Latch* ....10.00 - 15.00
   1548 *Monday Woman* ....10.00 - 15.00
Chess 1554, 1564, 1580, 1592, 1608, 1627..............7.00 - 12.00
Federal 12306 *Light Up Your Lamp* ....10.00 - 15.00

MAC & JAKE:
Meteor 5022 *Yakety Yak* (red label)........................50.00 - 75.00

LOU MAC:
Blue Lake 108 *Come Back Little Daddy* ....10.00 - 15.00
   114 *Slow Down* ....30.00 - 50.00
   117 *Albert Is His Name* ....10.00 - 15.00
   119 *Move Me* ....10.00 - 15.00

LEON MACH:
Lavender 1554 *You Hurt Me So* ....15.00 - 20.00

BILL MACK:
Imperial 8177 *Play My Boogie* ....20.00 - 30.00
   8200 *I'm Not Free* ....10.00 - 15.00
   8212 *That's The Way I Like You*......................10.00 - 15.00
   8225 *That's How I Feel* ....10.00 - 15.00
   8242 *Crazed For Love* ....10.00 - 15.00
   8278 *Sue-Suzie Boogie* ....15.00 - 20.00
   8294 *A Fool For You* ....10.00 - 15.00
Starday 231 *Kitty Kat*...50.00 - 75.00
   252 *Cat Just Got In Town* ....50.00 - 75.00
   280 *It's Saturday Night*...................................50.00 - 75.00
   313 *Cheatin' On Your Mind* ....20.00 - 30.00
   418 *Long, Long Train* ....15.00 - 20.00

BILLY MACK:
Lewis Records 1001 *Tribute To Jerry Lee* ....10.00 - 15.00

BOBBY MACK:
Tempus 1508 *She's My Little Baby* ....8.00 - 12.00

JEANI MACK:
Class 230 *Dirty Dishes* ....10.00 - 15.00
   242 *Super Duper*...10.00 - 15.00

LONNIE MACK:
Fraternity (LP) 1014 *Wham Of The Memphis Man* .30.00 - 50.00

PATTI MACK:
Cinema 101 *Handy Andy* ....30.00 - 50.00

WARNER MACK:
Decca 30471, 30841...5.00 - 10.00

VINCENT MACREE & THE RHYTHM KINGS:
Gametime 103 *Teen-Age Talk*.................................8.00 - 12.00

JOHNNY MADARA:
Bamboo 503 *Good Golly Miss Molly* ....10.00 - 15.00
   511 *A Story Untold*..10.00 - 15.00

JIMMIE MADDIN:
American International 525 *Bird Dog* ....20.00 - 30.00
   542 *Tongue Tied* ....30.00 - 30.00
Dot 15641 *Tongue Tied* ....10.00 - 20.00
Freedom 44007 *I'm Studyin' You* ....10.00 - 15.00
Imperial 5494 *Jeanie, Jeanie, Jeanie* ....10.00 - 15.00
   5496 *Shirley Purley*..10.00 - 15.00
Tampa 102 *Let 'Em Roll* ....10.00 - 15.00

MADDOX BROTHERS (& ROSE):
Columbia 21559 *The Death Of Rock And Roll* ....15.00 - 20.00
   40836 *Ugly And Slouchy*..................................10.00 - 15.00
   41020 *Stop Whistlin' Wolf* ....10.00 - 15.00
King (LP) 669 *A Collection Of Sacred Songs* ....25.00 - 40.00
   (LP) 677 *Maddox Brothers And Rose* ....40.00 - 60.00

ROSE MADDOX:
Capitol (LP) 1312 *One Rose* ....20.00 - 30.00
   (LP) 1548 *A Big Bouquet Of Roses*...................15.00 - 25.00
Columbia 21394 *Wild Wild Young Men* ....8.00 - 12.00
   21490 *Hey Little Dreamboat* ....10.00 - 15.00

MADDY BROTHERS:
Celestial 109 *Rockin' Party* ....10.00 - 15.00

THE MADISON BROTHERS:
Apt 25050 *Trusting In You* ....15.00 - 20.00
Cedargrove 314 *Trusting In You*..............................50.00 - 80.00
Sure 1002 *Give Me Your Heart*...............................50.00 - 80.00

THE MAGIC NOTES:
Blue Beat 51 *Rosabel*..50.00 - 80.00

THE MAGICS:
Debra 1003 *Chapel Bells* ....15.00 - 20.00

MAGIC SAM:
Chief 7013 *Mr. Charlie* ....15.00 - 20.00
   7017 *Square Dance Rock* ....10.00 - 15.00
   7026 *Do The Camel Walk* ....10.00 - 15.00
   7033 *Blue Light Boogie* ....10.00 - 15.00
Cobra 5013 *All Your Love*......................................30.00 - 50.00
   5021 *Look Watcha Done*..................................30.00 - 50.00
   5025 *All Night Love* ....30.00 - 50.00
   5029 *Twenty-One Days In Jail* ....25.00 - 40.00

THE MAGIC TONES:
King 4665 *When I Kneel Down To Pray* ....150.00 - 200.00
   4681 *How Can You Treat Me This Way* ....150.00 - 200.00

THE MAGNETS:
Groove 0058 *You Just Say The Word* ....15.00 - 20.00

THE MAGNIFICENT FOUR:
Blast 210 *The Closer You Are*................................8.00 - 12.00
Whale 506 *The Closer You Are* ....15.00 - 20.00

MAGNIFICENTS:
Dee Gee 3008 *My Heart Is Calling* ....8.00 - 12.00
Vee Jay 183 *Up On The Mountain*.........................10.00 - 20.00
   208 *Caddy Bo*..15.00 - 20.00
   235 *Off The Mountain* ....20.00 - 30.00
   281 *Don't Leave Me* ....25.00 - 40.00

MAHARAJAHS:
Flip 332 *Why Don't You Answer?* ....10.00 - 15.00

MOE MAHARREY:
Hi 2019 *I Cry For You* ....7.00 - 10.00

SIDNEY MAIDEN:
Dig 138 *Hand Me Down Baby*...............................50.00 - 75.00
Flash 101 *Everything Is Wrong* ....50.00 - 75.00
Imperial 5189 *Honey Bee Blues* ....100.00 - 150.00

MAJESTICS:
Bim 1 *How Long Will It Last*................................20.00 - 30.00
Chex 1000 *Give Me A Cigarette*............................20.00 - 30.00
   1004 *Unhappy And Blue* ....15.00 - 20.00
   1006 *Lonely Heart* ....10.00 - 15.00
Knight 105 *Pennies For A Beggar* ....75.00 - 100.00
Linda 111 *Strange World*......................................10.00 - 15.00
   121 *Girl Of My Dreams*................................20.00 - 30.00
Marlin 802 *Cave Man Rock*................................300.00 - up
NRC 502 *Please Don't Say No*.............................30.00 - 50.00
Pixie 6901 *Searching For A New Love*....................8.00 - 12.00
Sioux 91459 *Lone Stranger* ....10.00 - 15.00

THE MAJORS:
Imperial 5855 *Time Will Tell*..................................8.00 - 12.00
Original 1003 *Big Eyes* ....30.00 - 50.00

VINCENT MALOY:
End 1019 *Hubba Hubba Ding Bing*.......................15.00 - 20.00

GENE MALTAIS:
Decca 30387 *Crazy Baby*.....................................15.00 - 20.00
Lilac 3159 *The Raging Sea*...................................20.00 - 30.00

MANDELLS:
Chess 1794 *Who, Me?* ....8.00 - 12.00
Smart 323 *Darling I'm Home* ....50.00 - 80.00
   325 *I Don't Have You* ....20.00 - 30.00

THE MANHATTANS:
Big Mack 3911 *Why Should I Cry* ....20.00 - 30.00
Carnival (LP) 201 *Dedicated To You* ....50.00 - 80.00
   506, 509, 512 ....5.00 - 10.00
Ransom 787 *It Was A Night Like This*....................50.00 - 80.00

GEORGE MANIS:
Eclaire - *Hep, Two, Three* ....- - -

BARRY MANN:
ABC Paramount (LP) 399 *Who Put The Bomp* ....50.00 - 80.00

BILLY MANN:
Dig 120 *A Million Heartaches Ago* ....10.00 - 15.00

CARL MANN (& THE KOOL KATS):
Jaxon 502 *Gonna Rock & Roll Tonight*................150.00 - 200.00
Phillips 3546 *Rockin' Love* ....10.00 - 15.00
   (LP) 1960 *Like, Mann*................................150.00 - 200.00

CHUCK MANN:
Leona 3699 *Little Miss Muffet* ....7.00 - 10.00

FRANKIE MANN & THE METEORS:
Apt 25024 *Toe To Toe* ....- - -

GLORIA MANN & CARTER RAYS:
Jubilee 5142 *Goodnight, Sweetheart, Goodnight* ....15.00 - 20.00

SKIP MANNING:
Empire 508 *Ham 'N' Eggs* ....- - -

RED MANSEL & THE HILLBILLY BOYS:
Allstar 7160 *Johnny On The Spot* ....10.00 - 15.00

JOE MAPHIS:
Columbia 21518 *Guitar Rock & Roll* ....8.00 - 12.00
Republic 2006 *Water Baby Boogie* ....10.00 - 15.00

THE MAPLES:
Blue Lake 111 *I Must Forget You*........................150.00 - 300.00

THE MARATHONS:
Arvee (LP) 428 *Peanut Butter* ....40.00 - 70.00
   5027, 5038, 5408 ....5.00 - 10.00
JC 101 *Don't Know Why*......................................10.00 - 15.00
Sabrina 334 *Don't Know Why*...............................40.00 - 60.00

MARBLES:
Lucky 002 *Golden Girl* ....250.00 - up

THE MARCELS:
Colpix (LP) 416 *Blue Moon*..................................50.00 - 80.00
Jody 123 *Take Me Back* ....30.00 - 50.00
St. Clair 13711 *That Lucky Old Sun* ....10.00 - 20.00

MARIGOLDS:
Excello 2057 *Rollin' Stone* ....15.00 - 20.00
   2061 *Two Strangers* ....20.00 - 30.00
   2081 *It's You, Darling, It's You*........................25.00 - 40.00

MARKEES:
Gone 5028 *Along Came Love* ....10.00 - 15.00

THE MARKEETS:
Melatone 1005 *Tear Drops* ....50.00 - 80.00

MORTY MARKER & THE IMPALAS:
Back Beat 521 *Tear Down The House*....................10.00 - 15.00

MARKEYS:
20th Century 1210 *Eternal Love*..............................- - -
Satellite 107 *Last Night*..7.00 - 10.00

MARK IV/MARK FOUR:
Cosmic 704 45 RPM (78 rpm)...............................15.00 - 25.00
Pacific Challenger 1002 *Swingin' Hangout* ....10.00 - 20.00

ROOSEVELT MARKS ORCHESTRA With CLAYTON LOVE:
Bobbin 102, 108..5.00 - 10.00

THE MARQUEES:
Daysel 1001 *Close To Me* ....75.00 - 100.00
Grand 141 *The Bells*..75.00 - 100.00
Len 100 *I'm In Misery* ....25.00 - 40.00
Okeh 7096 *Wyatt Earp*..15.00 - 20.00
Warner Brothers 5139 *Until I Die* ....15.00 - 20.00

THE MARQUIS:
Rainbow 358 *I Don't Want Your Love* ....75.00 - 100.00

PERCY MARSHALL:
Marshall 16481 *Give Me My Guitar And My Traveling Shoes* ....10.00 - 15.00

MARTELLS:
Cessna 477 *Forgotten Spring*................................75.00 - 100.00

MARTELS:
Nasco 6026 *Where Did My Woman Go* ....10.00 - 15.00

MARTHA & THE VANDELLAS:
Gordy (LP) 902 *Come And Get These Memories* ..75.00 - 100.00
   (LP) 907 *Heat Wave* ....20.00 - 30.00
   (LP) 915 *Dance Party* ....20.00 - 30.00

BILLY MARTIN:
Lucky 0009 *If It's Lovin' That You Want* ....25.00 - 40.00

BOBBY MARTIN:
Belkay 600 *Jo Jo Rock And Roll* ....20.00 - 30.00

DEAN MARTIN:
Apollo 1088 *Oh Marie*.................................... - - -
    1116 *Santa Lucia* .... - - -
Capitol (EP) 1-401, 2-401 *Dean Martin Sings* ....15.00 - 20.00
    (EP) H-401 *Dean Martin Sings* (10 inch)..........40.00 - 70.00
    (EP) 1-481 *Sunny Italy*...........................15.00 - 20.00
    (EP) 1-533 *Living It Up*..........................50.00 - 75.00
    (EP) 1-576, 2-576 *Swingin' Down Yonder* ....15.00 - 20.00
    (EP) 1-701 *Memories Are Made Of This* ....15.00 - 20.00
    (EP) 1-752 *Pardners*.............................20.00 - 30.00
    (EP) 1-840 *Ten Thousand Bedrooms*................20.00 - 30.00
    (EP) 1-939 *Return To Me* ....15.00 - 20.00
PRO-987 *Sleep Warm* (promotional)....................50.00 - 75.00
    (EP) 1-1027 *Volare*..............................15.00 - 20.00
    1609 *I Met A Girl* (promotional).................50.00 - 75.00
    2160 *It's 1200 Miles From Texas To Palm Springs*
    ....50.00 - 75.00

(Note: See also the Jazz, Dance Bands, Etc. section for 78 RPM records by Dean Martin. While his earliest records were issued as 78s only, many are found in both 78 and 45 RPM formats.)
Reprise 40-046 (7 inch LP) *Country Style*............25.00 - 50.00
    200 *Sophia* (promotional)........................50.00 - 80.00
Reprise (most other issues)...........................4.00 - 7.00

GENE MARTIN:
Bakersfield 126 *I Wouldn't Give A Nickel* ....8.00 - 12.00

JANIS MARTIN:
Bella 1001 *Cracker Jack* ....10.00 - 15.00
RCA Victor (EP) 4093 *Just Squeeze Me* ....100.00 - 150.00
    6491 *Drugstore Rock & Roll*......................8.00 - 12.00
    6560 *Ooby Dooby*.................................20.00 - 30.00
    6652 *My Boy Elvis*...............................15.00 - 20.00
    6744 *Let's Elope Baby*...........................8.00 - 12.00
    6832 *Love Me To Pieces*..........................8.00 - 12.00
    6983 *Love And Kisses*............................8.00 - 12.00
    7104 *All Right Baby*.............................15.00 - 20.00
    7184 *Cracker Jack*...............................15.00 - 20.00
    7318 *Bang Bang* ....15.00 - 20.00

JERRY MARTIN:
Fredlo 5901 *Janet* ....50.00 - 75.00
"R" 507 *Lover's Promise*............................. - - -
    510 *Deep In My Heart* .... - - -

JIMMY MARTIN:
Jaxon 501 *Rock The Bop*.............................50.00 - 80.00

RIC MARTIN:
Condor 101/102 *I Travel The Road* .... - - -
    103/104 *Warm One*................................ - - -

SONNY MARTIN:
Felsted 8507 *Rockabye Baby*.........................8.00 - 12.00

WINK MARTINDALE:
Dot (LP) 3245 *Deck Of Cards* ....20.00 - 30.00
    15728 *All Love Broke Loose*......................7.00 - 10.00
OJ 1009 *Love's Got Me Thinkin'*.....................8.00 - 12.00

MARTINETS:
Success 110 *Baby Think It Over* ....8.00 - 12.00

MARTINIQUES:
Danceland 770 *Broken Hearted Me* ....20.00 - 30.00
    777 *Tonight Is Just Another Night*...............15.00 - 20.00
    1002 *I Need Love*................................15.00 - 20.00

MARTY:
Novelty 701 *Marty On Planet Mars* ....7.00 - 10.00
(Note: 78 RPM pressings exist.)

THE MARVELETTES:
Tamla (LP) 228 *Please Mr. Postman*..................50.00 - 80.00
    (LP) 229 *Smash Hits of 62* ....40.00 - 70.00
    (LP) 231 *Playboy* ....60.00 - 100.00
    (LP) 237 *The Marvelous* ....40.00 - 70.00

MARVELIERS:
Cougar 1868 *Down* ....50.00 - 80.00

MARVELLOS:
Exodus 6214 *She Told Me Lies*.......................25.00 - 40.00
Reprise 20088 *She Told Me Lies* ....15.00 - 20.00
Theron 117 *Calypso Mama*............................100.00 - 150.00

THE MAR-VELS/MARVELS/MARVELLS:
ABC Paramount 9771 *I Won't Have You Breaking My Heart*
    ....50.00 - 80.00
Laurie 3016 *I Shed So Many Tears* ....30.00 - 50.00
Love 5011 *Cherry Lips* ....15.00 - 20.00
Magnet 1005 *Lovely Charms* ....50.00 - 75.00
Mun Rab 1008 *Just Another Fool*.....................150.00 - 200.00
Tammy 1016 *Somewhere In Life* ....75.00 - 100.00
    1019 *My Guardian Angel*..........................40.00 - 60.00
Winn 1916 *For Sentimental Reasons* ....40.00 - 60.00

MARVELOWS:
ABC Paramount 10603 *A Friend*.......................7.00 - 10.00
    10629 *I Do*......................................7.00 - 10.00
    10708 *Shim Sham*.................................7.00 - 10.00
    10756 *Do It* ....7.00 - 10.00

MARVELLUS MICKEY:
Marlo 1535 *I Feel So Good* ....50.00 - 75.00

MARVIN & THE CHIRPS:
Tip Top 202 *I'll Miss You This Christmas*...........30.00 - 50.00

MARVIN & JOHNNY:
Crown (LP) 5381 *Marvin & Johnny*....................25.00 - 40.00
Modern 933 *Cherry Pie* ....10.00 - 15.00
    946 *Little Honey*................................7.00 - 10.00
    949 *Ko Ko Mo*....................................7.00 - 10.00
    952 *Baby Won't You Marry Me* ....7.00 - 10.00
    959 *Sugar Mama*..................................7.00 - 10.00
    968 *Will You Love Me* ....10.00 - 15.00
    974 *Ain't That Right*............................10.00 - 15.00
Specialty 479 *Baby Doll* ....10.00 - 15.00
    530 *Flip*..8.00 - 12.00
Swingin' 645 *Second Helping Of Cherry Pie*..........7.00 - 10.00

MARYLANDERS:
Jubilee 5079 *I'm A Sentimental Fool*................150.00 - 200.00
    5091 *Make Me Thrill Again*.......................100.00 - 150.00
    5114 *Good Old 99* (red plastic) ....150.00 - 300.00

THE MASCOTS:
Blast 206 *Once Upon A Love* ....15.00 - 20.00
King 5377 *The Story Of My Heart*....................15.00 - 20.00
    5435 *Lonely Rain* ....15.00 - 20.00
MGM 11959 *Please Have Mercy* .... - - -

JAMES MASK:
Bandera 1306 *Save Your Love* ....15.00 - 20.00

BONNIE JO MASON:
Annette 1000 *Ringo, I Love You* ....75.00 - 100.00

THE MASQUERADERS:
Boyd 1027 *Vanessa* ....80.00 - 120.00

THE MASQUERADES:
Formal 1011 *These Red Roses* ....20.00 - 30.00

THE MASTERS:
Bingo *1008 Lovely Way To Spend An Evening* ....15.00 - 20.00
End 1061 *Look Out* ....20.00 - 30.00
Len 103 *'Til I Return* ....40.00 - 70.00
Le Sage 714 *Crying My Heart Out* ....80.00 - 120.00

SAMMY MASTERS:
4 Star 1696 *Pink Cadillac* ....15.00 - 20.00
 1697 *Whop T Bop* ....15.00 - 20.00
Galahad 526 *On Tour In Heaven* ....5.00 - 8.00
Lode 108 *Rockin' Red Wing* ....7.00 - 10.00

MASTER-TONES:
Bruce 111 *Tell Me* ....150.00 - 250.00

MATADORS:
Keith 6502 *If You Left Me Today* ....10.00 - 15.00
Sue 700 *Vengeance* ....20.00 - 30.00
 701 *Be Good To Me* ....15.00 - 25.00

BILLY MATCH & STARFIRES:
Starfire 664 *I Want My Baby* ....10.00 - 15.00

LITTLE ARTHUR MATHEWS:
Dig 117 *Big Bad Bulldog* ....15.00 - 20.00
Federal 12232 *I'm Gonna Whale On You* ....15.00 - 20.00

JOHNNY MATHIS:
Columbia 40851, 40993 (78 rpm) ....7.00 - 12.00

MIKE MATHIS:
Blue River 203 *I Can't Get Loose* ....10.00 - 15.00

FAT MAN/FATS MATTHEWS (& THE FOUR KITTENS):
Imperial 5211 *When Boy Meets Girl* ....300.00 - up
 5235 *Down The Line* ....150.00 - 200.00

RAMON MAUPIN:
Fernwood 101 *Long Gone* ....50.00 - 75.00
 105 *Rockin' Rufus* ....50.00 - 75.00

HOWARD MAYBERRY:
Dixie 908 *Proof Of Love* ....50.00 - 80.00

(ARTHUR) LEE MAYE (& THE CROWNS):
Cash 1063 *Will You Be Mine* ....40.00 - 70.00
 1065 *All I Want Is Someone To Love* ....40.00 - 70.00
Dig 124 *This Is The Night for Love* ....50.00 - 80.00
 133 *A Fool's Prayer* ....50.00 - 80.00
Modern 944 *Set My Heart Free* ....200.00 - 300.00
RPM 424 *Truly* ....40.00 - 60.00
 429 *Love Me Always* ....50.00 - 80.00
 438 *Please Don't Leave Me* ....50.00 - 80.00
Specialty 573 *Gloria* ....30.00 - 50.00
Yvette 300 *Gloria* ....30.00 - 50.00

NATHANIEL MAYER:
Fortune (LP) 8014 *Going Back To The Village Of Love*
 ....80.00 - 120.00

PERCY MAYFIELD:
Chess 1599 *Double Dealing* ....15.00 - 20.00
Specialty 416 *Cry Baby* ....20.00 - 30.00
 432 *Louisiana* ....15.00 - 20.00
 439 *Lonesome Highway* ....15.00 - 20.00
 451 *River's Invitation* ....10.00 - 15.00
 460 *Lost Mind* ....10.00 - 15.00

 473 *The Bachelor Blues* ....10.00 - 15.00
 485 *Loose Lips* ....10.00 - 15.00
 499 *You Don't Exist No More* ....10.00 - 15.00
(Note: Earlier issues than those listed above are usually found as 78
 RPM records, valued at $5.00 to $10.00. 45 RPM counterparts of
 these lower numbers are valued at $15-20. Records pressed of
 colored vinyl are worth substantially more than prices quoted.)

JEAN MAYS:
Diamond 170 *Dew Drop Inn* ....10.00 - 15.00

MIKE McALISTER:
Hob Nob 441 *I Don't Dig It* ....7.00 - 10.00

LEON McAULIFF:
ABC Paramount (LP) 394 *Cozy Inn* ....20.00 - 30.00

DALE McBRIDE With GAYLON CHRISTIE & DOWNBEATS:
Fame 503 *It Might Have Been* ....15.00 - 20.00
Kobb 1500 *If You See My Julie* ....15.00 - 20.00

JERRY (BOOGIE) McCAIN (& HIS UPSTARTS):
Excello 2068 *Courtin' In A Cadillac* ....20.00 - 30.00
 2079 *If It Wasn't For My Baby* ....15.00 - 25.00
 2081 *Things Ain't Right* ....15.00 - 20.00
 2103 *Trying To Please* ....10.00 - 15.00
 2111 *Listen Young Girls* ....10.00 - 15.00
 2127 *The Jig's Up* ....10.00 - 15.00
Trumpet 217 *Wine O-Wine* ....50.00 - 75.00
 231 *Stay Out Of Automobiles* ....50.00 - 75.00

LITTLE JOHNNY McCALL:
Wow 1000 *My Love I Can't Hide* .... -   -

MAC McCLANAHAN:
Tiger 104 *That Nonsense Stuff* ....7.00 - 10.00

YUL McCLAY (See THE MONDELLOS)

HAZEL McCOLLUM With THE EL DORADOS:
Vee Jay 118 *Annie's Answer* (red plastic) ....200.00 - 300.00

JIMMY McCRACKLIN (& HIS BLUES BLASTERS):
Irma 102 *You're The One* ....8.00 - 12.00
 103 *Take A Chance* ....8.00 - 12.00
 107 *I'm The One* ....8.00 - 12.00
Mercury 71516 *George Slop* ....7.00 - 10.00
Modern 926 *Blues Blasters Boogie* ....15.00 - 20.00
 934 *Darling Share Your Love* ....15.00 - 20.00
 951 *Couldn't Be A Dream* ....10.00 - 15.00
 967 *That Ain't Right* ....8.00 - 12.00
Peacock 1605 *She's Gone* ....15.00 - 20.00
 1615 *She Felt Too Good* ....10.00 - 15.00
 1634 *I Cried* ....10.00 - 15.00
 1639 *My Story* ....10.00 - 15.00

JIM McCRORY:
Key 5803 *Parking Lot* ....30.00 - 50.00
 5805 *Rock Ya Baby* ....30.00 - 50.00

LLOYD McCULLOUGH:
Republic 7129 *Gonna Love My Baby* ....100.00 - 200.00

GENE McDANIELS:
Liberty (LP) 3146 *In Times Like These* ....25.00 - 40.00

LUKE McDANIEL(S):
King 1247 *Drive On* ....8.00 - 12.00
 1338 *Automobile Song* ....8.00 - 12.00
 1380 *Money Bag Woman* ....8.00 - 12.00
Trumpet 184 *No More* ....15.00 - 20.00

JIM McDONALD:
KCM 3700 *Let's Have A Ball*..................15.00 - 20.00

LONNIE McDONALD:
Howdy 1111 *Too Many Memories* ....- - -

SKEETS McDONALD:
Capitol (LP) 1040 *Goin' Steady With The Blues* .....40.00 - 60.00
   3461 *Heart Breakin' Mama*.................15.00 - 20.00
Capitol, most other issues ....4.00 - 8.00

TOM McDONALD:
Go-Far 962 *One Woman Man* ....20.00 - 30.00

BOB McFADDEN & DOR:
Brunswick (LP) 54056 *Songs Our Mummy Taught Us*
................40.00 - 60.00

RUTH McFADDEN (See also THE SUPREMES):
Old Town 1030 *School Boy* ....50.00 - 80.00

BROWNIE McGHEE (& HIS JOOK BLOCK BUSTERS):
Dot 1184 *Cheatin' And Lying* ....15.00 - 20.00
Encore 102 *High Price Blues* ....15.00 - 20.00
Folkways (LP) 2030 (10 inch) *Blues* ....- - -
  (LP) 2421 *Blues Of America* ....- - -
  (LP) 3557 *Blues* ....- - -
Harlem 2323 *Christina* ....30.00 - 50.00
  2329 *My Confession* ....30.00 - 50.00
Jackson 2304 *Mean Old Frisco* (red vinyl) .....80.00 - 120.00
Jax 304 *Key To The Highway* ....50.00 - 75.00
  310 *Dissatisfied Woman* ....50.00 - 75.00
  312 *Cherry Red* ....50.00 - 75.00
  322 *Pawnshop Blues* ....50.00 - 75.00
Old Town 1075 *She Loves So Easy* ....7.00 - 10.00
Red Robin 111 *Don't Dog Your Woman* ....75.00 - 100.00
Savoy 1177 *Anna Mae* ....15.00 - 20.00
  1185 *When It's Love Time* ....15.00 - 20.00
  1564 *Be My Friend* ....8.00 - 12.00
  (LP) 14019 *Back Country Blues* (with Sonny Terry)
................80.00 - 130.00
Sharp (LP) 2003 *Brownie McGhee*................100.00 - 150.00
(Many of Brownie McGhee's records were issued in 78 RPM format, for which see the **BLUES, RHYTHM & BLUES** section)

STICK McGHEE:
Atlantic 991 *Meet You In The Morning* ....50.00 - 80.00
(Note: Earlier numbers are usually found as 78 RPM records, which are listed in the Blues, etc., section of this book. 45 RPM records of these earlier issues would bring $50.00-$100.00 or more.)
Decca 48104 *Drinkin' Wine Spo-De-O-De* ....40.00 - 70.00
Essex 709 *My Little Rose*................10.00 - 15.00
Herald 553 *Money Fever* ....15.00 - 20.00
King 4610 *Head Happy With Wine* ....20.00 - 30.00
  4628 *Whiskey, Women And Loaded Dice* ....20.00 - 30.00
  4672 *Jungle Juice* ....20.00 - 30.00
  4700 *I'm Doin' All The Time* ....20.00 - 30.00
  4783 *Double Crossin' Liquor* ....15.00 - 20.00
  4800 *Get Your Mind Out Of The Gutter* ....15.00 - 20.00
Savoy 1148 *Things Have Changed*................15.00 - 20.00

BUTCH McGILLIS & THE ROCKATUNES:
Rock-A-Tune 1010 *Woman Fever*................50.00 - 100.00

WAYNE McGINNIS:
Meteor 5035 *Rock And Roll Rhythm* ....50.00 - 80.00

MEL McGONNIGLE:
Rocket 101 *Rattle Shakin' Mama*................80.00 - 130.00

LOWELL McGUIRE:
Nasco 6007 *Leave My Girlie Alone* ....15.00 - 20.00

ED McILWAIN (See THE TRAVELERS)

CHESTER McINTYRE:
Sarg 180 *I'm Gonna Rock With My Baby Tonight* .. 30.00 - 50.00

GENE McKAY:
Clark 238 *What I Say* ....15.00 - 20.00

L. C. McKINLEY (& HIS ORCHESTRA):
Bea & Baby 102 *Nit Wit* ....20.00 - 30.00
States 135 *Weeping Willow Blues* ....100.00 - 150.00
Vee Jay 133 *She's Five Feet Three* ....50.00 - 80.00
  159 *I'm So Satisfied* ....40.00 - 70.00

JOHN McKINNEY & THE PREMIERS:
Mad 1009 *Gee How I Love You* ....50.00 - 80.00

GENE McKOWN:
Aggie 101 *Rock-A-Billy Rhythm* ....40.00 - 60.00

BUTCH McLAREY:
Kliff 103 *Rockin' Hall* ....75.00 - 100.00

BETTE McLAURIN:
Derby 790 *I May Hate Myself in the Morning* ....20.00 - 30.00
  804 *My Heart Belongs To Only You* ....25.00 - 40.00

OSCAR McLOLLIE (& THE HONEYJUMPERS):
Crown (LP) 5016 *Oscar McLollie & The Honeyjumpers*
................30.00 - 50.00
Modern 902 *The Honey Jump* ....10.00 - 15.00
  915 *Be Cool My Heart* ....10.00 - 20.00
  920 *God Gave Us Christmas* ....8.00 - 12.00
  928 *Mama Don't Like* ....8.00 - 12.00
  938 *Wiggle Toe* ....8.00 - 12.00
  955 *Eternal Love* ....8.00 - 12.00
  970 *Convicted* ....8.00 - 12.00

CECIL McNABB:
King 5116 *Clock Tickin' Rhythm*................50.00 - 80.00

BIG JAY McNEELY:
King (LP) 530 ... *In 3-D*................75.00 - 100.00
Savoy (LP) 15045 (10 inch)................50.00 - 75.00

CLYDE McPHATTER (& THE DRIFTERS):
Atlantic (EP) 605 *Rock With Clyde McPhatter* .... 100.00 - 150.00
  (EP) 618 *Clyde McPhatter*................80.00 - 120.00
  1185 *Come What May* (78 rpm)................15.00 - 20.00
  1199 *A Lover's Question* (78 rpm) ....40.00 - 70.00
  2028 *Since You've Been Gone* (78 rpm) ....30.00 - 50.00
  2038 *There You Go* (78 rpm) ....30.00 - 50.00
  (LP) 8003 *Clyde McPhatter & The Drifters* (black label)
................100.00 - 150.00
  (LP) 8024 *Love Ballads* ....75.00 - 100.00
  (LP) 8031 *Clyde* ....75.00 - 100.00
King (LP) 559 *Clyde McPhatter With Billy Ward & His Dominoes*
................150.00 - 250.00
(Note: This album exists as Federal 559, which is considerably rarer than the King issue.)
MGM (LP) 3775 *Let's Start Over Again* ....40.00 - 70.00

CHANDOS McRILL:
Stardust 655 *Money Lovin' Woman* ....15.00 - 20.00

CARL McVOY:
Hi 2001 *Tootsie* ....15.00 - 20.00
  2002 *Little John's Gone* ....8.00 - 12.00
Phillips 3526 *Tootsie*................10.00 - 15.00

THE MEADOWLARKS (See also DON JULIAN):
RPM 399 *Love Only You* ....75.00 - 100.00
 406 *L.M.F.S.T.* ....80.00 - 130.00

MEDALLIONAIRES:
Mercury 71309 *Magic Moonlight* ....20.00 - 30.00

THE MEDALLIONS (See also VERNON GREEN):
Dooto (EP) 202 ....75.00 - 100.00
Dooto/Dootone 347 *Buick 59* ....15.00 - 25.00
 357 *The Telegram* ....15.00 - 25.00
 364 *Edna* ....20.00 - 30.00
 373 *My Pretty Baby* ....25.00 - 40.00
 379 *Dear Darling* ....20.00 - 30.00
 393 *I Want A Love* ....20.00 - 30.00
 400 *Shedding Tears For You* ....20.00 - 30.00
 419 *For Better Or For Worse* ....20.00 - 30.00
 446 *Magic Mountain* ....15.00 - 30.00
 454 *Behind The Door* ....10.00 - 20.00
(Note: Foregoing Dootone records, with multi-color labels, are
 reissues, valued substantially lower.)
Dootone (LP) unnumbered Rhythm & Blues Vocal Group Series
 album .... - - -
Essex 901 *I Know* ....100.00 - 150.00
Sarg 191 *I Love You True* ....10.00 - 15.00
 194 *Lovin' Time* ....10.00 - 15.00
Singular 1002 *A Broken Heart* ....25.00 - 40.00

THE MELLO DROPS:
Imperial 5325 *When I Grow Too Old To Dream* ...100.00 - 200.00

MELLO FELLOWS:
Lamp 8006 *My Friend Charlie* ....15.00 - 25.00

MELLO HARPS:
Do Re Mi 203 *Love Is A Vow* ....750.00 - up
Tin Pan Alley 145 *I Love Only You* ....75.00 - 100.00
 157 *What Good Are My Dreams* ....150.00 - 200.00
 159 *My Bleeding Heart* ....100.00 - 150.00

MELLO-KINGS:
Herald (EP) 451 *The Fabulous* ....100.00 - 200.00
 502 *Tonite, Tonite* ....15.00 - 20.00
 502 *Tonite, Tonite* (78 rpm) ....30.00 - 50.00
 507 *Chapel On The Hill* ....20.00 - 30.00
 518 *Valerie* ....20.00 - 30.00
 536 *Running To You* ....20.00 - 30.00
 536 *Chip Chip* (actually *Down In Cuba* by The Royal Holidays)
  ....40.00 - 60.00
 548 *Our Love Is Beautiful* ....20.00 - 30.00
 554 *I Promise* ....20.00 - 30.00
 561 *Till There Was You* ....20.00 - 30.00
 (LP) 1013 *Tonight-Tonight* ....150.00 - 300.00

MELLO-MOODS/MELLO MOODS:
Prestige 799 *Call On Me* ....200.00 - 300.00
 856 *I'm Lost* ....150.00 - 250.00
Red Robin 104 *I Couldn't Sleep A Wink Last Night* .. - -
(Note: The existence of Red Robin 104 in 45 RPM format has not
 been verified.)
Robin 105 *How Could You?* ....300.00 - up

MELLO-TONES/MELLOTONES:
Decca (EP) 2399 *Mellotones* ....75.00 - 100.00
 48318 *Man Loves Woman* ....100.00 - 150.00
 48319 *I'm Just Another One In Love With You* ...100.00 - 150.00
Fascination 1001 *Rosie Lee* ....50.00 - 80.00
Gee 1007 *Rosie Lee* ....10.00 - 15.00
 1037 *Rosie Lee* (78 rpm) ....10.00 - 15.00
 1040 *Ca-Sandra* ....15.00 - 20.00

Herald 502 *Tonite, Tonite* ....75.00 - 100.00
Lee Tone 700 *Prayer Of Love* (blue label) ....150.00 - 300.00

MELLOW KEYS:
Gee 1014 *I'm Not A Deceiver* ....15.00 - 20.00

MELLOWS:
Candelight 1011 *You're Gone* ....25.00 - 40.00
Celeste 3002 *My Darling* ....50.00 - 100.00
 3004 *I'm Yours* ....50.00 - 100.00
Jay Dee 793 *How Sentimental Can I Be* ....50.00 - 80.00
 797 *Smoke From Your Cigarette* ....30.00 - 50.00
 801 *I Still Care* ....50.00 - 80.00
 807 *Yesterday's Memories* ....50.00 - 80.00

MELO-AIRES:
Nasco 6019 *Indebted To You* ....10.00 - 15.00

MELODAIRES:
Flyright 915 *Now You Know* ....10.00 - 15.00

THE MELODEERS:
Studio 9908 *Wishing Is For Fools* ....10.00 - 15.00

MEL-O-DOTS:
Apollo 1192 *Just How Long* (colored plastic) ......800.00 - up

MELODY MAKERS:
Hollis 1001 *Let's Make Love Worthwhile* ....- - -
 1002 *The Nearness Of You* ....- - -

MELO GENTS:
Warner Bros. 5056 *Baby Be Mine* ....15.00 - 20.00

MELOTONES (See MELLOTONES)

RAY MELTON:
Image 1005 *Boppin' Guitar* ....30.00 - 50.00

MEMORIES:
Way-Lin 101 *Love Bells* ....75.00 - 100.00

"MEMORY LANE HITS BY THE ORIGINAL GROUPS":
Fire (LP) 100 ....75.00 - 100.00

MEMPHIS MINNIE & HER COMBO/With LITTLE JOE & HIS BAND:
Checker 771 *Me And My Chauffeur* (red plastic) . 150.00 - 250.00
J.O.B. 1101 *Kissing In The Dark* (red plastic) ......200.00 - 300.00

MEMPHIS SLIM & HIS/THE HOUSE ROCKERS/ ORCHESTRA:
Chess (LP) 1455 *Memphis Slim* ....50.00 - 100.00
Folkways (LP) 3524 *The Real Boogie Woogie* ....- - -
Mercury 70063 *Drivin' Me Mad* ....15.00 - 20.00
Money 212 *My Country Gal* ....10.00 - 20.00
United 138 *Back Alley* ....30.00 - 50.00
 156 *Five O'Clock Blues* ....15.00 - 25.00
 166 *This Is My Lucky Day* ....15.00 - 25.00
 176 *Sassy Mae* ....15.00 - 25.00
 182 *Four Years of Torment* ....15.00 - 20.00
 189 *Two Of a Kind* ....15.00 - 20.00
 201 *Blue and Lonesome* ....15.00 - 20.00
(Any of foregoing, if pressed of translucent red vinyl, command
 substantially higher prices)
Vee Jay 271 *Stroll On Little Girl* ....8.00 - 12.00
 294 *What's The Matter* ....8.00 - 12.00
 330 *Steppin' Out* ....8.00 - 12.00
 343 *The Come Back* ....8.00 - 12.00
 (LP) 1012 *Memphis Slim At The Gate Of Horn*. 40.00 - 60.00

WALLY MERCER:
Dot 1099 *Rock Around The Clock* ....30.00 - 50.00
 1120 *Looped* ....30.00 - 50.00

MERCY BABY:
Ace 528 *Rock And Roll Blues* ....20.00 - 30.00
   535 *Mercy's Blues* ....20.00 - 30.00
Mercy Baby 501 *You Ran Away* ....30.00 - 50.00
   502 *The Rock And Stomp* ....30.00 - 50.00
Ric 995 *Don't Lie To Me* ....10.00 - 15.00

MERCY DEE (See DEE)

MERRILL BROTHERS:
GM 102 *Mercy Blues* ....10.00 - 15.00

BIG MACEO MERRIWEATHER:
Fortune (LP) 3002 *Big Maceo Merriweather & John Lee Hooker*
....50.00 - 80.00

"MERRY CHRISTMAS BABY":
Hollywood (LP) 501 (Charles Brown, et al.) ....200.00 - up

METALLICS:
Baronet 2 *Need Your Love* ....15.00 - 20.00
   14 *Get Lost* ....15.00 - 20.00

THE METEORS:
Beltone 2041 *Let's Start Anew* ....50.00 - 80.00

THE METRONOMES:
Cadence 1339 *Dear Don* ....15.00 - 20.00
Maureen 1000 *My Dearest Darling* ....10.00 - 15.00
Specialty 472 *She's Gone* ....150.00 - up
Strand (LP) *The Metronomes Sing The Standard Hits*
....50.00 - 80.00

THE METROPOLITANS:
Junior 395 *So Much In Love* ....15.00 - 25.00

METROS:
Just 1502 *All Of My Life* ....50.00 - 80.00

THE METROTONES:
Reserve 114 *More And More* ....75.00 - 100.00
   116 *Please Come Back* ....50.00 - 80.00
(Note: above have black label*)*

LOUIE MEYERS (& THE ACES):
Abco 104 *Blusey* ....50.00 - 75.00

JOEY MICHAELS:
Arcade 150 *Sixteen Cats* ....20.00 - 30.00

MICKEY & SYLVIA:
Groove (EP) 18 *Love Is Strange* ....75.00 - 100.00
Rainbow 316 *Se Le Boom Run Dun* ....15.00 - 20.00
Vik (LP) 1102 *New Sounds* ....100.00 - 150.00

ELMON MICKLE (& HIS RHYTHM ACES):
Elko 003 *Flat Foot Sam* ....50.00 - 80.00
E.M. 132 *Lonesome Highway* ....30.00 - 50.00
EM & EP 133 *Short 'N' Fat* ....25.00 - 40.00
J Gems 1908 *Short 'N' Fat* ....15.00 - 25.00

GARY MIDDLETON:
Harlem 102 *Don't Be Shy* ....30.00 - 50.00

MIDNIGHTERS (See also HANK BALLARD):
Federal (LP) 295-90 (10 inch) *The Midnighters*....400.00 - up
   (EP) 333 *Midnighters Sing Their Greatest Hits*
....100.00 - 150.00
   (LP) 541 *Midnighters Sing Their Greatest Hits*
....100.00 - 200.00
   12169 *Work With Me Annie* ....15.00 - 20.00
   12185 *Sexy Ways* ....10.00 - 15.00
   12195 *Annie Had A Baby* ....10.00 - 15.00

12202, 12205, 12210, 12220, 12224, 12227,
   12230, 12240, 12243, 12251, 12260, 12270,
   12285, 12293, 12299, 12305, 12317, 12339....7.00 - 12.00
King (LP) 581 *...Greatest Hits... Vol. 2* ....100.00 - 150.00
Sarg 187 *Rockin' Romance* ....15.00 - 20.00

MIDNIGHTS:
Music City 746 *Hear My Plea* ....20.00 - 30.00
   762 *Cheating On Me* ....20.00 - 30.00

MIKE & THE UTOPIANS:
Cee Jay 574 *I Wish* ....100.00 - 150.00

BOBBY MILANO:
Challenge 59005 *Double Talking Baby* ....15.00 - 20.00

AMOS MILBURN (See also PARTY AFTER HOURS):
Aladdin (LP) 704 (10 inch) *Rockin' The Boogie* (red vinyl)
....250.00 - 500.00
   (LP) 810 *Rockin' The Boogie* ....200.00 - 400.00
   3105 *Boogie Woogie* ....50.00 - 75.00
   3124 *Trouble In Mind* ....50.00 - 75.00
   3125 *Flyin' Home* ....50.00 - 75.00
   3133 *Roll Mr. Jelly* ....50.00 - 75.00
   3146 *Button Your Lip* ....25.00 - 40.00
   3150 *Greyhound* ....20.00 - 30.00
   3159 *Rock Rock* ....20.00 - 30.00
   3164 *Let Me Go Home Whiskey* ....20.00 - 30.00
   3168, 3197, 3218, 3226, 3240, 3248, 3253, 3269,
    3293, 3320, 3332, 3363, 3383, 3420 ....8.00 - 15.00
(Note: Numbers lower than those listed here are usually found as 78
   RPM records; see Blues, etc. section. 45 RPM issues of such
   earlier numbers would bring more than $50.00.)
Motown (LP) 608 *Return of The Blues Boss* ....100.00 - 150.00
   1038 *I'll Make It Up To You Somehow* .... - -
Score (LP) 4012 *Let's Have A Party* ....80.00 - 130.00

MILLER SISTERS:
Ember 1004 *Guess Who* ....7.00 - 10.00
Flip 504 *I Knew You Would* ....80.00 - 120.00
Herald 455 *Until You're Mine* ....10.00 - 15.00
Onyx 507 *Sugar Daddy* ....15.00 - 20.00
Sun 230 *There's No Right Way To Do Me Wrong* ......100.00 - 150.00
   255 *Ten Cats Down* ....40.00 - 60.00
   504 *I Knew You Would* ....100.00 - 200.00

ARLIE MILLER:
Lucky 80 *Lou Ann* ....20.00 - 30.00

BUDDY MILLER:
Band Box 311 *Teen Twist* ....10.00 - 15.00
   322 *Little Bo Peep* ....10.00 - 15.00
   335 *With Tears In My Eyes* ....10.00 - 15.00
Gem 102 *Little Bo Peep* ....15.00 - 20.00
VEM 2226 *Teen Twist* ....15.00 - 20.00

CARL MILLER:
Lu 503 *Rhythm Guitar* ....100.00 - 200.00

CHUCK MILLER:
Mercury (LP) 20195 *After Hours* ....50.00 - 80.00

CLINT MILLER:
ABC Paramount 9878 *Bertha Lou* ....10.00 - 15.00
   9938 *Teenage Dance* ....10.00 - 15.00

DICK MILLER & HIS BAND/SOUTHERN RAMBLERS:
Aggie 1002 *Now I'm Gone* ....15.00 - 20.00
M & M - *Humpty Dumpty Love* .... - -

FRANKIE MILLER:
Audio Lab (LP) 1562 *Fine Country Singin'* ....75.00 - 100.00
Columbia 21314 *It's No Big Thing To Me* ....8.00 - 12.00
   21378 *You Don't Show Me Much* ....8.00 - 12.00
   21420 *Paid In Full*.....................................8.00 - 12.00
   21472 *Paint, Powder And Perfume* ....8.00 - 12.00
   21519 *Day By Day* ....7.00 - 10.00
Starday (LP) SLP-338 *Blackland Farmer* ....30.00 - 50.00
   457, 481, 496, 513, 525, 537, 550, 566, 655,
      673, 691, 709 ....5.00 - 10.00

JODY MILLER:
Capitol (LP) 2349 *Queen Of The House*.................20.00 - 40.00

ROGER MILLER:
Starday 356 *Can't Stop Lovin' You* ....15.00 - 30.00

SCOTT MILLER:
Grey Cliff 722 *I Got School* ....10.00 - 15.00

TAL MILLER:
Goldband 1059 *Life's Journey*.........................7.00 - 10.00
Hollywood 1094, 1097 ....8.00 - 12.00

WALTER MILLER With THE BARONS:
Meteor 5037 *My Last Mile* ....75.00 - 100.00

WARREN MILLER:
United Artists 104 *Everybody's Got A Baby But Me*
....25.00 - 40.00

LOU MILLET:
Republic 7130 *Slip Slip Slippin' In* ....75.00 - 100.00

THE MILLIONAIRES:
Davis 441 *Somebody's Lying* ....10.00 - 15.00

BOBBY MILTON & THE DEBUTONES:
Arrow 1009 *A Place In My Heart*......................20.00 - 30.00

BUDDY MILTON & THE TWILIGHTERS:
RPM 418 *Say Another Word* ....80.00 - 130.00
   419 *Ooh Wah* ....75.00 - 100.00

LITTLE MILTON (See LITTLE)

ROY MILTON:
Dooto (LP) 223 *Rock 'N' Roll Vs. Rhythm 'N' Blues*
....75.00 - 100.00
Dootone 363, 369..8.00 - 12.00
Specialty 429, 438, 464, 480, 538, 545 ....7.00 - 12.00
(Note: Copies pressed of red vinyl command higher prices. These
   and earlier issues are usually found as 78 rpm records.)

SAL MINEO:
Epic (LP) 3404 *Dino*..................................50.00 - 75.00

ROSS MININI:
Gulfstream 7269 *Oh Janet*............................20.00 - 30.00

JIMMY MINOR:
Mercury 71527 *I'm a Fool For You* ....7.00 - 10.00
   71623 *So Doggone Lonesome* ....7.00 - 10.00

MINOR BOPS:
Lamp 2012 *Need Your Love Tonight*....................40.00 - 60.00

THE MINOR CHORDS:
Lu Pine 112 *Many A Day*..............................10.00 - 15.00

MINORS:
Celeste 3007 *Jerry* ....200.00 - 300.00

MINOR TONES:
Music City 816 *Forever Darling* ....80.00 - 130.00

MINT JULEPS:
Herald 481 *Bells Of Love* ....50.00 - 80.00

MINTS:
Lin 5001 *Busy Body Rock* ....15.00 - 25.00
   5007 *Night Air* ....15.00 - 20.00

MIRACLES:
Baton 210 *A Lover's Chant* ....50.00 - 80.00
Cash 1008 *You're An Angel* ....30.00 - 50.00
End 1019 *Got A Job* ....15.00 - 20.00
   1029 *I Cry* ....15.00 - 20.00
Fury 1001 *I Love You So* ....100.00 - 150.00
   1002/1003 *Your Love* ....100.00 - 150.00
Motown 1/2 *Bad Girl* ....150.00 - up
Tamla (LP) 220 *Hi, We're The Miracles* ....100.00 - 300.00
   (LP) 223 *Cookin' With The Miracles*.............150.00 - 300.00
   (LP) 224 *Shop Around* ....80.00 - 120.00
   (LP) 236 *Christmas with* ....50.00 - 80.00
   (LP) 238 *The Fabulous..* ....50.00 - 80.00
   (LP) 245 *Doin' Mickey's Monkey*..................30.00 - 60.00
   54028 *The Feeling Is So Fine* ....40.00 - 60.00
   54034 *Shop Around*................................7.00 - 10.00
   54034 *Shop Around* (Master number on label and in wax reads:
      H-55518A2) ....75.00 - 100.00
   54044 *Mighty Good Lovin'* ....15.00 - 30.00
(Note: Above 45s, if original issues, will have the "striped" label
   design.)

BILLY MIRANDA:
Checker 957 *Run Rose* ....7.00 - 10.00

MISS PEACHES:
Groove 0009 *Calling Moody Field* ....8.00 - 12.00

BILLY MITCHELL:
Atlantic 974 *Bald Head Woman* ....30.00 - 60.00

BOBBY MITCHELL (& THE TOPPERS):
Imperial 5250 *One Friday Morning*....................50.00 - 75.00
   5270 *Baby's Gone* ....30.00 - 50.00
   5295 *Wedding Bells Are Ringing* ....50.00 - 75.00
   5309 *I'm A Young Man* ....40.00 - 60.00
   5326 *I Wish I Knew* ....25.00 - 40.00
   5346 *I Cried* ....15.00 - 20.00
   5378, 5392 ....8.00 - 12.00

FREDDIE MITCHELL:
Rock & Roll 609 *Three Strikes You're Out* ....8.00 - 12.00

JOHNNY MITCHELL (See THE MAJESTICS)

LEE MITCHELL:
Sharp 0862 *Rootie Tootie Baby* ....50.00 - 75.00

MARLON MITCHELL:
Vena 0100 *Ice Cold Baby* ....30.00 - 50.00

STANLEY MITCHELL & THE TORNADOS:
Chess 1649 *Four O'Clock In The Morning* ....30.00 - 50.00

TOMMIE MITCHELL:
Mercury 70930 *Little Mama* ....15.00 - 20.00

WILLIE MITCHELL:
Skipper 1001 *Lizzie Lou* ....8.00 - 12.00
Stomper Time 1160 *Tell It To Me Baby* ....15.00 - 20.00

MIXERS:
Bold 101 *You Said You're Leaving Me*.................80.00 - 120.00
   102 *Love And Kisses* ....80.00 - 120.00

HANK MIZELL:
Eko 506 *Jungle Rock* ....75.00 - 100.00
King 5236 *Jungle Rock*...........................30.00 - 50.00

BOBBY MIZZELL & LEE WAYNE:
20th Fox 160 *Same Thing*.........................15.00 - 20.00

THE MOHAWKS (See POPCORN & THE MOHAWKS)

RONNIE MOLLEEN:
King 5365 *Rockin' Up*..............................25.00 - 40.00

MONARCHS:
JAM 104 *This Old Heart* ....10.00 - 15.00
Melba 101 *In My Younger Days* ....10.00 - 15.00
Neil 101 *In My Younger Days* ....10.00 - 15.00
   103 *Always Be Faithful*....................15.00 - 20.00
Sound Stage 2502 *This Old Heart* ....7.00 - 10.00
Wing 90040 *Angels In The Sky*..................10.00 - 15.00

BOBBY MONCRIEF:
D 1014 *Don't Hold Me To A Vow* ....15.00 - 20.00

THE MONDELLOS:
Rhythm 102 *Come Back Home*.................80.00 - 130.00
   105 *Over The Rainbow* ....80.00 - 130.00
   106 *Daylight Saving Time* ....100.00 - 150.00
   109 *Hard To Please* ....80.00 - 130.00
   114 *My Heart*.................................300.00 - up
   1003 *One Hundred Years From Today* ....100.00 - 150.00

MONIQUES:
Centaur 105 *All The Way Now*.................10.00 - 20.00

MONITORS:
Aladdin 3309 *Tonight's The Night* ....30.00 - 50.00
Circus 219 *A Boy Friend's Prayer* ....30.00 - 50.00
Specialty 595 *Our School Days*................15.00 - 20.00
   622 *Closer To Heaven*......................25.00 - 40.00
   636 *Mama Linda*............................10.00 - 15.00

MONOGRAMS:
Saga 1000 *My Baby Dearest Darling* ....30.00 - 50.00

MONORAYS:
Nasco 6020 *It's Love Baby* ....8.00 - 12.00
Red Rocket 476 *My Guardian Angel*.......10.00 - 15.00
Tammy 1005 *My Guardian Angel* ....50.00 - 80.00

MONOTONES:
Argo 5290 *Book Of Love* ....8.00 - 12.00
   5290 *Book Of Love* (78 rpm) ....20.00 - 30.00
   5301 *Tom Foolery*...........................8.00 - 12.00
   5321 *The Legend Of Sleepy Hollow* ....10.00 - 15.00
   5339 *Fools Will Be Fools* ....15.00 - 20.00
Hull 735 *Reading The Book Of Love* ....20.00 - 30.00
   743 *Tattle Tale* ....10.00 - 15.00
Mascot 124 *Book Of Love*........................80.00 - 120.00

MARILYN MONROE:
RCA Victor (EP) 593 Selections From *"There's No Business Like Show Business"* ....30.00 - 50.00
   5745 *The River Of No Return* ....8.00 - 12.00
   20-5745 *"Who Is She?"* (promotional 78 RPM) ......25.00 - 50.00
   6033 *Heat Wave* ....10.00 - 15.00

SMILEY MONROE:
Vita 163 *Teen Age Doll* ....10.00 - 15.00

THE MONTAGUES:
Andex 4025 *I'm Happy* ....100.00 - 150.00

MONTCLAIRS:
Audicon 111 *Good Night*.........................15.00 - 20.00
Hi-Q 5001 *Golden Angel* ....25.00 - 50.00
Premium 404 *My Every Dream* ....75.00 - 100.00
Sonic 104 *All I Want Is Love* ....200.00 - up

THE MONTELS:
Universal 101 *Union Hall*.......................30.00 - 60.00

MONTEREYS:
Arwin 130 *Goodbye My Love* ....10.00 - 15.00
Dominion 1019 *First Kiss*........................20.00 - 30.00
East West 121 *I'll Love You Again* ....8.00 - 12.00
Impala 213 *Without A Girl*......................20.00 - 30.00
Nestor 15 *Someone Like You* ....300.00 - up
Planet 57 *Blast Off*..................................5.00 - 8.00
Rose 109 *You're The Girl For Me* ....15.00 - 30.00
Teen Age 1001 *Someone Like You* ....80.00 - 130.00
Trans American 1001 *Little Darlin'* ....150.00 - 200.00

JOE MONTGOMERY:
Abbott 189 *Cool Cat*................................. - -

LITTLE BROTHER MONTGOMERY (& HIS BOGALUSA BOYS/VICKSBURGERS):
Ebony 1000 *Cow Cow Blues*...................15.00 - 20.00
   1002 *Fever* ....15.00 - 20.00
   1005 *Pinetops Boogie* ....15.00 - 20.00
   1030 *Gonna Raise A Ruckus Tonight* ....15.00 - 20.00

THE MON-VALES:
Pen Joy 502 *Carol-Ann* ....20.00 - 30.00

THE MOODS:
Kool 1024 *High School Dance* ....10.00 - 15.00
   1029 *Opp-Sy-Do* ....7.00 - 10.00
   1032 *Only The Young*.......................7.00 - 10.00
Sarg 162 *Little Alice*...............................20.00 - 30.00
   176 *Easy Going* ....15.00 - 20.00
   179 *Let Me Have Your Love* ....20.00 - 30.00
   184 *Rockin' Santa Claus* ....15.00 - 25.00
   185 *On The Move* ....15.00 - 25.00
TNT 189 *It's Goodbye And Not Goodnight*............20.00 - 40.00

THE MOONBEAMS/MOONBEEMS:
Checker 912 *Cryin' The Blues* ....10.00 - 15.00
Great 100 *A Lover's Plea*........................15.00 - 25.00
Sapphire 1003 *Cryin' The Blues* ....20.00 - 30.00

GLEN MOONEY:
Fraternity 898 *Go Steady With Me*..........10.00 - 15.00

MOONGLOWS:
Champagne 7500 *I Just Can't Tell No Lie*............200.00 - 300.00
Chance 1147 *Baby, Please* (red plastic)..............400.00 - 800.00
   1150 *Just A Lonely Christmas* (red plastic) .....400.00 - 800.00
   1152 *Secret Love* (silver & blue label) ....250.00 - 400.00
   1152 *Secret Love* (yellow & black label).........150.00 - 200.00
   1156 *I Was Wrong* (black & white label) ....150.00 - 200.00
   1156 *I Was Wrong* (yellow & black label) ......100.00 - 150.00
1161 *My Gal* ....500.00 - up
Chess (LP) 1425 *Rock, Rock, Rock* (black label)....80.00 - 130.00
   (LP) 1430 *Look, It's The Moonglows* (black label) ....100.00 - 150.00
   1581 *Sincerely*.................................15.00 - 25.00
(Note: This, and numbers through 1669, are of the Silver Top label)
   1589 *Most Of All*.............................20.00 - 30.00
   1598 *Foolish Me* ....15.00 - 25.00
   1605 *In Love* ....25.00 - 40.00
   1611 *In My Diary*............................25.00 - 40.00

1619 *We Go Together*	15.00 -	20.00
1629 *When I'm With You*	15.00 -	20.00
1646 *I Knew From The Start*	15.00 -	20.00
1651 *I'm Afraid The Masquerade Is Over*	15.00 -	20.00
1661 *Please Send Me Someone To Love*	15.00 -	20.00
1669 *The Beating Of My Heart*	15.00 -	20.00
1681 *Too Late*	15.00 -	20.00

(Note: This, and subsequent issues, have all-blue labels, Chess vertical)

1689 *In The Middle Of The Night*	15.00 -	20.00
1701 *Sweeter Than Words*	15.00 -	20.00
1717 *I'll Never Stop Wanting You*	15.00 -	20.00
1770 *Junior*	10.00 -	15.00
(EP) 5123 *Look, It's The Moonglows*	100.00 -	200.00
Vee Jay (LP) 1052 *The Moonglows Meet The Flamingos*	75.00 -	100.00

MOONLIGHTERS:

Josie 843 *Broken Heart*	10.00 -	15.00
Tara 100 *Glow Of Love*	50.00 -	80.00
102 *Rock-A-Bayou Baby*	50.00 -	80.00

CECIL MOORE:

Sarg 150 *Walkin' Fever*	20.00 -	30.00
165 *Kathy*	20.00 -	30.00
192 *My Money's Gone*	15.00 -	20.00
206 *Diamond Back*	7.00 -	10.00

DONNY LEE MOORE:

Shelley 1000 *I'm Buggin Out Little Baby*	30.00 -	50.00

GENE MOORE & THE METRONOMES (See THE METRONOMES)

JIMMY MOORE & THE PEACOCKS/TABS:

Noble 711 *Tender Love*	300.00 -	up
720 *Oops!*	300.00 -	up

JOHNNY MOORE; JOHNNY MOORE'S COMBO/ THREE BLAZERS; JOHNNY MOORE with JIMMY HAGGETT BAND:

Aladdin 3106 *Cloudy Skies*	20.00 -	30.00
Blaze 101 *Every Time*	5.00 -	10.00
110 *Run Sinner Run*	5.00 -	10.00
Modern Hollywood 1001 *Strange Love*	10.00 -	15.00
1002 *Lonesome Train*	10.00 -	15.00
1012 *Diesel Drive*	10.00 -	15.00
1031 *Johnny Ace's Last Letter*	10.00 -	15.00
1045 *Christmas Eve Baby*	10.00 -	15.00
(Unnumbered) *Dragnet Blues*	15.00 -	25.00
Vaden III *Country Girl*	20.00 -	30.00

LATTIE MOORE:

ARC 8005 *Pretty Woman Blues*	15.00 -	25.00
Audio Lab (LP) 1573 *Country Side*	40.00 -	70.00
Speed 101 *Juke Joint Johnny*	50.00 -	80.00

MERRILL MOORE:

Capitol (EP) *Merrill Moore*	50.00 -	80.00
2226 *Big Bug Boogie*	8.00 -	12.00
2386 *Bartender's Blues*	8.00 -	12.00
2574 *House Of Blue Lights*	8.00 -	12.00
2691 *Snatchin' And Grabbin'*	7.00 -	10.00
(most other issues)	5.00 -	10.00

RONNIE MOORE:

Teen's Choice 7 *Sweet Shop Doll*	- -	-

RUDY MOORE:

Federal 12253 *I'm Mad With You*	10.00 -	15.00
12259 *Ring-A-Ling Dong*	10.00 -	15.00
12276 *Step It Up And Go*	15.00 -	20.00
12280 *Robbie Dobbie*	10.00 -	15.00

SCOTTY MOORE (TRIO):

Epic (LP) 24103 *The Guitar That Changed The World*	50.00 -	75.00
Fernwood 107 *Have Guitar Will Travel*	15.00 -	20.00

SPARKLE MOORE:

Fraternity 751 *Rock-A-Bop*	20.00 -	30.00
766 *Tiger*	15.00 -	25.00

MOOSE JOHN:

Ultra 102 *Wrong Doin' Woman*	20.00 -	30.00

PRENTICE MORELAND:

Dot 16173 *Sincerely*	8.00 -	12.00

RICHARD MORELAND:

Picture 6969 *Please Don't Ask Me*	10.00 -	15.00
7722 *Mailman Blues*	10.00 -	15.00

BILL MORGAN:

Delta 504 *She Gave Me Lovin'*	10.00 -	15.00

CHARLIE MORGAN:

Walmay 101 *South Of Chicago*	20.00 -	30.00

ROCKET MORGAN:

Zynn 502 *You're Humbuggin' Me*	15.00 -	20.00
507 *What Ya Gonna Do*	15.00 -	20.00
1003 *Walkin' Home*	15.00 -	20.00

JACKIE MORNINGSTAR:

Sandy 1018 *Rockin' To The Graveyard*	30.00 -	50.00

MOROCCANS:

Salem 1014 *Believe In Tomorrow*	30.00 -	50.00

MOROCCOS:

United 188 *Pardon My Tears*	50.00 -	80.00
193 *Somewhere Over The Rainbow*	50.00 -	80.00
204 *What Is A Teenager's Prayer*	60.00 -	100.00
207 *Sad Sad Hours*	80.00 -	130.00

TINY MORRIE:

Hurricane 6966 *Bernardine*	10.00 -	15.00

BOB MORRIS:

Cascade 5907 *Party Time*	8.00 -	12.00

ELMORE MORRIS:

Peacock 1660, 1668	7.00 -	12.00

GENE MORRIS:

Edmoral 1012 *Lovin' Honey*	30.00 -	50.00
Vik 0287 *Lovin' Honey*	15.00 -	20.00
Winston 1046 *If You Need My Love*	15.00 -	20.00

JIMMY MORRIS (See THE BELVEDERES)

LEO MORRIS:

Ivory 41465 *I Don't Need You*	15.00 -	20.00

ROD MORRIS:

Capitol 1882, 1946, 2022, 2301, 2424, 2541	5.00 -	10.00
Ludwig 1002 *Ghost Of Casey Jones*	8.00 -	12.00

BILL MORRISON:

TNT 9029 *Set Me Free*	75.00 -	100.00
9031 *Baby Be Good*	75.00 -	100.00

(Beware of repressings, some utilizing original stampers)

JIM MORRISON:

Arctic 5001 *Ready To Rock*	75.00 -	100.00

ELLA MAE MORSE:
Capitol (LP) 513 *Barrelhouse, Boogie & Blues* ......40.00 - 60.00

ROY MOSS:
Fascination 1002 *Wiggle Walking Baby* ....15.00 - 20.00
Mercury 70770 *You Nearly Lose Your Mind* ....20.00 - 30.00
     70858 *You Don't Know My Mind* ....20.00 - 30.00

DANNY MOTE:
Opal 001 *Done You Wrong* .... - - -

FRANK MOTLEY:
"DC" 0415 *Everybody Wants A Flat Top* ....8.00 - 12.00

"MOUNTAIN FROLIC":
Brunswick (LP) 5900 (10 inch) (various artists) .....30.00 - 50.00

JUNE MOY (& THE FEATHERS):
Showtime 1103 *Castle Of Dreams* ....80.00 - 130.00

MR. SAD HEAD:
RCA Victor 5089 *Sad Head Blues* ....30.00 - 50.00
     5388 *Black Diamond* ....30.00 - 50.00

MR. STRING BEAN:
Herald 418 *Pass The Juice Miss Lucy* ....30.00 - 50.00

MR. X:
Vita 152 *Rock Dock* .... - - -

MUDDY WATERS:
Chess (LP) 1427 *The Best Of Muddy Waters* ....50.00 - 80.00
     (LP) 1444 *Sings Big Bill* ....40.00 - 70.00
(Note: Above LPs have black label.)
     1509 *Country Boy* ....100.00 - 150.00
     1514 *Please Have Mercy* ....100.00 - 150.00
     1526 *Gone To Main Street* ....80.00 - 120.00
     1537 *Sad, Sad Day* ....80.00 - 120.00
     1542 *Turn The Lamp Down Low* ....75.00 - 100.00
     1550 *Blow Wind Blow* ....50.00 - 80.00
     1560 *She's So Pretty* ....40.00 - 60.00
(Note: Issues earlier than those above, i.e. lower numbers, are
     usually found as 78 RPM records, as listed in the Blues, etc.; see
     those sections. 45 RPM issues of such lower numbers are valued
     at $100.00 and up, with premium prices for records pressed of
     colored vinyl.)
     1571 *Oh Yeah* ....25.00 - 40.00
     1579 *I'm Ready* ....25.00 - 40.00
     1585 *Loving Man* ....30.00 - 50.00
     1596 *I Want To Be Loved* ....25.00 - 40.00
     1602 *Young Fashioned Ways* ....20.00 - 30.00
     1612 *Sugar Sweet* ....20.00 - 30.00
     1620 *All Aboard* ....15.00 - 20.00
     1630 *Diamonds At Your Feet* ....15.00 - 20.00
     1644, 1652, 1667, 1680, 1692, 1704, 1718, 1733,
         1739, 1748, 1758, 1765, 1774, 1796, 1819,
         1827, 1839, 1862 ....10.00 - 15.00

MOON MULLICAN:
Coral (LP) 57235 *Moon Over Mullican* ....150.00 - 200.00
     61994 *Jenny Lee* ....30.00 - 50.00
     62042 *Sweet Rockin' Music* ....30.00 - 50.00
Dixie - *Good Times Gonna Roll Again* .... - - -
King (LP) 555 *Moon Mullican Sings His All Time Greatest Hits*
     ....75.00 - 100.00
     (LP) 628 *16 Favorite Tunes* ....50.00 - 80.00
     917 *I Was Sorta Wonderin'* ....10.00 - 15.00
     947 *Without A Port Of Love* ....10.00 - 15.00
     965 *Cherokee Boogie* ....10.00 - 15.00
     984 *Heartless Lover* ....8.00 - 12.00
     1043 *Shoot The Moon* ....8.00 - 12.00

     1060 *Triflin' Woman Blues* ....10.00 - 15.00
     1152 *A Thousand And One Sleepless Nights* .....10.00 - 15.00
     1164 *Oogle, Oogle, Olglie* ....10.00 - 15.00
     1198 *Rocket To The Moon* ....10.00 - 15.00
     1244 *Grandpa Stole My Baby* ....10.00 - 15.00
     1337 *Good Deal, Lucille* ....10.00 - 15.00
     1366 *No Stranger* ....8.00 - 12.00
     1408 *You Got The Best Of Me* ....8.00 - 12.00
     1467, 4894, 4915, 4979 ....5.00 - 10.00
Starday (LP) SLP-267 *Mister Piano Man* ....75.00 - 100.00
     527, 545, 556, 594, 596 ....7.00 - 10.00

DEE MULLIN:
D 1066 *I've Really Got A Right To Cry* ....10.00 - 15.00

MUMBLES (See also WALTER HORTON):
RPM 338 *Black Gal* ....100.00 - 150.00

GENE MUMFORD & THE SERENADERS:
Whiz 1500 *Please Give Me One More Chance* ......80.00 - 130.00

MURFREESBORO:
Champion 1007 *Oh My Love* .... - - -

CHUCK MURPHY:
Columbia 21258 *Hocus Pocus* .... - - -
     21305 *Rhythm Hall* ....15.00 - 20.00

DON MURPHY:
Cosmopolitan 2264 *Mean Mama Blues* ....30.00 - 50.00

JIMMY MURPHY:
Columbia 21486 *Here Kitty Kitty* ....20.00 - 30.00
     21534 *Sixteen Tons Rock & Roll* ....20.00 - 30.00
     21569 *Baboon Boogie* ....25.00 - 40.00
Rev 3508 *I'm Gone Mama* ....10.00 - 15.00

THE MUSTANGS:
Vest 51 *Over The Rainbow* ....100.00 - 150.00

SAMMY MYERS:
Ace 536 *Sleeping In The Ground* ....15.00 - 20.00
Fury 1035 *Sad, Sad Lonesome Day* ....15.00 - 20.00

BIG BOY MYLES & THE SHA-WEES:
Specialty 564 *That Girl I Married* ....30.00 - 50.00
     590 *Hickory Dickory Dock* ....30.00 - 50.00

BILLY MYLES:
Ember 1026 *The Joker* ....8.00 - 12.00
     1026 *The Joker* (78 rpm) ....30.00 - 50.00

THE MYSTICS:
Chatam 350/351 *Teenage Sweetheart* ....200.00 - up
Laurie 3028 *Hushabye* ....10.00 - 15.00
     3038 *So Tenderly* ....10.00 - 15.00
     3047 *All Through The Night* ....10.00 - 15.00
     3058 *White Cliffs Of Dover* ....10.00 - 15.00
     3086 *Goodbye Mr. Blues* ....10.00 - 15.00
     3104 *Darling I Know How* ....10.00 - 15.00

CLIFF/CLIFFIE NASH:
Do Ra Me 5027 *I'll Never Know* ....7.00 - 10.00
     5028 *Jennie Lou* ....7.00 - 10.00
Kim 1048 *This Little Boy's Gone Lookin'* ....8.00 - 12.00

NATIVE BOYS:
Combo 113 *Strange Love* ....30.00 - 50.00
     115 *Tears* ....30.00 - 60.00
     119 *Laughing Love* ....40.00 - 70.00
     120 *Oh Let Me Dream* ....40.00 - 70.00
Modern 939 *Native Girl* ....75.00 - 125.00

JERRY NEAL:
Dot 15810 *I Hates Rabbits* ....15.00 -   20.00

MEREDITH NEAL:
Blaze 101 *Gertrude*..................50.00 -   80.00

TEX NEIGHBORS:
Emerald 2021 *Rockin' Beat* ....25.00 -   40.00

FRED NEIL:
Look 1002 *Don't Put The Blame On Me* ....10.00 -   15.00

FREDDY NEIL & FRIEND:
Brunswick 55177 *Listen Kitten* ....10.00 -   15.00

BILLY NELSON & FIVE WINGS:
Savoy 1183 *Walk Along*..................10.00 -   15.00

EARL NELSON (See THE PELICANS)

JAY NELSON:
Hollywood 1088 *Lover's Plea*..................10.00 -   15.00

JIMMIE/JIMMY (T-99) NELSON:
Chess 1877 *Tell Me Who* ....8.00 -   12.00
Music City 797 ....15.00 -   20.00
RPM 325 *T-99 Blues* ....100.00 -   150.00
   329 *Baby Child* ....100.00 -   150.00
   353 *Bad Habit* ....30.00 -   50.00
   368 *Little Rich Girl* ....30.00 -   50.00
   377 *Little Miss Teasin' Brown*..................30.00 -   50.00
   385 *Married Men Like Sport* ....30.00 -   50.00
   389 *Big Mouth* ....25.00 -   40.00
   397 *Cry Hard Luck* ....25.00 -   40.00

RICKY NELSON:
Imperial (EP) 153, 154, 155 *Ricky Nelson* ....20.00 -   40.00
   (EP) 156, 158, 159, 160, 161, 161, 162, 164 ......20.00 -   40.00
   5463 *Be Bop Baby* ....10.00 -   15.00
   5463 *Be Bop Baby* (78 rpm) ....20.00 -   30.00
   5483 *Stood Up* ....10.00 -   15.00
   5483 *Stood Up* (78 rpm) ....20.00 -   30.00
   5503 *Believe What You Say* ....7.00 -   10.00
   5503 *Believe What You Say* (78 rpm) ....30.00 -   50.00
   5528 *Poor Little Fool* ....7.00 -   10.00
   5528 *Poor Little Fool* (78 rpm) ....40.00 -   60.00
   5545 *Lonesome Town* ....7.00 -   10.00
   5545 *Lonesome Town* (78 rpm) ....50.00 -   100.00
   5565 *It's Late* ....7.00 -   10.00
   5565 *It's Late* (78 rpm)..................50.00 -   100.00
   (most other issues) ....5.00 -   10.00
   (LP) 9048 *Ricky* ....35.00 -   50.00
   (LP) *Ricky Nelson* ....35.00 -   50.00
   (LP) 9059 *More Songs By Ricky*..................35.00 -   50.00
   (LP) 9061 *Ricky Sings Again* ....35.00 -   50.00
   (LP) 9082 *Songs By Ricky* ....30.00 -   50.00
   Verve (LP) 2083 *Teen Time* ....100.00 -   200.00
   Verve (EP) 5048 *Ricky* ....100.00 -   150.00
   Verve 10047 *Teenager's Romance*..................15.00 -   20.00
   10047 *Teenager's Romance* (78 rpm) ....30.00 -   50.00
   10070 *You're My One And Only Love*................15.00 -   20.00
   10070 *You're My One And Only Love* (78 rpm).50.00 -   80.00

TOMMY NELSON:
Dixie 2014 *Hobo Bop* ....30.00 -   50.00

WILLIE NELSON:
Bellair 107 *Night Life* (red plastic) ....15.00 -   25.00
Betty 5702 *Misery Mansion* (red plastic) ....10.00 -   15.00
   5703 *Man With The Blues* ....7.00 -   10.00
Liberty (LP) 3308 *Here's Willie Nelson*..................20.00 -   40.00

THE NEONS:
Gone 5090 *Golden Dreams*..................15.00 -   20.00
Tetra 4444 *Kiss Me Quickly* ....15.00 -   20.00
   4449 *Road To Romance* ....15.00 -   20.00
Waldon 100 *My Lover*..................80.00 -   130.00

NERVOUS NORVUS:
Dot 15470 *Transfusion* ....5.00 -   8.00
   15485 *Ape Call* ....5.00 -   10.00
   15500 *The Fang* ....7.00 -   10.00
Embee 177 *I Like Girls* ....7.00 -   10.00

BILL NETTLES:
Starday 174 *Wine-O-Boogie* ....30.00 -   50.00

JOE NETTLES & THE SATELLITES:
Circle 1174 *Oh Baby*..................15.00 -   25.00

AARON NEVILLE:
Minit 618 *Show Me The Way* ....7.00 -   10.00

CARL NEWMAN & HIS NIGHT HAWKS:
Mar-vel 2350 *Rockin' And A-Boppin'* ....20.00 -   30.00
Trio 849 *Rockin' And A-Boppin'* ....75.00 -   100.00

JIMMY NEWMAN:
Dot 15766 *Carry On* ....15.00 -   20.00
MGM (LP) 3777 *This Is Jimmie Newman* ....25.00 -   50.00

NEWPORT RHYTHMAIRES:
Newport 101 *Mornin' Blues* ....15.00 -   20.00

THE NEWPORTS:
Kane 008 *If I Could Tonight* ....20.00 -   30.00
Kent 380 *The Wonder Of Love* ....20.00 -   30.00

THE NEWTONES:
Baton 260 *Remember The Night* ....150.00 -   up

NEW YORKERS (FIVE):
Danice 801 *Gloria My Darling*..................100.00 -   150.00
Wall 547 *Dream A Little Dream*..................20.00 -   30.00

NICK & THE STINGRAYS:
Mill Mont 1628 *Broken Hearted Baby* ....30.00 -   50.00

BETTY NICKELL & THE ROCKETS:
Abbey 102 *Hot Dog* ....20.00 -   30.00

NICKEY & THE NOBLES:
End 1098 *School Bells* ....10.00 -   15.00
Gone 5039 *School Bells* ....15.00 -   25.00

ROCKY NIGHT WITH HIS NIGHT CATS:
Pearl 708 *Teen Age Bop* ....50.00 -   75.00

THE NIGHTBEATS:
Zoom 002 *Lonesome Road Rock* ....10.00 -   20.00

NIGHT CAPS:
Vandan (LP) 8124 *Wine, Wine, Wine* ....100.00 -   200.00
(Note: Original pressings of the above LP are quite scarce, but a reissue has been extensively distributed.)

ROBERT NIGHTHAWK & THE NIGHTHAWKS BAND:
States 131 *Maggie Campbell* (red vinyl) ....200.00 -   300.00

NIGHT OWLS:
Bethlehem 3087 *Bells Ring*..................8.00 -   12.00
Cuca 1075 *Waitin' By The School* ....20.00 -   30.00
NRC 015 *You Shouldn't Oughta Done It* ....8.00 -   12.00

NIGHT RAIDERS (See MICKEY HAWKS)

NINO & THE EBBTIDES (See THE EBBTIDES)

NIPTONES:
Lorraine 1001 *Angie* ....10.00 - 15.00

NITECAPS:
Groove 0134 *A Kiss And A Vow* ....30.00 - 50.00
0147 *Sweet Thing*.................20.00 - 30.00
0158 *You May Not Know*....................20.00 - 30.00
0176 *In Each Corner Of My Heart*....................20.00 - 30.00

NITE RIDERS:
Apollo 460 *Women And Cadillacs* ....15.00 - 20.00
466 *Doctor Velvet* ....15.00 - 20.00
MGM 12487 *Sittin' Sippin' Coffee*....................10.00 - 15.00

FORD NIX & THE MOONSHINERS:
Clix 813 *Nine Times Out Of Ten* ....30.00 - 50.00

HOYLE NIX:
Bo-Kay 110 *I Don't Love-A Nobody* ....10.00 - 15.00
Caprock 105 *Coming Down From Denver*................7.00 - 10.00
109 *Big Ball's In Cowtown*.................................7.00 - 10.00

WILLIE NIX:
Chance 1163 *Nervous Wreck*...................................150.00 - 300.00
Checker 756 *Truckin' Little Woman*......................150.00 - 250.00
Sabre 104 *All By Myself*..80.00 - 120.00
Sun 179 *Baker Shop Boogie* ....200.00 - up

ELMORE NIXON:
Imperial 5388 *You Left Me* ....30.00 - 50.00
Post 2008 *Don't Do It*...30.00 - 50.00

ROY NIXON:
Dee Cee 714 *Hard Rockin' Daddy* ....20.00 - 30.00

EDDIE NOACK:
D 1019 *Have Blues-Will Travel*...............................20.00 - 30.00
1037 *Walk 'Em Off* ....15.00 - 20.00
1060 *A Thinking Man's Woman* ....10.00 - 15.00
TNT 110 *Too Hot To Handle* ....20.00 - 30.00

NOBELLS:
Mar 101 *Crying Over You* ....20.00 - 30.00

EDDIE NOBLE:
Suite 16 111 *Mean Old Blues* ....10.00 - 15.00

EMMY NOBLE:
Liberty 55122 *I Done Done* ....8.00 - 12.00

NOBLES:
Klik 305 *Poor Rock And Roll* ....50.00 - 80.00
Sapphire 151 *Do You Love Me* ....30.00 - 50.00

NOBLETONES:
C & M 182 *I Love You*...25.00 - 40.00
438 *I'm Crying*.................................15.00 - 20.00

SID NOEL:
Aladdin 3331 *Flying Saucer*....................................10.00 - 15.00

MISS FRANKIE NOLAN:
ABC Paramount 10231 *I Still Care* ....10.00 - 15.00

TERRY NOLAND:
Apt 25065 *Long Gone Baby* ....10.00 - 15.00
Brunswick (LP) 54041 *Terry Noland* ....75.00 - 125.00
55010 *Hypnotized* ....8.00 - 12.00
55036 *Patty Baby*.................................7.00 - 10.00
55054 *Oh Baby Look At Me*....................10.00 - 15.00
55069 *Crazy Dream*..................................8.00 - 12.00

55092 *There Was A Fungus Among Us* ....8.00 - 12.00
55122 *Guess I'm Gonna Fall*....................10.00 - 15.00

JIMMY NOLAN:
Imperial 5363 *Let's Try Again* ....10.00 - 20.00

LARRY NOLEN & HIS BANDITS:
Starday 668 *King Of The Ducktail Cats* ....30.00 - 50.00

THE NOMADS:
Northern 503 *Heart Attack*.....................................30.00 - 50.00

GENE NORMAN (& THE ROCKETS):
Snag 101 *Snaggle Tooth Ann* ....75.00 - 100.00
Soma 1156 *No Help Wanted* ....10.00 - 15.00

RAY NORMAN:
Nasco 6030 *Heartbreak Station* ....10.00 - 15.00

BOBBY NORRIS:
Capitol 3945 *I Went Rockin'* ....15.00 - 20.00

CHUCK NORRIS:
Atlantic 994 *Let Me Know* ....20.00 - 30.00

JOE NORRIS:
SOM 1001 *Rock Out Of This World* ....35.00 - 50.00

NOTATIONS:
Clarity 106 *I Just Want To Know* ....30.00 - 50.00
Wonder 100 *What A Night For Love* ....75.00 - 100.00

NOTEMAKERS:
Sotoplay 007 *It Hurts To Wonder* ....75.00 - 100.00

NOTES:
Capitol 3332 *Don't Leave Me Now* ....10.00 - 15.00
MGM 12338 *Trust In Me*..20.00 - 30.00
Sarg 177 *Little Girl* ....15.00 - 25.00

NOTE TORIALS:
Impala 201 *My Valerie*..100.00 - 150.00
Sunbeam 119 *My Valerie* ....40.00 - 60.00

ERNIE NOWLIN:
Missouri 640 *Tally Ho* ....10.00 - 15.00

BOBBY NUNN (See also LITTLE ESTHER):
Dootone 302 *Anticipating Blues* ....15.00 - 20.00

NUTMEGS:
Herald 452 *Story Untold* ....10.00 - 20.00
459 *Ship Of Love*....................................15.00 - 20.00
466 *Whispering Sorrows* ....15.00 - 20.00
475 *Key To The Kingdom* ....20.00 - 30.00
492 *A Love So Sure* ....20.00 - 30.00
538 *My Story* ....15.00 - 25.00
574 *Rip Van Winkle* ....8.00 - 12.00
Tel 1011 *A Dream Of Love* ....30.00 - 50.00

NU-TONES/NUTONES:
Cha Cha 716 *Sharon Lee* ....8.00 - 12.00
Combo 127 *At Midnite*..125.00 - 175.00
Hollywood Star 798 *Believe* ....300.00 - up

NU-TRENDS:
Lawn 216 *Together* ....200.00 - up

BOB OAKES & THE SULTANS:
Regent 7502 *You Gotta Rock And Roll*....................8.00 - 12.00

OCAPELLOS:
General 107 *The Stars*...30.00 - 50.00

OCTAVES:
Val 1001 *Mambo Carolyn* ....20.00 - 30.00

DOYLE O'DELL & THE CASS COUNTY BOYS:
Era (LP) 20004 ....25.00 - 40.00

JIM OERTLING:
Hammond 267 *Old Moss Back* ....30.00 - 60.00

LILLIAN OFFITT:
Chief 7012 *The Man Won't Work* ....8.00 - 12.00
    7015 *Oh Mama* ....7.00 - 10.00
    7029 *Shine On*...7.00 - 10.00
Excello 2104, 2124, 2139 ....5.00 - 8.00

THE OFF KEYS:
Rowe 003 *Our Wedding Day* ....15.00 - 20.00
Technicord 1001 *Our Wedding Day* ....10.00 - 15.00

LOUIS OGLETREE:
Parrot 822 *Tell It Like It Is*...............................50.00 - 100.00

JOHNNY O'KEEFE:
Brunswick 55067 *Shake Baby Shake*.......................20.00 - 30.00

JOHNNY OLENN (& THE JOKERS):
Glenco 7001 *Sally Let Your Bangs Hang* ....10.00 - 15.00
Liberty (LP) 3029 *Just Rollin' With Johnny Olenn* ....100.00 - 150.00
TNT 1016 *Sally Let Your Bangs Hang Down* ....50.00 - 75.00
    1018 *I Ain't Gonna Cry No More* ....50.00 - 75.00

OLE SONNY BOY:
Excello 2086 *Blues And Misery*............................30.00 - 50.00

BOBBY OLIVER:
Lucky Four 1004 *Where Do Dreams Go*................15.00 - 20.00
    1006 *Lucille* ....15.00 - 20.00

BIG DANNY OLIVER:
Trend 30-012 *Sapphire* ....7.00 - 10.00
    30-016 *Blues For The 49* ....7.00 - 10.00

SHADIE OLLER:
Summit 114 *Come To Me, Baby*...........................60.00 - 100.00

ROCKY OLSON:
Chess 1723 *Kansas City* ....8.00 - 12.00

OLYMPICS:
Arvee (LP) 423 *Doin' The Hully Gully* ....50.00 - 80.00
    (LP) 424 *Dance By The Light Of The Moon*.......50.00 - 80.00
    (LP) 429 *Party Time* ....50.00 - 80.00
Demon 1508 *Western Movies* (78 rpm)..................30.00 - 50.00

SLIM O'MARY:
Mar-Vel 20 *Row, Boy, Sink Or Swim* .... - -

THE ONBEATS:
Granite 302 *Catastrophe*.. - -

GRADIE O'NEAL:
Bella 2205 *Baby Oh Baby*..................................40.00 - 80.00

JOHNNY O'NEILL:
King 4599 *Johnny Feels The Blues* ....50.00 - 75.00

ONTARIOS:
Big Town 121 *Memories Of You* ....80.00 - 130.00

OPALS:
Apollo 462 *My Heart's Desire* ....50.00 - 75.00

"OPRY STARS-JAMBORIEE":
Mercury (LP) 20350 (various artists) ....20.00 - 30.00

GENE O'QUINN:
Capitol 1508 *Boogie Woogie Fever*.......................15.00 - 20.00
    1708 *Triflin' Woman*................................10.00 - 15.00

1821 *It's No Use* ....10.00 - 15.00
1943, 2050, 2075, 2210, 2344, 2490, 2655,
    2715, 2843, 2935 ....7.00 - 12.00

ROY ORBISON (& THE TEEN KINGS & THE ROSES):
MGM (most issues)..5.00 - 8.00
Monument (most issues) ....5.00 - 8.00
    (LP) 4002, 14002 *Lonely And Blue*................50.00 - 80.00
    (LP) 4007, 14007 *Crying* ....40.00 - 70.00
RCA Victor 7381 *Sweet And Innocent* ....15.00 - 20.00
    7447 *Almost Eighteen* ....15.00 - 20.00
Sun 242 *Ooby Dooby* ....30.00 - 50.00
    242 *Ooby Dooby* (78 rpm) ....50.00 - 100.00
    251 *Rock House* ....25.00 - 40.00
    251 *Rock House* (78 rpm) ....40.00 - 70.00
    265 *Devil Doll* ....25.00 - 40.00
    265 *Devil Doll* (78 rpm) ....40.00 - 70.00
    284 *Chicken Hearted* ....25.00 - 40.00
    284 *Chicken Hearted* (78 rpm) ....50.00 - 75.00
    (LP) 1260 *...at The Rock House* ....50.00 - 80.00

THE ORBITS:
Argo 5286 *Who Are You* ....7.00 - 10.00
Don-J 48796 *I'm Home* ....125.00 - 175.00
Flair-X 5000 *Message Of Love* ....8.00 - 12.00

ORCHIDS:
King 4661 *Oh Why*..100.00 - 150.00
    4663 *Beginning To Miss You* ....100.00 - 200.00
Parrot 815 *You're Everything To Me* ....50.00 - 100.00
    819 *You Said You Loved Me* ....50.00 - 100.00

ORIGINAL CASUALS:
Back Beat (EP) 40 *Three Kisses Past Midnight* .....50.00 - 80.00
    503 *So Tough* ....7.00 - 10.00
    510 *Don't Pass Me By* ....8.00 - 12.00
    514 *Three Kisses Past Midnight* ....8.00 - 12.00

THE ORIGINAL DELL-VIKINGS (See DELL-VIKINGS)

THE ORIGINAL PYRAMIDS:
Shell 304 *Ankle Bracelet* ....10.00 - 15.00

THE ORIGINALS (featuring TONY ALLEN):
Diamond 102 *At Times Like This* ....10.00 - 15.00
    116 *You And I*...10.00 - 15.00
Original Sound 10 *Wishing Star* ....7.00 - 10.00

ORIOLES:
Abner 1016 *Super Girl*......................................10.00 - 15.00
Jubilee (EP) 5000 *The Orioles Sing* ....400.00 - up
    5000 *It's Too Soon To Know* ....250.00 - up
    5005 *Deacon Jones* ....250.00 - up
    5016 *Forgive And Forget*............................200.00 - 400.00
    5017 *What Are You Doing New Year's Eve*.....150.00 - 200.00
    5025 *At Night* ....150.00 - 300.00
    5040 *I Crossed My Fingers* ....150.00 - 300.00
    5045 *Oh Holy Night* ....75.00 - 100.00
    5051 *I Miss You So* ....150.00 - 250.00
    5061 *I'm Just A Fool In Love* ....150.00 - 250.00
    5065 *Baby Please Don't Go* (red plastic) ....300.00 - up
    5071 *When You're Not Around*....................150.00 - 250.00
    5074 *Proud Of You* ....125.00 - 175.00
    5074 *Proud Of You* (red plastic) ....300.00 - up
    5082 *It's Over Because We're Through* ....150.00 - 200.00
    5084 *Gettin' Tired Tired Tired* ....150.00 - 200.00
    5092 *Don't Cry Baby* ....100.00 - 150.00
    5092 *Don't Cry Baby* (red plastic)................250.00 - up
    5102 *You Belong To Me* ....125.00 - 175.00
    5107 *Till Then* ....100.00 - 150.00

5107 *Till Then (red plastic)*	150.00 -	250.00
5108 *Hold Me, Thrill Me, Kiss Me*	50.00 -	80.00
5108 *Hold Me, Thrill Me, Kiss Me* (red plastic)	150.00 -	200.00
5115 *Bad Little Girl*	50.00 -	80.00
5115 *Bad Little Girl* (red plastic)	150.00 -	200.00
5120 *I Cover The Waterfront*	50.00 -	80.00
5120 *I Cover The Waterfront* (red plastic)	150.00 -	200.00
5122 *Crying In The Chapel*	25.00 -	50.00
5127 *Write And Tell Me Why*	30.00 -	60.00

(Note: See Blues, etc. section for 78 RPM records by **THE ORIOLES**, most of which 78s are not known to exist in 45 RPM format. 78 RPM counterparts of 45s listed here are worth only a small percentage of values for 45s.)

5134 *There's No One But You*	10.00 -	15.00
5137 *Secret Love*	10.00 -	15.00
5143 *Maybe You'll Be There*	20.00 -	30.00
5154 *In The Chapel In The Moonlight*	10.00 -	15.00
5161 *If You Believe*	10.00 -	15.00
5172 *Runaround*	10.00 -	15.00
5177 *I Love You Mostly*	10.00 -	15.00
5189 *I Need You Baby*	10.00 -	15.00
5221 *Moody Over You*	15.00 -	20.00
5363 *Tell Me So*	7.00 -	10.00
Vee Jay 196 *Happy Till The Letter*	10.00 -	15.00
228 *For All We Know*	10.00 -	15.00
244 *Sugar Girl*	50.00 -	80.00

ORLANDOS:
Cindy 3006 *Cloudburst*	40.00 -	60.00

TONY ORLANDO & THE MILOS:
Milo 101 *Ding Dong*	20.00 -	30.00

THE ORLONS:
Cameo (LP) *Not Me*	25.00 -	40.00

J. D. ORR & THE LONESOME VALLEY BOYS:
Summit 105 *Hula Hoop Boogie*	75.00 -	100.00

DAVID ORRELL:
Felsted 8515 *You're The One*	25.00 -	40.00

BOBBY OSBORN:
Knickerbocker 1312 *Bound To Happen*	-	-

THE OSBORNE BROTHERS & RED ALLEN:
MGM (LP) 3734	20.00 -	30.00

JIMMIE OSBORNE:
Audio Lab (LP) 1527 *Singing Songs He Wrote*	30.00 -	50.00

MILT OSHINS:
Pelvis 169 *All About Elvis*	10.00 -	20.00

THE OSPREYS:
East West 110 *It's Good To Me*	7.00 -	10.00

JOHNNY OTIS:
Capitol (LP) 940 *The Johnny Otis Show*	75.00 -	100.00
(EP) 1134 *Johnny Otis Show*	50.00 -	80.00
Dig (LP) 104 *Rock & Roll Hit Parade*	150.00 -	200.00
Peacock 1625, 1636	10.00 -	15.00

KEN OTTEY:
RCA Victory 7185 *Main Drag Saturday Night*	10.00 -	15.00

"OUR BEST TO YOU":
Everlast (LP) 201 (various artists)	50.00 -	100.00

THE OVATIONS:
Andie 5017 *My Lullaby*	10.00 -	15.00
Barry 101 *My Lullaby*	7.00 -	10.00
Epic 9470 *The Day We Fell In Love*	10.00 -	20.00

Goldwax 110 *Pretty Little Angel*	5.00 -	8.00
Josie 916 *Remembering*	7.00 -	10.00

DANNY OVERBEA:
Apex 7751 *Stop*	7.00 -	10.00
Checker 768 *Train, Train, Train*	30.00 -	50.00
774 *40 Cups Of Coffee*	25.00 -	40.00

(above, if pressed of translucent red plastic, bring considerably more)
784 *I Could-But I Won't*	10.00 -	20.00
796 *You're Mine*	10.00 -	20.00
808 *A Toast To Lovers*	10.00 -	15.00
816 *Do You Love Me*	10.00 -	15.00
Federal 12324 *Candy Bar*	10.00 -	20.00

KENNY OWEN:
Poplar 106 *I Got The Bug*	15.00 -	20.00

RUDY OWEN & THE RAVENS:
Startime 3287 *Pretty Linda*	10.00 -	15.00

BUCK OWENS (See also CORKY JONES):
Newstar 6418 *Hot Dog*	50.00 -	80.00
Pep 105 *It Don't Show On Me*	10.00 -	15.00
106 *The House Down The Block*	10.00 -	15.00
109 *There Goes My Love*	10.00 -	15.00

CLYDE OWENS:
Linco 1313 *Swing It Little Katy*	100.00 -	150.00

THE PACERS:
Calico 101 *I Found A Dream*	15.00 -	20.00
Guyden 2064 *How Sweet*	100.00 -	150.00

PACKARDS:
Paradise 105 *Dream Of Love*	60.00 -	100.00
Pla Bac 106 *Ladise*	300.00 -	up

THE PAGANS:
Music City 832 *Lover's Plea*	100.00 -	200.00
835 *Fool That I Am*	100.00 -	150.00

ALLEN PAGE & THE DELTONES:
Moon 301 *Honeysuckle*	20.00 -	30.00
302 *Dateless Night*	20.00 -	30.00
303 *She's The One That Got It*	20.00 -	30.00

PAGEANTS:
Arlen 731 *Saturday Romance*	10.00 -	15.00
Du-Well 101 *Saturday Romance*	30.00 -	50.00
Goldisc 3013 *Happy Together*	50.00 -	80.00

HAL PAIGE (& THE WAILERS):
Atlantic 996 *Break Of Day Blues*	30.00 -	50.00
1032 *Big Foot Mae*	20.00 -	40.00
Fury 1024 *After Hours Blues*	10.00 -	20.00
J & S 1601 *Thunder Bird*	30.00 -	50.00

"PAJAMA PARTY":
Roulette (LP) 20521 (various artists)	30.00 -	50.00

THE PALISADES:
Calico 113 *Close Your Eyes*	7.00 -	10.00
Debra 1003 *Chapel Bells*	30.00 -	50.00

TOMMY PALM:
Bob 101 *Stroll With Me Baby*	10.00 -	15.00

CLARENCE PALMER & THE JIVE BOMBERS (See THE JIVE BOMBERS)

PALMS:
States 157 *Darling Patricia*	50.00 -	80.00
United 208 *Tear Drops*	50.00 -	80.00

PALS:
Guyden 2019 *My Baby Likes To Rock*......................8.00 - 12.00
Turf 1000 *Summer Is Here* ....10.00 - 15.00

PAPA LIGHTFOOT:
Aladdin 3171 *P. L. Blues* ....75.00 - 100.00
    3304 *Jumpin' With Jarvis* ....25.00 - 50.00
Imperial 5289 *Mean Old Train* ....50.00 - 75.00
Savoy 1161 *Mean Old Train* ....20.00 - 30.00

THE PARADONS:
Milestone 2003 *Diamonds And Pearls* ....10.00 - 15.00
Warner Bros. 5186 *Take All Of Me* ....10.00 - 15.00

THE PARAGONS (See also THE JESTERS):
Musicraft 1102 *Wedding Bells*...........................8.00 - 12.00
    (LP) 8001 *The Paragons vs. The Harptones* ......40.00 - 60.00
Tap 500 *If* ....8.00 - 12.00
    503 *In Midst Of Night* ....10.00 - 15.00
    504 *These Are the Things I Love* ....20.00 - 30.00
Winley 215 *Florence* ....10.00 - 20.00
    220 *Let's Start All Over Again* ....15.00 - 25.00
    223 *Two Hearts Are Better Than One* ....15.00 - 25.00
    227 *Vows Of Love* ....10.00 - 20.00
    228 *Don't Cry Baby* ....15.00 - 25.00
    236 *Darling I Love You* ....20.00 - 30.00
    240 *So You Will Know* ....10.00 - 15.00
    250 *Kneel And Pray*...........................15.00 - 25.00

THE PARAKEETS (QUINTETTE):
Atlas 1068 *I Had A Love* ....50.00 - 75.00
    1069 *My Heart Tells Me* ....50.00 - 75.00
    1071 *Teenage Rose* ....15.00 - 20.00
    1075 *Love Was A Stranger To Me* ....25.00 - 50.00
Jubilee 5407 *Shangri-La*...............................8.00 - 12.00

KENNY PARCHMAN:
Jaxon - *Don't You Know* ....80.00 - 120.00
Lu 504 *Get It Off Your Mind* ....100.00 - 150.00

PARIS BROTHERS:
Brunswick 55132 *This Is It*............................8.00 - 12.00
Coral 62220 *Funny Feeling* ....5.00 - 8.00

(LITTLE) JUNIOR PARKER & HIS BAND/BLUE FLAMES/ORCHESTRA (See also LITTLE JUNIOR'S BLUE FLAMES):
Duke (LP) 76 *Driving Wheel* ....40.00 - 60.00
    120 *Dirty Friend Blues* ....15.00 - 20.00
    127 *Please Baby Blues*........................15.00 - 20.00
    137 *Backtracking* ....10.00 - 15.00
    147 *Driving Me* ....10.00 - 15.00
    157 *Mother-In-Law Blues* ....10.00 - 15.00
    164 *Next Time You See Me* ....8.00 - 12.00
    168 *Pretty Baby* ....7.00 - 10.00
Duke 177, 184, 193, 301, 324 ....5.00 - 10.00

TIM PARKER:
Emmons 1005 *That's Alright Mama* ....- - -

RAY PARKS:
Capitol 3580 You're Gonna Have To Bawl, That's All
....10.00 - 15.00

RAY PARKS & THE CANUCKS (See THE CANUCKS with Ray Parks)

THE PARLIAMENTS:
Flipp 100 *Lonely Island* ....15.00 - 25.00

FRED PARRIS & THE SATINS (See THE FIVE SATINS)

KENT PARRY & THE ROGUES:
Alton 600 *Stop Then Rock* ....10.00 - 15.00

DEAN PARRISH:
Warner Bros. 5436 *Come On Down* ....5.00 - 8.00

AL PARSONS:
- *Wait For Me Baby/Memories Of Yesterday*...............- - -

BILL PARSONS:
Starday 526 *Hot Red Volkswagen* ....8.00 - 12.00

GENE PARSONS:
Southfield 4501 *Night Club Rock & Roll* ....30.00 - 60.00

"PARTY AFTER HOURS":
Aladdin (LP) 703 (10 inch) (various artists) (red vinyl)
....300.00 - up

THE PASSIONS:
Audicon 102 *Just To Be With You* ....7.00 - 10.00
    105 *This Is My Love* ....7.00 - 10.00
    106 *Gloria*....................................7.00 - 10.00
    108 *Beautiful Dreamer* ....10.00 - 15.00
    112 *Made For Lovers*..........................15.00 - 20.00
Capitol 3963 *My Aching Heart* ....8.00 - 12.00
Diamond 146 *Sixteen Candles* ....10.00 - 15.00
Dore 505 *Tango Of Love* ....15.00 - 20.00
Era 1063 *My Aching Heart* ....10.00 - 20.00
Jubilee 5406 *One Is All It Took*........................10.00 - 15.00
Octavia 8005 *I've Gotta Know* ....80.00 - 120.00
Unique 79 *Too Many Memories*.........................7.00 - 10.00

THE PASTELS:
Argo 5287 *My One And Only Dream* ....10.00 - 15.00
    5314 *So Far Away*.............................10.00 - 15.00
Mascot 123 *Been So Long* ....50.00 - 80.00
United 196 *If You Put Your Arms Around Me* ....40.00 - 70.00

PAT AND DEE:
Dixie 2006 *Gee Whiz* ....25.00 - 50.00

GUS PATE & THE JOKERS:
Summit 111 *Man Alive* ....30.00 - 50.00

SONNY PATERSON & THE INVICTAS:
Jack Bee 1003 *Gone So Long* ....10.00 - 15.00

PRINCE PATRIDGE:
Big Moment 103/104 *Next Door Neighbors*............8.00 - 12.00
Cat 105 *Cooperation*..................................5.00 - 10.00
Crest 1006, 1022, 1009 ....5.00 - 10.00

FRANK PATT & ORCHESTRA:
Flash 117 *Gonna Hold On* ....8.00 - 12.00

JIMMY PATTON (WITH ANN JONES):
Halligan 001 *Okie's In The Pokie* ....80.00 - 120.00
Moon (LP) 101 *Make Room For The Blues*...........50.00 - 80.00
Sage 241 *Yah-I'm Movin'* ....50.00 - 80.00
Sims 103 *Guilty*......................................7.00 - 10.00
    104 *Teen-Age Heart*...........................20.00 - 30.00
    117 *Okie's In The Pokie*......................35.00 - 50.00
    (LP) 127 *Blue Darlin'*........................50.00 - 80.00

PAT PATTON:
King 4942 *Flip Kitten* ....10.00 - 20.00

BUNNY PAUL (See also THE HARPTONES):
Point 5 *Sweet Talk*...................................10.00 - 15.00

CLARENCE PAUL:
Hanover 4519 *May Heaven Bless You*........................7.00 - 10.00
Roulette 4196 *Falling In Love Again* ....8.00 - 12.00

JERRY PAUL:
Holiday 1001 *Step Out*..10.00 - 15.00

JOYCE PAUL:
Dot 15703 *Baby, You've Had It*................................ - - -

LEE PAXTON:
Spring Dale 102 *Tall Texas Women* ....20.00 - 30.00

DUSTY PAYNE (& HIS RHYTHM ROCKERS):
Bakersfield 119 *Long Time Gone* ....30.00 - 50.00
Fire 111 *I Want You*...40.00 - 80.00

HAL PAYNE:
Starday-*Honky Tonk Stomp* ....10.00 - 15.00

TOMMY PAYNE:
Felsted 8531 *I Go Ape*...10.00 - 15.00
XYZ 601 *Fire Engine Red Bandanna* ....7.00 - 10.00
   603 *Cruisin' Around*..7.00 - 10.00

PEACHEROOS:
Excello 2044 *Be-Bop Baby*....................................200.00 - up

THE PEACOCKS (See also JIMMY MOORE):
L&M 1002 *Bouquet Of Roses*...............................100.00 - 150.00

THE PEARLS:
Amber 2003 *It Must Be Love*..................................60.00 - 100.00
Atco 6057 *Shadows Of Love*...................................25.00 - 40.00
   6066 *Bells Of Love* ....30.00 - 50.00
On The Square 320 *Band Of Angels*........................ - - -
Onyx 503 *Let's You And I Go Steady*.....................20.00 - 30.00
   506 *Tree In The Meadow* ....25.00 - 40.00
   510 *Your Cheatin' Heart* ....10.00 - 15.00
   511 *Ice Cream Baby* ....15.00 - 20.00
   516 *The Wheel Of Love*......................................20.00 - 30.00

JIMMY PEARSON:
Dixie - *Nobody Cares/I'm Not Sure* .... - - -

RONNIE PEARSON:
Herald 500 *Hot Shot*...15.00 - 25.00
   514 *She Bops A Lot*..15.00 - 25.00
   516 *Flippin' Over You*...15.00 - 25.00

PEDIGO BROTHERS:
Atwell 100 *She's Gone* ....20.00 - 30.00

PAUL PEEK:
NRC 001 *The Rock Around* ....8.00 - 12.00
   002 *Sweet Skinny Jenny*......................................8.00 - 12.00
   008 *Olds-Mo-William*..7.00 - 10.00

CARROLL (WILD RED) PEGUES:
GM Record Co. 109 *Rhythm Feet* ....10.00 - 20.00

DANNY PEIL & THE APOLLOS:
Raynard 602 *Jungle Jump* ....10.00 - 15.00

MORRIS PEJOE:
Abco 106 *Maybe Blues*..30.00 - 50.00
Atomic H 410/411 *You Gone Away*.........................15.00 - 20.00
Checker 766 *Gonna Buy Me A Telephone*................80.00 - 120.00
   781 *Can't Get Along*...75.00 - 100.00
(above, pressed of red translucent vinyl, command higher prices)
Vee Jay 148 *You Gonna Need Me* ....50.00 - 80.00

PELICANS:
Class 209 *I Bow To You*..80.00 - 130.00

Imperial 5307 *Chimes*..300.00 - up
Parrot 793 *Aurelia*..500.00 - up
   793 *Aurelia* (red plastic) ....1000.00 - up

TRACY PENDARVIS:
Des Cant 1234 *First Love* ....7.00 - 10.00
Scott 1202 *It' Don't Pay* ....20.00 - 30.00
   1203 *All You Gotta Do*..20.00 - 30.00

PENGUINS:
Atlantic 1132 *Pledge Of Love* ....10.00 - 15.00
Dooto (EP) 201 *The Penguins* ....75.00 - 100.00
   (EP) 241, 243, 244 *Cool Cool Penguins*............75.00 - 100.00
   (LP) 242 *The Cool Cool Penguins* (yellow label)
   ....200.00 - 300.00
   (LP) 242 *The Cool Cool Penguins* (multi-colored label)
   ....50.00 - 75.00
   428 *That's How Much I Need You*.....................40.00 - 70.00
   432 *Sweet Love* ....30.00 - 50.00
   435 *Do Not Pretend* ....30.00 - 50.00
Dootone (LP) unnumbered Rhythm & Blues vocal group series
   album ....- - -
   345 *When I Am Gone* ....50.00 - 80.00
   348 *Earth Angel* ....10.00 - 20.00
   353 *Ookey Oook* ....10.00 - 20.00
   362 *Kiss A Fool Goodbye* ....30.00 - 50.00
Mercury 70610 *Be Mine Or Be A Fool*...................10.00 - 15.00
   70654 *It Only Happens With You* ....10.00 - 20.00
   70703 *Devil That I See*.......................................10.00 - 20.00
   70762 *A Christmas Prayer*..................................20.00 - 30.00
   70799 *My Troubles Are Not At An End* ....10.00 - 15.00
   70943 *Earth Angel* ....10.00 - 20.00
   71033 *Will You Be Mine* ....10.00 - 20.00
Power 7023 *Earth Angel* ....7.00 - 10.00
Wing 90076 *Peace of Mind* ....10.00 - 20.00

WILLIAM PENIX:
Daffan 116 *Dig That Crazy Driver*.........................30.00 - 50.00

LITTLE LAMBSIE PENN:
Atco 6082 *I Wanna Spend Christmas With Elvis* ...15.00 - 20.00

TONY PENN:
P.R.I. 101 *Shake Rattle And Roll* ....20.00 - 30.00
   7016 *I Don't Want To Stay Home*........................ - - -

DICK PENNER:
Sun 282 *Cindy Lou*...20.00 - 30.00

RAY PENNINGTON:
Lee 502 *Boogie Woogie Country Girl* ....30.00 - 50.00

HANK PENNY:
Audio Lab (LP) 1508 *Hank Penny Sings*................30.00 - 50.00
Decca 29926 *Rock Of Gibraltar* ....8.00 - 12.00

JOE PENNY:
Federal 12322 *Bip A Little, Bop A Lot* ....20.00 - 30.00
Sims 173 *Hatty Fatty* ....15.00 - 20.00

CURLEY PENROD:
QQ 703 *There's A Leak* ....15.00 - 20.00

THE PENTAGONS:
Caldwell 411 *Until Then* ....15.00 - 20.00
Donna 1337 *To Be Loved* ....7.00 - 10.00
Fleet International 100 *To Be Loved* ....30.00 - 50.00
Jamie 1201 *She's Mine* ....8.00 - 12.00
   1210 *I'm In Love* ....5.00 - 10.00

THE PEPPERS:
Chess 1577 *Rocking Chair Baby* ....100.00 - 150.00

THE PEREZ BROTHERS:
Wolfie 103 *Dream A Little Dream* ....10.00 - 15.00

THE PERFORMERS:
Allstar 714 *I'll Make You Understand* ....75.00 - 100.00
Tip Top 402 *Give Me Your Heart* ....15.00 - 20.00

CARL PERKINS:
Columbia (LP) 1234 *Whole Lotta Shakin'* ....100.00 - 150.00
   (EP) 12341 *Whole Lotta Shakin'* ....100.00 - 150.00
   41131 *Pink Pedal Pushers* ....10.00 - 15.00
   41207 *Levi Jacket* ....10.00 - 15.00
   41379 *Pointed Toe Shoes* ....10.00 - 15.00
Flip 501 *Movie Magg* ....150.00 - 300.00
Sun (EP) 115 *Blue Suede Shoes* ....75.00 - 100.00
   224 *Gone, Gone, Gone* ....40.00 - 60.00
   234 *Blue Suede Shoes* ....15.00 - 25.00
   234 *Blue Suede Shoes* (78 rpm) ....20.00 - 30.00
   235 *Tennessee/Sure To Fall* .... - -
(Note: Sun 235 may not have been issued.)
   243 *Boppin' The Blues* ....15.00 - 20.00
   243 *Boppin' The Blues* (78 rpm) ....20.00 - 30.00
   249 *Dixie Fried* ....15.00 - 20.00
   249 *Dixie Fried* (78 rpm) ....20.00 - 30.00
   261 *Matchbox* ....15.00 - 20.00
   261 *Matchbox* (78 rpm) ....25.00 - 40.00
   274 *That's Right* ....10.00 - 15.00
   274 *That's Right* (78 rpm) ....20.00 - 30.00
   287 *Glad All Over* ....10.00 - 15.00
   287 *Glad All Over* (78 rpm) ....20.00 - 30.00
   (LP) 1225 *Teen Beat (The Best of Carl Perkins)* ....50.00 - 80.00
   (LP) 1225 *The Dance Album of Carl Perkins* ..100.00 - up

JESSE PERKINS & THE BAD BOYS:
Savoy 1584 *Madly In Love* ....7.00 - 10.00

JOE PERKINS & ROOKIES:
King 5005 *Time Alone Will Tell* ....10.00 - 15.00
   5030 *A New Feeling* ....25.00 - 40.00

LAURA LEE PERKINS:
Imperial 5493 *Kiss Me Baby* ....10.00 - 15.00
   5507 *Don't Wait Up* ....10.00 - 15.00

REGGIE PERKINS:
Gem 1201 *Saturday Night Party* ....20.00 - 30.00
Ray Note 9 *Date Bait Baby* ....10.00 - 15.00

ROY PERKINS:
Meladee 111 *You're On My Mind* ....75.00 - 100.00
   112 *You're Gone* ....75.00 - 100.00
Mercury 71278 *Drop Top* ....8.00 - 12.00
RAM 122 *That's What The Mailman Has To Say* ...15.00 - 20.00

BERLIN PERRY & THE GLEAMS:
Ribbon 6902 *Put That Tear Back* ....50.00 - 75.00

BOB PERRY:
Top Rank 2063 *Juke Box* ....7.00 - 10.00

IKE PERRY & THE LYRICS:
Bridge 110 *Stairsteps to Heaven* ....50.00 - 75.00
Courier 828 *Don't Let It Get You Down* ....8.00 - 12.00

PAUL PERRY:
- *Got A Gal Named Dee* ....20.00 - 30.00

THE PERSIANS:
Gold Eagle 1813 *Gee What A Girl* ....7.00 - 10.00
Goldisc 1 *Vault Of Memories* ....8.00 - 12.00
   17 *Let's Get Married* ....7.00 - 10.00
RSVP 114 *Tears Of Love* ....15.00 - 20.00

PERSONALITIES:
Safari 1002 *Woe Woe Baby* ....50.00 - 80.00

PETE & JIMMY & THE RHYTHM KNIGHTS:
Castle 504 *So Wild* ....20.00 - 30.00

PETE PETERS:
- *Rockin' In My Sweet Baby's Arms* ....8.00 - 12.00

BOBBY PETERSON (QUINTET):
V-Tone 205, 214, 217, 221, 226 ....7.00 - 10.00

EARL PETERSON:
Columbia 21364 *Boogie Blues* ....10.00 - 15.00
Sun 197 *Boogie Blues* ....80.00 - 120.00

MIKE PETTIT & THE STAGS:
Anthem 601227 *It's A Reamer* ....15.00 - 20.00

DARYL PETTY:
Hornet 502 *The Day I Die* ....10.00 - 15.00

RONNIE PETTY:
Dee Jay 1006 *Cha Cha Joe* ....7.00 - 10.00

VI PETTY:
Nor Va-Jak 1325 *True Love Ways* ....25.00 - 40.00

PHANTOM:
Dot 16056 *Love Me* ....50.00 - 100.00
   16056 *Love Me* (with picture sleeve) ....100.00 - 150.00
Phantom 100 *I'm The Phantom* ....15.00 - 20.00

THE PHARAOS:
Donna 1327 *The Tender Touch* ....8.00 - 12.00

THE PHAROAHS:
Class 202 *Teenagers Love Song* ....75.00 - 100.00
Fascination 001 *Walking Sad* ....75.00 - 100.00

JOHNNY PHELPS:
Ski 5505 *Tom Katt* ....20.00 - 30.00

THE PHILADELPHIANS:
Campus 101 *The Love That I Lost* ....10.00 - 15.00
   103 *Church Bells* ....10.00 - 15.00
Guyden 2093 *My Love, My Love* ....15.00 - 20.00

THE PHILHARMONICS:
Future 2200 *Why Don't You Write Me* ....8.00 - 12.00

"PHILLIES' TODAY'S HITS":
Phillies (LP) 4004 ....80.00 - 130.00

"PHILLIP MORRIS COUNTRY MUSIC SHOW":
Columbia (LP) 1048 (various artists) ....30.00 - 50.00

BILL PHILLIPS:
Columbia 41218 *There's A Change In Me* ....10.00 - 15.00

CARL PHILLIPS:
Bobbin 110 *Wigwam Willie* ....75.00 - 125.00

CHARLIE PHILLIPS:
Coral 61970 *Be My Bride* ....10.00 - 15.00

EARL PHILLIPS:
Vee Jay 158 *Nothing But Love* ....25.00 - 40.00

MARVIN PHILLIPS:
Specialty 445 *Wine Woogie* ....20.00 - 30.00

PHIL PHILLIPS (WITH THE TWILIGHTS):
Clique 100 *Please Forgive Me* ....8.00 - 12.00
Khoury's 711 *Sea Of Love* ....80.00 - 130.00
Mercury 71465 *Sea Of Love* ....7.00 - 10.00
   71531 *Verdie Mae* ....8.00 - 12.00
   71550, 71611, 71649, 71657, 71746, 71817 ....5.00 - 8.00

LARRY PHILLIPSON:
Cinch 3858 *Bitter Feelings* ....7.00 - 10.00

PIANO RED:
Checker 911 *So Worried*......................10.00 - 15.00
Groove (EP) 3 *Jump Man Jump*............30.00 - 50.00
  (EP) 6 *Piano Red In Concert*...............30.00 - 50.00
  (EP) 7 *Piano Red In Concert*...............30.00 - 50.00
  (EP) 8 *Piano Red In Concert*...............30.00 - 50.00
  0023 *Decatur Street Blues*....................10.00 - 15.00
  0101 *Pay It No Mind*.............................10.00 - 15.00
  (LP) 0101 *Jump, Man, Jump*..............150.00 - 200.00
  0118 *Six O'Clock Boogie*......................10.00 - 15.00
  0126 *Red's Blues*...................................7.00 - 10.00
  0136 *Jumpin' With Daddy*....................10.00 - 15.00
  0145 *That's My Desire*.........................10.00 - 15.00
  0169 *Woo-Ee*..10.00 - 15.00
  (LP) 1002 *Piano Red In Concert*........150.00 - 200.00
  5000 *Red's Boogie*................................7.00 - 10.00
Jax 1000 *This Old World*.......................7.00 - 10.00
RCA Victor (EP) 587 *Rockin' With Red*....40.00 - 70.00
  4265 *Diggin' The Boogie*......................15.00 - 20.00
  4380 *Hey Good Lookin'*........................15.00 - 20.00
  4524 *Bouncin' With Red*.......................8.00 - 12.00
  4766 *The Sales Tax Boogie*..................8.00 - 12.00
  4957 *Daybreak*.....................................8.00 - 12.00
  5101 *Everybody's Boogie*.....................8.00 - 12.00
  5224 *She's Dynamite*............................8.00 - 12.00
  5337 *Decatur Street Boogie*..................8.00 - 12.00
  5544 *Right And Ready*..........................8.00 - 12.00
  6856 *Wild Fire*.....................................8.00 - 12.00
  6953 *Please Don't Talk About Me*.........8.00 - 12.00
  7065 *South*...7.00 - 10.00
  7217 *Comin' On*...................................7.00 - 10.00
  50-0099 *Rockin' With Red*....................7.00 - 10.00
  50-0106 *My Gal Jo*..............................15.00 - 20.00
  50-0118 *Jumpin' The Boogie*................10.00 - 15.00
  50-0130 *Layin' The Boogie*..................10.00 - 15.00

LEE PICKETT & THE SCREAMERS:
Jolt 331 *Fatty Patty* .... - - -

LITTLE "GUITAR" PICKETT:
Jack 101 *The Buzzard* ....10.00 - 15.00

PICO PETE:
Jet 100 *Hot Dog* ....15.00 - 20.00

WEBB PIERCE:
Decca 30045 *Teenage Boogie* ....10.00 - 15.00
King (LP) 648 *The One And Only* ....30.00 - 50.00

BILL PINKY & THE TURKS:
Phillips 3524 *After The Hop* ....10.00 - 15.00

PIPES:
Dootone 388 *Be Fair* ....75.00 - 100.00
  401 *You're An Angel*..........................75.00 - 100.00
Jacy 001 *Baby Please Don't Go* ....50.00 - 80.00

PIPS:
Brunswick 55048 *Whistle My Love* ....25.00 - 40.00
Huntom 2510 *Every Beat Of My Heart* ....50.00 - 80.00
Vee Jay 386 *Every Beat Of My Heart* .....10.00 - 15.00

PITCH PIKES:
Mercury 71099 *Zing Zing*.....................8.00 - 12.00
  71147 *How Will I Know* ....5.00 - 8.00

AL (DR. HORSE) PITTMAN:
Clown 3008 *Woman! You Talk Too Much* ....7.00 - 10.00

GLORIA JEAN PITTS:
Imperial 5406 *I Don't Stand No Quittin'* ....15.00 - 20.00

PLAIDS:
Liberty 55167 *Hungry For Your Love* ....25.00 - 40.00
Nasco 6011 *My Pretty Baby*..................8.00 - 12.00

THE PLANETS:
Aljon 1244 *Once In A Lifetime* ....80.00 - 120.00
Era 1038 *Never Again*...........................8.00 - 12.00
  1049 *Be Sure*......................................8.00 - 12.00

PLANTS (See also BABY WASHINGTON):
J & S 248 *I Searched The Seven Seas*......75.00 - 100.00
  1602 *Dear I Swear*...............................75.00 - 100.00
  1618 *From Me*......................................100.00 - 150.00

THE PLATTERS (See also LINDA HAYES):
Federal (LP) 349-549 *The Platters* ....300.00 - up
(Note: This album is the same as King 549 below. Copies have been found on the Federal label with King covers.)
  12153 *Give Thanks* ....75.00 - 100.00
  12164 *I'll Cry When You're Gone* ....80.00 - 130.00
  12181 *Roses Of Picardy*.......................75.00 - 100.00
  12188 *Tell The World* ....50.00 - 80.00
  12198 *Voo-Vee-Ah-Bee*.......................40.00 - 60.00
  12204 *Take Me Back*............................40.00 - 60.00
  12244 *Only You*...................................40.00 - 60.00
  12250 *Tell The World*...........................30.00 - 50.00
  12271 *Give Thanks* ....100.00 - 200.00
King (EP) 378 *The Platters*....................100.00 - 200.00
  (LP) 549 *The Platters*..........................150.00 - 200.00
  (LP) 651 *The Platters*..........................50.00 - 80.00
Mercury (EP) 3336, 3341.........................15.00 - 25.00
  (EP) 4029 *Vol. 1*.................................15.00 - 25.00
  (EP) 4030 *Vol. 2*.................................15.00 - 25.00
  (LP) 20146 *The Platters*.......................25.00 - 40.00
  (LP) 20216 *The Platters Vol. 2*............20.00 - 30.00
  (LP) 20298 *The Flying Platters*............20.00 - 30.00
  (LP) 20366 *Around The World* ....15.00 - 25.00
  (LP) 20410 *Remember When*................15.00 - 25.00
  (LP) 20472 *Encore Of Golden Hits* ......10.00 - 20.00
  70633 *Only You* (maroon label)............10.00 - 15.00
(copies of above having pink label bring somewhat more)
  70753 *The Great Pretender* (maroon label).......10.00 - 15.00
  70819 *The Magic Touch* (maroon label)............10.00 - 15.00
  70893 *My Prayer* (maroon label).....................10.00 - 15.00
  70948 *You'll Never Never Know* (maroon label)....10.00 - 15.00
  71011 *On My Word Of Honor* (maroon label)... 10.00 - 15.00
  71032 *I'm Sorry* (maroon label) ....10.00 - 15.00
  71093 *My Dream* ....7.00 - 10.00
  71184 *Only Because* ....7.00 - 10.00
(Note: 78 RPM issues of the foregoing titles usually command similar prices.)
Mercury 71246 *Helpless* ....8.00 - 12.00
  71289 *Twilight Time* ....7.00 - 10.00
  71289 *Twilight Time* (78 rpm) ....20.00 - 30.00
  71320, 71353, 71383, 71427, 71467, 71502,
    71538, 71563, 71624, 71656, 71697,
    71745, 71847, 71904 ....5.00 - 10.00
Power 7012 *Only You* ....7.00 - 10.00

PLAYBOYS:
Cat 108 *Tell Me*....................................15.00 - 20.00
  115 *Good Golly Miss Molly* ....15.00 - 20.00
SRC 1221 *Rave On* ....15.00 - 20.00
Tetra 4447 *One Question* ....30.00 - 50.00

THE PLURALS:
Wanger 185 *Donna My Dear* ....10.00 - 15.00
　　188 *Goodnight* ....10.00 - 15.00

BOBBY POE:
White Rock 1112 *Rock & Roll Record Girl* ....60.00 - 80.00

THE POET/POETS:
Flash 129 *Vowels Of Love* (black label) ....20.00 - 30.00
Hade 1001 *I'll Never Let You Go* ....15.00 - 20.00
Imperial 5664 *I'm In Love* ....8.00 - 12.00
Pull 129 *Vowels Of Love* ....50.00 - 75.00
Red Bird 10046 *Merry Christmas Baby* ....7.00 - 10.00
Spot 107 *Honey Chile* ....20.00 - 30.00

BOBBY POORE:
Beta 1003 *Heartbreak Of Love* ....10.00 - 15.00

(GROOVY) JOE POOVEY:
Dixie 733 *Careful Baby* ....75.00 - 100.00
　　2018 *Ten Long Fingers* ....100.00 - 150.00

POP CORN & THE MOHAWKS:
Motown 1002 *Shimmy Gully* ....10.00 - 15.00
　　1019 *Real Good Lovin'* ....15.00 - 20.00

POPPA/POPPY HOP:
Ivory 127 *My Woman Has A Black Cat Bone* ....10.00 - 20.00
　　133 *I Met A Strange Woman* ....10.00 - 15.00
　　134 *Merry Christmas Darling* ....10.00 - 15.00
　　135 *Be Careful With The Blues* ....10.00 - 15.00

WALTER POPULIST & THE TRUETONES:
Flame 10152 *Come Back To Me* ....8.00 - 12.00

BRUCE PORTER:
Lee - *Rattlesnake* ....15.00 - 20.00

ROCKY PORTER:
Stars 549(?) *First Sight* ....15.00 - 20.00

ROYCE PORTER (& THE KOUNTS):
D 1026 *Lookin'* ....30.00 - 50.00
Look 1001 *Yes I Do* ....40.00 - 60.00
Mercury 71314 *Good time* ....10.00 - 15.00
　　- *Lookin'* ....10.00 - 15.00
Spade 1931 *A Woman Can Make You Blue* ....100.00 - 150.00

THE PORTRAITS:
Capitol 4181 *Close To You* ....8.00 - 12.00

PORTUGESE JOE & THE TENNESSEE ROCKABILLIES:
Surf 5016 *Sugar Sugar Honey* ....- - -
　　5018 *Teen Age Riot* ....- - -

THE POSSESSIONS:
Britton 1003/1004 *No More Love* ....10.00 - 15.00

BOB POTTER:
Rural Rhythm *Leave A-Laughin'* ....- - -
Fox 409 *I'm A Real Glad Daddy* ....50.00 - 75.00

AUSTIN POWELL (& THE JAMES) QUINTET:
Atlantic 968 *What More Can I Ask?*.....................150.00 - 200.00
Decca 48206 *All This Can't Be True* ....75.00 - 100.00

CHRIS POWELL & THE (FIVE) BLUE FLAMES:
Columbia 39407 *My Love Is Gone* ....- - -
Groove 0105 *Break It Up* ....10.00 - 15.00
　　0111 *Something's Got To Give* ....8.00 - 12.00
　　0128 *Goodbye Little Girl* ....8.00 - 12.00
　　0144 *Moritat* ....5.00 - 8.00
Okeh 6875 *Darn That Dream* ....10.00 - 15.00
　　6900 *Blue Boy* ....10.00 - 15.00

DOUG POWELL:
Tip Top 713 *Jeannie With The Dark Blue Eyes*...... 20.00 - 30.00

JESSIE POWELL ORCHESTRA (See FLUFFY HUNTER)

SANDY POWELL:
Impala 211 *Pistol Packin' Mama* ....- - -

JACKIE POWERS:
Mopic 7708 *Heeby Jeeby Blues* .... 10.00 - 20.00

JETT POWERS:
Design 811 *Go, Girl, Go*.. 30.00 - 50.00

JOHNNY POWERS (with STAN GETZ & THE TOM CATS/& HIS ROCKETS):
Fox 916/917 *Rock, Rock* .... 75.00 - 100.00
Fortune 199 *Honey, Let's Go* .... 30.00 - 50.00
HI-Q 5044 *Honey, Let's Go* .... 15.00 - 20.00
Sun 327 *Be Mine, All Mine* .... 8.00 - 12.00

WAYNE POWERS:
Phillips 3523 *Point Of View*.................................... 8.00 - 12.00

PQ ROCK & ROLL (See MILT OSHINS)

BILLY PRAGER:
Crystal 106 *Do It Bop* .... 15.00 - 20.00

LYNN PRATT:
Hornet 1000 *Tom Cat Boogie* .... 80.00 - 120.00
　　1001 *I Don't Need*.. 75.00 - 100.00
　　1002 *Come Here Mama* .... 75.00 - 100.00

SCRAPPER PRATTS FALCONS:
Falcon 79492 *Guitar Man's Struggle* .... 15.00 - 20.00

THE PREACHERS:
Moonglow 5006 *Pain And Sorrow* .... 10.00 - 15.00

THE PRECISIONS:
Debra 1001 *Stop Leading Me On*............................ 8.00 - 12.00
Golden Crest 571 *Someone To Watch Over Me* ...... 8.00 - 12.00
Highland 300 *Eight Reasons Why (I Love You)*...... 50.00 - 80.00

PRE-HISTORICS:
Edsel 779 *Alley-Oop-Cha-Cha-Cha* .... 7.00 - 10.00

PRELUDES:
Cub 9005 *Kingdom Of Love* .... 30.00 - 50.00
Empire 103 *Don't Fall In Love Too Soon* .... 20.00 - 30.00
Octavia 8008 *A Place For You* .... 10.00 - 15.00

PRELUDES (FIVE):
Pik 230 *Starlight* .... 8.00 - 12.00

PREMEERS:
Herald 577 *Diary Of Our Love* .... 8.00 - 12.00

THE PREMIERS:
Alert 706 *Jolene*.. 20.00 - 30.00
Cindy 3008 *China Doll* .... 40.00 - 70.00
Dig 106 *New Moon* .... 30.00 - 50.00
　　113 *My Darling* .... 30.00 - 50.00
F-M 677 *Magic Of Love* .... 10.00 - 15.00
Gone 5009 *Valerie* .... 75.00 - 100.00
Mink 021 *Tonight* .... 10.00 - 15.00
Ondex 1711 *Speaking Of You* .... 25.00 - 40.00

RALPH PRESCOTT:
Lanor 564 *Hot Hot Lips* .... 8.00 - 12.00

ELVIS PRESLEY:

(Note: The collecting of Elvis' records and other Elvis collectibles involves intricacies beyond the scope of this book. Seemingly insignificant variations in labels or record jackets can mean wide price differences. Record sleeves may have values higher than the records themselves; the sleeves of records not listed here due to the minimal value of the records may be worth several dollars or more. The same is true of promotional copies of common records not otherwise worthy of inclusion herein. Also sought after are unofficial, "bootleg", and "fantasy" records - such as "Sun" records which were never originally produced by that company. Non-commercial issues, containing perhaps one track by Elvis, such as Armed Services radio transcriptions, are also in demand. Commercial issues which are often nothing more than repackagings of previously issued material, continue to proliferate with increasing emphasis on gimmickry such as colored vinyl and picture discs, and find a ready market, even at premium prices. Certain reissues, such as the higher-number maroon label EPs, command higher prices than their original issue counterparts. The listings below include only pre-1965 records issued commercially or promotionally; excluded are "bootleg" and spurious issues, foreign issues, recent reissues, etc.)

Those interested in pursuing the intricacies of Elvis Presley records (and peripheral collectibles) should consult one of the books dealing with same, such as *"The Official Price Guide To Memorabilia of Elvis Presley and The Beatles"*, by Osborne, Cox, and Lindsay.

Rainbow-*The Truth About Me* (78 rpm) .... 50.00 - 80.00

(Note: Above is a magazine insert record, often found affixed to another 78 RPM record to facilitate playing)

RCA Victor (EP-2 records) SPD -22 *Elvis Presley* 200.00 - up
  (EP 3 records) *SPD-23 Elvis Presley* .... 300.00 - up
  (EP) 7-37 *Perfect For Parties* .... 50.00 - 80.00

(Note: Above were issued for promotional purposes.)

  (EP) 747 *Elvis Presley* .... 25.00 - 50.00
  (EP) 821 *Heartbreak Hotel* .... 25.00 - 50.00
  (EP) 830 *Elvis Presley* .... 25.00 - 50.00
  (EP) 940 *The Real Elvis* .... 25.00 - 50.00
  (EP) 965 *Any Way You Want Me* .... 25.00 - 50.00
  (EP) 992 *Elvis Vol. 1* .... 25.00 - 40.00
  (EP) 993 *Elvis Vol. 2* .... 25.00 - 40.00
  (EP) 994 *Strictly Elvis* .... 25.00 - 40.00
  (LP) 1035 *Christmas Album* (MONO) .... 80.00 - 120.00
  (EP-2 Records) 1254 *Elvis Presley* (4 songs on each record)
  .... 100.00 - 150.00
  (EP-2 Records) 1254 *Elvis Presley*
  (6 songs on each record) .... 300.00 - up
  (EP) 1-1515 *Loving You* .... 20.00 - 30.00
  (EP) 2-1515 *Loving You, Vol. 2* .... 20.00 - 30.00
  (LP) 1254 *Elvis Presley* .... 40.00 - 70.00
  (LP) 1382 *Elvis* .... 40.00 - 70.00

(Note: A number of variations in label and cover of LPM-1382 exist, some of which are valuable.)

  (LP) 1515 *Loving You* .... 25.00 - 40.00
  (LP) 1707 *Elvis' Golden Records* .... 50.00 - 75.00
  (LP) 1884 *King Creole* .... 40.00 - 60.00
  (LP) 1951 *Elvis' Christmas Album* .... 40.00 - 70.00
  (LP) 1990 *For LP Fans Only* .... 50.00 - 75.00
  (LP) 2011 *A Date With Elvis* .... 50.00 - 75.00

(Note: Double-pocket version of this album, with 1960 calendar on back cover commands higher premium.)

  (LP) 2075 *50,000,000 Elvis Fans Can't Be Wrong*
  .... 40.00 - 60.00
  (LP) 2697 *It Happened At The World's Fair* ...... 40.00 - 60.00
  (LP) 3468 *Harum Scarum* .... 30.00 - 50.00
  (LP) 3558 *Frankie And Johnny* .... 30.00 - 50.00

  (LP) 3787 *Double Trouble* .... 30.00 - 50.00
  (LP) 3893 *Clambake* .... 60.00 - 100.00
  (LP) 3921 *Elvis' Gold Records, Vol. 4* .... 300.00 - up
  (LP) 3989 *Speedway* .... 500.00 - up

(Note: Foregoing EPs and LPs are all original MONO issues, with black labels having dog logo at top. LPs have "LPM-" prefix to catalog numbers. Subsequent pressings, including STEREO issues with "LPS-" prefixes, are worth substantially less.)

  (EP) 4006 *Love Me Tender* .... 20.00 - 30.00
  (EP) 4041 *Just For You* .... 20.00 - 30.00
  (EP) 4054 *Peace In The Valley* .... 20.00 - 30.00
  (EP) 4108 *Elvis Sings Christmas Songs* .... 20.00 - 30.00
  (EP) 4114 *Jailhouse Rock* .... 20.00 - 30.00
  (EP) 4319 *King Creole, Vol. 1* .... 20.00 - 30.00
  (EP) 4321 *King Creole, Vol. 2* .... 20.00 - 30.00
  (EP) 4325 *Elvis Sails* .... 30.00 - 50.00
  (EP) 4340 *Christmas With Elvis* .... 20.00 - 30.00
  (EP) 4368 *Follow That Dream* .... 20.00 - 30.00
  (EP) 4371 *Kid Galahad* .... 20.00 - 30.00
  (EP) 4382 *Viva Las Vegas* .... 20.00 - 30.00
  (EP) 4283 *Tickle Me* .... 20.00 - 30.00
  (EP) 4387 *Easy Come, Easy Go* .... 25.00 - 50.00
  (EP) 5088 *A Touch Of Gold* .... 100.00 - up
  (EP) 5101 *A Touch Of Gold, Vol. 2* .... 100.00 - up
  (EP) 5120 *The Real Elvis* .... 100.00 - up
  (EP) 5121 *Peace In The Valley* .... 100.00 - up
  (EP) 5122 *King Creole* .... 100.00 - up
  (EP) 5141 *A Touch Of Gold, Vol. 3* .... 100.00 - up

(Note: Foregoing EPs are maroon label issues. Subsequent issues, with black or orange labels are worth only about $15.00 to $30.00 each.)

  (EP) 5157 *Elvis Sails* .... 40.00 - 60.00
  6357 *Mystery Train* .... 20.00 - 30.00
  6357 *Mystery Train* (78 rpm) .... 40.00 - 60.00
  6380 *That's All Right* .... 20.00 - 30.00
  6380 *That's All Right* (78 rpm) .... 40.00 - 60.00
  6381 *Good Rockin' Tonight* .... 20.00 - 30.00
  6381 *Good Rockin' Tonight* (78 rpm) .... 50.00 - 75.00
  6382 *Milkcow Blues Boogie* .... 20.00 - 30.00
  6382 *Milkcow Blues Boogie* (78 rpm) .... 50.00 - 75.00
  6383 *Baby, Let's Play House* .... 20.00 - 30.00
  6383 *Baby, Let's Play House* (78 rpm) .... 50.00 - 75.00
  6420, 6540, 6604 .... 8.00 - 12.00
  6420 *Heartbreak Hotel* (78 rpm) .... 20.00 - 30.00
  6540 *I Want You, I Need You* (78 rpm) .... 20.00 - 30.00
  6604 *Hound Dog* (78 rpm) .... 20.00 - 30.00
  6636 *Blue Suede Shoes* .... 20.00 - 30.00
  6636 *Blue Suede Shoes* (78 rpm) .... 40.00 - 60.00
  6637 *I Got A Woman* .... 20.00 - 30.00
  6637 *I Got A Woman* (78 rpm) .... 40.00 - 60.00
  6638 *I'll Never Let You Go* .... 25.00 - 40.00
  6638 *I'll Never Let You Go* (78 rpm) .... 40.00 - 70.00
  6639 *Tryin' To Get To You* .... 25.00 - 40.00
  6639 *Tryin' To Get To You* (78 rpm) .... 40.00 - 70.00
  6640 *Blue Moon* .... 20.00 - 30.00
  6640 *Blue Moon* (78 rpm) .... 40.00 - 60.00
  6641 *Money Honey* .... 20.00 - 30.00
  6641 *Money Honey* (78 rpm) .... 40.00 - 60.00
  6642 *Shake, Rattle And Roll* .... 20.00 - 30.00
  6642 *Shake, Rattle And Roll* (78 rpm) .... 40.00 - 60.00
  6643 *Love Me Tender* .... 7.00 - 10.00
  6643 *Love Me Tender* (78 rpm) .... 15.00 - 30.00

RCA Victor 6800, 6870, 7000, 7035, 7150, 7240,
7280, 7410 .... 5.00 - 10.00
  6800 *Too Much* (78 rpm) .... 20.00 - 30.00
  6870 *All Shook Up* (78 rpm) .... 25.00 - 40.00
  7000 *Teddy Bear* (78 rpm) .... 30.00 - 50.00

7035 *Jailhouse Rock* (78 rpm) ....30.00 -   50.00
7150 *I Beg Of You* (78 rpm) ....30.00 -   50.00
7240 *Wear My Ring* (78 rpm) ....50.00 -   75.00
7280 *Hard Headed Woman* (78 rpm) ....50.00 - 100.00
7410 *I Got Stung* (78 rpm)............................150.00 - 300.00
(Note: The only copies seen of 7410 have come from jukebox operators.)
(Higher-numbered 78 rpm Canadian pressings exist.)
37-7850 *Surrender* (7 inches 33 1/3 RPM) ......200.00 -   up
37-7880 *I Feel So Bad* (7 inches 33 1/3 RPM).200.00 -   up
37-7908 *Little Sister* (7 inches 33 1/3 RPM) ....300.00 -   up
37-7968 *Can't Help Falling In Love* (7 inches 33 1/3 RPM)
....300.00 -   up
37-7992 *Good Luck Charm* (7 inches 33 1/3 RPM)
....300.00 -   up
37-8041 *She's Not You* (7 inches 33 1/3 RPM)..... -   -
37-8100 *Return To Sender* (7 inches 33 1/3 RPM) .....-   -
(Note: Above issues should not be confused with the usual 45 RPM issues, which have corresponding catalog numbers; the 45s are of nominal value only. Note the "37" prefix to catalog numbers.)
The 33 1/3 RPM issues listed here are quoted at widely varying prices, sometimes multiples of prices above, particularly for the later issues. It is doubted that such high prices are actually realized; these issues should be regarded as highly speculative.)
61-7740 *Stuck On You* (STEREO 45 RPM) .....200.00 -   up
61-7777 *It's Now Or Never* (STEREO 45 RPM)
....200.00 -   up
61-7850 *Surrender* (STEREO 45 RPM)...........200.00 -   up
61-7880 *I Feel So Bad* (STEREO 45 RPM) .....200.00 -   up
(Note: Above three issues should not be confused with the usual MONO 45 RPM issues, which have corresponding catalog numbers. Note the "61" prefix. The MONO 45s have only nominal value.)
68-7850 *Surrender* (7 inch STEREO 33 1/3 RPM)
....400.00 -   up
68-7880 *I Feel So Bad* (7 inch STEREO 33 1/3 RPM)
.... -   -   -
(Note: Above should not be confused with the usual 45 RPM records which have corresponding catalog numbers. Note the "68" prefix. Very high prices, sometimes multiples of prices above, have been quoted for these records, but whether such prices might actually be realized is subject to doubt. These records should be regarded as highly speculative.)
G8-MW-8705 *TV Guide Presents Elvis Presley* .... rare
(Note: Above is a special promotional record. Extremely high prices have been quoted for it, particularly where it is accompanied by the original printed material.)
Sun 209 *That's All Right*..500.00 - 800.00
210 *Good Rockin' Tonight*................................500.00 - 800.00
215 *Milkcow Blues Boogie* ....600.00 - 1200.00
217 *Baby, Let's Play House*..............................300.00 - 600.00
223 *Mystery Train* ....300.00 - 600.00
(Note: "The prices quoted herein are for records in excellent condition." It is particularly appropriate to restate this respecting the commercially issued RCA Victor records of Elvis Presley, because most such records are plentiful in worn (and in the case of EPs and LPs, coverless) condition, and are usually found in that state. Worn copies and coverless EPs and LPs are generally worth nominal sums at most, and are probably unsaleable at any price.)

JOHNNY PRESTON:
Mercury (EP) 3397 *Johnny Preston* ....30.00 -   50.00
(LP) 20592 *Running Bear*....................................50.00 -   80.00
(LP) 20609 *Come Rock With Me* ....50.00 -   80.00
Mercury 71728 *Rock 'N' Roll Guitar* ....8.00 -   12.00
Mercury (most other issues) ....5.00 -   8.00

PRESTOS:
Mercury 70747 *Til We Meet Again*........................ 15.00 -   25.00

THE PRETENDERS: (See also JIMMY JONES)
APT 25026 *Blue And Lonely* ....40.00 -   60.00
Bethlehem 3050 *Ding Dong Bells* .... 10.00 -   15.00
Central 2605 *Blue And Lonely* .... 200.00 -   up
Power Martin 1001 *Smile*.................................... 15.00 -   25.00
Rama 198 *Possessive Love* .... 25.00 -   40.00
Whirlin Disc 106 *Close Your Eyes* .... 20.00 -   30.00

PRETTY BOY:
Atlantic 1147 *Bip Bop Bip* .... 15.00 -   20.00
Big 617 *Rockin' The Mule* .... 15.00 -   20.00
Rhythm 1768 *Find My Baby*................................ 30.00 -   50.00

LLOYD PRICE:
ABC Paramount (LP) 277 *The Exciting Lloyd Price*
.... 20.00 -   30.00
(LP) 297 *Mr. Personality*.................................... 25.00 -   40.00
(LP) 315 *Sings The Blues* .... 25.00 -   40.00
9792 *Just Because* (78 rpm).............................. 10.00 -   15.00
9972 *Stagger Lee* (78 rpm) .... 20.00 -   30.00
9997 *Is It Really Love?* (78 rpm) .... 10.00 -   15.00
KRC 303 *Hello Little Girl* .... 7.00 -   10.00
Specialty 428 *Lawdy Miss Clawdy* .... 15.00 -   20.00
440 *Restless Heart* .... 10.00 -   20.00
452 *Ain't It A Shame?* .... 10.00 -   20.00
457 *So Long* .... 10.00 -   20.00
463 *Where You At?* .... 10.00 -   15.00
483 *Too Late For Tears* .... 10.00 -   15.00
494 *Walkin' The Track*...................................... 10.00 -   15.00
(Note: Above are found pressed of red plastic; these command higher prices.)
Specialty 535 *Oo-ee Baby*.................................. 15.00 -   30.00
571, 482, 602.. 5.00 -   10.00
(LP) 2105 *Lloyd Price* .... 50.00 -   80.00

MEL PRICE:
Dixie 2016 *Little Dog Blues* .... 30.00 -   50.00

NEDRA PRICE:
Ponca 101 *Let's Have a Party* .... 15.00 -   20.00

RAY PRICE:
Columbia (LP) 1015 *Ray Price Sings Heart Songs* 20.00 -   30.00
(LP) 1148 *Talk To Your Heart*............................ 20.00 -   30.00

RONNIE PRICE & VELVETS:
Carousel 1001 *White Bucks*................................ 10.00 -   15.00

THE PRIMETTES:
Lupine 120 *Tears Of Sorrow* .... 50.00 -   80.00

BOBBY PRINCE:
Chance 1128 *Tell Me Why, Why, Why* .... 25.00 -   40.00

PRISONAIRES:
Sun 186 *Just Walkin' In The Rain* .... 50.00 -   80.00
189 *My God Is Real* .... 100.00 - 150.00
191 *A Prisoner's Prayer* .... 100.00 - 200.00
207 *There Is Love In You* .... 500.00 -   up

JIMMY PRITCHETT:
Crystal 503 *That's The Way I Feel* .... 25.00 -   50.00

PRODIGALS:
Abner 1015 *Won't You Believe* .... 30.00 -   50.00
Falcon 1011 *Marsha* .... 10.00 -   15.00

PROFESSOR LONGHAIR:
Atlantic 1020 *In The Night* .... 50.00 - 100.00

Ebb 101 *Cry Pretty Baby* ....30.00 - 50.00
    106 *Look What You're Doin* ....25.00 - 40.00
    121 *Looka No Hair* ....25.00 - 40.00
Ron 326 *Cuttin' Out* ....7.00 - 10.00
    329 *Go To The Mardi Gras* ....7.00 - 10.00

PROPHETS:
Atco 6078 *Stormy* ....10.00 - 15.00
Jairick 201 *Little Miss Dreamer* ....40.00 - 60.00

PROWLERS:
Aragon 302 *Rock Me Baby* ....30.00 - 40.00

LEWIS PRUITT:
Peach 703 *Pretty Baby* ....30.00 - 50.00
    710 *This Little Girl* ....30.00 - 50.00

RALPH PRUITT with HIS RHYTHM BOYS:
Meridian 1506/1507 *Hey Mr. Porter* ....50.00 - 80.00

SNOOKY PRYOR:
J.O.B. 1014 *Cryin' Shame* ....150.00 - 300.00
    1126 *Boogie Twist* ....75.00 - 100.00
Parrot 807 *Crosstown Blues* ....150.00 - 300.00
Vee Jay 215 *Someone To Love Me* ....25.00 - 40.00

RED PRYSOCK:
Mercury (LP) 20088 *Rock 'N' Roll* ....50.00 - 80.00
    (LP) 20211 *Fruit Boots* ....30.00 - 60.00
    (LP) 20307 *The Beat* ....30.00 - 60.00
Red Robin 117 *Hard Rock* ....20.00 - 30.00

DENNIS PUCKETT:
Emerald 2018 *Rockin' Teens* ....35.00 - 50.00

DWIGHT PULLEN:
Carlton 455 *Sunglasses After Dark* ....40.00 - 70.00

WHITEY PULLEN:
Crown (LP) 332 *Country Music Star* ....25.00 - 40.00
    (LP) 5332 *Country Music Star* ....30.00 - 50.00
Sage 274 *Walk My Way Back Home* ....25.00 - 40.00
    283 *You'll Get Yours Someday* ....25.00 - 45.00
    294 *Let's Go Wild Tonight* ....30.00 - 50.00
    313 *Tuscaloosa Lucy* ....30.00 - 50.00

VERN PULLENS:
Spade 1927 *Bop Crazy Baby* ....100.00 - 200.00
- *Mama Don't Allow No Boppin'* ....100.00 - 200.00

THE PYRAMIDS:
C-Note 108 *Someday* ....300.00 - up
Cub 9112 *Cryin'* ....8.00 - 12.00
Davis 453 *At Any Cost* ....15.00 - 20.00
    457 *Before It's Too Late* ....15.00 - 25.00
Federal 12233 *Deep In My Heart For You* ......80.00 - 130.00
Hollywood 1047 *Someday* ....200.00 - up
Shell 711 *Ankle Bracelet* ....15.00 - 30.00

THE QUADRELLS:
Kudo 662 *It's All My Fault* ....25.00 - 40.00
Whirlin Disc 103 *Come To Me* ....25.00 - 40.00

THE QUAILS: (See also BILL ROBINSON)
DeLuxe 6085 *Things She Used To Do* ....20.00 - 30.00
Harvey 114, 116, 120 ....5.00 - 8.00

THE QUAILTONES: (See SAX KARI)

THE QUARTER NOTES:
DeLuxe 6116 *Loneliness* ....7.00 - 10.00
    6129 *My Fantasy* ....7.00 - 10.00
Dot 15685 *Like You Bug Me* ....8.00 - 12.00
Fox 2 *Teen Age Blues* ....10.00 - 15.00

DOUG QUATTLEBAUM:
Gotham 7519 *Don't Be Funny Baby* ....40.00 - 70.00

QUEENS (See also SHIRLEY GUNTER):
Flair 1050 *Oop Shoop* ....8.00 - 12.00

? (QUESTION MARK) & THE MYSTERIANS:
Cameo (LP) 2004 *96 Tears* ....25.00 - 40.00
Pa-Go-Go 102 *96 Tears* ....30.00 - 40.00

QUESTION MARKS:
Swingtime 346 *Another Soldier Gone* ....- - -
    346 *Another Soldier Gone* (78 rpm) ....75.00 - 100.00
(Note: Existence of Swing Time 346 in 45 RPM format, other than
    bootlegs, is not verified.)

ANDY QUINN:
Decca 30438 *Rock-A-Boogie* ....10.00 - 15.00
    30521 *Sweet Treat* ....10.00 - 15.00
    30843 *Sharon Lee* ....10.00 - 15.00

QUINNS:
Cyclone 111 *Oh Starlight* ....25.00 - 40.00

EDDIE QUINTEROS:
Brent 7009 *Come Dance With Me* ....15.00 - 20.00
    7014 *Slow Down Sandy* ....15.00 - 20.00

THE QUINTONES:
Chess 1685 *I Try So Hard* ....15.00 - 20.00
Gee 1009 *I'm Willing* ....200.00 - up
Hunt 321 *Down The Aisle Of Love* ....8.00 - 12.00
    322 *There'll Be No Sorrow* ....8.00 - 12.00
Park 57-112 *More Than A Notion* ....50.00 - 80.00
Red Top 108 *Down The Aisle Of Love* ....15.00 - 20.00
    116 *I Watch The Stars* ....15.00 - 20.00
    118 *Oh Heavenly Father* ....15.00 - 20.00

THE QUOTATIONS:
Verve 10245 *Imagination* ....7.00 - 10.00
    10252 *This Love Of Mine* ....10.00 - 15.00
    10261 *See You In September* ....10.00 - 15.00

DON RADER:
The Strate 8 1501 *Rockin' The Blues* ....75.00 - 100.00
    1507 *Rock & Roll Granpa* ....30.00 - 60.00

THE RADIANTS:
Dootone 451 *I'm Betting My Heart* ....8.00 - 12.00

JANICE RADO & THE SEQUINS:
Edsel 782 *I'm Coming Home* ....7.00 - 10.00

THE RAIDERS:
Van 00262 *Skipping Around* ....15.00 - 30.00

THE RAINBOWS:
Argyle 1012 *Stay* ....5.00 - 8.00
Dave 908 *I Know* ....8.00 - 12.00
    909 *It Wouldn't Be Right* ....8.00 - 12.00
Fire 1012 *Mary Lee* ....8.00 - 12.00
Hamilton 143 *They Say* ....7.00 - 10.00
Pilgrim 703 *Mary Lee* ....10.00 - 20.00
    711 *Shirley* ....50.00 - 80.00
Rama 209 *They Say* ....200.00 - 300.00
Red Robin 134 *Mary Lee* ....80.00 - 130.00

THE RAINDROPS/RAIN DROPS:
Capitol 4136 *Rain* ....8.00 - 12.00
Corsair 104 *Love Is Like A Mountain* ....15.00 - 30.00
Dore 561 *Love Is Like A Mountain* ....8.00 - 12.00
Hamilton 50021 *Without Love* ....8.00 - 12.00
Jubilee (LP) 5023 *The Raindrops* ....25.00 - 40.00

Sotoplay 0028 *I Still Love You* ....7.00 - 10.00
Spin It 104 *I Found Heaven In Love* ....30.00 - 50.00
    106 *Little One* ....30.00 - 50.00
Vega 105 *Dim Those Lights* ....30.00 - 50.00

CHRIS RAINER & THE ELRODS:
Red Head 1005 *Eleven O'Clock* ....10.00 - 15.00

JERRY RAINES:
Drew-Blan 1001 *Dangerous Redhead* ....15.00 - 20.00

MARVIN RAINWATER:
Crown (LP) 307 *Marvin Rainwater* ....15.00 - 30.00
MGM (EP) 1464 *Songs By Vol. 1* ....30.00 - 50.00
    (EP) 1465 *Songs By Vol. 2* ....30.00 - 50.00
    (EP) 1466 *Songs By Vol. 3* ....30.00 - 50.00
    (LP) 3534 *Songs By Marvin Rainwater* ....40.00 - 60.00
    (LP) 4046 *Gonna Find Me A Bluebird* ....40.00 - 60.00
    (LP) 3721 *Marvin Rainwater Sings With A Heart/A Beat*
    ....50.00 - 80.00
    12152 *Dem Low Down Blues* ....10.00 - 15.00
    12240 *Hot And Cold* ....20.00 - 30.00
    12412 *Gonna Find Me A Bluebird* (78 rpm) ......15.00 - 25.00
    12511 *My Brand Of Blues* ....8.00 - 12.00
    12609 *Baby, Don't Go* ....8.00 - 12.00
    12653 *Moanin' The Blues* ....8.00 - 12.00
    12665 *I Dig You Baby* ....8.00 - 12.00

RAJAHS:
Klik 7805 *I Fell In Love* ....100.00 - 150.00

RAMBLERS:
Federal 12286 *The Heaven And The Earth* ....40.00 - 60.00
Jax 319 *Search My Heart* (red plastic) ....250.00 - up
MGM 11850 *Vadunt-Un-Vada Song* ....80.00 - 130.00
    55006 *Bad Girl* ....50.00 - 75.00

JOHNNY RAMISTELLA:
Suede 1401 *Two By Two* .... - -

THE RAMS:
Flair 1066 *Sweet Thing* ....40.00 - 60.00

D.C. RAND & THE HOKERS:
Candy 003 *Shake It Up* ....15.00 - 20.00

BILLY RANDALL:
Savoy 1570 *Rowena* ....8.00 - 12.00

RANDY & THE RAINBOWS:
Rust 5059 *Denise* ....7.00 - 10.00
    5073 *Why Do Kids Grow Up* ....5.00 - 8.00
    5080 *Happy Teenager* ....5.00 - 8.00
    5091 *Little Star* ....5.00 - 8.00
    5101 *Joy Ride* ....7.00 - 10.00

WAYNE RANEY:
Decca 30212 *Shake Baby Shake* ....10.00 - 15.00
Decca, most other issues ....5.00 - 10.00
King (LP) 588 *Songs From The Hills* ....40.00 - 60.00
King (most issues) ....5.00 - 10.00
(Note: Earlier issues, pressed of red vinyl, bring somewhat more.)

RANNELS:
Boss 2122 *Boom Baby* ....100.00 - up

BOZO RATLIFF:
Space 100 *Rock Along Time* ....30.00 - 50.00

RAVENS:
Argo 5255 *Kneel And Pray* (ship logo) ....20.00 - 30.00
    5261 *A Simple Prayer* (ship logo) ....20.00 - 30.00
    5276 *Dear One* (ship logo) ....15.00 - 30.00
    5284 *Here Is My Heart* ....15.00 - 30.00

Columbia 6-903 *Time Takes Care Of Everything*... 75.00 - 100.00
    6-925 *I'm So Crazy For Love* ....80.00 - 120.00
    39112 *You Don't Have To Drop A Heart* ....80.00 - 120.00
    39194 *You're Always In My Dreams* ....80.00 - 130.00
    39408 *You Foolish Thing* ....100.00 - 150.00
Jubilee 5184 *Happy Go Lucky Baby* ....10.00 - 20.00
    5203 *Green Eyes* ....10.00 - 20.00
    5217 *On Chapel Hill* ....20.00 - 30.00
King (EP) 310 *The Ravens* ....150.00 - 200.00
Mercury 5764 *There's No Use Pretending* ....25.00 - 50.00
    5800 *Begin The Beguine* ....20.00 - 30.00
    5853 *Chloe* ....20.00 - 30.00
    8257 *Hey, Good Lookin'* ....75.00 - 100.00
    8291 *Write Me One Sweet Letter* ....40.00 - 70.00
    70060 *Don't Mention My Name* ....20.00 - 30.00
    70119 *Come A Little Bit Closer* ....10.00 - 15.00
    70307 *September Song* ....20.00 - 30.00
    70413 *Love Is No Dream* ....20.00 - 30.00
    70505 *White Christmas* ....10.00 - 20.00
    70554 *Old Man River* ....20.00 - 30.00
National 9111 *Count Every Star* ....200.00 - 300.00
Okeh 6825 *The Wiffenpoof Song* ....75.00 - 100.00
    6843 *Everything But You* ....75.00 - 100.00
    6888 *Mam'selle* ....80.00 - 130.00
Regent (LP) 6062 *Write Me A Letter* (green label). 50.00 - 80.00
Rendition (EP) 104 *The Ravens* ....300.00 - up
Savoy 1540 *White Christmas* ....10.00 - 15.00

THE RAVES:
Liberty 55103 *If I Knew The Way* ....7.00 - 10.00
Swade 104 *Tell Me One More Time* ....8.00 - 12.00

DANNY RAY:
Vin 1025 *Love Me* ....15.00 - 20.00

DAVID RAY:
Kliff 101 *Lonesome Baby Blues* ....100.00 - 200.00
    102 *Jitter Buggin' Baby* ....100.00 - 200.00

DON RAY:
Rodeo 129 *Rock 'N' Roll Blues* ....15.00 - 25.00
    130 *Imogene* ....15.00 - 25.00

GENE RAY:
Cowtown 802 *I'm Going To Hollywood* ....50.00 - 75.00

NELSON RAY:
Rebel 104 *Walkin' Shoes* .... - -

RAY & LAMAR:
Capa 103 *Won't Do* ....8.00 - 12.00

RAY & LINDA:
Starday 333 *Hey Doll Baby* .... - -

RAY & LINDY:
United Artists 171 *Angel Love* ....8.00 - 12.00

RAY-O-VACS:
Atco 6085 *Crying All Alone* ....10.00 - 15.00
Decca 48162 *Besame Mucho* ....20.00 - 40.00
    48197 *Goodnight My Love* ....30.00 - 50.00
    48211 *You Can Depend On Me* ....25.00 - 40.00
    48260 *Hands Across The Table* ....25.00 - 40.00
Josie 781 *I Still Love You* ....15.00 - 30.00
Jubilee 5098 *What Can I Say* ....30.00 - 50.00
    5124 *You Know* ....10.00 - 15.00

RAYS:
Argo 1074 *How Long Must I Wait* ....8.00 - 12.00
Cameo 117 *Silhouettes* (78 rpm) ....20.00 - 30.00
Chess 1613 *Tippity Top* ....15.00 - 20.00

1678 *How Long Must I Wait* ....10.00 - 15.00
(EP) 5120 *Tippity Top* ....100.00 - 150.00
Perri 1004 *Are You Happy Now* ....7.00 - 10.00
XYZ 100 *My Steady Girl* ....15.00 - 20.00
    102 *Silhouettes* ....30.00 - 50.00
    600 *Why Do You Look The Other Way* ....15.00 - 20.00
    605 *Mediterranean Moon* ....8.00 - 12.00
    607 *Magic Moon* ....8.00 - 12.00
    608 *Silver Starlight* ....8.00 - 12.00
    2001 *Elevator Operator* ....10.00 - 15.00

"RCA CAMDEN ROCKERS":
Camden (LP) 435 (various artists) ....30.00 - 50.00

R-DELLS:
Dade 1806 *You Know Baby* ....15.00 - 20.00

OTIS READ:
Nanc 1118/1119 *Come On Baby* ....8.00 - 12.00

BILL READER:
Voll-Para 100 *There Was A Time* ....8.00 - 12.00
   - *Remember You're Mine* .... - - -

JIMMY REAGAN & THE RHYTHM ROCKERS:
G&G 128 *Lonely, Lonely Heart* ....20.00 - 30.00

RICK REASON:
Mar-Vel 3300 *I Feel So Bad* .... - - -

JOHNNY REBB:
Bullseye 1027 *Rock On* ....10.00 - 15.00
Flame 154 *My Body Can't Take It* ....7.00 - 10.00

REBEL ROUSERS:
Memphis 107 *Thunder* ....7.00 - 10.00
    113 *Zombie Walks* ....7.00 - 10.00

THE REBELS:
Kings X 3362 *In My Heart* ....100.00 - 200.00
Marlee 009 *Wild Weekend* ....10.00 - 15.00

JOHNNY REDD:
Corallen - *Rockin' with Ruby* ....20.00 - 30.00

TEDDY REDELL:
Atco 6162 *Judy* ....8.00 - 12.00
Hi 2024 *Pipeliner* ....10.00 - 15.00
Vaden 110 *Knockin' On The Backside* .....30.00 - 50.00
    115 *Gold Dust* ....15.00 - 25.00
    116 *Judy* ....30.00 - 50.00
    301 *I Want To Hold You* ....10.00 - 15.00

RED JACKS:
Apt 25006 *Big Brown Eyes* ....5.00 - 8.00

TERRY REDMAN:
MGM 12735 *Come On Back* ....8.00 - 12.00

RED TOPPERS:
Dan 3214 *I Never Had A Girl Like You* .....5.00 - 8.00

REED BROTHERS & THE STINGERS:
Award 122/123 *Swamp Rock* ....20.00 - 30.00

A.C. REED:
Age 29101 *This Little Voice* ....5.00 - 8.00
    29103 *I Wanna Be Free* ....7.00 - 10.00
    29112 *Mean Cop* ....7.00 - 10.00
    29123 *Lotta Lovin'* ....7.00 - 10.00

AL REED:
Dot - *I Love Her So* ....8.00 - 12.00
TNT - *I Love Her So* ....20.00 - 30.00
Winner 700 *Top Notch Grade A* ....8.00 - 12.00

BOB REED & HIS BAND:
Melatone 1003 *I'm Leaving You* ....5.00 - 8.00

CHUCK REED:
Hit 101 *Talkin' No Trash* ....10.00 - 15.00

EARL REED:
Cherokee 779 *Flat Foot Sam* ....7.00 - 10.00

JAMES REED (& HIS BAND):
Big Town 117 *You Better Hold Me* ....30.00 - 40.00
Flair 1034 *This Is The End* ....50.00 - 80.00
    1042 *You Better Hold Me* ....30.00 - 50.00
Money 201 *My Love Is Real* ....20.00 - 30.00
Rhythm 1775 *I Wanna Know* ....80.00 - 130.00

JERRI REED:
Bango 500 *While You're Gone* ....5.00 - 8.00

JERRY REED:
Capitol 3882 *Bessie Baby* ....7.00 - 10.00

JIMMY REED:
Chance 1142 *High And Lonesome* ....100.00 - 150.00
Vee Jay 100 *High And Lonesome* (red plastic) .....150.00 - 200.00
    105 *Jimmie's Boogie* (red plastic) ......80.00 - 120.00
    119 *Boogie In The Dark* (red plastic) ...75.00 - 100.00
    132 *Pretty Thing* ....15.00 - 25.00
    153 *I Don't Go For That* ....8.00 - 12.00
    168 *Ain't That Lovin' You Baby* ....7.00 - 10.00
    186, 203, 236, 237, 248, 253, 270, 275, 287, 298,
        304, 314, 326, 333, 347, 357 ......5.00 - 10.00
    (LP) 1004 *I'm Jimmy Reed* (maroon label) ....30.00 - 40.00
    (LP) 1008 *Rockin' With Reed* (maroon label) ....30.00 - 40.00
    (LP) 1022 *Found Love* ....20.00 - 30.00
    (LP) 1025 *Now Appearing* ....15.00 - 20.00
    (LP) 1035 (2 records) *At Carnegie Hall* ....15.00 - 20.00
    (LP) 1039 *The Best Of Jimmy Reed* ....10.00 - 15.00
    (LP) 1050 *Just Jimmy Reed* ....10.00 - 15.00
    (LP) 1067, 1072, 1073 ....8.00 - 12.00

LULU REED:
King (most issues) ....5.00 - 10.00
    (LP) 604 *Blue And Moody* ....100.00 - 200.00

BILL REEDER:
Fernwood 121 *You're My Baby* .... - - -

BILL REESE QUINTET & THE CORONETS:
Sterling 903 *Don't Deprive Me* ....50.00 - 80.00

DANNY REEVES:
D 1206 *Bell Hop Blues/I'm A Hobo* ....50.00 - 80.00
San 1509 *Spunky Monkey* ....30.00 - 50.00

GLENN REEVES (& HIS ROCK BILLYS/TOWN & COUNTRY PLAYBOYS):
Atco 6080 *Drinkin' Wine Spo-Dee-O-Dee* ...15.00 - 20.00
Decca 30481 *My Tortured Heart* ....8.00 - 12.00
    30589 *Betty Bounce* ....8.00 - 12.00
    30780 *Tarzan* ....8.00 - 12.00
Republic 7121 *That'll Be Love* ....10.00 - 20.00
TNT 120 *I'm Johnny On The Spot* ....40.00 - 60.00
    129 *I Ain't Got Room To Rock* ....50.00 - 75.00

JIM REEVES:
Abbott (LP) 5001 *Jim Reeves Sings* ....150.00 - 300.00
RCA Victor (LP) 1256 *Singing Down The Lane* ....40.00 - 60.00
    (LP) 1410 *Bimbo* ....40.00 - 60.00
    (LP) 1576 *Jim Reeves* ....15.00 - 25.00
    (LP) 1685 *Girls I Have Known* ....15.00 - 25.00

PEARL REEVES & THE CONCORDS:
Harlem 2332 *I'm Not Ashamed* ....50.00 - 80.00

THE REFLECTIONS:
Golden World (LP) 300 *Just Like Romeo And Juliet*
....50.00 - 75.00

REGALS:
Aladdin 3266 *Run Pretty Baby* ....30.00 - 50.00
Atlantic 1062 *I'm So Lonely* ....10.00 - 15.00
Lavender 1452 *Yes My Love* ....8.00 - 12.00

REGENTS:
Cousins 1002 *Barbara-Ann* ....80.00 - 130.00
Gee (LP) 706 *Barbara-Ann* ....80.00 - 130.00
   1065 *Barbara Ann* ....7.00 - 10.00
   1071 *Laura My Darling* ....8.00 - 12.00
   1073 *Don't Be a Fool* ....8.00 - 12.00
   1075 *Oh Baby* ....8.00 - 12.00
Kayo 101 *No Hard Feelings* ....10.00 - 15.00

BILLY REINSFORD:
Hermitage 803 *Magnolia* ....25.00 - 40.00

THE RELATIONS:
Kape 504 *Until We Two Are One* ....7.00 - 10.00
Michele 506 *When We Get The Word* ......8.00 - 12.00
Utopia 12 *Don't Let Me Down This Weekend* ....10.00 - 15.00
Zell's 712 *Say You Love Me* ....7.00 - 10.00

BOBBY RELF (& THE LAURELS):
Cash 1019 *Our Love* ....15.00 - 20.00
Dot 15510 *Little Fool* ....15.00 - 25.00
Flair 1063 *Yours Alone* ....100.00 - 200.00

REMINISCENTS:
Day 1000 *Oh Let Me Dream* ....15.00 - 25.00

JOHNNY RENO:
Valley's Meadowlark 105-58 *Naughty Mama* ....15.00 - 20.00

RENOWNS:
Everest 19396 *Wild One* ....15.00 - 20.00

REVALONS:
Pet 802 *Dreams Are For Fools* ....30.00 - 50.00

REVELERS:
G & C 1617 *What Was Once Was Once* ...20.00 - 30.00

RE-VELS/REVELS:
Andie 5077 *Please* ....7.00 - 10.00
Chess 1708 *False Alarm* (blue label)............50.00 - 75.00
Norgolde 103 *Dead Man's Stroll* ....20.00 - 40.00
   103 *Midnight Stroll* ....8.00 - 12.00
   104 *Foo Man Choo* ....10.00 - 15.00
Sound 129 *You Lied To Me* ....30.00 - 50.00
   135 *Dream My Darling Dream* ....30.00 - 50.00
Teen 122 *So In Love* ....150.00 - 200.00

PAUL REVERE & THE RAIDERS:
Gardena 116 *Like Long Hair* ....8.00 - 12.00
   (LP) 1000 *Like Long Hair* ....100.00 - 150.00
Sane (LP) 1001 *Paul Revere & The Raiders* ....100.00 - 150.00

THE REVERES:
Glory 272 *Lenore* ....8.00 - 12.00

EDDIE REYNOLDS:
Dixie 838 *What Was It* ....30.00 - 50.00

BIG JACK REYNOLDS & HIS BLUE MEN:
Hi-Q 5036 *I Had A Little Dog* ....8.00 - 12.00

JODY REYNOLDS:
Demon 1507 *Endless Sleep* (78 rpm).............10.00 - 15.00
   1515 *Beulah Lee* ....8.00 - 12.00
   1524 *Stone Cold* ....8.00 - 12.00

WESLEY REYNOLDS:
Rose 108 *Trip To The Moon* ....25.00 - 40.00
   117 *Rag Mop* ....20.00 - 30.00

DARRELL RHODES:
Winston 1029 *Lu Lu*...................................150.00 - 250.00

JIMMY RHODES & THE SHUFFLES:
Cupid 5005 *I Wanna Go* ....8.00 - 12.00

SLIM RHODES:
Sun 216 *Uncertain Love* ....50.00 - 80.00
   225 *House Of Sin* ....100.00 - 150.00
   238 *Gonna Romp And Stomp* ....40.00 - 70.00
   256 *Do What I Do* ....20.00 - 30.00

TEXAS RED RHODES:
Echo 1001 *Go Cats Go* ....50.00 - 80.00

RHYTHM ACES:
Vee Jay 123 *I Wonder Why*........................75.00 - 100.00
   138 *Whisper To Me*.........................75.00 - 100.00
(Above, pressed of translucent red vinyl, bring substantially higher
   prices.)
   160 *That's My Sugar*.......................20.00 - 30.00
   417 *Be Mine* ....7.00 - 10.00

RHYTHM JESTERS:
Lectra 513 *Please Be Mine* ....8.00 - 12.00
Rama 213 *Rock Music*................................15.00 - 20.00

RHYTHM MASTERS:
Flip 314 *Baby We Two* ....250.00 - up

RHYTHM ROCKERS:
Cross Country 524 *Fiddle Bop* ....20.00 - 30.00
Oasis 104 *Thinkin' About You* ....30.00 - 50.00
Sun 248 *Fiddle Bop* ....30.00 - 50.00

RHYTHM ROCKETS:
Gulfstream 6654 *My Shadow* ....20.00 - 30.00

ELDON RICE:
El Rio 413 *Our Love Won't Die* ....75.00 - 100.00

CHARLIE RICH:
Groove 58-0025 *Big Boss Man* ....8.00 - 12.00
Phillips Int'l. (LP) 197 *Lonely Weekends* ....100.00 - 200.00

DAVE RICH:
RCA Victor 7334 *Rosie Let's Get Cozy* ....10.00 - 15.00

CLIFF RICHARD:
Capitol 4096 *Move It* ....10.00 - 15.00
   4154 *Livin' Lovin' Doll* ....10.00 - 15.00

RICHARD BROTHERS:
Strate 8 1500 *Stolen Property* ....50.00 - 80.00

JAY RICHARDS & THE BLUES KINGS:
Goldband 1101 *Hear Love Knockin'* ....10.00 - 15.00

JAPE RICHARDSON (See also BIG BOPPER):
Mercury 71219 *Crazy Blues* ....10.00 - 15.00
   71312 *A Teen-Age Moon* ....10.00 - 15.00

NOLAN RICHARDSON:
Jamaka 1005 *Money In The Bank* ....20.00 - 30.00

RICHIE (& THE ROYALS):
Rello 1 *And When I'm Near You* ....15.00 - 20.00
    3 *Be My Girl* ....30.00 - 50.00

PAT RICHMOND & THE FIRE BALLS:
Vulco 1500 *Don't Stop The Rockin'* ....50.00 - 80.00

RICKI & RIKATONES:
Manhattan 3201 *T.N.T.* ....10.00 - 15.00

JIMMY RICKS (& THE RAVENS):
Baton 236 *I'm A Fool To Want You* ....10.00 - 15.00
Mercury 70213 *Who'll Be The Fool* ....15.00 - 20.00

TOMMY RIDGELY:
Atlantic 1009 *Oh Lawdy*......................................25.00 - 40.00
    1039 *Jam Up* ....40.00 - 70.00
Herald (most issues) ....5.00 - 10.00
Imperial 5198 *Lavinia* ....50.00 - 100.00
    5203 *Looped* ....50.00 - 100.00
    5214 *Monkey Man* ....50.00 - 100.00
    5223 *Good Times* ....50.00 - 100.00
Ric (most issues) ....5.00 - 8.00

THE RIFFS:
Sunny 22 *Little Girl* ....40.00 - 60.00

BILLY LEE RILEY:
Brunswick 55085 *Is That All To The Ball (Mr. Hall)?*
....25.00 - 40.00
Home Of The Blues 223 *Flip, Flop And Fly* ....8.00 - 12.00
Sun 245 *Rock With Me Baby* ....30.00 - 50.00
    260 *Flying Saucer Rock & Roll* ....30.00 - 50.00
    277 *Red Hot* ....25.00 - 40.00
    289 *Baby Please Don't Go* ....40.00 - 60.00
    313 *Down By The Riverside* ....8.00 - 12.00
    322 *Got The Water Boiling* ....20.00 - 30.00

BOB RILEY:
Dot 15625 *Without Your Love* ....10.00 - 15.00
MGM 12612 *Wanda Jean* ....15.00 - 25.00
York - *Big Dog* ....15.00 - 25.00

OTIS RILEY:
Kappa 208 *Rock and Roll Riley* ....40.00 - 60.00
    209 *Little Miss Bibbity Bobbity Boom* ....20.00 - 30.00

RUSS RILEY & THE FIVE SOUNDS:
Aljon 115 *Tonight Must Live On* ....100.00 - 150.00

RINKY DINKS:
Atco 6121 *Early In The Morning* ....10.00 - 15.00
    6121 *Early In The Morning* (78 rpm) ....20.00 - 40.00
    6128 *Mighty Mighty Man* ....10.00 - 20.00
    6128 *Mighty Mighty Man* (78 rpm) ....25.00 - 50.00

CHUCK RIO:
Challenge 59019 *Denise* ....7.00 - 10.00

RIP-CHORDS:
Abco 105 *Let's Do The Razzle Dazzle* ....300.00 - up
(Above, pressed of translucent red vinyl, brings substantially more.)

GEORGE RITCHIE:
Smart 321 *But In A Million Years* ....10.00 - 15.00

THE RIVALS:
Darryl 722 *I Must See You Again* ....7.00 - 10.00
LuPine 118 *It's Gonna Work Out* ....7.00 - 10.00
Puff 1001 *Love Me*..15.00 - 20.00

LITTLE BOBBY RIVERA (& THE HEMLOCKS):
Fury 1004 *Cora Lee* (maroon label) ....30.00 - 50.00

CANDY RIVERS & THE FALCONS:
Flip 302 *You Are The Only One*............................100.00 - 150.00

CHUCK RIVERS:
Cenla 222 *All Alone At Night* ....20.00 - 30.00

CLIFF RIVERS:
Thanks! 1201 *True Lips* ....15.00 - 20.00

RIVERAS/RIVIERAS:
Algonquin 718 *A Night To Remember* ....80.00 - 120.00
Coed 503 *Count Every Star* ....8.00 - 12.00
    508 *Moonlight Serenade* ....8.00 - 12.00
    513 *Our Love* ....8.00 - 12.00
    522 *Since I Made You Cry* ....8.00 - 12.00
    529 *Blessing Of Love* ....8.00 - 12.00
    538 *My Friend*...8.00 - 12.00
    542 *Stay In My Heart* ....8.00 - 12.00
    561 *El Dorado*...15.00 - 30.00
    592 *Moonlight Cocktails* ....8.00 - 12.00
Riviera (LP) 701 *Campus Party* ....50.00 - 80.00

RIVILEERS:
Baton 200 *A Thousand Stars*................................30.00 - 50.00
    201 *Forever*..30.00 - 50.00
    205 *Eternal Love* ....40.00 - 70.00
    207 *For Sentimental Reasons* ....20.00 - 30.00
    209 *Don't Ever Leave Me* ....25.00 - 40.00
    241 *A Thousand Stars* ....10.00 - 15.00

THE RIVINGTONS:
Liberty (LP) 3282 *Doin' The Bird* ....40.00 - 70.00
    55610 *Cherry* ....10.00 - 15.00

ROAMERS:
Savoy 1147 *I'll Never Get Over You* ....10.00 - 15.00
    1149 *Women And Whiskey*..................................10.00 - 15.00
    1156 *Chop Chop Ching-A-Ling* ....10.00 - 15.00

JOHNNY ROANE:
Wagon 1004 *Dragstrip Baby* ....20.00 - 30.00

EDDIE ROBBINS:
David 1001 *Janice* ....8.00 - 12.00
Dot 15702 *A Girl Like You* ....10.00 - 15.00
Power 214 *A Girl Like You* ....20.00 - 30.00

MARTY ROBBINS:
Columbia (LP) 976 *The Song Of Robbins* ....20.00 - 40.00
    (LP) 1087 *Song Of The Islands*...........................20.00 - 30.00
    (LP) 1189 *Marty Robbins* ....20.00 - 30.00
    (EP) B-2116 *Singing The Blues* ....35.00 - 50.00
    (EP) B-2134 *A White Sportcoat* ....40.00 - 60.00
    2601 (LP) (10 inch) *Rock'n Roll'n Robbins* ....200.00 - 300.00
    21351 *That's All Right* ....10.00 - 15.00
    21446 *Maybelline*..10.00 - 15.00
    21461 *Pretty Mama*..8.00 - 12.00
    21477 *Tennessee Toddy* ....10.00 - 15.00
    40679 *Long Tall Sally*..15.00 - 20.00
    40706 *Respectfully Miss Brooks*..........................10.00 - 15.00
    40864 *A White Sport Coat* (78 rpm) ....10.00 - 15.00
    41013 *The Story Of My Life* (78 rpm).................15.00 - 25.00

MEL ROBBINS:
Argo 5340 *Save It* ....15.00 - 20.00

ROBERT & JOHNNY:
Old Town (most issues) ....7.00 - 10.00
Old Town 1052 *I Believe In You* (78 rpm).............15.00 - 20.00

BOBBY ROBERTS with THE BAD HABITS:
Hut 881 *Hop Skip And Jump* ....30.00 - 40.00
Sky 101 *Big Sandy* ....50.00 - 75.00

DENNIS ROBERTS:
Sims 145 *Mule Skinner Blues* ....7.00 - 10.00
Yucca 133 *Come On* ....7.00 - 10.00

DON "RED" ROBERTS:
Chart 643 *Don't Say Maybe* ....-   -   -
Rama 230 *Don't Say Maybe* ....15.00 - 20.00

LANCE ROBERTS:
Decca 30955 *Gonna Have Myself A Ball* ....10.00 - 15.00

LYNN ROBERTS & THE PHANTOMS:
Oriole 101 *I'll Be Around* ....80.00 - 130.00
(Above, pressed of translucent red vinyl, brings substantially more.)

SONNY ROBERTS & THE ECHOES:
Impala 1001 *I'll Never Let You Go* ....200.00 - up

WALTER ROBERTSON:
Flair 1053 *Sputterin' Blues* ....30.00 - 50.00

ROBINS:
Arvee 5001 *Just Like That* ....7.00 - 10.00
    5013 *Live Wire Suzie* ....7.00 - 10.00
Atco 6059 *Smokey Joe's Cafe* ....8.00 - 12.00
Crown 106 *I Made A Vow* ....150.00 - 200.00
    120 *The Key To My Heart* ....75.00 - 100.00
Knight 2008 *It's Never Too Late* ....10.00 - 15.00
Lavender 001 *White Cliffs Of Dover* ....10.00 - 15.00
    002 *Mary Lou* ....10.00 - 15.00
RCA Victor 5175 *A Fool Such As I* ....80.00 - 130.00
    5271 *Oh Why* ....75.00 - 100.00
    5434 *How Would You Know* ....80.00 - 130.00
    5489 *Empty Bottles* ....75.00 - 100.00
    5564 *Get It Off You Mind* ....75.00 - 100.00
Spark 103 *Riot In Cell Block Number Nine* ....30.00 - 50.00
    107 *Framed* ....30.00 - 50.00
    110 *If Tear Drops Were Kisses* ....50.00 - 100.00
    113 *One Kiss* ....50.00 - 100.00
    116 *I Must Be Dreaming* ....50.00 - 75.00
    122 *Smokey Joe's Cafe* ....40.00 - 60.00
Whippet 100 *Cherry Lips* ....15.00 - 25.00
    200 *Out Of The Picture* ....8.00 - 12.00
    201 *Hurt Me* ....10.00 - 15.00
    203 *That Old Black Magic* ....10.00 - 15.00
    206 *A Fool In Love* ....10.00 - 15.00
    208 *Every Night* ....10.00 - 15.00
    211 *In My Dreams* ....10.00 - 20.00
    212 *You Wanted Fun* ....10.00 - 15.00
    (LP) 703 *Rock & Roll With The Robins* ....150.00 - 200.00

BILL ROBINSON & THE QUAILS:
De Luxe 6030 *Lonely Star* ....75.00 - 100.00
    6047 *I Know She's Gone* ....75.00 - 100.00
    6057 *Somewhere Somebody Cares* ....50.00 - 80.00
    6059 *Heaven Is The Place* ....50.00 - 80.00
    6074 *Oh Sugar* ....40.00 - 60.00

DICK ROBINSON:
MCI 1006 *Boppin' Martian* ....20.00 - 40.00

FENTION/FENTON ROBINSON (& THE CASTLE ROCKERS/HIS DUKES):
Duke 190, 191, 312, 329 ....7.00 - 10.00
Meteor 5041 *Crying Out Loud* (black label) ....40.00 - 70.00
U.S.A. 842 *From My Heart* ....7.00 - 10.00

JERRY ROBINSON:
Epic 9234 *A Whole Lot Of Lovin'* ....30.00 - 60.00

JIMMY LEE ROBINSON:
Bandera 2510 *Twist It Baby* ....8.00 - 12.00

MARK ROBINSON:
Tee Gee 104 *Pretty Jane* ....10.00 - 15.00

SUGAR CHILE ROBINSON:
Capitol (LP) 589 *Boogie Woogie* ....75.00 - 100.00

CARSON ROBINSON:
MGM 12266 *Rockin' And Rollin' With Granmaw* . 25.00 - 40.00
(most other issues) ....5.00 - 10.00

THE ROB-ROYS: (See also NORMAN FOX)
Back Beat 501 *Tell Me Why* ....20.00 - 30.00

TOMMY ROCCO:
Razorback 102 *I'll Cry Awhile* ....7.00 - 10.00

ROCHELL & THE CANDLES:
Challenge 9158 *Each Night* ....10.00 - 15.00
Swingin' 623 *Once Upon A Time* ....8.00 - 12.00
    634 *So Far Away* ....8.00 - 12.00
    640 *Peg Of My Heart* ....8.00 - 12.00
    652 *A Long Time Ago* ....8.00 - 12.00

THE ROCK 'N' ROLLERS:
Ven 100 *For You* ....15.00 - 25.00

"ROCK & ROLL FOREVER":
Atlantic (LP) 8010 (various artists) ....40.00 - 80.00
    (LP) 8021 *Vol. 2* (various artists) ....40.00 - 80.00

"ROCK 'N' ROLL JAMBOREE":
End (LP) 302 *Rock 'N' Roll Jamboree*
(cover variations exist) ....50.00 - 100.00

"ROCK & ROLL SOCK HOP":
Score 4018 (various artists) ....75.00 - 100.00

"ROCK 'N' ROLL SPECTACULAR":
Dawn (LP) 1119 *Rock 'N' Roll Spectaculr* ....50.00 - 100.00

ROCK-A-FELLAS:
Southern Sound 112 *Dear Someone* ....10.00 - 15.00

ROCK A TEENS:
Doran 3515 *Woo-Hoo* ....25.00 - 50.00
Roulette 4192 *Woo-Hoo* ....5.00 - 10.00
    4217 *Doggone It Baby* ....10.00 - 15.00
    (LP) 25109 *Woo-Hoo* ....75.00 - 100.00

ROCK-A-TONES:
Whammy 7450 *One More Chance* ....-   -

ROCKERS (See also PAUL WINLEY):
Carter 3029 *Count Every Star* ....250.00 - up
Federal 12267 *What Am I To Do* ....30.00 - 50.00
    12273 *Down In The Bottom* ....20.00 - 30.00
Premium 401 *Angel Child* ....15.00 - 20.00

THE ROCKETEERS:
Herald 415 *Foolish One* ....150.00 - 200.00
(Above, pressed of translucent red vinyl, brings substantially more.)
M.J.C. 501 *My Reckless Heart* ....250.00 - up
Modern 999 *Talk It Over* ....10.00 - 15.00

ROCKETONES:
Melba 113 *Mexico* ....15.00 - 20.00

ROCKETS: (See also BILL BODAFORD)
Modern 992 *Be Lovey Dovey* ....10.00 - 15.00
    1021 *Johnny's House Party* ....10.00 - 15.00
Tri-Dec 25725 *My Rockin' Baby* ....20.00 - 30.00

ROCKETTES:
Parrot 789 *I Can't Forget* ....300.00 -   up

ROCKIN' BRADLEY:
Fire 1007 *Look Out*.................................20.00 -   30.00

THE ROCKING BROTHERS:
R & B 1309 *Rock It* ....8.00 -   12.00

ROCKIN' CHAIRS:
Recorte 401 *Rockin' Chair Boogie*........................10.00 -   15.00
  404 *Come Oh Baby* ....15.00 -   20.00

ROCKIN DUKES:
OJ 1007 *My Baby Left Me* ....100.00 - 150.00

"ROCKIN '50s"
Atlantic (LP) 8037 (various artists) ....30.00 -   50.00

ROCKING STOCKINGS:
Sun 1960 *Rockin-Lang-Syne*.......................10.00 -   15.00

ROCKIN' JESTERS:
Oklahoma - *I Was Too Blind* ....15.00 -   20.00

ROCKIN' KIDS:
Dot 15749 *Yea Yea (I'm In The Mood)* ....10.00 -   20.00

ROCKIN' REBELS:
Swan (LP) 509 *Wild Weekend* ....50.00 -   80.00

ROCKIN' RONALD:
End 1043 *Kansas City* ....20.00 -   30.00

ROCKIN' R'S:
Tempus 7541 *Crazy Baby*..........................10.00 -   15.00

ROCKIN' SAINTS:
Decca 31144 *Cheat On Me Baby*..........................20.00 -   30.00

(COUNT) ROCKIN' SIDNEY/SYDNEY (& HIS ALL STARS/DUKES):
Goldband 1158, 1159, 1162, 1170.......................5.00 -   10.00
Jin 110 *My Little Girl* ....15.00 -   20.00
  156, 164, 168, 170, 174, 177 ....5.00 -   10.00

THE ROCK-ITS:
Spangle 2010 *It's L-O-V-E* ....10.00 -   15.00

"ROCK, ROCK, ROCK":
Chess (LP) 1425 (black label) (From the motion picture; with
  Flamingos, Moonglows)........................40.00 -   80.00

ROD & TERRY:
Cuca 1206 *That's All Right*........................20.00 -   30.00

BUCK RODGERS:
Starday 245 *Little Rock Rock*..........................30.00 -   50.00

JIMMIE RODGERS:
Roulette 4015 *Honeycomb* (78 rpm).......................15.00 -   20.00
  4031 *Kisses Sweeter Than Wine* (78 rpm)..........15.00 -   20.00
  4045 *Oh-Oh, I'm Falling In Love Again* (78 rpm)
  ....15.00 -   20.00
  4070 *Secretly* (78 rpm) ....10.00 -   15.00
  4090 *Are You Really Mine* (78 rpm)...................10.00 -   15.00
  4116 *Bimbombey* (78 rpm) ....20.00 -   30.00

GENE RODGUE:
Richland 24 *Little Cajun Girl* ....25.00 -   50.00

TOMMY ROE (& BOBBY LEE TRAMMELL):
ABC Paramount (LP) 432 *Sheila* ....30.00 -   50.00
Crown (LP) 5323 *Tommy Roe And Bobby Lee*........20.00 -   30.00
Judd 1022 *Sheila*........................15.00 -   20.00

JESSE ROGERS:
Arcade 169 *Jump Cats Jump* ....20.00 -   30.00

JIMMY ROGERS (& HIS ROCKING FOUR/TRIO):
Chess 1506 *Back Door Friend*........................100.00 - 150.00
  1519 *The Last Time*........................100.00 - 150.00
  1543 *Act Like You Love Me* ....75.00 - 100.00
  1574 *Sloppy Drunk* ....50.00 -   80.00
  1616, 1643, 165⁹ ....10.00 -   20.00
  1687, 1721........................10.00 -   20.00

KENNETH/KENNY ROGERS:
Carlton 454 *That Crazy Feeling* ....15.00 -   20.00
Ken-Lee 102 *Jole Blon* ....7.00 -   10.00
Spade - *That Crazy Feeling* ....- -   -
- *We'll Always Have Each Other* ....- -   -

LELAN ROGERS:
Lynn 502 *Hold, Part 1/Part 2* ....8.00 -   12.00

ROY ROGERS:
RCA Victor (LP) 1439 *(& Dale Evans)*........................30.00 -   50.00
  (LP) 3041 (10 inch) *Souvenir Album* ....30.00 -   50.00

WELDON (& WANDA) ROGERS:
Imperial 5451 *So Long, Good Luck, And Goodbye* ....25.00 -   40.00
Je-Well 103 *This Son Is Just for You* ....100.00 - 200.00
  104 *Women Drivers* ....- -   -
  105 *Heaven's Back Door* ....- -   -
  107 *If I Had One Day To Live* ....- -   -
Peach 744 *If I Had One Day To Live* ....- -   -
  759 *How Times Have Changed* ....- -   -
  763 *I'm Hanging Up The Phone* ....- -   -

ROLLING CREW:
Aladdin 3301 *Home On Alcatraz*........................50.00 -   80.00

MIMI ROMAN:
Decca 29930 *Little Lovin'* ....10.00 -   20.00

RICH ROMAN:
CG 5003 *T.T.B.* ....10.00 -   15.00

ROMANCERS:
Bay-Tone 101 *You Don't Understand* ....10.00 -   15.00
Celebrity 701 *No Greater Love*........................15.00 -   25.00
Dootone 381 *I Still Remember* ....20.00 -   30.00
  404 *This Is Goodbye* ....20.00 -   30.00
Linda 119 *My Heart Cries* ....7.00 -   10.00
Marquee 711 *Take Me To Paradise* ....10.00 -   15.00
Palette 5075 *It Only Happens With You* ....10.00 -   15.00

THE ROMANS:
Juno 014 *You Are My Only Love* ....150.00 - 200.00
M.M.I. 1238 *Wild Ideas* ....40.00 -   70.00

ROMEOS:
Apollo 461 *I Beg You Please* ....150.00 - 200.00
  466 *Doctor Velvet* ....30.00 -   50.00
Atco 6107 *Fine Fine Baby*........................10.00 -   15.00
Fox 748/749 *Let's Be Partners* ....50.00 -   75.00
  845/846 *Moments To Remember* ....80.00 - 120.00

CHAN ROMERO:
Del-Fi 4119 *If I Had My Way* ....10.00 -   20.00
  4126 *My Little Ruby*........................10.00 -   20.00

RONETTES:
Colpix (LP) 486 *The Ronettes*........................75.00 - 100.00
Phillies (LP) 4006 *Presenting The Fabulous Ronettes*
  ....80.00 - 130.00

(Note: Some copies read "Ronnettes.")

RONNIE & THE HI-LITES:
Raven 8000 *Valarie* ....8.00 - 12.00
Win 250 *A Slow Dance* ....5.00 - 8.00
    251 *You Keep Me Guessin'*.................5.00 - 8.00
    252 *High School Romance* ....7.00 - 10.00

RONNIE & MARLENE:
Westport 144 *Marlene* ....10.00 - 15.00

RONNIE & ROY:
Capitol 4192 *Big Fat Sally* ....10.00 - 15.00

THE ROOSTERS:
Epic 9487 *Let's Try Again* ....7.00 - 10.00

ANDY ROSE:
Aamco 100 *Lov-A-Lov-A Love* ....15.00 - 20.00
    103 *My Devotion* ....15.00 - 20.00

THE ROSEBUDS:
Gee 1033 *Dearest Darling* ....8.00 - 12.00

ROSIE:
Brunswick (LP) 754102 *Lonely Blue Nights* ....40.00 - 80.00

DANNY ROSS:
Minor 107 *Look At You Go* ....30.00 - 50.00

DOCTOR/DR. ROSS (& HIS JUMP & JIVE BOYS/ ORBITS):
Chess 1504 *Dr. Ross Boogie* ....200.00 - 400.00
D.I.R. 101/102 *Industrial Boogie* ....20.00 - 30.00
Fortune 538 *Sugar Mama* ....30.00 - 50.00
    857 *Cat Squirrel* ....15.00 - 20.00
Hi-Q 5027 *Numbers Blues* ....15.00 - 20.00
    5033 *New York Breakdown* ....15.00 - 20.00
Sun 193 *Come Back Baby*.......................200.00 - 300.00
    212 *The Boogie Disease* ....200.00 - 300.00

JERRY ROSS:
Murco 1016 *Ever'body's Tryin'* ....40.00 - 70.00

LEE ROSS:
Liberty 55127 *Candy Lips* ....5.00 - 8.00

PATTY ROSS:
Aardell 107 *Rock It Davy, Rock It* .... - -

BOB ROUBIAN:
Prep 101 *Rocket To The Moon*.................8.00 - 12.00

ROULETTES:
Ebb 124 *The Way You Carry On* ....8.00 - 12.00

ROVERS:
Capitol 3078 *Why Oh-h* ....8.00 - 12.00
Music City 750 *Why-Ohh*.......................30.00 - 50.00
    780 *Salute to Johnny Ace* ....20.00 - 30.00
(Above, if pressed of translucent colored vinyl, bring substantially
    higher prices)
    792 *Whole Lot of Love* ....40.00 - 70.00

LYNN ROWE:
Hit 181 *Red Rover* ....15.00 - 20.00

PECK ROWELL:
Coin 101 *Take It Easy Greasy*.................. - -

ROXSTERS:
Art 175 *So Long*.................................30.00 - 40.00

ROYALE MONARCHS:
Dell 101 *Whole Lot Of Shakin' Goin' On* .... - -

ROYAL HALOS:
Aladdin 3460 *My Love Is True* ....15.00 - 25.00

ROYAL HAWK:
Flair 1013 *I Wonder Why*.......................20.00 - 30.00

THE ROYAL HOLIDAYS:
Carlton 472 *Margaret* ....10.00 - 15.00
Herald 536 *Down In Cuba* ....50.00 - 75.00
Penthouse 9357 *Margaret*.......................50.00 - 75.00

THE ROYAL JESTERS:
Cobra 2222 *Love Me* ....10.00 - 15.00
    7777 *I Want To Be Loved* ....10.00 - 15.00
Harlem 105 *My Angel Of Love* ....80.00 - 120.00

THE ROYAL JOKERS:
Atco 6052 *You Tickle Me, Baby*...............15.00 - 20.00
    6062 *Don't Leave Me Fanny* ....15.00 - 20.00
    6077 *She's Mine, All Mine*................15.00 - 20.00
Fortune 840 *Sweet Little Angel* ....15.00 - 20.00
Hi-Q 5004 *September In The Rain*...........15.00 - 20.00

THE ROYAL KINGS:
Forlin 502 *Peter-Peter* ....15.00 - 20.00

ROYAL KNIGHTS:
Radio City 1001 *There's Going To Be A Wedding*. 15.00 - 20.00

ROYAL LANCERS:
Citation 5004 *Angel In My Eyes* ....8.00 - 12.00

ROYAL NOTES:
Athena 201 *Come Dance With Me*...........10.00 - 15.00
Kellit 7032 *Three Speed Girl* ....40.00 - 60.00
    7034 *You Are My Love*...................40.00 - 60.00

ROYALS:
Federal 12064 *Every Beat Of My Heart*...............200.00 - 300.00
    12077 *Starting From Tonight* ....200.00 - 300.00
    12088 *Moonrise* ....200.00 - 300.00
    12098 *A Love In My Heart*..............150.00 - 250.00
(Note: Any of above, pressed of colored vinyl,
    command higher prices.)
    12113 *Are You Forgetting* ....80.00 - 130.00
    12121 *The Shrine Of St. Cecilia* ....80.00 - 130.00
    12133 *Get It* ....50.00 - 80.00
    12150 *Hello Miss Fine* ....50.00 - 80.00
    12160 *Someone Like You* ....50.00 - 80.00
    12169 *Work With Me Annie* ....25.00 - 50.00
Okeh 6832 *Dreams Of You* ....150.00 - 250.00
Venus 103 *Someday We'll Meet Again*................75.00 - 100.00

ROYAL TEENS:
ABC Paramount 9882 *Short Shorts* (78 rpm) ....20.00 - 30.00
Capitol 4261 *Believe Me*........................7.00 - 10.00
    4335 *Was It A Dream*....................10.00 - 15.00
    4402 *It's The Talk Of The Town* ....10.00 - 15.00
Mighty 109, 111, 112.............................8.00 - 12.00
Power 113 *Sittin' With My Baby*..............15.00 - 20.00
    215 *Short Shorts*..........................25.00 - 40.00

ROYALTONES:
Old Town 1018 *Crazy Love* ....15.00 - 25.00
    1028 *Latin Love* ....15.00 - 20.00

RUBY & THE ROMANTICS:
Kapp, most issues..................................5.00 - 8.00

DON RUBY:
Cub 9012 *Rockin' Piano, Outta Tune Guitar* ....25.00 - 40.00

LAWSON RUDD:
Harvest 709 *Shake This Town* ....15.00 - 25.00

RAY RUFF:
Bolo 741 *Pledge Of Love* ....8.00 - 12.00
Lin 5034 *Beatle Maniacs* ....10.00 - 15.00
   5035 *I Took A Liking To You* ....7.00 - 10.00
   5036 *In Dreamland* ....7.00 - 10.00
Norman 503 *Half-Pint Baby* ....7.00 - 10.00
   508 *Love Made A Fool Of You* ....7.00 - 10.00
   513 *Well Alright* ....7.00 - 10.00
   524 *My Gift To You* ....7.00 - 10.00
   528 *Lonely Hours* ....7.00 - 10.00
   539 *I'm Qualified* ....7.00 - 10.00

MISTER RUFFIN:
Spark 115 *Bring It On Back* ....15.00 - 25.00

RIFF RUFFIN:
Cash 1023 *If I Can't Have You* ....5.00 - 8.00

"RUMBLE":
Jubilee (LP) 1114 (various artists) ....30.00 - 50.00

THE RUNAROUNDS/RUN-A-ROUNDS:
Felsted 8710 *Send Her Back* ....8.00 - 12.00
KC 116 *Unbelievable* ....10.00 - 15.00

OTIS RUSH (& HIS BAND):
Chess 1751, 1775 ....7.00 - 10.00
Cobra 5000 *I Can't Quit You Baby* ....20.00 - 30.00
   5005 *Violent Love* ....15.00 - 20.00
   5010 *Groaning The Blues* ....20.00 - 30.00
   5015 *Jump Sister Bessie* ....15.00 - 20.00
   5023 *Three Times A Fool* ....20.00 - 30.00
   5027 *Checking On My Baby* ....15.00 - 20.00
   5030 *Double Trouble* ....15.00 - 20.00
   5032 *All Your Love* ....15.00 - 20.00

JIMMY RUSHING:
King 4588 *In The Moonlight* ....15.00 - 25.00

RUSS & THE STING-RAYS:
Carol 102 *Do The Surf* ....10.00 - 15.00

IRVIN RUSS:
Felco 201 *Crazy Alligator* ....50.00 - 75.00

BOBBY RUSSELL & THE IMPOLLOS:
Felsted 8520 *She's Gonna Be Sorry* ....8.00 - 12.00
Spar 740 *Roll Over Beethoven* ....15.00 - 20.00

JOY RUSSELL:
Nasco 7008 *My Little Honey Bee* ....5.00 - 10.00

TED RUSSELL:
Terock 1000 *Bright Lights* ....7.00 - 10.00

MARK RUSSO:
Crosley 218 *I'm Gonna Knock On Your Door* ...8.00 - 12.00

RUSTY & DOUG:
Hickory (LP) 103 *Rusty & Doug Sing "Louisiana Man" & Other
   Favorites* ....30.00 - 50.00
   1077 *Hey Mae* ....10.00 - 15.00
Hickory (most other issues) ....5.00 - 8.00

CATHY RYAN & THE ADMIRALS:
King 4792 *It's A Sad, Sad Feeling* ....20.00 - 40.00

CHARLEY RYAN:
4-Star 1749 *Hot Rod Guitar* ....8.00 - 12.00
Souvenir 101 *Hot Rod Lincoln* ....20.00 - 30.00

BOBBY RYDELL:
Cameo 160, 164 ....7.00 - 10.00
   (LP) 1006 *We Got Love* ....35.00 - 50.00
   (LP) 1007 *Bobby Sings, Bobby Sings* ....20.00 - 30.00
   (LP) 1009 *Bobby's Biggest Hits* ....20.00 - 30.00

JUNIOR RYDER AND THE PEACOCKS:
Duke 119 *Sad Story* ....20.00 - 30.00

FORREST RYE:
Fortune 172 *Wild Cat Boogie* ....10.00 - 15.00

RYTHM ROCKERS (See RHYTHM ROCKERS)

JOHNNY SABER:
Adonis 103 *Wish It Could Be Me* ....50.00 - 80.00

SABRES:
Bullseye 101 *You Can Depend On Me* ....75.00 - 100.00
Cal-West 45847 *Always Forever* ....75.00 - 125.00
Gala 114 *Hot Rod Kelly* ....40.00 - 60.00
Kil-Mac 1412 *Take Up The Slack, Daddy-O* ....15.00 - 20.00

THE SAFARIS:
Eldo 101 *Image Of A Girl* ....8.00 - 12.00
   105 *Summer Nights* ....10.00 - 15.00
   110 *In The Still On The Night* ....10.00 - 15.00
   113 *Garden Of Love* ....10.00 - 15.00

DOUG SAHM (& THE MARKAYS/PHAROAHS/ELL-KINGS) (See also LITTLE DOUG):
Harlem 107 *Why, Why, Why* ....30.00 - 50.00
   108 *Baby Tell Me* ....30.00 - 50.00
   113 *Slow Down* ....40.00 - 60.00
   116 *Sapphire* (possibly unissued) ....- - -
Personality 3504 *Baby What's On Your Mind* ...8.00 - 12.00
   Renner 212 *Big Hat* ....15.00 - 25.00
   215 *Crazy Crazy Feeling* ....20.00 - 30.00
   226 *Two Hearts in Love* ....15.00 - 20.00
   232 *Little Angel* ....15.00 - 20.00
   240 *Lucky Me* ....15.00 - 20.00
   247 *Mister Kool* ....20.00 - 30.00
Satin 100 *Crazy Daisy* ....50.00 - 75.00
Tribe (most issues) ....5.00 - 10.00
Warrior 507 *Crazy Daisy* ....75.00 - 100.00

SAIGONS:
Dootone 375 *You're Heavenly* ....75.00 - 100.00

SAILOR BOY:
Dig 116 *Country Hoe* ....20.00 - 30.00
   126 *What Have I Done Wrong?* ....20.00 - 30.00

NICKY ST. CLAIR: (See THE FIVE TROJANS)

ST. LOUIS JIMMY:
Duke 110 *Drinkin' Woman* ....75.00 - 100.00
Herald 407 *Hard Luck Boogie* ....80.00 - 130.00
Parrot 823 *Murder In The First Degree* ....75.00 - 100.00

ST. LOUIS MAC:
Bea & Baby 113 *Broken Heart* ....15.00 - 20.00

MAC SALES (See MAC & JAKE)

SAMMY SALVO:
Hickory 1138 *Don't Cast Your Spell On Me* ....10.00 - 15.00
Imperial 5615 *Marble Heart* ....7.00 - 10.00
Mark V 2391 *One Little Baby* ....25.00 - 40.00

SAM THE SHAM & THE PHAROAHS:
XL 906 *Wooly Bully* ....30.00 - 50.00

SAMMY & THE DEL-LARKS:
Ea-Jay 100 *I Never Will Forget* ....20.00 - 30.00

CLARENCE SAMUELS:
Apt 25028 *We're Going To The Hop* ....8.00 - 12.00
Excello 2093 *Chicken Hearted Woman* ....15.00 - 20.00
Lamp 8004 *Crazy With The Heart*...........................15.00 - 20.00
    8005 *Lightnin' Struck Me* ....15.00 - 20.00

BOBBY SANDERS:
Kaybo 618 *It Was You* ....30.00 - 50.00
Kent 382 *Maybe I'm Wrong* ....150.00 - up

CURLEY SANDERS (& THE SANTONES):
Concept - *Walking Blues* ....15.00 - 20.00
Jamboree 509 *Brand New Rock & Roll* ....15.00 - 20.00

HANK SANDERS:
Crest 1039 *How Much How Much*...........................15.00 - 20.00

SLIM SANDERS:
V-M 612 *All My Love* ....10.00 - 15.00

WILLIS SANDERS & THE (FABULOUS) EMBERS:
Jupiter 213 *Taking A Chance On You*......................80.00 - 130.00
    215 *I'll Be With You* ....150.00 - up
Millionaire 775 *Lovable You* ....40.00 - 70.00

BILLY SANDLIN:
Gala 110 *She's Mean* ....15.00 - 20.00

SANDMEN (See also CHUCK WILLIS):
Okeh 7052 *Somebody To Love* ....10.00 - 15.00

TOMMY SANDS:
RCA Victor 5435 *Love Pains* ....7.00 - 10.00
    5800 *Don't Drop It* ....5.00 - 8.00

FRANK SANDY & THE JACKALS:
M-G-M 12678 *Let's Go Rock 'N' Roll*....................20.00 - 30.00

RALPH SANFORD:
King 1403 *Oo-Ee-Baby* ....10.00 - 15.00

JOHNNY SARDO:
Chock Full Of Hits 104 *Romance In The Dark* ....20.00 - 30.00
Warner Bros. 5014 *I Wanna Rock* ....8.00 - 12.00

SATELLITES:
Class 234 *Heavenly Angel* ....15.00 - 20.00
Cupid 5004 *Linda Jean*...25.00 - 40.00
DMG 4001 *Dark Town Strutters' Ball* ....8.00 - 12.00
Malynn 234 *Heavenly Angel* ....8.00 - 12.00

SATINTONES:
Motown 1000 *My Beloved*.....................................30.00 - 50.00
    1006 *A Love That Can Never Be* ....40.00 - 60.00
    1006 *Angel* ....100.00 - 200.00
(Note: #1006 occurs with different titles, of which "Angel" is
    scarcer.)
    1020 *Zing Went The Strings Of My Heart* ....30.00 - 50.00
Tamla 54026 *Motor City* ....40.00 - 60.00

SATISFACTIONS:
Chesapeake 610 *We Will Walk Together*.................15.00 - 20.00

SAUCERS:
Felco 104 *Why Do I Dream* ....50.00 - 75.00
Kick 100 *Hi-Oom* (yellow label) ....25.00 - 50.00
    516 *Flossie Mae* ....50.00 - 80.00
Lynne 101 *Hello Darling*.......................................50.00 - 75.00

LITTLE BUTCHIE SAUNDERS & HIS BUDDIES:
Herald 485 *Lindy Lou* ....15.00 - 20.00
    491 *Great Big Heart* ....15.00 - 20.00

DUKE SAVAGE & ARRIBINS:
Argo 5346 *Your Love* ....15.00 - 20.00

GENE SAVAGE:
Big West 1109 *Big Machine* ....20.00 - 30.00

ASHTON SAVOY & HIS COMBO:
Hollywood 1081 *Juke Joint* ....20.00 - 30.00

JULES SAVOY & THE CHROMATICS:
Real 1320 *Would You* ....150.00 - up
    1321 *Lonesome Heart* ....150.00 - up
    1322 *Sugar Pie* ....150.00 - up
    1323 *Clap Clap* ....50.00 - 75.00

THE SAVOYS (See also SONNY BROOKS, AL SMITH):
Combo 75 *Darling Stay With Me*............................50.00 - 80.00
    81 *Evil Ways* ....30.00 - 50.00
Savoy 1188 *Say You're Mine* ....15.00 - 20.00

HENRY SAWYER & THE JUPITORS:
Planet-X 9621 *It Takes Two* ....500.00 - up

RAY SAWYER:
Sandy 1030 *Rockin' Satellite* ....15.00 - 20.00

SAXONS:
Contender 1313 *Is It True* ....20.00 - 30.00
Tampa 139 *My Love Is True* ....10.00 - 15.00

ALONZO SCALES:
Wing 90020 *My Baby Likes To Shuffle*..................20.00 - 30.00
    90049 *Hard Luck Child* ....20.00 - 30.00

SCALE-TONES:
Jay-Dee 810 *Everlasting Love* ....50.00 - 80.00

SCAMPS:
Peacock 1655 *Yes, My Baby* ....30.00 - 50.00

SCARLETS:
Cine Vista 1001 *Joannie* ....8.00 - 12.00
Fury 1036 *Truly Yours* ....10.00 - 15.00
Klik 7905 *She's Gone* ....40.00 - 70.00
Red Robin 128 *Dear One* ....50.00 - 80.00
    133 *Love Doll*...75.00 - 100.00
    135 *True Love* ....50.00 - 80.00
    138 *Kiss Me* ....100.00 - 150.00

MURRAY SCHAFF'S ARISTOCRATS:
Essex 366 *Believe Me* ....10.00 - 15.00
Sound 101 *Believe Me* ....15.00 - 20.00

STEVE SCHICKEL:
Mercury 70999 *Leave My Sideburns Be* ....10.00 - 15.00

TYRONE SCHMIDLING:
Andex 4022 *Honey Don't* ....50.00 - 75.00

THE SCHOLARS:
Cue 7927 *What Did I Do Wrong* ....7.00 - 10.00
Dot 15519 *If You Listened With Your Heart* ....7.00 - 10.00
Imperial 5449 *Beloved* ....10.00 - 15.00
    5459 *Eternally Yours* ....8.00 - 12.00
Ruby Ray 2 *Please Please* ....15.00 - 20.00

SCHOOLBOY CLEVE:
Feature 3013 *Strange Letter Blues*.........................50.00 - 80.00

SCHOOLBOYS:
Juanita 103 *Angel Of Love* ....25.00 - 50.00
Okeh 7076 *Shirley* (purple label)...........................10.00 - 15.00
    7085 *Mary* (purple label) ....10.00 - 15.00
    7090 *Pearl* (purple label) ....10.00 - 15.00

STEVE SCHULTE:
Felsted 8502 *Too Blue To Cry* ....8.00 - 12.00

DUANE SCHURB:
Enterprise 1226 *Rolly Polly* ....15.00 - 20.00

SCOOTERS:
Dawn 224 *Someday We'll Meet Again* ....60.00 - 100.00

SCOTT BROTHERS:
Fabor 117 *Yuggi Duggi*................................7.00 - 10.00

JACK SCOTT:
ABC Paramount 9818 *Baby She's Gone* ....25.00 - 40.00
   9860 *Two Timin' Woman*.......................25.00 - 40.00
Capitol (LP) 2035 *Burning Bridges*.................30.00 - 50.00
Carlton (LP) 107 *Jack Scott*.......................40.00 - 60.00
   (LP) 122 *What Am I Living For*...............50.00 - 80.00
   462, 483, 504, 514, 519 ....5.00 - 10.00
   (EP) 1070, 1071 *Presenting Jack Scott* ....50.00 - 100.00
   (EP) 1072 *Jack Scott Sings* ....50.00 - 100.00
Groove 58-0031, 58-0037, 58-0042 ....7.00 - 12.00
Guaranteed 211 *Go Wild Little Sadie* ....8.00 - 12.00
Jubilee 5606 *My Special Angel*.....................5.00 - 10.00
Sesac (LP) 4201/4202 *Soul Stirring* .... - - -
Top Rank (LP) 319, 619 *I Remember Hank Williams*
   ....50.00 - 75.00
   (LP) 326, 626 *What In The World's Come Over You*
   ....50.00 - 75.00
   2055, 2075, 2093 ....5.00 - 8.00

MABEL SCOTT:
Parrot 780 *Mabel's Blues* (red plastic) ....200.00 - up

RAY SCOTT (& THE SHADES):
Erwin 700 *Boppin' Wigwam Willie* ....150.00 - 250.00
Satellite 104 *You Drive Me Crazy* ....150.00 - 300.00
Stomper Time - *High Heel Sneakers*.................. - -
   1161 *Boy Meets Girl* ....30.00 - 50.00
Tri Ess 1001 *We Need Love* ....7.00 - 10.00

RODNEY SCOTT:
Canon 225 *Granny Went Rockin'* ....35.00 - 50.00
   231 *You're So Square* ....35.00 - 50.00

SANDY SCOTT:
Choice 5606 *Shake It Up* ....15.00 - 20.00

SHERREE SCOTT:
Robbins 101 *Whole Lotta Shakin'* ....20.00 - 30.00
Sherree Heart 1479 *Easy Payments*.....................20.00 - 30.00

TOMMY SCOTT:
Federal 10003 *Rockin' And Rollin'* ....10.00 - 15.00
   10011 *Tennessee*..............................10.00 - 15.00

LEVI SEABURY:
Blues Boy Kingdom 101 *Boogie Beat*....................40.00 - 60.00

EDDIE SEACREST:
KRC 5001 *Shakin' With A Flavor* ....15.00 - 20.00

THE SEARCHERS:
Class 223 *Wow Wow Baby* ....8.00 - 12.00

KELLY SEARS:
Quintet 104 *Barnyard Rock* ....5.00 - 8.00

DICK SEATON:
K-Ark - *Juke Box Rock* ....15.00 - 20.00

SEBASTIAN:
Mr. Maestro 801 *Darling I Do* ....20.00 - 30.00
Take 3 2002 *Darling I Do* ....8.00 - 12.00

SECRETS:
Decca 30350 *See You Next Year* ....8.00 - 12.00

NEIL SEDAKA:
Decca 30520 *Laura Lee* ....15.00 - 20.00
Guyden 2004 *Ring-A-Rockin'* ....10.00 - 15.00
Legion 133 *Ring-A-Rockin'* ....20.00 - 30.00
RCA Victor (EP) 433 *I Go Ape* ....75.00 - 100.00
   7473 *I Go Ape* ....10.00 - 15.00

THE SEDATES:
MRB 171 *Please Love Me Forever* ....10.00 - 15.00
Port 70004 *I Found* ....8.00 - 12.00
20th Century 1212 *I Found* ....10.00 - 15.00

ALVIE SELF:
Don-Ray 5960 *Let's Go Wild* ....20.00 - 30.00
   5963 *Young Singer*.....................15.00 - 25.00
Ford 1015 *Rain Dance* ....10.00 - 15.00

JIMMY SELF:
Coral 62009 *Oh Babe*.........................10.00 - 15.00

RONNIE SELF:
ABC Paramount 9714 *Pretty Bad Blues* ....35.00 - 50.00
   9768 *Sweet Love* ....35.00 - 50.00
Columbia (EP) 2149 *Ain't I'm A Dog*..........100.00 - 150.00
   40875 *Big Fool* ....15.00 - 20.00
   40989 *Ain't I'm A Dog*.................10.00 - 15.00
   41101 *Bop-A-Lena*......................10.00 - 15.00
   41166 *Date Bate* ....20.00 - 30.00
   41241 *Petrified*........................25.00 - 40.00
Decca 30958 *Big Town* ....7.00 - 10.00
   31131 *I've Been There* ....7.00 - 10.00

STEWART SELF:
Starrett 5709 *Mary Ellen*....................8.00 - 12.00

JOHNNY SELLERS:
Chance 1120 *Rock Me In The Cradle* ....40.00 - 60.00
   1123 *Mighty Lonesome* ....40.00 - 60.00
   1138 *Mirror Blues*.....................100.00 - 150.00
King 4498 *Don't Knock At My Door* ....40.00 - 80.00
   4567 *Heavyweight Mama* ....40.00 - 80.00

TOMMY SENA:
Valmont 904 *Let It Be Me*....................15.00 - 20.00

THE SENATORS:
Bristol 1916 *Scheming* ....80.00 - 130.00
Golden Crest 514 *Loretta*....................75.00 - 125.00
Winn 1917 *Wedding Bells* ....30.00 - 50.00

THE SENDERS:
Entra 711 *Pretty Little Pretty* ....40.00 - 70.00
Kent 320 *I Dream Of You* ....10.00 - 15.00
   324 *One More Kiss* ....25.00 - 40.00

SENIORS:
Excello 2130 *Why Did You Leave Me* ....10.00 - 15.00
Interlude 163 *It's Been A Long Time* .... - - -
Tetra 4446 *Evening Shadows Falling* ....40.00 - 60.00

CHARLES SENNS:
OJ 1014 *Gee Whiz Liz*........................30.00 - 50.00

THE SENSATIONAL DELLOS:
Mida 109 *Lost Love* ....15.00 - 20.00

SENSATIONS:
Argo (LP) 4022 *Let Me In*....................80.00 - 130.00
   5391 *A Part Of Me* ....7.00 - 10.00

Atco 6056 *Yes Sir That's My Baby* ....8.00 - 12.00

    6067 *Please Mr. Disc Jockey*.....................8.00 - 12.00

    6075 *My Heart Cries For You* ....8.00 - 12.00

    6083 *Little Wallflower* ....7.00 - 10.00

    6090 *My Debut To Love* ....8.00 - 12.00

THE SENTIMENTALS:

Checker 875 *I Want To Love You* ....7.00 - 10.00

Mint 801 *I Want To Love You*.........................15.00 - 20.00

    802 *Wedding Bells* ....15.00 - 20.00

    803 *I'm Your Fool Always* ....15.00 - 20.00

    805 *You're Mine* ....10.00 - 15.00

SEQUINS:

Red Robin 140 *Don't Fall In Love* ....80.00 - 130.00

SERENADERS:

Chock Full Of Hits 102 *I Wrote A Letter* ....50.00 - 75.00

De Luxe 6022 *Please, Please Forgive Me* ....100.00 - 150.00

M-G-M 12623 *Never Let Me Go* ....10.00 - 15.00

    12666 *Give Me A Girl* ....10.00 - 15.00

Red Robin 115 *I Want To Love You Baby*.............100.00 - 150.00

Riverside 4549 *Two Lovers Make One Fool* ....8.00 - 12.00

Swing Time 347 *Ain't Gonna Cry No More* ....200.00 - 300.00

Teen Life 9 *Gates Of Gold* ....150.00 - 250.00

V.I.P. 25002 *I'll Cry Tomorrow* ....15.00 - 20.00

THE SERENADES:

Chief 7002 *A Sinner In Love* ....50.00 - 80.00

SEVILLES:

Galaxy 721 *Charlena*......................................8.00 - 12.00

J-C 116 *Charlena* ....15.00 - 20.00

    118 *Louella* ....7.00 - 10.00

THE SHADES:

Aladdin 3453 *Dear Lori* ....80.00 - 130.00

THE SHADOWS:

Decca 28765 *No Use* ....50.00 - 80.00

    48307 *Tell Her* ....50.00 - 80.00

    48322 *Better Than Gold* ....50.00 - 80.00

Del-Fi 4109 *Under The Stars Of Love*....................10.00 - 15.00

Delta 1509 *There Stands The Glass*........................50.00 - 75.00

SHAKEY JAKE:

Artistic 1502 *Roll Your Money Maker*....................10.00 - 15.00

Prestige 807 *Jake's Blues* ....10.00 - 15.00

The Blues 303 *Respect Me Baby* ....7.00 - 10.00

THE SHANGRI-LAS:

Red Bird (LP) 20-101 *Leader Of The Pack* ....50.00 - 80.00

DEL SHANNON:

Big Top (LP) 1303 *Runaway*...............................40.00 - 70.00

    (LP) *Runaway* (STEREO) ....100.00 - up

    (LP) 1308 *Little Town Flirt* ....40.00 - 60.00

THE SHANTONES:

Trilyte 5001 *Come To Me* ....500.00 - up

THE SHANTONS:

Jay-Mar 164 *Lovers' March* ....100.00 - 150.00

    241 *Lucille* ....200.00 - up

Pam 112 *Why Don't You Believe Me* ....15.00 - 20.00

THE SHARPS:

Aladdin 3401 *What Will I Gain* ....15.00 - 20.00

Chess 1690 *Six Months, Three Weeks* ....8.00 - 12.00

Combo 146 *All My Love* ....30.00 - 50.00

Dot 15806 *All My Love* ....15.00 - 20.00

Jamie 1040 *Come On* .... 15.00 - 20.00

    1108 *Look At Me* .... 10.00 - 20.00

    1114 *Here's My Heart* .... 10.00 - 20.00

Lamp 2007 *Lock My Heart* .... 20.00 - 30.00

TAG 2200 *Six Months, Three Weeks* .... 20.00 - 40.00

Vik 0264 *Come On* .... 10.00 - 15.00

THE SHARPTONES/SHARP TONES:

Ace 133 *I'll Always Remember* .... 75.00 - 100.00

Post 2009 *Since I Fell For You* .... 100.00 - 150.00

LAWRENCE SHAUL:

Reed 1049 *Tutti Frutti* .... 20.00 - 40.00

BUDDY SHAW:

Starday 642 *Don't Sweep That Dirt On Me*............ 30.00 - 60.00

JOHN SHAW & THE SENSATIONAL DELLOS:

U-C 1031 *Why Did You Leave Me*...................... 100.00 - 200.00

SHA-WEEZ:

Aladdin 3170 *No One To Love Me* .... 300.00 - up

THE SH-BOOMS:

Cat 117 *Could It Be*................................... 15.00 - 20.00

JERRY SHEELY & THE VERSATILES:

Star 220 *Love Only Me*................................. 100.00 - 150.00

CHARLES (MAD DOG) SHEFFIELD:

Goldband 1045 *Mad Dog* .... 20.00 - 30.00

THE SHEIKS (See THE SHIEKS)

JIM SHELBY:

Barton 409 *I'm A Long Gone Daddy* .... 15.00 - 25.00

LeGrand 1013 *Why Should I Dance* .... - - -

THE SHELLS:

End 1022 *Sippin' Soda*................................ 50.00 - 80.00

    1050 *Whispering Winds* .... 15.00 - 20.00

Johnson 104 *Baby Oh Baby* .... 8.00 - 12.00

    106 *Pleading No More* .... 30.00 - 50.00

    107 *Explain It To Me* .... 8.00 - 12.00

    109 *Better Forget Him* .... 8.00 - 12.00

    110 *In The Dim Light Of Dark*............ 8.00 - 12.00

    112 *Sweetest One* .... 10.00 - 15.00

    119 *Deep In My Heart* .... 15.00 - 20.00

    120 *A Toast To Your Birthday* .... 15.00 - 20.00

    127 *On My Honor* .... 20.00 - 30.00

    332 *Explain It To Me* .... 10.00 - 15.00

Josie 912 *Our Wedding Day* .... 8.00 - 12.00

GARY SHELTON:

Mark 143 *Goodbye Little Darlin' Goodbye*............ 30.00 - 50.00

Mercury 71310 *Kissin' At The Drive-In* .... 8.00 - 12.00

ROSCOE SHELTON:

Excello 2146, 2167, 2170, 2176, 2181, 2192, 2198 . 5.00 - 10.00

    (LP) 8002 *Roscoe Shelton*................... 40.00 - 60.00

SHEP & THE LIMELITES:

Hull 740 *Daddy's Home* .... 20.00 - 30.00

    (LP) 1001 *Our Anniversary* .... 150.00 - 250.00

BUDDY SHEPPARD & THE HOLIDAYS:

Sabina 506 *My Love Is Real*....................... 15.00 - 20.00

    510 *That Background Sound*................ 15.00 - 20.00

SHANE SHEPPARD & THE LIMELITES:

APT 25046 *One Week From Today*.................... 15.00 - 20.00

THE SHEPPARDS:
Apex 7750 *Never Felt This Way Before* ....7.00 - 10.00
   7760 *Just Like You*..7.00 - 10.00
   7762 *Tragic*...7.00 - 10.00
PAM 1001 *Never Let Me Go* ....7.00 - 10.00
United 198 *Sherry*..50.00 - 80.00
Wes 7750 *The Glitter In Your Eyes* ....7.00 - 10.00

TONY SHERIDAN & THE BEAT BROTHERS:
Decca 31382 *My Bonnie/The Saints* ....300.00 - up
(Note: Prices as high as $1000.00 have been quoted for this Beatle
   record! Promotional copies are commoner than regular
   commercial copies.)

SHERIFF & REVELS:
Vee Jay 306 *Shambalor* ....10.00 - 15.00

SHERMAN & THE DARTS:
Fury 1014 *Remember (It's Only You And I)* ....25.00 - 40.00

BILL(Y) SHERRELL/SHERRILL (& THE DELL TONES):
Mercury 71679 *Like Makin' Love* ....5.00 - 8.00
See 1005 *Hear Her Rave On* ....15.00 - 20.00
Tyme 101 *Don't You Rock Me Daddy-O* ....20.00 - 40.00
   102 *Cadillac Baby* ....30.00 - 50.00
   104 *Kool Kat*...40.00 - 60.00
   106 *Rock On Baby* ....30.00 - 50.00

THE SHERRYS:
Guyden (LP) 503 *At The Hop With* ....75.00 - 100.00

SHERWOODS:
Johnson 111 *Little Big Horn* ....7.00 - 10.00
   121 *Sneakin' Around* ....7.00 - 10.00
Magnifico 105 *Happy Holiday* ....7.00 - 10.00

SHIEKS:
Amy 807 *Come On Back* ....75.00 - 100.00
Cat 116 *Walk That Walk* ....10.00 - 15.00
Ef-n-De 1000 *Give Me Another Chance* (red label)
   ....250.00 - up
Federal 12237 *Sentimental Heart* ....30.00 - 50.00
LeGrand 1013 *Why Should I Dance* ....7.00 - 10.00
   1016 *Too Much Alike* ....5.00 - 8.00

THE SHIELDS:
Continental 4072 *You Told A Lie*..........................200.00 - up
Dot 15805 *You Cheated*...10.00 - 20.00
   15856 *I'm Sorry Now*...10.00 - 20.00
   15940 *Play The Game Fair* ....15.00 - 20.00
Falcon 100 *You'll Be Coming Home Soon* ....40.00 - 70.00
Tender 506 *You Cheated* ....10.00 - 15.00
   513 *You Cheated*..8.00 - 12.00
   518 *I'm Sorry Now*...10.00 - 20.00
   521 *Play The Game Fair* ....10.00 - 15.00
   567 *I'm Sorry Now*..8.00 - 12.00
Transcontinental 1013 *You'll Be Coming Home Soon*
   ....50.00 - 80.00

THE SHINDIGS:
Mustang 3003 *Wolfman*..10.00 - 15.00

REESE SHIPLEY:
Valley 106 *Catfish Boogie* ....10.00 - 15.00

THE SHIRELLES:
Decca 30588 *I Met Him On A Sunday*.....................15.00 - 20.00
   30669 *My Love Is A Charm* ....10.00 - 15.00
   30761 *I Got The Message* ....10.00 - 15.00
Scepter (LP) 501 *Tonight's The Night*.....................75.00 - 100.00
   (LP) 504 *Baby It's You* ....50.00 - 80.00

   (LP) 507 *Greatest Hits*.....................................20.00 - 30.00
   1203 *Dedicated To The One I Love* ....10.00 - 15.00
   1205 *A Teardrop And A Lollipop*......................10.00 - 15.00
   1208 *Tonight's The Night* (pink & black label) . 10.00 - 15.00
   1211 *Will You Love Me Tomorrow* ....10.00 - 15.00
(Note: Above are white label)
   1220 *A Thing Of The Past* ....8.00 - 12.00
Scepter (most other issues) ....5.00 - 8.00
Tiara 6112 *I Met Him On A Sunday*.......................40.00 - 60.00

SHIRLEY & LEE:
Aladdin (LP) 807 *Let The Good Times Roll* ....200.00 - 300.00
   3153 *I'm Gone* ....25.00 - 40.00
   3173 *Baby* ....20.00 - 30.00
   3192 *So In Love* ....20.00 - 30.00
   3205 *The Proposal* ....20.00 - 30.00
   3222 *Lee Goofed* ....15.00 - 20.00
   3244 *Confessin'* ....15.00 - 20.00
   3289 *Feel So Good* ....15.00 - 20.00
   3302 *Lee's Dream* ....15.00 - 20.00
   3318, 3325, 3338, 3362, 3369, 3380, 3390..........8.00 - 12.00
Imperial (LP) 9179 *Let The Good Times Roll* ....80.00 - 120.00
Score (LP) 4023 *Let The Good Times Roll* ....100.00 - 150.00
Warwick (LP) 2028 *Let The Good Times Roll* ....50.00 - 80.00

RUFUS SHOFFNER:
American Artist - *Orbit Twist* ....35.00 - 50.00

TROY SHONDEL:
Everest (LP) 1206 *The Many Sides Of*...................50.00 - 80.00

THE SHONDELLS (See TOMMY JAMES)

SHOWCASES:
Galaxy 732 *This Love Was Real* ....200.00 - up

THE SHUFFLES:
Rayco 508 *Do You Remember* ....40.00 - 70.00

HAROLD SHUTTERS:
Golden Rod 204 *Rock 'N' Roll Mr. Moon* ....75.00 - 100.00
   300 *Bunny Honey* ....75.00 - 100.00

SHYTANS:
Bruce 110 *Skokiann* ....10.00 - 15.00

JERRY SIEFERT:
Note 10018 *Dirty White Bucks And The Tight Peg Pants*
   ....15.00 - 20.00

THE SILHOUETTES:
Ace 552 *I Sold My Heart To The Junkman*...............8.00 - 12.00
   563 *Evelyn*..50.00 - 80.00
Ember 1029 *Get A Job* ....8.00 - 12.00
   1029 *Get A Job* (78 rpm) ....20.00 - 30.00
   1032 *Headin' For The Poorhouse* ....8.00 - 12.00
   1032 *Headin' For The Poorhouse* (78 rpm)......10.00 - 20.00
   1037 *Bing Bong*..15.00 - 20.00
Grand 142 *Wish I Could Be There* ....50.00 - 75.00
Junior 391 *Get A Job*...100.00 - 200.00
(Note: Quotes as high as $500.00 have been noted for this record.)
Junior 396 *I Sold My Heart To The Junkman* ....20.00 - 30.00
   400 *Evelyn*...150.00 - 200.00
   593 *Get A Job*...20.00 - 30.00
(Note: Above should have brown label.)
   993 *Your Love* ....15.00 - 20.00
20th Fox 240 *Never*..8.00 - 12.00

BOB SILVA & THE SILVA-TONES:
Monarch 5281 *That's All I Want From You* ....10.00 - 15.00

SID SILVER:
Bakersfield 510 *Bumble Rumble* ....15.00 - 20.00

JOHNNIE SILVERS:
Sims 111 *Tuff Stuff* (blue label) ....30.00 - 50.00

SILVERTONES:
Joey 302 *Canadian Sunset* ....30.00 - 50.00

AL SIMMONS:
Dig 138 *Old Folks Boogie* ....15.00 - 20.00
　142 *You Ain't Too Old* ....15.00 - 20.00

GENE SIMMONS:
Sun 299 *Drinkin' Wine* ....80.00 - 120.00

MACK SIMMONS & HIS BOYS:
C.J. 607 *Jumping At The Cadillac* ....8.00 - 12.00

MORRIS SIMMONS:
Sandy 1027 *Shenandoah Valley* ....5.00 - 10.00

JERRY SIMMS:
RCA Victor 7483 *Dancing With A Memory* ....8.00 - 12.00

FRANK SIMON:
Audio Lab (LP) 1552 *Four Star Hits* ....25.00 - 40.00
4 Star 1647 *Sugar Plum Boogie* ....10.00 - 15.00

DONALD SIMPSON & THE ROCKENETTES:
Major 1002 *Save Me Your Love* ....75.00 - 100.00

HOKE SIMPSON:
Colonial 530 *Number One* ....10.00 - 15.00

CHUCK SIMS:
Spangle 2005 *Little Pigeon* ....15.00 - 20.00
Trend 30-000 *Little Pigeon* ....8.00 - 12.00

FRANKIE LEE SIMS:
Ace 524 *What Will Lucy Do* ....8.00 - 12.00
　527 *Hey Little Girl* ....8.00 - 12.00
　539 *I Warned You Baby* ....8.00 - 12.00
Specialty 459 *Lucy Mae Blues* ....15.00 - 25.00
　478 *I'm Long Gone* ....15.00 - 25.00
　487 *I'll Get Along Somehow* ....15.00 - 25.00
　(LP) 2124 *Lucy Mae Blues* ....75.00 - 100.00
Vin 1006 *Well Goodbye Baby* ....5.00 - 8.00

MAC SIMS:
Pacer 1201 *Drivin' Wheel* ....15.00 - 20.00

THE SINGING WANDERERS:
Decca 29298 *Wrong Party Again* ....50.00 - 75.00

BEBE SINGLETON with JEFF & THE NOTES:
Stentor 101 *The Shrine Of The Echoes* ....150.00 - up

CHARLIE SINGLETON:
Decca 48193 *Alligator Meat* ....20.00 - 40.00

EDDIE SINGLETON & THE CHROMATICS:
Amsco 3701 *Too Late* ....50.00 - 80.00
Brunswick 55080 *Too Late* ....15.00 - 25.00

JIMMY SINGLETON & THE ROYAL SATINS:
Devere 006 *Sally* ....150.00 - 200.00

SIR DOUGLAS QUINTET (See: DOUG SAHM)

BOBBY SISCO:
Chess 1650 *Go, Go, Go* ....50.00 - 75.00
Mar-Vel 111 *Honky Tonkin' Rhythm* ....40.00 - 60.00

GENE SISCO:
Dess 7001 *Grandma Rock And Roll* ....30.00 - 50.00
　7003 *Turning The Tables* ....30.00 - 50.00

THE SIX TEENS:
Flip 315 *A Casual Look* ....8.00 - 12.00
　315 *A Casual Look* (78 rpm) ....15.00 - 20.00
　317 *Send Me Flowers* ....8.00 - 12.00
　320 *My Special Guy* ....8.00 - 12.00
　322 *Arrow Of Love* ....8.00 - 12.00
　326 *My Surprise* ....8.00 - 12.00
　329 *My Secret* ....8.00 - 12.00
　333 *Love's Funny That Way* ....8.00 - 12.00
　338 *Baby-O* ....8.00 - 12.00
　346 *Heaven Knows I Love You* ....10.00 - 15.00
　350 *So Happy* ....10.00 - 15.00
　351 *Suddenly In Love* ....10.00 - 15.00
　(LP) 1001 *12 Flip Hits* (with Richard Berry, et al.)
　...50.00 - 80.00

SKEE BROTHERS:
Epic 9275 *Big Deal* ....15.00 - 20.00
Okeh 7108 *That's All She Wrote* ....15.00 - 20.00

EDDIE SKELTON:
Dixie 2011 *Keep It Swinging* ....75.00 - 100.00
Starday 294 *My Heart Gets Lonely* ....30.00 - 50.00
　315 *That's Love* ....30.00 - 50.00

BILL SKIDMORE III:
Crest 1040 *Date Bait* ....15.00 - 25.00

SKINNY DYNAMO:
Excello 2097 *So Long, So Long* ....15.00 - 25.00

MACY (SKIP) SKIPPER:
Light 2020 *Who Put The Squeeze* ....15.00 - 25.00

NORM SKYLAR:
Crest 1044 *Rock 'N' Roll Blues* ....15.00 - 20.00

SKYLARKS:
Decca 48241 *You And I* ....80.00 - 120.00

THE SKYLINERS:
Calico 103, 109, 117 ....7.00 - 12.00
　(LP) 3000 *The Skyliners* ....75.00 - 100.00
Colpix 188 *I'll Close My Eyes* ....8.00 - 12.00

THE SKYSCRAPERS:
Checker 779 *You Look Good To Me* (red plastic). 100.00 - 150.00
Mercury 70795 *I Thought You'd Care* ....10.00 - 15.00

THE SLADES:
Domino 100/200 *Baby* ....10.00 - 15.00
　500 *You Cheated* ....8.00 - 12.00
　800 *You Gambled* ....8.00 - 12.00
　900, 901 *Just You* ....10.00 - 15.00
　906 *It's Your Turn* ....10.00 - 15.00
　1000 *You Must Try* ....10.00 - 15.00
Liberty 55118 *Baby* ....7.00 - 10.00

SLICK SLAVIN:
Imperial 5540 *Speed Crazy* ....10.00 - 15.00

SLIM HARPO (See HARPO)

SLY FOX:
Spark 108 *Hoo-Doo Say* ....30.00 - 50.00
　112 *My Four Women* ....30.00 - 50.00

SMART TONES:
Herald 529 *Bob-O-Link* ....15.00 - 30.00

AL SMITH:
Goldband 1092 *If I Don't See You* ....8.00 - 12.00

AL SMITH & THE SAVOYS:
Combo 90 *Chop Chop Boom* ....40.00 - 60.00

AL SMITH COMBO (See HAZEL McCOLLUM with THE EL DORADOS)

ARTHUR SMITH:
M-G-M (LP) 236 (10 inch) *Foolish Questions* ....50.00 - 75.00
   (LP) 533 (10 inch) *Fingers On Fire* ....50.00 - 75.00
   (LP) 3301 (10 inch) *Specials* ....40.00 - 60.00
   (LP) 3525 *Fingers On Fire* ....40.00 - 60.00
   12544 *Teen-Aged Rebel* ....10.00 - 15.00

BILLY SMITH:
Red Head - *Tell Me Baby* ....- - -

BOBBY SMITH (& SPINNERS):
Fox 104 *She's Gone From Me* ....40.00 - 60.00
Tri-Phi 1018 *She Don't Love Me* ....8.00 - 12.00

BUDDY SMITH:
Hanover 4533 *Tennessee* ....10.00 - 15.00

CARL SMITH:
Columbia (LP) 959 *Sunday Down South* ....25.00 - 40.00
   (LP) 1022 *Smith's The Name* ....25.00 - 40.00
   (LP) 1172 *Let's Live A Little* ....25.00 - 40.00
   (LP) 2579 (10 inch) ....30.00 - 50.00
   (LP) 9023 (10 inch) *Soft And Tenderly* ....30.00 - 50.00
   (LP) 9025 (10 inch) *Sentimental Songs* ....30.00 - 50.00
   (EP) 9591, 10222 ....20.00 - 30.00

CHESTER SMITH:
Decca 30603 *You Gotta Move* ....10.00 - 15.00

DAPPA SMITH:
Peach 709 *China Doll* ....- - -

DAYTON SMITH:
Warrior 501 *What Will The Answer Be* ....15.00 - 20.00

FLOYD SMITH & THE MONTCLAIRS:
Fortune 540 *This Is A Miracle* ....15.00 - 25.00

GENE SMITH:
Rem 458 *I'm Gone* ....15.00 - 20.00

(LITTLE) GEORGE SMITH (& HIS HARMONICA):
Carolyn 1420 *Nobody Knows* ....7.00 - 10.00
J&M 001 *Go Ahead On Women* ....25.00 - 40.00
RPM 434 *Telephone Blues* ....20.00 - 30.00
   442 *Blues Stay Away* ....15.00 - 20.00
   456 *Love Life* ....15.00 - 20.00
   478 *You Don't Love Me* ....10.00 - 15.00

HANK SMITH & ROCKATUNES:
Rock-A-Tune 1012 *Rock 'N' Roll Hep Cat* ....50.00 - 80.00

HENRY SMITH:
Dot 1220 *Good Rocking Mama* ....30.00 - 50.00

HUEY (PIANO) SMITH & HIS CLOWNS:
Ace (EP) 104 *Having Fun With Huey Smith* ....30.00 - 60.00
   530 *Rocking Pneumonia & The Boogie Woogie Flu* (78 rpm)
   ....40.00 - 60.00
   538 *Just A Lonely Clown* (78 rpm) ....15.00 - 30.00
   (LP) 1004 *Having A Good Time* ....40.00 - 80.00
   (LP) 1015 *For Dancing* ....40.00 - 80.00
   (LP) 1027 *'Twas The Night Before Christmas* ...50.00 - 100.00
   8008 *Quiet As It's Kept* ....- - -

KENNY SMITH:
Rural Rhythm 507 *Walkin' By My Lonesome* ....15.00 - 20.00
   508 *You'll Come To Me* ....15.00 - 20.00

L. C. SMITH & THE SOUTHERN PLAYBOYS:
Wango (unnumbered) *Radio Boogie* ....50.00 - 80.00

LARRY SMITH (See THE CASTROES)

LENDON SMITH with THE JESTERS:
Meteor 5030 *Lost Love* ....40.00 - 60.00

MACK ALLEN SMITH:
Statue 602 *Such A Night* ....8.00 - 12.00
   607 *Mean Old Frisco* ....8.00 - 12.00

RAY SMITH (See also PAT CUPP):
Infinity 007 *Let Yourself Go* ....7.00 - 10.00
Judd (LP) 701 *Travelin' With Ray* ....100.00 - 150.00
Sun 298 *Right Behind You Baby* ....20.00 - 30.00
   308 *Why Why Why* ....15.00 - 20.00
   319 *Rockin' Bandit* ....10.00 - 15.00
   372 *Travelin' Salesman* ....7.00 - 10.00
   375 *Candy Doll* ....7.00 - 10.00
Tollie 9029 *Did We Have A Party* ....10.00 - 15.00

ROBERT SMITH:
Camelia 100 *Traveling Sam* ....20.00 - 30.00

ROBERT CURTIS SMITH:
Bluesville (LP) 1064 *Clarksville Blues* ....25.00 - 40.00

RONNIE/RONNY SMITH:
Brunswick 55137 *Lookie, Lookie, Lookie* ....10.00 - 15.00
Hamilton 50003 *My Babe* ....7.00 - 10.00
Imperial 5667 *Long Time No Love* ....7.00 - 10.00
   5679 *I Hear You Knocking* ....7.00 - 10.00

SAMMY SMITH:
Wee Rebel 102 *Alaska Rock* ....30.00 - 40.00

SHELBY SMITH:
Rebel 728 *Rockin' Mama* ....40.00 - 80.00
Smitty 55783 *What's On Your Mind* ....100.00 - 150.00

WARREN SMITH:
Sun 239 *Rock 'N' Roll Ruby* ....25.00 - 40.00
   250 *Ubangi Stomp* ....25.00 - 40.00
   268 *Miss Froggie* ....20.00 - 30.00
   286 *I've Got Love If You Want It* ....25.00 - 40.00
   314 *Sweet Sweet Girl* ....15.00 - 20.00

LONNIE SMITHSON:
Starday 330 *Me And The Blues* ....40.00 - 60.00

SMOKEY JOE:
Flip 228 *Signifying Monkey* ....40.00 - 60.00
Sun 228 *Signifying Monkey* ....75.00 - 100.00

SMOOTHTONES:
Jem 412 *Bring Back Your Love To Me* ....25.00 - 40.00
Okeh 7078 *Little Cupid* ....8.00 - 12.00

SMOKEY SMOTHERS:
Federal 12385, 12395, 12405, 12420, 12441,
   12466, 12488, 12503 ....5.00 - 10.00
King (LP) 779 ....50.00 - 80.00

THE SNAPPERS:
20th Fox 148 *If There Were* ....5.00 - 8.00

LESLIE SNEED:
Cascade 103 *Oh, Baby Doll* ....15.00 - 25.00

EDDIE SNOW:
Sun 226 *Ain't That Right* ....80.00 - 120.00

HANK SNOW:
RCA Victor (LP) 113 *Just Keep A-Movin'* ....20.00 - 30.00
   (LP) 1156 *Old Doc Brown* ....20.00 - 30.00

(LP) 1233 *Country Classics*	15.00 -	20.00
(LP) 1419 *Country & Western Jamboree*	15.00 -	20.00
(LP) 1435 *Country Guitar Vol. 2*	15.00 -	20.00
(LP) 3026 (10 inch) *Hank Snow*	20.00 -	30.00
(LP) 3070 (10 inch) *Hank Snow Sings*	15.00 -	25.00
(LP) 3131 (10 inch) *Hank Snow Salutes Jimmy Rodgers*	20.00 -	30.00
(LP) 3267 (10 inch) *Country Guitar*	15.00 -	25.00

VALAIDA SNOW:

Chess 1555 *If You Don't Mean It*	20.00 -	30.00

THE SOLATAIRES/SOLITAIRES:

Argo 5316 *Please Kiss This Letter*	8.00 -	12.00
Old Town 1000 *Blue Valentine*	100.00 -	150.00
1006 *Please Remember My Heart*	75.00 -	100.00
1006/1007 *Please Remember My Heart*	80.00 -	130.00

(Note: Later issues have #1006 on both sides.)
(Above, pressed of translucent red vinyl, bring substantially higher prices.)

Old Town 1008 *Lonely*	80.00 -	130.00
1010 *I Don't Stand A Ghost Of A Chance*	80.00 -	130.00
1012 *My Dear*	75.00 -	100.00
1014 *The Wedding*	40.00 -	70.00
1015 *Magic Rose*	40.00 -	70.00
1019 *The Honeymoon*	40.00 -	60.00
1026 *The Angels Sang*	30.00 -	60.00
1032 *Give Me One More Chance*	50.00 -	80.00
1034 *Please Kiss This Letter*	20.00 -	30.00
1044 *I Really Love You So*	75.00 -	100.00
1049 *No More Sorrows*	25.00 -	50.00
1059 *Please Remember My Heart*	15.00 -	20.00
1066 *Embraceable You*	15.00 -	20.00
1071 *Light A Candle In The Chapel*	15.00 -	20.00
1096 *Lonesome Lover*	15.00 -	20.00
1139 *The Time Is Here*	15.00 -	20.00

KING SOLOMON:

Big Town 102 *Mean Train*	30.00 -	50.00

SOLOTONES:

Excello 2060 *Front Page Blues*	50.00 -	80.00

SONICS:

Checker 922 *You Made Me Cry*	8.00 -	12.00
Groove 0112 *As I Live On*	50.00 -	80.00
Harvard 801 *This Broken Heart*	75.00 -	100.00
922 *You Made Me Cry*	15.00 -	20.00
X-Tra 107 *Once In A Lifetime*	250.00 -	up

SONNETS:

Herald 477 *Please Won't You Call Me*	15.00 -	30.00

SONNY GUITAR:

Yucca 136 *Betty Lou*	10.00 -	15.00

SONS OF THE PIONEERS:

Camden (LP) 413 *Wagons West*	15.00 -	25.00
RCAVictor (LP) 1130 *Favorites*	20.00 -	30.00
(LP) 1431 *How Great Thou Art*	20.00 -	30.00
(LP) 1483 *One Man's Songs*	20.00 -	30.00
(LP) 3032 (10 inch)	20.00 -	30.00
(LP) 3095 (10 inch)	20.00 -	30.00
(LP) 3162 (10 inch) *Western Classics*	20.00 -	30.00

SOOTHERS:

Port 70041 *I Believe In You*	10.00 -	15.00

THE SOPHOMORES:

Chord 1302 *What Can I Do*	15.00 -	20.00

Dawn 216 *Cool Cool Baby*	8.00 -	12.00
218 *I Get A Thrill*	8.00 -	12.00
223 *I Left My Sugar*	8.00 -	12.00
225 *Is There Someone For Me*	8.00 -	12.00
228 *If I Should Lose Your Love*	8.00 -	12.00
237 *Each Time I Hold You*	8.00 -	12.00
Epic 9259 *Charades*	5.00 -	8.00
Seeco (LP) 451 *The Sophomores*	50.00 -	80.00

THE SOUL STIRRERS featuring SAM COOKE:

Specialty (LP) 2106	40.00 -	70.00

SOUNDS:

Modern 975 *So Unnecessary*	15.00 -	25.00
981 *Sweet Sixteen*	15.00 -	20.00
Sarg 172 *Life*	15.00 -	20.00
181 *My Pillow Of Dreams*	15.00 -	20.00

SOUVENIERS:

Inferno 2001 *I Could Have Danced All Night*	25.00 -	40.00

RED SOVINE:

Decca 30239 *Juke Joint Johnny*	8.00 -	12.00

SPADES:

Major 1007 *Close To You*	15.00 -	30.00

DICK SPAIN:

Oasis 1001 *Straw Broom Boogie*	30.00 -	50.00

SPANIELS:

Chance 1141 *Baby It's You*	150.00 -	200.00
1141 *Baby It's You* (red plastic)	400.00 -	up
Neptune 125 *For Sentimental Reasons*	7.00 -	10.00
Vee Jay 101 *Baby It's You* (red plastic)	500.00 -	up
103 *The Bells Ring Out*	75.00 -	100.00
Vee Jay 103 *The Bells Ring Out* (red plastic)	300.00 -	up
107 *Goodnite Sweetheart, Goodnite*	50.00 -	80.00
107 *same, but red plastic*	200.00 -	up
116 *Let's Make Up* (red plastic)	200.00 -	up
116 *Let's Make Up* (black plastic)	30.00 -	50.00
131 *Don'cha Go*	20.00 -	30.00
131 *Don'cha Go* (red plastic)	200.00 -	up
154 *Painted Picture*	20.00 -	30.00
178 *False Love*	40.00 -	60.00
189 *Dear Heart*	40.00 -	60.00
202 *Since I Fell For You*	50.00 -	80.00
229 *You Gave Me Peace Of Mind*	20.00 -	30.00
246 *I.O.U.*	15.00 -	20.00
257 *I Need Your Kisses*	15.00 -	20.00
264 *I Lost You*	15.00 -	20.00
278 *Tina*	15.00 -	20.00
290 *Stormy Weather*	15.00 -	20.00
301 *Heart And Soul*	15.00 -	20.00
310 *Trees*	15.00 -	20.00
328 *100 Years From Today*	20.00 -	30.00
342 *People Will Say We're In Love*	40.00 -	60.00
350 *Bus Fare Home*	15.00 -	20.00
(LP) 1002 *Goodnight, It's Time To Go* (maroon label)	100.00 -	150.00
(LP) 1002 (black label)	50.00 -	75.00
(LP) 1024 *The Spaniels*	100.00 -	150.00

OTIS SPANN:

Checker 807 *It Must Have Been The Devil*	75.00 -	100.00

THE SPARKLETONES:

ABC Paramount 9837 *Boppin' Rock Boogie*	5.00 -	8.00
Paris 542 *Are You From Dixie?*	7.00 -	10.00

SPARKS:
Hull 723 *Danny Boy* ....80.00 - 130.00
   724 *Adreann*..................................20.00 - 30.00
RPM 417 *Make A Little Love* ....75.00 - 100.00

SPARKS OF RHYTHM:
Apollo 479 *Don't Love You Any More* ....50.00 - 80.00
   481 *Stars Are In The Sky* ....50.00 - 80.00
   541 *Everybody Rock And Go* ....15.00 - 20.00

JERRY SPARKS:
Fidelity 4058 *My Tears*................................7.00 - 10.00

SPARROWS:
Davis 456-45 *Love Me Tender* ....80.00 - 130.00
Jay Dee 783 *Tell Me Baby*......................100.00 - 150.00
   790 *I'll Be Lovin' You*...........................80.00 - 130.00

MERLE SPEARS:
Whit 711 *Gonna Move*.................................7.00 - 10.00

SPECK & DOYLE:
Syrup Bucket 1000 *Big Noise, Bright Lights*...........35.00 - 50.00

PHIL SPECTOR:
Phillies (LP) 100 *The Phil Spector Spectacular* (promotional, no jacket) ....300.00 - up
(Note: Prices of up to $4500.00 have been quoted for this LP!)

RONNIE SPEEKS & THE ELRODS:
King 5548 *What Is Your Technique*........................10.00 - 15.00

THE SPEIDELS:
Monte Carlo 101 *Oh Baby*......................................50.00 - 80.00

SPELLBINDERS:
Date 1556 *Since I Don't Have You* ....5.00 - 8.00

JIMMY SPELLMAN:
Dot 15607 *Doggonit* ....10.00 - 15.00
Viv 1005 *Lover Man*....................................8.00 - 12.00

SPENCER & SPENCER:
Gone 5053 *Stagger Lawrence* ....7.00 - 10.00

BOB SPENCER:
Epic 9139 *Roll, Hot Rod, Roll* ....15.00 - 20.00

CARL SPENCER & THE MELLOWS:
Candlelight 1012 *Farewell, Farewell*......................30.00 - 50.00

SONNY SPENCER:
Memo 17984 *Gilee* ....7.00 - 10.00

SPIDERS:
Imperial 5265 *I Didn't Want To Do It* ....40.00 - 60.00
   5280 *I'll Stop Crying* ....30.00 - 50.00
   5291 *I'm Slippin' In* ....30.00 - 50.00
(Note: Above are blue label with script letters.)
Imperial 5305 *The Real Thing* ....25.00 - 40.00
   5318 *She Keeps Me Wondering* ....25.00 - 40.00
   5331 *That's Enough* ....20.00 - 30.00
   5344 *Am I The One* ....20.00 - 30.00
   5354 *Bells In My Heart*............................15.00 - 25.00
   5366, 5376, 5393, 5405, 5423, 5714 ....8.00 - 15.00
   (LP) 9140 *I Didn't Want To Do It* ....80.00 - 130.00

SPIEDELS:
Crosley 201 *Dear Joan* ....20.00 - 30.00

THE SPINNERS (See also BOBBY SMITH):
Capitol 3955 *Lovers Prayer*..............................8.00 - 12.00
Rhythm 125 *My Love And Your Love*....................150.00 - 250.00

Tri-Phi 1001 *That's What Girls Are Made For* ....5.00 - 8.00
   1004 *Love (I Am So Glad I Found You)* ....5.00 - 8.00
   1007 *What Did She Use?* ....5.00 - 8.00
   1013 *I've Been Hurt*..............................5.00 - 8.00

SPLENDORS:
Jano 004 *An Island Called Romance* ....20.00 - 30.00
Taurus 101 *The Golden Years*........................40.00 - 60.00
   102 *Who Can It Be* ....10.00 - 15.00

THE SPORTTONES:
Munich 101 *So Sincere* ....250.00 - up

THE SPOTLIGHTERS:
Aladdin 3436 *Whisper* ....30.00 - 50.00
   3441 *This Is My Story* ....15.00 - 30.00
Imperial 5342 *It's Cold* ....50.00 - 80.00

SPROUTS:
Spangle 2002 *Teen Billy Baby* ....15.00 - 20.00

TOMMY SPURLIN:
Art 109 *One-Eyed Sam* ....50.00 - 80.00
Perfect 109 *Hang Loose* ....50.00 - 80.00

THE SPUTNIKS:
Class 217 *My Love Is Gone*............................15.00 - 20.00
   222 *Wait A Little While* ....10.00 - 15.00
Pam Mar 601 *My Love Is Gone* ....80.00 - 120.00

SPY DELS/SPYDELS:
Addit 1220 *We're In Love*..............................8.00 - 12.00
Cracker Jack 4001 *We'll Be Together*....................7.00 - 10.00
MZ 112 *No More Teasing*...............................10.00 - 15.00

SQUIRES:
Aladdin 3360 *Dreamy Eyes* ....20.00 - 30.00
Boss 2120 *It's Time* ....200.00 - up
Combo 35 *Let's Give Love A Try* ....100.00 - 150.00
   42 *My Little Girl** ....- - -
(*May exist in 78 rpm format only.)........................- - -
Congress 223 *Joyce*...................................20.00 - 30.00
Dice 478 *Every Word Of This Song* ....75.00 - 100.00
Gee 1082 *So Many Tears Ago*.........................10.00 - 15.00
Herald 580 *Why Should I Suffer*......................10.00 - 15.00
Kicks 1 *Lucy Lou* ....300.00 - up
Mambo 105 *Sindy* ....20.00 - 40.00
Vita 105 *Sindy*..25.00 - 40.00
   113 *Me And My Deal* ....20.00 - 30.00
   116 *Heavenly Angel* ....30.00 - 50.00
   128 *Breath Of Air* ....30.00 - 50.00

CLYDE STACY:
Bullseye 1004 *Baby Shame* ....8.00 - 12.00
   1008 *Honky Tonk Hardwood Floor*................15.00 - 20.00
   1014 *You Want Love* ....7.00 - 10.00
Candlelight 1015 *Hoy Hoy* ....15.00 - 20.00
   1018 *Dream Boy* ....10.00 - 15.00
G & H 101 *Baby Shame* ....10.00 - 15.00
Len 1015 *You're Satisfied*..............................10.00 - 15.00

SONNY STAFFORD:
Blue Moon 476 *Record Hop Blues* ....40.00 - 60.00

JOHNNY STANDLEY:
Magnolia 1003 *Rock & Roll Must Go*...................10.00 - 15.00

DOUG STANFORD:
D 1034 *Won't You Tell On Me* ....8.00 - 12.00

THE STANLEY BROTHERS:
Mercury (LP) 20349 *Country Pickin' And Singin'*. 20.00 - 40.00

RAY STANLEY:
Argo 5280 *Over A Coke* (ship logo label) ....10.00 - 15.00
Zephyr 011 *Pushin'* ....10.00 - 15.00
　022 *My Lovin' Baby*...10.00 - 15.00

STAR COMBO:
Skippy 102 *Mr. Rock And Roll* ....20.00 - 30.00

THE STARFIRES:
Atomic 1912 *Love Will Break Your Heart* ....8.00 - 12.00
Bargain 5003 *Love Will Break Your Heart*............15.00 - 20.00
Bernice 201 *Yearning For You* ....80.00 - 120.00
D & H 200 *These Foolish Things* ....20.00 - 30.00
Decca 30730 *Three Roses* ....10.00 - 15.00
　30916 *Love Is Here To Stay*..................................10.00 - 15.00

JOHNNY STARK:
Crystalette 709 *Roll Baby Roll* ....20.00 - 30.00
　713 *Cold Coffee* ....20.00 - 30.00
　715 *Rockin' Billy* ....20.00 - 30.00

DOC STARKES:
Linda 109 *Rockin' To School* ....30.00 - 50.00

THE STARLARKS:
Ancho 102 *Heavenly Father*.....................................40.00 - 60.00
Elm 001 *The Fountain Of Love* ....250.00 - up
Ember 1013 *The Fountain Of Love* ....15.00 - 20.00

THE STARLIGHTERS:
End 1031 *It's Twelve O'Clock*..................................50.00 - 75.00
　1049 *I Cried* ....15.00 - 20.00
　1072 *A Story Of Love*...50.00 - 75.00
Hi-Q 5016 *Zoom* ....15.00 - 20.00
Sun Coast 1001 *Until You Return* ....250.00 - up

STARLINGS:
Dawn 212 *I'm Just A Crying Fool*.........................150.00 - 200.00
　213 *I Gotta Go Now* ....75.00 - 100.00
Josie 760 *My Plea For Love* ....150.00 - 200.00

THE STARLITERS:
Combo 73 *Arline* (red label) ....80.00 - 130.00

STARLITES (See also JACKIE & THE STARLITES):
Ember 1011 *They Call Me A Dreamer* ....20.00 - 30.00
　1021 *Tears Are Just For Fools* ....15.00 - 25.00
Fury 1034 *Valarie* ....15.00 - 20.00
　1045 *Silver Lining* ....15.00 - 20.00
Peak 5000 *Missing You* ....40.00 - 60.00

ANDY STARR:
Arcade 115 *I Love My Baby* ....30.00 - 50.00
M-G-M 12263 *Rockin' Rollin' Stone* ....30.00 - 50.00
　12315 *She's A-Goin' Jessie* ....30.00 - 40.00
　12364 *Round And Round* ....50.00 - 75.00
　12421 *No Room For Your Kind*...............................30.00 - 40.00

BILLY STARR:
Imperial 8186 *Hound Dog* ....20.00 - 30.00
Twy-Lite 750 *I Wanta* ....40.00 - 80.00

FRANK/FRANKIE STARR:
Holiday Inn 104 *Knees Shakin'* ....15.00 - 20.00
Lin 5009 *Dig Them Squeaky Shoes* ....30.00 - 50.00
　5013 *Tell Me Why* ....8.00 - 12.00
　5033 *Me & The Fool*...8.00 - 12.00
Sims 212 *Elevator Baby* ....8.00 - 12.00
Star-Win 7003 *Elevator Boogie*...............................15.00 - 20.00

JIMMY STARR:
Debbie 101 *Oooh Crazy* ....7.00 - 10.00

JIMMY STAYTON:
Blue Hen 220 *Hot Hot Mama* ....100.00 - 150.00
　224 *You're Gonna Treat Me Right* ....100.00 - 150.00

SONNY STEELE:
Republic 2020 *Mine Mine Mine*..............................20.00 - 30.00

PAUL STEFEN & THE ROYAL LANCERS:
Citation 5004 *Say Mama*...10.00 - 15.00

STEVE STEPHENS:
Rebel 1314 *Weird Session* ....15.00 - 25.00

BIG WILL STEPHENS & T-MEN:
Corvet 1013 *Saturday Night* ....15.00 - 20.00

N. A. STEPHENSON:
Westwood 201 *Boogie Woogie Country Girl* ....150.00 - 200.00

DEBBIE STEVENS:
APT 25027 *If You Can't Rock Me* ....15.00 - 20.00

JULIE STEVENS & THE PREMIERS:
Dig 115 *Blue Mood*..8.00 - 12.00

RAY STEVENS:
Captil 4030 *Cat Pants* ....10.00 - 15.00

SCOTT STEVENS:
APT 25031 *Why Why Why*...10.00 - 15.00

SONNY STEVENSON:
Onda 111 *Bessie Lou* ....- - -

CHARLIE STEWART & THE GEMTONES:
Solid Gold 779 *Paradise Of Love* ....20.00 - 40.00

DON STEWART:
DAD 104 *More Than Words Can Tell*.........................- - -

FRANKLIN STEWART:
Lu 501 *That Long Black Train*..............................100.00 - 150.00

GENE STEWART:
King 5124 *Oh Baby, Dance With Me* ....10.00 - 15.00

REDD STEWART:
Audio Lab (LP) 1528 *Redd Stewart Sings* ....25.00 - 40.00

SANDY STEWART:
Atco 6137 *Playmates* ....5.00 - 8.00

VERNON STEWART:
Peach 751 *Mean Mean Baby*....................................20.00 - 30.00

WYNN STEWART:
Jackpot 48005 *Come On* ....8.00 - 12.00

ARBEE STIDHAM:
Abco 100 *Meet Me Halfway* ....25.00 - 40.00
　107 *When I Find My Baby* ....25.00 - 40.00
Checker 778 *I Don't Play* ....40.00 - 60.00 *
(* Copies pressed of red translucent vinyl bring considerably more.)
RCA Victor 47-4951 *I Found Out For Myself* ....15.00 - 20.00
　50-0003 *I Found Out For Myself*...........................20.00 - 30.00
　50-0024 *Falling Blues*...20.00 - 30.00
　50-0037 *Barbecue Lounge* ....20.00 - 30.00
　50-0083 *Any Time Ring My Bell* ....20.00 - 30.00
　50-0093 *Squeeze Me Baby*.......................................20.00 - 30.00
　50-0101 *You'll Be Sorry* ....20.00 - 30.00
(Note: #50-0003 through 50-0101 are orange plastic.)
States 164 *I Stayed Away Too Long*.......................50.00 - 80.00

STINTON BROS.:
Arko - *Diggin' That Rock And Roll* ....- - -

GARY STITES:
Carlton 508 *Shine That Ring*..7.00 - 12.00
    516 *Hey Little Girl*...7.00 - 12.00
    521 *Without Your Love*.................................7.00 - 12.00
    525 *Lawdy Miss Clawdy*..............................7.00 - 12.00
    529 *Hey, Hey*..7.00 - 12.00

TINY STOKES:
Big T 235 *Blackfoot Boogie*........................10.00 - 15.00

THE STOMPERS:
Gone 5120 *Forgive Me*..............................50.00 - 80.00
Landa 684 *Foolish One*.................................5.00 - 8.00
Souvenir 1003 *Blue Moon Of Kentucky*.................15.00 - 20.00

DOUG STONE:
Cee Dee 101 *Memphis Yodel Blues*.........................10.00 - 15.00

JEFF STONE:
Sarg 151 *Everybody Rock*.............................30.00 - 40.00

JERRY STONE with THE FOUR DOTS:
Freedom 44002 *My Baby (She Loves Me)*...............10.00 - 15.00
    44005 *Pleading For Your Love*..........................10.00 - 15.00

JIMMY STONE:
Gone 5001 *Found*..30.00 - 50.00

LAWRENCE STONE:
Dig 130 *Everytime*...7.00 - 10.00

BILLY STORM (See also THE VALIANTS):
Barbary Coast 1001 *The Way To My Heart*............40.00 - 60.00
Buena Vista (LP) 3315 *Billy Storm* (STEREO) ....100.00 - 150.00
Famous (LP) 504 *This Is The Night*........................50.00 - 80.00

WARREN STORM:
Nasco 6015 *Mama Mama Mama* (78 rpm).............15.00 - 20.00
    6025 *Troubles, Troubles*.....................................8.00 - 12.00
    6028 *So Long, So Long*......................................8.00 - 12.00
    6031 *Birmingham Jail*.......................................8.00 - 12.00
Rocko 512 *Oh Oh Baby*..................................8.00 - 12.00
Zynn 1019 *Blues Stop Knocking*..................... - -
    1021 *This Should Go On Forever*..................... - -
    1024 *Let Me Know*.. - -

STORMY HERMAN & HIS MIDNIGHT RAMBLERS:
Dooto 358 *Bad Luck*................................15.00 - 20.00

CARL STORY:
Columbia 21250 *Step It Up And Go*.........................8.00 - 12.00

JIMMY STRANGE & FLAHERTY'S CARAVAN:
Jenn 101 *Real Gone Daddy*.....................................25.00 - 35.00

STRANGERS:
King 4697 *I've Got Eyes*..40.00 - 80.00
    4709 *Blue Flowers*..150.00 - 200.00
    4728 *Hoping You'll Understand*.........................80.00 - 120.00
    4745 *Get It One More Time*.............................50.00 - 80.00
    4766 *Dreams Come True*..................................75.00 - 100.00
    4821 *Without A Friend*...................................50.00 - 80.00
Titan 1702, 1703, 1704...7.00 - 10.00

RON STRAWN:
Eko 503 *Drivin'*..50.00 - 80.00

RICHARD STREET & THE DISTANTS:
Harmon 1002 *Answer Me*........................15.00 - 20.00
Thelma TY 4 2282 *Answer Me*..............................20.00 - 30.00

JOHNNY STRICKLAND:
Roulette 4119 *She's Mine*.......................10.00 - 15.00
    4147 *I've Heard That Line Before*..........................8.00 - 12.00

    4221 *Sweet Talkin' Baby*.....................................8.00 - 12.00
    4335 *Fool's Hall Of Fame*...................................8.00 - 12.00

STRIDERS:
Apollo 480 *Hesitating Fool*...........................80.00 - 130.00

BOBBY STRIGO:
Renown 109 *The Pad*.....................................8.00 - 12.00

STRIKES:
Imperial 5443 *If You Can't Rock Me*.....................10.00 - 15.00
    5446 *Rockin'*...10.00 - 15.00
Lin 5006 *If You Can't Rock Me*...........................15.00 - 20.00

HENRY STROGIN:
Hank 5002 *Good Love*..................................8.00 - 12.00

STROLLERS:
Cub 9060 *Favors*...8.00 - 12.00
States 163 *In Your Dreams*..................................50.00 - 75.00

BARRETT STRONG:
Anna 1111 *Money* (78 rpm)....................................200.00 - up
(Note: The existence of this very late 78 RPM issue has been verified.)

NOLAN STRONG & THE DIABLOS:
Fortune 509/510 *An Old Fashioned Girl*...............15.00 - 20.00
    511 *The Wind*..15.00 - 20.00
    516 *Daddy Lookin' Strong*.............................15.00 - 20.00
    518 *Jump, Shake and Move*............................15.00 - 20.00
    519 *You Are*..15.00 - 20.00
    522 *Teardrop From Heaven* ....15.00 - 20.00
    525 *Can't We Talk This Over* ....10.00 - 15.00
    531 *I Am With You*.......................................15.00 - 20.00
    544 *Blue Moon* ....15.00 - 20.00
    553 *I Really Love You*....................................10.00 - 15.00
    556 *It's Because Of You*..................................10.00 - 15.00
    569 *You're Presentable*...................................10.00 - 15.00
    841 *Harriet*...20.00 - 30.00
    (LP) 8012 *Fortune Of Hits*.............................50.00 - 80.00
    (LP) 8015 *Mind Over Matter*..........................50.00 - 80.00
(Note: Fortune records were extensively reissued and repressed.)

RAY STRONG:
Rocket 754 *You're Gonna Reap What You Sow*......... - -

STUDENTS:
Checker 902 *I'm So Young*...............................8.00 - 12.00
    1004 *My Vow To You*......................................8.00 - 12.00
Note 10012 *I'm So Young* ....75.00 - 100.00
    10019 *My Vow To You*..................................75.00 - 100.00
Red Top 100 *My Heart Is An Open Door*...............50.00 - 80.00

GENE STUMP & BILL SWAIN:
Clix 830 *Stream Of Love*....................................... - -

THE STYLE KINGS:
Sotoplay 0011 *Kissing Behind The Moon* ....15.00 - 20.00
    0014 *House Party* ....10.00 - 15.00

STYLERS:
Kicks 2 *Gentle As A Teardrop* ....150.00 - 200.00
Gordy 7018 *Pushing Up Daisies* ....10.00 - 15.00

THE STYLISTS:
Rose 17 *One Room*..10.00 - 20.00

THE SUADES:
Spinning 6011 *Wrong Yo-Yo* ....15.00 - 20.00

SUBURBANS (See also ANN COLE):
Baton 227 *TV Baby* ....15.00 - 20.00
Gee 1076 *Love Me* ....8.00 - 12.00
Port 70011 *Alphabet Of Love*...............................10.00 - 15.00

SUGAR BOY (& HIS CANE-CUTTERS):
Checker 783 *Overboard* ....25.00 - 40.00
    787 *Jock-O-Mo* ....20.00 - 30.00
    795 *I Bowed On My Knees* ....15.00 - 20.00

SUGARCANE & HIS VIOLIN:
Eldo 103 *They Say You Never Can Miss* ....8.00 - 12.00

SUGARTONES/SUGAR-TONES:
Benida 5021 *Scandal* ....40.00 - 70.00
Cannon 391 *How Can I Pretend* ....10.00 - 15.00
    392 *How Can You Forget So Soon* ....10.00 - 15.00
Okeh 6814 *Your Fool Again* ....75.00 - 100.00
    6877 *Wishin'* ....80.00 - 130.00
    6992 *I Just Want To Dream* ....80.00 - 120.00

BRAD SUGGS:
Meteor 5034 *Bop, Baby, Bop* (black label)..............50.00 - 80.00

JERRY SULLIVAN:
Vee 100 *Ella Mae* ....20.00 - 30.00

SULTANS:
DeCade 101 *God Made An Angel* ....20.00 - 30.00
Duke 125 *How Deep Is The Ocean* ....30.00 - 50.00
    133 *I Cried My Heart Out* ....30.00 - 50.00
    135 *What Makes Me Feel This Way* ....30.00 - 50.00
    178 *If I Could Tell* ....15.00 - 20.00
Jam 103 *Toss In My Sleep* ....8.00 - 12.00
    107 *How Far Does A Friendship Go?* ....7.00 - 10.00
    113 *Don't Tie Me Down* ....7.00 - 10.00
Jubilee 5054 *You Captured My Heart* (78 rpm*) ...75.00 - 100.00
*(unknown in 45 rpm format)
    5077 *Don't Be Angry* ....300.00 - up
Tilt 782 *It'll Be Easy* ....10.00 - 15.00

GENE SUMMERS:
Capri 507 *Alabama Shake* ....8.00 - 12.00
Jan 100 *School Of Rock 'N' Roll* ....10.00 - 20.00
    102 *Gotta Lotta That* ....10.00 - 20.00
    106 *Twixteen* ....10.00 - 20.00

THE SUNBEAMS:
Acme 719 *Please Say You'll Be Mine* ....200.00 - up
Herald 451 *Tell Me Why* ....80.00 - 120.00

THE SUNDIALS:
Guyden 2065 *Chapel Of Love* ....75.00 - 100.00

THE SUNDOWNERS featuring WILBUR MARTIN:
T.R.C. 2839 *Live It Up* ....15.00 - 20.00

SUNNYLAND SLIM (TRIO) (& HIS BOYS/PLAYBOYS):
Blue Lake 105 *Going Back To Memphis*..............100.00 - 150.00
    107 *Shake It Baby* ....100.00 - 150.00
Club 51 106 *Be Mine Alone* ....80.00 - 120.00
Cobra 5006 *Highway 61* ....50.00 - 80.00
J.O.B. 1003 *Leaving Your Town*..................................- -
    1105 *Shake It Baby* ....100.00 - 150.00
    1108 *Four Day Bounce* ....100.00 - 150.00
Prestige 811 *Baby How Long* ....- -
    816 *I'm Prison Bound* ....- -

SUNRAYS:
Sun 293 *Lonely Hours* ....15.00 - 20.00

SUNSETS:
Petal 1040 *Lydia* ....15.00 - 25.00

THE SUPERBS:
Dore 704 *The Story Book of Love* ....10.00 - 15.00
    715 *Sad, Sad Day* ....10.00 - 20.00

    722 *My Heart Isn't In It* ....10.00 - 15.00
    727 *I Was Blind* ....8.00 - 12.00
Dore (most other issues) ....7.00 - 10.00
Heritage 103 *Rainbow Of Love* ....10.00 - 20.00
Melmar 121 *My Love For You* ....15.00 - 20.00

THE SUPERIORS:
Atco 6106 *Lost Love* ....10.00 - 20.00
Fal 301 *What Is Love?* ....20.00 - 30.00
Federal 12436 *I'm Sorry Baby* ....8.00 - 12.00
Main Line 104 *Lost Love* ....50.00 - 75.00
Real Fine 837 *Eternal Dream* ....75.00 - 100.00
Verve 10370 *What Would I Do* ....7.00 - 10.00

THE SUPREMES:
Ace 534 *Just For You And I*..................................15.00 - 20.00
APT 25055 *Another Chance To Love* ....15.00 - 20.00
Bernice 202 *Be My Love* ....50.00 - 75.00
Kitten 6969 *Could This Be You* ....100.00 - 150.00
Mark 129 *Snap, Crackle And Pop* ....250.00 - up
Mascot 126 *Little Sally Walker* ....50.00 - 75.00
Motown (LP) 606 *Meet The Supremes* (Note: Cover shows girls
    sitting on stools.)..................................150.00 - 200.00
    1027, 1034..................................10.00 - 15.00
    1040 *You Bring Back Memories* ....15.00 - 20.00
    1054 *Run, Run, Run* ....15.00 - 20.00
Old Town 1017 *Since My Baby's Been Gone*........30.00 - 50.00
    1024 *My Baby* ....40.00 - 60.00
Sara 1032 *I Lost My Job* ....100.00 - 150.00
Tamla 54038 *I Want A Guy*..................................40.00 - 60.00
    54045 *Who's Loving You* ....15.00 - 20.00
(Note: Above are Tamla label with horizontal lines.)

THE SURFARIS:
DFS 11/12 *Wipe-Out*..................................300.00 - up
(Note: Prices as high as $2,000.00 have been seen for this record!)
Princess 50 *Wipe-Out*..................................40.00 - 80.00

SURF RIDERS:
Nasco 6008 *Rocko Socko* ....15.00 - 20.00

SURRATT & SMITH:
Audio Lab (LP) 1565 *Songs Everybody Knows*......25.00 - 40.00

SURVIVORS:
Capitol 5102 *Pamela Jean* ....50.00 - 75.00

RONNIE STUTTON:
Mar-Vel 5000 *Country Rock And Roll*..................................- - -

DEL SWADE:
Production 65216 *Better Get Ready, Betty* ....20.00 - 30.00

SWALLOWS:
After Hours 104 *My Baby* ....300.00 - up
Chariot 104 *My Baby* ....300.00 - up
Federal 12319 *Angel Baby* ....15.00 - 20.00
    12328 *We Want To Rock*..................................10.00 - 15.00
    12329 *Beside You*..................................10.00 - 15.00
    12333 *Itchy Twitchy Feeling*..................................10.00 - 15.00
Guyden 2023 *You Must Try* ....30.00 - 50.00
King 4458 *Dearest* ....300.00 - up
    4466 *Since You've Been Gone Away* ....- -
(Note: The existence of above in 45 RPM format has not been
    verified; 78s are known.)
    4501 *Eternally*..................................125.00 - 175.00
    4515 *Roll Roll Pretty Baby* ....150.00 - 200.00
    4525 *Beside You*..................................75.00 - 100.00
    4533 *I Only Have Eyes For You* ....100.00 - 150.00
    4579 *Please Baby Please*..................................100.00 - 150.00

4612 *Laugh (Though You Want To Cry)* ....80.00 - 120.00
4632 *Nobodys Lovin' Me*................80.00 - 120.00
4656 *Trust Me* ....75.00 - 100.00
4676 *I'll Be Waiting*................80.00 - 120.00
(Note: First pressings of early King issues should not have the designation "High Fidelity" and should have the suffixes "A" or "AA" after the catalog numbers. Records pressed of colored plastic can bring substantially higher prices.)

JIMMY SWAN:
M-G-M 12226 *Hey, Baby, Baby*....................15.00 - 20.00
12348 *Country Cattin'*....................15.00 - 20.00
Trumpet 176 *Juke Joint Mama*....................15.00 - 20.00
177 *Triflin' On Me*....................15.00 - 25.00
197 *Losers Weepers*....................15.00 - 25.00
198 *Lonesome Daddy Blues*....................15.00 - 25.00

SWANNEE & THE ROCKABILLIES:
Clix 825 *Thrill Happy*.................... - - -

THE SWANS:
Ballad 1003 *Night Train*....................75.00 - 100.00
1007 *Santa Claus Boogie Song* ....50.00 - 75.00
Dot 16210 *Why Must I Cry*....................8.00 - 12.00
Fortune 813 *Wedding Bells, Oh Wedding Bells*.....150.00 - 300.00
822 *Mister Cool Breeze* ....80.00 - 130.00
Rainbow 233 *My True Love* ....400.00 - up
Steamboat 101 *Believe In Me* ....150.00 - 200.00

BOBBY SWANSON & THE SONICS:
Igloo 1003 *Rockin' Little Eskimo* ....100.00 - 150.00

HANK SWATLEY:
Aron 101 *Oakie Boogie* ....40.00 - 60.00

AL SWEATT:
Keen 289 *Little Red Wagon*....................30.00 - 50.00

JIM SWEENEY:
Date 1001 *The Midnight Hour*....................7.00 - 10.00

JIMMY SWEENEY (See: THE VARIETEERS)

THE SWINGING HEARTS:
Diamond 162 *Please Say It Isn't So* ....10.00 - 15.00
Lucky Four 1011 *Please Say It Isn't So* ....25.00 - 50.00
1025 *How Can I Love You* ....25.00 - 40.00
Magic Touch 2001 *You Speak Of Love* ....8.00 - 12.00
NRM 1002 *How Can I Love You* ....8.00 - 12.00
620 1002 *How Can I Love You*....................25.00 - 40.00 *
*(Above, pressed of colored vinyl, brings substantially more.)
1005 *Pony Rock* ....15.00 - 25.00
1009 *You Speak Of Love*....................20.00 - 30.00

THE SWINGING PHILLIES:
De Luxe 6171 *L-O-V-E* ....50.00 - 75.00

HAWARD/HOWARD SWORDS with THE BLUE LIGHT BOYS:
Meteor 5019 *You Will Have To Pay* ....25.00 - 40.00

THE SYCAMORES:
Groove 0121 *I'll Be Waiting*....................50.00 - 75.00

BOBBY SYKES:
Decca 30573 *Touch Of Loving* ....7.00 - 10.00

ROOSEVELT SYKES (& HIS HONEYDRIPPERS):
Crown (LP) 5287 *Roosevelt Sykes Sings The Blues* ....30.00 - 50.00
House Of Sound 505 *She's Jail Bait* ....15.00 - 20.00
Imperial 5347 *Sweet Old Chicago* ....30.00 - 50.00
5367 *Crazy Fox* ....30.00 - 50.00
Kent 384, 434....................5.00 - 10.00

RCA Victor 50-0025 *Stop Her Papa* ....30.00 - 50.00
50-0040 *My Baby Is Gone* ....30.00 - 50.00
(Note: Above two are made of orange plastic.)
United 120 *Heavy Heart* ....50.00 - 75.00
120 *Heavy Heart* (red plastic) ....80.00 - 120.00
129 *Security Blues* ....30.00 - 50.00
139 *Four O'Clock Blues* ....30.00 - 50.00
152 *Tell Me True*....................30.00 - 50.00
(Note: Above, if pressed of red vinyl, bring substantially more.)

SYLVIA & MICKEY:
Cat 102 *Speed Life* ....8.00 - 12.00

BOBBY SYSOM:
Blue Moon 304 *Big Time Mama*....................30.00 - 50.00

TABBYS:
Time 1008 *My Darling* ....10.00 - 15.00

TABS:
Dot 15887 *Avenue Of Tears* ....8.00 - 12.00
Gardena 110 *Never Forget* ....8.00 - 12.00
Nasco 6016 *Will We Meet Again* ....8.00 - 12.00
Noble 719 *Never Forget* ....50.00 - 75.00
720 *Oops* ....200.00 - up
Vee Jay 418, 446 ....5.00 - 8.00

DICK TACKER:
Kingston - *Rock All Night With Me* ....30.00 - 40.00

THE TADS:
Dot 15518 *Your Reason* ....10.00 - 15.00
Liberty Bell 9010 *Your Reason*....................15.00 - 20.00

TOM TALL (& HIS TOM CATS):
Crest 1038 *Stack-A-Records* ....25.00 - 40.00
1051 *High School Dance* ....10.00 - 15.00
Fabor 132 *Hot Rod Is Her Name* ....10.00 - 15.00

JOHNNY T. TALLEY:
Mercury 70902 *Lonesome Train*....................15.00 - 20.00

TAMPA RED:
RCA Victor 4275 *Boogie Woogie Woman* ....20.00 - 30.00
4898 *True Love* ....20.00 - 30.00
5134 *Too Late, Too Long*....................15.00 - 20.00
5273 *I'll Never Let You Go* ....15.00 - 20.00
50-0019 *Come On, If You're Coming* ....40.00 - 60.00
50-0027 *It's A Brand New Boogie* ....40.00 - 60.00
50-0041 *That's Her Own Business* ....40.00 - 60.00
50-0056 *It's Too Late Now* ....40.00 - 60.00
50-0084 *1950 Blues* ....40.00 - 60.00
(Note: Last five records are made of orange plastic.)

ROY TAN:
Dot 15551 *I Don't Like It*....................7.00 - 10.00
15551 *I Don't Like It* (78 rpm)....................15.00 - 20.00
15595 *Hot Rod Queen*....................8.00 - 12.00

TANGENTS:
Fresh 1 *I Can't Live Alone* ....10.00 - 15.00
2274 *That Lucky Old Sun* ....10.00 - 15.00

TANGIERS:
A-J 905 *The Plea* ....10.00 - 15.00
Class 224 *Don't Try*....................15.00 - 20.00
Decca 29603 *Tabarin*....................30.00 - 50.00
29971 *Oh, Baby!* ....30.00 - 50.00
Strand 25039 *Don't Stop The Music*....................10.00 - 15.00

ROY TANN (See ROY TAN)

THE TANTONES:
Lamp 2002 *No Matter* ....15.00 - 25.00
  2008 *So Afraid* ....20.00 - 30.00

TARHEEL SLIM (& LITTLE ANN):
Fire 1000, 1009 ....7.00 - 10.00
(Note: 78 rpm issues of above exist.)
Fury 1016 *Number 9 Train* ....15.00 - 20.00

FRANKIE TARO:
G&G 111 *Susy Ann* ....30.00 - 50.00

LEON D. TARVER & THE CHORDONES:
Checker 791 *I'm A Young Rooster* ....100.00 - 200.00

JOE TATE:
Roulette 4059 *Satellite Rock* ....10.00 - 15.00

BILL TAYLOR (& THE CYCLONES/& SMOKEY JO):
Flip 502 *Split Personality* ....100.00 - 150.00
Trophy 500 *Nelda Jane* ....8.00 - 12.00
  -*Wombie Zombie/I'm Young* .... - - -

WILD BILL TAYLOR:
Fame 502 *Study Hall Romance* ....80.00 - 130.00

BOB TAYLOR:
Yucca 110 *Don't Be Unfair* ....15.00 - 20.00

CARMEN TAYLOR (& THE BOLEROS):
Apollo 489 *Teen-Age Ball* ....20.00 - 30.00
Atlantic 1002 *Lovin' Daddy* ....20.00 - 30.00
  1041 *Freddie* ....50.00 - 80.00

EDDIE TAYLOR:
Vee Jay 149 *E.T. Blues* ....50.00 - 75.00
  185 *Big Town Playboy* ....30.00 - 50.00
  206 *Don't Knock At My Door* ....20.00 - 30.00
  267 *Lookin' For Trouble* ....20.00 - 30.00
Vivid 104 *I'm Sitting Here* ....7.00 - 10.00

FAITH TAYLOR & THE SWEET TEENS:
Bea & Baby 104 *Please Be Mine* ....10.00 - 15.00
  105 *Paper Route Baby* ....10.00 - 15.00
Federal 12334 *Your Candy Kisses* ....15.00 - 25.00

HOUND DOG TAYLOR:
Bea & Baby 112 *My Baby's Coming Home* ....15.00 - 20.00
Firma 626 *Alley Music* ....10.00 - 15.00

KIRK TAYLOR & THE MAJESTICS:
Bandera 2507 *From Out Of This World* ....10.00 - 20.00

KOKO TAYLOR:
Checker 1092 *I Got What It Takes* ....7.00 - 10.00
  1135, 1148 ....5.00 - 8.00
U.S.A. 745 *Honkey Tonky* ....5.00 - 8.00

MORRIS TAYLOR:
Key 5718 *Look-A-What* ....20.00 - 30.00

R. DEAN TAYLOR:
Mala 444 *Long Way To St. Louis* ....7.00 - 10.00

RAY TAYLOR AND ALABAMA PALS:
Clix 801 *Clocking My Card* ....15.00 - 20.00
  802 *Connie Lou* ....150.00 - 300.00

TED TAYLOR:
APT 25063 *Little Things Mean A Lot* ....7.00 - 10.00
Duke 304 *Since You're Home* ....10.00 - 20.00
  308 *Count The Stars* ....10.00 - 15.00
Laurie 3076 *You've Been Crying* ....8.00 - 12.00

Okeh 7154 *Pretending Love* ....7.00 - 10.00
  7171 *That's Life I Guess* ....7.00 - 10.00
Top Rank 2011 *I'm Saving My Love* ......15.00 - 20.00
  2076 *Darling, Take Me Back* ....8.00 - 12.00

TRUE TAYLOR:
Big 614 *True Or False* ....15.00 - 20.00

VERNON TAYLOR:
Dot 15632 *I've Got The Blues* ....10.00 - 15.00

WILLIAM TELL TAYLOR with JIMMY HEAP & THE MELODY MASTERS:
D 1051 *I Like It* ....10.00 - 15.00

THE TAYLOR TONES:
C & T 0001 *Too Young To Love* ....10.00 - 20.00
Starmaker 1926 *A Star* ....8.00 - 12.00

THE TEAM MATES:
Le Cam 701 *Sooner Or Later* ....8.00 - 12.00
  706 *If Only I Had Known* ....8.00 - 12.00
  707 *Once There Was A Time* ....10.00 - 15.00
  708 *Sylvia* ....10.00 - 15.00
Paula 220 *Most Of All* ....10.00 - 20.00
Soft 104 *Most Of All* ....20.00 - 30.00

THE TEARDROPS:
Colvin 777 *I Know* ....25.00 - 40.00
Josie 766 *The Stars Are Out Tonight* .....50.00 - 75.00
  771 *My Heart* ....75.00 - 100.00
  856 *We Won't Tell* ....8.00 - 12.00
  862 *Cry No More* ....8.00 - 12.00
  873 *Daddy's Little Girl* ....8.00 - 12.00
King 5004 *My Inspiration* ....15.00 - 20.00
  5037 *Don't Be Afraid To Love* ....10.00 - 15.00
Port 70019 *The Stars Are Out Tonight* ...7.00 - 10.00
Sampson 634 *Come Back To Me* .... - -
(Note: The existence of above in 45 RPM format has not been verified; 78s are known.)
Saxony 1007 *That's Why I'll Get By* ....7.00 - 10.00
  1008, 1009 ....5.00 - 8.00

THE TEARS:
Astronaut 5001 *She's Mine* ....15.00 - 25.00
Dig 112 *Until The Day I Die* ....15.00 - 20.00
Embassy 1005 *In The Palm Of My Hand* ....10.00 - 15.00

THE TEASERS:
Checker 800 *How Could You Hurt Me So* ....200.00 - 300.00
Checker 800 *Same, But Red Plastic* ....400.00 - up
Note 10002 *Why Oh Why* .... - - -

TED AND JOHNNY:
Peach 0566 *Teenage Party* ....10.00 - 15.00

TEDDY & THE CONTINENTALS:
Pik 235 *Tick Tick Tock* ....7.00 - 10.00
Richie 445 *Do You* ....20.00 - 30.00
  1001 *Tick Tick Tock* ....15.00 - 25.00

THE TEDDY BEARS:
Imperial 5562 *I Don't Need You Anymore* ....7.00 - 10.00
  5594 *Don't Go Away* ....7.00 - 10.00
  (LP) 9067 *The Teddy Bears Sing!* (MONO) ......50.00 - 75.00
  (LP) 12067 *The Teddy Bears Sing!* (STEREO) .....100.00 - 150.00

TEENAGE MOONLIGHTERS:
Mark 134 *I Want To Cry* ....400.00 - up

"TEENAGE PARTY"
Gee (LP) 702 (The Crows, Cleftones, et al.) ....50.00 - 80.00

THE TEENAGERS (featuring FRANKIE LYMON):

Gee (EP) 601 *The Teenagers Go Rockin'*	25.00 -	40.00
(EP) 602 *The Teenagers Go Romantic*	25.00 -	40.00
(LP) 701 *The Teenagers featuring Frankie Lymon (mono) (red label)*	100.00 -	150.00
Gee 1002, 1012	5.00 -	10.00
1002 *Why Do Fools Fall In Love* (78 rpm)	10.00 -	15.00
1012 *I Want You To Be My Girl* (78 rpm)	10.00 -	15.00

TEENANGELS:

Sun 388 (DJ) *Tell Me My Love*	10.00 -	15.00

THE TEENCHORDS (See LEWIS LYMON)

THE TEEN KINGS; TEEN KINGS (vocal, ROY ORBISON):

Bee 1114 *Tell Me If You Know*	300.00 -	up
Je-Well 101 *Ooby Dooby*	500.00 -	up
(Note: Prices as high as $2,500.00 have been seen for this record!)		
Willett 118 *My Greatest Wish*	50.00 -	75.00

TEENOS:

Dub 2839 *Love Only One*	15.00 -	20.00

TEEN QUEENS:

Crown (LP) 373 *Teen Queens*	30.00 -	60.00
(LP) 5022 *Eddie My Love*	50.00 -	80.00
Kent 348 *Eddie My Love*	5.00 -	8.00
RPM 453 *Eddie My Love*	10.00 -	15.00
453 *Eddie My Love* (78 rpm)	10.00 -	20.00
460, 464, 470, 484	7.00 -	10.00

THE TEEN TONES/TEENTONES:

Dandy Dan 2 *My Sweet*	25.00 -	40.00
Decca 30895 *Don't Call Me Baby, I'll Call You*	10.00 -	15.00
Nu-Clear unnumb. *Faded Love*	10.00 -	20.00
Rego 1004 *Love Is A Vow*	75.00 -	100.00
Swan 4040 *My Little Baby*	8.00 -	12.00
Tri-Disc 102 *I Feel So Happy*	7.00 -	10.00
Wynne 107 *Faded Love*	7.00 -	10.00

TELLERS:

Fire 1038 *Tears Fell From My Eyes*	10.00 -	15.00

BOB TEMPLE:

King 4958 *Come Back Come Back*	8.00 -	12.00

TEMPO MENTALS:

Ebb 112 *Dearest*	10.00 -	20.00

THE TEMPOS:

Bofuz 1106 *Why Don't You Write Me*	20.00 -	30.00
Climax 102 *See You In September*	7.00 -	10.00
105 *Crossroads Of Love*	7.00 -	10.00
Hi-Q 5005 *I'm Laughing At You*	10.00 -	15.00
Kapp 213 *I Got A Job*	7.00 -	10.00
Rhythm 121 *Promise Me*	80.00 -	120.00
USA 810 *Why Don't You Write Me*	8.00 -	12.00

TEMPO TONES:

Acme 102 *Find Yourself Another Fool*	15.00 -	20.00
103 *On Your Radio*	15.00 -	20.00
713 *Ride Along*	25.00 -	50.00
715 *In My Dreams*	80.00 -	130.00
718 *Come Into My Heart*	80.00 -	130.00

TEMPO TOPPERS (See also DEUCES OF RHYTHM):

Peacock 1628 *Always*	40.00 -	60.00

THE TEMPTATIONS:

Goldisc 3007 *Letter Of Devotion*	10.00 -	15.00
Gordy 7001 *Dream Come True*	15.00 -	20.00
7010, 7015, 7020	8.00 -	12.00

King 5118 *Standing Alone*	80.00 -	130.00
Miracle 5 *Oh Mother Of Mine*	15.00 -	20.00
12 *Check Yourself*	15.00 -	20.00
Parkway 803 *Birds 'N' Bees*	15.00 -	30.00
Savoy 1532 *Mister Juke Box*	10.00 -	15.00
1550 *Don't You Know*	10.00 -	15.00

TENDERFOOTS:

Federal 12214 *Kissing Bug*	15.00 -	20.00
12219 *My Confession*	30.00 -	50.00
12225 *Those Golden Bells*	30.00 -	50.00
12228 *Sindy*	25.00 -	50.00

TENDER SLIM:

Herald 571 *Don't Cut Out On Me*	7.00 -	10.00

TENNESSEE DRIFTER:

Maid 1000 *The Drifter*	100.00 -	150.00

TENNESSEE DRIFTERS:

Dot 1166 *Boogie Woogie Baby*	30.00 -	50.00
1187 *Corrine Corrina*	30.00 -	50.00

TENNESSEE JIM:

Choice 852 *My Baby She's Rockin'*	15.00 -	20.00

TERMITES:

Bee 1825 *Give Me Your Heart*	50.00 -	75.00

TERRACE TONES:

Apt 25016 *Words Of Wisdom*	20.00 -	30.00

TERRANS:

Graham 801 *Moonrise*	30.00 -	50.00

CLYDE TERRELL:

Excello 2151 *Poor Folk*	7.00 -	10.00

SISTER O. M. TERRELL:

Columbia 21092 *The Gambling Man*	10.00 -	15.00

DON TERRY:

Lin 5018 *Knees Shakin'*	50.00 -	80.00

DOSSIE TERRY:

King 5072 *I Got A Watch Dog*	15.00 -	20.00

FLASH TERRY:

Indigo 135 *Cool It*	15.00 -	20.00
Kent 310 *On My Way Back Home*	10.00 -	20.00
Suncoast 1003 *She's My Baby*	20.00 -	30.00

GENE TERRY & HIS DOWN BEATS:

Savoy 1559 *Fine Fine*	8.00 -	12.00

GORDON TERRY:

RCA Victor 7428 *It Ain't Right*	10.00 -	15.00
7632 *A Lotta Lotta Woman*	10.00 -	15.00

LARRY TERRY:

Testa 0006 *Hep Cat*	50.00 -	80.00

MARK TERRY:

Kem 2746 *Nobody's Darling*	-	-

SONNY TERRY (with BROWNIE McGHEE) (See also BROWNIE McGHEE):

Elektra (LP) 14 (10 inch) *Folk Blues*	20.00 -	30.00
Everest (LP) 206 *Sonny Terry*	20.00 -	30.00
Fantasy (LP) 3254 *Sonny Terry*	20.00 -	30.00
Folkways (LP) #35 (10 inch) *Harmonica*	-	-
(LP) 2006 (10 inch) *Washboard Band*	-	-
(LP) 2035 (10 inch) *Harmonica*	-	-
(LP) 2327 (10 inch) *Blues & Folksongs*	-	-
Gotham 517 *Four O'Clock Blues*	30.00 -	50.00
518 *Lonesome Room*	30.00 -	50.00

Gramercy 1004 *Hootin' Blues* (red plastic)..............80.00 - 120.00
Groove 0015 *Louise*..15.00 - 25.00
　　0135 *Hootin' Blues No. 2*...................................15.00 - 25.00
Harlem 2327 *Dangerous Woman* ....30.00 - 60.00
Jax 305 *I Don't Worry* (red vinyl) ....50.00 - 80.00
Josie 828 *Fast Freight Blues* ....8.00 - 12.00
Old Town 1023 *Uncle Bud*.................................15.00 - 20.00
RCA Victor 5492 *Hootin' And Jumpin'* ....15.00 - 20.00
　　5577 *I'm Gonna Rock My Wig* ....15.00 - 20.00
Red Robin 110 *Harmonica Hop* ....50.00 - 75.00
Riverside (LP) 12-644 *...And His Mouth Harp* ....20.00 - 30.00
Roulette (LP) 25074 *Folk Songs*........................15.00 - 20.00
Stinson (LP) 55 (10 inch) *Blues*.......................... -　-　　-

TERRY & THE PIRATES:
Chess 1696 *Talk About The Girl* ....10.00 - 15.00
Valli 100 *Talk About The Girl* ....20.00 - 30.00

JOE TEX:
Ace 550 *Mother's Advice* ....8.00 - 12.00
Checker (LP) 2993 *Hold On! It's Joe*...................30.00 - 50.00

THE TEXANS:
Gothic 001 *Rockin' Johnny Home* ....10.00 - 15.00
Infinity 001 *Green Grass Of Texas* ....10.00 - 15.00

TEXAS MATADORS:
IMA 101 *Flower Blossom* ....7.00 - 10.00

TEXAS RED (& JIMMY):
Bullseye 1009 *Coming Home* ....15.00 - 20.00
Checker 879 *Black Snake Blues* ....8.00 - 12.00

JOHN TEXIERA:
G & G 100 *Strike It Rich* ....15.00 - 20.00

RUDY THACKER:
Lucky 0012 *Black Train* ....30.00 - 50.00

CHUCK THARP & FIREBALLS:
Jaro 77029 *Long Long Ponytail*..............................20.00 - 30.00

SISTER ROSETTA THARPE:
Decca (LP) 5382 *The Wedding Ceremony of* ....50.00 - 75.00
Promenade (LP) 2234 *Spirituals In Rhythm* ....40.00 - 60.00

FRANK THAYER:
Outlaw 1 *Evening Shadows* ....15.00 - 20.00

THEMES (with JACK SNOW):
Excello 2152 *The Magic Of You*.............................15.00 - 20.00
Stork 001 *There's No Moon Out Tonight* ....8.00 - 12.00

JOE THERRIEN, JR. (& THE ROCKETS/SULLY TRIO):
Brunswick 55005 *Hey Babe, Let's Go Downtown* ..15.00 - 20.00
Brunswick 55017 *You're Long Gone* ....15.00 - 20.00
Jat 101 *I Ain't Gonna Be Around* ....20.00 - 30.00
Lido 505 *Hey Babe, Let's Go Downtown* ....20.00 - 30.00

FATSO THEUS & THE FLAIRS:
Aladdin *3324 Be Cool My Heart* ....100.00 - 150.00

ALEXANDER "MUDCAT" THOMAS:
NRC 062 *Step It Up And Go*................................8.00 - 12.00

B. J. THOMAS:
Pacemaker (LP) 3001 *So Lonesome I Could Cry* ....50.00 - 80.00

CLIFF THOMAS:
Phillips Int. 3521 *Treat Me Right* ....10.00 - 15.00

JERRY THOMAS (& THE RHYTHM ROCKERS):
Khoury's 708 *Baby Please* ....15.00 - 20.00
Orchid 274 *Jungle Dan*...15.00 - 20.00

JESSE THOMAS:
Elko 107 *Another Fool Like Me*.......................50.00 - 75.00
Hollywood 1072 *Cool Kind Lover*.........................15.00 - 20.00

KID THOMAS:
Federal 12298 *The Wolf Pack* ....50.00 - 80.00
T.R.C. 1012 *Rockin' This Joint Tonight* ....60.00 - 100.00

LAFAYETTE THOMAS:
Savoy 1574 *Lafayette's A-Comin'* ....10.00 - 15.00

MULE THOMAS:
Hollywood 1091 *Blow My Baby Back Home*..........30.00 - 40.00

PLAY BOY THOMAS:
Parrot 785 *No Doubt About It* ....50.00 - 75.00
Swing Time 340 *Too Much Pride*........................50.00 - 75.00

RUFUS THOMAS (JR.):
Chess 1517 *Juanita* ....150.00 - 300.00
Sun 181 *Bear Cat* ....80.00 - 130.00
　　188 *Tiger Man*...................................80.00 - 130.00

TAB(BY) THOMAS:
Delta 416 *Thinking Blues*.................................20.00 - 30.00
Excello 2212, 2222, 2281 ....5.00 - 8.00
Feature 3007 *Tomorrow* ....20.00 - 30.00
Rocko 511 *Too Late Blues* ....8.00 - 12.00
Zynn 1002 *My Baby's Got It*...............................10.00 - 15.00

AL THOMPSON:
Debonair 168 *Too Cool For That* ....15.00 - 20.00

BUDDY THOMPSON:
Atco 6095 *This Is The Night* ....10.00 - 15.00

CHUCK THOMPSON:
Granite 13775 *Tired Of Fooling Around* ....20.00 - 30.00

FRED THOMPSON:
Jim Dandy 4501 *Please Be Fair* ....5.00 - 8.00

HANK THOMPSON:
Capitol (LP) 418 (10 inch) *Brazos Valley Songs* .... 20.00 - 30.00
　　(LP) 418 *Brazos Valley Songs* ....20.00 - 30.00
　　(LP) 618 *North Of The Rio Grande* ....20.00 - 30.00
　　(LP) 729 *All Time Hits* ....15.00 - 20.00
　　(LP) 826 *Hank*...15.00 - 20.00
　　(LP) 975 *Dance Ranch*....................................15.00 - 20.00
　　(LP) 1246 *Songs For Rounders* ....15.00 - 20.00
　　3623 *Rockin' In The Congo* ....7.00 - 10.00

HAYDEN THOMPSON:
Phillips 3517 *Love My Baby* ....20.00 - 30.00
Profile 4015 *Whatcha Gonna Do*..........................20.00 - 30.00

JUNIOR THOMPSON:
JJ's 006 *Ooby Dooby* ....10.00 - 15.00
Meteor 5029 *Mama's Little Baby* (red label)........150.00 - 200.00
Tune (unnumbered) *How Come You Do Me?*.......200.00 - 300.00

KID GUITAR THOMPSON:
Dore 581 *My Baby Done Me Wrong*......................7.00 - 10.00

LORETTA THOMPSON:
Skoop 1050 ....20.00 - 30.00
United 214 *Hi De Ho Rock And Roll* ....15.00 - 20.00

SONNY THOMPSON:
King (LP) 568 *Moody Blues* ....75.00 - 100.00
King, most issues ....5.00 - 10.00

WILLIE MAE ("BIG MAMA") THORNTON:
Bay Tone 107 *Big Mama's Blues* ....7.00 - 10.00
Kent 424 *Before Day*..3.00 - 5.00

Peacock 1567 *All Fed Up* ....20.00 - 30.00
    1587 *Let Your Tears Fall Baby* ....20.00 - 30.00
    1603 *Mischievous Boogie* ....20.00 - 30.00
    1612 *Hound Dog*...50.00 - 80.00
    1621 *Cotton Picking Blues* ....15.00 - 20.00
  1626 *The Big Change* ....15.00 - 20.00
    1632 *I Smell A Rat* ....15.00 - 20.00
    1642 *Stop Hoppin' On Me* ....15.00 - 20.00
    1647 *Walking Blues* ....15.00 - 20.00
(Note: Above are red or maroon labels.)
Peacock 1650, 1654, 1681 ....7.00 - 12.00

"THOSE GOOD OLD MEMORIES":
Capitol (LP) 1414 (various artists) ....20.00 - 40.00

THRASHERS:
Mason's 178 *Jeannie* ....200.00 - up
  178 *Jeannie* (red plastic)......................75.00 - 100.00

THREE CHUCKLES:
Boulevard 100 *Run Around* ....20.00 - 30.00
Vik (LP) 1067 ....75.00 - 100.00
Vik (most issues) ....5.00 - 8.00
X (most issues) ....5.00 - 8.00

THREE D'S:
Dean 521 *Broken Hearted* ....10.00 - 15.00
Paris 511 *Crazy Little Woman* ....8.00 - 12.00
  514 *Jumpin' Jack*...................................7.00 - 10.00
Square 502 *Square* ....10.00 - 15.00

3 DOTS AND A DASH:
Imperial 5115 *Don't Cry Baby* ....150.00 - 200.00
  5164 *Let's Do It*...................................150.00 - 200.00

THREE FRIENDS:
Brunswick 55032 *Jinx* ....8.00 - 12.00
Cal-Gold 169 *Walkin' Shoes* ....40.00 - 70.00
Lido 500 *Blanche*....................................10.00 - 15.00
  502 *I'm Only A Boy* ....10.00 - 15.00

THE THREE HONEYDROPS:
Music City 813 *In The Summer* ....10.00 - 20.00
  814 *Rockin' Satellite*............................10.00 - 20.00

THREE OF US TRIO:
Pam 1001 *'Tis Love* ....20.00 - 30.00
Pam-Nor 501 *Busy Body Mama* ....- - -
York 3332 *Sugar Lump* ....20.00 - 40.00

THREE RAMBLERS:
Ozark 716 *Walking Talking Baby Doll*......15.00 - 20.00

THRILLERS:
Big Town 109 *The Drunkard* ....30.00 - 50.00
Herald 432 *Lizabeth* ....40.00 - 70.00
Thriller 3530* *I'm Gonna Live My Life Alone* ....- - -
(Note: *The existence of above in 45 RPM format has not been verified.)

THUNDERBIRDS:
De Luxe 6075 *Baby Let's Play House*......40.00 - 60.00
G.G. 103 *Love Is A Problem*....................30.00 - 50.00
Holiday 2609 *Mary*..................................40.00 - 60.00

BILLY TIDWELL:
KoBoCo 1009 *Folsom Prison Blues*...........10.00 - 20.00

TIFANOS:
Tifco 822 *It's Raining*..............................10.00 - 15.00

SONNY TIL (See ORIOLES)

BIG SON TILLIS & D.C. BENDER:
Elko 821 *Rocks Is My Pillow* ....75.00 - 100.00
  822 *Ten Long Years* ....75.00 - 100.00
  823 *Dayton Stomp* ....75.00 - 100.00

CLYDE TILLIS:
Cash 1054 *It Makes No Difference Now*.................8.00 - 12.00
Milmart 112 *You Can Do What You Wanna Do* ....10.00 - 20.00

MEL TILLIS:
Columbia 40944 *Juke Box Man*.......................8.00 - 12.00
  41026 *Hearts Of Stone* ....8.00 - 12.00
  41115 *Teen-Age Wedding* ....8.00 - 12.00

TINO & REVLONS:
Dearborn 525 *Rave On*...............................8.00 - 12.00
Dearborn (LP) 1004 *By Request at The Sway-Zee* .50.00 - 75.00
May 103 *Rave On* ....20.00 - 30.00

TITANS:
Class 244 *No Time* ....10.00 - 15.00
Fidelity 3016 *What Have I Done* ....10.00 - 15.00
Specialty 614 *Sweet Peach* ....8.00 - 12.00
  625 *Don't You Just Know It*................8.00 - 12.00
  632 *Arlene* ....8.00 - 12.00
Vita 148 *So Hard To Laugh, So Easy To Cry*........25.00 - 40.00
  158 *Look What You're Doing Baby*.................20.00 - 30.00

TITONES:
Scepter 1206 *Symbol Of Love* ....15.00 - 30.00
Wand 105 *Symbol of Love* ....7.00 - 10.00

BUD TITUS:
Sage 244 *Hocus Pocus*...............................15.00 - 25.00

"TODAY'S HITS":
Philles (LP) 4004 (various artists) ....80.00 - 130.00

FULLER TODD:
King 5048 *Old Fashioned* ....5.00 - 8.00
  5075 *Young Hearts Are True* ....8.00 - 12.00
  5111 *Top Ten Rock* ....8.00 - 12.00

JOHNNY TODD:
Modern 1003 *Pink Cadillac*......................20.00 - 30.00

TOKENS:
Gary 1006 *Doom-Lang* ....10.00 - 15.00
Laurie 3180 *Please Write* ....10.00 - 15.00
Melba 104 *I Love My Baby*......................7.00 - 10.00
RCA Victor (LP) 2514 *The Lion Sleeps Tonight*....25.00 - 40.00

TOMMIE TOLLESON:
Kool 1005 *A Girl Named Sue* ....15.00 - 20.00

TOM & JERRY:
Big 613 *Hey, Schoolgirl*...........................10.00 - 20.00
  616 *Our Song* ....15.00 - 20.00
  618 *That's My Story*............................15.00 - 20.00
  618 *Hey, Schoolgirl* (78 rpm) ....50.00 - 100.00
  621 *Baby Talk* ....15.00 - 20.00
Hunt 319 *That's My Story*.........................15.00 - 20.00

KENNY TOMERLIN:
Teen Ager 1001 *Crazy Little Teen*...........5.00 - 8.00

TONY & THE MASQUINS:
Ruthie 1000 *My Angel Eyes* ....30.00 - 50.00

TONY & THE RAINDROPS:
Chesapeake 609 *While Walking* ....25.00 - 40.00
Crosley 340 *My Heart Cried*....................300.00 - up

TONY & THE TECHNICS:
Chex 1010 *Ha Ha He Told On You* ....8.00 - 12.00

TONY & THE TWILIGHTERS/TWILITERS:
Jalynne 106 *Did You Make Up Your Mind* ....20.00 - 30.00
Red Top 127 *The Key To My Heart* ....50.00 - 80.00

JACKSON TOOMBS:
Excello 2083 *Kiss-A-Me-Quick* ....15.00 - 20.00

TOPICS:
Cross Country 102 *In A Little While* ....10.00 - 15.00
Perri 1007 *The Girl In My Dreams* ....15.00 - 20.00

THE TOP NOTES:
Atlantic 2066, 2080, 2097 ....5.00 - 10.00
   2115 *Always Late* ....8.00 - 12.00
Festival 1021 *Wait For Me Baby* ....8.00 - 12.00

TOPPERS (See also BOBBY MITCHELL):
ABC Paramount 9759 *Lonely* ....5.00 - 8.00
Jubilee 5136 *Baby Let Me Bang Your Box* ....15.00 - 20.00

TOPPS:
Red Robin 126 *Tippin'* ....50.00 - 75.00

THE TOPS:
Singular 712 *An Innocent Kiss* ....50.00 - 80.00

THE TORCHES:
Ring-O 302 *Darn Your Love* ....7.00 - 10.00

THE TOREADORS:
Midas 1001 *Do You Remember?* ....25.00 - 40.00

THE TORNADOS:
Bumble Bee 503 *Love In Your Life* ....10.00 - 15.00

TORQUAYS:
Holly 4701 *Pineapple Moon* ....10.00 - 15.00

JACKIE TORRELL:
Dude - *I'm Gonna Look* .... - - -

JOHNNY TORRENCE & THE JEWELS:
R & B 1306 *Rosalie* ....75.00 - 100.00

"TOWN HALL PARTY":
Columbia (LP) CL-1072 (various artists) ....30.00 - 50.00

TOWN THREE (See also WES VOIGHT):
De Luxe 6176 *Another Guy's Line* ....15.00 - 20.00
   6180 *I Want A Lover* ....15.00 - 20.00

THE TOYS:
Dyno Voice (LP) 9002 *Sing A Lover's Concerto* ....30.00 - 50.00

BUCK TRAIL:
Trail 100 *Knocked Out Joint On Mars* ....75.00 - 100.00

TRAILBLAZERS:
Watson 500 *Grandpa's Rock* ....35.00 - 50.00

TRAITS (See also ROY HEAD):
Renner 221 *Little Mama* ....15.00 - 20.00
   229 *Got My Mojo Working* ....15.00 - 20.00
TNT 164 *One More Time* ....30.00 - 50.00
   175 *Live It Up* ....30.00 - 50.00
   185 *Night Time Blues* ....30.00 - 50.00

BOBBY LEE TRAMMEL:
ABC Paramount 9890 *Shirley Lee* ....15.00 - 25.00
Alley 1001 *It's All Your Fault* ....7.00 - 10.00
Alley 1004 *Come On Baby* ....8.00 - 12.00
Atlanta 1501 *Sally Twist* ....5.00 - 8.00
   1502 *Come On* ....5.00 - 8.00
   Atlanta (LP) 1503 *"Arkansas Twist"* ....80.00 - 120.00
Fabor 127 *You Mostest Girl* ....8.00 - 12.00
   4038 *Shirley Lee* ....15.00 - 20.00
Radio 102 *You Mostest Girl* ....15.00 - 20.00
   114 *Should I Make Amends* ....10.00 - 20.00
Sims 183 *New Dance In France* ....7.00 - 10.00
Vaden 304 *Been A-Walking* ....20.00 - 30.00
Warrior 1554 *Woe Is Me* ....10.00 - 15.00

CARL TRANTHAM (& RHYTHM ALL STARS):
Lincoln 643 *Where There's A Will* ....50.00 - 80.00
Starday 361 *Our True Love* ....50.00 - 80.00

THE TRASHMEN:
Garrett (LP) 200 *Surfin' Bird* ....50.00 - 80.00

TRAVELERS:
Allison 922 *We Made A Promise* ....30.00 - 50.00
Andex 2011 *I'll Be Home For Christmas* ....8.00 - 12.00
   4006 *Why* ....8.00 - 12.00
   4033 *I Go For You* ....7.00 - 10.00
Atlas 1086 *Lenora* ....40.00 - 60.00
Decca 31215 *Ivy On The Old School Wall* ....7.00 - 10.00
   31282 *White Rose* ....10.00 - 15.00
Okeh 6959 *Why Darling Why* ....10.00 - 20.00
World Wide 8511 *Too Young* ....30.00 - 50.00

TRAVIS & BOB:
Sandy 1017 *We're Too Young* ....7.00 - 10.00
   1019 *Little Bitty Johnny* ....7.00 - 10.00
   1024 *Oh Yeah* ....7.00 - 10.00
   1029 *That's How Long* ....7.00 - 10.00

MERLE TRAVIS:
Capitol (LP) 891 *Back Home* ....30.00 - 50.00

"TREASURE CHEST OF MUSTY DUSTIES":
Fortune (LP) 8011 ....50.00 - 100.00
(reissues exist)

TREBLE CHORDS:
Decca 31015 *Teresa* ....15.00 - 30.00

TREMAINES:
Cash 100 *Jingle Jingle* ....200.00 - up
Kane 008 *Heavenly* ....20.00 - 40.00
   008 *Heavenly* (red plastic) ....50.00 - 75.00
Old Town 1051 *Jingle Jingle* ....15.00 - 20.00
Val 101 *Jingle Jingle* ....50.00 - 80.00
V-Tone 507 *Heavenly* ....8.00 - 12.00

TOMMY TREMBLE & THE SHADOWS:
Sound Tex 641013 *She Said* ....7.00 - 10.00

THE TREMONTS:
Brunswick 55217 *Legend Of Love* ....10.00 - 15.00
Pat Riccio 101 *Believe My Heart* ....25.00 - 40.00

TREND TONES:
Superb 100 *Never Again* ....10.00 - 20.00

THE TRENIERS:
Epic (EP) 7014 *"Go Go Go"* ....25.00 - 40.00
   (EP) 7114 *"Those Crazy Treniers"* ....25.00 - 40.00
Hermitage (LP) unnumbered *After Hours With...* ..25.00 - 50.00

TOMMY TRENT:
Allstar 7184 *Just For Tonight* ....7.00 - 10.00

THE TRENTONS:
Shepherd 2204 *Star Bright* ....40.00 - 60.00

GARY TREXLER:
Rev 3507 *Teen Baby* ....10.00 - 15.00

TREYS:
Bella 16 *Come To Me* ....10.00 - 15.00

TRIDELS/TRI-DELLS:
Eldo 104 *Little Do I Know* ....8.00 - 12.00
San Dee 1009 *Land Of Love* ....10.00 - 20.00

TRI-LADS:
Bullseye 1003 *Cherry Pie*.........................15.00 - 20.00

FRANK TRIOLO:
Flagship 106 *Ice Cream Baby*...................75.00 - 100.00

TRITONES/TRI-TONES:
Jamie 1035 *Blues In The Closet*................... - -
Miss Julie 6501 *Teardrops* ....50.00 - 75.00
Vita 171 *Teenage Angel* ....10.00 - 15.00
   173 *With This Ring* ....10.00 - 15.00

DELBERT TROILINDER:
Mist 1012 *So We Walked* ....10.00 - 15.00

THE TROJANS:
RPM 446 *As Long As I Have You*...............40.00 - 80.00
Tender 516 *Alone In This World* ....20.00 - 30.00

THE TROOPERS:
Lamp 2009 *My Resolution*........................40.00 - 70.00
Lummtone 101 *My Choice For A Mate*.......40.00 - 60.00

TROPHIES:
Challenge 9133 *Desire* ....10.00 - 15.00

TROUPERS:
Red Top 118 *Peter, Pumpkin Eater*...........10.00 - 20.00

TRUETONES:
Felsted 8625 *Singing Waters* ....25.00 - 40.00
Monument 4501 *Honey Honey*..................40.00 - 60.00

THE TRUMPETEERS:
Grand (LP) 7701 *The Last Supper*............... - -
Score (LP) 4021 *Milky White Way* ....100.00 - 150.00

TRU-TONES:
Chart 634 *Tears In My Eyes* ....150.00 - 200.00
Tru unnumbered *Darling I'm Sorry* ....20.00 - 30.00

ERNEST TUBB:
Decca (LP) 5301 (10 inch) *Favorites* ....20.00 - 30.00
   (LP) 5344 (10 inch) *The Old Rugged Cross*.......20.00 - 30.00
   (LP) 5336 (10 inch) *Sings Jimmy Rodgers Songs*
   ....30.00 - 50.00
   (LP) 8291 *Favorites*............................20.00 - 30.00
   (LP) 8553 *Daddy Of 'Em All* ....20.00 - 30.00

JUSTIN TUBB:
Decca 30606 *Rock It On Down To My House* ....8.00 - 12.00

ANITA TUCKER:
Capitol 3277 *Let's Make Love* ....7.00 - 10.00
   3452 *Handcuffed Heart* ....7.00 - 10.00

BILLY JOE TUCKER:
Dot 16240 *Boogie Woogie Bill* ....10.00 - 20.00
Maha 103 *Boogie Woogie Bill*..................30.00 - 50.00

ERNEST TUCKER:
Jubilee 5340 *Mirror, Mirror On The Wall* ....7.00 - 10.00

JACK TUCKER:
4-Star 1719 *Big Door*..............................10.00 - 15.00
Ozark 960 *Honeymoon Trip to Mars*.........10.00 - 15.00

ORRIN TUCKER:
White Rock 1115 *Been Lookin' For Love* .... 10.00 - 15.00

RICK TUCKER & THE TURKS:
Veeda 4005 *I'll Be There*.........................10.00 - 15.00

LEE TULLY:
Flair-X 3007 *Elwood Pretzel* .... 10.00 - 15.00

TUNE BLENDERS:
Federal 12201 *Oh Yes I Know* ..... 25.00 - 40.00

THE TUNEMASTERS:
Mark 7000 *It's All Over*.......................... 75.00 - 100.00
Tune 203 *Lover's Paradise* .... 10.00 - 15.00

TUNE ROCKERS:
Pet - *No Stoppin' This Boppin'* .... - - -
United Artists 139 *The Green Mosquito* (78 rpm)...... - - -
(Note: The existence of this record in 78 RPM form has not been
   verified; foreign 78s do exist.)

TUNE TONES:
Herald 524 *Please Baby Please* .... 10.00 - 15.00
   539 *She's Right For Me* .... 8.00 - 12.00

THE TUNE WEAVERS:
Casa Grande 101 *Little Boy* ..... 15.00 - 20.00
   3038 *This Can Be Love* .... 10.00 - 15.00
   4037 *"Happy, Happy Birthday Baby"*.............. 10.00 - 15.00
   4038 *This Can't Be Love*.................. 10.00 - 15.00
   4040 *There Stands My Love* .... 10.00 - 15.00
Checker 872 *Happy, Happy Birthday Baby*.............. 5.00 - 10.00
   872 *Happy, Happy Birthday Baby* (78 rpm)...... 20.00 - 30.00
(Note: Checker 872 occurs with two different flip sides.)

TURBANS:
Herald 458 *When You Dance* .... 7.00 - 10.00
   458 *When You Dance* (78 rpm)........... 15.00 - 20.00
   469 *Sister Sookey* .... 8.00 - 12.00
   478 *B-I-N-G-O (Bingo)*..................... 8.00 - 12.00
   486 *All Of My Love* .... 8.00 - 12.00
   495 *Valley Of Love*......................... 8.00 - 12.00
   510 *Congratulations* .... 8.00 - 12.00
Imperial 5807, 5828, 5847 .... 5.00 - 10.00
Money 209 *No No Cherry*...................... 40.00 - 70.00
   211 *When I Return* .... 10.00 - 15.00
(Note: Flip side of Money 211 is by The Turks.)
Parkway 820 *When You Dance* .... 8.00 - 12.00
Red Top 115 *Curfew Time* .... 15.00 - 20.00
Roulette 4281, 4326 .... 5.00 - 8.00

THE TURKS (See also RICK TUCKER):
Ball 101 *Emily*..................................... 7.00 - 10.00
Bally 1017 *This Heart Of Mine* .... 7.00 - 10.00
Cash 1042 *It Can't Be True* .... 7.00 - 10.00
Class 256 *Rockville U.S.A.* .... 5.00 - 8.00
Imperial 5783 *I'm A Fool*...................... 8.00 - 12.00
Knight 2005 *It Can't Be True* .... 5.00 - 10.00
Money 211 *Emily*................................ 10.00 - 15.00
(Note: Flip side of Money 211 is by The Turbans.)
   215 *I've Been Accused* .... 10.00 - 15.00

RICHARD TURLEY:
Fraternity 845 *Makin' Love To My Baby* .... 10.00 - 15.00

IKE TURNER & KINGS OF RHYTHM (See also BILLY GAYLES):
Cobra 5033 *Walking Down The Aisle* .... 8.00 - 12.00

IKE & TINA TURNER:
Sue 722 *That's All I Need* ....7.00 - 10.00
  (LP) 2003 *Ike & Tina Turner's Kings of Rhythm Dance*
  ....75.00 - 100.00
  (LP) 2004 *Dynamite!* ....100.00 - 150.00

JACK TURNER:
Hickory 1050 *Everybody's Rockin' But Me* ....15.00 - 20.00

JESSIE LEE TURNER:
Carlton 496 *The Little Space Girl*.............................5.00 - 8.00
  509 *Baby Please Don't Tease* ....5.00 - 8.00
Imperial 5649 *I'm The Little Space Girl's Father*.....7.00 - 10.00
Sudden 105 *The Elopers* ....5.00 - 8.00

(BIG) JOE TURNER:
Atlantic (EP) 536 *Joe Turner Sings* ....50.00 - 80.00
  (EP) 565 *Joe Turner* ....50.00 - 80.00
  (EP) 606 *Rock With Joe Turner* ....50.00 - 100.00
  982 *Still In Love* ....30.00 - 50.00
  1001 *Honey Hush* ....15.00 - 20.00
  1016 *TV Mama* ....10.00 - 15.00
  1026 *Shake, Rattle & Roll* ....15.00 - 25.00
  1040 *Well All Right* ....10.00 - 15.00
  1053 *Flip, Flop And Fly* ....10.00 - 15.00
  1069 *Midnight Cannonball*.......................10.00 - 15.00
  1080 *The Chicken And The Hawk* ....10.00 - 15.00
  (LP) 1234 *Boss Of The Blues*.................75.00 - 100.00
(foregoing have yellow labels; following have red labels)
  1088 *Corrine Corrina* ....10.00 - 15.00
  1100 *Rock A While* ....10.00 - 15.00
  1122 *Midnight Special Train* ....10.00 - 15.00
  1131 *After A While* ....8.00 - 12.00
  1146 *World Of Trouble* ....8.00 - 12.00
  1155 *Trouble In Mind* ....8.00 - 12.00
  1167 *Wee Baby Blues* ....8.00 - 12.00
  1184 *Blues In The Night* ....8.00 - 12.00
  2034 *Got You On My Mind*........................8.00 - 12.00
  2044 *Honey Hush* ....8.00 - 12.00
  2054 *My Little Honey Dripper* ....8.00 - 12.00
  2072 *My Reason For Living* ....8.00 - 12.00
  (LP) 1243 *Joe Turner Sings Kansas City Jazz* (black label)
  ....50.00 - 80.00
  (LP) 1332 *Big Joe Rides Again* ....50.00 - 80.00
  (LP) 8005 *Joe Turner* (black label) ....50.00 - 80.00
  (LP) 8023 *Rockin' The Blues*...................75.00 - 100.00
  (LP) 8033 *Big Joe Is Here* ....75.00 - 100.00
Crown (LP) 5295 *Joe Turner With Red Nelson*.......30.00 - 50.00
Decca 29711 *Piney Brown Blues* ....10.00 - 15.00
  29924 *Corrine, Corrina* ....10.00 - 15.00
Savoy (LP) 14012... *And The Blues*....................50.00 - 80.00
  (LP) 14016 *Careless Love* ....50.00 - 80.00

SAMMY TURNER:
Big Top (LP) 1301 *Lavender Blue Moods* ....40.00 - 70.00

TU TONES:
Lin 5021 *Saccharin Sally*...................................10.00 - 15.00

BILL TUTT:
Gilt-Edge 5082 *Monkey On My Back*.................... - -

THE TUXEDOS:
Forte 1414 *Yes, It's True* ....30.00 - 50.00

TV SLIM (See also OSCAR WILLS):
Checker 870 *Flat Foot Sam*................................10.00 - 15.00
  1029 *The Big Fight* ....7.00 - 10.00
Clif 103 *Flat Foot Sam* ....40.00 - 80.00

Speed 704 *Flat Foot Sam Meets Jim Dandy*..........10.00 - 15.00
  705 *My Ship Is Sinking* ....10.00 - 15.00
  706 *My Baby Is Gone*.............................10.00 - 15.00
  711 *Don't Reach 'Cross My Plate* ....10.00 - 15.00
  714, 715, 803, 807, 808, 810.......................7.00 - 10.00
  6865 *To Prove My Love* ....7.00 - 10.00

"TWELVE FLIP HITS"
Flip (LP) 1001 *(various artists)* ....50.00 - 100.00

THE TWIGS:
Hollywood 1015 *Chapel Of Memories* ....40.00 - 70.00
  1026 *Wonderful World*............................40.00 - 70.00

THE TWILIGHTERS (& DONALD RICHARDS) (See also BUDDY MILTON):
Bubble 1334 *My Silent Prayer*............................10.00 - 15.00
Caddy 103 *Eternally* ....80.00 - 120.00
Cholly 712 *Let There Be Love* ....250.00 - up
Dot 15526 *Eternally*...10.00 - 20.00
Ebb 117 *Live Like A King* ....15.00 - 30.00
Groove 0154 *Sittin' In A Corner* ....15.00 - 20.00
J-V-B 83 *How Many Times*................................300.00 - up
Marshall 702 *Please Tell Me You're Mine* (red plastic)
  ....250.00 - up
M-G-M 55011 *Little Did I Dream* ....80.00 - 120.00
  55014 *Half Angel* ....80.00 - 120.00
Morgil 105 *Tender Is My Love* ....20.00 - 30.00
Paloma 100 *You Better Make It* ....10.00 - 15.00
Pico 2801 *Eternally*..15.00 - 20.00
Pla Bac 1113 *Eternally* ....15.00 - 20.00
Red Top 127 *The Key To My Heart* ....50.00 - 80.00
Ricki 907 *Help Me* ....10.00 - 20.00
Sara 1048 *Restless Love* ....15.00 - 20.00
Specialty 548 *It's True* ....40.00 - 60.00
Spin 1 *Yes You Are*...50.00 - 100.00
Super 1003 *Please Come Home* ....8.00 - 12.00

TWILIGHTS:
Airport 101 *As I Remember* ....10.00 - 15.00
Felice 713 *Believe It Or Not* ....10.00 - 15.00
Finesse 1717 *My Heart Belongs Only To You* ....10.00 - 15.00
Harthon 134 *It's Been So Long* ....8.00 - 12.00
  135 *For The First Time* ....8.00 - 12.00
Six Star 1002 *Little Richard* ....5.00 - 8.00
Spenada 101 *Just Can't Let Her Go* ....30.00 - 60.00
Tuxedo 917 *I'm Falling For You* ....40.00 - 70.00

TWILITERS (See TWILIGHTERS)

CONWAY TWITTY:
ABC Paramount 10550 *My Baby Left Me* ....10.00 - 15.00
Mercury 71086 *I Need Your Lovin'* (maroon label) 15.00 - 20.00
  71148 *Shake It Up*..................................20.00 - 30.00
  71384 *Double Talk Baby* ....15.00 - 20.00
Metro (LP) 512 *It's Only Make Believe*................15.00 - 30.00
M-G-M (LP) 3744 *Conway Twitty Sings*...............50.00 - 80.00
  (LP) 3786 *Saturday Night* ....50.00 - 80.00
  (LP) 3818 *Lonely Blue Boy* ....40.00 - 70.00
  (LP) 3907 *The Rock And Roll Story*............40.00 - 70.00

THE TWYLIGHTS:
Rock'n 102 *Darling Let's Fall In Love* ....15.00 - 30.00

BIG "T" TYLER:
Aladdin 3384 *King Kong* ....10.00 - 15.00

FRANKIE TYLER:
Okeh 7103 *I Go Ape* ....15.00 - 20.00

JOHNNY TYLER:
Ekko 1000 *Devil's Hot Rod* (red plastic).................50.00 -   80.00
Rural Rhythm 515 *Lie To Me Baby* (red plastic).....50.00 -   80.00
Starday 263 *Lie To Me Baby* ....40.00 -   70.00

KIP TYLER (& HIS FLIPS):
Challenge 1014 *She Got Eyes*.....................10.00 -   15.00
        59008 *Ooh Yeah Baby* ....10.00 -   15.00
Ebb 154 *She's My Witch* ....15.00 -   20.00
    156 *Oh Linda* ....10.00 -   15.00
Starla 003 *Let's Monkey Around* ....10.00 -   15.00

RUCKUS TYLER:
Fabor 135 *Rollin' And A-Rockin'* ....30.00 -   50.00

T. TEXAS TYLER:
King (LP) 664 *T. Texas Tyler* ....15.00 -   30.00
    (LP) 721 ....15.00 -   30.00

TYMES:
Parkway (LP) 7032 *So Much In Love* ....40.00 -   80.00
(LP) 7038 *The Sound Of The Wonderful Tymes*........ -   -   -

UNFORGETTABLES:
Alan K 6901 *Little Mary* ....75.00 - 100.00
Pamela 204 *Oh, Wishing Well* ....80.00 - 130.00

THE UNIQUES:
Bliss 1004 *I'm So Unhappy* ....250.00 -   up
C-Way 2676 *I've Got A Secret* ....10.00 -   15.00
Demand 2936 *Merry Christmas, Darling*........15.00 -   20.00
        2940 *Times Change* ....15.00 -   20.00
Dot 16533 *Times Change* ....10.00 -   15.00
End 1012 *Tell The Angels* ....50.00 -   80.00
Gone 5113 *I'm So Unhappy* ....50.00 -   80.00
Lee unnumbered *Never Let Me Go* .... -   -   -
Lucky Four 1024 *Silvery Moon* ....80.00 - 130.00
Mr. Cee 100 *Look At Me* ....50.00 -   80.00
Peacock 1677 *Somewhere* ....15.00 -   20.00
        1695 *Picture Of My Baby* ....10.00 -   20.00
Pride 1018 *It's Got To Come From Your Heart*......20.00 -   30.00
    620 1003 *Pretty Baby* ....25.00 -   40.00
Tee Kay 112 *A Million Miles Away*....................15.00 -   20.00
World Pacific 808 *I Cross My Fingers* ....75.00 - 100.00

THE UNIQUE TEENS:
Dynamic 110 *Whatcha Know New* ....20.00 -   40.00
Hanover 4510 *Jeannie* ....10.00 -   15.00
Ivy 112 *Jeannie*...15.00 -   25.00

THE UNIVERSALS:
Ascot 2124 *Dear Ruth* ....40.00 -   60.00
Cora-Lee 101 *The Picture* ....15.00 -   20.00
Festival 1601 *Dreaming* ....15.00 -   25.00
Kerwood 712 *Never Was A Girl* ....30.00 -   60.00
Mark-X 7004 *Again*......................................40.00 -   70.00
Shepherd 2200 *A Love Only You Can Give*.............20.00 -   30.00
V-Tone 236 *If It Wasn't For Pride* ....10.00 -   15.00

THE UNKNOWNS:
Shield 7101 *One More Chance*............................8.00 -   12.00
X Tra 102 *One More Chance* ....150.00 - 200.00

THE UNTOUCHABLES:
Alan K 6901 *Little Mary*.................................100.00 - 150.00
Some copies of above credited to (See) **UNFORGETTABLES.**
Madison 128 *Poor Boy Needs A Preacher* ....7.00 -   10.00
    134 *Goodnight Sweetheart Goodnight* ....7.00 -   10.00
    139 *Sixty Minute Man* ....7.00 -   10.00
    147 *Do Your Best* ....7.00 -   10.00

UPFRONTS:
Lummtone 103 *It Took Time*...............................15.00 -   20.00
    104 *Too Far To Turn Around* ....15.00 -   20.00
    106 *When You Kiss Me* ....30.00 -   50.00
    107 *Send Me Someone To Love* ....15.00 -   20.00
    114 *Most Of The Pretty Young Girls* ....40.00 -   60.00

UPSETTERS:
Little Star 123 *Every Night About This Time*...........8.00 -   12.00
    128 *Valley Of Tears* ....8.00 -   12.00

UPSTARTS:
Apollo 468 *Feed Me Baby* ....15.00 -   30.00

THE UPTONES:
Lute 6025 *I'll Be There*.....................................8.00 -   12.00
    6029 *Be Mine* ....8.00 -   12.00
Magnum 714 *Dreaming* ....7.00 -   10.00
Watts 1080 *Dreaming* ....8.00 -   12.00

AL URBAN:
Sarg 148 *Lookin' For Money*.............................20.00 -   30.00
    158 *Won't Tell You Her Name* ....30.00 -   50.00

UTAH CARL:
Starday 301 *Lovin' You*....................................20.00 -   30.00

THE UTOPIANS:
Imperial 5861 *Dutch Treat* ....7.00 -   10.00
    5876 *Along My Lonely Way* .... -   -   -
    5921 *Let Love Come Later* ....7.00 -   10.00

VAL-CHORDS:
Gametime 104 *Candy Store Love* ....10.00 -   20.00

BLACKIE VALE:
Hurricane 100 *If I Had Me A Woman* ....40.00 -   60.00

RITCHIE VALENS:
Del-Fi (LP) PR-1 *Ritchie Valens* ....40.00 -   70.00
    (LP) 1201 *Ritchie Valens* ....50.00 -   80.00
    (LP) 1206 *Ritchie* ....40.00 -   70.00
    (LP) 1214 - *In Concert At Pacoima Jr. High*.....40.00 -   80.00
    (LP) 1225 *His Greatest Hits* ....20.00 -   30.00
    (LP) 1247 *His Greatest Hits, Vol. 2*.................20.00 -   30.00

VALENTINES:
Ludix 102 *Johnny One Heart* ....7.00 -   10.00
Old Town 1009 *Tonight Kathleen* ....150.00 - 200.00
Rama 171 *Lily Maebelle* (blue label) ....15.00 -   20.00
    181 *I Love You Darling* (blue label) ....30.00 -   50.00
    186 *Christmas Prayer* (blue label)...................80.00 - 120.00
    196 *The Woo Woo Train* ....20.00 -   30.00
    201 *I'll Never Let You Go* ....20.00 -   30.00
    208 *Nature's Creation* ....20.00 -   30.00
    228 *Don't Say Goodnight* ....20.00 -   30.00

THE VALENTINOS:
Brunswick 55171 *A Kiss From Your Lips* ....20.00 -   30.00
Sar 132, 137, 144, 152, 155 ....7.00 -   10.00

THE VALETS:
Jon 4025 *When I Met You* ....40.00 -   60.00
    4219 *You And You Alone* ....8.00 -   12.00
Vulcan 135 *You And You Alone* ....50.00 -   80.00

THE VALIANTS:
Andex 4026 *Please Wait, My Love* ....20.00 -   40.00
Ensign 4035 *Walkin' Girl* ....7.00 -   10.00
Fredlo 6208 *Susan Come Back* ....10.00 -   15.00
Keen 34004 *This Is The Night* ....8.00 -   12.00
    3-4007 *Walkin' Girl* ....10.00 -   15.00
    3-4026 *Please Wait My Love* ....15.00 -   20.00

Shar Dee 703 *Dear Cindy*.................................40.00 -   70.00
Speck 1001 *Wedding Bells* ....400.00 -   up

FRANKIE VALLE/VALLEY/VALLI/VALLY (& THE ROMANS/THE TRAVELLERS):

Cindy 3012 *Real*...50.00 -   80.00
Corona 1234 *My Mother's Eyes* ....75.00 -   100.00
Decca 30994 *Please Take A Chance* ....40.00 -   60.00
Mercury 70381 *Forgive And Forget* (maroon or pink label)
....50.00 -   75.00

VALQUINS:

Gaity 161 *Falling Star* ....300.00 -   up

VAL-TONES:

De Luxe 6084 *Tender Darling* ....50.00 -   75.00
Gcc 1004 *You Belong To My Heart*............80.00 -   130.00

VALUMES (See also THE VOLUMES):

Chex 1002 *I Love You*.................................40.00 -   60.00

AL VANCE:

Goldwax 116 *Every Woman I Know* ....7.00 -   10.00

THE VAN DYKES:

Atlantic 2161 *King Of Fools*.......................10.00 -   20.00
Decca 30654 *The Fixer*................................10.00 -   15.00
    30762 *Come On Baby*.............................20.00 -   30.00
    31036 *Better Come Back To Me* ....10.00 -   15.00
De Luxe 6193 *The Bells Are Ringing* ....7.00 -   10.00
Donna 1333 *Guardian Angel*........................10.00 -   15.00
Green Sea 101 *Rich Girl*...............................8.00 -   12.00
    105 *I'll Get By*...8.00 -   12.00
Hue 6500 *No Man Is An Island* ....10.00 -   15.00
King 5158 *The Bells Are Ringing* ....20.00 -   30.00
Spring 1113 *Guardian Angel*........................50.00 -   75.00

THE VANGUARDS:

Derby 854 *Don't Let It Happen Again* ....30.00 -   50.00
Dot 15791 *Baby Doll* ....8.00 -   12.00
Ivy 103 *Moonlight* ....30.00 -   50.00
Regency 743 *Tears Fall* ....50.00 -   80.00
Ruth 439 *Last Night* ....15.00 -   25.00

THE VAN KIRKS:

Flame 110 *I Don't Want You* .... -   -   -

ARNOLD VAN WINKLE:

Ruby 540 *A Rusty Old Dime*.........................15.00 -   20.00

THE VARIETEERS:

Hickory 1004 *I've Got A Woman's Love*.........75.00 -   100.00
    1014 *I Pay With Every Breath I Take*.........50.00 -   80.00
    1025 *Call My Gal, Miss Jones*....................50.00 -   80.00

VARNELLS:

Arnold 1003 *Who Created Love* ....15.00 -   20.00
    1006 *All Because* ....10.00 -   15.00

CHEEK-O VASS & THE SOLA-TEARS:

Twy-Lite 752 *Desert Party Blues* .... -   -   -

BOBBY VAUGHN:

Whiz 503 *Good Good Lovin'* ....8.00 -   12.00

DALE VAUGHN:

Von 480 *High Steppin'* ....100.00 -   150.00

DELL VAUGHN with THE FORTUNE AIRES:

Fortune - *Rock The Universe* ....15.00 -   20.00
Hi-Q 5044 *Rock The Universe* ....10.00 -   15.00

VECTORS:

Standard 700 *One Day* ....20.00 -   30.00

RUSS VEERS:

Trend 30010 *Warm As Toast* ....15.00 -   20.00

VELAIRES/VEL-AIRES:

Dino 100 *Forever Always* ....200.00 -   up
Jamie 1198 *Roll Over Beethoven* ....7.00 -   10.00
    1203 *Sticks And Stones* ....5.00 -   8.00
    1211 *Ubangi Stomp*..................................7.00 -   10.00
    1223 *Memory Tree*....................................7.00 -   10.00

GENE VELL:

Whiz 9001 *I Done Got Over* ....10.00 -   15.00

VELOURS:

Cub 9001 *Remember* ....10.00 -   15.00
    9014 *Crazy Love* ....10.00 -   15.00
    9029 *Blue Velvet* ....8.00 -   12.00
End 1090 *Lover Come Back* ....8.00 -   12.00
Gone 5092 *Can I Come Over Tonight* ....8.00 -   12.00
Onyx 501 *My Love Come Back*.....................60.00 -   100.00
    508 *Romeo* ....100.00 -   150.00
    512 *Can I Come Over Tonight* ....40.00 -   70.00
    515 *This Could Be The Night* ....20.00 -   30.00
Onyx 520 *Remember* ....30.00 -   50.00
Orbit 9001 *Remember* ....10.00 -   15.00
Studio 9902 *I Promise* ....10.00 -   15.00

VELS:

Amy 881 *In-Laws* ....15.00 -   20.00
Trebco 702 *Please Be Mine* ....40.00 -   60.00

THE VELTONES:

Coy 101 *Playboy* ....80.00 -   130.00
Kapp 268 *Playboy* ....25.00 -   40.00
Mercury 71526 *Fool In Love* ....10.00 -   20.00
Satellite 100 *Fool In Love* ....40.00 -   60.00
Vel (unnumbered) *Please Say You'll Be True* ....150.00 -   200.00
Wedgc 1013 *My Dear*...................................4000 -   60.00
Zara 901 *I Need You* ....10.00 -   15.00

VELVATONES:

Meteor 5042 *Real Gone Baby*.......................30.00 -   50.00
Nu Kat 110 *Impossible* ....15.00 -   25.00

CHUCK VELVET:

USA 1224 *Red Lipstick*.................................. -   -   -

VELVETEENS:

Laurie 3126 *I Thank You* ....7.00 -   10.00
Stark 102 *Teen Prayer* ....8.00 -   12.00
    105 *I Thank You* ....7.00 -   10.00
    12591 *Please Holy Father* .... -   -   -

VELVETEERS:

Spitfire 15 *Tell Me You're Mine* ....300.00 -   up

THE VELVETIERS:

Ric 958 *Oh Baby* ....50.00 -   80.00

THE VELVET KEYS:

King 5090 *My Baby's Gone* ....20.00 -   30.00
    5109 *Don't Take My Picture* ....20.00 -   30.00

VELVETONES:

Aladdin 3372 *The Glory Of Love*...................50.00 -   80.00
    3391 *I Found My Love* ....50.00 -   80.00
    3463 *My Every Thought*...........................50.00 -   80.00
Ascot 2117 *I Want Him So Bad* ....5.00 -   8.00
Coronet 4 *Don't Say You're Sorry Again* ......150.00 -   200.00
D 1049 *Penalty Of Love*...............................25.00 -   40.00
    1072 *Worried Over You* ....20.00 -   30.00
Deb 1008 *Stars Of Wonder* ....50.00 -   80.00

Imperial 5878 *The Glory Of Love*...................................7.00 - 10.00
Milmart 113 *A Prayer At Gettysburg* ....35.00 - 50.00

THE VELVETS:
Fury 1012 *I-I-I (Love You So-So-So)*...................10.00 - 15.00
Monument (most issues) ....5.00 - 8.00
Pilgrim 706 *I*...8.00 - 12.00
Plaid 101 *Everybody Knows* ....10.00 - 15.00
Red Robin 120 *They Tried*...................................50.00 - 75.00
   122 *I*..40.00 - 70.00
   127 *I Cried*...50.00 - 75.00
20th Fox 165 *If I Could Be With You* ....8.00 - 12.00

THE VELVITONES (See VELVETONES)

NICK VENET:
Imperial 5522 *Love In Be Bop Time* ....8.00 - 12.00
RCA Victor (EP) 4100 *Flippin'* ....20.00 - 30.00

VENTURES:
Blue Horizon 100 *Cookies And Cake* ....8.00 - 12.00

THE VERDICTS:
East Coast 103 *My Life's Desire* ....75.00 - 100.00

VERNALLS:
Ru Lu 6753 *Raindrops*..100.00 - 150.00

LARRY VERNE:
Era (LP) 104 *Mister Larry Verne* ....30.00 - 50.00

VERNON & CLIFF:
Dootone 443 *You Came Along* ....8.00 - 12.00

VERNON & THE JEWELS:
Kayo 5104 *The Thought Of You* ....8.00 - 12.00

RAY VERNON:
Rumble 1349 *Evil Angel*......................................8.00 - 12.00
Scottie 1320 *Vendetta*..10.00 - 20.00

THE VERSATILES (See also JERRY SHEELY):
Atlantic 2004 *Passing By*....................................8.00 - 12.00
Coaster 800 *In The Garden Of Love*.....................8.00 - 12.00
Peacock 1910 *The White Cliffs Of Dover*...............8.00 - 12.00
Ramco 3717 *Just Pretending*................................50.00 - 80.00
Rocal 1002 *Lundee Dundee*..................................20.00 - 30.00
Staff 210 *Cry Like A Baby* ....8.00 - 10.00

VERSATONES:
All Star 501 *Tight Skirt And Sweater* ....10.00 - 20.00
Atlantic 2210 *Tight Skirt And Sweater* ....7.00 - 10.00
Richie 4081 *Will She Return* ....80.00 - 130.00

THE VESTELLES:
Decca 30733 *Ditta Wa Do* ....5.00 - 8.00

THE VETS:
Swami 551 *Wipe The Tears From Your Eyes*...........7.00 - 10.00

THE VIBES:
ABC Paramount 9810 *Darling* ....10.00 - 20.00
Allied 10006 *What's Her Name* ....20.00 - 30.00
   10007 *Misunderstood*......................................20.00 - 30.00
Chariot 105 *Stop Torturing Me*............................300.00 - up
Perspective 5858 *Pretty Baby*..............................20.00 - 30.00
Rayna 103 *You Got Me Crying* ....10.00 - 15.00

THE VIBRA-HARPS:
Atco 6134 *It Must Be Magic*.................................8.00 - 12.00
Beech 713 *Walk Beside Me* ....25.00 - 40.00
Fury 1022 *The Only Love Of Mine*.........................80.00 - 130.00

VIBRANAIRES:
After Hours 103 *Doll Face* (red plastic) ....400.00 - up
Chariot 103 *Doll Face* ....400.00 - up

THE VICEROYS/VICE-ROYS:
Aladdin 3273 *Please Baby Please* ....60.00 - 100.00
Little Star 107 *I'm So Sorry* ....30.00 - 50.00
Original Sound 15 *Dreamy Eyes* ....10.00 - 15.00
Ramco 3715 *My Heart* ....100.00 - 200.00
Smash 1716 *I'm So Sorry* ....7.00 - 10.00

MAC VICKERY:
Abco 502 *Bell Bottom Jeans*................................- - -
Gone 5075 *Meant To Be* ....8.00 - 12.00
   5085 *Goin' Back To St. Louis* ....8.00 - 12.00

RAY VICT & THE BOP ROCKERS:
Goldband 1042 *Bop Stop Rock* ....20.00 - 30.00

THE VICTORIANS:
Saxony 103 *Heartbreaking Moon*..........................150.00 - 200.00
Selma 1002 *Wedding Bells* ....50.00 - 75.00
Specialty 411 *Don't Break My Heart Again*.........150.00 - 200.00
   420 *Part Time Sweetheart**..............................- - -
(Note: * Existence of Specialty 420 in 45 RPM format has not been verified; 78s are known.)

VIDALTONES:
Josie 900 *Forever*..10.00 - 20.00

THE VIDELS:
Early 702 *I Wish*..300.00 - up
JDS 5004 *Mister Lonely*......................................10.00 - 15.00
   5005 *She's Not Coming Home* ....10.00 - 15.00
Kapp 361 *I'll Keep On Waiting* ....8.00 - 12.00
   405 *A Letter From Ann* ....10.00 - 15.00
Rhody 2000 *Be My Girl*.......................................15.00 - 20.00

THE VIDEOS:
Casino 102 *Moonglow You Know*...........................15.00 - 25.00
   105 *Love Or Infatuation*..................................50.00 - 75.00
Gone 5107 *Trickle Trickle* ....8.00 - 12.00

VI-KINGS:
Del-Mann 544 *Rock A Little Bit*............................10.00 - 15.00

THE VILONS:
Aljon 1259 *Mother Nature* ....20.00 - 30.00
Lake 713 *Let Me In Your Life* ....10.00 - 15.00

DARRYL VINCENT:
Sandy 1016 *Daddy's Gone Batty*...........................20.00 - 30.00
   1020 *Wild Wild Party*......................................20.00 - 30.00

GENE VINCENT & THE BLUE CAPS:
Capitol (EP) 764 *Bluejean Bop! each part* ....50.00 - 75.00
(Note: The EP is actually three, together comprising the LP following. Although the EP catalog numbers have prefixes 1-, 2-, and 3- designating parts 1, 2, and 3, these prefixes are omitted here and in the case of other EPs in series.)
Capitol (LP) 764 *Bluejean Bop!* ....100.00 - 150.00
   (EP) 811 *Gene Vincent And The Blue Caps* (3 parts) (each)
      ....50.00 - 75.00
   (LP) 811 *Gene Vincent And The Blue Caps*.....100.00 - 150.00
   (EP) *Gene Vincent Rocks And The Blue Caps Roll* (3 parts) (each)
      ....50.00 - 75.00
   (LP) 970 *Gene Vincent Rocks And The Blues Caps Roll*
      ....75.00 - 100.00
   (EP) 985 *Hot Rod Gang* ....100.00 - 150.00
   (EP) 1059 *A Gene Vincent Record Date* (3 parts)
      ....50.00 - 75.00

(LP) 1059 *A Gene Vincent Record Date*.............80.00 - 120.00
(LP) 1207 *Sounds Like Gene Vincent*.................80.00 - 120.00
(LP) 1342 *Crazy Times*.........................80.00 - 120.00
3450 *Be Bop A Lula* (78 rpm)................15.00 - 20.00
3450 *Be Bop A Lula* ....8.00 - 12.00
3530 *Race With The Devil* ....7.00 - 10.00
3558 *Bluejean Bop*.............................8.00 - 12.00
3558 *Bluejean Bop* (78 rpm)................20.00 - 30.00
3617 *Crazy Legs* ....10.00 - 15.00
3678 *Five Days Five Days*....................10.00 - 15.00
3763 *Lotta Lovin'* ....8.00 - 12.00
3763 *Lotta Lovin'* (78 rpm) ....30.00 - 50.00
3839 *Dance To The Bop* (78 rpm) ....50.00 - 80.00
3839 *Dance To The Bop* ....10.00 - 15.00
3874 *I Gotta Baby*............................15.00 - 20.00
3959 *Baby Blue* ....15.00 - 20.00
4010 *Rocky Road Blues* ....15.00 - 25.00
4051 *Git It* ....15.00 - 25.00
4105 *Be Bop Boogie Boy* ....20.00 - 30.00
4153 *Who's Pushin' Your Swing* ....15.00 - 20.00
4237 *Right Now* ....15.00 - 25.00
4313 *Wild Cat* ....20.00 - 30.00
4442 *Pistol Packin' Mama* ....15.00 - 20.00
4525 *If You Want My Lovin'* ....15.00 - 20.00
4665 *Lucky Star* ....15.00 - 25.00
Challenge 59365 *Hurtin' For You Baby*...................7.00 - 10.00

VINES:
Cee-Jay 582 *I Must See You Again*.........................10.00 - 20.00

DOT VINSON:
M-G-M 12734 *Livin' With The Blues*.......................8.00 - 12.00

EDDIE "CLEANHEAD" VINSON (See also BATTLE OF THE BLUES):
Aamco (LP) 74 *Clean Heads Back In Town* ....30.00 - 50.00
King 4563 *I Need You Tonight* ....10.00 - 20.00
    4582 *Person To Person* ....10.00 - 20.00
(Note: Earlier issues, usually found as 78 RPM records valued at
$7.00-$10.00, may be found as 45s, valued at $20.00 to $40.00,
or more, if pressed of colored vinyl.)
Mercury 70334 *Old Man Boogie*.........................8.00 - 12.00
    70525 *Anxious Heart* ....7.00 - 10.00
(Note: Earlier issues, in the Mercury 2000 and 8000 series, are 78
RPM records, valued at $5.00-$10.00.)

VIOLINAIRES:
Drummond 4000 *Another Soldier Gone*................300.00 - up

THE VIPERS:
Duchess 102 *Little Miss Sweetness* ....15.00 - 20.00

THE V. I. P. S:
Carmel 44 *Long John* .... - -
Congress 211 *My Girl Cried* ....10.00 - 15.00

VISCOUNTS (See also SAMMY HAGAN):
Amy (LP) 8008 *Harlem Nocturne* ....30.00 - 50.00
Madison (LP) 1001 *The Viscounts* ....40.00 - 60.00
Mercury 71073 *My Girl*.........................7.00 - 10.00
Star-Fax 1002 *Wandering*......................300.00 - up

THE VISIONS:
Big Top 3092 *Tell Me You're Mine*......................10.00 - 15.00
    3119 *Secret World Of Tears* ....10.00 - 15.00
Elgey 1003 *Teenager's Life* ....10.00 - 15.00
R & R 3002 *It's You I Love* ....100.00 - 150.00

VISUALS:
Poplar 115 *Submarine Race* ....10.00 - 15.00
    117 *My Juanita* ....10.00 - 15.00
    121 *Please Don't Be Mad At Me* ....80.00 - 120.00

THE VITELLS:
Decca 31362 *Shirley* ....10.00 - 20.00

VITO & THE SALUTATIONS:
Harold 7009 *Gloria*.........................5.00 - 8.00
Kram 1202 *Your Way*........................10.00 - 20.00
Rayna 5009 *Gloria*.........................10.00 - 15.00
Wells 1008 *Can I Depend On You*............10.00 - 20.00

THE VOCALEERS:
Old Town 1089 *Love And Devotion* ....10.00 - 15.00
Paradise 113 *I Need Your Love So Bad*........15.00 - 20.00
Red Robin 113 *Be True* ....75.00 - 100.00
    114 *Is It A Dream* ....75.00 - 100.00
    119 *I Walk Alone* ....75.00 - 100.00
    125 *Love You*..........................75.00 - 100.00
    132 *Angel Face* ....75.00 - 100.00
Twistime 45-T-II *A Golden Tear* ....7.00 - 10.00
Vest 832 *Hear My Plea* ....40.00 - 60.00

VOCALTONES:
Apollo 488 *My Girl*.........................40.00 - 60.00
    492 *Darling* ....50.00 - 80.00
    497 *My Version Of Love* ....60.00 - 100.00
Cindy 3004 *Walkin' My Baby*................50.00 - 80.00
Juanita 100 *Walkin' With My Baby* ....40.00 - 60.00

VOICE MASTERS:
Anna 101 *Hope And Pray* ....15.00 - 25.00
    102 *Needed*............................15.00 - 25.00
Frisco 15235 *Two Lovers* ....15.00 - 25.00

VOICES:
Cash 1011 *Why* ....10.00 - 20.00
    1014 *My Love Grows Stronger* ....15.00 - 20.00
    1015 *I Want To Be Ready* ....15.00 - 20.00
    1016 *Santa Claus Boogie* ....15.00 - 20.00

VOICES FIVE:
Craft 111 *You're Driving Me Crazy* ....40.00 - 70.00
    116 *For Sentimental Reasons* ....40.00 - 70.00
Stere-O-Craft 111 *You're Driving Me Crazy* ....15.00 - 30.00

WES VOIGHT (See also TOWN THREE):
King 5211 *I'm Movin' In* ....15.00 - 20.00

VOILINAIRES (See VIOLINAIRES):

THE VOLCANOS:
Harthon 138, 146 ....5.00 - 8.00
Tailspin 1 *You Knock Me Out* ....20.00 - 40.00

VOLTONES:
Dynamic 108 *If She Should Call*..............200.00 - up

THE VOLUMES:
Chex 1002 *I Love You*.........................8.00 - 12.00
    1005 *Come Back Into My Heart* ....8.00 - 12.00
Ivy 104 *In My Heart*..........................10.00 - 15.00
Jaguar 3004 *I Won't Tell A Soul* ....50.00 - 80.00
    3006 *So Disappointed With Love*.......40.00 - 70.00
Jubilee 5446 *Teenage Paradise* ....7.00 - 10.00
    5454 *Our Song* ....7.00 - 10.00
Old Town 1154 *Why* ....10.00 - 15.00

THE VONDELLS:
Marvello 5003 *Errand Boy* ....15.00 - 20.00
    5006 *Valentino* ....15.00 - 20.00

THE VOWS:
Markay 103 *I Wanna A Chance* ....100.00 - up
   103 *Have You Heard* ....15.00 - 20.00
Sta Set 402 *Say You'll Be Mine* ....10.00 - 15.00
Tamara 506 *Dottie* ....10.00 - 15.00
   760 *When A Boy Loves A Girl* ....10.00 - 15.00

THE VOXPOPPERS:
Amp 3 1004 *The Last Drag* ....10.00 - 15.00
Mercury 71282 *The Last Drag* ....5.00 - 8.00
   71315 *Ping Pong Baby* ....7.00 - 10.00
Versailles 200 *A Blessing After All* ....8.00 - 12.00

THE VOYAGERS:
Titan 1712 *I Never Loved Anyone* ....10.00 - 15.00

LYNN VROOMAN:
Penguin 1010 *Let The Good Times Roll* ....15.00 - 20.00

WADE & DICK:
Sun 269 *Bop Bop Baby*....................................15.00 - 20.00
   269 *Bop Bop Baby* (78 rpm) ....20.00 - 30.00

DON WADE:
San 206 *Gone, Gone, Gone* ....30.00 - 50.00

MORRIS WADE:
Ransom 102 *Is It Too Late*..............................100.00 - 150.00

ROGER WADE:
Harmon 1003 *I Can Only Hurt You* ....15.00 - 20.00

RONNIE/RONNY WADE:
King 5061 *Gotta Make Her Mine*....................15.00 - 20.00
   5078 *I Know But I'll Never Tell* ....15.00 - 20.00
   5099 *Annie Don't Work* ....15.00 - 20.00
   5112 *All I Want*...15.00 - 20.00

CHARLIE WAGGONER:
Linco 503 *One Eyed Sam* ....25.00 - 40.00

PORTER WAGONER:
RCA Victor (LP) 1358 *Satisfied Man* ....20.00 - 30.00

THE WAILERS:
Columbia 40288 *Stop The Clock* ....30.00 - 60.00
Golden Crest (LP) 3075 *The Fabulous Wailers* ......40.00 - 70.00

HAPPY WAINWRIGHT:
Sandy 1004 *My Baby Don't Love Me No More* ......30.00 - 50.00

LES WALDROOP:
Flop 1012 *Got It Made In The Shade* ....20.00 - 30.00

JACKIE WALKER:
Imperial 5473 *Peggy Sue* ....10.00 - 15.00
   5490 *Only Teenagers Allowed*.....................8.00 - 12.00
   5521 *Good, Good Feelin'* ....8.00 - 12.00

LANIE WALKER:
Blue Hen 219 *Why Baby Why*..........................8.00 - 12.00
   230 *No Use Knocking* ....10.00 - 15.00

T-BONE WALKER:
Atlantic 1065 *T-Bone Shuffle*..........................20.00 - 30.00
   1074 *Play On Little Girl* ....20.00 - 30.00
   (LP) 8020 *T-Bone Blues* ....75.00 - 100.00
Capitol (LP) 370 *T-Bone Walker* (10 inch) ....75.00 - 100.00
   (LP) 1958 *The Great Blues Vocals & Guitar Of T-Bone Walker*
      ....40.00 - 60.00
Imperial 5171 *Cold Cold Boogie* (blue label)..........75.00 - 100.00
   5202 *Street Walking Woman* ....75.00 - 100.00
   5216 *Blue Mood* ....60.00 - 100.00
   5228 *Long Distance Blues* ....60.00 - 100.00

   5239 *Party Girl* ....50.00 - 80.00
   5284 *Wanderin' Heart* ....40.00 - 60.00
   5311 *High Society* ....40.00 - 60.00
   (LP) 9098 *T-Bone Walker Sings The Blues* ....80.00 - 130.00
   (LP) 9116 *Singing The Blues* ....80.00 - 130.00
   (LP) 9146 *I Get So Weary*.........................80.00 - 130.00

WAYNE WALKER:
Brunswick 55133 *You've Got Me* ....8.00 - 12.00
Columbia 40905 *A Teenage Love Affair*.........8.00 - 12.00
Everest 19380 *Love, Love, Love* ....8.00 - 12.00

"WALKIN' BY MYSELF":
Chess (LP) 1446 (various artists)......................30.00 - 60.00

SHADY WALL:
Decca 30539 *The New Raunchy*......................7.00 - 10.00

BILLY WALLACE (& THE BAMA DRIFTERS):
Deb 1003 *Don't Flirt With My Baby* ....10.00 - 15.00
Mercury 70876 *That's My Reward* ....15.00 - 25.00
   70957 *Mean Mistreatin' Baby* ....15.00 - 25.00

JOE WALLACE & THE OWLS:
Moon 304 *Leopard Man* ....30.00 - 50.00

VANN WALLS & THE ROCKETS:
Atlantic 988 *Open The Door*...........................40.00 - 80.00

WALTON & SILVER LAKE BOYS:
Lael 1137 *Man What A Party* ....75.00 - 100.00

JAMES WALTON & HIS BLUES KINGS:
Hi-Q 5029 *Miss Jessie James* ....5.00 - 10.00

SQUARE WALTON:
RCA Victor 5493 *Gimme Your Bank Roll* ....20.00 - 30.00
   5584 *Bad Hangover* ....20.00 - 30.00

THE WANDERERS:
Cub 9003 *A Teenage Quarrel* ....7.00 - 10.00
   9019 *Two Hearts* ....10.00 - 15.00
   9023 *Please* ....8.00 - 12.00
   9035 *I'm Not Ashamed*..............................8.00 - 12.00
   9054 *I Walked Through A Forest*...............8.00 - 12.00
   9075, 9089, 9094, 9099, 9109..................7.00 - 10.00
Onyx 518 *Thinking Of You* ....20.00 - 30.00
Orbit 9003 *A Teenage Quarrel* ....10.00 - 15.00
Savoy 1109 *We Could Find Happiness* ....100.00 - 200.00
United Artists 570 *After He Breaks Your Heart* ......8.00 - 12.00
   648 *I'll Know* ....10.00 - 15.00

BILLY WARD & HIS DOMINOES (See also The Dominoes & Clyde McPhatter):
Decca (EP) 2549 *Billy Ward & The Dominoes*.......75.00 - 100.00
   (LP) 8621 *Billy Ward & The Dominoes* ....75.00 - 125.00
   29933, 30043, 30149.................................7.00 - 10.00
   30420 *To Each His Own* ....10.00 - 15.00
Federal (LP) 295-94 (10-inch) ....1000.00 - up
(Note: * Regarded as one of the rarest albums, prices of $5,000.00, $10,000.00, and even $20,000.00 have been seen as estimates of its value.)
   (LP) 395-94 (12 inch) ....300.00 - 600.00
   (LP) 548 *Billy Ward & His Dominoes*..............80.00 - 130.00
   12139 *You Can't Keep A Good Man Down*.......30.00 - 50.00
   12162 *Until The Real Thing Comes Along* ....20.00 - 30.00
   12178 *Tootsie Roll* ....20.00 - 30.00
   12184 *Handwriting On The Wall*................20.00 - 30.00
   12193 *Above Jacob's Ladder*......................20.00 - 30.00
   12209 *Can't Do Sixty No More* ....15.00 - 20.00
   12218 *Cave Man* ....15.00 - 20.00

12263 *Bobby Sox Baby*	10.00 -	15.00
12301 *One Moment With You*	10.00 -	15.00
12308 *Have Mercy Baby*	10.00 -	15.00
Jubilee 5163 *Come To Me Baby*	8.00 -	12.00
5213 *Take Me Back To Heaven*	8.00 -	12.00

King (LP) 548 *Billy Ward & His Dominoes With Clyde McPhatter* ....50.00 - 100.00

(Note: King 548 is a repackaging of Federal 548, above.)

(LP) 733 *Billy Ward And His Dominoes*	50.00 -	100.00
1280 *Rags To Riches*	8.00 -	12.00
1281 *Christmas In Heaven*	20.00 -	30.00
1342 *Tenderly*	15.00 -	20.00
1364 *Three Coins In The Fountain*	8.00 -	12.00
1365 *Little Things Mean A Lot*	10.00 -	15.00
1492 *Learnin' The Blues*	10.00 -	15.00
1502 *Give Me You*	10.00 -	15.00
5463 *Lay In On The Line*	7.00 -	10.00
Liberty (LP) 3056 *Sea Of Glass*	20.00 -	30.00
(LP) 3083 *Yours Forever*	20.00 -	30.00

LEE WARD:
Gait 407 *The Defense Rest* ....15.00 - 25.00

LITTLE SAMMY WARD:
P-C 1091 *Begging For Love* .... - - -

WALTER WARD & THE CHALLENGERS:
Melatone 1002 *I Can't Tell*..........................80.00 - 130.00

WILLIE WARD:
Fee-Bee 233 *I'm A Madman*.........................15.00 - 20.00

EDDIE WARE & HIS BAND:
States 130 *Lonely Broken Heart* ....25.00 - 40.00

MERRILL WARNER:
Travel 505 *Don't Let Me Dream Tonight* ......20.00 - 30.00

BABY BOY WARREN:
Blue Lake 106 *Sante Fe* (red plastic) ....300.00 - 500.00
Drummond 3003 *Stop Breakin' Down* ....300.00 - 500.00

DOUG WARREN & THE RAYS:
Image 1011 *Around Midnight*.......................10.00 - 15.00

JOEY WARREN:
Superior 3305 *Goatee* ....5.00 - 10.00

WASHBOARD SAM:
Chess 1545 *Diggin' My Potatoes* ....75.00 - 100.00
RCA Victor 50-0023 *I'm Just Tired*...............30.00 - 50.00
50-0048 *Market Street Swing* ....30.00 - 50.00
50-0090 *Motherless Child Blues* ....30.00 - 50.00
(Note: Above RCA Victor records are made of orange plastic.)

BABY WASHINGTON (& THE PLANTS):
Checker 918 *I Hate To See You Go* ....7.00 - 10.00
J & S 1604 *There Must Be A Reason* ....15.00 - 20.00
1607 *Been A Long Time, Baby* ....10.00 - 15.00
1632 *I Hate To See You Go* ....10.00 - 15.00
Neptune 107 *Let's Love In The Moonlight* ......8.00 - 12.00
Sue (LP) 1014 *That's How Heartaches Are Made* ..30.00 - 50.00

DINAH WASHINGTON (See also THE RAVENS):
Mercury 70336 *Such A Night* ....8.00 - 12.00
70600 *If It's The Last Thing I Do* ....8.00 - 12.00
Mercury, most other issues ....5.00 - 10.00

LEROY WASHINGTON:
Excello 2144 *Wild Cherry* ....10.00 - 15.00
2172 *My True Life* ....10.00 - 15.00

CROWN PRINCE WATERFORD (See "PARTY AFTER HOURS", AND BLUES, ETC. section)

BILL/BILLY WATKINS:
Allied 10001 *Sandman Of Love* ....25.00 - 40.00
Chess 1786 *Where Is My Love* ....8.00 - 12.00
Robell 1001 *Little Things Mean A Lot* ....10.00 - 20.00
Tip-Toe 14321 *I Got Troubles* ....40.00 - 60.00

KATIE WATKINS:
Checker 879 *Snake Blues*..............................7.00 - 10.00

LACILLE WATKINS & THE VOLUMES (See THE VOLUMES)

VIOLA WATKINS:
Jubilee 5095 *Really Real* .... - - -

GENE WATSON & THE ROCKETS:
Tri-Dec 8357 *My Rockin' Baby* ....40.00 - 60.00

JIMMY WATSON:
Brunswick 55079 *Daisy* ....7.00 - 10.00

YOUNG JOHN WATSON:
Federal 12120 *Highway 60* ....75.00 - 100.00
12131 *Motor Head Baby*..............................75.00 - 100.00
12143 *I Got Eyes* ....50.00 - 75.00
12157 *What's Going On* ....40.00 - 60.00
12175 *Space Guitar* ....30.00 - 50.00

JOHNNY WATSON:
Cactus - *I'm Not Crazy* ....15.00 - 20.00

JOHNNY "GUITAR" WATSON:
Chess (LP) 1490 *The Blues Soul of...* ....50.00 - 75.00
Class 246 *One More Kiss*..............................7.00 - 10.00
Goth 101 *Rat Now* ....8.00 - 12.00
Jowat 118 *Baby Don't Leave* ....7.00 - 10.00
King (LP) 857 *Johnny "Guitar" Watson*..........50.00 - 80.00
RPM 423 *Hot Little Mama* ....10.00 - 20.00
431 *Don't Touch Me* ....10.00 - 15.00
436 *Someone Cares For Me* ....10.00 - 15.00
447 *Watson Oh Baby* ....10.00 - 15.00
455 *Three Hours Past Midnight* ....10.00 - 15.00
471 *She Moves Me* ....10.00 - 15.00

HUNTER WATTS:
Hammond 103 *Wild Man Rock*......................20.00 - 30.00

NOBLE ("THIN MAN") WATTS:
Baton 246, 249, 251, 254, 257, 266, 273 ....5.00 - 10.00

SLIM WATTS:
Starday 282 *Tu La Lou*.................................40.00 - 60.00

ALVIS WAYNE:
Westport 132 *Swing Bop Boogie* ....30.00 - 50.00
138 *Don't Mean Maybe, Baby* ....25.00 - 40.00
140 *You Are The One* ....20.00 - 30.00

BILLY WAYNE:
Hill Crest 778 *I Love My Baby*......................75.00 - 100.00

BOBBY WAYNE (with THE WARRIORS):
LV 101 *Sally Ann*..15.00 - 20.00
Mercury 71070 *Gone* ....7.00 - 10.00

DON WAYNE:
Swan 4024 *Let Me Be Your Plaything* ....10.00 - 15.00

GAYLON WAYNE:
Universal Artist 52071 *High School's On Fire* ......10.00 - 15.00

LITTLE JACKY WAYNE:
Rem 306 *White Felt Hat* ....75.00 - 100.00

JAMES WAYNE:
Aladdin 3234 *Crying In Vain* ....20.00 - 30.00
Imperial 5258 *Sweet Little Woman* ....30.00 - 50.00
Peacock 1672 *Please Be Mine* ....10.00 - 15.00

ROY WAYNE:
Clif 101 *Honey Won't You Listen* ....50.00 - 100.00

SCOTTY WAYNE:
Talent Scout 1008 *Only One* ....10.00 - 15.00
   1011 *Roobie Doobie* ....10.00 - 15.00

THOMAS WAYNE:
Fernwood 106 *You're The One That Done It* ....8.00 - 12.00
Fernwood 109, 111, 113, 122 ....5.00 - 10.00
Mercury 71287 *You're The One That Done It*..........5.00 - 8.00

WEE WILLIE WAYNE:
Imperial 5355 *Travelin' Mood*.............................30.00 - 50.00
   5368 *Good News*...10.00 - 15.00
   5737 *I Got To Be Careful* ....7.00 - 10.00
(LP) 9144 *Travelin' Mood*.....................................80.00 - 130.00

ALFY WEATHERBEE:
Roulette 4005 *49 Jukeboxes* ....7.00 - 10.00

JOE WEAVER & THE BLUENOTES/DON JUANS:
Fortune 825 *Baby, I Love You So* ....15.00 - 25.00
   832 *Baby Child* ....15.00 - 25.00
Jaguar 3011 *Lazy Susan* ....25.00 - 40.00

BOBBY WEBB (& THE JETS):
Jazzmar 1 *Feel The Same* ....15.00 - 20.00
Webb 429 *Tears Over You* ....15.00 - 20.00

BOOGIE BILL WEBB:
Imperial 5257 *Bad Dog* ....50.00 - 80.00

DON WEBB:
Brunswick 55158 *I'll Be Back Home* ....10.00 - 15.00

HOYT WEBB:
Ruby 320 *Baby Won't You Slow It Down*................20.00 - 30.00

ROLLIE WEBBER:
Virgelle 721 *Klickety Klack*..................................10.00 - 15.00

LEWIS WEBER:
Scottie 1304 *Queen Of Rock & Roll* ....25.00 - 40.00

WEBS:
Guyden 2090 *Question* ....20.00 - 30.00
Sotoplay 006 *Let Me Take You Home* ....80.00 - 130.00

KATIE WEBSTER:
Action 1000 *Close To My Heart*............................7.00 - 10.00
Rocko 503, 513...8.00 - 12.00
U.S.A. 736, 742 ....5.00 - 10.00
Zynn 505 *Hoowee, Sweet Daddy*...........................10.00 - 15.00

THE WEBTONES:
M-G-M 12724 *My Lost Love* ....10.00 - 15.00

RUSTY WELLINGTON (& HIS BLUE RANGERS):
Arcade 124 *I Want A Little Lovin'*.........................25.00 - 40.00
M-G-M 12581 *Rocking Chair On The Moon* ....15.00 - 30.00

ARDIS WELLS:
Azalea *132 Baby Doll* ....15.00 - 25.00

BILLY WELLS & THE CRESCENTS (See also THE CRESCENTS):
Reserve 105 *Julie* ....75.00 - 100.00

GLENN WELLS & THE BLENDS:
Jin 122 *Lesson In Love*..7.00 - 10.00

JUNIOR WELLS (& HIS EAGLE ROCKERS):
Chief 7005 *Two Headed Woman* ....10.00 - 15.00
   7008 *I Could Cry* ....10.00 - 15.00
   7016 *A Galloping Mule* ....10.00 - 15.00
   7021 *Universal Rock* ....10.00 - 15.00
   7030 *I'm a Stranger* ....10.00 - 15.00
   7034 *You Sure Look Good To Me*...................10.00 - 15.00
   7035 *It Hurts Me Too* ....10.00 - 15.00
   7038 *I Need Me A Car* ....10.00 - 15.00
Profile 4005 *I Could Cry*......................................10.00 - 15.00
   4011 *Come On In This House* ....10.00 - 15.00
   4013 *You Don't Care* ....10.00 - 15.00
Shad 5010 *So Tired* ....10.00 - 15.00
States 122 *Cut That Out* (red plastic) ....200.00 - 400.00
   134 *Junior's Wail* (red plastic) ....200.00 - 450.00
   139 *'Bout The Break Of Day* (red plastic) ....150.00 - 300.00
   143 *So All Alone* (red plastic) ....150.00 - 300.00

MARY WELLS:
Motown (LP) 600 *Bye Bye Baby - I Don't Want To Take A Chance* ....50.00 - 75.00
   (LP) 605 *The One Who Really Loves You* ....30.00 - 50.00
   (LP) 607 *Two Lovers And Other Hits* ....20.00 - 40.00

COY WERLEY:
Sundown 122 *Black Jack* ....15.00 - 30.00

JIMMY WERT:
Skyline 752 *Bingo Blues* ....30.00 - 40.00

JOE WEST:
Bandbox 276 *Maybe You're The One*......................7.00 - 10.00

PENNY WEST:
Ozark 102 *Needle In A Haystack*..............................- - -

SONNEE WEST:
Nor Va Jak 1956 *Rock Ola Ruby* ....200.00 - up

SONNY WEST:
Atlantic 1174 *Rave On*..15.00 - 20.00

SPEEDY WEST:
Capitol (LP) 1341 *Steel Guitar* ....20.00 - 30.00

KENT WESTBERRY:
Art 172 *My Baby Don't Rock Me*..............................- - -

WALT WESTBROOK:
Bobbin 106, 119..7.00 - 10.00

GEORGE WESTON:
Jackpot 48013 *Hey Little Car Hop* ....5.00 - 10.00
   48017 *Shelley Shelley* ....6.00 - 10.00
Talley 118 *Hold Still Baby*..................................10.00 - 15.00

THE WESTSIDERS:
Leopard 5004 *No Tears Left For Crying* ....10.00 - 20.00
United Artists 500 *No Tears Left For Crying* ....5.00 - 8.00

BOBBY WHEELER:
Diamond 101 *Rock & Roll Baby*...........................25.00 - 40.00

ONIE WHEELER:
Columbia 21371, 21418, 21454, 21500, 21523,
   40787, 40917...5.00 - 10.00
K-Ark 671 *Too Hot To Handle* ....10.00 - 15.00

Okeh 18022 *Run 'Em Off* ....8.00 - 12.00
　　18049 *Little Mama* ....10.00 - 15.00
Scottie 1325 *Too Hot To Handle* ....10.00 - 15.00

THE WHEELERS:
Cenco 107 *Once I Had A Girl* ....15.00 - 20.00

THE WHEELS:
Premium 405 *My Hearts Desire* ....15.00 - 20.00
　　408 *Teasin' Heart* ....25.00 - 40.00
　　410 *How Could I Ever Leave* ....50.00 - 75.00
Time 1003 *So Young And So In Love* ....15.00 - 25.00

THE WHIPS:
Flair 1025 *Pleading Heart* ....250.00 - up

WHIRLERS:
Port 70025 *Magic Mirror* ....8.00 - 12.00
Whirlin Disc 108 *Magic Mirror* ....25.00 - 40.00

THE WHIRLWINDS:
Guyden 2052 *Angel Love* ....8.00 - 12.00
Philips 40139 *At The Party* ....40.00 - 70.00

WHISPERS:
Dore 724 *The Happy One* ....8.00 - 12.00
　　729 *Never Again* ....8.00 - 12.00
　　735 *It Hurts So Much* ....7.00 - 10.00
　　740 *As I Sit Here* ....8.00 - 12.00
Gotham 7-309 *Fool Heart* ....40.00 - 70.00
　　7-312 *Are You Sorry* ....150.00 - 250.00

BOBBY WHITE:
End 1097 *Our Last Goodbye* ....20.00 - 30.00

BUDDY WHITE:
Milestone 2006 *Unlucky Man* ....8.00 - 12.00

DONNIE WHITE:
King 5122 *That's My Doll* ....10.00 - 15.00

FLOYD WHITE & THE DEALERS:
Criterion 1 *Cinderella* ....30.00 - 50.00
Tee Vee 302 *Pains Of Love* ....40.00 - 70.00

JOSH WHITE:
Decca (LP) 5082 *Ballads* (10 inch) ....20.00 - 30.00
　　(LP) 5247 *Ballads, Vol. 2* (10 inch)......20.00 - 30.00
　　(LP) 8665 *Josh White* ....40.00 - 60.00
Elektra (LP) 102 *Josh At Midnight* ....20.00 - 30.00
　　(LP) 114 *Josh* ....20.00 - 30.00
　　(LP) 123 *25th Anniversary Album* ....20.00 - 30.00
　　(LP) 158 *Chain Gang Songs* ....15.00 - 25.00
London (LP) 338 (10 inch) ....15.00 - 20.00
　　(LP) 1341 *Josh White Program* ....20.00 - 30.00
Mercury (LP) 25014 *Josh White Sings* (10 inch) ....15.00 - 20.00
　　(LP) 20203 *Josh White's Blues* ....20.00 - 30.00
Period (LP) 1209 *(And Big Bill Broonzy)*................40.00 - 60.00
Stinson (LP) 14 *Blues* (10 inch)................. - - -
　　(LP) 15 *Folk Songs* (10 inch)............... - - -

FUZZY WHITENER:
Starday 704(?) *Sugar Buggar* .... - - -

WILBUR WHITFIELD & THE PLEASERS:
Aladdin 3381 *P. B. Baby* ....15.00 - 30.00

RAY WHITLEY:
Vee Jay 433 *Yessirree-Yessirree* ....7.00 - 10.00

SLIM WHITMAN:
Imperial (EP) 106, 131, 132, 133, 134, 135,
　　136, 137 ....20.00 - 30.00
　　8134 *My Love Is Growing Stale* ....15.00 - 20.00

8144 *Bandera Waltz* ....10.00 - 15.00
8156 *China Doll* ....10.00 - 15.00
8163 *By The Waters Of The Minnetonka* .... 8.00 - 12.00
8169 *Keep It A Secret* .... 8.00 - 12.00
8180 *How Can I Tell?* ....10.00 - 15.00
8189 *Restless Heart* .... 8.00 - 12.00
8201 *Danny Boy* .... 7.00 - 10.00
8208 *Darlin' Don't Cry* .... 7.00 - 10.00
8220 *Stairway To Heaven* .... 7.00 - 10.00
8223 *Secret Love* .... 7.00 - 10.00
8236 *We Stood At The Altar* .... 7.00 - 10.00
(Note: Above are blue label with script lettering; following are red
　　label with script lettering.)
Imperial 8257 *Beautiful Dreamer* .... 7.00 - 10.00
　　8267 *The Singing Hills* .... 7.00 - 10.00
　　8281 *Cattle Call* .... 7.00 - 10.00
　　8290 *Roll On, Silvery Moon* .... 7.00 - 10.00
　　8298 *I'll Never Stop Loving You* .... 7.00 - 10.00
　　8299 *You Have My Heart* .... 7.00 - 10.00
　　8304, 8305, 8307, 8308, 8309, 8310, 8312, 8316,
　　　　8317, 8318, 8319, 8320, 8321, 8322, 8323,
　　　　8326, 8327, 8328, 8329 .... 5.00 - 10.00
　　5731, 5746, 5766, 5778, 5791, 5821, 5859, 5871,
　　　　5900, 5919, 5938, 5966 .... 5.00 - 8.00
　　(LP) 9003 *Slim Whitman Favorites* (maroon label)
　　　　..25.00 - 40.00
　　(LP) 9026 *Slim Whitman Sings* ....20.00 - 30.00
　　(LP) 9056 *Slim Whitman* ....15.00 - 25.00
　　(LP) 9064 *Country Favorites* ....15.00 - 25.00
RCA Victor (LP) 3217 *Sings & Yodels* (10 inch). 100.00 - 150.00
　　48-0145 *Birmingham Jail* ....20.00 - 30.00
(Note: Above is pressed of translucent green plastic.)

WHOOPING CRANES:
El Rey 1000 *Heart And Soul* .... 5.00 - 8.00

"WHOOPERS":
Jubilee (LP) 1119 *(The Dominoes, Orioles, et al.)* . 50.00 - 100.00

JOHNNY WICK:
United 116 *Jockey Jack Boogie* .... 75.00 - 100.00

WALLY WIGGINS:
Mercury 71645 *Maybe Someday* ....10.00 - 15.00

COYE WILCOX:
Azalea 124 *Zippy, Hippy, Dippy* ....10.00 - 15.00

THE WILD CHILDS:
Cascade 102 *I'm Leaving Town Baby* ....10.00 - 15.00

ARTIE WILKINS (See THE PALMS)

CHUCK WILEY:
United Artists 113 *Tear It Up* ....15.00 - 20.00

RICHARD WILKINSON:
Tone 1126 *Wicked Woman* .... 8.00 - 12.00

JESS WILLARD:
Ekko 1018 *Don't Hold Her So Close* ....10.00 - 15.00

SLIM WILLETT:
Audio Lab (LP) 1542 ....40.00 - 70.00
4-Star 1614 *Hadacol Corners* .... 8.00 - 12.00
Winston 1036 *Toolpusher* .... 7.00 - 10.00

WALLY WILLETTE:
Flag 118 *Eenie Meenie* ....75.00 - 100.00

AL WILLIAMS & THE BARDS:
Dawn 208 *I'm A Winedrinker* ....40.00 - 70.00

ANDRE WILLIAMS (& THE DON JUANS/FIVE DOLLARS/INSPIRATIONS):

Epic 9196 *Bacon Fat*	8.00 -	12.00
Fortune 824 *Pulling Time*	15.00 -	20.00
831 *Bacon Fat*	15.00 -	20.00
834 *Mean Jean*	15.00 -	20.00
837 *Jail Bait*	15.00 -	20.00
839 *Come On, Baby*	15.00 -	20.00
851 *Movin*	8.00 -	12.00
856 *Jail House Blues*	15.00 -	20.00
Ronald 1001 *Please Give Me A Chance*	10.00 -	15.00

BERNIE WILLIAMS:

Imperial 5360 *Don't Tease Me*	15.00 -	25.00

BILLY WILLIAMS:

Coral (LP) 57251 *Half Sweet, Half Beat*	25.00 -	40.00
61212 *Sh-Boom*	8.00 -	12.00
61264 *The Honeydripper*	8.00 -	12.00
61363 *Smoke From Your Cigarette*	8.00 -	12.00
61462 *The Glory Of Love*	8.00 -	12.00
61639 *You'll Reach A Star*	8.00 -	12.00
(most other issues)	5.00 -	10.00
Mercury 5866 *Azure*	8.00 -	12.00
5884 *It's Best We Say Goodbye*	8.00 -	12.00
5902 *That's What I'm Here For*	8.00 -	12.00
70012 *I Don't Know Why*	8.00 -	12.00
70094 *Pour Me A Glass Of Teardrops*	8.00 -	12.00
70180 *This Side Of Heaven*	8.00 -	12.00
(most other issues)	5.00 -	10.00
(LP) 20317 *Oh Yeah*	30.00 -	50.00
M-G-M 10928 *I Won't Cry Anymore*	10.00 -	15.00
10967 *You Made Me Love You*	10.00 -	15.00
11066 *It's Over*	10.00 -	15.00
11117 *I'll Never Fail You*	10.00 -	15.00
M-G-M (most other issues)	7.00 -	12.00

BOB WILLIAMS (See also THE CYCLONES):

Debonair 161 *My Goose Is Cooked*	5.00 -	8.00

BUZZ WILLIAMS:

Worthmore (DP) 185 *Blue Suede Shoes; Heartbreak Hotel* other cuts by other artist of no interest	7.00 -	10.00

CORA WILLIAMS with THE FOUR JACKS:

Federal 12079 *Sure Cure For The Blues*	75.00 -	100.00

EDDIE WILLIAMS:

Alcor 2013 *Have A Heart*	10.00 -	20.00
Baronet 4 *Never Too Late*	8.00 -	12.00
Corsair 402 *Tears Had Fallen*	8.00 -	12.00
Excello 2158 *You Broke Your Vows*	8.00 -	12.00
R-dell 114 *Never Too Late*	15.00 -	20.00

FLETCHER WILLIAMS:

Bullseye 1001 *Mary Lou*	7.00 -	10.00

HANK WILLIAMS:

M-G-M (LP) 107 *Hank Williams Sings* (10 inch)	40.00 -	60.00
(LP) 168 *Moanin' The Blues* (10 inch)	50.00 -	75.00
(LP) 202 *Memorial Album* (10 inch)	35.00 -	50.00
(LP) 203 *Hank Williams As Luke The Drifter* (10 inch)	75.00 -	100.00
(LP) 242 *Honky Tonkin'* (10 inch)	50.00 -	75.00
(LP) 243 *I Saw The Light* (10 inch)	50.00 -	75.00
(LP) 291 *Ramblin' Man* (10 inch)	15.00 -	20.00
(EP) 1014 *Crazy Heart*	15.00 -	20.00
(EP) 1076 *Move It On Over*	15.00 -	20.00
(EP) 1082 *There'll Be No Teardrops Tonight*	15.00 -	20.00
(EP) 1101, 1102 *Hank Williams Sings*	15.00 -	20.00

(EP) 1135, 1136 *Ramblin' Man*	35.00 -	50.00
(EP) 1165 *Luke The Drifter*	15.00 -	20.00
(EP) 1215, 1216, 1217 *Moanin' The Blues*	15.00 -	20.00
(EP) 1218 *I Saw The Light*	15.00 -	20.00
(EP) 1317, 1318, 1319 *Honky Tonkin'*	15.00 -	20.00
(EP) 1491, 1492, 1493 *Sing Me A Blue Song*	15.00 -	20.00
(EP) 1554, 1555, 1556 *The Immortal Hank Williams*	10.00 -	15.00
(LP) 3219 *Ramblin' Man*	40.00 -	70.00
(LP) 3267 *Hank Williams As Luke The Drifter*	50.00 -	80.00
(LP) 3272 *Memorial Album*	35.00 -	60.00
(LP) 3330 *Moanin' The Blues*	35.00 -	60.00
(LP) 3331 *I Saw The Light*	40.00 -	70.00
(LP) 3412 *Honky Tonkin'*	35.00 -	50.00
(LP) 3560 *Sing Me A Blue Song*	35.00 -	50.00
(LP) 3605 *The Immortal Hank Williams*	35.00 -	50.00
(LP) 3733 *The Unforgettable*	25.00 -	35.00
(LP) 3803 *The Lonesome Sound Of*	20.00 -	30.00

(Note: Above must have original yellow and black labels.)

M-G-M 30751, 30752, 30753, 30754 together comprise 45 RPM album set - 202, *Hank Williams Memorial Album*	30.00 -	40.00
30755, 30756, 30757, 30758 together comprise 45 RPM album set - 203, *Hank Williams As Luke The Drifter*	30.00 -	50.00

JIM(MIE) WILLIAMS:

Dub 2842 *You're Always Late*	15.00 -	25.00
Sun 270 *That Depends On You*	10.00 -	15.00

JODY WILLIAMS:

Argo 5274 *Lucky Lou*	8.00 -	12.00

PO' JOE WILLIAMS:

Atomic H (unnumbered) *Rock 'N' Roll Boogie*	20.00 -	30.00

LARRY WILLIAMS:

Specialty 608 *Short Fat Fannie*	7.00 -	10.00
608 *Short Fat Fannie* (78 rpm)	15.00 -	20.00
615 *Bony Moronie*	7.00 -	10.00
615 *Bony Moronie* (78 rpm)	15.00 -	25.00
626 *Dizzy, Miss Lizzy*	7.00 -	10.00
626 *Dizzy, Miss Lizzy* (78 rpm)	15.00 -	20.00
634 *Hootchy-Koo*	5.00 -	8.00
634 *Hootchy-Koo* (78 rpm)	10.00 -	15.00
647 *I Was A Fool*	5.00 -	8.00
647 *I Was A Fool* (78 rpm)	10.00 -	15.00
(LP) 2109 *Here's Larry Williams*	50.00 -	80.00

LAWTON WILLIAMS:

Colony 101 *Get On The Ball, Paul*	-	-

LESTER WILLIAMS:

Duke 123 *Let's Do It*	15.00 -	25.00
131 *Crazy 'Bout My Baby*	15.00 -	25.00
Imperial 5402 *McDonald's Daughter*	20.00 -	30.00

LEW WILLIAMS:

Imperial 5394 *Cat Talk*	20.00 -	30.00
5411 *Bop Bop Ba Doo Bop*	20.00 -	30.00
5429 *Centipede*	15.00 -	20.00
8306 *I'll Play Your Game*	15.00 -	20.00

MAURICE WILLIAMS & THE ZODIACS:

Herald (most issues)	5.00 -	10.00
(LP) 1014 *Stay*	75.00 -	100.00

MEL WILLIAMS (& THE MONTCLAIRS):

Decca 29370 *Lessons In Love*	10.00 -	15.00
29499 *Eternal Love*	10.00 -	15.00
29554 *God Gave Me You*	10.00 -	15.00

Dig (LP) 103 *All Through The Night*......................80.00 - 130.00
   107 *Here At My Phone* ....8.00 - 12.00
   114 *Hold Me* ....7.00 - 10.00
   123 *Don't Cry Baby* ....8.00 - 12.00
   128 *All Through The Night* ....8.00 - 12.00
   140 *Stand There Mountain* ....8.00 - 12.00
Federal 12236 *Lonely Heart* ....20.00 - 30.00
Rage 101 *Fools Fall In Love* ....50.00 - 80.00

MORRY WILLIAMS & THE KIDS:
Luck 102 *Time Runs Out* ....80.00 - 130.00
Tee Vee 301 *Are You My Girl Friend* ....60.00 - 100.00

OTIS WILLIAMS & HIS CHARMS/NEW GROUP:
De Luxe 6088, 6090, 6091, 6095, 6097, 6098, 6105,
  6115, 6130, 6137, 6138, 6149, 6158, 6165, 6174 ......7.00 - 12.00
  6093 *Ivory Tower* (78 rpm).................10.00 - 15.00
King (LP) 560 *Otis Williams & His Charms Sing All Time Hits*
  ....100.00 - 200.00
  (LP) 614 *This Is Otis Williams & The Charms*...75.00 - 100.00
  5323 *It's A Treat* ....8.00 - 12.00
  5332 *Silver Star* ....8.00 - 12.00
  5372 *Image Of A Girl* ....10.00 - 15.00
  (most other issues) ....5.00 - 10.00

PO' JO WILLIAMS (See PO' JOE WILLIAMS)

REBECCA WILLIAMS:
Lamp 2011 *Please Give Me A Match* ....7.00 - 10.00

ROBERT WILLIAMS & THE GROOVERS:
Tip Top 730 *Cranberry Blues* ....20.00 - 30.00

RON WILLIAMS (& THE CUSTOMS):
Imperial 5729 *On Top Of Old Smokey* ....7.00 - 10.00
  5800 *Don't Tell Me Maybe*................7.00 - 10.00
Pastel 404 *Hey Little Pearl* ....7.00 - 10.00
Ty-Tex 100 *Sue Sue Baby*.......................20.00 - 30.00

SONNY BOY WILLIAMS:
Duplex 9005 *Alice Mae Blues* ....15.00 - 20.00

SUGAR BOY WILLIAMS:
Herald 555 *Five Long Years* ....10.00 - 20.00

TONY WILLIAMS (See PLATTERS)

WAYNE WILLIAMS & THE SURE SHOTS:
Sure 1001 *Red Hot Mama*......................150.00 - 250.00

JAMES WILLIAMSON:
Chance 1131 *The Woman I Love* ....150.00 - 200.00

SONNY BOY WILLIAMSON:
Ace 511 *Boppin' With Sonny*....................10.00 - 15.00
Checker 824 *Don't Start Me To Talkin'* ....15.00 - 20.00
  834 *Let Me Explain*............................15.00 - 20.00
  847 *The Key To Your Door*.................10.00 - 20.00
  864 *Fattening Frogs For Snakes* ....10.00 - 20.00
  883, 894, 910, 927, 943, 956, 963, 975, 1003,
    1036, 1065, 1080, 1134 ....8.00 - 12.00
  (LP) 1437 *Sonny Boy Williamson* (black label) .80.00 - 120.00
RAM 2501 *Mailman, Mailman* ....7.00 - 10.00
RCA Victor 50-0005 *Little Girl* (orange plastic)....40.00 - 60.00
  50-0030 *Southern Dream* (orange plastic)........40.00 - 60.00
Trumpet 144 *West Memphis Blues* ....50.00 - 80.00
  145 *Pontiac Blues* ....30.00 - 50.00
  166 *Nine Below Zero* ....20.00 - 30.00
  168 *Stop Now Baby*............................20.00 - 30.00
  212 *Cat Hop*......................................20.00 - 30.00
  215 *Gettin' Out Of Town* ....20.00 - 30.00
  216 *Red Hot Kisses* ....15.00 - 20.00
  228 *Empty Bedroom*..........................15.00 - 20.00

CHUCK WILLIS (with THE ROYALS/& THE SANDMEN):
Atlantic (EP) 591 *It's Too Late* ....75.00 - 100.00
  (EP) 608, 609, *Rock With Chuck Willis* ....75.00 - 100.00
  (EP) 612 *What Am I Living For* ....80.00 - 130.00
  1130, 1168, 1179, 1192, 2029......................5.00 - 10.00
(Note: 78 RPM issues command somewhat higher premiums.)
Atlantic (LP) 8018 *The King Of The Stroll* (black label)
  ....50.00 - 80.00
Epic (LP) 3425 *Chuck Willis Wails The Blues* ....80.00 - 130.00
Okeh 6985 *I've Been Treated Wrong Too Long* .....30.00 - 50.00
  7015 *You're Still My Baby*.................8.00 - 12.00
  7041 *Change My Mind*........................8.00 - 12.00
  7051 *Lawdy Miss Mary*......................8.00 - 12.00
  7055 *I Can Tell* ....10.00 - 15.00
  7067 *It Were You* ....8.00 - 12.00

DON WILLIS:
Satellite 101 *Boppin' High School Baby* ....250.00 - up

HAL WILLIS:
Athens 704 *Walkin' Dream*....................15.00 - 20.00
Atlantic 1114 *My Pink Cadillac* ....40.00 - 70.00

LITTLE SON WILLIS:
Swing Time 304 *Operator Blues* ....100.00 - 150.00
  305 *Harlem Blues* ....- - -
  306 *Nothing But The Blues* ....- - -
  341 *Roll Me Over Slow*.......................- - -

RALPH WILLIS:
King 4611 *Why'd You Do It* ....100.00 - 150.00
  4631 *Door Bell Blues* ....100.00 - 150.00

RAY WILLIS:
Jane 103 *Whatta You Do* ....15.00 - 20.00

ROD WILLIS:
Chic 1010 *Somebody's Been Rockin' My Baby* ......15.00 - 20.00
NRC 020 *The Cat*...................................50.00 - 100.00

ROLLIE WILLIS & THE CONTENDERS:
Saxony 1001 *Whenever I Get Lonely*....................100.00 - 150.00

SLIM WILLIS:
C.J. 622, 627, 635 ....7.00 - 12.00

WILLOWS:
Club 1014 *This Is The End*......................30.00 - 50.00
Eldorado 508 *The First Taste Of Love* ....10.00 - 20.00
4 Star 1753 *Now That I Have You* ....40.00 - 70.00
Heidi 107 *Sit By The Fire* ....7.00 - 10.00
Melba (LP) 102 *Church Bells May Ring* ....80.00 - 130.00
  102 *Church Bells Are Ringing* ....40.00 - 70.00
  102 *Church Bells May Ring* ....10.00 - 15.00
  106 *My Angel* ....10.00 - 15.00
  115 *Little Darlin* ....10.00 - 20.00
Warwick 524 *My Dear Dearest Darling* ....10.00 - 15.00

BILLY JACK WILLS:
M-G-M 11966 *There's Good Rocking Tonight* ......20.00 - 30.00

BOB WILLS (& HIS TEXAS PLAYBOYS):
Columbia (LP) 9003 *Round Up* ....20.00 - 30.00
Harmony (LP) 7036 *Bob Wills Special* ....20.00 - 30.00
M-G-M (LP) 91 (10 inch) *Ranch House Favorites* 20.00 - 30.00

OSCAR WILLS: (See also TV SLIM)
Argo 5277 *Flatfoot Sam* (ship logo label) ....7.00 - 10.00

WILLY & RUTH:
Spark 105 *Love Me* ....15.00 - 20.00

ANDY WILSON:
Athens 700 *Little Mama* ....8.00 - 12.00
Back Beat 518 *Too Much Of Not Enough* ....7.00 - 10.00
Bullseye 1012 *Teenage Martha* ....15.00 - 20.00
   1020 *Worry Worry* ....15.00 - 20.00
   1023 *Little Boy Blue* ....15.00 - 20.00
Dot 1127 *Hillbilly Boogie* ....10.00 - 15.00

DALLAS WILSON:
Rodeo 127 *High Steppin' Daddy* ....15.00 - 25.00

DOYLE WILSON:
Lamp 2015 *Hey Hey* ....15.00 - 20.00

EASY DEAL WILSON:
Sims 112 *Gotta Have You* ....10.00 - 15.00
Viv 2 *There'll Come A Day* ....5.00 - 8.00

HENRY WILSON & THE BLUENOTES:
Colonial 7778 *It's Really Love* ....10.00 - 15.00
Dot 15692 *Mighty Low* ....15.00 - 20.00

HOP WILSON (& HIS TWO BUDDIES):
Goldband 1071 *Chicken Stuff* ....15.00 - 20.00
   1078 *Broke And Hungry* ....15.00 - 20.00

J. FRANK WILSON:
Josie (LP) 4006 *Last Kiss* ....40.00 - 70.00
Le Cam 722 *Last Kiss* ....20.00 - 30.00
Tamara 761 *Last Kiss* ....8.00 - 12.00

JACKIE WILSON:
Brunswick (LP) 54042 *He's So Fine* ....50.00 - 80.00
   (LP) 54045 *Lonely Teardrops* ....50.00 - 80.00
   55024 *Reet Petite* ....5.00 - 10.00
   55024 *Reet Petite* (78 rpm) ....20.00 - 30.00
   55052, 55070, 55086, 55105 ....5.00 - 10.00
   55105 *Lonely Teardrops* (78 rpm) ....50.00 - 80.00
   55124 *That's Why* ....5.00 - 8.00
   55124 *That's Why* (78 rpm) ....30.00 - 50.00
   (EP) 70045 *That's Why I Love You So* ....25.00 - 40.00
   (EP) 71042 *Jumpin' Jack* ....30.00 - 50.00

JIMMY WILSON (& THE BLUES BLASTERS):
Big Town 101 *Tin Pan Alley* ....7.00 - 10.00
   107 *Blues At Sundown* ....5.00 - 8.00
   113 *Mountain Climber* ....10.00 - 15.00
   115 *Trouble In My House* ....10.00 - 15.00
   123 *I've Found Out* ....10.00 - 15.00
Chart 610 *Alley Blues* ....15.00 - 25.00
   629 *Send Me The Key* ....15.00 - 25.00
Goldband 1074 *Big Wheel Rolling* ....10.00 - 15.00
   1091 *Could I Be Wrong* ....10.00 - 15.00
   1095 *That Is Why I'm Happy* ....10.00 - 15.00
Imperial 5549 *Big Wheel Rolling* ....8.00 - 12.00
Irma 108 *Blues In The Alley* ....10.00 - 20.00
Rhythm 1765 *Strangest Blues* ....40.00 - 60.00
7-11 2104 *Ethel Mae* ....30.00 - 50.00
   2105 *Crying Like A Baby Child* ....30.00 - 50.00

JOHNNY WILSON:
Coronado 001 *Twi-Light-Zone* ....20.00 - 30.00

PEANUTS WILSON:
Brunswick 55039 *Cast Iron Arm* ....75.00 - 100.00

TOM WILSON:
Crest 1007 *Can You Bop?* ....15.00 - 20.00

THE WIL-SONES:
Highland 1020 *Come On Mama* ....40.00 - 70.00

MAGGIE SUE WIMBERLEY:
Sun 229 *How Long* ....75.00 - 100.00

DANNY WINCHELL:
M-G-M 12577 *My Little Tree House* ....8.00 - 12.00
Recorte 406 *Jeannie* ....10.00 - 15.00
   410 *Don't Say You're Sorry* ....10.00 - 15.00
   415 *I've Chosen You* ....10.00 - 20.00

DON WINDLE:
Republic 7060 *Girl Down The Street* ....- - -

THE WINDSORS:
Back Beat 506 *My Gloria* ....200.00 - up
Wig Wag 103 *Carol Ann* ....25.00 - 40.00

PAUL WINLEY & THE ROCKERS:
Premium 401 *Angel Child* ....15.00 - 25.00

WINNERS:
Derby 802 *To Think We're Only Friends* ....15.00 - 25.00
Rainbow 331 *Can This Be Love* ....80.00 - 130.00

JACK WINSTON & THE HI-JACKS:
Jay Wing 5806 *It's Rock And Roll* ....40.00 - 80.00

JOHNNY WINTER (& THE CRYSTALIERS):
Frolic 501 *That's What Love Does* ....10.00 - 15.00
   503 *Ease My Pain* ....10.00 - 15.00
   509 *Gangster Of Love* ....10.00 - 15.00
   512 *I Won't Believe It* ....10.00 - 15.00
KRCO 106 *Creepy* ....20.00 - 30.00
   107 *One Night Of Love* ....20.00 - 30.00
Sonobeat 107 *Rollin' And Tumblin'* ....7.00 - 10.00

DON WINTERS:
Coin 102 *Pretty Moon* ....15.00 - 20.00

THE WISDOMS:
Gaity 169 *Lost In Dreams* ....300.00 - up

MAC WISEMAN:
Dot 15544 *Step It Up And Go* ....7.00 - 10.00

NORMAN WITCHER:
Poor Boy 102 *Somebody's Been Rocking My Boat* ....50.00 - 75.00

JIMMY WITHERSPOON (See also BATTLE OF THE BLUES):
Atlantic (LP) 1266 *New Orleans Blues* ....25.00 - 40.00
Checker 798 *Big Daddy* ....15.00 - 20.00
   810 *Waiting For Your Return* ....15.00 - 20.00
   826 *It Ain't No Sedan* ....15.00 - 20.00
Crown (LP) 5156 *Jimmy Witherspoon* ....30.00 - 50.00
   (LP) 5192 *Jimmy Witherspoon Sings The Blues* ......30.00 - 50.00
Federal 12095 *Foolish Prayer* ....50.00 - 80.00
   12099 *Lucille* ....50.00 - 80.00
   12107 *Corn Whiskey* ....50.00 - 80.00
   12118 *Jay's Blues* ....40.00 - 60.00
   12138 *East Mile* ....30.00 - 50.00
   12155 *Miss Mistreater* ....30.00 - 50.00
   12156 *Sad Life* ....50.00 - 80.00
   12173 *Just For You* ....15.00 - 25.00
   12188 *Highway To Happiness* ....15.00 - 25.00
   12189 *I Done Told You* ....15.00 - 25.00
HI Firecord (LP) 421 *At Monterey* ....10.00 - 15.00
King (LP) 634 *Jimmy Witherspoon* ....75.00 - 100.00
Pacific Jazz (LP) 1267 *Singin' The Blues* ....30.00 - 50.00
RCA Victor (LP) 1639 *Goin' To Kansas City Blues*
   ....20.00 - 30.00
   6977 *Who Baby Who* ....5.00 - 10.00

JIMMY WITTER:
Elvis 900 *If You Love My Woman* ....10.00 - 15.00
Neptune 118 *My Kind Of Woman* ....10.00 - 15.00

DICK WOLF:
Dale 101 *Spine Tinglin' Love* .... - - -

DANNY WOLFE:
Dot 15571 *Pretty Blue Jean Baby* ....8.00 - 12.00
    15667 *Let's Flat Get It* ....15.00 - 20.00
    15715 *Pucker Point* ....8.00 - 12.00

JIMMY WOLFORD:
Capitol 4606 *Goin' Steady With The Blues* ....8.00 - 12.00
4 Star 1714 *My Name Is Jimmy* ....30.00 - 40.00

BOBBY WOOD:
Pen 113 *Everybody's Searchin'* ....15.00 - 20.00

NORMAN WOOD:
Tamm 2015 *Black Lake Boogie* .... - - -

TOMMY WOOD:
D 1000 *Can't Play Hookey* ....20.00 - 30.00

JERRY WOODARD:
Fad 901 *Six Long Weeks* ....30.00 - 60.00
RCA Victor 7616 *Who's Gonna Rock My Baby* ....8.00 - 12.00
Reed 1017 *Who's Gonna Rock My Baby* ....20.00 - 30.00

BENNIE WOODS & THE FIVE DUKES:
Atlas 1040 *I Crossed My Fingers* .... 300.00 - up

BILL WOODS:
Bakersfield - *Phone Me, Baby* ....20.00 - 30.00
Fire 100 *Go Crazy Man* ....20.00 - 30.00

BOB WOODS:
Kingsport 100 *Greasy Corner Boogie* .... - - -
    110 *Sunshine Boogie* .... - - -

DONALD WOODS & THE VEL-AIRES:
Flip 303 *Let's Party Awhile* ....10.00 - 20.00
    306 *My Baby's Gone* ....20.00 - 30.00
    306 *Death Of An Angel* ....10.00 - 20.00
    309 *Stay With Me Always* ....15.00 - 25.00
    312 *Heaven In Your Arms* ....20.00 - 40.00

JOHNNY WOODS & FAMOUS RHYTHM ACES:
Bo-Kay 113 *Valley Of The Blues* .... - - -

SONNY WOODS (& THE DOWNBEATS/with THE TWIGS):
Hollywood 1015 *Chapel Of Memories* ....50.00 - 75.00
    1026 *Wonderful World* ....50.00 - 75.00
Peacock 1679 *So Many Tears* ....15.00 - 20.00
    1689 *Someday She'll Come Along* ....15.00 - 20.00

JOHNNY WOODSON & THE CRESCENDOS (See also THE CRESCENDOS):
Spry 108 *Dreamer From My Heart* ....150.00 - 250.00

DON WOODY:
Arco 4623 *Not I* ....15.00 - 20.00
Decca 30277 *Bird Dog* ....30.00 - 50.00

SHEB WOOLEY:
M-G-M (EP) 1188, 1189, 1190 *Sheb Wooley*..........20.00 - 30.00
    (EP) 1607 *Purple People Eater Plays Earth Music*
                                           .....20.00 - 30.00
    (EP) 1607 *The Purple People Eater* ....20.00 - 30.00
    (LP) 3299 *Sheb Wooley* ....35.00 - 50.00
    12651 *The Purple People Eater* ....7.00 - 10.00
    12651 *The Purple People Eater* (78 rpm) ....30.00 - 50.00
    (most other issues) ....5.00 - 10.00

JIMMY WORK:
All 502 *Tennessee Border*... - - -

WAYNE WORLEY:
Brent 7024 *Red Headed Woman* ....15.00 - 20.00
Elbridge 11016 *Red Headed Woman* ....30.00 - 40.00

JOHN WORTHAN:
Peach 711 *Too Too Many* ....75.00 - 100.00
    722 *The Cats Were Jumpin'* ....80.00 - 120.00

DOUG WRAY:
Epic 9322 *Goose Bumps* ....7.00 - 10.00

LINK WRAY (& HIS WRAYMEN):
Cadence 1347 *Rumble* ....7.00 - 10.00
    1347 *Rumble* (78 rpm) ....20.00 - 40.00
Epic (LP) 3661 *Link Wray And His Waymen*........50.00 - 80.00
    (most issues) ....5.00 - 10.00
Swan (most issues) ....5.00 - 10.00
Swan (LP) 510 *Jack The Ripper* ....50.00 - 80.00

LUCKY WRAY:
Starday 552 *It's Music She Says* ....50.00 - 75.00
    575 *Got Another Baby* ....50.00 - 75.00
    608 *Teenage Cutie* ....50.00 - 75.00

WRENS:
Rama 53 *Love's Something That's Made For Two* .... 300.00 - up
    65 *Eleven Roses* ....50.00 - 80.00
    105 *Eleven Roses* .... - -
    110 *Love's Something That's Made For Two* ...50.00 - 75.00
    174 *Serenade Of The Bells* ....80.00 - 130.00
    175 *Betty Jean* ....75.00 - 100.00
    184 *I Won't Come To Your Wedding* ....80.00 - 130.00
    194 *C'est La Vie*...........................50.00 - 75.00

DALE WRIGHT (& THE WRIGHT GUYS):
Fraternity 804, 818, 831, 837 ....5.00 - 10.00

JOHNNY WRIGHT with IKE TURNER:
RPM 443 *Suffocate* (red label)...............................15.00 - 20.00

STEVE WRIGHT:
Lin 5022 *Wild Wild Woman*...................................20.00 - 30.00

GENE WYATT:
Ebb 123 *Love Fever* ....15.00 - 20.00
Lucky Seven 101 *Music And Arithmetic*................20.00 - 30.00

JOHNNY WYATT & THE HI TONES:
Big Time 1927 *Wondering Why* ....100.00 - 150.00
Magnum 736 *Once Upon A Time* ....7.00 - 10.00
Swingin 643 *One Night With You* ....7.00 - 10.00

THE X-CITERS:
Carter 2764 *As We Danced* .... - - -

JIMMY YANCEY:
Atlantic (LP) 103 *Yancey Special* (10 inch)............50.00 - 75.00
    (LP) 130 *Jimmy & Mama Yancey*...................50.00 - 75.00
    (LP) 134 *Jimmy & Mama Yancey*...................50.00 - 75.00
(Note: Above two are 10-inch LPs.)
    (LP) 1231 *Pure Blues Jimmy & Mama Yancey* . 30.00 - 40.00

LAFAYETTE YARBOROUGH:
Bart (?) - *Comic Book Crazy*..............................30.00 - 40.00

MALCOLM YELVINGTON:
Sun 211 *Drinkin' Wine Spodee-O-Dee* ....100.00 - 150.00
    246 *Rocking With My Baby*...........................50.00 - 80.00

RUSTY YORK:
Chess 1730 *Sugaree* ....7.00 - 10.00
King 5103 *Shake 'Em Up Baby* ....10.00 - 15.00
    5511, 5587...........................5.00 - 10.00

Note 10021 *Sugaree* ....20.00 - 30.00
P.J. 100 *Sugaree* ....7.00 - 10.00
Sage - *Sadie Mae* ....10.00 - 15.00

BOBBY YOUNG:
Guyden 2087 *To Each His Own* ....100.00 - 150.00

CECIL YOUNG QUARTETTE:
King 4692 *Ooh Diga Gow* ....20.00 - 30.00
   4749 *Who Parked The Car* ....20.00 - 30.00

DONNIE YOUNG:
AmCan 407 *From Twelve To Seven* ....- - -
Decca 31077 *Shakin' The Blues* ....10.00 - 15.00

FARON YOUNG:
Capitol (LP) 778 *Sweethearts Or Strangers* ....20.00 - 30.00
   (LP) 1004 *The Object Of My Affection* ....20.00 - 30.00
   (LP) 1096 *This Is Faron Young* ....15.00 - 20.00
   (LP) 1185 *My Garden Of Prayer* ....15.00 - 20.00
   (LP) 1245 *Talk About Hits* ....10.00 - 15.00

GEORGE YOUNG:
Mercury 71259 *Can't Stop Me* ....15.00 - 20.00

MIGHTY JOE YOUNG:
Fire 1033 *Empty Arms* ....7.00 - 10.00

LENNY YOUNG & THE JAY BIRDS:
Jackpot 48006 *Joyce* ....7.00 - 10.00
Jay Scott 1001 *Loveable* ....20.00 - 30.00

LESTER YOUNG TRIO:
Aladdin (LP) 705 (10 inch) ....100.00 - 150.00

NELSON YOUNG:
Lucky 0002 *Rock Old Sputnick* ....40.00 - 60.00
Starday 341 *So Easy To Fall In Love* ....20.00 - 30.00

ROY YOUNG:
Can. Hall (?) - *Big Fat Mama/Just Keep It Up* ....- - -

YOUNGHEARTS:
Infinity 006 *Do Not Forsake Me* ....150.00 - 300.00

YOUNG JESSIE:
Modern 921 *I Smell A Rat* ....10.00 - 20.00
   961 *Mary Lou* ....10.00 - 15.00
   973 *Nothing Seems Right* ....8.00 - 12.00
   1002 *Don't Happen No More* ....8.00 - 12.00
   1010 *Oochie Coochie* ....7.00 - 10.00

YOUNG LADS:
Felice 712 *Night After Night* ....25.00 - 40.00
Neil 100 *Moonlight* ....20.00 - 30.00

THE YOUNG LIONS:
Dot 16172 *Little Girl* ....10.00 - 20.00
Tampa 158 *Oh Daddy* ....10.00 - 20.00
United Artists 177 *Maybe Someday* ....10.00 - 15.00

THE YOUNGSTERS:
Apt 25021 *Sweet Talk* ....7.00 - 10.00
Checker 917 *Lucky Sixteen* ....7.00 - 10.00

Empire 104 *Shattered Dreams* ....15.00 - 20.00
   107 *Counterfeit Heart* ....10.00 - 20.00
   109 *Dreamy Eyes* ....15.00 - 25.00
Lesley 1925 *You Told Another Lie* ....30.00 - 50.00

YOUNGTONES:
Brunswick 55089 *Oh Tell Me* ....20.00 - 30.00
X-Tra 104 *You I Adore* ....60.00 - 100.00
   110 *Patricia* ....25.00 - 40.00
   120/121 *Can I Come Over* ....40.00 - 60.00

"YOUR FAVORITE SINGING GROUPS":
Hull (LP) 1002 (various artists) ....80.00 - 130.00

"YOUR OLD FAVORITES":
Old Town (LP) 101 (various artists) ....50.00 - 100.00

EDDIE ZACK (& COUSIN RICHIE):
Columbia 21387 *Rocky Road Blues* ....15.00 - 20.00
   21441 *I'm Gonna Roll And Rock* ....15.00 - 20.00

FRANCIS ZAMBON:
Vamalco 503 *Our Love Will Last* ....7.00 - 10.00

HERB ZANE:
De Luxe 6099 *Let Me In Your Heart* ....10.00 - 15.00

TEX ZARIO:
Arcade 163 *Jukebox Cannonball* ....20.00 - 30.00
Skyrocket 1001 *Go Man Go, Get Gone* ....20.00 - 30.00

ZEBULONS:
Cub 9069 *Falling Water* ....10.00 - 20.00

DANNY ZELLA (& THE LARADOS/HIS ZELL ROCKS):
Dial 100 *Sapphire* ....10.00 - 15.00
Fox 10056/10057 *Wicked Ruby* ....7.00 - 10.00

BEN (JOE) ZEPPA (& THE ZEPHYRS):
Award 124 *Shame On You Miss Lindy* ....15.00 - 20.00
Era 1042 *Topsy Turvy* ....10.00 - 15.00
Metrol 9001 *Shame On You Miss Lindy* ....10.00 - 15.00
Specialty 577 *A Foolish Fool* ....15.00 - 30.00

GEORGE ZIMMERMAN & THE THRILLS:
JAB 103 *Whose Baby Are You* ....100.00 - 150.00

THE ZIRCONS:
Cool Sound 1030 *Silver Bells* ....8.00 - 12.00
Dot 15724 *Only One Love* ....7.00 - 10.00
Federal 12452 *No Twistin' On Sunday* ....7.00 - 10.00
   12478 *Get Up and Go To School* ....7.00 - 10.00
Heigh ho 607 *Where There's A Will* ....7.00 - 10.00
   608/609 *I Couldn't Stop Crying* ....7.00 - 10.00
MelloMood 1000 *Lonely Way* ....5.00 - 8.00
Winston 1020 *Only One Love* ....15.00 - 20.00
   1022 *Return My Love* ....15.00 - 20.00

THE ZODIACS (See also MAURICE WILLIAMS):
Cole 101 *Golly Gee* ....15.00 - 20.00
   102 *She's Mine* ....15.00 - 20.00
Soma 1410 *Another Little Darling* ....8.00 - 12.00
   1418 *Anything* ....8.00 - 12.00
Sphere Sound 707 *The Winds* ....7.00 - 10.00

Bibliography

Steven C. Barr, *The Almost Complete 78 Rpm Record Dating Guide*, Promar Printing (a division of Yesterday Once Again, P.O. Box 6773, Huntington Beach, California 92615), 1992. (A guide to dating 78 RPM records on virtually all U.S. and Canadian, and many foreign, labels)

Brian Case & Stan Britt, *The Illustrated Encyclopedia Of Jazz*, Harmony Books, New York, 1978. (Contains selective discography of albums, photos of album jackets, short biographies of over 400 jazz artists.)

Ken Clee, *The Directory Of American 45 RPM Records*, privately published by Stak-O-Wax, P.O. Box 11412, Philadelphia, Pennsylvania 19111. (Five volumes, loose-leaf format. Discography, or more properly, a collection of over 3,400 artist and label discographies. Records listed in order of release with titles of both sides. Over 4,000 pages, containing over a million listings. Kept current and updated with periodic supplements.)

Ron Dethlefson and Ray Wile, *Edison Disc Artists And Records*, 1910-1929, APM Press, 502 East 17th Street, Brooklyn, New York 11226, 1990. (Contains listings by title and artist for all Edison LP and 78 RPM records, photos of artists, all known label varieties, listings for many Edison Diamond Discs by title and artist, and photos of typical labels.)

Robert Dixon & John Godrich, *Recording The Blues*, Stein and Day, New York, 1970. (The story of recording companies; how and where they recorded the artists they recorded; many interesting reproductions and illustrations of record labels and record company promotional materials.)

Galen Gart, *The American Record Label Directory & Dating Guide, 1940-1959*, Big Nickel Publications, Milford, New Hampshire. (out of print)

John Godrich & Robert Dixon, *Blues & Gospel Records, 1902-1943*, Third Edition, Storyville Publications, Essex, England. (A massive discography, arranged alphabetically by artist, providing 78 RPM issue numbers, all songs recorded by each artist in chronological order, including unissued titles; recording dates, accompaniment personnels, recording locations, master numbers, "take" numbers. Prefatory material includes information about "race" labels and recording "field trips.")

Roger D. Kinkle, *The Complete Encyclopedia Of Popular Music And Jazz, 1900-1950*. Arlington House, New Rochelle, New York. 1974. (Four volumes, 2642 pages. Data on movie musicals; performers, with biographies; singers; composers; bandleaders; musicians; listings of 100 to 200 songs, most popular, for each year; representative recordings for each year; Broadway musicals; numerical listings of 9 major labels.)

Jeff A. Kreiter, *Group Collector's Record Price Guide*, Sixth Edition, published by the author, Jeff Kreiter, P.O. Box 127, Bridgeport, Ohio 43912, 1996. (Discography and price guide, listing 18,000 45 RPM vocal group records, 1950-1995. Main section organized by label. 468 pages.)

Mike Leadbitter & Neil Slaven, *Blues Records 1943-1966*, Oak Publications, New York, 1968. (Discography, containing the recorded work of over 1,000 artists. Recording dates, records issued, personnels, recording locations.)

Dan Mahoney, *The Columbia 13/14000-D Series*-A Numerical Listing, Walter C. Allen, Stanhope, New Jersey, 1961. (Interesting, in-depth treatment of the Columbia "Race" series, Artists, Song titles, master numbers, dates, and even quantities of records ordered.)

Neil Maken, *Hand-Cranked Phonographs-It All Started With Edison*, Promar Publishing (a division of Yesterday Once Again), P.O. Box 6773, Huntington Beach, California 92615. (An introduction to the old-style hand-wound phonograph and records, both cylinder and disc. Covers the major manufacturers of phonographs and records, describes the different types of cylinders. Particularly useful to novice collectors)

Bill C. Malone, *Country Music U.S.A.*, University of Texas Press, Austin, Texas, 1968.

Robert R. Olson and Eugene Earle, *Montgomery Ward*, privately published by Robert R. Olson, 2964 Stacie Way, Medford, Oregon 97504-9098. (Numerical listing of Montgomery Ward label, including artist index. 154 pages)

Oliver Read & Walter L. Welch, *From Tin Foil To Stereo: Evolution of the Phonograph,* Howard W. Sams, Inc., Indianapolis, Indiana, 1976. (In addition to detailed and scholarly treatment of its main subject, contains information about record companies and their corporate genealogy.) (A new edition, by Walter Welch and Leah Burt, is available, but full information is not at hand; enquire of Yesterday Once Again, listed in Sources section.)

Brian Rust, *The American Dance Band Discography, 1917-1942*, Arlington House Publishers, New Rochelle, New York, 1975. (Two volumes, 2066 Pages. Discography, providing 78 RPM issues numbers, all songs recorded by each artist/band in chronological order, including unissued titles; recording dates; personnels; recording locations; master numbers; "takes.") (Note: This set is out of print.)

Brian Rust, *The American Record Label Book*. DaCapo Press, Inc., 233 Spring Street, New York, New York, 10013. (Information about, and in most cases, photographs of, many American and some British labels up to about 1942.)

Brian Rust, *The Complete Entertainment Discography, From The Mid-1890s TO 1942*, DaCapo Press, Inc., 233 Spring Street, New York, New York 10013. (Covers the recorded output of celebrities and personalities. Includes brief biographies of artists, details of their 78-RPM record issues; unissued recordings; recording dates, locations, accompanying personnels.)

Brian Rust, *Jazz Records*, 1897-1942, Fifth Edition, Storyville Publications & Co., Ltd., 66 Fairfax Drive, Chigwell, Essex IG7 6HS, England. (Two massive volumes covering virtually all known 78-RPM records of jazz interest. In addition to the usual thorough discographical data, this set includes a song index. This, and the other discographies by Rust, above, cannot be praised too highly!) (out of print)

Claude Seary, *Columbia Records "A" Series*, privately published by Claude Seary, British Columbia, Canada. (Numerical listing of Columbia records from November, 1908 to December, 1923, with master numbers, issue dates. The complete series comprises five volumes, plus an artist index.)

Michael W. Sherman, *The Collector's Guide To Victor Records*, Monarch Record Enterprises, Dallas, Texas, 1992. (In-depth coverage of all domestic Victor issues, including earliest predecessor labels, affiliated labels; over 300 photographs, including over 100 in color; rarity guide to label varieties. A most interesting, high-quality book. 176 pages.)

Lou Silvani, *Collecting Rare Records*, Times Square Records, Box 391, Bronx, New York 10463, 1992. (A guide for the vocal group collector, it offers guidance as to desirability, scarcity, and how to recognize original issues, second pressings, reissues, and bootlegs. 320 pages.)

Allan Sutton and Kurt Nauck, *American Record Labels And Companies - An Encyclopedia, 1891-1943,* Mainspring Press, Denver, Colorado, 2000. (Detailed descriptions of over 400 pre-war labels, including label varieties, dates of production, record manufacturer histories and corporate genealogies. The book itself has no illustrations, but is accompanied by a CD-ROM with over 1,000 full color label illustrations of labels described in the book.)

Nick Tosches, *Country-The Biggest Music In America*, Stein and Day, New York, 1977 (Animated, knowledgeable treatment of the subject, and more rockabilly, blues, etc.)

Joel Whitburn, *Pop Memories, 1890-1954*, Record Research Inc., P.O. Box 200, Menomonee Falls, Wisconsin 53052. (Lists, by artist, "every recording to appear on America's popular music charts from 1890 through 1954." While this claim has been disputed, essentially because of a dearth of meaningful "charts" from the early years, the book is useful and fascinating.)

Joel Whitburn, *Top Country Singles, 1944-1997*, Record Research Inc., P.O. Box 200, Menomonee Falls, Wisconsin 53052. (Compiled from Billboard's country singles charts, it lists over 16,700 country singles.)

Joel Whitburn, *Top Pop Singles, 1955-1999*, Record Research Inc. P.O. Box 200, Menomonee Falls, Wisconsin 53052. (Lists, by artist, over 23,000 singles that appeared on *Billboard Magazine*'s pop singles charts, showing debut dates, peak positions on charts, biographical information for artists, etc.)

Publications

Antique Phonograph Monthly, Allen Koenigsberg, Editor, 502 East 17th Street, Brooklyn, New York 11226, Web site: www.phonobooks.com, e-mail: allenamet@aol.com.

(Early phonographs and recording processes; pioneer recording artists and their recordings. Advertising, mostly relating to phonographs, parts, repairs, and restoration; records, including cylinders.)

Discoveries, 700 East State Street, Iola, Wisconsin 54990. Phone: (715) 445-2214. Or 1 (800) 258-0929 to subscribe. (Large, monthly, with features, interviews, reviews, numerous ads offering records for direct sale and at auction, and a "Mailbox" section to encourage reader participation. Mainly rock 'n' roll, rhythm & blues of the 1950s and 1960s with efforts toward wider scope.)

Goldmine, 700 East State Street, Iola, Wisconsin 54990, Phone: (715) 445-2214. Or 1 (800) 258-0929.

(Large bi-weekly, with features, discographies, reviews, and an extensive auction/for sale section offering mainly rock 'n' roll, rhythm & blues, and later forms of music, of the 1950s to the present, including CDs)

I.A.J.R.C. Journal, (Quarterly publication of the International Association of Jazz Record Collectors; sent to members. Yearly dues: $35.00. Write to: Dick Peters, IAJRC, 12366 Quinlan Avenue, Port Charlotte, FL 33981. (Articles, research, and an excellent source of information on available reissues of jazz; the club itself offers to members low-priced LP and CD reissues of its own.)

Joslin's Jazz Journal, Gene Joslin, Editor and Publisher, Box 213, Parsons, Kansas 67357, Phone: (316) 421-4114

(Attractively produced quarterly tabloid, primarily of interest to collectors of jazz and dance band 78s and LPs. Contains articles, research, and reviews, in addition to advertisements and auctions.)

New Amberola Graphic, Martin F. Bryan, Editor, 213 Caledonia Street, St. Johnsbury, Vermont 05819. (Quarterly, concerned largely with artists, recordings, and phonographs of the very early days of recording, with a penchant for exploring the odd and curious. Of late, consisting of two sections, to accommodate a growing auction section - which regularly contains cylinders, as well as disc records.)

Record Finder, Walter Smith, Publisher, P.O. Box 1047, Glen Allen, Virginia 23060. Telephone: (804) 266-1154; Internet: www.recordfinders.com

(Monthly, featuring sales of 78s, 45s, and LPs of all styles, from easy listening and pop, to rock 'n' roll. Mostly a market place, which includes consignment sales. Its Internet site has a "Collector Wants" section, in which record seekers can have their wants listed inexpensively; a classified section; convention calendar; and articles.)

Rhythm And News, Bjorn Jentoft, Publisher, P. O. Box 184, Old Saybrook, Connecticut 06475 (sold on a "per issue" basis- no subscriptions, each issue has stories, research, discographies, graphics, and record for sale. Focus is rhythm and blues, and 1950s rock 'n' roll.)

78 Quarterly, Pete Whelan, Editor, P.O. Box 283, Key West, Florida 33041, Web site: 78quarterly.com.

(Published infrequently, title notwithstanding, this 96-page magazine explores the byways of record collecting, with emphasis on the rare and obscure in blues, and, to a lesser extent, jazz and country. One feature is an ongoing survey of the "rarest" records, which, although hardly scientific, is most interesting. A feature on rare labels, with lots of pictures; chronicles of an old-time collector; the history of a major "race" label; and a "jackpot" find are a few typical items: It's sort of like sitting in on a bull-session of some of the cognoscenti.)

VJM's Jazz & Blues Mart, Russ Shor, Editor, P.O. Box 8184, Radnor, Pennsylvania 19087. (Primarily an international marketplace for collectors of jazz, dance band, blues, and country 78s, and jazz LPs. Consisting mostly of offerings at auction, content of articles and editorials has been increasing. Quarterly.)

Sources

Following are some sources of publications, references, supplies, equipment, and services of interest to record collectors. The sources mentioned are not the only ones; others' advertisements may be found in the various collector publications. The listing of any source is not intended to be a recommendation. It is intended merely to provide information in response to common inquiries, and to spare me the burden of answering these inquiries individually.

Antique Phonograph Monthly, 502 East 17th Street, Brooklyn, New York 11226. Telephone: (718) 941-6835; Fax: (718) 941-1408; Web site: www.phonobooks.com; e-mail: allenamet@aol.com. In addition to publishing the magazine (See "Publications"), APM is an excellent source of reference materials and memorabilia pertaining to vintage phonographs, records, and recording artists; books, catalogs, manuals, magazines, discographies, posters, etc. Included are facsimiles and reprints of original catalogs, manuals, and sales materials.

Antique Phonograph Supply Company, Route 23, Box 123, Davenport Center, New York, 13751 Telephone: (607) 278-6218; Web site: www.antiquephono.com. Accessories, steel needles, parts for the maintenance, repair, and restoration of vintage phonographs; literature, sleeves for 78 RPM records. Issues a catalog of its offerings and services for $3.00.

Esoteric Sound, 4813 Wallbank Avenue, Downers Grove. Illinois 60515. Telephone/Fax: (630) - 960-9137; Web site: www.esotericsound.com; e-mail: esoterictt@aol.com. Specializes in high-performance audio equipment used for reproduction of vintage recordings: turntables (with up to six speeds, including "78" RPM), noise reduction equipment, equalizers, standard and custom styli, etc. Also provides digital editing, CD mastering with CEDAR noise reduction, and auctions vintage recordings.

Expert Stylus Company, P.O. Box 3, Ashtead, Surrey, England KT21 2QD, Stylus replacement service for all types of cartridges, for acoustical and electrical playing of various types of vintage records, laterally and vertically recorded.

Nauck's Vintage Records, 6323 Inway Drive, Spring, Texas 77389-3643. Telephone: (281) 370-7899; FAX: (281) 251-7023; e-mail: nauck@78rpm.com. Nauck's Resource Catalog offers a full line of collector books and discographies, record-collecting accessories, including multi-speed turntables and audio equipment.

Robert R. Olson, 2964 Stacie Way, Medford, Oregon 97504-9098. Researcher and compiler of numericals of various 78 RPM record labels of the 1920s and 1930s, particularly country series. Has published listings of Banner, Decca 5000 series, Grey Gull 4000 series, and Montgomery Ward (see Bibliography).

Record Research Inc., P.O. Box 200, Menomonee Falls, Wisconsin 53052. Telephone: (414) 251-5408. Fax: (414) 251-9452. Web site: RECORDRESEARCH.COM. Publisher of more than thirty books by Joel Whitburn on "charted" music (three of which are listed in the Bibliography, which see).

Shure Brothers, Inc., 222 Hartrey Avenue, Evanston, Illinois 60202-3696. Telephone: (800) 25 SHURE; FAX: (800) 347-4873; E-mail: sales@shure.com. Cartridges and styli; full line, featuring extra low force V15VxMR high performance cartridge - also specialized professional DJ cartridges and 78 RPM styli.

Something Special Enterprises, P.O. Box 74, Allison Park, Pennsylvania 15101. Telephone: (412) 487-2626; Fax: (412) 487-3369; e-mail: sseorder@aol.com. Record sleeves, plastic and paper (including 78-RPM sleeves); LP jackets, mailers, fillers, jewel cases, storage boxes, etc.

Sun Ripe Promotions, P.O. Box 29, Boyne Falls, Michigan 49713. Distributes books relating to music, record collecting, and memorabilia, primarily from the 1950s and later.

Laurie Wright, 66 Fairview Drive, Chigwell, Essex, England IG7 6HS. Former publisher of defunct Storyville magazine (vintage jazz and blues) and Storyville books continues to offer books and back issues from remaining stock (but not *Jazz Records* or *Blues & Gospel Records*). List available.

Yesterday Once Again, P.O. Box 6773, Huntington Beach, California 92615. Telephone: (714) 963-2474; Fax: (714) 963-1558; e-mail: yesterdayonceagain@yahoo.com. Books, including many on acoustical phonographs; needles; parts for the maintenance, repair and restoration of antique phonographs; has machine shop and repair service; reprints of literature and manuals for antique phonographs.

Tollie
Ca. 1964
Picture sleeve for Beatles (45) record.

TRIANGLE
Ca. 1924 (78)
Early Duke Ellington record

UNITED (red vinyl)
Mid-1950s (45)
Blues record by Memphis Slim

UNIVERSAL ZONOPHONE RECORD
Ca. 1904 (78) (one-sided)

UP-TO-DATE
Ca. 1924 (78)
Very scarce label

VEE JAY (red vinyl)
Early 1950s (45)
Classic, sought-after group record

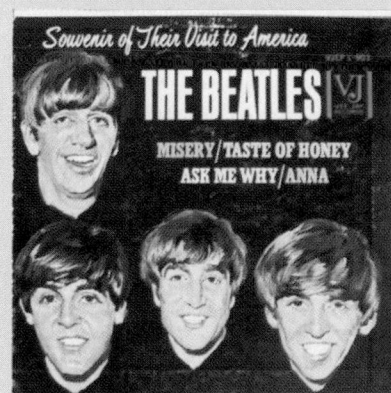

VEE JAY
Ca. 1965 jacket of Beatles EP

VERVE
Ca. 1957 (78)

VICTOR (special record)
Ca. 1927 (78)
Sought-after Jean Goldkette record

VISTA
Ca. 1960
Picture sleeve for Annette Funicello record

VOCALION
Ca. 1928 (78)

VOCALION
Ca. 1937 (78)
Sought-after Robert Johnson blues record

VOGUE (picture record)
Ca. 1947 (78)
Special purpose record

VOGUE (picture record)
Ca. 1947 (78)
The commonest Vogue record by Clyde McCoy

VOGUE (picture record)
Ca. 1947 (78)
Flipside of Vogue R707

VOGUE (picture record)
Ca. 1947 (78)
Lulu Belle & Scotty on Vogue R719

VOGUE (picture record)
Ca. 1947 (78)
Hour of Charm orchestra on Vogue R725

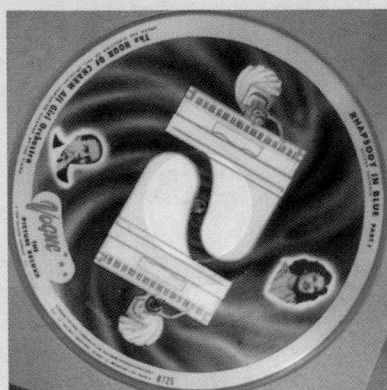

VOGUE (picture record)
Ca. 1947 (78)
Flip side of Vogue R725

VOGUE (picture record)
Ca. 1947 (78)
Flip side of Vogue R719

VOGUE (picture record)
Ca. 1947 (78)
Hour of Charm Orch. on Vogue R726

VOGUE (picture record)
Ca. 1947 (78)
Lulu Belle & Scotty on Vogue R720

VOGUE (picture record)
Ca. 1947 (78)
Flip side of Vogue R720

WORLD RECORD
Ca. 1918 (78)

YERKES DANCE RECORD
Ca. 1924 (78)

WELLING & McGHEE (See also McGHEE & WELLING):

Champion 16585 *The Hallelujah Side*	20.00	-	30.00
16598 *Nothing But The Blood*	20.00	-	30.00
16660 *Ring The Bells Of Heaven*	20.00	-	30.00
Gennett 6719 *Lonely Village Churchyard*	15.00	-	20.00
7096 *Picture From Life's Other Side*	15.00	-	20.00
Melotone 5-12-59 *The Maple On The Hill*	7.00	-	10.00
Oriole 8056 *The Lonely Village Churchyard*	7.00	-	10.00

(Note: The above titles on Melotone and Oriole, and those on Perfect, below, probably were issued contemporaneously on Banner, Conqueror, Melotone, Oriole, Perfect, Romeo.)

Paramount 3084 *In The Garden*	10.00	-	15.00
3093 *Haven Of Rest*	10.00	-	15.00
3102 *Are You Washed In The Blood*	10.00	-	15.00
3108 *My Mother's Bible*	10.00	-	15.00
3115 *At The Cross*	10.00	-	15.00
3157 *Too Many Parties And Too Many Pals*	10.00	-	15.00
3175 *I Love To Walk With Jesus*	10.00	-	15.00
3286 *Where Is My Mama*	10.00	-	15.00
3310 *Almost Persuaded*	15.00	-	20.00
Perfect 12769 *The Crime At Quiet Dell*	7.00	-	10.00
12801 *Sweet Hour Of Prayer*	7.00	-	10.00
Vocalion 5241 *The Hallelujah Side*	10.00	-	15.00
5251 *The Lilly Of The Valley*	10.00	-	15.00
5263 *The Nearer, The Sweeter*	10.00	-	15.00
5299 *Go By The Way Of The Cross*	10.00	-	15.00

WELLING & SCHANNEN/SHANNON:

Paramount 3127 *S.O.S. Vestris*	10.00	-	15.00
3134 *I'm A Child Of The King*	10.00	-	15.00
3142 *Are You A Christian?*	10.00	-	15.00

FRANK WELLING (& THE RED BRUSH ROWDIES):

Champion 16474 *My Little Mountain Home*	30.00	-	50.00
16562 *I Can't Think Of Everything*	30.00	-	50.00
16588 *The Old Man's Story*	30.00	-	50.00
16590 *Shake Hands With Mother Again*	30.00	-	50.00
16594 *The Little Old Crossroad Store*	30.00	-	50.00
16618 *Roll It Down Baby*	50.00	-	75.00
16652 *Daddy's Lullaby*	50.00	-	75.00
16697 *Daddy And Son*	50.00	-	75.00
Gennett 6616 *Yodelin' Daddy Blues*	25.00	-	40.00
6671 *I Wants My Lulu*	20.00	-	30.00
7111 *Little Pal*	20.00	-	30.00
7142 *That's A Plenty*	40.00	-	60.00
Paramount 3119 *The Last Mile*	35.00	-	50.00
3125 *She's My Mama, And I'm Her Daddy*	35.00	-	50.00
3216 *A Plea To Young Wives*	35.00	-	50.00
3287 *Busted Bank Blues*	40.00	-	60.00
Supertone 9083 *Yodelin' Daddy Blues*	10.00	-	15.00

WELLS BROTHERS STRING BAND:

Bluebird 7588 *Snow White Stone*	5.00	-	8.00

WENATCHEE MOUNTAINEERS:

Titles issued contemporaneously on Banner, Conqueror, Melotone, Oriole, Perfect, and Romeo: *Bring Your Roses To Your Mother; Britt's Reel; By The Sleepy Rio Grande; Dear Old Southern Moon; I Like Mountain Music; The Little Rose Covered Shack; Texas Rag; When It's Harvest Time* ....5.00 - 8.00

JOE WERNER & THE RAMBLERS:

Bluebird 7539, 7575, 7639, 7690, 7923	5.00	-	8.00

C. A. WEST:

Gennett 7098 *A Mother's Advice*	12.00	-	16.00
Supertone 9650 *Oh Willie Come Back*	5.00	-	8.00

CAL WEST:

Vocalion 5361 *Cal West's Yodeling Blues*	10.00	-	15.00

ED "JAKE" WEST:

Broadway 8109 *Waiting For The Train*	5.00	-	8.00
Challenge 813 *Waiting For The Train*	5.00	-	8.00
Paramount 3154 *Waiting For The Train*	5.00	-	8.00

WALTON WEST:

Champion 45161 *'Leven Miles From Leavenworth*	7.00	-	10.00
45170 *In That Vine Covered Chapel*	7.00	-	10.00

WESTERNERS:

Titles issued contemporaneously on Banner, Conqueror, Melotone, Oriole, Perfect, and Romeo: *Carry Me Back To The Lone Prairie; The Cowboy's Dream; Goin' Down To Santa Fe Town; Gol Darn Wheel; Good Old Turnip Greens; If Jesse James Rode Again; Is It True What They Say About Dixie?; My Gal On The Rio Grande; My Herdin' Song; Nobody To Love; Out On The Loco Range; Pretty Boy Floyd; Rancho Grande; Ridin' Down That Old Texas Trail; Roundup Time In Heaven; The Santa Fe Trail; Texas Star* ....5.00 - 10.00

Vocalion 02957 *Life's Evening Sun Is Sinking Low*	8.00	-	12.00
04222 *Honeysuckle Schottische*	5.00	-	8.00
04223 *Rancho Grande*	5.00	-	8.00
04310 *Old Rose Waltz*	5.00	-	8.00
04414 *Good Old Turnip Greens*	5.00	-	8.00

DON WESTON:

Champion 16748 *That Old Feather Bed On The Farm*	15.00	-	20.00
16764 *The Dying Cowgirl*	15.00	-	20.00
16779 *'Way Out West In Texas*	15.00	-	20.00
16825 *That Mother And Daddy Of Mine*	20.00	-	30.00
Champion 45053, 45101, 45107, 45110	5.00	-	10.00

WEST VIRGINIA COON HUNTERS:

Victor 20862 *Greasy String*	20.00	-	30.00

WEST VIRGINIA NIGHT OWLS:

Victor 21190 *Sweet Bird*	15.00	-	25.00
21533 *I'm Goin' To Walk On The Streets Of Glory*	15.00	-	25.00

WEST VIRGINIA RAIL SPLITTER:

Champion 15852 *In The Jailhouse Now*	10.00	-	15.00
15897 *Barney McCoy*	10.00	-	15.00
15943 *Old And Only In The Way*	10.00	-	15.00
15990 *The Habit*	10.00	-	15.00
16053 *Zeb Turney's Gal*	10.00	-	15.00
16095 *The Dying Ranger*	10.00	-	15.00

WEST VIRGINIA RAMBLERS:

Champion 16757 *O Dem Golden Slippers*	20.00	-	30.00
45017 *O Dem Golden Slippers*	7.00	-	10.00

WEST VIRGINIA RIDGE RUNNERS:

Superior 2794 *Dill Pickle Rag*	25.00	-	40.00

WEST VIRGINIA SNAKE HUNTERS:

Brunswick 119 *Standin' In The Need Of Prayer*	15.00	-	25.00

JIM WHALEN:

Champion 15545 *May I Sleep In Your Barn Tonight Mister?*	8.00	-	12.00

(FRANK) WHEELER & (MONROE) LAMB:
Victor 23537 *Jim Blake, The Engineer*....................10.00 - 15.00
   23755 *Will You Sometimes Think Of Me* ....20.00 - 30.00
   V40169 *Jolly Group Of Cowboys*........................10.00 - 15.00
   V40248 *Since The Preacher Made Us One*........10.00 - 15.00

WEBB WHIPPLE:
Okeh 45574 *Don't Hang Me In The Morning* ....10.00 - 15.00

WHITE BROTHERS:
Vocalion 04530 *The Fugitive's Lament* ....7.00 - 10.00
   04674 *Southern Moon*....................................7.00 - 10.00

WHITE & DAWSON:
Superior 2541 *On The Banks Of The Silvery Stream*......10.00 - 15.00

FIDDLIN' BOB WHITE:
Bell 1171 *Cripple Creek*....................................5.00 - 8.00
   1188 *Billy In The Low Ground* ....5.00 - 8.00

CLYDE WHITE:
Champion 16318 *Beside A Lonely River* ....10.00 - 15.00

GEORGE WHITE:
Okeh 45241, 45257, 45287, 45335, 45351...........5.00 - 10.00
Okeh 45382 *Dust Pan Blues*................................7.00 - 10.00
   45432 *Living In The Mountains*..........................7.00 - 10.00
   45502 *I Am Just A Gambler*..............................7.00 - 10.00

JOHN WHITE:
Romeo 5066 *Strawberry Roan* ....5.00 - 8.00

JOHNNIE/JOHNNY WHITE & HIS RHYTHM RIDERS:
Citation 102 *My Home In Tennessee* ....7.00 - 10.00
Fortune 145 *Mean And Evil Blues* ....5.00 - 8.00

REUBEN WHITE:
Challenge 336 *Old Sefus Brown* ....7.00 - 10.00

ZEB WHITE:
Vocalion 5189 *When You Were Sweet Sixteen* ....8.00 - 12.00

RED WHITEHEAD & DUTCH COLEMAN:
Vocalion 5414 *Booneville Stomp*...........................50.00 - 75.00

WHITE MOUNTAIN ORCHESTRA:
Victor 23619 *Maxwell's Old Rye Waltz* ....30.00 - 50.00
   V40185 *Leather Britches*...................................20.00 - 30.00

RAY WHITELY (& ODIS ELDER); WHITLEY'S RANGE RAMBLERS:
Titles issued contemporaneously on Banner, Conqueror, Melotone, Oriole, Perfect, and Romeo: *Have You Written Your Mother Lately; The Morror Castle Disaster; Pretty Boy Floyd; Old Wishing Well; Singing A Song In Sing Sing; Sittin' On The Old Settee* ....8.00 - 12.00
Decca 5078 *Big Bad Blues* ....10.00 - 15.00
   5132 *Wiley Post*..10.00 - 15.00
   5195 *Wah-Hoo*..7.00 - 10.00
   5205 *Blue Yodel Blues* ....7.00 - 10.00
   5285 *Travelin'* ....5.00 - 8.00
   5293 *You Took My Candy*................................5.00 - 8.00

J. B. WHITMIRE & THE BLUE SKY TRIO:
Bluebird 7132, 7844 ....5.00 - 10.00

(HENRY) WHITTER (& G. B. GRAYSON); WHITTER'S VIRGINIA BREAKDOWNERS; HENRY WHITTER & FIDDLER JOE: (See also GRAYSON & WHITTER)
Champion 15629 *Cluck Old Hen*.............................8.00 - 12.00
Gennett 6320 *Train Forty-Five* ....15.00 - 20.00
   6373 *I'll Never Be Yours* ....15.00 - 20.00

   6418 *Red Or Green*.......................................15.00 - 20.00
   6436 *Old Jimmy Sutton*..................................15.00 - 20.00
   6656 *Cluck Old Hen*......................................15.00 - 20.00
   6733 *Sally Goodin*...15.00 - 20.00
Herwin 75537 *Snow Storm* ....20.00 - 30.00
Okeh 40015 *Lonesome Road Blues* ....20.00 - 30.00
   40029 *Last Train Blues* ....10.00 - 15.00
   40063 *Little Brown Jug* ....10.00 - 15.00
   40064 *Tippy Two Step Blues*............................20.00 - 30.00
   40077 *Western County* ....15.00 - 20.00
   40109 *Sydney Allen*.......................................10.00 - 15.00
   40120 *Double Headed Train* ....10.00 - 15.00
   40143 *New River Train*....................................10.00 - 15.00
   40169 *The Drunkard's Child* ....10.00 - 15.00
   40187 *Rain Crow Bill Blues* ....10.00 - 15.00
   40211 *Nellie Gray*...10.00 - 15.00
   40229 *Broken Engagement Blues* ....10.00 - 15.00
   40237 *Ellen Smith* ....10.00 - 15.00
   40269 *Rabbit Race* ....10.00 - 15.00
   40296 *Keep My Skillet Good And Greasy* ....10.00 - 15.00
   40320 *Round-Town Girl* ....10.00 - 15.00
   40352 *The Long Tongued Woman* ....10.00 - 15.00
   40375 *Butcher Boy*..10.00 - 15.00
   40395 *My Darling's Black Mustache* ....12.00 - 18.00
   40403 *Goodbye, Old Booze* ....12.00 - 18.00
   45003 *Liza Jane* ....15.00 - 20.00
   45045 *The Heart Of Old Galax* ....15.00 - 20.00
   45046 *Put My Little Shoes Away* ....10.00 - 15.00
   45053 *Many Times With You I've Wondered* ....10.00 - 15.00
   45061 *Hand Me Down My Walking Cane* ....10.00 - 15.00
   45063 *The Burglar Man*...................................10.00 - 15.00
   45081 *George Collins* ....10.00 - 15.00
Victor 20878 *Whitter's Fox Chase* ....7.00 - 10.00
   V40061 *Poor Lost Boy*....................................15.00 - 20.00
   V40105 *Short Life Of Trouble* ....15.00 - 20.00
   V40135 *Little Maggie With A Dram Glass*........15.00 - 20.00
   V40235 *Tom Dooley*......................................15.00 - 20.00
   V40292 *Fox Chase No. 2* ....15.00 - 20.00

PETE WIGGINS:
Okeh 45295 *The Gay Caballero* ....5.00 - 8.00
   45412 *Everybody Does It In Hawaii*..................5.00 - 8.00

MILLER WIKEL:
Gennett 6566 *Frail Wildwood Flower* ....15.00 - 20.00
Paramount 3205 *Young Charlotte*..........................15.00 - 25.00

RILEY WILCOX:
Bell 1179 *The Broken Engagement* ....7.00 - 10.00

WILEY, ZEKE & HOMER:
Bluebird 7426 *Greenback Dollar, Part 3* ....5.00 - 8.00
   7452 *Someone To Love You When You're Old*.... 5.00 - 8.00
   7572 *I Will Never Turn Back* ....5.00 - 8.00
   7628 *Under The Old Kentucky Moon* ....5.00 - 8.00

WILKINS & SHARON:
Broadway 8204 *My Mother's Bible* ....7.00 - 10.00

FRANK WILKINS:
Broadway 8205 *The Last Mile* ....8.00 - 12.00

DOC WILLIAMS:
Wheeling 1017 *One Heart One Life* .... - - -

"DAD" WILLIAMS:
Brunswick 306 *Money Musk*...................................10.00 - 15.00